OXFORD R

T
Oxford
Guide to the
French
Language

The Oxford
Guide to the
French
Language

WILLIAM ROWLINSON

MICHAEL JANES

Oxford   New York

OXFORD UNIVERSITY PRESS

Oxford University Press, Walton Street, Oxford OX2 6DP

Oxford New York Toronto
Delhi Bombay Calcutta Madras Karachi
Kuala Lumpur Singapore Hong Kong Tokyo
Nairobi Dar es Salaam Cape Town
Melbourne Auckland Madrid

and associated companies in
Berlin Ibadan

Oxford is a trade mark of Oxford University Press

Grammar © Oxford University Press 1991
Dictionary © Oxford University Press 1988

First issued as an Oxford University Press paperback 1992

British Library Cataloguing in Publication Data
Data available
ISBN 0-19-282957-2

Library of Congress Cataloging in Publication Data
Rowlinson, W.
The Oxford guide to the French language / William Rowlinson,
Michael Janes.
p. cm.—(Oxford reference)
Includes French grammar and The Oxford paperback French dictionary.
1. French language—Grammar—1950- 2. French language—Dictionaries—
English. I. Janes, Michael. II. Rowlinson, W. French grammar. 1992.
III. Oxford paperback French dictionary.
1992. IV. Title. V. Series.
448.2'421—dc20   PC2105.R64   1992   91-45898
ISBN 0-19-282957-2

3 5 7 9 10 8 6 4

Printed in Great Britain by
Richard Clay Ltd.
Bungay, Suffolk

Contents

Grammar

Verbs

Modal verbs *64*
faire + infinitive and similar
constructions *71*
Impersonal verbs *74*

TENSE FORMATION

The tenses of French verbs are either *simple*, in which
case the verb is a single word, or *compound*, in which case
it is normally formed from a part of the verb **avoir**, *to
have*, followed by the past participle:

> simple tense: **je porte**, *I wear*
> compound tense: **j'ai porté**, *I have worn*

Regular verbs, what they are

Most French verbs are regular—that is they follow an
entirely predictable pattern. The pattern they follow is
determined by the way their infinitive ends. They divide
into three groups (known as conjugations), each with its
own infinitive ending:

> port**er**, *to wear*, first conjugation
> fin**ir**, *to finish*, second conjugation
> vend**re**, *to sell*, third conjugation

Most French verbs belong to the first conjugation,
whose infinitives all end in **-er**. All invented new verbs
are automatically first conjugation verbs. Verbs in the
second conjugation all have an infinitive ending **-ir**, and
those in the very small third conjugation all have an
infinitive ending **-re**.

Irregular verbs, what they are

Some French verbs are irregular, following no pattern.
In the simple tenses there is no way of predicting their

stems (the part of the verb to which endings are added) or, quite frequently, the endings that are added to them. In the compound tenses, however, it is only the past participle which is irregular. So, for example, with **vouloir** (irregular), *to want*:

present (simple tense)	*perfect (compound tense)*
je veux	**j'ai voulu**
tu veux	**tu as voulu**
il veut	**il a voulu**
nous voulons	**nous avons voulu**
vous voulez	**vous avez voulu**
ils veulent	**ils ont voulu**

▶ There is a table of all the common irregular verbs with their conjugation on page 242.

Simple-tense formation, regular verbs

To form each simple tense a fixed set of endings is added to the verb's stem. The stem is the infinitive minus its **-er**, **-ir** or **-re** ending. Each conjugation has a different set of verb endings.

> **porter** → **port-** → **je** porte, *I wear*
> **finir** → **fin-** → **je** fin**is**, *I finish*
> **vendre** → **vend-** → **je** vend**s**, *I sell*

The ending of the verb corresponds to the subject of the verb:

> **je** fin**is**, *I finish*
> **il** fin**it**, *he finishes*

▶ The complete tense-formation of regular verbs is given on pp. 4–12, with the verb endings printed in bold.

Compound-tense formation, all verbs

To form a compound tense you need to know a verb's past participle. The past participle of a regular verb is

formed by removing the **-er**, **-ir**, or **-re** of the infinitive.
To this stem is added **-é** (first conjugation), **-i** (second
conjugation), or **-u** (third conjugation):

infinitive		*past participle*
porter	→	port**é**
finir	→	fin**i**
vendre	→	vend**u**

The tenses of **avoir** used to form the compound tenses
are:

> perfect tense:
>   present of **avoir**: j'**ai** porté
>
> pluperfect tense:
>   imperfect of **avoir**: j'**avais** porté
>
> future perfect tense:
>   future of **avoir**: j'**aurai** porté
>
> conditional perfect tense:
>   conditional of **avoir**: j'**aurais** porté
>
> past anterior tense:
>   past historic of **avoir**: j'**eus** porté
>
> perfect subjunctive:
>   present subjunctive of **avoir**: j'**aie** porté
>
> pluperfect subjunctive:
>   imperfect subjunctive of **avoir**: j'**eusse** porté

▶ Some very common French verbs form their
compound tenses with **être** instead of **avoir**. See p. 12.

▶ In all the compound tenses the past participle may
sometimes agree with its subject or its direct object, in
gender and in number. See p. 14.

CONJUGATION OF -er VERBS

(First-conjugation verbs)

In all tenses **elle** (*she*), **on** (*one*) and singular nouns are
followed by the **il** form of the verb; **elles** (*they*, feminine)

and plural nouns are followed by the **ils** form of the verb.

infinitive	**port**er, *to wear*
present participle	**port**ant, *wearing*
past participle	**port**é, *worn*
imperative	**port**e, *wear...!*
	portons, *let's wear...*
	portez, *wear...!*

Simple tenses

present tense, *I wear, I am wearing*	je **port**e	nous **port**ons
	tu **port**es	vous **port**ez
	il **port**e	ils **port**ent
imperfect tense, *I wore, I was wearing, I used to wear*	je **port**ais	nous **port**ions
	tu **port**ais	vous **port**iez
	il **port**ait	ils **port**aient
past historic tense, *I wore*	je **port**ai	nous **port**âmes
	tu **port**as	vous **port**âtes
	il **port**a	ils **port**èrent
future tense, *I shall wear, I shall be wearing*	je **port**erai	nous **port**erons
	tu **port**eras	vous **port**erez
	il **port**era	ils **port**eront
conditional tense, *I should wear*	je **port**erais	nous **port**erions
	tu **port**erais	vous **port**eriez
	il **port**erait	ils **port**eraient
present subjunctive, *I wear, I may wear*	je **port**e	nous **port**ions
	tu **port**es	vous **port**iez
	il **port**e	ils **port**ent
imperfect subjunctive*, *I wore, I might wear*	je **port**asse	nous **port**assions
	tu **port**asses	vous **port**assiez
	il **port**ât	ils **port**assent

* archaic or literary

Compound tenses

perfect tense, *I wore, I have worn,* *I have been wearing*	j'**ai** porté tu **as** porté il **a** porté	nous **avons** porté vous **avez** porté ils **ont** porté
pluperfect tense, *I had worn, I had* *been wearing*	j'**avais** porté tu **avais** porté il **avait** porté	nous **avions** porté vous **aviez** porte ils **avaient** porté
future perfect tense, *I shall have worn, I* *shall have been* *wearing*	j'**aurai** porté tu **auras** porté il **aura** porté	nous **aurons** porté vous **aurez** porté ils **auront** porté
conditional perfect tense, *I should* *have worn*	j'**aurais** porté tu **aurais** porté il **aurait** porté	nous **aurions** porté vous **auriez** porté ils **auraient** porté
past anterior tense*, *I had worn*	j'**eus** porté tu **eus** porté il **eut** porté	nous **eûmes** porté vous **eûtes** porté ils **eurent** porté
perfect subjunctive, *I wore, I may* *have worn*	j'**aie** porté tu **aies** porté il **ait** porté	nous **ayons** porté vous **ayez** porté ils **aient** porté
pluperfect subjunctive*, *I* *had worn*	j'**eusse** porté tu **eusses** porté il **eût** porté	nous **eussions** porté vous **eussiez** porté ils **eussent** porté

Imperative of -er verbs

The **tu** form of the imperative of **-er** verbs (also verbs like **ouvrir**, see p. 29) has no **-s** except when followed by **y** or **en**:

> **donne-le-moi!**, *give it to me!*
> **donnes-en à ta sœur aussi!**, *give your sister some as well!*
> **vas-y!**, *go on!*

* archaic or literary

Spelling changes in some -er verbs

▶ Tenses with changes are given in detail in the verb tables on p. 239.

■ Verbs ending -e[CONSONANT]er change the **e** of the stem to **è** when a silent **e** follows:

> **mener → je mène**

They also make this change in the future and conditional, where the **e** that follows is soft rather than silent:

> **je mènerai; je mènerais**

■ verbs ending **-eter** and **-eler**, however, usually produce the open sound in the **e** by doubling the consonant:

> **jeter → je jette**
> **rappeler → je rappelle**

■ some verbs ending **-eter** and **-eler** follow the pattern of **mener**, changing the e to **è**:

> **acheter → j'achète**
> **geler → je gèle**

Most verbs that do this are, however, quite uncommon. The only ones you are at all likely to encounter are:

acheter, *buy*	**geler**, *freeze*
ciseler, *engrave*	**haleter**, *pant*
congeler, *(deep) freeze*	**modeler**, *model*
crocheter, *hook (up)*	**peler**, *peel*
déceler, *disclose*	**racheter**, *buy back,*
dégeler, *thaw*	*buy again*
démanteler, dismantle	

■ Verbs ending -é[CONSONANT]er change the **é** to **è** before a silent **e** in the same way, *except in the future and conditional tenses*:

espérer → j'espère, but
j'espéreral; j'espérerais

■ Verbs ending -cer and -ger change the c to ç and the g to ge before a and o. This keeps the c and the g soft:

commencer → nous commençons
manger → nous mangeons

■ Verbs ending -oyer and -uyer change the y to i before a silent e:

envoyer → j'envoie
appuyer → j'appuie

With verbs ending -ayer this change is optional:

payer → je paie or je paye

CONJUGATION OF -ir VERBS

(Second-conjugation verbs)

In all tenses elle (*she*), on (*one*), and singular nouns are followed by the il form of the verb; elles (*they*, feminine) and plural nouns are followed by the ils form of the verb.

infinitive	fin**ir**, *to finish*
present participle	fin**issant**, *finishing*
past participle	fin**i**, *finished*
imperative	fin**is**, *finish …!*
	fin**issons**, *let's finish …*
	fin**issez**, *finish …!*

Simple tenses

present tense,	je fin**is**	nous fin**issons**
I finish, I am	tu fin**is**	vous fin**issez**
finishing	il fin**it**	ils fin**issent**

imperfect tense, *I finished, I was finishing, I used to finish*	je fin**issais**	nous fin**issions**
	tu fin**issais**	vous fin**issiez**
	il fin**issait**	ils fin**issaient**
past historic tense, *I finished*	je fin**is**	nous fin**îmes**
	tu fin**is**	vous fin**îtes**
	il fin**it**	ils fin**irent**
future tense, *I shall finish, I shall be finishing*	je fin**irai**	nous fin**irons**
	tu fin**iras**	vous fin**irez**
	il fin**ira**	ils fin**iront**
conditional tense, *I should finish*	je fin**irais**	nous fin**irions**
	tu fin**irais**	vous fin**iriez**
	il fin**irait**	ils fin**iraient**
present subjunctive, *I finish, I may finish*	je fin**isse**	nous fin**issions**
	tu fin**isses**	vous fin**issiez**
	il fin**isse**	ils fin**issent**
imperfect subjunctive*, *I finished, I might finish*	je fin**isse**	nous fin**issions**
	tu fin**isses**	vous fin**issiez**
	il fin**ît**	ils fin**issent**

Compound tenses

perfect tense, *I finished, I have finished*	j'**ai** fini	nous **avons** fini
	tu **as** fini	vous **avez** fini
	il **a** fini	ils **ont** fini
pluperfect tense, *I had finished*	j'**avais** fini	nous **avions** fini
	tu **avais** fini	vous **aviez** fini
	il **avait** fini	ils **avaient** fini
future perfect tense, *I shall have finished*	j'**aurai** fini	nous **aurons** fini
	tu **auras** fini	vous **aurez** fini
	il **aura** fini	ils **auront** fini
conditional perfect tense, *I should have finished*	j'**aurais** fini	nous **aurions** fini
	tu **aurais** fini	vous **auriez** fini
	il **aurait** fini	ils **auraient** fini

* archaic or literary

past anterior tense*, *I had finished*	j'**eus** fini	nous **eûmes** fini
	tu **eus** fini	vous **eûtes** fini
	il **eut** fini	ils **eurent** fini
perfect subjunctive, *I finished, I may have finished*	j'**ale** fini	nous **ayons** fini
	tu **ales** fini	vous **ayez** fini
	il **alt** fini	ils **aient** fini
pluperfect subjunctive*, *I had finished*	j'**eusse** fini	nous **eussions** fini
	tu **eusses** fini	vous **eussiez** fini
	il **eût** fini	ils **eussent** fini

CONJUGATION OF -re VERBS

(Third-conjugation verbs)

In all tenses **elle** (*she*), **on** (*one*), and singular nouns are followed by the **il** form of the verb; **elles** (*they*, feminine) and plural nouns are followed by the **ils** form of the verb.

infinitive	vend**re**, *to sell*
present participle	vend**ant**, *selling*
past participle	vend**u**, *sold*
imperative	vend**s**, *sell ...!*
	vend**ons**, *let's sell ...*
	vend**ez**, *sell ...!*

Simple tenses

present tense, *I sell, I am selling*	je vend**s**	nous vend**ons**
	tu vend**s**	vous vend**ez**
	il vend	ils vend**ent**
imperfect tense, *I sold, I was selling, I used to sell*	je vend**ais**	nous vend**ions**
	tu vend**ais**	vous vend**iez**
	il vend**ait**	ils vend**aient**

* archaic or literary

past historic tense, I sold	je vend**is** tu vend**is** il vend**it**	nous vend**îmes** vous vend**îtes** ils vend**irent**
future tense, I shall sell, I shall be selling	je vend**rai** tu vend**ras** il vend**ra**	nous vend**rons** vous vend**rez** ils vend**ront**
conditional tense, I should sell	je vend**rais** tu vend**rais** il vend**rait**	nous vend**rions** vous vend**riez** ils vend**raient**
present subjunctive, I sell, I may sell	je vend**e** tu vend**es** il vend**e**	nous vend**ions** vous vend**iez** ils vend**ent**
imperfect subjunctive*, I sold, I might sell	je vend**isse** tu vend**isses** il vend**ît**	nous vend**issions** vous vend**issiez** ils vend**issent**

Compound tenses

perfect tense, I sold, I have sold, I have been selling	j'**ai** vendu tu **as** vendu il **a** vendu	nous **avons** vendu vous **avez** vendu ils **ont** vendu
pluperfect tense, I had sold, I had been selling	j'**avais** vendu tu **avais** vendu il **avait** vendu	nous **avions** vendu vous **aviez** vendu ils **avaient** vendu
future perfect tense, I shall have sold	j'**aurai** vendu tu **auras** vendu il **aura** vendu	nous **aurons** vendu vous **aurez** vendu ils **auront** vendu
conditional perfect tense, I should have sold	j'**aurais** vendu tu **aurais** vendu il **aurait** vendu	nous **aurions** vendu vous **auriez** vendu ils **auraient** vendu
past anterior tense*, I had sold	j'**eus** vendu tu **eus** vendu il **eut** vendu	nous **eûmes** vendu vous **eûtes** vendu ils **eurent** vendu

* archaic or literary

perfect subjunctive,	j'**aie** vendu	nous **ayons** vendu
I sold, I may have	tu **aies** vendu	vous **ayez** vendu
sold	il **ait** vendu	ils **aient** vendu
pluperfect	j'**eusse** vendu	nous **eussions** vendu
subjunctive*,	tu **eusses** vendu	vous **eussiez** vendu
I had sold	il **eût** vendu	ils **eussent** vendu

COMPOUND TENSES

▶ For the formation of the compound tenses see p. 3.

Compound tenses formed with être

Although most verbs form their compound tenses with
avoir as the auxiliary, two groups form these tenses with
être: reflexive verbs and a small number of common
verbs expressing motion or change of state.

■ Reflexive verbs

> **je me suis levé de bonne heure**, *I got up early*
> **tu t'étais couché tard?**, *you'd gone to bed late?*

▶ See p. 30 for the formation of reflexive verbs and p. 15
for their agreement.

■ 'Motion' verbs

This is a group of thirteen common (and a few more
quite uncommon) verbs mainly expressing some kind of
motion or change of state, and all intransitive (used
without a direct object):

arriver, *arrive*	**il est arrivé**
partir, *set off*	**il est parti**
entrer, *enter*	**il est entré**
sortir, *go out*	**il est sorti**
aller, *go*	**il est allé**
venir, *come*	**il est venu**

* archaic or literary

monter, *go up*	**il est monté**
descendre, *go down*	**il est descendu**
mourir, *die*	**il est mort**
naître, *be born*	**il est né**
rester, *stay*	**il est resté**
tomber, *fall*	**il est tombé**
retourner, *return*	**il est retourné**

Accourir and **passer** used intransitively may take either **être** or **avoir**:

elle est accourue/elle a accouru, *she ran up*

Except **convenir à** (*suit*), all compound verbs based on the above verbs also take **être** when used intransitively.

je suis parvenu à le faire, *I managed to do it*
il est devenu soldat, *he became a soldier*
but **cela ne lui a pas convenu**, *it didn't suit him*

▶ See p. 15 for the past-participle agreement with this group of verbs.

■ 'Motion' verbs used transitively

Some of the above verbs can also be used with a direct object (transitively). These verbs are:

descendre, *to take down, to get down, to go down*
monter, *to take up, to put up, to bring up, to go up*
entrer (or more usually its compound, **rentrer**), *to put in, to let in, to bring in*
retourner, *to turn (over)*
sortir, *to take out, to bring out*

When they are used this way they take **avoir**, not **être**:

il a sorti un billet de cent francs de son portefeuille, *he took a hundred-franc note from his wallet*
j'ai descendu l'escalier, *I came down the stairs*

■ Verbs of motion and change of state other than those listed above always take **avoir**, whether used transitively or intransitively.

> **tu as beaucoup changé, toi**, *you've changed a lot, you have*

Past-participle agreement in compound tenses

■ Verbs conjugated with **avoir**

In most cases the past participle of a verb conjugated with **avoir** does not change at all. However, if an **avoir** verb has a direct object, and this precedes the verb, the past participle agrees with that object in gender and number, adding **-e** for feminine singular, **-s** for masculine plural and **-es** for feminine plural.

> **tes papiers, je les ai trouvés**, *those papers of yours, I found them*
> – agreement, because direct object **les** precedes the verb
> **voilà les papiers que tu as cherchés**, *there are the papers you've been looking for*
> – agreement, because direct object **que**, referring to **les papiers**, precedes
> **quelle date as-tu choisie?**, *what date did you choose?*
> – agreement, because direct object **quelle date** precedes

Notice that there is no agreement with an indirect object, or with **en**, or with a direct object that does not precede the verb:

> **j'ai trouvé les papiers**, *I've found the papers*
> – no agreement, direct object **les papiers** follows

c'est à Sylvie que j'ai envoyé cet argent, *it's Sylvie I sent that money to*
> – no agreement with **que**: it is the indirect object, standing for **à Sylvie**. The direct object **cet argent** follows.

les gâteaux? J'en ai mangé deux, *the cakes? I've eaten two of them*
> – no agreement with **en**: it is not a true direct object

■ Verbs conjugated with **être**

□ Intransitive verbs of motion and change of state

The past participles of the thirteen 'motion' verbs and their compounds conjugated with **être** (see p. 12) agree with the subject in gender and number, adding **-e** for feminine singular, **-s** for masculine plural, **-es** for feminine plural:

> **elle est arrivée hier**, *she arrived yesterday*
> **elles étaient parties bien avant midi**, *they'd set off long before twelve o'clock*
> **ils seront déjà sortis**, *they'll already have gone out*

□ Reflexive verbs

The past participles of reflexive verbs agree in gender and number with the preceding direct object, which in most cases will correspond to the subject:

> **elle s'est levée tard**, *she got up late*
> **ils se sont dépêchés**, *they hurried*

In some cases, however, the reflexive is an indirect object, and then there is no agreement:

> **elle s'est dit, « pourquoi pas? »**, *she said to herself, why not?*
> **ils se sont écrit toutes les semaines**, *they wrote to each other every week*

> **elle s'est cassé la cheville**, *she broke her ankle*
> – **la cheville**, the ankle, is the direct object, **se** is an indirect object indicating whose ankle she broke

but notice:

> **quelle cheville s'est-il cassée?**, *which ankle has he broken?*
> – the agreement is with **quelle cheville**, which is the direct object, precedes, and is feminine.

■ Past participle used as an adjective

The past participle may also be used simply as an adjective, in which case, like any other adjective, it agrees with its noun:

> **elles sont épuisées mais contentes**, *they are exhausted but happy*

▶ See p. 38 for all the uses of the past participle.

USE OF TENSES

The present tense

French has only one form of the present tense, corresponding to both the present simple and the present continuous in English. So **je mange** translates both *I eat* and *I am eating*. There is no possible translation of *I am eating* using the present participle in French. If the continuing nature of the action needs to be stressed, **être en train de** is used:

> **mais je suis en train de déjeuner!**, *but I'm still eating my lunch!*

General uses of the present tense

■ As in English, the present is used not just to indicate what is going on at the moment:

je mange un œuf, *I'm eating an egg*

but also what habitually occurs:

je mange toujours un œuf au petit déjeuner,
I always have an egg for breakfast

■ It can also be used, again as in English, to indicate a future:

tu prends un œuf?, *are you having (going to have) an egg?*

■ The present tense is used much more frequently than in English to narrate a past series of events, not just in spoken French but in written French also:

1945. A Hiroshima, la bombe explose. Toute discussion est terminée ... *1945. In Hiroshima, the bomb exploded. All discussion was over*

This is called the historic present, and it is used to give more immediacy to past events. But see also p. 22.

Special uses of the present tense

■ Present tense with **depuis** (*for*), **depuis que** (*since*), **voilà ... que** (*since/for*) and **il y a ... que** (*since/for*)

☐ **Depuis, depuis que**

With the preposition **depuis** and after the conjunction **depuis que** a French present tense is used where in English we should expect a perfect:

je suis ici depuis deux jours, *I've been here (for) two days*

je le vois beaucoup plus souvent depuis que sa femme est partie, *I've seen him a lot more often since his wife's gone*

With **depuis** plus a negative, however, the tense is the same as in English:

> **je ne l'ai pas vu depuis deux jours**, *I haven't seen
> him for two days*

And where the action is already completed the tense with
depuis is also a past tense, as in English:

> **je l'ai terminé depuis deux heures**, *I finished it two
> hours ago*

▶ See also **depuis** + imperfect, p. 21.

☐ **Voilà … que, il y a … que**

All that has been said above about **depuis** also holds
good for the constructions **voilà … que** and **il y a …
que** (*since/for*):

> **voilà (il y a) deux jours que je suis ici**, *I've been
> here for two days*
> **voilà (il y a) deux jours que je ne l'ai pas vu**, *I
> haven't seen him for two days (it's two days
> since I've seen him)*

■ Present tense with **venir de**

With **venir de** (*to have just* done something) we find a
present tense of **venir** corresponding to a perfect in
English:

> **je viens de déjeuner**, *I've just had lunch*

The literal sense of the French is 'I'm coming from
having lunch' (present) rather than the English 'I have
just had lunch' (perfect). This French construction ('I'm
coming from') is a quite logical equivalent to **je vais
déjeuner**, *I'm going to have lunch* (see p. 24).

▶ See also **venir de** + imperfect, p. 21.

The perfect tense

The perfect has two main uses in French; as a 'true'
perfect and as a past narrative tense.

■ The 'true' perfect (= *I have done*)

As in English, the true perfect is used to speak of something that happened in the past and has some bearing on what is being talked about in the present:

> **j'ai mangé tous tes chocolats**, *I've eaten all your chocolates* (now there's going to be trouble!)
>
> **je suis tombé trois fois déjà**, *I've fallen over three times already* (and he's asking me to go on the ice again!)

It also corresponds to the English perfect continuous:

> **j'ai regardé la télévision tout l'après-midi**, *I've been watching television all afternoon*

Don't be tempted to use an imperfect for this—**je regardais la télévision** means *I was watching television* (when all at once something happened).

■ The past-action perfect (= *I did*)

In French, the perfect is also used for an action in past narrative, especially in speech, where English uses a simple past tense:

> **je me suis levé à sept heures, j'ai allumé la radio et je suis entré dans la salle de bains**, *I got up at seven o'clock, switched on the radio and went into the bathroom*

However, for repeated past actions, where the English simple past, *I went*, really means *I used to go* or *I would go*, French uses the imperfect:

> **on allait chaque année à Torremolinos. C'était affreux!**, *we went (= used to go) to Torremolinos every year. It was (= used to be) dreadful!*

▶ See general uses of the imperfect, below.

The imperfect tense

General uses of the imperfect

■ To indicate a repeated action:

> **il venait me chercher tous les matins à huit heures**, *he came and picked me up (used to come and pick me up; would come and pick me up) every morning at eight*

■ To indicate a continuing action (which is often then interrupted by a single action, for which the perfect or past historic is used):

> **j'épluchais des pommes de terre quand elle sonna à la porte**, *I was peeling potatoes when she rang the doorbell*

■ To indicate a continuing state of affairs:

> **j'ai regardé par la fenêtre. Il pleuvait**, *I looked out of the window. It was raining*

Imperfect or not? Choosing the right French past tense

In general, an English 'was ... ing' indicates an imperfect, and so does 'would ...', unless this has an 'if' involved or implied (*I wouldn't do that ... if I were you*), in which case the tense is the conditional—see p. 26. However, if a simple past tense is to be translated into French, you must consider whether this is one single action (past historic or perfect) or a repeated action (imperfect).

Special uses of the imperfect

■ Imperfect for a single action

More and more frequently the imperfect is used by modern writers at all levels (literature, magazines, newspapers) as a single-action tense to give greater immediacy to an event. Here the newspaper *Le Figaro* is recounting individual events—in the imperfect:

> **Côté cinéma, Bernard Borderie décidait de saisir la balle au bond. Il choisissait pour interpréter le rôle la toute jeune Michèle Mercier.** *For the film, Bernard Borderie decided to grab his opportunity. He chose a really young actress to play the part, Michèle Mercier.*

Clearly 'deciding' and 'choosing' were single, not continous or repeated, actions. The feeling behind these imperfect tenses seems to be: 'there he was, deciding, choosing …' Though this use of the imperfect should be recognized, it is not recommended that it be imitated.

■ Imperfect with **depuis** (*for*), **depuis que** (*since*), **voilà … que** (*since/for*) and **il y avait … que** (*since/for*)

Where English uses a pluperfect continuous (*I had been doing*) with these expressions, French uses an imperfect:

> **j'y étais depuis deux jours**, *I had been there (for) two days*
> **je le voyais beaucoup plus souvent depuis que sa femme était partie**, *I had been seeing him a lot more since his wife had gone*
> **voilà (il y avait) deux jours que j'étais là**, *I had been there for two days*

All the other rules that apply to these expressions used with the present (see pp. 17, 18) also apply when they are used with the imperfect.

■ Imperfect with **venir de** (*to have just*)

Where English uses a simple past of *have just* …, French uses an imperfect of **venir de**:

> **je venais de déjeuner**, *I had just had lunch*

▶ Compare **venir de** + present, p. 18.

■ Imperfect in **si** sentences

After **si** meaning *if*, the simple past in English always corresponds to an imperfect in French:

> **si j'avais ton numéro, je te téléphonerais**, *if I had your number I'd phone you*

Perfect or past historic are not possible after **si** meaning *if*; nor is the conditional, which you might be tempted to use because the main verb in such sentences is usually in the conditional.

However, as in English, the conditional can be used after **si** where it really means *whether*:

> **je ne savais pas s'il retéléphonerait**, *I didn't know if (whether) he would phone back*

▶ See also p. 26 for the conditional in **si** sentences.

The past historic tense

The past historic is mainly, though not exclusively, a written past narrative tense. In spoken French the perfect is usually used instead to recount past actions. However, the past historic can readily be heard in some French dialects and may also be used in standard spoken French where what is being narrated is clearly a self-contained story or a historical event.

Cases where the past historic is not used

■ The past historic is an alternative to the perfect as a narrative tense—it can never be substituted for the imperfect, or for the 'true' perfect (see p. 19).

■ In letter-writing and other personal writing the perfect, not the past historic, is normally used to narrate single actions in the past.

■ The present tense (known in this case as the historic present) may quite often be found with a past meaning, substituting for the past historic. The change to the present from the past historic (or vice versa, from the historic present to the past historic) is felt to lend more immediacy to a narrative at the point at which it occurs. The following example (here, historic present to past historic at the important moment) is taken from the magazine *Marie France*:

> Ensemble le soir, ils **font** la tournée des bistrots de la Butte, ce qui ne **va** pas sans dispute ni même sans coups ... A l'époque Picasso **est** un petit gars noiraud et rablé; immenses yeux noirs, larges épaules et des hanches fines ... Le coup de foudre **se produisit** sous une pluie battante: la jeune femme courait pour se mettre à l'abri, Picasso lui **barra** le passage en lui tendant un petit chat; elle **rit** et **accepta** sans plus de façon.
>
> *In the evenings they made the rounds of the Butte pubs together, not without rows, even blows. At the time Picasso was a swarthy, broad, stocky lad, with huge black eyes, big shoulders and narrow hips. Then, in a downpour of rain, came love at first sight: the girl was running for shelter, Picasso stood in her way offering her a kitten. She laughed, and accepted without more ado.*

The change to the past historic comes at **le coup de foudre se produisit**.

■ Future for past historic

The use of the future tense instead of the past historic for past narrative is a not uncommon journalistic device. See p. 25.

The future tense

Future tense and aller + infinitive

As well as the actual future tense (**je porterai** — *I shall wear*), there is a future formed with **aller**, just as in

English futurity may be expressed by 'I am going to':

> **je vais partir**, *I'm going to leave*

This is sometimes called the 'immediate future', but the ordinary future tense can also be used for immediate happenings, and **aller** + infinitive can be used for things well into the distant future:

> **le défilé aura lieu cet après-midi**, *the procession will take place this afternoon*
>
> **on va retourner à Torremolinos l'année prochaine**, *we're going to go to Torremolinos again next year*

In fact, **aller** + infinitive is used to stress present intention:

> **Monsieur le directeur va vous voir demain à dix heures**, *the manager will see you tomorrow at ten* (that's what he's just decided)

or the relationship of the future event to something that is happening in the present:

> **si tu ne fais pas attention, tu vas te couper le doigt**, *if you don't look out you'll cut our finger* (a direct consequence of not watching what you're doing!)

This will often involve an event not too far into the future, but this is not necessarily the case (note the Torremolinos example above).

Special uses of the future tense

■ Future after **quand, lorsque, dès que, aussitôt que, tant que, pendant que**

Clauses beginning *when* (**quand, lorsque**), *as soon as* (**aussitôt que, dès que**), *as long as* (**tant que**) or *whilst* (**pendant que**) have a present tense in English with futurity implied. In French the tense must be future:

dès que le magasin ouvrira, on sera à votre service, *as soon as the shop opens we shall be at your service*

With these time conjunctions French follows the strict time-logic of the situation, so that in sentences such as the following a future perfect must be used:

je te dirai quand elle sera partie, *I'll tell you when she's gone* (logically, *when she will have gone*)

Note that this strict time-logic does not extend to the conjunction **si**, *if*, which takes the same non-logical tense as English:

s'il est là quand je reviendrai, *if he's there when I get back* (present tense, **est**, not the more logical future)

■ Future as a past narrative tense

The use of the future for past narrative is also becoming more common, especially in newspaper writing. The aim is to heighten the effect with a sense of 'what was destined to happen next was ...' This example comes from *Le Figaro*:

Michèle **fera** tout pour échapper à cette cage dorée. Elle **finira** par quitter la France, **tentera** une nouvelle carrière aux États-Unis, **se lancera** dans la production, **se ruinera** avec une régularité métronomique pour «monter» des films qui n'**aboutiront** guère.

Michèle did everything possible to escape from this gilded cage. She ended up leaving France, tried a new career in the United States, launched herself into production, ruined herself over and over again putting on films that had little success.

An effect similar to that of the French could be obtained in English using *was to* with each verb, but it would be considerably more clumsy than the French futures are.

The conditional tenses (conditional and conditional perfect)

General uses of the conditional

■ The conditional can show future possibility (what might or might not happen if ...):

> **je ne ferais pas ça (si j'étais à ta place)**, *I shouldn't do that (if I were you)*

The 'if' clause may or may not be expressed.

■ The conditional can also show a 'future in the past'. In this use it indicates something that is to happen subsequently to some event narrated in a past tense (*would* is used for this in English):

> **elle m'a assuré qu'elle le ferait**, *she assured me she'd do it*

Conditional tenses used in si sentences

Conditional and conditional perfect tenses are very often found in sentences that include a clause beginning with **si**:

> **je serais content si elle venait**, *I'd be pleased if she came*
>
> **si elle était venue, j'aurais été tellement heureux**, *if she'd come I'd have been so happy*

The sequence is

> **si** + imperfect, + main clause conditional
> **si** + pluperfect, + main clause conditional perfect

▶ See also p. 22.

Special uses of the conditional tense

■ The conditional may express qualified possibility:

> **il serait peut-être temps de regarder votre avenir en face**, *it might perhaps be time to face your future*

■ The conditional may be used to avoid direct responsibility for the accuracy of a statement:

> **il resterait 30% de la population à fumer**, *there is said to be (appears to be) 30% of the population who still smoke*

■ The conditional may express a polite, hesitant request:

> **vous ne pourriez pas le revendre?**, *couldn't you perhaps sell it again?*

Literary tenses

One of the simple tenses, the imperfect subjunctive, and two of the compound tenses, the pluperfect subjunctive and the past anterior, are obsolescent or literary, to be recognized but not used.

The imperfect subjunctive

This is found in subjunctive clauses with a past meaning:

> **elle ne pensait pas qu'il le sût**, *she didn't think he knew it*

Everyday French would use a present subjunctive:

> **elle ne pensait pas qu'il le sache**

The pluperfect subjunctive

■ This is used where the verb has a pluperfect meaning:

> **il téléphona, bien qu'elle fût déjà partie**, *he telephoned, even though she had already left*

Here, everyday French would use a perfect subjunctive:

> **il téléphona, bien qu'elle soit déjà partie**

■ It is also used in literary French instead of the conditional perfect:

> **Rodrigue, qui l'eût cru? ... Chimène, qui l'eût dit? ...** *Rodrigue, who would have believed it?— Chimène, who would have said it?*
>
> (Corneille: *Le Cid*)

The past anterior

This is used with a pluperfect meaning after the conjunctions **quand, lorsque, dès que, aussitôt que**, but only when the verb in the main clause is in the past historic:

> **quand elle eut fini de parler, il se leva et sortit**, *when she had finished speaking, he got up and went out*

THE IMPERATIVE

The imperative is used to give orders or instructions or to express requests.

Formation of the imperative

The imperative has three forms, which are the same as the **tu**, **nous**, and **vous** parts of the present tense of the verb:

> **choisis**, *choose!*
> **choisissons**, *let's choose*
> **choisissez**, *choose!*

■ First conjugation (**-er**) verbs lose the final **-s** of the **tu** form of the imperative, unless followed by **y** or **en**:

> **donne-le-moi**, *give it to me*
> **donnes-en à ton amie**, *give some to your friend*
> **va à ta chambre!**, *go to your room!*

So do irregular verbs whose **tu** form of the present ends
in **-es**:

>**ouvre la porte**, *open the door*

▶ For form, order and position of pronoun objects with
the imperative, see p. 106.

■ In the negative the **ne** and **pas** etc. go round the verb
in the usual way:

>**ne choisissez pas encore**, *don't choose yet*

■ Third-person commands (*let him/her/it/them ...*) are
expressed by using **que** plus the present subjunctive:

>**qu'il le trouve lui-même**, *let him find it himself!*

Alternatives to the imperative

An imperative need not be used to express a command.
There are a number of other ways of doing it.

■ Politer than the imperative is **voulez-vous
(veux-tu) ...**, *will you/would you ...*, or **puis-je vous
prier de ...**, *would you be so kind as to ...*:

>**voulez-vous chercher mon sac?**, *would you look
for my bag?*
>**puis-je vous prier de me passer ma valise?**, *would
you be so kind as to pass me my case?*

■ The imperative of **vouloir** plus the infinitive is found
as an alternative to the imperative in formal language and
in the ending to formal letters:

>**veuillez signer ici**, *kindly sign here*
>**Veuillez agréer, chère madame, l'expression de
mes sentiments les plus distingués**, *Yours
sincerely*

■ In official notices and in recipes an infinitive, or
défense de ..., or **... interdit** may be found instead of
an imperative:

> **ne pas se pencher au dehors**, *do not lean out*
> **défense de fumer**, *no smoking*
> **entrée interdite**, *no entry*

■ The future tense may also express a command, as in English:

> **vous ferez exactement ce que je vous dirai**, *you'll do exactly what I say*

REFLEXIVE VERBS

Reflexive verbs are verbs whose direct or indirect object is the same as their subject (*he scratches himself; she allows herself a chocolate*). In French they consist of a simple verb preceded by a reflexive pronoun:

> **il arrête le train**, *he stops the train*—simple verb
> **le train s'arrête**, *the train stops (itself)*—reflexive verb

■ The reflexive pronouns

Apart from **se**, they are the same as the ordinary object pronouns:

> **me**, *(to) myself*
> **te**, *(to) yourself*
> **se**, *(to) himself, (to) herself, (to) itself, (to) oneself, (to) themselves*
> **nous**, *(to) ourselves*
> **vous**, *(to) yourself, (to) yourselves*

Me, **te**, and **se** become **m'**, **t'**, and **s'** before a vowel or **h** 'mute'. **Te** becomes **toi** when used with the imperative (see p. 107).

The reflexive pronoun corresponding to **on** is **se**:

> **on se blâme**, *we blame ourselves*

□ The reflexive pronouns are the same whether they are

direct or indirect objects, and stand before the verb in the same way as other object pronouns.

▶ For the order of object pronouns, including reflexives, see p. 106.

☐ Reflexive pronouns in the plural—**nous, vous, se**—as well as meaning *(to) ourselves, (to) yourselves, (to) themselves*, can also mean *(to) one another* or *(to) each other*. This includes **se** when it refers to **on** with a plural meaning *(we, you, people, etc.)*:

> **ils se détestent**, *they hate each other*
> **elles se téléphonent tous les soirs**, *they phone each other every evening*
> **on s'aime**, *we love one another*

If ambiguity might otherwise result, **l'un(e) l'autre / les un(e)s les autres** is added, where the reflexive is a direct object; or **l'un(e) à l'autre / les un(e)s aux autres**, where the reflexive is an indirect object:

> **nous nous sommes demandé, si ...,** *we wondered (asked ourselves) whether ...*
> **nous nous sommes demandé l'un à l'autre, si ...,** *we asked each other, whether ...*

■ Compound tenses of reflexive verbs are formed with **être**, not **avoir**.

In compound tenses the past participle of a reflexive verb agrees with a preceding direct object. Since direct object and subject are usually the same, this means that the past participle of a reflexive verb appears to agree with its subject. However, this is not always the case:

> **elle s'est lavée**, *she washed (herself)*
> **elle s'est lavé les cheveux**, *she washed her hair*

▶ See also p. 15.

■ A French reflexive verb may correspond to an English one:

> **il se gratte**, *he scratches himself*

but very often it does not:

> **elle s'assoit**, *she sits down*
> **il se lave**, *he washes*

■ Reflexive verbs are occasionally used in French where English uses a passive:

> **je m'étonne: je croyais que c'était gratuit**, *I'm surprised, I thought it was free*
> **cela ne se vend pas ici**, *it's not sold here*

► See p. 34 for this and other alternatives to the passive.

■ Reflexive verbs may sometimes have the sense of 'becoming':

> **je m'ennuie**, *I'm getting bored*
> **elle s'impatientait**, *she was becoming impatient*

THE PASSIVE

The passive forms of the tenses are those where the subject of the verb experiences the action rather than performs it (active: *he helped*; passive: *he was helped*).

Formation of the passive

The passive in English is formed with parts of the verb *to be* plus the past participle; in French it is formed in exactly the same way with parts of **être** plus the past participle:

> **elle est partout détestée**, *she is hated everywhere*
> **il était protégé par sa femme**, *he was protected by his wife*
> **la ville avait été abandonnée par ses habitants**, *the town had been abandoned by its inhabitants*

In the passive the past participle always agrees with
the subject, in the same way that an adjective would.

■ In English the 'doer' of the action is indicated by *by*
(as in this sentence you're reading). This is **par**, or
sometimes **de**, in French. **Par** is more specific:

> **il a été tué par sa femme**, *he was killed by his
> wife*
>
> **elle est bien vue de tout le monde**, *she is well
> regarded by everyone*

However, where *by* refers to the instrument used,
rather than the person doing the action, **de** is always
used in French:

> **il a été tué d'un coup de revolver**, *he was killed by
> a revolver shot*

■ In English, the indirect object of an active verb may
be made into the subject of the corresponding passive
verb:

> *someone gave the book to me → I was given the
> book*
>
> *Paul gave the book to me → I was given the book
> by Paul*

This is impossible in French. *I was given the book* can be
translated using **on**:

> **on m'a donné le livre** (literally, *someone has given
> me the book*)

However, in the second example, *I was given the book by
Paul*, where the 'doer' of the action is stated, the
sentence has to remain active in French:

> **Paul m'a donné le livre**

Or, if the English sentence stresses 'Paul':

> **c'est Paul qui m'a donné le livre**

Alternatives to the passive

The passive is frequently avoided in French, especially when the 'doer' of the action is not mentioned.

■ Most frequently **on** is used:

> **on l'avait abandonné**, *it had been abandoned*

■ Sometimes a reflexive verb may be used:

> **cela ne se fait pas!**, *that's not done!*
> **la porte s'ouvre**, *the door is (being) opened* (**la porte est ouverte** would mean *the door is— already—open*)

■ Or an active form may be preferred where English would use a passive:

> **ta lettre les a bouleversés**, *they've been shattered by your letter*

■ Occasionally, where the subject is a person, **se faire** is used:

> **il s'est fait renvoyer en Espagne**, *he's been sent (got himself sent) back to Spain*
> **on s'est fait congédier**, *we've been sacked*

PARTICIPLES

The present participle

Formation of the present participle

The present participle (in English, the *-ing* part of the verb) is formed in French by substituting **-ant** for **-ons** in the **nous** form of the present tense of the verb:

> **choisir → nous choisissons → choisissant**

There are only three present participles which are exceptions to this rule:

être: étant
avoir: ayant
savoir: sachant (but **savant** where the present
participle is used as an adjective: **un phoque
savant**, *a performing seal*)

Note also the two spellings of **fatiguant/fatigant**, the
second used adjectivally:

en fatiguant la salade, *whilst dressing the salad*
une journée fatigante, *an exhausting day*

Uses of the present participle

■ As an adjective

The present participle can be used as an adjective. When
it is so used, it behaves exactly as other adjectives. So it
agrees with its noun, and qualifying adverbs precede it:

l'année suivante, *the following year*
une femme incroyablement charmante, *an
incredibly charming woman*

■ As a verb

The present participle can also be used verbally in a
phrase with or without **en** (= *in*, *by*, *whilst*). When the
present participle is used verbally, pronoun objects stand
in front of it and adverbs after it, just as with any other
part of the verb:

**en la rencontrant un jour dans la rue, il lui a
adressé la parole**, *(on) meeting her one day in
the street, he spoke to her*

Negatives go round it, as they go round other parts of
the verb:

**ne sachant pas que vous étiez là, elle se tourna
vers moi**, *not knowing you were there, she
turned to me*

In this verbal use the present participle, since it is not an adjective, does not take adjective agreements.

□ With or without **en**

When the present participle is used verbally without **en**, the two actions (that of the present participle and that of the main verb) follow one another. When the participle is used with **en** the actions go on simultaneously:

> **se retournant, elle répondit …**, *turning round, she replied …*
>
> **en tombant, elle a entraîné une lampe**, *in falling (as she fell), she brought down a lamp*
>
> **comment s'est elle fait mal? — En tombant**, *how did she hurt herself? By falling (When she fell)*

En with a present participle usually corresponds to the English *on … ing, by … ing, in … ing, whilst … ing*.

□ With **tout en**

The addition of **tout** to the above construction (**tout en …**) draws attention to the fact that the two actions were going on together, often over a period of time. **Tout en** is usually translated as *whilst*:

> **tout en me parlant, il allumait sa pipe**, *whilst (all the time he was) speaking to me, he was lighting his pipe*

Tout en can also have the meaning of *whilst* (*on the one hand*):

> **tout en reconnaissant ce que vous avez fait, je dois vous dire que …**, *whilst recognizing what you have done, I have to tell you that …*

□ With verbs of motion

English can make a verbal phrase by using a verb of motion plus a preposition (*swim away*, *fly off*, *run out*).

French has no equivalent construction and uses a variety of strategies to deal with these concepts (**partir à la nage, s'envoler**, etc.). One of these is to make the preposition into a verb and then add a present participle with **en: sortir en courant**, *run out*. This present-participle construction is most frequently found with **courir**.

▶ See also translation problems, p. 233.

■ As a noun

Present participles are occasionally used as nouns. They add **-e** for feminine, **-(e)s** for plural forms: **l'occupant**, *occupier*; **la passante**, *(woman) passer-by*; **des anciens combattants**, *old soldiers*.

▶ The present participle can never be used in French with an auxiliary verb, as it is in English. *I am sleeping* has to be **je dors**. See p. 16.

The perfect participle

In English, the perfect participle is formed with the present participle of *to have* plus the past participle of the verb. In French the perfect participle is formed in an exactly parallel way, using the present participle of **avoir** plus the past participle of the verb:

> **ayant dit cela, elle s'assit**, *having said that, she sat down*

Verbs that form their compound tenses with **être** also form their perfect participle with **être**:

> **étant arrivée de très bonne heure, elle acheta un journal**, *having arrived very early, she bought a newspaper*
>
> **s'étant déjà baigné, il descendit directement prendre son petit déjeuner**, *having already bathed, he went straight down to breakfast.*

As the above examples show, the use of the perfect participle in French exactly parallels its use in English.

The past participle

Formation of the past participle

Past participles of regular verbs are formed by removing the ending of the infinitive (**-er**, **-ir**, **-re**) and adding **-é**, **-i**, **-u**:

> **porter** → **porté**, *carried*
> **choisir** → **choisi**, *chosen*
> **vendre** → **vendu**, *sold*

▶ For the past participles of irregular verbs see the verb list, p. 242.

Uses of the past participle

■ The past participle is used to form all the compound tenses.

▶ See p. 3 (compound tense formation), p. 14 (past-participle agreement).

■ The past participle is used with **être** to form the passive.

▶ See p. 32.

■ The past participle may be used adjectivally; it then agrees with its noun, takes an adverb qualification, etc., just like any other adjective:

> **elle était complètement épuisée**, *she was completely exhausted*

■ The past participle may also occasionally be used as a noun:

> **le reçu**, *receipt*
> **les rescapés**, *survivors*

■ French sometimes uses a past participle where English

would use a present participle. Mostly this is to describe positions of the body. Common examples are:

accoudé, *leaning (on one's elbows)*
agenouillé, *kneeling*
appuyé, *leaning*
assis, *sitting*

couché, *lying (e.g. in bed)*
étendu, *lying (outstretched)*
(sus)pendu, *hanging*

une seule lampe était suspendue au plafond, *just one lamp was hanging from the ceiling*
il était agenouillé devant l'autel, *he was kneeling before the altar*

THE SUBJUNCTIVE

The subjunctive, expressing doubt or unreality, barely exists any longer in English (*if I were you*; *if that be so*; *would that he were*). In French, though some of its tenses are literary or archaic, it is still in constant use in both the spoken and the written language.

The subjunctive is found in subordinate clauses beginning with **que** meaning *that*, though by no means all such clauses have a subjunctive. The subjunctive in French originally showed the speaker's attitude to an event in the light of his or her emotion (doubt, disbelief, pleasure, etc.). Nowadays it has become fixed as the form used after certain verbs or certain conjunctions, most of which still express some sort of emotion. In only a limited number of cases, however, noted below, is there still a choice between using or not using the subjunctive.

Formation of the subjunctive

The subjunctive has four tenses in French. Of these only the present subjunctive and, on the not very frequent occasions where a perfect meaning is necessary, the perfect subjunctive are in modern everyday use. The tenses are formed as follows:

■ Present subjunctive

The present subjunctive is formed from the **ils** form of the present tense with endings as follows:

choisir → ils choisissent → choisiss-

je choisisse	nous choisiss**ions**
tu choisiss**es**	vous choisiss**iez**
il choisisse	ils choisiss**ent**

This normally produces, as with **choisir** above, **nous** and **vous** forms identical with those of the imperfect tense. In the few cases where this would not be so, **nous** and **vous** forms of the imperfect tense are used for present subjunctive **nous** and **vous**:

prendre → ils prennent → prenn-

je prenne	**nous prenions**
tu prennes	**vous preniez**
il prenne	ils prennent

The following verbs do not follow this pattern:

> **aller, avoir, être, faire, falloir, pouvoir, savoir, valoir, vouloir**

▶ For the subjunctive forms of these verbs, see the list of irregular verbs, p. 242.

■ Perfect subjunctive

Use the present subjunctive of **avoir** or **être** with the past participle of the verb:

j'aie choisi	**nous ayons** choisi
tu aies choisi	**vous ayez** choisi
il ait choisi	**ils aient** choisi

je sois arrivé(e)	**nous soyons** arrivé(e)s
tu sois arrivé(e)	**vous soyez** arrivé(e)(s)
il soit arrivé	**ils soient** arrivés

■ Imperfect subjunctive

The imperfect subjunctive is based on the past historic tense, as follows:

-er verbs (past historic: **je portai**):

je port**asse**	nous port**assions**
tu port**asses**	vous port**assiez**
il port**ât**	ils port**assent**

-ir and **-re** verbs (past historic: **je choisis, je vendis**):

je vend**isse**	nous vend**issions**
tu vend**isses**	vous vend**issiez**
il vend**ît**	ils vend**issent**

Irregular verbs that form their past historic with **-us** etc. form their imperfect subjunctive with **-usse**:

être:	je f**usse**	nous f**ussions**
	tu f**usses**	vous f**ussiez**
	il f**ût**	ils f**ussent**

▶ See the irregular verb list, p. 242.

■ Pluperfect subjunctive

Formed from the imperfect subjunctive of **avoir** or **être** plus the past participle:

j'eusse choisi, etc.
je fusse parti, etc.

■ Future subjunctive

This tense does not exist. To express future meanings in subjunctive clauses, **devoir** must be used. See p. 67.

Uses of the subjunctive

■ The subjunctive is used after certain verbs; the ones listed are those most frequently met:

☐ Verbs of expectancy, wishing, wanting

vouloir que, *wish*; *want*
souhaiter que, *wish*
attendre que, *wait until*
désirer que, *want*
préférer que, *prefer*
aimer mieux que, *prefer*
il est préférable que, *it is preferable*
il vaut mieux que, *it is better*
il est important que, *it is important*

il est important que tu le saches, *it's important that you know*

With verbs of wishing, preferring, etc., English very often uses an infinitive dependent on an object—*they prefer us to go*. This is impossible in French and must always be translated by a dependent clause (= *they prefer that we should go*):

on préfère que nous partions, *they prefer us to go*
que voulez-vous qu'on fasse pour les jeunes chômeurs?, *what do you want us to do for the young unemployed?*

Note that **espérer que**, *hope*, does not take the subjunctive.

☐ Verbs of necessity

il faut que, *must*
il est nécessaire/urgent que, *it is necessary/ urgent*

il faut que vous vous débrouilliez tout seul, *you must sort it out on your own*

☐ Verbs of ordering, forbidding, allowing

ordonner que, *order*
dire que, *tell*

défendre que, *forbid*
permettre que, *allow*
s'opposer à ce que, *be opposed (to someone doing ...)*

je ne permets pas que vous voyagiez seule, *I shall not allow you to travel alone*

With **dire que** there is a difference in meaning according to whether the subjunctive is used or not:

dites au courrier qu'il part ce soir, *tell the courier he's leaving tonight* (piece of information)
dites au courrier qu'il parte ce soir, *tell the courier to leave tonight* (command)

☐ Verbs of possibility

il est possible que, *it is possible*
il se peut que, *it is possible*
il semble que, *it seems*
il paraît que, *it seems*
il est peu probable que, *it is improbable*
il est impossible que, *it is impossible*

se peut-il qu'elle soit déjà là?, *is it possible that she's there already?*

Note that **il est probable que**, *it is probable*, and **il me semble/me paraît que**, *it seems to me*, do not generally take the subjunctive.

☐ Verbs of surprise and incomprehension

s'étonner que, *be surprised*
être surpris/étonné que, *be surprised*
quelle chance que, *what luck*
il me paraît curieux/surprenant/incroyable etc.
que, *it seems odd/surprising/unbelievable*

je m'étonne qu'il y ait autant de chômeurs, *I'm surprised there are so many unemployed*

☐ Verbs of uncertainty

il n'est pas certain que, *it is not certain*
il n'est pas évident/vrai que, *it is not obvious/true*
je ne nie pas que, *I don't deny*
mettons/supposons que, *let us assume*

mettons que les réponses de ce sondage soient exactes, *let us assume that the replies to this poll are correct*

☐ Verbs of doubt and disbelief

douter que, *doubt*
il est douteux que,
    it is doubtful

penser que, *think*
croire que, *believe*
trouver, *think*   } in the
s'attendre à ce que, *expect*   negative or
être sûr/certain,   interrogative
    be sure/certain

je ne crois pas qu'elle t'ait dit des choses pareilles,
    I don't believe she said things like that to you

With the last five verbs above there is a difference in meaning according to whether the subjunctive is used or not:

je ne pense pas qu'il pleut, *I don't think it's raining*
    (I'm fairly sure it isn't)
je ne pense pas qu'il pleuve, *I don't <u>think</u> it's raining* (though it may be)

☐ Verbs of liking, pleasure, dislike, displeasure

aimer que, *like*
adorer que, *love*
ça me plaît que, *I'm glad*
être content/heureux/enchanté que, *be glad/happy/delighted*
détester que, *hate*

j'aime que vous chantiez comme ça, *I like you to sing like that*

☐ Verbs of regret and concern

regretter que, *be sorry*
être désolé que, *be sorry*
c'est dommage que, *it's a pity*
avoir peur que ... (ne), *be afraid*
craindre que ... (ne), *be afraid*, (and the related conjunctions **de peur que ... (ne)**, **de crainte que ... (ne)**, *for fear that*)
être fâché que, *be annoyed that*
avoir honte que, *be ashamed that*

je suis désolé qu'elle ne puisse pas venir, *I'm sorry she can't come*

▶ The use of **ne** with **avoir peur que, craindre que**, and **de peur/crainte que** is formal or literary. See p. 162.

■ The subjunctive is used after certain conjunctions. The common ones are:

☐ **bien que/quoique**, *although*

bien que tout le monde se connaisse au village, personne ne lui parlait, *although everyone knew each other in the village, no-one would speak to him*

☐ **afin que/pour que**, *so that; for*

ils ont tout fait pour qu'il vienne le plus souvent possible, *they did everything so (that) he would come as often as possible*

☐ **à moins que ... (ne)**, *unless*

il y aura une catastrophe à moins que vous ne cédiez la place, *there'll be a disaster unless you give way*

▶ The use of **ne** (without **pas**, and with no negative

meaning) is still quite commonly found after **à moins que**, although even here it is tending to disappear except in formal or literary language. See p. 163.

☐ **que**, *whether*; **que ... que**, *whether ... whether*; **soit que ... que**, *whether ... whether*

> **les Français aiment le rock, qu'il soit hard ou qu'il ne le soit pas**, *the French like rock, whether it's hard or not*
> **qu'on parte ou non**, *whether we leave or not*
> **soit qu'on parte ou qu'on reste**, *whether we leave or stay*

☐ **jusqu'à ce que / en attendant que**, *until*

> **restez là jusqu'à ce qu'elle vienne**, *wait there until she comes*

☐ **avant que ... (ne)**, *before*; **après que**, *after*

> **ne bougez pas avant qu'elle parte**, *don't move before she goes*

The subjunctive is nowadays very commonly used after **après que**, though not in careful or literary French.

▶ The use of **ne** after **avant que** is formal or literary. See p. 163.

☐ **pourvu que / à condition que**, *provided that*

> **oui, pourvu que vous le disiez au patron**, *yes, provided that you tell the boss*

☐ **si ... que**, *however*; **qui que**, *whoever*; **quoi que**, *whatever*

> **cet édifice, si imposant qu'il soit**, *this building, however impressive it may be*
> **qui qu'elle soit, quoi qu'elle dise, ne la crois pas**, *whoever she is, whatever she says, don't believe her*

▶ See also p. 233.

☐ **sans que,** *without*

> **faites-le, sans que nous en sachions rien,** *do it without us knowing anything about it*

☐ **de sorte que / de façon que / de manière que,** *so that* (= *with the inention that*)

> **on le fera, de sorte que vous puissiez voir toutes les possibilités,** *we'll do it, so that you can see all the possibilities*

Note that when these conjunctions express result, they are not followed by the subjunctive:

> **on l'a fait de sorte qu'ils ont pu voir toutes les possibilités,** *we did it in such a way that they could see all the possibilities*

■ The subjunctive is also used in the following cases:

☐ To relate back to a superlative, or to the adjectives **premier, dernier, seul, unique,** which convey a superlative idea

> **la Bretagne est la première province française qu'on ait dotée d'un programme d'action,** *Britanny is the first French province to have been provided with an action programme*

The subjunctive is not always found in these constructions.

☐ To express a 'required characteristic'

> **il cherchait quelque chose qui puisse le protéger,** *he was looking for something that could protect him*

With this construction the subjunctive is not used if the thing characterized is actually known to exist:

il cherchait la seule chose qui pouvait le protéger: son casque, *he was looking for the only thing that could protect him, his helmet*

☐ To express a third person command

que le ciel soit loué!, *heaven be praised!*

☐ In a second 'if' clause, where **que** is substituted for **si**

si tu veux nous accompagner, et que tu puisses être prêt avant huit heures, on t'emmènera, *if you want to go with us, and you can be ready by eight o'clock, we'll take you*

The substitution of **que** for the second **si** is not obligatory; a second **si** would not be followed by the subjunctive.

☐ Instead of a conditional perfect in literary French. The tense used is the pluperfect subjunctive

il ne l'eût pas fait, *he would not have done it*

Avoiding the subjunctive

Though the French use the subjunctive a great deal in everyday conversation, it is most frequently found after expressions of desire, necessity, and regret (**je veux que ...**, **il faut que ...**, **je suis désolé que ...**). Otherwise it tends to indicate high style, and expressions involving it are avoided wherever possible. So

il est possible qu'elle vienne aujourd'hui, *it's possible that she'll come today*

becomes

peut-être qu'elle va venir aujourd'hui, *perhaps she'll come today* and

> **on le fera demain, à moins qu'elle ne vienne aujourd'hui**, *we'll do it tomorrow, unless she comes today*

becomes

> **on le fera demain, si elle ne vient pas aujourd'hui**, *we'll do it tomorrow, if she doesn't come today*

and

> **donne-le-lui avant qu'elle parte**, *give it to her before she goes*

becomes

> **donne-le-lui avant son départ**, *give it to her before her departure*

■ The subjunctive is also avoided where both verbs would have the same subject, by using the appropriate preposition and a dependent infinitive. English frequently does this too:

> **je suis désolé d'apprendre la mauvaise nouvelle de cette façon**, *I'm sorry to hear (that I should hear) the bad news in this way* (instead of **je suis désolé que j'apprenne la mauvaise nouvelle de cette façon**)

▶ See p. 51 for the infinitive after verbs and pp. 51, 52 for the infinitive after adjectives.

■ In the same way, the subjunctive can be avoided with impersonal verbs by using a dependent infinitive:

> **il a fallu que je repense tout → il a fallu tout repenser**, *I had to rethink everything*

If there is any ambiguity about what the subject of the infinitive is, then a subjunctive clause must be used. The use of an indirect object with the main verb (**il m'a fallu tout repenser**) is literary.

THE INFINITIVE

The infinitive, what it is

Infinitives of French regular verbs end in **-er**, **-ir**, or **-re**, corresponding to the English *to ...* form of the verb:

> **porter**, *to wear*
> **choisir**, *to choose*
> **vendre**, *to sell*

The infinitive is the 'name' of the verb: it is really a sort of noun, and as such can be the subject or object of a verb, or stand after a preposition:

> **fumer, c'est dangereux**, *smoking is dangerous*
> **fumer, je le déteste**, *smoking, I hate it*
> **défense de fumer**, *no smoking*

Notice, in the examples above, that English usually uses the *-ing* form of the verb rather than the infinitive as the verbal noun.

Some infinitives have become true nouns and take an article. They are always masculine:

> **on peut apporter son manger**, *you may bring your own food* (**manger**, *to eat*)
> **un homme de savoir**, *a man of learning* (**savoir**, *to know*)

■ Pronoun objects stand in front of the infinitive:

> **pour le regarder**, *in order to look at it*

■ Both parts of a negative stand in front of the infinitive and its object pronouns:

un film à ne pas manquer, *a film not to be missed*
pour ne plus le regarder, *in order not to look at it any more*

The infinitive after a verb

Infinitives usually follow another verb, and in English they are joined to it by *to*. In French they are joined to it by **à, de**, or nothing at all. Which of these is used depends on the head verb, not on the infinitive, and it doesn't vary—it is always, for instance, **se mettre à** + infinitive (*begin to*), **essayer de** + infinitive (*try to*), **vouloir** + infinitive (*want to*).

▶ For the correct preposition to use with any verb (**à, de**, or nothing) see the alphabetical list on pp. 59–64.

■ It is normally impossible in French for an infinitive to depend on the object of another verb as it can in English:

> *I want Fred to listen to me*—Fred is the object of *want*, but Fred is also the subject of *listen*.

A subordinate clause has to be used for this in French (see p. 42):

> **je veux que Fred m'écoute**, *I want Fred to listen to me*

However, with a verb of perceiving (seeing, hearing, feeling, etc.) a construction similar to the English one is possible:

> **je l'ai regardé travailler**, *I watched him work*

▶ See also p. 232.

The infinitive after adjectives, nouns, and adverbs

Infinitives may also follow adjectives, nouns, and adverbial expressions of quantity (**beaucoup, trop**, etc.).

A preposition is used before the infinitive and in most
cases this is **de**:

> **je suis étonné de te voir**, *I'm surprised to see you*
> **je n'ai pas le temps de te parler**, *I haven't the time
> to speak to you*

Sometimes, however, the infinitive has a passive sense
(*to be done* rather than *to do*), and in this case **à** is used:

> **j'ai beaucoup à faire**, *I've a lot to do* (= *to be
> done*)
> **j'ai deux pièces à tapisser**, *I've two rooms to
> paper* (= *to be papered*)
> **c'est une pièce très difficile à tapisser**, *it's a very
> difficult room to paper* (= *to be papered*).
> Compare: **il est très difficile de tapisser cette
> pièce**, *it's very difficult to paper this room*

There are one or two exceptions to this. In spite of the
following infinitive having an active sense, **à** is always
used with:

> **disposé à**, *willing to*
> **lent à**, *slow to*
> **prêt à**, *ready to*
> **prompt à**, *prompt in*
>
> **vous êtes prêts à partir?**, *you're ready to go?*

and with **unique**, **seul**, **dernier** and the ordinal
numbers:

> **il était le seul à venir**, *he was the only one to
> come*

The infinitive after prepositions

▶ For infinitives following **à** and **de**:
after verbs, see pp. 55 and 56;
after adjectives, nouns and adverbs, see p. 51.

Infinitives may also follow the prepositions **après**, **par**, **sans**, and **pour**, and many compound prepositions formed with **de** (**au lieu de**, **avant de**, etc.):

> **sans bouger**, *without moving*
> **pour sortir**, *in order to go out*
> **je commence par citer Molière**, *I shall begin by quoting Molière*

■ In English, the part of the verb which follows a preposition is in almost all cases the present participle (*without looking*, *after eating*). In French it is always an infinitive, except after **en** where the present participle is used: **en retournant**, *on coming back*. See p. 35.

■ Always after **après**, and sometimes, according to meaning, after other prepositions, a perfect infinitive is used:

> **après l'avoir mangé**, *after eating (having eaten) it*
> **il est prison pour avoir volé une voiture**, *he's in prison for having stolen a car*

▶ For the perfect infinitive, see below.

Other uses of the infinitive

■ In literary French the infinitive may be found, preceded by **de**, instead of a past historic:

> **et Yves de répondre «Mais non»**, *and Yves replied 'Of course not'*

■ The infinitive may also be used as an imperative. See p. 29.

The perfect infinitive

The perfect infinitive is formed with the infinitive of **avoir** or **être** plus the past participle of the verb:

> **avoir porté**, *to have worn*
> **être parti**, *to have gone*
> **s'être dépêché**, *to have hurried*

Past participles make the same agreements as in the compound tenses of the verb.

As well as being used after **après** and other prepositions (see p. 53), the perfect infinitive is used after a number of verbs where logic demands it. Common ones are:

> **se souvenir de/se rappeler**, *remember*
> **remercier de**, *thank for*
> **regretter de/être désolé de**, *be sorry for*
> **pardonner (à quelqu'un) de**, *forgive (somebody) for*

Beware: the tense of the equivalent English verb may not be the logical one!

> **je me souviens de l'avoir dit**, *I remember saying (having said) it*
> **je vous remercie d'avoir téléphoné**, *thank you for phoning (having phoned)*
> **elle est désolée de nous avoir dérangés**, *she's sorry to have (for having) disturbed us*
> **peux-tu me pardonner de t'avoir tellement dérangé?**, *can you forgive me for upsetting (having upset) you so much?*

PREPOSITIONS AFTER VERBS

Prepositions with infinitives

In English a verb is linked to a following infinitive either by *to* (*I hope to go*) or by nothing at all (*I must go*). The constructions are invariable, we always use *hope + to*, *must* + *nothing*, whatever the infinitive that follows. The same is true of French, except that in French there are three possibilities, **de**, **à**, and nothing.

■ Verb + **de** + infinitive:

> **il essaye de la faire**, *he tries to do it*

This is by far the largest group and if a verb does not belong to one of the two other groups below, it should be assumed to take **de**.

■ Verb + nothing + infinitive

This is a relatively small group of rather common verbs. It includes:

☐ Verbs of expectancy (wanting, hoping)

> **j'espère vous revoir**, *I hope to see you again*

☐ Verbs of perception (seeing, hearing, feeling)

> **l'entends-tu venir?**, *can you hear him coming?*

☐ Verbs of liking and dislike

> **je déteste nager dans l'eau froide**, *I hate swimming in cold water*

☐ The modal verbs (**vouloir, pouvoir,** etc. See p. 64)

> **je ne sais pas nager**, *I can't swim*

☐ Intransitive verbs of motion (**aller, monter, sortir,** etc.)

> **va chercher ton père**, *go and look for your father*
> (note that the *and* used in English with these verbs is not used in French)

Pour may also be used with these verbs to stress the purpose of the action:

> **Il est entré dans le garage pour chercher une pelle**, *he went into the garage (in order) to look for a spade*

The most frequently met verbs taking an infinitive without a preposition are:

adorer, *adore*	**envoyer**, *send*	**prétendre**, *claim*
aimer (mieux), *prefer*	**espérer**, *hope*	**se rappeler**, *remember*
aller, *go*	**faillir**, *almost (do)*	**regarder**, *look at*
compter, *expect*	**faire**, *have (done)*	**rentrer**, *come in*
croire, *think*	**falloir**, *must*	**sembler**, *seem*
descendre, *come down*	**laisser**, *let*	**(se) sentir**, *feel*
désirer, *want*	**monter**, *go up*	**sortir**, *go out*
détester, *hate*	**oser**, *dare*	**souhaiter**, *wish*
devoir, *have to*	**paraître**, *seem*	**valoir mieux**, *be better*
écouter, *listen to*	**partir**, *go off*	**venir**, *come*
entendre, *hear*	**pouvoir**, *can*	**voir**, *see*
entrer, *come in*	**préférer**, *prefer*	**vouloir**, *want*

▶ For a fuller treatment of **faire** and **laisser** + infinitive see p. 71.

■ Verb + **à** + infinitive

This is also a small group of verbs. They are less heavily used, but still common. The **à** indicates aim or direction. The most frequently met verbs in this group are:

aider à, *help*	**chercher à**, *try*	**demander à**, *ask*
s'amuser à, *enjoy oneself*	**commencer à**, *begin*	**encourager à**, *encourage*
apprendre à, *learn*	**consentir à**, *consent*	**enseigner à**, *teach*
s'apprêter à, *get ready*	**consister à**, *consist (in)*	**forcer à**, *force*
arriver à, *manage*	**continuer à**, *continue*	**s'habituer à**, *get used*
s'attendre à, *expect*	**se décider à**, *decide; make up one's mind*	**hésiter à**, *hesitate*
avoir à, *have*		**s'intéresser à**, *be interested*
		inviter à, *invite*

se mettre à,	**perdre du temps à,**	**renoncer à,** *give up*
start	waste time	**rester à,** *be left*
obliger à, *force*	**persister à,**	**réussir à,** *manage*
parvenir à, *manage*	persist	**servir à,** *be used*
passer du temps à,	**pousser à,** *urge*	**songer à,** *think*
spend time	**(se) préparer à,**	**tarder à,** *be late*
penser à, *think*	prepare	**tenir à,** *be keen*

▶ See p. 59 for an alphabetical list of infinitive and noun constructions after verbs.

Prepositions with nouns and pronouns

Most French verbs have the same preposition before a following noun as their English equivalents. There are three main groups where this is not the case.

■ Verbs with a direct object where we should expect a preposition:

> **attendez-moi!,** *wait for me!*

The most frequently met verbs of this kind are:

approuver, *approve of*	**habiter,** *live at*
attendre, *wait for*	**mettre,** *put on*
chercher, *look for*	**payer,** *pay for*
demander, *ask for*	**regarder,** *look at*
écouter, *listen to*	**reprocher,** *blame for*
essayer, *try on*	

■ Verbs taking **de** where we should expect nothing:

> **elle joue du violon,** *she plays the violin*

The most frequently met verbs in this group are:

s'apercevoir de, *notice*	**discuter de,** *discuss*
s'approcher de,	**douter de,** *doubt*
approach	**se douter de,**
avoir besoin de, *need*	suspect
changer de, *change*	**s'emparer de,** *grab*

jouer de, *play*	**se méfier de**, *mistrust*
(*an instrument*)	**se servir de**, *use*
jouir de, *enjoy*	**se souvenir de**, *remember*
manquer de, *lack*	**se tromper de**, *mistake*

■ Verbs taking **à** where we should expect nothing:

elle joue au tennis, *she plays tennis*

The most frequently encountered verbs of this kind are:

assister à, *attend*	**renoncer à**, *renounce*
convenir à, *suit*	**répondre à**, *answer*
se fier à, *trust*	**résister à**, *resist*
jouer à, *play* (*a game*)	**ressembler à**, *resemble*
nuire à, *harm*	**succéder à**, *succeed*
(des)obéir à, (*dis*)*obey*	(*someone*)
pardonner à, *forgive*	**survivre à**, *outlive*
(dé)plaire à, (*dis*)*please*	**téléphoner à**, *telephone*

Also in this group are a number of verbs that take **à** with the noun at the same time as an infinitive with **de**:

j'ai dit à Jean-Pierre de ne pas sortir, *I told Jean-Pierre not to go out*

These verbs are:

commander à … de, *order*	**ordonner à … de**, *order*
conseiller à … de, *advise*	**permettre à … de**, *allow*
défendre à … de, *forbid*	**promettre à … de**, *promise*
demander à … de, *ask*	**proposer à … de**, *suggest*
dire à … de, *tell*	

■ Verbs taking **à** or **de** where English has an entirely different preposition:

je l'ai acheté au fermier, *I bought it from the farmer*

These verbs are:

acheter à, *buy from*
arracher à, *snatch from*
blâmer de, *blame for*
boire à, *drink from*
cacher à, *hide from*
croire à, *believe in*
demander à, *ask for ... from*
dépendre de, *depend on*
doter de, *equip with*
emprunter à, *borrow from*
enlever à, *take away from*
féliciter de, *congratulate on*
s'intéresser à, *be interested in*

louer de, *praise for*
manquer à, *be missed by*
penser à, *think about*
prendre à, *take from*
punir de, *punish for*
récompenser de, *reward for*
réfléchir à, *think about*
remercier de, *thank for*
rêver à, *dream about*
rire de, *laugh at*
servir à, *be used for*
songer à, *think about*
témoigner de, *bear witness to*
toucher à, *meddle with*
vivre de, *live on*
voler à, *steal from*

Alphabetical list of verb constructions with prepositions

The list includes both verbs + preposition + infinitive, and verbs + preposition + noun. Only 'problem' verbs are included. If a verb is not included, assume that:

■ with a noun it will take the same construction as in English

■ before an infinitive it will take **de**

Abbreviations used:

> qn—**quelqu'un**
> qch—**quelque chose**
> sb—somebody
> sth—something
> INF—infinitive

acheter à qn	*buy from sb*
adorer + INF	*adore to*
aider à + INF	*help to*
aimer + INF	*like to*
aimer mieux + INF	*prefer to*
aller + INF	*go and; be going to*
s'amuser à + INF	*have fun … ing*
s'apercevoir de qch	*notice sth*
apprendre qch à qn	*teach sb sth*
apprendre à qn à + INF	*teach sb to*
apprendre à + INF	*learn to*
s'apprêter à + INF	*prepare to*
s'approcher de qn	*approach sb*
arracher à qn	*snatch from sb*
arriver à + INF	*manage to*
assister à qch	*attend/witness sth*
attendre qn	*wait for sb*
s'attendre à + INF	*expect to*
avoir qch à + INF	*have sth to*
avoir besoin de + INF	*need to*
blâmer de qch	*blame for sth*
boire à qch	*drink from/to sth*
cacher à qn	*hide from sb*
changer de qch	*change sth*
chercher qch	*look for sth*
chercher à + INF	*try to*
commander à qn de + INF	*order sb to*
commencer à (sometimes **de**) + INF	*begin to*

compter + INF	*intend to*
conseiller à qn de + INF	*advise sb to*
consentir à + INF	*agree to*
consentir à qch	*agree to sth*
consister en/dans qch	*consist of sth*
consister à + INF	*consist in*
continuer à (sometimes **de**) + INF	*continue to*
convenir à qn	*suit sb*
croire qn	*believe sb*
croire à/en qn/qch	*believe in sb/sth; trust in sb/sth*
se décider à + INF	*decide to; make up your mind to*
défendre à qn de + INF	*forbid sb to*
demander qn/qch	*ask for sb/sth*
demander qch à qn	*ask sb for sth*
demander à + INF	*ask to*
demander à qn de + INF	*ask sb to*
dépendre de qn/qch	*depend on sb/sth*
déplaire à qn	*displease sb*
descendre + INF	*go down and*
désirer + INF	*want to*
désobéir à qn	*disobey sb*
détester + INF	*hate to; detest ... ing*
devoir + INF	*have to*
dire à qn de + INF	*tell sb to*
discuter de qch	*discuss sth*
doter de qch	*equip with sth*
douter de qch	*doubt sth*
se douter de qch	*suspect sth*
écouter qn/qch	*listen to sb/sth*
écouter qn + INF	*listen to sb ... ing*
s'emparer de qch	*grab sth*
emprunter à qn	*borrow from sb*
encourager à + INF	*encourage to*

enlever à qn	*take away from sb*
enseigner qch à qn	*teach sb sth*
entendre qn + INF	*hear sb … ing*
entrer + INF	*go/come in and*
envoyer qn + INF	*send sb to*
espérer + INF	*hope to*
essayer qch	*try sth on*
se fâcher de qch	*be annoyed about sth*
se fâcher contre qn	*be annoyed with sb*
faillir + INF	*almost do sth*
falloir + INF (**il faut**, etc.)	*must*
féliciter qn de qch	*congratulate sb on sth*
se fier à qn	*trust sb*
forcer à + INF	*force to*
habiter + PLACE	*live at/in*
habituer qn à + INF	*get sb used to … ing*
s'habituer à + INF	*get used to … ing*
hésiter à + INF	*hesitate to*
s'intéresser à qn/qch	*be interested in sb/sth*
s'intéresser à + INF	*be interested in … ing*
inviter qn à + INF	*invite sb to*
jouer à qch	*play (a game)*
jouer de qch	*play (an instrument)*
jouir de qch	*enjoy sth*
laisser + INF	*let*
louer de qch	*praise for sth*
manquer de qch	*lack sth*
manquer à qn	*be missed by sb*
se marier avec qn	*marry sb*
se méfier de qn	*mistrust sb*
mettre qch	*put sth on*
se mettre à + INF	*begin to*
monter + INF	*go up (stairs) and*
nuire à qch	*harm sth*
obéir à qn	*obey sb*
obliger qn à + INF	*force sb to*

ordonner à qn de + INF	*order sb to*
oser + INF	*dare to*
paraître + INF	*appear to*
pardonner qch à qn	*forgive sb for sth*
partir + INF	*go off and; go off to*
parvenir à + INF	*manage to*
passer du temps à + INF	*spend time … ing*
payer qch	*pay for sth*
penser à qn/qch	*think about sb/sth*
penser à + INF	*think of … ing*
perdre du temps à + INF	*waste time … ing*
permettre à qn de + INF	*allow sb to*
persister à + INF	*persist in … ing*
plaire à qn	*please sb*
pousser à + INF	*urge to*
pouvoir + INF	*be able to*
préférer + INF	*prefer to*
prendre à qn	*take from sb*
préparer qn à + INF	*prepare sb to*
se préparer à	*get ready to*
prétendre + INF	*claim to*
promettre à qn de + INF	*promise sb to*
proposer à qn de + INF	*suggest to sb that they should*
punir de qch	*punish for sth*
se rappeler + PERFECT INF	*remember … ing*
(*sometimes* **de** + PERF INF)	
récompenser de qch	*reward for sth*
réfléchir à qch	*think about sth*
regarder qn/qch	*look at sb/sth*
regarder qn + INF	*watch sb … ing*
remercier de qch	*thank for sth*
renoncer à qch	*give sth up*
renoncer à + INF	*give up … ing*
rentrer + INF	*come (back) in to*
répondre à qn/qch	*answer sb/sth*
reprocher qch à qn	*blame sb for sth*

résister à qch	*resist sth*
ressembler à qn/qch	*be like sb/sth*
rester à + INF	*remain to*
réussir à + INF	*manage to*
rêver à qn/qch	*dream about sb/sth*
rire de qn/qch	*laugh at sb/sth*
sembler + INF	*seem to*
sentir qch + INF	*feel sth ... ing*
se sentir + INF	*feel oneself ... ing*
servir à qch	*be used for sth*
servir à + INF	*be used to*
se servir de qch	*use sth*
songer à qn/qch	*think about sb/sth*
songer à + INF	*think about ... ing*
sortir + INF	*go out and*
souhaiter + INF	*want to*
se souvenir de qn/qch	*remember sb/sth*
succéder à qn	*succeed sb*
survivre à qn	*outlive sb*
tarder à + INF	*delay ... ing*
téléphoner à qn	*telephone sb*
témoigner de qch	*bear witness to sth*
tenir à + INF	*be keen to*
toucher à qch	*meddle with sth*
se tromper de qch	*mistake sth; be wrong about sth*
valoir mieux + INF	*be better to*
venir + INF	*come and; come to*
vivre de qch	*live on sth*
voir qn + INF	*see sb ... ing*
voler à qn	*steal from sb*
vouloir + INF	*want to*

MODAL VERBS

The modal verbs (auxiliary verbs of 'mood' like *can*, *must*, *will*, in English) always have a dependent infinitive:

je veux parler, *I want to speak*

Even if this infinitive is occasionally not expressed, it is always implied: **je veux bien!**, for instance, is really **je veux bien faire ce que tu as proposé!**

In French the five modal verbs are:

> **devoir**, *must*
> **falloir (il faut)**, *have to*
> **pouvoir**, *be allowed to*
> **savoir**, *can*
> **vouloir**, *will*

The meanings given above are in fact not really adequate. These verbs have a number of different meanings and shades of meaning in different uses of their various tenses. These are explained below.

Devoir

In its basic meaning **devoir** implies obligation, inner conviction, moral necessity (compare **falloir**, below). Its English equivalent is *have to* or *must*:

> **je dois rentrer**, *I must (have to) go home*

■ Present

As well as *have to*, **devoir** in the present tense also has the sense of *should, is supposed to, is probably ... ing*:

> **il doit être là**, *he should be there (by now)*

It can also mean *am to*:

> **je dois aller à Paris demain**, *I'm to go to Paris tomorrow*

■ Imperfect

As well as *used to have to*, the imperfect of **devoir** can also mean *was to, was due to*:

> **on devait faire la vaisselle tous les matins avant
> sept heures**, *we used to have to wash up every
> morning before seven o'clock*
> **dans trois jours la guerre devait éclater**, *in three
> days war was to break out*

■ Perfect

The basic meaning of the perfect is *had to* (or *has had to*);
the perfect also means *must have*:

> **j'ai dû prendre le train**, *I had to (I've had to) take
> the train*
> **il a dû partir plus tôt**, *he must have left earlier*

■ Pluperfect

The pluperfect meaning is *had had to*, or *must have* (*must
have* is the same as the perfect—English has no separate
pluperfect form of *must*):

> **comme la voiture était en panne, j'avais dû
> prendre le train**, *as the car was off the road, I'd
> had to take the train*
> **elle nous répondit qu'il avait dû partir plus tôt**, *she
> replied that he must have left earlier*

■ Conditional

The conditional means *would have to*, and also *ought to* or
should:

> **s'il devenait président, on devrait quitter le pays**, *if
> he became president we should have to leave
> the country*
> **cela devrait faire votre affaire**, *that ought to
> (should) do the job for you*

■ Conditional perfect

The conditional perfect means *would have had to*, and
also *ought to have* or *should have*:

> **s'il était devenu président, on aurait dû quitter le
> pays**, *if he had become president we should
> have had to leave the country*
> **il aurait dû répondre**, *he ought to have (should
> have) replied*

■ Present subjunctive

Verbs have no future subjunctive. The present
subjunctive of **devoir** is used where it is necessary to
give other verbs in the subjunctive a future meaning:

> **je suis désolé qu'elle doive te suivre par avion**,
> *I'm sorry she's going to fly out after you* (**qu'elle
> te suive** could mean she's already set out)

■ Note that **devoir** can be used impersonally, in all
tenses, as an extension of **il y a**:

> **il doit y avoir trois cents personnes**, *there must be
> three hundred people*

■ Used without a dependent infinitive, **devoir** means *to
owe*. In this sense it is not a modal verb:

> **je vous dois mille francs**, *I owe you a thousand
> francs*

Falloir

The basic meaning of **falloir** is *must* or *have to*, implying
external necessity or constraint. Compare **devoir**, above.

> **tu dois rentrer déjà? — Mais oui, il faut
> absolument rentrer: sinon, ma mère ne me
> permettra pas de sortir demain**, *you must go
> home already?—Yes, I've really got to or my
> mother won't let me come out tomorrow*

■ **Falloir** is always an impersonal verb, used only in the
il form (**il faut**, **il fallait**, etc.). The person need not be
expressed at all if it is obvious who is involved:

> **Pierre, il faut téléphoner à ta grand–mère**, *you must phone your grandmother, Pierre*

The real subject can be expressed by a dative:

> **il me faut partir**, *I have to go*

but this is rather formal, and spoken French prefers a subjunctive clause if it is necessary to say who is involved:

> **il faut que je parte**, *I've got to go*

Pouvoir

Pouvoir means basically *can* or *be allowed to*. Parts of the English verb *can* are missing and *be able to* or *be allowed to* has sometimes to be substituted when translating.

> **peut-on sortir par ici?**, *can we (are we allowed to) go out this way?*
> **l'eau est bonne, on pourra nager**, *the water's fine, we'll be able to go swimming*

As well as *be allowed to* and *can*, **pouvoir** can also mean *may*, either as the politer form of *can*, or expressing possibility:

> **puis-je parler à votre patron?**, *may I speak to your boss?*
> **il peut toujours venir**, *he may still come*

Note too the reflexive form, **se pouvoir**:

> **cela se peut**, *that's possible*

■ Perfect

Means *was able to* or *could* (in a past sense), or *may have*:

> **je n'ai pas pu ouvrir la boîte**, *I couldn't open the tin*

elle a pu se tromper de train, *she may have got
the wrong train*

■ Conditional

Means *would be able to* or *could* (in a conditional sense),
and also *might*:

si tu payais, je pourrais t'accompagner, *if you paid
I could (would be able to) come with you*
je crois qu'il pourrait neiger, *I think it might snow*

■ Conditional perfect

Means *would have been able to* or *could have*, also *might
have*:

si tu avais payé, j'aurais pu t'accompagner, *if
you'd paid, I could have (would have been able
to) come with you*
**elle aurait pu se présenter avant le
commencement du spectacle**, *she might have
turned up before the play started*

■ **Pouvoir** can be used impersonally as an extension of
il y a:

il pourrait y en avoir mille, *there might be a
thousand of them*

■ With verbs of perception (**entendre, voir, sentir**)
English uses *can* or *could* where French prefers the
simple verb:

je le voyais atterrir, *I could see it landing*

Savoir

Savoir means *can* in the sense of *know how to*. Compare
pouvoir above.

**l'eau est bonne, on peut nager — Mais moi, je ne
sais pas nager**, *the water's fine, we can go
swimming—But I can't swim*

■ Conditional

In careful or formal language, the negative conditional of **savoir** is used as a politer form of *I can't*. In this use the **pas** is always omitted:

> **je ne saurais faire cela**, *I don't really think I can do that*

With the full negative **je ne saurais pas** means *would not know how to, couldn't* (in a moral sense):

> **je ne saurais pas faire quelque chose comme ça**, *I couldn't do anything like that*

■ **Savoir** is most frequently found used without a dependent infinitive, meaning *to know*. In this use it is not a modal verb:

> **je sais qu'elle est là**, *I know she's there*

Vouloir

The basic meaning of **vouloir** is *to wish* or *want*:

> **je veux vous dire quelque chose**, *I want to tell you something*

It also means *will, be willing to*. **Bien** is used where English stresses *will*:

> **oui, je veux bien le faire**, *yes, I will do it*
> **la moto ne veut pas démarrer**, *the bike won't start*

It can also mean *attempt to* or *intend to*:

> **j'ai voulu l'embrasser**, *I tried to kiss her*
> **qu'est-ce qu'il veut faire?**, *what does he mean to do?*

■ Conditional, conditional perfect

As well as *should wish, should want* (conditional), and *should have wished, should have wanted* (conditional perfect), these tenses also have the meanings *should like* and *should have liked*:

> **je voudrais être à sa place**, *I'd like to be in her place*
>
> **j'aurais voulu la revoir**, *I'd have liked to see her again*

With this meaning **je voudrais** is a standard way of asking politely for things:

> **je voudrais deux cents grammes de pâté s'il vous plaît**, *I should like two hundred grams of pâté, please*

■ Vouloir may also be used as a polite form of the imperative.

▶ See p. 29.

FAIRE + INFINITIVE AND SIMILAR CONSTRUCTIONS

Faire + infinitive

Faire + infinitive means *to have something done, to get something done, to get someone to do something*:

> **j'ai fait téléphoner à ses parents**, *I've got someone to phone his parents*
>
> **elle a fait enlever ce qui restait du repas**, *she had what was left of the meal taken away*

■ Position of objects with **faire** + infinitive

☐ Noun objects of either verb follow both verbs

> **tu as fait jouer Pierre?**, *you got Pierre to play?*
>
> **tu as fait repeindre la porte?**, *you've had the door painted?*

☐ Pronoun objects of either verb come before both verbs

> **tu l'as fait jouer?**, *you got him to play?*
> **tu l'as fait repeindre?**, *you've had it painted?*

☐ If both verbs need a direct object, the object of **faire** becomes indirect (**à ...**), since in French a double direct object is impossible

> **les premières notes de la musique ont fait perdre à chacun son air désinvolte**, *the first notes of the music made everyone lose their air of detachment*

■ **Faire** + reflexive verbs

If the dependent verb is reflexive it loses its object pronoun:

> **je les ai fait asseoir** (not **s'asseoir**), *I got them to sit down*
> **elle les a fait taire**, *she shut them up*

So if you find a reflexive pronoun in this construction it must belong to **faire** (*have oneself ..., get oneself ...*):

> **elle s'est fait virer du lycée**, *she got herself thrown out of school*

■ Agreement of past participle of **faire**

In the **faire** + infinitive construction the past participle **fait** is invariable: it never agrees with a preceding direct object. See the last two examples above (**je les ai fait ..., elle s'est fait ...**).

Laisser, voir, entendre, sentir + infinitive

■ **Laisser** + infinitive means *to let something be done* or *to let someone do something*:

> **tu l'as déjà laissé revenir?**, *you've let her come back already?*

> **j'ai dû le laisser passer**, *I had to let him go through*

■ **Voir/entendre/sentir** + infinitive mean *to see/hear/ feel something happen*:

> **on l'a vu partir**, *we saw him go*
> **je me sens guérir**, *I can feel myself getting better*

■ All points made above with regard to **faire** concerning objects and past participle agreement may also apply to this group of verbs, though they are quite often ignored:

> **tu lui as laissé repeindre ta porte?**, or very often
> **tu l'as laissé repeindre ta porte?**, *you've let him paint your door?*

English equivalents of faire, etc. + infinitive

Some infinitive constructions of the verbs considered above are the equivalent of a simple verb or a verb plus preposition in English. The most common are:

> **entendre dire que**, *hear that*
> **entendre parler de**, *hear about*
> **faire entrer**, *let in; show in*
> **faire sortir**, *let out; show out*
> **faire venir**, *send for*
> **faire voir**, *show*
> **laisser tomber**, *drop*

Similar constructions with other verbs used with an infinitive are:

> **aller chercher**, *go for*
> **envoyer chercher**, *send for*
> **venir chercher**, *come for*
> **vouloir dire**, *mean*

IMPERSONAL VERBS

Impersonal verbs are verbs whose subject is **il** or **ce/cela** meaning *it* or *there*.

Impersonal verbs with il

These are of two kinds: those that are always constructed with **il,** and those where **il** is simply a temporary subject so that the real subject can be held back until later in the sentence.

■ Real subject **il**

In this group are:

☐ Weather verbs, e.g.

il pleut, *it's raining*
il neige, *it's snowing*
il gèle, *it's freezing*
il tonne, *it's thundering*
il fait du vent, *it's windy*
il fait du brouillard, *it's foggy*
il fait beau, *it's fine*
il fait mauvais, *the weather's bad*
il fait chaud/froid, *it's hot/cold*

☐ **Être** used with time of day

il est cinq heures, *it's five o'clock*
il est midi et demi, *it's half past twelve*
il est tard, *it's late*

☐ **Il y a,** *there is, there are*

il y a trente mille personnes dans le stade, *there are thirty thousand people in the stadium*

Il y a is always singular.

▶ **Il y a** can also be used with **devoir** and **pouvoir**: **il peut y avoir ...**, *there may be ...* See pp. 67 and 69.

□ A large number of other impersonal expressions, of which some of the commonest are:

> **il s'agit de**, *it's a question of; it's about*
> **il m'est arrivé de**, *I happened to*
> **il faut (que)**, *you (we, they, etc.) must/need*
> **il paraît que**, *it appears that*
> **il semble que**, *it seems that*
> **il suffit de**, *you only have to*
> **il vaut mieux**, *it's better to*

Notice also

> **il était une fois**, *once upon a time*

■ **Il** to hold back the real subject

Any verb can be used in this way; it remains singular, agreeing with **il**, even if the real subject is plural:

> **il pousse beaucoup de fleurs au Sahara**, *there are lots of flowers (that grow) in the Sahara*
> **il reste encore dix minutes**, *there are ten minutes still left*
> **il me manque de l'argent comptant**, *I need ready cash* (literally: *there is lacking to me ready cash*)

□ The real subject may be a noun, as in the examples above; or it may be a clause

> **il me brûlait les lèvres de demander à quoi ça servait**, *I was dying to ask what that was for*

□ The real subject may be an infinitive clause, following an adjective plus **de**. The pattern is: **il est** + adjective + **de** + infinitive clause

> **il est difficile de concevoir quelque chose de plus imposant**, *it is difficult to conceive of anything more impressive*

In spoken French **c'est** is often used instead of **il est** in this construction.

☐ The real subject may be a clause introduced by **que**, following an adjective. The pattern is: **il est** + adjective + **que** + clause

> **il est évident qu'elle mange trop**, *it's obvious that she eats too much*

Here too, **c'est** is often used instead of **il est** in spoken French.

Impersonal verbs with ce or cela/ça as subject

Ce (*it*) is used as the subject of **être**, and **cela/ça** (*it, that*) as the subject of any verb (including **être**), to stand for a previously expressed clause:

> **il est facile de mentir — Ah oui, c'est facile**, *it's easy to tell lies—Oh yes, it's easy* (**c'** refers back to **de mentir**)
>
> **si elle ment, c'est qu'elle ne veut pas vous parler de Jean-Claude**, *if she's lying, it's because she doesn't want to talk to you about Jean-Claude* (**c'** refers back to **si elle ment**)
>
> **tout ce que j'ai dit me paraît évident — Oui, cela prouve que tu es fou!**, *everything I've said seems obvious to me—Yes, that proves you're crazy!* (**cela** refers back to **tout ce que j'ai dit me paraît évident**)

C'est + adjective is also used extremely often in spoken French instead of **il est** + adjective:

> **c'est** (for: **il est**) **facile de mentir — Ah oui, c'est facile**

Articles

Articles are words like *a* and *the*. Nouns are rarely used without an article in French. If the noun has no article in English, it is most likely to have a definite article in French. There are, however, quite a number of exceptions to this—see below.

THE DEFINITE ARTICLE

The definite article (*the* in English) has four forms, **le**, **la**, or **l'** with singular nouns, **les** with plural nouns. **Le** is used before a masculine singular noun, **la** before a feminine singular noun, **l'** before a singular noun of either gender beginning with a vowel or **h** 'mute'*. **Les** is used before a plural noun of either gender:

> **le garçon**, *the boy*; **la fille**, *the girl*; **le haricot**, *the bean*
> **l'homme**, *the man*; **l'arbre**, *the tree*
> **les garçons**, *the boys*; **les filles**, *the girls*; **les haricots**, *the beans*;
> **les hommes**, *the men*; **les arbres**, *the trees*

Le and **les** compound with **à** and **de** to produce **au**, **aux** (*to the*) and **du**, **des** (*of the*), thus:

---

* In older French some **h**'s were pronounced and some were not, which accounts for **le haricot** and **l'homme**. There is no pronunciation difference in modern French (no **h**'s are pronounced), and there are no rules to decide whether an **h** is 'mute' or not.

$$à + le = au \qquad de + le = du$$
$$à + les = aux \qquad de + les = des$$

A la and **à l'**, **de la** and **de l'** do not change.

The same changes are found in the compound words **auquel, auxquels, auxquelles** (*to whom*; *to which*) and **duquel, desquels, desquelles** (*of whom*; *of which*).

Using the definite article

The definite article is used in French in a number of places where we should omit it in English.

■ When generalizing:

> **aimez-vous les animaux?**, *do you like animals?*
> (i.e. animals in general)

■ With abstract nouns:

> **c'est comme ça, la vie**, *life's like that*
> **l'amour de la patrie**, *love of country*

But not with abstract nouns after **avec** and **sans**:

> **avec difficulté**, *with difficulty*
> **sans occupation**, *unemployed*

■ With parts of the body, especially when used as the object of a verb:

> **levez le bras**, *raise your arm*

A reflexive indirect object pronoun is added in this construction when the action is done to, rather than with, the part of the body mentioned:

> **elle s'est lavé le visage**, *she has washed her face*

■ With names preceded by adjective or titles:

> **le très petit Jean-Pierre**, *tiny little Jean-Pierre*
> **le président Mitterrand**, *President Mitterrand*

■ With names of countries, areas, mountains, lakes:

> **l'Angleterre**, *England*; **la Corse**, *Corsica* (but **en Angleterre, d'Angleterre**, *in/from England*; **en Corse, de Corse**, *in/from Corsica*); **le Mont-Blanc**, *Mont Blanc*; **le lac Trasimène**, *Lake Trasimeno*

■ With names of languages:

> **j'apprends le français**, *I'm learning French*
> **tu parles bien le français**, *you speak French well*

The article is omitted, however, after **parler** where the name of the language follows without any other qualification:

> **il parle français**, *he speaks French*

■ With days, mealtimes, seasons, religious festivals:

> **je déteste le lundi**, *I hate Monday(s)*
> **tu prends le petit déjeuner?**, *do you want breakfast?*
> **c'est l'hiver qui revient**, *winter's back*
> **le vendredi saint**, *Good Friday*
> **la Toussaint**, *All Saints' Day* (but the article is omitted with **Pâques**, *Easter*, and often with **Noël**, *Christmas*)

■ With school subjects and games:

> **aimes-tu les maths?**, *do you like maths?*
> **ici, on joue au rugby**, *here they play rugby*
> **il déteste les sports**, *he hates games*

Definite article for indefinite article

The definite article is used in a number of places where we should use the indefinite article (*a, an*).

■ When expressing quantity after price:

douze francs le kilo, *twelve francs a kilo*
cent francs la bouteille, *a hundred francs a bottle*

■ When expressing speed:

cent vingt kilomètres à l'heure, *120 km an hour*
(note the addition of **à** in French)

■ French also uses a definite article in a number of set expressions where in English we should use an indefinite article or no article at all:

il s'est couché le dernier/le premier, *he went to bed last/first*
l'un d'eux, *one of them*
au lit, *in bed*
au régime, *on a diet*
à la maison, *at home*
à l'école, *at school*
à l'église, *in church*

Omission of the definite article

The definite article is omitted in French in forming an attributive noun (a noun used as an adjective):

du pâté de campagne, *country pâté*
un tronc d'arbre, *a tree trunk*
les fromages de France, *French cheeses*

Compare these with:

un goût de la campagne, *a taste of the countryside*
le tronc de l'arbre, *the trunk of the tree*
le nord de la France, *the north of France*

THE INDEFINITE AND PARTITIVE ARTICLES

It is convenient to consider these two forms of article together, since there is much similarity in their use in French.

The indefinite article, what it is

The indefinite article (*a, an, some/any* in English) has three forms: **un** with masculine singular nouns, **une** with feminine singular nouns, **des** with plural nouns:

> **un garçon**, *a boy*; **une fille**, *a girl*; **un haricot**, *a bean*
> **un homme**, *a man*; **un arbre**, *a tree*
> **des garçons**, *some boys*; **des arbres**, *some trees*

The partitive article, what it is

The partitive article (*some* in English, or *any* in questions and after negatives) has three forms, **du, de la**, and **de l'**. They are used before singular 'uncountable' nouns, i.e. nouns like *milk, sugar*, etc. that cannot normally be used in the plural. **Du** is used before a masculine noun, **de la** before a feminine noun, **de l'** before a noun of either gender beginning with a vowel or **h** 'mute':

> **du chocolat**, *some chocolate*
> **de la confiture**, *some jam*
> **de l'argent**, *some money*

The partitive is sometimes said to have a plural form, **des**. Strictly speaking, however, **des** is the plural of the indefinite article: the singular of **des vins** is **un vin**, not **du vin**.

Du/de la/des or le/la/les?

English sometimes does not use any article at all before nouns:

> **vous prenez du lait?**, *do you take milk?*
> **je déteste le lait**, *I hate milk*

This raises the problem of whether to use **du/de la/des** or **le/la/les** where English has a noun with no article. **Du/de la/des** particularizes, **le/la/les** generalizes: **du/de la/des** means 'some', **le/la/les** implies 'all'. So:

> **vous avez du jus d'orange?**, *do you have orange juice?* (i.e., some orange juice)
>
> **j'aime le jus d'orange**, *I like orange juice* (i.e., orange juice in general, all orange juice)
>
> **il y a des mouches dans ma soupe**, *there are flies in my soup* (some flies, not all the flies that exist)
>
> **je n'aime pas les mouches**, *I don't like flies* (all flies, any flies at all, not just some flies)

De for des, etc.

■ After a negative the indefinite article (**un/une/des**) and the partitive article (**du/de la/de l'**) become **de** (**d'** before a vowel or **h** 'mute'). English may use *any* for this:

> **j'ai du temps**, *I have time*
>
> **je n'ai pas de temps**, *I've no time* (*I haven't any time*)
>
> **il n'y a pas de pellicule dans l'appareil**, *there isn't any film in the camera*
>
> **je n'ai pas d'appareil**, *I don't have* (*haven't got*) *a camera*

Ne ... que is not regarded as negative as far as this rule is concerned:

> **je n'ai qu'un très vieil appareil**, *I've only a very old camera*

A negative *is* followed by an indefinite or partitive article if what is negated is the identity of the noun:

> **ce n'est pas un train, c'est un tramway**, *it isn't a train, it's a tram*

■ The plural indefinite article **des** becomes **de** (**d'** before a vowel or **h** 'mute') when the noun following is preceded by an adjective:

> **j'ai eu d'incroyables difficultés**, *I've had unbelievable difficulties*

This rule is often ignored where the meaning of the phrase centres on the noun rather than the adjective:

> **des jolies filles**, *pretty girls*

It is always ignored where the adjective + noun pair forms a set expression:

> **des petits pois**, *peas*
> **des petits pains**, *bread rolls*

Before the adjective **autres**, however, you must keep to **d'**:

> **d'autres voyageurs ont dit ...**, *other travellers have said ...*

■ After the preposition **de** (*of*) the partitive article **du/ de la/de l'** and the plural indefinite article **des** are always omitted:

> **j'ai besoin d'argent**, *I need* (*some*) *money*
> **c'était un grand cratère plein d'eau**, *it was a great crater full of* (*some*) *water*

This means that expressions of quantity, which all incorporate the preposition **de** (*of*), omit **du/de la/de l'/ des**:

> **un verre de vin**, *a glass of wine*
> **beaucoup de vin**, *a lot of wine*

But note that the definite article, meaning *the*, is NOT omitted in such cases:

je prendrai un verre du vin que vous avez là sur le buffet, *I'll have a glass of the wine you've got there on the sideboard*

Nor is the indefinite article in the singular omitted:

donnez-moi deux verres d'un vin doux naturel, *let me have two glasses of a dessert wine*

The expressions of quantity **encore** (*more*) and **bien** (*many*) are intensifying adverbs not incorporating the preposition **de** and are followed by **du/de la/des**:

encore du pain, s'il vous plaît!, *more bread please!*
bien des gens disent cela, *many people say that*

Omission of the indefinite article

The indefinite article is omitted in French in the following cases where, in the singular, it would be used in English.

■ In apposition (i.e., where a second noun is placed directly after a first one in order to explain it):

M. Duval, ancien combattant de la guerre de quatorze-dix-huit, *M. Duval, a veteran of the 14–18 war*

Definite articles, however, are not dropped in apposition:

M. Duval, l'ancien combattant dont nous parlons, *M. Duval, the veteran we're speaking about*

■ After **il est/elle est/**NOUN **est**, followed by the name of a profession:

il est menuisier, *he's a joiner*
son fils est avocat, *his son's a lawyer*

But not after **c'est**:

> **c'est un menuisier**, *he's a joiner*

■ After **quel!**:

> **quel imbécile!**, *what a fool!*

■ After **sans**:

> **les voyageurs sans billet**, *passengers without a ticket*

The partitive article is also omitted in this case, as in English:

> **une journée sans vin est une journée sans soleil**, *a day without wine is a day without sunshine*

■ In lists, both the indefinite article and the partitive article may be omitted, as in English:

> **on y voyait des moutons**, *sheep could be seen there*

but:

> **on y voyait moutons, vaches, porcs, poules, tous pêle-mêle**, *sheep, cattle, pigs, chickens could be seen there, all higgledy piggledy*

> **on nous offrait du mouton**, *we were offered lamb*

but:

> **on nous offrait mouton, porc, veau, bœuf ... toutes sortes de viandes**, *we were offered lamb, pork, veal, beef—all kinds of meat*

This use is rather literary.

Nouns

GENDER OF NOUNS

English has three genders: masculine, feminine, and neuter (*he, she, it*). French has only two: masculine and feminine. Most nouns denoting male people are masculine, most denoting female people are feminine. Names of inanimate objects may be either masculine or feminine. Unlike English nouns, French nouns make their gender obvious by means of the article in front of them and the adjectives that go with them.

The rules for gender in French are very far from watertight and there are many exceptions to all of them. As an overall rule of thumb for an unknown noun: if it ends in **-e** it is more likely to be feminine, if not it is more likely to be masculine.

Masculine groups

■ Workers, traders, animals, names of males are masculine:

> **le constructeur**, *builder*; **le boulanger**, *baker*; **le lion**, *lion*; **le fils**, *son*

Many but not all of these also have feminine forms: see p. 93. **Une autruche** (*ostrich*), **la baleine** (*whale*), **la girafe** (*giraffe*), **la panthère** (*panther*), **la souris** (*mouse*), **la fourmi** (*ant*) are always feminine.

■ Days, months, seasons, weights, measures, numerals, fractions, points of the compass, languages are masculine:

> **le vendredi**, *Friday*; **(le) janvier**, *January*; **le printemps**, *spring*; **le kilo**, *kilo*; **le kilomètre**, *kilometre*; **le douze**, *twelve*; **le quart**, *quarter*; **le sud**, *south*; **le français**, *French*

Exceptions: **la livre**, *pound*; **la tonne**, *(metric) ton*; **la moitié**, *half*

■ Trees, shrubs, metals are masculine:

> **le hêtre**, *beech*; **le laurier**, *laurel*; **le fer**, *iron*

Exceptions: **la bruyère**, *heather*; **la ronce**, *bramble*; **une aubépine**, *hawthorn*

■ Countries, rivers, vegetables and fruit not ending **-e** are masculine:

> **le Japon**, *Japan*; **le Nil**, *Nile*; **le chou**, *cabbage*; **le citron**, *lemon*

■ Most nouns of English origin are masculine:

> **le baby-foot**, *pin-table football*; **le hit-parade**, *hit parade*

Exception: **une interview**, *interview*

■ Words not normally nouns, when used as nouns, are masculine:

> **un joli rose**, *a pretty pink*
> **un oui suivi d'un non**, *a yes followed by a no*
> **on peut apporter son manger**, *you may bring your own food*

Exception: adjectives and participles used as nouns have the gender that their ending shows. So: **le passant, la passante**, *passer-by*; **une allée**, *path*; **la nouvelle**, *piece of news*; **la sortie**, *way out*

■ Nouns with the following endings are masculine:

-acle and **-icle**:

le spectacle, *show*; **un article**, *article*

-age:

le garage

Exceptions: **la cage**, *cage*; **une image**, *picture*;
la nage, *swimming*; **la page**, *page*; **la plage**,
beach; **la rage**, *rage, rabies*

-ail:

le travail, *work*

-asme and **-isme**:

le sarcasme, *sarcasm*; **le communisme**,
communism

-c:

le lac, *lake*

-é:

le péché, *sin*

-eau:

le bateau, *boat*

Exceptions: **une eau**, *water*; **la peau**, *skin*

-ège:

le collège, *secondary school*

-ème:

le poème, *poem*

Exception: **la crème**, *cream*

-er and **-ier**:

le clocher, *steeple*; **le papier**, *paper*

Exceptions: **la mer**, *sea*; **la cuiller**, *spoon* (also
spelled, and always pronounced, **cuillère**)

-ment:

le sentiment, *sentiment*

Exception: **la jument**, *mare*

-oir:

le couloir, *corridor*

-ou:

le trou, *hole*

■ Concrete nouns ending **-eur** are masculine:

>**le moteur**, *engine*

Abstract nouns ending **-eur** are feminine: **la grandeur**, *greatness*

■ Common traps! The following nouns ending **-e** look extremely feminine—they are all masculine:

>**le crime**, *crime*; **le disque**, *record*; **le groupe**, *group*; **le manque**, *lack*; **le mélange**, *mixture*; **le reste**, *remainder*; **le risque**, *risk*; **le silence**, *silence*; **le vice**, *vice*

Feminine groups

■ Feminine forms of traders, workers, animals; names of females:

>**la boulangère**, *baker*; **une électricienne**, *electrician*; **la lionne**, *lioness*; **la fille**, *girl*

Many feminine forms, for historical reasons, do not exist; many others (like **l'électricienne** above) are being newly coined; some (e.g. **la mairesse**, *mayoress*, i.e., *mayor's wife*) can still only refer to the wife of the male. In the animals group, no feminine forms exist of **un éléphant**, *elephant*, **un hippopotame**, *hippopotamus*, **le vautour**, *vulture*.

▶ See also p. 93 for the formation of feminine nouns.

■ Countries, rivers, vegetables and fruit ending **-e** are feminine:

>**la Hollande**, *Holland*; **la Tamise**, *Thames*; **la poire**, *pear*; **la carotte**, *carrot*; **la marguerite**, *daisy*

Exceptions: **le Mexique**, *Mexico*; **le Danube**; **le Rhône**; **le légume**, *vegetable*

■ Shops and trades, arts and sciences, religious festivals
are feminine:

> **la boucherie**, *butcher's*; **la menuiserie**, *joinery*; **la**
> **sculpture**, *sculpture*; **la chimie**, *chemistry*; **la**
> **Pentecôte**, *Whitsun*; **la Toussaint**, *All Saints' Day*

Exception: **un joyeux Noël**, *happy Christmas* (but **à la**
Noël, short for **à la fête** (*festival*) **de Noël**)

■ Nouns with the following endings are feminine:

> **-ace**:
> > **la grâce**, *grace*
> > Exception: **un espace**, *space*
>
> **-ade**:
> > **la baignade**, *bathing*
> > Exceptions: **le grade**, *grade*; **le stade**, *stadium*
>
> **-ance** (and the similarly pronounced endings
> **-anse, -ence, ense**):
> > **la dépendance**, *dependence*; **la danse**, *dance*;
> > **la conscience**, *conscience*; **la défense**,
> > *defence*
> > Exception: **le silence**, *silence*
>
> **-che**:
> > **la tâche**, *task*
> > Exceptions: **le manche**, *handle*; **le reproche**,
> > *reproach*; **le caniche**, *poodle*
>
> **-ée**:
> > **la matinée**, *morning*
> > Exceptions: **le musée**, *museum*; **le lycée**,
> > *sixth-form college*
>
> **-elle**:
> > **la querelle**, *quarrel*
>
> **-ère**:
> > **la lumière**, *light*
> > Exceptions: **le frère**, *brother*; **le père**, *father*;
> > **le cimetière**, *cemetery*; **le mystère**, *mystery*;
> > **le caractère**, *character*; **le cratère**, *crater*

-esse:

> **la faiblesse**, *weakness*

-ie:

> **la pluie**, *rain*
>
> Exceptions: **le génie**, *genius*; **un incendie**, *fire*;
> **le parapluie**, *umbrella*

-ine and **-une**:

> **la piscine**, *swimming pool*; **la fortune**, *fortune*

-ion:

> **la concentration**, *concentration*
>
> Exceptions: **le camion**, *lorry*; **un espion**, *spy*

-ison (and **-aison**):

> **la prison**, *prison*; **la maison**, *house*

-oire:

> **la foire**, *fair*
>
> Exceptions: **le laboratoire**, *laboratory*; **le**
> **pourboire**, *tip*; **un observatoire**,
> *observatory*; **l'ivoire**, *ivory*

-onne:

> **la couronne**, *crown*

-te (and **-tte**, **-ette**):

> **la date**, *date*; **la patte**, *paw*; **la buvette**, *bar*
>
> Exception: **le squelette**, *skeleton*

-té and **-tié**:

> **la beauté**, *beauty*; **la pitié**, *pity*
>
> Exceptions: **le côté**, *side*; **le comté**, *county*; **le**
> **traité**, *treaty*; **le pâté**, (*meat, fish*) *pâté*

-ure:

> **la nature**, *nature*
>
> Exceptions: **le murmure**, *murmur*; **le mercure**,
> *mercury*

Very many of the above are abstract nouns: most abstract nouns, whatever their endings, are in fact feminine.

■ Abstract nouns ending **-eur** are feminine:

> **la chaleur**, *heat*

> Exceptions: **le bonheur**, *happiness*; **le malheur**, *unhappiness*; **un honneur**, *honour*; **le déshonneur**, *dishonour*; **le labeur**, *labour*

Concrete nouns ending **-eur** are masculine: **le carburateur**, *carburettor*

■ Common traps! The following nouns ending in a consonant look extremely masculine—they are all feminine:

> **la chair**, *flesh*; **la clef**, *key*; **la croix**, *cross*; **la façon**, *way, manner*; **la faim**, *hunger*; **la soif**, *thirst*; **la souris**, *mouse*; **la vis**, *screw*

Nouns with different meanings according to gender

masculine	*feminine*
l'aide, *assistant* (*male*)	**l'aide**, *assistance; assistant* (*female*)
le crêpe, *crêpe*	**la crêpe**, *pancake*
le critique, *critic*	**la critique**, *criticism*
le faux, *forgery*	**la faux**, *scythe*
le livre, *book*	**la livre**, *pound*
le manche, *handle*	**la manche**, *sleeve* (**la Manche**, *English Channel*)
le manœuvre, *labourer*	**la manœuvre**, *manœuvre*
le mémoire, *memorandum*	**la mémoire**, *memory*
le mode, *method; way*	**la mode**, *fashion; manner*
le mort, *dead man*	**la mort**, *death*
le moule, *mould*	**la moule**, *mussel*
un office, *office; religious service*	**une office**, *pantry*

le **page**, *page*(*boy*)	la **page**, *page* (*of a book*)
le **pendule**, pendulum	la **pendule**, *clock*
le **physique**, physique	la **physique**, *physics*
le **poêle**, *stove*	la **poêle**, *frying pan*
le **poste**, *set* (*e.g. TV*); (*military*) *post*; (*fire, police*) *station*	la **poste**, *post* (= *mail*); *post office*
le **somme**, *nap*	la **somme**, *sum*
le **tour**, *trick; tour*	la **tour**, tower
le **trompette**, trumpeter	la **trompette**, *trumpet*
le **vapeur**, *steamer* (*boat*)	la **vapeur**, *steam*
le **vase**, *vase*	la **vase**, *mud; silt*
le **voile**, *veil*	la **voile**, *sail*

Gender of compound nouns

There are many exceptions, but

■ Compounds of two nouns or a noun plus adjective take the gender of the (first) noun:

> le **chou-fleur**, *cauliflower*

■ Compounds where the first element is part of a verb are masculine:

> le **tire-bouchon**, *corkscrew*

■ When in doubt about the gender of a compound noun, choose masculine.

FEMININE OF NOUNS

Professions, positions, nationalities, names of relationships, domestic animals (and a few wild ones) mostly have both masculine and feminine forms according to sex:

le vendeur, *salesman*	**la vendeuse**, *saleswoman*
le Français, *Frenchman*	**la Française**, *Frenchwoman*
le cousin, (*male*) *cousin*	**la cousine**, (*female*) *cousin*
le chien, *dog*	**la chienne**, *bitch*

With professions and positions the feminine form quite often still means *wife of the* ..., though this is not the case with the newer professions:

> **la mairesse**, *mayoress; wife of the mayor*
> **l'informaticienne**, (*female*) *computer programmer*

With animals, where two forms exist, the masculine form is used as the general term; the feminine form is only used where a specific distinction of sex is being made. Exception: **la chèvre** (general term for *goat*; masculine is **le bouc**, *billy-goat*)

■ The regular feminine endings are:

masculine noun	*feminine form*
-e	no change
le Russe, *Russian*	**la Russe**
-er	-ère
un ouvrier, *worker*	**une ouvrière**
-eur	-euse
le dormeur, *sleeper*	**la dormeuse**
-f	-ve
le veuf, *widower*	**la veuve**
-en, -on, -et	-enne, -onne, -ette
le chien, *dog*	**la chienne**
le Breton, *Breton*	**la Bretonne**
le cadet, *junior*	**la cadette**
-teur	-teuse: where the noun is based on the present participle of a verb

-trice: in all other cases

le menteur, *lier*	**la menteuse** (p.p. **mentant**)
le directeur, *director*	**la directrice** (p.p. **dirigeant**)
-x	**-se**
un époux, *spouse, husband*	**une épouse**

With other endings the feminine, where it exists, is formed by adding **-e**:

un ami, *friend*	**une amie**
un Anglais, *Englishman*	**une Anglaise**

■ Nouns with an irregular feminine form:

masculine	*feminine*
un abbé, *abbot*	**une abbesse**
un ambassadeur, *ambassador*	**une ambassadrice**
un âne, *donkey*	**une ânesse**
le canard, *drake*	**la canne**, *duck*
le chat, *cat*	**la chatte**
le comte, *count*	**la comtesse**
le compagnon, *companion*	**la compagne**
le copain, *pal*	**la copine**
le dieu, *god*	**la déesse**
le dindon, *turkey*	**la dinde**
le duc, *duke*	**la duchesse**
un empereur, *emperor*	**une impératrice**
le fils, *son*	**la fille**, *daughter*
le Grec, *Greek*	**la Grecque**
le héros, *hero*	**l'héroïne**
l'hôte, *host*	**l'hôtesse**
un inspecteur, *inspector*	**une inspectrice**
le jumeau, *twin*	**la jumelle**

le loup, *wolf*	la louve
le maître, *master*	la maîtresse
le mulet, *mule*	la mule
le nègre, *negro*	la négresse
le neveu, *nephew*	la nièce
le paysan, *peasant*	la paysanne
le pécheur, *sinner*	la pécheresse
le prêtre, *priest*	la prêtresse
le prince, *prince*	la princesse
le Suisse, *Swiss*	la Suissesse
le tigre, *tiger*	la tigresse
le traître, *traitor*	la traîtresse
le Turc, *Turk*	la Turque

■ Nouns with an entirely different feminine form.

As in English, the feminine form may be expressed by an entirely different word. Among the commonest of these are:

masculine	*feminine*
le cerf, *stag*	la biche, *hind*
le cheval, *horse*	la jument, *mare*
le coq, *cock*	la poule, *hen*
l'étalon, *stallion*	la jument, *mare*
le frère, *brother*	la sœur, *sister*
le garçon, *boy*	la fille, *girl*
l'homme, *man*	la femme, *woman*
le mari, *husband*	la femme, *wife*
l'oncle, *uncle*	la tante, *aunt*
le parrain, *godfather*	la marraine, *godmother*
le père, *father*	la mère, *mother*
le porc, *pig*	la truie, *sow*
le roi, *king*	la reine, *queen*
le serviteur, *servant*	la servante, *servant*
le taureau, *bull*	la vache, *cow*

■ Nouns unchanged in the feminine form:

un/une enfant, *child*

plus masculine nouns ending **-e**.

■ Nouns with only one gender, whatever the sex of the person they refer to:

un ange, *angel*

un amateur, *lover, amateur*

un assassin, *killer*

un auteur, *author*

le cadre, *executive*

la connaissance, *aquaintance*

le député, *MP*

le docteur, *doctor*

la dupe, *dupe*

un écrivain, *writer*

le facteur, *postman*

le guide, *guide*

un imposteur, *imposter*

un ingénieur, *engineer*

le juge, *judge*

le maire, *mayor*

le médecin, *doctor*

le ministre, *minister*

le peintre, *painter*

la personne, *person*

le poète, *poet*

le possesseur, *owner*

le professeur, *(secondary) teacher* (but, slang **le/la prof**)

la recrue, *recruit*

la sentinelle, *sentry*

le spectateur, *spectator*

le soldat, *soldier*

le témoin, *witness*

la vedette, *star*

la victime, *victim*

With professions, a specifically female form can be produced where needed by using **une femme** and adding the name of the profession attributively:

une femme auteur, *woman author, authoress*

Feminine forms of some of the above are now appearing in French (e.g., **une ministre**). They are not yet fully accepted and are at present best avoided.

For names of animals with only one gender (which is most animals), specifically male and female forms can be produced by using the adjectives **mâle, femelle**:

une souris mâle, *a male mouse*

un hamster femelle, *a female hamster*

PLURAL OF NOUNS
Plural formation

French nouns add **-s** to form their plural, except:

- Nouns ending **-s**, **-x**, **-z** remain unchanged:

le tas, *heap*	**les tas**
la croix, *cross*	**les croix**
le nez, *nose*	**les nez**

- Nouns ending **-au**, **-eau**, **-eu** add **-x**:

le tuyau, *drainpipe*	**les tuyaux**
le gâteau, *cake*	**les gâteaux**
le neveu, *nephew*	**les neveux**

Exceptions: **le bleu** (*bruise*) → **les bleus**; **le pneu** (*tyre*) → **les pneus**

- Nouns ending **-al** change their ending to **-aux**:

le journal, *newspaper*	**les journaux**

Exceptions: **le bal** (*dance*) → **les bals**; **le festival** (*festival*) → **les festivals**

- Four nouns ending **-ail** change it to **-aux** instead of adding **-s**:

le corail, *coral*	**les coraux**
l'émail, *enamel*	**les émaux**
le travail, *work*	**les travaux**
le vitrail, *stained-glass window*	**les vitraux**

- Seven nouns ending **-ou** add **-x** instead of **-s**:

le bijou, *jewel*	**les bijoux**
le caillou, *pebble*	**les cailloux**
le chou, *cabbage*	**les choux**
le genou, *knee*	**les genoux**
le hibou, *owl*	**les hiboux**
le joujou, *toy*	**les joujoux**
le pou, *louse*	**les poux**

■ Letter names remain unchanged in the plural:

> **cela s'écrit avec deux p**, *you write it with two p's*

■ Family names usually remain unchanged in the plural; historical names add an **-s**:

> **les Robinson**, *the Robinsons*
> **les Bourbons**, *the Bourbons*

■ Irregular plurals:

l'aïeul, *ancestor*	**les aïeux**
le bonhomme, *fellow*	**les bonshommes**
le ciel, *sky*	**les cieux**
l'œil, *eye*	**les yeux**
madame, *Mrs*	**mesdames**
mademoiselle, *Miss*	**mesdemoiselles**
monsieur, *Mr*	**messieurs**

■ The following nouns have an extra meaning in the plural:

le ciseau, *chisel*	**les ciseaux**, *chisels; scissors*
la lunette, *telescope*	**les lunettes**, *telescopes; spectacles*
la vacance, *vacancy*	**les vacances**, *vacancies; holidays*
la gage, *pledge*	**les gages**, *pledges; wages*
l'affaire, *affair*	**les affaires**, *affairs; business*

Plural of compound nouns

There are many exceptions, but the following rules may help.

■ Compound nouns written as a single word, the plural is **-s**:

le pourboire, *tip*   **les pourboires**

■ Compound nouns formed of an adjective plus a noun
or two nouns, both add **-s**:

la belle-mère, *mother-in-law* **les belles-mères**
le chou-fleur, *cauliflower*   **les choux-fleurs**

■ Compound nouns formed of a noun plus a
prepositional phrase, only the noun adds **-s**:

un arc-en-ciel, *rainbow*   **des arcs-en-ciel**

■ Compound nouns formed of a noun preceded by a
preposition, the plural is the same as the singular:

le hors-d'œuvre, *starter*   **les hors-d'œuvre**

■ Compound nouns formed of a verb plus its object
noun, the noun adds **-s**:

le tire-bouchon, *corkscrew* **les tire-bouchons**
un essuie-glace, *windscreen-* **des essuie-glaces**
wiper

But many compounds of this kind do not change in the
plural:

le coupe-circuit, *circuit-* **les coupe-circuit**
breaker

■ Compound nouns formed without a noun component,
the plural is the same as the singular:

le passe-partout, *master key* **les passe-partout**

Singular for plural

■ Plural (or usually plural) in English, but singular in
French are:

le bétail, *cattle*; **la famille**, *family*; **la police**, *police*

The verb that follows them must be singular:

la famille est à table, *the family are sitting down to a meal*

■ Singular in English, but plural in French are:

les funérailles, *funeral*; **les nouvelles**, *news*; and (usually) **les fiancailles**, *engagement*; **les progrès**, *progress*

The verb that follows them must be plural:

les funérailles sont lundi prochain, *the funeral is next Monday*

Pronouns

SUBJECT PRONOUNS

The subject pronouns are

singular	*plural*
je, *I*	**nous**, *we*
tu, *you*	**vous**, *you*
il, *he, it*; **elle**, *she, it*	**ils**, **elles**, *they*

Je becomes **j'** before a word beginning with a vowel or **h** 'mute'.

■ **Il** is used for a person or a thing when referring to a masculine noun, **elle** when referring to a feminine noun.

■ **Ils** (*they*) is used to refer to more than one masculine (people or things) or a mixture of masculines and feminines, **elles** (*they*) to refer to more than one feminine.

■ **Vous** can be either plural:

> **toi et ta famille, vous êtes déjà allés en Corse?**, *have you and your family already been to Corsica?*

or a formal or polite form of the singular:

> **voulez-vous ouvrir la fenêtre, monsieur?**, *will you please open the window (sir)?*

The polite **vous** is always used to strangers; **tu** is normally used to a close friend or colleague, a relation, a fellow-student. **Tu** is always used to address a child or an animal. Said to a stranger it may be purposely impolite. The same applies of course to all related forms (**ton, le tien**, etc.; **votre, le vôtre**, etc.).

■ The subject pronoun **on** takes the same form of the verb as **il**. It means *one* in the sense of 'people in general', and often corresponds to an indefinite *we* or *they* in English:

> **on part à trois heures trente-six**, *we leave at 3.36*
> **on écrit des choses vraiment incroyables**, *they write some really unbelievable things*

In spoken French **on** is almost always used instead of **nous**:

> **où on va ce soir?**, *where are we going tonight?*

On may be seen as feminine or plural when agreements are made, but it does not have to be:

> **ton père et moi, on était si fatigué(s)**, *we were so tired, your father and I*

▶ **On** is frequently used in French instead of the passive. See pp. 33, 34.

■ **Ce** (*this, that, it, those*) is used as an impersonal subject pronoun, but only with the verb **être**. In the plural **ce** is used with a plural form of **être** (**ce sont**, **c'étaient**, etc.):

> **c'est une Citroën**, *it's a Citroën*
> **ce sont des mouettes**, *those are seagulls*

With verbs other than **être** (and sometimes with **être** too), **cela** or the less formal **ça** is used:

> **ça (cela) ne se voit pas**, *that's (it's) not obvious*

▶ See also pp. 75, 76, and 225 for the use of **c'est** or **il est** + adjective and p. 84 and p. 224 for **c'est** or **il est** + noun.

▶ The stressed or disjunctive pronouns, **moi**, **toi**, etc. may also be used as subject pronouns in some circumstances. See p. 110.

OBJECT PRONOUNS

Forms of the object pronouns

■ The direct object pronouns are:

singular	*plural*
me, *me*	**nous**, *us*
te, *you*	**vous**, *you*
le, *him, it*; **la**, *her, it*	**les**, *them*

■ The indirect object pronouns are:

singular	*plural*
me, *to me*	**nous**, *to us*
te, *to you*	**vous**, *to you*
lui, *to him, to her, to it*	**leur**, *to them*

English often omits the *to* of the indirect object: *give it (to) me*. If you are not clear whether an English object without a *to* is indirect or not, simply insert the *to* and see if the sentence still makes sense.

■ The reflexive object pronouns are the same whether direct or indirect. They are:

singular	*plural*
me, (*to*) *myself*	**nous**, (*to*) *ourselves*
te, (*to*) *yourself*	**vous**, (*to*) *yourself/yourselves*
se, (*to*) *him-/her-/itself*	**se**, (*to*) *themselves*

▶ For the use of the reflexive pronouns see p. 30.

■ **Me, te, le, la, se** become **m', t', l', l', s'** before a vowel or **h** 'mute'.

Me and **te** become **moi** and **toi** in the positive imperative (**m'** and **t'** before a vowel). See p. 28 (formation of the imperative) and p. 106 (pronouns with the imperative).

■ **Y** (*to it, there*) and **en** (*of it, some*) are also treated as object pronouns. See p. 107.

Position of object pronouns

Object pronouns stand immediately before the verb (this includes infinitives, present participles, **voici** and **voilà**):

> **je t'explique le problème**, *I'll explain the problem to you*
>
> **je vais t'expliquer le problème**, *I'm going to explain the problem to you*
>
> **en t'expliquant le problème, j'éclaircirai tout**, *by explaining the problem to you, I'll make everything clear*
>
> **le voilà, le problème**, *that's it, that's the problem*

In the compound tenses they stand immediately before the auxiliary verb (**avoir** or **être**):

> **l'as-tu trouvé?**, *have you found it?*
>
> **je l'ai trouvé dans l'armoire**, *I found it in the cupboard*

Since they stand immediately before the verb, object pronouns follow the **ne** of a negative:

je ne l'ai pas trouvé, *I haven't found it*

▶ For the position of object pronouns with the imperative, see below.

Order of object pronouns

Where two object pronouns appear together they stand in this order:

me				
te	**le**			
se	**la**	**lui**		
nous	**les**	**leur**	**y**	**en**
vous				

je te l'apporte, *I'll bring it to you*
elle le lui a emprunté, *she's borrowed it from him*
il n'y en a pas, *there isn't any*

Pronouns from the first and third columns cannot appear together. In the rare cases where this would happen the dative object is expressed by **à** + a disjunctive pronoun:

on va vous présenter à elles, *we're going to introduce you to them* (not **'vous leur'**)

Order of pronouns with the imperative

■ With the negative imperative the order of pronouns is as above:

ne me l'explique pas!, *don't explain it to me!*

■ With the positive imperative, object pronouns follow the verb, are hyphenated to it and to each other, and stand in the following order:

	moi, m'		
	toi, t'		
le	lui		
la	nous	y	en
les	vous		
	leur		

So:

> **donne-les-lui**, *give them to him*
> **donnez-la-leur**, *give it to them*

Me and **te** become **moi** and **toi** in the positive imperative; before **en** they become **m'** and **t'** and are not followed by a hyphen:

> **donne-les-moi**, *give them to me*
> **donne-m'en**, *give me some*

The pronouns y and en

■ **Y** stands for **à, sur** or **dans** + a thing or things. In this sense it usually means *to, at, in it/them*:

> **je m'y oppose formellement**, *I'm absolutely opposed to it*
> **il ne s'y intéresse pas du tout**, *he's not in the least interested in it*

It can also mean *there*, in which case it is really an adverb, though it still behaves as an object pronoun as far as its position in the sentence is concerned:

> **on y sera bien ombragé**, *we'll be in the shade there*

■ **En** stands for **de** + a thing or things. In this sense it usually means *of, with, from it/them*:

> **nous en parlerons demain**, *we'll speak of it tomorrow*

> **trois voyageurs en sont descendus**, *three passengers got out of it*

It often means *of it*, *of them* with an expression of quantity:

> **j'en ai beaucoup**, *I've got a lot of it*
> **il y en a trois**, *there are three of them*

With expressions of quantity English frequently drops *of it/them*. This is impossible in French—the **en** must always be there:

> **il faudra en remplacer un**, *you'll have to replace one* (*of them*)

With expressions of quantity, **en** can also stand for **de** + persons:

> **combien de frères as-tu? — J'en ai trois**, *how many brothers have you?—I've got three*

En can also mean *some* or *any*:

> **tu en as? Alors, donne-m'en**, *have you got any? Well, give me some*

Object pronouns to complete the sense

We have an example above (**il faudra en remplacer un**) of **en** used to complete the sense in French where in English *of it/them* is often omitted. This also occurs with the pronouns **le** (= *it*) and **y**:

> **je te l'ai dit**, *I told you* (*so*)
> **vous êtes la fille de cet homme? — Non, je ne le suis pas**, *you are this man's daughter?—No, I'm not* (*it*)
> **oui, j'y vais**, *all right, I'm going* (*there*)
> **elle sera déjà partie, je le sais**, *she'll have gone, I know* (*it*)

However, with **savoir** this **le** may be dropped in a simple response to a statement:

> **elle est là — Oui, je (le) sais**, *she's there—Yes, I know*

DISJUNCTIVE PRONOUNS

The disjunctive, or stressed, pronouns are those that stand separated from ('disjoined from') verbs. There are no separate forms for these pronouns in English, ordinary subject or object pronouns being used. In French the disjunctive pronouns are:

moi, *me*		**nous**, *us*	
toi, *you*		**vous**, *you*	
lui, *him*		**eux**, *them* (masculine)	
elle, *her*		**elles**, *them* (feminine)	

The disjunctive corresponding to **on** is **soi**. It means *oneself, yourself*, and is only used after a preposition or **que** (see below). **Soi** in fact is the disjunctive that corresponds to all the indefinite pronouns (**chacun, tout le monde, personne**, etc.). See p. 127.

Disjunctives usually only refer to people, not to things. For the corresponding usage with things, see p. 112.

Use of the disjunctive pronouns

■ Disjunctives may stand completely alone in response to a question or statement:

> **qui l'a pris? — Moi!**, *who's taken it?—Me!*
> **tu l'as pris! — Moi?**, *you've taken it!—(What) me?*

■ They are used after prepositions:

> **comme nous**, *like us*
> **la plupart d'entre elles**, *most of them*
> **c'est à moi**, *it's mine* (*it belongs to me*)
> **chacun pour soi**, *each one for himself*

■ The preposition **à** plus a disjunctive pronoun is used with certain verbs instead of an indirect object, to refer to people. These verbs are:

> **penser/songer à**, *think about*
> **avoir affaire à**, *have business with; deal with*
> **prendre garde à**, *beware of*
>
> **je pense à toi**, *I'm thinking of you*

A disjunctive after **à** is also used with **venir** and **aller** where movement in space is indicated:

> **elle est venue volontiers à moi**, *she came to me willingly*

but not otherwise:

> **ce kilt ne te va pas du tout**, *that kilt really doesn't suit you*

■ Disjunctive pronouns are used to specify the individual parts of a plural subject. A subject pronoun may or may not appear as well:

> **eux et moi, on se voit souvent**, *they and I see each other a lot*
> **les enfants et lui se taquinent toujours**, *he and the children always tease each other*
> **qui l'a fait, lui ou son copain?**, *who did it, he or his pal?*

■ They are used to give a subject or object pronoun more emphasis:

> **moi, je ne suis pas d'accord**, *I don't agree*
> **je ne l'aime pas du tout, lui**, *I don't like **him** at all*

■ They are used after **c'est, c'était**, etc. In this sense the disjunctives may refer to things as well as people:

> **c'est toi?** *it's you?*
> **c'est eux/elles!**, *it's them!*

In careful speech or writing **ce sont eux/elles** is used.

■ They are used after **que** in comparatives and after **ne ... que**, *only*, and **ne ... ni ... ni**, *neither ... nor*:

> **elle est plus jolie que moi**, *she's prettier than me*
> **on parle toujours des choses qui n'intéressent que soi**, *we always talk about things that only interest ourselves*

■ They are used before a relative pronoun:

> **lui, qui ne sait absolument rien, a été promu capitaine**, *he, who knows absolutely nothing, has been promoted captain*
> **elle m'aime, moi qui n'ai pas un sou**, *she loves me, I who haven't a penny*

This usage is rather literary.

■ They are used instead of subject pronouns with **aussi** and **seul**:

> **lui seul est resté dans la chambre**, *he alone remained in the room*
> **eux aussi l'ont essayé**, *they tried it too*

■ They combine with **-même** to produce emphatic forms:

moi-même, *myself*	**nous-mêmes**, *ourselves*
toi-même, *yourself*	**vous-même(s)**, *yourself*; *yourselves*
lui-même, *himself*	**eux-mêmes**, *themselves*
elle-même, *herself*	**elles-mêmes**,
soi-même, *onself* etc.	*themselves*

> **tu l'as vraiment fait toi-même?**, *you really did it
> (all by) yourself?*

Substitutes for the disjunctive pronouns

The disjunctive pronouns are not normally used to refer
to things. For a preposition + *it/them* an adverb is
substituted:

> **sur lui → dessus**, *on it*
> **dans lui → dedans**, *in it*
> **derrière lui → derrière**, *behind it*
> **après lui → après**, *after it*
> **à côté de lui → à côté**, *beside it*
> etc.
>
> **qu'est-ce qu'il y a dessus? Et dedans?**, *what's on
> it? And in it?*

Alternatively a demonstrative pronoun may be used:

> **je n'ai jamais eu une moto comme celle-là**, *I've
> never had a bike like it*
> **cela seul est resté sur la table**, *it alone remained
> on the table*

RELATIVE PRONOUNS

Relative pronouns introduce a clause within the sentence
and usually relate it back to a noun in the main clause. In
English they are *who, whom, whose, which, that, what*. In
French they are:

> **qui**, *who, which, that*
> **que**, *whom, which, that*
>
> **ce qui, ce que**, *what*
>
> **lequel**, *which*
>
> **de qui** or **dont**, *of whom, whose*

> **duquel** or **dont**, *of which, whose*
> **à qui**, *to whom*
> **auquel**, *to which*

and the less common

> **ce dont**, *that of which*
> **ce à quoi**, *that to which*

Que and **ce que** become **qu'** and **ce qu'** before a vowel. **Qui** and **ce qui** never change.

Relatives are sometimes omitted in English. In French this is not possible and it is important to recognize that a sentence like 'the man you want to see is here' has a hidden relative (*who* or *that*):

> **le client que tu voulais voir est là**, *the customer (that/who) you wanted to see is here*

Qui and que

■ **Qui** is the subject of the clause it introduces, **que** is the direct object:

> **la femme qui parle**, *the woman who is speaking*
> **la femme que tu connais**, *the woman (that) you know*

So **que** will be followed by a subject noun or pronoun (**tu** above), and **qui** will be followed by a verb, possibly preceded by **ne** and/or an object pronoun.

■ **Que** may not be the object of the verb it introduces but of an infinitive depending on that verb. This is similar to English:

> **la femme que tu espères épouser**, *the woman that you hope to marry* (you hope to marry her, you don't 'hope' her, so **que** is actually the object of **épouser**, not of **espères**)

■ After **que** a noun subject and the verb are often inverted if nothing else follows in that clause:

> **voilà la liste que demande l'inspecteur**, *here's the list the inspector is asking for*

This does not happen with pronoun subjects, or if something else follows in the clause:

> **voilà la liste que vous demandez**, *here's the list you're asking for*
>
> **voilà la liste que l'inspecteur a demandée hier**, *here's the list the inspector asked for yesterday*

■ Beware! As well as being a relative, meaning *who*, *which*, *that*, **que** may also be a conjunction meaning *that* (this too may be omitted in English):

> **j'espère que tu te portes bien**, *I hope (that) you are well*

and it may also be part of a comparison, meaning *than*:

> **il est plus grand que toi**, *he's bigger than you*

Que = *what*, **qui** = *who*, and **lequel** = *which* may also introduce questions; here the question mark makes their meaning clear:

> **que dis-tu?**, *what are you saying?*

▶ See p. 118.

■ In order to avoid ambiguity **lequel** may sometimes be used instead of **qui/que**. This is because **lequel** shows gender and number:

> **j'ai écrit au père de sa femme, lequel est très riche**, *I've written to his wife's father, who is very rich*

▶ For the declension of **lequel** see p. 116.

Relative pronouns after prepositions

■ After prepositions **qui** is used for people (English *whom* or *that*). So *with/without/under whom* is **avec/sans/ sous qui**:

> **la femme avec qui je parle**, *the woman to whom I'm speaking* (*that I'm speaking to*)

Notice that in English (as in the bracketed version above) we try to avoid the old-fashioned and formal word *whom*. So we often use *that* as the relative and push the preposition to the end of the clause. This is impossible in French: the preposition must come immediately before the relative.

□ After the prepositions **parmi**, *among*, and **entre**, *between*, **lesquels/lesquelles** is used instead of **qui** for people

> **les mineurs parmi lesquels tu vis**, *the miners among whom you live*

▶ For the declension of **lequel** see p. 116.

□ **De + qui** usually becomes **dont**, *whose, of whom*.

The word order after **dont** (or **de qui** or **duquel**) is always subject, verb, rest of clause. This is not the case in English, where the object is placed immediately after the word *whose*:

> **voilà l'homme dont (de qui) tu as volé la voiture**, *there's the man whose car you stole*

English also drops the definite article (*whose car*) which French does not (**dont ... la voiture**).

Dont is used as the relative (for both people and things) with verbs that have an object preceded by **de**:

> **l'homme dont tu as besoin**, *the man you need* (= *of whom you have need*)

■ After prepositions **lequel** is used for things. So *with/ without/under which* is **avec/sans/sous lequel**. **Lequel** declines as follows:

	singular	*plural*
masculine	**lequel**	**lesquels**
feminine	**laquelle**	**lesquelles**

Lequel agrees in gender and number with the noun it refers back to.

□ **Lequel** combines with the prepositions **à** and **de** to produce the forms **auquel, auxquels, à laquelle, auxquelles** and **duquel, desquels, de laquelle, desquelles**

> **les autorités auxquelles j'écris**, *the authorities I'm writing to*
>
> **le pays duquel je parle**, *the country I'm speaking about*

However, the simpler word **dont**, *of which, whose*, is often substituted for **duquel** etc.

> **le pays dont je parle**, *the country I'm speaking of*
>
> **la voiture dont il a volé la radio**, *the car whose radio he stole*

Similarly, **où**, *where*, is often used instead of **auquel, dans lequel**, **sur lequel**, etc. where the meaning allows it:

> **la maison où (dans laquelle) il passe sa vie**, *the house where* (*in which*) *he spends his life*

▶ See p. 115 for the word order after **dont** and **duquel**.

■ In English *whose* can be used after a preposition: *the nurse, without whose efforts I shouldn't be here.* **Dont** cannot be used in this way in French: **de qui / duquel** must be used instead:

> **cette infirmière, sans les soins de qui je ne serais plus ici, ne travaille plus dans cet hôpital**, *that nurse, without whose efforts I should no longer be here, doesn't work in this hospital any more*

This construction is often clumsy in French, however, and is usually avoided:

> **sans les soins de cette infirmière, je ne serais plus ici; mais elle ne travaille plus dans cet hôpital**, *without that nurse's efforts I should no longer be here today; but she doesn't work in this hospital any more*

Ce qui, ce que, ce dont, ce à quoi

■ *What* as a relative is **ce qui** or **ce que**, **ce qui** being the subject form and **ce que** the object form, as with **qui** and **que**. These relative pronouns introduce noun clauses:

> **je ne comprends pas ce que tu dis**, *I don't understand what you're saying*

If the main verb following a noun clause introduced by **ce qui/ce que** is **être**, a comma and **ce** are introduced, like this:

> **ce qui est difficile, c'est de jouer de la cornemuse**, *what's difficult is playing the bagpipes*

This construction is extremely common.

■ **Ce qui** and **ce que** are used instead of **qui** and **que** as relatives after **tout**, *all, everything*:

> **tout ce que tu dis est incompréhensible**, *everything (that) you say is incomprehensible*

■ **Ce qui** and **ce que** can also mean *which*, where this refers to an idea rather than a specific thing:

> **il va jouer de la cornemuse, ce qui est très difficile**, *he's going to play the bagpipes, which is very difficult* (*which* refers not to bagpipes but to playing them)

After prepositions the form of the relative meaning *which*, and referring back to an idea, is **quoi**:

> **je lui ait tout expliqué, sans quoi il aurait été vraiment fâché**, *I've explained everything to him, without which he would have been really angry* (*which* refers to my having explained things to him)

■ When the verb used in the relative clause takes **à** or **de** before its object, *what* as a relative is **ce à quoi** (**à** verbs) or **ce dont** (**de** verbs):

> **ce à quoi je pense, c'est d'aller jouer à la pétanque**, *what I'm thinking of is going to play pétanque* (the verb is **penser à**)
> **je peux t'envoyer ce dont tu as besoin**, *I can send you what you need* (*what you have need of*) (the verb is **avoir besoin de**)

Ce à quoi and, especially, **ce dont** are only rarely met. **De quoi** is often used instead of the latter:

> **voilà de quoi tu as besoin**, *here's what you need*

INTERROGATIVE PRONOUNS

The interrogative pronouns in English are *who?*, *what?*, and *which?* In English they have the same forms in both direct and indirect questions:

> *who did it?*—direct question
> *I want to know who did it*—indirect question

In French they have somewhat different forms in direct and in indirect questions.

Interrogative pronouns in direct questions

Referring to people

■ As the subject of the sentence the interrogative pronoun referring to people is **qui est-ce qui** or just **qui**. Both mean *who*:

> **qui est-ce qui arrive?**, *who's coming?*
> **qui vous a dit ça?**, *who told you that?*

The interrogative pronoun **qui** is always masculine singular—even if you know that the people who turned up were feminine and plural, you still ask **qui est arrivé?**

■ As the object of the sentence the interrogative pronoun referring to people is **qui est-ce que** or just **qui**. Both mean *who* (in older or formal English, *whom*). The **que** changes to **qu'** before a vowel:

> **qui est-ce qu'on a élu?**, *who did they elect?*
> **qui as-tu envoyé?**, *who did you send?*

■ After a preposition the interrogative pronoun referring to people is **qui est-ce que** or just **qui**. Both mean *who(m)*. The **que** changes to **qu'** before a vowel:

> **pour qui avez-vous fait cela?**, *who did you do it for? (for whom did you do it?)*
> **de qui est-ce que tu parles?**, *who are you talking about? (about whom are you talking?)*

Notice that in English the preposition may (and usually does) go to the end of its clause. This is impossible in French—it must always stand before the interrogative pronoun.

■ The longer forms of the interrogatives are common in speech.

Referring to things

■ As the subject of the sentence the interrogative pronoun referring to things is **qu'est-ce qui**, *what*:

> **qu'est-ce qui arrive?**, *what's happening?*

Notice that there is no alternative form here.

■ As the object of the sentence the interrogative pronoun referring to things is **qu'est-ce que** or just **que**. Both mean *what*. In both, **que** changes to **qu'** before a vowel:

> **qu'est-ce qu'on a trouvé?**, *what did they find?*
> **qu'as-tu fait de mon pullover blanc?**, *what have you done with my white pullover?*

Notice also the form **qu'est-ce que c'est qu'un …?** (sometimes shortened to **qu'est-ce qu'un …?**) meaning *what's a …?*

> **qu'est-ce c'est qu'un ornithorynque?**, *what's a duck-billed platypus?*

■ After a preposition the interrogative pronoun referring to things is **quoi**, *what*:

> **avec quoi as-tu fait cela?**, *what did you do that with? (with what did you do that?)*

■ The longer forms of the interrogatives are common in speech.

Interrogative pronouns in indirect questions

Referring to people

■ The interrogative pronoun in indirect questions referring to people is always **qui**, *who(m)*, whether it is used as subject, object or after a preposition:

> **je ne sais pas qui sera président**, *I've no idea who will be president*

je me demande qui vous allez choisir, *I wonder who you'll choose*

dis-moi à qui tu penses, *tell me who you're thinking of*

Referring to things

■ As the subject of an indirect question, the interrogative pronoun referring to things is **ce qui**, *what*:

je ne sais pas ce qui se passe ici, *I don't know what's happening here*

■ As the object of an indirect question, the interrogative pronoun referring to things is **ce que**, *what*:

explique-moi ce que tu penses, *explain to me what you're thinking*

■ After prepositions, the interrogative pronoun in an indirect question referring to things is **quoi**, *what*:

demande-lui de quoi elle a besoin, *ask her what she needs*

The interrogative pronoun lequel

■ **Lequel** means *which* as an interrogative pronoun. It refers to both people and things and is used in both direct and indirect questions. It agrees with the noun it refers to in gender and number:

	singular	*plural*
masculine	**lequel**	**lesquels**
feminine	**laquelle**	**lesquelles**

Notice that both parts of the word change.

lequel des deux préfères-tu?, *which of the two do you prefer?*

il a répondu à trois questions — lesquelles?, *he's answered three questions—which (ones)?*

> **je ne sais pas lequel des deux je préfère**, *I don't
> know which of the two I prefer*

■ With the prepositions **à** and **de, lequel** forms the
following compounds:

	singular	*plural*
masculine	**auquel, duquel**	**auxquels, desquels**
feminine	**à laquelle, de laquelle**	**auxquelles, desquelles**

> **auquel des trois donnez-vous votre voix?**, *which of
> the three do you give your vote to?*

The interrogative adjective quel

■ The interrogative adjective corresponding to all the
above pronouns is **quel**, *which, what*. **Quel** agrees with
its noun in gender and number:

	singular	*plural*
masculine	**quel**	**quels**
feminine	**quelle**	**quelles**

> **avec quelle main l'as-tu fait?**, *which hand did you
> do it with?*
> **quels gens fréquente-t-il?**, *what (kind of) people
> does he go around with?*
> **je me demande à quel quai ça va arriver**, *I
> wonder which (what) platform it will arrive at*

■ With the verb **être, quel** may be divided from its
noun by the verb:

> **quels sont ces gens?**, *what (kind of) people are
> these? (who are these people?)*

► For questions introduced by other question-words see
p. 212. For the formation of direct and indirect questions
see pp. 211 and 213.

POSSESSIVE PRONOUNS

■ The forms of the possessive pronouns (*mine, yours,* etc. in English) are:

masc. sing.	*fem. sing.*	*masc. plural*	*fem. plural*	
le mien	**la mienne**	**les miens**	**les miennes**	*mine*
le tien	**la tienne**	**les tiens**	**les tiennes**	*yours*
le sien	**la sienne**	**les siens**	**les siennes**	*his, hers, its*
le nôtre	**la nôtre**	**les nôtres**		*ours*
le vôtre	**la vôtre**	**les vôtres**		*yours*
le leur	**la leur**	**les leurs**		*theirs*

> **ma mère et la vôtre sont parties ensemble**, *my mother and yours left together*

With **à**, **le/les** becomes **au/aux**; with **de**, **le/les** becomes **du/des**:

> **cet élève est un des miens**, *this pupil is one of mine*

■ **Le sien, la sienne, les sien(ne)s** do not agree with the *owner* of the object, but with the object itself. So **le sien** means either *his* or *hers*, referring to a masculine object, and **la sienne** means either *his* or *hers* referring to a feminine object:

> **mon argent, je l'ai toujours, mais Marie a dépensé tout le sien**, *I've still got my money, but Marie's spent all hers*

■ The possessive pronoun corresponding to **on** and other indefinite pronouns is **le sien**:

> **on s'occupe des siens**, *you look after your own (people)*

■ *It's mine, it's yours*, etc. may also be translated into French by **c'est à moi, c'est à toi**, etc. This use of

à + disjunctive pronoun is only possible after **être**, where it is extremely common.

There is a slight difference in meaning between **c'est à moi** and **c'est le mien**. **C'est le mien** distinguishes between objects possessed: 'that one is mine, maybe some other is yours'; **c'est à moi** emphasizes the ownership of the object 'that's mine (so give it me!)'.

DEMONSTRATIVE PRONOUNS

The demonstrative pronouns—English *this* (*one*), *that* (*one*), *those*—point things out. In French they are **celui**, *this one here; that one there*, specifying, or **ceci/cela**, *this one/that one*, not specifying.

■ The forms of **celui** are:

	masculine	*feminine*	
singular	**celui**	**celle**	*this, that, the one*
plural	**ceux**	**celles**	*these, those*

They agree in gender and number with the noun they refer to.

■ **Celui** does not stand alone. It may be followed by a preposition, by **qui/que** or by **-ci/-là**.

Celui + preposition

The preposition most frequently found after **celui** is **de**. **Celui de** means *that of* and is the equivalent of the English **'s**:

> **celui de Nicole est cassé**, *Nicole's is broken*
> **la voiture? C'est celle de mon ami**, *the car? It's my friend's*

■ Other prepositions are also found after **celui**:

>**quel tapis? — Celui devant la porte**, *which
carpet?—The one in front of the door*

Celui à is frequently encountered when shopping:

>**quels abricots? — Ceux à neuf francs**, *which
apricots?—The ones at nine francs*

Celui qui, celui que

Celui qui and **celui que** mean *the one who, the one that*
or in the plural *those who, those that*. The **qui** and **que**
are relative pronouns (see p. 112), so **celui qui** is the
subject of its clause and is followed by a verb, **celui que**
is the object and is followed by a pronoun or noun
subject, and then the verb:

>**celle qui habitait à côté de Jean-Luc a déménagé**,
>*the one who lived next to Jean-Luc has moved*
>**lesquels? Ceux que tu trouves difficiles?**, *which?
>Those you find difficult?*

■ The relatives **à qui** and **dont** are also found after
celui when the verb that follows takes **à** or **de**:

>**celui à qui je pense**, *the one I'm thinking of*
>(**penser à**)
>**celle dont tu parles**, *the one you're talking about*
>(**parler de**)

Celui-ci, celui-là

Celui-ci means *this one*, **celui-là** means *that one* when
you are making a specific contrast:

>**celui-ci est bleu, celui-là est plutôt vert**, *this one's
>blue, that one's more green*

Because **là** is often used to mean *here* as well as *there* in modern French, **celui-là** is losing its ability to point to something at a distance when it is not contrasted, as in the example above, with **celui-ci**. To indicate something at a distance, therefore, **celui là-bas**, *that one over there*, is now often used instead of **celui-là**.

■ **Celui-ci** can also mean *the latter*, **celui-là** *the former*:

> **tu connais Luc et son frère? Alors, celui-ci a demandé de tes nouvelles hier soir,** *you know Luc and his brother? Well, the latter asked (his brother asked) about you last night*

Notice that *the former/the latter* are only used in formal English, whereas **celui-là/celui-ci** can be used with this meaning in French at all levels.

Cela, ça, ceci

Sometimes called neuter demonstratives, **cela** (and its more colloquial form **ça**) means *that* or *this* or *it*, **ceci** means *this*. **Cela/ça** is used much more frequently than **ceci**.

■ **Cela/ça** and **ceci** may refer to ideas, **cela** to one already mentioned, **ceci** to one about to be produced:

> **j'ai entendu tout ce que tu as dit, mais cela est très difficile à comprendre,** *I've heard all you've been saying, but that's (it's) very difficult to understand*
> **ça se comprend!** *that's obvious!*
> **écoutez ceci,** *listen to this*

or they may refer to objects, so far unnamed in the case of **ceci**:

> **je t'ai apporté ceci, c'est un petit cadeau,** *I've brought you this, it's a little present*

already known in the case of **cela/ça**:

> **ça te plaît?**, *do you like it?*

■ Whereas **celui-là** distinguishes between a number of objects, **cela/ça** simply points. Compare:

> **cela m'appartient**, *that's mine* (pointing to a single object)
> **celui-là m'appartient**, *that one's mine* (pointing to one among a number of similar objects)

Ce

The pronoun **ce** is a weaker form of **cela/ceci**, used only with **être**, and meaning *it* or *that*:

> **qui est-ce? — C'est moi**, *who's that?—It's me*

Ce becomes **c'** before **e**, **ç** before **a**:

> **ç'a été le plus grand problème**, *that's been the greatest problem*

■ The pronoun **ce** when used as the subject of **être** can also be plural:

> **ce sont des baleines**, *those are whales*

▶ See pp. 224 and 225 for **c'est** versus **il est**.

INDEFINITE PRONOUNS

Indefinite pronouns (*somebody*, *something*, *anybody*, etc. in English) all take the third person (**il** form) of the verb in French, as in English. The forms of object pronouns, reflexives, possessives corresponding to indefinite pronouns are also the third person forms (**le, la, lui; se; son, sa, ses; le sien** and their plurals); the corresponding form of the disjunctive is **soi**:

> **chacun doit s'asseoir à sa propre place**,
> *everybody must sit down in his or her own place*

Some indefinites only function as pronouns, some can also be adjectives—see below. See also indefinite adjectives, p. 148.

Used only as pronouns

■ **Chacun** (fem. **chacune**), *each one, everybody*:

> **chacun doit prendre une feuille de papier**,
> *everybody must take a sheet of paper*

■ **Je ne sais quoi**, *something or other*

This phrase is used as if it were a simple pronoun. It may take an adjective, preceded by **de**:

> **elle a dit je ne sais quoi de complètement stupide**,
> *she said something or other completely stupid*

■ **N'importe qui**, *anyone (at all)*:

> **n'importe qui te dira ça**, *anyone (at all) will tell you that*
> **ne le dis pas à n'importe qui**, *don't tell just anyone*

■ **On**, *one, you, we, they, someone, people in general*:

> **on nous regarde**, *somebody's looking at us*
> **qu'est-ce qu'on va faire?**, *what are we going to do?*

▶ See also pp. 103, 109, and (**on** as a substitute for the passive) 34.

■ **Personne**, *nobody, not anybody*:

> **qui est là? — Personne**, *who's there—Nobody*
> **je n'y vois personne**, *I can't see anyone there*

Personne must have a **ne** with an associated verb, as in the second example above. See p. 159.

Any adjective with **personne** follows it, is masculine, and is preceded by **de**:

> **il n'y a personne de compétent**, *there is no one qualified*

■ **Quelque chose**, *something, anything*:

> **tu as vu quelque chose?**, *did you see anything?*
> **oui, il y a quelque chose qui bouge**, *yes, there's something moving*

Any adjective with **quelque chose** follows it, is masculine, and is preceded by **de**:

> **ça doit être quelque chose d'horrible!**, *it must be something horrible!*

The other **chose** compounds behave similarly:

> **autre chose**, *something else*
> **peu de chose**, *little*
> **pas grand-chose**, *not much*

■ **Quelqu'un**, *someone, anybody*:

> **il y a quelqu'un dans la grange**, *there's someone in the barn*
> **est-ce que tu entends quelqu'un?**, *can you hear anybody?*

Quelqu'un has masculine and feminine plural forms (**quelques-uns, quelques-unes**) but no feminine singular form (the masculine must be used even if you are aware that 'someone' is a woman):

> **il s'est déjà marié avec quelqu'un**, *he's already married somebody*

The plural form, **quelques-un(e)s**, must have an **en** with its associated verb when it is used as the direct object:

> **ces dames-là? oui, j'en connais quelques-unes**, *those ladies? yes, I know some of them*

Any adjective with **quelqu'un** follows it and is preceded by **de**:

> **je cherche quelqu'un de beau**, *I'm looking for someone handsome*

■ **Quiconque**, *whoever; any*:

> **quiconque dit cela, ment!**, *whoever says that is lying!*
>
> **il joue mieux que quiconque de ses amis**, *he plays better than any of his friends*

Qui que ce soit (qui/que) may be used, in rather less formal style, for **quiconque**. See p. 234.

■ **Rien**, *nothing, not anything*:

> **tu entends quelque chose? — Non, rien**, *can you hear anything?—No, nothing*
>
> **je n'entends absolument rien**, *I can hear absolutely nothing*

Rien must have a **ne** with an associated verb, as in the second example above. See p. 159.

Any adjective with **rien** follows it, is masculine, and is preceded by **de**:

> **ce n'est rien de spécial**, *it's nothing special*

■ **L'un** (fem. **l'une**), *(the) one*:

> **j'ai rencontré l'un d'eux en ville**, *I met one of them in town*
>
> **l'une chante, l'autre pas**, *one sings, the other doesn't*

As in the second example above, **l'un** is often followed later in the sentence by **l'autre**, *another, the other*. The plural is **les un(e)s ... les autres ...**

L'un(e) l'autre (plural **les un(e)s les autres**) is used to mean *one another, each other*:

> **ils se détestent l'un l'autre**, *they hate one another*

Used as both pronouns and adjectives

▶ For these indefinites used as adjectives, see p. 148.

■ **Aucun** (fem. **aucune**), *none, not any*:

> **tu as entendu ses disques? — Non, aucun,** *you've heard his records?—No, none of them*
> **il n'en a aucun,** *he hasn't any*

Aucun must have **en** before the verb when it is used as the direct object; it must also have a **ne** with an associated verb, as in the second example above. See p. 159.

Pas un (fem. **pas une**) and **nul** (fem. **nulle**) are found as alternatives to **aucun**, with the same meaning.

■ **Certains** (fem. **certaines**), *some (people)*:

> **certains ont dit qu'il a subtilisé l'argent,** *some people said he pinched the money*
> **certaines d'entre elles ont très bien parlé,** *some of them spoke very well*

Certain(e)s must have **en** before the verb when used as the direct object:

> **j'en connais certains,** *I know some of them*

■ **Plusieurs,** *several (people)*:

> **plusieurs sont venus sans savoir pourquoi,** *several came without knowing why*

Plusieurs must have **en** before the verb when used as the direct object:

> **il en a tué plusieurs,** *he killed several (of them)*

Any adjective with **plusieurs** follows it and is preceded by **de**:

> **il y en a plusieurs de verts,** *there are several green ones*

■ **Tous** (fem. **toutes**), *everybody, all*:

> **je vous connais tous**, *I know you all*
> **elles sont toutes là**, *they are all there*
> **tous sont venus à la réunion**, *all of them came to the meeting*

Tous usually follows the verb, as in the first two examples above, whether it refers to the subject or the object. It stands before the verb when it alone is the subject, as in the third example above.

■ **Tout**, *everything, all*:

> **tout est arrangé**, *all is arranged*
> **j'ai tout fait**, *I've done everything*

Adjectives

In French, adjectives are singular or plural and masculine or feminine according to the noun they refer to. To the basic masculine form **-e** is added to make the adjective feminine, **-s** to make it masculine plural, **-es** to make it feminine plural:

	singular	*plural*
masculine	**un stylo noir,** *a black pen*	**des stylos noirs**
feminine	**une boîte noire,** *a black box*	**des boîtes noires**

An adjective referring to two singular nouns is plural; if they are of different genders the adjective is masculine plural:

un complet et une cravate noirs, *a black suit and tie*

Adjectives usually follow their noun; but see p. 138, position of adjectives.

FEMININE OF ADJECTIVES

Adjectives whose masculine form ends in **-e** remain unchanged in the feminine:

> **un stylo rouge**, *a red pen*
> **une boîte rouge**, *a red box*

otherwise all adjectives add **-e** to form their feminine.

■ Additional changes are made by adjectives with the following endings. Many of these changes are identical to those made by nouns to form their feminines—see p. 93.

masculine adjective	*feminine adjective*
-c	**-que**
public, *public*	**publique**
except:	
blanc, *white*	**blanche**
franc, *frank*	**franche**
grec, *Greek*	**grecque**
sec, *dry*	**sèche**
-er	**-ère**
dernier, *last*	**dernière**
-eur	**-euse**
trompeur, *deceptive*	**trompeuse**
except:	
inférieur, *lower*	**inférieure**
supérieur, *higher*	**supérieure**
intérieur, *inner*	**intérieure**
extérieur, *outer*	**extérieure**
majeur, *major*	**majeure**
mineur, *minor*	**mineure**
meilleur, *better*	**meilleure**
and see **-teur** below	

masculine	feminine
-f	**-ve**
informatif, *informative*	**informative**
except:	
bref, *brief*	**brève**
-gu	**-guë** (the tréma, ¨, indicates that the **e** is pronounced separately from the **u**)
aigu, *sharp*	**aiguë**
-teur	**-teuse**: where the adjective is based on the present participle of a verb
menteur, *lying*	**menteuse** (**mentir**, p.p. **mentant**)
	-trice: in all other cases
conservateur, *conservative*	**conservatrice** (**conserver**, p.p. **conservant**).
-x	**-se**
heureux, *happy*	**heureuse**
except:	
doux, *gentle*	**douce**
faux, *false*	**fausse**
roux, *red-haired*	**rousse**
vieux, *old*	**vieille**

■ Adjectives with the following endings double the consonant of their ending before adding **-e**:

masculine	feminine
-el	**-elle**
officiel, *official*	**officielle**
-en	**-enne**
ancien, *former*	**ancienne**
-et	**-ette**
net, *clear*	**nette**
except:	
complet, *complete*	**complète**
concret, *concrete*	**concrète**

discret, *discreet*	discrète
inquiet, *worried*	inquiète
secret, *secret*	secrète
-eil	-eille
pareil, *similar*	pareille
-on	-onne
bon, *good*	bonne

■ The following adjectives have a special form used before a masculine singular noun beginning with a vowel or 'mute' **h**, and their feminine form is derived from this:

masculine	masc. before vowel	feminine
beau, *fine*	bel	belle
fou, *mad*	fol	folle
mou, *soft*	mol	molle
nouveau, *new*	nouvel	nouvelle
vieux, *old*	vieil	vieille

■ Other adjectives with irregular feminine forms:

masculine	feminine
bas, *low*	basse
bénin, *benign*	bénigne
épais, *thick*	épaisse
exprès, *explicit*	expresse
favori, *favourite*	favorite
frais, *fresh*	fraîche
gras, *greasy*	grasse
gros, *big*	grosse
gentil, *nice*	gentille
jumeau, *twin*	jumelle
las, *tired*	lasse
long, *long*	longue
malin, *cunning*	maligne
nul, *no*	nulle
paysan, *peasant*	paysanne
sot, *foolish*	sotte

■ The following adjectives are invariable—they make no agreement at all with either a feminine or a plural noun:

> **châtain**, *chestnut*
> **impromptu**, *impromptu*
> **k(h)aki**, *khaki*
> **marron**, *brown*
> **snob**, *snobbish*

and all compound colour-adjectives:

> **une voiture bleu clair**, *a light blue car*
> **une boîte vert foncé**, *a dark green box*

The following adjectives make plural but no feminine agreements:

> **chic** (m. and f. plural **chics**), *chic*
> **maximum** (m. and f. plural, **maximums**), *maximum*
> **minimum** (m. and f. plural **minimums**), *minimum*

PLURAL OF ADJECTIVES

■ All feminine and most masculine adjectives form their plural by adding **-s** to their singular form. This also applies where the feminine singular is irregular:

	singular	*plural*
masculine	**bon**, *good*	**bons**
feminine	**bonne**	**bonnes**

■ Adjectives ending as follows have irregular masculine plurals. Their feminine plurals are formed regularly by adding **-s** to the feminine singular.

masculine singular	*masculine plural*
-s, -x	no change
gris, *grey*	**gris**
faux, *false*	**faux**

-eau	-eaux
beau, *fine*	**beaux**
-al	-aux
brutal, *brutal*	**brutaux**
except:	
banal, *trite*	**banals**
fatal, *fatal*	**fatals**
final, *final*	**finals**
naval, *naval*	**navals**

▶ A number of adjectives are invariable, remaining unchanged in both their feminine and their plural forms. See p. 137.

POSITION OF ADJECTIVES

The usual position for an adjective in French is immediately after the noun:

> **une robe verte**, *a green dress*

Two or more adjectives after the noun are joined with **et**:

> **une robe verte et blanche**, *a green and white dress*

Adjectives are also found in front of the noun, however, and some adjectives are almost always found in this position:

> **une jolie robe verte et blanche**, *a pretty green and white dress*

Adjectives that commonly precede are:

> **beau**, *fine*
> **bon**, *good* (and **meilleur**, *better, best*)
> **court**, *short*

gentil, *nice*
grand, *big; tall*
gros, *big*
jeune, *young*
joli, *pretty*
long, *long*
mauvais, *bad* (and **pire**, *worse, worst*)
méchant, *nasty*
nouveau, *new*
petit, *little* (and **moindre**, *less, least*)
vaste, *vast*
vieux, *old*
vilain, *ugly*

If in doubt place these adjectives before the noun, and all others after.

■ Most adjectives can in fact be placed before or after their noun, with a small but distinct difference in meaning. Placing the adjective after the noun indicates an objective distinction, placing it before shows a subjective feeling. So:

> **le long de cette côte s'étire une interminable plage**, *along this coastline stretches an endless beach* (travel agent's language: 'endless' is gushing and imprecise—'that seems as though it might go on for ever'; **une plage interminable**, however, means that the beach is literally or apparently interminable (and therefore boring and tiresome)

This use of adjectives before the noun is very common in modern French writing at all levels to strengthen the emotional content. The effect is often lost in written English: in spoken English we usually get it by stressing the adjective in some way:

> **ces superbes peintures**, *these superb paintings*
> **une fantastique reproduction**, *a fantastic
>   reproduction*
> **cette magnifique vallée**, *this magnificent valley*
> **d'une rare qualité**, *of a really rare quality*

The adjectives listed on p. 138 above are rarely used as
distinguishers: this is why they usually go before the
noun. Some adjectives, however, such as colour
adjectives, are almost always used to make an objective
distinction and so they normally follow the noun.

■ There are some adjectives whose position is
completely fixed:

□ Numbers, both cardinal (*one, two, three,* etc.) and
ordinal (*first, second, third,* etc.), always precede the
noun.

> **les trois mousquetaires**, *the three musketeers*
> **le quatrième mousquetaire**, *the fourth musketeer*

But in the following cases where the number follows in
English it also follows in French.

> **numéro deux**, *number two*
> **page cinq**, *page five*
> **Henri quatre**, *Henri the Fourth*
> **acte trois**, *act three*

□ Demonstrative, possessive, and interrogative adjectives
always precede.

> **cet enfant-là**, *that child*
> **son parapluie**, *his umbrella*
> **quelle difficulté?**, *what difficulty?*

□ Indefinite adjectives like **chaque**, *each*, **tel**, *such*,
autre, *other*, always precede. See p. 148.

> **une telle personne**, *such a person*
> **chaque enfant**, *each child*

☐ Past participles used as adjectives always follow.

un verre cassé, *a broken glass*

☐ Adjectives of nationality always follow.

la révolution française, *the French revolution*

☐ Scientific and technical adjectives always follow.

l'acide chlorhydrique, *hydrochloric acid*

☐ Adjectives with a qualifying phrase always follow.

un bon champignon, *a good mushroom*
un champignon bon à manger, *an edible mushroom*

■ A small number of adjectives have quite different meanings according to whether they precede or follow the noun. They are:

ancien, *former / ancient*

un ancien professeur, *a former teacher*
des meubles anciens, *very old furniture*

certain, *certain* (= *I'm not sure what*) / *definite, (absolutely) sure*

un certain jour de mai, *a certain day (one day) in May*
il faut fixer le rendez-vous pour un jour certain, *we must fix the appointment for a definite day*

cher, *dear* (= *emotionally important*) / *dear* (= *expensive*)

mon cher Charles, *my dear Charles*
une lampe chère, *an expensive lamp*

dernier, *last* (*of a sequence*) / *last* (= *just gone*)

le dernier chèque de mon chéquier, *the last cheque in my chequebook*
dimanche dernier, *last Sunday*

divers, *various/varying*

> **j'ai eu diverses difficultés**, *I've had various difficulties*
> **on m'a donné des réponses diverses**, *I've been given varying replies*

même, *same/very*

> **la même chose**, *the same thing*
> **l'homme même**, *the very man*

Même before the article or before a pronoun means *even*:

> **même cet homme-là**, *even that man*
> **même vous**, *even you*

pauvre, *poor (= to be pitied)/poor (= not rich)*

> **ce pauvre enfant!**, *that poor child!*
> **une famille pauvre**, *a poor family*

propre, *own/clean*

> **mes propres mains**, *my own hands*
> **les mains propres**, *clean hands*

seul, *only/alone*

> **la seule solution**, *the only solution*
> **le roi seul a le droit de décider**, *the king alone has the right to decide* (this use is the equivalent of 'only the king', and **seul le roi** is equally possible)

vrai, *real (= genuine)/true (= not fictitious)*

> **un vrai mystère**, *a real mystery*
> **une histoire vraie**, *a true story*

COMPARATIVE AND SUPERLATIVE OF ADJECTIVES

■ English has two ways to form the comparative and superlative of adjectives:

> *fine*: *finer* (comparative), *finest* (superlative)
> *difficult*: *more difficult* (comparative), *most difficult* (superlative)

French forms the comparative and superlative in one way only, with **plus** (comparative) and **le/la/les plus** (superlative):

> **beau, plus beau, le plus beau**, *fine, finer, finest*
>
> **la voile est un plus beau sport que le tennis**, *sailing is a finer sport than tennis*
> **c'est le plus beau sport possible**, *it's the finest sport possible*
>
> **difficile, plus difficile, le plus difficule**, *difficult, more difficult, most difficult*
>
> **c'est une activité encore plus difficile**, *it's an even more difficult activity*
> **c'est l'activité la plus difficile de toutes**, *it's the most difficult activity of all*

■ The comparative or superlative comes in the same position, before or after the noun, that the adjective itself would take, and agrees in the same way as an ordinary adjective does. Notice that where it comes after the noun, the superlative adjective has its own definite article, independently of any article that already stands with the noun:

> **cette activité la plus difficile de toutes**, *this most difficult of all activities*

A superlative adjective immediately after a possessive (**mon, ma, mes; ton, ta, tes,** etc.) drops its definite article:

> **sa plus jolie jupe,** *her prettiest skirt*

■ The following comparative and superlative adjectives are exceptional:

> **bon, meilleur, le meilleur,** *good, better, best*

> **mauvais, plus mauvais, le plus mauvais,** or
> **mauvais, pire, le pire (pire, le pire** are nowadays only used in some set phrases: **le remède est pire que le mal,** *the cure is worse than the disease*)

> **petit, plus petit, le plus petit,** *small,* (*physically*) *smaller, smallest,* or
> **petit, moindre, le moindre,** *little, less* (= *of less importance*), *least*

■ Comparisons, as well as being expressed by **plus ... que,** *more ... than,* can also be expressed by:

> **moins ... que,** *less ... than*

> **ton journal est moins intéressant que le mien,**
> *your paper's less interesting than mine*

> **aussi ... que,** *as ... as*

> **elle est aussi riche que son père,** *she's as rich as her father*

> **pas aussi** (or **pas si**) **... que,** *not as ... as*

> **elle n'est pas (aus)si riche que son grand-père,**
> *she's not as rich as her grandfather*

■ *Than* after a comparative is **que:**

> **vous êtes plus jeune que moi?,** *you're younger than me?*

As after a comparative is also **que**:

> **elle n'est pas si vieille que lui**, *she's not as old as him*

In after a superlative is **de**:

> **le plus grand bâtiment du monde**, *the biggest building in the world*

By with either a comparative or a superlative is **de**:

> **il est de beaucoup le plus beau**, *he's by far the most handsome*

■ **Le/la/les moins** can also be used, like **le/la/les plus**, as a superlative:

> **l'enfant le moins gâté**, *the least spoiled child*

■ Where **plus** and **moins** are used to compare nouns rather than adjectives they are followed by **de**:

> **tu as plus de force que moi**, *you have more strength than I*
>
> **la ville a moins d'habitants qu'auparavant**, *the town has fewer inhabitants than formerly*

To express equal quantity **autant de**, *as much as*, is used:

> **elle a autant d'argent que son petit ami**, *she has as much money as her boyfriend*

More than, *less than* plus a quantity is also **plus de**, **moins de**:

> **il a plus de soixante ans**, *he's more than sixty*

■ *More and more* is **de plus en plus**, *less and less* **de moins en moins**:

> **le temps devient de plus en plus orageux**, *the weather's getting more and more stormy*
>
> **j'ai de moins en moins d'argent**, *I've less and less money*

▶ For the use of the subjunctive in a clause following a superlative, see p. 47.

DEMONSTRATIVE, POSSESSIVE, AND INTERROGATIVE ADJECTIVES

Demonstrative adjectives (*this*, *that* in English) and possessive adjectives (*my*, *your*, *his*, *her*, etc. in English) stand in exactly the same relationship to nouns as do definite and indefinite articles. They are in fact sometimes known as demonstrative and possessive articles.

■ The demonstrative adjective in French is **ce** (masculine singular), **cet** (masculine singular before a vowel or 'mute' **h**), **cette** (feminine singular), **ces** (plural):

> **ce jeune homme**, *this young man*
> **cet homme**, *this man*
> **cette fille**, *this girl*
> **ces gens**, *these people*

Where it is necessary to differentiate between *this* and *that*, **-ci** and **-là** are added to the following noun:

> **ce jeune homme-ci**, *this young man*
> **ces gens-là**, *those people*

However, just as French tends to use **là**, *there*, much more than **ici**, *here*, so **ce ... -là** is used in modern French in many cases where English would use *this*, with **ce ... là-bas** used for the more distant object:

> **tu sais quel train tu prends? Celui-là? — Non, ce train là-bas**, *do you know which train you're getting? This one?—No, that train (there)*

■ The possessive adjectives are:

with masc. sing. noun	with fem. sing. noun	with plur. noun	
mon	**ma**	**mes**	*my*
ton	**ta**	**tes**	*your*
son	**sa**	**ses**	*his, her, its*
	notre	**nos**	*our*
	votre	**vos**	*your*
	leur	**leurs**	*their*

Mon, ton, and **son** are also used before a feminine singular noun beginning with a vowel or 'mute' **h.**

> **c'est ma cassette,** *it's my cassette*
>
> **c'est ton orange,** *it's your orange* (**orange** is feminine)
>
> **c'est son pullover,** *it's his/her pullover*

Notice that **son, sa, ses,** like the rest of the possessives, have the gender of the object possessed, not of the person owning it. So **son pullover** is *his* or *her pullover*, **sa cassette** *his* or *her cassette*. Where it is necessary to differentiate, **à lui/à elle** are added:

> **c'est sa cassette à lui,** *it's his cassette*

■ The interrogative adjective in French is **quel?,** *which, what?* It agrees in gender and number with the noun that follows:

	singular	*plural*
masculine	**quel**	**quels**
feminine	**quelle**	**quelles**

> **quelle robe vas-tu porter?,** *which dress are you going to wear?*

Quel can be used to introduce an indirect question:

> **je ne sais pas quelle robe porter**, *I don't know what dress to wear*
>
> **je me demande quelle robe Sophie va porter**, *I wonder what dress Sophie will wear*

■ **Quel ...!** may also be an exclamation, meaning in the singular *what a ...!*, *what ...!*, in the plural *what ...!*

> **quel beau jour!**, *what a lovely day!*
> **quelle chance!**, *what luck!*
> **quelles vacances formidables!**, *what terrific holidays!*

INDEFINITE ADJECTIVES

Indefinite adjectives, as a group, include in English such words as *several, certain, such*. The indefinite adjectives in French are:

> **aucun, nul**, *no, not any*
> **autre**, *other*
> **certain**, *certain*
> **chaque**, *each*
> **même**, *same*
> **plusieurs**, *several*
> **quelque**, *some, any*
> **tel**, *such*
> **tout** (singular) *all, the whole of*; (plural) *all; every*

Chaque has no plural form, **plusieurs** no singular form. **Plusieurs** is unchanged in both masculine and feminine; **tel** and **tout** decline as follows:

	singular	*plural*
masculine	**tel; tout**	**tels; tous**
feminine	**telle; toute**	**telles; toutes**

Aucun and **nul** take **ne** with their verb, like negative adverbs: see p. 159.

■ **Chaque, plusieurs, quelque, aucun, nul,** and
certains (plural) are used without preceding article:

> **chaque employé sera payé la même somme,** *each*
> *worker will be paid the same amount*
> **plusieurs d'entre eux sont là,** *several of them are*
> *there*
> **j'y vois quelques problèmes,** *I can see some*
> *problems there*
> **c'est à cause de certaines difficultés,** *it's because*
> *of certain difficulties*

■ **Tout** has the article following, as with *all* in English
(but unlike the English usage with *every*):

> **tout le temps,** *all the time*
> **tous les soirs,** *every evening*

In the singular **tout** may be used without article to mean
all, any:

> **cela exclut tout progrès dans cette affaire,** *that*
> *excludes any progress in this matter*

■ **Autre** and **tel** stand after the article like other
adjectives. Notice that this is not the case with *such* in
English:

> **les autres hommes,** *the other men*
> **un autre homme,** *another man*
> **un tel homme,** *such a man*

Such may also be used in English adverbially to qualify
another adjective: *she has such big eyes*. In French this
must be the adverb form **tellement,** or **si,** both of which
mean *such* or *so*:

> **ses yeux sont tellement grands,** *her eyes are so*
> *big*
> **elle a de si grands yeux,** *she has such big eyes*

- **Même** has four meanings according to position:
- Before the article, *even*

> **même son secrétaire le dit**, *even his secretary says so*

- Before the noun, or after the verb, *same*

> **c'est exactement la même chose**, *it's exactly the same thing*
>
> **ces deux filles sont toujours les mêmes**, *those two girls are always the same*

- After the noun, *very*

> **voilà l'homme même que je cherchais**, *there's the very man I was looking for*

- Attached to a pronoun with a hyphen, *self*

> **il l'a fait lui-même**, *he did it himself*

NOUNS USED ADJECTIVALLY (ATTRIBUTIVE NOUNS)

English frequently uses nouns as adjectives: *a coffee pot, a steel saucepan, a box girder, a cat flap*. These imply something like 'used for', 'made from', 'in the form of', 'used by'. In French the adjectival (or attributive) noun is placed after the main noun, and joined to it with a preposition which makes clear this relationship. The prepositions used are **de**, **à**, and **en**:

de

- *of, appropriate for, belonging to*

> **un match de tennis**, *a tennis match* (= *a match of tennis*)

la route de Manieu, *the Manieu road* (= *the road appropriate for Manieu*)

les feuilles d'automne, *autumn leaves* (= *the leaves of autumn*)

des poulets de batterie, *battery hens* (= *belonging to a battery*)

□ *for the purpose of*

une salle d'attente, *a waiting room* (= *a room for the purpose of waiting*)

un effet de choc, *a shock effect* (= *an effect for the purpose of shocking*)

à

□ *to contain, intended for*

un pot à café, *a coffee pot* (= *a pot to contain coffee*. Compare **un pot de café**, *a pot of coffee*)

une boîte aux lettres, *a letter box* (= *a box intended for letters*)

Verbal nouns (the *-ing* form in English, the infinitive in French) use **à** with this meaning to transform themselves into adjectives:

une salle à manger, *a dining room* (= *a room intended for eating*)

une machine à laver, *a washing machine* (= *a machine intended for washing*)

□ *using, employing*

une poutre à caisson, *a box girder* (= *a girder using a box shape*)

un moulin à vent, *a windmill* (= a mill that uses wind)

□ *with, possessing*

un chien à pedigree, *a pedigree dog* (= a dog possessing pedigree)

en

☐ *made from*

> **une casserole en acier**, *a steel saucepan* (= *a saucepan made from steel*)
>
> **un bracelet en or**, *a gold bracelet* (= *a bracelet made from gold*)

De is sometimes used in this way, too:

> **une barre de fer**, *an iron bar*

☐ *in the form of*

> **un escalier en spirale**, *a spiral staircase* (= *a staircase in the form of a spiral*)

■ Sometimes, especially with modern words, the adjectival noun simply follows the main one, without any preposition, though often with a hyphen:

> **une cocotte-minute**, *a pressure cooker* ('*minute casserole*')
>
> **une bande-annonce**, *a film trailer* ('*advertisement reel*')

Adverbs

FORMATION OF ADVERBS

Adverbs formed from adjectives

■ Most French adverbs are formed by adding **-ment** to the feminine form of the adjective:

> **égal**, *equal* → feminine: **égale**
> → adverb: **également**, *equally*

■ If the masculine form of the adjective ends in a vowel, **-ment** is added to this masculine form:

> **vrai**, *real* → **vraiment**, *really*
> **forcé**, *forced* → **forcément**, *'forcedly'*, *necessarily*

Nouveau, mou, and **fou,** however, base their adverbs on their differing feminine forms **nouvelle, molle,** and **folle**:

> **nouveau** → **nouvellement**, *newly*
> **mou** → **mollement**, *softly*
> **fou** → **follement**, *madly*

■ Adjectives ending **-ent** and **-ant** form adverbs ending **-emment** and **-amment** (both pronounced as if they were spelled **-amment**):

> **récent → récemment**, *recently*
> **constant → constamment**, *constantly*

Exceptions: **lent → lentement**, *slowly*; **présent →
présentement**, *presently*

■ A number of adjectives that do not end in **é** follow the
pattern of **forcément**:

> **aveugle → aveuglément**, *blindly*
> **commun → communément**, *communally*
> **confus → confusément**, *confusedly*
> **énorme → énormément**, *enormously*
> **exprès → expressément**, *explicitly*
> **impuni**, *unpunished* **→ impunément**, *with impunity,
> scot-free*
> **intense**, *intense* **→ intensément**, *intensively*
> **précis → précisément**, *precisely*
> **profond → profondément**, *deeply*

■ The following adverbs are completely irregular in the
way they are formed from their adjectives:

> **bon → bien**, *well*
> **bref → brièvement**, *briefly*
> **continu → continûment**, *continuously*
> **gai → gaiement**, *gaily*
> **gentil → gentiment**, *kindly*
> **mauvais → mal**, *badly*
> **meilleur → mieux**, *better*
> **moindre → moins**, *less*
> **petit → peu**, *little*
> **traître → traîtreusement**, *treacherously*

Adverbs not formed from adjectives

There are also many adverbs in French which are not
formed from adjectives, mostly short words like **ainsi,
donc, dedans**:

ainsi c'est entendu?, *so it's agreed?*

Some of these relate to conjunctions:

ainsi, *thus*, conjunction → **ainsi**, *so*, adverb

some to prepositions:

dans, *in*, preposition → **dedans**, *inside*, adverb

some are independent:

donc, *then*, adverb

Adverb alternatives

■ Adjectives are used as adverbs in a number of fixed expressions:

bas, haut	**parler bas, parler haut**, *speak softly/loudly*
bon, mauvais	**sentir bon, sentir mauvais**, *smell good/bad*
cher	**coûter cher, payer cher**, *cost/pay a lot*
court	**s'arrêter court, couper court**, *stop/cut short*
dur	**travailler dur**, *work hard*
juste/faux	**chanter juste, chanter faux**, *sing on/off-key*
net	**refuser net**, *refuse point blank*

■ Adverb phrases commonly substitute for the longer and more cumbersome adverbs, and must be used where the adjective has no corresponding adverb, such as **content**, *happy*, *content*:

il me regarda d'un air content, *he looked at me contentedly*

— **Ah non, dit-il d'une voix triste**, *'Oh no,' he said sadly*

elle répondit à voix basse, *she answered softly*

je l'ai fait avec soin, *I did it carefully*

le régiment s'est battu avec beaucoup de courage, *the regiment fought very courageously*

elle l'a fait sans hésitation, *she did it unhesitatingly*

POSITION OF ADVERBS

Adverbs describe or modify a verb:

> **elle joue bien**, *she plays well* (adverb: **bien**)

or an adjective:

> **cela est complètement différent**, *that's completely different* (adverb: **complètement**)

or another adverb:

> **oui, très probablement**, *yes, very probably* (modifying adverb: **très**)

■ With adjectives and adverbs the modifying adverb stands immediately in front of the word it modifies, as in English. See the last two examples above.

■ With verbs:

□ In simple tenses adverbs usually stand immediately after the verb.

> **je connais intimement toute cette famille**, *I know all that family intimately*

□ In compound tenses adverbs follow the past participle if they take the stress.

> **je l'ai vu finalement**, *I saw him, in the end*
> **je lui ai finalement parlé**, *I finally <u>spoke</u> to him*

In practice this means that adverbs of place and precise adverbs of time (**aujourd'hui, demain, hier**, etc.) almost always stand after the past participle:

> **elle l'a mis là, sur le plancher**, *she's put it there, on the floor*
> **on l'a fait hier**, *we did it yesterday*

and short adverbs of degree (**bien, beaucoup, trop,** etc.) or imprecise adverbs of time (**déjà, souvent, bientôt**, etc.) stand before the past participle:

tu l'as très bien expliqué, *you explained it very well*

il est déjà arrivé, *he's already arrived*

☐ With a dependent infinitive the above points about adverbs with the past participle also apply.

je vais le faire finalement, *I'm finally going to do it*

je vais finalement lui parler, *I'm finally going to speak to him*

■ Adverbs, especially those of time and place, may be placed at the head of their clause for emphasis, as they sometimes are in English:

partout on voyait des coquelicots, *everywhere poppies could be seen*

jamais je ne fume, *I never smoke*

■ Interrogative adverbs stand at the head of their clause, of course:

quand reviendra-t-elle?, *when will she come back?*

▶ For the word order after interrogative adverbs, see p. 212.

COMPARATIVE AND SUPERLATIVE OF ADVERBS

In English the comparative and superlative are:

easily →comparative: *more easily*
superlative: *most easily*

In French the comparative and superlative of adverbs are formed in a similar way to those of adjectives (for which see p. 143):

facilement, *easily*

comparative **plus facilement**, *more easily*
superlative **le plus facilement**, *most easily*

c'est comme ça que tu le feras le plus facilement,
that's the way you'll do it most easily

■ The superlative adverb always starts **le** (never **la** or
les):

c'est elle qui le fera le plus facilement, *she's the
one who will do it most easily*

■ As with adjectives

moins ... que, *less ... than*
aussi ... que, *as ... as*
si ... que, *as* (after a negative)

can be used to form comparatives in the same way as
plus ... que:

elle part en vacances moins souvent que toi, *she
goes on holiday less often than you*
il ne conduit pas si vite que toi, *he doesn't drive
as fast as you*

Le moins ..., *the least ...*, can also be used in a
similar way to **le plus ...**, *the most ...*, to form a
superlative:

celui qui le fait le moins bien, *the one who does it
least well*

■ The following adverbs have irregular comparatives
and superlatives:

beaucoup, *much*   **plus, le plus**, *more, the most*
bien, *well*   **mieux, le mieux**, *better, the
best*
peu, *little*   **moins, le moins**, *less, the
least*

The comparative adverb **pis**, *worse*, corresponding to the comparative adjective **pire**, is now only used in a few set expressions:

> **tant pis pour lui!**, *so much the worse for him!*

NEGATIVE ADVERBS

The negative adverbs in French are

> **aucun**, *no, none*
> **guère**, *hardly*
> **jamais**, *never*
> **ni**, *neither; nor*
> **nul**, *no*
> **nulle part**, *nowhere*
> **nullement**, *in no way*
> **pas**, *not*
> **personne**, *nobody*
> **plus**, *no longer*
> **que**, *only*
> **rien**, *nothing*

Negating a verb

The normal position for all the negative adverbs is after the verb in simple tenses, and before the past participle in compound tenses. In addition, they all have **ne** before the verb and any accompanying object pronouns. **Ne** becomes **n'** before a vowel or 'mute' **h**:

> **je ne le lui donne jamais**, *I never give it to him*
> **je n'ai rien dit**, *I haven't said anything*

■ **Nulle part** and **personne** normally come after the past participle in compound tenses:

> **ils n'ont vu personne**, *they haven't seen anyone*
> **on ne le trouve nulle part**, *it is not found anywhere*

■ **Ni**

□ With two objects: the **ni** is repeated in front of each
object. Any pronoun object must be a disjunctive (see
p. 111)

> **je n'ai rencontré ni lui ni sa femme**, *I met neither
> him nor his wife*

□ With two subjects: the **ni** is repeated in front of each
subject. Any pronoun subject must be a disjunctive (see
p. 111). The verb is usually plural

> **ni lui ni sa femme n'étaient là**, *neither he nor his
> wife was (were) there*

□ With two verbs: the **ne** is repeated

> **il ne fume ni ne boit**, *he neither smokes nor drinks*

Neither without *nor* is **non plus**:

> **moi non plus**, *me neither!*
> **je ne l'ai pas vu non plus**, *I haven't seen him
> either*

■ **Que**, *only*, qualifying an object stands in front of the
object. A pronoun object must be a disjunctive (see
p. 111):

> **je n'aime que lui**, *I love only him*
> **je n'ai vraiment regardé que l'acteur principal**, *I
> only really looked at the main actor*

Que can also be made to qualify a verb by using the
verb as an infinitive in the construction **ne faire que**:

> **cet enfant ne fait que crier**, *that child only cries
> (does nothing but cry)*

Que can itself be negated with **pas**:

> **il n'y a pas que Pierre qui soit invité**, *it's not only
> Pierre who's been invited*

■ **Aucun** and **nul** are actually adjectives, agreeing with the noun they stand in front of. They are used only in the singular; **nul** has the feminine form **nulle**.

In all other respects **aucun** and **nul** are like the other negative adverbs.

■ **Personne, rien, ni ... ni...**, **aucun ...** and **nul ...** can stand as the subject of the sentence. The **ne** still appears before the verb (but beware—there is no **pas**!):

> **personne ne l'a entendu**, *nobody's heard it*

See indefinite pronouns, pp. 127 ff.

Negating an infinitive

■ With an infinitive both the **ne** and the negative adverb stand in front of the infinitive and its pronoun objects:

> **je peux ne pas venir**, *I may possibly not come* (as opposed to **je ne peux pas venir**, *I can't come*)

except in the case of those negative adverbs which follow the past participle (**personne, nulle part, ni, que, aucun, nul**), which also follow the infinitive:

> **je suis désolé de ne voir personne**, *I'm very sorry not to see anyone*
> **j'espère ne trouver ni difficultés ni problèmes**, *I hope to find neither difficulties nor problems*

■ **Sans** + infinitive can stand with all the negative adverbs, without a **ne**:

> **sans rien voir**, *without seeing anything*

Double negative adverbs

Plus and **jamais** can qualify another negative adverb. They stand in front of it:

> **je ne vois plus personne**, *I don't see anybody any more*
> **je n'achète jamais rien**, *I never buy anything*

Negatives with other parts of the sentence

■ *Not* with parts of the sentence other than the verb is either **pas** or **non**, or the stronger **non pas**. **Ne** does not appear in this case:

> **je veux des pommes, et non pas des pommes de terre!**, *I want apples, not potatoes!*

■ Most of the negative adverbs can be used without **ne** where no verb is expressed:

> **qui a téléphoné? — Personne**, *who phoned?— Nobody*
> **qu'est-ce que tu entends? — Plus rien**, *what can you hear?—Nothing any more*

Omission of ne and pas

■ **Ne** is omitted extremely frequently in spoken French:

> **Jean-Luc? Connais pas!**, *Jean-Luc? Don't know him!*
> **elle vient ce soir? — Oh, moi je sais pas**, *is she coming tonight?—Oh, I don't know*

■ **Pas** is omitted in literary French with the verbs **pouvoir, savoir, oser** + infinitive

> **je ne savais comment répondre**, *I did not know how to reply*

Non-negative ne

A non-negative **ne** is used in careful speech in clauses dependent on a number of expressions, mostly involving the subjunctive. The commonest are:

- Verbs of fearing: **avoir peur que, craindre que**

> **j'ai peur qu'elle ne soit déjà là**, *I'm afraid she may be there already*

- Conjunctions: **avant que, à moins que, de peur que, de crainte que**

> **je l'ai fait de peur qu'elle ne le fasse elle-même**, *I did it for fear she (in case she) might do it herself*

- Comparisons: **plus … que, moins … que**

> **il est moins habile que vous ne pensez**, *he is less clever than you think*

This **ne** has no negative meaning and is not used in everyday spoken French.

▶ See uses of the subjunctive, pp. 41 ff.

Prepositions

Alphabetical list of French prepositions and
their use *164*
Cross-reference list of English
prepositions *185*

Prepositions—words like *in*, *on*, *over*—stand in front of a
noun or pronoun to relate it to the rest of the sentence:

> **il chante toujours dans la salle de bain**, *he always*
> *sings in the bathroom* (preposition: **dans**, *in*)

■ Prepositions can also stand in front of a verb—*without*
looking, *by singing*. In English this part of a verb is the
-ing form. In French it is the infinitive:

> **sans regarder**, *without looking*

except with the preposition **en**, which is followed by a
present participle:

> **en chantant**, *by singing*

■ The prepositions **à** and **de** combine with the definite
article to form **au**, **aux** and **du**, **des**. See p. 77.

■ The prepositions **à**, **de**, and **en** are usually repeated if
they refer to more than one noun or pronoun. This is
often not the case in English:

> **j'ai parlé à lui et à ses voisins**, *I spoke to him and*
> *his neighbours*

ALPHABETICAL LIST OF FRENCH
PREPOSITIONS AND THEIR USE

The use of prepositions differs considerably from
language to language. Below we give an alphabetical list

of those French prepositions that may give difficulty, with their main and subsidiary meanings and examples of their use. The principal meaning (or meanings) is given first, with other meanings following in alphabetical order.

In addition, on p. 185 there is an alphabetical list of English prepositions with their various French equivalents, for cross-reference to the French list.

à, *at*

at (place)

> **on se retrouve à la gare routiere**, *we'll meet at the bus station*
> **à la maison**, *at home*
> **à l'école**, *at school*
> **au travail**, *at work*

at (time)

> **à midi et à une heure**, *at noon and at one o'clock*
> **au crépuscule**, *at twilight*
> **à l'aube**, *at dawn*
> **à Noël**, *at Christmas*

at (numbers)

> **à cent kilomètres à l'heure**, (*at*) *100 km. an hour*
> **à très peu de distance**, *at a very little distance*
> **ceux à vingt francs**, *those at 20 francs*

belonging to (English uses the possessive pronoun):

> **c'est à lui** (= it belongs to him), *it's his*

▶ See p. 123.

by

> **tu le reconnaîtras à sa moustache**, *you'll recognize him by his moustache*
> **des dentelles faites à la main** (= by hand), *hand-made lace*
> **cela se vend au kilo**, *we sell that by the kilo*

for (English uses an attributive noun)

> **un réservoir à essence** (= a tank for petrol), *a petrol tank*
> **un verre à vin** (= a glass for wine), *a wineglass* (compare **un verre de vin**, *a glass of wine*)

from

> **il l'a pris à ton frère**, *he took it from your brother* (and similarly **arracher à**, *snatch from*, **acheter à**, *buy from*, **boire à**, *drink from*, **cacher à**, *hide from*, **emprunter à**, *borrow from*, **voler à**, *steal from*)

in (place)

> **à la campagne**, *in the country* (but **en ville**, *in town*)
> **à la main**, *in my* (*her, your, etc.*) *hand*
> **au lit**, *in bed*
> **au ciel**, *in the sky*
> **au soleil**, *in the sun*
> **à Marseille**, *in Marseilles*
> **aux États-Unis**, *in the United States*
> **au Mexique**, *in Mexico* (but **en** with feminine singular countries: **en France**)

in (time)

> **au petit matin**, *in the early morning* (but without an adjective '*in*' with parts of the day is just **le**: **le matin**, *in the morning*; **l'après-midi**, *in the afternoon*; **le soir**, *in the evening*)
> **au XX° siècle**, *in the twentieth century*
> **au mois de mai**, *in* (*the month of*) *May* (but **en mai**, *in May*)
> **au printemps**, *in spring* (but **en** with the other seasons: **en été**, *in summer*)
> **à son tour**, *in* (*his*) *turn*

in (manner)

> **à voix basse**, *in a soft voice*
> **des champignons à la grecque**, *mushrooms cooked the Greek way*
> **des tripes à la mode de Caen**, *Caen-style tripe*

on

> **au menu**, *on the menu*
> **ces peintures au mur**, *those paintings on the wall*
> **marqué au front**, *marked on the forehead*
> **à bicyclette, à pied, à cheval**, *on a bicycle (by bicycle), on foot, on horseback*
> **à droite/gauche**, *on the right/left*
> **à la page dix-huit**, *on page 18*

to

> **je vais à la boulangerie**, *I'm going to the baker's*
> **elle va à Paris, aux États-Unis, au Portugal**, *she's going to Paris, the USA, Portugal* (but **en** with feminine singular countries: **elle va en Italie**, *she's going to Italy*)
> **j'ai parlé à ton prof**, *I've spoken to your teacher*
> **du matin au soir**, *from morning to (till) night*

using (English usually has an attributive noun)

> **un moteur à essence** (= using petrol), *a petrol engine*
> **un moulin à vent** (= using wind), *a windmill*
> **une locomotive à vapeur** (= using steam), *a steam locomotive*

with (= *containing, having*—English may use an attributive noun)

> **une pâté aux truffes** (= a pâté with truffles), *truffle pâté*
> **un chien à pedigree** (= a dog with a pedigree), *a pedigree dog*

l'homme au parapluie, *the man with the umbrella*
la femme aux yeux verts, *the woman with green eyes*

▶ For uses of **à** with verbs see p. 56.

▶ For **à** used after adjectives, nouns, and adverbs see p. 51.

à part, *except*

▶ See **au dehors de**, below.

à travers, *through*

▶ See **par**, p. 180.

après, *after*

after (time)

après trois heures, *after three o'clock*
après la guerre, *after the war*

after (place)

la troisième maison après la mairie, *the third house after the town hall*
elle court après lui, *she's running after him*

according to (notice the **d'**)

d'après Le Figaro, *according to Le Figaro*

▶ For **après** + perfect infinitive (*after ...ing*), see p. 53.

au-dehors de, *outside*

outside

ce chien reste au-dehors de la maison, *that dog stays outside the house*

The shorter form **hors de** locates less precisely:

> **ceux qui habitent hors de la ville**, *those who live (somewhere) outside the town*

Hors de also means *out of*:

> **elle était hors d'haleine**, *she was out of breath*

and **hors** means *except*:

> **personne hors lui**, *no one except him*

Except is, however, now more usually **à part**:

> **personne à part sa mère**, *no one except her mother*

au-dessous de, *under(neath), below*

▶ See **sous**, p. 183.

au-dessus de, *over*

over, above (physically)

> **le ciel au-dessus de la montagne**, *the sky over (above) the mountains*

Over, above with motion is **par-dessus**:

> **l'aigle vola par-dessus la montagne**, *the eagle flew over the mountains*

Where *over* implies *touching* it is **sur**:

> **une serviette sur le bras**, *with a towel over his arm*

above, over (= *more than*)

> **ne paie pas au-dessus de cent francs**, *don't pay above (more than) 100 francs*

auprès de, *beside*

beside (nearness)

> **elle se tenait auprès du lit,** *she was standing beside the bed*

beside (= *compared to*)

> **son frère jumeau n'est rien auprès de lui,** *his twin brother is nothing beside (compared to) him*

avant, *before*

before (time)

> **avant le commencement du jeu,** *before the beginning of the match*
> **avant de sortir,** *before going out* (note the **de** before an infinitive)

before (place in a sequence of places)

> **vous descendez avant Genève?,** *are you getting out before Geneva?*

The older, formal use of *before* to mean *in front of* is **devant**:

> **il s'agenouilla devant l'autel,** *he knelt before the altar*

avec, *with*

with (= *together with*)

> **tu viens avec nous?,** *are you coming with us?*

with (= *by means of*)

> **tu ne le feras pas avec un tire-bouchon,** *you won't manage it with a corkscrew*

chez, *at X's*

at (or to) the house or shop of (English usually uses a possessive)

> **on va chez le fruitier**, *we're going to the greengrocer's*
>
> **on se voit chez Chantal**, *see you at Chantal's*
>
> **faites comme chez vous**, *make yourself at home*

with (= as far as X is concerned)

> **chez elle on ne sait jamais où on en est**, *with her you never know where you are*

among

> **chez les Esquimaux on ne joue pas beaucoup de tennis**, *not much tennis is played among the Eskimos*

in (the works of)

> **ce mot ne se trouve pas chez Racine**, *that word isn't found in Racine*

contre, *against*

against (in both concrete and abstract senses)

> **l'échelle est contre le garage**, *the ladder is against the garage*
>
> **nous sommes tous contre la guerre**, *we are all against war*

for

> **tu veux échanger ça contre mon tourne-disques?**, *do you want to exchange that for my record player?*

dans, *in*

in, *into* (place)

> **on va dans le jardin**, *we're going into the garden*
> **il y a deux hommes dans sa vie**, *there are two men in her life*

in (time, = *at the end of*)

> **je serai de retour dans dix minutes**, *I'll be back in ten minutes* (= *ten minutes from now*)

In = *within the space of* is **en**:

> **je le ferai en dix minutes**, *I'll do it in* (*within the space of*) *ten minutes*

from

> **je l'ai pris dans le tiroir**, *I took it from the drawer*

▶ See also **à**, *from*, p. 166. The French have in mind the original position of the object, from which it is then taken, snatched, etc.

de, *of*

of (possession or relation—English often uses a possessive or an attributive noun)

> **la voiture de Pierre**, *Pierre's car* (*the car of Pierre*)
> **la première femme de mon oncle**, *my uncle's first wife* (*the first wife of my uncle*)
> **la porte du jardin**, *the garden gate* (*the gate of the garden*)
> **la route de Versailles**, *the Versailles road* (*the road of Versailles*)
> **une partie de plaisir**, *a pleasure party* (*a party of pleasure*)

les vacances de Noël, *the Christmas holidays (the holidays of Christmas)*

of (= *containing*)

un verre de vin, *a glass of wine*

of (appositional, = *that is*)

au mois de septembre, *in the month of September (the month that is September)*
la ville de Paris, *the city of Paris*

about (= *concerning*)

elle est folle de ses animaux, *she's mad about her animals*

by

elle est Française de naissance, *she's French by birth*
il arriva accompagné de sa femme, *he arrived accompanied by his wife*
il a été blessé d'une balle, *he has been hit by a bullet* (See p. 33 for the use of **de** with the passive)

from

d'où vient-il?, *where has he come from?*
il revient de Paris, *he's just come back from Paris*
de temps en temps, *from time to time*
elle est différente de sa sœur, *she's different from her sister*

in (manner)

d'une voix basse, *in a low voice* (but **à** if the article is not used: **à voix basse**, *in a low voice*)
d'une manière impolie, *in a rude manner*
d'une façon stupide, *in a stupid way*

Similarly,

d'un air fâché, *with an angry look*

in (after a superlative or superlative-type word—see p. 145)

> **le meilleur du monde**, *the best in the world*
> **le premier de sa classe**, *the first in its class*

made of (English usually uses an attributive noun)

> **un coussin de soie**, *a silk cushion (a cushion made of silk)*
> **un chapeau de paille**, *a straw hat (a hat made of straw)*

than (with a quantity following a comparison)

> **plus de cinq fois**, *more than five times*
> **les enfants de moins de treize ans**, *children below (of less than) thirteen years*

to

> **tu es libre d'assumer n'importe quoi**, *you are free to assume anything at all*

with

> **il est couvert de boue**, *he's covered with mud*
> **elle pleure de joie**, *she is weeping with joy*
> **il nous questionna d'un air soupçonneux**, *he questioned us with a suspicious look*

De is also used, with no equivalent word in English, in the following cases.

■ After expressions of quantity (this includes **un million**, *million*, and **un milliard**, *billion*, but not other numbers):

> **beaucoup de monde**, *a lot of people*
> **trop de questions**, *too many questions*
> **un million de chiens**, *a million dogs*

▶ See p. 83.

■ After **quelque chose, rien, personne**, etc.:

> **quelque chose de beau**, *something beautiful*
> **rien de spécial**, *nothing special*

▶ See pp. 128 ff.

■ To join two nouns where the second is used adjectivally (the attributive noun):

> **la salle de bain**, *the bathroom*
> **la salle de séjour**, *the sitting room*

▶ For **de** with verbs see p. 55.
▶ For **de** used after adjectives, nouns, and adverbs see p. 51.

depuis, *since*

since (a place or a point in time)

> **tu n'as rien mangé depuis ton arrivée**, *you haven't eaten anything since your arrival (since you got here)*
> **c'est le premier péage depuis Lyon**, *it's the first toll point since Lyons*

for (a length of time)

> **elle regarde la télévision depuis une demi-heure**, *she's been looking at television for half an hour*

▶ *For* with time may also be **pendant** or **pour**. See pp. 181, 182.
▶ For tenses with both the above meanings of **depuis** see pp. 17 and 21.

from (a place or a time), in **depuis ... jusqu'à**, *from ... to*

> **la côte méditerranéenne depuis Toulon jusqu'à Nice**, *the Mediterranean coast from Toulon to (as far as) Nice*

on est ouvert depuis huit heures du matin jusqu'à huit heures du soir, *we are open from eight in the morning until eight at night*

De ... à is less emphatic:

du matin au soir, *from morning to night*

from (a place, = *out from*)

le panorama depuis le sommet est extraordinaire, *the panorama from the summit is remarkable*

dès, *as soon as*

as soon as; no later than (with future time)

je le ferai dès demain, *I'll do it no later than tomorrow*
dès son arrivée, *as soon as she gets here*
dès maintenant, *from now on*

as far back as; ever since (a point in past time onwards)

dès son enfance elle était insupportable, *even as a child (ever since her childhood) she was unbearable*

devant, *in front of*

▶ See **avant**, p. 170.

en, *in*

En expresses *in* in a more abstract or less specific way than does **dans**. It is always used without an article:

en ville, *in town*
en question, *in question*

except in a very few set expressions beginning with a vowel or 'mute' **h**:

en l'absence de, *in the absence of*
en l'air, *in the air*
en l'an ..., *in (the year) ...*
en l'honneur de, *in honour of*

in

en réponse à votre lettre, *in reply to your letter*
des perles en forme de collier, *pearls in the form of a necklace*
elle sortit en colère, *she went out angry (in anger)*
la cuisine était peinte en vert, *the kitchen was painted (in) green*
habillé en short, *dressed in shorts*

in (time: months, seasons, years)

en février, *in February*
en été, en automne et en hiver, *in summer, autumn, and winter* (but **au printemps**, *in spring*)
en 1999, *in 1999* (but **en l'an 1999**—note the article)

in, into (languages)

en français, *in French*
traduisez ça en anglais, *translate that into English*

in, to (with feminine singular names of countries and of continents)

on va en France, *we're going to France*
nous en Europe, *we in Europe*

▶ Otherwise *in* or *to* with countries is **au/aux**. See **à**, pp. 166, 167.

in (time within which)

je le ferai en deux minutes, *I'll do it (I'll have it done) in two minutes*

In (= *at the end of which time*) is **dans**:

> **je le ferai dans deux minutes**, *I'll do it* (*I'll start the job*) *in two minutes*

▶ See **dans**, p. 172.

as (= *in the shape of, as if it were*)

> **Monsieur Charles, en parfait gentleman, les accueillit très poliment**, *Charles, as the perfect gentleman, welcomed them very politely*
> **il me traite toujours en enfant**, *he always treats me as a child*
> **elle était déguisée en duchesse**, *she was dressed as a duchess*

by (with a form of transport, usually when one is 'in' the vehicle)

> **nous y allons en avion**, *we're going by plane*
> **ceux qui roulent en auto et en moto**, *those who travel by car and by motorbike* (also **à moto**)

▶ See also **à** (p. 167) and **par** (p. 180) with this meaning.

by, whilst, on (followed by the present participle)

> **je l'ai rencontrée en sortant du supermarché**, *I met her* (*whilst I was*) *coming out of the supermarket*

▶ See present participle, p. 35.

in the form of (English sometimes uses an attributive noun)

> **une antenne en croix**, *an aerial in the form of a cross*
> **un escalier en spirale**, *a spiral staircase* (*in the form of a spiral*)

made of (English often uses an attributive noun)

> **une table en acajou**, *a mahogany table*

De is also used with this meaning (see p. 174). **En** tends to draw more attention to the material of which the article is made than does **de**:

> **un téléviseur en or**, *a golden television set*

on

> **j'ai un chat qui me suit en promenade**, *I've a cat that follows me on my walks*
> **on part en vacances**, *we're leaving on holiday*

entre, *between*

between (two people or things)

> **entre lui et moi**, *between him and me*
> **entre dix heures et minuit**, *between ten o'clock and midnight*

among(st) (more than two people or things)

> **ici vous êtes entre amis**, *here you are among friends*
> **on causait entre soi**, *people were talking among themselves*

> *Among(st)* is, however, more frequently **parmi**:

> **parmi tous ceux qui étaient là, elle était la seule à bouger**, *amongst all those who were there she was the only one to move*

of (after **de** (**d'entre**) in expressions of quantity before pronouns)

> **quatre d'entre eux**, *four of them*
> **beaucoup d'entre vous**, *many of you*

envers, *towards* (figurative)

▶ See **vers**, p. 185.

hors (de), *except; out of*

▶ See **au-dehors de**, p. 168.

par, *by*

by

> **on commence par discuter, on finit par se
> quereller**, *you begin by discussing, you end by
> falling out*
> **par la D565**, *by the D565 road*
> **par ici/là**, *(by) this/that way*

by (with passive)

> **elle a été blessée par son mari**, *she was injured
> by her husband*

▶ See passive, p. 33.

by (with a few forms of transport, as an alternative to **en**)

> **par le train**, *by train*
> **par le métro**, *by underground*
> **par avion**, *by plane*

from (= *out of*, reason)

> **elle ne fait rien par conviction**, *she does nothing
> from (out of) conviction*

on, to

> **il était étendu par terre**, *he was lying on the
> ground*
> **elle est tombée par terre**, *she fell over; she fell to
> the ground* (from a standing position). Compare:
> **l'avion est tombé à terre**, *the plane fell to the
> ground* (from a height)

on, in (weather)

> **par un jour froid d'hiver**, *on a cold winter's day*
> **par un temps superbe**, *in splendid weather*

per, a (after numbers)

> **cinquante fois par semaine**, *fifty times a week*
> **deux par personne**, *two per person*

through

> **elle m'a vu par la fenêtre**, *she saw me through the window*
> **il a longtemps erré par les rues de Paris**, *for a long time he wandered through the streets of Paris*

Through where some difficulty is implied is **à travers**:

> **il se fraya un chemin à travers la foule**, *he battled his way through the crowd*

via

> **tu peux aller par Lyon ou par Dijon**, *you can go via Lyons or Dijon*

parmi, *among(st)*

▶ See **entre**, p. 179.

pendant, *during*

during

> **pendant ma visite**, *during my visit*

for (a completed period of time in the past)

> **ce mois-ci il a chômé pendant treize jours**, *this month he was out of work for thirteen days*

▶ See also **pour** (p. 182) and **depuis** (p. 175) meaning *for* with time.

pour, *for*

for (= *in favour of*)

> **tu votes pour les socialistes?**, *are you voting for the socialists?*
>
> **il faut peser le pour et le contre**, *you've got to weigh the pros and cons*

for (= *on behalf of*)

> **morts pour la France**, *they died for France*
>
> **elle y répondra pour toi**, *she'll reply to it for you*

for (intention)

> **ceci est pour toi**, *this is for you*
>
> **l'avion part pour Paris à trois heures cinq**, *the plane leaves for Paris at 3.05*

for (= *because of*)

> **on vous donne une contravention pour avoir laissé votre voiture devant le commissariat**, *you've been given a parking ticket for having left (for leaving) your car in front of the police station*

for (= *in exchange for*)

> **qu'est-ce que tu me donnes pour mon vélo?**, *what will you give me for my bike?*

for (plus intended length of time)

> **tu y vas pour trois mois?**, *you're going for three months?*

▶ See also **depuis** (p. 175) and **pendant** (p. 181) meaning *for* with time.

for (+ *an amount*)

> **tu en as là pour trente minutes**, *you've enough work there for twenty minutes*

> **pour cent francs de sans-plomb, s'il vous plait**, *100 francs worth ('for 100 francs') of unleaded, please*

as for

> **pour moi, je voudrais bien le faire**, *as far as I'm concerned (as for me), I'd like to do it*

Quant à is also used in this sense:

> **quant à vous**, *as for you*

per

> **dix pour cent**, *ten per cent*

to (= *in order to*)

> **pour faire fonctionner la pompe, il faut d'abord sortir le robinet**, *(in order) to operate the pump, the nozzle must first be withdrawn*

to (after **trop** + adjective, *too ...*, **assez** + adjective, *... enough*, and the verb **suffire**, *to be enough*)

> **tu es trop jeune pour y entrer**, *you're too young to go in*
>
> **vous êtes assez informé pour savoir que ...**, *you're well enough informed to know that ...*
>
> **cela suffira pour vous donner une idée de nos pensées**, *that will be enough to give you an idea of our thoughts*

quant à, *as for*

▶ See **pour**, above.

sous, *under*

under

> **ton hamster est sous ma chaise**, *your hamster is under my chair*

Au-dessous de, *under*, implies *completely under* (= *underneath*), or means *below* in figurative senses:

> **les chiffres sont au-dessous de ce qu'on attendait**, *the figures are below what we expected*

in

> **tu ne peux pas sortir sous la pluie**, *you can't go out in the rain*
>
> **sous peu, l'avion décolla**, *shortly after (in a little while) the plane took off*
>
> **ils vécurent sous le règne de Louis XIV**, *they lived in the reign of Louis XIV*

sur, *on*

on, on to

> **je l'ai laissé sur le fauteuil**, *I left it on the armchair*
>
> **monte sur l'échelle**, *climb up (on to) the ladder*
>
> **elle était sur le point d'interrompre**, *she was about to interrupt (on the point of interrupting)*
>
> **assis sur le mur**, *sitting on the wall* (*on* = *hanging on* is **à**. See p. 167)
>
> **sur notre droite**, *on our right*
>
> **je n'ai pas d'argent sur moi**, *I haven't any money on me*

by

> **douze centimètres de haut sur dix centimètres de large**, *12 cm. high by 10 cm. wide*

over

> **son autorité sur vous est très restreinte**, *his authority over you is very limited*
>
> **le pont sur l'estuaire de la Seine**, *the bridge over the Seine estuary*

▶ See also **au-dessus de**, *over*, p. 169.

in

> **j'ai laissé la clé sur la porte**, *I've left the key in the door*

in, out of

> **une personne sur dix**, *one person in ten*
> **dix-neuf sur vingt**, *19 out of 20*

upon

> **sur quoi, elle claqua la porte**, *whereupon (upon which) she slammed the door*

vers, *towards*

towards (place or point in time)

> **il s'en va vers la plage**, *he goes off towards the beach*
> **vers la fin de l'après-midi**, *towards the end of the afternoon*

Towards (figurative) is **envers**:

> **il est très bien intentionné envers nous**, *he is very well intentioned towards us*

about (with time of day)

> **vers dix heures et demie**, *about half past ten*

CROSS-REFERENCE LIST OF ENGLISH PREPOSITIONS

Prepositions presenting problems of translation are listed. These prepositions are cross-referenced to the list of French prepositions starting on p. 164. It is dangerous to take a French meaning from this list without subsequently checking its usage in the French list.

for
  à, 166
  a length of time, **depuis**, 175
  a completed period, **pendant**, 181
  intention, **pour**, 182
  = *because of*, **pour**, 182
  = *in favour of*, **pour**, 182
  = *in exchange for*, **contre**, 171; **pour**, 182
  = *on behalf of*, **pour**, 182
  + amount, **pour**, 182
  + intended length of time, **pour**, 182

from
  à, 166
  dans, 172
  de, 172
  place (= *out from*), **depuis**, 176
  reason (= *out of*), **par**, 180

from ... to
  depuis ... jusqu'à, 175
  de ... à, 176

in
  abstract meanings, **en**, 176; 177
  after superlatives, **de**, 174
  countries, feminine singular, **en**, 177
    masculine or plural, **à**, 166; 167
  languages, **en**, 177
  manner, **à**, 167; **de**, 173
  place, **à**, 166
  sous, 184
  sur, 185
  time, **à**, 166
  time (months, seasons, years), **en**, 177
  time (= *at the end of*), **dans**, 172
  time (= *within the space of*), **en**, 172; 177

| Conjunctions

■ Conjunctions are joining-words. They may join nouns or pronouns:

> **lui et son chien**, *he and his dog* (conjunction: **et**)

or phrases:

> **en arrivant ou en partant**, *on arriving or leaving*
> (conjunction: **ou**)

or clauses:

> **elle chante, mais elle ne joue pas**, *she sings but*
> *she doesn't play* (conjunction: **mais**)

■ They may also introduce a subordinate clause:

> **je le ferai quand j'aurai de l'argent**, *I'll do it when*
> *I have money* (conjunction: **quand**)

Many of the conjunctions that introduce subordinate clauses in French are two-word phrases with **que** as the second word:

> **je lui ai téléphoné pendant qu'elle travaillait**,
> *I phoned her whilst she was working*
> (conjunction: **pendant que**)

Quite often the first word of the phrase is a preposition with the same English meaning as the conjunction:

> **avant**, *before*, preposition
> **avant que**, *before*, conjunction
>
> **sans**, *without*, preposition
> **sans que**, *without*, conjunction

It is important to distinguish these—the preposition

will stand before a noun or (sometimes) the infinitive of a verb:

> **sans effort**, *without effort*
> **sans me regarder**, *without looking at me*

The conjunction will introduce a subordinate clause:

> **je l'organiserai avant qu'on leur parle**, *I'll organize it before anyone speaks to them*

▶ Many subordinating conjunctions are followed by the subjunctive. See p. 45.

■ The following conjunctions may give problems:

☐ **aussi**, *so, therefore*

After **aussi**, verb and pronoun subject are inverted:

> **elle n'y montrait aucun intérêt, aussi est-il parti sans plus rien dire**, *she wasn't showing any interest, so he left without saying anything more*

Aussi can of course also be an adverb, meaning *also*.

☐ **ni**, *nor*

After **sans**, **ni** is used where in English we should use *or*:

> **sans père ni mère**, *without father or mother*

☐ **où**, *where*

After definite expressions of time **où** is used where in English we should use *when* or *that* or nothing at all:

> **l'instant où elle s'est retournée**, *the moment (when, that) she turned round*

See also **que** below.

☐ **que**, *that*

Que becomes **qu'** before a vowel in written French. In spoken French it frequently remains as **que**.

After indefinite expressions of time **que** is used where in English we use *when*

> **un jour qu'il faisait beau**, *one day when it was fine*

See also **où** above.

Que is often used to avoid repeating a conjunction

> **quand tu viendras à Dijon et que tu verras la maison, tu seras enchanté**, *when you come to Dijon and (when you) see the house you'll be delighted*

When **que** replaces the conjunction **si** in this way it is followed by the subjunctive. See p. 48.

Que in comparisons means *than*

> **il est plus fort que moi**, *he's stronger than me*

▶ **Que** can also be a relative pronoun. See p. 112.

■ Paired conjunctions.

These conjunctions are used in much the same way as in English. The common ones are:

ni ... ni, *neither ... nor*
non seulement ... mais encore, *not only ... but also*
et ... et, *both ... and*
ou (bien) ... ou (bien), *either ... or (else)*
soit ... soit, *either ... or*

> **je n'ai ni argent ni ma carte Visa**, *I've neither money nor my Visa card*
> **non seulement lui mais encore toute sa famille sont venus déjeuner**, *not only he but all his family came to lunch*
> **on lui a pris et son agenda et son sac à main**, *they took both her diary and her handbag*
> **ou vous lui demandez pardon, ou je vous tue**, *either you apologize to her or I kill you*

> **on voyagera soit par le train soit par avion**, *they'll travel either by train or by plane*

The last three pairs are used mostly in written French, a simple **et, ou,** or **ou bien** being used in the spoken language.

▶ For the use of **ne** with **ni ... ni** see p. 160.

Numbers, Time, Quantities

CARDINAL NUMBERS

The cardinal numbers are

0	zéro	24	vingt-quatre
1	un(e)	25	vingt-cinq
2	deux	26	vingt-six
3	trois	27	vingt-sept
4	quatre	28	vingt-huit
5	cinq	29	vingt-neuf
6	six	30	trente
7	sept	31	trente et un(e)
8	huit	32	trente-deux
9	neuf	40	quarante
10	dix	41	quarante et un(e)
11	onze	50	cinquante
12	douze	51	cinquante et un(e)
13	treize	60	soixante
14	quatorze	61	soixante et un(e)
15	quinze	70	soixante-dix
16	seize	71	soixante et onze
17	dix-sept	72	soixante-douze
18	dix-huit	80	quatre vingts
19	dix-neuf	81	quatre-vingt-un(e)
20	vingt	82	quatre-vingt-deux
21	vingt et un(e)	90	quatre-vingt-dix
22	vingt-deux	91	quatre-vingt-onze
23	vingt-trois	92	quatre-vingt-douze

100	cent	2 000	deux mille
101	cent un(e)	1 000 000	un million
200	deux cents	1 000 200	un million deux
201	deux cent un(e)		cents
1 000	mille	2 000 000	deux millions
1 001	mille un(e)	1 000 000 000	un milliard
1 002	mille deux	2 000 000 000	deux milliards

Thousands and millions are written with spaces (formerly sometimes with full stops) rather than, as in English, with commas. The comma is used for a decimal point—see p. 215.

■ There is no **-s** on the plural of **vingt** and **cent** when these are followed by another number.

■ There is never an **-s** on the plural of **mille** meaning *thousands*. **Le mille**, meaning *mile*, takes a plural **-s**.

■ **Million** and **milliard** are nouns. With a noun immediately following, they take **de**:

> **un million de soldats**, *a million soldiers*

but

> **un million deux cent mille soldats**, *1,200,000 soldiers*

All other numbers are adjectives. They are invariable, except that those ending in **un** agree with a following feminine noun (changing to **une**).

■ There is no **un** before **cent**, **mille**, meaning *one hundred*, *one thousand*:

> **mille francs**, *one thousand francs*

There is no **et** after **cent** or **mille**:

> **cent douze**, *a hundred and twelve*
> **mille un**, *one thousand and one*

except in the book title, ***Les mille et une nuits***, *A Thousand and One Nights*.

■ Figures are grouped in twos when you speak
telephone numbers:

> 33 56 08 = **trente-trois cinquante-six zéro huit**
> 445 35 71 = **quatre cent quarante-cinq trente-cinq
> soixante et onze**

■ In Belgium, Switzerland, and Canada **septante**,
octante or **huitante**, and **nonante** are used for 70, 80,
and 90.

■ The numbers **six** and **dix** have each three different
pronunciations. Before a consonant the **-x** is not
pronounced; before a vowel or **h** 'mute' it is pronounced
z; where **six** and **dix** stand after the noun (**chapitre six**)
or in dates (**le dix novembre**) the **-x** is pronounced **s**.

The final consonants of **cinq**, **sept**, **huit**, and **neuf** are
not normally pronounced before another consonant,
except in dates.

The **f** of **neuf** is pronounced **v** before the words **ans**,
years, and **heures**, *o'clock*; before other words beginning
with a vowel or **h** 'mute' it is pronounced **f**.

The **t** of **vingt** is usually pronounced in the numbers
21–29; it is not pronounced in dates: **le vin[gt] août**.

■ Before **huit** and **onze**, **le** does not become **l'**:

> **tu as le huit de trèfle?**, *do you have the eight of
> clubs?*
> **le onze juin**, *the eleventh of June*

This also applies to the ordinal forms:

> **le huitième**, *the eighth*
> **le onzième**, *the eleventh*

ORDINAL NUMBERS

Ordinal numbers (*first*, *second*, *third*, etc.) are formed by
removing the final **-e** of the cardinal number (if it ends in
-e) and adding **-ième**:

8, **huit** → 8th, **huitième**
12, **douze** → 12th, **douzième**
21, **vingt et un** → 21st, **vingt et unième**

Exceptions:

premier (fem: **première**), 1st
cinquième, 5th
neuvième, 9th

> **la première fois**, *the first time* (but **la trente et
> unième fois**, *the thirty-first time*)
> **le cinquième article**, *the fifth article*
> **le vingt-neuvième livre**, *the twenty-ninth book*

■ **Second** (fem: **seconde**) is an alternative to
deuxième, mainly used where there is no reference to a
third or subsequent thing or person. Notice though:

> **je suis en seconde**, *I'm in the fifth form* (French
> secondary schools count their classes in the
> opposite order to English schools)

■ Ordinals may be abbreviated thus **1er, 2e, 3e**, etc., or
1°, 2°, 3°, etc. The latter is short for the Latin *primo,
secundo, tertio,* etc.

■ When cardinal and ordinal numbers are used together
the order is the reverse of that in English:

> **les cinq premiers mois**, *the first five months*

■ French uses cardinal numbers where we use ordinal
numbers for days of the month and numbers of kings:

> **le vingt mai**, *the twentieth of May*
> **Henri quatre**, *Henri the Fourth*

However, for *first* French uses **premier**:

> **le premier septembre**, *the first of September*
> **Charles premier**, *Charles the First*

French, like English, uses cardinals for act, scene,

volume, and chapter numbers, but in all these cases uses **premier** for *one*:

> **acte premier**, *act one*
> **acte deux**, *act two*
> **chapitre premier**, *chapter one*

APPROXIMATE NUMBERS

Approximate numbers are formed in French by adding **-aine** to the cardinal number (the final **-e**, if any, is first dropped). They can only be based on 8, 15, tens up to 60, and 100. The resultant number is a feminine noun and is followed by **de**:

> **une quinzaine de francs**, *about fifteen francs*
> **une vingtaine de personnes**, *about twenty (a score of) people*
> **une cinquantaine de cahiers**, *about fifty exercise books*

■ **Mille**, *thousand*, forms **un millier**:

> **un millier de bateaux**, *about a thousand boats*

■ These nouns can be used in the plural:

> **des centaines de voitures**, *hundreds of cars*

■ **Une douzaine**, *a dozen*, though precise, is formed in the same way as the approximate numbers:

> **une douzaine d'œufs**, *a dozen eggs*

   Une quinzaine can also be used precisely to mean *a fortnight*, and **une huitaine** is sometimes found as an alternative to **une semaine**, *a week*.

FRACTIONS

Ordinal numbers are used to express fractions, as in English:

$^1/_5$ = **un cinquième**
$^3/_8$ = **trois huitièmes**

Exceptions:

·   **un quart** = $^1/_4$, **trois quarts** = $^3/_4$
un tiers = $^1/_3$, **deux tiers** = $^2/_3$
un demi = $^1/_2$

■ *Half* as a mathematical term is **le demi**:

les deux demis, *the two halves*

but in ordinary language, *half of* something is **la moitié de**:

la moitié du temps il ne fait rien, *half the time he does nothing*

Half as an adjective is **demi**. It is hyphenated to the noun and is invariable:

un demi-jour, *a half day*
une demi-heure, *a half hour* (but **un quart d'heure**, *quarter of an hour*)

La demie is *the half-hour*:

la demie sonne, *it's striking half past*

■ Decimals are expressed in French with a comma:

1·5 → **1,5 (un virgule cinq)**

■ The main mathematical signs are:

+ **plus**   ÷ **divisé par**
− **moins** ^{2} **au carré**
× **fois**   % **pour cent**

trois plus deux égalent cinq, *three plus two equals five*
dix au carré, *ten squared*
onze pour cent, *eleven per cent*

TIME AND DATE

Time of day

Quelle heure est-il?, *what time is it?*
Avez-vous l'heure, monsieur/madame? (politer!)
Il est:

> **une heure**, *one o'clock*
> **une heure cinq**, *five past one*
> **deux heures**, *two o'clock*
> **deux heures et** (or **un**) **quart**, *quarter past two*
> **trois heures et demie, trois heures trente**, *half past three*
> **quatre heures moins le** (or **moins un**) **quart**, *quarter to four*
> **cinq heures moins une (minute)**, *a minute to five*
> **midi**, *noon*
> **midi et demi, midi trente**, *half past twelve*
> **minuit**, *midnight*
> **minuit et demi, minuit trente**, *half past twelve*

■ **Heure(s)** is used where English uses *o'clock*. **Et demie** is used after hours, **et demi** after **midi**, **minuit**. With quarters the article **le** is used after **moins** but not after **et**.

■ The forms **trois heures trente**, etc. are adopted from the twenty-four hour clock, used in timetables and all official documents. This follows the pattern:

> **une heure dix**, 01h10
> **douze heures quarante-cinq**, 12h45
> **dix-neuf heures cinquante-cinq**, 19h55

■ French has no equivalents to *a.m.* and *p.m.* Where necessary, **du matin**, *in the morning*, **de l'après-midi**, *in the afternoon*, or **du soir**, *in the evening*, are added as appropriate:

trois heures du matin, *3 a.m.*

■ *In the morning (afternoon, evening)* is simply **le matin (l'après-midi, le soir)**. *At night* is **la nuit**. *Every morning* (etc.) is **tous les matins**.

Prepositions etc. with times of day

à, *at, by*

> **alors, on se revoit à trois heures précises**, *right, we'll meet at three o'clock sharp*
> **on sera là à midi**, *we'll be there by twelve*

à partir de, *from*

> **je serai dans le bureau à partir de neuf heures et demie**, *I shall be in the office from 9.30*

au bout de, *after*

> **au bout d'un petit instant elle recommença**, *after a moment she began again*

de ... à, *from ... to*

> **le restaurant est ouvert de midi à deux heures et demie**, *the restaurant is open from 12 to 2.30*

environ, *about*

> **il est environ sept heures** (or **sept heures environ**), *it's about seven o'clock*

jusqu'à, *until*

> **jusqu'à quatre heures de l'après-midi**, *until 4 p.m.*

pas plus tard que, *no later than*

> **il faut y arriver pas plus tard que deux heures et demie**, *you must get there no later than half past two*

passé, *past*

> **il est huit heures passées**, *it's past eight o'clock*

vers, *about*

> **il est parti vers les cinq heures,** *he left about five*

Days, months, seasons

days of the week	*months of the year*
dimanche, *Sunday*	**janvier,** *January*
lundi, *Monday*	**février,** *February*
mardi, *Tuesday*	**mars,** *March*
mercredi, *Wednesday*	**avril,** *April*
jeudi, *Thursday*	**mai,** *May*
vendredi, *Friday*	**juin,** *June*
samedi, *Saturday*	**juillet,** *July*
	août, *August*
today, etc.	**septembre,** *September*
avant-hier, *the day before*	**octobre,** *October*
yesterday	**novembre,** *November*
hier, *yesterday*	**décembre,** *December*
aujourd'hui, *today*	
demain, *tomorrow*	*seasons*
après-demain, *the day after*	**le printemps,** *spring*
tomorrow	**l'été,** *summer*
la veille, *the day before*	**l'automne,** *autumn*
le lendemain, *the day after*	**l'hiver,** *winter*

Days, months, and seasons are all masculine and are spelt with a small letter.

Parts of the day

hier, *yesterday*	
ce (cet), *this*	⎫ ⎧ **matin,** *morning*
demain, *tomorrow*	⎬ ⎨ **après-midi,** *afternoon*
dimanche, *Sunday* (etc.)	⎭ ⎩ **soir,** *evening*
le lendemain, *the day*	
after, in the …	

> **on vous verra dimanche soir**, *we'll see you Sunday evening*
>
> **cela est arrivé ce matin**, *that happened this morning*
>
> **on s'est brouillés le lendemain soir**, *they quarrelled the following evening*

The evening before is **la veille au soir**.

Cette nuit means either *tonight* or *last night*, according to context:

> **tu dormiras bien cette nuit!**, *you'll sleep well tonight!*
>
> **je n'ai pas dormi cette nuit**, *I didn't sleep last night*

Prepositions with days, months, seasons, etc.

■ *In* with months is **en** or **au mois de**:

> **en avril**, *in April*
>
> **au mois d'août**, *in August*

■ *In* with seasons is **en**, except **le printemps**:

> **en hiver**, *in winter*
>
> **au printemps**, *in spring*

■ *In* with years is **en** or **en l'an**. **Mil** is used instead of **mille** in writing years:

> **en l'an mil neuf cent quarante-cinq**, *in 1945*

In spoken French **dix-neuf** (etc.) is very often used for **mil neuf** (etc.):

> **en seize cent douze**, *in 1612*

In the eighties (etc.) is **dans les années quatre-vingt** (note spelling here: no **-s**, hyphen).

■ *In* with centuries is **au**:

> **au vingtième siècle**, *in the twentieth century*

■ *On* with days in the plural is **le**:

> **il ne travaille que le mercredi**, *he only works on Wednesdays*

■ *On* with days in the singular is not translated:

> **elle arrive mercredi**, *she's coming on Wednesday*
> **elle arrive mercredi matin**, *she's coming on Wednesday morning*

The date

The date is expressed with **le**, plus a cardinal number (except for **premier**, *first*), plus the month. *On* before a date is not translated:

> **on sera à Paris le quatorze juillet**, *we are going to be in Paris on the fourteenth of July*
> **nous sommes le premier juin**, *today's the first of June*

When the day is expressed, the article before the date is usually dropped:

> **lundi, vingt mai** or **le lundi vingt mai**, *Monday the twentieth of May*

MEASUREMENT

Length, breadth, height

> **Quelle est** $\left\{\begin{array}{l}\textbf{la longueur}\\ \textbf{la largeur}\\ \textbf{la hauteur}\end{array}\right\}$ **de cette pièce?**,
>
> *How* $\left\{\begin{array}{l}long\\ wide\\ high\end{array}\right\}$*is this room?*

— Elle a trois mètres dix de $\begin{Bmatrix} \textbf{long} \\ \textbf{large} \\ \textbf{haut} \end{Bmatrix}$, *It's*

3.10 *metres* $\begin{Bmatrix} long \\ wide \\ high \end{Bmatrix}$

■ **Faire** can be used instead of **avoir**:

elle fait trois mètres de long, *it's three metres long*

■ *By* in measurements is **sur**:

cette pièce fait trois mètres sur quatre, *this room is three metres by four*

Other common ways of expressing dimension

■ **Long** (etc.) **de**:

cette poutre est longue de trois mètres, *this beam is three metres long*
une poutre longue de trois mètres, *a beam three metres long*

■ **De longueur** (etc.):

cette poutre a trois mètres de longueur, *this beam is three metres long*
une poutre de trois mètres de longueur, *a beam three metres long*

■ **D'une longueur** (etc.) **de**:

cette poutre est d'une longueur de trois mètres, *this beam is three metres long*
une poutre d'une longueur de trois mètres, *a beam three metres long*

The same constructions can be used with **profond/la profondeur**, *deep/depth*, and **épais/l'épaisseur**, *thick/*

thickness, except the **de long** construction, which cannot be used with **épais** and **profond**.

Personal measurements

Quelle taille faites-vous?, *What size are you?*
Quelle est votre taille?, *What is your height?*

Quel est votre tour de $\left\{\begin{array}{c} \textbf{poitrine} \\ \textbf{taille} \\ \textbf{hanches} \end{array}\right\}$**?**, *What is your*

$\left\{\begin{array}{c} bust \\ waist \\ hip \end{array}\right\} size?$

Quelle pointure chaussez-vous/faites-vous?, *What is your shoe size?*

Notice the three meanings of **la taille**: *size, height, waist*. Only the context makes clear which is meant.

Word Order

Word order in French is generally the same as in English, except that:

- Adjectives usually follow their nouns. See p. 138.

- Object pronouns precede the verb. See p. 105.

- Adverbs follow the verb. See p. 156.

- Negatives stand in two parts around the verb. See p. 159.

- The 'strong' position in the French sentence is at the end, so where there are, for instance, two or more adverb phrases, the more important one goes to the end. Thus the answer to **quand l'as-tu retrouvé?** (*when did you find it?*) might be:

> **je l'ai retrouvé dans la voiture hier soir**, *I found it last night in the car*

English usage varies, but the more important phrase tends to come first in English, straight after the verb, as in the above example.

- Word order in direct and indirect questions is treated on pp. 211 and 213.

SPECIAL CASES

■ After direct speech, subject and 'saying' verb are inverted:

> **«Bonjour, dit-il, ça va?»**, *'Hello,' he said, 'How are you?'*
>
> **«Vraiment?» répondit l'agent**, *'Really?' the policeman replied*

Notice what happens in compound tenses:

> **«Bonjour, a-t-il dit, ça va?»**, *'Hello,' he said, 'How are you?'*
>
> **«Vraiment?» a répondu l'agent**, *'Really?' the policeman replied*

Although the pronoun inversion is like the question form (**a-t-il dit?**) the noun inversion is not (**l'agent a-t-il répondu?**).

■ In a clause beginning **peut-être**, *perhaps*, **à peine**, *scarcely*, or **aussi**, *therefore*, verb and subject pronoun are inverted:

> **peut-être a-t-elle froid**, *perhaps she's cold*
> **à peine son père était-il arrivé que le repas commença**, *his father had scarcely got there when the meal began*
> **maintenant tu me dis la vérité, aussi suis-je content**, *now you're telling me the truth, so I'm happy*

This inversion is literary, however. In everyday French it is avoided: **peut-être** would be placed after the verb, or the sentence would begin with **peut-être que**:

> **elle a peut-être froid**
> **peut-être qu'elle a froid**

A peine would similarly be placed after the verb, and **donc** would be substituted for **aussi**:

> **son père était à peine arrivé que le repas**
> **commença**
> **maintenant tu me dis la vérité, donc je suis**
> **content**

■ In exclamations after **comme** and **que** French has normal word order where English does not:

> **comme il est beau!**, *how handsome he is!*
> **que tu es bête!**, *how silly you are!*

■ After **dont** French always has normal word order where English sometimes does not:

> **le médecin dont tu connais la fille**, *the doctor*
> *whose daughter you know*
> **le médecin dont la fille est malade**, *the doctor*
> *whose daughter is ill*

▶ See also p. 115.

WORD ORDER IN DIRECT QUESTIONS

Simple questions

Simple questions are formed:

■ By a statement with an interrogative (rising) intonation. This is the commonest way to form a question in speech:

> **c'est une Française?**, *is she French?*

■ By prefixing **est-ce que** to the statement. This is also common in both speech and writing:

> **est-ce que vous prenez du sucre?**, *do you take*
> *sugar?*

■ By inverting verb and subject pronoun and putting a hyphen between them:

> **prenez-vous du café?**, *will you have some coffee?*

An extra **-t** is inserted where the verb ends in **-e** or **-a**:

> **a-t-il déjà dîné?**, *has he already eaten?*

In modern French there is, for most verbs, no inverted form of the interrogative with the **je** form of the present tense. **Est-ce que** or a simple question intonation is used.

Inversion is, however, still used with the **je** form of the present tense of **pouvoir**, **devoir**, **être**, and, occasionally, **avoir**:

> **puis-je vous revoir?**, *may I see you again?* (NB never **'peux-je'**)
> **que dois-je dire?**, *what am I to say?*
> **suis-je encore de tes amis?**, *am I still one of your friends?*
> **ai-je tout corrigé?**, *have I marked everything?*

■ By stating the noun subject and then asking the question about it using a pronoun. This produces the sequence noun, verb, hyphen, pronoun:

> **votre chien a-t-il déjà quitté la quarantaine?**, *has your dog already left quarantine?*

This construction is literary and is hardly ever found in everyday French.

Questions following question words (interrogative adverbs)

Questions following words such as **pourquoi**, *why*, **quand**, *when*, **où**, *where*, etc. are formed:

■ With a statement pronounced with an interrogative (rising) intonation, following the question word:

quand tu pars?, *when are you going?*

This construction is frowned upon in the written language but is extremely common in spoken French.

■ With the question word followed by **est-ce que** and a statement:

où est-ce que tu vas?, *where are you going?*

This is common in both written and spoken French.

■ With the question word followed by the verb, a hyphen and the subject pronoun:

comment as-tu fait cela?, *how did you do that?*

■ With the question word followed by the verb and the subject noun:

quand part le train de Marseille?, *when does the Marseilles train go?*

This form is not possible after **pourquoi** and often sounds clumsy in compound tenses. In these cases one of the other forms is used.

■ With the question word followed by the noun subject, the question then being asked about this using a pronoun:

pourquoi le train de Marseille part-il de cette voie?, *why does the Marseilles train leave from this platform?*

This construction is literary and is hardly ever found in everyday French.

▶ For questions introduced by the interrogative pronouns **qui, que**, etc. (*who, what*), see p. 119.

WORD ORDER IN INDIRECT QUESTIONS

An indirect question is one that is reported in some way (direct question: *why is he there?*, indirect question:

I don't know why he's there). As in English the word
order is: question word followed by normal order:

> **je ne sais pas pourquoi il est là**, *I don't know why
> he's there*

If the subject of the indirect question is a noun and the
verb would otherwise end the sentence, verb and noun
are inverted:

> **je me demande si ta copine est là**, *I wonder if
> your friend is there*
> **je me demande où est ta copine**, *I wonder where
> your friend is*

In this way French avoids leaving a weak word like **est**
in the strong position at the end of the sentence.

Punctuation

French punctuation is largely similar to English, with the following exceptions:

COMMAS

■ Commas are not used in writing large numbers in French. Where we would put a comma, modern French leaves a gap:

> English: 44,000,000   French: 44 000 000

■ Commas are used in decimals where we would use a decimal point or a full stop:

> English: 3·25 or 3.25   French: 3,25

CAPITAL LETTERS

Capitals are used much less frequently in French than in English. French uses small letters for:

■ Country adjectives:

> **il a l'air italien**, *he looks Italian*
> **une assiette anglaise**, *a plate of cold meats*

■ Language nouns:

> **elle parle français**, *she speaks French*

but not nouns of nationality:

> **c'est une Française**, *she's French*

■ Personal and professional titles, ranks:

> **monsieur Dubois** (but **M. Dubois**)
> **le docteur Artin**
> **le général Leclerc**

■ Street, square, avenue, etc., in names:

> **tu descends place de la Concorde**, *you get out at the Place de la Concorde*
> **la mer Méditerranée**, *the Mediterranean Sea*
> **elle demeure boulevard Raspail**, *she lives in the Boulevard Raspail*
> **7, rue Victor-Hugo**

■ Points of the compass:

> **le sud**, *the south*; **le nord**, *the north* (but **le Nord**, name of the region)

■ Names of days, months:

> **dimanche prochain**, *next Sunday*
> **en janvier dernier**, *last January*

■ Cheeses and wines named after places:

> **le camembert**, *Camembert*
> **le beaujolais**, *Beaujolais*

■ Quite often after an exclamation mark where the sense is not complete. There are two examples in the Daudet extract on p. 218 (in the section on inverted commas).

COLON AND DASH

Colon

The colon is used more frequently than in English. As well as being used as a long pause, intermediate between a semi-colon and a full stop (as in English), the colon is used where an amplification or explanation is to follow next. English often uses a dash for this, French hardly ever:

> **La seule solution: refaire le toit**, *The only solution—repair the roof*

Dash

■ Used at the beginning and end of parentheses, as in English:

> **Le patron parlait — il aimait beaucoup parler — et en même temps il tapait sur la table**, *The boss was speaking—he was very fond of speaking—and at the same time he was tapping on the table*

■ Used to mark off items in a list:

> **il sera nécessaire de**
> **— remplacer les poutres**
> **— refaire le toit**
> **— réparer les rebords des fenêtres**
> **— reconstruire les placards**

> *It will be necessary to*
> *replace the beams,*
> *redo the roof,*
> *repair the window-sills,*
> *remake the cupboards*

■ Used to indicate a change of speaker in direct speech (see below, inverted commas).

SUSPENSION POINTS (...)

These may indicate that the sentence breaks off, as in English. In French, they may also indicate that what is to come next is comic, incongruous, or unexpected. English often uses a dash here:

> **45 milliards de francs par mois … la moitié du budget de l'État!**, *45 billion francs a year—half the national budget!*

INVERTED COMMAS

These are printed « » or " ". Single inverted commas ' ', are almost never used in French.

Inverted commas are placed at the beginning and end of a section of dialogue. Within that dialogue change of speaker is indicated by a new paragraph beginning with a dash (—), but the inverted commas are not closed or reopened. Short phrases indicating who is speaking, together with any adverbial qualifications, (e.g., **répondit-il d'un air distrait**) are included within the dialogue without closing or reopening the inverted commas. Longer interpolations (of at least one complete sentence) do entail closing and reopening the inverted commas.

The following extract from Daudet's *Lettres de mon moulin* illustrates all these points:

> **«C'est fini … Je n'en fais plus.**
> **— Qu'est-ce qu'il y a donc, père Gaucher? demanda le prieur, qui se doutait bien un peu de ce qu'il y avait.**
> **— Ce qu'il y a, monseigneur? … Il y a que je bois, que je bois comme un misérable …**
> **— Mais je vous avais dit de compter vos gouttes.**
> **— Ah, bien oui! compter mes gouttes! c'est par gobelets qu'il faudrait compter maintenant … Que le feu de Dieu me brûle si je m'en mêle encore!»**

C'est le chapitre qui ne riait plus.
«Mais, malheureux, vous nous ruinez! criait
l'argentier en agitant son grand-livre.
— Préférez-vous que je me damne?»

'It's over. I'm not making any more.'

'What's the matter then, père Gaucher?' asked
the prior, who rather suspected what the matter
was.

'What's the matter, monseigneur? The matter is,
I'm drinking, drinking like a scoundrel.'

'But I told you to count your sips.'

'Oh yes, count my sips! It's cupfuls I'd have to
be counting now. May the fire of God consume me
if I have anything more to do with it!'

Now it was the chapter who were no longer
laughing.

'But, you wretched man, you're ruining us!'
cried the treasurer, waving his ledger.

'Would you rather I damned myself?'

Translation Problems

The following list is alphabetical. It includes items not covered in the body of the grammar, or treated in a number of different places and more conveniently brought together here. Translation problems not covered here should be tackled via the index, or, in the case of prepositions, the alphabetical lists on pp. 185 (English) and 164 (French).

-ING

The *-ing* form of the verb is basically the present participle, but it has other uses in English, few of which correspond to the French.

■ *-ing* as adjective (the *-ing* word stands in front of a noun):

the setting sun
the deciding factor

In this case the French word will also be an adjective. It may be a present participle used as an adjective, as in English:

le soleil couchant, *the setting sun* (**se coucher**, *set* →present participle **couchant**)

or it may be an ordinary adjective:

le facteur décisif, *the deciding factor*

▶ See present participle, p. 34.

■ *-ing* as a verb in a phrase:

he spoke, looking at me closely
getting off the bus, I saw Micheline

In this case the *-ing* word is translated by a present participle, usually preceded by **en**, *whilst*:

il parla, en me regardant de près, *he spoke, looking at me closely*
en descendant de l'autobus, j'ai vu Micheline, *getting off the bus, I saw Micheline*

This construction can only be used where both verbs have the same subject (*he* spoke and *he* looked at me, *I* got off and *I* saw her). Where the subjects are different, **qui** (or alternatively, after verbs of perception only, an infinitive) has to be used:

j'ai vu Micheline qui descendait de l'autobus, or
j'ai vu Micheline descendre de l'autobus, *I saw Micheline getting off the bus*

In this case the subjects are different (*I* saw, but *Micheline* got off).

▶ For more detail see p. 35.

■ -*ing* after a preposition:

> *without stopping*
> *before eating*

This is an infinitive:

> **sans parler**, *without speaking*
> **avant de manger**, *before eating*

With some prepositions, notably **après**, *after*, the sense may demand a perfect infinitive:

> **après avoir mangé**, *after eating*
> **après être sorti**, *after going out*

After the preposition **en**, *whilst*, *by*, *in*, a present participle is used:

> **en tournant**, *whilst turning*

▶ For more detail see pp. 52 (infinitives after prepositions) and 53 (perfect infinitive).

■ -*ing* in 'continuous' tenses: *I am running, I was running, I shall be running, I have been running*, etc.

French does not use a present participle for these: *I run* and *I am running* are the same in French: **je cours**, *I have been running* and *I have run* are the same, **j'ai couru**. Only in the case of the imperfect does a special 'continuous' tense exist: **je courais**, *I was running*.

If the continuous nature of an action needs to be emphasized (which is not usually the case), **être en train de** is used:

> **je serai en train de déjeuner**, *I shall be eating my lunch*

▶ For more details see p. 16.

Superficially similar to the above are sentences such as 'she was leaning on the fence', 'he was lying on the ground'. In this case, however, French views *lying*, *leaning,* etc. as adjectives and uses **être** plus a past participle:

> **elle était accoudée sur la clôture**, *she was leaning on the fence*
> **il était couché par terre**, *he was lying on the ground*

▶ For further details see p. 39.

■ *-ing* after a verb:

> *he begins typing*
> *she stops telephoning*
> *they love swimming*

This is an infinitive in French, preceded by the preposition appropriate to the main verb:

> **il commence à taper**, *he begins typing*
> **elle s'arrête de téléphoner**, *she stops telephoning*
> **ils adorent nager**, *they love swimming*

■ *-ing* after a verb with an object:

> *he stops her telephoning*
> *she heard him laughing*

This is also an infinitive in French, preceded by the preposition appropriate to the main verb:

> **il l'empêche de téléphoner**, *he stops her telephoning*
> **elle l'a entendu rire**, *she heard him laughing*

▶ For the prepositions that verbs take before an infinitive see p. 51.

■ *-ing* as subject of the sentence (the verbal noun):

> *walking tires me*
> *telephoning is easier*

This is an infinitive in French:

> **me promener me fatigue**, *walking tires me*
> **téléphoner est plus simple**, *telephoning is easier*

However, French prefers to avoid this use of the infinitive at the beginning of the sentence, and usually makes the infinitive depend on the other verb:

> **ça me fatigue de me promener**, *it tires me to walk*
> **c'est plus simple de téléphoner**, *it's easier to telephone*

▶ See also the infinitive as verbal noun, p. 50.

■ *-ing* as a noun

English uses *-ing* nouns for many sorts of activity and sports. These are translated by other nouns in French:

> *fishing*, **la pêche**
> *swimming*, **la natation**
> *singing*, **le chant**
> *horse-riding*, **l'équitation**

IT IS

It is with nouns and adjectives

■ Where *it is* refers to a noun that has already been mentioned, it is translated by **il est** or **elle est** according to the gender of that noun:

> **la clé? Elle est sur la porte**, *the key? It's in the door*
> **ma nouvelle robe, ah oui, elle est bleue**, *my new dress, yes, it's blue*

■ Where *it is* introduces a noun or pronoun, it is translated by **c'est**, whatever the gender of the noun or pronoun. The plural (*those are*) is **ce sont**:

> **c'est une Citroën**, *it's a Citroën*
> **c'est moi!**, *it's me!*
> **ce sont des mouettes**, *those are seagulls*

C'est is similarly used to introduce adverbial
expressions:

> **c'est à Noël qu'elle vient**, *it's at Christmas that
> she's coming*

■ Where *it is* refers back to something other than a noun
(a noun clause, a previous sentence, etc.), **c'est** is used.

> **il parle italien? Oui, c'est possible**, *he speaks
> Italian? Yes, it's possible*

■ Where *it is* introduces an adjective followed by **que** or
de, **il est** is used:

> **il est possible qu'il parle italien**, *it's possible that
> he speaks Italian*
> **il est difficile de traduire cela**, *it's difficult to
> translate that*

However, in the spoken language **c'est** is very often used
in this case too:

> **c'est possible qu'il parle Italien**, *it's possible he
> speaks Italian*

■ In all cases except the last **cela est** or the more casual
ça est may be used instead of **c'est**:

> **cela est possible**, *it's (that's) possible*

It is, with weather, time, etc.

■ *It* is **il** with:

□ Weather verbs, both simple verbs

> **il pleut**, *it's raining*
> **il neige**, *it's snowing*

and those constructed with **faire**

> **il fait du vent**, *it's windy*
> **il fait beau**, *it's fine*

☐ Time of day

> **il est cinq heures**, *it's five o'clock*
> **il est midi et demi**, *it's half past twelve*

☐ The time expressions: **tard**, *late*, **tôt**, *early*, **temps**,
time

> **il est tard**, *it's late*
> **il est temps de partir**, *it's time to go*
> **il est temps que tu partes**, *it's time you went*

■ With other time expressions **c'est** is used:

> **c'est dimanche**, *it's Sunday*
> **c'est janvier**, *it's January*
> **c'est le printemps**, *it's spring*
> **c'est le 18 mai**, *it's the 18th of May*

■ **Pouvoir**, *can*, and **devoir**, *ought to*, *should*, may be
introduced into these constructions:

> **ce doit être possible**, *it ought to be possible*
> **il peut neiger**, *it may snow*

▶ For further details see impersonal verbs, pp. 74 ff.

JUST (adverb)

■ *just = exactly*: **juste**; **justement**

> **tu as juste trois minutes**, *you have just three
> minutes*
> **c'est juste au-dessus de la porte**, *it's just above
> the door*
> **on a sonné juste au moment où je me mettais
> dans le bain**, *someone rang the bell just when I
> was getting into the bath*
> **voilà justement ce que je dis toujours**, *that's just
> what I always say*

■ *just* = *only*: **seul; seulement**

> **un seul**, *just one*
> **seulement deux, trois**, etc., *just two, three*, etc.
> **une seule fois**, *just once*

■ *just* in *have/had just*: **venir de** + infinitive

> **je viens de le faire**, *I've just done it*
> **on venait de l'ouvrir**, *they had just opened it*

▶ See pp. 18 and 21 for more details on tenses with **venir de**.

■ *just* in *just as* (= *equally*): **tout**

> **cela est tout aussi difficile**, *that's just as difficult*

■ *just* with a following verb: **ne faire que** + infinitive

> **elle n'a fait que pleurer**, *she just cried*

-SELF

■ *-self* as direct or indirect object: reflexive pronoun (**me, te, se**, etc.) before verb:

> **il s'est distingué**, *he distinguished himself*
> **je me disais la même chose**, *I was saying the same thing to myself*

▶ For further details see reflexive pronouns, p. 30.

■ *-self* as a strengthener of the subject: disjunctive pronoun + **-même** (**moi-même, toi-même**, etc.) placed after verb:

> **tu l'as fait toi-même?**, *you did it yourself?*

▶ For further details see disjunctive pronouns, p. 109 and disjunctives with **-même**, p. 111.

■ *-self* after preposition: disjunctive pronoun (**moi, toi,** etc.) with or without **-même**:

> **je ne parle que pour moi**, *I can only speak for myself*
> **il n'écrit que pour lui-même**, *he writes only for himself*

■ *oneself* is **soi(-même)**:

> **on ne peut pas le garder pour soi(-même)**, *one can't keep it for oneself*

▶ For further details on the use of **soi** see p. 109.

SINCE

■ Preposition: **depuis**

> **je t'attends depuis deux heures et demie**, *I've been waiting for you since half past two*
> **je t'attendais depuis deux heures et demie**, *I had been waiting for you since half past two*

The tenses with **depuis** are different from the English ones in positive statements: *have been … ing* = French present, *had been … ing* = French imperfect. With a negative the tense is the same as in English:

> **je ne l'ai pas vue depuis la boum**, *I haven't seen her since the party*

▶ **Depuis** can also mean *for*. For more details on tenses with **depuis** see pp. 17 and 21.

■ Adverb: **depuis**

> **tu l'a vue depuis?**, *have you seen her since?*

The adverb **depuis** does not affect the tense of the verb.

■ Time conjunction: **depuis que**

> **elle travaille depuis que son mari est mort**, *she has been working (has worked) ever since her husband died*
>
> **elle marchait depuis que la voiture était finalement tombée en panne**, *she had been walking (ever) since the car finally broke down*
>
> **je ne dors plus depuis qu'il est de retour**, *I'm not sleeping any more since he's back*

Tenses with **depuis que**, conjunction, are the same as with **depuis**, preposition, above.

▶ For further information on **depuis que** see pp. 17 and 21.

■ Conjunction expressing reason: **puisque**

> **puisqu'il est si impoli je ne lui parle plus**, *since he's so rude I don't speak to him any more*

SOON AND LATE

Soon, early

■ *soon*: **bientôt**

> **on sera bientôt là**, *we'll soon be there*

■ *soon = early*: **tôt**

> **on est arrivé beaucoup trop tôt**, *we got there much too soon (early)*

■ *early = in good time*: **de bonne heure**

> **on est arrivé de bonne heure**, *we got there early*

■ *sooner = earlier*: **plus tôt**

> **nous sommes arrivés plus tôt qu'eux**, *we arrived sooner (earlier) than they did*

■ *sooner* = *in preference*; *rather*: **plutôt**

> **plutôt lui que moi**, *sooner him than me*

Late

■ *late*, time of day: **tard**

> **il est très tard, rentrons**, *it's very late, let's go home*

■ *late*, = *after the appropriate time*: **tard**

> **maintenant il est trop tard**, *now it's too late*

■ *late*, referring to people: **en retard**

> **nous sommes en retard**, *we're late*

■ *late*, adjective: **tardif**

> **à cette heure tardive**, *at this late hour*

■ *late*, adjective, = *dead*: **feu**

> **le tombeau de feu son père**, *his late father's grave*

Feu is invariable. Note its position.

TIME(S)

■ *time(s)* = *occasion(s)*: **la/les fois**

> **pour la première fois**, *for the first time*

■ *time* = *length, amount of time*: **le temps**

> **malheureusement je n'ai pas le temps**,
> *unfortunately I haven't got (the) time*

■ *time* = *point in time*: **le moment**

> **tu es arrivé au bon moment?**, *you got there at the right time?*

On time is **à temps**:

> **il faut arriver à temps**, *you must get there on time*

■ *time* = *time of day*: **l'heure**

> **vous avez l'heure?**, *do you have the (right) time?*

■ *time* = *period*: **l'époque**

> **à cette époque j'étais toujours au lycée**, *at that time I was still at college*

TO BE

To be is translated by verbs other than **être** in the following cases:

■ Location: **se trouver**

> **le garage se trouve derrière la maison**, *the garage is (located) behind the house*

■ Physical states: **avoir**

> **j'ai chaud/froid/faim/soif/sommeil/peur/honte**, *I'm hot/cold/hungry/thirsty/tired/frightened/ashamed*

Similarly: *to be right/wrong* is **avoir raison/tort**.

■ Health: **aller**

> **comment allez-vous?**, *how are you?*
> **maman va beaucoup mieux**, *mother's much better*

■ Weather: **faire**

> **il fait chaud/froid/beau/mauvais/du vent/du brouillard**, *it's hot/cold/fine/bad/windy/foggy*

■ Age: **avoir**

> **elle a vingt et un ans**, *she's twenty-one (years old)*

▶ *I am to/I was to* is translated by **devoir**. See p. 65.

VERB + OBJECT + INFINITIVE

Sentences such as *I want her to go*, *I like her to talk* cannot be translated directly into French, as, with the exception of a very few verbs (see below), this verb + object + infinitive construction does not exist in French. A clause has to be used instead:

> **je veux qu'elle parte**, *I want her to go* (*'I want that she should go'*)
>
> **j'aime qu'il me gratte le dos**, *I like him to scratch my back* (*'I like that he scratches my back'*)

Both **vouloir que** and **aimer que** in the above examples take the subjunctive.

A similar construction used in English with verbs of perception consists of verb + object + infinitive/present participle (*I hear him speak/speaking*). This construction, with verbs of perception (**voir, entendre, sentir**, etc.), can be translated directly into French. A dependent infinitive is used:

> **je l'entends parler**, *I hear him speak(ing)*

▶ For further details see p. 42 (subjunctive) and p. 51 (dependent infinitive)

VERB + PREPOSITION COMBINATIONS

Many English verbs consist of a simple verb plus a preposition (*cry out, run away, run back*). This verb-plus-preposition construction is impossible in French and such verbs, sometimes called phrasal verbs, have to be translated in one of the following ways.

■ By a simple verb:

> **crispée de douleur, elle commença à crier**, *contorted with pain, she began to cry out* (*cry out*: **crier**)

> **à la nuit tombante ils se sont enfuis**, *at nightfall*
> *they ran away* (*run away*: **s'enfuir**)

■ By a verb based on the preposition, plus a dependent present participle (with **en**) or an adverb phrase:

> **ils sont retournés en courant**, *they ran back* (*run*
> *back*: **retourner en courant**, '*go back running*')
> **ils sont partis à la hâte**, *they hurried off* (*hurry off*:
> **partir à la hâte**, '*go off in a hurry*')

▶ For further details see p. 36.

■ Where the verb-phrase has an object, by a verb with a dependent infinitive:

> **laisse-le entrer!**, *let him in*

Several of these are based on **faire**:

> **faire entrer**, *show in*
> **faire sortir**, *show out*
> **faire venir**, *send for*

▶ See p. 73 for more details.

WHATEVER, WHOEVER

Whatever

■ Pronoun subject: **quoi qui, quoi que ce soit qui**; pronoun object: **quoi que** (all + subjunctive)

> **quoi qui bouge, ne tirez pas!**, *whatever moves,*
> *don't shoot*
> **quoi que ce soit qui ronge votre parquet, ce n'est**
> **pas des souris**, *whatever is eating your*
> *floorboards, it isn't mice*
> **quoi qu'il dise, je ne le crois pas**, *whatever he*
> *says* (*may say*), *I don't believe him*

■ Adjective: **quel que soit**

> **quel que soit l'argent qu'on vous offre**, *whatever money you are offered*
>
> **ne renoncez pas, quelles que soient les difficultés**, *don't give up, whatever the difficulties may be*

■ *Anything whatever* is **quoi que ce soit**, used as if it were a pronoun:

> **il ne se plaigne pas de quoi que ce soit**, *he doesn't complain about anything whatever (anything at all)*

Whoever

■ **Qui que ce soit qui** (subject), **qui que ce soit que** (object) both + subjunctive:

> **qui que ce soit qui vous ait dit cela, c'est complètement faux**, *whoever told you that, it's completely untrue*
>
> **qui que ce soit qu'on propose comme candidat, je ne voterai pas**, *whoever they put up as candidate, I shall not vote*

Quiconque may be used, in rather more formal style, for **qui que ce soit qui/que**. See p. 130.

Pronunciation Traps

To attempt to present the pronunciation of French as a whole in a grammar of this kind would be impossible and pointless. It is, however, useful to provide reference to those commonly used words whose pronunciation does not follow the usual patterns or with which learners consistently find pronunciation problems.

The following list gives such problem words alphabetically, with a very approximate imitated pronunciation followed by the exact pronunciation represented by the letters of the International Phonetic Alphabet. In general, related words show the same pronunciation changes (so **le sculpteur**, *sculptor*, is pronounced without a p, like **la sculpture**, listed below).

ail (m.), *garlic*	eye	aj
aile (f.), *wing*	el	ɛl
alcool (m.), *alcohol*	al-col	alkɔl
	(one o pronounced)	
amener, *bring*	am-nay	amne
Amiens (the town)	am-ya	amjɛ̃
automne (m.), *autumn*	oh-tonn	otɔn
	(m not pronounced)	
but, **automnal**,	oh-tom-nal	otɔmnal
autumnal	(m usually pronounced)	
bœuf (m.), *beef; ox*	berf	bœf
but plural **bœufs**,	berh	bø
cattle; oxen		
cent un, *101*; **cent onze**	son-ern; son-onz	sɑ̃ œ̃; sɑ̃ ɔ̃:z
111	(t not pronounced)	
chef (m.), chief, *head*	shef	ʃɛf
but, **chef d'œuvre**,	shed-er-vr	ʃɛdœ:vɽ
masterpiece	(f not pronounced)	

Christ (m.), *Christ*	creased (t pronounced)	krist
but **Jésus Christ**	jay-zoo-cree (t not pronounced)	ʒezy kri
condamner, *condemn*	con-da-nay (m not pronounced)	kɔ̃dɑne
cuiller (also spelled **cuillère**), (f.) *spoon*	kwee-yair (r pronounced)	kɥijɛ:r
dix, *10* (standing alone)	deese	dis
(before a consonant)	dee	di
(before a vowel)	deez	diz
dot, (f.) *dowry*	dot (t pronounced)	dɔt
emmener, *take away*	om-nay	ɑ̃mne
estomac (m.), *stomach*	esto-ma (c not pronounced)	ɛstɔma
eu, *had* (past participle of **avoir**)	ee (+ rounded lips)	y
fier, *proud*	fee-air (r pronounced)	fjɛ:r
fils (m.), *son*	feese (s pronounced)	fis
but **fils** (m. pl.), *wires*	feel (s not pronounced)	fil
hais, hait, *hate(s)* (**je**, **tu** and **il** form of present, **haïr**)	eh (i not pronounced separately)	ɛ
hélas, *alas*	ay-lars (s pronounced)	elɑ:s
jus (m.), *juice*	joo (s not pronounced)	ʒy
mademoiselle (f.), *miss*	mad-mwa-zel (first e not pronounced)	madmwazɛl
mille, *thousand*	meal (ll pronounced l)	mil

mœurs, (f. pl.), *manners*	merse (s usually pronounced)	mœrs
naïveté (f.), *naïvety*	na-eev-tay	naivte
neuf, *9*	nerf	nœf
but **neuf heures**	ner-vur	nœv œːr
and **neuf ans**	ner-von (f pronounced v)	nœv ã
notre, *our*; **votre**, *your*	notr; votr	nɔtr̥; vɔtr̥
but, **nôtre**, *ours*; **vôtre**, *yours*	note-r, vote-r (o lengthened)	noːtr̥; voːtr̥
œuf (m.), *egg*	erf	œf
but plural **œufs**, *eggs*	erh (fs not pronounced, vowel lengthened)	φ
oignon (m.), *onion*	on-yon	ɔɲɔ̃
os (m.), *bone*	os	ɔs
but plural **os**, *bones*	oh (s not pronounced, vowel lengthened)	o
poêle (m.), *stove*; (f.), *frying pan*	pwal	pwal
Reims, (*Rheims*, the town)	ranse	rɛ̃ːs
rhum (m.), *rum* and **Rome**, *Rome*	rom	rɔm
sandwich (m.), *sandwich*	*sond-witch*	sãdwitʃ
sceptique, *sceptical*	sep-teek (c not pronounced)	sɛptik
sculpture (f.), *sculpture*	skill-tour (p not pronounced)	skyltyːr
sens (m.), *sense*; *direction*	sonse (last s pronounced)	sãːs

six, *6* (standing alone)	cease	sis
(before a consonant)	sea	si
(before a vowel)	seas	siz
solennel, *solemn*	sol-a-nel	sɔlanɛl
	(first e pronounced a)	
tabac (m.),	ta-ba	taba
tobacco(nist's)	(c not pronounced)	
tiers (m.), *third*	tea-air	tjɛːr
	(s not pronounced)	
vieille (f.), *old*	vyay	vjɛːj
but **veille** (f.), *the day*	vay	vɛːj
before		
village (m.), *village*	vee-large	vilaːʒ
	(ll pronounced l)	
ville (f.), *town*	veel	vil
	(ll pronounced l)	
vingt, *20*	van	vɛ̃
but **vingt et un**, *21*	van-tay-ern	vɛ̃t e œ̃
vingt-deux, *22*, etc.	vant-der	vɛ̃t dø
	(t usually pronounced	
	from 21 on)	
wagon (m.), *carriage*	va-gon	vagɔ̃

Verb Tables

▶ See also pp. 7 and 8.

■ Verbs with infinitives ending **-e**[consonant]**er**:

□ changing the **-e** to **-è** before a mute or unstressed **e**. See p. 7 for a list of verbs in this group. Model: **acheter**, *to buy*:

present		past participle
j'achète	**nous achetons**	**acheté**
tu achètes	**vous achetez**	
il achète	**ils achètent**	

future	past historic
j'achèterai	**j'achetai**

□ doubling the consonant before a mute or unstressed **-e**. Model: **jeter**, *to throw*:

present		past participle
je jette	**nous jetons**	**jeté**
tu jettes	**vous jetez**	
il jette	**ils jettent**	

future	past historic
je jetterai	**je jetai**

■ Verbs with infinitives ending **-é[consonant]er**:

The **é** changes to **è** before a mute **e**, but not in the future or conditional. Model: **préférer**, *to prefer*:

present		past participle
je préfère	**nous préférons**	**préféré**
tu préfères	**vous préférez**	
il préfère	**ils préfèrent**	

future	past historic
je préférerai	**je préférai**

■ Verbs with infinitives ending **-yer**:

The **y** changes to **i** before a mute or unstressed **e**. The change is optional with **-ayer** verbs. Model: **appuyer**, *to lean*:

present		past participle
j'appuie	**nous appuyons**	**appuyé**
tu appuies	**vous appuyez**	
il appuie	**ils appuient**	

future	past historic
j'appuierai	**j'appuyai**

■ Verbs with infinitives ending **-cer**:

The **c** changes to **ç** before **a** and **o**. Model: **commencer**, *to begin*:

present		past participle
je commence	**nous commençons**	**commencé**
tu commences	**vous commencez**	
il commence	**ils commencent**	

future		past historic
je commencerai		**je commençai**

present participle	imperfect	
commençant	**je commençais**	**nous commencions**
	tu commençais	**vous commenciez**
	il commençait	**ils commençaient**

■ Verbs with infinitives ending **-ger**:

The **g** changes to **ge** before **a** and **o**. Model: **manger**, *to eat*:

present		past participle
je mange	**nous mangeons**	**mangé**
tu manges	**vous mangez**	
il mange	**ils mangent**	

future	past historic
je mangerai	**je mangeai**

present participle	imperfect	
mangeant	**je mangeais**	**nous mangions**
	tu mangeais	**vous mangiez**
	il mangeait	**ils mangeaient**

IRREGULAR VERBS

Verbs, including common compound verbs, are in alphabetical order. Verbs marked * are less common: some parts of these verbs are very rarely met.

Verbs marked † form their compound tenses with **être**.

The parts given are the infinitive, the full present tense, the past participle (from which all compound tenses may be formed, see p. 3), the **je** form of the future (from which the rest of the future and the conditional may be formed), and the **je** form of the past historic (from which the rest of the past historic may be formed). The endings for these last three tenses are:

	future	*conditional*	*past historic*		
je	-ai	-ais	-ai	-is	-us
tu	-as	-ais	-as	-is	-us
il	-a	-ait	-a	-it	-ut
nous	-ons	-ions	-âmes	-îmes	-ûmes
vous	-ez	-iez	-âtes	-îtes	-ûtes
ils	-ont	-aient	-èrent	-irent	-urent

The conditional endings are added to the future stem to form the conditional; the same endings are added to the **nous** form of the present (without its **-ons**) to form the imperfect.

For the formation of the present and imperfect subjunctive see pp. 40 and 41.

infinitive; present	past participle	future	past historic
*acquérir *acquire*			
j'acquiers	**acquis**	**j'acquerrai**	**j'acquis**
tu acquiers			
il acquiert			
nous acquérons			
vous acquérez			
ils acquièrent			

accueillir, *welcome* → **cueillir**

admettre, *admit* → **mettre**

aller† *go*			
je vais	**allé**	**j'irai**	**j'allai**
tu vas			
il va			
nous allons			
vous allez			
ils vont			

pres. subjunctive: **j'aille, nous allions**

apercevoir, *catch sight of* → **recevoir**

apparaître, *appear* → **connaître**

apprendre, *learn* → **prendre**

infinitive; present	past participle	future	past historic
s'asseoir† *sit down*			
je m'assieds	**assis**	**je**	**je m'assis**
tu t'assieds		**m'assiérai**	
il s'assied			
nous nous asseyons			
vous vous asseyez			
ils s'asseyent			

more colloquial form of present: **je m'assois, tu t'assois, il s'assoit, nous nous assoyons, vous vous assoyez, ils s'assoient**

atteindre, *reach* → **peindre**

avoir *have*			
j'ai	**eu**	**j'aurai**	**j'eus**
tu as			
il a			
nous avons			
vous avez			
ils ont			

pres. subjunctive: **j'aie, nous ayons**, pres. participle: **ayant**, imperative: **aie, ayons, ayez**

*battre
beat   regular except present: **je bats, tu bats, il bat, nous battons, vous battez, ils battent**

*se battre†, *fight* → **battre**

infinitive; present	past participle	future	past historic
boire *drink*			
je bois	**bu**	**je boirai**	**je bus**
tu bois			
il boit			
nous buvons			
vous buvez			
ils boivent			

*bouillir regular except present: **je bous, tu bous, il bout,**
  boil   **nous bouillons, vous bouillez, ils bouillent**

* combattre, *combat* → **battre**

commettre, *commit* → **mettre**

comprendre, *understand* → **prendre**

* concevoir, *conceive* → **recevoir**

conduire *drive*			
je conduis	**conduit**	**je conduirai**	**je conduisis**
tu conduis			
il conduit			
nous conduisons			
vous conduisez			
ils conduisent			
connaître *know*			
je connais	**connu**	**je connaîtrai**	**je connus**
tu connais			
il connaît			
nous connaissons			
vous connaissez			
ils connaissent			

infinitive; present	past participle	future	past historic
construire, *construct* → **conduire**			
* **contraindre**, *restrict* → **peindre**			
* **contredire**, *contradict* → **dire** (present: **vous contredisez**)			
* **convaincre**, *convince* → **vaincre**			
* **coudre** *sew*			
je couds	**cousu**	**je coudrai**	**je cousis**
tu couds			
il coud			
nous cousons			
vous cousez			
ils cousent			
courir *run*			
je cours	**couru**	**je courrai**	**je courus**
tu cours			
il court			
nous courons			
vous courez			
ils courent			
couvrir *cover*			
je couvre	**couvert**	**je couvrirai**	**je couvris**
tu couvres			
il couvre			
nous couvrons			
vous couvrez			
ils couvrent			
craindre, *fear* → **peindre**			

infinitive; present	past participle	future	past historic
croire *believe*			
je crois **tu crois** **il croit** **nous croyons** **vous croyez** **ils croient**	**cru**	**je croirai**	**je crus**
* croître *grow*			
je croîs **tu croîs** **il croît** **nous croissons** **vous croissez** **ils croissent**	**crû** (f.: **crue**)	**je croîtrai**	past hist. not used
* cueillir *gather*			
je cueille **tu cueilles** **il cueille** **nous cueillons** **vous cueillez** **ils cueillent**	**cueilli**	**je cueillerai**	**je cueillis**
* cuire, *cook* → **conduire**			
décevoir, *deceive* → **recevoir**			
découvrir, *discover* → **couvrir**			
décrire, *describe* → **écrire**			
* détruire, *destroy* → **conduire**			

infinitive; present	past participle	future	past historic
devoir			
must; owe			
je dois	**dû**	**je devrai**	**je dus**
tu dois	(f.: **due,**		
il doit	m. pl.: **dus,**		
nous devons	f. pl.: **dues)**		
vous devez			
ils doivent			
dire			
say			
je dis	**dit**	**je dirai**	**je dis**
tu dis			
il dit			
nous disons			
vous dites			
ils disent			
dormir, *sleep* → **partir**			
écrire			
write			
j'écris	**écrit**	**j'écrirai**	**j'écrivis**
tu écris			
il écrit			
nous écrivons			
vous écrivez			
ils écrivent			
★ **élire,** *elect* → **lire**			
★ **émouvoir,** *move; stir up* → **mouvoir** (past participle: **ému**)			
★ **s'enquérir†,** *enquire* → **acquérir**			

infinitive; present	past participle	future	past historic
envoyer *send*			
j'envoie	**envoyé**	**j'enverrai**	**j'envoyai**
tu envoies			
il envoie			
nous envoyons			
vous envoyez			
ils envoient			

éteindre, *switch off; put out* → **peindre**

être *be*			
je suis	**été**	**je serai**	**je fus**
tu es			
il est			
nous sommes			
vous êtes			
ils sont			

pres. subjunctive: **je sois, nous soyons,**
pres. participle: **étant,** imperative: **sois, soyons, soyez**

* étreindre, *embrace* → **peindre**

faire *do; make*			
je fais			
tu fais	**fait**	**je ferai**	**je fis**
il fait			
nous faisons			
vous faites			
ils font			

pres. subjunctive: **je fasse, nous fassions**

infinitive; present	past participle	future	past historic
falloir *must*; *be necessary*			
il faut	**fallu**	**il faudra**	**il fallut**
pres. subjunctive: **il faille**			
★ **fuir** *flee*			
je fuis	**fui**	**je fuirai**	**je fuis**
tu fuis			
il fuit			
nous fuyons			
vous fuyez			
ils fuient			
★ **haïr** *hate*			
je hais	**haï**	**je haïrai**	**je haïs**
tu hais			
il hait			
nous haïssons			
vous haïssez			
ils haïssent			
(past. historic: **nous haïmes, vous haïtes,** imperfect subjunctive: **il haït**—but all three forms are virtually unused)			

★ **s'inscrire**†, *have oneself registered* → **écrire**

interdire, *forbid* → **dire** (present: **vous interdisez**)

introduire, *introduce*; *put in* → **conduire**

joindre, *join* → **peindre**

infinitive; present	past participle	future	past historic
lire *read*			
je lis	**lu**	**je lirai**	**je lus**
tu lis			
il lit			
nous lisons			
vous lisez			
ils lisent			
*luire *shine*			
il luit	**lui**	**il luira**	past hist.
ils luisent	(no f.)		not used
mentir, *tell lies* → **partir**			
mettre *put*			
je mets	**mis**	**je mettrai**	**je mis**
tu mets			
il met			
nous mettons			
vous mettez			
ils mettent			
*moudre *grind*			
je mouds	**moulu**	**je moudrai**	**je moulus**
tu mouds			
il moud			
nous moulons			
vous moulez			
ils moulent			

infinitive; present	past participle	future	past historic
mourir† *die*			
je meurs **tu meurs** **il meurt** **nous mourons** **vous mourez** **ils meurent**	**mort**	**je mourrai**	**je mourus**

* mouvoir
  drive;
  propel			

je meus **tu meus** **il meut** **nous mouvons** **vous mouvez** **ils meuvent**	**mû** (f. **mue**)	**je mouvrai**	**je mus** (rare)

* naître†, *be born* → **connaître** (past participle: **né**, past historic: **je naquis**)

* nuire, *harm* → **cuire** (past participle: **nui**)

offrir, *offer* → **couvrir**

ouvrir, *open* → **couvrir**

* paître, *graze* → **connaître** (no past participle or past historic)

paraître, *appear* → **connaître**

infinitive; present	past participle	future	past historic
partir† *leave*			
je pars	**parti**	**je partirai**	**je partis**
tu pars			
il part			
nous partons			
vous partez			
ils partent			
peindre *paint*			
je peins	**peint**	**je peindrai**	**je peignis**
tu peins			
il peint			
nous peignons			
vous peignez			
ils peignent			
* plaindre, *pity* → **peindre**			
* plaire *please*			
je plais	**plu**	**je plairai**	**je plus**
tu plais			
il plaît			
nous plaisons			
vous plaisez			
ils plaisent			
pleuvoir *rain*			
il pleut	**plu**	**il pleuvra**	**il plut**
pres. subjunctive: **il pleuve**			
poursuivre, *pursue* → **suivre**			

infinitive; present	past participle	future	past historic
pouvoir			
can; be able			
je peux			
(puis-je?)	**pu**	**je pourrai**	**je pus**
tu peux			
il peut			
nous pouvons			
vous pouvez			
ils peuvent			
pres. subjunctive: **je puisse, nous puissions**			
prendre			
take			
je prends	**pris**	**je prendrai**	**je pris**
tu prends			
il prend			
nous prenons			
vous prenez			
ils prennent			
produire, *produce* → **conduire**			
*****promouvoir**, *promote:* only infinitive and past participle (**promu**) used			
recevoir			
receive			
je reçois	**reçu**	**je recevrai**	**je reçus**
tu reçois			
il reçoit			
nous recevons			
vous recevez			
ils reçoivent			
reconnaître, *recognize* → **connaître**			

infinitive; present	past participle	future	past historic

---

* réduire, *reduce* → **conduire**

---

* se repentir†, *repent* → **partir**

---

* résoudre
   resolve

je résous	résolu	je	je résolus
tu résous		résoudrai	
il résout			
nous résolvons			
vous résolvez			
ils résolvent			

---

* restreindre, *restrain; limit* → **peindre**

---

rire
   laugh

je ris	ri	je rirai	je ris
tu ris			
il rit			
nous rions			
vous riez			
ils rient			

---

* rompre
   break

je romps	rompu	je romprai	je rompis
tu romps			
il rompt			
nous rompons			
vous rompez			
ils rompent			

infinitive; present	past participle	future	past historic
savoir *know*			
je sais	**su**	**je saurai**	**je sus**
tu sais			
il sait			
nous savons			
vous savez			
ils savent			

pres. subjunctive: **je sache, nous sachions**
pres. participle: **sachant**; used as adjective, **savant**
imperative: **sache, sachons, sachez**

★ séduire, *seduce* → **conduire**

sentir, se sentir†, *feel* → **partir**

servir, *serve* → **partir**

sortir†, *go out* → **partir**

souffrir, *suffer* → **couvrir**

sourire, *smile* → **rire**

suffire, *be (quite) enough* → **lire**   (past participle: **suffi**, past historic: **je suffis**)

infinitive; present	past participle	future	past historic
suivre *follow*			
je suis	**suivi**	**je suivrai**	**je suivis**
tu suis			
il suit			
nous suivons			
vous suivez			
ils suivent			

surprendre, *surprise* → **prendre**

★ survivre, *survive* → **vivre**

infinitive; present	past participle	future	past historic

* se taire†, *be quiet* → **plaire** (present: **il se tait**)

tenir, *hold* → **venir**

traduire, *translate* → **conduire**

* vaincre
  defeat

je vaincs	vaincu	je vaincrai	je vainquis
tu vaincs			
il vainc			
nous vainquons			
vous vainquez			
ils vainquent			

* valoir
  be worth

je vaux	valu	je vaudrai	je valus
tu vaux			
il vaut			
nous valons			
vous valez			
ils valent			

pres. subjunctive: **je vaille, nous valions, ils vaillent**; forms other than **il** extremely uncommon in all tenses

venir†
  come

je viens	venu	je viendrai	je vins
tu viens			tu vins
il vient			il vint
nous venons			nous vînmes
vous venez			vous vîntes
ils viennent			ils vinrent

infinitive; present	past participle	future	past historic
* vêtir			
dress			
je vêts	**vêtu**	**je vêtirai**	**je vêtis**
tu vêts			
il vêt			
nous vêtons			
vous vêtez			
ils vêtent			

(present **nous vêtissons, vous vêtissez, ils vêtissent,** present part. **vêtissant,** and imperfect **je vêtissais** etc. are also found)

vivre			
live			
je vis	**vécu**	**je vivrai**	**je vécus**
tu vis			
il vit			
nous vivons			
vous vivez			
ils vivent			

voir			
see			
je vois	**vu**	**je verrai**	**je vis**
tu vois			
il voit			
nous voyons			
vous voyez			
ils voient			

infinitive; present	past participle	future	past historic
vouloir *want*			
je veux	**voulu**	**je voudrai**	**je voulus**
tu veux			
il veut			
nous voulons			
vous voulez			
ils veulent			

pres. subjunctive: **je veuille, nous voulions**
imperative: **veuille, veuillez** (= *would you kindly*)

Glossary of Grammatical Terms

Abstract Noun The name of something that is not a concrete object or person. Words such as *difficulty*, *hope*, *discussion* are abstract nouns.

Active See Passive.

Adjective A word describing a noun. *A big, blue, untidy painting*—*big, blue, untidy* are adjectives describing the noun *painting*.

Adverb A word that describes or modifies (i) a verb: *he did it gracefully* (adverb: *gracefully*), or (ii) an adjective: *a disgracefully large helping* (adverb: *disgracefully*), or (iii) another adverb: *she skated extraordinarily gracefully* (adverbs: *extraordinarily, gracefully*).

Agreement In French, adjectives agree with nouns, verbs agree with subject nouns or pronouns, pronouns agree with nouns, etc. This is a way of showing that something refers to or goes with something else. Agreement is by number (showing whether something is singular or plural) and by gender (showing whether something is masculine or feminine). For instance: **des chaussettes bleues**, *blue socks*: **-e** is added to the adjective because **chaussette** is feminine, **-s** is added to **bleue** because **chaussettes** is plural.

Apposition Two nouns or noun phrases are used together, the second one explaining the first: *the station master, a big man with a moustache, came in.* 'A big man with a moustache' is in apposition to 'the station master'.

Articles The little words like *a* and *the* that stand in front of nouns. In English, *the* is the definite article (it defines a particular item in a category: *the hat you've got on*); *a* or *an* is the indefinite article (it doesn't specify which item in a category: *wear a hat, any hat*); *some* is the partitive article (it specifies a part but not the whole of a category: *I'd like some mustard*).

Attributive Noun A noun used as an adjective: *a petrol pump*: 'petrol' is an attributive noun, telling us what sort of pump.

Auxiliary Verb A verb used to help form a compound tense. In *I am walking, he has walked* the auxiliary verbs are *to be* (*am*) and *to have* (*has*).

Cardinal Numbers The numbers used in counting (*one, two, three, four*, etc.). Compare with Ordinal Numbers.

Clause A self-contained section of a sentence containing a verb: *He came in and was opening his mail when the lights went out*—'he came in', 'and (he) was opening his mail', 'when the lights went out' are clauses.

Comparative With adjectives and adverbs, the form produced by adding *-er* or prefixing *more*: *bigger, more difficult, more easily*.

Compound Noun Noun formed from two or more separate words, usually hyphenated in French: **le tire-bouchon**, *corkscrew*—both English and French words are compound nouns.

Compound Tense Tense of a verb formed by a part of that verb preceded by an auxiliary verb (*am, have, shall*, etc.): *am walking; have walked; shall walk*.

Compound Verb Verb formed by the addition of a prefix (*un-, over-, de-, dis-*, etc.) to another verb: simple verbs: *wind, take*; compound verbs: *unwind, overtake*.

Conditional Perfect Tense The tense used to express what might have happened (if something else had occurred) and formed in English with *should have* (*I* *should have walked, we should have walked*) or *would have* (*you would have walked, he would have walked, they would have walked*).

Conditional Tense The tense used to express what might happen (if something else occurred) and formed in English with *should* (*I should walk, we should walk*) or *would* (*you would walk, he would walk, they would walk*).

Conjugation The pattern which a type of verb follows. There is only one regular conjugation in English: *to walk*: present, *I walk, he walks*; past, *he walked*; perfect, *he has walked*, etc.

Conjunction A word like *and, but, when, because* that starts a clause and joins it to the rest of the sentence.

Consonant A letter representing a sound that can only be used in conjunction with a vowel. In French, the vowels are **a, e, i, o, u, y**. All the other letters of the alphabet are consonants.

Definite Article See Articles.

Demonstrative Adjective An adjective that is used to point out a particular thing: *I'll have that cake; this cake is terrible; give me those cakes—that, this, those* are demonstrative adjectives.

Demonstrative Article Alternative name for Demonstrative Adjective.

Demonstrative Pronoun A pronoun that is used to point out a particular thing: *I'll have that; this is terrible; give me those—that, this, those* are demonstrative pronouns.

Direct Object The noun or pronoun that experiences the action of the verb: *he hits me*, direct object: *me*. See also Indirect Object.

Disjunctive Pronoun Also called Stressed Pronoun. A pronoun that does not stand directly with a verb as its subject or object: *Who said that? Me!—me* is a disjunctive pronoun. Disjunctives in French have different forms from ordinary personal pronouns.

Ending See Stem.

Feminine See Gender.

First Conjugation Verb In French, a verb whose infinitive ends in **-er**.

First Person See Third Person.

Future Perfect Tense The tense used to express what, at some future time, will be a past occurrence. Formed in English with *shall have* (*I shall have walked, we shall have walked*) and *will have* (*you will have walked, he will have walked, they will have walked*).

Future Tense The tense used to express a future occurrence and formed in English with *shall* (*I shall walk, we shall walk*) or *will* (*you will walk, he will walk, they will walk*).

Gender In French, a noun or pronoun may be either masculine or feminine: this is known as the gender of the noun or pronoun. The gender may correspond to the sex of the thing named, or may not. In English gender only shows in pronouns (*he, she, it,* etc.) and corresponds to the sex of the thing named. See Agreement.

Historic Present Present tense used to relate past events, often in order to make the narrative more vivid: *So then I go into the kitchen and what do I see?*

Imperative The form of the verb that expresses a command. In English it is usually the same as the infinitive without *to*: infinitive, *to walk*, imperative, *walk!*

Imperfect Subjunctive One of the past tenses of the French subjunctive. See Subjunctive.

Imperfect Tense A French past tense formed by adding a set of endings (**-ais, -ais, -ait**, etc.) to the **nous** form of the present tense minus its **-ons**. Often corresponds to the English past continuous: **je marchais**, *I was walking*.

Impersonal Verb A verb whose subject is an imprecise *it* or *there*: *it is raining*; *there's no need for that*.

Indefinite Adjectives Adjectives such as *each, such, some, other, every, several*.

Indefinite Article See Articles.

Indefinite Pronouns Pronouns such as *somebody, anybody, something, anything, everybody, nobody*.

Indirect Object The noun or pronoun at which the direct object is aimed. In English it either has or can have *to* in front of it: *I passed it (to) him*, indirect object *(to) him*; *I gave her my address (I gave my address to her)*, indirect object *(to) her*. In these examples *it* and *my address* are direct objects. See Direct Object.

Indirect Question A question (without a question mark) in a subordinate clause. It is introduced by some such expression as *I wonder if, do you know where, I'll tell him when*. Direct question: *When is he coming?* Indirect question: *I don't know when he's coming*.

Infinitive The basic part of the verb from which other parts are derived. In English, it is normally preceded by *to*: *to walk, to run*.

Interrogative The question form of the verb.

Interrogative Adjective A question word (in English *which* ...? or *what* ...?) used adjectivally with a following noun: *which book do you mean?*

Interrogative Adverb An adverb that introduces a direct question, in English *why?, when?, how?*, etc. In indirect questions the same words function as conjunctions, joining the question to the main clause. *Why do you say that?*—direct question, *why* is an interrogative adverb; *I don't know why you say that*—indirect question, *why* is a conjunction.

Interrogative Pronoun A pronoun that asks a question, in English *who?* and *what?*

Intransitive Of verbs: having no direct object.

Irregular Verb In French, a verb that does not follow the pattern of one of the three regular conjugations.

Main Clause A clause within a sentence that could stand on its own and still make sense. For example: *He came in when he was ready. He came in* is a main clause (it makes sense standing on its own); *when he was ready* is a subordinate clause (it can't stand on its own and still make sense).

Masculine See Gender.

Modal Verbs (literally 'verbs of mood') These are the auxiliary verbs (other than *have* and *be*) that always appear with a dependent infinitive: *I can walk, I must walk, I will walk*—*can, must, will* are modal verbs.

Noun A word that names a person or thing. *Peter, box, glory, indecision* are nouns.

Noun Clause A clause that is the equivalent of a noun within the sentence: *I don't want to catch whatever you've got* (*whatever you've got* is a clause for which we might substitute a noun, e.g., *measles*).

Number With nouns, pronouns, etc.—the state of being either singular or plural. See Agreement.

Object See Direct Object and Indirect Object.

Ordinal (Number) A number such as *first, second, third, fourth,* normally used adjectivally about one thing in a series.

Partitive Article See Articles.

Passive The basic tenses of a verb are active. Passive tenses are the set of tenses that are used in order to make the person or thing experiencing the action of the verb (normally the object) into the subject of the verb. Active (basic tense): *I discover it*, passive: *it is discovered (by me)*; active: *he ate them*, passive: *they were eaten (by him)*.

Past Anterior Tense A French tense equivalent in time to the pluperfect, formed with the past historic of **avoir** or **être** + past participle: **j'eus marché**, *I had walked*.

Past Historic Tense A French past tense used in writing narrative instead of the perfect; often eqivalent to the English simple past tense: **je marchai**, *I walked*.

Past Participle The part of the verb used to form compound past tenses. In English, it usually ends in *-ed*; verb: *to walk*; past participle: *walked*; perfect tense: *I have walked*.

Perfect Continuous In English, the past tense formed using *was + -ing*, implying that something was continuing to occur: *I was walking*.

Perfect Infinitive The past form of the infinitive, formed in English from *to have* + past participle: *to have walked*.

Perfect Participle The part of the verb that in English is formed by *having* + past participle: *having walked away, he now came back*: *having walked* is a perfect participle.

Perfect Tense The past tense that, in English, is formed by using *have* + past participle: *I have walked*.

Personal Pronouns Subject and object pronouns referring to people or things (*he, him, she, her, it*, etc.).

Phrasal Verb In English, a verb made by combining a simple verb with a preposition: *run out, jump up, stand down*.

Phrase A self-contained section of a sentence that does not contain a full verb. *Being late as usual, he arrived at* *a quarter past eleven*: *at a quarter past eleven* is a phrase; present and past participles are not full verbs, so *being late as usual* is also a phrase. Compare Clause.

Pluperfect Continuous In English, the equivalent tense to the pluperfect using *had been + -ing*, implying that something had been going on (when something else happened), e.g.: *I had been walking for an hour, when ...*

Pluperfect Tense The past tense, that, in English, is formed by using *had +* past participle: *I had walked.*

Possessive Adjective An adjective that indicates possession; in English, *my, your, her,* etc.: *that is my book.*

Possessive Article Alternative name for Possessive Adjective.

Possessive Pronoun A pronoun that indicates possession; in English, *mine, yours, hers,* etc.: *that book is mine.*

Preposition A word like *in, over, near, across* that stands in front of a noun or pronoun relating it to the rest of the sentence.

Present Continuous See Present Tense.

Present Participle The part of the verb that in English ends in *-ing*: *to walk*: present participle, *walking.*

Present Tense The tense of the verb that refers to things now happening regularly (simple present: *I walk*), or happening at the moment (present continuous: *I am walking*).

Pronoun A word such as *he, she, which, mine* that stands instead of a noun (usually already mentioned).

Reflexive Verbs Verbs whose object is the same as their subject: *he likes himself, she can dress herself. Himself, herself* are reflexive pronouns.

Relative Pronoun A pronoun that introduces a subordinate clause and at the same time allows that clause to function as an adjective or noun. In English the relative pronouns are *who(m)*, *which*, *whose*, *that*, and *what*. *Tell me what you know!*: *what you know* is a noun clause and the direct object of *tell me*. It is introduced by the relative pronoun *what*. *That's the lad who stole my wallet*: *who stole my wallet* is an adjectival clause describing *lad*. It is introduced by the relative pronoun *who*.

Second Conjugation Verb In French, a verb whose infinitive ends in **-ir**.

Second Person See Third Person.

Simple Tense A one-word tense of a verb: *I walk, I run* (as opposed to a compound tense: *I am walking, I was running*).

Stem The part of a verb to which endings indicating tense, person, etc. are added. Verb: *to walk*: stem, *walk-*: *he walk-s, he walk-ed*, etc.

Stressed Pronouns See Disjunctive Pronouns.

Subject (of verb, clause, or sentence) The noun or pronoun that initiates the action of the verb: *George walked*, subject: *George*; *he hit George*, subject: *he*.

Subjunctive In French, a set of tenses that express doubt or unlikelihood. The subjunctive still exists in only a few expressions in English: *If I were you* [but I'm not], *I'd go now* (*I were* is subjunctive—the normal past tense is *I was*).

Subordinate Clause A clause in a sentence that depends, in order to make sense, on a main clause. See Main Clause.

Subordinating Conjunction The conjunction that introduces a subordinate clause.

Superlative With adjectives and adverbs, the form produced by adding *-est* or prefixing *most*: *biggest, most difficult, most easily*.

Tense The form of a verb that indicates when the action takes place (e.g., present tense: *I walk*; past tense: *I walked*).

Third Conjugation Verb In French, a verb whose infinitive ends in **-re**.

Third Person *He, she, it, they* (and their derivatives, like *him, his, her, their*), or any noun. The first person is *I* or *we* (and their derivatives), the second person is *you* (and its derivatives).

Transitive Of verbs: having a direct object.

Verb The word that tells you what the subject of the clause does: *he goes*; *she dislikes me*; *have you eaten it?*, *they know nothing—goes, dislikes, have eaten, know* are verbs.

Verbal Noun Part of the verb (in English, usually the present participle) used as a noun: *smoking is bad for you*: verbal noun, *smoking*.

Vowel A letter representing a sound that can be pronounced by itself without the addition of other sounds. In French the vowels are **a, e, i, o, u, y**.

| Index

English prepositions should be looked up in the alphabetical list on page 185.

French prepositions should be looked up in the alphabetical list on page 164.

Irregular verbs should be looked up in the alphabetical list on page 242.

The preposition a verb takes before an infinitive or noun will be found in the alphabetical list of verbs on page 59.

Words offering problems of pronunciation should be looked up in the alphabetical list on page 235.

Definitions of grammatical terms will be found in the glossary on page 260.

Dictionary

Preface

This dictionary is written with speakers of both English and French in mind, and contains the most useful words and expressions of the English and French languages of today.

Indicators in brackets marking different uses of the same word together with a wide range of style and field labels guide the user towards the appropriate translation.

Common abbreviations, names of countries, and other useful geographical names are included.

Pronunciation is given by means of the International Phonetic Alphabet for all headwords and for those derived words whose pronunciation cannot easily be deduced from that of a headword.

For their valuable help and advice, I am grateful to Dr J. B. Sykes, Miss J. M. Hawkins, and Mrs J. Andrews, and to Mr H. Ferrar, Dr J. A. Hutchinson, and Professor J. Leblon who made many useful suggestions.

M. J.

March 1986

Préface

Ce dictionnaire s'adresse à tous ceux, francophones et anglophones, qui désirent connaître les mots et les expressions les plus courants du français et de l'anglais d'aujourd'hui.

Des indications en italique placées entre parenthèses distinguent chaque sens différent d'un même mot et guident l'usager dans son choix de la traduction juste. L'usager trouvera également dans ce dictionnaire les abréviations et les sigles les plus courants, et les noms géographiques les plus utiles.

La prononciation, qui est celle de l'Alphabet Phonétique International, est donnée pour chaque mot principal—ou mot vedette—d'un article et pour un mot dérivé lorsque la prononciation de celui-ci ne résulte pas de celle du mot principal.

Je tiens à remercier ici les personnes qui ont accepté de me faire profiter de leur compétence: le Dr J. B. Sykes, Miss J. M. Hawkins et Mrs J. Andrews, Mr H. Ferrar et le Dr J. A. Hutchinson, ainsi que le Professeur J. Leblon à qui je dois maintes suggestions.

M. J.

Mars 1986

Introduction

A swung dash (∼) is used within entries to represent a headword or that part of a headword preceding a vertical bar (|).

An obelisk (†) immediately following a verb headword in the French into English section indicates that the verb is listed in the tables of irregular verbs on p. 524. In English, the past tense and past participle are usually formed by the addition of *ed* to the infinitive (e.g. *jump*, *jumped*), although only *d* is added to a verb ending in a silent *e* (e.g. *move*, *moved*), and in a verb ending in *y* the *y* changes to *i* before the addition of *ed* (e.g. *carry*, *carried*). Irregular English past tenses and participles are given in the English into French text.

An asterisk immediately following a French word (e.g. qu'*) shows the form of that word used before a vowel or mute h.

In French, the plural of a noun is usually formed by the addition of *s* to the singular, whereas a noun ending in *s*, *x*, or *z* remains unchanged. In English, the plural is also formed by the addition of *s*, although *es* is added to form the plural of a noun ending in *ch*, *s*, *sh*, *ss*, *us*, *x*, or *z* (e.g. *sash*, *sashes*). In the case of a noun ending in *quy*, or *y* preceded by a consonant, *y* becomes *ies* (e.g. *baby*, *babies*). French and English plurals are listed when they do not follow these rules.

In general, the feminine of a French adjective is formed by the addition of *e* to the masculine, except that a masculine ending in *e* remains unchanged. In the English into French section, only the masculine form of a French adjective is shown. In the French headword list, the feminine of an adjective is given when the addition of *e* to the masculine affects pronunciation (e.g. *petit*, *petite*; *fatigant*, *fatigante*) or when there is some other change besides the addition of *e*, whether or not pronunciation is affected (e.g. *ambigu*, *ambiguë*; *dû*, *due*; *heureux*, *heureuse*).

Proprietary Terms

This dictionary includes some words which are, or are asserted to be, proprietary names or trade marks. Their inclusion does not imply that they have acquired for legal purposes a non-proprietary or general significance, nor is any other judgement implied concerning their legal status. In cases where the editor has some evidence that a word is used as a proprietary name or trade mark this is indicated by the letter (P.), but no judgement concerning the legal status of such words is made or implied thereby.

Introduction

Un *s* couché (~) figurant à l'intérieur d'un article remplace le mot
vedette de cet article ou la partie de ce mot qui précède une ligne
verticale (|).

Le symbole † placé après un verbe français renvoie le lecteur
aux tableaux des conjugaisons, page 524. En anglais, on forme
généralement le passé simple et le participe passé d'un verbe
régulier en ajoutant *ed* à l'infinitif (par exemple *jump, jumped*), ou
en ajoutant *d* à un infinitif se terminant par un *e* muet (par exemple
move, moved). Si l'infinitif se termine par un *y*, on change le *y* en
ied (par exemple *carry, carried*). Les passés simples et participes
passés irréguliers sont indiqués.

En français, le pluriel d'un nom se forme généralement par le
simple ajout d'un *s*; un nom qui se termine par *s, x,* ou *z* reste
toutefois invariable. En anglais aussi, on forme le pluriel en
ajoutant un *s*; toutefois, un nom se terminant par *ch, s, sh, ss, us,
x,* ou *z* prend *es* au pluriel (par exemple *sash, sashes*); et un nom
se terminant par *quy,* ou *y* précédé d'une consonne, change le *y* en
ies (par exemple *baby, babies*). En français et en anglais, sont
indiqués les pluriels qui ne suivent pas les règles précédentes.

En général, on forme le féminin d'un adjectif français en ajoutant
un *e* au masculin; toutefois, un adjectif masculin se terminant par
e ne varie pas. Dans la partie anglais-français, figure seulement la
forme masculine de l'adjectif français. Dans la partie français-
anglais, le féminin d'un adjectif est indiqué lorsque l'ajout d'un *e*
modifie la prononciation (par exemple *petit, petite; fatigant, fatigante*) ou lorsque la forme masculine subit un changement autre
que celui du simple ajout d'un *e* (par exemple *ambigu, ambiguë;
dû, due; heureux, heureuse*).

Marques déposées

Ce dictionnaire contient des termes qui sont ou qui ont été désignés
comme des marques déposées. La présence ou l'absence de cette
désignation ne peut toutefois être considérée comme ayant valeur
juridique.

Pronunciation of French

Phonetic symbols

Vowels

i	v*ie*		y	vêt*u*
e	pr*é*		ø	p*eu*
ɛ	l*ai*t		œ	p*eu*r
a	pl*a*t		ə	d*e*
ɑ	b*a*s		ɛ̃	mat*in*
ɔ	m*o*rt		ɑ̃	s*an*s
o	m*o*t		ɔ̃	b*on*
u	gen*ou*		œ̃	l*un*di

Consonants and semi-consonants

p	*p*ayer		ʒ	*j*e
b	*b*on		m	*m*ain
t	*t*erre		n	*n*ous
d	*d*ans		l	*l*ong
k	*c*ou		r	*r*ue
g	*g*ant		ɲ	a*gn*eau
f	*f*eu		ŋ	campi*ng*
v	*v*ous		j	*y*eux
s	*s*ale		w	*ou*i
z	*z*éro		ɥ	h*u*ile
ʃ	*ch*at			

Note: ' before the pronunciation of a word beginning with *h* indicates no liaison or elision.

Prononciation de l'anglais

Symboles phonétiques

Voyelles et diphtongues

iː	s*ee*		ə	*a*go
ɪ	s*i*t		eɪ	p*a*ge
e	t*e*n		əʊ	h*o*me
æ	h*a*t		aɪ	f*i*ve
ɑː	*ar*m		aɪə	f*ire*
ɔ	g*o*t		aʊ	n*ow*
ɔː	s*aw*		aʊə	fl*our*
ʊ	p*u*t		ɔɪ	j*oi*n
uː	t*oo*		ɪə	n*ear*
ʌ	c*u*p		eə	h*air*
ɜː	f*ur*		ʊə	p*oor*

Consonnes

p	*p*en		s	*s*o
b	*b*ad		z	*z*oo
t	*t*ea		ʃ	*sh*e
d	*d*ip		ʒ	mea*s*ure
k	*c*at		h	*h*ow
g	*g*ot		m	*m*an
tʃ	*ch*in		n	*n*o
dʒ	*J*une		ŋ	si*ng*
f	*f*all		l	*l*eg
v	*v*oice		r	*r*ed
θ	*th*in		j	*y*es
ð	*th*en		w	*w*et

Note: ' précède la syllabe accentuée.

Abbreviations · Abréviations

abbreviation	*abbr., abrév.*	abréviation
adjective(s)	*a. (adjs.)*	adjectif(s)
adverb(s)	*adv(s).*	adverbe(s)
American	*Amer.*	américain
anatomy	*anat.*	anatomie
approximately	*approx.*	approximativement
archaeology	*archaeol.,*	archéologie
	archéol.	
architecture	*archit.*	architecture
motoring	*auto.*	automobile
auxiliary	*aux.*	auxiliaire
aviation	*aviat.*	aviation
botany	*bot.*	botanique
commerce	*comm.*	commerce
conjunction(s)	*conj(s).*	conjonction(s)
cookery	*culin.*	culinaire
electricity	*electr., électr.*	électricité
feminine	*f.*	féminin
familiar	*fam.*	familier
figurative	*fig.*	figuré
geography	*geog., géog.*	géographie
geology	*geol., géol.*	géologie
grammar	*gram.*	grammaire
humorous	*hum.*	humoristique
interjection(s)	*int(s).*	interjection(s)
invariable	*invar.*	invariable
legal, law	*jurid.*	juridique
language	*lang.*	langue
masculine	*m.*	masculin
medicine	*med., méd.*	médecine
military	*mil.*	militaire
music	*mus.*	musique
noun(s)	*n(s).*	nom(s)
nautical	*naut.*	nautique
oneself	*o.s.*	se, soi-même
proprietary term	P.	marque déposée
pejorative	*pej., péj.*	péjoratif
philosophy	*phil.*	philosophie
photography	*photo.*	photographie
plural	*pl.*	pluriel
politics	*pol.*	politique
possessive	*poss.*	possessif

ABBREVIATIONS · ABRÉVIATIONS

past participle	*p.p.*	participe passé
prefix	*pref.*, *préf.*	préfixe
preposition(s)	*prep(s).*, *prép(s).*	préposition(s)
present participle	*pres. p.*	participe présent
pronoun	*pron.*	pronom
relative pronoun	*pron. rel.*	pronom relatif
psychology	*psych.*	psychologie
past tense	*p.t.*	passé
something	*qch.*	quelque chose
someone	*qn.*	quelqu'un
railway	*rail.*	chemin de fer
religion	*relig.*	religion
relative pronoun	*rel. pron.*	pronom relatif
school, scholastic	*schol.*, *scol.*	scolaire
singular	*sing.*	singulier
slang	*sl.*	argot
someone	*s.o.*	quelqu'un
something	*sth.*	quelque chose
technical	*techn.*	technique
television	*TV*	télévision
university	*univ.*	université
auxiliary verb	*v. aux.*	verbe auxiliaire
intransitive verb	*v.i.*	verbe intransitif
pronominal verb	*v. pr.*	verbe pronominal
transitive verb	*v.t.*	verbe transitif

FRANÇAIS-ANGLAIS
FRENCH-ENGLISH

A

a /a/ *voir* **avoir.**

à /a/ *prép.* (*à* + *le* = *au*, *à* + *les* = *aux*) in, at; (*direction*) to; (*temps*) at; (*jusqu'à*) to, till; (*date*) on; (*époque*) in; (*moyen*) by, on; (*prix*) for; (*appartenance*) of; (*mesure*) by. **donner**/*etc.* **~**, give/*etc.* to. **apprendre**/*etc.* **~**, learn/*etc.* to. **l'homme ~ la barbe**, the man with the beard. **~ la radio**, on the radio. **c'est ~ moi**/*etc.*, it is mine/*etc.* **c'est ~ vous**/*etc.* **de**, it is up to you/*etc.* to; (*en jouant*) it is your/*etc.* turn to. **dix km ~ l'heure**, ten km. an *ou* per hour.

abaissement /abɛsmɑ̃/ *n.m.* (*baisse*) drop, fall.

abaisser /abese/ *v.t.* lower; (*levier*) pull *ou* push down; (*fig.*) humiliate. **s'~** *v. pr.* go down, drop; (*fig.*) humiliate o.s. **s'~ à**, stoop to.

abandon /abɑ̃dɔ̃/ *n.m.* abandonment; desertion; (*sport*) withdrawal; (*naturel*) abandon. **à l'~**, in a state of neglect. **~ner** /-ɔne/ *v.t.* abandon, desert; (*renoncer à*) give up, abandon; (*céder*) give (**à**, to). **s'~ner à**, give o.s. up to.

abasourdir /abazurdir/ *v.t.* stun.

abat-jour /abaʒur/ *n.m. invar.* lampshade.

abats /aba/ *n.m. pl.* offal.

abattement /abatmɑ̃/ *n.m.* dejection; (*faiblesse*) exhaustion; (*comm.*) allowance.

abattis /abati/ *n.m. pl.* giblets.

abattoir /abatwar/ *n.m.* slaughterhouse.

abattre† /abatr/ *v.t.* knock down; (*arbre*) cut down; (*animal*) slaughter; (*avion*) shoot down; (*affaiblir*) weaken; (*démoraliser*) dishearten. **s'~** *v. pr.* come down, fall (down).

abbaye /abei/ *n.f.* abbey.

abbé /abe/ *n.m.* priest; (*supérieur d'une abbaye*) abbot.

abcès /apsɛ/ *n.m.* abscess.

abdi|quer /abdike/ *v.t./i.* abdicate. **~cation** *n.f.* abdication.

abdom|en /abdɔmɛn/ *n.m.* abdomen. **~inal** (*m. pl.* **~inaux**) *a.* abdominal.

abeille /abɛj/ *n.f.* bee.

aberrant, ~e /abɛrɑ̃, -t/ *a.* absurd.

aberration /abɛrasjɔ̃/ *n.f.* aberration; (*idée*) absurd idea.

abêtir /abetir/ *v.t.* make stupid.

abhorrer /abɔre/ *v.t.* loathe, abhor.

abîme /abim/ *n.m.* abyss.

abîmer /abime/ *v.t.* damage, spoil. **s'~** *v. pr.* get damaged *ou* spoilt.

abject /abʒɛkt/ *a.* abject.

abjurer /abʒyre/ *v.t.* abjure.

ablation /ablasjɔ̃/ *n.f.* removal.

ablutions /ablysjɔ̃/ *n.f. pl.* ablutions.

abnégation /abnegasjɔ̃/ *n.f.* self-sacrifice.

aboiement /abwamɑ̃/ *n.m.* bark(ing). **~s**, barking.

abois (aux) /(oz)abwa/ *adv.* at bay.

abol|ir /abɔlir/ *v.t.* abolish. **~ition** *n.f.* abolition.

abominable /abɔminabl/ *a.* abominable.

abond|ant, ~ante /abɔ̃dɑ̃, -t/ *a.* abundant, plentiful. **~amment** *adv.* abundantly. **~ance** *n.f.* abundance; (*prospérité*) affluence.

abonder /abɔ̃de/ *v.i.* abound (**en**, in).

abonn|er (s') /(s)abɔne/ *v. pr.* subscribe (**à**, to). **~é, ~ée** *n.m., f.* subscriber; season-ticket holder. **~ement** *n.m.* (*à un journal*) subscription; (*de bus, théâtre, etc.*) season-ticket.

abord /abɔr/ *n.m.* access. **~s**, surroundings. **d'~**, first.

abordable /abɔrdabl/ *a.* (*prix*) reasonable; (*personne*) approachable.

abordage /abɔrdaʒ/ *n.m.* (*accident: naut.*) collision. **prendre à l'~**, (*navire*) board, attack.

aborder /abɔrde/ *v.t.* approach; (*lieu*) reach; (*problème etc.*) tackle. —*v.i.* reach land.

aborigène /abɔriʒɛn/ *n.m.* aborigine, aboriginal.

aboutir /abutir/ *v.i.* succeed, achieve

a result. ～ à, end (up) in, lead to.
n'～ à rien, come to nothing.
aboutissement /abutismɑ̃/ *n.m.* outcome.
aboyer /abwaje/ *v.i.* bark.
abrasi|f, ～ve /abrazif, -v/ *a. & n.m.* abrasive.
abrégé /abreʒe/ *n.m.* summary.
abréger /abreʒe/ *v.t. (texte)* shorten, abridge; *(mot)* abbreviate, shorten; *(visite)* cut short.
abreuv|er /abrœve/ *v.t.* water; *(fig.)* overwhelm. **s'～er** *v. pr.* drink. **～oir** *n.m.* watering-place.
abréviation /abrevjɑsjɔ̃/ *n.f.* abbreviation.
abri /abri/ *n.m.* shelter. **à l'～,** under cover. **à l'～ de,** sheltered from.
abricot /abriko/ *n.m.* apricot.
abriter /abrite/ *v.t.* shelter; *(recevoir)* house. **s'～** *v. pr.* (take) shelter.
abroger /abrɔʒe/ *v.t.* repeal.
abrupt /abrypt/ *a.* steep, sheer; *(fig.)* abrupt.
abruti, ～e /abryti/ *n.m.,f. (fam.)* idiot.
abrutir /abrytir/ *v.t.* make *ou* drive stupid, dull the mind of.
absence /apsɑ̃s/ *n.f.* absence.
absent, ～e /apsɑ̃, -t/ *a.* absent, away; *(chose)* missing. —*n.m., f.* absentee.
～éisme /-teism/ *n.m.* absenteeism.
～éiste /-teist/ *n.m./f.* absentee.
absenter (s') /(s)apsɑ̃te/ *v. pr.* go *ou* be away; *(sortir)* go out, leave.
absinthe /apsɛ̃t/ *n.m.* absinthe.
absolu /apsɔly/ *a.* absolute. **～ment** *adv.* absolutely.
absolution /apsɔlysjɔ̃/ *n.f.* absolution.
absor|ber /apsɔrbe/ *v.t.* absorb; *(temps etc.)* take up. **～bant, ～bante** *a. (travail etc.)* absorbing; *(matière)* absorbent. **～ption** *n.f.* absorption.
absoudre /apsudr/ *v.t.* absolve.
absten|ir (s') /(s)apstənir/ *v. pr.* abstain. **s'～ir de,** refrain from. **～tion** /-ɑ̃sjɔ̃/ *n.f.* abstention.
abstinence /apstinɑ̃s/ *n.f.* abstinence.
abstr|aire /apstrɛr/ *v.t.* abstract. **～action** *n.f.* abstraction. **faire ～action de,** disregard. **～ait, ～aite** *a. & n.m.* abstract.
absurd|e /apsyrd/ *a.* absurd. **～ité** *n.f.* absurdity.
abus /aby/ *n.m.* abuse, misuse; *(injustice)* abuse.
abuser /abyze/ *v.t.* deceive. —*v.i.* go too far. **s'～** *v. pr.* be mistaken. **～ de,** abuse, misuse; *(profiter de)*

take advantage of; *(alcool etc.)* over-indulge in.
abusi|f, ～ve /abyzif, -v/ *a.* excessive, improper.
acabit /akabi/ *n.m.* ilk.
académicien, ～ne /akademisjɛ̃, -jɛn/ *n.m., f.* academician.
académ|ie /akademi/ *n.f.* academy; *(circonscription)* educational district. **A～ie,** Academy. **～ique** *a.* academic.
acajou /akaʒu/ *n.m.* mahogany.
acariâtre /akarjɑtr/ *a.* cantankerous.
accablement /akɑbləmɑ̃/ *n.m.* despondency.
accabl|er /akɑble/ *v.t.* overwhelm. **～er d'impôts,** burden with taxes. **～er d'injures,** heap insults upon. **～ant, ～ante** *a. (chaleur)* oppressive.
accalmie /akalmi/ *n.f.* lull.
accaparer /akapare/ *v.t.* monopolize; *(fig.)* take up all the time of.
accéder /aksede/ *v.i.* ～ à, reach; *(pouvoir, requête, trône, etc.)* accede to.
accélér|er /akselere/ *v.i. (auto.)* accelerate. —*v.t.,* **s'～er** *v. pr.* speed up. **～ateur** *n.m.* accelerator. **～ation** *n.f.* acceleration; speeding up.
accent /aksɑ̃/ *n.m.* accent; *(sur une syllabe)* stress, accent; *(ton)* tone. **mettre l'～ sur,** stress.
accent|uer /aksɑ̃tɥe/ *v.t. (lettre, syllabe)* accent; *(fig.)* emphasize, accentuate. **s'～uer** *v. pr.* become more pronounced, increase. **～uation** *n.f.* accentuation.
accept|er /aksɛpte/ *v.t.* accept. **～er de,** agree to. **～able** *a.* acceptable. **～ation** *n.f.* acceptance.
acception /aksɛpsjɔ̃/ *n.f.* meaning.
accès /aksɛ/ *n.m.* access; *(porte)* entrance; *(de fièvre)* attack; *(de colère)* fit; *(de joie)* (out)burst. **les ～ de,** *(voies)* the approaches to.
accessible /aksesibl/ *a.* accessible; *(personne)* approachable.
accession /aksɛsjɔ̃/ *n.f.* ～ à, accession to.
accessit /aksesit/ *n.m.* honourable mention.
accessoire /akseswar/ *a.* secondary. —*n.m.* accessory; *(théâtre)* prop.
accident /aksidɑ̃/ *n.m.* accident. **～ de train/d'avion,** train/plane crash. **～é** /-te/ *a.* damaged *ou* hurt (in an accident); *(terrain)* uneven, hilly.
accidentel, ～le /aksidɑ̃tɛl/ *a.* accidental.

acclam|er /aklame/ *v.t.* cheer, acclaim. **~ations** *n.f. pl.* cheers.

acclimat|er /aklimate/ *v.t.*, **s'~er** *v. pr.* acclimatize; (*Amer.*) acclimate. **~ation** *n.f.* acclimatization; (*Amer.*) acclimation.

accolade /akɔlad/ *n.f.* embrace; (*signe*) brace, bracket.

accommodant, ~e /akɔmɔdɑ̃, -t/ *a.* accommodating.

accommodement /akɔmɔdmɑ̃/ *n.m.* compromise.

accommoder /akɔmɔde/ *v.t.* adapt (**à**, to); (*cuisiner*) prepare; (*assaisonner*) flavour. **s'~ de,** put up with.

accompagn|er /akɔ̃paɲe/ *v.t.* accompany. **s'~er de,** be accompanied by. **~ateur, ~atrice** *n.m., f.* (*mus.*) accompanist; (*guide*) guide. **~ement** *n.m.* (*mus.*) accompaniment.

accompli /akɔ̃pli/ *a.* accomplished.

accompl|ir /akɔ̃plir/ *v.t.* carry out, fulfil. **s'~ir** *v. pr.* be carried out, happen. **~issement** *n.m.* fulfilment.

accord /akɔr/ *n.m.* agreement; (*harmonie*) harmony; (*mus.*) chord. **être d'~,** agree (**pour,** to). **se mettre d'~,** come to an agreement, agree. **d'~!,** all right!, OK!

accordéon /akɔrdeɔ̃/ *n.m.* accordion.

accord|er /akɔrde/ *v.t.* grant; (*couleurs etc.*) match; (*mus.*) tune. **s'~er** *v. pr.* agree. **s'~er avec,** (*s'entendre avec*) get on with. **~eur** *n.m.* tuner.

accoster /akɔste/ *v.t.* accost; (*navire*) come alongside.

accotement /akɔtmɑ̃/ *n.m.* roadside, verge; (*Amer.*) shoulder.

accoter (s') /(s)akɔte/ *v.pr.* lean (**à**, against).

accouch|er /akuʃe/ *v.i.* give birth (**de**, to); (*être en travail*) be in labour. —*v.t.* deliver. **~ement** *n.m.* childbirth; (*travail*) labour. (**médecin**) **~eur** *n.m.* obstetrician. **~euse** *n.f.* midwife.

accoud|er (s') /(s)akude/ *v. pr.* lean (one's elbows) on. **~oir** *n.m.* armrest.

accoupl|er /akuple/ *v.t.* couple; (*faire copuler*) mate. **s'~er** *v. pr.* mate. **~ement** *n.m.* mating; coupling.

accourir /akurir/ *v.i.* run up.

accoutrement /akutrəmɑ̃/ *n.m.* (strange) garb.

accoutumance /akutymɑ̃s/ *n.f.* habituation; (*méd.*) addiction.

accoutum|er /akutyme/ *v.t.* accus-
tom. **s'~er** *v. pr.* get accustomed. **~é** *a.* customary.

accréditer /akredite/ *v.t.* give credence to; (*personne*) accredit.

accroc /akro/ *n.m.* tear, rip; (*fig.*) hitch.

accroch|er /akrɔʃe/ *v.t.* (*suspendre*) hang up; (*attacher*) hook, hitch; (*déchirer*) catch; (*heurter*) hit; (*attirer*) attract. **s'~er** *v. pr.* cling, hang on; (*se disputer*) clash. **~age** *n.m.* hanging; hooking; (*auto.*) collision; (*dispute*) clash; (*mil.*) encounter.

accroissement /akrwasmɑ̃/ *n.m.* increase (**de,** in).

accroître /akrwatr/ *v.t.*, **s'~** *v. pr.* increase.

accroup|ir (s') /(s)akrupir/ *v. pr.* squat. **~i** *a.* squatting.

accueil /akœj/ *n.m.* reception, welcome.

accueill|ir† /akœjir/ *v.t.* receive, welcome; (*aller chercher*) meet. **~ant, ~ante** *a.* friendly.

acculer /akyle/ *v.t.* corner. **~ à,** force *ou* drive into *ou* against *ou* close to.

accumul|er /akymyle/ *v.t.*, **s'~er** *v. pr.* accumulate, pile up. **~ateur** *n.m.* accumulator. **~ation** *n.f.* accumulation.

accus /aky/ *n.m. pl.* (*fam.*) battery.

accusation /akyzasjɔ̃/ *n.f.* accusation; (*jurid.*) charge. **l'~,** (*magistrat*) the prosecution.

accus|er /akyze/ *v.t.* accuse; (*blâmer*) blame; (*jurid.*) charge; (*fig.*) show, emphasize. **~er réception,** acknowledge receipt. **~ateur, ~atrice** *a.* incriminating; *n.m., f.* accuser. **~é, ~ée** *a.* marked; *n.m., f.* accused.

acerbe /asɛrb/ *a.* bitter.

acéré /asere/ *a.* sharp.

achalandé /aʃalɑ̃de/ *a.* **bien ~,** well-stocked.

acharn|é /aʃarne/ *a.* relentless, ferocious. **~ement** *n.m.* relentlessness.

acharner (s') /(s)aʃarne/ *v. pr.* **s'~ sur,** set upon; (*poursuivre*) hound. **s'~ à faire,** struggle to do.

achat /aʃa/ *n.m.* purchase. **~s,** shopping. **faire l'~ de,** buy.

acheminer /aʃmine/ *v.t.* dispatch. **s'~ vers,** head for.

achet|er† /aʃte/ *v.t.* buy, purchase. **~er à,** buy from; (*pour*) buy for. **~eur, ~euse** *n.m., f.* buyer; (*client de magasin*) shopper.

achèvement /aʃɛvmɑ̃/ *n.m.* completion.

achever /aʃve/ *v.t.* finish (off). **s'~** *v. pr.* end.

acid|e /asid/ *a.* acid, sharp. —*n.m.* acid. **~ité** *n.f.* acidity. **~ulé** *a.* slightly acid.

acier /asje/ *n.m.* steel. **aciérie** *n.f.* steelworks.

acné /akne/ *n.f.* acne.

acolyte /akɔlit/ *n.m.* (*péj.*) associate.

acompte /akɔ̃t/ *n.m.* deposit, part-payment.

à-côté /akote/ *n.m.* side-issue. **~s,** (*argent*) extras.

à-coup /aku/ *n.m.* jolt, jerk. **par ~s,** by fits and starts.

acoustique /akustik/ *n.f.* acoustics. —*a.* acoustic.

acqu|érir† /akerir/ *v.t.* acquire, gain; (*biens*) purchase, acquire. **~éreur** *n.m.* purchaser. **~isition** *n.f.* acquisition; purchase.

acquiescer /akjese/ *v.i.* acquiesce, agree.

acquis, ~e /aki, -z/ *n.m.* experience. —*a.* acquired; (*fait*) established; (*faveurs*) secured. **~ à,** (*projet*) in favour of.

acquit /aki/ *n.m.* receipt. **par ~ de conscience,** for peace of mind.

acquitt|er /akite/ *v.t.* acquit; (*dette*) settle. **s'~er de,** (*promesse, devoir*) carry out. **s'~er envers,** repay. **~ement** *n.m.* acquittal; settlement.

âcre /ɑkr/ *a.* acrid.

acrobate /akrɔbat/ *n.m./f.* acrobat.

acrobatie /akrɔbasi/ *n.f.* acrobatics. **~ aérienne,** aerobatics. **acrobatique** /-tik/ *a.* acrobatic.

acte /akt/ *n.m.* act, action, deed; (*théâtre*) act; (*de naissance, mariage*) certificate. **~s,** (*compte rendu*) proceedings. **prendre ~ de,** note.

acteur /aktœr/ *n.m.* actor.

acti|f, ~ve /aktif, -v/ *a.* active. —*n.m.* (*comm.*) assets. **avoir à son ~f,** have to one's credit *ou* name. **~vement** *adv.* actively.

action /aksjɔ̃/ *n.f.* action; (*comm.*) share; (*jurid.*) action. **~naire** /-jɔnɛr/ *n.m./f.* shareholder.

actionner /aksjɔne/ *v.t.* work, activate.

activer /aktive/ *v.t.* speed up; (*feu*) boost. **s'~** *v. pr.* hurry, rush.

activiste /aktivist/ *n.m./f.* activist.

activité /aktivite/ *n.f.* activity. **en ~,** active.

actrice /aktris/ *n.f.* actress.

actualiser /aktɥalize/ *v.t.* update.

actualité /aktɥalite/ *n.f.* topicality; (*événements*) current events. **~s,** news. **d'~,** topical.

actuel, ~le /aktɥɛl/ *a.* present; (*d'actualité*) topical. **~lement** *adv.* at the present time.

acuité /akɥite/ *n.f.* acuteness.

acupunct|ure /akypɔ̃ktyr/ *n.f.* acupuncture. **~eur** *n.m.* acupuncturist.

adage /adaʒ/ *n.m.* adage.

adapt|er /adapte/ *v.t.* adapt; (*fixer*) fit. **s'~er** *v. pr.* adapt (o.s.); (*techn.*) fit. **~ateur, ~atrice** *n.m., f.* adapter; *n.m.* (*électr.*) adapter. **~ation** *n.f.* adaptation.

additif /aditif/ *n.m.* (*note*) rider; (*substance*) additive.

addition /adisjɔ̃/ *n.f.* addition; (*au café etc.*) bill; (*Amer.*) check. **~nel, ~nelle** /-jɔnɛl/ *a.* additional. **~ner** /-jɔne/ *v.t.* add; (*totaliser*) add (up).

adepte /adɛpt/ *n.m./f.* follower.

adéquat, ~e /adekwa, -t/ *a.* suitable.

adhérent, ~e /aderɑ̃, -t/ *n.m., f.* member.

adhé|rer /adere/ *v.i.* adhere, stick (à, to). **~rer à,** (*club etc.*) be a member of; (*s'inscrire à*) join. **~rence** *n.f.* adhesion. **~sif, ~sive** *a. & n.m.* adhesive. **~sion** *n.f.* membership; (*accord*) adherence.

adieu (*pl.* **~x**) /adjø/ *int. & n.m.* goodbye, farewell.

adipeu|x, ~se /adipø, -z/ *a.* fat; (*tissu*) fatty.

adjacent, ~e /adʒasɑ̃, -t/ *a.* adjacent.

adjectif /adʒɛktif/ *n.m.* adjective.

adjoindre /adʒwɛ̃dr/ *v.t.* add, attach; (*personne*) appoint. **s'~** *v. pr.* appoint.

adjoint, ~e /adʒwɛ̃, -t/ *n.m., f. & a.* assistant. **~ au maire,** deputy mayor.

adjudant /adʒydɑ̃/ *n.m.* warrant-officer.

adjuger /adʒyʒe/ *v.t.* award; (*aux enchères*) auction. **s'~** *v. pr.* take.

adjurer /adʒyre/ *v.t.* beseech.

admettre† /admɛtr/ *v.t.* let in, admit; (*tolérer*) allow; (*reconnaître*) admit; (*candidat*) pass.

administrati|f, ~ve /administratif, -v/ *a.* administrative.

administr|er /administre/ *v.t.* run, manage; (*justice, biens, etc.*) administer. **~ateur, ~atrice** *n.m.*, *f.* administrator, director. **~ation** *n.f.* administration. **A~ation,** Civil Service.

admirable /admirabl/ *a.* admirable.

admirati|f, ~ve /admiratif, -v/ *a.* admiring.

admir|er /admire/ *v.t.* admire. **~ateur, ~atrice** *n.m.*, *f.* admirer. **~ation** *n.f.* admiration.

admissible /admisibl/ *a.* admissible; (*candidat*) eligible.

admission /admisjɔ̃/ *n.f.* admission.

adolescen|t, ~te /adɔlesɑ̃, -t/ *n.m.*, *f.* adolescent. **~ce** *n.f.* adolescence.

adonner (s') /(s)adɔne/ *v. pr.* **s'~ à,** devote o.s. to; (*vice*) take to.

adopt|er /adɔpte/ *v.t.* adopt. **~ion** /-psjɔ̃/ *n.f.* adoption.

adopti|f, ~ve /adɔptif, -v/ *a.* adopted.

adorable /adɔrabl/ *a.* delightful, adorable.

ador|er /adɔre/ *v.t.* adore; (*relig.*) worship, adore. **~ation** *n.f.* adoration; worship.

adosser /adɔse/ *v.t.*, **s'~** *v. pr.* lean back (**à, contre,** against).

adoucir /adusir/ *v.t.* soften; (*boisson*) sweeten; (*personne*) mellow; (*chagrin*) ease. **s'~** *v. pr.* soften; mellow; ease; (*temps*) become milder.

adresse /adrɛs/ *n.f.* address; (*habileté*) skill.

adresser /adrese/ *v.t.* send; (*écrire l'adresse sur*) address; (*remarque etc.*) address. **s'~ à,** address; (*aller voir*) go and ask *ou* see; (*bureau*) enquire at; (*viser, intéresser*) be directed at.

adroit, ~e /adrwa, -t/ *a.* skilful, clever. **~ement** /-tmɑ̃/ *adv.* skilfully, cleverly.

aduler /adyle/ *v.t.* adulate.

adulte /adylt/ *n.m./f.* adult. —*a.* adult; (*plante, animal*) fully grown.

adultère /adyltɛr/ *a.* adulterous. —*n.m.* adultery.

advenir /advǝnir/ *v.i.* occur.

adverbe /advɛrb/ *n.m.* adverb.

adversaire /advɛrsɛr/ *n.m.* opponent, adversary.

adverse /advɛrs/ *a.* opposing.

adversité /advɛrsite/ *n.f.* adversity.

aérateur /aeratœr/ *n.m.* ventilator.

aér|er /aere/ *v.t.* air; (*texte*) lighten. **s'~er** *v. pr.* get some air. **~ation** *n.f.* ventilation. **~é** *a.* airy.

aérien, ~ne /aerjɛ̃, -jɛn/ *a.* air; (*photo*) aerial; (*câble*) overhead; (*fig.*) airy.

aérodrome /aerɔdrom/ *n.m.* aerodrome.

aérodynamique /aerɔdinamik/ *a.* streamlined, aerodynamic.

aérogare /aerɔgar/ *n.f.* air terminal.

aéroglisseur /aerɔglisœr/ *n.m.* hover craft.

aérogramme /aerɔgram/ *n.m.* airmail letter; (*Amer.*) aerogram.

aéronautique /aerɔnotik/ *a.* aeronautical. —*n.f.* aeronautics.

aéronavale /aerɔnaval/ *n.f.* Fleet Air Arm; (*Amer.*) Naval Air Force.

aéroport /aerɔpɔr/ *n.m.* airport.

aéroporté /aerɔpɔrte/ *a.* airborne.

aérosol /aerɔsɔl/ *n.m.* aerosol.

aérospat|ial (*m. pl.* **~iaux**) /aerɔspasjal, -jo/ *a.* aerospace.

affable /afabl/ *a.* affable.

affaibl|ir /afeblir/ *v.t.*, **s'~ir** *v. pr.* weaken. **~issement** *n.m.* weakening.

affaire /afɛr/ *n.f.* matter, affair; (*transaction*) deal; (*occasion*) bargain; (*firme*) business; (*jurid.*) case. **~s,** affairs; (*comm.*) business; (*effets*) belongings. **avoir ~ à,** (have to) deal with. **c'est mon ~, ce sont mes ~s,** that is my business.

affair|er (s') /(s)afere/ *v. pr.* bustle about. **~é** *a.* busy.

affaiss|er (s') /(s)afese/ *v.pr.* (*sol*) sink, subside; (*poutre*) sag; (*personne*) collapse. **~ement** /-ɛsmɑ̃/ *n.m.* subsidence.

affaler (s') /(s)afale/ *v. pr.* slump (down), collapse.

affam|er /afame/ *v.t.* starve. **~é** *a.* starving.

affect|é /afɛkte/ *a.* affected. **~ation**[1] *n.f.* affectation.

affect|er /afɛkte/ *v.t.* (*feindre, émouvoir*) affect; (*destiner*) assign; (*nommer*) appoint, post. **~ation**[2] *n.f.* assignment; appointment, posting.

affecti|f, ~ve /afɛktif, -v/ *a.* emotional.

affection /afɛksjɔ̃/ *n.f.* affection; (*maladie*) ailment. **~ner** /-jɔne/ *v.t.* be fond of.

affectueu|x, ~se /afɛktɥø, -z/ *a.* affectionate.

affermir /afɛrmir/ *v.t.* strengthen.

affiche /afiʃ/ *n.f.* (public) notice; (*publicité*) poster; (*théâtre*) bill.

affich|er /afiʃe/ *v.t.* post up, announce; (*sentiment etc.*) display. **~age** *n.m.* billposting; (*électronique*) display.

affilée (d') /(d)afile/ *adv*. in a row, at a stretch.

affiler /afile/ *v.t.* sharpen.

affil|ier (s') /(s)afilje/ *v. pr.* become affiliated. **~iation** *n.f.* affiliation.

affiner /afine/ *v.t.* refine.

affinité /afinite/ *n.f.* affinity.

affirmati|f, ~ve /afirmatif, -v/ *a.* affirmative. —*n.f.* affirmative.

affirm|er /afirme/ *v.t.* assert. **~ation** *n.f.* assertion.

affleurer /aflœre/ *v.i.* appear on the surface.

affliction /afliksjɔ̃/ *n.f.* affliction.

afflig|er /afliʒe/ *v.t.* grieve. **~é de,** afflicted with.

affluence /aflyɑ̃s/ *n.f.* crowd(s).

affluent /aflyɑ̃/ *n.m.* tributary.

affluer /aflye/ *v.i.* flood in; (*sang*) rush.

afflux /afly/ *n.m.* influx, flood; (*du sang*) rush.

affol|er /afɔle/ *v.t.* throw into a panic. **s'~er** *v. pr.* panic. **~ement** *n.m.* panic.

affranch|ir /afrɑ̃ʃir/ *v.t.* stamp; (*à la machine*) frank; (*esclave*) emancipate; (*fig.*) free. **~issement** *n.m.* (*tarif*) postage.

affréter /afrete/ *v.t.* charter.

affreu|x, ~se /afrø, -z/ *a.* (*laid*) hideous; (*mauvais*) awful. **~sement** *adv.* awfully, hideously.

affriolant, ~e /afrijɔlɑ̃, -t/ *a.* enticing.

affront /afrɔ̃/ *n.m.* affront.

affront|er /afrɔ̃te/ *v.t.* confront. **s'~er** *v. pr.* confront each other. **~ement** *n.m.* confrontation.

affubler /afyble/ *v.t.* rig out.

affût /afy/ *n.m.* **à l'~,** on the watch (**de,** for).

affûter /afyte/ *v.t.* sharpen.

afin /afɛ̃/ *prép. & conj.* **~ de/que,** in order to/that.

africain, ~e /afrikɛ̃, -ɛn/ *a. & n.m.,f.* African.

Afrique /afrik/ *n.f.* Africa. **~ du Sud,** South Africa.

agacer /agase/ *v.t.* irritate, annoy.

âge /ɑʒ/ *n.m.* age. **quel ~ avez- vous?,** how old are you? **~ adulte,** adulthood. **~ mûr,** middle age. **d'un certain ~,** past one's prime.

âgé /ɑʒe/ *a.* elderly. **~ de cinq ans**/*etc.,* five years/*etc.* old.

agence /aʒɑ̃s/ *n.f.* agency, bureau, office; (*succursale*) branch.

agenc|er /aʒɑ̃se/ *v.t.* organize, arrange. **~ement** *n.m.* organization.

agenda /aʒɛ̃da/ *n.m.* diary; (*Amer.*) datebook.

agenouiller (s') /(s)aʒnuje/ *v. pr.* kneel (down).

agent /aʒɑ̃/ *n.m.* agent; (*fonctionnaire*) official. **~ (de police),** policeman. **~ de change,** stockbroker.

agglomération /aglɔmerɑsjɔ̃/ *n.f.* built-up area, town.

aggloméré /aglɔmere/ *n.m.* (*bois*) chipboard.

agglomérer /aglɔmere/ *v.t.,* **s'~** *v. pr.* pile up.

agglutiner /aglytine/ *v.t.,* **s'~** *v. pr.* stick together.

aggraver /agrave/ *v.t.,* **s'~** *v. pr.* worsen.

agil|e /aʒil/ *a.* agile, nimble. **~ité** *n.f.* agility.

agir /aʒir/ *v.i.* act. **il s'agit de,** it is a matter of; (*il faut*) it is necessary to. **dans ce livre il s'agit de,** this book is about. **dont il s'agit,** in question.

agissements /aʒismɑ̃/ *n.m. pl.* (*péj.*) dealings.

agité /aʒite/ *a.* restless, fidgety; (*troublé*) agitated; (*mer*) rough.

agit|er /aʒite/ *v.t.* (*bras etc.*) wave; (*liquide*) shake; (*troubler*) agitate; (*discuter*) debate. **s'~er** *v. pr.* bustle about; (*enfant*) fidget; (*foule, pensées*) stir. **~ateur, ~atrice** *n.m., f.* agitator. **~ation** *n.f.* bustle; (*trouble*) agitation.

agneau (*pl.* **~x**) /aɲo/ *n.m.* lamb.

agonie /agɔni/ *n.f.* death throes.

agoniser /agɔnize/ *v.i.* be dying.

agraf|e /agraf/ *n.f.* hook; (*pour papiers*) staple. **~er** *v.t.* hook (up); staple. **~euse** *n.f.* stapler.

agrand|ir /agrɑ̃dir/ *v.t.* enlarge. **s'~ir** *v. pr.* expand, grow. **~issement** *n.m.* extension; (*de photo*) enlargement.

agréable /agreabl/ *a.* pleasant. **~ment** /-əmɑ̃/ *adv.* pleasantly.

agréer /agree/ *v.t.* accept. **~ à,** please.

agrég|ation /agregɑsjɔ̃/ *n.f.* agrégation (*highest examination for recruitment of teachers*). **~é, ~ée** /-ʒe/ *n.m., f.* agrégé (*teacher who has passed the agrégation*).

agrément /agremɑ̃/ *n.m.* charm; (*plaisir*) pleasure; (*accord*) assent.

agrémenter /agremɑ̃te/ *v.t.* embellish (**de,** with).

agrès /agrɛ/ *n.m. pl.* (gymnastics) apparatus.

agress|er /agrese/ *v.t.* attack. **~eur**

/-εsœr/ *n.m.* attacker; (*mil.*) aggres-
sor. **~ion** /-εsjɔ̃/ *n.f.* attack; (*mil.*)
aggression.
agressi|f, ~ve /agresif, -v/ *a.* aggres-
sive. **~vité** *n.f.* aggressiveness.
agricole /agrikɔl/ *a.* agricultural;
(*ouvrier etc.*) farm.
agriculteur /agrikyltœr/ *n.m.*
farmer.
agriculture /agrikyltyr/ *n.f.* agriculture, farming.
agripper /agripe/ *v.t.*, **s'~ à**, grab,
clutch.
agrumes /agrym/ *n.m. pl.* citrus
fruit(s).
aguerrir /agerir/ *v.t.* harden.
aguets (aux) /(oz)agε/ *adv.* on the
look-out.
aguicher /agiʃe/ *v.t.* entice.
ah /α/ *int.* ah, oh.
ahur|ir /ayrir/ *v.t.* dumbfound. **~isse-
ment** *n.m.* stupefaction.
ai /e/ *voir* **avoir.**
aide /εd/ *n.f.* help, assistance, aid.
—*n.m./f.* assistant. **à l'~ de,** with
the help of. **~ familiale,** home help.
~-mémoire *n.m. invar.* handbook
of facts. **~ sociale,** social security; (*Amer.*) welfare. **~ soignant,
~ soignante** *n.m.,f.* auxiliary nurse.
venir en ~ à, help.
aider /ede/ *v.t./i.* help, assist. **s'~ de,**
use.
aïe /aj/ *int.* ouch.
aïeul, ~e /ajœl/ *n.m.,f.* grandparent.
aïeux /ajø/ *n.m. pl.* forefathers.
aigle /εgl/ *n.m.* eagle.
aigr|e /εgr/ *a.* sour, sharp; (*fig.*) sharp.
~e-doux, ~e-douce *a.* bitter-sweet.
~eur *n.f.* sourness; (*fig.*) sharpness.
~eurs d'estomac, heartburn.
aigrir /egrir/ *v.t.* embitter; (*caractère*)
sour. **s'~** *v. pr.* turn sour; (*personne*)
become embittered.
aigu, ~ë /egy/ *a.* acute; (*objet*) sharp;
(*voix*) shrill.
aiguillage /egɥijaʒ/ *n.m.* (*rail.*) points;
(*rail., Amer.*) switches.
aiguille /egɥij/ *n.f.* needle; (*de montre*)
hand; (*de balance*) pointer.
aiguill|er /egɥije/ *v.t.* shunt; (*fig.*)
steer. **~eur** *n.m.* pointsman; (*Amer.*)
switchman. **~eur du ciel,** air traffic
controller.
aiguillon /egɥijɔ̃/ *n.m.* (*dard*) sting;
(*fig.*) spur. **~ner** /-jɔne/ *v.t.* spur on.
aiguiser /eg(ɥ)ize/ *v.t.* sharpen; (*fig.*)
stimulate.

ail (*pl.* **~s**) /aj/ *n.m.* garlic.
aile /εl/ *n.f.* wing.
ailé /ele/ *a.* winged.
aileron /εlrɔ̃/ *n.m.* (*de requin*) fin.
ailier /elje/ *n.m.* winger; (*Amer.*) end.
aille /aj/ *voir* **aller**[1].
ailleurs /ajœr/ *adv.* elsewhere. **d'~,**
besides, moreover. **par ~,** moreover,
furthermore. **partout ~,** everywhere
else.
ailloli /ajɔli/ *n.m.* garlic mayonnaise.
aimable /εmabl/ *a.* kind. **~ment**
/-əmã/ *adv.* kindly.
aimant[1] /εmã/ *n.m.* magnet. **~er**
/-te/ *v.t.* magnetize.
aimant[2], **~e** /εmã, -t/ *a.* loving.
aimer /eme/ *v.t.* like; (*d'amour*) love.
~ bien, quite like. **~ mieux** *ou* autant, prefer.
aine /εn/ *n.f.* groin.
aîné, ~e /ene/ *a.* eldest; (*entre deux*)
elder. —*n.m., f.* eldest (child); elder
(child). **~s** *n.m. pl.* elders. **il est mon
~,** he is my senior.
ainsi /ε̃si/ *adv.* thus; (*donc*) so. **~ que,**
as well as; (*comme*) as. **et ~ de suite,**
and so on.
air /εr/ *n.m.* air; (*mine*) look, air; (*mélo-
die*) tune. **~ conditionné,** air-
conditioning. **avoir l'~,** look (**de,**
like). **avoir l'~ de faire,** appear
to be doing. **en l'~,** (up) in the air;
(*promesses etc.*) empty.
aire /εr/ *n.f.* area. **~ d'atterrissage,**
landing-strip.
aisance /εzɑ̃s/ *n.f.* ease; (*richesse*)
affluence.
aise /εz/ *n.f.* joy. —*a.* **bien ~ de**/**que,**
delighted about/that. **à l'~,** (*sur un
siège*) comfortable; (*pas gêné*) at ease;
(*fortuné*) comfortably off. **mal à l'~,**
uncomfortable; ill at ease. **aimer ses
~s,** like one's comforts.
aisé /eze/ *a.* easy; (*fortuné*) well-off.
~ment *adv.* easily.
aisselle /εsεl/ *n.f.* armpit.
ait /ε/ *voir* **avoir.**
ajonc /aʒɔ̃/ *n.m.* gorse.
ajourn|er /aʒurne/ *v.t.* postpone; (*as-
semblée*) adjourn. **~ement** *n.m.* postponement; adjournment.
ajout /aʒu/ *n.m.* addition.
ajouter /aʒute/ *v.t.*, **s'~** *v. pr.* add (**à,**
to). **~ foi,** lend credence.
ajust|er /aʒyste/ *v.t.* adjust; (*coup*)
aim; (*cible*) aim at; (*adapter*) fit. **s'~er**
v. pr. fit. **~age** *n.m.* fitting. **~é** *a.*

close-fitting. ~ement *n.m.* adjustment. ~eur *n.m.* fitter.

alambic /alɑ̃bik/ *n.m.* still.

alanguir (s') /(s)alɑ̃gir/ *v. pr.* grow languid.

alarme /alarm/ *n.f.* alarm.

alarmer /alarme/ *v.t.* alarm. **s'~** *v. pr.* become alarmed (**de**, at).

albâtre /albɑtr/ *n.m.* alabaster.

albatros /albatros/ *n.m.* albatross.

albinos /albinos/ *n.m./f.* albino.

album /albɔm/ *n.m.* album.

alcali /alkali/ *n.m.* alkali.

alchim|ie /alʃimi/ *n.f.* alchemy. ~iste *n.m.* alchemist.

alcool /alkɔl/ *n.m.* alcohol; (*eau de vie*) brandy. ~ **à brûler**, methylated spirit. ~ique *a.* & *n.m./f.* alcoholic. ~isé *a.* (*boisson*) alcoholic. ~isme *n.m.* alcoholism.

alcootest /alkɔtɛst/ *n.m.* (P.) breath test; (*appareil*) breathalyser.

alcôve /alkov/ *n.f.* alcove.

aléa /alea/ *n.m.* hazard.

aléatoire /aleatwar/ *a.* uncertain.

alentour /alɑ̃tur/ *adv.* around. ~s *n.m. pl.* surroundings. **aux ~s de**, round about.

alerte /alɛrt/ *a.* agile. —*n.f.* alert.

alerter /alɛrte/ *v.t.* alert.

algarade /algarad/ *n.f.* altercation.

alg|èbre /alʒɛbr/ *n.f.* algebra. ~ébrique *a.* algebraic.

Alger /alʒe/ *n.m./f.* Algiers.

Algérie /alʒeri/ *n.f.* Algeria.

algérien, ~ne /alʒerjɛ̃, -jɛn/ *a.* & *n.m.*, *f.* Algerian.

algue /alg/ *n.f.* seaweed.

alias /aljɑs/ *adv.* alias.

alibi /alibi/ *n.m.* alibi.

aliéné, ~e /aljene/ *n.m.*, *f.* insane person.

alién|er /aljene/ *v.t.* alienate; (*céder*) give up. **s'~er** *v. pr.* alienate. ~ation *n.f.* alienation.

aligner /aliɲe/ *v.t.* (*objets*) line up, make lines of; (*chiffres*) string together. ~ **sur**, bring into line with. **s'~** *v. pr.* line up. **s'~ sur**, align o.s. on. **alignement** /-əmɑ̃/ *n.m.* alignment.

aliment /alimɑ̃/ *n.m.* food. ~aire /-tɛr/ *a.* food.

aliment|er /alimɑ̃te/ *v.t.* feed; (*fournir*) supply; (*fig.*) sustain. ~ation *n.f.* feeding; supply(ing); (*régime*) diet; (*aliments*) groceries.

alinéa /alinea/ *n.m.* paragraph.

aliter (s') /(s)alite/ *v. pr.* take to one's bed.

allaiter /alete/ *v.t.* feed, suckle.

allant /alɑ̃/ *n.m.* verve, drive.

allécher /aleʃe/ *v.t.* tempt.

allée /ale/ *n.f.* path, lane; (*menant à une maison*) drive(way). ~s **et venues**, comings and goings.

allégation /alegɑsjɔ̃/ *n.f.* allegation.

allég|er /aleʒe/ *v.t.* make lighter; (*poids*) lighten; (*fig.*) alleviate.

allégor|ie /alegɔri/ *n.f.* allegory. ~ique *a.* allegorical.

allègre /alɛgr/ *a.* gay; (*vif*) jaunty.

allégresse /alegrɛs/ *n.f.* gaiety.

alléguer /alege/ *v.t.* put forward.

alléluia /aleluja/ *n.m.* & *int.* alleluia.

Allemagne /almaɲ/ *n.f.* Germany. ~ **de l'Ouest**, West Germany.

allemand, ~e /almɑ̃, -d/ *a.* & *n.m.*, *f.* German. —*n.m.* (*lang.*) German.

aller[1]† /ale/ *v.i.* (*aux. être*) go. **s'en ~** *v. pr.* go away. ~ **à**, (*convenir à*) suit; (*s'adapter à*) fit. ~ **faire**, be going to do. **comment allez-vous?**, (**comment**) **ça va?**, how are you? **ça va!**, all right! **il va bien**, he is well. **allez-y!**, go on! **allez!**, come on!

aller[2] /ale/ *n.m.* outward journey; (*billet*) single (ticket); (*Amer.*) one-way (ticket). ~ **et retour**, return journey; (*Amer.*) round trip; (*billet*) return (ticket); (*Amer.*) round trip (ticket).

allerg|ie /alɛrʒi/ *n.f.* allergy. ~ique *a.* allergic.

alliage /aljaʒ/ *n.m.* alloy.

alliance /aljɑ̃s/ *n.f.* alliance; (*bague*) wedding-ring; (*mariage*) marriage.

allié, ~e /alje/ *n.m.*, *f.* ally; (*parent*) relative (by marriage).

allier /alje/ *v.t.* combine; (*pol.*) ally. **s'~** *v. pr.* combine; (*pol.*) become allied; (*famille*) become related (**à**, to).

alligator /aligatɔr/ *n.m.* alligator.

allô /alo/ *int.* hallo, hello.

allocation /alɔkɑsjɔ̃/ *n.f.* allowance. ~ **de chômage**, unemployment benefit. ~s **familiales**, family allowance.

allocution /alɔkysjɔ̃/ *n.f.* speech.

allongé /alɔ̃ʒe/ *a.* elongated.

allongement /alɔ̃ʒmɑ̃/ *n.m.* lengthening.

allonger /alɔ̃ʒe/ *v.t.* lengthen; (*bras, jambe*) stretch (out). **s'~** *v. pr.* get longer; (*s'étendre*) stretch (o.s.) out.

allouer /alwe/ *v.t.* allocate.

allum|er /alyme/ *v.t.* light; (*radio,*

lampe, *etc.*) switch on; (*pièce*) switch the light(s) on in; (*fig.*) arouse. **s'~er** *v. pr.* (*lumière*) come on. **~age** *n.m.* lighting; (*auto.*) ignition. **~e-gaz** *n.m. invar.* gas lighter.

allumette /alymɛt/ *n.f.* match.

allure /alyr/ *n.f.* speed, pace; (*démarche*) walk; (*prestance*) bearing; (*air*) look. **à toute ~**, at full speed. **avoir de l'~**, have style.

allusion /alyzjɔ̃/ *n.f.* hint (**à**, at), allusion (**à**, to). **faire ~ à**, hint at, allude to.

almanach /almana/ *n.m.* almanac.

aloi /alwa/ *n.m.* **de bon ~**, sterling; (*gaieté*) wholesome.

alors /alɔr/ *adv.* then. —*conj.* so, then. **~ que**, when, while; (*tandis que*) whereas.

alouette /alwɛt/ *n.f.* lark.

alourdir /alurdir/ *v.t.* weigh down.

aloyau (*pl.* **~x**) /alwajo/ *n.m.* sirloin.

alpage /alpaʒ/ *n.m.* mountain pasture.

Alpes /alp/ *n.f. pl.* **les ~**, the Alps.

alpestre /alpɛstr/ *a.* alpine.

alphab|et /alfabɛ/ *n.m.* alphabet. **~étique** *a.* alphabetical.

alphabétiser /alfabetize/ *v.t.* teach to read and write.

alpin, ~e /alpɛ̃, -in/ *a.* alpine.

alpinis|te /alpinist/ *n.m.|f.* mountaineer. **~me** *n.m.* mountaineering.

altér|er /altere/ *v.t.* falsify; (*abîmer*) spoil; (*donner soif à*) make thirsty. **s'~er** *v. pr.* deteriorate. **~ation** *n.f.* deterioration.

alternati|f, ~ve /altɛrnatif, -v/ *a.* alternating. —*n.f.* alternative. **~vement** *adv.* alternately.

altern|er /altɛrne/ *v.t.|i.* alternate. **~ance** *n.f.* alternation. **en ~ance**, alternately. **~é** *a.* alternate.

Altesse /altɛs/ *n.f.* Highness.

alt|ier, ~ière /altje, -jɛr/ *a.* haughty.

altitude /altityd/ *n.f.* altitude, height.

alto /alto/ *n.m.* viola.

altruiste /altrɥist/ *a.* altruistic. —*n.m.|f.* altruist.

aluminium /alyminjɔm/ *n.m.* aluminium; (*Amer.*) aluminum.

alvéole /alveɔl/ *n.f.* (*de ruche*) cell.

amabilité /amabilite/ *n.f.* kindness.

amadouer /amadwe/ *v.t.* win over.

amaigr|ir /amegrir/ *v.t.* make thin(ner). **~issant, ~issante** *a.* (*régime*) slimming.

amalgam|e /amalgam/ *n.m.* combi-

nation. **~er** *v.t.* combine, amalgamate.

amand|e /amɑ̃d/ *n.f.* almond; (*d'un fruit à noyau*) kernel.

amant /amɑ̃/ *n.m.* lover.

amarr|e /amar/ *n.f.* (mooring) rope. **~es**, moorings. **~er** *v.t.* moor.

amas /amɑ/ *n.m.* heap, pile.

amasser /amase/ *v.t.* amass, gather; (*empiler*) pile up. **s'~** *v. pr.* pile up; (*gens*) gather.

amateur /amatœr/ *n.m.* amateur. **~ de**, lover of. **d'~**, amateur; (*péj.*) amateurish. **~isme** *n.m.* amateurism.

amazone (en) /(ɑ̃n)amazon/ *adv.* sidesaddle.

ambages (sans) /(sɑ̃z)ɑ̃baʒ/ *adv.* in plain language.

ambassade /ɑ̃basad/ *n.f.* embassy.

ambassa|deur, ~drice /ɑ̃basadœr, -dris/ *n.m., f.* ambassador.

ambiance /ɑ̃bjɑ̃s/ *n.f.* atmosphere.

ambiant, ~e /ɑ̃bjɑ̃, -t/ *a.* surrounding.

ambidextre /ɑ̃bidɛkstr/ *a.* ambidextrous.

ambigu, ~ë /ɑ̃bigy/ *a.* ambiguous. **~ïté** /-ɥite/ *n.f.* ambiguity.

ambitieu|x, ~se /ɑ̃bisjø, -z/ *a.* ambitious.

ambition /ɑ̃bisjɔ̃/ *n.f.* ambition. **~ner** /-jɔne/ *v.t.* have as one's ambition (**de**, to).

ambivalent, ~e /ɑ̃bivalɑ̃, -t/ *a.* ambivalent.

ambre /ɑ̃br/ *n.m.* amber.

ambulanc|e /ɑ̃bylɑ̃s/ *n.f.* ambulance. **~ier, ~ière** *n.m., f.* ambulance driver.

ambulant, ~e /ɑ̃bylɑ̃, -t/ *a.* itinerant.

âme /ɑm/ *n.f.* soul. **~ sœur**, soul mate.

amélior|er /ameljɔre/ *v.t., s'~er* *v. pr.* improve. **~ation** *n.f.* improvement.

aménag|er /amenaʒe/ *v.t.* (*arranger*) fit out; (*transformer*) convert; (*installer*) fit up; (*territoire*) develop. **~ement** *n.m.* fitting out; conversion; fitting up; development; (*modification*) adjustment.

amende /amɑ̃d/ *n.f.* fine. **faire ~ honorable**, make an apology.

amend|er /amɑ̃de/ *v.t.* improve; (*jurid.*) amend. **s'~er** *v. pr.* mend one's ways. **~ement** *n.m.* (*de texte*) amendment.

amener /amne/ *v.t.* bring; (*causer*) bring about. **s'~** *v. pr.* (*fam.*) come along.

amenuiser (s') /(s)amənɥize/ *v. pr.* dwindle.

amer, amère /amɛr/ *a.* bitter.

américain, ~e /amerikɛ̃, -ɛn/ *a.* & *n.m., f.* American.

Amérique /amerik/ *n.f.* America. **~ du Nord/Sud,** North/South America.

amerrir /amerir/ *v.i.* land (on the sea).

amertume /amɛrtym/ *n.f.* bitterness.

ameublement /amœbləmɑ̃/ *n.m.* furniture.

ameuter /amøte/ *v.t.* draw a crowd of; (*fig.*) stir up.

ami, ~e /ami/ *n.m., f.* friend; (*de la nature, des livres, etc.*) lover. —*a.* friendly.

amiable /amjabl/ *a.* amicable. **à l'~** *adv.* amicably; *a.* amicable.

amiante /amjɑ̃t/ *n.m.* asbestos.

amic|al (*m. pl.* **~aux**) /amikal, -o/ *a.* friendly. **~alement** *adv.* in a friendly manner.

amicale /amikal/ *n.f.* association.

amidon /amidɔ̃/ *n.m.* starch. **~ner** /-ɔne/ *v.t.* starch.

amincir /amɛ̃sir/ *v.t.* make thinner. **s'~** *v. pr.* get thinner.

amir|al (*pl.* **~aux**) /amiral, -o/ *n.m.* admiral.

amitié /amitje/ *n.f.* friendship. **~s,** kind regards. **prendre en ~,** take a liking to.

ammoniac /amɔnjak/ *n.m.* (*gaz*) ammonia.

ammoniaque /amɔnjak/ *n.f.* (*eau*) ammonia.

amnésie /amnezi/ *n.f.* amnesia.

amnistie /amnisti/ *n.f.* amnesty.

amoindrir /amwɛ̃drir/ *v.t.* diminish.

amollir /amɔlir/ *v.t.* soften.

amonceler /amɔ̃sle/ *v.t.,* **s'~** *v. pr.* pile up.

amont (en) /(ɑ̃n)amɔ̃/ *adv.* upstream.

amorc|e /amɔrs/ *n.f.* bait; (*début*) start; (*explosif*) fuse, cap; (*de pistolet d'enfant*) cap. **~er** *v.t.* start; (*hameçon*) bait; (*pompe*) prime.

amorphe /amɔrf/ *a.* (*mou*) listless.

amortir /amɔrtir/ *v.t.* (*choc*) cushion; (*bruit*) deaden; (*dette*) pay off; (*objet acheté*) make pay for itself.

amour /amur/ *n.m.* love. **pour l'~ de,** for the sake of. **~-propre** *n.m.* self-respect.

amouracher (s') /(s)amuraʃe/ *v. pr.* become infatuated (**de,** with).

amoureu|x, ~se /amurø, -z/ *a.* (*ardent*) amorous; (*vie*) love. —*n.m., f.* lover. **~x de qn.,** in love with s.o.

amovible /amɔvibl/ *a.* removable.

ampère /ɑ̃pɛr/ *n.m.* amp(ere).

amphibie /ɑ̃fibi/ *a.* amphibious.

amphithéâtre /ɑ̃fiteɑtr/ *n.m.* amphitheatre; (*d'université*) lecture hall.

ample /ɑ̃pl/ *a.* ample; (*mouvement*) broad. **~ment** /-əmɑ̃/ *adv.* amply.

ampleur /ɑ̃plœr/ *n.f.* extent, size; (*de vêtement*) fullness.

amplif|ier /ɑ̃plifje/ *v.t.* amplify; (*fig.*) expand, develop. **s'~ier** *v. pr.* expand, develop. **~icateur** *n.m.* amplifier.

ampoule /ɑ̃pul/ *n.f.* (*électrique*) bulb; (*sur la peau*) blister; (*de médicament*) phial.

ampoulé /ɑ̃pule/ *a.* turgid.

amput|er /ɑ̃pyte/ *v.t.* amputate; (*fig.*) reduce. **~ation** *n.f.* amputation; (*fig.*) reduction.

amuse-gueule /amyzgœl/ *n.m. invar.* appetizer.

amus|er /amyze/ *v.t.* amuse; (*détourner l'attention de*) distract. **s'~er** *v. pr.* enjoy o.s.; (*jouer*) play. **~ement** *n.m.* amusement; (*passe-temps*) diversion. **~eur** *n.m.* (*péj.*) entertainer.

amusette /amyzɛt/ *n.f.* petty amusement.

amygdale /amidal/ *n.f.* tonsil.

an /ɑ̃/ *n.m.* year. **avoir dix/etc. ~s,** be ten/etc. years old.

anachronisme /anakrɔnism/ *n.m.* anachronism.

anagramme /anagram/ *n.f.* anagram.

analogie /analɔʒi/ *n.f.* analogy.

analogue /analɔg/ *a.* similar.

analphabète /analfabɛt/ *a.* & *n.m./f.* illiterate.

analy|se /analiz/ *n.f.* analysis; (*de sang*) test. **~ser** *v.t.* analyse. **~ste** *n.m./f.* analyst. **~tique** *a.* analytical.

ananas /anana(s)/ *n.m.* pineapple.

anarch|ie /anarʃi/ *n.f.* anarchy. **~ique** *a.* anarchic. **~iste** *n.m./f.* anarchist.

anatom|ie /anatɔmi/ *n.f.* anatomy. **~ique** *a.* anatomical.

ancestr|al (*m. pl.* **~aux**) /ɑ̃sɛstral, -o/ *a.* ancestral.

ancêtre /ɑ̃sɛtr/ *n.m.* ancestor.

anche /ɑ̃ʃ/ *n.f.* (*mus.*) reed.

anchois /ɑ̃ʃwa/ *n.m.* anchovy.

ancien, ~ne /ɑ̃sjɛ̃, -jɛn/ *a.* old; (*de jadis*) ancient; (*meuble*) antique; (*précédent*) former, ex-, old; (*dans une* *fonction*) senior. —*n.m., f.* senior person; (*par l'âge*) elder. ~ **combattant**, ex-serviceman. ~**nement** /-jɛnmɑ̃/ *adv.* formerly. ~**neté** /-jɛnte/ *n.f.* age; seniority.

ancr|e /ɑ̃kr/ *n.f.* anchor. **jeter/lever l'~e**, cast/weigh anchor. ~**er** *v.t.* anchor; (*fig.*) fix. **s'~er** *v. pr.* anchor.

andouille /ɑ̃duj/ *n.f.* sausage filled with chitterlings; (*idiot: fam.*) nitwit.

âne /ɑn/ *n.m.* donkey, ass; (*imbécile*) ass.

anéantir /aneɑ̃tir/ *v.t.* destroy; (*exterminer*) annihilate; (*accabler*) overwhelm.

anecdot|e /anɛkdɔt/ *n.f.* anecdote. ~**ique** *a.* anecdotal.

aném|ie /anemi/ *n.f.* anaemia. ~**ié**, ~**ique** *adjs.* anaemic.

ânerie /ɑnri/ *n.f.* stupidity; (*parole*) stupid remark.

ânesse /ɑnɛs/ *n.f.* she-ass.

anesthés|ie /anɛstezi/ *n.f.* (*opération*) anaesthetic. ~**ique** *a.* & *n.m.* (*substance*) anaesthetic.

ang|e /ɑ̃ʒ/ *n.m.* angel. **aux ~es**, in seventh heaven. ~**élique** *a.* angelic.

angélus /ɑ̃ʒelys/ *n.m.* angelus.

angine /ɑ̃ʒin/ *n.f.* sore throat, tonsillitis.

anglais, ~**e** /ɑ̃glɛ -z/ *a.* English. —*n.m., f.* Englishman, Englishwoman. —*n.m.* (*lang.*) English.

angle /ɑ̃gl/ *n.m.* angle; (*coin*) corner.

Angleterre /ɑ̃glətɛr/ *n.f.* England.

anglicisme /ɑ̃glisism/ *n.m.* anglicism.

angliciste /ɑ̃glisist/ *n.m./f.* English specialist.

anglo- /ɑ̃glɔ/ *préf.* Anglo-.

anglophone /ɑ̃glɔfɔn/ *a.* English-speaking. —*n.m./f.* English speaker.

anglo-saxon, ~**ne** /ɑ̃glɔsaksɔ̃, -ɔn/ *a.* & *n.m., f.* Anglo-Saxon.

angoiss|e /ɑ̃gwas/ *n.f.* anguish. ~**ant**, ~**ante** *a.* harrowing. ~**é** *a.* anguished. ~**er** *v.t.* cause anguish to.

anguille /ɑ̃gij/ *n.f.* eel.

anguleux, ~**se** /ɑ̃gylø, -z/ *a.* (*figure*) angular.

anicroche /anikrɔʃ/ *n.f.* snag.

anim|al (*pl.* ~**aux**) /animal, -o/ *n.m.* animal. —*a.* (*m. pl.* ~**aux**) animal.

animà|teur, ~**trice** /animatœr, -tris/ *n.m., f.* organizer, leader; (*TV*) compère; (*TV, Amer.*) master of ceremonies.

anim|é /anime/ *a.* lively; (*affairé*) busy; (*être*) animate. ~**ation** *n.f.*

liveliness; (*affairement*) activity; (*cinéma*) animation.

animer /anime/ *v.t.* liven up; (*mener*) lead; (*mouvoir, pousser*) drive; (*encourager*) spur on. **s'~** *v. pr.* liven up.

animosité /animozite/ *n.f.* animosity.

anis /anis/ *n.m.* (*parfum, boisson*) aniseed.

ankylos|er (s') /(s)ɑ̃kiloze/ *v. pr.* go stiff. ~**é** *a.* stiff.

annales /anal/ *n.f. pl.* annals.

anneau (*pl.* ~**x**) /ano/ *n.m.* ring; (*de chaîne*) link.

année /ane/ *n.f.* year.

annexe /anɛks/ *a.* attached; (*bâtiment*) adjoining. —*n.f.* annexe; (*Amer.*) annex.

annex|er /anɛkse/ *v.t.* annex; (*document*) attach. ~**ion** *n.f.* annexation.

annihiler /aniile/ *v.t.* annihilate.

anniversaire /anivɛrsɛr/ *n.m.* birthday; (*d'un événement*) anniversary. —*a.* anniversary.

annonc|e /anɔ̃s/ *n.f.* announcement; (*publicitaire*) advertisement; (*indice*) sign. ~**er** *v.t.* announce; (*dénoter*) indicate. **s'~er bien/mal**, look good/bad. ~**eur** *n.m.* advertiser; (*speaker*) announcer.

Annonciation /anɔ̃sjasjɔ̃/ *n.f.* **l'~**, the Annunciation.

annot|er /anɔte/ *v.t.* annotate. ~**ation** *n.f.* annotation.

annuaire /anɥɛr/ *n.m.* year-book. ~ **(téléphonique)**, (telephone) directory.

annuel, ~**le** /anɥɛl/ *a.* annual, yearly. ~**lement** *adv.* annually, yearly.

annuité /anɥite/ *n.f.* annual payment.

annulaire /anɥlɛr/ *n.m.* ring-finger.

annul|er /anɥle/ *v.t.* cancel; (*contrat*) nullify; (*jugement*) quash. **s'~er** *v. pr.* cancel each other out. ~**ation** *n.f.* cancellation.

anodin, ~**e** /anɔdɛ̃, -in/ *a.* insignificant; (*blessure*) harmless.

anomalie /anɔmali/ *n.f.* anomaly.

ânonner /ɑnɔne/ *v.t./i.* mumble, drone.

anonymat /anɔnima/ *n.m.* anonymity.

anonyme /anɔnim/ *a.* anonymous.

anorak /anɔrak/ *n.m.* anorak.

anorm|al (*m. pl.* ~**aux**) /anɔrmal, -o/ *a.* abnormal.

anse /ɑ̃s/ *n.f.* handle; (*baie*) cove.

antagonis|me /ɑ̃tagɔnism/ *n.m.*

antagonism. ∼te *n.m./f.* antagonist; *a.* antagonistic.

antan (d') /(d)ātā/ *a.* of long ago.

antarctique /ātarktik/ *a.* & *n.m.* Antarctic.

antécédent /ātesedā/ *n.m.* antecedent.

antenne /āten/ *n.f.* aerial; (*Amer.*) antenna; (*d'insecte*) antenna; (*succursale*) agency; (*mil.*) outpost; (*auto., méd.*) emergency unit. **à l'∼,** on the air. **sur l'∼ de,** on the wavelength of.

antérieur /āterjœr/ *a.* previous, earlier; (*placé devant*) front. **∼ à,** prior to. **∼ement** *adv.* earlier. **∼ement à,** prior to. **antériorité** /-jɔrite/ *n.f.* precedence.

anthologie /ātɔlɔʒi/ *n.f.* anthology.

anthropolo|gie /ātrɔpɔlɔʒi/ *n.f.* anthropology. **∼gue** *n.m./f.* anthropologist.

anthropophage /ātrɔpɔfaʒ/ *a.* cannibalistic. *—n.m./f.* cannibal.

anti- /āti/ *préf.* anti-.

antiaérien, ∼ne /ātiaerjē, -jεn/ *a.* anti-aircraft. **abri ∼,** air-raid shelter.

antiatomique /ātiatɔmik/ *a.* **abri ∼,** fall-out shelter.

antibiotique /ātibjɔtik/ *n.m.* antibiotic.

anticancéreu|x, ∼se /ātikāserø, -z/ *a.* (anti-)cancer.

antichambre /ātiʃābr/ *n.f.* waiting-room, antechamber.

anticipation /ātisipɑsjɔ̃/ *n.f.* **d'∼,** (*livre, film*) science fiction. **par ∼,** in advance.

anticipé /ātisipe/ *a.* early.

anticiper /ātisipe/ *v.t./i.* ∼ (**sur**), anticipate.

anticonceptionnel, ∼le /ātikɔ̃-sεpsjɔnεl/ *a.* contraceptive.

anticorps /ātikɔr/ *n.m.* antibody.

anticyclone /ātisyklon/ *n.m.* anticyclone.

antidater /ātidate/ *v.t.* backdate, antedate.

antidote /ātidɔt/ *n.m.* antidote.

antigel /ātiʒεl/ *n.m.* antifreeze.

antillais, ∼e /ātijε, -z/ *a.* & *n.m.*, *f.* West Indian.

Antilles /ātij/ *n.f. pl.* **les ∼,** the West Indies.

antilope /ātilɔp/ *n.f.* antelope.

antimite /ātimit/ *n.m.* moth repellent.

antipath|ie /ātipati/ *n.f.* antipathy. **∼ique** *a.* unpleasant.

antipodes /ātipɔd/ *n.m. pl.* antipodes. **aux ∼ de,** (*fig.*) poles apart from.

antiquaire /ātikεr/ *n.m./f.* antique dealer.

antiqu|e /ātik/ *a.* ancient. **∼ité** *n.f.* antiquity; (*objet*) antique.

antisémit|e /ātisemit/ *a.* anti-Semitic. **∼isme** *n.m.* anti-Semitism.

antiseptique /ātisεptik/ *a.* & *n.m.* antiseptic.

antithèse /ātitεz/ *n.f.* antithesis.

antivol /ātivɔl/ *n.m.* anti-theft lock *ou* device.

antre /ātr/ *n.m.* den.

anus /anys/ *n.m.* anus.

anxiété /āksjete/ *n.f.* anxiety.

anxieu|x, ∼se /āksjø, -z/ *a.* anxious. *—n.m., f.* worrier.

août /u(t)/ *n.m.* August.

apais|er /apeze/ *v.t.* appease, calm, soothe; (*douleur, colère*) soothe. **s'∼er** *v. pr.* (*tempête*) die down. **∼ement** *n.m.* appeasement; soothing. **∼ements** *n.m. pl.* reassurances.

apanage /apanaʒ/ *n.m.* **l'∼ de,** the privilege of.

aparté /aparte/ *n.m.* private exchange; (*théâtre*) aside. **en ∼,** in private.

apath|ie /apati/ *n.f.* apathy. **∼ique** *a.* apathetic.

apatride /apatrid/ *n.m./f.* stateless person.

apercevoir† /apεrsəvwar/ *v.t.* see. **s'∼ de,** notice. **s'∼ que,** notice *ou* realize that.

aperçu /apεrsy/ *n.m.* general view *ou* idea; (*intuition*) insight.

apéritif /aperitif/ *n.m.* aperitif.

à-peu-près /apøprε/ *n.m. invar.* approximation.

apeuré /apœre/ *a.* scared.

aphone /afɔn/ *a.* voiceless.

aphrodisiaque /afrɔdizjak/ *a.* & *n.m.* aphrodisiac.

aphte /aft/ *n.m.* mouth ulcer.

apit|oyer /apitwaje/ *v.t.* move (to pity). **s'∼oyer sur,** feel pity for. **∼oiement** *n.m.* pity.

aplanir /aplanir/ *v.t.* level; (*fig.*) smooth out.

aplatir /aplatir/ *v.t.* flatten (out). **s'∼** *v. pr.* (*s'allonger*) lie flat; (*s'humilier*) grovel; (*tomber: fam.*) fall flat on one's face.

aplomb /aplɔ̃/ *n.m.* balance; (*fig.*) self-possession. **d'∼,** (*en équilibre*) steady, balanced.

Apocalypse /apɔkalips/ *n.f.* Apocalypse. **apocalyptique** /-tik/ *a.* apocalyptic.

apogée /apɔʒe/ *n.m.* peak.

apologie /apɔlɔʒi/ *n.f.* vindication.

a posteriori /aposterjɔri/ *adv.* after the event.

apostolat /apostɔla/ *n.m.* proselytism; (*fig.*) calling.

apostroph|e /apostrɔf/ *n.f.* apostrophe; (*appel*) sharp address. ~**er** *v.t.* address sharply.

apothéose /apoteoz/ *n.f.* final triumph.

apôtre /apotr/ *n.m.* apostle.

apparaître† /aparɛtr/ *v.i.* appear. **il apparaît que,** it appears that.

apparat /apara/ *n.m.* pomp. **d'~,** ceremonial.

appareil /aparɛj/ *n.m.* apparatus; (*électrique*) appliance; (*anat.*) system; (*téléphonique*) phone; (*dentier*) brace; (*auditif*) hearing-aid; (*avion*) plane. ~(**-photo**), camera. ~ **électro-ménager,** household electrical appliance.

appareiller[1] /apareje/ *v.i.* (*navire*) cast off, put to sea.

appareiller[2] /apareje/ *v.t.* (*assortir*) match.

apparemment /aparamɑ̃/ *adv.* apparently.

apparence /aparɑ̃s/ *n.f.* appearance. **en ~,** outwardly; (*apparemment*) apparently.

apparent, ~e /aparɑ̃, -t/ *a.* apparent; (*visible*) conspicuous.

apparenté /aparɑ̃te/ *a.* related; (*semblable*) similar.

appariteur /aparitœr/ *n.m.* (*univ.*) attendant, porter.

apparition /aparisjɔ̃/ *n.f.* appearance; (*spectre*) apparition.

appartement /apartəmɑ̃/ *n.m.* flat; (*Amer.*) apartment.

appartenance /apartənɑ̃s/ *n.f.* membership (**à,** of), belonging (**à,** to).

appartenir† /apartənir/ *v.i.* belong (**à,** to). **il lui/vous/***etc.* **appartient de,** it is up to him/you/*etc.* to.

appât /apɑ/ *n.m.* bait; (*fig.*) lure. ~**er** /-te/ *v.t.* lure.

appauvrir /apovrir/ *v.t.* impoverish. **s'~** *v. pr.* grow impoverished.

appel /apɛl/ *n.m.* call; (*jurid.*) appeal; (*mil.*) call-up. **faire ~ à,** (*recourir à*) call on; (*invoquer*) appeal to; (*évoquer*) call up; (*exiger*) call for. **faire l'~,**

(*scol.*) call the register; (*mil.*) take a roll-call.

appelé /aple/ *n.m.* conscript.

appel|er /aple/ *v.t.* call; (*nécessiter*) call for. **s'~er** *v. pr.* be called. ~**é à,** (*désigné à*) marked out for. **en ~er à,** appeal to. **il s'appelle,** his name is. ~**lation** /apelɑsjɔ̃/ *n.f.* designation.

appendic|e /apẽdis/ *n.m.* appendix. ~**ite** *n.f.* appendicitis.

appentis /apɑ̃ti/ *n.m.* lean-to.

appesantir /apzɑ̃tir/ *v.t.* weigh down. **s'~** *v. pr.* grow heavier. **s'~ sur,** dwell upon.

appétissant, ~e /apetisɑ̃, -t/ *a.* appetizing.

appétit /apeti/ *n.m.* appetite.

applaud|ir /aplodir/ *v.t./i.* applaud. ~**ir à,** applaud. ~**issements** *n.m. pl.* applause.

applique /aplik/ *n.f.* wall lamp.

appliqué /aplike/ *a.* painstaking.

appliquer /aplike/ *v.t.* apply. **s'~** *v. pr.* apply o.s. (**à,** to). **s'~ à,** (*concerner*) apply to. **applicable** /-abl/ *a.* applicable. **application** /-ɑsjɔ̃/ *n.f.* application.

appoint /apwẽ/ *n.m.* contribution. **d'~,** extra. **faire l'~,** give the correct money.

appointements /apwẽtmɑ̃/ *n.m. pl.* salary.

apport /apɔr/ *n.m.* contribution.

apporter /aporte/ *v.t.* bring.

apposer /apoze/ *v.t.* affix.

appréciable /apresjabl/ *a.* appreciable.

appréc|ier /apresje/ *v.t.* appreciate; (*évaluer*) appraise. ~**iation** *n.f.* appreciation; appraisal.

appréhen|der /apreɑ̃de/ *v.t.* dread, fear; (*arrêter*) apprehend. ~**sion** *n.f.* apprehension.

apprendre† /aprɑ̃dr/ *v.t./i.* learn; (*être informé de*) hear of. ~ **qch. à qn.,** teach s.o. sth.; (*informer*) tell s.o. sth. ~ **à faire,** learn to do. ~ **à qn. à faire,** teach s.o. to do. ~ **que,** learn that; (*être informé*) hear that.

apprenti, ~e /aprɑ̃ti/ *n.m.,f.* apprentice.

apprentissage /aprɑ̃tisaʒ/ *n.m.* apprenticeship.

apprêter /aprete/ *v.t.,* **s'~** *v. pr.* prepare.

apprivoiser /aprivwaze/ *v.t.* tame.

approba|teur, ~trice /aprobatœr, -tris/ *a.* approving.

approbation /aprɔbɑsjɔ̃/ *n.f.* approval.

approchant, ~e /aprɔʃɑ̃, -t/ *a.* close, similar.

approche /aprɔʃ/ *n.f.* approach.

approché /aprɔʃe/ *a.* approximate.

approcher /aprɔʃe/ *v.t.* (*objet*) move near(er) (**de**, to); (*roi, artiste, etc.*) approach. —*v.i.* ~ (**de**), approach. **s'~ de**, approach, move near(er) to.

approfond|ir /aprɔfɔ̃dir/ *v.t.* deepen; (*fig.*) go into thoroughly. ~**i** *a.* thorough.

approprié /aprɔprije/ *a.* appropriate.

approprier (s') /(s)aprɔprije/ *v. pr.* appropriate.

approuver /apruve/ *v.t.* approve; (*trouver louable*) approve of; (*soutenir*) agree with.

approvisionn|er /aprɔvizjɔne/ *v.t.* supply. **s'~er** *v. pr.* stock up. ~**ement** *n.m.* supply.

approximati|f, ~ve /aprɔksimatif, -v/ *a.* approximate. ~**vement** *adv.* approximately.

approximation /aprɔksimɑsjɔ̃/ *n.f.* approximation.

appui /apɥi/ *n.m.* support; (*de fenêtre*) sill; (*pour objet*) rest. **à l'~ de**, in support of.

appuyer /apɥije/ *v.t.* lean, rest; (*presser*) press; (*soutenir*) support, back. —*v.i.* ~ **sur**, press (on); (*fig.*) stress. **s'~ sur**, lean on; (*compter sur*) rely on.

âpre /ɑpr/ *a.* harsh, bitter. ~ **au gain**, grasping.

après /aprɛ/ *prép.* after; (*au-delà de*) beyond. —*adv.* after(wards); (*plus tard*) later. ~ **avoir fait**, after doing. ~ **qu'il est parti**, after he left. ~ **coup**, after the event. **d'~**, (*selon*) according to. ~**-demain** *adv.* the day after tomorrow. ~**-guerre** *n.m.* post-war period. ~**-midi** *n.m./f. invar.* afternoon. ~**-ski** *n.m.* snow-boot (*worn when not skiing*).

a priori /aprijɔri/ *adv.* in principle, without going into the matter.

à-propos /aprɔpo/ *n.m.* timeliness; (*fig.*) presence of mind.

apte /apt/ *a.* capable (**à**, of).

aptitude /aptityd/ *n.f.* aptitude, ability.

aquarelle /akwarɛl/ *n.f.* watercolour, aquarelle.

aquarium /akwarjɔm/ *n.m.* aquarium.

aquatique /akwatik/ *a.* aquatic.

aqueduc /akdyk/ *n.m.* aqueduct.

arabe /arab/ *a.* Arab; (*lang.*) Arabic; (*désert*) Arabian. —*n.m./f.* Arab. —*n.m.* (*lang.*) Arabic.

Arabie /arabi/ *n.f.* ~ **Séoudite,** Saudi Arabia.

arable /arabl/ *a.* arable.

arachide /araʃid/ *n.f.* peanut.

araignée /areɲe/ *n.f.* spider.

arbitraire /arbitrɛr/ *a.* arbitrary.

arbitr|e /arbitr/ *n.m.* referee; (*cricket, tennis*) umpire; (*maître*) arbiter; (*jurid.*) arbitrator. ~**age** *n.m.* arbitration; (*sport*) refereeing. ~**er** *v.t.* (*match*) referee; (*jurid.*) arbitrate.

arborer /arbɔre/ *v.t.* display; (*vêtement*) sport.

arbre /arbr/ *n.m.* tree; (*techn.*) shaft.

arbrisseau (*pl.* ~**x**) /arbriso/ *n.m.* shrub.

arbuste /arbyst/ *n.m.* bush.

arc /ark/ *n.m.* (*arme*) bow; (*voûte*) arch. ~ **de cercle**, arc of a circle.

arcade /arkad/ *n.f.* arch. ~**s**, arcade, arches.

arc-boutant (*pl.* **arcs-boutants**) /arkbutɑ̃/ *n.m.* flying buttress.

arc-bouter (s') /(s)arkbute/ *v. pr.* lean (for support), brace o.s.

arceau (*pl.* ~**x**) /arso/ *n.m.* hoop; (*de voûte*) arch.

arc-en-ciel (*pl.* **arcs-en-ciel**) /arkɑ̃sjɛl/ *n.m.* rainbow.

archaïque /arkaik/ *a.* archaic.

arche /arʃ/ *n.f.* arch. ~ **de Noé**, Noah's ark.

archéolo|gie /arkeɔlɔʒi/ *n.f.* archaeology. ~**gique** *a.* archaeological. ~**gue** *n.m./f.* archaeologist.

archer /arʃe/ *n.m.* archer.

archet /arʃɛ/ *n.m.* (*mus.*) bow.

archétype /arketip/ *n.m.* archetype.

archevêque /arʃəvɛk/ *n.m.* archbishop.

archi- /arʃi/ *préf.* (*fam.*) tremendously.

archipel /arʃipɛl/ *n.m.* archipelago.

architecte /arʃitɛkt/ *n.m.* architect.

architecture /arʃitɛktyr/ *n.f.* architecture.

archiv|es /arʃiv/ *n.f. pl.* archives. ~**iste** *n.m./f.* archivist.

arctique /arktik/ *a. & n.m.* Arctic.

ardemment /ardamɑ̃/ *adv.* ardently.

ard|ent, ~ente /ardɑ̃, -t/ *a.* burning; (*passionné*) ardent; (*foi*) fervent. ~**eur** *n.f.* ardour; (*chaleur*) heat.

ardoise /ardwaz/ n.f. slate.

ardu /ardy/ a. arduous.

are /ar/ n.m. are (= 100 square metres).

arène /arɛn/ n.f. arena. ~(s), (pour courses de taureaux) bullring.

arête /arɛt/ n.f. (de poisson) bone; (bord) ridge.

argent /arʒɑ̃/ n.m. money; (métal) silver. ~ comptant, cash.

argenté /arʒɑ̃te/ a. silver(y); (métal) (silver-)plated.

argenterie /arʒɑ̃tri/ n.f. silverware.

argentin, ~e /arʒɑ̃tɛ̃, -in/ a. & n.m.,f. Argentinian, Argentine.

Argentine /arʒɑ̃tin/ n.f. Argentina.

argil|e /arʒil/ n.f. clay. ~eux, ~euse a. clayey.

argot /argo/ n.m. slang. ~ique /-ɔtik/ a. (terme) slang; (style) slangy.

arguer /argɥe/ v.i. ~ de, put forward as a reason.

argument /argymɑ̃/ n.m. argument. ~er /-te/ v.i. argue.

aride /arid/ a. arid, barren.

aristocrate /aristɔkrat/ n.m./f. aristocrat.

aristocrat|ie /aristɔkrasi/ n.f. aristocracy. ~ique /-atik/ a. aristocratic.

arithmétique /aritmetik/ n.f. arithmetic. —a. arithmetical.

armateur /armatœr/ n.m. shipowner.

armature /armatyr/ n.f. framework; (de tente) frame.

arme /arm/ n.f. arm, weapon. ~s, (blason) arms. ~ à feu, firearm.

armée /arme/ n.f. army. ~ de l'air, Air Force. ~ de terre, Army.

armement /arməmɑ̃/ n.m. arms.

armer /arme/ v.t. arm; (fusil) cock; (navire) equip; (renforcer) reinforce. ~ de, (garnir de) fit with. s'~ de, arm o.s. with.

armistice /armistis/ n.m. armistice.

armoire /armwar/ n.f. cupboard; (penderie) wardrobe.

armoiries /armwari/ n.f. pl. (coat of) arms.

armure /armyr/ n.f. armour.

arnica /arnika/ n.f. (méd.) arnica.

aromate /arɔmat/ n.m. herb, spice.

aromatique /arɔmatik/ a. aromatic.

aromatisé /arɔmatize/ a. flavoured.

arôme /arom/ n.m. aroma.

arpège /arpɛʒ/ n.m. arpeggio.

arpent|er /arpɑ̃te/ v.t. pace up and down; (terrain) survey. ~eur n.m. surveyor.

arqué /arke/ a. arched; (jambes) bandy.

arraché (à l') /(al)araʃe/ adv. with a struggle, after a hard struggle.

arrache-pied (d') /(d)araʃpje/ adv. relentlessly.

arracher /araʃe/ v.t. pull out; (plante) pull ou dig up; (cheveux, page) tear ou pull out; (par une explosion) blow off. ~ à, (enlever à) snatch from; (fig.) force ou wrest from. s'~ qch., fight over sth. **arrachage** /-aʒ/ n.m. pulling ou digging up.

arraisonner /arɛzɔne/ v.t. inspect.

arrangeant, ~e /arɑ̃ʒɑ̃, -t/ a. obliging.

arrangement /arɑ̃ʒmɑ̃/ n.m. arrangement.

arranger /arɑ̃ʒe/ v.t. arrange, fix up; (réparer) put right; (régler) sort out; (convenir à) suit. s'~ v. pr. (se mettre d'accord) come to an arrangement; (se débrouiller) manage (pour, to).

arrestation /arɛstasjɔ̃/ n.f. arrest.

arrêt /arɛ/ n.m. stopping (de, of); (lieu) stop; (pause) pause; (jurid.) decree. ~s, (mil.) arrest. à l'~, stationary. **faire un ~,** (make a) stop. ~ **de travail,** (grève) stoppage. **rester** ou **tomber en ~,** stop short.

arrêté /arete/ n.m. order.

arrêter /arete/ v.t./i. stop; (date, regard) fix; (appréhender) arrest. s'~ v. pr. stop. (s')~ **de faire,** stop doing.

arrhes /ar/ n.f. pl. deposit.

arrière /arjɛr/ n.m. back, rear; (football) back. —a. invar. back, rear. à l'~, in ou at the back. en ~, behind; (marcher) backwards. en ~ de, behind. ~-**boutique** n.f. back room (of the shop). ~-**garde** n.f. rearguard. ~-**goût** n.m. after-taste. ~-**grand-mère** n.f. great-grandmother. ~-**grand-père** (pl. ~-**grands-pères**) n.m. great-grandfather. ~-**pensée** n.f. ulterior motive. ~-**plan** n.m. background.

arriéré /arjere/ a. backward. —n.m. arrears.

arrimer /arime/ v.t. rope down; (cargaison) stow.

arrivage /arivaʒ/ n.m. consignment.

arrivant, ~e /arivɑ̃, -t/ n.m., f. new arrival.

arrivée /arive/ n.f. arrival; (sport) finish.

arriver /arive/ v.i. (aux. être) arrive, come; (réussir) succeed; (se produire) happen. ~ à, (atteindre) reach. ~ à

faire, manage to do. **en ~ à faire,** get to the stage of doing. **il arrive que,** it happens that. **il lui arrive de faire,** he (sometimes) does.

arriviste /arivist/ *n.m.|f.* self-seeker.

arrogan|t, ~te /arɔgã, -t/ *a.* arrogant. **~ce** *n.f.* arrogance.

arroger (s') /(s)arɔʒe/ *v. pr.* assume (without justification).

arrondir /arɔ̃dir/ *v.t.* (make) round; (*somme*) round off. **s'~** *v. pr.* become round(ed).

arrondissement /arɔ̃dismã/ *n.m.* district.

arros|er /aroze/ *v.t.* water; (*repas*) wash down; (*victoire*) celebrate with a drink. **~age** *n.m.* watering. **~oir** *n.m.* watering-can.

arsen|al (*pl.* **~aux**) /arsənal, -o/ *n.m.* arsenal; (*naut.*) dockyard.

arsenic /arsənik/ *n.m.* arsenic.

art /ar/ *n.m.* art. **~s et métiers,** arts and crafts. **~s ménagers,** domestic science.

artère /artɛr/ *n.f.* artery. (**grande) ~,** main road.

artériel, ~le /arterjɛl/ *a.* arterial.

arthrite /artrit/ *n.f.* arthritis.

artichaut /artiʃo/ *n.m.* artichoke.

article /artikl/ *n.m.* article; (*comm.*) item, article. **à l'~ de la mort,** at death's door. **~ de fond,** feature (article). **~s d'ameublement,** furnishings. **~s de voyage,** travel requisites *ou* goods.

articul|er /artikyle/ *v.t.*, **s'~er** *v. pr.* articulate. **~ation** *n.f.* articulation; (*anat.*) joint.

artifice /artifis/ *n.m.* contrivance.

artificiel, ~le /artifisjɛl/ *a.* artificial. **~lement** *adv.* artificially.

artill|erie /artijri/ *n.f.* artillery. **~eur** *n.m.* gunner.

artisan /artizã/ *n.m.* artisan, craftsman. **l'~ de,** (*fig.*) the architect of. **~al** (*m. pl.* **~aux**) /-anal, -o/ *a.* of *ou* by craftsmen, craft. **~at** /-ana/ *n.m.* craft; (*classe*) artisans.

artist|e /artist/ *n.m.|f.* artist; (*musicien, acteur*) performer. **~ique** *a.* artistic.

as[1] /a/ *voir* **avoir.**

as[2] /ɑs/ *n.m.* ace.

ascendant[1], **~e** /asãdã, -t/ *a.* ascending, upward.

ascendan|t[2] /asãdã/ *n.m.* influence. **~ts,** ancestors. **~ce** *n.f.* ancestry.

ascenseur /asãsœr/ *n.m.* lift; (*Amer.*) elevator.

ascension /asãsjɔ̃/ *n.f.* ascent. **A~,** Ascension.

ascète /asɛt/ *n.m.|f.* ascetic.

ascétique /asetik/ *a.* ascetic.

aseptique /asɛptik/ *a.* aseptic.

asiatique /azjatik/ *a.* & *n.m.|f.*, **Asiate** /azjat/ *n.m.|f.* Asian.

Asie /azi/ *n.f.* Asia.

asile /azil/ *n.m.* refuge; (*pol.*) asylum; (*pour malades, vieillards*) home.

aspect /aspɛ/ *n.m.* appearance; (*fig.*) aspect. **à l'~ de,** at the sight of.

asperge /aspɛrʒ/ *n.f.* asparagus.

asper|ger /aspɛrʒe/ *v.t.* spray. **~sion** *n.f.* spray(ing).

aspérité /asperite/ *n.f.* bump, rough edge.

asphalt|e /asfalt/ *n.m.* asphalt. **~er** *v.t.* asphalt.

asphyxie /asfiksi/ *n.f.* suffocation.

asphyxier /asfiksje/ *v.t.*, **s'~** *v. pr.* suffocate, asphyxiate.

aspic /aspik/ *n.m.* (*serpent*) asp.

aspirateur /aspiratœr/ *n.m.* vacuum cleaner.

aspir|er /aspire/ *v.t.* inhale; (*liquide*) suck up. —*v.i.* **~er à,** aspire to. **~ation** *n.f.* inhaling; suction; (*ambition*) aspiration.

aspirine /aspirin/ *n.f.* aspirin.

assagir /asaʒir/ *v.t.*, **s'~** *v. pr.* sober down.

assaill|ir /asajir/ *v.t.* assail. **~ant** *n.m.* assailant.

assainir /asenir/ *v.t.* clean up.

assaisonn|er /asɛzɔne/ *v.t.* season. **~ement** *n.m.* seasoning.

assassin /asasɛ̃/ *n.m.* murderer; (*pol.*) assassin.

assassin|er /asasine/ *v.t.* murder; (*pol.*) assassinate. **~at** *n.m.* murder; (*pol.*) assassination.

assaut /aso/ *n.m.* assault, onslaught. **donner l'~ à, prendre d'~,** storm.

assécher /aseʃe/ *v.t.* drain.

assemblée /asãble/ *n.f.* meeting; (*gens réunis*) gathering; (*pol.*) assembly.

assembl|er /asãble/ *v.t.* assemble, put together; (*réunir*) gather. **s'~er** *v. pr.* gather, assemble. **~age** *n.m.* assembly; (*combinaison*) collection; (*techn.*) joint.

assener /asene/ *v.t.* (*coup*) deal.

assentiment /asãtimã/ *n.m.* assent.

asseoir† /aswar/ *v.t.* sit (down), seat;

(*affermir*) establish; (*baser*) base. **s'~** *v. pr.* sit (down).

assermenté /asɛrmɑ̃te/ *a.* sworn.

assertion /asɛrsjɔ̃/ *n.f.* assertion.

asservir /asɛrvir/ *v.t.* enslave.

assez /ase/ *adv.* enough; (*plutôt*) quite, fairly. **~ grand/rapide/** *etc.*, big/ fast/*etc.* enough (**pour**, to). **~ de**, enough.

assid|u /asidy/ *a.* (*zélé*) assiduous; (*régulier*) regular. **~u auprès de**, attentive to. **~uité** /-ɥite/ *n.f.* assiduousness; regularity. **~ûment** *adv.* assiduously.

assiéger /asjeʒe/ *v.t.* besiege.

assiette /asjɛt/ *n.f.* plate; (*équilibre*) seat. **~ anglaise**, assorted cold-meats. **~ creuse/plate**, soup-/dinnerplate. **ne pas être dans son ~**, feel out of sorts.

assiettée /asjete/ *n.f.* plateful.

assigner /asiɲe/ *v.t.* assign; (*limite*) fix.

assimil|er /asimile/ *v.t.*, **s'~er** *v. pr.* assimilate. **~er à**, liken to; (*classer*) class as. **~ation** *n.f.* assimilation; likening; classification.

assis, ~e /asi, -z/ *voir* **asseoir.** —*a.* sitting (down), seated.

assise /asiz/ *n.f.* (*base*) foundation. **~s**, (*tribunal*) assizes; (*congrès*) meeting.

assistance /asistɑ̃s/ *n.f.* audience; (*aide*) assistance. **l'A~ (publique)**, government child care service.

assistant, ~e /asistɑ̃, -t/ *n.m.,f.* assistant; (*univ.*) assistant lecturer. **~s**, (*spectateurs*) members of the audience. **~ social, ~e sociale**, social worker.

assister /asiste/ *v.t.* assist. —*v.i.* **~ à**, attend, be (present) at; (*scène*) witness.

association /asɔsjɑsjɔ̃/ *n.f.* association.

associé, ~e /asɔsje/ *n.m.*, *f.* partner, associate. —*a.* associate.

associer /asɔsje/ *v.t.* associate; (*mêler*) combine. **~ qn. à**, have s.o. become involved with *ou* in. **s'~** *v. pr.* become associated, join forces (**à**, with); (*s'harmoniser*) combine (**à**, with). **s'~ à**, (*joie de qn.*) share in; (*opinion de qn.*) share.

assoiffé /aswafe/ *a.* thirsty.

assombrir /asɔ̃brir/ *v.t.* darken; (*fig.*) make gloomy. **s'~** *v. pr.* darken; become gloomy.

assommer /asɔme/ *v.t.* knock out;

(*tuer*) kill; (*animal*) stun; (*fig.*) overwhelm; (*ennuyer: fam.*) bore.

Assomption /asɔ̃psjɔ̃/ *n.f.* Assumption.

assorti /asɔrti/ *a.* matching; (*objets variés*) assorted.

assort|ir /asɔrtir/ *v.t.* match (**à**, with, to). **~ir de**, accompany with. **s'~ir** (**à**), match. **~iment** *n.m.* assortment.

assoup|ir (s') /(s)asupir/ *v. pr.* doze off; (*s'apaiser*) subside. **~i** *a.* dozing.

assouplir /asuplir/ *v.t.* make supple; (*fig.*) make flexible.

assourdir /asurdir/ *v.t.* (*personne*) deafen; (*bruit*) deaden.

assouvir /asuvir/ *v.t.* satisfy.

assujettir /asyʒetir/ *v.t.* subject, subdue. **~ à**, subject to.

assumer /asyme/ *v.t.* assume.

assurance /asyrɑ̃s/ *n.f.* (self-)assurance; (*garantie*) assurance; (*contrat*) insurance. **~s sociales**, National Insurance.

assuré, ~e /asyre/ *a.* certain, assured; (*sûr de soi*) (self-)confident, assured. —*n.m.*,*f.* insured. **~ment** *adv.* certainly.

assurer /asyre/ *v.t.* ensure; (*fournir*) provide; (*exécuter*) carry out; (*comm.*) insure; (*stabiliser*) steady; (*frontières*) make secure. **~ à qn. que**, assure s.o. that. **~ qn. de**, assure s.o. of. **s'~ de/que**, make sure of/that. **s'~ qch.**, (*se procurer*) secure *ou* ensure sth.

assureur /-œr/ *n.m.* insurer.

astérisque /asterisk/ *n.m.* asterisk.

asthm|e /asm/ *n.m.* asthma. **~atique** *a.* & *n.m.*/*f.* asthmatic.

asticot /astiko/ *n.m.* maggot.

astiquer /astike/ *v.t.* polish.

astre /astr/ *n.m.* star.

astreignant, ~e /astrɛɲɑ̃, -t/ *a.* exacting.

astreindre /astrɛ̃dr/ *v.t.* **~ qn. à qch.**, force sth. on s.o. **~ à faire**, force to do.

astringent, ~e /astrɛ̃ʒɑ̃, -t/ *a.* astringent.

astrolo|gie /astrɔlɔʒi/ *n.f.* astrology. **~gue** *n.m.*/*f.* astrologer.

astronaute /astrɔnot/ *n.m.*/*f.* astronaut.

astronom|ie /astrɔnɔmi/ *n.f.* astronomy. **~e** *n.m.*/*f.* astronomer. **~ique** *a.* astronomical.

astuce /astys/ *n.f.* smartness; (*truc*) trick; (*plaisanterie*) wisecrack.

astucieu|x, ~se /astysjø, -z/ *a.* smart, clever.

atelier /atəlje/ *n.m.* workshop; (*de peintre*) studio.

athé|e /ate/ *n.m.|f.* atheist. —*a.* atheistic. **~isme** *n.m.* atheism.

athl|ète /atlɛt/ *n.m.|f.* ˙athlete. **~étique** *a.* athletic. **~étisme** *n.m.* athletics.

atlantique /atlãtik/ *a.* Atlantic. —*n.m.* **A~,** Atlantic (Ocean).

atlas /atlɑs/ *n.m.* atlas.

atmosph|ère /atmɔsfɛr/ *n.f.* atmosphere. **~érique** *a.* atmospheric.

atome /atom/ *n.m.* atom.

atomique /atɔmik/ *a.* atomic.

atomiseur /atɔmizœr/ *n.m.* spray.

atout /atu/ *n.m.* trump (card); (*avantage*) great asset.

âtre /ɑtr/ *n.m.* hearth.

atroc|e /atrɔs/ *a.* atrocious. **~ité** *n.f.* atrocity.

atroph|ie /atrɔfi/ *n.f.* atrophy. **~ié** *a.* atrophied.

attabler (s') /(s)atable/ *v. pr.* sit down at table.

attachant, ~e /ataʃã, -t/ *a.* likeable.

attache /ataʃ/ *n.f.* (*agrafe*) fastener; (*lien*) tie. **à l'~,** (*chien*) on a leash.

attach|é, ~ée /ataʃe/ *a.* être **~é à,** (*aimer*) be attached to. —*n.m.,f.* (*pol.*) attaché. **~ement** *n.m.* attachment.

attacher /ataʃe/ *v.t.* tie (up); (*ceinture, robe, etc.*) fasten; (*étiquette*) attach. **~ à,** (*attribuer à*) attach to. —*v.i.* (*culin.*) stick. **s'~ à,** (*se lier à*) become attached to; (*se consacrer à*) apply o.s. to.

attaque /atak/ *n.f.* attack. **~ à main armée,** armed attack.

attaqu|er /atake/ *v.t./i.,* **s'~er à,** attack; (*problème, sujet*) tackle. **~ant, ~ante** *n.m., f.* attacker; (*football*) striker; (*football, Amer.*) forward.

attardé /atarde/ *a.* backward; (*idées*) outdated; (*en retard*) late.

attarder (s') /(s)atarde/ *v. pr.* linger.

atteindre† /atɛ̃dr/ *v.t.* reach; (*blesser*) hit; (*affecter*) affect.

atteint, ~e /atɛ̃, -t/ *a.* **~ de,** suffering from.

atteinte /atɛ̃t/ *n.f.* attack (à, on).

attel|er /atle/ *v.t.* (*cheval*) harness; (*remorque*) couple. **s'~er à,** get down to. **~age** *n.m.* harnessing; coupling; (*bêtes*) team.

attenant, ~e /atnã, -t/ *a.* **~ (à),** adjoining.

attendant (en) /(ãn)atãdã/ *adv.* meanwhile.

attendre /atãdr/ *v.t.* wait for, await; (*escompter*) expect. —*v.i.* wait. **~ que qn. fasse,** wait for s.o. to do. **s'~ à,** expect.

attendr|ir /atãdrir/ *v.t.* move (to pity). **s'~ir** *v. pr.* be moved to pity. **~issant, ~issante** *a.* moving.

attendu /atãdy/ *a.* (*escompté*) expected; (*espéré*) long-awaited. **~ que,** considering that.

attentat /atãta/ *n.m.* murder attempt. **~ (à la bombe),** (bomb) attack.

attente /atãt/ *n.f.* wait(ing); (*espoir*) expectation.

attenter /atãte/ *v.i.* **~ à,** make an attempt on; (*fig.*) violate.

attenti|f, ~ve /atãtif, -v/ *a.* attentive; (*scrupuleux*) careful. **~f à,** mindful of; (*soucieux*) careful of. **~vement** *adv.* attentively.

attention /atãsjõ/ *n.f.* attention. **~ (à)!,** watch out (for)! faire **~ à,** pay attention to; (*veiller à*) be careful of. **~né** /-jɔne/ *a.* considerate.

attentisme /atãtism/ *n.m.* wait-and-see policy.

atténuer /atenɥe/ *v.t.* (*violence*) tone down; (*douleur*) ease; (*faute*) mitigate. **s'~** *v. pr.* subside.

atterrer /atere/ *v.t.* dismay.

atterr|ir /aterir/ *v.i.* land. **~issage** *n.m.* landing.

attestation /atɛstasjõ/ *n.f.* certificate.

attester /atɛste/ *v.t.* testify to. **~ que,** testify that.

attifé /atife/ *a.* (*fam.*) dressed up.

attirail /atiraj/ *n.m.* (*fam.*) gear.

attirance /atirãs/ *n.f.* attraction.

attirant, ~e /atirã, -t/ *a.* attractive.

attirer /atire/ *v.t.* draw, attract; (*causer*) bring. **s'~** *v. pr.* bring upon o.s.; (*amis*) win.

attiser /atize/ *v.t.* (*feu*) poke; (*sentiment*) stir up.

attitré /atitre/ *a.* accredited; (*habituel*) usual.

attitude /atityd/ *n.f.* attitude; (*maintien*) bearing.

attraction /atraksjõ/ *n.f.* attraction.

attrape-nigaud /atrapnigo/ *n.m.* (*fam.*) con.

attraper /atrape/ *v.t.* catch; (*habitude, style*) pick up; (*duper*) take in; (*gronder: fam.*) tell off.

attrayant, ~e /atrɛjã, -t/ *a.* attractive.

attrib|uer /atribɥe/ *v.t.* award;

(donner) assign; (*imputer*) attribute.
s'~uer *v. pr.* claim. **~ution** *n.f.*
awarding; assignment. **~utions** *n.f.*
pl. attributions.
attrister /atriste/ *v.t.* sadden.
attroup|er (s') /(s)atrupe/ *v. pr.*
gather. **~ement** *n.m.* crowd.
au /o/ *voir* **à.**
aubaine /obɛn/ *n.f.* (stroke of) good
fortune.
aube /ob/ *n.f.* dawn, daybreak.
aubépine /obepin/ *n.f.* hawthorn.
auberg|e /obɛrʒ/ *n.f.* inn. **~e de jeu-
nesse,** youth hostel. **~iste** *n.m./f.*
innkeeper.
aubergine /obɛrʒin/ *n.f.* aubergine,
egg-plant.
aucun, ~e /okœ, okyn/ *a.* no, not any;
(*positif*) any. —*pron.* none, not any;
(*positif*) any. **~ des deux,** neither of
the two. **d'~s,** some. **~ement**
/okynmã/ *adv.* not at all.
audace /odas/ *n.f.* daring; (*impudence*)
audacity.
audacieu|x, ~se /odasjø, -z/ *a.* daring.
au-delà /odla/ *adv.,* **~ de** *prép.*
beyond.
au-dessous /odsu/ *adv.,* **~ de** *prép.*
below.
au-dessus /odsy/ *adv.,* **~ de** *prép.*
above.
au-devant (de) /odvã(də)/ *prép.* **aller
~ de qn.,** go to meet s.o.
audience /odjãs/ *n.f.* audience; (*d'un
tribunal*) hearing; (*intérêt*) attention.
audiotypiste /odjotipist/ *n.m./f.* audio
typist.
audio-visuel, ~le /odjovizɥɛl/ *a.*
audio-visual.
audi|teur, ~trice /oditœr, -tris/ *n.m.,
f.* listener.
audition /odisjõ/ *n.f.* hearing; (*théâtre,
mus.*) audition. **~ner** /-jɔne/ *v.t./i.*
audition.
auditoire /oditwar/ *n.m.* audience.
auditorium /oditɔrjɔm/ *n.m.* (*mus.,
radio*) recording studio.
auge /oʒ/ *n.f.* trough.
augment|er /ogmãte/ *v.t./i.* increase;
(*employé*) increase the pay of. **~ation**
n.f. increase. **~ation (de salaire),**
(pay) rise; (*Amer.*) raise.
augure /ogyr/ *n.m.* (*devin*) oracle. **de
bon/mauvais ~,** of good/ill omen.
augurer /ogyre/ *v.t.* predict (**de,**
from).
auguste /ogyst/ *a.* august.
aujourd'hui /oʒurdɥi/ *adv.* today.

aumône /omon/ *n.f.* alms.
aumônier /omonje/ *n.m.* chaplain.
auparavant /oparavã/ *adv.* before-
(hand).
auprès (de) /oprɛ(də)/ *prép.* by, next
to; (*comparé à*) compared with; (*s'a-
dressant à*) to.
auquel, ~le /okɛl/ *voir* **lequel.**
aura, aurait /ora, orɛ/ *voir* **avoir.**
auréole /oreɔl/ *n.f.* halo.
auriculaire /orikylɛr/ *n.m.* little
finger.
aurore /orɔr/ *n.f.* dawn.
ausculter /ɔskylte/ *v.t.* examine with
a stethoscope.
auspices /ospis/ *n.m. pl.* auspices.
aussi /osi/ *adv.* too, also; (*comparaison*) as; (*tellement*) so. —*conj.* (*donc*)
therefore. **~ bien que,** as well as.
aussitôt /osito/ *adv.* immediately. **~
que,** as soon as. **~ arrivé/levé**/*etc.*,
as soon as one has arrived/got up/*etc.*
aust|ère /ostɛr/ *a.* austere. **~érité** *n.f.*
austerity.
austral (*m. pl.* **~s**) /ostral/ *a.*
southern.
Australie /ostrali/ *n.f.* Australia.
australien, ~ne /ostraljɛ̃, -jɛn/ *a.* &
n.m., f. Australian.
autant /otã/ *adv.* (*travailler, manger,
etc.*) as much (**que,** as). **~ (de),** (*quantité*) as much (**que,** as); (*nombre*) as
many (**que,** as); (*tant*) so much; so
many. **~ faire,** one had better do.
d'~ plus que, all the more since. **en
faire ~,** do the same. **pour ~,** for all
that.
autel /otɛl/ *n.m.* altar.
auteur /otœr/ *n.m.* author. **~ de,**
(*action*) person who carried out *ou*
caused.
authentifier /otãtifje/ *v.t.* authenticate.
authenti|que /otãtik/ *a.* authentic.
~cité *n.f.* authenticity.
auto /oto/ *n.f.* car. **~s tamponneuses,**
dodgems, bumper cars.
auto- /oto/ *préf.* self-, auto-.
autobiographie /otobjɔgrafi/ *n.f.* autobiography.
autobus /otobys/ *n.m.* bus.
autocar /otɔkar/ *n.m.* coach.
autochtone /ɔtɔktɔn/ *n.m./f.* native.
autocollant, ~e /otɔkɔlã, -t/ *a.* self-
adhesive. —*n.m.* sticker.
autocratique /otɔkratik/ *a.* auto-
cratic.

autodéfense /otɔdefɑ̃s/ *n.f.* self-defence.

autodidacte /otɔdidakt/ *a.* & *n.m.lf.* self-taught (person).

auto-école /otɔekɔl/ *n.f.* driving school.

autographe /otɔgraf/ *n.m.* autograph.

automate /otɔmat/ *n.m.* automaton.

automatique /otɔmatik/ *a.* automatic. **~ment** *adv.* automatically.

automat|iser /otɔmatize/ *v.t.* automate. **~ion** /-masjɔ̃/ *n.f.*, **~isation** *n.f.* automation.

automne /otɔn/ *n.m.* autumn.

automobil|e /otɔmɔbil/ *a.* motor, car. —*n.f.* (motor) car. **l'~e**, (*sport*) motoring. **~iste** *n.m.lf.* motorist.

autonom|e /otɔnɔm/ *a.* autonomous. **~ie** *n.f.* autonomy.

autopsie /otɔpsi/ *n.f.* post-mortem, autopsy.

autorail /otɔraj/ *n.m.* railcar.

autorisation /otɔrizasjɔ̃/ *n.f.* permission, authorization; (*permis*) permit.

autoris|er /otɔrize/ *v.t.* authorize, permit; (*rendre possible*) allow (of). **~é** *a.* (*opinions*) authoritative.

autoritaire /otɔritɛr/ *a.* authoritarian.

autorité /otɔrite/ *n.f.* authority. **faire ~**, be authoritative.

autoroute /otɔrut/ *n.f.* motorway; (*Amer.*) highway.

auto-stop /otɔstɔp/ *n.m.* hitch-hiking. **faire de l'~**, hitch-hike. **prendre en ~**, give a lift to. **~peur**, **~peuse** *n.m.*, *f.* hitch-hiker.

autour /otur/ *adv.*, **~ de** *prép.* around. **tout ~**, all around.

autre /otr/ *a.* other. **un ~ jour**/*etc.*, another day/*etc.* —*pron.* **un ~, une ~**, another (one). **l'~**, the other (one). **les autres**, the others; (*autrui*) others. **d'~s**, (some) others. **~ chose/ part**, sth./somewhere else. **qn./rien d'~**, s.o./nothing else. **d'~ part**, on the other hand. **vous ~s Anglais**, you English. **d'un jour**/*etc.* **à l'~**, (*bientôt*) any day/*etc.* now.

autrefois /otrəfwa/ *adv.* in the past.

autrement /otrəmɑ̃/ *adv.* differently; (*sinon*) otherwise; (*plus*) far more.

Autriche /otriʃ/ *n.f.* Austria.

autrichien, ~ne /otriʃjɛ̃, -jɛn/ *a.* & *n.m.*, *f.* Austrian.

autruche /otryʃ/ *n.f.* ostrich.

autrui /otrɥi/ *pron.* others.

auvent /ovɑ̃/ *n.m.* canopy.

aux /o/ *voir* **à**.

auxiliaire /oksiljɛr/ *a.* auxiliary. —*n.m.lf.* (*assistant*) auxiliary. —*n.m.* (*gram.*) auxiliary.

auxquel|s, ~les /okɛl/ *voir* **lequel**.

aval (en) /(ɑ̃)aval/ *adv.* downstream.

avalanche /avalɑ̃ʃ/ *n.f.* avalanche.

avaler /avale/ *v.t.* swallow.

avance /avɑ̃s/ *n.f.* advance; (*sur un concurrent*) lead. **~ (de fonds)**, advance. **à l'~, d'~**, in advance. **en ~**, early; (*montre*) fast. **en ~ (sur)**, (*menant*) ahead (of).

avancement /avɑ̃smɑ̃/ *n.m.* promotion.

avanc|er /avɑ̃se/ *v.t.li.* move forward, advance; (*argent*) advance; (*montre*) be *ou* go fast; (*faire saillie*) jut out. **s'~er** *v. pr.* move forward, advance; (*se hasarder*) commit o.s. **~é, ~ée** *a.* advanced; *n.f.* projection.

avanie /avani/ *n.f.* affront.

avant /avɑ̃/ *prép.* & *adv.* before. —*a. invar.* front —*n.m.* front; (*football*) forward. **~ de faire**, before doing. **~ qu'il (ne) fasse**, before he does. **en ~**, (*mouvement*) forward. **en ~ (de)**, (*position, temps*) in front (of). **~ peu**, before long. **~ tout**, above all. **bien ~ dans**, very deep(ly) *ou* far into. **~-bras** *n.m. invar.* forearm. **~-centre** *n.m.* centre-forward. **~-coureur** *a. invar.* precursory, foreshadowing. **~-dernier, ~dernière** *a.* & *n.m.*, *f.* last but one. **~-garde** *n.f.* (*mil.*) vanguard; (*fig.*) avant-garde. **~-goût** *n.m.* foretaste. **~-guerre** *n.m.* pre-war period. **~-hier** /-tjɛr/ *adv.* the day before yesterday. **~poste** *n.m.* outpost. **~-première** *n.f.* preview. **~-veille** *n.f.* two days before.

avantag|e /avɑ̃taʒ/ *n.m.* advantage; (*comm.*) benefit. **~er** *v.t.* favour; (*embellir*) show off to advantage.

avantageu|x, ~se /avɑ̃taʒø, -z/ *a.* attractive.

avar|e /avar/ *a.* miserly. —*n.m.lf.* miser. **~e de**, sparing of. **~ice** *n.f.* avarice.

avarié /avarje/ *a.* (*aliment*) spoiled.

avaries /avari/ *n.f. pl.* damage.

avatar /avatar/ *n.m.* (*fam.*) misfortune.

avec /avɛk/ *prép.* with; (*envers*) towards. —*adv.* (*fam.*) with it *ou* them.

avenant, ~e /avnɑ̃, -t/ *a.* pleasing.

avenant (à l') /(al)avnɑ̃/ *adv.* in a similar style.

avènement /avɛnmɑ̃/ *n.m.* advent; (*d'un roi*) accession.

avenir /avnir/ *n.m.* future. **à l'~,** in future. **d'~,** with (future) prospects.

aventur|e /avɑ̃tyr/ *n.f.* adventure; (*sentimentale*) affair. **~eux, ~euse** *a.* adventurous; (*hasardeux*) risky. **~ier, ~ière** *n.m.,f.* adventurer.

aventurer (s') /(s)avɑ̃tyre/ *v. pr.* venture.

avenue /avny/ *n.f.* avenue.

avérer (s') /(s)avere/ *v. pr.* prove (to be).

averse /avɛrs/ *n.f.* shower.

aversion /avɛrsjɔ̃/ *n.f.* aversion.

avert|ir /avɛrtir/ *v.t.* inform; (*mettre en garde, menacer*) warn. **~i** *a.* informed. **~issement** *n.m.* warning.

avertisseur /avɛrtisœr/ *n.m.* (*auto.*) horn. **~ d'incendie,** fire-alarm.

aveu (*pl.* **~x**) /avø/ *n.m.* confession. **de l'~ de,** by the admission of.

aveugl|e /avœgl/ *a.* blind. **—***n.m./f.* blind man, blind woman. **~ement** *n.m.* blindness. **~ément** *adv.* blindly. **~er** *v.t.* blind.

aveuglette (à l') /(al)avœglɛt/ *adv.* (*à tâtons*) blindly.

avia|teur, ~trice /avjatœr, -tris/ *n.m.,f.* aviator.

aviation /avjɑsjɔ̃/ *n.f.* flying; (*industrie*) aviation; (*mil.*) air force. **d'~,** air.

avid|e /avid/ *a.* greedy (**de,** for); (*anxieux*) eager (**de,** for). **~e de faire,** eager to do. **~ité** *n.f.* greed; eagerness.

avilir /avilir/ *v.t.* degrade.

avion /avjɔ̃/ *n.m.* (aero)plane, aircraft. **~ à réaction,** jet.

aviron /avirɔ̃/ *n.m.* oar. **l'~,** (*sport*) rowing.

avis /avi/ *n.m.* opinion; (*renseignement*) notification; (*comm.*) advice. **être d'~ que,** be of the opinion that.

avisé /avize/ *a.* sensible. **bien-/mal ~ de,** well-/ill-advised to.

aviser /avize/ *v.t.* notice; (*informer*) advise. **—***v.i.* decide what to do (**à, about**). **s'~ de,** suddenly realize. **s'~ de faire,** take it into one's head to do.

aviver /avive/ *v.t.* revive.

avocat[1]**, ~e** /avɔka, -t/ *n.m.,f.* barrister; (*Amer.*) attorney; (*fig.*) advocate. **~ de la défense,** counsel for the defence.

avocat[2] /avɔka/ *n.m.* (*fruit*) avocado (pear).

avoine /avwan/ *n.f.* oats.

avoir† /avwar/ *v. aux.* have. **—***v.t.* have; (*obtenir*) get; (*duper: fam.*) take in. **—***n.m.* assets. **~ à faire,** have to do. **~ chaud/faim/***etc.***,** be hot/hungry/*etc.* **~ dix/***etc.* **ans,** be ten/*etc.* years old. **~ lieu,** take place. **~ lieu de,** have good reason to. **en ~ à *ou* contre,** have a grudge against. **en ~ assez,** have had enough. **en ~ pour une minute/***etc.***,** be busy for a minute/*etc.* **il en a pour cent francs,** it will cost him one hundred francs. **qu'est-ce que vous avez?,** what is the matter with you?

avoisin|er /avwazine/ *v.t.* border on. **~ant, ~ante** *a.* neighbouring.

avort|er /avɔrte/ *v.i.* (*projet etc.*) miscarry. (**se faire**) **~er,** have an abortion. **~é** *a.* abortive. **~ement** *n.m.* (*méd.*) abortion.

avorton /avɔrtɔ̃/ *n.m.* runt.

avou|er /avwe/ *v.t.* confess (to). **—***v.i.* confess. **~é** *a.* avowed; *n.m.* solicitor; (*Amer.*) attorney.

avril /avril/ *n.m.* April.

axe /aks/ *n.m.* axis; (*essieu*) axle; (*d'une politique*) main line(s), basis. **~ (routier),** main road.

axer /akse/ *v.t.* centre.

axiome /aksjom/ *n.m.* axiom.

ayant /ɛjɑ̃/ *voir* **avoir.**

azimuts /azimyt/ *n.m. pl.* **dans tous les ~,** (*fam.*) all over the place.

azote /azɔt/ *n.m.* nitrogen.

azur /azyr/ *n.m.* sky-blue.

B

baba /baba/ *n.m.* ~ (**au rhum**), rum baba.

babil /babi(l)/ *n.m.* babble. ~**ler** /-ije/ *v.i.* babble.

babines /babin/ *n.f. pl.* chops.

babiole /babjɔl/ *n.f.* knick-knack; (*bagatelle*) trifle.

bâbord /babɔr/ *n.m.* port (side).

babouin /babwɛ̃/ *n.m.* baboon.

bac[1] /bak/ *n.m.* (*fam.*) = **baccalauréat**.

bac[2] /bak/ *n.m.* (*bateau*) ferry; (*récipient*) tub; (*plus petit*) tray.

baccalauréat /bakalɔrea/ *n.m.* school leaving certificate.

bâch|e /baʃ/ *n.f.* tarpaulin. ~**er** *v.t.* cover (with a tarpaulin).

bachel|ier, ~ière /baʃəlje, -jɛr/ *n.m., f.* holder of the *baccalauréat*.

bachot /baʃo/ *n.m.* (*fam.*) = **baccalauréat**. ~**er** /-ɔte/ *v.i.* cram (for an exam).

bâcler /bakle/ *v.t.* botch (up).

bactérie /bakteri/ *n.f.* bacterium.

badaud, ~e /bado, -d/ *n.m., f.* (*péj.*) onlooker.

baderne /badɛrn/ *n.f.* (**vieille**) ~, (*péj.*) old fogey.

badigeon /badiʒɔ̃/ *n.m.* whitewash. ~**ner** /-ɔne/ *v.t.* whitewash; (*barbouiller*) daub.

badin, ~e /badɛ̃, -in/ *a.* lighthearted.

badine /badin/ *n.f.* cane.

badiner /badine/ *v.i.* joke (**sur, avec**, about).

baffe /baf/ *n.f.* (*fam.*) slap.

bafouer /bafwe/ *v.t.* scoff at.

bafouiller /bafuje/ *v.t./i.* stammer.

bâfrer /bafre/ *v.t./i.* (*fam.*) gobble.

bagage /bagaʒ/ *n.m.* bag; (*fig.*) (store of) knowledge. ~**s**, luggage, baggage. ~**s à main**, hand luggage.

bagarr|e /bagar/ *n.f.* fight. ~**er** *v.i.*, se ~**er** *v. pr.* fight.

bagatelle /bagatɛl/ *n.f.* trifle; (*somme*) trifling amount.

bagnard /baɲar/ *n.m.* convict.

bagnole /baɲɔl/ *n.f.* (*fam.*) car.

bagou(t) /bagu/ *n.m.* glib tongue.

bagu|e /bag/ *n.f.* (*anneau*) ring. ~**er** *v.t.* ring.

baguenauder (se) /(sə)bagnode/ *v. pr.* (*fam.*) stroll *ou* loaf about.

baguette /bagɛt/ *n.f.* stick; (*de chef d'orchestre*) baton; (*chinoise*) chopstick; (*magique*) wand; (*pain*) stick of bread. ~ **de tambour,** drumstick.

bahut /bay/ *n.m.* chest.

baie /bɛ/ *n.f.* (*géog.*) bay; (*fruit*) berry. ~ (**vitrée**), picture window.

baign|er /beɲe/ *v.t.* bathe; (*enfant*) bath. —*v.i.* ~**er dans,** soak in; (*être enveloppé dans*) be steeped in. se ~**er** *v. pr.* go swimming *ou* bathing. ~**é de,** bathed in; (*sang*) soaked in. ~**ade** /bɛɲad/ *n.f.* bathing, swimming. ~**eur, ~euse** /bɛɲœr, -øz/ *n.m., f.* bather.

baignoire /bɛɲwar/ *n.f.* bath(-tub).

bail (*pl.* **baux**) /baj, bo/ *n.m.* lease.

bâill|er /baje/ *v.i.* yawn; (*être ouvert*) gape. ~**ement** *n.m.* yawn.

bailleur /bajœr/ *n.m.* ~ **de fonds,** (*comm.*) backer.

bâillon /bajɔ̃/ *n.m.* gag. ~**ner** /bajɔne/ *v.t.* gag.

bain /bɛ̃/ *n.m.* bath; (*de mer*) bathe. ~(**s**) **de soleil,** sunbathing. ~**-marie** (*pl.* ~**s-marie**) *n.m.* double boiler. **dans le** ~, (*compromis*) involved; (*au courant*) in the picture. **prendre un** ~ **de foule,** mingle with the crowd.

baïonnette /bajɔnɛt/ *n.f.* bayonet.

baiser /beze/ *n.m.* kiss. —*v.t.* (*main*) kiss; (*duper: fam.*) con.

baisse /bɛs/ *n.f.* fall, drop. **en** ~, falling.

baisser /bese/ *v.t.* lower; (*radio, lampe, etc.*) turn down. —*v.i.* go down, fall; (*santé, forces*) fail. se ~ *v. pr.* bend down.

bajoues /baʒu/ *n.f. pl.* chops.

bal (*pl.* ~**s**) /bal/ *n.m.* dance; (*habillé*) ball; (*lieu*) dance-hall.

balad|e /balad/ *n.f.* stroll; (*en auto*) drive. ~**er** *v.t.* take for a stroll. se ~**er** *v. pr.* (go for a) stroll; (*excursionner*) wander around. se ~**er** (**en auto**), go for a drive.

balafr|e /balafr/ *n.f.* gash; (*cicatrice*) scar. ~**er** *v.t.* gash.

balai /balɛ/ *n.m.* broom. ~**-brosse** *n.m.* garden broom.

balance /balɑ̃s/ *n.f.* scales; (*équilibre*) balance.

balancer /balɑ̃se/ *v.t.* swing; (*douce-*

ment) sway; (*lancer*: *fam.*) chuck; (*se débarrasser de*: *fam.*) chuck out. —*v.i.*, se ~ *v. pr.* swing; sway. se ~ de, (*fam.*) not care about.

balancier /balãsje/ *n.m.* pendulum; (*de montre*) balance-wheel.

balançoire /balãswar/ *n.f.* swing; (*bascule*) see-saw.

balay|er /baleje/ *v.t.* sweep (up); (*chasser*) sweep away; (*se débarrasser de*) sweep aside. ~age *n.m.* sweeping. ~eur, ~euse *n.m.*, *f.* road sweeper. ~ures *n.f. pl.* sweepings.

balbut|ier /balbysje/ *v.t.*/*i.* stammer. ~iement *n.m.* stammering.

balcon /balkõ/ *n.m.* balcony; (*théâtre*) dress circle.

baldaquin /baldakẽ/ *n.m.* canopy.

baleine /balɛn/ *n.f.* whale.

balis|e /baliz/ *n.f.* beacon; (*bouée*) buoy; (*auto.*) (road) sign. ~er *v.t.* mark out (with beacons); (*route*) signpost.

balistique /balistik/ *a.* ballistic.

balivernes /balivɛrn/ *n.f. pl.* balderdash.

ballade /balad/ *n.f.* ballad.

ballant, ~e /balã, -t/ *a.* dangling.

ballast /balast/ *n.m.* ballast.

balle /bal/ *n.f.* (*projectile*) bullet; (*sport*) ball; (*paquet*) bale.

ballerine /balrin/ *n.f.* ballerina.

ballet /balɛ/ *n.m.* ballet.

ballon /balõ/ *n.m.* balloon; (*sport*) ball. ~ de football, football.

ballonné /balɔne/ *a.* bloated.

ballot /balo/ *n.m.* bundle; (*nigaud*: *fam.*) idiot.

ballottage /balɔtaʒ/ *n.m.* second ballot (*due to indecisive result*).

ballotter /balɔte/ *v.t.*/*i.* shake about, toss.

balnéaire /balneɛr/ *a.* seaside.

balourd, ~e /balur, -d/ *n.m.*, *f.* oaf. —*a.* oafish. ~ise /-diz/ *n.f.* (*gaffe*) blunder.

balustrade /balystrad/ *n.f.* railing(s).

bambin /bãbẽ/ *n.m.* tiny tot.

bambou /bãbu/ *n.m.* bamboo.

ban /bã/ *n.m.* round of applause. ~s, (*de mariage*) banns. mettre au ~ de, cast out from.

banal (*m. pl.* ~s) /banal/ *a.* commonplace, banal. ~ité *n.f.* banality.

banane /banan/ *n.f.* banana.

banc /bã/ *n.m.* bench; (*de poissons*) shoal. ~ des accusés, dock. ~ d'essai, test bed; (*fig.*) testing-ground.

bancaire /bãkɛr/ *a.* banking; (*chèque*) bank.

bancal (*m. pl.* ~s) /bãkal/ *a.* wobbly; (*personne*) bandy.

bandage /bãdaʒ/ *n.m.* bandage. ~ herniaire, truss.

bande[1] /bãd/ *n.f.* (*de papier etc.*) strip; (*rayure*) stripe; (*de film*) reel; (*radio*) band; (*pansement*) bandage. ~ (**magnétique**), tape. ~ dessinée, comic strip. ~ sonore, sound-track. par la ~, indirectly.

bande[2] /bãd/ *n.f.* (*groupe*) bunch, band, gang.

bandeau (*pl.* ~x) /bãdo/ *n.m.* headband; (*sur les yeux*) blindfold.

bander /bãde/ *v.t.* bandage; (*arc*) bend; (*muscle*) tense. ~ les yeux à, blindfold.

banderole /bãdrɔl/ *n.f.* banner.

bandit /bãdi/ *n.m.* bandit. ~isme /-tism/ *n.m.* crime.

bandoulière (en) /(ã)bãduljɛr/ *adv.* (slung) across one's shoulder.

banjo /bã(d)ʒo/ *n.m.* banjo.

banlieu|e /bãljø/ *n.f.* suburbs. de ~e, suburban. ~sard, ~sarde /-zar, -zard/ *n.m.*, *f.* (suburban) commuter.

bannière /banjɛr/ *n.f.* banner.

bannir /banir/ *v.t.* banish.

banque /bãk/ *n.f.* bank; (*activité*) banking. ~ d'affaires, merchant bank.

banqueroute /bãkrut/ *n.f.* (fraudulent) bankruptcy.

banquet /bãkɛ/ *n.m.* dinner; (*fastueux*) banquet.

banquette /bãkɛt/ *n.f.* seat.

banquier /bãkje/ *n.m.* banker.

bapt|ême /batɛm/ *n.m.* baptism; christening. ~iser *v.t.* baptize, christen; (*appeler*) christen.

baquet /bakɛ/ *n.m.* tub.

bar /bar/ *n.m.* (*lieu*) bar.

baragouin /baragwẽ/ *n.m.* gibberish, gabble. ~er /-wine/ *v.t.*/*i.* gabble; (*langue*) speak a few words of.

baraque /barak/ *n.f.* hut, shed; (*boutique*) stall; (*maison*: *fam.*) house. ~ments *n.m. pl.* huts.

baratin /baratẽ/ *n.m.* (*fam.*) sweet *ou* smooth talk. ~er /-ine/ *v.t.* (*fam.*) chat up; (*Amer.*) sweet-talk.

barbar|e /barbar/ *a.* barbaric. —*n.m.*/ *f.* barbarian. ~ie *n.f.* (*cruauté*) barbarity.

barbe /barb/ *n.f.* beard. ~ à **papa**, candy-floss; (*Amer.*) cotton candy. **la**

~!, (*fam.*) blast (it)! **quelle** ~!, (*fam.*) what a bore!

barbecue /barbəkju/ *n.m.* barbecue.

barbelés /barbəle/ *n.m. pl.* barbed wire.

barber /barbe/ *v.t.* (*fam.*) bore.

barbiche /barbiʃ/ *n.f.* goatee.

barbiturique /barbityrik/ *n.m.* barbiturate.

barboter[1] /barbɔte/ *v.i.* paddle, splash.

barboter[2] /barbɔte/ *v.t.* (*voler*: *fam.*) pinch.

barbouiller /barbuje/ *v.t.* (*peindre*) daub; (*souiller*) smear; (*griffonner*) scribble; (*estomac*: *fam.*) upset.

barbu /barby/ *a.* bearded.

barda /barda/ *n.m.* (*fam.*) gear.

barder /barde/ *v.i.* **ça va** ~, (*fam.*) sparks will fly.

barème /barɛm/ *n.m.* list, table; (*échelle*) scale.

baril /bari(l)/ *n.m.* barrel; (*de poudre*) keg.

bariolé /barjɔle/ *a.* motley.

barman /barman/ *n.m.* barman; (*Amer.*) bartender.

baromètre /barɔmɛtr/ *n.m.* barometer.

baron, ~**ne** /barɔ̃, -ɔn/ *n.m., f.* baron, baroness.

baroque /barɔk/ *a.* weird; (*archit.*, *art*) baroque.

baroud /barud/ *n.m.* ~ **d'honneur**, gallant last fight.

barque /bark/ *n.f.* (small) boat.

barrage /baraʒ/ *n.m.* dam; (*sur route*) road-block.

barre /bar/ *n.f.* bar; (*trait*) line, stroke; (*naut.*) helm.

barreau (*pl.* ~**x**) /baro/ *n.m.* bar; (*d'échelle*) rung. **le** ~, (*jurid.*) the bar.

barrer /bare/ *v.t.* block; (*porte*) bar; (*rayer*) cross out; (*naut.*) steer. **se** ~ *v. pr.* (*fam.*) hop it.

barrette /barɛt/ *n.f.* (hair-)slide.

barreur /barœr/ *n.m.* (*sport*) coxswain.

barricad|e /barikad/ *n.f.* barricade. ~**er** *v.t.* barricade. **se** ~**er** *v. pr.* barricade o.s.

barrière /barjɛr/ *n.f.* (*porte*) gate; (*clôture*) fence; (*obstacle*) barrier.

barrique /barik/ *n.f.* barrel.

baryton /baritɔ̃/ *n.m.* baritone.

bas, basse /ba, bas/ *a.* low; (*action*) base. —*n.m.* bottom; (*chaussette*) stocking. —*n.f.* (*mus.*) bass. —*adv.*

low. **à** ~, down with. **en** ~, down below; (*dans une maison*) downstairs. **en** ~ **de**, at the bottom of. **plus** ~, further *ou* lower down. ~**-côté** *n.m.* (*de route*) verge; (*Amer.*) shoulder. ~ **de laine**, nest-egg. ~**-fonds** *n.m. pl.* (*eau*) shallows; (*fig.*) dregs. ~**-relief** *n.m.* low relief. ~**-ventre** *n.m.* lower abdomen.

basané /bazane/ *a.* tanned.

bascule /baskyl/ *n.f.* (*balance*) scales. (**jeu de**) ~, see-saw. **cheval/fauteuil à** ~, rocking-horse/-chair.

basculer /baskyle/ *v.t./i.* topple over; (*benne*) tip up.

base /baz/ *n.f.* base; (*fondement*) basis; (*pol.*) rank and file. **de** ~, basic.

baser /baze/ *v.t.* base. **se** ~ **sur**, base o.s. on.

basilique /bazilik/ *n.f.* basilica.

basket(-ball) /baskɛt(bɔl)/ *n.m.* basketball.

basque /bask/ *a. & n.m./f.* Basque.

basse /bas/ *voir* **bas**.

basse-cour (*pl.* **basses-cours**) /baskur/ *n.f.* farmyard.

bassement /basmã/ *adv.* basely.

bassesse /basɛs/ *n.f.* baseness; (*action*) base act.

bassin /basɛ̃/ *n.m.* bowl; (*pièce d'eau*) pond; (*rade*) dock; (*géog.*) basin; (*anat.*) pelvis. ~ **houiller**, coalfield.

basson /basɔ̃/ *n.m.* bassoon.

bastion /bastjɔ̃/ *n.m.* bastion.

bat /ba/ *voir* **battre**.

bât /ba/ *n.m.* pack-saddle.

bataill|e /bataj/ *n.f.* battle; (*fig.*) fight. ~**er** *v.i.* fight. ~**eur**, ~**euse** *n.m., f.* fighter; *a.* fighting.

bataillon /batajɔ̃/ *n.m.* battalion.

bâtard, ~**e** /batar, -d/ *n.m., f.* bastard. —*a.* (*solution*) hybrid.

bateau (*pl.* ~**x**) /bato/ *n.m.* boat. ~**-mouche** (*pl.* ~**x-mouches**) *n.m.* river-boat, sightseeing boat.

bâti /bati/ *a.* **bien** ~, well-built. —*n.m.* frame.

batifoler /batifole/ *v.i.* fool about.

bâtiment /batimã/ *n.m.* building; (*navire*) vessel; (*industrie*) building trade.

bâtir /batir/ *v.t.* build; (*coudre*) baste.

bâtisse /batis/ *n.f.* (*péj.*) building.

bâton /batɔ̃/ *n.m.* stick. **à** ~**s rompus**, jumping from subject to subject. ~ **de rouge**, lipstick.

battage /bataʒ/ *n.m.* (*publicité*: *fam.*) (hard) plugging.

battant /batɑ̃/ *n.m.* (*vantail*) flap. **porte à deux ~s**, double door.

battement /batmɑ̃/ *n.m.* (*de cœur*) beat(ing); (*temps*) interval.

batterie /batri/ *n.f.* (*mil.*, *électr.*) battery; (*mus.*) drums. **~ de cuisine,** pots and pans.

batteur /batœr/ *n.m.* (*mus.*) drummer; (*culin.*) whisk.

battre† /batr/ *v.t.*/*i.* beat; (*blé*) thresh; (*cartes*) shuffle; (*parcourir*) scour; (*faire du bruit*) bang. **se ~** *v. pr.* fight. **~ des ailes,** flap its wings. **~ des mains,** clap. **~ en retraite,** beat a retreat. **~ la semelle,** stamp one's feet. **~ pavillon,** fly a flag. **~ son plein,** be in full swing.

baume /bom/ *n.m.* balm.

bavard, ~e /bavar, -d/ *a.* talkative. —*n.m.*, *f.* chatterbox.

bavard|er /bavarde/ *v.i.* chat; (*jacasser*) chatter, gossip. **~age** *n.m.* chatter, gossip.

bav|e /bav/ *n.f.* dribble, slobber; (*de limace*) slime. **~er** *v.i.* dribble, slobber. **~eux, ~euse** *a.* dribbling; (*omelette*) runny.

bav|ette /bavɛt/ *n.f.*, **~oir** *n.m.* bib.

bavure /bavyr/ *n.f.* smudge; (*erreur*) mistake. **sans ~,** flawless(ly).

bazar /bazar/ *n.m.* bazaar; (*objets*: *fam.*) clutter.

bazarder /bazarde/ *v.t.* (*vendre*: *fam.*) get rid of, flog.

béant, ~e /beɑ̃, -t/ *a.* gaping.

béat, ~e /bea, -t/ *a.* (*hum.*) blissful; (*péj.*) smug. **~itude** /-tityd/ *n.f.* (*hum.*) bliss.

beau *ou* **bel*, belle** (*m. pl.* **~x**) /bo, bɛl/ *a.* fine, beautiful; (*femme*) beautiful; (*homme*) handsome; (*grand*) big. —*n.f.* beauty; (*sport*) deciding game. **au ~ milieu,** right in the middle. **bel et bien,** well and truly. **de plus belle,** more than ever. **faire le ~,** sit up and beg. **on a ~ essayer/insister/etc.,** however much one tries/insists/*etc.*, it is no use trying/insisting/*etc.* **~x-arts** *n.m. pl.* fine arts. **~-fils** (*pl.* **~x-fils**) *n.m.* son-in-law; (*remariage*) stepson. **~-frère** (*pl.* **~x-frères**) *n.m.* brother-in-law. **~père** (*pl.* **~x-pères**) *n.m.* father-in-law; stepfather. **~x-parents** *n.m. pl.* parents-in-law.

beaucoup /boku/ *adv.* a lot, very much. —*pron.* many (people). **~ de,** (*nombre*) many; (*quantité*) a lot of. **pas ~ (de),** not many; (*quantité*) not

much. **~ plus**/*etc.*, much more/*etc.* **~ trop,** much too much. **de ~,** by far.

beauté /bote/ *n.f.* beauty. **en ~,** magnificently.

bébé /bebe/ *n.m.* baby.

bec /bɛk/ *n.m.* beak; (*de plume*) nib; (*de bouilloire*) spout; (*de casserole*) lip; (*bouche*: *fam.*) mouth. **~-de-cane** (*pl.* **~s-de-cane**) door handle. **~ de gaz,** gas lamp (*in street*).

bécane /bekan/ *n.f.* (*fam.*) bike.

bécasse /bekas/ *n.f.* woodcock.

bêche /bɛʃ/ *n.f.* spade.

bêcher /beʃe/ *v.t.* dig.

bécoter /bekɔte/ *v.t.*, **se ~** *v. pr.* (*fam.*) kiss.

becquée /beke/ *n.f.* **donner la ~ à,** feed.

becqueter /bɛkte/ *v.t.* peck (at).

bedaine /bədɛn/ *n.f.* paunch.

bedeau (*pl.* **~x**) /bədo/ *n.m.* beadle.

bedonnant, ~e /bədɔnɑ̃, -t/ *a.* paunchy.

beffroi /befrwa/ *n.m.* belfry.

bégayer /begeje/ *v.t.*/*i.* stammer.

bègue /bɛg/ *n.m.*/*f.* stammerer. **être ~,** stammer.

bégueule /begœl/ *a.* prudish.

béguin /begɛ̃/ *n.m.* **avoir le ~ pour,** (*fam.*) be sweet on.

beige /bɛʒ/ *a.* & *n.m.* beige.

beignet /bɛɲɛ/ *n.m.* fritter.

bel /bɛl/ *voir* **beau.**

bêler /bele/ *v.i.* bleat.

belette /bəlɛt/ *n.f.* weasel.

belge /bɛlʒ/ *a.* & *n.m.*/*f.* Belgian.

Belgique /bɛlʒik/ *n.f.* Belgium.

bélier /belje/ *n.m.* ram.

belle /bɛl/ *voir* **beau.**

belle|-fille (*pl.* **~s-filles**) /bɛlfij/ *n.f.* daughter-in-law; (*remariage*) stepdaughter. **~-mère** (*pl.* **~s-mères**) *n.f.* mother-in-law; stepmother. **~-sœur** (*pl.* **~s-sœurs**) *n.f.* sister-in-law.

belligérant, ~e /beliʒerɑ̃, -t/ *a.* & *n.m.* belligerent.

belliqueu|x, ~se /belikø, -z/ *a.* warlike.

belote /bəlɔt/ *n.f.* belote (*card game*).

belvédère /bɛlvedɛr/ *n.m.* (*lieu*) viewing spot, viewpoint.

bémol /bemɔl/ *n.m.* (*mus.*) flat.

bénédiction /benediksjɔ̃/ *n.f.* blessing.

bénéfice /benefis/ *n.m.* (*gain*) profit; (*avantage*) benefit.

bénéficiaire /benefisjɛr/ *n.m./f.* beneficiary.

bénéficier /benefisje/ *v.i.* ~ **de**, benefit from; (*jouir de*) enjoy, have.

bénéfique /benefik/ *a.* beneficial.

Bénélux /benelyks/ *n.m.* Benelux.

benêt /bənɛ/ *n.m.* simpleton.

bénévole /benevɔl/ *a.* voluntary.

bén|in, ~igne /benɛ̃, -iɲ/ *a.* mild, slight; (*tumeur*) benign.

bén|ir /benir/ *v.t.* bless. ~**it**, ~**ite** *a.* (*eau*) holy; (*pain*) consecrated.

bénitier /benitje/ *n.m.* holy-water stoup.

benjamin, ~e /bɛ̃ʒamɛ̃, -in/ *n.m., f.* youngest child.

benne /bɛn/ *n.f.* (*de grue*) scoop; (*amovible*) skip. ~ (**basculante**), dump truck.

benzine /bɛ̃zin/ *n.f.* benzine.

béotien, ~ne /beɔsjɛ̃, -jɛn/ *n.m., f.* philistine.

béquille /bekij/ *n.f.* crutch; (*de moto*) stand.

bercail /bɛrkaj/ *n.m.* fold.

berceau (*pl.* ~**x**) /bɛrso/ *n.m.* cradle.

bercer /bɛrse/ *v.t.* (*balancer*) rock; (*apaiser*) lull; (*leurrer*) delude.

berceuse /bɛrsøz/ *n.f.* lullaby.

béret /berɛ/ *n.m.* beret.

berge /bɛrʒ/ *n.f.* (*bord*) bank.

berg|er, ~ère /bɛrʒe, -ɛr/ *n.m., f.* shepherd, shepherdess. ~**erie** *n.f.* sheep-fold.

berline /bɛrlin/ *n.f.* (*auto.*) saloon; (*auto., Amer.*) sedan.

berlingot /bɛrlɛ̃go/ *n.m.* boiled sweet; (*emballage*) carton.

berne (en) /(ɑ̃)bɛrn/ *adv.* at half-mast.

berner /bɛrne/ *v.t.* hoodwink.

besogne /bəzɔɲ/ *n.f.* task, job, chore.

besogneu|x, ~se /bəzɔɲø, -z/ *a.* needy.

besoin /bəzwɛ̃/ *n.m.* need. **avoir ~ de**, need. **au ~**, if need be.

best|ial (*m. pl.* ~**iaux**) /bɛstjal, -jo/ *a.* bestial.

bestiaux /bɛstjo/ *n.m. pl.* livestock.

bestiole /bɛstjɔl/ *n.f.* creepy-crawly.

bétail /betaj/ *n.m.* farm animals.

bête[1] /bɛt/ *n.f.* animal. ~ **noire**, pet hate, pet peeve. ~ **sauvage**, wild beast.

bête[2] /bɛt/ *a.* stupid. ~**ment** *adv.* stupidly.

bêtise /betiz/ *n.f.* stupidity; (*action*) stupid thing.

béton /betɔ̃/ *n.m.* concrete. ~ **armé**, reinforced concrete. ~**nière** /-ɔnjɛr/ *n.f.* cement-mixer, concrete-mixer.

betterave /bɛtrav/ *n.f.* beetroot. ~ **sucrière**, sugar-beet.

beugler /bøgle/ *v.i.* bellow, low; (*radio*) blare.

beurr|e /bœr/ *n.m.* butter. ~**er** *v.t.* butter. ~**ier** *n.m.* butter-dish.

bévue /bevy/ *n.f.* blunder.

biais /bjɛ/ *n.m.* expedient; (*côté*) angle. **de ~, en ~**, at an angle. **de ~**, (*fig.*) indirectly.

biaiser /bjeze/ *v.i.* hedge.

bibelot /biblo/ *n.m.* curio.

biberon /bibrɔ̃/ *n.m.* (feeding-) bottle.

bible /bibl/ *n.f.* bible. **la B~**, the Bible.

bibliobus /biblijɔbys/ *n.m.* mobile library.

bibliograph|e /biblijɔgraf/ *n.m./f.* bibliographer. ~**ie** *n.f.* bibliography.

bibliophile /biblijɔfil/ *n.m./f.* book-lover.

biblioth|èque /biblijɔtɛk/ *n.f.* library; (*meuble*) bookcase; ~**écaire** *n.m./f.* librarian.

biblique /biblik/ *a.* biblical.

biceps /bisɛps/ *n.m.* biceps.

biche /biʃ/ *n.f.* doe.

bichonner /biʃɔne/ *v.t.* doll up.

bicoque /bikɔk/ *n.f.* shack.

bicyclette /bisiklɛt/ *n.f.* bicycle.

bide /bid/ *n.m.* (*ventre: fam.*) belly; (*théâtre: argot*) flop.

bidet /bidɛ/ *n.m.* bidet.

bidon /bidɔ̃/ *n.m.* can. —*a. invar.* (*fam.*) phoney. **ce n'est pas du ~**, (*fam.*) it's the truth.

bidonville /bidɔ̃vil/ *n.f.* shanty town.

bidule /bidyl/ *n.m.* (*fam.*) thing.

bien /bjɛ̃/ *adv.* well; (*très*) quite, very. —*n.m.* good; (*patrimoine*) possession. —*a. invar.* good; (*passable*) all right; (*en forme*) well; (*à l'aise*) comfortable; (*beau*) attractive; (*respectable*) nice, respectable. —*conj.* ~ **que**, (al)though. ~ **du**, (*quantité*) a lot of, much. ~ **des**, (*nombre*) many. **il l'a ~ fait**, (*intensif*) he did do it. **ce n'est pas ~ de**, it is not right to. ~ **sûr**, of course. ~**s de consommation**, consumer goods. ~-**aimé, ~-aimée** *a.* & *n.m., f.* beloved. ~-**être** *n.m.* well-being. ~-**fondé** *n.m.* soundness.

bienfaisan|t, ~te /bjɛ̃fəzɑ̃, -t/ *a.* beneficial. ~**ce** *n.f.* charity.

bienfait /bjɛ̃fɛ/ *n.m.* (kind) favour; (*avantage*) benefit.

bienfai|teur, ~trice /bjɛ̃fɛtœr, -tris/ *n.m., f.* benefactor.

bienheureu|x, ~se /bjɛ̃nœrø, -z/ *a.* blessed.

bienséan|t, ~te /bjɛ̃seɑ̃, ~t/ *a.* proper. **~ce** *n.f.* propriety.

bientôt /bjɛ̃to/ *adv.* soon. **à ~,** see you soon.

bienveillan|t, ~te /bjɛ̃vɛjɑ̃, -t/ *a.* kind(ly). **~ce** *n.f.* kind(li)ness.

bienvenu, ~e /bjɛ̃vny/ *a.* welcome. **—***n.f.* welcome. **—***n.m., f.* **être le ~, être la ~e,** be welcome. **souhaiter la ~e à,** welcome.

bière /bjɛr/ *n.f.* beer; (*cercueil*) coffin. **~ blonde,** lager. **~ brune,** stout, brown ale. **~ pression,** draught beer.

biffer /bife/ *v.t.* cross out.

bifteck /biftɛk/ *n.m.* steak.

bifur|quer /bifyrke/ *v.i.* branch off, fork. **~cation** *n.f.* fork, junction.

bigam|e /bigam/ *a.* bigamous. **—***n.m./f.* bigamist. **~ie** *n.f.* bigamy.

bigarré /bigare/ *a.* motley.

bigot, ~e /bigo, -ɔt/ *n.m., f.* religious fanatic. **—***a.* over-pious.

bigoudi /bigudi/ *n.m.* curler.

bijou (*pl.* **~x**) /biʒu/ *n.m.* jewel. **~terie** *n.f.* (*boutique*) jeweller's shop; (*bijoux*) jewellery. **~tier, ~tière** *n.m., f.* jeweller.

bikini /bikini/ *n.m.* bikini.

bilan /bilɑ̃/ *n.m.* outcome; (*d'une catastrophe*) (casualty) toll; (*comm.*) balance sheet. **faire le ~ de,** assess.

bile /bil/ *n.f.* bile. **se faire de la ~,** (*fam.*) worry.

bilieu|x, ~se /biljø, -z/ *a.* bilious; (*fig.*) irascible.

bilingue /bilɛ̃g/ *a.* bilingual.

billard /bijar/ *n.m.* billiards; (*table*) billiard-table.

bille /bij/ *n.f.* (*d'enfant*) marble; (*de billard*) billiard-ball.

billet /bijɛ/ *n.m.* ticket; (*lettre*) note. **~ (de banque),** (bank)note. **~ d'aller et retour,** return ticket; (*Amer.*) round trip ticket. **~ de faveur,** complimentary ticket. **~ simple,** single ticket; (*Amer.*) one-way ticket.

billion /biljɔ̃/ *n.m.* billion (= 10^{12}); (*Amer.*) trillion.

billot /bijo/ *n.m.* block.

bimensuel, ~le /bimɑ̃sɥɛl/ *a.* fortnightly, bimonthly.

bin|er /bine/ *v.t.* hoe. **~ette** *n.f.* hoe.

biochimie /bjoʃimi/ *n.f.* biochemistry.

biograph|ie /bjografi/ *n.f.* biography. **~e** *n.m./f.* biographer.

biolog|ie /bjolɔʒi/ *n.f.* biology. **~ique** *a.* biological. **~iste** *n.m./f.* biologist.

bipède /bipɛd/ *n.m.* biped.

bique /bik/ *n.f.* (nanny-)goat.

bis[1], **bise** /bi, biz/ *a.* greyish brown.

bis[2] /bis/ *a.invar.* (*numéro*) A, a. **—***n.m. & int.* encore.

bisbille (en) /(ɑ̃)bisbij/ *adv.* (*fam.*) at loggerheads.

biscornu /biskɔrny/ *a.* crooked; (*bizarre*) weird.

biscotte /biskɔt/ *n.f.* rusk.

biscuit /biskɥi/ *n.m.* (*salé*) biscuit; (*Amer.*) cracker; (*sucré*) biscuit; (*Amer.*) cookie. **~ de Savoie,** spongecake.

bise[1] /biz/ *n.f.* (*fam.*) kiss.

bise[2] /biz/ *n.f.* (*vent*) north wind.

bison /bizɔ̃/ *n.m.* (American) buffalo, bison.

bisser /bise/ *v.t.* encore.

bistouri /bisturi/ *n.m.* lancet.

bistre /bistr/ *a. & n.m.* dark brown.

bistro(t) /bistro/ *n.m.* café, bar.

bitume /bitym/ *n.m.* asphalt.

bizarre /bizar/ *a.* odd, peculiar. **~ment** *adv.* oddly. **~rie** *n.f.* peculiarity.

blafard, ~e /blafar, -d/ *a.* pale.

blagu|e /blag/ *n.f.* joke. **~e à tabac,** tobacco-pouch. **~er** *v.i.* joke; *v.t.* tease. **~eur, ~euse** *n.m., f.* joker; *a.* jokey.

blaireau (*pl.* **~x**) /blɛro/ *n.m.* shaving-brush; (*animal*) badger.

blâm|e /blɑm/ *n.m.* rebuke, blame. **~able** *a.* blameworthy. **~er** *v.t.* rebuke, blame.

blanc, blanche /blɑ̃, blɑ̃ʃ/ *a.* white; (*papier, page*) blank. **—***n.m.* white; (*espace*) blank. **—***n.m., f.* white man, white woman. **—***n.f.* (*mus.*) minim. **~ (de poulet),** breast, white meat (of the chicken). **le ~,** (*linge*) whites. **laisser en ~,** leave blank.

blancheur /blɑ̃ʃœr/ *n.f.* whiteness.

blanch|ir /blɑ̃ʃir/ *v.t.* whiten; (*linge*) launder; (*personne*: *fig.*) clear. **~ir (à la chaux),** whitewash. **—***v.i.* turn white. **~issage** *n.m.* laundering. **~isserie** *n.f.* laundry. **~isseur, ~isseuse** *n.m., f.* laundryman, laundress.

blas|er /blaze/ *v.t.* make blasé. **~é** *a.* blasé.

blason /blazɔ̃/ *n.m.* coat of arms.

blasph|ème /blasfɛm/ *n.m.* blasphemy. **~ématoire** *a.* blasphemous. **~émer** *v.t./i.* blaspheme.

blatte /blat/ *n.f.* cockroach.

blazer /blɛzœr/ *n.m.* blazer.

blé /ble/ *n.m.* wheat.

bled /blɛd/ *n.m.* (*fam.*) dump, hole.

blême /blɛm/ *a.* (sickly) pale.

bless|er /blese/ *v.t.* injure, hurt; (*mil.*) wound; (*offenser*) hurt, wound. **se ~er** *v. pr.* injure *ou* hurt o.s. **~ant, ~ante** /blɛsɑ̃, -t/ *a.* hurtful. **~é, ~ée** *n.m., f.* casualty, injured person.

blessure /blesyr/ *n.f.* wound.

blet, ~te /blɛ, blɛt/ *a.* over-ripe.

bleu /blø/ *a.* blue; (*culin.*) very rare. —*n.m.* blue; (*contusion*) bruise. **~(s)**, (*vêtement*) overalls. **~ir** *v.t./i.* turn blue.

bleuet /bløɛ/ *n.m.* cornflower.

bleuté /bløte/ *a.* slightly blue.

blind|er /blɛ̃de/ *v.t.* armour(-plate). **~é** *a.* armoured; *n.m.* armoured car, tank.

blizzard /blizar/ *n.m.* blizzard.

bloc /blɔk/ *n.m.* block; (*de papier*) pad; (*système*) unit; (*pol.*) bloc. **à ~**, hard, tight. **en ~**, all together. **~-notes** (*pl.* **~s-notes**) *n.m.* note-pad.

blocage /blɔkaʒ/ *n.m.* (*des prix*) freeze, freezing; (*des roues*) locking.

blocus /blɔkys/ *n.m.* blockade.

blond, ~e /blɔ̃, -d/ *a.* fair, blond. --*n.m., f.* fair-haired *ou* blond man *ou* woman. **~eur** /-dœr/ *n.f.* fairness.

bloquer /blɔke/ *v.t.* block; (*porte, machine*) jam; (*freins*) slam on; (*roues*) lock; (*prix, crédits*) freeze; (*grouper*) put together. **se ~** *v. pr.* jam; (*roues*) lock.

blottir (se) /(sə)blɔtir/ *v. pr.* snuggle, huddle.

blouse /bluz/ *n.f.* smock.

blouson /bluzɔ̃/ *n.m.* lumber-jacket; (*Amer.*) windbreaker.

blue-jean /bludʒin/ *n.m.* jeans.

bluff /blœf/ *n.m.* bluff. **~er** *v.t./i.* bluff.

boa /bɔa/ *n.m.* boa.

bobard /bɔbar/ *n.m.* (*fam.*) fib.

bobine /bɔbin/ *n.f.* reel; (*sur machine*) spool; (*électr.*) coil.

bocage /bɔkaʒ/ *n.m.* grove.

boc|al (*pl.* **~aux**) /bɔkal, -o/ *n.m.* jar.

bock /bɔk/ *n.m.* beer glass; (*contenu*) glass of beer.

bœuf (*pl.* **~s**) /bœf, bø/ *n.m.* ox; (*viande*) beef. **~s**, oxen.

bohème /bɔɛm/ *a. & n.m./f.* bohemian.

bohémien, ~ne /bɔemjɛ̃, -jɛn/ *n.m., f.* gypsy.

boire† /bwar/ *v.t./i.* drink; (*absorber*) soak up. **~ un coup**, have a drink.

bois¹ /bwa/ *voir* **boire.**

bois² /bwa/ *n.m.* (*matériau, forêt*) wood. **de ~, en ~**, wooden.

boisé /bwaze/ *a.* wooded.

bois|er /bwaze/ *v.t.* (*chambre*) panel. **~eries** *n.f. pl.* panelling.

boisson /bwasɔ̃/ *n.f.* drink.

boit /bwa/ *voir* **boire.**

boîte /bwat/ *n.f.* box; (*de conserves*) tin, can; (*firme: fam.*) firm. **~ à gants**, glove compartment. **~ aux lettres**, letter-box. **~ de nuit**, night-club. **~ postale**, post-office box.

boiter /bwate/ *v.i.* limp; (*meuble*) wobble.

boiteu|x, ~se /bwatø, -z/ *a.* lame; (*meuble*) wobbly.

boîtier /bwatje/ *n.m.* case.

bol /bɔl/ *n.m.* bowl. **un ~ d'air**, a breath of fresh air.

bolide /bɔlid/ *n.m.* racing car.

Bolivie /bɔlivi/ *n.f.* Bolivia.

bolivien, ~ne /bɔlivjɛ̃, -jɛn/ *a. & n.m., f.* Bolivian.

bombance /bɔ̃bɑ̃s/ *n.f.* faire **~**, (*fam.*) revel.

bombard|er /bɔ̃barde/ *v.t.* bomb; (*par obus*) shell; (*nommer: fam.*) appoint unexpectedly (as). **~er qn. de**, (*fig.*) bombard s.o. with. **~ement** *n.m.* bombing; shelling. **~ier** *n.m.* (*aviat.*) bomber.

bombe /bɔ̃b/ *n.f.* bomb; (*atomiseur*) spray, aerosol.

bombé /bɔ̃be/ *a.* rounded; (*route*) cambered.

bomber /bɔ̃be/ *v.t.* **~ la poitrine**, throw out one's chest.

bon, bonne /bɔ̃, bɔn/ *a.* good; (*qui convient*) right; (*prudent*) wise. **~ à/pour**, (*approprié*) fit to/for. —*n.m.* (*billet*) voucher, coupon; (*comm.*) bond. **du ~**, some good. **à quoi ~?**, what's the good *ou* point? **bonne année**, happy New Year. **~ anniversaire**, happy birthday. **~ appétit/voyage**, enjoy your meal/trip. **bonne chance/nuit**, good luck/night. **bonne femme**, (*péj.*) woman. **bonne-maman** (*pl.* **bonnes-mamans**) *n.f.* (*fam.*) granny. **~-papa** (*pl.* **~s-papas**) *n.m.* (*fam.*) grand-dad. **~ sens**, common sense. **~ vivant**, jolly fellow. **de bonne heure**, early.

bonasse /bɔnas/ *a.* weak.

bonbon /bɔ̃bɔ̃/ *n.m.* sweet; (*Amer.*) candy. **∼nière** /-ɔnjɛr/ *n.f.* sweet box; (*Amer.*) candy box.

bond /bɔ̃/ *n.m.* leap.

bonde /bɔ̃d/ *n.f.* plug; (*trou*) plug-hole.

bondé /bɔ̃de/ *a.* packed.

bondir /bɔ̃dir/ *v.i.* leap.

bonheur /bɔnœr/ *n.m.* happiness; (*chance*) (good) luck. **au petit ∼,** haphazardly. **par ∼,** luckily.

bonhomme[1] (*pl.* **bonshommes**) /bɔnɔm, bɔ̃zɔm/ *n.m.* fellow. **∼ de neige,** snowman.

bonhom|me[2] /bɔnɔm/ *a. invar.* good-hearted. **∼ie** *n.f.* good-heartedness.

boni /bɔni/ *n.m.* surplus.

boniment /bɔnimɑ̃/ *n.m.* smooth talk.

bonjour /bɔ̃ʒur/ *n.m. & int.* hallo, hello, good morning *ou* afternoon.

bon marché /bɔ̃marʃe/ *a. invar.* cheap. —*adv.* cheap(ly).

bonne[1] /bɔn/ *a.f. voir* **bon.**

bonne[2] /bɔn/ *n.f.* (*domestique*) maid. **∼ d'enfants,** nanny.

bonnement /bɔnmɑ̃/ *adv.* **tout ∼,** quite simply.

bonnet /bɔnɛ/ *n.m.* cap; (*de femme*) bonnet.

bonneterie /bɔnɛtri/ *n.f.* hosiery.

bonsoir /bɔ̃swar/ *n.m. & int.* good evening; (*en se couchant*) good night.

bonté /bɔ̃te/ *n.f.* kindness.

bonus /bɔnys/ *n.m.* (*auto.*) no claims bonus.

boom /bum/ *n.m.* (*comm.*) boom.

bord /bɔr/ *n.m.* edge; (*rive*) bank. **à ∼ (de),** on board. **au ∼ de la mer,** at the seaside. **au ∼ des larmes,** on the verge of tears. **∼ de la route,** roadside. **∼ du trottoir,** kerb; (*Amer.*) curb.

bordeaux /bɔrdo/ *n.m. invar.* Bordeaux (wine). —*a. invar.* maroon.

bordée /bɔrde/ *n.f.* **∼ d'injures,** torrent of abuse.

bordel /bɔrdɛl/ *n.m.* (*désordre: fam.*) shambles.

border /bɔrde/ *v.t.* line, border; (*tissu*) edge; (*personne, lit*) tuck in.

bordereau (*pl.* **∼x**) /bɔrdəro/ *n.m.* (*liste*) note, slip; (*facture*) invoice.

bordure /bɔrdyr/ *n.f.* border. **en ∼ de,** on the edge of.

borgne /bɔrɲ/ *a.* one-eyed; (*fig.*) shady.

borne /bɔrn/ *n.f.* boundary marker. **∼ (kilométrique),** (*approx.*) milestone. **∼s,** limits.

borné /bɔrne/ *a.* narrow; (*personne*) narrow-minded.

borner /bɔrne/ *v.t.* confine. **se ∼** *v. pr.* confine o.s. (**à,** to).

bosquet /bɔskɛ/ *n.m.* grove.

bosse /bɔs/ *n.f.* bump; (*de chameau*) hump. **avoir la ∼ de,** (*fam.*) have a gift for.

bosseler /bɔsle/ *v.t.* emboss; (*endommager*) dent.

bosser /bɔse/ *v.i.* (*fam.*) work (hard). —*v.t.* (*fam.*) work (hard) at.

bossu, ∼e /bɔsy/ *n.m., f.* hunchback.

botani|que /bɔtanik/ *n.f.* botany. —*a.* botanical. **∼ste** *n.m./f.* botanist.

bott|e /bɔt/ *n.f.* boot; (*de fleurs, légumes*) bunch; (*de paille*) bundle, bale; (*coup d'épée*) lunge. **∼ier** *n.m.* bootmaker.

botter /bɔte/ *v.t.* kick, boot.

bottillon /bɔtijɔ̃/ *n.m.* ankle boot.

Bottin /bɔtɛ̃/ *n.m.* (P.) phone book.

bouc /buk/ *n.m.* (billy-)goat; (*barbe*) goatee. **∼ émissaire,** scapegoat.

boucan /bukɑ̃/ *n.m.* (*fam.*) din.

bouche /buʃ/ *n.f.* mouth. **∼ bée,** open-mouthed. **∼ d'égout,** manhole. **∼ d'incendie,** (fire) hydrant. **∼ de métro,** entrance to the underground *ou* subway (*Amer.*).

bouché /buʃe/ *a.* (*temps*) overcast; (*personne: fam.*) dense.

bouchée /buʃe/ *n.f.* mouthful.

boucher[1] /buʃe/ *v.t.* block; (*bouteille*) cork. **se ∼** *v. pr.* get blocked. **se ∼ le nez,** hold one's nose.

bouch|er[2], **∼ère** /buʃe, -ɛr/ *n.m., f.* butcher. **∼erie** *n.f.* butcher's (shop); (*carnage*) butchery.

bouche-trou /buʃtru/ *n.m.* stop-gap.

bouchon /buʃɔ̃/ *n.m.* stopper; (*en liège*) cork; (*de bidon, tube*) cap; (*de pêcheur*) float; (*de circulation: fig.*) traffic jam.

boucle /bukl/ *n.f.* (*de ceinture*) buckle; (*forme*) loop; (*de cheveux*) curl. **∼ d'oreille,** ear-ring.

boucl|er /bukle/ *v.t.* fasten; (*terminer*) finish off; (*enfermer: fam.*) shut up; (*encercler*) seal off; (*budget*) balance. —*v.i.* curl. **∼é** *a.* (*cheveux*) curly.

bouclier /buklije/ *n.m.* shield.

bouddhiste /budist/ *a. & n.m./f.* Buddhist.

boud|er /bude/ *v.i.* sulk. —*v.t.* steer clear of. **∼erie** *n.f.* sulkiness. **∼eur, ∼euse** *a.* **∼eur, ∼euse** *a., n.m., f.* sulky (person).

boudin /budɛ̃/ *n.m.* black pudding.

boudoir /budwar/ *n.m.* boudoir.

boue /bu/ *n.f.* mud.

bouée /bwe/ *n.f.* buoy. ~ **de sauvetage,** lifebuoy.

boueu|x, ~se /bwø, -z/ *a.* muddy. —*n.m.* dustman; (*Amer.*) garbage collector.

bouff|e /buf/ *n.f.* (*fam.*) food, grub. ~**er** *v.t./i.* (*fam.*) eat; (*bâfrer*) gobble.

bouffée /bufe/ *n.f.* puff, whiff; (*méd.*) flush; (*d'orgueil*) fit.

bouffi /bufi/ *a.* bloated.

bouffon, ~ne /bufɔ̃ -ɔn/ *a.* farcical.

bouge /buʒ/ *n.m.* hovel; (*bar*) dive.

bougeoir /buʒwar/ *n.m.* candlestick.

bougeotte /buʒɔt/ *n.f.* **la ~,** (*fam.*) the fidgets.

bouger /buʒe/ *v.t./i.* move; (*agir*) stir. **se ~** *v. pr.* (*fam.*) move.

bougie /buʒi/ *n.f.* candle; (*auto.*) spark(ing)-plug.

bougon, ~ne /bugɔ̃, -ɔn/ *a.* grumpy. ~**ner** /-ɔne/ *v.i.* grumble.

bougre /bugr/ *n.m.* (*fam.*) fellow. **ce ~ de,** (*fam.*) that devil of a.

bouillabaisse /bujabɛs/ *n.f.* fish soup.

bouillie /buji/ *n.f.* porridge, baby food. **en ~,** crushed, mushy.

bouill|ir† /bujir/ *v.i.* boil. —*v.t.* (**faire**) ~**ir,** boil. ~**ant, ~ante** *a.* boiling.

bouilloire /bujwar/ *n.f.* kettle.

bouillon /bujɔ̃/ *n.m.* bubble; (*aliment*) broth. ~**ner** /-jɔne/ *v.i.* bubble.

bouillotte /bujɔt/ *n.f.* hot-water bottle.

boulang|er, ~ère /bulɑ̃ʒe, -ɛr/ *n.m.*, *f.* baker. ~**erie** *n.f.* bakery. ~**erie-pâtisserie** *n.f.* baker's and confectioner's shop.

boule /bul/ *n.f.* ball. ~**s,** (*jeu*) bowls. ~ **de neige,** snowball. **faire ~ de neige,** snowball.

bouleau (*pl.* ~**x**) /bulo/ *n.m.* (silver) birch.

bouledogue /buldɔg/ *n.m.* bulldog.

boulet /bulɛ/ *n.m.* (*de canon*) cannonball; (*de forçat*) ball and chain.

boulette /bulɛt/ *n.f.* (*de papier*) pellet; (*aliment*) meat ball.

boulevard /bulvar/ *n.m.* boulevard.

boulevers|er /bulvɛrse/ *v.t.* turn upside down; (*pays, plans*) disrupt; (*émouvoir*) distress, upset. ~**ement** *n.m.* upheaval.

boulier /bulje/ *n.m.* abacus.

boulimie /bulimi/ *n.f.* compulsive eating.

boulon /bulɔ̃/ *n.m.* bolt. ~**ner** /-ɔne/ *v.t.* bolt.

boulot[1] /bulo/ *n.m.* (*travail: fam.*) work.

boulot[2]**, ~te** /bulo, -ɔt/ *a.* (*rond: fam.*) dumpy.

boum /bum/ *n.m.* & *int.* bang. —*n.f.* (*réunion: argot*) party.

bouquet /bukɛ/ *n.m.* (*de fleurs*) bunch, bouquet; (*d'arbres*) clump. **c'est le ~!,** (*fam.*) that's the last straw!

bouquin /bukɛ̃/ *n.m.* (*fam.*) book. ~**er** /-ine/ *v.t./i.* (*fam.*) read. ~**iste** /-inist/ *n.m./f.* second-hand bookseller.

bourbeu|x, ~se /burbø, -z/ *a.* muddy.

bourbier /burbje/ *n.m.* mire.

bourde /burd/ *n.f.* blunder.

bourdon /burdɔ̃/ *n.m.* bumble-bee.

bourdonn|er /burdɔne/ *v.i.* buzz. ~**ement** *n.m.* buzzing.

bourg /bur/ *n.m.* (market) town.

bourgade /burgad/ *n.f.* village.

bourgeois, ~e /burʒwa, -z/ *a.* & *n.m.*, *f.* middle-class (person); (*péj.*) bourgeois. ~**ie** /-zi/ *n.f.* middle class(es).

bourgeon /burʒɔ̃/ *n.m.* bud. ~**ner** /-ɔne/ *v.i.* bud.

bourgogne /burgɔɲ/ *n.m.* burgundy. —*n.f.* **la B~,** Burgundy.

bourlinguer /burlɛ̃ge/ *v.i.* (*fam.*) travel about.

bourrade /burad/ *n.f.* prod.

bourrage /buraʒ/ *n.m.* ~ **de crâne,** brainwashing.

bourrasque /burask/ *n.f.* squall.

bourrati|f, ~ve /buratif, -v/ *a.* filling, stodgy.

bourreau (*pl.* ~**x**) /buro/ *n.m.* executioner. ~ **de travail,** workaholic.

bourrelet /burlɛ/ *n.m.* weather-strip, draught excluder; (*de chair*) roll of fat.

bourrer /bure/ *v.t.* cram (**de,** with); (*pipe*) fill. ~ **de,** (*nourriture*) stuff with. ~ **de coups,** thrash. ~ **le crâne à qn.,** fill s.o.'s head with nonsense.

bourrique /burik/ *n.f.* ass.

bourru /bury/ *a.* surly.

bours|e /burs/ *n.f.* purse; (*subvention*) grant. **la B~e,** the Stock Exchange. ~**ier, ~ière** *a.* Stock Exchange; *n.m.*, *f.* holder of a grant.

boursoufler /bursufle/ *v.t.,* **se ~** *v. pr.* puff up, swell.

bouscul|er /buskyle/ *v.t.* (*pousser*) jostle; (*presser*) rush; (*renverser*) knock over. ~**ade** *n.f.* rush; (*cohue*) crush.

bouse /buz/ *n.f.* (cow) dung.

bousiller /buzije/ *v.t.* (*fam.*) mess up.

boussole /busɔl/ *n.f.* compass.

bout /bu/ *n.m.* end; (*de langue, bâton*) tip; (*morceau*) bit. à ~, exhausted. à ~ de souffle, out of breath. à ~ portant, point-blank. au ~ de, (*après*) after. ~ filtre, filter-tip. venir à ~ de, (*finir*) manage to finish.

boutade /butad/ *n.f.* jest; (*caprice*) whim.

boute-en-train /butɑ̃trɛ̃/ *n.m. invar.* joker, live wire.

bouteille /butɛj/ *n.f.* bottle.

boutiqu|e /butik/ *n.f.* shop; (*de mode*) boutique. ~ier, ~ière *n.m., f.* (*péj.*) shopkeeper.

bouton /butɔ̃/ *n.m.* button; (*pustule*) pimple; (*pousse*) bud; (*de porte, radio, etc.*) knob. ~ de manchette, cufflink. ~-d'or *n.m.* (*pl.* ~s-d'or) buttercup. ~ner /-ɔne/ *v.t.* button (up). ~nière /-ɔnjɛr/ *n.f.* buttonhole. ~-pression (*pl.* ~s-pression) *n.m.* press-stud; (*Amer.*) snap.

boutonneu|x, ~se /butɔnø, -z/ *a.* pimply.

bouture /butyr/ *n.f.* (*plante*) cutting.

bovin, ~e /bɔvɛ̃, -in/ *a.* bovine. ~s *n.m. pl.* cattle.

bowling /bɔliŋ/ *n.m.* bowling; (*salle*) bowling-alley.

box (*pl.* ~ *ou* boxes) /bɔks/ *n.m.* lock-up garage; (*de dortoir*) cubicle; (*d'écurie*) (loose) box; (*jurid.*) dock.

box|e /bɔks/ *n.f.* boxing. ~er *v.t./i.* box. ~eur *n.m.* boxer.

boyau (*pl.* ~x) /bwajo/ *n.m.* gut; (*corde*) catgut; (*galerie*) gallery; (*de bicyclette*) tyre; (*Amer.*) tire.

boycott|er /bɔjkɔte/ *v.t.* boycott. ~age *n.m.* boycott.

bracelet /braslɛ/ *n.m.* bracelet; (*de montre*) strap.

braconn|er /brakɔne/ *v.i.* poach. ~ier *n.m.* poacher.

brad|er /brade/ *v.t.* sell off. ~erie *n.f.* open-air sale.

braguette /bragɛt/ *n.f.* fly, flies.

brailler /brɑje/ *v.t./i.* bawl.

braire /brɛr/ *v.i.* bray.

braise /brɛz/ *n.f.* embers.

braiser /breze/ *v.t.* braise.

brancard /brɑ̃kar/ *n.m.* stretcher; (*bras*) shaft. ~ier /-dje/ *n.m.* stretcher-bearer.

branch|e /brɑ̃ʃ/ *n.f.* branch. ~ages *n.m. pl.* (cut) branches.

branch|er /brɑ̃ʃe/ *v.t.* connect; (*électr.*) plug in. ~ement *n.m.* connection.

branchies /brɑ̃ʃi/ *n.f. pl.* gills.

brandir /brɑ̃dir/ *v.t.* brandish.

branle /brɑ̃l/ *n.m.* mettre en ~, donner le ~ à, set in motion. ~-bas *n.m. invar.* commotion.

branler /brɑ̃le/ *v.i.* be shaky. —*v.t.* shake.

braquer /brake/ *v.t.* aim; (*regard*) fix; (*roue*) turn; (*personne*) antagonize. —*v.i.* (*auto.*) turn (the wheel).

bras /bra/ *n.m.* arm. —*n.m. pl.* (*fig.*) labour, hands. à ~-le-corps *adv.* round the waist. ~ dessus bras dessous, arm in arm. ~ droit, (*fig.*) right-hand man. en ~ de chemise, in one's shirtsleeves.

brasier /brɑzje/ *n.m.* blaze.

brassard /brasar/ *n.m.* arm-band.

brasse /bras/ *n.f.* (breast-)stroke; (*mesure*) fathom.

brassée /brase/ *n.f.* armful.

brass|er /brase/ *v.t.* mix; (*bière*) brew; (*affaires*) handle a lot of. ~age *n.m.* mixing; brewing. ~erie *n.f.* brewery; (*café*) brasserie. ~eur *n.m.* brewer. ~eur d'affaires, big businessman.

brassière /brasjɛr/ *n.f.* (baby's) vest.

bravache /bravaʃ/ *n.m.* braggart.

bravade /bravad/ *n.f.* bravado.

brave /brav/ *a.* brave; (*bon*) good. ~ment *adv.* bravely.

braver /brave/ *v.t.* defy.

bravo /bravo/ *int.* bravo. —*n.m.* cheer.

bravoure /bravur/ *n.f.* bravery.

break /brɛk/ *n.m.* estate car; (*Amer.*) station-wagon.

brebis /brəbi/ *n.f.* ewe. ~ galeuse, black sheep.

brèche /brɛʃ/ *n.f.* gap, breach.

bredouille /brəduj/ *a.* empty-handed.

bredouiller /brəduje/ *v.t./i.* mumble.

bref, brève /brɛf, -v/ *a.* short, brief. —*adv.* in short. en ~, in short.

Brésil /brezil/ *n.m.* Brazil.

brésilien, ~ne /breziljɛ̃, -jɛn/ *a. & n.m., f.* Brazilian.

Bretagne /brətaɲ/ *n.f.* Brittany.

bretelle /brətɛl/ *n.f.* (shoulder-)strap; (*d'autoroute*) access road. ~s, (*pour pantalon*) braces; (*Amer.*) suspenders.

breton, ~ne /brətɔ̃, -ɔn/ *a. & n.m., f.* Breton.

breuvage /brœvaʒ/ *n.m.* beverage.

brève /brɛv/ *voir* bref.

brevet /brəvɛ/ *n.m.* diploma. ~ (d'invention), patent.

brevet|er /brəvte/ v.t. patent. ~é a. (diplômé) qualified.

bréviaire /brevjɛr/ n.m. breviary.

bribes /brib/ n.f. pl. bits, scraps.

bric-à-brac /brikabrak/ n.m. invar. bric-à-brac.

bricole /brikɔl/ n.f. trifle.

bricol|er /brikɔle/ v.i. do odd (do-it-yourself) jobs. —v.t. fix (up). ~age n.m. do-it-yourself (jobs). ~eur, ~euse n.m., f. handyman, handy-woman.

brid|e /brid/ n.f. bridle. **tenir en** ~e, keep in check. ~er v.t. (cheval) bridle; (fig.) keep in check, bridle.

bridge /bridʒ/ n.m. (cartes) bridge.

briève|ment /brijɛvmã/ adv. briefly. ~té n.f. brevity.

brigad|e /brigad/ n.f. (de police) squad; (mil.) brigade; (fig.) team. ~ier n.m. (de police) sergeant.

brigand /brigã/ n.m. robber. ~age /-daʒ/ n.m. robbery.

briguer /brige/ v.t. seek (after).

brill|ant, ~ante /brijã, -t/ a. (couleur) bright; (luisant) shiny; (remarquable) brilliant. —n.m. (éclat) shine; (diamant) diamond. ~amment adv. brilliantly.

briller /brije/ v.i. shine.

brim|er /brime/ v.t. bully; (contrarier) annoy. ~ade n.f. bullying; annoyance.

brin /brɛ̃/ n.m. (de corde) strand; (de muguet) sprig. ~ **d'herbe,** blade of grass. **un** ~ **de,** a bit of.

brindille /brɛ̃dij/ n.f. twig.

bringuebaler /brɛ̃gbale/ v.i. (fam.) wobble about.

brio /brijo/ n.m. brilliance.

brioche /brijɔʃ/ n.f. brioche (small round sweet cake); (ventre: fam.) tummy.

brique /brik/ n.f. brick.

briquer /brike/ v.t. polish.

briquet /brikɛ/ n.m. (cigarette-) lighter.

brisant /brizã/ n.m. reef.

brise /briz/ n.f. breeze.

bris|er /brize/ v.t. break; (fatiguer) exhaust. **se** ~er v. pr. break. ~e-lames n.m. invar. breakwater. ~eur de grève n.m. strike-breaker.

britannique /britanik/ a. British. —n.m./f. Briton. **les B**~s, the British.

broc /bro/ n.m. pitcher.

brocant|e /brɔkãt/ n.f. second-hand goods. ~eur, ~euse n.m., f. second-hand goods dealer.

broche /brɔʃ/ n.f. brooch; (culin.) spit.

broché /brɔʃe/ a. paperback(ed).

brochet /brɔʃɛ/ n.m. (poisson) pike.

brochette /brɔʃɛt/ n.f. skewer.

brochure /brɔʃyr/ n.f. brochure, booklet.

brod|er /brɔde/ v.t. embroider. —v.i. (fig.) embroider the truth. ~erie n.f. embroidery.

broncher /brɔ̃ʃe/ v.i. falter.

bronch|es /brɔ̃ʃ/ n.f. pl. bronchial tubes. ~ite n.f. bronchitis.

bronze /brɔ̃z/ n.m. bronze.

bronz|er /brɔ̃ze/ v.i., se ~er v. pr. get a (sun-)tan. ~age n.m. (sun-)tan. ~é a. (sun-)tanned.

brosse /brɔs/ n.f. brush. ~ **à dents,** toothbrush. ~ **à habits,** clothes-brush. **en** ~, (coiffure) in a crew cut.

brosser /brɔse/ v.t. brush; (fig.) paint.

brouette /bruɛt/ n.f. wheelbarrow.

brouhaha /bruaa/ n.m. hullabaloo.

brouillard /brujar/ n.m. fog.

brouille /bruj/ n.f. quarrel.

brouill|er /bruje/ v.t. mix up; (vue) blur; (œufs) scramble; (radio) jam; (amis) set at odds. **se** ~er v. pr. become confused; (ciel) cloud over; (amis) fall out. ~on¹, ~onne a. disorderly.

brouillon² /brujɔ̃/ n.m. (rough) draft.

broussailles /brusɑj/ n.f. pl. undergrowth.

brousse /brus/ n.f. la ~, the bush.

brouter /brute/ v.t./i. graze.

broutille /brutij/ n.f. (bagatelle) trifle.

broyer /brwaje/ v.t. crush; (moudre) grind.

bru /bry/ n.f. daughter-in-law.

bruin|e /brɥin/ n.f. drizzle. ~er v.i. drizzle.

bruire /brɥir/ v.i. rustle.

bruissement /brɥismã/ n.m. rustling.

bruit /brɥi/ n.m. noise; (fig.) rumour.

bruitage /brɥitaʒ/ n.m. sound effects.

brûlant, ~e /brylã, -t/ a. burning (hot); (sujet) red-hot; (ardent) fiery.

brûlé /bryle/ a. (démasqué: fam.) blown. —n.m. burning.

brûle-pourpoint (à) /(a)brylpurpwɛ̃/ adv. point-blank.

brûl|er /bryle/ v.t./i. burn; (essence) use (up); (signal) go through ou past (without stopping); (dévorer: fig.) con-

sume. se ∼er *v. pr.* burn o.s. ∼eur
n.m. burner.
brûlure /brylyr/ *n.f.* burn. ∼s d'estomac, heartburn.
brum|e /brym/ *n.f.* mist. ∼eux,
∼euse *a.* misty; (*idées*) hazy.
brun, ∼e /brœ̃, bryn/ *a.* brown,
dark. —*n.m.* brown. —*n.m.*, *f.* dark-
haired person. ∼ir /brynir/ *v.i.* turn
brown; (*se bronzer*) get a tan.
brusque /brysk/ *a.* (*soudain*) sudden,
abrupt; (*rude*) abrupt. ∼ment /-əmɑ̃/
adv. suddenly, abruptly.
brusquer /bryske/ *v.t.* rush.
brut /bryt/ *a.* (*diamant*) rough; (*soie*)
raw; (*pétrole*) crude; (*comm.*) gross.
brut|al (*m. pl.* ∼aux) /brytal, -o/ *a.*
brutal. ∼aliser *v.t.* treat roughly *ou*
violently, manhandle. ∼alité *n.f.*
brutality.
brute /bryt/ *n.f.* brute.
Bruxelles /brysɛl/ *n.m./f.* Brussels.
bruy|ant, ∼ante /brɥijɑ̃, -t/ *a.* noisy.
∼amment *adv.* noisily.
bruyère /bryjɛr/ *n.f.* heather.
bu /by/ *voir* **boire.**
bûche /byʃ/ *n.f.* log. **ramasser une** ∼,
(*fam.*) come a cropper.
bûcher¹ /byʃe/ *n.m.* (*supplice*) stake.
bûch|er² /byʃe/ *v.t./i.* (*fam.*) slog away
(at). ∼eur, ∼euse *n.m.*, *f.* (*fam.*)
slogger.
bûcheron /byʃrɔ̃/ *n.m.* woodcutter.
budg|et /bydʒɛ/ *n.m.* budget. ∼étaire
a. budgetary.
buée /bɥe/ *n.f.* mist, condensation.
buffet /byfɛ/ *n.m.* sideboard; (*table,
restaurant*) buffet.
buffle /byfl/ *n.m.* buffalo.
buis /bɥi/ *n.m.* (*arbre, bois*) box.
buisson /bɥisɔ̃/ *n.m.* bush.
buissonnière /bɥisɔnjɛr/ *a.f.* faire
l'école ∼, play truant; (*Amer.*) play
hooky.
bulbe /bylb/ *n.m.* bulb.
bulgare /bylgar/ *a. & n.m./f.* Bulgari-
an.
Bulgarie /bylgari/ *n.f.* Bulgaria.
bulldozer /buldozœr/ *n.m.* bulldozer.

bulle /byl/ *n.f.* bubble.
bulletin /byltɛ̃/ *n.m.* bulletin, report;
(*scol.*) report; (*billet*) ticket. ∼ (de
vote), ballot-paper. ∼ de salaire,
pay-slip.
buraliste /byralist/ *n.m./f.* tobacco-
ist; (*à la poste*) clerk.
bureau (*pl.* ∼x) /byro/ *n.m.* office;
(*meuble*) desk; (*comité*) board. ∼ de
location, booking-office; (*théâtre*)
box-office. ∼ de poste, post office. ∼
de tabac, tobacconist's (shop).
bureaucrate /byrokrat/ *n.m./f.* bureaucrat.
bureaucrat|ie /byrokrasi/ *n.f.* bur-
eaucracy. ∼ique /-tik/ *a.* bureau-
cratic.
bureautique /byrotik/ *n.f.* office auto-
mation.
burette /byrɛt/ *n.f.* (*de graissage*) oil-
can.
burlesque /byrlɛsk/ *a.* ludicrous;
(*théâtre*) burlesque.
bus /bys/ *n.m.* bus.
busqué /byske/ *a.* hooked.
buste /byst/ *n.m.* bust.
but /by(t)/ *n.m.* target; (*dessein*) aim,
goal; (*football*) goal. **avoir pour** ∼
de, aim to. de ∼ en blanc, point-
blank.
butane /bytan/ *n.f.* butane, Calor gas
(P.).
buté /byte/ *a.* obstinate.
buter /byte/ *v.i.* ∼ contre, knock
against; (*problème*) come up
against. —*v.t.* antagonize. se ∼ *v. pr.*
(*s'entêter*) become obstinate.
buteur /bytœr/ *n.m.* striker.
butin /bytɛ̃/ *n.m.* booty, loot.
butiner /bytine/ *v.i.* gather nectar.
butoir /bytwar/ *n.m.* ∼ (de porte),
doorstop.
butor /bytɔr/ *n.m.* (*péj.*) lout.
butte /byt/ *n.f.* mound. en ∼ à, exposed to.
buvard /byvar/ *n.m.* blotting-paper.
buvette /byvɛt/ *n.f.* (refreshment) bar.
buveu|r, ∼se /byvœr, -øz/ *n.m.*, *f.*
drinker.

C

c' /s/ *voir* **ce**[1].

ça /sa/ *pron.* it, that; (*pour désigner*) that; (*plus près*) this. ~ **va?**, (*fam.*) how's it going? ~ **va!**, (*fam.*) all right! **où** ~**?**, (*fam.*) where? **quand** ~**?**, (*fam.*) when?

çà /sa/ *adv.* ~ **et là**, here and there.

caban|e /kaban/ *n.f.* hut; (*à outils*) shed; (*à lapins*) hutch. ~**on** *n.m.* hut; (*en Provence*) cottage.

cabaret /kabarɛ/ *n.m.* night-club.

cabas /kaba/ *n.m.* shopping basket.

cabillaud /kabijo/ *n.m.* cod.

cabine /kabin/ *n.f.* (*à la piscine*) cubicle; (*à la plage*) (beach) hut; (*de bateau*) cabin; (*de pilotage*) cockpit; (*de camion*) cab; (*d'ascenseur*) cage. ~ **(téléphonique)**, phone-booth, phone-box.

cabinet /kabinɛ/ *n.m.* (*de médecin*) surgery; (*Amer.*) office; (*d'avocat*) office; (*clientèle*) practice; (*pol.*) Cabinet; (*pièce*) room. ~**s**, (*toilettes*) toilet. ~ **de toilette**, toilet.

câble /kabl/ *n.m.* cable; (*corde*) rope.

câbler /kable/ *v.t.* cable.

cabosser /kabose/ *v.t.* dent.

cabot|age /kabotaʒ/ *n.m.* coastal navigation. ~**eur** *n.m.* coaster.

cabotin, ~**e** /kabotɛ̃, -in/ *n.m., f.* (*théâtre*) ham; (*fig.*) play-actor. ~**age** /-inaʒ/ *n.m.* ham acting; (*fig.*) play-acting.

cabrer /kabre/ *v.t.*, **se** ~ *v. pr.* (*cheval*) rear up. **se** ~ **contre**, rebel against.

cabri /kabri/ *n.m.* kid.

cabriole /kabrijɔl/ *n.f.* caper; (*culbute*) somersault.

cabriolet /kabrijɔlɛ/ *n.m.* (*auto.*) convertible.

cacahuète /kakauɛt/ *n.f.* peanut.

cacao /kakao/ *n.m.* cocoa.

cachalot /kaʃalo/ *n.m.* sperm whale.

cachemire /kaʃmir/ *n.m.* cashmere.

cach|er /kaʃe/ *v.t.* hide, conceal (**à**, from). **se** ~**er** *v. pr.* hide; (*se trouver caché*) be hidden. ~**e-cache** *n.m. invar.* hide-and-seek. ~**e-nez** *n.m. invar.* scarf.

cachet /kaʃɛ/ *n.m.* seal; (*de la poste*) postmark; (*comprimé*) tablet; (*d'artiste*) fee; (*fig.*) style.

cacheter /kaʃte/ *v.t.* seal.

cachette /kaʃɛt/ *n.f.* hiding-place. **en** ~, in secret.

cachot /kaʃo/ *n.m.* dungeon.

cachott|eries /kaʃɔtri/ *n.f. pl.* secrecy. ~**ier**, ~**ière** *a.* secretive.

cactus /kaktys/ *n.m.* cactus.

cadavérique /kadaverik/ *a.* (*teint*) deathly pale.

cadavre /kadavr/ *n.m.* corpse.

cadeau (*pl.* ~**x**) /kado/ *n.m.* present, gift.

cadenas /kadna/ *n.m.* padlock. ~**ser** /-ase/ *v.t.* padlock.

cadenc|e /kadɑ̃s/ *n.f.* rhythm, cadence; (*de travail*) rate. **en** ~**e**, in time. ~**é** *a.* rhythmic(al).

cadet, ~**te** /kadɛ, -t/ *a.* youngest; (*entre deux*) younger. —*n.m., f.* youngest (child); younger (child). **il est mon** ~, he is my junior.

cadran /kadrɑ̃/ *n.m.* dial. ~ **solaire**, sundial.

cadre /kadr/ *n.m.* frame; (*milieu*) surroundings; (*limites*) scope; (*contexte*) framework. —*n.m./f.* (*personne: comm.*) executive. **les** ~**s**, (*comm.*) the managerial staff.

cadrer /kadre/ *v.i.* ~ **avec**, tally with. —*v.t.* (*photo*) centre.

cadu|c, ~**que** /kadyk/ *a.* obsolete.

cafard /kafar/ *n.m.* (*insecte*) cockroach. **avoir le** ~, (*fam.*) be feeling low.

caf|é /kafe/ *n.m.* coffee; (*bar*) café. ~**é au lait**, white coffee. ~**etier**, ~**etière** *n.m., f.* café owner; *n.f.* coffee-pot.

caféine /kafein/ *n.f.* caffeine.

cafouiller /kafuje/ *v.i.* (*fam.*) bumble, flounder.

cage /kaʒ/ *n.f.* cage; (*d'escalier*) well; (*d'ascenseur*) shaft.

cageot /kaʒo/ *n.m.* crate.

cagibi /kaʒibi/ *n.m.* storage room.

cagneu|x, ~**se** /kaɲø, -z/ *a.* knock-kneed.

cagnotte /kaɲɔt/ *n.f.* kitty.

cagoule /kagul/ *n.f.* hood.

cahier /kaje/ *n.m.* notebook; (*scol.*) exercise-book.

cahin-caha /kaɛ̃kaa/ *adv.* **aller** ~, (*fam.*) jog along.

cahot /kao/ *n.m.* bump, jolt. ~**er**

/kaɔte/ *v.t./i.* bump, jolt. **~eux,
~euse** /kaɔtø, -z/ *a.* bumpy.
caïd /kaid/ *n.m.* (*fam.*) big shot.
caille /kɑj/ *n.f.* quail.
cailler /kɑje/ *v.t./i.*, **se ~** *v. pr.* (*sang*)
clot; (*lait*) curdle.
caillot /kɑjo/ *n.m.* (blood) clot.
caillou (*pl.* **~x**) /kɑju/ *n.m.* stone;
(*galet*) pebble. **~teux, ~teuse** *a.*
stony. **~tis** *n.m.* gravel.
caisse /kɛs/ *n.f.* crate, case; (*tiroir,
machine*) till; (*guichet*) pay-desk; (*bureau*) office; (*mus.*) drum. **~ enregistreuse,** cash register. **~ d'épargne,**
savings bank.
caiss|ier, ~ière /kesje, -jɛr/ *n.m., f.*
cashier.
caisson /kɛsɔ̃/ *n.m.* (little) box.
cajol|er /kaʒɔle/ *v.t.* coax. **~eries** *n.f.
pl.* coaxing.
cake /kɛk/ *n.m.* fruit-cake.
calamité /kalamite/ *n.f.* calamity.
calcaire /kalkɛr/ *a.* (*sol*) chalky; (*eau*)
hard.
calciné /kalsine/ *a.* charred.
calcium /kalsjɔm/ *n.m.* calcium.
calcul /kalkyl/ *n.m.* calculation; (*scol.*)
arithmetic; (*différentiel*) calculus.
calcul|er /kalkyle/ *v.t.* calculate.
~ateur *n.m.* (*ordinateur*) computer,
calculator. **~atrice** *n.f.* (*ordinateur*)
calculator.
cale /kal/ *n.f.* wedge; (*de navire*) hold.
~ sèche, dry dock.
calé /kale/ *a.* (*fam.*) clever.
caleçon /kalsɔ̃/ *n.m.* underpants. **~
de bain,** (bathing) trunks.
calembour /kalɑ̃bur/ *n.m.* pun.
calendrier /kalɑ̃drije/ *n.m.* calendar;
(*fig.*) timetable.
calepin /kalpɛ̃/ *n.m.* notebook.
caler /kale/ *v.t.* wedge; (*moteur*)
stall. —*v.i.* stall.
calfeutrer /kalføtre/ *v.t.* stop up the
cracks of.
calibr|e /kalibr/ *n.m.* calibre; (*d'un
œuf, fruit*) grade. **~er** *v.t.* grade.
calice /kalis/ *n.m.* (*relig.*) chalice.
califourchon (à) /(a)kalifurʃɔ̃/ *adv.*
astride. —*prép.* **à ~ sur,** astride.
câlin, ~e /kɑlɛ̃, -in/ *a.* endearing,
cuddly. **~er** /-ine/ *v.t.* cuddle.
calmant /kalmɑ̃/ *n.m.* sedative.
calm|e /kalm/ *a.* calm —*n.m.* calm
(-ness). **~er** *v.t.*, **se ~er** *v. pr.*
(*personne*) calm (down); (*diminuer*)
ease.
calomn|ie /kalɔmni/ *n.f.* slander;

(*écrite*) libel. **~ier** *v.t.* slander; libel.
~ieux, ~ieuse *a.* slanderous; libel-
lous.
calorie /kalɔri/ *n.f.* calorie.
calorifuge /kalɔrifyʒ/ *a.* (heat-)insu-
lating. —*n.m.* lagging.
calot /kalo/ *n.m.* (*mil.*) forage-cap.
calotte /kalɔt/ *n.f.* (*relig.*) skullcap;
(*tape: fam.*) slap.
calqu|e /kalk/ *n.m.* tracing; (*fig.*) exact
copy. **~er** *v.t.* trace; (*fig.*) copy. **~er
sur,** model on.
calvaire /kalvɛr/ *n.m.* (*croix*) calvary;
(*fig.*) suffering.
calvitie /kalvisi/ *n.f.* baldness.
camarade /kamarad/ *n.m./f.* friend;
(*pol.*) comrade. **~ de jeu,** playmate.
~rie *n.f.* good companionship.
cambouis /kɑ̃bwi/ *n.m.* (engine) oil.
cambrer /kɑ̃bre/ *v.t.* arch. **se ~** *v. pr.*
arch one's back.
cambriol|er /kɑ̃brijɔle/ *v.t.* burgle.
~age *n.m.* burglary. **~eur, ~euse**
n.m., f. burglar.
cambrure /kɑ̃bryr/ *n.f.* curve.
camée /kame/ *n.m.* cameo.
camelot /kamlo/ *n.m.* street vendor.
camelote /kamlɔt/ *n.f.* junk.
camembert /kamɑ̃bɛr/ *n.m.* Camembert (cheese).
caméra /kamera/ *n.f.* (*cinéma, télévision*) camera.
caméra|man (*pl.* **~men**) /kamera-
man, -mɛn/ *n.m.* cameraman.
camion /kamjɔ̃/ *n.m.* lorry, truck. **~-
citerne** *n.m.* tanker. **~nage** /-jɔnaʒ/
n.m. haulage. **~nette** /-jɔnɛt/ *n.f.* van.
~neur /-jɔnœr/ *n.m.* lorry *ou* truck
driver; (*entrepreneur*) haulage contractor.
camisole /kamizɔl/ *n.f.* **~ (de force),**
strait-jacket.
camoufl|er /kamufle/ *v.t.* camouflage.
~age *n.m.* camouflage.
camp /kɑ̃/ *n.m.* camp; (*sport*) side.
campagn|e /kɑ̃paɲ/ *n.f.* country(side);
(*mil., pol.*) campaign. **~ard, ~arde**
a. country; *n.m., f.* countryman,
countrywoman.
campanile /kɑ̃panil/ *n.m.* belltower.
camp|er /kɑ̃pe/ *v.i.* camp. —*v.t.* plant
boldly; (*esquisser*) sketch. **se ~er** *v.
pr.* plant o.s. **~ement** *n.m.* encampment. **~eur, ~euse** *n.m., f.* camper.
camping /kɑ̃piŋ/ *n.m.* camping.
(terrain de) ~, campsite.
campus /kɑ̃pys/ *n.m.* campus.

camus, ~e /kamy, -z/ *a.* (*personne*) pug-nosed.

Canada /kanada/ *n.m.* Canada.

canadien, ~ne /kanadjɛ̃, -jɛn/ *a.* & *n.m.*, *f.* Canadian. —*n.f.* fur-lined jacket.

canaille /kanɑj/ *n.f.* rogue.

can|al (*pl.* ~**aux**) /kanal, -o/ *n.m.* (*artificiel*) canal; (*bras de mer*) channel; (*techn.*, *TV*) channel. **par le ~al de,** through.

canalisation /kanalizɑsjɔ̃/ *n.f.* (*tuyaux*) main(s).

canaliser /kanalize/ *v.t.* (*eau*) canalize; (*fig.*) channel.

canapé /kanape/ *n.m.* sofa.

canard /kanar/ *n.m.* duck.

canari /kanari/ *n.m.* canary.

cancans /kɑ̃kɑ̃/ *n.m. pl.* malicious gossip.

canc|er /kɑ̃sɛr/ *n.m.* cancer. **~éreux, ~éreuse** *a.* cancerous; *n.m.*, *f.* cancer victim.

cancre /kɑ̃kr/ *n.m.* dunce.

cancrelat /kɑ̃krəla/ *n.m.* cockroach.

candélabre /kɑ̃delabr/ *n.m.* candelabrum.

candeur /kɑ̃dœr/ *n.f.* naïvety.

candidat, ~e /kɑ̃dida, -t/ *n.m.*, *f.* candidate; (*à un poste*) applicant, candidate (**à,** for). ~**ure** /-tyr/ *n.f.* application; (*pol.*) candidacy.

candide /kɑ̃did/ *a.* naïve.

cane /kan/ *n.f.* (female) duck. ~**ton** *n.m.* duckling.

canette /kanɛt/ *n.f.* (*de bière*) bottle.

canevas /kanva/ *n.m.* canvas; (*plan*) framework, outline.

caniche /kaniʃ/ *n.m.* poodle.

canicule /kanikyl/ *n.f.* hot summer days.

canif /kanif/ *n.m.* penknife.

canin, ~e /kanɛ̃, -in/ *a.* canine.

caniveau (*pl.* ~**x**) /kanivo/ *n.m.* gutter.

canne /kan/ *n.f.* (walking-)stick. ~ **à pêche,** fishing-rod. ~ **à sucre,** sugarcane.

cannelle /kanɛl/ *n.f.* cinnamon.

cannibale /kanibal/ *a.* & *n.m./f.* cannibal.

canoë /kanɔe/ *n.m.* canoe; (*sport*) canoeing.

canon /kanɔ̃/ *n.m.* (big) gun; (*d'une arme*) barrel; (*principe, règle*) canon. ~**nade** /-ɔnad/ *n.f.* gunfire. ~**nier** /-ɔnje/ *n.m.* gunner.

cañon /kaɲɔ̃/ *n.m.* canyon.

canoniser /kanɔnize/ *v.t.* canonize.

canot /kano/ *n.m.* boat. ~ **de sauvetage,** lifeboat. ~ **pneumatique,** rubber dinghy.

canot|er /kanɔte/ *v.i.* boat. ~**age** *n.m.* boating.

cantate /kɑ̃tat/ *n.f.* cantata.

cantatrice /kɑ̃tatris/ *n.f.* opera singer.

cantine /kɑ̃tin/ *n.f.* canteen.

cantique /kɑ̃tik/ *n.m.* hymn.

canton /kɑ̃tɔ̃/ *n.m.* (*en France*) district; (*en Suisse*) canton.

cantonade (à la) /(ala)kɑ̃tɔnad/ *adv.* for all to hear.

cantonner /kɑ̃tɔne/ *v.t.* (*mil.*) billet. **se ~ dans,** confine o.s. to.

cantonnier /kɑ̃tɔnje/ *n.m.* roadman, road mender.

canular /kanylar/ *n.m.* practical joke.

caoutchou|c /kautʃu/ *n.m.* rubber; (*élastique*) rubber band. ~**c mousse,** foam rubber. ~**ter** *v.t.* rubberize. ~**teux, ~teuse** *a.* rubbery.

cap /kap/ *n.m.* cape, headland; (*direction*) course. **doubler** *ou* **franchir le ~ de,** go beyond (the point of). **mettre le ~ sur,** steer a course for.

capable /kapabl/ *a.* able, capable. ~ **de qch.,** capable of sth. ~ **de faire,** able to do, capable of doing.

capacité /kapasite/ *n.f.* ability; (*contenance*) capacity.

cape /kap/ *n.f.* cape.

capillaire /kapilɛr/ *a.* (*lotion, soins*) hair.

capilotade (en) /(ɑ̃)kapilɔtad/ *adv.* (*fam.*) reduced to a pulp.

capitaine /kapitɛn/ *n.m.* captain.

capit|al, ~ale (*m. pl.* ~**aux**) /kapital, -o/ *a.* major, fundamental; (*peine, lettre*) capital. —*n.m.* (*pl.* ~**aux**) (*comm.*) capital; (*fig.*) stock. ~**aux,** (*comm.*) capital. —*n.f.* (*ville, lettre*) capital.

capitalis|te /kapitalist/ *a.* & *n.m./f.* capitalist. ~**me** *n.m.* capitalism.

capiteu|x, ~se /kapitø, -z/ *a.* heady.

capitonner /kapitɔne/ *v.t.* pad.

capitul|er /kapityle/ *v.i.* capitulate. ~**ation** *n.f.* capitulation.

capor|al (*pl.* ~**aux**) /kapɔral, -o/ *n.m.* corporal.

capot /kapo/ *n.m.* (*auto.*) bonnet; (*auto., Amer.*) hood.

capote /kapɔt/ *n.f.* (*auto.*) hood; (*auto., Amer.*) convertible) top.

capoter /kapɔte/ *v.i.* overturn.

câpre /kɑpr/ *n.f.* (*culin.*) caper.

capric|e /kapris/ *n.m.* whim, caprice.
~ieux, ~ieuse *a.* capricious; (*appareil*) temperamental.
capsule /kapsyl/ *n.f.* capsule; (*de bouteille, pistolet*) cap.
capter /kapte/ *v.t.* (*eau*) tap; (*émission*) pick up; (*fig.*) win, capture.
captieu|x, ~se /kapsjø, -z/ *a.* specious.
capti|f, ~ve /kaptif, -v/ *a.* & *n.m., f.* captive.
captiver /kaptive/ *v.t.* captivate.
captur|e /kaptyr/ *n.f.* capture. **~er** *v.t.* capture.
capuch|e /kapyʃ/ *n.f.* hood. **~on** *n.m.* hood; (*de stylo*) cap.
caquet /kakɛ/ *n.m.* cackle.
caquet|er /kakte/ *v.i.* cackle. **~age** *n.m.* cackle.
car[1] /kar/ *conj.* because, for.
car[2] /kar/ *n.m.* coach; (*Amer.*) bus.
carabine /karabin/ *n.f.* rifle.
caracoler /karakɔle/ *v.i.* prance.
caract|ère /karaktɛr/ *n.m.* (*nature, lettre*) character. **~ères d'imprimerie,** block letters. **~ériel, ~érielle** *a.* character; *n.m., f.* disturbed child.
caractérisé /karakterize/ *a.* well-defined.
caractériser /karakterize/ *v.t.* characterize. **se ~ par,** be characterized by.
caractéristique /karakteristik/ *a.* & *n.f.* characteristic.
carafe /karaf/ *n.f.* decanter.
carambol|er (se) /(sə)karãbɔle/ *v. pr.* (*voitures*) smash into each other. **~age** *n.m.* multiple smash-up.
caramel /karamɛl/ *n.m.* caramel.
carapace /karapas/ *n.f.* shell.
carat /kara/ *n.m.* carat.
caravane /karavan/ *n.f.* (*auto.*) caravan; (*auto., Amer.*) trailer; (*convoi*) caravan.
carbone /karbɔn/ *n.m.* carbon. (**papier**) **~,** carbon (paper).
carboniser /karbɔnize/ *v.t.* burn (to ashes).
carburant /karbyrã/ *n.m.* (motor) fuel.
carburateur /karbyratœr/ *n.m.* carburettor; (*Amer.*) carburetor.
carcan /karkã/ *n.m.* (*contrainte*) yoke.
carcasse /karkas/ *n.f.* carcass; (*d'immeuble, de voiture*) frame.
cardiaque /kardjak/ *a.* heart. *—n.m./f.* heart patient.
cardin|al (*m. pl.* **~aux**) /kardinal, -o/

a. cardinal. *—n.m.* (*pl.* **~aux**) cardinal.
Carême /karɛm/ *n.m.* Lent.
carence /karãs/ *n.f.* inadequacy; (*manque*) deficiency.
carène /karɛn/ *n.f.* hull.
caressant, ~e /karɛsã, -t/ *a.* endearing.
caress|e /karɛs/ *n.f.* caress. **~er** /-ese/ *v.t.* caress, stroke; (*espoir*) cherish.
cargaison /kargɛzɔ̃/ *n.f.* cargo.
cargo /kargo/ *n.m.* cargo boat.
caricatur|e /karikatyr/ *n.f.* caricature. **~al** (*m. pl.* **~aux**) *a.* caricature-like.
car|ie /kari/ *n.f.* cavity. **la ~ie** (**dentaire**), tooth decay. **~ié** *a.* (*dent*) decayed.
carillon /karijɔ̃/ *n.m.* chimes; (*horloge*) chiming clock. **~ner** /-jɔne/ *v.i.* chime, peal.
carlingue /karlɛ̃g/ *n.f.* (*d'avion*) cabin.
carnage /karnaʒ/ *n.m.* carnage.
carnass|ier, ~ière /karnasje, -jɛr/ *a.* flesh-eating.
carnaval (*pl.* **~s**) /karnaval/ *n.m.* carnival.
carnet /karnɛ/ *n.m.* notebook; (*de tickets, chèques, etc.*) book. **~ de notes,** school report.
carotte /karɔt/ *n.f.* carrot.
carotter /karɔte/ *v.t.* (*argot*) swindle. **~ qch. à qn.,** (*argot*) wangle sth. from s.o.
carpe /karp/ *n.f.* carp.
carpette /karpɛt/ *n.f.* rug.
carré /kare/ *a.* (*forme, mesure*) square; (*fig.*) straightforward. *—n.m.* square; (*de terrain*) patch.
carreau (*pl.* **~x**) /karo/ *n.m.* (window) pane; (*par terre, au mur*) tile; (*dessin*) check; (*cartes*) diamonds. **à ~x,** check(ed).
carrefour /karfur/ *n.m.* crossroads.
carrel|er /karle/ *v.t.* tile. **~age** *n.m.* tiling; (*sol*) tiles.
carrelet /karlɛ/ *n.m.* (*poisson*) plaice.
carrément /karemã/ *adv.* straight; (*tout à fait: fam.*) definitely.
carrer (se) /(sə)kare/ *v. pr.* settle firmly.
carrière /karjɛr/ *n.f.* career; (*terrain*) quarry.
carrossable /karɔsabl/ *a.* suitable for vehicles.
carrosse /karɔs/ *n.m.* (horsedrawn) coach.
carross|erie /karɔsri/ *n.f.* (*auto.*)

body(work). **~ier** *n.m.* (*auto.*) body-builder.

carrousel /karuzɛl/ *n.m.* (*tournoiement*) merry-go-round.

carrure /karyr/ *n.f.* build.

cartable /kartabl/ *n.m.* satchel.

carte /kart/ *n.f.* card; (*géog.*) map; (*naut.*) chart; (*au restaurant*) menu. **~s,** (*jeu*) cards. **à la ~,** (*manger*) à la carte. **~ blanche,** a free hand. **~ des vins,** wine list. **~ grise,** (car) registration card. **~ postale,** post-card.

cartel /kartɛl/ *n.m.* cartel.

cartilage /kartilaʒ/ *n.m.* cartilage.

carton /kartɔ̃/ *n.m.* cardboard; (*boîte*) (cardboard) box. **~ à dessin,** portfolio. **faire un ~,** (*fam.*) take a pot-shot. **~nage** /-ɔnaʒ/ *n.m.* cardboard packing.

cartonné /kartɔne/ *a.* (*livre*) hard-back.

cartouch|e /kartuʃ/ *n.f.* cartridge; (*de cigarettes*) carton. **~ière** *n.f.* cart-ridge-belt.

cas /kɑ/ *n.m.* case. **au ~ où,** in case. **~ urgent,** emergency. **en aucun ~,** on no account. **en ~ de,** in the event of, in case of. **en tout ~,** in any case. **faire ~ de,** set great store by.

casan|ier, ~ière /kazanje, -jɛr/ *a.* home-loving.

casaque /kazak/ *n.f.* (*de jockey*) shirt.

cascade /kaskad/ *n.f.* waterfall; (*fig.*) spate.

cascadeur /kaskadœr/ *n.m.* stunt-man.

case /kɑz/ *n.f.* hut; (*compartiment*) pigeon-hole; (*sur papier*) square.

caser /kɑze/ *v.t.* (*mettre*) put; (*loger*) put up; (*dans un travail*) find a job for; (*marier*) marry off.

caserne /kazɛrn/ *n.f.* barracks.

casier /kɑzje/ *n.m.* pigeon-hole, compartment; (*meuble*) cabinet; (*à bouteilles*) rack. **~ judiciaire,** criminal record.

casino /kazino/ *n.m.* casino.

casqu|e /kask/ *n.m.* helmet; (*chez le coiffeur*) (hair-)drier. **~e (à écouteurs),** headphones. **~é** *a.* wearing a helmet.

casquette /kaskɛt/ *n.f.* cap.

cassant, ~e /kɑsɑ̃, -t/ *a.* brittle; (*brusque*) curt.

casse /kɑs/ *n.f.* (*objets*) breakages. **mettre à la ~,** scrap.

cass|er /kɑse/ *v.t./i.* break; (*annuler*)

annul; (*dégrader*) demote. **se ~er** *v. pr.* break. **~er la tête à,** (*fam.*) give a headache to. **~e-cou** *n.m. invar.* daredevil. **~e-croûte** *n.m. invar.* snack. **~e-noisettes** *ou* **~e-noix** *n.m. invar.* nutcrackers. **~e-pieds** *n.m./f. invar.* (*fam.*) pain (in the neck). **~e-tête** *n.m. invar.* (*problème*) headache.

casserole /kasrɔl/ *n.f.* saucepan.

cassette /kasɛt/ *n.f.* casket; (*de magnétophone*) cassette.

cassis /kasis/ *n.m.* black currant; (*sur une route*) dip.

cassoulet /kasulɛ/ *n.m.* stew (of beans and meat).

cassure /kasyr/ *n.f.* break.

caste /kast/ *n.f.* caste.

castor /kastɔr/ *n.m.* beaver.

castr|er /kastre/ *v.t.* castrate. **~ation** *n.f.* castration.

cataclysme /kataklism/ *n.m.* cata-clysm.

catalogu|e /katalɔg/ *n.m.* catalogue. **~er** *v.t.* catalogue; (*personne: péj.*) label.

catalyseur /katalizœr/ *n.m.* catalyst.

cataphote /katafɔt/ *n.m.* reflector.

cataplasme /kataplasm/ *n.m.* poul-tice.

catapult|e /katapylt/ *n.f.* catapult. **~er** *v.t.* catapult.

cataracte /katarakt/ *n.f.* cataract.

catastroph|e /katastrɔf/ *n.f.* disaster, catastrophe. **~ique** *a.* catastrophic.

catch /katʃ/ *n.m.* (all-in) wrestling. **~eur, ~euse** *n.m.,f.* (all-in) wrestler.

catéchisme /kateʃism/ *n.m.* cat-echism.

catégorie /kategɔri/ *n.f.* category.

catégorique /kategɔrik/ *a.* categori-cal.

cathédrale /katedral/ *n.f.* cathedral.

cathode /katɔd/ *n.f.* cathode.

catholi|que /katɔlik/ *a.* Catholic. **~cisme** *n.m.* Catholicism.

catimini (en) /(ɑ̃)katimini/ *adv.* on the sly.

cauchemar /koʃmar/ *n.m.* nightmare.

cause /koz/ *n.f.* cause; (*jurid.*) case. **à ~ de,** because of. **en ~,** (*en jeu, concerné*) involved. **pour ~ de,** on account of.

caus|er /koze/ *v.t.* cause. —*v.i.* chat. **~erie** *n.f.* talk. **~ette** *n.f.* **faire la ~ette,** have a chat.

caustique /kostik/ *a.* caustic.

cauteleu|x, ~se /kotlø, -z/ *a.* wily.

caution /kosjɔ̃/ *n.f.* surety; (*jurid.*) bail; (*appui*) backing. **sous ~,** on bail.

cautionn|er /kosjone/ *v.t.* guarantee; (*soutenir*) back. **~ement** *n.m.* (*somme*) guarantee.

cavalcade /kavalkad/ *n.f.* (*fam.*) stampede, rush.

cavalerie /kavalri/ *n.f.* (*mil.*) cavalry; (*au cirque*) horses.

caval|ier, ~ière /kavalje, -jɛr/ *a.* offhand. —*n.m.,f.* rider; (*pour danser*) partner. —*n.m.* (*échecs*) knight.

cave[1] /kav/ *n.f.* cellar.

cave[2] /kav/ *a.* sunken.

caveau (*pl.* **~x**) /kavo/ *n.m.* vault.

caverne /kavɛrn/ *n.f.* cave.

caviar /kavjar/ *n.m.* caviare.

cavité /kavite/ *n.f.* cavity.

ce[1]**, c'*** /sə, s/ *pron.* it, that. **c'est,** it *ou* that is. **ce sont,** they are. **c'est un chanteur/une chanteuse/** *etc.*, he/ she is a singer/*etc.* **ce qui, ce que,** what. **ce que c'est bon/***etc.***!,** how good/*etc.* it is! **tout ce qui, tout ce que,** everything that.

ce[2] *ou* **cet*** , **cette** (*pl.* **ces**) /sə, sɛt, se/ *a.* that; (*proximité*) this. **ces,** those; (*proximité*) these.

ceci /səsi/ *pron.* this.

cécité /sesite/ *n.f.* blindness.

céder /sede/ *v.t.* give up. —*v.i.* (*se rompre*) give way; (*se soumettre*) give in.

cédille /sedij/ *n.f.* cedilla.

cèdre /sɛdr/ *n.m.* cedar.

CEE *abrév.* (*Communauté économique européenne*) EEC.

ceinture /sɛtyr/ *n.f.* belt; (*taille*) waist; (*de bus, métro*) circle (line). **~ de sauvetage,** lifebelt. **~ de sécurité,** seat-belt.

ceinturer /sɛtyre/ *v.t.* seize round the waist; (*entourer*) surround.

cela /səla/ *pron.* it, that; (*pour désigner*) that. **~ va de soi,** it is obvious.

célèbre /selɛbr/ *a.* famous.

célébr|er /selebre/ *v.t.* celebrate. **~ation** *n.f.* celebration (**de,** of).

célébrité /selebrite/ *n.f.* fame; (*personne*) celebrity.

céleri /sɛlri/ *n.m.* (*en branches*) celery. **~(-rave),** celeriac.

céleste /selɛst/ *a.* celestial.

célibat /seliba/ *n.m.* celibacy.

célibataire /selibatɛr/ *a.* unmarried. —*n.m.* bachelor. —*n.f.* unmarried woman.

celle, celles /sɛl/ *voir* **celui.**

cellier /selje/ *n.m.* store-room (*for wine*).

cellophane /selɔfan/ *n.f.* (P.) Cellophane (P.).

cellul|e /selyl/ *n.f.* cell. **~aire** *a.* cell. **fourgon** *ou* **voiture ~aire,** prison van.

celui, celle (*pl.* **ceux, celles**) /səlɥi, sɛl, sø/ *pron.* the one. **~ de mon ami,** my friend's. **~-ci,** this (one). **~-là,** that (one). **ceux-ci,** these (ones). **ceux-là,** those (ones).

cendr|e /sɑ̃dr/ *n.f.* ash. **~é** *a.* (*couleur*) ashen.

cendrier /sɑ̃drije/ *n.m.* ashtray.

censé /sɑ̃se/ *a.* **être ~ faire,** be supposed to do.

censeur /sɑ̃sœr/ *n.m.* censor; (*scol.*) assistant headmaster.

censur|e /sɑ̃syr/ *n.f.* censorship. **~er** *v.t.* censor; (*critiquer*) censure.

cent (*pl.* **~s**) /sɑ̃/ (*generally* /sɑ̃t/ *pl.* /sɑ̃z/ *before vowel*) *a.* & *n.m.* (a) hundred. **~ un** /sɑ̃œ̃/ a hundred and one.

centaine /sɑ̃tɛn/ *n.f.* hundred. **une ~ (de),** (about) a hundred.

centenaire /sɑ̃tnɛr/ *n.m.* (*anniversaire*) centenary.

centième /sɑ̃tjɛm/ *a.* & *n.m./f.* hundredth.

centigrade /sɑ̃tigrad/ *a.* centigrade.

centilitre /sɑ̃tilitr/ *n.m.* centilitre.

centime /sɑ̃tim/ *n.m.* centime.

centimètre /sɑ̃timɛtr/ *n.m.* centimetre; (*ruban*) tape-measure.

centr|al, ~ale (*m. pl.* **~aux**) /sɑ̃tral, -o/ *a.* central. —*n.m.* (*pl.* **~aux**). **~al (téléphonique),** (telephone) exchange. —*n.f.* power-station. **~aliser** *v.t.* centralize.

centr|e /sɑ̃tr/ *n.m.* centre. **~e-ville** *n.m.* town centre. **~er** *v.t.* centre.

centupl|e /sɑ̃typl/ *n.m.* **le ~e (de),** a hundredfold. **au ~e,** a hundredfold. **~er** *v.t./i.* increase a hundredfold.

cep /sɛp/ *n.m.* vine stock.

cépage /sepaʒ/ *n.m.* (variety of) vine.

cependant /səpɑ̃dɑ̃/ *adv.* however.

céramique /seramik/ *n.f.* ceramic; (*art*) ceramics.

cerceau (*pl.* **~x**) /sɛrso/ *n.m.* hoop.

cercle /sɛrkl/ *n.m.* circle; (*cerceau*) hoop. **~ vicieux,** vicious circle.

cercueil /sɛrkœj/ *n.m.* coffin.

céréale /sereal/ *n.f.* cereal.

cérébr|al (*m. pl.* **~aux**) /serebral, -o/ *a.* cerebral.

cérémonial (*pl.* ~s) /seremɔnjal/ *n.m.* ceremonial.

cérémon|ie /seremɔni/ *n.f.* ceremony. ~**ie(s)**, (*façons*) fuss. ~**ieux**, ~**ieuse** *a.* ceremonious.

cerf /sɛr/ *n.m.* stag.

cerf-volant (*pl.* **cerfs-volants**) /sɛrvɔlɑ̃/ *n.m.* kite.

ceris|e /sriz/ *n.f.* cherry. ~**ier** *n.m.* cherry tree.

cerne /sɛrn/ *n.m.* ring.

cern|er /sɛrne/ *v.t.* surround; (*question*) define. **les yeux** ~**és**, with rings under one's eyes.

certain, ~**e** /sɛrtɛ̃, -ɛn/ *a.* certain; (*sûr*) certain, sure (**de**, of; **que**, that). —*pron.* ~**s**, certain people. **d'un** ~ **âge**, past one's prime. **un** ~ **temps**, some time.

certainement /sɛrtɛnmɑ̃/ *adv.* certainly.

certes /sɛrt/ *adv.* indeed.

certificat /sɛrtifika/ *n.m.* certificate.

certif|ier /sɛrtifje/ *v.t.* certify. ~**ier qch. à qn.**, assure s.o. of sth. ~**ié** *a.* (*professeur*) qualified.

certitude /sɛrtityd/ *n.f.* certainty.

cerveau (*pl.* ~**x**) /sɛrvo/ *n.m.* brain.

cervelas /sɛrvəla/ *n.m.* saveloy.

cervelle /sɛrvɛl/ *n.f.* brain.

ces /se/ *voir* **ce**².

césarienne /sezarjɛn/ *n.f.* Caesarean (section).

cessation /sɛsasjɔ̃/ *n.f.* suspension.

cesse /sɛs/ *n.f.* **n'avoir de** ~ **que,** have no rest until. **sans** ~, incessantly.

cesser /sese/ *v.t./i.* stop. ~ **de faire,** stop doing.

cessez-le-feu /seselfø/ *n.m. invar.* cease-fire.

cession /sɛsjɔ̃/ *n.f.* transfer.

c'est-à-dire /setadir/ *conj.* that is (to say).

cet, cette /sɛt/ *voir* **ce**².

ceux /sø/ *voir* **celui.**

chacal (*pl.* ~**s**) /ʃakal/ *n.m.* jackal.

chacun, ~**e** /ʃakœ̃, -yn/ *pron.* each (one), every one; (*tout le monde*) everyone.

chagrin /ʃagrɛ̃/ *n.m.* sorrow. **avoir du** ~, be distressed. ~**er** /-ine/ *v.t.* distress.

chahut /ʃay/ *n.m.* row, din. ~**er** /-te/ *v.i.* make a row; *v.t.* be rowdy with. ~**eur,** ~**euse** /-tœr, -tøz/ *n.m.*, *f.* rowdy.

chaîn|e /ʃɛn/ *n.f.* chain; (*de télévision*) channel. ~**e de montage/fabrica-tion,** assembly/production line. ~**e hi-fi,** hi-fi system. **en** ~**e,** (*accidents*) multiple. ~**ette** *n.f.* (small) chain. ~**on** *n.m.* link.

chair /ʃɛr/ *n.f.* flesh. **bien en** ~, plump. ~ **à saucisses,** sausage meat. **la** ~ **de poule,** goose-flesh.

chaire /ʃɛr/ *n.f.* (*d'église*) pulpit; (*univ.*) chair.

chaise /ʃɛz/ *n.f.* chair. ~ **longue,** (*siège pliant*) deck-chair.

chaland /ʃalɑ̃/ *n.m.* barge.

châle /ʃɑl/ *n.m.* shawl.

chalet /ʃalɛ/ *n.m.* chalet.

chaleur /ʃalœr/ *n.f.* heat; (*moins intense*) warmth; (*d'un accueil, d'une couleur*) warmth. ~**eux,** ~**euse** *a.* warm.

challenge /ʃalɑ̃ʒ/ *n.m.* contest.

chaloupe /ʃalup/ *n.f.* launch, boat.

chalumeau (*pl.* ~**x**) /ʃalymo/ *n.m.* blowlamp; (*Amer.*) blowtorch.

chalut /ʃaly/ *n.m.* trawl-net. ~**ier** /-tje/ *n.m.* trawler.

chamailler (se) /(sə)ʃamaje/ *v. pr.* squabble.

chambarder /ʃɑ̃barde/ *v.t.* (*fam.*) turn upside down.

chambre /ʃɑ̃br/ *n.f.* (bed)room; (*pol., jurid.*) chamber. ~ **à air,** inner tube. ~ **à coucher,** bedroom. ~ **à un lit/ deux lits,** single/double room. ~ **forte,** strong-room.

chambrer /ʃɑ̃bre/ *v.t.* (*vin*) bring to room temperature.

chameau (*pl.* ~**x**) /ʃamo/ *n.m.* camel.

chamois /ʃamwa/ *n.m.* chamois.

champ /ʃɑ̃/ *n.m.* field. ~ **de bataille,** battlefield. ~ **de courses,** race-course.

champagne /ʃɑ̃paɲ/ *n.m.* champagne.

champêtre /ʃɑ̃pɛtr/ *a.* rural.

champignon /ʃɑ̃piɲɔ̃/ *n.m.* mush-room.

champion, ~**ne** /ʃɑ̃pjɔ̃, -jɔn/ *n.m.*, *f.* champion. ~**nat** /-jɔna/ *n.m.* championship.

chance /ʃɑ̃s/ *n.f.* (good) luck; (*possibilité*) chance. **avoir de la** ~, be lucky. **une** ~, a stroke of luck.

chanceler /ʃɑ̃sle/ *v.i.* stagger; (*fig.*) falter.

chancelier /ʃɑ̃səlje/ *n.m.* chancellor.

chanceu|x, ~**se** /ʃɑ̃sø, -z/ *a.* lucky.

chancre /ʃɑ̃kr/ *n.m.* canker.

chandail /ʃɑ̃daj/ *n.m.* sweater.

chandelier /ʃɑ̃dəlje/ *n.m.* candlestick.

chandelle /ʃɑ̃dɛl/ *n.f.* candle.

change /ʃɑ̃ʒ/ *n.m.* (foreign) exchange.

changeant, ~e /ʃɑ̃ʒɑ̃, -t/ *a.* changeable.

changement /ʃɑ̃ʒmɑ̃/ *n.m.* change.

changer /ʃɑ̃ʒe/ *v.t./i.* change. **se ~** *v. pr.* change (one's clothes). **~ de nom/voiture,** change one's name/car. **~ de place/train,** change places/trains. **~ de direction,** change direction. **~ d'avis** *ou* **d'idée,** change one's mind.

changeur /ʃɑ̃ʒœr/ *n.m.* **~ automatique,** (money) change machine.

chanoine /ʃanwan/ *n.m.* canon.

chanson /ʃɑ̃sɔ̃/ *n.f.* song.

chant /ʃɑ̃/ *n.m.* singing; (*chanson*) song; (*religieux*) hymn.

chantage /ʃɑ̃taʒ/ *n.m.* blackmail.

chant|er /ʃɑ̃te/ *v.t./i.* sing. **si cela vous ~e,** (*fam.*) if you feel like it. **~eur, ~euse** *n.m., f.* singer.

chantier /ʃɑ̃tje/ *n.m.* building site. **~ naval,** shipyard. **mettre en ~,** get under way, start.

chantonner /ʃɑ̃tɔne/ *v.t./i.* hum.

chanvre /ʃɑ̃vr/ *n.m.* hemp.

chao|s /kao/ *n.m.* chaos. **~tique** /kaotik/ *a.* chaotic.

chaparder /ʃaparde/ *v.t.* (*fam.*) filch.

chapeau (*pl.* **~x**) /ʃapo/ *n.m.* hat; (*techn.*) cap.

chapelet /ʃaplɛ/ *n.m.* rosary; (*fig.*) string. **dire son ~,** tell one's beads, say the rosary.

chapelle /ʃapɛl/ *n.f.* chapel. **~ ardente,** chapel of rest.

chapelure /ʃaplyr/ *n.f.* breadcrumbs.

chaperon /ʃaprɔ̃/ *n.m.* chaperon. **~ner** /-ɔne/ *v.t.* chaperon.

chapiteau (*pl.* **~x**) /ʃapito/ *n.m.* (*de cirque*) big top; (*de colonne*) capital.

chapitre /ʃapitr/ *n.m.* chapter; (*fig.*) subject.

chapitrer /ʃapitre/ *v.t.* reprimand.

chaque /ʃak/ *a.* every, each.

char /ʃar/ *n.m.* (*mil.*) tank; (*de carnaval*) float; (*charrette*) cart; (*dans l'antiquité*) chariot.

charabia /ʃarabja/ *n.m.* (*fam.*) gibberish.

charade /ʃarad/ *n.f.* (*jeu*) charade.

charbon /ʃarbɔ̃/ *n.m.* coal. **~ de bois,** charcoal. **~nages** /-ɔnaʒ/ *n.m.pl.* coal-mines. **~nier** /-ɔnje/ *n.m.* coal-merchant.

charcut|erie /ʃarkytri/ *n.f.* pork-butcher's shop; (*aliments*) (cooked)

pork meats. **~ier, ~ière** *n.m., f.* pork-butcher.

chardon /ʃardɔ̃/ *n.m.* thistle.

charge /ʃarʒ/ *n.f.* load, burden; (*mil., électr., jurid.*) charge; (*mission*) responsibility. **~s,** expenses; (*de locataire*) service charges. **être à la ~ de,** be the responsibility of. **~s sociales,** social security contributions. **prendre en ~,** take charge of; (*transporter*) give a ride to.

chargé /ʃarʒe/ *a.* (*arbre*) laden; (*journée*) busy; (*langue*) coated.

charger /ʃarʒe/ *v.t.* load; (*attaquer*) charge; (*batterie*) charge. —*v.i.* (*attaquer*) charge. **se ~ de,** take charge *ou* care of. **~ qn. de,** weigh s.o. down with; (*tâche*) entrust s.o. with. **~ qn. de faire,** instruct s.o. to do. **chargement** /-əmɑ̃/ *n.m.* loading; (*objets*) load.

chariot /ʃarjo/ *n.m.* (*à roulettes*) trolley; (*charrette*) cart.

charitable /ʃaritabl/ *a.* charitable.

charité /ʃarite/ *n.f.* charity. **faire la ~,** give to charity. **faire la ~ à,** give to.

charlatan /ʃarlatɑ̃/ *n.m.* charlatan.

charmant, ~e /ʃarmɑ̃, -t/ *a.* charming.

charm|e /ʃarm/ *n.m.* charm. **~er** *v.t.* charm. **~eur, ~euse** *n.m., f.* charmer.

charnel, ~le /ʃarnɛl/ *a.* carnal.

charnier /ʃarnje/ *n.m.* mass grave.

charnière /ʃarnjɛr/ *n.f.* hinge. **à la ~ de,** at the meeting point between.

charnu /ʃarny/ *a.* fleshy.

charpent|e /ʃarpɑ̃t/ *n.f.* framework; (*carrure*) build. **~é a.** built.

charpentier /ʃarpɑ̃tje/ *n.m.* carpenter.

charpie (en) /(ɑ̃)ʃarpi/ *adv.* in(to) shreds.

charretier /ʃartje/ *n.m.* carter.

charrette /ʃarɛt/ *n.f.* cart.

charrier /ʃarje/ *v.t.* carry.

charrue /ʃary/ *n.f.* plough.

charte /ʃart/ *n.f.* charter.

charter /ʃartɛr/ *n.m.* charter flight.

chasse /ʃas/ *n.f.* hunting; (*au fusil*) shooting; (*poursuite*) chase; (*recherche*) hunt. **~ (d'eau),** (toilet) flush. **~ sous-marine,** underwater fishing.

châsse /ʃas/ *n.f.* shrine, reliquary.

chass|er /ʃase/ *v.t./i.* hunt; (*faire partir*) chase away; (*odeur, employé*) get rid of. ~e-neige *n.m. invar.* snow-plough. ~eur, ~euse *n.m., f.* hunter; *n.m.* page-boy; (*avion*) fighter.

châssis /ʃasi/ *n.m.* frame; (*auto.*) chassis.

chaste /ʃast/ *a.* chaste. ~té /-əte/ *n.f.* chastity.

chat, ~te /ʃa, ʃat/ *n.m., f.* cat.

châtaigne /ʃatɛɲ/ *n.f.* chestnut.

châtain /ʃatɛ̃/ *a. invar.* chestnut (brown).

château (*pl.* ~x) /ʃato/ *n.m.* castle; (*manoir*) manor. ~ d'eau, water-tower. ~ fort, fortified castle.

châtelain, ~e /ʃatlɛ̃, -ɛn/ *n.m., f.* lord of the manor, lady of the manor.

châtier /ʃatje/ *v.t.* chastise; (*style*) refine.

châtiment /ʃatimɑ̃/ *n.m.* punishment.

chaton /ʃatɔ̃/ *n.m.* (*chat*) kitten.

chatouill|er /ʃatuje/ *v.t.* tickle. ~ement *n.m.* tickling.

chatouilleu|x, ~se /ʃatujø, -z/ *a.* ticklish; (*susceptible*) touchy.

chatoyer /ʃatwaje/ *v.i.* glitter.

châtrer /ʃatre/ *v.t.* castrate.

chatte /ʃat/ *voir* **chat.**

chaud, ~e /ʃo, ʃod/ *a.* warm; (*brûlant*) hot; (*vif: fig.*) warm. —*n.m.* heat. **au** ~, in the warm(th). **avoir** ~, be warm; be hot. **il fait** ~, it is warm; it is hot. ~ement /-dmɑ̃/ *adv.* warmly; (*disputé*) hotly.

chaudière /ʃodjɛr/ *n.f.* boiler.

chaudron /ʃodrɔ̃/ *n.m.* cauldron.

chauffage /ʃofaʒ/ *n.m.* heating. ~ central, central heating.

chauffard /ʃofar/ *n.m.* reckless driver.

chauff|er /ʃofe/ *v.t./i.* heat (up). **se** ~er *v. pr.* warm o.s. (up). ~e-eau *n.m. invar.* water-heater.

chauffeur /ʃofœr/ *n.m.* driver; (*aux gages de qn.*) chauffeur.

chaum|e /ʃom/ *n.m.* (*de toit*) thatch. ~ière *n.f.* thatched cottage.

chaussée /ʃose/ *n.f.* road(way).

chauss|er /ʃose/ *v.t.* (*chaussures*) put on; (*enfant*) put shoes on (to). **se** ~er *v. pr.* put one's shoes on. ~er **bien,** (*aller*) fit well. ~er **du 35**/*etc.*, take a size 35/*etc.* shoe. ~e-pied *n.m.* shoe-horn. ~eur *n.m.* shoemaker.

chaussette /ʃosɛt/ *n.f.* sock.

chausson /ʃosɔ̃/ *n.m.* slipper. ~ (**aux pommes**), (apple) turnover.

chaussure /ʃosyr/ *n.f.* shoe.

chauve /ʃov/ *a.* bald.

chauve-souris (*pl.* **chauves-souris**) /ʃovsuri/ *n.f.* bat.

chauvin, ~e /ʃovɛ̃, -in/ *a.* chauvin-istic. —*n.m., f.* chauvinist. ~isme /-inism/ *n.m.* chauvinism.

chaux /ʃo/ *n.f.* lime.

chavirer /ʃavire/ *v.t./i.* (*bateau*) cap-size.

chef /ʃɛf/ *n.m.* leader, head; (*culin.*) chef; (*de tribu*) chief. ~ d'accusa-tion, (*jurid.*) charge. ~ d'équipe, foreman; (*sport*) captain. ~ d'État, head of State. ~ de famille, head of the family. ~ de file, (*pol.*) leader. ~ de gare, station-master. ~ d'orches-tre, conductor. ~ de service, depart-ment head. ~-lieu (*pl.* ~s-lieux) *n.m.* county town.

chef-d'œuvre (*pl.* **chefs-d'œuvre**) /ʃɛdœvr/ *n.m.* masterpiece.

cheik /ʃɛk/ *n.m.* sheikh.

chemin /ʃmɛ̃/ *n.m.* path, road; (*direc-tion, trajet*) way. **beaucoup de** ~ à **faire,** a long way to go. ~ de fer, railway. en *ou* par ~ de fer, by rail. ~ de halage, towpath. ~ vicinal, by-road. **se mettre en** ~, start out.

cheminée /ʃmine/ *n.f.* chimney; (*in-térieure*) fireplace; (*encadrement*) mantelpiece; (*de bateau*) funnel.

chemin|er /ʃmine/ *v.i.* plod; (*fig.*) pro-gress. ~ement *n.m.* progress.

cheminot /ʃmino/ *n.m.* railwayman; (*Amer.*) railroad man.

chemis|e /ʃmiz/ *n.f.* shirt; (*dossier*) folder; (*de livre*) jacket. ~e de nuit, night-dress. ~erie *n.f.* (*magasin*) man's shop. ~ette *n.f.* short-sleeved shirt.

chemisier /ʃmizje/ *n.m.* blouse.

chen|al (*pl.* ~aux) /ʃənal, -o/ *n.m.* channel.

chêne /ʃɛn/ *n.m.* oak.

chenil /ʃni(l)/ *n.m.* kennels.

chenille /ʃnij/ *n.f.* caterpillar.

chenillette /ʃnijɛt/ *n.f.* tracked ve-hicle.

cheptel /ʃɛptɛl/ *n.m.* livestock.

chèque /ʃɛk/ *n.m.* cheque. ~ de voy-age, traveller's cheque.

chéquier /ʃekje/ *n.m.* cheque book.

cher, chère /ʃɛr/ *a.* dear, expensive; (*aimé*) dear. —*adv.* (*coûter, payer*) a lot (of money). —*n.m., f.* **mon** ~, **ma chère,** my dear.

chercher /ʃɛrʃe/ *v.t.* look for; (*aide, paix, gloire*) seek. **aller** ~, go and get *ou* fetch, go for. ～ **à faire,** attempt to do. ～ **la petite bête,** be finicky.

chercheu|r, ～**se** /ʃɛrʃœr, -øz/ *n.m.,f.* research worker.

chèrement /ʃɛrmɑ̃/ *adv.* dearly.

chéri, ～**e** /ʃeri/ *a.* beloved. —*n.m.,f.* darling.

chérir /ʃerir/ *v.t.* cherish.

cherté /ʃɛrte/ *n.f.* high cost.

chéti|f, ～**ve** /ʃetif, -v/ *a.* puny.

chev|al (*pl.* ～**aux**) /ʃval, -o/ *n.m.* horse. ～**al** (**vapeur**), horsepower. à ～**al,** on horseback. à ～**al sur,** straddling. **faire du** ～**al,** ride (a horse).

chevaleresque /ʃvalrɛsk/ *a.* chivalrous.

chevalerie /ʃvalri/ *n.f.* chivalry.

chevalet /ʃvalɛ/ *n.m.* easel.

chevalier /ʃvalje/ *n.m.* knight.

chevalière /ʃvaljɛr/ *n.f.* signet-ring.

chevalin, ～**e** /ʃvalɛ̃, -in/ *a.* (*boucherie*) horse; (*espèce, regard*) equine.

chevauchée /ʃvoʃe/ *n.f.* (horse) ride.

chevaucher /ʃvoʃe/ *v.t.* straddle. —*v.i.,* **se** ～ *v. pr.* overlap.

chevelu /ʃəvly/ *a.* hairy.

chevelure /ʃəvlyr/ *n.f.* hair.

chevet /ʃvɛ/ *n.m.* **au** ～ **de,** at the bedside of.

cheveu (*pl.* ～**x**) /ʃvø/ *n.m.* (*poil*) hair. ～**x,** (*chevelure*) hair.

cheville /ʃvij/ *n.f.* ankle; (*fiche*) peg, pin; (*pour mur*) (wall) plug.

chèvre /ʃɛvr/ *n.f.* goat.

chevreau (*pl.* ～**x**) /ʃəvro/ *n.m.* kid.

chevreuil /ʃəvrœj/ *n.m.* roe(-deer); (*culin.*) venison.

chevron /ʃəvrɔ̃/ *n.m.* (*poutre*) rafter. à ～**s,** herring-bone.

chevronné /ʃəvrɔne/ *a.* experienced, seasoned.

chevroter /ʃəvrɔte/ *v.i.* quaver.

chewing-gum /ʃwiŋɡɔm/ *n.m.* chewing-gum.

chez /ʃe/ *prép.* at *ou* to the house of; (*parmi*) among; (*dans le caractère ou l'œuvre de*) in. ～ **le boucher**/*etc.,* at the butcher's/*etc.* ～ **soi,** at home; (*avec direction*) home. ～**-soi** *n.m. invar.* one's own house.

chic /ʃik/ *a. invar.* smart; (*gentil*) decent. —*n.m.* style. **avoir le** ～ **pour,** have the knack of. ～ (**alors**)!, great!

chicane /ʃikan/ *n.f.* zigzag; (*querelle*) quarrel.

chiche /ʃiʃ/ *a.* mean (**de,** with). ～

(**que je le fais**)!, (*fam.*) I bet you I will, can, *etc.*

chichis /ʃiʃi/ *n.m. pl.* (*fam.*) fuss.

chicorée /ʃikɔre/ *n.f.* (*frisée*) endive; (*à café*) chicory.

chien, ～**ne** /ʃjɛ̃, ʃjɛn/ *n.m.* dog. —*n.f.* dog, bitch. ～ **de garde,** watch-dog. ～**loup** *n.m.* (*pl.* ～**s-loups**) wolfhound.

chiffon /ʃifɔ̃/ *n.m.* rag.

chiffonner /ʃifɔne/ *v.t.* crumple; (*préoccuper*: *fam.*) bother.

chiffonnier /ʃifɔnje/ *n.m.* rag-and-bone man.

chiffre /ʃifr/ *n.m.* figure; (*code*) code. ～**s arabes**/**romains,** Arabic/Roman numerals. ～ **d'affaires,** turnover.

chiffrer /ʃifre/ *v.t.* set a figure to, assess; (*texte*) encode. **se** ～ **à,** amount to.

chignon /ʃiɲɔ̃/ *n.m.* bun, chignon.

Chili /ʃili/ *n.m.* Chile.

chilien, ～**ne** /ʃiljɛ̃, -jɛn/ *a. & n.m.,f.* Chilean.

chim|ère /ʃimɛr/ *n.f.* fantasy. ～**érique** *a.* fanciful.

chim|ie /ʃimi/ *n.f.* chemistry. ～**ique** *a.* chemical. ～**iste** *n.m.*/*f.* chemist.

chimpanzé /ʃɛ̃pɑ̃ze/ *n.m.* chimpanzee.

Chine /ʃin/ *n.f.* China.

chinois, ～**e** /ʃinwa, -z/ *a. & n.m.,f.* Chinese. —*n.m.* (*lang.*) Chinese.

chiot /ʃjo/ *n.m.* pup(py).

chiper /ʃipe/ *v.t.* (*fam.*) swipe.

chipoter /ʃipɔte/ *v.i.* (*manger*) nibble; (*discuter*) quibble.

chips /ʃips/ *n.m. pl.* crisps; (*Amer.*) chips.

chiquenaude /ʃiknod/ *n.f.* flick.

chiromanc|ie /kirɔmɑ̃si/ *n.f.* palmistry. ～**ien,** ～**ienne** *n.m.,f.* palmist.

chirurgic|al (*m. pl.* ～**aux**) /ʃiryɾʒikal, -o/ *a.* surgical.

chirurg|ie /ʃiryɾʒi/ *n.f.* surgery. ～**ie esthétique,** plastic surgery. ～**ien** *n.m.* surgeon.

chlore /klɔr/ *n.m.* chlorine.

choc /ʃɔk/ *n.m.* (*heurt*) impact, shock; (*émotion*) shock; (*collision*) crash; (*affrontement*) clash; (*méd.*) shock.

chocolat /ʃɔkɔla/ *n.m.* chocolate. ～ **au lait,** milk chocolate.

chœur /kœr/ *n.m.* chorus; (*chanteurs, nef*) choir. **en** ～, in chorus.

chois|ir /ʃwazir/ *v.t.* choose, select. ～**i** *a.* carefully chosen; (*passage*) selected.

choix /ʃwa/ *n.m.* choice, selection. **au**

~, according to preference. **de** ~, choice. **de premier** ~, top quality.

choléra /kɔlera/ *n.m.* cholera.

chômage /ʃomaʒ/ *n.m.* unemployment. **en** ~, unemployed. **mettre en** ~ **technique**, lay off.

chôm|er /ʃome/ *v.i.* be unemployed; (*usine*) lie idle. ~**eur**, ~**euse** *n.m., f.* unemployed person. **les** ~**eurs**, the unemployed.

chope /ʃɔp/ *n.f.* tankard.

choquer /ʃɔke/ *v.t.* shock; (*commotionner*) shake; (*verres*) clink.

choral, ~**e** (*m. pl.* ~**s**) /kɔral/ *a.* choral. —*n.f.* choir, choral society.

chorégraph|ie /kɔregrafi/ *n.f.* choreography. ~**e** *n.m./f.* choreographer.

choriste /kɔrist/ *n.m./f.* chorister.

chose /ʃoz/ *n.f.* thing. (**très**) **peu de** ~, nothing much.

chou (*pl.* ~**x**) /ʃu/ *n.m.* cabbage. ~ (**à la crème**), cream puff. ~**x de Bruxelles**, Brussels sprouts. **mon petit** ~, (*fam.*) my little dear.

choucas /ʃuka/ *n.m.* jackdaw.

chouchou, ~**te** /ʃuʃu, -t/ *n.m., f.* pet, darling.

choucroute /ʃukrut/ *n.f.* sauerkraut.

chouette¹ /ʃwɛt/ *n.f.* owl.

chouette² /ʃwɛt/ *a.* (*fam.*) super.

chou-fleur (*pl.* **choux-fleurs**) /ʃuflœr/ *n.m.* cauliflower.

choyer /ʃwaje/ *v.t.* pamper.

chrétien, ~**ne** /kretjɛ̃, -jɛn/ *a. & n.m., f.* Christian. ~**nement** /-jɛnmɑ̃/ *adv.* in a Christian way.

Christ /krist/ *n.m.* **le** ~, Christ.

christianisme /kristjanism/ *n.m.* Christianity.

chrom|e /krom/ *n.m.* chromium, chrome. ~**é** *a.* chromium-plated.

chromosome /krɔmozom/ *n.m.* chromosome.

chroniqu|e /krɔnik/ *a.* chronic. —*n.f.* (*rubrique*) column; (*nouvelles*) news; (*annales*) chronicle. ~**eur** *n.m.* columnist; (*historien*) chronicler.

chronolog|ie /krɔnɔlɔʒi/ *n.f.* chronology. ~**ique** *a.* chronological.

chronom|ètre /krɔnɔmɛtr/ *n.m.* stopwatch. ~**étrer** *v.t.* time.

chrysanthème /krizɑ̃tɛm/ *n.m.* chrysanthemum.

chuchot|er /ʃyʃɔte/ *v.t./i.* whisper. ~**ement** *n.m.* whisper(ing).

chuinter /ʃwɛ̃te/ *v.i.* hiss.

chut /ʃyt/ *int.* shush.

chute /ʃyt/ *n.f.* fall; (*déchet*) scrap. ~ (**d'eau**), waterfall. ~ **du jour**, nightfall. ~ **de pluie**, rainfall.

chuter /ʃyte/ *v.i.* (*fam.*) fall.

Chypre /ʃipr/ *n.f.* Cyprus.

-ci /si/ *adv.* (*après un nom précédé de ce, cette, etc.*) **cet homme-ci**, this man. **ces maisons-ci**, these houses.

ci- /si/ *adv.* here. **ci-après**, hereafter. **ci-contre**, opposite. **ci-dessous**, below. **ci-dessus**, above. **ci-gît**, here lies. **ci-inclus**, **ci-incluse**, **ci-joint**, **ci-jointe**, enclosed.

cible /sibl/ *n.f.* target.

ciboul|e /sibul/ *n.f.*, ~**ette** *n.f.* chive(s).

cicatrice /sikatris/ *n.f.* scar.

cicatriser /sikatrize/ *v.t.*, **se** ~ *v. pr.* heal (up).

cidre /sidr/ *n.m.* cider.

ciel (*pl.* **cieux**, **ciels**) /sjɛl, sjø/ *n.m.* sky; (*relig.*) heaven. **cieux**, (*relig.*) heaven.

cierge /sjɛrʒ/ *n.m.* candle.

cigale /sigal/ *n.f.* cicada.

cigare /sigar/ *n.m.* cigar.

cigarette /sigarɛt/ *n.f.* cigarette.

cigogne /sigɔɲ/ *n.f.* stork.

cil /sil/ *n.m.* (eye)lash.

ciller /sije/ *v.i.* blink.

cime /sim/ *n.f.* peak, tip.

ciment /simɑ̃/ *n.m.* cement. ~**er** /-te/ *v.t.* cement.

cimetière /simtjɛr/ *n.m.* cemetery. ~ **de voitures**, breaker's yard.

cinéaste /sineast/ *n.m./f.* film-maker.

ciné-club /sineklœb/ *n.m.* film society.

cinéma /sinema/ *n.m.* cinema. ~**tographique** *a.* cinema.

cinémathèque /sinematɛk/ *n.f.* film library; (*salle*) film theatre.

cinéphile /sinefil/ *n.m./f.* film buff.

cinétique /sinetik/ *a.* kinetic.

cinglant, ~**e** /sɛ̃glɑ̃, -t/ *a.* biting.

cinglé /sɛ̃gle/ *a.* (*fam.*) crazy.

cingler /sɛ̃gle/ *v.t.* lash.

cinq /sɛ̃k/ *a. & n.m.* five. ~**ième** *a. & n.m./f.* fifth.

cinquantaine /sɛ̃kɑ̃tɛn/ *n.f.* **une** ~ (**de**), about fifty.

cinquant|e /sɛ̃kɑ̃t/ *a. & n.m.* fifty. ~**ième** *a. & n.m./f.* fiftieth.

cintre /sɛ̃tr/ *n.m.* coat-hanger; (*archit.*) curve.

cintré /sɛ̃tre/ *a.* curved; (*chemise*) fitted.

cirage /siraʒ/ *n.m.* (wax) polish.

circoncision /sirkɔ̃sizjɔ̃/ *n.f.* circumcision.

circonférence /sirkɔ̃ferɑ̃s/ *n.f.* circumference.

circonflexe /sirkɔ̃flɛks/ *a.* circumflex.

circonscription /sirkɔ̃skripsjɔ̃/ *n.f.* district. ~ **(électorale)**, constituency.

circonscrire /sirkɔ̃skrir/ *v.t.* confine; *(sujet)* define.

circonspect /sirkɔ̃spɛkt/ *a.* circumspect.

circonstance /sirkɔ̃stɑ̃s/ *n.f.* circumstance; *(occasion)* occasion.

circonstancié /sirkɔ̃stɑ̃sje/ *a.* detailed.

circonvenir /sirkɔ̃vnir/ *v.t.* circumvent.

circuit /sirkɥi/ *n.m.* circuit; *(trajet)* tour, trip.

circulaire /sirkylɛr/ *a.* & *n.f.* circular.

circul|er /sirkyle/ *v.i.* circulate; *(train, automobile, etc.)* travel; *(piéton)* walk. **faire ~er**, *(badauds)* move on. **~ation** *n.f.* circulation; *(de véhicules)* traffic.

cire /sir/ *n.f.* wax.

ciré /sire/ *n.m.* oilskins.

cir|er /sire/ *v.t.* polish, wax. **~eur** *n.m.* bootblack. **~euse** *n.f.* *(appareil)* floor-polisher.

cirque /sirk/ *n.m.* circus; *(arène)* amphitheatre; *(désordre: fig.)* chaos.

cisaill|e(s) /sizaj/ *n.f. (pl.)* shears. **~er** *v.t.* prune.

ciseau *(pl. ~x)* /sizo/ *n.m.* chisel. **~x**, scissors.

ciseler /sizle/ *v.t.* chisel.

citadelle /sitadɛl/ *n.f.* citadel.

citadin, ~e /sitadɛ̃, -in/ *n.m., f.* city dweller. —*a.* city.

cité /site/ *n.f.* city. ~ **ouvrière,** (workers') housing estate. ~ **universitaire,** (university) halls of residence.

cit|er /site/ *v.t.* quote, cite; *(jurid.)* summon. **~ation** *n.f.* quotation; *(jurid.)* summons.

citerne /sitɛrn/ *n.f.* tank.

cithare /sitar/ *n.f.* zither.

citoyen, ~ne /sitwajɛ̃, -jɛn/ *n.m., f.* citizen. **~neté** *n.f.* citizenship.

citron /sitrɔ̃/ *n.m.* lemon. **~nade** /-ɔnad/ *n.f.* lemon squash *ou* drink, (still) lemonade.

citrouille /sitruj/ *n.f.* pumpkin.

civet /sivɛ/ *n.m.* stew. ~ **de lièvre/ lapin,** jugged hare/rabbit.

civette /sivɛt/ *n.f.* *(culin.)* chive(s).

civière /sivjɛr/ *n.f.* stretcher.

civil /sivil/ *a.* civil; *(non militaire)* civilian; *(poli)* civil. —*n.m.* civilian. **dans le ~,** in civilian life. **en ~,** in plain clothes.

civilisation /sivilizɑsjɔ̃/ *n.f.* civilization.

civiliser /sivilize/ *v.t.* civilize. **se ~** *v. pr.* become civilized.

civi|que /sivik/ *a.* civic. **~sme** *n.m.* civic sense.

clair /klɛr/ *a.* clear; *(éclairé)* light, bright; *(couleur)* light; *(liquide)* thin. —*adv.* clearly. —*n.m.* ~ **de lune,** moonlight. **le plus ~ de,** most of. **~ement** *adv.* clearly.

claire-voie (à) /(a)klɛrvwa/ *adv.* with slits to let the light through.

clairière /klɛrjɛr/ *n.f.* clearing.

clairon /klɛrɔ̃/ *n.m.* bugle. **~ner** /-ɔne/ *v.t.* trumpet (forth).

clairsemé /klɛrsəme/ *a.* sparse.

clairvoyant, ~e /klɛrvwajɑ̃, -t/ *a.* clear-sighted.

clamer /klame/ *v.t.* utter aloud.

clameur /klamœr/ *n.f.* clamour.

clan /klɑ̃/ *n.m.* clan.

clandestin, ~e /klɑ̃dɛstɛ̃, -in/ *a.* secret; *(journal)* underground.

clapet /klapɛ/ *n.m.* valve.

clapier /klapje/ *n.m.* (rabbit) hutch.

clapot|er /klapɔte/ *v.i.* lap. **~is** *n.m.* lapping.

claquage /klakaʒ/ *n.m.* strained muscle.

claque /klak/ *n.f.* slap.

claqu|er /klake/ *v.i.* bang; *(porte)* slam, bang; *(fouet)* snap, crack; *(se casser: fam.)* conk out. —*v.t.* *(porte)* slam, bang; *(gifler)* slap; *(fatiguer: fam.)* tire out. **~er des doigts,** snap one's fingers. **~er des mains,** clap one's hands. **il claque des dents,** his teeth are chattering. **~ement** *n.m.* bang(ing); slam(ming); snap(ping).

claquettes /klakɛt/ *n.f. pl.* tap-dancing.

clarifier /klarifje/ *v.t.* clarify.

clarinette /klarinɛt/ *n.f.* clarinet.

clarté /klarte/ *n.f.* light, brightness; *(netteté)* clarity.

classe /klɑs/ *n.f.* class; *(salle: scol.)* class(-room). **aller en ~,** go to school. ~ **ouvrière/moyenne,** working/ middle class. **faire la ~,** teach.

class|er /klɑse/ *v.t.* classify; *(par mérite)* grade; *(papiers)* file; *(affaire)* close. **se ~er premier/dernier,**

come first/last. **~ement** *n.m.* classification; grading; filing; (*rang*) place, grade; (*de coureur*) placing.

classeur /klɑsœr/ *n.m.* filing cabinet; (*chemise*) file.

classif|ier /klasifje/ *v.t.* classify. **~ication** *n.f.* classification.

classique /klasik/ *a.* classical; (*de qualité*) classic(al); (*habituel*) classic. —*n.m.* classic; (*auteur*) classical author.

clause /kloz/ *n.f.* clause.

claustration /klostrɑsjɔ̃/ *n.f.* confinement.

claustrophobie /klostrɔfɔbi/ *n.f.* claustrophobia.

clavecin /klavsɛ̃/ *n.m.* harpsichord.

clavicule /klavikyl/ *n.f.* collar-bone.

clavier /klavje/ *n.m.* keyboard.

clé, clef /kle/ *n.f.* key; (*outil*) spanner; (*mus.*) clef. —*a. invar.* key. **~ anglaise**, (monkey-)wrench. **~ de contact**, ignition key. **~ de voûte**, keystone.

clémen|t, ~te /klemɑ̃, -t/ *a.* (*doux*) mild; (*indulgent*) lenient. **~ce** *n.f.* mildness; leniency.

clémentine /klemɑ̃tin/ *n.f.* clementine.

clerc /klɛr/ *n.m.* (*d'avoué etc.*) clerk; (*relig.*) cleric.

clergé /klɛrʒe/ *n.m.* clergy.

cléric|al (*m. pl.* **~aux**) /klerikal, -o/ *a.* clerical.

cliché /kliʃe/ *n.m.* cliché; (*photo.*) negative.

client, ~e /klijɑ̃, -t/ *n.m.,f.* customer; (*d'un avocat*) client; (*d'un médecin*) patient; (*d'hôtel*) guest. **~èle** /-tɛl/ *n.f.* customers, clientele; (*d'un avocat*) clientele, clients, practice; (*d'un médecin*) practice, patients; (*soutien*) custom.

cligner /kliɲe/ *v.i.* **~ des yeux**, blink. **~ de l'œil**, wink.

clignot|er /kliɲɔte/ *v.i.* blink; (*lumière*) flicker; (*comme signal*) flash. **~ant** *n.m.* (*auto.*) indicator; (*auto., Amer.*) directional signal.

climat /klima/ *n.m.* climate. **~ique** /-tik/ *a.* climatic.

climatis|ation /klimatizɑsjɔ̃/ *n.f.* air-conditioning. **~é** *a.* air-conditioned.

clin d'œil /klɛ̃dœj/ *n.m.* wink. **en un ~**, in a flash.

clinique /klinik/ *a.* clinical. —*n.f.* (private) clinic.

clinquant, ~e /klɛ̃kɑ̃, -t/ *a.* showy. —*n.m.* (*lamelles*) tinsel.

clique /klik/ *n.f.* clique; (*mus., mil.*) band.

cliquet|er /klikte/ *v.i.* clink. **~is** *n.m.* clink(ing).

clivage /klivaʒ/ *n.m.* cleavage.

clochard, ~e /klɔʃar, -d/ *n.m., f.* tramp.

cloch|e¹ /klɔʃ/ *n.f.* bell. **~ette** *n.f.* bell.

cloche² /klɔʃ/ *n.f.* (*fam.*) idiot.

cloche-pied (à) /(a)klɔʃpje/ *adv.* hopping on one foot.

clocher¹ /klɔʃe/ *n.m.* bell-tower; (*pointu*) steeple. **de ~**, parochial.

clocher² /klɔʃe/ *v.i.* (*fam.*) be wrong.

cloison /klwazɔ̃/ *n.f.* partition; (*fig.*) barrier. **~ner** /-ɔne/ *v.t.* partition; (*personne*) cut off.

cloître /klwatr/ *n.m.* cloister.

cloîtrer (se) /(sə)klwatre/ *v. pr.* shut o.s. away.

clopin-clopant /klɔpɛ̃klɔpɑ̃/ *adv.* hobbling.

cloque /klɔk/ *n.f.* blister.

clore /klɔr/ *v.t.* close.

clos, ~e /klo, -z/ *a.* closed.

clôtur|e /klotyr/ *n.f.* fence; (*fermeture*) closure. **~er** *v.t.* enclose; (*festival, séance, etc.*) close.

clou /klu/ *n.m.* nail; (*furoncle*) boil; (*de spectacle*) star attraction. **~ de girofle**, clove. **les ~s**, (*passage*) zebra *ou* pedestrian crossing. **~er** *v.t.* nail down; (*fig.*) pin down. **~er qn. au lit**, keep s.o. confined to his bed.

clouté /klute/ *a.* studded.

clown /klun/ *n.m.* clown.

club /klœb/ *n.m.* club.

coaguler /kɔagyle/ *v.t./i.*, **se ~** *v. pr.* coagulate.

coaliser (se) /(sə)kɔalize/ *v. pr.* join forces.

coalition /kɔalisjɔ̃/ *n.f.* coalition.

coasser /kɔase/ *v.i.* croak.

cobaye /kɔbaj/ *n.m.* guinea-pig.

cocaïne /kɔkain/ *n.f.* cocaine.

cocarde /kɔkard/ *n.f.* rosette.

cocard|ier, ~ière /kɔkardje, -jɛr/ *a.* chauvinistic.

cocasse /kɔkas/ *a.* comical.

coccinelle /kɔksinɛl/ *n.f.* ladybird; (*Amer.*) ladybug.

cocher¹ /kɔʃe/ *v.t.* tick (off), check.

cocher² /kɔʃe/ *n.m.* coachman.

cochon, ~ne /kɔʃɔ̃, -ɔn/ *n.m.* pig. —*n.m., f.* (*personne*: *fam.*) pig. —*a.* (*fam.*) filthy. **~nerie** /-ɔnri/ *n.f.*

(*saleté*: *fam.*) filth; (*marchandise*: *fam.*) rubbish.

cocktail /kɔktɛl/ *n.m.* cocktail; (*réunion*) cocktail party.

cocon /kɔkɔ̃/ *n.m.* cocoon.

cocotier /kɔkɔtje/ *n.m.* coconut palm.

cocotte /kɔkɔt/ *n.f.* (*marmite*) casserole. ∼ **minute**, (P.) pressure-cooker. **ma** ∼, (*fam.*) my sweet, my dear.

cocu /kɔky/ *n.m.* (*fam.*) cuckold.

code /kɔd/ *n.m.* code. ∼**s, phares** ∼, dipped headlights. ∼ **de la route**, Highway Code. **se mettre en** ∼, dip one's headlights.

coder /kɔde/ *v.t.* code.

codifier /kɔdifje/ *v.t.* codify.

coéquip|ier, ∼**ière** /kɔekipje, -jɛr/ *n.m., f.* team-mate.

cœur /kœr/ *n.m.* heart; (*cartes*) hearts. **à** ∼ **ouvert**, (*opération*) open-heart; (*parler*) freely. **avoir bon** ∼, be kindhearted. **de bon** ∼, with a good heart. **par** ∼, by heart.

coexist|er /kɔɛgziste/ *v.i.* coexist. ∼**ence** *n.f.* coexistence.

coffre /kɔfr/ *n.m.* chest; (*pour argent*) safe; (*auto.*) boot; (*auto.*, *Amer.*) trunk. ∼**-fort** (*pl.* ∼**s-forts**) *n.m.* safe.

coffrer /kɔfre/ *v.t.* (*fam.*) lock up.

coffret /kɔfrɛ/ *n.m.* casket, box.

cognac /kɔnak/ *n.m.* cognac.

cogner /kɔne/ *v.t./i.* knock. **se** ∼ *v. pr.* knock o.s.

cohabit|er /kɔabite/ *v.i.* live together. ∼**ation** *n.f.* living together.

cohérent, ∼**e** /kɔerɑ̃, -t/ *a.* coherent.

cohésion /kɔezjɔ̃/ *n.f.* cohesion.

cohorte /kɔɔrt/ *n.f.* troop.

cohue /kɔy/ *n.f.* crowd.

coi, coite /kwa, -t/ *a.* silent.

coiffe /kwaf/ *n.f.* head-dress.

coiff|er /kwafe/ *v.t.* do the hair of; (*chapeau*) put on; (*surmonter*) cap. ∼**er qn. d'un chapeau**, put a hat on s.o. **se** ∼**er** *v. pr.* do one's hair. **se** ∼**er d'un chapeau**, put a hat on. ∼**é de**, wearing. **bien/mal** ∼**é**, with tidy/untidy hair. ∼**eur**, ∼**euse** *n.m., f.* hairdresser; *n.f.* dressing-table.

coiffure /kwafyr/ *n.f.* hairstyle; (*chapeau*) hat; (*métier*) hairdressing.

coin /kwɛ̃/ *n.m.* corner; (*endroit*) spot; (*cale*) wedge; (*pour graver*) die. **au** ∼ **du feu**, by the fireside. **dans le** ∼, locally. **du** ∼, local.

coincer /kwɛ̃se/ *v.t.* jam; (*caler*) wedge; (*attraper*: *fam.*) catch. **se** ∼ *v. pr.* get jammed.

coïncid|er /kɔɛ̃side/ *v.i.* coincide. ∼**ence** *n.f.* coincidence.

coing /kwɛ̃/ *n.m.* quince.

coite /kwat/ *voir* **coi.**

coke /kɔk/ *n.m.* coke.

col /kɔl/ *n.m.* collar; (*de bouteille*) neck; (*de montagne*) pass. ∼ **roulé**, polo-neck; (*Amer.*) turtle-neck.

coléoptère /kɔleɔptɛr/ *n.m.* beetle.

colère /kɔlɛr/ *n.f.* anger; (*accès*) fit of anger. **en** ∼, angry. **se mettre en** ∼, lose one's temper.

colér|eux, ∼**euse** /kɔlerø, -z/, ∼**ique** *adjs.* quick-tempered.

colifichet /kɔlifiʃɛ/ *n.m.* trinket.

colimaçon (en) /(ɑ̃)kɔlimasɔ̃/ *adv.* spiral.

colin /kɔlɛ̃/ *n.m.* (*poisson*) hake.

colique /kɔlik/ *n.f.* diarrhoea. ∼**s**, colic.

colis /kɔli/ *n.m.* parcel.

collabor|er /kɔlabɔre/ *v.i.* collaborate (**à**, on). ∼**er à**, (*journal*) contribute to. ∼**ateur**, ∼**atrice** *n.m., f.* collaborator; contributor. ∼**ation** *n.f.* collaboration (**à**, on); contribution (**à**, to).

collant, ∼**e** /kɔlɑ̃, -t/ *a.* skin-tight; (*poisseux*) sticky. —*n.m.* (*bas*) tights; (*de danseur*) leotard.

collation /kɔlasjɔ̃/ *n.f.* light meal.

colle /kɔl/ *n.f.* glue; (*en pâte*) paste; (*problème*: *fam.*) poser; (*scol.*, *argot*) detention.

collect|e /kɔlɛkt/ *n.f.* collection. ∼**er** *v.t.* collect.

collecteur /kɔlɛktœr/ *n.m.* (*égout*) main sewer.

collecti|f, ∼**ve** /kɔlɛktif, -v/ *a.* collective; (*billet*, *voyage*) group. ∼**vement** *adv.* collectively.

collection /kɔlɛksjɔ̃/ *n.f.* collection.

collectionn|er /kɔlɛksjɔne/ *v.t.* collect. ∼**eur**, ∼**euse** *n.m., f.* collector.

collectivité /kɔlɛktivite/ *n.f.* community.

coll|ège /kɔlɛʒ/ *n.m.* (secondary) school; (*assemblée*) college. ∼**égien**, ∼**égienne** *n.m., f.* schoolboy, school-girl.

collègue /kɔlɛg/ *n.m./f.* colleague.

coll|er /kɔle/ *v.t.* stick; (*avec colle liquide*) glue; (*affiche*) stick up; (*mettre*: *fam.*) stick; (*scol.*, *argot*) keep in; (*embarrasser*: *fam.*) stump. —*v.i.* stick (**à**, to); (*être collant*) be sticky. ∼**er à**, (*convenir à*) fit, correspond to. **être** ∼**é à**, (*examen*: *fam.*) fail.

collet /kɔlɛ/ *n.m.* (*piège*) snare. ∼

monté, prim and proper. **prendre qn. au ~**, collar s.o.

collier /kɔlje/ *n.m.* necklace; (*de chien*) collar.

colline /kɔlin/ *n.f.* hill.

collision /kɔlizjɔ̃/ *n.f.* (*choc*) collision; (*lutte*) clash.

colloque /kɔlɔk/ *n.m.* symposium.

colmater /kɔlmate/ *v.t.* seal; (*trou*) fill in.

colombe /kɔlɔ̃b/ *n.f.* dove.

Colombie /kɔlɔ̃bi/ *n.f.* Colombia.

colon /kɔlɔ̃/ *n.m.* settler; (*enfant*) child staying at a holiday camp.

colonel /kɔlɔnɛl/ *n.m.* colonel.

colon|ial, **~iale** (*m. pl.* **~iaux**) /kɔlɔnjal, -jo/ *a. & n.m., f.* colonial.

colon|ie /kɔlɔni/ *n.f.* colony. **~ de vacances**, children's holiday camp.

coloniser /kɔlɔnize/ *v.t.* colonize.

colonne /kɔlɔn/ *n.f.* column. **~ vertébrale**, spine. **en ~ par deux**, in double file.

color|er /kɔlɔre/ *v.t.* colour; (*bois*) stain. **~ant** *n.m.* colouring; stain. **~ation** *n.f.* (*couleur*) colour(ing).

colorier /kɔlɔrje/ *v.t.* colour (in).

coloris /kɔlɔri/ *n.m.* colour.

coloss|al (*m. pl.* **~aux**) /kɔlɔsal, -o/ *a.* colossal.

colosse /kɔlɔs/ *n.m.* giant.

colport|er /kɔlpɔrte/ *v.t.* hawk. **~eur**, **~euse** *n.m., f.* hawker.

colza /kɔlza/ *n.m.* rape(-seed).

coma /kɔma/ *n.m.* coma. **dans le ~**, in a coma.

combat /kɔ̃ba/ *n.m.* fight; (*sport*) match. **~s**, fighting.

combati|f, **~ve** /kɔ̃batif, -v/ *a.* eager to fight; (*esprit*) fighting.

combatt|re† /kɔ̃batr/ *v.t./i.* fight. **~ant**, **~ante** *n.m., f.* fighter; (*mil.*) combattant.

combien /kɔ̃bjɛ̃/ *adv.* **~ (de)**, (*quantité*) how much; (*nombre*) how many. **~ il a changé!**, (*comme*) how he has changed! **~ y a-t-il d'ici à . . .?**, how far is it to . . .?

combinaison /kɔ̃binɛzɔ̃/ *n.f.* combination; (*manigance*) scheme; (*de femme*) slip; (*bleu de travail*) boiler suit; (*Amer.*) overalls. **~ d'aviateur**, flying-suit.

combine /kɔ̃bin/ *n.f.* trick; (*fraude*) fiddle.

combiné /kɔ̃bine/ *n.m.* (*de téléphone*) receiver.

combiner /kɔ̃bine/ *v.t.* (*réunir*) combine; (*calculer*) devise.

comble[1] /kɔ̃bl/ *a.* packed.

comble[2] /kɔ̃bl/ *n.m.* height. **~s**, (*mansarde*) attic, loft. **c'est le ~!**, that's the last straw!

combler /kɔ̃ble/ *v.t.* fill; (*perte, déficit*) make good; (*désir*) fulfil; (*personne*) gratify. **~ qn. de cadeaux**/*etc.*, lavish gifts/*etc.* on s.o.

combustible /kɔ̃bystibl/ *n.m.* fuel.

combustion /kɔ̃bystjɔ̃/ *n.f.* combustion.

comédie /kɔmedi/ *n.f.* comedy. **~ musicale**, musical. **jouer la ~**, put on an act.

comédien, **~ne** /kɔmedjɛ̃, -jɛn/ *n.m., f.* actor, actress.

comestible /kɔmɛstibl/ *a.* edible. **~s** *n.m. pl.* foodstuffs.

comète /kɔmɛt/ *n.f.* comet.

comique /kɔmik/ *a.* comical; (*genre*) comic. *—n.m.* (*acteur*) comic; (*comédie*) comedy; (*côté drôle*) comical aspect.

comité /kɔmite/ *n.m.* committee.

commandant /kɔmɑ̃dɑ̃/ *n.m.* commander; (*armée de terre*) major. **~ (de bord)**, captain. **~ en chef**, Commander-in-Chief.

commande /kɔmɑ̃d/ *n.f.* (*comm.*) order. **~s**, (*d'avion etc.*) controls.

command|er /kɔmɑ̃de/ *v.t.* command; (*acheter*) order. *—v.i.* be in command. **~er à**, (*maîtriser*) control. **~er à qn. de**, command s.o. to. **~ement** *n.m.* command; (*relig.*) commandment.

commando /kɔmɑ̃do/ *n.m.* commando.

comme /kɔm/ *conj.* as. *—prép.* like. *—adv.* (*exclamation*) how. **~ ci comme ça**, so-so. **~ d'habitude**, **~ à l'ordinaire**, as usual. **~ il faut**, proper(ly). **~ pour faire**, as if to do. **~ quoi**, to the effect that. **qu'avez-vous ~ amis**/*etc.*?, what have you in the way of friends/*etc.*?

commémor|er /kɔmemɔre/ *v.t.* commemorate. **~ation** *n.f.* commemoration.

commenc|er /kɔmɑ̃se/ *v.t.* begin, start. **~er à faire**, begin *ou* start to do. **~ement** *n.m.* beginning, start.

comment /kɔmɑ̃/ *adv.* how. **~?**, (*répétition*) pardon?; (*surprise*) what? **~ est-il?**, what is he like?

commentaire /kɔmɑ̃tɛr/ *n.m.* comment; (*d'un texte*) commentary.

comment|er /kɔmãte/ *v.t.* comment on. **~ateur, ~atrice** *n.m., f.* commentator.

commérages /kɔmeraʒ/ *n.m. pl.* gossip.

commerçant, ~e /kɔmɛrsã, -t/ *a.* (*rue*) shopping; (*nation*) trading; (*personne*) business-minded. —*n.m., f.* shopkeeper.

commerce /kɔmɛrs/ *n.m.* trade, commerce; (*magasin*) business. **faire du ~,** trade.

commerc|ial (*m. pl.* **~iaux**) /kɔmɛrsjal, -jo/ *a.* commercial. **~ialiser** *v.t.* market.

commère /kɔmɛr/ *n.f.* gossip.

commettre† /kɔmɛtr/ *v.t.* commit.

commis /kɔmi/ *n.m.* (*de magasin*) assistant; (*de bureau*) clerk.

commissaire /kɔmisɛr/ *n.m.* (*sport*) steward. **~ (de police),** (police) superintendent. **~-priseur** (*pl.* **~s-priseurs**) *n.m.* auctioneer.

commissariat /kɔmisarja/ *n.m.* **~ (de police),** police station.

commission /kɔmisjɔ̃/ *n.f.* commission; (*course*) errand; (*message*) message. **~s,** shopping. **~naire** /-jɔnɛr/ *n.m.* errand-boy.

commod|e /kɔmɔd/ *a.* handy; (*facile*) easy. **pas ~e,** (*personne*) a difficult customer. —*n.f.* chest (of drawers). **~ité** *n.f.* convenience.

commotion /kɔmosjɔ̃/ *n.f.* **~ (cérébrale),** concussion. **~né** /-jɔne/ *a.* shaken.

commuer /kɔmɥe/ *v.t.* commute.

commun, ~e /kɔmœ̃, -yn/ *a.* common; (*effort, action*) joint; (*frais, pièce*) shared. —*n.f.* (*circonscription*) commune. **~s** *n.m. pl.* outhouses, outbuildings. **avoir** *ou* **mettre en ~,** share. **~al** (*m. pl.* **~aux**) /-ynal, -o/ *a.* of the commune, local. **~ément** /-ynemã/ *adv.* commonly.

communauté /kɔmynote/ *n.f.* community.

commune /kɔmyn/ *voir* **commun.**

communiant, ~e /kɔmynjã, -t/ *n.m., f.* (*relig.*) communicant.

communicati|f, ~ve /kɔmynikatif, -v/ *a.* communicative.

communication /kɔmynikasjɔ̃/ *n.f.* communication; (*téléphonique*) call. **~ interurbaine,** long-distance call.

commun|ier /kɔmynje/ *v.i.* (*relig.*) receive communion. **~ion** *n.f.* communion.

communiqué /kɔmynike/ *n.m.* communiqué.

communiquer /kɔmynike/ *v.t.* pass on, communicate; (*mouvement*) impart. —*v.i.* communicate. **se ~ à,** spread to.

communis|te /kɔmynist/ *a.* & *n.m./f.* communist. **~me** *n.m.* communism.

commutateur /kɔmytatœr/ *n.m.* (*électr.*) switch.

compact /kɔ̃pakt/ *a.* dense; (*voiture*) compact.

compagne /kɔ̃paɲ/ *n.f.* companion.

compagnie /kɔ̃paɲi/ *n.f.* company. **tenir ~ à,** keep company.

compagnon /kɔ̃paɲɔ̃/ *n.m.* companion; (*ouvrier*) workman. **~ de jeu,** playmate.

comparaître /kɔ̃parɛtr/ *v.i.* (*jurid.*) appear (*devant, before*).

compar|er /kɔ̃pare/ *v.t.* compare. **se ~er** *v. pr.* be compared. **~able** *a.* comparable. **~aison** *n.f.* comparison; (*littéraire*) simile. **~atif, ~ative** *a.* & *n.m.* comparative. **~é** *a.* comparative.

comparse /kɔ̃pars/ *n.m./f.* (*péj.*) stooge.

compartiment /kɔ̃partimã/ *n.m.* compartment. **~er** /-te/ *v.t.* divide up.

comparution /kɔ̃parysjɔ̃/ *n.f.* (*jurid.*) appearance.

compas /kɔ̃pa/ *n.m.* (pair of) compasses; (*boussole*) compass.

compassé /kɔ̃pase/ *a.* stilted.

compassion /kɔ̃pasjɔ̃/ *n.f.* compassion.

compatible /kɔ̃patibl/ *a.* compatible.

compatir /kɔ̃patir/ *v.i.* sympathize. **~ à,** share in.

compatriote /kɔ̃patrijɔt/ *n.m./f.* compatriot.

compens|er /kɔ̃pãse/ *v.t.* compensate for. **~ation** *n.f.* compensation.

compère /kɔ̃pɛr/ *n.m.* accomplice.

compéten|t, ~te /kɔpetã, -t/ *a.* competent. **~ce** *n.f.* competence.

compétiti|f, ~ve /kɔ̃petitif, -v/ *a.* competitive.

compétition /kɔ̃petisjɔ̃/ *n.f.* competition; (*sportive*) event. **de ~,** competitive.

compiler /kɔ̃pile/ *v.t.* compile.

complainte /kɔ̃plɛ̃t/ *n.f.* lament.

complaire (se) /(sə)kɔ̃plɛr/ *v. pr.* **se ~ dans,** delight in.

complaisan|t, ~te /kɔ̃plɛzã, -t/ *a.*

kind; (*indulgent*) indulgent. ～ce *n.f.* kindness; indulgence.

complément /kɔ̃plemɑ̃/ *n.m.* complement; (*reste*) rest. ～ (**d'objet**), (*gram.*) object. ～ **d'information**, further information. ～**aire** /-tɛr/ *a.* complementary; (*renseignements*) supplementary.

compl|et[1], ～**ète** /kɔ̃plɛ, -t/ *a.* complete; (*train, hôtel, etc.*) full. ～**ètement** *adv.* completely.

complet[2] /kɔ̃plɛ/ *n.m.* suit.

compléter /kɔ̃plete/ *v.t.* complete; (*agrémenter*) complement. **se** ～ *v. pr.* complement each other.

complex|e[1] /kɔ̃plɛks/ *a.* complex. ～**ité** *n.f.* complexity.

complex|e[2] /kɔ̃plɛks/ *n.m.* (*sentiment, bâtiments*) complex. ～**é** *a.* inhibited, hung up.

complication /kɔ̃plikɑsjɔ̃/ *n.f.* complication; (*complexité*) complexity.

complic|e /kɔ̃plis/ *n.m.* accomplice. ～**ité** *n.f.* complicity.

compliment /kɔ̃plimɑ̃/ *n.m.* compliment. ～**s**, (*félicitations*) congratulations. ～**er** /-te/ *v.t.* compliment.

compliqu|er /kɔ̃plike/ *v.t.* complicate. **se** ～**er** *v. pr.* become complicated. ～**é** *a.* complicated.

complot /kɔ̃plo/ *n.m.* plot. ～**er** /-ɔte/ *v.t./i.* plot.

comporter[1] /kɔ̃pɔrte/ *v.t.* contain; (*impliquer*) involve.

comport|er[2] (**se**) /(sə)kɔ̃pɔrte/ *v. pr.* behave; (*joueur*) perform. ～**ement** *n.m.* behaviour; (*de joueur*) performance.

composé /kɔ̃poze/ *a.* compound; (*guindé*) affected. —*n.m.* compound.

compos|er /kɔ̃poze/ *v.t.* make up, compose; (*chanson, visage*) compose; (*numéro*) dial. —*v.i.* (*scol.*) take an exam; (*transiger*) compromise. **se** ～**er de**, be made up *ou* composed of. ～**ant** *n.m.*, ～**ante** *n.f.* component.

composi|teur, ～**trice** /kɔ̃pozitœr, -tris/ *n.m.,f.* (*mus.*) composer.

composition /kɔ̃pozisjɔ̃/ *n.f.* composition; (*examen*) test, exam.

composter /kɔ̃pɔste/ *v.t.* (*billet*) punch.

compot|e /kɔ̃pɔt/ *n.f.* stewed fruit. ～**e de pommes**, stewed apples. ～**ier** *n.m.* fruit dish.

compréhensible /kɔ̃preɑ̃sibl/ *a.* understandable.

compréhensi|f, ～**ve** /kɔ̃preɑ̃sif, -v/ *a.* understanding.

compréhension /kɔ̃preɑ̃sjɔ̃/ *n.f.* understanding, comprehension.

comprendre† /kɔ̃prɑ̃dr/ *v.t.* understand; (*comporter*) comprise. **ça se comprend**, that is understandable.

comprimé /kɔ̃prime/ *n.m.* tablet.

compr|imer /kɔ̃prime/ *v.t.* compress; (*réduire*) reduce. ～**ession** *n.f.* compression; reduction.

compris, ～**e** /kɔ̃pri, -z/ *a.* included; (*d'accord*) agreed. ～ **entre**, (contained) between. **service** (**non**) ～, service (not) included, (not) including service. **tout** ～, (all) inclusive. **y** ～, including.

compromettre /kɔ̃prɔmɛtr/ *v.t.* compromise.

compromis /kɔ̃prɔmi/ *n.m.* compromise.

comptab|le /kɔ̃tabl/ *a.* accounting. —*n.m.* accountant. ～**ilité** *n.f.* accountancy; (*comptes*) accounts; (*service*) accounts department.

comptant /kɔ̃tɑ̃/ *adv.* (*payer*) (in) cash; (*acheter*) for cash.

compte /kɔ̃t/ *n.m.* count; (*facture, comptabilité*) account; (*nombre exact*) right number. ～**s**, (*justifications*) explanation. **à bon** ～, cheaply. **à son** ～, (*travailler*) for o.s., on one's own. **faire le** ～ **de**, count. **pour le** ～ **de**, on behalf of. **sur le** ～ **de**, about. ～ **à rebours**, countdown. ～**-gouttes** *n.m. invar.* (*méd.*) dropper. ～ **rendu**, report; (*de film, livre*) review.

compter /kɔ̃te/ *v.t.* count; (*prévoir*) reckon; (*facturer*) charge for; (*avoir*) have; (*classer*) consider. —*v.i.* (*calculer, importer*) count. ～ **avec**, reckon with. ～ **faire**, expect to do. ～ **parmi**, (*figurer*) be considered among. ～ **sur**, rely on.

compteur /kɔ̃tœr/ *n.m.* meter. ～ **de vitesse**, speedometer.

comptine /kɔ̃tin/ *n.f.* nursery rhyme; (*pour compter*) counting rhyme.

comptoir /kɔ̃twar/ *n.m.* counter; (*de café*) bar.

compulser /kɔ̃pylse/ *v.t.* examine.

comt|e, ～**esse** /kɔ̃t, -ɛs/ *n.m.,f.* count, countess.

comté /kɔ̃te/ *n.m.* county.

con, conne /kɔ̃, kɔn/ *a.* (*argot*) bloody foolish. —*n.m.,f.* (*argot*) bloody fool.

concave /kɔ̃kav/ *a.* concave.

concéder /kɔ̃sede/ *v.t.* grant, concede.

concentr|er /kɔ̃sɑ̃tre/ v.t., se ~er v. pr. concentrate. ~ation n.f. concentration. ~é a. concentrated; (lait) condensed; (personne) absorbed; n.m. concentrate.

concept /kɔ̃sɛpt/ n.m. concept.

conception /kɔ̃sɛpsjɔ̃/ n.f. conception.

concerner /kɔ̃sɛrne/ v.t. concern.

concert /kɔ̃sɛr/ n.m. concert. de ~, in unison.

concert|er /kɔ̃sɛrte/ v.t. organize, agree, prepare. se ~er v. pr. confer. ~é a. (plan etc.) concerted.

concerto /kɔ̃sɛrto/ n.m. concerto.

concession /kɔ̃sesjɔ̃/ n.f. concession; (terrain) plot.

concessionnaire /kɔ̃sesjɔnɛr/ n.m./f. (authorized) dealer.

concevoir† /kɔ̃svwar/ v.t. (imaginer, engendrer) conceive; (comprendre) understand.

concierge /kɔ̃sjɛrʒ/ n.m./f. caretaker.

concil|ier /kɔ̃silje/ v.t. reconcile. se ~ier v. pr. (s'attirer) win (over). ~iation n.f. conciliation.

concis, ~e /kɔ̃si, -z/ a. concise. ~ion /-zjɔ̃/ n.f. concision.

concitoyen, ~ne /kɔ̃sitwajɛ̃, -jɛn/ n.m., f. fellow citizen.

concl|ure† /kɔ̃klyr/ v.t./i. conclude. ~ure à, conclude in favour of. ~uant, ~uante a. conclusive. ~usion n.f. conclusion.

concombre /kɔ̃kɔ̃br/ n.m. cucumber.

concorde /kɔ̃kɔrd/ n.f. concord.

concord|er /kɔ̃kɔrde/ v.i. agree. ~ance n.f. agreement; (analogie) similarity. ~ant, ~ante a. in agreement.

concourir /kɔ̃kurir/ v.i. compete. ~ à, contribute towards.

concours /kɔ̃kur/ n.m. competition; (examen) competitive examination; (aide) aid; (de circonstances) combination.

concr|et, ~ète /kɔ̃krɛ, -t/ a. concrete. ~ètement adv. in concrete terms.

concrétiser /kɔ̃kretize/ v.t. give concrete form to. se ~ v. pr. materialize.

conçu /kɔ̃sy/ a. bien/mal ~, (appartement etc.) well/badly planned.

concurrenc|e /kɔ̃kyrɑ̃s/ n.f. competition. faire ~e à, compete with. ~er v.t. compete with.

concurrent, ~e /kɔ̃kyrɑ̃, -t/ n.m., f. competitor; (scol.) candidate. —a. competing.

condamn|er /kɔ̃dɑne/ v.t. (censurer, obliger) condemn; (jurid.) sentence; (porte) block up. ~ation n.f. condemnation; (peine) sentence. ~é a. (fichu) without hope, doomed.

condens|er /kɔ̃dɑse/ v.t., se ~er v. pr. condense. ~ation n.f. condensation.

condescendre /kɔ̃desɑ̃dr/ v.i. condescend (à, to).

condiment /kɔ̃dimɑ̃/ n.m. condiment.

condisciple /kɔ̃disipl/ n.m. classmate, schoolfellow.

condition /kɔ̃disjɔ̃/ n.f. condition. ~s, (prix) terms. à ~ de ou que, provided (that). sans ~, unconditional(ly). sous ~, conditionally. ~nel, ~nelle a. conditional.

conditionner /kɔ̃disjɔne/ v.t. condition; (emballer) package.

condoléances /kɔ̃dɔleɑ̃s/ n.f. pl. condolences.

conduc|teur, ~trice /kɔ̃dyktœr, -tris/ n.m., f. driver.

conduire† /kɔ̃dɥir/ v.t. lead; (auto.) drive; (affaire) conduct. —v.i. drive. se ~ v. pr. behave. ~ à, (accompagner à) take to.

conduit /kɔ̃dɥi/ n.m. (anat.) duct.

conduite /kɔ̃dɥit/ n.f. conduct; (auto.) driving; (tuyau) main. ~ à droite, (place) right-hand drive.

cône /kon/ n.m. cone.

confection /kɔ̃fɛksjɔ̃/ n.f. making. de ~, ready-made. la ~, the clothing industry. ~ner /-jɔne/ v.t. make.

confédération /kɔ̃federasjɔ̃/ n.f. confederation.

conférenc|e /kɔ̃ferɑ̃s/ n.f. conference; (exposé) lecture. ~e au sommet, summit conference. ~ier, ~ière n.m., f. lecturer.

conférer /kɔ̃fere/ v.t. give; (décerner) confer.

confess|er /kɔ̃fese/ v.t., se ~er v. pr. confess. ~eur n.m. confessor. ~ion n.f. confession; (religion) denomination. ~ionnal (pl. ~ionnaux) n.m. confessional. ~ionnel, ~ionnelle a. denominational.

confettis /kɔ̃feti/ n.m. pl. confetti.

confiance /kɔ̃fjɑ̃s/ n.f. trust. avoir ~ en, trust.

confiant, ~e /kɔ̃fjɑ̃, -t/ a. (assuré) confident; (sans défiance) trusting. ~ en ou dans, confident in.

confiden|t, ~te /kɔ̃fidɑ̃, -t/ n.m., f. confidant, confidante. ~ce n.f. confidence.

confidentiel, ~le /kɔ̃fidɑ̃sjɛl/ *a.* confidential.

confier /kɔ̃fje/ *v.t.* ~ **à qn.**, entrust s.o. with; (*secret*) confide to s.o. **se ~ à**, confide in.

configuration /kɔ̃figyrɑsjɔ̃/ *n.f.* configuration.

confiner /kɔ̃fine/ *v.t.* confine. —*v.i.* ~ **à**, border on. **se ~** *v. pr.* confine o.s. (**à, dans**, to).

confins /kɔ̃fɛ̃/ *n.m. pl.* confines.

confirm|er /kɔ̃firme/ *v.t.* confirm. **~ation** *n.f.* confirmation.

confis|erie /kɔ̃fizri/ *n.f.* sweet shop. **~eries**, confectionery. **~eur, ~euse** *n.m., f.* confectioner.

confis|quer /kɔ̃fiske/ *v.t.* confiscate. **~cation** *n.f.* confiscation.

confit, ~e /kɔ̃fi, -t/ *a.* (*culin.*) candied.

confiture /kɔ̃fityr/ *n.f.* jam.

conflit /kɔ̃fli/ *n.m.* conflict.

confondre /kɔ̃fɔ̃dr/ *v.t.* confuse, mix up; (*consterner, étonner*) confound. **se ~** *v. pr.* merge. **se ~ en excuses**, apologize profusely.

confondu /kɔ̃fɔ̃dy/ *a.* (*déconcerté*) overwhelmed, confounded.

conforme /kɔ̃fɔrm/ *a.* ~ **à**, in accordance with.

conformément /kɔ̃fɔrmemɑ̃/ *adv.* ~ **à**, in accordance with.

conform|er /kɔ̃fɔrme/ *v.t.* adapt. **se ~er à**, conform to. **~ité** *n.f.* conformity.

conformis|te /kɔ̃fɔrmist/ *a. & n.m./f.* conformist. **~me** *n.m.* conformism.

confort /kɔ̃fɔr/ *n.m.* comfort. **~able** /-tabl/ *a.* comfortable.

confrère /kɔ̃frɛr/ *n.m.* colleague.

confrérie /kɔ̃freri/ *n.f.* brotherhood.

confront|er /kɔ̃frɔ̃te/ *v.t.* confront; (*textes*) compare. **~ation** *n.f.* confrontation.

confus, ~e /kɔ̃fy, -z/ *a.* confused; (*gêné*) embarrassed.

confusion /kɔ̃fyzjɔ̃/ *n.f.* confusion; (*gêne*) embarrassment.

congé /kɔ̃ʒe/ *n.m.* holiday; (*arrêt momentané*) time off; (*mil.*) leave; (*avis de départ*) notice. **~ de maladie**, sick-leave. **jour de ~**, day off. **prendre ~ de**, take one's leave of.

congédier /kɔ̃ʒedje/ *v.t.* dismiss.

cong|eler /kɔ̃ʒle/ *v.t.* freeze. **~élateur** *n.m.* freezer.

congénère /kɔ̃ʒenɛr/ *n.m./f.* fellow creature.

congénit|al (*m. pl.* **~aux**) /kɔ̃ʒenital, -o/ *a.* congenital.

congère /kɔ̃ʒɛr/ *n.f.* snow-drift.

congestion /kɔ̃ʒɛstjɔ̃/ *n.f.* congestion. **~ cérébrale**, stroke, cerebral haemorrhage. **~ner** /-jɔne/ *v.t.* congest;, (*visage*) flush.

congrégation /kɔ̃gregɑsjɔ̃/ *n.f.* congregation.

congr|ès /kɔ̃grɛ/ *n.m.* congress. **~essiste** *n.m./f.* member of a congress, delegate.

conifère /kɔnifɛr/ *n.m.* conifer.

conique /kɔnik/ *a.* conic(al).

conjectur|e /kɔ̃ʒɛktyr/ *n.f.* conjecture. **~er** *v.t./i.* conjecture.

conjoint, ~e[1] /kɔ̃ʒwɛ̃, -t/ *n.m., f.* spouse.

conjoint, ~e[2] /kɔ̃ʒwɛ̃, -t/ *a.* joint. **~ement** /-tmɑ̃/ *adv.* jointly.

conjonction /kɔ̃ʒɔ̃ksjɔ̃/ *n.f.* conjunction.

conjoncture /kɔ̃ʒɔ̃ktyr/ *n.f.* circumstances; (*économique*) economic climate.

conjugaison /kɔ̃ʒygɛzɔ̃/ *n.f.* conjugation.

conjug|al (*m. pl.* **~aux**) /kɔ̃ʒygal, -o/ *a.* conjugal.

conjuguer /kɔ̃ʒyge/ *v.t.* (*gram.*) conjugate; (*efforts*) combine. **se ~** *v. pr.* (*gram.*) be conjugated.

conjur|er /kɔ̃ʒyre/ *v.t.* (*éviter*) avert; (*implorer*) entreat. **se ~er** *v. pr.* conspire. **~ation** *n.f.* conspiracy. **~é, ~ée** *n.m., f.* conspirator.

connaissance /kɔnɛsɑ̃s/ *n.f.* knowledge; (*personne*) acquaintance; (*science*) consciousness. **~s**, (*science*) knowledge. **faire la ~ de**, meet; (*personne connue*) get to know. **perdre ~**, lose consciousness. **sans ~**, unconscious.

connaisseur /kɔnɛsœr/ *n.m.* connoisseur.

connaître† /kɔnɛtr/ *v.t.* know; (*avoir*) have. **se ~** *v. pr.* (*se rencontrer*) meet. **faire ~**, make known. **s'y ~ à** *ou* **en**, know (all) about.

conne|cter /kɔnɛkte/ *v.t.* connect. **~xion** *n.f.* connection.

connexe /kɔnɛks/ *a.* related.

connivence /kɔnivɑ̃s/ *n.f.* connivance.

connotation /kɔnɔtɑsjɔ̃/ *n.f.* connotation.

connu /kɔny/ *a.* well-known.

conquér|ir /kɔ̃kerir/ v.t. conquer. **~ant, ~ante** n.m., f. conqueror.

conquête /kɔ̃kɛt/ n.f. conquest.

consacrer /kɔ̃sakre/ v.t. devote; (relig.) consecrate; (sanctionner) establish. **se ~** v. pr. devote o.s. (à, to).

consciemment /kɔ̃sjamɑ̃/ adv. consciously.

conscience /kɔ̃sjɑ̃s/ n.f. conscience; (perception) consciousness. **avoir/ prendre ~ de**, be/become aware of. **perdre ~**, lose consciousness.

consciencieu|x, ~se /kɔ̃sjɑ̃sjø, -z/ a. conscientious.

conscient, ~e /kɔ̃sjɑ̃, -t/ a. conscious. **~ de**, aware ou conscious of.

conscription /kɔ̃skripsjɔ̃/ n.f. conscription.

conscrit /kɔ̃skri/ n.m. conscript.

consécration /kɔ̃sekrasjɔ̃/ n.f. consecration.

consécuti|f, ~ve /kɔ̃sekytif, -v/ a. consecutive. **~f à**, following upon. **~vement** adv. consecutively.

conseil /kɔ̃sɛj/ n.m. (piece of) advice; (assemblée) council, committee; (séance) meeting; (personne) consultant. **~ d'administration**, board of directors. **~ des ministres**, Cabinet. **~ municipal**, town council.

conseiller[1] /kɔ̃seje/ v.t. advise. **~ à qn. de**, advise s.o. to. **~ qch. à qn.**, recommend sth. to s.o.

conseill|er[2], **~ère** /kɔ̃seje, -ɛjɛr/ n.m., f. adviser, counsellor. **~er municipal**, town councillor.

consent|ir /kɔ̃sɑ̃tir/ v.i. agree (à, to). —v.t. grant. **~ement** n.m. consent.

conséquence /kɔ̃sekɑ̃s/ n.f. consequence. **en ~**, consequently; (comme il convient) accordingly.

conséquent, ~e /kɔ̃sekɑ̃, -t/ a. logical; (important: fam.) sizeable. **par ~**, consequently.

conserva|teur, ~trice /kɔ̃sɛrvatœr, -tris/ a. conservative. —n.m., f. (pol.) conservative. —n.m. (de musée) curator. **~tisme** n.m. conservatism.

conservatoire /kɔ̃sɛrvatwar/ n.m. academy.

conserve /kɔ̃sɛrv/ n.f. tinned ou canned food. **en ~**, tinned, canned.

conserv|er /kɔ̃sɛrve/ v.t. keep; (en bon état) preserve; (culin.) preserve. **se ~er** v. pr. (culin.) keep. **~ation** n.f. preservation.

considérable /kɔ̃siderabl/ a. considerable.

considération /kɔ̃siderasjɔ̃/ n.f. consideration; (respect) regard. **prendre en ~**, take into consideration.

considérer /kɔ̃sidere/ v.t. consider; (respecter) esteem. **~ comme**, consider to be.

consigne /kɔ̃siɲ/ n.f. (de gare) left luggage (office); (Amer.) (baggage) checkroom; (scol.) detention; (somme) deposit; (ordres) orders. **~ automatique**, (left-luggage) lockers; (Amer.) (baggage) lockers.

consigner /kɔ̃siɲe/ v.t. (comm.) charge a deposit on; (écrire) record; (élève) keep in; (soldat) confine.

consistan|t, ~te /kɔ̃sistɑ̃, -t/ a. solid; (épais) thick. **~ce** n.f. consistency; (fig.) solidity.

consister /kɔ̃siste/ v.i. **~ en/dans**, consist of/in. **~ à faire**, consist in doing.

consol|er /kɔ̃sɔle/ v.t. console. **se ~er** v. pr. be consoled (de, for). **~ation** n.f. consolation.

consolider /kɔ̃sɔlide/ v.t. strengthen; (fig.) consolidate.

consomma|teur, ~trice /kɔ̃sɔmatœr, -tris/ n.m., f. (comm.) consumer; (dans un café) customer.

consommé[1] /kɔ̃sɔme/ a. consummate.

consommé[2] /kɔ̃sɔme/ n.m. (bouillon) consommé.

consomm|er /kɔ̃sɔme/ v.t. consume; (user) use, consume; (mariage) consummate. —v.i. drink. **~ation** n.f. consumption; consummation; (boisson) drink. **de ~ation**, (comm.) consumer.

consonne /kɔ̃sɔn/ n.f. consonant.

consortium /kɔ̃sɔrsjɔm/ n.m. consortium.

conspir|er /kɔ̃spire/ v.i. conspire. **~ateur, ~atrice** n.m., f. conspirator. **~ation** n.f. conspiracy.

conspuer /kɔ̃spɥe/ v.t. boo.

const|ant, ~ante /kɔ̃stɑ̃, -t/ a. constant. **~amment** /-amɑ̃/ adv. constantly. **~ance** n.f. constancy.

constat /kɔ̃sta/ n.m. (official) report.

constat|er /kɔ̃state/ v.t. note; (certifier) certify. **~ation** n.f. observation.

constellation /kɔ̃stelasjɔ̃/ n.f. constellation.

constellé /kɔ̃stele/ a. **~ de**, studded with.

constern|er /kɔ̃stɛrne/ v.t. dismay. **~ation** n.f. dismay.

constip|é /kɔ̃stipe/ a. constipated; (fig.) stilted. **~ation** n.f. constipation.

constituer /kɔ̃stitɥe/ v.t. make up, constitute; (organiser) form; (être) constitute. **se ~ prisonnier**, give o.s. up.

constituti|f, ~ve /kɔ̃stitytif, -v/ a. constituent.

constitution /kɔ̃stitysjɔ̃/ n.f. formation; (d'une équipe) composition; (pol., méd.) constitution. **~nel, ~nelle** /-jɔnɛl/ a. constitutional.

constructeur /kɔ̃stryktœr/ n.m. manufacturer.

constructi|f, ~ve /kɔ̃stryktif, -v/ a. constructive.

constr|uire† /kɔ̃strɥir/ v.t. build; (système, phrase, etc.) construct. **~uction** n.f. building; (structure) construction.

consul /kɔ̃syl/ n.m. consul. **~aire** a. consular. **~at** n.m. consulate.

consult|er /kɔ̃sylte/ v.t. consult. —v.i. (médecin) hold surgery; (Amer.) hold office hours. **se ~er** v. pr. confer. **~ation** n.f. consultation; (réception: méd.) surgery; (Amer.) office.

consumer /kɔ̃syme/ v.t. consume. **se ~** v. pr. be consumed.

contact /kɔ̃takt/ n.m. contact; (toucher) touch. **mettre/couper le ~**, (auto.) switch on/off the ignition. **prendre ~ avec**, get in touch with. **~er** v.t. contact.

contag|ieux, ~ieuse /kɔ̃taʒjø, -z/ a. contagious. **~ion** n.f. contagion.

container /kɔ̃tɛnɛr/ n.m. container.

contamin|er /kɔ̃tamine/ v.t. contaminate. **~ation** n.f. contamination.

conte /kɔ̃t/ n.m. tale.

contempl|er /kɔ̃tɑ̃ple/ v.t. contemplate. **~ation** n.f. contemplation.

contemporain, ~e /kɔ̃tɑ̃pɔrɛ̃, -ɛn/ a. & n.m., f. contemporary.

contenance /kɔ̃tnɑ̃s/ n.f. (contenu) capacity; (allure) bearing; (sangfroid) composure.

contenant /kɔ̃tnɑ̃/ n.m. container.

contenir† /kɔ̃tnir/ v.t. contain; (avoir une capacité de) hold. **se ~** v. pr. contain o.s.

content, ~e /kɔ̃tɑ̃, -t/ a. pleased (de, with). **~ de faire**, pleased to do.

content|er /kɔ̃tɑ̃te/ v.t. satisfy. **se ~er de**, content o.s. with. **~ement** n.m. contentment.

contentieux /kɔ̃tɑ̃sjø/ n.m. matters in dispute; (service) legal department.

contenu /kɔ̃tny/ n.m. (de contenant) contents; (de texte) content.

conter /kɔ̃te/ v.t. tell, relate.

contestataire /kɔ̃tɛstatɛr/ n.m./f. protester.

conteste (sans) /(sɑ̃)kɔ̃tɛst/ adv. indisputably.

contest|er /kɔ̃tɛste/ v.t. dispute; (univ.) protest against. —v.i. protest. **~able** a. debatable. **~ation** n.f. dispute; (univ.) protest.

conteu|r, ~se /kɔ̃tœr, -øz/ n.m., f. story-teller.

contexte /kɔ̃tɛkst/ n.m. context.

contigu, ~ë /kɔ̃tigy/ a. adjacent (à, to).

continent /kɔ̃tinɑ̃/ n.m. continent. **~al** (m. pl. **~aux**) /-tal, -to/ a. continental.

contingences /kɔ̃tɛ̃ʒɑ̃s/ n.f. pl. contingencies.

contingent /kɔ̃tɛ̃ʒɑ̃/ n.m. (mil.) contingent; (comm.) quota.

continu /kɔ̃tiny/ a. continuous.

continuel, ~le /kɔ̃tinɥɛl/ a. continual. **~lement** adv. continually.

contin|uer /kɔ̃tinɥe/ v.t. continue. —v.i. continue, go on. **~uer à ou de faire**, carry on ou go on ou continue doing. **~uation** n.f. continuation.

continuité /kɔ̃tinɥite/ n.f. continuity.

contorsion /kɔ̃tɔrsjɔ̃/ n.f. contortion.

contour /kɔ̃tur/ n.m. outline, contour. **~s**, (d'une route etc.) twists and turns, bends.

contourner /kɔ̃turne/ v.t. go round; (difficulté) get round.

contracepti|f, ~ve /kɔ̃trasɛptif, -v/ a. & n.m. contraceptive.

contraception /kɔ̃trasɛpsjɔ̃/ n.f. contraception.

contract|er /kɔ̃trakte/ v.t. (maladie, dette) contract; (muscle) tense, contract. **se ~er** v. pr. contract. **~é** a. tense. **~ion** /-ksjɔ̃/ n.f. contraction.

contractuel, ~le /kɔ̃traktɥɛl/ n.m., f. (agent) traffic warden.

contradiction /kɔ̃tradiksjɔ̃/ n.f. contradiction.

contradictoire /kɔ̃tradiktwar/ a. contradictory; (débat) open.

contraignant, ~e /kɔ̃trɛɲɑ̃, -t/ a. restricting.

contraindre† /kɔ̃trɛ̃dr/ v.t. compel.

contraint, ~e /kɔ̃trɛ̃, -t/ a. constrained. —n.f. constraint.

contraire /kɔ̃trɛr/ *a.* & *n.m.* opposite. ～ **à,** contrary to. **au ～,** on the contrary. ～**ment** *adv.* ～**ment à,** contrary to.

contralto /kɔ̃tralto/ *n.m.* contralto.

contrar|ier /kɔ̃trarje/ *v.t.* annoy; (*action*) frustrate. ～**iété** *n.f.* annoyance.

contrast|e /kɔ̃trast/ *n.m.* contrast. ～**er** *v.i.* contrast.

contrat /kɔ̃tra/ *n.m.* contract.

contravention /kɔ̃travɑ̃sjɔ̃/ *n.f.* (parking-)ticket. **en ～,** in contravention (**à,** of).

contre /kɔ̃tr(ə)/ *prép.* against; (*en échange de*) for. **tout ～,** close by. ～**attaque** *n.f.,* ～**attaquer** *v.t.* counterattack. ～**balancer** *v.t.* counterbalance. **à ～-jour** *adv.* against the (sun)light. ～**offensive** *n.f.* counteroffensive. **prendre le ～-pied,** do the opposite; (*opinion*) take the opposite view. **à ～-pied** *adv.* (*sport*) on the wrong foot. ～**-plaqué** *n.m.* plywood. ～**-révolution** *n.f.* counter-revolution. ～**-torpilleur** *n.m.* destroyer.

contreband|e /kɔ̃trəbɑ̃d/ *n.f.* contraband. **faire la ～e de, passer en ～e,** smuggle. ～**ier** *n.m.* smuggler.

contrebas (en) /(ɑ̃)kɔ̃trəba/ *adv.* & *prép.* **en ～ (de),** below.

contrebasse /kɔ̃trəbas/ *n.f.* double-bass.

contrecarrer /kɔ̃trəkare/ *v.t.* thwart.

contrecœur (à) /(a)kɔ̃trəkœr/ *adv.* reluctantly.

contrecoup /kɔ̃trəku/ *n.m.* consequence.

contredire† /kɔ̃trədir/ *v.t.* contradict. **se ～** *v. pr.* contradict o.s.

contrée /kɔ̃tre/ *n.f.* region, land.

contrefaçon /kɔ̃trəfasɔ̃/ *n.f.* (*objet imité, action*) forgery.

contrefaire /kɔ̃trəfɛr/ *v.t.* (*falsifier*) forge; (*parodier*) mimic; (*déguiser*) disguise.

contrefait, ～**e** /kɔ̃trəfɛ -t/ *a.* deformed.

contreforts /kɔ̃trəfɔr/ *n.m. pl.* foothills.

contremaître /kɔ̃trəmɛtr/ *n.m.* foreman.

contrepartie /kɔ̃trəparti/ *n.f.* compensation.

contrepoids /kɔ̃trəpwa/ *n.m.* counterbalance.

contrer /kɔ̃tre/ *v.t.* counter.

contresens /kɔ̃trəsɑ̃s/ *n.m.* misinter-

pretation; (*absurdité*) nonsense. **à ～,** the wrong way.

contresigner /kɔ̃trəsiɲe/ *v.t.* countersign.

contretemps /kɔ̃trətɑ̃/ *n.m.* hitch. **à ～,** at the wrong time.

contrevenir /kɔ̃trəvnir/ *v.i.* ～ **à,** contravene.

contribuable /kɔ̃tribɥabl/ *n.m./f.* taxpayer.

contribuer /kɔ̃tribɥe/ *v.t.* contribute (**à,** to, towards).

contribution /kɔ̃tribysjɔ̃/ *n.f.* contribution. ～**s,** (*impôts*) taxes; (*administration*) tax office.

contrit, ～**e** /kɔ̃tri, -t/ *a.* contrite.

contrôl|e /kɔ̃trol/ *n.m.* check; (*des prix, d'un véhicule*) control; (*poinçon*) hallmark. ～**e de soi-même,** self-control. ～**e des changes,** exchange control. ～**e des naissances,** birth-control. ～**er** *v.t.* check; (*surveiller, maîtriser*) control. **se ～er** *v. pr.* control o.s.

contrôleu|r, ～**se** /kɔ̃trolœr, -øz/ *n.m., f.* (bus) conductor *ou* conductress; (*de train*) (ticket) inspector.

contrordre /kɔ̃trɔrdr/ *n.m.* change of orders.

controvers|e /kɔ̃trɔvɛrs/ *n.f.* controversy. ～**é** *a.* controversial.

contumace (par) /(par)kɔ̃tymas/ *adv.* in one's absence.

contusion /kɔ̃tyzjɔ̃/ *n.f.* bruise. ～**né** /-jɔne/ *a.* bruised.

convaincre† /kɔ̃vɛ̃kr/ *v.t.* convince. ～ **qn. de faire,** persuade s.o. to do.

convalescen|t, ～**te** /kɔ̃valesɑ̃, -t/ *a.* & *n.m., f.* convalescent. ～**ce** *n.f.* convalescence. **être en ～ce,** convalesce.

convenable /kɔ̃vnabl/ *a.* (*correct*) decent, proper; (*approprié*) suitable.

convenance /kɔ̃vnɑ̃s/ *n.f.* **à sa ～,** to one's satisfaction. **les ～s,** the proprieties.

convenir† /kɔ̃vnir/ *v.i.* be suitable. ～ **à** suit. ～ **de/que,** (*avouer*) admit (to)/ that. ～ **de,** (*s'accorder sur*) agree (up)on. **il convient de,** it is advisable to; (*selon les bienséances*) it would be right to.

convention /kɔ̃vɑ̃sjɔ̃/ *n.f.* convention. ～**s,** (*convenances*) convention. **de ～,** conventional. ～**nel,** ～**nelle** /-jɔnɛl/ *a.* conventional.

convenu /kɔ̃vny/ *a.* agreed.

converger /kɔ̃vɛrʒe/ *v.i.* converge.

convers|er /kɔ̃vɛrse/ *v.i.* converse. **~ation** *n.f.* conversation.

conver|tir /kɔ̃vɛrtir/ *v.t.* convert (**à**, to; **en**, into). **se ~tir** *v. pr.* be converted, convert. **~sion** *n.f.* conversion. **~tible** *a.* convertible.

convexe /kɔ̃vɛks/ *a.* convex.

conviction /kɔ̃viksjɔ̃/ *n.f.* conviction.

convier /kɔ̃vje/ *v.t.* invite.

convive /kɔ̃viv/ *n.m./f.* guest.

convocation /kɔ̃vɔkasjɔ̃/ *n.f.* summons to attend; (*d'une assemblée*) convening; (*document*) notification to attend.

convoi /kɔ̃vwa/ *n.m.* convoy; (*train*) train. **~ (funèbre),** funeral procession.

convoit|er /kɔ̃vwate/ *v.t.* desire, covet, envy. **~ise** *n.f.* desire, envy.

convoquer /kɔ̃vɔke/ *v.t.* (*assemblée*) convene; (*personne*) summon.

convoy|er /kɔ̃vwaje/ *v.t.* escort. **~eur** *n.m.* escort ship. **~eur de fonds,** security guard.

convulsion /kɔ̃vylsjɔ̃/ *n.f.* convulsion.

coopérati|f, ~ve /kɔɔperatif, -v/ *a.* co-operative. —*n.f.* co-operative (society).

coopér|er /kɔɔpere/ *v.i.* co-operate (**à**, in). **~ation** *n.f.* co-operation.

coopter /kɔɔpte/ *v.t.* co-opt.

coordination /kɔɔrdinasjɔ̃/ *n.f.* co-ordination.

coordonn|er /kɔɔrdɔne/ *v.t.* co-ordinate. **~ées** *n.f. pl.* co-ordinates; (*adresse*: *fam.*) particulars.

copain /kɔpɛ̃/ *n.m.* (*fam.*) pal.

copeau (*pl.* **~x**) /kɔpo/ *n.m.* (*lamelle de bois*) shaving.

cop|ie /kɔpi/ *n.f.* copy; (*scol.*) paper. **~ier** *v.t./i.* copy. **~ier sur,** (*scol.*) copy *ou* crib from.

copieu|x, ~se /kɔpjø, -z/ *a.* copious.

copine /kɔpin/ *n.f.* (*fam.*) pal.

copiste /kɔpist/ *n.m./f.* copyist.

copropriété /kɔprɔprijete/ *n.f.* co-ownership.

copulation /kɔpylasjɔ̃/ *n.f.* copulation.

coq /kɔk/ *n.m.* cock. **~-à-l'âne** *n.m. invar.* abrupt change of subject.

coque /kɔk/ *n.f.* shell; (*de bateau*) hull.

coquelicot /kɔkliko/ *n.m.* poppy.

coqueluche /kɔklyʃ/ *n.f.* whooping cough.

coquet, ~te /kɔkɛ, -t/ *a.* flirtatious; (*élégant*) pretty; (*somme*: *fam.*) tidy. **~terie** /-tri/ *n.f.* flirtatiousness.

coquetier /kɔktje/ *n.m.* egg-cup.

coquillage /kɔkijaʒ/ *n.m.* shellfish; (*coquille*) shell.

coquille /kɔkij/ *n.f.* shell; (*faute*) misprint. **~ Saint-Jacques,** scallop.

coquin, ~e /kɔkɛ̃, -in/ *a.* naughty. —*n.m.,* *f.* rascal.

cor /kɔr/ *n.m.* (*mus.*) horn. **~ (au pied),** corn.

cor|ail (*pl.* **~aux**) /kɔraj, -o/ *n.m.* coral.

Coran /kɔrɑ̃/ *n.m.* Koran.

corbeau (*pl.* **~x**) /kɔrbo/ *n.m.* (*oiseau*) crow.

corbeille /kɔrbɛj/ *n.f.* basket. **~ à papier,** waste-paper basket.

corbillard /kɔrbijar/ *n.m.* hearse.

cordage /kɔrdaʒ/ *n.m.* rope.

corde /kɔrd/ *n.f.* rope; (*d'arc, de violon, etc.*) string. **~ à linge,** washing line. **~ à sauter,** skipping-rope. **~ raide,** tightrope. **~s vocales,** vocal cords.

cordée /kɔrde/ *n.f.* roped party.

cord|ial (*m. pl.* **~iaux**) /kɔrdjal, -jo/ *a.* warm, cordial. **~ialité** *n.f.* warmth.

cordon /kɔrdɔ̃/ *n.m.* string, cord. **~-bleu** (*pl.* **~s-bleus**) *n.m.* first-rate cook. **~ de police,** police cordon.

cordonnier /kɔrdɔnje/ *n.m.* shoe mender.

Corée /kɔre/ *n.f.* Korea.

coreligionnaire /kɔrəliʒjɔnɛr/ *n.m./f.* person of the same religion.

coriace /kɔrjas/ *a.* (*aliment*) tough. —*a. & n.m.* tenacious and tough (person).

corne /kɔrn/ *n.f.* horn.

cornée /kɔrne/ *n.f.* cornea.

corneille /kɔrnɛj/ *n.f.* crow.

cornemuse /kɔrnəmyz/ *n.f.* bagpipes.

corner[1] /kɔrne/ *v.t.* (*page*) make dog-eared. —*v.i.* (*auto.*) hoot; (*auto.*, *Amer.*) honk.

corner[2] /kɔrnɛr/ *n.m.* (*football*) corner.

cornet /kɔrnɛ/ *n.m.* (paper) cone; (*crème glacée*) cornet, cone.

corniaud /kɔrnjo/ *n.m.* (*fam.*) nitwit.

corniche /kɔrniʃ/ *n.f.* cornice; (*route*) cliff road.

cornichon /kɔrniʃɔ̃/ *n.m.* gherkin.

corollaire /kɔrɔlɛr/ *n.m.* corollary.

corporation /kɔrpɔrasjɔ̃/ *n.f.* professional body.

corporel, ~le /kɔrpɔrɛl/ *a.* bodily; (*châtiment*) corporal.

corps /kɔr/ *n.m.* body; (*mil.*, *pol.*) corps. **~ à corps,** hand to hand. **~**

électoral, electorate. ∼ **enseignant,** teaching profession. **faire** ∼ **avec,** form part of.

corpulen|t, ∼**te** /kɔrpylɑ̃, -t/ *a.* stout. ∼**ce** *n.f.* stoutness.

correct /kɔrɛkt/ *a.* proper, correct; (*exact*) correct. ∼**ement** *adv.* properly; correctly.

correc|teur, ∼**trice** /kɔrɛktœr, -tris/ *n.m.,f.* (*scol.*) examiner.

correction /kɔrɛksjɔ̃/ *n.f.* correction; (*punition*) beating.

corrélation /kɔrelɑsjɔ̃/ *n.f.* correlation.

correspondan|t, ∼**te** /kɔrɛspɔ̃dɑ̃, -t/ *a.* corresponding. —*n.m.,* *f.* correspondent. ∼**ce** *n.f.* correspondence; (*de train, d'autobus*) connection.

correspondre /kɔrɛspɔ̃dr/ *v.i.* (*s'accorder, écrire*) correspond; (*chambres*) communicate.

corrida /kɔrida/ *n.f.* bullfight.

corridor /kɔridɔr/ *n.m.* corridor.

corrig|er /kɔriʒe/ *v.t.* correct; (*devoir*) mark, correct; (*punir*) beat; (*guérir*) cure. **se** ∼**er de,** cure o.s. of. ∼**é** *n.m.* (*scol.*) correct version, model answer.

corroborer /kɔrɔbɔre/ *v.t.* corroborate.

corro|der /kɔrɔde/ *v.t.* corrode. ∼**sion** /-ozjɔ̃/ *n.f.* corrosion.

corromp|re|t /kɔrɔ̃pr/ *v.t.* corrupt; (*soudoyer*) bribe. ∼**u** *a.* corrupt.

corrosi|f, ∼**ve** /kɔrozif, -v/ *a.* corrosive.

corruption /kɔrypsjɔ̃/ *n.f.* corruption.

corsage /kɔrsaʒ/ *n.m.* bodice; (*chemisier*) blouse.

corsaire /kɔrsɛr/ *n.m.* pirate.

Corse /kɔrs/ *n.f.* Corsica.

corse /kɔrs/ *a.* & *n.m.|f.* Corsican.

corsé /kɔrse/ *a.* (*vin*) full-bodied; (*scabreux*) spicy.

corset /kɔrsɛ/ *n.m.* corset.

cortège /kɔrtɛʒ/ *n.m.* procession.

corvée /kɔrve/ *n.f.* chore.

cosaque /kɔzak/ *n.m.* Cossack.

cosmétique /kɔsmetik/ *n.m.* hair oil.

cosmique /kɔsmik/ *a.* cosmic.

cosmonaute /kɔsmɔnot/ *n.m.|f.* cosmonaut.

cosmopolite /kɔsmɔpɔlit/ *a.* cosmopolitan.

cosmos /kɔsmɔs/ *n.m.* (*espace*) (outer) space; (*univers*) cosmos.

cosse /kɔs/ *n.f.* (*de pois*) pod.

cossu /kɔsy/ *a.* well-to-do.

costaud, ∼**e** /kɔsto, -d/ *a.* (*fam.*) strong. —*n.m.* (*fam.*) strong man.

costum|e /kɔstym/ *n.m.* suit; (*théâtre*) costume. ∼**é** *a.* dressed up.

cote /kɔt/ *n.f.* (*classification*) mark; (*en Bourse*) quotation; (*de cheval*) odds; (*de candidat, acteur*) rating. ∼ **d'alerte,** danger level.

côte /kot/ *n.f.* (*littoral*) coast; (*pente*) hill; (*anat.*) rib; (*de porc*) chop. ∼ **à côte,** side by side. **la C**∼ **d'Azur,** the (French) Riviera.

côté /kote/ *n.m.* side; (*direction*) way. **à** ∼, nearby; (*voisin*) next-door. **à** ∼ **de,** next to; (*comparé à*) compared to; (*cible*) wide of. **aux** ∼**s de,** by the side of. **de** ∼, aside; (*regarder*) sideways. **de ce** ∼, this way. **du** ∼ **de,** towards; (*proximité*) near; (*provenance*) from.

coteau (*pl.* ∼**x**) /kɔto/ *n.m.* hill.

côtelette /kotlɛt/ *n.f.* chop.

coter /kɔte/ *v.t.* (*comm.*) quote; (*apprécier, noter*) rate.

coterie /kɔtri/ *n.f.* clique.

côt|ier, ∼**ière** /kotje, -jɛr/ *a.* coastal.

cotis|er /kɔtize/ *v.i.* pay one's contributions (**à,** to); (*à un club*) pay one's subscription. **se** ∼**er** *v. pr.* club together. ∼**ation** *n.f.* contribution(s); subscription.

coton /kɔtɔ̃/ *n.m.* cotton. ∼ **hydrophile,** cotton wool.

côtoyer /kotwaje/ *v.t.* skirt, run along; (*fréquenter*) rub shoulders with; (*fig.*) verge on.

cotte /kɔt/ *n.f.* (*d'ouvrier*) overalls.

cou /ku/ *n.m.* neck.

couchage /kuʃaʒ/ *n.m.* sleeping arrangements.

couchant /kuʃɑ̃/ *n.m.* sunset.

couche /kuʃ/ *n.f.* layer; (*de peinture*) coat; (*de bébé*) nappy. ∼**s,** (*méd.*) childbirth. ∼**s sociales,** social strata.

coucher /kuʃe/ *n.m.* ∼ (**du soleil**), sunset. —*v.t.* put to bed; (*loger*) put up; (*étendre*) lay down. ∼ (**par écrit**), inscribe. —*v.i.* sleep. **se** ∼ *v. pr.* go to bed; (*s'étendre*) lie down; (*soleil*) set. **couché** *a.* in bed; (*étendu*) lying down.

couchette /kuʃɛt/ *n.f.* (*rail.*) couchette; (*naut.*) bunk.

coucou /kuku/ *n.m.* cuckoo.

coude /kud/ *n.m.* elbow; (*de rivière etc.*) bend. ∼ **à coude,** side by side.

cou-de-pied (*pl.* **cous-de-pied**) /kudpje/ *n.m.* instep.

coudoyer /kudwaje/ *v.t.* rub shoulders with.

coudre† /kudr/ *v.t./i.* sew.

couenne /kwan/ *n.f.* (*de jambon*) rind.

couette /kwɛt/ *n.f.* duvet, continental quilt.

couffin /kufɛ̃/ *n.m.* Moses basket.

couiner /kwine/ *v.i.* squeak.

coulant, ~e /kulɑ̃, -t/ *a.* (*indulgent*) easy-going.

coulée /kule/ *n.f.* ~ **de lave**, lava flow.

couler[1] /kule/ *v.i.* flow, run; (*fromage, nez*) run; (*fuir*) leak. —*v.t.* (*sculpture, métal*) cast; (*vie*) pass, lead. **se ~** *v. pr.* (*se glisser*) slip.

couler[2] /kule/ *v.t./i.* (*bateau*) sink.

couleur /kulœr/ *n.f.* colour; (*peinture*) paint; (*cartes*) suit. **~s**, (*teint*) colour. **de ~**, (*homme, femme*) coloured. **en ~s**, (*télévision, film*) colour.

couleuvre /kulœvr/ *n.f.* (grass *ou* smooth) snake.

couliss|e /kulis/ *n.f.* (*de tiroir etc.*) runner. **~es**, (*théâtre*) wings. **à ~e**, (*porte, fenêtre*) sliding. **~er** *v.i.* slide.

couloir /kulwar/ *n.m.* corridor; (*de bus*) gangway; (*sport*) lane.

coup /ku/ *n.m.* blow; (*choc*) knock; (*sport*) stroke; (*de crayon, chance*) stroke; (*de fusil, pistolet*) shot; (*fois*) time; (*aux échecs*) move. **à ~ sûr**, definitely. **après ~**, after the event. **~ de chiffon**, wipe (with a rag). **~ de coude**, nudge. **~ de couteau**, stab. **~ d'envoi**, kick-off. **~ d'état**, (*pol.*) coup. **~ de feu**, shot. **~ de fil**, phone call. **~ de filet**, haul. **~ de frein**, sudden braking. **~ de grâce**, finishing blow. **~ de main**, helping hand. **~ d'œil**, glance. **~ de pied**, kick. **~ de poing**, punch. **~ de sang**, (*méd.*) stroke. **~ de soleil**, sunburn. **~ de sonnette**, ring (on a bell). **~ de téléphone**, telephone call. **~ de tête**, wild impulse. **~ de tonnerre**, thunderclap. **~ de vent**, gust of wind. **~ franc**, free kick. **~ sur coup**, in rapid succession. **d'un seul ~**, in one go. **du premier ~**, first go. **sale ~**, dirty trick. **sous le ~ de**, under the influence of. **sur le ~**, immediately.

coupable /kupabl/ *a.* guilty. —*n.m./f.* culprit.

coupe[1] /kup/ *n.f.* cup; (*de champagne*) goblet; (*à fruits*) dish.

coupe[2] /kup/ *n.f.* (*de vêtement etc.*) cut; (*dessin*) section. **~ de cheveux**, haircut.

coupé /kupe/ *n.m.* (*voiture*) coupé.

coup|er /kupe/ *v.t./i.* cut; (*arbre*) cut

down; (*arrêter*) cut off; (*voyage*) break; (*appétit*) take away; (*vin*) water down. **se ~er** *v. pr.* cut o.s.; (*routes*) intersect. **~er la parole à**, cut short. **~e-papier** *n.m. invar.* paper-knife.

couperosé /kuproze/ *a.* blotchy.

couple /kupl/ *n.m.* couple.

coupler /kuple/ *v.t.* couple.

couplet /kuplɛ/ *n.m.* verse.

coupole /kupɔl/ *n.f.* dome.

coupon /kupɔ̃/ *n.m.* (*étoffe*) remnant; (*billet, titre*) coupon.

coupure /kupyr/ *n.f.* cut; (*billet de banque*) note; (*de presse*) cutting. **~ (de courant)**, power cut.

cour /kur/ *n.f.* (court)yard; (*de roi*) court; (*tribunal*) court. **~ (de récréation)**, playground. **~ martiale**, court martial. **faire la ~ à**, court.

courag|e /kuraʒ/ *n.m.* courage. **~eux, ~euse** *a.* courageous.

couramment /kuramɑ̃/ *adv.* frequently; (*parler*) fluently.

courant[1], **~e** /kurɑ̃, -t/ *a.* standard, ordinary; (*en cours*) current.

courant[2] /kurɑ̃/ *n.m.* current. **~ d'air**, draught. **dans le ~ de**, in the course of. **être/mettre au ~ de**, know/tell about; (*à jour*) be/bring up to date on.

courbatur|e /kurbatyr/ *n.f.* ache. **~é** *a.* aching.

courbe /kurb/ *n.f.* curve. —*a.* curved.

courber /kurbe/ *v.t./i.*, **se ~** *v. pr.* bend.

coureu|r, ~se /kurœr, -øz/ *n.m., f.* (*sport*) runner. **~r automobile**, racing driver.

courge /kurʒ/ *n.f.* marrow; (*Amer.*) squash.

courgette /kurʒɛt/ *n.f.* courgette; (*Amer.*) zucchini.

courir† /kurir/ *v.i.* run; (*se hâter*) rush; (*nouvelles etc.*) go round. —*v.t.* (*risque*) run; (*danger*) face; (*épreuve sportive*) run *ou* compete in; (*fréquenter*) do the rounds of; (*filles*) chase.

couronne /kurɔn/ *n.f.* crown; (*de fleurs*) wreath.

couronn|er /kurɔne/ *v.t.* crown. **~ement** *n.m.* coronation, crowning; (*fig.*) crowning achievement.

courrier /kurje/ *n.m.* post, mail; (*de journal*) column.

courroie /kurwa/ *n.f.* strap; (*techn.*) belt.

courroux /kuru/ *n.m.* wrath.

cours /kur/ *n.m.* (*déroulement*) course;

(*leçon*) class; (*série de leçons*) course; (*prix*) price; (*cote*) rate; (*allée*) avenue. **au ~ de**, in the course of. **avoir ~**, (*monnaie*) be legal tender; (*fig.*) be current. **~ d'eau**, river, stream. **~ magistral**, (*univ.*) lecture. **en ~**, current; (*travail*) in progress. **en ~ de route**, on the way.

course /kurs/ *n.f.* run(ning); (*épreuve de vitesse*) race; (*entre rivaux: fig.*) race; (*de projectile*) flight; (*voyage*) journey; (*commission*) errand. **~s**, (*achats*) shopping; (*de chevaux*) races.

cours|ier, ~ière /kursje, -jɛr/ *n.m., f.* (*chasseur*) messenger.

court¹, ~e /kur, -t/ *a.* short. —*adv.* short. **à ~ de**, short of. **pris de ~**, caught unawares. **~-circuit** (*pl.* **~s-circuits**) *n.m.* short circuit.

court² /kur/ *n.m.* **~ (de tennis)**, (tennis) court.

court|ier, ~ière /kurtje, -jɛr/ *n.m., f.* broker.

courtisan /kurtizɑ̃/ *n.m.* courtier.

courtisane /kurtizan/ *n.f.* courtesan.

courtiser /kurtize/ *v.t.* court.

courtois, ~e /kurtwa, -z/ *a.* courteous. **~ie** /-zi/ *n.f.* courtesy.

couscous /kuskus/ *n.m.* couscous.

cousin, ~e /kuzɛ̃, -in/ *n.m., f.* cousin. **~ germain**, first cousin.

coussin /kusɛ̃/ *n.m.* cushion.

coût /ku/ *n.m.* cost.

couteau (*pl.* **~x**) /kuto/ *n.m.* knife. **~ à cran d'arrêt**, flick-knife.

coutellerie /kutɛlri/ *n.f.* (*magasin*) cutlery shop.

coût|er /kute/ *v.t./i.* cost. **~e que coûte**, at all costs. **~eux, ~euse** *a.* costly.

coutum|e /kutym/ *n.f.* custom. **~ier, ~ière** *a.* customary.

coutur|e /kutyr/ *n.f.* sewing; (*métier*) dressmaking; (*points*) seam. **~ier** *n.m.* fashion designer. **~ière** *n.f.* dressmaker.

couvée /kuve/ *n.f.* brood.

couvent /kuvɑ̃/ *n.m.* convent; (*de moines*) monastery.

couver /kuve/ *v.t.* (*œufs*) hatch; (*personne*) pamper; (*maladie*) be coming down with, be sickening for. —*v.i.* (*feu*) smoulder; (*mal*) be brewing.

couvercle /kuvɛrkl/ *n.m.* lid, cover.

couvert¹, ~e /kuvɛr, -t/ *a.* covered (**de**, with); (*habillé*) covered up; (*ciel*) overcast. —*n.m.* (*abri*) cover. **à ~**,

(*mil.*) under cover. **à ~ de**, (*fig.*) safe from.

couvert² /kuvɛr/ *n.m.* (*à table*) place-setting; (*prix*) cover charge. **~s**, (*couteaux etc.*) cutlery. **mettre le ~**, lay the table.

couverture /kuvɛrtyr/ *n.f.* cover; (*de lit*) blanket; (*toit*) roofing. **~ chauffante**, electric blanket.

couveuse /kuvøz/ *n.f.* **~ (artificielle)**, incubator.

couvreur /kuvrœr/ *n.m.* roofer.

couvr|ir† /kuvrir/ *v.t.* cover. **se ~ir** *v. pr.* (*s'habiller*) cover up; (*se coiffer*) put one's hat on; (*ciel*) become overcast. **~e-chef** *n.m.* hat. **~e-feu** (*pl.* **~e-feux**) *n.m.* curfew. **~e-lit** *n.m.* bedspread.

cow-boy /kɔbɔj/ *n.m.* cowboy.

crabe /krab/ *n.m.* crab.

crachat /kraʃa/ *n.m.* spit(tle).

cracher /kraʃe/ *v.i.* spit; (*radio*) crackle. —*v.t.* spit (out).

crachin /kraʃɛ̃/ *n.m.* drizzle.

crack /krak/ *n.m.* (*fam.*) wizard, ace, prodigy.

craie /krɛ/ *n.f.* chalk.

craindre† /krɛdr/ *v.t.* be afraid of, fear; (*être sensible à*) be easily damaged by.

crainte /krɛt/ *n.f.* fear. **de ~ de/que**, for fear of/that.

crainti|f, ~ve /krɛtif, -v/ *a.* timid.

cramoisi /kramwazi/ *a.* crimson.

crampe /krɑ̃p/ *n.f.* cramp.

crampon /krɑ̃pɔ̃/ *n.m.* (*de chaussure*) stud.

cramponner (se) /(sə)krɑ̃pɔne/ *v. pr.* **se ~ à**, cling to.

cran /krɑ̃/ *n.m.* (*entaille*) notch; (*trou*) hole; (*courage: fam.*) pluck.

crâne /krɑn/ *n.m.* skull.

crâner /krɑne/ *v.i.* (*fam.*) swank.

crapaud /krapo/ *n.m.* toad.

crapul|e /krapyl/ *n.f.* villain. **~eux, ~euse** *a.* sordid, foul.

craqu|er /krake/ *v.i.* crack, snap; (*plancher*) creak; (*couture*) split; (*fig.*) break down. —*v.t.* **~er une allumette**, strike a match. **~ement** *n.m.* crack(ing), snap(ping); creak(ing); striking.

crass|e /kras/ *n.f.* grime. **~eux, ~euse** *a.* grimy.

cratère /kratɛr/ *n.m.* crater.

cravache /kravaʃ/ *n.f.* horsewhip.

cravate /kravat/ *n.f.* tie.

crawl /krol/ *n.m.* (*nage*) crawl.

crayeu|x, ~se /krɛjø, -z/ a. chalky.

crayon /krɛjɔ̃/ n.m. pencil. **~ (de couleur)**, crayon. **~ à bille**, ballpoint pen.

créanc|ier, ~ière /kreɑ̃sje, -jɛr/ n.m., f. creditor.

créa|teur, ~trice /kreatœr, -tris/ a. creative. —n.m., f. creator.

création /kreɑsjɔ̃/ n.f. creation; (comm.) product.

créature /kreatyr/ n.f. creature.

crèche /krɛʃ/ n.f. day nursery; (relig.) crib.

crédibilité /kredibilite/ n.f. credibility.

crédit /kredi/ n.m. credit; (banque) bank. **~s**, funds. **à ~**, on credit. **faire ~**, give credit (à, to). **~er** /-te/ v.t. credit. **~eur, ~euse** /-tœr, -tøz/ a. in credit; n.m., f. person whose account is in credit.

credo /kredo/ n.m. creed.

crédule /kredyl/ a. credulous.

créer /kree/ v.t. create.

crémation /kremɑsjɔ̃/ n.f. cremation.

crème /krɛm/ n.f. cream; (dessert) cream dessert. —a. invar. cream. —n.m. (café) **~**, white coffee. **~ à raser**, shaving-cream.

crémeu|x, ~se /kremø, -z/ a. creamy.

crém|ier, ~ière /kremje, -jɛr/ n.m., f. dairyman, dairywoman. **~erie** /kremri/ n.f. dairy.

créneau (pl. **~x**) /kreno/ n.m. (trou) gap, slot. **faire un ~**, park between two cars.

créole /kreɔl/ n.m./f. Creole.

crêpe[1] /krɛp/ n.f. (galette) pancake. **~rie** n.f. pancake shop.

crêpe[2] /krɛp/ n.m. (tissu) crêpe; (matière) crêpe (rubber); (de deuil) black band.

crépit|er /krepite/ v.i. crackle. **~ement** n.m. crackling.

crépu /krepy/ a. frizzy.

crépuscule /krepyskyl/ n.m. twilight, dusk.

crescendo /kreʃɛndo/ adv. & n.m. invar. crescendo.

cresson /kresɔ̃/ n.m. (water)cress.

crête /krɛt/ n.f. crest; (de coq) comb.

crétin, ~e /kretɛ̃, -in/ n.m., f. cretin.

creuser /krøze/ v.t. dig; (évider) hollow out; (fig.) go deeply into. **se ~ (la cervelle)**, (fam.) rack one's brains.

creuset /krøze/ n.m. (lieu) melting-pot.

creu|x, ~se /krø, -z/ a. hollow. —n.m. hollow; (de l'estomac) pit.

crevaison /krəvɛzɔ̃/ n.f. puncture.

crevasse /krəvas/ n.f. crack; (de glacier) crevasse; (de la peau) chap.

crève-cœur /krɛvkœr/ n.m. invar. heart-break.

crever /krəve/ v.t./i. burst; (pneu) puncture, burst; (exténuer: fam.) exhaust; (mourir: fam.) die; (œil) put out.

crevette /krəvɛt/ n.f. **~ (grise)**, shrimp. **~ (rose)**, prawn.

cri /kri/ n.m. cry.

criant, ~e /krijɑ̃, -t/ a. glaring.

criard, ~e /krijar, -d/ a. (couleur) garish; (voix) bawling.

crible /kribl/ n.m. sieve, riddle.

criblé /krible/ a. **~ de**, riddled with.

cric /krik/ n.m. (auto.) jack.

crier /krije/ v.i. shout, cry (out); (grincer) creak. —v.t. (ordre) shout (out).

crim|e /krim/ n.m. crime; (meurtre) murder. **~inalité** n.f. crime. **~inel, ~inelle** a. criminal; n.m., f. criminal; (assassin) murderer.

crin /krɛ̃/ n.m. horsehair.

crinière /krinjɛr/ n.f. mane.

crique /krik/ n.f. creek.

criquet /krikɛ/ n.m. locust.

crise /kriz/ n.f. crisis; (méd.) attack; (de colère) fit. **~ cardiaque**, heart attack.

crisp|er /krispe/ v.t., **se ~er** v. pr. tense; (poings) clench. **~ation** n.f. tenseness; (spasme) twitch. **~é** a. tense.

crisser /krise/ v.i. crunch; (pneu) screech.

crist|al (pl. **~aux**) /kristal, -o/ n.m. crystal.

cristallin, ~e /kristalɛ̃, -in/ a. (limpide) crystal-clear.

cristalliser /kristalize/ v.t./i., **se ~** v. pr. crystallize.

critère /kritɛr/ n.m. criterion.

critérium /kriterjɔm/ n.m. eliminating heat.

critique /kritik/ a. critical. —n.f. criticism; (article) review. —n.m. critic. **la ~**, (personnes) critics.

critiquer /kritike/ v.t. criticize.

croc /kro/ n.m. (dent) fang; (crochet) hook.

croc-en-jambe (pl. **crocs-en-jambe**) /krɔkɑ̃ʒɑ̃b/ n.m. = **croche-pied**.

croche /krɔʃ/ *n.f.* quaver. **double ∼,** semiquaver.

croche-pied /krɔʃpje/ *n.m.* **faire un ∼ à,** trip up.

crochet /krɔʃɛ/ *n.m.* hook; (*détour*) detour; (*signe*) (square) bracket. **faire au ∼,** crochet.

crochu /krɔʃy/ *a.* hooked.

crocodile /krɔkɔdil/ *n.m.* crocodile.

crocus /krɔkys/ *n.m.* crocus.

croire† /krwar/ *v.t./i.* believe (**à, en,** in); (*estimer*) think, believe (**que,** that).

croisade /krwazad/ *n.f.* crusade.

croisé /krwaze/ *a.* (*veston*) double-breasted. *—n.m.* crusader.

croisée /krwaze/ *n.f.* window. **∼ des chemins,** crossroads.

crois|er[1] /krwaze/ *v.t.*, **se ∼er** *v. pr.* cross; (*passant, véhicule*) pass (each other). **∼ement** *n.m.* crossing; passing; (*carrefour*) crossroads.

crois|er[2] /krwaze/ *v.i.* (*bateau*) cruise. **∼eur** *n.m.* cruiser. **∼ière** *n.f.* cruise.

croissan|t[1], **∼te** /krwasɑ̃, -t/ *a.* growing. **∼ce** *n.f.* growth.

croissant[2] /krwasɑ̃/ *n.m.* crescent; (*pâtisserie*) croissant.

croître† /krwatr/ *v.i.* grow; (*lune*) wax.

croix /krwa/ *n.f.* cross. **∼ gammée,** swastika. **C∼-Rouge,** Red Cross.

croque-monsieur /krɔkməsjø/ *n.m. invar.* toasted ham and cheese sandwich.

croque-mort /krɔkmɔr/ *n.m.* undertaker's assistant.

croqu|er /krɔke/ *v.t./i.* crunch; (*dessiner*) sketch. **∼ant, ∼ante** *a.* crunchy.

croquet /krɔkɛ/ *n.m.* croquet.

croquette /krɔkɛt/ *n.f.* croquette.

croquis /krɔki/ *n.m.* sketch.

crosse /krɔs/ *n.f.* (*de fusil*) butt; (*d'évêque*) crook.

crotte /krɔt/ *n.f.* droppings.

crotté /krɔte/ *a.* muddy.

crottin /krɔtɛ̃/ *n.m.* (horse) dung.

crouler /krule/ *v.i.* collapse; (*être ruiné*) crumble.

croupe /krup/ *n.f.* rump; (*de colline*) brow. **en ∼,** pillion.

croupier /krupje/ *n.m.* croupier.

croupir /krupir/ *v.i.* stagnate.

croustill|er /krustije/ *v.i.* be crusty. **∼ant, ∼ante** *a.* crusty; (*fig.*) spicy.

croûte /krut/ *n.f.* crust; (*de fromage*) rind; (*de plaie*) scab.

croûton /krutɔ̃/ *n.m.* (*bout de pain*) crust; (*avec potage*) croûton.

croyable /krwajabl/ *a.* credible.

croyan|t, ∼te /krwajɑ̃, -t/ *n.m., f.* believer. **∼ce** *n.f.* belief.

CRS *abrév.* (*Compagnies républicaines de sécurité*) French state security police.

cru[1] /kry/ *voir* **croire.**

cru[2] /kry/ *a.* raw; (*lumière*) harsh; (*propos*) crude. *—n.m.* vineyard; (*vin*) wine.

crû /kry/ *voir* **croître.**

cruauté /kryote/ *n.f.* cruelty.

cruche /kryʃ/ *n.f.* pitcher.

cruc|ial (*m. pl.* **∼iaux**) /krysjal, -jo/ *a.* crucial.

crucif|ier /krysifje/ *v.t.* crucify. **∼ixion** *n.f.* crucifixion.

crucifix /krysifi/ *n.m.* crucifix.

crudité /krydite/ *n.f.* (*de langage*) crudeness. **∼s,** (*culin.*) raw vegetables *ou* fruit.

crue /kry/ *n.f.* rise in water level. **en ∼,** in spate.

cruel, ∼le /kryɛl/ *a.* cruel.

crûment /krymɑ̃/ *adv.* crudely.

crustacés /krystase/ *n.m. pl.* shellfish.

crypte /kript/ *n.f.* crypt.

Cuba /kyba/ *n.m.* Cuba.

cubain, ∼e /kybɛ̃, -ɛn/ *a. & n.m., f.* Cuban.

cub|e /kyb/ *n.m.* cube. *—a.* (*mètre etc.*) cubic. **∼ique** *a.* cubic.

cueill|ir† /kœjir/ *v.t.* pick, gather; (*personne: fam.*) pick up. **∼ette** *n.f.* picking, gathering.

cuill|er, ∼ère /kɥijɛr/ *n.f.* spoon. **∼erée** *n.f.* spoonful.

cuir /kɥir/ *n.m.* leather. **∼ chevelu,** scalp.

cuirassé /kɥirase/ *n.m.* battleship.

cuire /kɥir/ *v.t./i.* cook; (*picoter*) smart. **∼ (au four),** bake. **faire ∼,** cook.

cuisine /kɥizin/ *n.f.* kitchen; (*art*) cookery, cooking; (*aliments*) cooking. **faire la ∼,** cook.

cuisin|er /kɥizine/ *v.t./i.* cook; (*interroger: fam.*) grill. **∼ier, ∼ière** *n.m., f.* cook; *n.f.* (*appareil*) cooker, stove.

cuisse /kɥis/ *n.f.* thigh; (*de poulet, mouton*) leg.

cuisson /kɥisɔ̃/ *n.m.* cooking.

cuit, ∼e /kɥi, -t/ *a.* cooked. **bien ∼,** well done *ou* cooked.

cuivr|e /kɥivr/ *n.m.* copper. **∼e**

(jaune), brass. ~es, (*mus.*) brass. ~é
a. coppery.

cul /ky/ *n.m.* (*derrière: fam.*) backside,
bum; (*de pot etc.*) bottom.

culbut|e /kylbyt/ *n.f.* somersault;
(*chute*) tumble. ~er *v.i.* tumble; *v.t.*
knock over.

cul-de-sac (*pl.* **culs-de-sac**) /kydsak/
n.m. cul-de-sac.

culinaire /kylinɛr/ *a.* culinary; (*recette*) cooking.

culminer /kylmine/ *v.i.* reach the
highest point.

culot[1] /kylo/ *n.m.* (*audace: fam.*)
nerve, cheek.

culot[2] /kylo/ *n.m.* (*fond: techn.*) base.

culotte /kylɔt/ *n.f.* (short) trousers;
(*sport*) shorts; (*de femme*) knickers;
(*Amer.*) panties. ~ (**de cheval**), (riding) breeches.

culpabilité /kylpabilite/ *n.f.* guilt.

culte /kylt/ *n.m.* cult, worship; (*religion*) religion; (*protestant*) service.

cultivé /kyltive/ *a.* cultured.

cultiv|er /kyltive/ *v.t.* cultivate;
(*plantes*) grow. ~**ateur,** ~**atrice**
n.m., f. farmer.

culture /kyltyr/ *n.f.* cultivation; (*de
plantes*) growing; (*agriculture*) farming; (*éducation*) culture. ~**s,** (*ter-
rains*) lands under cultivation. ~
physique, physical training.

culturel, ~**le** /kyltyrɛl/ *a.* cultural.

cumuler /kymyle/ *v.t.* (*fonctions*) hold
simultaneously.

cupide /kypid/ *a.* avaricious.

cur|e /kyr/ *n.f.* (course of) treatment,
cure. ~**able** *a.* curable.

curé /kyre/ *n.m.* (parish) priest.

cur|er /kyre/ *v.t.* clean. ~**e-dent** *n.m.*
toothpick. ~**e-pipe** *n.m.* pipe-cleaner.

curieu|x, ~**se** /kyrjø, -z/ *a.* curious.
—*n.m., f.* (*badaud*) onlooker.
~**sement** *adv.* curiously.

curiosité /kyrjozite/ *n.f.* curiosity; (*objet*) curio; (*spectacle*) unusual sight.

cutané /kytane/ *a.* skin.

cuti-réaction /kytireaksjɔ̃/ *n.f.* skin
test.

cuve /kyv/ *n.f.* tank.

cuvée /kyve/ *n.f.* (*de vin*) vintage.

cuvette /kyvɛt/ *n.f.* bowl; (*de lavabo*)
(wash-)basin; (*des cabinets*) pan,
bowl.

cyanure /sjanyr/ *n.m.* cyanide.

cybernétique /sibɛrnetik/ *n.f.* cybernetics.

cycl|e /sikl/ *n.m.* cycle. ~**ique** *a.*
cyclic(al).

cyclis|te /siklist/ *n.m./f.* cyclist. —*a.*
cycle. ~**me** *n.m.* cycling.

cyclomoteur /syklɔmɔtœr/ *n.m.*
moped.

cyclone /syklon/ *n.m.* cyclone.

cygne /siɲ/ *n.m.* swan.

cylindr|e /silɛ̃dr/ *n.m.* cylinder.
~**ique** *a.* cylindrical.

cylindrée /silɛ̃dre/ *n.f.* (*de moteur*)
capacity.

cymbale /sɛ̃bal/ *n.f.* cymbal.

cyni|que /sinik/ *a.* cynical. —*n.m.*
cynic. ~**sme** *n.m.* cynicism.

cyprès /siprɛ/ *n.m.* cypress.

cypriote /siprijɔt/ *a. & n.m./f.* Cypriot.

D

d' /d/ *voir* de.

d'abord /dabɔr/ *adv.* first; (*au début*) at first.

dactylo /daktilo/ *n.f.* typist. ∼- (**graphie**) *n.f.* typing. ∼**graphe** *n.f.* typist. ∼**graphier** *v.t.* type.

dada /dada/ *n.m.* hobby-horse.

dahlia /dalja/ *n.m.* dahlia.

daigner /deɲe/ *v.t.* deign.

daim /dɛ̃/ *n.m.* (fallow) deer; (*cuir*) suede.

dais /dɛ/ *n.m.* canopy.

dall|e /dal/ *n.f.* paving stone, slab. ∼**age** *n.m.* paving.

daltonien, ∼ne /daltɔnjɛ̃, -jɛn/ *a.* colour-blind.

dame /dam/ *n.f.* lady; (*cartes, échecs*) queen. ∼**s**, (*jeu*) draughts; (*jeu*: *Amer.*) checkers.

damier /damje/ *n.m.* draught-board; (*Amer.*) checker-board. **à ∼,** chequered.

damn|er /dane/ *v.t.* damn. ∼**ation** *n.f.* damnation.

dancing /dãsiŋ/ *n.m.* dance-hall.

dandiner (se) /(sə)dãdine/ *v. pr.* waddle.

Danemark /danmark/ *n.m.* Denmark.

danger /dãʒe/ *n.m.* danger. **en ∼,** in danger. **mettre en ∼,** endanger.

dangereu|x, ∼se /dãʒrø, -z/ *a.* dangerous.

danois, ∼e /danwa, -z/ *a.* Danish. —*n.m.,f.* Dane. —*n.m.* (*lang.*) Danish.

dans /dã/ *prép.* in; (*mouvement*) into; (*à l'intérieur de*) inside, in; (*approximation*) about. ∼ **dix jours,** in ten days' time. **prendre/boire/***etc.* ∼, take/drink/*etc.* out of *ou* from.

dans|e /dãs/ *n.f.* dance; (*art*) dancing. ∼**er** *v.t./i.* dance. ∼**eur, ∼euse** *n.m.,* *f.* dancer.

dard /dar/ *n.m.* (*d'animal*) sting.

darder /darde/ *v.t.* shoot, cast forth.

dat|e /dat/ *n.f.* date. ∼**e limite,** deadline. ∼**er** *v.t./i.* date. **à ∼er de,** as from.

datt|e /dat/ *n.f.* (*fruit*) date. ∼**ier** *n.m.* date-palm.

dauphin /dofɛ̃/ *n.m.* (*animal*) dolphin.

davantage /davãtaʒ/ *adv.* more; (*plus longtemps*) longer. ∼ **de,** more. ∼ **que,** more than; longer than.

de, d' */də, d/ *prép.* (*de + le = du,* *de + les = des*) of; (*provenance*) from; (*moyen, manière*) with; (*agent*) by. —*article* some; (*interrogation*) any, some. **le livre ∼ mon ami,** my friend's book. **un pont ∼ fer,** an iron bridge. **dix mètres ∼ haut,** ten metres high. **du pain,** (some) bread. **des fleurs,** (some) flowers.

dé /de/ *n.m.* (*à jouer*) dice; (*à coudre*) thimble. ∼**s,** (*jeu*) dice.

débâcle /debakl/ *n.f.* (*mil.*) rout.

déball|er /debale/ *v.t.* unpack. ∼**age** *n.m.* unpacking.

débandade /debãdad/ *n.f.* (headlong) flight.

débarbouiller /debarbuje/ *v.t.* wash the face of. **se ∼** *v. pr.* wash one's face.

débarcadère /debarkadɛr/ *n.m.* landing-stage.

débardeur /debardœr/ *n.m.* docker.

débarqu|er /debarke/ *v.t./i.* disembark, land; (*arriver*: *fam.*) turn up. ∼**ement** *n.m.* disembarkation.

débarras /debara/ *n.m.* junk room. **bon ∼!,** good riddance!

débarrasser /debarase/ *v.t.* clear (**de,** of). ∼ **qn. de,** take from s.o.; (*défaut, ennemi*) rid s.o. of. **se ∼ de,** get rid of, rid o.s. of.

débat /deba/ *n.m.* debate.

débattre†[1] /debatr/ *v.t.* debate.

débattre†[2] **(se)** /(sə)debatr/ *v. pr.* struggle (to get free).

débauch|e /deboʃ/ *n.f.* debauchery; (*fig.*) profusion. ∼**er**[1] *v.t.* debauch.

débaucher[2] /deboʃe/ *v.t.* (*licencier*) lay off.

débil|e /debil/ *a.* weak. —*n.m./f.* moron. ∼**iter** *v.t.* debilitate.

débit /debi/ *n.m.* (rate of) flow; (*de magasin*) turnover; (*élocution*) delivery; (*de compte*) debit. ∼ **de tabac,** tobacconist's shop.

débi|ter /debite/ *v.t.* cut up; (*fournir*) produce; (*vendre*) sell; (*dire*: *péj.*) spout; (*compte*) debit. ∼**teur, ∼trice** *n.m.,f.* debtor; *a.* (*compte*) in debit.

débl|ayer /debleje/ *v.t.* clear. ∼**aiement** *n.m.* clearing.

débloquer /deblɔke/ *v.t.* (*prix, salaires*) free.

déboires /debwar/ *n.m. pl.* disappointments.

déboiser /debwaze/ *v.t.* clear (of trees).

déboîter /debwate/ *v.i.* (*véhicule*) pull out. —*v.t.* (*membre*) dislocate.

débonnaire /debɔnɛr/ *a.* easy-going.

débord|er /debɔrde/ *v.i.* overflow. —*v.t.* (*dépasser*) extend beyond. ~**er de**, (*joie etc.*) be overflowing with. ~**é** *a.* snowed under (**de**, with). ~**ement** *n.m.* overflowing.

débouché /debuʃe/ *n.m.* opening; (*comm.*) outlet; (*sortie*) end, exit.

déboucher /debuʃe/ *v.t.* (*bouteille*) uncork; (*évier*) unblock. —*v.i.* emerge (**de**, from). ~ **sur**, (*rue*) lead into.

débourser /deburse/ *v.t.* pay out.

déboussolé /debusɔle/ *a.* (*fam.*) disorientated, disoriented.

debout /dəbu/ *adv.* standing; (*levé*, *éveillé*) up. **être** ~, **se tenir** ~, be standing, stand. **se mettre** ~, stand up.

déboutonner /debutɔne/ *v.t.* unbutton. **se** ~ *v. pr.* unbutton o.s.; (*vêtement*) come undone.

débraillé /debrɑje/ *a.* slovenly.

débrancher /debrɑ̃ʃe/ *v.t.* unplug, disconnect.

débray|er /debreje/ *v.i.* (*auto.*) declutch; (*faire grève*) stop work. ~**age** /debrɛjaʒ/ *n.m.* (*pédale*) clutch; (*grève*) stoppage.

débridé /debride/ *a.* unbridled.

débris /debri/ *n.m. pl.* fragments; (*détritus*) rubbish, debris.

débrouill|er /debruje/ *v.t.* disentangle; (*problème*) sort out. **se** ~**er** *v. pr.* manage. ~**ard**, ~**arde** *a.* (*fam.*) resourceful.

débroussailler /debrusaje/ *v.t.* clear (of brushwood).

débusquer /debyske/ *v.t.* drive out.

début /deby/ *n.m.* beginning. **faire ses** ~**s**, (*en public*) make one's début.

début|er /debyte/ *v.i.* begin; (*dans un métier etc.*) start out. ~**ant**, ~**ante** *n.m.*, *f.* beginner.

deçà (en) /(ɑ̃)dəsa/ *adv.* this side. —*prép.* **en** ~ **de**, this side of.

décacheter /dekaʃte/ *v.t.* open.

décade /dekad/ *n.f.* ten days; (*décennie*) decade.

décaden|t, ~**te** /dekadɑ̃, -t/ *a.* decadent. ~**ce** *n.f.* decadence.

décalcomanie /dekalkɔmani/ *n.f.* transfer; (*Amer.*) decal.

décal|er /dekale/ *v.t.* shift. ~**age** *n.m.*

(*écart*) gap. ~**age horaire**, time difference.

décalquer /dekalke/ *v.t.* trace.

décamper /dekɑ̃pe/ *v.i.* clear off.

décanter /dekɑ̃te/ *v.t.* allow to settle. **se** ~ *v. pr.* settle.

décap|er /dekape/ *v.t.* scrape down; (*surface peinte*) strip. ~**ant** *n.m.* chemical agent; (*pour peinture*) paint stripper.

décapiter /dekapite/ *v.t.* behead.

décapotable /dekapɔtabl/ *a.* convertible.

décapsul|er /dekapsyle/ *v.t.* take the cap off. ~**eur** *n.m.* bottle-opener.

décéd|er /desede/ *v.i.* die. ~**é** *a.* deceased.

déceler /desle/ *v.t.* detect; (*démontrer*) reveal.

décembre /desɑ̃br/ *n.m.* December.

décennie /deseni/ *n.f.* decade.

déc|ent, ~**ente** /desɑ̃, -t/ *a.* decent. ~**emment** /-amɑ̃/ *adv.* decently. ~**ence** *n.f.* decency.

décentraliser /desɑ̃tralize/ *v.t.* decentralize.

déception /desɛpsjɔ̃/ *n.f.* disappointment.

décerner /desɛrne/ *v.t.* award.

décès /desɛ/ *n.m.* death.

décevoir† /desvwar/ *v.t.* disappoint.

déchaîn|er /deʃene/ *v.t.* (*violence etc.*) unleash; (*enthousiasme*) arouse a good deal of. **se** ~**er** *v. pr.* erupt. ~**ement** /-ɛnmɑ̃/ *n.m.* (*de passions*) outburst.

déchanter /deʃɑ̃te/ *v.i.* lose one's high hopes, become disillusioned.

décharge /deʃarʒ/ *n.f.* (*salve*) volley of shots. ~ (**électrique**), electrical discharge. ~ (**publique**), rubbish tip.

décharg|er /deʃarʒe/ *v.t.* unload; (*arme*, *accusé*) discharge. ~**er de**, release from. **se** ~**er** *v. pr.* (*batterie*, *pile*) go flat. ~**ement** *n.m.* unloading.

décharné /deʃarne/ *a.* bony.

déchausser (se) /(sə)deʃose/ *v. pr.* take off one's shoes.

déchéance /deʃeɑ̃s/ *n.f.* decay.

déchet /deʃɛ/ *n.m.* (*reste*) scrap; (*perte*) waste. ~**s**, (*ordures*) refuse.

déchiffrer /deʃifre/ *v.t.* decipher.

déchiqueter /deʃikte/ *v.t.* tear to shreds.

déchir|ant, ~**ante** /deʃirɑ̃, -t/ *a.* heart-breaking. ~**ement** *n.m.* heartbreak; (*conflit*) split.

déchir|er /deʃire/ *v.t.* tear; (*lacérer*)

tear up; (*arracher*) tear off *ou* out; (*diviser*) tear apart; (*oreilles*: *fig.*) split. **se ～er** *v. pr.* tear. **～ure** *n.f.* tear.

déch|oir /deʃwar/ *v.i.* demean o.s. **～oir de**, (*rang*) lose, fall from. **～u** *a.* fallen.

décibel /desibɛl/ *n.m.* decibel.

décid|er /deside/ *v.t.* decide on; (*persuader*) persuade. **～er que/de**, decide that/to. *—v.i.* decide. **～er de qch.**, decide on sth. **se ～er** *v. pr.* make up one's mind (**à**, to). **～é** *a.* (*résolu*) determined; (*fixé*, *marqué*) decided. **～ément** *adv.* certainly.

décim|al, **～ale** (*m. pl.* **～aux**) /desimal, -o/ *a.* & *n.f.* decimal.

décimer /desime/ *v.t.* decimate.

décimètre /desimɛtr/ *n.m.* decimetre.

décisi|f, **～ve** /desizif, -v/ *a.* decisive.

décision /desizjɔ̃/ *n.f.* decision.

déclar|er /deklare/ *v.t.* declare; (*naissance*) register. **se ～er** *v. pr.* (*feu*) break out. **～er forfait**, (*sport*) withdraw. **～ation** *n.f.* declaration; (*commentaire politique*) statement.

déclasser /deklɑse/ *v.t.* (*coureur*) relegate; (*hôtel*) downgrade.

déclench|er /deklɑ̃ʃe/ *v.t.* (*techn.*) release, set off; (*lancer*) launch; (*provoquer*) trigger off. **se ～er** *v. pr.* (*techn.*) go off.

déclic /deklik/ *n.m.* click; (*techn.*) trigger mechanism.

déclin /deklɛ̃/ *n.m.* decline.

décliner[1] /dekline/ *v.i.* decline.

décliner[2] /dekline/ *v.t.* (*refuser*) decline; (*dire*) state.

déclivité /deklivite/ *n.f.* slope.

décocher /dekɔʃe/ *v.t.* (*coup*) fling; (*regard*) shoot.

décoder /dekɔde/ *v.t.* decode.

décoiffer /dekwafe/ *v.t.* (*ébouriffer*) disarrange the hair of. **se ～** *v. pr.* take off one's hat.

décoll|er[1] /dekɔle/ *v.i.* (*avion*) take off. **～age** *n.m.* take-off.

décoller[2] /dekɔle/ *v.t.* unstick.

décolleté /dekɔlte/ *a.* low-cut. *—n.m.* low neckline.

décolor|er /dekɔlɔre/ *v.t.* fade; (*cheveux*) bleach. **se ～er** *v. pr.* fade. **～ation** *n.f.* bleaching.

décombres /dekɔ̃br/ *n.m. pl.* rubble.

décommander /dekɔmɑ̃de/ *v.t.* cancel.

décompos|er /dekɔ̃poze/ *v.t.* break up; (*substance*) decompose; (*visage*) con-

tort. **se ～er** *v. pr.* (*pourrir*) decompose. **～ition** *n.f.* decomposition.

décompt|e /dekɔ̃t/ *n.m.* deduction; (*détail*) breakdown. **～er** *v.t.* deduct.

déconcerter /dekɔ̃sɛrte/ *v.t.* disconcert.

déconfiture /dekɔ̃fityr/ *n.f.* collapse, ruin.

décongestionner /dekɔ̃ʒɛstjɔne/ *v.t.* relieve congestion in.

déconseill|er /dekɔ̃seje/ *v.t.* **～er qch. à qn.**, advise s.o. against sth. **～é** *a.* not advisable, inadvisable.

décontenancer /dekɔ̃tnɑ̃se/ *v.t.* disconcert.

décontracter /dekɔ̃trakte/ *v.t.*, **se ～** *v. pr.* relax.

déconvenue /dekɔ̃vny/ *n.f.* disappointment.

décor /dekɔr/ *n.m.* (*paysage*, *théâtre*) scenery; (*cinéma*) set; (*cadre*) setting; (*de maison*) décor.

décorati|f, **～ve** /dekɔratif, -v/ *a.* decorative.

décor|er /dekɔre/ *v.t.* decorate. **～ateur**, **～atrice** *n.m.*, *f.* (interior) decorator. **～ation** *n.f.* decoration.

décortiquer /dekɔrtike/ *v.t.* shell; (*fig.*) dissect.

découdre (**se**) /(sə)dekudr/ *v. pr.* come unstitched.

découler /dekule/ *v.i.* **～ de**, follow from.

découp|er /dekupe/ *v.t.* cut up; (*viande*) carve; (*détacher*) cut out. **se ～er sur**, stand out against. **～age** *n.m.* (*image*) cut-out. **～ure** *n.f.* (*morceau*) piece cut out.

décourag|er /dekuraʒe/ *v.t.* discourage. **se ～er** *v. pr.* become discouraged. **～ement** *n.m.* discouragement.

décousu /dekuzy/ *a.* (*idées etc.*) disjointed.

découvert, **～e** /dekuvɛr, -t/ *a.* (*tête etc.*) bare; (*terrain*) open. *—n.m.* (*de compte*) overdraft. *—n.f.* discovery. **à ～**, exposed; (*fig.*) openly. **à la ～e de**, in search of.

découvrir† /dekuvrir/ *v.t.* discover; (*enlever ce qui couvre*) uncover; (*voir*) see; (*montrer*) reveal. **se ～** *v. pr.* uncover o.s.; (*se décoiffer*) take one's hat off; (*ciel*) clear.

décrasser /dekrase/ *v.t.* clean.

décrépit, **～e** /dekrepi, -t/ *a.* decrepit.

décret /dekrɛ/ *n.m.* decree. **～er** /-ete/ *v.t.* decree.

décrier /dekrije/ *v.t.* disparage.

décrire† /dekrir/ *v.t.* describe.

décroch|er /dekrɔʃe/ *v.t.* unhook; (*obtenir*: *fam.*) get. —*v.i.* (*abandonner*: *fam.*) give up. ∼**er (le téléphone)**, pick up the phone. ∼**é** *a.* (*téléphone*) off the hook.

décroître /dekrwatr/ *v.i.* decrease.

décrypter /dekripte/ *v.t.* decipher.

déçu /desy/ *a.* disappointed.

déculotter (se) /(sə)dekylɔte/ *v. pr.* take one's trousers off.

décupl|e /dekypl/ *n.m.* **au** ∼**e**, tenfold. **le** ∼**e de**, ten times. ∼**er** *v.t./i.* increase tenfold.

dédaign|er /dedeɲe/ *v.t.* scorn. ∼**er de faire**, consider it beneath one to do. ∼**eux**, ∼**euse** /dedeɲø, -z/ *a.* scornful.

dédain /dedɛ̃/ *n.m.* scorn.

dédale /dedal/ *n.m.* maze.

dedans /dədɑ̃/ *adv. & n.m.* inside. **au** ∼ **(de)**, **en** ∼, on the inside.

dédicac|e /dedikas/ *n.f.* dedication, inscription; ∼**er** *v.t.* dedicate, inscribe.

dédier /dedje/ *v.t.* dedicate.

dédire (se) /(sə)dedir/ *v. pr.* go back on one's word.

dédit /dedi/ *n.m.* (*comm.*) penalty.

dédommag|er /dedɔmaʒe/ *v.t.* compensate (**de**, for). ∼**ement** *n.m.* compensation.

dédouaner /dedwane/ *v.t.* clear through customs.

dédoubler /deduble/ *v.t.* split into two. ∼ **un train**, put on a relief train.

déd|uire† /dedɥir/ *v.t.* deduct; (*conclure*) deduce. ∼**uction** *n.f.* deduction.

déesse /deɛs/ *n.f.* goddess.

défaillance /defajɑ̃s/ *n.f.* weakness; (*évanouissement*) black-out; (*panne*) failure.

défaill|ir /defajir/ *v.i.* faint; (*forces etc.*) fail. ∼**ant**, ∼**ante** *a.* (*personne*) faint; (*candidat*) defaulting.

défaire† /defɛr/ *v.t.* undo; (*valise*) unpack; (*démonter*) take down; (*débarrasser*) rid. **se** ∼ *v. pr.* come undone. **se** ∼ **de**, rid o.s. of.

défait, ∼**e**[1] /defɛ, -t/ *a.* (*cheveux*) ruffled; (*visage*) haggard.

défaite[2] /defɛt/ *n.f.* defeat.

défaut /defo/ *n.m.* fault, defect; (*d'un verre, diamant etc.*) flaw; (*carence*) lack; (*pénurie*) shortage. **à** ∼ **de**, for lack of. **en** ∼, at fault. **faire** ∼, (*argent etc.*) be lacking. **par** ∼, (*jurid.*) in one's absence.

défav|eur /defavœr/ *n.f.* disfavour. ∼**orable** *a.* unfavourable.

défavoriser /defavɔrize/ *v.t.* put at a disadvantage.

défection /defɛksjɔ̃/ *n.f.* desertion. **faire** ∼, desert.

défect|ueux, ∼**ueuse** /defɛktɥø, -z/ *a.* faulty, defective. ∼**uosité** *n.f.* faultiness; (*défaut*) fault.

défendre /defɑ̃dr/ *v.t.* defend; (*interdire*) forbid. ∼ **à qn. de**, forbid s.o. to. **se** ∼ *v. pr.* defend o.s.; (*se débrouiller*) manage; (*se protéger*) protect o.s. **se** ∼ **de**, (*refuser*) refrain from.

défense /defɑ̃s/ *n.f.* defence; (*d'éléphant*) tusk. ∼ **de fumer**/*etc.*, no smoking/*etc.*

défenseur /defɑ̃sœr/ *n.m.* defender.

défensi|f, ∼**ve** /defɑ̃sif, -v/ *a. & n.f.* defensive.

déféren|t, ∼**te** /deferɑ̃, -t/ *a.* deferential. ∼**ce** *n.f.* deference.

déférer /defere/ *v.t.* (*jurid.*) refer. —*v.i.* ∼ **à**, (*avis etc.*) defer to.

déferler /defɛrle/ *v.i.* (*vagues*) break; (*violence etc.*) erupt.

défi /defi/ *n.m.* challenge; (*refus*) defiance. **mettre au** ∼, challenge.

défiance /defjɑ̃s/ *n.f.* mistrust.

déficience /defisjɑ̃s/ *n.f.* deficiency.

déficit /defisit/ *n.m.* deficit. ∼**aire** *a.* in deficit.

défier /defje/ *v.t.* challenge; (*braver*) defy. **se** ∼ **de**, mistrust.

défigurer /defigyre/ *v.t.* disfigure; (*gâter*) spoil; (*texte*) deface.

défilé[1] /defile/ *n.m.* procession; (*mil.*) parade, march past; (*fig.*) (continual) stream.

défilé[2] /defile/ *n.m.* (*géog.*) gorge.

défiler /defile/ *v.i.* march (past); (*visiteurs*) stream; (*images*) flash by. **se** ∼ *v. pr.* (*fam.*) sneak off.

défini /defini/ *a.* definite.

définir /definir/ *v.t.* define.

définiti|f, ∼**ve** /definitif, -v/ *a.* final; (*permanent*) definitive. **en** ∼**ve**, in the final analysis. ∼**vement** *adv.* definitively, permanently.

définition /definisjɔ̃/ *n.f.* definition; (*de mots croisés*) clue.

déflagration /deflagrasjɔ̃/ *n.f.* explosion.

déflation /deflasjɔ̃/ *n.f.* deflation. ∼**niste** /-jɔnist/ *a.* deflationary.

défoncer /defɔ̃se/ *v.t.* (*porte etc.*) break down; (*route, terrain*) dig up; (*lit*) break the springs of.

déform|er /defɔrme/ *v.t.* put out of shape; (*membre*) deform; (*faits, pensée*) distort. **~ation** *n.f.* loss of shape; deformation; distortion.

défouler (se) /(sə)defule/ *v. pr.* let off steam.

défraîchir (se) /(sə)defreʃir/ *v. pr.* become faded.

défrayer /defreje/ *v.t.* (*payer*) pay the expenses of.

défricher /defriʃe/ *v.t.* clear (for cultivation).

défunt, ~e /defœ̃, -t/ *a.* (*mort*) late. —*n.m., f.* deceased.

dégagé /degaʒe/ *a.* clear; (*manières*) free and easy.

dégag|er /degaʒe/ *v.t.* (*exhaler*) give off; (*désencombrer*) clear; (*délivrer*) free; (*faire ressortir*) bring out. —*v.i.* (*football*) kick the ball (down the pitch *ou* field). **se ~er** *v. pr.* free o.s.; (*ciel, rue*) clear; (*odeur etc.*) emanate. **~ement** *n.m.* giving off; clearing; freeing; (*espace*) clearing; (*football*) clearance.

dégainer /degene/ *v.t./i.* draw.

dégarnir /degarnir/ *v.t.* clear, empty. **se ~** *v. pr.* clear, empty; (*crâne*) go bald.

dégâts /dega/ *n.m. pl.* damage.

dégel /deʒɛl/ *n.m.* thaw. **~er** /deʒle/ *v.t./i.* thaw (out). (**faire**) **~er,** (*culin.*) thaw.

dégénér|er /deʒenere/ *v.i.* degenerate. **~é, ~ée** *a.* & *n.m., f.* degenerate.

dégingandé /deʒɛ̃gɑ̃de/ *a.* gangling.

dégivrer /deʒivre/ *v.t.* (*auto.*) de-ice; (*frigo*) defrost.

dégonfl|er /degɔ̃fle/ *v.t.* let down, deflate. **se ~er** *v. pr.* (*fam.*) get cold feet. **~é** *a.* (*pneu*) flat; (*lâche: fam.*) yellow.

dégorger /degɔrʒe/ *v.i.* **faire ~,** (*culin.*) soak.

dégouliner /deguline/ *v.i.* trickle.

dégourdi /degurdi/ *a.* smart.

dégourdir /degurdir/ *v.t.* (*membre, liquide*) warm up. **se ~** (**les jambes**), stretch one's legs.

dégoût /degu/ *n.m.* disgust.

dégoût|er /degute/ *v.t.* disgust. **~er qn. de qch.,** put s.o. off sth. **se ~er de,** get sick of. **~ant, ~ante** *a.* disgusting.

dégoutter /degute/ *v.i.* drip.

dégradé /degrade/ *n.m.* (*de couleurs*) gradation.

dégrader /degrade/ *v.t.* degrade; (*abî-*

mer) damage. **se ~** *v. pr.* (*se détériorer*) deteriorate.

dégrafer /degrafe/ *v.t.* unhook.

dégraisser /degrese/ *v.t.* (*vêtement*) remove the grease from.

degré /dəgre/ *n.m.* degree; (*d'escalier*) step.

dégrever /degrəve/ *v.t.* reduce the tax on.

dégringol|er /degrɛ̃gɔle/ *v.i.* tumble (down). —*v.t.* rush down. **~ade** *n.f.* tumble.

dégriser /degrize/ *v.t.* sober up.

dégrossir /degrosir/ *v.t.* (*bois*) trim; (*projet*) rough out.

déguenillé /dɛgnije/ *a.* ragged.

déguerpir /degɛrpir/ *v.i.* clear off.

dégueulasse /degœlas/ *a.* (*argot*) disgusting, lousy.

déguis|er /degize/ *v.t.* disguise. **se ~er** *v. pr.* disguise o.s.; (*au carnaval etc.*) dress up. **~ement** *n.m.* disguise; (*de carnaval etc.*) fancy dress.

dégust|er /degyste/ *v.t.* taste, sample; (*savourer*) enjoy. **~ation** *n.f.* tasting, sampling.

déhancher (se) /(sə)deɑ̃ʃe/ *v. pr.* sway one's hips.

dehors /dəɔr/ *adv.* & *n.m.* outside. —*n.m. pl.* (*aspect de qn.*) exterior. **au ~ (de),** outside. **en ~ de,** outside; (*hormis*) apart from. **jeter/ mettre**/*etc.* **~,** throw/put/ *etc.* out.

déjà /deʒa/ *adv.* already; (*avant*) before, already.

déjeuner /deʒœne/ *v.i.* (have) lunch; (*le matin*) (have) breakfast. —*n.m.* lunch. (**petit**) **~,** breakfast.

déjouer /deʒwe/ *v.t.* thwart.

delà /dəla/ *adv.* & *prép.* **au ~ (de), en ~ (de), par ~,** beyond.

délabrer (se) /(sə)delabre/ *v. pr.* become dilapidated.

délacer /delase/ *v.t.* undo.

délai /delɛ/ *n.m.* time-limit; (*attente*) wait; (*sursis*) extension (of time). **sans ~,** without delay.

délaisser /delese/ *v.t.* desert.

délass|er /delase/ *v.t.,* **se ~er** *v. pr.* relax. **~ement** *n.m.* relaxation.

délation /delasjɔ̃/ *n.f.* informing.

délavé /delave/ *a.* faded.

délayer /deleje/ *v.t.* mix (with liquid); (*idée*) drag out.

délecter (se) /(sə)delɛkte/ *v. pr.* **se ~ de,** delight in.

délégation /delegasjɔ̃/ *n.f.* delegation.

délégu|er /delege/ *v.t.* delegate. ∼**é**, ∼**ée** *n.m.*, *f.* delegate.

délester /deleste/ *v.t.* (*route*) relieve congestion on.

délibéré /delibere/ *a.* deliberate; (*résolu*) determined. ∼**ment** *adv.* deliberately.

délibér|er /delibere/ *v.i.* deliberate. ∼**ation** *n.f.* deliberation.

délicat, ∼**e** /delika, -t/ *a.* delicate; (*plein de tact*) tactful; (*exigeant*) particular. ∼**ement** /-tmã/ *adv.* delicately; tactfully. ∼**esse** /-tɛs/ *n.f.* delicacy; tact. ∼**esses** /-tɛs/ *n.f. pl.* (kind) attentions.

délice /delis/ *n.m.* delight. ∼**s** *n.f. pl.* delights.

délicieu|x, ∼**se** /delisjø, -z/ *a.* (*au goût*) delicious; (*charmant*) delightful.

délié /delje/ *a.* fine, slender; (*agile*) nimble.

délier /delje/ *v.t.* untie; (*délivrer*) free. **se** ∼ *v. pr.* come untied.

délimit|er /delimite/ *v.t.* determine, demarcate. ∼**ation** *n.f.* demarcation.

délinquan|t, ∼**te** /delɛ̃kã, -t/ *a. & n.m.*, *f.* delinquent. ∼**ce** *n.f.* delinquency.

délire /delir/ *n.m.* delirium; (*fig.*) frenzy.

délir|er /delire/ *v.i.* be delirious (**de**, with); (*déraisonner*) rave. ∼**ant**, ∼**ante** *a.* delirious; (*frénétique*) frenzied.

délit /deli/ *n.m.* offence, crime.

délivr|er /delivre/ *v.t.* free, release; (*pays*) deliver; (*remettre*) issue. ∼**ance** *n.f.* release; deliverance; issue.

déloger /delɔʒe/ *v.t.* force out.

déloy|al (*m. pl.* ∼**aux**) /delwajal, -jo/ *a.* disloyal; (*procédé*) unfair.

delta /dɛlta/ *n.m.* delta.

déluge /delyʒ/ *n.m.* flood; (*pluie*) downpour.

déluré /delyre/ *a.* smart, sharp.

démagogue /demagɔg/ *n.m./f.* demagogue.

demain /dmɛ̃/ *adv.* tomorrow.

demande /dmãd/ *n.f.* request; (*d'emploi*) application; (*exigence*) demand. ∼ **en mariage**, proposal (of marriage).

demandé /dmãde/ *a.* in demand.

demander /dmãde/ *v.t.* ask for; (*chemin*, *heure*) ask; (*emploi*) apply for; (*nécessiter*) require. ∼ **que/si**, ask

that/if. ∼ **qch. à qn.**, ask s.o. for sth. ∼ **à qn. de**, ask s.o. to. ∼ **en mariage**, propose to. **se** ∼ **si/où/** *etc.*, wonder if/where/*etc.*

démang|er /demãʒe/ *v.t./i.* itch. ∼**eaison** *n.f.* itch(ing).

démanteler /demãtle/ *v.t.* break up.

démaquill|er (**se**) /(sə)demakije/ *v. pr.* remove one's make-up. ∼**ant** *n.m.* make-up remover.

démarcation /demarkasjõ/ *n.f.* demarcation.

démarche /demarʃ/ *n.f.* walk, gait; (*procédé*) step. **faire des** ∼**s auprès de**, make approaches to.

démarcheu|r, ∼**se** /demarʃœr, -øz/ *n.m.*, *f.* (door-to-door) canvasser.

démarquer /demarke/ *v.t.* (*prix*) mark down.

démarr|er /demare/ *v.i.* (*moteur*) start (up); (*partir*) move off; (*fig.*) get moving. —*v.t.* (*fam.*) get moving. ∼**age** *n.m.* start. ∼**eur** *n.m.* starter.

démasquer /demaske/ *v.t.* unmask.

démêler /demele/ *v.t.* disentangle.

démêlés /demele/ *n.m. pl.* trouble.

déménag|er /demenaʒe/ *v.i.* move (house). —*v.t.* (*meubles*) remove. ∼**ement** *n.m.* move; (*de meubles*) removal. ∼**eur** *n.m.* removal man; (*Amer.*) furniture mover.

démener (**se**) /(sə)demne/ *v. pr.* move about wildly; (*fig.*) exert o.s.

démen|t, ∼**te** /demã, -t/ *a.* insane. —*n.m.*, *f.* lunatic. ∼**ce** *n.f.* insanity.

démenti /demãti/ *n.m.* denial.

démentir /demãtir/ *v.t.* refute; (*ne pas être conforme à*) belie. ∼ **que**, deny that.

démesuré /deməzyre/ *a.* inordinate.

démettre /demɛtr/ *v.t.* (*poignet etc.*) dislocate. ∼ **qn. de**, dismiss s.o. from. **se** ∼ *v. pr.* resign (**de**, from).

demeurant (**au**) /(o)dəmœrã/ *adv.* after all, for all that.

demeure /dəmœr/ *n.f.* residence. **mettre en** ∼ **de**, order to.

demeurer /dəmœre/ *v.i.* live; (*rester*) remain.

demi, ∼**e** /dmi/ *a.* half(-). —*n.m.*, *f.* half. —*n.m.* (*bière*) (half-pint) glass of beer; (*football*) half-back. —*n.f.* (*à l'horloge*) half-hour. —*adv.* à ∼, half; (*ouvrir*, *fermer*) half-way. **une heure et** ∼**e**, an hour and a half; (*à l'horloge*) half past one. **une** ∼**-journée/-livre/** *etc.*, half a day/pound/*etc.*, a half-day/pound/*etc.* ∼**-cercle** *n.m.* semicircle.

~**-finale** *n.f.* semi-final. ~**-frère** *n.m.* stepbrother. ~**-heure** *n.f.* half-hour, half an hour. ~**-jour** *n.m.* half-light. à ~**-mot** *adv.* without having to express every word. ~**-pension** *n.f.* half-board. ~**-pensionnaire** *n.m.f.* day-boarder. ~**-sel** *a. invar.* slightly salted. ~**-sœur** *n.f.* stepsister. ~**-tarif** *n.m.* half-fare. ~**-tour** *n.m.* about turn; (*auto.*) U-turn. **faire** ~**-tour**, turn back.

démis, ~**e** /demi, -z/ *a.* dislocated.

démission /demisjɔ̃/ *n.f.* resignation. ~**ner** /-jɔne/ *v.i.* resign.

démobiliser /demɔbilize/ *v.t.* demobilize.

démocrate /demɔkrat/ *n.m.f.* democrat. —*a.* democratic.

démocrat|ie /demɔkrasi/ *n.f.* democracy. ~**ique** /-atik/ *a.* democratic.

démodé /demɔde/ *a.* old-fashioned.

demoiselle /dǝmwazɛl/ *n.f.* young lady; (*célibataire*) spinster. ~ **d'honneur**, bridesmaid.

démol|ir /demɔlir/ *v.t.* demolish. ~**ition** *n.f.* demolition.

démon /demɔ̃/ *n.m.* demon.

démoniaque /demɔnjak/ *a.* fiendish.

démonstra|teur, ~**trice** /demɔ̃stratœr, -tris/ *n.m., f.* demonstrator. ~**tion** /-asjɔ̃/ *n.f.* demonstration; (*de force*) show.

démonstrati|f, ~**ve** /demɔ̃stratif, -v/ *a.* demonstrative.

démonter /demɔ̃te/ *v.t.* take apart, dismantle; (*installation*) take down; (*fig.*) disconcert. **se** ~ *v. pr.* come apart.

démontrer /demɔ̃tre/ *v.t.* show, demonstrate.

démoraliser /demɔralize/ *v.t.* demoralize.

démuni /demyni/ *a.* impoverished. ~ **de**, without.

démunir /demynir/ *v.t.* ~ **de**, deprive of. **se** ~ **de**, part with.

démystifier /demistifje/ *v.t.* enlighten.

dénaturer /denatyre/ *v.t.* (*faits etc.*) distort.

dénégation /denegasjɔ̃/ *n.f.* denial.

dénicher /deniʃe/ *v.t.* (*trouver*) dig up; (*faire sortir*) flush out.

dénier /denje/ *v.t.* deny.

dénigr|er /denigre/ *v.t.* denigrate. ~**ement** *n.m.* denigration.

dénivellation /denivɛlasjɔ̃/ *n.f.* (*pente*) slope.

dénombrer /denɔ̃bre/ *v.t.* count; (*énumérer*) enumerate.

dénomination /denɔminasjɔ̃/ *n.f.* designation.

dénommer /denɔme/ *v.t.* name.

dénonc|er /denɔ̃se/ *v.t.* denounce; (*scol.*) tell on. **se** ~**er** *v. pr.* give o.s. up. ~**iateur**, ~**iatrice** *n.m., f.* informer; (*scol.*) tell-tale. ~**iation** *n.f.* denunciation.

dénoter /denɔte/ *v.t.* denote.

dénouement /denumɑ̃/ *n.m.* outcome; (*théâtre*) dénouement.

dénouer /denwe/ *v.t.* unknot, undo. **se** ~ *v.pr.* (*nœud*) come undone.

dénoyauter /denwajote/ *v.t.* stone; (*Amer.*) pit.

denrée /dɑ̃re/ *n.f.* foodstuff.

dens|e /dɑ̃s/ *a.* dense. ~**ité** *n.f.* density.

dent /dɑ̃/ *n.f.* tooth; (*de roue*) cog. **faire ses** ~**s**, teethe. ~**aire** /-tɛr/ *a.* dental.

dentelé /dɑ̃tle/ *a.* jagged.

dentelle /dɑ̃tɛl/ *n.f.* lace.

dentier /dɑ̃tje/ *n.m.* denture.

dentifrice /dɑ̃tifris/ *n.m.* toothpaste.

dentiste /dɑ̃tist/ *n.m.f.* dentist.

dentition /dɑ̃tisjɔ̃/ *n.f.* teeth.

dénud|er /denyde/ *v.t.* bare. ~**é** *a.* bare.

dénué /denɥe/ *a.* ~ **de**, devoid of.

dénuement /denymɑ̃/ *n.m.* destitution.

déodorant /deɔdɔɑ̃/ *a.m. & n.m.* (**produit**) ~, deodorant.

dépann|er /depane/ *v.t.* repair; (*fig.*) help out. ~**age** *n.m.* repair. **de** ~**age**, (*service etc.*) breakdown. ~**euse** *n.f.* breakdown lorry; (*Amer.*) wrecker.

dépareillé /depareje/ *a.* odd, not matching.

déparer /depare/ *v.t.* mar.

départ /depar/ *n.m.* departure; (*sport*) start. **au** ~, at the outset.

départager /departaʒe/ *v.t.* settle the matter between.

département /departǝmɑ̃/ *n.m.* department.

départir (se) /(sǝ)departir/ *v. pr.* **se** ~ **de**, depart from.

dépassé /depase/ *a.* outdated.

dépass|er /depase/ *v.t.* go past, pass; (*véhicule*) overtake; (*excéder*) exceed; (*rival*) surpass; (*dérouter: fam.*) be beyond. —*v.i.* stick out; (*véhicule*) overtake. ~**ement** *n.m.* overtaking.

dépays|er /depeize/ *v.t.* disorientate, disorient. ~**ement** *n.m.* disorientation; (*changement*) change of scenery.

dépecer /depəse/ *v.t.* carve up.

dépêch|e /depɛʃ/ *n.f.* dispatch; (*télégraphique*) telegram. **~er**[1] /-eʃe/ *v.t.* dispatch.

dépêcher[2] **(se)** /(sə)depeʃe/ *v. pr.* hurry (up).

dépeigné /depeɲe/ *a.* dishevelled.

dépeindre /depɛ̃dr/ *v.t.* depict.

dépendance /depɑ̃dɑ̃s/ *n.f.* dependence; (*bâtiment*) outbuilding.

dépendre /depɑ̃dr/ *v.t.* take down. —*v.i.* depend (**de**, on). **~ de**, (*appartenir à*) belong to.

dépens (aux) /(o)depɑ̃/ *prép.* **aux ~ de,** at the expense of.

dépens|e /depɑ̃s/ *n.f.* expense; expenditure. **~er** *v.t./i.* spend; (*énergie etc.*) expend. **se ~er** *v. pr.* exert o.s.

dépens|ier, ~ière /depɑ̃sje, -jɛr/ *a.* **être ~ier,** be a spendthrift.

dépérir /deperir/ *v.i.* wither.

dépeupler /depœple/ *v.t.* depopulate. **se ~** *v. pr.* become depopulated.

déphasé /defaze/ *a.* (*fam.*) out of touch.

dépist|er /depiste/ *v.t.* detect; (*criminel*) track down; (*poursuivant*) throw off the scent. **~age** *n.m.* detection.

dépit /depi/ *n.m.* resentment. **en ~ de,** despite. **~é** /-te/ *a.* vexed.

déplacé /deplase/ *a.* out of place.

déplac|er /deplase/ *v.t.* move. **se ~er** *v. pr.* move; (*voyager*) travel. **~ement** *n.m.* moving; travel(ling).

déplaire /deplɛr/ *v.i.* **~ à,** (*irriter*) displease. **ça me déplaît,** I dislike that. **se ~** *v. pr.* dislike it.

déplaisant, ~e /deplɛzɑ̃, -t/ *a.* unpleasant, disagreeable.

déplaisir /deplezir/ *n.m.* displeasure.

dépliant /deplijɑ̃/ *n.m.* leaflet.

déplier /deplije/ *v.t.* unfold.

déplor|er /deplɔre/ *v.t.* (*trouver regrettable*) deplore; (*mort*) lament. **~able** *a.* deplorable.

dépl|oyer /deplwaje/ *v.t.* (*ailes, carte*) spread; (*courage*) display; (*armée*) deploy. **~oiement** *n.m.* display; deployment.

déport|er /depɔrte/ *v.t.* (*exiler*) deport; (*dévier*) carry off course. **~ation** *n.f.* deportation.

déposer /depoze/ *v.t.* put down; (*laisser*) leave; (*passager*) drop; (*argent*) deposit; (*installation*) dismantle; (*plainte*) lodge; (*armes*) lay

down; (*roi*) depose. —*v.i.* (*jurid.*) testify. **se ~** *v. pr.* settle.

dépositaire /depozitɛr/ *n.m./f.* (*comm.*) agent.

déposition /depozisjɔ̃/ *n.f.* (*jurid.*) statement.

dépôt /depo/ *n.m.* (*garantie, lie*) deposit; (*entrepôt*) warehouse; (*d'autobus*) depot; (*d'ordures*) dump. **laisser en ~,** give for safe keeping.

dépotoir /depɔtwar/ *n.m.* rubbish dump.

dépouille /depuj/ *n.f.* skin, hide. **~ (mortelle),** mortal remains. **~s,** (*butin*) spoils.

dépouillé /depuje/ *a.* bare. **~ de,** bereft of.

dépouiller /depuje/ *v.t.* go through; (*votes*) count; (*écorcher*) skin. **~ de,** strip of.

dépourvu /depurvy/ *a.* **~ de,** devoid of. **prendre au ~,** catch unawares.

déprav|er /deprave/ *v.t.* deprave. **~ation** *n.f.* depravity.

dépréc|ier /depresje/ *v.t.,* **se ~ier** *v. pr.* depreciate. **~iation** *n.f.* depreciation.

déprédations /depredasjɔ̃/ *n.f. pl.* damage.

dépr|imer /deprime/ *v.t.* depress. **~ession** *n.f.* depression.

depuis /dəpɥi/ *prép.* since; (*durée*) for; (*à partir de*) from. —*adv.* (ever) since. **~ que,** since. **~ quand attendez-vous?,** how long have you been waiting?

députation /depytasjɔ̃/ *n.f.* deputation.

député, ~e /depyte/ *n.m., f.* Member of Parliament.

déraciner /derasine/ *v.t.* uproot.

déraill|er /deraje/ *v.i.* be derailed. **faire ~er,** derail. **~ement** *n.m.* derailment. **~eur** *n.m.* (*de vélo*) gear mechanism, *dérailleur.*

déraisonnable /derɛzɔnabl/ *a.* unreasonable.

déraisonner /derɛzɔne/ *v.i.* talk nonsense.

dérang|er /derɑ̃ʒe/ *v.t.* (*gêner*) bother, disturb; (*dérégler*) upset, disrupt. **se ~er** *v. pr.* put o.s. out. **ça vous ~e si . . .?,** do you mind if . . .? **~ement** *n.m.* bother; (*désordre*) disorder, upset. **en ~ement,** out of order.

dérap|er /derape/ *v.i.* skid; (*fig.*) get out of control. **~age** *n.m.* skid.

déréglé /deregle/ *a.* (*vie*) dissolute.

dérégler /deregle/ *v.t.* put out of order. **se ~** *v. pr.* go wrong.

dérider /deride/ *v.t.* cheer up.

dérision /derizjɔ̃/ *n.f.* mockery. **par ~**, derisively.

dérisoire /derizwar/ *a.* derisory.

dérivatif /derivatif/ *n.m.* distraction.

dériv|e /deriv/ *n.f.* **aller à la ~e**, drift. **~er**[1] *v.i.* (*bateau*) drift; *v.t.* (*détourner*) divert.

dériv|er[2] /derive/ *v.i.* **~er de**, derive from. **~é** *a.* derived; *n.m.* derivative; (*techn.*) by-product.

dern|ier, ~ière /dɛrnje, -jɛr/ *a.* last; (*nouvelles, mode*) latest; (*étage*) top. *—n.m., f.* last (one). **ce ~ier**, the latter. **en ~ier**, last. **le ~ier cri**, the latest fashion.

dernièrement /dɛrnjɛrmɑ̃/ *adv.* recently.

dérobade /derɔbad/ *n.f.* evasion, dodge.

dérobé /derɔbe/ *a.* hidden. **à la ~e**, stealthily.

dérober /derɔbe/ *v.t.* steal; (*cacher*) hide (à, from). **se ~** *v. pr.* slip away. **se ~ à**, (*obligation*) shy away from; (*se cacher à*) hide from.

dérogation /derɔgasjɔ̃/ *n.f.* exemption.

déroul|er /derule/ *v.t.* (*fil etc.*) unwind. **se ~er** *v. pr.* unwind; (*avoir lieu*) take place; (*récit, paysage*) unfold. **~ement** *n.m.* (*d'une action*) development.

déroute /derut/ *n.f.* (*mil.*) rout.

dérouter /derute/ *v.t.* re-route; (*fig.*) disconcert.

derrière /dɛrjɛr/ *prép. & adv.* behind. *—n.m.* back, rear; (*postérieur*) behind. **de ~**, back, rear; (*pattes*) hind. **par ~**, (from) behind, at the back *ou* rear.

des /de/ *voir* **de**.

dès /dɛ/ *prép.* (right) from, from the time of. **~ lors**, from then on. **~ que**, as soon as.

désabusé /dezabyze/ *a.* disillusioned.

désaccord /dezakɔr/ *n.m.* disagreement. **~é** /-de/ *a.* out of tune.

désaffecté /dezafɛkte/ *a.* disused.

désaffection /dezafɛksjɔ̃/ *n.f.* alienation (**pour, from**).

désagréable /dezagreabl/ *a.* unpleasant.

désagréger (se) /(sə)dezagreʒe/ *v. pr.* disintegrate.

désagrément /dezagremɑ̃/ *n.m.* annoyance.

désaltérer /dezaltere/ *v.i.*, **se ~** *v. pr.* quench one's thirst.

désamorcer /dezamɔrse/ *v.t.* (*situation, obus*) defuse.

désappr|ouver /dezapruve/ *v.t.* disapprove of. **~obation** *n.f.* disapproval.

désarçonner /dezarsɔne/ *v.t.* disconcert, throw; (*jockey*) unseat, throw.

désarm|er /dezarme/ *v.t./i.* disarm. **~ement** *n.m.* (*pol.*) disarmament.

désarroi /dezarwa/ *n.m.* confusion.

désarticuler /dezartikyle/ *v.t.* (*déboiter*) dislocate.

désastr|e /dezastr/ *n.m.* disaster. **~eux, ~euse** *a.* disastrous.

désavantag|e /dezavɑ̃taʒ/ *n.m.* disadvantage. **~er** *v.t.* put at a disadvantage. **~eux, ~euse** *a.* disadvantageous.

désaveu (*pl.* **~x**) /dezavø/ *n.m.* repudiation.

désavouer /dezavwe/ *v.t.* repudiate.

désaxé, ~e /dezakse/ *a. & n.m., f.* unbalanced (person).

descendan|t, ~te /desɑ̃dɑ̃, -t/ *n.m., f.* descendant. **~ce** *n.f.* descent; (*enfants*) descendants.

descendre /desɑ̃dr/ *v.i.* (*aux. être*) go down; (*venir*) come down; (*passager*) get off *ou* out; (*nuit*) fall. **~ de**, (*être issu de*) be descended from. *—v.t.* (*aux. avoir*) (*escalier etc.*) go *ou* come down; (*objet*) take down; (*abattre*) shoot down.

descente /desɑ̃t/ *n.f.* descent; (*pente*) (downward) slope; (*raid*) raid. **~ de lit**, bedside rug.

descripti|f, ~ve /dɛskriptif, -v/ *a.* descriptive.

description /dɛskripsjɔ̃/ *n.f.* description.

désemparé /dezɑ̃pare/ *a.* distraught; (*navire*) crippled.

désemplir /dezɑ̃plir/ *v.i.* **ne pas ~**, be always crowded.

désenchanté /dezɑ̃ʃɑ̃te/ *a.* disenchanted.

désenfler /dezɑ̃fle/ *v.i.* go down.

déséquilibre /dezekilibr/ *n.m.* imbalance. **en ~**, unsteady.

déséquilibr|er /dezekilibre/ *v.t.* throw off balance. **~é, ~ée** *a. & n.m., f.* unbalanced (person).

désert[1], **~e** /dezɛr, -t/ *a.* deserted.

désert[2] /dezɛr/ *n.m.* desert. **~ique** /-tik/ *a.* desert.

désert|er /dezɛrte/ *v.t./i.* desert. **~eur**
n.m. deserter. **~ion** /-ɛrsjɔ̃/ *n.f.* desertion.

désespér|er /dezɛspere/ *v.i.*, **se ~er**
v. pr. despair. **~er de**, despair of.
~ant, ~ante *a.* utterly disheart-
ening. **~é** *a.* in despair; (*état, cas*)
hopeless; (*effort*) desperate. **~ément**
adv. desperately.

désespoir /dezɛspwar/ *n.m.* despair.
au ~, in despair.

déshabill|er /dezabije/ *v.t.*, **se ~er** *v.
pr.* undress, get undressed. **~é** *a.*
undressed; *n.m.* négligé.

déshabituer (se) /(sə)dezabitɥe/ *v. pr.*
se ~ de, get out of the habit of.

désherb|er /dezɛrbe/ *v.t.* weed. **~ant**
n.m. weed-killer.

déshériter /dezerite/ *v.t.* disinherit;
(*désavantager*) deprive.

déshonneur /dezɔnœr/ *n.m.* dishonour.

déshonor|er /dezɔnɔre/ *v.t.* dis-
honour. **~ant, ~ante** *a.* dis-
honourable.

déshydrater /dezidrate/ *v.t.*, **se ~** *v.
pr.* dehydrate.

désignation /deziɲɑsjɔ̃/ *n.f.* designation.

désigner /deziɲe/ *v.t.* (*montrer*) point
to *ou* out; (*élire*) appoint; (*signifier*)
indicate.

désillusion /dezilyzjɔ̃/ *n.f.* disillusion-
ment.

désinence /dezinɑ̃s/ *n.f.* (*gram.*) ending.

désinfect|er /dezɛ̃fɛkte/ *v.t.* disinfect.
~ant *n.m.* disinfectant.

désintégrer /dezɛ̃tegre/ *v.t.*, **se ~** *v.
pr.* disintegrate.

désintéressé /dezɛ̃terese/ *a.* disinterested.

désintéresser (se) /(sə)dezɛ̃terese/ *v.
pr.* **se ~ de**, lose interest in.

désintoxiquer /dezɛ̃tɔksike/ *v.t.* cure
of an addiction.

désinvolt|e /dezɛ̃vɔlt/ *a.* casual. **~ure**
n.f. casualness.

désir /dezir/ *n.m.* wish, desire; (*convoitise*) desire.

désirer /dezire/ *v.t.* want; (*convoiter*)
desire. **~ faire**, want *ou* wish to do.

désireu|x, ~se /dezirø, -z/ *a.* **~x de**,
anxious to.

désist|er (se) /(sə)deziste/ *v. pr.* with-
draw. **~ement** *n.m.* withdrawal.

désobéir /dezɔbeir/ *v.i.* **~ (à)**, disobey.

désobéissan|t, ~te /dezɔbeisɑ̃, -t/ *a.*
disobedient. **~ce** *n.f.* disobedience.

désobligeant, ~e /dezɔbliʒɑ̃, -t/ *a.* disagreeable, unkind.

désodorisant /dezɔdɔrizɑ̃/ *n.m.* air
freshener.

désœuvr|é /dezœvre/ *a.* idle. **~ement**
n.m. idleness.

désolé /dezɔle/ *a.* (*région*) desolate.

désol|er /dezɔle/ *v.t.* distress. **être ~é**,
(*regretter*) be sorry. **~ation** *n.f.* distress.

désopilant, ~e /dezɔpilɑ̃, -t/ *a.* hilarious.

désordonné /dezɔrdɔne/ *a.* untidy;
(*mouvements*) uncoordinated.

désordre /dezɔrdr/ *n.m.* disorder;
(*de vêtements, cheveux*) untidiness.
mettre en ~, make untidy.

désorganiser /dezɔrganize/ *v.t.* disorganize.

désorienter /dezɔrjɑ̃te/ *v.t.* disorientate, disorient.

désormais /dezɔrmɛ/ *adv.* from now
on.

désosser /dezɔse/ *v.t.* bone.

despote /dɛspɔt/ *n.m.* despot.

desquels, desquelles /dekɛl/ *voir* lequel.

dessaisir (se) /(sə)desezir/ *v. pr.* **se ~
de**, relinquish, part with.

dessaler /desale/ *v.t.* (*culin.*) soak.

dessécher /deseʃe/ *v.t.*, **se ~** *v. pr.* dry
out *ou* up.

dessein /desɛ̃/ *n.m.* intention. **à ~**,
intentionally.

desserrer /desere/ *v.t.* loosen. **se ~** *v.
pr.* come loose.

dessert /desɛr/ *n.m.* dessert.

desserte /desɛrt/ *n.f.* (*transports*) service, servicing.

desservir /desɛrvir/ *v.t./i.* clear away;
(*autobus*) provide a service to, serve.

dessin /desɛ̃/ *n.m.* drawing; (*motif*)
design; (*contour*) outline. **~ animé**,
(*cinéma*) cartoon. **~ humoristique**,
cartoon.

dessin|er /desine/ *v.t./i.* draw; (*fig.*)
outline. **se ~er** *v. pr.* appear, take
shape. **~ateur, ~atrice** *n.m., f.*
artist; (*industriel*) draughtsman.
~ateur de mode, fashion designer.

dessoûler /desule/ *v.t./i.* sober up.

dessous /dsu/ *adv.* underneath. *—n.m.*
under-side, underneath. *—n.m. pl.*
underclothes. **du ~**, bottom; (*voisins*)
downstairs. **en ~**, **par ~**, underneath. **avoir le ~**, get the worst of it.

~**-de-plat** *n.m. invar.* (heat-resistant) table-mat.

dessus /dsy/ *adv.* on top (of it), on it. —*n.m.* top. **du** ~, top; (*voisins*) upstairs. **en** ~, above. **par** ~, over (it). **avoir le** ~, get the upper hand. ~**-de-lit** *n.m. invar.* bedspread.

destin /dɛstɛ̃/ *n.m.* (*sort*) fate; (*avenir*) destiny.

destinataire /dɛstinatɛr/ *n.m./f.* addressee.

destination /dɛstinasjɔ̃/ *n.f.* destination; (*emploi*) purpose. **à** ~ **de,** (going) to.

destinée /dɛstine/ *n.f.* (*sort*) fate; (*avenir*) destiny.

destiner /dɛstine/ *v.t.* ~ **à,** intend for; (*vouer*) destine for; (*affecter*) earmark for. **être destiné à faire,** be intended to do; (*condamné, obligé*) be destined to do. **se** ~ **à,** (*carrière*) intend to take up.

destit|uer /dɛstitɥe/ *v.t.* dismiss (from office). ~**ution** *n.f.* dismissal.

destruc|teur, ~**trice** /dɛstryktœr, -tris/ *a.* destructive.

destruction /dɛstryksjɔ̃/ *n.f.* destruction.

dés|uet, ~**uète** /desɥɛ, -t/ *a.* outdated.

désunir /dezynir/ *v.t.* divide.

détachant /detaʃɑ̃/ *n.m.* stain-remover.

détach|é /detaʃe/ *a.* detached. ~**ement** *n.m.* detachment.

détacher /detaʃe/ *v.t.* untie; (*ôter*) remove, detach; (*déléguer*) send (on assignment *ou* secondment). **se** ~ *v. pr.* come off, break away; (*nœud etc.*) come undone; (*ressortir*) stand out.

détail /detaj/ *n.m.* detail; (*de compte*) breakdown; (*comm.*) retail. **au** ~, (*vendre etc.*) retail. **de** ~, (*prix etc.*) retail. **en** ~, in detail.

détaillé /detaje/ *a.* detailed.

détaill|er /detaje/ *v.t.* (*articles*) sell in small quantities, split up. ~**ant,** ~**ante** *n.m., f.* retailer.

détaler /detale/ *v.i.* (*fam.*) make tracks, run off.

détaxer /detakse/ *v.t.* reduce the tax on.

détect|er /detɛkte/ *v.t.* detect. ~**eur** *n.m.* detector. ~**ion** /-ksjɔ̃/ *n.f.* detection.

détective /detɛktiv/ *n.m.* detective.

déteindre /detɛ̃dr/ *v.i.* (*couleur*) run (**sur,** on to). ~ **sur,** (*fig.*) rub off on.

détend|re /detɑ̃dr/ *v.t.* slacken;

(*ressort*) release; (*personne*) relax. **se** ~**re** *v. pr.* become slack, slacken; be released; relax. ~**u** *a.* (*calme*) relaxed.

détenir† /detnir/ *v.t.* hold; (*secret, fortune*) possess.

détente /detɑ̃t/ *n.f.* relaxation; (*pol.*) détente; (*saut*) spring; (*gâchette*) trigger; (*relâchement*) release.

déten|teur, ~**trice** /detɑ̃tœr, -tris/ *n.m., f.* holder.

détention /detɑ̃sjɔ̃/ *n.f.* ~ **préventive,** custody.

détenu, ~**e** /detny/ *n.m., f.* prisoner.

détergent /detɛrʒɑ̃/ *n.m.* detergent.

détérior|er /deterjɔre/ *v.t.* damage. **se** ~**er** *v. pr.* deteriorate. ~**ation** *n.f.* damaging; deterioration.

détermin|er /detɛrmine/ *v.t.* determine. **se** ~**er** *v. pr.* make up one's mind (**à,** to). ~**ation** *n.f.* determination. ~**é** *a.* (*résolu*) determined; (*précis*) definite.

déterrer /detere/ *v.t.* dig up.

détersif /detɛrsif/ *n.m.* detergent.

détestable /detɛstabl/ *a.* foul.

détester /detɛste/ *v.t.* hate. **se** ~ *v. pr.* hate each other.

déton|er /detɔne/ *v.i.* explode, detonate. ~**ateur** *n.m.* detonator. ~**ation** *n.f.* explosion, detonation.

détonner /detɔne/ *v.i.* clash.

détour /detur/ *n.m.* bend; (*crochet*) detour; (*fig.*) roundabout means.

détourné /deturne/ *a.* roundabout.

détourn|er /deturne/ *v.t.* divert; (*tête, yeux*) turn away; (*avion*) hijack; (*argent*) embezzle. **se** ~**er de,** stray from. ~**ement** *n.m.* diversion; hijack(ing); embezzlement.

détrac|teur, ~**trice** /detraktœr, -tris/ *n.m., f.* critic.

détraquer /detrake/ *v.t.* break, put out of order; (*estomac*) upset. **se** ~ *v. pr.* (*machine*) go wrong.

détrempé /detrɑ̃pe/ *a.* saturated.

détresse /detrɛs/ *n.f.* distress.

détriment /detrimɑ̃/ *n.m.* detriment.

détritus /detritys/ *n.m. pl.* rubbish.

détroit /detrwa/ *n.m.* strait.

détromper /detrɔ̃pe/ *v.t.* undeceive, enlighten.

détruire† /detrɥir/ *v.t.* destroy.

dette /dɛt/ *n.f.* debt.

deuil /dœj/ *n.m.* mourning; (*perte*) bereavement. **porter le** ~, be in mourning.

deux /dø/ *a. & n.m.* two. ~ **fois,** twice.

tous (les) ∼, both. ∼**-pièces** *n.m. invar.* (*vêtement*) two-piece. ∼**-points** *n.m. invar.* (*gram.*) colon. ∼**-roues** *n.m. invar.* two-wheeled vehicle.

deuxième /døzjɛm/ *a.* & *n.m./f.* second. ∼**ment** *adv.* secondly.

dévaler /devale/ *v.t./i.* hurtle down.

dévaliser /devalize/ *v.t.* rob, clean out.

dévaloriser /devalɔrize/ *v.t.*, **se** ∼ *v. pr.* reduce in value.

déval|uer /devalɥe/ *v.t.*, **se** ∼**uer** *v. pr.* devalue. ∼**uation** *n.f.* devaluation.

devancer /dəvɑ̃se/ *v.t.* be *ou* go ahead of; (*arriver*) arrive ahead of; (*prévenir*) anticipate.

devant /dvɑ̃/ *prép.* in front of; (*distance*) ahead of; (*avec mouvement*) past; (*en présence de*) before; (*face à*) in the face of. —*adv.* in front; (*à distance*) ahead. —*n.m.* front. **de** ∼, front. **par** ∼, at *ou* from the front, in front.

devanture /dvɑ̃tyr/ *n.f.* shop front; (*étalage*) shop-window.

dévaster /devaste/ *v.t.* devastate.

déveine /devɛn/ *n.f.* bad luck.

développ|er /devlɔpe/ *v.t.*, **se** ∼**er** *v. pr.* develop. ∼**ement** *n.m.* development; (*de photos*) developing.

devenir† /dəvnir/ *v.i.* (*aux. être*) become. **qu'est-il devenu?**, what has become of him?

déverser /devɛrse/ *v.t.*, **se** ∼ *v. pr.* empty out, pour out.

dévêtir /devetir/ *v.t.*, **se** ∼ *v. pr.* undress.

déviation /devjɑsjɔ̃/ *n.f.* diversion.

dévider /devide/ *v.t.* unwind.

dévier /devje/ *v.t.* divert; (*coup*) deflect. —*v.i.* (*ballon, balle*) veer; (*personne*) deviate.

devin /dəvɛ̃/ *n.m.* fortune-teller.

deviner /dvine/ *v.t.* guess; (*prévoir*) foretell; (*apercevoir*) distinguish.

devinette /dvinɛt/ *n.f.* riddle.

devis /dvi/ *n.m.* estimate.

dévisager /devizaʒe/ *v.t.* stare at.

devise /dviz/ *n.f.* motto. ∼**s**, (*monnaie*) (foreign) currency.

dévisser /devise/ *v.t.* unscrew.

dévoiler /devwale/ *v.t.* reveal.

devoir[1] /dvwar/ *n.m.* duty; (*scol.*) homework; (*fait en classe*) exercise.

devoir†[2] /dvwar/ *v.t.* owe. —*v. aux.* ∼ **faire**, (*nécessité*) must do, have (got) to do; (*intention*) be due to do. ∼ **être**, (*probabilité*) must be. **vous devriez,**

you should. **il aurait dû,** he should have.

dévorer /devɔre/ *v.t.* devour.

dévot, ∼**e** /devo, -ɔt/ *a.* devout.

dévotion /devosjɔ̃/ *n.f.* (*relig.*) devotion.

dévou|er (se) /(sə)devwe/ *v. pr.* devote o.s. (**à,** to); (*se sacrifier*) sacrifice o.s. ∼**é** *a.* devoted. ∼**ement** /-vumɑ̃/ *n.m.* devotion.

dévoyé, ∼**e** /devwaje/ *a.* & *n.m.*, *f.* delinquent.

dextérité /dɛksterite/ *n.f.* skill.

diab|ète /djabɛt/ *n.m.* diabetes. ∼**étique** *a.* & *n.m./f.* diabetic.

diab|le /djɑbl/ *n.m.* devil. ∼**olique** *a.* diabolical.

diagnosti|c /djagnɔstik/ *n.m.* diagnosis. ∼**quer** *v.t.* diagnose.

diagon|al, ∼**ale** (*m. pl.* ∼**aux**) /djagɔnal, -o/ *a.* & *n.f.* diagonal. **en** ∼**ale,** diagonally.

diagramme /djagram/ *n.m.* diagram; (*graphique*) graph.

dialecte /djalɛkt/ *n.m.* dialect.

dialogu|e /djalɔg/ *n.m.* dialogue. ∼**er** *v.i.* (*pol.*) have a dialogue.

diamant /djamɑ̃/ *n.m.* diamond.

diamètre /djamɛtr/ *n.m.* diameter.

diapason /djapazɔ̃/ *n.m.* tuning-fork.

diaphragme /djafragm/ *n.m.* diaphragm.

diapositive /djapozitiv/ *n.f.* (colour) slide.

diarrhée /djare/ *n.f.* diarrhoea.

dictat|eur /diktatœr/ *n.m.* dictator. ∼**ure** *n.f.* dictatorship.

dict|er /dikte/ *v.t.* dictate. ∼**ée** *n.f.* dictation.

diction /diksjɔ̃/ *n.f.* diction.

dictionnaire /diksjɔnɛr/ *n.m.* dictionary.

dicton /diktɔ̃/ *n.m.* saying.

dièse /djɛz/ *n.m.* (*mus.*) sharp.

diesel /djezɛl/ *n.m.* & *a. invar.* diesel.

diète /djɛt/ *n.f.* (starvation) diet.

diététicien, ∼**ne** /djetetisjɛ̃, -jɛn/ *n.m.*, *f.* dietician.

diététique /djetetik/ *n.f.* dietetics. —*a.* **produit** *ou* **aliment** ∼, health food.

dieu (*pl.* ∼**x**) /djø/ *n.m.* god. **D**∼, God.

diffam|er /difame/ *v.t.* slander; (*par écrit*) libel. ∼**ation** *n.f.* slander; libel.

différé (en) /(ɑ̃)difere/ *adv.* (*émission*) recorded.

différemment /diferamɑ̃/ *adv.* differently.

différence /diferãs/ *n.f.* difference. **à la ~ de,** unlike.

différencier /diferãsje/ *v.t.* differentiate. **se ~ de,** (*différer de*) differ from.

différend /diferã/ *n.m.* difference (of opinion).

différent, ~e /diferã, -t/ *a.* different (**de,** from).

différentiel, ~le /diferãsjɛl/ *a.* & *n.m.* differential.

différer[1] /difere/ *v.t.* postpone.

différer[2] /difere/ *v.i.* differ.

difficile /difisil/ *a.* difficult. **~ment** *adv.* with difficulty.

difficulté /difikylte/ *n.f.* difficulty.

difform|e /difɔrm/ *a.* deformed. **~ité** *n.f.* deformity.

diffus, ~e /dify, -z/ *a.* diffuse.

diffus|er /difyze/ *v.t.* broadcast; (*lumière, chaleur*) diffuse. **~ion** *n.f.* broadcasting; diffusion.

dig|érer /diʒere/ *v.t.* digest; (*endurer: fam.*) stomach. **~este, ~estible** *adjs.* digestible. **~estion** *n.f.* digestion.

digesti|f, ~ve /diʒɛstif, -v/ *a.* digestive. —*n.m.* after-dinner liqueur.

digit|al (*m. pl.* **~aux**) /diʒital, -o/ *a.* digital.

digne /diɲ/ *a.* (*noble*) dignified; (*honnête*) worthy. **~ de,** worthy of. **~ de foi,** trustworthy.

dignitare /diɲiter/ *n.m.* dignitary.

dignité /diɲite/ *n.f.* dignity.

digression /digresjɔ̃/ *n.f.* digression.

digue /dig/ *n.f.* dike.

dilapider /dilapide/ *v.t.* squander.

dilat|er /dilate/ *v.t.*, **se ~er** *v. pr.* dilate. **~ation** /-asjɔ̃/ *n.f.* dilation.

dilemme /dilɛm/ *n.m.* dilemma.

dilettante /diletãt/ *n.m., f.* amateur.

diligence[1] /diliʒãs/ *n.f.* (*voiture à chevaux*) stage-coach.

diligen|t, ~te /diliʒã, -t/ *a.* prompt, diligent. **~ce**[2] *n.f.* diligence.

diluer /dilɥe/ *v.t.* dilute.

dimanche /dimãʃ/ *n.m.* Sunday.

dimension /dimãsjɔ̃/ *n.f.* (*taille*) size; (*mesure*) dimension.

dimin|uer /diminɥe/ *v.t.* reduce, decrease; (*plaisir, courage, etc.*) lessen; (*dénigrer*) lessen. —*v.i.* decrease. **~ution** *n.f.* decrease (**de,** in).

diminutif /diminytif/ *n.m.* diminutive; (*surnom*) pet name *ou* form.

dinde /dɛ̃d/ *n.f.* turkey.

dindon /dɛ̃dɔ̃/ *n.m.* turkey.

dîn|er /dine/ *n.m.* dinner. —*v.i.* have dinner. **~eur, ~euse** *n.m., f.* diner.

dingue /dɛ̃g/ *a.* (*fam.*) crazy.

dinosaure /dinozɔr/ *n.m.* dinosaur.

diocèse /djɔsɛz/ *n.m.* diocese.

diphtérie /difteri/ *n.f.* diphtheria.

diphtongue /diftɔ̃g/ *n.f.* diphthong.

diplomate /diplɔmat/ *n.m.* diplomat. —*a.* diplomatic.

diplomat|ie /diplɔmasi/ *n.f.* diplomacy. **~ique** /-atik/ *a.* diplomatic.

diplôm|e /diplom/ *n.m.* certificate, diploma; (*univ.*) degree. **~é** *a.* qualified.

dire† /dir/ *v.t.* say; (*secret, vérité, heure*) tell; (*penser*) think. **~ que,** say that. **~ à qn. que/de,** tell s.o. that/to. **se ~** *v. pr.* (*mot*) be said; (*fatigué etc.*) say that one is. **ça me/vous/***etc.* **dit de faire,** I/you/*etc.* feel like doing. **on dirait que,** it would seem that, it seems that.

direct /dirɛkt/ *a.* direct. **en ~,** (*émission*) live. **~ement** *adv.* directly.

direc|teur, ~trice /dirɛktœr, -tris/ *n.m., f.* director; (*chef de service*) manager, manageress; (*d'école*) headmaster, headmistress.

direction /dirɛksjɔ̃/ *n.f.* (*sens*) direction; (*de société etc.*) management; (*auto.*) steering. **en ~ de,** (going) to.

directive /dirɛktiv/ *n.f.* instruction.

dirigeant, ~e /diriʒã, -t/ *n.m., f.* (*pol.*) leader; (*comm.*) manager. —*a.* (*classe*) ruling.

diriger /diriʒe/ *v.t.* run, manage, direct; (*véhicule*) steer; (*orchestre*) conduct; (*braquer*) aim; (*tourner*) turn. **se ~** *v. pr.* guide o.s. **se ~ vers,** make one's way to.

dis /di/ *voir* **dire.**

discern|er /disɛrne/ *v.t.* discern. **~ement** *n.m.* discernment.

disciple /disipl/ *n.m.* disciple.

disciplin|e /disiplin/ *n.f.* discipline. **~aire** *a.* disciplinary. **~er** *v.t.* discipline.

discontinu /diskɔ̃tiny/ *a.* intermittent.

discontinuer /diskɔ̃tinɥe/ *v.i.* **sans ~,** without stopping.

discordant, ~e /diskɔrdã, -t/ *a.* discordant.

discorde /diskɔrd/ *n.f.* discord.

discothèque /diskɔtɛk/ *n.f.* record library; (*club*) disco(thèque).

discourir /diskurir/ *v.i.* (*péj.*) hold forth, ramble on.

discours /diskur/ *n.m.* speech.

discréditer /diskredite/ *v.t.* discredit.

discr|et, **~ète** /diskrɛ, -t/ *a.* discreet.
~ètement *adv.* discreetly.
discrétion /diskresjɔ̃/ *n.f.* discretion.
à ~, as much as one desires.
discrimination /diskriminasjɔ̃/ *n.f.*
discrimination.
disculper /diskylpe/ *v.t.* exonerate.
discussion /diskysjɔ̃/ *n.f.* discussion;
(*querelle*) argument.
discuté /diskyte/ *a.* controversial.
discuter /diskyte/ *v.t.* discuss; (*contester*) question. —*v.i.* (*parler*) talk;
(*répliquer*) argue. **~ de,** discuss.
disette /dizɛt/ *n.f.* (food) shortage.
diseuse /dizøz/ *n.f.* **~ de bonne aventure,** fortune-teller.
disgrâce /disgrɑs/ *n.f.* disgrace.
disgracieu|x, **~se** /disgrasjø, -z/ *a.*
ungainly.
disjoindre /disʒwɛ̃dr/ *v.t.* take apart.
se ~ *v. pr.* come apart.
dislo|quer /disloke/ *v.t.* (*membre*) dis-
locate; (*machine etc.*) break (apart).
se ~quer *v. pr.* (*parti, cortège*) break
up; (*meuble*) come apart. **~cation** *n.f.*
(*anat.*) dislocation.
dispar|aître† /disparɛtr/ *v.i.* disap-
pear; (*mourir*) die. **faire ~aître,** get
rid of. **~ition** *n.f.* disappearance;
(*mort*) death. **~u,** **~ue** *a.* (*soldat etc.*)
missing; *n.m.*, *f.* missing person;
(*mort*) dead person.
disparate /disparat/ *a.* ill-assorted.
disparité /disparite/ *n.f.* disparity.
dispensaire /dispɑ̃sɛr/ *n.m.* clinic.
dispense /dispɑ̃s/ *n.f.* exemption.
dispenser /dispɑ̃se/ *v.t.* exempt (**de,**
from). **se ~ de (faire),** avoid (doing).
disperser /disperse/ *v.t.* (*éparpiller*)
scatter; (*répartir*) disperse. **se ~** *v.
pr.* disperse.
disponib|le /disponibl/ *a.* available.
~ilité *n.f.* availability.
disposé /dispoze/ *a.* **bien/mal ~,** in a
good/bad mood. **~ à,** prepared to. **~
envers,** disposed towards.
disposer /dispoze/ *v.t.* arrange. **~ à,**
(*engager à*) incline to. —*v.i.* **~ de,**
have at one's disposal. **se ~ à,** prepare to.
dispositif /dispozitif/ *n.m.* device;
(*plan*) plan of action. **~ antiparasite,**
suppressor.
disposition /dispozisjɔ̃/ *n.f.* arrangement; (*humeur*) mood; (*tendance*)
tendency. **~s,** (*préparatifs*) arrangements; (*aptitude*) aptitude. **à la ~ de,**
at the disposal of.

disproportionné /disproporsjɔne/ *a.*
disproportionate.
dispute /dispyt/ *n.f.* quarrel.
disputer /dispyte/ *v.t.* (*match*) play;
(*course*) run in; (*prix*) fight for (**à qn.,**
with s.o.); (*gronder: fam.*) tell off. **se
~** *v. pr.* quarrel; (*se battre pour*) fight
over; (*match*) be played.
disquaire /diskɛr/ *n.m./f.* record dealer.
disqualif|ier /diskalifje/ *v.t.* disqual-
ify. **~ication** *n.f.* disqualification.
disque /disk/ *n.m.* (*mus.*) record;
(*sport*) discus; (*cercle*) disc, disk. **~tte**
/-ɛt/ *n.f.* floppy disk.
dissection /disɛksjɔ̃/ *n.f.* dissection.
dissemblable /disɑ̃blabl/ *a.* dissimilar.
disséminer /disemine/ *v.t.* scatter.
disséquer /diseke/ *v.t.* dissect.
dissertation /disɛrtasjɔ̃/ *n.f.* (*scol.*)
essay.
disserter /disɛrte/ *v.i.* **~ sur,** comment upon.
dissiden|t, **~te** /disidɑ̃, -t/ *a. & n.m.,
f.* dissident. **~ce** *n.f.* dissidence.
dissimul|er /disimyle/ *v.t.* conceal (**à,**
from). **se ~er** *v. pr.* conceal o.s. **~a-
tion** *n.f.* concealment; (*fig.*) deceit.
dissipé /disipe/ *a.* (*élève*) unruly.
dissip|er /disipe/ *v.t.* (*fumée, crainte*)
dispel; (*fortune*) squander; (*personne*)
lead into bad ways. **se ~er** *v. pr.*
disappear. **~ation** *n.f.* squandering;
(*indiscipline*) misbehaviour.
dissolu /disoly/ *a.* dissolute.
dissolution /disolysjɔ̃/ *n.f.* dissolution.
dissolvant /disolvɑ̃/ *n.m.* solvent;
(*pour ongles*) nail polish remover.
dissonant, **~e** /disonɑ̃, -t/ *a.* discordant.
dissoudre† /disudr/ *v.t.,* **se ~** *v. pr.*
dissolve.
dissua|der /disɥade/ *v.t.* dissuade (**de,**
from). **~sion** /-ɥazjɔ̃/ *n.f.* dissuasion.
distance /distɑ̃s/ *n.f.* distance; (*écart*)
gap. **à ~,** at **ou** from a distance.
distancer /distɑ̃se/ *v.t.* leave behind.
distant, **~e** /distɑ̃, -t/ *a.* distant.
distendre /distɑ̃dr/ *v.t.,* **se ~** *v. pr.*
distend.
distill|er /distile/ *v.t.* distil. **~ation**
n.f. distillation.
distillerie /distilri/ *n.f.* distillery.
distinct, **~e** /distɛ̃(kt), -ɛkt/ *a.* distinct. **~ement** /-ɛktəmɑ̃/ *adv.* dis-
tinctly.

distincti|f, ∼ve /distɛ̃ktif, -v/ *a.* distinctive.

distinction /distɛ̃ksjɔ̃/ *n.f.* distinction.

distingué /distɛ̃ge/ *a.* distinguished.

distinguer /distɛ̃ge/ *v.t.* distinguish.

distraction /distraksjɔ̃/ *n.f.* absent-mindedness; (*oubli*) lapse; (*passe-temps*) distraction.

distraire† /distrɛr/ *v.t.* amuse; (*rendre inattentif*) distract. **se ∼** *v. pr.* amuse o.s.

distrait, ∼e /distrɛ, -t/ *a.* absent-minded.

distrib|uer /distribɥe/ *v.t.* hand out, distribute; (*répartir, amener*) distribute; (*courrier*) deliver. **∼uteur** *n.m.* (*auto., comm.*) distributor. **∼uteur** (*automatique*), vending-machine. **∼ution** *n.f.* distribution; (*du courrier*) delivery; (*acteurs*) cast.

district /distrikt/ *n.m.* district.

dit¹, dites /di, dit/ *voir* **dire**.

dit², ∼e /di, dit/ *a.* (*décidé*) agreed; (*surnommé*) called.

divag|uer /divage/ *v.i.* rave. **∼ations** *n.f. pl.* ravings.

divan /divɑ̃/ *n.m.* divan.

divergen|t, ∼te /divɛrʒɑ̃, -t/ *a.* divergent. **∼ce** *n.f.* divergence.

diverger /divɛrʒe/ *v.i.* diverge.

divers, ∼e /divɛr, -s/ *a.* (*varié*) diverse; (*différent*) various. **∼ement** /-səmɑ̃/ *adv.* variously.

diversifier /divɛrsifje/ *v.t.* diversify.

diversion /divɛrsjɔ̃/ *n.f.* diversion.

diversité /divɛrsite/ *n.f.* diversity.

divert|ir /divɛrtir/ *v.t.* amuse. **se ∼ir** *v. pr.* amuse o.s. **∼issement** *n.m.* amusement.

dividende /dividɑ̃d/ *n.m.* dividend.

divin, ∼e /divɛ̃, -in/ *a.* divine.

divinité /divinite/ *n.f.* divinity.

divis|er /divize/ *v.t.*, **se ∼er** *v. pr.* divide. **∼ion** *n.f.* division.

divorc|e /divɔrs/ *n.m.* divorce. **∼é, ∼ée** *a.* divorced; *n.m., f.* divorcee. **∼er** *v.i.* **∼er (d'avec)**, divorce.

divulguer /divylge/ *v.t.* divulge.

dix /dis/ (/di/ *before consonant*, /diz/ *before vowel*) *a. & n.m.* ten. **∼ième** /dizjɛm/ *a. & n.m./f.* tenth.

dix-huit /dizɥit/ *a. & n.m.* eighteen. **∼ième** *a. & n.m./f.* eighteenth.

dix-neu|f /diznœf/ *a. & n.m.* nineteen. **∼vième** *a. & n.m./f.* nineteenth.

dix-sept /disɛt/ *a. & n.m.* seventeen. **∼ième** *a. & n.m./f.* seventeenth.

dizaine /dizɛn/ *n.f.* (about) ten.

docile /dɔsil/ *a.* docile.

dock /dɔk/ *n.m.* dock.

docker /dɔkɛr/ *n.m.* docker.

doct|eur /dɔktœr/ *n.m.* doctor. **∼oresse** *n.f.* lady doctor.

doctorat /dɔktɔra/ *n.m.* doctorate.

doctrin|e /dɔktrin/ *n.f.* doctrine. **∼aire** *a.* doctrinaire.

document /dɔkymɑ̃/ *n.m.* document. **∼aire** /-tɛr/ *a. & n.m.* documentary.

documentaliste /dɔkymɑ̃talist/ *n.m./f.* information officer.

document|er /dɔkymɑ̃te/ *v.t.* document. **se ∼er** *v. pr.* collect information. **∼ation** *n.f.* information, literature. **∼é** *a.* well-documented.

dodeliner /dɔdline/ *v.i.* **∼ de la tête**, sway one's head, nod.

dodo /dɔdo/ *n.m.* **faire ∼**, (*langage enfantin*) go to sleep.

dodu /dɔdy/ *a.* plump.

dogm|e /dɔgm/ *n.m.* dogma. **∼atique** *a.* dogmatic.

doigt /dwa/ *n.m.* finger. **∼ de pied**, toe.

doigté /dwate/ *n.m.* (*mus.*) fingering, touch; (*adresse*) tact.

doigtier /dwatje/ *n.m.* finger-stall.

dois, doit /dwa/ *voir* **devoir²**.

doléances /dɔleɑ̃s/ *n.f. pl.* grievances.

dollar /dɔlar/ *n.m.* dollar.

domaine /dɔmɛn/ *n.m.* estate, domain; (*fig.*) domain.

dôme /dom/ *n.m.* dome.

domestique /dɔmɛstik/ *a.* domestic. —*n.m./f.* servant.

domestiquer /dɔmɛstike/ *v.t.* domesticate.

domicile /dɔmisil/ *n.m.* home. **à ∼**, at home; (*livrer*) to the home.

domicilié /dɔmisilje/ *a.* resident.

domin|er /dɔmine/ *v.t./i.* dominate; (*surplomber*) tower over, dominate; (*équipe*) dictate the game (to). **∼ant, ∼ante** *a.* dominant; *n.f.* dominant feature. **∼ation** *n.f.* domination.

domino /dɔmino/ *n.m.* domino.

dommage /dɔmaʒ/ *n.m.* (*tort*) harm. **∼(s)**, (*dégâts*) damage. **c'est ∼**, it is a pity. **∼s-intérêts** *n.m. pl.* (*jurid.*) damages.

dompt|er /dɔ̃te/ *v.t.* tame. **∼eur, ∼euse** *n.m., f.* tamer.

don /dɔ̃/ *n.m.* (*cadeau, aptitude*) gift.

dona|teur, ∼trice /dɔnatœr, -tris/ *n.m., f.* donor.

donation /dɔnasjɔ̃/ *n.f.* donation.

donc /dɔ̃(k)/ *conj.* so, then; (*par consé-quent*) so, therefore.

donjon /dɔ̃ʒɔ̃/ *n.m.* (*tour*) keep.

donné /dɔne/ *a.* (*fixé*) given; (*pas cher: fam.*) dirt cheap. **étant ~ que,** given that.

données /dɔne/ *n.f. pl.* (*de science*) data; (*de problème*) facts.

donner /dɔne/ *v.t.* give; (*distribuer*) give out; (*récolte etc.*) produce. —*v.i.* **~ sur,** look out on to. **~ dans,** (*piège*) fall into. **ça donne soif/faim,** it makes one thirsty/hungry. **~ à répa-rer/**etc.*, take to be repaired/*etc.* **~ lieu à,** give rise to. **se ~ à,** devote o.s. to. **se ~ du mal,** go to a lot of trouble (**pour faire,** to do).

donneu|r, **~se** /dɔnœr, -øz/ *n.m., f.* (*de sang*) donor.

dont /dɔ̃/ *pron. rel.* (*chose*) whose, of which; (*personne*) whose; (*partie d'un tout*) of whom; (*chose*) of which; (*provenance*) from which; (*manière*) in which. **le père ~ la fille,** the father whose daughter. **ce ~,** what. **~ il a besoin,** which he needs. **l'enfant ~ il est fier,** the child he is proud of.

doper /dɔpe/ *v.t.* dope. **se ~** *v. pr.* take dope.

doré /dɔre/ *a.* (*couleur d'or*) golden.

dorénavant /dɔrenavɑ̃/ *adv.* hence-forth.

dorer /dɔre/ *v.t.* gild; (*culin.*) brown; (*peau*) tan.

dorloter /dɔrlɔte/ *v.t.* pamper.

dorm|ir† /dɔrmir/ *v.i.* sleep; (*être en-dormi*) be asleep. **~eur,** **~euse** *n.m., f.* sleeper.

dortoir /dɔrtwar/ *n.m.* dormitory.

dorure /dɔryr/ *n.f.* gilding.

dos /do/ *n.m.* back; (*de livre*) spine. **à ~ de,** riding on. **de ~,** from behind. **~ crawlé,** backstroke.

dos|e /doz/ *n.f.* dose. **~age** *n.m.* (*mélange*) mixture. **faire le ~age de,** measure out; balance. **~er** *v.t.* meas-ure out; (*équilibrer*) balance.

dossard /dɔsar/ *n.m.* (*sport*) number.

dossier /dɔsje/ *n.m.* (*documents*) file; (*de chaise*) back.

dot /dɔt/ *n.f.* dowry.

doter /dɔte/ *v.t.* **~ de,** equip with.

douan|e /dwan/ *n.f.* customs. **~ier,** **~ière** *a.* customs; *n.m., f.* customs officer.

doubl|e /dubl/ *a. & adv.* double. —*n.m.* (*copie*) duplicate; (*sosie*) double. **le ~e** (**de**), twice as much *ou* as many (as).

~e décimètre, ruler. **~ement**[1] *adv.* doubly.

doubl|er /duble/ *v.t./i.* double; (*dé-passer*) overtake; (*vêtement*) line; (*film*) dub; (*classe*) repeat; (*cap*) round. **~ement**[2] *n.m.* doubling. **~ure** *n.f.* (*étoffe*) lining; (*acteur*) understudy.

douce /dus/ *voir* **doux.**

douceâtre /dusɑtr/ *a.* sickly sweet.

doucement /dusmɑ̃/ *adv.* gently.

douceur /dusœr/ *n.f.* (*mollesse*) soft-ness; (*de climat*) mildness; (*de per-sonne*) gentleness; (*joie, plaisir*) sweetness. **~s,** (*friandises*) sweet things. **en ~,** smoothly.

douch|e /duʃ/ *n.f.* shower. **~er** *v.t.* give a shower to. **se ~er** *v. pr.* have *ou* take a shower.

doué /dwe/ *a.* gifted. **~ de,** endowed with.

douille /duj/ *n.f.* (*électr.*) socket.

douillet, **~te** /dujɛ, -t/ *a.* cosy, comfortable; (*personne: péj.*) soft.

doul|eur /dulœr/ *n.f.* pain; (*chagrin*) grief. **~oureux,** **~oureuse** *a.* pain-ful.

doute /dut/ *n.m.* doubt. **sans ~,** no doubt. **sans aucun ~,** without doubt.

douter /dute/ *v.i.* **~ de,** doubt. **se ~ de,** suspect.

douteu|x, **~se** /dutø, -z/ *a.* doubtful.

douve /duv/ *n.f.* moat.

Douvres /duvr/ *n.m./f.* Dover.

doux, douce /du, dus/ *a.* (*moelleux*) soft; (*sucré*) sweet; (*clément, pas fort*) mild; (*pas brusque, bienveillant*) gentle.

douzaine /duzɛn/ *n.f.* about twelve; (*douze*) dozen. **une ~ d'œufs/**etc.*, a dozen eggs/*etc.*

douz|e /duz/ *a. & n.m.* twelve. **~ième** *a. & n.m./f.* twelfth.

doyen, **~ne** /dwajɛ̃, -jɛn/ *n.m., f.* dean; (*en âge*) most senior person.

dragée /draʒe/ *n.f.* sugared almond.

dragon /dragɔ̃/ *n.m.* dragon.

dragu|e /drag/ *n.f.* (*bateau*) dredger. **~er** *v.t.* (*rivière*) dredge; (*filles: fam.*) chat up, try to pick up.

drainer /drene/ *v.t.* drain.

dramatique /dramatik/ *a.* dra-matic. —*n.f.* (*television*) drama.

dramatiser /dramatize/ *v.t.* dramat-ize.

dramaturge /dramatyrʒ/ *n.m./f.* dramatist.

drame /dram/ *n.m.* drama.

drap /dra/ *n.m.* sheet; (*tissu*) (woollen) cloth.

drapeau (*pl.* ~x) /drapo/ *n.m.* flag.

draper /drape/ *v.t.* drape.

draperies /drapri/ *n.f. pl.* (*tentures*) hangings.

dress|er /drese/ *v.t.* put up, erect; (*tête*) raise; (*animal*) train; (*liste*) draw up. **se ~er** *v. pr.* (*bâtiment etc.*) stand; (*personne*) draw o.s. up. **~er l'oreille,** prick up one's ears. **~age** /drɛsaʒ/ *n.m.* training. **~eur, ~euse** /drɛsœr, -øz/ *n.m., f.* trainer.

dribbler /drible/ *v.t./i.* (*football*) dribble.

drogue /drɔg/ *n.f.* drug. **la ~,** drugs.

drogu|er /drɔge/ *v.t.* (*malade*) drug heavily, dose up; (*victime*) drug. **se ~er** *v. pr.* take drugs. **~é, ~ée** *n.m., f.* drug addict.

drogu|erie /drɔgri/ *n.f.* hardware and chemist's shop; (*Amer.*) drugstore. **~iste** *n.m./f.* owner of a *droguerie*.

droit[1], **~e** /drwa, -t/ *a.* (*non courbe*) straight; (*loyal*) upright; (*angle*) right. *—adv.* straight. *—n.f.* straight line.

droit[2], **~e** /drwa, -t/ *a.* (*contraire de gauche*) right. **à ~e,** on the right; (*direction*) (to the) right. **la ~e,** the right (side); (*pol.*) the right (wing). **~ier, ~ière** /-tje, -tjɛr/ *a. & n.m., f.* right-handed (person).

droit[3] /drwa/ *n.m.* right. **~(s),** (*taxe*) duty; (*d'inscription*) fee(s). **le ~,** (*jurid.*) law. **avoir ~ à,** be entitled to. **avoir le ~ de,** be allowed to. **~ d'auteur,** copyright. **~s d'auteur,** royalties.

drôle /drol/ *a.* funny. **~ d'air,** funny look. **~ment** *adv.* funnily; (*extrêmement: fam.*) dreadfully.

dromadaire /drɔmadɛr/ *n.m.* dromedary.

dru /dry/ *a.* thick. **tomber ~,** fall thick and fast.

drugstore /drœgstɔr/ *n.m.* drugstore.

du /dy/ *voir* **de.**

dû, due /dy/ *voir* **devoir**[2]. *—a.* due. *—n.m.* due; (*argent*) dues. **~ à,** due to.

duc, duchesse /dyk, dyʃɛs/ *n.m., f.* duke, duchess.

duel /dɥɛl/ *n.m.* duel.

dûment /dymã/ *adv.* duly.

dune /dyn/ *n.f.* dune.

duo /dɥo/ *n.m.* (*mus.*) duet; (*fig.*) duo.

dup|e /dyp/ *n.f.* dupe. **~er** *v.t.* dupe.

duplex /dyplɛks/ *n.m.* split-level apartment; (*Amer.*) duplex; (*émission*) link-up.

duplicata /dyplikata/ *n.m. invar.* duplicate.

duplicateur /dyplikatœr/ *n.m.* duplicator.

duplicité /dyplisite/ *n.f.* duplicity.

duquel /dykɛl/ *voir* **lequel.**

dur /dyr/ *a.* hard; (*sévère*) harsh, hard; (*viande*) tough, hard; (*col, brosse*) stiff. *—adv.* hard. *—n.m.* tough guy. **~ d'oreille,** hard of hearing.

durable /dyrabl/ *a.* lasting.

durant /dyrã/ *prép.* during; (*mesure de temps*) for.

durc|ir /dyrsir/ *v.t./i.*, **se ~ir** *v. pr.* harden. **~issement** *n.m.* hardening.

durée /dyre/ *n.f.* length; (*période*) duration.

durement /dyrmã/ *adv.* harshly.

durer /dyre/ *v.i.* last.

dureté /dyrte/ *n.f.* hardness; (*sévérité*) harshness.

duvet /dyvɛ/ *n.m.* down; (*sac*) (down-filled) sleeping-bag.

dynami|que /dinamik/ *a.* dynamic. **~sme** *n.m.* dynamism.

dynamit|e /dinamit/ *n.f.* dynamite. **~er** *v.t.* dynamite.

dynastie /dinasti/ *n.f.* dynasty.

dysenterie /disãtri/ *n.f.* dysentery.

E

eau (*pl.* ~**x**) /o/ *n.f.* water. ~ **courante/dormante**, running/ still water. ~ **de Cologne**, eau-de-Cologne. ~ **dentifrice**, mouthwash. ~ **de toilette**, toilet water. ~**-de-vie** (*pl.* ~**x-de-vie**) *n.f.* brandy. ~ **douce/salée**, fresh/salt water. ~**-forte** (*pl.* ~**x-fortes**) *n.f.* etching. ~ **potable**, drinking water.

ébahir /ebair/ *v.t.* dumbfound.

ébats /eba/ *n.m. pl.* frolics.

ébattre (s') /(s)ebatr/ *v. pr.* frolic.

ébauch|e /eboʃ/ *n.f.* outline. ~**er** *v.t.* outline. **s'**~**er** *v. pr.* form.

ébène /ebɛn/ *n.f.* ebony.

ébéniste /ebenist/ *n.m.* cabinet-maker.

éberlué /ebɛrlɥe/ *a.* flabbergasted.

éblou|ir /ebluir/ *v.t.* dazzle. ~**issement** *n.m.* dazzle, dazzling; (*malaise*) dizzy turn.

éboueur /ebwœr/ *n.m.* dustman; (*Amer.*) garbage collector.

ébouillanter /ebujɑ̃te/ *v.t.* scald.

éboul|er (s') /(s)ebule/ *v. pr.* crumble, collapse. ~**ement** *n.m.* landslide. ~**is** *n.m. pl.* fallen rocks and earth.

ébouriffé /eburife/ *a.* dishevelled.

ébranler /ebrɑ̃le/ *v.t.* shake. **s'**~ *v. pr.* move off.

ébrécher /ebreʃe/ *v.t.* chip.

ébriété /ebrijete/ *n.f.* intoxication.

ébrouer (s') /(s)ebrue/ *v. pr.* shake o.s.

ébruiter /ebrɥite/ *v.t.* spread about.

ébullition /ebylisjɔ̃/ *n.f.* boiling. **en** ~, boiling.

écaille /ekaj/ *n.f.* (*de poisson*) scale; (*de peinture, roc*) flake; (*matière*) tortoiseshell.

écailler /ekaje/ *v.t.* (*poisson*) scale. **s'**~ *v. pr.* flake (off).

écarlate /ekarlat/ *a. & n.f.* scarlet.

écarquiller /ekarkije/ *v.t.* ~ **les yeux**, open one's eyes wide.

écart /ekar/ *n.m.* gap; (*de prix etc.*) difference; (*embardée*) swerve; (*de conduite*) lapse (**de**, in). **à l'**~, out of the way. **tenir à l'**~, (*participant*) keep out of things. **à l'**~ **de**, away from.

écarté /ekarte/ *a.* (*lieu*) remote.

écartement /ekartəmɑ̃/ *n.m.* gap.

écarter /ekarte/ *v.t.* (*objets*) move apart; (*ouvrir*) open; (*éliminer*) dismiss. ~ **qch. de**, move sth. away from. ~ **qn. de**, keep s.o. away from. **s'**~ *v. pr.* (*s'éloigner*) move away; (*quitter son chemin*) move aside. **s'**~ **de**, stray from.

ecclésiastique /eklezjastik/ *a.* ecclesiastical. —*n.m.* clergyman.

écervelé, ~**e** /esɛrvəle/ *a.* scatter-brained. —*n.m., f.* scatter-brain.

échafaud /eʃafo/ *n.m.* scaffold.

échafaudage /eʃafodaʒ/ *n.m.* scaffolding; (*amas*) heap.

échalote /eʃalɔt/ *n.f.* shallot.

échancr|é /eʃɑ̃kre/ *a.* (*robe*) low-cut. ~**ure** *n.f.* low neckline.

échang|e /eʃɑ̃ʒ/ *n.m.* exchange. **en** ~**e** (**de**), in exchange (for). ~**er** *v.t.* exchange (**contre**, for).

échangeur /eʃɑ̃ʒœr/ *n.m.* (*auto.*) interchange.

échantillon /eʃɑ̃tijɔ̃/ *n.m.* sample. ~**nage** /-jɔnaʒ/ *n.m.* range of samples.

échappatoire /eʃapatwar/ *n.f.* (*clever*) way out.

échappée /eʃape/ *n.f.* (*sport*) breakaway; (*vue*) vista.

échappement /eʃapmɑ̃/ *n.m.* exhaust.

échapper /eʃape/ *v.i.* ~ **à**, escape; (*en fuyant*) escape (from). **s'**~ *v. pr.* escape. ~ **des mains de** *ou* **à**, slip out of the hands of. **l'**~ **belle**, have a narrow *ou* lucky escape.

écharde /eʃard/ *n.f.* splinter.

écharpe /eʃarp/ *n.f.* scarf; (*de maire*) sash. **en** ~, (*bras*) in a sling.

écharper /eʃarpe/ *v.t.* cut to pieces.

échasse /eʃas/ *n.f.* stilt.

échauffer /eʃofe/ *v.t.* heat; (*fig.*) excite. **s'**~ *v. pr.* warm up.

échauffourée /eʃofure/ *n.f.* (*mil.*) skirmish; (*bagarre*) scuffle.

échéance /eʃeɑ̃s/ *n.f.* due date (for payment); (*délai*) deadline; (*obligation*) (financial) commitment.

échéant (le cas) /(ləkɑz)eʃeɑ̃/ *adv.* if the occasion arises, possibly.

échec /eʃɛk/ *n.m.* failure. ~**s**, (*jeu*) chess. ~ **et mat**, checkmate. **en** ~, in check.

échelle /eʃɛl/ *n.f.* ladder; (*dimension*) scale.

échelon /eʃlɔ̃/ *n.m.* rung; (*de fonctionnaire*) grade; (*niveau*) level.

échelonner /eʃlɔne/ *v.t.* spread out, space out.

échevelé /eʃəvle/ *a.* dishevelled.

échine /eʃin/ *n.f.* backbone.

échiquier /eʃikje/ *n.m.* chessboard.

écho /eko/ *n.m.* echo. ~s, (*dans la presse*) gossip.

échoppe /eʃɔp/ *n.f.* stall.

échouer[1] /eʃwe/ *v.i.* fail.

échouer[2] /eʃwe/ *v.t.* (*bateau*) ground. —*v.i.*, s'~ *v. pr.* run aground.

éclabouss|er /eklabuse/ *v.t.* splash. ~ure *n.f.* splash.

éclair /eklɛr/ *n.m.* (flash of) lightning; (*fig.*) flash; (*gâteau*) éclair. —*a. invar.* lightning.

éclairage /eklɛraʒ/ *n.m.* lighting; (*point de vue*) light.

éclaircie /eklɛrsi/ *n.f.* sunny interval.

éclairc|ir /eklɛrsir/ *v.t.* make lighter; (*mystère*) clear up. s'~ir *v. pr.* (*ciel*) clear; (*mystère*) become clearer. ~issement *n.m.* clarification.

éclairer /eklere/ *v.t.* light (up); (*personne*) give some light to; (*fig.*) enlighten; (*situation*) throw light on. —*v.i.* give light. s'~ *v. pr.* become clearer. s'~ à la bougie, use candle-light.

éclaireu|r, ~se /eklɛrœr, -øz/ *n.m., f.* (boy) scout, (girl) guide. —*n.m.* (*mil.*) scout.

éclat /ekla/ *n.m.* fragment; (*de lumière*) brightness; (*de rire*) (out)burst; (*splendeur*) brilliance.

éclatant, ~e /eklatɑ̃, -t/ *a.* brilliant.

éclat|er /eklate/ *v.i.* burst; (*exploser*) go off; (*verre*) shatter; (*guerre*) break out; (*groupe*) split up. ~er de rire, burst out laughing. ~ement *n.m.* bursting; (*de bombe*) explosion; (*scission*) split.

éclipse /eklips/ *n.f.* eclipse.

éclipser /eklipse/ *v.t.* eclipse. s'~ *v. pr.* (*fam.*) slip away.

éclopé /eklɔpe/ *a.* lame.

écl|ore /eklɔr/ *v.i.* (*œuf*) hatch; (*fleur*) open. ~osion *n.f.* hatching; opening.

écluse /eklyz/ *n.f.* (*de canal*) lock.

écœurer /ekœre/ *v.t.* sicken.

école /ekɔl/ *n.f.* school. ~ maternelle primaire/secondaire, nursery/primary/secondary school. ~ normale, teachers' training college.

écol|ier, ~ière /ekɔlje, -jɛr/ *n.m., f.* schoolboy, schoolgirl.

écolog|ie /ekɔlɔʒi/ *n.f.* ecology. ~ique *a.* ecological.

éconduire /ekɔ̃dɥir/ *v.t.* dismiss.

économe /ekɔnɔm/ *a.* thrifty. —*n.m./f.* bursar.

économ|ie /ekɔnɔmi/ *n.f.* economy. ~ies, (*argent*) savings. une ~ie de, (*gain*) a saving of. ~ie politique, economics. ~ique *a.* (*pol.*) economic; (*bon marché*) economical. ~iser *v.t./i.* save. ~iste *n.m./f.* economist.

écoper /ekɔpe/ *v.t.* bail out. ~ (de), (*fam.*) get.

écorce /ekɔrs/ *n.f.* bark; (*de fruit*) peel.

écorch|er /ekɔrʃe/ *v.t.* graze; (*animal*) skin. s'~er *v. pr.* graze o.s. ~ure *n.f.* graze.

écossais, ~e /ekɔsɛ, -z/ *a.* Scottish. —*n.m., f.* Scot.

Écosse /ekɔs/ *n.f.* Scotland.

écosser /ekɔse/ *v.t.* shell.

écot /eko/ *n.m.* share.

écouler[1] /ekule/ *v.t.* dispose of, sell.

écoul|er[2] (s') /(s)ekule/ *v. pr.* flow (out), run (off); (*temps*) pass. ~ement *n.m.* flow.

écourter /ekurte/ *v.t.* shorten.

écoute /ekut/ *n.f.* listening. à l'~ (de), listening in (to). aux ~s, attentive.

écout|er /ekute/ *v.t.* listen to; (*radio*) listen (in) to. —*v.i.* listen. ~eur *n.m.* earphones; (*de téléphone*) receiver.

écran /ekrɑ̃/ *n.m.* screen.

écrasant, ~e /ekrazɑ̃, -t/ *a.* overwhelming.

écraser /ekraze/ *v.t.* crush; (*piéton*) run over. s'~ *v. pr.* crash (contre, into).

écrémer /ekreme/ *v.t.* skim.

écrevisse /ekrəvis/ *n.f.* crayfish.

écrier (s') /(s)ekrije/ *v. pr.* exclaim.

écrin /ekrɛ̃/ *n.m.* case.

écrire† /ekrir/ *v.t./i.* write; (*orthographier*) spell. s'~ *v. pr.* (*mot*) be spelt.

écrit /ekri/ *n.m.* document; (*examen*) written paper. par ~, in writing.

écriteau (*pl.* ~x) /ekrito/ *n.m.* notice.

écriture /ekrityr/ *n.f.* writing. ~s, (*comm.*) accounts. l'É~ (sainte), the Scriptures.

écrivain /ekrivɛ̃/ *n.m.* writer.

écrou /ekru/ *n.m.* nut.

écrouer /ekrue/ *v.t.* imprison.

écrouler (s') /(s)ekrule/ *v. pr.* collapse.

écueil /ekœj/ *n.m.* reef; (*fig.*) danger.

écuelle /ekɥɛl/ *n.f.* bowl.

éculé /ekyle/ a. (*soulier*) worn at the heel; (*fig.*) well-worn.

écume /ekym/ n.f. foam; (*culin.*) scum.

écum|er /ekyme/ v.t. skim; (*piller*) plunder. —v.i. foam. **~oire** n.f. skimmer.

écureuil /ekyrœj/ n.m. squirrel.

écurie /ekyri/ n.f. stable.

écusson /ekysõ/ n.m. badge.

écuy|er, ~ère /ekuije, -jɛr/ n.m., f. (horse) rider.

édenté /edɑ̃te/ a. toothless.

édifice /edifis/ n.m. building.

édif|ier /edifje/ v.t. construct; (*porter à la vertu, éclairer*) edify. **~ication** n.f. construction; edification.

édit /edi/ n.m. edict.

édi|ter /edite/ v.t. publish; (*annoter*) edit. **~teur, ~trice** n.m., f. publisher; editor.

édition /edisjõ/ n.f. edition; (*industrie*) publishing.

éditor|ial (*pl.* **~iaux**) /editɔrjal, -jo/ n.m. editorial.

édredon /edrədõ/ n.m. eiderdown.

éducati|f, ~ve /edykatif, -v/ a. educational.

éducation /edykasjõ/ n.f. education; (*dans la famille*) upbringing; (*manières*) manners.

éduquer /edyke/ v.t. educate; (*à la maison*) bring up.

effac|é /efase/ a. (*modeste*) unassuming. **~ement** n.m. unassuming manner; (*suppression*) erasure.

effacer /efase/ v.t. (*gommer*) rub out; (*par lavage*) wash out; (*souvenir etc.*) erase. **s'~** v. pr. fade; (*s'écarter*) step aside.

effar|er /efare/ v.t. alarm. **~ement** n.m. alarm.

effaroucher /efaruʃe/ v.t. scare away.

effecti|f¹, ~ve /efɛktif, -v/ a. effective. **~vement** adv. effectively; (*en effet*) indeed.

effectif² /efɛktif/ n.m. size, strength. **~s,** numbers.

effectuer /efɛktɥe/ v.t. carry out, make.

efféminé /efemine/ a. effeminate.

effervescen|t, ~te /efɛrvesɑ̃, -t/ a. (*agité*) excited. **~ce** n.f. excitement.

effet /efɛ/ n.m. effect; (*impression*) impression. **~s,** (*habits*) clothes, things. **en ~,** indeed. **faire de l'~,** have an effect, be effective.

effeuiller /efœje/ v.t. remove the leaves *ou* petals from.

efficac|e /efikas/ a. effective; (*personne*) efficient. **~ité** n.f. effectiveness; efficiency.

effigie /efiʒi/ n.f. effigy.

effilé /efile/ a. slender, tapering.

effilocher (s') /(s)efiloʃe/ v. pr. fray.

efflanqué /eflɑ̃ke/ a. emaciated.

effleurer /eflœre/ v.t. touch lightly; (*sujet*) touch on; (*se présenter à*) occur to.

effondr|er (s') /(s)efõdre/ v. pr. collapse. **~ement** n.m. collapse.

efforcer (s') /(s)eforse/ v. pr. try (hard) (**de,** to).

effort /efɔr/ n.m. effort.

effraction /efraksjõ/ n.f. **entrer par ~,** break in.

effranger (s') /(s)efrɑ̃ʒe/ v. pr. fray.

effray|er /efreje/ v.t. frighten; (*décourager*) put off. **s'~er** v. pr. be frightened. **~ant, ~ante** a. frightening; (*fig.*) frightful.

effréné /efrene/ a. wild.

effriter (s') /(s)efrite/ v. pr. crumble.

effroi /efrwa/ n.m. dread.

effronté /efrõte/ a. impudent.

effroyable /efrwajabl/ a. dreadful.

effusion /efyzjõ/ n.f. **~ de sang,** bloodshed.

égailler (s') /(s)egaje/ v. pr. disperse.

ég|al, ~ale (*m. pl.* **~aux**) /egal, -o/ a. equal; (*surface, vitesse*) even. —n.m., f. equal. **ça m'est/lui est ~al,** it is all the same to me/him.

également /egalmɑ̃/ adv. equally; (*aussi*) as well.

égaler /egale/ v.t. equal.

égaliser /egalize/ v.t./i. (*sport*) equalize; (*niveler*) level out.

égalit|é /egalite/ n.f. equality; (*de surface, d'humeur*) evenness. **à ~é (de points),** equal. **~aire** a. egalitarian.

égard /egar/ n.m. regard. **~s,** consideration. **à cet ~,** in this respect. **à l'~ de,** with regard to; (*envers*) towards.

égar|er /egare/ v.t. mislay; (*tromper*) lead astray. **s'~er** v. pr. get lost; (*se tromper*) go astray. **~ement** n.m. loss; (*affolement*) confusion.

égayer /egeje/ v.t. (*personne*) cheer up; (*pièce*) brighten up.

égide /eʒid/ n.f. aegis.

églefin /egləfɛ̃/ n.m. haddock.

église /egliz/ n.f. church.

égoïs|te /egɔist/ a. selfish. —n.m./f. egoist. **~me** n.m. selfishness, egoism.

égorger /egɔrʒe/ v.t. slit the throat of.

égosiller (s') /(s)egozije/ v. pr. shout one's head off.

égout /egu/ n.m. sewer.

égoutt|er /egute/ v.t./i., **s'~er** v. pr. (vaisselle) drain. **~oir** n.m. draining-board; (panier) dish drainer.

égratign|er /egratiɲe/ v.t. scratch. **~ure** n.f. scratch.

égrener /egrəne/ v.t. (raisins) pick off; (notes) sound one by one.

Égypte /eʒipt/ n.f. Egypt.

égyptien, ~ne /eʒipsjɛ̃, -jɛn/ a. & n.m., f. Egyptian.

eh /e/ int. hey. **~ bien**, well.

éhonté /eɔ̃te/ a. shameless.

éjecter /eʒɛkte/ v.t. eject.

élabor|er /elabɔre/ v.t. elaborate. **~ation** n.f. elaboration.

élaguer /elage/ v.t. prune.

élan[1] /elɑ̃/ n.m. (sport) run-up; (vitesse) momentum; (fig.) surge.

élan[2] /elɑ̃/ n.m. (animal) moose.

élancé /elɑ̃se/ a. slender.

élancer (s') /(s)elɑ̃se/ v. pr. leap forward, dash; (se dresser) soar.

élarg|ir /elarʒir/ v.t., **s'~ir** v. pr. widen. **~issement** n.m. widening.

élasti|que /elastik/ a. elastic. —n.m. elastic band; (tissu) elastic. **~cité** n.f. elasticity.

élec|teur, ~trice /elɛktœr, -tris/ n.m., f. voter, elector.

élection /elɛksjɔ̃/ n.f. election.

élector|al (m. pl. **~aux**) /elɛktɔral, -o/ a. (réunion etc.) election; (collège) electoral.

électorat /elɛktɔra/ n.m. electorate, voters.

électricien /elɛktrisjɛ̃/ n.m. electrician.

électricité /elɛktrisite/ n.f. electricity.

électrifier /elɛktrifje/ v.t. electrify.

électrique /elɛktrik/ a. electric(al).

électrocuter /elɛktrɔkyte/ v.t. electrocute.

électron /elɛktrɔ̃/ n.m. electron.

électronique /elɛktrɔnik/ a. electronic. —n.f. electronics.

électrophone /elɛktrɔfɔn/ n.m. record-player.

élég|ant, ~ante /elegɑ̃, -t/ a. elegant. **~amment** adv. elegantly. **~ance** n.f. elegance.

élément /elemɑ̃/ n.m. element; (meuble) unit. **~aire** /-ter/ a. elementary.

éléphant /elefɑ̃/ n.m. elephant.

élevage /ɛlvaʒ/ n.m. (stock-)breeding.

élévation /elevasjɔ̃/ n.f. raising; (hausse) rise; (plan) elevation.

élève /elɛv/ n.m./f. pupil.

élevé /elve/ a. high; (noble) elevated. **bien ~**, well-mannered.

élever /elve/ v.t. raise; (enfants) bring up, raise; (animal) breed. **s'~** v. pr. rise; (dans le ciel) soar up. **s'~ à**, amount to.

éleveu|r, ~se /ɛlvœr, -øz/ n.m., f. (stock-)breeder.

éligible /eliʒibl/ a. eligible.

élimé /elime/ a. worn thin.

élimin|er /elimine/ v.t. eliminate. **~ation** n.f. elimination. **~atoire** a. eliminating; n.f. (sport) heat.

élire† /elir/ v.t. elect.

élision /elizjɔ̃/ n.f. (gram.) elision.

élite /elit/ n.f. élite.

elle /ɛl/ pron. she; (complément) her; (chose) it. **~-même** pron. herself; itself.

elles /ɛl/ pron. they; (complément) them. **~-mêmes** pron. themselves.

ellip|se /elips/ n.f. ellipse. **~tique** a. elliptical.

élocution /elɔkysjɔ̃/ n.f. diction.

élog|e /elɔʒ/ n.m. praise. **faire l'~e de**, praise. **~ieux, ~ieuse** a. laudatory.

éloigné /elwaɲe/ a. distant. **~ de**, far away from.

éloign|er /elwaɲe/ v.t. take away ou remove (**de**, from); (personne aimée) estrange (**de**, from); (danger) ward off; (visite) put off. **s'~er** v. pr. go ou move away (**de**, from); (affectivement) become estranged (**de**, from). **~ement** n.m. removal; (distance) distance; (oubli) estrangement.

éloquen|t, ~te /elɔkɑ̃, -t/ a. eloquent. **~ce** n.f. eloquence.

élu, ~e /ely/ a. elected. —n.m.,f. (pol.) elected representative.

élucider /elyside/ v.t. elucidate.

éluder /elyde/ v.t. elude.

émacié /emasje/ a. emaciated.

ém|ail (pl. **~aux**) /emaj, -o/ n.m. enamel.

émaillé /emaje/ a. enamelled. **~ de**, studded with.

émancip|er /emɑ̃sipe/ v.t. emancipate. **s'~er** v. pr. become emancipated. **~ation** n.f. emancipation.

éman|er /emane/ v.i. emanate. **~ation** n.f. emanation.

émarger /emarʒe/ v.t. initial.

emball|er /ɑ̃bale/ v.t. pack, wrap; (personne: fam.) enthuse. **s'~er** v. pr.

(*moteur*) race; (*cheval*) bolt; (*personne*) get carried away. ~**age** *n.m.* package, wrapping.

embarcadère /ɑ̃barkadɛr/ *n.m.* landing-stage.

embarcation /ɑ̃barkɑsjɔ̃/ *n.f.* boat.

embardée /ɑ̃barde/ *n.f.* swerve.

embargo /ɑ̃bargo/ *n.m.* embargo.

embarqu|er /ɑ̃barke/ *v.t.* embark; (*charger*) load; (*emporter: fam.*) cart off. —*v.i.*, **s'~er** *v. pr.* board, embark. **s'~er dans**, embark upon. ~**ement** *n.m.* embarkation; loading.

embarras /ɑ̃bara/ *n.m.* obstacle; (*gêne*) embarrassment; (*difficulté*) difficulty.

embarrasser /ɑ̃barase/ *v.t.* clutter (up); (*gêner dans les mouvements*) hinder; (*fig.*) embarrass. **s'~ de**, burden o.s. with.

embauch|e /ɑ̃boʃ/ *n.f.* hiring; (*emploi*) employment. ~**er** *v.t.* hire, take on.

embaumer /ɑ̃bome/ *v.t./i.* (make) smell fragrant; (*cadavre*) embalm.

embellir /ɑ̃belir/ *v.t.* brighten up; (*récit*) embellish.

embêt|er /ɑ̃bete/ *v.t.* (*fam.*) annoy. **s'~er** *v. pr.* (*fam.*) get bored. ~**ant**, ~**ante** *a.* (*fam.*) annoying. ~**ement** /ɑ̃bɛtmɑ̃/ *n.m.* (*fam.*) annoyance.

emblée (d') /(d)ɑ̃ble/ *adv.* right away.

emblème /ɑ̃blɛm/ *n.m.* emblem.

emboîter /ɑ̃bwate/ *v.t.*, **s'~** *v. pr.* fit together. **(s')~ dans**, fit into. **~ le pas à qn.**, (*imiter*) follow suit.

embonpoint /ɑ̃bɔ̃pwɛ̃/ *n.m.* stoutness.

embouchure /ɑ̃buʃyr/ *n.f.* (*de fleuve*) mouth; (*mus.*) mouthpiece.

embourber (s') /(s)ɑ̃burbe/ *v. pr.* get bogged down.

embourgeoiser (s') /(s)ɑ̃burʒwaze/ *v. pr.* become middle-class.

embouteillage /ɑ̃butɛjaʒ/ *n.m.* traffic jam.

emboutir /ɑ̃butir/ *v.t.* (*heurter*) crash into.

embranchement /ɑ̃brɑ̃ʃmɑ̃/ *n.m.* (*de routes*) junction.

embraser /ɑ̃brɑze/ *v.t.* set on fire, fire. **s'~** *v. pr.* flare up.

embrass|er /ɑ̃brase/ *v.t.* kiss; (*adopter, contenir*) embrace. **s'~er** *v. pr.* kiss. ~**ades** *n.f. pl.* kissing.

embrasure /ɑ̃brɑzyr/ *n.f.* opening.

embray|er /ɑ̃breje/ *v.i.* let in the clutch. ~**age** /ɑ̃brɛjaʒ/ *n.m.* clutch.

embrigader /ɑ̃brigade/ *v.t.* enrol.

embrocher /ɑ̃brɔʃe/ *v.t.* (*viande*) spit.

embrouiller /ɑ̃bruje/ *v.t.* mix up; (*fils*) tangle. **s'~** *v. pr.* get mixed up.

embroussaillé /ɑ̃brusaje/ *a.* (*poils, chemin*) bushy.

embryon /ɑ̃brijɔ̃/ *n.m.* embryo. ~**naire** /-jɔnɛr/ *a.* embryonic.

embûches /ɑ̃byʃ/ *n.f. pl.* traps.

embuer /ɑ̃bɥe/ *v.t.* mist up.

embuscade /ɑ̃byskad/ *n.f.* ambush.

embusquer (s') /(s)ɑ̃byske/ *v. pr.* lie in ambush.

éméché /emeʃe/ *a.* tipsy.

émeraude /ɛmrod/ *n.f.* emerald.

émerger /emɛrʒe/ *v.i.* emerge; (*fig.*) stand out.

émeri /ɛmri/ *n.m.* emery.

émerveill|er /emɛrveje/ *v.t.* amaze. **s'~er de**, marvel at, be amazed at. ~**ement** /-vɛjmɑ̃/ *n.m.* amazement, wonder.

émett|re† /emɛtr/ *v.t.* give out; (*message*) transmit; (*timbre, billet*) issue; (*opinion*) express. ~**eur** *n.m.* transmitter.

émeut|e /emøt/ *n.f.* riot. ~**ier**, ~**ière** *n.m., f.* rioter.

émietter /emjete/ *v.t.*, **s'~** *v. pr.* crumble.

émigrant, ~**e** /emigrɑ̃, -t/ *n.m., f.* emigrant.

émigré, ~**e** /emigre/ *n.m., f.* exile.

émigr|er /emigre/ *v.i.* emigrate. ~**ation** *n.f.* emigration.

émin|ent, ~**ente** /eminɑ̃, -t/ *a.* eminent. ~**emment** /-amɑ̃/ *adv.* eminently. ~**ence** *n.f.* eminence; (*colline*) hill.

émissaire /emisɛr/ *n.m.* emissary.

émission /emisjɔ̃/ *n.f.* emission; (*de message*) transmission; (*de timbre*) issue; (*programme*) broadcast.

emmagasiner /ɑ̃magazine/ *v.t.* store.

emmanchure /ɑ̃mɑ̃ʃyr/ *n.f.* armhole.

emmêler /ɑ̃mele/ *v.t.* tangle.

emménager /ɑ̃menaʒe/ *v.i.* move in. **~ dans**, move into.

emmener /ɑ̃mne/ *v.t.* take; (*comme prisonnier*) take away.

emmerder /ɑ̃mɛrde/ *v.t.* (*argot*) bother. **s'~** *v. pr.* (*argot*) get bored.

emmitoufler /ɑ̃mitufle/ *v.t.*, **s'~** *v. pr.* wrap up (warmly).

emmurer /ɑ̃myre/ *v.t.* trap, wall in.

émoi /emwa/ *n.m.* excitement.

émoluments /emɔlymɑ̃/ *n.m.pl.* remuneration.

émonder /emɔ̃de/ *v.t.* prune.

émoti|f, ~**ve** /emɔtif, -v/ *a.* emotional.

émotion /emosjɔ̃/ *n.f.* emotion; (*peur*) fright. **∼nel**, **∼nelle** /-jɔnɛl/ *a.* emotional.

émousser /emuse/ *v.t.* blunt.

émouv|oir /emuvwar/ *v.t.* move. **s'∼oir** *v. pr.* be moved. **∼ant**, **∼ante** *a.* moving.

empailler /ɑ̃paje/ *v.t.* stuff.

empaler /ɑ̃pale/ *v.t.* impale.

empaqueter /ɑ̃pakte/ *v.t.* package.

emparer (s') /(s)ɑ̃pare/ *v. pr.* **s'∼ de**, seize.

empâter (s') /(s)ɑ̃pɑte/ *v. pr.* fill out, grow fatter.

empêchement /ɑ̃pɛʃmɑ̃/ *n.m.* hitch, difficulty.

empêcher /ɑ̃peʃe/ *v.t.* prevent. **∼ de faire**, prevent *ou* stop (from) doing. **il ne peut pas s'∼ de penser**, he cannot help thinking.

empeigne /ɑ̃pɛɲ/ *n.f.* upper.

empereur /ɑ̃prœr/ *n.m.* emperor.

empeser /ɑ̃pəze/ *v.t.* starch.

empester /ɑ̃pɛste/ *v.t.* make stink, stink out; (*essence etc.*) stink of. *–v.i.* stink.

empêtrer (s') /(s)ɑ̃petre/ *v. pr.* become entangled.

emphase /ɑ̃faz/ *n.f.* pomposity.

empiéter /ɑ̃pjete/ *v.i.* **∼ sur**, encroach upon.

empiffrer (s') /(s)ɑ̃pifre/ *v. pr.* (*fam.*) gorge o.s.

empiler /ɑ̃pile/ *v.t.*, **s'∼** *v. pr.* pile (up).

empire /ɑ̃pir/ *n.m.* empire; (*fig.*) control.

empirer /ɑ̃pire/ *v.i.* worsen.

empirique /ɑ̃pirik/ *a.* empirical.

emplacement /ɑ̃plasmɑ̃/ *n.m.* site.

emplâtre /ɑ̃plɑtr/ *n.m.* (*méd*) plaster.

emplette /ɑ̃plɛt/ *n.f.* purchase. **∼s**, shopping.

emplir /ɑ̃plir/ *v.t.*, **s'∼** *v. pr.* fill.

emploi /ɑ̃plwa/ *n.m.* use; (*travail*) job. **∼ du temps**, timetable. **l'∼**, (*pol.*) employment.

employ|er /ɑ̃plwaje/ *v.t.* use; (*personne*) employ. **s'∼er** *v. pr.* be used. **s'∼er à**, devote o.s. to. **∼é**, **∼ée** *n.m.*, *f.* employee. **∼eur**, **∼euse** *n.m.*, *f.* employer.

empocher /ɑ̃pɔʃe/ *v.t.* pocket.

empoign|er /ɑ̃pwaɲe/ *v.t.* grab. **s'∼er** *v. pr.* have a row. **∼ade** *n.f.* row.

empoisonn|er /ɑ̃pwazɔne/ *v.t.* poison; (*empuantir*) stink out; (*embêter: fam.*) annoy. **∼ement** *n.m.* poisoning.

emport|é /ɑ̃pɔrte/ *a.* quick-tempered. **∼ement** *n.m.* anger.

emporter /ɑ̃pɔrte/ *v.t.* take (away); (*entraîner*) carry away; (*prix*) carry off; (*arracher*) tear off. **∼ un chapeau/***etc.*, (*vent*) blow off a hat/*etc.* **s'∼** *v. pr.* lose one's temper. **l'∼**, get the upper hand (**sur**, of).

empourpré /ɑ̃purpre/ *a.* crimson.

empreint, **∼e** /ɑ̃prɛ̃, -t/ *a.* **∼ de**, marked with. *–n.f.* mark. **∼e (digitale)**, fingerprint. **∼e de pas**, footprint.

empress|er (s') /(s)ɑ̃prese/ *v. pr.* **s'∼er auprès de**, be attentive to. **s'∼er de**, hasten to. **∼é** *a.* eager, attentive. **∼ement** /ɑ̃prɛsmɑ̃/ *n.m.* eagerness.

emprise /ɑ̃priz/ *n.f.* influence.

emprisonn|er /ɑ̃prizɔne/ *v.t.* imprison. **∼ement** *n.m.* imprisonment.

emprunt /ɑ̃prœ̃/ *n.m.* loan. **faire un ∼**, take out a loan.

emprunté /ɑ̃prœ̃te/ *a.* awkward.

emprunt|er /ɑ̃prœ̃te/ *v.t.* borrow (**à**, from); (*route*) take; (*fig.*) assume. **∼eur**, **∼euse** *n.m.*, *f.* borrower.

empuantir /ɑ̃pɥɑtir/ *v.t.* make stink, stink out.

ému /emy/ *a.* moved; (*apeuré*) nervous; (*joyeux*) excited.

émulation /emylasjɔ̃/ *n.f.* emulation.

émule /emyl/ *n.m./f.* imitator.

émulsion /emylsjɔ̃/ *n.f.* emulsion.

en[1] /ɑ̃/ *prép.* in; (*avec direction*) to; (*manière, état*) in, on; (*moyen de transport*) by; (*composition*) made of. **∼ cadeau/médecin/***etc.*, as a present/doctor/*etc.* **∼ guerre**, at war. **∼ faisant**, by *ou* on *ou* while doing.

en[2] /ɑ̃/ *pron.* of it, of them; (*moyen*) with it; (*cause*) from it; (*lieu*) from there. **∼ avoir/vouloir/***etc.*, have/want/*etc.* some. **ne pas ∼ avoir/vouloir/***etc.*, not have/want/*etc.* any. **où ∼ êtes-vous?**, where are you up to?, how far have you got?

encadr|er /ɑ̃kadre/ *v.t.* frame; (*entourer d'un trait*) circle; (*entourer*) surround. **∼ement** *n.m.* framing; (*de porte*) frame.

encaissé /ɑ̃kese/ *a.* steep-sided.

encaiss|er /ɑ̃kese/ *v.t.* (*argent*) collect; (*chèque*) cash; (*coups: fam.*) take. **∼eur** /ɑ̃kesœr/ *n.m.* debt-collector.

en-cas /ɑ̃kɑ/ *n.m.* (stand-by) snack.

encastrer /ɑ̃kastre/ *v.t.* embed.

encaustiqu|e /ãkɔstik/ *n.f.* wax polish. **~er** *v.t.* wax.

enceinte[1] /ãsɛ̃t/ *a.f.* pregnant.

enceinte[2] /ãsɛ̃t/ *n.f.* wall; (*espace*) enclosure.

encens /ãsã/ *n.m.* incense.

encercler /ãsɛrkle/ *v.t.* surround.

enchaîn|er /ãʃene/ *v.t.* chain (up); (*coordonner*) link (up). —*v.i.* continue. **s'~er** *v. pr.* be linked (up). **~ement** /ãʃɛnmã/ *n.m.* (*suite*) chain; (*liaison*) link(ing).

enchant|er /ãʃãte/ *v.t.* delight; (*ensorceler*) enchant. **~é** *a.* (*ravi*) delighted. **~ement** *n.m.* delight; (*magie*) enchantment.

enchâsser /ãʃase/ *v.t.* set.

enchère /ãʃɛr/ *n.f.* bid. **mettre** *ou* **vendre aux ~s**, sell by auction.

enchevêtrer /ãʃvetre/ *v.t.* tangle. **s'~** *v. pr.* become tangled.

enclave /ãklav/ *n.f.* enclave.

enclencher /ãklãʃe/ *v.t.* engage.

enclin, ~e /ãklɛ̃, -in/ *a.* **~ à**, inclined to.

enclore /ãklɔr/ *v.t.* enclose.

enclos /ãklo/ *n.m.* enclosure.

enclume /ãklym/ *n.f.* anvil.

encoche /ãkɔʃ/ *n.f.* notch.

encoignure /ãkɔɲyr/ *n.f.* corner.

encoller /ãkɔle/ *v.t.* paste.

encolure /ãkɔlyr/ *n.f.* neck.

encombr|er /ãkɔ̃bre/ *v.t.* clutter (up); (*gêner*) hamper. **s'~er de**, burden o.s. with. **~ant, ~ante** *a.* cumbersome. **~ement** *n.m.* congestion; (*auto.*) traffic jam; (*volume*) bulk.

encontre de (à l') /(al)ãkɔ̃trədə/ *prép.* against.

encore /ãkɔr/ *adv.* (*toujours*) still; (*de nouveau*) again; (*de plus*) more; (*aussi*) also. **~ mieux/plus grand/** *etc.*, even better/larger/*etc.* **~ une heure/un café/***etc.*, another hour/coffee/*etc.* **pas ~**, not yet. **si ~**, if only.

encourag|er /ãkuraʒe/ *v.t.* encourage. **~ement** *n.m.* encouragement.

encourir /ãkurir/ *v.t.* incur.

encrasser /ãkrase/ *v.t.* clog up (with dirt).

encr|e /ãkr/ *n.f.* ink. **~er** *v.t.* ink.

encrier /ãkrije/ *n.m.* ink-well.

encroûter (s') /(s)ãkrute/ *v. pr.* become doggedly set in one's ways. **s'~ dans**, sink into.

encylopéd|ie /ãsiklɔpedi/ *n.f.* encyclopaedia. **~ique** *a.* encyclopaedic.

endetter /ãdete/ *v.t.*, **s'~** *v. pr.* get into debt.

endeuiller /ãdœje/ *v.t.* plunge into mourning.

endiablé /ãdjable/ *a.* wild.

endiguer /ãdige/ *v.t.* dam; (*fig.*) check.

endimanché /ãdimãʃe/ *a.* in one's Sunday best.

endive /ãdiv/ *n.f.* chicory.

endoctrin|er /ãdɔktrine/ *v.t.* indoctrinate. **~ement** *n.m.* indoctrination.

endommager /ãdɔmaʒe/ *v.t.* damage.

endorm|ir /ãdɔrmir/ *v.t.* send to sleep; (*atténuer*) allay. **s'~ir** *v. pr.* fall asleep. **~i** *a.* asleep; (*apathique*) sleepy.

endosser /ãdɔse/ *v.t.* (*vêtement*) put on; (*assumer*) assume; (*comm.*) endorse.

endroit /ãdrwa/ *n.m.* place; (*de tissu*) right side. **à l'~**, the right way round, right side out.

end|uire /ãdɥir/ *v.t.* coat. **~uit** *n.m.* coating.

endurance /ãdyrãs/ *n.f.* endurance.

endurant, ~e /ãdyrã, -t/ *a.* tough.

endurcir /ãdyrsir/ *v.t.* harden. **s'~** *v. pr.* become hard(ened).

endurer /ãdyre/ *v.t.* endure.

énerg|ie /enɛrʒi/ *n.f.* energy. **~étique** *a.* energy. **~ique** *a.* energetic.

énerver /enɛrve/ *v.t.* irritate. **s'~** *v. pr.* get worked up.

enfance /ãfãs/ *n.f.* childhood; (*début*) infancy.

enfant /ãfã/ *n.m./f.* child. **~ en bas âge**, infant. **~illage** /-tijaʒ/ *n.m.* childishness. **~in, ~ine** /-tɛ̃, -tin/ *a.* childlike; (*puéril*) childish; (*jeu, langage*) children's.

enfanter /ãfãte/ *v.t./i.* give birth (to).

enfer /ãfɛr/ *n.m.* hell.

enfermer /ãfɛrme/ *v.t.* shut up. **s'~** *v. pr.* shut o.s. up.

enferrer (s') /(s)ãfere/ *v. pr.* become entangled.

enfiévré /ãfjevre/ *a.* feverish.

enfilade /ãfilad/ *n.f.* string, row.

enfiler /ãfile/ *v.t.* (*aiguille*) thread; (*anneaux*) string; (*vêtement*) slip on; (*rue*) take; (*insérer*) insert.

enfin /ãfɛ̃/ *adv.* at last, finally; (*en dernier lieu*) finally; (*somme toute*) after all; (*résignation, conclusion*) well.

enflammer /ãflame/ *v.t.* set fire to; (*méd.*) inflame. **s'~** *v. pr.* catch fire.

enfl|er /ãfle/ v.t./i., **s'∼er** v. pr. swell. **∼é** a. swollen. **∼ure** n.f. swelling.

enfoncer /ãfɔ̃se/ v.t. (épingle etc.) push ou drive in; (chapeau) push down; (porte) break down; (mettre) thrust, put. —v.i., **s'∼** v. pr. sink (**dans**, into).

enfouir /ãfwir/ v.t. bury.

enfourcher /ãfurʃe/ v.t. mount.

enfourner /ãfurne/ v.t. put in the oven.

enfreindre /ãfrɛ̃dr/ v.t. infringe.

enfuir† (**s'**) /(s)ãfɥir/ v. pr. run off.

enfumer /ãfyme/ v.t. fill with smoke.

engageant, ∼e /ãgaʒã, -t/ a. attractive.

engag|er /ãgaʒe/ v.t. (lier) bind, commit; (embaucher) take on; (commencer) start; (introduire) insert; (entraîner) involve; (encourager) urge; (investir) invest. **s'∼er** v. pr. (promettre) commit o.s.; (commencer) start; (soldat) enlist; (concurrent) enter. **s'∼er à faire**, undertake to do. **s'∼er dans**, (voie) enter. **∼ement** n.m. (promesse) promise; (pol., comm.) commitment; (début) start; (inscription: sport) entry.

engelure /ãʒlyr/ n.f. chilblain.

engendrer /ãʒãdre/ v.t. beget; (causer) generate.

engin /ãʒɛ̃/ n.m. machine; (outil) instrument; (projectile) missile. **∼ explosif**, explosive device.

englober /ãglɔbe/ v.t. include.

engloutir /ãglutir/ v.t. swallow (up). **s'∼** v. pr. (navire) be engulfed.

engorger /ãgɔrʒe/ v.t. block.

engou|er (**s'**) /(s)ãgwe/ v. pr. **s'∼er de**, become infatuated with. **∼ement** /-umã/ n.m. infatuation.

engouffrer /ãgufre/ v.t. devour. **s'∼ dans**, rush into (with force).

engourd|ir /ãgurdir/ v.t. numb. **s'∼ir** v. pr. go numb. **∼i** a. numb.

engrais /ãgrɛ/ n.m. manure; (chimique) fertilizer.

engraisser /ãgrese/ v.t. fatten. **s'∼** v. pr. get fat.

engrenage /ãgrənaʒ/ n.m. gears; (fig.) chain (of events).

engueuler /ãgœle/ v.t. (argot) curse, swear at, hurl abuse at.

enhardir (**s'**) /(s)ãardir/ v. pr. become bolder.

énième /ɛnjɛm/ a. (fam.) umpteenth.

énigm|e /enigm/ n.f. riddle, enigma. **∼atique** a. enigmatic.

enivrer /ãnivre/ v.t. intoxicate. **s'∼** v. pr. get drunk.

enjamb|er /ãʒãbe/ v.t. step over; (pont) span. **∼ée** n.f. stride.

enjeu (pl. **∼x**) /ãʒø/ n.m. stake(s).

enjôler /ãʒole/ v.t. wheedle.

enjoliver /ãʒɔlive/ v.t. embellish.

enjoliveur /ãʒɔlivœr/ n.m. hub-cap.

enjoué /ãʒwe/ a. cheerful.

enlacer /ãlase/ v.t. entwine.

enlaidir /ãledir/ v.t. make ugly. —v.i. grow ugly.

enlèvement /ãlɛvmã/ n.m. removal; (rapt) kidnapping.

enlever /ãlve/ v.t. (emporter) take (away), remove (**à**, from); (vêtement) take off, remove; (tache, organe) take out, remove; (kidnapper) kidnap; (gagner) win.

enliser (**s'**) /(s)ãlize/ v. pr. get bogged down.

enneig|é /ãneʒe/ a. snow-covered. **∼ement** /ãnɛʒmã/ n.m. snow conditions.

ennemi /ɛnmi/ n.m. & a. enemy. **∼ de**, (fig.) hostile to.

ennui /ãnɥi/ n.m. boredom; (tracas) trouble, worry.

ennuyer /ãnɥije/ v.t. bore; (irriter) annoy; (préoccuper) worry. **s'∼** v. pr. get bored.

ennuyeu|x, ∼se /ãnɥijø, -z/ a. boring; (fâcheux) annoying.

énoncé /enɔ̃se/ n.m. wording, text; (gram.) utterance.

énoncer /enɔ̃se/ v.t. express, state.

enorgueillir (**s'**) /(s)ãnɔrgœjir/ v. pr. **s'∼ de**, pride o.s. on.

énorm|e /enɔrm/ a. enormous. **∼ément** adv. enormously. **∼ément de**, an enormous amount of. **∼ité** n.f. enormous size; (atrocité) enormity; (bévue) enormous blunder.

enquérir (**s'**) /(s)ãkerir/ v. pr. **s'∼ de**, enquire about.

enquêt|e /ãkɛt/ n.f. investigation; (jurid.) inquiry; (sondage) survey. **∼er** /-ete/ v.i. **∼er** (**sur**), investigate. **∼eur, ∼euse** n.m., f. investigator.

enraciné /ãrasine/ a. deep-rooted.

enrag|er /ãraʒe/ v.i. be furious. **faire ∼er**, annoy. **∼é** a. furious; (chien) mad; (fig.) fanatical. **∼eant, ∼eante** a. infuriating.

enrayer /ãreje/ v.t. check.

enregistr|er /ãrʒistre/ v.t. note, record; (mus.) record. (**faire**) **∼er**, (bagages) register, check in. **∼ement**

n.m. recording; (*des bagages*) registration.

enrhumer (s') /(s)ɑ̃ryme/ *v. pr.* catch a cold.

enrich|ir /ɑ̃riʃir/ *v.t.* enrich. **s'~ir** *v. pr.* grow rich(er). **~issement** *n.m.* enrichment.

enrober /ɑ̃rɔbe/ *v.t.* coat (**de,** with).

enrôler /ɑ̃role/ *v.t.,* **s'~** *v. pr.* enlist, enrol.

enrou|er (s') /(s)ɑ̃rwe/ *v. pr.* become hoarse. **~é** *a.* hoarse.

enrouler /ɑ̃rule/ *v.t.,* **s'~** *v. pr.* wind. **s'~ dans une couverture,** roll o.s. up in a blanket.

ensabler /ɑ̃sɑble/ *v.t.,* **s'~** *v. pr.* (*port*) silt up.

ensanglanté /ɑ̃sɑ̃glɑte/ *a.* bloodstained.

enseignant, ~e /ɑ̃sɛɲɑ̃, -t/ *n.m., f.* teacher. —*a.* teaching.

enseigne /ɑ̃sɛɲ/ *n.f.* sign.

enseignement /ɑ̃sɛɲmɑ̃/ *n.m.* teaching; (*instruction*) education.

enseigner /ɑ̃seɲe/ *v.t./i.* teach. **~ qch. à qn.,** teach s.o. sth.

ensemble /ɑ̃sɑ̃bl/ *adv.* together. —*n.m.* unity; (*d'objets*) set; (*mus.*) ensemble. **dans l'~,** on the whole. **d'~,** (*idée etc.*) general. **l'~ de,** (*totalité*) all of, the whole of.

ensemencer /ɑ̃smɑ̃se/ *v.t.* sow.

enserrer /ɑ̃sere/ *v.t.* grip (tightly).

ensevelir /ɑ̃səvlir/ *v.t.* bury.

ensoleill|é /ɑ̃sɔleje/ *a.* sunny. **~ement** /ɑ̃sɔlɛjmɑ̃/ *n.m.* (period of) sunshine.

ensommeillé /ɑ̃sɔmeje/ *a.* sleepy.

ensorceler /ɑ̃sɔrsəle/ *v.t.* bewitch.

ensuite /ɑ̃sɥit/ *adv.* next, then; (*plus tard*) later.

ensuivre (s') /(s)ɑ̃sɥivr/ *v. pr.* follow.

entaill|e /ɑ̃taj/ *n.f.* notch; (*blessure*) gash. **~er** *v.t.* notch; gash.

entamer /ɑ̃tame/ *v.t.* start; (*inciser*) cut into; (*ébranler*) shake.

entass|er /ɑ̃tase/ *v.t.,* **s'~er** *v. pr.* pile up. **(s')~er dans,** cram (together) into. **~ement** *n.m.* (*tas*) pile.

entendement /ɑ̃tɑ̃dmɑ̃/ *n.m.* understanding.

entendre /ɑ̃tɑ̃dr/ *v.t.* hear; (*comprendre*) understand; (*vouloir*) intend, mean; (*vouloir dire*) mean. **s'~** *v. pr.* (*être d'accord*) agree. **~ dire que,** hear that. **~ parler de,** hear of. **s'~ (bien),** get on (avec, with). **(cela) s'entend,** of course.

entendu /ɑ̃tɑ̃dy/ *a.* (*convenu*) agreed; (*sourire, air*) knowing. **bien ~,** of course. **(c'est) ~!,** all right!

entente /ɑ̃tɑ̃t/ *n.f.* understanding. **à double ~,** with a double meaning.

entériner /ɑ̃terine/ *v.t.* ratify.

enterr|er /ɑ̃tere/ *v.t.* bury. **~ement** /ɑ̃tɛrmɑ̃/ *n.m.* burial, funeral.

entêtant, ~e /ɑ̃tɛtɑ̃, -t/ *a.* heady.

en-tête /ɑ̃tɛt/ *n.m.* heading. **à ~,** headed.

entêt|é /ɑ̃tete/ *a.* stubborn. **~ement** /ɑ̃tɛtmɑ̃/ *n.m.* stubbornness.

entêter (s') /(s)ɑ̃tete/ *v. pr.* persist (**à, dans,** in).

enthousias|me /ɑ̃tuzjasm/ *n.m.* enthusiasm. **~mer** *v.t.* enthuse. **s'~mer pour,** enthuse over. **~te** *a.* enthusiastic.

enticher (s') /(s)ɑ̃tiʃe/ *v. pr.* **s'~ de,** become infatuated with.

ent|ier, ~ière /ɑ̃tje, -jɛr/ *a.* whole; (*absolu*) absolute; (*entêté*) unyielding. —*n.m.* whole. **en ~ier,** entirely. **~ièrement** *adv.* entirely.

entité /ɑ̃tite/ *n.f.* entity.

entonner /ɑ̃tɔne/ *v.t.* start singing.

entonnoir /ɑ̃tɔnwar/ *n.m.* funnel; (*trou*) crater.

entorse /ɑ̃tɔrs/ *n.f.* sprain. **~ à,** (*loi*) infringement of.

entortiller /ɑ̃tɔrtije/ *v.t.* wrap (up); (*enrouler*) wind, wrap; (*duper*) deceive.

entourage /ɑ̃turaʒ/ *n.m.* circle of family and friends; (*bordure*) surround.

entourer /ɑ̃ture/ *v.t.* surround (**de,** with); (*réconforter*) rally round. **~ de,** (*écharpe etc.*) wrap round.

entracte /ɑ̃trakt/ *n.m.* interval.

entraide /ɑ̃trɛd/ *n.f.* mutual aid.

entraider (s') /(s)ɑ̃trede/ *v. pr.* help each other.

entrailles /ɑ̃traj/ *n.f. pl.* entrails.

entrain /ɑ̃trɛ̃/ *n.m.* zest, spirit.

entraînant, ~e /ɑ̃trɛnɑ̃, -t/ *a.* rousing.

entraînement /ɑ̃trɛnmɑ̃/ *n.m.* (*sport*) training.

entraîn|er /ɑ̃trene/ *v.t.* carry away *ou* along; (*emmener, influencer*) lead; (*impliquer*) entail; (*sport*) train; (*roue*) drive. **~eur** /ɑ̃trɛnœr/ *n.m.* trainer.

entrav|e /ɑ̃trav/ *n.f.* hindrance. **~er** *v.t.* hinder.

entre /ɑ̃tr(ə)/ *prép.* between; (*parmi*) among(st). **~ autres,** among other things. **l'un d' ~ nous/vous/eux,** one of us/you/them.

entrebâillé /ɑ̃trəbɑje/ *a.* ajar.

entrechoquer (s') /(s)ɑ̃trəʃɔke/ *v. pr.* knock against each other.

entrecôte /ɑ̃trəkot/ *n.f.* rib steak.

entrecouper /ɑ̃trəkupe/ *v.t.* ∼ **de,** intersperse with.

entrecroiser (s') /(s)ɑ̃trəkrwaze/ *v. pr.* (*routes*) intersect.

entrée /ɑ̃tre/ *n.f.* entrance; (*accès*) admission, entry; (*billet*) ticket; (*culin.*) first course; (*de données: techn.*) input. ∼ **interdite,** no entry.

entrefaites (sur ces) /(syrsez)ɑ̃trəfɛt/ *adv.* at that moment.

entrejambes /ɑ̃trəʒɑ̃b/ *n.m.* crotch.

entrelacer /ɑ̃trəlase/ *v.t.*, **s'**∼ *v. pr.* intertwine.

entremêler /ɑ̃trəmele/ *v.t.*, **s'**∼ *v. pr.* (inter)mingle.

entremets /ɑ̃trəmɛ/ *n.m.* dessert.

entre|mettre (s') /(s)ɑ̃trəmɛtr/ *v. pr.* intervene. ∼**mise** *n.f.* intervention. **par l'**∼**mise de,** through.

entreposer /ɑ̃trəpoze/ *v.t.* store.

entrepôt /ɑ̃trəpo/ *n.m.* warehouse.

entreprenant, ∼**e** /ɑ̃trəprənɑ̃, -t/ *a.* enterprising.

entreprendre† /ɑ̃trəprɑ̃dr/ *v.t.* start on; (*personne*) buttonhole. ∼ **de faire,** undertake to do.

entrepreneur /ɑ̃trəprənœr/ *n.m.* ∼ **(de bâtiments),** (building) contractor.

entreprise /ɑ̃trəpriz/ *n.f.* undertaking; (*société*) firm.

entrer /ɑ̃tre/ *v.i.* (*aux. être*) go in, enter; (*venir*) come in, enter. ∼ **dans,** go *ou* come into, enter; (*club*) join. ∼ **en colère,** become angry. ∼ **en collision,** collide (**avec,** with). **faire** ∼, (*personne*) show in. **laisser** ∼, let in.

entresol /ɑ̃trəsɔl/ *n.m.* mezzanine.

entre-temps /ɑ̃trətɑ̃/ *adv.* meanwhile.

entretenir† /ɑ̃trətnir/ *v.t.* maintain; (*faire durer*) keep alive. ∼ **qn. de,** converse with s.o. about. **s'**∼ *v. pr.* speak (**de,** about; **avec,** to).

entretien /ɑ̃trətjɛ̃/ *n.m.* maintenance; (*discussion*) talk; (*audience*) interview.

entrevoir /ɑ̃trəvwar/ *v.t.* make out; (*brièvement*) glimpse.

entrevue /ɑ̃trəvy/ *n.f.* interview.

entrouvrir /ɑ̃truvrir/ *v.t.* half-open.

énumér|er /enymere/ *v.t.* enumerate. ∼**ation** *n.f.* enumeration.

envah|ir /ɑ̃vair/ *v.t.* invade, overrun;

(*douleur, peur*) overcome. ∼**isseur** *n.m.* invader.

enveloppe /ɑ̃vlɔp/ *n.f.* envelope; (*emballage*) covering; (*techn.*) casing.

envelopper /ɑ̃vlɔpe/ *v.t.* wrap (up); (*fig.*) envelop.

envenimer /ɑ̃vnime/ *v.t.* (*plaie*) make septic; (*fig.*) embitter. **s'**∼ *v. pr.* turn septic; become embittered.

envergure /ɑ̃vɛrgyr/ *n.f.* wing-span; (*importance*) scope; (*qualité*) calibre.

envers /ɑ̃vɛr/ *prép.* toward(s), to. —*n.m.* (*de tissu*) wrong side. **à l'**∼, upside down; (*pantalon*) back to front; (*chaussette*) inside out.

envie /ɑ̃vi/ *n.f.* desire, wish; (*jalousie*) envy. **avoir** ∼ **de,** want, feel like. **avoir** ∼ **de faire,** want to do, feel like doing.

envier /ɑ̃vje/ *v.t.* envy.

envieu|x, ∼**se** /ɑ̃vjø, -z/ *a.* & *n.m., f.* envious (person).

environ /ɑ̃virɔ̃/ *adv.* (round) about. ∼**s** *n.m. pl.* surroundings. **aux** ∼**s de,** round about.

environnement /ɑ̃virɔnmɑ̃/ *n.m.* environment.

environn|er /ɑ̃virɔne/ *v.t.* surround. ∼**ant,** ∼**ante** *a.* surrounding.

envisager /ɑ̃vizaʒe/ *v.t.* consider. ∼ **de faire,** consider doing.

envoi /ɑ̃vwa/ *n.m.* dispatch; (*paquet*) consignment.

envol /ɑ̃vɔl/ *n.m.* flight; (*d'avion*) take-off.

envoler (s') /(s)ɑ̃vɔle/ *v. pr.* fly away; (*avion*) take off; (*papiers*) blow away.

envoûter /ɑ̃vute/ *v.t.* bewitch.

envoyé, ∼**e** /ɑ̃vwaje/ *n.m., f.* envoy; (*de journal*) correspondent.

envoyer† /ɑ̃vwaje/ *v.t.* send; (*lancer*) throw; (*gifle, coup*) give.

enzyme /ɑ̃zim/ *n.m.* enzyme.

épagneul, ∼**e** /epaɲœl/ *n.m., f.* spaniel.

épais, ∼**se** /epɛ, -s/ *a.* thick; (*corps*) thickset. ∼**seur** /-sœr/ *n.f.* thickness.

épaissir /epesir/ *v.t./i.*, **s'**∼ *v. pr.* thicken.

épanch|er (s') /(s)epɑ̃ʃe/ *v. pr.* pour out one's feelings; (*liquide*) pour out. ∼**ement** *n.m.* outpouring.

épanoui /epanwi/ *a.* (*joyeux*) beaming, radiant.

épan|ouir (s') /(s)epanwir/ *v. pr.* (*fleur*) open out; (*visage*) beam; (*personne*) blossom. ∼**ouissement** *n.m.* (*éclat*) blossoming, full bloom.

épargne /eparɲ/ *n.f.* saving; (*somme*) savings.

épargn|er /eparɲe/ *v.t./i.* save; (*ne pas tuer*) spare. **~er qch. à qn.**, spare s.o. sth. **~ant, ~ante** *n.m., f.* saver.

éparpiller /eparpije/ *v.t.* scatter; (*efforts*) dissipate. **s'~** *v. pr.* scatter.

épars, ~e /epar, -s/ *a.* scattered.

épat|er /epate/ *v.t.* (*fam.*) amaze. **~ant, ~ante** *a.* (*fam.*) amazing.

épaule /epol/ *n.f.* shoulder.

épauler /epole/ *v.t.* (*arme*) raise; (*aider*) support.

épave /epav/ *n.f.* wreck.

épée /epe/ *n.f.* sword.

épeler /ɛple/ *v.t.* spell.

éperdu /eperdy/ *a.* wild, frantic. **~ment** *adv.* wildly, frantically.

éperon /eprɔ̃/ *n.m.* spur. **~ner** /-ɔne/ *v.t.* spur (on).

épervier /epɛrvje/ *n.m.* sparrowhawk.

éphémère /efemɛr/ *a.* ephemeral.

éphéméride /efemerid/ *n.f.* tear-off calendar.

épi /epi/ *n.m.* (*de blé*) ear. **~ de cheveux,** tuft of hair.

épic|e /epis/ *n.f.* spice. **~é** *a.* spicy. **~er** *v.t.* spice.

épic|ier, ~ière /episje, -jɛr/ *n.m., f.* grocer. **~erie** *n.f.* grocery shop; (*produits*) groceries.

épidémie /epidemi/ *n.f.* epidemic.

épiderme /epidɛrm/ *n.m.* skin.

épier /epje/ *v.t.* spy on; (*occasion*) watch out for.

épilep|sie /epilɛpsi/ *n.f.* epilepsy. **~tique** *a. & n.m./f.* epileptic.

épiler /epile/ *v.t.* remove unwanted hair from; (*sourcils*) pluck.

épilogue /epilɔg/ *n.m.* epilogue; (*fig.*) outcome.

épinard /epinar/ *n.m.* (*plante*) spinach. **~s,** (*nourriture*) spinach.

épin|e /epin/ *n.f.* thorn, prickle; (*d'animal*) prickle, spine. **~eux, ~euse** *a.* thorny.

épingl|e /epɛ̃gl/ *n.f.* pin. **~e de nourrice, ~e de sûreté,** safety-pin. **~er** *v.t.* pin; (*arrêter: fam.*) nab.

épique /epik/ *a.* epic.

épisod|e /epizɔd/ *n.m.* episode. **à ~es,** serialized. **~ique** *a.* occasional.

épitaphe /epitaf/ *n.f.* epitaph.

épithète /epitɛt/ *n.f.* epithet.

épître /epitr/ *n.f.* epistle.

éploré /eplɔre/ *a.* tearful.

épluch|er /eplyʃe/ *v.t.* peel; (*examiner: fig.*) scrutinize. **~age** *n.m.* peeling;

(*fig.*) scrutiny. **~ure** *n.f.* piece of peel *ou* peeling. **~ures** *n.f. pl.* peelings.

épointer /epwɛ̃te/ *v.t.* blunt.

épong|e /epɔ̃ʒ/ *n.f.* sponge. **~er** *v.t.* (*liquide*) sponge up; (*surface*) sponge (down); (*front*) mop.

épopée /epɔpe/ *n.f.* epic.

époque /epɔk/ *n.f.* time, period. **à l'~,** at the time. **d'~,** period.

épouse /epuz/ *n.f.* wife.

épouser[1] /epuze/ *v.t.* marry.

épouser[2] /epuze/ *v.t.* (*forme, idée*) assume, embrace, adopt.

épousseter /epuste/ *v.t.* dust.

époustouflant, ~e /epustuflɑ̃, -t/ *a.* (*fam.*) staggering.

épouvantable /epuvɑ̃tabl/ *a.* appalling. **~ment** /-əmɑ̃/ *adv.* appallingly.

épouvantail /epuvɑ̃taj/ *n.m.* scarecrow.

épouvant|e /epuvɑ̃t/ *n.f.* terror. **~er** *v.t* terrify.

époux /epu/ *n.m.* husband. **les ~,** the married couple.

éprendre (s') /(s)eprɑ̃dr/ *v. pr.* **s'~ de,** fall in love with.

épreuve /eprœv/ *n.f.* test; (*sport*) event; (*malheur*) ordeal; (*photo.*) print; (*d'imprimerie*) proof. **mettre à l'~,** put to the test.

éprouvé /epruve/ *a.* (well-)proven.

éprouv|er /epruve/ *v.t.* test; (*ressentir*) experience; (*affliger*) distress. **~ant, ~ante** *a.* testing.

éprouvette /epruvɛt/ *n.f.* test-tube.

épuis|er /epɥize/ *v.t.* (*fatiguer, user*) exhaust. **s'~er** *v. pr.* become exhausted. **~é** *a.* exhausted; (*livre*) out of print. **~ement** *n.m.* exhaustion.

épuisette /epɥizɛt/ *n.f.* fishing-net.

épur|er /epyre/ *v.t.* purify; (*pol.*) purge. **~ation** *n.f.* purification; (*pol.*) purge.

équat|eur /ekwatœr/ *n.m.* equator. **~orial** (*m. pl.* **~oriaux**) *a.* equatorial.

équation /ekwasjɔ̃/ *n.f.* equation.

équerre /ekɛr/ *n.f.* (set) square. **d'~,** square.

équilibr|e /ekilibr/ *n.m.* balance. **être** *ou* **se tenir en ~e,** (*personne*) balance; (*objet*) be balanced. **~é** *a.* well-balanced. **~er** *v.t.* balance. **s'~er** *v. pr.* (*forces etc.*) counterbalance each other.

équilibriste /ekilibrist/ *n.m./f.* tightrope walker.

équinoxe /ekinɔks/ *n.m.* equinox.

équipage /ekipaʒ/ *n.m.* crew.

équipe /ekip/ *n.f.* team. **~ de nuit/ jour,** night/day shift.

équipée /ekipe/ *n.f.* escapade.

équipement /ekipmɑ̃/ *n.m.* equipment. **~s,** (*installations*) amenities, facilities.

équiper /ekipe/ *v.t.* equip (**de,** with). **s'~** *v. pr.* equip o.s.

équip|ier, **~ière** /ekipje, -jɛr/ *n.m.,f.* team member.

équitable /ekitabl/ *a.* fair. **~ment** /-əmɑ̃/ *adv.* fairly.

équitation /ekitasjɔ̃/ *n.f.* (horse-)riding.

équité /ekite/ *n.f.* equity.

équivalen|t, **~te** /ekivalɑ̃, -t/ *a.* equivalent. **~ce** *n.f.* equivalence.

équivaloir /ekivalwar/ *v.i.* **~ à,** be equivalent to.

équivoque /ekivɔk/ *a.* equivocal; (*louche*) questionable. *—n.f.* ambiguity.

érable /erabl/ *n.m.* maple.

érafl|er /erafle/ *v.t.* scratch. **~ure** *n.f.* scratch.

éraillé /erɑje/ *a.* (*voix*) raucous.

ère /ɛr/ *n.f.* era.

érection /erɛksjɔ̃/ *n.f.* erection.

éreinter /erẽte/ *v.t.* exhaust; (*fig.*) criticize severely.

ergoter /ɛrgɔte/ *v.i.* quibble.

ériger /eriʒe/ *v.t.* erect. (**s'**)**~ en,** set (o.s.) up as.

ermitage /ɛrmitaʒ/ *n.m.* retreat.

ermite /ɛrmit/ *n.m.* hermit.

éroder /erɔde/ *v.t.* erode.

érosion /erozjɔ̃/ *n.f.* erosion.

éroti|que /erɔtik/ *a.* erotic. **~sme** *n.m.* eroticism.

errer /ɛre/ *v.i.* wander.

erreur /ɛrœr/ *n.f.* mistake, error. **dans l'~,** mistaken. **par ~,** by mistake.

erroné /ɛrɔne/ *a.* erroneous.

érudit, **~e** /erydi, -t/ *a.* scholarly. *—n.m., f.* scholar. **~ion** /-sjɔ̃/ *n.f.* scholarship.

éruption /erypsjɔ̃/ *n.f.* eruption; (*méd.*) rash.

es /ɛ/ *voir* **être.**

escabeau (*pl.* **~x**) /ɛskabo/ *n.m.* stepladder; (*tabouret*) stool.

escadre /ɛskadr/ *n.f.* (*naut.*) squadron.

escadrille /ɛskadrij/ *n.f.* (*aviat.*) flight, squadron.

escadron /ɛskadrɔ̃/ *n.m.* (*mil.*) squadron.

escalad|e /ɛskalad/ *n.f.* climbing; (*pol., comm.*) escalation. **~er** *v.t.* climb.

escale /ɛskal/ *n.f.* (*d'avion*) stopover; (*port*) port of call.

escalier /ɛskalje/ *n.m.* stairs. **~ mécanique** *ou* **roulant,** escalator.

escalope /ɛskalɔp/ *n.f.* escalope.

escamotable /ɛskamɔtabl/ *a.* (*techn.*) retractable.

escamoter /ɛskamɔte/ *v.t.* make vanish; (*éviter*) dodge.

escargot /ɛskargo/ *n.m.* snail.

escarmouche /ɛskarmuʃ/ *n.f.* skirmish.

escarpé /ɛskarpe/ *a.* steep.

escarpin /ɛskarpẽ/ *n.m.* pump.

esclaffer (s') /(s)ɛsklafe/ *v. pr.* guffaw, burst out laughing.

esclandre /ɛsklɑ̃dr/ *n.m.* scene.

esclav|e /ɛsklav/ *n.m./f.* slave. **~age** *n.m.* slavery.

escompte /ɛskɔ̃t/ *n.m.* discount.

escompter /ɛskɔ̃te/ *v.t.* expect; (*comm.*) discount.

escort|e /ɛskɔrt/ *n.f.* escort. **~er** *v.t.* escort. **~eur** *n.m.* escort (ship).

escouade /ɛskwad/ *n.f.* squad.

escrim|e /ɛskrim/ *n.f.* fencing. **~eur, ~euse** *n.m., f.* fencer.

escrimer (s') /(s)ɛskrime/ *v. pr.* struggle.

escroc /ɛskro/ *n.m.* swindler.

escroqu|er /ɛskrɔke/ *v.t.* swindle. **~er qch. à qn.,** swindle s.o. out of sth. **~erie** *n.f.* swindle.

espace /ɛspas/ *n.m.* space. **~s verts,** gardens, parks.

espacer /ɛspase/ *v.t.* space out. **s'~** *v. pr.* become less frequent.

espadrille /ɛspadrij/ *n.f.* canvas sandal.

Espagne /ɛspaɲ/ *n.f.* Spain.

espagnol, **~e** /ɛspaɲɔl/ *a.* Spanish. *—n.m., f.* Spaniard. *—n.m.* (*lang.*) Spanish.

espèce /ɛspɛs/ *n.f.* kind, sort; (*race*) species. **~s,** (*argent*) cash. **~ d'idiot/de brute/***etc.***!,** you idiot/ brute/*etc.*!

espérance /ɛsperɑ̃s/ *n.f.* hope.

espérer /ɛspere/ *v.t.* hope for. **~ faire/que,** hope to do/that. *—v.i.* hope. **~ en,** have faith in.

espiègle /ɛspjɛgl/ *a.* mischievous.

espion, **~ne** /ɛspjɔ̃, -jɔn/ *n.m., f.* spy.

espionn|er /ɛspjɔne/ *v.t./i.* spy (on). **~age** *n.m.* espionage, spying.

esplanade /ɛsplanad/ *n.f.* esplanade.

espoir /ɛspwar/ *n.m.* hope.

esprit /ɛspri/ *n.m.* spirit; (*intellect*) mind; (*humour*) wit. **perdre l'~**, lose one's mind. **reprendre ses ~s**, come to.

Esquimau, ~de (*m. pl. ~x*) /ɛskimo, -d/ *n.m., f.* Eskimo.

esquinter /ɛskɛ̃te/ *v.t.* (*fam.*) ruin.

esquiss|e /ɛskis/ *n.f.* sketch; (*fig.*) suggestion. **~er** *v.t.* sketch; (*geste etc.*) make an attempt at.

esquiv|e /ɛskiv/ *n.f.* (*sport*) dodge. **~er** *v.t.* dodge. **s'~er** *v. pr.* slip away.

essai /ɛsɛ/ *n.m.* testing; (*épreuve*) test, trial; (*tentative*) try; (*article*) essay. **à l'~**, on trial.

essaim /ɛsɛ̃/ *n.m.* swarm. **~er** /eseme/ *v.i.* swarm; (*fig.*) spread.

essayage /ɛsɛjaʒ/ *n.m.* (*de vêtement*) fitting.

essayer /eseje/ *v.t./i.* try; (*vêtement*) try (on); (*voiture etc.*) try (out). **~ de faire,** try to do.

essence[1] /esɑ̃s/ *n.f.* (*carburant*) petrol; (*Amer.*) gas.

essence[2] /esɑ̃s/ *n.f.* (*nature, extrait*) essence.

essentiel, ~le /esɑ̃sjɛl/ *a.* essential. —*n.m.* **l'~,** the main thing; (*quantité*) the main part. **~lement** *adv.* essentially.

essieu (*pl. ~x*) /esjø/ *n.m.* axle.

essor /esɔr/ *n.m.* expansion.

essor|er /esɔre/ *v.t.* (*linge*) spin-dry; (*en tordant*) wring. **~euse** *n.f.* spin-drier.

essouffler /esufle/ *v.t.* make breathless. **s'~** *v. pr.* get out of breath.

ess|uyer[1] /esɥije/ *v.t.* wipe. **s'~uyer** *v. pr.* dry *ou* wipe o.s. **~uie-glace** *n.m. invar.* windscreen wiper; (*Amer.*) windshield wiper. **~uie-mains** *n.m. invar.* hand-towel.

essuyer[2] /esɥije/ *v.t.* (*subir*) suffer.

est[1] /ɛ/ *voir* être.

est[2] /ɛst/ *n.m.* east. —*a. invar.* east; (*partie*) eastern; (*direction*) easterly.

estampe /ɛstɑ̃p/ *n.f.* print.

estampille /ɛstɑ̃pij/ *n.f.* stamp.

esthète /ɛstɛt/ *n.m./f.* aesthete.

esthéticienne /ɛstetisjɛn/ *n.f.* beautician.

esthétique /ɛstetik/ *a.* aesthetic.

estimable /ɛstimabl/ *a.* worthy.

estime /ɛstim/ *n.f.* esteem.

estim|er /ɛstime/ *v.t.* (*objet*) value; (*calculer*) estimate; (*respecter*) es-

teem; (*considérer*) consider. **~ation** *n.f.* valuation; (*calcul*) estimation.

estiv|al (*m. pl. ~aux*) /ɛstival, -o/ *a.* summer. **~ant, ~ante** *n.m., f.* summer visitor, holiday-maker.

estomac /ɛstɔma/ *n.m.* stomach.

estomper (s') /(s)ɛstɔ̃pe/ *v. pr.* become blurred.

estrade /ɛstrad/ *n.f.* platform.

estragon /ɛstragɔ̃/ *n.m.* tarragon.

estrop|ier /ɛstrɔpje/ *v.t.* cripple; (*fig.*) mangle. **~ié, ~iée** *n.m., f.* cripple.

estuaire /ɛstɥɛr/ *n.m.* estuary.

estudiantin, ~e /ɛstydjɑ̃tɛ̃, -in/ *a.* student.

esturgeon /ɛstyrʒɔ̃/ *n.m.* sturgeon.

et /e/ *conj.* and. **~ moi/lui**/*etc.*?, what about me/him/*etc.*?

étable /etabl/ *n.f.* cow-shed.

établi /etabli/ *n.m.* work-bench.

établir /etablir/ *v.t.* establish; (*liste, facture*) draw up; (*personne, camp, record*) set up. **s'~** *v. pr.* (*personne*) establish o.s. **s'~ épicier**/*etc.*, set (o.s.) up as a grocer/*etc.*

établissement /etablismɑ̃/ *n.m.* (*bâtiment, institution*) establishment.

étage /etaʒ/ *n.m.* floor, storey; (*de fusée*) stage. **à l'~,** upstairs. **au premier ~,** on the first floor.

étager (s') /(s)etaʒe/ *v. pr.* rise at different levels.

étagère /etaʒɛr/ *n.f.* shelf; (*meuble*) shelving unit.

étai /etɛ/ *n.m.* prop, buttress.

étain /etɛ̃/ *n.m.* tin; (*alliage*) pewter.

étais, était /etɛ/ *voir* être.

étal (*pl. ~s*) /etal/ *n.m.* stall.

étalag|e /etalaʒ/ *n.m.* display; (*vitrine*) shop-window. **~iste** *n.m./f.* window-dresser.

étaler /etale/ *v.t.* spread; (*journal*) spread (out); (*vacances*) stagger; (*exposer*) display. **s'~** *v. pr.* (*s'étendre*) stretch out; (*tomber: fam.*) fall flat.

étalon /etalɔ̃/ *n.m.* (*cheval*) stallion; (*modèle*) standard.

étanche /etɑ̃ʃ/ *a.* watertight; (*montre*) waterproof.

étancher /etɑ̃ʃe/ *v.t.* (*soif*) quench; (*sang*) stem.

étang /etɑ̃/ *n.m.* pond.

étant /etɑ̃/ *voir* être.

étape /etap/ *n.f.* stage; (*lieu d'arrêt*) stopover.

état /eta/ *n.m.* state; (*liste*) statement; (*métier*) profession; (*nation*) State. **en bon/mauvais ~,** in good/bad condition. **en ~ de**, in a position to. **en ~ de marche**, in working order. **~ civil**, civil status. **~ de choses**, situation. **~-major** (*pl.* **~s-majors**) *n.m.* (*officiers*) staff. **faire ~ de**, (*citer*) mention.

étatisé /etatize/ *a.* State-controlled.

États-Unis /etazyni/ *n.m. pl.* **~ (d'Amérique)**, United States (of America).

étau (*pl.* **~x**) /eto/ *n.m.* vice.

étayer /eteje/ *v.t.* prop up.

été[1] /ete/ *voir* **être**.

été[2] /ete/ *n.m.* summer.

étein|dre† /etɛ̃dr/ *v.t.* put out, extinguish; (*lumière, radio, gaz*) turn off. **s'~dre** *v. pr.* (*feu*) go out; (*mourir*) die. **~t, ~te** /etɛ̃, -t/ *a.* (*feu*) out; (*volcan*) extinct.

étendard /etɑ̃dar/ *n.m.* standard.

étendre /etɑ̃dr/ *v.t.* spread; (*journal, nappe*) spread out; (*bras, jambes*) stretch (out); (*linge*) hang out; (*agrandir*) extend. **s'~** *v. pr.* (*s'allonger*) stretch out; (*se propager*) spread; (*plaine etc.*) stretch. **s'~ sur**, (*sujet*) dwell on.

étendu, **~e** /etɑ̃dy/ *a.* extensive. —*n.f.* area; (*d'eau*) stretch; (*importance*) extent.

éternel, **~le** /etɛrnɛl/ *a.* eternal. **~lement** *adv.* eternally.

éterniser (**s'**) /(s)etɛrnize/ *v. pr.* (*durer*) drag on.

éternité /etɛrnite/ *n.f.* eternity.

étern|uer /etɛrnɥe/ *v.i.* sneeze. **~uement** /-ymɑ̃/ *n.m.* sneeze.

êtes /ɛt/ *voir* **être**.

éther /etɛr/ *n.m.* ether.

Éthiopie /etjɔpi/ *n.f.* Ethiopia.

éthique /etik/ *a.* ethical. —*n.f.* ethics.

ethn|ie /ɛtni/ *n.f.* ethnic group. **~ique** *a.* ethnic.

étinceler /etɛ̃sle/ *v.i.* sparkle.

étincelle /etɛ̃sɛl/ *n.f.* spark.

étioler (**s'**) /(s)etjɔle/ *v. pr.* wilt.

étiqueter /etikte/ *v.t.* label.

étiquette /etikɛt/ *n.f.* label; (*protocole*) etiquette.

étirer /etire/ *v.t.*, **s'~** *v. pr.* stretch.

étoffe /etɔf/ *n.f.* fabric.

étoffer /etɔfe/ *v.t.*, **s'~** *v. pr.* fill out.

étoil|e /etwal/ *n.f.* star. **à la belle ~e**, in the open. **~e de mer**, starfish. **~é** *a.* starry.

étonn|er /etɔne/ *v.t.* amaze. **s'~er** *v. pr.* be amazed (**de**, at). **~ant, ~ante**

a. amazing. **~ement** *n.m.* amazement.

étouff|er /etufe/ *v.t./i.* suffocate; (*sentiment, révolte*) stifle; (*feu*) smother; (*bruit*) muffle. **on ~e**, it is stifling. **s'~er** *v. pr.* suffocate; (*en mangeant*) choke. **~ant, ~ante** *a.* stifling.

étourd|i, ~ie /eturdi/ *a.* unthinking, scatter-brained. —*n.m., f.* scatter-brain. **~erie** *n.f.* thoughtlessness; (*acte*) thoughtless act.

étourd|ir /eturdir/ *v.t.* stun; (*griser*) make dizzy. **~issant, ~issante** *a.* stunning. **~issement** *n.m.* (*syncope*) dizzy spell.

étourneau (*pl.* **~x**) /eturno/ *n.m.* starling.

étrange /etrɑ̃ʒ/ *a.* strange. **~ment** *adv.* strangely. **~té** *n.f.* strangeness.

étrang|er, ~ère /etrɑ̃ʒe, -ɛr/ *a.* strange, unfamiliar; (*d'un autre pays*) foreign. —*n.m., f.* foreigner; (*inconnu*) stranger. **à l'~er**, abroad. **de l'~er**, from abroad.

étrangler /etrɑ̃gle/ *v.t.* strangle; (*fureur, col*) choke. **s'~** *v. pr.* choke.

être† /ɛtr/ *v.i.* be. —*v. aux.* (*avec aller, sortir, etc.*) have. **~ donné/ fait/etc.**, (*passif*) be given/done/etc. —*n.m.* (*personne, créature*) being. **~ médecin/ tailleur/etc.**, be a doctor/a tailor/ etc. **~ à qn.**, be s.o.'s. **c'est à faire**, it needs to be *ou* should be done. **est-ce qu'il travaille?**, is he working?, does he work? **vous travaillez, n'est-ce pas?**, you are working, aren't you?, you work, don't you? **il est deux heures/etc.**, it is two o'clock/etc. **nous sommes le six mai**, it is the sixth of May.

étrein|dre /etrɛ̃dr/ *v.t.* grasp; (*ami*) embrace. **~te** /-ɛ̃t/ *n.f.* grasp; embrace.

étrenner /etrene/ *v.t.* use for the first time.

étrennes /etrɛn/ *n.f. pl.* (*cadeau*) New Year's gift.

étrier /etrije/ *n.m.* stirrup.

étriqué /etrike/ *a.* tight; (*fig.*) narrow.

étroit, **~e** /etrwa, -t/ *a.* narrow; (*vêtement*) tight; (*liens, surveillance*) close. **à l'~**, cramped. **~ement** /-tmɑ̃/ *adv.* closely. **~esse** /-tɛs/ *n.f.* narrowness.

étude /etyd/ *n.f.* study; (*bureau*) office. (**salle d'**)**~**, (*scol.*) prep room; (*scol.*, *Amer.*) study hall. **à l'~**, under consideration. **faire des ~s (de)**, study.

étudiant, ~e /etydjɑ̃, -t/ *n.m.*, *f.* student.

étudier /etydje/ *v.t.*/*i.* study.

étui /etɥi/ *n.m.* (*à lunettes etc.*) case; (*de revolver*) holster.

étymologie /etimɔlɔʒi/ *n.f.* etymology.

eu, eue /y/ *voir* **avoir.**

eucalyptus /økaliptys/ *n.m.* eucalyptus.

euphémisme /øfemism/ *n.m.* euphemism.

euphorie /øfɔri/ *n.f.* euphoria.

Europe /ørɔp/ *n.f.* Europe.

européen, ~ne /ørɔpeɛ̃, -ɛɛn/ *a.* & *n.m.*, *f.* European.

euthanasie /øtanazi/ *n.f.* euthanasia.

eux /ø/ *pron.* they; (*complément*) them. ~-**mêmes** *pron.* themselves.

évac|uer /evakɥe/ *v.t.* evacuate. ~**uation** *n.f.* evacuation.

évad|er (s') /(s)evade/ *v. pr.* escape. ~**é,** ~**ée** *a.* escaped; *n.m.*, *f.* escaped prisoner.

éval|uer /evalɥe/ *v.t.* assess. ~**uation** *n.f.* assessment.

évang|ile /evɑ̃ʒil/ *n.m.* gospel. **l'Évangile,** the Gospel. ~**élique** *a.* evangelical.

évan|ouir (s') /(s)evanwir/ *v. pr.* faint; (*disparaître*) vanish. ~**ouissement** *n.m.* (*syncope*) fainting fit.

évapor|er /evapɔre/ *v.t.*, **s'**~**er** *v. pr.* evaporate. ~**ation** *n.f.* evaporation.

évasi|f, ~**ve** /evazif, -v/ *a.* evasive.

évasion /evazjɔ̃/ *n.f.* escape; (*par le rêve etc.*) escapism.

évêché /eveʃe/ *n.m.* see, bishopric.

éveil /evɛj/ *n.m.* awakening. **donner l'**~ **à,** arouse the suspicions of. **en** ~**,** alert.

éveill|er /eveje/ *v.t.* awake(n); (*susciter*) arouse. **s'**~**er** *v. pr.* awake(n); be aroused. ~**é** *a.* awake; (*intelligent*) alert.

événement /evɛnmɑ̃/ *n.m.* event.

éventail /evɑ̃taj/ *n.m.* fan; (*gamme*) range.

éventé /evɑ̃te/ *a.* (*gâté*) stale.

éventrer /evɑ̃tre/ *v.t.* (*sac etc.*) rip open.

éventualité /evɑ̃tɥalite/ *n.f.* possibility. **dans cette** ~**,** in that event.

éventuel, ~**le** /evɑ̃tɥɛl/ *a.* possible. ~**lement** *adv.* possibly.

évêque /evɛk/ *n.m.* bishop.

évertuer (s') /(s)evɛrtɥe/ *v. pr.* **s'**~ **à,** struggle hard to.

éviction /eviksjɔ̃/ *n.f.* eviction.

évidemment /evidamɑ̃/ *adv.* obviously; (*bien sûr*) of course.

évidence /evidɑ̃s/ *n.f.* obviousness; (*fait*) obvious fact. **être en** ~**,** be conspicuous. **mettre en** ~**,** (*fait*) highlight.

évident, ~e /evidɑ̃, -t/ *a.* obvious, evident.

évider /evide/ *v.t.* hollow out.

évier /evje/ *n.m.* sink.

évincer /evɛ̃se/ *v.t.* oust.

éviter /evite/ *v.t.* avoid (**de faire,** doing). ~ **à qn.,** (*dérangement etc.*) spare s.o.

évoca|teur, ~**trice** /evɔkatœr, -tris/ *a.* evocative.

évocation /evɔkasjɔ̃/ *n.f.* evocation.

évolué /evɔlɥe/ *a.* highly developed.

évol|uer /evɔlɥe/ *v.i.* develop; (*se déplacer*) manœuvre; (*Amer.*) maneuver. ~**ution** *n.f.* development; (*d'une espèce*) evolution; (*déplacement*) movement.

évoquer /evɔke/ *v.t.* call to mind, evoke.

ex- /ɛks/ *préf.* ex-.

exacerber /ɛgzasɛrbe/ *v.t.* exacerbate.

exact, ~e /ɛgza(kt), -akt/ *a.* exact, accurate; (*correct*) correct; (*personne*) punctual. ~**ement** /-ktəmɑ̃/ *adv.* exactly. ~**itude** /-ktityd/ *n.f.* exactness; punctuality.

ex aequo /ɛgzeko/ *adv.* (*classer*) equal. **être** ~**,** be equally placed.

exagéré /ɛgzaʒere/ *a.* excessive.

exagér|er /ɛgzaʒere/ *v.t.*/*i.* exaggerate; (*abuser*) go too far. ~**ation** *n.f.* exaggeration.

exaltation /ɛgzaltasjɔ̃/ *n.f.* elation.

exalté, ~e /ɛgzalte/ *n.m.*, *f.* fanatic.

exalter /ɛgzalte/ *v.t.* excite; (*glorifier*) exalt.

examen /ɛgzamɛ̃/ *n.m.* examination; (*scol.*) exam(ination).

examin|er /ɛgzamine/ *v.t.* examine. ~**ateur,** ~**atrice** *n.m.*, *f.* examiner.

exaspér|er /ɛgzaspere/ *v.t.* exasperate. ~**ation** *n.f.* exasperation.

exaucer /ɛgzose/ *v.t.* grant; (*personne*) grant the wish(es) of.

excavation /ɛkskavasjɔ̃/ *n.f.* excavation.

excédent /ɛksedɑ̃/ *n.m.* surplus. ~ **de bagages,** excess luggage. ~**aire** /-tɛr/ *a.* excess, surplus.

excéder[1] /ɛksede/ *v.t.* (*dépasser*) exceed.

excéder[2] /ɛksede/ *v.t.* (*agacer*) irritate.

excellen|t, ~te /ɛksɛlɑ̃, -t/ a. excellent. **~ce** n.f. excellence.

exceller /ɛksele/ v.i. excel (**dans**, in).

excentri|que /ɛksɑ̃trik/ a. & n.m./f. eccentric. **~cité** n.f. eccentricity.

excepté /ɛksɛpte/ a. & prép. except.

excepter /ɛksɛpte/ v.t. except.

exception /ɛksɛpsjɔ̃/ n.f. exception. **à l'~ de**, except for. **d'~**, exceptional. **faire ~**, be an exception. **~nel, ~nelle** /-jɔnɛl/ a. exceptional. **~nellement** /-jɔnɛlmɑ̃/ adv. exceptionally.

excès /ɛksɛ/ n.m. excess. **~ de vitesse**, speeding.

excessi|f, ~ve /ɛksesif, -v/ a. excessive. **~vement** adv. excessively.

excitant /ɛksitɑ̃/ n.m. stimulant.

excit|er /ɛksite/ v.t. excite; (encourager) exhort (**à**, to); (irriter: fam.) annoy. **~ation** n.f. excitement.

exclam|er (s') /(s)ɛksklame/ v. pr. exclaim. **~ation** n.f. exclamation.

exclu|re† /ɛksklyr/ v.t. exclude; (expulser) expel; (empêcher) preclude. **~sion** n.f. exclusion.

exclusi|f, ~ve /ɛksklyzif, -v/ a. exclusive. **~vement** adv. exclusively. **~vité** n.f. (comm.) exclusive rights. **en ~vité à**, (film) (showing) exclusively at.

excommunier /ɛkskɔmynje/ v.t. excommunicate.

excrément(s) /ɛkskremɑ̃/ n.m. (pl.). excrement.

excroissance /ɛkskrwasɑ̃s/ n.f. (out)growth, excrescence.

excursion /ɛkskyrsjɔ̃/ n.f. excursion; (à pied) hike.

excuse /ɛkskyz/ n.f. excuse. **~s**, apology. **faire des ~s**, apologize.

excuser /ɛkskyze/ v.t. excuse. **s'~** v. pr. apologize (**de**, for). **je m'excuse**, (fam.) excuse me.

exécrable /ɛgzekrabl/ a. abominable.

exécrer /ɛgzekre/ v.t. loathe.

exécut|er /ɛgzekyte/ v.t. carry out, execute; (mus.) perform; (tuer) execute. **~ion** /-sjɔ̃/ n.f. execution; (mus.) performance.

exécuti|f, ~ve /ɛgzekytif, -v/ a. & n.m. (pol.) executive.

exemplaire /ɛgzɑ̃plɛr/ a. exemplary. —n.m. copy.

exemple /ɛgzɑ̃pl/ n.m. example. **par ~**, for example.

exempt, ~e /ɛgzɑ̃, -t/ a. **~ de**, exempt from.

exempt|er /ɛgzɑ̃te/ v.t. exempt (**de, from**). **~ion** /-psjɔ̃/ n.f. exemption.

exercer /ɛgzɛrse/ v.t. exercise; (influence, contrôle) exert; (métier) work at; (former) train, exercise. **s'~ (à)**, practise.

exercice /ɛgzɛrsis/ n.m. exercise; (mil.) drill; (de métier) practice. **en ~**, in office; (médecin) in practice.

exhaler /ɛgzale/ v.t. emit.

exhausti|f, ~ve /ɛgzostif, -v/ a. exhaustive.

exhiber /ɛgzibe/ v.t. exhibit.

exhibitionniste /ɛgzibisjɔnist/ n.m./f. exhibitionist.

exhorter /ɛgzɔrte/ v.t. exhort.

exigence /ɛgziʒɑ̃s/ n.f. demand.

exig|er /ɛgziʒe/ v.t. demand. **~eant, ~eante** a. demanding.

exigu, ~ë /ɛgzigy/ a. tiny.

exil /ɛgzil/ n.m. exile. **~é, ~ée** n.m., f. exile. **~er** v.t. exile. **s'~er** v. pr. go into exile.

existence /ɛgzistɑ̃s/ n.f. existence.

exist|er /ɛgziste/ v.i. exist. **~ant, ~ante** a. existing.

exode /ɛgzɔd/ n.m. exodus.

exonér|er /ɛgzɔnere/ v.t. exempt (**de, from**). **~ation** n.f. exemption.

exorbitant, ~e /ɛgzɔrbitɑ̃, -t/ a. exorbitant.

exorciser /ɛgzɔrsize/ v.t. exorcize.

exotique /ɛgzɔtik/ a. exotic.

expansi|f, ~ve /ɛkspɑ̃sif, -v/ a. expansive.

expansion /ɛkspɑ̃sjɔ̃/ n.f. expansion.

expatr|ier (s') /(s)ɛkspatrije/ v. pr. leave one's country. **~ié, ~iée** n.m., f. expatriate.

expectative /ɛkspɛktativ/ n.f. **dans l'~**, still waiting.

expédient, ~e /ɛkspedjɑ̃, -t/ a. & n.m. expedient.

expéd|ier /ɛkspedje/ v.t. send, dispatch; (tâche) dispatch. **~iteur, ~itrice** n.m., f. sender. **~ition** n.f. dispatch; (voyage) expedition.

expéditi|f, ~ve /ɛkspeditif, -v/ a. quick.

expérience /ɛkspɛrjɑ̃s/ n.f. experience; (scientifique) experiment.

expérimenté /ɛksperimɑ̃te/ a. experienced.

expériment|er /ɛksperimɑ̃te/ v.t. test, experiment with. **~al** (m. pl. **~aux**) a. experimental. **~ation** n.f. experimentation.

expert, ~e /ɛkspɛr, -t/ a. expert.

—*n.m.* expert; (*d'assurances*) valuer; (*Amer.*) appraiser. **~-comptable** (*pl.* **~s-comptables**) *n.m.* accountant.

expertis|e /ɛkspɛrtiz/ *n.f.* expert appraisal. **~er** *v.t.* appraise.

expier /ɛkspje/ *v.t.* atone for.

expir|er /ɛkspire/ *v.i.* breathe out; (*finir, mourir*) expire. **~ation** *n.f.* expiry.

explicati|f, ~ve /ɛksplikatif, -v/ *a.* explanatory.

explication /ɛksplikasjɔ̃/ *n.f.* explanation; (*fig.*) discussion; (*scol.*) commentary.

explicite /ɛksplisit/ *a.* explicit.

expliquer /ɛksplike/ *v.t.* explain. **s'~** *v. pr.* explain o.s.; (*discuter*) discuss things; (*être compréhensible*) be understandable.

exploit /ɛksplwa/ *n.m.* exploit.

exploitant /ɛksplwatɑ̃/ *n.m.* farmer.

exploit|er /ɛksplwate/ *v.t.* (*personne*) exploit; (*ferme*) run; (*champs*) work. **~ation** *n.f.* exploitation; running; working; (*affaire*) concern. **~eur, ~euse** *n.m., f.* exploiter.

explor|er /ɛksplore/ *v.t.* explore. **~ateur, ~atrice** *n.m., f.* explorer. **~ation** *n.f.* exploration.

explos|er /ɛksploze/ *v.i.* explode. **faire ~er**, explode; (*bâtiment*) blow up. **~ion** *n.f.* explosion.

explosi|f, ~ve /ɛksplozif, -v/ *a. & n.m.* explosive.

export|er /ɛksporte/ *v.t.* export. **~ateur, ~atrice** *n.m., f.* exporter; *a.* exporting. **~ation** *n.f.* export.

exposant, ~e /ɛkspozɑ̃, -t/ *n.m., f.* exhibitor.

exposé /ɛkspoze/ *n.m.* talk; (*d'une action*) account.

expos|er /ɛkspoze/ *v.t.* display, show; (*expliquer*) explain; (*soumettre, mettre en danger*) expose (à, to); (*vie*) endanger. **~é au nord**/*etc.*, facing north/*etc.* **s'~er à**, expose o.s. to.

exposition /ɛkspozisjɔ̃/ *n.f.* display; (*salon*) exhibition. **~ à**, exposure to.

exprès[1] /ɛksprɛ/ *adv.* specially; (*délibérément*) on purpose.

expr|ès[2], **~esse** /ɛksprɛs/ *a.* express. **~essément** *adv.* expressly.

express /ɛksprɛs/ *a. & n.m. invar.* (**café**) **~**, espresso. (**train**) **~**, fast train.

expressi|f, ~ve /ɛkspresif, -v/ *a.* expressive.

expression /ɛksprɛsjɔ̃/ *n.f.* expression.

exprimer /ɛksprime/ *v.t.* express. **s'~** *v. pr.* express o.s.

expuls|er /ɛkspylse/ *v.t.* expel; (*locataire*) evict; (*joueur*) send off. **~ion** *n.f.* expulsion; eviction.

expurger /ɛkspyrʒe/ *v.t.* expurgate.

exquis, ~e /ɛkski, -z/ *a.* exquisite.

extase /ɛkstaz/ *n.f.* ecstasy.

extasier (**s'**) /(s)ɛkstazje/ *v. pr.* **s'~ sur**, be ecstatic about.

extensible /ɛksɑ̃sibl/ *a.* expandable, extendible.

extensi|f, ~ve /ɛkstɑ̃sif, -v/ *a.* extensive.

extension /ɛkstɑ̃sjɔ̃/ *n.f.* extension; (*expansion*) expansion.

exténuer /ɛkstenɥe/ *v.t.* exhaust.

extérieur /ɛksterjœr/ *a.* outside; (*signe, gaieté*) outward; (*politique*) foreign. —*n.m.* outside, exterior; (*de personne*) exterior. **à l'~** (**de**), outside. **~ement** *adv.* outwardly.

extérioriser /ɛksterjorize/ *v.t.* show.

extermin|er /ɛkstɛrmine/ *v.t.* exterminate. **~ation** *n.f.* extermination.

externe /ɛkstɛrn/ *a.* external. —*n.m./f.* (*scol.*) day pupil.

extincteur /ɛkstɛ̃ktœr/ *n.m.* fire extinguisher.

extinction /ɛkstɛ̃ksjɔ̃/ *n.f.* extinction. **~ de voix**, loss of voice.

extirper /ɛkstirpe/ *v.t.* eradicate.

extor|quer /ɛkstorke/ *v.t.* extort. **~sion** *n.f.* extortion.

extra /ɛkstra/ *a. invar.* first-rate. —*n.m. invar.* (*repas*) (special) treat.

extra- /ɛkstra/ *préf.* extra-.

extrad|er /ɛkstrade/ *v.t.* extradite. **~ition** *n.f.* extradition.

extr|aire† /ɛkstrɛr/ *v.t.* extract. **~action** *n.f.* extraction.

extrait /ɛkstrɛ/ *n.m.* extract.

extraordinaire /ɛkstraordinɛr/ *a.* extraordinary.

extravagan|t, ~te /ɛkstravagɑ̃, -t/ *a.* extravagant. **~ce** *n.f.* extravagance.

extraverti, ~e /ɛkstravɛrti/ *n.m., f.* extrovert.

extrême /ɛkstrɛm/ *a. & n.m.* extreme. **E~-Orient** *n.m.* Far East. **~ment** *adv.* extremely.

extrémiste /ɛkstremist/ *n.m., f.* extremist.

extrémité /ɛkstremite/ *n.f.* extremity, end; (*misère*) dire straits. **~s,** (*excès*) extremes.

exubéran|t, ∼te /ɛgzyberã, -t/ *a.* exuberant. **∼ce** *n.f.* exuberance.

exulter /ɛgzylte/ *v.i.* exult.

F

F *abrév.* (*franc, francs*) franc, francs.
fable /fɑbl/ *n.f.* fable.
fabrique /fabrik/ *n.f.* factory.
fabri|quer /fabrike/ *v.t.* make; (*industriellement*) manufacture; (*fig.*) make up. **∼cant, ∼cante** *n.m., f.* manufacturer. **∼cation** *n.f.* making; manufacture.
fabuleu|x, ∼se /fabylø, -z/ *a.* fabulous.
façade /fasad/ *n.f.* front; (*fig.*) façade.
face /fas/ *n.f.* face; (*d'un objet*) side. **en ∼ (de), d'en ∼,** opposite. **en ∼ de,** (*fig.*) faced with. **∼ à,** facing; (*fig.*) faced with. **faire ∼ à,** face.
facétie /fasesi/ *n.f.* joke.
facette /fasɛt/ *n.f.* facet.
fâch|er /fɑʃe/ *v.t.* anger. **se ∼er** *v. pr.* get angry; (*se brouiller*) fall out. **∼é** *a.* angry; (*désolé*) sorry.
fâcheu|x, ∼se /fɑʃø, -z/ *a.* unfortunate.
facil|e /fasil/ *a.* easy; (*caractère*) easygoing. **∼ement** *adv.* easily. **∼ité** *n.f.* easiness; (*aisance*) ease; (*aptitude*) ability; (*possibilité*) facility.
faciliter /fasilite/ *v.t.* facilitate.
façon /fasɔ̃/ *n.f.* way; (*de vêtement*) cut. **∼s,** (*chichis*) fuss. **de cette ∼,** in this way. **de ∼ à,** so as to. **de toute ∼,** anyway.
façonner /fasɔne/ *v.t.* shape; (*faire*) make.
facteur¹ /faktœr/ *n.m.* postman.
facteur² /faktœr/ *n.m.* (*élément*) factor.
factice /faktis/ *a.* artificial.
faction /faksjɔ̃/ *n.f.* faction. **de ∼,** (*mil.*) on guard.
factur|e /faktyr/ *n.f.* bill; (*comm.*) invoice. **∼er** *v.t.* invoice.
facultati|f, ∼ve /fakyltatif, -v/ *a.* optional.
faculté /fakylte/ *n.f.* faculty; (*possibilité*) power; (*univ.*) faculty.
fade /fad/ *a.* insipid.
fagot /fago/ *n.m.* bundle of firewood.
fagoter /fagɔte/ *v.t.* (*fam.*) rig out.
faibl|e /fɛbl/ *a.* weak; (*espoir, quantité, écart*) slight; (*revenu, intensité*) low. —*n.m.* weakling; (*penchant, défaut*) weakness. **∼e d'esprit,** feeble-minded. **∼esse** *n.f.* weakness. **∼ir** *v.i.* weaken.
faïence /fajɑ̃s/ *n.f.* earthenware.
faille /faj/ *n.f.* (*géog.*) fault; (*fig.*) flaw.
faillir /fajir/ *v.i.* **j'ai failli acheter**/*etc.*, I almost bought/*etc.*
faillite /fajit/ *n.f.* bankruptcy; (*fig.*) collapse.
faim /fɛ̃/ *n.f.* hunger. **avoir ∼,** be hungry.
fainéant, ∼e /feneɑ̃, -t/ *a.* idle. —*n.m., f.* idler.
faire† /fɛr/ *v.t.* make; (*activité*) do; (*rêve, chute, etc.*) have; (*mesure*) be; (*dire*) say. —*v.i.* do; (*paraître*) look. **se ∼** *v. pr.* (*petit etc.*) make o.s.; (*amis, argent*) make; (*illusions*) have; (*devenir*) become. **∼ du rugby/du violon**/*etc.*, play rugby/the violin/*etc.* **∼ construire/punir**/*etc.*, have *ou* get built/punished/*etc.* **∼ pleurer/tomber**/*etc.*, make cry/fall/*etc.* **se ∼ tuer**/*etc.*, get killed/*etc.* **il fait beau/chaud**/*etc.*, it is fine/hot/*etc.* **∼ l'idiot,** play the fool. **ne ∼ que pleurer**/*etc.*, (*faire continuellement*) do nothing but cry/*etc.* **ça ne fait rien,** it doesn't matter. **se ∼ à,** get used to. **s'en ∼,** worry. **ça se fait,** that is done. **∼part** *n.m. invar.* announcement.
fais, fait¹ /fɛ/ *voir* **faire.**
faisable /fəzabl/ *a.* feasible.
faisan /fəzɑ̃/ *n.m.* pheasant.
faisceau (*pl.* **∼x**) /fɛso/ *n.m.* (*rayon*) beam; (*fagot*) bundle.
fait², **∼e** /fɛ, fɛt/ *a.* done; (*fromage*) ripe; (*homme*) grown. **∼ pour,** made for. **tout ∼,** ready made.
fait³ /fɛ/ *n.m.* fact; (*événement*) event. **au ∼ (de),** informed (of). **de ce ∼,** therefore. **du ∼ de,** on account of. **∼ divers,** (trivial) news item. **∼ nouveau,** new development. **sur le ∼,** in the act.
faîte /fɛt/ *n.m.* top; (*fig.*) peak.
faites /fɛt/ *voir* **faire.**
faitout /fɛtu/ *n.m.* stew-pot.
falaise /falɛz/ *n.f.* cliff.
falloir† /falwar/ *v.i.* **il faut qch.**/**qn.,** we, you, *etc.* need sth./s.o. **il lui faut du pain,** he needs bread. **il faut rester,** we, you, *etc.* have to *ou* must stay. **il faut que j'y aille,** I have to

ou must go. **il faudrait que tu
partes,** you should leave. **il fallait le
faire,** we, you, *etc.* should have done
it. **il s'en faut de beaucoup que je
sois,** I am far from being.

falsifier /falsifje/ *v.t.* falsify.

famélique /famelik/ *a.* starving.

fameu|x, ~**se** /famø, -z/ *a.* famous;
(*excellent*: *fam.*) first-rate. ~**sement**
adv. (*fam.*) extremely.

famil|ial (*m. pl.* ~**iaux**) /familjal, -jo/
a. family.

familiar|iser /familjarize/ *v.t.*
familiarize (**avec,** with). **se** ~**iser**
v. pr. familiarize o.s. ~**isé** *a.* familiar.
~**ité** *n.f.* familiarity.

famil|ier, ~**ière** /familje, -jɛr/ *a.*
familiar; (*amical*) informal. —*n.m.*
regular visitor. ~**ièrement** *adv.* informally.

famille /famij/ *n.f.* family. **en** ~, with
one's family.

famine /famin/ *n.f.* famine.

fan|al (*pl.* ~**aux**) /fanal, -o/ *n.m.* lan-
tern, light.

fanati|que /fanatik/ *a.* fanatical.
—*n.m./f.* fanatic. ~**sme** *n.m.* fanati-
cism.

faner (se) /(sə)fane/ *v. pr.* fade.

fanfare /fɑ̃far/ *n.f.* brass band; (*musique*) fanfare.

fanfaron, ~**ne** /fɑ̃farɔ̃, -ɔn/ *a.* boastful. —*n.m., f.* boaster.

fanion /fanjɔ̃/ *n.m.* pennant.

fantaisie /fɑ̃tezi/ *n.f.* imagination, fantasy; (*caprice*) whim. **(de)** ~, (*boutons
etc.*) fancy.

fantaisiste /fɑ̃tezist/ *a.* unorthodox.

fantasme /fɑ̃tasm/ *n.m.* fantasy.

fantasque /fɑ̃task/ *a.* whimsical.

fantassin /fɑ̃tasɛ̃/ *n.m.* infantryman.

fantastique /fɑ̃tastik/ *a.* fantastic.

fantoche /fɑ̃tɔʃ/ *n.m. & a.* puppet.

fantôme /fɑ̃tom/ *n.m.* ghost. —*a.* (*péj.*)
bogus.

faon /fɑ̃/ *n.m.* fawn.

farc|e[1] /fars/ *n.f.* (practical) joke;
(*théâtre*) farce. ~**eur,** ~**euse** *n.m., f.*
joker.

farc|e[2] /fars/ *n.f.* (*hachis*) stuffing. ~**ir**
v.t. stuff.

fard /far/ *n.m.* make-up. ~**er** /-de/ *v.t.,*
se ~**er** *v. pr.* make up.

fardeau (*pl.* ~**x**) /fardo/ *n.m.* burden.

farfelu, ~**e** /farfəly/ *a. & n.m., f.* eccentric.

farin|e /farin/ *n.f.* flour. ~**e d'avoine,**
oatmeal. ~**eux,** ~**euse** *a.* floury.

farouche /faruʃ/ *a.* shy; (*peu sociable*)
unsociable; (*violent*) fierce. ~**ment**
adv. fiercely.

fart /far(t)/ *n.m.* (ski) wax. ~**er** /farte/
v.t. (*skis*) wax.

fascin|er /fasine/ *v.t.* fascinate. ~**a-
tion** *n.f.* fascination.

fascis|te /faʃist/ *a. & n.m./f.* fascist.
~**me** *n.m.* fascism.

fasse /fas/ *voir* **faire.**

faste /fast/ *n.m.* splendour.

fastidieu|x, ~**se** /fastidjø, -z/ *a.* tedi-
ous.

fat|al (*m. pl.* ~**als**) /fatal/ *a.* inevitable;
(*mortel*) fatal. ~**alement** *adv.* inevitably. ~**alité** *n.f.* (*destin*) fate.

fataliste /fatalist/ *n.m./f.* fatalist.

fatidique /fatidik/ *a.* fateful.

fatigant, ~**e** /fatigɑ̃, -t/ *a.* tiring; (*ennuyeux*) tiresome.

fatigue /fatig/ *n.f.* fatigue, tiredness.

fatigu|er /fatige/ *v.t.* tire; (*yeux, mo-
teur*) strain. —*v.i.* (*moteur*) labour. **se**
~**er** *v. pr.* get tired, tire (**de,** of). ~**é**
a. tired.

fatras /fatra/ *n.m.* jumble.

faubourg /fobur/ *n.m.* suburb.

fauché /foʃe/ *a.* (*fam.*) broke.

faucher /foʃe/ *v.t.* (*herbe*) mow; (*voler*:
fam.) pinch. ~ **qn.,** (*véhicule, tir*) mow
s.o. down.

faucille /fosij/ *n.f.* sickle.

faucon /fokɔ̃/ *n.m.* falcon, hawk.

faudra, faudrait /fodra, fodrɛ/ *voir*
falloir.

faufiler (se) /(sə)fofile/ *v. pr.* edge
one's way.

faune /fon/ *n.f.* wildlife, fauna.

faussaire /fosɛr/ *n.m.* forger.

fausse /fos/ *voir* **faux**[2].

faussement /fosmɑ̃/ *adv.* falsely.

fausser /fose/ *v.t.* buckle; (*fig.*) distort.
~ **compagnie à,** sneak away from.

fausseté /foste/ *n.f.* falseness.

faut /fo/ *voir* **falloir.**

faute /fot/ *n.f.* mistake; (*responsabilité*) fault; (*délit*) offence; (*péché*) sin.
en ~, at fault. ~ **de,** for want of. ~
de quoi, failing which.

fauteuil /fotœj/ *n.m.* armchair; (*de
président*) chair; (*théâtre*) seat. ~ **roulant,** wheelchair.

fauti|f, ~**ve** /fotif, -v/ *a.* guilty; (*faux*)
faulty. —*n.m., f.* guilty party.

fauve /fov/ *a.* (*couleur*) fawn. —*n.m.*
wild cat.

faux[1] /fo/ *n.f.* scythe.

faux[2]**, fausse** /fo, fos/ *a.* false; (*falsifié*)

fake, forged; (*numéro, calcul*) wrong; (*voix*) out of tune. **c'est ~!**, that is wrong! **il est ~ de**, it is wrong to. —*adv.* (*chanter*) out of tune. —*n.m.* forgery. **fausse couche**, miscarriage. **~-filet** *n.m.* sirloin. **~-monnayeur** *n.m.* forger.

faveur /favœr/ *n.f.* favour. **de ~**, (*régime*) preferential. **en ~ de**, in favour of.

favorable /favɔrabl/ *a.* favourable.

favori, ~te /favɔri, -t/ *a. & n.m.*, *f.* favourite. **~tisme** *n.m.* favouritism.

favoris /favɔri/ *n.m. pl.* side-whiskers.

favoriser /favɔrize/ *v.t.* favour.

fébrile /febril/ *a.* feverish.

fécond, ~e /fekɔ̃, -d/ *a.* fertile. **~er** /-de/ *v.t.* fertilize. **~ité** /-dite/ *n.f.* fertility.

fécule /fekyl/ *n.f.* starch.

fédér|al (*m. pl.* **~aux**) /federal, -o/ *a.* federal.

fédération /federasjɔ̃/ *n.f.* federation.

fée /fe/ *n.f.* fairy.

féer|ie /fe(e)ri/ *n.f.* magical spectacle. **~ique** *a.* magical.

feindre† /fɛ̃dr/ *v.t.* feign. **~ de**, pretend to.

feinte /fɛ̃t/ *n.f.* feint.

fêler /fele/ *v.t.*, **se ~** *v. pr.* crack.

félicité /felisite/ *n.f.* bliss.

félicit|er /felisite/ *v.t.* congratulate (**de**, on). **~ations** *n.f. pl.* congratulations (**pour**, on).

félin, ~e /felɛ̃, -in/ *a. & n.m.* feline.

fêlure /felyr/ *n.f.* crack.

femelle /fəmɛl/ *a. & n.f.* female.

fémin|in, ~ine /feminɛ̃, -in/ *a.* feminine; (*sexe*) female; (*mode, équipe*) women's. —*n.m.* feminine. **~ité** *n.f.* femininity.

féministe /feminist/ *n.m./f.* feminist.

femme /fam/ *n.f.* woman; (*épouse*) wife. **~ de chambre**, chambermaid. **~ de ménage**, cleaning lady.

fémur /femyr/ *n.m.* thigh-bone.

fendiller /fɑ̃dije/ *v.t.*, **se ~** *v. pr.* crack.

fendre /fɑ̃dr/ *v.t.* (*couper*) split; (*fissurer*) crack; (*foule*) push through. **se ~** *v. pr.* crack.

fenêtre /fənɛtr/ *n.f.* window.

fenouil /fənuj/ *n.m.* fennel.

fente /fɑ̃t/ *n.f.* (*ouverture*) slit, slot; (*fissure*) crack.

féod|al (*m. pl.* **~aux**) /feɔdal, -o/ *a.* feudal.

fer /fɛr/ *n.m.* iron. **~ (à repasser)**, iron. **~ à cheval**, horseshoe. **~**

blanc (*pl.* **~s-blancs**) *n.m.* tinplate. **~ de lance**, spearhead.

fera, ferait /fəra, fərɛ/ *voir* **faire**.

ferme¹ /fɛrm/ *a.* firm. —*adv.* (*travailler*) hard. **~ment** /-əmɑ̃/ *adv.* firmly.

ferme² /fɛrm/ *n.f.* farm; (*maison*) farm(house).

fermé /fɛrme/ *a.* closed; (*gaz, radio, etc.*) off.

ferment /fɛrmɑ̃/ *n.m.* ferment.

ferment|er /fɛrmɑ̃te/ *v.i.* ferment. **~ation** *n.f.* fermentation.

fermer /fɛrme/ *v.t./i.* close, shut; (*cesser d'exploiter*) close *ou* shut down; (*gaz, radio, etc.*) turn off. **se ~** *v. pr.* close, shut.

fermeté /fɛrməte/ *n.f.* firmness.

fermeture /fɛrmətyr/ *n.f.* closing; (*dispositif*) catch. **~ annuelle**, annual closure. **~ éclair**, (P.) zip(-fastener); (*Amer.*) zipper.

ferm|ier, ~ière /fɛrmje, -jɛr/ *n.m.* farmer. —*n.f.* farmer's wife. —*a.* farm.

fermoir /fɛrmwar/ *n.m.* clasp.

féroc|e /ferɔs/ *a.* ferocious. **~ité** *n.f.* ferocity.

ferraille /fɛraj/ *n.f.* scrap-iron.

ferré /fɛre/ *a.* (*canne*) steel-tipped. **~ en** *ou* **sur**, (*fam.*) clued up on.

ferrer /fɛre/ *v.t.* (*cheval*) shoe.

ferronnerie /fɛrɔnri/ *n.f.* ironwork.

ferroviaire /fɛrɔvjɛr/ *a.* rail(way).

ferry-boat /fɛribot/ *n.m.* ferry.

fertil|e /fɛrtil/ *a.* fertile. **~ en**, (*fig.*) rich in. **~iser** *v.t.* fertilize. **~ité** *n.f.* fertility.

ferv|ent, ~ente /fɛrvɑ̃, -t/ *a.* fervent. —*n.m., f.* enthusiast (**de**, of). **~eur** *n.f.* fervour.

fesse /fɛs/ *n.f.* buttock.

fessée /fese/ *n.f.* spanking.

festin /fɛstɛ̃/ *n.m.* feast.

festival (*pl.* **~s**) /fɛstival/ *n.m.* festival.

festivités /fɛstivite/ *n.f. pl.* festivities.

festoyer /fɛstwaje/ *v.i.* feast.

fête /fɛt/ *n.f.* holiday; (*religieuse*) feast; (*du nom*) name-day; (*réception*) party; (*en famille*) celebration; (*foire*) fair; (*folklorique*) festival. **~ des Mères**, Mother's Day. **~ foraine**, fun-fair. **faire la ~**, make merry.

fêter /fete/ *v.t.* celebrate; (*personne*) give a celebration for.

fétiche /fetiʃ/ *n.m.* fetish; (*fig.*) mascot.

fétide /fetid/ *a.* fetid.

feu¹ (*pl.* **~x**) /fø/ *n.m.* fire; (*lumière*)

light; (*de réchaud*) burner. **~x (rouges)**, (traffic) lights. **à ~ doux**, on a low flame. **du ~**, (*pour cigarette*) a light. **~ d'artifice**, firework display. **~ de joie**, bonfire. **~ de position**, sidelight. **mettre le ~ à**, set fire to. **prendre ~**, catch fire.

feu² /fø/ *a. invar.* (*mort*) late.

feuillage /fœjaʒ/ *n.m.* foliage.

feuille /fœj/ *n.f.* leaf; (*de papier, bois, etc.*) sheet; (*formulaire*) form.

feuillet /fœjɛ/ *n.m.* leaf.

feuilleter /fœjte/ *v.t.* leaf through.

feuilleton /fœjtɔ̃/ *n.m.* (*à suivre*) serial; (*histoire complète*) series.

feuillu /fœjy/ *a.* leafy.

feutre /føtr/ *n.m.* felt; (*chapeau*) felt hat; (*crayon*) felt-tipped pen.

feutré /føtre/ *a.* (*bruit*) muffled.

fève /fɛv/ *n.f.* broad bean.

février /fevrije/ *n.m.* February.

fiable /fjabl/ *a.* reliable.

fiacre /fjakr/ *n.m.* hackney cab.

fiançailles /fjɑ̃saj/ *n.f. pl.* engagement.

fianc|er (se) /(sə)fjɑ̃se/ *v. pr.* become engaged (**avec**, to). **~é, ~ée** *a.* engaged; *n.m.* fiancé; *n.f.* fiancée.

fibre /fibr/ *n.f.* fibre. **~ de verre**, fibreglass.

ficeler /fisle/ *v.t.* tie up.

ficelle /fisɛl/ *n.f.* string.

fiche /fiʃ/ *n.f.* (index) card; (*formulaire*) form, slip; (*électr.*) plug.

ficher¹ /fiʃe/ *v.t.* (*enfoncer*) drive (**dans**, into).

ficher² /fiʃe/ *v.t.* (*faire: fam.*) do; (*donner: fam.*) give; (*mettre: fam.*) put. **se ~ de**, (*fam.*) make fun of. **~ le camp**, (*fam.*) clear off. **il s'en fiche**, (*fam.*) he couldn't care less.

fichier /fiʃje/ *n.m.* file.

fichu¹ /fiʃy/ *a.* (*mauvais: fam.*) rotten; (*fini: fam.*) done for.

fichu² /fiʃy/ *n.m.* (head)scarf.

ficti|f, ~ve /fiktif, -v/ *a.* fictitious.

fiction /fiksjɔ̃/ *n.f.* fiction.

fidèle /fidɛl/ *a.* faithful. —*n.m./f.* (*client*) regular; (*relig.*) believer. **~s**, (*à l'église*) congregation. **~ment** *adv.* faithfully.

fidélité /fidelite/ *n.f.* fidelity.

fiel /fjɛl/ *n.m.* gall.

fier¹, fière /fjɛr/ *a.* proud (**de**, of). **fièrement** *adv.* proudly. **~té** *n.f.* pride.

fier² (se) /(sə)fje/ *v. pr.* **se ~ à**, trust.

fièvre /fjɛvr/ *n.f.* fever.

fiévreu|x, ~se /fjevrø, -z/ *a.* feverish.

figé /fiʒe/ *a.* fixed, set; (*manières*) stiff.

figer /fiʒe/ *v.t./i.*, **se ~** *v. pr.* congeal. **~ sur place**, petrify.

fignoler /fiɲɔle/ *v.t.* refine (upon), finish off meticulously.

figu|e /fig/ *n.f.* fig. **~ier** *n.m.* fig-tree.

figurant, ~e /figyrɑ̃, -t/ *n.m., f.* (*cinéma*) extra.

figure /figyr/ *n.f.* face; (*forme, personnage*) figure; (*illustration*) picture.

figuré /figyre/ *a.* (*sens*) figurative. **au ~**, figuratively.

figurer /figyre/ *v.i.* appear. —*v.t.* represent. **se ~** *v. pr.* imagine.

fil /fil/ *n.m.* thread; (*métallique, électrique*) wire; (*de couteau*) edge; (*tissu*) linen. **au ~ de**, with the passing of. **au ~ de l'eau**, with the current. **~ de fer**, wire.

filament /filamɑ̃/ *n.m.* filament.

filature /filatyr/ *n.f.* (textile) mill; (*surveillance*) shadowing.

file /fil/ *n.f.* line; (*voie: auto.*) lane. **~ (d'attente)**, queue; (*Amer.*) line. **en ~ indienne**, in single file. **se mettre en ~**, line up.

filer /file/ *v.t.* spin; (*suivre*) shadow. **~ qch. à qn.**, (*fam.*) slip s.o. sth. —*v.i.* (*bas*) ladder, run; (*liquide*) run; (*aller vite: fam.*) speed along, fly by; (*partir: fam.*) dash off.

filet /file/ *n.m.* net; (*d'eau*) trickle; (*de viande*) fillet. **~ (à bagages)**, (luggage) rack. **~ à provisions**, string bag (*for shopping*).

fil|ial, ~iale (*m. pl.* **~iaux**) /filjal, -jo/ *a.* filial. —*n.f.* subsidiary (company).

filière /filjɛr/ *n.f.* (official) channels; (*de trafiquants*) network. **passer par ou suivre la ~**, (*employé*) work one's way up.

filigrane /filigran/ *n.m.* watermark.

filin /filɛ̃/ *n.m.* rope.

fille /fij/ *n.f.* girl; (*opposé à fils*) daughter. **~-mère** (*pl.* **~s-mères**) *n.f.* (*péj.*) unmarried mother.

fillette /fijet/ *n.f.* little girl.

filleul /fijœl/ *n.m.* godson. **~e** *n.f.* god-daughter.

film /film/ *n.m.* film. **~ d'épouvante muet/parlant**, horror/silent/talking film. **~ dramatique**, drama. **~er** *v.t.* film.

filon /filɔ̃/ *n.m.* (*géol.*) seam; (*situation*) source of wealth.

fils /fis/ *n.m.* son.

filtr|e /filtr/ *n.m.* filter. **~er** *v.t./i.* filter; (*personne*) screen.

fin[1] /fɛ̃/ *n.f.* end. **à la ~**, finally. **en ~ de compte**, all things considered. **~ de semaine**, weekend. **mettre ~ à**, put an end to. **prendre ~**, come to an end.

fin[2], **fine** /fɛ̃, fin/ *a.* fine; (*tranche, couche*) thin; (*taille*) slim; (*plat*) exquisite; (*esprit, vue*) sharp. —*adv.* (*couper*) finely. **~es herbes**, herbs.

fin|al, ~ale[1] (*m. pl.* **~aux** *ou* **~als**) /final, -o/ *a.* final. —*n.f.* (*sport*) final; (*gram.*) final syllable. —*n.m.* (*pl.* **~aux** *ou* **~als**) (*mus.*) finale. **~ale- ment** *adv.* finally; (*somme toute*) after all.

finale[2] /final/ *n.m.* (*mus.*) finale.

finaliste /finalist/ *n.m./f.* finalist.

financ|e /finɑ̃s/ *n.f.* finance. **~er** *v.t.* finance. **~ier, ~ière** *a.* financial; *n.m.* financier.

finement /finmɑ̃/ *adv.* finely; (*avec habileté*) cleverly.

finesse /finɛs/ *n.f.* fineness; (*de taille*) slimness; (*acuité*) sharpness. **~s**, (*de langue*) niceties.

fini /fini/ *a.* finished; (*espace*) finite. —*n.m.* finish.

finir /finir/ *v.t./i.* finish, end; (*arrêter*) stop; (*manger*) finish (up). **en ~ avec**, have done with. **~ par faire**, end up doing.

finition /finisjɔ̃/ *n.f.* finish.

finlandais, ~e /fɛ̃lɑ̃dɛ, -z/ *a.* Finnish. —*n.m., f.* Finn.

Finlande /fɛ̃lɑ̃d/ *n.f.* Finland.

finnois, ~e /finwa, -z/ *a.* Finnish. —*n.m.* (*lang.*) Finnish.

fiole /fjɔl/ *n.f.* phial.

firme /firm/ *n.f.* firm.

fisc /fisk/ *n.m.* tax authorities. **~al** (*m. pl.* **~aux**) *a.* tax, fiscal. **~alité** *n.f.* tax system.

fission /fisjɔ̃/ *n.f.* fission.

fissur|e /fisyr/ *n.f.* crack. **~er** *v.t.*, **se ~er** *v. pr.* crack.

fiston /fistɔ̃/ *n.m.* (*fam.*) son.

fixation /fiksasjɔ̃/ *n.f.* fixing; (*complexe*) fixation.

fixe /fiks/ *a.* fixed; (*stable*) steady. **à heure ~**, at a set time.

fixer /fikse/ *v.t.* fix. **~ (du regard)**, stare at. **se ~** *v. pr.* (*s'installer*) settle down. **être fixé**, (*personne*) have made up one's mind.

flacon /flakɔ̃/ *n.m.* bottle.

flageolet /flaʒɔlɛ/ *n.m* (*haricot*) (dwarf) kidney bean.

flagrant, ~e /flagrɑ̃, -t/ *a.* flagrant. **en ~ délit**, in the act.

flair /flɛr/ *n.m.* (sense of) smell; (*fig.*) intuition. **~er** /flere/ *v.t.* sniff at; (*fig.*) sense.

flamand, ~e /flamɑ̃, -d/ *a.* Flemish. —*n.m.* (*lang.*) Flemish. —*n.m., f.* Fleming.

flamant /flamɑ̃/ *n.m.* flamingo.

flambant /flɑ̃bɑ̃/ *adv.* **~ neuf**, brand-new.

flambeau (*pl.* **~x**) /flɑ̃bo/ *n.m.* torch.

flambée /flɑ̃be/ *n.f.* blaze; (*fig.*) explosion.

flamber /flɑ̃be/ *v.i.* blaze. —*v.t.* (*aiguille*) sterilize; (*volaille*) singe.

flamboyer /flɑ̃bwaje/ *v.i.* blaze.

flamme /flam/ *n.f.* flame; (*fig.*) ardour.

flammèche /flamɛʃ/ *n.f.* spark.

flan /flɑ̃/ *n.m.* custard-pie.

flanc /flɑ̃/ *n.m.* side; (*d'animal, d'armée*) flank.

flancher /flɑ̃ʃe/ *v.i.* (*fam.*) give in.

Flandre(s) /flɑ̃dr/ *n.f.* (*pl.*) Flanders.

flanelle /flanɛl/ *n.f.* flannel.

flân|er /flane/ *v.i.* stroll. **~erie** *n.f.* stroll.

flanquer /flɑ̃ke/ *v.t.* flank; (*jeter: fam.*) chuck; (*donner: fam.*) give.

flaque /flak/ *n.f.* (*d'eau*) puddle; (*de sang*) pool.

flash (*pl.* **~es**) /flaʃ/ *n.m.* (*photo.*) flash; (*information*) news flash.

flasque /flask/ *a.* flabby.

flatt|er /flate/ *v.t.* flatter. **se ~er de**, pride o.s. on. **~erie** *n.f.* flattery. **~eur, ~euse** *a.* flattering; *n.m., f.* flatterer.

fléau (*pl.* **~x**) /fleo/ *n.m.* (*désastre*) scourge; (*personne*) bane.

flèche /flɛʃ/ *n.f.* arrow; (*de clocher*) spire.

flécher /fleʃe/ *v.t.* mark *ou* signpost (with arrows).

fléchette /fleʃɛt/ *n.f.* dart.

fléchir /fleʃir/ *v.t.* bend; (*personne*) move. —*v.i.* (*faiblir*) weaken; (*poutre*) sag, bend.

flegmatique /flɛgmatik/ *a.* phlegmatic.

flegme /flɛgm/ *n.m.* composure.

flemm|e /flɛm/ *n.f.* (*fam.*) laziness. **~ard, ~arde** *a.* (*fam.*) lazy; *n.m., f.* (*fam.*) lazy-bones.

flétrir /fletrir/ *v.t.*, **se ~** *v. pr.* wither.

fleur /flœr/ *n.f.* flower; (*d'un arbre*)

blossom. **à ~ de terre/d'eau,** just above the ground/water. **à ~s,** flowery. **~ de l'âge,** prime of life.

fleur|ir /flœrir/ v.i. flower; (*arbre*) blossom; (*fig.*) flourish. —v.t. adorn with flowers. **~i** a. in flower; (*fig.*) flowery.

fleuriste /flœrist/ n.m.|f. florist.

fleuve /flœv/ n.m. river.

flexible /flɛksibl/ a. flexible.

flexion /flɛksjɔ̃/ n.f. (*anat.*) flexing.

flic /flik/ n.m. (*fam.*) cop.

flirt /flœrt/ n.m. flirtation. **~er** v.i. flirt. **~eur, ~euse** n.m., f. flirt.

flocon /flɔkɔ̃/ n.m. flake.

floraison /flɔrɛzɔ̃/ n.f. flowering.

flor|al (m. pl. **~aux**) /flɔral, -o/ a. floral.

floralies /flɔrali/ n.f. pl. flower-show.

flore /flɔr/ n.f. flora.

florissant, ~e /flɔrisã, -t/ a. flourishing.

flot /flo/ n.m. flood, stream. **être à ~,** be afloat. **les ~s,** the waves.

flottant, ~e /flɔtã, -t/ a. (*vêtement*) loose; (*indécis*) indecisive.

flotte /flɔt/ n.f. fleet; (*pluie: fam.*) rain.

flottement /flɔtmã/ n.m. (*incertitude*) indecision.

flott|er /flɔte/ v.i. float; (*drapeau*) flutter; (*nuage, parfum, pensées*) drift; (*pleuvoir: fam.*) rain. **~eur** n.m. float.

flou /flu/ a. (*vague*) fuzzy.

fluct|uer /flyktɥe/ v.i. fluctuate. **~uation** n.f. fluctuation.

fluet, ~te /flyɛ, -t/ a. slender; (*voice*) thin.

fluid|e /flɥid/ a. & n.m. fluid. **~ité** n.f. fluidity.

fluor /flyɔr/ n.m. (*pour les dents*) fluoride.

fluorescent, ~e /flyɔresã, -t/ a. fluorescent.

flût|e /flyt/ n.f. flute; (*verre*) champagne glass. **~iste** n.m.|f. flautist; (*Amer.*) flutist.

fluv|ial (m. pl. **~iaux**) /flyvjal, -jo/ a. river.

flux /fly/ n.m. flow. **~ et reflux,** ebb and flow.

fluxion /flyksjɔ̃/ n.f. **~ de poitrine,** pneumonia.

foc|al (m. pl. **~aux**) /fɔkal, -o/ a. focal.

fœtus /fetys/ n.m. foetus.

foi /fwa/ n.f. faith; (*promesse*) word. **être de bonne/mauvaise ~,** be acting in good/bad faith. **ma ~!,** well (indeed)!

foie /fwa/ n.m. liver. **~ gras,** foie gras.

foin /fwɛ̃/ n.m. hay.

foire /fwar/ n.f. fair. **faire la ~,** (*fam.*) make merry.

fois /fwa/ n.f. time. **une ~,** once. **deux ~,** twice. **à la ~,** at the same time. **des ~,** (*parfois*) sometimes.

foison /fwazɔ̃/ n.f. abundance. **à ~,** in abundance. **~ner** /-ɔne/ v.i. abound (**de,** in).

fol /fɔl/ voir fou.

folâtrer /fɔlatre/ v.i. frolic.

folichon, ~ne /fɔliʃɔ̃, -ɔn/ a. **pas ~,** (*fam.*) not much fun.

folie /fɔli/ n.f. madness; (*bêtise*) foolish thing, folly.

folklor|e /fɔlklɔr/ n.m. folklore. **~ique** a. folk; (*fam.*) picturesque.

folle /fɔl/ voir fou.

follement /fɔlmã/ adv. madly.

fomenter /fɔmãte/ v.t. foment.

fonc|er¹ /fɔ̃se/ v.t.|i. darken. **~é** a. dark.

foncer² /fɔ̃se/ v.i. (*fam.*) dash along. **~ sur,** (*fam.*) charge at.

fonc|ier, ~ière /fɔ̃sje, -jɛr/ a. fundamental; (*comm.*) real estate. **~ièrement** adv. fundamentally.

fonction /fɔ̃ksjɔ̃/ n.f. function; (*emploi*) position. **~s,** (*obligations*) duties. **en ~ de,** according to. **~ publique,** civil service.

fonctionnaire /fɔ̃ksjɔnɛr/ n.m.|f. civil servant.

fonctionnel, ~le /fɔ̃ksjɔnɛl/ a. functional.

fonctionn|er /fɔ̃ksjɔne/ v.i. work. **faire ~er,** work. **~ement** n.m. working.

fond /fɔ̃/ n.m. bottom; (*de salle, magasin, etc.*) back; (*essentiel*) basis; (*contenu*) content; (*plan*) background. **à ~,** thoroughly. **au ~,** basically. **de ~,** (*bruit*) background; (*sport*) longdistance. **de ~ en comble,** from top to bottom.

fondament|al (m. pl. **~aux**) /fɔ̃damãtal, -o/ a. fundamental.

fondation /fɔ̃dasjɔ̃/ n.f. foundation.

fond|er /fɔ̃de/ v.t. found; (*baser*) base (**sur,** on). (**bien**) **~é,** well-founded. **~é à,** justified in. **se ~er sur,** be guided by, place one's reliance on. **~ateur, ~atrice** n.m., f. founder.

fonderie /fɔ̃dri/ n.f. foundry.

fondre /fɔ̃dr/ v.t.|i. melt; (*dans l'eau*) dissolve; (*mélanger*) merge. **se ~** v. pr. merge. **faire ~,** melt; dissolve. **~**

en larmes, burst into tears. ~ **sur,** swoop on.

fondrière /fɔ̃drijɛr/ *n.f.* pot-hole.

fonds /fɔ̃/ *n.m.* fund. —*n.m. pl.* (*capitaux*) funds. ~ **de commerce,** business.

fondu /fɔ̃dy/ *a.* melted; (*métal*) molten.

font /fɔ̃/ *voir* **faire.**

fontaine /fɔ̃tɛn/ *n.f.* fountain; (*source*) spring.

fonte /fɔ̃t/ *n.f.* melting; (*fer*) cast iron. ~ **des neiges,** thaw.

foot /fut/ *n.m.* (*fam.*) football.

football /futbol/ *n.m.* football. ~**eur** *n.m.* footballer.

footing /futiŋ/ *n.m.* fast walking.

forage /fɔraʒ/ *n.m.* drilling.

forain /fɔrɛ̃/ *n.m.* fairground entertainer. **(marchand)** ~, stall-holder (*at a fair or market*).

forçat /fɔrsa/ *n.m.* convict.

force /fɔrs/ *n.f.* force; (*physique*) strength; (*hydraulique etc.*) power. ~**s,** (*physiques*) strength. **à** ~ **de,** by sheer force of. **de** ~, **par la** ~, by force. ~ **de dissuasion,** deterrent. ~ **de frappe,** strike force, deterrent. ~ **de l'âge,** prime of life. ~**s de l'ordre,** police (force).

forcé /fɔrse/ *a.* forced; (*inévitable*) inevitable.

forcément /fɔrsemɑ̃/ *adv.* necessarily; (*évidemment*) obviously.

forcené, ~**e** /fɔrsəne/ *a.* frenzied. —*n.m.,f.* maniac.

forceps /fɔrsɛps/ *n.m.* forceps.

forcer /fɔrse/ *v.t.* force (**à faire,** to do); (*voix*) strain. —*v.i.* (*exagérer*) overdo it. **se** ~ *v. pr.* force o.s.

forcir /fɔrsir/ *v.i.* fill out.

forer /fɔre/ *v.t.* drill.

forest|**ier,** ~**ière** /fɔrɛstje, -jɛr/ *a.* forest.

foret /fɔrɛ/ *n.m.* drill.

forêt /fɔrɛ/ *n.f.* forest.

forfait /fɔrfɛ/ *n.m.* (*comm.*) inclusive price. ~**aire** /-tɛr/ *a.* (*prix*) inclusive.

forge /fɔrʒ/ *n.f.* forge.

forger /fɔrʒe/ *v.t.* forge; (*inventer*) make up.

forgeron /fɔrʒərɔ̃/ *n.m.* blacksmith.

formaliser (se) /(sə)fɔrmalize/ *v. pr.* take offence (**de,** at).

formalité /fɔrmalite/ *n.f.* formality.

format /fɔrma/ *n.m.* format.

formation /fɔrmasjɔ̃/ *n.f.* formation; (*de médecin etc.*) training; (*culture*) education.

forme /fɔrm/ *n.f.* form; (*contour*) shape, form. ~**s,** (*de femme*) figure. **en** ~, (*sport*) in good shape, on form. **en** ~ **de,** in the shape of.

formel, ~**le** /fɔrmɛl/ *a.* formal; (*catégorique*) positive. ~**lement** *adv.* positively.

former /fɔrme/ *v.t.* form; (*instruire*) train. **se** ~ *v. pr.* form.

formidable /fɔrmidabl/ *a.* fantastic.

formulaire /fɔrmylɛr/ *n.m.* form.

formul|**e** /fɔrmyl/ *n.f.* formula; (*expression*) expression; (*feuille*) form. ~**er** *v.t.* formulate.

fort[1], ~**e** /fɔr, -t/ *a.* strong; (*grand*) big; (*pluie*) heavy; (*bruit*) loud; (*pente*) steep; (*élève*) clever. —*adv.* (*frapper*) hard; (*parler*) loud; (*très*) very; (*beaucoup*) very much. —*n.m.* strong point. **au plus** ~ **de,** at the height of.

fort[2] /fɔr/ *n.m.* (*mil.*) fort.

fortement /fɔrtəmɑ̃/ *adv.* strongly; (*frapper*) hard; (*beaucoup*) greatly.

forteresse /fɔrtərɛs/ *n.f.* fortress.

fortifiant /fɔrtifjɑ̃/ *n.m.* tonic.

fortif|**ier** /fɔrtifje/ *v.t.* fortify. ~**ication** *n.f.* fortification.

fortuit, ~**e** /fɔrtɥi, -t/ *a.* fortuitous.

fortune /fɔrtyn/ *n.f.* fortune. **de** ~, (*improvisé*) makeshift. **faire** ~, make one's fortune.

fortuné /fɔrtyne/ *a.* wealthy.

forum /fɔrɔm/ *n.m.* forum.

fosse /fos/ *n.f.* pit; (*tombe*) grave. ~ **d'aisances,** cesspool.

fossé /fose/ *n.m.* ditch; (*fig.*) gulf.

fossette /fosɛt/ *n.f.* dimple.

fossile /fosil/ *n.m.* fossil.

fossoyeur /foswajœr/ *n.m.* gravedigger.

fou *ou* **fol*, folle** /fu, fɔl/ *a.* mad; (*course,* *regard*) wild; (*énorme: fam.*) tremendous. —*n.m.* madman; (*bouffon*) jester. —*n.f.* madwoman. **le** ~ **rire,** the giggles.

foudre /fudr/ *n.f.* lightning.

foudroy|**er** /fudrwaje/ *v.t.* strike by lightning; (*électr.*) electrocute; (*maladie etc.*) strike down; (*atterrer*) stagger. ~**ant,** ~**ante** *a.* staggering; (*mort, maladie*) violent.

fouet /fwɛ/ *n.m.* whip; (*culin.*) whisk.

fouetter /fwete/ *v.t.* whip; (*crème etc.*) whisk.

fougère /fuʒɛr/ *n.f.* fern.

fougu|**e** /fug/ *n.f.* ardour. ~**eux,** ~**euse** *a.* ardent.

fouill|**e** /fuj/ *n.f.* search; (*archéol.*) excavation. ~**er** *v.t./i.* search; (*creuser*) dig. ~**er dans,** (*tiroir*) rummage through.

fouillis /fuji/ *n.m.* jumble.

fouine /fwin/ *n.f.* beech-marten.

fouiner /fwine/ *v.i.* nose about.

foulard /fular/ *n.m.* scarf.

foule /ful/ *n.f.* crowd. **une ~ de,** (*fig.*) a mass of.

foulée /fule/ *n.f.* stride.

fouler /fule/ *v.t.* press; (*sol*) tread; (*membre*) sprain. **se ~** *v. pr.* (*fam.*) exert o.s.

foulure /fulyr/ *n.f.* sprain.

four /fur/ *n.m.* oven; (*de potier*) kiln; (*théâtre*) flop. **~ à micro-ondes,** microwave oven. **~ crématoire,** crematorium.

fourbe /furb/ *a.* deceitful.

fourbu /furby/ *a.* exhausted.

fourche /furʃ/ *n.f.* fork; (*à foin*) pitchfork.

fourchette /furʃɛt/ *n.f.* fork; (*comm.*) margin.

fourchu /furʃy/ *a.* forked.

fourgon /furgɔ̃/ *n.m.* van; (*wagon*) wagon. **~ mortuaire,** hearse.

fourgonnette /furgɔnɛt/ *n.f.* (small) van.

fourmi /furmi/ *n.f.* ant. **des ~s,** (*méd.*) pins and needles.

fourmilière /furmiljɛr/ *n.f.* anthill.

fourmiller /furmije/ *v.i.* swarm (**de,** with).

fournaise /furnɛz/ *n.f.* (*feu, endroit*) furnace.

fourneau (*pl.* ~**x**) /furno/ *n.m.* stove.

fournée /furne/ *n.f.* batch.

fourni /furni/ *a.* (*épais*) thick.

fourn|ir /furnir/ *v.t.* supply, provide; (*client*) supply; (*effort*) put in. ~**ir à qn.,** supply s.o. with. **se ~ir chez,** shop at. ~**isseur** *n.m.* supplier. ~**iture** *n.f.* supply.

fourrage /furaʒ/ *n.m.* fodder.

fourré[1] /fure/ *n.m.* thicket.

fourré[2] /fure/ *a.* (*vêtement*) fur-lined; (*gâteau etc.*) filled (*with jam, cream, etc.*).

fourreau (*pl.* ~**x**) /furo/ *n.m.* sheath.

fourr|er /fure/ *v.t.* (*mettre: fam.*) stick. ~**e-tout** *n.m. invar.* junk room; (*sac*) holdall.

fourreur /furœr/ *n.m.* furrier.

fourrière /furjɛr/ *n.f.* (*lieu*) pound.

fourrure /furyr/ *n.f.* fur.

fourvoyer (se) /(sə)furvwaje/ *v. pr.* go astray.

foutaise /futɛz/ *n.f.* (*argot*) rubbish.

foutre /futr/ *v.t.* (*argot*) = **ficher**[2].

foyer /fwaje/ *n.m.* home; (*âtre*) hearth; (*club*) club; (*d'étudiants*) hostel; (*théâtre*) foyer; (*photo.*) focus; (*centre*) centre.

fracas /fraka/ *n.m.* din; (*de train*) roar; (*d'objet qui tombe*) crash.

fracass|er /frakase/ *v.t.,* **se ~er** *v. pr.* smash. ~**ant,** ~**ante** *a.* (*bruyant, violent*) shattering.

fraction /fraksjɔ̃/ *n.f.* fraction. ~**ner** /-jɔne/ *v.t.,* **se ~ner** *v. pr.* split (up).

fractur|e /fraktyr/ *n.f.* fracture. ~**er** *v.t.* (*os*) fracture; (*porte etc.*) break open.

fragil|e /fraʒil/ *a.* fragile. ~**ité** *n.f.* fragility.

fragment /fragmɑ̃/ *n.m.* bit, fragment. ~**aire** /-tɛr/ *a.* fragmentary. ~**er** /-te/ *v.t.* split, fragment.

frai /frɛ/ *n.m.* spawn.

fraîche /frɛʃ/ *voir* **frais**[1].

fraîchement /frɛʃmɑ̃/ *adv.* (*récemment*) freshly; (*avec froideur*) coolly.

fraîcheur /frɛʃœr/ *n.f.* coolness; (*nouveauté*) freshness.

fraîchir /freʃir/ *v.i.* freshen.

frais[1], **fraîche** /frɛ, -ʃ/ *a.* fresh; (*temps, accueil*) cool; (*peinture*) wet. —*adv.* (*récemment*) newly. —*n.m.* **mettre au ~,** put in a cool place. **~ et dispos,** fresh. **il fait ~,** it is cool.

frais[2] /frɛ/ *n.m. pl.* expenses; (*droits*) fees. **~ généraux,** (*comm.*) overheads, running expenses.

frais|e /frɛz/ *n.f.* strawberry. ~**ier** *n.m.* strawberry plant.

frambois|e /frɑ̃bwaz/ *n.f.* raspberry. ~**ier** *n.m.* raspberry bush.

fran|c[1], ~**che** /frɑ̃, -ʃ/ *a.* frank; (*regard*) open; (*net*) clear; (*cassure*) clean; (*libre*) free; (*véritable*) downright. ~**c-maçon** (*pl.* ~**cs-maçons**) *n.m.* Freemason. ~**c-maçonnerie** *n.f.* Freemasonry.

franc[2] /frɑ̃/ *n.m.* franc.

français, ~**e** /frɑ̃sɛ, -z/ *a.* French. —*n.m.,* *f.* Frenchman, Frenchwoman. —*n.m.* (*lang.*) French.

France /frɑ̃s/ *n.f.* France.

franche /frɑ̃ʃ/ *voir* **franc**[1].

franchement /frɑ̃ʃmɑ̃/ *adv.* frankly; (*nettement*) clearly; (*tout à fait*) really.

franchir /frɑ̃ʃir/ *v.t.* (*obstacle*) get over; (*traverser*) cross; (*distance*) cover; (*limite*) exceed.

franchise /frɑ̃ʃiz/ *n.f.* frankness; (*douanière*) exemption (from duties).

franco /frɑ̃ko/ *adv.* postage paid.

franco- /frɑ̃ko/ *préf.* Franco-.

francophone /frɑ̃kɔfɔn/ *a.* French-speaking. *—n.m./f.* French speaker.

frange /frɑ̃ʒ/ *n.f.* fringe.

franquette (à la bonne) /(alabɔn) frɑ̃kɛt/ *adv.* informally.

frappant, ~e /frapɑ̃, -t/ *a.* striking.

frappe /frap/ *n.f.* (*de courrier etc.*) typing; (*de dactylo*) touch.

frapp|er /frape/ *v.t./i.* strike; (*battre*) hit, strike; (*monnaie*) mint; (*à la porte*) knock, bang. **~é de panique,** panic-stricken.

frasque /frask/ *n.f.* escapade.

fratern|el, ~elle /fratɛrnɛl/ *a.* brotherly. **~iser** *v.i.* fraternize. **~ité** *n.f.* brotherhood.

fraude /frod/ *n.f.* fraud; (*à un examen*) cheating.

fraud|er /frode/ *v.t./i.* cheat. **~eur, ~euse** *n.m., f.* cheat; (*criminel*) defrauder.

frauduleu|x, ~se /frodylø, -z/ *a.* fraudulent.

frayer /freje/ *v.t.* open up. **se ~ un passage,** force one's way (**dans,** through).

frayeur /frejœr/ *n.f.* fright.

fredaine /frədɛn/ *n.f.* escapade.

fredonner /frədɔne/ *v.t.* hum.

freezer /frizœr/ *n.m.* freezer.

frégate /fregat/ *n.f.* frigate.

frein /frɛ̃/ *n.m.* brake. **mettre un ~ à,** curb.

frein|er /frene/ *v.t.* slow down; (*modérer, enrayer*) curb. *—v.i.* (*auto.*) brake. **~age** /frɛnaʒ/ *n.m.* braking.

frelaté /frəlate/ *a.* adulterated.

frêle /frɛl/ *a.* frail.

frelon /frəlɔ̃/ *n.m.* hornet.

frémir /fremir/ *v.i.* shudder, shake; (*feuille, eau*) quiver.

frêne /frɛn/ *n.m.* ash.

fréné|sie /frenezi/ *n.f.* frenzy. **~tique** *a.* frenzied.

fréqu|ent, ~ente /frekɑ̃, -t/ *a.* frequent. **~emment** /-amɑ̃/ *adv.* frequently. **~ence** *n.f.* frequency.

fréquenté /frekɑ̃te/ *a.* crowded.

fréquent|er /frekɑ̃te/ *v.t.* frequent; (*école*) attend; (*personne*) see. **~ation** *n.f.* frequenting. **~ations** *n.f. pl.* acquaintances.

frère /frɛr/ *n.m.* brother.

fresque /frɛsk/ *n.f.* fresco.

fret /frɛ/ *n.m.* freight.

frétiller /fretije/ *v.i.* wriggle.

friable /frijabl/ *a.* crumbly.

friand, ~e /frijɑ̃, -d/ *a.* **~ de,** fond of.

friandise /frijɑ̃diz/ *n.f.* sweet; (*Amer.*) candy; (*gâteau*) cake.

fric /frik/ *n.m.* (*fam.*) money.

fric-frac /frikfrak/ *n.m.* (*fam.*) break-in.

friche (en) /(ɑ̃)friʃ/ *adv.* fallow. **être en ~,** lie fallow.

friction /friksjɔ̃/ *n.f.* friction; (*massage*) rub-down. **~ner** /-jɔne/ *v.t.* rub (down).

frigidaire /friʒidɛr/ *n.m.* (P.) refrigerator.

frigid|e /friʒid/ *a.* frigid. **~ité** *n.f.* frigidity.

frigo /frigo/ *n.m.* (*fam.*) fridge.

frigorif|ier /frigɔrifje/ *v.t.* refrigerate. **~ique** *a.* (*vitrine etc.*) refrigerated.

frileu|x, ~se /frilø, -z/ *a.* sensitive to cold.

frimousse /frimus/ *n.f.* (sweet) face.

fringale /frɛ̃gal/ *n.f.* (*fam.*) ravenous appetite.

fringant, ~e /frɛ̃gɑ̃, -t/ *a.* dashing.

fringues /frɛ̃g/ *n.f. pl.* (*fam.*) togs.

friper /fripe/ *v.t.,* **se ~** *v. pr.* crumple.

frip|ier, ~ière /fripje, -jɛr/ *n.m., f.* second-hand clothes dealer.

fripon, ~ne /fripɔ̃, -ɔn/ *n.m., f.* rascal. *—a.* rascally.

fripouille /fripuj/ *n.f.* rogue.

frire /frir/ *v.t./i.* fry. **faire ~,** fry.

frise /friz/ *n.f.* frieze.

fris|er[1] /frize/ *v.t./i.* (*cheveux*) curl; (*personne*) curl the hair of. **~é** *a.* curly.

friser[2] /frize/ *v.t.* (*surface*) skim.

frisquet /friskɛ/ *a.m.* (*fam.*) chilly.

frisson /frisɔ̃/ *n.m.* (*de froid*) shiver; (*de peur*) shudder. **~ner** /-ɔne/ *v.i.* shiver; shudder.

frit, ~e /fri, -t/ *a.* fried. *—n.f.* chip.

friteuse /fritøz/ *n.f.* (deep) fryer.

friture /frityr/ *n.f.* fried fish; (*huile*) (frying) oil *ou* fat.

frivol|e /frivɔl/ *a.* frivolous. **~ité** *n.f.* frivolity.

froid, ~e /frwa, -d/ *a.* & *n.m.* cold. **avoir/prendre ~,** be/catch cold. **il fait ~,** it is cold. **~ement** /-dmɑ̃/ *adv.* coldly; (*calculer*) coolly. **~eur** /-dœr/ *n.f.* coldness.

froisser /frwase/ *v.t.* crumple; (*fig.*) offend. **se ~** *v. pr.* crumple; (*fig.*) take offence.

frôler /frole/ *v.t.* brush against, skim; (*fig.*) come close to.

fromag|e /frɔmaʒ/ *n.m.* cheese. **~er**, **~ère** *a.* cheese; *n.m.,f.* cheese maker; (*marchand*) cheesemonger. **~erie** *n.f.* (*local*) cheese factory.

froment /frɔmã/ *n.m.* wheat.

froncer /frɔ̃se/ *v.t.* gather. **~ les sourcils**, frown.

fronde /frɔ̃d/ *n.f.* sling; (*fig.*) revolt.

front /frɔ̃/ *n.m.* forehead; (*mil., pol.*) front. **de ~**, at the same time; (*de face*) head-on; (*côte à côte*) abreast. **faire ~ à**, face up to. **~al** (*m. pl.* **~aux**) /-tal, -to/ *a.* frontal.

front|ière /frɔ̃tjɛr/ *n.f.* border, frontier. **~alier**, **~alière** *a.* border, frontier.

frott|er /frɔte/ *v.t./i.* rub; (*allumette*) strike. **~ement** *n.m.* rubbing.

frouss|e /frus/ *n.f.* (*fam.*) fear. **avoir la ~e**, (*fam.*) be scared. **~ard**, **~arde** *n.m., f.* (*fam.*) coward.

fructifier /fryktifje/ *v.i.* bear fruit.

fructueu|x, **~se** /fryktɥø, -z/ *a.* fruitful.

frug|al (*m. pl.* **~aux**) /frygal, -o/ *a.* frugal. **~alité** *n.f.* frugality.

fruit /frɥi/ *n.m.* fruit. **des ~s**, (some) fruit. **~s de mer**, seafood. **~é** /-te/ *a.* fruity. **~ier**, **~ière** /-tje, -tjɛr/ *a.* fruit; *n.m., f.* fruiterer.

fruste /fryst/ *a.* coarse.

frustr|er /frystre/ *v.t.* frustrate. **~ation** *n.f.* frustration.

fuel /fjul/ *n.m.* fuel oil.

fugiti|f, **~ve** /fyʒitif, -v/ *a.* (*passager*) fleeting. —*n.m., f.* fugitive.

fugue /fyg/ *n.f.* (*mus.*) fugue. **faire une ~**, abscond.

fuir† /fɥir/ *v.i.* flee, run away; (*temps*) fly; (*eau, robinet, etc.*) leak. —*v.t.* (*éviter*) shun.

fuite /fɥit/ *n.f.* flight; (*de liquide, d'une nouvelle*) leak. **en ~**, on the run. **mettre en ~**, put to flight. **prendre la ~**, take (to) flight.

fulgurant, **~e** /fylgyrã, -t/ *a.* (*vitesse*) lightning.

fumée /fyme/ *n.f.* smoke; (*vapeur*) steam.

fum|er /fyme/ *v.t./i.* smoke; (*soupe*) steam. **~e-cigarette** *n.m. invar.* cigarette-holder. **~é** *a.* (*poisson, verre*) smoked. **~eur**, **~euse** *n.m., f.* smoker.

fumet /fymɛ/ *n.m.* aroma.

fumeu|x, **~se** /fymø, -z/ *a.* (*confus*) hazy.

fumier /fymje/ *n.m.* manure.

fumiste /fymist/ *n.m.* heating engineer. —*n.m./f.* (*employé: fam.*) shirker.

funambule /fynãbyl/ *n.m./f.* tightrope walker.

funèbre /fynɛbr/ *a.* funeral; (*fig.*) gloomy.

funérailles /fyneraj/ *n.f. pl.* funeral.

funéraire /fynerɛr/ *a.* funeral.

funeste /fynɛst/ *a.* fatal; (*fig.*) disastrous.

funiculaire /fynikylɛr/ *n.m.* funicular.

fur /fyr/ *n.m.* **au ~ et à mesure**, as one goes along, progressively. **au ~ et à mesure que**, as.

furet /fyrɛ/ *n.m.* ferret.

fureter /fyrte/ *v.i.* nose (about).

fureur /fyrœr/ *n.f.* fury; (*passion*) passion. **avec ~**, furiously; passionately. **mettre en ~**, infuriate.

furie /fyri/ *n.f.* fury; (*femme*) shrew.

furieu|x, **~se** /fyrjø, -z/ *a.* furious.

furoncle /fyrɔ̃kl/ *n.m.* boil.

furti|f, **~ve** /fyrtif, -v/ *a.* furtive.

fusain /fyzɛ̃/ *n.m.* (*crayon*) charcoal; (*arbre*) spindle-tree.

fuseau (*pl.* **~x**) /fyzo/ *n.m.* ski trousers; (*pour filer*) spindle. **~ horaire**, time zone.

fusée /fyze/ *n.f.* rocket.

fuselage /fyzlaʒ/ *n.m.* fuselage.

fuser /fyze/ *v.i.* issue forth.

fusible /fyzibl/ *n.m.* fuse.

fusil /fyzi/ *n.m.* rifle, gun; (*de chasse*) shotgun. **~ mitrailleur**, machine-gun.

fusill|er /fyzije/ *v.t.* shoot. **~ade** *n.f.* shooting.

fusion /fyzjɔ̃/ *n.f.* fusion; (*comm.*) merger. **~ner** /-jɔne/ *v.t./i.* merge.

fut /fy/ *voir* **être**.

fût /fy/ *n.m.* (*tonneau*) barrel; (*d'arbre*) trunk.

futaie /fytɛ/ *n.f.* forest.

futé /fyte/ *a.* cunning.

futil|e /fytil/ *a.* futile. **~ité** *n.f.* futility.

futur /fytyr/ *a. & n.m.* future. **~e maman**, mother-to-be.

fuyant, **~e** /fɥijã, -t/ *a.* (*front, ligne*) receding; (*personne*) evasive.

fuyard, **~e** /fɥijar, -d/ *n.m., f.* runaway.

G

gabardine /gabardin/ *n.f.* gabardine.

gabarit /gabari/ *n.m.* dimension; (*patron*) template; (*fig.*) calibre.

gâcher /gɑʃe/ *v.t.* (*gâter*) spoil; (*gaspiller*) waste.

gâchette /gɑʃɛt/ *n.f.* trigger.

gâchis /gɑʃi/ *n.m.* mess; (*gaspillage*) waste.

gadoue /gadu/ *n.f.* sludge; (*neige*) slush.

gaff|e /gaf/ *n.f.* blunder. **faire ~e**, (*fam.*) be careful (à, of). **~er** *v.i.* blunder.

gag /gag/ *n.m.* gag.

gage /gaʒ/ *n.m.* pledge; (*de jeu*) forfeit. **~s**, (*salaire*) wages. **en ~ de**, as a token of. **mettre en ~**, pawn.

gager /gaʒe/ *v.t.* wager (**que**, that).

gageure /gaʒyr/ *n.f.* wager (against all the odds).

gagn|er /gaɲe/ *v.t.* (*match, prix, etc.*) win; (*argent, pain*) earn; (*temps, terrain*) gain; (*atteindre*) reach; (*convaincre*) win over. —*v.i.* win; (*fig.*) gain. **~er sa vie**, earn one's living. **~ant, ~ante**, *a.* winning; *n.m., f.* winner. **~e-pain** *n.m. invar.* job.

gai /ge/ *a.* cheerful; (*ivre*) merry. **~ement** *adv.* cheerfully. **~eté** *n.f.* cheerfulness. **~etés** *n.f. pl.* delights.

gaillard, **~e** /gajar, -d/ *a.* hale and hearty; (*grivois*) coarse. —*n.m.* hale and hearty fellow; (*type: fam.*) fellow.

gain /gɛ̃/ *n.m.* (*salaire*) earnings; (*avantage*) gain; (*économie*) saving. **~s**, (*comm.*) profits; (*au jeu*) winnings.

gaine /gɛn/ *n.f.* (*corset*) girdle; (*étui*) sheath.

gala /gala/ *n.m.* gala.

galant, **~e** /galɑ̃, -t/ *a.* courteous; (*scène, humeur*) romantic.

galaxie /galaksi/ *n.f.* galaxy.

galb|e /galb/ *n.m.* curve. **~é** *a.* shapely.

gale /gal/ *n.f.* (*de chat etc.*) mange.

galère /galɛr/ *n.f.* (*navire*) galley.

galerie /galri/ *n.f.* gallery; (*théâtre*) circle; (*de voiture*) roof-rack.

galet /galɛ/ *n.m.* pebble.

galette /galɛt/ *n.f.* flat cake.

galeu|x, **~se** /galø, -z/ *a.* (*animal*) mangy.

galimatias /galimatja/ *n.m.* gibberish.

Galles /gal/ *n.f. pl.* **le pays de ~**, Wales.

gallois, **~e** /galwa, -z/ *a.* Welsh. —*n.m.* Welshman, Welshwoman. —*n.m.* (*lang.*) Welsh.

galon /galɔ̃/ *n.m.* braid; (*mil.*) stripe.

galop /galo/ *n.m.* gallop. **aller au ~**, gallop. **~ d'essai**, trial run. **~er** /-ɔpe/ *v.i.* (*cheval*) gallop; (*personne*) run.

galopade /galɔpad/ *n.f.* wild rush.

galopin /galɔpɛ̃/ *n.m.* (*fam.*) rascal.

galvaniser /galvanize/ *v.t.* galvanize.

galvauder /galvode/ *v.t.* debase (through misuse).

gambad|e /gɑ̃bad/ *n.f.* leap. **~er** *v.i.* leap about.

gamelle /gamɛl/ *n.f.* (*de soldat*) mess bowl *ou* tin; (*d'ouvrier*) food-box.

gamin, **~e** /gamɛ̃, -in/ *a.* playful. —*n.m., f.* (*fam.*) kid.

gamme /gam/ *n.f.* (*mus.*) scale; (*série*) range.

gang /gɑ̃g/ *n.m.* gang.

gangrène /gɑ̃grɛn/ *n.f.* gangrene.

gangster /gɑ̃gstɛr/ *n.m.* gangster; (*escroc*) crook.

gant /gɑ̃/ *n.m.* glove. **~ de toilette**, face-flannel, face-cloth. **~é** /-gɑ̃te/ *a.* (*personne*) wearing gloves.

garag|e /garaʒ/ *n.m.* garage. **~iste** *n.m.* garage owner; (*employé*) garage mechanic.

garant, **~e** /garɑ̃, -t/ *n.m., f.* guarantor. —*n.m.* guarantee. **se porter ~ de**, guarantee.

garant|ie /garɑ̃ti/ *n.f.* guarantee; (*protection*) safeguard. **~ies**, (*de police d'assurance*) cover. **~ir** *v.t.* guarantee; (*protéger*) protect (**de**, from).

garçon /garsɔ̃/ *n.m.* boy; (*célibataire*) bachelor. **~ (de café)**, waiter. **~ d'honneur**, best man.

garçonnière /garsɔnjɛr/ *n.f.* bachelor flat.

garde[1] /gard/ *n.f.* guard; (*d'enfants, de bagages*) care; (*service*) guard (duty); (*infirmière*) nurse. **de ~**, on duty. **~ à vue**, (police) custody. **mettre en ~**, warn. **prendre ~**, be careful (à, of).

garde[2] /gard/ *n.m.* (*personne*) guard;

(*de propriété, parc*) warden. ~ **champêtre**, village policeman. ~ **du corps**, bodyguard.

gard|er /garde/ *v.t.* (*conserver, maintenir*) keep; (*vêtement*) keep on; (*surveiller*) look after; (*défendre*) guard. **se ~er** *v. pr.* (*denrée*) keep. **~er le lit**, stay in bed. **se ~er de faire**, be careful not to do. **~e-à-vous** *int.* (*mil.*) attention. **~e-boue** *n.m. invar.* mudguard. **~e-chasse** (*pl.* **~es-chasses**) *n.m.* gamekeeper. **~e-fou** *n.m.* railing. **~e-manger** *n.m. invar.* (food) safe; (*placard*) larder. **~e-robe** *n.f.* wardrobe.

garderie /gardəri/ *n.f.* day nursery.

gardien, ~ne /gardjɛ̃, -jɛn/ *n.m.,f.* (*de prison, réserve*) warden; (*d'immeuble*) caretaker; (*de musée*) attendant; (*garde*) guard. **~ de but**, goalkeeper. **~ de la paix**, policeman. **~ de nuit**, night watchman. **~ne d'enfants**, child-minder, baby-sitter.

gare[1] /gar/ *n.f.* (*rail.*) station. **~ routière**, coach station; (*Amer.*) bus station.

gare[2] /gar/ *int.* **~ à**, watch out for. **~ à toi**, watch out.

garer /gare/ *v.t.*, **se ~** *v. pr.* park. **se ~ (de)**, get out of the way (of).

gargariser (se) /(sə)gargarize/ *v. pr.* gargle.

gargarisme /gargarism/ *n.m.* gargle.

gargouille /garguj/ *n.f.* (water)spout; (*sculptée*) gargoyle.

gargouiller /garguje/ *v.i.* gurgle.

garnement /garnəmã/ *n.m.* rascal.

garn|ir /garnir/ *v.t.* fill; (*décorer*) decorate; (*couvrir*) cover; (*doubler*) line; (*culin.*) garnish. **se ~ir** *v. pr.* (*lieu*) fill. **~i** *a.* (*plat*) served with vegetables. **bien ~i**, (*rempli*) well-filled.

garnison /garnizɔ̃/ *n.f.* garrison.

garniture /garnityr/ *n.f.* (*légumes*) vegetables; (*ornement*) trimming; (*de voiture*) trim.

gars /ga/ *n.m.* (*fam.*) fellow.

gas-oil /gazɔjl/ *n.m.* diesel oil.

gaspill|er /gaspije/ *v.t.* waste. **~age** *n.m.* waste.

gastrique /gastrik/ *a.* gastric.

gastronom|e /gastronɔm/ *n.m.*,*f.* gourmet. **~ie** *n.f.* gastronomy.

gâteau (*pl.* **~x**) /gato/ *n.m.* cake. **~ sec**, biscuit; (*Amer.*) cookie.

gâter /gate/ *v.t.* spoil. **se ~** *v. pr.* (*dent, viande*) go bad; (*temps*) get worse.

gâterie /gatri/ *n.f.* little treat.

gâteu|x, ~se /gatø, -z/ *a.* senile.

gauch|e[1] /goʃ/ *a.* left. **à ~e**, on the left; (*direction*) (to the) left. **la ~e**, the left (side); (*pol.*) the left (wing). **~er, ~ère** *a.* & *n.m.*, *f.* left-handed (person). **~iste** *a.* & *n.m.*/*f.* (*pol.*) leftist.

gauche[2] /goʃ/ *a.* (*maladroit*) awkward. **~rie** *n.f.* awkwardness.

gauchir /goʃir/ *v.t.*/*i.*, **se ~** *v. pr.* warp.

gaufre /gofr/ *n.f.* waffle.

gaufrette /gofrɛt/ *n.f.* wafer.

gaulois, ~e /golwa, -z/ *a.* Gallic; (*fig.*) bawdy. —*n.m.*,*f.* Gaul.

gausser (se) /(sə)gose/ *v. pr.* **se ~ de**, deride, scoff at.

gaver /gave/ *v.t.* force-feed; (*fig.*) cram. **se ~ de**, gorge o.s. with.

gaz /gaz/ *n.m. invar.* gas. **~ lacrymogène**, tear-gas.

gaze /gaz/ *n.f.* gauze.

gazelle /gazɛl/ *n.f.* gazelle.

gazer /gaze/ *v.i.* (*marcher*: *fam.*) be ou go all right.

gazette /gazɛt/ *n.f.* newspaper.

gazeu|x, ~se /gazø, -z/ *a.* (*boisson*) fizzy.

gazomètre /gazɔmɛtr/ *n.m.* gasometer.

gazon /gazɔ̃/ *n.m.* lawn, grass.

gazouiller /gazuje/ *v.i.* (*oiseau*) chirp; (*bébé*) babble.

geai /ʒɛ/ *n.m.* jay.

géant, ~e /ʒeã, -t/ *a.* & *n.m.*, *f.* giant.

geindre /ʒɛ̃dr/ *v.i.* groan.

gel /ʒɛl/ *n.m.* frost; (*pâte*) gel; (*comm.*) freezing.

gélatine /ʒelatin/ *n.f.* gelatine.

gel|er /ʒəle/ *v.t.*/*i.* freeze. **~é** *a.* frozen; (*membre abîmé*) frostbitten. **~ée** *n.f.* frost; (*culin.*) jelly. **~ée blanche**, hoar-frost.

gélule /ʒelyl/ *n.f.* (*méd.*) capsule.

gém|ir /ʒemir/ *v.i.* groan. **~issement** *n.m.* groan(ing).

gênant, ~e /ʒɛnã, -t/ *a.* embarrassing; (*irritant*) annoying.

gencive /ʒãsiv/ *n.f.* gum.

gendarme /ʒãdarm/ *n.m.* policeman, gendarme. **~rie** /-əri/ *n.f.* police force; (*local*) police station.

gendre /ʒãdr/ *n.m.* son-in-law.

gène /ʒɛn/ *n.m.* gene.

gêne /ʒɛn/ *n.f.* discomfort; (*confusion*) embarrassment; (*dérangement*) trouble. **dans la ~**, in financial straits.

généalogie /ʒenealɔʒi/ *n.f.* genealogy.

gên|er /ʒene/ v.t. bother, disturb; (*troubler*) embarrass; (*encombrer*) hamper; (*bloquer*) block. **se ~er** v. pr. put o.s. out. **~é** a. embarrassed.

génér|al (m. pl. **~aux**) /ʒeneral, -o/ a. general. —n.m. (pl. **~aux**) general. **en ~al**, in general. **~alement** adv. generally.

généralis|er /ʒeneralize/ v.t./i. generalize. **se ~er** v. pr. become general. **~ation** n.f. generalization.

généraliste /ʒeneralist/ n.m./f. general practitioner.

généralité /ʒeneralite/ n.f. majority. **~s**, general points.

génération /ʒenerɑsjɔ̃/ n.f. generation.

génératrice /ʒeneratris/ n.f. generator.

généreu|x, **~se** /ʒenerø, -z/ a. generous. **~sement** adv. generously.

générique /ʒenerik/ n.m. (*cinéma*) credits.

générosité /ʒenerozite/ n.f. generosity.

genêt /ʒənɛ/ n.m. (*plante*) broom.

génétique /ʒenetik/ a. genetic. —n.f. genetics.

Genève /ʒənɛv/ n.m./f. Geneva.

gén|ial (m. pl. **~iaux**) /ʒenjal, -jo/ a. brilliant.

génie /ʒeni/ n.m. genius. **~ civil**, civil engineering.

génisse /ʒenis/ n.f. heifer.

génit|al (m. pl. **~aux**) /ʒenital, -o/ a. genital.

génocide /ʒenɔsid/ n.m. genocide.

genou (pl. **~x**) /ʒnu/ n.m. knee. **à ~x**, kneeling. **se mettre à ~x**, kneel.

genre /ʒɑ̃r/ n.m. sort, kind; (*attitude*) manner; (*gram.*) gender. **~ de vie**, life-style.

gens /ʒɑ̃/ n.m./f. pl. people.

genti|l, **~lle** /ʒɑ̃ti, -j/ a. kind, nice; (*agréable*) nice; (*sage*) good. **~llesse** /-jɛs/ n.f. kindness. **~ment** adv. kindly.

géograph|ie /ʒeɔgrafi/ n.f. geography. **~e** n.m./f. geographer. **~ique** a. geographical.

geôl|ier, **~ière** /ʒolje, -jɛr/ n.m., f. gaoler, jailer.

géolo|gie /ʒeɔlɔʒi/ n.f. geology. **~gique** a. geological. **~gue** n.m./f. geologist.

géomètre /ʒeɔmɛtr/ n.m. surveyor.

géométr|ie /ʒeɔmetri/ n.f. geometry. **~ique** a. geometric.

géranium /ʒeranjɔm/ n.m. geranium.

géran|t, **~te** /ʒerɑ̃, -t/ n.m., f. manager, manageress. **~t d'immeuble**, landlord's agent. **~ce** n.f. management.

gerbe /ʒɛrb/ n.f. (*de fleurs*, *d'eau*) spray; (*de blé*) sheaf.

ger|cer /ʒɛrse/ v.t./i., **se ~cer** v. pr. chap. **~çure** n.f. chap.

gérer /ʒere/ v.t. manage.

germanique /ʒɛrmanik/ a. Germanic.

germ|e /ʒɛrm/ n.m. germ. **~er** v.i. germinate.

gésir /ʒezir/ v.i. be lying.

gestation /ʒɛstasjɔ̃/ n.f. gestation.

geste /ʒɛst/ n.m. gesture.

gesticul|er /ʒɛstikyle/ v.i. gesticulate. **~ation** n.f. gesticulation.

gestion /ʒɛstjɔ̃/ n.f. management.

geyser /ʒezɛr/ n.m. geyser.

ghetto /gɛto/ n.m. ghetto.

gibecière /ʒibsjɛr/ n.f. shoulder-bag.

gibet /ʒibɛ/ n.m. gallows.

gibier /ʒibje/ n.m. (*animaux*) game.

giboulée /ʒibule/ n.f. shower.

gicl|er /ʒikle/ v.i. squirt. **faire ~er**, squirt. **~ée** n.f. squirt.

gifl|e /ʒifl/ n.f. slap (in the face). **~er** v.t. slap.

gigantesque /ʒigɑ̃tɛsk/ a. gigantic.

gigot /ʒigo/ n.m. leg (of mutton).

gigoter /ʒigɔte/ v.i. (*fam.*) wriggle.

gilet /ʒilɛ/ n.m. waistcoat; (*cardigan*) cardigan. **~ (de corps)**, vest. **~ de sauvetage**, life-jacket.

gin /dʒin/ n.m. gin.

gingembre /ʒɛ̃ʒɑ̃br/ n.m. ginger.

girafe /ʒiraf/ n.f. giraffe.

giroflée /ʒirɔfle/ n.f. wallflower.

girouette /ʒirwɛt/ n.f. weathercock, weather-vane.

gisement /ʒizmɑ̃/ n.m. deposit.

gitan, **~e** /ʒitɑ̃, -an/ n.m., f. gypsy.

gîte /ʒit/ n.m. (*maison*) home; (*abri*) shelter.

givr|e /ʒivr/ n.m. (hoar-)frost. **~er** v.t., **se ~er** v. pr. frost (up).

glace /glas/ n.f. ice; (*crème*) ice-cream; (*vitre*) window; (*miroir*) mirror; (*verre*) glass.

glac|er /glase/ v.t. freeze; (*gâteau*, *boisson*) ice; (*papier*) glaze; (*pétrifier*) chill. **se ~er** v. pr. freeze. **~é** a. (*vent*, *accueil*) icy.

glac|ial (m. pl. **~iaux**) /glasjal, -jo/ a. icy.

glacier /glasje/ n.m. (*géog.*) glacier; (*vendeur*) ice-cream man.

glacière /glasjɛr/ n.f. icebox.
glaçon /glasɔ̃/ n.m. block of ice; (pour boisson) ice-cube; (sur le toit) icicle.
glaïeul /glajœl/ n.m. gladiolus.
glaise /glɛz/ n.f. clay.
gland /glɑ̃/ n.m. acorn; (ornement) tassel.
glande /glɑ̃d/ n.f. gland.
glaner /glane/ v.t. glean.
glapir /glapir/ v.i. yelp.
glas /glɑ/ n.m. knell.
glissant, ~e /glisɑ̃, -t/ a. slippery.
gliss|er /glise/ v.i. slide; (sur l'eau) glide; (déraper) slip; (véhicule) skid. —v.t., se ~er v. pr. slip (dans, into). ~ade n.f. sliding; (endroit) slide. ~ement n.m. sliding; gliding; (fig.) shift. ~ement de terrain, landslide.
glissière /glisjɛr/ n.f. groove. à ~, (porte, système) sliding.
glob|al (m. pl. ~aux) /glɔbal, -o/ a. (entier, général) overall. ~alement adv. as a whole.
globe /glɔb/ n.m. globe. ~ oculaire, eyeball. ~ terrestre, globe.
globule /glɔbyl/ n.m. (du sang) corpuscle.
gloire /glwar/ n.f. glory.
glorieu|x, ~se /glɔrjø, -z/ a. glorious. ~sement adv. gloriously.
glorifier /glɔrifje/ v.t. glorify.
glossaire /glɔsɛr/ n.m. glossary.
glouss|er /gluse/ v.i. chuckle; (poule) cluck. ~ement n.m. chuckle; cluck.
glouton, ~ne /glutɔ̃, -ɔn/ a. gluttonous. —n.m., f. glutton.
gluant, ~e /glyɑ̃, -t/ a. sticky.
glucose /glykoz/ n.m. glucose.
glycérine /gliserin/ n.f. glycerine.
glycine /glisin/ n.f. wistaria.
gnome /gnom/ n.m. gnome.
goal /gol/ n.m. goalkeeper.
gobelet /gɔblɛ/ n.m. tumbler, mug.
gober /gɔbe/ v.t. swallow (whole).
godasse /gɔdas/ n.f. (fam.) shoe.
godet /gɔdɛ/ n.m. (small) pot.
goéland /gɔelɑ̃/ n.m. (sea)gull.
goélette /gɔelɛt/ n.f. schooner.
gogo /gogo/ n.m. (fam.) sucker.
gogo (à) /(a)gogo/ adv. (fam.) galore, in abundance.
goguenard, ~e /gɔgnar, -d/ a. mocking.
goguette (en) /(ɑ̃)gɔgɛt/ adv. (fam.) having a binge ou spree.
goinfr|e /gwɛ̃fr/ n.m. (glouton: fam.) pig. se ~er v. pr. (fam.) stuff o.s. like a pig (de, with).

golf /gɔlf/ n.m. golf.
golfe /gɔlf/ n.m. gulf.
gomm|e /gɔm/ n.f. rubber; (Amer.) eraser; (résine) gum. ~er v.t. rub out.
gond /gɔ̃/ n.m. hinge.
gondol|e /gɔ̃dɔl/ n.f. gondola. ~ier n.m. gondolier.
gondoler (se) /(sə)gɔ̃dɔle/ v. pr. warp; (rire: fam.) split one's sides.
gonfl|er /gɔ̃fle/ v.t./i. swell; (ballon, pneu) pump up, blow up; (exagérer) inflate. se ~er v. pr. swell. ~é a. swollen; (courageux: fam.) plucky. ~ement n.m. swelling. ~eur n.m. air pump.
gong /gɔ̃g/ n.m. gong.
gorge /gɔrʒ/ n.f. throat; (poitrine) breast; (vallée) gorge.
gorgée /gɔrʒe/ n.f. sip, gulp.
gorg|er /gɔrʒe/ v.t. fill (de, with). se ~er v. pr. gorge o.s. (de, with). ~é de, full of.
gorille /gɔrij/ n.m. gorilla; (garde: fam.) bodyguard.
gosier /gozje/ n.m. throat.
gosse /gɔs/ n.m./f. (fam.) kid.
gothique /gɔtik/ a. Gothic.
goudron /gudrɔ̃/ n.m. tar. ~ner /-ɔne/ v.t. tar.
gouffre /gufr/ n.m. gulf, abyss.
goujat /guʒa/ n.m. lout, boor.
goulot /gulo/ n.m. neck.
goulu, ~e /guly/ a. gluttonous. —n.m., f. glutton.
gourde /gurd/ n.f. (à eau) flask; (idiot: fam.) chump.
gourdin /gurdɛ̃/ n.m. club, cudgel.
gourer (se) /(sə)gure/ v. pr. (fam.) make a mistake.
gourmand, ~e /gurmɑ̃, -d/ a. greedy. —n.m., f. glutton. ~ise /-diz/ n.f. greed; (mets) delicacy.
gourmet /gurmɛ/ n.m. gourmet.
gourmette /gurmɛt/ n.f. chain bracelet.
gousse /gus/ n.f. ~ d'ail, clove of garlic.
goût /gu/ n.m. taste.
goûter /gute/ v.t. taste; (apprécier) enjoy. —v.i. have tea. —n.m. tea, snack. ~ à ou de, taste.
goutt|e /gut/ n.f. drop; (méd.) gout. ~er v.i. drip.
gouttelette /gutlɛt/ n.f. droplet.
gouttière /gutjɛr/ n.f. gutter.
gouvernail /guvɛrnaj/ n.m. rudder; (barre) helm.

gouvernante /guvɛrnɑ̃t/ n.f. governess.

gouvernement /guvɛrnəmɑ̃/ n.m. government. ~**al** (m. pl. ~**aux**) /-tal, -to/ a. government.

gouvern|er /guvɛrne/ v.t./i. govern. ~**eur** n.m. governor.

grâce /grɑs/ n.f. (charme) grace; (faveur) favour; (relig.) grace. ~ **à**, thanks to.

gracier /grasje/ v.t. pardon.

gracieu|x, ~**se** /grasjø, -z/ a. graceful; (gratuit) free. ~**sement** adv. gracefully; free (of charge).

gracile /grasil/ a. slender.

gradation /gradɑsjɔ̃/ n.f. gradation.

grade /grad/ n.m. rank.

gradé /grade/ n.m. non-commissioned officer.

gradin /gradɛ̃/ n.m. tier, step. **en** ~**s**, terraced.

graduel, ~**le** /gradɥɛl/ a. gradual.

grad|uer /gradɥe/ v.t. (règle etc.) graduate. ~**uation** n.f. graduation.

graffiti /grafiti/ n.m. pl. graffiti.

grain /grɛ̃/ n.m. grain; (de café) bean; (de chapelet) bead. ~ **de beauté**, mole; (sur le visage) beauty spot. ~ **de raisin**, grape.

graine /grɛn/ n.f. seed.

graissage /grɛsaʒ/ n.m. lubrication.

graiss|e /grɛs/ n.f. fat; (lubrifiant) grease. ~**er** v.t. grease. ~**eux**, ~**euse** a. greasy.

gramm|aire /gramɛr/ n.f. grammar. ~**atical** (m. pl. ~**aticaux**) a. grammatical.

gramme /gram/ n.m. gram.

grand, ~**e** /grɑ̃, -d/ a. big, large; (haut) tall; (mérite, distance, ami) great; (bruit) loud; (plus âgé) big. —adv. (ouvrir) wide. —n.m., f. (adulte) grown-up; (enfant) older child. **au** ~ **air**, in the open air. **au** ~ **jour**, in broad daylight; (fig.) in the open. **de** ~**e envergure**, large-scale. **en** ~**e partie**, largely. ~**e banlieue**, outer suburbs. **G**~**e-Bretagne** n.f. Great Britain. **pas** ~-**chose**, not much. ~**e école**, university. ~ **ensemble**, housing estate. ~**es lignes**, (rail.) main lines. ~ **magasin**, department store. ~-**mère** (pl. ~**s-mères**) n.f. grandmother. ~**s-parents** n.m. pl. grandparents. ~-**père** (pl. ~**s-pères**) n.m. grandfather. ~**e personne**, grownup. ~ **public**, general public. ~-**rue** n.f. high street. ~**e surface**, hyper-

market. ~**es vacances**, summer holidays.

grandement /grɑ̃dmɑ̃/ adv. greatly.

grandeur /grɑ̃dœr/ n.f. greatness; (dimension) size.

grandiose /grɑ̃djoz/ a. grandiose.

grandir /grɑ̃dir/ v.i. grow; (bruit) grow louder. —v.t. magnify; (personne) make taller.

grange /grɑ̃ʒ/ n.f. barn.

granit /granit/ n.m. granite.

granulé /granyle/ n.m. granule.

graphique /grafik/ a. graphic. —n.m. graph.

grappe /grap/ n.f. cluster. ~ **de raisin**, bunch of grapes.

gras, ~**se** /grɑ, -s/ a. fat; (aliment) fatty; (surface) greasy; (épais) thick; (caractères) bold. —n.m. (culin.) fat. **faire la** ~**se matinée**, sleep late. ~**sement payé**, highly paid.

gratification /gratifikɑsjɔ̃/ n.f. bonus.

gratifier /gratifje/ v.t. favour, reward (**de**, with).

gratin /gratɛ̃/ n.m. baked dish with cheese topping; (élite: fam.) upper crust.

gratis /gratis/ adv. free.

gratitude /gratityd/ n.f. gratitude.

gratt|er /grate/ v.t./i. scratch; (avec un outil) scrape. **se** ~**er** v. pr. scratch o.s. **ça me** ~**e**, (fam.) it itches. ~**e-ciel** n.m. invar. skyscraper. ~**oir** n.m. scraper.

gratuit, ~**e** /gratɥi, -t/ a. free; (acte) gratuitous. ~**ement** /-tmɑ̃/ adv. free (of charge).

gravats /gravɑ/ n.m. pl. rubble.

grave /grav/ a. serious; (solennel) grave; (voix) deep; (accent) grave. ~**ment** adv. seriously; gravely.

grav|er /grave/ v.t. engrave; (sur bois) carve. ~**eur** n.m. engraver.

gravier /gravje/ n.m. gravel; (morceau) bit of gravel.

gravillon /gravijɔ̃/ n.m. gravel; (morceau) bit of gravel. ~**s**, gravel.

gravir /gravir/ v.t. climb.

gravitation /gravitɑsjɔ̃/ n.f. gravitation.

gravité /gravite/ n.f. gravity.

graviter /gravite/ v.i. revolve.

gravure /gravyr/ n.f. engraving; (de tableau, photo) print, plate.

gré /gre/ n.m. (volonté) will; (goût) taste. **à son** ~, (agir) as one likes. **de bon** ~, willingly.

grec, ~que /grɛk/ *a.* & *n.m.*, *f.* Greek. —*n.m.* (*lang.*) Greek.

Grèce /grɛs/ *n.f.* Greece.

greff|e /grɛf/ *n.f.* graft; (*d'organe*) transplant. **~er** /grefe/ *v.t.* graft; transplant.

greffier /grefje/ *n.m.* clerk of the court.

grégaire /gregɛr/ *a.* gregarious.

grêle[1] /grɛl/ *a.* (*maigre*) spindly; (*voix*) shrill.

grêl|e[2] /grɛl/ *n.f.* hail. **~er** /grele/ *v.i.* hail. **~on** *n.m.* hailstone.

grelot /grəlo/ *n.m.* (little) bell.

grelotter /grəlote/ *v.i.* shiver.

grenade[1] /grənad/ *n.f.* (*fruit*) pomegranate.

grenade[2] /grənad/ *n.f.* (*explosif*) grenade.

grenat /grəna/ *a. invar.* dark red.

grenier /grənje/ *n.m.* attic; (*pour grain*) loft.

grenouille /grənuj/ *n.f.* frog.

grésiller /grezije/ *v.i.* sizzle; (*radio*) crackle.

grève[1] /grɛv/ *n.f.* strike. **se mettre en ~,** go on strike. **~ du zèle,** work-to-rule; (*Amer.*) rule-book slow-down. **~ perlée,** go-slow; (*Amer.*) slow-down strike. **~ sauvage,** wildcat strike.

grève[2] /grɛv/ *n.f.* (*rivage*) shore.

gréviste /grevist/ *n.m./f.* striker.

gribouill|er /gribuje/ *v.t./i.* scribble. **~is** /-ji/ *n.m.* scribble.

grief /grijɛf/ *n.m.* grievance.

grièvement /grijɛvmɑ̃/ *adv.* seriously.

griff|e /grif/ *n.f.* claw; (*de couturier*) label. **~er** *v.t.* scratch, claw.

griffonner /grifone/ *v.t./i.* scrawl.

grignoter /griɲote/ *v.t./i.* nibble.

gril /gril/ *n.m.* grill, grid(iron).

grillade /grijad/ *n.f.* (*viande*) grill.

grillage /grijaʒ/ *n.m.* wire netting.

grille /grij/ *n.f.* railings; (*portail*) (metal) gate; (*de fenêtre*) bars; (*de cheminée*) grate; (*fig.*) grid.

grill|er /grije/ *v.t./i.* burn; (*ampoule*) blow; (*feu rouge*) go through. (**faire**) **~er,** (*pain*) toast; (*viande*) grill; (*café*) roast. **~e-pain** *n.m. invar.* toaster.

grillon /grijɔ̃/ *n.m.* cricket.

grimace /grimas/ *n.f.* (funny) face; (*de douleur, dégoût*) grimace.

grimer /grime/ *v.t.*, **se ~** *v. pr.* make up.

grimper /grɛ̃pe/ *v.t./i.* climb.

grinc|er /grɛ̃se/ *v.i.* creak. **~er des**

dents, grind one's teeth. **~ement** *n.m.* creak(ing).

grincheu|x, ~se /grɛ̃ʃø, -z/ *a.* grumpy.

gripp|e /grip/ *n.f.* influenza, flu. **être ~é,** have (the) flu; (*mécanisme*) be seized up *ou* jammed.

gris, ~e /gri, -z/ *a.* grey; (*saoul*) tipsy.

grisaille /grizaj/ *n.f.* greyness, gloom.

griser /grize/ *v.t.* intoxicate.

grisonner /grizone/ *v.i.* go grey.

grive /griv/ *n.f.* (*oiseau*) thrush.

grivois, ~e /grivwa, -z/ *a.* bawdy.

grog /grɔg/ *n.m.* grog.

grogn|er /grɔɲe/ *v.i.* growl; (*cochon*) grunt. **~ement** *n.m.* growl; grunt.

grognon, ~ne /grɔɲɔ̃, -ɔn/ *a.* grumpy.

groin /grwɛ̃/ *n.m.* snout.

grommeler /grɔmle/ *v.t./i.* mutter.

grond|er /grɔ̃de/ *v.i.* rumble; (*chien*) growl; (*conflit etc.*) be brewing. —*v.t.* scold. **~ement** *n.m.* rumbling; growling.

groom /grum/ *n.m.* page(-boy).

gros, ~se /gro, -s/ *a.* big, large; (*gras*) fat; (*important*) great; (*épais*) thick; (*lourd*) heavy. —*adv.* (*beaucoup*) a lot. —*n.m.*, *f.* fat man, fat woman. —*n.m.* le **~ de,** the bulk of. **de ~,** (*comm.*) wholesale. **en ~,** roughly; (*comm.*) wholesale. **~ bonnet,** (*fam.*) bigwig. **~ lot,** jackpot. **~ mot,** rude word. **~ titre,** headline.

groseille /grozɛj/ *n.f.* (red *ou* white) currant. **~ à maquereau,** gooseberry.

grosse /gros/ *voir* **gros.**

grossesse /grosɛs/ *n.f.* pregnancy.

grosseur /grosœr/ *n.f.* (*volume*) size; (*enflure*) lump.

gross|ier, ~ière /grosje, -jɛr/ *a.* coarse, rough; (*imitation, instrument*) crude; (*vulgaire*) coarse; (*insolent*) rude; (*erreur*) gross. **~ièrement** *adv.* (*sommairement*) roughly; (*vulgairement*) coarsely. **~ièreté** *n.f.* coarseness; crudeness; rudeness; (*mot*) rude word.

grossir /grosir/ *v.t./i.* swell; (*personne*) put on weight; (*au microscope*) magnify; (*augmenter*) grow; (*exagérer*) magnify.

grossiste /grosist/ *n.m./f.* wholesaler.

grosso modo /grosomɔdo/ *adv.* roughly.

grotesque /grɔtɛsk/ *a.* grotesque; (*ridicule*) ludicrous.

grotte /grɔt/ *n.f.* cave, grotto.

grouill|er /gruje/ *v.i.* be swarming
(**de**, with). **~ant, ~ante** *a.* swarm-
ing.

groupe /grup/ *n.m.* group. **~ électrogène**, generating set. **~ scolaire**,
school block.

group|er /grupe/ *v.t.*, **se ~er** *v. pr.*
group (together). **~ement** *n.m.*
grouping.

grue /gry/ *n.f.* (*machine, oiseau*) crane.

grumeau (*pl.* **~x**) /grymo/ *n.m.* lump
(*in gravy, soup, etc.*).

gruyère /gryjɛr/ *n.m.* gruyère
(cheese).

gué /ge/ *n.m.* ford. **passer** *ou* **traverser à ~**, ford.

guenille /gǝnij/ *n.f.* rag.

guenon /gǝnɔ̃/ *n.f.* female monkey.

guépard /gepar/ *n.m.* cheetah.

guêp|e /gɛp/ *n.f.* wasp. **~ier** /gepje/
n.m. wasp's nest; (*fig.*) trap.

guère /gɛr/ *adv.* (**ne**) **~**, hardly. **il n'y
a ~ de pain**, there is hardly any
bread.

guéridon /geridɔ̃/ *n.m.* pedestal table.

guérill|a /gerija/ *n.f.* guerrilla war-
fare. **~ero** /-jero/ *n.m.* guerrilla.

guér|ir /gerir/ *v.t.* (*personne, maladie,
mal*) cure (**de**, of); (*plaie, membre*)
heal. *—v.i.* get better. **~ir de**, recover
from. **~ison** *n.f.* curing; healing;
(*de personne*) recovery. **~isseur,
~isseuse** *n.m., f.* healer.

guérite /gerit/ *n.f.* (*mil.*) sentry-box.

guerre /gɛr/ *n.f.* war. **en ~**, at war.
faire la ~, wage war (**à**, against). **~
civile**, civil war. **~ d'usure**, war of
attrition.

guerr|ier, ~ière /gɛrje, -jɛr/ *a.* war-
like. *—n.m., f.* warrior.

guet /gɛ/ *n.m.* watch. **faire le ~**, be
on the watch. **~-apens** /gɛtapɑ̃/ *n.m.
invar.* ambush.

guetter /gete/ *v.t.* watch; (*attendre*)
watch out for.

guetteur /gɛtœr/ *n.m.* look-out.

gueule /gœl/ *n.f.* mouth; (*figure: fam.*)
face.

gueuler /gœle/ *v.i.* (*fam.*) bawl.

gueuleton /gœltɔ̃/ *n.m.* (*repas: fam.*)
blow-out, slap-up meal.

gui /gi/ *n.m.* mistletoe.

guichet /giʃɛ/ *n.m.* window, counter;
(*de gare*) ticket-office (window); (*de
théâtre*) box-office (window).

guide /gid/ *n.m.* guide. *—n.f.* (*fille
scout*) girl guide. **~s** *n.f. pl.* (*rênes*)
reins.

guider /gide/ *v.t.* guide.

guidon /gidɔ̃/ *n.m.* handlebars.

guignol /giɲɔl/ *n.m.* puppet; (*personne*) clown; (*spectacle*) puppet-
show.

guillemets /gijmɛ/ *n.m. pl.* quotation
marks, inverted commas.

guilleret, ~te /gijrɛ, -t/ *a.* sprightly,
jaunty.

guillotin|e /gijɔtin/ *n.f.* guillotine.
~er *v.t.* guillotine.

guimauve /gimov/ *n.f.* marshmallow.

guindé /gɛ̃de/ *a.* stilted.

guirlande /girlɑ̃d/ *n.f.* garland.

guise /giz/ *n.f.* **à sa ~**, as one pleases.
en ~ de, by way of.

guitar|e /gitar/ *n.f.* guitar. **~iste**
n.m./f. guitarist.

guttur|al (*m. pl.* **~aux**) /gytyral, -o/
a. guttural.

gym /ʒim/ *n.f.* gym.

gymnas|e /ʒimnɑz/ *n.m.* gym(na-
sium). **~te** /-ast/ *n.m./f.* gymnast.
~tique /-astik/ *n.f.* gymnastics.

gynécolo|gie /ʒinekɔlɔʒi/ *n.f.* gynae-
cology. **~gique** *a.* gynaecological.
~gue *n.m./f.* gynaecologist.

H

habile /abil/ *a.* skilful, clever. ~**té** *n.f.* skill.

habill|er /abije/ *v.t.* dress (**de**, in); (*équiper*) clothe; (*recouvrir*) cover (**de**, with). **s'~er** *v. pr.* dress (o.s.), get dressed; (*se déguiser*) dress up. ~**é** *a.* (*costume*) dressy. ~**ement** *n.m.* clothing.

habit /abi/ *n.m.* dress, outfit; (*de cérémonie*) tails. ~**s**, clothes.

habitable /abitabl/ *a.* (in)habitable.

habitant, ~e /abitɑ̃, -t/ *n.m., f.* (*de maison*) occupant; (*de pays*) inhabitant.

habitat /abita/ *n.m.* housing conditions; (*d'animal*) habitat.

habitation /abitasjɔ̃/ *n.f.* living; (*logement*) house.

habit|er /abite/ *v.i.* live. *—v.t.* live in; (*planète, zone*) inhabit. ~**é** *a.* (*terre*) inhabited.

habitude /abityd/ *n.f.* habit. **avoir l'~ de faire,** be used to doing. **d'~,** usually.

habitué, ~e /abitɥe/ *n.m., f.* regular visitor: (*client*) regular.

habituel, ~le /abitɥɛl/ *a.* usual. ~**lement** *adv.* usually.

habituer /abitɥe/ *v.t.* ~ **à,** accustom to. **s'~ à,** get used to.

hache /ʿaʃ/ *n.f.* axe.

haché /ʿaʃe/ *a.* (*phrases*) jerky.

hacher /ʿaʃe/ *v.t.* mince; (*au couteau*) chop; (*fig.*) cut to pieces.

hachette /ʿaʃɛt/ *n.f.* hatchet.

hachis /ʿaʃi/ *n.m.* minced meat; (*Amer.*) ground meat.

hachisch /ʿaʃiʃ/ *n.m.* hashish.

hachoir /ʿaʃwar/ *n.m.* (*appareil*) mincer; (*couteau*) chopper.

hagard, ~e /ʿagar, -d/ *a.* wild (-looking).

haie /ʿɛ/ *n.f.* hedge; (*rangée*) row; (*de coureur*) hurdle.

haillon /ʿajɔ̃/ *n.m.* rag.

hain|e /ʿɛn/ *n.f.* hatred. ~**eux, ~euse** *a.* full of hatred.

haïr /ʿair/ *v.t.* hate.

hâl|e /ʿal/ *n.m.* (sun-)tan. ~**é** *a.* (sun-)tanned.

haleine /alɛn/ *n.f.* breath.

hal|er /ʿale/ *v.t.* tow. ~**age** *n.m.* towing.

haleter /ʿalte/ *v.i.* pant.

hall /ʿol/ *n.m.* hall; (*de gare*) concourse.

halle /ʿal/ *n.f.* (covered) market. ~**s**, (main) food market.

hallucination /alysinɑsjɔ̃/ *n.f.* hallucination.

halo /ʿalo/ *n.m.* halo.

halte /ʿalt/ *n.f.* stop; (*repos*) break; (*escale*) stopping place. *—int.* stop; (*mil.*) halt. **faire ~,** stop.

halt|ère /altɛr/ *n.m.* dumb-bell. ~**érophilie** *n.f.* weight-lifting.

hamac /ʿamak/ *n.m.* hammock.

hameau (*pl.* ~**x**) /ʿamo/ *n.m.* hamlet.

hameçon /amsɔ̃/ *n.m.* (fish-)hook.

hanche /ʿɑ̃ʃ/ *n.f.* hip.

hand-ball /ʿɑ̃dbal/ *n.m.* handball.

handicap /ʿɑ̃dikap/ *n.m.* handicap. ~**é, ~ée** *a. & n.m., f.* handicapped (person). ~**er** *v.t.* handicap.

hangar /ʿɑ̃gar/ *n.m.* shed; (*pour avions*) hangar.

hanneton /ʿantɔ̃/ *n.m.* May-bug.

hanter /ʿɑ̃te/ *v.t.* haunt.

hantise /ʿɑ̃tiz/ *n.f.* obsession (**de**, with).

happer /ʿape/ *v.t.* snatch, catch.

haras /ʿarɑ/ *n.m.* stud-farm.

harasser /ʿarase/ *v.t.* exhaust.

harceler /ʿarsəle/ *v.t.* harass.

hardi /ʿardi/ *a.* bold. ~**esse** /-djɛs/ *n.f.* boldness. ~**ment** *adv.* boldly.

hareng /ʿarɑ̃/ *n.m.* herring.

hargn|e /ʿarɲ/ *n.f.* (aggressive) bad temper. ~**eux, ~euse** *a.* bad-tempered.

haricot /ʿariko/ *n.m.* bean. ~ **vert,** French *ou* string bean; (*Amer.*) green bean.

harmonica /armɔnika/ *n.m.* harmonica.

harmon|ie /armɔni/ *n.f.* harmony. ~**ieux, ~ieuse** *a.* harmonious.

harmoniser /armɔnize/ *v.t.*, **s'~** *v. pr.* harmonize.

harnacher /ʿarnaʃe/ *v.t.* harness.

harnais /ʿarnɛ/ *n.m.* harness.

harp|e /ʿarp/ *n.f.* harp. ~**iste** *n.m./f.* harpist.

harpon /ʿarpɔ̃/ *n.m.* harpoon. ~**ner** /-ɔne/ *v.t.* harpoon; (*arrêter: fam.*) detain.

hasard /'azar/ *n.m.* chance; (*coïncidence*) coincidence. ~s, (*risques*) hazards. au ~, (*choisir etc.*) at random; (*flâner*) aimlessly. ~eux, ~euse /-dø, -z/ *a.* risky.

hasarder /'azarde/ *v.t.* risk; (*remarque*) venture. se ~ dans, risk going into. se ~ à faire, risk doing.

haschisch /'aʃiʃ/ *n.m.* hashish.

hâte /'at/ *n.f.* haste. à la ~, en ~, hurriedly. avoir ~ de, be eager to.

hâter /'ate/ *v.t.* hasten. se ~ *v. pr.* hurry (de, to).

hâti|f, ~ve /'atif, -v/ *a.* hasty; (*précoce*) early.

hauss|e /'os/ *n.f.* rise (de, in). en ~e, rising. ~er *v.t.* raise; (*épaules*) shrug. se ~er *v. pr.* stand up, raise o.s. up.

haut, ~e /'o, 'ot/ *a.* high; (*de taille*) tall. —*adv.* high; (*parler*) loud(ly); (*lire*) aloud. —*n.m.* top. à ~e voix, aloud. des ~s et des bas, ups and downs. en ~, (*regarder, jeter*) up; (*dans une maison*) upstairs. en ~ (de), at the top (of). ~ en couleur, colourful. plus ~, further up, higher up; (*dans un texte*) above. ~-de-forme (*pl.* ~s-de-forme) *n.m.* top hat. ~-fourneau (*pl.* ~s-fourneaux) *n.m.* blast-furnace. ~-le-cœur *n.m. invar.* nausea. ~-parleur *n.m.* loudspeaker.

hautain, ~e /'otɛ̃, -ɛn/ *a.* haughty.

hautbois /'obwa/ *n.m.* oboe.

hautement /'otmɑ̃/ *adv.* highly.

hauteur /'otœr/ *n.f.* height; (*colline*) hill; (*arrogance*) haughtiness. à la ~, (*fam.*) up to it. à la ~ de, level with; (*tâche, situation*) equal to.

hâve /'av/ *a.* gaunt.

havre /'avr/ *n.m.* haven.

Haye (La) /(la)'ɛ/ *n.f.* The Hague.

hayon /'ɛjɔ̃/ *n.m.* (*auto.*) rear opening, tail-gate.

hebdomadaire /ɛbdɔmadɛr/ *a. & n.m.* weekly.

héberg|er /ebɛrʒe/ *v.t.* accommodate. ~ement *n.m.* accommodation.

hébéter /ebete/ *v.t.* stupefy.

hébraïque /ebraik/ *a.* Hebrew.

hébreu (*pl.* ~x) /ebrø/ *a.m.* Hebrew. —*n.m.* (*lang.*) Hebrew.

hécatombe /ekatɔ̃b/ *n.f.* slaughter.

hectare /ɛktar/ *n.m.* hectare (= *10,000 square metres*).

hégémonie /eʒemɔni/ *n.f.* hegemony.

hein /'ɛ̃/ *int.* (*fam.*) eh.

hélas /'elas/ *int.* alas. —*adv.* sadly.

héler /'ele/ *v.t.* hail.

hélice /elis/ *n.f.* propeller.

hélicoptère /elikɔptɛr/ *n.m.* helicopter.

héliport /elipɔr/ *n.m.* heliport.

helvétique /ɛlvetik/ *a.* Swiss.

hémisphère /emisfɛr/ *n.m.* hemisphere.

hémorragie /emɔraʒi/ *n.f.* haemorrhage.

hémorroïde /emɔrɔid/ *n.f.* pile.

henn|ir /'enir/ *v.i.* neigh. ~issement *n.m.* neigh.

hep /'ɛp/ *int.* hey.

herbage /ɛrbaʒ/ *n.m.* pasture.

herb|e /ɛrb/ *n.f.* grass; (*méd., culin.*) herb. en ~e, green; (*fig.*) budding. ~eux, ~euse *a.* grassy.

herbicide /ɛrbisid/ *n.m.* weedkiller.

hérédit|é /eredite/ *n.f.* heredity. ~aire *a.* hereditary.

héré|sie /erezi/ *n.f.* heresy. ~tique *a.* heretical; *n.m./f.* heretic.

hériss|er /'erise/ *v.t.*, se ~er *v. pr.* bristle. ~er qn., ruffle s.o. ~é *a.* bristling (de, with).

hérisson /'erisɔ̃/ *n.m.* hedgehog.

héritage /eritaʒ/ *n.m.* inheritance; (*spirituel etc.*) heritage.

hérit|er /erite/ *v.t./i.* inherit (de, from). ~er de qch., inherit sth. ~ier, ~ière *n.m., f.* heir, heiress.

hermétique /ɛrmetik/ *a.* airtight; (*fig.*) unfathomable. ~ment *adv.* hermetically.

hermine /ɛrmin/ *n.f.* ermine.

hernie /'ɛrni/ *n.f.* hernia.

héroïne[1] /erɔin/ *n.f.* (*femme*) heroine.

héroïne[2] /erɔin/ *n.f.* (*drogue*) heroin.

héroï|que /erɔik/ *a.* heroic. ~sme *n.m.* heroism.

héron /'erɔ̃/ *n.m.* heron.

héros /'ero/ *n.m.* hero.

hésit|er /ezite/ *v.i.* hesitate (à, to). en ~ant, hesitantly. ~ant, ~ante *a.* hesitant. ~ation *n.f.* hesitation.

hétéroclite /eterɔklit/ *a.* heterogeneous.

hétérogène /eterɔʒɛn/ *a.* heterogeneous.

hêtre /'ɛtr/ *n.m.* beech.

heure /œr/ *n.f.* time; (*mesure de durée*) hour; (*scol.*) period. quelle ~ est-il?, what time is it? il est dix/*etc.* ~s, it is ten/*etc.* o'clock. à l'~, (*venir, être*) on time. d'~ en heure, hourly. ~ avancée, late hour. ~ d'affluence,

~ **de pointe,** rush-hour. ~ **indue,** ungodly hour. ~**s creuses,** off-peak periods. ~**s supplémentaires,** overtime.

heureusement /œrøzmɑ̃/ *adv.* fortunately.

heureu|x, ~se /œrø, -z/ *a.* happy; (*chanceux*) lucky, fortunate.

heurt /'œr/ *n.m.* collision; (*conflit*) clash.

heurter /'œrte/ *v.t.* (*cogner*) hit; (*mur etc.*) bump into, hit; (*choquer*) offend. **se ~ à,** bump into, hit; (*fig.*) come up against.

hexagone /ɛgzagɔn/ *n.m.* hexagon.

hiberner /ibɛrne/ *v.i.* hibernate.

hibou (*pl.* ~**x**) /'ibu/ *n.m.* owl.

hideu|x, ~se /'idø, -z/ *a.* hideous.

hier /jɛr/ *adv.* yesterday. ~ **soir,** last night, yesterday evening.

hiérarch|ie /'jerarʃi/ *n.f.* hierarchy. ~**ique** *a.* hierarchical.

hi-fi /'ifi/ *a. invar.* & *n.f.* (*fam.*) hi-fi.

hilare /ilar/ *a.* merry.

hilarité /ilarite/ *n.f.* laughter.

hindou, ~e /ɛ̃du/ *a.* & *n.m.,f.* Hindu.

hippi|que /ipik/ *a.* horse, equestrian. ~**sme** *n.m.* horse-riding.

hippodrome /ipɔdrom/ *n.m.* racecourse.

hippopotame /ipɔpɔtam/ *n.m.* hippopotamus.

hirondelle /irɔ̃dɛl/ *n.f.* swallow.

hirsute /irsyt/ *a.* shaggy.

hispanique /ispanik/ *a.* Spanish, Hispanic.

hisser /'ise/ *v.t.* hoist, haul. **se ~** *v. pr.* raise o.s.

histoire /istwar/ *n.f.* (*récit, mensonge*) story; (*étude*) history; (*affaire*) business. ~(**s**), (*chichis*) fuss. ~**s,** (*ennuis*) trouble.

historien, ~ne /istɔrjɛ̃, -jɛn/ *n.m., f.* historian.

historique /istɔrik/ *a.* historical.

hiver /ivɛr/ *n.m.* winter. ~**nal** (*m. pl.* ~**naux**) *a.* winter; (*glacial*) wintry. ~**ner** *v.i.* winter.

H.L.M. /'aʃɛlɛm/ *n.m./f.* (= *habitation à loyer modéré*) block of council flats; (*Amer.*) (government-sponsored) low-cost apartment building.

hocher /'ɔʃe/ *v.t.* ~ **la tête,** (*pour dire oui*) nod; (*pour dire non*) shake one's head.

hochet /'ɔʃɛ/ *n.m.* rattle.

hockey /'ɔkɛ/ *n.m.* hockey. ~ **sur glace,** ice hockey.

hold-up /'ɔldœp/ *n.m. invar.* (*attaque*) hold-up.

hollandais, ~e /'ɔlɑ̃dɛ, -z/ *a.* Dutch. —*n.m., f.* Dutchman, Dutchwoman. —*n.m.* (*lang.*) Dutch.

Hollande /'ɔlɑ̃d/ *n.f.* Holland.

homard /'ɔmar/ *n.m.* lobster.

homicide /ɔmisid/ *n.m.* homicide. ~ **involontaire,** manslaughter.

hommage /ɔmaʒ/ *n.m.* tribute, homage. ~**s,** (*salutations*) respects. **en ~ de,** as a token of.

homme /ɔm/ *n.m.* man; (*espèce*) man(kind). ~ **d'affaires,** businessman. ~ **de la rue,** man in the street. ~ **d'État,** statesman. ~ **de paille,** stooge. ~**-grenouille** (*pl.* ~**s-grenouilles**) *n.m.* frogman. ~ **politique,** politician.

homog|ène /ɔmɔʒɛn/ *a.* homogeneous. ~**énéité** *n.f.* homogeneity.

homologue /ɔmɔlɔg/ *n.m./f.* counterpart.

homologuer /ɔmɔlɔge/ *v.t.* recognize (officially), validate.

homonyme /ɔmɔnim/ *n.m.* (*personne*) namesake.

homosex|uel, ~uelle /ɔmɔsɛksɥɛl/ *a.* & *n.m., f.* homosexual. ~**ualité** *n.f.* homosexuality.

Hongrie /'ɔ̃gri/ *n.f.* Hungary.

hongrois, ~e /'ɔ̃grwa, -z/ *a.* & *n.m., f.* Hungarian.

honnête /ɔnɛt/ *a.* honest; (*satisfaisant*) fair. ~**ment** *adv.* honestly; fairly. ~**té** *n.f.* honesty.

honneur /ɔnœr/ *n.m.* honour; (*mérite*) credit. **d'~,** (*invité, place*) of honour; (*membre*) honorary. **en ~,** in favour. **en quel ~?,** (*fam.*) why? **faire ~ à,** (*équipe, famille*) bring credit to.

honorable /ɔnɔrabl/ *a.* honourable; (*convenable*) respectable. ~**ment** /-əmɑ̃/ *adv.* honourably; respectably.

honoraire /ɔnɔrɛr/ *a.* honorary. ~**s** *n.m. pl.* fees.

honorer /ɔnɔre/ *v.t.* honour; (*faire honneur à*) do credit to. **s'~ de,** pride o.s. on.

honorifique /ɔnɔrifik/ *a.* honorary.

hont|e /'ɔ̃t/ *n.f.* shame. **avoir ~e,** be ashamed (**de,** of). **faire ~e à,** make ashamed. ~**eux, ~euse** *a.* (*personne*) ashamed (**de,** of); (*action*) shameful. ~**eusement** *adv.* shamefully.

hôpit|al (*pl.* ~**aux**) /ɔpital, -o/ *n.m.* hospital.

hoquet /'ɔkɛ/ *n.m.* hiccup. **le ~,** (the) hiccups. **~er** /'ɔkte/ *v.i.* hiccup.

horaire /ɔrɛr/ *a.* hourly. —*n.m.* timetable.

horizon /ɔrizɔ̃/ *n.m.* horizon; (*perspective*) view.

horizont|al (*m. pl.* **~aux**) /ɔrizɔ̃tal, -o/ *a.* horizontal. **~alement** *adv.* horizontally.

horloge /ɔrlɔʒ/ *n.f.* clock. **~rie** *n.f.* (*magasin*) watchmaker's shop.

horlog|er, **~ère** /ɔrlɔʒe, -ɛr/ *n.m.,* f. watchmaker.

hormis /'ɔrmi/ *prép.* save.

hormone /ɔrmɔn/ *n.f.* hormone.

horoscope /ɔrɔskɔp/ *n.m.* horoscope.

horreur /ɔrœr/ *n.f.* horror. **avoir ~ de,** detest.

horrible /ɔribl/ *a.* horrible. **~ment** /-əmã/ *adv.* horribly.

horrifier /ɔrifje/ *v.t.* horrify.

hors /'ɔr/ *prép.* **~ de,** out of; (*à l'extérieur de*) outside. **~-bord** *n.m. invar.* speedboat. **~ d'atteinte,** out of reach. **~ d'haleine,** out of breath. **~ d'œuvre** *n.m. invar.* hors-d'œuvre. **~ de prix,** exorbitant. **~ de soi,** beside o.s. **~-jeu** *a. invar.* offside. **~-la-loi** *n.m. invar.* outlaw. **~ pair,** outstanding. **~-taxe** *a. invar.* dutyfree.

hortensia /ɔrtɑ̃sja/ *n.m.* hydrangea.

horticulture /ɔrtikyltyr/ *n.f.* horticulture.

hospice /ɔspis/ *n.m.* home.

hospital|ier, **~ière**[1] /ɔspitalje, -jɛr/ *a.* hospitable. **~ité** *n.f.* hospitality.

hospital|ier, **~ière**[2] /ɔspitalje, -jɛr/ *a.* (*méd.*) hospital. **~iser** *v.t.* take to hospital.

hostie /ɔsti/ *n.f.* (*relig.*) host.

hostil|e /ɔstil/ *a.* hostile. **~ité** *n.f.* hostility.

hôte /ot/ *n.m.* (*maître*) host; (*invité*) guest.

hôtel /otɛl/ *n.m.* hotel. **~ (particulier),** (private) mansion. **~ de ville,** town hall. **~ier,** **~ière** /otəlje, -jɛr/ *a.* hotel; *n.m.,* f. hotelier. **~lerie** *n.f.* hotel business; (*auberge*) country hotel.

hôtesse /otɛs/ *n.f.* hostess. **~ de l'air,** air hostess.

hotte /'ɔt/ *n.f.* basket; (*de cuisinière*) hood.

houblon /'ublɔ̃/ *n.m.* **le ~,** hops.

houill|e /'uj/ *n.f.* coal. **~e blanche,**

hydroelectric power. ~er, **~ère** *a.* coal; *n.f.* coalmine.

houl|e /'ul/ *n.f.* (*de mer*) swell. **~eux,** **~euse** *a.* stormy.

houppette /'upɛt/ *n.f.* powder-puff.

hourra /'ura/ *n.m.* & *int.* hurrah.

housse /'us/ *n.f.* dust-cover.

houx /'u/ *n.m.* holly.

hublot /'yblo/ *n.m.* porthole.

huche /'yʃ/ *n.f.* **~ à pain,** bread-bin.

huer /'ɥe/ *v.t.* boo. **huées** *n.f. pl.* boos.

huil|e /ɥil/ *n.f.* oil; (*personne: fam.*) bigwig. **~er** *v.t.* oil. **~eux,** **~euse** *a.* oily.

huissier /ɥisje/ *n.m.* (*appariteur*) usher; (*jurid.*) bailiff.

huit /'ɥi(t)/ *a.* eight. —*n.m.* eight. **~ jours,** a week. **~aine** /'ɥitɛn/ *n.f.* about eight; (*semaine*) week. **~ième** /'ɥitjɛm/ *a.* & *n.m.f.* eighth.

huître /ɥitr/ *n.f.* oyster.

humain, **~e** /ymɛ̃, ymɛn/ *a.* human; (*compatissant*) humane. **~ement** /ymɛnmã/ *adv.* humanly; humanely.

humanitaire /ymanitɛr/ *a.* humanitarian.

humanité /ymanite/ *n.f.* humanity.

humble /œbl/ *a.* humble.

humecter /ymɛkte/ *v.t.* moisten.

humer /'yme/ *v.t.* smell.

humeur /ymœr/ *n.f.* mood, humour; (*tempérament*) temper. **de bonne/ mauvaise ~,** in a good/bad mood.

humid|e /ymid/ *a.* damp; (*chaleur, climat*) humid; (*lèvres, yeux*) moist. **~ité** *n.f.* humidity.

humil|ier /ymilje/ *v.t.* humiliate. **~iation** *n.f.* humiliation.

humilité /ymilite/ *n.f.* humility.

humorist|e /ymɔrist/ *n.m.f.* humorist. **~ique** *a.* humorous.

humour /ymur/ *n.m.* humour; (*sens*) sense of humour.

huppé /'ype/ *a.* (*fam.*) high-class.

hurl|er /'yrle/ *v.t./i.* howl. **~ement** *n.m.* howl(ing).

hurluberlu /yrlybɛrly/ *n.m.* scatterbrain.

hutte /'yt/ *n.f.* hut.

hybride /ibrid/ *a.* & *n.m.* hybrid.

hydrate /idrat/ *n.m.* **~ de carbone,** carbohydrate.

hydraulique /idrolik/ *a.* hydraulic.

hydravion /idravjɔ̃/ *n.m.* seaplane.

hydro-électrique /idroelɛktrik/ *a.* hydroelectric.

hydrogène /idrɔʒɛn/ *n.m.* hydrogen.

hyène /jɛn/ *n.f.* hyena.

hyg|iène /iʒjɛn/ *n.f.* hygiene. **~i-énique** *a.* /iʒjenik/ hygienic.

hymne /imn/ *n.m.* hymn. **~ national,** national anthem.

hyper- /ipɛr/ *préf.* hyper-.

hypermarché /ipɛrmarʃe/ *n.m.* (*supermarché*) hypermarket.

hypertension /ipɛrtɑ̃sjɔ̃/ *n.f.* high blood-pressure.

hypno|se /ipnoz/ *n.f.* hypnosis. **~tique** /-ɔtik/ *a.* hypnotic. **~tisme** /-ɔtism/ *n.m.* hypnotism.

hypnotis|er /ipnɔtize/ *v.t.* hypnotize. **~eur** *n.m.* hypnotist.

hypocrisie /ipɔkrizi/ *n.f.* hypocrisy.

hypocrite /ipɔkrit/ *a.* hypocritical. —*n.m./f.* hypocrite.

hypoth|èque /ipɔtɛk/ *n.f.* mortgage. **~équer** *v.t.* mortgage.

hypoth|èse /ipɔtɛz/ *n.f.* hypothesis. **~étique** *a.* hypothetical.

hystér|ie /isteri/ *n.f.* hysteria. **~ique** *a.* hysterical.

I

iceberg /isbɛrg/ *n.m.* iceberg.

ici /isi/ *adv.* (*espace*) here; (*temps*) now.
d'~ demain, by tomorrow. **d'~ là**,
in the meantime. **d'~ peu**, shortly.
~ même, in this very place.

icône /ikon/ *n.f.* icon.

idé|al (*m. pl.* **~aux**) /ideal, -o/ *a.*
ideal. —*n.m.* (*pl.* **~aux**) ideal. **~a-
liser** *v.t.* idealize.

idéalis|te /idealist/ *a.* idealistic.
—*n.m./f.* idealist. **~me** *n.m.* idealism.

idée /ide/ *n.f.* idea; (*esprit*) mind. **~
fixe**, obsession. **~ reçue**, conventional opinion.

identif|ier /idɑ̃tifje/ *v.t.*, **s'~ier** *v. pr.*
identify (**à**, with). **~ication** *n.f.* identification.

identique /idɑ̃tik/ *a.* identical.

identité /idɑ̃tite/ *n.f.* identity.

idéolog|ie /ideɔlɔʒi/ *n.f.* ideology.
~ique *a.* ideological.

idiom|e /idjom/ *n.m.* idiom. **~atique**
/idjɔmatik/ *a.* idiomatic.

idiot, **~e** /idjo, idjɔt/ *a.* idiotic. —*n.m.*,
f. idiot. **~ie** /idjɔsi/ *n.f.* idiocy; (*acte,
parole*) idiotic thing.

idiotisme /idjɔtism/ *n.m.* idiom.

idolâtrer /idɔlɑtre/ *v.t.* idolize.

idole /idɔl/ *n.f.* idol.

idyllique /idilik/ *a.* idyllic.

if /if/ *n.m.* (*arbre*) yew.

igloo /iglu/ *n.m.* igloo.

ignare /iɲar/ *a.* ignorant. —*n.m./f.*
ignoramus.

ignoble /iɲɔbl/ *a.* vile.

ignoran|t, **~te** /iɲɔrɑ̃, -t/ *a.* ignor-
ant. —*n.m.*, *f.* ignoramus. **~ce** *n.f.*
ignorance.

ignorer /iɲɔre/ *v.t.* not know; (*personne*) ignore.

il /il/ *pron.* he; (*chose*) it. **~ est vrai**/*etc.*
que, it is true/*etc.* that. **~ neige**/
pleut/*etc.*, it is snowing/raining/*etc.*
~ y a, there is; (*pluriel*) there are;
(*temps*) ago; (*durée*) for.

île /il/ *n.f.* island. **~ déserte**, desert
island. **~s anglo-normandes**, Chan-
nel Islands. **~s Britanniques**, British Isles.

illég|al (*m. pl.* **~aux**) /ilegal, -o/ *a.*
illegal. **~alité** *n.f.* illegality.

illégitim|e /ileʒitim/ *a.* illegitimate.
~ité *n.f.* illegitimacy.

illettré, **~e** /iletre/ *a.* & *n.m.*, *f.* illiterate.

illicite /ilisit/ *a.* illicit.

illimité /ilimite/ *a.* unlimited.

illisible /ilizibl/ *a.* illegible; (*livre*) un-
readable.

illogique /ilɔʒik/ *a.* illogical.

illumin|er /ilymine/ *v.t.*, **s'~er** *v. pr.*
light up. **~ation** *n.f.* illumination. **~é**
a. (*monument*) floodlit.

illusion /ilyzjɔ̃/ *n.f.* illusion. **se faire
des ~s**, delude o.s. **~ner** /-jɔne/ *v.t.*
delude. **~niste** /-jɔnist/ *n.m./f.* con-
juror.

illusoire /ilyzwar/ *a.* illusory.

illustre /ilystr/ *a.* illustrious.

illustr|er /ilystre/ *v.t.* illustrate.
s'~er *v. pr.* become famous. **~ation**
n.f. illustration. **~é** *a.* illustrated;
n.m. illustrated magazine.

îlot /ilo/ *n.m.* island; (*de maisons*)
block.

ils /il/ *pron.* they.

imag|e /imaʒ/ *n.f.* picture; (*métaphore*)
image; (*reflet*) reflection. **~é** *a.* full of
imagery.

imaginaire /imaʒinɛr/ *a.* imaginary.

imaginati|f, **~ve** /imaʒinatif, -v/ *a.*
imaginative.

imagin|er /imaʒine/ *v.t.* imagine; (*in-
venter*) think up. **s'~er** *v. pr.* imagine
(**que**, that). **~ation** *n.f.* imagination.

imbattable /ɛ̃batabl/ *a.* unbeatable.

imbécil|e /ɛ̃besil/ *a.* idiotic. —*n.m./f.*
idiot. **~lité** *n.f.* idiocy; (*action*) idiotic
thing.

imbiber /ɛ̃bibe/ *v.t.* soak (**de**, with).
s'~ *v. pr.* become soaked.

imbriqué /ɛ̃brike/ *a.* (*lié*) linked.

imbu /ɛ̃by/ *a.* **~ de**, full of.

imbuvable /ɛ̃byvabl/ *a.* undrinkable;
(*personne*: *fam.*) insufferable.

imit|er /imite/ *v.t.* imitate; (*person-
nage*) impersonate; (*faire comme*) do
the same as; (*document*) copy.
~ateur, **~atrice** *n.m.*, *f.* imitator;
impersonator. **~ation** *n.f.* imitation;
impersonation.

immaculé /imakyle/ *a.* spotless.

immangeable /ɛ̃mɑ̃ʒabl/ *a.* inedible.

immatricul|er /imatrikyle/ *v.t.* regis-
ter. (**se**) **faire ~er**, register. **~ation**
n.f. registration.

immédiat, ∼e /imedja, -t/ *a.* immediate. —*n.m.* **dans l'∼,** for the moment.
∼ement /-tmã/ *adv.* immediately.

immens|e /imãs/ *a.* immense.
∼ément *adv.* immensely. **∼ité** *n.f.*
immensity.

immer|ger /imɛrʒe/ *v.t.* immerse.
s'∼ger *v. pr.* submerge. **∼sion** *n.f.*
immersion.

immeuble /imœbl/ *n.m.* block of flats,
building. **∼ (de bureaux),** (office)
building *ou* block.

immigr|er /imigre/ *v.i.* immigrate.
∼ant, ∼ante *a.* & *n.m.,f.* immigrant.
∼ation *n.f.* immigration. **∼é, ∼ée** *a.*
& *n.m., f.* immigrant.

imminen|t, ∼te /iminã, -t/ *a.* immin-
ent. **∼ce** *n.f.* imminence.

immiscer (s') /(s)imise/ *v. pr.* interfere (**dans,** in).

immobil|e /imɔbil/ *a.* still, motionless.
∼ité *n.f.* stillness; (*inaction*) immob-
ility.

immobil|ier, ∼ière /imɔbilje, -jɛr/
a. property. **agence ∼ière,** estate
agent's office; (*Amer.*) real estate
office. **agent ∼ier,** estate agent;
(*Amer.*) real estate agent.

immobilis|er /imɔbilize/ *v.t.* immobil-
ize; (*stopper*) stop. **s'∼er** *v. pr.* stop.
∼ation *n.f.* immobilization.

immodéré /imɔdere/ *a.* immoderate.

immoler /imɔle/ *v.t.* sacrifice.

immonde /imɔ̃d/ *a.* filthy.

immondices /imɔ̃dis/ *n.f. pl.* refuse.

immor|al (*m. pl.* **∼aux**) /imɔral, -o/ *a.*
immoral. **∼alité** *n.f.* immorality.

immortaliser /imɔrtalize/ *v.t.* immor-
talize.

immort|el, ∼elle /imɔrtɛl/ *a.* immor-
tal. **∼alité** *n.f.* immortality.

immuable /imɥabl/ *a.* unchanging.

immunis|er /imynize/ *v.t.* immunize.
∼é contre, (*à l'abri de*) immune to.

immunité /imynite/ *n.f.* immunity.

impact /ɛ̃pakt/ *n.m.* impact.

impair[1] /ɛ̃pɛr/ *a.* (*numéro*) odd.

impair[2] /ɛ̃pɛr/ *n.m.* blunder.

impardonnable /ɛ̃pardɔnabl/ *a.* unforgivable.

imparfait, ∼e /ɛ̃parfɛ, -t/ *a.* & *n.m.*
imperfect.

impart|ial (*m. pl.* **∼iaux**) /ɛ̃parsjal,
-jo/ *a.* impartial. **∼ialité** *n.f.* impar-
tiality.

impasse /ɛ̃pas/ *n.f.* (*rue*) dead end;
(*situation*) deadlock.

impassible /ɛ̃pasibl/ *a.* impassive.

impat|ient, ∼iente /ɛ̃pasjã, -t/ *a.* im-
patient. **∼iemment** /-jamã/ *adv.* im-
patiently. **∼ience** *n.f.* impatience.

impatienter /ɛ̃pasjãte/ *v.t.* annoy. **s'∼**
v. pr. lose patience (**contre,** with).

impayable /ɛ̃pɛjabl/ *a.* (killingly)
funny, hilarious.

impayé /ɛ̃peje/ *a.* unpaid.

impeccable /ɛ̃pekabl/ *a.* impeccable.

impénétrable /ɛ̃penetrabl/ *a.* impenetrable.

impénitent, ∼e /ɛ̃penitã, -t/ *a.* unre-
pentant.

impensable /ɛ̃pãsabl/ *a.* unthinkable.

impérati|f, ∼ve /ɛ̃peratif, -v/ *a.* im-
perative. —*n.m.* requirement; (*gram.*)
imperative.

impératrice /ɛ̃peratris/ *n.f.* empress.

imperceptible /ɛ̃pɛrsɛptibl/ *a.* imperceptible.

imperfection /ɛ̃pɛrfɛksjɔ̃/ *n.f.* imperfection.

impér|ial (*m. pl.* **∼iaux**) /ɛ̃perjal, -jo/
a. imperial. **∼ialisme** *n.m.* imperial-
ism.

impériale /ɛ̃perjal/ *n.f.* upper deck.

impérieu|x, ∼se /ɛ̃perjø, -z/ *a.* imperi-
ous; (*pressant*) pressing.

impérissable /ɛ̃perisabl/ *a.* undying.

imperméable /ɛ̃pɛrmeabl/ *a.* impervious (**à,** to); (*manteau, tissu*) waterproof. —*n.m.* raincoat.

impersonnel, ∼le /ɛ̃pɛrsɔnɛl/ *a.* impersonal.

impertinen|t, ∼te /ɛ̃pɛrtinã, -t/ *a.* im-
pertinent. **∼ce** *n.f.* impertinence.

imperturbable /ɛ̃pɛrtyrbabl/ *a.* unshakeable.

impét|ueux, ∼ueuse /ɛ̃petɥø, -z/ *a.*
impetuous. **∼uosité** *n.f.* impetuosity.

impie /ɛ̃pi/ *a.* ungodly.

impitoyable /ɛ̃pitwajabl/ *a.* merciless.

implacable /ɛ̃plakabl/ *a.* implacable.

implant|er /ɛ̃plãte/ *v.t.* establish.
s'∼er *v. pr.* become established.
∼ation *n.f.* establishment.

implication /ɛ̃plikasjɔ̃/ *n.f.* implication.

implicite /ɛ̃plisit/ *a.* implicit.

impliquer /ɛ̃plike/ *v.t.* imply (**que,**
that). **∼ dans,** implicate in.

implorer /ɛ̃plɔre/ *v.t.* implore.

impoli /ɛ̃pɔli/ *a.* impolite. **∼tesse**
n.f. impoliteness; (*remarque*) impolite
remark.

impondérable /ɛ̃pɔ̃derabl/ *a.* & *n.m.*
imponderable.

impopulaire /ɛ̃pɔpylɛr/ *a.* unpopular.
importance /ɛ̃pɔrtɑ̃s/ *n.f.* importance; (*taille*) size; (*ampleur*) extent.
important, ∼**e** /ɛ̃pɔrtɑ̃, -t/ *a.* important; (*en quantité*) considerable, sizeable, big. —*n.m.* l'∼, the important thing.
import|er[1] /ɛ̃pɔrte/ *v.t.* (*comm.*) import. ∼**ateur,** ∼**atrice** *n.m., f.* importer; *a.* importing. ∼**ation** *n.f.* import.
import|er[2] /ɛ̃pɔrte/ *v.i.* matter, be important (à, to). **il** ∼**e que,** it is important that. **n'**∼**e, peu** ∼**e,** it does not matter. **n'**∼**e comment,** anyhow. **n'**∼**e où,** anywhere. **n'**∼**e qui,** anybody. **n'**∼**e quoi,** anything.
importun, ∼**e** /ɛ̃pɔrtœ̃, -yn/ *a.* troublesome. —*n.m., f.* nuisance. ∼**er** /-yne/ *v.t.* trouble.
imposant, ∼**e** /ɛ̃pozɑ̃, -t/ *a.* imposing.
imposer /ɛ̃poze/ *v.t.* impose (à, on); (*taxer*) tax. **s'**∼ *v. pr.* (*action*) be essential; (*se faire reconnaître*) stand out.
impossibilité /ɛ̃pɔsibilite/ *n.f.* impossibility. **dans l'**∼ **de,** unable to.
impossible /ɛ̃pɔsibl/ *a.* & *n.m.* impossible.
impost|eur /ɛ̃pɔstœr/ *n.m.* impostor. ∼**ure** *n.f.* imposture.
impôt /ɛ̃po/ *n.m.* tax. ∼**s,** (*contributions*) tax(ation), taxes. ∼ **sur le revenu,** income tax.
impotent, ∼**e** /ɛ̃pɔtɑ̃, -t/ *a.* crippled. —*n.m., f.* cripple.
impraticable /ɛ̃pratikabl/ *a.* (*route*) impassable.
imprécis, ∼**e** /ɛ̃presi, -z/ *a.* imprecise. ∼**ion** /-izjɔ̃/ *n.f.* imprecision.
imprégner /ɛ̃preɲe/ *v.t.* fill (**de,** with); (*imbiber*) impregnate (**de,** with). **s'**∼ **de,** become filled with; (*s'imbiber*) become impregnated with.
imprenable /ɛ̃prənabl/ *a.* impregnable.
impresario /ɛ̃presarjo/ *n.m.* manager.
impression /ɛ̃presjɔ̃/ *n.f.* impression; (*de livre*) printing.
impressionn|er /ɛ̃presjɔne/ *v.t.* impress. ∼**able** *a.* impressionable. ∼**ant,** ∼**ante** *a.* impressive.
imprévisible /ɛ̃previzibl/ *a.* unpredictable.
imprévoyance /ɛ̃prevwajɑ̃s/ *n.f.* lack of foresight.
imprévu /ɛ̃prevy/ *a.* unexpected. —*n.m.* unexpected incident.

imprim|er /ɛ̃prime/ *v.t.* print; (*marquer*) imprint; (*transmettre*) impart. ∼**ante** *n.f.* (*d'un ordinateur*) printer. ∼**é** *a.* printed; *n.m.* (*formulaire*) printed form. ∼**erie** *n.f.* (*art*) printing; (*lieu*) printing works. ∼**eur** *n.m.* printer.
improbable /ɛ̃prɔbabl/ *a.* unlikely, improbable.
impromptu /ɛ̃prɔ̃pty/ *a.* & *adv.* impromptu.
impropr|e /ɛ̃prɔpr/ *a.* incorrect. ∼**e à,** unfit for. ∼**iété** *n.f.* incorrectness; (*erreur*) error.
improvis|er /ɛ̃prɔvize/ *v.t./i.* improvise. ∼**ation** *n.f.* improvisation.
improviste (à l') /(al)ɛ̃prɔvist/ *adv.* unexpectedly.
imprud|ent, ∼**ente** /ɛ̃prydɑ̃, -t/ *a.* careless. **il est** ∼**ent de,** it is unwise to. ∼**emment** /-amɑ̃/ *adv.* carelessly. ∼**ence** *n.f.* carelessness; (*acte*) careless action.
impuden|t, ∼**te** /ɛ̃pydɑ̃, -t/ *a.* impudent. ∼**ce** *n.f.* impudence.
impuissan|t, ∼**te** /ɛ̃pɥisɑ̃, -t/ *a.* helpless; (*méd.*) impotent. ∼**t à,** powerless to. ∼**ce** *n.f.* helplessness; (*méd.*) impotence.
impulsi|f, ∼**ve** /ɛ̃pylsif, -v/ *a.* impulsive.
impulsion /ɛ̃pylsjɔ̃/ *n.f.* (*poussée, influence*) impetus; (*instinct, mouvement*) impulse.
impunément /ɛ̃pynemɑ̃/ *adv.* with impunity.
impuni /ɛ̃pyni/ *a.* unpunished.
impur /ɛ̃pyr/ *a.* impure. ∼**eté** *n.f.* impurity.
imputer /ɛ̃pyte/ *v.t.* ∼ **à,** impute to.
inabordable /inabɔrdabl/ *a.* (*prix*) prohibitive.
inacceptable /inaksɛptabl/ *a.* unacceptable; (*scandaleux*) outrageous.
inaccessible /inaksesibl/ *a.* inaccessible.
inaccoutumé /inakutyme/ *a.* unaccustomed.
inachevé /inaʃve/ *a.* unfinished.
inacti|f, ∼**ve** /inaktif, -v/ *a.* inactive.
inaction /inaksjɔ̃/ *n.f.* inactivity.
inadapté, ∼**e** /inadapte/ *n.m., f.* (*psych.*) maladjusted person.
inadmissible /inadmisibl/ *a.* unacceptable.
inaltérable /inalterabl/ *a.* stable, that does not deteriorate; (*sentiment*) unfailing.

inanimé /inanime/ *a.* (*évanoui*) un-conscious; (*mort*) lifeless; (*matière*) inanimate.

inaperçu /inapɛrsy/ *a.* unnoticed.

inappréciable /inapresjabl/ *a.* invaluable.

inapte /inapt/ *a.* unsuited (à, to). ~ à faire, incapable of doing.

inarticulé /inartikyle/ *a.* inarticulate.

inattendu /inatɑ̃dy/ *a.* unexpected.

inattenti|f, ~ve /inatɑ̃tif, -v/ *a.* inattentive (à, to).

inattention /inatɑ̃sjɔ̃/ *n.f.* inattention.

inaugur|er /inogyre/ *v.t.* inaugurate. ~ation *n.f.* inauguration.

inaugur|al (*m. pl.* ~aux) /inogyral, -o/ *a.* inaugural.

incalculable /ɛ̃kalkylabl/ *a.* incalculable.

incapable /ɛ̃kapabl/ *a.* incapable (de qch., of sth.). ~ de faire, unable to do, incapable of doing. —*n.m./f.* incompetent.

incapacité /ɛ̃kapasite/ *n.f.* incapacity. dans l'~ de, unable to.

incarcérer /ɛ̃karsere/ *v.t.* incarcerate.

incarn|er /ɛ̃karne/ *v.t.* embody. ~ation *n.f.* embodiment, incarnation.

incartade /ɛ̃kartad/ *n.f.* indiscretion, misdeed, prank.

incassable /ɛ̃kasabl/ *a.* unbreakable.

incendiaire /ɛ̃sɑ̃djɛr/ *a.* incendiary. —*n.m./f.* arsonist.

incend|ie /ɛ̃sɑ̃di/ *n.m.* fire. ~ie criminel, arson. ~ier *v.t.* set fire to.

incert|ain, ~aine /ɛ̃sɛrtɛ̃, -ɛn/ *a.* uncertain; (*contour*) vague. ~itude *n.f.* uncertainty.

incessamment /ɛ̃sɛsamɑ̃/ *adv.* immediately.

incessant, ~e /ɛ̃sɛsɑ̃, -t/ *a.* incessant.

incest|e /ɛ̃sɛst/ *n.m.* incest. ~ueux, ~ueuse *a.* incestuous.

inchangé /ɛ̃ʃɑ̃ʒe/ *a.* unchanged.

incidence /ɛ̃sidɑ̃s/ *n.f.* effect.

incident /ɛ̃sidɑ̃/ *n.m.* incident. ~ technique, technical hitch.

incinér|er /ɛ̃sinere/ *v.t.* incinerate; (*mort*) cremate. ~ateur *n.m.* incinerator.

incis|er /ɛ̃size/ *v.t.* (*abcès etc.*) lance. ~ion *n.f.* lancing; (*entaille*) incision.

incisi|f, ~ve /ɛ̃sizif, -v/ *a.* incisive.

incit|er /ɛ̃site/ *v.t.* incite (à, to). ~ation *n.f.* incitement.

inclinaison /ɛ̃klinɛzɔ̃/ *n.f.* incline; (*de la tête*) tilt.

inclination[1] /ɛ̃klinɑsjɔ̃/ *n.f.* (*penchant*) inclination.

inclin|er /ɛ̃kline/ *v.t.* tilt, lean; (*courber*) bend; (*inciter*) encourage (à, to). —*v.i.* ~er à, be inclined to. s'~er *v. pr.* (*se courber*) bow down; (*céder*) give in; (*chemin*) slope. ~er la tête, (*approuver*) nod; (*révérence*) bow. ~ation[2] *n.f.* (*de la tête*) nod; (*du buste*) bow.

incl|ure /ɛ̃klyr/ *v.t.* include; (*enfermer*) enclose. jusqu'au lundi ~us, up to and including Monday. ~usion *n.f.* inclusion.

incognito /ɛ̃kɔɲito/ *adv.* incognito.

incohéren|t, ~te /ɛ̃kɔerɑ̃, -t/ *a.* incoherent. ~ce *n.f.* incoherence.

incolore /ɛ̃kɔlɔr/ *a.* colourless; (*crème, verre*) clear.

incomber /ɛ̃kɔ̃be/ *v.i.* il vous/*etc.* incombe de, it is your/*etc.* responsibility to.

incommode /ɛ̃kɔmɔd/ *a.* awkward.

incommoder /ɛ̃kɔmɔde/ *v.t.* inconvenience.

incomparable /ɛ̃kɔ̃parabl/ *a.* incomparable.

incompatib|le /ɛ̃kɔ̃patibl/ *a.* incompatible. ~ilité *n.f.* incompatibility.

incompéten|t, ~te /ɛ̃kɔ̃petɑ̃, -t/ *a.* incompetent. ~ce *n.f.* incompetence.

incompl|et, ~ète /ɛ̃kɔ̃plɛ, -t/ *a.* incomplete.

incompréhensible /ɛ̃kɔ̃preɑ̃sibl/ *a.* incomprehensible.

incompréhens|if, ~ive /ɛ̃kɔ̃preɑ̃sif, -v/ *a.* lacking in understanding. ~ion *n.f.* lack of understanding.

incompris, ~e /ɛ̃kɔ̃pri, -z/ *a.* misunderstood.

inconcevable /ɛ̃kɔ̃svabl/ *a.* inconceivable.

inconciliable /ɛ̃kɔ̃siljabl/ *a.* irreconcilable.

inconditionnel, ~le /ɛ̃kɔ̃disjɔnɛl/ *a.* unconditional.

inconfort /ɛ̃kɔ̃fɔr/ *n.m.* discomfort. ~able /-tabl/ *a.* uncomfortable.

incongru /ɛ̃kɔ̃gry/ *a.* unseemly.

inconnu, ~e /ɛ̃kɔny/ *a.* unknown (à, to). —*n.m.,f.* stranger. —*n.m.* l'~, the unknown. —*n.f.* unknown (quantity).

inconsc|ient, ~iente /ɛ̃kɔ̃sjɑ̃, -t/ *a.* unconscious (de, of); (*fou*) mad. —*n.m.* (*psych.*) subconscious. ~iemment /-jamɑ̃/ *adv.* unconsciously. ~ience *n.f.* unconsciousness; (*folie*) madness.

inconsidéré /ɛ̃kɔ̃sidere/ *a.* thoughtless.

inconsolable /ɛ̃kɔ̃sɔlabl/ *a.* inconsolable.

inconstan|t, ∼te /ɛ̃kɔ̃stɑ̃, -t/ *a.* fickle. **∼ce** *n.f.* fickleness.

incontest|able /ɛ̃kɔ̃tɛstabl/ *a.* indisputable. **∼é** *a.* undisputed.

incontinen|t, ∼te /ɛ̃kɔ̃tinɑ̃, -t/ *a.* incontinent. **∼ce** *n.f.* incontinence.

incontrôlable /ɛ̃kɔ̃trolabl/ *a.* unverifiable.

inconvenan|t, ∼te /ɛ̃kɔ̃vnɑ̃, -t/ *a.* improper. **∼ce** *n.f.* impropriety.

inconvénient /ɛ̃kɔ̃venjɑ̃/ *n.m.* disadvantage; (*risque*) risk; (*objection*) objection.

incorpor|er /ɛ̃kɔrpɔre/ *v.t.* incorporate; (*mil.*) enlist. **∼ation** *n.f.* incorporation; (*mil.*) enlistment.

incorrect /ɛ̃kɔrɛkt/ *a.* (*faux*) incorrect; (*malséant*) improper; (*impoli*) impolite.

incorrigible /ɛ̃kɔriʒibl/ *a.* incorrigible.

incrédul|e /ɛ̃kredyl/ *a.* incredulous. **∼ité** *n.f.* incredulity.

incriminer /ɛ̃krimine/ *v.t.* incriminate.

incroyable /ɛ̃krwajabl/ *a.* incredible.

incroyant, ∼e /ɛ̃krwajɑ̃, -t/ *n.m., f.* non-believer.

incrust|er /ɛ̃kryste/ *v.t.* (*décorer*) inlay (**de**, with). **s'∼er dans,** become embedded in. **∼ation** *n.f.* inlay.

inculp|er /ɛ̃kylpe/ *v.t.* charge (**de**, with). **∼ation** *n.f.* charge. **∼é, ∼ée** *n.m., f.* accused.

inculquer /ɛ̃kylke/ *v.t.* instil (**à**, into).

inculte /ɛ̃kylt/ *a.* uncultivated; (*cheveux*) unkempt; (*personne*) uneducated.

incurable /ɛ̃kyrabl/ *a.* incurable.

incursion /ɛ̃kyrsjɔ̃/ *n.f.* incursion.

incurver /ɛ̃kyrve/ *v.t.*, **s'∼** *v. pr.* curve.

Inde /ɛ̃d/ *n.f.* India.

indécen|t, ∼te /ɛ̃desɑ̃, -t/ *a.* indecent. **∼ce** *n.f.* indecency.

indéchiffrable /ɛ̃deʃifrabl/ *a.* indecipherable.

indécis, ∼e /ɛ̃desi, -z/ *a.* indecisive; (*qui n'a pas encore pris de décision*) undecided. **∼ion** /-izjɔ̃/ *n.f.* indecision.

indéfini /ɛ̃defini/ *a.* indefinite; (*vague*) undefined. **∼ment** *adv.* indefinitely. **∼ssable** *a.* indefinable.

indélébile /ɛ̃delebil/ *a.* indelible.

indélicat, ∼e /ɛ̃delika, -t/ *a.* (*malhonnête*) unscrupulous.

indemne /ɛ̃dɛmn/ *a.* unharmed.

indemniser /ɛ̃dɛmnize/ *v.t.* indemnify, compensate.

indemnité /ɛ̃dɛmnite/ *n.f.* indemnity; (*allocation*) allowance.

indéniable /ɛ̃denjabl/ *a.* undeniable.

indépend|ant, ∼ante /ɛ̃depɑ̃dɑ̃, -t/ *a.* independent. **∼amment** *adv.* independently. **∼amment de,** apart from. **∼ance** *n.f.* independence.

indescriptible /ɛ̃dɛskriptibl/ *a.* indescribable.

indésirable /ɛ̃dezirabl/ *a.* & *n.m./f.* undesirable.

indestructible /ɛ̃dɛstryktibl/ *a.* indestructible.

indétermination /ɛ̃detɛrminɑsjɔ̃/ *n.f.* indecision.

indéterminé /ɛ̃detɛrmine/ *a.* unspecified.

index /ɛ̃dɛks/ *n.m.* forefinger; (*liste*) index. **∼er** *v.t.* index.

indica|teur, ∼trice /ɛ̃dikatœr, -tris/ *n.m.*, *f.* (police) informer. —*n.m.* (*livre*) guide; (*techn.*) indicator.

indicati|f, ∼ve /ɛ̃dikatif, -v/ *a.* indicative (**de**, of). —*n.m.* (*radio*) signature tune; (*téléphonique*) dialling code; (*gram.*) indicative.

indication /ɛ̃dikɑsjɔ̃/ *n.f.* indication; (*renseignement*) information; (*directive*) instruction.

indice /ɛ̃dis/ *n.m.* sign; (*dans une enquête*) clue; (*des prix*) index; (*d'octane, de salaire*) rating.

indien, ∼ne /ɛ̃djɛ̃, -jɛn/ *a.* & *n.m., f.* Indian.

indifféremment /ɛ̃diferamɑ̃/ *adv.* equally.

indifféren|t, ∼te /ɛ̃diferɑ̃, -t/ *a.* indifferent (**à**, to). **ça m'est ∼t,** it makes no difference to me. **∼ce** *n.f.* indifference.

indigène /ɛ̃diʒɛn/ *a.* & *n.m./f.* native.

indigen|t, ∼te /ɛ̃diʒɑ̃, -t/ *a.* poor. **∼ce** *n.f.* poverty.

indigest|e /ɛ̃diʒɛst/ *a.* indigestible. **∼ion** *n.f.* indigestion.

indignation /ɛ̃diɲɑsjɔ̃/ *n.f.* indignation.

indign|e /ɛ̃diɲ/ *a.* unworthy (**de**, of); (*acte*) vile. **∼ité** *n.f.* unworthiness; (*acte*) vile act.

indigner /ɛ̃diɲe/ *v.t.* make indignant. **s'∼** *v. pr.* become indignant (**de**, at).

indiqu|er /ɛ̃dike/ *v.t.* show, indicate; (*renseigner sur*) point out, tell; (*déterminer*) give, state, appoint. ~**er du doigt**, point to *ou* out *ou* at. ~**é** *a.* (*heure*) appointed; (*opportun*) appropriate; (*conseillé*) recommended.

indirect /ɛ̃dirɛkt/ *a.* indirect.

indiscipliné /ɛ̃disipline/ *a.* unruly.

indiscr|et, ~ète /ɛ̃diskrɛ, -t/ *a.* indiscreet; (*curieux*) inquisitive. ~**étion** *n.f.* indiscretion; inquisitiveness.

indiscutable /ɛ̃diskytabl/ *a.* unquestionable.

indispensable /ɛ̃dispɑ̃sabl/ *a.* indispensable. **il est ~ que**, it is essential that.

indispos|er /ɛ̃dispoze/ *v.t.* make unwell. ~**er (contre soi)**, (*mécontenter*) antagonize. ~**é** *a.* unwell. ~**ition** *n.f.* indisposition.

indistinct, ~e /ɛ̃distɛ̃(kt), -ɛ̃kt/ *a.* indistinct. ~**ement** /-ɛ̃ktəmɑ̃/ *adv.* indistinctly; (*également*) without distinction.

individ|u /ɛ̃dividy/ *n.m.* individual. ~**ualiser** *v.t.* individualize. ~**ualiste** *n.m./f.* individualist.

individuel, ~le /ɛ̃dividɥɛl/ *a.* individual; (*propriété, opinion*) personal. ~**lement** *adv.* individually.

indivisible /ɛ̃divizibl/ *a.* indivisible.

Indochine /ɛ̃dɔʃin/ *n.f.* Indo-China.

indolen|t, ~te /ɛ̃dɔlɑ̃, -t/ *a.* indolent. ~**ce** *n.f.* indolence.

indolore /ɛ̃dɔlɔr/ *a.* painless.

Indonésie /ɛ̃dɔnezi/ *n.f.* Indonesia.

indonésien, ~ne /ɛ̃dɔnezjɛ̃, -jɛn/ *a.* & *n.m., f.* Indonesian.

induire /ɛ̃dɥir/ *v.t.* infer (**de**, from). **~ en erreur**, mislead.

indulgen|t, ~te /ɛ̃dylʒɑ̃, -t/ *a.* indulgent; (*clément*) lenient. ~**ce** *n.f.* indulgence; leniency.

industr|ie /ɛ̃dystri/ *n.f.* industry. ~**ialisé** *a.* industrialized.

industriel, ~le /ɛ̃dystrijɛl/ *a.* industrial. —*n.m.* industrialist. ~**lement** *adv.* industrially.

inébranlable /inebrɑ̃labl/ *a.* unshakeable.

inédit, ~e /inedi, -t/ *a.* unpublished; (*fig.*) original.

ineffable /inefabl/ *a.* sublime.

inefficace /inefikas/ *a.* ineffective.

inég|al (*m. pl.* ~**aux**) /inegal, -o/ *a.* unequal; (*irrégulier*) uneven. ~**alé** *a.* unequalled. ~**alité** *n.f.* (*injustice*)

inequality; (*irrégularité*) unevenness; (*différence*) difference (**de**, between).

inéluctable /inelyktabl/ *a.* inescapable.

inept|e /inɛpt/ *a.* inept, absurd. ~**ie** /inɛpsi/ *n.f.* ineptitude.

inépuisable /inepɥizabl/ *a.* inexhaustible.

inert|e /inɛrt/ *a.* inert; (*mort*) lifeless. ~**ie** /inɛrsi/ *n.f.* inertia.

inespéré /inɛspere/ *a.* unhoped for.

inestimable /inɛstimabl/ *a.* priceless.

inévitable /inevitabl/ *a.* inevitable.

inexact, ~e /inɛgza(kt), -akt/ *a.* (*imprécis*) inaccurate; (*incorrect*) incorrect.

inexcusable /inɛkskyzabl/ *a.* unforgivable.

inexistant, ~e /inɛgzistɑ̃, -t/ *a.* nonexistent.

inexorable /inɛgzɔrabl/ *a.* inexorable.

inexpérience /inɛksperjɑ̃s/ *n.f.* inexperience.

inexpli|cable /inɛksplikabl/ *a.* inexplicable. ~**qué** *a.* unexplained.

inextricable /inɛkstrikabl/ *a.* inextricable.

infaillible /ɛ̃fajibl/ *a.* infallible.

infâme /ɛ̃fɑm/ *a.* vile.

infamie /ɛ̃fami/ *n.f.* infamy; (*action*) vile action.

infanterie /ɛ̃fɑ̃tri/ *n.f.* infantry.

infantile /ɛ̃fɑ̃til/ *a.* infantile.

infarctus /ɛ̃farktys/ *n.m.* coronary (thrombosis).

infatigable /ɛ̃fatigabl/ *a.* tireless.

infect /ɛ̃fɛkt/ *a.* revolting.

infect|er /ɛ̃fɛkte/ *v.t.* infect. **s'~er** *v. pr.* become infected. ~**ion** /-ksjɔ̃/ *n.f.* infection; (*odeur*) stench.

infectieu|x, ~se /ɛ̃fɛksjø, -z/ *a.* infectious.

inférieur, ~e /ɛ̃ferjœr/ *a.* (*plus bas*) lower; (*moins bon*) inferior (**à**, to). —*n.m., f.* inferior. **~ à**, (*plus petit que*) smaller than.

infériorité /ɛ̃ferjɔrite/ *n.f.* inferiority.

infern|al (*m. pl.* ~**aux**) /ɛ̃fɛrnal, -o/ *a.* infernal.

infester /ɛ̃fɛste/ *v.t.* infest.

infid|èle /ɛ̃fidɛl/ *a.* unfaithful. ~**élité** *n.f.* unfaithfulness; (*acte*) infidelity.

infiltr|er (s') /(s)ɛ̃filtre/ *v. pr.* **s'~er** (**dans**), (*personnes, idées, etc.*) infiltrate; (*liquide*) percolate. ~**ation** *n.f.* infiltration.

infime /ɛ̃fim/ *a.* tiny.

infini /ɛ̃fini/ *a.* infinite. —*n.m.*

infinity. **à l'~,** endlessly. **~ment**
adv. infinitely.

infinité /ɛ̃finite/ *n.f.* **une ~ de,** an
infinite amount of.

infinitif /ɛ̃finitif/ *n.m.* infinitive.

infirm|e /ɛ̃firm/ *a. & n.m./f.* disabled
(person). **~ité** *n.f.* disability.

infirmer /ɛ̃firme/ *v.t.* invalidate.

infirm|erie /ɛ̃firməri/ *n.f.* sick-bay,
infirmary. **~ier** *n.m.* (male) nurse.
~ière *n.f.* nurse.

inflammable /ɛ̃flamabl/ *a.* (in)flam-
mable.

inflammation /ɛ̃flamɑsjɔ̃/ *n.f.* inflammation.

inflation /ɛ̃flasjɔ̃/ *n.f.* inflation.

inflexible /ɛ̃flɛksibl/ *a.* inflexible.

inflexion /ɛ̃flɛksjɔ̃/ *n.f.* inflexion.

infliger /ɛ̃fliʒe/ *v.t.* inflict; (*sanction*)
impose.

influen|ce /ɛ̃flyɑ̃s/ *n.f.* influence.
~çable *a.* easily influenced. **~cer**
v.t. influence.

influent, ~e /ɛ̃flyɑ̃, -t/ *a.* influential.

influer /ɛ̃flye/ *v.i.* **~ sur,** influence.

informa|teur, ~trice /ɛ̃fɔrmatœr,
-tris/ *n.m., f.* informant.

informaticien, ~ne /ɛ̃fɔrmatisjɛ̃,
-jɛn/ *n.m., f.* computer scientist.

information /ɛ̃fɔrmɑsjɔ̃/ *n.f.* information; (*jurid.*) inquiry. **une ~,** (some)
information; (*nouvelle*) (some) news.
les ~s, the news.

informati|que /ɛ̃fɔrmatik/ *n.f.* com-
puter science; (*techniques*) data processing. **~ser** *v.t.* computerize.

informe /ɛ̃fɔrm/ *a.* shapeless.

informer /ɛ̃fɔrme/ *v.t.* inform (**de,**
about, of). **s'~** *v. pr.* enquire (**de,**
about).

infortun|e /ɛ̃fɔrtyn/ *n.f.* misfortune.
~é, ~ée *a.* wretched; *n.m., f.* wretch.

infraction /ɛ̃fraksjɔ̃/ *n.f.* offence. **~ à,**
breach of.

infranchissable /ɛ̃frɑ̃ʃisabl/ *a.* impassable; (*fig.*) insuperable.

infrarouge /ɛ̃fraruʒ/ *a.* infra-red.

infructueu|x, ~se /ɛ̃fryktɥø, -z/ *a.*
fruitless.

infus|er /ɛ̃fyze/ *v.t./i.* infuse, brew.
~ion *n.f.* herb-tea, infusion.

ingénier (s') /(s)ɛ̃ʒenje/ *v. pr.* **s'~ à,**
strive to.

ingénieur /ɛ̃ʒenjœr/ *n.m.* engineer.

ingén|ieux, ~ieuse /ɛ̃ʒenjø, -z/ *a.* in-
genious. **~iosité** *n.f.* ingenuity.

ingénu /ɛ̃ʒeny/ *a.* naïve.

ingér|er (s') /(s)ɛ̃ʒere/ *v. pr.* **s'~er**

dans, interfere in. **~ence** *n.f.* interference.

ingrat, ~e /ɛ̃gra, -t/ *a.* ungrateful;
(*pénible*) thankless; (*disgracieux*) unattractive. **~itude** /-tityd/ *n.f.* ingratitude.

ingrédient /ɛ̃gredjɑ̃/ *n.m.* ingredient.

inguérissable /ɛ̃gerisabl/ *a.* incurable.

ingurgiter /ɛ̃gyrʒite/ *v.t.* swallow.

inhabité /inabite/ *a.* uninhabited.

inhabituel, ~le /inabitɥɛl/ *a.* unusual.

inhalation /inalɑsjɔ̃/ *n.f.* inhaling.

inhérent, ~e /inerɑ̃, -t/ *a.* inherent
(**à,** in).

inhibition /inibisjɔ̃/ *n.f.* inhibition.

inhospital|ier, ~ière /inɔspitalje,
-jɛr/ *a.* inhospitable.

inhumain, ~e /inymɛ̃, -ɛn/ *a.* inhuman.

inhum|er /inyme/ *v.t.* bury. **~ation**
n.f. burial.

inimaginable /inimaʒinabl/ *a.* unimaginable.

inimitié /inimitje/ *n.f.* enmity.

ininterrompu /inɛ̃terɔ̃py/ *a.* continuous, uninterrupted.

iniqu|e /inik/ *a.* iniquitous. **~ité** *n.f.*
iniquity.

init|ial (*m. pl.* **~iaux**) /inisjal, -jo/ *a.*
initial. **~ialement** *adv.* initially.

initiale /inisjal/ *n.f.* initial.

initiative /inisjativ/ *n.f.* initiative.

init|ier /inisje/ *v.t.* initiate. **s'~ier**
v. pr. become initiated (**à,** into).
~iateur, ~iatrice *n.m., f.* initiator.
~iation *n.f.* initiation.

inject|er /ɛ̃ʒɛkte/ *v.t.* inject. **~é de**
sang, bloodshot. **~ion** /-ksjɔ̃/ *n.f.* injection.

injur|e /ɛ̃ʒyr/ *n.f.* insult. **~ier** *v.t.* in-
sult. **~ieux, ~ieuse** *a.* insulting.

injust|e /ɛ̃ʒyst/ *a.* unjust, unfair. **~ice**
n.f. injustice.

inlassable /ɛ̃lɑsabl/ *a.* tireless.

inné /ine/ *a.* innate.

innocen|t, ~te /inɔsɑ̃, -t/ *a. & n.m., f.*
innocent. **~ce** *n.f.* innocence.

innocenter /inɔsɑ̃te/ *v.t.* (*disculper*)
clear, prove innocent.

innombrable /inɔ̃brabl/ *a.* countless.

innov|er /inɔve/ *v.i.* innovate. **~a-**
teur, ~atrice *n.m., f.* innovator. **~a-**
tion *n.f.* innovation.

inoccupé /inɔkype/ *a.* unoccupied.

inoculer /inɔkyle/ *v.t.* **~ qch. à qn.,**
infect s.o. with sth.

inodore /inɔdɔr/ *a.* odourless.

inoffensi|f, ~ve /inɔfɑ̃sif, -v/ *a.* harmless.

inond|er /inɔ̃de/ *v.t.* flood; (*mouiller*) soak; (*envahir*) inundate (**de,** with). **~é de soleil,** bathed in sunlight. **~ation** *n.f.* flood; (*action*) flooding.

inopérant, ~e /inɔperɑ̃, -t/ *a.* inoperative.

inopportun, ~e /inɔpɔrtœ̃, -yn/ *a.* inopportune.

inoubliable /inublijabl/ *a.* unforgettable.

inouï /inwi/ *a.* incredible.

inoxydable /inɔksidabl/ *a.* (*couteau*) stainless-steel. **acier ~,** stainless steel.

inqualifiable /ɛ̃kalifjabl/ *a.* unspeakable.

inqu|iet, ~iète /ɛ̃kjɛ, ɛ̃kjɛt/ *a.* worried. —*n.m., f.* worrier.

inquiét|er /ɛ̃kjete/ *v.t.* worry. **s'~er** worry (**de,** about). **~ant, ~ante** *a.* worrying.

inquiétude /ɛ̃kjetyd/ *n.f.* anxiety, worry.

inquisition /ɛ̃kizisjɔ̃/ *n.f.* inquisition.

insalubre /ɛ̃salybr/ *a.* unhealthy.

insanité /ɛ̃sanite/ *n.f.* insanity.

insatiable /ɛ̃sasjabl/ *a.* insatiable.

inscription /ɛ̃skripsjɔ̃/ *n.f.* inscription; (*immatriculation*) enrolment.

inscrire† /ɛ̃skrir/ *v.t.* write (down); (*graver, tracer*) inscribe; (*personne*) enrol; (*sur une liste*) put down. **s'~** *v. pr.* put one's name down. **s'~ à,** (*école*) enrol at; (*club, parti*) join; (*examen*) enter for. **s'~ dans le cadre de,** come within the framework of.

insecte /ɛ̃sɛkt/ *n.m.* insect.

insecticide /ɛ̃sɛktisid/ *n.m.* insecticide.

insécurité /ɛ̃sekyrite/ *n.f.* insecurity.

insensé /ɛ̃sɑ̃se/ *a.* senseless.

insensib|le /ɛ̃sɑ̃sibl/ *a.* insensitive (**à,** to); (*graduel*) imperceptible. **~ilité** *n.f.* insensitivity.

inséparable /ɛ̃separabl/ *a.* inseparable.

insérer /ɛ̃sere/ *v.t.* insert. **s'~ dans,** be part of.

insidieu|x, ~se /ɛ̃sidjø, -z/ *a.* insidious.

insigne /ɛ̃siɲ/ *n.m.* badge. **~(s),** (*d'une fonction*) insignia.

insignifian|t, ~te /ɛ̃siɲifjɑ̃, -t/ *a.* insignificant. **~ce** *n.f.* insignificance.

insinuation /ɛ̃sinɥasjɔ̃/ *n.f.* insinuation.

insinuer /ɛ̃sinɥe/ *v.t.* insinuate. **s'~ dans,** penetrate.

insipide /ɛ̃sipid/ *a.* insipid.

insistan|t, ~te /ɛ̃sistɑ̃, -t/ *a.* insistent. **~ce** *n.f.* insistence.

insister /ɛ̃siste/ *v.i.* insist (**pour faire,** on doing). **~ sur,** stress.

insociable /ɛ̃sɔsjabl/ *a.* unsociable.

insolation /ɛ̃sɔlasjɔ̃/ *n.f.* (*méd.*) sunstroke.

insolen|t, ~te /ɛ̃sɔlɑ̃, -t/ *a.* insolent. **~ce** *n.f.* insolence.

insolite /ɛ̃sɔlit/ *a.* unusual.

insoluble /ɛ̃sɔlybl/ *a.* insoluble.

insolvable /ɛ̃sɔlvabl/ *a.* insolvent.

insomnie /ɛ̃sɔmni/ *n.f.* insomnia.

insonoriser /ɛ̃sɔnɔrize/ *v.t.* soundproof.

insoucian|t, ~te /ɛ̃susjɑ̃, -t/ *a.* carefree. **~ce** *n.f.* unconcern.

insoumission /ɛ̃sumisjɔ̃/ *n.f.* rebelliousness.

insoutenable /ɛ̃sutnabl/ *a.* unbearable; (*argument*) untenable.

inspec|ter /ɛ̃spɛkte/ *v.t.* inspect. **~teur, ~trice** *n.m., f.* inspector. **~tion** /-ksjɔ̃/ *n.f.* inspection.

inspir|er /ɛ̃spire/ *v.t.* inspire. —*v.i.* breathe in. **~er à qn.,** inspire s.o. with. **s'~er de,** be inspired by. **~ation** *n.f.* inspiration; (*respiration*) breath.

instab|le /ɛ̃stabl/ *a.* unstable; (*meuble, équilibre*) unsteady. **~ilité** *n.f.* instability; unsteadiness.

install|er /ɛ̃stale/ *v.t.* install; (*gaz, meuble*) put in; (*étagère*) put up; (*équiper*) fit out. **s'~er** *v. pr.* settle (down); (*emménager*) settle in. **s'~er comme,** set o.s. up as. **~ation** *n.f.* installation; (*de local*) fitting out; (*de locataire*) settling in. **~ations** *n.f. pl.* (*appareils*) fittings.

instance /ɛ̃stɑ̃s/ *n.f.* authority; (*prière*) entreaty. **avec ~,** with insistence. **en ~ de,** in the course of, on the point of.

instant /ɛ̃stɑ̃/ *n.m.* moment, instant. **à l'~,** this instant.

instantané /ɛ̃stɑ̃tane/ *a.* instantaneous; (*café*) instant. —*n.m.* snapshot.

instaur|er /ɛ̃stɔre/ *v.t.* institute. **~ation** *n.f.* institution.

instiga|teur, ~trice /ɛ̃stigatœr, -tris/

n.m., f. instigator. ~**tion** /-ɑsjɔ̃/ *n.f.* instigation.

instinct /ɛ̃stɛ̃/ *n.m.* instinct. **d'~,** instinctively.

instincti|f, ~**ve** /ɛ̃stɛ̃ktif, -v/ *a.* instinctive. ~**vement** *adv.* instinctively.

instituer /ɛ̃stitɥe/ *v.t.* establish.

institut /ɛ̃stity/ *n.m.* institute. ~ **de beauté,** beauty parlour. ~ **universitaire de technologie,** polytechnic, technical college.

institu|teur, ~**trice** /ɛ̃stitytœr, -tris/ *n.m., f.* primary-school teacher.

institution /ɛ̃stitysjɔ̃/ *n.f.* institution; (*école*) private school.

instructi|f, ~**ve** /ɛ̃stryktif, -v/ *a.* instructive.

instruction /ɛ̃stryksjɔ̃/ *n.f.* education; (*document*) directive. ~**s,** (*ordres, mode d'emploi*) instructions.

instruire† /ɛ̃strɥir/ *v.t.* teach, educate. ~ **de,** inform of. **s'~** *v. pr.* educate o.s. **s'~ de,** enquire about.

instruit, ~**e** /ɛ̃strɥi, -t/ *a.* educated.

instrument /ɛ̃strymɑ̃/ *n.m.* instrument; (*outil*) implement.

insu /ɛ̃sy/ *n.m.* **à l'~ de,** without the knowledge of.

insubordination /ɛ̃sybɔrdinɑsjɔ̃/ *n.f.* insubordination.

insuffisan|t, ~**te** /ɛ̃syfizɑ̃, -t/ *a.* inadequate; (*en nombre*) insufficient. ~**ce** *n.f.* inadequacy.

insulaire /ɛ̃sylɛr/ *a.* island. —*n.m./f.* islander.

insuline /ɛ̃sylin/ *n.f.* insulin.

insult|e /ɛ̃sylt/ *n.f.* insult. ~**er** *v.t.* insult.

insupportable /ɛ̃sypɔrtabl/ *a.* unbearable.

insurg|er (s') /(s)ɛ̃syrʒe/ *v. pr.* rebel. ~**é,** ~**ée** *a. & n.m., f.* rebel.

insurmontable /ɛ̃syrmɔ̃tabl/ *a.* insurmountable.

insurrection /ɛ̃syrɛksjɔ̃/ *n.f.* insurrection.

intact /ɛ̃takt/ *a.* intact.

intangible /ɛ̃tɑ̃ʒibl/ *a.* intangible.

intarissable /ɛ̃tarisabl/ *a.* inexhaustible.

intégr|al (*m. pl.* ~**aux**) /ɛ̃tegral, -o/ *a.* complete; (*édition*) unabridged. ~**alement** *adv.* in full. ~**alité** *n.f.* whole. **dans son ~alité,** in full.

intègre /ɛ̃tɛgr/ *a.* upright.

intégr|er /ɛ̃tegre/ *v.t.,* **s'~er** *v. pr.* integrate. ~**ation** *n.f.* integration.

intégrité /ɛ̃tegrite/ *n.f.* integrity.

intellect /ɛ̃telɛkt/ *n.m.* intellect. ~**uel,** ~**uelle** *a. & n.m., f.* intellectual.

intelligence /ɛ̃teliʒɑ̃s/ *n.f.* intelligence; (*compréhension*) understanding; (*complicité*) complicity.

intellig|ent, ~**ente** /ɛ̃teliʒɑ̃, -t/ *a.* intelligent. ~**emment** /-amɑ̃/ *adv.* intelligently.

intelligible /ɛ̃teliʒibl/ *a.* intelligible.

intempérance /ɛ̃tɑ̃perɑ̃s/ *n.f.* intemperance.

intempéries /ɛ̃tɑ̃peri/ *n.f. pl.* severe weather.

intempesti|f, ~**ve** /ɛ̃tɑ̃pɛstif, -v/ *a.* untimely.

intenable /ɛ̃tnabl/ *a.* unbearable; (*position*) untenable.

intendan|t, ~**te** /ɛ̃tɑ̃dɑ̃, -t/ *n.m.* (*mil.*) quartermaster. —*n.m., f.* (*scol.*) bursar. ~**ce** *n.f.* (*scol.*) bursar's office.

intens|e /ɛ̃tɑ̃s/ *a.* intense; (*circulation*) heavy. ~**ément** *adv.* intensely. ~**ifier** *v.t.,* **s'~ifier** *v. pr.* intensify. ~**ité** *n.f.* intensity.

intensi|f, ~**ve** /ɛ̃tɑ̃sif, -v/ *a.* intensive.

intenter /ɛ̃tɑ̃te/ *v.t.* ~ **un procès** *ou* **une action,** institute proceedings (**à, contre,** against).

intention /ɛ̃tɑ̃sjɔ̃/ *n.f.* intention (**de faire,** of doing). **à l'~ de qn.,** for s.o. ~**né** /-jɔne/ *a.* **bien/mal** ~**né,** well-/ill-intentioned.

intentionnel, ~**le** /ɛ̃tɑ̃sjɔnɛl/ *a.* intentional.

inter- /ɛ̃tɛr/ *préf.* inter-.

interaction /ɛ̃tɛraksjɔ̃/ *n.f.* interaction.

intercaler /ɛ̃tɛrkale/ *v.t.* insert.

intercéder /ɛ̃tɛrsede/ *v.i.* intercede.

intercept|er /ɛ̃tɛrsɛpte/ *v.t.* intercept. ~**ion** /-psjɔ̃/ *n.f.* interception.

interchangeable /ɛ̃tɛrʃɑ̃ʒabl/ *a.* interchangeable.

interdiction /ɛ̃tɛrdiksjɔ̃/ *n.f.* ban. ~ **de fumer,** no smoking.

interdire† /ɛ̃tɛrdir/ *v.t.* forbid; (*officiellement*) ban, prohibit. ~ **à qn. de faire,** forbid s.o. to do; (*empêcher*) prevent s.o. from doing.

interdit, ~**e** /ɛ̃tɛrdi, -t/ *a.* (*étonné*) nonplussed.

intéressant, ~**e** /ɛ̃terɛsɑ̃, -t/ *a.* interesting; (*avantageux*) attractive.

intéressé, ~**e** /ɛ̃terese/ *a.* (*en cause*) concerned; (*égoïste*) selfish. —*n.m., f.* person concerned.

intéresser /ɛ̃terese/ *v.t.* interest; (*con-*

cerner) concern. **s'~ à,** be interested in.

intérêt /ɛterɛ/ *n.m.* interest; *(égoïsme)* self-interest. **~(s),** *(comm.)* interest. **vous avez ~ à,** it is in your interest to.

interférence /ɛtɛrferɑ̃s/ *n.f.* interference.

intérieur, ~e /ɛterjœr/ *a.* inner, inside; *(vol, politique)* domestic; *(vie, calme)* inner. —*n.m.* interior; *(de boîte, tiroir)* inside. **à l'~ (de),** inside *(fig.)* within. **~ement** *adv.* inwardly.

intérim /ɛterim/ *n.m.* interim. **assurer l'~,** deputize **(de,** for). **par ~,** acting. **~aire** *a.* temporary, interim.

interjection /ɛtɛrʒɛksjɔ̃/ *n.f.* interjection.

interlocu|teur, ~trice /ɛtɛrlɔkytœr, -tris/ *n.m., f.* **son ~teur,** the person one is speaking to.

interloquer /ɛtɛrlɔke/ *v.t.* take aback.

intermède /ɛtɛrmɛd/ *n.m.* interlude.

intermédiaire /ɛtɛrmedjɛr/ *a.* intermediate. —*n.m./f.* intermediary.

interminable /ɛtɛrminabl/ *a.* endless.

intermittent, ~e /ɛtɛrmitɑ̃, -t/ *a.* intermittent.

internat /ɛtɛrna/ *n.m.* boarding-school.

internation|al *(m. pl. ~aux)* /ɛtɛrnasjɔnal, -o/ *a.* international.

interne /ɛtɛrn/ *a.* internal. —*n.m./f.* *(scol.)* boarder.

intern|er /ɛtɛrne/ *v.t.* *(pol.)* intern; *(méd.)* confine. **~ement** *n.m.* *(pol.)* internment.

interpell|er /ɛtɛrpele/ *v.t.* shout to; *(apostropher)* shout at; *(interroger)* question. **~ation** *n.f.* *(pol.)* questioning.

interphone /ɛtɛrfɔn/ *n.m.* intercom.

interposer (s') /(s)ɛtɛrpoze/ *v. pr.* intervene.

interpr|ète /ɛtɛrprɛt/ *n.m./f.* interpreter; *(artiste)* performer. **~étariat** *n.m.* interpreting.

interprét|er /ɛtɛrprete/ *v.t.* interpret; *(jouer)* play; *(chanter)* sing. **~ation** *n.f.* interpretation; *(d'artiste)* performance.

interrogati|f, ~ve /ɛtɛrɔgatif, -v/ *a. & n.m.* interrogative.

interrogatoire /ɛtɛrɔgatwar/ *n.m.* interrogation.

interro|ger /ɛtɛrɔʒe/ *v.t.* question; *(élève)* test. **~gateur, ~gatrice** *a.*

questioning. **~gation** *n.f.* question; *(action)* questioning; *(épreuve)* test.

interr|ompre† /ɛtɛrɔ̃pr/ *v.t.* break off, interrupt; *(personne)* interrupt. **s'~ompre** *v. pr.* break off. **~upteur** *n.m.* switch. **~uption** *n.f.* interruption; *(arrêt)* break.

intersection /ɛtɛrsɛksjɔ̃/ *n.f.* intersection.

interstice /ɛtɛrstis/ *n.m.* crack.

interurbain /ɛtɛryrbɛ̃/ *n.m.* long-distance telephone service.

intervalle /ɛtɛrval/ *n.m.* space; *(temps)* interval. **dans l'~,** in the meantime.

interven|ir† /ɛtɛrvənir/ *v.i.* intervene; *(survenir)* occur; *(méd.)* operate. **~tion** /-vɑ̃sjɔ̃/ *n.f.* intervention; *(méd.)* operation.

intervertir /ɛtɛrvɛrtir/ *v.t.* invert.

interview /ɛtɛrvju/ *n.f.* interview. **~er** /-ve/ *v.t.* interview.

intestin /ɛtɛstɛ̃/ *n.m.* intestine.

intim|e /ɛtim/ *a.* intimate; *(fête, vie)* private; *(dîner)* quiet. —*n.m./f.* intimate friend. **~ement** *adv.* intimately. **~ité** *n.f.* intimacy; *(vie privée)* privacy.

intimid|er /ɛtimide/ *v.t.* intimidate. **~ation** *n.f.* intimidation.

intituler /ɛtityle/ *v.t.* entitle. **s'~** *v. pr.* be entitled.

intolérable /ɛtɔlerabl/ *a.* intolerable.

intoléran|t, ~te /ɛtɔlerɑ̃, -t/ *a.* intolerant. **~ce** *n.f.* intolerance.

intonation /ɛtɔnɑsjɔ̃/ *n.f.* intonation.

intoxiqué, ~e /ɛtɔksike/ *n.m., f.* *(par la drogue, le tabac, etc.)* addict.

intoxi|quer /ɛtɔksike/ *v.t.* poison; *(pol.)* brainwash. **~cation** *n.f.* poisoning; *(pol.)* brainwashing.

intraduisible /ɛtradɥizibl/ *a.* untranslatable.

intraitable /ɛtrɛtabl/ *a.* inflexible.

intransigean|t, ~te /ɛtrɑ̃siʒɑ̃, -t/ *a.* intransigent. **~ce** *n.f.* intransigence.

intransiti|f, ~ve /ɛtrɑ̃zitif, -v/ *a.* intransitive.

intraveineu|x, ~se /ɛtravɛnø, -z/ *a.* intravenous.

intrépide /ɛtrepid/ *a.* fearless.

intrigu|e /ɛtrig/ *n.f.* intrigue; *(théâtre)* plot. **~er** *v.t./i.* intrigue.

intrinsèque /ɛtrɛ̃sɛk/ *a.* intrinsic.

introduction /ɛtrɔdyksjɔ̃/ *n.f.* introduction.

introduire† /ɛtrɔdɥir/ *v.t.* introduce, bring in; *(insérer)* put in, insert. **~ ~**

qn., show s.o. in. **s'~ dans**, get into, enter.

introspecti|f, **~ve** /ɛ̃trɔspɛktif, -v/ *a.* introspective.

introuvable /ɛ̃truvabl/ *a.* that cannot be found.

introverti, **~e** /ɛ̃trɔvɛrti/ *n.m., f.* introvert. —*a.* introverted.

intrus, **~e** /ɛ̃try, -z/ *n.m., f.* intruder. **~ion** /-zjɔ̃/ *n.f.* intrusion.

intuiti|f, **~ve** /ɛ̃tɥitif, -v/ *a.* intuitive.

intuition /ɛ̃tɥisjɔ̃/ *n.f.* intuition.

inusable /inyzabl/ *a.* hard-wearing.

inusité /inyzite/ *a.* uncommon.

inutil|e /inytil/ *a.* useless; (*vain*) needless. **~ement** *adv.* needlessly. **~ité** *n.f.* uselessness.

inutilisable /inytilizabl/ *a.* unusable.

invalid|e /ɛ̃valid/ *a. & n.m.|f.* disabled (person). **~ité** *n.f.* disablement.

invariable /ɛ̃varjabl/ *a.* invariable.

invasion /ɛ̃vazjɔ̃/ *n.f.* invasion.

invectiv|e /ɛ̃vɛktiv/ *n.f.* invective. **~er** *v.t.* abuse.

invend|able /ɛ̃vɑ̃dabl/ *a.* unsaleable. **~u** *a.* unsold.

inventaire /ɛ̃vɑ̃tɛr/ *n.m.* inventory; (*recensement*) survey. **faire l'~ de**, take stock of.

invent|er /ɛ̃vɑ̃te/ *v.t.* invent. **~eur** *n.m.* inventor. **~ion** /ɛ̃vɑ̃sjɔ̃/ *n.f.* invention.

inventi|f, **~ve** /ɛ̃vɑ̃tif, -v/ *a.* inventive.

inverse /ɛ̃vɛrs/ *a.* opposite; (*ordre*) reverse. —*n.m.* reverse. **~ment** /-əmɑ̃/ *adv.* conversely.

invers|er /ɛ̃vɛrse/ *v.t.* reverse, invert. **~ion** *n.f.* inversion.

investigation /ɛ̃vɛstigɑsjɔ̃/ *n.f.* investigation.

invest|ir /ɛ̃vɛstir/ *v.t.* invest. **~issement** *n.m.* (*comm.*) investment.

investiture /ɛ̃vɛstityr/ *n.f.* nomination.

invétéré /ɛ̃vetere/ *a.* inveterate.

invincible /ɛ̃vɛ̃sibl/ *a.* invincible.

invisible /ɛ̃vizibl/ *a.* invisible.

invit|er /ɛ̃vite/ *v.t.* invite (à, to). **~ation** *n.f.* invitation. **~é**, **~ée** *n.m., f.* guest.

invivable /ɛ̃vivabl/ *a.* unbearable.

involontaire /ɛ̃vɔlɔ̃tɛr/ *a.* involuntary.

invoquer /ɛ̃vɔke/ *v.t.* call upon, invoke; (*alléguer*) plead.

invraisembl|able /ɛ̃vrɛsɑ̃blabl/ *a.* improbable; (*incroyable*) incredible. **~ance** *n.f.* improbability.

invulnérable /ɛ̃vylnerabl/ *a.* invulnerable.

iode /jɔd/ *n.m.* iodine.

ira, irait /ira, irɛ/ *voir* **aller**[1].

Irak /irak/ *n.m.* Iraq. **~ien**, **~ienne** *a. & n.m., f.* Iraqi.

Iran /irɑ̃/ *n.m.* Iran. **~ien**, **~ienne** /iranjɛ̃, -jɛn/ *a. & n.m., f.* Iranian.

irascible /irasibl/ *a.* irascible.

iris /iris/ *n.m.* iris.

irlandais, **~e** /irlɑ̃dɛ, -z/ *a.* Irish. —*n.m., f.* Irishman, Irishwoman.

Irlande /irlɑ̃d/ *n.f.* Ireland.

iron|ie /irɔni/ *n.f.* irony. **~ique** *a.* ironic(al).

irraisonné /irɛzɔne/ *a.* irrational.

irréalisable /irealizabl/ *a.* (*projet*) unworkable.

irrécupérable /irekyperabl/ *a.* irretrievable, beyond recall.

irréel, **~le** /ireɛl/ *a.* unreal.

irréfléchi /irefleʃi/ *a.* thoughtless.

irréfutable /irefytabl/ *a.* irrefutable.

irrégul|ier, **~ière** /iregylje, -jɛr/ *a.* irregular. **~arité** *n.f.* irregularity.

irrémédiable /iremedjabl/ *a.* irreparable.

irremplaçable /irɑ̃plasabl/ *a.* irreplaceable.

irréparable /ireparabl/ *a.* beyond repair.

irréprochable /ireprɔʃabl/ *a.* flawless.

irrésistible /irezistibl/ *a.* irresistible; (*drôle*) hilarious.

irrésolu /irezɔly/ *a.* indecisive.

irrespirable /irɛspirabl/ *a.* stifling.

irresponsable /irɛspɔ̃sabl/ *a.* irresponsible.

irréversible /irevɛrsibl/ *a.* irreversible.

irrévocable /irevɔkabl/ *a.* irrevocable.

irrigation /irigɑsjɔ̃/ *n.f.* irrigation.

irriguer /irige/ *v.t.* irrigate.

irrit|er /irite/ *v.t.* irritate. **s'~er de**, be annoyed at. **~able** *a.* irritable. **~ation** *n.f.* irritation.

irruption /irypsjɔ̃/ *n.f.* **faire ~ dans**, burst into.

Islam /islam/ *n.m.* Islam.

islamique /islamik/ *a.* Islamic.

islandais, **~e** /islɑ̃dɛ, -z/ *a.* Icelandic. —*n.m., f.* Icelander. —*n.m.* (*lang.*) Icelandic.

Islande /islɑ̃d/ *n.f.* Iceland.

isolé /izɔle/ *a.* isolated. **~ment** *adv.* in isolation.

isol|er /izɔle/ *v.t.* isolate; (*électr.*) insulate. **s'~er** *v. pr.* isolate o.s. **~ant** *n.m.* insulating material. **~ation** *n.f.* insulation. **~ement** *n.m.* isolation.

isoloir /izɔlwar/ *n.m.* polling booth.

Isorel /izɔrɛl/ *n.m.* (P.) hardboard.

isotope /izɔtɔp/ *n.m.* isotope.

Israël /israɛl/ *n.m.* Israel.

israélien, ~ne /israeljɛ̃, -jɛn/ *a.* & *n.m.,f.* Israeli.

israélite /israelit/ *a.* Jewish. —*n.m./f.* Jew, Jewess.

issu /isy/ *a.* **être ~ de**, come from.

issue /isy/ *n.f.* exit; (*résultat*) outcome;

(*fig.*) solution. **à l'~ de**, at the conclusion of. **rue** *ou* **voie sans ~**, dead end.

isthme /ism/ *n.m.* isthmus.

Italie /itali/ *n.f.* Italy.

italien, ~ne /italjɛ̃, -jɛn/ *a.* & *n.m.,f.* Italian. —*n.m.* (*lang.*) Italian.

italique /italik/ *n.m.* italics.

itinéraire /itinerɛr/ *n.m.* itinerary, route.

itinérant, ~e /itinerɑ̃, -t/ *a.* itinerant.

ivoire /ivwar/ *n.m.* ivory.

ivr|e /ivr/ *a.* drunk. **~esse** *n.f.* drunkenness. **~ogne** *n.m.* drunk(ard).

J

j' /ʒ/ *voir* **je.**
jacasser /ʒakase/ *v.i.* chatter.
jachère (en) /(ã)ʒaʃɛr/ *adv.* fallow.
jacinthe /ʒasɛ̃t/ *n.f.* hyacinth.
jade /ʒad/ *n.m.* jade.
jadis /ʒadis/ *adv.* long ago.
jaillir /ʒajir/ *v.i.* (*liquide*) spurt (out); (*lumière*) stream out; (*apparaître, fuser*) burst forth.
jais /ʒɛ/ *n.m.* **(noir) de ~,** jet-black.
jalon /ʒalɔ̃/ *n.m.* (*piquet*) marker. **~ner** /-ɔne/ *v.t.* mark (out).
jalou|x, ~se /ʒalu, -z/ *a.* jealous. **~ser** *v.t.* be jealous of. **~sie** *n.f.* jealousy; (*store*) (venetian) blind.
jamais /ʒamɛ/ *adv.* ever. **(ne) ~,** never. **il ne boit ~,** he never drinks. **à ~,** for ever. **si ~,** if ever.
jambe /ʒãb/ *n.f.* leg.
jambon /ʒãbɔ̃/ *n.m.* ham. **~neau** (*pl.* **~neaux**) /-ɔno/ *n.m.* knuckle of ham.
jante /ʒãt/ *n.f.* rim.
janvier /ʒãvje/ *n.m.* January.
Japon /ʒapɔ̃/ *n.m.* Japan.
japonais, ~e /japɔnɛ, -z/ *a. & n.m., f.* Japanese. —*n.m.* (*lang.*) Japanese.
japper /ʒape/ *v.i.* yelp.
jaquette /ʒakɛt/ *n.f.* (*de livre, femme*) jacket; (*d'homme*) morning coat.
jardin /ʒardɛ̃/ *n.m.* garden. **~ d'enfants,** nursery (school). **~ public,** public park.
jardin|er /ʒardine/ *v.i.* garden. **~age** *n.m.* gardening. **~ier, ~ière** *n.m., f.* gardener; *n.f.* (*meuble*) plant-stand. **~ière de légumes,** mixed vegetables.
jargon /ʒargɔ̃/ *n.m.* jargon.
jarret /ʒarɛ/ *n.m.* back of the knee.
jarretelle /ʒartɛl/ *n.f.* suspender; (*Amer.*) garter.
jarretière /ʒartjɛr/ *n.f.* garter.
jaser /ʒaze/ *v.i.* jabber.
jasmin /ʒasmɛ̃/ *n.m.* jasmine.
jatte /ʒat/ *n.f.* bowl.
jaug|e /ʒoʒ/ *n.f.* capacity; (*de navire*) tonnage; (*compteur*) gauge. **~er** *v.t.* gauge.
jaun|e /ʒon/ *a. & n.m.* yellow. **~e d'œuf,** (egg) yolk. **~ir** *v.t./i.* turn yellow.
jaunisse /ʒonis/ *n.f.* jaundice.
javelot /ʒavlo/ *n.m.* javelin.

jazz /dʒaz/ *n.m.* jazz.
je, j'* /ʒə, ʒ/ *pron.* I.
jean /dʒin/ *n.m.* jeans.
jeep /(d)ʒip/ *n.f.* jeep.
jerrycan /(d)ʒerikan/ *n.m.* jerrycan.
jersey /ʒɛrzɛ/ *n.m.* jersey.
Jersey /ʒɛrzɛ/ *n.f.* Jersey.
Jésus /ʒezy/ *n.m.* Jesus.
jet¹ /ʒɛ/ *n.m.* throw; (*de liquide, vapeur*) jet; (*de lumière*) flash. **~ d'eau,** fountain.
jet² /dʒɛt/ *n.m.* (*avion*) jet.
jetée /ʒte/ *n.f.* pier.
jeter /ʒte/ *v.t.* throw; (*au rebut*) throw away; (*regard, ancre, lumière*) cast; (*cri*) utter; (*bases*) lay. **~ un coup d'œil,** have *ou* take a look (**à,** at). **se ~ contre,** (*heurter*) bash into. **se ~ dans,** (*fleuve*) flow into. **se ~ sur,** (*se ruer sur*) rush at.
jeton /ʒtɔ̃/ *n.m.* token; (*pour compter*) counter.
jeu (*pl.* **~x**) /ʒø/ *n.m.* game; (*amusement*) play; (*au casino etc.*) gambling; (*théâtre*) acting; (*série*) set; (*de lumière, ressort*) play. **en ~,** (*honneur*) at stake; (*forces*) at work. **~ de cartes,** (*paquet*) pack of cards. **~ d'échecs,** (*boîte*) chess set. **~ de mots,** pun. **~ télévisé,** television quiz.
jeudi /ʒødi/ *n.m.* Thursday.
jeun (à) /(a)ʒœ̃/ *adv.* without food.
jeune /ʒœn/ *a.* young; (*cadet*) younger. —*n.m./f.* young person. **~ fille,** girl. **~s mariés,** newly-weds. **les ~s,** young people.
jeûn|e /ʒøn/ *n.m.* fast. **~er** *v.i.* fast.
jeunesse /ʒœnɛs/ *n.f.* youth; (*apparence*) youthfulness. **la ~,** (*jeunes*) the young.
joaill|ier, ~ière /ʒɔaje, -jɛr/ *n.m., f.* jeweller. **~erie** *n.f.* jewellery; (*magasin*) jeweller's shop.
jockey /ʒɔkɛ/ *n.m.* jockey.
joie /ʒwa/ *n.f.* joy.
joindre† /ʒwɛ̃dr/ *v.t.* join; (*mains, pieds*) put together; (*efforts*) combine; (*dans une enveloppe*) enclose. **se ~ à,** join.
joint, ~e /ʒwɛ̃, -t/ *a.* (*efforts*) joint; (*pieds*) together. —*n.m.* joint; (*ligne*)

join; (*de robinet*) washer. ~**ure** /-tyr/ *n.f.* joint; (*ligne*) join.

joker /ʒɔkɛr/ *n.m.* (*carte*) joker.

joli /ʒɔli/ *a.* pretty, nice; (*somme, profit*) nice. **c'est bien** ~ **mais**, that is all very well but. ~**ment** *adv.* prettily; (*très: fam.*) awfully.

jonc /ʒɔ̃/ *n.m.* (bul)rush.

joncher /ʒɔ̃ʃe/ *v.t.* litter (**de**, with).

jonction /ʒɔ̃ksjɔ̃/ *n.f.* junction.

jongl|er /ʒɔ̃gle/ *v.i.* juggle. ~**eur**, ~**euse** *n.m.,*, *f.* juggler.

jonquille /ʒɔ̃kij/ *n.f.* daffodil.

Jordanie /ʒɔrdani/ *n.f.* Jordan.

joue /ʒu/ *n.f.* cheek.

jouer /ʒwe/ *v.t.i.* play; (*théâtre*) act; (*au casino etc.*) gamble; (*fonctionner*) work; (*film, pièce*) put on; (*cheval*) back; (*être important*) count. ~ **à** *ou* **de,** play. ~ **la comédie**, put on an act. **se** ~ **de**, make light of.

jouet /ʒwɛ/ *n.m.* toy; (*personne: fig.*) plaything; (*victime*) victim.

joueu|r, ~**se** /ʒwœr, -øz/ *n.m.,*, *f.* player; (*parieur*) gambler.

joufflu /ʒufly/ *a.* chubby-cheeked; (*visage*) chubby.

joug /ʒu/ *n.m.* yoke.

jouir /ʒwir/ *v.i.* ~ **de,** enjoy.

jouissance /ʒwisɑ̃s/ *n.f.* pleasure; (*usage*) use.

joujou (*pl.* ~**x**) /ʒuʒu/ *n.m.* (*fam.*) toy.

jour /ʒur/ *n.m.* day; (*opposé à nuit*) day(time); (*lumière*) daylight; (*aspect*) light; (*ouverture*) gap. **de nos** ~**s**, nowadays. **du** ~ **au lendemain**, overnight. **il fait** ~, it is (day)light. ~ **chômé** *ou* **férié**, public holiday. ~ **de fête,** holiday. ~ **ouvrable,** ~ **de travail,** working day. **mettre à** ~, update. **mettre au** ~, uncover.

journ|al (*pl.* ~**aux**) /ʒurnal, -o/ *n.m.* (news)paper; (*spécialisé*) journal; (*intime*) diary; (*radio*) news. ~**al de bord,** log-book.

journal|ier, ~**ière** /ʒurnalje, -jɛr/ *a.* daily.

journalis|te /ʒurnalist/ *n.m.f.* journalist. ~**me** *n.m.* journalism.

journée /ʒurne/ *n.f.* day.

journellement /ʒurnɛlmɑ̃/ *adv.* daily.

jov|ial (*m. pl.* ~**iaux**) /ʒɔvjal, -jo/ *a.* jovial.

joyau (*pl.* ~**x**) /ʒwajo/ *n.m.* gem.

joyeu|x, ~**se** /ʒwajø, -z/ *a.* merry, joyful. ~**x anniversaire,** happy birthday. ~**sement** *adv.* merrily.

jubilé /ʒybile/ *n.m.* jubilee.

jubil|er /ʒybile/ *v.i.* be jubilant. ~**ation** *n.f.* jubilation.

jucher /ʒyʃe/ *v.t.,* **se** ~ *v. pr.* perch.

judaï|que /ʒydaik/ *a.* Jewish. ~**sme** *n.m.* Judaism.

judas /ʒyda/ *n.m.* peep-hole.

judiciaire /ʒydisjɛr/ *a.* judicial.

judicieu|x, ~**se** /ʒydisjø, -z/ *a.* judicious.

judo /ʒydo/ *n.m.* judo.

juge /ʒyʒ/ *n.m.* judge; (*arbitre*) referee. ~ **de paix,** Justice of the Peace. ~ **de touche,** linesman.

jugé (au) /(o)ʒyʒe/ *adv.* by guesswork.

jugement /ʒyʒmɑ̃/ *n.m.* judgement; (*criminel*) sentence.

jugeote /ʒyʒɔt/ *n.f.* (*fam.*) gumption, common sense.

juger /ʒyʒe/ *v.t.i.* judge; (*estimer*) consider (**que,** that). ~ **de,** judge.

juguler /ʒygyle/ *v.t.* stifle, check.

jui|f, ~**ve** /ʒɥif, -v/ *a.* Jewish. —*n.m., f.* Jew, Jewess.

juillet /ʒɥijɛ/ *n.m.* July.

juin /ʒɥɛ̃/ *n.m.* June.

jum|eau, ~**elle** (*m. pl.* ~**eaux**) /ʒymo, -ɛl/ *a. & n.m., f.* twin. ~**elage** *n.m.* twinning. ~**eler** *v.t.* (*villes*) twin.

jumelles /ʒymɛl/ *n.f. pl.* binoculars.

jument /ʒymɑ̃/ *n.f.* mare.

jungle /ʒœ̃gl/ *n.f.* jungle.

junte /ʒœ̃t/ *n.f.* junta.

jupe /ʒyp/ *n.f.* skirt.

junior /ʒynjɔr/ *n.m.f. & a.* junior.

jupon /ʒypɔ̃/ *n.m.* slip, petticoat.

juré, ~**e** /ʒyre/ *n.m., f.* juror. —*a.* sworn.

jurer /ʒyre/ *v.t.* swear (**que,** that). —*v.i.* (*pester*) swear; (*contraster*) clash (**avec,** with). ~ **de qch./de faire,** swear to sth./to do.

juridiction /ʒyridiksjɔ̃/ *n.f.* jurisdiction; (*tribunal*) court of law.

juridique /ʒyridik/ *a.* legal.

juriste /ʒyrist/ *n.m.f.* legal expert.

juron /ʒyrɔ̃/ *n.m.* swear-word.

jury /ʒyri/ *n.m.* jury.

jus /ʒy/ *n.m.* juice; (*de viande*) gravy; (*café: fam.*) coffee.

jusque /ʒysk(ə)/ *prép.* **jusqu'à,** (up) to, as far as; (*temps*) until, till; (*limite*) up to; (*y compris*) even. **jusqu'à ce que,** until. **jusqu'en,** until. **jusqu'où?,** how far? ~ **dans,** ~ **sur,** as far as.

juste /ʒyst/ *a.* fair, just; (*légitime*) just; (*correct, exact*) right; (*vrai*) true; (*vêtement*) tight; (*quantité*) on the

short side. —*adv*. rightly, correctly;
(*chanter*) in tune; (*seulement, exactement*) just. (**un peu**) ~, (*calculer,
mesurer*) a bit fine *ou* close. **au** ~,
exactly. **c'était** ~, (*presque raté*) it
was a close thing.

justement /ʒystəmã/ *adv*. just; (*avec
justice ou justesse*) justly.

justesse /ʒystɛs/ *n.f.* accuracy. **de** ~,
just, narrowly.

justice /ʒystis/ *n.f.* justice; (*autorités*)
law; (*tribunal*) court.

justif|ier /ʒystifje/ *v.t.* justify. —*v.i.*
~**ier de**, prove. **se** ~**ier** *v. pr.* justify
o.s. ~**iable** *a*. justifiable. ~**ication**
n.f. justification.

juteu|x, ~se /ʒytø, -z/ *a*. juicy.

juvénile /ʒyvenil/ *a*. youthful.

juxtaposer /ʒykstapoze/ *v.t.* juxtapose.

K

kaki /kaki/ *a. invar.* & *n.m.* khaki.
kaléidoscope /kaleidɔskɔp/ *n.m.* kaleidoscope.
kangourou /kɑ̃guru/ *n.m.* kangaroo.
karaté /karate/ *n.m.* karate.
kart /kart/ *n.m.* go-cart.
kascher /kaʃɛr/ *a. invar.* kosher.
képi /kepi/ *n.m.* kepi.
kermesse /kɛrmɛs/ *n.f.* fair; (*de charité*) fête.
kérosène /kerozɛn/ *n.m.* kerosene, aviation fuel.
kibboutz /kibuts/ *n.m.* kibbutz.
kidnapp|er /kidnape/ *v.t.* kidnap. **~eur**, **~euse** *n.m.*, *f.* kidnapper.

kilo /kilo/ *n.m.* kilo.
kilogramme /kilɔgram/ *n.m.* kilogram.
kilohertz /kilɔɛrts/ *n.m.* kilohertz.
kilom|ètre /kilɔmɛtr/ *n.m.* kilometre. **~étrage** *n.m.* (*approx.*) mileage.
kilowatt /kilɔwat/ *n.m.* kilowatt.
kinésithérapie /kineziterapi/ *n.f.* physiotherapy.
kiosque /kjɔsk/ *n.m.* kiosk. **~ à musique,** bandstand.
klaxon /klaksɔn/ *n.m.* (P.) (*auto.*) horn. **~ner** /-e/ *v.i.* sound one's horn.
knock-out /nɔkawt/ *n.m.* knock-out.
kyste /kist/ *n.m.* cyst.

L

l', la /l, la/ *voir* **le.**

-là /la/ *adv. (après un nom précédé de ce, cette, etc.)* **cet homme-là,** that man. **ces maisons-là,** those houses.

là /la/ *adv.* there; *(ici)* here; *(chez soi)* in; *(temps)* then. **c'est ~ que,** this is where. **~ où,** where. **~-bas** *adv.* over there. **~-dedans** *adv.* inside, in there. **~-dessous** *adv.* underneath, under there. **~dessus** *adv.* on there. **~haut** *adv.* up there; *(à l'étage)* upstairs.

label /labɛl/ *n.m. (comm.)* seal.

labeur /labœr/ *n.m.* toil.

labo /labo/ *n.m. (fam.)* lab.

laboratoire /labɔratwar/ *n.m.* laboratory.

laborieu|x, ~se /labɔrjø, -z/ *a.* laborious; *(personne)* industrious. **classes/masses ~ses,** working classes/masses.

labour /labur/ *n.m.* ploughing; *(Amer.)* plowing. **~er** *v.t./i.* plough; *(Amer.)* plow. **être ~é,** *(déchiré)* be furrowed. **~eur** *n.m.* ploughman; *(Amer.)* plowman.

labyrinthe /labirɛ̃t/ *n.m.* maze.

lac /lak/ *n.m.* lake.

lacer /lase/ *v.t.* lace up.

lacérer /lasere/ *v.t.* tear (up).

lacet /lasɛ/ *n.m.* (shoe-)lace; *(de route)* sharp bend, zigzag.

lâche /lɑʃ/ *a.* cowardly; *(détendu)* loose. —*n.m./f.* coward. **~ment** *adv.* in a cowardly way.

lâcher /lɑʃe/ *v.t.* let go of; *(abandonner)* give up; *(laisser)* leave; *(libérer)* release; *(parole)* utter; *(desserrer)* loosen. —*v.i.* give way. **~ prise,** let go.

lâcheté /lɑʃte/ *n.f.* cowardice.

laconique /lakɔnik/ *a.* laconic.

lacté /lakte/ *a.* milk.

lacune /lakyn/ *n.f.* gap.

ladite /ladit/ *voir* **ledit.**

lagune /lagyn/ *n.f.* lagoon.

laïc /laik/ *n.m.* layman.

laid, ~e /lɛ, lɛd/ *a.* ugly; *(action)* vile. **~eur** /lɛdœr/ *n.f.* ugliness.

lain|e /lɛn/ *n.f.* wool. **de ~e,** woollen. **~age** *n.m.* woollen garment.

laïque /laik/ *a.* secular; *(habit, per-sonne)* lay. —*n.m./f.* layman, laywoman.

laisse /lɛs/ *n.f.* lead, leash.

laisser /lese/ *v.t.* leave. **~ qn. faire,** let s.o. do. **~ qch. à qn.,** let s.o. have sth., leave s.o. sth. **~ tomber,** drop. **se ~ aller,** let o.s. go. **~-aller** *n.m. invar.* carelessness. **laissez-passer** *n.m. invar.* pass.

lait /lɛ/ *n.m.* milk. **frère/sœur de ~,** foster-brother/-sister. **~age** /lɛtaʒ/ *n.m.* milk product. **~eux, ~euse** /lɛtø, -z/ *a.* milky.

lait|ier, ~ière /letje, lɛtjɛr/ *a.* dairy. —*n.m., f.* dairyman, dairywoman. —*n.m. (livreur)* milkman. **~erie** /lɛtri/ *n.f.* dairy.

laiton /lɛtɔ̃/ *n.m.* brass.

laitue /lety/ *n.f.* lettuce.

lama /lama/ *n.m.* llama.

lambeau *(pl. ~x)* /lãbo/ *n.m.* shred. **en ~x,** in shreds.

lambin, ~e /lãbɛ̃, -in/ *a. (fam.)* sluggish. —*n.m., f. (fam.)* dawdler.

lambris /lãbri/ *n.m.* panelling.

lame /lam/ *n.f.* blade; *(lamelle)* strip; *(vague)* wave. **~ de fond,** ground swell.

lamelle /lamɛl/ *n.f.* (thin) strip.

lamentable /lamãtabl/ *a.* deplorable.

lament|er (se) /(sə)lamãte/ *v. pr.* moan. **~ation(s)** *n.f. (pl.)* moaning.

laminé /lamine/ *a.* laminated.

lampadaire /lãpadɛr/ *n.m.* standard lamp; *(de rue)* street lamp.

lampe /lãp/ *n.f.* lamp; *(de radio)* valve; *(Amer.)* vacuum tube. **~ (de poche),** torch; *(Amer.)* flashlight. **~ de chevet,** bedside lamp.

lampion /lãpjɔ̃/ *n.m.* (Chinese) lantern.

lance /lãs/ *n.f.* spear; *(de tournoi)* lance; *(tuyau)* hose; *(bout de tuyau)* nozzle.

lanc|er /lãse/ *v.t.* throw; *(avec force)* hurl; *(navire, idée, personne)* launch; *(émettre)* give out; *(regard)* cast; *(moteur)* start. **se ~er** *v. pr. (sport)* gain momentum; *(se précipiter)* rush. **se ~er dans,** launch into. —*n.m.* throw; *(action)* throwing. **~ement** *n.m.* throwing; *(de navire)* launching. **~e-missiles** *n.m. invar.* missile launcher. **~e-pierres** *n.m. invar.* catapult.

lancinant, ~e /lãsinã, -t/ *a.* haunting; (*douleur*) throbbing.

landau /lãdo/ *n.m.* pram; (*Amer.*) baby carriage.

lande /lãd/ *n.f.* heath, moor.

langage /lãgaʒ/ *n.m.* language.

lang|e /lãʒ/ *n.f.* baby's blanket. **~er** *v.t.* (*bébé*) change.

langoureu|x, ~se /lãgurø, -z/ *a.* languid.

langoust|e /lãgust/ *n.f.* (spiny) lobster. **~ine** *n.f.* (Norway) lobster.

langue /lãg/ *n.f.* tongue; (*idiome*) language. **de ~ anglaise/française,** English-/French-speaking. **~ maternelle,** mother tongue.

languette /lãgɛt/ *n.f.* tongue.

langueur /lãgœr/ *n.f.* languor.

langu|ir /lãgir/ *v.i.* languish. **~issant, ~issante** *a.* languid.

lanière /lanjɛr/ *n.f.* strap.

lanterne /lãtɛrn/ *n.f.* lantern; (*électrique*) lamp; (*de voiture*) sidelight.

laper /lape/ *v.t./i.* lap.

lapider /lapide/ *v.t.* stone.

lapin /lapɛ̃/ *n.m.* rabbit.

laps /laps/ *n.m.* **~ de temps,** lapse of time.

lapsus /lapsys/ *n.m.* slip (of the tongue).

laquais /lakɛ/ *n.m.* lackey.

laqu|e /lak/ *n.f.* lacquer. **~er** *v.t.* lacquer.

laquelle /lakɛl/ *voir* **lequel.**

larcin /larsɛ̃/ *n.m.* theft.

lard /lar/ *n.m.* (pig's) fat; (*viande*) bacon.

large /larʒ/ *a.* wide, broad; (*grand*) large; (*non borné*) (*généreux*) generous. *—adv.* (*mesurer*) broadly; (*voir*) big. *—n.m.* **de ~,** (*mesure*) wide. **le ~,** (*mer*) the open sea. **au ~ de,** (*en face de: naut.*) off. **~ d'esprit,** broad-minded. **~ment** /-əmã/ *adv.* widely; (*ouvrir*) wide; (*amplement*) amply; (*généreusement*) generously; (*au moins*) easily.

largesse /larʒɛs/ *n.f.* generosity.

largeur /larʒœr/ *n.f.* width, breadth; (*fig.*) breadth.

larguer /large/ *v.t.* drop. **~ les amarres,** cast off.

larme /larm/ *n.f.* tear; (*goutte: fam.*) drop.

larmoyant, ~e /larmwajã, -t/ *a.* tearful.

larron /larɔ̃/ *n.m.* thief.

larve /larv/ *n.f.* larva.

larvé /larve/ *a.* latent.

laryngite /larɛ̃ʒit/ *n.f.* laryngitis.

larynx /larɛ̃ks/ *n.m.* larynx.

las, ~se /lɑ, lɑs/ *a.* weary.

lascar /laskar/ *n.m.* (*fam.*) fellow.

lasci|f, ~ve /lasif, -v/ *a.* lascivious.

laser /lazɛr/ *n.m.* laser.

lasse /lɑs/ *voir* **las.**

lasser /lɑse/ *v.t.* weary. **se ~** *v. pr.* weary (**de,** of).

lassitude /lɑsityd/ *n.f.* weariness.

lasso /laso/ *n.m.* lasso.

latent, ~e /latã, -t/ *a.* latent.

latér|al (*m. pl.* **~aux**) /lateral, -o/ *a.* lateral.

latin, ~e /latɛ̃, -in/ *a. & n.m., f.* Latin. *—n.m.* (*lang.*) Latin.

latitude /latityd/ *n.f.* latitude.

latrines /latrin/ *n.f. pl.* latrine(s).

latte /lat/ *n.f.* lath; (*de plancher*) board.

lauréat, ~e /lɔrea, -t/ *a.* prizewinning. *—n.m.,f.* prize-winner.

laurier /lɔrje/ *n.m.* laurel; (*culin.*) bay-leaves.

lavable /lavabl/ *a.* washable.

lavabo /lavabo/ *n.m.* wash-basin. **~s,** toilet(s).

lavage /lavaʒ/ *n.m.* washing. **~ de cerveau,** brainwashing.

lavande /lavãd/ *n.f.* lavender.

lave /lav/ *n.f.* lava.

lav|er /lave/ *v.t.* wash; (*injure etc.*) avenge. **se ~er** *v. pr.* wash (o.s.) (**se**) **~er de,** clear (o.s.) of. **~e-glace** *n.m.* windscreen washer. **~eur de carreaux,** window-cleaner. **~e-vaisselle** *n.m. invar.* dishwasher.

laverie /lavri/ *n.f.* **~ (automatique),** launderette; (*Amer.*) laundromat.

lavette /lavɛt/ *n.f.* dishcloth.

lavoir /lavwar/ *n.m.* wash-house.

laxati|f, ~ve /laksatif, -v/ *a. & n.m.* laxative.

laxisme /laksism/ *n.m.* laxity.

layette /lɛjɛt/ *n.f.* baby clothes.

le *ou* **l'*, la** *ou* **l'*** (*pl.* **les**) /lə, l, la, le/ *article* the; (*mesure*) a, per. *—pron.* (*homme*) him; (*femme*) her; (*chose, animal*) it. **les** *pron.* them. **aimer ~ thé/la France,** like tea/France. **~ matin,** in the morning. **il sort ~ mardi,** he goes out on Tuesdays. **levez ~ bras,** raise your arm. **je ~ connais,** I know him. **je ~ sais,** I know (it).

lécher /leʃe/ *v.t.* lick.

lèche-vitrines /lɛʃvitrin/ *n.m.* **faire du ~,** (*fam.*) go window-shopping.

leçon /ləsɔ̃/ *n.f.* lesson. **faire la ~ à,** lecture.

lec|teur, ~trice /lɛktœr, -tris/ *n.m., f.* reader; (*univ.*) foreign language assistant.

lecture /lɛktyr/ *n.f.* reading.

ledit, ladite (*pl.* **lesdit(e)s**) /lədi, ladit, ledi(t)/ *a.* the aforesaid.

lég|al (*m. pl.* **~aux**) /legal, -o/ *a.* legal. **~alement** *adv.* legally. **~aliser** *v.t.* legalize. **~alité** *n.f.* legality; (*loi*) law.

légation /legɑsjɔ̃/ *n.f.* legation.

légend|e /leʒɑ̃d/ *n.f.* (*histoire, inscription*) legend. **~aire** *a.* legendary.

lég|er, ~ère /leʒe, -ɛr/ *a.* light; (*bruit, faute, maladie*) slight; (*café, argument*) weak; (*imprudent*) thoughtless; (*frivole*) fickle. **à la ~ère,** thoughtlessly. **~èrement** /-ɛrmɑ̃/ *adv.* lightly; (*agir*) thoughtlessly; (*un peu*) slightly. **~èreté** /-ɛrte/ *n.f.* lightness; thoughtlessness.

légion /leʒjɔ̃/ *n.f.* legion. **~naire** /-jɔnɛr/ *n.m.* (*mil.*) legionnaire.

législati|f, ~ve /leʒislatif, -v/ *a.* legislative.

législation /leʒislɑsjɔ̃/ *n.f.* legislation.

legislature /leʒislatyr/ *n.f.* term of office.

légitim|e /leʒitim/ *a.* legitimate. **en état de ~e défense,** acting in self-defence. **~ité** *n.f.* legitimacy.

legs /lɛg/ *n.m.* legacy.

léguer /lege/ *v.t.* bequeath.

légume /legym/ *n.m.* vegetable.

lendemain /lɑ̃dmɛ̃/ *n.m.* **le ~,** the next day, the day after; (*fig.*) the future. **le ~ de,** the day after. **le ~ matin/soir,** the next morning/evening.

lent, ~e /lɑ̃, lɑ̃t/ *a.* slow. **~ement** /lɑ̃tmɑ̃/ *adv.* slowly. **~eur** /lɑ̃tœr/ *n.f.* slowness.

lentille[1] /lɑ̃tij/ *n.f.* (*plante*) lentil.

lentille[2] /lɑ̃tij/ *n.f.* (*verre*) lens.

léopard /leɔpar/ *n.m.* leopard.

lèpre /lɛpr/ *n.f.* leprosy.

lépreu|x, ~se /leprø, -z/ *a.* leprous. —*n.m., f.* leper.

lequel, laquelle (*pl.* **lesquel(le)s**) /ləkɛl, lakɛl, lekɛl/ *pron.* (*à + lequel = auquel, à + lesquel(le)s = aux-quel(le)s; de + lequel = duquel, de + lesquel(le)s = desquel(le)s*) which; (*interrogatif*) which (one); (*personne*) who; (*complément indirect*) whom.

les /le/ *voir* **le.**

lesbienne /lɛsbjɛn/ *n.f.* lesbian.

léser /leze/ *v.t.* wrong.

lésiner /lezine/ *v.i.* be stingy (**sur,** with).

lésion /lezjɔ̃/ *n.f.* lesion.

lesquels, lesquelles /lekɛl/ *voir* **lequel.**

lessiv|e /lesiv/ *n.f.* washing-powder; (*linge, action*) washing. **~er** *v.t.* wash.

lest /lɛst/ *n.m.* ballast. **~er** *v.t.* ballast.

leste /lɛst/ *a.* nimble; (*grivois*) coarse.

létharg|ie /letarʒi/ *n.f.* lethargy. **~ique** *a.* lethargic.

lettre /lɛtr/ *n.f.* letter. **à la ~,** literally. **en toutes ~s,** in full. **~ exprès,** express letter. **les ~s,** (*univ.*) (the) arts.

lettré /letre/ *a.* well-read.

leucémie /løsemi/ *n.f.* leukaemia.

leur /lœr/ *a.* (*f. invar.*) their. —*pron.* (to) them. **le ~, la ~, les ~s,** theirs.

leurr|e /lœr/ *n.m.* illusion; (*duperie*) deception. **~er** *v.t.* delude.

levé /ləve/ *a.* (*debout*) up.

levée /ləve/ *n.f.* lifting; (*de courrier*) collection; (*de troupes, d'impôts*) levying.

lever /ləve/ *v.t.* lift (up), raise; (*interdiction*) lift; (*séance*) close; (*armée, impôts*) levy. —*v.i.* (*pâte*) rise. **se ~** *v. pr.* get up; (*soleil, rideau*) rise; (*jour*) break. —*n.m.* **~ du jour,** daybreak. **~ du rideau,** (*théâtre*) curtain (up). **~ du soleil,** sunrise.

levier /ləvje/ *n.m.* lever; (*pour soulever*) crowbar.

lèvre /lɛvr/ *n.f.* lip.

lévrier /levrije/ *n.m.* greyhound.

levure /ləvyr/ *n.f.* yeast.

lexicographie /lɛksikɔgrafi/ *n.f.* lexicography.

lexique /lɛksik/ *n.m.* vocabulary; (*glossaire*) lexicon.

lézard /lezar/ *n.m.* lizard.

lézard|e /lezard/ *n.f.* crack. **se ~er** *v. pr.* crack.

liaison /ljɛzɔ̃/ *n.f.* connection; (*transport*) link; (*contact*) contact; (*gram., mil.*) liaison; (*amoureuse*) affair.

liane /ljan/ *n.f.* jungle vine.

liasse /ljas/ *n.f.* bundle.

Liban /libɑ̃/ *n.m.* Lebanon.

libanais, ~e /libanɛ, -z/ *a. & n.m., f.* Lebanese.

libeller /libele/ *v.t.* write, draw up.

libellule /libelyl/ *n.f.* dragonfly.

libér|al (*m. pl.* **~aux**) /liberal, -o/ *a.*

liberal. **~alement** *adv.* liberally.
~alisme *n.m.* liberalism. **~alité**
n.f. liberality.

libér|er /libere/ *v.t.* (*personne*) free,
release; (*pays*) liberate, free. **se ~er**
v. pr. free o.s. **~ateur, ~atrice** *a.*
liberating; *n.m., f.* liberator. **~ation**
n.f. release; (*de pays*) liberation.

liberté /libɛrte/ *n.f.* freedom, liberty;
(*loisir*) free time. **en ~ provisoire**,
on bail. **être/mettre en ~**, be/set
free.

libertin, ~e /libɛrtɛ̃, -in/ *a.* & *n.m., f.*
libertine.

librair|e /librɛr/ *n.m./f.* bookseller.
~ie /-eri/ *n.f.* bookshop.

libre /libr/ *a.* free; (*place, pièce*)
vacant, free; (*passage*) clear; (*école*)
private (*usually religious*). **~ de
qch./de faire**, free from sth./to do.
~-échange *n.m.* free trade. **~ment**
/-əmã/ *adv.* freely. **~-service** (*pl.* **~s-
services**) *n.m.* self-service.

Libye /libi/ *n.f.* Libya.

libyen, ~ne /libjɛ̃, -jɛn/ *a.* & *n.m., f.*
Libyan.

licence /lisãs/ *n.f.* licence; (*univ.*)
degree.

licencié, ~e /lisãsje/ *n.m., f.* **~ ès
lettres/sciences**, Bachelor of Arts/
Science.

licenc|ier /lisãsje/ *v.t.* lay off, dismiss.
~iement *n.m.* dismissal.

licencieu|x, ~se /lisãsjø, -z/ *a.*
licentious, lascivious.

lichen /likɛn/ *n.m.* lichen.

licite /lisit/ *a.* lawful.

licorne /likɔrn/ *n.f.* unicorn.

lie /li/ *n.f.* dregs.

liège /ljɛʒ/ *n.m.* cork.

lien /ljɛ̃/ *n.m.* (*rapport*) link; (*attache*)
bond, tie; (*corde*) rope.

lier /lje/ *v.t.* tie (up), bind; (*relier*) link;
(*engager, unir*) bind. **~ conver-
sation**, strike up a conversation. **se
~ avec**, make friends with. **très lié
avec**, very friendly with.

lierre /ljɛr/ *n.m.* ivy.

lieu (*pl.* **~x**) /ljø/ *n.m.* place. **~x**,
(*locaux*) premises; (*d'un accident*)
scene. **au ~ de**, instead of. **en premier ~**, firstly. **en dernier ~**, lastly.
~ commun, commonplace.

lieutenant /ljøtnã/ *n.m.* lieutenant.

lièvre /ljɛvr/ *n.m.* hare.

ligament /ligamã/ *n.m.* ligament.

ligne /liɲ/ *n.f.* line; (*trajet*) route;
(*formes*) lines; (*de femme*) figure.

en ~, (*joueurs etc.*) lined up; (*personne au téléphone*) connected.

lignée /liɲe/ *n.f.* ancestry, line.

ligoter /ligɔte/ *v.t.* tie up.

ligu|e /lig/ *n.f.* league. **se ~er** *v. pr.*
form a league (**contre**, against).

lilas /lila/ *n.m.* & *a. invar.* lilac.

limace /limas/ *n.f.* slug.

limande /limãd/ *n.f.* (*poisson*) dab.

lim|e /lim/ *n.f.* file. **~er** *v.t.* file.

limier /limje/ *n.m.* bloodhound; (*policier*) sleuth.

limitation /limitasjɔ̃/ *n.f.* limitation.
~ de vitesse, speed limit.

limit|e /limit/ *n.f.* limit; (*de jardin,
champ*) boundary. **—a.** (*vitesse, âge*)
maximum; (*cas*) extreme. **~er** *v.t.*
limit; (*délimiter*) form the border of.

limoger /limɔʒe/ *v.t.* dismiss.

limonade /limɔnad/ *n.f.* lemonade.

limpid|e /lɛ̃pid/ *a.* limpid, clear. **~ité**
n.f. clearness.

lin /lɛ̃/ *n.m.* flax.

linceul /lɛ̃sœl/ *n.m.* shroud.

linéaire /lineɛr/ *a.* linear.

linge /lɛ̃ʒ/ *n.m.* linen; (*lessive*) washing; (*torchon*) cloth. **~ (de corps)**,
underwear. **~rie** *n.f.* underwear.

lingot /lɛ̃go/ *n.m.* ingot.

linguiste /lɛ̃gɥist/ *n.m./f.* linguist.

linguistique /lɛ̃gɥistik/ *a.* linguistic. **—*n.f.*** linguistics.

lino /lino/ *n.m.* lino.

linoléum /linɔleɔm/ *n.m.* linoleum.

lion, ~ne /ljɔ̃, ljɔn/ *n.m., f.* lion,
lioness.

liquéfier /likefje/ *v.t.*, **se ~** *v. pr.*
liquefy.

liqueur /likœr/ *n.f.* liqueur.

liquide /likid/ *a.* & *n.m.* liquid. (**argent**) **~**, ready money.

liquid|er /likide/ *v.t.* liquidate;
(*vendre*) sell. **~ation** *n.f.* liquidation;
(*vente*) (clearance) sale.

lire[1]† /lir/ *v.t./i.* read.

lire[2] /lir/ *n.f.* lira.

lis[1] /li/ *voir* **lire**[1].

lis[2] /lis/ *n.m.* (*fleur*) lily.

lisible /lizibl/ *a.* legible; (*roman etc.*)
readable.

lisière /lizjɛr/ *n.f.* edge.

liss|e /lis/ *a.* smooth. **~er** *v.t.* smooth.

liste /list/ *n.f.* list.

lit[1] /li/ *voir* **lire**[1].

lit[2] /li/ *n.m.* (*de personne, fleuve*) bed.
~ de camp, camp-bed. **~ d'enfant**,
cot. **~ d'une personne**, single bed.

litanie /litani/ *n.f.* litany.

literie /litri/ *n.f.* bedding.

litière /litjɛr/ *n.f.* (*paille*) litter.

litige /litiʒ/ *n.m.* dispute.

litre /litr/ *n.m.* litre.

littéraire /literɛr/ *a.* literary.

littér|al (*m. pl.* ~**aux**) /literal, -o/ *a.* literal. ~**alement** *adv.* literally.

littérature /literatyr/ *n.f.* literature.

littor|al (*pl.* ~**aux**) /litɔral, -o/ *n.m.* coast.

liturg|ie /lityrʒi/ *n.f.* liturgy. ~**ique** *a.* liturgical.

livide /livid/ *a.* (*blême*) pallid; (*bleu*) livid.

livraison /livrɛzɔ̃/ *n.f.* delivery.

livre[1] /livr/ *n.m.* book. ~ **de bord**, log-book. ~ **de poche**, paperback.

livre[2] /livr/ *n.f.* (*monnaie*, *poids*) pound.

livrée /livre/ *n.f.* livery.

livr|er /livre/ *v.t.* deliver; (*abandonner*) give over (**à**, to); (*secret*) give away. ~**é à soi-même**, left to o.s. **se** ~**er à**, give o.s. over to; (*actes*, *boisson*) indulge in; (*se confier à*) confide in; (*effectuer*) carry out.

livret /livrɛ/ *n.m.* book; (*mus.*) libretto. ~ **scolaire**, school report (book).

livreu|r, ~**se** /livrœr, -øz/ *n.m.*, *f.* delivery boy *ou* girl.

lobe /lɔb/ *n.m.* lobe.

loc|al[1] (*m. pl.* ~**aux**) /lɔkal, -o/ *a.* local. ~**alement** *adv.* locally.

loc|al[2] (*pl.* ~**aux**) /lɔkal, -o/ *n.m.* premises. ~**aux**, premises.

localisé /lɔkalize/ *a.* localized.

localité /lɔkalite/ *n.f.* locality.

locataire /lɔkatɛr/ *n.m./f.* tenant; (*de chambre*, *d'hôtel*) lodger.

location /lɔkasjɔ̃/ *n.f.* (*de maison*) renting; (*de voiture*) hiring, renting; (*de place*) booking, reservation; (*par propriétaire*) renting out; hiring out. **en** ~, (*voiture*) on hire, rented.

lock-out /lɔkawt/ *n.m. invar.* lockout.

locomotion /lɔkɔmosjɔ̃/ *n.f.* locomotion.

locomotive /lɔkɔmɔtiv/ *n.f.* engine, locomotive.

locution /lɔkysjɔ̃/ *n.f.* phrase.

logarithme /lɔgaritm/ *n.m.* logarithm.

loge /lɔʒ/ *n.f.* (*de concierge*) lodge; (*d'acteur*) dressing-room; (*de spectateur*) box.

logement /lɔʒmɑ̃/ *n.m.* accommodation; (*appartement*) flat; (*habitat*) housing.

log|er /lɔʒe/ *v.t.* accommodate. —*v.i.*, **se** ~**er** *v. pr.* live. (**trouver à**) **se** ~**er**, find accommodation. **être** ~**é**, live. **se** ~**er dans**, (*balle*) lodge itself in.

logeu|r, ~**se** /lɔʒœr, -øz/ *n.m.*, *f.* landlord, landlady.

logiciel /lɔʒisjɛl/ *n.m.* software.

logique /lɔʒik/ *a.* logical. —*n.f.* logic. ~**ment** *adv.* logically.

logis /lɔʒi/ *n.m.* dwelling.

logistique /lɔʒistik/ *n.f.* logistics.

loi /lwa/ *n.f.* law.

loin /lwɛ̃/ *adv.* far (away). **au** ~, far away. **de** ~, from far away; (*de beaucoup*) by far. ~ **de là**, far from it. **plus** ~, further.

lointain, ~**e** /lwɛ̃tɛ̃, -ɛn/ *a.* distant. —*n.m.* distance.

loir /lwar/ *n.m.* dormouse.

loisir /lwazir/ *n.m.* (spare) time. ~**s**, spare time; (*distractions*) spare time activities.

londonien, ~**ne** /lɔ̃dɔnjɛ̃, -jɛn/ *a.* London. —*n.m.*, *f.* Londoner.

Londres /lɔ̃dr/ *n.m./f.* London.

long, ~**ue** /lɔ̃, lɔ̃g/ *a.* long. —*n.m.* **de** ~, (*mesure*) long. **à la** ~**ue**, in the end. **à** ~ **terme**, long-term. **de** ~ **en large**, back and forth. **à** ~ **faire**, a long time doing. (**tout**) **le** ~ **de**, (all) along.

longer /lɔ̃ʒe/ *v.t.* go along; (*limiter*) border.

longévité /lɔ̃ʒevite/ *n.f.* longevity.

longitude /lɔ̃ʒityd/ *n.f.* longitude.

longtemps /lɔ̃tɑ̃/ *adv.* a long time. **avant** ~, before long. **trop** ~, too long.

longue /lɔ̃g/ *voir* **long**.

longuement /lɔ̃gmɑ̃/ *adv.* at length.

longueur /lɔ̃gœr/ *n.f.* length. ~**s**, (*de texte etc.*) over-long parts. **à** ~ **de journée**, all day long. ~ **d'onde**, wavelength.

lopin /lɔpɛ̃/ *n.m.* ~ **de terre**, patch of land.

loquace /lɔkas/ *a.* talkative.

loque /lɔk/ *n.f.* ~**s**, rags. ~ (**humaine**), (human) wreck.

loquet /lɔkɛ/ *n.m.* latch.

lorgner /lɔrɲe/ *v.t.* eye.

lorgnon /lɔrɲɔ̃/ *n.m.* eyeglasses.

lors de /lɔrdə/ *prép.* at the time of.

lorsque /lɔrsk(ə)/ *conj.* when.

losange /lɔzɑ̃ʒ/ *n.m.* diamond.

lot /lo/ *n.m.* prize; (*portion*, *destin*) lot.

loterie /lɔtri/ *n.f.* lottery.

lotion /losjɔ̃/ *n.f.* lotion.

lotissement /lɔtismã/ *n.m.* building plot.

louable /lwabl/ *a.* praiseworthy.

louange /lwãʒ/ *n.f.* praise.

louche[1] /luʃ/ *a.* shady, dubious.

louche[2] /luʃ/ *n.f.* ladle.

loucher /luʃe/ *v.i.* squint.

louer[1] /lwe/ *v.t.* (*maison*) rent; (*voiture*) hire, rent; (*place*) book, reserve; (*propriétaire*) rent out; hire out.

louer[2] /lwe/ *v.t.* (*approuver*) praise (**de**, for). **se ~ de**, congratulate o.s. on.

loufoque /lufɔk/ *a.* (*fam.*) crazy.

loup /lu/ *n.m.* wolf.

loupe /lup/ *n.f.* magnifying glass.

louper /lupe/ *v.t.* (*manquer*: *fam.*) miss; (*bâcler*: *fam.*) mess up.

lourd, ~e /lur, -d/ *a.* heavy; (*chaleur*) close; (*faute*) gross. **~ement** /-dəmã/ *adv.* heavily. **~eur** /-dœr/ *n.f.* heaviness.

lourdaud, ~e /lurdo, -d/ *a.* loutish. —*n.m., f.* lout, oaf.

loutre /lutr/ *n.f.* otter.

louve /luv/ *n.f.* she-wolf.

louveteau (*pl.* **~x**) /luvto/ *n.m.* (*scout*) Cub (Scout).

loy|al (*m. pl.* **~aux**) /lwajal, -o/ *a.* loyal; (*honnête*) fair. **~alement** *adv.* loyally; fairly. **~auté** *n.f.* loyalty; fairness.

loyer /lwaje/ *n.m.* rent.

lu /ly/ *voir* **lire**[1].

lubie /lybi/ *n.f.* whim.

lubrif|ier /lybrifje/ *v.t.* lubricate. **~iant** *n.m.* lubricant.

lubrique /lybrik/ *a.* lewd.

lucarne /lykarn/ *n.f.* skylight.

lucid|e /lysid/ *a.* lucid. **~ité** *n.f.* lucidity.

lucrati|f, ~ve /lykratif, -v/ *a.* lucrative. **à but non ~f,** non-profit-making.

lueur /lɥœr/ *n.f.* (*faint*) light, glimmer; (*fig.*) glimmer, gleam.

luge /lyʒ/ *n.f.* toboggan.

lugubre /lygybr/ *a.* gloomy.

lui /lɥi/ *pron.* him; (*sujet*) he; (*chose*) it; (*objet indirect*) (to) him; (*femme*) (to) her; (*chose*) (to) it. **~-même** *pron.* himself; itself.

luire† /lɥir/ *v.i.* shine; (*reflet humide*) glisten; (*reflet chaud, faible*) glow.

lumbago /lɔ̃bago/ *n.m.* lumbago.

lumière /lymjɛr/ *n.f.* light. **~s,** (*connaissances*) knowledge. **faire (toute) la ~ sur,** clear up.

luminaire /lyminɛr/ *n.m.* lamp.

lumineu|x, ~se /lyminø, -z/ *a.* luminous; (*éclairé*) illuminated; (*source, rayon*) (of) light; (*vif*) bright.

lunaire /lynɛr/ *a.* lunar.

lunatique /lynatik/ *a.* temperamental.

lunch /lœntʃ/ *n.m.* buffet lunch.

lundi /lœ̃di/ *n.m.* Monday.

lune /lyn/ *n.f.* moon. **~ de miel,** honeymoon.

lunette /lynɛt/ *n.f.* **~s,** glasses; (*de protection*) goggles. **~ arrière,** (*auto.*) rear window. **~ d'approche,** telescope. **~s de soleil,** sun-glasses.

luron /lyrɔ̃/ *n.m.* **gai** *ou* **joyeux ~,** (*fam.*) quite a lad.

lustre /lystr/ *n.m.* (*éclat*) lustre; (*objet*) chandelier.

lustré /lystre/ *a.* shiny.

luth /lyt/ *n.m.* lute.

lutin /lytɛ̃/ *n.m.* goblin.

lutrin /lytrɛ̃/ *n.m.* lectern.

lutt|e /lyt/ *n.f.* fight, struggle; (*sport*) wrestling. **~er** *v.i.* fight, struggle; (*sport*) wrestle. **~eur, ~euse** *n.m., f.* fighter; (*sport*) wrestler.

luxe /lyks/ *n.m.* luxury. **de ~,** luxury; (*produit*) de luxe.

Luxembourg /lyksãbur/ *n.m.* Luxemburg.

lux|er /lykse/ *v.t.* dislocate. **~ation** *n.f.* dislocation.

luxueu|x, ~se /lyksɥø, -z/ *a.* luxurious.

luxure /lyksyr/ *n.f.* lust.

luxuriant, ~e /lyksyrjã, -t/ *a.* luxuriant.

luzerne /lyzɛrn/ *n.f.* (*plante*) lucerne, alfalfa.

lycée /lise/ *n.m.* (secondary) school. **~n, ~nne** /-ɛ̃, -ɛn/ *n.m., f.* pupil (at secondary school).

lynch|er /lɛ̃ʃe/ *v.t.* lynch. **~age** *n.m.* lynching.

lynx /lɛ̃ks/ *n.m.* lynx.

lyre /lir/ *n.f.* lyre.

lyri|que /lirik/ *a.* (*poésie*) lyric; (*passionné*) lyrical. **artiste/théâtre ~que,** opera singer/house. **~sme** *n.m.* lyricism.

lys /lis/ *n.m.* lily.

M

m' /m/ *voir* me.

ma /ma/ *voir* mon.

macabre /makabr/ *a.* gruesome, macabre.

macadam /makadam/ *n.m.* (*goudronné*) Tarmac (P.).

macaron /makarɔ̃/ *n.m.* (*gâteau*) macaroon; (*insigne*) badge.

macaronis /makarɔni/ *n.m. pl.* macaroni.

macédoine /masedwan/ *n.f.* mixed vegetables. ~ **de fruits,** fruit salad.

macérer /masere/ *v.t./i.* soak; (*dans du vinaigre*) pickle.

Mach /mak/ *n.m.* (**nombre de**) ~, Mach (number).

mâchefer /mɑʃfɛr/ *n.m.* clinker.

mâcher /mɑʃe/ *v.t.* chew. **ne pas** ~ **ses mots,** not mince one's words.

machiavélique /makjavelik/ *a.* machiavellian.

machin /maʃɛ̃/ *n.m.* (*chose: fam.*) thing; (*personne: fam.*) what's-his-name.

machin|al (*m. pl.* ~**aux**) /maʃinal, -o/ *a.* automatic. ~**alement** *adv.* automatically.

machinations /maʃinɑsjɔ̃/ *n.f. pl.* machinations.

machine /maʃin/ *n.f.* machine; (*d'un train, navire*) engine. ~ **à écrire,** typewriter. ~ **à laver/coudre,** washing-/sewing-machine. ~ **à sous,** fruit machine; (*Amer.*) slot-machine. ~**-outil** (*pl.* ~**s-outils**) *n.f.* machine tool. ~**rie** *n.f.* machinery.

machiner /maʃine/ *v.t.* plot.

machiniste /maʃinist/ *n.m.* (*théâtre*) stage-hand; (*conducteur*) driver.

macho /ma(t)ʃo/ *n.m.* (*fam.*) macho.

mâchoire /mɑʃwar/ *n.f.* jaw.

maçon /masɔ̃/ *n.m.* builder; (*poseur de briques*) bricklayer. ~**nerie** /-ɔnri/ *n.f.* brickwork; (*pierres*) stonework, masonry.

maçonnique /masɔnik/ *a.* Masonic.

macrobiotique /makrɔbjɔtik/ *a.* macrobiotic.

maculer /makyle/ *v.t.* stain.

Madagascar /madagaskar/ *n.f.* Madagascar.

madame (*pl.* **mesdames**) /madam, medam/ *n.f.* madam. **M**~ *ou* **Mme** Dupont, Mrs Dupont. **bonsoir, mesdames,** good evening, ladies.

madeleine /madlɛn/ *n.f.* madeleine (*small shell-shaped sponge-cake*).

mademoiselle (*pl.* **mesdemoiselles**) /madmwazɛl, medmwazɛl/ *n.f.* miss. **M**~ *ou* **Mlle Dupont,** Miss Dupont. **bonsoir, mesdemoiselles,** good evening, ladies.

madère /madɛr/ *n.m.* (*vin*) Madeira.

madone /madɔn/ *n.f.* madonna.

madré /madre/ *a.* wily.

madrig|al (*pl.* ~**aux**) /madrigal, -o/ *n.m.* madrigal.

maestro /maɛstro/ *n.m.* maestro.

maf(f)ia /mafja/ *n.f.* Mafia.

magasin /magazɛ̃/ *n.m.* shop, store; (*entrepôt*) warehouse; (*d'une arme etc.*) magazine.

magazine /magazin/ *n.m.* magazine; (*émission*) programme.

magicien, ~**ne** /maʒisjɛ̃, -jɛn/ *n.m., f.* magician.

magie /maʒi/ *n.f.* magic.

magique /maʒik/ *a.* magic; (*mystérieux*) magical.

magistr|al (*m. pl.* ~**aux**) /maʒistral, -o/ *a.* masterly; (*grand: hum.*) colossal. ~**alement** *adv.* in a masterly fashion.

magistrat /maʒistra/ *n.m.* magistrate.

magistrature /maʒistratyr/ *n.f.* judiciary.

magnanim|e /maɲanim/ *a.* magnanimous. ~**ité** *n.f.* magnanimity.

magnat /magna/ *n.m.* tycoon, magnate.

magner (se) /(sə)maɲe/ *v. pr.* (*argot*) hurry.

magnésie /maɲezi/ *n.f.* magnesia.

magnéti|que /maɲetik/ *a.* magnetic. ~**ser** *v.t.* magnetize. ~**sme** *n.m.* magnetism.

magnétophone /maɲetɔfɔn/ *n.m.* tape recorder. ~ **à cassettes,** cassette recorder.

magnétoscope /maɲetɔskɔp/ *n.m.* video-recorder.

magnifi|que /maɲifik/ *a.* magnificent. ~**cence** *n.f.* magnificence.

magnolia /maɲɔlja/ *n.m.* magnolia.

magot /mago/ *n.m.* (*fam.*) hoard (of money).

mahométan, ~e /maɔmetɑ̃, -an/ *a.* & *n.m.*, *f.* Muhammedan.

mai /mɛ/ *n.m.* May.

maigr|e /mɛgr/ *a.* thin; (*viande, joue*) lean; (*yaourt*) low-fat; (*fig.*) poor, meagre. **faire ~e**, abstain from meat. **~ement** *adv.* poorly. **~eur** *n.f.* thinness; leanness; (*fig.*) meagreness.

maigrir /megrir/ *v.i.* get thin(ner); (*en suivant un régime*) slim. —*v.t.* make thin(ner).

maille /mɑj/ *n.f.* stitch; (*de filet*) mesh. **~ filée**, ladder, run.

maillet /majɛ/ *n.m.* mallet.

maillon /majɔ̃/ *n.m.* link.

maillot /majo/ *n.m.* (*de danseur*) tights; (*tricot*) jersey; (*de bébé*) swaddling-clothes. **~ (de corps)**, vest. **~ de bain**, swim-suit; (*d'homme*) (swimming) trunks.

main /mɛ̃/ *n.f.* hand. **avoir la ~ heureuse**, be lucky. **donner la ~ à qn.**, hold s.o.'s hand. **en ~s propres**, in person. **~ courante**, handrail. **~-d'œuvre** (*pl.* **~s-d'œuvre**) *n.f.* labour; (*ensemble d'ouvriers*) labour force. **~-forte** *n.f. invar.* assistance. **sous la ~**, handy. **vol/attaque à ~ armée**, armed robbery/attack.

maint, ~e /mɛ̃, mɛ̃t/ *a.* many a. **~s**, many.

maintenant /mɛ̃tnɑ̃/ *adv.* now; (*de nos jours*) nowadays.

maintenir† /mɛ̃tnir/ *v.t.* keep, maintain; (*soutenir*) hold up; (*affirmer*) maintain. **se ~** *v. pr.* (*continuer*) persist; (*rester*) remain.

maintien /mɛ̃tjɛ̃/ *n.m.* (*attitude*) bearing; (*conservation*) maintenance.

maire /mɛr/ *n.m.* mayor.

mairie /meri/ *n.f.* town hall; (*administration*) town council.

mais /mɛ/ *conj.* but. **~ oui, ~ si**, of course. **~ non**, definitely not.

maïs /mais/ *n.m.* maize; (*Amer.*) corn.

maison /mɛzɔ̃/ *n.f.* house; (*foyer*) home; (*immeuble*) building. **~ (de commerce)**, firm. —*a. invar.* (*culin.*) home-made. **à la ~**, at home. **rentrer** *ou* **aller à la ~**, go home. **~ des jeunes**, youth centre. **~ de repos, ~ de convalescence**, convalescent home. **~ de retraite**, old people's home.

maisonnée /mɛzɔne/ *n.f.* household.

maisonnette /mɛzɔnɛt/ *n.f.* small house, cottage.

maître /mɛtr/ *n.m.* master. **~ (d'école)**, schoolmaster. **~ de**, in control of. **se rendre ~ de**, gain control of; (*incendie*) bring under control. **~ assistant/de conférences**, junior/senior lecturer. **~ chanteur**, blackmailer. **~ d'hôtel**, head waiter; (*domestique*) butler. **~ nageur**, swimming instructor.

maîtresse /mɛtrɛs/ *n.f.* mistress. **~ (d'école)**, schoolmistress. —*a.f.* (*idée, poutre, qualité*) main. **~ de**, in control of.

maîtris|e /metriz/ *n.f.* mastery; (*univ.*) master's degree. **~ (de soi)**, self-control. **~er** *v.t.* master; (*incendie*) control; (*personne*) subdue. **se ~er** *v. pr.* control o.s.

majesté /maʒɛste/ *n.f.* majesty.

majestueu|x, ~se /maʒɛstɥø, -z/ *a.* majestic. **~sement** *adv.* majestically.

majeur /maʒœr/ *a.* major; (*jurid.*) of age. —*n.m.* middle finger. **en ~e partie**, mostly. **la ~e partie de**, most of.

major|er /maʒɔre/ *v.t.* increase. **~ation** *n.f.* increase (**de**, in).

majorit|é /maʒɔrite/ *n.f.* majority. **en ~é**, chiefly. **~aire** *a.* majority. **être ~aire**, be in the majority.

Majorque /maʒɔrk/ *n.f.* Majorca.

majuscule /maʒyskyl/ *a.* capital. —*n.f.* capital letter.

mal¹ /mal/ *adv.* badly; (*incorrectement*) wrong(ly). **~ (à l'aise)**, uncomfortable. **aller ~**, (*malade*) be bad. **c'est ~ de**, it is wrong *ou* bad to. **entendre/comprendre ~**, not hear/understand properly. **~ famé**, of ill repute. **~ fichu**, (*personne: fam.*) feeling lousy.

mal² (*pl.* **maux**) /mal, mo/ *n.m.* evil; (*douleur*) pain, ache; (*maladie*) disease; (*effort*) trouble; (*dommage*) harm; (*malheur*) misfortune. **avoir ~ à la tête/aux dents/à la gorge**, have a headache/a toothache/a sore throat. **avoir le ~ de mer/du pays**, be seasick/homesick. **faire du ~ à**, hurt, harm.

malade /malad/ *a.* sick, ill; (*bras, gorge*) bad; (*plante*) diseased. — *n.m./f.* sick person; (*d'un médecin*) patient.

maladie /maladi/ *n.f.* illness, disease; (*fig.*) mania.

maladi|f, ~ve /maladif, -v/ *a.* sickly; (*peur*) morbid.

maladresse /maladrɛs/ *n.f.* clumsiness; (*erreur*) blunder.

maladroit, ~e /maladrwa, -t/ *a.* & *n.m., f.* clumsy (person).

malais, ~e[1] /malɛ, -z/ *a.* & *n.m., f.* Malay.

malaise[2] /malɛz/ *n.m.* feeling of faintness *ou* dizziness; (*fig.*) uneasiness, malaise.

malaisé /maleze/ *a.* difficult.

Malaysia /malɛzja/ *n.f.* Malaysia.

malaria /malarja/ *n.f.* malaria.

malaxer /malakse/ *v.t.* (*pétrir*) knead; (*mêler*) mix.

malchanc|e /malʃãs/ *n.f.* misfortune. **~eux, ~euse** *a.* unlucky.

mâle /mɑl/ *a.* male; (*viril*) manly. —*n.m.* male.

malédiction /malediksjɔ̃/ *n.f.* curse.

maléfice /malefis/ *n.m.* evil spell.

maléfique /malefik/ *a.* evil.

malencontreu|x, ~se /malãkɔ̃trø, -z/ *a.* unfortunate.

mal-en-point /malãpwɛ̃/ *a. invar.* in a bad way.

malentendu /malãtãdy/ *n.m.* misunderstanding.

malfaçon /malfasɔ̃/ *n.f.* fault.

malfaisant, ~e /malfəzã, -t/ *a.* harmful.

malfaiteur /malfɛtœr/ *n.m.* criminal.

malformation /malfɔrmasjɔ̃/ *n.f.* malformation.

malgache /malgaʃ/ *a.* & *n.m./f.* Malagasy.

malgré /malgre/ *prép.* in spite of, despite. **~ tout,** after all.

malhabile /malabil/ *a.* clumsy.

malheur /malœr/ *n.m.* misfortune; (*accident*) accident.

malheureu|x, ~se /malœrø, -z/ *a.* unhappy; (*regrettable*) unfortunate; (*sans succès*) unlucky; (*insignifiant*) wretched. —*n.m., f.* (poor) wretch. **~sement** *adv.* unfortunately.

malhonnête /malɔnɛt/ *a.* dishonest; (*impoli*) rude. **~té** *n.f.* dishonesty; rudeness; (*action*) dishonest action.

malic|e /malis/ *n.f.* mischievousness; (*méchanceté*) malice. **~ieux, ~ieuse** *a.* mischievous.

mal|in, ~igne /malɛ̃, -iɲ/ *a.* clever, smart; (*méchant*) malicious; (*tumeur*) malignant; (*difficile*: *fam.*) difficult. **~ignité** *n.f.* malignancy.

malingre /malɛ̃gr/ *a.* puny.

malintentionné /malɛ̃tãsjɔne/ *a.* malicious.

malle /mal/ *n.f.* (*valise*) trunk; (*auto.*) boot; (*auto., Amer.*) trunk.

malléable /maleabl/ *a.* malleable.

mallette /malɛt/ *n.f.* (small) suitcase.

malmener /malməne/ *v.t.* manhandle, handle roughly.

malodorant, ~e /malɔdɔrã, -t/ *a.* smelly, foul-smelling.

malotru /malɔtry/ *n.m.* boor.

malpoli /malpɔli/ *a.* impolite.

malpropre /malprɔpr/ *a.* dirty. **~té** /-əte/ *n.f.* dirtiness.

malsain, ~e /malsɛ̃, -ɛn/ *a.* unhealthy.

malt /malt/ *n.m.* malt.

maltais, ~e /maltɛ, -z/ *a.* & *n.m., f.* Maltese.

Malte /malt/ *n.f.* Malta.

maltraiter /maltrete/ *v.t.* ill-treat.

malveillan|t, ~te /malvɛjã, -t/ *a.* malevolent. **~ce** *n.f.* malevolence.

maman /mamã/ *n.f.* mum(my), mother.

mamelle /mamɛl/ *n.f.* teat; (*de femme*) breast.

mamelon /mamlɔ̃/ *n.m.* (*colline*) hillock.

mamie /mami/ *n.f.* (*fam.*) granny.

mammifère /mamifɛr/ *n.m.* mammal.

mammouth /mamut/ *n.m.* mammoth.

manche[1] /mãʃ/ *n.f.* sleeve; (*sport, pol.*) round. **la M~,** the Channel.

manche[2] /mãʃ/ *n.m.* (*d'un instrument*) handle. **~ à balai,** broomstick.

manchette /mãʃɛt/ *n.f.* cuff; (*de journal*) headline.

manchot[1] **, ~e** /mãʃo, -ɔt/ *a.* & *n.m., f.* one-armed (person); (*sans bras*) armless (person).

manchot[2] /mãʃo/ *n.m.* (*oiseau*) penguin.

mandarin /mãdarɛ̃/ *n.m.* (*fonctionnaire*) mandarin.

mandarine /mãdarin/ *n.f.* tangerine, mandarin (orange).

mandat /mãda/ *n.m.* (*postal*) money order; (*pol.*) mandate; (*procuration*) proxy; (*de police*) warrant. **~aire** /-tɛr/ *n.m.* (*représentant*) representative. **~er** /-te/ *v.t.* (*pol.*) delegate.

manège /manɛʒ/ *n.m.* riding-school; (*à la foire*) merry-go-round; (*manœuvre*) wiles, ploy.

manette /manɛt/ *n.f.* lever.

mangeable /mãʒabl/ *a.* edible.

mangeaille /mãʒaj/ *n.f.* (*fam.*) (bad) food.

mangeoire /mãʒwar/ *n.f.* trough.

mang|er /mɑ̃ʒe/ *v.t./i.* eat; (*fortune*) go through; (*essence*, *gaz*) consume, go through. —*n.m.* food. **donner à ~er à**, feed. **~eur, ~euse** *n.m.*, *f.* eater.

mangue /mɑ̃g/ *n.f.* mango.

maniable /manjabl/ *a.* easy to handle.

maniaque /manjak/ *a.* fussy. —*n.m./f.* fuss-pot; (*fou*) maniac. **un ~ de**, a maniac for.

manie /mani/ *n.f.* habit; (*obsession*) mania.

man|ier /manje/ *v.t.* handle. **~iement** *n.m.* handling.

manière /manjɛr/ *n.f.* way, manner. **~s**, (*politesse*) manners; (*chichis*) fuss. **de cette ~**, in this way. **de ~ à**, so as to. **de toute ~**, anyway, in any case.

maniéré /manjere/ *a.* affected.

manif /manif/ *n.f.* (*fam.*) demo.

manifestant, ~e /manifɛstɑ̃, -t/ *n.m.*, *f.* demonstrator.

manifeste /manifɛst/ *a.* obvious. —*n.m.* manifesto.

manifest|er¹ /manifɛste/ *v.t.* show, manifest. **se ~er** *v. pr.* (*sentiment*) show itself; (*apparaître*) appear. **~ation**¹ *n.f.* expression, demonstration, manifestation; (*de maladie*) appearance.

manifest|er² /manifɛste/ *v.i.* (*pol.*) demonstrate. **~ation**² *n.f.* (*pol.*) demonstration; (*événement*) event.

maniganc|e /manigɑ̃s/ *n.f.* little plot. **~er** *v.t.* plot.

manipul|er /manipyle/ *v.t.* handle; (*péj.*) manipulate. **~ation** *n.f.* handling; (*péj.*) manipulation.

manivelle /manivɛl/ *n.f.* crank.

manne /man/ *n.f.* (*aubaine*) godsend.

mannequin /mankɛ̃/ *n.m.* (*personne*) model; (*statue*) dummy.

manœuvr|e¹ /manœvr/ *n.f.* manœuvre. **~er** *v.t./i.* manœuvre; (*machine*) operate.

manœuvre² /manœvr/ *n.m.* (*ouvrier*) labourer.

manoir /manwar/ *n.m.* manor.

manque /mɑ̃k/ *n.m.* lack (**de**, of); (*vide*) gap. **~s**, (*défauts*) faults. **~ à gagner**, loss of profit.

manqué /mɑ̃ke/ *a.* (*écrivain etc.*) failed.

manquement /mɑ̃kmɑ̃/ *n.m.* **~ à**, breach of.

manquer /mɑ̃ke/ *v.t.* miss; (*gâcher*) spoil; (*examen*) fail. —*v.i.* be short *ou* lacking; (*absent*) be absent; (*en moins*, *disparu*) be missing; (*échouer*) fail. **~ à**, (*devoir*) fail in. **~ de**, be short of, lack. **il/ça lui manque**, he misses him/it. **~ (de) faire**, (*faillir*) nearly do. **ne pas ~ de**, not fail to.

mansarde /mɑ̃sard/ *n.f.* attic.

manteau (*pl.* **~x**) /mɑ̃to/ *n.m.* coat.

manucur|e /manykyr/ *n.m./f.* manicurist. **~er** *v.t.* manicure.

manuel, ~le /manɥɛl/ *a.* manual. —*n.m.* (*livre*) manual. **~lement** *adv.* manually.

manufactur|e /manyfaktyr/ *n.f.* factory. **~er** *v.t.* manufacture.

manuscrit, ~e /manyskri, -t/ *a.* handwritten. —*n.m.* manuscript.

manutention /manytɑ̃sjɔ̃/ *n.f.* handling.

mappemonde /mapmɔ̃d/ *n.f.* world map; (*sphère*) globe.

maquereau (*pl.* **~x**) /makro/ *n.m.* (*poisson*) mackerel.

maquette /makɛt/ *n.f.* (scale) model.

maquill|er /makije/ *v.t.* make up; (*truquer*) fake. **se ~er** *v. pr.* make (o.s.) up. **~age** *n.m.* make-up.

maquis /maki/ *n.m.* (*paysage*) scrub; (*mil.*) Maquis, underground.

maraîch|er, ~ère /mareʃe, -ɛʃɛr/ *n.m.*, *f.* market gardener; (*Amer.*) truck farmer.

marais /marɛ/ *n.m.* marsh.

marasme /marasm/ *n.m.* slump.

marathon /maratɔ̃/ *n.m.* marathon.

marbre /marbr/ *n.m.* marble.

marc /mar/ *n.m.* (*eau-de-vie*) marc. **~ de café**, coffee-grounds.

marchand, ~e /marʃɑ̃, -d/ *n.m.*, *f.* trader; (*de charbon*, *vins*) merchant. —*a.* (*valeur*) market. **~ de couleurs**, ironmonger; (*Amer.*) hardware merchant. **~ de journaux**, newsagent. **~ de légumes**, greengrocer. **~ de poissons**, fishmonger.

marchand|er /marʃɑ̃de/ *v.t.* haggle over. —*v.i.* haggle. **~age** *n.m.* haggling.

marchandise /marʃɑ̃diz/ *n.f.* goods.

marche /marʃ/ *n.f.* (*démarche*, *trajet*) walk; (*rythme*) pace; (*mil.*, *mus.*) march; (*d'escalier*) step; (*sport*) walking; (*de machine*) working; (*de véhicule*) running; (*de maladie*) course. **en ~**, (*train etc.*) moving. **faire ~ arrière**, (*véhicule*) reverse. **mettre en ~**, start (up). **se mettre en ~**, start moving.

marché /marʃe/ *n.m.* market;

(*contrat*) deal. **faire son ~,** do one's shopping. **~ aux puces,** flea market. **M~ commun,** Common Market. **~ noir,** black market.

marchepied /marʃəpje/ *n.m.* (*de train, camion*) step.

march|er /marʃe/ *v.i.* walk; (*aller*) go; (*fonctionner*) work, run; (*prospérer*) go well; (*consentir: fam.*) agree. **~er** (**au pas**), (*mil.*) march. **faire ~er qn.,** pull s.o.'s leg. **~eur, ~euse** *n.m., f.* walker.

mardi /mardi/ *n.m.* Tuesday. **M~ gras,** Shrove Tuesday.

mare /mar/ *n.f.* (*étang*) pond; (*flaque*) pool.

marécag|e /marekaʒ/ *n.m.* marsh. **~eux, ~euse** *a.* marshy.

maréch|al (*pl.* **~aux**) /mareʃal, -o/ *n.m.* marshal. **~al-ferrant** (*pl.* **~aux-ferrants**) blacksmith.

marée /mare/ *n.f.* tide; (*poissons*) fresh fish. **~ noire,** oil-slick.

marelle /marɛl/ *n.f.* hopscotch.

margarine /margarin/ *n.f.* margarine.

marge /marʒ/ *n.f.* margin. **en ~ de,** (*à l'écart de*) on the fringe(s) of.

margin|al, ~ale (*m. pl.* **~aux**) /marʒinal, -o/ *a.* marginal. *—n.m., f.* drop-out.

marguerite /margərit/ *n.f.* daisy.

mari /mari/ *n.m.* husband.

mariage /marjaʒ/ *n.m.* marriage; (*cérémonie*) wedding.

marié, ~e /marje/ *a.* married. *—n.m.* (bride)groom. *—n.f.* bride. **les ~s,** the bride and groom.

marier /marje/ *v.t.* marry. **se ~** *v. pr.* get married, marry. **se ~ avec,** marry, get married to.

marin, ~e /marɛ̃, -in/ *a.* sea. *—n.m.* sailor. *—n.f.* navy. **~e marchande,** merchant navy.

mariner /marine/ *v.t./i.* marinate.

marionnette /marjɔnɛt/ *n.f.* puppet; (*à fils*) marionette.

maritalement /maritalmɑ̃/ *adv.* as husband and wife.

maritime /maritim/ *a.* maritime, coastal; (*droit, agent*) shipping.

marmaille /marmaj/ *n.f.* (*enfants: fam.*) brats.

marmelade /marməlad/ *n.f.* stewed fruit.

marmite /marmit/ *n.f.* (cooking-)pot.

marmonner /marmɔne/ *v.t./i.* mumble.

marmot /marmo/ *n.m.* (*fam.*) kid.

marmotter /marmɔte/ *v.t./i.* mumble.

Maroc /marɔk/ *n.m.* Morocco.

marocain, ~e /marɔkɛ̃, -ɛn/ *a. & n.m., f.* Moroccan.

maroquinerie /marɔkinri/ *n.f.* (*magasin*) leather goods shop.

marotte /marɔt/ *n.f.* fad, craze.

marquant, ~e /markɑ̃, -t/ *a.* outstanding.

marque /mark/ *n.f.* mark; (*de produits*) brand, make; (*score*) score. **de ~,** (*comm.*) brand-name; (*fig.*) important. **~ de fabrique,** trade mark. **~ déposée,** registered trade mark.

marqué /marke/ *a.* marked.

marquer /marke/ *v.t.* mark; (*indiquer*) show; (*écrire*) note down; (*point, but*) score; (*joueur*) mark; (*animal*) brand. *—v.i.* (*trace*) leave a mark; (*événement*) stand out.

marquis, ~e[1] /marki, -z/ *n.m., f.* marquis, marchioness.

marquise[2] /markiz/ *n.f.* (*auvent*) glass awning.

marraine /marɛn/ *n.f.* godmother.

marrant, ~e /marɑ̃, -t/ *a.* (*fam.*) funny.

marre /mar/ *adv.* **en avoir ~,** (*fam.*) be fed up (**de,** with).

marrer (se) /(sə)mare/ *v. pr.* (*fam.*) laugh, have a (good) laugh.

marron /marɔ̃/ *n.m.* chestnut; (*couleur*) brown; (*coup: fam.*) thump. *—a. invar.* brown. **~ d'Inde,** horse-chestnut.

mars /mars/ *n.m.* March.

marsouin /marswɛ̃/ *n.m.* porpoise.

marteau (*pl.* **~x**) /marto/ *n.m.* hammer. **~ (de porte),** (door) knocker. **~ piqueur** *ou* **pneumatique,** pneumatic drill.

marteler /martəle/ *v.t.* hammer.

mart|ial (*m. pl.* **~iaux**) /marsjal, -jo/ *a.* martial.

martien, ~ne /marsjɛ̃, -jɛn/ *a. & n.m., f.* Martian.

martyr, ~e[1] /martir/ *n.m., f.* martyr. *—a.* martyred. **~iser** *v.t.* martyr; (*fig.*) batter.

martyre[2] /martir/ *n.m.* (*souffrance*) martyrdom.

marxis|te /marksist/ *a. & n.m./f.* Marxist. **~me** *n.m.* Marxism.

mascarade /maskarad/ *n.f.* masquerade.

mascotte /maskɔt/ *n.f.* mascot.

masculin, ~e /maskylɛ̃, -in/ *a.* masculine; (*sexe*) male; (*mode, équipe*) men's. —*n.m.* masculine. ~**ité** /-inite/ *n.f.* masculinity.

masochis|te /mazɔʃist/ *n.m.|f.* masochist. ~**me** *n.m.* masochism.

masqu|e /mask/ *n.m.* mask. ~**er** *v.t.* mask (à, from); (*lumière*) block (off).

massacr|e /masakr/ *n.m.* massacre. ~**er** *v.t.* massacre; (*abîmer*: *fam.*) spoil.

massage /masaʒ/ *n.m.* massage.

masse /mas/ *n.f.* (*volume*) mass; (*gros morceau*) lump, mass; (*outil*) sledgehammer. **en** ~, (*vendre*) in bulk; (*venir*) in force; (*production*) mass. **la** ~, (*foule*) the masses. **une** ~ **de,** (*fam.*) masses of.

masser[1] /mase/ *v.t.*, **se** ~ *v. pr.* (*gens, foule*) mass.

mass|er[2] /mase/ *v.t.* (*pétrir*) massage. ~**eur,** ~**euse** *n.m.,* f. masseur, masseuse.

massi|f, ~**ve** /masif, -v/ *a.* massive; (*or, argent*) solid. —*n.m.* (*de fleurs*) clump; (*géog.*) massif. ~**vement** *adv.* (*en masse*) in large numbers.

massue /masy/ *n.f.* club, bludgeon.

mastic /mastik/ *n.m.* putty.

mastiquer /mastike/ *v.t.* (*mâcher*) chew.

masturb|er (se) /(sə)mastyrbe/ *v. pr.* masturbate. ~**ation** *n.f.* masturbation.

masure /mazyr/ *n.f.* hovel.

mat /mat/ *a.* (*couleur*) matt; (*bruit*) dull. **être** ~, (*aux échecs*) be checkmate.

mât /mɑ/ *n.m.* mast; (*pylône*) pole.

match /matʃ/ *n.m.* match; (*Amer.*) game. (**faire**) ~ **nul,** tie, draw. ~ **retour,** return match.

matelas /matla/ *n.m.* mattress.

matelasser /matlase/ *v.t.* pad; (*tissu*) quilt.

matelot /matlo/ *n.m.* sailor.

mater /mate/ *v.t.* (*personne*) subdue; (*réprimer*) stifle.

matérialiser (se) /(sə)materjalize/ *v. pr.* materialize.

matérialiste /materjalist/ *a.* materialistic. —*n.m.|f.* materialist.

matériaux /materjo/ *n.m. pl.* materials.

matériel, ~**le** /materjɛl/ *a.* material. —*n.m.* equipment, materials; (*d'un ordinateur*) hardware.

maternel, ~**le** /matɛrnɛl/ *a.* motherly, maternal; (*rapport de parenté*) maternal. —*n.f.* nursery school.

maternité /matɛrnite/ *n.f.* maternity hospital; (*état de mère*) motherhood.

mathémati|que /matematik/ *a.* mathematical. —*n.f. pl.* mathematics. ~**cien,** ~**cienne** *n.m.,* f. mathematician.

maths /mat/ *n.f. pl.* (*fam.*) maths.

matière /matjer/ *n.f.* matter; (*produit*) material; (*sujet*) subject. **en** ~ **de,** as regards. ~ **plastique,** plastic. ~**s grasses,** fat.

matin /matɛ̃/ *n.m.* morning.

matin|al (*m. pl.* ~**aux**) /matinal, -o/ *a.* morning; (*de bonne heure*) early.

matinée /matine/ *n.f.* morning; (*spectacle*) matinée.

matou /matu/ *n.m.* tom-cat.

matraqu|e /matrak/ *n.f.* (*de police*) truncheon; (*Amer.*) billy (club); (*de malfaiteur*) cosh, club. ~**er** *v.t.* club, beat; (*message*) plug.

matrice /matris/ *n.f.* womb; (*techn.*) matrix.

matrimon|ial (*m. pl.* ~**iaux**) /matrimɔnjal, -jo/ *a.* matrimonial.

maturité /matyrite/ *n.f.* maturity.

maudire† /modir/ *v.t.* curse.

maudit, ~**e** /modi, -t/ *a.* (*fam.*) damned.

maugréer /mogree/ *v.i.* grumble.

mausolée /mozɔle/ *n.m.* mausoleum.

maussade /mosad/ *a.* gloomy.

mauvais, ~**e** /mɔvɛ, -z/ *a.* bad; (*erroné*) wrong; (*malveillant*) evil; (*désagréable*) nasty, bad; (*mer*) rough. —*n.m.* **le** ~, the bad. **il fait** ~, the weather is bad. ~**e herbe,** weed. ~**e langue,** gossip. ~**e passe,** tight spot. ~ **traitements,** ill-treatment.

mauve /mov/ *a. & n.m.* mauve.

mauviette /movjɛt/ *n.f.* weakling.

maux /mo/ *voir* **mal**[2].

maxim|al (*m. pl.* ~**aux**) /maksimal, -o/ *a.* maximum.

maxime /maksim/ *n.f.* maxim.

maximum /maksimɔm/ *a. & n.m.* maximum. **au** ~, as much as possible; (*tout au plus*) at most.

mayonnaise /majɔnɛz/ *n.f.* mayonnaise.

mazout /mazut/ *n.m.* heating oil.

me, m'* /mə, m/ *pron.* me; (*indirect*) (to) me; (*réfléchi*) myself.

méandre /meɑ̃dr/ *n.m.* meander.

mec /mek/ *n.m.* (*fam.*) bloke, guy.

mécanicien /mekanisjɛ̃/ *n.m.* mechanic; (*rail.*) train driver.

mécani|que /mekanik/ *a.* mechanical; (*jouet*) clockwork. —*n.f.* mechanics; (*mécanisme*) mechanism. **~ser** *v.t.* mechanize.

mécanisme /mekanism/ *n.m.* mechanism.

méch|ant, ~ante /meʃɑ̃, -t/ *a.* (*cruel*) wicked; (*désagréable*) nasty; (*enfant*) naughty; (*chien*) vicious; (*sensationnel*: *fam.*) terrific. —*n.m., f.* (*enfant*) naughty child. **~amment** *adv.* wickedly. **~anceté** *n.f.* wickedness; (*action*) wicked action.

mèche /mɛʃ/ *n.f.* (*de cheveux*) lock; (*de bougie*) wick; (*d'explosif*) fuse.

méconnaissable /mekɔnɛsabl/ *a.* unrecognizable.

méconn|aître /mekɔnɛtr/ *v.t.* be ignorant of; (*mésestimer*) underestimate. **~aissance** *n.f.* ignorance. **~u** *a.* unrecognized.

mécontent, ~e /mekɔ̃tɑ̃, -t/ *a.* dissatisfied (**de,** with); (*irrité*) annoyed (**de,** at, with). **~ement** /-tmɑ̃/ *n.m.* dissatisfaction; annoyance. **~er** /-te/ *v.t.* dissatisfy; (*irriter*) annoy.

médaill|e /medaj/ *n.f.* medal; (*insigne*) badge; (*bijou*) medallion. **~é, ~ée** *n.m., f.* medal holder.

médaillon /medajɔ̃/ *n.m.* medallion; (*bijou*) locket.

médecin /mɛdsɛ̃/ *n.m.* doctor.

médecine /mɛdsin/ *n.f.* medicine.

média|teur, ~trice /medjatœr, -tris/ *n.m., f.* mediator.

médiation /medjɑsjɔ̃/ *n.f.* mediation.

médic|al (*m. pl.* **~aux**) /medikal, -o/ *a.* medical.

médicament /medikamɑ̃/ *n.m.* medicine.

médicin|al (*m. pl.* **~aux**) /medisinal, -o/ *a.* medicinal.

médico-lég|al (*m. pl.* **~aux**) /medikɔlegal, -o/ *a.* forensic.

médiév|al (*m. pl.* **~aux**) /medjeval, -o/ *a.* medieval.

médiocr|e /medjɔkr/ *a.* mediocre, poor. **~ement** *adv.* (*peu*) not very; (*mal*) in a mediocre way. **~ité** *n.f.* mediocrity.

médire /medir/ *v.i.* **~ de,** speak ill of.

médisance /medizɑ̃s/ *n.f.* **~(s),** malicious gossip.

méditati|f, ~ve /meditatif, -v/ *a.* (*pensif*) thoughtful.

médit|er /medite/ *v.t./i.* meditate. **~er de,** plan to. **~ation** *n.f.* meditation.

Méditerranée /mediterane/ *n.f.* **la ~,** the Mediterranean.

méditerranéen, ~ne /mediteraneɛ̃, -ɛn/ *a.* Mediterranean.

médium /medjɔm/ *n.m.* (*personne*) medium.

méduse /medyz/ *n.f.* jellyfish.

meeting /mitiŋ/ *n.m.* meeting.

méfait /mefɛ/ *n.m.* misdeed. **les ~s de,** (*conséquences*) the ravages of.

méfian|t, ~te /mefjɑ̃, -t/ *a.* distrustful. **~ce** *n.f.* distrust.

méfier (se) /(sə)mefje/ *v. pr.* be wary *ou* careful. **se ~ de,** distrust, be wary of.

mégarde (par) /(par)megard/ *adv.* by accident, accidentally.

mégère /meʒɛr/ *n.f.* (*femme*) shrew.

mégot /mego/ *n.m.* (*fam.*) cigarette-end.

meilleur, ~e /mɛjœr/ *a. & adv.* better (**que,** than). **le ~ livre**/*etc.*, the best book/*etc.* **mon ~ ami**/*etc.*, my best friend/*etc.* —*n.m., f.* best (one). **~ marché,** cheaper.

mélancol|ie /melɑ̃kɔli/ *n.f.* melancholy. **~ique** *a.* melancholy.

mélang|e /melɑ̃ʒ/ *n.m.* mixture, blend. **~er** *v.t.*, **se ~er** *v. pr.* mix, blend; (*embrouiller*) mix up.

mélasse /melas/ *n.f.* treacle; (*Amer.*) molasses.

mêlée /mele/ *n.f.* scuffle; (*rugby*) scrum.

mêler /mele/ *v.t.* mix (**à,** with); (*qualités*) combine; (*embrouiller*) mix up. **~ à,** (*impliquer dans*) involve in. **se ~** *v. pr.* mix; combine. **se ~ à,** (*se joindre à*) join. **se ~ de,** meddle in.

mélod|ie /melɔdi/ *n.f.* melody. **~ieux, ~ieuse** *a.* melodious. **~ique** *a.* melodic.

mélodram|e /melɔdram/ *n.m.* melodrama. **~atique** *a.* melodramatic.

mélomane /melɔman/ *n.m./f.* music lover.

melon /mlɔ̃/ *n.m.* melon. (**chapeau**) **~,** bowler (hat).

membrane /mɑ̃bran/ *n.f.* membrane.

membre[1] /mɑ̃br/ *n.m.* limb.

membre[2] /mɑ̃br/ *n.m.* (*adhérent*) member.

même /mɛm/ *a.* same. **ce livre**/*etc.* **~,** this very book/*etc.* **la bonté**/*etc.* **~,** kindness/*etc.* itself. —*pron.* same (one). —*adv.* even. **à ~,** (*sur*) directly on. **à ~ de,** in a position to. **de ~,** (*aussi*) too; (*de la même façon*) likewise. **de ~ que,** just as. **en ~ temps,** at the same time.

mémé /meme/ *n.f.* (*fam.*) granny.

mémoire /memwar/ *n.f.* memory. —*n.m.* (*requête*) memorandum; (*univ.*) dissertation. **~s,** (*souvenirs écrits*) memoirs. **à la ~ de,** to the memory of. **de ~,** from memory.

mémorable /memɔrabl/ *a.* memorable.

mémorandum /memɔrɑ̃dɔm/ *n.m.* memorandum.

mémor|ial (*pl.* **~iaux**) /memɔrjal, -jo/ *n.m.* memorial.

menac|e /mənas/ *n.f.* threat. **~er** *v.t.* threaten (**de faire,** to do).

ménage /menaʒ/ *n.m.* (married) couple; (*travail*) housework. **se mettre en ~,** set up house.

ménagement /menaʒmɑ̃/ *n.m.* care and consideration.

ménag|er[1], **~ère** /menaʒe, -ɛr/ *a.* household, domestic. —*n.f.* housewife.

ménager[2] /menaʒe/ *v.t.* treat with tact; (*utiliser*) be sparing in the use of; (*organiser*) prepare (carefully).

ménagerie /menaʒri/ *n.f.* menagerie.

mendiant, ~e /mɑ̃djɑ̃, -t/ *n.m., f.* beggar.

mendicité /mɑ̃disite/ *n.f.* begging.

mendier /mɑ̃dje/ *v.t.* beg for. —*v.i.* beg.

menées /məne/ *n.f. pl.* schemings.

mener /məne/ *v.t.* lead; (*entreprise, pays*) run. —*v.i.* lead. **~ à,** (*accompagner à*) take to. **~ à bien,** see through.

meneur /mənœr/ *n.m.* (*chef*) (ring)-leader. **~ de jeu,** compère; (*Amer.*) master of ceremonies.

méningite /menɛ̃ʒit/ *n.f.* meningitis.

ménopause /menɔpoz/ *n.f.* menopause.

menotte /mənɔt/ *n.f.* (*fam.*) hand. **~s,** handcuffs.

mensong|e /mɑ̃sɔ̃ʒ/ *n.m.* lie; (*action*) lying. **~er, ~ère** *a.* untrue.

menstruation /mɑ̃stryɑsjɔ̃/ *n.f.* menstruation.

mensualité /mɑ̃sɥalite/ *n.f.* monthly payment.

mensuel, ~le /mɑ̃sɥɛl/ *a.* & *n.m.* monthly. **~lement** *adv.* monthly.

mensurations /mɑ̃syrɑsjɔ̃/ *n.f. pl.* measurements.

ment|al (*m. pl.* **~aux**) /mɑ̃tal, -o/ *a.* mental.

mentalité /mɑ̃talite/ *n.f.* mentality.

menteu|r, ~se /mɑ̃tœr, -z/ *n.m., f.* liar. —*a.* untruthful.

menthe /mɑ̃t/ *n.f.* mint.

mention /mɑ̃sjɔ̃/ *n.f.* mention; (*annotation*) note; (*scol.*) grade. **~ bien,** (*scol.*) distinction. **~ner** /-jɔne/ *v.t.* mention.

mentir† /mɑ̃tir/ *v.i.* lie.

menton /mɑ̃tɔ̃/ *n.m.* chin.

menu[1] /məny/ *n.m.* (*carte*) menu; (*repas*) meal.

menu[2] /məny/ *a.* (*petit*) tiny; (*fin*) fine; (*insignifiant*) minor. —*adv.* (*couper*) fine.

menuis|ier /mənɥizje/ *n.m.* carpenter, joiner. **~erie** *n.f.* carpentry, joinery.

méprendre (se) /(sə)meprɑ̃dr/ *v. pr.* **se ~ sur,** be mistaken about.

mépris /mepri/ *n.m.* contempt, scorn (**de,** for). **au ~ de,** in defiance of.

méprisable /meprizabl/ *a.* despicable.

méprise /mepriz/ *n.f.* mistake.

mépris|er /meprize/ *v.t.* scorn, despise. **~ant, ~ante** *a.* scornful.

mer /mɛr/ *n.f.* sea; (*marée*) tide. **en haute ~,** on the open sea.

mercenaire /mɛrsənɛr/ *n.m. & a.* mercenary.

merci /mɛrsi/ *int.* thank you, thanks (**de, pour,** for). —*n.f.* mercy. **~ beaucoup, ~ bien,** thank you very much.

merc|ier, ~ière /mɛrsje, -jɛr/ *n.m., f.* haberdasher; (*Amer.*) notions merchant. **~erie** *n.f.* haberdashery; (*Amer.*) notions store.

mercredi /mɛrkrədi/ *n.m.* Wednesday. **~ des Cendres,** Ash Wednesday.

mercure /mɛrkyr/ *n.m.* mercury.

merde /mɛrd/ *int.* (*fam.*) oh hell.

mère /mɛr/ *n.f.* mother. **~ de famille,** mother.

méridien /meridjɛ̃/ *n.m.* meridian.

méridion|al, ~ale (*m. pl.* **~aux**) /meridjɔnal, -o/ *a.* southern. —*n.m.,f.* southerner.

meringue /mərɛ̃g/ *n.f.* meringue.

mérite /merit/ *n.m.* merit.

mérit|er /merite/ *v.t.* deserve. **~ant, ~ante** *a.* deserving.

méritoire /meritwar/ *a.* commendable.

merlan /mɛrlɑ̃/ *n.m.* whiting.

merle /mɛrl/ *n.m.* blackbird.

merveille /mɛrvɛj/ *n.f.* wonder, marvel. **à ∼**, wonderfully.

merveilleu|x, ∼se /mɛrvɛjø, -z/ *a.* wonderful, marvellous. **∼sement** *adv.* wonderfully.

mes /me/ *voir* **mon**.

mésange /mezɑ̃ʒ/ *n.f.* tit(mouse).

mésaventure /mezavɑ̃tyr/ *n.f.* misadventure.

mesdames /medam/ *voir* **madame**.

mesdemoiselles /medmwazɛl/ *voir* **mademoiselle**.

mésentente /mezɑ̃tɑ̃t/ *n.f.* disagreement.

mesquin, ∼e /mɛskɛ̃, -in/ *a.* mean. **∼erie** /-inri/ *n.f.* meanness.

mess /mɛs/ *n.m.* (*mil.*) mess.

messag|e /mesaʒ/ *n.m.* message. **∼er, ∼ère** *n.m.,f.* messenger.

messe /mɛs/ *n.f.* (*relig.*) mass.

Messie /mesi/ *n.m.* Messiah.

messieurs /mesjø/ *voir* **monsieur**.

mesure /məzyr/ *n.f.* measurement; (*quantité, étalon*) measure; (*disposition*) measure, step; (*cadence*) time; (*modération*) moderation. **à ∼ que**, as. **dans la ∼ où**, in so far as. **dans une certaine ∼**, to some extent. **en ∼ de**, in a position to.

mesuré /məzyre/ *a.* measured; (*personne*) moderate.

mesurer /məzyre/ *v.t.* measure; (*juger*) assess; (*argent, temps*) ration. **∼ à** *ou* **sur**, match to. **se ∼ avec**, pit o.s. against.

met /mɛ/ *voir* **mettre**.

métabolisme /metabɔlism/ *n.m.* metabolism.

mét|al (*pl.* **∼aux**) /metal, -o/ *n.m.* metal. **∼allique** *a.* (*objet*) metal; (*éclat etc.*) metallic.

métallurg|ie /metalyrʒi/ *n.f.* (*industrie*) steel *ou* metal industry. **∼iste** *n.m.* steel *ou* metal worker.

métamorphos|e /metamɔrfoz/ *n.f.* metamorphosis. **∼er** *v.t.*, **se ∼er** *v. pr.* transform.

métaphor|e /metafɔr/ *n.f.* metaphor. **∼ique** *a.* metaphorical.

météo /meteo/ *n.f.* (*bulletin*) weather forecast.

météore /meteɔr/ *n.m.* meteor.

météorolog|ie /meteɔrɔlɔʒi/ *n.f.* meteorology; (*service*) weather bureau. **∼ique** *a.* weather; (*études etc.*) meteorological.

méthod|e /metɔd/ *n.f.* method; (*ouvrage*) course, manual. **∼ique** *a.* methodical.

méticuleu|x, ∼se /metikylø, -z/ *a.* meticulous.

métier /metje/ *n.m.* job; (*manuel*) trade; (*intellectuel*) profession; (*expérience*) skill. **∼ (à tisser)**, loom.

métis, ∼se /metis/ *a. & n.m., f.* half-caste.

métrage /metraʒ/ *n.m.* length. **court ∼**, short film. **long ∼**, full-length film.

mètre /mɛtr/ *n.m.* metre; (*règle*) rule. **∼ à ruban**, tape-measure.

métreur /metrœr/ *n.m.* quantity surveyor.

métrique /metrik/ *a.* metric.

métro /metro/ *n.m.* underground; (*à Paris*) Métro.

métropol|e /metrɔpɔl/ *n.f.* metropolis; (*pays*) mother country. **∼itain, ∼itaine** *a.* metropolitan.

mets[1] /mɛ/ *n.m.* dish.

mets[2] /mɛ/ *voir* **mettre**.

mettable /mɛtabl/ *a.* wearable.

metteur /mɛtœr/ *n.m.* **∼ en scène**, (*théâtre*) producer; (*cinéma*) director.

mettre† /mɛtr/ *v.t.* put; (*vêtement*) put on; (*radio, gaz, etc.*) put *ou* switch on; (*table*) lay; (*pendule*) set; (*temps*) take; (*installer*) put in; (*supposer*) suppose. **se ∼** *v. pr.* put o.s.; (*objet*) go; (*porter*) wear. **∼ bas**, give birth. **∼ qn. en boîte**, pull s.o.'s leg. **∼ en cause** *ou* **en question**, question. **∼ en colère**, make angry. **∼ en valeur**, highlight; (*un bien*) exploit. **se ∼ à**, (*entrer dans*) get *ou* go into. **se ∼ à faire**, start doing. **se ∼ à l'aise**, make o.s. comfortable. **se ∼ à table**, sit down at the table. **se ∼ au travail**, set to work. **(se) ∼ en ligne**, line up.

meuble /mœbl/ *n.m.* piece of furniture. **∼s**, furniture.

meubler /mœble/ *v.t.* furnish; (*fig.*) fill. **se ∼** *v. pr.* buy furniture.

meugl|er /møgle/ *v.i.* moo. **∼ement(s)** *n.m.* (*pl.*) mooing.

meule /møl/ *n.f.* (*de foin*) haystack; (*à moudre*) millstone.

meun|ier, ∼ière /mønje -jɛr/ *n.m., f.* miller.

meurs, meurt /mœr/ *voir* **mourir**.

meurtr|e /mœrtr/ *n.m.* murder. **∼ier, ∼ière** *a.* deadly; *n.m.* murderer; *n.f.* murderess.

meurtr|ir /mœrtrir/ *v.t.* bruise. **∼issure** *n.f.* bruise.

meute /møt/ *n.f.* (*troupe*) pack.

mexicain, ~e /mɛksikɛ̃, -ɛn/ *a.* & *n.m.*, *f.* Mexican.

Mexique /mɛksik/ *n.m.* Mexico.

mi- /mi/ *préf.* mid-, half-. **à ~-chemin**, half-way. **à ~-côte**, half-way up the hill. **la ~-juin**/*etc.*, mid-June/*etc.*

miaou /mjau/ *n.m.* mew.

miaul|er /mjole/ *v.i.* mew. **~ement** *n.m.* mew.

miche /miʃ/ *n.f.* round loaf.

micro /mikro/ *n.m.* microphone, mike.

micro- /mikro/ *préf.* micro-

microbe /mikrɔb/ *n.m.* germ.

microfilm /mikrɔfilm/ *n.m.* micro-film.

micro-onde /mikroɔ̃d/ *n.f.* micro-wave.

microphone /mikrɔfɔn/ *n.m.* micro-phone.

microplaquette /mikroplakɛt/ *n.f.* (micro)chip.

microscop|e /mikroskɔp/ *n.m.* micro-scope. **~ique** *a.* microscopic.

microsillon /mikrosijɔ̃/ *n.m.* long-playing record.

midi /midi/ *n.m.* twelve o'clock, mid-day, noon; (*déjeuner*) lunch-time; (*sud*) south. **le M~**, the South of France.

mie /mi/ *n.f.* soft part (of the loaf).

miel /mjɛl/ *n.m.* honey.

mielleu|x, ~se /mjɛlø, -z/ *a.* unctuous.

mien, ~ne /mjɛ̃, mjɛn/ *pron.* **le ~, la ~ne, les ~(ne)s,** mine.

miette /mjɛt/ *n.f.* crumb; (*fig.*) scrap. **en ~s,** in pieces.

mieux /mjø/ *adv.* & *a. invar.* better (**que,** than). **le** *ou* **la** *ou* **les ~,** (the) best. —*n.m.* best; (*progrès*) improve-ment. **faire de son ~,** do one's best. **faire ~ de,** be better off to. **le ~ serait de,** the best thing would be to.

mièvre /mjɛvr/ *a.* genteel and insipid.

mignon, ~ne /miɲɔ̃, -ɔn/ *a.* pretty.

migraine /migrɛn/ *n.f.* headache.

migration /migrɑsjɔ̃/ *n.f.* migration.

mijoter /miʒote/ *v.t./i.* simmer; (*tramer*: *fam.*) cook up.

mil /mil/ *n.m.* a thousand.

milic|e /milis/ *n.f.* militia. **~ien** *n.m.* militiaman.

milieu (*pl.* **~x**) /miljø/ *n.m.* middle; (*environnement*) environment; (*groupe*) circle; (*mesure*) medium; (*voie*) middle way; (*criminel*) under-world. **au ~ de,** in the middle of.

militaire /militɛr/ *a.* military. —*n.m.* soldier.

milit|er /milite/ *v.i.* be a militant. **~er pour,** militate in favour of. **~ant, ~ante** *n.m.*, *f.* militant.

mille[1] /mil/ *a.* & *n.m. invar.* a thou-sand. **deux ~,** two thousand.

mille[2] /mil/ *n.m.* **~ (marin),** (naut-ical) mile.

millénaire /milenɛr/ *n.m.* millen-nium.

mille-pattes /milpat/ *n.m. invar.* centipede.

millésime /milezim/ *n.m.* year.

millet /mijɛ/ *n.m* millet.

milliard /miljar/ *n.m.* thousand million, billion. **~aire** /-dɛr/ *n.m.*/*f.* multimillionaire.

millier /milje/ *n.m.* thousand. **un ~ (de),** about a thousand.

millimètre /milimɛtr/ *n.m.* milli-metre.

million /miljɔ̃/ *n.m.* million. **deux ~s (de),** two million. **~naire** /-jɔnɛr/ *n.m.*/*f.* millionaire.

mim|e /mim/ *n.m.*/*f.* (*personne*) mime. —*n.m.* (*art*) mime. **~er** *v.t.* mime; (*singer*) mimic.

mimique /mimik/ *n.f.* (*expressive*) gestures.

mimosa /mimoza/ *n.m.* mimosa.

minable /minabl/ *a.* shabby.

minaret /minarɛ/ *n.m.* minaret.

minauder /minode/ *v.i.* simper.

minc|e /mɛ̃s/ *a.* thin; (*svelte, insigni-fiant*) slim. —*int.* dash (it). **~eur** *n.f.* thinness; slimness.

mine[1] /min/ *n.f.* expression; (*allure*) appearance. **avoir bonne ~,** look well. **faire ~ de,** make as if to.

mine[2] /min/ *n.f.* (*exploitation, explo-sif*) mine; (*de crayon*) lead. **~ de char-bon,** coal-mine.

miner /mine/ *v.t.* (*saper*) undermine; (*garnir d'explosifs*) mine.

minerai /minrɛ/ *n.m.* ore.

minér|al (*m. pl.* **~aux**) /mineral, -o/ *a.* mineral. —*n.m.* (*pl.* **~aux**) mineral.

minet, ~te /minɛ, -t/ *n.m.*, *f.* (*chat*: *fam.*) puss(y).

mineur[1], **~e** /minœr/ *a.* minor; (*jurid.*) under age. —*n.m.*, *f.* (*jurid.*) minor.

mineur[2] /minœr/ *n.m.* (*ouvrier*) miner.

mini- /mini/ *préf.* mini-.

miniature /minjatyr/ *n.f.* & *a.* minia-ture.

minibus /minibys/ *n.m.* minibus.
min|ier, ~ière /minje, -jɛr/ *a.* mining.
minim|al (*m. pl.* **~aux**) /minimal, -o/ *a.* mimimum.
minime /minim/ *a.* minor. —*n.m./f.* (*sport*) junior.
minimiser /minimize/ *v.t.* minimize.
minimum /minimɔm/ *a.* & *n.m.* minimum. **au ~,** (*pour le moins*) at the very least.
minist|ère /ministɛr/ *n.m.* ministry; (*gouvernement*) government. **~ère de l'Intérieur,** Home Office; (*Amer.*) Department of the Interior. **~ériel, ~érielle** *a.* ministerial, government.
ministre /ministr/ *n.m.* minister. **~ de l'Intérieur,** Home Secretary; (*Amer.*) Secretary of the Interior.
minorer /minɔre/ *v.t.* reduce.
minorit|é /minɔrite/ *n.f.* minority. **~aire** *a.* minority. **être ~aire,** be in the minority.
Minorque /minɔrk/ *n.f.* Minorca.
minuit /minɥi/ *n.m.* midnight.
minuscule /minyskyl/ *a.* minute. —*n.f.* (*lettre*) **~,** small letter.
minut|e /minyt/ *n.f.* minute. **~er** *v.t.* time (to the minute).
minuterie /minytri/ *n.f.* time-switch.
minutie /minysi/ *n.f.* meticulousness.
minutieu|x, ~se /minysjø, -z/ *a.* meticulous. **~sement** *adv.* meticulously.
mioche /mjɔʃ/ *n.m., f.* (*fam.*) youngster, kid.
mirabelle /mirabɛl/ *n.f.* (mirabelle) plum.
miracle /mirɑkl/ *n.m.* miracle.
miraculeu|x, ~se /mirakylø, -z/ *a.* miraculous. **~sement** *adv.* miraculously.
mirage /miraʒ/ *n.m.* mirage.
mirobolant, ~e /mirɔbɔlɑ̃, -t/ *a.* (*fam.*) marvellous.
miroir /mirwar/ *n.m.* mirror.
miroiter /mirwate/ *v.i.* gleam, shimmer.
mis, ~e¹ /mi, miz/ *voir* **mettre.** —*a.* **bien ~,** well-dressed.
mise² /miz/ *n.f.* putting; (*argent*) stake; (*tenue*) attire. **~ à feu,** blast-off. **~ au point,** adjustment; (*fig.*) clarification. **~ de fonds,** capital outlay. **~ en garde,** warning. **~ en scène,** (*théâtre*) production; (*cinéma*) direction.
miser /mize/ *v.t.* (*argent*) bet, stake (**sur,** on). **~ sur,** (*compter sur: fam.*) bank on.

misérable /mizerabl/ *a.* miserable, wretched; (*indigent*) poverty-stricken; (*minable*) seedy. —*n.m./f.* wretch.
mis|ère /mizɛr/ *n.f.* (grinding) poverty; (*malheur*) misery. **~éreux, ~éreuse** *n.m., f.* pauper.
miséricorde /mizerikɔrd/ *n.f.* mercy.
missel /misɛl/ *n.m.* missal.
missile /misil/ *n.m.* missile.
mission /misjɔ̃/ *n.m.* mission. **~naire** /-jɔnɛr/ *n.m./f.* missionary.
missive /misiv/ *n.f.* missive.
mistral /mistral/ *n.m. invar.* (*vent*) mistral.
mitaine /mitɛn/ *n.f.* mitten.
mit|e /mit/ *n.f.* (clothes-)moth. **~é** *a.* moth-eaten.
mi-temps /mitɑ̃/ *n.f. invar.* (*repos: sport*) half-time; (*période: sport*) half. **à ~,** part time.
miteu|x, ~se /mitø, -z/ *a.* shabby.
mitigé /mitiʒe/ *a.* (*modéré*) lukewarm; (*mélange: fam.*) mixed.
mitrail|le /mitrɑj/ *n.f.* gunfire. **~er** *v.t.* machine-gun.
mitraill|ette /mitrɑjɛt/ *n.f.* sub-machine-gun. **~euse** *n.f.* machine-gun.
mi-voix (à) /(a)mivwa/ *adv.* in an undertone.
mixeur /miksœr/ *n.m.* liquidizer, blender.
mixte /mikst/ *a.* mixed; (*usage*) dual; (*tribunal*) joint; (*école*) coeducational.
mixture /mikstyr/ *n.f.* (*péj.*) mixture.
mobile¹ /mɔbil/ *a.* mobile; (*pièce*) moving; (*fête*) movable; (*feuillet*) loose. —*n.m.* (*art*) mobile.
mobile² /mɔbil/ *n.m.* (*raison*) motive.
mobilier /mɔbilje/ *n.m.* furniture.
mobilis|er /mɔbilize/ *v.t.* mobilize. **~ation** *n.f.* mobilization.
mobilité /mɔbilite/ *n.f.* mobility.
mobylette /mɔbilɛt/ *n.f.* (P.) moped.
mocassin /mɔkasɛ̃/ *n.m.* moccasin.
moche /mɔʃ/ *a.* (*laid: fam.*) ugly; (*mauvais: fam.*) lousy.
modalité /mɔdalite/ *n.f.* mode.
mode¹ /mɔd/ *n.f.* fashion; (*coutume*) custom. **à la ~,** fashionable.
mode² /mɔd/ *n.m.* method, mode; (*genre*) way. **~ d'emploi,** directions (for use).
modèle /mɔdɛl/ *n.m. & a.* model. **~ réduit,** (small-scale) model.
modeler /mɔdle/ *v.t.* model (**sur,** on). **se ~ sur,** model o.s. on.

modéré, ~e /mɔdere/ a. & n.m., f. moderate. **~ment** adv. moderately.

modér|er /mɔdere/ v.t. moderate. **se ~er** v. pr. restrain o.s. **~ateur, ~atrice** a. moderating. **~ation** n.f. moderation.

modern|e /mɔdɛrn/ a. modern. —n.m. modern style. **~iser** v.t. modernize.

modest|e /mɔdɛst/ a. modest. **~ement** adv. modestly. **~ie** n.f. modesty.

modicité /mɔdisite/ n.f. lowness.

modif|ier /mɔdifje/ v.t. modify. **se ~ier** v. pr. alter. **~ication** n.f. modification.

modique /mɔdik/ a. low.

modiste /mɔdist/ n.f. milliner.

module /mɔdyl/ n.m. module.

modul|er /mɔdyle/ v.t./i. modulate. **~ation** n.f. modulation.

moelle /mwal/ n.f. marrow. **~ épinière,** spinal cord.

moelleu|x, ~se /mwalø, -z/ a. soft; (onctueux) smooth.

mœurs /mœr(s)/ n.f. pl. (morale) morals; (habitudes) customs; (manières) ways.

moi /mwa/ pron. me; (indirect) (to) me; (sujet) I. —n.m. self. **~-même** pron. myself.

moignon /mwaɲɔ̃/ n.m. stump.

moindre /mwɛ̃dr/ a. (moins grand) less(er). **le** ou **la ~, les ~s,** the slightest, the least.

moine /mwan/ n.m. monk.

moineau (pl. **~x**) /mwano/ n.m. sparrow.

moins /mwɛ̃/ adv. less (**que,** than). —prép. (soustraction) minus. **~ de,** (quantité) less, not so much (**que,** as); (objets, personnes) fewer, not so many (**que,** as). **~ de dix francs/d'une livre**/etc., less than ten francs/one pound/etc. **le** ou **la** ou **les ~,** the least. **le ~ grand/haut,** the smallest/ lowest. **au ~, du ~,** at least. **de ~,** less. **en ~,** less; (manquant) missing. **une heure ~ dix,** ten to one. **à ~ que,** unless.

mois /mwa/ n.m. month.

mois|i /mwazi/ a. mouldy. —n.m. mould. **de ~i,** (odeur, goût) musty. **~ir** v.i. go mouldy. **~issure** n.f. mould.

moisson /mwasɔ̃/ n.f. harvest.

moissonn|er /mwasɔne/ v.t. harvest, reap. **~eur, ~euse** n.m., f. harvester. **~euse-batteuse** (pl. **~euses-batteuses**) n.f. combine harvester.

moit|e /mwat/ a. sticky, clammy. **~eur** n.f. stickiness.

moitié /mwatje/ n.f. half; (milieu) halfway mark. **à ~,** half-way. **à ~ vide/ fermé**/etc., half empty/closed/etc. **à ~ prix,** at half-price. **la ~ de,** half (of).

moka /mɔka/ n.m. (gâteau) coffee cream cake.

mol /mɔl/ voir **mou.**

molaire /mɔlɛr/ n.f. molar.

molécule /mɔlekyl/ n.f. molecule.

molester /mɔlɛste/ v.t. manhandle, rough up.

molle /mɔl/ voir **mou.**

moll|ement /mɔlmã/ adv. softly; (faiblement) feebly. **~esse** n.f. softness; (faiblesse, indolence) feebleness.

mollet /mɔlɛ/ n.m. (de jambe) calf.

molletonné /mɔltɔne/ a. (fleece-) lined.

mollir /mɔlir/ v.i. soften; (céder) yield.

mollusque /mɔlysk/ n.m. mollusc.

môme /mom/ n.m./f. (fam.) kid.

moment /mɔmã/ n.m. moment; (période) time. (**petit**) **~,** short while. **au ~ où,** when. **du ~ où** ou **que,** seeing that. **en ce ~,** at the moment.

momentané /mɔmãtane/ a. momentary. **~ment** adv. momentarily; (en ce moment) at present.

momie /mɔmi/ n.f. mummy.

mon, ma ou **mon*** (pl. **mes**) /mɔ̃, ma, mɔ̃n, me/ a. my.

Monaco /mɔnako/ n.f. Monaco.

monarchie /mɔnarʃi/ n.f. monarchy.

monarque /mɔnark/ n.m. monarque.

monastère /mɔnastɛr/ n.m. monastery.

monceau (pl. **~x**) /mɔ̃so/ n.m. heap, pile.

mondain, ~e /mɔ̃dɛ̃, -ɛn/ a. society, social.

monde /mɔ̃d/ n.m. world. **du ~,** (a lot of) people; (quelqu'un) somebody. **le** (**grand**) **~,** (high) society.

mond|ial (m. pl. **~iaux**) /mɔ̃djal, -jo/ a. world; (influence) worldwide. **~ialement** adv. the world over.

monégasque /mɔnegask/ a. & n.m./f. Monegasque.

monétaire /mɔnetɛr/ a. monetary.

mongolien, ~ne /mɔ̃gɔljɛ̃, -jɛn/ n.m., f. & a. (méd.) mongol.

moni|teur, ~trice /mɔnitœr, -tris/ n.m., f. instructor, instructress; (de colonie de vacances) assistant, minder; (Amer.) (camp) counselor.

monnaie /mɔnɛ/ *n.f.* currency; (*pièce*) coin; (*appoint*) change. **faire la ~ de**, get change for. **faire à qn. la ~ de**, give s.o. change for. **menue** *ou* **petite ~**, small change.

monnayer /mɔneje/ *v.t.* convert into cash.

mono /mɔno/ *a. invar.* mono.

monocle /mɔnɔkl/ *n.m.* monocle.

monocorde /mɔnɔkɔrd/ *a.* monotonous.

monogramme /mɔnɔgram/ *n.m.* monogram.

monologue /mɔnɔlɔg/ *n.m.* monologue.

monopol|e /mɔnɔpɔl/ *n.m.* monopoly. **~iser** *v.t.* monopolize.

monosyllabe /mɔnɔsilab/ *n.m.* monosyllable.

monoton|e /mɔnɔtɔn/ *a.* monotonous. **~ie** *n.f.* monotony.

monseigneur /mɔ̃sɛɲœr/ *n.m.* Your *ou* His Grace.

monsieur (*pl.* **messieurs**) /məsjø, mesjø/ *n.m.* gentleman. **M~** *ou* **M. Dupont**, Mr Dupont. **Messieurs** *ou* **MM. Dupont**, Messrs Dupont. **oui ~**, yes; (*avec déférence*) yes, sir.

monstre /mɔ̃str/ *n.m.* monster. —*a.* (*fam.*) colossal.

monstr|ueux, ~ueuse /mɔ̃stryø, -z/ *a.* monstrous. **~uosité** *n.f.* monstrosity.

mont /mɔ̃/ *n.m.* mount.

montage /mɔ̃taʒ/ *n.m.* (*assemblage*) assembly; (*cinéma*) editing.

montagn|e /mɔ̃taɲ/ *n.f.* mountain; (*région*) mountains. **~es russes**, roller-coaster. **~ard, ~arde** *n.m., f.* mountain dweller. **~eux, ~euse** *a.* mountainous.

montant[1], **~e** /mɔ̃tɑ̃, -t/ *a.* rising; (*robe*) high-necked.

montant[2] /mɔ̃tɑ̃/ *n.m.* amount; (*pièce de bois*) upright.

mont-de-piété (*pl.* **monts-de-piété**) /mɔ̃dpjete/ *n.m.* pawnshop.

monte-charge /mɔ̃tʃarʒ/ *n.m. invar.* service lift; (*Amer.*) dumb waiter.

montée /mɔ̃te/ *n.f.* ascent, climb; (*de prix*) rise; (*côte*) hill.

monter /mɔ̃te/ *v.i.* (*aux. être*) go *ou* come up; (*grimper*) climb; (*prix, mer*) rise. **~ à**, (*cheval*) mount. **~ dans**, (*train*) get on to; (*voiture*) get into. **~ sur**, (*colline*) climb up; (*trône*) ascend. —*v.t.* (*aux. avoir*) go *ou* come up; (*objet*) take *ou* bring up; (*cheval,*

garde) mount; (*société*) set up. **~ à cheval**, (*sport*) ride. **~ en flèche**, soar. **~ en graine**, go to seed.

monteu|r, ~se /mɔ̃tœr, -øz/ *n.m., f.* (*techn.*) fitter; (*cinéma*) editor.

monticule /mɔ̃tikyl/ *n.m.* mound.

montre /mɔ̃tr/ *n.f.* watch. **~-bracelet** (*pl.* **~s-bracelets**) *n.f.* wrist-watch. **faire ~ de**, show.

montrer /mɔ̃tre/ *v.t.* show (**à**, to). **se ~** *v. pr.* show o.s.; (*être*) be; (*s'avérer*) prove to be. **~ du doigt**, point to.

monture /mɔ̃tyr/ *n.f.* (*cheval*) mount; (*de lunettes*) frame; (*de bijou*) setting.

monument /mɔnymɑ̃/ *n.m.* monument. **~ aux morts**, war memorial. **~al** (*m. pl.* **~aux**) /-tal, -to/ *a.* monumental.

moqu|er (se) /(sə)mɔke/ *v. pr.* **se ~er de**, make fun of. **je m'en ~e**, (*fam.*) I couldn't care less. **~erie** *n.f.* mockery. **~eur, ~euse** *a.* mocking.

moquette /mɔkɛt/ *n.f.* fitted carpet; (*Amer.*) wall-to-wall carpeting.

mor|al, ~ale /mɔral/ (*m. pl.* **~aux**) /mɔral, -o/ *a.* moral. —*n.m.* (*pl.* **~aux**) morale. —*n.f.* moral code; (*mœurs*) morals; (*de fable*) moral. **faire la ~ale à**, lecture. **~alement** *adv.* morally. **~alité** *n.f.* morality; (*de fable*) moral.

moralisa|teur, ~trice /mɔralizatœr, -tris/ *a.* moralizing.

morbide /mɔrbid/ *a.* morbid.

morceau (*pl.* **~x**) /mɔrso/ *n.m.* piece, bit; (*de sucre*) lump; (*de viande*) cut; (*passage*) passage.

morceler /mɔrsəle/ *v.t.* fragment.

mordant, ~e /mɔrdɑ̃, -t/ *a.* scathing; (*froid*) biting. —*n.m.* (*énergie*) vigour, punch.

mordiller /mɔrdije/ *v.t.* nibble.

mord|re /mɔrdr/ *v.t./i.* bite. **~re sur**, overlap into. **~u, ~ue** *n.m., f.* (*fam.*) fan; *a.* bitten. **~u de**, (*fam.*) crazy about.

morfondre (se) /(sə)mɔrfɔ̃dr/ *v. pr.* mope, wait anxiously.

morgue[1] /mɔrg/ *n.f.* morgue, mortuary.

morgue[2] /mɔrg/ *n.f.* (*attitude*) haughtiness.

moribond, ~e /mɔribɔ̃, -d/ *a.* dying.

morne /mɔrn/ *a.* dull.

morose /mɔroz/ *a.* morose.

morphine /mɔrfin/ *n.f.* morphine.

mors /mɔr/ *n.m.* (*de cheval*) bit.

morse[1] /mɔrs/ *n.m.* walrus.

morse[2] /mɔrs/ *n.m.* (*code*) Morse code.

morsure /mɔrsyr/ *n.f.* bite.

mort[1] /mɔr/ *n.f.* death.

mort[2], **~e** /mɔr, -t/ *a.* dead. —*n.m., f.* dead man, dead woman. **les ~s,** the dead. **~ de fatigue,** dead tired. **~-né** *a.* stillborn.

mortadelle /mɔrtadɛl/ *n.f.* mortadella.

mortalité /mɔrtalite/ *n.f.* death rate.

mortel, ~le /mɔrtɛl/ *a.* mortal; (*accident*) fatal; (*poison, silence*) deadly. —*n.m., f.* mortal. **~lement** *adv.* mortally.

mortier /mɔrtje/ *n.m.* mortar.

mortifier /mɔrtifje/ *v.t.* mortify.

mortuaire /mɔrtɥɛr/ *a.* (*cérémonie*) funeral; (*avis*) death.

morue /mɔry/ *n.f.* cod.

mosaïque /mɔzaik/ *n.f.* mosaic.

Moscou /mɔsku/ *n.m./f.* Moscow.

mosquée /mɔske/ *n.f.* mosque.

mot /mo/ *n.m.* word; (*lettre, message*) line, note. **~ d'ordre,** watchword. **~ de passe,** password. **~s croisés,** crossword (puzzle).

motard /mɔtar/ *n.m.* (*fam.*) police motorcyclist.

motel /mɔtɛl/ *n.m.* motel.

moteur[1] /mɔtœr/ *n.m.* engine, motor.

mo|teur[2], **~trice** /mɔtœr, -tris/ *a.* (*nerf*) motor; (*force*) driving.

motif /mɔtif/ *n.m.* reason; (*jurid.*) motive; (*dessin*) pattern.

motion /mɔsjɔ̃/ *n.f.* motion.

motiv|er /mɔtive/ *v.t.* motivate; (*justifier*) justify. **~ation** *n.f.* motivation.

moto /mɔto/ *n.f.* motor cycle. **~cycliste** *n.m./f.* motor-cyclist.

motoriser /mɔtɔrize/ *v.t.* motorize.

motrice /mɔtris/ *voir* **moteur**[2].

motte /mɔt/ *n.f.* lump; (*de terre*) clod. **~ de gazon,** turf.

mou *ou* **mol*, molle** /mu, mɔl/ *a.* soft; (*faible, indolent*) feeble. —*n.m.* **du ~,** slack. **avoir du ~,** be slack.

mouchard, ~e /muʃar, -d/ *n.m., f.* informer; (*scol.*) sneak. **~er** /-de/ *v.t.* (*fam.*) inform on.

mouche /muʃ/ *n.f.* fly.

moucher (se) /(sə)muʃe/ *v. pr.* blow one's nose.

moucheron /muʃrɔ̃/ *n.m.* midge.

moucheté /muʃte/ *a.* speckled.

mouchoir /muʃwar/ *n.m.* handkerchief; (*en papier*) tissue.

moudre /mudr/ *v.t.* grind.

moue /mu/ *n.f.* long face. **faire la ~,** pull a long face.

mouette /mwɛt/ *n.f.* (sea)gull.

moufle /mufl/ *n.f.* (*gant*) mitten.

mouill|er /muje/ *v.t.* wet, make wet. **se ~er** *v. pr.* get (o.s.) wet. **~er** (*l'ancre*), anchor. **~é** *a.* wet.

moulage /mulaʒ/ *n.m.* cast.

moul|e[1] /mul/ *n.m.* mould. **~er** *v.t.* mould; (*statue*) cast.

moule[2] /mul/ *n.f.* (*coquillage*) mussel.

moulin /mulɛ̃/ *n.m.* mill; (*moteur: fam.*) engine. **~ à vent,** windmill.

moulinet /mulinɛ/ *n.m.* (*de canne à pêche*) reel.

moulu /muly/ *a.* ground; (*fatigué: fam.*) dead beat.

moulure /mulyr/ *n.f.* moulding.

mourant, ~e /murɑ̃, -t/ *a.* dying. —*n.m., f.* dying person.

mourir† /murir/ *v.i.* (*aux. être*) die. **~ d'envie de,** be dying to. **~ de faim,** be starving. **~ d'ennui,** be dead bored.

mousquetaire /muskətɛr/ *n.m.* musketeer.

mousse[1] /mus/ *n.f.* moss; (*écume*) froth, foam; (*de savon*) lather; (*dessert*) mousse.

mousse[2] /mus/ *n.m.* ship's boy.

mousseline /muslin/ *n.f.* muslin.

mousser /muse/ *v.i.* froth, foam; (*savon*) lather.

mousseu|x, ~se /musø, -z/ *a.* frothy. —*n.m.* sparkling wine.

mousson /musɔ̃/ *n.f.* monsoon.

moustach|e /mustaʃ/ *n.f.* moustache. **~es,** (*d'animal*) whiskers. **~u** *a.* wearing a moustache.

moustiquaire /mustikɛr/ *n.f.* mosquito-net.

moustique /mustik/ *n.m.* mosquito.

moutarde /mutard/ *n.f.* mustard.

mouton /mutɔ̃/ *n.m.* sheep; (*peau*) sheepskin; (*viande*) mutton.

mouvant, ~e /muvɑ̃, -t/ *a.* changing; (*terrain*) shifting.

mouvement /muvmɑ̃/ *n.m.* movement; (*agitation*) bustle; (*en gymnastique*) exercise; (*impulsion*) impulse; (*de colère*) outburst; (*tendance*) tendency. **en ~,** in motion.

mouvementé /muvmɑ̃te/ *a.* eventful.

mouvoir† /muvwar/ *v.t.* drive; (*membre*) move. **se ~** *v. pr.* move.

moyen[1], **~ne** /mwajɛ̃, -jɛn/ *a.* average; (*médiocre*) poor. —*n.f.* average; (*scol.*) pass-mark. **de taille ~ne,** medium-sized. **~ âge,** Middle Ages. **~ne**

d'âge, average age. **M~-Orient** *n.m.* Middle East. **~nement** /-jɛnmɑ̃/ *adv.* moderately.

moyen[2] /mwajɛ̃/ *n.m.* means, way. **~s,** means; (*dons*) abilities. **au ~ de,** by means of. **il n'y a pas ~ de,** it is not possible to.

moyennant /mwajɛnɑ̃/ *prép.* (*pour*) for; (*grâce à*) with.

moyeu (*pl.* **~x**) /mwajø/ *n.m.* hub.

mû, mue[1] /my/ *a.* driven (**par,** by).

mue[2] /my/ *n.f.* moulting; (*de voix*) breaking of the voice.

muer /mɥe/ *v.i.* moult; (*voix*) break. **se ~ en,** change into.

muet, ~te /mɥɛ, -t/ *a.* (*personne*) dumb; (*fig.*) speechless (**de,** with); (*silencieux*) silent. —*n.m., f.* dumb person.

mufle /myfl/ *n.m.* nose, muzzle; (*personne: fam.*) boor, lout.

mugir /myʒir/ *v.i.* (*vache*) moo; (*bœuf*) bellow; (*fig.*) howl.

muguet /mygɛ/ *n.m.* lily of the valley.

mule /myl/ *n.f.* (she-)mule; (*pantoufle*) mule.

mulet /mylɛ/ *n.m.* (he-)mule.

multi- /mylti/ *préf.* multi-.

multicolore /myltikɔlɔr/ *a.* multi-coloured.

multination|al, ~ale (*m. pl.* **~aux**) /myltinasjɔnal, -o/ *a.* & *n.f.* multi-national.

multiple /myltipl/ *a.* & *n.m.* multiple.

multiplicité /myltiplisite/ *n.f.* multiplicity, abundance.

multipl|ier /myltiplije/ *v.t.,* **se ~ier** *v. pr.* multiply. **~ication** *n.f.* multiplication.

multitude /myltityd/ *n.f.* multitude, mass.

municip|al (*m. pl.* **~aux** /mynisipal, -o/ *a.* municipal; (*conseil*) town. **~ alité** *n.f.* (*ville*) municipality; (*conseil*) town council.

munir /mynir/ *v.t.* **~ de,** provide with. **se ~ de,** provide o.s. with.

munitions /mynisjɔ̃/ *n.f. pl.* ammu-nition.

mur /myr/ *n.m.* wall. **~ du son,** sound barrier.

mûr /myr/ *a.* ripe; (*personne*) mature.

muraille /myrɑj/ *n.f.* (high) wall.

mur|al (*m. pl.* **~aux** /myral, -o/ *a.* wall; (*tableau*) mural.

mûre /myr/ *n.f.* blackberry.

muret /myrɛ/ *n.m.* low wall.

mûrir /myrir/ *v.t./i.* ripen; (*personne, projet*) mature.

murmur|e /myrmyr/ *n.m.* murmur. **~er** *v.t./i.* murmur.

musc /mysk/ *n.m.* musk.

muscade /myskad/ *n.f.* nutmeg.

muscl|e /myskl/ *n.m.* muscle. **~é** *a.* muscular, brawny.

muscul|aire /myskylɛr/ *a.* muscular. **~ature** *n.f.* muscles.

museau (*pl.* **~x**) /myzo/ *n.m.* muzzle; (*de porc*) snout.

musée /myze/ *n.m.* museum; (*de pein-ture*) art gallery.

museler /myzle/ *v.t.* muzzle.

muselière /myzəljɛr/ *n.f.* muzzle.

musette /myzɛt/ *n.f.* haversack.

muséum /myzeɔm/ *n.m.* (natural his-tory) museum.

music|al (*m. pl.* **~aux**) /myzikal, -o/ *a.* musical.

music-hall /myzikol/ *n.m.* variety theatre.

musicien, ~ne /myzisjɛ̃, -jɛn/ *a.* musical. —*n.m., f.* musician.

musique /myzik/ *n.f.* music; (*or-chestre*) band.

musulman, ~e /myzylmɑ̃, -an/ *a.* & *n.m., f.* Muslim.

mutation /mytasjɔ̃/ *n.f.* change; (*bio-logique*) mutation.

muter /myte/ *v.t.* transfer.

mutil|er /mytile/ *v.t.* mutilate. **~a-tion** *n.f.* mutilation. **~é, ~ée** *a.* & *n.m., f.* disabled (person).

mutin, ~e /mytɛ̃, -in/ *a.* saucy. —*n.m., f.* rebel.

mutin|er (se) /(sə)mytine/ *v. pr.* mutiny. **~é** *a.* mutinous. **~erie** *n.f.* mutiny.

mutisme /mytism/ *n.m.* silence.

mutuel, ~le /mytɥɛl/ *a.* mutual. —*n.f.* Friendly Society; (*Amer.*) bene-fit society. **~lement** *adv.* mutually; (*l'un l'autre*) each other.

myop|e /mjɔp/ *a.* short-sighted. **~ie** *n.f.* short-sightedness.

myosotis /mjozɔtis/ *n.m.* forget-me-not.

myriade /mirjad/ *n.f.* myriad.

myrtille /mirtij/ *n.f.* bilberry; (*Amer.*) blueberry.

mystère /mistɛr/ *n.m.* mystery.

mystérieu|x, ~se /misterjø, -z/ *a.* mysterious.

mystif|ier /mistifje/ *v.t.* deceive, hoax. **~ication** *n.f.* hoax.

mysti|que /mistik/ *a.* mystic(al).

—*n.m./f.* mystic. —*n.f.* (*puissance*) mystique. **~cisme** *n.m.* mysticism. **myth|e** /mit/ *n.m.* myth. **~ique** *a.* mythical.

mytholog|ie /mitɔlɔʒi/ *n.f.* mythology. **~ique** *a.* mythological. **mythomane** /mitɔman/ *n.m./f.* compulsive liar (and fantasizer).

N

n' /n/ *voir* **ne.**

nacr|e /nakr/ *n.f.* mother-of-pearl.
~é *a.* pearly.

nage /naʒ/ *n.f.* swimming; (*manière*)
(swimming) stroke. **à la ~,** by swimming. **traverser à la ~,** swim across.
en ~, sweating.

nageoire /naʒwar/ *n.f.* fin.

nag|er /naʒe/ *v.t./i.* swim. **~eur,**
~euse *n.m, f.* swimmer.

naguère /nagɛr/ *adv.* not long ago.

naï|f, ~ve /naif, -v/ *a.* naïve. —*n.m.,*
f. innocent.

nain, ~e /nɛ̃, nɛn/ *n.m., f. & a.* dwarf.

naissance /nɛsɑ̃s/ *n.f.* birth; (*de rivière*) source. **donner ~ à,** give birth
to.

naître† /nɛtr/ *v.i.* be born; (*résulter*)
arise (**de,** from). **faire ~,** (*susciter*)
give rise to.

naïveté /naivte/ *n.f.* naïvety.

nana /nana/ *n.f.* (*fam.*) girl.

nanti /nɑ̃ti/ *a.* affluent.

nantir /nɑ̃tir/ *v.t.* **~ de,** provide with.

naphtaline /naftalin/ *n.f.* mothballs.

nappe /nap/ *n.f.* table-cloth; (*d'eau*)
sheet; (*de brouillard, gaz*) layer.

napperon /naprɔ̃/ *n.m.* (cloth) table-
mat. **~ (individuel),** place-mat.

narcotique /narkɔtik/ *a. & n.m.* narcotic.

narguer /narge/ *v.t.* mock.

narine /narin/ *n.f.* nostril.

narquois, ~e /narkwa, -z/ *a.* derisive.

narr|er /nare/ *v.t.* narrate. **~ateur,**
~atrice *n.m.,f.* narrator. **~ation** *n.f.*
narrative; (*action*) narration; (*scol.*)
composition.

nas|al (*m. pl.* **~aux**) /nazal, -o/ *a.*
nasal.

naseau (*pl.* **~x**) /nazo/ *n.m.* nostril.

nasiller /nazije/ *v.i.* have a nasal
twang.

nat|al (*m. pl.* **~als**) /natal/ *a.* native.

natalité /natalite/ *n.f.* birth rate.

natation /natasjɔ̃/ *n.f.* swimming.

nati|f, ~ve /natif, -v/ *a.* native.

nation /nɑsjɔ̃/ *n.f.* nation.

nation|al, ~ale (*m. pl.* **~aux**)
/nasjɔnal, -o/ *a.* national. —*n.f.* trunk-
road; (*Amer.*) highway. **~aliser** *v.t.*
nationalize. **~alisme** *n.m.* national-
ism.

nationalité /nasjɔnalite/ *n.f.* nationality.

Nativité /nativite/ *n.f.* **la ~,** the Nativity.

natte /nat/ *n.f.* (*de cheveux*) plait; (*tapis
de paille*) mat.

naturaliser /natyralize/ *v.t.* natural-
ize.

nature /natyr/ *n.f.* nature. —*a. invar.*
(*eau, omelette, etc.*) plain. **de ~ à,**
likely to. **en ~,** in kind. **~ morte,**
still life.

naturel, ~le /natyrɛl/ *a.* natural.
—*n.m.* nature; (*simplicité*) natural-
ness. **~lement** *adv.* naturally.

naufrag|e /nofraʒ/ *n.m.* (ship)wreck.
faire ~e, be shipwrecked; (*bateau*)
be wrecked. **~é, ~ée** *a. & n.m., f.*
shipwrecked (person).

nauséabond, ~e /nozeabɔ̃, -d/ *a.*
nauseating.

nausée /noze/ *n.f.* nausea.

nautique /notik/ *a.* nautical; (*sports*)
aquatic.

naval (*m. pl.* **~s**) /naval/ *a.* naval.

navet /navɛ/ *n.m.* turnip; (*film, tableau*) dud.

navette /navɛt/ *n.f.* shuttle (service). **faire la ~,** shuttle back and
forth.

navigable /navigabl/ *a.* navigable.

navig|uer /navige/ *v.i.* sail; (*avion*)
fly; (*piloter*) navigate. **~ateur** *n.m.*
seafarer; (*d'avion*) navigator. **~ation**
n.f. navigation; (*trafic*) shipping.

navire /navir/ *n.m.* ship.

navré /navre/ *a.* sorry (**de,** to).

navrer /navre/ *v.t.* upset.

ne, n'* /nə, n/ *adv.* **~ pas,** not. **~
jamais,** never. **~ plus,** (*temps*) no
longer, not any more. **~ que,** only.
je crains qu'il ne parte, (*sans valeur
négative*) I am afraid he will leave.

né, née /ne/ *voir* **naître.** —*a. & n.m.,f.*
born. **il est ~,** he was born. **premier-/
dernier-~,** first-/last-born.

néanmoins /neɑ̃mwɛ̃/ *adv.* nevertheless.

néant /neɑ̃/ *n.m.* nothingness; (*aucun*)
none.

nébuleu|x, ~se /nebylø, -z/ *a.* nebu-
lous.

nécessaire /nesesɛr/ *a.* necessary.

—*n.m.* (*sac*) bag; (*trousse*) kit. **le** ~, (*l'indispensable*) the necessities. **faire le** ~, do what is necessary. ~**ment** *adv.* necessarily.

nécessité /nesesite/ *n.f.* necessity.

nécessiter /nesesite/ *v.t.* necessitate.

nécrologie /nekrɔlɔʒi/ *n.f.* obituary.

néerlandais, ~**e** /neɛrlɑ̃dɛ, -z/ *a.* Dutch. —*n.m., f.* Dutchman, Dutchwoman. —*n.m.* (*lang.*) Dutch.

nef /nɛf/ *n.f.* nave.

néfaste /nefast/ *a.* harmful (**à,** to); (*funeste*) ill-fated.

négati|f, ~**ve** /negatif, -v/ *a.* & *n.m., f.* negative.

négation /negɑsjɔ̃/ *n.f.* negation.

négligé /negliʒe/ *a.* (*tenue, travail*) slovenly. —*n.m.* (*tenue*) négligé.

négligeable /negliʒabl/ *a.* negligible, insignificant.

négligen|t, ~**te** /negliʒɑ̃, -t/ *a.* careless, negligent. ~**ce** *n.f.* carelessness, negligence; (*erreur*) omission.

négliger /negliʒe/ *v.t.* neglect; (*ne pas tenir compte de*) disregard. **se** ~ *v. pr.* neglect o.s.

négoc|e /negɔs/ *n.m.* business. ~**iant,** ~**iante** *n.m., f.* merchant.

négoc|ier /negɔsje/ *v.t./i.* negotiate. ~**iable** *a.* negotiable. ~**iateur,** ~**iatrice** *n.m., f.* negotiator. ~**iation** *n.f.* negotiation.

nègre[1] /nɛgr/ *a.* (*musique etc.*) Negro.

nègre[2] /nɛgr/ *n.m.* (*écrivain*) ghost writer.

neig|e /nɛʒ/ *n.f.* snow. ~**eux,** ~**euse** *a.* snowy.

neiger /neʒe/ *v.i.* snow.

nénuphar /nenyfar/ *n.m.* water-lily.

néologisme /neɔlɔʒism/ *n.m.* neologism.

néon /neɔ̃/ *n.m.* neon.

néo-zélandais, ~**e** /neɔzelɑ̃dɛ, -z/ *a.* New Zealand. —*n.m., f.* New Zealander.

nerf /nɛr/ *n.m.* nerve; (*vigueur: fam.*) stamina.

nerv|eux, ~**euse** /nɛrvø, -z/ *a.* nervous; (*irritable*) nervy; (*centre, cellule*) nerve-; (*voiture*) responsive. ~**eusement** *adv.* nervously. ~**osité** *n.f.* nervousness; (*irritabilité*) touchiness.

nervure /nɛrvyr/ *n.f.* (*bot.*) vein.

net, ~**te** /nɛt/ *a.* (*clair, distinct*) clear; (*propre*) clean; (*soigné*) neat; (*prix, poids*) net. —*adv.* (*s'arrêter*) dead; (*refuser*) flatly; (*parler*) plainly; (*se casser*) clean. ~**tement** *adv.* clearly; (*certainement*) definitely.

netteté /nɛtte/ *n.f.* clearness.

nettoy|er /nɛtwaje/ *v.t.* clean. ~**age** *n.m.* cleaning. ~**age à sec,** dry-cleaning.

neuf[1] /nœf/ (/nœv/ *before heures, ans*) *a.* & *n.m.* nine.

neu|f[2], ~**ve** /nœf, -v/ *a.* & *n.m.* new. **à** ~**f,** (*refaire*) like new. **du** ~**f,** (*fait nouveau*) some new development.

neutr|e /nøtr/ *a.* neutral; (*gram.*) neuter. —*n.m.* (*gram.*) neuter. ~**alité** *n.f.* neutrality.

neutron /nøtrɔ̃/ *n.m.* neutron.

neuve /nœv/ *voir* **neuf**[2].

neuvième /nœvjɛm/ *a.* & *n.m./f.* ninth.

neveu (*pl.* ~**x**) /nəvø/ *n.m.* nephew.

névros|e /nevroz/ *n.f.* neurosis. ~**é,** ~**ée** *a.* & *n.m., f.* neurotic.

nez /ne/ *n.m.* nose. ~ **à nez,** face to face. ~ **épaté,** flat nose.

ni /ni/ *conj.* neither, nor. ~ **grand ni petit,** neither big nor small. ~ **l'un ni l'autre ne fument,** neither (one nor the other) smokes.

niais, ~**e** /njɛ, -z/ *a.* silly. —*n.m., f.* simpleton. ~**erie** /-zri/ *n.f.* silliness.

niche /niʃ/ *n.f.* (*de chien*) kennel; (*cavité*) niche; (*farce*) trick.

nichée /niʃe/ *n.f.* brood.

nicher /niʃe/ *v.i.* nest. **se** ~ *v. pr.* nest; (*se cacher: fam.*) hide.

nickel /nikel/ *n.m.* nickel.

nicotine /nikɔtin/ *n.f.* nicotine.

nid /ni/ *n.m.* nest. ~ **de poule,** pothole.

nièce /njɛs/ *n.f.* niece.

nier /nje/ *v.t.* deny.

nigaud, ~**e** /nigo, -d/ *a.* silly. —*n.m., f.* silly idiot.

nippon, ~**e** /nipɔ̃, -ɔn/ *a.* & *n.m., f.* Japanese.

niveau (*pl.* ~**x**) /nivo/ *n.m.* level; (*compétence*) standard. **au** ~, up to standard. ~ **à bulle,** spirit-level. ~ **de vie,** standard of living.

nivel|er /nivle/ *v.t.* level. ~**lement** /-ɛlmɑ̃/ *n.m.* levelling.

noble /nɔbl/ *a.* noble. —*n.m./f.* nobleman, noblewoman.

noblesse /nɔblɛs/ *n.f.* nobility.

noce /nɔs/ *n.f.* wedding; (*personnes*) wedding guests. ~**s,** wedding. **faire la** ~, (*fam.*) make merry.

noci|f, ~**ve** /nɔsif, -v/ *a.* harmful.

noctambule /nɔktɑ̃byl/ *n.m./f.* night-owl, late-night reveller.

nocturne /nɔktyrn/ *a.* nocturnal.

Noël /nɔɛl/ *n.m.* Christmas.

nœud[1] /nø/ *n.m.* knot; (*ornemental*) bow. ~s, (*fig.*) ties. ~ **coulant,** noose. ~ **papillon,** bow-tie.

nœud[2] /nø/ *n.m.* (*naut.*) knot.

noir, ~e /nwar/ *a.* black; (*obscur, sombre*) dark; (*triste*) gloomy. —*n.m.* black; (*obscurité*) dark. —*n.m., f.* (*personne*) Black. —*n.f.* (*mus.*) crotchet. ~**ceur** *n.f.* blackness; (*indignité*) vileness.

noircir /nwarsir/ *v.t./i.,* **se** ~ *v. pr.* blacken.

nois|ette /nwazɛt/ *n.f.* hazel-nut. ~**etier** *n.m.* hazel.

noix /nwa/ *n.f.* nut; (*du noyer*) walnut; (*de beurre*) knob.

nom /nɔ̃/ *n.m.* name; (*gram.*) noun. **au** ~ **de,** on behalf of. ~ **de famille,** surname. ~ **de jeune fille,** maiden name. ~ **propre,** proper noun.

nomade /nɔmad/ *a.* nomadic. —*n.m./f.* nomad.

nombre /nɔ̃br/ *n.m.* number. **au** ~ **de,** (*parmi*) among; (*l'un de*) one of. **en (grand)** ~, in large numbers.

nombreu|x, ~**se** /nɔ̃brø, -z/ *a.* numerous; (*important*) large.

nombril /nɔ̃bri/ *n.m.* navel.

nomin|al (*m. pl.* ~**aux**) /nɔminal, -o/ *a.* nominal.

nomination /nɔminasjɔ̃/ *n.f.* appointment.

nommément /nɔmemã/ *adv.* by name.

nommer /nɔme/ *v.t.* name; (*élire*) appoint. **se** ~ *v. pr.* (*s'appeler*) be called.

non /nɔ̃/ *adv.* no; (*pas*) not. —*n.m. invar.* no. ~ **(pas) que,** not that. **il vient,** ~**?,** he is coming, isn't he? **moi** ~ **plus,** neither am, do, can, *etc.* I.

non- /nɔ̃/ *préf.* non-.

nonante /nɔnɑ̃t/ *a. & n.m.* ninety.

nonchalance /nɔ̃ʃalɑ̃s/ *n.f.* nonchalance.

non-sens /nɔ̃sɑ̃s/ *n.m.* absurdity.

nord /nɔr/ *n.m.* north. —*a. invar.* north; (*partie*) northern; (*direction*) northerly. ~-**africain,** ~-**africaine** *a. & n.m., f.* North African. ~-**est** *n.m* north-east. ~-**ouest** *n.m.* north-west.

nordique /nɔrdik/ *a. & n.m./f.* Scandinavian.

norm|al, ~**ale** (*m. pl.* ~**aux**) /nɔrmal, -o/ *a.* normal. —*n.f.* normality; (*norme*) norm; (*moyenne*) average. ~**alement** *adv.* normally.

normand, ~**e** /nɔrmã, -d/ *a. & n.m., f.* Norman.

Normandie /nɔrmãdi/ *n.f.* Normandy.

norme /nɔrm/ *n.f.* norm; (*de production*) standard.

Norvège /nɔrvɛʒ/ *n.f.* Norway.

norvégien, ~**ne** /nɔrveʒjɛ̃, -jɛn/ *a. & n.m., f.* Norwegian.

nos /no/ *voir* **notre.**

nostalg|ie /nɔstalʒi/ *n.f.* nostalgia. ~**ique** *a.* nostalgic.

notable /nɔtabl/ *a. & n.m.* notable.

notaire /nɔtɛr/ *n.m.* notary.

notamment /nɔtamã/ *adv.* notably.

notation /nɔtasjɔ̃/ *n.f.* notation; (*remarque*) remark.

note /nɔt/ *n.f.* (*remarque*) note; (*chiffrée*) mark; (*facture*) bill; (*mus.*) note. ~ **(de service),** memorandum. **prendre** ~ **de,** take note of.

not|er /nɔte/ *v.t.* note, notice; (*écrire*) note (down); (*devoir*) mark. **bien/mal** ~**é,** (*employé etc.*) highly/poorly rated.

notice /nɔtis/ *n.f.* note; (*mode d'emploi*) directions.

notif|ier /nɔtifje/ *v.t.* notify. ~**ication** *n.f.* notification.

notion /nosjɔ̃/ *n.f.* notion.

notoire /nɔtwar/ *a.* well-known; (*criminel*) notorious.

notre (*pl.* **nos**) /nɔtr, no/ *a.* our.

nôtre /notr/ *pron.* **le** *ou* **la** ~, **les** ~**s,** ours.

nouer /nwe/ *v.t.* tie, knot; (*relations*) strike up.

noueu|x, ~**se** /nwø, -z/ *a.* gnarled.

nougat /nuga/ *n.m.* nougat.

nouille /nuj/ *n.f.* (*idiot: fam.*) idiot.

nouilles /nuj/ *n.f. pl.* noodles.

nounours /nunurs/ *n.m.* teddy bear.

nourri /nuri/ *a.* intense.

nourrice /nuris/ *n.f.* child-minder; (*qui allaite*) wet-nurse.

nourr|ir /nurir/ *v.t.* feed; (*faire vivre*) feed, provide for; (*sentiment: fig.*) nourish. —*v.i.* be nourishing. **se** ~**ir** *v. pr.* eat. **se** ~**ir de,** feed on. ~**issant,** ~**issante** *a.* nourishing.

nourrisson /nurisɔ̃/ *n.m.* infant.

nourriture /nurityr/ *n.f.* food; (*régime*) diet.

nous /nu/ *pron.* we; (*complément*) us; (*indirect*) (to) us; (*réfléchi*) ourselves; (*l'un l'autre*) each other. ~-**mêmes** *pron.* ourselves.

nouveau *ou* **nouvel*, nouvelle**[1] (*m.*

pl. ~x) /nuvo, nuvɛl/ *a.* & *n.m.* new.
—*n.m.,f.* (*élève*) new boy, new girl. **de**
~, **à** ~, again. **du** ~, (*fait nouveau*)
some new development. **nouvel an,**
new year. ~x **mariés,** newly-weds.
~-**né,** ~-**née** *a.* new-born; *n.m., f.*
new-born baby. ~ **venu, nouvelle**
venue, newcomer. **Nouvelle**
Zélande, New Zealand.
nouveauté /nuvote/ *n.f.* novelty;
(*chose*) new thing.
nouvelle² /nuvɛl/ *n.f.* (piece of)
news; (*récit*) short story. ~s, news.
nouvellement /nuvɛlmɑ̃/ *adv.* newly,
recently.
novembre /nɔvɑ̃br/ *n.m.* November.
novice /nɔvis/ *a.* inexperienced.
—*n.m./f.* novice.
noyade /nwajad/ *n.f.* drowning.
noyau (*pl.* ~x) /nwajo/ *n.m.* (*de fruit*)
stone; (*de cellule*) nucleus; (*groupe*)
group; (*centre*: *fig.*) core.
noy|er¹ /nwaje/ *v.t.* drown; (*inonder*)
flood. **se** ~**er** *v. pr.* drown; (*volon-*
tairement) drown o.s. ~**é,** ~**ée** *n.m.,*
f. drowning person; (*mort*) drowned
person.
noyer² /nwaje/ *n.m.* (*arbre*) walnut-
tree.
nu /ny/ *a.* naked; (*mains, mur, fil*)
bare. —*n.m.* nude. **(se) mettre à** ~,
strip. ~-**pieds** *adv.* barefoot; *n.m.pl.*
beach shoes. ~-**tête** *adv.* bareheaded.
nuag|e /nɥaʒ/ *n.m.* cloud. ~**eux,**
~**euse** *a.* cloudy.
nuance /nɥɑ̃s/ *n.f.* shade; (*de sens*)
nuance; (*différence*) difference.

nuancer /nɥɑ̃se/ *v.t.* (*opinion*) qualify.
nucléaire /nyklɛɛr/ *a.* nuclear.
nudis|te /nydist/ *n.m./f.* nudist. ~**me**
n.m. nudism.
nudité /nydite/ *n.f.* (*de personne*)
nudity; (*de chambre etc.*) bareness.
nuée /nɥe/ *n.f.* (*foule*) host.
nuire† /nɥir/ *v.i.* ~ **à,** harm.
nuisible /nɥizibl/ *a.* harmful.
nuit /nɥi/ *n.f.* night. **cette** ~, tonight;
(*hier*) last night. **il fait** ~, it is dark.
~ **blanche,** sleepless night. **la** ~, **de**
~, at night.
nul, ~**le** /nyl/ *a.* (*aucun*) no; (*zéro*)
nil; (*qui ne vaut rien*) useless; (*non*
valable) null. —*pron.* no one. ~
autre, no one else. ~**le part,**
nowhere. ~**lement** *adv.* not at all.
~**lité** *n.f.* uselessness; (*personne*) useless person.
numéraire /nymerɛr/ *n.m.* cash.
numér|al (*pl.* ~**aux**) /nymeral, -o/
n.m. numeral.
numérique /nymerik/ *a.* numerical;
(*montre, horloge*) digital.
numéro /nymero/ *n.m.* number; (*de*
journal) issue; (*spectacle*) act. ~**ter**
/-ɔte/ *v.t.* number.
nupt|ial (*m. pl.* ~**iaux**) /nypsjal, -jo/
a. wedding.
nuque /nyk/ *n.f.* nape (of the neck).
nurse /nœrs/ *n.f.* (children's) nurse.
nutriti|f, ~**ve** /nytritif, -v/ *a.* nu-
tritious; (*valeur*) nutritional.
nutrition /nytrisjɔ̃/ *n.f.* nutrition.
nylon /nilɔ̃/ *n.m.* nylon.
nymphe /nɛ̃f/ *n.f.* nymph.

O

oasis /ɔazis/ *n.f.* oasis.

obéir /ɔbeir/ *v.i.* obey. ~ **à**, obey. **être obéi**, be obeyed.

obéissan|t, ~te /ɔbeisɑ̃, -t/ *a.* obedient. ~**ce** *n.f.* obedience.

obèse /ɔbɛz/ *a.* obese.

obésité /ɔbezite/ *n.f.* obesity.

object|er /ɔbʒɛkte/ *v.t.* put forward (as an excuse). ~**er que**, object that. ~**ion** /-ksjɔ̃/ *n.f.* objection.

objecti|f, ~ve /ɔbʒɛktif, -v/ *a.* objective. −*n.m.* objective. ~**vement** *adv.* objectively. ~**vité** *n.f.* objectivity.

objet /ɔbʒɛ/ *n.m.* object; (*sujet*) subject. **être** *ou* **faire l'**~ **de**, be the subject of; (*recevoir*) receive. ~**s de toilette**, toilet requisites. ~**s trouvés**, lost property; (*Amer.*) lost and found.

obligation /ɔbligɑsjɔ̃/ *n.f.* obligation; (*comm.*) bond.

obligatoire /ɔbligatwar/ *a.* compulsory. ~**ment** *adv.* of necessity; (*fam.*) inevitably.

obligean|t, ~te /ɔbliʒɑ̃, -t/ *a.* obliging, kind. ~**ce** *n.f.* kindness.

oblig|er /ɔbliʒe/ *v.t.* compel, oblige (**à faire**, to do); (*aider*) oblige. **être ~é de**, have to. ~**é à qn.**, obliged to s.o. (**de**, for).

oblique /ɔblik/ *a.* oblique. **en** ~, at an angle.

obliquer /ɔblike/ *v.i.* turn off.

oblitérer /ɔblitere/ *v.t.* (*timbre*) cancel.

oblong, ~ue /ɔblɔ̃, -g/ *a.* oblong.

obsc|ène /ɔpsɛn/ *a.* obscene. ~**énité** *n.f.* obscenity.

obscur /ɔpskyr/ *a.* dark; (*confus, humble*) obscure.

obscurcir /ɔpskyrsir/ *v.t.* darken; (*fig.*) obscure. **s'**~ *v. pr.* (*ciel etc.*) darken.

obscurité /ɔpskyrite/ *n.f.* dark(ness); (*passage, situation*) obscurity.

obséd|er /ɔpsede/ *v.t.* obsess. ~**ant, ~ante** *a.* obsessive. ~**é, ~ée** *n.m.,f.* maniac.

obsèques /ɔpsɛk/ *n.f. pl.* funeral.

observation /ɔpsɛrvɑsjɔ̃/ *n.f.* observation; (*reproche*) criticism; (*obéissance*) observance.

observatoire /ɔpsɛrvatwar/ *n.m.* observatory; (*mil.*) observation post.

observ|er /ɔpsɛrve/ *v.t.* observe; (*surveiller*) watch, observe. **faire ~er qch.**, point sth. out (**à**, to). ~**ateur, ~atrice** *a.* observant; *n.m., f.* observer.

obsession /ɔpsesjɔ̃/ *n.f.* obsession.

obstacle /ɔpstakl/ *n.m.* obstacle. **faire** ~ **à**, stand in the way of.

obstétrique /ɔpstetrik/ *n.f.* obstetrics.

obstin|é /ɔpstine/ *a.* obstinate. ~**ation** *n.f.* obstinacy.

obstiner (s') /(s)ɔpstine/ *v. pr.* persist (**à**, in).

obstruction /ɔpstryksjɔ̃/ *n.f.* obstruction. **faire de l'**~, obstruct.

obstruer /ɔpstrye/ *v.t.* obstruct.

obten|ir† /ɔptənir/ *v.t.* get, obtain. ~**tion** /-ɑ̃sjɔ̃/ *n.f.* obtaining.

obturateur /ɔptyratœr/ *n.m.* (*photo.*) shutter.

obtus, ~e /ɔpty, -z/ *a.* obtuse.

obus /ɔby/ *n.m.* shell.

occasion /ɔkazjɔ̃/ *n.f.* opportunity (**de faire**, of doing); (*circonstance*) occasion; (*achat*) bargain; (*article non neuf*) second-hand buy. **à l'**~, sometimes. **d'**~, second-hand. ~**nel, ~nelle** /-jɔnɛl/ *a.* occasional.

occasionner /ɔkazjone/ *v.t.* cause.

occident /ɔksidɑ̃/ *n.m.* west. ~**al, ~ale** (*m. pl.* ~**aux**) /-tal, -to/ *a.* western. −*n.m., f.* westerner.

occulte /ɔkylt/ *a.* occult.

occupant, ~e /ɔkypɑ̃, -t/ *n.m.,f.* occupant. −*n.m.* (*mil.*) forces of occupation.

occupation /ɔkypɑsjɔ̃/ *n.f.* occupation.

occupé /ɔkype/ *a.* busy; (*place, pays*) occupied; (*téléphone*) engaged; (*Amer.*) busy.

occuper /ɔkype/ *v.t.* occupy; (*ouvrier*) employ; (*poste*) hold. **s'**~ *v. pr.* (*s'affairer*) keep busy (**à faire**, doing). **s'**~ **de**, (*personne, problème*) take care of; (*bureau, firme*) be in charge of.

occurrence (en l') /(ɑ̃l)ɔkyrɑ̃s/ *adv.* in this case.

océan /ɔseɑ̃/ *n.m.* ocean.

ocre /ɔkr/ *a. invar.* ochre.

octane /ɔktan/ *n.m.* octane.

octave /ɔktav/ *n.f.* (*mus.*) octave.

octobre /ɔktɔbr/ *n.m.* October.

octogone /ɔktɔgɔn/ *n.m.* octagon.

octroyer /ɔktrwaje/ *v.t.* grant.

oculaire /ɔkylɛr/ *a.* ocular.

oculiste /ɔkylist/ *n.m./f.* eye-specialist.

ode /ɔd/ *n.f.* ode.

odeur /ɔdœr/ *n.f.* smell.

odieu|x, ~se /ɔdjø, -z/ *a.* odious.

odorant, ~e /ɔdɔrɑ̃, -t/ *a.* sweet-smelling.

odorat /ɔdɔra/ *n.m.* (sense of) smell.

œcuménique /ekymenik/ *a.* ecumenical.

œil (*pl.* **yeux**) /œj, jø/ *n.m.* eye. **à l'~**, (*fam.*) free. **à mes yeux**, in my view. **faire de l'~ à**, make eyes at. **faire les gros yeux à**, scowl at. **fermer l'~**, shut one's eyes. **~ poché**, black eye. **yeux bridés**, slit eyes.

œillade /œjad/ *n.f.* wink.

œillères /œjɛr/ *n.f. pl.* blinkers.

œillet /œjɛ/ *n.m.* (*plante*) carnation; (*trou*) eyelet.

œuf (*pl.* **~s**) /œf, ø/ *n.m.* egg. **~ à la coque/dur/sur le plat**, boiled/hard-boiled/fried egg.

œuvre /œvr/ *n.f.* (*ouvrage, travail*) work. **~** (**de bienfaisance**), charity. **être à l'~**, be at work. **mettre en ~**, (*moyens*) implement.

œuvrer /œvre/ *v.i.* work.

offense /ɔfɑ̃s/ *n.f.* insult; (*péché*) offence.

offens|er /ɔfɑ̃se/ *v.t.* offend. **s'~er de**, take offence at. **~ant, ~ante** *a.* offensive.

offensi|f, ~ve /ɔfɑ̃sif, -v/ *a. & n.f.* offensive.

offert, ~e /ɔfɛr, -t/ *voir* **offrir.**

office /ɔfis/ *n.m.* office; (*relig.*) service; (*de cuisine*) pantry. **d'~**, automatically.

officiel, ~le /ɔfisjɛl/ *a. & n.m., f.* official. **~lement** *adv.* officially.

officier[1] /ɔfisje/ *n.m.* officer.

officier[2] /ɔfisje/ *v.i.* (*relig.*) officiate.

officieu|x, ~se /ɔfisjø, -z/ *a.* unofficial. **~sement** *adv.* unofficially.

offrande /ɔfrɑ̃d/ *n.f.* offering.

offrant /ɔfrɑ̃/ *n.m.* **au plus ~**, to the highest bidder.

offre /ɔfr/ *n.f.* offer; (*aux enchères*) bid. **l'~ et la demande**, supply and demand. **~s d'emploi**, (*dans un journal*) jobs advertised, situations vacant.

offrir† /ɔfrir/ *v.t.* offer (**de faire**, to

do); (*cadeau*) give; (*acheter*) buy. **s'~** *v. pr.* offer o.s. (**comme**, as); (*spectacle*) present itself; (*s'acheter*) treat o.s. to. **~ à boire à**, offer a drink to.

offusquer /ɔfyske/ *v.t.* offend.

ogive /ɔʒiv/ *n.f.* (*atomique etc.*) warhead.

ogre /ɔgr/ *n.m.* ogre.

oh /o/ *int.* oh.

oie /wa/ *n.f.* goose.

oignon /ɔɲɔ̃/ *n.m.* (*légume*) onion; (*de tulipe etc.*) bulb.

oiseau (*pl.* **~x**) /wazo/ *n.m.* bird.

oisi|f, ~ve /wazif, -v/ *a.* idle. **~veté** *n.f.* idleness.

oléoduc /ɔleɔdyk/ *n.m.* oil pipeline.

oliv|e /ɔliv/ *n.f. & a. invar.* olive. **~ier** *n.m.* olive-tree.

olympique /ɔlɛ̃pik/ *a.* Olympic.

ombrag|e /ɔ̃braʒ/ *n.m.* shade. **prendre ~e de**, take offence at. **~é** *a.* shady. **~eux, ~euse** *a.* easily offended.

ombre /ɔ̃br/ *n.f.* (*pénombre*) shade; (*contour*) shadow; (*soupçon: fig.*) hint, shadow. **dans l'~**, (*secret*) in the dark. **faire de l'~ à qn.**, be in s.o.'s light.

ombrelle /ɔ̃brɛl/ *n.f.* parasol.

omelette /ɔmlɛt/ *n.f.* omelette.

omettre† /ɔmɛtr/ *v.t.* omit.

omission /ɔmisjɔ̃/ *n.f.* omission.

omnibus /ɔmnibys/ *n.m.* slow train.

omoplate /ɔmɔplat/ *n.f.* shoulder-blade.

on /ɔ̃/ *pron.* we, you, one; (*les gens*) people, they; (*quelqu'un*) someone. **~ dit**, people say, they say, it is said (**que**, that).

once /ɔ̃s/ *n.f.* ounce.

oncle /ɔ̃kl/ *n.m.* uncle.

onctueu|x, ~se /ɔ̃ktɥø, -z/ *a.* smooth.

onde /ɔ̃d/ *n.f.* wave. **~s courtes/longues**, short/long wave. **sur les ~s**, on the radio.

ondée /ɔ̃de/ *n.f.* shower.

on-dit /ɔ̃di/ *n.m. invar.* rumour.

ondul|er /ɔ̃dyle/ *v.i.* undulate; (*cheveux*) be wavy. **~ation** *n.f.* wave, undulation. **~é** *a.* (*chevelure*) wavy.

onéreu|x, ~se /ɔnerø, -z/ *a.* costly.

ongl|e /ɔ̃gl/ *n.m.* (finger-)nail. **avoir l'~ée**, have frozen fingertips.

ont /ɔ̃/ *voir* **avoir.**

ONU *abrév.* (*Organisation des nations unies*) UN.

onyx /ɔniks/ *n.m.* onyx.

onz|e /ɔ̃z/ *a.* & *n.m.* eleven. **~ième** *a.* & *n.m./f.* eleventh.

opale /ɔpal/ *n.f.* opal.

opa|que /ɔpak/ *a.* opaque. **~cité** *n.f.* opaqueness.

opéra /ɔpera/ *n.m.* opera; (*édifice*) opera-house. **~-comique** (*pl.* **~s-comiques**) *n.m.* light opera.

opérateur /ɔperatœr/ *n.m.* (*caméra-man*) cameraman.

opération /ɔperasjɔ̃/ *n.f.* operation; (*comm.*) deal.

opérationnel, ~le /ɔperasjɔnɛl/ *a.* operational.

opératoire /ɔperatwar/ *a.* (*méd.*) surgical.

opérer /ɔpere/ *v.t.* (*personne*) operate on; (*kyste etc.*) remove; (*exécuter*) carry out, make. —*v.i.* (*méd.*) operate; (*faire effet*) work. **s'~** *v. pr.* (*se produire*) occur.

opérette /ɔperɛt/ *n.f.* operetta.

opiner /ɔpine/ *v.i.* nod.

opiniâtre /ɔpinjɑtr/ *a.* obstinate.

opinion /ɔpinjɔ̃/ *n.f.* opinion.

opium /ɔpjɔm/ *n.m.* opium.

opportun, ~e /ɔpɔrtœ̃, -yn/ *a.* opportune. **~ité** /-ynite/ *n.f.* opportuneness.

opposant, ~e /ɔpozɑ̃, -t/ *n.m., f.* opponent.

opposé /ɔpoze/ *a.* (*sens, angle, etc.*) opposite; (*factions*) opposing; (*intérêts*) conflicting. —*n.m.* opposite. **à l'~,** (*opinion etc.*) contrary (**de,** to). **être ~ à,** be opposed to.

opposer /ɔpoze/ *v.t.* (*objets*) place opposite each other; (*personnes*) oppose; (*contraster*) contrast; (*résistance, argument*) put up. **s'~** *v. pr.* (*personnes*) confront each other; (*styles*) contrast. **s'~ à,** oppose.

opposition /ɔpozisjɔ̃/ *n.f.* opposition. **faire ~ à,** oppose.

oppress|er /ɔprese/ *v.t.* oppress. **~ant, ~ante** *a.* oppressive. **~eur** *n.m.* oppressor. **~ion** *n.f.* oppression.

opprimer /ɔprime/ *v.t.* oppress.

opter /ɔpte/ *v.i.* **~ pour,** opt for.

opticien, ~ne /ɔptisjɛ̃, -jɛn/ *n.m., f.* optician.

optimis|te /ɔptimist/ *n.m./f.* optimist. —*a.* optimistic. **~me** *n.m.* optimism.

optimum /ɔptimɔm/ *a.* & *n.m.* optimum.

option /ɔpsjɔ̃/ *n.f.* option.

optique /ɔptik/ *a.* (*verre*) optical. —*n.f.* (*perspective*) perspective.

opulen|t, ~te /ɔpylɑ̃, -t/ *a.* opulent. **~ce** *n.f.* opulence.

or[1] /ɔr/ *n.m.* gold. **d'~,** golden. **en ~,** gold; (*occasion*) golden.

or[2] /ɔr/ *conj.* now, well.

oracle /ɔrakl/ *n.m.* oracle.

orag|e /ɔraʒ/ *n.m.* (thunder)storm. **~eux, ~euse** *a.* stormy.

oraison /ɔrɛzɔ̃/ *n.f.* prayer.

or|al (*m. pl.* **~aux**) /ɔral, -o/ *a.* oral. —*n.m.* (*pl.* **~aux**) oral.

orang|e /ɔrɑ̃ʒ/ *n.f.* & *a. invar.* orange. **~é** *a.* orange-coloured. **~er** *n.m.* orange(-tree).

orangeade /ɔrɑ̃ʒad/ *n.f.* orangeade.

orateur /ɔratœr/ *n.m.* speaker.

oratorio /ɔratɔrjo/ *n.m.* oratorio.

orbite /ɔrbit/ *n.f.* orbit; (*d'œil*) socket.

orchestr|e /ɔrkɛstr/ *n.m.* orchestra; (*de jazz*) band; (*parterre*) stalls. **~er** *v.t.* orchestrate.

orchidée /ɔrkide/ *n.f.* orchid.

ordinaire /ɔrdinɛr/ *a.* ordinary; (*habituel*) usual; (*qualité*) standard. —*n.m.* l'**~,** the ordinary; (*nourriture*) the standard fare. **d'~, à l'~,** usually. **~ment** *adv.* usually.

ordinateur /ɔrdinatœr/ *n.m.* computer.

ordination /ɔrdinasjɔ̃/ *n.f.* (*relig.*) ordination.

ordonnance /ɔrdɔnɑ̃s/ *n.f.* (*ordre, décret*) order; (*de médecin*) prescription; (*soldat*) orderly.

ordonné /ɔrdɔne/ *a.* orderly.

ordonner /ɔrdɔne/ *v.t.* order (**à qn. de,** s.o. to); (*agencer*) arrange; (*méd.*) prescribe; (*prêtre*) ordain.

ordre /ɔrdr/ *n.m.* order; (*propreté*) tidiness. **aux ~s de qn.,** at s.o.'s disposal. **avoir de l'~,** be tidy. **de premier ~,** first-rate. **l'~ du jour,** (*programme*) agenda. **mettre en ~,** tidy (up).

ordure /ɔrdyr/ *n.f.* filth. **~s,** (*détritus*) rubbish; (*Amer.*) garbage.

oreille /ɔrɛj/ *n.f.* ear.

oreiller /ɔreje/ *n.m.* pillow.

oreillons /ɔrɛjɔ̃/ *n.m. pl.* mumps.

orfèvr|e /ɔrfɛvr/ *n.m.* goldsmith, silversmith. **~erie** *n.f.* goldsmith's *ou* silversmith's trade.

organe /ɔrgan/ *n.m.* organ; (*porte-parole*) mouthpiece.

organigramme /ɔrganigram/ *n.m.* flow chart.

organique /ɔrganik/ *a.* organic.
organisation /ɔrganizɑsjɔ̃/ *n.f.* organization.
organis|er /ɔrganize/ *v.t.* organize. **s'~er** *v. pr.* organize o.s. **~ateur, ~atrice** *n.m., f.* organizer.
organisme /ɔrganism/ *n.m.* body, organism.
organiste /ɔrganist/ *n.m./f.* organist.
orgasme /ɔrgasm/ *n.m.* orgasm.
orge /ɔrʒ/ *n.f.* barley.
orgelet /ɔrʒəlɛ/ *n.m.* (*furoncle*) sty.
orgie /ɔrʒi/ *n.f.* orgy.
orgue /ɔrg/ *n.m.* organ. **~s** *n.f. pl.* organ. **~ de Barbarie,** barrel-organ.
orgueil /ɔrgœj/ *n.m.* pride.
orgueilleu|x, ~se /ɔrgœjø, -z/ *a.* proud.
Orient /ɔrjɑ̃/ *n.m.* **l'~,** the Orient.
orientable /ɔrjɑ̃tabl/ *a.* adjustable.
orient|al, ~ale (*m. pl.* **~aux**) /ɔrjɑ̃tal, -o/ *a.* eastern; (*de l'Orient*) oriental. —*n.m., f.* Oriental.
orientation /ɔrjɑ̃tɑsjɔ̃/ *n.f.* direction; (*d'une politique*) course; (*de maison*) aspect. **~ professionnelle,** careers advisory service.
orienté /ɔrjɑ̃te/ *a.* (*partial*) slanted, tendentious.
orienter /ɔrjɑ̃te/ *v.t.* position; (*personne*) direct. **s'~** *v. pr.* (*se repérer*) find one's bearings. **s'~ vers,** turn towards.
orifice /ɔrifis/ *n.m.* orifice.
originaire /ɔriʒinɛr/ *a.* **être ~ de,** be a native of.
origin|al, ~ale (*m. pl.* **~aux**) /ɔriʒinal, -o/ *a.* original; (*curieux*) eccentric. —*n.m.* original. —*n.m., f.* eccentric. **~alité** *n.f.* originality; eccentricity.
origine /ɔriʒin/ *n.f.* origin. **à l'~,** originally. **d'~,** (*pièce, pneu*) original.
originel, ~le /ɔriʒinɛl/ *a.* original.
orme /ɔrm/ *n.m.* elm.
ornement /ɔrnəmɑ̃/ *n.m.* ornament. **~al** (*m. pl.* **~aux**) /-tal, -to/ *a.* ornamental.
orner /ɔrne/ *v.t.* decorate.
ornière /ɔrnjɛr/ *n.f.* rut.
ornithologie /ɔrnitɔlɔʒi/ *n.f.* ornithology.
orphelin, ~e /ɔrfəlɛ̃, -in/ *n.m., f.* orphan. —*a.* orphaned. **~at** /-ina/ *n.m.* orphanage.
orteil /ɔrtɛj/ *n.m.* toe.
orthodox|e /ɔrtɔdɔks/ *a.* orthodox. **~ie** *n.f.* orthodoxy.

orthograph|e /ɔrtɔgraf/ *n.f.* spelling. **~ier** *v.t.* spell.
orthopédique /ɔrtɔpedik/ *a.* orthopaedic.
ortie /ɔrti/ *n.f.* nettle.
os (*pl.* **os**) /ɔs, o/ *n.m.* bone.
OS *abrév. voir* **ouvrier spécialisé.**
oscill|er /ɔsile/ *v.i.* sway; (*techn.*) oscillate; (*hésiter*) waver, fluctuate. **~ation** *n.f.* (*techn.*) oscillation; (*variation*) fluctuation.
oseille /ozɛj/ *n.f.* (*plante*) sorrel.
os|er /oze/ *v.t./i.* dare. **~é** *a.* daring.
osier /ozje/ *n.m.* wicker.
ossature /ɔsatyr/ *n.f.* frame.
ossements /ɔsmɑ̃/ *n.m. pl.* bones.
osseu|x, ~se /ɔsø, -z/ *a.* bony; (*tissu*) bone.
ostensible /ɔstɑ̃sibl/ *a.* conspicuous, obvious.
ostentation /ɔstɑ̃tɑsjɔ̃/ *n.f.* ostentation.
otage /otaʒ/ *n.m.* hostage.
otarie /otari/ *n.f.* sea-lion.
ôter /ote/ *v.t.* remove (**à qn.,** from s.o.); (*déduire*) take away.
otite /otit/ *n.f.* ear infection.
ou /u/ *conj.* or. **~ bien,** or else. **~ vous ou moi,** either you or me.
où /u/ *adv. & pron.* where; (*dans lequel*) in which; (*sur lequel*) on which; (*auquel*) at which. **d'~,** from which; (*pour cette raison*) hence. **d'~?,** from where? **par ~,** through which. **par ~?,** which way? **~ qu'il soit,** wherever he may be. **le jour ~,** the day when.
ouate /wat/ *n.f.* cotton wool; (*Amer.*) absorbent cotton.
oubli /ubli/ *n.m.* forgetfulness; (*trou de mémoire*) lapse of memory; (*négligence*) oversight. **l'~,** (*tomber dans, sauver de*) oblivion.
oublier /ublije/ *v.t.* forget. **s'~** *v. pr.* forget o.s.; (*chose*) be forgotten.
oublieu|x, ~se /ublijø, -z/ *a.* forgetful (**de,** of).
ouest /wɛst/ *n.m.* west. —*a. invar.* west; (*partie*) western; (*direction*) westerly.
ouf /uf/ *int.* phew.
oui /wi/ *adv.* yes.
ouï-dire (**par**) /(par)widir/ *adv.* by hearsay.
ouïe /wi/ *n.f.* hearing.
ouïes /wi/ *n.f. pl.* gills.
ouille /uj/ *int.* ouch.
ouïr /wir/ *v.t.* hear.

ouragan /uragã/ *n.m.* hurricane.

ourler /urle/ *v.t.* hem.

ourlet /urlɛ/ *n.m.* hem.

ours /urs/ *n.m.* bear. **~ blanc,** polar bear. **~ en peluche,** teddy bear.

ouste /ust/ *int.* (*fam.*) scram.

outil /uti/ *n.m.* tool.

outillage /utijaʒ/ *n.m.* tools; (*d'une usine*) equipment.

outiller /utije/ *v.t.* equip.

outrage /utraʒ/ *n.m* (grave) insult.

outrag|er /utraʒe/ *v.t.* offend. **~eant, ~eante** *a.* offensive.

outranc|e /utrãs/ *n.f.* excess. **à ~e,** to excess; (*guerre*) all-out. **~ier, ~ière** *a.* excessive.

outre /utr/ *prép.* besides. **en ~,** besides. **~-mer** *adv.* overseas. **~ mesure,** excessively.

outrepasser /utrəpase/ *v.t.* exceed.

outrer /utre/ *v.t.* exaggerate; (*indigner*) incense.

outsider /awtsajdœr/ *n.m.* outsider.

ouvert, ~e /uver, -t/ *voir* **ouvrir.** —*a.* open; (*gaz, radio, etc.*) on. **~ement** /-təmã/ *adv.* openly.

ouverture /uvɛrtyr/ *n.f.* opening; (*mus.*) overture. **~s,** (*offres*) overtures. **~ d'esprit,** open-mindedness.

ouvrag|e /uvraʒ/ *n.m.* (*travail, livre*) work; (*couture*) needlework. **~é** *a.* finely worked.

ouvreuse /uvrøz/ *n.f.* usherette.

ouvr|ier, ~ière /uvrije, -jɛr/ *n.m., f.* worker. —*a.* working-class; (*conflit*) industrial; (*syndicat*) workers'. **~ier qualifié/spécialisé,** skilled/ unskilled worker.

ouvr|ir† /uvrir/ *v.t.* open (up); (*gaz, radio, etc.*) turn *ou* switch on. —*v.i.* open (up). **s'~ir** *v. pr.* open (up). **s'~ir à qn.,** open one's heart to s.o. **~e-boîte(s)** *n.m.* tin-opener. **~e-bouteille(s)** *n.m.* bottle-opener.

ovaire /ovɛr/ *n.m.* ovary.

ovale /ɔval/ *a.* & *n.m.* oval.

ovation /ɔvasjɔ̃/ *n.f.* ovation.

oxygène /ɔksiʒɛn/ *n.m.* oxygen.

oxygéner (**s'**) /(s)ɔksiʒene/ *v. pr.* (*fam.*) get some fresh air.

P

pachyderme /paʃidɛrm/ *n.m.* elephant.

pacifier /pasifje/ *v.t.* pacify.

pacifique /pasifik/ *a.* peaceful; (*personne*) peaceable; (*géog.*) Pacific. —*n.m.* P~, Pacific (Ocean).

pacifiste /pasifist/ *n.m./f.* pacifist.

pacotille /pakɔtij/ *n.f.* trash.

pacte /pakt/ *n.m.* pact.

pactiser /paktize/ *v.i.* ~ **avec,** be in league *ou* agreement with.

paddock /padɔk/ *n.m.* paddock.

pag|aie /pagɛ/ *n.f.* paddle. ~**ayer** *v.i.* paddle.

pagaille /pagaj/ *n.f.* mess, shambles.

page /paʒ/ *n.f.* page. **être à la** ~, be up to date.

pagode /pagɔd/ *n.f.* pagoda.

paie /pɛ/ *n.f.* pay.

paiement /pɛmɑ̃/ *n.m.* payment.

païen, ~**ne** /pajɛ̃, -jɛn/ *a. & n.m., f.* pagan.

paillasse /pajas/ *n.f.* straw mattress; (*d'un évier*) draining-board.

paillasson /pajasɔ̃/ *n.m.* doormat.

paille /paj/ *n.f.* straw; (*défaut*) flaw.

paillette /pajɛt/ *n.f.* (*sur robe*) sequin; (*de savon*) flake. ~**s d'or,** gold-dust.

pain /pɛ̃/ *n.m.* bread; (*unité*) loaf (of bread); (*de savon etc.*) bar. ~ **d'épice,** gingerbread. ~ **grillé,** toast.

pair[1] /pɛr/ *a.* (*nombre*) even.

pair[2] /pɛr/ *n.m.* (*personne*) peer. **au** ~, (*jeune fille etc.*) au pair. **de** ~, together (**avec,** with).

paire /pɛr/ *n.f.* pair.

paisible /pezibl/ *a.* peaceful.

paître /pɛtr/ *v.i.* (*brouter*) graze.

paix /pɛ/ *n.f.* peace; (*papier*) peace treaty.

Pakistan /pakistɑ̃/ *n.m.* Pakistan.

pakistanais, ~**e** /pakistanɛ, -z/ *a. & n.m., f.* Pakistani.

palace /palas/ *n.m.* luxury hotel.

palais[1] /palɛ/ *n.m.* palace. **P**~ **de Justice,** Law Courts. ~ **des sports,** sports stadium.

palais[2] /palɛ/ *n.m.* (*anat.*) palate.

palan /palɑ̃/ *n.m.* hoist.

pâle /pɑl/ *a.* pale.

Palestine /palɛstin/ *n.f.* Palestine.

palestinien, ~**ne** /palɛstinjɛ̃, -jɛn/ *a. & n.m., f.* Palestinian.

palet /palɛ/ *n.m.* (*hockey*) puck.

paletot /palto/ *n.m.* thick jacket.

palette /palɛt/ *n.f.* palette.

pâleur /pɑlœr/ *n.f.* paleness.

palier /palje/ *n.m.* (*d'escalier*) landing; (*étape*) stage; (*de route*) level stretch.

pâlir /pɑlir/ *v.t./i.* (turn) pale.

palissade /palisad/ *n.f.* fence.

pallier /palje/ *v.i.* ~ **à,** alleviate.

palmarès /palmarɛs/ *n.m.* list of prize-winners.

palm|e /palm/ *n.f.* palm leaf; (*symbole*) palm; (*de nageur*) flipper. ~**ier** *n.m.* palm(-tree).

palmé /palme/ *a.* (*patte*) webbed.

pâlot, ~**te** /pɑlo, -ɔt/ *a.* pale.

palourde /palurd/ *n.f.* clam.

palper /palpe/ *v.t.* feel.

palpit|er /palpite/ *v.i.* (*battre*) pound, palpitate; (*frémir*) quiver. ~**ations** *n.f. pl.* palpitations.

paludisme /palydism/ *n.m.* malaria.

pâmer (se) /(sə)pɑme/ *v. pr.* swoon.

pamphlet /pɑflɛ/ *n.m.* satirical pamphlet.

pamplemousse /pɑpləmus/ *n.m.* grapefruit.

pan[1] /pɑ/ *n.m.* piece; (*de chemise*) tail.

pan[2] /pɑ/ *int.* bang.

panacée /panase/ *n.f.* panacea.

panache /panaʃ/ *n.m.* plume; (*bravoure*) gallantry; (*allure*) panache.

panaché /panaʃe/ *a.* (*bariolé, mélangé*) motley. —*n.m.* shandy. **bière** ~**e, demi** ~, shandy.

pancarte /pɑkart/ *n.f.* sign; (*de manifestant*) placard.

pancréas /pɑkreas/ *n.m.* pancreas.

pané /pane/ *a.* breaded.

panier /panje/ *n.m.* basket. ~ **à provisions,** shopping basket. ~ **à salade,** (*fam.*) police van.

paniqu|e /panik/ *n.f.* panic. ~**er** *v.i.,* **se** ~**er** *v. pr.* panic.

panne /pan/ *n.f.* breakdown. **être en** ~, have broken down. **être en** ~ **sèche,** have run out of petrol *ou* gas (*Amer.*). ~ **de courant,** power failure.

panneau (*pl.* ~**x**) /pano/ *n.m.* sign; (*publicitaire*) hoarding; (*de porte etc.*) panel. ~ (**d'affichage**), notice-board. ~ (**de signalisation**), road sign.

panoplie /panɔpli/ *n.f.* (*jouet*) outfit; (*gamme*) range.

panoram|a /panɔrama/ *n.m.* panorama. **~ique** *a.* panoramic.

panse /pɑ̃s/ *n.f.* paunch.

pans|er /pɑ̃se/ *v.t.* (*plaie*) dress; (*personne*) dress the wound(s) of; (*cheval*) groom. **~ement** *n.m.* dressing. **~ement adhésif**, sticking-plaster.

pantalon /pɑ̃talɔ̃/ *n.m.* (pair of) trousers. **~s**, trousers.

panthère /pɑ̃tɛr/ *n.f.* panther.

pantin /pɑ̃tɛ̃/ *n.m.* puppet.

pantomime /pɑ̃tɔmim/ *n.f.* mime; (*spectacle*) mime show.

pantoufle /pɑ̃tufl/ *n.f.* slipper.

paon /pɑ̃/ *n.m.* peacock.

papa /papa/ *n.m.* dad(dy).

papauté /papote/ *n.f.* papacy.

pape /pap/ *n.m.* pope.

paperass|e /papras/ *n.f.* **~e(s)**, (*péj.*) papers. **~erie** *n.f.* (*péj.*) papers; (*tracasserie*) red tape.

papet|ier /paptje, -jɛr/ *n.m.*, *f.* stationer. **~erie** /papetri/ *n.f.* (*magasin*) stationer's shop.

papier /papje/ *n.m.* paper; (*formulaire*) form. **~ à lettres**, writing-paper. **~ aluminium**, tin foil. **~ buvard**, blotting-paper. **~ calque**, tracing-paper. **~ carbone**, carbon paper. **~ collant**, sticky tape. **~ de verre**, sandpaper. **~ hygiénique**, toilet-paper. **~ journal**, newspaper. **~ mâché**, papier mâché. **~ peint**, wallpaper.

papillon /papijɔ̃/ *n.m.* butterfly; (*contravention*) parking-ticket. **~ (de nuit)**, moth.

papot|er /papote/ *v.i.* prattle. **~age** *n.m.* prattle.

paprika /paprika/ *n.m.* paprika.

Pâque /pɑk/ *n.f.* Passover.

paquebot /pakbo/ *n.m.* liner.

pâquerette /pɑkrɛt/ *n.f.* daisy.

Pâques /pɑk/ *n.f. pl.* & *n.m.* Easter.

paquet /pakɛ/ *n.m.* packet; (*de cartes*) pack; (*colis*) parcel. **un ~ de**, (*tas*) a mass of.

par /par/ *prép.* by; (*à travers*) through; (*motif*) out of, from; (*provenance*) from. **commencer/finir ~ qch.**, begin/end with sth. **commencer/finir ~ faire**, begin by/end up (by) doing. **~ an/mois/***etc.*, a *ou* per year/month/*etc.* **~ avion**, (*lettre*) (by) airmail. **~-ci, par-là**, here and there. **~ contre**, on the other hand.

~ hasard, by chance. **~ ici/là**, this/that way. **par inadvertance**, inadvertently. **~ intermittence**, intermittently. **~ l'intermédiaire de**, through. **~ malheur** *ou* **malchance**, unfortunately. **~ miracle**, miraculously. **~ moments**, at times. **~ opposition à**, as opposed to.

parabole /parabɔl/ *n.f.* (*relig.*) parable.

parachever /paraʃve/ *v.t.* perfect.

parachut|e /paraʃyt/ *n.m.* parachute. **~er** *v.t.* parachute. **~iste** *n.m./f.* parachutist; (*mil.*) paratrooper.

parad|e /parad/ *n.f.* parade; (*sport*) parry; (*réplique*) reply. **~er** *v.i.* show off.

paradis /paradi/ *n.m.* paradise.

paradox|e /paradɔks/ *n.m.* paradox. **~al** (*m. pl.* **~aux**) *a.* paradoxical.

paraffine /parafin/ *n.f.* paraffin wax.

parages /paraʒ/ *n.m. pl.* area, vicinity.

paragraphe /paragraf/ *n.m.* paragraph.

paraître† /parɛtr/ *v.i.* appear; (*sembler*) seem, appear; (*ouvrage*) be published, come out. **faire ~**, (*ouvrage*) bring out.

parallèle /paralɛl/ *a.* parallel; (*illégal*) unofficial. —*n.m.* parallel. —*n.f.* parallel (line). **~ment** *adv.* parallel (à, to).

paraly|ser /paralize/ *v.t.* paralyse. **~sie** *n.f.* paralysis. **~tique** *a.* & *n.m./f.* paralytic.

paramètre /paramɛtr/ *n.m.* parameter.

paranoïa /paranɔja/ *n.f.* paranoia.

parapet /parapɛ/ *n.m.* parapet.

paraphe /paraf/ *n.m.* signature.

paraphrase /parafraz/ *n.f.* paraphrase.

parapluie /paraplɥi/ *n.m.* umbrella.

parasite /parazit/ *n.m.* parasite. **~s**, (*radio*) interference. —*a.* parasitic.

parasol /parasɔl/ *n.m.* sunshade.

paratonnerre /paratɔnɛr/ *n.m.* lightning-conductor *ou* -rod.

paravent /paravɑ̃/ *n.m.* screen.

parc /park/ *n.m.* park; (*de bétail*) pen; (*de bébé*) play-pen; (*entrepôt*) depot. **~ de stationnement**, car-park.

parcelle /parsɛl/ *n.f.* fragment; (*de terre*) plot.

parce que /parskə/ *conj.* because.

parchemin /parʃəmɛ̃/ *n.m.* parchment.

parcimon|ie /parsimɔni/ *n.f.* **avec**

~ie, parsimoniously. **~ieux, ~ieuse** *a.* parsimonious.

parcmètre /parkmɛtr/ *n.m.* parking-meter.

parcourir† /parkurir/ *v.t.* travel *ou* go through; (*distance*) travel; (*des yeux*) glance at *ou* over.

parcours /parkur/ *n.m.* route; (*voyage*) journey.

par-delà /pardəla/ *prép.* & *adv.* beyond.

par-derrière /pardɛrjɛr/ *prép.* & *adv.* behind, at the back *ou* rear (of).

par-dessous /pardsu/ *prép.* & *adv.* under(neath).

pardessus /pardəsy/ *n.m.* overcoat.

par-dessus /pardsy/ *prép.* & *adv.* over. **~ bord,** overboard. **~ le marché,** into the bargain. **~ tout,** above all.

par-devant /pardvɑ̃/ *adv.* at *ou* from the front, in front.

pardon /pardɔ̃/ *n.m.* forgiveness. **(je vous demande) ~!,** (I am) sorry!; (*pour demander qch.*) excuse me!

pardonn|er /pardɔne/ *v.t.* forgive. **~er qch. à qn.,** forgive s.o. for sth. **~able** *a.* forgivable.

paré /pare/ *a.* ready.

pare-balles /parbal/ *a. invar.* bullet-proof.

pare-brise /parbriz/ *n.m. invar.* windscreen; (*Amer.*) windshield.

pare-chocs /parʃɔk/ *n.m. invar.* bumper.

pareil, ~le /parɛj/ *a.* similar (à, to); (*tel*) such (a). —*n.m., f.* equal. —*adv.* (*fam.*) the same. **c'est ~,** it is the same. **vos ~s,** (*péj.*) those of your type, those like you. **~lement** *adv.* the same.

parement /parmɑ̃/ *n.m.* facing.

parent, ~e /parɑ̃, -t/ *a.* related (**de,** to). —*n.m., f.* relative, relation. **~s** (*père et mère*) *n.m. pl.* parents.

parenté /parɑ̃te/ *n.f.* relationship.

parenthèse /parɑ̃tɛz/ *n.f.* bracket, parenthesis; (*fig.*) digression.

parer¹ /pare/ *v.t.* (*coup*) parry. —*v.i.* **~ à,** deal with.

parer² /pare/ *v.t.* (*orner*) adorn.

paress|e /parɛs/ *n.f.* laziness. **~er** /-ese/ *v.i.* laze (about). **~eux, ~euse** *a.* lazy; *n.m., f.* lazybones.

parfaire /parfɛr/ *v.t.* perfect.

parfait, ~e /parfɛ, -t/ *a.* perfect. **~ement** /-tmɑ̃/ *adv.* perfectly; (*bien sûr*) certainly.

parfois /parfwa/ *adv.* sometimes.

parfum /parfœ̃/ *n.m.* scent; (*substance*) perfume, scent; (*goût*) flavour.

parfum|er /parfyme/ *v.t.* perfume; (*gâteau*) flavour. **se ~er** *v. pr.* put on one's perfume. **~é** *a.* fragrant; (*savon*) scented. **~erie** *n.f.* (*produits*) perfumes; (*boutique*) perfume shop.

pari /pari/ *n.m.* bet.

par|ier /parje/ *v.t.* bet. **~ieur, ~ieuse** *n.m., f.* punter, better.

Paris /pari/ *n.m./f.* Paris.

parisien, ~ne /parizjɛ̃, -jɛn/ *a.* Paris, Parisian. —*n.m., f.* Parisian.

parit|é /parite/ *n.f.* parity. **~aire** *a.* (*commission*) joint.

parjur|e /parʒyr/ *n.m.* perjury. —*n.m./f.* perjurer. **se ~er** *v. pr.* perjure o.s.

parking /parkiŋ/ *n.m.* car-park; (*Amer.*) parking-lot; (*stationnement*) parking.

parlement /parləmɑ̃/ *n.m.* parliament. **~aire** /-tɛr/ *a.* parliamentary; *n.m./f.* Member of Parliament; (*fig.*) negotiator. **~er** /-te/ *v.i.* negotiate.

parl|er /parle/ *v.i.* talk, speak (à, to). —*v.t.* (*langue*) speak; (*politique, affaires, etc.*) talk. **se ~er** *v. pr.* (*langue*) be spoken. —*n.m.* speech; (*dialecte*) dialect. **~ant, ~ante** *a.* (*film*) talking; (*fig.*) eloquent. **~eur, ~euse** *n.m., f.* talker.

parmi /parmi/ *prép.* among(st).

parod|ie /parɔdi/ *n.f.* parody. **~ier** *v.t.* parody.

paroi /parwa/ *n.f.* wall; (*cloison*) partition (wall).

paroiss|e /parwas/ *n.f.* parish. **~ial** (*m. pl.* **~iaux**) *a.* parish. **~ien, ~ienne** *n.m., f.* parishioner.

parole /parɔl/ *n.f.* (*mot, promesse*) word; (*langage*) speech. **demander la ~,** ask to speak. **prendre la ~,** (begin to) speak.

paroxysme /parɔksism/ *n.m.* height, highest point.

parquer /parke/ *v.t., se ~ v. pr.* (*auto.*) park.

parquet /parkɛ/ *n.m.* floor; (*jurid.*) public prosecutor's department.

parrain /parɛ̃/ *n.m.* godfather; (*fig.*) sponsor. **~er** /-ene/ *v.t.* sponsor.

pars, part¹ /par/ *voir* **partir.**

parsemer /parsəme/ *v.t.* strew (**de,** with).

part² /par/ *n.f.* share, part. **à ~,** (*de côté*) aside; (*séparément*) apart; (*excepté*) apart from. **d'autre ~,** on the other hand; (*de plus*) moreover. **de la ~ de**, from. **de toutes ~s**, from all sides. **d'une ~**, on the one hand. **faire ~ à qn.**, inform s.o. (**de**, of). **prendre ~ à**, take part in; (*joie, douleur*) share.

partag|e /partaʒ/ *n.m.* dividing; sharing out; (*part*) share. **~er** *v.t.* divide; (*distribuer*) share out; (*avoir en commun*) share. **se ~er qch.**, share sth.

partance (en) /(ɑ̃)partɑ̃s/ *adv.* about to depart.

partant /partɑ̃/ *n.m.* (*sport*) starter.

partenaire /partənɛr/ *n.m./f.* partner.

parterre /partɛr/ *n.m.* flower-bed; (*théâtre*) stalls.

parti /parti/ *n.m.* (*pol.*) party; (*en mariage*) match; (*décision*) decision. **~ pris**, prejudice. **prendre ~ pour**, side with.

part|ial (*m. pl.* **~iaux**) /parsjal, -jo/ *a.* biased. **~ialité** *n.f.* bias.

participe /partisip/ *n.m.* (*gram.*) participle.

particip|er /partisipe/ *v.i.* **~er à**, take part in, participate in; (*profits, frais*) share; (*spectacle*) appear in. **~ant, ~ante** *n.m., f.* participant (**à**, in); (*à un concours*) entrant. **~ation** *n.f.* participation; sharing; (*d'un artiste*) appearance.

particularité /partikylarite/ *n.f.* particularity.

particule /partikyl/ *n.f.* particle.

particul|ier, ~ière /partikylje, -jɛr/ *a.* (*spécifique*) particular; (*bizarre*) peculiar; (*privé*) private. —*n.m.* private individual. **en ~ier**, in particular; (*en privé*) in private. **~ier à**, peculiar to. **~ièrement** *adv.* particularly.

partie /parti/ *n.f.* part; (*cartes, sport*) game; (*jurid.*) party; (*sortie*) outing, party. **en ~**, partly. **faire ~ de**, be part of; (*adhérer à*) belong to. **~ intégrante**, integral part.

partiel, ~le /parsjɛl/ *a.* partial. —*n.m.* (*univ.*) class examination. **~lement** *adv.* partially, partly.

partir† /partir/ *v.i.* (*aux. être*) go; (*quitter un lieu*) leave, go; (*tache*) come out; (*bouton*) come off; (*coup de feu*) go off; (*commencer*) start. **à ~ de**, from.

partisan, ~e /partizɑ̃, -an/ *n.m., f.* supporter. —*n.m.* (*mil.*) partisan. **être ~ de**, be in favour of.

partition /partisjɔ̃/ *n.f.* (*mus.*) score.

partout /partu/ *adv.* everywhere. **~ où**, wherever.

paru /pary/ *voir* **paraître**.

parure /paryr/ *n.f.* adornment; (*bijoux*) (set of) jewels, jewellery.

parution /parysjɔ̃/ *n.f.* publication.

parvenir† /parvənir/ *v.i.* (*aux. être*) **~ à**, reach; (*résultat*) achieve. **~ à faire**, manage to do.

parvenu, ~e /parvəny/ *n.m., f.* upstart.

parvis /parvi/ *n.m.* (*place*) square.

pas¹ /pɑ/ *adv.* not. (**ne**) **~**, not. **je ne sais ~**, I do not know. **~ de sucre/livres/etc.**, no sugar/books/etc. **~ du tout**, not at all. **~ encore**, not yet. **~ mal**, not bad; (*beaucoup*) quite a lot (**de**, of). **~ vrai?**, (*fam.*) isn't that so?

pas² /pɑ/ *n.m.* step; (*bruit*) footstep; (*trace*) footprint; (*vitesse*) pace; (*de vis*) thread. **à deux ~ (de)**, close by. **au ~**, at a walking pace; (*véhicule*) very slowly. **au ~ (cadencé)**, in step. **~ de la porte**, doorstep.

passable /pɑsabl/ *a.* tolerable. **~ment** /-əmɑ̃/ *adv.* (*pas trop mal*) tolerably; (*beaucoup*) quite a bit.

passage /pɑsaʒ/ *n.m.* passing, passage; (*traversée*) crossing; (*arrivée*) arrival; (*visite*) visit; (*chemin*) way, passage; (*d'une œuvre*) passage. **de ~**, (*voyageur*) visiting. **~ à niveau**, level crossing. **~ clouté**, pedestrian crossing. **~ interdit**, (*panneau*) no thoroughfare. **~ souterrain**, subway; (*Amer.*) underpass.

passag|er, ~ère /pɑsaʒe, -ɛr/ *a.* temporary. —*n.m., f.* passenger. **~er clandestin**, stowaway.

passant, ~e /pɑsɑ̃, -t/ *a.* (*rue*) busy. —*n.m., f.* passer-by. —*n.m.* (*anneau*) loop.

passe /pɑs/ *n.f.* pass. **bonne/mauvaise ~**, good/bad patch. **en ~ de**, on the road to. **~-montagne** *n.m.* Balaclava. **~-partout** *n.m. invar.* master-key; *a. invar.* for all occasions. **~-temps** *n.m. invar.* pastime.

passé /pɑse/ *a.* (*révolu*) past; (*dernier*) last; (*fini*) over; (*fané*) faded. —*prép.* after. —*n.m.* past. **~ de mode**, out of fashion.

passeport /pɑspɔr/ *n.m.* passport.

passer /pɑse/ *v.i.* (*aux. être ou avoir*) pass; (*aller*) go; (*venir*) come; (*temps*) pass (by), go by; (*film*) be shown;

(*couleur*) fade. —*v.t.* (*aux. avoir*) pass, cross; (*donner*) pass, hand; (*mettre*) put; (*oublier*) overlook; (*enfiler*) slip on; (*dépasser*) go beyond; (*temps*) spend, pass; (*film*) show; (*examen*) take; (*commande*) place; (*soupe*) strain. se ~ *v. pr.* happen, take place. laisser ~, let through; (*occasion*) miss. ~ à tabac, (*fam.*) beat up. ~ devant, (*édifice*) go past. ~ en fraude, smuggle. ~ outre, take no notice (à, of). ~ pour, (*riche etc.*) be taken to be. ~ sur, (*détail*) pass over. ~ un coup de fil à qn., give s.o. a ring. se ~ de, go *ou* do without.

passerelle /pɑsrɛl/ *n.f.* footbridge; (*pour accéder à un avion, à un navire*) gangway.

passible /pasibl/ *a.* ~ de, liable to.

passi|f, ~ve /pasif, -v/ *a.* passive. —*n.m.* (*comm.*) liabilities. ~vité *n.f.* passiveness.

passion /pɑsjɔ̃/ *n.f.* passion.

passionn|er /pɑsjone/ *v.t.* fascinate. se ~er pour, have a passion for. ~é *a.* passionate. être ~é de, have a passion for. ~ément *adv.* passionately.

passoire /pɑswar/ *n.f.* (à *thé*) strainer; (à *légumes*) colander.

pastel /pastɛl/ *n.m. & a. invar.* pastel.

pastèque /pastɛk/ *n.f.* water-melon.

pasteur /pastœr/ *n.m.* (*relig.*) minister.

pasteuriser /pastœrize/ *v.t.* pasteurize.

pastiche /pastiʃ/ *n.m.* pastiche.

pastille /pastij/ *n.f.* (*bonbon*) pastille, lozenge.

pastis /pastis/ *n.m.* aniseed liqueur.

pastor|al (*m. pl.* ~aux) /pastɔral, -o/ *a.* pastoral.

patate /patat/ *n.f.* (*fam.*) potato.

patauger /patoʒe/ *v.i.* splash about.

pâte /pɑt/ *n.f.* paste; (*farine*) dough; (à *tarte*) pastry; (à *frire*) batter. ~s (*alimentaires*), pasta. ~ à modeler, Plasticine (P.). ~ dentifrice, toothpaste.

pâté /pɑte/ *n.m.* (*culin.*) pâté; (*d'encre*) ink-blot. ~ de maisons, block of houses. ~ en croûte, meat pie.

pâtée /pɑte/ *n.f.* feed, mash.

patelin /patlɛ̃/ *n.m.* (*fam.*) village.

patent, ~e[1] /patɑ̃, -t/ *a.* patent.

patent|e[2] /patɑ̃t/ *n.f.* trade licence. ~é *a.* licensed.

patère /patɛr/ *n.f.* (coat) peg.

patern|el, ~elle /patɛrnɛl/ *a.* paternal. ~ité *n.f.* paternity.

pâteu|x, ~se /pɑtø, -z/ *a.* pasty; (*langue*) coated.

pathétique /patetik/ *a.* moving. —*n.m.* pathos.

patholog|ie /patɔlɔʒi/ *n.f.* pathology. ~ique *a.* pathological.

pat|ient, ~iente /pasjɑ̃, -t/ *a. & n.m., f.* patient. ~iemment /-jamɑ̃/ *adv.* patiently. ~ience *n.f.* patience.

patienter /pasjɑ̃te/ *v.i.* wait.

patin /patɛ̃/ *n.m.* skate. ~ à roulettes, roller-skate.

patin|er /patine/ *v.i.* skate; (*voiture*) spin. ~age *n.m.* skating. ~eur, ~euse *n.m., f.* skater.

patinette /patinɛt/ *n.f.* scooter.

patinoire /patinwar/ *n.f.* skating-rink.

pâtir /pɑtir/ *v.i.* suffer (de, from).

pâtiss|ier, ~ière /pɑtisje, -jɛr/ *n.m., f.* pastry-cook, cake shop owner. ~erie *n.f.* cake shop; (*gâteau*) pastry; (*art*) cake making.

patois /patwa/ *n.m.* patois.

patraque /patrak/ *a.* (*fam.*) peaky, out of sorts.

patrie /patri/ *n.f.* homeland.

patrimoine /patrimwan/ *n.m.* heritage.

patriot|e /patrijɔt/ *a.* patriotic. —*n.m./f.* patriot. ~ique *a.* patriotic. ~isme *n.m.* patriotism.

patron[1], ~ne /patrɔ̃, -ɔn/ *n.m., f.* employer, boss; (*propriétaire*) owner, boss; (*saint*) patron saint. ~al (*m. pl.* ~aux) /-ɔnal, -o/ *a.* employers'. ~at /-ɔna/ *n.m.* employers.

patron[2] /patrɔ̃/ *n.m.* (*couture*) pattern.

patronage /patrɔnaʒ/ *n.m.* patronage; (*foyer*) youth club.

patronner /patrɔne/ *v.t.* support.

patrouill|e /patruj/ *n.f.* patrol. ~er *v.i.* patrol.

patte /pat/ *n.f.* leg; (*pied*) foot; (*de chat*) paw; (*main: fam.*) hand; (*de poche, d'enveloppe*) flap. ~s, (*favoris*) sideburns.

pâturage /pɑtyraʒ/ *n.m.* pasture.

pâture /pɑtyr/ *n.f.* food.

paume /pom/ *n.f.* (*de main*) palm.

paumé, ~e /pome/ *n.m., f.* (*fam.*) wretch, loser.

paumer /pome/ *v.t.* (*fam.*) lose.

paupière /popjɛr/ *n.f.* eyelid.

pause /poz/ *n.f.* pause; (*halte*) break.

pauvre /povr/ *a.* poor. —*n.m./f.* poor

man, poor woman. ~**ment** /-əmɑ̃/ *adv.* poorly. ~**té** /-ɑte/ *n.f.* poverty.

pavaner (se) /(sə)pavane/ *v. pr.* strut.

pav|er /pave/ *v.t.* pave; (*chaussée*) cobble. ~**é** *n.m.* paving-stone; cobble(-stone).

pavillon[1] /pavijɔ̃/ *n.m.* house; (*de gardien*) lodge.

pavillon[2] /pavijɔ̃/ *n.m.* (*drapeau*) flag.

pavoiser /pavwaze/ *v.t.* deck with flags. —*v.i.* put out the flags.

pavot /pavo/ *n.m.* poppy.

payant, ~e /pɛjɑ̃, -t/ *a.* (*billet*) for which a charge is made; (*spectateur*) (fee-)paying; (*rentable*) profitable.

payer /peje/ *v.t./i.* pay; (*service, travail, etc.*) pay for; (*acheter*) buy (à, for). **se ~** *v. pr.* (*s'acheter*) buy o.s. **faire ~ à qn.**, (*cent francs etc.*) charge s.o. (**pour**, for). **se ~ la tête de**, make fun of.

pays /pei/ *n.m.* country; (*région*) region; (*village*) village. **du ~**, local. **les P~-Bas**, the Netherlands. **le ~ de Galles**, Wales.

paysage /peizaʒ/ *n.m.* landscape.

paysan, ~ne /peizɑ̃, -an/ *n.m., f.* farmer, country person; (*péj.*) peasant. —*a.* (*agricole*) farming; (*rural*) country.

PCV (en) /(ɑ̃)peseve/ *adv.* **appeler** *ou* **téléphoner en ~**, reverse the charges; (*Amer.*) call collect.

PDG *abrév. voir* **président directeur général.**

péage /peaʒ/ *n.m.* toll; (*lieu*) tollgate.

peau (*pl.* ~**x**) /po/ *n.f.* skin; (*cuir*) hide. **~ de chamois**, chamois (-leather). **~ de mouton**, sheepskin. **P~-Rouge** (*pl.* **P~x-Rouges**) *n.m./f.* Red Indian.

pêche[1] /pɛʃ/ *n.f.* peach.

pêche[2] /pɛʃ/ *n.f.* (*activité*) fishing; (*poissons*) catch. **~ à la ligne**, angling.

péché /peʃe/ *n.m.* sin.

péch|er /peʃe/ *v.i.* sin. **~er par timidité**/*etc.*, be too timid/*etc.* **~eur, ~eresse** *n.m., f.* sinner.

pêch|er /peʃe/ *v.t.* (*poisson*) catch; (*dénicher: fam.*) dig up. —*v.i.* fish. **~eur** *n.m.* fisherman; (*à la ligne*) angler.

pécule /pekyl/ *n.m.* (*économies*) savings.

pécuniaire /pekynjɛr/ *a.* financial.

pédago|gie /pedagɔʒi/ *n.f.* education. **~gique** *a.* educational. **~gue** *n.m./f.* teacher.

pédal|e /pedal/ *n.f.* pedal. **~er** *v.i.* pedal.

pédalo /pedalo/ *n.m.* pedal boat.

pédant, ~e /pedɑ̃, -t/ *a.* pedantic.

pédéraste /pederast/ *n.m.* homosexual.

pédiatre /pedjatr/ *n.m./f.* paediatrician.

pédicure /pedikyr/ *n.m./f.* chiropodist.

pedigree /pedigri/ *n.m.* pedigree.

pègre /pɛgr/ *n.f.* underworld.

peign|e /pɛɲ/ *n.m.* comb. **~er** /peɲe/ *v.t.* comb; (*personne*) comb the hair of. **se ~er** *v. pr.* comb one's hair.

peignoir /pɛɲwar/ *n.m.* dressing-gown.

peindre† /pɛ̃dr/ *v.t.* paint.

peine /pɛn/ *n.f.* sadness, sorrow; (*effort, difficulté*) trouble; (*punition*) punishment; (*jurid.*) sentence. **avoir de la ~**, feel sad. **ce n'est pas la ~ de faire**, it is not worth (while) doing.

peine (à) /(a)pɛn/ *adv.* hardly.

peiner /pene/ *v.i.* struggle. —*v.t.* sadden.

peintre /pɛ̃tr/ *n.m.* painter. **~ en bâtiment**, house painter.

peinture /pɛ̃tyr/ *n.f.* painting; (*matière*) paint. **~ à l'huile**, oil-painting.

péjorati|f, ~ve /peʒɔratif, -v/ *a.* pejorative.

pelage /pəlaʒ/ *n.m.* coat, fur.

pêle-mêle /pɛlmɛl/ *adv.* in confusion.

peler /pəle/ *v.t./i.* peel.

pèlerin /pɛlrɛ̃/ *n.m.* pilgrim. **~age** /-inaʒ/ *n.m.* pilgrimage.

pèlerine /pɛlrin/ *n.f.* cape.

pélican /pelikɑ̃/ *n.m.* pelican.

pelle /pɛl/ *n.f.* shovel; (*d'enfant*) spade. **~tée** *n.f.* shovelful.

pellicule /pelikyl/ *n.f.* film. **~s**, (*méd.*) dandruff.

pelote /pəlɔt/ *n.f.* ball; (*d'épingles*) pincushion.

peloton /plɔtɔ̃/ *n.m.* troop, squad; (*sport*) pack. **~ d'exécution**, firing-squad.

pelotonner (se) /(sə)plɔtɔne/ *v. pr.* curl up.

pelouse /pluz/ *n.f.* lawn.

peluche /plyʃ/ *n.f.* (*tissu*) plush. **en ~**, (*lapin, chien*) fluffy, furry.

pelure /plyr/ *n.f.* peeling.

pén|al (*m. pl.* ~**aux**) /penal, -o/ *a.* penal. **~aliser** *v.t.* penalize. **~alité** *n.f.* penalty.

penalt|y (*pl.* ~ies) /penalti/ *n.m.* penalty (kick).

penaud, ~e /pəno, -d/ *a.* sheepish.

penchant /pãʃã/ *n.m.* inclination; (*goût*) liking (**pour**, for).

pench|er /pãʃe/ *v.t.* tilt. —*v.i.* lean (over), tilt. **se ~er** *v. pr.* lean (forward). **~er pour**, favour. **se ~er sur**, (*problème etc.*) examine.

pendaison /pãdɛzɔ̃/ *n.f.* hanging.

pendant¹ /pãdã/ *prép.* (*au cours de*) during; (*durée*) for. **~ que**, while.

pendant², ~e /pãdã, -t/ *a.* hanging; (*question etc.*) pending. —*n.m.* (*contrepartie*) matching piece (**de**, to). **~ d'oreille**, drop ear-ring.

pendentif /pãdãtif/ *n.m.* pendant.

penderie /pãdri/ *n.f.* wardrobe.

pend|re /pãdr/ *v.t./i.* hang. **se ~re** *v. pr.* hang (**à**, from); (*se tuer*) hang o.s. **~re la crémaillère**, have a house-warming. **~u, ~ue** *a.* hanging (**à**, from); *n.m.*, *f.* hanged man, hanged woman.

pendul|e /pãdyl/ *n.f.* clock. —*n.m.* pendulum. **~ette** *n.f.* (travelling) clock.

pénétr|er /penetre/ *v.i.* **~er** (**dans**), enter. —*v.t.* penetrate. **se ~er de**, become convinced of. **~ant, ~ante** *a.* penetrating.

pénible /penibl/ *a.* difficult; (*douloureux*) painful; (*fatigant*) tiresome. **~ment** /-əmã/ *adv.* with difficulty; (*cruellement*) painfully.

péniche /peniʃ/ *n.f.* barge.

pénicilline /penisilin/ *n.f.* penicillin.

péninsule /penɛ̃syl/ *n.f.* peninsula.

pénis /penis/ *n.m.* penis.

pénitence /penitãs/ *n.f.* (*peine*) penance; (*regret*) penitence; (*fig.*) punishment. **faire ~**, repent.

péniten|cier /penitãsje/ *n.m.* penitentiary. **~tiaire** /-sjɛr/ *a.* prison.

pénombre /penɔ̃br/ *n.f.* half-light.

pensée¹ /pãse/ *n.f.* thought.

pensée² /pãse/ *n.f.* (*fleur*) pansy.

pens|er /pãse/ *v.t./i.* think. **~er à**, (*réfléchir à*) think about; (*se souvenir de, prévoir*) think of. **~er faire**, think of doing. **~eur** *n.m.* thinker.

pensi|f, ~ve /pãsif, -v/ *a.* pensive.

pension /pãsjɔ̃/ *n.f.* (*scol.*) boarding-school; (*repas, somme*) board; (*allocation*) pension. **~ (de famille)**, guest-house. **~ alimentaire**, (*jurid.*) alimony. **~naire** /-jɔnɛr/ *n.m./f.* boarder; (*d'hôtel*) guest. **~nat** /-jɔna/ *n.m.* boarding-school.

pente /pãt/ *n.f.* slope. **en ~**, sloping.

Pentecôte /pãtkot/ *n.f.* Whitsun.

pénurie /penyri/ *n.f.* shortage.

pépé /pepe/ *n.m.* (*fam.*) grandad.

pépier /pepje/ *v.i.* chirp.

pépin /pepɛ̃/ *n.m.* (*graine*) pip; (*ennui: fam.*) hitch; (*parapluie: fam.*) brolly.

pépinière /pepinjɛr/ *n.f.* (tree) nursery.

perçant, ~e /pɛrsã, -t/ *a.* (*froid*) piercing; (*yeux*) keen.

percée /pɛrse/ *n.f.* opening; (*attaque*) breakthrough.

perce-neige /pɛrsənɛʒ/ *n.m./f. invar.* snowdrop.

percepteur /pɛrsɛptœr/ *n.m.* tax-collector.

perceptible /pɛrsɛptibl/ *a.* perceptible.

perception /pɛrsɛpsjɔ̃/ *n.f.* perception; (*d'impôts*) collection.

percer /pɛrse/ *v.t.* pierce; (*avec perceuse*) drill; (*mystère*) penetrate; (*dent*) cut. —*v.i.* break through.

perceuse /pɛrsøz/ *n.f.* drill.

percevoir† /pɛrsəvwar/ *v.t.* perceive; (*impôt*) collect.

perche /pɛrʃ/ *n.f.* (*bâton*) pole.

perch|er /pɛrʃe/ *v.t.*, **se ~er** *v. pr.* perch. **~oir** *n.m.* perch.

percussion /pɛrkysjɔ̃/ *n.f.* percussion.

percuter /pɛrkyte/ *v.t.* strike; (*véhicule*) crash into.

perd|re /pɛrdr/ *v.t./i.* lose; (*gaspiller*) waste; (*ruiner*) ruin. **se ~re** *v. pr.* get lost; (*rester inutilisé*) go to waste. **~ant, ~ante** *a.* losing; *n.m.*, *f.* loser. **~u** *a.* (*endroit*) isolated; (*moments*) spare; (*malade*) finished.

perdreau (*pl.* **~x**) /pɛrdro/ *n.m.* (young) partridge.

perdrix /pɛrdri/ *n.f.* partridge.

père /pɛr/ *n.m.* father.

péremptoire /perãptwar/ *a.* peremptory.

perfection /pɛrfɛksjɔ̃/ *n.f.* perfection.

perfectionn|er /pɛrfɛksjɔne/ *v.t.* improve. **se ~er en anglais**/*etc.*, improve one's English/*etc.* **~é** *a.* sophisticated. **~ement** *n.m.* improvement.

perfectionniste /pɛrfɛksjɔnist/ *n.m./f.* perfectionist.

perfid|e /pɛrfid/ *a.* perfidious, treacherous. **~ie** *n.f.* perfidy.

perfor|er /pɛrfɔre/ *v.t.* perforate; (*billet, bande*) punch. **~ateur** *n.m.*

(*appareil*) punch. ~**ation** *n.f.* perforation; (*trou*) hole.

performan|ce /pɛrfɔrmɑ̃s/ *n.f.* performance. ~**t**, ~**te** *a.* high-performance, successful.

péricliter /periklite/ *v.i.* decline, be in rapid decline.

péril /peril/ *n.m.* peril.

périlleu|x, ~**se** /perijø, -z/ *a.* perilous.

périmé /perime/ *a.* expired; (*désuet*) outdated.

périmètre /perimɛtr/ *n.m.* perimeter.

périod|e /perjɔd/ *n.f.* period. ~**ique** *a.* periodic(al); *n.m.* (*journal*) periodical.

péripétie /peripesi/ *n.f.* (unexpected) event, adventure.

périphér|ie /periferi/ *n.f.* periphery; (*banlieue*) outskirts. ~**ique** *a.* peripheral; *n.m.* (**boulevard**) ~, ring road.

périple /peripl/ *n.m.* journey.

pér|ir /perir/ *v.i.* perish, die. ~**issable** *a.* perishable.

périscope /periskɔp/ *n.m.* periscope.

perle /pɛrl/ *n.f.* (*bijou*) pearl; (*boule*) bead.

permanence /pɛrmanɑ̃s/ *n.f.* permanence; (*bureau*) duty office; (*scol.*) study room. **de** ~, on duty. **en** ~, permanently.

permanent, ~**e** /pɛrmanɑ̃, -t/ *a.* permanent; (*spectacle*) continuous; (*comité*) standing. —*n.f.* (*coiffure*) perm.

perméable /pɛrmeabl/ *a.* permeable; (*personne*) susceptible (**à**, to).

permettre† /pɛrmɛtr/ *v.t.* allow, permit. ~ **à qn. de**, allow *ou* permit s.o. to. **se** ~ **de**, take the liberty to.

permis, ~**e** /pɛrmi, -z/ *a.* allowed. —*n.m.* licence, permit. ~ **de conduire**, driving-licence.

permission /pɛrmisjɔ̃/ *n.f.* permission; (*mil.*) leave.

permut|er /pɛrmyte/ *v.t.* change round. ~**ation** *n.f.* permutation.

pernicieu|x, ~**se** /pɛrnisjø, -z/ *a.* pernicious.

Pérou /peru/ *n.m.* Peru.

perpendiculaire /pɛrpɑ̃dikylɛr/ *a.* & *n.f.* perpendicular.

perpétrer /pɛrpetre/ *v.t.* perpetrate.

perpétuel, ~**le** /pɛrpetɥɛl/ *a.* perpetual.

perpétuer /pɛrpetɥe/ *v.t.* perpetuate.

perpétuité (**à**) /(a)pɛrpetɥite/ *adv.* for life.

perplex|e /pɛrplɛks/ *a.* perplexed. ~**ité** *n.f.* perplexity.

perquisition /pɛrkizisjɔ̃/ *n.f.* (police) search. ~**ner** /-jɔne/ *v.t./i.* search.

perron /pɛrɔ̃/ *n.m.* (front) steps.

perroquet /pɛrɔkɛ/ *n.m.* parrot.

perruche /peryʃ/ *n.f.* budgerigar.

perruque /peryk/ *n.f.* wig.

persan, ~**e** /pɛrsɑ̃, -an/ *a.* & *n.m.* (*lang.*) Persian.

persécut|er /pɛrsekyte/ *v.t.* persecute. ~**ion** /-ysjɔ̃/ *n.f.* persecution.

persévér|er /pɛrsevere/ *v.i.* persevere. ~**ance** *n.f.* perseverance.

persienne /pɛrsjɛn/ *n.f.* (outside) shutter.

persil /pɛrsi/ *n.m.* parsley.

persistan|t, ~**te** /pɛrsistɑ̃, -t/ *a.* persistent; (*feuillage*) evergreen. ~**ce** *n.f.* persistence.

persister /pɛrsiste/ *v.i.* persist (**à faire**, in doing).

personnage /pɛrsɔnaʒ/ *n.m.* character; (*important*) personality.

personnalité /pɛrsɔnalite/ *n.f.* personality.

personne /pɛrsɔn/ *n.f.* person. ~**s**, people. —*pron.* (*quelqu'un*) anybody. (**ne**) ~, nobody.

personnel, ~**le** /pɛrsɔnɛl/ *a.* personal; (*égoïste*) selfish. —*n.m.* staff. ~**lement** *adv.* personally.

personnifier /pɛrsɔnifje/ *v.t.* personify.

perspective /pɛrspɛktiv/ *n.f.* (*art*) perspective; (*vue*) view; (*possibilité*) prospect; (*point de vue*) viewpoint, perspective.

perspicac|e /pɛrspikas/ *a.* shrewd. ~**ité** *n.f.* shrewdness.

persua|der /pɛrsɥade/ *v.t.* persuade (**de faire**, to do). ~**sion** /-ɥazjɔ̃/ *n.f.* persuasion.

persuasi|f, ~**ve** /pɛrsɥazif, -v/ *a.* persuasive.

perte /pɛrt/ *n.f.* loss; (*ruine*) ruin. **à** ~ **de vue**, as far as the eye can see. ~ **de**, (*temps*, *argent*) waste of.

pertinen|t, ~**te** /pɛrtinɑ̃, -t/ *a.* pertinent; (*esprit*) judicious. ~**ce** *n.f.* pertinence.

perturb|er /pɛrtyrbe/ *v.t.* disrupt; (*personne*) perturb. ~**ateur**, ~**atrice** *a.* disruptive; *n.m.*, *f.* disruptive element. ~**ation** *n.f.* disruption.

pervenche /pɛrvɑ̃ʃ/ *n.f.* periwinkle.

pervers, ~**e** /pɛrvɛr, -s/ *a.* perverse; (*dépravé*) perverted. ~**ion** /-sjɔ̃/ *n.f.* perversion.

pervert|ir /pɛrvɛrtir/ *v.t.* pervert. **~i,
~ie** *n.m., f.* pervert.
pes|ant, ~ante /pəzã, -t/ *a.* heavy.
~amment *adv.* heavily. **~anteur**
n.f. heaviness. **la ~anteur,** (*force*)
gravity.
pèse-personne /pɛzpɛrsɔn/ *n.m.*
(bathroom) scales.
pes|er /pəze/ *v.t./i.* weigh. **~er sur,**
bear upon. **~ée** *n.f.* weighing; (*effort*)
pressure.
peseta /pezeta/ *n.f.* peseta.
pessimis|te /pesimist/ *a.* pessi-
mistic. *—n.m.* pessimist. **~me** *n.m.*
pessimism.
peste /pɛst/ *n.f.* plague; (*personne*)
pest.
pester /pɛste/ *v.i.* **~ (contre),** curse.
pestilentiel, ~le /pɛstilãsjɛl/ *a.* fetid,
stinking.
pétale /petal/ *n.m.* petal.
pétanque /petãk/ *n.f.* bowls.
pétarader /petarade/ *v.i.* backfire.
pétard /petar/ *n.m.* banger.
péter /pete/ *v.i.* (*fam.*) go bang; (*casser*:
fam.) snap.
pétill|er /petije/ *v.i.* (*feu*) crackle; (*eau,
yeux*) sparkle. **~ant, ~ante** *a.*
(*gazeux*) fizzy.
petit, ~e /pti, -t/ *a.* small; (*avec
nuance affective*) little; (*jeune*) young,
small; (*faible*) slight; (*mesquin*)
petty. *—n.m.,f.* little child; (*scol.*) junior. **~s,** (*de chat*) kittens; (*de chien*)
pups. **en ~,** in miniature. **~ ami,**
boy-friend. **~e amie,** girl-friend. **~ à
petit,** little by little. **~es annonces,**
small ads. **~e cuiller,** teaspoon. **~
déjeuner,** breakfast. **~-enfant**
(*pl.* **~s-enfants**) *n.m.* grandchild.
~e-fille (*pl.* **~es-filles**) *n.f.* grand-
daughter. **~-fils** (*pl.* **~s-fils**) *n.m.*
grandson. **~ pain,** roll. **~-pois** (*pl.*
~s-pois) *n.m.* garden pea. **~e vérole,**
smallpox.
petitesse /ptitɛs/ *n.f.* smallness; (*péj.*)
meanness.
pétition /petisjɔ̃/ *n.f.* petition.
pétrifier /petrifje/ *v.t.* petrify.
pétrin /petrɛ̃/ *n.m.* (*situation*: *fam.*)
fix.
pétrir /petrir/ *v.t.* knead.
pétrol|e /petrɔl/ *n.m.* (*brut*) oil; (*pour
lampe etc.*) paraffin. **~ier, ~ière** *a.*
oil; *n.m.* (*navire*) oil-tanker.
pétulant, ~e /petylã, -t/ *a.* exuberant,
full of high spirits.
peu /pø/ *adv.* **~ (de),** (*quantité*) little,

not much; (*nombre*) few, not many.
~ intéressant/*etc.*, not very interest-
ing/*etc.* *—pron.* few. *—n.m.* little. **un
~ (de),** a little. **à ~ près,** more or
less. **de ~,** only just. **~ à peu,** gradu-
ally. **~ après/avant,** shortly after/
before. **~ de chose,** not much. **~
nombreux,** few. **~ souvent,** seldom.
peuplade /pœplad/ *n.f.* tribe.
peuple /pœpl/ *n.m.* people.
peupler /pœple/ *v.t.* populate.
peuplier /pœplije/ *n.m.* poplar.
peur /pœr/ *n.f.* fear. **avoir ~,** be afraid
(**de,** of). **de ~ de,** for fear of. **faire ~
à,** frighten. **~eux, ~euse** *a.* fearful,
timid.
peut /pø/ *voir* **pouvoir**[1].
peut-être /pøtɛtr/ *adv.* perhaps,
maybe. **~ que,** perhaps, maybe.
peux /pø/ *voir* **pouvoir**[1].
phallique /falik/ *a.* phallic.
phantasme /fãtasm/ *n.m.* fantasy.
phare /far/ *n.m.* (*tour*) lighthouse; (*de
véhicule*) headlight.
pharmaceutique /farmasøtik/ *a.*
pharmaceutical.
pharmac|ie /farmasi/ *n.f.* (*magasin*)
chemist's (shop); (*Amer.*) pharmacy;
(*science*) pharmacy. **~ien, ~ienne**
n.m., f. chemist, pharmacist.
pharyngite /farɛ̃ʒit/ *n.f.* pharyngitis.
phase /faz/ *n.f.* phase.
phénomène /fenɔmɛn/ *n.m.* phenomenon; (*original*: *fam.*) eccentric.
philanthrop|e /filãtrɔp/ *n.m./f.* phil-
anthropist. **~ique** *a.* philanthropic.
philatél|ie /filateli/ *n.f.* philately.
~iste *n.m./f.* philatelist.
philharmonique /filarmɔnik/ *a.* philharmonic.
Philippines /filipin/ *n.f. pl.* **les ~,** the
Philippines.
philosoph|e /filɔzɔf/ *n.m./f.* philo-
sopher. *—a.* philosophical. **~ie** *n.f.*
philosophy. **~ique** *a.* philosophical.
phobie /fɔbi/ *n.f.* phobia.
phonétique /fɔnetik/ *a.* phonetic.
phonographe /fɔnɔgraf/ *n.m.* gramophone; (*Amer.*) phonograph.
phoque /fɔk/ *n.m.* (*animal*) seal.
phosphate /fɔsfat/ *n.m.* phosphate.
phosphore /fɔsfɔr/ *n.m.* phosphorus.
photo /fɔto/ *n.f.* photo; (*art*) photo-
graphy.
photocop|ie /fɔtɔkɔpi/ *n.f.* photocopy.
~ier *v.t.* photocopy.
photogénique /fɔtɔʒenik/ *a.* photogenic.

photograph|e /fɔtɔgraf/ *n.m./f.* photographer. **~ie** *n.f.* photograph; (*art*) photography. **~ier** *v.t.* photograph. **~ique** *a.* photographic.

phrase /frɑz/ *n.f.* sentence.

physicien, ~ne /fizisjɛ̃, -jɛn/ *n.m., f.* physicist.

physiologie /fizjɔlɔʒi/ *n.f.* physiology.

physionomie /fizjɔnɔmi/ *n.f.* face.

physique¹ /fizik/ *a.* physical. —*n.m.* physique. **au ~**, physically. **~ment** *adv.* physically.

physique² /fizik/ *n.f.* physics.

piailler /pjɑje/ *v.i.* squeal, squawk.

pian|o /pjano/ *n.m.* piano. **~iste** *n.m./f.* pianist.

pic /pik/ *n.m.* (*outil*) pickaxe; (*sommet*) peak; (*oiseau*) woodpecker. **à ~**, (*verticalement*) sheer; (*couler*) straight to the bottom.

pichenette /piʃnɛt/ *n.f.* flick.

pichet /piʃɛ/ *n.m.* pitcher.

pickpocket /pikpɔkɛt/ *n.m.* pickpocket.

pick-up /pikœp/ *n.m. invar.* record-player.

picorer /pikɔre/ *v.t./i.* peck.

picot|er /pikɔte/ *v.t.* prick; (*yeux*) make smart. **~ement** *n.m.* pricking; smarting.

pie /pi/ *n.f.* magpie.

pièce /pjɛs/ *n.f.* piece; (*chambre*) room; (*pour raccommoder*) patch; (*écrit*) document. **~ (de monnaie)**, coin. **~ (de théâtre)**, play. **dix francs**/*etc.* **(la) ~**, ten francs/*etc.* each. **~ de rechange**, spare part. **~ détachée**, part. **~ d'identité**, identity paper.

pied /pje/ *n.m.* foot; (*de meuble*) leg; (*de lampe*) base; (*de salade*) plant. **à ~**, on foot. **au ~ de la lettre**, literally. **avoir ~**, have a footing. **comme un ~**, (*fam.*) terribly. **mettre sur ~**, set up. **~ bot**, club-foot. **un ~ d'égalité**, an equal footing. **~-noir** (*pl.* **~s-noirs**) *n.m.* Algerian Frenchman.

piédest|al (*pl.* **~aux**) /pjedɛstal, -o/ *n.m.* pedestal.

piège /pjɛʒ/ *n.m.* trap.

piég|er /pjeʒe/ *v.t.* trap; (*avec explosifs*) booby-trap. **lettre/voiture ~ée**, letter-/car-bomb.

pierr|e /pjɛr/ *n.f.* stone. **~e d'achoppement**, stumbling-block. **~e de touche**, touchstone. **~e tombale**, tombstone. **~eux, ~euse** *a.* stony.

piété /pjete/ *n.f.* piety.

piétiner /pjetine/ *v.i.* stamp one's feet; (*ne pas avancer*: *fig.*) mark time. —*v.t.* trample (on).

piéton /pjetɔ̃/ *n.m.* pedestrian. **~nier, ~nière** /-ɔnje, -jɛr/ *a.* pedestrian.

piètre /pjɛtr/ *a.* wretched.

pieu (*pl.* **~x**) /pjø/ *n.m.* post, stake.

pieuvre /pjœvr/ *n.f.* octopus.

pieu|x, ~se /pjø, -z/ *a.* pious.

pif /pif/ *n.m.* (*fam.*) nose.

pigeon /piʒɔ̃/ *n.m.* pigeon.

piger /piʒe/ *v.t./i.* (*fam.*) understand.

pigment /pigmɑ̃/ *n.m.* pigment.

pignon /piɲɔ̃/ *n.m.* (*de maison*) gable.

pile /pil/ *n.f.* (*tas, pilier*) pile; (*électr.*) battery; (*atomique*) pile. —*adv.* (*s'arrêter*: *fam.*) dead. **à dix heures ~**, (*fam.*) at ten on the dot. **~ ou face?**, heads or tails?

piler /pile/ *v.t.* pound.

pilier /pilje/ *n.m.* pillar.

pill|er /pije/ *v.t.* loot. **~age** *n.m.* looting. **~ard, ~arde** *n.m., f.* looter.

pilonner /pilɔne/ *v.t.* pound.

pilori /pilɔri/ *n.m.* pillory.

pilot|e /pilɔt/ *n.m.* pilot; (*auto.*) driver. —*a.* pilot. **~er** *v.t.* (*aviat., naut.*) pilot; (*auto.*) drive; (*fig.*) guide.

pilule /pilyl/ *n.f.* pill.

piment /pimɑ̃/ *n.m.* pepper, pimento; (*fig.*) spice. **~é** /-te/ *a.* spicy.

pimpant, ~e /pɛ̃pɑ̃, -t/ *a.* spruce.

pin /pɛ̃/ *n.m.* pine.

pinard /pinar/ *n.m.* (*vin*: *fam.*) plonk, cheap wine.

pince /pɛ̃s/ *n.f.* (*outil*) pliers; (*levier*) crowbar; (*de crabe*) pincer; (*à sucre*) tongs. **~ (à épiler)**, tweezers. **~ (à linge)**, (clothes-)peg.

pinceau (*pl.* **~x**) /pɛ̃so/ *n.m.* paintbrush.

pinc|er /pɛ̃se/ *v.t.* pinch; (*arrêter*: *fam.*) pinch. **se ~er le doigt**, catch one's finger. **~é** *a.* (*ton, air*) stiff. **~ée** *n.f.* pinch (**de**, of).

pincettes /pɛ̃sɛt/ *n.f. pl.* (fire) tongs.

pinède /pinɛd/ *n.f.* pine forest.

pingouin /pɛ̃gwɛ̃/ *n.m.* penguin; (*au sens strict*) auk.

ping-pong /piŋpɔ̃g/ *n.m.* table tennis, ping-pong.

pingre /pɛ̃gr/ *a.* miserly.

pinson /pɛ̃sɔ̃/ *n.m.* chaffinch.

pintade /pɛ̃tad/ *n.f.* guinea-fowl.

pioch|e /pjɔʃ/ *n.f.* pick(axe). **~er** *v.t./i.* dig; (*étudier*: *fam.*) study hard, slog away (at).

pion /pjɔ̃/ *n.m.* (*de jeu*) piece; (*échecs*) pawn; (*scol.*, *péj.*) supervisor.

pionnier /pjɔnje/ *n.m.* pioneer.

pipe /pip/ *n.f.* pipe. **fumer la ~,** smoke a pipe.

pipe-line /piplin/ *n.m.* pipeline.

piquant, ~e /pikɑ̃, -t/ *a.* (*barbe etc.*) prickly; (*goût*) pungent; (*détail etc.*) spicy. —*n.m.* prickle; (*de hérisson*) spine, prickle; (*fig.*) piquancy.

pique[1] /pik/ *n.f.* (*arme*) pike.

pique[2] /pik/ *n.m.* (*cartes*) spades.

piqué /pike/ *a.* (*couvre-lit*) quilted; (*vin*) sour; (*visage*) pitted.

pique-niqu|e /piknik/ *n.m.* picnic. **~er** *v.i.* picnic.

piquer /pike/ *v.t.* prick; (*langue*) burn, sting; (*abeille etc.*) sting; (*serpent etc.*) bite; (*enfoncer*) stick; (*coudre*) (machine-)stitch; (*curiosité*) excite; (*crise*) have; (*voler: fam.*) pinch. —*v.i.* (*avion*) dive; (*goût*) be hot. **~ une tête,** plunge headlong. **se ~ de,** pride o.s. on.

piquet /pikɛ/ *n.m.* stake; (*de tente*) peg. **au ~,** (*scol.*) in the corner. **~ de grève,** (*strike*) picket.

piqueter /pikte/ *v.t.* dot.

piqûre /pikyr/ *n.f.* prick; (*d'abeille etc.*) sting; (*de serpent etc.*) bite; (*point*) stitch; (*méd.*) injection, shot, jab; (*trou*) hole.

pirate /pirat/ *n.m.* pirate. **~ de l'air,** hijacker. **~rie** *n.f.* piracy.

pire /pir/ *a.* worse (**que,** than). **le ~ livre/***etc.*, the worst book/*etc.* —*n.m.* **le ~,** the worst (thing). **au ~,** at worst.

pirogue /pirɔg/ *n.f.* canoe, dug-out.

pirouette /pirwɛt/ *n.f.* pirouette.

pis[1] /pi/ *n.m* (*de vache*) udder.

pis[2] /pi/ *a. invar. & adv.* worse. —*n.m.* **le ~,** the worst.

pis-aller /pizale/ *n.m. invar.* stop-gap, temporary expedient.

piscine /pisin/ *n.f.* swimming-pool.

pissenlit /pisɑ̃li/ *n.m.* dandelion.

pistache /pistaʃ/ *n.f.* pistachio.

piste /pist/ *n.f.* track; (*de personne, d'animal*) track, trail; (*aviat.*) runway; (*de cirque*) ring; (*de patinage*) rink; (*de danse*) floor; (*sport*) racetrack. **~ cyclable,** cycle-track; (*Amer.*) bicycle path.

pistolet /pistɔlɛ/ *n.m.* gun, pistol; (*de peintre*) spray-gun.

piston /pistɔ̃/ *n.m.* (*techn.*) piston.

pistonner /pistɔne/ *v.t.* (*fam.*) recommend, pull strings for.

piteu|x, ~se /pitø, -z/ *a.* pitiful.

pitié /pitje/ *n.f.* pity. **il me fait ~, j'ai ~ de lui,** I pity him.

piton /pitɔ̃/ *n.m.* (*à crochet*) hook; (*sommet pointu*) peak.

pitoyable /pitwajabl/ *a.* pitiful.

pitre /pitr/ *n.m.* clown.

pittoresque /pitɔrɛsk/ *a.* picturesque.

pivot /pivo/ *n.m.* pivot. **~er** /-ɔte/ *v.i.* revolve; (*personne*) swing round.

pizza /pidza/ *n.f.* pizza.

placage /plakaʒ/ *n.m.* (*en bois*) veneer; (*sur un mur*) facing.

placard /plakar/ *n.m.* cupboard; (*affiche*) poster. **~er** /-de/ *v.t.* (*affiche*) post up; (*mur*) cover with posters.

place /plas/ *n.f.* place; (*espace libre*) room, space; (*siège*) seat, place; (*prix d'un trajet*) fare; (*esplanade*) square; (*emploi*) position; (*de parking*) space. **à la ~ de,** instead of. **en ~, à sa ~,** in its place. **faire ~ à,** give way to.

plac|er /plase/ *v.t.* place; (*invité, spectateur*) seat; (*argent*) invest. **se ~er** *v. pr.* (*personne*) take up a position; (*troisième etc.: sport*) come (in). **~é** *a.* (*sport*) placed. **bien ~é pour,** in a position to. **~ement** *n.m.* (*d'argent*) investment.

placide /plasid/ *a.* placid.

plafond /plafɔ̃/ *n.m.* ceiling.

plage /plaʒ/ *n.f.* beach; (*station*) (seaside) resort; (*aire*) area.

plaid /plɛd/ *n.m.* travelling-rug.

plaider /plede/ *v.t./i.* plead.

plaid|oirie /plɛdwari/ *n.f.* (*defence*) speech. **~oyer** *n.m.* plea.

plaie /plɛ/ *n.f.* wound; (*personne: fam.*) nuisance.

plaignant, ~e /plɛɲɑ̃, -t/ *n.m.,f.* plaintiff.

plaindre† /plɛ̃dr/ *v.t.* pity. **se ~** *v. pr.* complain (**de,** about). **se ~ de,** (*souffrir de*) complain of.

plaine /plɛn/ *n.f.* plain.

plaint|e /plɛ̃t/ *n.f.* complaint; (*gémissement*) groan. **~if, ~ive** *a.* plaintive.

plaire† /plɛr/ *v.i.* **~ à,** please. **ça lui plaît,** he likes it. **elle lui plaît,** he likes her, she pleases him. **se ~** *v. pr.* (*à Londres etc.*) like *ou* enjoy it. **se ~ à faire,** like *ou* enjoy doing.

plaisance /plɛzɑ̃s/ *n.f.* **la (navigation de) ~,** yachting.

plaisant, ~e /plɛzɑ̃, -t/ *a.* pleasant; (*drôle*) amusing.

plaisant|er /plɛzɑ̃te/ v.i. joke. ~**erie** n.f. joke. ~**in** n.m. joker.

plaisir /plezir/ n.m. pleasure. **faire** ~ **à**, please.

plan[1] /plɑ̃/ n.m. plan; (de ville) map; (surface, niveau) plane. ~ **d'eau**, expanse of water. **premier** ~, foreground. **dernier** ~, background.

plan[2], ~**e** /plɑ̃, plan/ a. flat.

planche /plɑ̃ʃ/ n.f. board, plank; (gravure) plate; (de potager) bed. ~ **à repasser**, ironing-board.

plancher /plɑ̃ʃe/ n.m. floor.

plan|er /plane/ v.i. glide. ~**er sur**, (mystère, danger) hang over. ~**eur** n.m. (avion) glider.

planète /planɛt/ n.f. planet.

planif|ier /planifje/ v.t. plan. ~**ication** n.f. planning.

planqu|e /plɑ̃k/ n.f. (fam.) hide-out; (emploi: fam.) cushy job. ~**er** v.t., **se** ~**er** v. pr. hide.

plant /plɑ̃/ n.m. seedling; (de légumes) bed.

plante /plɑ̃t/ n.f. plant. ~ **des pieds**, sole (of the foot).

plant|er /plɑ̃te/ v.t. (plante etc.) plant; (enfoncer) drive in; (installer) put up; (mettre) put. **rester** ~**é**, stand still, remain standing. ~**ation** n.f. planting; (de tabac etc.) plantation.

planton /plɑ̃tɔ̃/ n.m. (mil.) orderly.

plantureu|x, ~**se** /plɑ̃tyrø, -z/ a. abundant.

plaque /plak/ n.f. plate; (de marbre) slab; (insigne) badge; (commémorative) plaque. ~ **chauffante**, hotplate. ~ **minéralogique**, number-plate.

plaqu|er /plake/ v.t. (bois) veneer; (bijou) plate; (cheveux) plaster; (aplatir) flatten; (rugby) tackle; (abandonner: fam.) ditch. ~**age** n.m. (rugby) tackle.

plasma /plasma/ n.m. plasma.

plastic /plastik/ n.m. plastic explosive.

plastique /plastik/ a. & n.m. plastic. **en** ~, plastic.

plastiquer /plastike/ v.t. blow up.

plastron /plastrɔ̃/ n.m. shirt-front.

plat[1], ~**e** /pla, -t/ a. flat. —n.m. (de main) flat. **à** ~ adv. (poser) flat; a. (batterie, pneu) flat. **à** ~ **ventre**, flat on one's face.

plat[2] /pla/ n.m. (culin.) dish; (partie de repas) course.

platane /platan/ n.m. plane(-tree).

plateau (pl. ~**x**) /plato/ n.m. tray; (d'électrophone) turntable, deck; (de

balance) pan; (géog.) plateau. ~ **de fromages**, cheeseboard.

plate-bande (pl. **plates-bandes**) /platbɑ̃d/ n.f. flower-bed.

plate-forme (pl. **plates-formes**) /platfɔrm/ n.f. platform.

platine[1] /platin/ n.m. platinum.

platine[2] /platin/ n.f. (de tourne-disque) turntable.

platitude /platityd/ n.f. platitude.

platonique /platɔnik/ a. platonic.

plâtr|e /plɑtr/ n.m. plaster; (méd.) (plaster) cast. ~**er** v.t. plaster; (membre) put in plaster.

plausible /plozibl/ a. plausible.

plébiscite /plebisit/ n.m. plebiscite.

plein, ~**e** /plɛ̃, plɛn/ a. full (**de**, of); (total) complete. —n.m. **faire le** ~ (**d'essence**), fill up (the tank). **à** ~, to the full. **à** ~ **temps**, full-time. **en** ~ **air**, in the open air. **en** ~ **milieu**/ **visage**, right in the middle/the face. **en** ~**e nuit**/etc., in the middle of the night/etc. ~ **les mains**, all over one's hands.

pleinement /plɛnmɑ̃/ adv. fully.

pléthore /pletɔr/ n.f. over-abundance, plethora.

pleurer /plœre/ v.i. cry, weep (**sur**, over); (yeux) water. —v.t. mourn.

pleurésie /plœrezi/ n.f. pleurisy.

pleurnicher /plœrniʃe/ v.i. (fam.) snivel.

pleurs (en) /(ɑ̃)plœr/ adv. in tears.

pleuvoir† /pløvwar/ v.i. rain; (fig.) rain ou shower down. **il pleut**, it is raining. **il pleut à verse** ou **à torrents**, it is pouring.

pli /pli/ n.m. fold; (de jupe) pleat; (de pantalon) crease; (enveloppe) cover; (habitude) habit. (**faux**) ~, crease.

pliant, ~**e** /plijɑ̃, -t/ a. folding; (parapluie) telescopic. —n.m. folding stool, camp-stool.

plier /plije/ v.t. fold; (courber) bend; (personne) submit (**à**, to). —v.i. bend; (personne) submit. **se** ~ v. pr. fold. **se** ~ **à**, submit to.

plinthe /plɛ̃t/ n.f. skirting-board; (Amer.) baseboard.

plisser /plise/ v.t. crease; (yeux) screw up; (jupe) pleat.

plomb /plɔ̃/ n.m. lead; (fusible) fuse. ~**s**, (de chasse) lead shot. **de** ou **en** ~, lead. **de** ~, (ciel) leaden.

plomb|er /plɔ̃be/ v.t. (dent) fill. ~**age** n.m. filling.

plomb|ier /plɔ̃bje/ *n.m.* plumber. **~erie** *n.f.* plumbing.

plongeant, ~e /plɔ̃ʒɑ̃, -t/ *a.* plunging.

plongeoir /plɔ̃ʒwar/ *n.m.* diving-board.

plongeon /plɔ̃ʒɔ̃/ *n.m.* dive.

plong|er /plɔ̃ʒe/ *v.i.* dive; (*route*) plunge. —*v.t.* plunge. **se ~er** *v. pr.* plunge (**dans**, into). **~ée** *n.f.*, (*lecture*) immersed in. **~ée** *n.f.* diving. **en ~ée**, (*sous-marin*) submerged. **~eur, ~euse** *n.m.,f.* diver; (*employé*) dishwasher.

plouf /pluf/ *n.m. & int.* splash.

ployer /plwaje/ *v.t./i.* bend.

plu /ply/ *voir* **plaire, pleuvoir.**

pluie /plɥi/ *n.f.* rain; (*averse*) shower. **~ battante/diluvienne**, driving/torrential rain.

plumage /plymaʒ/ *n.m.* plumage.

plume /plym/ *n.f.* feather; (*stylo*) pen; (*pointe*) nib.

plumeau (*pl.* **~x**) /plymo/ *n.m.* feather duster.

plumer /plyme/ *v.t.* pluck.

plumet /plymɛ/ *n.m.* plume.

plumier /plymje/ *n.m.* pencil box.

plupart /plypar/ *n.f.* most. **la ~ des**, (*gens, cas, etc.*) most. **la ~ du temps**, most of the time.

pluriel, ~le /plyrjɛl/ *a. & n.m.* plural. **au ~**, (*nom*) plural.

plus[1] /ply/ *adv. de négation.* (**ne**) **~**, (*temps*) no longer, not any more. (**ne**) **~ de**, (*quantité*) no more. **je n'y vais ~**, I do not go there any longer *ou* any more. (**il n'y a**) **~ de pain**, (there is) no more bread.

plus[2] /ply/ (/plyz/ *before vowel*, /plys/ *in final position*) *adv.* more (**que**, than). **~ âgé/tard**/*etc.*, older/later/*etc.* **~ beau**/*etc.*, more beautiful/*etc.* **le ~**, the most. **le ~ beau**/*etc.*, the most beautiful; (*de deux*) the more beautiful. **le ~ de**, (*gens etc.*) most. **~ de**, (*pain etc.*) more; (*dix jours etc.*) more than. **il est ~ de huit heures**/*etc.* it is after eight/*etc.* o'clock. **de ~**, more (**que**, than); (*en outre*) moreover. (**âgés**) **de ~ de** (*huit ans etc.*) over, more than. **de ~ en plus**, more and more. **en ~**, extra. **en ~ de**, in addition to. **~ ou moins**, more or less.

plus[3] /plys/ *conj.* plus.

plusieurs /plyzjœr/ *a. & pron.* several.

plus-value /plyvaly/ *n.f.* (*bénéfice*) profit.

plutôt /plyto/ *adv.* rather (**que**, than).

pluvieu|x, ~se /plyvjø, -z/ *a.* rainy.

pneu (*pl.* **~s**) /pnø/ *n.m.* tyre; (*lettre*) express letter. **~matique** *a.* (*gonflable*) inflatable; *n.m.* tyre; (*lettre*) express letter.

pneumonie /pnømɔni/ *n.f.* pneumonia.

poche /pɔʃ/ *n.f.* pocket; (*sac*) bag. **~s**, (*sous les yeux*) bags.

pocher /pɔʃe/ *v.t.* (*œuf*) poach.

pochette /pɔʃɛt/ *n.f.* pack(et), envelope; (*sac*) bag, pouch; (*d'allumettes*) book; (*de disque*) sleeve; (*mouchoir*) pocket handkerchief.

podium /pɔdjɔm/ *n.m.* rostrum.

poêle[1] /pwal/ *n.f.* **~ (à frire)**, frying-pan.

poêle[2] /pwal/ *n.m.* stove.

poème /pɔɛm/ *n.m.* poem.

poésie /pɔezi/ *n.f.* poetry; (*poème*) poem.

poète /pɔɛt/ *n.m.* poet.

poétique /pɔetik/ *a.* poetic.

poids /pwa/ *n.m.* weight. **~ coq**/ **lourd/plume**, bantamweight/ heavyweight/featherweight. **~ lourd**, (*camion*) lorry, juggernaut; (*Amer.*) truck.

poignant, ~e /pwaɲɑ̃, -t/ *a.* poignant.

poignard /pwaɲar/ *n.m.* dagger. **~er** /-de/ *v.t.* stab.

poigne /pwaɲ/ *n.f.* grip.

poignée /pwaɲe/ *n.f.* handle; (*quantité*) handful. **~ de main**, handshake.

poignet /pwaɲɛ/ *n.m.* wrist; (*de chemise*) cuff.

poil /pwal/ *n.m.* hair; (*pelage*) fur; (*de brosse*) bristle. **~s**, (*de tapis*) pile. **à ~**, (*fam.*) naked. **~u** *a.* hairy.

poinçon /pwɛ̃sɔ̃/ *n.m.* awl; (*marque*) hallmark. **~ner** /-ɔne/ *v.t.* (*billet*) punch. **~neuse** /-ɔnøz/ *n.f.* punch.

poing /pwɛ̃/ *n.m.* fist.

point[1] /pwɛ̃/ *n.m.* point; (*note: scol.*) mark; (*tache*) spot, dot; (*de couture*) stitch. **~ (final)**, full stop, period. **à ~**, (*culin.*) medium; (*arriver*) at the right time. **faire le ~**, take stock. **mettre au ~**, (*photo*) focus; (*technique*) perfect; (*fig.*) clear up. **~ culminant**, peak. **~ de repère**, landmark. **~ de suture**, (*méd.*) stitch. **~ de vue**, point of view. **~ d'interrogation/d'exclamation**, question/exclamation mark. **~ du jour**, daybreak. **~ mort**, (*auto.*) neutral. **~**

virgule, semicolon. **sur le ~ de,** about to.

point[2] /pwɛ̃/ *adv.* **(ne) ~,** not.

pointe /pwɛ̃t/ *n.f.* point, tip; (*clou*) tack; (*de grille*) spike; (*fig.*) touch (**de,** of). **de ~,** (*industrie*) highly advanced. **en ~,** pointed. **sur la ~ des pieds,** on tiptoe.

pointer[1] /pwɛ̃te/ *v.t.* (*cocher*) tick off. —*v.i.* (*employé*) clock in *ou* out. **se ~ v. pr.** (*fam.*) turn up.

pointer[2] /pwɛ̃te/ *v.t.* (*diriger*) point, aim.

pointillé /pwɛ̃tije/ *n.m.* dotted line. —*a.* dotted.

pointilleu|x, ~se /pwɛ̃tijø, -z/ *a.* fastidious, particular.

pointu /pwɛ̃ty/ *a.* pointed; (*aiguisé*) sharp.

pointure /pwɛ̃tyr/ *n.f.* size.

poire /pwar/ *n.f.* pear.

poireau (*pl.* **~x**) /pwaro/ *n.m.* leek.

poirier /pwarje/ *n.m.* pear-tree.

pois /pwa/ *n.m.* pea; (*dessin*) dot.

poison /pwazɔ̃/ *n.m.* poison.

poisseu|x, ~se /pwasø, -z/ *a.* sticky.

poisson /pwasɔ̃/ *n.m.* fish. **~ rouge,** goldfish.

poissonn|ier, ~ière /pwasɔnje, -jɛr/ *n.m.*, *f.* fishmonger. **~erie** *n.f.* fish shop.

poitrail /pwatraj/ *n.m.* breast.

poitrine /pwatrin/ *n.f.* chest; (*seins*) bosom; (*culin.*) breast.

poivr|e /pwavr/ *n.m.* pepper. **~é** *a.* peppery. **~ière** *n.f.* pepper-pot.

poivron /pwavrɔ̃/ *n.m.* pepper, capsicum.

poivrot, ~e /pwavro, -ɔt/ *n.m.*, *f.* (*fam.*) drunkard.

poker /pɔkɛr/ *n.m.* poker.

polaire /pɔlɛr/ *a.* polar.

polariser /pɔlarize/ *v.t.* polarize.

pôle /pol/ *n.m.* pole.

polémique /pɔlemik/ *n.f.* argument. —*a.* controversial.

poli /pɔli/ *a.* (*personne*) polite. **~ment** *adv.* politely.

polic|e[1] /pɔlis/ *n.f.* police; (*discipline*) (law and) order. **~ier, ~ière** *a.* police; (*roman*) detective; *n.m.* policeman.

police[2] /pɔlis/ *n.f.* (*d'assurance*) policy.

polio(myélite) /pɔljo(mjelit)/ *n.f.* polio(myelitis).

polir /pɔlir/ *v.t.* polish.

polisson, ~ne /pɔlisɔ̃, -ɔn/ *a.* naughty. —*n.m.*, *f.* rascal.

politesse /pɔlites/ *n.f.* politeness; (*parole*) polite remark.

politicien, ~ne /pɔlitisjɛ̃, -jɛn/ *n.m.*, *f.* (*péj.*) politician.

politi|que /pɔlitik/ *a.* political. —*n.f.* politics; (*ligne de conduite*) policy. **~ser** *v.t.* politicize.

pollen /pɔlɛn/ *n.m.* pollen.

poll|uer /pɔlɥe/ *v.t.* pollute. **~ution** *n.f.* pollution.

polo /pɔlo/ *n.m.* polo; (*vêtement*) sports shirt, tennis shirt.

Pologne /pɔlɔɲ/ *n.f.* Poland.

polonais, ~e /pɔlɔnɛ, -z/ *a.* Polish. —*n.m.*, *f.* Pole. —*n.m.* (*lang.*) Polish.

poltron, ~ne /pɔltrɔ̃, -ɔn/ *a.* cowardly. —*n.m.*, *f.* coward.

polycopier /pɔlikɔpje/ *v.t.* duplicate, stencil.

polygamie /pɔligami/ *n.f.* polygamy.

polyglotte /pɔliglɔt/ *n.m.*/*f.* polyglot.

polyvalent, ~e /pɔlivalɑ̃, -t/ *a.* varied; (*personne*) versatile.

pommade /pɔmad/ *n.f.* ointment.

pomme /pɔm/ *n.f.* apple; (*d'arrosoir*) rose. **~ d'Adam,** Adam's apple. **~ de terre,** potato. **~s frites,** chips; (*Amer.*) French fries.

pommeau (*pl.* **~x**) /pɔmo/ *n.m.* (*de canne*) knob.

pommette /pɔmɛt/ *n.f.* cheek-bone.

pommier /pɔmje/ *n.m.* apple-tree.

pompe /pɔ̃p/ *n.f.* pump; (*splendeur*) pomp. **~ à incendie,** fire-engine. **~s funèbres,** undertaker's.

pomper /pɔ̃pe/ *v.t.*/*i.* pump; (*épuiser*: *fam.*) tire out.

pompeu|x, ~se /pɔ̃pø, -z/ *a.* pompous.

pompier /pɔ̃pje/ *n.m.* fireman.

pompiste /pɔ̃pist/ *n.m.*/*f.* petrol pump attendant; (*Amer.*) gas station attendant.

pompon /pɔ̃pɔ̃/ *n.m.* pompon.

pomponner /pɔ̃pɔne/ *v.t.* deck out.

poncer /pɔ̃se/ *v.t.* rub down.

ponctuation /pɔ̃ktɥasjɔ̃/ *n.f.* punctuation.

ponct|uel, ~uelle /pɔ̃ktɥɛl/ *a.* punctual. **~ualité** *n.f.* punctuality.

ponctuer /pɔ̃ktɥe/ *v.t.* punctuate.

pondéré /pɔ̃dere/ *a.* level-headed.

pondre /pɔ̃dr/ *v.t.*/*i.* lay.

poney /pɔnɛ/ *n.m.* pony.

pont /pɔ̃/ *n.m.* bridge; (*de navire*) deck; (*de graissage*) ramp. **faire le ~,** take the extra day(s) off (*between holi-*

days). ~ **aérien,** airlift. ~**-levis** *(pl.* ~**s-levis)** *n.m.* drawbridge.

ponte /pɔ̃t/ *n.f.* laying (of eggs).

pontife /pɔ̃tif/ *n.m.* **(souverain)** ~, pope.

pontific|al *(m. pl.* ~**aux)** /pɔ̃tifikal, -o/ *a.* papal.

pop /pɔp/ *n.m. & a. invar. (mus.)* pop.

popote /pɔpɔt/ *n.f. (fam.)* cooking.

populace /pɔpylas/ *n.f.* rabble.

popul|aire /pɔpylɛr/ *a.* popular; *(expression)* colloquial; *(quartier, origine)* working-class. ~**arité** *n.f.* popularity.

population /pɔpylasjɔ̃/ *n.f.* population.

populeu|x, ~**se** /pɔpylø, -z/ *a.* populous.

porc /pɔr/ *n.m.* pig; *(viande)* pork.

porcelaine /pɔrsəlɛn/ *n.f.* china, porcelain.

porc-épic *(pl.* **porcs-épics)** /pɔrkepik/ *n.m.* porcupine.

porche /pɔrʃ/ *n.m.* porch.

porcherie /pɔrʃəri/ *n.f.* pigsty.

por|e /pɔr/ *n.m.* pore. ~**eux,** ~**euse** *a.* porous.

pornograph|ie /pɔrnɔgrafi/ *n.f.* pornography. ~**ique** *a.* pornographic.

port[1] /pɔr/ *n.m.* port, harbour. **à bon** ~, safely. ~ **maritime,** seaport.

port[2] /pɔr/ *n.m. (transport)* carriage; *(d'armes)* carrying; *(de barbe)* wearing.

portail /pɔrtaj/ *n.m.* portal.

portant, ~**e** /pɔrtɑ̃, -t/ *a.* **bien/mal** ~, in good/bad health.

portati|f, ~**ve** /pɔrtatif, -v/ *a.* portable.

porte /pɔrt/ *n.f.* door; *(passage)* doorway; *(de jardin, d'embarquement)* gate. **mettre à la** ~, throw out. ~ **d'entrée,** front door. ~**-fenêtre** *(pl.* ~**s-fenêtres)** *n.f.* French window.

porté /pɔrte/ *a.* ~ **à,** inclined to. ~ **sur,** fond of.

portée /pɔrte/ *n.f. (d'une arme)* range; *(de voûte)* span; *(d'animaux)* litter; *(impact)* significance; *(mus.)* stave. **à** ~ **de,** within reach of.

portefeuille /pɔrtəfœj/ *n.m.* wallet; *(de ministre)* portfolio.

portemanteau *(pl.* ~**x)** /pɔrtmɑ̃to/ *n.m.* coat *ou* hat stand.

port|er /pɔrte/ *v.t.* carry; *(vêtement, bague)* wear; *(fruits, responsabilité, nom)* bear; *(coup)* strike; *(amener)* bring; *(inscrire)* enter. —*v.i. (bruit)*

carry; *(coup)* hit home. ~**er sur,** rest on; *(concerner)* bear on. **se** ~**er bien,** be *ou* feel well. **se** ~**er candidat,** stand as a candidate. ~**er aux nues,** praise to the skies. ~**e-avions** *n.m. invar.* aircraft-carrier. ~**e-bagages** *n.m. invar.* luggage rack. ~**e-bonheur** *n.m. invar. (objet)* charm. ~**e-clefs** *n.m. invar.* key-ring. ~**e-documents** *n.m. invar.* attaché case, document wallet. ~**e-monnaie** *n.m. invar.* purse. ~**e-parole** *n.m. invar.* spokesman. ~**e-voix** *n.m. invar.* megaphone.

porteu|r, ~**se** /pɔrtœr, -øz/ *n.m., f. (de nouvelles)* bearer; *(méd.)* carrier. —*n.m. (rail.)* porter.

portier /pɔrtje/ *n.m.* door-man.

portière /pɔrtjɛr/ *n.f.* door.

portillon /pɔrtijɔ̃/ *n.m.* gate.

portion /pɔrsjɔ̃/ *n.f.* portion.

portique /pɔrtik/ *n.m.* portico; *(sport)* crossbar.

porto /pɔrto/ *n.m.* port (wine).

portrait /pɔrtrɛ/ *n.m.* portrait. ~**-robot** *(pl.* ~**s-robots)** *n.m.* identikit, photofit.

portuaire /pɔrtɥɛr/ *a.* port.

portugais, ~**e** /pɔrtygɛ, -z/ *a. & n.m., f.* Portuguese. —*n.m. (lang.)* Portuguese.

Portugal /pɔrtygal/ *n.m.* Portugal.

pose /poz/ *n.f.* installation; *(attitude)* pose; *(photo.)* exposure.

posé /poze/ *a.* calm.

poser /poze/ *v.t.* put (down); *(installer)* install, put in; *(mine, fondations)* lay; *(question)* ask; *(problème)* pose. —*v.i. (modèle)* pose. **se** ~ *v. pr. (avion, oiseau)* land; *(regard)* alight; *(se présenter)* arise. ~ **sa candidature,** apply (à, for).

positi|f, ~**ve** /pozitif, -v/ *a.* positive.

position /pozisjɔ̃/ *n.f.* position.

poss|éder /pɔsede/ *v.t.* possess; *(propriété)* own, possess. ~**esseur** *n.m.* possessor; owner.

possessi|f, ~**ve** /pɔsesif, -v/ *a.* possessive.

possession /pɔsesjɔ̃/ *n.f.* possession. **prendre** ~ **de,** take possession of.

possibilité /pɔsibilite/ *n.f.* possibility.

possible /pɔsibl/ *a.* possible. —*n.m.* **le** ~, what is possible. **faire son** ~, do one's utmost. **le plus tard/etc.** ~, as late/etc. as possible. **pas** ~, impossible.

post- /pɔst/ *préf.* post-.

post|al (*m. pl.* ~**aux**) /pɔstal, -o/ *a.* postal.

poste[1] /pɔst/ *n.f.* (*service*) post; (*bureau*) post office. ~ **aérienne**, air-mail. **mettre à la** ~, post. **Postes et Télécommunications**, Post Office. **P**~**s, Télégraphes, Téléphones**, Post Office.

poste[2] /pɔst/ *n.m.* (*lieu, emploi*) post; (*de radio, télévision*) set; (*téléphone*) extension (number). ~ **d'essence**, petrol *ou* gas (*Amer.*) station. ~ **de pilotage**, cockpit. ~ **de police**, police station.

poster[1] /pɔste/ *v.t.* (*lettre, personne*) post.

poster[2] /pɔstɛr/ *n.m.* poster.

postérieur /pɔsterjœr/ *a.* later; (*partie*) back. ~ **à**, after. —*n.m.* (*fam.*) posterior.

postérité /pɔsterite/ *n.f.* posterity.

posthume /pɔstym/ *a.* posthumous.

postiche /pɔstiʃ/ *a.* false.

post|ier, ~**ière** /pɔstje, -jɛr/ *n.m., f.* postal worker.

post-scriptum /pɔstskriptɔm/ *n.m. invar.* postscript.

postul|er /pɔstyle/ *v.t.* apply for; (*principe*) postulate. ~**ant**, ~**ante** *n.m., f.* applicant.

posture /pɔstyr/ *n.f.* posture.

pot /po/ *n.m.* pot; (*en carton*) carton; (*en verre*) jar; (*chance: fam.*) luck; (*boisson: fam.*) drink. ~**-au-feu** /pɔtofø/ *n.m. invar.* (*plat*) beef stew. ~ **de chambre**, chamber-pot. ~ **d'échappement**, exhaust-pipe. ~**-de-vin** (*pl.* ~**s-de-vin**) *n.m.* bribe.

potable /pɔtabl/ *a.* drinkable.

potage /pɔtaʒ/ *n.m.* soup.

potag|er, ~**ère** /pɔtaʒe, -ɛr/ *a.* vegetable. —*n.m.* vegetable garden.

pote /pɔt/ *n.m.* (*fam.*) chum.

poteau (*pl.* ~**x**) /pɔto/ *n.m.* post; (*télégraphique*) pole. ~ **indicateur**, signpost.

potelé /pɔtle/ *a.* plump.

potence /pɔtɑ̃s/ *n.f.* gallows.

potentiel, ~**le** /pɔtɑ̃sjɛl/ *a. & n.m.* potential.

pot|erie /pɔtri/ *n.f.* pottery; (*objet*) piece of pottery. ~**ier** *n.m.* potter.

potins /pɔtɛ̃/ *n.m. pl.* gossip.

potion /posjɔ̃/ *n.f.* potion.

potiron /pɔtirɔ̃/ *n.m.* pumpkin.

pou (*pl.* ~**x**) /pu/ *n.m.* louse.

poubelle /pubɛl/ *n.f.* dustbin; (*Amer.*) garbage can.

pouce /pus/ *n.m.* thumb; (*de pied*) big toe; (*mesure*) inch.

poudr|e /pudr/ *n.f.* powder. ~**e** (**à canon**), gunpowder. **en** ~**e**, (*lait*) powdered; (*chocolat*) drinking. ~**er** *v.t.* powder. ~**eux**, ~**euse** *a.* powdery.

poudrier /pudrije/ *n.m.* (powder) compact.

poudrière /pudrijɛr/ *n.f.* (*région*) powder-keg.

pouf /puf/ *n.m.* pouffe.

pouffer /pufe/ *v.i.* guffaw.

pouilleu|x, ~**se** /pujø, -z/ *a.* filthy.

poulailler /pulaje/ *n.m.* (hen-)coop.

poulain /pulɛ̃/ *n.m.* foal.

poule /pul/ *n.f.* hen; (*culin.*) fowl; (*femme: fam.*) tart; (*rugby*) group.

poulet /pulɛ/ *n.m.* chicken.

pouliche /puliʃ/ *n.f.* filly.

poulie /puli/ *n.f.* pulley.

pouls /pu/ *n.m.* pulse.

poumon /pumɔ̃/ *n.m.* lung.

poupe /pup/ *n.f.* stern.

poupée /pupe/ *n.f.* doll.

poupon /pupɔ̃/ *n.m.* baby. ~**nière** /-ɔnjɛr/ *n.f.* crèche, day nursery.

pour /pur/ *prép.* for; (*envers*) to; (*à la place de*) on behalf of; (*comme*) as. ~ **cela**, for that reason. ~ **cent**, per cent. ~ **de bon**, for good. ~ **faire**, (in order) to do. ~ **que**, so that. ~ **moi**, as for me. ~ **petit**/*etc.* **qu'il soit**, however small/*etc.* he may be. **trop poli**/*etc.* ~, too polite/*etc.* to. **le** ~ **et le contre**, the pros and cons.

pourboire /purbwar/ *n.m.* tip.

pourcentage /pursɑ̃taʒ/ *n.m.* percentage.

pourchasser /purʃase/ *v.t.* pursue.

pourparlers /purparle/ *n.m. pl.* talks.

pourpre /purpr/ *a. & n.m.* crimson; (*violet*) purple.

pourquoi /purkwa/ *conj. & adv.* why. —*n.m. invar.* reason.

pourra, pourrait /pura, purɛ/ *voir* **pouvoir**[1].

pourr|ir /purir/ *v.t./i.* rot. ~**i** *a.* rotten. ~**iture** *n.f.* rot.

poursuite /pursɥit/ *n.f.* pursuit (**de**, of). ~**s**, (*jurid.*) legal action.

poursuiv|re† /pursɥivr/ *v.t.* pursue; (*continuer*) continue (with). ~**re** (**en justice**), (*au criminel*) prosecute; (*au civil*) sue. —*v.i.*, **se** ~**re** *v. pr.* continue. ~**ant**, ~**ante** *n.m., f.* pursuer.

pourtant /purtɑ̃/ *adv.* yet.

pourtour /purtur/ *n.m.* perimeter.

pourv|oir† /purvwar/ *v.t.* ~**oir de,** provide with. —*v.i.* ~**oir à,** provide for. ~**u de,** supplied with. ~**oyeur,** ~**oyeuse** *n.m., f.* supplier.

pourvu que /purvyk(ə)/ *conj.* (*condition*) provided (that); (*souhait*) let us hope (that).

pousse /pus/ *n.f.* growth; (*bourgeon*) shoot.

poussé /puse/ *a.* (*études*) advanced.

poussée /puse/ *n.f.* pressure; (*coup*) push; (*de prix*) upsurge; (*méd.*) outbreak.

pousser /puse/ *v.t.* push; (*du coude*) nudge; (*cri*) let out; (*soupir*) heave; (*continuer*) continue; (*exhorter*) urge (à, to); (*forcer*) drive (à, to); (*amener*) bring (à, to). —*v.i.* push; (*grandir*) grow. **se** ~ *v. pr.* move over *ou* up.

poussette /pusɛt/ *n.f.* push-chair; (*Amer.*) (baby) stroller.

pouss|ière /pusjɛr/ *n.f.* dust. ~**i-éreux,** ~**iéreuse** *a.* dusty.

poussi|f, ~**ve** /pusif, -v/ *a.* short-winded, wheezing.

poussin /pusɛ̃/ *n.m.* chick.

poutre /putr/ *n.f.* beam; (*en métal*) girder.

pouvoir¹† /puvwar/ *v. aux.* (*possibilité*) can, be able; (*permission, éventualité*) may, can. **il peut/pouvait/pourrait venir,** he can/could/might come. **je n'ai pas pu,** I could not. **j'ai pu faire,** (*réussi à*) I managed to do. **je n'en peux plus,** I am exhausted. **il se peut que,** it may be that.

pouvoir² /puvwar/ *n.m.* power; (*gouvernement*) government. **au** ~, in power. ~**s publics,** authorities.

prairie /preri/ *n.f.* meadow.

praline /pralin/ *n.f.* sugared almond.

praticable /pratikabl/ *a.* practicable.

praticien, ~**ne** /pratisjɛ̃, -jɛn/ *n.m., f.* practitioner.

pratiquant, ~**e** /pratikã, -t/ *a.* practising. —*n.m., f.* church-goer.

pratique /pratik/ *a.* practical. —*n.f.* practice; (*expérience*) experience. **la** ~ **du golf/du cheval,** golfing/riding. ~**ment** *adv.* in practice; (*presque*) practically.

pratiquer /pratike/ *v.t./i.* practise; (*sport*) play; (*faire*) make.

pré /pre/ *n.m.* meadow.

pré- /pre/ *préf.* pre-.

préalable /prealabl/ *a.* preliminary, prior. —*n.m.* precondition. **au** ~, first.

préambule /preãbyl/ *n.m.* preamble.

préau (*pl.* ~**x**) /preo/ *n.m.* (*scol.*) covered playground.

préavis /preavi/ *n.m.* (advance) notice.

précaire /prekɛr/ *a.* precarious.

précaution /prekosjɔ̃/ *n.f.* (*mesure*) precaution; (*prudence*) caution.

précéd|ent, ~**ente** /presedã, -t/ *a.* previous. —*n.m.* precedent. ~**emment** /-amã/ *adv.* previously.

précéder /presede/ *v.t./i.* precede.

précepte /presɛpt/ *n.m.* precept.

précep|teur, ~**trice** /presɛptœr, -tris/ *n.m., f.* tutor.

prêcher /preʃe/ *v.t./i.* preach.

précieu|x, ~**se** /presjø, -z/ *a.* precious.

précipice /presipis/ *n.m.* abyss, chasm.

précipit|é /presipite/ *a.* hasty. ~**amment** *adv.* hastily. ~**ation** *n.f.* haste.

précipiter /presipite/ *v.t.* throw, precipitate; (*hâter*) hasten. **se** ~ *v. pr.* rush (**sur,** at, on to); (*se jeter*) throw o.s; (*s'accélérer*) speed up.

préci|s, ~**e** /presi, -z/ *a.* precise; (*mécanisme*) accurate. —*n.m.* summary. **dix heures/***etc.* ~**es,** ten o'clock/*etc.* sharp. ~**ément** /-zemã/ *adv.* precisely.

préciser /presize/ *v.t./i.* specify. **se** ~ *v. pr.* become clear(er).

précision /presizjɔ̃/ *n.f.* precision; (*détail*) detail.

précoc|e /prekɔs/ *a.* early; (*enfant*) precocious. ~**ité** *n.f.* earliness; precociousness

préconçu /prekɔ̃sy/ *a.* preconceived.

préconiser /prekɔnize/ *v.t.* advocate.

précurseur /prekyrsœr/ *n.m.* forerunner.

prédécesseur /predesesœr/ *n.m.* predecessor.

prédicateur /predikatœr/ *n.m.* preacher.

prédilection /predilɛksjɔ̃/ *n.f.* preference.

préd|ire† /predir/ *v.t.* predict. ~**iction** *n.f.* prediction.

prédisposer /predispoze/ *v.t.* predispose.

prédominant, ~**e** /predɔminã, -t/ *a.* predominant.

prédominer /predɔmine/ *v.i.* predominate.

préfabriqué /prefabrike/ *a.* prefabricated.

préface /prefas/ *n.f.* preface.

préfecture /prefɛktyr/ *n.f.* prefecture. **∼ de police,** police headquarters.

préférence /preferɑ̃s/ *n.f.* preference. **de ∼,** preferably. **de ∼ à,** in preference to.

préférentiel, ∼le /preferɑ̃sjɛl/ *a.* preferential.

préfér|er /prefere/ *v.t.* prefer (à, to). **∼er faire,** prefer to do. **∼able** *a.* preferable. **∼é, ∼ée** *a.* & *n.m., f.* favourite.

préfet /prefɛ/ *n.m.* prefect. **∼ de police,** prefect *ou* chief of police.

préfixe /prefiks/ *n.m.* prefix.

préhistorique /preistɔrik/ *a.* prehistoric.

préjudic|e /preʒydis/ *n.m.* harm, prejudice. **porter ∼e à,** harm. **∼iable** *a.* harmful.

préjugé /preʒyʒe/ *n.m.* prejudice.

préjuger /preʒyʒe/ *v.i.* **∼ de,** prejudge.

prélasser (se) /(sə)prelɑse/ *v. pr.* loll (about).

prél|ever /prelve/ *v.t.* deduct; (*sang*) take. **∼èvement** *n.m.* deduction. **∼èvement de sang,** blood sample.

préliminaire /preliminɛr/ *a.* & *n.m.* preliminary.

prélude /prelyd/ *n.m.* prelude.

prématuré /prematyre/ *a.* premature. —*n.m.* premature baby.

prémédit|er /premedite/ *v.t.* premeditate. **∼ation** *n.f.* premeditation.

prem|ier, ∼ière /prəmje, -jɛr/ *a.* first; (*rang*) front, first; (*enfance*) early; (*nécessité, souci*) prime; (*qualité*) top, prime; (*état*) original. —*n.m., f.* first (one). —*n.m.* (*date*) first; (*étage*) first floor. —*n.f.* (*rail.*) first class; (*exploit jamais vu*) first; (*cinéma, théâtre*) première. **de ∼ier ordre,** first-rate. **en ∼ier,** first. **∼ier jet,** first draft. **∼ier ministre,** Prime Minister.

premièrement /prəmjɛrmɑ̃/ *adv.* firstly.

prémisse /premis/ *n.f.* premiss.

prémonition /premɔnisjɔ̃/ *n.f.* premonition.

prémunir /premynir/ *v.t.* protect.

prenant, ∼e /prənɑ̃, -t/ *a.* (*activité*) engrossing.

prénatal (*m. pl.* ∼s) /prenatal/ *a.* antenatal; (*Amer.*) prenatal.

prendre† /prɑ̃dr/ *v.t.* take; (*attraper*) catch, get; (*acheter*) get; (*repas*) have; (*engager, adopter*) take on; (*poids, voix*) put on; (*chercher*) pick up;

(*panique, colère*) take hold of. —*v.i.* (*liquide*) set; (*feu*) catch; (*vaccin*) take; (*aller*) go. **se ∼ en glace,** freeze over. **se ∼ pour,** think one is. **s'en ∼ à,** attack; (*rendre responsable*) blame. **s'y ∼,** set about (it).

preneu|r, ∼se /prənœr, -øz/ *n.m., f.* buyer.

prénom /prenɔ̃/ *n.m.* first name. **∼mer** /-ɔme/ *v.t.* call. **se ∼mer** *v. pr.* be called.

préoccup|er /preɔkype/ *v.t.* worry; (*absorber*) preoccupy. **se ∼er de,** be worried about; be preoccupied about. **∼ation** *n.f.* worry; (*idée fixe*) preoccupation.

préparatifs /preparatif/ *n.m. pl.* preparations.

préparatoire /preparatwar/ *a.* preparatory.

prépar|er /prepare/ *v.t.* prepare; (*repas, café*) make. **se ∼er** *v. pr.* prepare o.s.; (*être proche*) be brewing. **∼er à qn.,** (*surprise*) have (got) in store for s.o. **∼ation** *n.f.* preparation.

prépondéran|t, ∼te /prepɔ̃derɑ̃, -t/ *a.* dominant. **∼ce** *n.f.* dominance.

prépos|er /prepoze/ *v.t.* put in charge (à, of). **∼é, ∼ée** *n.m., f.* employee; (*des postes*) postman, postwoman.

préposition /prepozisjɔ̃/ *n.f.* preposition.

préretraite /prerətrɛt/ *n.f.* early retirement.

prérogative /prerɔgativ/ *n.f.* prerogative.

près /prɛ/ *adv.* near, close. **∼ de,** near (to), close to; (*presque*) nearly. **à cela ∼,** apart from that. **de ∼,** closely.

présag|e /prezaʒ/ *n.m.* foreboding, omen. **∼er** *v.t.* forebode.

presbyte /prɛsbit/ *a.* long-sighted, far-sighted.

presbytère /prɛsbitɛr/ *n.m.* presbytery.

prescr|ire† /prɛskrir/ *v.t.* prescribe. **∼iption** *n.f.* prescription.

préséance /preseɑ̃s/ *n.f.* precedence.

présence /prezɑ̃s/ *n.f.* presence; (*scol.*) attendance.

présent, ∼e /prezɑ̃, -t/ *a.* present. —*n.m.* (*temps, cadeau*) present. **à ∼,** now.

présent|er /prezɑ̃te/ *v.t.* present; (*personne*) introduce (à, to); (*montrer*) show. **se ∼er** *v. pr.* introduce o.s. (à, to); (*aller*) go; (*apparaître*) appear; (*candidat*) come forward; (*occasion* *etc.*) arise. **se ~er à,** (*examen*) sit for; (*élection*) stand for. **se ~er bien,** look good. **~able** *a.* presentable. **~ateur, ~atrice** *n.m., f.* presenter. **~ation** *n.f.* presentation; introduction.

préserv|er /prezɛrve/ *v.t.* protect. **~ation** *n.f.* protection, preservation.

présiden|t, ~te /prezidɑ̃, -t/ *n.m., f.* president; (*de firme, comité*) chairman, chairwoman. **~t directeur général,** managing director. **~ce** *n.f.* presidency; chairmanship.

présidentiel, ~le /prezidɑ̃sjɛl/ *a.* presidential.

présider /prezide/ *v.t.* preside over. —*v.i.* preside.

présomption /prezɔ̃psjɔ̃/ *n.f.* presumption.

présomptueu|x, ~se /prezɔ̃ptɥø, -z/ *a.* presumptuous.

presque /prɛsk(ə)/ *adv.* almost, nearly. **~ jamais,** hardly ever. **~ rien,** hardly anything.

presqu'île /prɛskil/ *n.f.* peninsula.

pressant, ~e /prɛsɑ̃, -t/ *a.* pressing, urgent; (*personne*) pressing.

presse /prɛs/ *n.f.* (*journaux, appareil*) press.

pressent|ir /presɑ̃tir/ *v.t.* sense. **~iment** *n.m.* presentiment.

press|er /prese/ *v.t.* squeeze, press; (*appuyer sur, harceler*) press; (*hâter*) hasten; (*inciter*) urge (**de,** to). —*v.i.* (*temps*) press; (*affaire*) be pressing. **se ~er** *v. pr.* (*se hâter*) hurry; (*se grouper*) crowd. **~é** *a.* in a hurry; (*air*) hurried. **citron ~é,** lemon juice. **orange ~ée,** orange juice. **~e-papiers** *n.m. invar.* paperweight.

pressing /presiŋ/ *n.m.* steam pressing; (*magasin*) dry-cleaner's.

pression /presjɔ̃/ *n.f.* pressure. —*n.m.|f.* (*bouton*) press-stud; (*Amer.*) snap.

pressoir /preswar/ *n.m.* press.

pressuriser /presyrize/ *v.t.* pressurize.

prestance /prɛstɑ̃s/ *n.f.* (imposing) presence.

prestation /prɛstasjɔ̃/ *n.f.* allowance; (*d'artiste etc.*) performance.

prestidigita|teur, ~trice /prɛstidiʒitatœr, -tris/ *n.m., f.* conjuror. **~tion** /-asjɔ̃/ *n.f.* conjuring.

prestig|e /prɛstiʒ/ *n.m.* prestige. **~ieux, ~ieuse** *a.* prestigious.

présumer /prezyme/ *v.t.* presume.

prêt¹, ~e /prɛ, -t/ *a.* ready (**à qch.,**

for sth., **à faire,** to do). **~-à-porter** /prɛtaporte/ *n.m. invar.* ready-to-wear clothes.

prêt² /prɛ/ *n.m.* loan.

prétendant /pretɑ̃dɑ̃/ *n.m.* (*amoureux*) suitor.

prétend|re /pretɑ̃dr/ *v.t.* claim (**que,** that); (*vouloir*) intend. **~re qn. riche/etc.,** claim that s.o. is rich/*etc.* **~u** *a.* so-called. **~ument** *adv.* supposedly, allegedly.

prétent|ieux, ~ieuse /pretɑ̃sjø, -z/ *a.* pretentious. **~ion** *n.f.* pretentiousness; (*exigence*) claim.

prêt|er /prete/ *v.t.* lend (**à,** to); (*attribuer*) attribute. —*v.i.* **~er à,** be open to. **~er attention,** pay attention. **~er serment,** take an oath. **~eur, ~euse** /pretœr, -øz/ *n.m., f.* (money-) lender. **~eur sur gages,** pawnbroker.

prétext|e /pretɛkst/ *n.m.* pretext, excuse. **~er** *v.t.* plead.

prêtre /prɛtr/ *n.m.* priest.

prêtrise /pretriz/ *n.f.* priesthood.

preuve /prœv/ *n.f.* proof. **faire ~ de,** show.

prévaloir /prevalwar/ *v.i.* prevail.

prévenan|t, ~te /prɛvnɑ̃, -t/ *a.* thoughtful. **~ce(s)** *n.f.* (*pl.*) thoughtfulness.

prévenir† /prɛvnir/ *v.t.* (*menacer*) warn; (*informer*) tell; (*éviter, anticiper*) forestall.

préventi|f, ~ve /prevɑ̃tif, -v/ *a.* preventive.

prévention /prevɑ̃sjɔ̃/ *n.f.* prevention; (*préjugé*) prejudice. **~ routière,** road safety.

prévenu, ~e /prɛvny/ *n.m., f.* defendant.

prév|oir† /prevwar/ *v.t.* foresee; (*temps*) forecast; (*organiser*) plan (for), provide for; (*envisager*) allow (for). **~u pour,** (*jouet etc.*) designed for. **~isible** *a.* foreseeable. **~ision** *n.f.* prediction; (*météorologique*) forecast.

prévoyan|t, ~te /prevwajɑ̃, -t/ *a.* showing foresight. **~ce** *n.f.* foresight.

prier /prije/ *v.i.* pray. —*v.t.* pray to; (*implorer*) beg (**de,** to); (*demander à*) ask (**de,** to). **je vous en prie,** please; (*il n'y a pas de quoi*) don't mention it.

prière /prijɛr/ *n.f.* prayer; (*demande*) request. **~ de,** (*vous êtes prié de*) will you please.

primaire /primɛr/ *a.* primary.

primauté /primote/ *n.f.* primacy.

prime /prim/ *n.f.* free gift; (*d'employé*) bonus; (*subvention*) subsidy; (*d'assurance*) premium.

primé /prime/ *a.* prize-winning.

primer /prime/ *v.t./i.* excel.

primeurs /primœr/ *n.f. pl.* early fruit and vegetables.

primevère /primvɛr/ *n.f.* primrose.

primiti|f, **∼ve** /primitif, -v/ *a.* primitive; (*originel*) original. —*n.m.*, *f.* primitive.

primord|ial (*m. pl.* **∼iaux**) /primɔrdjal, -jo/ *a.* essential.

princ|e /prɛ̃s/ *n.m.* prince. **∼esse** *n.f.* princess. **∼ier**, **∼ière** *a.* princely.

princip|al (*m. pl.* **∼aux**) /prɛ̃sipal, -o/ *a.* main, principal. —*n.m.* (*pl.* **∼aux**) headmaster; (*chose*) main thing. **∼alement** *adv.* mainly.

principauté /prɛ̃sipote/ *n.f.* principality.

principe /prɛ̃sip/ *n.m.* principle. **en ∼**, theoretically; (*d'habitude*) as a rule.

printan|ier, **∼ière** /prɛ̃tanje, -jɛr/ *a.* spring(-like).

printemps /prɛ̃tɑ̃/ *n.m.* spring.

priorit|é /prijɔrite/ *n.f.* priority; (*auto.*) right of way. **∼aire** *a.* priority. **être ∼aire**, have priority.

pris, **∼e**[1] /pri, -z/ *voir* **prendre**. —*a.* (*place*) taken; (*crème*) set; (*personne*, *journée*) busy; (*gorge*) infected. **∼ de**, (*peur*, *fièvre*, *etc.*) stricken with. **∼ de panique**, panic-stricken.

prise[2] /priz/ *n.f.* hold, grip; (*animal etc. attrapé*) catch; (*mil.*) capture. **∼** (*de courant*), (*mâle*) plug; (*femelle*) socket. **aux ∼s avec**, at grips with. **∼ de conscience**, awareness. **∼ de contact**, first contact, initial meeting. **∼ de position**, stand. **∼ de sang**, blood test. **∼ de vues**, filming.

priser /prize/ *v.t.* (*estimer*) prize.

prisme /prism/ *n.m.* prism.

prison /prizɔ̃/ *n.f.* prison, gaol, jail; (*réclusion*) imprisonment. **∼nier**, **∼nière** /-ɔnje, -jɛr/ *n.m.*, *f.* prisoner.

privé /prive/ *a.* private. —*n.m.* (*comm.*) private sector. **en ∼**, **dans le ∼**, in private.

priv|er /prive/ *v.t.* **∼er de**, deprive of. **se ∼er de**, go without. **∼ation** *n.f.* deprivation; (*sacrifice*) hardship.

privil|ège /privilɛʒ/ *n.m.* privilege. **∼égié**, **∼égiée** *a. & n.m.,f.* privileged (person).

prix /pri/ *n.m.* price; (*récompense*) prize. **à tout ∼**, at all costs. **au ∼ de**, (*fig.*) at the expense of. **∼ coûtant**, **∼ de revient**, cost price. **∼ fixe**, set price; (*repas*) set meal.

pro- /pro/ *préf.* pro-.

probab|le /prɔbabl/ *a.* probable, likely. **∼ilité** *n.f.* probability. **∼lement** *adv.* probably.

probant, **∼e** /prɔbɑ̃, -t/ *a.* convincing, conclusive.

probité /prɔbite/ *n.f.* integrity.

problème /prɔblɛm/ *n.m.* problem.

procéd|er /prɔsede/ *v.i.* proceed. **∼er à**, carry out. **∼é** *n.m.* process; (*conduite*) behaviour.

procédure /prɔsedyr/ *n.f.* procedure.

procès /prɔsɛ/ *n.m.* (*criminel*) trial; (*civil*) lawsuit, proceedings. **∼-verbal** (*pl.* **∼-verbaux**) *n.m.* report; (*contravention*) ticket.

procession /prɔsesjɔ̃/ *n.f.* procession.

processus /prɔsesys/ *n.m.* process.

prochain, **∼e** /prɔʃɛ̃, -ɛn/ *a.* (*suivant*) next; (*proche*) imminent; (*avenir*) near. —*n.m.* fellow. **∼ement** /-ɛnmɑ̃/ *adv.* soon.

proche /prɔʃ/ *a.* near, close; (*avoisinant*) neighbouring; (*parent*, *ami*) close. **∼ de**, close *ou* near to. **être ∼**, (*imminent*) be approaching. **∼s** *n.m. pl.* close relations. **P∼-Orient** *n.m.* Near East.

proclam|er /prɔklame/ *v.t.* declare, proclaim. **∼ation** *n.f.* declaration, proclamation.

procréation /prɔkreasjɔ̃/ *n.f.* procreation.

procuration /prɔkyrasjɔ̃/ *n.f.* proxy.

procurer /prɔkyre/ *v.t.* bring (à, to). **se ∼** *v. pr.* obtain.

procureur /prɔkyrœr/ *n.m.* public prosecutor.

prodig|e /prɔdiʒ/ *n.m.* marvel; (*personne*) prodigy. **∼ieux**, **∼ieuse** *a.* tremendous, prodigious.

prodigu|e /prɔdig/ *a.* wasteful. **∼er** *v.t.* **∼er à**, lavish on.

producti|f, **∼ve** /prɔdyktif, -v/ *a.* productive. **∼vité** *n.f.* productivity.

prod|uire† /prɔdɥir/ *v.t.* produce. **se ∼uire** *v. pr.* (*survenir*) happen. **∼ucteur**, **∼uctrice** *a.* producing; *n.m.*, *f.* producer. **∼uction** *n.f.* production; (*produit*) product.

produit /prɔdɥi/ *n.m.* product. **∼s**, (*de la terre*) produce. **∼ chimique**, chemical. ∼s **alimentaires,** food-stuffs.

proéminent, ∼e /prɔeminã, -t/ *a.* prominent.

prof /prɔf/ *n.m. (fam.)* teacher.

profane /prɔfan/ *a.* secular. —*n.m./f.* lay person.

profaner /prɔfane/ *v.t.* desecrate.

proférer /prɔfere/ *v.t.* utter.

professer[1] /prɔfese/ *v.t. (déclarer)* profess.

professer[2] /prɔfese/ *v.t./i. (enseigner)* teach.

professeur /prɔfɛsœr/ *n.m.* teacher; *(univ.)* lecturer; *(avec chaire)* professor.

profession /prɔfɛsjɔ̃/ *n.f.* occupation; *(intellectuelle)* profession. ∼**nel,** ∼**nelle** /-jɔnɛl/ *a.* professional; *(école)* vocational; *n.m., f.* professional.

professorat /prɔfɛsɔra/ *n.m.* teaching.

profil /prɔfil/ *n.m.* profile.

profiler (se) /(sə)prɔfile/ *v. pr.* be outlined.

profit /prɔfi/ *n.m.* profit. **au** ∼ **de,** in aid of. ∼**able** /-tabl/ *a.* profitable.

profiter /prɔfite/ *v.i.* ∼ **à,** benefit. ∼ **de,** take advantage of.

profond, ∼e /prɔfɔ̃, -d/ *a.* deep; *(sentiment, intérêt)* profound; *(causes)* underlying. **au plus** ∼ **de,** in the depths of. ∼**ément** /-demã/ *adv.* deeply; *(différent, triste)* profoundly; *(dormir)* soundly. ∼**eur** /-dœr/ *n.f.* depth.

profusion /prɔfyzjɔ̃/ *n.f.* profusion.

progéniture /prɔʒenityr/ *n.f.* offspring.

programmation /prɔgramasjɔ̃/ *n.f.* programming.

programm|e /prɔgram/ *n.m.* programme; *(matières: scol.)* syllabus; *(informatique)* program. ∼**e (d'études),** curriculum. ∼**er** *v.t.* *(ordinateur)* program; *(émission)* bill. ∼**eur,** ∼**euse** *n.m., f.* computer programmer.

progrès /prɔgrɛ/ *n.m. & n.m.pl.* progress.

progress|er /prɔgrese/ *v.i.* progress. ∼**ion** /-ɛsjɔ̃/ *n.f.* progression.

progressi|f, ∼**ve** /prɔgresif, -v/ *a.* progressive. ∼**vement** *adv.* progressively.

progressiste /prɔgresist/ *a.* progressive.

prohib|er /prɔibe/ *v.t.* prohibit. ∼**ition** *n.f.* prohibition.

prohibiti|f, ∼**ve** /prɔibitif, -v/ *a.* prohibitive.

proie /prwa/ *n.f.* prey. **en** ∼ **à,** tormented by.

projecteur /prɔʒɛktœr/ *n.m.* floodlight; *(mil.)* searchlight; *(cinéma)* projector.

projectile /prɔʒɛktil/ *n.m.* missile.

projection /prɔʒɛksjɔ̃/ *n.f.* projection; *(séance)* show.

projet /prɔʒɛ/ *n.m.* plan; *(ébauche)* draft. ∼ **de loi,** bill.

projeter /prɔʒte/ *v.t.* plan **(de,** to); *(film)* project, show; *(jeter)* hurl, project.

prolét|aire /prɔletɛr/ *n.m./f.* proletarian. ∼**ariat** *n.m.* proletariat. ∼**arien,** ∼**arienne** *a.* proletarian.

prolifér|er /prɔlifere/ *v.i.* proliferate. ∼**ation** *n.f.* proliferation.

prolifique /prɔlifik/ *a.* prolific.

prologue /prɔlɔg/ *n.m.* prologue.

prolongation /prɔlɔ̃gasjɔ̃/ *n.f.* extension. ∼**s,** *(football)* extra time.

prolong|er /prɔlɔ̃ʒe/ *v.t.* prolong. **se** ∼**er** *v. pr.* continue, extend. ∼**é** *a.* prolonged. ∼**ement** *n.m.* extension.

promenade /prɔmnad/ *n.f.* walk; *(à bicyclette, à cheval)* ride; *(en auto)* drive, ride. **faire une** ∼, go for a walk.

promen|er /prɔmne/ *v.t.* take for a walk. ∼**er sur qch.,** *(main, regard)* run over sth. **se** ∼**er** *v. pr.* walk. **(aller) se** ∼**er,** go for a walk. ∼**eur,** ∼**euse** *n.m., f.* walker.

promesse /prɔmɛs/ *n.f.* promise.

promett|re† /prɔmɛtr/ *v.t./i.* promise. ∼**re (beaucoup),** be promising. **se** ∼**re de,** resolve to. ∼**eur,** ∼**euse** *a.* promising.

promontoire /prɔmɔ̃twar/ *n.m.* headland.

promoteur /prɔmɔtœr/ *n.m. (immobilier)* property developer.

prom|ouvoir /prɔmuvwar/ *v.t.* promote. **être** ∼**u,** be promoted. ∼**otion** *n.f.* promotion; *(univ.)* year; *(comm.)* special offer.

prompt, ∼**e** /prɔ̃, -t/ *a.* swift.

prôner /prone/ *v.t.* extol; *(préconiser)* preach, advocate.

pronom /prɔnɔ̃/ *n.m.* pronoun. ∼**inal** *(m. pl.* ∼**inaux)** /-ɔminal, -o/ *a.* pronominal.

prononc|er /prɔnɔ̃se/ *v.t.* pronounce; *(discours)* make. **se** ∼**er** *v. pr. (mot)* be pronounced; *(personne)* make a

decision (**pour**, in favour of). ~**é** *a.*
pronounced. ~**iation** *n.f.* pronunciation.

pronosti|c /prɔnɔstik/ *n.m.* forecast.
~**quer** *v.t.* forecast.

propagande /prɔpagãd/ *n.f.* propaganda.

propag|er /prɔpaʒe/ *v.t.*, **se** ~**er**
v. pr. spread. ~**ation** /-gasjɔ̃/ *n.f.*
spread(ing).

proph|ète /prɔfɛt/ *n.m.* prophet. ~**é-
tie** /-esi/ *n.f.* prophecy. ~**étique** *a.*
prophetic. ~**étiser** *v.t./i.* prophesy.

propice /prɔpis/ *a.* favourable.

proportion /prɔpɔrsjɔ̃/ *n.f.* proportion; (*en mathématiques*) ratio.
~**né** /-jɔne/ *a.* proportionate (**à**, to).
~**nel**, ~**nelle** /-jɔnɛl/ *a.* proportional.
~**ner** /-jɔne/ *v.t.* proportion.

propos /prɔpo/ *n.m.* intention; (*sujet*)
subject. —*n.m. pl.* (*paroles*) remarks.
à ~, at the right time; (*dans un dialogue*) by the way. **à** ~ **de**, about.

propos|er /prɔpoze/ *v.t.* propose;
(*offrir*) offer. **se** ~**er** *v. pr.* volunteer
(**pour**, to); (*but*) set o.s. **se** ~**er de
faire**, propose to do. ~**ition** *n.f.* proposal; (*affirmation*) proposition;
(*gram.*) clause.

propre¹ /prɔpr/ *a.* clean; (*soigné*) neat;
(*honnête*) decent. ~**ment**¹ /-əmã/ *adv.*
cleanly; neatly; decently.

propre² /prɔpr/ *a.* (*à soi*) own; (*sens*)
literal. ~ **à**, (*qui convient*) suited
to; (*spécifique*) peculiar to. ~**ment**²
/-əmã/ *adv.* strictly. **le bureau**/*etc.*
~**ment dit**, the office/*etc.* itself.

propreté /prɔprəte/ *n.f.* cleanliness;
(*netteté*) neatness.

propriétaire /prɔprijetɛr/ *n.m./f.*
owner; (*comm.*) proprietor; (*qui loue*)
landlord, landlady.

propriété /prɔprijete/ *n.f.* property;
(*d'un terme*) propriety.

propuls|er /prɔpylse/ *v.t.* propel.
~**ion** *n.f.* propulsion.

prosaïque /prozaik/ *a.* prosaic.

proscr|ire /prɔskrir/ *v.t.* proscribe.
~**it**, ~**ite** *a.* proscribed; *n.m.,f.* (*exilé*)
exile.

prose /proz/ *n.f.* prose.

prospec|ter /prɔspɛkte/ *v.t.* prospect.
~**teur**, ~**trice** *n.m.,* *f.* prospector.
~**tion** /-ksjɔ̃/ *n.f.* prospecting.

prospectus /prɔspɛktys/ *n.m.* leaflet.

prosp|ère /prɔspɛr/ *a.* flourishing,
thriving. ~**érer** *v.i.* thrive, prosper.
~**érité** *n.f.* prosperity.

prostern|er (se) /(sə)prɔstɛrne/ *v. pr.*
bow down. ~**é** *a.* prostrate.

prostit|uée /prɔstitɥe/ *n.f.* prostitute.
~**ution** *n.f.* prostitution.

prostré /prɔstre/ *a.* prostrate.

protagoniste /prɔtagɔnist/ *n.m.* protagonist.

protec|teur, ~**trice** /prɔtɛktœr, -tris/
n.m.,f. protector. —*a.* protective.

protection /prɔtɛksjɔ̃/ *n.f.* protection;
(*fig.*) patronage.

protég|er /prɔteʒe/ *v.t.* protect; (*fig.*)
patronize. **se** ~**er** *v. pr.* protect o.s.
~**é** *n.m.* protégé. ~**ée** *n.f.* protégée.

protéine /prɔtein/ *n.f.* protein.

protestant, ~**e** /prɔtɛstã, -t/ *a. & n.m.,*
f. Protestant.

protest|er /prɔtɛste/ *v.t./i.* protest. ~**a-
tion** *n.f.* protest.

protocole /prɔtɔkɔl/ *n.m.* protocol.

prototype /prɔtɔtip/ *n.m.* prototype.

protubéran|t, ~**te** /prɔtyberã, -t/ *a.*
bulging. ~**ce**, *n.f.* protuberance.

proue /pru/ *n.f.* bow, prow.

prouesse /pruɛs/ *n.f.* feat, exploit.

prouver /pruve/ *v.t.* prove.

provenance /prɔvnãs/ *n.f.* origin. **en**
~ **de**, from.

provenç|al, ~**ale** (*m. pl.* ~**aux**)
/prɔvãsal, -o/ *a. & n.m.,f.* Provençal.

Provence /prɔvãs/ *n.f.* Provence.

provenir† /prɔvnir/ *v.i.* ~ **de**, come
from.

proverb|e /prɔvɛrb/ *n.m.* proverb.
~**ial** (*m. pl.* ~**iaux**) *a.* proverbial.

providence /prɔvidãs/ *n.f.* providence.

provinc|e /prɔvɛ̃s/ *n.f.* province. **de**
~**e**, provincial. **la** ~**e**, the provinces.
~**ial**, ~**iale** (*m. pl.* ~**iaux**) *a. & n.m.,*
f. provincial.

proviseur /prɔvizœr/ *n.m.* headmaster.

provision /prɔvizjɔ̃/ *n.f.* supply, store;
(*acompte*) deposit. ~**s**, (*achats*) shopping; (*vivres*) provisions.

provisoire /prɔvizwar/ *a.* temporary.
~**ment** *adv.* temporarily.

provo|quer /prɔvɔke/ *v.t.* cause; (*ex-
citer*) arouse; (*défier*) provoke. ~**cant**,
~**cante** *a.* provocative. ~**cation** *n.f.*
provocation.

proximité /prɔksimite/ *n.f.* proximity.
à ~ **de**, close to.

prude /pryd/ *a.* prudish. —*n.f.* prude.

prud|ent, ~**ente** /prydã, -t/ *a.* cautious; (*sage*) wise. **soyez** ~**ent**, be
careful. ~**emment** /-amã/ *adv.* cau-

tiously; wisely. ~**ence** *n.f.* caution;
wisdom.
prune /pryn/ *n.f.* plum.
pruneau (*pl.* ~**x**) /pryno/ *n.m.* prune.
prunelle¹ /prynɛl/ *n.f.* (*pupille*) pupil.
prunelle² /prynɛl/ *n.f.* (*fruit*) sloe.
psaume /psom/ *n.m.* psalm.
pseudo- /psødɔ/ *préf.* pseudo-.
pseudonyme /psødɔnim/ *n.m.*
pseudonym.
psychanalys|e /psikanaliz/ *n.f.*
psychoanalysis. ~**er** *v.t.* psycho-
analyse. ~**te** /-st/ *n.m./f.* psycho-
analyst.
psychiatr|e /psikjatr/ *n.m./f.* psy-
chiatrist. ~**ie** *n.f.* psychiatry. ~**ique**
a. psychiatric.
psychique /psiʃik/ *a.* mental, psychological.
psycholo|gie /psikɔlɔʒi/ *n.f.* psy-
chology. ~**gique** *a.* psychological.
~**gue** *n.m./f.* psychologist.
PTT *abrév.* (*Postes, Télégraphes, Téléphones*) Post Office.
pu /py/ *voir* **pouvoir**¹.
puant, ~**e** /pɥɑ̃, -t/ *a.* stinking. ~**eur**
/-tœr/ *n.f.* stink.
puberté /pybɛrte/ *n.f.* puberty.
publi|c, ~**que** /pyblik/ *a.* public.
—*n.m.* public; (*assistance*) audience.
en ~**c**, in public.
publicit|é /pyblisite/ *n.f.* publicity, ad-
vertising; (*annonce*) advertisement;
(*intérêt général*) publicity. ~**aire** *a.*
publicity.
publ|ier /pyblije/ *v.t.* publish. ~**ica-
tion** *n.f.* publication.
publiquement /pyblikmɑ̃/ *adv.* pub-
licly.
puce¹ /pys/ *n.f.* flea.
puce² /pys/ *n.f.* (*électronique*) chip.
pud|eur /pydœr/ *n.f.* modesty. ~**ique**
a. modest.
pudibond, ~**e** /pydibɔ̃, -d/ *a.* prudish.
puer /pɥe/ *v.i.* stink. —*v.t.* stink of.
puéricultrice /pɥerikyltris/ *n.f.*
children's nurse.
puéril /pɥeril/ *a.* puerile.
puis /pɥi/ *adv.* then.
puiser /pɥize/ *v.t.* draw (**qch. dans,**
sth. from). —*v.i.* ~ **dans qch.,** dip
into sth.

puisque /pɥisk(ə)/ *conj.* since, as.
puissance /pɥisɑ̃s/ *n.f.* power. **en** ~
a. potential; *adv.* potentially.
puiss|ant, ~**ante** /pɥisɑ̃, -t/ *a.* power-
ful. ~**amment** *adv.* powerfully.
puits /pɥi/ *n.m.* well; (*de mine*) shaft.
pull(-over) /pyl(ɔvɛr)/ *n.m.* pullover.
pulpe /pylp/ *n.f.* pulp.
pulsation /pylsasjɔ̃/ *n.f.* (heart)beat.
pulvéris|er /pylverize/ *v.t.* pulverize;
(*liquide*) spray. ~**ateur** *n.m.* spray.
punaise /pynɛz/ *n.f.* (*insecte*) bug;
(*clou*) drawing-pin; (*Amer.*) thumbtack.
pun|ir /pynir/ *v.t.* punish. ~**ition** *n.f.*
punishment.
pupille¹ /pypij/ *n.f.* (*de l'œil*) pupil.
pupille² /pypij/ *n.m./f.* (*enfant*) ward.
pupitre /pypitr/ *n.m.* (*scol.*) desk. ~ **à
musique,** music stand.
pur /pyr/ *a.* pure; (*whisky*) neat. ~**e-
ment** *adv.* purely. ~**eté** *n.f.* purity.
~**-sang** *n.m.* *invar.* (*cheval*)
thoroughbred.
purée /pyre/ *n.f.* purée; (*de pommes de
terre*) mashed potatoes.
purgatoire /pyrgatwar/ *n.m.* purgatory.
purg|e /pyrʒ/ *n.f.* purge. ~**er** *v.t.* (*pol.,
méd.*) purge; (*peine: jurid.*) serve.
purif|ier /pyrifje/ *v.t.* purify. ~**ica-
tion** *n.f.* purification.
purin /pyrɛ̃/ *n.m.* (liquid) manure.
puritain, ~**e** /pyritɛ̃, -ɛn/ *n.m.,f.* puritan. —*a.* puritanical.
pus /py/ *n.m.* pus.
pustule /pystyl/ *n.f.* pimple.
putain /pytɛ̃/ *n.f.* (*fam.*) whore.
putréfier (**se**) /(sə)pytrefje/ *v. pr.*
putrefy.
puzzle /pœzl/ *n.m.* jigsaw (puzzle).
P-V *abrév.* (*procès-verbal*) ticket,
traffic fine.
pygmée /pigme/ *n.m.* pygmy.
pyjama /piʒama/ *n.m.* pyjamas. **un** ~,
a pair of pyjamas.
pylône /pilon/ *n.m.* pylon.
pyramide /piramid/ *n.f.* pyramid.
Pyrénées /pirene/ *n.f.pl.* **les** ~, the
Pyrenees.
pyromane /pirɔman/ *n.m./f.* arsonist.

Q

QI *abrév.* (*quotient intellectuel*) IQ.

qu' /k/ *voir* que.

quadrill|er /kadrije/ *v.t.* (*zone*) comb, control. **~age** *n.m.* (*mil.*) control. **~é** *a.* (*papier*) squared.

quadrupède /kadrypɛd/ *n.m.* quadruped.

quadrupl|e /kadrypl/ *a. & n.m.* quadruple. **~er** *v.t./i.* quadruple. **~és, ~ées** *n.m., f. pl.* quadruplets.

quai /ke/ *n.m.* (*de gare*) platform; (*de port*) quay; (*de rivière*) embankment.

qualificatif /kalifikatif/ *n.m.* (*épithète*) term.

qualif|ier /kalifje/ *v.t.* qualify; (*décrire*) describe (**de**, as). **se ~ier** *v. pr.* qualify (**pour**, for). **~ication** *n.f.* qualification; description. **~ié** *a.* qualified; (*main-d'œuvre*) skilled.

qualit|é /kalite/ *n.f.* quality; (*titre*) occupation. **en ~é de**, in one's capacity as. **~atif, ~ative** *a.* qualitative.

quand /kɑ̃/ *conj. & adv.* when. **~ même**, all the same. **~ (bien) même**, even if.

quant (à) /kɑ̃t(a)/ *prép.* as for.

quantit|é /kɑ̃tite/ *n.f.* quantity. **une ~é de**, a lot of. **~atif, ~ative** *a.* quantitative.

quarantaine /karɑ̃tɛn/ *n.f.* (*méd.*) quarantine. **une ~ (de)**, about forty.

quarant|e /karɑ̃t/ *a. & n.m.* forty. **~ième** *a. & n.m./f.* fortieth.

quart /kar/ *n.m.* quarter; (*naut.*) watch. **~ (de litre)**, quarter litre. **~ de finale**, quarter-final. **~ d'heure**, quarter of an hour.

quartier /kartje/ *n.m.* neighbourhood, district; (*de lune, bœuf*) quarter; (*de fruit*) segment. **~s**, (*mil.*) quarters. **de ~, du ~**, local. **~ général**, headquarters.

quartz /kwarts/ *n.m.* quartz.

quasi- /kazi/ *préf.* quasi-.

quasiment /kazimɑ̃/ *adv.* almost.

quatorz|e /katɔrz/ *a. & n.m.* fourteen. **~ième** *a. & n.m./f.* fourteenth.

quatre /katr(ə)/ *a. & n.m.* four. **~-vingt(s)** *a. & n.m.* eighty. **~-vingt-dix** *a. & n.m.* ninety.

quatrième /katrijɛm/ *a. & n.m./f.* fourth. **~ment** *adv.* fourthly.

quatuor /kwatɥɔr/ *n.m.* quartet.

que, qu'* /kə, k/ *conj.* that; (*comparaison*) than. **qu'il vienne**, let him come. **qu'il vienne ou non**, whether he comes or not. **ne faire ~ demander/etc.**, only ask/etc. —*adv.* (*ce*) **~ tu es bête, qu'est-ce ~ tu es bête**, how silly you are. **~ de**, what a lot of. —*pron. rel.* (*personne*) that, whom; (*chose*) that, which; (*temps, moment*) when; (*interrogatif*) what. **un jour/etc. ~**, one day/etc. when. **~ faites-vous?, qu'est-ce ~ vous faites?**, what are you doing?

Québec /kebɛk/ *n.m.* Quebec.

quel, ~le /kɛl/ *a.* what; (*interrogatif*) which, what; (*qui*) who. —*pron.* which. **~ dommage**, what a pity. **~ qu'il soit**, (*chose*) whatever *ou* whichever it may be; (*personne*) whoever he may be.

quelconque /kɛlkɔ̃k/ *a.* any, some; (*banal*) ordinary; (*médiocre*) poor.

quelque /kɛlkə/ *a.* some. **~s**, a few, some. —*adv.* (*environ*) some. **et ~**, (*fam.*) and a bit. **~ chose**, something; (*interrogation*) anything. **~ part**, somewhere. **~ peu**, somewhat.

quelquefois /kɛlkəfwa/ *adv.* sometimes.

quelques|-uns, ~-unes /kɛlkəzœ̃, -yn/ *pron.* some, a few.

quelqu'un /kɛlkœ̃/ *pron.* someone, somebody; (*interrogation*) anyone, anybody.

quémander /kemɑ̃de/ *v.t.* beg for.

qu'en-dira-t-on /kɑ̃diratɔ̃/ *n.m. invar.* gossip.

querell|e /kərɛl/ *n.f.* quarrel. **~eur, ~euse** *a.* quarrelsome.

quereller (se) /(sə)kərele/ *v. pr.* quarrel.

question /kɛstjɔ̃/ *n.f.* question; (*affaire*) matter, question. **en ~**, in question; (*en jeu*) at stake. **il est ~ de**, (*cela concerne*) it is about; (*on parle de*) there is talk of. **il n'en est pas ~**, it is out of the question. **~ner** /-jɔne/ *v.t.* question.

questionnaire /kɛstjɔnɛr/ *n.m.* questionnaire.

quêt|e /kɛt/ *n.f.* (*relig.*) collection. **en ~e de**, in search of. **~er** /kete/ *v.i.* collect money; *v.t.* seek.

queue /kø/ *n.f.* tail; (*de poêle*) handle; (*de fruit*) stalk; (*de fleur*) stem; (*file*) queue; (*file: Amer.*) line; (*de train*) rear. **faire la ~**, queue (up); (*Amer.*) line up. **~ de cheval**, pony-tail.

qui /ki/ *pron. rel.* (*personne*) who; (*chose*) which, that; (*interrogatif*) who; (*après prép.*) whom; (*quiconque*) whoever. **à ~ est ce stylo**/*etc.?*, whose pen/*etc.* is this? **qu'est-ce ~?**, what? **~ est-ce qui?**, who? **~ que ce soit,** anyone.

quiche /kiʃ/ *n.f.* quiche.

quiconque /kikɔ̃k/ *pron.* whoever; (*n'importe qui*) anyone.

quiétude[1] /kjetyd/ *n.f.* quiet.

quille[1] /kij/ *n.f.* (*de bateau*) keel.

quille[2] /kij/ *n.f.* (*jouet*) skittle.

quincaill|ier, **~ière** /kɛ̃kɑje, -jɛr/ *n.m., f.* hardware dealer. **~erie** *n.f.* hardware; (*magasin*) hardware shop.

quinine /kinin/ *n.f.* quinine.

quinquenn|al (*m.pl.* **~aux**) /kɛ̃kenal, -o/ *a.* five-year.

quint|al (*pl.* **~aux**) /kɛ̃tal, -o/ *n.m.* quintal (= *100 kg.*).

quintette /kɛ̃tɛt/ *n.m.* quintet.

quintupl|e /kɛ̃typl/ *a.* fivefold. —*n.m.* quintuple. **~er** *v.t./i.* increase fivefold. **~és, ~ées,** *n.m., f. pl.* quintuplets.

quinzaine /kɛ̃zɛn/ *n.f.* **une ~ (de),** about fifteen.

quinz|e /kɛ̃z/ *a. & n.m.* fifteen. **~e jours,** two weeks. **~ième** *a. & n.m.*/*f.* fifteenth.

quiproquo /kiprɔko/ *n.m.* misunderstanding.

quittance /kitɑ̃s/ *n.f.* receipt.

quitte /kit/ *a.* quits (**envers,** with). **~ à faire,** even if it means doing.

quitter /kite/ *v.t.* leave; (*vêtement*) take off. **se ~** *v. pr.* part.

quoi /kwa/ *pron.* what; (*après prép.*) which. **de ~ vivre/manger**/*etc.*, (*assez*) enough to live on/ to eat/*etc.* **de ~ écrire,** sth. to write with, what is necessary to write with. **~ que,** whatever. **~ que ce soit,** anything.

quoique /kwak(ə)/ *conj.* (al)though.

quolibet /kɔlibɛ/ *n.m.* gibe.

quorum /k(w)ɔrɔm/ *n.m.* quorum.

quota /k(w)ɔta/ *n.m.* quota.

quote-part (*pl.* **quotes-parts**) /kɔtpar/ *n.f.* share.

quotidien, ~ne /kɔtidjɛ̃, -jɛn/ *a.* daily; (*banal*) everyday. —*n.m.* daily (paper). **~nement** /-jɛnmɑ̃/ *adv.* daily.

quotient /kɔsjɑ̃/ *n.m.* quotient.

R

rabâcher /rabaʃe/ *v.t.* keep repeating.

rabais /rabɛ/ *n.m.* (price) reduction.

rabaisser /rabese/ *v.t.* (*déprécier*) belittle; (*réduire*) reduce.

rabat /raba/ *n.m.* flap. **~-joie** *n.m. invar.* killjoy.

rabattre /rabatr/ *v.t.* pull *ou* put down; (*diminuer*) reduce; (*déduire*) take off. **se ~** *v. pr.* (*se refermer*) close; (*véhicule*) cut in, turn sharply. **se ~ sur,** fall back on.

rabbin /rabɛ̃/ *n.m.* rabbi.

rabibocher /rabiboʃe/ *v.t.* (*fam.*) reconcile.

rabiot /rabjo/ *n.m.* (*fam.*) extra.

râblé /rable/ *a.* stocky, sturdy.

rabot /rabo/ *n.m.* plane. **~er** /-ɔte/ *v.t.* plane.

raboteu|x, ~se /rabotø, -z/ *a.* uneven.

rabougri /rabugri/ *a.* stunted.

rabrouer /rabrue/ *v.t.* snub.

racaille /rakaj/ *n.f.* rabble.

raccommoder /rakɔmɔde/ *v.t.* mend; (*personnes*: *fam.*) reconcile.

raccompagner /rakɔ̃paɲe/ *v.t.* see *ou* take back (home).

raccord /rakɔr/ *n.m.* link; (*de papier peint*) join. **~ (de peinture),** touch-up.

raccord|er /rakɔrde/ *v.t.* connect, join. **~ement** *n.m.* connection.

raccourci /rakursi/ *n.m.* short cut. **en ~,** in brief.

raccourcir /rakursir/ *v.t.* shorten. —*v.i.* get shorter.

raccrocher /rakrɔʃe/ *v.t.* hang back up; (*personne*) grab hold of; (*relier*) connect. **~ (le récepteur),** hang up. **se ~ à,** cling to; (*se relier à*) be connected to *ou* with.

raccroc (par) /(par)rakro/ *adv.* by a stroke of luck, by a fluke.

rac|e /ras/ *n.f.* race; (*animale*) breed. **de ~e,** pure-bred. **~ial** (*m. pl.* **~iaux**) *a.* racial.

rachat /raʃa/ *n.m.* buying (back); (*de pécheur*) redemption.

racheter /raʃte/ *v.t.* buy (back); (*davantage*) buy more; (*nouvel objet*) buy another; (*pécheur*) redeem; (*défaut*) make up for. **se ~** *v. pr.* make amends.

racine /rasin/ *n.f.* root.

racis|te /rasist/ *a. & n.m./f.* racist. **~me** *n.m.* racism.

raclée /rakle/ *n.f.* (*fam.*) thrashing.

racler /rakle/ *v.t.* scrape. **se ~ la gorge,** clear one's throat.

racol|er /rakɔle/ *v.t.* solicit. **~age** *n.m.* soliciting.

racontars /rakɔ̃tar/ *n.m. pl.* (*fam.*) gossip, stories.

raconter /rakɔ̃te/ *v.t.* (*histoire*) tell, relate; (*vacances etc.*) tell about. **~ à qn. que,** tell s.o. that, say to s.o. that.

racorni /rakɔrni/ *a.* hard(ened).

radar /radar/ *n.m.* radar.

rade /rad/ *n.f.* harbour. **en ~,** (*personne*: *fam.*) stranded, behind.

radeau (*pl.* **~x**) /rado/ *n.m.* raft.

radiateur /radjatœr/ *n.m.* radiator; (*électrique*) heater.

radiation /radjasjɔ̃/ *n.f.* (*énergie*) radiation.

radic|al (*m. pl.* **~aux**) /radikal, -o/ *a.* radical. —*n.m.* (*pl.* **~aux**) radical.

radier /radje/ *v.t.* cross off.

radieu|x, ~se /radjø, -z/ *a.* radiant.

radin, ~e /radɛ̃, -in/ *a.* (*fam.*) stingy.

radio /radjo/ *n.f.* radio; (*radiographie*) X-ray.

radioacti|f, ~ve /radjoaktif, -v/ *a.* radioactive. **~vité** *n.f.* radioactivity.

radiodiffus|er /radjodifyze/ *v.t.* broadcast. **~ion** *n.f.* broadcasting.

radiograph|ie /radjografi/ *n.f.* (*photographie*) X-ray. **~ier** *v.t.* X-ray. **~ique** *a.* X-ray.

radiologue /radjolɔg/ *n.m./f.* radiographer.

radiophonique /radjofɔnik/ *a.* radio.

radis /radi/ *n.m.* radish.

radoter /radɔte/ *v.i.* (*fam.*) talk drivel.

radouc|ir (se) /(sə)radusir/ *v. pr.* calm down; (*temps*) become milder. **~issement** *n.m.* (*du temps*) milder weather.

rafale /rafal/ *n.f.* (*de vent*) gust; (*tir*) burst of gunfire.

raffermir /rafɛrmir/ *v.t.* strengthen. **se ~** *v. pr.* become stronger.

raffin|é /rafine/ *a.* refined. **~ement** *n.m.* refinement.

raffin|er /rafine/ *v.t.* refine. **~age** *n.m.* refining. **~erie** *n.f.* refinery.

raffoler /rafɔle/ *v.i.* ~ **de,** be extremely fond of.

raffut /rafy/ *n.m.* (*fam.*) din.

rafiot /rafjo/ *n.m.* (*fam.*) boat.

rafistoler /rafistɔle/ *v.t.* (*fam.*) patch up.

rafle /rɑfl/ *n.f.* (police) raid.

rafler /rɑfle/ *v.t.* grab, swipe.

rafraîch|ir /rafreʃir/ *v.t.* cool (down); (*raviver*) brighten up; (*personne, mémoire*) refresh. **se ~ir** *v. pr.* (*se laver*) freshen up; (*boire*) refresh o.s.; (*temps*) get cooler. ~**issant,** ~**issante** *a.* refreshing.

rafraîchissement /rafreʃismɑ̃/ *n.m.* (*boisson*) cold drink. ~**s,** (*fruits etc.*) refreshments.

ragaillardir /ragajardir/ *v.t.* (*fam.*) buck up.

rag|e /raʒ/ *n.f.* rage; (*maladie*) rabies. **faire ~e,** rage. ~**e de dents,** raging toothache. ~**er** *v.i.* rage. ~**eur,** ~**euse** *a.* ill-tempered.

ragot(s) /rago/ *n.m.* (*pl.*) (*fam.*) gossip.

ragoût /ragu/ *n.m.* stew.

raid /rɛd/ *n.m.* (*mil.*) raid; (*sport*) rally.

raid|e /rɛd/ *a.* stiff; (*côte*) steep; (*corde*) tight; (*cheveux*) straight. —*adv.* (*en pente*) steeply. ~**eur** *n.f.* stiffness; steepness.

raidir /redir/ *v.t.,* **se ~** *v. pr.* stiffen; (*position*) harden; (*corde*) tighten.

raie[1] /rɛ/ *n.f.* line; (*bande*) strip; (*de cheveux*) parting.

raie[2] /rɛ/ *n.f.* (*poisson*) skate.

raifort /rɛfɔr/ *n.m.* horse-radish.

rail /rɑj/ *n.m.* (*barre*) rail. **le ~,** (*transport*) rail.

raill|er /rɑje/ *v.t.* mock (at). ~**erie** *n.f.* mocking remark. ~**eur,** ~**euse** *a.* mocking.

rainure /renyr/ *n.f.* groove.

raisin /rezɛ̃/ *n.m.* ~**(s),** grapes. ~ **sec,** raisin.

raison /rezɔ̃/ *n.f.* reason. **à ~ de,** at the rate of. **avec ~,** rightly. **avoir ~,** be right (**de faire,** to do). **avoir ~ de qn.,** get the better of s.o. **donner ~ à,** prove right. **en ~ de,** (*cause*) because of.

raisonnable /rezɔnabl/ *a.* reasonable, sensible.

raisonn|er /rezɔne/ *v.i.* reason. —*v.t.* (*personne*) reason with. ~**ement** *n.m.* reasoning; (*propositions*) argument.

rajeunir /raʒœnir/ *v.t.* make (look) younger; (*moderniser*) modernize;

(*méd.*) rejuvenate. —*v.i.* look younger.

rajout /raʒu/ *n.m.* addition. ~**er** /-te/ *v.t.* add.

rajust|er /raʒyste/ *v.t.* straighten; (*salaires*) (re)adjust. ~**ement** *n.m.* (re)adjustment.

râl|e /rɑl/ *n.m.* (*de blessé*) groan. ~**er** *v.i.* groan; (*protester: fam.*) moan.

ralent|ir /ralɑ̃tir/ *v.t./i.,* **se ~ir** *v. pr.* slow down. ~**i** *a.* slow; *n.m.* (*cinéma*) slow motion. **être** *ou* **tourner au ~i,** tick over, idle.

rall|ier /ralje/ *v.t.* rally; (*rejoindre*) rejoin. **se ~ier** *v. pr.* rally. **se ~ier à,** (*avis*) come over to. ~**iement** *n.m.* rallying.

rallonge /ralɔ̃ʒ/ *n.f.* (*de table*) extension. ~ **de,** (*supplément de*) extra.

rallonger /ralɔ̃ʒe/ *v.t.* lengthen.

rallumer /ralyme/ *v.t.* light (up) again; (*lampe*) switch on again; (*ranimer: fig.*) revive.

rallye /rali/ *n.m.* rally.

ramassé /ramase/ *a.* squat; (*concis*) concise.

ramass|er /ramase/ *v.t.* pick up; (*récolter*) gather; (*recueillir*) collect. **se ~er** *v. pr.* draw o.s. together, curl up. ~**age** *n.m.* (*cueillette*) gathering. ~**age scolaire,** school bus service.

rambarde /rɑ̃bard/ *n.f.* guard-rail.

rame /ram/ *n.f.* (*aviron*) oar; (*train*) train; (*perche*) stake.

rameau (*pl.* ~**x**) /ramo/ *n.m.* branch.

ramener /ramne/ *v.t.* bring back. ~ **à,** (*réduire à*) reduce to. **se ~** *v. pr.* (*fam.*) turn up. **se ~ à,** (*problème*) come down to.

ram|er /rame/ *v.i.* row. ~**eur,** ~**euse** *n.m.,f.* rower.

ramif|ier (se) /(sə)ramifje/ *v. pr.* ramify. ~**ication** *n.f.* ramification.

ramollir /ramɔlir/ *v.t.,* **se ~** *v. pr.* soften.

ramon|er /ramɔne/ *v.t.* sweep. ~**eur** *n.m.* (chimney-)sweep.

rampe /rɑ̃p/ *n.f.* banisters; (*pente*) ramp. ~ **de lancement,** launching pad.

ramper /rɑ̃pe/ *v.i.* crawl.

rancart /rɑ̃kar/ *n.m.* **mettre** *ou* **jeter au ~,** (*fam.*) scrap.

ranc|e /rɑ̃s/ *a.* rancid. ~**ir** *v.i.* go *ou* turn rancid.

rancœur /rɑ̃kœr/ *n.f.* resentment.

rançon /rɑ̃sɔ̃/ *n.f.* ransom. ~**ner** /-ɔne/ *v.t.* hold to ransom.

rancun|e /rɑ̃kyn/ *n.f.* grudge. **~ier, ~ière** *a.* vindictive.

randonnée /rɑ̃dɔne/ *n.f.* walk; (*en auto, vélo*) ride.

rang /rɑ̃/ *n.m.* row; (*hiérarchie, condition*) rank. **se mettre en ~s,** line up.

rangée /rɑ̃ʒe/ *n.f.* row.

rang|er /rɑ̃ʒe/ *v.t.* put away; (*chambre etc.*) tidy (up); (*disposer*) place; (*véhicule*) park. **se ~er** *v. pr.* (*véhicule*) park; (*s'écarter*) stand aside; (*s'assagir*) settle down. **se ~er à,** (*avis*) accept. **~ement** *n.m.* (*de chambre*) tidying (up); (*espace*) storage space.

ranimer /ranime/ *v.t.*, **se ~** *v. pr.* revive.

rapace[1] /rapas/ *n.m.* bird of prey.

rapace[2] /rapas/ *a.* grasping.

rapatr|ier /rapatrije/ *v.t.* repatriate. **~iement** *n.m.* repatriation.

râp|e /rɑp/ *n.f.* (*culin.*) grater; (*lime*) rasp. **~er** *v.t.* grate; (*bois*) rasp.

râpé /rɑpe/ *a.* threadbare.

rapetisser /raptise/ *v.t.* make smaller. *—v.i.* get smaller.

râpeu|x, ~se /rɑpø, -z/ *a.* rough.

rapid|e /rapid/ *a.* fast, rapid. *—n.m.* express (train). **~ement** *adv.* fast, rapidly. **~ité** *n.f.* speed.

rapiécer /rapjese/ *v.t.* patch.

rappel /rapɛl/ *n.m.* recall; (*deuxième avis*) reminder; (*de salaire*) back pay.

rappeler /raple/ *v.t.* call back; (*diplomate, réserviste*) recall; (*évoquer*) remind, recall. **~ qch. à qn.,** (*redire*) remind s.o. of sth. **se ~** *v. pr.* remember, recall.

rapport /rapɔr/ *n.m.* connection; (*compte rendu*) report; (*profit*) yield. **~s,** (*relations*) relations. **en ~ avec,** (*accord*) in keeping with. **mettre/se mettre en ~ avec,** put/get in touch with. **par ~ à,** in relation to.

rapport|er /rapɔrte/ *v.t.* bring back; (*profit*) bring in; (*dire, répéter*) report. *—v.i.* (*comm.*) bring in a good return; (*mouchard: fam.*) tell tales. **se ~er à,** relate to. **s'en ~er à,** rely on. **~eur, ~euse** *n.m.,f.* (*mouchard*) telltale; *n.m.* (*instrument*) protractor.

rapproch|er /raprɔʃe/ *v.t.* bring closer (**de,** to); (*réconcilier*) bring together; (*comparer*) compare. **se ~er** *v. pr.* get closer *ou* come closer (**de,** to); (*personnes, pays*) come together; (*s'apparenter*) be close (**de,** to). **~é** *a.* close. **~ement** *n.m.* reconciliation;

(*rapport*) connection; (*comparaison*) parallel.

rapt /rapt/ *n.m.* abduction.

raquette /rakɛt/ *n.f.* (*de tennis*) racket; (*de ping-pong*) bat.

rare /rar/ *a.* rare; (*insuffisant*) scarce. **~ment** *adv.* rarely, seldom. **~té** *n.f.* rarity; scarcity; (*objet*) rarity.

raréfié /rarefje/ *a.* rarefied.

raréfier (se) /(sə)rarefje/ *v. pr.* (*nourriture etc.*) become scarce.

ras, ~e /rɑ, rɑz/ *a.* (*herbe, poil*) short. **à ~ de,** very close to. **en avoir ~ le bol,** (*fam.*) be really fed up. **~e campagne,** open country.

ras|er /rɑze/ *v.t.* shave; (*cheveux, barbe*) shave off; (*frôler*) skim; (*abattre*) raze; (*ennuyer: fam.*) bore. **se ~er** *v. pr.* shave. **~age** *n.m.* shaving. **~eur, ~euse** *n.m.,f.* (*fam.*) bore.

rasoir /rɑzwar/ *n.m.* razor.

rassas|ier /rasazje/ *v.t.* satisfy. **être ~ié de,** have had enough of.

rassembl|er /rasɑ̃ble/ *v.t.* gather; (*courage*) muster. **se ~er** *v. pr.* gather. **~ement** *n.m.* gathering.

rasseoir (se) /(sə)raswar/ *v. pr.* sit down again.

rass|is, ~ise *ou* **~ie** /rasi, -z/ *a.* (*pain*) stale.

rassurer /rasyre/ *v.t.* reassure.

rat /ra/ *n.m.* rat.

ratatiner (se) /(sə)ratatine/ *v. pr.* shrivel up.

rate /rat/ *n.f.* spleen.

râteau (*pl.* **~x**) /rɑto/ *n.m.* rake.

râtelier /rɑtəlje/ *n.m.* (*de bétail*) (stable-)rack; (*support*) rack.

rat|er /rate/ *v.t./i.* miss; (*gâcher*) spoil; (*échouer*) fail. **~é, ~ée** *n.m., f.* (*personne*) failure. **avoir des ~és,** (*auto.*) backfire.

ratif|ier /ratifje/ *v.t.* ratify. **~ication** *n.f.* ratification.

ration /rasjɔ̃/ *n.f.* ration.

rationaliser /rasjonalize/ *v.t.* rationalize.

rationnel, ~le /rasjonɛl/ *a.* rational.

rationn|er /rasjone/ *v.t.* ration. **~ement** *n.m.* rationing.

ratisser /ratise/ *v.t.* rake; (*fouiller*) comb.

rattacher /rataʃe/ *v.t.* tie up again; (*relier*) link; (*incorporer*) join.

rattrapage /ratrapaʒ/ *n.m.* **~ scolaire,** remedial classes.

rattraper /ratrape/ *v.t.* catch; (*rejoin-*

dre) catch up with; (*retard, erreur*) make up for. **se ~** *v. pr.* catch up; (*se dédommager*) make up for it. **se ~ à**, catch hold of.

ratur|e /ratyr/ *n.f.* deletion. **~er** *v.t.* delete.

rauque /rok/ *a.* raucous, harsh.

ravager /ravaʒe/ *v.t.* devastate, ravage.

ravages /ravaʒ/ *n.m. pl.* **faire des ~**, wreak havoc.

raval|er /ravale/ *v.t.* (*façade etc.*) clean; (*humilier*) lower. **~ement** *n.m.* cleaning.

ravauder /ravode/ *v.t.* mend.

ravi /ravi/ *a.* delighted (**que,** that).

ravier /ravje/ *n.m.* hors-d'œuvre dish.

ravigoter /ravigɔte/ *v.t.* (*fam.*) buck up.

ravin /ravɛ̃/ *n.m.* ravine.

ravioli /ravjɔli/ *n.m. pl.* ravioli.

ravir /ravir/ *v.t.* delight. **~ à qn.**, (*enlever*) rob s.o. of.

raviser (se) /(sə)ravize/ *v. pr.* change one's mind.

ravissant, ~e /ravisɑ̃, -t/ *a.* beautiful.

ravisseu|r, ~se /ravisœr, -øz/ *n.m.,f.* kidnapper.

ravitaill|er /ravitaje/ *v.t.* provide with supplies; (*avion*) refuel. **se ~er** *v. pr.* stock up. **~ement** *n.m.* provision of supplies (**de,** to); refuelling; (*denrées*) supplies.

raviver /ravive/ *v.t.* revive.

rayé /reje/ *a.* striped.

rayer /reje/ *v.t.* scratch; (*biffer*) cross out.

rayon /rɛjɔ̃/ *n.m.* ray; (*planche*) shelf; (*de magasin*) department; (*de roue*) spoke; (*de cercle*) radius. **~ d'action**, range. **~ de miel**, honeycomb. **~ X**, X-ray.

rayonn|er /rɛjɔne/ *v.i.* radiate; (*de joie*) beam; (*se déplacer*) tour around (*from a central point*). **~ement** *n.m.* (*éclat*) radiance; (*influence*) influence; (*radiations*) radiation.

rayure /rɛjyr/ *n.f.* scratch; (*dessin*) stripe. **à ~s,** striped.

raz-de-marée /rɑdmare/ *n.m. invar.* tidal wave. **~ électoral,** landslide.

re- /rə/ *préf.* re-.

ré- /re/ *préf.* re-.

réacteur /reaktœr/ *n.m.* jet engine; (*nucléaire*) reactor.

réaction /reaksjɔ̃/ *n.f.* reaction. **~ en chaîne,** chain reaction. **~naire** /-jɔnɛr/ *a. & n.m./f.* reactionary.

réadapter /readapte/ *v.t., se ~* *v. pr.* readjust.

réaffirmer /reafirme/ *v.t.* reaffirm.

réagir /reaʒir/ *v.i.* react.

réalis|er /realize/ *v.t.* carry out; (*effort, bénéfice, achat*) make; (*rêve*) fulfil; (*film*) produce, direct; (*capital*) realize; (*se rendre compte de*: *fam.*) realize. **se ~er** *v. pr.* materialize. **~ateur, ~atrice** *n.m., f.* (*cinéma*) director; (*TV*) producer. **~ation** *n.f.* realization; (*œuvre*) achievement.

réalis|te /realist/ *a.* realistic. **—**n.m./f. realist. **~me** *n.m.* realism.

réalité /realite/ *n.f.* reality.

réanim|er /reanime/ *v.t.* resuscitate. **~ation** *n.f.* resuscitation.

réapparaître /reaparɛtr/ *v.i.* reappear.

réarm|er (se) /(sə)rearme/ *v. pr.* rearm. **~ement** *n.m.* rearmament.

rébarbati|f, ~ve /rebarbatif, -v/ *a.* forbidding, off-putting.

rebâtir /rəbɑtir/ *v.t.* rebuild.

rebattu /rəbaty/ *a.* hackneyed.

rebelle /rəbɛl/ *a.* rebellious; (*soldat*) rebel. **—**n.m./f. rebel.

rebeller (se) /(sə)rəbele/ *v. pr.* rebel, hit back defiantly.

rébellion /rebeljɔ̃/ *n.f.* rebellion.

rebiffer (se) /(sə)rəbife/ *v. pr.* (*fam.*) rebel.

rebond /rəbɔ̃/ *n.m.* bounce; (*par ricochet*) rebound. **~ir** /-dir/ *v.i.* bounce; rebound.

rebondi /rəbɔ̃di/ *a.* chubby.

rebondissement /rəbɔ̃dismɑ̃/ *n.m.* (new) development.

rebord /rəbɔr/ *n.m.* edge. **~ de la fenêtre,** window-ledge.

rebours (à) /(a)rəbur/ *adv.* the wrong way.

rebrousser /rəbruse/ *v.t.* **~ chemin,** turn back.

rebuffade /rəbyfad/ *n.f.* rebuff.

rébus /rebys/ *n.m.* rebus.

rebut /rəby/ *n.m.* **mettre** *ou* **jeter au ~,** scrap.

rebut|er /rəbyte/ *v.t.* put off. **~ant, ~ante** *a.* off-putting.

récalcitrant, ~e /rekalsitrɑ̃, -t/ *a.* stubborn.

recal|er /rəkale/ *v.t.* (*fam.*) fail. **être ~é,** fail.

récapitul|er /rekapityle/ *v.t./i.* recapitulate. **~ation** *n.f.* recapitulation.

recel /rəsɛl/ *n.m.* receiving. **~er**

/rəs(ə)le/ *v.t.* (*objet volé*) receive; (*cacher*) conceal.

récemment /resamã/ *adv.* recently.

recens|er /rəsãse/ *v.t.* (*population*) take a census of; (*objets*) list. **∼ement** *n.m.* census; list.

récent, ∼e /resã, -t/ *a.* recent.

récépissé /resepise/ *n.m.* receipt.

récepteur /reseptœr/ *n.m.* receiver.

récepti|f, ∼ve /reseptif, -v/ *a.* receptive.

réception /resepsjɔ̃/ *n.f.* reception. **∼ de,** (*lettre etc.*) receipt of. **∼niste** /-jɔnist/ *n.m./f.* receptionist.

récession /resesjɔ̃/ *n.f.* recession.

recette /rəsɛt/ *n.f.* (*culin.*) recipe; (*argent*) takings. **∼s,** (*comm.*) receipts.

receveu|r, ∼se /rəsvœr, -øz/ *n.m., f.* (*d'autobus*) (bus-)conductor, (bus-)conductress; (*des impôts*) tax collector.

recevoir† /rəsvwar/ *v.t.* receive; (*obtenir*) get, receive. **être reçu (à),** pass. —*v.i.* (*médecin*) receive patients. **se ∼** *v. pr.* (*tomber*) land.

rechange (de) /(də)rəʃɑ̃ʒ/ *a.* (*roue, vêtements, etc.*) spare; (*politique etc.*) alternative.

réchapper /reʃape/ *v.i.* **∼ de** *ou* **à,** come through, survive.

recharg|e /rəʃarʒ/ *n.f.* (*de stylo*) refill. **∼er** *v.t.* refill; (*batterie*) recharge.

réchaud /reʃo/ *n.m.* stove.

réchauff|er /reʃofe/ *v.t.* warm up. **se ∼er** *v. pr.* warm o.s. up; (*temps*) get warmer. **∼ement** *n.m.* (*de température*) rise (**de,** in).

rêche /rɛʃ/ *a.* harsh.

recherche /rəʃɛrʃ/ *n.f.* search (**de,** for); (*raffinement*) elegance. **∼(s),** (*univ.*) research. **∼s,** (*enquête*) investigations.

recherch|er /rəʃɛrʃe/ *v.t.* search for. **∼é** *a.* in great demand; (*élégant*) elegant. **∼é pour meurtre,** wanted for murder.

rechigner /rəʃiɲe/ *v.i.* **∼ à,** balk at.

rechut|e /rəʃyt/ *n.f.* (*méd.*) relapse. **∼er** *v.i.* relapse.

récidiv|e /residiv/ *n.f.* second offence. **∼er** *v.i.* commit a second offence.

récif /resif/ *n.m.* reef.

récipient /resipjã/ *n.m.* container.

réciproque /resiprɔk/ *a.* mutual, reciprocal. **∼ment** *adv.* each other; (*inversement*) conversely.

récit /resi/ *n.m.* (*compte rendu*) account, story; (*histoire*) story.

récital (*pl.* **∼s**) /resital/ *n.m.* recital.

récit|er /resite/ *v.t.* recite. **∼ation** *n.f.* recitation.

réclame /reklam/ *n.f.* advertising; (*annonce*) advertisement.

réclam|er /reklame/ *v.t.* call for, demand; (*revendiquer*) claim. —*v.i.* complain. **∼ation** *n.f.* complaint.

reclus, ∼e /rəkly, -z/ *n.m., f.* recluse. —*a.* cloistered.

réclusion /reklyzjɔ̃/ *n.f.* imprisonment.

recoin /rəkwɛ̃/ *n.m.* nook.

récolt|e /rekɔlt/ *n.f.* (*action*) harvest; (*produits*) crop, harvest; (*fig.*) crop. **∼er** *v.t.* harvest, gather; (*fig.*) collect.

recommand|er /rəkɔmãde/ *v.t.* recommend; (*lettre*) register. **∼ation** *n.f.* recommendation.

recommencer /rəkɔmãse/ *v.t./i.* (*reprendre*) begin *ou* start again; (*refaire*) repeat.

récompens|e /rekɔ̃pãs/ *n.f.* reward; (*prix*) award. **∼er** *v.t.* reward (**de,** for).

réconcil|ier /rekɔ̃silje/ *v.t.* reconcile. **se ∼ier** *v. pr.* become reconciled. **∼iation** *n.f.* reconciliation.

reconduire† /rəkɔ̃dɥir/ *v.t.* see home; (*à la porte*) show out; (*renouveler*) renew.

réconfort /rekɔ̃fɔr/ *n.m.* comfort. **∼er** /-te/ *v.t.* comfort.

reconnaissable /rəkɔnɛsabl/ *a.* recognizable.

reconnaissan|t, ∼te /rəkɔnɛsã, -t/ *a.* grateful (**de,** for). **∼ce** *n.f.* gratitude; (*fait de reconnaître*) recognition; (*mil.*) reconnaissance.

reconnaître† /rəkɔnɛtr/ *v.t.* recognize; (*admettre*) admit (**que,** that); (*mil.*) reconnoitre. **se ∼** *v. pr.* (*s'orienter*) find one's bearings.

reconstituant /rəkɔ̃stitɥã/ *n.m.* tonic.

reconstituer /rəkɔ̃stitɥe/ *v.t.* reconstitute; (*crime*) reconstruct.

reconstr|uire† /rəkɔ̃strɥir/ *v.t.* rebuild. **∼uction** *n.f.* rebuilding.

reconversion /rəkɔ̃vɛrsjɔ̃/ *n.f.* (*de main-d'œuvre*) redeployment.

record /rəkɔr/ *n.m. & a. invar.* record.

recouper /rəkupe/ *v.t.* confirm. **se ∼** *v. pr.* check, tally, match up.

recourbé /rəkurbe/ *a.* curved; (*nez*) hooked.

recourir /rəkurir/ *v.i.* **∼ à,** resort to.

recours /rəkur/ *n.m.* resort. **avoir ∼ à,** have recourse to, resort to.

recouvrer /rəkuvre/ v.t. recover.

recouvrir† /rəkuvrir/ v.t. cover.

récréation /rekreɑsjɔ̃/ n.f. recreation; (scol.) playtime.

récrier (se) /(sə)rekrije/ v. pr. cry out.

récrimination /rekriminɑsjɔ̃/ n.f. recrimination.

recroqueviller (se) /(sə)rəkrɔkvije/ v. pr. curl up.

recrudescence /rəkrydesɑ̃s/ n.f. new outbreak.

recrue /rəkry/ n.f. recruit.

recrut|er /rəkryte/ v.t. recruit. ~e-ment n.m. recruitment.

rectang|le /rɛktɑ̃gl/ n.m. rectangle. ~ulaire a. rectangular.

rectif|ier /rɛktifje/ v.t. correct, rectify. ~ication n.f. correction.

recto /rɛkto/ n.m. front of the page.

reçu /rəsy/ voir **recevoir**. —n.m. receipt. —a. accepted; (candidat) successful.

recueil /rəkœj/ n.m. collection.

recueill|ir† /rəkœjir/ v.t. collect; (prendre chez soi) take in. **se** ~ir v. pr. meditate. ~ement n.m. meditation. ~i a. meditative.

recul /rəkyl/ n.m. retreat; (éloignement) distance; (déclin) decline. (mouvement de) ~, backward movement. ~ade n.f. retreat.

reculé /rəkyle/ a. remote.

reculer /rəkyle/ v.t./i. move back; (véhicule) reverse; (armée) retreat; (diminuer) decline; (différer) postpone. ~ **devant,** (fig.) shrink from.

reculons (à) /(a)rəkylɔ̃/ adv. backwards.

récupér|er /rekypere/ v.t./i. recover; (vieux objets) salvage. ~ation n.f. recovery; salvage.

récurer /rekyre/ v.t. scour.

récuser /rekyze/ v.t. challenge. **se** ~ v. pr. state that one is not qualified to judge.

recycl|er /rəsikle/ v.t. (personne) retrain; (chose) recycle. **se** ~er v. pr. retrain. ~age n.m. retraining; recycling.

rédac|teur, ~trice /redaktœr, -tris/ n.m., f. writer, editor. **le** ~teur en chef,** the editor (in chief).

rédaction /redaksjɔ̃/ n.f. writing; (scol.) composition; (personnel) editorial staff.

reddition /redisjɔ̃/ n.f. surrender.

redevance /rədvɑ̃s/ n.f. (de télévision) licence fee.

rédiger /rediʒe/ v.t. write; (contrat) draw up.

redire† /rədir/ v.t. repeat. **avoir** ou **trouver à** ~ **à,** find fault with.

redondant, ~e /rədɔ̃dɑ̃, -t/ a. superfluous.

redonner /rədɔne/ v.t. give back; (davantage) give more.

redoubl|er /rəduble/ v.t./i. increase; (classe: scol.) repeat. ~er de prudence/etc., be more careful/etc. ~e-ment n.m. (accroissement) increase (de, in).

redout|er /rədute/ v.t. dread. ~able a. formidable.

redoux /rədu/ n.m. milder weather.

redress|er /rədrese/ v.t. straighten (out ou up); (situation) right, redress. **se** ~er v. pr. (personne) straighten (o.s) up; (se remettre debout) stand up; (pays, économie) recover. ~ement /rədrɛsmɑ̃/ n.m. (relèvement) recovery.

réduction /redyksjɔ̃/ n.f. reduction.

réduire† /reduir/ v.t. reduce (à, to). **se** ~ **à,** (revenir à) come down to.

réduit¹, ~e /redui, -t/ a. (objet) small-scale; (limité) limited.

réduit² /redui/ n.m. recess.

réédu|quer /reedyke/ v.t. (personne) rehabilitate; (membre) re-educate. ~cation n.f. rehabilitation; re-education.

réel, ~le /reɛl/ a. real. —n.m. reality. ~lement adv. really.

réexpédier /reɛkspedje/ v.t. forward; (retourner) send back.

refaire† /rəfɛr/ v.t. do again; (erreur, voyage) make again; (réparer) do up, redo.

réfection /refɛksjɔ̃/ n.f. repair.

réfectoire /refɛktwar/ n.m. refectory.

référence /referɑ̃s/ n.f. reference.

référendum /referɛ̃dɔm/ n.m. referendum.

référer /refere/ v.i. **en** ~ **à,** refer the matter to. **se** ~ **à,** refer to.

refermer /rəfɛrme/ v.t., **se** ~, v. pr. close (again).

refiler /rəfile/ v.t. (fam.) palm off (à, on).

réfléch|ir /refleʃir/ v.i. think (à, about). —v.t. reflect. **se** ~ir v. pr. be reflected. ~i a. (personne) thoughtful; (verbe) reflexive.

refl|et /rəflɛ/ n.m. reflection; (lumière) light. ~éter /-ete/ v.t. reflect. **se** ~éter v. pr. be reflected.

réflexe /reflɛks/ *a. & n.m.* reflex.

réflexion /reflɛksjɔ̃/ *n.f.* reflection; (*pensée*) thought, reflection. **à la** ～, on second thoughts.

refluer /rəflye/ *v.i.* flow back; (*foule*) retreat.

reflux /rəfly/ *n.m.* (*de marée*) ebb.

refondre /rəfɔ̃dr/ *v.t.* recast.

réform|e /reform/ *n.f.* reform. ～**ateur**, ～**atrice** *n.m., f.* reformer. ～**er** *v.t.* reform; (*soldat*) invalid (out of the army). **se** ～**er** *v. pr.* mend one's ways.

refoul|er /rəfule/ *v.t.* force back; (*désir*) repress. ～**é** *a.* repressed. ～**ement** *n.m.* repression.

réfractaire /refraktɛr/ *a.* **être** ～ **à**, resist.

refrain /rəfrɛ̃/ *n.m.* chorus.

refréner /rəfrene/ *v.t.* curb, check.

réfrigér|er /refriʒere/ *v.t.* refrigerate. ～**ateur** *n.m.* refrigerator.

refroid|ir /rəfrwadir/ *v.t./i.* cool (down). **se** ～**ir** *v. pr.* (*personne, temps*) get cold; (*ardeur*) cool (off). ～**issement** *n.m.* cooling; (*rhume*) chill.

refuge /rəfyʒ/ *n.m.* refuge; (*chalet*) mountain hut.

réfug|ier (se) /(sə)refyʒje/ *v. pr.* take refuge. ～**ié**, ～**iée** *n.m., f.* refugee.

refus /rəfy/ *n.m.* refusal. ～**er** /-ze/ *v.t.* refuse (**de**, to); (*recaler*) fail. **se** ～**er à**, (*évidence etc.*) reject.

réfuter /refyte/ *v.t.* refute.

regagner /rəgaɲe/ *v.t.* regain; (*revenir à*) get back to.

regain /rəgɛ̃/ *n.m.* ～ **de**, renewal of.

régal (*pl.* ～**s**) /regal/ *n.m.* treat. ～**er** *v.t.* treat (**de**, to). **se** ～**er** *v. pr.* treat o.s. (**de**, to).

regard /rəgar/ *n.m.* (*expression, coup d'œil*) look; (*fixe*) stare; (*vue, œil*) eye. **au** ～ **de**, in regard to. **en** ～ **de**, compared with.

regardant, ～**e** /rəgardɑ̃, -t/ *a.* careful (with money).

regarder /rəgarde/ *v.t.* look at; (*observer*) watch; (*considérer*) consider; (*concerner*) concern. ～ (**fixement**), stare at. —*v.i.* look. ～ **à**, (*qualité etc.*) pay attention to. ～ **vers**, (*maison*) face. **se** ～ *v. pr.* (*personnes*) look at each other.

régates /regat/ *n.f. pl.* regatta.

régénérer /reʒenere/ *v.t.* regenerate.

régen|t, ～**te** /reʒɑ̃, -t/ *n.m., f.* regent. ～**ce** *n.f.* regency.

régenter /reʒɑ̃te/ *v.t.* rule.

régie /reʒi/ *n.f.* (*entreprise*) public corporation.

regimber /rəʒɛ̃be/ *v.i.* balk.

régime /reʒim/ *n.m.* system; (*pol.*) regime; (*méd.*) diet; (*de moteur*) speed; (*de bananes*) bunch.

régiment /reʒimɑ̃/ *n.m.* regiment.

région /reʒjɔ̃/ *n.f.* region. ～**al** (*m. pl.* ～**aux**) /-jɔnal, -o/ *a.* regional.

régir /reʒir/ *v.t.* govern.

régisseur /reʒisœr/ *n.m.* (*théâtre*) stage-manager.

registre /rəʒistr/ *n.m.* register.

réglage /reglaʒ/ *n.m.* adjustment.

règle /rɛgl/ *n.f.* rule; (*instrument*) ruler. ～**s**, (*de femme*) period. **en** ～, in order. ～ **à calculer**, slide-rule.

réglé /regle/ *a.* (*vie*) ordered.

règlement /rɛgləmɑ̃/ *n.m.* regulation; (*règles*) regulations; (*solution, paiement*) settlement. ～**aire** /-tɛr/ *a.* (*uniforme*) regulation.

réglement|er /rɛgləmɑ̃te/ *v.t.* regulate. ～**ation** *n.f.* regulation.

régler /regle/ *v.t.* settle; (*machine*) adjust; (*personne*) settle up with; (*papier*) rule. —*v.i.* (*payer*) settle (up). ～ **son compte à**, settle a score with.

réglisse /reglis/ *n.f.* liquorice.

règne /rɛɲ/ *n.m.* reign; (*végétal, animal, minéral*) kingdom.

régner /reɲe/ *v.i.* reign.

regorger /rəgɔrʒe/ *v.i.* ～ **de**, be overflowing with.

regret /rəgrɛ/ *n.m.* regret. **à** ～, with regret.

regrett|er /rəgrete/ *v.t.* regret; (*personne*) miss. ～**able** *a.* regrettable.

regrouper /rəgrupe/ *v.t.*, **se** ～ *v. pr.* gather (together).

régulariser /regylarize/ *v.t.* regularize.

régulation /regylasjɔ̃/ *n.f.* regulation.

régul|ier, ～**ière** /regylje, -jɛr/ *a.* regular; (*qualité, vitesse*) steady, even; (*ligne, paysage*) even; (*légal*) legal; (*honnête*) honest. ～**arité** *n.f.* regularity; steadiness; evenness. ～**ièrement** *adv.* regularly; (*d'ordinaire*) normally.

réhabilit|er /reabilite/ *n.f.* rehabilitate. ～**ation** *n.f.* rehabilitation.

rehausser /rəose/ *v.t.* raise; (*faire valoir*) enhance.

rein /rɛ̃/ *n.m.* kidney. ～**s**, (*dos*) small of the back.

reine /rɛn/ *n.f.* queen. ～**-claude** *n.f.* greengage.

réinsertion /reɛ̃sɛrsjɔ̃/ *n.f.* reintegration, rehabilitation.

réitérer /reitere/ *v.t.* repeat.

rejaillir /rəʒajir/ *v.i.* ~ **sur,** rebound on.

rejet /rəʒɛ/ *n.m.* rejection.

rejeter /rəʒte/ *v.t.* throw back; (*refuser*) reject; (*vomir*) bring up; (*déverser*) discharge. ~ **une faute** /*etc.* **sur qn.,** shift the blame for a mistake/*etc.* on to s.o.

rejeton(s) /rəʒtɔ̃/ *n.m.* (*pl.*) (*fam.*) offspring.

rejoindre† /rəʒwɛ̃dr/ *v.t.* go back to, rejoin; (*rattraper*) catch up with; (*rencontrer*) join, meet. se ~ *v. pr.* (*personnes*) meet; (*routes*) join, meet.

réjoui /reʒwi/ *a.* joyful.

réjou|ir /reʒwir/ *v.t.* delight. se ~ir *v. pr.* be delighted (**de qch.,** at sth.). ~issances *n.f. pl.* festivities. ~issant, ~issante *a.* cheering.

relâche /rəlaʃ/ *n.m.* (*repos*) respite. faire ~, (*théâtre*) close.

relâché /rəlaʃe/ *a.* lax.

relâch|er /rəlaʃe/ *v.t.* slacken; (*personne*) release; (*discipline*) relax. se ~er *v. pr.* slacken. ~ement *n.m.* slackening.

relais /rəlɛ/ *n.m.* relay. ~ (**routier**), roadside café.

relanc|e /rəlɑ̃s/ *n.f.* boost. ~er *v.t.* boost, revive; (*renvoyer*) throw back.

relati|f, ~ve /rəlatif, -v/ *a.* relative.

relation /rəlasjɔ̃/ *n.f.* relation(ship); (*ami*) acquaintance; (*récit*) account. ~s, relations. en ~ avec qn., in touch with s.o.

relativement /rəlativmɑ̃/ *adv.* relatively. ~ à, in relation to.

relativité /rəlativite/ *n.f.* relativity.

relax|er (se) /(sə)rəlakse/ *v. pr.* relax. ~ation *n.f.* relaxation.

relayer /rəleje/ *v.t.* relieve; (*émission*) relay. se ~ *v. pr.* take over from one another.

reléguer /rəlege/ *v.t.* relegate.

relent /rəlɑ̃/ *n.m.* stench.

relève /rəlɛv/ *n.f.* relief. **prendre** *ou* **assurer la** ~, take over (**de,** from).

relevé /rəlve/ *n.m.* list; (*de compte*) statement; (*de compteur*) reading.

relèvement /rəlɛvmɑ̃/ *n.m.* recovery.

relever /rəlve/ *v.t.* pick up; (*personne tombée*) help up; (*remonter*) raise; (*col*) turn up; (*manches*) roll up; (*sauce*) season; (*goût*) bring out; (*compteur*)

read; (*défi*) accept; (*relayer*) relieve; (*remarquer, noter*) note; (*rebâtir*) rebuild. ~ **qn. de,** relieve s.o. of. —*v.i.* ~ **de,** (*dépendre de*) be the concern of; (*méd.*) recover from. se ~ *v. pr.* (*personne*) get up (again); (*pays, économie*) recover.

relief /rəljɛf/ *n.m.* relief. **mettre en** ~, highlight.

relier /rəlje/ *v.t.* link (**à,** to); (*ensemble*) link together; (*livre*) bind.

religieu|x, ~se /rəliʒjø, -z/ *a.* religious. —*n.m.* monk. —*n.f.* nun.

religion /rəliʒjɔ̃/ *n.f.* religion.

reliquat /rəlika/ *n.m.* residue.

relique /rəlik/ *n.f.* relic.

reliure /rəljyr/ *n.f.* binding.

reluire /rəlɥir/ *v.i.* shine. **faire** ~, shine.

reluisant, ~e /rəlɥizɑ̃, -t/ *a.* shiny. **peu** *ou* **pas** ~, not brilliant.

reman|ier /rəmanje/ *v.t.* revise; (*ministère*) reshuffle. ~iement *n.m.* revision; reshuffle.

remarier (se) /(sə)rəmarje/ *v. pr.* remarry.

remarquable /rəmarkabl/ *a.* remarkable.

remarque /rəmark/ *n.f.* remark.

remarquer /rəmarke/ *v.t.* notice; (*dire*) say. **faire** ~, point out (**à,** to). **se faire** ~, attract attention.

remblai /rɑ̃blɛ/ *n.m.* embankment.

rembourrer /rɑ̃bure/ *v.t.* pad.

rembours|er /rɑ̃burse/ *v.t.* repay; (*billet, frais*) refund. ~ement *n.m.* repayment; refund.

remède /rəmɛd/ *n.m.* remedy; (*médicament*) medicine.

remédier /rəmedje/ *v.i.* ~ **à,** remedy.

remémorer (se) /(sə)rəmemɔre/ *v. pr.* recall.

remerc|ier /rəmɛrsje/ *v.t.* thank (**de,** for); (*licencier*) dismiss. ~iements *n.m. pl.* thanks.

remettre† /rəmɛtr/ *v.t.* put back; (*vêtement*) put back on; (*donner*) hand (over); (*devoir, démission*) hand in; (*restituer*) give back; (*différer*) put off; (*ajouter*) add; (*se rappeler*) remember; (*peine*) remit. se ~ *v. pr.* (*guérir*) recover. se ~ **à,** go back to. se ~ **à faire,** start doing again. **s'en** ~ **à,** leave it to. ~ **en cause** *ou* **en question,** call into question.

remise[1] /rəmiz/ *n.f.* (*abri*) shed.

remise[2] /rəmiz/ *n.f.* (*rabais*) discount; (*livraison*) delivery; (*ajournement*) postponement. ~ **en cause** *ou* **en question,** calling into question.

remiser /rəmize/ *v.t.* put away.

rémission /remisjɔ̃/ *n.f.* remission.

remontant /rəmɔ̃tã/ *n.m.* tonic.

remontée /rəmɔ̃te/ *n.f.* ascent; (*d'eau, de prix*) rise. ~ **mécanique,** ski-lift.

remont|er /rəmɔ̃te/ *v.i.* go *ou* come (back) up; (*prix, niveau*) rise (again); (*revenir*) go back. —*v.t.* (*rue etc.*) go *ou* come (back) up; (*relever*) raise; (*montre*) wind up; (*objet démonté*) put together again; (*personne*) buck up. ~**epente** *n.m.* ski-lift.

remontoir /rəmɔ̃twar/ *n.m.* winder.

remontrer /rəmɔ̃tre/ *v.t.* show again.

remords /rəmɔr/ *n.m.* remorse. **avoir un** *ou* **des** ~, feel remorse.

remorqu|e /rəmɔrk/ *n.f.* (*véhicule*) trailer. **en** ~**e,** on tow. ~**er** *v.t.* tow.

remorqueur /rəmɔrkœr/ *n.m.* tug.

remous /rəmu/ *n.m.* eddy; (*de bateau*) backwash; (*fig.*) turmoil.

rempart /rãpar/ *n.m.* rampart.

remplaçant, ~**e** /rãplasã, -t/ *n.m., f.* replacement; (*joueur*) reserve.

remplac|er /rãplase/ *v.t.* replace. ~**e-ment** *n.m.* replacement.

rempli /rãpli/ *a.* full (**de,** of).

rempl|ir /rãplir/ *v.t.* fill (up); (*formulaire*) fill (in *ou* out); (*tâche, condition*) fulfil. **se** ~**ir** *v. pr.* fill (up). ~**issage** *n.m.* filling; (*de texte*) padding.

remporter /rãpɔrte/ *v.t.* take back; (*victoire*) win.

remuant, ~**e** /rəmɥã, -t/ *a.* restless.

remue-ménage /rəmymenaʒ/ *n.m. invar.* commotion, bustle.

remuer /rəmɥe/ *v.t./i.* move; (*thé, café*) stir; (*gigoter*) fidget; (*dent*) be loose. **se** ~ *v. pr.* move.

rémunér|er /remynere/ *v.t.* pay. ~**a-tion** *n.f.* payment.

renâcler /rənɑkle/ *v.i.* snort. ~ **à,** balk at, jib at.

ren|aître /rənɛtr/ *v.i.* be reborn; (*sentiment*) be revived. ~**aissance** *n.f.* rebirth.

renard /rənar/ *n.m.* fox.

renchérir /rãʃerir/ *v.i.* become dearer. ~ **sur,** go one better than.

rencontr|er /rãkɔ̃tr/ *n.f.* meeting; (*de routes*) junction; (*mil.*) encounter; (*match*) match; (*Amer.*) game. ~**er** *v.t.* meet; (*heurter*) strike; (*trouver*) find. **se** ~**er** *v. pr.* meet.

rendement /rãdmã/ *n.m.* yield; (*travail*) output.

rendez-vous /rãdevu/ *n.m.* appointment; (*d'amoureux*) date; (*lieu*) meeting-place.

rendormir (se) /(sə)rãdɔrmir/ *v. pr.* go back to sleep.

rendre /rãdr/ *v.t.* give back, return; (*donner en retour*) return; (*son, monnaie*) give; (*hommage*) pay; (*justice*) dispense; (*jugement*) pronounce; (*expression*) render. ~ **heureux/possible/***etc.*, make happy/possible/ *etc.* —*v.i.* (*terres*) yield; (*vomir*) vomit. **se** ~ *v. pr.* (*capituler*) surrender; (*aller*) go (**à,** to); (*ridicule, utile, etc.*) make o.s. ~ **compte de,** report on. ~ **des comptes à,** be accountable to. ~ **justice à qn.,** do s.o. justice. ~ **service (à),** help. ~ **visite à,** visit. **se** ~ **compte de,** realize.

rendu /rãdy/ *a.* (*fatigué*) exhausted. **être** ~, (*arrivé*) have arrived.

rêne /rɛn/ *n.f.* rein.

renégat, ~**e** /rənega, -t/ *n.m., f.* renegade.

renfermé /rãfɛrme/ *n.m.* stale smell. **sentir le** ~, smell stale.

renferm|er /rãfɛrme/ *v.t.* contain. **se** ~**er (en soi-même),** withdraw (into o.s.).

renfl|é /rãfle/ *a.* bulging. ~**ement** *n.m.* bulge.

renflouer /rãflue/ *v.t.* refloat.

renfoncement /rãfɔ̃smã/ *n.m.* recess.

renforcer /rãfɔrse/ *v.t.* reinforce.

renfort /rãfɔr/ *n.m.* reinforcement. **de** ~, (*armée, personnel*) back-up.

renfrogn|er (se) /(sə)rãfrɔɲe/ *v. pr.* scowl. ~**é** *a.* surly, sullen.

rengaine /rãgɛn/ *n.f.* old song.

renier /rənje/ *v.t.* (*personne, pays*) disown, deny; (*foi*) renounce.

renifler /rənifle/ *v.t./i.* sniff.

renne /rɛn/ *n.m.* reindeer.

renom /rənɔ̃/ *n.m.* renown; (*réputation*) reputation. ~**mé** /-ɔme/ *a.* famous. ~**mée** /-ɔme/ *n.f.* fame; reputation.

renonc|er /rənɔ̃se/ *v.i.* ~**er à,** (*habitude, ami, etc.*) give up, renounce. ~**er à faire,** give up (all thought of) doing. ~**ement** *n.m.*, ~**iation** *n.f.* renunciation.

renouer /rənwe/ *v.t.* tie up (again); (*reprendre*) renew. —*v.i.* ~ **avec,** start up again with.

renouveau (*pl.* ~**x**) /rənuvo/ *n.m.* revival.

renouvel|er /rənuvle/ *v.t.* renew;

(*réitérer*) repeat. **se** ~**er** *v. pr.* be renewed; be repeated. ~**lement** /-vɛlmɑ̃/ *n.m.* renewal.

rénov|er /renɔve/ *v.t.* (*édifice*) renovate; (*institution*) reform. ~**ation** *n.f.* renovation; reform.

renseignement /rɑ̃sɛɲmɑ̃/ *n.m.* ~(**s**), information.

renseigner /rɑ̃seɲe/ *v.t.* inform, give information to. **se** ~ *v. pr.* enquire, make enquiries, find out.

rentab|le /rɑ̃tabl/ *a.* profitable. ~**ilité** *n.f.* profitability.

rent|e /rɑ̃t/ *n.f.* (private) income; (*pension*) pension, annuity. ~**ier**, ~**ière** *n.m., f.* person of private means.

rentrée /rɑ̃tre/ *n.f.* return; (*d'un acteur*) come-back; (*parlementaire*) reopening; (*scol.*) start of the new year.

rentrer /rɑ̃tre/ (*aux. être*) *v.i.* go *ou* come back home, return home; (*entrer*) go *ou* come in; (*entrer à nouveau*) go *ou* come back in; (*revenu*) come in; (*élèves*) go back. ~ **dans**, (*heurter*) smash into. —*v.t.* (*aux. avoir*) bring in; (*griffes*) draw in; (*vêtement*) tuck in.

renverse (à la) /(ala)rɑ̃vɛrs/ *adv.* backwards.

renvers|er /rɑ̃vɛrse/ *v.t.* knock over *ou* down; (*piéton*) knock down; (*liquide*) upset, spill; (*mettre à l'envers*) turn upside down; (*gouvernement*) overturn; (*inverser*) reverse; (*étonner: fam.*) astound. **se** ~**er** *v. pr.* (*véhicule*) overturn; (*verre, vase*) fall over. ~**ement** *n.m.* (*pol.*) overthrow.

renv|oi /rɑ̃vwa/ *n.m.* return; dismissal; expulsion; postponement; reference; (*rot*) belch. ~**oyer†** *v.t.* send back, return; (*employé*) dismiss; (*élève*) expel; (*ajourner*) postpone; (*référer*) refer; (*réfléchir*) reflect.

réorganiser /reɔrganize/ *v.t.* reorganize.

réouverture /reuvɛrtyr/ *n.f.* reopening.

repaire /rəpɛr/ *n.m.* den.

répandre /repɑ̃dr/ *v.t.* (*liquide*) spill; (*étendre, diffuser*) spread; (*lumière, sang*) shed; (*odeur*) give off. **se** ~ *v. pr.* spread; (*liquide*) spill. **se** ~ **en**, (*injures etc.*) pour forth, launch forth into.

répandu /repɑ̃dy/ *a.* (*courant*) widespread.

répar|er /repare/ *v.t.* repair, mend; (*faute*) make amends for; (*remédier*

à) put right. ~**ateur** *n.m.* repairer. ~**ation** *n.f.* repair; (*compensation*) compensation.

repartie /rəparti/ *n.f.* retort.

repartir† /rəpartir/ *v.i.* start (up) again; (*voyageur*) set off again; (*s'en retourner*) go back.

répart|ir /repartir/ *v.t.* distribute; (*partager*) share out; (*étaler*) spread. ~**ition** *n.f.* distribution.

repas /rəpɑ/ *n.m.* meal.

repass|er /rəpɑse/ *v.i.* come *ou* go back. —*v.t.* (*linge*) iron; (*leçon*) go over; (*couteau*) sharpen. ~**age** *n.m.* ironing.

repêcher /rəpeʃe/ *v.t.* fish out; (*candidat*) allow to pass.

repentir /rəpɑ̃tir/ *n.m.* repentance. **se** ~ *v. pr.* (*relig.*) repent (**de**, of). **se** ~ **de**, (*regretter*) regret.

répercu|ter /repɛrkyte/ *v.t.* (*bruit*) echo. **se** ~**ter** *v. pr.* echo. **se** ~**ter sur**, have repercussions on. ~**ssion** *n.f.* repercussion.

repère /rəpɛr/ *n.m.* mark; (*jalon*) marker; (*fig.*) landmark.

repérer /repere/ *v.t.* locate, spot. **se** ~ *v. pr.* find one's bearings.

répert|oire /repɛrtwar/ *n.m.* index; (*artistique*) repertoire. ~**orier** *v.t.* index.

répéter /repete/ *v.t.* repeat. —*v.t./i.* (*théâtre*) rehearse. **se** ~ *v. pr.* be repeated; (*personne*) repeat o.s.

répétition /repetisjɔ̃/ *n.f.* repetition; (*théâtre*) rehearsal.

repiquer /rəpike/ *v.t.* (*plante*) plant out; (*photo, texte*) touch up.

répit /repi/ *n.m.* rest, respite.

replacer /rəplase/ *v.t.* replace.

repl|i /rəpli/ *n.m.* fold; (*retrait*) withdrawal. ~**ier** *v.t.* fold (up); (*ailes, jambes*) tuck in. **se** ~**ier** *v. pr.* withdraw (**sur soi-même**, into o.s.).

répliqu|e /replik/ *n.f.* reply; (*riposte*) retort; (*discussion*) objection; (*théâtre*) line(s); (*copie*) replica. ~**er** *v.t./i.* reply; (*riposter*) retort; (*objecter*) answer back.

répondant, ~e /repɔ̃dɑ̃, -t/ *n.m., f.* guarantor. **avoir du** ~, have money behind one.

répondre /repɔ̃dr/ *v.t.* (*remarque etc.*) reply with. ~ **que**, answer *ou* reply that. —*v.i.* answer, reply; (*être insolent*) answer back; (*réagir*) respond (**à**, to). ~ **à**, answer. ~ **de**, answer for.

réponse /repõs/ *n.f.* answer, reply; (*fig.*) response.

report /rəpɔr/ *n.m.* (*transcription*) transfer; (*renvoi*) postponement.

reportage /rəpɔrtaʒ/ *n.m.* report; (*en direct*) commentary.

reporter[1] /rəpɔrte/ *v.t.* take back; (*ajourner*) put off; (*transcrire*) transfer. **se ~ à,** refer to.

reporter[2] /rəpɔrtɛr/ *n.m.* reporter.

repos /rəpo/ *n.m.* rest; (*paix*) peace; (*tranquillité*) peace and quiet; (*moral*) peace of mind.

repos|er /rəpoze/ *v.t.* put down again; (*délasser*) rest. −*v.i.* rest (**sur,** on). **se ~er** *v. pr.* rest. **se ~er sur,** rely on. **~ant, ~ante** *a.* restful.

repoussant, ~e /rəpusã, -t/ *a.* repulsive.

repousser /rəpuse/ *v.t.* push back; (*écarter*) push away; (*dégoûter*) repel; (*décliner*) reject; (*ajourner*) put back. −*v.i.* grow again.

répréhensible /repreãsibl/ *a.* blameworthy.

reprendre† /rəprãdr/ *v.t.* take back; (*retrouver*) regain; (*souffle*) get back; (*évadé*) recapture; (*recommencer*) resume; (*redire*) repeat; (*modifier*) alter; (*blâmer*) reprimand. **~ du pain**/*etc.*, take some more bread/*etc.* −*v.i.* (*recommencer*) resume; (*affaires*) pick up. **se ~** *v. pr.* (*se ressaisir*) pull o.s. together; (*se corriger*) correct o.s.

représailles /rəprezaj/ *n.f. pl.* reprisals.

représentati|f, ~ve /rəprezãtatif, -v/ *a.* representative.

représent|er /rəprezãte/ *v.t.* represent; (*théâtre*) perform. **se ~er** *v. pr.* (*s'imaginer*) imagine. **~ant, ~ante** *n.m., f.* representative. **~ation** *n.f.* representation; (*théâtre*) performance.

réprimand|e /reprimãd/ *n.f.* reprimand. **~er** *v.t.* reprimand.

répr|imer /reprime/ *v.t.* repress. **~ession** *n.f.* repression.

repris /rəpri/ *n.m.* **~ de justice,** ex-convict.

reprise /rəpriz/ *n.f.* resumption; (*théâtre*) revival; (*télévision*) repeat; (*de tissu*) darn, mend; (*essor*) recovery; (*comm.*) part-exchange, trade-in. **à plusieurs ~s,** on several occasions.

repriser /rəprize/ *v.t.* darn, mend.

réprobation /reprɔbasjõ/ *n.f.* condemnation.

reproch|e /rəprɔʃ/ *n.m.* reproach, blame. **~er** *v.t.* **~er qch. à qn.,** reproach *ou* blame s.o. for sth.

reprod|uire† /rəprɔdɥir/ *v.t.* reproduce. **se ~uire** *v. pr.* reproduce; (*arriver*) recur. **~ucteur, ~uctrice** *a.* reproductive. **~uction** *n.f.* reproduction.

réprouver /repruve/ *v.t.* condemn.

reptile /rɛptil/ *n.m.* reptile.

repu /rəpy/ *a.* satiated.

républi|que /repyblik/ *n.f.* republic. **~que populaire,** people's republic. **~cain, ~caine** *a. & n.m., f.* republican.

répudier /repydje/ *v.t.* repudiate.

répugnance /repyɲãs/ *n.f.* repugnance; (*hésitation*) reluctance.

répugn|er /repyɲe/ *v.i.* **~er à,** be repugnant to. **~er à faire,** be reluctant to do. **~ant, ~ante** *a.* repulsive.

répulsion /repylsjõ/ *n.f.* repulsion.

réputation /repytasjõ/ *n.f.* reputation.

réputé /repyte/ *a.* renowned. **~ pour être,** reputed to be.

requérir /rəkerir/ *v.t.* require, demand.

requête /rəkɛt/ *n.f.* request; (*jurid.*) petition.

requiem /rekɥijɛm/ *n.m. invar.* requiem.

requin /rəkɛ̃/ *n.m.* shark.

requis, ~e /rəki, -z/ *a.* required.

réquisition /rekizisjõ/ *n.f.* requisition. **~ner** /-jɔne/ *v.t.* requisition.

rescapé, ~e /rɛskape/ *n.m., f.* survivor. −*a.* surviving.

rescousse /rɛskus/ *n.f.* **à la ~,** to the rescue.

réseau (*pl.* **~x**) /rezo/ *n.m.* network.

réservation /rezɛrvasjõ/ *n.f.* reservation.

réserve /rezɛrv/ *n.f.* reserve; (*restriction*) reservation, reserve; (*indienne*) reservation; (*entrepôt*) store-room. **en ~,** in reserve. **les ~s,** (*mil.*) the reserves.

réserv|er /rezɛrve/ *v.t.* reserve; (*place*) book, reserve. **se ~er le droit de,** reserve the right to. **~é** *a.* (*personne, place*) reserved.

réserviste /rezɛrvist/ *n.m.* reservist.

réservoir /rezɛrvwar/ *n.m.* tank; (*lac*) reservoir.

résidence /rezidãs/ *n.f.* residence.

résident, ~e /rezidã, -t/ *n.m., f.* resident foreigner. ~**iel**, ~**ielle** /-sjɛl/ *a.* residential.

résider /rezide/ *v.i.* reside.

résidu /rezidy/ *n.m.* residue.

résign|er (se) /(sə)reziɲe/ *v. pr.* resign o.s. ~**ation** *n.f.* resignation.

résilier /rezilje/ *v.t.* terminate.

résille /rezij/ *n.f.* (hair-)net.

résine /rezin/ *n.f.* resin.

résistance /rezistɑ̃s/ *n.f.* resistance; (*fil électrique*) element.

résistant, ~**e** /rezistɑ̃, -t/ *a.* tough.

résister /reziste/ *v.i.* resist. ~ **à**, resist (*examen, chaleur*) stand up to.

résolu /rezɔly/ *voir* **résoudre**. —*a.* resolute. ~ **à**, resolved to. ~**ment** *adv.* resolutely.

résolution /rezɔlysjɔ̃/ *n.f.* resolution.

résonance /rezɔnɑ̃s/ *n.f.* resonance.

résonner /rezɔne/ *v.i.* resound.

résor|ber /rezɔrbe/ *v.t.* reduce. **se** ~**ber** *v. pr.* be reduced. ~**ption** *n.f.* reduction.

résoudre† /rezudr/ *v.t.* solve; (*décider*) decide on. ~ **de, se** ~ **à**, resolve to.

respect /rɛspɛ/ *n.m.* respect.

respectab|le /rɛspɛktabl/ *a.* respectable. ~**ilité** *n.f.* respectability.

respecter /rɛspɛkte/ *v.t.* respect. **faire** ~, (*loi, décision*) enforce.

respecti|f, ~**ve** /rɛspɛktif, -v/ *a.* respective. ~**vement** *adv.* respectively.

respectueu|x, ~**se** /rɛspɛktɥø, -z/ *a.* respectful.

respir|er /rɛspire/ *v.i.* breathe; (*se reposer*) get one's breath. —*v.t.* breathe; (*exprimer*) radiate. ~**ation** *n.f.* breathing; (*haleine*) breath. ~**atoire** *a.* breathing.

resplend|ir /rɛsplɑ̃dir/ *v.i.* shine. ~**issant**, ~**issante** *a.* radiant.

responsabilité /rɛspɔ̃sabilite/ *n.f.* responsibility; (*légale*) liability.

responsable /rɛspɔ̃sabl/ *a.* responsible (**de**, for). ~ **de**, (*chargé de*) in charge of. —*n.m./f.* person in charge; (*coupable*) person responsible.

resquiller /rɛskije/ *v.i.* get in without paying; (*dans la queue*) jump the queue.

ressaisir (se) /(sə)rəsezir/ *v. pr.* pull o.s. together.

ressasser /rəsase/ *v.t.* (*rabâcher, ruminer*) keep going over.

ressembl|er /rəsɑ̃ble/ *v.i.* ~**er à**, resemble, look like. **se** ~**er** *v. pr.* look alike. ~**ance** *n.f.* resemblance. ~**ant**,

~**ante** *a.* (*photo etc.*) true to life; (*pareil*) alike.

ressemeler /rəsəmle/ *v.t.* sole.

ressentiment /rəsɑ̃timɑ̃/ *n.m.* resentment.

ressentir /rəsɑ̃tir/ *v.t.* feel. **se** ~ **de**, feel the effects of.

resserre /rəsɛr/ *n.f.* shed.

resserrer /rəsere/ *v.t.* tighten; (*contracter*) contract. **se** ~ *v. pr.* tighten; contract; (*route etc.*) narrow.

resservir /rəsɛrvir/ *v.i.* come in useful (again).

ressort /rəsɔr/ *n.m.* (*objet*) spring; (*fig.*) energy. **du** ~ **de**, within the jurisdiction *ou* scope of. **en dernier** ~, in the last resort.

ressortir† /rəsɔrtir/ *v.i.* go *ou* come back out; (*se voir*) stand out. **faire** ~, bring out. ~ **de**, (*résulter*) result *ou* emerge from.

ressortissant, ~**e** /rəsɔrtisɑ̃, -t/ *n.m.*, *f.* national.

ressource /rəsurs/ *n.f.* resource. ~**s**, resources.

ressusciter /resysite/ *v.i.* come back to life.

restant, ~**e** /rɛstɑ̃, -t/ *a.* remaining. —*n.m.* remainder.

restaur|ant /rɛstɔrɑ̃/ *n.m.* restaurant. ~**ateur**, ~**atrice** *n.m.*, *f.* restaurant owner.

restaur|er /rɛstɔre/ *v.t.* restore. **se** ~**er** *v. pr.* eat. ~**ation** *n.f.* restoration; (*hôtellerie*) catering.

reste /rɛst/ *n.m.* rest; (*d'une soustraction*) remainder. ~**s**, remains (**de**, of); (*nourriture*) left-overs. **un** ~ **de** pain/*etc.*, some left-over bread/*etc.* **au** ~, **du** ~, moreover, besides.

rest|er /rɛste/ *v.i.* (*aux. être*) stay, remain; (*subsister*) be left, remain. **il** ~**e** **du pain**/*etc.*, there is some bread/*etc.* left (over). **il me** ~**e du pain,** I have some bread left (over). **il me** ~**e à**, it remains for me to. **en** ~**er à**, go no further than. **en** ~**er là**, stop there.

restit|uer /rɛstitɥe/ *v.t.* (*rendre*) return, restore; (*son*) reproduce. ~**u- tion** *n.f.* return.

restreindre† /rɛstrɛ̃dr/ *v.i.* restrict. **se** ~ *v. pr.* (*dans les dépenses*) cut down.

restricti|f, ~**ve** /rɛstriktif, -v/ *a.* restrictive.

restriction /rɛstriksjɔ̃/ *n.f.* restriction; (*réticence*) reservation.

résultat /rezylta/ *n.m.* result.

résulter /rezylte/ *v.i.* ~ **de,** result from.

résum|er /rezyme/ *v.t.*, **se** ~**er** *v. pr.* summarize. ~**é** *n.m.* summary. **en** ~**é,** in short.

résurrection /rezyrɛksjɔ̃/ *n.f.* resurrection; (*renouveau*) revival.

rétabl|ir /retablir/ *v.t.* restore; (*personne*) restore to health. **se** ~**ir** *v. pr.* be restored; (*guérir*) recover. ~**issement** *n.m.* restoring; (*méd.*) recovery.

retaper /rətape/ *v.t.* (*maison etc.*) do up. **se** ~ *v. pr.* (*guérir*) get back on one's feet.

retard /rətar/ *n.m.* lateness; (*sur un programme*) delay; (*infériorité*) backwardness. **avoir du** ~**,** be late; (*montre*) be slow. **en** ~**,** late; (*retardé*) backward. **en** ~ **sur,** behind. **rattraper** *ou* **combler son** ~**,** catch up.

retardataire /rətardatɛr/ *n.m./f.* late comer. —*a.* (*arrivant*) late.

retardé /rətarde/ *a.* backward.

retardement (à) /(a)rətardəmɑ̃/ *a.* (*bombe etc.*) delayed-action.

retarder /rətarde/ *v.t.* delay; (*sur un programme*) set back; (*montre*) put back. —*v.i.* (*montre*) be slow.

retenir† /rətnir/ *v.t.* hold back; (*haleine, attention, prisonnier*) hold; (*eau, chaleur*) retain, hold; (*garder*) keep; (*retarder*) detain; (*réserver*) book; (*se rappeler*) remember; (*déduire*) deduct; (*accepter*) accept. **se** ~ *v. pr.* (*se contenir*) restrain o.s. **se** ~ **à,** hold on to. **se** ~ **de,** stop o.s. from.

rétention /retɑ̃sjɔ̃/ *n.f.* retention.

retent|ir /rətɑ̃tir/ *v.i.* ring out (**de,** with). ~**issant,** ~**issante** *a.* resounding. ~**issement** *n.m.* (*effet, répercussion*) effect.

retenue /rətny/ *n.f.* restraint; (*somme*) deduction; (*scol.*) detention.

réticen|t, ~**te** /retisɑ̃, -t/ *a.* (*hésitant*) reluctant; (*réservé*) reticent. ~**ce** *n.f.* reluctance; reticence.

rétif, ~**ve** /retif, -v/ *a.* restive, recalcitrant.

rétine /retin/ *n.f.* retina.

retiré /rətire/ *a.* secluded.

retirer /rətire/ *v.t.* (*sortir*) take out; (*ôter*) take off; (*argent, candidature*) withdraw; (*avantage*) derive. ~ **à qn.,** take away from s.o. **se** ~ *v. pr.* withdraw, retire.

retombées /rətɔ̃be/ *n.f. pl.* fall-out.

retomber /rətɔ̃be/ *v.i.* fall; (*à nouveau*) fall again. ~ **dans,** (*erreur etc.*) fall back into.

rétorquer /retɔrke/ *v.t.* retort.

rétorsion /retɔrsjɔ̃/ *n.f.* retaliation.

retouch|e /rətuʃ/ *n.f.* touch-up; alteration. ~**er** *v.t.* touch up; (*vêtement*) alter.

retour /rətur/ *n.m.* return. **être de** ~**,** be back (**de,** from). ~ **en arrière,** flashback.

retourner /rəturne/ *v.t.* (*aux. avoir*) turn over; (*vêtement*) turn inside out; (*lettre, compliment*) return; (*émouvoir: fam.*) upset. —*v.i.* (*aux. être*) go back, return. **se** ~ *v. pr.* turn round; (*dans son lit*) twist and turn. **s'en** ~**,** go back. **se** ~ **contre,** turn against.

retracer /rətrase/ *v.t.* retrace.

rétracter /retrakte/ *v.t.*, **se** ~ *v. pr.* retract.

retrait /rətrɛ/ *n.m.* withdrawal; (*des eaux*) ebb, receding. **être (situé) en** ~**,** be set back.

retraite /rətrɛt/ *n.f.* retirement; (*pension*) (retirement) pension; (*fuite, refuge*) retreat. **en** ~**,** retired. **mettre à la** ~**,** pension off. **prendre sa** ~**,** retire.

retraité, ~**e** /rətrete/ *a.* retired. —*n.m., f.* (old-age) pensioner, senior citizen.

retrancher /rətrɑ̃ʃe/ *v.t.* remove; (*soustraire*) deduct. **se** ~ *v. pr.* (*mil.*) entrench o.s.

retransm|ettre /rətrɑ̃smɛtr/ *v.t.* broadcast. ~**ission** *n.f.* broadcast.

rétrécir /retresir/ *v.t.* narrow; (*vêtement*) take in. —*v.i.*, **se** ~ *v. pr.* (*tissu*) shrink; (*rue*) narrow.

rétrib|uer /retribɥe/ *v.t.* pay. ~**ution** *n.f.* payment.

rétrograd|e /retrograd/ *a.* retrograde. ~**er** *v.i.* (*reculer*) fall back, recede; *v.t.* demote.

rétrospectivement /retrɔspɛktivmɑ̃/ *adv.* in retrospect.

retrousser /rətruse/ *v.t.* pull up.

retrouvailles /rətruvɑj/ *n.f. pl.* reunion.

retrouver /rətruve/ *v.t.* find (again); (*rejoindre*) meet (again); (*forces, calme*) regain; (*se rappeler*) remember. **se** ~ *v. pr.* find o.s. (back); (*se réunir*) meet (again). **s'y** ~**,** (*s'orienter*) find one's way.

rétroviseur /retrovizœr/ *n.m.* (*auto.*) (rear-view) mirror.

réunion /reynjɔ̃/ *n.f.* meeting; (*d'objets*) collection.

réunir /reynir/ *v.t.* gather, collect; (*rapprocher*) bring together; (*convoquer*) call together; (*raccorder*) join; (*qualités*) combine. **se ~** *v. pr.* meet.

réussi /reysi/ *a.* successful.

réussir /reysir/ *v.i.* succeed, be successful (**à faire**, in doing). **~ à qn.**, work well for s.o.; (*climat etc.*) agree with s.o. —*v.t.* make a success of.

réussite /reysit/ *n.f.* success.

revaloriser /rəvalɔrize/ *v.t.* revalue.

revanche /rəvɑ̃ʃ/ *n.f.* revenge; (*sport*) return *ou* revenge match. **en ~**, on the other hand.

rêvasser /rɛvase/ *v.i.* day-dream.

rêve /rɛv/ *n.m.* dream. **faire un ~**, have a dream.

revêche /rəvɛʃ/ *a.* ill-tempered.

réveil /revɛj/ *n.m.* awakening; (*pendule*) alarm-clock.

réveill|er /reveje/ *v.t.*, **se ~er** *v. pr.* wake (up); (*fig.*) awaken. **~é** *a.* awake. **~e-matin** *n.m. invar.* alarm-clock.

réveillon /revɛjɔ̃/ *n.m.* midnight meal (on Christmas Eve *ou* New Year's Eve). **~ner** /-jɔne/ *v.i.* celebrate the *réveillon*.

révél|er /revele/ *v.t.* reveal. **se ~er** *v. pr.* be revealed. **se ~er facile**/*etc.*, prove easy/*etc.* **~ateur, ~atrice** *a.* revealing. **~ation** *n.f.* revelation.

revenant /rəvnɑ̃/ *n.m.* ghost.

revendi|quer /rəvɑ̃dike/ *v.t.* claim. **~catif, ~cative** *a.* (*mouvement etc.*) in support of one's claims. **~cation** *n.f.* claim; (*action*) claiming.

revend|re /rəvɑ̃dr/ *v.t.* sell (again). **~eur, ~euse** *n.m., f.* dealer.

revenir† /rəvnir/ *v.i.* (*aux. être*) come back, return (**à**, to). **~ à**, (*activité*) go back to; (*se résumer à*) come down to; (*échoir à*) fall to; (*coûter*) cost. **~ à soi**, come to. **~ de**, (*maladie, surprise*) get over. **~ sur ses pas**, retrace one's steps.

revente /rəvɑ̃t/ *n.f.* resale.

revenu /rəvny/ *n.m.* income; (*d'un état*) revenue.

rêver /reve/ *v.t./i.* dream.

réverbération /revɛrberasjɔ̃/ *n.f.* reflection, reverberation.

réverbère /revɛrber/ *n.m.* street lamp.

révérenc|e /reverɑ̃s/ *n.f.* reverence; (*salut d'homme*) bow; (*salut de femme*) curtsy. **~ieux, ~ieuse** *a.* reverent.

révérend, ~e /reverɑ̃, -d/ *a. & n.m.* reverend.

rêverie /rɛvri/ *n.f.* day-dream; (*activité*) day-dreaming.

revers /rəvɛr/ *n.m.* reverse; (*de main*) back; (*d'étoffe*) wrong side; (*de veste*) lapel; (*tennis*) backhand; (*fig.*) setback.

réversible /reversibl/ *a.* reversible.

revêt|ir /rəvetir/ *v.t.* cover; (*habit*) put on; (*prendre, avoir*) assume. **~ement** /-vɛtmɑ̃/ *n.m.* covering; (*de route*) surface.

rêveu|r, ~se /rɛvœr, -øz/ *a.* dreamy. —*n.m., f.* dreamer.

revigorer /rəvigɔre/ *v.t.* revive.

revirement /rəvirmɑ̃/ *n.m.* sudden change.

révis|er /revize/ *v.t.* revise; (*véhicule*) overhaul. **~ion** *n.f.* revision; overhaul.

revivre† /rəvivr/ *v.i.* live again. —*v.t.* relive. **faire ~**, revive.

révocation /revɔkasjɔ̃/ *n.f.* repeal; (*d'un fonctionnaire*) dismissal.

revoir† /rəvwar/ *v.t.* see (again); (*réviser*) revise. **au ~**, goodbye.

révolte /revɔlt/ *n.f.* revolt.

révolt|er /revɔlte/ *v.t.*, **se ~er** *v. pr.* revolt. **~ant, ~ante** *a.* revolting. **~é, ~ée** *n.m., f.* rebel.

révolu /revɔly/ *a.* past.

révolution /revɔlysjɔ̃/ *n.f.* revolution. **~naire** /-jɔnɛr/ *a. & n.m./f.* revolutionary. **~ner** /-jɔne/ *v.t.* revolutionize.

revolver /revɔlvɛr/ *n.m.* revolver, gun.

révoquer /revɔke/ *v.t.* repeal; (*fonctionnaire*) dismiss.

revue /rəvy/ *n.f.* (*examen, défilé*) review; (*magazine*) magazine; (*spectacle*) variety show.

rez-de-chaussée /redʃose/ *n.m. invar.* ground floor; (*Amer.*) first floor.

RF *abrév.* (*République Française*) French Republic.

rhabiller (se) /(sə)rabije/ *v. pr.* get dressed (again), dress (again).

rhapsodie /rapsɔdi/ *n.f.* rhapsody.

rhétorique /retɔrik/ *n.f.* rhetoric. —*a.* rhetorical.

rhinocéros /rinɔserɔs/ *n.m.* rhinoceros.

rhubarbe /rybarb/ *n.f.* rhubarb.

rhum /rɔm/ *n.m.* rum.

rhumatis|me /rymatism/ *n.m.* rheumatism. **∼ant, ∼ante** /-zɑ̃, -t/ *a.* rheumatic.

rhume /rym/ *n.m.* cold. **∼ des foins,** hay fever.

ri /ri/ *voir* **rire.**

riant, ∼e /rjɑ̃, -t/ *a.* cheerful.

ricaner /rikane/ *v.i.* snigger, giggle.

riche /riʃ/ *a.* rich (**en,** in). —*n.m./f.* rich person. **∼ment** *adv.* richly.

richesse /riʃɛs/ *n.f.* wealth; (*de sol, décor*) richness. **∼s,** wealth.

ricoch|er /rikɔʃe/ *v.i.* rebound, ricochet. **∼et** *n.m.* rebound, ricochet.

rictus /riktys/ *n.m.* grin, grimace.

rid|e /rid/ *n.f.* wrinkle; (*sur l'eau*) ripple. **∼er** *v.t.* wrinkle; (*eau*) ripple.

rideau (*pl.* **∼x**) /rido/ *n.m.* curtain; (*métallique*) shutter; (*fig.*) screen. **∼ de fer,** (*pol.*) Iron Curtain.

ridicul|e /ridikyl/ *a.* ridiculous. —*n.m.* absurdity. **le ∼e,** ridicule. **∼iser** *v.t.* ridicule.

rien /rjɛ̃/ *pron.* (**ne**) **∼,** nothing. —*n.m.* trifle. **de ∼!,** (*fam.*) don't mention it! **∼ d'autre/de plus,** nothing else/ more. **∼ du tout,** nothing at all. **∼ que,** just, only.

rieu|r, ∼se /rjœr, rjøz/ *a.* merry.

rigid|e /riʒid/ *a.* rigid; (*muscle*) stiff. **∼ité** *n.f.* rigidity; stiffness.

rigole /rigɔl/ *n.f.* channel.

rigol|er /rigɔle/ *v.i.* laugh; (*s'amuser*) have some fun; (*plaisanter*) joke. **∼ade** *n.f.* fun.

rigolo, ∼te /rigɔlo, -ɔt/ *a.* (*fam.*) funny. —*n.m.,f.* (*fam.*) joker.

rigoureu|x, ∼se /rigurø, -z/ *a.* rigorous; (*hiver*) harsh. **∼sement** *adv.* rigorously.

rigueur /rigœr/ *n.f.* rigour. **à la ∼,** at a pinch. **être de ∼,** be the rule.

rim|e /rim/ *n.f.* rhyme. **∼er** *v.i.* rhyme (**avec,** with). **cela ne ∼e à rien,** it makes no sense.

rin|cer /rɛ̃se/ *v.t.* rinse. **∼çage** *n.m.* rinse; (*action*) rinsing.

ring /riŋ/ *n.m.* boxing ring.

ripost|e /ripɔst/ *n.f.* retort; (*mil.*) reprisal. **∼er** *v.i.* retaliate; *v.t.* retort (**que,** that). **∼er à,** (*attaque*) counter; (*insulte etc.*) reply to.

rire† /rir/ *v.i.* laugh (**de,** at); (*plaisanter*) joke; (*s'amuser*) have fun. —*n.m.* laugh. **∼s, le ∼,** laughter.

risée /rize/ *n.f.* **la ∼ de,** the laughing-stock of.

risible /rizibl/ *a.* laughable.

risqu|e /risk/ *n.m.* risk. **∼é** *a.* risky; (*osé*) daring. **∼er** *v.t.* risk. **∼er de faire,** stand a good chance of doing. **se ∼er à/dans,** venture to/into.

rissoler /risɔle/ *v.t./i.* brown.

ristourne /risturn/ *n.f.* discount.

rite /rit/ *n.m.* rite.

rituel, ∼le /rituɛl/ *a.* & *n.m.* ritual.

rivage /rivaʒ/ *n.m.* shore.

riv|al, ∼ale (*m. pl.* **∼aux**) /rival, -o/ *n.m., f.* rival. —*a.* rival. **∼aliser** *v.i.* compete (**avec,** with). **∼alité** *n.f.* rivalry.

rive /riv/ *n.f.* (*de fleuve*) bank; (*de lac*) shore.

riv|er /rive/ *v.t.* rivet. **∼et** *n.m.* rivet.

riverain, ∼e /rivrɛ̃, -ɛn/ *a.* riverside. —*n.m., f.* riverside resident; (*d'une rue*) resident.

rivière /rivjɛr/ *n.f.* river.

rixe /riks/ *n.f.* brawl.

riz /ri/ *n.m.* rice. **∼ière** /rizjɛr/ *n.f.* paddy(-field), rice field.

robe /rɔb/ *n.f.* (*de femme*) dress; (*de juge*) robe; (*de cheval*) coat. **∼ de chambre,** dressing-gown.

robinet /rɔbinɛ/ *n.m.* tap; (*Amer.*) faucet.

robot /rɔbo/ *n.m.* robot.

robuste /rɔbyst/ *a.* robust. **∼sse** /-ɛs/ *n.f.* robustness.

roc /rɔk/ *n.m.* rock.

rocaill|e /rɔkɑj/ *n.f.* rocky ground; (*de jardin*) rockery. **∼eux, ∼euse** *a.* (*terrain*) rocky.

roch|e /rɔʃ/ *n.f.* rock. **∼eux, ∼euse** *a.* rocky.

rocher /rɔʃe/ *n.m.* rock.

rock /rɔk/ *n.m.* (*mus.*) rock.

rod|er /rɔde/ *v.t.* (*auto.*) run in; (*auto., Amer.*) break in. **∼age** *n.m.* running in; breaking in.

rôd|er /rode/ *v.i.* roam; (*suspect*) prowl. **∼eur, ∼euse** *n.m.,f.* prowler.

rogne /rɔɲ/ *n.f.* (*fam.*) anger.

rogner /rɔɲe/ *v.t.* trim; (*réduire*) cut.

rognon /rɔɲɔ̃/ *n.m.* (*culin.*) kidney.

rognures /rɔɲyr/ *n.f. pl.* scraps.

roi /rwa/ *n.m.* king. **les Rois mages,** the Magi.

roitelet /rwatlɛ/ *n.m.* wren.

rôle /rol/ *n.m.* role, part.

romain, ∼e /rɔmɛ̃, -ɛn/ *a.* & *n.m., f.* Roman. —*n.f.* (*laitue*) cos.

roman /rɔmɑ̃/ *n.m.* novel; (*fig.*) story; (*genre*) fiction.

romance /rɔmɑ̃s/ *n.f.* sentimental ballad.

romanc|ier, ~ière /rɔmɑ̃sje, -jɛr/ *n.m.,f.* novelist.

romanesque /rɔmanɛsk/ *a.* romantic; (*incroyable*) incredible.

romanichel, ~le /rɔmaniʃɛl/ *n.m.,f.* gypsy.

romanti|que /rɔmɑ̃tik/ *a. & n.m./f.* romantic. **~sme** *n.m.* romanticism.

rompre† /rɔ̃pr/ *v.t./i.* break; (*relations*) break off; (*fiancés*) break it off. **se ~** *v. pr.* break.

rompu /rɔ̃py/ *a.* (*exténué*) exhausted.

ronces /rɔ̃s/ *n.f. pl.* brambles.

ronchonner /rɔ̃ʃɔne/ *v.i.* (*fam.*) grumble.

rond, ~e[1] /rɔ̃, rɔ̃d/ *a.* round; (*gras*) plump; (*ivre: fam.*) tight. —*n.m.* (*cercle*) ring; (*tranche*) slice. **~ement** /rɔ̃dmɑ̃/ *adv.* briskly; (*franchement*) straight. **~eur** /rɔ̃dœr/ *n.f.* roundness; (*franchise*) frankness; (*embonpoint*) plumpness. **~-point** (*pl.* **~s-points**) *n.m.* roundabout; (*Amer.*) traffic circle.

ronde[2] /rɔ̃d/ *n.f.* round(s); (*de policier*) beat; (*mus.*) semibreve.

rondelet, ~te /rɔ̃dlɛ, -t/ *a.* chubby.

rondelle /rɔ̃dɛl/ *n.f.* (*techn.*) washer; (*tranche*) slice.

rondin /rɔ̃dɛ̃/ *n.m.* log.

ronfl|er /rɔ̃fle/ *v.i.* snore; (*moteur*) hum. **~ement(s)** *n.m.* (*pl.*) snoring; humming.

rong|er /rɔ̃ʒe/ *v.t.* gnaw (at); (*vers, acide*) eat into; (*personne: fig.*) consume. **se ~er les ongles,** bite one's nails. **~eur** *n.m.* rodent.

ronronn|er /rɔ̃rɔne/ *v.i.* purr. **~ement** *n.m.* purr(ing).

roquette /rɔkɛt/ *n.f.* rocket.

rosaire /rozɛr/ *n.m.* rosary.

rosbif /rɔsbif/ *n.m.* roast beef.

rose /roz/ *n.f.* rose. —*a.* pink; (*situation, teint*) rosy. —*n.m.* pink.

rosé /roze/ *a.* pinkish; (*vin*) rosé. —*n.m.* rosé.

roseau (*pl.* **~x**) /rozo/ *n.m.* reed.

rosée /roze/ *n.f.* dew.

roseraie /rozrɛ/ *n.f.* rose garden.

rosette /rozɛt/ *n.f.* rosette.

rosier /rozje/ *n.m.* rose-bush.

rosse /rɔs/ *a.* (*fam.*) nasty.

rosser /rɔse/ *v.t.* thrash.

rossignol /rɔsiɲɔl/ *n.m.* nightingale.

rot /ro/ *n.m.* (*fam.*) burp.

rotati|f, ~ve /rɔtatif, -v/ *a.* rotary.

rotation /rɔtasjɔ̃/ *n.f.* rotation.

roter /rɔte/ *v.i.* (*fam.*) burp.

rotin /rɔtɛ̃/ *n.m.* (rattan) cane.

rôt|ir /rotir/ *v.t./i.,* **se ~ir** *v. pr.* roast. **~i** *n.m.* roasting meat; (*cuit*) roast. **~i de porc,** roast pork.

rôtisserie /rotisri/ *n.f.* grill-room.

rôtissoire /rotiswar/ *n.f.* (roasting) spit.

rotule /rɔtyl/ *n.f.* kneecap.

rouage /rwaʒ/ *n.m.* (*techn.*) (working) part. **~s,** (*d'une organisation: fig.*) wheels.

roucouler /rukule/ *v.i.* coo.

roue /ru/ *n.f.* wheel. **~ (dentée),** cog(-wheel).

roué /rwe/ *a.* wily, calculating.

rouer /rwe/ *v.t.* **~ de coups,** thrash.

rouet /rwɛ/ *n.m.* spinning-wheel.

rouge /ruʒ/ *a.* red; (*fer*) red-hot. —*n.m.* red; (*vin*) red wine; (*fard*) rouge. **~ (à lèvres,** lipstick. —*n.m./f.* (*pol.*) red. **~-gorge** (*pl.* **~s-gorges**) *n.m.* robin.

rougeole /ruʒɔl/ *n.f.* measles.

rougeoyer /ruʒwaje/ *v.i.* glow (red).

rougeur /ruʒœr/ *n.f.* redness; (*tache*) red blotch; (*gêne, honte*) red face.

rougir /ruʒir/ *v.t./i.* turn red; (*de honte*) blush.

rouill|e /ruj/ *n.f.* rust. **~é** *a.* rusty. **~er** *v.i.,* **se ~er** *v. pr.* get rusty, rust.

roulant, ~e /rulɑ̃, -t/ *a.* (*meuble*) on wheels; (*escalier*) moving.

rouleau (*pl.* **~x**) /rulo/ *n.m.* roll; (*outil, vague*) roller. **~ à pâtisserie,** rolling-pin. **~ compresseur,** steamroller.

roulement /rulmɑ̃/ *n.m.* rotation; (*bruit*) rumble; (*d'yeux, de tambour*) roll. **~ à billes,** ball-bearing.

rouler /rule/ *v.t./i.* roll; (*ficelle, manches*) roll up; (*duper: fam.*) cheat; (*véhicule, train*) go, travel; (*conducteur*) drive. **se ~** *v. pr.* roll (over).

roulette /rulɛt/ *n.f.* (*de meuble*) castor; (*de dentiste*) drill; (*jeu*) roulette.

roulis /ruli/ *n.m.* rolling.

roulotte /rulɔt/ *n.f.* caravan.

roumain, ~e /rumɛ̃, -ɛn/ *a. & n.m.,f.* Romanian.

Roumanie /rumani/ *n.f.* Romania.

roupiller /rupije/ *v.i.* (*fam.*) sleep.

rouquin, ~e /rukɛ̃, -in/ *a.* (*fam.*) red-haired. —*n.m.,f.* (*fam.*) redhead.

rouspéter /ruspete/ *v.i.* (*fam.*) grumble, moan, complain.

rousse /rus/ *voir* **roux.**

roussir /rusir/ *v.t.* scorch. —*v.i.* turn brown.

route /rut/ *n.f.* road; (*naut., aviat.*) route; (*direction*) way; (*voyage*) journey; (*chemin: fig.*) path. **en ~,** on the way. **en ~!,** let's go! **mettre en ~,** start. **~ nationale,** trunk road, main road. **se mettre en ~,** set out.

rout|ier, ~ière /rutje, -jɛr/ *a.* road. —*n.m.* long-distance lorry driver *ou* truck driver (*Amer.*); (*restaurant*) roadside café.

routine /rutin/ *n.f.* routine.

rou|x, ~sse /ru, rus/ *a.* red, reddish-brown; (*personne*) red-haired. —*n.m., f.* redhead.

roy|al (*m. pl.* **~aux**) /rwajal, -jo/ *a.* royal; (*total: fam.*) thorough. **~alement** *adv.* royally.

royaume /rwajom/ *n.m.* kingdom. **R~-Uni** *n.m.* United Kingdom.

royauté /rwajote/ *n.f.* royalty.

ruade /ryad, rɥad/ *n.f.* kick.

ruban /rybã/ *n.m.* ribbon; (*de magnétophone*) tape; (*de chapeau*) band. **~ adhésif,** sticky tape.

rubéole /rybeɔl/ *n.f.* German measles.

rubis /rybi/ *n.m.* ruby; (*de montre*) jewel.

rubrique /rybrik/ *n.f.* heading; (*article*) column.

ruche /ryʃ/ *n.f.* beehive.

rude /ryd/ *a.* rough; (*pénible*) tough; (*grossier*) crude; (*fameux: fam.*) tremendous. **~ment** *adv.* (*frapper etc.*) hard; (*traiter*) harshly; (*très: fam.*) awfully.

rudiment|s /rydimã/ *n.m. pl.* rudiments. **~aire** /-tɛr/ *a.* rudimentary.

rudoyer /rydwaje/ *v.t.* treat harshly.

rue /ry/ *n.f.* street.

ruée /rɥe/ *n.f.* rush.

ruelle /rɥɛl/ *n.f.* alley.

ruer /rɥe/ *v.i.* (*cheval*) kick. **se ~ dans/vers,** rush into/towards. **se ~ sur,** pounce on.

rugby /rygbi/ *n.m.* Rugby.

rugby|man (*pl.* **~men**) /rygbiman, -mɛn/ *n.m.* Rugby player.

rug|ir /ryʒir/ *v.i.* roar. **~issement** *n.m.* roar.

rugueu|x, ~se /rygø, -z/ *a.* rough.

ruin|e /rɥin/ *n.f.* ruin. **~er** *v.t.* ruin.

ruineu|x, ~se /rɥinø, -z/ *a.* ruinous.

ruisseau (*pl.* **~x**) /rɥiso/ *n.m.* stream; (*rigole*) gutter.

ruisseler /rɥisle/ *v.i.* stream.

rumeur /rymœr/ *n.f.* (*nouvelle*) rumour; (*son*) murmur, hum; (*protestation*) rumblings.

ruminer /rymine/ *v.t./i.* (*méditer*) meditate.

rupture /ryptyr/ *n.f.* break; (*action*) breaking; (*de contrat*) breach; (*de pourparlers*) breakdown.

rur|al (*m. pl.* **~aux**) /ryral, -o/ *a.* rural.

rus|e /ryz/ *n.f.* cunning; (*perfidie*) trickery. **une ~e,** a trick, a ruse. **~é** *a.* cunning.

russe /rys/ *a. & n.m./f.* Russian. —*n.m.* (*lang.*) Russian.

Russie /rysi/ *n.f.* Russia.

rustique /rystik/ *a.* rustic.

rustre /rystr/ *n.m.* lout, boor.

rutilant, ~e /rytilã, -t/ *a.* sparkling, gleaming.

rythm|e /ritm/ *n.m.* rhythm; (*vitesse*) rate; (*de la vie*) pace. **~é, ~ique** *adjs.* rhythmical.

S

s' /s/ *voir* **se.**

sa /sa/ *voir* **son**[1].

SA *abrév.* (*société anonyme*) PLC.

sabbat /saba/ *n.m.* sabbath.

sabl|e /sɑbl/ *n.m.* sand. **~es mouvants,** quicksands. **~er** *v.t.* sand. **~eux, ~euse, ~onneux, ~onneuse** *adjs.* sandy.

sablier /sɑblije/ *n.m.* (*culin.*) egg-timer.

saborder /sabɔrde/ *v.t.* (*navire*) scuttle.

sabot /sabo/ *n.m.* (*de cheval etc.*) hoof; (*chaussure*) clog; (*de frein*) shoe.

sabot|er /sabɔte/ *v.t.* sabotage; (*bâcler*) botch. **~age** *n.m.* sabotage; (*acte*) act of sabotage. **~eur, ~euse** *n.m., f.* saboteur.

sabre /sɑbr/ *n.m.* sabre.

sac /sak/ *n.m.* bag; (*grand, en toile*) sack. **mettre à ~,** (*maison*) ransack; (*ville*) sack. **~ à dos,** rucksack. **~ à main,** handbag. **~ de couchage,** sleeping-bag.

saccad|e /sakad/ *n.f.* jerk. **~é** *a.* jerky.

saccager /sakaʒe/ *v.t.* (*ville, pays*) sack; (*maison*) ransack; (*bouleverser*) wreck.

saccharine /sakarin/ *n.f.* saccharin.

sacerdoce /sasɛrdɔs/ *n.m.* priesthood; (*fig.*) vocation.

sachet /saʃɛ/ *n.m.* (small) bag; (*de shampooing etc.*) sachet. **~ de thé,** tea-bag.

sacoche /sakɔʃ/ *n.f.* bag; (*d'élève*) satchel; (*de moto*) saddle-bag.

sacquer /sake/ *v.t.* (*renvoyer*: *fam.*) sack.

sacr|e /sakr/ *n.m.* (*de roi*) coronation; (*d'évêque*) consecration. **~er** *v.t.* crown; consecrate.

sacré /sakre/ *a.* sacred; (*maudit*: *fam.*) damned.

sacrement /sakrəmɑ̃/ *n.m.* sacrament.

sacrifice /sakrifis/ *n.m.* sacrifice.

sacrifier /sakrifje/ *v.t.* sacrifice. **se ~** *v. pr.* sacrifice o.s.

sacrilège /sakrilɛʒ/ *n.m.* sacrilege. —*a.* sacrilegious.

sacristain /sakristɛ̃/ *n.m.* sexton.

sacristie /sakristi/ *n.f.* vestry.

sacro-saint, ~e /sakrɔsɛ̃, -t/ *a.* sacrosanct.

sadi|que /sadik/ *a.* sadistic. —*n.m./f.* sadist. **~sme** *n.m.* sadism.

safari /safari/ *n.m.* safari.

sagace /sagas/ *a.* shrewd.

sage /saʒ/ *a.* wise; (*docile*) good; (*modeste*) sober. —*n.m.* wise man. **~-femme** (*pl.* **~s-femmes**) *n.f.* midwife. **~ment** *adv.* wisely; (*docilement*) quietly. **~sse** /-ɛs/ *n.f.* wisdom; (*docilité*) good behaviour.

saignant, ~e /sɛɲɑ̃, -t/ *a.* (*culin.*) rare.

saign|er /seɲe/ *v.t./i.* bleed. **~ée** *n.f.* bleeding; (*perte*: *fig.*) heavy sacrifice. **~ement** *n.m.* bleeding. **~ement de nez,** nosebleed.

saill|ie /saji/ *n.f.* projection. **faire ~ie,** project. **~ant, ~ante** *a.* projecting; (*remarquable*) salient.

sain, ~e /sɛ̃, sɛn/ *a.* healthy; (*moralement*) sane. **~ et sauf,** safe and sound. **~ement** /sɛnmɑ̃/ *adv.* healthily; (*juger*) sanely.

saindoux /sɛ̃du/ *n.m.* lard.

saint, ~e /sɛ̃, sɛ̃t/ *a.* holy; (*bon, juste*) saintly. —*n.m., f.* saint. **S~-Esprit** *n.m.* Holy Spirit. **S~-Siège** *n.m.* Holy See. **S~-Sylvestre** *n.f.* New Year's Eve. **Sainte Vierge,** Blessed Virgin.

sainteté /sɛ̃tte/ *n.f.* holiness; (*de mariage, lieu*) sanctity.

sais /sɛ/ *voir* **savoir.**

saisie /sezi/ *n.f.* (*jurid.*) seizure.

sais|ir /sezir/ *v.t.* grab (hold of), seize; (*occasion, biens*) seize; (*comprendre*) grasp; (*frapper*) strike. **~i de,** (*peur*) stricken by, overcome by. **se ~ir de,** seize. **~issant, ~issante** *a.* (*spectacle*) gripping.

saison /sɛzɔ̃/ *n.f.* season. **~nier, ~nière** /-ɔnje, -jɛr/ *a.* seasonal.

sait /sɛ/ *voir* **savoir.**

salad|e /salad/ *n.f.* salad; (*laitue*) lettuce; (*désordre*: *fam.*) mess. **~ier** *n.m.* salad bowl.

salaire /salɛr/ *n.m.* wages, salary.

salaisons /salɛzɔ̃/ *n.f. pl.* salt meat *ou* fish.

salami /salami/ *n.m.* salami.

salarié, ~e /salarje/ *a.* wage-earning. —*n.m., f.* wage-earner.

salaud /salo/ *n.m.* (*argot*) bastard.

sale /sal/ *a.* dirty, filthy; (*mauvais*) nasty.

sal|er /sale/ *v.t.* salt. ∼**é** *a.* (*goût*) salty; (*plat*) salted; (*viande, poisson*) salt; (*grivois: fam.*) spicy; (*excessif: fam.*) steep.

saleté /salte/ *n.f.* dirtiness; (*crasse*) dirt; (*action*) dirty trick; (*obscénité*) obscenity. ∼(**s**), (*camelote*) rubbish. ∼**s**, (*détritus*) mess.

salière /saljɛr/ *n.f.* salt-cellar.

salin, ∼**e** /salɛ̃, -in/ *a.* saline.

sal|ir /salir/ *v.t.* (make) dirty; (*réputation*) tarnish. **se** ∼**ir** *v. pr.* get dirty. ∼**issant**, ∼**issante** *a.* dirty; (*étoffe*) easily dirtied.

salive /saliv/ *n.f.* saliva.

salle /sal/ *n.f.* room; (*grande, publique*) hall; (*d'hôpital*) ward; (*théâtre, cinéma*) auditorium. ∼ **à manger**, dining-room. ∼ **d'attente**, waiting-room. ∼ **de bains**, bathroom. ∼ **de séjour**, living-room.

salon /salɔ̃/ *n.m.* lounge; (*de coiffure, beauté*) salon; (*exposition*) show. ∼ **de thé**, tea-room.

salope /salɔp/ *n.f.* (*argot*) bitch.

saloperie /salɔpri/ *n.f.* (*action: fam.*) dirty trick; (*camelote: fam.*) rubbish.

salopette /salɔpɛt/ *n.f.* dungarees; (*d'ouvrier*) overalls.

saltimbanque /saltɛ̃bɑ̃k/ *n.m./f.* (street *ou* fairground) acrobat.

salubre /salybr/ *a.* healthy.

saluer /salɥe/ *v.t.* greet; (*en partant*) take one's leave of; (*de la tête*) nod to; (*de la main*) wave to; (*mil.*) salute.

salut /saly/ *n.m.* greeting; (*de la tête*) nod; (*de la main*) wave; (*mil.*) salute; (*sauvegarde, rachat*) salvation. —*int.* (*bonjour: fam.*) hallo; (*au revoir: fam.*) bye-bye.

salutaire /salytɛr/ *a.* salutary.

salutation /salytɑsjɔ̃/ *n.f.* greeting.

salve /salv/ *n.f.* salvo.

samedi /samdi/ *n.m.* Saturday.

sanatorium /sanatɔrjɔm/ *n.m.* sanatorium.

sanctifier /sɑ̃ktifje/ *v.t.* sanctify.

sanction /sɑ̃ksjɔ̃/ *n.f.* sanction. ∼**ner** /-jɔne/ *v.t.* sanction; (*punir*) punish.

sanctuaire /sɑ̃ktɥɛr/ *n.m.* sanctuary.

sandale /sɑ̃dal/ *n.f.* sandal.

sandwich /sɑ̃dwitʃ/ *n.m.* sandwich.

sang /sɑ̃/ *n.m.* blood. ∼**-froid** *n.m. invar.* calm, self-control.

sanglant, ∼**e** /sɑ̃glɑ̃, -t/ *a.* bloody.

sangl|e /sɑ̃gl/ *n.f.* strap. ∼**er** *v.t.* strap.

sanglier /sɑ̃glije/ *n.m.* wild boar.

sanglot /sɑ̃glo/ *n.m.* sob. ∼**er** /-ɔte/ *v.i.* sob.

sangsue /sɑ̃sy/ *n.f.* leech.

sanguin, ∼**e** /sɑ̃gɛ̃, -in/ *a.* (*groupe etc.*) blood; (*caractère*) fiery.

sanguinaire /sɑ̃ginɛr/ *a.* bloodthirsty.

sanitaire /sanitɛr/ *a.* health; (*conditions*) sanitary; (*appareils, installations*) bathroom, sanitary.

sans /sɑ̃/ *prép.* without. ∼ **que vous le sachiez**, without your knowing. ∼**abri** /sɑ̃zabri/ *n.m./f. invar.* homeless person. ∼ **ça**, ∼ **quoi**, otherwise. ∼ **arrêt**, non-stop. ∼ **encombre/faute/ tarder**, without incident/fail/delay. ∼ **fin/goût/limite**, endless/tasteless/ limitless. ∼**-gêne** *a.invar.* inconsiderate, thoughtless; *n.m. invar.* thoughtlessness. ∼ **importance/pareil/ précédent / travail**, unimportant/ unparalleled / unprecedented / unemployed. ∼ **plus**, but no more than that, but nothing more.

santé /sɑ̃te/ *n.f.* health.

saoul, ∼**e** /su, sul/ *voir* **soûl**.

saper /sape/ *v.t.* undermine.

sapeur /sapœr/ *n.m.* (*mil.*) sapper. ∼**pompier** (*pl.* ∼**s-pompiers**) *n.m.* fireman.

saphir /safir/ *n.m.* sapphire.

sapin /sapɛ̃/ *n.m.* fir(-tree). ∼ **de Noël**, Christmas tree.

sarbacane /sarbakan/ *n.f.* (*jouet*) peashooter.

sarcas|me /sarkasm/ *n.m.* sarcasm. ∼**tique** *a.* sarcastic.

sarcler /sarkle/ *v.t.* weed.

sardine /sardin/ *n.f.* sardine.

sardonique /sardɔnik/ *a.* sardonic.

sarment /sarmɑ̃/ *n.m.* vine shoot.

sas /sɑ(s)/ *n.m.* (*naut., aviat.*) airlock.

satané /satane/ *a.* (*fam.*) blasted.

satanique /satanik/ *a.* satanic.

satellite /satelit/ *n.m.* satellite.

satin /satɛ̃/ *n.m.* satin.

satir|e /satir/ *n.f.* satire. ∼**ique** *a.* satirical.

satisfaction /satisfaksjɔ̃/ *n.f.* satisfaction.

satis|faire† /satisfɛr/ *v.t.* satisfy. —*v.i.* ∼**faire à**, satisfy. ∼**faisant**, ∼**faisante** *a.* (*acceptable*) satisfactory. ∼**fait**, ∼**faite** *a.* satisfied (**de**, with).

satur|er /satyre/ *v.t.* saturate. ∼**ation** *n.f.* saturation.

sauc|e /sos/ *n.f.* sauce; (*jus de viande*)

gravy. **~e tartare,** tartar sauce.
~ière *n.f.* sauce-boat.
saucisse /sosis/ *n.f.* sausage.
saucisson /sosisɔ̃/ *n.m.* (cold) sausage.
sauf[1] /sof/ *prép.* except. **~ erreur/**
imprévu, barring error/the unforeseen.
sau|f[2], **~ve** /sof, sov/ *a.* safe, un-
harmed. **~f-conduit** *n.m.* safe conduct.
sauge /soʒ/ *n.f.* (*culin.*) sage.
saugrenu /sogrəny/ *a.* preposterous,
ludicrous.
saule /sol/ *n.m.* willow. **~ pleureur,**
weeping willow.
saumâtre /somatr/ *a.* briny.
saumon /somɔ̃/ *n.m.* salmon. *—a.*
invar. salmon-pink.
saumure /somyr/ *n.f.* brine.
sauna /sona/ *n.m.* sauna.
saupoudrer /sopudre/ *v.t.* sprinkle.
saut /so/ *n.m.* jump, leap. **faire un ~**
chez, pop round to. **le ~,** (*sport*)
jumping. **~ en hauteur/longueur,**
high/long jump. **~ périlleux,** somersault.
sauté /sote/ *a.* & *n.m.* (*culin.*) sauté.
saut|er /sote/ *v.i.* jump, leap; (*exploser*)
blow up; (*fusible*) blow; (*se détacher*)
come off. *—v.t.* jump (over); (*page,*
classe) skip. **faire ~er,** (*détruire*)
blow up; (*fusible*) blow; (*casser*) break;
(*renvoyer: fam.*) kick out. **~er à la**
corde, skip. **~er aux yeux,** be obvious. **~e-mouton** *n.m.* leap-frog.
sauterelle /sotrɛl/ *n.f.* grasshopper.
sautiller /sotije/ *v.i.* hop.
sautoir /sotwar/ *n.m.* (*sport*) jumping
area.
sauvage /sovaʒ/ *a.* wild; (*primitif,*
cruel) savage; (*farouche*) unsociable;
(*illégal*) unauthorized. *—n.m./f.* unsociable person; (*brute*) savage. **~rie**
n.f. savagery.
sauve /sov/ *voir* **sauf**[2].
sauvegard|e /sovgard/ *n.f.* safeguard.
~er *v.t.* safeguard.
sauv|er /sove/ *v.t.* save; (*d'un danger*)
rescue, save; (*matériel*) salvage. **se**
~er *v. pr.* (*fuir*) run away; (*partir:*
fam.) go (away). **~e-qui-peut** *n.m.*
invar. stampede. **~etage** *n.m.* rescue;
salvage. **~eteur** *n.m.* rescuer. **~eur**
n.m. saviour.
sauvette (à la) /(ala)sovɛt/ *adv.*
hastily; (*vendre*) illicitly.
savamment /savamɑ̃/ *adv.* learnedly;
(*avec habileté*) skilfully.

savan|t, ~e /savɑ̃, -t/ *a.* learned;
(*habile*) skilful. *—n.m.* scientist.
saveur /savœr/ *n.f.* flavour.
savoir[†] /savwar/ *v.t.* know; (*pouvoir*)
be able to; (*apprendre*) hear. *—n.m.*
learning. **à ~,** namely. **faire ~ à qn.**
que, inform s.o. that. **je ne saurais**
pas, I could not, I cannot. (**pas**) **que**
je sache, (not) as far as I know.
savon /savɔ̃/ *n.m.* soap; (*réprimande:*
fam.) dressing down. **~ner** /-ɔne/ *v.t.*
soap. **~nette** /-ɔnɛt/ *n.f.* bar of soap.
~neux, ~neuse /-ɔnø, -z/ *a.* soapy.
savour|er /savure/ *v.t.* savour. **~eux,**
~euse *a.* tasty; (*fig.*) spicy.
saxophone /saksɔfɔn/ *n.m.* saxophone.
scabreu|x, ~se /skabrø, -z/ *a.* risky;
(*indécent*) obscene.
scalpel /skalpɛl/ *n.m.* scalpel.
scalper /skalpe/ *v.t.* scalp.
scandal|e /skɑ̃dal/ *n.m.* scandal;
(*tapage*) uproar; (*en public*) noisy
scene. **faire ~e,** shock people. **~eux,**
~euse *a.* scandalous. **~iser** *v.t.* scandalize, shock.
scander /skɑ̃de/ *v.t.* (*vers*) scan; (*slo-*
gan) chant.
scandinave /skɑ̃dinav/ *a.* & *n.m./f.*
Scandinavian.
Scandinavie /skɑ̃dinavi/ *n.f.* Scandinavia.
scaphandr|e /skafɑ̃dr/ *n.m.* diving-
suit; (*aviat.*) spacesuit. **~e auto-**
nome, aqualung. **~ier** *n.m.* diver.
scarabée /skarabe/ *n.m.* beetle.
scarlatine /skarlatin/ *n.f.* scarlet
fever.
scarole /skarɔl/ *n.f.* endive.
sceau (*pl.* **~x**) /so/ *n.m.* seal.
scélérat /selera/ *n.m.* scoundrel.
scell|er /sele/ *v.t.* seal; (*fixer*) cement.
~és *n.m. pl.* seals.
scénario /senarjo/ *n.m.* scenario.
scène /sɛn/ *n.f.* scene; (*estrade, art*
dramatique) stage. **mettre en ~,**
(*pièce*) stage.
scepti|que /sɛptik/ *a.* sceptical.
—n.m./f. sceptic. **~cisme** *n.m.* scepti-
cism.
sceptre /sɛptr/ *n.m.* sceptre.
schéma /ʃema/ *n.m.* diagram. **~tique**
a. diagrammatic; (*sommaire*) sketchy.
schisme /ʃism/ *n.m.* schism.
schizophrène /skizɔfrɛn/ *a.* & *n.m./f.*
schizophrenic.
scie /si/ *n.f.* saw.
sciemment /sjamɑ̃/ *adv.* knowingly.

scien|ce /sjãs/ *n.f.* science; (*savoir*) knowledge. **∼ce-fiction** *n.f.* science fiction. **∼tifique** *a.* scientific; *n.m./f.* scientist.

scier /sje/ *v.t.* saw.

scinder /sɛ̃de/ *v.t.*, **se ∼** *v. pr.* split.

scintill|er /sɛ̃tije/ *v.i.* glitter; (*étoile*) twinkle. **∼ement** *n.m.* glittering; twinkling.

scission /sisjɔ̃/ *n.f.* split.

sciure /sjyr/ *n.f.* sawdust.

sclérose /skleroz/ *n.f.* sclerosis.

scol|aire /skɔlɛr/ *a.* school. **∼arisation** *n.f.*, **∼arité** *n.f.* schooling. **∼arisé** *a.* provided with schooling.

scorbut /skɔrbyt/ *n.m.* scurvy.

score /skɔr/ *n.m.* score.

scories /skɔri/ *n.f. pl.* slag.

scorpion /skɔrpjɔ̃/ *n.m.* scorpion.

scotch[1] /skɔtʃ/ *n.m.* (*boisson*) Scotch (whisky).

scotch[2] /skɔtʃ/ *n.m.* (P.) Sellotape (P.); (*Amer.*) Scotch (tape) (P.).

scout, ∼e /skut/ *n.m. & a.* scout.

script /skript/ *n.m.* (*écriture*) printing.

scrupul|e /skrypyl/ *n.m.* scruple. **∼eusement** *adv.* scrupulously. **∼eux, ∼euse** *a.* scrupulous.

scruter /skryte/ *v.t.* examine, scrutinize.

scrutin /skrytɛ̃/ *n.m.* (*vote*) ballot; (*opération électorale*) poll.

sculpt|er /skylte/ *v.t.* sculpture, carve. **∼eur** *n.m.* sculptor. **∼ure** *n.f.* sculpture.

se, s'* /sə, s/ *pron.* himself; (*femelle*) herself; (*indéfini*) oneself; (*non humain*) itself; (*pl.*) themselves; (*réciproque*) each other, one another. **∼ parler**, (*indirect*) speak to o.s. **∼ faire**, (*passif*) be done. **∼ laver les mains**, (*possessif*) wash one's hands.

séance /seãs/ *n.f.* session; (*cinéma, théâtre*) show. **∼ de pose**, sitting. **∼ tenante**, forthwith.

séant, ∼e /seã, -t/ *a.* seemly.

seau (*pl.* **∼x**) /so/ *n.m.* bucket, pail.

sec, sèche /sɛk, sɛʃ/ *a.* dry; (*fruits*) dried; (*coup, bruit*) sharp; (*cœur*) hard; (*whisky*) neat; (*Amer.*) straight. —*adv.* (*frapper, pleuvoir*) hard. —*n.m.* **à ∼**, (*sans eau*) dry. **au ∼**, in a dry place.

sécateur /sekatœr/ *n.m.* (pruning) shears.

sécession /sesesjɔ̃/ *n.f.* secession. **faire ∼**, secede.

sèche /sɛʃ/ *voir* **sec**. **∼ment** *adv.* drily.

sèche-cheveux /sɛʃʃəvø/ *n.m. invar.* hair-drier.

sécher /seʃe/ *v.t./i.* dry; (*cours: fam.*) skip; (*ignorer: argot*) be stumped. **se ∼** *v. pr.* dry o.s.

sécheresse /seʃrɛs/ *n.f.* dryness; (*temps sec*) drought.

séchoir /seʃwar/ *n.m.* drier.

second, ∼e[1] /sgɔ̃, -d/ *a. & n.m.*, *f.* second. —*n.m.* (*adjoint*) second in command; (*étage*) second floor. —*n.f.* (*transport*) second class.

secondaire /sgɔ̃dɛr/ *a.* secondary.

seconde[2] /sgɔ̃d/ *n.f.* (*instant*) second.

seconder /sgɔ̃de/ *v.t.* assist.

secouer /skwe/ *v.t.* shake; (*poussière, torpeur*) shake off. **se ∼**, (*fam.*) shake o.s. out of it.

secour|ir /skurir/ *v.t.* assist, help. **∼able** *a.* helpful. **∼iste** *n.m./f.* first-aid worker.

secours /skur/ *n.m.* assistance, help; (*mil.*) relief. —*n.m. pl.* (*méd.*) first aid; (*mil.*) relief. **au ∼!**, help! **de ∼**, emergency; (*équipe, opération*) rescue.

secousse /skus/ *n.f.* jolt, jerk; (*morale*) shock; (*séisme*) tremor.

secr|et, ∼ète /səkrɛ, -t/ *a.* secret. —*n.m.* secret; (*discrétion*) secrecy. **en ∼et**, in secret, secretly.

secrétaire /skretɛr/ *n.m./f.* secretary. —*n.m.* (*meuble*) writing-desk. **∼ d'État**, junior minister.

secrétariat /skretarja/ *n.m.* secretarial work; (*bureau*) secretary's office; (*d'un organisme*) secretariat.

sécrét|er /sekrete/ *v.t.* secrete. **∼ion** /-sjɔ̃/ *n.f.* secretion.

sect|e /sɛkt/ *n.f.* sect. **∼aire** *a.* sectarian.

secteur /sɛktœr/ *n.m.* area; (*mil., comm.*) sector; (*circuit: électr.*) mains.

section /sɛksjɔ̃/ *n.f.* section; (*transports publics*) fare stage; (*mil.*) platoon. **∼ner** /-jɔne/ *v.t.* sever.

séculaire /sekylɛr/ *a.* age-old.

sécul|ier, ∼ière /sekylje, -jɛr/ *a.* secular.

sécuriser /sekyrize/ *v.t.* reassure.

sécurité /sekyrite/ *n.f.* security; (*absence de danger*) safety. **en ∼**, safe, secure. **S∼ sociale**, social services, social security services.

sédatif /sedatif/ *n.m.* sedative.

sédentaire /sedãtɛr/ *a.* sedentary.

sédiment /sedimã/ *n.m.* sediment.

séditieu|x, ~se /sedisjø, -z/ *a.* seditious.

sédition /sedisjɔ̃/ *n.f.* sedition.

séd|uire† /sedɥir/ *v.t.* charm; (*plaire à*) appeal to; (*abuser de*) seduce. **~ucteur, ~uctrice** *a.* seductive; *n.m., f.* seducer. **~uction** *n.f.* seduction; (*charme*) charm. **~uisant, ~uisante** *a.* attractive.

segment /sɛgmɑ̃/ *n.m.* segment.

ségrégation /segregasjɔ̃/ *n.f.* segregation.

seigle /sɛgl/ *n.m.* rye.

seigneur /sɛɲœr/ *n.m.* lord. **le S~,** the Lord.

sein /sɛ̃/ *n.m.* breast; (*fig.*) bosom. **au ~ de,** in the midst of.

Seine /sɛn/ *n.f.* Seine.

séisme /seism/ *n.m.* earthquake.

seiz|e /sɛz/ *a. & n.m.* sixteen. **~ième** *a. & n.m./f.* sixteenth.

séjour /seʒur/ *n.m.* stay; (*pièce*) living-room. **~ner** *v.i.* stay.

sel /sɛl/ *n.m.* salt; (*piquant*) spice.

sélect /selɛkt/ *a.* select.

sélecti|f, ~ve /selɛktif, -v/ *a.* selective.

sélection /selɛksjɔ̃/ *n.f.* selection. **~ner** /-jɔne/ *v.t.* select.

self(-service) /sɛlf(sɛrvis)/ *n.m.* self-service.

selle /sɛl/ *n.f.* saddle.

seller /sele/ *v.t.* saddle.

sellette /selɛt/ *n.f.* **sur la ~,** under examination.

selon /slɔ̃/ *prép.* according to (**que,** whether).

semailles /smɑj/ *n.f. pl.* sowing; (*époque*) seed-time.

semaine /smɛn/ *n.f.* week. **en ~,** in the week.

sémantique /semɑ̃tik/ *a.* semantic. —*n.f.* semantics.

sémaphore /semafɔr/ *n.m.* (*appareil*) semaphore.

semblable /sɑ̃blabl/ *a.* similar (**à,** to). **de ~s propos**/*etc.*, (*tels*) such remarks/*etc.* —*n.m.* fellow (creature).

semblant /sɑ̃blɑ̃/ *n.m.* **faire ~ de,** pretend to. **un ~ de,** a semblance of.

sembl|er /sɑ̃ble/ *v.i.* seem (**à,** to; **que,** that). **il me ~e que,** it seems to me that.

semelle /smɛl/ *n.f.* sole.

semence /smɑ̃s/ *n.f.* seed; (*clou*) tack. **~s,** (*graines*) seed.

sem|er /sme/ *v.t.* sow; (*jeter, parsemer*) strew; (*répandre*) spread; (*personne*:

fam.) lose. **~eur, ~euse** *n.m., f.* sower.

semestr|e /smɛstr/ *n.m.* half-year; (*univ.*) semester. **~iel, ~ielle** *a.* half-yearly.

semi- /səmi/ *préf.* semi-.

séminaire /seminɛr/ *n.m.* (*relig.*) seminary; (*univ.*) seminar.

semi-remorque /səmirəmɔrk/ *n.m.* articulated lorry; (*Amer.*) semi(-trailer).

semis /səmi/ *n.m.* (*terrain*) seedbed; (*plant*) seedling.

sémit|e /semit/ *a.* Semitic. —*n.m./f.* Semite. **~ique** *a.* Semitic.

semonce /səmɔ̃s/ *n.f.* reprimand. **coup de ~,** warning shot.

semoule /smul/ *n.f.* semolina.

sénat /sena/ *n.m.* senate. **~eur** /-tœr/ *n.m.* senator.

sénil|e /senil/ *a.* senile. **~ité** *n.f.* senility.

sens /sɑ̃s/ *n.m.* sense; (*signification*) meaning, sense; (*direction*) direction. **à mon ~,** to my mind. **à ~ unique,** (*rue etc.*) one-way. **ça n'a pas de ~,** that does not make sense. **~ commun,** common sense. **~ giratoire,** roundabout; (*Amer.*) rotary. **~ interdit,** no entry; (*rue*) one-way street.

sensation /sɑ̃sasjɔ̃/ *n.f.* feeling, sensation. **faire ~,** create a sensation. **~nel, ~nelle** /-jɔnɛl/ *a.* sensational.

sensé /sɑ̃se/ *a.* sensible.

sensibiliser /sɑ̃sibilize/ *v.t.* **~ à,** make sensitive to.

sensib|le /sɑ̃sibl/ *a.* sensitive (**à,** to); (*appréciable*) noticeable. **~ilité** *n.f.* sensitivity. **~lement** *adv.* noticeably; (*à peu près*) more or less.

sensoriel, ~le /sɑ̃sɔrjɛl/ *a.* sensory.

sens|uel, ~uelle /sɑ̃sɥɛl/ *a.* sensuous; (*sexuel*) sensual. **~ualité** *n.f.* sensuousness; sensuality.

sentence /sɑ̃tɑ̃s/ *n.f.* (*jurid.*) sentence; (*adage*) maxim.

senteur /sɑ̃tœr/ *n.f.* scent.

sentier /sɑ̃tje/ *n.m.* path.

sentiment /sɑ̃timɑ̃/ *n.m.* feeling. **avoir le ~ de,** be aware of.

sentiment|al (*m. pl.* **~aux**) /sɑ̃timɑ̃tal, -o/ *a.* sentimental. **~alité** *n.f.* sentimentality.

sentinelle /sɑ̃tinɛl/ *n.f.* sentry.

sentir† /sɑ̃tir/ *v.t.* feel; (*odeur*) smell; (*goût*) taste; (*pressentir*) sense; (*supporter: fam.*) bear. **~ la lavande**/*etc.*, smell of lavender/ *etc.* —*v.i.* smell. **se**

~ **fier/mieux**/*etc.*, feel proud/ better/*etc.*

séparé /separe/ *a.* separate. ~**ment** *adv.* separately.

sépar|er /separe/ *v.t.* separate; (*en deux*) split. **se** ~**er** *v. pr.* separate, part (**de**, from); (*se détacher*) split. **se** ~**er de**, (*se défaire de*) part with. ~**ation** *n.f.* separation.

sept /sɛt/ *a.* & *n.m.* seven.

septante /sɛptɑ̃t/ *a.* & *n.m.* (*en Belgique, Suisse*) seventy.

septembre /sɛptɑ̃br/ *n.m.* September.

septentrion|al (*m. pl.* ~**aux**) /sɛptɑ̃trijɔnal, -o/ *a.* northern.

septième /sɛtjɛm/ *a.* & *n.m./f.* seventh.

sépulcre /sepylkr/ *n.m.* (*relig.*) sepulchre.

sépulture /sepyltyr/ *n.f.* burial; (*lieu*) burial place.

séquelles /sekɛl/ *n.f. pl.* (*de guerre*) aftermath.

séquence /sekɑ̃s/ *n.f.* sequence.

séquestrer /sekɛstre/ *v.t.* confine (illegally), lock away.

sera, serait /sra, srɛ/ *voir* **être**.

serein, ~e /sərɛ̃, -ɛn/ *a.* serene.

sérénade /serenad/ *n.f.* serenade.

sérénité /serenite/ *n.f.* serenity.

sergent /sɛrʒɑ̃/ *n.m.* sergeant.

série /seri/ *n.f.* series; (*d'objets*) set. **de** ~, (*véhicule etc.*) standard. **fabrication** *ou* **production en** ~, mass production.

sérieu|x, ~se /serjø, -z/ *a.* serious; (*digne de foi*) reliable; (*authentique*) genuine; (*chances, raison*) good. —*n.m.* seriousness. **garder/perdre son** ~**x**, keep/be unable to keep a straight face. **prendre au** ~**x**, take seriously. ~**sement** *adv.* seriously.

serin /srɛ̃/ *n.m.* canary.

seringue /srɛ̃g/ *n.f.* syringe.

serment /sɛrmɑ̃/ *n.m.* oath; (*promesse*) pledge.

sermon /sɛrmɔ̃/ *n.m.* sermon. ~**ner** /-ɔne/ *v.t.* (*fam.*) lecture.

serpe /sɛrp/ *n.f.* bill(hook).

serpent /sɛrpɑ̃/ *n.m.* snake. ~ **à sonnettes**, rattlesnake.

serpenter /sɛrpɑ̃te/ *v.i.* meander.

serpentin /sɛrpɑ̃tɛ̃/ *n.m.* streamer.

serpillière /sɛrpijɛr/ *n.f.* floorcloth.

serre[1] /sɛr/ *n.f.* (*local*) greenhouse.

serre[2] /sɛr/ *n.f.* (*griffe*) claw.

serré /sere/ *a.* (*habit, nœud, programme*) tight; (*personnes*) packed, crowded; (*lutte, mailles*) close; (*cœur*) heavy.

serrer /sere/ *v.t.* (*saisir*) grip; (*presser*) squeeze; (*vis, corde, ceinture*) tighten; (*poing*) clench; (*pieds*) pinch; (*rangs*) close; (*embrasser*) hug; (*rapprocher*) squeeze up. ~ **qn.**, (*vêtement*) be tight on s.o. —*v.i.* ~ **à droite**, keep over to the right. **se** ~ *v. pr.* (*se rapprocher*) squeeze (up) (**contre**, against). ~ **de près**, follow closely. ~ **la main à**, shake hands with.

serrur|e /seryr/ *n.f.* lock. ~**ier** *n.m.* locksmith.

sertir /sɛrtir/ *v.t.* (*bijou*) set.

sérum /serɔm/ *n.m.* serum.

servante /sɛrvɑ̃t/ *n.f.* (maid)servant.

serveu|r, ~se /sɛrvœr, -øz/ *n.m., f.* waiter, waitress; (*au bar*) barman, barmaid.

serviable /sɛrvjabl/ *a.* helpful.

service /sɛrvis/ *n.m.* service; (*fonction, temps de travail*) duty; (*pourboire*) service (charge). **être de** ~, be on duty. **rendre un** ~**/mauvais** ~ **à qn.**, do s.o. a favour/disservice. ~ **d'ordre**, (*policiers*) police.

serviette /sɛrvjɛt/ *n.f.* (*de toilette*) towel; (*sac*) briefcase. ~ (**de table**), serviette; (*Amer.*) napkin.

servile /sɛrvil/ *a.* servile.

servir† /sɛrvir/ *v.t./i.* serve; (*être utile*) be of use, serve. ~ **qn.** (**à table**), wait on s.o. **ça sert à**, (*outil, récipient, etc.*) it is used for. **ça me sert à/de**, I use it for/as. ~ **de**, serve as, be used as. ~ **à qn. de guide**/*etc.*, act as a guide/*etc.* for s.o. **se** ~ *v. pr.* (*à table*) help o.s. (**de**, to). **se** ~ **de**, use.

serviteur /sɛrvitœr/ *n.m.* servant.

servitude /sɛrvityd/ *n.f.* servitude.

ses /se/ *voir* **son**[1].

session /sesjɔ̃/ *n.f.* session.

seuil /sœj/ *n.m.* doorstep; (*entrée*) doorway; (*fig.*) threshold.

seul, ~e /sœl/ *a.* alone, on one's own; (*unique*) only. **un** ~ **travail**/*etc.*, only one job/*etc.* **pas un** ~ **ami**/*etc.*, not a single friend/*etc.* —*n.m., f.* **le** ~, **la** ~**e**, the only one. **un** ~, **une** ~**e**, only one. **pas un** ~, not (a single) one.

seulement /sœlmɑ̃/ *adv.* only.

sève /sɛv/ *n.f.* sap.

sév|ère /sevɛr/ *a.* severe. ~**èrement** *adv.* severely. ~**érité** /-erite/ *n.f.* severity.

sévices /sevis/ *n.m. pl.* cruelty.

sévir /sevir/ *v.i.* (*fléau*) rage. ~ **contre,** punish.

sevrer /səvre/ *v.t.* wean.

sexe /sɛks/ *n.m.* sex; (*organes*) sex organs.

sex|uel, ~**uelle** /sɛksɥɛl/ *a.* sexual. ~**ualité** *n.f.* sexuality.

seyant, ~**e** /sɛjɑ̃, -t/ *a.* becoming.

shampooing /ʃɑ̃pwɛ̃/ *n.m.* shampoo.

shérif /ʃerif/ *n.m.* sheriff.

short /ʃɔrt/ *n.m.* (pair of) shorts.

si[1] (**s'** *before il, ils*) /si, s/ *conj.* if; (*interrogation indirecte*) if, whether. ~ **on partait?,** (*suggestion*) what about going? **s'il vous** *ou* **te plaît,** please. ~ **oui,** if so. ~ **seulement,** if only.

si[2] /si/ *adv.* (*tellement*) so; (*oui*) yes. **un** ~ **bon repas,** such a good meal. **pas** ~ **riche que,** not as rich as. ~ **habile qu'il soit,** however skilful he may be. ~ **bien que,** with the result that.

siamois, ~**e** /sjamwa, -z/ *a.* Siamese.

Sicile /sisil/ *n.f.* Sicily.

sida /sida/ *n.m.* (*méd.*) AIDS.

sidérer /sidere/ *v.t.* (*fam.*) stagger.

sidérurgie /sideryrʒi/ *n.f.* iron and steel industry.

siècle /sjɛkl/ *n.m.* century; (*époque*) age.

siège /sjɛʒ/ *n.m.* seat; (*mil.*) siege. ~ **éjectable,** ejector seat. ~ **social,** head office, headquarters.

siéger /sjeʒe/ *v.i.* (*assemblée*) sit.

sien, ~**ne** /sjɛ̃, sjɛn/ *pron.* **le** ~**, la** ~**ne, les** ~(**ne**)**s,** his; (*femme*) hers; (*chose*) its. **les** ~**s,** (*famille*) one's family.

sieste /sjɛst/ *n.f.* siesta.

siffl|er /sifle/ *v.i.* whistle; (*avec un sifflet*) blow one's whistle; (*serpent, gaz*) hiss. —*v.t.* (*air*) whistle; (*chien*) whistle to *ou* for; (*acteur*) hiss; (*signaler*) blow one's whistle for. ~**e-ment** *n.m.* whistling. **un** ~**ement,** a whistle.

sifflet /siflɛ/ *n.m.* whistle. ~**s,** (*huées*) boos.

siffloter /siflɔte/ *v.t./i.* whistle.

sigle /sigl/ *n.m.* abbreviation, acronym.

sign|al (*pl.* ~**aux**) /siɲal, -o/ *n.m.* signal. ~**aux lumineux,** (*auto.*) traffic signals.

signal|er /siɲale/ *v.t.* indicate; (*par une sonnerie, un écriteau*) signal; (*dénoncer, mentionner*) report; (*faire remarquer*) point out. **se** ~**er par,**

distinguish o.s. by. ~**ement** *n.m.* description.

signalisation /siɲalizasjɔ̃/ *n.f.* signalling, signposting; (*signaux*) signals.

signataire /siɲatɛr/ *n.m./f.* signatory.

signature /siɲatyr/ *n.f.* signature; (*action*) signing.

signe /siɲ/ *n.m.* sign; (*de ponctuation*) mark. **faire** ~ **à,** beckon (**de,** to); (*contacter*) contact. **faire** ~ **que non,** shake one's head. **faire** ~ **que oui,** nod.

signer /siɲe/ *v.t.* sign. **se** ~ *v. pr.* (*relig.*) cross o.s.

significati|f, ~**ve** /siɲifikatif, -v/ *a.* significant.

signification /siɲifikasjɔ̃/ *n.f.* meaning.

signifier /siɲifje/ *v.t.* mean, signify; (*faire connaître*) make known (**à,** to).

silenc|e /silɑ̃s/ *n.m.* silence; (*mus.*) rest. **garder le** ~**e,** keep silent. ~**ieux,** ~**ieuse** *a.* silent; *n.m.* (*auto.*) silencer; (*auto., Amer.*) muffler.

silex /silɛks/ *n.m.* flint.

silhouette /silwɛt/ *n.f.* outline, silhouette.

silicium /silisjɔm/ *n.m.* silicon.

sillage /sijaʒ/ *n.m.* (*trace d'eau*) wake.

sillon /sijɔ̃/ *n.m.* furrow; (*de disque*) groove.

sillonner /sijɔne/ *v.t.* criss-cross.

silo /silo/ *n.m.* silo.

simagrées /simagre/ *n.f. pl.* fuss, pretence.

simil|aire /similɛr/ *a.* similar. ~**itude** *n.f.* similarity.

simple /sɛ̃pl/ *a.* simple; (*non double*) single. —*n.m.* (*tennis*) singles. ~ **d'esprit** *n.m./f.* simpleton. ~ **particulier,** ordinary individual. ~ **soldat,** private. ~**ment** /-əmɑ̃/ *adv.* simply.

simplicité /sɛ̃plisite/ *n.f.* simplicity; (*naïveté*) simpleness.

simplif|ier /sɛ̃plifje/ *v.t.* simplify. ~**ication** *n.f.* simplification.

simulacre /simylakr/ *n.m.* pretence, sham.

simul|er /simyle/ *v.t.* simulate. ~**ation** *n.f.* simulation.

simultané /simyltane/ *a.* simultaneous. ~**ment** *adv.* simultaneously.

sinc|ère /sɛ̃sɛr/ *a.* sincere. ~**èrement** *adv.* sincerely. ~**érité** *n.f.* sincerity.

singe /sɛ̃ʒ/ *n.m.* monkey, ape.

singer /sɛ̃ʒe/ *v.t.* mimic, ape.

singeries /sɛ̃ʒri/ *n.f. pl.* antics.

singulariser (se) /(sə)sɛ̃gylarize/ *v. pr.* make o.s. conspicuous.

singul|ier, ~ière /sɛ̃gylje, -jɛr/ *a.* peculiar, remarkable; (*gram.*) singular. *—n.m.* (*gram.*) singular. **~arité** *n.f.* peculiarity. **~ièrement** *adv.* peculiarly; (*beaucoup*) remarkably.

sinistre[1] /sinistr/ *a.* sinister.

sinistr|e[2] /sinistr/ *n.m.* disaster; (*incendie*) blaze; (*dommages*) damage. **~é** *a.* disaster-stricken; *n.m.*, *f.* disaster victim.

sinon /sinɔ̃/ *conj.* (*autrement*) otherwise; (*sauf*) except (**que**, that); (*si ce n'est*) if not.

sinueu|x, ~se /sinɥø, -z/ *a.* winding; (*fig.*) tortuous.

sinus /sinys/ *n.m.* (*anat.*) sinus.

sionisme /sjonism/ *n.m.* Zionism.

siphon /sifɔ̃/ *n.m.* siphon.

sirène[1] /sirɛn/ *n.f.* (*appareil*) siren.

sirène[2] /sirɛn/ *n.f.* (*femme*) mermaid.

sirop /siro/ *n.m.* syrup; (*boisson*) cordial.

siroter /sirɔte/ *v.t.* sip.

sirupeu|x, ~se /sirypø, -z/ *a.* syrupy.

sis, ~e /si, siz/ *a.* situated.

site /sit/ *n.m.* setting; (*pittoresque*) beauty spot; (*emplacement*) site; (*monument etc.*) place of interest.

sitôt /sito/ *adv.* **~ entré**/*etc.*, immediately after coming in/*etc.* **~ que**, as soon as. **pas de ~**, not for a while.

situation /situɑsjɔ̃/ *n.f.* situation, position. **~ de famille**, marital status.

situ|er /situe/ *v.t.* situate, locate. **se ~er** *v. pr.* (*se trouver*) be situated. **~é** *a.* situated.

six /sis/ (/si/ *before consonant,* /siz/ *before vowel*) *a.* & *n.m.* six. **~ième** /sizjɛm/ *a.* & *n.m./f.* sixth.

sketch (*pl.* **~es**) /skɛtʃ/ *n.m.* (*théâtre*) sketch.

ski /ski/ *n.m.* (*patin*) ski; (*sport*) skiing. **faire du ~**, ski.

sk|ier /skje/ *v.i.* ski. **~ieur, ~ieuse** *n.m.*, *f.* skier.

slalom /slalɔm/ *n.m.* slalom.

slave /slav/ *a.* Slav; (*lang.*) Slavonic. *—n.m./f.* Slav.

slip /slip/ *n.m.* (*d'homme*) (under)-pants; (*de femme*) knickers; (*Amer.*) panties. **~ de bain**, (swimming) trunks; (*du bikini*) briefs.

slogan /slɔgã/ *n.m.* slogan.

smoking /smɔkiŋ/ *n.m.* evening *ou* dinner suit, dinner-jacket.

snack(-bar) /snak(bar)/ *n.m.* snack-bar.

snob /snɔb/ *n.m./f.* snob. *—a.* snobbish. **~isme** *n.m.* snobbery.

sobr|e /sɔbr/ *a.* sober. **~iété** *n.f.* sobriety.

sobriquet /sɔbrikɛ/ *n.m.* nickname.

sociable /sɔsjabl/ *a.* sociable.

soc|ial (*m. pl.* **~iaux**) /sɔsjal, -jo/ *a.* social.

socialis|te /sɔsjalist/ *n.m./f.* socialist. **~me** *n.m.* socialism.

sociétaire /sɔsjetɛr/ *n.m./f.* (society) member.

société /sɔsjete/ *n.f.* society; (*compagnie, firme*) company.

sociolo|gie /sɔsjɔlɔʒi/ *n.f.* sociology. **~gique** *a.* sociological. **~gue** *n.m./f.* sociologist.

socle /sɔkl/ *n.m.* (*de colonne, statue*) plinth; (*de lampe*) base.

socquette /sɔkɛt/ *n.f.* ankle sock.

soda /sɔda/ *n.m.* (fizzy) drink.

sodium /sɔdjɔm/ *n.m.* sodium.

sœur /sœr/ *n.f.* sister.

sofa /sɔfa/ *n.m.* sofa.

soi /swa/ *pron.* oneself. **en ~**, in itself. **~-disant** *a. invar.* so-called, self-styled; *adv.* supposedly.

soie /swa/ *n.f.* silk.

soif /swaf/ *n.f.* thirst. **avoir ~**, be thirsty.

soigné /swaɲe/ *a.* tidy, neat.

soigner /swaɲe/ *v.t.* look after, take care of; (*tenue, style*) take care over; (*maladie*) treat. **se ~** *v. pr.* look after o.s.

soigneu|x, ~se /swaɲø, -z/ *a.* careful (**de**, about); (*ordonné*) tidy. **~sement** *adv.* carefully.

soi-même /swamɛm/ *pron.* oneself.

soin /swɛ̃/ *n.m.* care; (*ordre*) tidiness. **~s**, care; (*méd.*) treatment. **avoir** *ou* **prendre ~ de qn./de faire**, take care of s.o./to do.

soir /swar/ *n.m.* evening.

soirée /sware/ *n.f.* evening; (*réception*) party. **~ dansante**, dance.

soit /swa/ *voir* être. *—conj.* (*à savoir*) that is to say. **~ . . . soit**, either . . . or.

soixantaine /swasãtɛn/ *n.f.* **une ~ (de)**, about sixty.

soixant|e /swasãt/ *a.* & *n.m.* sixty. **~e-dix** *a.* & *n.m.* seventy. **~e-dixième** *a.* & *n.m./f.* seventieth. **~ième** *a.* & *n.m./f.* sixtieth.

soja /sɔʒa/ *n.m.* (*graines*) soya beans; (*plante*) soya.

sol /sɔl/ *n.m.* ground; (*de maison*) floor; (*terrain agricole*) soil.

solaire /sɔlɛr/ *a.* solar; (*rayons, lumière*) sun's; (*huile, filtre*) sun.

soldat /sɔlda/ *n.m.* soldier.

solde¹ /sɔld/ *n.f.* (*salaire*) pay.

solde² /sɔld/ *n.m.* (*comm.*) balance. **~s,** (*articles*) sale goods. **en ~,** (*acheter etc.*) at sale price. **les ~s,** the sales.

solder /sɔlde/ *v.t.* sell off at sale price; (*compte*) settle. **se ~ par,** (*aboutir à*) end in.

sole /sɔl/ *n.f.* (*poisson*) sole.

soleil /sɔlɛj/ *n.m.* sun; (*chaleur*) sunshine; (*fleur*) sunflower. **il fait du ~,** it is sunny.

solennel, ~le /sɔlanɛl/ *a.* solemn.

solennité /sɔlanite/ *n.f.* solemnity.

solex /sɔlɛks/ *n.m.* (P.) moped.

solfège /sɔlfɛʒ/ *n.m.* elementary musical theory.

solid|aire /sɔlidɛr/ *a.* (*mécanismes*) interdependent; (*personnes*) who show solidarity. **~arité** *n.f.* solidarity.

solidariser (se) /(sə)sɔlidarize/ *v. pr.* show solidarity (**avec,** with).

solid|e /sɔlid/ *a.* solid. —*n.m.* (*corps*) solid. **~ement** *adv.* solidly. **~ité** *n.f.* solidity.

solidifier /sɔlidifje/ *v.t.,* **se ~** *v. pr.* solidify.

soliste /sɔlist/ *n.m./f.* soloist.

solitaire /sɔlitɛr/ *a.* solitary. —*n.m./f.* (*ermite*) hermit; (*personne insociable*) loner.

solitude /sɔlityd/ *n.f.* solitude.

solive /sɔliv/ *v.i.* joist.

sollicit|er /sɔlisite/ *v.t.* request; (*attirer, pousser*) prompt; (*tenter*) tempt. **~ation** *n.f.* earnest request.

sollicitude /sɔlisityd/ *n.f.* concern.

solo /sɔlo/ *n.m. & a. invar.* (*mus.*) solo.

solstice /sɔlstis/ *n.m.* solstice.

soluble /sɔlybl/ *a.* soluble.

solution /sɔlysjɔ̃/ *n.f.* solution.

solvable /sɔlvabl/ *a.* solvent.

solvant /sɔlvɑ̃/ *n.m.* solvent.

sombre /sɔ̃br/ *a.* dark; (*triste*) sombre.

sombrer /sɔ̃bre/ *v.i.* sink (**dans,** into).

sommaire /sɔmɛr/ *a.* summary; (*tenue, repas*) scant. —*n.m.* summary.

sommation /sɔmasjɔ̃/ *n.f.* (*mil.*) warning; (*jurid.*) summons.

somme¹ /sɔm/ *n.f.* sum. **en ~, ~**

toute, in short. **faire la ~ de,** add (up), total (up).

somme² /sɔm/ *n.m.* (*sommeil*) nap.

sommeil /sɔmɛj/ *n.m.* sleep; (*besoin de dormir*) drowsiness. **avoir ~,** be *ou* feel sleepy. **~ler** /-meje/ *v.i.* doze; (*fig.*) lie dormant.

sommelier /sɔməlje/ *n.m* wine waiter.

sommer /sɔme/ *v.t.* summon.

sommes /sɔm/ *voir* **être.**

sommet /sɔmɛ/ *n.m.* top; (*de montagne, gloire*) summit; (*de triangle*) apex.

sommier /sɔmje/ *n.m.* bed springs.

somnambule /sɔmnɑ̃byl/ *n.m.* sleepwalker.

somnifère /sɔmnifɛr/ *n.m.* sleeping-pill.

somnolen|t, ~te /sɔmnɔlɑ̃, -t/ *a.* drowsy. **~ce** *n.f.* drowsiness.

somnoler /sɔmnɔle/ *v.i.* doze.

sompt|ueux, ~ueuse /sɔ̃ptɥø, -z/ *a.* sumptuous. **~uosité** *n.f.* sumptuousness.

son¹, **sa** *ou* **son*** (*pl.* **ses**) /sɔ̃, sa, sɔ̃n, se/ *a.* his; (*femme*) her; (*chose*) its; (*indéfini*) one's.

son² /sɔ̃/ *n.m.* (*bruit*) sound.

son³ /sɔ̃/ *n.m.* (*de blé*) bran.

sonate /sɔnat/ *n.f.* sonata.

sonde /sɔ̃d/ *n.f.* (*pour les forages*) drill; (*méd.*) probe.

sond|er /sɔ̃de/ *v.t.* sound; (*terrain*) drill; (*personne*) sound out. **~age** *n.m.* sounding; drilling. **~age** (**d'opinion,** (opinion) poll.

song|e /sɔ̃ʒ/ *n.m.* dream. **~er** *v.i.* dream; *v.t.* **~er que,** think that. **~er à,** think about. **~eur, ~euse** *a.* pensive.

sonnantes /sɔnɑ̃t/ *a.f. pl.* **à six/etc. heures ~,** on the stroke of six/etc.

sonné /sɔne/ *a.* (*fam.*) crazy.

sonner /sɔne/ *v.t./i.* ring; (*clairon, glas*) sound; (*heure*) strike; (*domestique*) ring for. **midi sonné,** well past noon. **~ de,** (*clairon etc.*) sound, blow.

sonnerie /sɔnri/ *n.f.* ringing; (*de clairon*) sound; (*mécanisme*) bell.

sonnet /sɔnɛ/ *n.m.* sonnet.

sonnette /sɔnɛt/ *n.f.* bell.

sonor|e /sɔnɔr/ *a.* resonant; (*onde, effets, etc.*) sound. **~ité** *n.f.* resonance; (*d'un instrument*) tone.

sonoris|er /sɔnɔrize/ *v.t.* (*salle*) wire for sound. **~ation** *n.f.* (*matériel*) sound equipment.

sont /sɔ̃/ *voir* **être.**

sophistiqué /sɔfistike/ *a.* sophisticated.

soporifique /sɔpɔrifik/ *a.* soporific.

sorbet /sɔrbɛ/ *n.m.* water-ice.

sorcellerie /sɔrsɛlri/ *n.f.* witchcraft.

sorc|ier /sɔrsje/ *n.m.* sorcerer. ∼**ière** *n.f.* witch.

sordide /sɔrdid/ *a.* sordid; (*lieu*) squalid.

sort /sɔr/ *n.m.* (*destin, hasard*) fate; (*condition*) lot; (*maléfice*) spell.

sortant, ∼**e** /sɔrtɑ̃, -t/ *a.* (*président etc.*) outgoing.

sorte /sɔrt/ *n.f.* sort, kind. **de** ∼ **que,** so that. **en quelque** ∼, in a way. **faire en** ∼ **que,** see to it that.

sortie /sɔrti/ *n.f.* departure, exit; (*porte*) exit; (*promenade*) outing; (*invective*) outburst; (*parution*) appearance; (*de disque, gaz*) release; (*d'un ordinateur*) output. ∼**s,** (*argent*) outgoings.

sortilège /sɔrtilɛʒ/ *n.m.* (magic) spell.

sortir† /sɔrtir/ *v.i.* (*aux. être*) go out, leave; (*venir*) come out; (*aller au spectacle etc.*) go out; (*livre, film*) come out; (*plante*) come up. ∼ **de,** (*pièce*) leave; (*milieu social*) come from; (*limites*) go beyond. —*v.t.* (*aux. avoir*) take out; (*livre, modèle*) bring out; (*dire: fam.*) come out with. ∼ **d'affaire, (s')en** ∼, get out of an awkward situation. ∼ **du commun** *ou* **de l'ordinaire,** be out of the ordinary.

sosie /sɔzi/ *n.m.* double.

sot, ∼**te** /so, sɔt/ *a.* foolish.

sottise /sɔtiz/ *n.f.* foolishness; (*action, remarque*) foolish thing.

sou /su/ *n.m.* ∼**s,** money. **pas un** ∼, not a penny. **sans le** ∼, without a penny.

soubresaut /subrəso/ *n.m.* (sudden) start.

souche /suʃ/ *n.f.* (*d'arbre*) stump; (*de famille, vigne*) stock; (*de carnet*) counterfoil.

souci[1] /susi/ *n.m.* (*inquiétude*) worry; (*préoccupation*) concern. **se faire du** ∼, worry.

souci[2] /susi/ *n.m.* (*plante*) marigold.

soucier (se) /(sə)susje/ *v. pr.* **se** ∼ **de,** be concerned about.

soucieu|x, ∼**se** /susjø, -z/ *a.* concerned (**de,** about).

soucoupe /sukup/ *n.f.* saucer.

soudain, ∼**e** /sudɛ̃, -ɛn/ *a.* sudden. —*adv.* suddenly. ∼**ement** /-ɛnmɑ̃/

adv. suddenly. ∼**eté** /-ɛnte/ *n.f.* suddenness.

soude /sud/ *n.f.* soda.

soud|er /sude/ *v.t.* solder, weld. **se** ∼**er** *v. pr.* (*os*) knit (together). ∼**ure** *n.f.* soldering, welding; (*substance*) solder.

soudoyer /sudwaje/ *v.t.* bribe.

souffle /sufl/ *n.m.* blow, puff; (*haleine*) breath; (*respiration*) breathing; (*explosion*) blast; (*vent*) breath of air.

soufflé /sufle/ *n.m.* (*culin.*) soufflé.

souffl|er /sufle/ *v.i.* blow; (*haleter*) puff. —*v.t.* (*bougie*) blow out; (*poussière, fumée*) blow; (*par explosion*) destroy; (*chuchoter*) whisper. ∼**er son rôle à,** prompt. ∼**eur,** ∼**euse** *n.m., f.* (*théâtre*) prompter.

soufflet /suflɛ/ *n.m.* (*instrument*) bellows.

souffrance /sufrɑ̃s/ *n.f.* suffering. **en** ∼, (*affaire*) pending.

souffr|ir† /sufrir/ *v.i.* suffer (**de,** from). —*v.t.* (*endurer*) suffer; (*admettre*) admit of. **il ne peut pas le** ∼**ir,** he cannot stand *ou* bear him. ∼**ant,** ∼**ante** *a.* unwell.

soufre /sufr/ *n.m.* sulphur.

souhait /swɛ/ *n.m.* wish. **nos** ∼**s de,** (*vœux*) good wishes for.

souhait|er /swete/ *v.t.* (*bonheur etc.*) wish for. ∼**er qch. à qn.,** wish s.o. sth. ∼**er que/faire,** hope that/to do. ∼**able** /swɛtabl/ *a.* desirable.

souiller /suje/ *v.t.* soil.

soûl, ∼**e** /su, sul/ *a.* drunk. —*n.m.* **tout son** ∼, as much as one can.

soulag|er /sulaʒe/ *v.t.* relieve. ∼**ement** *n.m.* relief.

soûler /sule/ *v.t.* make drunk. **se** ∼ *v. pr.* get drunk.

soulèvement /sulɛvmɑ̃/ *n.m.* uprising.

soulever /sulve/ *v.t.* lift, raise; (*exciter*) stir; (*question, poussière*) raise. **se** ∼ *v. pr.* lift *ou* raise o.s. up; (*se révolter*) rise up.

soulier /sulje/ *n.m.* shoe.

souligner /suliɲe/ *v.t.* underline; (*taille, yeux*) emphasize.

soum|ettre† /sumɛtr/ *v.t.* (*dompter, assujettir*) subject (**à,** to); (*présenter*) submit (**à,** to). **se** ∼**ettre** *v. pr.* submit (**à,** to). ∼**is,** ∼**ise** *a.* submissive. ∼**ission** *n.f.* submission.

soupape /supap/ *n.f.* valve.

soupçon /supsɔ̃/ *n.m.* suspicion. **un** ∼ **de,** (*fig.*) a touch of. ∼**ner** /-ɔne/ *v.t.*

suspect. **~neux, ~neuse** /-ɔnø, -z/ *a.* suspicious.

soupe /sup/ *n.f.* soup.

souper /supe/ *n.m.* supper. —*v.i.* have supper.

soupeser /supəze/ *v.t.* judge the weight of; (*fig.*) weigh up.

soupière /supjɛr/ *n.f.* (soup) tureen.

soupir /supir/ *n.m.* sigh. **~er** *v.i.* sigh.

soupir|ail (*pl.* **~aux**) /supiraj, -o/ *n.m.* small basement window.

soupirant /supirɑ̃/ *n.m.* suitor.

souple /supl/ *a.* supple; (*règlement, caractère*) flexible. **~sse** /-ɛs/ *n.f.* suppleness; flexibility.

source /surs/ *n.f.* source; (*eau*) spring. **~ thermale**, hot springs.

sourcil /sursi/ *n.m.* eyebrow.

sourciller /sursije/ *v.i.* bat an eyelid.

sourd, ~e /sur, -d/ *a.* deaf; (*bruit, douleur*) dull; (*caché*) secret, hidden. —*n.m., f.* deaf person. **faire la ~e oreille**, turn a deaf ear. **~-muet** (*pl.* **~s-muets**), **~e-muette** (*pl.* **~es-muettes**) *a.* deaf and dumb; *n.m., f.* deaf mute.

sourdine /surdin/ *n.f.* (*mus.*) mute. **en ~**, quietly.

souricière /surisjɛr/ *n.f.* mousetrap; (*fig.*) trap.

sourire /surir/ *n.m.* smile. —*v.i.* smile (à, at). **~ à**, (*fortune*) smile on.

souris /suri/ *n.f.* mouse.

sournois, ~e /surnwa, -z/ *a.* sly, underhand. **~ement** /-zmɑ̃/ *adv.* slyly.

sous /su/ *prép.* under, beneath. **~ la main**, handy. **~ la pluie**, in the rain. **~ peu**, shortly. **~ terre**, underground.

sous- /su/ *préf.* (*subordination*) sub-; (*insuffisance*) under-.

sous-bois /subwa/ *n.m. invar.* undergrowth.

souscr|ire /suskrir/ *v.i.* **~ire à**, subscribe to. **~iption** *n.f.* subscription.

sous-entend|re /suzɑ̃tɑ̃dr/ *v.t.* imply. **~u** *n.m.* insinuation.

sous-estimer /suzɛstime/ *v.t.* underestimate.

sous-jacent, ~e /suʒasɑ̃, -t/ *a.* underlying.

sous-marin, ~e /sumarɛ̃, -in/ *a.* underwater. —*n.m.* submarine.

sous-officier /suzɔfisje/ *n.m.* non-commissioned officer.

sous-préfecture /suprefɛktyr/ *n.f.* sub-prefecture.

sous-produit /suprɔdɥi/ *n.m.* by-product.

soussigné, ~e /susiɲe/ *a. & n.m., f.* undersigned.

sous-sol /susɔl/ *n.m.* (*cave*) basement.

sous-titr|e /sutitr/ *n.m.* subtitle. **~er** *v.t.* subtitle.

soustr|aire† /sustrɛr/ *v.t.* remove; (*déduire*) subtract. **se ~aire à**, escape from. **~action** *n.f.* (*déduction*) subtraction.

sous-traiter /sutrete/ *v.t.* subcontract.

sous-verre /suvɛr/ *n.m. invar.* picture frame, glass mount.

sous-vêtement /suvɛtmɑ̃/ *n.m.* undergarment. **~s**, underwear.

soutane /sutan/ *n.f.* cassock.

soute /sut/ *n.f.* (*de bateau*) hold. **~ à charbon**, coal-bunker.

soutenir† /sutnir/ *v.t.* support; (*fortifier, faire durer*) sustain; (*résister à*) withstand. **~ que**, maintain that. **se ~ v. pr.** (*se tenir debout*) support o.s.

soutenu /sutny/ *a.* (*constant*) sustained; (*style*) lofty.

souterrain, ~e /sutɛrɛ̃, -ɛn/ *a.* underground. —*n.m.* underground passage, subway.

soutien /sutjɛ̃/ *n.m.* support. **~-gorge** (*pl.* **~s-gorge**) *n.m.* bra.

soutirer /sutire/ *v.t.* **~ à qn.**, extract from s.o.

souvenir[1] /suvnir/ *n.m.* memory, recollection; (*objet*) memento; (*cadeau*) souvenir.

souvenir[2]† **(se)** /(sə)suvnir/ *v. pr.* **se ~ de**, remember. **se ~ que**, remember that.

souvent /suvɑ̃/ *adv.* often.

souverain, ~e /suvrɛ̃, -ɛn/ *a.* sovereign; (*extrême: péj.*) supreme. —*n.m., f.* sovereign. **~ pontife**, pope. **~eté** /-ɛnte/ *n.f.* sovereignty.

soviétique /sɔvjetik/ *a.* Soviet. —*n.m./f.* Soviet citizen.

soyeu|x, ~se /swajø, -z/ *a.* silky.

spacieu|x, ~se /spasjø, -z/ *a.* spacious.

spaghetti /spageti/ *n.m. pl.* spaghetti.

sparadrap /sparadra/ *n.m.* sticking-plaster; (*Amer.*) adhesive tape *ou* bandage.

spasm|e /spasm/ *n.m.* spasm. **~odique** *a.* spasmodic.

spat|ial (*m. pl.* **~iaux**) /spasjal, -jo/ *a.* space.

spatule /spatyl/ *n.f.* spatula.

speaker, ∼**ine** /spikœr, -rin/ *n.m., f.* announcer.

spéc|ial (*m. pl.* ∼**iaux**) /spesjal, -jo/ *a.* special; (*singulier*) peculiar. ∼**iale- ment** *adv.* especially; (*exprès*) speci- ally.

spécialis|er (se) /(sə)spesjalize/ *v. pr.* specialize (**dans,** in). ∼**ation** *n.f.* specialization.

spécialiste /spesjalist/ *n.m./f.* special- ist.

spécialité /spesjalite/ *n.f.* speciality; (*Amer.*) specialty.

spécif|ier /spesifje/ *v.t.* specify. ∼**ica- tion** *n.f.* specification.

spécifique /spesifik/ *a.* specific.

spécimen /spesimɛn/ *n.m.* specimen.

spectacle /spɛktakl/ *n.m.* sight, spec- tacle; (*représentation*) show.

spectaculaire /spɛktakylɛr/ *a.* spec- tacular.

specta|teur, ∼**trice** /spɛktatœr, -tris/ *n.m., f.* onlooker; (*sport*) spectator. **les** ∼**teurs,** (*théâtre*) the audience.

spectre /spɛktr/ *n.m.* (*revenant*) spectre; (*images*) spectrum.

spécul|er /spekyle/ *v.i.* speculate. ∼**a- teur,** ∼**atrice** *n.m., f.* speculator. ∼**a- tion** *n.f.* speculation.

spéléologie /speleɔlɔʒi/ *n.f.* cave exploration, pot-holing; (*Amer.*) spelunking

sperme /spɛrm/ *n.m.* sperm.

sph|ère /sfɛr/ *n.f.* sphere. ∼**érique** *a.* spherical.

sphinx /sfɛ̃ks/ *n.m.* sphinx.

spirale /spiral/ *n.f.* spiral.

spirite /spirit/ *n.m./f.* spiritualist.

spirituel, ∼**le** /spirityɛl/ *a.* spiritual; (*amusant*) witty.

spiritueux /spirityø/ *n.m.* (*alcool*) spirit.

splend|ide /splɑ̃did/ *a.* splendid. ∼**eur** *n.f.* splendour.

spongieu|x, ∼**se** /spɔ̃ʒjø, -z/ *a.* spongy.

spontané /spɔ̃tane/ *a.* spontaneous. ∼**ité** *n.f.* spontaneity. ∼**ment** *adv.* spontaneously.

sporadique /spɔradik/ *a.* sporadic.

sport /spɔr/ *n.m.* sport. —*a. invar.* (*vêtements*) casual. **veste/voiture de** ∼, sports jacket/car.

sporti|f, ∼**ve** /spɔrtif, -v/ *a.* sporting; (*résultats*) sports. —*n.m.* sports- man. —*n.f.* sportswoman.

spot /spɔt/ *n.m.* spotlight.

sprint /sprint/ *n.m.* sprint. ∼**er** *v.i.* sprint; *n.m.* /-œr/ sprinter.

square /skwar/ *n.m.* (public) garden.

squelett|e /skəlɛt/ *n.m.* skeleton. ∼**ique** /-etik/ *a.* skeletal.

stabiliser /stabilize/ *v.t.* stabilize.

stab|le /stabl/ *a.* stable. ∼**ilité** *n.f.* stability.

stade[1] /stad/ *n.m.* (*sport*) stadium.

stade[2] /stad/ *n.m.* (*phase*) stage.

stag|e /staʒ/ *n.m.* training period. ∼**iaire** *a.* & *n.m./f.* trainee.

stagn|er /stagne/ *v.i.* stagnate. ∼**ant,** ∼**ante** *a.* stagnant. ∼**ation** *n.f.* stag- nation.

stand /stɑ̃d/ *n.m.* stand, stall. ∼ **de tir,** (shooting-)range.

standard[1] /stɑ̃dar/ *n.m.* switchboard. ∼**iste** /-dist/ *n.m./f.* switchboard operator.

standard[2] /stɑ̃dar/ *a. invar.* standard. ∼**iser** /-dize/ *v.t.* standardize.

standing /stɑ̃diŋ/ *n.m.* status, stand- ing. **de** ∼, (*hôtel etc.*) luxury.

star /star/ *n.f.* (*actrice*) star.

starter /startɛr/ *n.m.* (*auto.*) choke.

station /stasjɔ̃/ *n.f.* station; (*halte*) stop. ∼ **balnéaire,** seaside resort. ∼ **debout,** standing position. ∼ **de taxis,** taxi rank; (*Amer.*) taxi stand. ∼**-service** (*pl.* ∼**s-service**) *n.f.* ser- vice station. ∼ **thermale,** spa.

stationnaire /stasjɔnɛr/ *a.* station- ary.

stationn|er /stasjɔne/ *v.i.* park. ∼**e- ment** *n.m.* parking.

statique /statik/ *a.* static.

statistique /statistik/ *n.f.* statistic; (*science*) statistics. —*a.* statistical.

statue /staty/ *n.f.* statue.

statuer /statɥe/ *v.i.* ∼ **sur,** rule on.

statu quo /statykwo/ *n.m.* status quo.

stature /statyr/ *n.f.* stature.

statut /staty/ *n.m.* status. ∼**s,** (*règles*) statutes. ∼**aire** /-tɛr/ *a.* statutory.

steak /stɛk/ *n.m.* steak.

stencil /stɛnsil/ *n.m.* stencil.

sténo /steno/ *n.f.* (*personne*) steno- grapher; (*sténographie*) shorthand.

sténodactylo /stenɔdaktilo/ *n.f.* short- hand typist; (*Amer.*) stenographer.

sténographie /stenɔgrafi/ *n.f.* short- hand.

stéréo /stereo/ *n.f. & a. invar.* stereo. ∼**phonique** /-eɔfɔnik/ *a.* stereo- phonic.

stéréotyp|e /stereɔtip/ *n.m.* stereo- type. ∼**é** *a.* stereotyped.

stéril|e /steril/ *a.* sterile. ∼**ité** *n.f.* sterility.

stérilis|er /steriliz/ *v.t.* sterilize. **~ation** *n.f.* sterilization.

stéthoscope /stetɔskɔp/ *n.m.* stethoscope.

stigmat|e /stigmat/ *n.m.* mark, stigma. **~iser** *v.t.* stigmatize.

stimul|er /stimyle/ *v.t.* stimulate. **~ant** *n.m.* stimulus; (*médicament*) stimulant. **~ation** *n.f.* stimulation.

stipul|er /stipyle/ *v.t.* stipulate. **~ation** *n.f.* stipulation.

stock /stɔk/ *n.m.* stock. **~er** *v.t.* stock. **~iste** *n.m.* stockist; (*Amer.*) dealer.

stoïque /stɔik/ *a.* stoical. —*n.m./f.* stoic.

stop /stɔp/ *int.* stop. —*n.m.* stop sign; (*feu arrière*) brake light. **faire du ~**, (*fam.*) hitch-hike.

stopper /stɔpe/ *v.t./i.* stop; (*vêtement*) mend, reweave.

store /stɔr/ *n.m.* blind; (*Amer.*) shade; (*de magasin*) awning.

strabisme /strabism/ *n.m.* squint.

strapontin /strapɔ̃tɛ̃/ *n.m.* folding seat, jump seat.

stratagème /strataʒɛm/ *n.m.* stratagem.

stratég|ie /strateʒi/ *n.f.* strategy. **~ique** *a.* strategic.

strict /strikt/ *a.* strict; (*tenue, vérité*) plain. **~ement** *adv.* strictly.

strident, ~e /stridɑ̃, -t/ *a.* shrill.

str|ie /stri/ *n.f.* streak. **~ier** *v.t.* streak.

strip-tease /striptiz/ *n.m.* strip-tease.

strophe /strɔf/ *n.f.* stanza.

structur|e /stryktyr/ *n.f.* structure. **~al** (*m. pl.* **~aux**) *a.* structural. **~er** *v.t.* structure.

studieu|x, ~se /stydjø, -z/ *a.* studious; (*période*) devoted to study.

studio /stydjo/ *n.m.* (*d'artiste, de télévision, etc.*) studio; (*logement*) studio flat, bed-sitter.

stupéf|ait, ~aite /stypefɛ, -t/ *a.* amazed. **~action** *n.f.* amazement.

stupéf|ier /stypefje/ *v.t.* amaze. **~iant, ~iante** *a.* amazing; *n.m.* drug, narcotic.

stupeur /stypœr/ *n.f.* amazement; (*méd.*) stupor.

stupid|e /stypid/ *a.* stupid. **~ité** *n.f.* stupidity.

styl|e /stil/ *n.m.* style. **~isé** *a.* stylized.

stylé /stile/ *a.* well-trained.

stylo /stilo/ *n.m.* pen. **~ à bille,** ball-point pen. **~ à encre,** fountain-pen.

su /sy/ *voir* savoir.

suave /sɥav/ *a.* sweet.

subalterne /sybaltɛrn/ *a.* & *n.m./f.* subordinate.

subconscient, ~e /sypkɔ̃sjɑ̃, -t/ *a.* & *n.m.* subconscious.

subdiviser /sybdivize/ *v.t.* subdivide.

subir /sybir/ *v.t.* suffer; (*traitement, expériences*) undergo.

subit, ~e /sybi, -t/ *a.* sudden. **~ement** /-tmɑ̃/ *adv.* suddenly.

subjecti|f, ~ve /sybʒɛktif, -v/ *a.* subjective. **~vité** *n.f.* subjectivity.

subjonctif /sybʒɔ̃ktif/ *a.* & *n.m.* subjunctive.

subjuguer /sybʒyge/ *v.t.* (*charmer*) captivate.

sublime /syblim/ *a.* sublime.

sublimer /syblime/ *v.t.* sublimate.

submer|ger /sybmɛrʒe/ *v.t.* submerge; (*fig.*) overwhelm. **~sion** *n.f.* submersion.

subordonné, ~e /sybɔrdɔne/ *a.* & *n.m., f.* subordinate.

subord|onner /sybɔrdɔne/ *v.t.* subordinate (**à,** to). **~ination** *n.f.* subordination.

subreptice /sybrɛptis/ *a.* surreptitious.

subside /sybzid/ *n.m.* grant.

subsidiaire /sypsidjɛr/ *a.* subsidiary.

subsist|er /sybziste/ *v.i.* subsist; (*durer, persister*) exist. **~ance** *n.f.* subsistence.

substance /sypstɑ̃s/ *n.f.* substance.

substantiel, ~le /sypstɑ̃sjɛl/ *a.* substantial.

substantif /sypstɑ̃tif/ *n.m.* noun.

substit|uer /sypstitɥe/ *v.t.* substitute (**à, for**). **se ~uer à,** (*remplacer*) substitute for; (*évincer*) take over from. **~ution** *n.f.* substitution.

subterfuge /sypterfyʒ/ *n.m.* subterfuge.

subtil /syptil/ *a.* subtle. **~ité** *n.f.* subtlety.

subtiliser /syptilize/ *v.t.* steal.

subvenir /sybvənir/ *v.i.* **~ à,** provide for.

subvention /sybvɑ̃sjɔ̃/ *n.f.* subsidy. **~ner** /-jɔne/ *v.t.* subsidize.

subversi|f, ~ve /sybvɛrsif, -v/ *a.* subversive.

subversion /sybvɛrsjɔ̃/ *n.f.* subversion.

suc /syk/ *n.m.* juice.

succédané /syksedane/ *n.m.* substitute (**de, for**).

succéder /syksede/ *v.i.* **~ à,** succeed. **se ~** *v. pr.* succeed one another.

succès /syksɛ/ *n.m.* success. **à ~**, (*film, livre, etc.*) successful. **avoir du ~**, be a success.

successeur /syksesœr/ *n.m.* successor.

successi|f, **~ve** /syksesif, -v/ *a.* successive. **~vement** *adv.* successively.

succession /syksesjɔ̃/ *n.f.* succession.

succinct, ~e /syksɛ̃, -t/ *a.* succinct.

succion /syksjɔ̃/ *n.f.* suction.

succomber /sykɔ̃be/ *v.i.* die. **~ à**, succumb to.

succulent, ~e /sykylɑ̃, -t/ *a.* succulent.

succursale /sykyrsal/ *n.f.* (*comm.*) branch.

sucer /syse/ *v.t.* suck.

sucette /sysɛt/ *n.f.* (*bonbon*) lollipop; (*tétine*) dummy; (*Amer.*) pacifier.

sucr|e /sykr/ *n.m.* sugar. **~e d'orge**, barley sugar. **~e en poudre**, castor sugar; (*Amer.*) finely ground sugar. **~ier, ~ière** *a.* sugar; *n.m.* (*récipient*) sugar-bowl.

sucr|er /sykre/ *v.t.* sugar, sweeten. **~é** *a.* sweet; (*additionné de sucre*) sweetened.

sucreries /sykrəri/ *n.f. pl.* sweets.

sud /syd/ *n.m.* south. —*a. invar.* south; (*partie*) southern; (*direction*) southerly. **~-africain, ~africaine** *a.* & *n.m.*, *f.* South African. **~-est** *n.m.* south-east. **~-ouest** *n.m.* south-west.

Suède /sɥɛd/ *n.f.* Sweden.

suédois, ~e /sɥedwa, -z/ *a.* Swedish. —*n.m.*, *f.* Swede. —*n.m.* (*lang.*) Swedish.

suer /sɥe/ *v.t./i.* sweat.

sueur /sɥœr/ *n.f.* sweat. **en ~**, sweating.

suff|ire† /syfir/ *v.i.* be enough (**à qn.**, for s.o.). **il ~it de faire**, one only has to do. **il ~it d'une goutte pour**, a drop is enough to. **~ire à**, (*besoin*) satisfy. **se ~ire à soi-même**, be self-sufficient.

suffis|ant, ~ante /syfizɑ̃, -t/ *a.* sufficient; (*vaniteux*) conceited. **~amment** *adv.* sufficiently. **~amment de**, sufficient. **~ance** *n.f.* (*vanité*) conceit.

suffixe /syfiks/ *n.m.* suffix.

suffo|quer /syfɔke/ *v.t./i.* choke, suffocate. **~cation** *n.f.* (*asphyxie*) feeling of suffocation.

suffrage /syfraʒ/ *n.m.* (*voix: pol.*) vote; (*modalité*) suffrage.

sugg|érer /sygʒere/ *v.t.* suggest. **~estion** /-ʒɛstjɔ̃/ *n.f.* suggestion.

suggesti|f, **~ve** /sygʒɛstif, -v/ *a.* suggestive.

suicid|e /sɥisid/ *n.m.* suicide. **~aire** *a.* suicidal.

suicid|er (se) /(sə)sɥiside/ *v. pr.* commit suicide. **~é, ~ée** *n.m.*, *f.* suicide.

suie /sɥi/ *n.f.* soot.

suint|er /sɥɛ̃te/ *v.i.* ooze. **~ement** *n.m.* oozing.

suis /sɥi/ *voir* **être, suivre**.

Suisse /sɥis/ *n.f.* Switzerland.

suisse /sɥis/ *a.* & *n.m.* Swiss. **~sse** /-ɛs/ *n.f.* Swiss (woman).

suite /sɥit/ *n.f.* continuation, rest; (*d'un film*) sequel; (*série*) series; (*appartement, escorte*) suite; (*résultat*) consequence; (*cohérence*) order. **~s**, (*de maladie*) after-effects. **à la ~, de ~**, (*successivement*) in succession. **à la ~ de**, (*derrière*) behind. **à la ~ de, par ~ de**, as a result of. **faire ~ (à)**, follow. **par la ~**, afterwards.

suivant¹, **~e** /sɥivɑ̃, -t/ *a.* following, next. —*n.m.*, *f.* following *ou* next person.

suivant² /sɥivɑ̃/ *prép.* (*selon*) according to.

suivi /sɥivi/ *a.* steady, sustained; (*cohérent*) consistent. **peu/très ~**, (*cours*) poorly/well-attended.

suivre† /sɥivr/ *v.t./i.* follow; (*comprendre*) keep up (with), follow. **se ~** *v. pr.* follow each other. **faire ~**, (*courrier etc.*) forward.

sujet¹, **~te** /syʒɛ, -t/ *a.* **~ à**, liable *ou* subject to. —*n.m.*, *f.* (*gouverné*) subject.

sujet² /syʒɛ/ *n.m.* (*matière, individu*) subject; (*motif*) cause; (*gram.*) subject. **au ~ de**, about.

sujétion /syʒesjɔ̃/ *n.f.* (*obligation*) constraint; (*esclavage*) subjection.

sulfurique /sylfyrik/ *a.* sulphuric.

sultan /syltɑ̃/ *n.m.* sultan.

summum /sɔmɔm/ *n.m.* height.

superbe /sypɛrb/ *a.* superb.

supercarburant /sypɛrkarbyrɑ̃/ *n.m.* high-octane petrol; (*Amer.*) high-octane gasoline.

supercherie /sypɛrʃəri/ *n.f.* trickery.

superficie /sypɛrfisi/ *n.f.* area.

superficiel, ~le /sypɛrfisjɛl/ *a.* superficial.

superflu /sypɛrfly/ *a.* superfluous. —*n.m.* (*excédent*) surplus.

supérieur, ~e /syperjœr/ *a.* (*plus*

haut) upper; (*quantité, nombre*) greater (**à,** than); (*études, principe*) higher (**à,** than); (*meilleur, hautain*) superior (**à,** to). —*n.m., f.* superior.

supériorité /syperjɔrite/ *n.f.* superiority.

superlati|f, ~ve /sypɛrlatif, -v/ *a. & n.m.* superlative.

supermarché /sypɛrmarʃe/ *n.m.* supermarket.

superposer /sypɛrpoze/ *v.t.* superimpose.

superpuissance /sypɛrpɥisɑ̃s/ *n.f.* superpower.

supersonique /sypɛrsɔnik/ *a.* supersonic.

superstit|ion /sypɛrstisjɔ̃/ *n.f.* superstition. **~ieux, ~ieuse** *a.* superstitious.

superviser /sypɛrvize/ *v.t.* supervise.

supplanter /syplɑ̃te/ *v.t.* supplant.

suppléan|t, ~te /sypleɑ̃, -t/ *n.m., f.* (temporary) replacement. —*a.* temporary. **~ce** *n.f.* (*fonction*) temporary appointment.

suppléer /syplee/ *v.t.* (*remplacer*) replace; (*ajouter*) supply. —*v.i.* **~ à,** (*compenser*) make up for.

supplément /syplemɑ̃/ *n.m.* (*argent*) extra charge; (*de livre*) supplement. **en ~,** extra. **un ~ de,** (*travail etc.*) extra. **~aire** /-tɛr/ *a.* extra, additional.

supplic|e /syplis/ *n.m.* torture. **~ier** *v.t.* torture.

supplier /syplije/ *v.t.* beg, beseech (**de,** to).

support /sypɔr/ *n.m.* support; (*publicitaire: fig.*) medium.

support|er[1] /sypɔrte/ *v.t.* (*endurer*) bear; (*subir*) suffer; (*soutenir*) support; (*résister à*) withstand. **~able** *a.* bearable.

supporter[2] /sypɔrtɛr/ *n.m.* (*sport*) supporter.

suppos|er /sypoze/ *v.t.* suppose; (*impliquer*) imply. **à ~er que,** supposing that. **~ition** *n.f.* supposition.

suppr|imer /syprime/ *v.t.* get rid of, remove; (*annuler*) cancel; (*mot*) delete. **~imer à qn.,** (*enlever*) take away from s.o. **~ession** *n.f.* removal; cancellation; deletion.

suprématie /sypremasi/ *n.f.* supremacy.

suprême /syprɛm/ *a.* supreme.

sur /syr/ *prép.* on, upon; (*pardessus*) over; (*au sujet de*) about, on; (*pro-*

portion) out of; (*mesure*) by. **aller/ tourner/etc. ~,** go/turn/*etc.* towards. **mettre/jeter/etc. ~,** put/throw/*etc.* on to. **~-le-champ** *adv.* immediately. **~ le qui-vive,** on the alert. **~ mesure,** made to measure. **~ place,** on the spot.

sur- /syr/ *préf.* over-.

sûr /syr/ *a.* certain, sure; (*sans danger*) safe; (*digne de confiance*) reliable; (*main*) steady; (*jugement*) sound.

surabondance /syrabɔ̃dɑ̃s/ *n.f.* superabundance.

suranné /syrane/ *a.* outmoded.

surcharg|e /syrʃarʒ/ *n.f.* overloading; (*poids*) extra load. **~er** *v.t.* overload; (*texte*) alter.

surchauffer /syrʃofe/ *v.t.* overheat.

surchoix /syrʃwa/ *a. invar.* of finest quality.

surclasser /syrklase/ *v.t.* outclass.

surcroît /syrkrwa/ *n.m.* increase (**de,** in), additional amount (**de,** of). **de ~,** in addition.

surdité /syrdite/ *n.f.* deafness.

sureau (*pl.* **~x**) /syro/ *n.m.* (*arbre*) elder.

surélever /syrɛlve/ *v.t.* raise.

sûrement /syrmɑ̃/ *adv.* certainly; (*sans danger*) safely.

surench|ère /syrɑ̃ʃɛr/ *n.f.* higher bid. **~érir** *v.i.* bid higher (**sur,** than).

surestimer /syrɛstime/ *v.t.* overestimate.

sûreté /syrte/ *n.f.* safety; (*garantie*) surety; (*d'un geste*) steadiness. **être en ~,** be safe. **S~ (nationale),** *division of French Ministère de l'Intérieur in charge of police.*

surexcité /syrɛksite/ *a.* very excited.

surf /syrf/ *n.m.* surf-riding.

surface /syrfas/ *n.f.* surface. **faire ~,** (*sous-marin etc.*) surface.

surfait, ~e /syrfɛ, -t/ *a.* overrated.

surgelé /syrʒəle/ *a.* (deep-)frozen.

surgir /syrʒir/ *v.i.* appear (suddenly).

surhomme /syrɔm/ *n.m.* superman.

surhumain, ~e /syrymɛ̃, -ɛn/ *a.* superhuman.

surlendemain /syrlɑ̃dmɛ̃/ *n.m.* **le ~,** two days later. **le ~ de,** two days after.

surmen|er /syrməne/ *v.t.,* **se ~er** *v. pr.* overwork. **~age** *n.m.* overworking; (*méd.*) overwork.

surmonter /syrmɔ̃te/ *v.t.* (*vaincre*) overcome, surmount; (*être au-dessus de*) surmount, top.

surnager /syrnaʒe/ *v.i.* float.
surnaturel, ∼**le** /syrnatyrɛl/ *a.*
supernatural.
surnom /syrnɔ̃/ *n.m.* nickname.
∼**mer** /-ɔme/ *v.t.* nickname.
surnombre (en) /(ɑ̃)syrnɔ̃br/ *adv.* too
many. **il est en** ∼, he is one too many.
surpasser /syrpɑse/ *v.t.* surpass.
surpeuplé /syrpœple/ *a.* overpopu-
lated.
surplomb /syrplɔ̃/ *n.m.* overhang.
en ∼, overhanging. ∼**er** /-be/ *v.t./i.*
overhang.
surplus /syrply/ *n.m.* surplus.
surpr|endre† /syrprɑ̃dr/ *v.t.* (*étonner*)
surprise; (*prendre au dépourvu*)
catch, surprise; (*entendre*) overhear; (*découvrir*) discover. ∼**enant,**
∼**enante** *a.* surprising. ∼**is,** ∼**ise**
a. surprised (**de,** at).
surprise /syrpriz/ *n.f.* surprise. ∼-
partie (*pl.* ∼**s-parties**) *n.f.* party.
surréalisme /syrrealism/ *n.m.* surrealism.
sursaut /syrso/ *n.m.* start, jump. **en**
∼, with a start. ∼ **de,** (*regain*) burst
of. ∼**er** /-te/ *v.i.* start, jump.
sursis /syrsi/ *n.m.* reprieve; (*mil.*) de-
ferment. **deux ans (de prison) avec**
∼, a two-year suspended sentence.
surtaxe /syrtaks/ *n.f.* surcharge.
surtout /syrtu/ *adv.* especially,
mainly; (*avant tout*) above all. ∼ **pas,**
certainly not.
surveillant, ∼**e** /syrvɛjɑ̃, -t/ *n.m., f.*
(*de prison*) warder; (*au lycée*) supervisor (in charge of discipline).
surveill|er /syrveje/ *v.t.* watch; (*tra-
vaux, élèves*) supervise. ∼**ance** *n.f.*
watch; supervision; (*de la police*) surveillance.
survenir /syrvənir/ *v.i.* occur, come
about; (*personne*) turn up.
survêtement /syrvɛtmɑ̃/ *n.m.* (*sport*)
track suit.
survie /syrvi/ *n.f.* survival.
survivance /syrvivɑ̃s/ *n.f.* survival.
surviv|re† /syrvivr/ *v.i.* survive. ∼**re**
à, (*conflit etc.*) survive; (*personne*) outlive. ∼**ant,** ∼**ante** *a.* surviving; *n.m.,*
f. survivor.
survol /syrvɔl/ *n.m.* **le** ∼ **de,** flying
over. ∼**er** *v.t.* fly over; (*livre*) skim
through.
survolté /syrvɔlte/ *a.* (*surexcité*)
worked up.
susceptib|le /sysɛptibl/ *a.* touchy.
∼**le de faire,** (*possibilité*) liable to

do; (*capacité*) able to do. ∼**ilité** *n.f.*
susceptibility.
susciter /sysite/ *v.t.* (*éveiller*) arouse;
(*occasionner*) create.
suspect, ∼**e** /syspɛ(kt), -ɛkt/ *a.* suspect, suspicious. ∼ **de,** suspected
of. —*n.m., f.* suspect. ∼**er** /-ɛkte/ *v.t.*
suspect.
suspend|re /syspɑ̃dr/ *v.t.* (*arrêter, dif-
férer, destituer*) suspend; (*accrocher*)
hang (up). **se** ∼**re à,** hang from. ∼**u**
à, hanging from.
suspens (en) /(ɑ̃)syspɑ̃/ *adv.* (*affaire*)
in abeyance; (*dans l'indécision*) in
suspense.
suspense /syspɑ̃s/ *n.m.* suspense.
suspension /syspɑ̃sjɔ̃/ *n.f.* suspension; (*lustre*) chandelier.
suspicion /syspisjɔ̃/ *n.f.* suspicion.
susurrer /sysyre/ *v.t./i.* murmur.
sutur|e /sytyr/ *n.f.* (*méd.*) stitching.
∼**er** *v.t.* stitch (up).
svelte /svɛlt/ *a.* slender.
S.V.P. *abrév. voir* **s'il vous plaît.**
syllabe /silab/ *n.f.* syllable.
symbol|e /sɛ̃bɔl/ *n.m.* symbol. ∼**ique**
a. symbolic(al). ∼**iser** *v.t.* symbolize.
symétr|ie /simetri/ *n.f.* symmetry.
∼**ique** *a.* symmetrical.
sympath|ie /sɛ̃pati/ *n.f.* (*goût*) liking;
(*affinité*) affinity; (*condoléances*) sym-
pathy. ∼**ique** *a.* nice, pleasant.
sympathis|er /sɛ̃patize/ *v.i.* get on
well (**avec,** with). ∼**ant,** ∼**ante** *n.m.,*
f. sympathizer.
symphon|ie /sɛ̃fɔni/ *n.f.* symphony.
∼**ique** *a.* symphonic; (*orchestre*) sym-
phony.
symposium /sɛ̃pozjɔm/ *n.m.* symposium.
sympt|ôme /sɛ̃ptom/ *n.m.* symptom.
∼**omatique** /-ɔmatik/ *a.* sympto-
matic.
synagogue /sinagɔg/ *n.f.* synagogue.
synchroniser /sɛ̃krɔnize/ *v.t.* synchronize.
syncope /sɛ̃kɔp/ *n.f.* (*méd.*) black-out.
syncoper /sɛ̃kɔpe/ *v.t.* syncopate.
syndic|at /sɛ̃dika/ *n.m.* (trade) union.
∼**at d'initiative,** tourist office.
∼**al** (*m. pl.* ∼**aux**) *a.* (trade-)union.
∼**aliste** *n.m./f.* trade-unionist; *a.*
(trade-)union.
syndiqué, ∼**e** /sɛ̃dike/ *n.m., f.* (trade-)
union member.
syndrome /sɛ̃drom/ *n.m.* syndrome.
synonyme /sinɔnim/ *a.* synonym-
ous. —*n.m.* synonym.

syntaxe /sɛ̃taks/ *n.f.* syntax.
synthèse /sɛ̃tɛz/ *n.f.* synthesis.
synthétique /sɛ̃tetik/ *a.* synthetic.
syphilis /sifilis/ *n.f.* syphilis.
Syrie /siri/ *n.f.* Syria.

syrien, ∼ne /sirjɛ̃, -jɛn/ *a.* & *n.m., f.* Syrian.
systématique /sistematik/ *a.* systematic. **∼ment** *adv.* systematically.
système /sistɛm/ *n.m.* system.

T

t' /t/ *voir* **te.**

ta /ta/ *voir* **ton¹.**

tabac /taba/ *n.m.* tobacco; (*magasin*) tobacconist's shop. —*a. invar.* buff. **~ à priser,** snuff.

tabasser /tabase/ *v.t.* (*fam.*) beat up.

tabernacle /tabɛrnakl/ *n.m.* tabernacle.

table /tabl/ *n.f.* table. **à ~!,** come and eat! **faire ~ rase,** make a clean sweep (**de,** of). **~ de nuit,** bedside table. **~ des matières,** table of contents. **~ roulante,** (tea-)trolley; (*Amer.*) (serving) cart.

tableau (*pl.* **~x**) /tablo/ *n.m.* picture; (*peinture*) painting; (*panneau*) board; (*graphique*) chart; (*liste*) list. **~ (noir),** blackboard. **~ d'affichage,** noticeboard. **~ de bord,** dashboard.

tabler /table/ *v.i.* **~ sur,** count on.

tablette /tablɛt/ *n.f.* shelf. **~ de chocolat,** bar of chocolate.

tablier /tablije/ *n.m.* apron; (*de pont*) platform; (*de magasin*) shutter.

tabou /tabu/ *n.m.* & *a.* taboo.

tabouret /taburɛ/ *n.m.* stool.

tabulateur /tabylatœr/ *n.m.* tabulator.

tac /tak/ *n.m.* **du ~ au tac,** tit for tat.

tache /taʃ/ *n.f.* mark, spot; (*salissure*) stain. **faire ~ d'huile,** spread. **~ de rousseur,** freckle.

tâche /tɑʃ/ *n.f.* task, job.

tacher /taʃe/ *v.t.* stain. **se ~** *v. pr.* (*personne*) get stains on one's clothes.

tâcher /tɑʃe/ *v.i.* **~ de faire,** try to do.

tacheté /taʃte/ *a.* spotted.

tacite /tasit/ *a.* tacit.

taciturne /tasityrn/ *a.* taciturn.

tact /takt/ *n.m.* tact.

tactile /taktil/ *a.* tactile.

tactique /taktik/ *a.* tactical. —*n.f.* tactics. **une ~,** a tactic.

taie /tɛ/ *n.f.* **~ d'oreiller,** pillowcase.

taillader /tɑjade/ *v.t.* gash, slash.

taille¹ /tɑj/ *n.f.* (*ceinture*) waist; (*hauteur*) height; (*grandeur*) size. **de ~,** sizeable.

taille² /tɑj/ *n.f.* cutting; pruning; (*forme*) cut. **~er** *v.t.* cut; (*arbre*) prune; (*crayon*) sharpen; (*vêtement*) cut out. **se ~er** *v. pr.* (*argot*) clear off. **~e-crayon(s)** *n.m. invar.* pencil-sharpener.

tailleur /tɑjœr/ *n.m.* tailor; (*costume*) lady's suit.

taillis /tɑji/ *n.m.* copse.

taire† /tɛr/ *v.t.* say nothing about. **se ~** *v. pr.* be silent *ou* quiet; (*devenir silencieux*) fall silent. **faire ~,** silence.

talc /talk/ *n.m.* talcum powder.

talent /talɑ̃/ *n.m.* talent. **~ueux, ~ueuse** /-tɥø, -z/ *a.* talented.

taloche /talɔʃ/ *n.f.* (*fam.*) slap (in the face).

talon /talɔ̃/ *n.m.* heel; (*de chèque*) stub.

talonner /talɔne/ *v.t.* follow hard on the heels of.

talus /taly/ *n.m.* embankment.

tambour /tɑ̃bur/ *n.m.* drum; (*personne*) drummer; (*porte*) revolving door.

tambourin /tɑ̃burɛ̃/ *n.m.* tambourine.

tambouriner /tɑ̃burine/ *v.t./i.* drum (**sur,** on).

tamis /tami/ *n.m.* sieve. **~er** /-ze/ *v.t.* sieve.

Tamise /tamiz/ *n.f.* Thames.

tamisé /tamize/ *a.* (*lumière*) subdued.

tampon /tɑ̃pɔ̃/ *n.m.* (*pour boucher*) plug; (*ouate*) wad, pad; (*timbre*) stamp; (*de train*) buffer. **~ hygiénique,** tampon.

tamponner /tɑ̃pɔne/ *v.t.* crash into; (*timbrer*) stamp; (*plaie*) dab; (*mur*) plug. **se ~** *v. pr.* (*véhicules*) crash into each other.

tandem /tɑ̃dɛm/ *n.m.* (*bicyclette*) tandem; (*personnes: fig.*) duo.

tandis que /tɑ̃dik(ə)/ *conj.* while.

tangage /tɑ̃gaʒ/ *n.m.* pitching.

tangente /tɑ̃ʒɑ̃t/ *n.f.* tangent.

tangible /tɑ̃ʒibl/ *a.* tangible.

tango /tɑ̃go/ *n.m.* tango.

tanguer /tɑ̃ge/ *v.i.* pitch.

tanière /tanjɛr/ *n.f.* den.

tank /tɑ̃k/ *n.m.* tank.

tann|er /tane/ *v.t.* tan. **~é** *a.* (*visage*) tanned, weather-beaten.

tant /tɑ̃/ *adv.* (*travailler, manger, etc.*) so much. **~ (de),** (*quantité*) so much; (*nombre*) so many. **~ que,** as long as; (*autant que*) as much as. **en ~ que,** (*comme*) as. **~ mieux!,** fine!, all the better! ∼ **pis!**, too bad!, it can't be helped.

tante /tãt/ *n.f.* aunt.

tantôt /tãto/ *adv.* sometimes; (*cet après-midi*) this afternoon.

tapag|e /tapaʒ/ *n.m.* din. ∼**eur**, ∼**euse** *a.* rowdy; (*tape-à-l'œil*) flashy.

tapant, ∼**e** /tapã, -t/ *a.* (*précis*) sharp.

tape /tap/ *n.f.* slap. ∼**-à-l'œil** *a. invar.* flashy, tawdry.

taper /tape/ *v.t.* bang; (*enfant*) slap; (*emprunter*: *fam.*) touch for money. ∼ (à la machine), type. —*v.i.* (*cogner*) bang; (*soleil*) beat down. ∼ **dans**, (*puiser dans*) dig into. ∼ **sur**, thump; (*critiquer*: *fam.*) knock. se ∼ *v. pr.* (*repas*: *fam.*) put away; (*corvée*: *fam.*) do.

tapioca /tapjɔka/ *n.m.* tapioca.

tap|ir (se) /(sə)tapir/ *v. pr.* crouch. ∼**i** *a.* crouching.

tapis /tapi/ *n.m.* carpet; (*petit*) rug; (*pour meuble*) cloth. ∼**-brosse** *n.m.* doormat. ∼ **de sol**, ground-sheet. ∼ **roulant**, (*pour objets*) conveyor belt.

tapiss|er /tapise/ *v.t.* (wall)paper; (*fig.*) cover (**de**, with). ∼**erie** *n.f.* tapestry; (*papier peint*) wallpaper. ∼**ier**, ∼**ière** *n.m.*, *f.* (*décorateur*) interior decorator; (*qui recouvre un siège*) upholsterer.

tapoter /tapɔte/ *v.t.* tap, pat.

taquin, ∼**e** /takɛ̃, -in/ *a.* fond of teasing. —*n.m.*, *f.* tease(r). ∼**er** /-ine/ *v.t.* tease. ∼**erie(s)** /-inri/ *n.f.* (*pl.*) teasing.

tarabiscoté /tarabiskɔte/ *a.* overelaborate.

tard /tar/ *adv.* late. **au plus** ∼, at the latest. **plus** ∼, later.

tarder /tarde/ *v.i.* (*être lent à venir*) be a long time coming. ∼ (à faire), take a long time (doing), delay (doing). **il me tarde de,** I long to.

tardi|f, ∼**ve** /tardif, -v/ *a.* late; (*regrets*) belated.

tare /tar/ *n.f.* (*défaut*) defect.

taré /tare/ *a.* (*méd.*) degenerate.

targette /tarʒɛt/ *n.f.* bolt.

targuer (se) /(sə)targe/ *v. pr.* se ∼ **de**, boast about.

tarif /tarif/ *n.m.* tariff; (*de train, taxi*) fare. ∼**s postaux**, postage *ou* postal rates. ∼**aire** *a.* tariff.

tarir /tarir/ *v.t./i.*, **se** ∼ *v. pr.* dry up.

tarte /tart/ *n.f.* tart; (*Amer.*) (open) pie. —*a. invar.* (*sot*: *fam.*) stupid; (*laid*: *fam.*) ugly.

tartin|e /tartin/ *n.f.* slice of bread (and butter). ∼**er** *v.t.* spread.

tartre /tartr/ *n.m.* (*bouilloire*) fur, calcium deposit; (*dents*) tartar.

tas /tɑ/ *n.m.* pile, heap. **un** *ou* **des** ∼ **de**, (*fam.*) lots of.

tasse /tɑs/ *n.f.* cup. ∼ **à thé**, teacup.

tasser /tɑse/ *v.t.* pack, squeeze; (*terre*) pack (down). se ∼ *v. pr.* (*terrain*) sink; (*se serrer*) squeeze up.

tâter /tɑte/ *v.t.* feel; (*fig.*) sound out. —*v.i.* ∼ **de**, try out.

tatillon, ∼**ne** /tatijɔ̃, -jɔn/ *a.* finicky.

tâtonn|er /tɑtɔne/ *v.i.* grope about. ∼**ements** *n.m. pl.* (*essais*) trial and error.

tâtons (à) /(a)tɑtɔ̃/ *adv.* **avancer** *ou* **marcher à** ∼, grope one's way along.

tatou|er /tatwe/ *v.t.* tattoo. ∼**age** *n.m.* (*dessin*) tattoo.

taudis /todi/ *n.m.* hovel.

taule /tol/ *n.f.* (*fam.*) prison.

taup|e /top/ *n.f.* mole. ∼**inière** *n.f.* molehill.

taureau (*pl.* ∼**x**) /tɔro/ *n.m.* bull.

taux /to/ *n.m.* rate.

taverne /tavɛrn/ *n.f.* tavern.

tax|e /taks/ *n.f.* tax. ∼**e sur la valeur ajoutée,** value added tax. ∼**er** *v.t.* tax; (*produit*) fix the price of. ∼**er qn. de,** accuse s.o. of.

taxi /taksi/ *n.m.* taxi(-cab); (*personne*: *fam.*) taxi-driver.

taxiphone /taksifɔn/ *n.m.* pay phone.

Tchécoslovaquie /tʃekɔslɔvaki/ *n.f.* Czechoslovakia.

tchèque /tʃɛk/ *a. & n.m./f.* Czech.

te, t'* /tə, t/ *pron.* you; (*indirect*) (to) you; (*réfléchi*) yourself.

technicien, ∼**ne** /tɛknisjɛ̃, -jɛn/ *n.m.*, *f.* technician.

technique /tɛknik/ *a.* technical. —*n.f.* technique. ∼**ment** *adv.* technically.

technolog|ie /tɛknɔlɔʒi/ *n.f.* technology. ∼**ique** *a.* technological.

teck /tɛk/ *n.m.* teak.

teindre† /tɛdr/ *v.t.* dye. **se** ∼ *v. pr.* (*personne*) dye one's hair.

teint /tɛ̃/ *n.m.* complexion.

teint|e /tɛ̃t/ *n.f.* shade, tint. **une** ∼**e de,** (*fig.*) a tinge of. ∼**er** *v.t.* (*papier, verre, etc.*) tint; (*bois*) stain.

teintur|e /tɛ̃tyr/ *n.f.* dyeing; (*produit*) dye. ∼**erie** *n.f.* (*boutique*) drycleaner's (and dyer's). ∼**ier**, ∼**ière** *n.m.*, *f.* dry-cleaner (and dyer).

tel, ∼**le** /tɛl/ *a.* such. **un** ∼ **livre**/*etc.*, such a book/*etc.* **un** ∼ **chagrin**/*etc.*, such sorrow/*etc.* ~ **que,** such as, like; (*ainsi que*) (just) as. ~ **ou tel,** such-and-such. ~ **quel,** (just) as it is.

télé /tele/ *n.f.* (*fam.*) TV.

télécommander /telekɔmɑ̃de/ *v.t.* operate by remote control.

télécommunications /telekɔmynikɑsjɔ̃/ *n.f. pl.* telecommunications.

télégramme /telegram/ *n.m.* telegram.

télégraph|e /telegraf/ *n.m.* telegraph. ~**ier** *v.t./i.* ~**ier (à),** cable. ~**ique** *a.* telegraphic; (*fil, poteau*) telegraph.

téléguid|er /telegide/ *v.t.* control by radio. ~**é** *a.* radio-controlled.

télématique /telematik/ *n.f.* computer communications.

télépathie /telepati/ *n.f.* telepathy.

téléphérique /teleferik/ *n.m.* cable-car.

téléphon|e /telefɔn/ *n.m.* (tele)phone. ~**e rouge,** (*pol.*) hot line. ~**er** *v.t./i.* ~**er (à),** (tele)phone. ~**ique** *a.* (tele)phone. ~**iste** *n.m./f.* operator.

télescop|e /teleskɔp/ *n.m.* telescope. ~**ique** *a.* telescopic.

télescoper /teleskɔpe/ *v.t.* smash into. **se** ~ *v. pr.* (*véhicules*) smash into each other.

télésiège /telesjɛʒ/ *n.m.* chair-lift.

téléski /teleski/ *n.m.* ski tow.

téléspecta|teur, ~**trice** /telespɛktatœr, -tris/ *n.m.,f.* (television) viewer.

télévis|er /televize/ *v.t.* televise. ~**eur** *n.m.* television set.

télévision /televizjɔ̃/ *n.f.* television.

télex /telɛks/ *n.m.* telex.

telle /tɛl/ *voir* **tel.**

tellement /tɛlmɑ̃/ *adv.* (*tant*) so much; (*si*) so. ~ **de,** (*quantité*) so much; (*nombre*) so many.

témér|aire /temerɛr/ *a.* rash. ~**ité** *n.f.* rashness.

témoignage /temwaɲaʒ/ *n.m.* testimony, evidence; (*récit*) account. ~ **de,** (*sentiment*) token of.

témoigner /temwaɲe/ *v.i.* testify (**de,** to). —*v.t.* show. ~ **que,** testify that.

témoin /temwɛ̃/ *n.m.* witness; (*sport*) baton. **être** ~ **de,** witness. ~ **oculaire,** eyewitness.

tempe /tɑ̃p/ *n.f.* (*anat.*) temple.

tempérament /tɑ̃peramɑ̃/ *n.m.* temperament; (*physique*) constitution. **à** ~, (*acheter*) on hire-purchase; (*Amer.*) on the installment plan.

tempérance /tɑ̃perɑ̃s/ *n.f.* temperance.

température /tɑ̃peratyr/ *n.f.* temperature.

tempér|er /tɑ̃pere/ *v.t.* temper. ~**é** *a.* (*climat*) temperate.

tempête /tɑ̃pɛt/ *n.f.* storm. ~ **de neige,** snowstorm.

tempêter /tɑ̃pete/ *v.i.* (*crier*) rage.

temple /tɑ̃pl/ *n.m.* temple; (*protestant*) church.

temporaire /tɑ̃pɔrɛr/ *a.* temporary. ~**ment** *adv.* temporarily.

temporel, ~**le** /tɑ̃pɔrɛl/ *a.* temporal.

temporiser /tɑ̃pɔrize/ *v.i.* play for time.

temps[1] /tɑ̃/ *n.m.* time; (*gram.*) tense; (*étape*) stage. **à** ~ **partiel/plein,** part-/full-time. **ces derniers** ~, lately. **dans le** ~, at one time. **dans quelque** ~, in a while. **de** ~ **en temps,** from time to time. ~ **d'arrêt,** pause.

temps[2] /tɑ̃/ *n.m.* (*atmosphère*) weather. ~ **de chien,** filthy weather.

tenace /tənas/ *a.* stubborn.

ténacité /tenasite/ *n.f.* stubbornness.

tenaille(s) /tənɑj/ *n.f. (pl.)* pincers.

tenanc|ier, ~**ière** /tənɑ̃sje, -jɛr/ *n.m., f.* keeper (**de,** of).

tenant /tənɑ̃/ *n.m.* (*partisan*) supporter; (*d'un titre*) holder.

tendance /tɑ̃dɑ̃s/ *n.f.* tendency; (*opinions*) leanings; (*évolution*) trend. **avoir** ~ **à,** have a tendency to, tend to.

tendon /tɑ̃dɔ̃/ *n.m.* tendon.

tendre[1] /tɑ̃dr/ *v.t.* stretch; (*piège*) set; (*bras*) stretch out; (*main*) hold out; (*cou*) crane; (*tapisserie*) hang. ~ **à qn.,** hold out to s.o. —*v.i.* ~ **à,** tend to. ~ **l'oreille,** prick up one's ears.

tendre[2] /tɑ̃dr/ *a.* tender; (*couleur, bois*) soft. ~**ment** /-əmɑ̃/ *adv.* tenderly. ~**sse** /-ɛs/ *n.f.* tenderness. ~**té** /-əte/ *n.f.* (*de viande*) tenderness.

tendu /tɑ̃dy/ *a.* (*corde*) tight; (*personne, situation*) tense; (*main*) outstretched.

tén|èbres /tenɛbr/ *n.f. pl.* darkness. ~**ébreux,** ~**ébreuse** *a.* dark.

teneur /tənœr/ *n.f.* content.

tenir† /tənir/ *v.t.* hold; (*pari, promesse, hôtel*) keep; (*place*) take up; (*propos*) utter; (*rôle*) play. ~ **de,** (*avoir reçu de*) have got from. ~ **pour,** regard as. ~ **propre/chaud**/*etc.*, keep clean/warm/*etc.* —*v.i.* hold. ~ **à,** be attached to. ~ **à faire,** be anxious to do. ~ **dans,** fit into. ~ **de qn.,** take after s.o. **se** ~ *v. pr.* (*rester*) remain; (*debout*) stand; (*avoir lieu*) be held. **se** ~ **à,**

hold on to. **se ~ bien,** behave o.s.
s'en ~ à, (*se limiter à*) confine o.s. to.
~ bon, stand firm. **~ compte de,**
take into account. **~ le coup,** hold
out. **~ tête à,** stand up to. **tiens!,**
(*surprise*) hey!

tennis /tenis/ *n.m.* tennis; (*terrain*)
tennis-court. —*n.m. pl.* (*chaussures*)
sneakers. **~ de table,** table tennis.

ténor /tenɔr/ *n.m.* tenor.

tension /tɑ̃sjɔ̃/ *n.f.* tension. **avoir de
la ~,** have high blood-pressure.

tentacule /tɑ̃takyl/ *n.m.* tentacle.

tentative /tɑ̃tativ/ *n.f.* attempt.

tente /tɑ̃t/ *n.f.* tent.

tenter[1] /tɑ̃te/ *v.t.* try (**de faire,** to do).

tent|er[2] /tɑ̃te/ *v.t.* (*allécher*) tempt. **~é
de,** tempted to. **~ation** *n.f.* temp-
tation.

tenture /tɑ̃tyr/ *n.f.* (wall) hanging;
(*collectif*) drapery.

tenu /təny/ *voir* **tenir.** —*a.* **bien ~,**
well-kept. **~ de,** obliged to.

ténu /teny/ *a.* (*fil etc.*) fine; (*cause,
nuance*) tenuous.

tenue /təny/ *n.f.* (*habillement*) dress;
(*de sport*) clothes; (*de maison*) upkeep;
(*conduite*) (good) behaviour; (*maintien*) posture. **~ de soirée,** evening
dress.

ter /tɛr/ *a. invar.* (*numéro*) B, b.

térébenthine /terebɑ̃tin/ *n.f.* turpentine.

tergiverser /tɛrʒivɛrse/ *v.i.* procrastinate.

terme /tɛrm/ *n.m.* (*mot*) term; (*date
limite*) time-limit; (*fin*) end; (*date de
loyer*) term. **à long/court ~,** long-/
short-term. **en bons ~s,** on good
terms (**avec,** with).

termin|al, ~ale (*m. pl.* **~aux**)
/tɛrminal, -o/ *a.* terminal. (**classe**)
~ale, sixth form; (*Amer.*) twelfth
grade. —*n.m.* (*pl.* **~aux**) terminal.

termin|er /tɛrmine/ *v.t./i.* finish;
(*soirée, débat*) end, finish. **se ~er**
v. pr. end (**par,** with). **~aison** *n.f.*
(*gram.*) ending.

terminologie /tɛrminɔlɔʒi/ *n.f.* terminology.

terminus /tɛrminys/ *n.m.* terminus.

terne /tɛrn/ *a.* dull, drab.

ternir /tɛrnir/ *v.t./i.,* **se ~** *v. pr.* tarnish.

terrain /tɛrɛ̃/ *n.m.* ground; (*parcelle*)
piece of land; (*à bâtir*) plot. **~ d'aviation,** airfield. **~ de camping,** campsite. **~ de golf,** golf-course. **~ de**

jeu, playground. **~ vague,** waste
ground; (*Amer.*) vacant lot.

terrasse /tɛras/ *n.f.* terrace; (*de café*)
pavement area.

terrassement /tɛrasmɑ̃/ *n.m.* excavation.

terrasser /tɛrase/ *v.t.* floor, overwhelm.

terrassier /tɛrasje/ *n.m.* navvy, labourer, ditch-digger.

terre /tɛr/ *n.f.* (*planète, matière*) earth;
(*étendue, pays*) land; (*sol*) ground; (*domaine*) estate. **à ~,** (*naut.*) ashore.
par ~, (*tomber, jeter*) to the ground;
(*s'asseoir, poser*) on the ground. **~
(cuite),** (baked) clay. **~-à-terre** *a.
invar.* matter-of-fact, down-to-earth.
~-plein *n.m.* (*auto.*) earth platform,
central reservation.

terreau /tɛro/ *n.m. invar.* compost.

terrer (se) /(sə)tɛre/ *v. pr.* hide o.s.,
dig o.s. in.

terrestre /tɛrɛstr/ *a.* land; (*de notre
planète*) earth's; (*fig.*) earthly.

terreur /tɛrœr/ *n.f.* terror.

terreu|x, ~se /tɛrø, -z/ *a.* earthy; (*sale*)
grubby.

terrible /tɛribl/ *a.* terrible; (*formidable: fam.*) terrific.

terrien, ~ne /tɛrjɛ̃, -jɛn/ *n.m., f.* earth-
dweller.

terrier /tɛrje/ *n.m.* (*trou de lapin etc.*)
burrow; (*chien*) terrier.

terrifier /tɛrifje/ *v.t.* terrify.

terrine /tɛrin/ *n.f.* (*culin.*) terrine.

territ|oire /tɛritwar/ *n.m.* territory.
~orial (*m. pl.* **~oriaux**) *a.* territorial.

terroir /tɛrwar/ *n.m.* (*sol*) soil; (*région*)
region. **du ~,** rural.

terroriser /tɛrɔrize/ *v.t.* terrorize.

terroris|te /tɛrɔrist/ *n.m./f.* terrorist.
~me *n.m.* terrorism.

tertre /tɛrtr/ *n.m.* mound.

tes /te/ *voir* **ton**[1].

tesson /tesɔ̃/ *n.m.* **~ de bouteille,**
piece of broken bottle.

test /tɛst/ *n.m.* test. **~er** *v.t.* test.

testament /tɛstamɑ̃/ *n.m.* (*jurid.*)
will; (*politique, artistique*) testament.
Ancien/Nouveau T~, Old/New
Testament.

testicule /tɛstikyl/ *n.m.* testicle.

tétanos /tetanos/ *n.m.* tetanus.

têtard /tɛtar/ *n.m.* tadpole.

tête /tɛt/ *n.f.* head; (*figure*) face; (*cheveux*) hair; (*cerveau*) brain. **à la ~
de,** at the head of. **à ~ reposée,** in a

leisurely moment. **de ~**, (*calculer*) in one's head. **en ~**, (*sport*) in the lead. **faire la ~**, sulk. **faire une ~**, (*football*) head the ball. **~-à-queue** *n.m. invar.* (*auto.*) spin. **~-à-tête** *n.m. invar.* tête-à-tête. **en ~-à-tête**, in private.

tétée /tete/ *n.f.* feed.

téter /tete/ *v.t./i.* suck.

tétine /tetin/ *n.f.* (*mamelle*) teat; (*sucette*) dummy; (*Amer.*) pacifier.

têtu /tety/ *a.* stubborn.

texte /tɛkst/ *n.m.* text; (*de leçon*) subject; (*morceau choisi*) passage.

textile /tɛkstil/ *n.m.* & *a.* textile.

textuel, ~le /tɛkstɥɛl/ *a.* literal.

texture /tɛkstyr/ *n.f.* texture.

thaïlandais, ~e /tailɑ̃dɛ, -z/ *a.* & *n.m., f.* Thai.

Thaïlande /tailɑ̃d/ *n.f.* Thailand.

thé /te/ *n.m.* tea.

théâtr|al (*m. pl.* **~aux**) /teatral, -o/ *a.* theatrical.

théâtre /teatr/ *n.m.* theatre; (*jeu forcé*) play-acting; (*d'un crime*) scene. **faire du ~**, act.

théière /tejɛr/ *n.f.* teapot.

thème /tɛm/ *n.m.* theme; (*traduction: scol.*) prose, translation (*into the foreign language*).

théolog|ie /teɔlɔʒi/ *n.f.* theology. **~ien** *n.m.* theologian. **~ique** *a.* theological.

théorème /teɔrɛm/ *n.m.* theorem.

théor|ie /teɔri/ *n.f.* theory. **~icien, ~icienne** *n.m., f.* theorist. **~ique** *a.* theoretical.

thérap|ie /terapi/ *n.f.* therapy. **~eutique** *a.* therapeutic.

thermique /tɛrmik/ *a.* thermal.

thermomètre /tɛrmɔmɛtr/ *n.m.* thermometer.

thermonucléaire /tɛrmɔnykleɛr/ *a.* thermonuclear.

thermos /tɛrmos/ *n.m./f.* (P.) Thermos (P.) (flask).

thermostat /tɛrmɔsta/ *n.m.* thermostat.

thésauriser /tezɔrize/ *v.t./i.* hoard.

thèse /tɛz/ *n.f.* thesis.

thon /tɔ̃/ *n.m.* (*poisson*) tuna.

thrombose /trɔ̃boz/ *n.f.* thrombosis.

thym /tɛ̃/ *n.m.* thyme.

thyroïde /tirɔid/ *n.f.* thyroid.

tibia /tibja/ *n.m.* shin-bone.

tic /tik/ *n.m.* (*contraction*) twitch; (*manie*) mannerism.

ticket /tikɛ/ *n.m.* ticket.

tic-tac /tiktak/ *n.m. invar.* (*de pendule*) tick(ing).

tiède /tjɛd/ *a.* lukewarm; (*atmosphère*) mild. **tiédeur** /tjedœr/ *n.f.* lukewarmness; mildness.

tiédir /tjedir/ *v.t./i.* (**faire**) **~**, warm slightly.

tien, ~ne /tjɛ̃, tjɛn/ *pron.* **le ~**, **la ~ne**, **les ~(ne)s**, yours.

tiens, tient /tjɛ̃/ *voir* **tenir.**

tiercé /tjɛrse/ *n.m.* place-betting.

tier|s, ~ce /tjɛr, -s/ *a.* third. —*n.m.* (*fraction*) third; (*personne*) third party. **T~s-Monde** *n.m.* Third World.

tige /tiʒ/ *n.f.* (*bot.*) stem, stalk; (*en métal*) shaft.

tignasse /tiɲas/ *n.f.* mop of hair.

tigre /tigr/ *n.m.* tiger. **~sse** /-ɛs/ *n.f.* tigress.

tigré /tigre/ *a.* spotted; (*rayé*) striped.

tilleul /tijœl/ *n.m.* lime(-tree), linden (-tree); (*infusion*) lime tea.

timbale /tɛ̃bal/ *n.f.* (*gobelet*) (metal) tumbler.

timbr|e /tɛ̃br/ *n.m.* stamp; (*sonnette*) bell; (*de voix*) tone. **~e-poste** (*pl.* **~es-poste**) *n.m.* postage stamp. **~er** *v.t.* stamp.

timbré /tɛ̃bre/ *a.* (*fam.*) crazy.

timid|e /timid/ *a.* timid. **~ité** *n.f.* timidity.

timoré /timɔre/ *a.* timorous.

tintamarre /tɛ̃tamar/ *n.m.* din.

tint|er /tɛ̃te/ *v.i.* ring; (*clefs*) jingle. **~ement** *n.m.* ringing; jingling.

tique /tik/ *n.f.* (*insecte*) tick.

tir /tir/ *n.m.* (*sport*) shooting; (*action de tirer*) firing; (*feu, rafale*) fire. **~ à l'arc**, archery. **~ forain**, shooting-gallery.

tirade /tirad/ *n.f.* soliloquy.

tirage /tiraʒ/ *n.m.* (*de photo*) printing; (*de journal*) circulation; (*de livre*) edition; (*de loterie*) draw; (*de cheminée*) draught.

tiraill|er /tiraje/ *v.t.* pull (away) at; (*harceler*) plague. **~é entre,** (*possibilités etc.*) torn between. **~ement** *n.m.* (*douleur*) gnawing pain; (*conflit*) conflict.

tiré /tire/ *a.* (*traits*) drawn.

tire-bouchon /tirbuʃɔ̃/ *n.m.* corkscrew.

tirelire /tirlir/ *n.f.* money-box; (*Amer.*) coin-bank.

tirer /tire/ *v.t.* pull; (*navire*) tow, tug; (*langue*) stick out; (*conclusion, trait, rideaux*) draw; (*coup de feu*) fire;

(*gibier*) shoot; (*photo*) print. ∼ **de**, (*sortir*) take *ou* get out of; (*extraire*) extract from; (*plaisir, nom*) derive from. —*v.i.* shoot, fire (**sur**, at). ∼ **sur**, (*couleur*) verge on; (*corde*) pull at. se ∼ *v. pr.* (*fam.*) clear off. se ∼ **de**, get out of. **s'en** ∼, (*en réchapper: fam.*) pull through; (*réussir: fam.*) cope. ∼ **à sa fin**, be drawing to a close. ∼ **au clair**, clarify. ∼ **au sort**, draw lots (for). ∼ **parti de**, take advantage of. ∼ **profit de**, profit from.

tiret /tirɛ/ *n.m.* dash.

tireur /tirœr/ *n.m.* gunman. ∼ **d'élite**, marksman. ∼ **isolé**, sniper.

tiroir /tirwar/ *n.m.* drawer. ∼-**caisse** (*pl.* ∼**s-caisses**) *n.m.* till.

tisane /tizan/ *n.f.* herb-tea.

tison /tizɔ̃/ *n.m.* ember.

tisonnier /tizɔnje/ *n.m.* poker.

tiss|er /tise/ *v.t.* weave. ∼**age** *n.m.* weaving. ∼**erand** /tisrɑ̃/ *n.m.* weaver.

tissu /tisy/ *n.m.* fabric, material; (*biologique*) tissue. **un** ∼ **de**, (*fig.*) a web of. ∼-**éponge** (*pl.* ∼**s-éponge**) *n.m.* towelling.

titre /titr/ *n.m.* title; (*diplôme*) qualification; (*comm.*) bond. ∼**s**, (*droits*) claims. (**gros**) ∼**s**, headlines. **à ce** ∼, (*pour cette qualité*) as such. **à** ∼ **d'exemple**, as an example. **à juste** ∼, rightly. **à** ∼ **privé**, in a private capacity. ∼ **de propriété**, title-deed.

titré /titre/ *a.* titled.

titrer /titre/ *v.t.* (*journal*) give as a headline.

tituber /titybe/ *v.i.* stagger.

titul|aire /titylɛr/ *a.* **être** ∼**aire**, have tenure. **être** ∼**aire de**, hold. —*n.m./f.* (*de permis etc.*) holder. ∼**ariser** *v.t.* give tenure to.

toast /tost/ *n.m.* piece of toast; (*allocution*) toast.

toboggan /tɔbɔgɑ̃/ *n.m.* (*traîneau*) toboggan; (*glissière*) slide; (*auto.*) flyover; (*auto., Amer.*) overpass.

toc /tɔk/ *int.* ∼ **toc!**, knock knock!

tocsin /tɔksɛ̃/ *n.m.* alarm (bell).

toge /tɔʒ/ *n.f.* (*de juge etc.*) gown.

tohu-bohu /tɔybɔy/ *n.m.* hubbub.

toi /twa/ *pron.* you; (*réfléchi*) yourself. **lève-**∼, stand up.

toile /twal/ *n.f.* cloth; (*sac, tableau*) canvas; (*coton*) cotton. ∼ **d'araignée**, cobweb. ∼ **de fond**, backdrop, backcloth.

toilette /twalɛt/ *n.f.* washing; (*habillement*) clothes, dress. ∼**s**, (*cabinets*) toilet(s). **de** ∼, (*articles, savon, etc.*) toilet. **faire sa** ∼, wash (and get ready).

toi-même /twamɛm/ *pron.* yourself.

toiser /twaze/ *v.t.* ∼ **qn.**, look s.o. up and down.

toison /twazɔ̃/ *n.f.* (*laine*) fleece.

toit /twa/ *n.m.* roof. ∼ **ouvrant**, (*auto.*) sun-roof.

toiture /twatyr/ *n.f.* roof.

tôle /tol/ *n.f.* (*plaque*) iron sheet. ∼ **ondulée**, corrugated iron.

tolérable /tɔlerabl/ *a.* tolerable.

toléran|t, ∼**te** /tɔlerɑ̃, -t/ *a.* tolerant. ∼**ce** *n.f.* tolerance; (*importations: comm.*) allowance.

tolérer /tɔlere/ *v.t.* tolerate; (*importations: comm.*) allow.

tollé /tɔle/ *n.m.* hue and cry.

tomate /tɔmat/ *n.f.* tomato.

tombe /tɔ̃b/ *n.f.* grave; (*avec monument*) tomb.

tombeau (*pl.* ∼**x**) /tɔ̃bo/ *n.m.* tomb.

tombée /tɔ̃be/ *n.f.* ∼ **de la nuit**, nightfall.

tomber /tɔ̃be/ *v.i.* (*aux. être*) fall; (*fièvre, vent*) drop; (*enthousiasme*) die down. **faire** ∼, knock over; (*gouvernement*) bring down. ∼ **à l'eau**, (*projet*) fall through. ∼ **bien** *ou* **à point**, come at the right time. ∼ **en panne**, break down. ∼ **en syncope**, faint. ∼ **sur**, (*trouver*) run across.

tombola /tɔ̃bɔla/ *n.f.* tombola; (*Amer.*) lottery.

tome /tɔm/ *n.m.* volume.

ton[1], **ta** *ou* **ton*** (*pl.* **tes**) /tɔ̃, ta, tɔ̃, te/ *a.* your.

ton[2] /tɔ̃/ *n.m.* tone; (*gamme: mus.*) key; (*hauteur de la voix*) pitch. **de bon** ∼, in good taste.

tonalité /tɔnalite/ *n.f.* tone; (*téléphone*) dialling tone; (*téléphone: Amer.*) dial tone.

tond|re /tɔ̃dr/ *v.t.* (*herbe*) mow; (*mouton*) shear; (*cheveux*) clip. ∼**euse** *n.f.* shears; clippers. ∼**euse (à gazon)**, (lawn-)mower.

tonifier /tɔnifje/ *v.t.* tone up.

tonique /tɔnik/ *a.* & *n.m.* tonic.

tonne /tɔn/ *n.f.* ton(ne).

tonneau (*pl.* ∼**x**) /tɔno/ *n.m.* (*récipient*) barrel; (*naut.*) ton; (*culbute*) somersault.

tonnelle /tɔnɛl/ *n.f.* bower.

tonner /tɔne/ *v.i.* thunder.

tonnerre /tɔnɛr/ *n.m.* thunder.

tonte /tɔ̃t/ *n.f.* (*de gazon*) mowing; (*de moutons*) shearing.

tonton /tɔ̃tɔ̃/ *n.m.* (*fam.*) uncle.

tonus /tɔnys/ *n.m.* energy.

top /tɔp/ *n.m.* (*signal pour marquer un instant précis*) stroke.

topo /tɔpo/ *n.m.* (*fam.*) talk, oral report.

toquade /tɔkad/ *n.f.* craze; (*pour une personne*) infatuation.

toque /tɔk/ *n.f.* (fur) hat; (*de jockey*) cap.

toqué /tɔke/ *a.* (*fam.*) crazy.

torche /tɔrʃ/ *n.f.* torch.

torcher /tɔrʃe/ *v.t.* (*fam.*) wipe.

torchon /tɔrʃɔ̃/ *n.m.* cloth, duster; (*pour la vaisselle*) tea-towel; (*Amer.*) dish-towel.

tordre /tɔrdr/ *v.t.* twist; (*linge*) wring. **se ∼** *v. pr.* twist, bend; (*de douleur*) writhe. **se ∼ (de rire)**, split one's sides.

tordu /tɔrdy/ *a.* twisted, bent; (*esprit*) warped.

tornade /tɔrnad/ *n.f.* tornado.

torpeur /tɔrpœr/ *n.f.* lethargy.

torpill|e /tɔrpij/ *n.f.* torpedo. **∼er** *v.t.* torpedo.

torrent /tɔrɑ̃/ *n.m.* torrent. **∼iel, ∼ielle** /-sjɛl/ *a.* torrential.

torride /tɔrid/ *a.* torrid.

torsade /tɔrsad/ *n.f.* twist.

torse /tɔrs/ *n.m.* chest; (*sculpture*) torso.

tort /tɔr/ *n.m.* wrong. **à ∼**, wrongly. **avoir ∼**, be wrong (**de faire**, to do). **donner ∼ à**, prove wrong. **faire (du) ∼ à**, harm.

torticolis /tɔrtikɔli/ *n.m.* stiff neck.

tortiller /tɔrtije/ *v.t.* twist, twirl. **se ∼** *v. pr.* wriggle, wiggle.

tortionnaire /tɔrsjɔnɛr/ *n.m.* torturer.

tortue /tɔrty/ *n.f.* tortoise; (*de mer*) turtle.

tortueu|x, ∼se /tɔrtyø, -z/ *a.* tortuous.

tortur|e(s) /tɔrtyr/ *n.f.* (*pl.*) torture. **∼er** *v.t.* torture.

tôt /to/ *adv.* early. **plus ∼**, earlier. **au plus ∼**, at the earliest. **le plus ∼ possible**, as soon as possible. **∼ ou tard**, sooner or later.

tot|al (*m. pl.* **∼aux**) /tɔtal, -o/ *a.* total. —*n.m.* (*pl.* **∼aux**) total. —*adv.* (*fam.*) to conclude, in short. **au ∼al**, all in all. **∼alement** *adv.* totally. **∼aliser** *v.t.* total.

totalitaire /tɔtalitɛr/ *a.* totalitarian.

totalité /tɔtalite/ *n.f.* entirety. **la ∼ de**, all of.

toubib /tubib/ *n.m.* (*fam.*) doctor.

touchant, ∼e /tuʃɑ̃, -t/ *a.* (*émouvant*) touching.

touche /tuʃ/ *n.f.* (*de piano*) key; (*de peintre*) touch. (**ligne de**) **∼**, touch-line. **une ∼ de**, a touch of.

toucher[1] /tuʃe/ *v.t.* touch; (*émouvoir*) move, touch; (*contacter*) get in touch with; (*cible*) hit; (*argent*) draw; (*chèque*) cash; (*concerner*) affect. —*v.i.* **∼ à**, touch; (*question*) touch on; (*fin, but*) approach. **se ∼** *v. pr.* (*lignes*) touch.

toucher[2] /tuʃe/ *n.m.* (*sens*) touch.

touffe /tuf/ *n.f.* (*de poils, d'herbe*) tuft; (*de plantes*) clump.

touffu /tufy/ *a.* thick, bushy; (*fig.*) complex.

toujours /tuʒur/ *adv.* always; (*encore*) still; (*en tout cas*) anyhow. **pour ∼**, for ever.

toupet /tupɛ/ *n.m.* (*culot: fam.*) cheek, nerve.

toupie /tupi/ *n.f.* (*jouet*) top.

tour[1] /tur/ *n.f.* tower; (*immeuble*) tower block; (*échecs*) rook.

tour[2] /tur/ *n.m.* (*mouvement, succession, tournure*) turn; (*excursion*) trip; (*à pied*) walk; (*en auto*) drive; (*artifice*) trick; (*circonférence*) circumference; (*techn.*) lathe. **∼ (de piste)**, lap. **à ∼ de rôle**, in turn. **à mon**/*etc.* **∼**, when it is my/*etc.* turn. **c'est mon**/ *etc.* **∼ de**, it is my/*etc.* turn to. **faire le ∼ de**, go round; (*question*) survey. **∼ d'horizon**, survey. **∼ de passe-passe**, sleight of hand. **∼ de taille**, waist measurement.

tourbe /turb/ *n.f.* peat.

tourbillon /turbijɔ̃/ *n.m.* whirlwind; (*d'eau*) whirlpool; (*fig.*) whirl, swirl. **∼ner** /-jɔne/ *v.i.* whirl, swirl.

tourelle /turɛl/ *n.f.* turret.

tourisme /turism/ *n.m.* tourism. **faire du ∼**, do some sightseeing.

tourist|e /turist/ *n.m./f.* tourist. **∼ique** *a.* tourist; (*route*) scenic.

tourment /turmɑ̃/ *n.m.* torment. **∼er** /-te/ *v.t.* torment. **se ∼er** *v. pr.* worry.

tournage /turnaʒ/ *n.m.* (*cinéma*) shooting.

tournant[1], **∼e** /turnɑ̃, -t/ *a.* (*qui pivote*) revolving.

tournant[2] /turnɑ̃/ *n.m.* bend; (*fig.*) turning-point.

tourne-disque /turnədisk/ *n.m.* record-player.

tournée /turne/ *n.f.* (*voyage, consommations*) round; (*théâtre*) tour. **faire la ~,** make the rounds (**de,** of).

tourner /turne/ *v.t.* turn; (*film*) shoot, make. —*v.i.* turn; (*toupie, tête*) spin; (*moteur, usine*) run. **se ~** *v. pr.* turn. **~ au froid,** turn cold. **~ autour de,** go round; (*personne, maison*) hang around; (*terre*) revolve round; (*question*) centre on. **~ de l'œil,** (*fam.*) faint. **~ en dérision,** mock. **~ en ridicule,** ridicule. **~ mal,** turn out badly.

tournesol /turnəsɔl/ *n.m.* sunflower.

tournevis /turnəvis/ *n.m.* screwdriver.

tourniquet /turnikɛ/ *n.m.* (*barrière*) turnstile.

tournoi /turnwa/ *n.m.* tournament.

tournoyer /turnwaje/ *v.i.* whirl.

tournure /turnyr/ *n.f.* turn; (*locution*) turn of phrase.

tourterelle /turtərɛl/ *n.f.* turtle-dove.

Toussaint /tusɛ̃/ *n.f.* **la ~,** All Saints' Day.

tousser /tuse/ *v.i.* cough.

tout[1], **~e** *a.* (*pl.* **tous, toutes**) /tu, tut/ *a.* all; (*n'importe quel*) any; (*tout à fait*) entirely. **~ le pays**/*etc.*, the whole country/*etc.*, all the country/*etc.* **~e la nuit/journée,** the whole night/day. **tous les jours/mois**/*etc.*, every day/ month/*etc.* —*pron.* everything, all. **tous** /tus/, **toutes,** all. **prendre ~,** take everything, take it all. **~ ce que,** all that. **~ le monde,** everyone. **tous les deux, toutes les deux,** both of them. —*adv.* (*très*) very; (*tout à fait*) quite. **~ au bout/début**/*etc.*, right at the end/beginning/*etc.* **~ en chantant/marchant**/*etc.*, while singing/ walking/*etc.* **~ à coup,** all of a sudden. **~ à fait,** quite, completely. **~ à l'heure,** in a moment; (*passé*) a moment ago. **~ au** *ou* **le long de,** throughout. **~ au plus/moins,** at most/ least. **~ de même,** all the same. **~ de suite,** straight away. **~ entier,** whole. **~ le contraire,** quite the opposite. **~ neuf,** brand-new. **~ nu,** stark naked. **~ près,** nearby. **~-puissant, ~e-puissante** *a.* omnipotent. **~ seul,** alone.

tout[2] /tu/ *n.m.* (*ensemble*) whole. **en ~,** in all.

tout-à-l'égout /tutalegu/ *n.m.* main drainage.

toutefois /tutfwa/ *adv.* however.

toux /tu/ *n.f.* cough.

toxicomane /tɔksikɔman/ *n.m.*/*f.* drug addict.

toxine /tɔksin/ *n.f.* toxin.

toxique /tɔksik/ *a.* toxic.

trac /trak/ *n.m.* **le ~,** nerves; (*théâtre*) stage fright.

tracas /traka/ *n.m.* worry. **~ser** /-se/ *v.t.*, **se ~ser** *v. pr.* worry.

trace /tras/ *n.f.* trace, mark; (*d'animal, de pneu*) tracks; (*vestige*) trace. **sur la ~ de,** on the track of. **~s de pas,** footprints.

tracé /trase/ *n.m.* (*ligne*) line; (*plan*) layout.

tracer /trase/ *v.t.* draw, trace; (*écrire*) write; (*route*) mark out.

trachée(-artère) /traʃe(artɛr)/ *n.f.* windpipe.

tract /trakt/ *n.m.* leaflet.

tractations /traktasjɔ̃/ *n.f. pl.* dealings.

tracteur /traktœr/ *n.m.* tractor.

traction /traksjɔ̃/ *n.f.* (*sport*) press-up, push-up.

tradition /tradisjɔ̃/ *n.f.* tradition. **~nel, ~nelle** /-jɔnɛl/ *a.* traditional.

trad|**uire**† /traduir/ *v.t.* translate; (*sentiment*) express. **~uire en justice,** take to court. **~ucteur, ~uctrice** *n.m.,* *f.* translator. **~uction** *n.f.* translation.

trafic /trafik/ *n.m.* (*commerce, circulation*) traffic.

trafiqu|**er** /trafike/ *v.i.* traffic. —*v.t.* (*fam.*) doctor. **~ant, ~ante** *n.m., f.* trafficker; (*d'armes, de drogues*) dealer.

tragédie /traʒedi/ *n.f.* tragedy.

tragique /traʒik/ *a.* tragic. **~ment** *adv.* tragically.

trah|**ir** /trair/ *v.t.* betray. **~ison** *n.f.* betrayal; (*crime*) treason.

train /trɛ̃/ *n.m.* (*rail.*) train; (*allure*) pace; (*ensemble*) set. **en ~,** (*en forme*) in shape. **en ~ de faire,** (busy) doing. **mettre en ~,** start up. **~ d'atterrissage,** undercarriage. **~ de vie,** lifestyle.

traînard, ~e /trɛnar, -d/ *n.m.,f.* slowcoach; (*Amer.*) slowpoke; (*en marchant*) straggler.

traîne /trɛn/ *n.f.* (*de robe*) train. **à la**

~, lagging behind; (*en remorque*) in tow.

traîneau (*pl.* ~x) /trɛno/ *n.m.* sledge.

traînée /trene/ *n.f.* (*trace*) trail; (*bande*) streak; (*femme*: *péj.*) prostitute.

traîner /trene/ *v.t.* drag (along); (*véhicule*) pull. —*v.i.* (*pendre*) trail; (*rester en arrière*) trail behind; (*flâner*) hang about; (*papiers, affaires*) lie around. ~ (en longueur), drag on. se ~ *v. pr.* (*par terre*) crawl. (faire) ~ en longueur, drag out. ~ ses mots *ou* sa voix, drawl.

train-train /trɛtrɛ̃/ *n.m.* routine.

traire† /trɛr/ *v.t.* milk.

trait /trɛ/ *n.m.* line; (*en dessinant*) stroke; (*caractéristique*) feature, trait; (*acte*) act. ~s, (*du visage*) features. avoir ~ à, relate to. d'un ~, (*boire*) in one gulp. ~ d'union, hyphen; (*fig.*) link.

traite /trɛt/ *n.f.* (*de vache*) milking; (*comm.*) draft. d'une seule ~, in one go, at a stretch.

traité /trete/ *n.m.* (*pacte*) treaty; (*ouvrage*) treatise.

traitement /trɛtmɑ̃/ *n.m.* treatment; (*salaire*) salary. ~ de données, data processing. ~ de texte, word processing.

traiter /trete/ *v.t.* treat; (*affaire*) deal with; (*données, produit*) process. ~ qn. de lâche/*etc.*, call s.o. a coward/ *etc.* —*v.i.* deal (avec, with). ~ de, (*sujet*) deal with.

traiteur /trɛtœr/ *n.m.* caterer.

traître, ~sse /trɛtr, -ɛs/ *a.* treacherous. —*n.m./f.* traitor.

trajectoire /traʒɛktwar/ *n.f.* path.

trajet /traʒɛ/ *n.m.* distance; (*voyage*) journey; (*itinéraire*) route.

trame /tram/ *n.f.* (*de récit etc.*) framework.

tramer /trame/ *v.t.* plot; (*complot*) hatch.

tramway /tramwɛ/ *n.m.* tram; (*Amer.*) streetcar.

tranchant, ~e /trɑ̃ʃɑ̃, -t/ *a.* sharp. —*n.m.* cutting edge.

tranche /trɑ̃ʃ/ *n.f.* (*rondelle*) slice; (*bord*) edge; (*partie*) portion.

tranchée /trɑ̃ʃe/ *n.f.* trench.

tranch|er[1] /trɑ̃ʃe/ *v.t.* cut; (*question*) decide. —*v.i.* (*décider*) decide. ~é *a.* (*net*) clear-cut.

trancher[2] /trɑ̃ʃe/ *v.i.* (*contraster*) contrast (sur, with).

tranquill|e /trɑ̃kil/ *a.* quiet; (*esprit*) at rest; (*conscience*) clear. être/laisser ~e, be/leave in peace. ~ement *adv.* quietly. ~ité *n.f.* (peace and) quiet; (*d'esprit*) peace of mind.

tranquillisant /trɑ̃kilizɑ̃/ *n.m.* tranquillizer.

tranquilliser /trɑ̃kilize/ *v.t.* reassure.

transaction /trɑ̃zaksjɔ̃/ *n.f.* transaction.

transatlantique /trɑ̃zatlɑ̃tik/ *n.m.* transatlantic liner; (*chaise*) deckchair.

transborder /trɑ̃sbɔrde/ *v.t.* transfer, transship.

transcend|er /trɑ̃sɑ̃de/ *v.t.* transcend. ~ant, ~ante *a.* transcendent.

transcr|ire /trɑ̃skrir/ *v.t.* transcribe. ~iption *n.f.* transcription; (*copie*) transcript.

transe /trɑ̃s/ *n.f.* en ~, in a trance; (*fig.*) very excited. dans les ~s, in sheer agony (de, over).

transférer /trɑ̃sfere/ *v.t.* transfer.

transfert /trɑ̃sfɛr/ *n.m.* transfer.

transform|er /trɑ̃sfɔrme/ *v.t.* change; (*radicalement*) transform; (*vêtement*) alter. se ~er *v. pr.* change; be transformed. (se) ~er en, turn into. ~ateur *n.m.* transformer. ~ation *n.f.* change; transformation.

transfuge /trɑ̃sfyʒ/ *n.m.* renegade.

transfusion /trɑ̃sfyzjɔ̃/ *n.f.* transfusion.

transgresser /trɑ̃sgrese/ *v.t.* disobey.

transiger /trɑ̃siʒe/ *v.i.* compromise.

transir /trɑ̃zir/ *v.t.* numb.

transistor /trɑ̃zistɔr/ *n.m.* (*dispositif, poste de radio*) transistor.

transit /trɑ̃zit/ *n.m.* transit. ~er *v.t./i.* pass in transit.

transiti|f, ~ve /trɑ̃zitif, -v/ *a.* transitive.

transi|tion /trɑ̃zisjɔ̃/ *n.f.* transition. ~toire *a.* (*provisoire*) transitional; (*fugitif*) fleeting.

translucide /trɑ̃slysid/ *a.* translucent.

transm|ettre† /trɑ̃smɛtr/ *v.t.* pass on; (*techn.*) transmit; (*radio*) broadcast. ~ission *n.f.* transmission; (*radio*) broadcasting.

transparaître /trɑ̃sparɛtr/ *v.i.* show (through).

transparen|t, ~te /trɑ̃sparɑ̃, -t/ *a.* transparent. ~ce *n.f.* transparency.

transpercer /trɑ̃spɛrse/ *v.t.* pierce.

transpir|er /trãspire/ v.i. perspire.
~**ation** n.f. perspiration.

transplant|er /trãsplãte/ v.t. trans-
plant. ~**ation** n.f. transplantation;
(greffe) transplant.

transport /trãspɔr/ n.m. trans-
port(ation); (sentiment) rapture. **les
~s,** transport. **les ~s en commun,**
public transport.

transport|er /trãspɔrte/ v.t. trans-
port; (à la main) carry. **se ~er** v. pr.
take o.s. (à, to). ~**eur** n.m. haulier;
(Amer.) trucker.

transposer /trãspoze/ v.t. transpose.

transvaser /trãsvaze/ v.t. decant.

transvers|al (m. pl. ~**aux**)
/trãsvɛrsal, -o/ a. cross, transverse.

trap|èze /trapɛz/ n.m. (sport) trapeze.
~**éziste** /-ezist/ n.m./f. trapeze artist.

trappe /trap/ n.f. trapdoor.

trappeur /trapœr/ n.m. trapper.

trapu /trapy/ a. stocky.

traquenard /traknar/ n.m. trap.

traquer /trake/ v.t. track down.

traumatis|me /tromatism/ n.m.
trauma. ~**ant,** ~**ante** /-zã, -t/ a.
traumatic.

trav|ail (pl. ~**aux**) /travaj, -o/ n.m.
work; (emploi, poste) job; (façonnage)
working. ~**aux,** work. **en** ~**ail,**
(femme) in labour. ~**ail à la chaîne,**
production-line work. ~**ail à la pièce**
ou **à la tâche,** piece-work. ~**ail noir,**
(fam.) moonlighting. ~**aux forcés,**
hard labour. ~**aux ménagers,**
housework.

travaill|er /travaje/ v.i. work; (se dé-
former) warp. ~**er à,** (livre etc.) work
on. —v.t. (façonner) work; (étudier)
work at ou on; (tourmenter) worry.
~**eur,** ~**euse** n.m./f. worker; a. hard-
working.

travailliste /travajist/ a. Labour.
—n.m./f. Labour party member.

travée /trave/ n.f. (rangée) row.

travers /travɛr/ n.m. (défaut) failing.
à ~, through. **au ~ (de),** through.
de ~, (chapeau, nez) crooked; (mal)
badly, the wrong way; (regarder)
askance. **en ~ (de),** across.

traverse /travɛrs/ n.f. (rail.) sleeper;
(rail., Amer.) tie.

traversée /travɛrse/ n.f. crossing.

traverser /travɛrse/ v.t. cross; (transpercer) go (right) through; (période,
forêt) go ou pass through.

traversin /travɛrsɛ̃/ n.m. bolster.

travestir /travɛstir/ v.t. disguise;
(vérité) misrepresent.

trébucher /trebyʃe/ v.i. stumble, trip
(over). **faire ~,** trip (up).

trèfle /trɛfl/ n.m. (plante) clover;
(cartes) clubs.

treillage /trɛjaʒ/ n.m. trellis.

treillis[1] /treji/ n.m. trellis; (en métal)
wire mesh.

treillis[2] /treji/ n.m. (tenue militaire)
combat uniform.

treiz|e /trɛz/ a. & n.m. thirteen.
~**ième** a. & n.m./f. thirteenth.

tréma /trema/ n.m. (gram.) diaeresis.

trembl|er /trãble/ v.i. shake, tremble;
(lumière, voix) quiver. ~**ement** n.m.
shaking; (frisson) shiver. ~**ement de
terre,** earthquake.

trembloter /trãblote/ v.i. quiver.

trémousser (se) /(sə)tremuse/ v. pr.
wriggle, wiggle.

trempe /trãp/ n.f. (caractère) calibre.

tremper /trãpe/ v.t./i. soak; (plonger)
dip; (acier) temper. **se ~** v. pr. (se
baigner) have a dip.

tremplin /trãplɛ̃/ n.m. springboard.

trentaine /trãtɛn/ n.f. **une ~ (de),**
about thirty.

trent|e /trãt/ a. & n.m. thirty. ~**ième**
a. & n.m./f. thirtieth.

trépider /trepide/ v.i. vibrate.

trépied /trepje/ n.m. tripod.

trépigner /trepiɲe/ v.i. stamp one's
feet.

très /trɛ/ (/trɛz/ before vowel) adv.
very. **~ aimé/estimé,** much liked/
esteemed.

trésor /trezɔr/ n.m. treasure; (ressources: comm.) finances. **le T~,** the
revenue department.

trésorerie /trezɔrri/ n.f. (bureaux)
accounts department; (du Trésor)
revenue office; (argent) finances;
(gestion) accounts.

trésor|ier, ~**ière** /trezɔrje, -jɛr/ n.m.,
f. treasurer.

tressaill|ir /tresajir/ v.i. shake,
quiver; (sursauter) start. ~**ement**
n.m. quiver; start.

tressauter /tresote/ v.i. (sursauter)
start.

tresse /trɛs/ n.f. braid, plait.

tresser /trese/ v.t. braid, plait.

tréteau (pl. ~**x**) /treto/ n.m. trestle.
~**x,** (théâtre) stage.

treuil /trœj/ n.m. winch.

trêve /trɛv/ n.f. truce; (fig.) respite.

tri /tri/ n.m. (classement) sorting;

(*sélection*) selection. **faire le ~ de,** sort; select. **~age** /-jaʒ/ *n.m.* sorting.

triang|le /trijɑ̃gl/ *n.m.* triangle. **~ulaire** *a.* triangular.

trib|al (*m. pl.* **~aux**) /tribal, -o/ *a.* tribal.

tribord /tribɔr/ *n.m.* starboard.

tribu /triby/ *n.f.* tribe.

tribulations /tribylɑsjɔ̃/ *n.f. pl.* tribulations.

tribun|al (*m. pl.* **~aux**) /tribynal, -o/ *n.m.* court. **~al d'instance,** magistrates' court.

tribune /tribyn/ *n.f.* (public) gallery; (*dans un stade*) grandstand; (*d'orateur*) rostrum; (*débat*) forum.

tribut /triby/ *n.m.* tribute.

tributaire /tribytɛr/ *a.* **~ de,** dependent on.

trich|er /triʃe/ *v.i.* cheat. **~erie** *n.f.* cheating. **une ~erie,** piece of trickery. **~eur, ~euse** *n.m., f.* cheat.

tricolore /trikɔlɔr/ *a.* red, white, and blue; (*français*: *fig.*) French.

tricot /triko/ *n.m.* knitting; (*pull*) sweater. **en ~,** knitted. **~ de corps,** vest; (*Amer.*) undershirt. **~er** /-ɔte/ *v.t./i.* knit.

trictrac /triktrak/ *n.m.* backgammon.

tricycle /trisikl/ *n.m.* tricycle.

trier /trije/ *v.t.* (*classer*) sort; (*choisir*) select.

trilogie /trilɔʒi/ *n.f.* trilogy.

trimbaler /trɛ̃bale/ *v.t.,* **se ~** *v. pr.* (*fam.*) trail around.

trimer /trime/ *v.i.* (*fam.*) slave.

trimestr|e /trimɛstr/ *n.m.* quarter; (*scol.*) term. **~iel, ~ielle** *a.* quarterly; (*bulletin*) end-of-term.

tringle /trɛ̃gl/ *n.f.* rod.

Trinité /trinite/ *n.f.* **la ~,** (*dogme*) the Trinity; (*fête*) Trinity.

trinquer /trɛ̃ke/ *v.i.* clink glasses.

trio /trijo/ *n.m.* trio.

triomph|e /trijɔ̃f/ *n.m.* triumph. **~al** (*m. pl.* **~aux**) *a.* triumphant.

triomph|er /trijɔ̃fe/ *v.i.* triumph (**de,** over); (*jubiler*) be triumphant. **~ant, ~ante** *a.* triumphant.

trip|es /trip/ *n.f. pl.* (*mets*) tripe; (*entrailles*: *fam.*) guts. **~ier, ~ière** *n.m., f.* tripe butcher.

triple /tripl/ *a.* triple, treble. —*n.m.* **le ~,** three times as much (**de,** as). **~ment** /-əmɑ̃/ *adv.* trebly.

tripl|er /triple/ *v.t./i.* triple, treble. **~és, ~ées** *n.m., f. pl.* triplets.

tripot /tripo/ *n.m.* gambling den.

tripoter /tripɔte/ *v.t.* (*fam.*) fiddle with. —*v.i.* (*fam.*) fiddle about.

trique /trik/ *n.f.* cudgel.

triste /trist/ *a.* sad; (*rue, temps, couleur*) gloomy; (*lamentable*) wretched, dreadful. **~ment** /-əmɑ̃/ *adv.* sadly. **~sse** /-ɛs/ *n.f.* sadness; gloominess.

triturer /trityre/ *v.t.* (*pâte*) knead.

triv|ial (*m. pl.* **~iaux**) /trivjal, -jo/ *a.* coarse. **~ialité** *n.f.* coarseness.

troc /trɔk/ *n.m.* exchange.

troène /trɔɛn/ *n.m.* (*bot.*) privet.

trognon /trɔɲɔ̃/ *n.m.* (*de pomme*) core.

trois /trwa/ *a.* & *n.m.* three. **~ième** /-zjɛm/ *a.* & *n.m./f.* third. **~ièmement** /-zjɛmmɑ̃/ *adv.* thirdly.

trolleybus /trɔlɛbys/ *n.m.* trolleybus.

trombe /trɔ̃b/ *n.f.* **~ d'eau,** downpour.

trombone /trɔ̃bɔn/ *n.m.* (*mus.*) trombone; (*agrafe*) paper-clip.

trompe /trɔ̃p/ *n.f.* (*d'éléphant*) trunk; (*mus.*) horn.

tromp|er /trɔ̃pe/ *v.t.* deceive, mislead; (*déjouer*) elude. **se ~er** *v. pr.* be mistaken. **se ~er de route/train**/*etc.*, take the wrong road/train/*etc.* **~erie** *n.f.* deception. **~eur, ~euse** *a.* (*personne*) deceitful; (*chose*) deceptive.

trompette /trɔ̃pɛt/ *n.f.* trumpet.

tronc /trɔ̃/ *n.m.* trunk; (*boîte*) collection box.

tronçon /trɔ̃sɔ̃/ *n.m.* section. **~ner** /-ɔne/ *v.t.* cut into sections.

trôn|e /tron/ *n.m.* throne. **~er** *v.i.* occupy the place of honour.

tronquer /trɔ̃ke/ *v.t.* truncate.

trop /tro/ *adv.* (*grand, loin, etc.*) too; (*boire, marcher, etc.*) too much. **~ (de),** (*quantité*) too much; (*nombre*) too many. **de ~, en ~,** too much; too many. **de ~,** (*intrus*) in the way. **~-plein** *n.m.* excess; (*dispositif*) overflow.

trophée /trɔfe/ *n.m.* trophy.

tropic|al (*m. pl.* **~aux**) /trɔpikal, -o/ *a.* tropical.

tropique /trɔpik/ *n.m.* tropic. **~s,** tropics.

troquer /trɔke/ *v.t.* exchange.

trot /tro/ *n.m.* trot. **aller au ~,** trot. **au ~,** (*fam.*) on the double.

trotter /trɔte/ *v.i.* trot.

trotteuse /trɔtøz/ *n.f.* (*aiguille de montre*) second hand.

trottiner /trɔtine/ *v.i.* patter along.

trottinette /trɔtinɛt/ *n.f.* (*jouet*) scooter.

trottoir /trɔtwar/ *n.m.* pavement; (*Amer.*) sidewalk. ~ **roulant,** moving walkway.

trou /tru/ *n.m.* hole; (*moment*) gap; (*lieu: péj.*) dump. ~ **(de mémoire),** lapse (of memory). ~ **de la serrure,** keyhole.

trouble /trubl/ *a.* (*eau, image*) unclear; (*louche*) shady. —*n.m.* agitation. ~**s,** (*pol.*) disturbances; (*méd.*) trouble.

troubl|er /truble/ *v.t.* disturb; (*eau*) make cloudy; (*inquiéter*) trouble. **se** ~**er** *v. pr.* (*personne*) become flustered. ~**fête** *n.m./f. invar.* killjoy.

trouée /true/ *n.f.* gap, open space; (*mil.*) breach (**dans,** in).

trouer /true/ *v.t.* make a hole *ou* holes in.

trouille /truj/ *n.f.* **avoir la** ~, (*fam.*) be scared.

troupe /trup/ *n.f.* troop; (*d'acteurs*) troupe. ~**s,** (*mil.*) troops.

troupeau (*pl.* ~**x**) /trupo/ *n.m.* herd; (*de moutons*) flock.

trousse /trus/ *n.f.* case, bag; (*de réparations*) kit. **aux** ~**s de,** on the tail of.

trousseau (*pl.* ~**x**) /truso/ *n.m.* (*de clefs*) bunch; (*de mariée*) trousseau.

trouvaille /truvɑj/ *n.f.* find.

trouver /truve/ *v.t.* find; (*penser*) think. **aller/venir** ~, (*rendre visite à*) go/come and see. **se** ~ *v. pr.* find o.s.; (*être*) be; (*se sentir*) feel. **il se trouve que,** it happens that. **se** ~ **mal,** faint.

truand /tryɑ̃/ *n.m.* gangster.

truc /tryk/ *n.m.* (*moyen*) way; (*artifice*) trick; (*chose: fam.*) thing. ~**age** *n.m.* = **truquage.**

truchement /tryʃmɑ̃/ *n.m.* **par le** ~ **de,** through.

truculent, ~**e** /trykylɑ̃, -t/ *a.* colourful.

truelle /tryɛl/ *n.f.* trowel.

truffe /tryf/ *n.f.* (*champignon*) truffle; (*nez*) nose.

truffer /tryfe/ *v.t.* (*fam.*) fill, pack (**de,** with).

truie /trɥi/ *n.f.* (*animal*) sow.

truite /trɥit/ *n.f.* trout.

truqu|er /tryke/ *v.t.* fix, rig; (*photo, texte*) fake. ~**age** *n.m.* fixing; faking; (*cinéma*) special effect.

trust /trœst/ *n.m* (*comm.*) trust.

tsar /tsar/ *n.m.* tsar, czar.

tsigane /tsigan/ *a.* & *n.m./f.* (Hungarian) gypsy.

tu[1] /ty/ *pron.* (*parent, ami, enfant, etc.*) you.

tu[2] /ty/ *voir* **taire.**

tuba /tyba/ *n.m.* (*mus.*) tuba; (*sport*) snorkel.

tube /tyb/ *n.m.* tube.

tubercul|eux, ~**euse** /tybɛrkylø, -z/ *a.* **être** ~**eux,** have tuberculosis. ~**ose** *n.f.* tuberculosis.

tubulaire /tybylɛr/ *a.* tubular.

tubulure /tybylyr/ *n.f.* tubing.

tu|er /tɥe/ *v.t.* kill; (*d'une balle*) shoot, kill; (*épuiser*) exhaust. **se** ~**er** *v. pr.* kill o.s.; (*accident*) be killed. ~**é,** ~**ée** *n.m., f.* person killed. ~**eur,** ~**euse** *n.m., f.* killer.

tuerie /tyri/ *n.f.* slaughter.

tue-tête (à) /(a)tytɛt/ *adv.* at the top of one's voice.

tuile /tɥil/ *n.f.* tile; (*malchance: fam.*) (stroke of) bad luck.

tulipe /tylip/ *n.f.* tulip.

tuméfié /tymefje/ *a.* swollen.

tumeur /tymœr/ *n.f.* tumour.

tumult|e /tymylt/ *n.m.* commotion; (*désordre*) turmoil. ~**ueux,** ~**ueuse** *a.* turbulent.

tunique /tynik/ *n.f.* tunic.

Tunisie /tynizi/ *n.f.* Tunisia.

tunisien, ~**ne** /tynizjɛ̃, -jɛn/ *a.* & *n.m., f.* Tunisian.

tunnel /tynɛl/ *n.m.* tunnel.

turban /tyrbɑ̃/ *n.m.* turban.

turbine /tyrbin/ *n.f.* turbine.

turbulen|t, ~**te** /tyrbylɑ̃, -t/ *a.* boisterous, turbulent. ~**ce** *n.f.* turbulence.

tur|c, ~**que** /tyrk/ *a.* Turkish. —*n.m., f.* Turk. —*n.m.* (*lang.*) Turkish.

turf /tyrf/ *n.m.* **le** ~, the turf. ~**iste** *n.m./f.* racegoer.

Turquie /tyrki/ *n.f.* Turkey.

turquoise /tyrkwaz/ *a. invar.* turquoise.

tutelle /tytɛl/ *n.f.* (*jurid.*) guardianship; (*fig.*) protection.

tu|teur, ~**trice** /tytœr, -tris/ *n.m., f.* (*jurid.*) guardian. —*n.m.* (*bâton*) stake.

tut|oyer /tytwaje/ *v.t.* address familiarly (using *tu*). ~**oiement** *n.m.* use of (familiar) *tu.*

tuyau (*pl.* ~**x**) /tɥijo/ *n.m.* pipe; (*conseil: fam.*) tip. ~ **d'arrosage,** hosepipe. ~**ter** *v.t.* (*fam.*) give a tip to. ~**terie** *n.f.* piping.

TVA *abrév.* (*taxe sur la valeur ajoutée*) VAT.

tympan /tɛ̃pɑ̃/ *n.m.* ear-drum.
type /tip/ *n.m.* (*modèle*) type; (*traits*)
features; (*individu*: *fam.*) bloke,
guy. —*a. invar.* typical. **le ~ même
de,** a classic example of.
typhoïde /tifɔid/ *n.f.* typhoid (fever).
typhon /tifɔ̃/ *n.m.* typhoon.

typhus /tifys/ *n.m.* typhus.
typique /tipik/ *a.* typical. **~ment** *adv.*
typically.
tyran /tirɑ̃/ *n.m.* tyrant.
tyrann|ie /tirani/ *n.f.* tyranny. **~ique**
a. tyrannical. **~iser** *v.t.* oppress,
tyrannize.

U

ulcère /ylsɛr/ n.m. ulcer.

ulcérer /ylsere/ v.t. (vexer) embitter, gall.

ultérieur /ylterjœr/ a., **~ement** adv. later.

ultimatum /yltimatɔm/ n.m. ultimatum.

ultime /yltim/ a. final.

ultra- /yltra/ préf. ultra-.

un, une /œ̃, yn/ a. one; (indéfini) a, an. **~ enfant**, /œ̃nɑ̃fɑ̃/ a child. —pron. & n.m., f. one. **l'~**, one. **les ~s**, some. **l'~ et l'autre, les ~s les autres**, each other. **l'~ ou l'autre**, either. **la ~e**, (de journal) front page. **~ autre**, another.

unanim|e /ynanim/ a. unanimous. **~ité** n.f. unanimity. **à l'~ité**, unanimously.

uni /yni/ a. united; (couple) close; (surface) smooth; (sans dessins) plain.

unième /ynjɛm/ a. -first. **vingt et ~**, twenty-first. **cent ~**, one hundred and first.

unif|ier /ynifje/ v.t. unify. **~ication** n.f. unification.

uniform|e /ynifɔrm/ n.m. uniform. —a. uniform. **~ément** adv. uniformly. **~iser** v.t. standardize. **~ité** n.f. uniformity.

unilatér|al (m. pl. **~aux**) /ynilateral, -o/ a. unilateral.

union /ynjɔ̃/ n.f. union. **l'U~ soviétique**, the Soviet Union.

unique /ynik/ a. (seul) only; (prix, voie) one; (incomparable) unique. **~ment** adv. only, solely.

unir /ynir/ v.t., **s'~** v. pr. unite, join.

unisson (à l') /(al)ynisɔ̃/ adv. in unison.

unité /ynite/ n.f. unit; (harmonie) unity.

univers /ynivɛr/ n.m. universe.

universel, ~le /ynivɛrsɛl/ a. universal.

universit|é /ynivɛrsite/ n.f. university. **~aire** a. university; n.m./f. academic.

uranium /yranjɔm/ n.m. uranium.

urbain, ~e /yrbɛ̃, -ɛn/ a. urban.

urbanisme /yrbanism/ n.m. town planning; (Amer.) city planning.

urgence /yrʒɑ̃s/ n.f. (cas) emergency; (de situation, tâche, etc.) urgency. **d'~** a. emergency; adv. urgently.

urgent, ~e /yrʒɑ̃, -t/ a. urgent.

urin|e /yrin/ n.f. urine. **~er** v.i. urinate.

urinoir /yrinwar/ n.m. urinal.

urne /yrn/ n.f. (électorale) ballot-box; (vase) urn. **aller aux ~s**, go to the polls.

URSS abrév. (Union des Républiques Socialistes Soviétiques) USSR.

usage /yzaʒ/ n.m. use; (coutume) custom; (de langage) usage. **à l'~ de**, for. **d'~**, (habituel) customary. **faire ~ de**, make use of.

usagé /yzaʒe/ a. worn.

usager /yzaʒe/ n.m. user.

usé /yze/ a. worn (out); (banal) trite.

user /yze/ v.t. wear (out); (consommer) use (up). —v.i. **~ de**, use. **s'~** v. pr. (tissu etc.) wear (out).

usine /yzin/ n.f. factory; (de métallurgie) works.

usité /yzite/ a. common.

ustensile /ystɑ̃sil/ n.m. utensil.

usuel, ~le /yzɥɛl/ a. ordinary, everyday.

usure /yzyr/ n.f. (détérioration) wear (and tear).

usurper /yzyrpe/ v.t. usurp.

utérus /yterys/ n.m. womb, uterus.

utile /ytil/ a. useful. **~ment** adv. usefully.

utilis|er /ytilize/ v.t. use. **~able** a. usable. **~ation** n.f. use.

utilitaire /ytiliter/ a. utilitarian.

utilité /ytilite/ n.f. use(fulness).

utop|ie /ytɔpi/ n.f. Utopia; (idée) Utopian idea. **~ique** a. Utopian.

V

va /va/ *voir* **aller**[1].

vacanc|e /vakɑ̃s/ *n.f.* (*poste*) vacancy. **∼es,** holiday(s); (*Amer.*) vacation. **en ∼es,** on holiday. **∼ier, ∼ière** *n.m., f.* holidaymaker; (*Amer.*) vacationer.

vacant, ∼e /vakɑ̃, -t/ *a.* vacant.

vacarme /vakarm/ *n.m.* uproar.

vaccin /vaksɛ̃/ *n.m.* vaccine; (*inoculation*) vaccination.

vaccin|er /vaksine/ *v.t.* vaccinate. **∼ation** *n.f.* vaccination.

vache /vaʃ/ *n.f.* cow. —*a.* (*méchant: fam.*) nasty. **∼ment** *adv.* (*très: fam.*) damned; (*pleuvoir, manger, etc.: fam.*) a hell of a lot. **∼r** /-e/ *n.m.* cowherd. **∼rie** *n.f.* (*fam.*) nastiness; (*chose: fam.*) nasty thing.

vacill|er /vasije/ *v.i.* sway, wobble; (*lumière*) flicker; (*fig.*) falter. **∼ant, ∼ante** *a.* (*mémoire, démarche*) shaky.

vadrouiller /vadruje/ *v.i.* (*fam.*) wander about.

va-et-vient /vaevjɛ̃/ *n.m. invar.* to and fro motion; (*de personnes*) comings and goings.

vagabond, ∼e /vagabɔ̃, -d/ *n.m., f.* vagrant, vagabond. **∼er** /-de/ *v.i.* wander.

vagin /vaʒɛ̃/ *n.m.* vagina.

vagir /vaʒir/ *v.i.* cry.

vague[1] /vag/ *a.* vague. —*n.m.* vagueness. **il est resté dans le ∼,** he was vague about it. **∼ment** *adv.* vaguely.

vague[2] /vag/ *n.f.* wave. **∼ de fond,** ground swell. **∼ de froid,** cold spell.

vaill|ant, ∼ante /vajɑ̃, -t/ *a.* brave; (*vigoureux*) healthy. **∼amment** /-amɑ̃/ *adv.* bravely. **∼ance** *n.f.* bravery.

vaille /vaj/ *voir* **valoir.**

vain, ∼e /vɛ̃, vɛn/ *a.* vain. **en ∼,** in vain. **∼ement** /vɛnmɑ̃/ *adv.* vainly.

vain|cre† /vɛ̃kr/ *v.t.* defeat; (*surmonter*) overcome. **∼cu, ∼cue** *n.m., f.* (*sport*) loser. **∼queur** *n.m.* victor; (*sport*) winner.

vais /vɛ/ *voir* **aller**[1].

vaisseau (*pl.* **∼x**) /vɛso/ *n.m.* ship; (*veine*) vessel. **∼ spatial,** spaceship.

vaisselle /vɛsɛl/ *n.f.* crockery; (*à laver*) dishes. **faire la ∼,** do the washing-up, wash the dishes.

val (*pl.* **∼s** *ou* **vaux**) /val, vo/ *n.m.* valley.

valable /valabl/ *a.* valid; (*de qualité*) worthwhile.

valet /valɛ/ *n.m.* (*cartes*) jack. **∼ (de chambre),** manservant. **∼ de ferme,** farm-hand.

valeur /valœr/ *n.f.* value; (*mérite*) worth, value. **∼s,** (*comm.*) stocks and shares. **avoir de la ∼,** be valuable.

valid|e /valid/ *a.* (*personne*) fit; (*billet*) valid. **∼er** *v.t.* validate. **∼ité** *n.f.* validity.

valise /valiz/ *n.f.* (suit)case. **faire ses ∼s,** pack (one's bags).

vallée /vale/ *n.f.* valley.

vallon /valɔ̃/ *n.m.* (small) valley. **∼né** /-ɔne/ *a.* undulating.

valoir† /valwar/ *v.i.* be worth; (*s'appliquer*) apply. **∼ qch.,** be worth sth.; (*être aussi bon que*) be as good as sth. —*v.t.* **∼ qch. à qn.,** bring s.o. sth. **se ∼** *v. pr.* (*être équivalents*) be as good as each other. **faire ∼,** put forward to advantage; (*droit*) assert. **∼ la peine, ∼ le coup,** be worth it. **ça ne vaut rien,** it is no good. **∼ mieux faire,** be better to do.

valoriser /valɔrize/ *v.t.* increase the worth of.

vals|e /vals/ *n.f.* waltz. **∼er** *v.i.* waltz.

valve /valv/ *n.f.* valve.

vampire /vɑ̃pir/ *n.m.* vampire.

vandal|e /vɑ̃dal/ *n.m./f.* vandal. **∼isme** *n.m.* vandalism.

vanille /vanij/ *n.f.* vanilla.

vanit|é /vanite/ *n.f.* vanity. **∼eux, ∼euse** *a.* vain, conceited.

vanne /van/ *n.f.* (*d'écluse*) sluice (-gate).

vant|ail (*pl.* **∼aux**) /vɑ̃taj, -o/ *n.m.* door, flap.

vantard, ∼e /vɑ̃tar, -d/ *a.* boastful; *n.m., f.* boaster. **∼ise** /-diz/ *n.f.* boastfulness; (*acte*) boast.

vanter /vɑ̃te/ *v.t.* praise. **se ∼** *v. pr.* boast (**de,** about).

va-nu-pieds /vanypje/ *n.m./f. invar.* vagabond, beggar.

vapeur[1] /vapœr/ *n.f.* (*eau*) steam; (*brume, émanation*) vapour.

vapeur[2] /vapœr/ *n.m.* (*bateau*) steamer.

vaporeu|x, ~se /vapɔrø, -z/ *a.* hazy; (*léger*) filmy, flimsy.

vaporis|er /vapɔrize/ *v.t.* spray. **~a-teur** *n.m.* spray.

vaquer /vake/ *v.i.* **~ à,** attend to.

varappe /varap/ *n.f.* rock climbing.

vareuse /varøz/ *n.f.* (*d'uniforme*) tunic.

variable /varjabl/ *a.* variable; (*temps*) changeable.

variante /varjɑ̃t/ *n.f.* variant.

varicelle /varisɛl/ *n.f.* chicken-pox.

varices /varis/ *n.f. pl.* varicose veins.

var|ier /varje/ *v.t./i.* vary. **~iation** *n.f.* variation. **~ié** *a.* (*non monotone, étendu*) varied; (*divers*) various.

variété /varjete/ *n.f.* variety. **~s,** (*spectacle*) variety.

variole /varjɔl/ *n.f.* smallpox.

vase[1] /vɑz/ *n.m.* vase.

vase[2] /vɑz/ *n.f.* (*boue*) silt, mud.

vaseu|x, ~se /vɑzø, -z/ *a.* (*confus: fam.*) woolly, hazy.

vasistas /vazistɑs/ *n.m.* fanlight, hinged panel (*in door or window*).

vaste /vast/ *a.* vast, huge.

vaudeville /vodvil/ *n.m.* vaudeville, light comedy.

vau-l'eau (à) /(a)volo/ *adv.* on the road to ruin.

vaurien, ~ne /vorjɛ̃, -jɛn/ *n.m., f.* good-for-nothing.

vautour /votur/ *n.m.* vulture.

vautrer (se) /(sə)votre/ *v. pr.* sprawl. **se ~ dans,** (*vice, boue*) wallow in.

va-vite (à la) /(ala)vavit/ *adv.* (*fam.*) in a hurry.

veau (*pl.* **~x**) /vo/ *n.m.* calf; (*viande*) veal.

vécu /veky/ *voir* **vivre.** —*a.* (*réel*) true, real.

vedette[1] /vədɛt/ *n.f.* (*artiste*) star. **en ~,** (*objet*) in a prominent position; (*personne*) in the limelight.

vedette[2] /vədɛt/ *n.f.* (*bateau*) launch.

végét|al (*m. pl.* **~aux**) /veʒetal, -o/ *a.* plant. —*n.m.* (*pl.* **~aux**) plant.

végétarien, ~ne /veʒetarjɛ̃, -jɛn/ *n.m., f.* vegetarian.

végétation /veʒetasjɔ̃/ *n.f.* vegetation. **~s,** (*méd.*) adenoids.

végéter /veʒete/ *v.i.* vegetate.

véhémen|t, ~te /veemɑ̃, -t/ *a.* vehement. **~ce** *n.f.* vehemence.

véhicul|e /veikyl/ *n.m.* vehicle. **~er** *v.t.* convey.

veille[1] /vɛj/ *n.f.* **la ~ (de),** the day before. **la ~ de Noël,** Christmas Eve. **à la ~ de,** on the eve of.

veille[2] /vɛj/ *n.f.* (*état*) wakefulness.

veillée /veje/ *n.f.* evening (gathering); (*mortuaire*) vigil, wake.

veiller /veje/ *v.i.* stay up *ou* awake. **~ à,** attend to. **~ sur,** watch over. —*v.t.* (*malade*) watch over.

veilleur /vɛjœr/ *n.m.* **~ de nuit,** night-watchman.

veilleuse /vɛjøz/ *n.f.* night-light; (*de véhicule*) sidelight; (*de réchaud*) pilot-light.

veinard, ~e /vɛnar, -d/ *n.m., f.* (*fam.*) lucky devil.

veine[1] /vɛn/ *n.f.* (*anat.*) vein; (*nervure, filon*) vein.

veine[2] /vɛn/ *n.f.* (*chance: fam.*) luck. **avoir de la ~,** (*fam.*) be lucky.

vélo /velo/ *n.m.* bicycle, bike; (*activité*) cycling.

vélodrome /velodrɔm/ *n.m.* velodrome, cycle-racing track.

vélomoteur /velomotœr/ *n.m.* moped.

velours /vlur/ *n.m.* velvet. **~ côtelé, ~ à côtes,** corduroy.

velouté /vəlute/ *a.* smooth. —*n.m.* smoothness.

velu /vəly/ *a.* hairy.

venaison /vənɛzɔ̃/ *n.f.* venison.

vendang|e(s) /vɑ̃dɑ̃ʒ/ *n.f.* (*pl.*) grape harvest. **~er** *v.i.* pick the grapes. **~eur, ~euse** *n.m., f.* grape-picker.

vendetta /vɑ̃deta/ *n.f.* vendetta.

vendeu|r, ~se /vɑ̃dœr, -øz/ *n.m., f.* shop assistant; (*marchand*) salesman, saleswoman; (*jurid.*) vendor, seller.

vendre /vɑ̃dr/ *v.t.,* **se ~** *v. pr.* sell. **à ~,** for sale.

vendredi /vɑ̃drədi/ *n.m.* Friday. **V~ saint,** Good Friday.

vénéneu|x, ~se /venenø, -z/ *a.* poisonous.

vénérable /venerabl/ *a.* venerable.

vénérer /venere/ *v.t.* revere.

vénérien, ~ne /venerjɛ̃, -jɛn/ *a.* venereal.

vengeance /vɑ̃ʒɑ̃s/ *n.f.* revenge, vengeance.

veng|er /vɑ̃ʒe/ *v.t.* avenge. **se ~er** *v. pr.* take (one's) revenge (**de,** for). **~eur, ~eresse** *a.* vengeful; *n.m., f.* avenger.

ven|in /vənɛ̃/ *n.m.* venom. **~imeux, ~imeuse** *a.* poisonous, venomous.

venir† /vənir/ *v.i.* (*aux. être*) come (**de,** from). **~ faire,** come to do. **venez faire,** come and do. **il vient/venait**

d'arriver, he has/had just arrived.
en ~ à, (question, conclusion, etc.)
come to. **en ~ aux mains,** come to
blows. **faire ~,** send for. **il m'est
venu à l'esprit** ou **à l'idée que,** it
occurred to me that.

vent /vã/ n.m. wind. **être dans le ~,**
(fam.) be with it. **il fait du ~,** it is
windy.

vente /vãt/ n.f. sale. **~ (aux enchères),** auction. **en ~,** on ou for
sale. **~ de charité,** (charity) bazaar.

ventil|er /vãtile/ v.t. ventilate. **~a-
teur** n.m. fan, ventilator. **~ation** n.f.
ventilation.

ventouse /vãtuz/ n.f. (dispositif) suction pad; (pour déboucher l'évier etc.)
plunger.

ventre /vãtr/ n.m. belly, stomach;
(utérus) womb. **avoir/prendre du
~,** have/develop a paunch.

ventriloque /vãtrilɔk/ n.m./f. ventriloquist.

ventru /vãtry/ a. pot-bellied.

venu /vəny/ voir venir. —a. **bien ~,**
(à propos) timely. **mal ~,** untimely.
être mal ~ de faire, have no grounds
for doing.

venue /vəny/ n.f. coming.

vêpres /vepr/ n.f. pl. vespers.

ver /ver/ n.m. worm; (des fruits, de la
viande) maggot.

véranda /verãda/ n.f. veranda.

verb|e /verb/ n.m. (gram.) verb. **~al**
(m. pl. **~aux**) a. verbal.

verbeu|x, ~se /verbø, -z/ a. verbose.

verdâtre /verdatr/ a. greenish.

verdict /verdikt/ n.m. verdict.

verdir /verdir/ v.i. turn green.

verdoyant, ~e /verdwajã, -t/ a. green,
verdant.

verdure /verdyr/ n.f. greenery.

véreu|x, ~se /verø, -z/ a. maggoty,
wormy; (malhonnête: fig.) shady.

verger /verʒe/ n.m. orchard.

vergla|s /vergla/ n.m. (black) ice;
(Amer.) sleet. **~cé** a. icy.

vergogne (sans) /(sã)vergɔɲ/ a.
shameless. —adv. shamelessly.

véridique /veridik/ a. truthful.

vérif|ier /verifje/ v.t. check, verify;
(compte) audit; (confirmer) confirm.
~ication n.f. check(ing), verifica-
tion.

véritable /veritabl/ a. true, real; (authentique) real. **~ment** /-əmã/ adv.
really.

vérité /verite/ n.f. truth; (de tableau,
roman) trueness to life. **en ~,** in fact.

vermeil, ~le /vermej/ a. bright red,
vermilion.

vermicelle(s) /vermisɛl/ n.m. (pl.)
vermicelli.

vermine /vermin/ n.f. vermin.

vermoulu /vermuly/ a. wormeaten.

vermouth /vermut/ n.m. (apéritif)
vermouth.

verni /verni/ a. (fam.) lucky.

vernir /vernir/ v.t. varnish.

vernis /verni/ n.m. varnish; (de poterie) glaze. **~ à ongles,** nail polish
ou varnish.

vernisser /vernise/ v.t. glaze.

verra, verrait /vera, verɛ/ voir voir.

verre /ver/ n.m. glass. **prendre** ou
boire un ~, have a drink. **~ de
contact,** contact lens. **~ dépoli/gros-
sissant,** frosted/magnifying glass.
~rie n.f. (objets) glassware.

verrière /verjer/ n.f. (toit) glass roof;
(paroi) glass wall.

verrou /veru/ n.m. bolt. **sous les ~s,**
behind bars.

verrouiller /veruje/ v.t. bolt.

verrue /very/ n.f. wart.

vers[1] /ver/ prép. towards; (temps)
about.

vers[2] /ver/ n.m. (ligne) line. **les ~,**
(poésie) verse.

versant /versã/ n.m. slope, side.

versatile /versatil/ a. fickle.

verse (à) /(a)vers/ adv. in torrents.

versé /verse/ a. **~ dans,** versed in.

vers|er /verse/ v.t./i. pour; (larmes,
sang) shed; (basculer) overturn;
(payer) pay. **~ement** n.m. payment.

verset /versɛ/ n.m. (relig.) verse.

version /versjɔ̃/ n.f. version; (traduction) translation.

verso /verso/ n.m. back (of the page).

vert, ~e /ver, -t/ a. green; (vieillard)
sprightly. —n.m. green.

vertèbre /vertebr/ n.f. vertebra.

vertement /vertəmã/ adv. sharply.

vertic|al, ~ale (m. pl. **~aux**)
/vertikal, -o/ a. & n.f. vertical. **à la
~ale, ~alement** adv. vertically.

vertig|e /vertiʒ/ n.m. dizziness. **~es,**
dizzy spells. **avoir le** ou **un ~e,** feel
dizzy. **~ineux, ~ineuse** a. dizzy;
(très grand) staggering.

vertu /verty/ n.f. virtue. **en ~ de,** by
virtue of. **~eux, ~euse** /-tɥø, -z/ a.
virtuous.

verve /verv/ n.f. spirit, wit.

vessie /vesi/ *n.f.* bladder.

veste /vɛst/ *n.f.* jacket.

vestiaire /vɛstjɛr/ *n.m.* cloakroom; (*sport*) changing-room.

vestibule /vɛstibyl/ *n.m.* hall.

vestige /vɛstiʒ/ *n.m.* (*objet*) relic; (*trace*) vestige.

veston /vɛstɔ̃/ *n.m.* jacket.

vêtement /vɛtmɑ̃/ *n.m.* article of clothing. **~s**, clothes.

vétéran /veterɑ̃/ *n.m.* veteran.

vétérinaire /veterinɛr/ *n.m.|f.* veterinary surgeon, (*Amer.*) veterinarian. —*a.* veterinary.

vétille /vetij/ *n.f.* trifle.

vêt|ir /vetir/ *v.t.*, **se ~ir** *v. pr.* dress. **~u** *a.* dressed (**de**, in).

veto /veto/ *n.m. invar.* veto.

vétuste /vetyst/ *a.* dilapidated.

veu|f, ~ve /vœf, -v/ *a.* widowed. —*n.m.* widower. —*n.f.* widow.

veuille /vœj/ *voir* **vouloir**.

veule /vøl/ *a.* feeble.

veut, veux /vø/ *voir* **vouloir**.

vexation /vɛksasjɔ̃/ *n.f.* humiliation.

vex|er /vɛkse/ *v.t.* upset, hurt. **se ~er** *v. pr.* be upset, be hurt. **~ant, ~ante** *a.* upsetting.

via /vja/ *prép.* via.

viable /vjabl/ *a.* viable.

viaduc /vjadyk/ *n.m.* viaduct.

viande /vjɑ̃d/ *n.f.* meat.

vibr|er /vibre/ *v.i.* vibrate; (*être ému*) thrill. **~ant, ~ante** *a.* (*émouvant*) vibrant. **~ation** *n.f.* vibration.

vicaire /vikɛr/ *n.m.* curate.

vice /vis/ *n.m.* (*moral*) vice; (*défectuosité*) defect.

vice- /vis/ *préf.* vice-.

vice versa /vis(e)vɛrsa/ *adv.* vice versa.

vicier /visje/ *v.t.* taint.

vicieu|x, ~se /visjø, -z/ *a.* depraved. —*n.m., f.* pervert.

vicin|al (*pl.* **~aux**) /visinal, -o/ *a.m.* **chemin ~al**, by-road, minor road.

vicomte /vikɔ̃t/ *n.m.* viscount.

victime /viktim/ *n.f.* victim; (*d'un accident*) casualty.

vict|oire /viktwar/ *n.f.* victory; (*sport*) win. **~orieux, ~orieuse** *a.* victorious; (*équipe*) winning.

victuailles /viktɥaj/ *n.f. pl.* provisions.

vidang|e /vidɑ̃ʒ/ *n.f.* emptying; (*auto.*) oil change; (*dispositif*) waste pipe. **~er** *v.t.* empty.

vide /vid/ *a.* empty. —*n.m.* emptiness,

void; (*trou, manque*) gap; (*espace sans air*) vacuum. **à ~**, empty.

vidéo /video/ *a. invar.* video.

vider /vide/ *v.t.* empty; (*poisson*) gut; (*lieu*) vacate; (*expulser*: *fam.*) throw out. **se ~** *v. pr.* empty.

vie /vi/ *n.f.* life; (*durée*) lifetime. **à ~, pour la ~,** for life. **donner la ~ à,** give birth to. **en ~,** alive. **~ chère,** high cost of living.

vieil /vjɛj/ *voir* **vieux**.

vieillard /vjɛjar/ *n.m.* old man.

vieille /vjɛj/ *voir* **vieux**.

vieillesse /vjɛjɛs/ *n.f.* old age.

vieill|ir /vjejir/ *v.i.* grow old, age; (*mot, idée*) become old-fashioned. —*v.t.* age. **~issement** *n.m.* ageing.

viens, vient /vjɛ̃/ *voir* **venir**.

vierge /vjɛrʒ/ *n.f.* virgin. —*a.* virgin; (*feuille, film*) blank.

vieux *ou* **vieil*, vieille** (*m. pl.* **vieux**) /vjø, vjɛj/ *a.* old. —*n.m.* old man. —*n.f.* old woman. **les ~,** old people. **mon ~,** (*fam.*) old man *ou* boy. **ma vieille,** (*fam.*) old girl, dear. **vieille fille,** (*péj.*) spinster. **~ garçon,** bachelor. **~ jeu** *a. invar.* old-fashioned.

vif, vive /vif, viv/ *a.* lively; (*émotion, vent*) keen; (*froid*) biting; (*lumière*) bright; (*douleur, parole*) sharp; (*souvenir, style, teint*) vivid; (*succès, impatience*) great. **brûler/enterrer ~,** burn/bury alive.

vigie /viʒi/ *n.f.* look-out.

vigilan|t, ~te /viʒilɑ̃, -t/ *a.* vigilant. **~ce** *n.f.* vigilance.

vigne /viɲ/ *n.f.* (*plante*) vine; (*vignoble*) vineyard.

vigneron, ~ne /viɲrɔ̃, -ɔn/ *n.m., f.* wine-grower.

vignette /viɲɛt/ *n.f.* (*étiquette*) label; (*auto.*) road tax sticker.

vignoble /viɲɔbl/ *n.m.* vineyard.

vigoureu|x, ~se /vigurø, -z/ *a.* vigorous, sturdy.

vigueur /vigœr/ *n.f.* vigour. **être/ entrer en ~,** (*loi*) be/come into force. **en ~,** (*terme*) in use.

vil /vil/ *a.* vile, base.

vilain, ~e /vilɛ̃, -ɛn/ *a.* (*mauvais*) nasty; (*laid*) ugly.

villa /vila/ *n.f.* (detached) house.

village /vilaʒ/ *n.m.* village.

villageois, ~e /vilaʒwa, -z/ *a.* village. —*n.m., f.* villager.

ville /vil/ *n.f.* town; (*importante*) city. **~ d'eaux,** spa.

vin /vɛ̃/ *n.m.* wine. ~ **d'honneur,** reception. ~ **ordinaire,** table wine.

vinaigre /vinɛgr/ *n.m.* vinegar.

vinaigrette /vinɛgrɛt/ *n.f.* oil and vinegar dressing, vinaigrette.

vindicati|f, ~ve /vɛ̃dikatif, -v/ *a.* vindictive.

vingt /vɛ̃/ (/vɛ̃t/ *before vowel and in numbers 22–29*) *a. & n.m.* twenty. **~ième** *a. & n.m./f.* twentieth.

vingtaine /vɛ̃tɛn/ *n.f.* **une ~ (de),** about twenty.

vinicole /vinikɔl/ *a.* wine(-growing).

vinyle /vinil/ *n.m.* vinyl.

viol /vjɔl/ *n.m.* (*de femme*) rape; (*de lieu, loi*) violation.

violacé /vjɔlase/ *a.* purplish.

viol|ent, ~ente /vjɔlɑ̃, -t/ *a.* violent. **~emment** /-amɑ̃/ *adv.* violently. **~ence** *n.f.* violence; (*acte*) act of violence.

violenter /vjɔlɑ̃te/ *v.t.* rape.

viol|er /vjɔle/ *v.t.* rape; (*lieu, loi*) violate. **~ation** *n.f.* violation.

violet, ~te /vjɔlɛ, -t/ *a. & n.m.* purple. —*n.f.* violet.

violon /vjɔlɔ̃/ *n.m.* violin. **~iste** /-ɔnist/ *n.m./f.* violinist.

violoncell|e /vjɔlɔ̃sɛl/ *n.m.* cello. **~iste** /-elist/ *n.m./f.* cellist.

vipère /vipɛr/ *n.f.* viper, adder.

virage /viraʒ/ *n.m.* bend; (*de véhicule*) turn; (*changement d'attitude*: *fig.*) change of course.

virée /vire/ *n.f.* (*fam.*) trip, outing.

vir|er /vire/ *v.i.* turn; (*avion*) bank. **~er au rouge**/etc., turn red/*etc.* —*v.t.* (*argent*) transfer; (*expulser*: *fam.*) throw out. **~ement** *n.m.* (*comm.*) (credit) transfer.

virevolter /virvɔlte/ *v.i.* spin round, swing round.

virginité /virʒinite/ *n.f.* virginity.

virgule /virgyl/ *n.f.* comma; (*dans un nombre*) (decimal) point.

viril /viril/ *a.* manly, virile. **~ité** *n.f.* manliness, virility.

virtuel, ~le /virtɥɛl/ *a.* virtual. **~lement** *adv.* virtually.

virtuos|e /virtɥoz/ *n.m./f.* virtuoso. **~ité** *n.f.* virtuosity.

virulen|t, ~te /virylɑ̃, -t/ *a.* virulent. **~ce** *n.f.* virulence.

virus /virys/ *n.m.* virus.

vis[1] /vi/ *voir* **vivre, voir.**

vis[2] /vis/ *n.f.* screw.

visa /viza/ *n.m.* visa.

visage /vizaʒ/ *n.m.* face.

vis-à-vis /vizavi/ *adv.* face to face, opposite. **~ de,** opposite; (*à l'égard de*) with respect to. —*n.m. invar.* (*personne*) person opposite.

viscères /visɛr/ *n.m. pl.* intestines.

visée /vize/ *n.f.* aim.

viser /vize/ *v.t.* aim at; (*concerner*) be aimed at; (*timbrer*) stamp. —*v.i.* aim. **~ à,** aim at; (*mesure, propos*) be aimed at.

visib|le /vizibl/ *a.* visible. **~ilité** *n.f.* visibility. **~lement** *adv.* visibly.

visière /vizjɛr/ *n.f.* (*de casquette*) peak; (*de casque*) visor.

vision /vizjɔ̃/ *n.f.* vision.

visionnaire /vizjɔnɛr/ *a. & n.m./f.* visionary.

visionn|er /vizjɔne/ *v.t.* view. **~euse** *n.f.* (*appareil*) viewer.

visite /vizit/ *n.f.* visit; (*examen*) examination; (*personne*) visitor. **de ~,** (*heure, carte*) visiting. **~ guidée,** guided tour.

visit|er /vizite/ *v.t.* visit; (*examiner*) examine. **~eur, ~euse** *n.m.,* f. visitor.

vison /vizɔ̃/ *n.m.* mink.

visqueu|x, ~se /viskø, -z/ *a.* viscous.

visser /vise/ *v.t.* screw (on).

visuel, ~le /vizɥɛl/ *a.* visual.

vit /vi/ *voir* **vivre, voir.**

vit|al (*m. pl.* **~aux**) /vital, -o/ *a.* vital. **~alité** *n.f.* vitality.

vitamine /vitamin/ *n.f.* vitamin.

vite /vit/ *adv.* fast, quickly; (*tôt*) soon. **~!,** quick!

vitesse /vitɛs/ *n.f.* speed; (*régime*: *auto.*) gear. **à toute ~,** at top speed. **en ~,** in a hurry, quickly.

vitic|ole /vitikɔl/ *a.* wine. **~ulteur** *n.m.* wine-grower. **~ulture** *n.f.* wine-growing.

vitrage /vitraʒ/ *n.m.* (*vitres*) windows.

vitr|ail (*pl.* **~aux**) /vitraj, -o/ *n.m.* stained-glass window.

vitr|e /vitr/ *n.f.* (window) pane; (*de véhicule*) window. **~é** *a.* glass, glazed. **~er** *v.t.* glaze.

vitrine /vitrin/ *n.f.* (shop) window; (*meuble*) display cabinet.

vivable /vivabl/ *a.* (*personne*) easy to live with; (*maison*) liveable.

vivace /vivas/ *a.* (*plante, sentiment*) perennial.

vivacité /vivasite/ *n.f.* liveliness; (*agilité*) quickness; (*d'émotion, de l'air*) keenness; (*de souvenir, style, teint*) vividness.

vivant, ~e /vivã, -t/ *a.* (*doué de vie, en usage*) living; (*en vie*) alive, living; (*actif, vif*) lively. —*n.m.* de son ~, in one's lifetime. **les ~s,** the living.

vivats /viva/ *n.m. pl.* cheers.

vive[1] /viv/ *voir* **vif.**

vive[2] /viv/ *int.* ~ le roi/président/ etc.!, long live the king/president/ etc.! ~(nt) les vacances!, hurrah for the holidays!

vivement /vivmã/ *adv.* (*vite, sèchement*) sharply; (*avec éclat*) vividly; (*beaucoup*) greatly. ~ la fin!, roll on the end, I'll be glad when it's the end!

viveur /vivœr/ *n.m.* pleasure-seeker.

vivier /vivje/ *n.m.* fish-pond.

vivifier /vivifje/ *v.t.* invigorate.

vivisection /vivisɛksjɔ̃/ *n.f.* vivisection.

vivoter /vivɔte/ *v.i.* plod on, get by.

vivre† /vivr/ *v.i.* live. ~ de, (*nourriture*) live on. —*v.t.* (*vie*) live; (*période, aventure*) live through. ~s *n.m. pl.* supplies. **faire ~,** (*famille etc.*) support. ~ encore, be still alive.

vlan /vlã/ *int.* bang.

vocabulaire /vɔkabylɛr/ *n.m.* vocabulary.

voc|al (*m. pl.* ~aux) /vɔkal, -o/ *a.* vocal.

vocalise /vɔkaliz/ *n.f.* voice exercise.

vocation /vɔkasjɔ̃/ *n.f.* vocation.

vodka /vɔdka/ *n.f.* vodka.

vœu (*pl.* ~x) /vø/ *n.m.* (*souhait*) wish; (*promesse*) vow.

vogue /vɔg/ *n.f.* fashion, vogue.

voguer /vɔge/ *v.i.* sail.

voici /vwasi/ *prép.* here is, this is; (*au pluriel*) here are, these are. **me ~,** here I am. ~ un an, (*temps passé*) a year ago. ~ un an que, it is a year since.

voie /vwa/ *n.f.* (*route*) road; (*chemin*) way; (*moyen*) means, way; (*partie de route*) lane; (*rails*) track; (*quai*) platform. **en ~ de,** in the process of. **en ~ de développement,** (*pays*) developing. **par la ~ des airs,** by air. ~ de dégagement, slip-road. ~ ferrée, railway; (*Amer.*) railroad. ~ lactée, Milky Way. ~ navigable, waterway. ~ publique, public highway. ~ sans issue, cul-de-sac, dead end.

voilà /vwala/ *prép.* there is, that is; (*au pluriel*) there are, those are; (*voici*) here is; here are. **le ~,** there he is. ~!, right!; (*en offrant qch.*) there you are! ~ un an, (*temps passé*) a

year ago. ~ un an que, it is a year since.

voilage /vwalaʒ/ *n.m.* net curtain.

voile[1] /vwal/ *n.f.* (*de bateau*) sail; (*sport*) sailing.

voile[2] /vwal/ *n.m.* veil; (*tissu léger et fin*) net.

voil|er[1] /vwale/ *v.t.* veil. **se ~er** *v. pr.* (*devenir flou*) become hazy. ~é *a.* (*terme, femme*) veiled; (*flou*) hazy.

voiler[2] /vwale/ *v.t.*, **se ~** *v. pr.* (*roue etc.*) buckle.

voilier /vwalje/ *n.m.* sailing-ship.

voilure /vwalyr/ *n.f.* sails.

voir† /vwar/ *v.t./i.* see. **se ~** *v. pr.* (*être visible*) show; (*se produire*) be seen; (*se trouver*) find o.s.; (*se fréquenter*) see each other. **ça n'a rien à ~ avec,** that has nothing to do with. **faire ~,** laisser ~, show. **je ne peux pas le ~,** (*fam.*) I cannot stand him. ~ trouble, have blurred vision. **voyons!,** (*irritation*) come on!

voire /vwar/ *adv.* indeed.

voirie /vwari/ *n.f.* (*service*) highway maintenance.

voisin, ~e /vwazɛ̃, -in/ *a.* (*proche*) neighbouring; (*adjacent*) next (**de,** to); (*semblable*) similar (**de,** to). —*n.m.,f.* neighbour.

voisinage /vwazinaʒ/ *n.m.* neighbourhood; (*proximité*) proximity.

voiture /vwatyr/ *n.f.* (motor) car; (*wagon*) coach, carriage. **en ~!,** all aboard! ~ à cheval, horse-drawn carriage. ~ de course, racing-car. ~ d'enfant, pram; (*Amer.*) baby carriage. ~ de tourisme, private car.

voix /vwa/ *n.f.* voice; (*suffrage*) vote. **à ~ basse,** in a whisper.

vol[1] /vɔl/ *n.m.* (*d'avion, d'oiseau*) flight; (*groupe d'oiseaux etc.*) flock, flight. **à ~ d'oiseau,** as the crow flies. ~ libre, hang-gliding. ~ plané, gliding.

vol[2] /vɔl/ *n.m.* (*délit*) theft; (*hold-up*) robbery. ~ à la tire, pick-pocketing.

volage /vɔlaʒ/ *a.* flighty.

volaille /vɔlaj/ *n.f.* **la ~,** (*poules etc.*) poultry. **une ~,** a fowl.

volant[1], **~e** /vɔlã, -t/ *a.* (*soucoupe etc.*) flying.

volant[2] /vɔlã/ *n.m.* (steering-)wheel; (*de jupe*) flounce.

volatile /vɔlatil/ *n.m.* fowl.

volcan /vɔlkã/ *n.m.* volcano. **~ique** /-anik/ *a.* volcanic.

volée /vɔle/ *n.f.* flight; (*oiseaux*) flight,

flock; (*de personnes*) swarm; (*de coups, d'obus*) volley; (*raclée*) beating. **à toute ~**, with full force. **de ~, à la ~**, in flight.

voler[1] /vɔle/ *v.i.* (*oiseau etc.*) fly.

vol|er[2] /vɔle/ *v.t./i.* steal (**à**, from). **~er qn.**, rob s.o. **~eur, ~euse** *n.m.*, *f.* thief; *a.* thieving.

volet /vɔlɛ/ *n.m.* (*de fenêtre*) shutter; (*de document*) (folded *ou* tear-off) section.

voleter /vɔlte/ *v.i.* flutter.

volière /vɔljɛr/ *n.f.* aviary.

volontaire /vɔlɔ̃tɛr/ *a.* voluntary; (*personne*) self-willed. —*n.m./f.* volunteer. **~ment** *adv.* voluntarily; (*exprès*) intentionally.

volonté /vɔlɔ̃te/ *n.f.* (*faculté, intention*) will; (*souhait*) wish; (*énergie*) willpower. **à ~**, (*à son gré*) at will. **bonne ~**, goodwill. **mauvaise ~**, ill will.

volontiers /vɔlɔ̃tje/ *adv.* (*de bon gré*) with pleasure, willingly, gladly; (*ordinairement*) readily.

volt /vɔlt/ *n.m.* volt. **~age** *n.m.* voltage.

volte-face /vɔltəfas/ *n.f. invar.* about-face. **faire ~**, turn round.

voltige /vɔltiʒ/ *n.f.* acrobatics.

voltiger /vɔltiʒe/ *v.i.* flutter.

volubile /vɔlybil/ *a.* voluble.

volume /vɔlym/ *n.m.* volume.

volumineu|x, ~se /vɔlyminø, -z/ *a.* bulky.

volupt|é /vɔlypte/ *n.f.* sensual pleasure. **~ueux, ~ueuse** *a.* voluptuous.

vom|ir /vɔmir/ *v.t./i.* vomit. **~i** *n.m.* vomit. **~issement(s)** *n.m.* (*pl.*) vomiting.

vont /vɔ̃/ *voir* **aller**[1].

vorace /vɔras/ *a.* voracious.

vos /vo/ *voir* **votre**.

vote /vɔt/ *n.m.* (*action*) voting; (*d'une loi*) passing; (*suffrage*) vote.

vot|er /vɔte/ *v.i.* vote. —*v.t.* vote for; (*adopter*) pass; (*crédits*) vote. **~ant, ~ante** *n.m.*, *f.* voter.

votre (*pl.* **vos**) /vɔtr, vo/ *a.* your.

vôtre /votr/ *pron.* **le** *ou* **la ~, les ~s**, yours.

vouer /vwe/ *v.t.* dedicate (**à**, to); (*promettre*) vow. **~ à l'échec**, doom to failure.

vouloir† /vulwar/ *v.t.* want (**faire**, to do). **ça ne veut pas bouger**/*etc.*, it will not move/*etc.* **je voudrais/voudrais bien venir**/ *etc.*, I should *ou* would like/really like to come/*etc.* **je**

veux bien venir/*etc.*, I am happy to come/*etc.* **voulez-vous attendre**/ *etc.?*, will you wait/*etc.?* **veuillez attendre**/*etc.*, kindly wait/*etc.* **~ absolument faire**, insist on doing. **comme** *ou* **si vous voulez**, if you like *ou* wish. **en ~ à qn.**, have a grudge against s.o.; (*être en colère contre*) be annoyed with s.o. **ne pas ~ de qch.**/**qn.**, not want sth./s.o. **~ dire**, mean. **~ du bien à**, wish well.

voulu /vuly/ *a.* (*délibéré*) intentional; (*requis*) required.

vous /vu/ *pron.* (*sujet, complément*) you; (*indirect*) (to) you; (*réfléchi*) yourself; (*pl.*) yourselves; (*l'un l'autre*) each other. **~-même** *pron.* yourself. **~-mêmes** *pron.* yourselves.

voûte /vut/ *n.f.* (*plafond*) vault; (*porche*) archway.

voûté /vute/ *a.* bent, stooped.

vouv|oyer /vuvwaje/ *v.t.* address politely (using *vous*). **~oiement** *n.m.* use of (polite) *vous*.

voyage /vwajaʒ/ *n.m.* journey, trip; (*par mer*) voyage. **~(s)**, (*action*) travelling. **de ~**, (*compagnon etc.*) travelling. **~ organisé**, (package) tour.

voyag|er /vwajaʒe/ *v.i.* travel. **~eur, ~euse** *n.m.*, *f.* traveller.

voyant[1], **~e** /vwajɑ̃, -t/ *a.* gaudy. —*n.f.* (*femme*) clairvoyant.

voyant[2] /vwajɑ̃/ *n.m.* (*signal*) (warning) light.

voyelle /vwajɛl/ *n.f.* vowel.

voyou /vwaju/ *n.m.* hooligan.

vrac (en) /(ɑ̃)vrak/ *adv.* in disorder; (*sans emballage, au poids*) loose, in bulk.

vrai /vrɛ/ *a.* true; (*réel*) real. —*n.m.* truth. **à ~ dire**, to tell the truth.

vraiment /vrɛmɑ̃/ *adv.* really.

vraisembl|able /vrɛsɑ̃blabl/ *a.* likely. **~ablement** *adv.* very likely. **~ance** *n.f.* likelihood, plausibility.

vrille /vrij/ *n.f.* (*aviat.*) spin.

vromb|ir /vrɔ̃bir/ *v.i.* hum. **~issement** *n.m.* humming.

vu /vy/ *voir* **voir**. —*a.* **bien/mal ~**, well/not well thought of. —*prép.* in view of. **~ que**, seeing that.

vue /vy/ *n.f.* (*spectacle*) sight; (*sens*) (eye)sight; (*panorama, idée*) view. **avoir en ~**, have in mind. **à ~**, (*tirer, payable*) at sight. **de ~**, by sight. **perdre de ~**, lose sight of. **en ~**, (*proche*) in sight; (*célèbre*) in the pub-

lic eye. **en ~ de faire,** with a view
to doing.
vulg|aire /vylgɛr/ *a.* (*grossier*) vulgar;
(*ordinaire*) common. **~arité** *n.f.* vul-
garity.

vulgariser /vylgarize/ *v.t.* popularize.
vulnérab|le /vylnerabl/ *a.* vulner-
able. **~ilité** *n.f.* vulnerability.

W

wagon /vagɔ̃/ *n.m.* (*de voyageurs*) carriage; (*Amer.*) car; (*de marchandises*)
wagon; (*Amer.*) freight car. **~-lit** (*pl.*
~s-lits) *n.m.* sleeping-car, sleeper.
~-restaurant (*pl.* **~s-restaurants**)
n.m. dining-car.
wallon, ~ne /walɔ̃, -ɔn/ *a.* & *n.m.*, *f.*
Walloon.

waters /watɛr/ *n.m. pl.* toilet.
watt /wat/ *n.m.* watt.
w.-c. /(dublə)vese/ *n.m. pl.* toilet.
week-end /wikɛnd/ *n.m.* weekend.
western /wɛstɛrn/ *n.m.* western.
whisk|y (*pl.* **~ies**) /wiski/ *n.m.*
whisky.

X

xénophob|e /ksenɔfɔb/ *a.* xeno-
phobic. —*n.m.|f.* xenophobe. **~ie** *n.f.*
xenophobia.

xérès /gzerɛs/ *n.m.* sherry.
xylophone /ksilɔfɔn/ *n.m.* xylophone.

Y

y /i/ *adv.* & *pron.* there; (*dessus*) on it;
(*pl.*) on them; (*dedans*) in it; (*pl.*) in
them. **s'~ habituer,** (*à cela*) get used
to it. **s'~ attendre,** expect it. **~
penser,** think of it. **il ~ entra,** (*dans
cela*) he entered it. **j'~ courus,** (*vers
cela*) I ran to it. **ça ~ est,** that is it.
~ être pour qch., have sth. to do
with it.
yacht /jɔt/ *n.m.* yacht.

yaourt /jaur(t)/ *n.m.* yoghurt.
yeux /jø/ *voir* œil.
yiddish /(j)idiʃ/ *n.m.* Yiddish.
yoga /jɔga/ *n.m.* yoga.
yougoslave /jugɔslav/ *a.* & *n.m.|f.*
Yugoslav.
Yougoslavie /jugɔslavi/ *n.f.* Yugo-
slavia.
yo-yo /jojo/ *n.m. invar.* (P.) yo-yo (P.).

Z

zèbre /zɛbr/ *n.m.* zebra.
zébré /zebre/ *a.* striped.
zèle /zɛl/ *n.m.* zeal.
zélé /zele/ *a.* zealous.
zénith /zenit/ *n.m.* zenith.
zéro /zero/ *n.m.* nought, zero; (*température*) zero; (*dans un numéro*) 0; (*football*) nil; (*football*: *Amer.*) zero; (*personne*) nonentity. **(re)partir de** ~, start from scratch.
zeste /zɛst/ *n.m.* peel.
zézayer /zezeje/ *v.i.* lisp.
zigzag /zigzag/ *n.m.* zigzag. **en** ~, zigzag. ~**uer** /-e/ *v.i.* zigzag.

zinc /zɛ̃g/ *n.m.* (*métal*) zinc; (*comptoir*: *fam.*) bar.
zodiaque /zɔdjak/ *n.m.* zodiac.
zona /zona/ *n.m.* (*méd.*) shingles.
zone /zon/ *n.f.* zone, area; (*faubourgs*) shanty town. ~ **bleue,** restricted parking zone.
zoo /zo(o)/ *n.m.* zoo.
zoolog|ie /zɔɔlɔʒi/ *n.f.* zoology. ~**ique** *a.* zoological. ~**iste** *n.m./f.* zoologist.
zoom /zum/ *n.m.* zoom lens.
zut /zyt/ *int.* blast (it), (oh) hell.

ANGLAIS-FRANÇAIS
ENGLISH-FRENCH

A

a /eɪ, *unstressed* ə/ *a.* (*before vowel* **an** /æn, ən/) un(e). **ten pence ~ kilo,** dix pence le kilo. **once ~ year,** une fois par an.

aback /ə'bæk/ *adv.* **taken ~,** déconcerté, interdit.

abandon /ə'bændən/ *v.t.* abandonner. —*n.* désinvolture *f.* **~ed** *a.* (*behaviour*) débauché. **~ment** *n.* abandon *m.*

abase /ə'beɪs/ *v.t.* humilier.

abashed /ə'bæʃt/ *a.* confus.

abate /ə'beɪt/ *v.i.* se calmer. —*v.t.* diminuer. **~ment** *n.* diminution *f.*

abattoir /'æbətwɑː(r)/ *n.* abattoir *m.*

abbey /'æbɪ/ *n.* abbaye *f.*

abb|ot /'æbət/ *n.* abbé *m.* **~ess** *n.* abbesse *f.*

abbreviat|e /ə'briːvɪeɪt/ *v.t.* abréger. **~ion** /-'eɪʃn/ *n.* abréviation *f.*

abdicat|e /'æbdɪkeɪt/ *v.t./i.* abdiquer. **~ion** /-'keɪʃn/ *n.* abdication *f.*

abdom|en /'æbdəmən/ *n.* abdomen *m.* **~inal** /-'dɒmɪnl/ *a.* abdominal.

abduct /æb'dʌkt/ *v.t.* enlever. **~ion** /-kʃn/ *n.* rapt *m.* **~or** *n.* ravisseu|r, -se *m., f.*

aberration /æbə'reɪʃn/ *n.* aberration *f.*

abet /ə'bet/ *v.t.* (*p.t.* **abetted**) (*jurid.*) encourager.

abeyance /ə'beɪəns/ *n.* **in ~,** (*matter*) en suspens; (*custom*) en désuétude.

abhor /əb'hɔː(r)/ *v.t.* (*p.t.* **abhorred**) exécrer. **~rence** /-'hɒrəns/ *n.* horreur *f.* **~rent** /-'hɒrənt/ *a.* exécrable.

abide /ə'baɪd/ *v.t.* (*p.t.* **abided**) supporter. —*v.i.* (*old use*; *p.t.* **abode**) demeurer. **~ by,** rester fidèle à.

abiding /ə'baɪdɪŋ/ *a.* éternel.

ability /ə'bɪlətɪ/ *n.* aptitude *f.* (**to do,** à faire); (*talent*) talent *m.*

abject /'æbdʒekt/ *a.* abject.

ablaze /ə'bleɪz/ *a.* en feu. **~ with,** (*anger etc.*: *fig.*) enflammé de.

abl|e /'eɪbl/ *a.* (**-er, -est**) capable (**to,** de). **be ~e,** pouvoir; (*know how to*) savoir. **~y** *adv.* habilement.

ablutions /ə'bluːʃnz/ *n. pl.* ablutions *f. pl.*

abnormal /æb'nɔːml/ *a.* anormal. **~ity** /-'mælətɪ/ *n.* anomalie *f.* **~ly** *adv.* (*unusually*) exceptionnellement.

aboard /ə'bɔːd/ *adv.* à bord. —*prep.* à bord de.

abode /ə'bəʊd/ *see* **abide.** —*n.* (*old use*) demeure *f.*

aboli|sh /ə'bɒlɪʃ/ *v.t.* supprimer, abolir. **~tion** /æbə'lɪʃn/ *n.* suppression *f.*, abolition *f.*

abominable /ə'bɒmɪnəbl/ *a.* abominable.

abominat|e /ə'bɒmɪneɪt/ *v.t.* exécrer. **~ion** /-'neɪʃn/ *n.* abomination *f.*

aboriginal /æbə'rɪdʒənl/ *a. & n.* aborigène (*m.*).

aborigines /æbə'rɪdʒiːz/ *n. pl.* aborigènes *m. pl.*

abort /ə'bɔːt/ *v.t.* faire avorter. —*v.i.* avorter. **~ive** *a.* (*attempt etc.*) manqué.

abortion /ə'bɔːʃn/ *n.* avortement *m.* **have an ~,** se faire avorter. **~ist** *n.* avorteu|r, -se *m., f.*

abound /ə'baʊnd/ *v.i.* abonder (**in,** en).

about /ə'baʊt/ *adv.* (*approximately*) environ; (*here and there*) çà et là; (*all round*) partout, autour; (*nearby*) dans les parages; (*of rumour*) en circulation. —*prep.* au sujet de; (*round*) autour de; (*somewhere in*) dans. **~face, ~-turn** *ns.* (*fig.*) volteface *f. invar.* **~ here,** par ici. **be ~ to,** être sur le point de. **how** *or* **what ~ leaving,** si on partait. **talk ~,** parler de.

above /ə'bʌv/ *adv.* au-dessus; (*on page*) ci-dessus. —*prep.* au-dessus de. **he is not ~ lying,** il n'est pas incapable de mentir. **~ all,** pardessus tout. **~board** *a.* honnête.

abrasion /ə'breɪʒn/ *n.* frottement *m.*; (*injury*) écorchure *f.*

abrasive /ə'breɪsɪv/ *a.* abrasif; (*irritating*: *fig.*) agaçant. —*n.* abrasif *m.*

abreast /ə'brest/ *adv.* de front. **keep ~ of,** se tenir au courant de.

abridge /əˈbrɪdʒ/ *v.t.* abréger. ~ment
n. abrégement *m.*, réduction *f.*; (*abridged text*) abrégé *m.*

abroad /əˈbrɔːd/ *adv.* à l'étranger; (*far
and wide*) de tous côtés.

abrupt /əˈbrʌpt/ *a.* (*sudden, curt*)
brusque; (*steep*) abrupt. ~ly *adv.*
(*suddenly*) brusquement; (*curtly,
rudely*) avec brusquerie. ~ness *n.*
brusquerie *f.*

abscess /ˈæbses/ *n.* abcès *m.*

abscond /əbˈskɒnd/ *v.i.* s'enfuir.

absen|t[1] /ˈæbsənt/ *a.* absent; (*look
etc.*) distrait. ~ce *n.* absence *f.*; (*lack*)
manque *m.* **in the ~ce of,** à défaut de.
~tly *adv.* distraitement. ~t-minded
a. distrait. ~t-mindedness *n.*
distraction *f.*

absent[2] /əbˈsent/ *v. pr.* ~ **o.s.,** s'absenter.

absentee /æbsənˈtiː/ *n.* absent(e) *m.*
(*f.*). ~ism *n.* absentéisme *m.*

absinthe /ˈæbsɪnθ/ *n.* absinthe *f.*

absolute /ˈæbsəluːt/ *a.* absolu; (*coward
etc.*: *fam.*) véritable. ~ly *adv.* absolument.

absolution /æbsəˈluːʃn/ *n.* absolution
f.

absolve /əbˈzɒlv/ *v.t.* (*from sin*) absoudre (**from,** de); (*from vow etc.*)
délier (**from,** de).

absor|b /əbˈsɔːb/ *v.t.* absorber. ~ption
n. absorption *f.*

absorbent /əbˈsɔːbənt/ *a.* absorbant.
~ **cotton,** (*Amer.*) coton hydrophile
m.

abst|ain /əbˈsteɪn/ *v.i.* s'abstenir
(**from,** de). ~ention /-ˈstenʃn/ *n.* ab-
stention *f.*; (*from drink*) abstinence *f.*

abstemious /əbˈstiːmɪəs/ *a.* sobre.

abstinen|ce /ˈæbstɪnəns/ *n.* abstinence
f. ~t *a.* sobre.

abstract[1] /ˈæbstrækt/ *a.* abstrait.
—*n.* (*quality*) abstrait *m.*; (*summary*)
résumé *m.*

abstract[2] /əbˈstrækt/ *v.t.* retirer,
extraire. ~ion /-kʃn/ *n.* extraction *f.*;
(*idea*) abstraction *f.*

abstruse /əbˈstruːs/ *a.* obscur.

absurd /əbˈsɜːd/ *a.* absurde. ~ity *n.*
absurdité *f.*

abundan|t /əˈbʌndənt/ *a.* abondant.
~ce *n.* abondance *f.* ~tly *adv.* (*entirely*) tout à fait.

abuse[1] /əˈbjuːz/ *v.t.* (*misuse*) abuser de;
(*ill-treat*) maltraiter; (*insult*) injurier.

abus|e[2] /əˈbjuːs/ *n.* (*misuse*) abus *m.*

(*of,* de); (*insults*) injures *f. pl.* ~ive
a. injurieux.

abut /əˈbʌt/ *v.i.* (*p.t.* **abutted**) être
contigu (**on,** à).

abysmal /əˈbɪzməl/ *a.* (*great*) profond;
(*bad*: *fam.*) exécrable.

abyss /əˈbɪs/ *n.* abîme *m.*

academic /ækəˈdemɪk/ *a.* universitaire; (*scholarly*) intellectuel; (*pej.*)
théorique. —*n.* universitaire *m./f.*
~ally /-lɪ/ *adv.* intellectuellement.

academ|y /əˈkædəmɪ/ *n.* (*school*) école
f. **A~y,** (*society*) Académie *f.* ~ician
/-ˈmɪʃn/ *n.* académicien(ne) *m.* (*f.*).

accede /əkˈsiːd/ *v.i.* ~ **to,** (*request, post,
throne*) accéder à.

accelerat|e /əkˈseləreɪt/ *v.t.* ac-
célérer. —*v.i.* (*speed up*) s'accélérer; (*auto.*) accélérer. ~ion
/-ˈreɪʃn/ *n.* accélération *f.*

accelerator /əkˈseləreɪtə(r)/ *n.* (*auto.*)
accélérateur *m.*

accent[1] /ˈæksənt/ *n.* accent *m.*

accent[2] /ækˈsent/ *v.t.* accentuer.

accentuat|e /əkˈsentʃʊeɪt/ *v.t.* accen-
tuer. ~ion /-ˈeɪʃn/ *n.* accentuation *f.*

accept /əkˈsept/ *v.t.* accepter. ~able *a.*
acceptable. ~ance *n.* acceptation *f.*;
(*approval, favour*) approbation *f.*

access /ˈækses/ *n.* accès *m.* (**to sth.,** à
qch.; **to s.o.,** auprès de qn.). ~ible
/əkˈsesəbl/ *a.* accessible.

accession /ækˈseʃn/ *n.* accession *f.*;
(*thing added*) nouvelle acquisition *f.*

accessory /əkˈsesərɪ/ *a.* accessoire.
—*n.* accessoire *m.*; (*person*: *jurid.*)
complice *m./f.*

accident /ˈæksɪdənt/ *n.* accident *m.*;
(*chance*) hasard *m.* ~al /-ˈdentl/ *a.*
accidentel, fortuit. ~ally /-ˈdentəlɪ/
adv. involontairement.

acclaim /əˈkleɪm/ *v.t.* acclamer. —*n.*
acclamation(s) *f.* (*pl.*).

acclimat|e /ˈæklɪmeɪt/ *v.t./i.* (*Amer.*)
(s')acclimater. ~ion /-ˈmeɪʃn/ *n.*
(*Amer.*) acclimatation *f.*

acclimatiz|e /əˈklaɪmətaɪz/ *v.t./i.*
(s')acclimater. ~ation /-ˈzeɪʃn/ *n.*
acclimatation *f.*

accolade /ˈækəleɪd/ *n.* (*of knight*) accolade *f.*; (*praise*) louange *f.*

accommodat|e /əˈkɒmədeɪt/ *v.t.*
loger, avoir de la place pour;
(*adapt*) adapter; (*supply*) fournir;
(*oblige*) obliger. ~ing *a.* obligeant. ~ion /-ˈdeɪʃn/ *n.* (*living-
premises*) logement *m.*; (*rented
rooms*) chambres *f. pl.*

accompan|y /ə'kʌmpəni/ v.t. accompagner. **∼iment** n. accompagnement m. **∼ist** n. accompagna|teur, -trice m., f.

accomplice /ə'kʌmplis/ n. complice m./f.

accomplish /ə'kʌmplɪʃ/ v.t. (perform) accomplir; (achieve) réaliser. **∼ed** a. accompli. **∼ment** n. accomplissement m. **∼ments** n.pl. (abilities) talents m. pl.

accord /ə'kɔːd/ v.i. concorder. —v.t. accorder. —n. accord m. **of one's own ∼**, de sa propre initiative. **∼ance** n. **in ∼ance with**, conformément à.

according /ə'kɔːdɪŋ/ adv. **∼ to**, selon, suivant. **∼ly** adv. en conséquence.

accordion /ə'kɔːdɪən/ n. accordéon m.

accost /ə'kɒst/ v.t. aborder.

account /ə'kaʊnt/ n. (comm.) compte m.; (description) compte rendu m.; (importance) importance f. —v.t. considérer. **∼ for**, rendre compte de, expliquer. **on ∼ of**, à cause de. **on no ∼**, en aucun cas. **take into ∼**, tenir compte de. **∼able** a. responsable (**for**, de). **∼ability** /-ə'bɪləti/ n. responsabilité f.

accountan|t /ə'kaʊntənt/ n. comptable m./f., expert-comptable m. **∼cy** n. comptabilité f.

accoutrements /ə'kuːtrəmənts/ n. pl. équipement m.

accredited /ə'kredɪtɪd/ a. accrédité.

accrue /ə'kruː/ v.i. s'accumuler. **∼ to**, (come to) revenir à.

accumulat|e /ə'kjuːmjʊleɪt/ v.t./i. (s')accumuler. **∼ion** /-'leɪʃn/ n. accumulation f.

accumulator /ə'kjuːmjʊleɪtə(r)/ n. (battery) accumulateur m.

accura|te /'ækjərət/ a. exact, précis. **∼cy** n. exactitude f., précision f. **∼tely** adv. exactement, avec précision.

accus|e /ə'kjuːz/ v.t. accuser. **the ∼ed**, l'accusé(e) m.(f.). **∼ation** /ækjuː'zeɪʃn/ n. accusation f.

accustom /ə'kʌstəm/ v.t. accoutumer. **∼ed** a. accoutumé. **become ∼ed to**, s'accoutumer à.

ace /eɪs/ n. (card, person) as m.

ache /eɪk/ n. douleur f., mal m. —v.i. faire mal. **my leg ∼s**, ma jambe me fait mal, j'ai mal à la jambe.

achieve /ə'tʃiːv/ v.t. réaliser, accomplir; (success) obtenir. **∼ment** n. ré-

alisation f. (of, de); (feat) exploit m., réussite f.

acid /'æsɪd/ a. & n. acide (m.). **∼ity** /ə'sɪdəti/ n. acidité f.

acknowledge /ək'nɒlɪdʒ/ v.t. reconnaître. **∼ (receipt of)**, accuser réception de. **∼ment** n. reconnaissance f.; accusé de réception m.

acme /'ækmɪ/ n. sommet m.

acne /'æknɪ/ n. acné f.

acorn /'eɪkɔːn/ n. (bot.) gland m.

acoustic /ə'kuːstɪk/ a. acoustique. **∼s** n. pl. acoustique f.

acquaint /ə'kweɪnt/ v.t. **∼ s.o. with sth.**, mettre qn. au courant de qch. **be ∼ed with**, (person) connaître; (fact) savoir. **∼ance** n. (knowledge, person) connaissance f.

acquiesce /ækwɪ'es/ v.i. consentir. **∼nce** n. consentement m.

acqui|re /ə'kwaɪə(r)/ v.t. acquérir; (habit) prendre. **∼sition** /ækwɪ'zɪʃn/ n. acquisition f. **∼sitive** /ə'kwɪzətɪv/ a. avide, âpre au gain.

acquit /ə'kwɪt/ v.t. (p.t. acquitted) acquitter. **∼ o.s. well**, bien s'en tirer. **∼tal** n. acquittement m.

acre /'eɪkə(r)/ n. (approx.) demi-hectare m. **∼age** n. superficie f.

acrid /'ækrɪd/ a. âcre.

acrimon|ious /ækrɪ'məʊnɪəs/ a. acerbe, acrimonieux. **∼y** /'ækrɪmənɪ/ n. acrimonie f.

acrobat /'ækrəbæt/ n. acrobate m./f. **∼ic** /-'bætɪk/ a. acrobatique. **∼ics** /-'bætɪks/ n. pl. acrobatie f.

acronym /'ækrənɪm/ n. sigle m.

across /ə'krɒs/ adv. & prep. (side to side) d'un côté à l'autre (de); (on the other side) de l'autre côté (de); (crosswise) en travers (de), à travers. **go or walk ∼**, traverser.

act /ækt/ n. (deed, theatre) acte m.; (in variety show) numéro m.; (decree) loi f. —v.i. agir; (theatre) jouer; (function) marcher; (pretend) jouer la comédie. —v.t. (part, role) jouer. **∼ as**, servir de. **∼ing** a. (temporary) intérimaire; n. (theatre) jeu m.

action /'ækʃn/ n. action f.; (mil.) combat m. **out of ∼**, hors de service. **take ∼**, agir.

activate /'æktɪveɪt/ v.t. (machine) actionner.

activ|e /'æktɪv/ a. actif; (interest) vif; (volcano) en activité. **∼ity** /-'tɪvəti/ n. activité f.

ac|tor /'aektə(r)/ *n.* acteur *m.* ~tress *n.* actrice *f.*

actual /'æktʃuəl/ *a.* réel; (*example*) concret. the ~ pen which, le stylo même que. ~ity /-'ælətɪ/ *n.* réalité *f.* ~ly *adv.* (*in fact*) en réalité, réellement.

actuary /'æktʃuərɪ/ *n.* actuaire *m.*/*f.*

acumen /'ækjumen, *Amer.* ə'kju:mən/ *n.* perspicacité *f.*

acupunctur|e /'ækjupʌŋktʃə(r)/ *n.* acupuncture *f.* ~ist *n.* acupuncteur *m.*

acute /ə'kju:t/ *a.* aigu; (*mind*) pénétrant; (*emotion*) intense, vif; (*shortage*) grave. ~ly *adv.* vivement. ~ness *n.* intensité *f.*

ad /æd/ *n.* (*fam.*) annonce *f.*

AD *abbr.* après J.-C.

adamant /'ædəmənt/ *a.* inflexible.

Adam's apple /'ædəmz'æpl/ *n.* pomme d'Adam *f.*

adapt /ə'dæpt/ *v.t.*/*i.* (s')adapter. ~ation /-'teɪʃn/ *n.* adaptation *f.* ~or *n.* (*electr.*) adaptateur *m.*

adaptab|le /ə'dæptəbl/ *a.* souple. ~ility /-'bɪlətɪ/ *n.* souplesse *f.*

add /æd/ *v.t.*/*i.* ajouter. ~ (up), (*total*) additionner. ~ up to, (*total*) s'élever à. ~ing machine, machine à calculer *f.*

adder /'ædə(r)/ *n.* vipère *f.*

addict /'ædɪkt/ *n.* intoxiqué(e) *m.* (*f.*); (*fig.*) fanatique *m.*/*f.*

addict|ed /ə'dɪktɪd/ *a.* ~ed to, (*drink*) adonné à. be ~ed to, (*fig.*) être un fanatique de. ~ion /-kʃn/ *n.* (*med.*) dépendance *f.*; (*fig.*) manie *f.* ~ive *a.* (*drug etc.*) qui crée une dépendance.

addition /ə'dɪʃn/ *n.* addition *f.* in ~, en outre. ~al /-ʃənl/ *a.* supplémentaire.

additive /'ædɪtɪv/ *n.* additif *m.*

address /ə'dres/ *n.* adresse *f.*; (*speech*) allocution *f.* —*v.t.* adresser; (*speak to*) s'adresser à. ~ee /ædre'si:/ *n.* destinataire *m.*/*f.*

adenoids /'ædɪnɔɪdz/ *n. pl.* végétations (adénoïdes) *f. pl.*

adept /'ædept, *Amer.* ə'dept/ *a.* & *n.* expert (at, en) (*m.*).

adequa|te /'ædɪkwət/ *a.* suffisant; (*satisfactory*) satisfaisant. ~cy *n.* quantité suffisante *f.*; (*of person*) compétence *f.* ~tely *adv.* suffisamment.

adhere /əd'hɪə(r)/ *v.i.* adhérer (to, à). ~ to, (*fig.*) respecter. ~nce /-rəns/ *n.* adhésion *f.*

adhesion /əd'hi:ʒn/ *n.* (*grip*) adhérence *f.*; (*support*: *fig.*) adhésion *f.*

adhesive /əd'hi:sɪv/ *a.* & *n.* adhésif (*m.*).

ad infinitum /ædɪnfɪ'naɪtəm/ *adv.* à l'infini.

adjacent /ə'dʒeɪsnt/ *a.* contigu (to, à).

adjective /'ædʒɪktɪv/ *n.* adjectif *m.*

adjoin /ə'dʒɔɪn/ *v.t.* être contigu à.

adjourn /ə'dʒɜːn/ *v.t.* ajourner. —*v.t.*/*i.* ~ (the meeting), suspendre la séance. ~ to, (*go*) se retirer à.

adjudicate /ə'dʒu:dɪkeɪt/ *v.t.*/*i.* juger.

adjust /ə'dʒʌst/ *v.t.* (*machine*) régler; (*prices*) (r)ajuster; (*arrange*) rajuster, arranger. —*v.t.*/*i.* ~ (o.s.) to, s'adapter à. ~able *a.* réglable. ~ment *n.* (*techn.*) réglage *m.*; (*of person*) adaptation *f.*

ad lib /æd'lɪb/ *v.i.* (*p.t.* ad libbed) (*fam.*) improviser.

administer /əd'mɪnɪstə(r)/ *v.t.* administrer.

administration /ədmɪnɪ'streɪʃn/ *n.* administration *f.*

administrator /əd'mɪnɪstreɪtə(r)/ *n.* administra|teur, -trice *m.*, *f.*

administrative /əd'mɪnɪstrətɪv/ *a.* administratif.

admirable /'ædmərəbl/ *a.* admirable.

admiral /'ædmərəl/ *n.* amiral *m.*

admir|e /əd'maɪə(r)/ *v.t.* admirer. ~ation /ædmə'reɪʃn/ *n.* admiration *f.* ~er *n.* admira|teur, -trice *m.*, *f.*

admissible /əd'mɪsəbl/ *a.* admissible.

admission /əd'mɪʃn/ *n.* admission *f.*; (*to museum, theatre, etc.*) entrée *f.*; (*confession*) aveu *m.*

admit /əd'mɪt/ *v.t.* (*p.t.* admitted) laisser entrer; (*acknowledge*) reconnaître, admettre. ~ to, avouer. ~tance *n.* entrée *f.* ~tedly *adv.* il est vrai (que).

admonish /əd'mɒnɪʃ/ *v.t.* réprimander.

ado /ə'du:/ *n.* (*fuss*) cérémonies *f. pl.*; (*excitement*) agitation *f.*

adolescen|t /ædə'lesnt/ *n.* & *a.* adolescent(e) (*m.* (*f.*)). ~ce *n.* adolescence *f.*

adopt /ə'dɒpt/ *v.t.* adopter. ~ed *a.* (*child*) adoptif. ~ion /-pʃn/ *n.* adoption *f.*

adoptive /ə'dɒptɪv/ *a.* adoptif.

ador|e /ə'dɔː(r)/ *v.t.* adorer. ~able *a.* adorable. ~ation /ædə'reɪʃn/ *n.* adoration *f.*

adorn /ə'dɔːn/ *v.t.* orner. ~ment *n.* ornement *m.*

adrift /ə'drɪft/ *a.* & *adv.* à la dérive.

adroit /əˈdrɔɪt/ *a.* adroit.

adulation /ædjuˈleɪʃn/ *n.* adulation *f.*

adult /ˈædʌlt/ *a. & n.* adulte (*m.*/*f.*). **~hood** *n.* condition d'adulte *f.*

adulterate /əˈdʌltəreɪt/ *v.t.* falsifier, frelater, altérer.

adulter|y /əˈdʌltəri/ *n.* adultère *m.* **~er**, **~ess** *ns.* épou/x, -se adultère *m.*, *f.* **~ous** *a.* adultère.

advance /ədˈvɑːns/ *v.t.* avancer. —*v.i.* (s')avancer; (*progress*) avancer. —*n.* avance *f.* —*a.* (*payment*) anticipé. **in ~**, à l'avance. **~d** *a.* avancé; (*studies*) supérieur. **~ment** *n.* avancement *m.*

advantage /ədˈvɑːntɪdʒ/ *n.* avantage *m.* **take ~ of**, profiter de; (*person*) exploiter. **~ous** /ædvənˈteɪdʒəs/ *a.* avantageux.

advent /ˈædvənt/ *n.* arrivée *f.*

Advent /ˈædvənt/ *n.* Avent *m.*

adventur|e /ədˈventʃə(r)/ *n.* aventure *f.* **~er** *n.* explora|teur, -trice *m.*, *f.*; (*pej.*) aventur|ier, -ière *m.*, *f.* **~ous** *a.* aventureux.

adverb /ˈædvɜːb/ *n.* adverbe *m.*

adversary /ˈædvəsəri/ *n.* adversaire *m.*/*f.*

advers|e /ˈædvɜːs/ *a.* défavorable. **~ity** /ədˈvɜːsəti/ *n.* adversité *f.*

advert /ˈædvɜːt/ *n.* (*fam.*) annonce *f.* **~isement** /ədˈvɜːtɪsmənt/ *n.* publicité *f.*; (*in paper etc.*) annonce *f.*

advertise /ˈædvətaɪz/ *v.t.*/*i.* faire de la publicité (pour); (*sell*) mettre une annonce (pour vendre). **~ for**, (*seek*) chercher (par voie d'annonce). **~r** /-ə(r)/ *n.* annonceur *m.*

advice /ədˈvaɪs/ *n.* conseil(s) *m.* (*pl.*); (*comm.*) avis *m.*

advis|e /ədˈvaɪz/ *v.t.* conseiller; (*inform*) aviser. **~e against**, déconseiller. **~able** *a.* conseillé, prudent (**to**, de). **~er** *n.* conseill|er, -ère *m.*, *f.* **~ory** *a.* consultatif.

advocate[1] /ˈædvəkət/ *n.* (*jurid.*) avocat *m.*

advocate[2] /ˈædvəkeɪt/ *v.t.* recommander.

aegis /ˈiːdʒɪs/ *n.* égide *f.*

aeon /ˈiːən/ *n.* éternité *f.*

aerial /ˈeərɪəl/ *a.* aérien. —*n.* antenne *f.*

aerobatics /eərəˈbætɪks/ *n. pl.* acrobatie aérienne *f.*

aerodrome /ˈeərədrəʊm/ *n.* aérodrome *m.*

aerodynamic /eərəʊdaɪˈnæmɪk/ *a.* aérodynamique.

aeroplane /ˈeərəpleɪn/ *n.* avion *m.*

aerosol /ˈeərəsɒl/ *n.* atomiseur *m.*

aesthetic /iːsˈθetɪk, *Amer.* esˈθetɪk/ *a.* esthétique.

afar /əˈfɑː(r)/ *adv.* **from ~**, de loin.

affable /ˈæfəbl/ *a.* affable.

affair /əˈfeə(r)/ *n.* (*matter*) affaire *f.*; (*romance*) liaison *f.*

affect /əˈfekt/ *v.t.* affecter. **~ation** /æfekˈteɪʃn/ *n.* affectation *f.* **~ed** *a.* affecté.

affection /əˈfekʃn/ *n.* affection *f.*

affectionate /əˈfekʃənət/ *a.* affectueux.

affiliat|e /əˈfɪlɪeɪt/ *v.t.* affilier. **~ed company**, filiale *f.* **~ion** /-ˈeɪʃn/ *n.* affiliation *f.*

affinity /əˈfɪnəti/ *n.* affinité *f.*

affirm /əˈfɜːm/ *v.t.* affirmer. **~ation** /æfəˈmeɪʃn/ *n.* affirmation *f.*

affirmative /əˈfɜːmətɪv/ *a.* affirmatif. —*n.* affirmative *f.*

affix /əˈfɪks/ *v.t.* apposer.

afflict /əˈflɪkt/ *v.t.* affliger. **~ion** /-kʃn/ *n.* affliction *f.*, détresse *f.*

affluen|t /ˈæfluənt/ *a.* riche. **~ce** *n.* richesse *f.*

afford /əˈfɔːd/ *v.t.* avoir les moyens d'acheter; (*provide*) fournir. **~ to do**, avoir les moyens de faire; (*be able*) se permettre de faire. **can you ~ the time?**, avez-vous le temps?

affray /əˈfreɪ/ *n.* rixe *f.*

affront /əˈfrʌnt/ *n.* affront *m.* —*v.t.* insulter.

afield /əˈfiːld/ *adv.* **far ~**, loin.

afloat /əˈfləʊt/ *adv.* à flot.

afoot /əˈfʊt/ *adv.* **sth. is ~**, il se trame *or* se prépare qch.

aforesaid /əˈfɔːsed/ *a.* susdit.

afraid /əˈfreɪd/ *a.* **be ~**, avoir peur (**of**, **to**, **de**; **that**, que); (*be sorry*) regretter. **I am ~ that**, (*regret to say*) je regrette de dire que.

afresh /əˈfreʃ/ *adv.* de nouveau.

Africa /ˈæfrɪkə/ *n.* Afrique *f.* **~n** *a. & n.* africain(e) (*m.* (*f.*)).

after /ˈɑːftə(r)/ *adv. & prep.* après. —*conj.* après que. **~ doing**, après avoir fait. **~-effect** *n.* suite *f.* **~ the manner of**, d'après. **be ~**, (*seek*) chercher.

aftermath /ˈɑːftəmɑːθ/ *n.* suites *f. pl.*

afternoon /ɑːftəˈnuːn/ *n.* après-midi *m.*/*f. invar.*

afters /ˈɑːftəz/ *n. pl.* (*fam.*) dessert *m.*

aftershave /'ɑːftəʃeɪv/ *n.* lotion après-rasage *f.*

afterthought /'ɑːftəθɔːt/ *n.* réflexion après coup *f.*

afterwards /'ɑːftəwədz/ *adv.* après, par la suite.

again /ə'gen/ *adv.* de nouveau, encore une fois; (*besides*) en outre.

against /ə'genst/ *prep.* contre. ~ **the law,** illégal.

age /eɪdʒ/ *n.* âge *m.* —*v.t./i.* (*pres. p.* **ageing**) vieillir. ~**s,** (*fam.*) une éternité. **of** ~, (*jurid.*) majeur. **ten years of** ~, âgé de dix ans. ~**less** *a.* toujours jeune.

aged[1] /'eɪdʒd/ *a.* ~ **six,** âgé de six ans.

aged[2] /'eɪdʒɪd/ *a.* âgé, vieux.

agen|cy /'eɪdʒənsɪ/ *n.* agence *f.*; (*means*) entremise *f.* ~**t** *n.* agent *m.*

agenda /ə'dʒendə/ *n.* ordre du jour *m.*

agglomeration /əglɒmə'reɪʃn/ *n.* agglomération *f.*

aggravat|e /'ægrəveɪt/ *v.t.* (*make worse*) aggraver; (*annoy*: *fam.*) exaspérer. ~**ion** /-'veɪʃn/ *n.* aggravation *f.*; exaspération *f.*; (*trouble*: *fam.*) ennuis *m. pl.*

aggregate /'ægrɪgət/ *a.* & *n.* total (*m.*).

aggress|ive /ə'gresɪv/ *a.* agressif. ~**ion** /-ʃn/ *n.* agression *f.* ~**iveness** *n.* agressivité *f.* ~**or** *n.* agresseur *m.*

aggrieved /ə'griːvd/ *a.* peiné..

aghast /ə'gɑːst/ *a.* horrifié..

agil|e /'ædʒaɪl, *Amer.* 'ædʒl/ *a.* agile. ~**ity** /ə'dʒɪlətɪ/ *n.* agilité *f.*

agitat|e /'ædʒɪteɪt/ *v.t.* agiter. ~**ion** /-'teɪʃn/ *n.* agitation *f.* ~**or** *n.* agita|teur, -trice *m., f.*

agnostic /æg'nɒstɪk/ *a.* & *n.* agnostique (*m./f.*).

ago /ə'gəʊ/ *adv.* il y a. **a month** ~, il y a un mois. **long** ~, il y a longtemps.

agog /ə'gɒg/ *a.* impatient, en émoi.

agon|y /'ægənɪ/ *n.* grande souffrance *f.*; (*mental*) angoisse *f.* ~**ize** *v.i.* souffrir. ~**ized** *a.* angoissé. ~**izing** *a.* angoissant.

agree /ə'griː/ *v.t./i.* être *or* se mettre d'accord; (*of figures*) concorder. ~ **that,** reconnaître que. ~ **to do,** accepter de faire. ~ **to sth.,** accepter qch. ~ **with,** (*of food etc.*) convenir à. ~**d** *a.* (*time, place*) convenu. **be** ~**d,** être d'accord.

agreeable /ə'griːəbl/ *a.* agréable. **be** ~, (*willing*) être d'accord.

agreement /ə'griːmənt/ *n.* accord *m.* **in** ~, d'accord.

agricultur|e /'ægrɪkʌltʃə(r)/ *n.* agriculture *f.* ~**al** /-'kʌltʃərəl/ *a.* agricole.

aground /ə'graʊnd/ *adv.* **run** ~, (*of ship*) (s')échouer.

ahead /ə'hed/ *adv.* (*in front*) en avant, devant; (*in advance*) à l'avance. ~ **of s.o.,** devant qn.; en avance sur qn. ~ **of time,** en avance.

aid /eɪd/ *v.t.* aider. —*n.* aide *f.* **in** ~ **of,** au profit de.

aide /eɪd/ *n.* (*Amer.*) aide *m./f.*

AIDS /eɪdz/ *n.* (*med.*) sida *m.*

ail /eɪl/ *v.t.* **what** ~**s you?,** qu'avez-vous? ~**ing** *a.* souffrant. ~**ment** *n.* maladie *f.*

aim /eɪm/ *v.t.* diriger; (*gun*) braquer (**at,** sur). —*v.i.* viser. —*n.* but *m.* ~ **at,** viser. ~ **to,** avoir l'intention de. **take** ~, viser. ~**less** *a.*, ~**lessly** *adv.* sans but.

air /eə(r)/ *n.* air *m.* —*v.t.* aérer; (*views*) exposer librement. —*a.* (*base etc.*) aérien. ~**-conditioned** *a.* climatisé. ~**-conditioning** *n.* climatisation *f.* ~ **force/hostess,** armée/hôtesse de l'air *f.* ~**mail,** poste aérienne *f.* **by** ~**mail,** par avion. ~ **raid,** attaque aérienne *f.* **by** ~, par avion. **in the** ~, (*rumour*) répandu; (*plan*) incertain. **on the** ~, sur l'antenne.

airborne /'eəbɔːn/ *a.* en (cours de) vol; (*troops*) aéroporté.

aircraft /'eəkrɑːft/ *n. invar.* avion *m.* ~**-carrier** *n.* porteavions *m. invar.*

airfield /'eəfiːld/ *n.* terrain d'aviation *m.*

airgun /'eəgʌn/ *n.* carabine à air comprimé *f.*

airlift /'eəlɪft/ *n.* pont aérien *m.*

airline /'eəlaɪn/ *n.* ligne aérienne *f.* ~**r** /-ə(r)/ *n.* avion de ligne *m.*

airlock /'eəlɒk/ *n.* (*in pipe*) bulle d'air *f.*; (*chamber*: *techn.*) sas *m.*

airman /'eəmən/ *n.* (*pl.* -**men**) aviateur *m.*

airplane /'eəpleɪn/ *n.* (*Amer.*) avion *m.*

airport /'eəpɔːt/ *n.* aéroport *m.*

airsickness /'eəsɪknɪs/ *n.* mal de l'air *m.*

airtight /'eətaɪt/ *a.* hermétique.

airways /'eəweɪz/ *n. pl.* compagnie d'aviation *f.*

airworthy /'eəwɜːðɪ/ *a.* en état de navigation.

airy /'eərɪ/ *a.* (-**ier, -iest**) bien aéré; (*manner*) désinvolte.

aisle /aɪl/ *n.* (*of church*) nef latérale *f.*; (*gangway*) couloir *m.*

ajar /ə'dʒɑ:(r)/ *adv. & a.* entr'ouvert.

akin /ə'kɪn/ *a.* ~ **to,** apparenté à.

alabaster /'æləbɑ:stə(r)/ *n.* albâtre *m.*

à la carte /ɑːlɑː'kɑːt/ *adv. & a. (culin.)* à la carte.

alacrity /ə'lækrətɪ/ *n.* empressement *m.*

alarm /ə'lɑːm/ *n.* alarme *f.; (clock)* réveil *m.* —*v.t.* alarmer. ~**-clock** *n.* réveil *m.,* réveille-matin *m. invar.* ~**ist** *n.* alarmiste *m./f.*

alas /ə'læs/ *int.* hélas.

albatross /'ælbətrɒs/ *n.* albatros *m.*

albino /æl'biːnəʊ, Amer.* æl'baɪnəʊ/ *n. (pl.* -os) albinos *m./f.*

album /'ælbəm/ *n.* album *m.*

alchem|y /'ælkɪmɪ/ *n.* alchimie *f.* ~**ist** *n.* alchimiste *m.*

alcohol /'ælkəhɒl/ *n.* alcool *m.* ~**ic** /-'hɒlɪk/ *a.* alcoolique; *(drink)* alcoolisé; *n.* alcoolique *m./f.* ~**ism** *n.* alcoolisme *m.*

alcove /'ælkəʊv/ *n.* alcôve *f.*

ale /eɪl/ *n.* bière *f.*

alert /ə'lɜːt/ *a. (lively)* vif; *(watchful)* vigilant. —*n.* alerte *f.* —*v.t.* alerter. **on the** ~, sur le qui-vive. ~**ness** *n.* vivacité *f.;* vigilance *f.*

algebra /'ældʒɪbrə/ *n.* algèbre *f.* ~**ic** /-'breɪɪk/ *a.* algébrique.

Algeria /æl'dʒɪərɪə/ *n.* Algérie *f.* ~**n** *a. & n.* algérien(ne) *(m. (f.)).*

alias /'eɪlɪəs/ *n. (pl.* -ases) faux nom *m.* —*adv.* alias.

alibi /'ælɪbaɪ/ *n. (pl.* -is) alibi *m.*

alien /'eɪlɪən/ *n. & a.* étrang|er, -ère *(m., f.).*

alienat|e /'eɪlɪəneɪt/ *v.t.* aliéner. ~**e one's friends**/*etc.,* s'aliéner ses amis/ *etc.* ~**ion** /-'neɪʃn/ *n.* aliénation *f.*

alight[1] /ə'laɪt/ *v.i. (person)* descendre; *(bird)* se poser.

alight[2] /ə'laɪt/ *a.* en feu, allumé.

align /ə'laɪn/ *v.t.* aligner. ~**ment** *n.* alignement *m.*

alike /ə'laɪk/ *a.* semblable. —*adv.* de la même façon. **look** *or* **be** ~, se ressembler.

alimony /'ælɪmənɪ, Amer.* -məʊnɪ/ *n.* pension alimentaire *f.*

alive /ə'laɪv/ *a.* vivant. ~ **to,** sensible à, sensibilisé à. ~ **with,** grouillant de.

alkali /'ælkəlaɪ/ *n. (pl.* -is) alcali *m.*

all /ɔːl/ *a.* tout(e), tous, toutes. —*pron.* tous, toutes; *(everything)* tout. —*adv.* tout. ~ **(the) men,** tous les hommes. ~ **of it,** (le) tout. ~ **but,** presque. ~-

clear *n.* fin d'alerte *f.* ~ **in,** *(exhausted)* épuisé. ~ **out,** à fond. ~**-out** *a. (effort)* maximum. ~ **over,** partout *(sur or* dans); *(finished)* fini. ~ **right,** bien; *(consenting)* bon! ~ **round,** dans tous les domaines; *(for all)* pour tous. ~**-round** *a.* général. ~ **there,** *(alert)* éveillé. ~ **the same,** tout de même.

allay /ə'leɪ/ *v.t.* calmer.

allegation /ælɪ'geɪʃn/ *n.* allégation *f.*

allege /ə'ledʒ/ *v.t.* prétendre. ~**dly** /-ɪdlɪ/ *adv.* d'après ce qu'on dit.

allegiance /ə'liːdʒəns/ *n.* fidélité *f.*

allegor|y /'ælɪgərɪ, Amer.* -gɔːrɪ/ *n.* allégorie *f.* ~**ical** /-'gɒrɪkl/ *a.* allégorique.

alleluia /ælɪ'luːjə/ *int. & n.* alléluia *(m.).*

allerg|y /'ælədʒɪ/ *n.* allergie *f.* ~**ic** /ə'lɜːdʒɪk/ *a.* allergique.

alleviate /ə'liːvɪeɪt/ *v.t.* alléger.

alley /'ælɪ/ *n. (street)* ruelle *f.; (in park)* allée *f.*

alliance /ə'laɪəns/ *n.* alliance *f.*

allied /'ælaɪd/ *a.* allié.

alligator /'ælɪgeɪtə(r)/ *n.* alligator *m.*

allocat|e /'æləkeɪt/ *v.t. (assign)* attribuer; *(share out)* distribuer. ~**ion** /-'keɪʃn/ *n.* allocation *f.*

allot /ə'lɒt/ *v.t. (p.t.* **allotted)** attribuer. ~**ment** *n.* attribution *f.; (share)* partage *m.; (land)* parcelle de terre *f. (louée pour la culture).*

allow /ə'laʊ/ *v.t.* permettre; *(grant)* accorder; *(reckon on)* prévoir; *(agree)* reconnaître. ~ **s.o. to,** permettre à qn. de. ~ **for,** tenir compte de.

allowance /ə'laʊəns/ *n.* allocation *f.,* indemnité *f.* **make** ~**s for,** être indulgent envers; *(take into account)* tenir compte de.

alloy /'ælɔɪ/ *n.* alliage *m.*

allude /ə'luːd/ *v.i.* ~ **to,** faire allusion à.

allure /ə'lʊə(r)/ *v.t.* attirer.

allusion /ə'luːʒn/ *n.* allusion *f.*

ally[1] /'ælaɪ/ *n.* allié(e) *m. (f.).*

ally[2] /ə'laɪ/ *v.t.* allier. ~ **o.s. with,** s'allier à *or* avec.

almanac /'ɔːlmənæk/ *n.* almanach *m.*

almighty /ɔːl'maɪtɪ/ *a.* tout-puissant; *(very great: fam.)* sacré, formidable. —*n.* **the A**~, le Tout-Puissant.

almond /'ɑːmənd/ *n.* amande *f.*

almost /'ɔːlməʊst/ *adv.* presque.

alms /ɑːmz/ *n.* aumône *f.*

alone /ə'ləʊn/ *a. & adv.* seul.

along /ə'lɒŋ/ *prep.* le long de. —*adv.*

come ∼, venir. go *or* walk ∼, passer.
all ∼, (*time*) tout le temps, depuis le
début. ∼ **with**, avec.
alongside /əlɒŋ'saɪd/ *adv.* (*naut.*) bord
à bord. come ∼, accoster. —*prep.* le
long de.
aloof /ə'lu:f/ *adv.* à l'écart. —*a.* distant.
∼ness *n.* réserve *f.*
aloud /ə'laʊd/ *adv.* à haute voix.
alphabet /'ælfəbet/ *n.* alphabet *m.* ∼i-
cal /-'betɪkl/ *a.* alphabétique.
alpine /'ælpaɪn/ *a.* (*landscape*) alpestre; (*climate*) alpin.
Alpine /'ælpaɪn/ *a.* des Alpes.
Alps /ælps/ *n. pl.* the ∼, les Alpes
f. pl.
already /ɔ:l'redɪ/ *adv.* déjà.
Alsatian /æl'seɪʃn/ *n.* (*dog*) berger allemand *m.*
also /'ɔ:lsəʊ/ *adv.* aussi.
altar /'ɔ:ltə(r)/ *n.* autel *m.*
alter /'ɔ:ltə(r)/ *v.t./i.* changer. ∼ation
/-'reɪʃn/ *n.* changement *m.*; (*to garment*) retouche *f.*
alternate[1] /ɔ:l'tɜ:nət/ *a.* alterné, alter-
natif. ∼ **days**/*etc.*, (*first one then the
other*) tous les deux jours/*etc.* ∼ly
adv. tour à tour.
alternate[2] /'ɔ:ltəneɪt/ *v.i.* alterner.
—*v.t.* faire alterner.
alternative /ɔ:l'tɜ:nətɪv/ *a.* autre; (*policy*) de rechange. —*n.* alternative *f.*,
choix *m.* ∼ly *adv.* comme alternative.
or ∼ly, ou alors.
although /ɔ:l'ðəʊ/ *conj.* bien que.
altitude /'æltɪtju:d/ *n.* altitude *f.*
altogether /ɔ:ltə'geðə(r)/ *adv.* (*completely*) tout à fait; (*on the whole*) à
tout prendre.
altruist /'æltru:ɪst/ *n.* altruiste *m./f.*
∼ic /-'ɪstɪk/ *a.* altruiste.
aluminium /ælju'mɪnɪəm/ (*Amer.*
aluminum /ə'lu:mɪnəm/) *n.* aluminium *m.*
always /'ɔ:lweɪz/ *adv.* toujours.
am /æm/ *see* be.
a.m. /eɪ'em/ *adv.* du matin.
amalgamate /ə'mælgəmeɪt/ *v.t./i.*
(s')amalgamer; (*comm.*) fusionner.
amass /ə'mæs/ *v.t.* amasser.
amateur /'æmətə(r)/ *n.* amateur *m.*
—*a.* (*musician etc.*) amateur *invar.*
∼ish *a.* (*pej.*) d'amateur. ∼ishly *adv.*
en amateur.
amaz|e /ə'meɪz/ *v.t.* stupéfier. ∼ed *a.*
stupéfait. ∼ement *n.* stupéfaction *f.*
∼ingly *adv.* étonnamment.

ambassador /æm'bæsədə(r)/ *n.* am-
bassadeur *m.*
amber /'æmbə(r)/ *n.* ambre *m.*; (*auto.*)
feu orange *m.*
ambidextrous /æmbɪ'dekstrəs/ *a.* ambidextre.
ambigu|ous /æm'bɪgjʊəs/ *a.* ambigu.
∼ity /-'gju:ətɪ/ *n.* ambiguïté *f.*
ambit /'æmbɪt/ *n.* limites *f. pl.*
ambiti|on /æm'bɪʃn/ *n.* ambition *f.*
∼ous *a.* ambitieux.
ambivalent /æm'bɪvələnt/ *a.* ambigu,
ambivalent.
amble /'æmbl/ *v.i.* marcher sans se
presser, s'avancer lentement.
ambulance /'æmbjʊləns/ *n.* ambulance *f.*
ambush /'æmbʊʃ/ *n.* embuscade *f.*
—*v.t.* tendre une embuscade à.
amen /ɑ:'men/ *int.* amen.
amenable /ə'mi:nəbl/ *a.* obligeant. ∼
to, (*responsive*) sensible à.
amend /ə'mend/ *v.t.* modifier, corriger.
∼ment *n.* (*to rule*) amendement *m.*
amends /ə'mendz/ *n. pl.* **make** ∼, réparer son erreur.
amenities /ə'mi:nətɪz/ *n. pl.* (*pleasant
features*) attraits *m. pl.*; (*facilities*)
aménagements *m. pl.*
America /ə'merɪkə/ *n.* Amérique *f.* ∼n
a. & n. américain(e) (*m. (f.)).* ∼nism
n. américanisme *m.* ∼nize *v.t.* amé-
ricaniser.
amiable /'eɪmɪəbl/ *a.* aimable.
amicable /'æmɪkəbl/ *a.* amical.
amid(st) /ə'mɪd(st)/ *prep.* au milieu de.
amiss /ə'mɪs/ *a.* & *adv.* mal. **sth.** ∼,
qch. qui ne va pas.
ammonia /ə'məʊnɪə/ *n.* (*gas*) ammoniac *m.*; (*water*) ammoniaque *f.*
ammunition /æmjʊ'nɪʃn/ *n.* munitions *f. pl.*
amnesia /æm'ni:zɪə/ *n.* amnésie *f.*
amnesty /'æmnəstɪ/ *n.* amnistie *f.*
amok /ə'mɒk/ *adv.* **run** ∼, devenir fou
furieux; (*crowd*) se déchaîner.
among(st) /ə'mʌŋ(st)/ *prep.* parmi,
entre. ∼ **the crowd**, (*in the middle
of*) parmi la foule. ∼ **the English**/
etc., (*race, group*) chez les Anglais/*etc.*
∼ **ourselves**/*etc.*, entre nous/*etc.*
amoral /eɪ'mɒrəl/ *a.* amoral.
amorous /'æmərəs/ *a.* amoureux.
amorphous /ə'mɔ:fəs/ *a.* amorphe.
amount /ə'maʊnt/ *n.* quantité *f.*; (*total*)
montant *m.*; (*sum of money*) somme
f. —*v.i.* ∼ **to**, (*add up to*) s'élever à;
(*be equivalent to*) revenir à.

amp /æmp/ *n.* (*fam.*) ampère *m.*

ampere /'æmpeə(r)/ *n.* ampère *m.*

amphibi|an /æm'fɪbɪən/ *n.* amphibie *m.* ~**ous** *a.* amphibie.

amphitheatre /'æmfɪθɪətə(r)/ *n.* amphithéâtre *m.*

ampl|e /'æmpl/ *a.* (**-er, -est**) (*enough*) (bien) assez de; (*large, roomy*) ample. ~**y** *adv.* amplement.

amplif|y /'æmplɪfaɪ/ *v.t.* amplifier. ~**ier** *n.* amplificateur *m.*

amputat|e /'æmpjʊteɪt/ *v.t.* amputer. ~**ion** /-'teɪʃn/ *n.* amputation *f.*

amuck /ə'mʌk/ *see* **amok.**

amuse /ə'mjuːz/ *v.t.* amuser. ~**ment** *n.* amusement *m.*, divertissement *m.* ~ **arcade,** salle de jeux *f.*

an /æn, *unstressed* ən/ *see* **a.**

anachronism /ə'nækrənɪzəm/ *n.* anachronisme *m.*

anaem|ia /ə'niːmɪə/ *n.* anémie *f.* ~**ic** *a.* anémique.

anaesthetic /ænɪs'θetɪk/ *n.* anesthésique *m.* **give an** ~, faire une anesthésie (**to,** à).

anagram /'ænəgræm/ *n.* anagramme *f.*

analogy /ə'nælədʒɪ/ *n.* analogie *f.*

analys|e (*Amer.* **analyze**) /'ænəlaɪz/ *v.t.* analyser. ~**t** /-ɪst/ *n.* analyste *m.*/*f.*

analysis /ə'næləsɪs/ *n.* (*pl.* **-yses** /-əsiːz/) analyse *f.*

analytic(al) /ænə'lɪtɪk(l)/ *a.* analytique.

anarch|y /'ænəkɪ/ *n.* anarchie *f.* ~**ist** *n.* anarchiste *m.*/*f.*

anathema /ə'næθəmə/ *n.* **that is** ~ **to me,** j'ai cela en abomination.

anatom|y /ə'nætəmɪ/ *n.* anatomie *f.* ~**ical** /ænə'tɒmɪkl/ *a.* anatomique.

ancest|or /'ænsestə(r)/ *n.* ancêtre *m.* ~**ral** /-'sestrəl/ *a.* ancestral.

ancestry /'ænsestrɪ/ *n.* ascendance *f.*

anchor /'æŋkə(r)/ *n.* ancre *f.* —*v.t.* mettre à l'ancre. —*v.i.* jeter l'ancre.

anchovy /'æntʃəvɪ/ *n.* anchois *m.*

ancient /'eɪnʃənt/ *a.* ancien.

ancillary /æn'sɪlərɪ/ *a.* auxiliaire.

and /ænd, *unstressed* ən(d)/ *conj.* et. **go** ~ **see him,** allez le voir. **richer** ~ **richer,** de plus en plus riche.

anecdote /'ænɪkdəʊt/ *n.* anecdote *f.*

anew /ə'njuː/ *adv.* de *or* à nouveau.

angel /'eɪndʒl/ *n.* ange *m.* ~**ic** /æn'dʒelɪk/ *a.* angélique.

anger /'æŋgə(r)/ *n.* colère *f.* —*v.t.* mettre en colère, fâcher.

angle[1] /'æŋgl/ *n.* angle *m.*

angle[2] /'æŋgl/ *v.i.* pêcher (à la ligne). ~ **for,** (*fig.*) quêter. ~**r** /-ə(r)/ *n.* pêcheu|r, -se *m.*, *f.*

Anglican /'æŋglɪkən/ *a.* & *n.* anglican(e) (*m.* (*f.*)).

Anglo- /'æŋgləʊ/ *pref.* anglo-.

Anglo-Saxon /'æŋgləʊ'sæksn/ *a.* & *n.* anglo-saxon(ne) (*m.* (*f.*)).

angr|y /'æŋgrɪ/ *a.* (**-ier, -iest**) fâché, en colère. **get** ~**y,** se fâcher, se mettre en colère (**with,** contre). ~**ily** *adv.* en colère.

anguish /'æŋgwɪʃ/ *n.* angoisse *f.*

angular /'æŋgjʊlə(r)/ *a.* (*features*) anguleux.

animal /'ænɪml/ *n.* & *a.* animal (*m.*).

animate[1] /'ænɪmət/ *a.* animé.

animat|e[2] /'ænɪmeɪt/ *v.t.* animer. ~**ion** /-'meɪʃn/ *n.* animation *f.*

animosity /ænɪ'mɒsətɪ/ *n.* animosité *f.*

aniseed /'ænɪsiːd/ *n.* anis *m.*

ankle /'æŋkl/ *n.* cheville *f.* ~ **sock,** socquette *f.*

annals /'ænlz/ *n. pl.* annales *f. pl.*

annex /ə'neks/ *v.t.* annexer. ~**ation** /ænek'seɪʃn/ *n.* annexion *f.*

annexe /'æneks/ *n.* annexe *f.*

annihilate /ə'naɪəleɪt/ *v.t.* anéantir.

anniversary /ænɪ'vɜːsərɪ/ *n.* anniversaire *m.*

annotat|e /'ænəteɪt/ *v.t.* annoter. ~**ion** /-'teɪʃn/ *n.* annotation *f.*

announce /ə'naʊns/ *v.t.* annoncer. ~**ment** *n.* annonce *f.* ~**r** /-ə(r)/ *n.* (*radio,* TV) speaker(ine) *m.* (*f.*).

annoy /ə'nɔɪ/ *v.t.* agacer, ennuyer. ~**ance** *n.* contrariété *f.* ~**ed** *a.* fâché (**with,** contre). **get** ~**ed,** se fâcher. ~**ing** *a.* ennuyeux.

annual /'ænjʊəl/ *a.* annuel. —*n.* publication annuelle *f.* ~**ly** *adv.* annuellement.

annuity /ə'njuːətɪ/ *n.* rente (viagère) *f.*

annul /ə'nʌl/ *v.t.* (*p.t.* **annulled**) annuler. ~**ment** *n.* annulation *f.*

anoint /ə'nɔɪnt/ *v.t.* oindre.

anomal|y /ə'nɒməlɪ/ *n.* anomalie *f.* ~**ous** *a.* anormal.

anon /ə'nɒn/ *adv.* (*old use*) bientôt.

anonym|ous /ə'nɒnɪməs/ *a.* anonyme. ~**ity** /ænə'nɪmətɪ/ *n.* anonymat *m.*

anorak /'ænəræk/ *n.* anorak *m.*

another /ə'nʌðə(r)/ *a.* & *pron.* un(e) autre. ~ **coffee,** (*one more*) encore un café. ~ **ten minutes,** encore dix minutes.

answer /'ɑːnsə(r)/ *n.* réponse *f.*; (*solution*) solution *f.* —*v.t.* répondre à;

(*prayer*) exaucer. —*v.i.* répondre. ~ **the door,** ouvrir la porte. ~ **back,** répondre. ~ **for,** répondre de. ~**able** *a.* responsable (**for,** de; **to,** devant).

ant /ænt/ *n.* fourmi *f.*

antagonis|m /æn'tægənizəm/ *n.* antagonisme *m.* ~**tic** /-'nistik/ *a.* antagoniste.

antagonize /æn'tægənaiz/ *v.t.* provoquer l'hostilité de.

Antarctic /æn'tɑːktik/ *a.* & *n.* antarctique (*m.*).

ante/'ænti/ *pref.* anti-, anté-.

antecedent /ænti'siːdnt/ *n.* antécédent *m.*

antelope /'æntiləup/ *n.* antilope *f.*

antenatal /'æntineitl/ *a.* prénatal.

antenna /æn'tenə/ *n.* (*pl.* -ae /-iː/) (*of insect*) antenne *f.*; (*pl.* -as; *aerial: Amer.*) antenne *f.*

anthem /'ænθəm/ *n.* (*relig.*) motet *m.*; (*of country*) hymne national *m.*

anthill /'ænthil/ *n.* fourmilière *f.*

anthology /æn'θɒlədʒi/ *n.* anthologie *f.*

anthropolog|y /ænθrə'pɒlədʒi/ *n.* anthropologie *f.* ~**ist** *n.* anthropologue *m.*/*f.*

anti/'ænti/ *pref.* anti-. ~**-aircraft** *a.* antiaérien.

antibiotic /æntibai'ɒtik/ *n.* antibiotique *m.*

antibody /'æntibɒdi/ *n.* anticorps *m.*

antic /'æntik/ *n.* bouffonnerie *f.*

anticipat|e /æn'tisipeit/ *v.t.* (*foresee, expect*) prévoir, s'attendre à; (*forestall*) devancer. ~**ion** /-'peiʃn/ *n.* attente *f.* **in** ~**ion of,** en prévision *or* attente de.

anticlimax /ænti'klaimæks/ *n.* (*letdown*) déception *f.*; (*event*) événement de moindre importance *m.* **it was an** ~, ça n'a pas répondu à l'attente.

anticlockwise /ænti'klɒkwaiz/ *adv.* & *a.* dans le sens inverse des aiguilles d'une montre.

anticyclone /ænti'saikləun/ *n.* anticyclone *m.*

antidote /'æntidəut/ *n.* antidote *m.*

antifreeze /'æntifriːz/ *n.* antigel *m.*

antipathy /æn'tipəθi/ *n.* antipathie *f.*

antiquarian /ænti'kweəriən/ *a.* (*bookseller*) spécialisé dans le livre ancien.

antiquated /'æntikweitid/ *a.* vieillot, suranné.

antique /æn'tiːk/ *a.* (*old*) ancien; (*from antiquity*) antique. —*n.* objet ancien *m.*, antiquité *f.* ~ **dealer,** antiquaire

m./*f.* ~ **shop,** magasin d'antiquités *m.*

antiquity /æn'tikwəti/ *n.* antiquité *f.*

anti-Semiti|c /æntisi'mitik/ *a.* antisémite. ~**sm** /-'semitizəm/ *n.* antisémitisme *m.*

antiseptic /ænti'septik/ *a.* & *n.* antiseptique (*m.*).

antisocial /ænti'səuʃl/ *a.* asocial, antisocial; (*unsociable*) insociable.

antithesis /æn'tiθəsis/ *n.* (*pl.* -eses /-əsiːz/) antithèse *f.*

antlers /'æntləz/ *n. pl.* bois *m. pl.*

anus /'einəs/ *n.* anus *m.*

anvil /'ænvil/ *n.* enclume *f.*

anxiety /æŋ'zaiəti/ *n.* (*worry*) anxiété *f.*; (*eagerness*) impatience *f.*

anxious /'æŋkʃəs/ *a.* (*troubled*) anxieux; (*eager*) impatient (**to,** de). ~**ly** *adv.* anxieusement; impatiemment.

any /'eni/ *a.* (*some*) du, de l', de la, des; (*after negative*) de, d'; (*every*) tout; (*no matter which*) n'importe quel. **at** ~ **moment,** à tout moment. **have you** ~ **water?**, avez-vous de l'eau? —*pron.* (*no matter which one*) n'importe lequel; (*someone*) quelqu'un; (*any amount of it or them*) en. **I do not have** ~, je n'en ai pas. —*adv.* (*a little*) un peu. **not** ~, nullement.

anybody /'enibɒdi/ *pron.* n'importe qui; (*somebody*) quelqu'un; (*after negative*) personne. **he did not see** ~, il n'a vu personne.

anyhow /'enihau/ *adv.* de toute façon; (*badly*) n'importe comment.

anyone /'eniwʌn/ *pron.* = **anybody.**

anything /'eniθiŋ/ *pron.* n'importe quoi; (*something*) quelque chose; (*after negative*) rien. **he did not see** ~, il n'a rien vu. ~ **but,** (*cheap etc.*) nullement. ~ **you do,** tout ce que tu fais.

anyway /'eniwei/ *adv.* de toute façon.

anywhere /'eniweə(r)/ *adv.* n'importe où; (*somewhere*) quelque part; (*after negative*) nulle part. **he does not go** ~, il ne va nulle part. ~ **you go,** partout où tu vas, où que tu ailles. ~ **else,** partout ailleurs.

apace /ə'peis/ *adv.* rapidement.

apart /ə'pɑːt/ *adv.* (*on or to one side*) à part; (*separated*) séparé; (*into pieces*) en pièces. ~ **from,** à part, excepté. **ten metres** ~, (*distant*) à dix mètres l'un de l'autre. **come** ~, se séparer;

(*machine*) se démonter. **keep ~,** séparer. **take ~,** démonter.

apartment /ə'pɑːtmənt/ *n.* (*Amer.*) appartement *m.* **~s,** logement *m.*

apath|y /'æpəθɪ/ *n.* apathie *f.* **~etic** /-'θetɪk/ *a.* apathique.

ape /eɪp/ *n.* singe *m.* —*v.t.* singer.

aperitif /ə'perətɪf/ *n.* apéritif *m.*

aperture /'æpətʃə(r)/ *n.* ouverture *f.*

apex /'eɪpeks/ *n.* sommet *m.*

aphrodisiac /æfrə'dɪzɪæk/ *a.* & *n.* aphrodisiaque (*m.*).

apiece /ə'piːs/ *adv.* chacun.

aplomb /ə'plɒm/ *n.* sang-froid *m.*

Apocalypse /ə'pɒkəlɪps/ *n.* Apocalypse *f.* **apocalyptic** /-'lɪptɪk/ *a.* apocalyptique.

apologetic /əpɒlə'dʒetɪk/ *a.* (*tone etc.*) d'excuse. **be ~,** s'excuser. **~ally** /-lɪ/ *adv.* en s'excusant.

apologize /ə'pɒlədʒaɪz/ *v.i.* s'excuser (**for,** de; **to,** auprès de).

apology /ə'pɒlədʒɪ/ *n.* excuses *f. pl.*; (*defence of belief*) apologie *f.*

apople|xy /'æpəpleksɪ/ *n.* apoplexie *f.* **~ctic** /-'plektɪk/ *a.* apoplectique.

Apostle /ə'pɒsl/ *n.* apôtre *m.*

apostrophe /ə'pɒstrəfɪ/ *n.* apostrophe *f.*

appal /ə'pɔːl/ *v.t.* (*p.t.* **appalled**) épouvanter. **~ling** *a.* épouvantable.

apparatus /æpə'reɪtəs/ *n.* (*machine* & *anat.*) appareil *m.*

apparel /ə'pærəl/ *n.* habillement *m.*

apparent /ə'pærənt/ *a.* apparent. **~ly** *adv.* apparemment.

apparition /æpə'rɪʃn/ *n.* apparition *f.*

appeal /ə'piːl/ *n.* appel *m.*; (*attractiveness*) attrait *m.*, charme *m.* —*v.i.* (*jurid.*) faire appel. **~ to s.o.,** (*beg*) faire appel à qn.; (*attract*) plaire à qn. **~ to s.o. for sth.,** demander qch. à qn. **~ing** *a.* (*attractive*) attirant.

appear /ə'pɪə(r)/ *v.i.* apparaître; (*arrive*) se présenter; (*seem, be published*) paraître; (*theatre*) jouer. **~ance** *n.* apparition *f.*; (*aspect*) apparence *f.*

appease /ə'piːz/ *v.t.* apaiser.

append /ə'pend/ *v.t.* joindre.

appendage /ə'pendɪdʒ/ *n.* appendice *m.*

appendicitis /əpendɪ'saɪtɪs/ *n.* appendicite *f.*

appendix /ə'pendɪks/ *n.* (*pl.* **-ices** /-ɪsiːz/) appendice *m.*

appertain /æpə'teɪn/ *v.i.* **~ to,** se rapporter à.

appetite /'æpɪtaɪt/ *n.* appétit *m.*

appetizer /'æpɪtaɪzə(r)/ *n.* (*snack*) amuse-gueule *m. invar.*; (*drink*) apéritif *m.*

appetizing /'æpɪtaɪzɪŋ/ *a.* appétissant.

applau|d /ə'plɔːd/ *v.t./i.* applaudir; (*decision*) applaudir à. **~se** *n.* applaudissements *m. pl.*

apple /'æpl/ *n.* pomme *f.* **~-tree** *n.* pommier *m.*

appliance /ə'plaɪəns/ *n.* appareil *m.*

applicable /'æplɪkəbl/ *a.* applicable.

applicant /'æplɪkənt/ *n.* candidat(e) *m.* (*f.*) (**for,** à).

application /æplɪ'keɪʃn/ *n.* application *f.*; (*request, form*) demande *f.*; (*for job*) candidature *f.*

apply /ə'plaɪ/ *v.t.* appliquer. —*v.i.* **~ to,** (*refer*) s'appliquer à; (*ask*) s'adresser à. **~ for,** (*job, grant*) demander. **~ o.s. to,** s'appliquer à.

applied *a.* appliqué.

appoint /ə'pɔɪnt/ *v.t.* (*to post*) nommer; (*fix*) désigner. **well-~ed** *a.* bien équipé. **~ment** *n.* nomination *f.*; (*meeting*) rendez-vous *m. invar.*; (*job*) poste *m.*

apportion /ə'pɔːʃn/ *v.t.* répartir.

apprais|e /ə'preɪz/ *v.t.* évaluer. **~al** *n.* évaluation *f.*

appreciable /ə'priːʃəbl/ *a.* appréciable.

appreciat|e /ə'priːʃɪeɪt/ *v.t.* (*like*) apprécier; (*understand*) comprendre; (*be grateful for*) être reconnaissant de. —*v.i.* prendre de la valeur. **~ion** /-'eɪʃn/ *n.* appréciation *f.*; (*gratitude*) reconnaissance *f.*; (*rise*) augmentation *f.* **~ive** /ə'priːʃɪətɪv/ *a.* reconnaissant.

apprehen|d /æprɪ'hend/ *v.t.* (*arrest, fear*) appréhender; (*understand*) comprendre. **~sion** *n.* appréhension *f.*

apprehensive /æprɪ'hensɪv/ *a.* inquiet. **be ~ of,** craindre.

apprentice /ə'prentɪs/ *n.* apprenti *m.* —*v.t.* mettre en apprentissage. **~ship** *n.* apprentissage *m.*

approach /ə'prəʊtʃ/ *v.t.* (s')approcher de; (*accost*) aborder. —*v.i.* (s')approcher. —*n.* approche *f.* **an ~ to,** (*problem*) une façon d'aborder; (*person*) une démarche auprès de. **~able** *a.* accessible; (*person*) abordable.

appropriate[1] /ə'prəʊprɪət/ *a.* approprié, propre. **~ly** *adv.* à propos.

appropriate[2] /ə'prəʊprɪeɪt/ *v.t.* s'approprier.

approval /əˈpruːvl/ *n.* approbation *f.* **on ∼**, à *or* sous condition.

approv|e /əˈpruːv/ *v.t./i.* approuver. **∼e of**, approuver. **∼ingly** *adv.* d'un air *or* d'un ton approbateur.

approximate[1] /əˈprɒksɪmət/ *a.* approximatif. **∼ly** *adv.* approximativement.

approximat|e[2] /əˈprɒksɪmeɪt/ *v.t.* se rapprocher de. **∼ion** /-ˈmeɪʃn/ *n.* approximation *f.*

apricot /ˈeɪprɪkɒt/ *n.* abricot *m.*

April /ˈeɪprəl/ *n.* avril *m.* **make an ∼ fool of**, faire un poisson d'avril à.

apron /ˈeɪprən/ *n.* tablier *m.*

apse /æps/ *n.* (*of church*) abside *f.*

apt /æpt/ *a.* (*suitable*) approprié; (*pupil*) doué. **be ∼ to**, avoir tendance à. **∼ly** *adv.* à propos.

aptitude /ˈæptɪtjuːd/ *n.* aptitude *f.*

aqualung /ˈækwəlʌŋ/ *n.* scaphandre autonome *m.*

aquarium /əˈkweərɪəm/ *n.* (*pl.* **-ums**) aquarium *m.*

aquatic /əˈkwætɪk/ *a.* aquatique; (*sport*) nautique.

aqueduct /ˈækwɪdʌkt/ *n.* aqueduc *m.*

aquiline /ˈækwɪlaɪn/ *a.* aquilin.

Arab /ˈærəb/ *n.* & *a.* arabe (*m./f.*). **∼ic** *a.* & *n.* (*lang.*) arabe (*m.*). **∼ic numerals**, chiffres arabes *m. pl.*

Arabian /əˈreɪbɪən/ *a.* arabe.

arable /ˈærəbl/ *a.* arable.

arbiter /ˈɑːbɪtə(r)/ *n.* arbitre *m.*

arbitrary /ˈɑːbɪtrərɪ/ *a.* arbitraire.

arbitrat|e /ˈɑːbɪtreɪt/ *v.i.* arbitrer. **∼ion** /-ˈtreɪʃn/ *n.* arbitrage *m.* **∼or** *n.* arbitre *m.*

arc /ɑːk/ *n.* arc *m.*

arcade /ɑːˈkeɪd/ *n.* (*shops*) galerie *f.*; (*arches*) arcades *f. pl.*

arcane /ɑːˈkeɪn/ *a.* mystérieux.

arch[1] /ɑːtʃ/ *n.* arche *f.*; (*in church etc.*) arc *m.*; (*of foot*) voûte plantaire *f.* — *v.t./i.* (s')arquer.

arch[2] /ɑːtʃ/ *a.* (*playful*) malicieux.

arch- /ɑːtʃ/ *pref.* (*hypocrite etc.*) grand, achevé.

archaeolog|y /ɑːkɪˈɒlədʒɪ/ *n.* archéologie *f.* **∼ical** /-əˈlɒdʒɪkl/ *a.* archéologique. **∼ist** *n.* archéologue *m./f.*

archaic /ɑːˈkeɪɪk/ *a.* archaïque.

archbishop /ɑːtʃˈbɪʃəp/ *n.* archevêque *m.*

arch-enemy /ɑːtʃˈenəmɪ/ *n.* ennemi numéro un *m.*

archer /ˈɑːtʃə(r)/ *n.* archer *m.* **∼y** *n.* tir à l'arc *m.*

archetype /ˈɑːkɪtaɪp/ *n.* archétype *m.*, modèle *m.*

archipelago /ɑːkɪˈpeləgəʊ/ *n.* (*pl.* **-os**) archipel *m.*

architect /ˈɑːkɪtekt/ *n.* architecte *m.*

architectur|e /ˈɑːkɪtektʃə(r)/ *n.* architecture *f.* **∼al** /-ˈtektʃərəl/ *a.* architectural.

archiv|es /ˈɑːkaɪvz/ *n. pl.* archives *f. pl.* **∼ist** /-ɪvɪst/ *n.* archiviste *m./f.*

archway /ˈɑːtʃweɪ/ *n.* voûte *f.*

Arctic /ˈɑːktɪk/ *a.* & *n.* arctique (*m.*). **arctic** *a.* glacial.

ardent /ˈɑːdnt/ *a.* ardent. **∼ly** *adv.* ardemment.

ardour /ˈɑːdə(r)/ *n.* ardeur *f.*

arduous /ˈɑːdjʊəs/ *a.* ardu.

are /ɑː(r)/ *see* be.

area /ˈeərɪə/ *n.* (*surface*) superficie *f.*; (*region*) région *f.*; (*district*) quartier *m.*; (*fig.*) domaine *m.*

arena /əˈriːnə/ *n.* arène *f.*

aren't /ɑːnt/ = **are not.**

Argentin|a /ɑːdʒənˈtiːnə/ *n.* Argentine *f.* **∼e** /ˈɑːdʒəntaɪn/, **∼ian** /-ˈtɪnɪən/ *a.* & *n.* argentin(e) (*m.* (*f.*)).

argu|e /ˈɑːgjuː/ *v.i.* (*quarrel*) se disputer; (*reason*) argumenter. —*v.t.* (*debate*) discuter. **∼e that**, alléguer que. **∼able** /-ʊəbl/ *a.* discutable.

argument /ˈɑːgjʊmənt/ *n.* dispute *f.*; (*reasoning*) argument *m.* **∼ative** /-ˈmentətɪv/ *a.* raisonneur, contrariant.

arid /ˈærɪd/ *a.* aride.

arise /əˈraɪz/ *v.i.* (*p.t.* **arose**, *p.p.* **arisen**) se présenter; (*old use*) se lever. **∼ from**, résulter de.

aristocracy /ærɪˈstɒkrəsɪ/ *n.* aristocratie *f.*

aristocrat /ˈærɪstəkræt, *Amer.* əˈrɪstəkræt/ *n.* aristocrate *m./f.* **∼ic** /-ˈkrætɪk/ *a.* aristocratique.

arithmetic /əˈrɪθmətɪk/ *n.* arithmétique *f.*

ark /ɑːk/ *n.* (*relig.*) arche *f.*

arm[1] /ɑːm/ *n.* bras *m.* **∼ in arm**, bras dessus bras dessous. **∼-band** *n.* brassard *m.*

arm[2] /ɑːm/ *v.t.* armer. **∼ed robbery**, vol à main armée *m.*

armament /ˈɑːməmənt/ *n.* armement *m.*

armchair /ˈɑːmtʃeə(r)/ *n.* fauteuil *m.*

armful /ˈɑːmfʊl/ *n.* brassée *f.*

armistice /ˈɑːmɪstɪs/ *n.* armistice *m.*

armlet /ˈɑːmlɪt/ *n.* brassard *m.*

armour /ˈɑːmə(r)/ *n.* armure *f.*; (*on

tanks etc.) blindage *m*. ~-**clad**, ~-**ed** *adjs*. blindé.

armoury /'ɑːmərɪ/ *n*. arsenal *m*.

armpit /'ɑːmpɪt/ *n*. aisselle *f*.

arms /ɑːmz/ *n. pl*. (*weapons*) armes *f. pl*.

army /'ɑːmɪ/ *n*. armée *f*.

aroma /ə'rəʊmə/ *n*. arôme *m*. ~**tic** /ærə'mætɪk/ *a*. aromatique.

arose /ə'rəʊz/ *see* **arise**.

around /ə'raʊnd/ *adv*. (tout) autour; (*here and there*) çà et là. —*prep*. autour de. ~ **here**, par ici.

arouse /ə'raʊz/ *v.t*. (*awaken*, *cause*) éveiller; (*excite*) exciter.

arpeggio /ɑː'pedʒɪəʊ/ *n*. (*pl*. -**os**) arpège *m*.

arrange /ə'reɪndʒ/ *v.t*. arranger; (*time*, *date*) fixer. ~ **to**, s'arranger pour. ~**ment** *n*. arrangement *m*. **make** ~**ments**, prendre des dispositions.

array /ə'reɪ/ *v.t*. (*mil*.) déployer; (*dress*) vêtir. —*n*. **an** ~ **of**, (*display*) un étalage impressionnant de.

arrears /ə'rɪəz/ *n. pl*. arriéré *m*. **in** ~, (*rent*) arriéré. **he is in** ~, il a des paiements en retard.

arrest /ə'rest/ *v.t*. arrêter; (*attention*) retenir. —*n*. arrestation *f*. **under** ~, en état d'arrestation.

arrival /ə'raɪvl/ *n*. arrivée *f*. **new** ~, arrivant(e) *m*. (*f*.).

arrive /ə'raɪv/ *v.i*. arriver.

arrogan|t /'ærəgənt/ *a*. arrogant. ~**ce** *n*. arrogance *f*. ~**tly** *adv*. avec arrogance.

arrow /'ærəʊ/ *n*. flèche *f*.

arsenal /'ɑːsənl/ *n*. arsenal *m*.

arsenic /'ɑːsnɪk/ *n*. arsenic *m*.

arson /'ɑːsn/ *n*. incendie criminel *m*. ~**ist** *n*. incendiaire *m./f*.

art[1] /ɑːt/ *n*. art *m*.; (*fine arts*) beaux arts *m. pl*. ~**s**, (*univ*.) lettres *f. pl*. ~ **gallery**, (*public*) musée (d'art) *m*.; (*private*) galerie (d'art) *f*. ~ **school**, école des beaux arts *f*.

art[2] /ɑːt/ (*old use*, *with thou*) = **are**.

artefact /'ɑːtɪfækt/ *n*. objet fabriqué *m*.

arter|y /'ɑːtərɪ/ *n*. artère *f*. ~**ial** /-'tɪərɪəl/ *a*. artériel. ~**ial road**, route principale *f*.

artful /'ɑːtfl/ *a*. astucieux, rusé. ~**ness** *n*. astuce *f*.

arthriti|s /ɑː'θraɪtɪs/ *n*. arthrite *f*. ~**c** /-ɪtɪk/ *a*. arthritique.

artichoke /'ɑːtɪtʃəʊk/ *n*. artichaut *m*.

article /'ɑːtɪkl/ *n*. article *m*. ~ **of**

clothing, vêtement *m*. ~**d** *a*. (*jurid*.) en stage.

articulate[1] /ɑː'tɪkjʊlət/ *a*. (*person*) capable de s'exprimer clairement; (*speech*) distinct.

articulat|e[2] /ɑː'tɪkjʊleɪt/ *v.t./i*. articuler. ~**ed lorry**, semi-remorque *m*. ~**ion** /-'leɪʃn/ *n*. articulation *f*.

artifice /'ɑːtɪfɪs/ *n*. artifice *m*.

artificial /ɑːtɪ'fɪʃl/ *a*. artificiel. ~**ity** /-ʃɪ'ælətɪ/ *n*. manque de naturel *m*.

artillery /ɑː'tɪlərɪ/ *n*. artillerie *f*.

artisan /ɑːtɪ'zæn/ *n*. artisan *m*.

artist /'ɑːtɪst/ *n*. artiste *m./f*. ~**ic** /-'tɪstɪk/ *a*. artistique. ~**ry** *n*. art *m*.

artiste /ɑː'tiːst/ *n*. (*entertainer*) artiste *m./f*.

artless /'ɑːtlɪs/ *a*. ingénu, naïf.

arty /'ɑːtɪ/ *a*. (*fam*., *péj*.) qui est du genre artiste.

as /æz, *unstressed* əz/ *adv. & conj*. comme; (*while*) pendant que. ~ **you get older**, en vieillissant. ~ **a gift**, en cadeau. ~ **tall as**, aussi grand que. ~ **for**, ~ **to**, quant à. ~ **much**, ~ **many**, autant (as, que). ~ **soon as**, aussitôt que. ~ **well**, aussi (as, bien que).

asbestos /æz'bestɒs/ *n*. amiante *f*.

ascend /ə'send/ *v.t*. gravir; (*throne*) monter sur. —*v.i*. monter. ~**ant** *n*. **in the** ~**ant**, qui monte.

ascent /ə'sent/ *n*. (*climbing*) ascension *f*.; (*slope*) côte *f*.

ascertain /æsə'teɪn/ *v.t*. s'assurer de. ~ **that**, s'assurer que.

ascetic /ə'setɪk/ *a*. ascétique. —*n*. ascète *m./f*.

ascribe /ə'skraɪb/ *v.t*. attribuer.

ash[1] /æʃ/ *n*. ~(-**tree**), frêne *m*.

ash[2] /æʃ/ *n*. cendre *f*. **A**~ **Wednesday**, Mercredi des Cendres *m*. ~**en** *a*. cendreux.

ashamed /ə'ʃeɪmd/ *a*. **be** ~, avoir honte, être honteux (**of**, de).

ashore /ə'ʃɔː(r)/ *adv*. à terre.

ashtray /'æʃtreɪ/ *n*. cendrier *m*.

Asia /'eɪʃə, *Amer*. 'eɪʒə/ *n*. Asie *f*. ~**n** *a. &. n*. asiatique (*m./f*.). ~**tic** /-ɪ'ætɪk/ *a*. asiatique.

aside /ə'saɪd/ *adv*. de côté. —*n*. aparté *m*. ~ **from**, (*Amer*.) à part.

asinine /'æsɪnaɪn/ *a*. stupide.

ask /ɑːsk/ *v.t./i*. demander; (*a question*) poser; (*invite*) inviter. ~ **s.o. sth.**, demander qch. à qn. ~ **about**, (*thing*) se renseigner sur; (*person*) demander des nouvelles de. ~ **for**, demander.

askance /ə'skæns/ *adv.* **look ~ at,** regarder avec méfiance.

askew /ə'skju:/ *adv.* & *a.* de travers.

asleep /ə'sli:p/ *a.* endormi; (*numb*) engourdi. —*adv.* **fall ~,** s'endormir.

asp /æsp/ *n.* (*snake*) aspic *m.*

asparagus /ə'spærəgəs/ *n.* (*plant*) asperge *f.*; (*culin.*) asperges *f. pl.*

aspect /'æspekt/ *n.* aspect *m.*; (*direction*) orientation *f.*

aspersions /ə'spɜ:ʃnz/ *n. pl.* **cast ~ on,** calomnier.

asphalt /'æsfælt, *Amer.* 'æsfɔ:lt/ *n.* asphalte *m.* —*v.t.* asphalter.

asphyxia /æs'fɪksɪə/ *n.* asphyxie *f.*

asphyxiat|e /əs'fɪksɪeɪt/ *v.t./i.* (s')asphyxier. **~ion** /-'eɪʃn/ *n.* asphyxie *f.*

aspir|e /əs'paɪə(r)/ *v.i.* **~e to,** aspirer à. **~ation** /æspə'reɪʃn/ *n.* aspiration *f.*

aspirin /'æsprɪn/ *n.* aspirine *f.*

ass /æs/ *n.* âne *m.*; (*person: fam.*) idiot(e) *m.* (*f.*).

assail /ə'seɪl/ *v.t.* assaillir. **~ant** *n.* agresseur *m.*

assassin /ə'sæsɪn/ *n.* assassin *m.*

assassinat|e /ə'sæsɪneɪt/ *v.t.* assassiner. **~ion** /-'neɪʃn/ *n.* assassinat *m.*

assault /ə'sɔ:lt/ *n.* (*mil.*) assaut *m.*; (*jurid.*) agression *f.* —*v.t.* (*person: jurid.*) agresser.

assembl|e /ə'sembl/ *v.t.* (*things*) assembler; (*people*) rassembler. —*v.i.* s'assembler, se rassembler. **~age** *n.* assemblage *m.*

assembly /ə'semblɪ/ *n.* assemblée *f.* **~ line,** chaîne de montage *f.*

assent /ə'sent/ *n.* assentiment *m.* —*v.i.* consentir.

assert /ə'sɜ:t/ *v.t.* affirmer; (*one's rights*) revendiquer. **~ion** /-ʃn/ *n.* affirmation *f.* **~ive** *a.* affirmatif, péremptoire.

assess /ə'ses/ *v.t.* évaluer; (*payment*) déterminer le montant de. **~ment** *n.* évaluation *f.* **~or** *n.* (*valuer*) expert *m.*

asset /'æset/ *n.* (*advantage*) atout *m.* **~s,** (*comm.*) actif *m.*

assiduous /ə'sɪdjʊəs/ *a.* assidu.

assign /ə'saɪn/ *v.t.* (*allot*) assigner. **~ s.o. to,** (*appoint*) affecter qn. à.

assignment /ə'saɪnmənt/ *n.* (*task*) mission *f.*, tâche *f.*

assimilat|e /ə'sɪməleɪt/ *v.t./i.* (s')assimiler. **~ion** /-'leɪʃn/ *n.* assimilation *f.*

assist /ə'sɪst/ *v.t./i.* aider. **~ance** *n.* aide *f.*

assistant /ə'sɪstənt/ *n.* aide *m./f.*; (*in shop*) vendeu|r, -se *m.*, *f.* —*a.* (*manager etc.*) adjoint.

associat|e[1] /ə'səʊʃɪeɪt/ *v.t.* associer. —*v.i.* **~e with,** fréquenter. **~ion** /-'eɪʃn/ *n.* association *f.* **A~ion football,** football *m.*

associate[2] /ə'səʊʃɪət/ *n.* & *a.* associé(e) (*m.* (*f.*)).

assort|ed /ə'sɔ:tɪd/ *a.* divers; (*foods*) assortis. **~ment** *n.* assortiment *m.* **an ~ment of guests/** etc., des invités/etc. divers.

assume /ə'sju:m/ *v.t.* supposer, présumer; (*power, attitude*) prendre; (*role, burden*) assumer.

assumption /ə'sʌmpʃn/ *n.* (*sth. supposed*) supposition *f.*

assurance /ə'ʃʊərəns/ *n.* assurance *f.*

assur|e /ə'ʃʊə(r)/ *v.t.* assurer. **~d** *a.* assuré. **~dly** /-rɪdlɪ/ *adv.* assurément.

asterisk /'æstərɪsk/ *n.* astérisque *m.*

astern /ə'stɜ:n/ *adv.* à l'arrière.

asthma /'æsmə/ *n.* asthme *m.* **~tic** /-'mætɪk/ *a.* & *n.* asthmatique (*m./f.*).

astonish /ə'stɒnɪʃ/ *v.t.* étonner. **~ingly** *adv.* étonnamment. **~ment** *n.* étonnement *m.*

astound /ə'staʊnd/ *v.t.* stupéfier.

astray /ə'streɪ/ *adv.* & *a.* **go ~,** s'égarer. **lead ~,** égarer.

astride /ə'straɪd/ *adv.* & *prep.* à califourchon (sur).

astringent /ə'strɪndʒənt/ *a.* astringent; (*severe: fig.*) austère. —*n.* astringent *m.*

astrolog|y /ə'strɒlədʒɪ/ *n.* astrologie *f.* **~er** *n.* astrologue *m.*

astronaut /'æstrənɔ:t/ *n.* astronaute *m./f.*

astronom|y /ə'strɒnəmɪ/ *n.* astronomie *f.* **~er** *n.* astronome *m.* **~ical** /æstrə'nɒmɪkl/ *a.* astronomique.

astute /ə'stju:t/ *a.* astucieux. **~ness** *n.* astuce *f.*

asunder /ə'sʌndə(r)/ *adv.* en morceaux; (*in two*) en deux.

asylum /ə'saɪləm/ *n.* asile *m.*

at /æt, *unstressed* ət/ *prep.* à. **~ the doctor's/**etc., chez le médecin/etc. **surprised ~,** (*cause*) étonné de. **angry ~,** fâché contre. **not ~ all,** pas du tout. **no wind/**etc. **~ all,** (*of any kind*) pas le moindre vent/etc. **~ night,** la nuit. **~ once,** tout de suite; (*simultaneously*) à la fois. **~ sea,** en mer. **~ times,** parfois.

ate /et/ *see* **eat.**

atheis|t /'eɪθɪɪst/ *n.* athée *m./f.* ∼**m**
/-zəm/ *n.* athéisme *m.*

athlet|e /'æθliːt/ *n.* athlète *m./f.* ∼**ic**
/-'letɪk/ *a.* athlétique. ∼**ics** /-'letɪks/
n. pl. athlétisme *m.*

Atlantic /ət'læntɪk/ *a.* atlantique. —*n.*
∼ (**Ocean**), Atlantique *m.*

atlas /'ætləs/ *n.* atlas *m.*

atmospher|e /'ætməsfɪə(r)/ *n.* atmos-
phère *f.* ∼**ic** /-'ferɪk/ *a.* atmos-
phérique.

atmospherics /ætməs'ferɪks/ *n. pl.*
parasites *m. pl.*

atom /'ætəm/ *n.* atome *m.* ∼**ic** /ə'tɒmɪk/
a. atomique. ∼**(ic) bomb**, bombe
atomique *f.*

atomize /'ætəmaɪz/ *v.t.* atomiser. ∼**r**
/-ə(r)/ *n.* atomiseur *m.*

atone /ə'təʊn/ *v.i.* ∼ **for**, expier.
∼**ment** *n.* expiation *f.*

atrocious /ə'trəʊʃəs/ *a.* atroce.

atrocity /ə'trɒsəti/ *n.* atrocité *f.*

atrophy /'ætrəfɪ/ *n.* atrophie *f.* —*v.t./i.*
(s')atrophier.

attach /ə'tætʃ/ *v.t./i.* (s')attacher;
(*letter*) joindre (**to**, à). ∼**ed** *a.* **be**
∼**ed to**, (*like*) être attaché à. **the**
∼**ed letter**, la lettre ci-jointe.
∼**ment** *n.* (*accessory*) accessoire *m.*;
(*affection*) attachement *m.*

attaché /ə'tæʃeɪ/ *n.* (*pol.*) attaché(e) *m.*
(*f.*). ∼ **case**, mallette *f.*

attack /ə'tæk/ *n.* attaque *f.* —*v.t./i.*
attaquer. ∼**er** *n.* agresseur *m.*, atta-
quant(e) *m.* (*f.*).

attain /ə'teɪn/ *v.t.* atteindre (à); (*gain*)
acquérir. ∼**able** *a.* accessible.
∼**ment** *n.* acquisition *f.* (**of**, de).
∼**ments**, réussites *f. pl.*

attempt /ə'tempt/ *v.t.* tenter. —*n.* tentative *f.* **an** ∼ **on s.o.'s life**, un attentat contre qn.

attend /ə'tend/ *v.t.* assister à; (*class*)
suivre; (*school, church*) aller à; (*escort*) accompagner. —*v.i.* assister. ∼
(**to**), (*look after*) s'occuper de. ∼**ance**
n. présence *f.*; (*people*) assistance *f.*

attendant /ə'tendənt/ *n.* employé(e)
m. (*f.*); (*servant*) serviteur *m.*

attention /ə'tenʃn/ *n.* attention *f.*; ∼!,
(*mil.*) garde-à-vous! **pay** ∼, faire *or*
prêter attention (**to**, à).

attentive /ə'tentɪv/ *a.* attentif; (*considerate*) attentionné. ∼**ly** *adv.* attentivement. ∼**ness** *n.* attention *f.*

attenuate /ə'tenjʊeɪt/ *v.t.* atténuer.

attest /ə'test/ *v.t./i.* ∼ (**to**), attester.
∼**ation** /æte'steɪʃn/ *n.* attestation *f.*

attic /'ætɪk/ *n.* grenier *m.*

attire /ə'taɪə(r)/ *n.* vêtements *m. pl.*
—*v.t.* vêtir.

attitude /'ætɪtjuːd/ *n.* attitude *f.*

attorney /ə'tɜːnɪ/ *n.* mandataire *m.*;
(*Amer.*) avocat *m.*

attract /ə'trækt/ *v.t.* attirer. ∼**ion**
/-kʃn/ *n.* attraction *f.*; (*charm*) attrait
m.

attractive /ə'træktɪv/ *a.* attrayant,
séduisant. ∼**ly** *adv.* agréablement.
∼**ness** *n.* attrait *m.*, beauté *f.*

attribute[1] /ə'trɪbjuːt/ *v.t.* ∼ **to**, attribuer à.

attribute[2] /'ætrɪbjuːt/ *n.* attribut *m.*

attrition /ə'trɪʃn/ *n.* **war of** ∼, guerre
d'usure *f.*

aubergine /'əʊbəʒiːn/ *n.* aubergine *f.*

auburn /'ɔːbən/ *a.* châtain roux *invar.*

auction /'ɔːkʃn/ *n.* vente aux enchères
f. —*v.t.* vendre aux enchères. ∼**eer**
/-ə'nɪə(r)/ *n.* commissaire-priseur *m.*

audaci|ous /ɔː'deɪʃəs/ *a.* audacieux.
∼**ty** /-æsəti/ *n.* audace *f.*

audible /'ɔːdəbl/ *a.* audible.

audience /'ɔːdɪəns/ *n.* auditoire *m.*;
(*theatre, radio*) public *m.*; (*interview*)
audience *f.*

audiotypist /'ɔːdɪəʊ'taɪpɪst/ *n.* audiotypiste *m./f.*

audio-visual /ɔːdɪəʊ'vɪʒʊəl/ *a.* audio-
visuel.

audit /'ɔːdɪt/ *n.* vérification des comptes *f.* —*v.t.* vérifier.

audition /ɔː'dɪʃn/ *n.* audition *f.* —*v.t./i.*
auditionner.

auditor /'ɔːdɪtə(r)/ *n.* commissaire aux
comptes *m.*

auditorium /ɔːdɪ'tɔːrɪəm/ *n.* (*of theatre
etc.*) salle *f.*

augment /ɔːg'ment/ *v.t.* augmenter.

augur /'ɔːgə(r)/ *v.i.* ∼ **well/ill**, être
de bon/mauvais augure.

august /ɔː'gʌst/ *a.* auguste.

August /'ɔːgəst/ *n.* août *m.*

aunt /ɑːnt/ *n.* tante *f.*

au pair /əʊ'peə(r)/ *n.* jeune fille au pair
f.

aura /'ɔːrə/ *n.* atmosphère *f.*

auspices /'ɔːspɪsɪz/ *n. pl.* auspices
m. pl., égide *f.*

auspicious /ɔː'spɪʃəs/ *a.* favorable.

auster|e /ɔː'stɪə(r)/ *a.* austère. ∼**ity**
/-erətɪ/ *n.* austérité *f.*

Australia /ɒ'streɪlɪə/ *n.* Australie *f.*
∼**n** *a.* & *n.* australien(ne) (*m.* (*f.*)).

Austria /'ɒstrɪə/ *n.* Autriche *f.* ∼**n**
a. & *n.* autrichien(ne) (*m.* (*f.*)).

authentic /ɔː'θentɪk/ *a.* authentique. ~**ity** /-ən'tɪsətɪ/ *n.* authenticité *f.*

authenticate /ɔː'θentɪkeɪt/ *v.t.* authentifier.

author /'ɔːθə(r)/ *n.* auteur *m.* ~**ess** *n.* femme auteur *f.* ~**ship** *n.* (*origin*) paternité *f.*

authoritarian /ɔːθɒrɪ'teərɪən/ *a.* autoritaire.

authorit|y /ɔː'θɒrətɪ/ *n.* autorité *f.*; (*permission*) autorisation *f.* ~**ative** /-ɪtətɪv/ *a.* (*trusted*) autorisé; (*manner*) autoritaire.

authoriz|e /'ɔːθəraɪz/ *v.t.* autoriser. ~**ation** /-'zeɪʃn/ *n.* autorisation *f.*

autistic /ɔː'tɪstɪk/ *a.* autistique.

autobiography /ɔːtəbaɪ'ɒɡrəfɪ/ *n.* autobiographie *f.*

autocracy /ɔː'tɒkrəsɪ/ *n.* autocratie *f.*

autocrat /'ɔːtəkræt/ *n.* autocrate *m.* ~**ic** /-'krætɪk/ *a.* autocratique.

autograph /'ɔːtəɡrɑːf/ *n.* autographe *m.* —*v.t.* signer, dédicacer.

automat|e /'ɔːtəmeɪt/ *v.t.* automatiser. ~**ion** /-'meɪʃn/ *n.* automatisation *f.*

automatic /ɔːtə'mætɪk/ *a.* automatique. ~**ally** /-klɪ/ *adv.* automatiquement.

automaton /ɔː'tɒmətən/ *n.* (*pl.* -**s** *or collectively* -**ta**) automate *m.*

automobile /'ɔːtəməbiːl/ *n.* (*Amer.*) auto(mobile) *f.*

autonom|y /ɔː'tɒnəmɪ/ *n.* autonomie *f.* ~**ous** *a.* autonome.

autopsy /'ɔːtɒpsɪ/ *n.* autopsie *f.*

autumn /'ɔːtəm/ *n.* automne *m.* ~**al** /-'tʌmnəl/ *a.* automnal.

auxiliary /ɔːɡ'zɪlɪərɪ/ *a.* & *n.* auxiliaire (*m./f.*). ~ (**verb**), auxiliaire *m.*

avail /ə'veɪl/ *v.t.* ~ **o.s. of**, profiter de. —*n.* **of no** ~, inutile. **to no** ~, sans résultat.

availab|le /ə'veɪləbl/ *a.* disponible. ~**ility** /-'bɪlətɪ/ *n.* disponibilité *f.*

avalanche /'ævəlɑːnʃ/ *n.* avalanche *f.*

avaric|e /'ævərɪs/ *n.* avarice *f.* ~**ious** /-'rɪʃəs/ *a.* avare.

avenge /ə'vendʒ/ *v.t.* venger. ~ **o.s.**, se venger (**on**, de).

avenue /'ævənjuː/ *n.* avenue *f.*; (*line of approach*: *fig.*) voie *f.*

average /'ævərɪdʒ/ *n.* moyenne *f.* —*a.* moyen. —*v.t./i.* faire la moyenne de; (*produce, do*) faire en moyenne. **on** ~, en moyenne.

avers|e /ə'vɜːs/ *a.* **be** ~**e to**, répugner à. ~**ion** /-ʃn/ *n.* aversion *f.*

avert /ə'vɜːt/ *v.t.* (*turn away*) détourner; (*ward off*) éviter.

aviary /'eɪvɪərɪ/ *n.* volière *f.*

aviation /eɪvɪ'eɪʃn/ *n.* aviation *f.*

aviator /'eɪvɪeɪtə(r)/ *n.* (*old use*) avia|teur, -trice *m.*, *f.*

avid /'ævɪd/ *a.* avide.

avocado /ævə'kɑːdəʊ/ *n.* (*pl.* -**os**) avocat *m.*

avoid /ə'vɔɪd/ *v.t.* éviter. ~**able** *a.* évitable. ~**ance** *n.* **the** ~**ance of s.o./sth. is . . .,** éviter qn./qch., c'est . . .

avuncular /ə'vʌŋkjʊlə(r)/ *a.* avunculaire.

await /ə'weɪt/ *v.t.* attendre.

awake /ə'weɪk/ *v.t./i.* (*p.t.* **awoke**, *p.p.* **awoken**) (s')éveiller. —*a.* **be** ~, ne pas dormir, être (r)éveillé.

awaken /ə'weɪkən/ *v.t./i.* (s')éveiller.

award /ə'wɔːd/ *v.t.* attribuer. —*n.* récompense *f.*, prix *m.*; (*scholarship*) bourse *f.*

aware /ə'weə(r)/ *a.* averti. ~ **of**, conscient de. **become** ~ **of**, prendre conscience de. ~**ness** *n.* conscience *f.*

awash /ə'wɒʃ/ *a.* inondé (**with**, de).

away /ə'weɪ/ *adv.* (*far*) (au) loin; (*absent*) absent, parti; (*persistently*) sans arrêt; (*entirely*) complètement. **six kilometres** ~, à six kilomètres (de distance). —*a.* & *n.* ~ (**match**), match à l'extérieur *m.*

awe /ɔː/ *n.* crainte (révérencielle) *f.* ~-**inspiring**, ~**some** *adjs.* terrifiant; (*sight*) imposant. ~-**struck** *a.* terrifié.

awful /'ɔːfl/ *a.* affreux. ~**ly** /'ɔːflɪ/ *adv.* (*badly*) affreusement; (*very*: *fam.*) rudement.

awhile /ə'waɪl/ *adv.* quelque temps.

awkward /'ɔːkwəd/ *a.* difficile; (*inconvenient*) inopportun; (*clumsy*) maladroit; (*embarrassing*) gênant; (*embarrassed*) gêné. ~**ly** *adv.* maladroitement; avec gêne. ~**ness** *n.* maladresse *f.*; (*discomfort*) gêne *f.*

awning /'ɔːnɪŋ/ *n.* auvent *m.*; (*of shop*) store *m.*

awoke, awoken /ə'wəʊk, ə'wəʊkən/ *see* **awake.**

awry /ə'raɪ/ *adv.* **go** ~, mal tourner. **sth. is** ~, qch. ne va pas.

axe /æks/ *n.* hache *f.* —*v.t.* (*pres. p.* **axing**) réduire; (*eliminate*) supprimer; (*employee*) renvoyer.

axiom /'æksɪəm/ *n.* axiome *m.*

axis /'æksɪs/ *n.* (*pl.* **axes** /-siːz/) axe *m.*

axle /'æksl/ *n.* essieu *m.*

ay(e) /aɪ/ *adv.* & *n.* oui (*m. invar.*).

B

BA *abbr. see* **Bachelor of Arts.**
babble /'bæbl/ *v.i.* babiller; (*stream*) gazouiller. —*n.* babillage *m.*
baboon /bə'bu:n/ *n.* babouin *m.*
baby /'beɪbɪ/ *n.* bébé *m.* ~ **carriage,** (*Amer.*) voiture d'enfant *f.* ~**-sit** *v.i.* garder les enfants. ~**-sitter** *n.* babysitter *m.*/*f.*
babyish /'beɪbɪʃ/ *a.* enfantin.
bachelor /'bætʃələ(r)/ *n.* célibataire *m.* **B**~ **of Arts/Science,** licencié(e) ès lettres/sciences *m.* (*f.*).
back /bæk/ *n.* (*of person, hand, page, etc.*) dos *m.*; (*of house*) derrière *m.*; (*of vehicle*) arrière *m.*; (*of room*) fond *m.*; (*of chair*) dossier *m.*; (*football*) arrière *m.* —*a.* de derrière, arrière *invar.*; (*taxes*) arriéré. —*adv.* en arrière; (*returned*) de retour, rentré. —*v.t.* (*support*) appuyer; (*bet on*) miser sur; (*vehicle*) faire reculer. —*v.i.* (*of person, vehicle*) reculer. **at the** ~ **of beyond,** au diable. **in** ~ **of,** (*Amer.*) derrière. ~**-bencher** *n.* (*pol.*) membre sans portefeuille *m.* ~ **down,** abandonner, se dégonfler. ~ **number,** vieux numéro *m.* ~ **out,** se dégager, se dégonfler. ~ **up,** (*support*) appuyer. ~**-up** *n.* appui *m.*; (*Amer., fam.*) embouteillage *m.*; *a.* de réserve.
backache /'bækeɪk/ *n.* mal de reins *m.*, mal aux reins *m.*
backbiting /'bækbaɪtɪŋ/ *n.* médisance *f.*
backbone /'bækbəʊn/ *n.* colonne vertébrale *f.*
backchat /'bæktʃæt/ *n.* réplique (impertinente) *f.*
backdate /bæk'deɪt/ *v.t.* antidater.
backer /'bækə(r)/ *n.* partisan *m.*; (*comm.*) bailleur de fonds *m.*
backfire /bæk'faɪə(r)/ *v.i.* (*auto.*) pétarader; (*fig.*) mal tourner.
backgammon /bæk'gæmən/ *n.* trictrac *m.*
background /'bækgraʊnd/ *n.* fond *m.*, arrière-plan *m.*; (*context*) contexte *m.*; (*environment*) milieu *m.*; (*experience*) formation *f.* —*a.* (*music, noise*) de fond.
backhand /'bækhænd/ *n.* revers *m.* ~**ed** *a.* équivoque. ~**ed stroke,** re-

vers *m.* ~**er** *n.* revers *m.*; (*bribe: sl.*) pot de vin *m.*
backing /'bækɪŋ/ *n.* appui *m.*
backlash /'bæklæʃ/ *n.* choc en retour *m.*, répercussions *f. pl.*
backlog /'bæklɒg/ *n.* accumulation (de travail) *f.*
backside /'bæksaɪd/ *n.* (*buttocks: fam.*) derrière *m.*
backstage /bæk'steɪdʒ/ *a. & adv.* dans les coulisses.
backstroke /'bækstrəʊk/ *n.* dos crawlé *m.*
backtrack /'bæktræk/ *v.i.* rebrousser chemin; (*change one's opinion*) faire marche arrière.
backward /'bækwəd/ *a.* (*step etc.*) en arrière; (*retarded*) arriéré.
backwards /'bækwədz/ *adv.* en arrière; (*walk*) à reculons; (*read*) à l'envers; (*fall*) à la renverse. **go** ~ **and forwards,** aller et venir.
backwater /'bækwɔ:tə(r)/ *n.* (*pej.*) trou perdu *m.*
bacon /'beɪkən/ *n.* lard *m.*; (*in rashers*) bacon *m.*
bacteria /bæk'tɪərɪə/ *n. pl.* bactéries *f. pl.* ~**l** *a.* bactérien.
bad /bæd/ *a.* (**worse, worst**) mauvais; (*wicked*) méchant; (*ill*) malade; (*accident*) grave; (*food*) gâté. **feel** ~, se sentir mal. ~ **language,** gros mots *m. pl.* ~**-mannered** *a.* mal élevé. ~**-tempered** *a.* grincheux. ~**ly** *adv.* mal; (*hurt*) grièvement. **want** ~**ly,** avoir grande envie de.
badge /bædʒ/ *n.* insigne *m.*; (*of identity*) plaque *f.*
badger /'bædʒə(r)/ *n.* blaireau *m.* —*v.t.* harceler.
badminton /'bædmɪntən/ *n.* badminton *m.*
baffle /'bæfl/ *v.t.* déconcerter.
bag /bæg/ *n.* sac *m.* ~**s,** (*luggage*) bagages *m. pl.*; (*under eyes*) poches *f. pl.* —*v.t.* (*p.t.* **bagged**) mettre en sac; (*take: fam.*) s'adjuger. ~**s of,** (*fam.*) beaucoup de.
baggage /'bægɪdʒ/ *n.* bagages *m. pl.*
baggy /'bægɪ/ *a.* (*trousers etc.*) qui fait des poches.
bagpipes /'bægpaɪps/ *n. pl.* cornemuse *f.*

Bahamas /bə'hɑːməz/ *n. pl.* **the ~**, les Bahamas *f. pl.*

bail[1] /beɪl/ *n.* caution *f.* **on ~**, sous caution. —*v.t.* mettre en liberté (provisoire) sous caution. **~ out**, (*fig.*) sortir d'affaire.

bail[2] /beɪl/ *n.* (*cricket*) bâtonnet *m.*

bail[3] /beɪl/ *v.t.* (*naut.*) écoper.

bailiff /'beɪlɪf/ *n.* huissier *m.*

bait /beɪt/ *n.* appât *m.* —*v.t.* appâter; (*fig.*) tourmenter.

bak|e /beɪk/ *v.t.* (faire) cuire (au four). —*v.i.* cuire (au four); (*person*) faire du pain *or* des gâteaux. **~er** *n.* boulang|er, -ère *m.,f.* **~ing** *n.* cuisson *f.* **~ing-powder** *n.* levure *f.*

bakery /'beɪkərɪ/ *n.* boulangerie *f.*

Balaclava /bælə'klɑːvə/ *n.* **~** (**helmet**), passe-montagne *m.*

balance /'bæləns/ *n.* équilibre *m.*; (*scales*) balance *f.*; (*outstanding sum*: *comm.*) solde *m.*; (*of payments, of trade*) balance *f.*; (*remainder*) reste *m.* —*v.t.* tenir en équilibre; (*weigh up & comm.*) balancer; (*budget*) équilibrer. —*v.i.* être en équilibre. **~d** *a.* équilibré.

balcony /'bælkənɪ/ *n.* balcon *m.*

bald /bɔːld/ *a.* (**-er, -est**) chauve; (*tyre*) lisse; (*fig.*) simple. **~ing** *a.* be **~ing**, perdre ses cheveux. **~ly** *adv.* (*speak*) crûment. **~ness** *n.* calvitie *f.*

balderdash /'bɔːldədæʃ/ *n.* balivernes *f. pl.*

bale[1] /beɪl/ *n.* (*of cotton*) balle *f.*; (*of straw*) botte *f.*

bale[2] /beɪl/ *v.i.* **~ out**, sauter en parachute.

baleful /'beɪlfʊl/ *a.* sinistre.

balk /bɔːk/ *v.t.* contrecarrer. —*v.i.* **~ at**, reculer devant.

ball[1] /bɔːl/ *n.* (*golf, tennis, etc.*) balle *f.*; (*football*) ballon *m.*; (*croquet, billiards, etc.*) boule *f.*; (*of wool*) pelote *f.*; (*sphere*) boule *f.* **~-bearing** *n.* roulement à billes *m.* **~-cock** *n.* robinet à flotteur *m.* **~-point** *n.* stylo à bille *m.*

ball[2] /bɔːl/ *n.* (*dance*) bal *m.*

ballad /'bæləd/ *n.* ballade *f.*

ballast /'bæləst/ *n.* lest *m.*

ballerina /bælə'riːnə/ *n.* ballerine *f.*

ballet /'bæleɪ/ *n.* ballet *m.*

ballistic /bə'lɪstɪk/ *a.* **~ missile**, engin balistique *m.*

balloon /bə'luːn/ *n.* ballon *m.*

ballot /'bælət/ *n.* scrutin *m.* **~** (**paper**), bulletin de vote *m.* **~-box** *n.* urne *f.* —*v.i.* (*p.t.* **balloted**) (*pol.*) voter. —*v.t.* (*members*) consulter par voie de scrutin.

ballroom /'bɔːlrʊm/ *n.* salle de bal *f.*

ballyhoo /bælɪ'huː/ *n.* (*publicity*) battage *m.*; (*uproar*) tapage *m.*

balm /bɑːm/ *n.* baume *m.* **~y** *a.* (*fragrant*) embaumé; (*mild*) doux; (*crazy*: *sl.*) dingue.

baloney /bə'ləʊnɪ/ *n.* (*sl.*) idioties *f. pl.*, calembredaines *f. pl.*

balustrade /bælə'streɪd/ *n.* balustrade *f.*

bamboo /bæm'buː/ *n.* bambou *m.*

bamboozle /bæm'buːzl/ *v.t.* (*cheat*: *sl.*) entortiller; (*confuse*: *sl.*) embrouiller.

ban /bæn/ *v.t.* (*p.t.* **banned**) interdire. **~ from**, exclure de. —*n.* interdiction *f.*

banal /bə'nɑːl, Amer.* 'beɪnl/ *a.* banal. **~ity** /-ælətɪ/ *n.* banalité *f.*

banana /bə'nɑːnə/ *n.* banane *f.*

band /bænd/ *n.* (*strip, group of people*) bande *f.*; (*mus.*) orchestre *m.*; (*mil.*) fanfare *f.* —*v.i.* **~ together**, se liguer.

bandage /'bændɪdʒ/ *n.* pansement *m.* —*v.t.* bander, panser.

bandit /'bændɪt/ *n.* bandit *m.*

bandstand /'bændstænd/ *n.* kiosque à musique *m.*

bandwagon /'bændwægən/ *n.* **climb on the ~**, prendre le train en marche.

bandy[1] /'bændɪ/ *v.t.* **~ about**, (*rumours, ideas, etc.*) faire circuler.

bandy[2] /'bændɪ/ *a.* (**-ier, -iest**) bancal.

bane /beɪn/ *n.* fléau *m.* **~ful** *a.* funeste.

bang /bæŋ/ *n.* (*blow, noise*) coup (violent) *m.*; (*explosion*) détonation *f.*; (*of door*) claquement *m.* —*v.t./i.* frapper; (*door*) claquer. —*int.* vlan. —*adv.* (*fam.*) exactement. **~ in the middle**, en plein milieu.

banger /'bæŋə(r)/ *n.* (*firework*) pétard *m.*; (*culin., sl.*) saucisse *f.* (**old**) **~**, (*car*: *sl.*) guimbarde *f.*

bangle /'bæŋgl/ *n.* bracelet *m.*

banish /'bænɪʃ/ *v.t.* bannir.

banisters /'bænɪstəz/ *n. pl.* rampe (d'escalier) *f.*

banjo /'bændʒəʊ/ (*pl.* **-os**) banjo *m.*

bank[1] /bæŋk/ *n.* (*of river*) rive *f.*; (*of earth*) talus *m.*; (*of sand*) banc *m.* —*v.t.* (*earth*) amonceler; (*fire*) couvrir. —*v.i.* (*aviat.*) virer.

bank[2] /bæŋk/ *n.* banque *f.* —*v.t.* mettre en banque. —*v.i.* **~ with**, avoir un compte à. **~ account**, compte en banque *m.* **~ holiday**, jour férié *m.* **~ on**, compter sur.

bank|ing /'bæŋkɪŋ/ *n.* opérations bancaires *f. pl.*; (*as career*) la banque. **~er** *n.* banquier *m.*

banknote /'bæŋknəʊt/ *n.* billet de banque *m.*

bankrupt /'bæŋkrʌpt/ *a.* be **~**, être en faillite. **go ~,** faire faillite. —*n.* failli(e) *m.* (*f.*). —*v.t.* mettre en faillite. **~cy** *n.* faillite *f.*

banner /'bænə(r)/ *n.* bannière *f.*

banns /bænz/ *n. pl.* bans *m. pl.*

banquet /'bæŋkwɪt/ *n.* banquet *m.*

bantamweight /'bæntəmweɪt/ *n.* poids coq *m.*

banter /'bæntə(r)/ *n.* plaisanterie *f.* —*v.i.* plaisanter.

bap /bæp/ *n.* petit pain *m.*

baptism /'bæptɪzəm/ *n.* baptême *m.*

Baptist /'bæptɪst/ *n.* baptiste *m.*/*f.*

baptize /bæp'taɪz/ *v.t.* baptiser.

bar /bɑː(r)/ *n.* (*of metal*) barre *f.*; (*on window & jurid.*) barreau *m.*; (*of chocolate*) tablette *f.*; (*pub*) bar *m.*; (*counter*) comptoir *m.*, bar *m.*; (*division: mus.*) mesure *f.*; (*fig.*) obstacle *m.* —*v.t.* (*p.t.* **barred**) (*obstruct*) barrer; (*prohibit*) interdire; (*exclude*) exclure. —*prep.* sauf. **~ of soap,** savonnette *f.*

Barbados /bɑː'beɪdɒs/ *n.* Barbade *f.*

barbarian /bɑː'beərɪən/ *n.* barbare *m.*/*f.*

barbari|c /bɑː'bærɪk/ *a.* barbare. **~ty** /-ətɪ/ *n.* barbarie *f.*

barbarous /'bɑːbərəs/ *a.* barbare.

barbecue /'bɑːbɪkjuː/ *n.* barbecue *m.* —*v.t.* griller, rôtir (au barbecue).

barbed /bɑːbd/ *a.* **~ wire,** fil de fer barbelé *m.*

barber /bɑː'bə(r)/ *n.* coiffeur *m.* (*pour hommes*).

barbiturate /bɑː'bɪtjʊrət/ *n.* barbiturique *m.*

bare /beə(r)/ *a.* (**-er, -est**) (*not covered or adorned*) nu; (*cupboard*) vide; (*mere*) simple. —*v.t.* mettre à nu.

bareback /'beə(r)bæk/ *adv.* à cru.

barefaced /'beə(r)feɪst/ *a.* éhonté.

bareheaded /'beə(r)hedɪd/ *a.* nu-tête *invar.*

barely /'beə(r)lɪ/ *adv.* à peine.

bargain /'bɑːgɪn/ *n.* (*deal*) marché *m.*; (*cheap thing*) occasion *f.* —*v.i.* négocier; (*haggle*) marchander. **~ for,** (*expect*) s'attendre à.

barge /bɑːdʒ/ *n.* chaland *m.* —*v.i.* **~ in,** interrompre; (*into room*) faire irruption.

baritone /'bærɪtəʊn/ *n.* baryton *m.*

bark[1] /bɑːk/ *n.* (*of tree*) écorce *f.*

bark[2] /bɑːk/ *n.* (*of dog*) aboiement *m.* —*v.i.* aboyer.

barley /'bɑːlɪ/ *n.* orge *f.* **~ sugar,** sucre d'orge *m.* **~-water** *n.* orgeat *m.*

barmaid /'bɑːmeɪd/ *n.* serveuse *f.*

barman /'bɑːmən/ *n.* (*pl.* **-men**) barman *m.*

barmy /'bɑːmɪ/ *a.* (*sl.*) dingue.

barn /bɑːn/ *n.* grange *f.*

barometer /bə'rɒmɪtə(r)/ *n.* baromètre *m.*

baron /'bærən/ *n.* baron *m.* **~ess** *n.* baronne *f.*

baroque /bə'rɒk, *Amer.* bə'rəʊk/ *a. & n.* baroque (*m.*).

barracks /'bærəks/ *n. pl.* caserne *f.*

barrage /'bærɑːʒ, *Amer.* bə'rɑːʒ/ *n.* (*barrier*) barrage *m.*; (*mil.*) tir de barrage *m.*

barrel /'bærəl/ *n.* tonneau *m.*; (*of oil*) baril *m.*; (*of gun*) canon *m.* **~-organ** *n.* orgue de Barbarie *m.*

barren /'bærən/ *a.* stérile.

barricade /bærɪ'keɪd/ *n.* barricade *f.* —*v.t.* barricader.

barrier /'bærɪə(r)/ *n.* barrière *f.*

barring /'bɑːrɪŋ/ *prep.* sauf.

barrister /'bærɪstə(r)/ *n.* avocat *m.*

barrow /'bærəʊ/ *n.* charrette à bras *f.*; (*wheelbarrow*) brouette *f.*

barter /'bɑːtə(r)/ *n.* troc *m.*, échange *m.* —*v.t.* troquer, échanger.

base /beɪs/ *n.* base *f.* —*v.t.* baser (**on,** sur; **in,** à). —*a.* bas, ignoble. **~less** *a.* sans fondement.

baseball /'beɪsbɔːl/ *n.* base-ball *m.*

baseboard /'beɪsbɔːd/ *n.* (*Amer.*) plinthe *f.*

basement /'beɪsmənt/ *n.* sous-sol *m.*

bash /bæʃ/ *v.t.* cogner. —*n.* coup (violent) *m.* **have a ~ at,** (*sl.*) s'essayer à. **~ed in,** enfoncé. **~ing** *n.* (*thrashing*) raclée *f.*

bashful /'bæʃfl/ *a.* timide.

basic /'beɪsɪk/ *a.* fondamental, élémentaire. **~ally** /-klɪ/ *adv.* au fond.

basilica /bə'zɪlɪkə/ *n.* basilique *f.*

basin /'beɪsn/ *n.* (*for liquids*) cuvette *f.*; (*for food*) bol *m.*; (*for washing*) lavabo *m.*; (*of river*) bassin *m.*

basis /'beɪsɪs/ *n.* (*pl.* **bases** /-siːz/) base *f.*

bask /bɑːsk/ *v.i.* se chauffer.

basket /'bɑːskɪt/ *n.* corbeille *f.*; (*with handle*) panier *m.*

basketball /'bɑːskɪtbɔːl/ *n.* basket (-ball) *m.*

Basque /bɑːsk/ *a.* & *n.* basque (*m.*/*f.*).

bass[1] /beɪs/ *a.* (*mus.*) bas, grave. —*n.* (*pl.* **basses**) basse *f.*

bass[2] /bæs/ *n. invar.* (*freshwater fish*) perche *f.*; (*sea*) bar *m.*

bassoon /bə'suːn/ *n.* basson *m.*

bastard /'bɑːstəd/ *n.* bâtard(e) *m.* (*f.*).; (*sl.*) sal|aud, -ope *m.*, *f.*

baste[1] /beɪst/ *v.t.* (*sew*) bâtir.

baste[2] /beɪst/ *v.t.* (*culin.*) arroser.

bastion /'bæstɪən/ *n.* bastion *m.*

bat[1] /bæt/ *n.* (*cricket etc.*) batte *f.*; (*table tennis*) raquette *f.* —*v.t.* (*p.t.* **batted**) (*ball*) frapper. **not ~ an eyelid**, ne pas sourciller.

bat[2] /bæt/ *n.* (*animal*) chauve-souris *f.*

batch /bætʃ/ *n.* (*of people*) fournée *f.*; (*of papers*) paquet *m.*; (*of goods*) lot *m.*

bated /'beɪtɪd/ *a.* **with ~ breath**, en retenant son souffle.

bath /bɑːθ/ *n.* (*pl.* **-s** /bɑːðz/) bain *m.*; (*tub*) baignoire *f.* **the ~s**, (*washing*) les bains (publics); (*swimming*) la piscine. —*v.t.* donner un bain à. —*v.i.* prendre un bain.

bathe /beɪð/ *v.t.* baigner. —*v.i.* se baigner; (*Amer.*) prendre un bain. —*n.* bain (de mer) *m.* **~r** /-ə(r)/ *n.* baigneu|r, -se *m.*, *f.*

bathing /'beɪðɪŋ/ *n.* baignade *f.* **~-costume** *n.* maillot de bain *m.*

bathrobe /'bæθrəʊb/ *m.* (*Amer.*) robe de chambre *f.*

bathroom /'bɑːθrʊm/ *n.* salle de bains *f.*

baton /'bætən/ *n.* (*mus.*, *mil.*) bâton *m.*

battalion /bə'tæljən/ *n.* bataillon *m.*

batter /'bætə(r)/ *v.t.* (*strike*) battre; (*ill-treat*) maltraiter. —*n.* (*culin.*) pâte (à frire) *f.* **~ed** *a.* (*pan*, *car*) cabossé; (*face*) meurtri. **~ing** *n.* **take a ~ing**, subir des coups.

battery /'bætərɪ/ *n.* (*mil.*, *auto.*) batterie *f.*; (*of torch*, *radio*) pile *f.*

battle /'bætl/ *n.* bataille *f.*; (*fig.*) lutte *f.* —*v.i.* se battre.

battleaxe /'bætələæks/ *n.* (*woman*: *fam.*) harpie *f.*

battlefield /'bætlfiːld/ *n.* champ de bataille *m.*

battlements /'bætlmənts/ *n. pl.* (*crenellations*) créneaux *m. pl.*; (*wall*) remparts *m. pl.*

battleship /'bætlʃɪp/ *n.* cuirassé *m.*

baulk /bɔːk/ *v.t.*/*i.* = **balk**.

bawd|y /'bɔːdɪ/ *a.* (**-ier**, **-iest**) paillard. **~iness** *n.* paillardise *f.*

bawl /bɔːl/ *v.t.*/*i.* brailler.

bay[1] /beɪ/ *n.* (*bot.*) laurier *m.*

bay[2] /beɪ/ *n.* (*geog.*, *archit.*) baie *f.*; (*area*) aire *f.* **~ window**, fenêtre en saillie *f.*

bay[3] /beɪ/ *n.* (*bark*) aboiement *m.* —*v.i.* aboyer. **at ~**, aux abois. **keep** or **hold at ~**, tenir à distance.

bayonet /'beɪənɪt/ *n.* baïonnette *f.*

bazaar /bə'zɑː(r)/ *n.* (*shop*, *market*) bazar *m.*; (*sale*) vente *f.*

bazooka /bə'zuːkə/ *n.* bazooka *m.*

BC *abbr.* (*before Christ*) avant J.-C.

be /biː/ *v.i.* (*present tense* **am**, **are**, **is**; *p.t.* **was**, **were**; *p.p.* **been**) être. **~ hot/right**/*etc.*, avoir chaud/raison/ *etc.* **he is 30**, (*age*) il a 30 ans. **it is fine/cold**/*etc.*, (*weather*) il fait beau/ froid/*etc.* **how are you?**, (*health*) comment allez-vous? **he is to come**, (*must*) il doit venir. **how much is it?**, (*cost*) ça fait or c'est combien? **~ reading/walking**/*etc.*, (*aux.*) lire/marcher/*etc.* **have been to**, avoir été à, être allé à.

beach /biːtʃ/ *n.* plage *f.*

beachcomber /'biːtʃkəʊmə(r)/ *n.* ramasseu|r, -se d'épaves *m.*, *f.*

beacon /'biːkən/ *n.* (*lighthouse*) phare *m.*; (*marker*) balise *f.*

bead /biːd/ *n.* perle *f.*

beak /biːk/ *n.* bec *m.*

beaker /'biːkə(r)/ *n.* gobelet *m.*

beam /biːm/ *n.* (*timber*) poutre *f.*; (*of light*) rayon *m.*; (*of torch*) faisceau *m.* —*v.i.* (*radiate*) rayonner. —*v.t.* (*broadcast*) diffuser. **~ing** *a.* radieux.

bean /biːn/ *n.* haricot *m.*; (*of coffee*) grain *m.*

beano /'biːnəʊ/ *n.* (*pl.* **-os**) (*sl.*) fête *f.*

bear[1] /beə(r)/ *n.* ours *m.*

bear[2] /beə(r)/ *v.t.* (*p.t.* **bore**, *p.p.* **borne**) (*carry*, *show*, *feel*) porter; (*endure*, *sustain*) supporter; (*child*) mettre au monde. —*v.i.* **~ left**/*etc.*, (*go*) prendre à gauche/*etc.* **~ in mind**, tenir compte de. **~ on**, se rapporter à. **~ out**, corroborer. **~ up!**, courage! **~able** *a.* supportable. **~er** *n.* por-teu|r, -se *m.*, *f.*

beard /bɪəd/ *n.* barbe *f.* **~ed** *a.* barbu.

bearing /'beərɪŋ/ *n.* (*behaviour*) maintien *m.*; (*relevance*) rapport *m.* **get one's ~s**, s'orienter.

beast /biːst/ *n.* bête *f.*; (*person*) brute *f.*

beastly /ˈbiːstlɪ/ *a.* (-ier, -iest) (*fam.*) détestable.

beat /biːt/ *v.t./i.* (*p.t.* **beat**, *p.p.* **beaten**) battre. —*n.* (*of drum, heart*) battement *m.*; (*mus.*) mesure *f.*; (*of policeman*) ronde *f.* ~ **a retreat**, battre en retraite. ~ **up**, tabasser. **it** ~**s me**, (*fam.*) ça me dépasse. ~**er** *n.* batteur *m.* ~**ing** *n.* raclée *f.*

beautician /bjuːˈtɪʃn/ *n.* esthéticien(ne) *m.* (*f.*).

beautiful /ˈbjuːtɪfl/ *a.* beau. ~**ly** /-flɪ/ *adv.* merveilleusement.

beautify /ˈbjuːtɪfaɪ/ *v.t.* embellir.

beauty /ˈbjuːtɪ/ *n.* beauté *f.* ~ **parlour**, institut de beauté *m.* ~ **spot**, grain de beauté *m.*; (*fig.*) site pittoresque *m.*

beaver /ˈbiːvə(r)/ *n.* castor *m.*

became /bɪˈkeɪm/ *see* **become**.

because /bɪˈkɒz/ *conj.* parce que. ~ **of**, à cause de.

beck /bek/ *n.* **at the** ~ **and call of**, aux ordres de.

beckon /ˈbekən/ *v.t./i.* ~ (**to**), faire signe à.

become /bɪˈkʌm/ *v.t./i.* (*p.t.* **became**, *p.p.* **become**) devenir; (*befit*) convenir à. **what has** ~ **of her?**, qu'est-elle devenue?

becoming /bɪˈkʌmɪŋ/ *a.* (*seemly*) bienséant; (*clothes*) seyant.

bed /bed/ *n.* lit *m.*; (*layer*) couche *f.*; (*of sea*) fond *m.*; (*of flowers*) parterre *m.* **go to** ~, (aller) se coucher. —*v.i.* (*p.t.* **bedded**). ~ **down**, se coucher. ~**ding** *n.* literie *f.*

bedbug /ˈbedbʌg/ *n.* punaise *f.*

bedclothes /ˈbedkləʊðz/ *n. pl.* couvertures *f. pl.* et draps *m. pl.*

bedevil /bɪˈdevl/ *v.t.* (*p.t.* **bedevilled**) (*confuse*) embrouiller; (*plague*) tourmenter.

bedlam /ˈbedləm/ *n.* chahut *m.*

bedpost /ˈbedpəʊst/ *n.* colonne de lit *f.*

bedraggled /bɪˈdrægld/ *a.* (*untidy*) débraillé.

bedridden /ˈbedrɪdn/ *a.* cloué au lit.

bedroom /ˈbedrʊm/ *n.* chambre à coucher *f.*

bedside /ˈbedsaɪd/ *n.* chevet *m.* ~ **book**, livre de chevet *m.*

bedsit, bedsitter /bedˈsɪt, -ə(r)/ *ns.* (*fam.*) = **bed-sitting-room**.

bed-sitting-room /bedˈsɪtɪŋrʊm/ *n.* chambre meublée *f.*, studio *m.*

bedspread /ˈbedspred/ *n.* dessus-de-lit *m. invar.*

bedtime /ˈbedtaɪm/ *n.* heure du coucher *f.*

bee /biː/ *n.* abeille *f.* **make a** ~**-line for**, aller tout droit vers.

beech /biːtʃ/ *n.* hêtre *m.*

beef /biːf/ *n.* bœuf *m.* —*v.i.* (*grumble*: *sl.*) rouspéter.

beefburger /ˈbiːfbɜːgə(r)/ *n.* hamburger *m.*

beefeater /ˈbiːfiːtə(r)/ *n.* hallebardier *m.*

beefy /ˈbiːfɪ/ *a.* (-ier, -iest) musclé.

beehive /ˈbiːhaɪv/ *n.* ruche *f.*

been /biːn/ *see* **be**.

beer /bɪə(r)/ *n.* bière *f.* ~**y** *a.* (*person, room*) qui sent la bière.

beet /biːt/ *n.* (*plant*) betterave *f.*

beetle /ˈbiːtl/ *n.* scarabée *m.*

beetroot /ˈbiːtruːt/ *n. invar.* (*culin.*) betterave *f.*

befall /bɪˈfɔːl/ *v.t.* (*p.t.* **befell**, *p.p.* **befallen**) arriver à.

befit /bɪˈfɪt/ *v.t.* (*p.t.* **befitted**) convenir à, seoir à.

before /bɪˈfɔː(r)/ *prep.* (*time*) avant; (*place*) devant. —*adv.* avant; (*already*) déjà. —*conj.* ~ **leaving**, avant de partir. ~ **he leaves**, avant qu'il (ne) parte.

beforehand /bɪˈfɔːhænd/ *adv.* à l'avance, avant.

befriend /bɪˈfrend/ *v.t.* offrir son amitié à, aider.

beg /beg/ *v.t.* (*p.t.* **begged**) (*entreat*) supplier (**to do**, de faire). ~ (**for**), (*money, food*) mendier; (*request*) solliciter, demander. —*v.i.* ~ (**for alms**), mendier. **it is going** ~**ging**, personne n'en veut.

began /bɪˈgæn/ *see* **begin**.

beget /bɪˈget/ *v.t.* (*p.t.* **begot**, *p.p.* **begotten**, *pres. p.* **begetting**) engendrer.

beggar /ˈbegə(r)/ *n.* mendiant(e) *m.* (*f.*).; (*sl.*) individu *m.*

begin /bɪˈgɪn/ *v.t./i.* (*p.t.* **began**, *p.p.* **begun**, *pres. p.* **beginning**) commencer (**to do**, à faire). ~**ner** *n.* débutant(e) *m.* (*f.*). ~**ning** *n.* commencement *m.*, début *m.*

begrudge /bɪˈgrʌdʒ/ *v.t.* (*envy*) envier; (*give unwillingly*) donner à contrecœur. ~ **doing**, faire à contrecœur.

beguile /bɪˈgaɪl/ *v.t.* tromper.

begun /bɪˈgʌn/ *see* **begin**.

behalf /bɪˈhɑːf/ *n.* **on** ~ **of**, pour; (*as*

behave /bɪˈheɪv/ *v.i.* se conduire. ～ (o.s.), se conduire bien.

behaviour /bɪˈheɪvjə(r)/ *n.* conduite *f.*, comportement *m.*

behead /bɪˈhed/ *v.t.* décapiter.

behind /bɪˈhaɪnd/ *prep.* derrière; (*in time*) en retard sur. —*adv.* derrière; (*late*) en retard. —*n.* (*buttocks*) derrière *m.*

behold /bɪˈhəʊld/ *v.t.* (*p.t.* **beheld**) (*old use*) voir.

beholden /bɪˈhəʊldən/ *a.* redevable (**to**, à; **for**, de).

beige /beɪʒ/ *a.* & *n.* beige (*m.*).

being /ˈbiːɪŋ/ *n.* (*person*) être *m.* **bring into** ～, créer. **come into** ～, prendre naissance.

belated /bɪˈleɪtɪd/ *a.* tardif.

belch /beltʃ/ *v.i.* faire un renvoi. —*v.t.* ～ **out**, (*smoke*) vomir. —*n.* renvoi *m.*

belfry /ˈbelfrɪ/ *n.* beffroi *m.*

Belgi|um /ˈbeldʒəm/ *n.* Belgique *f.* ～**an** *a.* & *n.* belge (*m./f.*).

belie /bɪˈlaɪ/ *v.t.* démentir.

belief /bɪˈliːf/ *n.* croyance *f.*; (*trust*) confiance *f.*; (*faith: relig.*) foi *f.*

believ|e /bɪˈliːv/ *v.t./i.* croire. ～**e in**, croire à; (*deity*) croire en. ～**able** *a.* croyable. ～**er** *n.* croyant(e) *m.* (*f.*).

belittle /bɪˈlɪtl/ *v.t.* déprécier.

bell /bel/ *n.* cloche *f.*; (*small*) clochette *f.*; (*on door*) sonnette *f.*; (*of phone*) sonnerie *f.*

belligerent /bɪˈlɪdʒərənt/ *a.* & *n.* belligérant(e) (*m.* (*f.*)).

bellow /ˈbeləʊ/ *v.t./i.* beugler.

bellows /ˈbeləʊz/ *n. pl.* soufflet *m.*

belly /ˈbelɪ/ *n.* ventre *m.* ～**-ache** *n.* mal au ventre *m.*

bellyful /ˈbelɪfʊl/ *n.* **have a** ～, en avoir plein le dos.

belong /bɪˈlɒŋ/ *v.i.* ～ **to**, appartenir à; (*club*) être membre de.

belongings /bɪˈlɒŋɪŋz/ *n. pl.* affaires *f. pl.*

beloved /bɪˈlʌvɪd/ *a.* & *n.* bienaimé(e) (*m.* (*f.*)).

below /bɪˈləʊ/ *prep.* au-dessous de; (*fig.*) indigne de. —*adv.* en dessous; (*on page*) ci-dessous.

belt /belt/ *n.* ceinture *f.*; (*techn.*) courroie *f.*; (*fig.*) région *f.* —*v.t.* (*hit: sl.*) rosser. —*v.i.* (*rush: sl.*) filer à toute allure.

bemused /bɪˈmjuːzd/ *a.* (*confused*) stupéfié; (*thoughtful*) pensif.

bench /bentʃ/ *n.* banc *m.*; (*working-table*) établi *m.* **the** ～, (*jurid.*) la magistrature (assise).

bend /bend/ *v.t./i.* (*p.t.* **bent**) (se) courber; (*arm, leg*) plier. —*n.* courbe *f.*; (*in road*) virage *m.*; (*of arm, knee*) pli *m.* ～ **down** *or* **over**, se pencher.

beneath /bɪˈniːθ/ *prep.* sous, audessous de; (*fig.*) indigne de. —*adv.* (au-)dessous.

benediction /benɪˈdɪkʃn/ *n.* bénédiction *f.*

benefactor /ˈbenɪfæktə(r)/ *n.* bienfai|teur, -trice *m.*, *f.*

beneficial /benɪˈfɪʃl/ *a.* avantageux, favorable.

benefit /ˈbenɪfɪt/ *n.* avantage *m.*; (*allowance*) allocation *f.* —*v.t.* (*p.t.* **benefited**, *pres. p.* **benefiting**) (*be useful to*) profiter à; (*do good to*) faire du bien à. ～ **from**, tirer profit de.

benevolen|t /bɪˈnevələnt/ *a.* bienveillant. ～**ce** *n.* bienveillance *f.*

benign /bɪˈnaɪn/ *a.* (*kindly*) bienveillant; (*med.*) bénin.

bent /bent/ *see* **bend**. —*n.* (*talent*) aptitude *f.*; (*inclination*) penchant *m.* —*a.* tordu; (*sl.*) corrompu. ～ **on doing**, décidé à faire.

bequeath /bɪˈkwiːð/ *v.t.* léguer.

bequest /bɪˈkwest/ *n.* legs *m.*

bereave|d /bɪˈriːvd/ *a.* **the** ～**d wife**/*etc.*, la femme/*etc.* du disparu. ～**ment** *n.* deuil *m.*

bereft /bɪˈreft/ *a.* ～ **of**, dénué de.

beret /ˈbereɪ/ *n.* béret *m.*

Bermuda /bəˈmjuːdə/ *n.* Bermudes *f. pl.*

berry /ˈberɪ/ *n.* baie *f.*

berserk /bəˈsɜːk/ *a.* **go** ～, devenir fou furieux.

berth /bɜːθ/ *n.* (*in train, ship*) couchette *f.*; (*anchorage*) mouillage *m.* —*v.i.* mouiller. **give a wide** ～ **to**, éviter.

beseech /bɪˈsiːtʃ/ *v.t.* (*p.t.* **besought**) implorer, supplier.

beset /bɪˈset/ *v.t.* (*p.t.* **beset**, *pres. p.* **besetting**) (*attack*) assaillir; (*surround*) entourer.

beside /bɪˈsaɪd/ *prep.* à côté de. ～ **o.s.**, hors de soi. ～ **the point**, sans rapport.

besides /bɪˈsaɪdz/ *prep.* en plus de; (*except*) excepté. —*adv.* en plus.

besiege /bɪˈsiːdʒ/ *v.t.* assiéger.

best /best/ *a.* meilleur. **the** ～ **book**

/etc., le meilleur livre/etc. —adv. (the)
~, (sing etc.) le mieux. —n. the ~
(one), le meilleur, la meilleure. ~
man, garçon d'honneur m. the ~
part of, la plus grande partie de. the
~ thing is to . . ., le mieux est de . . .
do one's ~, faire de son mieux. make
the ~ of, s'accommoder de.

bestow /bɪˈstəʊ/ v.t. accorder.

best-seller /bestˈselə(r)/ n. best-seller
m., succès de librairie m.

bet /bet/ n. pari m. —v.t./i. (p.t. bet or
betted, pres. p. betting) parier.

betray /bɪˈtreɪ/ v.t. trahir. ~al n.
trahison f.

betrothed /bɪˈtrəʊðd/ n. fiancé(e)
m. (f.).

better /ˈbetə(r)/ a. meilleur. —adv.
mieux. —v.t. (improve) améliorer; (do
better than) surpasser. —n. one's
~s, ses supérieurs m. pl. I had ~
go, je ferais mieux de partir. the
~ part of, la plus grande partie
de. get ~, s'améliorer; (recover) se
remettre. get the ~ of, l'emporter
sur.

betting-shop /ˈbetɪŋʃɒp/ n. bureau de
P.M.U. m.

between /bɪˈtwiːn/ prep. entre. —adv.
in ~, au milieu.

beverage /ˈbevərɪdʒ/ n. boisson f.

bevy /ˈbevɪ/ n. essaim m.

beware /bɪˈweə(r)/ v.i. prendre garde
(of, à).

bewilder /bɪˈwɪldə(r)/ v.t. désorienter,
embarrasser. ~ment n. désorienta-
tion f.

bewitch /bɪˈwɪtʃ/ v.t. enchanter.

beyond /bɪˈjɒnd/ prep. au-delà de;
(doubt, reach) hors de; (besides) excepté. —adv. au-delà. it is ~ me, ça
me dépasse.

bias /ˈbaɪəs/ n. (inclination) penchant
m.; (prejudice) préjugé m. —v.t. (p.t.
biased) influencer. ~ed a. partial.

bib /bɪb/ n. bavoir m.

Bible /ˈbaɪbl/ n. Bible f.

biblical /ˈbɪblɪkl/ a. biblique.

bibliography /bɪblɪˈɒɡrəfɪ/ n. biblio-
graphie f.

bicarbonate /baɪˈkɑːbənət/ n. bicarbonate m.

biceps /ˈbaɪseps/ n. biceps m.

bicker /ˈbɪkə(r)/ v.i. se chamailler.

bicycle /ˈbaɪsɪkl/ n. bicyclette f. —v.i.
faire de la bicyclette.

bid[1] /bɪd/ n. (at auction) offre f.,
enchère f.; (attempt) tentative f.

—v.t./i. (p.t. & p.p. bid, pres. p.
bidding) (offer) faire une offre or
une enchère (de). the highest ~der,
le plus offrant.

bid[2] /bɪd/ v.t. (p.t. bade /bæd/, p.p.
bidden or bid, pres. p. bidding)
ordonner; (say) dire. ~ding n. ordre
m.

bide /baɪd/ v.t. ~ one's time, attendre
le bon moment.

biennial /baɪˈenɪəl/ a. biennal.

bifocals /baɪˈfəʊklz/ n. pl. lunettes
bifocales f. pl.

big /bɪɡ/ a. (bigger, biggest) grand; (in
bulk) gros; (generous: sl.) généreux.
—adv. (fam.) en grand; (earn: fam.)
gros. ~headed a. prétentieux. think
~, (fam.) voir grand.

bigam|y /ˈbɪɡəmɪ/ n. bigamie f. ~ist n.
bigame m./f. ~ous a. bigame.

bigot /ˈbɪɡət/ n. fanatique m./f. ~ed
a. fanatique. ~ry n. fanatisme m.

bigwig /ˈbɪɡwɪɡ/ n. (fam.) gros bonnet
m., ponte m.

bike /baɪk/ n. (fam.) vélo m.

bikini /bɪˈkiːnɪ/ n. (pl. -is) bikini m.

bilberry /ˈbɪlbərɪ/ n. myrtille f.

bile /baɪl/ n. bile f.

bilingual /baɪˈlɪŋɡwəl/ a. bilingue.

bilious /ˈbɪlɪəs/ a. bilieux.

bill[1] /bɪl/ n. (invoice) facture f.; (in
hotel, for gas, etc.) note f.; (in restaurant) addition f.; (of sale) acte m.;
(pol.) projet de loi m.; (banknote:
Amer.) billet de banque m. —v.t. (person: comm.) envoyer la facture à;
(theatre) mettre à l'affiche.

bill[2] /bɪl/ n. (of bird) bec m.

billboard /ˈbɪlbɔːd/ n. panneau d'affichage m.

billet /ˈbɪlɪt/ n. cantonnement m. —v.t.
(p.t. billeted) cantonner (on, chez).

billiards /ˈbɪljədz/ n. billard m.

billion /ˈbɪljən/ n. billion m.; (Amer.)
milliard m.

billy-goat /ˈbɪlɪɡəʊt/ n. bouc m.

bin /bɪn/ n. (for rubbish, litter) boîte
(à ordures) f.; (for bread) huche f.,
coffre m.

bind /baɪnd/ v.t. (p.t. bound) lier;
(book) relier; (jurid.) obliger. —n.
(bore: sl.) plaie f. be ~ing on, être
obligatoire pour.

binding /ˈbaɪndɪŋ/ n. reliure f.

binge /bɪndʒ/ n. go on a ~, (spree: sl.)
faire la bringue.

bingo /ˈbɪŋɡəʊ/ n. loto m.

binoculars /bɪˈnɒkjʊləz/ n. pl. jumelles f. pl.

biochemistry /baɪəʊˈkemɪstrɪ/ n. biochimie f.

biograph|y /baɪˈɒɡrəfɪ/ n. biographie f. ~**er** n. biographe m./f.

biolog|y /baɪˈɒlədʒɪ/ n. biologie f. ~**ical** /-əˈlɒdʒɪkl/ a. biologique. ~**ist** n. biologiste m./f.

biped /ˈbaɪped/ n. bipède m.

birch /bɜːtʃ/ n. (tree) bouleau m.; (whip) verge f., fouet m.

bird /bɜːd/ n. oiseau m.; (fam.) individu m.; (girl: sl.) poule f.

Biro /ˈbaɪərəʊ/ n. (pl. -os) (P.) stylo à bille m., Bic m. (P.).

birth /bɜːθ/ n. naissance f. ~ **certificate**, acte de naissance m. ~**control** n. contrôle des naissances m. ~**rate** n. natalité f.

birthday /ˈbɜːθdeɪ/ n. anniversaire m.

birthmark /ˈbɜːθmɑːk/ n. tache de vin f., envie f.

birthright /ˈbɜːθraɪt/ n. patrimoine m.

biscuit /ˈbɪskɪt/ n. biscuit m.; (Amer.) petit pain (au lait) m.

bisect /baɪˈsekt/ v.t. couper en deux.

bishop /ˈbɪʃəp/ n. évêque m.

bit[1] /bɪt/ n. morceau m.; (of horse) mors m.; (of tool) mèche f. **a** ~, (a little) un peu.

bit[2] /bɪt/ see bite.

bitch /bɪtʃ/ n. chienne f.; (woman: fam.) garce f. —v.i. (grumble: fam.) râler. ~**y** a. (fam.) vache.

bite /baɪt/ v.t./i. (p.t. bit, p.p. bitten) mordre. —n. morsure f.; (mouthful) bouchée f. ~ **one's nails**, se ronger les ongles. **have a** ~, manger un morceau.

biting /ˈbaɪtɪŋ/ a. mordant.

bitter /ˈbɪtə(r)/ a. amer; (weather) glacial, âpre. —n. bière anglaise f. ~**ly** adv. amèrement. **it is** ~**ly cold**, il fait un temps glacial. ~**ness** n. amertume f.

bitty /ˈbɪtɪ/ a. décousu.

bizarre /bɪˈzɑː(r)/ a. bizarre.

blab /blæb/ v.i. (p.t. blabbed) jaser.

black /blæk/ a. (-er, -est) noir. —n. (colour) noir m. **B**~, (person) Noir(e) m. (f.). —v.t. noircir; (goods) boycotter. ~ **and blue**, couvert de bleus. ~ **eye**, œil poché m. ~ **list**, liste noire f. ~ **market**, marché noir m. ~ **sheep**, brebis galeuse f. ~ **spot**, point noir m.

blackberry /ˈblækbərɪ/ n. mûre f.

blackbird /ˈblækbɜːd/ n. merle m.

blackboard /ˈblækbɔːd/ n. tableau noir m.

blackcurrant /ˈblækkʌrənt/ n. cassis m.

blacken /ˈblækən/ v.t./i. noircir.

blackguard /ˈblægɑːd, Amer. ˈblægəd/ n. canaille f.

blackleg /ˈblækleg/ n. jaune m.

blacklist /ˈblæklɪst/ v.t. mettre sur la liste noire or à l'index.

blackmail /ˈblækmeɪl/ n. chantage m. —v.t. faire chanter. ~**er** n. maîtrechanteur m.

blackout /ˈblækaʊt/ n. panne d'électricité f.; (med.) syncope f.

blacksmith /ˈblæksmɪθ/ n. forgeron m.

bladder /ˈblædə(r)/ n. vessie f.

blade /bleɪd/ n. (of knife etc.) lame f.; (of propeller, oar) pale f. ~ **of grass**, brin d'herbe m.

blame /bleɪm/ v.t. accuser. —n. faute f. ~ **s.o. for sth.**, reprocher qch. à qn. **he is to** ~, il est responsable (for, de). ~**less** a. irréprochable.

bland /blænd/ a. (-er, -est) (gentle) doux; (insipid) fade.

blank /blæŋk/ a. blanc; (look) vide; (cheque) en blanc. —n. blanc m. ~ (**cartridge**), cartouche à blanc f.

blanket /ˈblæŋkɪt/ n. couverture f.; (layer: fig.) couche f. —v.t. (p.t. blanketed) recouvrir.

blare /bleə(r)/ v.t./i. beugler. —n. vacarme m., beuglement m.

blarney /ˈblɑːnɪ/ n. boniment m.

blasé /ˈblɑːzeɪ/ a. blasé.

blaspheme /blæsˈfiːm/ v.t./i. blasphémer.

blasphem|y /ˈblæsfəmɪ/ n. blasphème m. ~**ous** a. blasphématoire; (person) blasphémateur.

blast /blɑːst/ n. explosion f.; (wave of air) souffle m.; (of wind) rafale f.; (noise from siren etc.) coup m. —v.t. (blow up) faire sauter. ~**ed** a. (fam.) maudit, fichu. ~**furnace** n. haut fourneau m. ~ **off**, être mis à feu. ~-**off** n. mise à feu f.

blatant /ˈbleɪtnt/ a. (obvious) flagrant; (shameless) éhonté.

blaze[1] /bleɪz/ n. flamme f.; (conflagration) incendie m.; (fig.) éclat m. —v.i. (fire) flamber; (sky, eyes, etc.) flamboyer.

blaze[2] /bleɪz/ v.t. ~ **a trail**, montrer or marquer la voie.

blazer /'bleɪzə(r)/ n. blazer m.

bleach /bliːtʃ/ n. décolorant m.; (for domestic use) eau de Javel f. —v.t./i. blanchir; (hair) décolorer.

bleak /bliːk/ a. (-er, -est) morne.

bleary /'blɪərɪ/ a. (eyes) voilé.

bleat /bliːt/ n. bêlement m. —v.i. bêler.

bleed /bliːd/ v.t./i. (p.t. bled) saigner.

bleep /bliːp/ n. bip m. ～er n. bip m.

blemish /'blemɪʃ/ n. tare f., défaut m.; (on reputation) tache f. —v.t. entacher.

blend /blend/ v.t./i. (se) mélanger. —n. mélange m.

bless /bles/ v.t. bénir. **be ～ed with,** avoir le bonheur de posséder. ～**ing** n. bénédiction f.; (benefit) avantage m.; (stroke of luck) chance f.

blessed /'blesɪd/ a. (holy) saint; (damned: fam.) sacré.

blew /bluː/ see blow[1].

blight /blaɪt/ n. (disease: bot.) rouille f.; (fig.) fléau m.

blighter /'blaɪtə(r)/ n. (sl.) type m.

blind /blaɪnd/ a. aveugle. —v.t. aveugler. —n. (on window) store m.; (deception) feinte f. **be ～ to,** ne pas voir. ～ **alley,** impasse f. ～ **man,** aveugle m. ～**ers** n. pl. (Amer.) œillères f. pl. ～**ly** adv. aveuglément. ～**ness** n. cécité f.

blindfold /'blaɪndfəʊld/ a. & adv. les yeux bandés. —n. bandeau m. —v.t. bander les yeux à.

blink /blɪŋk/ v.i. cligner des yeux; (of light) clignoter.

blinkers /'blɪŋkəz/ n. pl. œillères f. pl.

bliss /blɪs/ n. félicité f. ～**ful** a. bienheureux. ～**fully** adv. joyeusement, merveilleusement.

blister /'blɪstə(r)/ n. ampoule f. —v.i. se couvrir d'ampoules.

blithe /blaɪð/ a. joyeux.

blitz /blɪts/ n. (aviat.) raid éclair m. —v.t. bombarder.

blizzard /'blɪzəd/ n. tempête de neige f.

bloated /'bləʊtɪd/ a. gonflé.

bloater /'bləʊtə(r)/ n. hareng saur m.

blob /blɒb/ n. (drop) (grosse) goutte f.; (stain) tache f.

bloc /blɒk/ n. bloc m.

block /blɒk/ n. bloc m.; (buildings) pâté de maisons m.; (in pipe) obstruction f. ～ (of flats), immeuble m. —v.t. bloquer. ～ **letters,** majuscules f. pl. ～**age** n. obstruction f.

blockade /blɒ'keɪd/ n. blocus m. —v.t. bloquer.

blockhead /'blɒkhed/ n. imbécile m./f.

bloke /bləʊk/ n. (fam.) type m.

blond /blɒnd/ a. & n. blond (m.).

blonde /blɒnd/ a. & n. blonde (f.).

blood /blʌd/ n. sang m. —a. (donor, bath, etc.) de sang; (bank, poisoning, etc.) du sang; (group, vessel) sanguin. ～**-curdling** a. à tourner le sang. ～**less** a. (fig.) pacifique. ～**-pressure** n. tension artérielle f.

bloodhound /'blʌdhaʊnd/ n. limier m.

bloodshed /'blʌdʃed/ n. effusion de sang f.

bloodshot /'blʌdʃɒt/ a. injecté de sang.

bloodstream /'blʌdstriːm/ n. sang m.

bloodthirsty /'blʌdθɜːstɪ/ a. sanguinaire.

bloody /'blʌdɪ/ a. (-ier, -iest) sanglant; (sl.) sacré. —adv. (sl.) vachement. ～**-minded** a. (fam.) hargneux, obstiné.

bloom /bluːm/ n. fleur f. —v.i. fleurir; (fig.) s'épanouir.

bloomer /'bluːmə(r)/ n. (sl.) gaffe f.

blossom /'blɒsəm/ n. fleur(s) f. (pl.). —v.i. fleurir; (person: fig.) s'épanouir.

blot /blɒt/ n. tache f. —v.t. (p.t. blotted) tacher; (dry) sécher. ～ **out,** effacer. ～**ter,** ～**ting-paper** ns. buvard m.

blotch /blɒtʃ/ n. tache f. ～**y** a. couvert de taches.

blouse /blaʊz/ n. chemisier m.

blow[1] /bləʊ/ v.t./i. (p.t. blew, p.p. blown) souffler; (fuse) (faire) sauter; (squander: sl.) perdre. ～ **one's nose,** se moucher. ～ **a whistle,** siffler. ～ **away** or **off,** emporter. ～**-dry** v.t. sécher. ～ **out,** (candle) souffler. ～**out** n. (of tyre) éclatement m. ～ **over,** passer. ～ **up,** (faire) sauter; (tyre) gonfler.

blow[2] /bləʊ/ n. coup m.

blowlamp /'bləʊlæmp/ n. chalumeau m.

blown /bləʊn/ see blow[1].

blowtorch /'bləʊtɔːtʃ/ n. (Amer.) chalumeau m.

blowy /'bləʊɪ/ a. **it is ～,** il y a du vent.

blowzy /'blaʊzɪ/ a. débraillé.

blubber /'blʌbə(r)/ n. graisse de baleine f.

bludgeon /'blʌdʒən/ n. gourdin m. —v.t. matraquer.

blue /bluː/ a. (-er, -est) bleu. —n. bleu m. **come out of the ～,** être inattendu. **have the ～s,** avoir le cafard.

bluebell /'blu:bel/ *n.* jacinthe des bois *f.*

bluebottle /'blu:bɒtl/ *n.* mouche à viande *f.*

blueprint /'blu:prɪnt/ *n.* plan *m.*

bluff[1] /blʌf/ *v.t./i.* bluffer. —*n.* bluff *m.*

bluff[2] /blʌf/ *a.* (*person*) brusque.

blunder /'blʌndə(r)/ *v.i.* faire une gaffe; (*move*) avancer à tâtons. —*n.* gaffe *f.*

blunt /blʌnt/ *a.* (*knife*) émoussé; (*person*) brusque. —*v.t.* émousser. ~**ly** *adv.* carrément. ~**ness** *n.* brusquerie *f.*

blur /blɜː(r)/ *n.* tache floue *f.* —*v.t.* (*p.t.* **blurred**) rendre flou.

blurb /blɜːb/ *n.* résumé publicitaire *m.*

blurt /blɜːt/ *v.t.* ~ **out**, lâcher, dire.

blush /blʌʃ/ *v.i.* rougir. —*n.* rougeur *f.*

bluster /'blʌstə(r)/ *v.i.* (*wind*) faire rage; (*swagger*) fanfaronner. ~**y** *a.* à bourrasques.

boar /bɔː(r)/ *n.* sanglier *m.*

board /bɔːd/ *n.* planche *f.*; (*for notices*) tableau *m.*; (*food*) pension *f.*; (*committee*) conseil *m.* —*v.t./i.* monter à bord (de). **on** ~, à bord. ~ **up**, boucher. ~ **with**, être en pension chez. ~**er** *n.* pensionnaire *m./f.* ~**ing-house** *n.* pension (de famille) *f.* ~**ing-school** *n.* pensionnat *m.*, pension *f.*

boast /bəʊst/ *v.i.* se vanter. —*v.t.* s'enorgueillir de. —*n.* vantardise *f.* ~**er** *n.* vantard(e) *m.* (*f.*). ~**ful** *a.* vantard. ~**fully** *adv.* en se vantant.

boat /bəʊt/ *n.* bateau *m.*; (*small*) canot *m.* **in the same** ~, logé à la même enseigne. ~**ing** *n.* canotage *m.*

boatswain /'bəʊsn/ *n.* maître d'équipage *m.*

bob[1] /bɒb/ *v.i.* (*p.t.* **bobbed**). ~ **up and down**, monter et descendre.

bob[2] /bɒb/ *n. invar.* (*sl.*) shilling *m.*

bobbin /'bɒbɪn/ *n.* bobine *f.*

bobby /'bɒbɪ/ *n.* (*fam.*) flic *m.*

bobsleigh /'bɒbsleɪ/ *n.* bob(sleigh) *m.*

bode /bəʊd/ *v.i.* ~ **well/ill**, être de bon/mauvais augure.

bodice /'bɒdɪs/ *n.* corsage *m.*

bodily /'bɒdɪlɪ/ *a.* physique, corporel. —*adv.* physiquement; (*in person*) en personne.

body /'bɒdɪ/ *n.* corps *m.*; (*mass*) masse *f.*; (*organization*) organisme *m.* ~(**work**), (*auto.*) carrosserie *f.* **the main** ~ **of**, le gros de.

bodyguard /'bɒdɪgɑːd/ *n.* garde du corps *m.*

boffin /'bɒfɪn/ *n.* (*sl.*) chercheu/r, -se (scientifique) *m., f.*

bog /bɒg/ *n.* marécage *m.* —*v.t.* (*p.t.* **bogged**). **get** ~**ged down**, s'embourber.

boggle /'bɒgl/ *v.i.* **the mind** ~**s**, on est stupéfait.

bogus /'bəʊgəs/ *a.* faux.

bogy /'bəʊgɪ/ *n.* (*annoyance*) embêtement *m.* ~(**man**), croquemitaine *m.*

boil[1] /bɔɪl/ *n.* furoncle *m.*

boil[2] /bɔɪl/ *v.t./i.* (faire) bouillir. ~ **down to**, se ramener à. ~ **over**, déborder. ~**ing hot**, bouillant. ~**ed** *a.* (*egg*) à la coque; (*potatoes*) à l'eau.

boiler /'bɔɪlə(r)/ *n.* chaudière *f.* ~ **suit**, bleu (de travail) *m.*

boisterous /'bɔɪstərəs/ *a.* tapageur.

bold /bəʊld/ *a.* (**-er, -est**) hardi. ~**ness** *n.* hardiesse *f.*

Bolivia /bə'lɪvɪə/ *n.* Bolivie *f.* ~**n** *a.* & *n.* bolivien(ne) (*m.* (*f.*)).

bollard /'bɒləd/ *n.* (*on road*) borne *f.*

bolster /'bəʊlstə(r)/ *n.* traversin *m.* —*v.t.* soutenir.

bolt /bəʊlt/ *n.* verrou *m.*; (*for nut*) boulon *m.*; (*lightning*) éclair *m.* —*v.t.* (*door etc.*) verrouiller; (*food*) engouffrer. —*v.i.* se sauver. ~ **upright**, tout droit.

bomb /bɒm/ *n.* bombe *f.* —*v.t.* bombarder. ~**er** *n.* (*aircraft*) bombardier *m.*; (*person*) plastiqueur *m.*

bombard /bɒm'bɑːd/ *v.t.* bombarder.

bombastic /bɒm'bæstɪk/ *a.* grandiloquent.

bombshell /'bɒmʃel/ *n.* **be a** ~, tomber comme une bombe.

bona fide /bəʊnə'faɪdɪ/ *a.* de bonne foi.

bonanza /bə'nænzə/ *n.* aubaine *f.*

bond /bɒnd/ *n.* (*agreement*) engagement *m.*; (*link*) lien *m.*; (*comm.*) obligation *f.*, bon *m.* **in** ~, (entreposé) en douane.

bondage /'bɒndɪdʒ/ *n.* esclavage *m.*

bone /bəʊn/ *n.* os *m.*; (*of fish*) arête *f.* —*v.t.* désosser. ~**-dry** *a.* tout à fait sec. ~ **idle**, paresseux comme une couleuvre.

bonfire /'bɒnfaɪə(r)/ *n.* feu *m.*; (*for celebration*) feu de joie *m.*

bonnet /'bɒnɪt/ *n.* (*hat*) bonnet *m.*; (*of vehicle*) capot *m.*

bonus /'bəʊnəs/ *n.* prime *f.*

bony /'bəʊnɪ/ *a.* (**-ier, -iest**) (*thin*) osseux; (*meat*) plein d'os; (*fish*) plein d'arêtes.

boo /buː/ *int.* hou. —*v.t.*/*i.* huer. —*n.* huée *f.*

boob /buːb/ *n.* (*blunder*: *sl.*) gaffe *f.* —*v.i.* (*sl.*) gaffer.

booby /'buːbɪ/ *n.* nigaud(e) *m.* (*f.*) ∼ **trap**, engin piégé *m.* ∼**-trap** *v.t.* (*p.t.* -**trapped**) piéger.

book /bʊk/ *n.* livre *m.*; (*of tickets etc.*) carnet *m.* ∼**s**, (*comm.*) comptes *m. pl.* —*v.t.* (*reserve*) retenir; (*write down*) inscrire. —*v.i.* retenir des places. ∼**able** *a.* qu'on peut retenir. (**fully**) ∼**ed**, complet. ∼**ing office**, guichet *m.*

bookcase /'bʊkkeɪs/ *n.* bibliothèque *f.*

bookkeeping /'bʊkkiːpɪŋ/ *n.* comptabilité *f.*

booklet /'bʊklɪt/ *n.* brochure *f.*

bookmaker /'bʊkmeɪkə(r)/ *n.* bookmaker *m.*

bookseller /'bʊkselə(r)/ *n.* libraire *m.*/*f.*

bookshop /'bʊkʃɒp/ *n.* librairie *f.*

bookstall /'bʊkstɔːl/ *n.* kiosque (à journaux) *m.*

boom /buːm/ *v.i.* (*gun, wind, etc.*) gronder; (*trade*) prospérer. —*n.* grondement *m.*; (*comm.*) boom *m.*, prospérité *f.*

boon /buːn/ *n.* (*benefit*) aubaine *f.*

boor /bʊə(r)/ *n.* rustre *m.* ∼**ish** *a.* rustre.

boost /buːst/ *v.t.* développer, stimuler; (*morale*) remonter; (*price*) augmenter; (*publicize*) faire de la réclame pour. —*n.* **give a** ∼ **to,** = **boost.**

boot /buːt/ *n.* botte *f.*, chaussure (montante) *f.*; (*of vehicle*) coffre *m.* **get the** ∼, (*sl.*) être mis à la porte.

booth /buːð/ *n.* (*for telephone*) cabine *f.*; (*at fair*) baraque *f.*

booty /'buːtɪ/ *n.* butin *m.*

booze /buːz/ *v.i.* (*fam.*) boire (beaucoup). —*n.* (*fam.*) alcool *m.*; (*spree*) beuverie *f.*

border /'bɔːdə(r)/ *n.* (*edge*) bord *m.*; (*frontier*) frontière *f.*; (*in garden*) bordure *f.* —*v.i.* ∼ **on,** (*be next to, come close to*) être voisin de, avoisiner.

borderline /'bɔːdəlaɪn/ *n.* ligne de démarcation *f.* ∼ **case,** cas limite *m.*

bore[1] /bɔː(r)/ *see* **bear**[2].

bore[2] /bɔː(r)/ *v.t.*/*i.* (*techn.*) forer.

bore[3] /bɔː(r)/ *v.t.* ennuyer. —*n.* raseu|r, -se *m.*, *f.*; (*thing*) ennui *m.* **be**

∼**d,** s'ennuyer. ∼**dom** *n.* ennui *m.*

boring *a.* ennuyeux.

born /bɔːn/ *a.* né. **be** ∼, naître.

borne /bɔːn/ *see* **bear**[2].

borough /'bʌrə/ *n.* municipalité *f.*

borrow /'bɒrəʊ/ *v.t.* emprunter (**from,** à). ∼**ing** *n.* emprunt *m.*

Borstal /'bɔːstl/ *n.* maison d'éducation surveillée *f.*

bosom /'bʊzəm/ *n.* sein *m.* ∼ **friend,** ami(e) intime *m.* (*f.*).

boss /bɒs/ *n.* (*fam.*) patron(ne) *m.* (*f.*) —*v.t.* ∼ (**about**), (*fam.*) donner des ordres à, régenter.

bossy /'bɒsɪ/ *a.* autoritaire.

botan|y /'bɒtənɪ/ *n.* botanique *f.* ∼**ical** /bə'tænɪkl/ *a.* botanique. ∼**ist** *n.* botaniste *m.*/*f.*

botch /bɒtʃ/ *v.t.* bâcler, saboter.

both /bəʊθ/ *a.* les deux. —*pron.* tous *or* toutes (les) deux, l'un(e) et l'autre. —*adv.* à la fois.

bother /'bɒðə(r)/ *v.t.* (*annoy, worry*) ennuyer; (*disturb*) déranger. —*v.i.* se déranger. —*n.* ennui *m.*; (*effort*) peine *f.* ∼ **about,** (*deal with*) s'occuper de; (*worry about*) s'inquiéter de. ∼ **doing** *or* **to do,** prendre la peine de faire.

bottle /'bɒtl/ *n.* bouteille *f.*; (*for baby*) biberon *m.* —*v.t.* mettre en bouteille(s). ∼**-opener** *n.* ouvre-bouteille(s) *m.* ∼ **up,** étouffer.

bottleneck /'bɒtlnek/ *n.* (*traffic jam*) bouchon *m.*

bottom /'bɒtəm/ *n.* fond *m.*; (*of hill, page, etc.*) bas *m.*; (*buttocks*) derrière *m.* —*a.* inférieur, du bas. ∼**less** *a.* insondable.

bough /baʊ/ *n.* rameau *m.*

bought /bɔːt/ *see* **buy.**

boulder /'bəʊldə(r)/ *n.* rocher *m.*

boulevard /'buːləvɑːd/ *n.* boulevard *m.*

bounce /baʊns/ *v.i.* rebondir; (*person*) faire des bonds, bondir; (*cheque*: *sl.*) être refusé. —*v.t.* faire rebondir. —*n.* rebond *m.*

bouncing /'baʊnsɪŋ/ *a.* robuste.

bound[1] /baʊnd/ *v.i.* (*leap*) bondir. —*n.* bond *m.*

bound[2] /baʊnd/ *see* **bind.** —*a.* **be** ∼ **for,** être en route pour, aller vers. ∼ **to,** (*obliged*) obligé de; (*certain*) sûr de.

boundary /'baʊndrɪ/ *n.* limite *f.*

bound|s /baʊndz/ *n. pl.* limites *f. pl.* **out of** ∼**s,** interdit. ∼**ed by,** limité par. ∼**less** *a.* sans bornes.

bountiful /'baʊntɪfl/ a. généreux.
bouquet /bʊ'keɪ/ n. bouquet m.
bout /baʊt/ n. période f.; (med.) accès m.; (boxing) combat m.
boutique /buː'tiːk/ n. boutique (de mode) f.
bow[1] /baʊ/ n. (weapon) arc m.; (mus.) archet m.; (knot) nœud m. **~-legged** a. aux jambes arquées. **~-tie** n. nœud papillon m.
bow[2] /baʊ/ n. (with head) salut m.; (with body) révérence f. —v.t./i. (s')incliner.
bow[3] /baʊ/ n. (naut.) proue f.
bowels /'baʊəlz/ n. pl. intestins m. pl.; (fig.) entrailles f. pl.
bowl[1] /bəʊl/ n. cuvette f.; (for food) bol m.
bowl[2] /bəʊl/ n. (ball) boule f. —v.t./i. (cricket) lancer. **~ over**, bouleverser. **~ing** n. jeu de boules m. **~ing-alley** n. bowling m.
bowler[1] /'bəʊlə(r)/ n. (cricket) lanceur m.
bowler[2] /'bəʊlə(r)/ n. **~ (hat)**, (chapeau) melon m.
box[1] /bɒks/ n. boîte f.; (theatre) loge f. —v.t. mettre en boîte. **~ in**, enfermer. **~-office** n. bureau de location m.
box[2] /bɒks/ v.t./i. (sport) boxer. **~ s.o.'s ears**, gifler qn. **~ing** n. boxe f. **Boxing Day**, le lendemain de Noël.
boy /bɔɪ/ n. garçon m. **~-friend** n. (petit) ami m. **~hood** n. enfance f. **~ish** a. enfantin, de garçon.
boycott /'bɔɪkɒt/ v.t. boycotter. —n. boycottage m.
bra /brɑː/ n. soutien-gorge m.
brace /breɪs/ n. (fastener) attache f.; (dental) appareil m. **~s**, (for trousers) bretelles f. pl. —v.t. soutenir. **~ o.s.**, rassembler ses forces.
bracelet /'breɪslɪt/ n. bracelet m.
bracing /'breɪsɪŋ/ a. vivifiant.
bracken /'brækən/ n. fougère f.
bracket /'brækɪt/ n. (for shelf etc.) tasseau m., support m.; (group) tranche f. **(round) ~**, (printing sign) parenthèse f. **(square) ~**, crochet m. —v.t. (p.t. **bracketed**) mettre entre parenthèses or crochets.
brag /bræg/ v.i. (p.t. **bragged**) se vanter.
braid /breɪd/ n. (trimming) galon m.; (of hair) tresse f.
Braille /breɪl/ n. braille m.
brain /breɪn/ n. cerveau m. **~s**, (fig.)

intelligence f. —v.t. assommer. **~-child** n. invention personnelle f. **~-drain** n. exode des cerveaux m. **~less** a. stupide.
brainwash /'breɪnwɒʃ/ v.t. faire un lavage de cerveau à.
brainwave /'breɪnweɪv/ n. idée géniale f., trouvaille f.
brainy /'breɪnɪ/ a. (-ier, -iest) intelligent.
braise /breɪz/ v.t. braiser.
brake /breɪk/ n. (auto. & fig.) frein m. —v.t./i. freiner.
bramble /'bræmbl/ n. ronce f.
bran /bræn/ n. (husks) son m.
branch /brɑːntʃ/ n. branche f.; (of road) embranchement m.; (comm.) succursale f. —v.i. **~ (off)**, bifurquer.
brand /brænd/ n. marque f. —v.t. **~ s.o. as**, donner à qn. la réputation de. **~-new** a. tout neuf.
brandish /'brændɪʃ/ v.t. brandir.
brandy /'brændɪ/ n. cognac m.
brash /bræʃ/ a. effronté.
brass /brɑːs/ n. cuivre m. **get down to ~ tacks**, en venir aux choses sérieuses. **top ~**, (sl.) gros bonnets m. pl.
brassière /'bræsɪə(r), Amer. brə'zɪər/ n. soutien-gorge m.
brat /bræt/ n. (child: pej.) môme m./f.; (ill-behaved) garnement m.
bravado /brə'vɑːdəʊ/ n. bravade f.
brave /breɪv/ a. (-er, -est) courageux, brave. —n. (Red Indian) brave m. —v.t. braver. **~ry** /-ərɪ/ n. courage m.
bravo /'brɑːvəʊ/ int. bravo.
brawl /brɔːl/ n. bagarre f. —v.i. se bagarrer.
brawn /brɔːn/ n. muscles m. pl. **~y** a. musclé.
bray /breɪ/ n. braiment m. —v.i. braire.
brazen /'breɪzn/ a. effronté.
brazier /'breɪzɪə(r)/ n. brasero m.
Brazil /brə'zɪl/ n. Brésil m. **~ian** a. & n. brésilien(ne) (m. (f.)).
breach /briːtʃ/ n. violation f.; (of contract) rupture f.; (gap) brèche f. —v.t. ouvrir une brèche dans.
bread /bred/ n. pain m. **~ and butter**, tartine f. **~-winner** n. soutien de famille m.
breadcrumbs /'bredkrʌmz/ n. pl. (culin.) chapelure f.
breadline /'bredlaɪn/ n. **on the ~**, dans l'indigence.
breadth /bretθ/ n. largeur f.

break /breɪk/ v.t. (p.t. **broke**, p.p. **broken**) casser; (*smash into pieces*) briser; (*vow, silence, rank, etc.*) rompre; (*law*) violer; (*a record*) battre; (*news*) révéler; (*journey*) interrompre; (*heart, strike, ice*) briser. —v.i. (se) casser; se briser. —n. cassure f., rupture f.; (*in relationship, continuity*) rupture f.; (*interval*) interruption f.; (*for coffee*) pause f.; (*luck: fam.*) chance f. **~ down** v.i. (*collapse*) s'effondrer; (*fail*) échouer; (*machine*) tomber en panne; v.t. (*door*) enfoncer; (*analyse*) analyser. **~-in** n. cambriolage m. **~ off**, (se) détacher; (*suspend*) rompre. **~ out**, (*fire, war, etc.*) éclater. **~ up**, (*end*) (faire) cesser; (*marriage*) (se) briser; (*crowd*) (se) disperser; (*schools*) entrer en vacances. **~able** a. cassable. **~age** n. casse f.

breakdown /'breɪkdaʊn/ n. (*techn.*) panne f.; (*med.*) dépression f.; (*of figures*) analyse f. —a. (*auto.*) de dépannage.

breaker /'breɪkə(r)/ n. (*wave*) brisant m.

breakfast /'brekfəst/ n. petit déjeuner m.

breakthrough /'breɪkθruː/ n. percée f.

breakwater /'breɪkwɔːtə(r)/ n. brise-lames m. invar.

breast /brest/ n. sein m.; (*chest*) poitrine f. **~-stroke** n. brasse f.

breath /breθ/ n. souffle m., haleine f. **out of ~**, essoufflé. **under one's ~**, tout bas.

breathalyser /'breθəlaɪzə(r)/ n. alcootest m.

breath|e /briːð/ v.t./i. respirer. **~ing** n. respiration f.

breather /'briːðə(r)/ n. moment de repos m.

breathtaking /'breθteɪkɪŋ/ a. à vous couper le souffle.

bred /bred/ see **breed**.

breeches /'brɪtʃɪz/ n. pl. culotte f.

breed /briːd/ v.t. (p.t. **bred**) élever; (*give rise to*) engendrer. —v.i. se reproduire. —n. race f. **~er** n. éleveur m. **~ing** n. élevage m.; (*fig.*) éducation f.

breez|e /briːz/ n. brise f. **~y** a. (*weather*) frais; (*cheerful*) jovial; (*casual*) désinvolte.

Breton /'bretn/ a. & n. breton(ne) (m. (f.)).

brevity /'brevətɪ/ n. brièveté f.

brew /bruː/ v.t. (*beer*) brasser; (*tea*)

faire infuser. —v.i. fermenter; infuser; (*fig.*) se préparer. —n. décoction f. **~er** n. brasseur m. **~ery** n. brasserie f.

bribe /braɪb/ n. pot-de-vin m. —v.t. soudoyer, acheter. **~ry** /-ərɪ/ n. corruption f.

brick /brɪk/ n. brique f. —v.t. **~ up**, murer.

bricklayer /'brɪkleɪə(r)/ n. maçon m.

bridal /'braɪdl/ a. nuptial.

bride /braɪd/ n. mariée f.

bridegroom /'braɪdgrʊm/ n. marié m.

bridesmaid /'braɪdzmeɪd/ n. demoiselle d'honneur f.

bridge[1] /brɪdʒ/ n. pont m.; (*of nose*) arête f. —v.t. **~ a gap**, combler une lacune.

bridge[2] /brɪdʒ/ n. (*cards*) bridge m.

bridle /'braɪdl/ n. bride f. —v.t. brider. **~-path** n. allée cavalière f.

brief[1] /briːf/ a. (-er, -est) bref. **~ly** adv. brièvement. **~ness** n. brièveté f.

brief[2] /briːf/ n. instructions f. pl.; (*jurid.*) dossier m. —v.t. donner des instructions à.

briefcase /'briːfkeɪs/ n. serviette f.

briefs /briːfs/ n. pl. slip m.

brigad|e /brɪ'geɪd/ n. brigade f. **~ier** /-ə'dɪə(r)/ n. général de brigade m.

bright /braɪt/ a. (-er, -est) brillant, vif; (*day, room*) clair; (*cheerful*) gai; (*clever*) intelligent. **~ly** adv. brillamment. **~ness** n. éclat m.

brighten /'braɪtn/ v.t. égayer. —v.i. (*weather*) s'éclaircir; (*of face*) s'éclairer.

brillian|t /'brɪljənt/ a. brillant; (*light*) éclatant. **~ce** n. éclat m.

brim /brɪm/ n. bord m. —v.i. (p.t. **brimmed**). **~ over**, déborder.

brine /braɪn/ n. saumure f.

bring /brɪŋ/ v.t. (p.t. **brought**) (*thing*) apporter; (*person, vehicle*) amener. **~ about**, provoquer. **~ back**, rapporter; ramener. **~ down**, faire tomber; (*shoot down, knock down*) abattre. **~ off**, réussir. **~ out**, (*take out*) sortir; (*show*) faire ressortir; (*book*) publier. **~ round or to**, ranimer. **~ to bear**, (*pressure etc.*) exercer. **~ up**, élever; (*med.*) vomir; (*question*) soulever.

brink /brɪŋk/ n. bord m.

brisk /brɪsk/ a. (-er, -est) vif. **~ness** n. vivacité f.

bristl|e /'brɪsl/ n. poil m. —v.i. se hérisser. **~ing with**, hérissé de.

Britain /'brɪtn/ n. Grande-Bretagne f.
British /'brɪtɪʃ/ a. britannique. **the ~,** les Britanniques m. pl.
Briton /'brɪtn/ n. Britannique m./f.
Brittany /'brɪtənɪ/ n. Bretagne f.
brittle /'brɪtl/ a. fragile.
broach /brəʊtʃ/ v.t. entamer.
broad /brɔːd/ a. (-er, -est) large; (*daylight, outline*) grand. **~ bean,** fève f. **~-minded** a. large d'esprit. **~ly** adv. en gros.
broadcast /'brɔːdkɑːst/ v.t./i. (p.t. **broadcast**) diffuser; (*person*) parler à la télévision *or* à la radio. —n. émission f.
broaden /'brɔːdn/ v.t./i. (s')élargir.
broccoli /'brɒkəlɪ/ n. *invar.* brocoli m.
brochure /'brəʊʃə(r)/ n. brochure f.
broke /brəʊk/ see **break.** —a. (*penniless: sl.*) fauché.
broken /'brəʊkən/ see **break.** —a. **~ English,** mauvais anglais m. **~-hearted** a. au cœur brisé.
broker /'brəʊkə(r)/ n. courtier m.
brolly /'brɒlɪ/ n. (*fam.*) pépin m.
bronchitis /brɒŋ'kaɪtɪs/ n. bronchite f.
bronze /brɒnz/ n. bronze m. —v.t./i. (se) bronzer.
brooch /brəʊtʃ/ n. broche f.
brood /bruːd/ n. nichée f., couvée f. —v.i. couver; (*fig.*) méditer tristement. **~y** a. mélancolique.
brook[1] /brʊk/ n. ruisseau m.
brook[2] /brʊk/ v.t. souffrir.
broom /bruːm/ n. balai m.
broomstick /'bruːmstɪk/ n. manche à balai m.
broth /brɒθ/ n. bouillon m.
brothel /'brɒθl/ n. maison close f.
brother /'brʌðə(r)/ n. frère m. **~hood** n. fraternité f. **~-in-law** n. (*pl.* **~s-in-law**) beau-frère m. **~ly** a. fraternel.
brought /brɔːt/ see **bring.**
brow /braʊ/ n. front m.; (*of hill*) sommet m.
browbeat /'braʊbiːt/ v.t. (p.t. **-beat,** p.p. **-beaten**) intimider.
brown /braʊn/ a. (-er, -est) brun. —n. brun m. —v.t./i. brunir; (*culin.*) (faire) dorer. **be ~ed off,** (*sl.*) en avoir ras le bol.
Brownie /'braʊnɪ/ n. jeannette f.
browse /braʊz/ v.i. feuilleter; (*animal*) brouter.
bruise /bruːz/ n. bleu m. —v.t. (*hurt*) faire un bleu à; (*fruit*) abîmer. **~d** a. couvert de bleus.

brunch /brʌntʃ/ n. petit déjeuner copieux m. (*pris comme déjeuner*).
brunette /bruː'net/ n. brunette f.
brunt /brʌnt/ n. **the ~ of,** le plus fort de.
brush /brʌʃ/ n. brosse f.; (*skirmish*) accrochage m.; (*bushes*) broussailles f. pl. —v.t. brosser. **~ against,** effleurer. **~ aside,** écarter. **~ off,** (*reject: fam.*) envoyer promener. **~ up (on),** se remettre à.
Brussels /'brʌslz/ n. Bruxelles m./f. **~ sprouts,** choux de Bruxelles m. pl.
brutal /'bruːtl/ a. brutal. **~ity** /-'tælətɪ/ n. brutalité f.
brute /bruːt/ n. brute f. **by ~ force,** par la force.
B.Sc. abbr. see **Bachelor of Science.**
bubble /'bʌbl/ n. bulle f. —v.i. bouillonner. **~ over,** déborder.
buck[1] /bʌk/ n. mâle m. —v.i. ruer. **~ up,** (*sl.*) prendre courage; (*hurry: sl.*) se grouiller.
buck[2] /bʌk/ n. (*Amer., sl.*) dollar m.
buck[3] /bʌk/ n. **pass the ~ to,** renvoyer la balle à, rejeter la responsabilité sur.
bucket /'bʌkɪt/ n. seau m.
buckle /'bʌkl/ n. boucle f. —v.t./i. (*fasten*) (se) boucler; (*bend*) voiler. **~ down to,** s'atteler à.
bud /bʌd/ n. bourgeon m. —v.i. (p.t. **budded**) bourgeonner.
Buddhis|t /'bʊdɪst/ a. & n. bouddhiste (m./f.). **~m** /-ɪzəm/ n. bouddhisme m.
budding /'bʌdɪŋ/ a. (*talent etc.*) naissant; (*film star etc.*) en herbe.
buddy /'bʌdɪ/ n. (*fam.*) copain m.
budge /bʌdʒ/ v.t./i. (faire) bouger.
budgerigar /'bʌdʒərɪgɑː(r)/ n. perruche f.
budget /'bʌdʒɪt/ n. budget m. —v.i. (p.t. **budgeted**). **~ for,** prévoir (dans son budget).
buff /bʌf/ n. (*colour*) chamois m.; (*Amer., fam.*) fanatique m./f. **in the ~,** tout nu.
buffalo /'bʌfələʊ/ n. (*pl.* **-oes** *or* **-o**) buffle m.; (*Amer.*) bison m.
buffer /'bʌfə(r)/ n. tampon m. **~ zone,** zone tampon f.
buffet[1] /'bʊfeɪ/ n. (*meal, counter*) buffet m.
buffet[2] /'bʌfɪt/ n. (*blow*) soufflet m. —v.t. (p.t. **buffeted**) souffleter.
buffoon /bə'fuːn/ n. bouffon m.
bug /bʌg/ n. (*insect*) punaise f.; (*any small insect*) bestiole f.; (*germ: sl.*)

microbe *m.*; (*device*: *sl.*) micro *m.*; (*defect*: *sl.*) défaut *m.* —*v.t.* (*p.t.* bugged) mettre des micros dans; (*Amer.*, *sl.*) embêter.

bugle /'bju:gl/ *n.* clairon *m.*

build /bɪld/ *v.t./i.* (*p.t.* built) bâtir, construire. —*n.* carrure *f.* ~ up, (*increase*) augmenter, monter; (*accumulate*) (s')accumuler. ~up *n.* accumulation *f.*; (*fig.*) publicité *f.* ~er *n.* entrepreneur *m.*; (*workman*) ouvrier *m.*

building /'bɪldɪŋ/ *n.* bâtiment *m.*; (*dwelling*) immeuble *m.* ~ society, caisse d'épargne-logement *f.*

built /bɪlt/ *see* build. ~-in *a.* encastré. ~-up area, agglomération *f.*, zone urbanisée *f.*

bulb /bʌlb/ *n.* oignon *m.*; (*electr.*) ampoule *f.* ~ous *a.* bulbeux.

Bulgaria /bʌl'geərɪə/ *n.* Bulgarie *f.* ~n *a.* & *n.* bulgare (*m.*/*f.*).

bulg|e /bʌldʒ/ *n.* renflement *m.*; (*in numbers*) augmentation temporaire *f.* —*v.i.* se renfler, être renflé. be ~ing with, être gonflé *or* bourré de.

bulk /bʌlk/ *n.* grosseur *f.* in ~, en gros; (*loose*) en vrac. the ~ of, la majeure partie de. ~y *a.* gros.

bull /bʊl/ *n.* taureau *m.* ~'s-eye *n.* centre (de la cible) *m.*

bulldog /'bʊldɒg/ *n.* bouledogue *m.*

bulldoze /'bʊldəʊz/ *v.t.* raser au bulldozer. ~r /-ə(r)/ *n.* bulldozer *m.*

bullet /'bʊlɪt/ *n.* balle *f.* ~-proof *a.* pare-balles *invar.*; (*vehicle*) blindé.

bulletin /'bʊlɪtɪn/ *n.* bulletin *m.*

bullfight /'bʊlfaɪt/ *n.* corrida *f.*

bullion /'bʊljən/ *n.* or *or* argent en lingots *m.*

bullring /'bʊlrɪŋ/ *n.* arène *f.*

bully /'bʊlɪ/ *n.* brute *f.*; tyran *m.* —*v.t.* (*treat badly*) brutaliser; (*persecute*) tyranniser; (*coerce*) forcer (**into**, à).

bum[1] /bʌm/ *n.* (*sl.*) derrière *m.*

bum[2] /bʌm/ *n.* (*Amer.*, *sl.*) vagabond(e) *m.* (*f.*).

bumble-bee /'bʌmblbi:/ *n.* bourdon *m.*

bump /bʌmp/ *n.* choc *m.*; (*swelling*) bosse *f.* —*v.t./i.* cogner, heurter. ~ along, cahoter. ~ into, (*hit*) rentrer dans; (*meet*) tomber sur. ~y *a.* cahoteux.

bumper /'bʌmpə(r)/ *n.* pare-chocs *m.* *invar.* —*a.* exceptionnel.

bumpkin /'bʌmpkɪn/ *n.* rustre *m.*

bumptious /'bʌmpʃəs/ *a.* prétentieux.

bun /bʌn/ *n.* (*cake*) petit pain au lait *m.*; (*hair*) chignon *m.*

bunch /bʌntʃ/ *n.* (*of flowers*) bouquet *m.*; (*of keys*) trousseau *m.*; (*of people*) groupe *m.*: (*of bananas*) régime *m.* ~ of grapes, grappe de raisin *f.*

bundle /'bʌndl/ *n.* paquet *m.* —*v.t.* mettre en paquet; (*push*) pousser.

bung /bʌŋ/ *n.* bonde *f.* —*v.t.* boucher; (*throw*: *sl.*) flanquer.

bungalow /'bʌŋgələʊ/ *n.* bungalow *m.*

bungle /'bʌŋgl/ *v.t.* gâcher.

bunion /'bʌnjən/ *n.* (*med.*) oignon *m.*

bunk[1] /bʌŋk/ *n.* couchette *f.* ~- beds *n. pl.* lits superposés *m. pl.*

bunk[2] /bʌŋk/ *n.* (*bunkum*: *sl.*) foutaise(s) *f.* (*pl.*).

bunker /'bʌŋkə(r)/ *n.* (*mil.*) bunker *m.*

bunkum /'bʌŋkəm/ *n.* balivernes *f. pl.*, foutaise(s) *f.* (*pl.*).

bunny /'bʌnɪ/ *n.* (*children's use*) (Jeannot) lapin *m.*

buoy /bɔɪ/ *n.* bouée *f.* —*v.t.* ~ up, (*hearten*) soutenir, encourager.

buoyan|t /'bɔɪənt/ *a.* (*cheerful*) gai. ~cy *n.* gaieté *f.*

burden /'bɜ:dn/ *n.* fardeau *m.* —*v.t.* accabler. ~some *a.* lourd.

bureau /'bjʊərəʊ/ *n.* (*pl.* -eaux /-əʊz/) bureau *m.*

bureaucracy /bjʊə'rɒkrəsɪ/ *n.* bureaucratie *f.*

bureaucrat /'bjʊərəkræt/ *n.* bureaucrate *m.*/*f.* ~ic /-'krætɪk/ *a.* bureaucratique.

burglar /'bɜ:glə(r)/ *n.* cambrioleur *m.* ~ize *v.t.* (*Amer.*) cambrioler. ~y *n.* cambriolage *m.*

burgle /'bɜ:gl/ *v.t.* cambrioler.

Burgundy /'bɜ:gəndɪ/ *n.* (*wine*) bourgogne *m.*

burial /'berɪəl/ *n.* enterrement *m.*

burlesque /bɜ:'lesk/ *n.* (*imitation*) parodie *f.*

burly /'bɜ:lɪ/ *a.* (-ier, -iest) costaud, solidement charpenté.

Burm|a /'bɜ:mə/ *n.* Birmanie *f.* ~ese /-'mi:z/ *a.* & *n.* birman(e) (*m.* (*f.*)).

burn /bɜ:n/ *v.t./i.* (*p.t.* burned *or* burnt) brûler. —*n.* brûlure *f.* ~ down *or* be burned down, être réduit en cendres. ~er *n.* brûleur *m.* ~ing *a.* (*fig.*) brûlant.

burnish /'bɜ:nɪʃ/ *v.t.* polir.

burnt /bɜ:nt/ *see* burn.

burp /bɜ:p/ *n.* (*fam.*) rot *m.* —*v.i.* (*fam.*) roter.

burrow /'bʌrəʊ/ *n.* terrier *m.* —*v.t.* creuser.

bursar /'bɜːsə(r)/ *n.* économe *m.*/*f.*

bursary /'bɜːsərɪ/ *n.* bourse *f.*

burst /bɜːst/ *v.t./i.* (*p.t.* **burst**) crever, (faire) éclater. —*n.* explosion *f.*; (*of laughter*) éclat *m.*; (*surge*) élan *m.* ∼ **into tears,** fondre en larmes. ∼ **out laughing,** éclater de rire.

bury /'berɪ/ *v.t.* (*person etc.*) enterrer; (*hide, cover*) enfouir; (*engross, thrust*) plonger.

bus /bʌs/ *n.* (*pl.* **buses**) (auto)bus *m.* —*v.i.* (*p.t.* **bussed**) prendre l'autobus. ∼-**stop** *n.* arrêt d'autobus *m.*

bush /bʊʃ/ *n.* buisson *m.*; (*land*) brousse *f.* ∼**y** *a.* broussailleux.

business /'bɪznɪs/ *n.* (*task, concern*) affaire *f.*; (*commerce*) affaires *f. pl.*; (*line of work*) métier *m.*; (*shop*) commerce *m.* **he has no** ∼ **to,** il n'a pas le droit de. **that's none of your** ∼**!,** ça ne vous regarde pas! ∼ **man,** homme d'affaires *m.*

businesslike /'bɪznɪslaɪk/ *a.* sérieux.

busker /'bʌskə(r)/ *n.* musicien(ne) des rues *m.* (*f.*).

bust[1] /bʌst/ *n.* buste *m.*; (*bosom*) poitrine *f.*

bust[2] /bʌst/ *v.t./i.* (*p.t.* **busted** *or* **bust**) (*burst*: *sl.*) crever; (*break*: *sl.*) (se) casser. —*a.* (*broken, finished*: *sl.*) fichu. ∼-**up** *n.* (*sl.*) engueulade *f.* **go** ∼, (*sl.*) faire faillite.

bustl|**e** /'bʌsl/ *v.i.* s'affairer. —*n.* affairement *m.*, remue-ménage *m.* ∼**ing** *a.* (*place*) bruyant, animé.

bus|**y** /'bɪzɪ/ *a.* (**-ier, -iest**) occupé; (*street*) animé; (*day*) chargé. —*v.t.* ∼**y o.s. with,** s'occuper à. ∼**ily** *adv.* activement.

busybody /'bɪzɪbɒdɪ/ *n.* **be a** ∼, faire la mouche du coche.

but /bʌt, *unstressed* bət/ *conj.* mais. —*prep.* sauf. —*adv.* (*only*) seulement. ∼ **for,** sans. **nobody** ∼, personne d'autre que.

butane /'bjuːteɪn/ *n.* butane *m.*

butcher /'bʊtʃə(r)/ *n.* boucher *m.* —*v.t.* massacrer. ∼**y** *n.* boucherie *f.*, massacre *m.*

butler /'bʌtlə(r)/ *n.* maître d'hôtel *m.*

butt /bʌt/ *n.* (*of gun*) crosse *f.*; (*of cigarette*) mégot *m.*; (*target*) cible *f.* —*v.i.* ∼ **in,** interrompre.

butter /'bʌtə(r)/ *n.* beurre *m.* —*v.t.* beurrer. ∼-**bean** *n.* haricot blanc *m.* ∼-**fingers** *n.* maladroit(e) *m.* (*f.*).

buttercup /'bʌtəkʌp/ *n.* bouton d'or *m.*

butterfly /'bʌtəflaɪ/ *n.* papillon *m.*

buttock /'bʌtək/ *n.* fesse *f.*

button /'bʌtn/ *n.* bouton *m.* —*v.t./i.* ∼ (**up**), (se) boutonner.

buttonhole /'bʌtnhəʊl/ *n.* boutonnière *f.* —*v.t.* accrocher.

buttress /'bʌtrɪs/ *n.* contrefort *m.* —*v.t.* soutenir.

buxom /'bʌksəm/ *a.* bien en chair.

buy /baɪ/ *v.t.* (*p.t.* **bought**) acheter (**from,** à); (*believe*: *sl.*) croire, avaler. —*n.* achat *m.* ∼**er** *n.* acheteur, -se *m.*, *f.*

buzz /bʌz/ *n.* bourdonnement *m.* —*v.i.* bourdonner. ∼ **off,** (*sl.*) fiche(r) le camp. ∼**er** *n.* sonnerie *f.*

by /baɪ/ *prep.* par, de; (*near*) à côté de; (*before*) avant; (*means*) en, à, par. ∼ **bike,** à vélo. ∼ **car,** en auto. ∼ **day,** de jour. ∼ **the kilo,** au kilo. ∼ **running**/*etc.*, en courant/*etc.* ∼ **sea,** par mer. —*adv.* (*near*) tout près. ∼ **and large,** dans l'ensemble. ∼**election** *n.* élection partielle *f.* ∼-**law** *n.* arrêté *m.*; (*of club etc.*) statut *m.* ∼ **o.s.,** tout seul. ∼-**product** *n.* sous-produit *m.* ∼-**road** *n.* chemin de traverse *m.*

bye(-bye) /baɪ('baɪ)/ *int.* (*fam.*) au revoir, salut.

bygone /'baɪgɒn/ *a.* passé.

bypass /'baɪpɑːs/ *n.* route qui contourne *f.* —*v.t.* contourner.

bystander /'baɪstændə(r)/ *n.* spectateur, -trice *m.*, *f.*

byword /'baɪwɜːd/ *n.* **be a** ∼ **for,** être connu pour.

C

cab /kæb/ *n.* taxi *m.*; (*of lorry, train*) cabine *f.*

cabaret /'kæbəreɪ/ *n.* spectacle (de cabaret) *m.*

cabbage /'kæbɪdʒ/ *n.* chou *m.*

cabin /'kæbɪn/ *n.* (*hut*) cabane *f.*; (*in ship, aircraft*) cabine *f.*

cabinet /'kæbɪnɪt/ *n.* (petite) armoire *f.*, meuble de rangement *m.*; (*for filing*) classeur *m.* **C~**, (*pol.*) cabinet *m.* **~-maker** *n.* ébéniste *m.*

cable /'keɪbl/ *n.* câble *m.* —*v.t.* câbler. **~-car** *n.* téléphérique *m.* **~ railway,** funiculaire *m.*

caboose /kə'buːs/ *n.* (*rail., Amer.*) fourgon *m.*

cache /kæʃ/ *n.* (*place*) cachette *f.* **a ~ of arms,** des armes cachées.

cackle /'kækl/ *n.* caquet *m.* —*v.i.* caqueter.

cactus /'kæktəs/ *n.* (*pl.* **-ti** /-taɪ/ *or* **-tuses**) cactus *m.*

cad /kæd/ *n.* malotru *m.* **~dish** *a.* grossier.

caddie /'kædɪ/ *n.* (*golf*) caddie *m.*

caddy /'kædɪ/ *n.* boîte à thé *f.*

cadence /'keɪdns/ *n.* cadence *f.*

cadet /kə'det/ *n.* élève officier *m.*

cadge /kædʒ/ *v.t.* se fairer payer, écornifler. —*v.i.* quémander. **~ money from,** taper. **~r** /-ə(r)/ *n.* écornifleu|r, -se *m.*, *f.*

Caesarean /sɪ'zeərɪən/ *a.* **~ (section),** césarienne *f.*

café /'kæfeɪ/ *n.* café(-restaurant) *m.*

cafeteria /kæfɪ'tɪərɪə/ *n.* cafétéria *f.*

caffeine /'kæfiːn/ *n.* caféine *f.*

cage /keɪdʒ/ *n.* cage *f.* —*v.t.* mettre en cage.

cagey /'keɪdʒɪ/ *a.* (*secretive: fam.*) peu communicatif.

Cairo /'kaɪərəʊ/ *n.* le Caire *m.*

cajole /kə'dʒəʊl/ *v.t.* cajoler.

cake /keɪk/ *n.* gâteau *m.* **~d** *a.* durci. **~d with,** raidi par.

calamit|y /kə'læmətɪ/ *n.* calamité *f.* **~ous** *a.* désastreux.

calcium /'kælsɪəm/ *n.* calcium *m.*

calculat|e /'kælkjʊleɪt/ *v.t.*/*i.* calculer; (*Amer.*) supposer. **~ed** *a.* (*action*) délibéré. **~ing** *a.* calculateur. **~ion** /-'leɪʃn/ *n.* calcul *m.* **~or** *n.* calculatrice *f.*

calculus /'kælkjʊləs/ *n.* (*pl.* **-li** /-laɪ/ *or* **-luses**) calcul *m.*

calendar /'kælɪndə(r)/ *n.* calendrier *m.*

calf[1] /kɑːf/ *n.* (*pl.* **calves**) (*young cow or bull*) veau *m.*

calf[2] /kɑːf/ *n.* (*pl.* **calves**) (*of leg*) mollet *m.*

calibre /'kælɪbə(r)/ *n.* calibre *m.*

calico /'kælɪkəʊ/ *n.* calicot *m.*

call /kɔːl/ *v.t.*/*i.* appeler. **~ (in** *or* **round),** (*visit*) passer. —*n.* appel *m.*; (*of bird*) cri *m.*; visite *f.* **be ~ed,** (*named*) s'appeler. **be on ~,** être de garde. **~ back,** rappeler; (*visit*) repasser. **~-box** *n.* cabine téléphonique *f.* **~ for,** (*require*) demander; (*fetch*) passer prendre. **~-girl** *n.* call-girl *f.* **~ off,** annuler. **~ out (to),** appeler. **~ on,** (*visit*) passer chez; (*appeal to*) faire appel à. **~ up,** appeler (au téléphone); (*mil.*) mobiliser, appeler. **~er** *n.* visiteu|r, -se *m.*, *f.* **~ing** *n.* vocation *f.*

callous /'kæləs/ *a.*, **~ly** *adv.* sans pitié. **~ness** *n.* manque de pitié *m.*

callow /'kæləʊ/ *a.* (**-er, -est**) inexpérimenté.

calm /kɑːm/ *a.* (**-er, -est**) calme. —*n.* calme *m.* —*v.t.*/*i.* **~ (down),** (se) calmer. **~ness** *n.* calme *m.*

calorie /'kælərɪ/ *n.* calorie *f.*

camber /'kæmbə(r)/ *n.* (*of road*) bombement *m.*

came /keɪm/ *see* **come.**

camel /'kæml/ *n.* chameau *m.*

cameo /'kæmɪəʊ/ *n.* (*pl.* **-os**) camée *m.*

camera /'kæmərə/ *n.* appareil(-photo) *m.*; (*for moving pictures*) caméra *f.* **~man** *n.* (*pl.* **-men**) caméraman *m.*

camouflage /'kæməflɑːʒ/ *n.* camouflage *m.* —*v.t.* camoufler.

camp[1] /kæmp/ *n.* camp *m.* —*v.i.* camper. **~-bed** *n.* lit de camp *m.* **~er** *n.* campeu|r, -se *m.*, *f.* **~ing** *n.* camping *m.*

camp[2] /kæmp/ *a.* (*mannered*) affecté; (*vulgar*) de mauvais goût.

campaign /kæm'peɪn/ *n.* campagne *f.* —*v.i.* faire campagne.

campsite /'kæmpsaɪt/ *n.* (*for holidaymakers*) camping *m.*

campus /'kæmpəs/ *n.* (*pl.* **-puses**) campus *m.*

can¹ /kæn/ *n.* bidon *m.*; (*sealed container for food*) boîte *f.* —*v.t.* (*p.t.* **canned**) mettre en boîte. ~ **it!**, (*Amer.*, *sl.*) ferme-la! ~**ned music**, musique de fond enregistrée *f.* ~**opener** *n.* ouvreboîte(s) *m.*

can² /kæn, *unstressed* kən/ *v. aux.* (*be able to*) pouvoir; (*know how to*) savoir.

Canad|a /'kænədə/ *n.* Canada *m.* ~**ian** /kə'neɪdɪən/ *a.* & *n.* canadien(ne) (*m.* (*f.*)).

canal /kə'næl/ *n.* canal *m.*

canary /kə'neərɪ/ *n.* canari *m.*

cancel /'kænsl/ *v.t./i.* (*p.t.* **cancelled**) (*call off, revoke*) annuler; (*cross out*) barrer; (*a stamp*) oblitérer. ~ **out**, (se) neutraliser. ~**lation** /-ə'leɪʃn/ *n.* annulation *f.*; oblitération *f.*

cancer /'kænsə(r)/ *n.* cancer *m.* ~**ous** *a.* cancéreux.

candid /'kændɪd/ *a.* franc. ~**ness** *n.* franchise *f.*

candida|te /'kændɪdeɪt/ *n.* candidat(e) *m.* (*f.*). ~**cy** /-əsɪ/ *n.* candidature *f.*

candle /'kændl/ *n.* bougie *f.*, chandelle *f.*; (*in church*) cierge *m.*

candlestick /'kændlstɪk/ *n.* bougeoir *m.*, chandelier *m.*

candour /'kændə(r)/ *n.* franchise *f.*

candy /'kændɪ/ *n.* (*Amer.*) bonbon(s) *m.* (*pl.*) ~**-floss** *n.* barbe à papa *f.*

cane /keɪn/ *n.* canne *f.*; (*for baskets*) rotin *m.*; (*for punishment: schol.*) baguette *f.*, bâton *m.* —*v.t.* donner des coups de baguette *or* de bâton à, fustiger.

canine /'keɪnaɪn/ *a.* canin.

canister /'kænɪstə(r)/ *n.* boîte *f.*

cannabis /'kænəbɪs/ *n.* cannabis *m.*

cannibal /'kænɪbl/ *n.* cannibale *m.*|*f.* ~**ism** *n.* cannibalisme *m.*

cannon /'kænən/ *n.* (*pl.* ~ *or* ~**s**) canon *m.* ~**-ball** *n.* boulet de canon *m.*

cannot /'kænət/ = **can not.**

canny /'kænɪ/ *a.* rusé, madré.

canoe /kə'nuː/ *n.* (*sport*) canoë *m.*, kayak *m.* —*v.i.* faire du canoë *or* du kayak. ~**ist** *n.* canoéiste *m.*|*f.*

canon /'kænən/ *n.* (*clergyman*) chanoine *m.*; (*rule*) canon *m.*

canonize /'kænənaɪz/ *v.t.* canoniser.

canopy /'kænəpɪ/ *n.* dais *m.*; (*over doorway*) marquise *f.*

cant /kænt/ *n.* jargon *m.*

can't /kɑːnt/ = **can not.**

cantankerous /kæn'tæŋkərəs/ *a.* acariâtre, grincheux.

canteen /kæn'tiːn/ *n.* (*restaurant*) cantine *f.*; (*flask*) bidon *m.*

canter /'kæntə(r)/ *n.* petit galop *m.* —*v.i.* aller au petit galop.

canvas /'kænvəs/ *n.* toile *f.*

canvass /'kænvəs/ *v.t./i.* (*comm., pol.*) solliciter des commandes *or* des voix (de). ~**ing** *n.* (*comm.*) démarchage *m.*; (*pol.*) démarchage électoral *m.*

canyon /'kænjən/ *n.* cañon *m.*

cap /kæp/ *n.* (*hat*) casquette *f.*; (*of bottle, tube*) bouchon *m.*, (*of beer or milk bottle*) capsule *f.*; (*of pen*) capuchon *m.*; (*for toy gun*) amorce *f.* —*v.t.* (*p.t.* **capped**) (*bottle*) capsuler; (*outdo*) surpasser. ~**ped with**, coiffé de.

capab|le /'keɪpəbl/ *a.* (*person*) capable (**of**, de), compétent. **be ~le of**, (*of situation, text, etc.*) être susceptible de. ~**ility** /-'bɪlətɪ/ *n.* capacité *f.* ~**ly** *adv.* avec compétence.

capacity /kə'pæsətɪ/ *n.* capacité *f.* **in one's ~ as,** en sa qualité de.

cape¹ /keɪp/ *n.* (*cloak*) cape *f.*

cape² /keɪp/ *n.* (*geog.*) cap *m.*

caper¹ /'keɪpə(r)/ *v.i.* gambader. —*n.* (*prank*) farce *f.*; (*activity: sl.*) affaire *f.*

caper² /'keɪpə(r)/ *n.* (*culin.*) câpre *f.*

capital /'kæpɪtl/ *a.* capital. —*n.* (*town*) capitale *f.*; (*money*) capital *m.* ~ (**letter**), majuscule *f.*

capitalis|t /'kæpɪtəlɪst/ *a.* & *n.* capitaliste (*m.*|*f.*). ~**m** /-zəm/ *n.* capitalisme *m.*

capitalize /'kæpɪtəlaɪz/ *v.i.* ~ **on**, tirer profit de.

capitulat|e /kə'pɪtʃʊleɪt/ *v.i.* capituler. ~**ion** /-'leɪʃn/ *n.* capitulation *f.*

capricious /kə'prɪʃəs/ *a.* capricieux.

capsize /kæp'saɪz/ *v.t./i.* (faire) chavirer.

capsule /'kæpsjuːl/ *n.* capsule *f.*

captain /'kæptɪn/ *n.* capitaine *m.* —*v.t.* commander, être le capitaine de.

caption /'kæpʃn/ *n.* (*for illustration*) légende *f.*; (*heading*) soustitre *m.*

captivate /'kæptɪveɪt/ *v.t.* captiver.

captiv|e /'kæptɪv/ *a.* & *n.* capti|f, -ve (*m.*, *f.*). ~**ity** /-'tɪvətɪ/ *n.* captivité *f.*

capture /'kæptʃə(r)/ *v.t.* (*person, animal*) prendre, capturer; (*attention*) retenir. —*n.* capture *f.*

car /kɑː(r)/ *n.* voiture *f.*, auto *f.* ~**park** *n.* parking *m.* ~**-wash** *n.* station de lavage *f.*, lave-auto *m.*

carafe /kə'ræf/ *n.* carafe *f.*

caramel /'kærəmel/ *n.* caramel *m.*

carat /'kærət/ *n*. carat *m*.

caravan /'kærəvæn/ *n*. caravane *f*.

carbohydrate /kɑːbəʊ'haɪdreɪt/ *n*. hydrate de carbone *m*.

carbon /'kɑːbən/ *n*. carbone *m*. ~ **copy,** ~ **paper,** carbone *m*.

carburettor /kɑːbjʊ'retə(r)/ *n*. carburateur *m*.

carcass /'kɑːkəs/ *n*. carcasse *f*.

card /kɑːd/ *n*. carte *f*. ~**-index** *n*. fichier *m*.

cardboard /'kɑːdbɔːd/ *n*. carton *m*.

cardiac /'kɑːdɪæk/ *a*. cardiaque.

cardigan /'kɑːdɪgən/ *n*. cardigan *m*.

cardinal /'kɑːdɪnl/ *a*. cardinal. —*n*. (*relig*.) cardinal *m*.

care /keə(r)/ *n*. (*attention*) soin *m*., attention *f*.; (*worry*) souci *m*.; (*protection*) garde *f*. —*v.i.* ~ **about,** s'intéresser à. ~ **for,** s'occuper de; (*invalid*) soigner. ~ **to** *or* **for,** aimer, vouloir. **I don't** ~, ça m'est égal. **take** ~ **of,** s'occuper de.

career /kə'rɪə(r)/ *n*. carrière *f*. —*v.i.* aller à toute vitesse.

carefree /'keəfriː/ *a*. insouciant.

careful /'keəfl/ *a*. soigneux; (*cautious*) prudent. ~**!**, attention! ~**ly** *adv*. avec soin.

careless /'keəlɪs/ *a*. négligent; (*work*) peu soigné. ~ **about,** peu soucieux de. ~**ly** *adv*. négligemment. ~**ness** *n*. négligence *f*.

caress /kə'res/ *n*. caresse *f*. —*v.t.* caresser.

caretaker /'keəteɪkə(r)/ *n*. gardien(ne) *m*. (*f*.).

cargo /'kɑːgəʊ/ *n*. (*pl*. **-oes**) cargaison *f*. ~ **boat,** cargo *m*.

Caribbean /kærɪ'biːən/ *a*. caraïbe. —*n*. **the** ~, les Antilles *f. pl*.

caricature /'kærɪkətjʊə(r)/ *n*. caricature *f*. —*v.t.* caricaturer.

caring /'keərɪŋ/ *a*. (*mother, son, etc*.) aimant. —*n*. affection *f*.

carnage /'kɑːnɪdʒ/ *n*. carnage *m*.

carnal /'kɑːnl/ *a*. charnel.

carnation /kɑː'neɪʃn/ *n*. œillet *m*.

carnival /'kɑːnɪvl/ *n*. carnaval *m*.

carol /'kærəl/ *n*. chant (de Noël) *m*.

carouse /kə'raʊz/ *v.i.* faire la fête.

carp[1] /kɑːp/ *n. invar*. carpe *f*.

carp[2] /kɑːp/ *v.i.* ~ (**at**), critiquer.

carpent|er /'kɑːpɪntə(r)/ *n*. charpentier *m*.; (*for light woodwork, furniture*) menuisier *m*. ~**ry** *n*. charpenterie *f*.; menuiserie *f*.

carpet /'kɑːpɪt/ *n*. tapis *m*. —*v.t.* (*p.t.* carpeted) recouvrir d'un tapis. ~**sweeper** *n*. balai mécanique *m*. **on the** ~, (*fam*.) sur la sellette.

carriage /'kærɪdʒ/ *n*. (*rail. & horse-drawn*) voiture *f*.; (*of goods*) transport *m*.; (*cost*) port *m*.

carriageway /'kærɪdʒweɪ/ *n*. chaussée *f*.

carrier /'kærɪə(r)/ *n*. transporteur *m*.; (*med*.) porteu|r, -se *m*., *f*. ~ (**bag**), sac en plastique *m*.

carrot /'kærət/ *n*. carotte *f*.

carry /'kærɪ/ *v.t./i.* porter; (*goods*) transporter; (*involve*) comporter. **be carried away,** s'emballer. ~**cot** *n*. porte-bébé *m*. ~ **off,** enlever; (*prize*) remporter. ~ **on,** continuer; (*behave*: *fam*.) se conduire (mal). ~ **out,** (*an order, plan*) exécuter; (*duty*) accomplir; (*task*) effectuer.

cart /kɑːt/ *n*. charrette *f*. —*v.t.* transporter; (*heavy object*: *sl*.) trimballer.

cartilage /'kɑːtɪlɪdʒ/ *n*. cartilage *m*.

carton /'kɑːtn/ *n*. (*box*) carton *m*.; (*of yoghurt, cream*) pot *m*.; (*of cigarettes*) cartouche *f*.

cartoon /kɑː'tuːn/ *n*. dessin (humoristique) *m*.; (*cinema*) dessin animé *m*. ~**ist** *n*. dessina|teur, -trice *m*., *f*.

cartridge /'kɑːtrɪdʒ/ *n*. cartouche *f*.

carve /kɑːv/ *v.t.* tailler; (*meat*) découper.

cascade /kæs'keɪd/ *n*. cascade *f*. —*v.i.* tomber en cascade.

case[1] /keɪs/ *n*. cas *m*.; (*jurid*.) affaire *f*.; (*phil*.) arguments *m. pl*. **in** ~ **he comes,** au cas où il viendrait. **in** ~ **of,** en cas de.

case[2] /keɪs/ *n*. (*crate*) caisse *f*.; (*for camera, cigarettes, spectacles, etc*.) étui *m*.; (*suitcase*) valise *f*.

cash /kæʃ/ *n*. argent *m*. —*a*. (*price etc*.) (au) comptant. —*v.t.* encaisser. ~ **a cheque,** (*person*) encaisser un chèque; (*bank*) payer un chèque. **pay** ~**/in** ~, payer comptant/en espèces. ~ **desk,** caisse *f*. ~ **in (on),** profiter (de).

cashew /'kæʃuː/ *n*. noix de cajou *f*.

cashier /kæ'ʃɪə(r)/ *n*. caiss|ier, -ière *m*., *f*.

cashmere /kæʃ'mɪə(r)/ *n*. cachemire *m*.

casino /kə'siːnəʊ/ *n*. (*pl*. **-os**) casino *m*.

cask /kɑːsk/ *n*. tonneau *m*.

casket /'kɑːskɪt/ *n*. (*box*) coffret *m*.; (*coffin*: *Amer*.) cercueil *m*.

casserole /'kæsərəʊl/ *n.* (*utensil*) cocotte *f.*; (*stew*) daube *f.*

cassette /kə'set/ *n.* cassette *f.*

cast /kɑːst/ *v.t.* (*p.t.* **cast**) (*throw*) jeter; (*glance, look*) jeter; (*shadow*) projeter; (*vote*) donner; (*metal*) couler. **~** (**off**), (*shed*) se dépouiller de.—*n.* (*theatre*) distribution *f.*; (*of dice*) coup *m.*; (*mould*) moule *m.*; (*med.*) plâtre *m.* **~ iron,** fonte *f.* **~-iron** *a.* de fonte; (*fig.*) solide. **~-offs** *n. pl.* vieux vêtements *m. pl.*

castanets /kæstə'nets/ *n. pl.* castagnettes *f. pl.*

castaway /'kɑːstəweɪ/ *n.* naufragé(e) *m.* (*f.*).

caste /kɑːst/ *n.* caste *f.*

castle /'kɑːsl/ *n.* château *m.*; (*chess*) tour *f.*

castor /'kɑːstə(r)/ *n.* (*wheel*) roulette *f.* **~ sugar,** sucre en poudre *m.*

castrat|e /kæ'streɪt/ *v.t.* châtrer. **~ion** /-ʃn/ *n.* castration *f.*

casual /'kæʒʊəl/ *a.* (*remark*) fait au hasard; (*meeting*) fortuit; (*attitude*) désinvolte; (*work*) temporaire; (*clothes*) sport *invar.* **~ly** *adv.* par hasard; (*carelessly*) avec désinvolture.

casualty /'kæʒʊəltɪ/ *n.* (*dead*) mort(e) *m.* (*f.*).; (*injured*) blessé(e) *m.* (*f.*); (*accident victim*) accidenté(e) *m.* (*f.*).

cat /kæt/ *n.* chat *m.* **C~'s-eyes** *n. pl.* (P.) cataphotes *m. pl.* (P.).

cataclysm /'kætəklɪzəm/ *n.* cataclysme *m.*

catalogue /'kætəlɒg/ *n.* catalogue *m.* —*v.t.* cataloguer.

catalyst /'kætəlɪst/ *n.* catalyseur *m.*

catapult /'kætəpʌlt/ *n.* lancepierres *m. invar.* —*v.t.* catapulter.

cataract /'kætərækt/ *n.* (*waterfall* & *med.*) cataracte *f.*

catarrh /kə'tɑː(r)/ *n.* rhume *m.*, catarrhe *m.*

catastroph|e /kə'tæstrəfɪ/ *n.* catastrophe *f.* **~ic** /kætə'strɒfɪk/ *a.* catastrophique.

catch /kætʃ/ *v.t.* (*p.t.* **caught**) attraper; (*grab*) prendre, saisir; (*catch unawares*) surprendre; (*jam, trap*) prendre; (*understand*) saisir. —*v.i.* prendre; (*get stuck*) se prendre (**in,** dans). —*n.* capture *f.*, prise *f.*; (*on door*) loquet *m.*; (*fig.*) piège *m.* **~ fire,** prendre feu. **~ on,** (*fam.*) prendre, devenir populaire. **~-phrase** *n.* slo-

gan *m.* **~ sight of,** apercevoir. **~ up,** se rattraper. **~ up** (**with**), rattraper.

catching /'kætʃɪŋ/ *a.* contagieux.

catchment /'kætʃmənt/ *n.* **~ area,** circonscription (administrative) *f.*

catchy /'kætʃɪ/ *a.* facile à retenir.

catechism /'kætɪkɪzəm/ *n.* catéchisme *m.*

categorical /kætɪ'gɒrɪkl/ *a.* catégorique.

category /'kætɪgərɪ/ *n.* catégorie *f.*

cater /'keɪtə(r)/ *v.i.* s'occuper de la nourriture. **~ for,** (*pander to*) satisfaire; (*of magazine etc.*) s'adresser à. **~er** *n.* traiteur *m.*

caterpillar /'kætəpɪlə(r)/ *n.* chenille *f.*

cathedral /kə'θiːdrəl/ *n.* cathédrale *f.*

catholic /'kæθəlɪk/ *a.* universel. **C~** *a.* & *n.* catholique (*m.*/*f.*). **~ism** /kə'θɒlɪsɪzəm/ *n.* catholicisme *m.*

cattle /'kætl/ *n. pl.* bétail *m.*

catty /'kætɪ/ *a.* méchant.

caucus /'kɔːkəs/ *n.* comité électoral *m.*

caught /kɔːt/ *see* **catch.**

cauldron /'kɔːldrən/ *n.* chaudron *m.*

cauliflower /'kɒlɪflaʊə(r)/ *n.* choufleur *m.*

cause /kɔːz/ *n.* cause *f.*; (*reason*) raison *f.*, motif *m.* —*v.t.* causer. **~ sth. to grow/move/***etc.*, faire pousser/bouger/*etc.* qch.

causeway /'kɔːzweɪ/ *n.* chaussée *f.*

caustic /'kɔːstɪk/ *a.* & *n.* caustique (*m.*).

cauti|on /'kɔːʃn/ *n.* prudence *f.*; (*warning*) avertissement *m.* —*v.t.* avertir. **~ous** *a.* prudent. **~ously** *adv.* prudemment.

cavalier /kævə'lɪə(r)/ *a.* cavalier.

cavalry /'kævəlrɪ/ *n.* cavalerie *f.*

cave /keɪv/ *n.* caverne *f.*, grotte *f.* —*v.i.* **~ in,** s'effondrer.

caveman /'keɪvmæn/ *n.* (*pl.* **-men**) homme des cavernes *m.*

cavern /'kævən/ *n.* caverne *f.*

caviare, *Amer.* **caviar** /'kævɪɑː(r)/ *n.* caviar *m.*

caving /'keɪvɪŋ/ *n.* spéléologie *f.*

cavity /'kævətɪ/ *n.* cavité *f.*

cavort /kə'vɔːt/ *v.i.* gambader.

cease /siːs/ *v.t.*/*i.* cesser. **~-fire** *n.* cessez-le-feu *m. invar.* **without ~,** sans cesse. **~less** *a.* incessant.

cedar /'siːdə(r)/ *n.* cèdre *m.*

cede /siːd/ *v.t.* céder.

cedilla /sɪ'dɪlə/ *n.* cédille *f.*

ceiling /'siːlɪŋ/ *n.* plafond *m.*

celebrat|e /'selɪbreɪt/ *v.t.* (*perform, glorify*) célébrer; (*event*) fêter, célébrer. —*v.i.* **we shall ~e**, on va fêter ça. **~ion** /-'breɪʃn/ *n.* fête *f.*

celebrated /'selɪbreɪtɪd/ *a.* célèbre.

celebrity /sɪ'lebrətɪ/ *n.* célébrité *f.*

celery /'selərɪ/ *n.* céleri *m.*

celiba|te /'selɪbət/ *a.* **be ~te**, vivre dans le célibat. **~cy** *n.* célibat *m.*

cell /sel/ *n.* cellule *f.*; (*electr.*) élément *m.*

cellar /'selə(r)/ *n.* cave *f.*

cell|o /'tʃeləʊ/ *n.* (*pl.* **-os**) violoncelle *m.* **~ist** *n.* violoncelliste *m.*/*f.*

Cellophane /'seləfeɪn/ *n.* (P.) cellophane *f.* (P.).

Celt /kelt/ *n.* Celte *m.*/*f.* **~ic** *a.* celtique, celte.

cement /sɪ'ment/ *n.* ciment *m.* —*v.t.* cimenter. **~-mixer** *n.* bétonnière *f.*

cemetery /'semətrɪ/ *n.* cimetière *m.*

cenotaph /'senətɑːf/ *n.* cénotaphe *m.*

censor /'sensə(r)/ *n.* censeur *m.* —*v.t.* censurer. **~ship** *n.* censure *f.*

censure /'senʃə(r)/ *n.* blâme *m.* —*v.t.* blâmer.

census /'sensəs/ *n.* recensement *m.*

cent /sent/ *n.* (*coin*) cent *m.*

centenary /sen'tiːnərɪ, *Amer.* 'sentənərɪ/ *n.* centenaire *m.*

centigrade /'sentɪgreɪd/ *a.* centigrade.

centilitre /'sentɪliːtə(r)/ *n.* centilitre *m.*

centimetre /'sentɪmiːtə(r)/ *n.* centimètre *m.*

centipede /'sentɪpiːd/ *n.* millepattes *m. invar.*

central /'sentrəl/ *a.* central. **~ heating**, chauffage central *m.* **~ize** *v.t.* centraliser. **~ly** *adv.* (*situated*) au centre.

centre /'sentə(r)/ *n.* centre *m.* —*v.t.* (*p.t.* **centred**) centrer. —*v.i.* **~ on**, tourner autour de. **~forward** *n.* avant-centre *m.*

centrifugal /sen'trɪfjʊgl/ *a.* centrifuge.

century /'sentʃərɪ/ *n.* siècle *m.*

ceramic /sɪ'ræmɪk/ *a.* (*art*) céramique; (*object*) en céramique.

cereal /'sɪərɪəl/ *n.* céréale *f.*

cerebral /'serɪbrəl, *Amer.* sə'riːbrəl/ *a.* cérébral.

ceremonial /serɪ'məʊnɪəl/ *a.* de cérémonie. —*n.* cérémonial *m.*

ceremon|y /'serɪmənɪ/ *n.* cérémonie *f.* **~ious** /-'məʊnɪəs/ *a.* solennel.

certain /'sɜːtn/ *a.* certain. **for ~**, avec certitude. **make ~ of**, s'assurer de.

~ly *adv.* certainement. **~ty** *n.* certitude *f.*

certificate /sə'tɪfɪkət/ *n.* certificat *m.*

certify /'sɜːtɪfaɪ/ *v.t.* certifier.

cessation /se'seɪʃn/ *n.* cessation *f.*

cesspit, cesspool /'sespɪt, 'sespuːl/ *ns.* fosse d'aisances *f.*

chafe /tʃeɪf/ *v.t.* frotter (contre).

chaff /tʃɑːf/ *v.t.* taquiner.

chaffinch /'tʃæfɪntʃ/ *n.* pinson *m.*

chagrin /'ʃægrɪn/ *n.* vif dépit *m.*

chain /tʃeɪn/ *n.* chaîne *f.* —*v.t.* enchaîner. **~ reaction,** réaction en chaîne *f.* **~-smoke** *v.i.* fumer de manière ininterrompue. **~ store**, magasin à succursales multiples *m.*

chair /tʃeə(r)/ *n.* chaise *f.*; (*armchair*) fauteuil *m.*; (*univ.*) chaire *f.* —*v.t.* (*preside over*) présider.

chairman /'tʃeəmən/ *n.* (*pl.* **-men**) président(e) *m.* (*f.*).

chalet /'ʃæleɪ/ *n.* chalet *m.*

chalk /tʃɔːk/ *n.* craie *f.* **~y** *a.* crayeux.

challeng|e /'tʃælɪndʒ/ *n.* défi *m.*; (*task*) gageure *f.* —*v.t.* (*summon*) défier (**to do**, de faire); (*question truth of*) contester. **~er** *n.* (*sport*) challenger *m.* **~ing** *a.* stimulant.

chamber /'tʃeɪmbə(r)/ *n.* (*old use*) chambre *f.* **~ music**, musique de chambre *f.* **~-pot** *n.* pot de chambre *m.*

chambermaid /'tʃeɪmbəmeɪd/ *n.* femme de chambre *f.*

chamois /'ʃæmɪ/ *n.* **~(-leather)**, peau de chamois *f.*

champagne /ʃæm'peɪn/ *n.* champagne *m.*

champion /'tʃæmpɪən/ *n.* champion(ne) *m.* (*f.*). —*v.t.* défendre. **~ship** *n.* championnat *m.*

chance /tʃɑːns/ *n.* (*luck*) hasard *m.*; (*opportunity*) occasion *f.*; (*likelihood*) chances *f. pl.*; (*risk*) risque *m.* —*a.* fortuit. —*v.t.* **~ doing**, prendre le risque de faire. **~ it**, risquer le coup.

chancellor /'tʃɑːnsələ(r)/ *n.* chancelier *m.* **C~ of the Exchequer**, Chancelier de l'Échiquier.

chancy /'tʃɑːnsɪ/ *a.* risqué.

chandelier /ʃændə'lɪə(r)/ *n.* lustre *m.*

change /tʃeɪndʒ/ *v.t.* (*alter*) changer; (*exchange*) échanger (**for**, contre); (*money*) changer. **~ trains/one's dress/etc.**, (*by substitution*) changer de train/de robe/*etc.* —*v.i* changer; (*change clothes*) se changer. —*n.* changement *m.*; (*money*) monnaie *f.*

a ~ **of clothes,** des vêtements de rechange. ~ **one's mind,** changer d'avis. ~ **over,** passer (**to,** à). ~**-over** n. passage m. ~**able** a. changeant; (*weather*) variable.

channel /'tʃænl/ n. chenal m.; (*TV*) chaîne f., canal m.; (*medium, agency*) canal m.; (*groove*) rainure f. —v.t. (p.t. **channelled**) (*direct*) canaliser. **the (English) C~,** la Manche. **the C~ Islands,** les îles anglo-normandes f. pl.

chant /tʃɑːnt/ n. (*relig.*) psalmodie f.; (*of demonstrators*) chant (scandé) m. —v.t./i. psalmodier; scander (des slogans).

chao|s /'keɪɒs/ n. chaos m. ~**tic** /-'ɒtɪk/ a. chaotique.

chap[1] /tʃæp/ n. (*man: fam.*) type m.

chap[2] /tʃæp/ n. gerçure f. —v.t./i. (p.t. **chapped**) (se) gercer.

chapel /'tʃæpl/ n. chapelle f.; (*Nonconformist*) église (nonconformiste) f.

chaperon /'ʃæpərəʊn/ n. chaperon m. —v.t. chaperonner.

chaplain /'tʃæplɪn/ n. aumônier m.

chapter /'tʃæptə(r)/ n. chapitre m.

char[1] /tʃɑː(r)/ n. (*fam.*) femme de ménage f.

char[2] /tʃɑː(r)/ v.t. (p.t. **charred**) carboniser.

character /'kærəktə(r)/ n. caractère m.; (*in novel, play*) personnage m. **of good ~,** de bonne réputation. ~**ize** v.t. caractériser.

characteristic /kærəktə'rɪstɪk/ a. & n. caractéristique (f.). ~**ally** adv. typiquement.

charade /ʃə'rɑːd/ n. charade f.

charcoal /'tʃɑːkəʊl/ n. charbon (de bois) m.

charge /tʃɑːdʒ/ n. prix m.; (*mil.*) charge f.; (*jurid.*) inculpation f., accusation f.; (*task, custody*) charge f. ~**s,** frais m. pl. —v.t. faire payer; (*ask*) demander (**for,** pour); (*enemy, gun*) charger; (*jurid.*) inculper, accuser. —v.i. foncer, se précipiter. **in ~ of,** responsable de. **take ~ of,** prendre en charge, se charger de. ~**able to,** (*comm.*) aux frais de.

chariot /'tʃærɪət/ n. char m.

charisma /kə'rɪzmə/ n. magnétisme m.

charit|y /'tʃærətɪ/ n. charité f.; (*society*) fondation charitable f. ~**able** a. charitable.

charlatan /'ʃɑːlətən/ n. charlatan m.

charm /tʃɑːm/ n. charme m.; (*trinket*)

amulette f. —v.t. charmer. ~**ing** a. charmant.

chart /tʃɑːt/ n. (*naut.*) carte (marine) f.; (*table*) tableau m., graphique m. —v.t. (*route*) porter sur la carte.

charter /'tʃɑːtə(r)/ n. charte f. ~ (**flight**), charter m. —v.t. affréter. ~**ed accountant,** expert-comptable m.

charwoman /'tʃɑːwʊmən/ n. (pl. -**women**) femme de ménage f.

chase /tʃeɪs/ v.t. poursuivre. —v.i. courir (**after,** après). —n. chasse f. ~ **away** or **off,** chasser.

chasm /'kæzəm/ n. abîme m.

chassis /'ʃæsɪ/ n. châssis m.

chaste /tʃeɪst/ a. chaste.

chastise /tʃæ'staɪz/ v.t. châtier.

chastity /'tʃæstətɪ/ n. chasteté f.

chat /tʃæt/ n. causette f. —v.i. (p.t. **chatted**) bavarder. **have a ~,** bavarder. ~**ty** a. bavard.

chatter /'tʃætə(r)/ n. bavardage m. —v.i. bavarder. **his teeth are** ~**ing,** il claque des dents.

chatterbox /'tʃætəbɒks/ n. bavard(e) m. (f.).

chauffeur /'ʃəʊfə(r)/ n. chauffeur (de particulier) m.

chauvinis|t /'ʃəʊvɪnɪst/ n. chauvin(e) m. (f.). **male ~t,** (*pej.*) phallocrate m. ~**m** /-zəm/ n. chauvinisme m.

cheap /tʃiːp/ a. (-**er,** -**est**) bon marché invar.; (*fare, rate*) réduit; (*worthless*) sans valeur. ~**er,** meilleur marché. invar. ~(**ly**) adv. à bon marché. ~**ness** n. bas prix m.

cheapen /'tʃiːpən/ v.t. déprécier.

cheat /tʃiːt/ v.i. tricher; (*by fraud*) frauder. —v.t. (*defraud*) frauder; (*deceive*) tromper. —n. escroc m.

check[1] /tʃek/ v.t./i. vérifier; (*tickets*) contrôler; (*stop*) enrayer, arrêter; (*restrain*) contenir; (*rebuke*) réprimander; (*tick off*: *Amer.*) cocher. —n. vérification f.; contrôle m.; (*curb*) frein m.; (*chess*) échec m.; (*bill:* *Amer.*) addition f.; (*cheque:* *Amer.*) chèque m. ~ **in,** signer le registre; (*at airport*) passer à l'enregistrement. ~ **out,** régler sa note. ~**-up** n. examen médical m.

check[2] /tʃek/ n. (*pattern*) carreaux m. pl. ~**ed** a. à carreaux.

checkmate /'tʃekmeɪt/ n. échec et mat m.

checkroom /'tʃekrʊm/ n. (*Amer.*) vestiaire m.

cheek /tʃiːk/ n. joue f.; (*impudence*) culot m. ~y a. effronté.

cheer /tʃɪə(r)/ n. gaieté f. ~s, acclamations f. pl. —int. à votre santé. —v.t. acclamer, applaudir. ~ (up), (*gladden*) remonter le moral à. ~ up, prendre courage. ~ful a. gai. ~fulness n. gaieté f.

cheerio /tʃɪərɪ'əʊ/ int. (*fam.*) salut.

cheerless /'tʃɪəlɪs/ a. morne.

cheese /tʃiːz/ n. fromage m.

cheetah /'tʃiːtə/ n. guépard m.

chef /ʃef/ n. (*cook*) chef m.

chemical /'kemɪkl/ a. chimique. —n. produit chimique m.

chemist /'kemɪst/ n. pharmacien(ne) m. (f.).; (*scientist*) chimiste m./f. ~'s shop, pharmacie f. ~ry n. chimie f.

cheque /tʃek/ n. chèque m. ~-book n. chéquier m.

chequered /'tʃekəd/ a. (*pattern*) à carreaux; (*fig.*) mouvementé.

cherish /'tʃerɪʃ/ v.t. chérir; (*hope*) nourrir, caresser.

cherry /'tʃerɪ/ n. cerise f.

chess /tʃes/ n. échecs m. pl. ~-board n. échiquier m.

chest /tʃest/ n. (*anat.*) poitrine f.; (*box*) coffre m. ~ of drawers, commode f.

chestnut /'tʃesnʌt/ n. châtaigne f.; (*edible*) marron m., châtaigne f.

chew /tʃuː/ v.t. mâcher. ~ing-gum n. chewing-gum m.

chic /ʃiːk/ a. chic *invar*.

chick /tʃɪk/ n. poussin m.

chicken /'tʃɪkɪn/ n. poulet m. —a. (*sl.*) froussard. —v.i. ~ out, (*sl.*) se dégonfler. ~-pox n. varicelle f.

chicory /'tʃɪkərɪ/ n. (*for salad*) endive f.; (*in coffee*) chicorée f.

chief /tʃiːf/ n. chef m. —a. principal. ~ly adv. principalement.

chilblain /'tʃɪlbleɪn/ n. engelure f.

child /tʃaɪld/ n. (*pl.* children /'tʃɪldrən/) enfant m./f. ~hood n. enfance f. ~ish a. enfantin. ~less a. sans enfants. ~like a. innocent, candide.

childbirth /'tʃaɪldbɜːθ/ n. accouchement m.

Chile /'tʃɪlɪ/ n. Chili m. ~an a. & n. chilien(ne) (m. (f.)).

chill /tʃɪl/ n. froid m.; (*med.*) refroidissement m. —a. froid. —v.t. (*person*) donner froid à; (*wine*) rafraîchir; (*food*) mettre au frais. ~y a. froid; (*sensitive to cold*) frileux. be or feel ~y, avoir froid.

chilli /'tʃɪlɪ/ n. (*pl.* -ies) piment m.

chime /tʃaɪm/ n. carillon m. —v.t./i. carillonner.

chimney /'tʃɪmnɪ/ n. cheminée f. ~-sweep n. ramoneur m.

chimpanzee /tʃɪmpæn'ziː/ n. chimpanzé m.

chin /tʃɪn/ n. menton m.

china /'tʃaɪnə/ n. porcelaine f.

Chin|a /'tʃaɪnə/ n. Chine f. ~ese /-'niːz/ a. & n. chinois(e) (m. (f.)).

chink[1] /tʃɪŋk/ n. (*slit*) fente f.

chink[2] /tʃɪŋk/ n. tintement m. —v.t./i. (faire) tinter.

chip /tʃɪp/ n. (*on plate etc.*) ébréchure f.; (*piece*) éclat m.; (*culin.*) frite f.; (*microchip*) microplaquette f., puce f. —v.t./i. (*p.t.* chipped) (s')ébrécher. ~ in, (*fam.*) dire son mot; (*with money: fam.*) contribuer. (potato) ~s, (*Amer.*) chips m. pl.

chipboard /'tʃɪpbɔːd/ n. aggloméré m.

chiropodist /kɪ'rɒpədɪst/ n. pédicure m./f.

chirp /tʃɜːp/ n. pépiement m. —v.i. pépier.

chirpy /'tʃɜːpɪ/ a. gai.

chisel /'tʃɪzl/ n. ciseau m. —v.t. (*p.t.* chiselled) ciseler.

chit /tʃɪt/ n. note f., mot m.

chit-chat /'tʃɪttʃæt/ n. bavardage m.

chivalr|y /'ʃɪvlrɪ/ n. galanterie f. ~ous a. chevaleresque.

chives /tʃaɪvz/ n. pl. ciboulette f.

chlorine /'klɔːriːn/ n. chlore m.

choc-ice /'tʃɒkaɪs/ n. esquimau m.

chock /tʃɒk/ n. cale f. ~-a-block, ~-full adjs. archiplein.

chocolate /'tʃɒklət/ n. chocolat m.

choice /tʃɔɪs/ n. choix m. —a. de choix.

choir /'kwaɪə(r)/ n. chœur m.

choirboy /'kwaɪəbɔɪ/ n. jeune choriste m.

choke /tʃəʊk/ v.t./i. (s')étrangler. —n. starter m. ~ (up), boucher.

cholera /'kɒlərə/ n. choléra m.

cholesterol /kə'lestərɒl/ n. cholestérol m.

choose /tʃuːz/ v.t./i. (*p.t.* chose, *p.p.* chosen) choisir. ~ to do, décider de faire.

choosy /'tʃuːzɪ/ a. (*fam.*) exigeant.

chop /tʃɒp/ v.t./i. (*p.t.* chopped) (*wood*) couper (à la hache); (*food*) hacher. —n. (*meat*) côtelette f. ~ down, abattre. ~per n. hachoir m.; (*sl.*) hélicoptère m.

choppy /'tʃɒpɪ/ a. (*sea*) agité.

chopstick /'tʃɒpstɪk/ *n.* baguette *f.*

choral /'kɔːrəl/ *a.* choral.

chord /kɔːd/ *n.* (*mus.*) accord *m.*

chore /tʃɔː(r)/ *n.* travail (routinier) *m.*; (*unpleasant task*) corvée *f.*

choreographer /kɒrɪ'ɒgrəfə(r)/ *n.* chorégraphe *m./f.*

chortle /'tʃɔːtl/ *n.* gloussement *m.* —*v.i.* glousser.

chorus /'kɔːrəs/ *n.* chœur *m.*; (*of song*) refrain *m.*

chose, chosen /tʃəʊz, 'tʃəʊzn/ *see* **choose.**

Christ /kraɪst/ *n.* le Christ *m.*

christen /'krɪsn/ *v.t.* baptiser. ∼**ing** *n.* baptême *m.*

Christian /'krɪstʃən/ *a.* & *n.* chrétien(ne) (*m.* (*f.*)). ∼ **name,** prénom *m.* ∼**ity** /-stɪ'ænətɪ/ *n.* christianisme *m.*

Christmas /'krɪsməs/ *n.* Noël *m.* —*a.* (*card, tree, etc.*) de Noël. ∼**box** *n.* étrennes *f. pl.* ∼ **Day/Eve,** le jour/la veille de Noël.

chrome /krəʊm/ *n.* chrome *m.*

chromium /'krəʊmɪəm/ *n.* chrome *m.*

chromosome /'krəʊməsəʊm/ *n.* chromosome *m.*

chronic /'krɒnɪk/ *a.* (*situation, disease*) chronique; (*bad: fam.*) affreux.

chronicle /'krɒnɪkl/ *n.* chronique *f.*

chronolog|y /krə'nɒlədʒɪ/ *n.* chronologie *f.* ∼**ical** /krɒnə'lɒdʒɪkl/ *a.* chronologique.

chrysanthemum /krɪ'sænθəməm/ *n.* chrysanthème *m.*

chubby /'tʃʌbɪ/ *a.* (-**ier, -iest**) dodu, potelé.

chuck /tʃʌk/ *v.t.* (*fam.*) lancer. ∼ **away** *or* **out,** (*fam.*) balancer.

chuckle /'tʃʌkl/ *n.* gloussement *m.* —*v.i.* glousser, rire.

chuffed /tʃʌft/ *a.* (*sl.*) bien content.

chum /tʃʌm/ *n.* cop|ain, -ine *m.*, *f.* ∼**my** *a.* amical. ∼**my with,** copain avec.

chunk /tʃʌŋk/ *n.* (gros) morceau *m.*

chunky /'tʃʌŋkɪ/ *a.* trapu.

church /'tʃɜːtʃ/ *n.* église *f.*

churchyard /'tʃɜːtʃjɑːd/ *n.* cimetière *m.*

churlish /'tʃɜːlɪʃ/ *a.* grossier.

churn /'tʃɜːn/ *n.* baratte *f.*; (*milk-can*) bidon *m.* —*v.t.* baratter. ∼ **out,** produire (en série).

chute /ʃuːt/ *n.* glissière *f.*; (*for rubbish*) vide-ordures *m. invar.*

chutney /'tʃʌtnɪ/ *n.* condiment (de fruits) *m.*

cider /'saɪdə(r)/ *n.* cidre *m.*

cigar /sɪ'gɑː(r)/ *n.* cigare *m.*

cigarette /sɪgə'ret/ *n.* cigarette *f.* ∼**holder** *n.* fume-cigarette *m. invar.*

cinder /'sɪndə(r)/ *n.* cendre *f.*

cine-camera /'sɪnɪkæmərə/ *n.* caméra *f.*

cinema /'sɪnəmə/ *n.* cinéma *m.*

cinnamon /'sɪnəmən/ *n.* cannelle *f.*

cipher /'saɪfə(r)/ *n.* (*numeral, code*) chiffre *m.*; (*person*) nullité *f.*

circle /'sɜːkl/ *n.* cercle *m.*; (*theatre*) balcon *m.* —*v.t.* (*go round*) faire le tour de; (*word, error, etc.*) entourer d'un cercle. —*v.i.* décrire des cercles.

circuit /'sɜːkɪt/ *n.* circuit *m.*

circuitous /sɜː'kjuːɪtəs/ *a.* indirect.

circular /'sɜːkjʊlə(r)/ *a.* & *n.* circulaire (*f.*).

circulat|e /'sɜːkjʊleɪt/ *v.t./i.* (faire) circuler. ∼**ion** /-'leɪʃn/ *n.* circulation *f.*; (*of newspaper*) tirage *m.*

circumcis|e /'sɜːkəmsaɪz/ *v.t.* circoncire. ∼**ion** /-'sɪʒn/ *n.* circoncision *f.*

circumference /sɜː'kʌmfərəns/ *n.* circonférence *f.*

circumflex /'sɜːkəmfleks/ *n.* circonflexe *m.*

circumspect /'sɜːkəmspekt/ *a.* circonspect.

circumstance /'sɜːkəmstəns/ *n.* circonstance *f.* ∼**s,** (*financial*) situation financière *f.*

circus /'sɜːkəs/ *n.* cirque *m.*

cistern /'sɪstən/ *n.* réservoir *m.*

citadel /'sɪtədel/ *n.* citadelle *f.*

cit|e /saɪt/ *v.t.* citer. ∼**ation** /-'teɪʃn/ *n.* citation *f.*

citizen /'sɪtɪzn/ *n.* citoyen(ne) *m.* (*f.*); (*of town*) habitant(e) *m.* (*f.*). ∼**ship** *n.* citoyenneté *f.*

citrus /'sɪtrəs/ *a.* ∼ **fruit(s),** agrumes *m. pl.*

city /'sɪtɪ/ *n.* (grande) ville *f.* **the C**∼, la Cité de Londres.

civic /'sɪvɪk/ *a.* civique. ∼ **centre,** centre administratif *m.* ∼**s** *n. pl.* instruction civique *f.*

civil /'sɪvl/ *a.* civil; (*rights*) civique; (*defence*) passif. **C**∼ **Servant,** fonctionnaire *m./f.* **C**∼ **Service,** fonction publique *f.* ∼ **war,** guerre civile *f.* ∼**ity** /sɪ'vɪlətɪ/ *n.* civilité *f.*

civilian /sɪ'vɪlɪən/ *a.* & *n.* civil(e) (*m.* (*f.*)).

civiliz|e /'sɪvəlaɪz/ v.t. civiliser. **~a-tion** /-'zeɪʃn/ n. civilisation f.

civvies /'sɪvɪz/ n. pl. **in ~**, (sl.) en civil.

clad /klæd/ see **clothe**.

claim /kleɪm/ v.t. revendiquer, réclamer; (assert) prétendre. —n. revendication f., prétention f.; (assertion) affirmation f.; (right) droit m.

claimant /'kleɪmənt/ n. (of social benefits) demandeur m.

clairvoyant /kleə'vɔɪənt/ n. voyant(e) m. (f.).

clam /klæm/ n. palourde f.

clamber /'klæmbə(r)/ v.i. grimper.

clammy /'klæmɪ/ a. (-ier, -iest) moite.

clamour /'klæmə(r)/ n. clameur f., cris m. pl. —v.i. **~ for**, demander à grands cris.

clamp /klæmp/ n. agrafe f.; (large) crampon m.; (for carpentry) serre-joint(s) m. —v.t. serrer. **~ down on**, sévir contre.

clan /klæn/ n. clan m.

clandestine /klæn'destɪn/ a. clandestin.

clang /klæŋ/ n. son métallique m.

clanger /'klæŋə(r)/ n. (sl.) bévue f.

clap /klæp/ v.t./i. (p.t. **clapped**) applaudir; (put forcibly) mettre. —n. applaudissement m.; (of thunder) coup m. **~ one's hands**, battre des mains.

claptrap /'klæptræp/ n. baratin m.

claret /'klærət/ n. bordeaux rouge m.

clarif|y /'klærɪfaɪ/ v.t./i. (se) clarifier. **~ication** /-ɪ'keɪʃn/ n. clarification f.

clarinet /klærɪ'net/ n. clarinette f.

clarity /'klærətɪ/ n. clarté f.

clash /klæʃ/ n. choc m.; (fig.) conflit m. —v.i. (metal objects) s'entrechoquer; (fig.) se heurter.

clasp /klɑːsp/ n. (fastener) fermoir m., agrafe f. —v.t. serrer.

class /klɑːs/ n. classe f. —v.t. classer.

classic /'klæsɪk/ a. & n. classique (m.). **~s**, (univ.) les humanités f. pl. **~al** a. classique.

classif|y /'klæsɪfaɪ/ v.t. classifier. **~ication** /-ɪ'keɪʃn/ n. classification f. **~ied** a. (information etc.) secret. **~ied advertisement**, petite annonce f.

classroom /'klɑːsrʊm/ n. salle de classe f.

classy /'klɑːsɪ/ a. (sl.) chic invar.

clatter /'klætə(r)/ n. cliquetis m. —v.i. cliqueter.

clause /klɔːz/ n. clause f.; (gram.) proposition f.

claustrophob|ia /klɔːstrə'fəʊbɪə/ n. claustrophobie f. **~ic** a. & n. claustrophobe (m.|f.).

claw /klɔː/ n. (of animal, small bird) griffe f.; (of bird of prey) serre f.; (of lobster) pince f. —v.t. griffer.

clay /kleɪ/ n. argile f.

clean /kliːn/ a. (-er, -est) propre; (shape, stroke, etc.) net. —adv. complètement. —v.t. nettoyer. —v.i. **~ up**, faire le nettoyage. **~-shaven** a. glabre. **~er** n. femme de ménage f.; (of clothes) teinturier, -ière m., f. **~ly** adv. proprement; (sharply) nettement.

cleanliness /'klenlɪnɪs/ n. propreté f.

cleans|e /klenz/ v.t. nettoyer; (fig.) purifier. **~ing cream**, crème démaquillante f.

clear /klɪə(r)/ a. (-er, -est) clair; (glass) transparent; (profit) net; (road) dégagé. —adv. complètement. —v.t. (free) dégager (of, de); (table) débarrasser; (jump over) franchir; (debt) liquider; (jurid.) disculper. **~ (away or off)**, (remove) enlever. —v.i. (fog) se dissiper. **~ of**, (away from) à l'écart de. **~ off** or **out**, (sl.) décamper. **~ out**, (clean) nettoyer. **~ up**, (tidy) ranger; (mystery) éclaircir; (of weather) s'éclaircir. **~ly** adv. clairement.

clearance /'klɪərəns/ n. (permission) autorisation f.; (space) dégagement m. **~ sale**, soldes m. pl.

clearing /'klɪərɪŋ/ n. clairière f.

clearway /'klɪəweɪ/ n. route à stationnement interdit f.

cleavage /'kliːvɪdʒ/ n. clivage m.; (fig.) naissance des seins f.

clef /klef/ n. (mus.) clé f.

cleft /kleft/ n. fissure f.

clemen|t /'klemənt/ a. clément. **~cy** n. clémence f.

clench /klentʃ/ v.t. serrer.

clergy /'klɜːdʒɪ/ n. clergé m. **~man** n. (pl. **-men**) ecclésiastique m.

cleric /'klerɪk/ n. clerc m. **~al** a. (relig.) clérical; (of clerks) de bureau, d'employé.

clerk /klɑːk, Amer. klɜːk/ n. employé(e) de bureau m. (f.).

clever /'klevə(r)/ a. (-er, -est) intelligent; (skilful) habile. **~ly** adv. intelligemment; habilement. **~ness** n. intelligence f.

cliché /'kliːʃeɪ/ n. cliché m.

click /klɪk/ n. déclic m. —v.i. faire

un déclic; (*people*: *sl.*) s'entendre, se plaire.

client /'klaɪənt/ *n.* client(e) *m.* (*f.*).

clientele /kliːən'tel/ *n.* clientèle *f.*

cliff /klɪf/ *n.* falaise *f.*

climat|e /'klaɪmɪt/ *n.* climat *m.* ~**ic** /-'mætɪk/ *a.* climatique.

climax /'klaɪmæks/ *n.* point culminant *m.*; (*sexual*) orgasme *m.*

climb /klaɪm/ *v.t.* (*stairs*) monter, grimper; (*tree, ladder*) monter *or* grimper à; (*mountain*) faire l'ascension de. —*v.i.* monter, grimper. —*n.* montée *f.* ~ **down**, (*fig.*) en rabattre. ~**er** *n.* (*sport*) alpiniste *m./f.*

clinch /klɪntʃ/ *v.t.* (*a deal*) conclure.

cling /klɪŋ/ *v.i.* (*p.t.* **clung**) se cramponner (**to**, à); (*stick*) coller.

clinic /'klɪnɪk/ *n.* centre médical *m.*; (*private*) clinique *f.*

clinical /'klɪnɪkl/ *a.* clinique.

clink /klɪŋk/ *n.* tintement *m.* —*v.t./i.* (faire) tinter.

clinker /'klɪŋkə(r)/ *n.* mâchefer *m.*

clip[1] /klɪp/ *n.* (*for paper*) trombone *m.*; (*for hair*) barrette *f.*; (*for tube*) collier *m.* —*v.t.* (*p.t.* **clipped**) attacher (**to**, à).

clip[2] /klɪp/ *v.t.* (*p.t.* **clipped**) (*cut*) couper. —*n.* coupe *f.*; (*of film*) extrait *m.*; (*blow*: *fam.*) taloche *f.* ~**ping** *n.* coupure *f.*

clippers /'klɪpəz/ *n. pl.* tondeuse *f.*; (*for nails*) pince à ongles *f.*

clique /kliːk/ *n.* clique *f.*

cloak /kləʊk/ *n.* (grande) cape *f.*, manteau ample *m.*

cloakroom /'kləʊkrʊm/ *n.* vestiaire *m.*; (*toilet*) toilettes *f. pl.*

clobber /'klɒbə(r)/ *n.* (*sl.*) affaires *f. pl.* —*v.t.* (*hit*: *sl.*) rosser.

clock /klɒk/ *n.* pendule *f.*; (*large*) horloge *f.* —*v.i.* ~ **in** *or* **out**, pointer. ~ **up**, (*miles etc.*: *fam.*) faire. ~**-tower** *n.* clocher *m.*

clockwise /'klɒkwaɪz/ *a. & adv.* dans le sens des aiguilles d'une montre.

clockwork /'klɒkwɜːk/ *n.* mécanisme *m.* —*a.* mécanique.

clod /klɒd/ *n.* (*of earth*) motte *f.*; (*person*: *fam.*) lourdaud(e) *m.* (*f.*).

clog /klɒg/ *n.* sabot *m.* —*v.t./i.* (*p.t.* **clogged**) (se) boucher.

cloister /'klɔɪstə(r)/ *n.* cloître *m.*

close[1] /kləʊs/ *a.* (**-er, -est**) (*near*) proche (**to**, de); (*link, collaboration*) étroit; (*friend*) intime; (*order, match*) serré; (*weather*) lourd.

~ **together,** (*crowded*) serrés. —*adv.* (tout) près. —*n.* (*street*) impasse *f.* ~ **by,** ~ **at hand,** tout près. ~**-up** *n.* gros plan *m.* **have a** ~ **shave,** l'échapper belle. ~**ly** *adv.* (*follow*) de près. ~**ness** *n.* proximité *f.*

close[2] /kləʊz/ *v.t.* fermer. —*v.i.* se fermer; (*of shop etc.*) fermer; (*end*) (se) terminer. —*n.* fin *f.* ~**d shop,** organisation qui exclut les travailleurs non syndiqués *f.*

closet /'klɒzɪt/ *n.* (*Amer.*) placard *m.*

closure /'kləʊʒə(r)/ *n.* fermeture *f.*

clot /klɒt/ *n.* (*of blood*) caillot *m.*; (*in sauce*) grumeau *m.*; (*sl.*) imbécile *m./f.* —*v.t./i.* (*p.t.* **clotted**) (se) coaguler.

cloth /klɒθ/ *n.* tissu *m.*; (*duster*) linge *m.*; (*table-cloth*) nappe *f.*

cloth|e /kləʊð/ *v.t.* (*p.t.* **clothed** *or* **clad**) vêtir. ~**ing** *n.* vêtements *m. pl.*

clothes /kləʊðz/ *n. pl.* vêtements *m. pl.*, habits *m. pl.*

cloud /klaʊd/ *n.* nuage *m.* —*v.i.* se couvrir (de nuages); (*become gloomy*) s'assombrir. ~**y** *a.* (*sky*) couvert; (*liquid*) trouble.

cloudburst /'klaʊdbɜːst/ *n.* trombe d'eau *f.*

clout /klaʊt/ *n.* (*blow*) coup de poing *m.*; (*power*: *fam.*) pouvoir effectif *m.* —*v.t.* frapper.

clove /kləʊv/ *n.* clou de girofle *m.* ~ **of garlic,** gousse d'ail *f.*

clover /'kləʊvə(r)/ *n.* trèfle *m.*

clown /klaʊn/ *n.* clown *m.* —*v.i.* faire le clown.

cloy /klɔɪ/ *v.t.* écœurer.

club /klʌb/ *n.* (*group*) club *m.*; (*weapon*) massue *f.* ~**s,** (*cards*) trèfle *m.* —*v.t./i.* (*p.t.* **clubbed**) matraquer. ~ **together,** (*share costs*) se cotiser.

cluck /klʌk/ *v.i.* glousser.

clue /kluː/ *n.* indice *m.*; (*in crossword*) définition *f.* **he does not have a** ~, **he is** ~**less,** (*fam.*) il n'en a pas la moindre idée.

clump /klʌmp/ *n.* massif *m.*

clums|y /'klʌmzɪ/ *a.* (**-ier, -iest**) maladroit; (*tool*) peu commode. ~**iness** *n.* maladresse *f.*

clung /klʌŋ/ *see* **cling.**

cluster /'klʌstə(r)/ *n.* (petit) groupe *m.* —*v.i.* se grouper.

clutch /klʌtʃ/ *v.t.* (*hold*) serrer fort; (*grasp*) saisir. —*v.i.* ~ **at,** (*try to* *grasp*) essayer de saisir. —*n.* étreinte *f.*; (*auto.*) embrayage *m.*

clutter /'klʌtə(r)/ *n.* désordre *m.*, fouillis *m.* —*v.t.* encombrer.

coach /kəʊtʃ/ *n.* autocar *m.*; (*of train*) wagon *m.*; (*horse-drawn*) carrosse *m.*; (*sport*) entraîneu|r, -se *m.*, *f.* —*v.t.* donner des leçons (particulières) à; (*sport*) entraîner.

coagulate /kəʊˈægjʊleɪt/ *v.t./i.* (se) coaguler.

coal /kəʊl/ *n.* charbon *m.*

coalfield /'kəʊlfiːld/ *n.* bassin houiller *m.*

coalition /kəʊəˈlɪʃn/ *n.* coalition *f.*

coarse /kɔːs/ *a.* (**-er, -est**) grossier. **~ness** *n.* caractère grossier *m.*

coast /kəʊst/ *n.* côte *f.* —*v.i.* (*car, bicycle*) descendre en roue libre. **~al** *a.* côtier.

coaster /'kəʊstə(r)/ *n.* (*ship*) caboteur *m.*; (*mat*) dessous de verre *m.*

coastguard /'kəʊstɡɑːd/ *n.* gardecôte *m.*

coastline /'kəʊstlaɪn/ *n.* littoral *m.*

coat /kəʊt/ *n.* manteau *m.*; (*of animal*) pelage *m.*; (*of paint*) couche *f.* —*v.t.* enduire, couvrir; (*with chocolate*) enrober (**with**, de). **~ of arms**, armoiries *f. pl.* **~ing** *n.* couche *f.*

coax /kəʊks/ *v.t.* amadouer.

cob /kɒb/ *n.* (*of corn*) épi *m.*

cobble[1] /'kɒbl/ *n.* pavé *m.* **~-stone** *n.* pavé *m.*

cobble[2] /'kɒbl/ *v.t.* rapetasser.

cobbler /'kɒblə(r)/ *n.* (*old use*) cordonnier *m.*

cobweb /'kɒbweb/ *n.* toile d'araignée *f.*

cocaine /kəʊˈkeɪn/ *n.* cocaïne *f.*

cock /kɒk/ *n.* (*oiseau*) mâle *m.*; (*rooster*) coq *m.* —*v.t.* (*gun*) armer; (*ears*) dresser. **~-and-bull story**, histoire à dormir debout *f.* **~eyed** *a.* (*askew: sl.*) de travers.

cockerel /'kɒkərəl/ *n.* jeune coq *m.*

cockle /'kɒkl/ *n.* (*culin.*) coque *f.*

cockney /'kɒknɪ/ *n.* Cockney *m./f.*

cockpit /'kɒkpɪt/ *n.* poste de pilotage *m.*

cockroach /'kɒkrəʊtʃ/ *n.* cafard *m.*

cocksure /kɒkˈʃʊə(r)/ *a.* sûr de soi.

cocktail /'kɒkteɪl/ *n.* cocktail *m.* **fruit ~**, macédoine (de fruits) *f.*

cocky /'kɒkɪ/ *a.* (**-ier, -iest**) trop sûr de soi, arrogant.

cocoa /'kəʊkəʊ/ *n.* cacao *m.*

coconut /'kəʊkənʌt/ *n.* noix de coco *f.*

cocoon /kəˈkuːn/ *n.* cocon *m.*

COD *abbr.* (*cash on delivery*) paiement à la livraison *m.*

cod /kɒd/ *n. invar.* morue *f.* **~-liver oil**, huile de foie de morue *f.*

coddle /'kɒdl/ *v.t.* dorloter.

code /kəʊd/ *n.* code *m.* —*v.t.* coder.

codify /'kəʊdɪfaɪ/ *v.t.* codifier.

coeducational /kəʊedʒʊˈkeɪʃənl/ *a.* (*school, teaching*) mixte.

coerc|e /kəʊˈɜːs/ *v.t.* contraindre. **~ion** /-ʃn/ *n.* contrainte *f.*

coexist /kəʊɪɡˈzɪst/ *v.i.* coexister. **~ence** *n.* coexistence *f.*

coffee /'kɒfɪ/ *n.* café *m.* **~ bar**, café *m.*, cafétéria *f.* **~-pot** *n.* cafetière *f.* **~-table** *n.* table basse *f.*

coffer /'kɒfə(r)/ *n.* coffre *m.*

coffin /'kɒfɪn/ *n.* cercueil *m.*

cog /kɒɡ/ *n.* dent *f.*; (*fig.*) rouage *m.*

cogent /'kəʊdʒənt/ *a.* convaincant; (*relevant*) pertinent.

cognac /'kɒnjæk/ *n.* cognac *m.*

cohabit /kəʊˈhæbɪt/ *v.i.* vivre en concubinage.

coherent /kəʊˈhɪərənt/ *a.* cohérent.

coil /kɔɪl/ *v.t./i.* (s')enrouler. —*n.* rouleau *m.*; (*one ring*) spire *f.*

coin /kɔɪn/ *n.* pièce (de monnaie) *f.* —*v.t.* (*word*) inventer. **~age** *n.* monnaie *f.*; (*fig.*) invention *f.*

coincide /kəʊɪnˈsaɪd/ *v.i.* coïncider.

coinciden|ce /kəʊˈɪnsɪdəns/ *n.* coïncidence *f.* **~tal** /-ˈdentl/ *a.* dû à une coïncidence.

coke /kəʊk/ *n.* coke *m.*

colander /'kʌləndə(r)/ *n.* passoire *f.*

cold /kəʊld/ *a.* (**-er, -est**) froid. **be** *or* **feel ~**, avoir froid. **it is ~**, il fait froid. —*n.* froid *m.*; (*med.*) rhume *m.* **~-blooded** *a.* sans pitié. **~ cream**, crème de beauté *f.* **~ feet**, la frousse. **~-shoulder** *v.t.* snober. **~ness** *n.* froideur *f.*

coleslaw /'kəʊlslɔː/ *n.* salade de chou cru *f.*

colic /'kɒlɪk/ *n.* coliques *f. pl.*

collaborat|e /kəˈlæbəreɪt/ *v.i.* collaborer. **~ion** /-ˈreɪʃn/ *n.* collaboration *f.* **~or** *n.* collabora|teur, -trice *m., f.*

collage /'kɒlɑːʒ/ *n.* collage *m.*

collapse /kəˈlæps/ *v.i.* s'effondrer; (*med.*) avoir un malaise. —*n.* effondrement *m.*

collapsible /kəˈlæpsəbl/ *a.* pliant.

collar /'kɒlə(r)/ *n.* col *m.*; (*of dog*) collier *m.* —*v.t.* (*appropriate: sl.*) piquer. **~-bone** *n.* clavicule *f.*

colleague /'kɒliːg/ *n.* collègue *m./f.*

collect /kə'lekt/ *v.t.* rassembler; (*pick up*) ramasser; (*call for*) passer prendre; (*money, rent*) encaisser; (*taxes*) percevoir; (*as hobby*) collectionner. —*v.i.* se rassembler; (*dust*) s'amasser. —*adv.* **call ~,** (*Amer.*) téléphoner en PCV. **~ion** /-kʃn/ *n.* collection *f.*; (*in church*) quête *f.*; (*of mail*) levée *f.* **~or** *n.* (*as hobby*) collectionneu|r, -se *m., f.*

collective /kə'lektɪv/ *a.* collectif.

college /'kɒlɪdʒ/ *n.* (*for higher education*) institut *m.,* école *f.*; (*within university*) collège *m.* **be in ~,** être en faculté.

collide /kə'laɪd/ *v.i.* entrer en collision (**with,** avec).

colliery /'kɒlɪərɪ/ *n.* houillère *f.*

collision /kə'lɪʒn/ *n.* collision *f.*

colloquial /kə'ləʊkwɪəl/ *a.* familier. **~ism** *n.* expression familière *f.*

collusion /kə'luːʒn/ *n.* collusion *f.*

colon /'kəʊlən/ *n.* (*gram.*) deux-points *m. invar.*; (*anat.*) côlon *m.*

colonel /'kɜːnl/ *n.* colonel *m.*

colonize /'kɒlənaɪz/ *v.t.* coloniser.

colon|y /'kɒlənɪ/ *n.* colonie *f.* **~ial** /kə'ləʊnɪəl/ *a. & n.* colonial(e) (*m. (f.)*).

colossal /kə'lɒsl/ *a.* colossal.

colour /'kʌlə(r)/ *n.* couleur *f.* —*a.* (*photo etc.*) en couleur; (*TV set*) couleur *invar.* —*v.t.* colorer; (*with crayon*) colorier. **~-blind** *a.* daltonien. **~ful** *a.* coloré.

coloured /'kʌləd/ *a.* (*person, pencil*) de couleur. —*n.* personne de couleur *f.*

colt /kəʊlt/ *n.* poulain *m.*

column /'kɒləm/ *n.* colonne *f.*

columnist /'kɒləmnɪst/ *n.* journaliste chroniqueur *m.*

coma /'kəʊmə/ *n.* coma *m.*

comb /kəʊm/ *n.* peigne *m.* —*v.t.* peigner; (*search*) ratisser. **~ one's hair,** se peigner.

combat /'kɒmbæt/ *n.* combat *m.* —*v.t.* (*p.t.* **combated**) combattre. **~ant** /-ətənt/ *n.* combattant(e) *m. (f.).*

combination /kɒmbɪ'neɪʃn/ *n.* combinaison *f.*

combine[1] /kəm'baɪn/ *v.t./i.* (se) combiner, (s')unir.

combine[2] /'kɒmbaɪn/ *n.* (*comm.*) trust *m.,* cartel *m.* **~ harvester,** moissonneuse-batteuse *f.*

combustion /kəm'bʌstʃən/ *n.* combustion *f.*

come /kʌm/ *v.i.* (*p.t.* **came,** *p.p.* **come**) venir; (*occur*) arriver. **~ about,** arriver. **~ across,** rencontrer *or* trouver par hasard. **~ away** *or* **off,** se détacher, partir. **~ back,** revenir. **~-back** *n.* rentrée *f.*; (*retort*) réplique *f.* **~ by,** obtenir. **~ down,** descendre; (*price*) baisser. **~-down** *n.* humiliation *f.* **~ in,** entrer. **~ in for,** recevoir. **~ into,** (*money*) hériter de. **~ off,** (*succeed*) réussir; (*fare*) s'en tirer. **~ out,** sortir. **~ round** *or* **to,** revenir à soi. **~ through,** s'en tirer (indemne de). **~ to,** (*amount*) revenir à. **~ up,** monter; (*fig.*) se présenter. **~-uppance** *n.* (*fam.*) punition (méritée) *f.* **~ up with,** (*find*) trouver; (*produce*) produire.

comedian /kə'miːdɪən/ *n.* comique *m.*

comedy /'kɒmədɪ/ *n.* comédie *f.*

comely /'kʌmlɪ/ *a.* (**-ier, -iest**) (*old use*) avenant, beau.

comet /'kɒmɪt/ *n.* comète *f.*

comfort /'kʌmfət/ *n.* confort *m.*; (*consolation*) réconfort *m.* —*v.t.* consoler. **one's ~s,** ses aises. **~able** *a.* (*chair, car, etc.*) confortable; (*person*) à l'aise, bien; (*wealthy*) aisé.

comforter /'kʌmfətə(r)/ *n.* (*baby's dummy*) sucette *f.*; (*quilt*: *Amer.*) édredon *m.*

comfy /'kʌmfɪ/ *a.* (*fam.*) = **comfortable.**

comic /'kɒmɪk/ *a.* comique. —*n.* (*person*) comique *m.*; (*periodical*) comic *m.* **~ strip,** bande dessinée *f.* **~al** *a.* comique.

coming /'kʌmɪŋ/ *n.* arrivée *f.* —*a.* à venir. **~s and goings,** allées et venues *f. pl.*

comma /'kɒmə/ *n.* virgule *f.*

command /kə'mɑːnd/ *n.* (*authority*) commandement *m.*; (*order*) ordre *m.*; (*mastery*) maîtrise *f.* —*v.t.* commander (**s.o. to,** à qn. de); (*be able to use*) disposer de; (*require*) nécessiter; (*respect*) inspirer. **~er** *n.* commandant *m.* **~ing** *a.* imposant.

commandeer /kɒmən'dɪə(r)/ *v.t.* réquisitionner.

commandment /kə'mɑːndmənt/ *n.* commandement *m.*

commando /kə'mɑːndəʊ/ *n.* (*pl.* **-os**) commando *m.*

commemorat|e /kə'meməreɪt/ *v.t.* commémorer. **~ion** /-'reɪʃn/ *n.* commémoration *f.* **~ive** /-ətɪv/ *a.* commémoratif.

commence /kə'mens/ *v.t./i.* commencer. ∼**ment** *n.* commencement *m.*; (*univ., Amer.*) cérémonie de distribution des diplômes *f.*

commend /kə'mend/ *v.t.* (*praise*) louer; (*entrust*) confier. ∼**able** *a.* louable. ∼**ation** /kɒmen'deɪʃn/ *n.* éloge *m.*

commensurate /kə'menʃərət/ *a.* proportionné.

comment /'kɒment/ *n.* commentaire *m.* —*v.i.* faire des commentaires. ∼ **on,** commenter.

commentary /'kɒməntrɪ/ *n.* commentaire *m.*; (*radio, TV*) reportage *m.*

commentat|e /'kɒmənteɪt/ *v.i.* faire un reportage. ∼**or** *n.* commenta|teur, -trice *m., f.*

commerce /'kɒmɜːs/ *n.* commerce *m.*

commercial /kə'mɜːʃl/ *a.* commercial; (*traveller*) de commerce. ∼**ize** *v.t.* commercialiser.

commiserat|e /kə'mɪzəreɪt/ *v.i.* ∼**e with,** s'apitoyer sur le sort de. ∼**ion** /-'reɪʃn/ *n.* commisération *f.*

commission /kə'mɪʃn/ *n.* commission *f.*; (*order for work*) commande *f.* —*v.t.* (*order*) commander; (*mil.*) nommer officier. ∼ **to do,** charger de faire. **out of** ∼, hors service. ∼**er** *n.* préfet (de police) *m.*

commissionaire /kəmɪʃə'neə(r)/ *n.* commissionnaire *m.*

commit /kə'mɪt/ *v.t.* (*p.t.* **committed**) commettre; (*entrust*) confier. ∼ **o.s.,** s'engager. ∼ **to memory,** apprendre par cœur. ∼**ment** *n.* engagement *m.*

committee /kə'mɪtɪ/ *n.* comité *m.*

commodity /kə'mɒdətɪ/ *n.* produit *m.*, article *m.*

common /'kɒmən/ *a.* (**-er, -est**) (*shared by all*) còmmun; (*usual*) courant, commun; (*vulgar*) vulgaire, commun. —*n.* terrain communal *m.* ∼ **law,** droit coutumier *m.* **C**∼ **Market,** Marché Commun *m.* ∼**-room** *n.* (*schol.*) salle commune *f.* ∼ **sense,** bon sens *m.* **House of C**∼**s,** Chambre des Communes *f.* **in** ∼, en commun. ∼**ly** *adv.* communément.

commoner /'kɒmənə(r)/ *n.* rotur|ier, -ière *m., f.*

commonplace /'kɒmənpleɪs/ *a.* banal. —*n.* banalité *f.*

Commonwealth /'kɒmənwelθ/ *n.* **the** ∼, le Commonwealth *m.*

commotion /kə'məʊʃn/ *n.* agitation *f.*, remue-ménage *m. invar.*

communal /'kɒmjʊnl/ *a.* (*shared*) commun; (*life*) collectif.

commune /'kɒmjuːn/ *n.* (*group*) communauté *f.*

communicat|e /kə'mjuːnɪkeɪt/ *v.t./i.* communiquer. ∼**ion** /-'keɪʃn/ *n.* communication *f.* ∼**ive** /-ətɪv/ *a.* communicatif.

communion /kə'mjuːnɪən/ *n.* communion *f.*

communiqué /kə'mjuːnɪkeɪ/ *n.* communiqué *m.*

Communis|t /'kɒmjʊnɪst/ *n.* communiste *m./f.* ∼**m** /-zəm/ *n.* communisme *m.*

community /kə'mjuːnətɪ/ *n.* communauté *f.*

commute /kə'mjuːt/ *v.i.* faire la navette. —*v.t.* (*jurid.*) commuer. ∼**r** /-ə(r)/ *n.* banlieusard(e) *m.* (*f.*).

compact[1] /kəm'pækt/ *a.* compact.

compact[2] /'kɒmpækt/ *n.* (*lady's case*) poudrier *m.*

companion /kəm'pænjən/ *n.* comp|agnon, -agne *m., f.* ∼**ship** *n.* camaraderie *f.*

company /'kʌmpənɪ/ *n.* (*companionship, firm*) compagnie *f.*; (*guests*) invité(e)s *m.* (*f.*) *pl.*

comparable /'kɒmpərəbl/ *a.* comparable.

compar|e /kəm'peə(r)/ *v.t.* comparer (**with, to,** à). ∼**ed with** *or* **to,** en comparaison de. —*v.i.* être comparable. ∼**ative** /-'pærətɪv/ *a.* (*study, form*) comparatif; (*comfort etc.*) relatif. ∼**atively** /-'pærətɪvlɪ/ *adv.* relativement.

comparison /kəm'pærɪsn/ *n.* comparaison *f.*

compartment /kəm'pɑːtmənt/ *n.* compartiment *m.*

compass /'kʌmpəs/ *n.* (*for direction*) boussole *f.*; (*scope*) portée *f.* ∼(**es**), (*for drawing*) compas *m.*

compassion /kəm'pæʃn/ *n.* compassion *f.* ∼**ate** *a.* compatissant.

compatib|le /kəm'pætəbl/ *a.* compatible. ∼**ility** /-'bɪlətɪ/ *n.* compatibilité *f.*

compatriot /kəm'pætrɪət/ *n.* compatriote *m./f.*

compel /kəm'pel/ *v.t.* (*p.t.* **compelled**) contraindre. ∼**ling** *a.* irrésistible.

compendium /kəm'pendɪəm/ *n.* abrégé *m.*, resumé *m.*

compensat|e /'kɒmpənseɪt/ *v.t./i.* (*financially*) dédommager (**for,** de). ∼**e for sth.,** compenser qch. ∼**ion** /-'seɪʃn/ *n.* compensation *f.*; (*financial*) dédommagement *m.*

compère /'kɒmpeə(r)/ n. anima|teur, -trice m., f. —v.t. animer.

compete /kəm'piːt/ v.i. concourir. ~ with, rivaliser avec.

competen|t /'kɒmpɪtənt/ a. compétent. ~ce n. compétence f.

competition /kɒmpə'tɪʃn/ n. (contest) concours m.; (sport) compétition f.; (comm.) concurrence f.

competitive /kəm'petətɪv/ a. (prices) concurrentiel, compétitif. ~ examination, concours m.

competitor /kəm'petɪtə(r)/ n. concurrent(e) m. (f.).

compile /kəm'paɪl/ v.t. (list) dresser; (book) rédiger. ~r /-ə(r)/ n. ré-dac|teur, -trice m., f.

complacen|t /kəm'pleɪsnt/ a. content de soi. ~cy n. contentement de soi m.

complain /kəm'pleɪn/ v.i. se plaindre (about, of, de).

complaint /kəm'pleɪnt/ n. plainte f.; (in shop etc.) réclamation f.; (illness) maladie f.

complement /'kɒmplɪmənt/ n. complément m. —v.t. compléter. ~ary /-'mentrɪ/ a. complémentaire.

complet|e /kəm'pliːt/ a. complet; (finished) achevé; (downright) parfait. —v.t. achever; (a form) remplir. ~ely adv. complètement. ~ion /-ʃn/ n. achèvement m.

complex /'kɒmpleks/ a. complexe. —n. (psych., archit.) complexe m. ~ity /kəm'pleksətɪ/ n. complexité f.

complexion /kəm'plekʃn/ n. (of face) teint m.; (fig.) caractère m.

compliance /kəm'plaɪəns/ n. (agreement) conformité f.

complicat|e /'kɒmplɪkeɪt/ v.t. compliquer. ~ed a. compliqué. ~ion /-'keɪʃn/ n. complication f.

complicity /kəm'plɪsətɪ/ n. complicité f.

compliment /'kɒmplɪmənt/ n. compliment m. —v.t. /'kɒmplɪment/ complimenter.

complimentary /kɒmplɪ'mentrɪ/ a. (offert) à titre gracieux; (praising) flatteur.

comply /kəm'plaɪ/ v.i. ~ with, se conformer à, obéir à.

component /kəm'pəʊnənt/ n. (of machine etc.) pièce f.; (chemical substance) composant m.; (element: fig.) composante f. —a. constituant.

compose /kəm'pəʊz/ v.t. composer. ~

o.s., se calmer. ~d a. calme. ~r /-ə(r)/ n. (mus.) compositeur m.

composition /kɒmpə'zɪʃn/ n. composition f.

compost /'kɒmpɒst, Amer. 'kɒmpəʊst/ n. compost m.

composure /kəm'pəʊʒə(r)/ n. calme m.

compound¹ /'kɒmpaʊnd/ n. (substance, word) composé m.; (enclosure) enclos m. —a. composé.

compound² /kəm'paʊnd/ v.t. (problem etc.) aggraver.

comprehen|d /kɒmprɪ'hend/ v.t. comprendre. ~sion n. compréhension f.

comprehensive /kɒmprɪ'hensɪv/ a. étendu, complet; (insurance) tous-risques invar. ~ school, collège d'enseignement secondaire m.

compress /kəm'pres/ v.t. comprimer. ~ion /-ʃn/ n. compression f.

comprise /kəm'praɪz/ v.t. comprendre, inclure.

compromise /'kɒmprəmaɪz/ n. compromis m. —v.t. compromettre. —v.i. transiger.

compulsion /kəm'pʌlʃn/ n. contrainte f.

compulsive /kəm'pʌlsɪv/ a. (psych.) compulsif; (liar, smoker) invétéré.

compulsory /kəm'pʌlsərɪ/ a. obligatoire.

compunction /kəm'pʌŋkʃn/ n. scrupule m.

computer /kəm'pjuːtə(r)/ n. ordinateur m. ~ science, informatique f. ~ize v.t. informatiser.

comrade /'kɒmr(e)ɪd/ n. camarade m./f. ~ship n. camaraderie f.

con¹ /kɒn/ v.t. (p.t. conned) (sl.) escroquer. —n. (sl.) escroquerie f. ~ man, (sl.) escroc m.

con² /kɒn/ see pro.

concave /'kɒŋkeɪv/ a. concave.

conceal /kən'siːl/ v.t. dissimuler. ~ment n. dissimulation f.

concede /kən'siːd/ v.t. concéder. —v.i. céder.

conceit /kən'siːt/ n. suffisance f. ~ed a. suffisant.

conceivabl|e /kən'siːvəbl/ a. concevable. ~y adv. this may ~y be done, il est concevable que cela puisse se faire.

conceive /kən'siːv/ v.t./i. concevoir. ~ of, concevoir.

concentrat|e /'kɒnsntreɪt/ v.t./i. (se) concentrer. ~ion /-'treɪʃn/ n. concentration f.

concept /'kɒnsept/ n. concept m. ~**ual** /kən'septʃʊəl/ a. notionnel.

conception /kən'sepʃn/ n. conception f.

concern /kən'sɜːn/ n. (interest, business) affaire f.; (worry) inquiétude f.; (firm: comm.) entreprise f., affaire f. —v.t. concerner. ~ **o.s. with**, be ~**ed with**, s'occuper de. ~**ing** prep. en ce qui concerne.

concerned /kən'sɜːnd/ a. inquiet.

concert /'kɒnsət/ n. concert m. **in** ~, ensemble.

concerted /kən'sɜːtɪd/ a. concerté.

concertina /kɒnsə'tiːnə/ n. concertina m.

concerto /kən'tʃeətəʊ/ n. (pl. -os) concerto m.

concession /kən'seʃn/ n. concession f.

conciliate /kən'sɪlɪeɪt/ v.t. (soothe) apaiser; (win over) se concilier (l'amitié de).

concise /kən'saɪs/ a. concis. ~**ly** adv. avec concision. ~**ness** n. concision f.

conclu|de /kən'kluːd/ v.t. conclure. —v.i. se terminer. ~**ding** a. final. ~**sion** n. conclusion f.

conclusive /kən'kluːsɪv/ a. concluant. ~**ly** adv. de manière concluante.

concoct /kən'kɒkt/ v.t. confectionner; (invent: fig.) fabriquer. ~**ion** /-kʃn/ n. mélange m.

concourse /'kɒnkɔːs/ n. (rail.) hall m.

concrete /'kɒŋkriːt/ n. béton m. —a. concret. —v.t. bétonner.

concur /kən'kɜː(r)/ v.i. (p.t. concurred) être d'accord.

concurrently /kən'kʌrəntlɪ/ adv. simultanément.

concussion /kən'kʌʃn/ n. commotion (cérébrale) f.

condemn /kən'dem/ v.t. condamner. ~**ation** /kɒndem'neɪʃn/ n. condamnation f.

condens|e /kən'dens/ v.t./i. (se) condenser. ~**ation** /kɒnden'seɪʃn/ n. condensation f.; (mist) buée f.

condescend /kɒndɪ'send/ v.i. condescendre.

condiment /'kɒndɪmənt/ n. condiment m.

condition /kən'dɪʃn/ n. condition f. —v.t. conditionner. **on** ~ **that**, à condition que. ~**al** a. conditionnel. **be** ~**al upon**, dépendre de.

condolences /kən'dəʊlənsɪz/ n. pl. condoléances f. pl.

condom /'kɒndəm/ n. préservatif m.

condominium /kɒndə'mɪnɪəm/ n. (Amer.) copropriété f.

condone /kən'dəʊn/ v.t. pardonner, fermer les yeux sur.

conducive /kən'djuːsɪv/ a. ~ **to**, favorable à.

conduct[1] /kən'dʌkt/ v.t. conduire; (orchestra) diriger.

conduct[2] /'kɒndʌkt/ n. conduite f.

conduct|or /kən'dʌktə(r)/ n. chef d'orchestre m.; (of bus) receveur m. ~**ress** n. receveuse f.

cone /kəʊn/ n. cône m.; (of ice-cream) cornet m.

confectioner /kən'fekʃənə(r)/ n. confiseu|r, -se m., f. ~**y** n. confiserie f.

confederate /kən'fedərət/ n. (accomplice) complice m./f.

confederation /kənfedə'reɪʃn/ n. confédération f.

confer /kən'fɜː(r)/ v.t./i. (p.t. conferred) conférer.

conference /'kɒnfərəns/ n. conférence f.

confess /kən'fes/ v.t./i. avouer; (relig.) (se) confesser. ~**ion** /-ʃn/ n. confession f.

confessional /kən'feʃənl/ n. confessionnal m.

confetti /kən'fetɪ/ n. confettis m. pl.

confide /kən'faɪd/ v.t. confier. —v.i. ~ **in**, se confier à.

confiden|t /'kɒnfɪdənt/ a. sûr. ~**ce** n. (trust) confiance f.; (boldness) confiance en soi f.; (secret) confidence f. ~**ce trick**, escroquerie f. **in** ~**ce**, en confidence.

confidential /kɒnfɪ'denʃl/ a. confidentiel.

confine /kən'faɪn/ v.t. enfermer; (limit) limiter. ~**ment** n. détention f.; (med.) couches f. pl.

confines /'kɒnfaɪnz/ n. pl. confins m. pl.

confirm /kən'fɜːm/ v.t. confirmer. ~**ation** /kɒnfə'meɪʃn/ n. confirmation f. ~**ed** a. (bachelor) endurci.

confiscat|e /'kɒnfɪskeɪt/ v.t. confisquer. ~**ion** /-'keɪʃn/ n. confiscation f.

conflagration /kɒnflə'greɪʃn/ n. incendie m.

conflict[1] /'kɒnflɪkt/ n. conflit m.

conflict[2] /kən'flɪkt/ v.i. être en contradiction. ~**ing** a. contradictoire.

conform /kən'fɔːm/ v.t./i. (se) conformer. ~**ist** n. conformiste m./f.

confound /kən'faʊnd/ v.t. confondre. ~ed a. (fam.) sacré.

confront /kən'frʌnt/ v.t. se trouver en face de; (danger) affronter. ~ **with,** confronter avec. ~ation /kɒnfrʌn'teɪʃn/ n. confrontation f.

confus|e /kən'fjuːz/ v.t. embrouiller; (mistake, confound) confondre. **become** ~ed, s'embrouiller. **I am** ~ed, je m'y perds. ~ing a. déroutant. ~ion /-ʒn/ n. confusion f.

congeal /kən'dʒiːl/ v.t./i. (se) figer.

congenial /kən'dʒiːnɪəl/ a. sympathique.

congenital /kən'dʒenɪtl/ a. congénital.

congest|ed /kən'dʒestɪd/ a. encombré; (med.) congestionné. ~ion /-stʃən/ n. (traffic) encombrement(s) m. (pl.); (med.) congestion f.

congratulat|e /kən'grætjʊleɪt/ v.t. féliciter (on, de). ~ions /-'leɪʃnz/ n. pl. félicitations f. pl.

congregat|e /'kɒngrɪgeɪt/ v.i. se rassembler. ~ion /-'geɪʃn/ n. assemblée f.

congress /'kɒngres/ n. congrès m. **C~,** (Amer.) Congrès m.

conic(al) /'kɒnɪk(l)/ a. conique.

conifer /'kɒnɪfə(r)/ n. conifère m.

conjecture /kən'dʒektʃə(r)/ n. conjecture f. —v.t./i. conjecturer.

conjugal /'kɒndʒʊgl/ a. conjugal.

conjugat|e /'kɒndʒʊgeɪt/ v.t. conjuguer. ~ion /-'geɪʃn/ n. conjugaison f.

conjunction /kən'dʒʌŋkʃn/ n. conjonction f. **in ~ with,** conjointement avec.

conjur|e /'kʌndʒə(r)/ v.i. faire des tours de passe-passe. —v.t. ~e **up,** faire apparaître. ~or n. prestidigita|teur, -trice m., f.

conk /kɒŋk/ v.i. ~ **out,** (sl.) tomber en panne.

conker /'kɒŋkə(r)/ n. (horse-chestnut fruit: fam.) marron m.

connect /kə'nekt/ v.t./i. (se) relier; (install, wire up to mains) brancher. ~ **with,** (of train) assurer la correspondance avec. ~ed a. lié. **be** ~ed **with,** avoir rapport à; (deal with) avoir des rapports avec.

connection /kə'nekʃn/ n. rapport m.; (rail.) correspondance f.; (phone call) communication f.; (electr.) contact m.; (joining piece) raccord m. ~s, (comm.) relations f. pl.

conniv|e /kə'naɪv/ v.i. ~e **at,** se faire

le complice de. ~ance n. connivence f.

connoisseur /kɒnə'sɜː(r)/ n. connaisseur m.

connot|e /kə'nəʊt/ v.t. impliquer. ~ation /kɒnə'teɪʃn/ n. connotation f.

conquer /'kɒŋkə(r)/ v.t. vaincre; (country) conquérir. ~or n. conquérant m.

conquest /'kɒŋkwest/ n. conquête f.

conscience /'kɒnʃəns/ n. conscience f.

conscientious /kɒnʃɪ'enʃəs/ a. consciencieux.

conscious /'kɒnʃəs/ a. conscient; (deliberate) voulu. ~ly adv. consciemment. ~ness n. conscience f.; (med.) connaissance f.

conscript[1] /kən'skrɪpt/ v.t. recruter par conscription. ~ion /-pʃn/ n. conscription f.

conscript[2] /'kɒnskrɪpt/ n. conscrit m.

consecrate /'kɒnsɪkreɪt/ v.t. consacrer.

consecutive /kən'sekjʊtɪv/ a. consécutif. ~ly adv. consécutivement.

consensus /kən'sensəs/ n. consensus m.

consent /kən'sent/ v.i. consentir. —n. consentement m.

consequence /'kɒnsɪkwəns/ n. conséquence f.

consequent /'kɒnsɪkwənt/ a. résultant. ~ly adv. par conséquent.

conservation /kɒnsə'veɪʃn/ n. préservation f.

conservationist /kɒnsə'veɪʃənɪst/ n. partisan(e) de la défense de l'environnement m. (f.).

conservative /kən'sɜːvətɪv/ a. conservateur; (estimate) modeste. **C~** a. & n. conserva|teur, -trice (m. (f.)).

conservatory /kən'sɜːvətrɪ/ n. (greenhouse) serre f.

conserve /kən'sɜːv/ v.t. conserver.

consider /kən'sɪdə(r)/ v.t. considérer; (allow for) tenir compte de. ~ation /-'reɪʃn/ n. considération f.; (respect) égard(s) m. (pl.). ~ing prep. compte tenu de.

considerabl|e /kən'sɪdərəbl/ a. considérable; (much) beaucoup de. ~ly adv. beaucoup, considérablement.

considerate /kən'sɪdərət/ a. prévenant, attentionné.

consign /kən'saɪn/ v.t. (entrust) confier; (send) expédier. ~ment n. envoi m.

consist /kən'sɪst/ v.i. consister (of, en; in doing, à faire).

consisten|t /kən'sɪstənt/ *a.* cohérent. **~t with,** conforme à. **~cy** *n.* (*of liquids*) consistance *f.*; (*fig.*) cohérence *f.* **~tly** *adv.* régulièrement.

consol|e /kən'səʊl/ *v.t.* consoler. **~ation** /kɒnsə'leɪʃn/ *n.* consolation *f.*

consolidat|e /kən'sɒlɪdeɪt/ *v.t./i.* (se) consolider. **~ion** /-'deɪʃn/ *n.* consolidation *f.*

consonant /'kɒnsənənt/ *n.* consonne *f.*

consort[1] /'kɒnsɔːt/ *n.* époux *m.*, épouse *f.*

consort[2] /kən'sɔːt/ *v.i.* **~ with,** fréquenter.

consortium /kən'sɔːtɪəm/ *n.* (*pl.* **-tia**) consortium *m.*

conspicuous /kən'spɪkjʊəs/ *a.* (*easily seen*) en évidence; (*showy*) voyant; (*noteworthy*) remarquable.

conspiracy /kən'spɪrəsɪ/ *n.* conspiration *f.*

conspire /kən'spaɪə(r)/ *v.i.* (*person*) comploter (**to do,** de faire), conspirer; (*events*) conspirer (**to do,** à faire).

constable /'kʌnstəbl/ *n.* agent de police *m.*, gendarme *m.*

constant /'kɒnstənt/ *a.* incessant; (*unchanging*) constant; (*friend*) fidèle. **~ly** *adv.* constamment.

constellation /kɒnstə'leɪʃn/ *n.* constellation *f.*

consternation /kɒnstə'neɪʃn/ *n.* consternation *f.*

constipat|e /'kɒnstɪpeɪt/ *v.t.* constiper. **~ion** /-'peɪʃn/ *n.* constipation *f.*

constituency /kən'stɪtjʊənsɪ/ *n.* circonscription électorale *f.*

constituent /kən'stɪtjʊənt/ *a.* constitutif. *—n.* élément constitutif *m.*; (*pol.*) élec|teur, -trice *m.*, *f.*

constitut|e /'kɒnstɪtjuːt/ *v.t.* constituer. **~ion** /-'tjuːʃn/ *n.* constitution *f.* **~ional** /-'tjuːʃənl/ *a.* constitutionnel; *n.* promenade *f.*

constrain /kən'streɪn/ *v.t.* contraindre.

constraint /kən'streɪnt/ *n.* contrainte *f.*

constrict /kən'strɪkt/ *v.t.* resserrer; (*movement*) gêner. **~ion** /-kʃn/ *n.* resserrement *m.*

construct /kən'strʌkt/ *v.t.* construire. **~ion** /-kʃn/ *n.* construction *f.*

constructive /kən'strʌktɪv/ *a.* constructif.

construe /kən'struː/ *v.t.* interpréter.

consul /'kɒnsl/ *n.* consul *m.* **~ar** /-jʊlə(r)/ *a.* consulaire.

consulate /'kɒnsjʊlət/ *n.* consulat *m.*

consult /kən'sʌlt/ *v.t.* consulter. *—v.i.* **~ with,** conférer avec. **~ation** /kɒnsl'teɪʃn/ *n.* consultation *f.*

consultant /kən'sʌltənt/ *n.* conseil|ler, -ère *m.*, *f.*; (*med.*) spécialiste *m.*/*f.*

consume /kən'sjuːm/ *v.t.* consommer; (*destroy*) consumer. **~r** /-ə(r)/ *n.* consomma|teur, -trice *m.*, *f.* *—a.* (*society*) de consommation.

consumerism /kən'sjuːmərɪzəm/ *n.* protection des consommateurs *f.*

consummate /'kɒnsəmeɪt/ *v.t.* consommer.

consumption /kən'sʌmpʃn/ *n.* consommation *f.*; (*med.*) phtisie *f.*

contact /'kɒntækt/ *n.* contact *m.*; (*person*) relation *f.* *—v.t.* contacter. **~ lenses,** verres de contact *m. pl.*

contagious /kən'teɪdʒəs/ *a.* contagieux.

contain /kən'teɪn/ *v.t.* contenir. **~ o.s.,** se contenir. **~er** *n.* récipient *m.*; (*for transport*) container *m.*

contaminat|e /kən'tæmɪneɪt/ *v.t.* contaminer. **~ion** /-'neɪʃn/ *n.* contamination *f.*

contemplat|e /'kɒntempleɪt/ *v.t.* (*gaze at*) contempler; (*think about*) envisager. **~ion** /-'pleɪʃn/ *n.* contemplation *f.*

contemporary /kən'temprərɪ/ *a. & n.* contemporain(e) (*m.* (*f.*)).

contempt /kən'tempt/ *n.* mépris *m.* **~ible** *a.* méprisable. **~uous** /-tʃʊəs/ *a.* méprisant.

contend /kən'tend/ *v.t.* soutenir. *—v.i.* **~ with,** (*compete*) rivaliser avec; (*face*) faire face à. **~er** *n.* adversaire *m.*, *f.*

content[1] /kən'tent/ *a.* satisfait. *—v.t.* contenter. **~ed** *a.* satisfait. **~ment** *n.* contentement *m.*

content[2] /'kɒntent/ *n.* contenu *m.* **~s,** contenu *m.*

contention /kən'tenʃn/ *n.* dispute *f.*; (*claim*) affirmation *f.*

contest[1] /'kɒntest/ *n.* (*competition*) concours *m.*; (*fight*) combat *m.*

contest[2] /kən'test/ *v.t.* contester; (*compete for or in*) disputer. **~ant** *n.* concurrent(e) *m.* (*f.*).

context /'kɒntekst/ *n.* contexte *m.*

continent /'kɒntɪnənt/ *n.* continent *m.* **the C~,** l'Europe (continentale) *f.* **~al** /-'nentl/ *a.* continental; européen.

contingen|t /kən'tɪndʒənt/ *a.* **be ~t upon,** dépendre de. *—n.* (*mil.*) contingent *m.* ∼**cy** *n.* éventualité *f.* ∼**cy plan,** plan d'urgence *m.*

continual /kən'tınjʊəl/ *a.* continuel. ∼**ly** *adv.* continuellement.

continu|e /kən'tınju:/ *v.t./i.* continuer; (*resume*) reprendre. ∼**ance** *n.* continuation *f.* ∼**ation** /-ʊ'eıʃn/ *n.* continuation *f.*; (*after interruption*) reprise *f.*; (*new episode*) suite *f.* ∼**ed** *a.* continu.

continuity /kɒntı'nju:ətı/ *n.* continuité *f.*

continuous /kən'tınjʊəs/ *a.* continu. ∼**ly** *adv.* sans interruption, continûment.

contort /kən'tɔ:t/ *v.t.* tordre. ∼ **o.s.,** se contorsionner. ∼**ion** /-ʃn/ *n.* torsion *f.*; contorsion *f.* ∼**ionist** /-ʃənıst/ *n.* contorsionniste *m./f.*

contour /'kɒntʊə(r)/ *n.* contour *m.*

contraband /'kɒntrəbænd/ *n.* contrebande *f.*

contraception /kɒntrə'sepʃn/ *n.* contraception *f.*

contraceptive /kɒntrə'septıv/ *a.* & *n.* contraceptif (*m.*).

contract[1] /'kɒntrækt/ *n.* contrat *m.*

contract[2] /kən'trækt/ *v.t./i.* (se) contracter. ∼**ion** /-kʃn/ *n.* contraction *f.*

contractor /kən'træktə(r)/ *n.* entrepreneur *m.*

contradict /kɒntrə'dıkt/ *v.t.* contredire. ∼**ion** /-kʃn/ *n.* contradiction *f.* ∼**ory** *a.* contradictoire.

contralto /kən'træltəʊ/ *n.* (*pl.* -**os**) contralto *m.*

contraption /kən'træpʃn/ *n.* (*fam.*) engin *m.*, truc *m.*

contrary[1] /'kɒntrərı/ *a.* contraire (**to,** à). —*n.* contraire *m.* —*adv.* ∼ **to,** contrairement à. **on the** ∼, au contraire.

contrary[2] /kən'treərı/ *a.* entêté.

contrast[1] /'kɒntrɑ:st/ *n.* contraste *m.*

contrast[2] /kən'trɑ:st/ *v.t./i.* contraster. ∼**ing** *a.* contrasté.

contraven|e /kɒntrə'vi:n/ *v.t.* enfreindre. ∼**tion** /-'venʃn/ *n.* infraction *f.*

contribut|e /kən'trıbju:t/ *v.t.* donner. —*v.i.* ∼ **to,** contribuer à; (*take part*) participer à; (*newspaper*) collaborer à. ∼**ion** /kɒntrı'bju:ʃn/ *n.* contribution *f.* ∼**or** *n.* collabora|teur, -trice *m.*,*f.*

contrivance /kən'traıvəns/ *n.* (*device*) appareil *m.*, truc *m.*

contrive /kən'traıv/ *v.t.* imaginer. ∼ **to do,** trouver moyen de faire.

control /kən'trəʊl/ *v.t.* (*p.t.* **controlled**) (*a firm etc.*) diriger; (*check*) contrôler; (*restrain*) maîtriser. —*n.* contrôle *m.*; (*mastery*) maîtrise *f.* ∼**s,** commandes *f. pl.*; (*knobs*) boutons *m. pl.* **have under** ∼, (*event*) avoir en main. **in** ∼ **of,** maître de.

controversial /kɒntrə'vɜ:ʃl/ *a.* discutable, discuté.

controversy /'kɒntrəvɜ:sı/ *n.* controverse *f.*

conurbation /kɒnɜ:'beıʃn/ *n.* agglomération *f.*, conurbation *f.*

convalesce /kɒnvə'les/ *v.i.* être en convalescence. ∼**nce** *n.* convalescence *f.* ∼**nt** *a.* & *n.* convalescent(e) (*m.* (*f.*)). ∼**nt home,** maison de convalescence *f.*

convector /kən'vektə(r)/ *n.* radiateur à convection *m.*

convene /kən'vi:n/ *v.t.* convoquer. —*v.i.* se réunir.

convenience /kən'vi:nıəns/ *n.* commodité *f.* ∼**s,** toilettes *f. pl.* **all modern** ∼**s,** tout le confort moderne. **at your** ∼, quand cela vous conviendra, à votre convenance.

convenient /kən'vi:nıənt/ *a.* commode, pratique; (*time*) bien choisi. **be** ∼ **for,** convenir à. ∼**ly** *adv.* (*arrive*) à propos. ∼**ly situated,** bien situé.

convent /'kɒnvənt/ *n.* couvent *m.*

convention /kən'venʃn/ *n.* (*assembly, agreement*) convention *f.*; (*custom*) usage *m.* ∼**al** *a.* conventionnel.

converge /kən'vɜ:dʒ/ *v.i.* converger.

conversant /kən'vɜ:snt/ *a.* **be** ∼ **with,** connaître; (*fact*) savoir; (*machinery*) s'y connaître en.

conversation /kɒnvə'seıʃn/ *n.* conversation *f.* ∼**al** *a.* (*tone etc.*) de la conversation. ∼**alist** *n.* causeu|r, -se *m.*, *f.*

converse[1] /kən'vɜ:s/ *v.i.* s'entretenir, converser (**with,** avec).

converse[2] /'kɒnvɜ:s/ *a.* & *n.* inverse (*m.*). ∼**ly** *adv.* inversement.

conver|t[1] /kən'vɜ:t/ *v.t.* convertir; (*house*) aménager. ∼**sion** /-ʃn/ *n.* conversion *f.* ∼**tible** *a.* convertible. —*n.* (*car*) décapotable *f.*

convert[2] /'kɒnvɜ:t/ *n.* converti(e) *m.* (*f.*).

convex /'kɒnveks/ *a.* convexe.

convey /kən'veı/ *v.t.* (*wishes, order*) transmettre; (*goods, people*) transporter; (*idea, feeling*) communiquer.

~ance n. transport m. **~or belt,** tapis roulant m.

convict[1] /kən'vɪkt/ v.t. déclarer coupable. **~ion** /-kʃn/ n. condamnation f.; (opinion) conviction f.

convict[2] /'kɒnvɪkt/ n. forçat m.

convinc|e /kən'vɪns/ v.t. convaincre. **~ing** a. convaincant.

convivial /kən'vɪvɪəl/ a. joyeux.

convoke /kən'vəʊk/ v.t. convoquer.

convoluted /'kɒnvəluːtɪd/ a. (argument etc.) compliqué.

convoy /'kɒnvɔɪ/ n. convoi m.

convuls|e /kən'vʌls/ v.t. convulser; (fig.) bouleverser. **be ~ed with laughter,** se tordre de rire. **~ion** /-ʃn/ n. convulsion f.

coo /kuː/ v.i. roucouler.

cook /kʊk/ v.t./i. (faire) cuire; (of person) faire la cuisine. —n. cuisin|ier, -ière m., f. **~ up,** (fam.) fabriquer.

cooker /'kʊkə(r)/ n. (stove) cuisinière f.; (apple) pomme à cuire f.

cookery /'kʊkərɪ/ n. cuisine f.

cookie /'kʊkɪ/ n. (Amer.) biscuit m.

cool /kuːl/ a. (-er, -est) frais; (calm) calme; (unfriendly) froid. —n. fraîcheur f.; (calmness: sl.) sangfroid m. —v.t./i. rafraîchir. **in the ~,** au frais. **~er** n. (for food) glacière f. **~ly** adv. calmement; froidement. **~ness** n. fraîcheur f.; froideur f.

coop /kuːp/ n. poulailler m. —v.t. **~ up,** enfermer.

co-operat|e /kəʊ'ɒpəreɪt/ v.i. coopérer. **~ion** /-'reɪʃn/ n. coopération f.

co-operative /kəʊ'ɒpərətɪv/ a. coopératif. —n. coopérative f.

co-opt /kəʊ'ɒpt/ v.t. coopter.

co-ordinat|e /kəʊ'ɔːdmeɪt/ v.t. coordonner. **~ion** /-'neɪʃn/ n. coordination f.

cop /kɒp/ v.t. (p.t. **copped**) (sl.) piquer. —n. (policeman: sl.) flic m.

cope /kəʊp/ v.i. (fam.) se débrouiller. **~ with,** s'occuper de.

copious /'kəʊpɪəs/ a. copieux.

copper[1] /'kɒpə(r)/ n. cuivre m.; (coin) sou m. —a. de cuivre.

copper[2] /'kɒpə(r)/ n. (sl.) flic m.

coppice, copse /'kɒpɪs, kɒps/ ns. taillis m.

copulat|e /'kɒpjʊleɪt/ v.i. s'accoupler. **~ion** /-'leɪʃn/ n. copulation f.

copy /'kɒpɪ/ n. copie f.; (of book, newspaper) exemplaire m.; (print: photo.) épreuve f. —v.t./i. copier.

copyright /'kɒpɪraɪt/ n. droit d'auteur m., copyright m.

coral /'kɒrəl/ n. corail m.

cord /kɔːd/ n. (petite) corde f.; (of curtain, pyjamas, etc.) cordon m.; (electr.) cordon électrique m.; (fabric) velours côtelé m.

cordial /'kɔːdɪəl/ a. cordial. —n. (fruit-flavoured drink) sirop m.

cordon /'kɔːdn/ n. cordon m. —v.t. **~ off,** mettre un cordon autour de.

corduroy /'kɔːdərɔɪ/ n. velours côtelé m., velours à côtes m.

core /kɔː(r)/ n. (of apple) trognon m.; (of problem) cœur m.; (techn.) noyau m. —v.t. vider.

cork /kɔːk/ n. liège m.; (for bottle) bouchon m. —v.t. boucher.

corkscrew /'kɔːkskruː/ n. tirebouchon m.

corn[1] /kɔːn/ n. blé m.; (maize: Amer.) maïs m.; (seed) grain m.

corn[2] /kɔːn/ n. (hard skin) cor m.

cornea /'kɔːnɪə/ n. cornée f.

corned /kɔːnd/ a. **~ beef,** corned-beef m.

corner /'kɔːnə(r)/ n. coin m.; (bend in road) virage m.; (football) corner m. —v.t. coincer, acculer; (market) accaparer. —v.i. prendre un virage. **~-stone** n. pierre angulaire f.

cornet /'kɔːnɪt/ n. cornet m.

cornflakes /'kɔːnfleɪks/ n. pl. céréales f. pl. (flocons de maïs).

cornflour /'kɔːnflaʊə(r)/ n. farine de maïs f.

cornice /'kɔːnɪs/ n. corniche f.

cornucopia /kɔːnjʊ'kəʊpɪə/ n. corne d'abondance f.

Corn|wall /'kɔːnwəl/ n. Cornouailles f. **~ish** a. de Cornouailles.

corny /'kɔːnɪ/ a. (-ier, -iest) (trite: fam.) rebattu; (mawkish: fam.) à l'eau de rose.

corollary /kə'rɒlərɪ, Amer. 'kɒrələrɪ/ n. corollaire m.

coronary /'kɒrənərɪ/ n. infarctus m.

coronation /kɒrə'neɪʃn/ n. couronnement m.

coroner /'kɒrənə(r)/ n. coroner m.

corporal[1] /'kɔːpərəl/ n. caporal m.

corporal[2] /'kɔːpərəl/ a. **~ punishment,** châtiment corporel m.

corporate /'kɔːpərət/ a. en commun; (body) constitué.

corporation /kɔːpə'reɪʃn/ n. (comm.) société f.; (of town) municipalité f.; (abdomen: fam.) bedaine f.

corps /kɔː(r)/ n. (pl. **corps** /kɔːz/) corps m.

corpse /kɔːps/ n. cadavre m.

corpulent /'kɔːpjʊlənt/ a. corpulent.

corpuscle /'kɔːpʌsl/ n. globule m.

corral /kəˈrɑːl/ n. (Amer.) corral m.

correct /kəˈrekt/ a. (right) exact, juste, correct; (proper) correct. **you are ~,** vous avez raison. —v.t. corriger. **~ion** /-kʃn/ n. correction f.

correlat|e /'kɒrəleɪt/ v.t./i. (faire) correspondre. **~ion** /-'leɪʃn/ n. corrélation f.

correspond /kɒrɪˈspɒnd/ v.i. correspondre. **~ence** n. correspondance f. **~ent** n. correspondant(e) m. (f.).

corridor /'kɒrɪdɔː(r)/ n. couloir m.

corroborate /kəˈrɒbəreɪt/ v.t. corroborer.

corro|de /kəˈrəʊd/ v.t./i. (se) corroder. **~sion** n. corrosion f.

corrosive /kəˈrəʊsɪv/ a. corrosif.

corrugated /'kɒrəgeɪtɪd/ a. ondulé. **~ iron,** tôle ondulée f.

corrupt /kəˈrʌpt/ a. corrompu. —v.t. corrompre. **~ion** /-pʃn/ n. corruption f.

corset /'kɔːsɪt/ n. (boned) corset m.; (elasticated) gaine f.

Corsica /'kɔːsɪkə/ n. Corse f.

cos /kɒs/ n. laitue romaine f.

cosh /kɒʃ/ n. matraque f. —v.t. matraquer.

cosmetic /kɒzˈmetɪk/ n. produit de beauté m. —a. cosmétique; (fig., pej.) superficiel.

cosmic /'kɒzmɪk/ a. cosmique.

cosmonaut /'kɒzmənɔːt/ n. cosmonaute m./f.

cosmopolitan /kɒzməˈpɒlɪt(ə)n/ a. & n. cosmopolite (m./f.).

cosmos /'kɒzmɒs/ n. cosmos m.

Cossack /'kɒsæk/ n. cosaque m.

cosset /'kɒsɪt/ v.t. (p.t. **cosseted**) dorloter.

cost /kɒst/ v.t. (p.t. **cost**) coûter; (p.t. **costed**) établir le prix de. —n. coût m. **~s,** (jurid.) dépens m. pl. **at all ~s,** à tout prix. **to one's ~,** à ses dépens.

co-star /'kəʊstɑː(r)/ n. partenaire m./f.

costly /'kɒstlɪ/ a. (-ier, -iest) coûteux; (valuable) précieux.

costume /'kɒstjuːm/ n. costume m.

cos|y /'kəʊzɪ/ a. (-ier, -iest) confortable, intime. —n. couvrethéière m. **~iness** n. confort m.

cot /kɒt/ n. lit d'enfant m.; (camp-bed: Amer.) lit de camp m.

cottage /'kɒtɪdʒ/ n. petite maison de campagne f.; (thatched) chaumière f. **~ cheese,** fromage blanc (maigre) m. **~ industry,** activité artisanale f. **~ pie,** hachis Parmentier m.

cotton /'kɒtn/ n. coton m. —v.i. **~ on,** (sl.) piger. **~ candy,** (Amer.) barbe à papa f. **~ wool,** coton hydrophile m.

couch /kaʊtʃ/ n. divan m. —v.t. (express) formuler.

couchette /kuːˈʃet/ n. couchette f.

cough /kɒf/ v.i. tousser. —n. toux f. **~ up,** (sl.) cracher, payer.

could /kʊd, unstressed kəd/ p.t. of **can**[2].

couldn't /'kʊdnt/ = **could not.**

council /'kaʊnsl/ n. conseil m. **~ house,** maison construite par la municipalité f., (approx.) H.L.M. m./f.

councillor /'kaʊnsələ(r)/ n. conseill|er, -ère municipal(e) m., f.

counsel /'kaʊnsl/ n. conseil m. —n. invar. (jurid.) avocat(e) m. (f.). **~lor** n. conseill|er, -ère m., f.

count[1] /kaʊnt/ v.t./i. compter. —n. compte m. **~ on,** compter sur.

count[2] /kaʊnt/ n. (nobleman) comte m.

countdown /'kaʊntdaʊn/ n. compte à rebours m.

countenance /'kaʊntɪnəns/ n. mine f. —v.t. admettre, approuver.

counter[1] /'kaʊntə(r)/ n. comptoir m.; (in bank etc.) guichet m.; (token) jeton m.

counter[2] /'kaʊntə(r)/ adv. **~ to,** à l'encontre de. —a. opposé. —v.t. opposer; (blow) parer. —v.i. riposter.

counter /'kaʊntə(r)/ pref. contre-.

counteract /kaʊntərˈækt/ v.t. neutraliser.

counter-attack /'kaʊntərətæk/ n. contre-attaque f. —v.t./i. contre-attaquer.

counterbalance /'kaʊntəbæləns/ n. contrepoids m. —v.t. contre-balancer.

counter-clockwise /kaʊntəˈklɒkwaɪz/ a. & adv. (Amer.) dans le sens inverse des aiguilles d'une montre.

counterfeit /'kaʊntəfɪt/ a. & n. faux (m.). —v.t. contrefaire.

counterfoil /'kaʊntəfɔɪl/ n. souche f.

counterpart /'kaʊntəpɑːt/ n. équivalent m.; (person) homologue m./f.

counter-productive /kaʊntəprə-

'dʌktɪv/ *a.* (*measure*) qui produit l'effet contraire.

countersign /'kaʊntəsaɪn/ *v.t.* contresigner.

countess /'kaʊntɪs/ *n.* comtesse *f.*

countless /'kaʊntlɪs/ *a.* innombrable.

countrified /'kʌntrɪfaɪd/ *a.* rustique.

country /'kʌntrɪ/ *n.* (*land*, *region*) pays *m.*; (*homeland*) patrie *f.*; (*countryside*) campagne *f.* **~ dance**, danse folklorique *f.*

countryman /'kʌntrɪmən/ *n.* (*pl.* **-men**) campagnard *m.*; (*fellow citizen*) compatriote *m.*

countryside /'kʌntrɪsaɪd/ *n.* campagne *f.*

county /'kaʊntɪ/ *n.* comté *m.*

coup /kuː/ *n.* (*pol.*) coup d'état *m.*

coupé /'kuːpeɪ/ *n.* (*car*) coupé *m.*

couple /'kʌpl/ *n.* (*people*, *animals*) couple *m.* —*v.t./i.* (s')accoupler. **a ~** (**of**), (*two or three*) deux ou trois.

coupon /'kuːpɒn/ *n.* coupon *m.*

courage /'kʌrɪdʒ/ *n.* courage *m.* **~ous** /kə'reɪdʒəs/ *a.* courageux.

courgette /kʊə'ʒet/ *n.* courgette *f.*

courier /'kʊrɪə(r)/ *n.* messag|er, -ère *m.*, *f.*; (*for tourists*) guide *m.*

course /kɔːs/ *n.* cours *m.*; (*series*) série *f.*; (*culin.*) plat *m.*; (*for golf*) terrain *m.*; (*fig.*) voie *f.* **in due ~**, en temps utile. **of ~**, bien sûr.

court /kɔːt/ *n.* cour *f.*; (*tennis*) court *m.* —*v.t.* faire la cour à; (*danger*) rechercher. **~ martial**, (*pl.* **courts martial**) conseil de guerre *m.* **~-martial** *v.t.* (*p.t.* **-martialled**) faire passer en conseil de guerre.

courteous /'kɜːtɪəs/ *a.* courtois.

courtesan /kɔːtɪ'zæn, *Amer.* 'kɔːtɪzn/ *n.* (*old use*) courtisane *f.*

courtesy /'kɜːtəsɪ/ *n.* courtoisie *f.* **by ~ of**, avec la permission de.

courtier /'kɔːtɪə(r)/ *n.* (*old use*) courtisan *m.*

courtyard /'kɔːtjɑːd/ *n.* cour *f.*

cousin /'kʌzn/ *n.* cousin(e) *m.* (*f.*). **first ~**, cousin(e) germain(e) *m.* (*f.*).

cove /kəʊv/ *n.* anse *f.*, crique *f.*

covenant /'kʌvənənt/ *n.* convention *f.*

Coventry /'kɒvntrɪ/ *n.* **send to ~**, mettre en quarantaine.

cover /'kʌvə(r)/ *v.t.* couvrir. —*n.* (*for bed*, *book*, *etc.*) couverture *f.*; (*lid*) couvercle *m.*; (*for furniture*) housse *f.*; (*shelter*) abri *m.* **~ charge**, couvert *m.* **~ up**, cacher. **~-up** *n.* tentative pour cacher la vérité *f.* **take ~**, se

mettre à l'abri. **~ing** *n.* enveloppe *f.* **~ing letter**, lettre *f.* (*jointe à un document*).

coverage /'kʌvərɪdʒ/ *n.* reportage *m.*

covet /'kʌvɪt/ *v.t.* convoiter.

cow /kaʊ/ *n.* vache *f.*

coward /'kaʊəd/ *n.* lâche *m.*/*f.* **~ly** *a.* lâche.

cowardice /'kaʊədɪs/ *n.* lâcheté *f.*

cowboy /'kaʊbɔɪ/ *n.* cow-boy *m.*

cower /'kaʊə(r)/ *v.i.* se recroqueviller (sous l'effet de la peur).

cowshed /'kaʊʃed/ *n.* étable *f.*

cox /kɒks/ *n.* barreur *m.* —*v.t.* barrer.

coxswain /'kɒksn/ *n.* barreur *m.*

coy /kɔɪ/ *a.* (**-er**, **-est**) (faussement) timide, qui fait le *or* la timide.

cozy /'kəʊzɪ/ *Amer.* = **cosy**.

crab /kræb/ *n.* crabe *m.* —*v.i.* (*p.t.* **crabbed**) rouspéter. **~-apple** *n.* pomme sauvage *f.*

crack /kræk/ *n.* fente *f.*; (*in glass*) fêlure *f.*; (*noise*) craquement *m.*; (*joke*: *sl.*) plaisanterie *f.* —*a.* (*fam.*) d'élite. —*v.t./i.* (*break partially*) (se) fêler; (*split*) (se) fendre; (*nut*) casser; (*joke*) raconter; (*problem*) résoudre. **~ down on**, (*fam.*) sévir contre. **~ up**, (*fam.*) craquer. **get ~ing**, (*fam.*) s'y mettre.

cracked /krækt/ *a.* (*sl.*) cinglé.

cracker /'krækə(r)/ *n.* pétard *m.*; (*culin.*) biscuit (salé) *m.*

crackers /'krækəz/ *a.* (*sl.*) cinglé.

crackle /'krækl/ *v.i.* crépiter. —*n.* crépitement *m.*

crackpot /'krækpɒt/ *n.* cinglé(e) *m.* (*f.*).

cradle /'kreɪdl/ *n.* berceau *m.* —*v.t.* bercer.

craft[1] /krɑːft/ *n.* métier artisanal *m.*; (*technique*) art *m.*; (*cunning*) ruse *f.*

craft[2] /krɑːft/ *n. invar.* (*boat*) bateau *m.*

craftsman /'krɑːftsmən/ *n.* (*pl.* **-men**) artisan *m.* **~ship** *n.* art *m.*

crafty /'krɑːftɪ/ *a.* (**-ier**, **-iest**) rusé.

crag /kræg/ *n.* rocher à pic *m.* **~gy** *a.* à pic; (*face*) rude.

cram /kræm/ *v.t./i.* (*p.t.* **crammed**). **~** (**for an exam**), bachoter. **~ into**, (*pack*) (s')entasser dans. **~ with**, (*fill*) bourrer de.

cramp /kræmp/ *n.* crampe *f.*

cramped /kræmpt/ *a.* à l'étroit.

cranberry /'krænbərɪ/ *n.* canneberge *f.*

crane /kreɪn/ n. grue f. —v.t. (neck) tendre.

crank[1] /kræŋk/ n. (techn.) manivelle f.

crank[2] /kræŋk/ n. excentrique m./f. ~y a. excentrique.

cranny /'krænɪ/ n. fissure f.

craps /kræps/ n. **shoot** ~, (Amer.) jouer aux dés.

crash /kræʃ/ n. accident m.; (noise) fracas m.; (of thunder) coup m.; (of firm) faillite f. —v.t./i. avoir un accident (avec); (of plane) s'écraser; (two vehicles) se percuter. —a. (course) intensif. ~helmet n. casque (anti-choc) m. ~ **into,** rentrer dans. ~-**land** v.i. atterrir en catastrophe.

crass /kræs/ a. grossier.

crate /kreɪt/ n. cageot m.

crater /'kreɪtə(r)/ n. cratère m.

cravat /krə'væt/ n. foulard m.

crav|e /kreɪv/ v.t./i. ~ (for), désirer ardemment. ~**ing** n. envie irrésistible f.

crawl /krɔːl/ v.i. ramper; (vehicle) se traîner. —n. (pace) pas m.; (swimming) crawl m. **be** ~**ing with,** grouiller de.

crayfish /'kreɪfɪʃ/ n. invar. écrevisse f.

crayon /'kreɪən/ n. crayon m.

craze /kreɪz/ n. engouement m.

crazed /kreɪzd/ a. affolé.

craz|y /'kreɪzɪ/ a. (-ier, -iest) fou. ~**y about,** (person) fou de; (thing) fana or fou de. ~**iness** n. folie f. ~**y paving,** dallage irrégulier m.

creak /kriːk/ n. grincement m. —v.i. grincer. ~**y** a. grinçant.

cream /kriːm/ n. crème f. —a. crème invar. —v.t. écrémer. ~ **cheese,** fromage frais m. ~**y** a. crémeux.

crease /kriːs/ n. pli m. —v.t./i. (se) froisser.

creat|e /kriː'eɪt/ v.t. créer. ~**ion** /-ʃn/ n. création f. ~**ive** a. créateur. ~**or** n. créa|teur, -trice m., f.

creature /'kriːtʃə(r)/ n. créature f.

crèche /kreʃ/ n. crèche f.

credence /'kriːdns/ n. foi f.

credentials /krɪ'denʃlz/ n. pl. (identity) pièces d'identité f. pl.; (competence) références f. pl.

credib|le /'kredəbl/ a. (excuse etc.) croyable, plausible. ~**ility** /-'bɪlətɪ/ n. crédibilité f.

credit /'kredɪt/ n. crédit m.; (honour) honneur m. **in** ~, créditeur. ~**s,** (cinema) générique m. —a. (balance) créditeur. —v.t. (p.t. **credited**) croire; (comm.) créditer. ~ **card,** carte de crédit f. ~ **s.o. with,** attribuer à qn. ~**or** n. créanc|ier, -ière m., f.

creditable /'kredɪtəbl/ a. méritoire, honorable.

credulous /'kredjʊləs/ a. crédule.

creed /kriːd/ n. credo m.

creek /kriːk/ n. crique f. **up the** ~, (sl.) dans le pétrin.

creep /kriːp/ v.i. (p.t. **crept**) ramper; (fig.) se glisser. —n. (person: sl.) pauvre type m. **give s.o. the** ~**s,** faire frissonner qn. ~**y** a. qui fait frissonner.

cremat|e /krɪ'meɪt/ v.t. incinérer. ~**ion** /-ʃn/ n. incinération f.

crematorium /kremə'tɔːrɪəm/ n. (pl. -**ia**) crématorium m.

Creole /'kriːəʊl/ n. créole m./f.

crêpe /kreɪp/ n. crêpe m. ~ **paper,** papier crêpon m.

crept /krept/ see **creep.**

crescendo /krɪ'ʃendəʊ/ n. (pl. -**os**) crescendo m.

crescent /'kresnt/ n. croissant m.; (fig.) rue en demi-lune f.

cress /kres/ n. cresson m.

crest /krest/ n. crête f.; (coat of arms) armoiries f. pl.

Crete /kriːt/ n. Crète f.

cretin /'kretɪn, Amer. 'kriːtn/ n. crétin(e) m. (f.). ~**ous** a. crétin.

crevasse /krɪ'væs/ n. crevasse f.

crevice /'krevɪs/ n. fente f.

crew /kruː/ n. équipage m.; (gang) équipe f. ~ **cut,** coupe en brosse f.

crib[1] /krɪb/ n. lit d'enfant m.

crib[2] /krɪb/ v.t./i. (p.t. **cribbed**) copier. —n. (schol., fam.) traduction f., aide-mémoire m. invar.

crick /krɪk/ n. (in neck) torticolis m.

cricket[1] /'krɪkɪt/ n. (sport) cricket m. ~**er** n. joueur de cricket m.

cricket[2] /'krɪkɪt/ n. (insect) grillon m.

crime /kraɪm/ n. crime m.; (minor) délit m.; (acts) criminalité f.

criminal /'krɪmɪnl/ a. & n. criminel(le) (m. (f.)).

crimp /krɪmp/ v.t. (hair) friser.

crimson /'krɪmzn/ a. & n. cramoisi (m.).

cring|e /krɪndʒ/ v.i. reculer; (fig.) s'humilier. ~**ing** a. servile.

crinkle /'krɪŋkl/ v.t./i. (se) froisser. —n. pli m.

cripple /'krɪpl/ n. infirme m./f. —v.t. estropier; (fig.) paralyser.

crisis /'kraɪsɪs/ *n.* (*pl.* **crises** /-siːz/) crise *f.*

crisp /krɪsp/ *a.* (**-er, -est**) (*culin.*) croquant; (*air, reply*) vif. ⁓s *n. pl.* chips *m. pl.*

criss-cross /'krɪskrɒs/ *a.* entrecroisé. —*v.t./i.* (s')entrecroiser.

criterion /kraɪ'tɪərɪən/ *n.* (*pl.* **-ia**) critère *m.*

critic /'krɪtɪk/ *n.* critique *m.* ⁓**al** *a.* critique. ⁓**ally** *adv.* d'une manière critique; (*ill*) gravement.

criticism /'krɪtɪsɪzəm/ *n.* critique *f.*

criticize /'krɪtɪsaɪz/ *v.t./i.* critiquer.

croak /krəʊk/ *n.* coassement *m.* —*v.i.* coasser.

crochet /'krəʊʃeɪ/ *n.* crochet *m.* —*v.t.* faire au crochet.

crock /krɒk/ *n.* (*person: fam.*) croulant *m.*; (*car: fam.*) guimbarde *f.*

crockery /'krɒkərɪ/ *n.* vaisselle *f.*

crocodile /'krɒkədaɪl/ *n.* crocodile *m.*

crocus /'krəʊkəs/ *n.* (*pl.* **-uses**) crocus *m.*

crony /'krəʊnɪ/ *n.* cop|ain, -ine *m., f.*

crook /krʊk/ *n.* (*criminal: fam.*) escroc *m.*; (*stick*) houlette *f.*

crooked /'krʊkɪd/ *a.* tordu; (*winding*) tortueux; (*askew*) de travers; (*dishonest: fig.*) malhonnête. ⁓**ly** *adv.* de travers.

croon /kruːn/ *v.t./i.* chantonner.

crop /krɒp/ *n.* récolte *f.*; (*fig.*) quantité *f.* —*v.t.* (*p.t.* **cropped**) couper. —*v.i.* ⁓ **up**, se présenter.

cropper /'krɒpə(r)/ *n.* **come a** ⁓, (*sl.*) ramasser une bûche.

croquet /'krəʊkeɪ/ *n.* croquet *m.*

croquette /krəʊ'ket/ *n.* croquette *f.*

cross /krɒs/ *n.* croix *f.*; (*hybrid*) hybride *m.* —*v.t./i.* traverser; (*legs, animals*) croiser; (*cheque*) barrer; (*paths*) se croiser. —*a.* en colère, fâché (**with**, contre). ⁓ **off** *or* **out**, rayer. ⁓ **s.o.'s mind**, venir à l'esprit de qn. **talk at** ⁓ **purposes**, parler sans se comprendre. ⁓**ly** *adv.* avec colère.

crossbar /'krɒsbɑː(r)/ *n.* barre transversale *f.*

cross-examine /krɒsɪg'zæmɪn/ *v.t.* faire subir un examen contradictoire à.

cross-eyed /'krɒsaɪd/ *a.* **be** ⁓, loucher.

crossfire /'krɒsfaɪə(r)/ *n.* feux croisés *m. pl.*

crossing /'krɒsɪŋ/ *n.* (*by boat*) traversée *f.*; (*on road*) passage clouté *m.*

cross-reference /krɒs'refrəns/ *n.* renvoi *m.*

crossroads /'krɒsrəʊdz/ *n.* carrefour *m.*

cross-section /krɒs'sekʃn/ *n.* coupe transversale *f.*; (*sample: fig.*) échantillon *m.*

crosswise /'krɒswaɪz/ *adv.* en travers.

crossword /'krɒswɜːd/ *n.* mots croisés *m. pl.*

crotch /krɒtʃ/ *n.* (*of garment*) entrejambes *m. invar.*

crotchet /'krɒtʃɪt/ *n.* (*mus.*) noire *f.*

crotchety /'krɒtʃɪtɪ/ *a.* grincheux.

crouch /kraʊtʃ/ *v.i.* s'accroupir.

crow /krəʊ/ *n.* corbeau *m.* —*v.i.* (*of cock*) (*p.t.* **crew**) chanter; (*fig.*) jubiler. **as the** ⁓ **flies**, à vol d'oiseau.

crowbar /'krəʊbɑː(r)/ *n.* levier *m.*

crowd /kraʊd/ *n.* foule *f.* —*v.i.* affluer. —*v.t.* remplir. ⁓ **into**, (s')entasser dans. ⁓**ed** *a.* plein.

crown /kraʊn/ *n.* couronne *f.*; (*top part*) sommet *m.* —*v.t.* couronner. **C**⁓ **Court**, Cour d'assises *f.* **C**⁓ **prince**, prince héritier *m.*

crucial /'kruːʃl/ *a.* crucial.

crucifix /'kruːsɪfɪks/ *n.* crucifix *m.*

crucif|y /'kruːsɪfaɪ/ *v.t.* crucifier. ⁓**ixion** /-'fɪkʃn/ *n.* crucifixion *f.*

crude /kruːd/ *a.* (**-er, -est**) (*raw*) brut; (*rough, vulgar*) grossier.

cruel /krʊəl/ *a.* (**crueller, cruellest**) cruel. ⁓**ty** *n.* cruauté *f.*

cruet /'kruːɪt/ *n.* huilier *m.*

cruis|e /kruːz/ *n.* croisière *f.* —*v.i.* (*ship*) croiser; (*tourists*) faire une croisière; (*vehicle*) rouler. ⁓**er** *n.* croiseur *m.* ⁓**ing speed**, vitesse de croisière *f.*

crumb /krʌm/ *n.* miette *f.*

crumble /'krʌmbl/ *v.t./i.* (s')effriter; (*bread*) (s')émietter; (*collapse*) s'écrouler.

crummy /'krʌmɪ/ *a.* (**-ier, -iest**) (*sl.*) moche, minable.

crumpet /'krʌmpɪt/ *n.* (*culin.*) petite crêpe (grillée) *f.*

crumple /'krʌmpl/ *v.t./i.* (se) froisser.

crunch /krʌntʃ/ *v.t.* croquer. —*n.* (*event*) moment critique *m.*

crusade /kruː'seɪd/ *n.* croisade *f.* ⁓**r** /-ə(r)/ *n.* (*knight*) croisé *m.*; (*fig.*) militant(e) *m.* (*f.*).

crush /krʌʃ/ *v.t.* écraser; (*clothes*) froisser. —*n.* (*crowd*) presse *f.* **a** ⁓ **on**, (*sl.*) le béguin pour. **orange** ⁓, orange pressée *f.*

crust /krʌst/ n. croûte f. ~y a. croustillant.

crutch /krʌtʃ/ n. béquille f.; (*crotch*) entre-jambes m. *invar.*

crux /krʌks/ n. the ~ of, (*problem etc.*) le nœud de.

cry /kraɪ/ n. cri m. —v.i. (*weep*) pleurer; (*call out*) crier. ~-baby n. pleurnicheu|r, -se m., f. ~ off, abandonner.

crying /ˈkraɪɪŋ/ a. (*evil etc.*) flagrant. a ~ shame, une vraie honte.

crypt /krɪpt/ n. crypte f.

cryptic /ˈkrɪptɪk/ a. énigmatique.

crystal /ˈkrɪstl/ n. cristal m. ~lize v.t./i. (se) cristalliser.

cub /kʌb/ n. petit m. C~ (Scout), louveteau m.

Cuba /ˈkjuːbə/ n. Cuba m. ~n a. & n. cubain(e) (m. (f.)).

cubby-hole /ˈkʌbɪhəʊl/ n. cagibi m.

cub|e /kjuːb/ n. cube m. ~ic a. cubique; (*metre etc.*) cube.

cubicle /ˈkjuːbɪkl/ n. (*in room, hospital, etc.*) box m.; (*at swimming-pool*) cabine f.

cuckoo /ˈkʊkuː/ n. coucou m.

cucumber /ˈkjuːkʌmbə(r)/ n. concombre m.

cuddl|e /ˈkʌdl/ v.t. serrer dans ses bras. —v.i. (kiss and) ~e, s'embrasser. —n. caresse f. ~y a. câlin, caressant.

cudgel /ˈkʌdʒl/ n. gourdin m.

cue[1] /kjuː/ n. signal m.; (*theatre*) réplique f.

cue[2] /kjuː/ n. (*billiards*) queue f.

cuff /kʌf/ n. manchette f. —v.t. gifler. ~-link n. bouton de manchette m. off the ~, impromptu.

cul-de-sac /ˈkʌldəsæk/ n. (pl. culs-de-sac) impasse f.

culinary /ˈkʌlɪnərɪ/ a. culinaire.

cull /kʌl/ v.t. (*select*) choisir; (*kill*) abattre sélectivement.

culminat|e /ˈkʌlmɪneɪt/ v.i. ~e in, terminer par. ~ion /-ˈneɪʃn/ n. point culminant m.

culprit /ˈkʌlprɪt/ n. coupable m./f.

cult /kʌlt/ n. culte m.

cultivat|e /ˈkʌltɪveɪt/ v.t. cultiver. ~ion /-ˈveɪʃn/ n. culture f.

cultural /ˈkʌltʃərəl/ a. culturel.

culture /ˈkʌltʃə(r)/ n. culture f. ~d a. cultivé.

cumbersome /ˈkʌmbəsəm/ a. encombrant.

cumulative /ˈkjuːmjʊlətɪv/ a. cumulatif.

cunning /ˈkʌnɪŋ/ a. rusé. —n. astuce f., ruse f.

cup /kʌp/ n. tasse f.; (*prize*) coupe f. C~ Final, finale de la coupe f. ~-tie n. match de coupe m.

cupboard /ˈkʌbəd/ n. placard m., armoire f.

cupful /ˈkʌpfʊl/ n. tasse f.

Cupid /ˈkjuːpɪd/ n. Cupidon m.

curable /ˈkjʊərəbl/ a. guérissable.

curate /ˈkjʊərət/ n. vicaire m.

curator /kjʊəˈreɪtə(r)/ n. (*of museum*) conservateur m.

curb[1] /kɜːb/ n. (*restraint*) frein m. —v.t. (*desires etc.*) refréner; (*price increase etc.*) freiner.

curb[2] /kɜːb/ n. (*kerb: Amer.*) bord du trottoir m.

curdle /ˈkɜːdl/ v.t./i. (se) cailler.

curds /kɜːdz/ n. pl. lait caillé m.

cure[1] /kjʊə(r)/ v.t. guérir; (*fig.*) éliminer. —n. (*recovery*) guérison f.; (*remedy*) remède m.

cure[2] /kjʊə(r)/ v.t. (*culin.*) fumer, saler.

curfew /ˈkɜːfjuː/ n. couvre-feu m.

curio /ˈkjʊərɪəʊ/ n. (pl. -os) curiosité f., bibelot m.

curi|ous /ˈkjʊərɪəs/ a. curieux. ~osity /-ˈɒsətɪ/ n. curiosité f.

curl /kɜːl/ v.t./i. (*hair*) boucler. —n. boucle f. ~ up, se pelotonner; (*shrivel*) se racornir.

curler /ˈkɜːlə(r)/ n. bigoudi m.

curly /ˈkɜːlɪ/ a. (-ier, -iest) bouclé.

currant /ˈkʌrənt/ n. raisin de Corinthe m.; (*berry*) groseille f.

currency /ˈkʌrənsɪ/ n. (*money*) monnaie f.; (*acceptance*) cours m.

current /ˈkʌrənt/ a. (*common*) courant; (*topical*) actuel; (*year etc.*) en cours. —n. courant m. ~ events, actualité f. ~ly adv. actuellement.

curriculum /kəˈrɪkjʊləm/ n. (pl. -la) programme scolaire m.

curry[1] /ˈkʌrɪ/ n. curry m., cari m.

curry[2] /ˈkʌrɪ/ v.t. ~ favour with, chercher les bonnes grâces de.

curse /kɜːs/ n. malédiction f.; (*oath*) juron m. —v.t. maudire. —v.i. (*swear*) jurer.

cursory /ˈkɜːsərɪ/ a. (trop) rapide.

curt /kɜːt/ a. brusque.

curtail /kɜːˈteɪl/ v.t. écourter, raccourcir; (*expenses etc.*) réduire.

curtain /'kɜ:tn/ *n.* rideau *m.*

curtsy /'kɜ:tsɪ/ *n.* révérence *f.* —*v.i.* faire une révérence.

curve /kɜ:v/ *n.* courbe *f.* —*v.t./i.* (se) courber; (*of road*) tourner.

cushion /'kʊʃn/ *n.* coussin *m.* —*v.t.* (*a blow*) amortir; (*fig.*) protéger.

cushy /'kʊʃɪ/ *a.* (-ier, -iest) (*job etc.*: *fam.*) pépère.

custard /'kʌstəd/ *n.* crème anglaise *f.*; (*set*) crème renversée *f.*

custodian /kʌ'stəʊdɪən/ *n.* gardien(ne) *m.* (*f.*).

custody /'kʌstədɪ/ *n.* garde *f.*; (*jurid.*) détention préventive *f.*

custom /'kʌstəm/ *n.* coutume *f.*; (*patronage*: *comm.*) clientèle *f.* ~**ary** *a.* d'usage.

customer /'kʌstəmə(r)/ *n.* client(e) *m.* (*f.*).

customs /'kʌstəmz/ *n. pl.* douane *f.* —*a.* douanier. ~ **officer,** douanier *m.*

cut /kʌt/ *v.t./i.* (*p.t.* cut, *pres. p.* cutting) couper; (*hedge, jewel*) tailler; (*prices etc.*) réduire. —*n.* coupure *f.*; (*of clothes*) coupe *f.*; (*piece*) morceau *m.*; réduction *f.* ~ **back** *or* **down** (on), réduire. ~-**back** *n.* réduction *f.* ~ **in,** (*auto.*) se rabattre. ~ **off,** couper; (*fig.*) isoler. ~ **out,** découper; (*leave out*) supprimer. ~-**price** *a.* à prix réduit. ~ **short,** (*visit*) écourter. ~

up, couper; (*carve*) découper. ~ **up about,** démoralisé par.

cute /kju:t/ *a.* (-er, -est) (*fam.*) astucieux; (*Amer.*) mignon.

cuticle /'kju:tɪkl/ *n.* petites peaux *f. pl.* (*de l'ongle*).

cutlery /'kʌtlərɪ/ *n.* couverts *m. pl.*

cutlet /'kʌtlɪt/ *n.* côtelette *f.*

cutting /'kʌtɪŋ/ *a.* cinglant. —*n.* (*from newspaper*) coupure *f.*; (*plant*) bouture *f.* ~ **edge,** tranchant *m.*

cyanide /'saɪənaɪd/ *n.* cyanure *m.*

cybernetics /saɪbə'netɪks/ *n.* cybernétique *f.*

cycl|e /'saɪkl/ *n.* cycle *m.*; (*bicycle*) vélo *m.* —*v.i.* aller à vélo. ~**ing** *n.* cyclisme *m.* ~**ist** *n.* cycliste *m./f.*

cyclic(al) /'saɪklɪk(l)/ *a.* cyclique.

cyclone /'saɪkləʊn/ *n.* cyclone *m.*

cylind|er /'sɪlɪndə(r)/ *n.* cylindre *m.* ~**rical** /-'lɪndrɪkl/ *a.* cylindrique.

cymbal /'sɪmbl/ *n.* cymbale *f.*

cynic /'sɪnɪk/ *n.* cynique *m./f.* ~**al** *a.* cynique. ~**ism** /-sɪzəm/ *n.* cynisme *m.*

cypress /'saɪprəs/ *n.* cyprès *m.*

Cypr|us /'saɪprəs/ *n.* Chypre *f.* ~**iot** /'sɪprɪət/ *a.* & *n.* cypriote (*m./f.*).

cyst /sɪst/ *n.* kyste *m.*

czar /zɑ:(r)/ *n.* tsar *m.*

Czech /tʃek/ *a.* & *n.* tchèque (*m./f.*).

Czechoslovak /tʃekə'sləʊvæk/ *a.* & *n.* tchécoslovaque (*m./f.*). ~**ia** /-slə'vækɪə/ *n.* Tchécoslovaquie *f.*

D

dab /dæb/ v.t. (p.t. **dabbed**) tamponner. —n. **a ~ of**, un petit coup de. **~ sth. on**, appliquer qch. à petits coups sur.

dabble /'dæbl/ v.i. **~ in**, se mêler un peu de. **~r** /-ə(r)/ n. amateur m.

dad /dæd/ n. (fam.) papa m. **~dy** n. (children's use) papa m.

daffodil /'dæfədɪl/ n. jonquille f.

daft /dɑːft/ a. (-er, -est) idiot.

dagger /'dægə(r)/ n. poignard m.

dahlia /'deɪlɪə/ n. dahlia m.

daily /'deɪlɪ/ a. quotidien. —adv. tous les jours. —n. (newspaper) quotidien m.; (charwoman: fam.) femme de ménage f.

dainty /'deɪntɪ/ a. (-ier, -iest) délicat.

dairy /'deərɪ/ n. (on farm) laiterie f.; (shop) crémerie f. —a. laitier.

daisy /'deɪzɪ/ n. pâquerette f.

dale /deɪl/ n. vallée f.

dally /'dælɪ/ v.i. lanterner.

dam /dæm/ n. barrage m. —v.t. (p.t. **dammed**) endiguer.

damag|e /'dæmɪdʒ/ n. dégâts m. pl., dommages m. pl.; (harm: fig.) préjudice m. **~es**, (jurid.) dommages et intérêts m. pl. —v.t. abîmer; (fig.) nuire à. **~ing** a. nuisible.

dame /deɪm/ n. (old use) dame f.; (Amer., sl.) fille f.

damn /dæm/ v.t. (relig.) damner; (swear at) maudire;. (condemn: fig.) condamner. —int. zut, merde. —n. **not care a ~**, s'en moquer éperdument. —a. sacré. —adv. rudement. **~ation** /-'neɪʃn/ n. damnation f.

damp /dæmp/ n. humidité f. —a. (-er, -est) humide. —v.t. humecter; (fig.) refroidir. **~en** v.t. = **damp**. **~ness** n. humidité f.

damsel /'dæmzl/ n. demoiselle f.

dance /dɑːns/ v.t./i. danser. —n. danse f.; (gathering) bal m. **~ hall**, dancing m., salle de danse f. **~r** /-ə(r)/ n. danseu|r, -se m., f.

dandelion /'dændɪlaɪən/ n. pissenlit m.

dandruff /'dændrʌf/ n. pellicules f. pl.

dandy /'dændɪ/ n. dandy m.

Dane /deɪn/ n. Danois(e) m. (f.).

danger /'deɪndʒə(r)/ n. danger m.; (risk) risque m. **be in ~ of**, risquer de. **~ous** a. dangereux.

dangle /'dæŋgl/ v.t./i. (se) balancer, (laisser) pendre.

Danish /'deɪnɪʃ/ a. danois. —n. (lang.) danois m.

dank /dæŋk/ a. (-er, -est) humide et froid.

dapper /'dæpə(r)/ a. élégant.

dare /deə(r)/ v.t. **~ (to) do**, oser faire. **~ s.o. to do**, défier qn. de faire. —n. défi m. **I ~ say**, je suppose (**that**, que).

daredevil /'deədevl/ n. casse-cou m. invar.

daring /'deərɪŋ/ a. audacieux.

dark /dɑːk/ a. (-er, -est) obscur, sombre, noir; (colour) foncé, sombre; (skin) brun, foncé; (gloomy) sombre. —n. noir m.; (nightfall) tombée de la nuit f. **~ horse**, individu aux talents inconnus m. **~-room** n. chambre noire f. **in the ~**, (fig.) dans l'ignorance (**about**, de). **~ness** n. obscurité f.

darken /'dɑːkən/ v.t./i. (s')assombrir.

darling /'dɑːlɪŋ/ a. & n. chéri(e) (m. (f.)).

darn /dɑːn/ v.t. repriser.

dart /dɑːt/ n. fléchette f. **~s**, (game) fléchettes f. pl. —v.i. s'élancer.

dartboard /'dɑːtbɔːd/ n. cible f.

dash /dæʃ/ v.i. se précipiter. —v.t. jeter (avec violence); (hopes) briser. —n. ruée f.; (stroke) tiret m. **a ~ of**, un peu de. **~ off**, (leave) partir en vitesse.

dashboard /'dæʃbɔːd/ n. tableau de bord m.

dashing /'dæʃɪŋ/ a. fringant.

data /'deɪtə/ n. pl. données f. pl. **~ processing**, informatique f.

date[1] /deɪt/ n. date f.; (meeting: fam.) rendez-vous m. —v.t./i. dater; (go out with: fam.) sortir avec. **to ~**, à ce jour. **~d** /-ɪd/ a. démodé.

date[2] /deɪt/ n. (fruit) datte f.

daub /dɔːb/ v.t. barbouiller.

daughter /'dɔːtə(r)/ n. fille f. **~-in-law** n. (pl. **~s-in-law**) belle-fille f.

daunt /dɔːnt/ v.t. décourager.

dauntless /'dɔːntlɪs/ a. intrépide.

dawdle /'dɔːdl/ v.i. lambiner. **~r** /-ə(r) / n. lambin(e) m. (f.).

dawn /dɔːn/ *n.* aube *f.* —*v.i.* poindre; (*fig.*) naître.

day /deɪ/ *n.* jour *m.*; (*whole day*) journée *f.*; (*period*) époque *f.* **~break** *n.* point du jour *m.* **~dream** *n.* rêverie *f.*; *v.i.* rêvasser. **the ~ before**, la veille. **the following** *or* **next ~**, le lendemain.

daylight /ˈdeɪlaɪt/ *n.* jour *m.*

daytime /ˈdeɪtaɪm/ *n.* jour *m.*, journée *f.*

daze /deɪz/ *v.t.* étourdir; (*with drugs*) hébéter. —*n.* **in a ~**, étourdi; hébété.

dazzle /ˈdæzl/ *v.t.* éblouir.

deacon /ˈdiːkən/ *n.* diacre *m.*

dead /ded/ *a.* mort; (*numb*) engourdi. —*adv.* complètement. —*n.* **in the ~ of**, au cœur de. **the ~**, les morts. **~ beat**, éreinté. **~ end**, impasse *f.* **~-pan** *a.* impassible. **in ~ centre**, au beau milieu. **stop ~**, s'arrêter pile. **the race was a ~ heat**, ils ont été classés ex aequo.

deaden /ˈdedn/ *v.t.* (*sound, blow*) amortir; (*pain*) calmer.

deadline /ˈdedlaɪn/ *n.* date limite *f.*

deadlock /ˈdedlɒk/ *n.* impasse *f.*

deadly /ˈdedlɪ/ *a.* (**-ier, -iest**) mortel; (*weapon*) meurtrier.

deaf /def/ *a.* (**-er, -est**) sourd. **~-aid** *n.* appareil acoustique *m.* **~ness** *n.* surdité *f.*

deafen /ˈdefn/ *v.t.* assourdir.

deal /diːl/ *v.t.* (*p.t.* **dealt**) donner; (*a blow*) porter. —*v.i.* (*trade*) commercer. —*n.* affaire *f.*; (*cards*) donne *f.* **a great** *or* **good ~**, beaucoup (of, de). **~ in**, faire le commerce de. **~ with**, (*handle, manage*) s'occuper de; (*be about*) traiter de. **~er** *n.* marchand(e) *m.* (*f.*).; (*agent*) concessionnaire *m.*/*f.*

dealings /ˈdiːlɪŋz/ *n. pl.* relations *f. pl.*

dean /diːn/ *n.* doyen *m.*

dear /dɪə(r)/ *a.* (**-er, -est**) cher. —*n.* (my) **~**, mon cher, ma chère; (*darling*) (mon) chéri, (ma) chérie. —*adv.* cher. —*int.* **oh ~**!, oh mon Dieu! **~ly** *adv.* tendrement; (*pay*) cher.

dearth /dɜːθ/ *n.* pénurie *f.*

death /deθ/ *n.* mort *f.* **~ certificate**, acte de décès *m.* **~ duty**, droits de succession *m. pl.* **~ penalty**, peine de mort *f.* **it is a ~-trap**, (*place, vehicle*) il y a un danger de mort. **~ly** *a.* de mort, mortel.

debar /dɪˈbaː(r)/ *v.t.* (*p.t.* **debarred**) exclure.

debase /dɪˈbeɪs/ *v.t.* avilir.

debat|e /dɪˈbeɪt/ *n.* discussion *f.* —*v.t.* discuter. **~e whether**, se demander si. **~able** *a.* discutable.

debauch /dɪˈbɔːtʃ/ *v.t.* débaucher. **~ery** *n.* débauche *f.*

debilitate /dɪˈbɪlɪteɪt/ *v.t.* débiliter.

debility /dɪˈbɪlətɪ/ *n.* débilité *f.*

debit /ˈdebɪt/ *n.* débit *m.* **in ~**, débiteur. —*a.* (*balance*) débiteur. —*v.t.* (*p.t.* **debited**) débiter.

debris /ˈdeɪbriː/ *n.* débris *m. pl.*

debt /det/ *n.* dette *f.* **in ~**, endetté. **~or** *n.* débi|teur, -trice *m.*, *f.*

debunk /diːˈbʌŋk/ *v.t.* (*fam.*) démythifier.

decade /ˈdekeɪd/ *n.* décennie *f.*

decaden|t /ˈdekədənt/ *a.* décadent. **~ce** *n.* décadence *f.*

decanter /dɪˈkæntə(r)/ *n.* carafe *f.*

decapitate /dɪˈkæpɪteɪt/ *v.t.* décapiter.

decay /dɪˈkeɪ/ *v.i.* se gâter, pourrir; (*fig.*) décliner. —*n.* pourriture *f.*; (*of tooth*) carie *f.*; (*fig.*) déclin *m.*

deceased /dɪˈsiːst/ *a.* décédé. —*n.* défunt(e) *m.* (*f.*).

deceit /dɪˈsiːt/ *n.* tromperie *f.* **~ful** *a.* trompeur. **~fully** *adv.* d'une manière trompeuse.

deceive /dɪˈsiːv/ *v.t.* tromper.

December /dɪˈsembə(r)/ *n.* décembre *m.*

decen|t /ˈdiːsnt/ *a.* décent, convenable; (*good: fam.*) (assez) bon; (*kind: fam.*) gentil. **~cy** *n.* décence *f.* **~tly** *adv.* décemment.

decentralize /diːˈsentrəlaɪz/ *v.t.* décentraliser.

decept|ive /dɪˈseptɪv/ *a.* trompeur. **~ion** /-pʃn/ *n.* tromperie *f.*

decibel /ˈdesɪbel/ *n.* décibel *m.*

decide /dɪˈsaɪd/ *v.t.*/*i.* décider. **~ on**, se décider pour. **~ to do**, décider de faire. **~d** /-ɪd/ *a.* (*firm*) résolu; (*clear*) net. **~dly** /-ɪdlɪ/ *adv.* résolument; nettement.

decimal /ˈdesɪml/ *a.* décimal. —*n.* décimale *f.* **~ point**, virgule *f.*

decimate /ˈdesɪmeɪt/ *v.t.* décimer.

decipher /dɪˈsaɪfə(r)/ *v.t.* déchiffrer.

decision /dɪˈsɪʒn/ *n.* décision *f.*

decisive /dɪˈsaɪsɪv/ *a.* (*conclusive*) décisif; (*firm*) décidé. **~ly** *adv.* d'une façon décidée.

deck[1] /dek/ *n.* pont *m.*; (*of cards: Amer.*) jeu *m.* **~-chair** *n.* chaise longue *f.* **top ~**, (*of bus*) impériale *f.*

deck[2] /dek/ *v.t.* (*adorn*) orner.

declar|e /dɪ'kleə(r)/ v.t. déclarer. **~ation** /deklə'reɪʃn/ n. déclaration f.

decline /dɪ'klaɪn/ v.t./i. refuser (poliment); (deteriorate) décliner; (fall) baisser. —n. déclin m.; baisse f.

decode /diː'kəʊd/ v.t. décoder.

decompos|e /diːkəm'pəʊz/ v.t./i. (se) décomposer. **~ition** /-ɒmpə'zɪʃn/ n. décomposition f.

décor /'deɪkɔː(r)/ n. décor m.

decorat|e /'dekəreɪt/ v.t. décorer; (room) tapisser. **~ion** /-'reɪʃn/ n. décoration f. **~ive** /-ətɪv/ a. décoratif.

decorator /'dekəreɪtə(r)/ n. peintre en bâtiment m. (**interior**) **~**, décora|teur, -trice d'appartements m., f.

decorum /dɪ'kɔːrəm/ n. décorum m.

decoy[1] /'diːkɔɪ/ n. (bird) appeau m.; (trap) piège m., leurre m.

decoy[2] /dɪ'kɔɪ/ v.t. attirer, appâter.

decrease /dɪ'kriːs/ v.t./i. diminuer. —n. /'diːkriːs/ diminution f.

decree /dɪ'kriː/ n. (pol., relig.) décret m.; (jurid.) jugement m. —v.t. (p.t. **decreed**) décréter.

decrepit /dɪ'krepɪt/ a. (building) délabré; (person) décrépit.

decry /dɪ'kraɪ/ v.t. dénigrer.

dedicat|e /'dedɪkeɪt/ v.t. dédier. **~e o.s. to**, se consacrer à. **~ed** a. dévoué. **~ion** /-'keɪʃn/ n. dévouement m.; (in book) dédicace f.

deduce /dɪ'djuːs/ v.t. déduire.

deduct /dɪ'dʌkt/ v.t. déduire. **~ion** /-kʃn/ n. déduction f.

deed /diːd/ n. acte m.

deem /diːm/ v.t. juger.

deep /diːp/ a. (**-er, -est**) profond. —adv. profondément. **~ in thought**, absorbé dans ses pensées. **~ into the night**, tard dans la nuit. **~-freeze** n. congélateur m.; v.t. surgeler. **~ly** adv. profondément.

deepen /'diːpən/ v.t. approfondir. —v.i. devenir plus profond; (mystery, night) s'épaissir.

deer /dɪə(r)/ n. invar. cerf m.

deface /dɪ'feɪs/ v.t. dégrader.

defamation /defə'meɪʃn/ n. diffamation f.

default /dɪ'fɔːlt/ v.i. (jurid) faire défaut. —n. **by ~**, (jurid.) par défaut. **win by ~**, gagner par forfait.

defeat /dɪ'fiːt/ v.t. vaincre; (thwart) faire échouer. —n. défaite f.; (of plan etc.) échec m.

defect[1] /'diːfekt/ n. défaut m. **~ive** /dɪ'fektɪv/ a. défectueux.

defect[2] /dɪ'fekt/ v.i. faire défection. **~ to**, passer à. **~or** n. transfuge m./f.

defence /dɪ'fens/ n. défense f. **~less** a. sans défense.

defend /dɪ'fend/ v.t. défendre. **~ant** n. (jurid.) accusé(e) m. (f.).

defensive /dɪ'fensɪv/ a. défensif. —n. défensive f.

defer /dɪ'fɜː(r)/ v.t. (p.t. **deferred**) (postpone) différer, remettre.

deferen|ce /'defərəns/ n. déférence f. **~tial** /-'renʃl/ a. déférent.

defian|ce /dɪ'faɪəns/ n. défi m. **in ~ce of**, au mépris de. **~t** a. de défi. **~tly** adv. d'un air de défi.

deficien|t /dɪ'fɪʃnt/ a. insuffisant. **be ~t in**, manquer de. **~cy** n. insuffisance f.; (fault) défaut m.

deficit /'defɪsɪt/ n. déficit m.

defile /dɪ'faɪl/ v.t. souiller.

define /dɪ'faɪn/ v.t. définir.

definite /'defɪnɪt/ a. précis; (obvious) net; (firm) catégorique; (certain) certain. **~ly** adv. certainement; (clearly) nettement.

definition /defɪ'nɪʃn/ n. définition f.

definitive /dɪ'fɪnətɪv/ a. définitif.

deflat|e /dɪ'fleɪt/ v.t. dégonfler. **~ion** /-ʃn/ n. dégonflement m.; (comm.) déflation f.

deflect /dɪ'flekt/ v.t./i. (faire) dévier.

deform /dɪ'fɔːm/ v.t. déformer. **~ed** a. difforme. **~ity** n. difformité f.

defraud /dɪ'frɔːd/ v.t. (state, customs) frauder. **~ s.o. of sth.**, escroquer qch. à qn.

defray /dɪ'freɪ/ v.t. payer.

defrost /diː'frɒst/ v.t. dégivrer.

deft /deft/ a. (**-er, -est**) adroit. **~ness** n. adresse f.

defunct /dɪ'fʌŋkt/ a. défunt.

defuse /diː'fjuːz/ v.t. désamorcer.

defy /dɪ'faɪ/ v.t. défier; (attempts) résister à.

degenerate[1] /dɪ'dʒenəreɪt/ v.i. dégénérer (**into**, en).

degenerate[2] /dɪ'dʒenərət/ a. & n. dégénéré(e) (m. (f.)).

degrad|e /dɪ'greɪd/ v.t. dégrader. **~ation** /degrə'deɪʃn/ n. dégradation f.; (state) déchéance f.

degree /dɪ'griː/ n. degré m.; (univ.) diplôme universitaire m.; (Bachelor's degree) licence f. **higher ~**, (univ.) maîtrise f., doctorat m. **to such a ~ that**, à tel point que.

dehydrate /diː'haɪdreɪt/ v.t./i. (se) déshydrater.

de-ice /diːˈaɪs/ v.t. dégivrer.
deign /deɪn/ v.t. ~ **to do**, daigner faire.
deity /ˈdiːɪtɪ/ n. divinité f.
deject|ed /dɪˈdʒektɪd/ a. abattu. ~**ion**
/-kʃn/ n. abattement m.
delay /dɪˈleɪ/ v.t. retarder. —v.i.
tarder. —n. (lateness, time overdue)
retard m.; (waiting) délai m.
delectable /dɪˈlektəbl/ a. délectable,
très agréable.
delegate[1] /ˈdelɪɡət/ n. délégué(e) m.
(f.).
delegat|e[2] /ˈdelɪɡeɪt/ v.t. déléguer.
~**ion** /-ˈɡeɪʃn/ n. délégation f.
delet|e /dɪˈliːt/ v.t. rayer. ~**ion** /-ʃn/
n. rature f.
deliberate[1] /dɪˈlɪbərət/ a. délibéré;
(steps, manner) mesuré. ~**ly** adv. exprès, délibérément.
deliberat|e[2] /dɪˈlɪbəreɪt/ v.i. délibérer.
—v.t. considérer. ~**ion** /-ˈreɪʃn/ n.
délibération f.
delica|te /ˈdelɪkət/ a. délicat. ~**cy** n.
délicatesse f.; (food) mets délicat or
raffiné m.
delicatessen /delɪkəˈtesn/ n. épicerie
fine f., charcuterie f.
delicious /dɪˈlɪʃəs/ a. délicieux.
delight /dɪˈlaɪt/ n. grand plaisir m.,
joie f., délice m. (f. in pl.); (thing)
délice m. (f. in pl.). —v.t. réjouir.
—v.i. ~ **in**, prendre plaisir à. ~**ed**
a. ravi. ~**ful** a. charmant, très
agréable.
delinquen|t /dɪˈlɪŋkwənt/ a. & n. délin-
quant(e) (m. (f.)). ~**cy** n. délinquance
f.
deliri|ous /dɪˈlɪrɪəs/ a. **be** ~**ous**,
délirer. ~**um** n. délire m.
deliver /dɪˈlɪvə(r)/ v.t. (message) remettre; (goods) livrer; (letters) distribuer; (free) délivrer; (utter)
prononcer; (med.) accoucher; (a blow)
porter. ~**ance** n. délivrance f. ~**y** n.
livraison f.; distribution f.; accouchement m.
delta /ˈdeltə/ n. delta m.
delu|de /dɪˈluːd/ v.t. tromper. ~**de**
o.s., se faire des illusions. ~**sion**
/-ʒn/ n. illusion f.
deluge /ˈdeljuːdʒ/ n. déluge m. —v.t.
inonder (**with**, de).
de luxe /dəˈlʌks/ a. de luxe.
delve /delv/ v.i. fouiller.
demagogue /ˈdeməɡɒɡ/ n. démagogue
m./f.
demand /dɪˈmɑːnd/ v.t. exiger. —n.
exigence f.; (claim) revendication f.;

(comm.) demande f. **in** ~, recherché.
~**ing** a. exigeant.
demarcation /diːmɑːˈkeɪʃn/ n. démarcation f.
demean /dɪˈmiːn/ v.t. ~ **o.s.**,
s'abaisser, s'avilir.
demeanour /dɪˈmiːnə(r)/ n. comportement m.
demented /dɪˈmentɪd/ a. dément.
demerara /deməˈreərə/ n. (brown sugar) cassonade f.
demise /dɪˈmaɪz/ n. décès m.
demo /ˈdeməʊ/ n. (pl. -os) (demon-
stration: fam.) manif f.
demobilize /diːˈməʊbəlaɪz/ v.t. démobiliser.
democracy /dɪˈmɒkrəsɪ/ n. démocratie
f.
democrat /ˈdeməkræt/ n. démocrate
m./f. ~**ic** /-ˈkrætɪk/ a. démocratique.
demoli|sh /dɪˈmɒlɪʃ/ v.t. démolir.
~**tion** /deməˈlɪʃn/ n. démolition f.
demon /ˈdiːmən/ n. démon m.
demonstrat|e /ˈdemənstreɪt/ v.t. dé-
montrer. —v.i. (pol.) manifester.
~**ion** /-ˈstreɪʃn/ n. démonstration f.;
(pol.) manifestation f. ~**or** n. manifes-
tant(e) m. (f.).
demonstrative /dɪˈmɒnstrətɪv/ a. dé-
monstratif.
demoralize /dɪˈmɒrəlaɪz/ v.t. démoraliser.
demote /dɪˈməʊt/ v.t. rétrograder.
demure /dɪˈmjʊə(r)/ a. modeste.
den /den/ n. antre m.
denial /dɪˈnaɪəl/ n. dénégation f.; (statement) démenti m.
denigrate /ˈdenɪɡreɪt/ v.t. dénigrer.
denim /ˈdenɪm/ n. toile de coton f.
~**s**, (jeans) blue-jeans m. pl.
Denmark /ˈdenmɑːk/ n. Danemark m.
denomination /dɪnɒmɪˈneɪʃn/ n.
(relig.) confession f.; (money) valeur
f.
denote /dɪˈnəʊt/ v.t. dénoter.
denounce /dɪˈnaʊns/ v.t. dénoncer.
dens|e /dens/ a. (-er, -est) dense; (per-
son) obtus. ~**ely** adv. (packed etc.)
très. ~**ity** n. densité f.
dent /dent/ n. bosse f. —v.t. cabosser.
there is a ~ **in the car door**, la
portière est cabossée.
dental /ˈdentl/ a. dentaire; (surgeon)
dentiste.
dentist /ˈdentɪst/ n. dentiste m./f. ~**ry**
n. art dentaire m.
denture /ˈdentʃə(r)/ n. dentier m.
denude /dɪˈnjuːd/ v.t. dénuder.

denunciation /dɪnʌnsɪ'eɪʃn/ *n.* dénonciation *f.*

deny /dɪ'naɪ/ *v.t.* nier (**that,** que); (*rumour*) démentir; (*disown*) renier; (*refuse*) refuser.

deodorant /diː'əʊdərənt/ *n.* & *a.* déodorant (*m.*).

depart /dɪ'pɑːt/ *v.i.* partir. ∼ **from,** (*deviate*) s'écarter de.

department /dɪ'pɑːtmənt/ *n.* département *m.*; (*in shop*) rayon *m.*; (*in office*) service *m.* ∼ **store,** grand magasin *m.*

departure /dɪ'pɑːtʃə(r)/ *n.* départ *m.* a ∼ **from,** (*custom, diet, etc.*) une entorse à.

depend /dɪ'pend/ *v.i.* dépendre (**on,** de). ∼ **on,** (*rely on*) compter sur. ∼**able** *a.* sûr. ∼**ence** *n.* dépendance *f.* ∼**ent** *a.* dépendant. be ∼**ent on,** dépendre de.

dependant /dɪ'pendənt/ *n.* personne à charge *f.*

depict /dɪ'pɪkt/ *v.t.* (*describe*) dépeindre; (*in picture*) représenter.

deplete /dɪ'pliːt/ *v.t.* (*reduce*) réduire; (*use up*) épuiser.

deplor|**e** /dɪ'plɔː(r)/ *v.t.* déplorer. ∼**able** *a.* déplorable.

deploy /dɪ'plɔɪ/ *v.t.* déployer.

depopulate /diː'pɒpjʊleɪt/ *v.t.* dépeupler.

deport /dɪ'pɔːt/ *v.t.* expulser. ∼**ation** /diːpɔː'teɪʃn/ *n.* expulsion *f.*

depose /dɪ'pəʊz/ *v.t.* déposer.

deposit /dɪ'pɒzɪt/ *v.t.* (*p.t.* **deposited**) déposer. —*n.* dépôt *m.*; (*of payment*) acompte *m.*; (*against damage*) caution *f.*; (*on bottle etc.*) consigne *f.* ∼**or** *n.* (*comm.*) déposant(e) *m.* (*f.*), épargnant(e) *m.* (*f.*).

depot /'depəʊ, *Amer.* 'diːpəʊ/ *n.* dépôt *m.*; (*Amer.*) gare (routière) *f.*

deprav|**e** /dɪ'preɪv/ *v.t.* dépraver. ∼**ity** /-'prævətɪ/ *n.* dépravation *f.*

deprecate /'deprəkeɪt/ *v.t.* désapprouver.

depreciat|**e** /dɪ'priːʃɪeɪt/ *v.t./i.* (se) déprécier. ∼**ion** /-'eɪʃn/ *n.* dépréciation *f.*

depress /dɪ'pres/ *v.t.* (*sadden*) déprimer; (*push down*) appuyer sur. become ∼**ed,** se décourager. ∼**ion** /-ʃn/ *n.* dépression *f.*

deprivation /deprɪ'veɪʃn/ *n.* privation *f.*

deprive /dɪ'praɪv/ *v.t.* ∼ **of,** priver de. ∼**d** *a.* (*child etc.*) déshérité.

depth /depθ/ *n.* profondeur *f.* be out of one's ∼, perdre pied; (*fig.*) être perdu. in the ∼s of, au plus profond de.

deputation /depjʊ'teɪʃn/ *n.* députation *f.*

deputize /'depjʊtaɪz/ *v.i.* assurer l'intérim (**for,** de). —*v.t.* (*Amer.*) déléguer, nommer.

deputy /'depjʊtɪ/ *n.* suppléant(e) *m.* (*f.*). —*a.* adjoint. ∼ **chairman,** vice-président *m.*

derail /dɪ'reɪl/ *v.t.* faire dérailler. be ∼**ed,** dérailler. ∼**ment** *n.* déraillement *m.*

deranged /dɪ'reɪndʒd/ *a.* (*mind*) dérangé.

derelict /'derəlɪkt/ *a.* abandonné.

deri|**de** /dɪ'raɪd/ *v.t.* railler. ∼**sion** /-'rɪʒn/ *n.* dérision *f.* ∼**sive** *a.* (*laughter, person*) railleur.

derisory /dɪ'raɪsərɪ/ *a.* (*scoffing*) railleur; (*offer etc.*) dérisoire.

derivative /dɪ'rɪvətɪv/ *a.* & *n.* dérivé (*m.*).

deriv|**e** /dɪ'raɪv/ *v.t.* ∼**e from,** tirer de. —*v.i.* ∼**e from,** dériver de. ∼**ation** /derɪ'veɪʃn/ *n.* dérivation *f.*

derogatory /dɪ'rɒgətrɪ/ *a.* (*word*) péjoratif; (*remark*) désobligeant.

derv /dɜːv/ *n.* gas-oil *m.*, gazole *m.*

descend /dɪ'send/ *v.t./i.* descendre. be ∼**ed from,** descendre de. ∼**ant** *n.* descendant(e) *m.* (*f.*).

descent /dɪ'sent/ *n.* descente *f.*; (*lineage*) origine *f.*

descri|**be** /dɪ'skraɪb/ *v.t.* décrire. ∼**ption** /-'skrɪpʃn/ *n.* description *f.* ∼**ptive** /-'skrɪptɪv/ *a.* descriptif.

desecrat|**e** /'desɪkreɪt/ *v.t.* profaner. ∼**ion** /-'kreɪʃn/ *n.* profanation *f.*

desert[1] /'dezət/ *n.* désert *m.* —*a.* désertique. ∼ **island,** île déserte *f.*

desert[2] /dɪ'zɜːt/ *v.t./i.* déserter. ∼**ed** *a.* désert. ∼**er** *n.* déserteur *m.* ∼**ion** /-ʃn/ *n.* désertion *f.*

deserts /dɪ'zɜːts/ *n. pl.* one's ∼, ce qu'on mérite.

deserv|**e** /dɪ'zɜːv/ *v.t.* mériter. ∼**edly** /-ɪdlɪ/ *adv.* à juste titre. ∼**ing** *a.* (*person*) méritant; (*action*) méritoire.

design /dɪ'zaɪn/ *n.* (*sketch*) dessin *m.*, plan *m.*; (*construction*) conception *f.*; (*pattern*) motif *m.*; (*style of dress*) modèle *m.*, (*aim*) dessein *m.* —*v.t.* (*sketch*) dessiner; (*devise, intend*) concevoir. ∼**er** *n.* dessina|teur, -trice *m.*, *f.*

designat|e /'dezɪgneɪt/ v.t. désigner. **∼ion** /-'neɪʃn/ n. désignation f.

desir|e /dɪ'zaɪə(r)/ n. désir m. —v.t. désirer. **∼able** a. désirable. **∼ability** /-ə'bɪlɪtɪ/ n. attrait m.

desk /desk/ n. bureau m.; (of pupil) pupitre m.; (in hotel) réception f.; (in bank) caisse f.

desolat|e /'desələt/ a. (place) désolé; (bleak: fig.) morne. **∼ion** /-'leɪʃn/ n. désolation f.

despair /dɪ'speə(r)/ n. désespoir m. —v.i. désespérer (of, de).

desperate /'despərət/ a. désespéré; (criminal) prêt à tout. **be ∼ for**, avoir une envie folle de. **∼ly** adv. désespérément.

desperation /despə'reɪʃn/ n. désespoir m.

despicable /dɪ'spɪkəbl/ a. méprisable, infâme.

despise /dɪ'spaɪz/ v.t. mépriser.

despite /dɪ'spaɪt/ prep. malgré.

desponden|t /dɪ'spɒndənt/ a. découragé. **∼cy** n. découragement m.

despot /'despɒt/ n. despote m.

dessert /dɪ'zɜːt/ n. dessert m. **∼-spoon** n. cuiller à dessert f.

destination /destɪ'neɪʃn/ n. destination f.

destine /'destɪn/ v.t. destiner.

destiny /'destɪnɪ/ n. destin m.

destitute /'destɪtjuːt/ a. indigent. **∼ of**, dénué de.

destr|oy /dɪ'strɔɪ/ v.t. détruire; (animal) abattre. **∼uction** n. destruction f. **∼uctive** a. destructeur.

destroyer /dɪ'strɔɪə(r)/ n. (warship) contre-torpilleur m.

detach /dɪ'tætʃ/ v.t. détacher. **∼able** a. détachable. **∼ed** a. détaché. **∼ed house**, maison individuelle f.

detachment /dɪ'tætʃmənt/ n. détachement m.

detail /'diːteɪl/ n. détail m. —v.t. exposer en détail; (troops) détacher. **∼ed** a. détaillé.

detain /dɪ'teɪn/ v.t. retenir; (in prison) détenir. **∼ee** /diːteɪ'niː/ n. détenu(e) m. (f.).

detect /dɪ'tekt/ v.t. découvrir; (perceive) distinguer; (mine) détecter. **∼ion** /-kʃn/ n. découverte f.; détection f. **∼or** n. détecteur m.

detective /dɪ'tektɪv/ n. policier m.; (private) détective m.

detention /dɪ'tenʃn/ n. détention f.; (schol.) retenue f.

deter /dɪ'tɜː(r)/ v.t. (p.t. **deterred**) dissuader (**from**, de).

detergent /dɪ'tɜːdʒənt/ a. & n. détergent (m.).

deteriorat|e /dɪ'tɪərɪəreɪt/ v.i. se détériorer. **∼ion** /-'reɪʃn/ n. détérioration f.

determin|e /dɪ'tɜːmɪn/ v.t. déterminer. **∼e to do**, décider de faire. **∼ation** /-'neɪʃn/ n. détermination f. **∼ed** a. déterminé. **∼ed to do**, décidé à faire.

deterrent /dɪ'terənt, Amer. dɪ'tɜːrənt/ n. force de dissuasion f.

detest /dɪ'test/ v.t. détester. **∼able** a. détestable.

detonat|e /'detəneɪt/ v.t./i. (faire) détoner. **∼ion** /-'neɪʃn/ n. détonation f. **∼or** n. détonateur m.

detour /'diːtʊə(r)/ n. détour m.

detract /dɪ'trækt/ v.i. **∼ from**, (lessen) diminuer.

detriment /'detrɪmənt/ n. détriment m. **∼al** /-'mentl/ a. préjudiciable (**to**, à).

devalu|e /diː'væljuː/ v.t. dévaluer. **∼ation** /-jʊ'eɪʃn/ n. dévaluation f.

devastat|e /'devəsteɪt/ v.t. dévaster; (overwhelm: fig.) accabler. **∼ing** a. accablant.

develop /dɪ'veləp/ v.t./i. (p.t. **developed**) (se) développer; (contract) contracter; (build on, transform) exploiter, aménager; (appear) se manifester. **∼ into**, devenir. **∼ing country**, pays en voie de développement m. **∼ment** n. développement m. (**new**) **∼ment**, fait nouveau m.

deviant /'diːvɪənt/ a. anormal. —n. (psych.) déviant m.

deviat|e /'diːvɪeɪt/ v.i. dévier. **∼e from**, (norm) s'écarter de. **∼ion** /-'eɪʃn/ n. déviation f.

device /dɪ'vaɪs/ n. appareil m.; (scheme) procédé m.

devil /'devl/ n. diable m. **∼ish** a. diabolique.

devious /'diːvɪəs/ a. tortueux. **he is ∼**, il a l'esprit tortueux.

devise /dɪ'vaɪz/ v.t. inventer; (plan, means) combiner, imaginer.

devoid /dɪ'vɔɪd/ a. **∼ of**, dénué de.

devolution /diːvə'luːʃn/ n. décentralisation f.; (of authority, power) délégation f. (**to**, à).

devot|e /dɪ'vəʊt/ v.t. consacrer. **∼ed** a. dévoué. **∼edly** adv. avec

dévouement. ∼**ion** /-ʃn/ *n.* dévouement *m.*; (*relig.*) dévotion *f.* ∼**ions,**
(*relig.*) dévotions *f. pl.*

devotee /devə'tiː/ *n.* ∼ **of,** passionné(e)
de *m.* (*f.*).

devour /dɪ'vaʊə(r)/ *v.t.* dévorer.

devout /dɪ'vaʊt/ *a.* (*person*) dévot;
(*prayer*) fervent.

dew /djuː/ *n.* rosée *f.*

dexterity /dek'sterətɪ/ *n.* dextérité *f.*

diabet|es /daɪə'biːtiːz/ *n.* diabète *m.*
∼**ic** /-'betɪk/ *a.* & *n.* diabétique (*m.*/*f.*).

diabolical /daɪə'bɒlɪkl/ *a.* diabolique;
(*bad: fam.*) atroce.

diagnose /'daɪəgnəʊz/ *v.t.* diagnosti-
quer.

diagnosis /daɪəg'nəʊsɪs/ *n.* (*pl.* -oses)
/-siːz/ diagnostic *m.*

diagonal /daɪ'ægənl/ *a.* diagonal. −*n.*
diagonale *f.* ∼**ly** *adv.* en diagonale.

diagram /'daɪəgræm/ *n.* schéma *m.*

dial /'daɪəl/ *n.* cadran *m.* −*v.t.* (*p.t.*
dialled) (*number*) faire; (*person*) appeler. ∼**ling tone,** (*Amer.*) ∼ **tone,**
tonalité *f.*

dialect /'daɪəlekt/ *n.* dialecte *m.*

dialogue /'daɪəlɒg/ *n.* dialogue *m.*

diameter /daɪ'æmɪtə(r)/ *n.* diamètre
m.

diamond /'daɪəmənd/ *n.* diamant *m.*;
(*shape*) losange *m.*; (*baseball*) terrain
m. ∼**s,** (*cards*) carreau *m.*

diaper /'daɪəpə(r)/ *n.* (*baby's nappy*:
Amer.) couche *f.*

diaphragm /'daɪəfræm/ *n.* diaphragme *m.*

diarrhoea /daɪə'rɪə/ *n.* diarrhée *f.*

diary /'daɪərɪ/ *n.* (*for appointments etc.*)
agenda *m.*; (*for private thoughts*) journal intime *m.*

dice /daɪs/ *n. invar.* dé *m.* −*v.t.* (*food*)
couper en dés.

dicey /'daɪsɪ/ *a.* (*fam.*) risqué.

dictat|e /dɪk'teɪt/ *v.t./i.* dicter. ∼**ion**
/-ʃn/ *n.* dictée *f.*

dictates /'dɪkteɪts/ *n. pl.* préceptes
m. pl.

dictator /dɪk'teɪtə(r)/ *n.* dictateur *m.*
∼**ship** *n.* dictature *f.*

dictatorial /dɪktə'tɔːrɪəl/ *a.* dictatorial.

diction /'dɪkʃn/ *n.* diction *f.*

dictionary /'dɪkʃənrɪ/ *n.* dictionnaire
m.

did /dɪd/ *see* do.

diddle /'dɪdl/ *v.t.* (*sl.*) escroquer.

didn't /'dɪdnt/ = **did not.**

die[1] /daɪ/ *v.i.* (*pres. p.* **dying**) mourir.

∼ **down,** diminuer. ∼ **out,** disparaître. **be dying to,** mourir d'envie
de.

die[2] /daɪ/ *n.* (*metal mould*) matrice *f.*,
étampe *f.*

die-hard /'daɪhɑːd/ *n.* réactionnaire
m./*f.*

diesel /'diːzl/ *n.* diesel *m.* ∼ **engine,**
moteur diesel *m.*

diet /'daɪət/ *n.* (*habitual food*) alimentation *f.*; (*restricted*) régime *m.* −*v.i.*
suivre un régime.

diet|etic /daɪə'tetɪk/ *a.* diététique.
∼**ician** *n.* diététicien(ne) *m.* (*f.*).

differ /'dɪfə(r)/ *v.i.* différer; (*disagree*)
ne pas être d'accord.

differen|t /'dɪfrənt/ *a.* différent. ∼**ce** *n.*
différence *f.*; (*disagreement*) différend
m. ∼**tly** *adv.* différemment (**from,**
de).

differential /dɪfə'renʃl/ *a.* & *n.* différentiel (*m.*).

differentiate /dɪfə'renʃɪeɪt/ *v.t.* différencier. −*v.i.* faire la différence
(**between,** entre).

difficult /'dɪfɪkəlt/ *a.* difficile. ∼**y** *n.*
difficulté *f.*

diffiden|t /'dɪfɪdənt/ *a.* qui manque
d'assurance. ∼**ce** *n.* manque d'assurance *m.*

diffuse[1] /dɪ'fjuːs/ *a.* diffus.

diffus|e[2] /dɪ'fjuːz/ *v.t.* diffuser. ∼**ion**
/-ʒn/ *n.* diffusion *f.*

dig /dɪg/ *v.t./i.* (*p.t.* dug, *pres. p.* **digging**) creuser; (*thrust*) enfoncer. −*n.*
(*poke*) coup de coude *m.*; (*remark*)
coup de patte *m.*; (*archaeol.*) fouilles
f. pl. ∼**s,** (*lodgings: fam.*) chambre
meublée *f.* ∼ **up,** déterrer.

digest[1] /dɪ'dʒest/ *v.t./i.* digérer.
∼**ible** *a.* digestible. ∼**ion** /-stʃən/ *n.*
digestion *f.*

digest[2] /'daɪdʒest/ *n.* sommaire *m.*

digestive /dɪ'dʒestɪv/ *a.* digestif.

digger /'dɪgə(r)/ *n.* (*techn.*) pelleteuse
f.

digit /'dɪdʒɪt/ *n.* chiffre *m.*

digital /'dɪdʒɪtl/ *a.* (*clock*) numérique,
à affichage numérique.

dignif|y /'dɪgnɪfaɪ/ *v.t.* donner de la
dignité à. ∼**ied** *a.* digne.

dignitary /'dɪgnɪtərɪ/ *n.* dignitaire *m.*

dignity /'dɪgnɪtɪ/ *n.* dignité *f.*

digress /daɪ'gres/ *v.i.* faire une digression ∼ **from,** s'écarter de. ∼**ion**
/-ʃn/ *n.* digression *f.*

dike /daɪk/ *n.* digue *f.*

dilapidated /dɪ'læpɪdeɪtɪd/ *a.* délabré.

dilat|e /daɪˈleɪt/ v.t./i. (se) dilater. ∼**ion** /-ʃn/ n. dilatation f.

dilatory /ˈdɪlətərɪ/ a. dilatoire.

dilemma /dɪˈlemə/ n. dilemme m.

dilettante /dɪlɪˈtæntɪ/ n. dilettante m./f.

diligen|t /ˈdɪlɪdʒənt/ a. assidu. ∼**ce** n. assiduité f.

dilly-dally /ˈdɪlɪdælɪ/ v.i. (fam.) lanterner.

dilute /daɪˈljuːt/ v.t. diluer.

dim /dɪm/ a. (**dimmer, dimmest**) (weak) faible; (dark) sombre; (indistinct) vague; (fam.) stupide. —v.t./i. (p.t. **dimmed**) (light) (s')atténuer. ∼**ly** adv. (shine) faiblement; (remember) vaguement. ∼**ness** n. faiblesse f.; (of room etc.) obscurité f.

dime /daɪm/ n. (in USA, Canada) pièce de dix cents f.

dimension /daɪˈmenʃn/ n. dimension f.

diminish /dɪˈmɪnɪʃ/ v.t./i. diminuer.

diminutive /dɪˈmɪnjʊtɪv/ a. minuscule. —n. diminutif m.

dimple /ˈdɪmpl/ n. fossette f.

din /dɪn/ n. vacarme m.

dine /daɪn/ v.i. dîner. ∼**r** /-ə(r)/ n. dîneu|r, -se m., f.; (rail.) wagon-restaurant m.; (Amer.) restaurant à service rapide m.

dinghy /ˈdɪŋgɪ/ n. canot m.; (inflatable) canot pneumatique m.

ding|y /ˈdɪndʒɪ/ a. (**-ier, -iest**) miteux, minable. ∼**iness** n. aspect miteux or minable m.

dining-room /ˈdaɪnɪŋrʊm/ n. salle à manger f.

dinner /ˈdɪnə(r)/ n. (evening meal) dîner m.; (lunch) déjeuner m. ∼-**jacket** n. smoking m.

dinosaur /ˈdaɪnəsɔː(r)/ n. dinosaure m.

dint /dɪnt/ n. **by** ∼ **of,** à force de.

diocese /ˈdaɪəsɪs/ n. diocèse m.

dip /dɪp/ v.t./i. (p.t. **dipped**) plonger. —n. (slope) déclivité f.; (in sea) bain rapide m. ∼ **into,** (book) feuilleter; (savings) puiser dans. ∼ **one's headlights,** se mettre en code.

diphtheria /dɪfˈθɪərɪə/ n. diphtérie f.

diphthong /ˈdɪfθɒŋ/ n. diphtongue f.

diploma /dɪˈpləʊmə/ n. diplôme m.

diplomacy /dɪˈpləʊməsɪ/ n. diplomatie f.

diplomat /ˈdɪpləmæt/ n. diplomate m./f. ∼**ic** /-ˈmætɪk/ a. (pol.) diplomatique; (person: fig.) diplomate.

dire /daɪə(r)/ a. (**-er, -est**) affreux; (need, poverty) extrême.

direct /dɪˈrekt/ a. direct. —adv. directement. —v.t. diriger; (letter, remark) adresser; (a play) mettre en scène. ∼ **s.o. to,** indiquer à qn. le chemin de. ∼**ness** n. franchise f.

direction /dɪˈrekʃn/ n. direction f.; (theatre) mise en scène f. ∼**s,** indications f. pl. ∼**s for use,** mode d'emploi m.

directly /dɪˈrektlɪ/ adv. directement; (at once) tout de suite. —conj. (fam.) dès que.

director /dɪˈrektə(r)/ n. direc|teur, -trice m., f.; (theatre) metteur en scène m.

directory /dɪˈrektərɪ/ n. (phone book) annuaire m.

dirt /dɜːt/ n. saleté f. ∼ **cheap,** (sl.) très bon marché invar. ∼-**track** n. (sport) cendrée f.

dirty /ˈdɜːtɪ/ a. (**-ier, -iest**) sale; (word) grossier. —v.t./i. (se) salir.

disability /dɪsəˈbɪlətɪ/ n. infirmité f.

disable /dɪsˈeɪbl/ v.t. rendre infirme. ∼**d** a. infirme.

disadvantage /dɪsədˈvɑːntɪdʒ/ n. désavantage m. ∼**d** a. déshérité.

disagree /dɪsəˈgriː/ v.i. ne pas être d'accord (**with,** avec). ∼ **with s.o.,** (food, climate) ne pas convenir à qn. ∼**ment** n. désaccord m.; (quarrel) différend m.

disagreeable /dɪsəˈgriːəbl/ a. désagréable.

disappear /dɪsəˈpɪə(r)/ v.i. disparaître. ∼**ance** n. disparition f.

disappoint /dɪsəˈpɔɪnt/ v.t. décevoir. ∼**ment** n. déception f.

disapprov|e /dɪsəˈpruːv/ v.i. ∼**e (of),** désapprouver. ∼**al** n. désapprobation f.

disarm /dɪsˈɑːm/ v.t./i. désarmer. ∼**ament** n. désarmement m.

disarray /dɪsəˈreɪ/ n. désordre m.

disast|er /dɪˈzɑːstə(r)/ n. désastre m. ∼**rous** a. désastreux.

disband /dɪsˈbænd/ v.t./i. (se) disperser.

disbelief /dɪsbɪˈliːf/ n. incrédulité f.

disc /dɪsk/ n. disque m. ∼ **jockey,** disc-jockey m., animateur m.

discard /dɪˈskɑːd/ v.t. se débarrasser de; (beliefs etc.) abandonner.

discern /dɪˈsɜːn/ v.t. discerner. ∼**ible** a. perceptible. ∼**ing** a. perspicace.

discharge[1] /dɪsˈtʃɑːdʒ/ v.t. (unload)

décharger; (*liquid*) déverser; (*duty*) remplir; (*dismiss*) renvoyer; (*prisoner*) libérer. —*v.i.* (*of pus*) s'écouler.

discharge[2] /'dɪstʃɑ:dʒ/ *n.* (*of pus*) écoulement *m.*; (*dismissal*) renvoi *m.*

disciple /dɪ'saɪpl/ *n.* disciple *m.*

disciplinarian /dɪsəplɪ'neərɪən/ *n.* personne qui fait régner la discipline *f.*

disciplin|e /'dɪsɪplɪn/ *n.* discipline *f.* —*v.t.* discipliner; (*punish*) punir. ∼**ary** *a.* disciplinaire.

disclaim /dɪs'kleɪm/ *v.t.* désavouer. ∼**er** *n.* démenti *m.*

disclos|e /dɪs'kləʊz/ *v.t.* révéler. ∼**ure** /-ʒə(r)/ *n.* révélation *f.*

disco /'dɪskəʊ/ *n.* (*pl.* -os) (*club*: *fam.*) discothèque *f.*, disco *m.*

discol|our /dɪs'kʌlə(r)/ *v.t./i.* (se) décolorer. ∼**oration** /-'reɪʃn/ *n.* décoloration *f.*

discomfort /dɪs'kʌmfət/ *n.* gêne *f.*

disconcert /dɪskən'sɜ:t/ *v.t.* déconcerter.

disconnect /dɪskə'nekt/ *v.t.* détacher; (*unplug*) débrancher; (*cut off*) couper.

discontent /dɪskən'tent/ *n.* mécontentement *m.* ∼**ed** *a.* mécontent.

discontinue /dɪskən'tɪnju:/ *v.t.* interrompre, cesser.

discord /'dɪskɔ:d/ *n.* discorde *f.*; (*mus.*) dissonance *f.* ∼**ant** /-'skɔ:dənt/ *a.* discordant.

discothèque /'dɪskətek/ *n.* discothèque *f.*

discount[1] /'dɪskaʊnt/ *n.* rabais *m.*

discount[2] /dɪs'kaʊnt/ *v.t.* ne pas tenir compte de.

discourage /dɪ'skʌrɪdʒ/ *v.t* décourager.

discourse /'dɪskɔ:s/ *n.* discours *m.*

discourteous /dɪs'kɜ:tɪəs/ *a.* impoli, peu courtois.

discover /dɪ'skʌvə(r)/ *v.t.* découvrir. ∼**y** *n.* découverte *f.*

discredit /dɪs'kredɪt/ *v.t.* (*p.t.* **discredited**) discréditer. —*n.* discrédit *m.*

discreet /dɪ'skri:t/ *a.* discret. ∼**ly** *adv.* discrètement.

discrepancy /dɪ'skrepənsɪ/ *n.* contradiction *f.*, incohérence *f.*

discretion /dɪ'skreʃn/ *n.* discrétion *f.*

discriminat|e /dɪ'skrɪmɪneɪt/ *v.t./i.* distinguer. ∼**e against**, établir une discrimination contre. ∼**ing** *a.* (*person*) qui a du discernement. ∼**ion** /-'neɪʃn/ *n.* discernement *m.*; (*bias*) discrimination *f.*

discus /'dɪskəs/ *n.* disque *m.*

discuss /dɪ'skʌs/ *v.t.* (*talk about*) discuter de; (*argue about, examine critically*) discuter. ∼**ion** /-ʃn/ *n.* discussion *f.*

disdain /dɪs'deɪn/ *n.* dédain *m.* ∼**ful** *a.* dédaigneux.

disease /dɪ'zi:z/ *n.* maladie *f.* ∼**d** *a.* malade.

disembark /dɪsɪm'bɑ:k/ *v.t./i.* débarquer.

disembodied /dɪsɪm'bɒdɪd/ *a.* désincarné.

disenchant /dɪsɪn'tʃɑ:nt/ *v.t.* désenchanter. ∼**ment** *n.* désenchantement *m.*

disengage /dɪsɪn'geɪdʒ/ *v.t.* dégager. ∼**ment** *n.* dégagement *m.*

disentangle /dɪsɪn'tæŋgl/ *v.t.* démêler.

disfavour /dɪs'feɪvə(r)/ *n.* défaveur *f.*

disfigure /dɪs'fɪgə(r)/ *v.t.* défigurer.

disgrace /dɪs'greɪs/ *n.* (*shame*) honte *f.*; (*disfavour*) disgrâce *f.* —*v.t.* déshonorer. ∼**d** *a.* (*in disfavour*) disgracié. ∼**ful** *a.* honteux.

disgruntled /dɪs'grʌntld/ *a.* mécontent.

disguise /dɪs'gaɪz/ *v.t.* déguiser. —*n.* déguisement *m.* **in** ∼, déguisé.

disgust /dɪs'gʌst/ *n.* dégoût *m.* —*v.t.* dégoûter. ∼**ing** *a.* dégoûtant.

dish /dɪʃ/ *n.* plat *m.* —*v.t.* ∼ **out**, (*fam.*) distribuer. ∼ **up**, servir. **the** ∼**es**, (*crockery*) la vaisselle.

dishcloth /'dɪʃklɒθ/ *n.* lavette *f.*; (*for drying*) torchon *m.*

dishearten /dɪs'hɑ:tn/ *v.t.* décourager.

dishevelled /dɪ'ʃevld/ *a.* échevelé.

dishonest /dɪs'ɒnɪst/ *a.* malhonnête. ∼**y** *n.* malhonnêteté *f.*

dishonour /dɪs'ɒnə(r)/ *n.* déshonneur *m.* —*v.t.* déshonorer. ∼**able** *a.* déshonorant. ∼**ably** *adv.* avec déshonneur.

dishwasher /'dɪʃwɒʃə(r)/ *n.* lave-vaisselle *m. invar.*

disillusion /dɪsɪ'lu:ʒn/ *v.t.* désillusionner. ∼**ment** *n.* désillusion *f.*

disincentive /dɪsɪn'sentɪv/ *n.* **be a** ∼ **to**, décourager.

disinclined /dɪsɪn'klaɪnd/ *a.* ∼ **to**, peu disposé à.

disinfect /dɪsɪn'fekt/ *v.t.* désinfecter. ∼**ant** *n.* désinfectant *m.*

disinherit /dɪsɪn'herɪt/ *v.t.* déshériter.

disintegrate /dɪs'ɪntɪgreɪt/ *v.t./i.* (se) désintégrer.

disinterested /dɪsˈɪntrəstɪd/ *a.* désintéressé.

disjointed /dɪsˈdʒɔɪntɪd/ *a.* (*talk*) décousu.

disk /dɪsk/ *n.* = **disc.**

dislike /dɪsˈlaɪk/ *n.* aversion *f.* —*v.t.* ne pas aimer.

dislocat|e /ˈdɪsləkeɪt/ *v.t.* (*limb*) disloquer. ~**ion** /-ˈkeɪʃn/ *n.* dislocation *f.*

dislodge /dɪsˈlɒdʒ/ *v.t.* (*move*) déplacer; (*drive out*) déloger.

disloyal /dɪsˈlɔɪəl/ *a.* déloyal. ~**ty** *n.* déloyauté *f.*

dismal /ˈdɪzməl/ *a.* morne, triste.

dismantle /dɪsˈmæntl/ *v.t.* démonter, défaire.

dismay /dɪsˈmeɪ/ *n.* consternation *f.* —*v.t.* consterner.

dismiss /dɪsˈmɪs/ *v.t.* renvoyer; (*from mind*) écarter. ~**al** *n.* renvoi *m.*

dismount /dɪsˈmaʊnt/ *v.i.* descendre, mettre pied à terre.

disobedien|t /dɪsəˈbiːdɪənt/ *a.* désobéissant. ~**ce** *n.* désobéissance *f.*

disobey /dɪsəˈbeɪ/ *v.t.* désobéir à. —*v.i.* désobéir.

disorder /dɪsˈɔːdə(r)/ *n.* désordre *m.*; (*ailment*) trouble(s) *m.* (*pl.*). ~**ly** *a.* désordonné.

disorganize /dɪsˈɔːɡənaɪz/ *v.t.* désorganiser.

disorientate /dɪsˈɔːrɪənteɪt/ *v.t.* désorienter.

disown /dɪsˈəʊn/ *v.t.* renier.

disparaging /dɪˈspærɪdʒɪŋ/ *a.* désobligeant. ~**ly** *adv.* de façon désobligeante.

disparity /dɪˈspærətɪ/ *n.* disparité *f.*, écart *m.*

dispassionate /dɪˈspæʃənət/ *a.* impartial; (*unemotional*) calme.

dispatch /dɪˈspætʃ/ *v.t.* (*send, complete*) expédier; (*troops*) envoyer. —*n.* expédition *f.*; envoi *m.*; (*report*) dépêche *f.* ~**-rider** *n.* estafette *f.*

dispel /dɪˈspel/ *v.t.* (*p.t.* **dispelled**) dissiper.

dispensary /dɪˈspensərɪ/ *n.* pharmacie *f.*, officine *f.*

dispense /dɪˈspens/ *v.t.* distribuer; (*medicine*) préparer. —*v.i.* ~ **with**, se passer de. ~**r** /-ə(r)/ *n.* (*container*) distributeur *m.*

dispers|e /dɪˈspɜːs/ *v.t./i.* (se) disperser. ~**al** *n.* dispersion *f.*

dispirited /dɪˈspɪrɪtɪd/ *a.* découragé, abattu.

displace /dɪsˈpleɪs/ *v.t.* déplacer.

display /dɪˈspleɪ/ *v.t.* montrer, exposer; (*feelings*) manifester. —*n.* exposition *f.*; manifestation *f.*; (*comm.*) étalage *m.*; (*of computer*) visuel *m.*

displeas|e /dɪsˈpliːz/ *v.t.* déplaire à. ~**ed with**, mécontent de. ~**ure** /-ˈpleʒə(r)/ *n.* mécontentement *m.*

disposable /dɪˈspəʊzəbl/ *a.* à jeter.

dispos|e /dɪˈspəʊz/ *v.t.* disposer. —*v.i.* ~**e of**, se débarrasser de. **well** ~**ed to**, bien disposé envers. ~**al** *n.* (*of waste*) évacuation *f.* **at s.o.'s** ~**al**, à la disposition de qn.

disposition /dɪspəˈzɪʃn/ *n.* disposition *f.*; (*character*) naturel *m.*

disproportionate /dɪsprəˈpɔːʃənət/ *a.* disproportionné.

disprove /dɪsˈpruːv/ *v.t.* réfuter.

dispute /dɪˈspjuːt/ *v.t.* contester. —*n.* discussion *f.*; (*pol.*) conflit *m.* **in** ~, contesté.

disqualif|y /dɪsˈkwɒlɪfaɪ/ *v.t.* rendre inapte; (*sport*) disqualifier. ~**y from driving**, retirer le permis à. ~**ication** /-ɪˈkeɪʃn/ *n.* disqualification *f.*

disquiet /dɪsˈkwaɪət/ *n.* inquiétude *f.* ~**ing** *a.* inquiétant.

disregard /dɪsrɪˈɡɑːd/ *v.t.* ne pas tenir compte de. —*n.* indifférence *f.* (**for**, à).

disrepair /dɪsrɪˈpeə(r)/ *n.* mauvais état *m.*, délabrement *m.*

disreputable /dɪsˈrepjʊtəbl/ *a.* peu recommandable.

disrepute /dɪsrɪˈpjuːt/ *n.* discrédit *m.*

disrespect /dɪsrɪˈspekt/ *n.* manque de respect *m.* ~**ful** *a.* irrespectueux.

disrupt /dɪsˈrʌpt/ *v.t.* (*disturb, break up*) perturber; (*plans*) déranger. ~**ion** /-pʃn/ *n.* perturbation *f.* ~**ive** *a.* perturbateur.

dissatisf|ied /dɪsˈsætɪsfaɪd/ *a.* mécontent. ~**action** /dɪsætɪsˈfækʃn/ *n.* mécontentement *m.*

dissect /dɪˈsekt/ *v.t.* disséquer. ~**ion** /-kʃn/ *n.* dissection *f.*

disseminate /dɪˈsemɪneɪt/ *v.t.* disséminer. **dissent** /dɪˈsent/ *v.i.* différer (**from**, de). —*n.* dissentiment *m.*

dissertation /dɪsəˈteɪʃn/ *n.* (*univ.*) mémoire *m.*

disservice /dɪsˈsɜːvɪs/ *n.* mauvais service *m.*

dissident /ˈdɪsɪdənt/ *a.* & *n.* dissident(e) (*m.* (*f.*)).

dissimilar /dɪˈsɪmɪlə(r)/ *a.* dissemblable, différent.

dissipate /ˈdɪsɪpeɪt/ *v.t./i.* se dissiper;

(*efforts*) gaspiller. ~d /-ɪd/ *a.* (*person*)
débauché.

dissociate /dɪˈsəʊʃɪeɪt/ *v.t.* dissocier.
~ **o.s. from,** se désolidariser de.

dissolute /ˈdɪsəljuːt/ *a.* dissolu.

dissolution /dɪsəˈluːʃn/ *n.* dissolution
f.

dissolve /dɪˈzɒlv/ *v.t./i.* (se) dissoudre.

dissuade /dɪˈsweɪd/ *v.t.* dissuader.

distance /ˈdɪstəns/ *n.* distance *f.* **from
a** ~, de loin. **in the** ~, au loin.

distant /ˈdɪstənt/ *a.* éloigné, lointain;
(*relative*) éloigné; (*aloof*) distant.

distaste /dɪsˈteɪst/ *n.* dégoût *m.* ~**ful**
a. désagréable.

distemper /dɪˈstempə(r)/ *n.* (*paint*) badigeon *m.*; (*animal disease*) maladie
f. —*v.t.* badigeonner.

distend /dɪˈstend/ *v.t./i.* (se) distendre.

distil /dɪˈstɪl/ *v.t.* (*p.t.* **distilled**) dis-
tiller. ~**lation** /-ˈleɪʃn/ *n.* distillation
f.

distillery /dɪˈstɪlərɪ/ *n.* distillerie *f.*

distinct /dɪˈstɪŋkt/ *a.* distinct; (*marked*) net. ~**ion** /-kʃn/ *n.* distinction *f.*;
(*in exam*) mention très bien *f.* ~**ive**
a. distinctif. ~**ly** *adv.* (*see*) distincte-
ment; (*forbid*) expressément; (*mark-
edly*) nettement.

distinguish /dɪˈstɪŋgwɪʃ/ *v.t./i.* distinguer. ~**ed** *a.* distingué.

distort /dɪˈstɔːt/ *v.t.* déformer. ~**ion**
/-ʃn/ *n.* distorsion *f.*; (*of facts*) déformation *f.*

distract /dɪˈstrækt/ *v.t.* distraire.
~**ed** *a.* (*distraught*) éperdu. ~**ing**
a. gênant. ~**ion** /-kʃn/ *n.* (*lack of
attention, entertainment*) distraction
f.

distraught /dɪˈstrɔːt/ *a.* éperdu.

distress /dɪˈstres/ *n.* douleur *f.*;
(*poverty, danger*) détresse *f.* —*v.t.*
peiner. ~**ing** *a.* pénible.

distribut|e /dɪˈstrɪbjuːt/ *v.t.* distri-
buer. ~**ion** /-ˈbjuːʃn/ *n.* distribution *f.*
~**or** *n.* distributeur *m.*

district /ˈdɪstrɪkt/ *n.* région *f.*; (*of town*)
quartier *m.*

distrust /dɪsˈtrʌst/ *n.* méfiance *f.* —*v.t.*
se méfier de.

disturb /dɪˈstɜːb/ *v.t.* déranger; (*alarm,
worry*) troubler. ~**ance** *n.* dérangement *m.* (**of,** de); (*noise*) tapage *m.*
~**ances** *n. pl.* (*pol.*) troubles *m. pl.*
~**ed** *a.* troublé. ~**ing** *a.* troublant.

disused /dɪsˈjuːzd/ *a.* désaffecté.

ditch /dɪtʃ/ *n.* fossé *m.* —*v.t.* (*sl.*) abandonner.

dither /ˈdɪðə(r)/ *v.i.* hésiter.

ditto /ˈdɪtəʊ/ *adv.* idem.

divan /dɪˈvæn/ *n.* divan *m.*

div|e /daɪv/ *v.i.* plonger; (*rush*) se pré-
cipiter. —*n.* plongeon *m.*; (*of plane*)
piqué *m.*; (*place: sl.*) bouge *m.* ~**er** *n.*
plongeu|r, -se *m., f.* ~**ing-board** *n.*
plongeoir *m.* ~**ing-suit** *n.* scaphandre *m.*

diverge /daɪˈvɜːdʒ/ *v.i.* diverger.

divergent /daɪˈvɜːdʒənt/ *a.* divergent.

diverse /daɪˈvɜːs/ *a.* divers.

diversify /daɪˈvɜːsɪfaɪ/ *v.t.* diversifier.

diversity /daɪˈvɜːsətɪ/ *n.* diversité *f.*

diver|t /daɪˈvɜːt/ *v.t.* détourner; (*traffic*)
dévier. ~**sion** /-ʃn/ *n.* détournement
m.; (*distraction*) diversion *f.*; (*of
traffic*) déviation *f.*

divest /daɪˈvest/ *v.t.* ~ **of,** (*strip of*)
priver de, déposséder de.

divide /dɪˈvaɪd/ *v.t./i.* (se) diviser.

dividend /ˈdɪvɪdend/ *n.* dividende *m.*

divine /dɪˈvaɪn/ *a.* divin.

divinity /dɪˈvɪnətɪ/ *n.* divinité *f.*

division /dɪˈvɪʒn/ *n.* division *f.*

divorce /dɪˈvɔːs/ *n.* divorce *m.* (**from,**
d'avec). —*v.t./i.* divorcer (d'avec). ~**d**
a. divorcé.

divorcee /dɪvɔːˈsiː, *Amer.* dɪvɔːˈseɪ/ *n.*
divorcé(e) *m.* (*f.*).

divulge /daɪˈvʌldʒ/ *v.t.* divulguer.

DIY *abbr.* do-it-yourself.

dizz|y /ˈdɪzɪ/ *a.* (**-ier, -iest**) vertigineux.
be *or* **feel** ~**y,** avoir le vertige.
~**iness** *n.* vertige *m.*

do /duː/ *v.t./i.* (3 *sing. present tense*
does; *p.t.* **did**; *p.p.,* **done**) faire; (*progress, be suitable*) aller; (*be enough*)
suffire; (*swindle: sl.*) avoir. **well
done!,** bravo! **well done,** (*culin.*) bien
cuit. **done for,** (*fam.*) fichu. —*v. aux.*
~ **you see?,** voyez-vous? **I** ~ **not
smoke,** je ne fume pas. **don't you?,**
doesn't he?, *etc.,* n'est-ce pas? —*n.*
(*pl.* **dos** *or* **do's**) soirée *f.,* fête *f.* ~
away with, supprimer. ~ **in,** (*sl.*)
tuer. ~**-it-yourself** *n.* bricolage *m.*;
a. (*shop, book*) de bricolage. ~ **out,**
(*clean*) nettoyer. ~ **up,** (*fasten*)
fermer; (*house*) refaire. ~ **with,**
(*want, need*) aimer bien avoir. ~
without, se passer de.

docile /ˈdəʊsaɪl/ *a.* docile.

dock[1] /dɒk/ *n.* dock *m.* —*v.t./i.* (se)
mettre à quai. ~**er** *n.* docker *m.*

dock[2] /dɒk/ *n.* (*jurid.*) banc des accusés *m.*

dock[3] /dɒk/ *v.t.* (*money*) retrancher.

dockyard /'dɒkjɑːd/ n. chantier naval m.

doctor /'dɒktə(r)/ n. médecin m., docteur m.; (univ.) docteur m. —v.t. (cat) châtrer; (fig.) altérer.

doctorate /'dɒktərət/ n. doctorat m.

doctrine /'dɒktrɪn/ n. doctrine f.

document /'dɒkjʊmənt/ n. document m. ~ary /-'mentrɪ/ a. & n. documentaire (m.).

doddering /'dɒdərɪŋ/ a. gâteux.

dodge /dɒdʒ/ v.t. esquiver. —v.i. faire un saut de côté. —n. (fam.) truc m.

dodgems /'dɒdʒəmz/ n. pl. autos tamponneuses f. pl.

dodgy /'dɒdʒɪ/ a. (-ier, -iest) (fam.) épineux, délicat.

doe /dəʊ/ n. (deer) biche f.

does /dʌz/ see **do**.

doesn't /'dʌznt/ = **does not**.

dog /dɒg/ n. chien m. —v.t. (p.t. dogged) poursuivre. ~-collar n. (fam.) (faux) col d'ecclésiastique m. ~-eared a. écorné.

dogged /'dɒgɪd/ a. obstiné.

dogma /'dɒgmə/ n. dogme m. ~tic /-'mætɪk/ a. dogmatique.

dogsbody /'dɒgzbɒdɪ/ n. factotum m., bonne à tout faire f.

doily /'dɔɪlɪ/ n. napperon m.

doings /'duːɪŋz/ n. pl. (fam.) activités f. pl., occupations f. pl.

doldrums /'dɒldrəmz/ n. pl. **be in the** ~, (person) avoir le cafard.

dole /dəʊl/ v.t. ~ **out**, distribuer. —n. (fam.) indemnité de chômage f. **on the** ~, (fam.) au chômage.

doleful /'dəʊlfl/ a. triste, morne.

doll /dɒl/ n. poupée f. —v.t. ~ **up**, (fam.) bichonner.

dollar /'dɒlə(r)/ n. dollar m.

dollop /'dɒləp/ n. (of food etc.: fam.) gros morceau m.

dolphin /'dɒlfɪn/ n. dauphin m.

domain /də'meɪn/ n. domaine m.

dome /dəʊm/ n. dôme m.

domestic /də'mestɪk/ a. familial; (trade, flights, etc.) intérieur; (animal) domestique. ~ **science**, arts ménagers m. pl. ~ated a. (animal) domestiqué.

domesticity /dɒme'stɪsətɪ/ n. vie de famille f.

dominant /'dɒmɪnənt/ a. dominant.

dominat|e /'dɒmɪneɪt/ v.t./i. dominer. ~ion /-'neɪʃn/ n. domination f.

domineer /dɒmɪ'nɪə(r)/ v.i. être dominateur or autoritaire.

dominion /də'mɪnjən/ n. (British pol.) dominion m.

domino /'dɒmɪnəʊ/ n. (pl. -oes) domino m. ~es, (game) dominos m. pl.

don[1] /dɒn/ v.t. (p.t. donned) revêtir, endosser.

don[2] /dɒn/ n. professeur d'université m.

donat|e /dəʊ'neɪt/ v.t. faire don de. ~ion /-ʃn/ n. don m.

done /dʌn/ see **do**.

donkey /'dɒŋkɪ/ n. âne m. ~-**work** n. travail pénible et ingrat m.

donor /'dəʊnə(r)/ n. dona|teur, -trice m., f.; (of blood) donneu|r, -se m., f.

don't /dəʊnt/ = **do not**.

doodle /'duːdl/ v.i. griffonner.

doom /duːm/ n. (ruin) ruine f.; (fate) destin m. —v.t. **be** ~ed **to**, être destiné or condamné à. ~ed **(to failure)**, voué à l'échec.

door /dɔː(r)/ n. porte f.; (of vehicle) portière f., porte f.

doorman /'dɔːmən/ n. (pl. -men) portier m.

doormat /'dɔːmæt/ n. paillasson m.

doorstep /'dɔːstep/ n. pas de (la) porte m., seuil m.

doorway /'dɔːweɪ/ n. porte f.

dope /dəʊp/ n. (fam.) drogue f.; (idiot: sl.) imbécile m./f. —v.t. doper. ~y a. (foolish: sl.) imbécile.

dormant /'dɔːmənt/ a. en sommeil.

dormitory /'dɔːmɪtrɪ, Amer. 'dɔːmɪtɔːrɪ/ n. dortoir m.; (univ., Amer.) résidence f.

dormouse /'dɔːmaʊs/ n. (pl. -mice) loir m.

dos|e /dəʊs/ n. dose f. ~age n. dose f.; (on label) dosologie f.

doss /dɒs/ v.i. (sl.) roupiller. ~-**house** n. asile de nuit m.

dot /dɒt/ n. point m. **on the** ~, (fam.) à l'heure pile.

dote /dəʊt/ v.i. ~ **on**, être gaga de.

dotted /'dɒtɪd/ a. (fabric) à pois. ~ **line**, ligne en pointillés f. ~ **with**, parsemé de.

dotty /'dɒtɪ/ a. (-ier, -iest) (fam.) cinglé, dingue.

double /'dʌbl/ a. double; (room, bed) pour deux personnes. —adv. deux fois. —n. double m. ~s, (tennis) double m. —v.t./i. doubler; (fold) plier en deux. **at** or **on the** ~, au pas de course. ~-**bass** n. (mus.) contrebasse f. ~-**breasted** a. croisé. ~ **chin**, double menton m. ~-**cross** v.t.

tromper. **~-dealing** n. double jeu m.
~-decker n. autobus à impériale m.
~ Dutch, baragouin m. **doubly** adv.
doublement.

doubt /daʊt/ n. doute m. —v.t. douter
de. **~** if or that, douter que. **~ful** a.,
incertain, douteux; (person) qui a des
doutes. **~less** adv. sans doute.

dough /dəʊ/ n. pâte f.; (money: sl.) fric
m.

doughnut /ˈdəʊnʌt/ n. beignet m.

douse /daʊs/ v.t. arroser; (lumière)
éteindre.

dove /dʌv/ n. colombe f.

Dover /ˈdəʊvə(r)/ n. Douvres m./f.

dowdy /ˈdaʊdɪ/ a. (-ier, -iest) (clothes)
sans chic, monotone.

down[1] /daʊn/ n. (fluff) duvet m.

down[2] /daʊn/ adv. en bas; (of sun)
couché; (lower) plus bas; —prep. en
bas de; (along) le long de. —v.t. (knock
down, shoot down) abattre; (drink)
vider. **come** or **go ~**, descendre.
~-and-out n. clochard(e) m. (f.) **~-
hearted** a. découragé. **~ payment**,
acompte m. **~-to-earth** a. terre-à-
terre invar. **~ under**, aux antipodes.
~ with, à bas.

downcast /ˈdaʊnkɑːst/ a. démoralisé.

downfall /ˈdaʊnfɔːl/ n. chute f.

downgrade /daʊnˈgreɪd/ v.t. déclasser.

downhill /daʊnˈhɪl/ adv. **go ~**,
descendre.

downpour /ˈdaʊnpɔː(r)/ n. grosse
averse f.

downright /ˈdaʊnraɪt/ a. (utter) véritable; (honest) franc. —adv. carrément.

downs /daʊnz/ n. pl. région de collines
f.

downstairs /daʊnˈsteəz/ adv. en
bas. —a. d'en bas.

downstream /ˈdaʊnstriːm/ adv. en
aval.

downtown /ˈdaʊntaʊn/ a. (Amer.) du
centre de la ville. **~ Boston** etc., le
centre de Boston/etc.

downtrodden /ˈdaʊntrɒdn/ a. oppri-
mé.

downward /ˈdaʊnwəd/ a. & adv., **~s**
adv. vers le bas.

dowry /ˈdaʊərɪ/ n. dot f.

doze /dəʊz/ v.i. sommeiller. **~ off**,
s'assoupir. —n. somme m.

dozen /ˈdʌzn/ n. douzaine f. **~s of**,
(fam.) des dizaines de.

Dr abbr. (Doctor) Docteur.

drab /dræb/ a. terne.

draft[1] /drɑːft/ n. (outline) brouillon
m.; (comm.) traite f. —v.t. faire le
brouillon de; (draw up) rédiger. **the
~**, (mil., Amer.) la conscription.

draft[2] /drɑːft/ n. (Amer.) = **draught**.

drag /dræg/ v.t./i. (p.t. **dragged**)
traîner; (river) draguer; (pull away)
arracher. —n. (task: fam.) corvée f.;
(person: fam.) raseu|r, -se m., f.;
(clothes: sl.) travesti m.

dragon /ˈdrægən/ n. dragon m.

dragon-fly /ˈdrægənflaɪ/ n. libellule f.

drain /dreɪn/ v.t. (land) drainer; (vegetables) égoutter; (tank, glass) vider;
(use up) épuiser. **~ (off)**, (liquid) faire
écouler. —v.i. **~ (off)**, (of liquid) s'é-
couler. —n. (sewer) égout m. **~(-pipe)**,
tuyau d'écoulement m. **be a ~ on**,
pomper. **~ing-board** n. égouttoir m.

drama /ˈdrɑːmə/ n. art dramatique m.,
théâtre m.; (play, event) drame m.
~tic /drəˈmætɪk/ a. dramatique.
~tist /ˈdræmətɪst/ n. dramaturge m.
~tize /ˈdræmətaɪz/ v.t. adapter pour
la scène; (fig.) dramatiser.

drank /dræŋk/ see **drink**.

drape /dreɪp/ v.t. draper. **~s** n. pl.
(Amer.) rideaux m. pl.

drastic /ˈdræstɪk/ a. sévère.

draught /drɑːft/ n. courant d'air m.
~s, (game) dames f. pl. **~ beer**, bière
(à la) pression f. **~y** a. plein de courants d'air.

draughtsman /ˈdrɑːftsmən/ n. (pl.
-men) dessina|teur, -trice industri-
el(le) m., f.

draw /drɔː/ v.t. (p.t. **drew**, p.p. **drawn**)
(pull) tirer; (attract) attirer; (pass)
passer; (picture) dessiner; (line)
tracer. —v.i. dessiner; (sport) faire
match nul; (come, move) venir. —n.
(sport) match nul m.; (in lottery) tirage
au sort m. **~ back**, (recoil) reculer.
~ in, (days) diminuer. **~ near**,
(s')approcher (**to**, de). **~ out**,
(money) retirer. **~ up** v.i. (stop)
s'arrêter; v.t. (document) dresser;
(chair) approcher.

drawback /ˈdrɔːbæk/ n. inconvénient
m.

drawbridge /ˈdrɔːbrɪdʒ/ n. pont-
levis m.

drawer /drɔː(r)/ n. tiroir m.

drawers /drɔːz/ n. pl. culotte f.

drawing /ˈdrɔːɪŋ/ n. dessin m. **~-pin**
n. punaise f. **~-room** n. salon m.

drawl /drɔːl/ n. voix traînante f.

drawn /drɔːn/ *see* **draw.** —*a.* (*features*) tiré; (*match*) nul.

dread /dred/ *n.* terreur *f.*, crainte *f.* —*v.t.* redouter.

dreadful /'dredfl/ *a.* épouvantable, affreux. ~**ly** *adv.* terriblement.

dream /driːm/ *n.* rêve *m.* —*v.t./i.* (*p.t.* **dreamed** *or* **dreamt**) rêver. —*a.* (*ideal*) de ses rêves. ~ **up,** imaginer. ~**er** *n.* rêveu|r, -se *m., f.* ~**y** *a.* rêveur.

drear|y /'drɪərɪ/ *a.* (**-ier, -iest**) triste; (*boring*) monotone. ~**iness** *n.* tristesse *f.*; monotonie *f.*

dredge /dredʒ/ *n.* drague *f.* —*v.t./i.* draguer. ~**r** /-ə(r)/ *n.* dragueur *m.*

dregs /dregz/ *n. pl.* lie *f.*

drench /drentʃ/ *v.t.* tremper.

dress /dres/ *n.* robe *f.*; (*clothing*) tenue *f.* —*v.t./i.* (s')habiller; (*food*) assaisonner; (*wound*) panser. ~ **circle,** premier balcon *m.* ~ **up as,** se déguiser en. **get** ~**ed,** s'habiller.

dresser /'dresə(r)/ *n.* buffet *m.*

dressing /'dresɪŋ/ *n.* (*sauce*) assaisonnement *m.*; (*bandage*) pansement *m.* ~**-gown** *n.* robe de chambre *f.* ~**room** *n.* (*sport*) vestiaire *m.*; (*theatre*) loge *f.* ~**table** *n.* coiffeuse *f.*

dressmak|er /'dresmeɪkə(r)/ *n.* couturière *f.* ~**ing** *n.* couture *f.*

dressy /'dresɪ/ *a.* (**-ier, -iest**) chic *invar.*

drew /druː/ *see* **draw.**

dribble /'drɪbl/ *v.i.* couler goutte à goutte; (*person*) baver; (*football*) dribbler.

dribs and drabs /drɪbzn'dræbz/ *n. pl.* petites quantités *f. pl.*

dried /draɪd/ *a.* (*fruit etc.*) sec.

drier /'draɪə(r)/ *n.* séchoir *m.*

drift /drɪft/ *v.i.* aller à la dérive; (*pile up*) s'amonceler. —*n.* dérive *f.*; amoncellement *m.*; (*of events*) tournure *f.*; (*meaning*) sens *m.* ~ **towards,** glisser vers. ~**er** *n.* personne sans but dans la vie *f.*

driftwood /'drɪftwʊd/ *n.* bois flotté *m.*

drill /drɪl/ *n.* (*tool*) perceuse *f.*; (*training*) exercice *m.*; (*procedure*: *fam.*) marche à suivre *f.* (**pneumatic**) ~, marteau pneumatique *m.* —*v.t.* percer; (*train*) entraîner. —*v.i.* être à l'exercice.

drily /'draɪlɪ/ *adv.* sèchement.

drink /drɪŋk/ *v.t./i.* (*p.t.* **drank,** *p.p.* **drunk**) boire. —*n.* (*liquid*) boisson *f.*; (*glass of alcohol*) verre *m.* **a** ~ **of**

water, un verre d'eau. ~**able** *a.* (*not unhealthy*) potable; (*palatable*) buvable. ~**er** *n.* buveu|r, -se *m., f.* ~**ing water,** eau potable *f.*

drip /drɪp/ *v.i.* (*p.t.* **dripped**) (dé)goutter; (*washing*) s'égoutter. —*n.* goutte *f.*; (*person*: *sl.*) lavette *f.* ~**-dry** *v.t.* laisser égoutter; *a.* sans repassage.

dripping /'drɪpɪŋ/ *n.* (*Amer.* ~**s**) graisse de rôti *f.*

drive /draɪv/ *v.t.* (*p.t.* **drove,** *p.p.* **driven**) chasser, pousser; (*vehicle*) conduire; (*machine*) actionner. —*v.i.* conduire. —*n.* promenade en voiture *f.*; (*private road*) allée *f.*; (*fig.*) énergie *f.*; (*psych.*) instinct *m.*; (*pol.*) campagne *f.* ~ **at,** en venir à. ~ **away,** (*of car*) partir. ~ **in,** (*force in*) enfoncer. ~ **mad,** rendre fou.

drivel /'drɪvl/ *n.* radotage *m.*

driver /'draɪvə(r)/ *n.* conduc|teur, -trice *m., f.*, chauffeur *m.*

driving /'draɪvɪŋ/ *n.* conduite *f.* ~ **licence,** permis de conduire *m.* ~ **rain,** pluie battante *f.* ~ **school,** auto-école *f.*

drizzle /'drɪzl/ *n.* bruine *f.* —*v.i.* bruiner.

dromedary /'drɒmədərɪ, (*Amer.*) 'drɒmədərɪ/ *n.* dromadaire *m.*

drone /drəʊn/ *n.* (*noise*) bourdonnement *m.*; (*bee*) faux bourdon *m.* —*v.i.* bourdonner; (*fig.*) parler d'une voix monotone.

drool /druːl/ *v.i.* baver.

droop /druːp/ *v.i.* pencher, tomber.

drop /drɒp/ *n.* goutte *f.*; (*fall, lowering*) chute *f.* —*v.t./i.* (*p.t.* **dropped**) (laisser) tomber; (*decrease, lower*) baisser. ~ (**off**), (*person from car*) déposer. ~ **a line,** écrire un mot (**to,** à). ~ **in,** passer (**on,** chez). ~ **off,** (*doze*) s'assoupir. ~ **out,** se retirer (**of,** de); (*of student*) abandonner. ~**out** *n.* marginal(e) *m.* (*f.*), raté(e) *m.* (*f.*).

droppings /'drɒpɪŋz/ *n. pl.* crottes *f. pl.*

dross /drɒs/ *n.* déchets *m. pl.*

drought /draʊt/ *n.* sécheresse *f.*

drove /drəʊv/ *see* **drive.**

droves /drəʊvz/ *n. pl.* foule(s) *f.* (*pl.*).

drown /draʊn/ *v.t./i.* (se) noyer.

drowsy /'draʊzɪ/ *a.* somnolent. **be** *or* **feel** ~, avoir envie de dormir.

drudge /drʌdʒ/ *n.* esclave du travail

m. **~ry** /-ərɪ/ *n.* travail pénible et ingrat *m.*

drug /drʌg/ *n.* drogue *f.*; (*med.*) médicament *m.* —*v.t.* (*p.t.* **drugged**) droguer. **~ addict**, drogué(e) *m.* (*f.*).

drugstore /ˈdrʌgstɔː(r)/ *n.* (*Amer.*) drugstore *m.*

drum /drʌm/ *n.* tambour *m.*; (*for oil*) bidon *m.* —*v.i.* (*p.t.* **drummed**) tambouriner. —*v.t.* **~ into s.o.**, répéter sans cesse à qn. **~ up**, (*support*) susciter; (*business*) créer. **~mer** *n.* tambour *m.*

drumstick /ˈdrʌmstɪk/ *n.* baguette de tambour *f.*; (*of chicken*) pilon *m.*

drunk /drʌŋk/ *see* **drink**. —*a.* ivre. **get ~**, s'enivrer. —*n.*, **~ard** *n.* ivrogne(sse) *m.* (*f.*). **~en** *a.* ivre; (*habitually*) ivrogne. **~enness** *n.* ivresse *f.*

dry /draɪ/ *a.* (**drier, driest**) sec; (*day*) sans pluie. —*v.t./i.* sécher. **be** *or* **feel ~**, avoir soif. **~-clean** *v.t.* nettoyer à sec. **~-cleaner** *n.* teinturier *m.* **~ up**, (*dry dishes*) essuyer la vaisselle; (*of supplies*) (se) tarir; (*be silent: fam.*) se taire. **~ness** *n.* sécheresse *f.*

dual /ˈdjuːəl/ *a.* double. **~ carriageway**, route à quatre voies *f.*

dub /dʌb/ *v.t.* (*p.t.* **dubbed**) (*film*) doubler; (*nickname*) surnommer.

dubious /ˈdjuːbɪəs/ *a.* douteux. **be ~ about sth.**, (*person*) douter de qch.

duchess /ˈdʌtʃɪs/ *n.* duchesse *f.*

duck /dʌk/ *n.* canard *m.* —*v.i.* se baisser subitement. —*v.t.* (*head*) baisser; (*person*) plonger dans l'eau. **~ling** *n.* caneton *m.*

duct /dʌkt/ *n.* conduit *m.*

dud /dʌd/ *a.* (*tool etc.: sl.*) mal fichu; (*coin: sl.*) faux; (*cheque: sl.*) sans provision. —*n.* **be a ~**, (*not work: sl.*) ne pas marcher.

dude /duːd/ *n.* (*Amer.*) dandy *m.*

due /djuː/ *a.* (*owing*) dû; (*expected*) attendu; (*proper*) qui convient. —*adv.* **~ east**/*etc.*, droit vers l'est/*etc.* —*n.* dû *m.* **~s**, droits *m. pl.*; (*of club*) cotisation *f.* **~ to**, à cause de; (*caused by*) dû à.

duel /ˈdjuːəl/ *n.* duel *m.*

duet /djuːˈet/ *n.* duo *m.*

duffel /ˈdʌfl/ *a.* **~ bag**, sac de marin *m.* **~ coat**, duffel-coat *m.*

dug /dʌg/ *see* **dig**.

duke /djuːk/ *n.* duc *m.*

dull /dʌl/ *a.* (**-er, -est**) ennuyeux; (*colour*) terne; (*weather*) morne;

(*sound*) sourd; (*stupid*) bête. —*v.t.* (*pain*) amortir; (*mind*) engourdir.

duly /ˈdjuːlɪ/ *adv.* comme il convient; (*in due time*) en temps voulu.

dumb /dʌm/ *a.* (**-er, -est**) muet; (*stupid: fam.*) bête.

dumbfound /dʌmˈfaʊnd/ *v.t.* sidérer, ahurir.

dummy /ˈdʌmɪ/ *n.* (*comm.*) article factice *m.*; (*of tailor*) mannequin *m.*; (*of baby*) sucette *f.* —*a.* factice. **~ run**, essai *m.*

dump /dʌmp/ *v.t.* déposer; (*abandon: fam.*) se débarrasser de. —*n.* tas d'ordures *m.*; (*refuse tip*) décharge *f.*; (*mil.*) dépôt *m.*; (*dull place: fam.*) trou *m.* **be in the ~s**, (*fam.*) avoir le cafard.

dumpling /ˈdʌmplɪŋ/ *n.* boulette de pâte *f.*

dumpy /ˈdʌmpɪ/ *a.* (**-ier, -iest**) boulot, rondelet.

dunce /dʌns/ *n.* cancre *m.*, âne *m.*

dune /djuːn/ *n.* dune *f.*

dung /dʌŋ/ *n.* (*excrement*) bouse *f.*, crotte *f.*; (*manure*) fumier *m.*

dungarees /dʌŋgəˈriːz/ *n. pl.* (*overalls*) salopette *f.*; (*jeans: Amer.*) jean *m.*

dungeon /ˈdʌndʒən/ *n.* cachot *m.*

dunk /dʌŋk/ *v.t.* tremper.

duo /ˈdjuːəʊ/ *n.* duo *m.*

dupe /djuːp/ *v.t.* duper. —*n.* dupe *f.*

duplicate[1] /ˈdjuːplɪkət/ *n.* double *m.* —*a.* identique.

duplicat|e[2] /ˈdjuːplɪkeɪt/ *v.t.* faire un double de; (*on machine*) polycopier. **~or** *n.* duplicateur *m.*

duplicity /djuːˈplɪsətɪ/ *n.* duplicité *f.*

durable /ˈdjʊərəbl/ *a.* (*tough*) résistant; (*enduring*) durable.

duration /djʊˈreɪʃn/ *n.* durée *f.*

duress /djʊˈres/ *n.* contrainte *f.*

during /ˈdjʊərɪŋ/ *prep.* pendant.

dusk /dʌsk/ *n.* crépuscule *m.*

dusky /ˈdʌskɪ/ *a.* (**-ier, -iest**) foncé.

dust /dʌst/ *n.* poussière *f.* —*v.t.* épousseter; (*sprinkle*) saupoudrer. **~-jacket** *n.* jaquette *f.*

dustbin /ˈdʌstbɪn/ *n.* poubelle *f.*

duster /ˈdʌstə(r)/ *n.* chiffon *m.*

dustman /ˈdʌstmən/ *n.* (*pl.* **-men**) éboueur *m.*, boueux *m.*

dustpan /ˈdʌstpæn/ *n.* pelle à poussière *f.*

dusty /ˈdʌstɪ/ *a.* (**-ier, -iest**) poussiéreux.

Dutch /dʌtʃ/ *a.* hollandais. —*n.* (*lang.*)

hollandais *m.* **go** ~, partager les frais. ~**man** *n.* Hollandais *m.* ~**woman** *n.* Hollandaise *f.*

dutiful /'dju:tɪfl/ *a.* obéissant.

dut|y /'dju:tɪ/ *n.* devoir *m.*; (*tax*) droit *m.* ~**ies**, (*of official etc.*) fonctions *f. pl.* ~**y-free** *a.* horstaxe. **on** ~**y**, de service.

duvet /'du:veɪ/ *n.* couette *f.*, courte-pointe *f.*

dwarf /dwɔ:f/ *n.* (*pl.* **-fs**) nain(e) *m.* (*f.*). —*v.t.* rapetisser.

dwell /dwel/ *v.i.* (*p.t.* **dwelt**) de-meurer. ~ **on**, s'étendre sur. ~**er** *n.*

habitant(e) *m.* (*f.*). ~**ing** *n.* habitation *f.*

dwindle /'dwɪndl/ *v.i.* diminuer.

dye /daɪ/ *v.t.* (*pres. p.* **dyeing**) tein-dre. —*n.* teinture *f.*

dying /'daɪɪŋ/ *see* **die**[1].

dynamic /daɪ'næmɪk/ *a.* dynamique.

dynamism /'daɪnəmɪzəm/ *n.* dyna-misme *m.*

dynamite /'daɪnəmaɪt/ *n.* dynamite *f.* —*v.t.* dynamiter.

dynasty /'dɪnəstɪ, *Amer.* 'daɪnəstɪ/ *n.* dynastie *f.*

dysentery /'dɪsəntrɪ/ *n.* dysenterie *f.*

E

each /iːtʃ/ *a.* chaque. —*pron.* cha-
cun(e). ~ **one,** chacun(e). ~ **other,**
l'un(e) l'autre, les un(e)s les autres.
know ~ other, se connaître. **love ~**
other, s'aimer.

eager /ˈiːɡə(r)/ *a.* impatient **(to,** de);
(*supporter, desire*) ardent. **be ~ to,**
(*want*) avoir envie de. ~ **for,** avide de.
~**ly** *adv.* avec impatience *or* ardeur.
~**ness** *n.* impatience *f.*, désir *m.*,
ardeur *f.*

eagle /ˈiːɡl/ *n.* aigle *m.*

ear[1] /ɪə(r)/ *n.* oreille *f.* ~**-drum** *n.*
tympan *m.* ~**-ring** *n.* boucle d'oreille
f.

ear[2] /ɪə(r)/ *n.* (*of corn*) épi *m.*

earache /ˈɪəreɪk/ *n.* mal à l'oreille *m.*,
mal d'oreille *m.*

earl /ɜːl/ *n.* comte *m.*

early /ˈɜːlɪ/ (**-ier, -iest**) *adv.* tôt, de
bonne heure; (*ahead of time*) en
avance. —*a.* premier; (*hour*) matinal;
(*fruit*) précoce; (*retirement*) anticipé.
have an ~ dinner, dîner tôt. **in ~**
summer, au début de l'été.

earmark /ˈɪəmɑːk/ *v.t.* destiner, réserver (**for,** à).

earn /ɜːn/ *v.t.* gagner; (*interest:* comm.)
rapporter. ~ **s.o. sth.,** (*bring*) valoir
qch. à qn.

earnest /ˈɜːnɪst/ *a.* sérieux. **in ~,**
sérieusement.

earnings /ˈɜːnɪŋz/ *n. pl.* salaire *m.*;
(*profits*) bénéfices *m. pl.*

earphone /ˈɪəfəʊn/ *n.* écouteur *m.*

earshot /ˈɪəʃɒt/ *n.* **within ~,** à portée
de voix.

earth /ɜːθ/ *n.* terre *f.* —*v.t.* (*electr.*)
mettre à la terre. **why/how/ where**
on ~? . . ., pourquoi/ comment/où
diable? . . . ~**ly** *a.* terrestre.

earthenware /ˈɜːθnweə(r)/ *n.* faïence
f.

earthquake /ˈɜːθkweɪk/ *n.* tremblement de terre *m.*

earthy /ˈɜːθɪ/ *a.* (*of earth*) terreux;
(*coarse*) grossier.

earwig /ˈɪəwɪɡ/ *n.* perce-oreille *m.*

ease /iːz/ *n.* aisance *f.*, facilité *f.*; (*comfort*) bien-être *m.* —*v.t./i.* (se) calmer;
(*relax*) (se) détendre; (*slow down*) ralentir; (*slide*) glisser. **at ~,** à l'aise;
(*mil.*) au repos. **with ~,** aisément.

easel /ˈiːzl/ *n.* chevalet *m.*

east /iːst/ *n.* est *m.* —*a.* d'est. —*adv.*
vers l'est. **the E~,** (*Orient*) l'Orient
m. ~**erly** *a.* d'est. ~**ern** *a.* de l'est,
oriental. ~**ward** *a.* à l'est. ~**wards**
adv. vers l'est.

Easter /ˈiːstə(r)/ *n.* Pâques *f. pl.* (*or m.*
sing.). ~ **egg,** œuf de Pâques *m.*

easy /ˈiːzɪ/ *a.* (**-ier, -iest**) facile;
(*relaxed*) aisé. ~ **chair,** fauteuil *m.*
go ~ with, (*fam.*) y aller doucement
avec. **take it ~,** ne pas se fatiguer.

easily *adv.* facilement.

easygoing /iːzɪˈɡəʊɪŋ/ *a.* (*with people*)
accommodant; (*relaxed*) décontracté.

eat /iːt/ *v.t./i.* (*p.t.* **ate,** *p.p.* **eaten**)
manger. ~ **into,** ronger. ~**able** *a.*
mangeable. ~**er** *n.* mangeu|r, -se *m.*,
f.

eau-de-Cologne /əʊdəkəˈləʊn/ *n.* eau
de Cologne *f.*

eaves /iːvz/ *n. pl.* avant-toit *m.*

eavesdrop /ˈiːvzdrɒp/ *v.i.* (*p.t.*
-dropped). ~ **(on),** écouter en
cachette.

ebb /eb/ *n.* reflux *m.* —*v.i.* refluer;
(*fig.*) décliner.

ebony /ˈebənɪ/ *n.* ébène *f.*

ebullient /ɪˈbʌlɪənt/ *a.* exubérant.

eccentric /ɪkˈsentrɪk/ *a. & n.* excentrique (*m./f.*). ~**ity** /eksenˈtrɪsətɪ/ *n.*
excentricité *f.*

ecclesiastical /ɪkliːzɪˈæstɪkl/ *a.* ecclésiastique.

echo /ˈekəʊ/ *n.* (*pl.* **-oes**) écho *m.*
—*v.t./i.* (*p.t.* **echoed,** *pres. p.* **echo-
ing**) (se) répercuter; (*fig.*) répéter.

eclipse /ɪˈklɪps/ *n.* éclipse *f.* —*v.t.*
éclipser.

ecology /iːˈkɒlədʒɪ/ *n.* écologie *f.*

economic /iːkəˈnɒmɪk/ *a.* économique;
(*profitable*) rentable. ~**al** *a.* économique; (*person*) économe. ~**s** *n.* économie politique *f.*

economist /ɪˈkɒnəmɪst/ *n.* économiste
m./f.

econom|y /ɪˈkɒnəmɪ/ *n.* économie *f.*
~**ize** *v.i.* ~ **(on),** économiser.

ecstasy /ˈekstəsɪ/ *n.* extase *f.*

ecstatic /ɪkˈstætɪk/ *a.* extasié. ~**ally**
adv. avec extase.

ecumenical /iːkjuːˈmenɪkl/ *a.* œcuménique.

eddy /'edɪ/ *n.* tourbillon *m.*
edge /edʒ/ *n.* bord *m.*; (*of town*) abords *m. pl.*; (*of knife*) tranchant *m.* —*v.t.* border. —*v.i.* (*move*) se glisser. **have the ~ on**, (*fam.*) l'emporter sur. **on ~**, énervé.
edging /'edʒɪŋ/ *n.* bordure *f.*
edgy /'edʒɪ/ *a.* énervé.
edible /'edɪbl/ *a.* mangeable; (*not poisonous*) comestible.
edict /'iːdɪkt/ *n.* décret *m.*
edifice /'edɪfɪs/ *n.* édifice *m.*
edify /'edɪfaɪ/ *v.t.* édifier.
edit /'edɪt/ *v.t.* (*p.t.* **edited**) (*newspaper*) diriger; (*prepare text of*) mettre au point, préparer; (*write*) rédiger; (*cut*) couper.
edition /ɪ'dɪʃn/ *n.* édition *f.*
editor /'edɪtə(r)/ *n.* (*writer*) rédac|teur, -trice *m.*, *f.*; (*annotator*) édi|teur, -trice *m.*, *f.* **the ~ (in chief)**, le rédacteur en chef. **~ial** /-'tɔːrɪəl/ *a.* de la rédaction; *n.* éditorial *m.*
educat|e /'edʒʊkeɪt/ *v.t.* instruire; (*mind, public*) éduquer. **~ed** *a.* instruit. **~ion** /-'keɪʃn/ *n.* éducation *f.*; (*schooling*) enseignement *m.* **~ional** /-'keɪʃənl/ *a.* pédagogique, éducatif.
EEC *abbr.* (*European Economic Community*) CEE *f.*
eel /iːl/ *n.* anguille *f.*
eerie /'ɪərɪ/ *a.* (**-ier**, **-iest**) sinistre.
effect /ɪ'fekt/ *n.* effet *m.* —*v.t.* effectuer. **come into ~**, entrer en vigueur. **take ~**, agir.
effective /ɪ'fektɪv/ *a.* efficace; (*striking*) frappant; (*actual*) effectif. **~ly** *adv.* efficacement; de manière frappante; effectivement. **~ness** *n.* efficacité *f.*
effeminate /ɪ'femɪnət/ *a.* efféminé.
effervescent /efə'vesnt/ *a.* effervescent.
efficien|t /ɪ'fɪʃnt/ *a.* efficace; (*person*) compétent. **~cy** *n.* efficacité *f.*; compétence *f.* **~tly** *adv.* efficacement.
effigy /'efɪdʒɪ/ *n.* effigie *f.*
effort /'efət/ *n.* effort *m.* **~less** *a.* facile.
effrontery /ɪ'frʌntərɪ/ *n.* effronterie *f.*
effusive /ɪ'fjuːsɪv/ *a.* expansif.
e.g. /iː'dʒiː/ *abbr.* par exemple.
egalitarian /ɪgælɪ'teərɪən/ *a.* égalitaire. —*n.* égalitariste *m./f.*
egg[1] /eg/ *n.* œuf *m.* **~-cup** *n.* coquetier *m.* **~-plant** *n.* aubergine *f.*
egg[2] /eg/ *v.t.* **~ on**, (*fam.*) inciter.
eggshell /'egʃel/ *n.* coquille d'œuf *f.*
ego /'egəʊ/ *n.* (*pl.* **-os**) moi *m.* **~(t)ism** *n.* égoïsme *m.* **~(t)ist** *n.* égoïste *m./f.*

Egypt /'iːdʒɪpt/ *n.* Égypte *f.* **~ian** /ɪ'dʒɪpʃn/ *a.* & *n.* égyptien(ne) (*m.* (*f.*)).
eh /eɪ/ *int.* (*fam.*) hein.
eiderdown /'aɪdədaʊn/ *n.* édredon *m.*
eight /eɪt/ *a.* & *n.* huit (*m.*). **eighth** /eɪtθ/ *a.* & *n.* huitième (*m./f.*).
eighteen /eɪ'tiːn/ *a.* & *n.* dix-huit (*m.*). **~th** *a.* & *n.* dix-huitième (*m./f.*).
eight|y /'eɪtɪ/ *a.* & *n.* quatre-vingts (*m.*) **~ieth** *a.* & *n.* quatre-vingtième (*m./f.*).
either /'aɪðə(r)/ *a.* & *pron.* l'un(e) ou l'autre; (*with negative*) ni l'un(e) ni l'autre; (*each*) chaque. —*adv.* non plus. —*conj.* **~ . . . or**, ou (bien) . . . ou (bien); (*with negative*) ni . . . ni.
eject /ɪ'dʒekt/ *v.t.* éjecter.
eke /iːk/ *v.t.* **~ out**, faire durer; (*living*) gagner difficilement.
elaborate[1] /ɪ'læbərət/ *a.* compliqué, recherché.
elaborate[2] /ɪ'læbəreɪt/ *v.t.* élaborer. —*v.i.* préciser. **~ on**, s'étendre sur.
elapse /ɪ'læps/ *v.i.* s'écouler.
elastic /ɪ'læstɪk/ *a.* & *n.* élastique (*m.*). **~ band**, élastique *m.* **~ity** /elæ'stɪsətɪ/ *n.* élasticité *f.*
elated /ɪ'leɪtɪd/ *a.* fou de joie.
elbow /'elbəʊ/ *n.* coude *m.*
elder[1] /'eldə(r)/ *a.* & *n.* aîné(e) (*m.* (*f.*)).
elder[2] /'eldə(r)/ *n.* (*tree*) sureau *m.*
elderly /'eldəlɪ/ *a.* (assez) âgé.
eldest /'eldɪst/ *a.* & *n.* aîné(e) (*m.* (*f.*)).
elect /ɪ'lekt/ *v.t.* élire. —*a.* (*president etc.*) futur. **~ to do**, choisir de faire. **~ion** /-kʃn/ *n.* élection *f.*
elector /ɪ'lektə(r)/ *n.* élec|teur, -trice *m.*, *f.* **~al** *a.* électoral. **~ate** *n.* électorat *m.*
electric /ɪ'lektrɪk/ *a.* électrique. **~ blanket**, couverture chauffante *f.* **~al** *a.* électrique.
electrician /ɪlek'trɪʃn/ *n.* électricien *m.*
electricity /ɪlek'trɪsətɪ/ *n.* électricité *f.*
electrify /ɪ'lektrɪfaɪ/ *v.t.* électrifier.
electrocute /ɪ'lektrəkjuːt/ *v.t.* électrocuter.
electron /ɪ'lektrɒn/ *n.* électron *m.*
electronic /ɪlek'trɒnɪk/ *a.* électronique. **~s** *n.* électronique *f.*
elegan|t /'elɪgənt/ *a.* élégant. **~ce** *n.* élégance *f.* **~tly** *adv.* élégamment.
element /'elɪmənt/ *n.* élément *m.*; (*of heater etc.*) résistance *f.* **~ary** /-'mentrɪ/ *a.* élémentaire.
elephant /'elɪfənt/ *n.* éléphant *m.*

elevat|e /'elɪveɪt/ *v.t.* élever. ∼**ion** /-'veɪʃn/ *n.* élévation *f.*

elevator /'eləveɪtə(r)/ *n.* (*Amer.*) ascenseur *m.*

eleven /ɪ'levn/ *a.* & *n.* onze (*m.*). ∼**th** *a.* & *n.* onzième (*m.*/*f.*).

elf /elf/ (*pl.* **elves**) lutin *m.*

elicit /ɪ'lɪsɪt/ *v.t.* obtenir (**from**, de).

eligible /'elɪdʒəbl/ *a.* admissible (**for**, à). **be** ∼ **for**, (*entitled to*) avoir droit à.

eliminat|e /ɪ'lɪmɪneɪt/ *v.t.* éliminer. ∼**ion** /-'neɪʃn/ *n.* élimination *f.*

élite /eɪ'liːt/ *n.* élite *f.*

ellip|se /ɪ'lɪps/ *n.* ellipse *f.* ∼**tical** *a.* elliptique.

elm /elm/ *n.* orme *m.*

elocution /elə'kjuːʃn/ *n.* élocution *f.*

elongate /'iːlɒŋgeɪt/ *v.t.* allonger.

elope /ɪ'ləʊp/ *v.i.* s'enfuir. ∼**ment** *n.* fugue (amoureuse) *f.*

eloquen|t /'eləkwənt/ *a.* éloquent. ∼**ce** *n.* éloquence *f.* ∼**tly** *adv.* avec éloquence.

else /els/ *adv.* d'autre. **everybody** ∼, tous les autres. **nobody** ∼, personne d'autre. **nothing** ∼, rien d'autre. **or** ∼, ou bien. **somewhere** ∼, autre part. ∼**where** *adv.* ailleurs.

elucidate /ɪ'luːsɪdeɪt/ *v.t.* élucider.

elude /ɪ'luːd/ *v.t.* échapper à; (*question*) éluder.

elusive /ɪ'luːsɪv/ *a.* insaisissable.

emaciated /ɪ'meɪʃɪeɪtɪd/ *a.* émacié.

emanate /'eməneɪt/ *v.i.* émaner.

emancipat|e /ɪ'mænsɪpeɪt/ *v.t.* émanciper. ∼**ion** /-'peɪʃn/ *n.* émancipation *f.*

embalm /ɪm'bɑːm/ *v.t.* embaumer.

embankment /ɪm'bæŋkmənt/ *n.* (*of river*) quai *m.*; (*of railway*) remblai *m.*, talus *m.*

embargo /ɪm'bɑːgəʊ/ *n.* (*pl.* -**oes**) embargo *m.*

embark /ɪm'bɑːk/ *v.t.*/*i.* (s')embarquer. ∼ **on**, (*business etc.*) se lancer dans; (*journey*) commencer. ∼**ation** /embɑː'keɪʃn/ *n.* embarquement *m.*

embarrass /ɪm'bærəs/ *v.t.* embarrasser, gêner. ∼**ment** *n.* embarras *m.*, gêne *f.*

embassy /'embəsɪ/ *n.* ambassade *f.*

embed /ɪm'bed/ *v.t.* (*p.t.* **embedded**) encastrer.

embellish /ɪm'belɪʃ/ *v.t.* embellir. ∼**ment** *n.* enjolivement *m.*

embers /'embəz/ *n. pl.* braise *f.*

embezzle /ɪm'bezl/ *v.t.* détourner.

∼**ment** *n.* détournement de fonds *m.* ∼**r** /-ə(r)/ *n.* escroc *m.*

embitter /ɪm'bɪtə(r)/ *v.t.* (*person*) aigrir; (*situation*) envenimer.

emblem /'embləm/ *n.* emblème *m.*

embod|y /ɪm'bɒdɪ/ *v.t.* incarner, exprimer; (*include*) contenir. ∼**iment** *n.* incarnation *f.*

emboss /ɪm'bɒs/ *v.t.* (*metal*) repousser; (*paper*) gaufrer.

embrace /ɪm'breɪs/ *v.t.*/*i.* (s')embrasser. —*n.* étreinte *f.*

embroider /ɪm'brɔɪdə(r)/ *v.t.* broder. ∼**y** *n.* broderie *f.*

embroil /ɪm'brɔɪl/ *v.t.* mêler (**in**, à).

embryo /'embrɪəʊ/ *n.* (*pl.* -**os**) embryon *m.* ∼**nic** /-'ɒnɪk/ *a.* embryonnaire.

emend /ɪ'mend/ *v.t.* corriger.

emerald /'emərəld/ *n.* émeraude *f.*

emerge /ɪ'mɜːdʒ/ *v.i.* apparaître. ∼**nce** /-əns/ *n.* apparition *f.*

emergency /ɪ'mɜːdʒənsɪ/ *n.* (*crisis*) crise *f.*; (*urgent case:* *med.*) urgence *f.* ∼ **exit**, sortie de secours *f.* **in an** ∼, en cas d'urgence.

emery /'emərɪ/ *n.* émeri *m.*

emigrant /'emɪgrənt/ *n.* émigrant(e) *m.* (*f.*).

emigrat|e /'emɪgreɪt/ *v.i.* émigrer. ∼**ion** /-'greɪʃn/ *n.* émigration *f.*

eminen|t /'emɪnənt/ *a.* éminent. ∼**ce** *n.* éminence *f.* ∼**tly** *adv.* éminemment, parfaitement.

emissary /'emɪsərɪ/ *n.* émissaire *m.*

emi|t /ɪ'mɪt/ *v.t.* (*p.t.* **emitted**) émettre. ∼**ssion** *n.* émission *f.*

emotion /ɪ'məʊʃn/ *n.* émotion *f.* ∼**al** *a.* (*person, shock*) émotif; (*speech, scene*) émouvant.

emotive /ɪ'məʊtɪv/ *a.* émotif.

emperor /'empərə(r)/ *n.* empereur *m.*

emphasis /'emfəsɪs/ *n.* (*on word*) accent *m.* **lay** ∼ **on**, mettre l'accent sur, accorder une importance à.

emphasize /'emfəsaɪz/ *v.t.* souligner; (*syllable*) insister sur.

emphatic /ɪm'fætɪk/ *a.* catégorique; (*manner*) énergique.

empire /'empaɪə(r)/ *n.* empire *m.*

empirical /ɪm'pɪrɪkl/ *a.* empirique.

employ /ɪm'plɔɪ/ *v.t.* employer. ∼**er** *n.* employeu|r, -se *m.*, *f.* ∼**ment** *n.* emploi *m.* ∼**ment agency,** agence de placement *f.*

employee /emplɔɪ'iː/ *n.* employé(e) *m.* (*f.*).

empower /ɪm'paʊə(r)/ *v.t.* autoriser (**to do**, à faire).

empress /'emprɪs/ *n.* impératrice *f.*
empt|y /'emptɪ/ *a.* (-ier, -iest) vide; (*promise*) vain. —*v.t./i.* (se) vider. **on an ~y stomach**, à jeun. **~ies** *n. pl.* bouteilles vides *f. pl.* **~iness** *n.* vide *m.*
emulate /'emjʊleɪt/ *v.t.* imiter.
emulsion /ɪ'mʌlʃn/ *n.* émulsion *f.*
enable /ɪ'neɪbl/ *v.t.* **~ s.o. to**, permettre à qn. de.
enamel /ɪ'næml/ *n.* émail *m.* —*v.t.* (*p.t.* **enamelled**) émailler.
enamoured /ɪ'næməd/ *a.* **be ~ of**, aimer beaucoup, être épris de.
encampment /ɪn'kæmpmənt/ *n.* campement *m.*
encase /ɪn'keɪs/ *v.t.* (*cover*) recouvrir (**in**, de); (*enclose*) enfermer (**in**, dans).
enchant /ɪn'tʃɑːnt/ *v.t.* enchanter. **~ing** *a.* enchanteur. **~ment** *n.* enchantement *m.*
encircle /ɪn'sɜːkl/ *v.t.* encercler.
enclave /'enkleɪv/ *n.* enclave *f.*
enclose /ɪn'kləʊz/ *v.t.* (*land*) clôturer; (*with letter*) joindre. **~d** *a.* (*space*) clos; (*market*) couvert; (*with letter*) ci-joint.
enclosure /ɪn'kləʊʒə(r)/ *n.* enceinte *f.*; (*comm.*) pièce jointe *f.*
encompass /ɪn'kʌmpəs/ *v.t.* (*include*) inclure.
encore /'ɒŋkɔː(r)/ *int. & n.* bis (*m.*).
encounter /ɪn'kaʊntə(r)/ *v.t.* rencontrer. —*n.* rencontre *f.*
encourage /ɪn'kʌrɪdʒ/ *v.t.* encourager. **~ment** *n.* encouragement *m.*
encroach /ɪn'krəʊtʃ/ *v.i.* **~ upon**, empiéter sur.
encumber /ɪn'kʌmbə(r)/ *v.t.* encombrer.
encyclical /ɪn'sɪklɪkl/ *n.* encyclique *f.*
encyclopaed|ia /ɪnsaɪklə'piːdɪə/ *n.* encyclopédie *f.* **~ic** *a.* encyclopédique.
end /end/ *n.* fin *f.*; (*farthest part*) bout *m.* —*v.t./i.* (se) terminer. **~ up doing**, finir par faire. **come to an ~**, prendre fin. **no ~ of**, (*fam.*) énormément de. **on ~**, (*upright*) debout; (*in a row*) de suite.
endanger /ɪn'deɪndʒə(r)/ *v.t.* mettre en danger.
endear|ing /ɪn'dɪərɪŋ/ *a.* attachant. **~ment** *n.* parole tendre *f.*
endeavour /ɪn'devə(r)/ *n.* effort *m.* —*v.i.* s'efforcer (**to**, de).
ending /'endɪŋ/ *n.* fin *f.*
endive /'endɪv/ *n.* chicorée *f.*

endless /'endlɪs/ *a.* interminable; (*times*) innombrable; (*patience*) infini.
endorse /ɪn'dɔːs/ *v.t.* (*document*) endosser; (*action*) approuver. **~ment** *n.* (*auto.*) contravention *f.*
endow /ɪn'daʊ/ *v.t.* doter. **~ment** *n.* dotation *f.* (**of**, de).
endur|e /ɪn'djʊə(r)/ *v.t.* supporter. —*v.i.* durer. **~able** *a.* supportable. **~ance** *n.* endurance *f.* **~ing** *a.* durable.
enemy /'enəmɪ/ *n. & a.* ennemi(e) (*m. (f.)*).
energetic /enə'dʒetɪk/ *a.* énergique.
energy /'enədʒɪ/ *n.* énergie *f.*
enforce /ɪn'fɔːs/ *v.t.* appliquer, faire respecter; (*impose*) imposer (**on**, à). **~d** *a.* forcé.
engage /ɪn'geɪdʒ/ *v.t.* engager. —*v.i.* **~ in**, se lancer dans. **~d** *a.* fiancé; (*busy*) occupé. **get ~d**, se fiancer. **~ment** *n.* fiançailles *f. pl.*; (*meeting*) rendez-vous *m.*; (*undertaking*) engagement *m.*
engaging /ɪn'geɪdʒɪŋ/ *a.* engageant, séduisant.
engender /ɪn'dʒendə(r)/ *v.t.* engendrer.
engine /'endʒɪn/ *n.* moteur *m.*; (*of train*) locomotive *f.*; (*of ship*) machine *f.* **~-driver** *n.* mécanicien *m.*
engineer /endʒɪ'nɪə(r)/ *n.* ingénieur *m.*; (*appliance repairman*) dépanneur *m.* —*v.t.* (*contrive: fam.*) machiner. **~ing** *n.* (*mechanical*) mécanique *f.*; (*road-building etc.*) génie *m.*
England /'ɪŋglənd/ *n.* Angleterre *f.*
English /'ɪŋglɪʃ/ *a.* anglais. —*n.* (*lang.*) anglais *m.* **~-speaking** *a.* anglophone. **the ~**, les Anglais *m. pl.* **~man** *n.* Anglais *m.* **~woman** *n.* Anglaise *f.*
engrav|e /ɪn'greɪv/ *v.t.* graver. **~ing** *n.* gravure *f.*
engrossed /ɪn'grəʊst/ *a.* absorbé (**in**, par).
engulf /ɪn'gʌlf/ *v.t.* engouffrer.
enhance /ɪn'hɑːns/ *v.t.* rehausser; (*price, value*) augmenter.
enigma /ɪ'nɪgmə/ *n.* énigme *f.* **~tic** /enɪg'mætɪk/ *a.* énigmatique.
enjoy /ɪn'dʒɔɪ/ *v.t.* aimer (*doing*, faire); (*benefit from*) jouir de. **~ o.s.**, s'amuser. **~able** *a.* agréable. **~ment** *n.* plaisir *m.*
enlarge /ɪn'lɑːdʒ/ *v.t./i.* (s')agrandir. **~ upon**, s'étendre sur. **~ment** *n.* agrandissement *m.*

enlighten /ɪnˈlaɪtn/ *v.t.* éclairer. ∼**ment** *n.* édification *f.*; (*information*) éclaircissements *m. pl.*

enlist /ɪnˈlɪst/ *v.t.* (*person*) recruter; (*fig.*) obtenir. —*v.i.* s'engager.

enliven /ɪnˈlaɪvn/ *v.t.* animer.

enmity /ˈenmətɪ/ *n.* inimitié *f.*

enormity /ɪˈnɔːmətɪ/ *n.* énormité *f.*

enormous /ɪˈnɔːməs/ *a.* énorme. ∼**ly** *adv.* énormément.

enough /ɪˈnʌf/ *adv. & n.* assez. —*a.* assez de. ∼ **glasses/time/***etc.*, assez de verres/de temps/*etc.* **have** ∼ **of,** en avoir assez de.

enquir|e /ɪnˈkwaɪə(r)/ *v.t./i.* demander. ∼**e about,** se renseigner sur. ∼**y** *n.* demande de renseignements *f.*

enrage /ɪnˈreɪdʒ/ *v.t.* mettre en rage, rendre furieux.

enrich /ɪnˈrɪtʃ/ *v.t.* enrichir.

enrol /ɪnˈrəʊl/ *v.t./i.* (*p.t.* **enrolled**) (s')inscrire. ∼**ment** *n.* inscription *f.*

ensconce /ɪnˈskɒns/ *v.t.* ∼ **o.s.,** bien s'installer.

ensemble /ɒnˈsɒmbl/ *n.* (*clothing &* *mus.*) ensemble *m.*

ensign /ˈensən, ˈensaɪn/ *n.* (*flag*) pavillon *m.*

enslave /ɪnˈsleɪv/ *v.t.* asservir.

ensue /ɪnˈsjuː/ *v.i.* s'ensuivre.

ensure /ɪnˈʃʊə(r)/ *v.t.* assurer. ∼ **that,** (*ascertain*) s'assurer que.

entail /ɪnˈteɪl/ *v.t.* entraîner.

entangle /ɪnˈtæŋgl/ *v.t.* emmêler.

enter /ˈentə(r)/ *v.t.* (*room, club, etc.*) entrer dans; (*note down, register*) inscrire. —*v.i.* entrer (**into,** dans). ∼ **for,** s'inscrire à.

enterprise /ˈentəpraɪz/ *n.* entreprise *f.*; (*boldness*) initiative *f.*

enterprising /ˈentəpraɪzɪŋ/ *a.* entreprenant.

entertain /entəˈteɪn/ *v.t.* amuser, divertir; (*guests*) recevoir; (*ideas*) considérer. ∼**er** *n.* artiste *m./f.* ∼**ment** *n.* amusement *m.*, divertissement *m.*; (*performance*) spectacle *m.*

enthral /ɪnˈθrɔːl/ *v.t.* (*p.t.* **enthralled**) captiver.

enthuse /ɪnˈθjuːz/ *v.i.* ∼ **over,** s'enthousiasmer pour.

enthusias|m /ɪnˈθjuːzɪæzəm/ *n.* enthousiasme *m.* ∼**tic** /-ˈæstɪk/ *a.* enthousiaste. ∼**tically** *adv.* /-ˈæstɪklɪ/ *adv.* avec enthousiasme.

enthusiast /ɪnˈθjuːzɪæst/ *n.* fervent(e) *m.(f.)*, passionné(e) *m.(f.)* (**for,** de).

entice /ɪnˈtaɪs/ *v.t.* attirer. ∼ **to do,** entraîner à faire. ∼**ment** *n.* (*attraction*) attrait *m.*

entire /ɪnˈtaɪə(r)/ *a.* entier. ∼**ly** *adv.* entièrement.

entirety /ɪnˈtaɪərətɪ/ *n.* **in its** ∼, en entier.

entitle /ɪnˈtaɪtl/ *v.t.* donner droit à (**to sth.,** à qch.; **to do,** de faire). ∼**d** *a.* (*book*) intitulé. **be** ∼**d to sth.,** avoir droit à qch. ∼**ment** *n.* droit *m.*

entity /ˈentətɪ/ *n.* entité *f.*

entrails /ˈentreɪlz/ *n. pl.* entrailles *f. pl.*

entrance[1] /ˈentrəns/ *n.* (*entering, way in*) entrée *f.* (**to,** de); (*right to enter*) admission *f.*

entrance[2] /ɪnˈtrɑːns/ *v.t.* transporter.

entrant /ˈentrənt/ *n.* (*sport*) concurrent(e) *m.* (*f.*); (*in exam*) candidat(e) *m.* (*f.*).

entreat /ɪnˈtriːt/ *v.t.* supplier.

entrench /ɪnˈtrentʃ/ *v.t.* (*mil.*) retrancher; (*fig.*) ancrer.

entrust /ɪnˈtrʌst/ *v.t.* confier.

entry /ˈentrɪ/ *n.* (*entrance*) entrée *f.*; (*word on list*) mot inscrit *m.* ∼ **form,** feuille d'inscription *f.*

entwine /ɪnˈtwaɪn/ *v.t.* entrelacer.

enumerate /ɪˈnjuːməreɪt/ *v.t.* énumérer.

enunciate /ɪˈnʌnsɪeɪt/ *v.t.* (*word*) articuler; (*ideas*) énoncer.

envelop /ɪnˈveləp/ *v.t.* (*p.t.* **enveloped**) envelopper.

envelope /ˈenvələʊp/ *n.* enveloppe *f.*

enviable /ˈenvɪəbl/ *a.* enviable.

envious /ˈenvɪəs/ *a.* envieux (**of sth.,** de qch.). ∼ **of s.o.,** jaloux de qn. ∼**ly** *adv.* avec envie.

environment /ɪnˈvaɪərənmənt/ *n.* milieu *m.*; (*ecological*) environnement *m.* ∼**al** /-ˈmentl/ *a.* du milieu; de l'environnement.

envisage /ɪnˈvɪzɪdʒ/ *v.t.* envisager.

envoy /ˈenvɔɪ/ *n.* envoyé(e) *m.* (*f.*).

envy /ˈenvɪ/ *n.* envie *f.* —*v.t.* envier.

enzyme /ˈenzaɪm/ *n.* enzyme *m.*

ephemeral /ɪˈfemərəl/ *a.* éphémère.

epic /ˈepɪk/ *n.* épopée *f.* —*a.* épique.

epidemic /epɪˈdemɪk/ *n.* épidémie *f.*

epilep|sy /ˈepɪlepsɪ/ *n.* épilepsie *f.* ∼**tic** /-ˈleptɪk/ *a. & n.* épileptique (*m.(f.)*).

epilogue /ˈepɪlɒg/ *n.* épilogue *m.*

episode /ˈepɪsəʊd/ *n.* épisode *m.*

epistle /ɪˈpɪsl/ *n.* épître *f.*

epitaph /ˈepɪtɑːf/ *n.* épitaphe *f.*

epithet /ˈepɪθet/ *n.* épithète *f.*

epitom|e /ɪˈpɪtəmɪ/ *n.* (*embodiment*)

modèle *m.*; (*summary*) résumé *m.*
~ize *v.t.* incarner.

epoch /'iːpɒk/ *n.* époque *f.* ~-**making** *a.* qui fait époque.

equal /'iːkwəl/ *a.* égal. —*n.* égal(e) *m.* (*f.*). —*v.t.* (*p.t.* **equalled**) égaler. ~ **to,** (*task*) à la hauteur de. ~**ity** /ɪ'kwɒlətɪ/ *n.* égalité *f.* ~**ly** *adv.* également; (*just as*) tout aussi.

equalize /'iːkwəlaɪz/ *v.t./i.* égaliser. ~**r** /-ə(r)/ *n.* (*goal*) but égalisateur *m.*

equanimity /ekwə'nɪmətɪ/ *n.* égalité d'humeur *f.*, calme *m.*

equate /ɪ'kweɪt/ *v.t.* assimiler, égaler (**with,** à).

equation /ɪ'kweɪʒn/ *n.* équation *f.*

equator /ɪ'kweɪtə(r)/ *n.* équateur *m.* ~**ial** /ekwə'tɔːrɪəl/ *a.* équatorial.

equilibrium /iːkwɪ'lɪbrɪəm/ *n.* équilibre *m.*

equinox /'iːkwɪnɒks/ *n.* équinoxe *m.*

equip /ɪ'kwɪp/ *v.t.* (*p.t.* **equipped**) équiper (**with,** de). ~**ment** *n.* équipement *m.*

equitable /'ekwɪtəbl/ *a.* équitable.

equity /'ekwətɪ/ *n.* équité *f.*

equivalen|t /ɪ'kwɪvələnt/ *a.* & *n.* équivalent (*m.*). ~**ce** *n.* équivalence *f.*

equivocal /ɪ'kwɪvəkl/ *a.* équivoque.

era /'ɪərə/ *n.* ère *f.*, époque *f.*

eradicate /ɪ'rædɪkeɪt/ *v.t.* supprimer, éliminer.

erase /ɪ'reɪz/ *v.t.* effacer. ~**r** /-ə(r)/ *n.* (*rubber*) gomme *f.*

erect /ɪ'rekt/ *a.* droit. —*v.t.* ériger. ~**ion** /-kʃn/ *n.* érection *f.*

ermine /'ɜːmɪn/ *n.* hermine *f.*

ero|de /ɪ'rəʊd/ *v.t.* ronger. ~**sion** *n.* érosion *f.*

erotic /ɪ'rɒtɪk/ *a.* érotique. ~**ism** /-sɪzəm/ *n.* érotisme *m.*

err /ɜː(r)/ *v.i.* (*be mistaken*) se tromper; (*sin*) pécher.

errand /'erənd/ *n.* course *f.*

erratic /ɪ'rætɪk/ *a.* (*uneven*) irrégulier; (*person*) capricieux.

erroneous /ɪ'rəʊnɪəs/ *a.* erroné.

error /'erə(r)/ *n.* erreur *f.*

erudit|e /'eruːdaɪt, *Amer.* 'erjʊdaɪt/ *a.* érudit. ~**ion** /-'dɪʃn/ *n.* érudition *f.*

erupt /ɪ'rʌpt/ *v.i.* (*volcano*) entrer en éruption; (*fig.*) éclater. ~**ion** /-pʃn/ *n.* éruption *f.*

escalat|e /'eskəleɪt/ *v.t./i.* (s')intensifier; (*of prices*) monter en flèche. ~**ion** /-'leɪʃn/ *n.* escalade *f.*

escalator /'eskəleɪtə(r)/ *n.* escalier mécanique *m.*, escalator *m.*

escapade /eskə'peɪd/ *n.* fredaine *f.*

escape /ɪ'skeɪp/ *v.i.* s'échapper (**from a place,** d'un lieu). —*v.t.* échapper à. —*n.* fuite *f.*, évasion *f.*; (*of gas etc.*) fuite *f.* ~ **from s.o.,** échapper à qn. ~ **to,** s'enfuir dans. **have a lucky** *or* **narrow** ~, l'échapper belle.

escapism /ɪ'skeɪpɪzəm/ *n.* évasion (de la réalité) *f.*

escort[1] /'eskɔːt/ *n.* (*guard*) escorte *f.*; (*of lady*) cavalier *m.*

escort[2] /ɪ'skɔːt/ *v.t.* escorter.

Eskimo /'eskɪməʊ/ *n.* (*pl.* **-os**) Esquimau(de) *m.* (*f.*).

especial /ɪ'speʃl/ *a.* particulier. ~**ly** *adv.* particulièrement.

espionage /'espɪənɑːʒ/ *n.* espionnage *m.*

esplanade /esplə'neɪd/ *n.* esplanade *f.*

espresso /e'spresəʊ/ *n.* (*pl.* **-os**) (*café*) express *m.*

essay /'eseɪ/ *n.* essai *m.*; (*schol.*) rédaction *f.*; (*univ.*) dissertation *f.*

essence /'esns/ *n.* essence *f.*; (*main point*) essentiel *m.*

essential /ɪ'senʃl/ *a.* essentiel. —*n. pl.* **the** ~**s,** l'essentiel *m.* ~**ly** *adv.* essentiellement.

establish /ɪ'stæblɪʃ/ *v.t.* établir; (*business, state*) fonder. ~**ment** *n.* établissement *m.*; fondation *f.* **the E**~**ment,** les pouvoirs établis.

estate /ɪ'steɪt/ *n.* (*land*) propriété *f.*; (*possessions*) biens *m. pl.*; (*inheritance*) succession *f.*; (*district*) cité *f.*, complexe *m.* ~ **agent,** agent immobilier *m.* ~ **car,** break *m.*

esteem /ɪ'stiːm/ *v.t.* estimer. —*n.* estime *f.*

estimate[1] /'estɪmət/ *n.* (*calculation*) estimation *f.*; (*comm.*) devis *m.*

estimat|e[2] /'estɪmeɪt/ *v.t.* estimer. ~**ion** /-'meɪʃn/ *n.* jugement *m.*; (*high regard*) estime *f.*

estuary /'estʃʊərɪ/ *n.* estuaire *m.*

etc. /et'setərə/ *adv.* etc.

etching /'etʃɪŋ/ *n.* eau-forte *f.*

eternal /ɪ'tɜːnl/ *a.* éternel.

eternity /ɪ'tɜːnətɪ/ *n.* éternité *f.*

ether /'iːθə(r)/ *n.* éther *m.*

ethereal /ɪ'θɪərɪəl/ *a.* éthéré.

ethic /'eθɪk/ *n.* éthique *f.* ~**s,** moralité *f.* ~**al** *a.* éthique.

Ethiopia /iːθɪ'əʊpɪə/ *n.* Éthiopie *f.* ~**n** *a.* & *n.* éthiopien(ne) (*m.*(*f.*)).

ethnic /'eθnɪk/ *a.* ethnique.

ethos /'iːθɒs/ *n.* génie *m.*

etiquette /'etɪket/ *n.* étiquette *f.*

etymology /etɪ'mɒlədʒɪ/ *n.* étymologie *f.*

eucalyptus / juːkə'lɪptəs/ *n.* (*pl.* -tuses) eucalyptus *m.*

eulogy /'juːlədʒɪ/ *n.* éloge *m.*

euphemism /'juːfəmɪzəm/ *n.* euphémisme *m.*

euphoria /juːˈfɔːrɪə/ *n.* euphorie *f.*

Europe /'jʊərəp/ *n.* Europe *f.* ~**an** /-'pɪən/ *a.* & *n.* européen(ne) (*m.* (*f.*)).

euthanasia /juːθə'neɪzɪə/ *n.* euthanasie *f.*

evacuat|e /ɪ'vækjʊeɪt/ *v.t.* évacuer. ~**ion** /-'eɪʃn/ *n.* évacuation *f.*

evade /ɪ'veɪd/ *v.t.* esquiver.

evaluate /ɪ'væljʊeɪt/ *v.t.* évaluer.

evangelical /iːvæn'dʒelɪkl/ *a.* évangélique.

evangelist /ɪ'vændʒəlɪst/ *n.* évangéliste *m.*

evaporat|e /ɪ'væpəreɪt/ *v.i.* s'évaporer. ~**ed milk**, lait concentré *m.* ~**ion** /-'reɪʃn/ *n.* évaporation *f.*

evasion /ɪ'veɪʒn/ *n.* fuite *f.* (**of**, devant; (*excuse*) subterfuge *m.*

evasive /ɪ'veɪsɪv/ *a.* évasif.

eve /iːv/ *n.* veille *f.* (**of**, de).

even /'iːvn/ *a.* régulier; (*surface*) uni; (*equal, unvarying*) égal; (*number*) pair. —*v.t./i.* ~ (**out** *or* **up**), (s')égaliser. —*adv.* même. ~ **better**/*etc.*, (*still*) encore mieux/ *etc.* **get** ~ **with**, se venger de. ~**ly** *adv.* régulièrement; (*equally*) de manière égale.

evening /'iːvnɪŋ/ *n.* soir *m.*; (*whole evening, event*) soirée *f.*

event /ɪ'vent/ *n.* événement *m.*; (*sport*) épreuve *f.* **in the** ~ **of**, en cas de. ~**ful** *a.* mouvementé.

eventual /ɪ'ventʃʊəl/ *a.* final, définitif. ~**ity** /-'ælətɪ/ *n.* éventualité *f.* ~**ly** *adv.* en fin de compte; (*in future*) un jour ou l'autre.

ever /'evə(r)/ *adv.* jamais; (*at all times*) toujours. ~ **since** *prep.* & *adv.* depuis; *conj.* depuis que. ~ **so**, (*fam.*) vraiment.

evergreen /'evəgriːn/ *n.* arbre à feuilles persistantes *m.*

everlasting /evə'lɑːstɪŋ/ *a.* éternel.

every /'evrɪ/ *a.* chaque. ~ **one**, chacun(e). ~ **other day,** un jour sur deux, tous les deux jours.

everybody /'evrɪbɒdɪ/ *pron.* tout le monde.

everyday /'evrɪdeɪ/ *a.* quotidien.

everyone /'evrɪwʌn/ *pron.* tout le monde.

everything /'evrɪθɪŋ/ *pron.* tout.

everywhere /'evrɪweə(r)/ *adv.* partout. ~ **he goes,** partout où il va.

evict /ɪ'vɪkt/ *v.t.* expulser. ~**ion** /-kʃn/ *n.* expulsion *f.*

evidence /'evɪdəns/ *n.* (*proof*) preuve(s) *f.* (*pl.*).; (*certainty*) évidence *f.*; (*signs*) signes *m. pl.*; (*testimony*) témoignage *m.* **give** ~, témoigner. **in** ~, en vue.

evident /'evɪdənt/ *a.* évident. ~**ly** *adv.* de toute évidence.

evil /'iːvl/ *a.* mauvais. —*n.* mal *m.*

evo|ke /ɪ'vəʊk/ *v.t.* évoquer. ~**cative** /ɪ'vɒkətɪv/ *a.* évocateur.

evolution /iːvə'luːʃn/ *n.* évolution *f.*

evolve /ɪ'vɒlv/ *v.i.* se développer, évoluer. —*v.t.* développer.

ewe /juː/ *n.* brebis *f.*

ex- /eks/ *pref.* ex-, ancien.

exacerbate /ɪg'zæsəbeɪt/ *v.t.* exacerber.

exact[1] /ɪg'zækt/ *a.* exact. ~**ly** *adv.* exactement. ~**ness** *n.* exactitude *f.*

exact[2] /ɪg'zækt/ *v.t.* exiger (**from**, de). ~**ing** *a.* exigeant.

exaggerat|e /ɪg'zædʒəreɪt/ *v.t./i.* exagérer. ~**ion** /-'reɪʃn/ *n.* exagération *f.*

exalt /ɪg'zɔːlt/ *v.t.* (*in rank*) élever; (*praise*) exalter.

exam /ɪg'zæm/ *n.* (*fam.*) examen *m.*

examination /ɪgzæmɪ'neɪʃn/ *n.* examen *m.*

examine /ɪg'zæmɪn/ *v.t.* examiner; (*witness etc.*) interroger. ~**r** /-ə(r)/ *n.* examina|teur, -trice *m., f.*

example /ɪg'zɑːmpl/ *n.* exemple *m.* **for** ~, par exemple. **make an** ~ **of,** punir pour l'exemple.

exasperat|e /ɪg'zæspəreɪt/ *v.t.* exaspérer. ~**ion** /-'reɪʃn/ *n.* exaspération *f.*

excavat|e /'ekskəveɪt/ *v.t.* creuser; (*uncover*) déterrer. ~**ions** /-'veɪʃnz/ *n. pl.* (*archaeol.*) fouilles *f. pl.*

exceed /ɪk'siːd/ *v.t.* dépasser. ~-**ingly** *adv.* extrêmement.

excel /ɪk'sel/ *v.i.* (*p.t.* **excelled**) exceller. —*v.t.* surpasser.

excellen|t /'eksələnt/ *a.* excellent. ~**ce** *n.* excellence *f.* ~**tly** *adv.* admirablement, parfaitement.

except /ɪk'sept/ *prep.* sauf, excepté. —*v.t.* excepter. ~ **for**, à part. ~**ing** *prep.* sauf, excepté.

exception /ɪk'sepʃn/ n. exception f. **take ~ to**, s'offenser de.

exceptional /ɪk'sepʃənl/ a. exceptionnel. **~ly** adv. exceptionnellement.

excerpt /'eksɜːpt/ n. extrait m.

excess[1] /ɪk'ses/ n. excès m.

excess[2] /'ekses/ a. excédentaire. **~ fare**, supplément m. **~ luggage**, excédent de bagages m.

excessive /ɪk'sesɪv/ a. excessif. **~ly** adv. excessivement.

exchange /ɪks'tʃeɪndʒ/ v.t. échanger. —n. échange m.; (between currencies) change m. (**telephone**) **~**, central (téléphonique) m.

exchequer /ɪks'tʃekə(r)/ n. (British pol.) Échiquier m.

excise /'eksaɪz/ n. impôt (indirect) m.

excit|e /ɪk'saɪt/ v.t. exciter; (enthuse) enthousiasmer. **~able** a. excitable. **~ed** a. excité. **get ~ed**, s'exciter. **~ement** n. excitation f. **~ing** a. passionnant.

exclaim /ɪk'skleɪm/ v.t./i. exclamer, s'écrier.

exclamation /eksklə'meɪʃn/ n. exclamation f. **~ mark** or **point** (Amer.), point d'exclamation m.

exclu|de /ɪk'skluːd/ v.t. exclure. **~sion** n. exclusion f.

exclusive /ɪk'skluːsɪv/ a. (rights etc.) exclusif; (club etc.) sélect; (news item) en exclusivité. **~ of service**/etc., service/etc. non compris. **~ly** adv. exclusivement.

excommunicate /ekskə'mjuːnɪkeɪt/ v.t. excommunier.

excrement /'ekskrəmənt/ n. excrément(s) m. (pl.).

excruciating /ɪk'skruːʃɪeɪtɪŋ/ a. atroce, insupportable.

excursion /ɪk'skɜːʃn/ n. excursion f.

excus|e[1] /ɪk'skjuːz/ v.t. excuser. **~e from**, (exempt) dispenser de. **~e me!**, excusez-moi!, pardon! **~able** a. excusable.

excuse[2] /ɪk'skjuːs/ n. excuse f.

ex-directory /eksdɪ'rektərɪ/ a. qui n'est pas dans l'annuaire.

execute /'eksɪkjuːt/ v.t. exécuter.

execution /eksɪ'kjuːʃn/ n. exécution f. **~er** n. bourreau m.

executive /ɪg'zekjʊtɪv/ n. (pouvoir) exécutif m.; (person) cadre m. —a. exécutif.

exemplary /ɪg'zemplərɪ/ a. exemplaire.

exemplify /ɪg'zemplɪfaɪ/ v.t. illustrer.

exempt /ɪg'zempt/ a. exempt (**from**, de). —v.t. exempter. **~ion** /-pʃn/ n. exemption f.

exercise /'eksəsaɪz/ n. exercice m. —v.t. exercer; (restraint, patience) faire preuve de. —v.i. prendre de l'exercice. **~ book**, cahier m.

exert /ɪg'zɜːt/ v.t. exercer. **~ o.s.**, se dépenser, faire des efforts. **~ion** /-ʃn/ n. effort m.

exhaust /ɪg'zɔːst/ v.t. épuiser. —n. (auto.) (pot d')échappement m. **~ed** a. épuisé. **~ion** /-stʃən/ n. épuisement m.

exhaustive /ɪg'zɔːstɪv/ a. complet.

exhibit /ɪg'zɪbɪt/ v.t. exposer; (fig.) faire preuve de. —n. objet exposé m. **~or** n. exposant(e) m. (f.).

exhibition /eksɪ'bɪʃn/ n. exposition f.; (act of showing) démonstration f. **~ist** n. exhibitionniste m./f.

exhilarat|e /ɪg'zɪləreɪt/ v.t. transporter de joie; (invigorate) stimuler. **~ion** /-'reɪʃn/ n. joie f.

exhort /ɪg'zɔːt/ v.t. exhorter (**to**, à).

exhume /eks'hjuːm/ v.t. exhumer.

exile /'eksaɪl/ n. exil m.; (person) exilé(e) m. (f.). —v.t. exiler.

exist /ɪg'zɪst/ v.i. exister. **~ence** n. existence f. **be in ~ence**, exister.

exit /'eksɪt/ n. sortie f.

exodus /'eksədəs/ n. exode m.

exonerate /ɪg'zɒnəreɪt/ v.t. disculper, innocenter.

exorbitant /ɪg'zɔːbɪtənt/ a. exorbitant.

exorcize /'eksɔːsaɪz/ v.t. exorciser.

exotic /ɪg'zɒtɪk/ a. exotique.

expan|d /ɪk'spænd/ v.t./i. (develop) (se) développer; (extend) (s')étendre; (metal, liquid) (se) dilater. **~sion** n. développement m.; dilatation f.; (pol., comm.) expansion f.

expanse /ɪk'spæns/ n. étendue f.

expatriate /eks'pætrɪət, Amer. eks'peɪtrɪət/ a. & n. expatrié(e) (m. (f.)).

expect /ɪk'spekt/ v.t. attendre, s'attendre à; (suppose) supposer; (demand) exiger; (baby) attendre. **~ to do**, compter faire. **~ation** /ekspek'teɪʃn/ n. attente f.

expectan|t /ɪk'spektənt/ a. **~t look**, air d'attente m. **~t mother**, future mère f. **~cy** n. attente f.

expedient /ɪk'spiːdɪənt/ a. opportun. —n. expédient m.

expedite /'ekspɪdaɪt/ v.t. hâter.

expedition /ekspɪˈdɪʃn/ *n.* expédition *f.*

expel /ɪkˈspel/ *v.t.* (*p.t.* **expelled**) expulser; (*from school*) renvoyer.

expend /ɪkˈspend/ *v.t.* dépenser. **~able** *a.* remplaçable.

expenditure /ɪkˈspendɪtʃə(r)/ *n.* dépense(s) *f.* (*pl.*).

expense /ɪkˈspens/ *n.* dépense *f.*, frais *m. pl.* **at s.o.'s ~**, aux dépens de qn.

expensive /ɪkˈspensɪv/ *a.* cher, coûteux; (*tastes, habits*) de luxe. **~ly** *adv.* coûteusement.

experience /ɪkˈspɪərɪəns/ *n.* expérience *f.*; (*adventure*) aventure *f.* —*v.t.* (*undergo*) connaître; (*feel*) éprouver. **~d** *a.* expérimenté.

experiment /ɪkˈsperɪmənt/ *n.* expérience *f.* —*v.i.* faire une expérience. **~al** /-ˈmentl/ *a.* expérimental.

expert /ˈekspɜːt/ *n.* expert(e) *m.* (*f.*). —*a.* expert. **~ly** *adv.* habilement.

expertise /ekspɜːˈtiːz/ *n.* compétence *f.* (**in**, en).

expir|e /ɪkˈspaɪə(r)/ *v.i.* expirer. **~ed** *a.* périmé. **~y** *n.* expiration *f.*

expl|ain /ɪkˈspleɪn/ *v.t.* expliquer. **~anation** /ekspləˈneɪʃn/ *n.* explication *f.* **~anatory** /-ˈænətərɪ/ *a.* explicatif.

expletive /ɪkˈspliːtɪv, *Amer.* ˈekspləʔɪv/ *n.* juron *m.*

explicit /ɪkˈsplɪsɪt/ *a.* explicite.

explo|de /ɪkˈspləʊd/ *v.t./i.* (faire) exploser. **~sion** *n.* explosion *f.* **~sive** *a.* & *n.* explosif (*m.*).

exploit[1] /ˈeksplɔɪt/ *n.* exploit *m.*

exploit[2] /ɪkˈsplɔɪt/ *v.t.* exploiter. **~ation** /eksplɔɪˈteɪʃn/ *n.* exploitation *f.*

exploratory /ɪkˈsplɒrətrɪ/ *a.* (*talks: pol.*) exploratoire.

explor|e /ɪkˈsplɔː(r)/ *v.t.* explorer; (*fig.*) examiner. **~ation** /ekspləˈreɪʃn/ *n.* exploration *f.* **~er** *n.* explora|teur, -trice *m., f.*

exponent /ɪkˈspəʊnənt/ *n.* interprète *m.* (**of**, de).

export[1] /ɪkˈspɔːt/ *v.t.* exporter. **~er** *n.* exportateur *m.*

export[2] /ˈekspɔːt/ *n.* exportation *f.*

expos|e /ɪkˈspəʊz/ *v.t.* exposer; (*disclose*) dévoiler. **~ure** /-ʒə(r)/ *n.* exposition *f.*; (*photo.*) pose *f.* **die of ~ure**, mourir de froid.

expound /ɪkˈspaʊnd/ *v.t.* exposer.

express[1] /ɪkˈspres/ *a.* formel, exprès; (*letter*) exprès *invar.* —*adv.* (*by express post*) (par) exprès. —*n.* (*train*) rapide *m.*; (*less fast*) express *m.* **~ly** *adv.* expressément.

express[2] /ɪkˈspres/ *v.t.* exprimer. **~ion** /-ʃn/ *n.* expression *f.* **~ive** *a.* expressif.

expulsion /ɪkˈspʌlʃn/ *n.* expulsion *f.*; (*from school*) renvoi *m.*

expurgate /ˈekspəgeɪt/ *v.t.* expurger.

exquisite /ˈekskwɪzɪt/ *a.* exquis. **~ly** *adv.* d'une façon exquise.

ex-serviceman /eksˈsɜːvɪsmən/ *n.* (*pl.* -**men**) ancien combattant *m.*

extant /ekˈstænt/ *a.* existant.

extempore /ekˈstempərɪ/ *a.* & *adv.* impromptu.

exten|d /ɪkˈstend/ *v.t.* (*increase*) étendre, agrandir; (*arm, leg*) étendre; (*prolong*) prolonger; (*house*) agrandir; (*grant*) offrir. —*v.i.* (*stretch*) s'étendre; (*in time*) se prolonger. **~sion** *n.* (*of line, road*) prolongement *m.*; (*in time*) prolongation *f.*; (*building*) annexe *f.*; (*of phone*) appareil supplémentaire *m.*; (*phone number*) poste *m.*

extensive /ɪkˈstensɪv/ *a.* vaste; (*study*) profond; (*damage etc.*) important. **~ly** *adv.* (*much*) beaucoup; (*very*) très.

extent /ɪkˈstent/ *n.* (*size, scope*) étendue *f.*; (*degree*) mesure *f.* **to such an ~ that**, à tel point que.

extenuate /ɪkˈstenjʊeɪt/ *v.t.* atténuer.

exterior /ɪkˈstɪərɪə(r)/ *a.* & *n.* extérieur (*m.*).

exterminat|e /ɪkˈstɜːmɪneɪt/ *v.t.* exterminer. **~ion** /-ˈneɪʃn/ *n.* extermination *f.*

external /ɪkˈstɜːnl/ *a.* extérieur; (*cause, medical use*) externe. **~ly** *adv.* extérieurement.

extinct /ɪkˈstɪŋkt/ *a.* (*species*) disparu; (*volcano, passion*) éteint. **~ion** /-kʃn/ *n.* extinction *f.*

extinguish /ɪkˈstɪŋgwɪʃ/ *v.t.* éteindre. **~er** *n.* extincteur *m.*

extol /ɪkˈstəʊl/ *v.t.* (*p.t.* **extolled**) exalter, chanter les louanges de.

extort /ɪkˈstɔːt/ *v.t.* extorquer (**from**, à). **~ion** /-ʃn/ *n.* (*jurid.*) extorsion (de fonds) *f.*

extortionate /ɪkˈstɔːʃənət/ *a.* exorbitant.

extra /ˈekstrə/ *a.* de plus, supplémentaire. —*adv.* plus (que d'habitude). **~ strong**, extra-fort. —*n.* (*additional thing*) supplément *m.*; (*cinema*) figurant(e) *m.* (*f.*). ~ **charge,** supplément *m.* ~ **time,** (*football*) prolongation *f.*

extra /'ekstrə/ *pref.* extra-.

extract[1] /ɪk'strækt/ *v.t.* extraire; (*promise, tooth*) arracher; (*fig.*) obtenir. ~**ion** /-kʃn/ *n.* extraction *f.*

extract[2] /'ekstrækt/ *n.* extrait *m.*

extra-curricular /ekstrəkə'rɪkjʊlə(r)/ *a.* hors programme.

extradit|**e** /'ekstrədaɪt/ *v.t.* extrader. ~**ion** /-'dɪʃn/ *n.* extradition *f.*

extramarital /ekstrə'mærɪtl/ *a.* extraconjugal.

extramural /ekstrə'mjʊərəl/ *a.* (*univ.*) hors faculté.

extraordinary /ɪk'strɔːdnrɪ/ *a.* extraordinaire.

extravagan|**t** /ɪk'strævəgənt/ *a.* extravagant; (*wasteful*) prodigue. ~**ce** *n.* extravagance *f.*; prodigalité *f.*

extrem|**e** /ɪk'striːm/ *a.* & *n.* extrême (*m.*). ~**ely** *adv.* extrêmement. ~**ist** *n.* extrémiste *m.*/*f.*

extremity /ɪk'stremətɪ/ *n.* extrémité *f.*

extricate /'ekstrɪkeɪt/ *v.t.* dégager.

extrovert /'ekstrəvɜːt/ *n.* extraverti(e) *m.* (*f.*).

exuberan|**t** /ɪg'zjuːbərənt/ *a.* exubérant. ~**ce** *n.* exubérance *f.*

exude /ɪg'zjuːd/ *v.t.* (*charm etc.*) manifester libéralement.

exult /ɪg'zʌlt/ *v.i.* exulter.

eye /aɪ/ *n.* œil *m.* (*pl.* yeux). —*v.t.* (*p.t.* eyed, *pres. p.* eyeing) regarder. **keep an** ~ **on,** surveiller. ~**-opener** *n.* révélation *f.* ~**-shadow** *n.* fard à paupières *m.*

eyeball /'aɪbɔːl/ *n.* globe oculaire *m.*

eyebrow /'aɪbraʊ/ *n.* sourcil *m.*

eyeful /'aɪfʊl/ *n.* **get an** ~, (*fam.*) se rincer l'œil.

eyelash /'aɪlæʃ/ *n.* cil *m.*

eyelet /'aɪlɪt/ *n.* œillet *m.*

eyelid /'aɪlɪd/ *n.* paupière *f.*

eyesight /'aɪsaɪt/ *n.* vue *f.*

eyesore /'aɪsɔː(r)/ *n.* horreur *f.*

eyewitness /'aɪwɪtnɪs/ *n.* témoin oculaire *m.*

F

fable /'feɪbl/ *n.* fable *f.*

fabric /'fæbrɪk/ *n.* (*cloth*) tissu *m.*

fabrication /fæbrɪ'keɪʃn/ *n.* (*invention*) invention *f.*

fabulous /'fæbjʊləs/ *a.* fabuleux; (*marvellous*: *fam.*) formidable.

façade /fə'sɑːd/ *n.* façade *f.*

face /feɪs/ *n.* visage *m.*, figure *f.*; (*aspect*) face *f.*; (*of clock*) cadran *m.* —*v.t.* être en face de; (*confront*) faire face à, affronter. —*v.i.* se tourner; (*of house*) être exposé. **~flannel** *n.* gant de toilette *m.* **~lift** *n.* lifting *m.* **~ to face**, face à face. **~ up to**, faire face à. **in the ~ of, ~d with**, face à. **make a (funny) ~**, faire une grimace.

faceless /'feɪslɪs/ *a.* anonyme.

facet /'fæsɪt/ *n.* facette *f.*

facetious /fə'siːʃəs/ *a.* facétieux.

facial /'feɪʃl/ *a.* de la face, facial. —*n.* soin du visage *m.*

facile /'fæsaɪl, *Amer.* 'fæsl/ *a.* facile, superficiel.

facilitate /fə'sɪlɪteɪt/ *v.t.* faciliter.

facilit|y /fə'sɪlətɪ/ *n.* facilité *f.* **~ies**, (*equipment*) équipements *m. pl.*

facing /'feɪsɪŋ/ *n.* parement *m.*

facsimile /fæk'sɪməlɪ/ *n.* facsimilé *m.*

fact /fækt/ *n.* fait *m.* **as a matter of ~, in ~**, en fait.

faction /'fækʃn/ *n.* faction *f.*

factor /'fæktə(r)/ *n.* facteur *m.*

factory /'fæktərɪ/ *n.* usine *f.*

factual /'fæktʃʊəl/ *a.* basé sur les faits.

faculty /'fækltɪ/ *n.* faculté *f.*

fad /fæd/ *n.* manie *f.*, folie *f.*

fade /feɪd/ *v.i.* (*sound*) s'affaiblir; (*memory*) s'évanouir; (*flower*) se faner; (*material*) déteindre; (*colour*) passer.

fag /fæg/ *n.* (*chore*: *fam.*) corvée *f.*; (*cigarette*: *sl.*) sèche *f.*; (*homosexual*: *Amer.*: *sl.*) pédé *m.*

fagged /fægd/ *a.* (*tired*) éreinté.

fail /feɪl/ *v.i.* échouer; (*grow weak*) (s'af)faiblir; (*run short*) manquer; (*engine etc.*) tomber en panne. —*v.t.* (*exam*) échouer à; (*candidate*) refuser, recaler; (*disappoint*) décevoir. **~ s.o.**, (*of words etc.*) manquer à qn. **~ to do**, (*not do*) ne pas faire; (*not be able*) ne pas réussir à faire. **without ~**, à coup sûr.

failing /'feɪlɪŋ/ *n.* défaut *m.* —*prep.* à défaut de.

failure /'feɪljə(r)/ *n.* échec *m.*; (*person*) raté(e) *m.* (*f.*).; (*breakdown*) panne *f.* **~ to do**, (*inability*) incapacité de faire *f.*

faint /feɪnt/ *a.* (**-er, -est**) léger, faible. —*v.i.* s'évanouir. —*n.* évanouissement *m.* **feel ~**, (*ill*) se trouver mal. **the ~est idea**, la moindre idée. **~hearted** *a.* timide. **~ly** *adv.* (*weakly*) faiblement; (*slightly*) légèrement. **~ness** *n.* faiblesse *f.*

fair[1] /feə(r)/ *n.* foire *f.* **~-ground** *n.* champ de foire *f.*

fair[2] /feə(r)/ *a.* (**-er, -est**) (*hair, person*) blond; (*skin etc.*) clair; (*just*) juste, équitable; (*weather*) beau; (*amount*) raisonnable. —*adv.* (*play*) loyalement. **~ play**, le fair-play. **~ly** *adv.* (*justly*) équitablement; (*rather*) assez. **~ness** *n.* justice *f.*

fairy /'feərɪ/ *n.* fée *f.* **~ story, ~-tale** *n.* conte de fées *m.*

faith /feɪθ/ *n.* foi. *f.* **~-healer** *n.* guérisseu|r, -se *m.*, *f.*

faithful /'feɪθfl/ *a.* fidèle. **~ly** *adv.* fidèlement. **~ness** *n.* fidélité *f.*

fake /feɪk/ *n.* (*forgery*) faux *m.*; (*person*) imposteur *m.* **it is a ~**, c'est faux. —*a.* faux. —*v.t.* (*copy*) faire un faux de; (*alter*) falsifier, truquer; (*illness*) simuler.

falcon /'fɔːlkən/ *n.* faucon *m.*

fall /fɔːl/ *v.i.* (*p.t.* **fell**, *p.p.* **fallen**) tomber. —*n.* chute *f.*; (*autumn*: *Amer.*) automne *m.* **~ back on**, se rabattre sur. **~ down** *or* **off**, tomber. **~ for**, (*person*: *fam.*) tomber amoureux de; (*a trick*: *fam.*) se laisser prendre à. **~ in**, (*mil.*) se mettre en rangs. **~ off**, (*decrease*) diminuer. **~ out**, se brouiller (**with**, avec). **~-out** *n.* retombées *f. pl.* **~ over**, tomber (par terre). **~ short**, être insuffisant. **~ through**, (*plans*) tomber à l'eau.

fallacy /'fæləsɪ/ *n.* erreur *f.*

fallible /'fæləbl/ *a.* faillible.

fallow /'fæləʊ/ *a.* en jachère.

false /fɔːls/ *a.* faux. **~hood** *n.* mensonge *m.* **~ly** *adv.* faussement. **~ness** *n.* fausseté *f.*

falsetto /fɔːl'setəʊ/ n. (pl. -os) fausset m.

falsify /'fɔːlsɪfaɪ/ v.t. falsifier.

falter /'fɔːltə(r)/ v.i. vaciller.

fame /feɪm/ n. renommée f.

famed /feɪmd/ a. renommé.

familiar /fə'mɪlɪə(r)/ a. familier. **be ~ with**, connaître. **~ity** /-'ærətɪ/ n. familiarité f. **~ize** v.t. familiariser.

family /'fæməlɪ/ n. famille f. —a. de famille, familial.

famine /'fæmɪn/ n. famine f.

famished /'fæmɪʃt/ a. affamé.

famous /'feɪməs/ a. célèbre. **~ly** adv. (very well: fam.) à merveille.

fan[1] /fæn/ n. ventilateur m.; (hand-held) éventail m. —v.t. (p.t. **fanned**) éventer; (fig.) attiser. —v.i. **~ out**, se déployer en éventail. **~ belt**, courroie de ventilateur f.

fan[2] /fæn/ n. (of person) admira|teur, -trice m., f.; (enthusiast) fervent(e) m. (f.), passionné(e) m. (f.).

fanatic /fə'nætɪk/ n. fanatique m./f. **~al** a. fanatique. **~ism** /-sɪzəm/ n. fanatisme m.

fancier /'fænsɪə(r)/ n. (dog/etc.) **~**, amateur (de chiens/etc.) m.

fanciful /'fænsɪfl/ a. fantaisiste.

fancy /'fænsɪ/ n. (whim, fantasy) fantaisie f.; (liking) goût m. —a. (buttons etc.) fantaisie invar.; (prices) extravagant; (impressive) impressionnant. —v.t. s'imaginer; (want: fam.) avoir envie de; (like: fam.) aimer. **take a ~ to s.o.**, se prendre d'affection pour qn. **it took my ~**, ça m'a plu. **~ dress**, travesti m.

fanfare /'fænfeə(r)/ n. fanfare f.

fang /fæŋ/ n. (of dog etc.) croc m.; (of snake) crochet m.

fanlight /'fænlaɪt/ n. imposte f.

fantastic /fæn'tæstɪk/ a. fantastique.

fantas|y /'fæntəsɪ/ n. fantaisie f.; (day-dream) fantasme m. **~ize** v.i. faire des fantasmes.

far /fɑː(r)/ adv. loin; (much) beaucoup; (very) très. —a. lointain; (end, side) autre. **~ away, ~ off**, au loin. **as ~ as**, (up to) jusqu'à. **as ~ as I know**, autant que je sache. **~-away** a. lointain. **the Far East**, l'Extrême-Orient m. **~-fetched** a. bizarre, exagéré. **~-reaching** a. de grande portée.

farc|e /fɑːs/ n. farce f. **~ical** a. ridicule, grotesque.

fare /feə(r)/ n. (prix du) billet m.; (food) nourriture f. —v.i. (progress) aller; (manage) se débrouiller.

farewell /feə'wel/ int. & n. adieu (m.).

farm /fɑːm/ n. ferme f. —v.t. cultiver. —v.i. être fermier. **~ out**, céder en sous-traitance. **~er** n. fermier m. **~ing** n. agriculture f.

farmhouse /'fɑːmhaʊs/ n. ferme f.

farmyard /'fɑːmjɑːd/ n. basse cour f.

farth|er /'fɑːðə(r)/ adv. plus loin. —a. plus éloigné. **~est** adv. le plus loin; a. le plus éloigné.

fascinat|e /'fæsɪneɪt/ v.t. fasciner. **~ion** /-'neɪʃn/ n. fascination f.

Fascis|t /'fæʃɪst/ n. fasciste m./f. **~m** /-zəm/ n. fascisme m.

fashion /'fæʃn/ n. (current style) mode f.; (manner) façon f. —v.t. façonner. **~ designer**, couturier m. **~able** a., **~ably** adv. à la mode.

fast[1] /fɑːst/ a. (-er, -est) rapide; (colour) grand teint invar., fixe; (firm) fixe, solide. —adv. vite; (firmly) ferme. **be ~**, (clock etc.) avancer. **~ asleep**, profondément endormi.

fast[2] /fɑːst/ v.i. (go without food) jeûner. —n. jeûne m.

fasten /'fɑːsn/ v.t./i. (s')attacher. **~er, ~ing** ns. attache f., fermeture f.

fastidious /fə'stɪdɪəs/ a. difficile.

fat /fæt/ n. graisse f.; (on meat) gras m. —a. (fatter, fattest) gros, gras; (meat) gras; (sum, volume: fig.) gros. **a ~ lot**, (sl.) bien peu (of, de). **~-head** n. (fam.) imbécile m., f. **~ness** n. corpulence f.

fatal /'feɪtl/ a. mortel; (fateful, disastrous) fatal. **~ity** /fə'tælətɪ/ n. mort m. **~ly** adv. mortellement.

fatalist /'feɪtəlɪst/ n. fataliste m./f.

fate /feɪt/ n. (controlling power) destin m., sort m.; (one's lot) sort m. **~ful** a. fatidique.

fated /'feɪtɪd/ a. destiné (to, à).

father /'fɑːðə(r)/ n. père m. **~- in-law** n. (pl. **~s-in-law**) beau-père m. **~hood** n. paternité f. **~ly** a. paternel.

fathom /'fæðəm/ n. brasse f. (= 1,8 m.). —v.t. **~ (out)**, comprendre.

fatigue /fə'tiːg/ n. fatigue f. —v.t. fatiguer.

fatten /'fætn/ v.t./i. engraisser. **~ing** a. qui fait grossir.

fatty /'fætɪ/ a. gras; (tissue) adipeux. —n. (person: fam.) gros(se) m. (f.).

fatuous /'fætʃʊəs/ a. stupide.

faucet /'fɔːsɪt/ n. (Amer.) robinet m.

fault /fɔːlt/ n. (defect, failing) défaut

m.; (*blame*) faute *f.*; (*geol.*) faille *f.* —*v.t.* ~ **sth./s.o.**, trouver des défauts à qch./chez qn. **at** ~, fautif. ~**less** *a.* irréprochable. ~**y** *a.* défectueux.

fauna /'fɔːnə/ *n.* faune *f.*

favour /'feɪvə(r)/ *n.* faveur *f.* —*v.t.* favoriser; (*support*) être en faveur de; (*prefer*) préférer. **do s.o. a** ~, rendre service à qn. ~**able** *a.* favorable. ~**ably** *adv.* favorablement.

favourit|e /'feɪvərɪt/ *a. & n.* favori(te) (*m.* (*f.*)). ~**ism** *n.* favoritisme *m.*

fawn[1] /fɔːn/ *n.* faon *m.* —*a.* fauve.

fawn[2] /fɔːn/ *v.i.* ~ **on**, flatter bassement, flagorner.

FBI *abbr.* (*Federal Bureau of Investigation*) (*Amer.*) service d'enquêtes du Ministère de la Justice *m.*

fear /fɪə(r)/ *n.* crainte *f.*, peur *f.*; (*fig.*) risque *m.* —*v.t.* craindre. **for** ~ **of/— that**, de peur de/que. ~**ful** *a.* (*terrible*) affreux; (*timid*) craintif. ~**less** *a.* intrépide. ~**lessness** *n.* intrépidité *f.*

fearsome /'fɪəsəm/ *a.* redoutable.

feasib|le /'fiːzəbl/ *a.* faisable; (*likely*) plausible. ~**ility** /-'bɪlətɪ/ *n.* possibilité *f.*; plausibilité *f.*

feast /fiːst/ *n.* festin *m.*; (*relig.*) fête *f.* —*v.i.* festoyer. —*v.t.* régaler. ~ **on**, se régaler de.

feat /fiːt/ *n.* exploit *m.*

feather /'feðə(r)/ *n.* plume *f.* —*v.t.* ~ **one's nest**, s'enrichir. ~ **duster**, plumeau *m.*

featherweight /'feðəweɪt/ *n.* poids plume *m. invar.*

feature /'fiːtʃə(r)/ *n.* caractéristique *f.*; (*of person, face*) trait *m.*; (*film*) long métrage *m.*; (*article*) article vedette *m.* —*v.t.* représenter; (*give prominence to*) mettre en vedette. —*v.i.* figurer (**in**, dans).

February /'februərɪ/ *n.* février *m.*

feckless /'feklɪs/ *a.* inepte.

fed /fed/ *see* **feed**. —*a.* **be** ~ **up**, (*fam.*) en avoir marre (**with**, de).

federa|l /'fedərəl/ *a.* fédéral. ~**tion** /-'reɪʃn/ *n.* fédération *f.*

fee /fiː/ *n.* (*for entrance*) prix *m.* ~(**s**), (*of doctor etc.*) honoraires *m. pl.*; (*of actor, artist*) cachet *m.*; (*for tuition*) frais *m. pl.*; (*for enrolment*) droits *m. pl.*

feeble /'fiːbl/ *a.* (-**er**, -**est**) faible. ~**minded** *a.* faible d'esprit.

feed /fiːd/ *v.t.* (*p.t.* **fed**) nourrir, donner à manger à; (*suckle*) allaiter; (*supply*)

alimenter. —*v.i.* se nourrir (**on**, de). —*n.* nourriture *f.*; (*of baby*) tétée *f.* **feedback** /'fiːdbæk/ *n.* réaction(s) *f.* (*pl.*).

feel /fiːl/ *v.t.* (*p.t.* **felt**) (*touch*) tâter; (*be conscious of*) sentir; (*experience*) éprouver; (*think*) estimer. —*v.i.* (*tired, lonely, etc.*) se sentir. ~ **hot/ thirsty**/*etc.*, avoir chaud/ soif/*etc.* ~ **as if**, avoir l'impression que. ~ **awful**, (*ill*) se sentir malade. ~ **like**, (*want: fam.*) avoir envie de.

feeler /'fiːlə(r)/ *n.* antenne *f.* **put out a** ~, lancer un ballon d'essai.

feeling /'fiːlɪŋ/ *n.* sentiment *m.*; (*physical*) sensation *f.*

feet /fiːt/ *see* **foot**.

feign /feɪn/ *v.t.* feindre.

feint /feɪnt/ *n.* feinte *f.*

felicitous /fə'lɪsɪtəs/ *a.* heureux.

feline /'fiːlaɪn/ *a.* félin.

fell[1] /fel/ *v.t.* (*cut down*) abattre.

fell[2] /fel/ *see* **fall**.

fellow /'feləʊ/ *n.* compagnon *m.*, camarade *m.*; (*of society*) membre *m.*; (*man: fam.*) type *m.* ~**countryman** *n.* compatriote *m.* ~**passenger**, ~**traveller** *n.* compagnon de voyage *m.* ~**ship** *n.* camaraderie *f.*; (*group*) association *f.*

felony /'felənɪ/ *n.* crime *m.*

felt[1] /felt/ *n.* feutre *m.*

felt[2] /felt/ *see* **feel**.

female /'fiːmeɪl/ *a.* (*animal etc.*) femelle; (*voice, sex, etc.*) féminin. —*n.* femme *f.*; (*animal*) femelle *f.*

feminin|e /'femənɪn/ *a. & n.* féminin (*m.*). ~**ity** /-'nɪnətɪ/ *n.* féminité *f.*

feminist /'femɪnɪst/ *n.* féministe *m./f.*

fenc|e /fens/ *n.* barrière *f.*; (*person: jurid.*) receleu|r, -se *m.*, *f.* —*v.t.* ~**e** (**in**), clôturer. —*v.i.* (*sport*) faire de l'escrime. ~**er** *n.* escrimeu|r, -se *m.*, *f.* ~**ing** *n.* escrime *f.*

fend /fend/ *v.i.* ~ **for o.s.**, se débrouiller tout seul. —*v.t.* ~ **off**, (*blow, attack*) parer.

fender /'fendə(r)/ *n.* (*for fireplace*) garde-feu *m. invar.*; (*mudguard: Amer.*) garde-boue *m. invar.*

fennel /'fenl/ *n.* (*culin.*) fenouil *m.*

ferment[1] /fə'ment/ *v.t./i.* (faire) fermenter. ~**ation** /fɜːmen'teɪʃn/ *n.* fermentation *f.*

ferment[2] /'fɜːment/ *n.* ferment *m.*; (*excitement: fig.*) agitation *f.*

fern /fɜːn/ *n.* fougère *f.*

feroc|ious /fəˈrəʊʃəs/ a. féroce. ~**ity** /-ˈrɒsətɪ/ n. férocité f.

ferret /ˈferɪt/ n. (animal) furet m. —v.i. (p.t. **ferreted**) fureter. —v.t. ~ **out**, dénicher.

ferry /ˈferɪ/ n. ferry(-boat) m., bac m. —v.t. transporter.

fertil|e /ˈfɜːtaɪl, Amer. ˈfɜːtl/ a. fertile; (person, animal) fécond. ~**ity** /fəˈtɪlətɪ/ n. fertilité f.; fécondité f. ~**ize** /-əlaɪz/ v.t. fertiliser; féconder.

fertilizer /ˈfɜːtəlaɪzə(r)/ n. engrais m.

fervent /ˈfɜːvənt/ a. fervent.

fervour /ˈfɜːvə(r)/ n. ferveur f.

fester /ˈfestə(r)/ v.i. (wound) suppurer; (fig.) rester sur le cœur.

festival /ˈfestɪvl/ n. festival m.; (relig.) fête f.

festiv|e /ˈfestɪv/ a. de fête, gai. ~**e season**, période des fêtes f. ~**ity** /feˈstɪvətɪ/ n. réjouissances f. pl.

festoon /feˈstuːn/ v.i. ~ **with**, orner de.

fetch /fetʃ/ v.t. (go for) aller chercher; (bring person) amener; (bring thing) apporter; (be sold for) rapporter.

fête /feɪt/ n. fête f. —v.t. fêter.

fetid /ˈfetɪd/ a. fétide.

fetish /ˈfetɪʃ/ n. (object) fétiche m.; (psych.) obsession f.

fetter /ˈfetə(r)/ v.t. enchaîner. ~**s** n. pl. chaînes f. pl.

feud /fjuːd/ n. querelle f.

feudal /ˈfjuːdl/ a. féodal.

fever /ˈfiːvə(r)/ n. fièvre f. ~**ish** a. fiévreux.

few /fjuː/ a. & n. peu (de). ~ **books**, peu de livres. **they are** ~, ils sont peu nombreux. **a** ~ a. quelques; n. quelques-un(e)s. **a good** ~, **quite a** ~, (fam.) bon nombre (de). ~**er** a. & n. moins (de). **be** ~**er**, être moins nombreux (**than**, que). ~**est** a. & n. le moins (de).

fiancé /fɪˈɒnseɪ/ n. fiancé m.

fiancée /fɪˈɒnseɪ/ n. fiancée f.

fiasco /fɪˈæskəʊ/ n. (pl. -os) fiasco m.

fib /fɪb/ n. mensonge m. ~**ber** n. menteu|r, -se m., f.

fibre /ˈfaɪbə(r)/ n. fibre f.

fibreglass /ˈfaɪbəɡlɑːs/ n. fibre de verre f.

fickle /ˈfɪkl/ a. inconstant.

fiction /ˈfɪkʃn/ n. fiction f. (**works of**) ~, romans m. pl. ~**al** a. fictif.

fictitious /fɪkˈtɪʃəs/ a. fictif.

fiddle /ˈfɪdl/ n. (fam.) violon m.; (swindle: sl.) combine f. —v.i. (sl.)

frauder. —v.t. (sl.) falsifier. ~ **with**, (fam.) tripoter. ~**r** /-ə(r)/ n. (fam.) violoniste m./f.

fidelity /fɪˈdelətɪ/ n. fidélité f.

fidget /ˈfɪdʒɪt/ v.i. (p.t. **fidgeted**) remuer sans cesse. —n. **be a** ~, être remuant. ~ **with**, tripoter. ~**y** a. remuant.

field /fiːld/ n. champ m.; (sport) terrain m.; (fig.) domaine m. —v.t. (ball: cricket) bloquer. ~**-day** n. grande occasion f. ~**-glasses** n. pl. jumelles f. pl. **F~ Marshal**, maréchal m.

fieldwork /ˈfiːldwɜːk/ n. travaux pratiques m. pl.

fiend /fiːnd/ n. démon m. ~**ish** a. diabolique.

fierce /fɪəs/ a. (-er, -est) féroce; (storm, attack) violent. ~**ness** n. férocité f.; violence f.

fiery /ˈfaɪərɪ/ a. (-ier, -iest) (hot) ardent; (spirited) fougueux.

fiesta /fɪˈestə/ n. fiesta f.

fifteen /fɪfˈtiːn/ a. & n. quinze (m.). ~**th** a. & n. quinzième (m./f.).

fifth /fɪfθ/ a. & n. cinquième (m./f.). ~ **column**, cinquième colonne f.

fift|y /ˈfɪftɪ/ a. & n. cinquante (m.). ~**ieth** a. & n. cinquantième (m./f.). **a** ~**y-fifty chance**, (equal) une chance sur deux.

fig /fɪɡ/ n. figue f.

fight /faɪt/ v.i. (p.t. **fought**) se battre; (struggle: fig.) lutter; (quarrel) se disputer. —v.t. se battre avec; (evil etc.: fig.) lutter contre. —n. (struggle) lutte f.; (quarrel) dispute f.; (brawl) bagarre f.; (mil.) combat m. ~ **back**, se défendre. ~ **over sth.**, se disputer qch. ~ **shy of**, fuir devant. ~**er** n. (brawler, soldier) combattant m.; (fig.) battant m.; (aircraft) chasseur m. ~**ing** n. combats m. pl.

figment /ˈfɪɡmənt/ n. invention f.

figurative /ˈfɪɡjərətɪv/ a. figuré.

figure /ˈfɪɡə(r)/ n. (number) chiffre m.; (diagram) figure f.; (shape) forme f.; (of woman) ligne f. ~**s**, arithmétique f. —v.t. s'imaginer. —v.i. (appear) figurer. ~ **out**, comprendre. ~**-head** n. (person with no real power) prête-nom m. ~ **of speech**, façon de parler f. **that** ~**s**, (Amer., fam.) c'est logique.

filament /ˈfɪləmənt/ n. filament m.

filch /fɪltʃ/ v.t. voler, piquer.

fil|e[1] /faɪl/ n. (tool) lime f. —v.t. limer. ~**ings** n. pl. limaille f.

file[2] /faɪl/ n. dossier m., classeur m.;

(*row*) file *f.* —*v.t.* (*papers*) classer.
—*v.i.* ∼ **in**, entrer en file. ∼
past, défiler devant.

fill /fɪl/ *v.t./i.* (se) remplir. —*n.* **eat
one's** ∼, manger à sa faim. **have had
one's** ∼, en avoir assez. ∼ **in**, (*form*)
remplir. ∼ **out**, (*get fat*) grossir. ∼
up, (*auto.*) faire le plein (d'essence).

fillet /'fɪlɪt, *Amer.* fɪ'leɪ/ *n.* filet *m.* —*v.t.*
(*p.t.* **filleted**) découper en filets.

filling /'fɪlɪŋ/ *n.* (*of tooth*) plombage *m.*
∼ **station**, station-service *f.*

filly /'fɪlɪ/ *n.* pouliche *f.*

film /fɪlm/ *n.* film *m.*; (*photo.*) pellicule
f. —*v.t.* filmer. ∼**goer** *n.* cinéphile
m./f. ∼ **star**, vedette de cinéma *f.*

filter /'fɪltə(r)/ *n.* filtre *m.*; (*traffic
signal*) flèche *f.* —*v.t./i.* filtrer; (*of
traffic*) suivre la flèche. ∼**-tip** *n.* bout
filtre *m.*

filth /fɪlθ/ *n.* saleté *f.* ∼**iness** *n.* saleté
f. ∼**y** *a.* sale.

fin /fɪn/ *n.* (*of fish, seal*) nageoire *f.*; (*of
shark*) aileron *m.*

final /'faɪnl/ *a.* dernier; (*conclusive*) définitif. —*n.* (*sport*) finale *f.* ∼**ist** *n.*
finaliste *m./f.* ∼**ly** *adv.* (*lastly, at last*)
enfin, finalement; (*once and for all*)
définitivement.

finale /fɪ'nɑːlɪ/ *n.* (*mus.*) final(e) *m.*

finalize /'faɪnəlaɪz/ *v.t.* mettre au point,
fixer.

financ|e /'faɪnæns/ *n.* finance *f.* —*a.*
financier. —*v.t.* financer. ∼**ier**
/-'nænsɪə(r)/ *n.* financier *m.*

financial /faɪ'nænʃl/ *a.* financier. ∼**ly**
adv. financièrement.

find /faɪnd/ *v.t.* (*p.t.* **found**) trouver;
(*sth. lost*) retrouver. —*n.* trouvaille *f.*
∼ **out** *v.t.* découvrir; *v.i.* se renseigner (**about**, sur). ∼**ings** *n. pl.*
conclusions *f. pl.*

fine[1] /faɪn/ *n.* amende *f.* —*v.t.* condamner à une amende.

fine[2] /faɪn/ *a.* (**-er, -est**) fin; (*excellent*)
beau. —*adv.* (très) bien; (*small*) fin.
∼ **arts**, beaux-arts *m. pl.* ∼**ly** *adv.*
(*admirably*) magnifiquement; (*cut*)
fin.

finery /'faɪnərɪ/ *n.* atours *m. pl.*

finesse /fɪ'nes/ *n.* finesse *f.*

finger /'fɪŋɡə(r)/ *n.* doigt *m.* —*v.t.*
palper. ∼**-nail** *n.* ongle *m.* ∼**stall** *n.*
doigtier *m.*

fingerprint /'fɪŋɡəprɪnt/ *n.* empreinte
digitale *f.*

fingertip /'fɪŋɡətɪp/ *n.* bout du doigt
m.

finicking, finicky /'fɪnɪkɪŋ, 'fɪnɪkɪ/
adjs. méticuleux.

finish /'fɪnɪʃ/ *v.t./i.* finir. —*n.* fin *f.*; (*of
race*) arrivée *f.*; (*appearance*) finition
f. ∼ **doing**, finir de faire. ∼ **up doing**,
finir par faire. ∼ **up in**, (*land up in*)
se retrouver à.

finite /'faɪnaɪt/ *a.* fini.

Fin|land /'fɪnlənd/ *n.* Finlande *f.*
∼**n** *n.* Finlandais(e) *m.* (*f.*). ∼**nish** *a.*
finlandais; *n.* (*lang.*) finnois *m.*

fir /fɜː(r)/ *n.* sapin *m.*

fire /'faɪə(r)/ *n.* feu *m.*; (*conflagration*)
incendie *m.* —*v.t.* (*bullet etc.*) tirer;
(*dismiss*) renvoyer; (*fig.*) enflammer. —*v.i.* tirer (**at**, sur). ∼ **a gun**,
tirer un coup de revolver *or* de fusil.
∼ **brigade**, pompiers *m. pl.* ∼
engine *n.* voiture de pompiers *f.*
∼**-escape** *n.* escalier de secours *m.* ∼
station, caserne de pompiers *f.*

firearm /'faɪərɑːm/ *n.* arme à feu *f.*

firecracker /'faɪəkrækə(r)/ *n.* (*Amer.*)
pétard *m.*

firelight /'faɪəlaɪt/ *n.* lueur du feu *f.*

fireman /'faɪəmən/ *n.* (*pl.* **-men**) pompier *m.*

fireplace /'faɪəpleɪs/ *n.* cheminée *f.*

fireside /'faɪəsaɪd/ *n.* coin du feu *m.*

firewood /'faɪəwʊd/ *n.* bois de chauffage *m.*

firework /'faɪəwɜːk/ *n.* feu d'artifice *m.*

firing-squad /'faɪərɪŋskwɒd/ *n.*
peloton d'exécution *m.*

firm[1] /fɜːm/ *n.* firme *f.*, société *f.*

firm[2] /fɜːm/ *a.* (**-er, -est**) ferme; (*belief*)
solide. ∼**ly** *adv.* fermement. ∼**ness**
n. fermeté *f.*

first /fɜːst/ *a.* premier. —*n.* prem|ier,
-ière *m.*, *f.* —*adv.* d'abord, premièrement; (*arrive etc.*) le premier, la première. **at** ∼, d'abord. **at** ∼ **hand**, de
première main. **at** ∼ **sight**, à première vue. ∼ **aid**, premiers soins
m. pl. ∼**class** *a.* de première classe.
∼ **floor**, (*Amer.*) rez-de-chaussée *m.*
invar. **F**∼ **Lady**, (*Amer.*) épouse du
Président *f.* ∼ **name**, prénom *m.* ∼ **of
all**, tout d'abord. ∼**-rate** *a.* excellent.
∼**ly** *adv.* premièrement.

fiscal /'fɪskl/ *a.* fiscal.

fish /fɪʃ/ *n.* (*usually invar.*) poisson
m. —*v.i.* pêcher. ∼ **for**, (*cod etc.*)
pêcher. ∼ **out**, (*from water*) repêcher;
(*take out: fam.*) sortir. ∼ **shop**, pois-
sonnerie *f.* ∼**ing** *n.* pêche *f.* **go** ∼**ing**,
aller à la pêche. ∼**ing rod**, canne

à pêche *f*. **~y** *a*. de poisson; (*fig.*) louche.

fisherman /'fɪʃəmən/ *n*. (*pl*. **-men**) *n*. pêcheur *m*.

fishmonger /'fɪʃmʌŋgə(r)/ *n*. poisson-n|ier, -ière *m*., *f*.

fission /'fɪʃn/ *n*. fission *f*.

fist /fɪst/ *n*. poing *m*.

fit[1] /fɪt/ *n*. (*bout*) accès *m*., crise *f*.

fit[2] /fɪt/ *a*. (**fitter, fittest**) en bonne santé; (*proper*) convenable; (*good enough*) bon; (*able*) capable. —*v.t./i.* (*p.t.* **fitted**) (*clothes*) aller (à); (*match*) s'accorder (avec); (*put or go in or on*) (s')adapter (**to**, à); (*install*) poser. —*n*. **be a good ~,** (*dress*) être à la bonne taille. **~ out, ~ up,** équiper. **~ness** *n*. santé *f*.; (*of remark*) justesse *f*.

fitful /'fɪtfl/ *a*. irrégulier.

fitment /'fɪtmənt/ *n*. meuble fixe *m*.

fitting /'fɪtɪŋ/ *a*. approprié.

fittings /'fɪtɪŋz/ *n. pl*. (*in house*) installations *f. pl*.

five /faɪv/ *a*. & *n*. cinq (*m*.).

fiver /'faɪvə(r)/ *n*. (*fam.*) billet de cinq livres *m*.

fix /fɪks/ *v.t.* (*make firm, attach, decide*) fixer; (*mend*) réparer; (*deal with*) arranger. —*n*. **in a ~,** dans le pétrin. **~ s.o. up with sth.,** trouver qch. à qn. **~ed** *a*. fixe.

fixation /fɪk'seɪʃn/ *n*. fixation *f*.

fixture /'fɪkstʃə(r)/ *n*. (*sport*) match *m*. **~s,** (*in house*) installations *f. pl*.

fizz /fɪz/ *v.i.* pétiller. —*n*. pétillement *m*. **~y** *a*. gazeux.

fizzle /'fɪzl/ *v.i.* pétiller. **~ out,** (*plan etc.*) finir en queue de poisson.

flab /flæb/ *n*. (*fam.*) corpulence *f*. **~by** /'flæbɪ/ *a*. flasque.

flabbergast /'flæbəgɑːst/ *v.t.* sidérer, ahurir.

flag[1] /flæg/ *n*. drapeau *m*.; (*naut.*) pavillon *m*. —*v.t.* (*p.t.* **flagged**) **~ (down),** faire signe de s'arrêter à. **~-pole** *n*. mât *m*.

flag[2] /flæg/ *v.i.* (*p.t.* **flagged**) (*weaken*) faiblir; (*sick person*) s'affaiblir; (*droop*) dépérir.

flagon /'flægən/ *n*. bouteille *f*.

flagrant /'fleɪgrənt/ *a*. flagrant.

flagstone /'flægstəʊn/ *n*. dalle *f*.

flair /fleə(r)/ *n*. flair *m*.

flak|e /fleɪk/ *n*. flocon *m*.; (*of paint, metal*) écaille *f*. —*v.i.* s'écailler. **~y** *a*. (*paint*) écailleux.

flamboyant /flæm'bɔɪənt/ *a*. (*colour*) éclatant; (*manner*) extravagant.

flame /fleɪm/ *n*. flamme *f*. —*v.i.* flamber.

flamingo /flə'mɪŋgəʊ/ *n*. (*pl*. **-os**) flamant (rose) *m*.

flammable /'flæməbl/ *a*. inflammable.

flan /flæn/ *n*. tarte *f*.; (*custard tart*) flan *m*.

flank /flæŋk/ *n*. flanc *m*. —*v.t.* flanquer.

flannel /'flænl/ *n*. flannelle *f*.; (*for face*) gant de toilette *m*.

flannelette /flænə'let/ *n*. pilou *m*.

flap /flæp/ *v.i.* (*p.t.* **flapped**) battre. —*v.t.* **~ its wings,** battre des ailes. —*n*. (*of pocket*) rabat *m*.; (*of table*) abattant *m*. **get into a ~,** (*fam.*) s'affoler.

flare /fleə(r)/ *v.i.* **~ up,** s'enflammer, flamber; (*fighting*) éclater; (*person*) s'emporter. —*n*. flamboiement *m*.; (*mil.*) fusée éclairante *f*.; (*in skirt*) évasement *m*. **~d** *a*. (*skirt*) évasé.

flash /flæʃ/ *v.i.* briller; (*on and off*) clignoter. —*v.t.* faire briller; (*aim torch*) diriger (**at**, sur); (*flaunt*) étaler. —*n*. éclair *m*., éclat *m*.; (*of news, camera*) flash *m*. **~ past,** passer à toute vitesse.

flashback /'flæʃbæk/ *n*. retour en arrière *m*.

flashlight /'flæʃlaɪt/ *n*. (*torch*) lampe électrique *f*.

flashy /'flæʃɪ/ *a*. voyant.

flask /flɑːsk/ *n*. flacon *m*.; (*vacuum flask*) thermos *m.*/*f. invar.* (P.).

flat /flæt/ *a*. (**flatter, flattest**) plat; (*tyre*) à plat; (*refusal*) catégorique; (*fare, rate*) fixe. —*adv*. (*say*) carrément. —*n*. (*rooms*) appartement *m*.; (*tyre: fam.*) crevaison *f*.; (*mus.*) bémol *m*. **~ out,** à toute vitesse. **~ly** *adv*. catégoriquement. **~ness** *n*. égalité *f*.

flatten /'flætn/ *v.t./i.* (s')aplatir.

flatter /'flaetə(r)/ *v.t.* flatter. **~er** *n*. flatteu|r, -se *m*., *f*. **~ing** *a*. flatteur. **~y** *n*. flatterie *f*.

flatulence /'flætjʊləns/ *n*. flatulence *f*.

flaunt /flɔːnt/ *v.t.* étaler, afficher.

flautist /'flɔːtɪst/ *n*. flûtiste *m.*/*f*.

flavour /'fleɪvə(r)/ *n*. goût *m*.; (*of ice-cream etc.*) parfum *m*. —*v.t.* parfumer, assaisonner. **~ing** *n*. arôme synthétique *m*.

flaw /flɔː/ *n*. défaut *m*. **~ed** *a*. imparfait. **~less** *a*. parfait.

flax /flæks/ *n*. lin *m*. **~en** *a*. de lin.

flea /fliː/ *n*. puce *f*. **~ market,** (*hum.*) marché aux puces *m*.

fleck /flek/ n. petite tache f.

fled /fled/ see **flee**.

fledged /fledʒd/ a. **fully-~**, (doctor etc.) diplômé; (member, citizen) à part entière.

flee /fliː/ v.i. (p.t. **fled**) s'enfuir. —v.t. s'enfuir de; (danger) fuir.

fleece /fliːs/ n. toison f. —v.t. voler.

fleet /fliːt/ n. (naut., aviat.) flotte f. **a ~ of vehicles**, un parc automobile.

fleeting /ˈfliːtɪŋ/ a. très bref.

Flemish /ˈflemɪʃ/ a. flamand. —n. (lang.) flamand m.

flesh /fleʃ/ n. chair f. **one's (own) ~ and blood**, les siens m. pl. **~y** a. charnu.

flew /fluː/ see **fly²**.

flex¹ /fleks/ v.t. (knee etc.) fléchir; (muscle) faire jouer.

flex² /fleks/ n. (electr.) fil souple m.

flexib|le /ˈfleksəbl/ a. flexible. **~ility** /-ˈbɪlətɪ/ n. flexibilité f.

flexitime /ˈfleksɪtaɪm/ n. horaire variable m.

flick /flɪk/ n. petit coup m. —v.t. donner un petit coup à. **~-knife** n. couteau à cran d'arrêt m.

flicker /ˈflɪkə(r)/ v.i. vaciller. —n. vacillement m.; (light) lueur f.

flier /ˈflaɪə(r)/ n. = **flyer**.

flies /flaɪz/ n. pl. (on trousers: fam.) braguette f.

flight¹ /flaɪt/ n. (of bird, plane, etc.) vol m. **~-deck** n. poste de pilotage m. **~ of stairs**, escalier m.

flight² /flaɪt/ n. (fleeing) fuite f. **put to ~**, mettre en fuite. **take (to) ~**, prendre la fuite.

flighty /ˈflaɪtɪ/ a. (-ier, -iest) frivole, volage.

flimsy /ˈflɪmzɪ/ a. (-ier, -iest) (pej.) mince, peu solide.

flinch /flɪntʃ/ v.i. (wince) broncher; (draw back) reculer.

fling /flɪŋ/ v.t. (p.t. **flung**) jeter. —n. **have a ~**, faire la fête.

flint /flɪnt/ n. silex m.; (for lighter) pierre f.

flip /flɪp/ v.t. (p.t. **flipped**) donner un petit coup à. —n. chiquenaude f. **~ through**, feuilleter. **the ~ side**, (of record) l'autre face f.

flippant /ˈflɪpənt/ a. désinvolte.

flipper /ˈflɪpə(r)/ n. (of seal etc.) nageoire f.; (of swimmer) palme f.

flirt /flɜːt/ v.i. flirter. —n. flirteu|r, -se m., f. **~ation** /-ˈteɪʃn/ n. flirt m.

flit /flɪt/ v.i. (p.t. **flitted**) voltiger.

float /fləʊt/ v.t./i. (faire) flotter. —n. flotteur m.; (cart) char m.

flock /flɒk/ n. (of sheep etc.) troupeau m.; (of people) foule f. —v.i. venir en foule.

flog /flɒg/ v.t. (p.t. **flogged**) (beat) fouetter; (sell: sl.) vendre.

flood /flʌd/ n. inondation f.; (fig.) flot m. —v.t. inonder. —v.i. (building etc.) être inondé; (river) déborder; (people, fig.) affluer.

floodlight /ˈflʌdlaɪt/ n. projecteur m. —v.t. (p.t. **floodlit**) illuminer.

floor /flɔː(r)/ n. sol m., plancher m.; (for dancing) piste f.; (storey) étage m. —v.t. (knock down) terrasser; (baffle) stupéfier.

flop /flɒp/ v.i. (p.t. **flopped**) s'agiter faiblement; (drop) s'affaler; (fail: sl.) échouer. —n. (sl.) échec m., fiasco m. **~py** a. lâche, flasque.

flora /ˈflɔːrə/ n. flore f.

floral /ˈflɔːrəl/ a. floral.

florid /ˈflɒrɪd/ a. fleuri.

florist /ˈflɒrɪst/ n. fleuriste m./f.

flounce /flaʊns/ n. volant m.

flounder¹ /ˈflaʊndə(r)/ v.i. patauger (avec difficulté).

flounder² /ˈflaʊndə(r)/ n. (fish: Amer.) flet m., plie f.

flour /ˈflaʊə(r)/ n. farine f. **~y** a. farineux.

flourish /ˈflʌrɪʃ/ v.i. prospérer. —v.t. brandir. —n. geste élégant m.; (curve) fioriture f.

flout /flaʊt/ v.t. faire fi de.

flow /fləʊ/ v.i. couler; (circulate) circuler; (traffic) s'écouler; (hang loosely) flotter. —n. (of liquid, traffic) écoulement m.; (of tide) flux m.; (of orders, words: fig.) flot m. **~ chart**, organigramme m. **~ in**, affluer. **~ into**, (of river) se jeter dans.

flower /ˈflaʊə(r)/ n. fleur f. —v.i. fleurir. **~-bed** n. plate-bande f. **~ed** a. à fleurs. **~y** a. fleuri.

flown /fləʊn/ see **fly²**.

flu /fluː/ n. (fam.) grippe f.

fluctuat|e /ˈflʌktʃʊeɪt/ v.i. varier. **~ion** /-ˈeɪʃn/ n. variation f.

flue /fluː/ n. (duct) tuyau m.

fluen|t /ˈfluːənt/ a. (style) aisé. **be ~t (in a language)**, parler (une langue) couramment. **~cy** n. facilité f. **~tly** adv. avec facilité; (lang.) couramment.

fluff /flʌf/ n. peluche(s) f. (pl.); (down) duvet m. **~y** a. pelucheux.

fluid /'fluːɪd/ a. & n. fluide (m.).

fluke /fluːk/ n. coup de chance m.

flung /flʌŋ/ see **fling**.

flunk /flʌŋk/ v.t./i. (Amer., fam.) être collé (à).

fluorescent /fluəˈresnt/ a. fluorescent.

fluoride /'fluəraɪd/ n. (in toothpaste, water) fluor m.

flurry /'flʌrɪ/ n. (squall) rafale f.; (fig.) agitation f.

flush[1] /flʌʃ/ v.i. rougir. —v.t. nettoyer à grande eau. —n. (blush) rougeur f.; (fig.) excitation f. —a. ~ **with**, (level with) au ras de. ~ **the toilet,** tirer la chasse d'eau.

flush[2] /flʌʃ/ v.t. ~ **out**, chasser.

fluster /'flʌstə(r)/ v.t. énerver.

flute /fluːt/ n. flûte f.

flutter /'flʌtə(r)/ v.i. voleter; (of wings) battre. —n. (of wings) battement m.; (fig.) agitation f.

flux /flʌks/ n. changement continuel m.

fly[1] /flaɪ/ n. mouche f.

fly[2] /flaɪ/ v.i. (p.t. **flew**, p.p. **flown**) voler; (of passengers) voyager en avion; (of flag) flotter; (rush) aller à toute vitesse. —v.t. (aircraft) piloter; (passengers, goods) transporter par avion; (flag) arborer. —n. (of trousers) braguette f.

flyer /'flaɪə(r)/ n. aviateur m.; (circular: Amer.) prospectus m.

flying /'flaɪɪŋ/ a. (saucer etc.) volant. —n. (activity) aviation f. ~ **buttress,** arc-boutant m. **with** ~ **colours,** haut la main. ~ **start,** excellent départ m. ~ **visit,** visite éclair f. (a. invar.).

flyover /'flaɪəʊvə(r)/ n. (road) toboggan m., saut-de-mouton m.

flyweight /'flaɪweɪt/ n. poids mouche m.

foal /fəʊl/ n. poulain m.

foam /fəʊm/ n. écume f., mousse f. —v.i. écumer, mousser. ~ (**rubber**) n. caoutchouc mousse m.

fob /fɒb/ v.t. (p.t. **fobbed**). ~ **off on (to) s.o.,** (palm off) refiler à qn. ~ **s.o. off with,** amener qn. à accepter par la ruse.

focal /'fəʊkl/ a. focal.

focus /'fəʊkəs/ n. (pl. -**cuses** or -**ci** /-saɪ/) foyer m.; (fig.) centre m. —v.t./i. (p.t. **focused**) (faire) converger; (instrument) mettre au point; (fig.) (se) concentrer. **be in/out of** ~, être/ne pas être au point.

fodder /'fɒdə(r)/ n. fourrage m.

foe /fəʊ/ n. ennemi(e) m.(f.).

foetus /'fiːtəs/ n. (pl. -**tuses**) fœtus m.

fog /fɒg/ n. brouillard m. —v.t./i. (p.t. **fogged**) (window etc.) (s')embuer. ~-**horn** n. (naut.) corne de brume f. ~**gy** a. brumeux. **it is** ~**gy**, il fait du brouillard.

fog(e)y /'fəʊgɪ/ n. (old) ~, vieille baderne f.

foible /'fɔɪbl/ n. faiblesse f.

foil[1] /fɔɪl/ n. (tin foil) papier d'aluminium m.; (fig.) repoussoir m.

foil[2] /fɔɪl/ v.t. (thwart) déjouer.

foist /fɔɪst/ v.t. imposer (on, à).

fold[1] /fəʊld/ v.t./i. (se) plier; (arms) croiser; (fail) s'effondrer. —n. pli m. ~**er** n. (file) chemise f.; (leaflet) dépliant m. ~**ing** a. pliant.

fold[2] /fəʊld/ n. (for sheep) parc à moutons m.; (relig.) bercail m.

foliage /'fəʊlɪdʒ/ n. feuillage m.

folk /fəʊk/ n. gens m. pl. ~**s**, parents m. pl. —a. folklorique.

folklore /'fəʊklɔː(r)/ n. folklore m.

follow /'fɒləʊ/ v.t./i. suivre. **it** ~**s that,** il s'ensuit que. ~ **suit,** en faire autant. ~ **up,** (letter etc.) donner suite à. ~**er** n. partisan m. ~**ing** n. partisans m. pl.; a. suivant; prep. à la suite de.

folly /'fɒlɪ/ n. sottise f.

foment /fəʊˈment/ v.t. fomenter.

fond /fɒnd/ a. (-**er**, -**est**) (loving) affectueux; (hope) cher. **be** ~ **of,** aimer. ~**ness** n. affection f.; (for things) attachement m.

fondle /'fɒndl/ v.t. caresser.

food /fuːd/ n. nourriture f. —a. alimentaire. ~ **processor,** robot (ménager) m.

fool /fuːl/ n. idiot(e) m. (f.). —v.t. duper. —v.i. faire l'idiot.

foolhardy /'fuːlhɑːdɪ/ a. téméraire.

foolish /'fuːlɪʃ/ a. idiot. ~**ly** adv. sottement. ~**ness** n. sottise f.

foolproof /'fuːlpruːf/ a. infaillible.

foot /fʊt/ n. (pl. **feet**) pied m.; (measure) pied m. (= 30.48 cm.); (of stairs, page) bas m. —v.t. (bill) payer. ~-**bridge** n. passerelle f. **on** ~, à pied. **on** or **to one's feet,** debout. **under s.o.'s feet,** dans les jambes de qn.

footage /'fʊtɪdʒ/ n. (of film) métrage m.

football /'fʊtbɔːl/ n. (ball) ballon m.; (game) football m. ~ **pools,** paris sur les matchs de football m. pl. ~**er** n. footballeur m.

foothills /'fʊthɪlz/ *n. pl.* contreforts *m. pl.*

foothold /'fʊthəʊld/ *n.* prise *f.*

footing /'fʊtɪŋ/ *n.* prise (de pied) *f.,* équilibre *m.;* (*fig.*) situation *f.* **on an equal ∼,** sur un pied d'égalité.

footlights /'fʊtlaɪts/ *n. pl.* rampe *f.*

footman /'fʊtmən/ *n.* (*pl.* **-men**) valet de pied *m.*

footnote /'fʊtnəʊt/ *n.* note (en bas de la page) *f.*

footpath /'fʊtpɑ:θ/ *n.* sentier *m.;* (*at the side of the road*) chemin *m.*

footprint /'fʊtprɪnt/ *n.* empreinte (de pied) *f.*

footsore /'fʊtsɔ:(r)/ *a.* **be ∼,** avoir les pieds douloureux.

footstep /'fʊtstep/ *n.* pas *m.*

footwear /'fʊtweə(r)/ *n.* chaussures *f. pl.*

for /fɔ:(r), *unstressed* fə(r)/ *prep.* pour; (*in spite of*) malgré; (*during*) pendant; (*before*) avant. —*conj.* car. **a liking ∼,** le goût de. **he has been away ∼,** il est absent depuis. **∼ ever,** pour toujours. **∼ good,** pour de bon.

forage /'fɒrɪdʒ/ *v.i.* fourrager. —*n.* fourrage *m.*

foray /'fɒreɪ/ *n.* incursion *f.*

forbade /fə'bæd/ *see* **forbid.**

forbear /fɔ:'beə(r)/ *v.t./i.* (*p.t.* **forbore,** *p.p.* **forborne**) s'abstenir. **∼ance** *n.* patience *f.*

forbid /fə'bɪd/ *v.t.* (*p.t.* **forbade,** *p.p.* **forbidden**) interdire, défendre (**s.o. to do,** à qn. de faire). **∼ s.o. sth.,** interdire *or* défendre qch. à qn. **you are ∼den to leave,** il vous est interdit de partir.

forbidding /fə'bɪdɪŋ/ *a.* menaçant.

force /fɔ:s/ *n.* force *f.* —*v.t.* forcer. **∼ into,** faire entrer de force. **∼ on,** imposer à. **come into ∼,** entrer en vigueur. **the ∼s,** les forces armées *f. pl.* **∼d** *a.* forcé. **∼ful** *a.* énergique.

force-feed /'fɔ:sfi:d/ *v.t.* (*p.t.* **-fed**) nourrir de force.

forceps /'fɔ:seps/ *n. invar.* forceps *m.*

forcibl|e /'fɔ:səbl/ *a.,* **∼y** *adv.* de force.

ford /fɔ:d/ *n.* gué *m.* —*v.t.* passer à gué.

fore /fɔ:(r)/ *a.* antérieur. —*n.* **to the ∼,** en évidence.

forearm /'fɔ:rɑ:m/ *n.* avant-bras *m. invar.*

foreboding /fɔ:'bəʊdɪŋ/ *n.* pressentiment *m.*

forecast /'fɔ:kɑ:st/ *v.t.* (*p.t.* **forecast**) prévoir. —*n.* prévision *f.*

forecourt /'fɔ:kɔ:t/ *n.* (*of garage*) devant *m.;* (*of station*) cour *f.*

forefathers /'fɔ:fɑ:ðəz/ *n. pl.* aïeux *m. pl.*

forefinger /'fɔ:fɪŋɡə(r)/ *n.* index *m.*

forefront /'fɔ:frʌnt/ *n.* premier rang *m.*

foregone /'fɔ:ɡɒn/ *a.* **∼ conclusion,** résultat à prévoir *m.*

foreground /'fɔ:ɡraʊnd/ *n.* premier plan *m.*

forehead /'fɒrɪd/ *n.* front *m.*

foreign /'fɒrən/ *a.* étranger; (*trade*) extérieur; (*travel*) à l'étranger. **∼er** *n.* étrang|er, -ère *m., f.*

foreman /'fɔ:mən/ *n.* (*pl.* **-men**) contremaître *m.*

foremost /'fɔ:məʊst/ *a.* le plus éminent. —*adv.* **first and ∼,** tout d'abord.

forensic /fə'rensɪk/ *a.* médico-légal. **∼ medicine,** médecine légale *f.*

forerunner /'fɔ:rʌnə(r)/ *n.* précurseur *m.*

foresee /fɔ:'si:/ *v.t.* (*p.t.* **-saw,** *p.p.* **-seen**) prévoir. **∼able** *a.* prévisible.

foreshadow /fɔ:'ʃædəʊ/ *v.t.* présager, laisser prévoir.

foresight /'fɔ:saɪt/ *n.* prévoyance *f.*

forest /'fɒrɪst/ *n.* forêt *f.*

forestall /fɔ:'stɔ:l/ *v.t.* devancer.

forestry /'fɒrɪstrɪ/ *n.* sylviculture *f.*

foretaste /'fɔ:teɪst/ *n.* avant-goût *m.*

foretell /fɔ:'tel/ *v.t.* (*p.t.* **foretold**) prédire.

forever /fə'revə(r)/ *adv.* toujours.

forewarn /fɔ:'wɔ:n/ *v.t.* avertir.

foreword /'fɔ:wɜ:d/ *n.* avant-propos *m. invar.*

forfeit /'fɔ:fɪt/ *n.* (*penalty*) peine *f.;* (*in game*) gage *m.* —*v.t.* perdre.

forgave /fə'ɡeɪv/ *see* **forgive.**

forge[1] /fɔ:dʒ/ *v.i.* **∼ ahead,** aller de l'avant, avancer.

forge[2] /fɔ:dʒ/ *n.* forge *f.* —*v.t.* (*metal, friendship*) forger; (*copy*) contrefaire, falsifier. **∼r** /-ə(r)/ *n.* faussaire *m.* **∼ry** /-ərɪ/ *n.* faux *m.,* contrefaçon *f.*

forget /fə'ɡet/ *v.t./i.* (*p.t.* **forgot,** *p.p.* **forgotten**) oublier. **∼-me-not** *n.* myosotis *m.* **∼ o.s.,** s'oublier. **∼ful** *a.* distrait. **∼ful of,** oublieux de.

forgive /fə'ɡɪv/ *v.t.* (*p.t.* **forgave,** *p.p.* **forgiven**) pardonner (**s.o. for sth.,** qch. à qn.). **∼ness** *n.* pardon *m.*

forgo /fɔ:'ɡəʊ/ *v.t.* (*p.t.* **forwent,** *p.p.* **forgone**) renoncer à.

fork /fɔ:k/ *n.* fourchette *f.;* (*for digging*

etc.) fourche *f.*; (*in road*) bifurcation *f.* −*v.i.* (*road*) bifurquer. **~-lift truck,** chariot élévateur *m.* **~ out,** (*sl.*) payer. **~ed** *a.* fourchu.

forlorn /fə'lɔːn/ *a.* triste, abandonné. **~ hope,** mince espoir *m.*

form /fɔːm/ *n.* forme *f.*; (*document*) formulaire *m.*; (*schol.*) classe *f.* −*v.t./i.* (se) former.

formal /'fɔːml/ *a.* officiel, en bonne et due forme; (*person*) compassé, cérémonieux; (*dress*) de cérémonie; (*denial, grammar*) formel. **~ity** /-'mælətɪ/ *n.* cérémonial *m.*; (*requirement*) formalité *f.* **~ly** *adv.* officiellement.

format /'fɔːmæt/ *n.* format *m.*

formation /fɔː'meɪʃn/ *n.* formation *f.*

formative /'fɔːmətɪv/ *a.* formateur.

former /'fɔːmə(r)/ *a.* ancien; (*first of two*) premier. −*n.* the **~,** celui-là, celle-là. **~ly** *adv.* autrefois.

formidable /'fɔːmɪdəbl/ *a.* redoutable, terrible.

formula /'fɔːmjʊlə/ *n.* (*pl.* -ae /-iː/ *or* -as) formule *f.*

formulate /'fɔːmjʊleɪt/ *v.t.* formuler.

forsake /fə'seɪk/ *v.t.* (*p.t.* forsook, *p.p.* forsaken) abandonner.

fort /fɔːt/ *n.* (*mil.*) fort *m.*

forte /'fɔːteɪ/ *n.* (*talent*) fort *m.*

forth /fɔːθ/ *adv.* en avant. **go back and ~,** aller et venir.

forthcoming /fɔːθ'kʌmɪŋ/ *a.* à venir, prochain; (*sociable: fam.*) communicatif.

forthright /'fɔːθraɪt/ *a.* direct.

forthwith /fɔːθ'wɪθ/ *adv.* sur-le-champ.

fortif|y /'fɔːtɪfaɪ/ *v.t.* fortifier. **~ication** /-ɪ'keɪʃn/ *n.* fortification *f.*

fortitude /'fɔːtɪtjuːd/ *n.* courage *m.*

fortnight /'fɔːtnaɪt/ *n.* quinze jours *m. pl.*, quinzaine *f.* **~ly** *a.* bimensuel; *adv.* tous les quinze jours.

fortress /'fɔːtrɪs/ *n.* forteresse *f.*

fortuitous /fɔː'tjuːɪtəs/ *a.* fortuit.

fortunate /'fɔːtʃənət/ *a.* heureux. **be ~,** avoir de la chance. **~ly** *adv.* heureusement.

fortune /'fɔːtʃuːn/ *n.* fortune *f.* **~-teller** *n.* diseuse de bonne aventure *f.* **have the good ~ to,** avoir la chance de.

fort|y /'fɔːtɪ/ *a. & n.* quarante (*m.*). **~y winks,** un petit somme. **~ieth** *a. & n.* quarantième (*m./f.*).

forum /'fɔːrəm/ *n.* forum *m.*

forward /'fɔːwəd/ *a.* en avant; (*ad-*

vanced) précoce; (*pert*) effronté. −*n.* (*sport*) avant *m.* −*adv.* en avant. −*v.t.* (*letter*) faire suivre; (*goods*) expédier; (*fig.*) favoriser. **come ~,** se présenter. **go ~,** avancer. **~ness** *n.* précocité *f.*

forwards /'fɔːwədz/ *adv.* en avant.

fossil /'fɒsl/ *n. & a.* fossile (*m.*).

foster /'fɒstə(r)/ *v.t.* (*promote*) encourager; (*child*) élever. **~child** *n.* enfant adoptif *m.* **~mother** *n.* mère adoptive *f.*

fought /fɔːt/ *see* **fight.**

foul /faʊl/ *a.* (-er, -est) (*smell, weather, etc.*) infect; (*place, action*) immonde; (*language*) ordurier. −*n.* (*football*) faute *f.* −*v.t.* souiller, encrasser. **~-mouthed** *a.* au langage ordurier. **~ play,** jeu irrégulier *m.*; (*crime*) acte criminel *m.* **~ up,** (*sl.*) gâcher.

found[1] /faʊnd/ *see* **find.**

found[2] /faʊnd/ *v.t.* fonder. **~ation** /-'deɪʃn/ *n.* fondation *f.*; (*basis*) fondement *m.* **~er**[1] *n.* fonda|teur, -trice *m., f.*

founder[2] /'faʊndə(r)/ *v.i.* sombrer.

foundry /'faʊndrɪ/ *n.* fonderie *f.*

fountain /'faʊntɪn/ *n.* fontaine *f.* **~pen** *n.* stylo à encre *m.*

four /fɔː(r)/ *a. & n.* quatre (*m.*). **~fold** *a.* quadruple; *adv.* au quadruple. **~th** *a. & n.* quatrième (*m./f.*).

foursome /'fɔːsəm/ *n.* partie à quatre *f.*

fourteen /fɔː'tiːn/ *a. & n.* quatorze (*m.*). **~th** *a. & n.* quatorzième (*m./f.*).

fowl /faʊl/ *n.* volaille *f.*

fox /fɒks/ *n.* renard *m.* −*v.t.* (*baffle*) mystifier; (*deceive*) tromper.

foyer /'fɔɪeɪ/ *n.* (*hall*) foyer *m.*

fraction /'frækʃn/ *n.* fraction *f.*

fracture /'fræktʃə(r)/ *n.* fracture *f.* −*v.t./i.* (se) fracturer.

fragile /'frædʒaɪl, *Amer.* 'frædʒəl/ *a.* fragile.

fragment /'frægmənt/ *n.* fragment *m.* **~ary** *a.* fragmentaire.

fragran|t /'freɪgrənt/ *a.* parfumé. **~ce** *n.* parfum *m.*

frail /freɪl/ *a.* (-er, -est) frêle.

frame /freɪm/ *n.* charpente *f.*; (*of picture*) cadre *m.*; (*of window*) châssis *m.*; (*of spectacles*) monture *f.* −*v.t.* encadrer; (*fig.*) formuler; (*jurid., sl.*) monter un coup contre. **~ of mind,** humeur *f.*

framework /'freɪmwɜːk/ *n.* structure *f.*; (*context*) cadre *m.*

franc /fræŋk/ *n.* franc *m.*

France /frɑːns/ *n.* France *f.*

franchise /'fræntʃaɪz/ *n.* (*pol.*) droit de vote *m.*; (*comm.*) concession *f.*

Franco- 'fræŋkəʊ/ *pref.* franco-.

frank[1] /fræŋk/ *a.* franc. **~ly** *adv.* franchement. **~ness** *n.* franchise *f.*

frank[2] /fræŋk/ *v.t.* affranchir.

frantic /'fræntɪk/ *a.* frénétique. **~ with,** fou de.

fratern|al /frə'tɜːnl/ *a.* fraternel. **~ity** *n.* (*bond*) fraternité *f.*; (*group, club*) confrérie *f.*

fraternize /'frætənaɪz/ *v.i.* fraterniser (**with,** avec).

fraud /frɔːd/ *n.* (*deception*) fraude *f.*; (*person*) imposteur *m.* **~ulent** *a.* frauduleux.

fraught /frɔːt/ *a.* (*tense*) tendu. **~ with,** chargé de.

fray[1] /freɪ/ *n.* rixe *f.*

fray[2] /freɪ/ *v.t./i.* (s')effilocher.

freak /friːk/ *n.* phénomène *m.* —*a.* anormal. **~ish** *a.* anormal.

freckle /'frekl/ *n.* tache de rousseur *f.* **~d** *a.* couvert de taches de rousseur.

free /friː/ *a.* (**freer** /'friːə(r)/, **freest** /'friːɪst/) libre; (*gratis*) gratuit; (*lavish*) généreux. —*v.t.* (*p.t.* **freed**) libérer; (*clear*) dégager. **a ~ hand,** carte blanche *f.* **~ kick,** coup franc *m.* **~ lance,** collabora|teur, -trice indépendant(e) *m., f.* **~ of charge,** gratuit(ement). **~-range** *a.* (*eggs*) de ferme. **~ly** *adv.* librement.

freedom /'friːdəm/ *n.* liberté *f.*

Freemason /'friːmeɪsn/ *n.* franc-maçon *m.* **~ry** *n.* franc-maçonnerie *f.*

freeway /'friːweɪ/ *n.* (*Amer.*) autoroute *f.*

freez|e /friːz/ *v.t./i.* (*p.t.* **froze,** *p.p.* **frozen**) geler; (*culin.*) (se) congeler; (*wages etc.*) bloquer. —*n.* gel *m.*; blocage *m.* **~er** *n.* congélateur *m.* **~ing** *a.* glacial. **below ~ing,** au-dessous de zéro.

freight /freɪt/ *n.* fret *m.* **~er** *n.* (*ship*) cargo *m.*

French /frentʃ/ *a.* français. —*n.* (*lang.*) français *m.* **~-speaking** *a.* francophone. **~ window** *n.* porte-fenêtre *f.* **the ~,** les Français *m. pl.* **~man** *n.* Français *m.* **~woman** *n.* Française *f.*

frenz|y /'frenzɪ/ *n.* frénésie *f.* **~ied** *a.* frénétique.

frequen|t[1] /'friːkwənt/ *a.* fréquent. **~cy** *n.* fréquence *f.* **~tly** *adv.* fréquemment.

frequent[2] /frɪ'kwent/ *v.t.* fréquenter.

fresco /'freskəʊ/ *n.* (*pl.* **-os**) fresque *f.*

fresh /freʃ/ *a.* (**-er, -est**) frais; (*different, additional*) nouveau; (*cheeky: fam.*) culotté. **~ water,** eau douce *f.* **~ly** *adv.* nouvellement. **~ness** *n.* fraîcheur *f.*

freshen /'freʃn/ *v.i.* (*weather*) fraîchir. **~ up,** (*person*) se rafraîchir.

fret /fret/ *v.i.* (*p.t.* **fretted**) se tracasser. **~ful** *a.* ronchon, insatisfait.

friar /'fraɪə(r)/ *n.* moine *m.*, frère *m.*

friction /'frɪkʃn/ *n.* friction *f.*

Friday /'fraɪdɪ/ *n.* vendredi *m.*

fridge /frɪdʒ/ *n.* frigo *m.*

fried /fraɪd/ *see* **fry.** —*a.* frit.

friend /frend/ *n.* ami(e) *m.* (*f.*). **~ship** *n.* amitié *f.*

friendl|y /'frendlɪ/ *a.* (**-ier, -iest**) amical, gentil. **F~y Society,** mutuelle *f.*, société de prévoyance *f.* **~iness** *n.* gentillesse *f.*

frieze /friːz/ *n.* frise *f.*

frigate /'frɪgət/ *n.* frégate *f.*

fright /fraɪt/ *n.* peur *f.*; (*person, thing*) horreur *f.* **~ful** *a.* affreux. **~fully** *adv.* affreusement.

frighten /'fraɪtn/ *v.t.* effrayer. **~ off,** faire fuir. **~ed** *a.* effrayé. **be ~ed,** avoir peur (**of,** de).

frigid /'frɪdʒɪd/ *a.* froid, glacial; (*psych.*) frigide. **~ity** /-'dʒɪdətɪ/ *n.* frigidité *f.*

frill /frɪl/ *n.* (*trimming*) fanfreluche *f.* **with no ~s,** très simple.

fringe /frɪndʒ/ *n.* (*edging, hair*) frange *f.*; (*of area*) bordure *f.*; (*of society*) marge *f.* **~ benefits,** avantages sociaux *m. pl.*

frisk /frɪsk/ *v.t.* (*search*) fouiller.

frisky /'frɪskɪ/ *a.* (**-ier, -iest**) fringant, frétillant.

fritter[1] /'frɪtə(r)/ *n.* beignet *m.*

fritter[2] /'frɪtə(r)/ *v.t.* **~ away,** gaspiller.

frivol|ous /'frɪvələs/ *a.* frivole. **~ity** /-'vɒlətɪ/ *n.* frivolité *f.*

frizzy /'frɪzɪ/ *a.* crépu, crêpelé.

fro /frəʊ/ *see* **to and fro.**

frock /frɒk/ *n.* robe *f.*

frog /frɒg/ *n.* grenouille *f.* **a ~ in one's throat,** un chat dans la gorge.

frogman /'frɒgmən/ *n.* (*pl.* **-men**) homme-grenouille *m.*

frolic /'frɒlɪk/ *v.i.* (*p.t.* **frolicked**) s'ébattre. —*n.* ébats *m. pl.*

from /frɒm, *unstressed* frəm/ *prep.* de; (*with time, prices, etc.*) à partir de, de; (*out of*) dans; (*habit, conviction, etc.*)

par; (*according to*) d'après. **take ~**, (*away from*) prendre à.

front /frʌnt/ *n.* (*of car, train, etc.*) avant *m.*; (*of garment, building*) devant *m.*; (*mil., pol.*) front *m.*; (*of book, pamphlet, etc.*) début *m.*; (*appearance*: *fig.*) façade *f.* —*a.* de devant, avant *invar.*; (*first*) premier. **~ door**, porte d'entrée *f.* **in ~ (of)**, devant. **~age** *n.* façade *f.* **~al** *a.* frontal; (*attack*) de front.

frontier /ˈfrʌntɪə(r)/ *n.* frontière *f.*

frost /frɒst/ *n.* gel *m.*, gelée *f.*; (*on glass etc.*) givre *m.* —*v.t./i.* (se) givrer. **~-bite** *n.* gelure *f.* **~bitten** *a.* gelé. **~ed** *a.* (*glass*) dépoli. **~ing** *n.* (*icing*: *Amer.*) glace *f.* **~y** *a.* (*weather, welcome*) glacial; (*window*) givré.

froth /frɒθ/ *n.* mousse *f.*, écume *f.* —*v.i.* mousser, écumer. **~y** *a.* mousseux.

frown /fraʊn/ *v.i.* froncer les sourcils. —*n.* froncement de sourcils *m.* **~ on**, désapprouver.

froze, frozen /frəʊz, ˈfrəʊzn/ *see* **freeze.**

frugal /ˈfruːɡl/ *a.* (*person*) économe; (*meal, life*) frugal. **~ly** *adv.* (*live*) simplement.

fruit /fruːt/ *n.* fruit *m.*; (*collectively*) fruits *m. pl.* **~ machine**, machine à sous *f.* **~ salad**, salade de fruits *f.* **~erer** *n.* fruit|ier, -ière *m., f.* **~y** *a.* (*taste*) fruité.

fruit|ful /ˈfruːtfl/ *a.* fécond; (*fig.*) fructueux. **~less** *a.* stérile.

fruition /fruːˈɪʃn/ *n.* **come to ~**, se réaliser.

frustrat|e /frʌˈstreɪt/ *v.t.* (*plan*) faire échouer; (*person*: *psych.*) frustrer; (*upset*: *fam.*) exaspérer. **~ion** /-ʃn/ *n.* (*psych.*) frustration *f.*; (*disappointment*) déception *f.*

fry[1] /fraɪ/ *v.t./i.* (*p.t.* **fried**) (faire) frire. **~ing-pan** *n.* poêle (à frire) *f.*

fry[2] /fraɪ/ *n.* **the small ~**, le menu fretin.

fuddy-duddy /ˈfʌdɪdʌdɪ/ *n.* **be a ~**, (*sl.*) être vieux jeu *invar.*

fudge /fʌdʒ/ *n.* fondant *m.*

fuel /ˈfjuːəl/ *n.* combustible *m.*; (*for car engine*) carburant *m.* —*v.t.* (*p.t.* **fuelled**) alimenter en combustible.

fugitive /ˈfjuːdʒətɪv/ *n. & a.* fugiti|f, -ve (*m., f.*).

fugue /fjuːɡ/ *n.* (*mus.*) fugue *f.*

fulfil /fʊlˈfɪl/ *v.t.* (*p.t.* **fulfilled**) accomplir, réaliser; (*condition*) remplir. **~ o.s.**, s'épanouir. **~ling** *a.* satisfaisant. **~ment** *n.* réalisation *f.*; épanouissement *m.*

full /fʊl/ *a.* (**-er, -est**) plein; (*bus, hotel*) complet; (*programme*) chargé; (*price*) entier; (*skirt*) ample. —*n.* **in ~**, intégral(ement). **write in ~**, écrire en toutes lettres. **to the ~**, complètement. **be ~ (up)**, n'avoir plus faim. **~ back**, (*sport*) arrière *m.* **~ moon**, pleine lune *f.* **~-scale** *a.* (*drawing etc.*) grandeur nature *invar.*; (*fig.*) de grande envergure. **at ~ speed**, à toute vitesse. **~ stop**, point *m.* **~-time** *a. & adv.* à plein temps. **~y** *adv.* complètement.

fulsome /ˈfʊlsəm/ *a.* excessif.

fumble /ˈfʌmbl/ *v.i.* tâtonner, fouiller. **~ with**, tripoter.

fume /fjuːm/ *v.i.* rager. **~s** *n. pl.* exhalaisons *f. pl.*, vapeurs *f. pl.*

fumigate /ˈfjuːmɪɡeɪt/ *v.t.* désinfecter.

fun /fʌn/ *n.* amusement *m.* **for ~**, pour rire. **~-fair** *n.* fête foraine *f.* **make ~ of**, se moquer de.

function /ˈfʌŋkʃn/ *n.* (*purpose, duty*) fonction *f.*; (*event*) réunion *f.*, cérémonie *f.* —*v.i.* fonctionner. **~al** *a.* fonctionnel.

fund /fʌnd/ *n.* fonds *m.* —*v.t.* fournir les fonds pour.

fundamental /fʌndəˈmentl/ *a.* fondamental.

funeral /ˈfjuːnərəl/ *n.* enterrement *m.*, funérailles *f. pl.* —*a.* funèbre.

fungus /ˈfʌŋɡəs/ *n.* (*pl.* **-gi** /-ɡaɪ/) (*plant*) champignon *m.*; (*mould*) moisissure *f.*

funicular /fjuːˈnɪkjʊlə(r)/ *n.* funiculaire *m.*

funk /fʌŋk/ *m.* **be in a ~**, (*afraid*: *sl.*) avoir la frousse; (*depressed*: *Amer., sl.*) être déprimé.

funnel /ˈfʌnl/ *n.* (*for pouring*) entonnoir *m.*; (*of ship*) cheminée *f.*

funn|y /ˈfʌnɪ/ *a.* (**-ier, -iest**) drôle; (*odd*) bizarre. **~y business**, affaire louche *f.* **~ily** *adv.* drôlement; bizarrement.

fur /fɜː(r)/ *n.* fourrure *f.*; (*in kettle*) tartre *m.*

furious /ˈfjʊərɪəs/ *a.* furieux. **~ly** *adv.* furieusement.

furnace /ˈfɜːnɪs/ *n.* fourneau *m.*

furnish /ˈfɜːnɪʃ/ *v.t.* (*with furniture*) meubler; (*supply*) fournir. **~ings** *n. pl.* ameublement *m.*

furniture /ˈfɜːnɪtʃə(r)/ *n.* meubles *m. pl.*, mobilier *m.*

furrier /ˈfʌrɪə(r)/ *n.* fourreur *m.*

furrow /'fʌrəʊ/ *n.* sillon *m.*

furry /'fɜːrɪ/ *a.* (*animal*) à fourrure; (*toy*) en peluche.

furth|er /'fɜːðə(r)/ *a.* plus éloigné; (*additional*) supplémentaire. —*adv.* plus loin; (*more*) davantage. —*v.t.* avancer. ～**est** *a.* le plus éloigné; *adv.* le plus loin.

furthermore /'fɜːðəmɔː(r)/ *adv.* en outre, de plus.

furtive /'fɜːtɪv/ *a.* furtif.

fury /'fjʊərɪ/ *n.* fureur *f.*

fuse[1] /fjuːz/ *v.t./i.* (*melt*) fondre; (*unite*: *fig.*) fusionner. —*n.* fusible *m.*, plomb *m.* ～ **the lights** *etc.*, faire sauter les plombs.

fuse[2] /fjuːz/ *n.* (*of bomb*) amorce *f.*

fuselage /'fjuːzəlɑːʒ/ *n.* fuselage *m.*

fusion /'fjuːʒn/ *n.* fusion *f.*

fuss /fʌs/ *n.* histoire(s) *f.* (*pl.*), agitation *f.* —*v.i.* s'agiter. **make a ～ of,** faire grand cas de. ～**y** *a.* (*finicky*) tatillon; (*hard to please*) difficile.

fusty /'fʌstɪ/ *a.* (**-ier, -iest**) qui sent le renfermé.

futile /'fjuːtaɪl/ *a.* futile, vain.

future /'fjuːtʃə(r)/ *a.* futur. —*n.* avenir *m.*; (*gram.*) futur *m.* **in ～,** à l'avenir.

fuzz /fʌz/ *n.* (*fluff*, *growth*) duvet *m.*; (*police*: *sl.*) flics *m. pl.*

fuzzy /'fʌzɪ/ *a.* (*hair*) crépu; (*photograph*) flou; (*person*: *fam.*) à l'esprit confus.

G

gabardine /ˈgæbəˈdiːn/ n. gabardine f.
gabble /ˈgæbl/ v.t./i. bredouiller. —n. baragouin m.
gable /ˈgeɪbl/ n. pignon m.
gad /gæd/ v.i. (p.t. gadded). ~ about, se promener, aller çà et là.
gadget /ˈgædʒɪt/ n. gadget m.
Gaelic /ˈgeɪlɪk/ n. gaélique m.
gaffe /gæf/ n. (blunder) gaffe f.
gag /gæg/ n. bâillon m.; (joke) gag m. —v.t. (p.t. gagged) bâillonner.
gaiety /ˈgeɪətɪ/ n. gaieté f.
gaily /ˈgeɪlɪ/ adv. gaiement.
gain /geɪn/ v.t. gagner; (speed, weight) prendre. —v.i. (of clock) avancer. —n. acquisition f.; (profit) gain m. ~ful a. profitable.
gainsay /geɪnˈseɪ/ v.t. (p.t. gainsaid) (formal) contredire.
gait /geɪt/ n. démarche f.
gala /ˈgɑːlə/ n. (festive occasion) gala m.; (sport) concours m.
galaxy /ˈgæləksɪ/ n. galaxie f.
gale /geɪl/ n. forte rafale de vent f., tempête f.
gall /gɔːl/ n. bile f.; (fig.) fiel m.; (impudence: sl.) culot m. ~bladder n. vésicule biliaire f.
gallant /ˈgælənt/ a. (brave) courageux; (chivalrous) galant. ~ry n. courage m.
galleon /ˈgælɪən/ n. galion m.
gallery /ˈgælərɪ/ n. galerie f.
galley /ˈgælɪ/ n. (ship) galère f.
Gallic /ˈgælɪk/ a. français. ~ism /-sɪzəm/ n. gallicisme m.
gallivant /ˈgælɪˈvænt/ v.i. (fam.) se promener, aller çà et là.
gallon /ˈgælən/ n. gallon m. (imperial = 4.546 litres; Amer. = 3.785 litres).
gallop /ˈgæləp/ n. galop m. —v.i. (p.t. galloped) galoper.
gallows /ˈgæləʊz/ n. potence f.
galore /gəˈlɔː(r)/ adv. en abondance, à gogo.
galosh /gəˈlɒʃ/ n. (overshoe) caoutchouc m.
galvanize /ˈgælvənaɪz/ v.t. galvaniser.
gambit /ˈgæmbɪt/ n. (opening) ~, (move) première démarche f.; (ploy) stratagème m.
gamble /ˈgæmbl/ v.t./i. jouer. —n.

(venture) entreprise risquée f.; (bet) pari m.; (risk) risque m. ~e on, miser sur. ~er n. joueu|r, -se m., f. ~ing n. jeu m.
game¹ /geɪm/ n. jeu m.; (football) match m.; (tennis) partie f.; (animals, birds) gibier m. —a. (brave) brave. ~ for, prêt à.
game² /geɪm/ a. (lame) estropié.
gamekeeper /ˈgeɪmkiːpə(r)/ n. gardechasse m.
gammon /ˈgæmən/ n. jambon fumé m.
gamut /ˈgæmət/ n. gamme f.
gamy /ˈgeɪmɪ/ a. faisandé.
gang /gæŋ/ n. bande f.; (of workmen) équipe f. —v.i. ~ up, se liguer (on, against, contre).
gangling /ˈgæŋglɪŋ/ a. dégingandé, grand et maigre.
gangrene /ˈgæŋgriːn/ n. gangrène f.
gangster /ˈgæŋstə(r)/ n. gangster m.
gangway /ˈgæŋweɪ/ n. passage m.; (aisle) allée f.; (of ship) passerelle f.
gaol /dʒeɪl/ n. prison f. —v.t. mettre en prison. ~er n. geôlier m.
gaolbird /ˈdʒeɪlbɜːd/ n. récidiviste m./f.
gap /gæp/ n. trou m., vide m.; (in time) intervalle m.; (in education) lacune f.; (difference) écart m.
gap|e /geɪp/ v.i. rester bouche bée. ~ing a. béant.
garage /ˈgærɑːʒ, Amer. gəˈrɑːʒ/ n. garage m. —v.t. mettre au garage.
garb /gɑːb/ n. costume m.
garbage /ˈgɑːbɪdʒ/ n. ordures f. pl.
garble /ˈgɑːbl/ v.t. déformer.
garden /ˈgɑːdn/ n. jardin m. —v.i. jardiner. ~er n. jardin|ier, -ière m., f. ~ing n. jardinage m.
gargle /ˈgɑːgl/ v.i. se gargariser. —n. gargarisme m.
gargoyle /ˈgɑːgɔɪl/ n. gargouille f.
garish /ˈgeərɪʃ/ a. voyant, criard.
garland /ˈgɑːlənd/ n. guirlande f.
garlic /ˈgɑːlɪk/ n. ail m.
garment /ˈgɑːmənt/ n. vêtement m.
garnish /ˈgɑːnɪʃ/ v.t. garnir (with, de). —n. garniture f.
garret /ˈgærət/ n. mansarde f.
garrison /ˈgærɪsn/ n. garnison f.
garrulous /ˈgærələs/ a. loquace.
garter /ˈgɑːtə(r)/ n. jarretière f.
gas /gæs/ n. (pl. gases) gaz m.; (med.)

anesthésique *m.*; (*petrol*: *Amer.*, *fam.*) essence *f.* —*a.* (*mask*, *pipe*) à gaz. —*v.t.* asphyxier; (*mil.*) gazer. —*v.i.* (*fam.*) bavarder.

gash /gæʃ/ *n.* entaille *f.* —*v.t.* entailler.

gasoline /ˈgæsəliːn/ *n.* (*petrol*: *Amer.*) essence *f.*

gasometer /gəˈsɒmɪtə(r)/ *n.* gazomètre *m.*

gasp /gɑːsp/ *v.i.* haleter; (*in surprise*: *fig.*) avoir le souffle coupé. —*n.* halètement *m.*

gassy /ˈgæsɪ/ *a.* gazeux.

gastric /ˈgæstrɪk/ *a.* gastrique.

gastronomy /gæˈstrɒnəmɪ/ *n.* gastronomie *f.*

gate /geɪt/ *n.* porte *f.*; (*of metal*) grille *f.*; (*barrier*) barrière *f.*

gatecrash /ˈgeɪtkræʃ/ *v.t./i.* venir sans invitation (à).

gateway /ˈgeɪtweɪ/ *n.* porte *f.*

gather /ˈgæðə(r)/ *v.t.* (*people, objects*) rassembler; (*pick up*) ramasser; (*flowers*) cueillir; (*fig.*) comprendre; (*sewing*) froncer. —*v.i.* (*people*) se rassembler; (*crowd*) se former; (*pile up*) s'accumuler. ~ **speed**, prendre de la vitesse. ~**ing** *n.* rassemblement *m.*

gaudy /ˈgɔːdɪ/ *a.* (-ier, -iest) voyant, criard.

gauge /geɪdʒ/ *n.* jauge *f.*, indicateur *m.* —*v.t.* jauger, évaluer.

gaunt /gɔːnt/ *a.* (*lean*) émacié; (*grim*) lugubre.

gauntlet /ˈgɔːntlɪt/ *n.* **run the ~ of**, subir (l'assaut de).

gauze /gɔːz/ *n.* gaze *f.*

gave /geɪv/ *see* **give**.

gawky /ˈgɔːkɪ/ *a.* (-ier, -iest) gauche, maladroit.

gawp (*or* **gawk**) /gɔːp, gɔːk/ *v.i.* ~ (**at**), regarder bouche bée.

gay /geɪ/ *a.* (-er, -est) (*joyful*) gai; (*fam.*) homosexuel.

gaze /geɪz/ *v.i.* ~ (**at**), regarder (fixement). —*n.* regard (fixe) *m.*

gazelle /gəˈzel/ *n.* gazelle *f.*

gazette /gəˈzet/ *n.* journal (officiel) *m.*

GB *abbr.* *see* **Great Britain**.

gear /gɪə(r)/ *n.* équipement *m.*; (*techn.*) engrenage *m.*; (*auto.*) vitesse *f.* —*v.t.* adapter. **in ~**, en prise. **out of ~**, au point mort.

gearbox /ˈgɪəbɒks/ *n.* (*auto.*) boîte de vitesses *f.*

geese /giːs/ *see* **goose**.

geezer /ˈgiːzə(r)/ *n.* (*sl.*) type *m.*

gel /dʒel/ *n.* gelée *f.*

gelatine /ˈdʒelətiːn/ *n.* gélatine *f.*

gelignite /ˈdʒelɪgnaɪt/ *n.* nitro glycérine *f.*

gem /dʒem/ *n.* pierre précieuse *f.*

gender /ˈdʒendə(r)/ *n.* genre *m.*

gene /dʒiːn/ *n.* gène *m.*

genealogy /dʒiːnɪˈælədʒɪ/ *n.* généalogie *f.*

general /ˈdʒenrəl/ *a.* général. —*n.* général *m.* ~ **election**, élections législatives *f. pl.* ~ **practitioner**, (*med.*) généraliste *m.* **in ~**, en général. ~**ly** *adv.* généralement.

generaliz|e /ˈdʒenrəlaɪz/ *v.t./i.* généraliser. ~**ation** /-ˈzeɪʃn/ *n.* généralisation *f.*

generate /ˈdʒenəreɪt/ *v.t.* produire.

generation /dʒenəˈreɪʃn/ *n.* génération *f.*

generator /ˈdʒenəreɪtə(r)/ *n.* (*electr.*) groupe électrogène *m.*

gener|ous /ˈdʒenərəs/ *a.* généreux; (*plentiful*) copieux. ~**osity** /-ˈrɒsətɪ/ *n.* générosité *f.*

genetic /dʒɪˈnetɪk/ *a.* génétique. ~**s** *n.* génétique *f.*

Geneva /dʒɪˈniːvə/ *n.* Genève *m.*/*f.*

genial /ˈdʒiːnɪəl/ *a.* affable, sympathique; (*climate*) doux.

genital /ˈdʒenɪtl/ *a.* génital. ~**s** *n. pl.* organes génitaux *m. pl.*

genius /ˈdʒiːnɪəs/ *n.* (*pl.* -uses) génie *m.*

genocide /ˈdʒenəsaɪd/ *n.* génocide *m.*

gent /dʒent/ *n.* (*sl.*) monsieur *m.*

genteel /dʒenˈtiːl/ *a.* distingué.

gentl|e /ˈdʒentl/ *a.* (-er, -est) (*mild, kind*) doux; (*slight*) léger; (*hint*) discret. ~**eness** *n.* douceur *f.* ~**y** *adv.* doucement.

gentleman /ˈdʒentlmən/ *n.* (*pl.* -men) (*man*) monsieur *m.*; (*well bred*) gentleman *m.*

genuine /ˈdʒenjʊm/ *a.* (*true*) véritable; (*person, belief*) sincère.

geograph|y /dʒɪˈɒgrəfɪ/ *n.* géographie *f.* ~**er** *n.* géographe *m.*/*f.* ~**ical** /dʒɪəˈgræfɪkl/ *a.* géographique.

geolog|y /dʒɪˈɒlədʒɪ/ *n.* géologie *f.* ~**ical** /dʒɪəˈlɒdʒɪkl/ *a.* géologique. ~**ist** *n.* géologue *m.*/*f.*

geometr|y /dʒɪˈɒmətrɪ/ *n.* géométrie *f.* ~**ic(al)** /dʒɪəˈmetrɪk(l)/ *a.* géométrique.

geranium /dʒəˈreɪnɪəm/ *n.* géranium *m.*

geriatric /dʒerɪˈætrɪk/ *a.* gériatrique.

germ /dʒɜːm/ *n.* (*rudiment, seed*) germe *m.*; (*med.*) microbe *m.*

German /'dʒɜːmən/ *a.* & *n.* allemand(e) (*m.* (*f.*)); (*lang.*) allemand *m.* ~ **measles,** rubéole *f.* ~ **shepherd,** (*dog*: *Amer.*) berger allemand *m.* ~**ic** /dʒə'mænɪk/ *a.* germanique. ~**y** *n.* Allemagne *f.*

germinate /'dʒɜːmɪneɪt/ *v.t./i.* (faire) germer.

gestation /dʒe'steɪʃn/ *n.* gestation *f.*

gesticulate /dʒe'stɪkjʊleɪt/ *v.i.* gesticuler.

gesture /'dʒestʃə(r)/ *n.* geste *m.*

get /get/ *v.t.* (*p.t.* & *p.p.* got, *p.p. Amer.* gotten, *pres. p.* getting) avoir, obtenir, recevoir; (*catch*) prendre; (*buy*) acheter, prendre; (*find*) trouver; (*fetch*) aller chercher; (*understand*: *sl.*) comprendre. ~ **s.o. to do sth.,** faire faire qch. à qn. —*v.i.* aller, arriver (**to**, à); (*become*) devenir; (*start*) se mettre (**to**, à); (*manage*) parvenir (**to**, à). ~ **married/ready**/*etc.*, se marier/se préparer/*etc.* ~ **about,** (*person*) se déplacer. ~ **across,** (*cross*) traverser. ~ **along** *or* **by,** (*manage*) se débrouiller. ~ **along** *or* **on,** (*progress*) avancer. ~ **along** *or* **on with,** s'entendre avec. ~ **at,** (*reach*) parvenir à. **what are you** ~**ting at?,** où veux-tu en venir? ~ **away,** partir; (*escape*) s'échapper. ~ **back** *v.i.* revenir; *v.t.* (*recover*) récupérer. ~ **by** *or* **through,** (*pass*) passer. ~ **down** *v.t./i.* descendre; (*depress*) déprimer. ~ **in,** entrer, arriver. ~ **off** *v.i.* (*from car etc.*) descendre; (*leave*) partir; (*jurid.*) être acquitté; *v.t.* (*remove*) enlever. ~ **on,** (*on train etc.*) monter; (*succeed*) réussir. ~ **on with,** continuer. ~ **out,** sortir. ~ **out of,** (*fig.*) se soustraire à. ~ **over,** (*illness*) se remettre de. ~ **round,** (*rule*) contourner; (*person*) entortiller. ~ **through,** (*finish*) finir. ~ **up** *v.i.* se lever; *v.t.* (*climb*: *bring*) monter. ~**-up** *n.* (*clothes*: *fam.*) mise *f.*

getaway /'getəweɪ/ *n.* fuite *f.*

geyser /'giːzə(r)/ *n.* chauffe-eau *m. invar.*; (*geol.*) geyser *m.*

Ghana /'gɑːnə/ *n.* Ghana *m.*

ghastly /'gɑːstlɪ/ *a.* (**-ier, -iest**) affreux; (*pale*) blême.

gherkin /'gɜːkɪn/ *n.* cornichon *m.*

ghetto /'getəʊ/ *n.* (*pl.* **-os**) ghetto *m.*

ghost /gəʊst/ *n.* fantôme *m.* ~**ly** *a.* spectral.

ghoulish /'guːlɪʃ/ *a.* morbide.

giant /'dʒaɪənt/ *n.* & *a.* géant (*m.*).

gibberish /'dʒɪbərɪʃ/ *n.* baragouin *m.*, charabia *m.*

gibe /dʒaɪb/ *n.* raillerie *f.* —*v.i.* ~ (**at**), railler.

giblets /'dʒɪblɪts/ *n. pl.* abattis *m. pl.*, abats *m. pl.*

gidd|y /'gɪdɪ/ *a.* (**-ier, -iest**) vertigineux. **be** *or* **feel** ~**y,** avoir le vertige. ~**iness** *n.* vertige *m.*

gift /gɪft/ *n.* cadeau *m.*; (*ability*) don *m.* ~**-wrap** *v.t.* (*p.t.* **-wrapped**) faire un paquet-cadeau de.

gifted /'gɪftɪd/ *a.* doué.

gig /gɪg/ *n.* (*fam.*) séance de jazz *f.*

gigantic /dʒaɪ'gæntɪk/ *a.* gigantesque.

giggle /'gɪgl/ *v.i.* ricaner (sottement), glousser. —*n.* ricanement *m.* **the** ~**s,** le fou rire.

gild /gɪld/ *v.t.* dorer.

gills /gɪlz/ *n. pl.* ouïes *f. pl.*

gilt /gɪlt/ *a.* doré. —*n.* dorure *f.* ~**-edged** *a.* (*comm.*) de tout repos.

gimmick /'gɪmɪk/ *n.* truc *m.*

gin /dʒɪn/ *n.* gin *m.*

ginger /'dʒɪndʒə(r)/ *n.* gingembre *m.* —*a.* roux. ~ **ale,** ~ **beer,** boisson gazeuse au gingembre *f.*

gingerbread /'dʒɪndʒəbred/ *n.* pain d'épice *m.*

gingerly /'dʒɪndʒəlɪ/ *adv.* avec précaution.

gipsy /'dʒɪpsɪ/ *n.* = **gypsy.**

giraffe /dʒɪ'rɑːf/ *n.* girafe *f.*

girder /'gɜːdə(r)/ *n.* poutre *f.*

girdle /'gɜːdl/ *n.* (*belt*) ceinture *f.*; (*corset*) gaine *f.*

girl /gɜːl/ *n.* (*petite*) fille *f.*; (*young woman*) (jeune) fille *f.* ~**-friend** *n.* amie *f.*; (*of boy*) petite amie *f.* ~**hood** *n.* enfance *f.*, jeunesse *f.* ~**ish** *a.* de (jeune) fille.

giro /'dʒaɪərəʊ/ *n.* (*pl.* **-os**) virement bancaire *m.*

girth /gɜːθ/ *n.* circonférence *f.*

gist /dʒɪst/ *n.* essentiel *m.*

give /gɪv/ *v.t.* (*p.t.* **gave,** *p.p.* **given**) donner; (*gesture*) faire; (*laugh, sigh, etc.*) pousser. —*v.i.* donner; (*yield*) céder; (*stretch*) se détendre. —*n.* élasticité *f.* ~ **away,** donner; (*secret*) trahir. ~ **back,** rendre. ~ **in,** (*yield*) se rendre. ~ **off,** dégager. ~ **out** *v.t.* distribuer; *v.i.* (*become used up*) s'épuiser. ~ **over,** (*devote*) consacrer; (*stop*: *fam.*) cesser. ~ **up** *v.t./i.* (*renounce*) renoncer (à); (*yield*) céder.

~ **o.s. up**, se rendre. ~ **way**, céder; (*collapse*) s'effondrer.

given /'gɪvn/ *see* give. —*a.* donné. ~ **name**, prénom *m.*

glacier /'glæsɪə(r), *Amer.* 'gleɪʃə(r)/ *n.* glacier *m.*

glad /glæd/ *a.* content. ~**ly** *adv.* avec plaisir.

gladden /'glædn/ *v.t.* réjouir.

glade /gleɪd/ *n.* clairière *f.*

gladiolus /glædɪ'əʊləs/ *n.* (*pl.* **-li** /-laɪ/) glaïeul *m.*

glam|our /'glæmə(r)/ *n.* enchantement *m.*, séduction *f.* ~**orize** *v.t.* rendre séduisant. ~**orous** *a.* séduisant, ensorcelant.

glance /glɑːns/ *n.* coup d'œil *m.* —*v.i.* ~ **at**, jeter un coup d'œil à.

gland /glænd/ *n.* glande *f.*

glar|e /gleə(r)/ *v.i.* briller très fort. —*n.* éclat (aveuglant) *m.*; (*stare*: *fig.*) regard furieux *m.* ~**e at**, regarder d'un air furieux. ~**ing** *a.* éblouissant; (*obvious*) flagrant.

glass /glɑːs/ *n.* verre *m.*; (*mirror*) miroir *m.* ~**es**, (*spectacles*) lunettes *f. pl.* ~**y** *a.* vitreux.

glaze /gleɪz/ *v.t.* (*door etc.*) vitrer; (*pottery*) vernisser. —*n.* vernis *m.*

gleam /gliːm/ *n.* lueur *f.* —*v.i.* luire.

glean /gliːn/ *v.t.* glaner.

glee /gliː/ *n.* joie *f.* ~ **club**, chorale *f.* ~**ful** *a.* joyeux.

glen /glen/ *n.* vallon *m.*

glib /glɪb/ *a.* (*person*: *pej.*) qui a la parole facile *or* du bagou; (*reply, excuse*) désinvolte, spécieux. ~**ly** *adv.* avec désinvolture.

glide /glaɪd/ *v.i.* glisser; (*of plane*) planer. ~**r** /-ə(r)/ *n.* planeur *m.*

glimmer /'glɪmə(r)/ *n.* lueur *f.* —*v.i.* luire.

glimpse /glɪmps/ *n.* aperçu *m.* **catch a** ~ **of**, entrevoir.

glint /glɪnt/ *n.* éclair *m.* —*v.i.* étinceler.

glisten /'glɪsn/ *v.i.* briller, luire.

glitter /'glɪtə(r)/ *v.i.* scintiller. —*n.* scintillement *m.*

gloat /gləʊt/ *v.i.* jubiler (**over**, à l'idée de).

global /'gləʊbl/ *a.* (*world-wide*) mondial; (*all-embracing*) global.

globe /gləʊb/ *n.* globe *m.*

gloom /gluːm/ *n.* obscurité *f.*; (*sadness*: *fig.*) tristesse *f.* ~**y** *a.* triste; (*pessimistic*) pessimiste.

glorif|y /'glɔːrɪfaɪ/ *v.t.* glorifier.

a ~**ied waitress**/*etc.*, à peine plus qu'une serveuse/*etc.*

glorious /'glɔːrɪəs/ *a.* splendide; (*deed, hero, etc.*) glorieux.

glory /'glɔːrɪ/ *n.* gloire *f.*; (*beauty*) splendeur *f.* —*v.i.* ~ **in**, s'enorgueillir de.

gloss /glɒs/ *n.* lustre *m.*, brillant *m.* —*a.* brillant. —*v.i.* ~ **over**, (*make light of*) glisser sur; (*cover up*) dissimuler. ~**y** *a.* brillant.

glossary /'glɒsərɪ/ *n.* glossaire *m.*

glove /glʌv/ *n.* gant *m.* ~ **compartment**, (*auto.*) vide-poches *m. invar.* ~**d** *a.* ganté.

glow /gləʊ/ *v.i.* rougeoyer; (*person, eyes*) rayonner. —*n.* rougeoiement *m.*, éclat *m.* ~**ing** *a.* (*account etc.*) enthousiaste.

glucose /'gluːkəʊs/ *n.* glucose *m.*

glue /gluː/ *n.* colle *f.* —*v.t.* (*pres. p.* **gluing**) coller.

glum /glʌm/ *a.* (**glummer, glummest**) triste, morne.

glut /glʌt/ *n.* surabondance *f.*

glutton /'glʌtn/ *n.* glouton(ne) *m.* (*f.*). ~**ous** *a.* glouton. ~**y** *n.* gloutonnerie *f.*

glycerine /'glɪsəriːn/ *n.* glycérine *f.*

gnarled /nɑːld/ *a.* noueux.

gnash /næʃ/ *v.t.* ~ **one's teeth**, grincer des dents.

gnat /næt/ *n.* (*fly*) cousin *m.*

gnaw /nɔː/ *v.t.*/*i.* ronger.

gnome /nəʊm/ *n.* gnome *m.*

go /gəʊ/ *v.i.* (*p.t.* **went**, *p.p.* **gone**) aller; (*leave*) partir; (*work*) marcher; (*become*) devenir; (*be sold*) se vendre; (*vanish*) disparaître. ~ **riding/shopping**/*etc.*, faire du cheval/les courses/*etc.* —*n.* (*pl.* **goes**) (*try*) coup *m.*; (*success*) réussite *f.*; (*turn*) tour *m.*; (*energy*) dynamisme *m.* **be** ~**ing to do**, aller faire. ~ **across**, traverser. ~ **ahead!**, allez-y! ~**-ahead** *n.* feu vert *m.*; *a.* dynamique. ~ **away**, s'en aller. ~ **back**, retourner; (*go home*) rentrer. ~ **back on**, (*promise etc.*) revenir sur. ~ **bad** *or* **off**, se gâter. ~**-between** *n.* intermédiaire *m.*/*f.* ~ **by**, (*pass*) passer. ~ **down**, descendre; (*sun*) se coucher. ~ **for**, aller chercher; (*like*) aimer; (*attack*: *sl.*) attaquer. ~ **in**, (r)entrer. ~ **in for**, (*exam*) se présenter à. ~**-kart** *n.* kart *m.* ~ **off**, partir; (*explode*) sauter; (*ring*) sonner. ~ **on**, continuer; (*happen*) se passer. ~ **out**, sortir;

(light, fire) s'éteindre. ∿ **over,** *(cross)* traverser; *(pass)* passer. ∿ **over** *or* **through,** *(check)* examiner; *(search)* fouiller. ∿ **round,** *(be enough)* suffire. ∿-**slow** *n.* grève perlée *f.* ∿ **through,** *(suffer)* subir. ∿ **under,** *(sink)* couler; *(fail)* échouer. ∿ **up,** monter. ∿ **without,** se passer de. **on the** ∿, actif.

goad /gəʊd/ *v.t.* aiguillonner.

goal /gəʊl/ *n.* but *m.* ∿-**post** *n.* poteau de but *m.*

goalkeeper /'gəʊlkiːpə(r)/ *n.* gardien de but *m.*

goat /gəʊt/ *n.* chèvre *f.*

goatee /gəʊ'tiː/ *n.* barbiche *f.*

gobble /'gɒbl/ *v.t.* engouffrer.

goblet /'gɒblɪt/ *n.* verre à pied *m.*

goblin /'gɒblɪn/ *n.* lutin *m.*

God /gɒd/ *n.* Dieu *m.* ∿-**forsaken** *a.* perdu.

god /gɒd/ *n.* dieu *m.* ∿**dess** *n.* déesse *f.* ∿**ly** *a.* dévot.

god|child /'gɒdtʃaɪld/ *n.* *(pl.* -**children)** filleul(e) *m. (f.).* ∿**daughter** *n.* filleule *f.* ∿**father** *n.* parrain *m.* ∿**mother** *n.* marraine *f.* ∿**son** *n.* filleul *m.*

godsend /'gɒdsend/ *n.* aubaine *f.*

goggle /'gɒgl/ *v.i.* ∿ **(at),** regarder avec de gros yeux.

goggles /'gɒglz/ *n. pl.* lunettes (protectrices) *f. pl.*

going /'gəʊɪŋ/ *n.* **it is slow/hard** ∿, c'est lent/difficile. —*a. (price, rate)* actuel. ∿**s-on** *n. pl.* activités (bizarres) *f. pl.*

gold /gəʊld/ *n.* or *m.* —*a.* en or, d'or. ∿-**mine** *n.* mine d'or *f.*

golden /'gəʊldən/ *a.* d'or; *(in colour)* doré; *(opportunity)* unique. ∿ **wedding,** noces d'or *f. pl.*

goldfish /'gəʊldfɪʃ/ *n. invar.* poisson rouge *m.*

gold-plated /gəʊld'pleɪtɪd/ *a.* plaqué or.

goldsmith /'gəʊldsmɪθ/ *n.* orfèvre *m.*

golf /gɒlf/ *n.* golf *m.* ∿-**course** *n.* terrain de golf *m.* ∿**er** *n.* joueu|r, -se de golf *m., f.*

golly /'gɒlɪ/ *int.* mince, zut.

gondol|a /'gɒndələ/ *n.* gondole *f.* ∿**ier** /-'lɪə(r)/ *n.* gondolier *m.*

gone /gɒn/ *see* **go.** —*a.* parti. ∿ **six o'clock,** six heures passées.

gong /gɒŋ/ *n.* gong *m.*

good /gʊd/ *a.* **(better, best)** bon; *(weather)* beau; *(well-behaved)* sage. —*n.* bien *m.* **as** ∿ **as,** *(almost)* pratiquement. **be** ∿ **with,** savoir s'y prendre avec. **do** ∿, faire du bien. **feel** ∿, se sentir bien. ∿-**for-nothing** *a. & n.* propre à rien *(m./f.).* **G**∿ **Friday,** Vendredi saint *m.* ∿-**afternoon,** ∿-**morning** *ints.* bonjour. ∿-**evening** *int.* bonsoir. ∿-**looking** *a.* joli. ∿ **name,** réputation *f.* ∿-**night** *int.* bonsoir, bonne nuit. **it is** ∿ **for you,** ça vous fait du bien. **it is no** ∿ **shouting**/*etc.*, ça ne sert à rien de crier/*etc.* ∿**ness** *n.* bonté *f.* **my** ∿**ness!**, mon Dieu!

goodbye /gʊd'baɪ/ *int. & n.* au revoir *(m. invar.).*

goods /gʊdz/ *n. pl.* marchandises *f. pl.*

goodwill /gʊd'wɪl/ *n.* bonne volonté *f.*

goody /'gʊdɪ/ *n. (fam.)* bonne chose *f.* ∿-**goody** *n.* petit(e) saint(e) *m. (f.).*

gooey /'guːɪ/ *a. (sl.)* poisseux.

goof /guːf/ *v.i. (Amer.)* gaffer.

goose /guːs/ *n. (pl.* **geese)** oie *f.* ∿-**flesh,** ∿-**pimples** *ns.* chair de poule *f.*

gooseberry /'gʊzbərɪ/ *n.* groseille à maquereau *f.*

gore[1] /gɔː(r)/ *n. (blood)* sang *m.*

gore[2] /gɔː(r)/ *v.t.* encorner.

gorge /gɔːdʒ/ *n. (geog.)* gorge *f.* —*v.t.* ∿ **o.s.,** se gorger.

gorgeous /'gɔːdʒəs/ *a.* magnifique, splendide, formidable.

gorilla /gə'rɪlə/ *n.* gorille *m.*

gormless /'gɔːmlɪs/ *a. (sl.)* stupide.

gorse /gɔːs/ *n. invar.* ajonc(s) *m. (pl.).*

gory /'gɔːrɪ/ *a.* **(-ier, -iest)** sanglant; *(horrific: fig.)* horrible.

gosh /gɒʃ/ *int.* mince (alors).

gospel /'gɒspl/ *n.* évangile *m.* **the G**∿, l'Évangile *m.*

gossip /'gɒsɪp/ *n.* bavardage(s) *m. (pl.),* commérage(s) *m. (pl.); (person)* bavard(e) *m. (f.).* —*v.i. (p.t.* **gossiped)** bavarder. ∿**y** *a.* bavard.

got /gɒt/ *see* **get.** —**have** ∿, avoir. **have** ∿ **to do,** devoir faire.

Gothic /'gɒθɪk/ *a.* gothique.

gouge /gaʊdʒ/ *v.t.* ∿ **out,** arracher.

gourmet /'gʊəmeɪ/ *n.* gourmet *m.*

gout /gaʊt/ *n. (med.)* goutte *f.*

govern /'gʌvn/ *v.t./i.* gouverner. ∿**ess** /-ənɪs/ *n.* gouvernante *f.* ∿**or** /-ənə(r)/ *n.* gouverneur *m.*

government /'gʌvənmənt/ *n.* gouvernement *m.* ∿**al** /-'mentl/ *a.* gouvernemental.

gown /gaʊn/ *n.* robe *f.; (of judge, teacher)* toge *f.*

GP *abbr. see* **general practitioner.**

grab /græb/ *v.t.* (*p.t.* **grabbed**) saisir.

grace /greɪs/ *n.* grâce *f.* —*v.t.* (*honour*) honorer; (*adorn*) orner. **~ful** *a.* gracieux.

gracious /'greɪʃəs/ *a.* (*kind*) bienveillant; (*elegant*) élégant.

gradation /grə'deɪʃn/ *n.* gradation *f.*

grade /greɪd/ *n.* catégorie *f.*; (*of goods*) qualité *f.*; (*on scale*) grade *m.*; (*school mark*) note *f.*; (*class: Amer.*) classe *f.* —*v.t.* classer; (*school work*) noter. **~ school,** (*Amer.*) école primaire *f.*

gradient /'greɪdɪənt/ *n.* (*slope*) inclinaison *f.*

gradual /'grædʒʊəl/ *a.* progressif, graduel. **~ly** *adv.* progressivement, peu à peu.

graduate[1] /'grædʒʊət/ *n.* (*univ.*) licencié(e) *m.* (*f.*), diplômé(e) *m.* (*f.*).

graduat|e[2] /'grædʒʊeɪt/ *v.i.* obtenir son diplôme. —*v.t.* graduer. **~ion** /-'eɪʃn/ *n.* remise de diplômes *f.*

graffiti /grə'fiːtiː/ *n. pl.* graffiti *m. pl.*

graft[1] /grɑːft/ *n.* (*med., bot.*) greffe *f.* —*v.t.* greffer.

graft[2] /grɑːft/ *n.* (*bribery: fam.*) corruption *f.*

grain /greɪn/ *n.* (*seed, quantity, texture*) grain *m.*; (*in wood*) fibre *f.*

gram /græm/ *n.* gramme *m.*

gramm|ar /'græmə(r)/ *n.* grammaire *f.* **~atical** /grə'mætɪkl/ *a.* grammatical.

gramophone /'græməfəʊn/ *n.* phonographe *m.*

grand /grænd/ *a.* (**-er, -est**) magnifique; (*duke, chorus*) grand. **~ piano,** piano à queue *m.*

grand|child /'græn(d)tʃaɪld/ *n.* (*pl.* **-children**) petit(e)-enfant *m.* (*f.*). **~daughter** *n.* petite-fille *f.* **~father** *n.* grand-père *m.* **~-mother** *n.* grand-mère *f.* **~-parents** *n. pl.* grands-parents *m. pl.* **~son** *n.* petit-fils *m.*

grandeur /'grændʒə(r)/ *n.* grandeur *f.*

grandiose /'grændɪəʊs/ *a.* grandiose.

grandstand /'græn(d)stænd/ *n.* tribune *f.*

granite /'grænɪt/ *n.* granit *m.*

granny /'grænɪ/ *n.* (*fam.*) grand-maman *f.*, mémé *f.*, mamie *f.*

grant /grɑːnt/ *v.t.* (*give*) accorder; (*request*) accéder à; (*admit*) admettre (**that,** que). —*n.* subvention *f.*; (*univ.*) bourse *f.* **take sth. for ~ed,** considérer qch. comme une chose acquise.

granulated /'grænjʊleɪtɪd/ *a.* **~ sugar,** sucre semoule *m.*

granule /'grænjuːl/ *n.* granule *m.*

grape /greɪp/ *n.* grain de raisin *m.* **~s,** raisin(s) *m.* (*pl.*).

grapefruit /'greɪpfruːt/ *n. invar.* pamplemousse *m.*

graph /grɑːf/ *n.* graphique *m.*

graphic /'græfɪk/ *a.* (*arts etc.*) graphique; (*fig.*) vivant, explicite.

grapple /græpl/ *v.i.* **~ with,** affronter, être aux prises avec.

grasp /grɑːsp/ *v.t.* saisir. —*n.* (*hold*) prise *f.*; (*strength of hand*) poigne *f.*; (*reach*) portée *f.*; (*fig.*) compréhension *f.*

grasping /'grɑːspɪŋ/ *a.* rapace.

grass /grɑːs/ *n.* herbe *f.* **~ roots,** peuple *m.*; (*pol.*) base *f.* **~-roots** *a.* populaire. **~y** *a.* herbeux.

grasshopper /'grɑːshɒpə(r)/ *n.* sauterelle *f.*

grassland /'grɑːslænd/ *n.* prairie *f.*

grate[1] /greɪt/ *n.* (*fireplace*) foyer *m.*; (*frame*) grille *f.*

grate[2] /greɪt/ *v.t.* râper. —*v.i.* grincer. **~ one's teeth,** grincer des dents. **~r** /-ə(r)/ *n.* râpe *f.*

grateful /'greɪtfl/ *a.* reconnaissant. **~ly** *adv.* avec reconnaissance.

gratif|y /'grætɪfaɪ/ *v.t.* satisfaire; (*please*) faire plaisir à. **~ied** *a.* très heureux. **~ying** *a.* agréable.

grating /'greɪtɪŋ/ *n.* grille *f.*

gratis /'greɪtɪs, 'grætɪs/ *a. & adv.* gratis (*a. invar.*).

gratitude /'grætɪtjuːd/ *n.* gratitude *f.*

gratuitous /grə'tjuːɪtəs/ *a.* gratuit.

gratuity /grə'tjuːətɪ/ *n.* (*tip*) pourboire *m.*; (*bounty: mil.*) prime *f.*

grave[1] /greɪv/ *n.* tombe *f.* **~- digger** *n.* fossoyeur *m.*

grave[2] /greɪv/ *a.* (**-er, -est**) (*serious*) grave. **~ly** *adv.* gravement.

grave[3] /grɑːv/ *a.* **~ accent,** accent grave *m.*

gravel /'grævl/ *n.* gravier *m.*

gravestone /'greɪvstəʊn/ *n.* pierre tombale *f.*

graveyard /'greɪvjɑːd/ *n.* cimetière *m.*

gravitat|e /'grævɪteɪt/ *v.i.* graviter. **~ion** /-'teɪʃn/ *n.* gravitation *f.*

gravity /'grævətɪ/ *n.* (*seriousness*) gravité *f.*; (*force*) pesanteur *f.*

gravy /'greɪvɪ/ *n.* jus (de viande) *m.*

graze[1] /greɪz/ *v.t./i.* (*eat*) paître.

graze[2] /greɪz/ *v.t.* (*touch*) frôler; (*scrape*) écorcher. —*n.* écorchure *f.*

greas|e /griːs/ *n.* graisse *f.* —*v.t.*
graisser. **~e-proof paper,** papier sul-
furisé *m.* **~y** *a.* graisseux.

great /greɪt/ *a.* (**-er, -est**) grand; (*very
good: fam.*) magnifique. **~ Britain,**
Grande-Bretagne *f.* **~-grandfather**
n. arrière-grand-père *m.* **~-grand-
mother** *n.* arrière-grand-mère *f.* **~ly**
adv. (*very*) très; (*much*) beaucoup.
~ness *n.* grandeur *f.*

Greece /griːs/ *n.* Grèce *f.*

greed /griːd/ *n.* avidité *f.*; (*for food*)
gourmandise *f.* **~y** *a.* avide; gourmand.

Greek /griːk/ *a. & n.* grec(que) (*m.* (*f.*));
(*lang.*) grec *m.*

green /griːn/ *a.* (**-er, -est**) vert; (*fig.*)
naïf. —*n.* vert *m.*; (*grass*) pelouse *f.*
~s, légumes verts *m. pl.* **~ belt,** zone
de verdure *f.* **~ light,** feu vert *m.* **the
~ pound,** la livre verte. **~ery** *n.*
verdure *f.*

greengage /ˈgriːngeɪdʒ/ *n.* (*plum*)
reine-claude *f.*

greengrocer /ˈgriːngrəʊsə(r)/ *n.* mar-
chand(e) de fruits et légumes *m.* (*f.*).

greenhouse /ˈgriːnhaʊs/ *n.* serre *f.*

greet /griːt/ *v.t.* (*receive*) accueillir;
(*address politely*) saluer. **~ing** *n.* accueil *m.* **~ings** *n. pl.* compliments *m.
pl.*; (*wishes*) vœux *m. pl.*

gregarious /grɪˈgeərɪəs/ *a.* (*instinct*)
grégaire; (*person*) sociable.

grenade /grɪˈneɪd/ *n.* grenade *f.*

grew /gruː/ *see* **grow.**

grey /greɪ/ *a.* (**-er, -est**) gris; (*fig.*)
triste. —*n.* gris *m.* —*v.i.* (*hair, person*)
grisonner.

greyhound /ˈgreɪhaʊnd/ *n.* lévrier *m.*

grid /grɪd/ *n.* grille *f.*; (*network: electr.*)
réseau *m.*; (*culin.*) gril *m.*

grief /griːf/ *n.* chagrin *m.* **come to
~,** (*person*) avoir un malheur; (*fail*)
tourner mal.

grievance /ˈgriːvns/ *n.* grief *m.*

grieve /griːv/ *v.t./i.* (s')affliger. **~ for,**
pleurer.

grill /grɪl/ *n.* (*cooking device*) gril *m.*;
(*food*) grillade *f.* —*v.t./i.* griller; (*in-
terrogate*) cuisiner.

grille /grɪl/ *n.* grille *f.*

grim /grɪm/ *a.* (**grimmer, grimmest**)
sinistre.

grimace /grɪˈmeɪs/ *n.* grimace *f.* —*v.i.*
grimacer.

grim|e /graɪm/ *n.* crasse *f.* **~y** *a.* cras-
seux.

grin /grɪn/ *v.i.* (*p.t.* **grinned**) sourire.
—*n.* (large) sourire *m.*

grind /graɪnd/ *v.t.* (*p.t.* **ground**)
écraser; (*coffee*) moudre; (*sharpen*)
aiguiser. —*n.* corvée *f.* **~ one's teeth,**
grincer des dents.

grip /grɪp/ *v.t.* (*p.t.* **gripped**) saisir;
(*interest*) passionner. —*n.* prise *f.*;
(*strength of hand*) poigne *f.* **come to
~s,** en venir aux prises.

gripe /graɪp/ *n.* **~s,** (*med.*) coliques *f.
pl.* —*v.i.* (*grumble: sl.*) râler.

grisly /ˈgrɪzlɪ/ *a.* (**-ier, -iest**) macabre,
horrible.

gristle /ˈgrɪsl/ *n.* cartilage *m.*

grit /grɪt/ *n.* gravillon *m.*, sable *m.*;
(*fig.*) courage *m.* —*v.t.* (*p.t.* **gritted**)
(*road*) sabler; (*teeth*) serrer.

grizzle /ˈgrɪzl/ *v.i.* (*cry*) pleurnicher.

groan /grəʊn/ *v.i.* gémir. —*n.* gémissement *m.*

grocer /ˈgrəʊsə(r)/ *n.* épic|ier, -ière
m., f. **~ies** *n. pl.* (*goods*) épicerie *f.*
~y *n.* (*shop*) épicerie *f.*

grog /grɒg/ *n.* grog *m.*

groggy /ˈgrɒgɪ/ *a.* (*weak*) faible; (*unsteady*) chancelant; (*ill*) mal fichu.

groin /grɔɪn/ *n.* aine *f.*

groom /gruːm/ *n.* marié *m.*; (*for
horses*) valet d'écurie *m.* —*v.t.* (*horse*)
panser; (*fig.*) préparer.

groove /gruːv/ *n.* (*for door etc.*) rainure
f.; (*in record*) sillon *m.*

grope /grəʊp/ *v.i.* tâtonner. **~ for,**
chercher à tâtons.

gross /grəʊs/ *a.* (**-er, -est**) (*coarse*)
grossier; (*comm.*) brut. —*n. invar.*
grosse *f.* **~ly** *adv.* grossièrement;
(*very*) extrêmement.

grotesque /grəʊˈtesk/ *a.* grotesque,
horrible.

grotto /ˈgrɒtəʊ/ *n.* (*pl.* **-oes**) grotte *f.*

grotty /ˈgrɒtɪ/ *a.* (*sl.*) moche.

grouch /graʊtʃ/ *v.i.* (*grumble: fam.*)
rouspéter, râler.

ground[1] /graʊnd/ *n.* terre *f.*, sol *m.*;
(*area*) terrain *m.*; (*reason*) raison *f.*;
(*electr., Amer.*) masse *f.* **~s,** terres *f.
pl.*, parc *m.*; (*of coffee*) marc *m.* —*v.t./i.*
(*naut.*) échouer; (*aircraft*) retenir au
sol. **~ floor,** rez-de-chaussée *m. invar.* **~less** *a.* sans fondement. **~
swell,** lame de fond *f.*

ground[2] /graʊnd/ *see* **grind.**

grounding /ˈgraʊndɪŋ/ *n.* connaissances (de base) *f. pl.*

groundsheet /ˈgraʊndʃiːt/ *n.* tapis de
sol *m.*

groundwork /ˈgraʊndwɜːk/ n. travail préparatoire m.

group /gruːp/ n. groupe m. —v.t./i. (se) grouper.

grouse[1] /graʊs/ n. invar. (bird) coq de bruyère m., grouse f.

grouse[2] /graʊs/ v.i. (grumble: fam.) rouspéter, râler.

grove /grəʊv/ n. bocage m.

grovel /ˈgrɒvl/ v.i. (p.t. **grovelled**) ramper. ~**ling** a. rampant.

grow /grəʊ/ v.i. (p.t. **grew**, p.p. **grown**) grandir; (of plant) pousser; (become) devenir. —v.t. cultiver. ~ **up,** devenir adulte. ~**er** n. cultiva|teur, -trice m., f.

growl /graʊl/ v.i. grogner. —n. grognement m.

grown /grəʊn/ see **grow**. —a. adulte. ~-**up** a. & n. adulte (m./f.).

growth /grəʊθ/ n. croissance f.; (in numbers) accroissement m.; (of hair, tooth) pousse f.; (med.) tumeur f.

grub /grʌb/ n. (larva) larve f.; (food: sl.) bouffe f.

grubby /ˈgrʌbɪ/ a. (-ier, -iest) sale.

grudge /grʌdʒ/ v.t. ~ **doing,** faire à contrecœur. ~ **s.o. sth.,** (success, wealth) en vouloir à qn. de qch. —n. rancune f. **have a** ~ **against,** en vouloir à. **grudgingly** adv. à contrecœur.

gruelling /ˈgruːəlɪŋ/ a. exténuant.

gruesome /ˈgruːsəm/ a. macabre.

gruff /grʌf/ a. (-er, -est) bourru.

grumble /ˈgrʌmbl/ v.i. ronchonner, grogner (at, après).

grumpy /ˈgrʌmpɪ/ a. (-ier, -iest) grincheux, grognon.

grunt /grʌnt/ v.i. grogner. —n. grognement m.

guarant|ee /gærənˈtiː/ n. garantie f. —v.t. garantir. ~**or** n. garant(e) m. (f.).

guard /gɑːd/ v.t. protéger; (watch) surveiller. —v.i. ~ **against,** se protéger contre. —n. (vigilance, mil. group) garde f.; (person) garde m.; (on train) chef de train m. ~**ian** n. gardien(ne) m. (f.); (of orphan) tu|teur, -trice m., f.

guarded /ˈgɑːdɪd/ a. prudent.

guerrilla /gəˈrɪlə/ n. guérillero m. ~ **warfare,** guérilla f.

guess /ges/ v.t./i. deviner; (suppose) penser. —n. conjecture f.

guesswork /ˈgeswɜːk/ n. conjectures f. pl.

guest /gest/ n. invité(e) m. (f.); (in hotel) client(e) m. (f.). ~-**house** n. pension f.

guffaw /gəˈfɔː/ n. gros rire m. —v.i. s'esclaffer, rire bruyamment.

guidance /ˈgaɪdns/ n. (advice) conseils m. pl.; (information) information f.

guide /gaɪd/ n. (person, book) guide m. —v.t. guider. ~**d** /-ɪd/ a. ~**d missile,** missile téléguidé m. ~-**lines** n. pl. grandes lignes f. pl.

Guide /gaɪd/ n. (girl) guide f.

guidebook /ˈgaɪdbʊk/ n. guide m.

guild /gɪld/ n. corporation f.

guile /gaɪl/ n. ruse f.

guillotine /ˈgɪlətiːn/ n. guillotine f.; (for paper) massicot m.

guilt /gɪlt/ n. culpabilité f. ~**y** a. coupable.

guinea-pig /ˈgɪnɪpɪg/ n. cobaye m.

guise /gaɪz/ n. apparence f.

guitar /gɪˈtɑː(r)/ n. guitare f. ~**ist** n. guitariste m./f.

gulf /gʌlf/ n. (part of sea) golfe m.; (hollow) gouffre m.

gull /gʌl/ n. mouette f., goéland m.

gullet /ˈgʌlɪt/ n. gosier m.

gullible /ˈgʌləbl/ a. crédule.

gully /ˈgʌlɪ/ n. (ravine) ravine f.; (drain) rigole f.

gulp /gʌlp/ v.t. ~ (**down**), avaler en vitesse. —v.i. (from fear etc.) avoir un serrement de gorge. —n. gorgée f.

gum[1] /gʌm/ n. (anat.) gencive f.

gum[2] /gʌm/ n. (from tree) gomme f.; (glue) colle f.; (for chewing) chewing-gum m. —v.t. (p.t. **gummed**) gommer.

gumboil /ˈgʌmbɔɪl/ n. abcès dentaire m.

gumboot /ˈgʌmbuːt/ n. botte de caoutchouc f.

gumption /ˈgʌmpʃn/ n. (fam.) initiative f., courage m., audace f.

gun /gʌn/ n. (pistol) pistolet m.; (rifle) fusil m.; (large) canon m. —v.t. (p.t. **gunned**). ~ **down,** abattre. ~**ner** n. artilleur m.

gunfire /ˈgʌnfaɪə(r)/ n. fusillade f.

gunge /gʌndʒ/ n. (sl.) crasse f.

gunman /ˈgʌnmən/ n. (pl. -**men**) bandit armé m.

gunpowder /ˈgʌnpaʊdə(r)/ n. poudre à canon f.

gunshot /ˈgʌnʃɒt/ n. coup de feu m.

gurgle /ˈgɜːgl/ n. glouglou m. —v.i. glouglouter.

guru /ˈgʊruː/ n. (pl. -**us**) gourou m.

gush /gʌʃ/ v.i. ~ (out), jaillir. —n. jaillissement m.

gust /gʌst/ n. rafale f.; (of smoke) bouffée f. ~y a. venteux.

gusto /'gʌstəʊ/ n. enthousiasme m.

gut /gʌt/ n. boyau m. ~s, boyaux m. pl., ventre m.; (courage: fam.) cran m. —v.t. (p.t. gutted) (fish) vider; (of fire) dévaster.

gutter /'gʌtə(r)/ n. (on roof) gouttière f.; (in street) caniveau m.

guttural /'gʌtərəl/ a. guttural.

guy /gaɪ/ n. (man: fam.) type m.

guzzle /'gʌzl/ v.t./i. (eat) bâfrer; (drink: Amer.) boire d'un trait.

gym /dʒɪm/ n. (fam.) gymnase m.; (fam.) gym(nastique) f. ~-slip n. tunique f. ~nasium n. gymnase m.

gymnast /'dʒɪmnæst/ n. gymnaste m./f. ~ics /-'næstɪks/ n. pl. gymnastique f.

gynaecolog|y /gaɪnɪ'kɒlədʒɪ/ n. gynécologie f. ~ist n. gynécologue m./f.

gypsy /'dʒɪpsɪ/ n. bohémien(ne) m. (f.).

gyrate /dʒaɪ'reɪt/ v.i. tournoyer.

H

haberdashery /hæbə'dæʃərɪ/ *n.* mercerie *f.*

habit /'hæbɪt/ *n.* habitude *f.*; (*costume: relig.*) habit *m.* **be in/get into the ~ of,** avoir/prendre l'habitude de.

habit|able /'hæbɪtəbl/ *a.* habitable. **~ation** /-'teɪʃn/ *n.* habitation *f.*

habitat /'hæbɪtæt/ *n.* habitat *m.*

habitual /hə'bɪtʃʊəl/ *a.* (*usual*) habituel; (*smoker, liar*) invétéré. **~ly** *adv.* habituellement.

hack[1] /hæk/ *n.* (*old horse*) haridelle *f.*; (*writer*) nègre *m.*, écrivailleu|r, -se *m., f.*

hack[2] /hæk/ *v.t.* hacher, tailler.

hackneyed /'hæknɪd/ *a.* rebattu.

had /hæd/ *see* have.

haddock /'hædək/ *n. invar.* églefin *m.* **smoked ~,** haddock *m.*

haemorrhage /'hemərɪdʒ/ *n.* hémorragie *f.*

haemorrhoids /'hemərɔɪdz/ *n. pl.* hémorroïdes *f. pl.*

hag /hæg/ *n.* (vieille) sorcière *f.*

haggard /'hægəd/ *a.* (*person*) qui a le visage défait; (*face, look*) défait, hagard.

haggle /'hægl/ *v.i.* marchander. **~ over,** (*object*) marchander; (*price*) discuter.

Hague (The) /(ðə)'heɪg/ *n.* La Haye.

hail[1] /heɪl/ *v.t.* (*greet*) saluer; (*taxi*) héler. —*v.i.* **~ from,** venir de.

hail[2] /heɪl/ *n.* grêle *f.* —*v.i.* grêler.

hailstone /'heɪlstəʊn/ *n.* grêlon *m.*

hair /heə(r)/ *n.* (*on head*) cheveux *m. pl.*; (*on body, of animal*) poils *m. pl.*; (*single strand on head*) cheveu *m.*; (*on body*) poil *m.* **~-do** *n.* (*fam.*) coiffure *f.* **~-raising** *a.* horrifique. **~-style** *n.* coiffure *f.*

hairbrush /'heəbrʌʃ/ *n.* brosse à cheveux *f.*

haircut /'heəkʌt/ *n.* coupe de cheveux *f.* **have a ~,** se faire couper les cheveux.

hairdresser /'heədresə(r)/ *n.* coiffeu|r, -se *m., f.*

hairpin /'heəpɪn/ *n.* épingle à cheveux *f.*

hairy /'heərɪ/ *a.* (-ier, -iest) poilu; (*terrifying: sl.*) horrifique.

hake /heɪk/ *n. invar.* colin *m.*

hale /heɪl/ *a.* vigoureux.

half /hɑːf/ *n.* (*pl.* **halves**) moitié *f.*, demi(e) *m.* (*f.*). —*a.* demi. —*adv.* à moitié. **~ a dozen,** une demi-douzaine. **~ an hour,** une demi-heure. **~-back** *n.* (*sport*) demi *m.* **~-caste** *n.* métis(se) *m.* (*f.*). **~-hearted** *a.* tiède. **at ~-mast** *adv.* en berne. **~-term** *n.* congé de (de)mi-trimestre *m.* **~-time** *n.* mi-temps *f.* **~-way** *adv.* à mi-chemin. **~-wit** *n.* imbécile *m./f.*

halibut /'hælɪbət/ *n. invar.* (*fish*) flétan *m.*

hall /hɔːl/ *n.* (*room*) salle *f.*; (*entrance*) vestibule *m.*; (*mansion*) manoir *m.*; (*corridor*) couloir *m.* **~ of residence,** foyer d'étudiants *m.*

hallelujah /hælɪ'luːjə/ *int. & n.* = **alleluia.**

hallmark /'hɔːlmɑːk/ *n.* (*on gold etc.*) poinçon *m.*; (*fig.*) sceau *m.*

hallo /hə'ləʊ/ *int. & n.* bonjour (*m.*). **~!,** (*telephone*) allô!; (*surprise*) tiens!

hallow /'hæləʊ/ *v.t.* sanctifier.

Hallowe'en /hæləʊ'iːn/ *n.* la veille de la Toussaint.

hallucination /həluːsɪ'neɪʃn/ *n.* hallucination *f.*

halo /'heɪləʊ/ *n.* (*pl.* **-oes**) auréole *f.*

halt /hɔːlt/ *n.* halte *f.* —*v.t./i.* (s')arrêter.

halve /hɑːv/ *v.t.* diviser en deux; (*time etc.*) réduire de moitié.

ham /hæm/ *n.* jambon *m.*; (*theatre: sl.*) cabotin(e) *m.* (*f.*).

hamburger /'hæmbɜːgə(r)/ *n.* hamburger *m.*

hamlet /'hæmlɪt/ *n.* hameau *m.*

hammer /'hæmə(r)/ marteau *m.* —*v.t./i.* marteler, frapper; (*defeat*) battre à plate couture.

hammock /'hæmək/ *n.* hamac *m.*

hamper[1] /'hæmpə(r)/ *n.* panier *m.*

hamper[2] /'hæmpə(r)/ *v.t.* gêner.

hamster /'hæmstə(r)/ *n.* hamster *m.*

hand /hænd/ *n.* main *f.*; (*of clock*) aiguille *f.*; (*writing*) écriture *f.*; (*worker*) ouvr|ier, -ière *m., f.*; (*cards*) jeu *m.* **(helping) ~,** coup de main *m.* —*v.t.* donner. **at ~,** proche. **~-luggage** *n.* bagages à main *m. pl.* **~ in** *or* **over,** remettre. **~ out,** distribuer. **~-out** *n.* prospectus *m.*; (*money*) aumône *f.* on ~, disponible. **on one's ~s**, (*fig.*) sur les bras. **on the one ~ . . . on the other ~**, d'une part . . . d'autre part. **to ~**, à portée de la main.

handbag /'hændbæg/ *n.* sac à main *m.*

handbook /'hændbʊk/ *n.* manuel *m.*

handcuffs /'hændkʌfs/ *n. pl.* menottes *f. pl.*

handful /'hændfʊl/ *n.* poignée *f.*; (*person*: *fam.*) personne difficile *f.*

handicap /'hændıkæp/ *n.* handicap *m.* —*v.t.* (*p.t.* **handicapped**) handicaper.

handicraft /'hændıkrɑːft/ *n.* travaux manuels *m. pl.*, artisanat *m.*

handiwork /'hændıwɜːk/ *n.* ouvrage *m.*

handkerchief /'hæŋkətʃıf/ *n.* (*pl.* **-fs**) mouchoir *m.*

handle /'hændl/ *n.* (*of door etc.*) poignée *f.*; (*of implement*) manche *m.*; (*of cup etc.*) anse *f.*; (*of pan etc.*) queue *f.* —*v.t.* manier; (*deal with*) s'occuper de; (*touch*) toucher à.

handlebar /'hændlbɑː(r)/ *n.* guidon *m.*

handshake /'hændʃeık/ *n.* poignée de main *f.*

handsome /'hænsəm/ *a.* (*goodlooking*) beau; (*generous*) généreux; (*large*) considérable.

handwriting /'hændraıtıŋ/ *n.* écriture *f.*

handy /'hændı/ *a.* (**-ier, -iest**) (*useful*) commode, utile; (*person*) adroit; (*near*) accessible.

handyman /'hændımæn/ *n.* (*pl.* **-men**) bricoleur *m.*; (*servant*) homme à tout faire *m.*

hang /hæŋ/ *v.t.* (*p.t.* **hung**) suspendre, accrocher; (*p.t.* **hanged**) (*criminal*) pendre. —*v.i.* pendre. —*n.* **get the ~ of doing**, trouver le truc pour faire. **~ about**, traîner. **~-gliding** *n.* vol libre *m.* **~ on**, (*hold out*) tenir bon; (*wait*: *sl.*) attendre. **~ out** *v.i.* pendre; (*live*: *sl.*) crécher; *v.t.* (*washing*) étendre. **~ up**, (*telephone*) raccrocher. **~-up** *n.* (*sl.*) complexe *m.*

hangar /'hæŋə(r)/ *n.* hangar *m.*

hanger /'hæŋə(r)/ *n.* (*for clothes*) cintre *m.* **~-on** *n.* parasite *m.*

hangover /'hæŋəʊvə(r)/ *n.* (*after drinking*) gueule de bois *f.*

hanker /'hæŋkə(r)/ *v.i.* **~ after**, avoir envie de. **~ing** *n.* envie *f.*

hanky-panky /'hæŋkıpæŋkı/ *n.* (*trickery*: *sl.*) manigances *f. pl.*

haphazard /hæp'hæzəd/ *a.*, **~ly** *adv.* au petit bonheur, au hasard.

hapless /'hæplıs/ *a.* infortuné.

happen /'hæpən/ *v.i.* arriver, se passer. **he ~s (often) to do**, il lui arrive (souvent) de faire. **he ~s to know that**, il se trouve qu'il sait que. **~ing** *n.* événement *m.*

happ|y /'hæpı/ *a.* (**-ier, -iest**) heureux. **~y medium** *or* **mean**, juste milieu *m.* **~ily** *adv.* joyeusement; (*fortunately*) heureusement. **~iness** *n.* bonheur *m.* **~y-go-lucky** *a.* insouciant.

harass /'hærəs/ *v.t.* harceler. **~ment** *n.* harcèlement *m.*

harbour /'hɑːbə(r)/ *n.* port *m.* —*v.t.* (*shelter*) héberger.

hard /hɑːd/ *a.* (**-er, -est**) dur; (*difficult*) difficile, dur. —*adv.* dur; (*think*) sérieusement; (*pull*) fort. **~-boiled egg**, œuf dur *m.* **~ by**, tout près. **~ done by**, mal traité. **~-headed** *a.* réaliste. **~ of hearing**, dur d'oreille. **~ shoulder**, accotement stabilisé *m.* **~ up**, (*fam.*) fauché. **~-working** *a.* travailleur. **~ness** *n.* dureté *f.*

hardboard /'hɑːdbɔːd/ *n.* Isorel *m.* (P.).

harden /'hɑːdn/ *v.t./i.* durcir.

hardly /'hɑːdlı/ *adv.* à peine. **~ ever**, presque jamais.

hardship /'hɑːdʃıp/ *n.* **~(s)**, épreuves *f. pl.*, souffrance *f.*

hardware /'hɑːdweə(r)/ *n.* (*metal goods*) quincaillerie *f.*; (*machinery, of computer*) matériel *m.*

hardy /'hɑːdı/ *a.* (**-ier, -iest**) résistant.

hare /heə(r)/ *n.* lièvre *m.* **~-brained** *a.* écervelé.

hark /hɑːk/ *v.i.* écouter. **~ back to**, revenir sur.

harm /hɑːm/ *n.* (*hurt*) mal *m.*; (*wrong*) tort *m.* —*v.t.* (*hurt*) faire du mal à; (*wrong*) faire du tort à; (*object*) endommager. **there is no ~ in**, il n'y a pas de mal à. **~ful** *a.* nuisible. **~less** *a.* inoffensif.

harmonica /hɑː'mɒnıkə/ *n.* harmonica *m.*

harmon|y /'hɑːmənı/ *n.* harmonie *f.* **~ious** /-'məʊnıəs/ *a.* harmonieux. **~ize** *v.t./i.* (s')harmoniser.

harness /'hɑːnıs/ *n.* harnais *m.* —*v.t.* (*horse*) harnacher; (*control*) maîtriser; (*use*) exploiter.

harp /hɑːp/ *n.* harpe *f.* —*v.i.* **~ on (about)**, rabâcher. **~ist** *n.* harpiste *m./f.*

harpoon /hɑː'puːn/ *n.* harpon *m.*

harpsichord /'hɑːpsɪkɔːd/ n. clavecin m.

harrowing /'hærəʊɪŋ/ a. déchirant, qui déchire le cœur.

harsh /hɑːʃ/ a. (-er, -est) dur, rude; (taste) âpre; (sound) rude, âpre. ~ly adv. durement. ~ness n. dureté f.

harvest /'hɑːvɪst/ n. moisson f., récolte f. —v.t. moissonner, récolter. ~er n. moissonneuse f.

has /hæz/ see have.

hash /hæʃ/ n. (culin.) hachis m.; (fig.) gâchis m. **make a ~ of**, (bungle: sl.) saboter.

hashish /'hæʃiːʃ/ n. ha(s)chisch m.

hassle /'hæsl/ n. (fam.) difficulté(s) f. (pl.); (bother, effort: fam.) mal m., peine f.; (quarrel: fam.) chamaillerie f. —v.t. (harass: fam.) harceler.

haste /heɪst/ n. hâte f. **in ~**, à la hâte. **make ~**, se hâter.

hasten /'heɪsn/ v.t./i. (se) hâter.

hast|y /'heɪstɪ/ a. (-ier, -iest) précipité. ~ily adv. à la hâte.

hat /hæt/ n. chapeau m. **a ~ trick**, trois succès consécutifs.

hatch[1] /hætʃ/ n. (for food) passe-plat m.; (naut.) écoutille f.

hatch[2] /hætʃ/ v.t./i. (faire) éclore.

hatchback /'hætʃbæk/ n. voiture avec hayon arrière f.

hatchet /'hætʃɪt/ n. hachette f.

hate /heɪt/ n. haine f. —v.t. haïr. ~ful a. haïssable.

hatred /'heɪtrɪd/ n. haine f.

haughty /'hɔːtɪ/ a. (-ier, -iest) hautain.

haul /hɔːl/ v.t. traîner, tirer; (goods) camionner. —n. (of thieves) butin m.; (catch) prise f.; (journey) voyage m. ~age n. camionnage m. ~ier n. camionneur m.

haunt /hɔːnt/ v.t. hanter. —n. endroit favori m.

have /hæv/ v.t. (3 sing. present tense has; p.t. had) avoir; (meal, bath, etc.) prendre; (walk, dream, etc.) faire. — v. aux. avoir; (with aller, partir, etc. & pronominal verbs) être. **~ it out with**, s'expliquer avec. **~ just done**, venir de faire. **~ sth. done**, faire faire qch. **~ to do**, devoir faire. **the ~s and have-nots**, les riches et les pauvres m. pl.

haven /'heɪvn/ n. havre m., abri m.

haversack /'hævəsæk/ n. musette f.

havoc /'hævək/ n. ravages m. pl.

haw /hɔː/ see hum.

hawk[1] /hɔːk/ n. faucon m.

hawk[2] /hɔːk/ v.t. colporter. ~er n. colporteu|r, -se m., f.

hawthorn /'hɔːθɔːn/ n. aubépine f.

hay /heɪ/ n. foin m. **~ fever**, rhume des foins m.

haystack /'heɪstæk/ n. meule de foin f.

haywire /'heɪwaɪə(r)/ a. **go ~**, (plans) se désorganiser; (machine) se détraquer.

hazard /'hæzəd/ n. risque m. —v.t. risquer, hasarder. ~ous a. hasardeux, risqué.

haze /heɪz/ n. brume f.

hazel /'heɪzl/ n. (bush) noisetier m. **~-nut** n. noisette f.

hazy /'heɪzɪ/ a. (-ier, -iest) (misty) brumeux; (fig.) flou, vague.

he /hiː/ pron. il; (emphatic) lui. —n. mâle m.

head /hed/ n. tête f.; (leader) chef m.; (of beer) mousse f. —a. principal. —v.t. être à la tête de. —v.i. **~ for**, se diriger vers. **~-dress** n. coiffure f.; (lady's) coiffe f. **~-on** a. & adv. de plein fouet. **~s or tails?**, pile ou face? **~ the ball**, faire une tête. **~ waiter**, maître d'hôtel m. ~er n. (football) tête f.

headache /'hedeɪk/ n. mal de tête m.

heading /'hedɪŋ/ n. titre m.; (subject category) rubrique f.

headlamp /'hedlæmp/ n. phare m.

headland /'hedlənd/ n. cap m.

headlight /'hedlaɪt/ n. phare m.

headline /'hedlaɪn/ n. titre m.

headlong /'hedlɒŋ/ adv. (in a rush) à toute allure.

head|master /hed'mɑːstə(r)/ n. (of school) directeur m. ~mistress n. directrice f.

headphone /'hedfəʊn/ n. écouteur m. **~s**, casque (à écouteurs) m.

headquarters /'hedkwɔːtəz/ n. pl. siège m., bureau central m.; (mil.) quartier général m.

headstrong /'hedstrɒŋ/ a. têtu.

headway /'hedweɪ/ n. progrès m. (pl.). **make ~**, faire des progrès.

heady /'hedɪ/ a. (-ier, -iest) (wine) capiteux; (exciting) grisant.

heal /hiːl/ v.t./i. guérir.

health /helθ/ n. santé f. ~y a. sain; (person) en bonne santé.

heap /hiːp/ n. tas m. —v.t. entasser. **~s of**, (fam.) des tas de.

hear /hɪə(r)/ v.t./i. (p.t. heard /hɜːd/) entendre. **hear, hear!**, bravo! ~

from, recevoir des nouvelles de. ~
of *or* **about,** entendre parler de. **not**
~ **of,** (*refuse to allow*) ne pas entendre
parler de. ~**ing** *n.* ouïe *f.*; (*of witness*)
audition *f.* ~**ing-aid** *n.* appareil acoustique *m.*

hearsay /'hɪəseɪ/ *n.* ouï-dire *m. invar.*
from ~, par ouï-dire.

hearse /hɜːs/ *n.* corbillard *m.*

heart /hɑːt/ *n.* cœur *m.* ~**s,** (*cards*)
cœur *m.* **at** ~, au fond. **by** ~, par
cœur. ~ **attack,** crise cardiaque *f.* ~-
break *n.* chagrin *m.* ~**breaking** *a.*
navrant. **be** ~-**broken,** avoir le cœur
brisé. ~-**to-heart** *a.* à cœur ouvert.
lose ~, perdre courage.

heartache /'hɑːteɪk/ *n.* chagrin *m.*

heartburn /'hɑːtbɜːn/ *n.* brûlures d'estomac *f. pl.*

hearten /'hɑːtn/ *v.t.* encourager.

heartfelt /'hɑːtfelt/ *a.* sincère.

hearth /hɑːθ/ *n.* foyer *m.*

heartless /'hɑːtlɪs/ *a.* cruel.

heart|y /'hɑːtɪ/ *a.* (**-ier, -iest**) (*sincere*)
chaleureux; (*meal*) gros. ~**ily** *adv.*
(*eat*) avec appétit.

heat /hiːt/ *n.* chaleur *f.*; (*excitement*:
fig.) feu *m.*; (*contest*) éliminatoire *f.*
—*v.t./i.* chauffer. ~ **stroke,** insolation *f.* ~ **wave,** vague de chaleur *f.*
~**er** *n.* radiateur *m.* ~**ing** *n.* chauffage *m.*

heated /'hiːtɪd/ *a.* (*fig.*) passionné.

heath /hiːθ/ *n.* (*area*) lande *f.*

heathen /'hiːðn/ *n.* païen(ne) *m.* (*f.*).

heather /'heðə(r)/ *n.* bruyère *f.*

heave /hiːv/ *v.t./i.* (*lift*) (se) soulever;
(*a sigh*) pousser; (*throw*: *fam.*) lancer;
(*retch*) avoir des nausées.

heaven /'hevn/ *n.* ciel *m.* ~**ly** *a.*
céleste; (*pleasing*: *fam.*) divin.

heav|y /'hevɪ/ *a.* (**-ier, -iest**) lourd;
(*cold, work, etc.*) gros; (*traffic*) dense.
~**ily** *adv.* lourdement; (*smoke, drink*)
beaucoup.

heavyweight /'hevɪweɪt/ *n.* poids
lourd *m.*

Hebrew /'hiːbruː/ *a.* hébreu (*m. only*),
hébraïque. —*n.* (*lang.*) hébreu *m.*

heckle /'hekl/ *v.t.* (*speaker*) interrompre, interpeller.

hectic /'hektɪk/ *a.* très bousculé, trépi-
dant, agité.

hedge /hedʒ/ *n.* haie *f.* —*v.t.* entourer. —*v.i.* (*in answering*) répondre
évasivement.

hedgehog /'hedʒhɒg/ *n.* hérisson *m.*

heed /hiːd/ *v.t.* faire attention à. —*n.*

pay ~ **to,** faire attention à. ~**less** *a.*
~**less of,** inattentif à.

heel /hiːl/ *n.* talon *m.*; (*man*: *sl.*) salaud
m. **down at** ~, (*Amer.*) **down at the**
~**s,** miteux.

hefty /'heftɪ/ *a.* (**-ier, -iest**) gros, lourd.

heifer /'hefə(r)/ *n.* génisse *f.*

height /haɪt/ *n.* hauteur *f.*; (*of person*)
taille *f.*; (*of plane, mountain*) altitude
f.; (*of fame, glory*) apogée *m.*; (*of joy,
folly, pain*) comble *m.*

heighten /'haɪtn/ *v.t.* (*raise*) rehausser;
(*fig.*) augmenter.

heinous /'heɪnəs/ *a.* atroce.

heir /eə(r)/ *n.* héritier *m.* ~**ess** *n.*
héritière *f.*

heirloom /'eəluːm/ *n.* bijou (meuble,
tableau, *etc.*) de famille *m.*

held /held/ *see* **hold**[1].

helicopter /'helɪkɒptə(r)/ *n.* hélicoptère *m.*

heliport /'helɪpɔːt/ *n.* héliport *m.*

hell /hel/ *n.* enfer *m.* ~-**bent** *a.*
acharné (**on,** à). ~**ish** *a.* infernal.

hello /hə'ləʊ/ *int. & n.* = **hallo.**

helm /helm/ *n.* (*of ship*) barre *f.*

helmet /'helmɪt/ *n.* casque *m.*

help /help/ *v.t./i.* aider. —*n.* aide *f.*;
(*employees*) personnel *m.*; (*charwoman*) femme de ménage *f.* ~ **o.s.
to,** se servir de. **he cannot** ~ **laughing,** il ne peut pas s'empêcher de
rire. ~**er** *n.* aide *m.*/*f.* ~**ful** *a.* utile;
(*person*) serviable. ~**less** *a.* impuissant.

helping /'helpɪŋ/ *n.* portion *f.*

helter-skelter /heltə'skeltə(r)/ *n.*
toboggan *m.* —*adv.* pêle-mêle.

hem /hem/ *n.* ourlet *m.* —*v.t.* (*p.t.*
hemmed) ourler. ~ **in,** enfermer.

hemisphere /'hemɪsfɪə(r)/ *n.* hémisphère *m.*

hemp /hemp/ *n.* chanvre *m.*

hen /hen/ *n.* poule *f.*

hence /hens/ *adv.* (*for this reason*)
d'où; (*from now*) d'ici. ~**forth** *adv.*
désormais.

henchman /'hentʃmən/ *n.* (*pl.* -**men**)
acolyte *m.*, homme de main *m.*

henpecked /'henpekt/ *a.* dominé *or*
harcelé par sa femme.

her /hɜː(r)/ *pron.* la, l'*; (*after prep.*)
elle. (**to**) ~, lui. **I know** ~, je la
connais. —*a.* son, sa, *pl.* ses.

herald /'herəld/ *v.t.* annoncer.

heraldry /'herəldrɪ/ *n.* héraldique *f.*

herb /hɜːb, *Amer.* ɜːb/ *n.* herbe *f.* ~**s,**
(*culin.*) fines herbes *f. pl.*

herd /hɜːd/ *n.* troupeau *m.* —*v.t./i.* ~ **together**, (s')entasser.

here /hɪə(r)/ *adv.* ici. ~!, (*take this*) tenez! ~ **is**, ~ **are**, voici. ~**abouts** *adv.* par ici.

hereafter /hɪər'ɑːftə(r)/ *adv.* après; (*in book*) ci-après.

hereby /hɪə'baɪ/ *adv.* par le présent acte; (*in letter*) par la présente.

hereditary /hə'redɪtərɪ/ *a.* héréditaire.

heredity /hə'redətɪ/ *n.* hérédité *f.*

here|sy /'herəsɪ/ *n.* hérésie *f.* ~**tic** *n.* hérétique *m./f.*

herewith /hɪə'wɪð/ *adv.* (*comm.*) avec ceci, ci-joint.

heritage /'herɪtɪdʒ/ *n.* patrimoine *m.*, héritage *m.*

hermetic /hɜː'metɪk/ *a.* hermétique.

hermit /'hɜːmɪt/ *n.* ermite *m.*

hernia /'hɜːnɪə/ *n.* hernie *f.*

hero /'hɪərəʊ/ *n.* (*pl.* **-oes**) héros *m.* ~**ine** /'herəʊɪn/ *n.* héroïne *f.* ~**ism** /'herəʊɪzəm/ *n.* héroïsme *m.*

heroic /hɪ'rəʊɪk/ *a.* héroïque.

heroin /'herəʊɪn/ *n.* héroïne *f.*

heron /'herən/ *n.* héron *m.*

herring /'herɪŋ/ *n.* hareng *m.*

hers /hɜːz/ *poss. pron.* le sien, la sienne, les sien(ne)s. **it is** ~, c'est à elle *or* le sien.

herself /hɜː'self/ *pron.* elle-même; (*reflexive*) se; (*after prep.*) elle.

hesitant /'hezɪtənt/ *a.* hésitant.

hesitat|e /'hezɪteɪt/ *v.i.* hésiter. ~**ion** /-'teɪʃn/ *n.* hésitation *f.*

het /het/ *a.* ~ **up**, (*sl.*) énervé.

heterogeneous /hetərə'dʒiːnɪəs/ *a.* hétérogène.

hew /hjuː/ *v.t.* (*p.p.* **hewn**) tailler.

hexagon /'heksəgən/ *n.* hexagone *m.* ~**al** /-'ægənl/ *a.* hexagonal.

hey /heɪ/ *int.* dites donc.

heyday /'heɪdeɪ/ *n.* apogée *m.*

hi /haɪ/ *int.* (*greeting*: *Amer.*) salut.

hibernat|e /'haɪbəneɪt/ *v.i.* hiberner. ~**ion** /-'neɪʃn/ *n.* hibernation *f.*

hiccup /'hɪkʌp/ *n.* hoquet *m.* —*v.i.* hoqueter. (**the**) ~**s**, le hoquet.

hide[1] /haɪd/ *v.t.* (*p.t.* **hid**, *p.p.* **hidden**) cacher (**from**, à). —*v.i.* se cacher (**from**, de). **go into hiding**, se cacher. ~-**out** *n.* (*fam.*) cachette *f.*

hide[2] /haɪd/ *n.* (*skin*) peau *f.*

hideous /'hɪdɪəs/ *a.* (*dreadful*) atroce; (*ugly*) hideux.

hiding /'haɪdɪŋ/ *n.* (*thrashing*: *fam.*) correction *f.*

hierarchy /'haɪərɑːkɪ/ *n.* hiérarchie *f.*

hi-fi /haɪ'faɪ/ *a.* & *n.* hi-fi *a.* & *f. invar.*; (*gramophone*) chaîne hi-fi *f.*

high /haɪ/ *a.* (**-er**, **-est**) haut; (*price, number*) élevé; (*priest, speed*) grand; (*voice*) aigu. —*n.* **a** (**new**) ~, (*recorded level*) un record. —*adv.* haut. ~-**handed** *a.* autoritaire. ~-**jump**, saut en hauteur *m.* ~-**rise building**, tour *f.* ~ **road**, grand-route *f.* ~ **school**, lycée *m.* **in the** ~ **season**, en pleine saison. ~-**speed** *a.* ultra-rapide. ~ **spot**, (*fam.*) point culminant *m.* ~ **street**, grand-rue *f.* ~-**strung** *a.* (*Amer.*) nerveux. ~ **tea**, goûter dînatoire *m.* ~**er education**, enseignement supérieur *m.*

highbrow /'haɪbraʊ/ *a.* & *n.* intellectuel(le) (*m.* (*f.*)).

highlight /'haɪlaɪt/ *n.* (*vivid moment*) instant remarquable *m.* —*v.t.* (*emphasize*) souligner.

highly /'haɪlɪ/ *adv.* extrêmement; (*paid*) très bien. ~-**strung** *a.* nerveux. **speak/think** ~ **of**, dire/penser du bien de.

Highness /'haɪnɪs/ *n.* Altesse *f.*

highway /'haɪweɪ/ *n.* route nationale *f.*

hijack /'haɪdʒæk/ *v.t.* détourner. —*n.* détournement *m.* ~**er** *n.* pirate (de l'air) *m.*

hike /haɪk/ *n.* excursion à pied *f.* —*v.i.* aller à pied. ~**r** /-ə(r)/ *n.* excursionniste *m./f.*

hilarious /hɪ'leərɪəs/ *a.* (*funny*) désopilant.

hill /hɪl/ *n.* colline *f.*; (*slope*) côte *f.* ~-**billy** *n.* (*Amer.*) péquenaud(e) *m.* (*f.*). ~**y** *a.* accidenté.

hillside /'hɪlsaɪd/ *n.* coteau *m.*

hilt /hɪlt/ *n.* (*of sword*) garde *f.* **to the** ~, tout à fait, au maximum.

him /hɪm/ *pron.* le, l'*; (*after prep.*) lui. (**to**) ~, lui. **I know** ~, je le connais.

himself /hɪm'self/ *pron.* lui-même; (*reflexive*) se; (*after prep.*) lui.

hind /haɪnd/ *a.* de derrière.

hind|er /'hɪndə(r)/ *v.t.* (*hamper*) gêner; (*prevent*) empêcher. ~**rance** *n.* obstacle *m.*, gêne *f.*

hindsight /'haɪndsaɪt/ *n.* **with** ~, rétrospectivement.

Hindu /hɪn'duː/ *n.* & *a.* hindou(e) (*m.* (*f.*)). ~**ism** /'hɪnduːɪzəm/ *n.* hindouisme *m.*

hinge /hɪndʒ/ *n.* charnière *f.* —*v.i.* ~ **on**, (*depend on*) dépendre de.

hint /hɪnt/ *n.* allusion *f.*; (*advice*) con-

seil *m.* —*v.t.* laisser entendre. —*v.i.*
~ **at,** faire allusion à.

hip /hɪp/ *n.* hanche *f.*

hippie /'hɪpɪ/ *n.* hippie *m.*/*f.*

hippopotamus /hɪpə'pɒtəməs/ *n.* (*pl.*
-**muses**) hippopotame *m.*

hire /'haɪə(r)/ *v.t.* (*thing*) louer; (*person*) engager. —*n.* location *f.* ~-**purchase** *n.* achat à crédit *m.*, vente à
crédit. *f.*

hirsute /'hɜːsjuːt/ *a.* hirsute.

his /hɪz/ *a.* son, sa, *pl.* ses. —*poss. pron.*
le sien, la sienne, les sien(ne)s. **it is**
~, c'est à lui *or* le sien.

hiss /hɪs/ *n.* sifflement *m.* —*v.t.*/*i.*
siffler.

historian /hɪ'stɔːrɪən/ *n.* historien(ne)
m. (*f.*).

histor|y /'hɪstərɪ/ *n.* histoire *f.* **make**
~**y,** entrer dans l'histoire. ~**ic(al)**
/hɪ'stɒrɪk(l)/ *a.* historique.

histrionic /hɪstrɪ'ɒnɪk/ *a.* théâtral.

hit /hɪt/ *v.t.* (*p.t.* **hit,** *pres. p.* **hitting**)
frapper; (*knock against, collide with*)
heurter; (*find*) trouver; (*affect*)
toucher. —*v.i.* ~ **on,** (*find*) tomber
sur. —*n.* (*blow*) coup *m.*; (*fig.*) succès
m. ~ **it off,** s'entendre bien (**with,**
avec). ~-**or-miss** *a.* fait au petit
bonheur.

hitch /hɪtʃ/ *v.t.* (*fasten*) accrocher.
—*n.* (*snag*) anicroche *f.* ~ **a lift,** ~-
hike *v.i.* faire de l'auto-stop. ~-**hiker**
n. auto-stoppeu|r, -se *m.*,*f.* ~ **up,** (*pull
up*) remonter.

hitherto /hɪðə'tuː/ *adv.* jusqu'ici.

hive /haɪv/ *n.* ruche *f.* —*v.t.* ~ **off,**
séparer; (*industry*) dénationaliser.

hoard /hɔːd/ *v.t.* amasser. —*n.* réserve(s) *f.* (*pl.*); (*of money*) magot *m.*,
trésor *m.*

hoarding /'hɔːdɪŋ/ *n.* panneau d'affichage *m.*

hoar-frost /'hɔːfrɒst/ *n.* givre *m.*

hoarse /hɔːs/ *a.* (-**er,** -**est**) enroué.
~**ness** *n.* enrouement *m.*

hoax /həʊks/ *n.* canular *m.* —*v.t.* faire
un canular à.

hob /hɒb/ *n.* plaque chauffante *f.*

hobble /'hɒbl/ *v.i.* clopiner.

hobby /'hɒbɪ/ *n.* passe-temps *m. invar.*
~-**horse** *n.* (*fig.*) dada *m.*

hob-nob /'hɒbnɒb/ *v.i.* (*p.t.* **hob-
nobbed**). ~ **with,** frayer avec.

hock[1] /hɒk/ *n.* vin du Rhin *m.*

hock[2] /hɒk/ *v.t.* (*pawn: sl.*) mettre au
clou.

hockey /'hɒkɪ/ *n.* hockey *m.*

hodgepodge /'hɒdʒpɒdʒ/ *n.* fatras *m.*

hoe /həʊ/ *n.* binette *f.* —*v.t.* (*pres. p.*
hoeing) biner.

hog /hɒg/ *n.* cochon *m.* —*v.t.* (*p.t.* **hog-
ged**) (*fam.*) accaparer.

hoist /hɔɪst/ *v.t.* hisser. —*n.* palan *m.*

hold[1] /həʊld/ *v.t.* (*p.t.* **held**) tenir; (*contain*) contenir; (*interest, breath, etc.*)
retenir; (*possess*) avoir; (*believe*)
maintenir. —*v.i.* (*of rope, weather,
etc.*) tenir. —*n.* prise *f.* **get** ~ **of,** saisir;
(*fig.*) trouver. ~ **back,** (*contain*) retenir; (*hide*) cacher. ~ **on,** (*stand
firm*) tenir bon; (*wait*) attendre. ~
on to, (*keep*) garder; (*cling to*) se
cramponner à. ~ **one's tongue,** se
taire. ~ **out** *v.t.* (*offer*) offrir; *v.i.*
(*resist*) tenir le coup. ~ **up,** (*support*)
soutenir; (*delay*) retarder; (*rob*) attaquer. ~-**up** *n.* retard *m.*; (*of traffic*)
bouchon *m.*; (*robbery*) hold-up *m. in-
var.* ~ **with,** approuver. ~**er** *n.* dé-
ten|teur, -trice *m.*,*f.*; (*of post*) titulaire
m./*f.*; (*for object*) support *m.*

hold[2] /həʊld/ *n.* (*of ship*) cale *f.*

holdall /'həʊldɔːl/ *n.* (*bag*) fourre-tout
m. invar.

holding /'həʊldɪŋ/ *n.* (*possession, land*)
possession *f.*

hole /həʊl/ *n.* trou *m.* —*v.t.* trouer.

holiday /'hɒlədeɪ/ *n.* vacances *f. pl.*;
(*public*) jour férié *m.*; (*day off*) congé
m. —*v.i.* passer ses vacances. ~-
maker *n.* vacanc|ier, -ière *m.*,*f.*

holiness /'həʊlɪnɪs/ *n.* sainteté *f.*

Holland /'hɒlənd/ *n.* Hollande *f.*

hollow /'hɒləʊ/ *a.* creux; (*fig.*) faux.
—*n.* creux *m.* —*v.t.* creuser.

holly /'hɒlɪ/ *n.* houx *m.*

holster /'həʊlstə(r)/ *n.* étui de revolver
m.

holy /'həʊlɪ/ *a.* (-**ier,** -**iest**) saint, sacré;
(*water*) bénit. **H**~ **Ghost, H**~ **Spirit,**
Saint-Esprit *m.*

homage /'hɒmɪdʒ/ *n.* hommage *m.*

home /həʊm/ *n.* maison *f.*, foyer *m.*;
(*institution*) maison *f.*; (*for soldiers,
workers*) foyer *m.*; (*country*) pays natal *m.* —*a.* de la maison, du foyer;
(*of family*) de famille; (*pol.*) national,
intérieur; (*match, visit*) à domicile.
—*adv.* (**at**) ~, à la maison, chez soi.
come *or* **go** ~, rentrer; (*from abroad*)
rentrer dans son pays. **feel at** ~
with, être à l'aise avec. **H**~ **Coun-
ties,** région autour de Londres *f.*
H~ **Office,** ministère de l'Intérieur
m. **H**~ **Secretary,** ministre de

l'Intérieur *m.* ~ **town,** ville natale *f.* ~ **truth,** vérité bien sentie *f.* ~**less** *a.* sans abri.

homeland /'həʊmlænd/ *n.* patrie *f.*

homely /'həʊmlɪ/ *a.* (**-ier, -iest**) simple; (*person: Amer.*) assez laid.

homesick /'həʊmsɪk/ *a.* **be** ~, avoir le mal du pays.

homeward /'həʊmwəd/ *a.* (*journey*) de retour.

homework /'həʊmwɜːk/ *n.* devoirs *m. pl.*

homicide /'hɒmɪsaɪd/ *n.* homicide *m.*

homogeneous /hɒmə'dʒiːnɪəs/ *a.* homogène.

homosexual /hɒmə'sekʃʊəl/ *a.* & *n.* homosexuel(le) (*m.* (*f.*)).

honest /'ɒnɪst/ *a.* honnête; (*frank*) franc. ~**ly** *adv.* honnêtement; franchement. ~**y** *n.* honnêteté *f.*

honey /'hʌnɪ/ *n.* miel *m.*; (*person: fam.*) chéri(e) *m.* (*f.*).

honeycomb /'hʌnɪkəʊm/ *n.* rayon de miel *m.*

honeymoon /'hʌnɪmuːn/ *n.* lune de miel *f.*

honk /hɒŋk/ *v.i.* klaxonner.

honorary /'ɒnərərɪ/ *a.* (*person*) honoraire; (*duties*) honorifique.

honour /'ɒnə(r)/ *n.* honneur *m.* —*v.t.* honorer. ~**able** *a.* honorable.

hood /hʊd/ *n.* capuchon *m.*; (*car roof*) capote *f.*; (*car engine cover: Amer.*) capot *m.*

hoodlum /'huːdləm/ *n.* voyou *m.*

hoodwink /'hʊdwɪŋk/ *v.t.* tromper.

hoof /huːf/ *n.* (*pl.* **-fs**) sabot *m.*

hook /hʊk/ *n.* crochet *m.*; (*on garment*) agrafe *f.*; (*for fishing*) hameçon *m.* —*v.t./i.* (s')accrocher; (*garment*) (s')agrafer. **off the** ~, tiré d'affaire; (*phone*) décroché.

hooked /hʊkt/ *a.* crochu. ~ **on,** (*sl.*) adonné à.

hooker /'hʊkə(r)/ *n.* (*rugby*) talonneur *m.*; (*Amer., sl.*) prostituée *f.*

hookey /'hʊkɪ/ *n.* **play** ~, (*Amer., sl.*) faire l'école buissonnière.

hooligan /'huːlɪɡən/ *n.* voyou *m.*

hoop /huːp/ *n.* (*toy etc.*) cerceau *m.*

hooray /huː'reɪ/ *int.* & *n.* = **hurrah.**

hoot /huːt/ *n.* (h)ululement *m.*; coup de klaxon *m.*; huée *f.* —*v.i.* (*owl*) (h)ululer; (*of car*) klaxonner; (*jeer*) huer. ~**er** *n.* klaxon *m.* (P.); (*of factory*) sirène *f.*

Hoover /'huːvə(r)/ *n.* (P.) aspirateur *m.* —*v.t.* passer à l'aspirateur.

hop[1] /hɒp/ *v.i.* (*p.t.* **hopped**) sauter (à cloche-pied). —*n.* saut *m.*; (*flight*) étape *f.* ~ **in,** (*fam.*) monter. ~ **it,** (*sl.*) décamper. ~ **out,** (*fam.*) descendre.

hop[2] /hɒp/ *n.* ~(**s**), houblon *m.*

hope /həʊp/ *n.* espoir *m.* —*v.t./i.* espérer. ~ **for,** espérer (avoir). ~**ful** *a.* encourageant. **be** ~**ful** (**that**), avoir bon espoir (que). ~**fully** *adv.* avec espoir; (*it is hoped*) on l'espère. ~**less** *a.* sans espoir; (*useless: fig.*) nul. ~**lessly** *adv.* sans espoir *m.*

hopscotch /'hɒpskɒtʃ/ *n.* marelle *f.*

horde /hɔːd/ *n.* horde *f.*, foule *f.*

horizon /hə'raɪzn/ *n.* horizon *m.*

horizontal /hɒrɪ'zɒntl/ *a.* horizontal.

hormone /'hɔːməʊn/ *n.* hormone *f.*

horn /hɔːn/ *n.* corne *f.*; (*of car*) klaxon *m.* (P.); (*mus.*) cor *m.* —*v.i.* ~ **in,** (*sl.*) interrompre. ~**y** *a.* (*hands*) calleux.

hornet /'hɔːnɪt/ *n.* frelon *m.*

horoscope /'hɒrəskəʊp/ *n.* horoscope *m.*

horrible /'hɒrəbl/ *a.* horrible.

horrid /'hɒrɪd/ *a.* horrible.

horrific /hə'rɪfɪk/ *a.* horrifiant.

horr|or /'hɒrə(r)/ *n.* horreur *f.* —*a.* (*film etc.*) d'épouvante. ~**ify** *v.t.* horrifier.

hors-d'œuvre /ɔː'dɜːvrə/ *n.* hors d'œuvre *m. invar.*

horse /hɔːs/ *n.* cheval *m.* ~- **chestnut** *n.* marron (d'Inde) *m.* ~**-radish** *n.* raifort *m.* ~ **sense,** (*fam.*) bon sens *m.*

horseback /'hɔːsbæk/ *n.* **on** ~, à cheval.

horseman /'hɔːsmən/ *n.* (*pl.* **-men**) cavalier *m.*

horsepower /'hɔːspaʊə(r)/ *n.* (*unit*) cheval (vapeur) *m.*

horseshoe /'hɔːsʃuː/ *n.* fer à cheval *m.*

horsy /'hɔːsɪ/ *a.* (*face etc.*) chevalin.

horticultur|e /'hɔːtɪkʌltʃə(r)/ *n.* horticulture *f.* ~**al** /-'kʌltʃərəl/ *a.* horticole.

hose /həʊz/ *n.* (*tube*) tuyau *m.* —*v.t.* arroser. ~**-pipe** *n.* tuyau *m.*

hosiery /'həʊzɪərɪ/ *n.* bonneterie *f.*

hospice /'hɒspɪs/ *n.* hospice *m.*

hospit|able /hɒ'spɪtəbl/ *a.* hospitalier. ~**ably** *adv.* avec hospitalité. ~**ality** /-'tælətɪ/ *n.* hospitalité *f.*

hospital /'hɒspɪtl/ *n.* hôpital *m.*

host[1] /həʊst/ *n.* (*master of house*) hôte *m.* ~**ess** *n.* hôtesse *f.*

host[2] /həʊst/ *n.* **a** ~ **of,** une foule de.

host[3] /həʊst/ n. (relig.) hostie f.

hostage /'hɒstɪdʒ/ n. otage m.

hostel /'hɒstl/ n. foyer m.

hostil|e /'hɒstaɪl/ a. hostile. **~ity** /hɒ'stɪlətɪ/ n. hostilité f.

hot /hɒt/ a. (**hotter, hottest**) chaud; (culin.) épicé; (news) récent. **be** or **feel ~**, avoir chaud. **it is ~**, il fait chaud. —v.t./i. (p.t. **hotted**). **~ up**, (fam.) chauffer. **~ dog**, hot-dog m. **~ line**, téléphone rouge m. **~ shot**, (Amer., sl.) crack m. **~-water bottle**, bouillotte f. **in ~ water**, (fam.) dans le pétrin. **~ly** adv. vivement.

hotbed /'hɒtbed/ n. foyer m.

hotchpotch /'hɒtʃpɒtʃ/ n. fatras m.

hotel /həʊ'tel/ n. hôtel m. **~ier** /-ɪeɪ/ n. hôtel|ier, -ière m., f.

hothead /'hɒthed/ n. tête brûlée f. **~ed** a. impétueux.

hotplate /'hɒtpleɪt/ n. plaque chauffante f.

hound /haʊnd/ n. chien courant m. —v.t. poursuivre.

hour /'aʊə(r)/ n. heure f. **~ly** a. & adv. toutes les heures. **~ly pay**, salaire horaire m. **paid ~ly**, payé à l'heure.

house[1] /haʊs/ n. (pl. **-s** /'haʊzɪz/) n. maison f.; (theatre) salle f.; (pol.) chambre f. **~-proud** a. méticuleux. **~-warming** n. pendaison de la crémaillère f.

house[2] /haʊz/ v.t. loger; (of building) abriter; (keep) garder.

housebreaking /'haʊsbreɪkɪŋ/ n. cambriolage m.

household /'haʊshəʊld/ n. (house, family) ménage m. **~er** n. occupant(e) m. (f.); (owner) propriétaire m./f.

housekeep|er /'haʊskiːpə(r)/ n. gouvernante f. **~ing** n. ménage m.

housewife /'haʊswaɪf/ n. (pl. **-wives**) ménagère f.

housework /'haʊswɜːk/ n. ménage m., travaux de ménage m. pl.

housing /'haʊzɪŋ/ n. logement m.

hovel /'hɒvl/ n. taudis m.

hover /'hɒvə(r)/ v.i. (bird, threat, etc.) planer; (loiter) rôder.

hovercraft /'hɒvəkrɑːft/ n. aéroglisseur m.

how /haʊ/ adv. comment. **~ long/tall is . . . ?**, quelle est la longueur/hauteur de . . . ? **~ pretty!**, comme or que c'est joli! **~ about a walk?**, si on faisait une promenade? **~ are you?**, comment allez-vous? **~ do you do?**, (in-

troduction) enchanté. **~ many?, ~ much?**, combien?

however /haʊ'evə(r)/ adv. de quelque manière que; (nevertheless) cependant. **~ small/delicate/etc. it may be**, quelque petit/délicat/etc. que ce soit.

howl /haʊl/ n. hurlement m. —v.i. hurler.

howler /'haʊlə(r)/ n. (fam.) bévue f.

HP abbr. see **hire-purchase**.

hp abbr. see **horsepower**.

hub /hʌb/ n. moyeu m.; (fig.) centre m. **~-cap** n. enjoliveur m.

hubbub /'hʌbʌb/ n. vacarme m.

huddle /'hʌdl/ v.i. se blottir.

hue[1] /hjuː/ n. (colour) teinte f.

hue[2] /hjuː/ n. **~ and cry**, clameur f.

huff /hʌf/ n. **in a ~**, fâché, vexé.

hug /hʌg/ v.t. (p.t. **hugged**) serrer dans ses bras; (keep close to) serrer. —n. étreinte f.

huge /hjuːdʒ/ a. énorme. **~ly** adv. énormément.

hulk /hʌlk/ n. (of ship) épave f.; (person) mastodonte m.

hull /hʌl/ n. (of ship) coque f.

hullo /hə'ləʊ/ int. & n. = **hallo**.

hum /hʌm/ v.t./i. (p.t. **hummed**) (person) fredonner; (insect) bourdonner; (engine) vrombir. —n. bourdonnement m.; vrombissement m. **~ (or hem) and haw** (or **ha**), bafouiller.

human /'hjuːmən/ a. humain. —n. être humain m. **~itarian** /-mænɪ'teərɪən/ a. humanitaire.

humane /hjuː'meɪn/ a. humain, plein d'humanité.

humanity /hjuː'mænətɪ/ n. humanité f.

humbl|e /'hʌmbl/ a. (**-er, -est**) humble. —v.t. humilier. **~y** adv. humblement.

humbug /'hʌmbʌg/ n. (false talk) charlatanisme m.

humdrum /'hʌmdrʌm/ a. monotone.

humid /'hjuːmɪd/ a. humide. **~ity** /-'mɪdətɪ/ n. humidité f.

humiliat|e /hjuː'mɪlɪeɪt/ v.t. humilier. **~ion** /-'eɪʃn/ n. humiliation f.

humility /hjuː'mɪlətɪ/ n. humilité f.

humorist /'hjuːmərɪst/ humoriste m./f.

hum|our /'hjuːmə(r)/ n. humour m.; (mood) humeur f. —v.t. ménager. **~orous** a. humoristique; (person) plein d'humour. **~orously** adv. avec humour.

hump /hʌmp/ *n.* bosse *f.* —*v.t.* voûter. **the ~,** (*sl.*) le cafard.
hunch[1] /hʌntʃ/ *v.t.* voûter.
hunch[2] /hʌntʃ/ *n.* petite idée *f.*
hunchback /'hʌntʃbæk/ *n.* bossu(e) *m.* (*f.*).
hundred /'hʌndrəd/ *a.* & *n.* cent (*m.*). **~s of,** des centaines de. **~fold** *a.* centuple; *adv.* au centuple. **~th** *a.* & *n.* centième (*m.*/*f.*).
hundredweight /'hʌndrədweɪt/ *n.* 50.8 kg.; (*Amer.*) 45.36 kg.
hung /hʌŋ/ *see* **hang.**
Hungar|y /'hʌŋgərɪ/ *n.* Hongrie *f.* **~ian** /-'geərɪən/ *a.* & *n.* hongrois(e) (*m.* (*f.*)).
hunger /'hʌŋgə(r)/ *n.* faim *f.* —*v.i.* **~ for,** avoir faim de. **~-strike** *n.* grève de la faim *f.*
hungr|y /'hʌŋgrɪ/ *a.* (**-ier, -iest**) affamé. **be ~y,** avoir faim. **~ily** *adv.* avidement.
hunk /hʌŋk/ *n.* gros morceau *m.*
hunt /hʌnt/ *v.t.*/*i.* chasser. —*n.* chasse *f.* **~ for,** chercher. **~er** *n.* chasseur *m.* **~ing** *n.* chasse *f.*
hurdle /'hɜ:dl/ *n.* (*sport*) haie *f.*; (*fig.*) obstacle *m.*
hurl /hɜ:l/ *v.t.* lancer.
hurrah, hurray /hʊ'rɑ:, hʊ'reɪ/ *int.* & *n.* hourra (*m.*).
hurricane /'hʌrɪkən, *Amer.* 'hʌrɪkeɪn/ *n.* ouragan *m.*
hurried /'hʌrɪd/ *a.* précipité. **~ly** *adv.* précipitamment.
hurry /'hʌrɪ/ *v.i.* se dépêcher, se presser. —*v.t.* presser, activer. —*n.* hâte *f.* **in a ~,** pressé.
hurt /hɜ:t/ *v.t.*/*i.* (*p.t.* **hurt**) faire mal (à); (*injure, offend*) blesser. —*a.* blessé. —*n.* mal *m.* **~ful** *a.* blessant.
hurtle /'hɜ:tl/ *v.t.* lancer. —*v.i.* **~ along,** avancer à toute vitesse.
husband /'hʌzbənd/ *n.* mari *m.*
hush /hʌʃ/ *v.t.* faire taire. —*n.* silence *m.* **~-hush** *a.* (*fam.*) ultra-secret. **~ up,** (*news etc.*) étouffer.
husk /hʌsk/ *n.* (*of grain*) enveloppe *f.*

husky /'hʌskɪ/ *a.* (**-ier, -iest**) (*hoarse*) enroué; (*burly*) costaud.
hustle /'hʌsl/ *v.t.* (*push, rush*) bousculer. —*v.i.* (*work busily*: *Amer.*) se démener. —*n.* bousculade *f.* **~ and bustle,** agitation *f.*
hut /hʌt/ *n.* cabane *f.*
hutch /hʌtʃ/ *n.* clapier *m.*
hyacinth /'haɪəsɪnθ/ *n.* jacinthe *f.*
hybrid /'haɪbrɪd/ *a.* & *n.* hybride (*m.*).
hydrangea /haɪ'dreɪndʒə/ *n.* hortensia *m.*
hydrant /'haɪdrənt/ *n.* (**fire**) **~,** bouche d'incendie *f.*
hydraulic /haɪ'drɔ:lɪk/ *a.* hydraulique.
hydroelectric /haɪdrəʊɪ'lektrɪk/ *a.* hydro-électrique.
hydrogen /'haɪdrədʒən/ *n.* hydrogène *m.* **~ bomb,** bombe à hydrogène *f.*
hyena /haɪ'i:nə/ *n.* hyène *f.*
hygiene /'haɪdʒi:n/ *n.* hygiène *f.*
hygienic /haɪ'dʒi:nɪk/ *a.* hygiénique.
hymn /hɪm/ *n.* cantique *m.*, hymne *m.*
hyper- /'haɪpə(r)/ *pref.* hyper-.
hypermarket /'haɪpəmɑ:kɪt/ *n.* hypermarché *m.*
hyphen /'haɪfn/ *n.* trait d'union *m.* **~ate** *v.t.* mettre un trait d'union à.
hypno|sis /hɪp'nəʊsɪs/ *n.* hypnose *f.* **~tic** /-'nɒtɪk/ *a.* hypnotique.
hypnot|ize /'hɪpnətaɪz/ *v.t.* hypnotiser. **~ism** *n.* hypnotisme *m.*
hypochondriac /haɪpə'kɒndrɪæk/ *n.* malade imaginaire *m.*/*f.*
hypocrisy /hɪ'pɒkrəsɪ/ *n.* hypocrisie *f.*
hypocrit|e /'hɪpəkrɪt/ *n.* hypocrite *m.*/*f.* **~ical** /-'krɪtɪkl/ *a.* hypocrite.
hypodermic /haɪpə'dɜ:mɪk/ *a.* hypodermique. —*n.* seringue hypodermique *f.*
hypothe|sis /haɪ'pɒθəsɪs/ *n.* (*pl.* **-theses** /-si:z/) hypothèse *f.* **~tical** /-ə'θetɪkl/ *a.* hypothétique.
hyster|ia /hɪ'stɪərɪə/ *n.* hystérie *f.* **~ical** /-erɪkl/ *a.* hystérique; (*person*) surexcité.
hysterics /hɪ'sterɪks/ *n. pl.* crise de nerfs *or* de rire *f.*

I

I /aɪ/ *pron.* je, j'*; (*stressed*) moi.
ice /aɪs/ *n.* glace *f.*; (*on road*) verglas
m. —*v.t.* (*cake*) glacer. —*v.i.* ~ (**up**),
(*window*) se givrer; (*river*) geler. ~-
cream *n.* glace *f.* ~-**cube** *n.* glaçon
m. ~ **hockey**, hockey sur glace *m.* ~
lolly, glace (sur bâtonnet) *f.*
iceberg /'aɪsbɜ:g/ *n.* iceberg *m.*
Iceland /'aɪslənd/ *n.* Islande *f.* ~**er** *n.*
Islandais(e) *m.* (*f.*). ~**ic** /-'lændɪk/ *a.*
islandais; *n.* (*lang.*) islandais *m.*
icicle /'aɪsɪkl/ *n.* glaçon *m.*
icing /'aɪsɪŋ/ *n.* (*sugar*) glace *f.*
icon /'aɪkɒn/ *n.* icône *f.*
icy /'aɪsɪ/ *a.* (-**ier**, -**iest**) (*hands, wind*)
glacé; (*road*) verglacé; (*manner, wel-
come*) glacial.
idea /aɪ'dɪə/ *n.* idée *f.*
ideal /aɪ'dɪəl/ *a.* idéal. —*n.* idéal *m.*
~**ize** *v.t.* idéaliser. ~**ly** *adv.* idéale-
ment.
idealis|t /aɪ'dɪəlɪst/ *n.* idéaliste *m.*/*f.*
~**m** /-zəm/ *n.* idéalisme *m.* ~**tic**
/-'lɪstɪk/ *a.* idéaliste.
identical /aɪ'dentɪkl/ *a.* identique.
identif|y /aɪ'dentɪfaɪ/ *v.t.* identifier.
—*v.i.* ~**y with**, s'identifier à. ~**ication** /-ɪ'keɪʃn/ *n.* identification *f.*
identikit /aɪ'dentɪkɪt/ *n.* portrait robot
m.
identity /aɪ'dentətɪ/ *n.* identité *f.*
ideolog|y /aɪdɪ'ɒlədʒɪ/ *n.* idéologie *f.*
~**ical** /-ə'lɒdʒɪkl/ *a.* idéologique.
idiocy /'ɪdɪəsɪ/ *n.* idiotie *f.*
idiom /'ɪdɪəm/ *n.* expression idiomatique *f.*; (*language*) idiome *m.* ~**atic**
/-'mætɪk/ *a.* idiomatique.
idiosyncrasy /ɪdɪə'sɪŋkrəsɪ/ *n.* particularité *f.*
idiot /'ɪdɪət/ *n.* idiot(e) *m.* (*f.*). ~**ic**
/-'ɒtɪk/ *a.* idiot.
idle /'aɪdl/ *a.* (-**er**, -**est**) désœuvré, oisif;
(*lazy*) paresseux; (*unemployed*) sans
travail; (*machine*) au repos; (*fig.*)
vain. —*v.i.* (*engine*) tourner au ralenti. —*v.t.* ~ **away**, gaspiller. ~**ness**
n. oisiveté *f.* ~**r** /-ə(r)/ *n.* oisi|f, -ve *m.*,
f.
idol /'aɪdl/ *n.* idole *f.* ~**ize** *v.t.* idolâtrer.
idyllic /ɪ'dɪlɪk, *Amer.* aɪ'dɪlɪk/ *a.*
idyllique.
i.e. *abbr.* c'est-à-dire.
if /ɪf/ *conj.* si.

igloo /'ɪglu:/ *n.* igloo *m.*
ignite /ɪg'naɪt/ *v.t.*/*i.* (s')enflammer.
ignition /ɪg'nɪʃn/ *n.* (*auto.*) allumage
m. ~ (**switch**), contact *m.*
ignoramus /ɪgnə'reɪməs/ *n.* (*pl.*
-**muses**) ignare *m.*/*f.*
ignoran|t /'ɪgnərənt/ *a.* ignorant (**of**,
de). ~**ce** *n.* ignorance *f.* ~**tly** *adv.* par
ignorance.
ignore /ɪg'nɔ:(r)/ *v.t.* ne faire *or* prêter
aucune attention à; (*person in street
etc.*) faire semblant de ne pas voir.
ilk /ɪlk/ *n.* (*kind: fam.*) acabit *m.*
ill /ɪl/ *a.* malade; (*bad*) mauvais.
—*adv.* mal. —*n.* mal *m.* ~**advised** *a.*
peu judicieux. ~ **at ease**, mal à l'aise.
~-**bred** *a.* mal élevé. ~-**fated** *a.* malheureux. ~-**gotten** *a.* mal acquis.
~-**natured** *a.* désagréable. ~-**treat**
v.t. maltraiter. ~ **will**, malveillance
f.
illegal /ɪ'li:gl/ *a.* illégal.
illegible /ɪ'ledʒəbl/ *a.* illisible.
illegitima|te /ɪlɪ'dʒɪtɪmət/ *a.* illégi-
time. ~**cy** *n.* illégitimité *f.*
illitera|te /ɪ'lɪtərət/ *a.* & *n.* illettré(e)
(*m.* (*f.*)), analphabète *m.*/*f.* ~**cy** *n.*
analphabétisme *m.*
illness /'ɪlnɪs/ *n.* maladie *f.*
illogical /ɪ'lɒdʒɪkl/ *a.* illogique.
illuminat|e /ɪ'lu:mɪneɪt/ *v.t.* éclairer;
(*decorate with lights*) illuminer. ~**ion**
/-'neɪʃn/ *n.* éclairage *m.*; illumination
f.
illusion /ɪ'lu:ʒn/ *n.* illusion *f.*
illusory /ɪ'lu:sərɪ/ *a.* illusoire.
illustrat|e /'ɪləstreɪt/ *v.t.* illustrer.
~**ion** /-'streɪʃn/ *n.* illustration *f.* ~**ive**
/-ətɪv/ *a.* qui illustre.
illustrious /ɪ'lʌstrɪəs/ *a.* illustre.
image /'ɪmɪdʒ/ *n.* image *f.* (**public**) ~,
(*of firm, person*) image de marque *f.*
~**ry** /-ərɪ/ *n.* images *f. pl.*
imaginary /ɪ'mædʒɪnərɪ/ *a.* imaginaire.
imaginat|ion /ɪmædʒɪ'neɪʃn/ *n.*
imagination *f.* ~**ive** /ɪ'mædʒɪnətɪv/ *a.*
plein d'imagination.
imagin|e /ɪ'mædʒɪn/ *v.t.* (*picture to o.s.*)
(s')imaginer; (*suppose*) imaginer.
~**able** *a.* imaginable.
imbalance /ɪm'bæləns/ *n.* déséquilibre
m.

imbecil|e /'ɪmbəsiːl/ *n. & a.* imbécile (*m.|f.*). **~ity** /-'sɪlətɪ/ *n.* imbécillité *f.*

imbibe /ɪm'baɪb/ *v.t.* absorber.

imbue /ɪm'bjuː/ *v.t.* imprégner.

imitat|e /'ɪmɪteɪt/ *v.t.* imiter. **~ion** /-'teɪʃn/ *n.* imitation *f.* **~or** *n.* imita|teur, -trice *m., f.*

immaculate /ɪ'mækjʊlət/ *a.* (*room, dress, etc.*) impeccable.

immaterial /ɪmə'tɪərɪəl/ *a.* sans importance (**to**, pour; **that**, que).

immature /ɪmə'tjʊə(r)/ *a.* pas mûr.

immediate /ɪ'miːdɪət/ *a.* immédiat. **~ly** *adv.* immédiatement; *conj.* dès que.

immens|e /ɪ'mens/ *a.* immense. **~ely** *adv.* extrêmement, immensément. **~ity** *n.* immensité *f.*

immers|e /ɪ'mɜːs/ *v.t.* plonger, immerger. **~ion** /-ɜːʃn/ *n.* immersion *f.* **~ion heater**, chauffe-eau (électrique) *m. invar.*

immigr|ate /'ɪmɪɡreɪt/ *v.i.* immigrer. **~ant** *n. & a.* immigré(e) (*m.* (*f.*)); (*newly-arrived*) immigrant(e) (*m.* (*f.*)). **~ation** /-'ɡreɪʃn/ *n.* immigration *f.*

imminen|t /'ɪmɪnənt/ *a.* imminent. **~ce** *n.* imminence *f.*

immobil|e /ɪ'məʊbaɪl, *Amer.* ɪ'məʊbl/ *a.* immobile. **~ize** /-əlaɪz/ *v.t.* immobiliser.

immoderate /ɪ'mɒdərət/ *a.* immodéré.

immodest /ɪ'mɒdɪst/ *a.* impudique.

immoral /ɪ'mɒrəl/ *a.* immoral. **~ity** /ɪmə'rælətɪ/ *n.* immoralité *f.*

immortal /ɪ'mɔːtl/ *a.* immortel. **~ity** /-'tælətɪ/ *n.* immortalité *f.* **~ize** *v.t.* immortaliser.

immun|e /ɪ'mjuːn/ *a.* immunisé (**from, to**, contre). **~ity** *n.* immunité *f.*

immuniz|e /'ɪmjʊnaɪz/ *v.t.* immuniser. **~ation** /-'zeɪʃn/ *n.* immunisation *f.*

imp /ɪmp/ *n.* lutin *m.*

impact /'ɪmpækt/ *n.* impact *m.*

impair /ɪm'peə(r)/ *v.t.* détériorer.

impale /ɪm'peɪl/ *v.t.* empaler.

impart /ɪm'pɑːt/ *v.t.* communiquer, transmettre.

impartial /ɪm'pɑːʃl/ *a.* impartial. **~ity** /-ɪ'ælətɪ/ *n.* impartialité *f.*

impassable /ɪm'pɑːsəbl/ *a.* (*barrier etc.*) infranchissable; (*road*) impraticable.

impasse /'æmpɑːs, *Amer.* 'ɪmpæs/ *n.* impasse *f.*

impassioned /ɪm'pæʃnd/ *a.* passionné.

impassive /ɪm'pæsɪv/ *a.* impassible.

impatien|t /ɪm'peɪʃnt/ *a.* impatient. **~ce** *n.* impatience *f.* **~tly** *adv.* impatiemment.

impeach /ɪm'piːtʃ/ *v.t.* mettre en accusation.

impeccable /ɪm'pekəbl/ *a.* impeccable.

impede /ɪm'piːd/ *v.t.* gêner.

impediment /ɪm'pedɪmənt/ *n.* obstacle *m.* (**speech**) **~**, défaut d'élocution *m.*

impel /ɪm'pel/ *v.t.* (*p.t.* **impelled**) pousser, forcer (**to do**, à faire).

impending /ɪm'pendɪŋ/ *a.* imminent.

impenetrable /ɪm'penɪtrəbl/ *a.* impénétrable.

imperative /ɪm'perətɪv/ *a.* nécessaire; (*need etc.*) impérieux. *—n.* (*gram.*) impératif *m.*

imperceptible /ɪmpə'septəbl/ *a.* **imperfect** /ɪm'pɜːfɪkt/ *a.* imparfait; (*faulty*) défectueux. **~ion** /-ə'fekʃn/ *n.* imperfection *f.*

imperial /ɪm'pɪərɪəl/ *a.* impérial; (*measure*) légal (au Royaume Uni). **~ism** *n.* impérialisme *m.*

imperil /ɪm'perəl/ *v.t.* (*p.t.* **imperilled**) mettre en péril.

imperious /ɪm'pɪərɪəs/ *a.* impérieux.

impersonal /ɪm'pɜːsənl/ *a.* impersonnel.

impersonat|e /ɪm'pɜːsəneɪt/ *v.t.* se faire passer pour; (*mimic*) imiter. **~ion** /-'neɪʃn/ *n.* imitation *f.* **~or** *n.* imita|teur, -trice *m., f.*

impertinen|t /ɪm'pɜːtɪnənt/ *a.* impertinent. **~ce** *n.* impertinence *f.* **~tly** *adv.* avec impertinence.

impervious /ɪm'pɜːvɪəs/ *a.* **~ to**, imperméable à.

impetuous /ɪm'petʃʊəs/ *a.* impétueux.

impetus /'ɪmpɪtəs/ *n.* impulsion *f.*

impinge /ɪm'pɪndʒ/ *v.i.* **~ on**, affecter; (*encroach*) empiéter sur.

impish /'ɪmpɪʃ/ *a.* espiègle.

implacable /ɪm'plækəbl/ *a.* implacable.

implant /ɪm'plɑːnt/ *v.t.* implanter.

implement[1] /'ɪmplɪmənt/ *n.* (*tool*) outil *m.*; (*utensil*) ustensile *m.*

implement[2] /'ɪmplɪment/ *v.t.* exécuter, mettre en pratique.

implicat|e /'ɪmplɪkeɪt/ *v.t.* impliquer. **~ion** /-'keɪʃn/ *n.* implication *f.*

implicit /ɪm'plɪsɪt/ *a.* (*implied*) implicite; (*unquestioning*) absolu.

implore /ɪm'plɔː(r)/ *v.t.* implorer.

impl|y /ɪm'plaɪ/ *v.t.* (*assume, mean*)

impliquer; (*insinuate*) laisser entendre. ~**ied** *a.* implicite.
impolite /ɪmpə'laɪt/ *a.* impoli.
imponderable /ɪm'pɒndərəbl/ *a.* & *n.*
impondérable (*m.*).
import[1] /ɪm'pɔːt/ *v.t.* importer. ~**ation**
/-'teɪʃn/ *n.* importation *f.* ~**er** *n.* im-
porta|teur, -trice *m.*, *f.*
import[2] /'ɪmpɔːt/ *n.* (*article*) importation *f.*; (*meaning*) sens *m.*
importan|t /ɪm'pɔːtnt/ *a.* important.
~**ce** *n.* importance *f.*
impos|e /ɪm'pəʊz/ *v.t.* imposer. —*v.i.*
~**e on,** abuser de l'amabilité de.
~**ition** /-ə'zɪʃn/ *n.* imposition *f.*;
(*fig.*) dérangement *m.*
imposing /ɪm'pəʊzɪŋ/ *a.* imposant.
impossib|le /ɪm'pɒsəbl/ *a.* impossible.
~**ility** /-'bɪləti/ *n.* impossibilité *f.*
impostor /ɪm'pɒstə(r)/ *n.* imposteur *m.*
impoten|t /'ɪmpətənt/ *a.* impuissant.
~**ce** *n.* impuissance *f.*
impound /ɪm'paʊnd/ *v.t.* confisquer,
saisir.
impoverish /ɪm'pɒvərɪʃ/ *v.t.* appauvrir.
impracticable /ɪm'præktɪkəbl/ *a.* impraticable.
impractical /ɪm'præktɪkl/ *a.* (*Amer.*)
peu pratique.
imprecise /ɪmprɪ'saɪs/ *a.* imprécis.
impregnable /ɪm'pregnəbl/ *a.* imprenable; (*fig.*) inattaquable.
impregnate /'ɪmpregneɪt/ *v.t.* imprégner (**with,** de).
impresario /ɪmprɪ'sɑːrɪəʊ/ *n.* (*pl.* -os)
impresario *m.*
impress /ɪm'pres/ *v.t.* impressionner;
(*imprint*) imprimer. ~ **on s.o.,** faire
comprendre à qn.
impression /ɪm'preʃn/ *n.* impression
f. ~**able** *a.* impressionnable.
impressive /ɪm'presɪv/ *a.* impressionnant.
imprint[1] /'ɪmprɪnt/ *n.* empreinte *f.*
imprint[2] /ɪm'prɪnt/ *v.t.* imprimer.
imprison /ɪm'prɪzn/ *v.t.* emprisonner.
~**ment** *n.* emprisonnement *m.*, prison *f.*
improbab|le /ɪm'prɒbəbl/ *a.* (*not
likely*) improbable; (*incredible*)
invraisemblable. ~**ility** /-'bɪləti/ *n.*
improbabilité *f.*
impromptu /ɪm'prɒmptjuː/ *a.* & *adv.*
impromptu.
improp|er /ɪm'prɒpə(r)/ *a.* incon-
venant, indécent; (*wrong*) incorrect.
~**riety** /-ə'praɪəti/ *n.* inconvenance *f.*

improve /ɪm'pruːv/ *v.t./i.* (s')amé-
liorer. ~**ment** *n.* amélioration *f.*
improvis|e /'ɪmprəvaɪz/ *v.t./i.* impro-
viser. ~**ation** /-'zeɪʃn/ *n.* improvisa-
tion *f.*
imprudent /ɪm'pruːdnt/ *a.* imprudent.
impuden|t /'ɪmpjʊdənt/ *a.* impudent.
~**ce** *n.* impudence *f.*
impulse /'ɪmpʌls/ *n.* impulsion *f.* **on**
~**,** sur un coup de tête.
impulsive /ɪm'pʌlsɪv/ *a.* impulsif. ~**ly**
adv. par impulsion.
impunity /ɪm'pjuːnəti/ *n.* impunité *f.*
with ~**,** impunément.
impur|e /ɪm'pjʊə(r)/ *a.* impur. ~**ity** *n.*
impureté *f.*
impute /ɪm'pjuːt/ *v.t.* imputer.
in /ɪn/ *prep.* dans, à, en. —*adv.* (*inside*)
dedans; (*at home*) là, à la maison;
(*in fashion*) à la mode. ~ **the box/
garden,** dans la boîte/le jardin. ~
Paris/school, à Paris/ l'école. ~ **win-
ter/English,** en hiver/anglais. ~ **India,** en Inde. ~ **Japan,** au Japon. ~ **a
firm manner/voice,** d'une manière/
voix ferme. ~ **an hour,** (*at end of*)
au bout d'une heure. ~ **an hour('s
time),** dans une heure. **in (the space
of) an hour,** en une heure. ~ **doing,**
en faisant. ~ **the evening,** le soir.
one ~ **ten,** un sur dix. **the best** ~**,**
le meilleur de. **we are** ~ **for,** on va
avoir. ~**laws** *n. pl.* (*fam.*) beaux-
parents *m. pl.* ~**patient** *n.* malade
hospitalisé(e) *m./f.* **the** ~**s and outs
of,** les tenants et aboutissants de. ~
so far as, dans la mesure où.
inability /ɪnə'bɪləti/ *n.* incapacité *f.* (**to
do,** de faire).
inaccessible /ɪnæk'sesəbl/ *a.* inaccessible.
inaccurate /ɪn'ækjərət/ *a.* inexact.
inaction /ɪn'ækʃn/ *n.* inaction *f.*
inactiv|e /ɪn'æktɪv/ *a.* inactif. ~**ity**
/-'tɪvəti/ *n.* inaction *f.*
inadequa|te /ɪn'ædɪkwət/ *a.* insuf-
fisant. ~**cy** *n.* insuffisance *f.*
inadmissible /ɪnəd'mɪsəbl/ *a.* inadmissible.
inadvertently /ɪnəd'vɜːtəntlɪ/ *adv.* par
mégarde.
inadvisable /ɪnəd'vaɪzəbl/ *a.* décon-
seillé, pas recommandé.
inane /ɪ'neɪn/ *a.* inepte.
inanimate /ɪn'ænɪmət/ *a.* inanimé.
inappropriate /ɪnə'prəʊprɪət/ *a.* inopportun.

inarticulate /maːˈtɪkjʊlət/ a. qui a du mal à s'exprimer.

inasmuch as /məzˈmʌtʃəz/ adv. en ce sens que; (*because*) vu que.

inattentive /məˈtentɪv/ a. inattentif.

inaugural /ɪˈnɔːgjʊrəl/ a. inaugural.

inaugurat|e /ɪˈnɔːgjʊreɪt/ v.t. (*open, begin*) inaugurer; (*person*) investir. ∼**ion** /-ˈreɪʃn/ n. inauguration f.; investiture f.

inauspicious /mɔːˈspɪʃəs/ a. peu propice.

inborn /ɪnˈbɔːn/ a. inné.

inbred /ɪnˈbred/ a. (*inborn*) inné.

incalculable /ɪnˈkælkjʊləbl/ a. incalculable.

incapable /ɪnˈkeɪpəbl/ a. incapable.

incapacit|y /ɪnkəˈpæsətɪ/ n. incapacité f. ∼**ate** v.t. rendre incapable (*de travailler etc.*).

incarcerate /ɪnˈkɑːsəreɪt/ v.t. incarcérer.

incarnat|e /ɪnˈkɑːneɪt/ a. incarné. ∼**ion** /-ˈneɪʃn/ n. incarnation f.

incendiary /ɪnˈsendɪərɪ/ a. incendiaire. —n. (*bomb*) bombe incendiaire f.

incense¹ /ˈɪnsens/ n. encens m.

incense² /ɪnˈsens/ v.t. mettre en fureur.

incentive /ɪnˈsentɪv/ n. motivation f.; (*payment*) prime (d'encouragement) f.

inception /ɪnˈsepʃn/ n. début m.

incessant /ɪnˈsesnt/ a. incessant. ∼**ly** adv. sans cesse.

incest /ˈɪnsest/ n. inceste m. ∼**uous** /ɪnˈsestjʊəs/ a. incestueux.

inch /ɪntʃ/ n. pouce m. (= 2.54 cm.). —v.i. avancer doucement.

incidence /ˈɪnsɪdəns/ n. fréquence f.

incident /ˈɪnsɪdənt/ n. incident m.; (*in play, film, etc.*) épisode m.

incidental /ɪnsɪˈdentl/ a. accessoire. ∼**ly** adv. accessoirement; (*by the way*) à propos.

incinerat|e /ɪnˈsɪnəreɪt/ v.t. incinérer. ∼**or** n. incinérateur m.

incipient /ɪnˈsɪpɪənt/ a. naissant.

incision /ɪnˈsɪʒn/ n. incision f.

incisive /ɪnˈsaɪsɪv/ a. incisif.

incite /ɪnˈsaɪt/ v.t. inciter, pousser. ∼**ment** n. incitation f.

inclement /ɪnˈklemənt/ a. inclément, rigoureux.

inclination /ɪnklɪˈneɪʃn/ n. (*propensity, bowing*) inclination f.

incline¹ /ɪnˈklaɪn/ v.t./i. incliner. **be ∼d to,** avoir tendance à.

incline² /ˈɪnklaɪn/ n. pente f.

inclu|de /ɪnˈkluːd/ v.t. comprendre, inclure. ∼**ding** prep. (y) compris. ∼**sion** n. inclusion f.

inclusive /ɪnˈkluːsɪv/ a. & adv. inclus, compris. **be ∼ of,** comprendre, inclure.

incognito /ɪnkɒgˈniːtəʊ/ adv. incognito.

incoherent /ɪnkəʊˈhɪərənt/ a. incohérent.

income /ˈɪnkʌm/ n. revenu m. **∼ tax,** impôt sur le revenu m.

incoming /ˈɪnkʌmɪŋ/ a. (*tide*) montant; (*tenant etc.*) nouveau.

incomparable /ɪnˈkɒmprəbl/ a. incomparable.

incompatible /ɪnkəmˈpætəbl/ a. incompatible.

incompeten|t /ɪnˈkɒmpɪtənt/ a. incompétent. ∼**ce** n. incompétence f.

incomplete /ɪnkəmˈpliːt/ a. incomplet.

incomprehensible /ɪnkɒmprɪˈhensəbl/ a. incompréhensible.

inconceivable /ɪnkənˈsiːvəbl/ a. inconcevable.

inconclusive /ɪnkənˈkluːsɪv/ a. peu concluant.

incongruous /ɪnˈkɒŋgrʊəs/ a. déplacé, incongru.

inconsequential /ɪnkɒnsɪˈkwenʃl/ a. sans importance.

inconsiderate /ɪnkənˈsɪdərət/ a. (*person*) qui ne se soucie pas des autres; (*act*) irréfléchi.

inconsisten|t /ɪnkənˈsɪstənt/ a. sans cohérence, inconséquent; (*at variance*) contradictoire. ∼**t with,** incompatible avec. ∼**cy** n. inconséquence f. ∼**cies,** contradictions f. pl.

inconspicuous /ɪnkənˈspɪkjʊəs/ a. peu en évidence.

incontinen|t /ɪnˈkɒntɪnənt/ a. incontinent. ∼**ce** n. incontinence f.

inconvenien|t /ɪnkənˈviːnɪənt/ a. incommode, peu pratique; (*time*) mal choisi. **be ∼t for,** ne pas convenir à. ∼**ce** n. dérangement m.; (*drawback*) inconvénient m.; v.t. déranger.

incorporate /ɪnˈkɔːpəreɪt/ v.t. incorporer; (*include*) contenir.

incorrect /ɪnkəˈrekt/ a. inexact.

incorrigible /ɪnˈkɒrɪdʒəbl/ a. incorrigible.

incorruptible /ɪnkəˈrʌptəbl/ a. incorruptible.

increas|e[1] /ɪnˈkriːs/ v.t./i. augmenter. ~**ing** a. croissant. ~**ingly** adv. de plus en plus.

increase[2] /ˈɪnkriːs/ n. augmentation f. **(in, of, de).**

incredible /ɪnˈkredəbl/ a. incroyable.

incredulous /ɪnˈkredjʊləs/ a. incrédule.

increment /ˈɪnkrəmənt/ n. augmentation f.

incriminat|e /ɪnˈkrɪmɪneɪt/ v.t. incriminer. ~**ing** a. compromettant.

incubat|e /ˈɪnkjʊbeɪt/ v.t. (eggs) couver. ~**ion** /-ˈbeɪʃn/ n. incubation f. ~**or** n. couveuse f.

inculcate /ˈɪnkʌlkeɪt/ v.t. inculquer.

incumbent /ɪnˈkʌmbənt/ n. (pol., relig.) titulaire m./f.

incur /ɪnˈkɜːr/ v.t. (p.t. **incurred**) encourir; (debts) contracter.

incurable /ɪnˈkjʊərəbl/ a. incurable.

incursion /ɪnˈkɜːʃn/ n. incursion f.

indebted /ɪnˈdetɪd/ a. ~ **to s.o.**, redevable à qn. **(for, de).**

indecen|t /ɪnˈdiːsnt/ a. indécent. ~**cy** n. indécence f.

indecision /ɪndɪˈsɪʒn/ n. indécision f.

indecisive /ɪndɪˈsaɪsɪv/ a. indécis.

indeed /ɪnˈdiːd/ adv. en effet, vraiment.

indefinable /ɪndɪˈfaɪnəbl/ a. indéfinissable.

indefinite /ɪnˈdefɪnɪt/ a. indéfini; (time) indéterminé. ~**ly** adv. indéfiniment.

indelible /ɪnˈdeləbl/ a. indélébile.

indemni|fy /ɪnˈdemnɪfaɪ/ v.t. (compensate) indemniser **(for, de)**; (safeguard) garantir. ~**ty** /-nətɪ/ n. indemnité f.; garantie f.

indent /ɪnˈdent/ v.t. (text) renfoncer. ~**ation** /-ˈteɪʃn/ n. (outline) découpure f.

independen|t /ɪndɪˈpendənt/ a. indépendant. ~**ce** n. indépendance f. ~**tly** adv. de façon indépendante. ~**tly of**, indépendamment de.

indescribable /ɪndɪˈskraɪbəbl/ a. indescriptible.

indestructible /ɪndɪˈstrʌktəbl/ a. indestructible.

indeterminate /ɪndɪˈtɜːmɪnət/ a. indéterminé.

index /ˈɪndeks/ n. (pl. **indexes**) (figure) indice m.; (in book) index m.; (in library) catalogue m. −v.t. classer. ~ **finger** index m. ~**linked** a. indexé.

India /ˈɪndɪə/ n. Inde f. ~**n** a. & n. indien(ne) (m. (f.)). ~**n summer**, été de la Saint-Martin m.

indicat|e /ˈɪndɪkeɪt/ v.t. indiquer. ~**ion** /-ˈkeɪʃn/ n. indication f. ~**or** n. (device) indicateur m.; (on vehicle) clignotant m.; (board) tableau m.

indicative /ɪnˈdɪkətɪv/ a. indicatif. −n. (gram.) indicatif m.

indict /ɪnˈdaɪt/ v.t. accuser. ~**ment** n. accusation f.

indifferen|t /ɪnˈdɪfrənt/ a. indifférent; (not good) médiocre. ~**ce** n. indifférence f.

indigenous /ɪnˈdɪdʒɪnəs/ a. indigène.

indigest|ion /ɪndɪˈdʒestʃən/ n. indigestion f. ~**ible** /-təbl/ a. indigeste.

indign|ant /ɪnˈdɪgnənt/ a. indigné. ~**ation** /-ˈneɪʃn/ n. indignation f.

indigo /ˈɪndɪgəʊ/ n. indigo m.

indirect /ɪndɪˈrekt/ a. indirect. ~**ly** adv. indirectement.

indiscr|eet /ɪndɪˈskriːt/ a. indiscret; (not wary) imprudent. ~**etion** /-eʃn/ n. indiscrétion f.

indiscriminate /ɪndɪˈskrɪmɪnət/ a. qui manque de discernement; (random) fait au hasard. ~**ly** adv. sans discernement; au hasard.

indispensable /ɪndɪˈspensəbl/ a. indispensable.

indispos|ed /ɪndɪˈspəʊzd/ a. indisposé, souffrant. ~**ition** /-əˈzɪʃn/ n. indisposition f.

indisputable /ɪndɪˈspjuːtəbl/ a. incontestable.

indistinct /ɪndɪˈstɪŋkt/ a. indistinct.

indistinguishable /ɪndɪˈstɪŋgwɪʃəbl/ a. indifférenciable.

individual /ɪndɪˈvɪdʒʊəl/ a. individuel. −n. individu m. ~**ist** n. individualiste m./f. ~**ity** /-ˈælətɪ/ n. individualité f. ~**ly** adv. individuellement.

indivisible /ɪndɪˈvɪzəbl/ a. indivisible.

Indo-China /ɪndəʊˈtʃaɪnə/ n. Indochine f.

indoctrinat|e /ɪnˈdɒktrɪneɪt/ v.t. endoctriner. ~**ion** /-ˈneɪʃn/ n. endoctrinement m.

indolen|t /ˈɪndələnt/ a. indolent. ~**ce** n. indolence f.

indomitable /ɪnˈdɒmɪtəbl/ a. indomptable.

Indonesia /ɪndəʊˈniːzɪə/ n. Indonésie f. ~**n** a. & n. indonésien(ne) (m. (f.)).

indoor /ˈɪndɔː(r)/ a. (clothes etc.)

d'intérieur; (*under cover*) couvert. ~s /ɪnˈdɔːz/ *adv.* à l'intérieur.

induce /ɪnˈdjuːs/ *v.t.* (*influence*) persuader; (*cause*) provoquer. ~ment *n.* encouragement *m.*

induct /ɪnˈdʌkt/ *v.t.* investir, installer; (*mil.*, *Amer.*) incorporer.

indulge /ɪnˈdʌldʒ/ *v.t.* (*desires*) satisfaire; (*person*) se montrer indulgent pour, gâter. −*v.i.* ~ **in**, se livrer à, s'offrir.

indulgen|t /ɪnˈdʌldʒənt/ *a.* indulgent. ~ce *n.* indulgence *f.*

industrial /ɪnˈdʌstrɪəl/ *a.* industriel; (*unrest etc.*) ouvrier; (*action*) revendicatif. ~ist *n.* industriel *m.* ~ized *a.* industrialisé.

industrious /ɪnˈdʌstrɪəs/ *a.* travailleur, appliqué.

industry /ˈɪndəstrɪ/ *n.* industrie *f.*; (*zeal*) application *f.*

inebriated /ɪˈniːbrɪeɪtɪd/ *a.* ivre.

inedible /ɪnˈedɪbl/ *a.* (*food*) immangeable.

ineffective /ɪnɪˈfektɪv/ *a.* inefficace; (*person*) incapable.

ineffectual /ɪnɪˈfektʃʊəl/ *a.* inefficace; (*person*) incapable.

inefficien|t /ɪnɪˈfɪʃnt/ *a.* inefficace; (*person*) incompétent. ~cy *n.* inefficacité *f.*; incompétence *f.*

ineligible /ɪnˈelɪdʒəbl/ *a.* inéligible. be ~ **for**, ne pas avoir droit à.

inept /ɪˈnept/ *a.* (*absurd*) inepte; (*out of place*) mal à propos.

inequality /ɪnɪˈkwɒlətɪ/ *n.* inégalité *f.*

inert /ɪˈnɜːt/ *a.* inerte.

inertia /ɪˈnɜːʃə/ *n.* inertie *f.*

inescapable /ɪnɪˈskeɪpəbl/ *a.* inéluctable.

inevitabl|e /ɪnˈevɪtəbl/ *a.* inévitable. ~y *adv.* inévitablement.

inexact /ɪnɪɡˈzækt/ *a.* inexact.

inexcusable /ɪnɪkˈskjuːzəbl/ *a.* inexcusable.

inexhaustible /ɪnɪɡˈzɔːstəbl/ *a.* inépuisable.

inexorable /ɪnˈeksərəbl/ *a.* inexorable.

inexpensive /ɪnɪkˈspensɪv/ *a.* bon marché *invar.*, pas cher.

inexperience /ɪnɪkˈspɪərɪəns/ *n.* inexpérience *f.* ~d *a.* inexpérimenté.

inexplicable /ɪnɪkˈsplɪkəbl/ *a.* inexplicable.

inextricable /ɪnɪkˈstrɪkəbl/ *a.* inextricable.

infallib|le /ɪnˈfæləbl/ *a.* infaillible. ~ility /-ˈbɪlətɪ/ *n.* infaillibilité *f.*

infam|ous /ˈɪnfəməs/ *a.* infâme. ~y *n.* infamie *f.*

infan|t /ˈɪnfənt/ *n.* nourrisson *m.*, petit(e) enfant *m./f.* ~cy *n.* petite enfance *f.*; (*fig.*) enfance *f.*

infantile /ˈɪnfəntaɪl/ *a.* infantile.

infantry /ˈɪnfəntrɪ/ *n.* infanterie *f.*

infatuat|ed /ɪnˈfætʃʊeɪtɪd/ *a.* ~ed with, engoué de. ~ion /-ˈeɪʃn/ *n.* engouement *m.*, béguin *m.*

infect /ɪnˈfekt/ *v.t.* infecter. ~ s.o. with, communiquer à qn. ~ion /-kʃn/ *n.* infection *f.*

infectious /ɪnˈfekʃəs/ *a.* (*person, disease & fig.*) contagieux.

infer /ɪnˈfɜː(r)/ *v.t.* (*p.t.* inferred) déduire. ~ence /ˈɪnfərəns/ *n.* déduction *f.*

inferior /ɪnˈfɪərɪə(r)/ *a.* inférieur (**to**, à); (*work, product*) de qualité inférieure. −*n.* inférieur(e) *m.* (*f.*). ~ity /-ˈɒrətɪ/ *n.* infériorité *f.*

infernal /ɪnˈfɜːnl/ *a.* infernal. ~ly *adv.* (*fam.*) atrocement.

inferno /ɪnˈfɜːnəʊ/ *n.* (*pl.* -os) (*hell*) enfer *m.*; (*blaze*) incendie *m.*

infertil|e /ɪnˈfɜːtaɪl, *Amer.* ɪnˈfɜːtl/ *a.* infertile. ~ity /-əˈtɪlətɪ/ *n.* infertilité *f.*

infest /ɪnˈfest/ *v.t.* infester.

infidelity /ɪnfɪˈdelətɪ/ *n.* infidélité *f.*

infighting /ˈɪnfaɪtɪŋ/ *n.* querelles internes *f. pl.*

infiltrat|e /ˈɪnfɪltreɪt/ *v.t./i.* s'infiltrer (dans). ~ion /-ˈtreɪʃn/ *n.* infiltration *f.*

infinite /ˈɪnfɪnɪt/ *a.* infini. ~ly *adv.* infiniment.

infinitesimal /ɪnfɪnɪˈtesɪml/ *a.* infinitésimal.

infinitive /ɪnˈfɪnətɪv/ *n.* infinitif *m.*

infinity /ɪnˈfɪnətɪ/ *n.* infinité *f.*

infirm /ɪnˈfɜːm/ *a.* infirme. ~ity *n.* infirmité *f.*

infirmary /ɪnˈfɜːmərɪ/ *n.* hôpital *m.*; (*sick-bay*) infirmerie *f.*

inflam|e /ɪnˈfleɪm/ *v.t.* enflammer. ~mable /-ˈæməbl/ *a.* inflammable. ~mation /-əˈmeɪʃn/ *n.* inflammation *f.*

inflammatory /ɪnˈflæmətrɪ/ *a.* incendiaire.

inflate /ɪnˈfleɪt/ *v.t.* (*balloon, prices, etc.*) gonfler.

inflation /ɪnˈfleɪʃn/ *n.* inflation *f.* ~ary *a.* inflationniste.

inflection /ɪnˈflekʃn/ *n.* inflexion *f.*; (*suffix: gram.*) désinence *f.*

inflexible /ɪnˈfleksəbl/ *a.* inflexible.
inflict /ɪnˈflɪkt/ *v.t.* infliger (**on**, à).
influence /ˈɪnfluəns/ *n.* influence *f.* —*v.t.* influencer. **under the ~,** (*drunk*: *fam.*) en état d'ivresse.
influential /ɪnfluˈenʃl/ *a.* influent.
influenza /ɪnfluˈenzə/ *n.* grippe *f.*
influx /ˈɪnflʌks/ *n.* afflux *m.*
inform /ɪnˈfɔːm/ *v.t.* informer. **keep ~ed,** tenir au courant. **~ant** *n.* informa|teur, -trice *m.*, *f.* **~er** *n.* indica|teur, -trice *m.*, *f.*
informal /ɪnˈfɔːml/ *a.* (*simple*) simple, sans cérémonie; (*unofficial*) officieux; (*colloquial*) familier. **~ity** /-ˈmælətɪ/*n.* simplicité *f.* **~ly** *adv.* sans cérémonie.
information /ɪnfəˈmeɪʃn/ *n.* renseignement(s) *m.* (*pl.*), information(s) *f.* (*pl.*).
informative /ɪnˈfɔːmətɪv/*a.* instructif.
infra-red /ɪnfrəˈred/ *a.* infrarouge.
infrequent /ɪnˈfriːkwənt/ *a.* peu fréquent. **~ly** *adv.* rarement.
infringe /ɪnˈfrɪndʒ/ *v.t.* contrevenir à. **~ on,** empiéter sur. **~ment** *n.* infraction *f.*
infuriate /ɪnˈfjʊərɪeɪt/ *v.t.* exaspérer, rendre furieux.
infus|e /ɪnˈfjuːz/ *v.t.* infuser. **~ion** /-ʒn/ *n.* infusion *f.*
ingen|ious /ɪnˈdʒiːnɪəs/ *a.* ingénieux. **~uity** /-ɪˈnjuːətɪ/ *n.* ingéniosité *f.*
ingenuous /ɪnˈdʒenjʊəs/ *a.* ingénu.
ingot /ˈɪŋgət/ *n.* lingot *m.*
ingrained /ɪnˈgreɪnd/ *a.* enraciné.
ingratiate /ɪnˈgreɪʃɪeɪt/ *v.t.* **~ o.s. with,** gagner les bonnes grâces de.
ingratitude /ɪnˈgrætɪtjuːd/ *n.* ingratitude *f.*
ingredient /ɪnˈgriːdɪənt/ *n.* ingrédient *m.*
inhabit /ɪnˈhæbɪt/ *v.t.* habiter. **~able** *a.* habitable. **~ant** *n.* habitant(e) *m.* (*f.*).
inhale /ɪnˈheɪl/ *v.t.* inhaler; (*tobacco smoke*) avaler.
inherent /ɪnˈhɪərənt/ *a.* inhérent. **~ly** *adv.* en soi, intrinsèquement.
inherit /ɪnˈherɪt/ *v.t.* hériter (de). **~ance** *n.* héritage *m.*
inhibit /ɪnˈhɪbɪt/ *v.t.* (*hinder*) gêner; (*prevent*) empêcher. **be ~ed,** avoir des inhibitions. **~ion** /-ˈbɪʃn/ *n.* inhibition *f.*
inhospitable /ɪnhɒˈspɪtəbl/ *a.* inhospitalier.
inhuman /ɪnˈhjuːmən/ *a.* (*brutal, not human*) inhumain. **~ity** /-ˈmænətɪ/ *n.* inhumanité *f.*
inhumane /ɪnhjuːˈmeɪn/ *a.* (*unkind*) inhumain.
inimitable /ɪˈnɪmɪtəbl/ *a.* inimitable.
iniquit|ous /ɪˈnɪkwɪtəs/ *a.* inique. **~y** /-ətɪ/ *n.* iniquité *f.*
initial /ɪˈnɪʃl/ *n.* initiale *f.* —*v.t.* (*p.t.* **initialled**) parapher. —*a.* initial. **~ly** *adv.* initialement.
initiat|e /ɪˈnɪʃɪeɪt/ *v.t.* (*begin*) amorcer; (*scheme*) lancer; (*person*) initier (**into**, à). **~ion** /-ˈeɪʃn/ *n.* initiation *f.*; (*start*) amorce *f.*
initiative /ɪˈnɪʃətɪv/ *n.* initiative *f.*
inject /ɪnˈdʒekt/ *v.t.* injecter; (*new element*: *fig.*) insuffler. **~ion** /-kʃn/ *n.* injection *f.*, piqûre *f.*
injunction /ɪnˈdʒʌŋkʃn/ *n.* (*court order*) ordonnance *f.*
injure /ˈɪndʒə(r)/ *v.t.* blesser; (*do wrong to*) nuire à.
injury /ˈɪndʒərɪ/ *n.* (*physical*) blessure *f.*; (*wrong*) préjudice *m.*
injustice /ɪnˈdʒʌstɪs/ *n.* injustice *f.*
ink /ɪŋk/ *n.* encre *f.* **~-well** *n.* encrier *m.* **~y** *a.* taché d'encre.
inkling /ˈɪŋklɪŋ/ *n.* petite idée *f.*
inland /ˈɪnlənd/ *a.* intérieur. —*adv.* à l'intérieur. **I~ Revenue,** fisc *m.*
inlay[1] /ɪnˈleɪ/ *v.t.* (*p.t.* **inlaid**) incruster.
inlay[2] /ˈɪnleɪ/ *n.* incrustation *f.*
inlet /ˈɪnlet/ *n.* bras de mer *m.*; (*techn.*) arrivée *f.*
inmate /ˈɪnmeɪt/ *n.* (*of asylum*) interné(e) *m.* (*f.*); (*of prison*) détenu(e) *m.* (*f.*).
inn /ɪn/ *n.* auberge *f.*
innards /ˈɪnədz/ *n. pl.* (*fam.*) entrailles *f. pl.*
innate /ɪˈneɪt/ *a.* inné.
inner /ˈɪnə(r)/ *a.* intérieur, interne; (*fig.*) profond, intime. **~most** *a.* le plus profond.
innings /ˈɪnɪŋz/ *n. invar.* tour de batte *m.*; (*fig.*) tour *m.*
innkeeper /ˈɪnkiːpə(r)/ *n.* aubergiste *m./f.*
innocen|t /ˈɪnəsnt/ *a.* & *n.* innocent(e) (*m.* (*f.*)). **~ce** *n.* innocence *f.*
innocuous /ɪˈnɒkjʊəs/ *a.* inoffensif.
innovat|e /ˈɪnəveɪt/ *v.i.* innover. **~ion** /-ˈveɪʃn/ *n.* innovation *f.* **~or** *n.* innova|teur, -trice *m.*, *f.*
innuendo /ɪnjuːˈendəʊ/ *n.* (*pl.* **-oes**) insinuation *f.*

innumerable /ɪ'nju:mərəbl/ *a.* innombrable.

inoculat|e /ɪ'nɒkjʊleɪt/ *v.t.* inoculer. ~**ion** /-'leɪʃn/ *n.* inoculation *f.*

inoffensive /mə'fensɪv/ *a.* inoffensif.

inoperative /ɪn'ɒpərətɪv/ *a.* inopérant.

inopportune /ɪn'ɒpətjuːn/ *a.* inopportun.

inordinate /ɪ'nɔːdɪnət/ *a.* excessif. ~**ly** *adv.* excessivement.

input /'ɪmpʊt/ *n.* (*data*) données *f. pl.*; (*computer process*) entrée *f.*; (*power*: *electr.*) énergie *f.*

inquest /'ɪnkwest/ *n.* enquête *f.*

inquir|e /ɪn'kwaɪə(r)/ *v.i.* faire une enquête. ~**y** *n.* enquête *f.*

inquisition /ɪnkwɪ'zɪʃn/ *n.* inquisition *f.*

inquisitive /ɪn'kwɪzətɪv/ *a.* curieux; (*prying*) indiscret.

inroad /'ɪnrəʊd/ *n.* incursion *f.*

insan|e /ɪn'seɪn/ *a.* fou. ~**ity** /ɪn'sænəti/ *n.* folie *f.*, démence *f.*

insanitary /ɪn'sænɪtrɪ/ *a.* insalubre, malsain.

insatiable /ɪn'seɪʃəbl/ *a.* insatiable.

inscri|be /ɪn'skraɪb/ *v.t.* inscrire; (*book*) dédicacer. ~**ption** /-ɪpʃn/ *n.* inscription *f.*; dédicace *f.*

inscrutable /ɪn'skruːtəbl/ *a.* impénétrable.

insect /'ɪnsekt/ *n.* insecte *m.*

insecticide /ɪn'sektɪsaɪd/ *n.* insecticide *m.*

insecur|e /ɪnsɪ'kjʊə(r)/ *a.* (*not firm*) peu solide; (*unsafe*) peu sûr; (*worried*) anxieux. ~**ity** *n.* insécurité *f.*

insemination /ɪnsemɪ'neɪʃn/ *n.* insémination *f.*

insensible /ɪn'sensəbl/ *a.* insensible; (*unconscious*) inconscient.

insensitive /ɪn'sensətɪv/ *a.* insensible.

inseparable /ɪn'seprəbl/ *a.* inséparable.

insert[1] /ɪn'sɜːt/ *v.t.* insérer. ~**ion** /-ʃn/ *n.* insertion *f.*

insert[2] /'ɪnsɜːt/ *n.* insertion *f.*

inshore /ɪn'ʃɔːr/ *a.* côtier.

inside /ɪn'saɪd/ *n.* intérieur *m.* ~**(s)**, (*fam.*) entrailles *f. pl.* —*a.* intérieur. —*adv.* à l'intérieur, dedans. —*prep.* à l'intérieur de; (*of time*) en moins de. ~ **out**, à l'envers; (*thoroughly*) à fond.

insidious /ɪn'sɪdɪəs/ *a.* insidieux.

insight /'ɪnsaɪt/ *n.* (*perception*) perspicacité *f.*; (*idea*) aperçu *m.*

insignia /ɪn'sɪɡnɪə/ *n. pl.* insignes *m. pl.*

insignificant /ɪnsɪɡ'nɪfɪkənt/ *a.* insignifiant.

insincer|e /ɪnsɪn'sɪə(r)/ *a.* peu sincère. ~**ity** /-'serəti/ *n.* manque de sincérité *m.*

insinuat|e /ɪn'sɪnjʊeɪt/ *v.t.* insinuer. ~**ion** /-'eɪʃn/ *n.* insinuation *f.*

insipid /ɪn'sɪpɪd/ *a.* insipide.

insist /ɪn'sɪst/ *v.t./i.* insister. ~ **on**, affirmer; (*demand*) exiger. ~ **on doing**, insister pour faire.

insisten|t /ɪn'sɪstənt/ *a.* insistant. ~**ce** *n.* insistance *f.* ~**tly** *adv.* avec insistance.

insolen|t /'ɪnsələnt/ *a.* insolent. ~**ce** *n.* insolence *f.*

insoluble /ɪn'sɒljʊbl/ *a.* insoluble.

insolvent /ɪn'sɒlvənt/ *a.* insolvable.

insomnia /ɪn'sɒmnɪə/ *n.* insomnie *f.* ~**c** /-ɪæk/ *n.* insomniaque *m./f.*

inspect /ɪn'spekt/ *v.t.* inspecter; (*tickets*) contrôler. ~**ion** /-kʃn/ *n.* inspection *f.*; contrôle *m.* ~**or** *n.* inspec|teur, -trice *m., f.*; (*on train, bus*) contrôleu|r, -se *m., f.*

inspir|e /ɪn'spaɪə(r)/ *v.t.* inspirer. ~**ation** /-ə'reɪʃn/ *n.* inspiration *f.*

instability /ɪnstə'bɪləti/ *n.* instabilité *f.*

install /ɪn'stɔːl/ *v.t.* installer. ~**ation** /-ə'leɪʃn/ *n.* installation *f.*

instalment /ɪn'stɔːlmənt/ *n.* (*payment*) acompte *m.*, versement *m.*; (*of serial*) épisode *m.*

instance /'ɪnstəns/ *n.* exemple *m.*; (*case*) cas *m.* **for ~**, par exemple. **in the first ~**, en premier lieu.

instant /'ɪnstənt/ *a.* immédiat; (*food*) instantané. —*n.* instant *m.* ~**ly** *adv.* immédiatement.

instantaneous /ɪnstən'teɪnɪəs/ *a.* instantané.

instead /ɪn'sted/ *adv.* plutôt. ~ **of doing**, au lieu de faire. ~ **of s.o.**, à la place de qn.

instep /'ɪnstep/ *n.* cou-de-pied *m.*

instigat|e /'ɪnstɪɡeɪt/ *v.t.* provoquer. ~**ion** /-'ɡeɪʃn/ *n.* instigation *f.* ~**or** *n.* instiga|teur, -trice *m., f.*

instil /ɪn'stɪl/ *v.t.* (*p.t.* **instilled**) inculquer; (*inspire*) insuffler.

instinct /'ɪnstɪŋkt/ *n.* instinct *m.* ~**ive** /ɪn'stɪŋktɪv/ *a.* instinctif.

institut|e /'ɪnstɪtjuːt/ *n.* institut *m.* —*v.t.* instituer; (*inquiry etc.*) entamer. ~**ion** /-'tjuːʃn/ *n.* institution *f.*; (*school, hospital*) établissement *m.*

instruct /ɪn'strʌkt/ *v.t.* instruire; (*or-*

der) ordonner. ∼ **s.o. in sth.,** enseigner qch. à qn. ∼**ion** /-kʃn/ *n.* instruction *f.* ∼**ions** /-kʃnz/ *n. pl.* (*for use*) mode d'emploi *m.* ∼**ive** *a.* instructif. ∼**or** *n.* instructeur *m.,* professeur *m.*

instrument /'ɪnstrʊmənt/ *n.* instrument *m.*

instrumental /ɪnstrʊ'mentl/ *a.* instrumental. **be** ∼ **in,** contribuer à. ∼**ist** *n.* instrumentaliste *n.|f.*

insubordinat|e /ɪnsə'bɔːdɪnət/ *a.* insubordonné. ∼**ion** /-'neɪʃn/ *n.* insubordination *f.*

insufferable /ɪn'sʌfrəbl/ *a.* intolérable, insupportable.

insufficient /ɪnsə'fɪʃnt/ *a.* insuffisant. ∼**ly** *adv.* insuffisamment.

insular /'ɪnsjʊlə(r)/ *a.* insulaire; (*mind, person: fig.*) borné.

insulat|e /'ɪnsjʊleɪt/ *v.t.* (*room, wire, etc.*) isoler. ∼**ing tape,** chatterton *m.* ∼**ion** /-'leɪʃn/ *n.* isolation *f.*

insulin /'ɪnsjʊlɪn/ *n.* insuline *f.*

insult[1] /ɪn'sʌlt/ *v.t.* insulter.

insult[2] /'ɪnsʌlt/ *n.* insulte *f.*

insuperable /ɪn'sjuːprəbl/ *a.* insurmontable.

insur|e /ɪn'ʃʊə(r)/ *v.t.* assurer. ∼**e that,** (*ensure: Amer.*) s'assurer que. ∼**ance** *n.* assurance *f.*

insurmountable /ɪnsə'maʊntəbl/ *a.* insurmontable.

insurrection /ɪnsə'rekʃn/ *n.* insurrection *f.*

intact /ɪn'tækt/ *a.* intact.

intake /'ɪnteɪk/ *n.* admission(s) *f.* (*pl.*); (*techn.*) prise *f.*

intangible /ɪn'tændʒəbl/ *a.* intangible.

integral /'ɪntɪgrəl/ *a.* intégral. **be an** ∼ **part of,** faire partie intégrante de.

integrat|e /'ɪntɪgreɪt/ *v.t./i.* (s')intégrer. ∼**ion** /-'greɪʃn/ *n.* intégration *f.*; (*racial*) déségrégation *f.*

integrity /ɪn'tegrətɪ/ *n.* intégrité *f.*

intellect /'ɪntəlekt/ *n.* intelligence *f.* ∼**ual** /-'lektʃʊəl/ *a. & n.* intellectuel(le) (*m.* (*f.*)).

intelligen|t /ɪn'telɪdʒənt/ *a.* intelligent. ∼**ce** *n.* intelligence *f.*; (*mil.*) renseignements *m. pl.* ∼**tly** *adv.* intelligemment.

intelligentsia /ɪntelɪ'dʒentsɪə/ *n.* intelligentsia *f.*

intelligible /ɪn'telɪdʒəbl/ *a.* intelligible.

intemperance /ɪn'tempərəns/ *n.* (*drunkenness*) ivrognerie *f.*

intend /ɪn'tend/ *v.t.* destiner. ∼ **to do,** avoir l'intention de faire. ∼**ed** *a.* intentionnel; *n.* (*future spouse: fam.*) promis(e) *m.* (*f.*).

intens|e /ɪn'tens/ *a.* intense; (*person*) passionné. ∼**ely** *adv.* (*to live etc.*) intensément; (*very*) extrêmement. ∼**ity** *n.* intensité *f.*

intensif|y /ɪn'tensɪfaɪ/ *v.t.* intensifier. ∼**ication** /-ɪ'keɪʃn/ *n.* intensification *f.*

intensive /ɪn'tensɪv/ *a.* intensif. **in** ∼ **care,** en réanimation.

intent /ɪn'tent/ *n.* intention *f.* —*a.* attentif. ∼ **on,** absorbé par. ∼ **on doing,** résolu à faire. ∼**ly** *adv.* attentivement.

intention /ɪn'tenʃn/ *n.* intention *f.* ∼**al** *a.* intentionnel.

inter /ɪn'tɜː(r)/ *v.t.* (*p.t.* **interred**) enterrer.

inter /'ɪntə(r)/ *pref.* inter-.

interact /ɪntə'rækt/ *v.i.* avoir une action réciproque. ∼**ion** /-kʃn/ *n.* interaction *f.*

intercede /ɪntə'siːd/ *v.i.* intercéder.

intercept /ɪntə'sept/ *v.t.* intercepter. ∼**ion** /-pʃn/ *n.* interception *f.*

interchange /'ɪntətʃeɪndʒ/ *n.* (*road junction*) échangeur *m.*

interchangeable /ɪntə'tʃeɪndʒəbl/ *a.* interchangeable.

intercom /'ɪntəkɒm/ *n.* interphone *m.*

interconnected /ɪntəkə'nektɪd/ *a.* (*facts, events, etc.*) lié.

intercourse /'ɪntəkɔːs/ *n.* (*sexual, social*) rapports *m. pl.*

interest /'ɪntrəst/ *n.* intérêt *m.*; (*stake*) intérêts *m. pl.* —*v.t.* intéresser. ∼**ed** *a.* intéressé. **be** ∼**ed in,** s'intéresser à. ∼**ing** *a.* intéressant.

interfer|e /ɪntə'fɪə(r)/ *v.i.* se mêler des affaires des autres. ∼**e in,** s'ingérer dans. ∼**ence** *n.* ingérence *f.*; (*radio*) parasites *m. pl.*

interim /'ɪntərɪm/ *n.* intérim *m.* —*a.* intérimaire.

interior /ɪn'tɪərɪə(r)/ *n.* intérieur *m.* —*a.* intérieur.

interjection /ɪntə'dʒekʃn/ *n.* interjection *f.*

interlock /ɪntə'lɒk/ *v.t./i.* (*techn.*) (s')emboîter, (s')enclencher.

interloper /'ɪntələʊpə(r)/ *n.* intrus(e) *m.* (*f.*).

interlude /'ɪntəluːd/ *n.* intervalle *m.*; (*theatre, mus.*) intermède *m.*

intermarr|iage /ɪntə'mærɪdʒ/ *n.* mariage entre membres de races différentes *m.* ~**y** *v.i.* se marier (entre eux).

intermediary /ɪntə'miːdɪərɪ/ *a. & n.* intermédiaire (*m./f.*).

intermediate /ɪntə'miːdɪət/ *a.* intermédiaire; (*exam etc.*) moyen.

interminable /ɪn'tɜːmɪnəbl/ *a.* interminable.

intermission /ɪntə'mɪʃn/ *n.* pause *f.*; (*theatre etc.*) entracte *m.*

intermittent /ɪntə'mɪtnt/ *a.* intermittent. ~**ly** *adv.* par intermittence.

intern[1] /ɪn'tɜːn/ *v.t.* interner. ~**ee** /-'niː/ *n.* interné(e) *m.* (*f.*). ~**ment** *n.* internement *m.*

intern[2] /'ɪntɜːn/ *n.* (*doctor: Amer.*) interne *m./f.*

internal /ɪn'tɜːnl/ *a.* interne; (*domestic: pol.*) intérieur. ~**ly** *adv.* intérieurement.

international /ɪntə'næʃnəl/ *a. & n.* international (*m.*).

interplay /'ɪntəpleɪ/ *n.* jeu *m.*, interaction *f.*

interpolate /ɪn'tɜːpəleɪt/ *v.t.* interpoler.

interpret /ɪn'tɜːprɪt/ *v.t./i.* interpréter. ~**ation** /-'teɪʃn/ *n.* interprétation *f.* ~**er** *n.* interprète *m./f.*

interrelated /ɪntərɪ'leɪtɪd/ *a.* en corrélation, lié.

interrogat|e /ɪn'terəgeɪt/ *v.t.* interroger. ~**ion** /-'geɪʃn/ *n.* interrogation *f.* (**of,** de); (*session of questions*) interrogatoire *m.*

interrogative /ɪntə'rɒgətɪv/ *a. & n.* interrogatif (*m.*).

interrupt /ɪntə'rʌpt/ *v.t.* interrompre. ~**ion** /-pʃn/ *n.* interruption *f.*

intersect /ɪntə'sekt/ *v.t./i.* (*lines, roads*) (se) couper. ~**ion** /-kʃn/ *n.* intersection *f.*; (*crossroads*) croisement *m.*

interspersed /ɪntə'spɜːst/ *a.* (*scattered*) dispersé. ~ **with,** parsemé de.

intertwine /ɪntə'twaɪn/ *v.t./i.* (s')entrelacer.

interval /'ɪntəvl/ *n.* intervalle *m.*; (*theatre*) entracte *m.* **at** ~**s,** par intervalles.

interven|e /ɪntə'viːn/ *v.i.* intervenir; (*of time*) s'écouler (**between,** entre). ~**tion** /-'venʃn/ *n.* intervention *f.*

interview /'ɪntəvjuː/ *n.* (*with reporter*) interview *f.*; (*for job etc.*) entrevue

f. —*v.t.* interviewer. ~**er** *n.* interviewer *m.*

intestin|e /ɪn'testɪn/ *n.* intestin *m.* ~**al** *a.* intestinal.

intima|te[1] /'ɪntɪmət/ *a.* intime; (*detailed*) profond. ~**cy** *n.* intimité *f.* ~**tely** *adv.* intimement.

intimate[2] /'ɪntɪmeɪt/ *v.t.* (*state*) annoncer; (*imply*) suggérer.

intimidat|e /ɪn'tɪmɪdeɪt/ *v.t.* intimider. ~**ion** /-'deɪʃn/ *n.* intimidation *f.*

into /'ɪntuː, *unstressed* 'ɪntə/ *prep.* (*put, go, fall, etc.*) dans; (*divide, translate, etc.*) en.

intolerable /ɪn'tɒlərəbl/ *a.* intolérable.

intoleran|t /ɪn'tɒlərənt/ *a.* intolérant. ~**ce** *n.* intolérance *f.*

intonation /ɪntə'neɪʃn/ *n.* intonation *f.*

intoxicat|e /ɪn'tɒksɪkeɪt/ *v.t.* enivrer. ~**ed** *a.* ivre. ~**ion** /-'keɪʃn/ *n.* ivresse *f.*

intra/'ɪntrə/ *pref.* intra-.

intractable /ɪn'træktəbl/ *a.* très difficile.

intransigent /ɪn'trænsɪdʒənt/ *a.* intransigeant.

intransitive /ɪn'trænsətɪv/ *a.* (*verb*) intransitif.

intravenous /ɪntrə'viːnəs/ *a.* (*med.*) intraveineux.

intrepid /ɪn'trepɪd/ *a.* intrépide.

intrica|te /'ɪntrɪkət/ *a.* complexe. ~**cy** *n.* complexité *f.*

intrigu|e /ɪn'triːg/ *v.t./i.* intriguer. —*n.* intrigue *f.* ~**ing** *a.* très intéressant; (*curious*) curieux.

intrinsic /ɪn'trɪnsɪk/ *a.* intrinsèque. ~**ally** /-klɪ/ *adv.* intrinsèquement.

introduce /ɪntrə'djuːs/ *v.t.* (*bring in, insert*) introduire; (*programme, question*) présenter. ~ **s.o. to,** (*person*) présenter qn. à.

introduct|ion /ɪntrə'dʌkʃn/ *n.* introduction *f.*; (*to person*) présentation *f.* ~**ory** /-tərɪ/ *a.* (*letter, words*) d'introduction.

introspective /ɪntrə'spektɪv/ *a.* introspectif.

introvert /'ɪntrəvɜːt/ *n.* introverti(e) *m.* (*f.*).

intru|de /ɪn'truːd/ *v.i.* (*person*) s'imposer (**on s.o.,** à qn.), déranger. ~**der** *n.* intrus(e) *m.* (*f.*). ~**sion** *n.* intrusion *f.*

intuit|ion /ɪntjuː'ɪʃn/ *n.* intuition *f.* ~**ive** /ɪn'tjuːɪtɪv/ *a.* intuitif.

inundat|e /'ɪnʌndeɪt/ *v.t.* inonder. **~ion** /-'deɪʃn/ *n.* inondation *f.*

invade /ɪn'veɪd/ *v.t.* envahir. **~r** /-ə(r)/ *n.* envahisseu|r, -se *m., f.*

invalid[1] /'ɪnvəlɪd/ *n.* malade *m./f.*; (*disabled*) infirme *m./f.*

invalid[2] /ɪn'vælɪd/ *a.* non valable. **~ate** *v.t.* invalider.

invaluable /ɪn'væljʊəbl/ *a.* inestimable.

invariabl|e /ɪn'veərɪəbl/ *a.* invariable. **~y** *adv.* invariablement.

invasion /ɪn'veɪʒn/ *n.* invasion *f.*

invective /ɪn'vektɪv/ *n.* invective *f.*

inveigh /ɪn'veɪ/ *v.i.* invectiver.

inveigle /ɪn'veɪgl/ *v.t.* persuader.

invent /ɪn'vent/ *v.t.* inventer. **~ion** /-enʃn/ *n.* invention *f.* **~ive** *a.* inventif. **~or** *n.* inven|teur, -trice *m., f.*

inventory /'ɪnvəntrɪ/ *n.* inventaire *m.*

inverse /ɪn'vɜ:s/ *a.* & *n.* inverse (*m.*). **~ly** *adv.* inversement.

inver|t /ɪn'vɜ:t/ *v.t.* intervertir. **~ted commas,** guillemets *m. pl.* **~sion** *n.* inversion *f.*

invest /ɪn'vest/ *v.t.* investir; (*time, effort*: *fig.*) consacrer. *—v.i.* faire un investissement. **~ in,** (*buy*: *fam.*) se payer. **~ment** *n.* investissement *m.* **~or** *n.* actionnaire *m./f.*

investigat|e /ɪn'vestɪgeɪt/ *v.t.* étudier; (*crime etc.*) enquêter sur. **~ion** /-'geɪʃn/ *n.* investigation *f.* **under ~ion,** à l'étude. **~or** *n.* (*police*) enquêteu|r, -se *m., f.*

inveterate /ɪn'vetərət/ *a.* invétéré.

invidious /ɪn'vɪdɪəs/ *a.* (*hateful*) odieux; (*unfair*) injuste.

invigilat|e /ɪn'vɪdʒɪleɪt/ *v.i.* (*schol.*) être de surveillance. **~or** *n.* surveillant(e) *m. (f.).*

invigorate /ɪn'vɪgəreɪt/ *v.t.* vivifier; (*encourage*) stimuler.

invincible /ɪn'vɪnsəbl/ *a.* invincible.

invisible /ɪn'vɪzəbl/ *a.* invisible.

invit|e /ɪn'vaɪt/ *v.t.* inviter; (*ask for*) demander. **~ation** /ɪnvɪ'teɪʃn/ *n.* invitation *f.* **~ing** *a.* (*meal, smile, etc.*) engageant.

invoice /'ɪnvɔɪs/ *n.* facture *f.* *—v.t.* facturer.

invoke /ɪn'vəʊk/ *v.t.* invoquer.

involuntary /ɪn'vɒləntrɪ/ *a.* involontaire.

involve /ɪn'vɒlv/ *v.t.* entraîner. **~d** *a.* (*complex*) compliqué; (*at stake*) en jeu. **~d in,** mêlé à. **~ment** *n.* participation *f.* (**in,** à).

invulnerable /ɪn'vʌlnərəbl/ *a.* invulnérable.

inward /'ɪnwəd/ *a.* & *adv.* vers l'intérieur; (*feeling etc.*) intérieur. **~ly** *adv.* intérieurement. **~s** *adv.* vers l'intérieur.

iodine /'aɪədi:n/ *n.* iode *m.*; (*antiseptic*) teinture d'iode *f.*

iota /aɪ'əʊtə/ *n.* (*amount*) brin *m.*

IOU /aɪəʊ'ju:/ *abbr.* (*I owe you*) reconnaissance de dette *f.*

IQ /aɪ'kju:/ *abbr.* (*intelligence quotient*) QI *m.*

Iran /ɪ'rɑ:n/ *n.* Iran *m.* **~ian** /ɪ'reɪnɪən/ *a.* & *n.* iranien(ne) (*m. (f.)*).

Iraq /ɪ'rɑ:k/ *n.* Irak *m.* **~i** *a.* & *n.* irakien(ne) (*m. (f.)*).

irascible /ɪ'ræsəbl/ *a.* irascible.

irate /aɪ'reɪt/ *a.* en colère, furieux.

ire /'aɪə(r)/ *n.* courroux *m.*

Ireland /'aɪələnd/ *n.* Irlande *f.*

iris /'aɪərɪs/ *n.* (*anat., bot.*) iris *m.*

Irish /'aɪərɪʃ/ *a.* irlandais. *—n.* (*lang.*) irlandais *m.* **~man** *n.* Irlandais *m.* **~woman** *n.* Irlandaise *f.*

irk /ɜ:k/ *v.t.* ennuyer. **~some** *a.* ennuyeux.

iron /'aɪən/ *n.* fer *m.*; (*appliance*) fer (à repasser) *m.* *—a.* de fer. *—v.t.* repasser. **I~ Curtain,** rideau de fer *m.* **~ out,** faire disparaître. **~ing-board** *n.* planche à repasser *f.*

ironic(al) /aɪ'rɒnɪk(l)/ *a.* ironique.

ironmonger /'aɪənmʌŋgə(r)/ *n.* quincailler *m.* **~y** *n.* quincaillerie *f.*

ironwork /'aɪənwɜ:k/ *n.* ferronnerie *f.*

irony /'aɪərənɪ/ *n.* ironie *f.*

irrational /ɪ'ræʃənl/ *a.* irrationnel; (*person*) pas rationnel.

irreconcilable /ɪrekən'saɪlbl/ *a.* irréconciliable; (*incompatible*) inconciliable.

irrefutable /ɪ'refjʊtəbl/ *a.* irréfutable.

irregular /ɪ'regjʊlə(r)/ *a.* irrégulier. **~ity** /-'lærətɪ/ *n.* irrégularité *f.*

irrelevan|t /ɪ'reləvənt/ *a.* sans rapport (**to,** avec). **~ce** *n.* manque de rapport *m.*

irreparable /ɪ'repərəbl/ *a.* irréparable, irrémédiable.

irreplaceable /ɪrɪ'pleɪsəbl/ *a.* irremplaçable.

irrepressible /ɪrɪ'presəbl/ *a.* irrépressible.

irresistible /ɪrɪ'zɪstəbl/ *a.* irrésistible.

irresolute /ɪ'rezəlu:t/ *a.* irrésolu.

irrespective /ɪrɪ'spektɪv/ *a.* **~ of,** sans tenir compte de.

irresponsible /ɪrɪ'spɒnsəbl/ a. irresponsable.

irretrievable /ɪrɪ'triːvəbl/ a. irréparable.

irreverent /ɪ'revərənt/ a. irrévérencieux.

irreversible /ɪrɪ'vɜːsəbl/ a. irréversible; (*decision*) irrévocable.

irrevocable /ɪ'revəkəbl/ a. irrévocable.

irrigat|e /'ɪrɪgeɪt/ v.t. irriguer. **~ion** /-'geɪʃn/ n. irrigation f.

irritable /'ɪrɪtəbl/ a. irritable.

irritat|e /'ɪrɪteɪt/ v.t. irriter. **~ion** /-'teɪʃn/ n. irritation f.

is /ɪz/ see **be**.

Islam /'ɪzlɑːm/ n. Islam m. **~ic** /ɪz'læmɪk/ a. islamique.

island /'aɪlənd/ n. île f. **traffic ~**, refuge m. **~er** n. insulaire m./f.

isle /aɪl/ n. île f.

isolat|e /'aɪsəleɪt/ v.t. isoler. **~ion** /-'leɪʃn/ n. isolement m.

isotope /'aɪsətəʊp/ n. isotope m.

Israel /'ɪzreɪl/ n. Israël m. **~i** /ɪz'reɪlɪ/ a. & n. israélien(ne) (m. (f.)).

issue /'ɪʃuː/ n. question f.; (*outcome*) résultat m.; (*of magazine etc.*) numéro m.; (*of stamps etc.*) émission f.; (*offspring*) descendance f. —v.t. distribuer, donner; (*stamps etc.*) émettre; (*book*) publier. —v.i. **~ from**, sortir de. **at ~**, en cause. **take**

~, engager une controverse.

isthmus /'ɪsməs/ n. isthme m.

it /ɪt/ pron. (*subject*) il, elle; (*object*) le, la, l'*; (*impersonal subject*) il; (*non-specific*) ce, c'*, cela, ça. **~ is**, (*quiet, my book, etc.*) c'est. **~ is cold/warm/late**/etc., il fait froid/ chaud/tard/etc. **that's ~**, c'est ça. **who is ~?**, qui est-ce? **of ~**, **from ~**, en. **in ~**, **at ~**, **to ~**, y.

italic /ɪ'tælɪk/ a. italique. **~s** n. pl. italique m.

Ital|y /'ɪtəlɪ/ n. Italie f. **~ian** /ɪ'tælɪən/ a. & n. italien(ne) (m. (f.)); (*lang.*) italien m.

itch /ɪtʃ/ n. démangeaison f. —v.i. démanger. **my arm ~es**, mon bras me démange. **I am ~ing to**, ça me démange de. **~y** a. qui démange.

item /'aɪtəm/ n. article m., chose f.; (*on agenda*) question f. **news ~**, fait divers m. **~ize** v.t. détailler.

itinerant /aɪ'tɪnərənt/ a. itinérant; (*musician, actor*) ambulant.

itinerary /aɪ'tɪnərərɪ/ n. itinéraire m.

its /ɪts/ a. son, sa, pl. ses.

it's /ɪts/ = **it is, it has**.

itself /ɪt'self/ pron. lui-même, elle-même; (*reflexive*) se.

ivory /'aɪvərɪ/ n. ivoire m. **~ tower**, tour d'ivoire f.

ivy /'aɪvɪ/ n. lierre m.

J

jab /dʒæb/ v.t. (p.t. **jabbed**) (thrust) enfoncer; (prick) piquer. —n. coup m.; (injection) piqûre f.

jabber /'dʒæbə(r)/ v.i. jacasser, bavarder; (indistinctly) bredouiller. —n. bavardage m.

jack /dʒæk/ n. (techn.) cric m.; (cards) valet m. —v.t. ~ **up**, soulever (avec un cric).

jackal /'dʒækɔːl/ n. chacal m.

jackass /'dʒækæs/ n. âne m.

jackdaw /'dʒækdɔː/ n. choucas m.

jacket /'dʒækɪt/ n. veste f., veston m.; (of book) jaquette f.

jack-knife /'dʒæknaɪf/ n. couteau pliant m.—v.i. (lorry) faire un tête-à-queue.

jackpot /'dʒækpɒt/ n. gros lot m. **hit the ~,** gagner le gros lot.

jade /dʒeɪd/ n. (stone) jade m.

jaded /'dʒeɪdɪd/ a. blasé.

jagged /'dʒægɪd/ a. dentelé.

jail /dʒeɪl/ n. & v.t. = gaol.

jalopy /dʒə'lɒpɪ/ n. vieux tacot m.

jam[1] /dʒæm/ n. confiture f.

jam[2] /dʒæm/ v.t./i. (p.t. **jammed**) (wedge, become wedged) coincer; (cram) (s')entasser; (street etc.) encombrer; (thrust) enfoncer; (radio) brouiller. —n. foule f.; (of traffic) embouteillage m.; (situation: fam.) pétrin m. ~**-packed** a. (fam.) bourré.

Jamaica /dʒə'meɪkə/ n. Jamaïque f.

jangle /'dʒæŋgl/ n. cliquetis m. —v.t./i. (faire) cliqueter.

janitor /'dʒænɪtə(r)/ n. concierge m.

January /'dʒænjʊərɪ/ n. janvier m.

Japan /dʒə'pæn/ n. Japon m. ~**ese** /dʒæpə'niːz/ a. & n. japonais(e) (m. (f.)); (lang.) japonais m.

jar[1] /dʒɑː(r)/ n. pot m., bocal m.

jar[2] /dʒɑː(r)/ v.i. (p.t. **jarred**) grincer; (of colours etc.) détonner. —v.t. ébranler. —n. son discordant m. ~**ring** a. discordant.

jar[3] /dʒɑː(r)/ n. **on the ~,** (ajar) entr'ouvert.

jargon /'dʒɑːgən/ n. jargon m.

jasmine /'dʒæsmɪn/ n. jasmin m.

jaundice /'dʒɔːndɪs/ n. jaunisse f.

jaundiced /'dʒɔːndɪst/ a. (envious) envieux; (bitter) aigri.

jaunt /dʒɔːnt/ n. (trip) balade f.

jaunty /'dʒɔːntɪ/ a. (-ier, -iest) (cheerful, sprightly) allègre.

javelin /'dʒævlɪn/ n. javelot m.

jaw /dʒɔː/ n. mâchoire f. —v.i. (talk: sl.) jacasser.

jay /dʒeɪ/ n. geai m. ~**-walk** v.i. traverser la chaussée imprudemment.

jazz /dʒæz/ n. jazz m. —v.t. ~ **up**, animer. ~**y** a. tape-à-l'œil invar.

jealous /'dʒeləs/ a. jaloux. ~**y** n. jalousie f.

jeans /dʒiːnz/ n. pl. (blue-)jean m.

jeep /dʒiːp/ n. jeep f.

jeer /dʒɪə(r)/ v.t./i. ~ **(at),** railler; (boo) huer. —n. raillerie f.; huée f.

jell /dʒel/ v.i. (set: fam.) prendre. ~**ied** a. en gelée.

jelly /'dʒelɪ/ n. gelée f.

jellyfish /'dʒelɪfɪʃ/ n. méduse f.

jeopard|y /'dʒepədɪ/ n. péril m. ~**ize** v.t. mettre en péril.

jerk /dʒɜːk/ n. secousse f.; (fool: sl.) idiot m.; (creep: sl.) salaud m. —v.t. donner une secousse à. ~**ily** adv. par saccades. ~**y** a. saccadé.

jersey /'dʒɜːzɪ/ n. (garment) chandail m., tricot m.; (fabric) jersey m.

jest /dʒest/ n. plaisanterie f. —v.i. plaisanter. ~**er** n. bouffon m.

Jesus /'dʒiːzəs/ n. Jésus m.

jet[1] /dʒet/ n. (mineral) jais m. ~**-black** a. de jais.

jet[2] /dʒet/ n. (stream) jet m.; (plane) avion à réaction m., jet m. ~ **lag,** fatigue due au décalage horaire f. ~**-propelled** a. à réaction.

jettison /'dʒetɪsn/ v.t. jeter à la mer; (aviat.) larguer; (fig.) abandonner.

jetty /'dʒetɪ/ n. (breakwater) jetée f.

Jew /dʒuː/ n. Juif m. ~**ess** n. Juive f.

jewel /'dʒuːəl/ n. bijou m. ~**led** a. orné de bijoux. ~**ler** n. bijout|ier, -ière m., f. ~**lery** n. bijoux m. pl.

Jewish /'dʒuːɪʃ/ a. juif.

Jewry /'dʒʊərɪ/ n. les Juifs m. pl.

jib /dʒɪb/ v.i. (p.t. **jibbed**) regimber (at, devant). —n. (sail) foc m.

jiffy /'dʒɪfɪ/ n. (fam.) instant m.

jig /dʒɪg/ n. (dance) gigue f.

jiggle /'dʒɪgl/ v.t. secouer légèrement.

jigsaw /'dʒɪgsɔː/ n. puzzle m.

jilt /dʒɪlt/ v.t. laisser tomber.

jingle /'dʒɪŋgl/ v.t./i. (faire) tinter. —n. tintement m.

jinx /dʒɪŋks/ n. (person: fam.) porte-malheur m. invar.; (spell: fig.) mauvais sort m.

jitter|s /'dʒɪtəz/ n. pl. **the ~s,** (fam.) la frousse f. **~y** /-ərɪ/ a. **be ~y,** (fam.) avoir la frousse.

job /dʒɒb/ n. travail m.; (post) poste m. **have a ~ doing,** avoir du mal à faire. **it is a good ~ that,** heureusement que. **~less** a. sans travail, au chômage.

jobcentre /'dʒɒbsentə(r)/ n. agence (nationale) pour l'emploi f.

jockey /'dʒɒkɪ/ n. jockey m. —v.i. (manœuvre) manœuvrer.

jocular /'dʒɒkjʊlə(r)/ a. jovial.

jog /dʒɒg/ v.t. (p.t. **jogged**) pousser; (memory) rafraîchir. —v.i. faire du jogging. **~ging** n. jogging m.

join /dʒɔɪn/ v.t. joindre, unir; (club) devenir membre de; (political group) adhérer à; (army) s'engager dans. **~ s.o.,** (in activity) se joindre à qn.; (meet) rejoindre qn. —v.i. (roads etc.) se rejoindre. —n. joint m. **~ in,** participer (à). **~ up,** (mil.) s'engager.

joiner /'dʒɔɪnə(r)/ n. menuisier m.

joint /dʒɔɪnt/ a. commun. —n. (join) joint m.; (anat.) articulation f.; (culin.) rôti m.; (place: sl.) boîte f. **~ author,** coauteur m. **out of ~,** déboîté. **~ly** adv. conjointement.

joist /dʒɔɪst/ n. solive f.

jok|e /dʒəʊk/ n. plaisanterie f.; (trick) farce f. —v.i. plaisanter. **~er** n. blagueu|r, -se m., f.; (cards) joker m. **~ingly** adv. pour rire.

joll|y /'dʒɒlɪ/ a. (-ier, -iest) gai. —adv. (fam.) rudement. **~ification** /-fɪ'keɪʃn/, **~ity** ns. réjouissances f. pl.

jolt /dʒəʊlt/ v.t./i. (vehicle, passenger) cahoter; (shake) secouer. —n. cahot m.; secousse f.

Jordan /'dʒɔːdn/ n. Jordanie f.

jostle /'dʒɒsl/ v.t./i. (push) bousculer; (push each other) se bousculer.

jot /dʒɒt/ n. brin m. —v.t. (p.t. **jotted**) noter. **~ter** n. (pad) bloc-notes m.

journal /'dʒɜːnl/ n. journal m. **~ism** n. journalisme m. **~ist** n. journaliste m./ f. **~ese** /ə'liːz/ n. jargon des journalistes m.

journey /'dʒɜːnɪ/ n. voyage m.; (distance) trajet m. —v.i. voyager.

jovial /'dʒəʊvɪəl/ a. jovial.

joy /dʒɔɪ/ n. joie f. **~-ride** n. balade en voiture f. **~ful, ~ous** adjs. joyeux.

jubil|ant /'dʒuːbɪlənt/ a. débordant de joie. **be ~ant,** jubiler. **~ation** /-'leɪʃn/ n. jubilation f.

jubilee /'dʒuːbɪliː/ n. jubilé m.

Judaism /'dʒuːdeɪɪzəm/ n. judaïsme m.

judder /'dʒʌdə(r)/ v.i. vibrer. —n. vibration f.

judge /dʒʌdʒ/ n. juge m. —v.t. juger. **~ment** n. jugement m.

judic|iary /dʒuː'dɪʃərɪ/ n. magistrature f. **~ial** a. judiciaire.

judicious /dʒuː'dɪʃəs/ a. judicieux.

judo /'dʒuːdəʊ/ n. judo m.

jug /dʒʌg/ n. cruche f., pichet m.

juggernaut /'dʒʌgənɔːt/ n. (lorry) poids lourd m., mastodonte m.

juggle /'dʒʌgl/ v.t./i. jongler (avec). **~r** /-ə(r)/ n. jongleu|r, -se m., f.

juic|e /dʒuːs/ n. jus m. **~y** a. juteux; (details etc.: fam.) croustillant.

juke-box /'dʒuːkbɒks/ n. jukebox m.

July /dʒuː'laɪ/ n. juillet m.

jumble /'dʒʌmbl/ v.t. mélanger. —n. (muddle) mélange m. **~ sale,** vente (de charité) f.

jumbo /'dʒʌmbəʊ/ a. **~ jet,** avion géant m., jumbo-jet m.

jump /dʒʌmp/ v.t./i. sauter; (start) sursauter; (of price etc.) faire un bond. —n. saut m.; sursaut m.; (increase) hausse f. **~ at,** sauter sur. **~ the gun,** agir prématurément. **~ the queue,** resquiller.

jumper /'dʒʌmpə(r)/ n. pull(-over) m.; (dress: Amer.) robe chasuble f.

jumpy /'dʒʌmpɪ/ a. nerveux.

junction /'dʒʌŋkʃn/ n. jonction f.; (of roads etc.) embranchement m.

juncture /'dʒʌŋktʃə(r)/ n. moment m.; (state of affairs) conjoncture f.

June /dʒuːn/ n. juin m.

jungle /'dʒʌŋgl/ n. jungle f.

junior /'dʒuːnɪə(r)/ a. (in age) plus jeune (**to,** que); (in rank) subalterne; (school) élémentaire; (executive, doctor) jeune. —n. cadet(te) m. (f.); (schol.) petit(e) élève m./f.; (sport) junior m./f.

junk /dʒʌŋk/ n. bric-à-brac m. invar.; (poor material) camelote f. —v.t. (Amer., sl.) balancer. **~shop** n. boutique de brocanteur f.

junkie /'dʒʌŋkɪ/ n. (sl.) drogué(e) m. (f.).

junta /'dʒʌntə/ n. junte f.

jurisdiction /dʒʊərɪs'dɪkʃn/ *n.* juridiction *f.*

jurisprudence /dʒʊərɪs'pruːdəns/ *n.* jurisprudence *f.*

juror /'dʒʊərə(r)/ *n.* juré *m.*

jury /'dʒʊərɪ/ *n.* jury *m.*

just /dʒʌst/ *a.* (*fair*) juste. —*adv.* juste, exactement; (*only*, *slightly*) juste; (*simply*) tout simplement. he has/had ∼ left/*etc.*, il vient/venait de partir/*etc.* have ∼ missed, avoir manqué de peu. ∼ as tall/*etc.*, tout aussi grand/ *etc.* (as, que). ∼ listen!, écoutez donc! ∼ly *adv.* avec justice.

justice /'dʒʌstɪs/ *n.* justice *f.* J∼ of the Peace, juge de paix *m.*

justifiabl|e /dʒʌstɪ'faɪəbl/ *a.* justifiable. ∼y *adv.* avec raison.

justif|y /'dʒʌstɪfaɪ/ *v.t.* justifier. ∼ication /-ɪ'keɪʃn/ *n.* justification *f.*

jut /dʒʌt/ *v.i.* (*p.t.* jutted). ∼ out, faire saillie, dépasser.

juvenile /'dʒuːvənaɪl/ *a.* (*youthful*) juvénile; (*childish*) puéril; (*delinquent*) jeune; (*court*) pour enfants. —*n.* jeune *m./f.*

juxtapose /dʒʌkstə'pəʊz/ *v.t.* juxtaposer.

K

kaleidoscope /kəˈlaɪdəskəʊp/ *n*. kaléidoscope *m*.

kangaroo /kæŋɡəˈruː/ *n*. kangourou *m*.

karate /kəˈrɑːtɪ/ *n*. karaté *m*.

kebab /kəˈbæb/ *n*. brochette *f*.

keel /kiːl/ *n*. (*of ship*) quille *f*. —*v.i*. ∼ **over**, chavirer.

keen /kiːn/ *a*. (**-er, -est**) (*interest, wind, feeling, etc*.) vif; (*mind, analysis*) pénétrant; (*edge, appetite*) aiguisé; (*eager*) enthousiaste. **be** ∼ **on**, (*person, thing: fam*.) aimer beaucoup. **be** ∼ **to do** *or* **on doing**, tenir beaucoup à faire. ∼**ly** *adv*. vivement; avec enthousiasme. ∼**ness** *n*. vivacité *f*.; enthousiasme *m*.

keep /kiːp/ *v.t*. (*p.t*. **kept**) garder; (*promise, shop, etc*.) tenir; (*family*) entretenir; (*animals*) élever; (*rule etc*.) respecter; (*celebrate*) célébrer; (*delay*) retenir; (*prevent*) empêcher; (*conceal*) cacher. —*v.i*. (*food*) se garder; (*remain*) rester. ∼ **(on)**, continuer (**doing**, à faire). —*n*. subsistance *f*.; (*of castle*) donjon *m*. **for** ∼**s**, (*fam*.) pour toujours. ∼ **back** *v.t*. retenir; *v.i*. ne pas s'approcher. ∼ **in/out**, empêcher d'entrer/de sortir. ∼ **up**, (se) maintenir. ∼ **up (with)**, suivre. ∼**er** *n*. gardien(ne) *m*. (*f*.).

keeping /ˈkiːpɪŋ/ *n*. garde *f*. **in** ∼ **with**, en accord avec.

keepsake /ˈkiːpseɪk/ *n*. (*thing*) souvenir *m*.

keg /keɡ/ *n*. tonnelet *m*.

kennel /ˈkenl/ *n*. niche *f*.

Kenya /ˈkenjə/ *n*. Kenya *m*.

kept /kept/ *see* **keep**.

kerb /kɜːb/ *n*. bord du trottoir *m*.

kerfuffle /kəˈfʌfl/ *n*. (*fuss: fam*.) histoire(s) *f*. (*pl*.).

kernel /ˈkɜːnl/ *n*. amande *f*.

kerosene /ˈkerəsiːn/ *n*. (*aviation fuel*) kérosène *m*.; (*paraffin*) pétrole (lampant) *m*.

ketchup /ˈketʃəp/ *n*. ketchup *m*.

kettle /ˈketl/ *n*. bouilloire *f*.

key /kiː/ *n*. clef *f*.; (*of piano etc*.) touche *f*. —*a*. clef (*f. invar*.). ∼**ring** *n*. porte-clefs *m. invar*. —*v.t*. ∼ **up**, surexciter.

keyboard /ˈkiːbɔːd/ *n*. clavier *m*.

keyhole /ˈkiːhəʊl/ *n*. trou de la serrure *m*.

keynote /ˈkiːnəʊt/ *n*. (*of speech etc*.) note dominante *f*.

keystone /ˈkiːstəʊn/ *n*. (*archit., fig*.) clef de voûte *f*.

khaki /ˈkɑːkɪ/ *a*. kaki *invar*.

kibbutz /kɪˈbʊts/ *n*. (*pl*. **-im** /-iːm/) *n*. kibboutz *m*.

kick /kɪk/ *v.t./i*. donner un coup de pied (à); (*of horse*) ruer. —*n*. coup de pied *m*.; ruade *f*.; (*of gun*) recul *m*.; (*thrill: fam*.) (malin) plaisir *m*. ∼**off** *n*. coup d'envoi *m*. ∼ **out**, (*fam*.) flanquer dehors. ∼ **up**, (*fuss, racket: fam*.) faire.

kid /kɪd/ *n*. (*goat, leather*) chevreau *m*.; (*child: sl*.) gosse *m./f*. —*v.t./i*. (*p.t*. **kidded**) blaguer.

kidnap /ˈkɪdnæp/ *v.t*. (*p.t*. **kidnapped**) enlever, kidnapper. ∼**ping** *n*. enlèvement *m*.

kidney /ˈkɪdnɪ/ *n*. rein *m*.; (*culin*.) rognon *m*.

kill /kɪl/ *v.t*. tuer; (*fig*.) mettre fin à. —*n*. mise à mort *f*. ∼**er** *n*. tueu|r, -se *m*., *f*. ∼**ing** *n*. massacre *m*., meurtre *m*.; *a*. (*funny: fam*.) tordant; (*tiring: fam*.) tuant.

killjoy /ˈkɪldʒɔɪ/ *n*. rabat-joie *m. invar*., trouble-fête *m./f. invar*.

kiln /kɪln/ *n*. four *m*.

kilo /ˈkiːləʊ/ *n*. (*pl*. **-os**) kilo *m*.

kilogram /ˈkɪləɡræm/ *n*. kilogramme *m*.

kilohertz /ˈkɪləhɜːts/ *n*. kilohertz *m*.

kilometre /ˈkɪləmiːtə(r)/ *n*. kilomètre *m*.

kilowatt /ˈkɪləwɒt/ *n*. kilowatt *m*.

kilt /kɪlt/ *n*. kilt *m*.

kin /kɪn/ *n*. parents *m. pl*.

kind[1] /kaɪnd/ *n*. genre *m*., sorte *f*., espèce *f*. **in** ∼, en nature *f*. ∼ **of**, (*somewhat: fam*.) un peu. **be two of a** ∼, se rassembler.

kind[2] /kaɪnd/ *a*. (**-er, -est**) gentil, bon. ∼**-hearted** *a*. bon. ∼**ness** *n*. bonté *f*.

kindergarten /ˈkɪndəɡɑːtn/ *n*. jardin d'enfants *m*.

kindle /ˈkɪndl/ *v.t./i*. (s')allumer.

kindly /ˈkaɪndlɪ/ *a*. (**-ier, -iest**) bienveillant. —*adv*. avec bonté. ∼

wait/*etc.*, voulez-vous avoir la bonté d'attendre/*etc.*
kindred /'kɪndrɪd/ *a.* apparenté. ∼ **spirit,** personne qui a les mêmes goûts *f.*, âme sœur *f.*
kinetic /kɪ'netɪk/ *a.* cinétique.
king /kɪŋ/ *n.* roi *m.* ∼**-size(d)** *a.* extra-long, géant.
kingdom /'kɪŋdəm/ *n.* royaume *m.*; (*bot.*) règne *m.*
kink /kɪŋk/ *n.* (*in rope*) entortillement *m.*, déformation *f.*; (*fig.*) perversion *f.* ∼**y** *a.* (*fam.*) perverti.
kiosk /'ki:ɒsk/ *n.* kiosque *m.* **tele-phone** ∼, cabine téléphonique *f.*
kip /kɪp/ *n.* (*sl.*) roupillon *m.* −*v.i.* (*p.t.* **kipped**) (*sl.*) roupiller.
kipper /'kɪpə(r)/ *n.* hareng fumé *m.*
kiss /kɪs/ *n.* baiser *m.* −*v.t./i.* (s')embrasser.
kit /kɪt/ *n.* équipement *m.*; (*clothing*) affaires *f. pl.*; (*set of tools etc.*) trousse *f.*; (*for assembly*) kit *m.* −*v.t.* (*p.t.* **kitted**). ∼ **out,** équiper.
kitbag /'kɪtbæg/ *n.* sac *m.* (*de marin etc.*).
kitchen /'kɪtʃɪn/ *n.* cuisine *f.* ∼ **garden,** jardin potager *m.*
kitchenette /kɪtʃɪ'net/ *n.* kitchenette *f.*
kite /kaɪt/ *n.* (*toy*) cerf-volant *m.*
kith /kɪθ/ *n.* ∼ **and kin,** parents et amis *m. pl.*
kitten /'kɪtn/ *n.* chaton *m.*
kitty /'kɪtɪ/ *n.* (*fund*) cagnotte *f.*
knack /næk/ *n.* truc *m.*, chic *m.*
knapsack /'næpsæk/ *n.* sac à dos *m.*
knave /neɪv/ *n.* (*cards*) valet *m.*
knead /ni:d/ *v.t.* pétrir.
knee /ni:/ *n.* genou *m.* ∼**s-up** *n.* (*fam.*) fête *f.*, soirée (dansante) *f.*
kneecap /'ni:kæp/ *n.* rotule *f.*
kneel /ni:l/ *v.i.* (*p.t.* **knelt**). ∼ (**down**), s'agenouiller.
knell /nel/ *n.* glas *m.*
knew /nju:/ *see* **know.**
knickers /'nɪkəz/ *n. pl.* (*woman's undergarment*) culotte *f.*, slip *m.*
knife /naɪf/ *n.* (*pl.* **knives**) couteau *m.* −*v.t.* poignarder.

knight /naɪt/ *n.* chevalier *m.*; (*chess*) cavalier *m.* −*v.t.* faire *or* armer chevalier. ∼**hood** *n.* titre de chevalier *m.*
knit /nɪt/ *v.t./i.* (*p.t.* **knitted** *or* **knit**) tricoter; (*bones etc.*) (se) souder. ∼ **one's brow,** froncer les sourcils. ∼**ting** *n.* tricot *m.*
knitwear /'nɪtweə(r)/ *n.* tricots *m. pl.*
knob /nɒb/ *n.* bouton *m.*
knock /nɒk/ *v.t./i.* frapper, cogner; (*criticize: sl.*) critiquer. −*n.* coup *m.* ∼ **about** *v.t.* malmener; *v.i.* vadrouiller. ∼ **down,** (*chair, pedestrian*) renverser; (*demolish*) abattre; (*reduce*) baisser. ∼**-down** *a.* (*price*) très bas. ∼**-kneed** *a.* cagneux. ∼ **off** *v.t.* faire tomber; (*fam.*) expédier; *v.i.* (*fam.*) s'arrêter de travailler. ∼ **out,** (*by blow*) assommer; (*tire*) épuiser. ∼**-out** *n.* (*boxing*) knock-out *m.* ∼ **over,** renverser. ∼ **up,** (*meal etc.*) préparer en vitesse. ∼**er** *n.* heurtoir *m.*
knot /nɒt/ *n.* nœud *m.* −*v.t.* (*p.t.* **knotted**) nouer. ∼**ty** /'nɒtɪ/ *a.* noueux; (*problem*) épineux.
know /nəʊ/ *v.t./i.* (*p.t.* **knew,** *p.p.* **known**) savoir (that, que); (*person, place*) connaître. −*n.* **in the** ∼, (*fam.*) dans le secret, au courant. ∼ **about,** (*cars etc.*) s'y connaître en. ∼**-all,** (*Amer.*) ∼**-it-all** *n.* je-sais-tout *m.*/*f.* ∼**-how** *n.* technique *f.* ∼ **of,** connaître, avoir entendu parler de. ∼**ingly** *adv.* (*consciously*) sciemment.
knowledge /'nɒlɪdʒ/ *n.* connaissance *f.*; (*learning*) connaissances *f. pl.* ∼**a-ble** *a.* bien informé.
known /nəʊn/ *see* **know.** −*a.* connu; (*recognized*) reconnu.
knuckle /'nʌkl/ *n.* articulation du doigt *f.* −*v.i.* ∼ **under,** céder.
Koran /kə'rɑːn/ *n.* Coran *m.*
Korea /kə'rɪə/ *n.* Corée *f.*
kosher /'kəʊʃə(r)/ *a.* kascher *invar.*
kowtow /kaʊ'taʊ/ *v.i.* se prosterner (**to,** devant).
kudos /'kju:dɒs/ *n.* (*fam.*) gloire *f.*

L

lab /læb/ *n.* (*fam.*) labo *m.*

label /'leɪbl/ *n.* étiquette *f.* —*v.t.* (*p.t.* **labelled**) étiqueter.

laboratory /lə'bɒrətrɪ, *Amer.* 'læbrətɔːrɪ/ *n.* laboratoire *m.*

laborious /lə'bɔːrɪəs/ *a.* laborieux.

labour /'leɪbə(r)/ *n.* travail *m.*; (*workers*) main-d'œuvre *f.* —*v.i.* peiner. —*v.t.* insister sur. **in ∼**, en train d'accoucher, en couches. **∼ed** *a.* laborieux.

Labour /'leɪbə(r)/ *n.* le parti travailliste *m.* —*a.* travailliste.

labourer /'leɪbərə(r)/ *n.* manœuvre *m.*; (*on farm*) ouvrier agricole *m.*

labyrinth /'læbərɪnθ/ *n.* labyrinthe *m.*

lace /leɪs/ *n.* dentelle *f.*; (*of shoe*) lacet *m.* —*v.t.* (*fasten*) lacer; (*drink*) arroser.

lacerate /'læsəreɪt/ *v.t.* lacérer.

lack /læk/ *n.* manque *m.* —*v.t.* manquer de. **be ∼ing**, manquer (**in**, de). **for ∼ of**, à défaut de.

lackadaisical /lækə'deɪzɪkl/ *a.* indolent, apathique.

lackey /'lækɪ/ *n.* laquais *m.*

laconic /lə'kɒnɪk/ *a.* laconique.

lacquer /'lækə(r)/ *n.* laque *f.*

lad /læd/ *n.* garçon *m.*, gars *m.*

ladder /'lædə(r)/ *n.* échelle *f.*; (*in stocking*) maille filée *f.* —*v.t./i.* (*stocking*) filer.

laden /'leɪdn/ *a.* chargé (**with**, de).

ladle /'leɪdl/ *n.* louche *f.*

lady /'leɪdɪ/ *n.* dame *f.* **∼ friend**, amie *f.* **∼-in-waiting** *n.* dame d'honneur *f.* **young ∼**, jeune femme *or* fille *f.* **∼like** *a.* distingué.

lady|bird /'leɪdɪbɜːd/ *n.* coccinelle *f.* **∼bug** *n.* (*Amer.*) coccinelle *f.*

lag[1] /læg/ *v.i.* (*p.t.* **lagged**) traîner. —*n.* (*interval*) décalage *m.*

lag[2] /læg/ *v.t.* (*p.t.* **lagged**) (*pipes*) calorifuger.

lager /'lɑːgə(r)/ *n.* bière blonde *f.*

lagoon /lə'guːn/ *n.* lagune *f.*

laid /leɪd/ *see* **lay**[2].

lain /leɪn/ *see* **lie**[2].

lair /leə(r)/ *n.* tanière *f.*

laity /'leɪətɪ/ *n.* laïques *m. pl.*

lake /leɪk/ *n.* lac *m.*

lamb /læm/ *n.* agneau *m.*

lambswool /'læmzwʊl/ *n.* laine d'agneau *f.*

lame /leɪm/ *a.* (**-er, -est**) boiteux; (*excuse*) faible. **∼ly** *adv.* (*argue*) sans conviction.

lament /lə'ment/ *n.* lamentation *f.* —*v.t./i.* se lamenter (sur). **∼able** *a.* lamentable.

laminated /'læmɪneɪtɪd/ *a.* laminé.

lamp /læmp/ *n.* lampe *f.*

lamp-post /'læmppəʊst/ *n.* réverbère *m.*

lampshade /'læmpʃeɪd/ *n.* abat-jour *m. invar.*

lance /lɑːns/ *n.* lance *f.* —*v.t.* (*med.*) inciser.

lancet /'lɑːnsɪt/ *n.* bistouri *m.*

land /lænd/ *n.* terre *f.*; (*plot*) terrain *m.*; (*country*) pays *m.* —*a.* terrestre; (*policy, reform*) agraire. —*v.t./i.* débarquer; (*aircraft*) (se) poser, (faire) atterrir; (*fall*) tomber; (*obtain*) décrocher; (*put*) mettre; (*a blow*) porter. **∼-locked** *a.* sans accès à la mer. **∼ up**, se retrouver.

landed /'lændɪd/ *a.* foncier.

landing /'lændɪŋ/ *n.* débarquement *m.*; (*aviat.*) atterrissage *m.*; (*top of stairs*) palier *m.* **∼-stage** *n.* débarcadère *m.*

land|lady /'lændleɪdɪ/ *n.* propriétaire *f.*; (*of inn*) patronne *f.* **∼lord** *n.* propriétaire *m.*; patron *m.*

landmark /'lændmɑːk/ *n.* (point de) repère *m.*

landscape /'læn(d)skeɪp/ *n.* paysage *m.* —*v.t.* aménager.

landslide /'lændslaɪd/ *n.* glissement de terrain *m.*; (*pol.*) raz-de-marée (électoral) *m. invar.*

lane /leɪn/ *n.* (*path, road*) chemin *m.*; (*strip of road*) voie *f.*; (*of traffic*) file *f.*; (*aviat.*) couloir *m.*

language /'læŋgwɪdʒ/ *n.* langue *f.*; (*speech, style*) langage *m.*

languid /'læŋgwɪd/ *a.* languissant.

languish /'læŋgwɪʃ/ *v.i.* languir.

lank /læŋk/ *a.* grand et maigre.

lanky /'læŋkɪ/ *a.* (**-ier, -iest**) dégingandé, grand et maigre.

lantern /'læntən/ *n.* lanterne *f.*

lap[1] /læp/ *n.* genoux *m. pl.*; (*sport*) tour (de piste) *m.* —*v.t./i.* (*p.t.* **lapped**). **∼ over**, (se) chevaucher.

lap² /læp/ *v.t.* (*p.t.* **lapped**). ~ **up**, laper. —*v.i.* (*waves*) clapoter.

lapel /lə'pel/ *n.* revers *m.*

lapse /læps/ *v.i.* (*decline*) se dégrader; (*expire*) se périmer. —*n.* défaillance *f.*, erreur *f.*; (*of time*) intervalle *m.* ~ **into**, retomber dans.

larceny /'lɑːsənɪ/ *n.* vol simple *m.*

lard /lɑːd/ *n.* saindoux *m.*

larder /'lɑːdə(r)/ *n.* garde-manger *m. invar.*

large /lɑːdʒ/ *a.* (**-er, -est**) grand, gros. **at** ~, en liberté; (*as a whole*) en général. ~**ly** *adv.* en grande mesure. ~**ness** *n.* grandeur *f.*

lark¹ /lɑːk/ *n.* (*bird*) alouette *f.*

lark² /lɑːk/ *n.* (*bit of fun: fam.*) rigolade *f.* —*v.i.* (*fam.*) rigoler.

larva /'lɑːvə/ *n.* (*pl.* **-vae** /-viː/) larve *f.*

laryngitis /lærɪn'dʒaɪtɪs/ *n.* laryngite *f.*

larynx /'lærɪŋks/ *n.* larynx *m.*

lascivious /lə'sɪvɪəs/ *a.* lascif.

laser /'leɪzə(r)/ *n.* laser *m.*

lash /læʃ/ *v.t.* fouetter. —*n.* coup de fouet *m.*; (*eyelash*) cil *m.* ~ **out**, (*spend*) dépenser follement. ~ **out against**, attaquer.

lashings /'læʃɪŋz/ *n. pl.* ~ **of**, (*cream etc.: sl.*) des masses de.

lass /læs/ *n.* jeune fille *f.*

lasso /læ'suː/ *n.* (*pl.* **-os**) lasso *m.*

last¹ /lɑːst/ *a.* dernier. —*adv.* en dernier; (*most recently*) la dernière fois. —*n.* dern|ier, -ière *m., f.*; (*remainder*) reste *m.* **at** (**long**) ~, enfin. ~ **night**, hier soir. **the** ~ **straw**, le comble. **the** ~ **word**, le mot de la fin. **on its** ~ **legs**, sur le point de rendre l'âme. ~**ly** *adv.* en dernier lieu.

last² /lɑːst/ *v.i.* durer. ~**ing** *a.* durable.

latch /lætʃ/ *n.* loquet *m.*

late /leɪt/ *a.* (**-er, -est**) (*not on time*) en retard; (*recent*) récent; (*former*) ancien; (*hour, fruit, etc.*) tardif; (*deceased*) défunt. **the late Mrs X**, feu Mme X. ~**st** /-ɪst/, (*last*) dernier. — *adv.* (*not early*) tard; (*not on time*) en retard. **in** ~ **July**, fin juillet. **of** ~, dernièrement. ~**ness** *n.* retard *m.*; (*of event*) heure tardive *f.*

lately /'leɪtlɪ/ *adv.* dernièrement.

latent /'leɪtnt/ *a.* latent.

lateral /'lætərəl/ *a.* latéral.

lathe /leɪð/ *n.* tour *m.*

lather /'lɑːðə(r)/ *n.* mousse *f.* —*v.t.* savonner. —*v.i.* mousser.

Latin /'lætɪn/ *n.* (*lang.*) latin *m.* —*a.* latin.

latitude /'lætɪtjuːd/ *n.* latitude *f.*

latrine /lə'triːn/ *n.* latrines *f. pl.*

latter /'lætə(r)/ *a.* dernier. —*n.* **the** ~, celui-ci, celle-ci. ~**-day** *a.* moderne. ~**ly** *adv.* dernièrement.

lattice /'lætɪs/ *n.* treillage *m.*

laudable /'lɔːdəbl/ *a.* louable.

laugh /lɑːf/ *v.i.* rire (**at, de**). —*n.* rire *m.* ~**able** *a.* ridicule. ~**ingstock** *n.* objet de risée *m.*

laughter /'lɑːftə(r)/ *n.* (*act*) rire *m.*; (*sound of laughs*) rires *m. pl.*

launch¹ /lɔːntʃ/ *v.t.* lancer. —*n.* lancement *m.* ~ (**out**) **into**, se lancer dans.

launch² /lɔːntʃ/ *n.* (*boat*) vedette *f.*

laund|er /'lɔːndə(r)/ *v.t.* blanchir. ~**ress** *n.* blanchisseuse *f.*

launderette /lɔːn'dret/ *n.* laverie automatique *f.*

laundry /'lɔːndrɪ/ *n.* (*place*) blanchisserie *f.*; (*clothes*) linge *m.*

laurel /'lɒrəl/ *n.* laurier *m.*

lava /'lɑːvə/ *n.* lave *f.*

lavatory /'lævətrɪ/ *n.* cabinets *m. pl.*

lavender /'lævəndə(r)/ *n.* lavande *f.*

lavish /'lævɪʃ/ *a.* (*person*) prodigue; (*plentiful*) copieux; (*lush*) somptueux. —*v.t.* prodiguer (**on**, à). ~**ly** *adv.* copieusement.

law /lɔː/ *n.* loi *f.*; (*profession, subject of study*) droit *m.* ~**-abiding** *a.* respectueux des lois. ~ **and order**, l'ordre public. ~**ful** *a.* légal. ~**fully** *adv.* légalement. ~**less** *a.* sans loi.

lawcourt /'lɔːkɔːt/ *n.* tribunal *m.*

lawn /lɔːn/ *n.* pelouse *f.*, gazon *m.* ~-**mower** *n.* tondeuse à gazon *f.* ~ **tennis**, tennis (sur gazon) *m.*

lawsuit /'lɔːsuːt/ *n.* procès *m.*

lawyer /'lɔːjə(r)/ *n.* avocat *m.*

lax /læks/ *a.* négligent; (*morals etc.*) relâché. ~**ity** *n.* négligence *f.*

laxative /'læksətɪv/ *n.* laxatif *m.*

lay¹ /leɪ/ *a.* (*non-clerical*) laïque; (*opinion etc.*) d'un profane.

lay² /leɪ/ *v.t.* (*p.t.* **laid**) poser, mettre; (*trap*) tendre; (*table*) mettre; (*plan*) former; (*eggs*) pondre. —*v.i.* pondre. ~ **down**, (dé)poser; (*condition*) (im)poser. ~ **hold of**, saisir. ~ **off** *v.t.* (*worker*) licencier; *v.i.* (*fam.*) arrêter. ~-**off** *n.* licenciement *m.* ~ **on**, (*provide*) fournir. ~ **out**, (*design*) dessiner; (*display*) disposer; (*money*) dépenser. ~ **up**, (*store*) amasser. ~ **waste**, ravager.

lay³ /leɪ/ *see* **lie**².

layabout /'leɪəbaʊt/ *n.* fainéant(e) *m.* (*f.*).

lay-by /'leɪbaɪ/ *n.* (*pl.* -bys) petite aire de stationnement *f.*

layer /'leɪə(r)/ *n.* couche *f.*

layman /'leɪmən/ *n.* (*pl.* -men) profane *m.*

layout /'leɪaʊt/ *n.* disposition *f.*

laze /leɪz/ *v.i.* paresser.

laz|y /'leɪzɪ/ *a.* (-ier, -iest) paresseux. ~iness *n.* paresse *f.* ~y-bones *n.* flemmard(e) *m.* (*f.*).

lead¹ /liːd/ *v.t./i.* (*p.t.* led) mener; (*team etc.*) diriger; (*life*) mener; (*induce*) amener. ~ to, conduire à, mener à. — *n.* avance *f.*; (*clue*) indice *m.*; (*leash*) laisse *f.*; (*theatre*) premier rôle *m.*; (*wire*) fil *m.*; (*example*) exemple *m.* **in the ~**, en tête. **~ away**, emmener. **~ up to**, (*come to*) en venir à; (*precede*) précéder.

lead² /led/ *n.* plomb *m.*; (*of pencil*) mine *f.* ~en *a.* de plomb.

leader /'liːdə(r)/ *n.* chef *m.*; (*of country, club, etc.*) dirigeant(e) *m.* (*f.*); (*leading article*) éditorial *m.* ~ship *n.* direction *f.*

leading /'liːdɪŋ/ *a.* principal. **~ article**, éditorial *m.*

leaf /liːf/ *n.* (*pl.* leaves) feuille *f.*; (*of table*) rallonge *f.* —*v.i.* **~ through**, feuilleter. ~y *a.* feuillu.

leaflet /'liːflɪt/ *n.* prospectus *m.*

league /liːg/ *n.* ligue *f.*; (*sport*) championnat *m.* **in ~ with**, de mèche avec.

leak /liːk/ *n.* fuite *f.* —*v.i.* fuir; (*news: fig.*) s'ébruiter. —*v.t.* répandre; (*fig.*) divulguer. ~age *n.* fuite *f.* ~y *a.* qui a une fuite.

lean¹ /liːn/ *a.* (-er, -est) maigre. —*n.* (*of meat*) maigre *m.* ~ness *n.* maigreur *f.*

lean² /liːn/ *v.t./i.* (*p.t.* leaned *or* leant /lent/) (*rest*) (s')appuyer; (*slope*) pencher. **~ over**, (*of person*) se pencher. ~to *n.* appentis *m.*

leaning /'liːnɪŋ/ *a.* penché. —*n.* tendance *f.*

leap /liːp/ *v.i.* (*p.t.* leaped *or* leapt /lept/) bondir. —*n.* bond *m.* ~-frog *n.* saute-mouton *m. invar.*; *v.i.* (*p.t.* -frogged) sauter (over, par-dessus). **~ year**, année bissextile *f.*

learn /lɜːn/ *v.t./i.* (*p.t.* learned *or* learnt) apprendre (**to do**, à faire). ~er *n.* débutant(e) *m.* (*f.*).

learn|ed /'lɜːnɪd/ *a.* érudit. ~ing *n.* érudition *f.*, connaissances *f. pl.*

lease /liːs/ *n.* bail *m.* —*v.t.* louer à bail.

leash /liːʃ/ *n.* laisse *f.*

least /liːst/ *a.* **the ~**, (*smallest amount of*) le moins de; (*slightest*) le *or* la moindre. —*n.* le moins. —*adv.* le moins; (*with adjective*) le *or* la moins. **at ~**, au moins.

leather /'leðə(r)/ *n.* cuir *m.*

leave /liːv/ *v.t.* (*p.t.* left) laisser; (*depart from*) quitter. —*n.* (*holiday*) congé *m.*; (*consent*) permission *f.* **be left (over)**, rester. **~ alone**, (*thing*) ne pas toucher à; (*person*) laisser tranquille. **~ out**, omettre. **on ~**, (*mil.*) en permission. **take one's ~**, prendre congé (**of**, de).

leavings /'liːvɪŋz/ *n. pl.* restes *m. pl.*

Leban|on /'lebənən/ *n.* Liban *m.* ~ese /-'niːz/ *a.* & *n.* libanais(e) (*m.* (*f.*)).

lecher /'letʃə(r)/ *n.* débauché *m.* ~ous *a.* lubrique. ~y *n.* lubricité *f.*

lectern /'lektən/ *n.* lutrin *m.*

lecture /'lektʃə(r)/ *n.* cours *m.*, conférence *f.*; (*rebuke*) réprimande *f.* —*v.t./i.* faire un cours *or* une conférence (à); (*rebuke*) réprimander. ~r /-ə(r)/ *n.* conférenc|ier, -ière *m.*, *f.*, (*univ.*) enseignant(e) *m.* (*f.*).

led /led/ *see* **lead**¹.

ledge /ledʒ/ *n.* rebord *m.*, saillie *f.*

ledger /'ledʒə(r)/ *n.* grand livre *m.*

lee /liː/ *n.* côté sous le vent *m.*

leech /liːtʃ/ *n.* sangsue *f.*

leek /liːk/ *n.* poireau *m.*

leer /lɪə(r)/ *v.i.* **~ (at)**, lorgner. —*n.* regard sournois *m.*

leeway /'liːweɪ/ *n.* (*naut.*) dérive *f.*; (*fig.*) liberté d'action *f.* **make up ~**, rattraper le retard.

left¹ /left/ *see* **leave**. **~ luggage (office)**, consigne *f.* ~overs *n. pl.* restes *m. pl.*

left² /left/ *a.* gauche. —*adv.* à gauche. —*n.* gauche *f.* **~-hand** *a.* à *or* de gauche. **~-handed** *a.* gaucher. **~-wing** *a.* (*pol.*) de gauche.

leftist /'leftɪst/ *n.* gauchiste *m.*/*f.*

leg /leg/ *n.* jambe *f.*; (*of animal*) patte *f.*; (*of table*) pied *m.*; (*of chicken*) cuisse *f.*; (*of lamb*) gigot *m.*; (*of journey*) étape *f.*

legacy /'legəsɪ/ *n.* legs *m.*

legal /'liːgl/ *a.* légal; (*affairs etc.*) juridique. ~ity /liː'gælətɪ/ *n.* légalité *f.* ~ly *adv.* légalement.

legalize /'liːgəlaɪz/ *v.t.* légaliser.

legation /lɪ'geɪʃn/ *n.* légation *f.*

legend /'ledʒənd/ *n.* légende *f.* ~ary *a.* légendaire.

leggings /'legɪŋz/ *n. pl.* jambières *f. pl.*

legib|le /'ledʒəbl/ *a.* lisible. ~ility /-'bɪlətɪ/ *n.* lisibilité *f.* ~ly *adv.* lisiblement.

legion /'li:dʒən/ *n.* légion *f.*

legislat|e /'ledʒɪsleɪt/ *v.i.* légiférer. ~ion /-'leɪʃn/ *n.* (*body of laws*) législation *f.*; (*law*) loi *f.*

legislat|ive /'ledʒɪslətɪv/ *a.* législatif. ~ure /-eɪtʃə(r)/ *n.* corps législatif *m.*

legitima|te /lɪ'dʒɪtɪmət/ *a.* légitime. ~cy *n.* légitimité *f.*

leisure /'leʒə(r)/ *n.* loisir(s) *m.* (*pl.*). at one's ~, à tête reposée. ~ly *a.* lent; *adv.* sans se presser.

lemon /'lemən/ *n.* citron *m.*

lemonade /lemə'neɪd/ *n.* (*fizzy*) limonade *f.*; (*still*) citronnade *f.*

lend /lend/ *v.t.* (*p.t.* **lent**) prêter; (*contribute*) donner. ~ **itself to**, se prêter à. ~**er** *n.* prêteu|r, -se *m.*, *f.* ~**ing** *n.* prêt *m.*

length /leŋθ/ *n.* longueur *f.*; (*in time*) durée *f.*; (*section*) morceau *m.* **at** ~, (*at last*) enfin. **at** (**great**) ~, longuement. ~**y** *a.* long.

lengthen /'leŋθən/ *v.t./i.* (s')allonger.

lengthways /'leŋθweɪz/ *adv.* dans le sens de la longueur.

lenien|t /'li:nɪənt/ *a.* indulgent. ~**cy** *n.* indulgence *f.* ~**tly** *adv.* avec indulgence.

lens /lenz/ *n.* lentille *f.*; (*of spectacles*) verre *m.*; (*photo.*) objectif *m.*

lent /lent/ *see* **lend**.

Lent /lent/ *n.* Carême *m.*

lentil /'lentl/ *n.* (*bean*) lentille *f.*

leopard /'lepəd/ *n.* léopard *m.*

leotard /'li:əʊtɑːd/ *n.* collant *m.*

leper /'lepə(r)/ *n.* lépreu|x, -se *m.*, *f.*

leprosy /'leprəsɪ/ *n.* lèpre *f.*

lesbian /'lezbɪən/ *n.* lesbienne *f.* —*a.* lesbien.

lesion /'li:ʒn/ *n.* lésion *f.*

less /les/ *a.* (*in quantity etc.*) moins de (**than**, que). —*adv.*, *n.* & *prep.* moins. ~ **than**, (*with numbers*) moins de. **work**/*etc.* ~ **than**, travailler/*etc.* moins que. **ten pounds**/*etc.* ~, dix livres/*etc.* de moins. ~ **and less**, de moins en moins. ~**er** *a.* moindre.

lessen /'lesn/ *v.t./i.* diminuer.

lesson /'lesn/ *n.* leçon *f.*

lest /lest/ *conj.* de peur que *or* de.

let /let/ *v.t.* (*p.t.* **let**, *pres. p.* **letting**) laisser; (*lease*) louer. —*v. aux.* ~ **us**

do, ~'s **do**, faisons. ~ **him do**, qu'il fasse. —*n.* location *f.* ~ **alone**, (*thing*) ne pas toucher à; (*person*) laisser tranquille. ~ **down**, baisser; (*deflate*) dégonfler; (*fig.*) décevoir. ~**-down** *n.* déception *f.* ~ **go** *v.t.* lâcher; *v.i.* lâcher prise. ~ **in**/**out**, laisser *or* faire entrer/sortir. ~ **o.s. in for**, (*task*) s'engager à; (*trouble*) s'attirer. ~ **off**, (*explode*, *fire*) faire éclater *or* partir; (*excuse*) dispenser. ~ **up**, (*fam.*) s'arrêter. ~**-up** *n.* répit *m.*

lethal /'li:θl/ *a.* mortel; (*weapon*) meurtrier.

letharg|y /'leθədʒɪ/ *n.* léthargie *f.* ~**ic** /lɪ'θɑːdʒɪk/ *a.* léthargique.

letter /'letə(r)/ *n.* lettre *f.* ~**-box** *n.* boîte à *or* aux lettres *f.* ~**ing** *n.* (*letters*) caractères *m. pl.*

lettuce /'letɪs/ *n.* laitue *f.*, salade *f.*

leukaemia /luː'kiːmɪə/ *n.* leucémie *f.*

level /'levl/ *a.* plat, uni; (*on surface*) horizontal; (*in height*) au même niveau (**with**, que); (*in score*) à égalité. —*n.* niveau *m.* —*v.t.* (*p.t.* **levelled**) niveler; (*aim*) diriger. **be on the** ~, (*fam.*) être franc. ~ **crossing**, passage à niveau *m.* ~**headed** *a.* équilibré.

lever /'liːvə(r)/ *n.* levier *m.* —*v.t.* soulever au moyen d'un levier.

leverage /'liːvərɪdʒ/ *n.* influence *f.*

levity /'levətɪ/ *n.* légèreté *f.*

levy /'levɪ/ *v.t.* (*tax*) (pré)lever. —*n.* impôt *m.*

lewd /ljuːd/ *a.* (-er, -est) obscène.

lexicography /leksɪ'kɒgrəfɪ/ *n.* lexicographie *f.*

lexicon /'leksɪkən/ *n.* lexique *m.*

liable /'laɪəbl/ *a.* **be** ~ **to do**, avoir tendance à faire, pouvoir faire. ~ **to**, (*illness etc.*) sujet à; (*fine*) passible de. ~ **for**, responsable de.

liabilit|y /laɪə'bɪlətɪ/ *n.* responsabilité *f.*; (*fam.*) handicap *m.* ~**ies**, (*debts*) dettes *f. pl.*

liais|e /lɪ'eɪz/ *v.i.* (*fam.*) faire la liaison. ~**on** /-ɒn/ *n.* liaison *f.*

liar /'laɪə(r)/ *n.* menteu|r, -se *m.*, *f.*

libel /'laɪbl/ *n.* diffamation *f.* —*v.t.* (*p.t.* **libelled**) diffamer.

liberal /'lɪbərəl/ *a.* libéral; (*generous*) généreux, libéral. ~**ly** *adv.* libéralement.

Liberal /'lɪbərəl/ *a.* & *n.* (*pol.*) libéral(e) (*m. f.*).

liberat|e /'lɪbəreɪt/ *v.t.* libérer. ~**ion** /-'reɪʃn/ *n.* libération *f.*

libert|y /'lɪbətɪ/ *n.* liberté *f.* **at ~y to**, libre de. **take ~ies**, prendre des libertés.

librar|y /'laɪbrərɪ/ *n.* bibliothèque *f.* **~ian** /-'breərɪən/ *n.* bibliothécaire *m./f.*

libretto /lɪ'bretəʊ/ *n.* (*pl.* -os) (*mus.*) livret *m.*

Libya /'lɪbɪə/ *n.* Libye *f.* **~n** *a.* & *n.* libyen(ne) (*m.(f.)*).

lice /laɪs/ *see* louse.

licence /'laɪsns/ *n.* permis *m.*; (*for television*) redevance *f.*; (*comm.*) licence *f.*; (*liberty: fig.*) licence *f.* **~ plate**, plaque minéralogique *f.*

license /'laɪsns/ *v.t.* accorder un permis à, autoriser.

licentious /laɪ'senʃəs/ *a.* licencieux.

lichen /'laɪkən/ *n.* lichen *m.*

lick /lɪk/ *v.t.* lécher; (*defeat: sl.*) rosser. —*n.* coup de langue *m.* **~ one's chops**, se lécher les babines.

licorice /'lɪkərɪs/ *n.* (*Amer.*) réglisse *f.*

lid /lɪd/ *n.* couvercle *m.*

lido /'laɪdəʊ/ *n.* (*pl.* -os) piscine en plein air *f.*

lie[1] /laɪ/ *n.* mensonge *m.* —*v.i.* (*p.t.* lied, *pres. p.* lying) (*tell lies*) mentir. **give the ~ to**, démentir.

lie[2] /laɪ/ *v.i.* (*p.t.* lay, *p.p.* lain, *pres. p.* lying) s'allonger; (*remain*) rester; (*be*) se trouver, être; (*in grave*) reposer. **be lying**, être allongé. **~ down**, s'allonger. **~ in, have a ~-in**, faire la grasse matinée. **~ low**, se cacher.

lieu /ljuː/ *n.* **in ~ of**, au lieu de.

lieutenant /lef'tenənt, *Amer.* luː'tenənt/ *n.* lieutenant *m.*

life /laɪf/ *n.* (*pl.* lives) vie *f.* **~ cycle**, cycle de vie *m.* **~-guard** *n.* sauveteur *m.* **~-jacket** *n.* gilet de sauvetage *m.* **~-size(d)** *a.* grandeur nature *invar.*

lifebelt /'laɪfbelt/ *n.* bouée de sauvetage *f.*

lifeboat /'laɪfbəʊt/ *n.* canot de sauvetage *m.*

lifebuoy /'laɪfbɔɪ/ *n.* bouée de sauvetage *f.*

lifeless /'laɪflɪs/ *a.* sans vie.

lifelike /'laɪflaɪk/ *a.* très ressemblant.

lifelong /'laɪflɒŋ/ *a.* de toute la vie.

lifetime /'laɪftaɪm/ *n.* vie *f.* **in one's ~**, de son vivant.

lift /lɪft/ *v.t.* lever; (*steal: fam.*) voler. —*v.i.* (*of fog*) se lever. —*n.* (*in building*) ascenseur *m.* **give a ~ to**, em-

mener (en voiture). **~-off** *n.* (*aviat.*) décollage *m.*

ligament /'lɪgəmənt/ *n.* ligament *m.*

light[1] /laɪt/ *n.* lumière *f.*; (*lamp*) lampe *f.*; (*for fire, on vehicle, etc.*) feu *m.*; (*headlight*) phare *m.* —*a.* (*not dark*) clair. —*v.t.* (*p.t.* lit *or* lighted) allumer; (*room etc.*) éclairer; (*match*) frotter. **bring to ~**, révéler. **come to ~**, être révélé. **~ up** *v.i.* s'allumer; *v.t.* (*room*) éclairer. **~-year** *n.* année-lumière *f.*

light[2] /laɪt/ *a.* (-er, -est) (*not heavy*) léger. **~-fingered** *a.* chapardeur. **~-headed** *a.* (*dizzy*) qui a un vertige; (*frivolous*) étourdi. **~hearted** *a.* gai. **~ly** *adv.* légèrement. **~ness** *n.* légèreté *f.*

lighten[1] /'laɪtn/ *v.t.* (*give light to*) éclairer; (*make brighter*) éclaircir.

lighten[2] /'laɪtn/ *v.t.* (*make less heavy*) alléger.

lighter /'laɪtə(r)/ *n.* briquet *m.*; (*for stove*) allume-gaz *m. invar.*

lighthouse /'laɪthaʊs/ *n.* phare *m.*

lighting /'laɪtɪŋ/ *n.* éclairage *m.*

lightning /'laɪtnɪŋ/ *n.* éclair(s) *m.* (*pl.*), foudre *f.* —*a.* éclair *invar.*

lightweight /'laɪtweɪt/ *a.* léger. —*n.* (*boxing*) poids léger *m.*

like[1] /laɪk/ *a.* semblable, pareil. —*prep.* comme. —*conj.* (*fam.*) comme. —*n.* pareil *m.* **be ~minded**, avoir les mêmes sentiments. **the ~s of you**, des gens comme vous.

like[2] /laɪk/ *v.t.* aimer (bien). **~s** *n. pl.* goûts *m. pl.* **I should ~**, je voudrais, j'aimerais. **would you ~?**, voulez-vous? **~able** *a.* sympathique.

likel|y /'laɪklɪ/ *a.* (-ier, -iest) probable. —*adv.* probablement. **he is ~y to do**, il fera probablement. **not ~y!**, (*fam.*) pas question! **~ihood** *n.* probabilité *f.*

liken /'laɪkən/ *v.t.* comparer.

likeness /'laɪknɪs/ *n.* ressemblance *f.*

likewise /'laɪkwaɪz/ *adv.* de même.

liking /'laɪkɪŋ/ *n.* (*for thing*) penchant *m.*; (*for person*) affection *f.*

lilac /'laɪlək/ *n.* lilas *m.* —*a.* lilas *invar.*

lily /'lɪlɪ/ *n.* lis *m.*, lys *m.* **~ of the valley**, muguet *m.*

limb /lɪm/ *n.* membre *m.* **out on a ~**, isolé (et vulnérable).

limber /'lɪmbə(r)/ *v.i.* **~ up**, faire des exercices d'assouplissement.

limbo /'lɪmbəʊ/ *n.* **be in ~**, (*forgotten*) être tombé dans l'oubli.

lime[1] /laɪm/ *n.* chaux *f.*

lime[2] /laɪm/ *n.* (*fruit*) lime *f.*, citron vert *m.*

lime[3] /laɪm/ *n.* ~(**-tree**), tilleul *m.*

limelight /'laɪmlaɪt/ *n.* **in the** ~, en vedette.

limerick /'lɪmərɪk/ *n.* poème humoristique *m.* (*de cinq vers*).

limit /'lɪmɪt/ *n.* limite *f.* —*v.t.* limiter. ~**ed company**, société anonyme *f.* ~**ation** /-'teɪʃn/ *n.* limitation *f.*

limousine /'lɪməziːn/ *n.* (*car*) limousine *f.*

limp[1] /lɪmp/ *v.i.* boiter. —*n.* **have a** ~, boiter.

limp[2] /lɪmp/ *a.* (**-er, -est**) mou.

limpid /'lɪmpɪd/ *a.* limpide.

linctus /'lɪŋktəs/ *n.* sirop *m.*

line[1] /laɪn/ *n.* ligne *f.*; (*track*) voie *f.*; (*wrinkle*) ride *f.*; (*row*) rangée *f.*, file *f.*; (*of poem*) vers *m.*; (*rope*) corde *f.*; (*of goods*) gamme *f.*; (*queue: Amer.*) queue *f.* —*v.t.* (*paper*) régler; (*streets etc.*) border. **in** ~ **for**, sur le point de recevoir. **in** ~ **with**, en accord avec. ~ **up**, (s')aligner; (*in queue*) faire la queue.

line[2] /laɪn/ *v.t.* (*garment*) doubler; (*fill*) remplir, garnir.

lineage /'lɪnɪdʒ/ *n.* lignée *f.*

linear /'lɪnɪə(r)/ *a.* linéaire.

linen /'lɪnɪn/ *n.* (*sheets etc.*) linge *m.*; (*material*) lin *m.*, toile de lin *f.*

liner /'laɪnə(r)/ *n.* paquebot *m.*

linesman /'laɪnzmən/ *n.* (*football*) juge de touche *m.*

linger /'lɪŋgə(r)/ *v.i.* s'attarder; (*smells etc.*) persister.

lingerie /'lænʒərɪ/ *n.* lingerie *f.*

lingo /'lɪŋgəʊ/ *n.* (*pl.* **-os**) (*hum., fam.*) jargon *m.*

linguist /'lɪŋgwɪst/ *n.* linguiste *m./f.*

linguistic /lɪŋ'gwɪstɪk/ *a.* linguistique. ~**s** *n.* linguistique *f.*

lining /'laɪnɪŋ/ *n.* doublure *f.*

link /lɪŋk/ *n.* lien *m.*; (*of chain*) maillon *m.* —*v.t.* relier; (*relate*) (re)lier. ~ **up**, (*of roads*) se rejoindre. ~**age** *n.* lien *m.*

links /lɪŋks/ *n. invar.* terrain de golf *m.*

lino /'laɪnəʊ/ *n.* (*pl.* **-os**) lino *m.*

linoleum /lɪ'nəʊlɪəm/ *n.* linoléum *m.*

lint /lɪnt/ *n.* (*med.*) tissu ouaté *m.*; (*fluff*) peluche(s) *f.* (*pl.*).

lion /'laɪən/ *n.* lion *m.* **take the** ~**'s share**, se tailler la part du lion. ~**ess** *n.* lionne *f.*

lip /lɪp/ *n.* lèvre *f.*; (*edge*) rebord *m.* ~-**read** *v.t./i.* lire sur les lèvres. **pay** ~-**service to**, n'approuver que pour la forme.

lipstick /'lɪpstɪk/ *n.* rouge (à lèvres) *m.*

liquefy /'lɪkwɪfaɪ/ *v.t./i.* (se) liquéfier.

liqueur /lɪ'kjʊə(r)/ *n.* liqueur *f.*

liquid /'lɪkwɪd/ *n. & a.* liquide (*m.*). ~**ize** *v.t.* passer au mixeur. ~**izer** *n.* mixeur *m.*

liquidat|e /'lɪkwɪdeɪt/ *v.t.* liquider. ~**ion** /-'deɪʃn/ *n.* liquidation *f.*

liquor /'lɪkə(r)/ *n.* alcool *m.*

liquorice /'lɪkərɪs/ *n.* réglisse *f.*

lira /'lɪərə/ *n.* (*pl.* **lire** /'lɪəreɪ/ *or* **liras**) lire *f.*

lisp /lɪsp/ *n.* zézaiement *m.* —*v.i.* zézayer. **with a** ~, en zézayant.

list[1] /lɪst/ *n.* liste *f.* —*v.t.* inscrire, dresser la liste de.

list[2] /lɪst/ *v.i.* (*ship*) gîter.

listen /'lɪsn/ *v.i.* écouter. ~ **to**, ~ **in** (**to**), écouter. ~**er** *n.* audi|teur, -trice *m./f.*

listless /'lɪstlɪs/ *a.* apathique.

lit /lɪt/ *see* **light**[1].

litany /'lɪtənɪ/ *n.* litanie *f.*

literal /'lɪtərəl/ *a.* littéral; (*person*) prosaïque. ~**ly** *adv.* littéralement.

literary /'lɪtərərɪ/ *a.* littéraire.

litera|te /'lɪtərət/ *a.* qui sait lire et écrire. ~**cy** *n.* capacité de lire et écrire *f.*

literature /'lɪtrətʃə(r)/ *n.* littérature *f.*; (*fig.*) documentation *f.*

lithe /laɪð/ *a.* souple, agile.

litigation /lɪtɪ'geɪʃn/ *n.* litige *m.*

litre /'liːtə(r)/ *n.* litre *m.*

litter /'lɪtə(r)/ *n.* détritus *m. pl.*, papiers *m. pl.*; (*animals*) portée *f.* —*v.t.* éparpiller; (*make untidy*) laisser des détritus dans. ~-**bin** *n.* poubelle *f.* ~**ed with**, jonché de.

little /'lɪtl/ *a.* petit; (*not much*) peu de. —*n.* peu *m.* —*adv.* peu. **a** ~, un peu (de).

liturgy /'lɪtədʒɪ/ *n.* liturgie *f.*

live[1] /laɪv/ *a.* vivant; (*wire*) sous tension; (*broadcast*) en direct. **be a** ~ **wire**, être très dynamique.

live[2] /lɪv/ *v.t./i.* vivre; (*reside*) habiter, vivre. ~ **down**, faire oublier. ~ **it up**, mener la belle vie. ~ **on**, (*feed o.s. on*) vivre de; (*continue*) survivre. ~ **up to**, se montrer à la hauteur de.

livelihood /'laɪvlɪhʊd/ *n.* moyens d'existence *m. pl.*

livel|y /'laɪvlɪ/ *a.* (**-ier, -iest**) vif, vivant. **~iness** *n.* vivacité *f.*

liven /'laɪvn/ *v.t./i.* ~ **up,** (s')animer; (*cheer up*) (s')égayer.

liver /'lɪvə(r)/ *n.* foie *m.*

livery /'lɪvərɪ/ *n.* livrée *f.*

livestock /'laɪvstɒk/ *n.* bétail *m.*

livid /'lɪvɪd/ *a.* livide; (*angry*: *fam.*) furieux.

living /'lɪvɪŋ/ *a.* vivant. —*n.* vie *f.* ~-**room** *n.* salle de séjour *f.*

lizard /'lɪzəd/ *n.* lézard *m.*

llama /'lɑːmə/ *n.* lama *m.*

load /ləʊd/ *n.* charge *f.*; (*loaded goods*) chargement *m.*, charge *f.*; (*weight, strain*) poids *m.* ~**s of,** (*fam.*) des masses de. —*v.t.* charger. ~**ed** *a.* (*dice*) pipé; (*wealthy*: *sl.*) riche.

loaf[1] /ləʊf/ *n.* (*pl.* **loaves**) pain *m.*

loaf[2] /ləʊf/ *v.i.* ~ (**about**), fainéanter. ~**er** *n.* fainéant(e) *m.* (*f.*).

loam /ləʊm/ *n.* terreau *m.*

loan /ləʊn/ *n.* prêt *m.*; (*money borrowed*) emprunt *m.* —*v.t.* (*lend*: *fam.*) prêter.

loath /ləʊθ/ *a.* peu disposé (**to,** à).

loath|e /ləʊð/ *v.t.* détester. ~**ing** *n.* dégoût *m.* ~**some** *a.* dégoûtant.

lobby /'lɒbɪ/ *n.* entrée *f.*, vestibule *m.*; (*pol.*) lobby *m.*, groupe de pression *m.* —*v.t.* faire pression sur.

lobe /ləʊb/ *n.* lobe *m.*

lobster /'lɒbstə(r)/ *n.* homard *m.*

local /'ləʊkl/ *a.* local; (*shops etc.*) du quartier. —*n.* personne du coin *f.*; (*pub*: *fam.*) pub du coin *m.* ~ **government,** administration locale *f.* ~**ly** *adv.* localement; (*nearby*) dans les environs.

locale /ləʊ'kɑːl/ *n.* lieu *m.*

locality /ləʊ'kælətɪ/ *n.* (*district*) région *f.*; (*position*) lieu *m.*

localized /'ləʊkəlaɪzd/ *a.* localisé.

locat|e /ləʊ'keɪt/ *v.t.* (*situate*) situer; (*find*) repérer. ~**ion** /-ʃn/ *n.* emplacement *m.* **on** ~**ion,** (*cinema*) en extérieur.

lock[1] /lɒk/ *n.* mèche (de cheveux) *f.*

lock[2] /lɒk/ *n.* (*of door etc.*) serrure *f.*; (*on canal*) écluse *f.* —*v.t./i.* fermer à clef; (*wheels*: *auto.*) (se) bloquer. ~ **in** *or* **up,** (*person*) enfermer. ~ **out,** (*by mistake*) enfermer dehors. ~**out** *n.* lockout *m. invar.*

locker /'lɒkə(r)/ *n.* casier *m.*

locket /'lɒkɪt/ *n.* médaillon *m.*

locksmith /'lɒksmɪθ/ *n.* serrurier *m.*

locomotion /ləʊkə'məʊʃn/ *n.* locomotion *f.*

locomotive /'ləʊkəməʊtɪv/ *n.* locomotive *f.*

locum /'ləʊkəm/ *n.* (*doctor etc.*) remplaçant(e) *m.* (*f.*).

locust /'ləʊkəst/ *n.* criquet *m.*, sauterelle *f.*

lodge /lɒdʒ/ *n.* (*house*) pavillon (de gardien *or* de chasse) *m.*; (*of porter*) loge *f.* —*v.t.* loger; (*money, complaint*) déposer. —*v.i.* être logé (**with,** chez); (*become fixed*) se loger. ~**r** /-ə(r)/ *n.* locataire *m.*/*f.*, pensionnaire *m.*/*f.*

lodgings /'lɒdʒɪŋz/ *n.* chambre (meublée) *f.*; (*flat*) logement *m.*

loft /lɒft/ *n.* grenier *m.*

lofty /'lɒftɪ/ *a.* (**-ier, -iest**) (*tall, noble*) élevé; (*haughty*) hautain.

log /lɒg/ *n.* (*of wood*) bûche *f.* ~(-**book**), (*naut.*) journal de bord *m.* —*v.t.* (*p.t.* **logged**) noter; (*distance*) parcourir.

logarithm /'lɒgərɪðəm/ *n.* logarithme *m.*

loggerheads /'lɒgəhedz/ *n. pl.* **at** ~, en désaccord.

logic /'lɒdʒɪk/ *a.* logique. ~**al** *a.* logique. ~**ally** *adv.* logiquement.

logistics /lə'dʒɪstɪks/ *n.* logistique *f.*

logo /'ləʊgəʊ/ *n.* (*pl.* **-os**) (*fam.*) emblème *m.*

loin /lɔɪn/ *n.* (*culin.*) filet *m.* ~**s,** reins *m. pl.*

loiter /'lɔɪtə(r)/ *v.i.* traîner.

loll /lɒl/ *v.i.* se prélasser.

loll|ipop /'lɒlɪpɒp/ *n.* sucette *f.* ~**y** *n.* (*fam.*) sucette *f.*; (*sl.*) fric *m.*

London /'lʌndən/ *n.* Londres *m.*/*f.* ~**er** *n.* Londonien(ne) *m.* (*f.*).

lone /ləʊn/ *a.* solitaire. ~**r** /-ə(r)/ *n.* solitaire *m.*/*f.* ~**some** *a.* solitaire.

lonely /'ləʊnlɪ/ *a.* (**-ier, -iest**) solitaire; (*person*) seul, solitaire.

long[1] /lɒŋ/ *a.* (**-er, -est**) long. —*adv.* longtemps. **how** ~ **is?,** quelle est la longueur de?; (*in time*) quelle est la durée de? **how** ~**?,** combien de temps? **he will not be** ~, il n'en a pas pour longtemps. **a** ~ **time,** longtemps. **as** *or* **so** ~ **as,** pourvu que. **before** ~, avant peu. **do no** ~**er,** ne plus faire. ~-**distance** *a.* (*flight*) sur long parcours; (*phone call*) interurbain. ~ **face,** grimace *f.* ~ **johns,** (*fam.*) caleçon long *m.* ~ **jump,** saut en longueur *m.* ~-**playing record,** microsillon *m.* ~-**range**

a. à longue portée; (*forecast*) à long terme. ∿-**sighted** *a.* presbyte. ∿-**standing** *a.* de longue date. ∿-**suffering** *a.* très patient. ∿-**term** *a.* à long terme. ∿ **wave,** grandes ondes *f. pl.* ∿-**winded** *a.* (*speaker etc.*) verbeux.

long² /lɒŋ/ *v.i.* avoir bien *or* très envie (**for, to,** de). ∿ **for s.o.,** (*pine for*) languir après qn. ∿**ing** *n.* envie *f.*; (*nostalgia*) nostalgie *f.*

longevity /lɒnˈdʒevətɪ/ *n.* longévité *f.*

longhand /ˈlɒŋhænd/ *n.* écriture courante *f.*

longitude /ˈlɒndʒɪtjuːd/ *n.* longitude *f.*

loo /luː/ *n.* (*fam.*) toilettes *f. pl.*

look /lʊk/ *v.t./i.* regarder; (*seem*) avoir l'air. —*n.* regard *m.*; (*appearance*) air *m.*, aspect *m.* (**good**) ∿**s,** beauté *f.* ∿ **after,** s'occuper de, soigner. ∿ **at,** regarder. ∿ **down on,** mépriser. ∿ **for,** chercher. ∿ **forward to,** attendre avec impatience. ∿ **in on,** passer voir. ∿ **into,** examiner. ∿ **like,** ressembler à, avoir l'air de. ∿ **out,** faire attention. ∿ **out for,** chercher; (*watch*) guetter. ∿-**out** *n.* (*mil.*) poste de guet *m.*; (*person*) guetteur *m.* ∿ **round,** se retourner. ∿ **up,** (*word*) chercher; (*visit*) passer voir. ∿ **up to,** respecter. ∿**ing-glass** *n.* glace *f.*

loom¹ /luːm/ *n.* métier à tisser *m.*

loom² /luːm/ *v.i.* surgir; (*event etc.: fig.*) paraître imminent.

loony /ˈluːnɪ/ *n. & a.* (*sl.*) fou, folle (*m., f.*).

loop /luːp/ *n.* boucle *f.* —*v.t.* boucler.

loophole /ˈluːphəʊl/ *n.* (*in rule*) échappatoire *f.*

loose /luːs/ *a.* (**-er, -est**) (*knot etc.*) desserré; (*page etc.*) détaché; (*clothes*) ample, lâche; (*lax*) relâché; (*not packed*) en vrac; (*inexact*) vague; (*pej.*) immoral. **at a** ∿ **end,** (*Amer.*) **at** ∿ **ends,** désœuvré. ∿**ly** *adv.* sans serrer; (*roughly*) vaguement.

loosen /ˈluːsn/ *v.t.* (*slacken*) desserrer; (*untie*) défaire.

loot /luːt/ *n.* butin *m.* —*v.t.* piller. ∿**er** *n.* pillard(e) *m.* (*f.*). ∿**ing** *n.* pillage *m.*

lop /lɒp/ *v.t.* (*p.t.* **lopped**). ∿ **off,** couper.

lop-sided /lɒpˈsaɪdɪd/ *a.* de travers.

lord /lɔːd/ *n.* seigneur *m.*; (*British title*) lord *m.* **the L**∿, le Seigneur. (**good**) **L**∿**!,** mon Dieu! ∿**ly** *a.* noble; (*haughty*) hautain.

lore /lɔː(r)/ *n.* traditions *f. pl.*

lorry /ˈlɒrɪ/ *n.* camion *m.*

lose /luːz/ *v.t./i.* (*p.t.* **lost**) perdre. **get lost,** se perdre. ∿**r** /-ə(r)/ *n.* perdant(e) *m.* (*f.*).

loss /lɒs/ *n.* perte *f.* **be at a** ∿, être perplexe. **be at a** ∿ **to,** être incapable de.

lost /lɒst/ *see* **lose.** —*a.* perdu. ∿ **property,** (*Amer.*) ∿ **and found,** objets trouvés *m. pl.*

lot¹ /lɒt/ *n.* (*fate*) sort *m.*; (*at auction*) lot *m.*; (*land*) lotissement *m.*

lot² /lɒt/ *n.* **the** ∿, (le) tout *m.*; (*people*) tous *m. pl.,* toutes *f. pl.* **a** ∿ (**of**), ∿**s** (**of**), (*fam.*) beaucoup (de). **quite a** ∿ (**of**), (*fam.*) pas mal (de).

lotion /ˈləʊʃn/ *n.* lotion *f.*

lottery /ˈlɒtərɪ/ *n.* loterie *f.*

loud /laʊd/ *a.* (**-er, -est**) bruyant, fort. —*adv.* fort. ∿ **hailer,** portevoix *m. invar.* **out** ∿, tout haut. ∿**ly** *adv.* fort.

loudspeaker /laʊdˈspiːkə(r)/ *n.* haut-parleur *m.*

lounge /laʊndʒ/ *v.i.* paresser. —*n.* salon *m.* ∿ **suit,** complet *m.*

louse /laʊs/ *n.* (*pl.* **lice**) pou *m.*

lousy /ˈlaʊzɪ/ *a.* (**-ier, -iest**) pouilleux; (*bad: sl.*) infect.

lout /laʊt/ *n.* rustre *m.*

lovable /ˈlʌvəbl/ *a.* adorable.

love /lʌv/ *n.* amour *m.*; (*tennis*) zéro *m.* —*v.t.* aimer; (*like greatly*) aimer (beaucoup) (**to do,** faire). **in** ∿, amoureux (**with,** de). ∿ **affair,** liaison amoureuse *f.*

lovely /ˈlʌvlɪ/ *a.* (**-ier, -iest**) joli; (*delightful: fam.*) très agréable.

lover /ˈlʌvə(r)/ *n.* amant *m.*; (*devotee*) amateur *m.* (**of,** de).

lovesick /ˈlʌvsɪk/ *a.* amoureux.

loving /ˈlʌvɪŋ/ *a.* affectueux.

low¹ /ləʊ/ *v.i.* meugler.

low² /ləʊ/ *a. & adv.* (**-er, -est**) bas. —*n.* (*low pressure*) dépression *f.* **reach a** (**new**) ∿, atteindre son niveau le plus bas. ∿-**cut** *a.* décolleté. ∿-**down** *a.* méprisable; *n.* (*fam.*) renseignements *m. pl.* ∿-**key** *a.* modéré; (*discreet*) discret.

lowbrow /ˈləʊbraʊ/ *a.* peu intellectuel.

lower /ˈləʊə(r)/ *a. & adv. see* **low².** —*v.t.* baisser. ∿ **o.s.,** s'abaisser.

lowlands /ˈləʊləndz/ *n. pl.* plaine(s) *f.* (*pl.*).

lowly /ˈləʊlɪ/ *a.* (**-ier, -iest**) humble.

loyal /ˈlɔɪəl/ *a.* loyal. ∿**ly** *adv.* loyalement. ∿**ty** *n.* loyauté *f.*

lozenge /'lɒzɪndʒ/ n. (shape) losange m.; (tablet) pastille f.

LP abbr. see **long-playing record.**

Ltd. abbr. (Limited) SA.

lubric|ate /'lu:brɪkeɪt/ v.t. graisser, lubrifier. ∼**ant** n. lubrifiant m. ∼**ation** /-'keɪʃn/ n. graissage m.

lucid /'lu:sɪd/ a. lucide. ∼**ity** /lu:'sɪdətɪ/ n. lucidité f.

luck /lʌk/ n. chance f. **bad** ∼, malchance f.

luck|y /'lʌkɪ/ a. (-ier, -iest) qui a de la chance, heureux; (event) heureux; (number) qui porte bonheur. ∼**ily** adv. heureusement.

lucrative /'lu:krətɪv/ a. lucratif.

lucre /'lu:kə(r)/ n. (pej.) lucre m.

ludicrous /'lu:dɪkrəs/ a. ridicule.

lug /lʌg/ v.t. (p.t. **lugged**) traîner.

luggage /'lʌgɪdʒ/ n. bagages m. pl. ∼-**rack** n. porte-bagages m. invar.

lukewarm /'lu:kwɔ:m/ a. tiède.

lull /lʌl/ v.t. (soothe, send to sleep) endormir. —n. accalmie f.

lullaby /'lʌləbaɪ/ n. berceuse f.

lumbago /lʌm'beɪgəʊ/ n. lumbago m.

lumber /'lʌmbə(r)/ n. bric-à-brac m. invar.; (wood) bois de charpente m. —v.t. ∼ **s.o. with,** (chore etc.) coller à qn.

lumberjack /'lʌmbədʒæk/ n. (Amer.) bûcheron m.

luminous /'lu:mɪnəs/ a. lumineux.

lump /lʌmp/ n. morceau m.; (swelling on body) grosseur f.; (in liquid) grumeau m. —v.t. ∼ **together,** réunir. ∼ **sum,** somme globale f. ∼**y** a. (sauce) grumeleux; (bumpy) bosselé.

lunacy /'lu:nəsɪ/ n. folie f.

lunar /'lu:nə(r)/ a. lunaire.

lunatic /'lu:nətɪk/ n. fou, folle m., f.

lunch /lʌntʃ/ n. déjeuner m. —v.i. déjeuner.

luncheon /'lʌntʃən/ n. déjeuner m. ∼ **meat,** (approx.) saucisson m. ∼ **voucher,** chèque-repas m.

lung /lʌŋ/ n. poumon m.

lunge /lʌndʒ/ n. mouvement brusque en avant m. —v.i. s'élancer (**at,** sur).

lurch[1] /lɜ:tʃ/ n. **leave in the** ∼, planter là, laisser en plan.

lurch[2] /lɜ:tʃ/ v.i. (person) tituber.

lure /lʊə(r)/ v.t. appâter, attirer. —n. (attraction) attrait m., appât m.

lurid /'lʊərɪd/ a. choquant, affreux; (gaudy) voyant.

lurk /lɜ:k/ v.i. se cacher; (in ambush) s'embusquer; (prowl) rôder.

luscious /'lʌʃəs/ a. appétissant.

lush /lʌʃ/ a. luxuriant. —n. (Amer., fam.) ivrogne(sse) m. (f.).

lust /lʌst/ n. luxure f.; (fig.) convoitise f. —v.i. ∼ **after,** convoiter.

lustre /'lʌstə(r)/ n. lustre m.

lusty /'lʌstɪ/ a. (-ier, -iest) robuste.

lute /lu:t/ n. (mus.) luth m.

Luxemburg /'lʌksəmbɜ:g/ n. Luxembourg m.

luxuriant /lʌg'ʒʊərɪənt/ a. luxuriant.

luxurious /lʌg'ʒʊərɪəs/ a. luxueux.

luxury /'lʌkʃərɪ/ n. luxe m. —a. de luxe.

lye /laɪ/ n. lessive (alcaline) f.

lying /'laɪɪŋ/ see **lie**[1], **lie**[2]. —n. le mensonge m.

lynch /lɪntʃ/ v.t. lyncher.

lynx /lɪŋks/ n. lynx m.

lyre /'laɪə(r)/ n. (mus.) lyre f.

lyric /'lɪrɪk/ a. lyrique. ∼**s** n. pl. paroles f. pl. ∼**al** a. lyrique. ∼**ism** /-sɪzəm/ n. lyrisme m.

M

MA *abbr. see* **Master of Arts.**

mac /mæk/ *n.* (*fam.*) imper *m.*

macabre /məˈkɑːbrə/ *a.* macabre.

macaroni /mækəˈrəʊnɪ/ *n.* macaronis *m. pl.*

macaroon /mækəˈruːn/ *n.* macaron *m.*

mace /meɪs/ *n.* (*staff*) masse *f.*

Mach /mɑːk/ *n.* ~ **(number),** (nombre de) Mach *m.*

machiavellian /mækɪəˈvelɪən/ *a.* machiavélique.

machinations /mækɪˈneɪʃnz/ *n. pl.* machinations *f. pl.*

machine /məˈʃiːn/ *n.* machine *f.* —*v.t.* (*sew*) coudre à la machine; (*techn.*) usiner. ~**-gun** *n.* mitrailleuse *f.*; *v.t.* (*p.t.* **-gunned**) mitrailler. ~ **readable** *a.* en langage machine. ~ **tool,** machine-outil *f.*

machinery /məˈʃiːnərɪ/ *n.* machinerie *f.*; (*working parts & fig.*) mécanisme(s) *m.* (*pl.*).

machinist /məˈʃiːnɪst/ *n.* (*operator*) opéra|teur, -trice sur machine *m., f.*; (*on sewing-machine*) piqueu/r, -se *m., f.*

macho /ˈmætʃəʊ/ *n.* (*pl.* **-os**) macho *m.*

mackerel /ˈmækrəl/ *n. invar.* (*fish*) maquereau *m.*

mackintosh /ˈmækɪntɒʃ/ *n.* imperméable *m.*

macrobiotic /mækrəʊbaɪˈɒtɪk/ *a.* macrobiotique.

mad /mæd/ *a.* (**madder, maddest**) fou; (*foolish*) insensé; (*dog etc.*) enragé; (*angry: fam.*) furieux. **be ~ about,** se passionner pour; (*person*) être fou de. **like ~,** comme un fou. ~**ly** *adv.* (*interested, in love, etc.*) follement; (*frantically*) comme un fou. ~**ness** *n.* folie *f.*

Madagascar /mædəˈgæskə(r)/ *n.* Madagascar *f.*

madam /ˈmædəm/ *n.* madame *f.*; (*unmarried*) mademoiselle *f.*

madcap /ˈmædkæp/ *a. & n.* écervelé(e) (*m.* (*f.*)).

madden /ˈmædn/ *v.t.* exaspérer.

made /meɪd/ *see* **make.** ~ **to measure,** fait sur mesure.

Madeira /məˈdɪərə/ *n.* (*wine*) madère *m.*

madhouse /ˈmædhaʊs/ *n.* (*fam.*) maison de fous *f.*

madman /ˈmædmən/ *n.* (*pl.* **-men**) fou *m.*

madonna /məˈdɒnə/ *n.* madone *f.*

madrigal /ˈmædrɪɡl/ *n.* madrigal *m.*

maestro /ˈmaɪstrəʊ/ *n.* (*pl.* **maestri** /-striː/) maestro *m.*

Mafia /ˈmæfɪə/ *n.* maf(f)ia *f.*

magazine /mæɡəˈziːn/ *n.* revue *f.*, magazine *m.*; (*of gun*) magasin *m.*

magenta /məˈdʒentə/ *a.* rouge violacé.

maggot /ˈmæɡət/ *n.* ver *m.*, asticot *m.* ~**y** *a.* véreux.

Magi /ˈmeɪdʒaɪ/ *n. pl.* **the ~,** les Rois mages *m. pl.*

magic /ˈmædʒɪk/ *n.* magie *f.* —*a.* magique. ~**al** *a.* magique.

magician /məˈdʒɪʃn/ *n.* magicien(ne) *m.* (*f.*).

magistrate /ˈmædʒɪstreɪt/ *n.* magistrat *m.*

magnanim|ous /mæɡˈnænɪməs/ *a.* magnanime. ~**ity** /-əˈnɪmətɪ/ *n.* magnanimité *f.*

magnate /ˈmæɡneɪt/ *n.* magnat *m.*

magnesia /mæɡˈniːʃə/ *n.* magnésie *f.*

magnet /ˈmæɡnɪt/ *n.* aimant *m.* ~**ic** /-ˈnetɪk/ *a.* magnétique. ~**ism** *n.* magnétisme *m.* ~**ize** *v.t.* magnétiser.

magnificen|t /mæɡˈnɪfɪsnt/ *a.* magnifique. ~**ce** *n.* magnificence *f.*

magnif|y /ˈmæɡnɪfaɪ/ *v.t.* grossir; (*sound*) amplifier; (*fig.*) exagérer. ~**ication** /-ɪˈkeɪʃn/ *n.* grossissement *m.*; amplification *f.* ~**ier** *n.*, ~**ying glass,** loupe *f.*

magnitude /ˈmæɡnɪtjuːd/ *n.* (*importance*) ampleur *f.*; (*size*) grandeur *f.*

magnolia /mæɡˈnəʊlɪə/ *n.* magnolia *m.*

magnum /ˈmæɡnəm/ *n.* magnum *m.*

magpie /ˈmæɡpaɪ/ *n.* pie *f.*

mahogany /məˈhɒɡənɪ/ *n.* acajou *m.*

maid /meɪd/ *n.* (*servant*) bonne *f.*; (*girl: old use*) jeune fille *f.*

maiden /ˈmeɪdn/ *n.* (*old use*) jeune fille *f.* —*a.* (*aunt*) célibataire; (*voyage*) premier. ~ **name,** nom de jeune fille *m.* ~**hood** *n.* virginité *f.* ~**ly** *a.* virginal.

mail[1] /meɪl/ *n.* poste *f.*; (*letters*) courrier *m.* —*a.* (*bag, van*) postal. —*v.t.* envoyer par la poste. ~**ing list,** liste d'adresses *f*. ~ **order,** vente par correspondance *f*.

mail[2] /meɪl/ *n*. (*armour*) cotte de mailles *f*.

mailman /'meɪlmæn/ *n*. (*pl*. **-men**) (*Amer*.) facteur *m*.

maim /meɪm/ *v.t.* mutiler.

main[1] /meɪn/ *a*. principal. —*n*. **in the** ~, en général. **a** ~ **road,** une grande route. ~**ly** *adv*. principalement, surtout.

main[2] /meɪn/ *n*. (**water/gas**) ~, conduite d'eau/de gaz *f*. **the** ~**s,** (*electr*.) le secteur.

mainland /'meɪnlənd/ *n*. continent *m*.

mainspring /'meɪnsprɪŋ/ *n*. ressort principal *m*.; (*motive*: *fig*.) mobile principal *m*.

mainstay /'meɪnsteɪ/ *n*. soutien *m*.

mainstream /'meɪnstriːm/ *n*. tendance principale *f*., ligne *f*.

maintain /meɪn'teɪn/ *v.t.* (*continue, keep, assert*) maintenir; (*house, machine, family*) entretenir; (*rights*) soutenir.

maintenance /'meɪntənəns/ *n*. (*care*) entretien *m*.; (*continuation*) maintien *m*.; (*allowance*) pension alimentaire *f*.

maisonette /meɪzə'net/ *n*. duplex *m*.

maize /meɪz/ *n*. maïs *m*.

majestic /mə'dʒestɪk/ *a*. majestueux.

majesty /'mædʒəsti/ *n*. majesté *f*.

major /'meɪdʒə(r)/ *a*. majeur. —*n*. commandant *m*. —*v.i.* ~ **in,** (*univ*., *Amer*.) se spécialiser en. ~ **road,** route à priorité *f*.

Majorca /mə'dʒɔːkə/ *n*. Majorque *f*.

majority /mə'dʒɒrəti/ *n*. majorité *f*. —*a*. majoritaire. **the** ~ **of people,** la plupart des gens.

make /meɪk/ *v.t./i*. (*p.t.* **made**) faire; (*manufacture*) fabriquer; (*friends*) se faire; (*money*) gagner, se faire; (*decision*) prendre; (*destination*) arriver à; (*cause to be*) rendre. ~ **s.o. do sth.,** obliger qn. à faire qch., faire faire qch. à qn. —*n*. fabrication *f*.; (*brand*) marque *f*. **be made of,** être fait de. ~ **o.s. at home,** se mettre à l'aise. ~ **it,** arriver; (*succeed*) réussir. **I** ~ **it two o'clock,** j'ai deux heures. **I cannot** ~ **anything of it,** je n'y comprends rien. ~ **as if to,** faire mine de. ~ **believe,** faire semblant. ~**-believe** *a*. feint, illusoire; *n*. fantaisie *f*. ~ **do,** (*manage*) se débrouiller (**with,** avec). ~ **do with,** (*content o.s.*) se contenter

de. ~ **for,** se diriger vers. ~ **good** *v.i.* réussir; *v.t.* compenser; (*repair*) réparer. ~ **off,** filer (**with,** avec). ~ **out** *v.t.* distinguer; (*understand*) comprendre; (*draw up*) faire; (*assert*) prétendre; *v.i.* (*fam*.) se débrouiller. ~ **over,** céder (**to,** à); (*convert*) transformer. ~ **up** *v.t.* faire, former; (*story*) inventer; (*deficit*) combler; *v.i.* se réconcilier. ~ **up** (**one's face**), se maquiller. ~**-up** *n*. maquillage *m*.; (*of object*) constitution *f*.; (*psych*.) caractère *m*. ~ **up for,** compenser; (*time*) rattraper. ~ **up one's mind,** se décider. ~ **up to,** se concilier les bonnes grâces de.

maker /'meɪkə(r)/ *n*. fabricant *m*.

makeshift /'meɪkʃɪft/ *n*. expédient *m*. —*a*. provisoire.

making /'meɪkɪŋ/ *n*. **be the** ~ **of,** faire le succès de. **he has the** ~**s of,** il a l'étoffe de.

maladjusted /mælə'dʒʌstɪd/ *a*. inadapté.

maladministration /mælədmɪnɪ'streɪʃn/ *n*. mauvaise gestion *f*.

malaise /mæ'leɪz/ *n*. malaise *m*.

malaria /mə'leərɪə/ *n*. malaria *f*.

Malay /mə'leɪ/ *a*. & *n*. malais(e) (*m*. (*f*.)). ~**sia** *n*. Malaysia *f*.

male /meɪl/ *a*. (*voice, sex*) masculin; (*bot*., *techn*.) mâle. —*n*. mâle *m*.

malevolen|t /mə'levələnt/ *a*. malveillant. ~**ce** *n*. malveillance *f*.

malform|ation /mælfɔː'meɪʃn/ *n*. malformation *f*. ~**ed** *a*. difforme.

malfunction /mæl'fʌŋkʃn/ *n*. mauvais fonctionnement *m*. —*v.i.* mal fonctionner.

malice /'mælɪs/ *n*. méchanceté *f*.

malicious /mə'lɪʃəs/ *a*. méchant. ~**ly** *adv*. méchamment.

malign /mə'laɪn/ *a*. pernicieux. —*v.t.* calomnier.

malignan|t /mə'lɪgnənt/ *a*. malveillant; (*tumour*) malin. ~**cy** *n*. malveillance *f*.; malignité *f*.

malinger /mə'lɪŋgə(r)/ *v.i.* feindre la maladie. ~**er** *n*. simula|teur, -trice *m*., *f*.

malleable /'mælɪəbl/ *a*. malléable.

mallet /'mælɪt/ *n*. maillet *m*.

malnutrition /mælnjuː'trɪʃn/ *n*. sous-alimentation *f*.

malpractice /mæl'præktɪs/ *n*. faute professionnelle *f*.

malt /mɔːlt/ *n*. malt *m*. ~ **whisky,** whisky pur malt *m*.

Malt|a /'mɔːltə/ *n.* Malte *f.* ～**ese** /-'tiːz/ *a.* & *n.* maltais(e) (*m.* (*f.*)).

maltreat /mæl'triːt/ *v.t.* maltraiter. ～**ment** *n.* mauvais traitement *m.*

mammal /'mæml/ *n.* mammifère *m.*

mammoth /'mæməθ/ *n.* mammouth *m.* —*a.* monstre.

man /mæn/ *n.* (*pl.* **men**) homme *m.*; (*in sports team*) joueur *m.*; (*chess*) pièce *f.* —*v.t.* (*p.t.* **manned**) pourvoir en hommes; (*ship*) armer; (*guns*) servir; (*be on duty at*) être de service à. ～**-hour** *n.* heure de main-d'œuvre *f.* ～**-hunt** *n.* chasse à l'homme *f.* ～ **in the street,** homme de la rue *m.* ～**made** *a.* artificiel. ～**-of-war** *n.* navire de guerre *m.* ～**-sized** *a.* grand. ～ **to man,** d'homme à homme.

manage /'mænɪdʒ/ *v.t.* diriger; (*shop, affairs*) gérer; (*handle*) manier. **I could** ～ **another drink,** (*fam.*) je prendrais bien encore un verre. —*v.i.* se débrouiller. ～ **to do,** réussir à faire. ～**able** *a.* (*tool, size, person, etc.*) maniable; (*job*) faisable. ～**ment** *n.* direction *f.*; (*of shop*) gestion *f.* **managing director,** directeur général *m.*

manager /'mænɪdʒə(r)/ *n.* directeur *m.*; (*of shop*) gérant *m.*; (*of actor*) impresario *m.* ～**ess** /-'res/ *n.* directrice *f.*; gérante *f.* ～**ial** /-'dʒɪərɪəl/ *a.* directorial. ～**ial staff,** cadres *m. pl.*

mandarin /'mændərɪn/ *n.* mandarin *m.*; (*orange*) mandarine *f.*

mandate /'mændeɪt/ *n.* mandat *m.*

mandatory /'mændətrɪ/ *a.* obligatoire.

mane /meɪn/ *n.* crinière *f.*

manful /'mænfl/ *a.* courageux.

mangle[1] /'mæŋgl/ *n.* (*for wringing*) essoreuse *f.*; (*for smoothing*) calandre *f.*

mangle[2] /'mæŋgl/ *v.t.* mutiler.

mango /'mæŋgəʊ/ *n.* (*pl.* **-oes**) mangue *f.*

mangy /'meɪndʒɪ/ *a.* galeux.

manhandle /'mænhændl/ *v.t.* maltraiter, malmener.

manhole /'mænhəʊl/ *n.* trou d'homme *m.*, regard *m.*

manhood /'mænhʊd/ *n.* âge d'homme *m.*; (*quality*) virilité *f.*

mania /'meɪnɪə/ *n.* manie *f.* ～**c** /-ræk/ *n.* maniaque *m./f.*, fou *m.*, folle *f.*

manicur|e /'mænɪkjʊə(r)/ *n.* soin des mains *m.* —*v.t.* soigner, manucurer. ～**ist** *n.* manucure *m./f.*

manifest /'mænɪfest/ *a.* manifeste.

—*v.t.* manifester. ～**ation** /-'steɪʃn/ *n.* manifestation *f.*

manifesto /mænɪ'festəʊ/ *n.* (*pl.* **-os**) manifeste *m.*

manifold /'mænɪfəʊld/ *a.* multiple.

manipulat|e /mə'nɪpjʊleɪt/ *v.t.* (*tool, person*) manipuler. ～**ion** /-'leɪʃn/ *n.* manipulation *f.*

mankind /mæn'kaɪnd/ *n.* genre humain *m.*

manly /'mænlɪ/ *a.* viril.

manner /'mænə(r)/ *n.* manière *f.*; (*attitude*) attitude *f.*; (*kind*) sorte *f.* ～**s,** (*social behaviour*) manières *f. pl.* ～**ed** *a.* maniéré.

mannerism /'mænərɪzəm/ *n.* trait particulier *m.*

manœuvre /mə'nuːvə(r)/ *n.* manœuvre *f.* —*v.t./i.* manœuvrer.

manor /'mænə(r)/ *n.* manoir *m.*

manpower /'mænpaʊə(r)/ *n.* main-d'œuvre *f.*

manservant /'mænsɜːvənt/ *n.* (*pl.* **menservants**) domestique *m.*

mansion /'mænʃn/ *n.* château *m.*

manslaughter /'mænslɔːtə(r)/ *n.* homicide involontaire *m.*

mantelpiece /'mæntlpiːs/ *n.* (*shelf*) cheminée *f.*

manual /'mænjʊəl/ *a.* manuel. —*n.* (*handbook*) manuel *m.*

manufacture /mænjʊ'fæktʃə(r)/ *v.t.* fabriquer. —*n.* fabrication *f.* ～**r** /-ə(r) / *n.* fabricant *m.*

manure /mə'njʊə(r)/ *n.* fumier *m.*

manuscript /'mænjʊskrɪpt/ *n.* manuscrit *m.*

many /'menɪ/ *a.* & *n.* beaucoup (de). **a great** *or* **good** ～, un grand nombre (de). ～ **a,** bien des.

map /mæp/ *n.* carte *f.*; (*of streets etc.*) plan *m.* —*v.t.* (*p.t.* **mapped**) faire la carte de. ～ **out,** (*route*) tracer; (*arrange*) organiser.

maple /'meɪpl/ *n.* érable *m.*

mar /mɑː(r)/ *v.t.* (*p.t.* **marred**) gâter; (*spoil beauty of*) déparer.

marathon /'mærəθən/ *n.* marathon *m.*

marauding /mə'rɔːdɪŋ/ *a.* pillard.

marble /'mɑːbl/ *n.* marbre *m.*; (*for game*) bille *f.*

March /mɑːtʃ/ *n.* mars *m.*

march /mɑːtʃ/ *v.i.* (*mil.*) marcher (au pas). ～ **off/etc.,** partir/etc. allégrement. —*v.t.* ～ **off,** (*lead away*) emmener. —*n.* marche *f.* ～**past** *n.* défilé *m.*

mare /'meə(r)/ *n.* jument *f.*

margarine /mɑːdʒəˈriːn/ n. margarine f.

margin /ˈmɑːdʒɪn/ n. marge f. **~al** a. marginal; (*increase etc.*) léger, faible. **~al seat**, (*pol.*) siège chaudement disputé m. **~ally** adv. très peu.

marigold /ˈmærɪɡəʊld/ n. souci m.

marijuana /mærɪˈwɑːnə/ n. marijuana f.

marina /məˈriːnə/ n. marina f.

marinate /ˈmærɪneɪt/ v.t. mariner.

marine /məˈriːn/ a. marin. —n. (*shipping*) marine f.; (*sailor*) fusilier marin m.

marionette /mærɪəˈnet/ n. marionnette f.

marital /ˈmærɪtl/ a. conjugal. **~ status**, situation de famille f.

maritime /ˈmærɪtaɪm/ a. maritime.

mark¹ /mɑːk/ n. (*currency*) mark m.

mark² /mɑːk/ n. marque f.; (*trace*) trace f., marque f.; (*schol.*) note f.; (*target*) but m. —v.t. marquer; (*exam*) corriger. **~ out**, délimiter; (*person*) désigner. **~ time**, marquer le pas. **~er** n. marque f. **~ing** n. (*marks*) marques f. pl.

marked /mɑːkt/ a. marqué. **~ly** /-ɪdlɪ/ adv. visiblement.

market /ˈmɑːkɪt/ n. marché m. —v.t. (*sell*) vendre; (*launch*) commercialiser. **~ garden**, jardin maraîcher m. **on the ~**, en vente. **~ing** n. marketing m.

marksman /ˈmɑːksmən/ n. (*pl.* -men) tireur d'élite m.

marmalade /ˈmɑːməleɪd/ n. confiture d'oranges f.

maroon /məˈruːn/ n. bordeaux m. *invar.* —a. bordeaux *invar.*

marooned /məˈruːnd/ a. abandonné; (*snow-bound etc.*) bloqué.

marquee /mɑːˈkiː/ n. grande tente f.; (*awning: Amer.*) marquise f.

marquis /ˈmɑːkwɪs/ n. marquis m.

marriage /ˈmærɪdʒ/ n. mariage m. **~able** a. nubile, mariable.

marrow /ˈmærəʊ/ n. (*of bone*) moelle f.; (*vegetable*) courge f.

marr|y /ˈmærɪ/ v.t. épouser; (*give or unite in marriage*) marier. —v.i. se marier. **~ied** a. marié; (*life*) conjugal. **get ~ied**, se marier.

marsh /mɑːʃ/ n. marais m. **~y** a. marécageux.

marshal /ˈmɑːʃl/ n. maréchal m.; (*at event*) membre du service d'ordre m. —v.t. (*p.t.* **marshalled**) rassembler.

marshmallow /mɑːʃˈmæləʊ/ n. guimauve f.

martial /ˈmɑːʃl/ a. martial. **~ law**, loi martiale f.

Martian /ˈmɑːʃn/ a. & n. martien(ne) (m. (f.)).

martyr /ˈmɑːtə(r)/ n. martyr(e) m. (f.). —v.t. martyriser. **~dom** n. martyre m.

marvel /ˈmɑːvl/ n. merveille f. —v.i. (*p.t.* **marvelled**) s'émerveiller (**at**, de).

marvellous /ˈmɑːvələs/ a. merveilleux.

Marxis|t /ˈmɑːksɪst/ a. & n. marxiste (m./f.). **~m** /-zəm/ n. marxisme m.

marzipan /ˈmɑːzɪpæn/ n. pâte d'amandes f.

mascara /mæˈskɑːrə/ n. mascara m.

mascot /ˈmæskət/ n. mascotte f.

masculin|e /ˈmæskjʊlɪn/ a. & n. masculin (m.). **~ity** /-ˈlɪnətɪ/ n. masculinité f.

mash /mæʃ/ n. pâtée f.; (*potatoes: fam.*) purée f. —v.t. écraser. **~ed potatoes**, purée (de pommes de terre) f.

mask /mɑːsk/ n. masque m. —v.t. masquer.

masochis|t /ˈmæsəkɪst/ n. masochiste m./f. **~m** /-zəm/ n. masochisme m.

mason /ˈmeɪsn/ n. (*builder*) maçon m. **~ry** n. maçonnerie f.

Mason /ˈmeɪsn/ n. maçon m. **~ic** /məˈsɒnɪk/ a. maçonnique.

masquerade /mɑːskəˈreɪd/ n. mascarade f. —v.i. **~ as**, se faire passer pour.

mass¹ /mæs/ n. (*relig.*) messe f.

mass² /mæs/ n. masse f. —v.t./i. (se) masser. **~-produce** v.t. fabriquer en série. **the ~es**, les masses f. pl.

massacre /ˈmæsəkə(r)/ n. massacre m. —v.t. massacrer.

massage /ˈmæsɑːʒ, *Amer.* məˈsɑːʒ/ n. massage m. —v.t. masser.

masseu|r /mæˈsɜː(r)/ n. masseur m. **~se** /-ɜːz/ n. masseuse f.

massive /ˈmæsɪv/ a. (*large*) énorme; (*heavy*) massif.

mast /mɑːst/ n. mât m.; (*for radio, TV*) pylône m.

master /ˈmɑːstə(r)/ n. maître m.; (*in secondary school*) professeur m. —v.t. maîtriser, dominer. **~-key** n. passepartout m. *invar.* **~mind** n. (*of scheme etc.*) cerveau m.; v.t. diriger.

M~ of Arts/*etc.*, titulaire d'une maîtrise ès lettres/ *etc.* *m.*/*f.* **~-stroke** *n.* coup de maître *m.* **~y** *n.* maîtrise *f.*

masterly /'mɑːstəlɪ/ *a.* magistral.

masterpiece /'mɑːstəpiːs/ *n.* chef-d'œuvre *m.*

masturbat|e /'mæstəbeɪt/ *v.i.* se masturber. **~ion** /-'beɪʃn/ *n.* masturbation *f.*

mat /mæt/ *n.* (petit) tapis *m.*, natte *f.*; (*at door*) paillasson *m.*

match¹ /mætʃ/ *n.* allumette *f.*

match² /mætʃ/ *n.* (*sport*) match *m.*; (*equal*) égal(e) *m.* (*f.*); (*marriage*) mariage *m.*; (*s.o. to marry*) parti *m.* —*v.t.* opposer; (*go with*) aller avec; (*cups etc.*) assortir; (*equal*) égaler. —*v.i.* (*be alike*) être assorti. **~ing** *a.* assorti.

matchbox /'mætʃbɒks/ *n.* boîte à allumettes *f.*

mate¹ /meɪt/ *n.* camarade *m.*/*f.*; (*of animal*) compagnon *m.*, compagne *f.*; (*assistant*) aide *m.*/*f* —*v.t.*/*i.* (s')accoupler (**with**, avec).

mate² /meɪt/ *n.* (*chess*) mat *m.*

material /mə'tɪərɪəl/ *n.* matière *f.*; (*fabric*) tissu *m.*; (*for building*) matériau(x) *m.* (*pl.*). **~s**, (*equipment*) matériel *m.* —*a.* matériel; (*fig.*) important. **~istic** /-'lɪstɪk/ *a.* matérialiste.

materialize /mə'tɪərɪəlaɪz/ *v.i.* se matérialiser, se réaliser.

maternal /mə'tɜːnl/ *a.* maternel.

maternity /mə'tɜːnətɪ/ *n.* maternité *f.* —*a.* (*clothes*) de grossesse. **~ hospital**, maternité *f.*

mathematic|s /mæθə'mætɪks/ *n.* & *n. pl.* mathématiques *f. pl.* **~ian** /-ə'tɪʃn/ *n.* mathématicien(ne) *m.* (*f.*). **~al** *a.* mathématique.

maths /mæθs/ (*Amer.* **math** /mæθ/) *n.* & *n. pl.* (*fam.*) maths *f. pl.*

matinée /'mætɪneɪ/ *n.* matinée *f.*

matriculat|e /mə'trɪkjʊleɪt/ *v.t.*/*i.* (s')inscrire. **~ion** /-'leɪʃn/ *n.* inscription *f.*

matrimon|y /'mætrɪmənɪ/ *n.* mariage *m.* **~ial** /-'məʊnɪəl/ *a.* matrimonial.

matrix /'meɪtrɪks/ *n.* (*pl.* **matrices** /-ɪsiːz/) matrice *f.*

matron /'meɪtrən/ *n.* (*married, elderly*) dame âgée *f.*; (*in hospital: former use*) infirmière-major *f.* **~ly** *a.* d'âge mûr; (*manner*) très digne.

matt /mæt/ *a.* mat.

matted /'mætɪd/ *a.* (*hair*) emmêlé.

matter /'mætə(r)/ *n.* (*substance*) matière *f.*; (*affair*) affaire *f.*; (*pus*) pus *m.* —*v.i.* importer. **as a ~ of fact**, en fait. **it does not ~**, ça ne fait rien. **~-of-fact** *a.* terre à terre *invar.* **no ~**, peu importe. **what is the ~?**, qu'est-ce qu'il y a?

matting /'mætɪŋ/ *n.* natte(s) *f.* (*pl.*).

mattress /'mætrɪs/ *n.* matelas *m.*

matur|e /mə'tjʊə(r)/ *a.* mûr. —*v.t.*/*i.* (se) mûrir. **~ity** *n.* maturité *f.*

maul /mɔːl/ *v.t.* déchiqueter.

Mauritius /mə'rɪʃəs/ *n.* île Maurice *f.*

mausoleum /mɔːsə'lɪəm/ *n.* mausolée *m.*

mauve /məʊv/ *a.* & *n.* mauve (*m.*).

mawkish /'mɔːkɪʃ/ *a.* mièvre.

maxim /'mæksɪm/ *n.* maxime *f.*

maxim|um /'mæksɪməm/ *a.* & *n.* (*pl.* **-ima**) maximum (*m.*). **~ize** *v.t.* porter au maximum.

may /meɪ/ *v. aux.* (*p.t.* **might**) pouvoir. **he ~/might come**, il peut/pourrait venir. **you might have**, vous auriez pu. **you ~ leave**, vous pouvez partir. **~ I smoke?**, puis-je fumer? **~ he be happy**, qu'il soit heureux. **I ~ or might as well stay**, je ferais aussi bien de rester.

May /meɪ/ *n.* mai *m.* **~ Day**, le Premier Mai.

maybe /'meɪbiː/ *adv.* peut-être.

mayhem /'meɪhem/ *n.* (*havoc*) ravages *m. pl.*

mayonnaise /meɪə'neɪz/ *n.* mayonnaise *f.*

mayor /meə(r)/ *n.* maire *m.* **~ess** *n.* (*wife*) femme du maire *f.*

maze /meɪz/ *n.* labyrinthe *m.*

me /miː/ *pron.* me, m'*; (*after prep.*) moi. (**to**) **~**, me, m'*. **he knows ~**, il me connaît.

meadow /'medəʊ/ *n.* pré *m.*

meagre /'miːɡə(r)/ *a.* maigre.

meal¹ /miːl/ *n.* repas *m.*

meal² /miːl/ *n.* (*grain*) farine *f.*

mealy-mouthed /miːlɪ'maʊðd/ *a.* mielleux.

mean¹ /miːn/ *a.* (**-er, -est**) (*poor*) misérable; (*miserly*) avare; (*unkind*) méchant. **~ness** *n.* avarice *f.*; méchanceté *f.*

mean² /miːn/ *a.* moyen. —*n.* milieu *m.*; (*average*) moyenne *f.* **in the ~ time**, en attendant.

mean³ /miːn/ *v.t.* (*p.t.* **meant**) vouloir dire, signifier; (*involve*) entraîner. **be**

meant for, être destiné à. ~ **to do,** avoir l'intention de faire.

meander /mɪˈændə(r)/ v.i. faire des méandres.

meaning /ˈmiːnɪŋ/ n. sens m., signification f. ~**ful** a. significatif. ~**less** a. dénué de sens.

means /miːnz/ n. moyen(s) m. (pl.). —n. pl. (wealth) moyens financiers m. pl. **by all** ~, certainement. **by no** ~, nullement.

meant /ment/ see **mean³**.

mean|time /ˈmiːntaɪm/, ~**while** advs. en attendant.

measles /ˈmiːzlz/ n. rougeole f.

measly /ˈmiːzlɪ/ a. (sl.) minable.

measurable /ˈmeʒərəbl/ a. mesurable.

measure /ˈmeʒə(r)/ n. mesure f.; (ruler) règle f. —v.t./i. mesurer. ~ **up to,** être à la hauteur de. ~**d** a. mesuré. ~**ment** n. mesure f.

meat /miːt/ n. viande f. ~**y** a. de viande; (fig.) substantiel.

mechanic /mɪˈkænɪk/ n. mécanicien(ne) m. (f.).

mechanic|al /mɪˈkænɪkl/ a. mécanique. ~**s** n. (science) mécanique f.; n. pl. mécanisme m.

mechan|ism /ˈmekənɪzəm/ n. mécanisme m. ~**ize** v.t. mécaniser.

medal /ˈmedl/ n. médaille f. ~**list** n. médaillé(e) m. (f.). **be a gold** ~**list,** être médaille d'or.

medallion /mɪˈdælɪən/ n. (medal, portrait, etc.) médaillon m.

meddle /ˈmedl/ v.i. (interfere) se mêler (**in,** de); (tinker) toucher (**with,** à). ~**some** a. importun.

media /ˈmiːdɪə/ see **medium.** —n. pl. **the** ~, les media m. pl.

mediat|e /ˈmiːdɪeɪt/ v.i. servir d'intermédiaire. ~**ion** /-ˈeɪʃn/ n. médiation f. ~**or** n. média|teur, -trice m., f.

medical /ˈmedɪkl/ a. médical; (student) en médecine. —n. (fam.) visite médicale f.

medicat|ed /ˈmedɪkeɪtɪd/ a. médical. ~**ion** /-ˈkeɪʃn/ n. médicaments m. pl.

medicin|e /ˈmedsn/ n. (science) médecine f.; (substance) médicament m. ~**al** /mɪˈdɪsɪnl/ a. médicinal.

medieval /medɪˈiːvl/ a. médiéval.

mediocr|e /miːdɪˈəʊkə(r)/ a. médiocre. ~**ity** /-ˈɒkrətɪ/ n. médiocrité f.

meditat|e /ˈmedɪteɪt/ v.t./i. méditer. ~**ion** /-ˈteɪʃn/ n. méditation f.

Mediterranean /medɪtəˈreɪnɪən/ a. méditerranéen. —n. **the** ~, la Méditerranée f.

medium /ˈmiːdɪəm/ n. (pl. **media**) milieu m.; (for transmitting data etc.) support m.; (pl. **mediums**) (person) médium m. —a. moyen.

medley /ˈmedlɪ/ n. mélange m.; (mus.) pot-pourri m.

meek /miːk/ a. (-er, -est) doux.

meet /miːt/ v.t. (p.t. met) rencontrer; (see again) retrouver; (fetch) (aller) chercher; (be introduced to) faire la connaissance de; (face, satisfy) faire face à. —v.i. se rencontrer; (see each other again) se retrouver; (in session) se réunir.

meeting /ˈmiːtɪŋ/ n. réunion f.; (between two people) rencontre f.

megaphone /ˈmegəfəʊn/ n. portevoix m. invar.

melanchol|y /ˈmelənkəlɪ/ n. mélancolie f. —a. mélancolique. ~**ic** /-ˈkɒlɪk/ a. mélancolique.

mellow /ˈmeləʊ/ a. (-er, -est) (fruit) mûr; (sound, colour) moelleux, doux; (person) mûri. —v.t./i. (mature) mûrir; (soften) (s')adoucir.

melodious /mɪˈləʊdɪəs/ a. mélodieux.

melodrama /ˈmelədrɑːmə/ n. mélodrame m. ~**tic** /-əˈmætɪk/ a. mélodramatique.

melod|y /ˈmelədɪ/ n. mélodie f. ~**ic** /mɪˈlɒdɪk/ a. mélodique.

melon /ˈmelən/ n. melon m.

melt /melt/ v.t./i. (faire) fondre. ~**ing-pot** n. creuset m.

member /ˈmembə(r)/ n. membre m. **M**~ **of Parliament,** député m. ~**ship** n. adhésion f.; (members) membres m. pl.; (fee) cotisation f.

membrane /ˈmembreɪn/ n. membrane f.

memento /mɪˈmentəʊ/ n. (pl. -oes) (object) souvenir m.

memo /ˈmeməʊ/ n. (pl. -os) (fam.) note f.

memoir /ˈmemwɑː(r)/ n. (record, essay) mémoire m.

memorable /ˈmemərəbl/ a. mémorable.

memorandum /meməˈrændəm/ n. (pl. -ums) note f.

memorial /mɪˈmɔːrɪəl/ n. monument m. —a. commémoratif.

memorize /ˈmeməraɪz/ v.t. apprendre par cœur.

memory /ˈmemərɪ/ n. (faculty) mémoire f.; (thing remembered) souvenir *m.* from ~, de mémoire. in ~ of, à la mémoire de.

men /men/ *see* **man.**

menac|e /'menəs/ *n.* menace *f.*; (*nuisance*) peste *f.* —*v.t.* menacer. ~**ingly** *adv.* d'un ton menaçant.

menagerie /mɪ'nædʒərɪ/ *n.* ménagerie *f.*

mend /mend/ *v.t.* réparer; (*darn*) raccommoder. —*n.* raccommodage *m.* ~ one's ways, s'amender. on the ~, en voie de guérison.

menfolk /'menfəʊk/ *n.* hommes *m. pl.*

menial /'miːnɪəl/ *a.* servile.

meningitis /menɪn'dʒaɪtɪs/ *n.* méningite *f.*

menopause /'menəpɔːz/ *n.* ménopause *f.*

menstruation /menstrʊ'eɪʃn/ *n.* menstruation *f.*

mental /'mentl/ *a.* mental; (*hospital*) psychiatrique.

mentality /men'tælətɪ/ *n.* mentalité *f.*

menthol /'menθɒl/ *n.* menthol *m.* —*a.* mentholé.

mention /'menʃn/ *v.t.* mentionner. —*n.* mention *f.* don't ~ it!, il n'y a pas de quoi!, je vous en prie!

mentor /'mentɔː(r)/ *n.* mentor *m.*

menu /'menjuː/ *n.* menu *m.*

mercantile /'mɜːkəntaɪl/ *a.* commercial.

mercenary /'mɜːsɪnərɪ/ *a. & n.* mercenaire (*m.*).

merchandise /'mɜːtʃəndaɪz/ *n.* marchandise *f. pl.*

merchant /'mɜːtʃənt/ *n.* marchand *m.* —*a.* (*ship, navy*) marchand. ~ **bank,** banque de commerce *f.*

merciful /'mɜːsɪfl/ *a.* miséricordieux. ~**ly** *adv.* (*fortunately*: *fam.*) Dieu merci.

merciless /'mɜːsɪlɪs/ *a.* impitoyable, implacable.

mercury /'mɜːkjʊrɪ/ *n.* mercure *m.*

mercy /'mɜːsɪ/ *n.* pitié *f.* at the ~ of, à la merci de.

mere /mɪə(r)/ *a.* simple. ~**ly** *adv.* simplement.

merest /'mɪərɪst/ *a.* moindre.

merge /mɜːdʒ/ *v.t./i.* (se) mêler (**with,** à); (*companies*: *comm.*) fusionner. ~**r** /-ə(r)/ *n.* fusion *f.*

meridian /mə'rɪdɪən/ *n.* méridien *m.*

meringue /mə'ræŋ/ *n.* meringue *f.*

merit /'merɪt/ *n.* mérite *m.* —*v.t.* (*p.t.* **merited**) mériter.

mermaid /'mɜːmeɪd/ *n.* sirène *f.*

merriment /'merɪmənt/ *n.* gaieté *f.*

merry /'merɪ/ *a.* (**-ier, -iest**) gai. **make ~,** faire la fête. ~**-go-round** *n.* manège *m.* ~**-making** *n.* réjouissances *f. pl.* **merrily** *adv.* gaiement.

mesh /meʃ/ *n.* maille *f.*; (*fabric*) tissu à mailles *m.*; (*network*) réseau *m.*

mesmerize /'mezməraɪz/ *v.t.* hypnotiser.

mess /mes/ *n.* désordre *m.*, gâchis *m.*; (*dirt*) saleté *f.*; (*mil.*) mess *m.* —*v.t.* ~ up, gâcher. —*v.i.* ~ about, s'amuser; (*dawdle*) traîner. ~ with, (*tinker with*) tripoter. make a ~ of, gâcher.

message /'mesɪdʒ/ *n.* message *m.*

messenger /'mesɪndʒə(r)/ *n.* messager *m.*

Messiah /mɪ'saɪə(r)/ *n.* Messie *m.*

Messrs /'mesəz/ *n. pl.* ~ **Smith,** Messieurs *or* MM. Smith.

messy /'mesɪ/ *a.* (**-ier, -iest**) en désordre; (*dirty*) sale.

met /met/ *see* **meet.**

metabolism /mɪ'tæbəlɪzəm/ *n.* métabolisme *m.*

metal /'metl/ *n.* métal *m.* —*a.* de métal. ~**lic** /mɪ'tælɪk/ *a.* métallique; (*paint, colour*) métallisé.

metallurgy /mɪ'tælədʒɪ, *Amer.* 'metələ:dʒɪ/ *n.* métallurgie *f.*

metamorphosis /metə'mɔːfəsɪs/ *n.* (*pl.* **-phoses** /-siːz/) métamorphose *f.*

metaphor /'metəfə(r)/ *n.* métaphore *f.* ~**ical** /-'fɒrɪkl/ *a.* métaphorique.

mete /miːt/ *v.t.* ~ out, donner, distribuer; (*justice*) rendre.

meteor /'miːtɪə(r)/ *n.* météore *m.*

meteorolog|y /miːtɪə'rɒlədʒɪ/ *n.* météorologie *f.* ~**ical** /-ə'lɒdʒɪkl/ *a.* météorologique.

meter[1] /'miːtə(r)/ *n.* compteur *m.*

meter[2] /'miːtə(r)/ *n.* (*Amer.*) = **metre.**

method /'meθəd/ *n.* méthode *f.*

methodical /mɪ'θɒdɪkl/ *a.* méthodique.

Methodist /'meθədɪst/ *n. & a.* méthodiste (*m./f.*).

methylated /'meθɪleɪtɪd/ *a.* ~ **spirit,** alcool à brûler *m.*

meticulous /mɪ'tɪkjʊləs/ *a.* méticuleux.

metre /'miːtə(r)/ *n.* mètre *m.*

metric /'metrɪk/ *a.* métrique. ~**ation** /-'keɪʃn/ *n.* adoption du système métrique *f.*

metropol|is /mə'trɒpəlɪs/ *n.* (*city*) métropole *f.* ~**itan** /metrə'pɒlɪtən/ *a.* métropolitain.

mettle /'metl/ *n.* courage *m.*

mew /mjuː/ *n.* miaulement *m.* —*v.i.* miauler.

mews /mjuːz/ *n. pl.* (*dwellings*) appartements chic aménagés dans des anciennes écuries *m. pl.*

Mexic|o /'meksɪkəʊ/ *n.* Mexique *m.* ~**an** *a.* & *n.* mexicain(e) (*m.* (*f.*)).

miaow /miːˈaʊ/ *n.* & *v.i.* = **mew.**

mice /maɪs/ *see* **mouse.**

mickey /'mɪkɪ/ *n.* **take the** ~ **out of,** (*sl.*) se moquer de.

micro /'maɪkrəʊ/ *pref.* micro-.

microbe /'maɪkrəʊb/ *n.* microbe *m.*

microchip /'maɪkrəʊtʃɪp/ *n.* microplaquette *f.*, puce *f.*

microfilm /'maɪkrəʊfɪlm/ *n.* microfilm *m.*

microphone /'maɪkrəfəʊn/ *n.* microphone *m.*

microprocessor /maɪkrəʊˈprəʊsesə(r)/ *n.* microprocesseur *m.*

microscop|e /'maɪkrəskəʊp/ *n.* microscope *m.* ~**ic** /-'skɒpɪk/ *a.* microscopique.

microwave /'maɪkrəʊweɪv/ *n.* micro-onde *f.* ~ **oven,** four à micro-ondes *m.*

mid /mɪd/ *a.* **in** ~ **air**/*etc.*, en plein ciel/*etc.* **in** ~ **March**/*etc.*, à la mi-mars/*etc.* **in** ~ **ocean**/*etc.*, au milieu de l'océan/*etc.*

midday /mɪd'deɪ/ *n.* midi *m.*

middle /'mɪdl/ *a.* du milieu; (*quality*) moyen. —*n.* milieu *m.* **in the** ~ **of,** au milieu de. ~**aged** *a.* d'un certain âge. **M**~ **Ages,** moyen âge *m.* ~ **class,** classe moyenne *f.* ~**class** *a.* bourgeois. **M**~ **East,** Proche-Orient *m.* **middleman** /'mɪdlmæn/ *n.* (*pl.* -**men**) intermédiaire *m.*

middling /'mɪdlɪŋ/ *a.* moyen.

midge /mɪdʒ/ *n.* moucheron *m.*

midget /'mɪdʒɪt/ *n.* nain(e) *m.* (*f.*). —*a.* minuscule.

Midlands /'mɪdləndz/ *n. pl.* région du centre de l'Angleterre *f.*

midnight /'mɪdnaɪt/ *n.* minuit *f.*

midriff /'mɪdrɪf/ *n.* ventre *m.*

midst /mɪdst/ *n.* **in the** ~ **of,** au milieu de. **in our** ~, parmi nous.

midsummer /mɪd'sʌmə(r)/ *n.* milieu de l'été *m.*; (*solstice*) solstice d'été *m.*

midway /mɪd'weɪ/ *adv.* à mi-chemin.

midwife /'mɪdwaɪf/ *n.* (*pl.* -**wives**) sage-femme *f.*

midwinter /mɪd'wɪntə(r)/ *n.* milieu de l'hiver *m.*

might[1] /maɪt/ *n.* puissance *f.* ~**y** *a.* puissant; (*very great*: *fam.*) très grand; *adv.* (*fam.*) rudement.

might[2] /maɪt/ *see* **may.**

migraine /'miːgreɪn, *Amer.* 'maɪgreɪn/ *n.* migraine *f.*

migrant /'maɪgrənt/ *a.* & *n.* (*bird*) migrateur (*m.*); (*worker*) migrant(e) (*m.* (*f.*)).

migrat|e /maɪ'greɪt/ *v.i.* émigrer. ~**ion** /-ʃn/ *n.* migration *f.*

mike /maɪk/ *n.* (*fam.*) micro *m.*

mild /maɪld/ *a.* (-er, -est) doux; (*illness*) bénin. ~**ly** *adv.* doucement. ~**ness** *n.* douceur *f.*

mildew /'mɪldjuː/ *n.* moisissure *f.*

mile /maɪl/ *n.* mille *m.* (= *1.6 km.*). ~**s too big**/*etc.*, (*fam.*) beaucoup trop grand/*etc.* ~**age** *n.* (*loosely*) kilométrage *m.*

milestone /'maɪlstəʊn/ *n.* borne *f.*; (*event, stage*: *fig.*) jalon *m.*

militant /'mɪlɪtənt/ *a.* & *n.* militant(e) (*m.* (*f.*)).

military /'mɪlɪtrɪ/ *a.* militaire.

militate /'mɪlɪteɪt/ *v.i.* militer.

militia /mɪ'lɪʃə/ *n.* milice *f.*

milk /mɪlk/ *n.* lait *m.* —*a.* (*product*) laitier. —*v.t.* (*cow etc.*) traire; (*fig.*) exploiter. ~ **shake,** milk-shake *m.* ~**y** *a.* (*diet*) lacté; (*colour*) laiteux; (*tea etc.*) au lait. **M**~**y Way,** Voie lactée *f.*

milkman /'mɪlkmən, *Amer.* 'mɪlkmæn/ *n.* (*pl.* -**men**) laitier *m.*

mill /mɪl/ *n.* moulin *m.*; (*factory*) usine *f.* —*v.t.* moudre. —*v.i.* ~ **around,** tourner en rond; (*crowd*) grouiller. ~**er** *n.* meunier *m.*

millennium /mɪ'lenɪəm/ *n.* (*pl.* -**ums**) millénaire *m.*

millet /'mɪlɪt/ *n.* millet *m.*

milli /'mɪlɪ/ *pref.* milli-.

millimetre /'mɪlɪmiːtə(r)/ *n.* millimètre *m.*

milliner /'mɪlɪnə(r)/ *n.* modiste *f.*

million /'mɪljən/ *n.* million *m.* **a** ~ **pounds,** un million de livres. ~**aire** /-'neə(r)/ *n.* millionnaire *m.*

millstone /'mɪlstəʊn/ *n.* meule *f.*; (*burden*: *fig.*) boulet *m.*

mime /maɪm/ *n.* (*actor*) mime *m.*/*f.*; (*art*) (art du) mime *m.* —*v.t.*/*i.* mimer.

mimic /'mɪmɪk/ *v.t.* (*p.t.* **mimicked**) imiter. —*n.* imita|teur, -trice *m.*, *f.* ~**ry** *n.* imitation *f.*

minaret /mɪnə'ret/ *n.* minaret *m.*

mince /mɪns/ *v.t.* hacher. —*n.* viande hachée *f.* ~ **pie,** tarte aux fruits confits *f.* **not to** ~ **matters,** ne pas mâcher ses mots. **~r** /-ə(r)/ *n.* (*machine*) hachoir *m.*

mincemeat /'mɪnsmiːt/ *n.* hachis de fruits confits *m.* **make ~ of,** anéantir, pulvériser.

mind /maɪnd/ *n.* esprit *m.*; (*sanity*) raison *f.*; (*opinion*) avis *m.* —*v.t.* (*have charge of*) s'occuper de; (*heed*) faire attention à. **be on s.o.'s ~,** préoccuper qn. **I do not ~ the noise**/*etc.*, le bruit/*etc.* ne me dérange pas. **I do not ~,** ça m'est égal. **~ful** *a.* attentif (**of,** à). **~less** *a.* irréfléchi.

minder /'maɪndə(r)/ *n.* gardien(ne) *m.* (*f.*).

mine[1] /maɪn/ *poss. pron.* le mien, la mienne, les mien(ne)s. **it is ~,** c'est à moi *or* le mien.

min|e[2] /maɪn/ *n.* mine *f.* —*v.t.* extraire; (*mil.*) miner. **~er** *n.* mineur *m.* **~ing** *n.* exploitation minière *f.*; *a.* minier.

minefield /'maɪnfiːld/ *n.* champ de mines *m.*

mineral /'mɪnərəl/ *n.* & *a.* minéral (*m.*). **~ (water),** (*fizzy soft drink*) boisson gazeuse *f.* **~ water,** (*natural*) eau minérale *f.*

minesweeper /'maɪnswiːpə(r)/ *n.* (*ship*) dragueur de mines *m.*

mingle /'mɪŋgl/ *v.t./i.* (se) mêler (**with,** à).

mingy /'mɪndʒɪ/ *a.* (*fam.*) radin.

mini /'mɪnɪ/ *pref.* mini-.

miniature /'mɪnɪtʃə(r)/ *a.* & *n.* miniature (*f.*).

minibus /'mɪnɪbʌs/ *n.* minibus *m.*

minicab /'mɪnɪkæb/ *n.* taxi *m.*

minim /'mɪnɪm/ *n.* blanche *f.*

minim|um /'mɪnɪməm/ *a.* & *n.* (*pl.* -ima) minimum (*m.*). **~al** *a.* minimal. **~ize** *v.t.* minimiser.

minist|er /'mɪnɪstə(r)/ *n.* ministre *m.* **~erial** /-'stɪərɪəl/ *a.* ministériel. **~ry** *n.* ministère *m.*

mink /mɪŋk/ *n.* vison *m.*

minor /'maɪnə(r)/ *a.* petit, mineur. —*n.* (*jurid.*) mineur(e) *m.* (*f.*).

minority /maɪ'nɒrətɪ/ *n.* minorité *f.* —*a.* minoritaire.

minster /'mɪnstə(r)/ *n.* église abbatiale *f.*

minstrel /'mɪnstrəl/ *n.* ménestrel *m.*, jongleu|r, -se *m.*, *f.*

mint[1] /mɪnt/ *n.* **the M~,** l'Hôtel de la Monnaie *m.* **a ~,** une fortune. —*v.t.* frapper. **in ~ condition,** à l'état neuf.

mint[2] /mɪnt/ *n.* (*plant*) menthe *f.*; (*sweet*) pastille de menthe *f.*

minus /'maɪnəs/ *prep.* moins; (*without*: *fam.*) sans. —*n.* (*sign*) moins *m.* **~ sign,** moins *m.*

minute[1] /'mɪnɪt/ *n.* minute *f.* **~s,** (*of meeting*) procès-verbal *m.*

minute[2] /maɪ'njuːt/ *a.* (*tiny*) minuscule; (*detailed*) minutieux.

mirac|le /'mɪrəkl/ *n.* miracle *m.* **~ulous** /mɪ'rækjʊləs/ *a.* miraculeux.

mirage /'mɪrɑːʒ/ *n.* mirage *m.*

mire /maɪə(r)/ *n.* fange *f.*

mirror /'mɪrə(r)/ *n.* miroir *m.*, glace *f.* —*v.t.* refléter.

mirth /mɜːθ/ *n.* gaieté *f.*

misadventure /mɪsəd'ventʃə(r)/ *n.* mésaventure *f.*

misanthropist /mɪs'ænθrəpɪst/ *n.* misanthrope *m.*/*f.*

misapprehension /mɪsæprɪ'henʃn/ *n.* malentendu *m.*

misbehav|e /mɪsbɪ'heɪv/ *v.i.* se conduire mal. **~iour** *n.* mauvaise conduite *f.*

miscalculat|e /mɪs'kælkjʊleɪt/ *v.t.* mal calculer. —*v.i.* se tromper. **~ion** /-'leɪʃn/ *n.* erreur de calcul *f.*

miscarr|y /mɪs'kærɪ/ *v.i.* faire une fausse couche. **~iage** /-ɪdʒ/ *n.* fausse couche *f.* **~iage of justice,** erreur judiciaire *f.*

miscellaneous /mɪsə'leɪnɪəs/ *a.* divers.

mischief /'mɪstʃɪf/ *n.* (*foolish conduct*) espièglerie *f.*; (*harm*) mal *m.* **get into ~,** faire des sottises.

mischievous /'mɪstʃɪvəs/ *a.* espiègle; (*malicious*) méchant.

misconception /mɪskən'sepʃn/ *n.* idée fausse *f.*

misconduct /mɪs'kɒndʌkt/ *n.* mauvaise conduite *f.*

misconstrue /mɪskən'struː/ *v.t.* mal interpréter.

misdeed /mɪs'diːd/ *n.* méfait *m.*

misdemeanour /mɪsdɪ'miːnə(r)/ *n.* (*jurid.*) délit *m.*

misdirect /mɪsdɪ'rekt/ *v.t.* (*person*) mal renseigner.

miser /'maɪzə(r)/ *n.* avare *m.*/*f.* **~ly** *a.* avare.

miserable /'mɪzrəbl/ *a.* (*sad*) malheureux; (*wretched*) misérable; (*unpleasant*) affreux.

misery /'mɪzərɪ/ *n.* (*unhappiness*) malheur *m.*; (*pain*) souffrances *f. pl.*;

misfire | 398 | **model**

(*poverty*) misère *f.*; (*person*: *fam.*) grincheu|x, -se *m.*, *f.*

misfire /mɪsˈfaɪə(r)/ *v.i.* (*plan etc.*) rater; (*engine*) avoir des ratés.

misfit /ˈmɪsfɪt/ *n.* inadapté(e) *m.* (*f.*).

misfortune /mɪsˈfɔːtʃuːn/ *n.* malheur *m.*

misgiving /mɪsˈgɪvɪŋ/ *n.* (*doubt*) doute *m.*; (*apprehension*) crainte *f.*

misguided /mɪsˈgaɪdɪd/ *a.* (*foolish*) imprudent; (*mistaken*) erroné. **be ~,** (*person*) se tromper.

mishap /ˈmɪshæp/ *n.* mésaventure *f.*, contretemps *m.*

misinform /mɪsɪnˈfɔːm/ *v.t.* mal renseigner.

misinterpret /mɪsɪnˈtɜːprɪt/ *v.t.* mal interpréter.

misjudge /mɪsˈdʒʌdʒ/ *v.t.* mal juger.

mislay /mɪsˈleɪ/ *v.t.* (*p.t.* **mislaid**) égarer.

mislead /mɪsˈliːd/ *v.t.* (*p.t.* **misled**) tromper. **~ing** *a.* trompeur.

mismanage /mɪsˈmænɪdʒ/ *v.t.* mal gérer. **~ment** *n.* mauvaise gestion *f.*

misnomer /mɪsˈnəʊmə(r)/ *n.* terme impropre *m.*

misplace /mɪsˈpleɪs/ *v.t.* mal placer; (*lose*) égarer.

misprint /ˈmɪsprɪnt/ *n.* faute d'impression *f.*, coquille *f.*

misrepresent /mɪsreprɪˈzent/ *v.t.* présenter sous un faux jour.

miss¹ /mɪs/ *v.t./i.* manquer; (*deceased person etc.*) regretter. **he ~es her/Paris**/*etc.*, elle/Paris/ *etc.* lui manque. **I ~ you,** tu me manques. —*n.* coup manqué *m.* **it was a near ~,** on l'a échappé belle *or* de peu. **~ out,** omettre.

miss² /mɪs/ *n.* (*pl.* **misses**) mademoiselle *f.* (*pl.* mesdemoiselles). **M~ Smith,** Mademoiselle *or* Mlle Smith.

misshapen /mɪsˈʃeɪpən/ *a.* difforme.

missile /ˈmɪsaɪl/ *n.* (*mil.*) missile *m.*; (*object thrown*) projectile *m.*

missing /ˈmɪsɪŋ/ *a.* (*after disaster*) disparu. **be ~,** (*not present, lost*) manquer.

mission /ˈmɪʃn/ *n.* mission *f.*

missionary /ˈmɪʃənrɪ/ *n.* missionnaire *m.*/*f.*

missive /ˈmɪsɪv/ *n.* missive *f.*

misspell /mɪsˈspel/ *v.t.* (*p.t.* **misspelt** *or* **misspelled**) mal écrire.

mist /mɪst/ *n.* brume *f.*; (*on window*) buée *f.* —*v.t./i.* (s')embuer.

mistake /mɪˈsteɪk/ *n.* erreur *f.*, faute *f.* —*v.t.* (*p.t.* **mistook**, *p.p.* **mistaken**) mal comprendre; (*choose wrongly*) se tromper de. **~ for,** prendre pour. **~n** /-ən/ *a.* erroné. **be ~n,** se tromper. **~nly** /-ənlɪ/ *adv.* par erreur.

mistletoe /ˈmɪsltəʊ/ *n.* gui *m.*

mistreat /mɪsˈtriːt/ *v.t.* maltraiter.

mistress /ˈmɪstrɪs/ *n.* maîtresse *f.*

mistrust /mɪsˈtrʌst/ *v.t.* se méfier de. —*n.* méfiance *f.*

misty /ˈmɪstɪ/ *a.* (-ier, -iest) brumeux; (*window*) embué.

misunderstand /mɪsʌndəˈstænd/ *v.t.* (*p.t.* **-stood**) mal comprendre. **~ing** *n.* malentendu *m.*

misuse¹ /mɪsˈjuːz/ *v.t.* mal employer; (*power etc.*) abuser de.

misuse² /mɪsˈjuːs/ *n.* mauvais emploi *m.*; (*unfair use*) abus *m.*

mite /maɪt/ *n.* (*child*) pauvre petit(e) *m.* (*f.*).

mitigate /ˈmɪtɪgeɪt/ *v.t.* atténuer.

mitten /ˈmɪtn/ *n.* moufle *f.*

mix /mɪks/ *v.t./i.* (se) mélanger. —*n.* mélange *m.* **~ up,** mélanger; (*bewilder*) embrouiller; (*mistake, confuse*) confondre (**with,** avec). **~-up** *n.* confusion *f.* **~ with,** (*people*) fréquenter. **~er** *n.* (*culin.*) mélangeur *m.* **be a good ~er,** être sociable.

mixed /mɪkst/ *a.* (*school etc.*) mixte; (*assorted*) assorti. **be ~up,** (*fam.*) avoir des problèmes.

mixture /ˈmɪkstʃə(r)/ *n.* mélange *m.*; (*for cough*) sirop *m.*

moan /ˈməʊn/ *n.* gémissement *m.* —*v.i.* gémir; (*complain*) grogner. **~er** *n.* (*grumbler*) grognon *m.*

moat /məʊt/ *n.* douve(s) *f.* (*pl.*).

mob /mɒb/ *n.* (*crowd*) cohue *f.*; (*gang*: *sl.*) bande *f.* —*v.t.* (*p.t.* **mobbed**) assiéger.

mobil|e /ˈməʊbaɪl/ *a.* mobile. **~e home,** caravane *f.* —*n.* mobile *m.* **~ity** /-ˈbɪlətɪ/ *n.* mobilité *f.*

mobiliz|e /ˈməʊbɪlaɪz/ *v.t./i.* mobiliser. **~ation** /-ˈzeɪʃn/ *n.* mobilisation *f.*

moccasin /ˈmɒkəsɪn/ *n.* mocassin *m.*

mocha /ˈməʊkə/ *n.* moka *m.*

mock /mɒk/ *v.t./i.* se moquer (de). —*a.* faux. **~-up** *n.* maquette *f.*

mockery /ˈmɒkərɪ/ *n.* moquerie *f.* **a ~ of,** une parodie de.

mode /məʊd/ *n.* (*way, method*) mode *m.*; (*fashion*) mode *f.*

model /ˈmɒdl/ *n.* modèle *m.*; (*of toy*) modèle réduit *m.*; (*artist's*) modèle

m.; (*for fashion*) mannequin *m.* —
a. modèle; (*car etc.*) modèle réduit
invar. —*v.t.* (*p.t.* **modelled**) modeler;
(*clothes*) présenter. —*v.i.* être mannequin; (*pose*) poser. ∼**ling** *n.* métier
de mannequin *m.*

moderate[1] /'mɒdərət/ *a.* & *n.* mo-
déré(e) (*m.* (*f.*)). ∼**ly** *adv.* (*in moderation*) modérément; (*fairly*) moyenne-
ment.

moderat|e[2] /'mɒdəreɪt/ *v.t./i.* (se) mo-
dérer. ∼**ion** /-'reɪʃn/ *n.* modération *f.*
in ∼**ion**, avec modération.

modern /'mɒdn/ *a.* moderne. ∼ **languages**, langues vivantes *f. pl.*
∼**ize** *v.t.* moderniser.

modest /'mɒdɪst/ *a.* modeste. ∼**y** *n.*
modestie *f.*

modicum /'mɒdɪkəm/ *n.* **a** ∼ **of**, un
peu de.

modif|y /'mɒdɪfaɪ/ *v.t.* modifier.
∼**ication** /-ɪ'keɪʃn/ *n.* modification *f.*

modulat|e /'mɒdjʊleɪt/ *v.t./i.* moduler.
∼**ion** /-'leɪʃn/ *n.* modulation *f.*

module /'mɒdjuːl/ *n.* module *m.*

mohair /'məʊheə(r)/ *n.* mohair *m.*

moist /mɔɪst/ *a.* (**-er, -est**) humide,
moite. ∼**ure** /'mɔɪstʃə(r)/ *n.* humidité *f.*

moisten /'mɔɪsn/ *v.t.* humecter.

molar /'məʊlə(r)/ *n.* molaire *f.*

molasses /mə'læsɪz/ *n.* mélasse *f.*

mold /məʊld/ *n.* (*Amer.*) = **mould.**

mole[1] /məʊl/ *n.* grain de beauté *m.*

mole[2] /məʊl/ *n.* (*animal*) taupe *f.*

molecule /'mɒlɪkjuːl/ *n.* molécule *f.*

molest /mə'lest/ *v.t.* (*pester*) impor-
tuner; (*ill-treat*) molester.

mollusc /'mɒləsk/ *n.* mollusque *m.*

mollycoddle /'mɒlɪkɒdl/ *v.t.* dorloter,
chouchouter.

molten /'məʊltən/ *a.* en fusion.

mom /mɒm/ *n.* (*Amer.*) maman *f.*

moment /'məʊmənt/ *n.* moment *m.*

momentar|y /'məʊməntrɪ, *Amer.*-terɪ/
a. momentané. ∼**ily** /*Amer.* məʊmən'-
terəlɪ/ *adv.* momentanément; (*soon:
Amer.*) très bientôt.

momentous /mə'mentəs/ *a.* important.

momentum /mə'mentəm/ *n.* élan *m.*

Monaco /'mɒnəkəʊ/ *n.* Monaco *f.*

monarch /'mɒnək/ *n.* monarque *m.*
∼**y** *n.* monarchie *f.*

monast|ery /'mɒnəstrɪ/ *n.* monastère
m. ∼**ic** /mə'næstɪk/ *a.* monastique.

Monday /'mʌndɪ/ *n.* lundi *m.*

monetarist /'mʌnɪtərɪst/ *n.* moné-
tariste *m.*/*f.*

monetary /'mʌnɪtrɪ/ *a.* monétaire.

money /'mʌnɪ/ *n.* argent *m.* ∼**s,**
sommes d'argent *f. pl.* ∼**-box** *n.* tire-
lire *f.* ∼**-lender** *n.* prêteu|r, -se *m.*, *f.*
∼ **order**, mandat *m.* ∼**-spinner** *n.*
mine d'or *f.*

mongol /'mɒŋgl/ *n.* & *a.* (*med.*) mon-
golien(ne) (*m.* (*f.*)).

mongrel /'mʌŋgrəl/ *n.* (chien) bâtard
m.

monitor /'mɒnɪtə(r)/ *n.* (*pupil*) chef de
classe *m.*; (*techn.*) moniteur *m.* —*v.t.*
contrôler; (*a broadcast*) écouter.

monk /mʌŋk/ *n.* moine *m.*

monkey /'mʌŋkɪ/ *n.* singe *m.* ∼**-nut**
n. cacahuète *f.* ∼**-wrench** *n.* clef à
molette *f.*

mono /'mɒnəʊ/ *n.* (*pl.* **-os**) mono *f.*
—*a.* mono *invar.*

monocle /'mɒnəkl/ *n.* monocle *m.*

monogram /'mɒnəgræm/ *n.* monogramme *m.*

monologue /'mɒnəlɒg/ *n.* monologue
m.

monopol|y /mə'nɒpəlɪ/ *n.* monopole
m. ∼**ize** *v.t.* monopoliser.

monosyllab|le /'mɒnəsɪləbl/ *n.* mono-
syllabe *m.* ∼**ic** /-'læbɪk/ *a.* monosylla-
bique.

monotone /'mɒnətəʊn/ *n.* ton uniforme *m.*

monoton|ous /mə'nɒtənəs/ *a.* mono-
tone. ∼**y** *n.* monotonie *f.*

monsoon /mɒn'suːn/ *n.* mousson *f.*

monst|er /'mɒnstə(r)/ *n.* monstre *m.*
∼**rous** *a.* monstrueux.

monstrosity /mɒn'strɒsətɪ/ *n.* mons-
truosité *f.*

month /mʌnθ/ *n.* mois *m.*

monthly /'mʌnθlɪ/ *a.* mensuel. —*adv.*
mensuellement. —*n.* (*periodical*)
mensuel *m.*

monument /'mɒnjʊmənt/ *n.* monument *m.* ∼**al** /-'mentl/ *a.* monumental.

moo /muː/ *n.* meuglement *m.* —*v.i.*
meugler.

mooch /muːtʃ/ *v.i.* (*sl.*) flâner. —*v.t.*
(*Amer., sl.*) se procurer.

mood /muːd/ *n.* humeur *f.* **in a good/
bad** ∼, de bonne/mauvaise humeur.
∼**y** *a.* d'humeur changeante; (*sullen*)
maussade.

moon /muːn/ *n.* lune *f.*

moon|light /'muːnlaɪt/ *n.* clair de lune
m. ∼**lit** *a.* éclairé par la lune.

moonlighting /'muːnlaɪtɪŋ/ *n.* (*fam.*) travail noir *m.*

moor[1] /mʊə(r)/ *n.* lande *f.*

moor[2] /mʊə(r)/ *v.t.* amarrer. **~ings** *n. pl.* (*chains etc.*) amarres *f. pl.*; (*place*) mouillage *m.*

moose /muːs/ *n. invar.* élan *m.*

moot /muːt/ *a.* discutable. —*v.t.* (*question*) soulever.

mop /mɒp/ *n.* balai à franges *m.* —*v.t.* (*p.t.* **mopped**). **~** (**up**), éponger. **~ of** hair, tignasse *f.*

mope /məʊp/ *v.i.* se morfondre.

moped /'məʊped/ *n.* cyclomoteur *m.*

moral /'mɒrəl/ *a.* moral. —*n.* morale *f.* **~s**, moralité *f.* **~ize** *v.i.* moraliser. **~ly** *adv.* moralement.

morale /mə'rɑːl/ *n.* moral *m.*

morality /mə'rælətɪ/ *n.* moralité *f.*

morass /mə'ræs/ *n.* marais *m.*

morbid /'mɔːbɪd/ *a.* morbide.

more /mɔː(r)/ *a.* (*a greater amount of*) plus de (**than**, que). —*n. & adv.* plus (**than**, que). (**some**) **~** tea/ pens/ etc., (*additional*) encore du thé/des stylos/*etc.* **no ~ bread**/ *etc.*, plus de pain/*etc.* **I want no ~, I do not want any ~**, je n'en veux plus. **~ or less**, plus ou moins.

moreover /mɔː'rəʊvə(r)/ *adv.* de plus, en outre.

morgue /mɔːɡ/ *n.* morgue *f.*

moribund /'mɒrɪbʌnd/ *a.* moribond.

morning /'mɔːnɪŋ/ *n.* matin *m.*; (*whole morning*) matinée *f.*

Morocc|o /mə'rɒkəʊ/ *n.* Maroc *m.* **~an** *a. & n.* marocain(e) (*m.* (*f.*)).

moron /'mɔːrɒn/ *n.* crétin(e) *m.* (*f.*).

morose /mə'rəʊs/ *a.* morose.

morphine /'mɔːfiːn/ *n.* morphine *f.*

Morse /mɔːs/ *n.* **~** (**code**), morse *m.*

morsel /'mɔːsl/ *n.* petit morceau *m.*; (*of food*) bouchée *f.*

mortal /'mɔːtl/ *a. & n.* mortel(le) (*m.* (*f.*)). **~ity** /mɔː'tælətɪ/ *n.* mortalité *f.*

mortar /'mɔːtə(r)/ *n.* mortier *m.*

mortgage /'mɔːɡɪdʒ/ *n.* prêt hypothécaire *m.*, emprunt-logement *m.* —*v.t.* hypothéquer.

mortify /'mɔːtɪfaɪ/ *v.t.* mortifier.

mortuary /'mɔːtʃərɪ/ *n.* morgue *f.*

mosaic /məʊ'zeɪɪk/ *n.* mosaïque *f.*

Moscow /'mɒskəʊ/ *n.* Moscou *m.*/*f.*

Moses /'məʊzɪz/ *a.* **~ basket**, couffin *m.*

mosque /mɒsk/ *n.* mosquée *f.*

mosquito /mə'skiːtəʊ/ *n.* (*pl.* **-oes**) moustique *m.*

moss /mɒs/ *n.* mousse *f.* **~y** *a.* moussu.

most /məʊst/ *a.* (*the greatest amount of*) le plus de; (*the majority of*) la plupart de. —*n.* le plus. —*adv.* (le) plus; (*very*) fort. **~ of**, la plus grande partie de; (*majority*) la plupart de. **at ~**, tout au plus. **for the ~ part**, pour la plupart. **make the ~ of**, profiter de. **~ly** *adv.* surtout.

motel /məʊ'tel/ *n.* motel *m.*

moth /mɒθ/ *n.* papillon de nuit *m.*; (*in cloth*) mite *f.* **~-ball** *n.* boule de naphtaline *f.* **~-eaten** *a.* mité.

mother /'mʌðə(r)/ *n.* mère *f.* —*v.t.* entourer de soins maternels, materner. **~hood** *n.* maternité *f.* **~-in-law** *n.* (*pl.* **~s-in-law**) belle-mère *f.* **~-of-pearl** *n.* nacre *f.* **M~'s Day**, la fête des mères. **~-to-be** *n.* future maman *f.* **~ tongue**, langue maternelle *f.*

motherly /'mʌðəlɪ/ *a.* maternel.

motif /məʊ'tiːf/ *n.* motif *m.*

motion /'məʊʃn/ *n.* mouvement *m.*; (*proposal*) motion *f.* —*v.t.*/*i.* **~** (**to**) s.o. to, faire signe à qn. de. **~less** *a.* immobile.

motivat|e /'məʊtɪveɪt/ *v.t.* motiver. **~ion** /-'veɪʃn/ *n.* motivation *f.*

motive /'məʊtɪv/ *n.* motif *m.*

motley /'mɒtlɪ/ *a.* bigarré.

motor /'məʊtə(r)/ *n.* moteur *m.*; (*car*) auto *f.* —*a.* (*anat.*) moteur; (*boat*) à moteur. —*v.i.* aller en auto. **~ bike**, (*fam.*) moto *f.* **~ car**, auto *f.* **~ cycle**, motocyclette *f.* **~-cyclist** *n.* motocycliste *m.*/*f.* **~ing** *n.* (*sport*) l'automobile *f.* **~ized** *a.* motorisé. **~ vehicle**, véhicule automobile *m.*

motorist /'məʊtərɪst/ *n.* automobiliste *m.*/*f.*

motorway /'məʊtəweɪ/ *n.* autoroute *f.*

mottled /'mɒtld/ *a.* tacheté.

motto /'mɒtəʊ/ *n.* (*pl.* **-oes**) devise *f.*

mould[1] /məʊld/ *n.* moule *m.* —*v.t.* mouler; (*influence*) former. **~ing** *n.* (*on wall etc.*) moulure *f.*

mould[2] /məʊld/ *n.* (*fungus, rot*) moisissure *f.* **~y** *a.* moisi.

moult /məʊlt/ *v.i.* muer.

mound /maʊnd/ *n.* monticule *m.*, tertre *m.*; (*pile: fig.*) tas *m.*

mount[1] /maʊnt/ *n.* (*hill*) mont *m.*

mount[2] /maʊnt/ *v.t.*/*i.* monter. —*n.* monture *f.* **~ up**, s'accumuler; (*add up*) chiffrer (**to**, à).

mountain /'maʊntɪn/ *n.* montagne *f.* **~ous** *a.* montagneux.

mountaineer /maʊntɪ'nɪə(r)/ n. alpiniste m./f. ~ing n. alpinisme m.

mourn /mɔːn/ v.t./i. ~ (for), pleurer. ~er n. personne qui suit le cortège funèbre f. ~ing n. deuil m.

mournful /'mɔːnfl/ a. triste.

mouse /maʊs/ n. (pl. **mice**) souris f.

mousetrap /'maʊstræp/ n. souricière f.

mousse /muːs/ n. (dish) mousse f.

moustache /mə'staːʃ, Amer. 'mʌstæʃ/ n. moustache f.

mousy /'maʊsɪ/ a. (hair) d'un brun terne; (fig.) timide.

mouth[1] /maʊθ/ n. bouche f.; (of dog, cat, etc.) gueule f. ~-organ n. harmonica m.

mouth[2] /maʊð/ v.t. dire.

mouthful /'maʊθfʊl/ n. bouchée f.

mouthpiece /'maʊθpiːs/ n. (mus.) embouchure f.; (person: fig.) porte-parole m. invar.

mouthwash /'maʊθwɒʃ/ n. eau dentifrice f.

movable /'muːvəbl/ a. mobile.

move /muːv/ v.t./i. remuer, (se) déplacer, bouger; (incite) pousser; (emotionally) émouvoir; (propose) proposer; (depart) partir; (act) agir. ~ (out), déménager. —n. mouvement m.; (in game) coup m.; (player's turn) tour m.; (procedure: fig.) démarche f.; (house change) déménagement m. ~ back, (faire) reculer. ~ forward or on, (faire) avancer. ~ in, emménager. ~ over, se pousser. on the ~, en marche.

movement /'muːvmənt/ n. mouvement m.

movie /'muːvɪ/ n. (Amer.) film m. the ~s, le cinéma.

moving /'muːvɪŋ/ a. en mouvement; (touching) émouvant.

mow /məʊ/ v.t. (p.p. **mowed** or **mown**) (corn etc.) faucher; (lawn) tondre. ~ down, faucher. ~er n. (for lawn) tondeuse f.

MP abbr. see **Member of Parliament**.

Mr /'mɪstə(r)/ n. (pl. **Messrs**). ~ Smith, Monsieur or M. Smith.

Mrs /'mɪsɪz/ n. (pl. **Mrs**). ~ Smith, Madame or Mme Smith. the ~ Smith, Mesdames or Mmes Smith.

Ms /mɪz/ n. (title of married or unmarried woman). ~ Smith, Madame or Mme Smith.

much /mʌtʃ/ a. beaucoup de. —adv. & n. beaucoup.

muck /mʌk/ n. fumier m.; (dirt: fam.) saleté f. —v.i. ~ about, (sl.) s'amuser. ~ about with, (sl.) tripoter. ~ in, (sl.) participer. —v.t. ~ up, (sl.) gâcher. ~y a. sale.

mucus /'mjuːkəs/ n. mucus m.

mud /mʌd/ n. boue f. ~dy a. couvert de boue.

muddle /'mʌdl/ v.t. embrouiller. —v.i. ~ through, se débrouiller. —n. désordre m., confusion f.; (mixup) confusion f.

mudguard /'mʌdgaːd/ n. garde-boue m. invar.

muff /mʌf/ n. manchon m.

muffin /'mʌfɪn/ n. muffin m. (petit pain rond et plat).

muffle /'mʌfl/ v.t. emmitoufler; (sound) assourdir. ~r /-ə(r)/ n. (scarf) cache-nez m. invar.

mug /mʌg/ n. tasse f.; (in plastic, metal) gobelet m.; (for beer) chope f.; (face: sl.) gueule f.; (fool: sl.) idiot(e) m. (f.) —v.t. (p.t. **mugged**) agresser. ~ger n. agresseur m. ~ging n. agression f.

muggy /'mʌgɪ/ a. lourd.

Muhammadan /mə'hæmɪdən/ a. & n. mahométan(e) (m.(f.)).

mule /mjuːl/ n. (male) mulet m.; (female) mule f.

mull[1] /mʌl/ v.t. (wine) chauffer.

mull[2] /mʌl/ v.t. ~ over, ruminer.

multi /'mʌltɪ/ pref. multi-.

multicoloured /'mʌltɪkʌləd/ a. multicolore.

multifarious /mʌltɪ'feərɪəs/ a. divers.

multinational /mʌltɪ'næʃnəl/ a. & n. multinational(e) (f.).

multiple /'mʌltɪpl/ a. & n. multiple (m.).

multipl|y /'mʌltɪplaɪ/ v.t./i. (se) multiplier. ~ication /-ɪ'keɪʃn/ n. multiplication f.

multitude /'mʌltɪtjuːd/ n. multitude f.

mum[1] /mʌm/ a. **keep ~**, (fam.) garder le silence.

mum[2] /mʌm/ n. (fam.) maman f.

mumble /'mʌmbl/ v.t./i. marmotter, marmonner.

mummy[1] /'mʌmɪ/ n. (embalmed body) momie f.

mummy[2] /'mʌmɪ/ n. (mother: fam.) maman f.

mumps /mʌmps/ n. oreillons m. pl.

munch /mʌntʃ/ v.t./i. mastiquer.

mundane /mʌnˈdeɪn/ *a.* banal.

municipal /mjuːˈnɪsɪpl/ *a.* municipal. **~ity** /-ˈpælətɪ/ *n.* municipalité *f.*

munitions /mjuːˈnɪʃnz/ *n. pl.* munitions *f. pl.*

mural /ˈmjʊərəl/ *a.* mural. —*n.* peinture murale *f.*

murder /ˈmɜːdə(r)/ *n.* meurtre *m.* —*v.t.* assassiner; (*ruin: fam.*) massacrer. **~er** *n.* meurtrier *m.*, assassin *m.* **~ess** *n.* meurtrière *f.* **~ous** *a.* meurtrier.

murky /ˈmɜːkɪ/ *a.* (-**ier**, -**iest**) (*night, plans, etc.*) sombre, ténébreux; (*liquid*) épais, sale.

murmur /ˈmɜːmə(r)/ *n.* murmure *m.* —*v.t./i.* murmurer.

muscle /ˈmʌsl/ *n.* muscle *m.* —*v.i.* **~ in,** (*Amer., sl.*) s'introduire de force (**on,** dans).

muscular /ˈmʌskjʊlə(r)/ *a.* musculaire; (*brawny*) musclé.

muse /mjuːz/ *v.i.* méditer.

museum /mjuːˈzɪəm/ *n.* musée *m.*

mush /mʌʃ/ *n.* (*pulp, soft food*) bouillie *f.* **~y** *a.* mou.

mushroom /ˈmʌʃrʊm/ *n.* champignon *m.* —*v.i.* pousser comme des champignons.

music /ˈmjuːzɪk/ *n.* musique *f.* **~al** *a.* musical; (*instrument*) de musique; (*talented*) doué pour la musique; *n.* comédie musicale *f.*

musician /mjuːˈzɪʃn/ *n.* musicien(ne) *m.* (*f.*).

musk /mʌsk/ *n.* musc *m.*

Muslim /ˈmʊzlɪm/ *a.* & *n.* musulman(e) (*m.* (*f.*)).

muslin /ˈmʌzlɪn/ *n.* mousseline *f.*

mussel /ˈmʌsl/ *n.* moule *f.*

must /mʌst/ *v. aux.* devoir. **you ~ go,** vous devez partir, il faut que vous partiez. **he ~ be old,** il doit être vieux. **I ~ have done it,** j'ai dû le faire. —*n.* **be a ~,** (*fam.*) être obligatoire.

mustard /ˈmʌstəd/ *n.* moutarde *f.*

muster /ˈmʌstə(r)/ *v.t./i.* (se) rassembler.

musty /ˈmʌstɪ/ *a.* (-**ier**, -**iest**) (*room, etc.*) qui sent le moisi; (*smell, taste*) de moisi.

mutation /mjuːˈteɪʃn/ *n.* mutation *f.*

mute /mjuːt/ *a.* & *n.* muet(te) (*m.* (*f.*)). **~d** /-ɪd/ *a.* (*colour, sound*) sourd, atténué; (*criticism*) voilé.

mutilat|e /ˈmjuːtɪleɪt/ *v.t.* mutiler. **~ion** /-ˈleɪʃn/ *n.* mutilation *f.*

mutin|y /ˈmjuːtɪnɪ/ *n.* mutinerie *f.* —*v.i.* se mutiner. **~ous** *a.* (*sailor etc.*) mutiné; (*fig.*) rebelle.

mutter /ˈmʌtə(r)/ *v.t./i.* marmonner, murmurer.

mutton /ˈmʌtn/ *n.* mouton *m.*

mutual /ˈmjuːtʃʊəl/ *a.* mutuel; (*common to two or more: fam.*) commun. **~ly** *adv.* mutuellement.

muzzle /ˈmʌzl/ *n.* (*snout*) museau *m.*; (*device*) muselière *f.*; (*of gun*) gueule *f.* —*v.t.* museler.

my /maɪ/ *a.* mon, ma, *pl.* mes.

myopic /maɪˈɒpɪk/ *a.* myope.

myriad /ˈmɪrɪəd/ *n.* myriade *f.*

myself /maɪˈself/ *pron.* moi-même; (*reflexive*) me, m'*; (*after prep.*) moi.

mysterious /mɪˈstɪərɪəs/ *a.* mystérieux.

mystery /ˈmɪstərɪ/ *n.* mystère *m.*

mystic /ˈmɪstɪk/ *a.* & *n.* mystique (*m.*/*f.*). **~al** *a.* mystique. **~ism** /-sɪzəm/ *n.* mysticisme *m.*

mystif|y /ˈmɪstɪfaɪ/ *v.t.* laisser perplexe. **~ication** /-ɪˈkeɪʃn/ *n.* perplexité *f.*

mystique /mɪˈstiːk/ *n.* mystique *f.*

myth /mɪθ/ *n.* mythe *m.* **~ical** *a.* mythique.

mythology /mɪˈθɒlədʒɪ/ *n.* mythologie *f.*

N

nab /næb/ v.t. (p.t. **nabbed**) (arrest: sl.) épingler, attraper.

nag /næg/ v.t./i. (p.t. **nagged**) critiquer; (pester) harceler.

nagging /'nægɪŋ/ a. persistant.

nail /neɪl/ n. clou m.; (of finger, toe) ongle m. —v.t. clouer. ~ polish, vernis à ongles m. on the ~, (pay) sans tarder, tout de suite.

naïve /naɪ'iːv/ a. naïf.

naked /'neɪkɪd/ a. nu. to the ~ eye, à l'œil nu. ~ly adv. à nu. ~ness n. nudité f.

name /neɪm/ n. nom m.; (fig.) réputation f. —v.t. nommer; (fix) fixer. be ~d after, porter le nom de. ~less a. sans nom, anonyme.

namely /'neɪmlɪ/ adv. à savoir.

namesake /'neɪmseɪk/ n. (person) homonyme m.

nanny /'nænɪ/ n. bonne d'enfants f. ~-goat n. chèvre f.

nap /næp/ n. somme m. —v.i. (p.t. **napped**) faire un somme. **catch** ~ping, prendre au dépourvu.

nape /neɪp/ n. nuque f.

napkin /'næpkɪn/ n. (at meals) serviette f.; (for baby) couche f.

nappy /'næpɪ/ n. couche f.

narcotic /naː'kɒtɪk/ a. & n. narcotique (m.).

narrat|e /nə'reɪt/ v.t. raconter. ~ion /-ʃn/ n. narration f. ~or n. narra|teur, -trice m., f.

narrative /'nærətɪv/ n. récit m.

narrow /'nærəʊ/ a. (-er, -est) étroit. —v.t./i. (se) rétrécir; (limit) (se) limiter. ~ly adv. étroitement; (just) de justesse. ~-minded a. à l'esprit étroit; (ideas etc.) étroit. ~ness n. étroitesse f.

nasal /'neɪzl/ a. nasal.

nast|y /'nɑːstɪ/ a. (-ier, -iest) mauvais, désagréable; (malicious) méchant. ~ily adv. désagréablement; méchamment. ~iness n. (malice) méchanceté f.

nation /'neɪʃn/ n. nation f. ~-wide a. dans l'ensemble du pays.

national /'næʃnəl/ a. national. —n. ressortissant(e) m. (f.). ~ **anthem**, hymne national m. ~**ism** n. nationa-

lisme m. ~**ize** v.t. nationaliser. ~ly adv. à l'échelle nationale.

nationality /næʃə'nælətɪ/ n. nationalité f.

native /'neɪtɪv/ n. (local inhabitant) autochtone m./f.; (non-European) indigène m./f. —a. indigène; (country) natal; (inborn) inné. be a ~ of, être originaire de. ~ **language**, langue maternelle f. ~ **speaker of French**, personne de langue maternelle française f.

Nativity /nə'tɪvətɪ/ n. the ~, la Nativité f.

natter /'nætə(r)/ v.i. bavarder.

natural /'nætʃrəl/ a. naturel. ~ **history**, histoire naturelle f. ~**ist** n. naturaliste m./f. ~**ly** adv. (normally, of course) naturellement; (by nature) de nature.

naturaliz|e /'nætʃrəlaɪz/ v.t. naturaliser. ~**ation** /-'zeɪʃn/ n. naturalisation f.

nature /'neɪtʃə(r)/ n. nature f.

naught /nɔːt/ n. (old use) rien m.

naught|y /'nɔːtɪ/ a. (-ier, -iest) vilain, méchant; (indecent) grivois. ~**ily** adv. mal.

nause|a /'nɔːsɪə/ n. nausée f. ~**ous** a. nauséabond.

nauseate /'nɔːsɪeɪt/ v.t. écœurer.

nautical /'nɔːtɪkl/ a. nautique.

naval /'neɪvl/ a. (battle etc.) naval; (officer) de marine.

nave /neɪv/ n. (of church) nef f.

navel /'neɪvl/ n. nombril m.

navigable /'nævɪɡəbl/ a. navigable.

navigat|e /'nævɪɡeɪt/ v.t. (sea etc.) naviguer sur; (ship) piloter. —v.i. naviguer. ~**ion** /-'ɡeɪʃn/ n. navigation f. ~**or** n. navigateur m.

navvy /'nævɪ/ n. terrassier m.

navy /'neɪvɪ/ n. marine f. ~ **(blue)**, bleu marine invar.

near /nɪə(r)/ adv. près. —prep. près de. —a. proche. —v.t. approcher de. **draw** ~, (s')approcher (to, de). ~**by** adv. tout près. **N~ East**, Proche-Orient m. ~ **to**, près de. ~**ness** n. proximité f.

nearby /nɪə'baɪ/ a. proche.

nearly /'nɪəlɪ/ adv. presque. **not** ~

as pretty/*etc.* **as,** loin d'être aussi joli/*etc.* que.

neat /niːt/ *a.* (**-er, -est**) soigné, net; (*room etc.*) bien rangé; (*clever*) habile; (*whisky, brandy, etc.*) sec. **~ly** *adv.* avec soin; habilement. **~ness** *n.* netteté *f.*

nebulous /'nebjʊləs/ *a.* nébuleux.

necessar|y /'nesəsərɪ/ *a.* nécessaire. **~ies** *n. pl.* nécessaire *m.* **~ily** *adv.* nécessairement.

necessitate /nɪ'sesɪteɪt/ *v.t.* nécessiter.

necessity /nɪ'sesətɪ/ *n.* nécessité *f.*; (*thing*) chose indispensable *f.*

neck /nek/ *n.* cou *m.*; (*of dress*) encolure *f.* **~ and neck,** à égalité.

necklace /'neklɪs/ *n.* collier *m.*

neckline /'neklaɪn/ *n.* encolure *f.*

necktie /'nektaɪ/ *n.* cravate *f.*

nectarine /'nektərɪn/ *n.* brugnon *m.*, nectarine *f.*

need /niːd/ *n.* besoin *m.* —*v.t.* avoir besoin de; (*demand*) demander. **you ~ not come,** vous n'êtes pas obligé de venir. **~less** *a.* inutile. **~lessly** *adv.* inutilement.

needle /'niːdl/ *n.* aiguille *f.* —*v.t.* (*annoy: fam.*) asticoter, agacer.

needlework /'niːdlwɜːk/ *n.* couture *f.*; (*object*) ouvrage (à l'aiguille) *m.*

needy /'niːdɪ/ *a.* (**-ier, -iest**) nécessiteux, indigent.

negation /nɪ'geɪʃn/ *n.* négation *f.*

negative /'negətɪv/ *a.* négatif. —*n.* (*of photograph*) négatif *m.*; (*word: gram.*) négation *f.* **in the ~,** (*answer*) par la négative; (*gram.*) à la forme négative. **~ly** *adv.* négativement.

neglect /nɪ'glekt/ *v.t.* négliger, laisser à l'abandon. —*n.* manque de soins *m.* (**state of**) **~,** abandon *m.* **~ to do,** négliger de faire. **~ful** *a.* négligent.

négligé /'neglɪʒeɪ/ *n.* négligé *m.*

negligen|t /'neglɪdʒənt/ *a.* négligent. **~ce** *n.* négligence *f.*

negligible /'neglɪdʒəbl/ *a.* négligeable.

negotiable /nɪ'gəʊʃəbl/ *a.* négociable.

negotiat|e /nɪ'gəʊʃɪeɪt/ *v.t./i.* négocier. **~ion** /-'eɪʃn/ *n.* négociation *f.* **~or** *n.* négocia|teur, -trice *m., f.*

Negr|o /'niːgrəʊ/ *n.* (*pl.* **-oes**) Noir *m.* —*a.* noir; (*art, music*) nègre. **~ess** *n.* Noire *f.*

neigh /neɪ/ *n.* hennissement *m.* —*v.i.* hennir.

neighbour /'neɪbə(r)/ *n.* voisin(e) *m.* (*f.*). **~hood** *n.* voisinage *m.*, quartier

m. in the ~hood of, aux alentours de. **~ing** *a.* voisin.

neighbourly /'neɪbəlɪ/ *a.* amical.

neither /'naɪðə(r)/ *a. & pron.* aucun(e) des deux, ni l'un(e) ni l'autre. —*adv.* ni. —*conj.* (ne) non plus. **~ big nor small,** ni grand ni petit. **~ shall I come,** je ne viendrai pas non plus.

neon /'niːɒn/ *n.* néon *m.* —*a.* (*lamp etc.*) au néon.

nephew /'nevjuː, *Amer.* 'nefjuː/ *n.* neveu *m.*

nerve /nɜːv/ *n.* nerf *m.*; (*courage*) courage *m.*; (*calm*) sang-froid *m.*; (*impudence: fam.*) culot *m.* **~s,** (*before exams etc.*) le trac *m.* **~racking** *a.* éprouvant.

nervous /'nɜːvəs/ *a.* nerveux. **be** *or* **feel ~,** (*afraid*) avoir peur. **~ly** *adv.* (*tensely*) nerveusement; (*timidly*) craintivement. **~ness** *n.* nervosité *f.*; (*fear*) crainte *f.*

nervy /'nɜːvɪ/ *a.* = **nervous**; (*Amer., fam.*) effronté.

nest /nest/ *n.* nid *m.* —*v.i.* nicher. **~egg** *n.* pécule *m.*

nestle /'nesl/ *v.i.* se blottir.

net[1] /net/ *n.* filet *m.* —*v.t.* (*p.t.* **netted**) prendre au filet. **~ting** *n.* (*nets*) filets *m. pl.*; (*wire*) treillis *m.*; (*fabric*) voile *m.*

net[2] /net/ *a.* (*weight etc.*) net.

netball /'netbɔːl/ *n.* netball *m.*

Netherlands /'neðələndz/ *n. pl.* **the ~,** les Pays-Bas *m. pl.*

nettle /'netl/ *n.* ortie *f.*

network /'netwɜːk/ *n.* réseau *m.*

neuro|sis /njʊə'rəʊsɪs/ *n.* (*pl.* **-oses** /-siːz/) névrose *f.* **~tic** /-'rɒtɪk/ *a. & n.* névrosé(e) (*m.* (*f.*)).

neuter /'njuːtə(r)/ *a. & n.* neutre (*m.*). —*v.t.* (*castrate*) châtrer.

neutral /'njuːtrəl/ *a.* neutre. **~ (gear),** (*auto.*) point mort *m.* **~ity** /-'trælətɪ/ *n.* neutralité *f.*

neutron /'njuːtrɒn/ *n.* neutron *m.* **~ bomb,** bombe à neutrons *f.*

never /'nevə(r)/ *adv.* (ne) jamais; (*not: fam.*) (ne) pas. **he ~ refuses,** il ne refuse jamais. **I ~ saw him,** (*fam.*) je ne l'ai pas vu. **~ again,** plus jamais. **~ mind,** (*don't worry*) ne vous en faites pas; (*it doesn't matter*) peu importe. **~ending** *a.* interminable.

nevertheless /nevəðə'les/ *adv.* néanmoins, toutefois.

new /njuː/ *a.* (**-er, -est**) nouveau; (*brand-new*) neuf. **~born** *a.*

nouveau-né. **~-laid egg**, œuf frais *m*.
~ moon, nouvelle lune *f*. **~ year**,
nouvel an *m*. **N~ Year's Day**, le jour
de l'an. **N~ Year's Eve**, la Saint-
Sylvestre. **N~ Zealand**, Nouvelle-
Zélande *f*. **N~ Zealander**, Néo-Zélan-
dais(e) *m*. (*f*.). **~ness** *n*. nouveauté *f*.

newcomer /'njuːkʌmə(r)/ *n*. nouveau
venu *m*., nouvelle venue *f*.

newfangled /njuːˈfæŋgld/ *a*. (*pej*.)
moderne, neuf.

newly /'njuːlɪ/ *adv*. nouvellement. **~-
weds** *n*. *pl*. nouveaux mariés *m*. *pl*.

news /njuːz/ *n*. nouvelle(s) *f*. (*pl*.);
(*radio*, *press*) informations *f*. *pl*.;
(*TV*) actualités *f*. *pl*., informations
f. *pl*. **~caster**, **~-reader** *ns*.
speaker(ine) *m*. (*f*.).

newsagent /'njuːzeɪdʒənt/ *n*. mar-
chand(e) de journaux *m*. (*f*.).

newsletter /'njuːzletə(r)/ *n*. bulletin
m.

newspaper /'njuːspeɪpə(r)/ *n*. journal
m.

newsreel /'njuːzriːl/ *n*. actualités *f*. *pl*.

newt /njuːt/ *n*. triton *m*.

next /nekst/ *a*. prochain; (*adjoining*)
voisin; (*following*) suivant. —*adv*.
la prochaine fois; (*afterwards*) ensuite. —*n*. suivant(e) *m*. (*f*.). **~ door**,
à côté (**to**, **de**). **~door** *a*. d'à côté. **~
of kin**, parent le plus proche *m*. **~
to**, à côté de.

nib /nɪb/ *n*. bec *m*., plume *f*.

nibble /'nɪbl/ *v.t./i*. grignoter.

nice /naɪs/ *a*. (**-er**, **-est**) agréable, bon;
(*kind*) gentil; (*pretty*) joli; (*respectable*)
bien *invar*.; (*subtle*) délicat. **~ly** *adv*.
agréablement; gentiment; (*well*) bien.

nicety /'naɪsətɪ/ *n*. subtilité *f*.

niche /nɪtʃ, niːʃ/ *n*. (*recess*) niche *f*.;
(*fig*.) place *f*., situation *f*.

nick /nɪk/ *n*. petite entaille *f*. —*v.t*.
(*steal*, *arrest*: *sl*.) piquer. **in the ~ of
time**, juste à temps.

nickel /'nɪkl/ *n*. nickel *m*.; (*Amer*.)
pièce de cinq cents *f*.

nickname /'nɪkneɪm/ *n*. surnom *m*.;
(*short form*) diminutif *m*. —*v.t*. surnommer.

nicotine /'nɪkətiːn/ *n*. nicotine *f*.

niece /niːs/ *n*. nièce *f*.

nifty /'nɪftɪ/ *a*. (*fam*.) chic *invar*.

Nigeria /naɪˈdʒɪərɪə/ *n*. Nigéria *m*./*f*.
~n *a*. & *n*. nigérian(e) (*m*. (*f*.)).

niggardly /'nɪgədlɪ/ *a*. chiche.

niggling /'nɪglɪŋ/ *a*. (*person*) tatillon;
(*detail*) insignifiant.

night /naɪt/ *n*. nuit *f*.; (*evening*) soir
m. —*a*. de nuit. **~-cap** *n*. boisson *f*.
(*avant d'aller se coucher*). **~-club** *n*.
boîte de nuit *f*. **~-dress**, **~-gown**
ns. chemise de nuit *f*. **~life** *n*. vie
nocturne *f*. **~-school** *n*. cours du soir
m. *pl*. **~-time** *n*. nuit *f*. **~-watchman**
n. veilleur de nuit *m*.

nightfall /'naɪtfɔːl/ *n*. tombée de la
nuit *f*.

nightingale /'naɪtɪŋgeɪl/ *n*. rossignol
m.

nightly /'naɪtlɪ/ *a*. & *adv*. (de) chaque
nuit *or* soir.

nightmare /'naɪtmeə(r)/ *n*. cauchemar
m.

nil /nɪl/ *n*. rien *m*.; (*sport*) zéro *m*.
—*a*. (*chances*, *risk*, *etc*.) nul.

nimble /'nɪmbl/ *a*. (**-er**, **-est**) agile.

nin|e /naɪn/ *a*. & *n*. neuf (*m*.). **~th** *a*.
& *n*. neuvième (*m*./*f*.).

nineteen /naɪnˈtiːn/ *a*. & *n*. dix-neuf
(*m*.). **~th** *a*. & *n*. dix-neuvième (*m*./*f*.).

ninet|y /'naɪntɪ/ *a*. & *n*. quatre-vingt-
dix (*m*.). **~ieth** *a*. & *n*. quatre-vingt-
dixième (*m*./*f*.).

nip /nɪp/ *v.t./i*. (*p.t*. **nipped**) (*pinch*)
pincer; (*rush*: *sl*.) courir. —*n*. pincement *m*.; (*cold*) fraîcheur *f*.

nipper /'nɪpə(r)/ *n*. (*sl*.) gosse *m*./*f*.

nipple /'nɪpl/ *n*. bout de sein *m*.; (*of
baby's bottle*) tétine *f*.

nippy /'nɪpɪ/ *a*. (**-ier**, **-iest**) (*fam*.)
alerte; (*chilly*: *fam*.) frais.

nitrogen /'naɪtrədʒən/ *n*. azote *m*.

nitwit /'nɪtwɪt/ *n*. (*fam*.) imbécile *m*./*f*.

no /nəʊ/ *a*. aucun(e); pas de. —*adv*.
non. —*n*. (*pl*. **noes**) non *m*. *invar*.
~ man/*etc*., aucun homme/*etc*. **~
money**/**time**/*etc*., pas d'argent/de
temps/*etc*. **~ man's land**, no
man's land *m*. **~ one = nobody**.
~ smoking/**entry**, défense de
fumer/d'entrer. **~ way!**, (*Amer*.,
fam.) pas question!

nob|le /'nəʊbl/ *a*. (**-er**, **-est**) noble.
~ility /-ˈbɪlətɪ/ *n*. noblesse *f*.

nobleman /'nəʊblmən/ *n*. (*pl*. **-men**)
noble *m*.

nobody /'nəʊbədɪ/ *pron*. (ne) personne. —*n*. nullité *f*. **he knows ~**, il
ne connaît personne. **~ is there**,
personne n'est là.

nocturnal /nɒkˈtɜːnl/ *a*. nocturne.

nod /nɒd/ *v.t./i*. (*p.t*. **nodded**). **~ (one's
head)**, faire un signe de tête. —*n*.
signe de tête *m*.

noise /nɔɪz/ *n.* bruit *m.* **~less** *a.* silencieux.

nois|y /'nɔɪzɪ/ *a.* (**-ier, -iest**) bruyant. **~ily** *adv.* bruyamment.

nomad /'nəʊmæd/ *n.* nomade *m./f.* **~ic** /-'mædɪk/ *a.* nomade.

nominal /'nɒmɪnl/ *a.* symbolique, nominal; (*value*) nominal.

nominat|e /'nɒmɪneɪt/ *v.t.* nommer; (*put forward*) proposer. **~ion** /-'neɪʃn/ *n.* nomination *f.*

non /nɒn/ *pref.* non-.

non-commissioned /nɒnkə'mɪʃnd/ *a.* **~ officer,** sous-officier *m.*

non-committal /nɒnkə'mɪtl/ *a.* évasif.

nondescript /'nɒndɪskrɪpt/ *a.* indéfinissable.

none /nʌn/ *pron.* aucun(e). **~ of us,** aucun de nous. **I have ~,** je n'en ai pas. **~ of,** pas une seule partie de. —*adv.* **~ too,** (ne) pas tellement. **he is ~ the happier,** il n'en est pas plus heureux.

nonentity /nɒ'nentətɪ/ *n.* nullité *f.*

non-existent /nɒnɪg'zɪstənt/ *a.* inexistant.

nonplussed /nɒn'plʌst/ *a.* perplexe, déconcerté.

nonsens|e /'nɒnsəns/ *n.* absurdités *f. pl.* **~ical** /-'sensɪkl/ *a.* absurde.

non-smoker /nɒn'sməʊkə(r)/ *n.* non-fumeur *m.*

non-stop /nɒn'stɒp/ *a.* (*train, flight*) direct. —*adv.* sans arrêt.

noodles /'nuːdlz/ *n. pl.* nouilles *f. pl.*

nook /nʊk/ *n.* (re)coin *m.*

noon /nuːn/ *n.* midi *m.*

noose /nuːs/ *n.* nœud coulant *m.*

nor /nɔː(r)/ *adv.* ni. —*conj.* (ne) non plus. **~ shall I come,** je ne viendrai pas non plus.

norm /nɔːm/ *n.* norme *f.*

normal /'nɔːml/ *a.* normal. **~ity** /nɔː'mælətɪ/ *n.* normalité *f.* **~ly** *adv.* normalement.

Norman /'nɔːmən/ *a. & n.* normand(e) (*m., f.*). **~dy** *n.* Normandie *f.*

north /nɔːθ/ *n.* nord *m.* —*a.* nord *invar.*, du nord. —*adv.* vers le nord. **N~ America,** Amérique du Nord *f.* **N~ American** *a. & n.* nord-américain(e) (*m. (f.)*). **~-east** *n.* nord-est *m.* **~erly** /'nɔːðəlɪ/ *a.* du nord. **~ward** *a.* au nord. **~wards** *adv.* vers le nord. **~-west** *n.* nord-ouest *m.*

northern /'nɔːðən/ *a.* du nord. **~er** *n.* habitant(e) du nord *m.* (*f.*).

Norw|ay /'nɔːweɪ/ *n.* Norvège *f.*

~egian /nɔː'wiːdʒən/ *a. & n.* norvégien(ne) (*m.* (*f.*)).

nose /nəʊz/ *n.* nez *m.* —*v.i.* **~ about,** fouiner.

nosebleed /'nəʊzbliːd/ *n.* saignement de nez *m.*

nosedive /'nəʊzdaɪv/ *n.* piqué *m.*

nostalg|ia /nɒ'stældʒə/ *n.* nostalgie *f.* **~ic** *a.* nostalgique.

nostril /'nɒstrəl/ *n.* narine *f.*; (*of horse*) naseau *m.*

nosy /'nəʊzɪ/ *a.* (**-ier, -iest**) (*fam.*) curieux, indiscret.

not /nɒt/ *adv.* (ne) pas. **I do ~ know,** je ne sais pas. **~ at all,** pas du tout. **~ yet,** pas encore. **I suppose ~,** je suppose que non.

notable /'nəʊtəbl/ *a.* notable. —*n.* (*person*) notable *m.*

notably /'nəʊtəblɪ/ *adv.* notamment.

notary /'nəʊtərɪ/ *n.* notaire *m.*

notation /nəʊ'teɪʃn/ *n.* notation *f.*

notch /nɒtʃ/ *n.* entaille *f.* —*v.t.* **~ up,** (*score etc.*) marquer.

note /nəʊt/ *n.* note *f.*; (*banknote*) billet *m.*; (*short letter*) mot *m.* —*v.t.* noter; (*notice*) remarquer.

notebook /'nəʊtbʊk/ *n.* carnet *m.*

noted /'nəʊtɪd/ *a.* éminent.

notepaper /'nəʊtpeɪpə(r)/ *n.* papier à lettres *m.*

noteworthy /'nəʊtwɜːðɪ/ *a.* remarquable.

nothing /'nʌθɪŋ/ *pron.* (ne) rien. —*n.* rien *m.*; (*person*) nullité *f.* —*adv.* nullement. **he eats ~,** il ne mange rien. **~ big**/*etc.*, rien de grand/*etc.* **~ else,** rien d'autre. **~ much,** pas grand-chose.

notice /'nəʊtɪs/ *n.* avis *m.*, annonce *f.*; (*poster*) affiche *f.* (**advance**) **~,** préavis *m.* **~ (of dismissal),** congé *m.* —*v.t.* remarquer, observer. **~-board** *n.* tableau d'affichage *m.* **take ~,** faire attention (**of,** à).

noticeabl|e /'nəʊtɪsəbl/ *a.* visible. **~y** *adv.* visiblement.

notif|y /'nəʊtɪfaɪ/ *v.t.* (*inform*) aviser; (*make known*) notifier. **~ication** /-ɪ'keɪʃn/ *n.* avis *m.*

notion /'nəʊʃn/ *n.* notion *f.*, **~s,** (*sewing goods etc.: Amer.*) mercerie *f.*

notor|ious /nəʊ'tɔːrɪəs/ *a.* (tristement) célèbre. **~iety** /-ə'raɪətɪ/ *n.* notoriété *f.* **~iously** *adv.* notoirement.

notwithstanding /nɒtwɪθ'stændɪŋ/ *prep.* malgré. —*adv.* néanmoins.

nougat /'nuːgaː/ *n.* nougat *m.*

nought /nɔ:t/ *n.* zéro *m.*

noun /naʊn/ *n.* nom *m.*

nourish /'nʌrɪʃ/ *v.t.* nourrir. **~ment** *n.* nourriture *f.*

novel /'nɒvl/ *n.* roman *m.* —*a.* nouveau. **~ist** *n.* romanc|ier, -ière *m.*, *f.* **~ty** *n.* nouveauté *f.*

November /nəʊ'vembə(r)/ *n.* novembre *m.*

novice /'nɒvɪs/ *n.* novice *m.|f.*

now /naʊ/ *adv.* maintenant. —*conj.* maintenant que. **just ~**, maintenant; (*a moment ago*) tout à l'heure. **~ and again**, **~ and then**, de temps à autre.

nowadays /'naʊədeɪz/ *adv.* de nos jours.

nowhere /'nəʊweə(r)/ *adv.* nulle part.

nozzle /'nɒzl/ *n.* (*tip*) embout *m.*; (*of hose*) lance *f.*

nuance /'nju:ɑ:ns/ *n.* nuance *f.*

nuclear /'nju:klɪə(r)/ *a.* nucléaire.

nucleus /'nju:klɪəs/ *n.* (*pl.* -**lei** /-lɪaɪ/) noyau *m.*

nud|e /nju:d/ *a.* nu. —*n.* nu *m.* **in the ~e**, tout nu. **~ity** *n.* nudité *f.*

nudge /nʌdʒ/ *v.t.* pousser du coude. —*n.* coup de coude *m.*

nudis|t /'nju:dɪst/ *n.* nudiste *m.|f.* **~m** /-zəm/ *n.* nudisme *m.*

nuisance /'nju:sns/ *n.* (*thing*, *event*) ennui *m.*; (*person*) peste *f.* **be a ~**, être ennuyeux.

null /nʌl/ *a.* nul. **~ify** *v.t.* infirmer.

numb /nʌm/ *a.* engourdi. —*v.t.* engourdir.

number /'nʌmbə(r)/ *n.* nombre *m.*; (*of ticket*, *house*, *page*, *etc.*) numéro *m.* —*v.t.* numéroter; (*count*, *include*) compter. **~-plate** *n.* plaque d'immatriculation *f.*

numerate /'nju:mərət/ *a.* qui a une bonne connaissance des mathématiques.

numeral /'nju:mərəl/ *n.* chiffre *m.*

numerical /nju:'merɪkl/ *a.* numérique.

numerous /'nju:mərəs/ *a.* nombreux.

nun /nʌn/ *n.* religieuse *f.*

nurs|e /nɜ:s/ *n.* infirmière *f.*, infirmier *m.*; (*nanny*) nurse *f.* —*v.t.* soigner; (*hope etc.*) nourrir. **~ing home**, clinique *f.*

nursemaid /'nɜ:smeɪd/ *n.* bonne d'enfants *f.*

nursery /'nɜ:sərɪ/ *n.* chambre d'enfants *f.*; (*for plants*) pépinière *f.* (**day**) **~**, crèche *f.* **~ rhyme**, chanson enfantine *f.*, comptine *f.* **~ school**, (école) maternelle *f.*

nurture /'nɜ:tʃə(r)/ *v.t.* élever.

nut /nʌt/ *n.* (*walnut*, *Brazil nut*, *etc.*) noix *f.*; (*hazelnut*) noisette *f.*; (*peanut*) cacahuète *f.*; (*techn.*) écrou *m.*; (*sl.*) idiot(e) *m.* (*f.*).

nutcrackers /'nʌtkrækəz/ *n. pl.* casse-noix *m. invar.*

nutmeg /'nʌtmeg/ *n.* muscade *f.*

nutrient /'nju:trɪənt/ *n.* substance nutritive *f.*

nutrit|ion /nju:'trɪʃn/ *n.* nutrition *f.* **~ious** *a.* nutritif.

nuts /nʌts/ *a.* (*crazy*: *sl.*) cinglé.

nutshell /'nʌtʃel/ *n.* coquille de noix *f.* **in a ~**, en un mot.

nylon /'naɪlɒn/ *n.* nylon *m.* **~s**, bas nylon *m. pl.*

O

oaf /əʊf/ *n.* (*pl.* **oafs**) lourdaud(e) *m.* (*f.*).

oak /əʊk/ *n.* chêne *m.*

OAP *abbr.* (*old-age pensioner*) retraité(e) *m.* (*f.*), personne âgée *f.*

oar /ɔː(r)/ *n.* aviron *m.*, rame *f.*

oasis /əʊ'eɪsɪs/ *n.* (*pl.* **oases** /-siːz/) oasis *f.*

oath /əʊθ/ *n.* (*promise*) serment *m.*; (*swear-word*) juron *m.*

oatmeal /'əʊtmiːl/ *n.* farine d'avoine *f.*, flocons d'avoine *m. pl.*

oats /əʊts/ *n. pl.* avoine *f.*

obedien|t /ə'biːdɪənt/ *a.* obéissant. ~**ce** *n.* obéissance *f.* ~**tly** *adv.* docilement, avec soumission.

obes|e /əʊ'biːs/ *a.* obèse. ~**ity** *n.* obésité *f.*

obey /ə'beɪ/ *v.t./i.* obéir (à).

obituary /ə'bɪtʃʊərɪ/ *n.* nécrologie *f.*

object[1] /'ɒbdʒɪkt/ *n.* (*thing*) objet *m.*; (*aim*) but *m.*, objet *m.*; (*gram.*) complément (d'objet) *m.* **money/** *etc.* **is no** ~, l'argent/*etc.* ne pose pas de problèmes.

object[2] /əb'dʒekt/ *v.i.* protester. —*v.t.* ~ **that**, objecter que. ~ **to**, désapprouver, protester contre. ~**ion** /-kʃn/ *n.* objection *f.*; (*drawback*) inconvénient *m.*

objectionable /əb'dʒekʃnəbl/ *a.* désagréable.

objectiv|e /əb'dʒektɪv/ *a.* objectif. —*n.* objectif *m.* ~**ity** /ɒbdʒek'tɪvətɪ/ *n.* objectivité *f.*

obligat|e /'ɒblɪgeɪt/ *v.t.* obliger. ~**ion** /-'geɪʃn/ *n.* obligation *f.* **under an** ~**ion to s.o.**, redevable à qn. (**for, de**).

obligatory /ə'blɪgətrɪ/ *a.* obligatoire.

oblig|e /ə'blaɪdʒ/ *v.t.* obliger. ~**e to do**, obliger à faire. ~**ed** *a.* obligé (**to, de**). ~**ed to s.o.**, redevable à qn. ~**ing** *a.* obligeant. ~**ingly** *adv.* obligeamment.

oblique /ə'bliːk/ *a.* oblique; (*reference etc.: fig.*) indirect.

obliterat|e /ə'blɪtəreɪt/ *v.t.* effacer. ~**ion** /-'reɪʃn/ *n.* effacement *m.*

oblivion /ə'blɪvɪən/ *n.* oubli *m.*

oblivious /ə'blɪvɪəs/ *a.* (*unaware*) inconscient (**to, of,** de).

oblong /'ɒblɒŋ/ *a.* oblong. —*n.* rectangle *m.*

obnoxious /əb'nɒkʃəs/ *a.* odieux.

oboe /'əʊbəʊ/ *n.* hautbois *m.*

obscen|e /əb'siːn/ *a.* obscène. ~**ity** /-enətɪ/ *n.* obscénité *f.*

obscur|e /əb'skjʊə(r)/ *a.* obscur. —*v.t.* obscurcir; (*conceal*) cacher. ~**ely** *adv.* obscurément. ~**ity** *n.* obscurité *f.*

obsequious /əb'siːkwɪəs/ *a.* obséquieux.

observan|t /əb'zɜːvənt/ *a.* observateur. ~**ce** *n.* observance *f.*

observatory /əb'zɜːvətrɪ/ *n.* observatoire *m.*

observ|e /əb'zɜːv/ *v.t.* observer; (*remark*) remarquer. ~**ation** /ɒbzə'veɪʃn/ *n.* observation *f.* ~**er** *n.* observa|teur, -trice *m.*, *f.*

obsess /əb'ses/ *v.t.* obséder. ~**ion** /-ʃn/ *n.* obsession *f.* ~**ive** *a.* obsédant; (*psych.*) obsessionnel.

obsolete /'ɒbsəliːt/ *a.* dépassé.

obstacle /'ɒbstəkl/ *n.* obstacle *m.*

obstetric|s /əb'stetrɪks/ *n.* obstétrique *f.* ~**ian** /ɒbstɪ'trɪʃn/ *n.* médecin accoucheur *m.*

obstina|te /'ɒbstɪnət/ *a.* obstiné. ~**cy** *n.* obstination *f.* ~**tely** *adv.* obstinément.

obstruct /əb'strʌkt/ *v.t.* (*block*) boucher; (*congest*) encombrer; (*hinder*) entraver. ~**ion** /-kʃn/ *n.* (*act*) obstruction *f.*; (*thing*) obstacle *m.*; (*traffic jam*) encombrement *m.*

obtain /əb'teɪn/ *v.t.* obtenir. —*v.i.* avoir cours. ~**able** *a.* disponible.

obtrusive /əb'truːsɪv/ *a.* importun; (*thing*) trop en évidence.

obtuse /əb'tjuːs/ *a.* obtus.

obviate /'ɒbvɪeɪt/ *v.t.* éviter.

obvious /'ɒbvɪəs/ *a.* évident, manifeste. ~**ly** *adv.* manifestement.

occasion /ə'keɪʒn/ *n.* occasion *f.*; (*big event*) événement *m.* —*v.t.* occasionner. **on** ~, à l'occasion.

occasional /ə'keɪʒənl/ *a.* fait, pris, *etc.* de temps en temps; (*visitor etc.*) qui vient de temps en temps. ~**ly** *adv.* de temps en temps. **very** ~**ly**, rarement.

occult /ɒ'kʌlt/ *a.* occulte.

occupation /ɒkjʊ'peɪʃn/ n. (*activity*, *occupying*) occupation f.; (*job*) métier m., profession f. ~**al** a. professionnel, du métier.

occup|y /'ɒkjʊpaɪ/ v.t. occuper. ~**ant**, ~**ier** ns. occupant(e) m. (f.).

occur /ə'kɜ:(r)/ v.i. (*p.t.* **occurred**) se produire; (*arise*) se présenter. ~ **to s.o.,** venir à l'esprit de qn.

occurrence /ə'kʌrəns/ n. événement m. **the** ~ **of,** l'existence de. **of frequent** ~, qui arrive souvent.

ocean /'əʊʃn/ n. océan m.

o'clock /ə'klɒk/ adv. **it is six** ~/ etc., il est six heures/etc.

octagon /'ɒktəgən/ n. octogone m.

octane /'ɒkteɪn/ n. octane m.

octave /'ɒktɪv/ n. octave f.

October /ɒk'təʊbə(r)/ n. octobre m.

octopus /'ɒktəpəs/ n. (*pl.* **-puses**) pieuvre f.

odd /ɒd/ a. (**-er, -est**) bizarre; (*number*) impair; (*left over*) qui reste; (*not of set*) dépareillé; (*occasional*) fait, pris, *etc.* de temps en temps. ~ **jobs,** menus travaux m. pl. **twenty** ~, vingt et quelques. ~**ity** n. bizarrerie f.; (*thing*) curiosité f. ~**ly** adv. bizarrement.

oddment /'ɒdmənt/ n. fin de série f.

odds /ɒdz/ n. pl. chances f. pl.; (*in betting*) cote f. **at** ~, en désaccord. **it makes no** ~, ça ne fait rien. ~ **and ends,** des petites choses.

ode /əʊd/ n. ode f.

odious /'əʊdɪəs/ a. odieux.

odour /'əʊdə(r)/ n. odeur f. ~**less** a. inodore.

of /ɒv, *unstressed* əv/ prep. de. ~ **the,** du, de la, *pl.* des. ~ **it,** ~ **them,** en. **a friend** ~ **mine,** un de mes amis. **six** ~ **them,** six d'entre eux. **the fifth** ~ **June**/ etc., le cinq juin/etc.

off /ɒf/ adv. parti, absent; (*switched off*) fermé, éteint; (*taken off*) enlevé, détaché; (*cancelled*) annulé; (*food*) mauvais. —prep. de; (*distant from*) éloigné de. **be** ~, (*leave*) partir. **be better** ~, (*in a better position, richer*) être mieux. **a day** ~, un jour de congé. **20%** ~, une réduction de 20%. **take sth.** ~, (*a surface*) prendre qch. sur. **on the** ~ **chance (that),** au cas où. ~ **colour,** (*ill*) patraque. ~ **color,** (*improper*: *Amer.*) scabreux. ~**-licence** n. débit de vins m. ~**-load** v.t. décharger. ~**-putting** a. (*fam.*) rebutant. ~**-stage** a. &

adv. dans les coulisses. ~**-white** a. blanc cassé *invar.*

offal /'ɒfl/ n. abats m. pl.

offence /ə'fens/ n. délit m. **give** ~ **to,** offenser. **take** ~, s'offenser (at, de).

offend /ə'fend/ v.t. offenser; (*fig.*) choquer. **be** ~**ed,** s'offenser (at, de). ~**er** n. délinquant(e) m. (f.).

offensive /ə'fensɪv/ a. offensant; (*disgusting*) dégoûtant; (*weapon*) offensif. —n. offensive f.

offer /'ɒfə(r)/ v.t. (*p.t.* **offered**) offrir. —n. offre f. **on** ~, en promotion. ~**ing** n. offrande f.

offhand /ɒf'hænd/ a. désinvolte. —adv. à l'improviste.

office /'ɒfɪs/ n. bureau m.; (*duty*) fonction f.; (*surgery*: *Amer.*) cabinet m. **good** ~**s,** bons offices m. pl. **in** ~, au pouvoir.

officer /'ɒfɪsə(r)/ n. (*army etc.*) officier m.; (*policeman*) agent m.

official /ə'fɪʃl/ a. officiel. —n. officiel m.; (*civil servant*) fonctionnaire m. f. ~**ly** adv. officiellement.

officiate /ə'fɪʃɪeɪt/ v.i. (*priest*) officier; (*president*) présider. ~ **as,** faire fonction de.

officious /ə'fɪʃəs/ a. trop zélé.

offing /'ɒfɪŋ/ n. **in the** ~, en perspective.

offset /'ɒfset/ v.t. (*p.t.* **-set,** *pres. p.* **-setting**) compenser.

offshoot /'ɒfʃuːt/ n. rejeton m.

offshore /ɒf'ʃɔː(r)/ a. côtier.

offside /ɒf'saɪd/ a. (*sport*) hors jeu *invar.*

offspring /'ɒfsprɪŋ/ n. *invar.* progéniture f.

often /'ɒfn/ adv. souvent. **how** ~?, combien de fois? **every so** ~, de temps en temps.

ogle /'əʊgl/ v.t. lorgner.

ogre /'əʊgə(r)/ n. ogre m.

oh /əʊ/ int. oh, ah.

oil /ɔɪl/ n. huile f.; (*petroleum*) pétrole m.; (*for heating*) mazout m. —v.t. graisser. ~**-painting** n. peinture à l'huile f. ~**-tanker** n. pétrolier m. ~**y** a. graisseux.

oilfield /'ɔɪlfiːld/ n. gisement pétrolifère m.

oilskins /'ɔɪlskɪnz/ n. pl. ciré m.

ointment /'ɔɪntmənt/ n. pommade f., onguent m.

OK /əʊ'keɪ/ a. & adv. (*fam.*) bien.

old /əʊld/ a. (**-er, -est**) vieux; (*person*) vieux, âgé; (*former*) ancien. **how** ~ **is**

he?, quel âge a-t-il? **he is eight years ~**, il a huit ans. **of ~**, jadis. **~ age**, vieillesse *f.* **~ boy**, ancien élève *m.*; (*fellow: fam.*) vieux *m.* **~er**, **~est**, (*son etc.*) aîné. **~-fashioned** *a.* démodé; (*person*) vieux jeu *invar.* **~ maid**, vieille fille *f.* **~ man**, vieillard *m.*, vieux *m.* **~-time** *a.* ancien. **~ woman**, vieille *f.*

olive /'ɒlɪv/ *n.* olive *f.* —*a.* olive *invar.* **~ oil**, huile d'olive *f.*

Olympic /ə'lɪmpɪk/ *a.* olympique. **~s** *n. pl.*, **~ Games**, Jeux olympiques *m. pl.*

omelette /'ɒmlɪt/ *n.* omelette *f.*

omen /'əʊmen/ *n.* augure *m.*

ominous /'ɒmɪnəs/ *a.* de mauvais augure; (*fig.*) menaçant.

omi|t /ə'mɪt/ *v.t.* (*p.t.* **omitted**) omettre. **~ssion** *n.* omission *f.*

omnipotent /ɒm'nɪpətənt/ *a.* omnipotent.

on /ɒn/ *prep.* sur. —*adv.* en avant; (*switched on*) allumé, ouvert; (*machine*) en marche; (*put on*) mis; (*happening*) en cours. **~ foot/time/etc.**, à pied/l'heure/*etc.* **~ doing**, en faisant. **~ Tuesday**, mardi. **~ Tuesdays**, le mardi. **walk/etc. ~**, continuer à marcher/*etc.* **be ~**, (*of film*) passer. **be ~ at**, (*fam.*) être après. **~ and off**, de temps en temps.

once /wʌns/ *adv.* une fois; (*formerly*) autrefois. —*conj.* une fois que. **all at ~**, tout à coup. **~-over** *n.* (*fam.*) coup d'œil rapide *m.*

oncoming /'ɒnkʌmɪŋ/ *a.* (*vehicle etc.*) qui approche.

one /wʌn/ *a. & n.* un(e) (*m.* (*f.*)). —*pron.* un(e) *m.* (*f.*); (*impersonal*) on. **~ (and only)**, seul (et unique). **a big/red/etc. ~**, un(e) grand(e)/ rouge/*etc.* **this/that ~**, celui-ci/-là, celle-ci/-là. **~ another**, l'un(e) l'autre. **~-eyed**, borgne. **~-off** *a.* (*fam.*), **~ of a kind**, (*Amer.*) unique, exceptionnel. **~sided** *a.* (*biased*) partial; (*unequal*) inégal. **~-way** *a.* (*street*) à sens unique; (*ticket*) simple.

oneself /wʌn'self/ *pron.* soi-même; (*reflexive*) se.

onion /'ʌnjən/ *n.* oignon *m.*

onlooker /'ɒnlʊkə(r)/ *n.* specta|teur, -trice *m.*, *f.*

only /'əʊnlɪ/ *a.* seul. **an ~ son/etc.**, un fils/*etc.* unique. —*adv. & conj.* seulement. **he ~ has six**, il n'en a que

six, il en a six seulement. **~ too**, extrêmement.

onset /'ɒnset/ *n.* début *m.*

onslaught /'ɒnslɔːt/ *n.* attaque *f.*

onus /'əʊnəs/ *n.* **the ~ is on me/ etc.**, c'est ma/*etc.* responsabilité (**to**, de).

onward(s) /'ɒnwəd(z)/ *adv.* en avant.

onyx /'ɒnɪks/ *n.* onyx *m.*

ooze /uːz/ *v.i.* suinter.

opal /'əʊpl/ *n.* opale *f.*

opaque /əʊ'peɪk/ *a.* opaque.

open /'əʊpən/ *a.* ouvert; (*view*) dégagé; (*free to all*) public; (*undisguised*) manifeste; (*question*) en attente. —*v.t./i.* (s')ouvrir; (*of shop, play*) ouvrir. **in the ~ air**, en plein air. **~-ended** *a.* sans limite (*de durée etc.*); (*system*) qui peut évoluer. **~-heart** *a.* (*surgery*) à cœur ouvert. **keep ~ house**, tenir table ouverte. **~ out or up**, (s')ouvrir. **~-plan** *a.* sans cloisons. **~ secret**, secret de Polichinelle *m.*

opener /'əʊpənə(r)/ *n.* ouvre-boîte(s) *m.*, ouvre-bouteille(s) *m.*

opening /'əʊpənɪŋ/ *n.* ouverture *f.*; (*job*) débouché *m.*, poste vacant *m.*

openly /'əʊpənlɪ/ *adv.* ouvertement.

opera /'ɒpərə/ *n.* opéra *m.* **~ glasses** *n. pl.* jumelles *f. pl.* **~tic** /ɒpə'rætɪk/ *a.* d'opéra.

operat|e /'ɒpəreɪt/ *v.t./i.* opérer; (*techn.*) (faire) fonctionner. **~e on**, (*med.*) opérer. **~ion** /-'reɪʃn/ *n.* opération *f.* **in ~ion**, en vigueur; (*techn.*) en service. **~or** *n.* opéra|teur, -trice *m.*, *f.*; (*telephonist*) standardiste *m.*/*f.*

operational /ɒpə'reɪʃənl/ *a.* opérationnel.

operative /'ɒpərətɪv/ *a.* (*med.*) opératoire; (*law etc.*) en vigueur.

operetta /ɒpə'retə/ *n.* opérette *f.*

opinion /ə'pɪnjən/ *n.* opinion *f.*, avis *m.* **~ated** *a.* dogmatique.

opium /'əʊpɪəm/ *n.* opium *m.*

opponent /ə'pəʊnənt/ *n.* adversaire *m.*/*f.*

opportune /'ɒpətjuːn/ *a.* opportun.

opportunist /ɒpə'tjuːnɪst/ *n.* opportuniste *m.*/*f.*

opportunity /ɒpə'tjuːnətɪ/ *n.* occasion *f.* (**to do**, de faire).

oppos|e /ə'pəʊz/ *v.t.* s'opposer à. **~ed to**, opposé à. **~ing** *a.* opposé.

opposite /'ɒpəzɪt/ *a.* opposé. —*n.* contraire *m.*, opposé *m.* —*adv.* en face.

—prep. ~ **(to)**, en face de. **one's** ~ **number,** son homologue *m.|f.*

opposition /ˌɒpə'zɪʃn/ *n.* opposition *f.*; (*mil.*) résistance *f.*

oppress /ə'pres/ *v.t.* opprimer. ~**ion** /-ʃn/ *n.* oppression *f.* ~**ive** *a.* (*cruel*) oppressif; (*heat*) oppressant. ~**or** *n.* oppresseur *m.*

opt /ɒpt/ *v.i.* ~ **for,** opter pour. ~ **out,** refuser de participer (**of,** à). ~ **to do,** choisir de faire.

optical /'ɒptɪkl/ *a.* optique. ~ **illusion,** illusion d'optique *f.*

optician /ɒp'tɪʃn/ *n.* opticien(ne) *m.* (*f.*).

optimis|t /'ɒptɪmɪst/ *n.* optimiste *m.|f.* ~**m** /-zəm/ *n.* optimisme *m.* ~**tic** /-'mɪstɪk/ *a.* optimiste. ~**tically** /-'mɪstɪklɪ/ *adv.* avec optimisme.

optimum /'ɒptɪməm/ *a.* & *n.* (*pl.* -ima) optimum (*m.*).

option /'ɒpʃn/ *n.* choix *m.*, option *f.*

optional /'ɒpʃənl/ *a.* facultatif.

opulen|t /'ɒpjʊlənt/ *a.* opulent. ~**ce** *n.* opulence *f.*

or /ɔː(r)/ *conj.* ou; (*with negative*) ni.

oracle /'ɒrəkl/ *n.* oracle *m.*

oral /'ɔːrəl/ *a.* oral. *—n.* (*examination*: *fam.*) oral *m.*

orange /'ɒrɪndʒ/ *n.* (*fruit*) orange *f.* *—a.* (*colour*) orange *invar.*

orangeade /ɒrɪndʒ'eɪd/ *n.* orangeade *f.*

orator /'ɒrətə(r)/ *n.* ora|teur, -trice *m.*, *f.* ~**y** /-trɪ/ *n.* rhétorique *f.*

oratorio /ɒrə'tɔːrɪəʊ/ *n.* (*pl.* -os) oratorio *m.*

orbit /'ɔːbɪt/ *n.* orbite *f.* *—v.t.* graviter autour de, orbiter.

orchard /'ɔːtʃəd/ *n.* verger *m.*

orchestra /'ɔːkɪstrə/ *n.* orchestre *m.* ~**l** /-'kestrəl/ *a.* orchestral.

orchestrate /'ɔːkɪstreɪt/ *v.t.* orchestrer.

orchid /'ɔːkɪd/ *n.* orchidée *f.*

ordain /ɔː'deɪn/ *v.t.* décréter (**that,** que); (*relig.*) ordonner.

ordeal /ɔː'diːl/ *n.* épreuve *f.*

order /'ɔːdə(r)/ *n.* ordre *m.*; (*comm.*) commande *f.* *—v.t.* ordonner; (*goods etc.*) commander. **in** ~, (*tidy*) en ordre; (*document*) en règle; (*fitting*) de règle. **in** ~ **that,** pour que. **in** ~ **to,** pour. ~ **s.o. to,** ordonner à qn. de.

orderly /'ɔːdəlɪ/ *a.* (*tidy*) ordonné; (*not unruly*) discipliné. *—n.* (*mil.*) planton *m.*; (*med.*) garçon de salle *m.*

ordinary /'ɔːdɪnrɪ/ *a.* (*usual*) ordinaire; (*average*) moyen.

ordination /ɔːdɪ'neɪʃn/ *n.* (*relig.*) ordination *f.*

ore /ɔː(r)/ *n.* minerai *m.*

organ /'ɔːgən/ *n.* organe *m.*; (*mus.*) orgue *m.* ~**ist** *n.* organiste *m.|f.*

organic /ɔː'gænɪk/ *a.* organique.

organism /'ɔːgənɪzəm/ *n.* organisme *m.*

organiz|e /'ɔːgənaɪz/ *v.t.* organiser. ~**ation** /-'zeɪʃn/ *n.* organisation *f.* ~**er** *n.* organisa|teur, -trice *m.*, *f.*

orgasm /'ɔːgæzəm/ *n.* orgasme *m.*

orgy /'ɔːdʒɪ/ *n.* orgie *f.*

Orient /'ɔːrɪənt/ *n.* **the** ~, l'Orient *m.* ~**al** /-'entl/ *n.* Oriental(e) *m.* (*f.*).

oriental /ɔːrɪ'entl/ *a.* oriental.

orient(at|e) /'ɔːrɪənt(eɪt)/ *v.t.* orienter. ~**ion** /-'teɪʃn/ *n.* orientation *f.*

orifice /'ɒrɪfɪs/ *n.* orifice *m.*

origin /'ɒrɪdʒɪn/ *n.* origine *f.*

original /ə'rɪdʒənl/ *a.* (*first*) originel; (*not copied*) original. ~**ity** /-'nælətɪ/ *n.* originalité *f.* ~**ly** *adv.* (*at the outset*) à l'origine; (*write etc.*) originalement.

originat|e /ə'rɪdʒɪneɪt/ *v.i.* prendre naissance. *—v.t.* être l'auteur de. ~**e from,** provenir de; (*person*) venir de. ~**or** *n.* auteur *m.*

ornament /'ɔːnəmənt/ *n.* (*decoration*) ornement *m.*; (*object*) objet décoratif *m.* ~**al** /-'mentl/ *a.* ornemental. ~**ation** /-en'teɪʃn/ *n.* ornementation *f.*

ornate /ɔː'neɪt/ *a.* richement orné.

ornithology /ɔːnɪ'θɒlədʒɪ/ *n.* ornithologie *f.*

orphan /'ɔːfn/ *n.* orphelin(e) *m.* (*f.*). *—v.t.* rendre orphelin. ~**age** *n.* orphelinat *m.*

orthodox /'ɔːθədɒks/ *a.* orthodoxe. ~**y** *n.* orthodoxie *f.*

orthopaedic /ɔːθə'piːdɪk/ *a.* orthopédique.

oscillate /'ɒsɪleɪt/ *v.i.* osciller.

ostensibl|e /ɒs'tensəbl/ *a.* apparent, prétendu. ~**y** *adv.* apparemment, prétendument.

ostentati|on /ɒsten'teɪʃn/ *n.* ostentation *f.* ~**ous** *a.* prétentieux.

osteopath /'ɒstɪəpæθ/ *n.* chiropracteur *m.*

ostracize /'ɒstrəsaɪz/ *v.t.* frapper d'ostracisme.

ostrich /'ɒstrɪtʃ/ *n.* autruche *f.*

other /'ʌðə(r)/ *a.* autre. *—n.* & *pron.* autre *m.|f.* *—adv.* ~ **than,** autrement que. **(some)** ⁓**s,** d'autres. **the** ⁓ **one,** l'autre *m.jf.*

otherwise /'ʌðəwaɪz/ *adv.* autrement.

otter /'ɒtə(r)/ *n.* loutre *f.*

ouch /aʊtʃ/ *int.* aïe!

ought /ɔːt/ *v. aux.* devoir. **you** ⁓ **to stay,** vous devriez rester. **he** ⁓ **to succeed,** il devrait réussir. **I** ⁓ **to have done it,** j'aurais dû le faire.

ounce /aʊns/ *n.* once *f.* (= *28.35 g.*).

our /'aʊə(r)/ *a.* notre, *pl.* nos.

ours /'aʊəz/ *poss. pron.* le *or* la nôtre, les nôtres.

ourselves /aʊə'selvz/ *pron.* nous-mêmes; (*reflexive & after prep.*) nous.

oust /aʊst/ *v.t.* évincer.

out /aʊt/ *adv.* dehors; (*gone out*) sorti; (*light*) éteint; (*in blossom*) épanoui; (*tide*) bas; (*secret*) révélé; (*sun*) levé. **be** ⁓, (*wrong*) se tromper. **be** ⁓ **to,** être résolu à. **run**/*etc.* ⁓, sortir en courant/ *etc.* ⁓**-and-out** *a.* absolu. ⁓ **of,** hors de; (*without*) sans, à court de. ⁓ **of pity**/*etc.,* par pitié/*etc.* **made** ⁓ **of,** fait en *or* de. **take** ⁓ **of,** prendre dans. **5** ⁓ **of 6,** 5 sur 6. ⁓ **of date,** démodé; (*not valid*) périmé. ⁓ **of doors,** dehors. ⁓ **of hand,** (*situation*) dont on n'est plus maître. ⁓ **of line,** (*impertinent*: *Amer.*) incorrect. ⁓ **of one's mind,** dément. ⁓ **of order,** (*broken*) en panne. ⁓ **of place,** (*object, remark*) déplacé. ⁓ **of the way,** écarté. ⁓**-patient** *n.* malade en consultation externe *m.jf.*

outbid /aʊt'bɪd/ *v.t.* (*p.t.* **-bid,** *pres. p.* **-bidding**) enchérir sur.

outboard /'aʊtbɔːd/ *a.* (*motor*) hors-bord *invar.*

outbreak /'aʊtbreɪk/ *n.* (*of war etc.*) début *m.*; (*of violence, boils*) éruption *f.*

outburst /'aʊtbɜːst/ *n.* explosion *f.*

outcast /'aʊtkɑːst/ *n.* paria *m.*

outcome /'aʊtkʌm/ *n.* résultat *m.*

outcry /'aʊtkraɪ/ *n.* tollé *m.*

outdated /aʊt'deɪtɪd/ *a.* démodé.

outdo /aʊt'duː/ *v.t.* (*p.t.* **-did,** *p.p.* **-done**) surpasser.

outdoor /'aʊtdɔː(r)/ *a.* de *or* en plein air. ⁓**s** /-'dɔːz/ *adv.* dehors.

outer /'aʊtə(r)/ *a.* extérieur. ⁓ **space,** espace (cosmique) *m.*

outfit /'aʊtfɪt/ *n.* (*articles*) équipement *m.*; (*clothes*) tenue *f.*; (*group*: *fam.*) équipe *f.* ⁓**ter** *n.* spécialiste de confection *m.jf.*

outgoing /'aʊtgəʊɪŋ/ *a.* (*minister, ten-*

ant) sortant; (*sociable*) ouvert. ⁓**s** *n. pl.* dépenses *f. pl.*

outgrow /aʊt'grəʊ/ *v.t.* (*p.t.* **-grew,** *p.p.* **-grown**) (*person*) grandir plus vite que; (*clothes*) devenir trop grand pour.

outhouse /'aʊthaʊs/ *n.* appentis *m.*; (*of mansion*) dépendance *f.*; (*Amer.*) cabinets extérieurs *m. pl.*

outing /'aʊtɪŋ/ *n.* sortie *f.*

outlandish /aʊt'lændɪʃ/ *a.* bizarre, étrange.

outlaw /'aʊtlɔː/ *n.* hors-la-loi *m. invar.* —*v.t.* proscrire.

outlay /'aʊtleɪ/ *n.* dépenses *f. pl.*

outlet /'aʊtlet/ *n.* (*for water, gases*) sortie *f.*; (*for goods*) débouché *m.*; (*for feelings*) exutoire *m.*

outline /'aʊtlaɪn/ *n.* contour *m.*; (*summary*) esquisse *f.* ⁓**s,** grandes lignes *f. pl.* —*v.t.* tracer le contour de; (*summarize*) exposer sommairement.

outlive /aʊt'lɪv/ *v.t.* survivre à.

outlook /'aʊtlʊk/ *n.* perspective *f.*

outlying /'aʊtlaɪŋ/ *a.* écarté.

outmoded /aʊt'məʊdɪd/ *a.* démodé.

outnumber /aʊt'nʌmbə(r)/ *v.t.* surpasser en nombre.

outpost /'aʊtpəʊst/ *n.* avant-poste *m.*

output /'aʊtpʊt/ *n.* rendement *m.*; (*of computer*) sortie *f.*

outrage /'aʊtreɪdʒ/ *n.* atrocité *f.*; (*scandal*) scandale *m.* —*v.t.* (*morals*) outrager; (*person*) scandaliser.

outrageous /aʊt'reɪdʒəs/ *a.* scandaleux, atroce.

outright /aʊt'raɪt/ *adv.* complètement; (*at once*) sur le coup; (*frankly*) carrément. —*a.* /'aʊtraɪt/ complet; (*refusal*) net.

outset /'aʊtset/ *n.* début *m.*

outside[1] /aʊt'saɪd/ *n.* extérieur *m.* —*adv.* (au) dehors. —*prep.* en dehors de; (*in front of*) devant.

outside[2] /'aʊtsaɪd/ *a.* extérieur.

outsider /aʊt'saɪdə(r)/ *n.* étrang|er, -ère *m., f.*; (*sport*) outsider *m.*

outsize /'aʊtsaɪz/ *a.* grande taille *invar.*

outskirts /'aʊtskɜːts/ *n. pl.* banlieue *f.*

outspoken /aʊt'spəʊkən/ *a.* franc.

outstanding /aʊt'stændɪŋ/ *a.* exceptionnel; (*not settled*) en suspens.

outstretched /əʊt'stretʃt/ *a.* (*arm*) tendu.

outstrip /aʊt'strɪp/ *v.t.* (*p.t.* **-stripped**) devancer, surpasser.

outward /'aʊtwəd/ *a. & adv.* vers l'extérieur; (*sign etc.*) extérieur; (*journey*)

d'aller. **~ly** *adv.* extérieurement. **~s**
adv. vers l'extérieur.

outweigh /aʊt'weɪ/ *v.t.* (*exceed in importance*) l'emporter sur.

outwit /aʊt'wɪt/ *v.t.* (*p.t.* **-witted**) duper, être plus malin que.

oval /'əʊvl/ *n. & a.* ovale (*m.*).

ovary /'əʊvərɪ/ *n.* ovaire *m.*

ovation /ə'veɪʃn/ *n.* ovation *f.*

oven /'ʌvn/ *n.* four *m.*

over /'əʊvə(r)/ *prep.* sur, au-dessus de; (*across*) de l'autre côté de; (*during*) pendant; (*more than*) plus de. —*adv.* (par-)dessus; (*ended*) fini; (*past*) passé; (*too*) trop; (*more*) plus. **jump**/*etc.* **~**, sauter/*etc.* par-dessus. **~ the radio,** à la radio. **ask ~**, inviter chez soi. **he has some ~**, il lui en reste. **all ~ (the table)**, partout (sur la table). **~ and over**, à maintes reprises. **~ here**, par ici. **~ there**, là-bas.

over /'əʊvə(r)/ *pref.* sur-, trop.

overall[1] /'əʊvərɔːl/ *n.* blouse *f.* **~s**, bleu(s) de travail *m.* (*pl.*).

overall[2] /əʊvər'ɔːl/ *a.* global, d'ensemble; (*length, width*) total. —*adv.* globalement.

overawe /əʊvər'ɔː/ *v.t.* intimider.

overbalance /əʊvə'bæləns/ *v.t./i.* (faire) basculer.

overbearing /əʊvə'beərɪŋ/ *a.* autoritaire.

overboard /'əʊvəbɔːd/ *adv.* par-dessus bord.

overbook /əʊvə'bʊk/ *v.t.* accepter trop de réservations pour.

overcast /'əʊvəkɑːst/ *a.* couvert.

overcharge /əʊvə'tʃɑːdʒ/ *v.t.* **~ s.o. (for)**, faire payer trop cher à qn.

overcoat /'əʊvəkəʊt/ *n.* pardessus *m.*

overcome /əʊvə'kʌm/ *v.t.* (*p.t.* **-came**, *p.p.* **-come**) triompher de; (*difficulty*) surmonter, triompher de. **~ by**, accablé de.

overcrowded /əʊvə'kraʊdɪd/ *a.* bondé; (*country*) surpeuplé.

overdo /əʊvə'duː/ *v.t.* (*p.t.* **-did**, *p.p.* **-done**) exagérer; (*culin.*) trop cuire. **~ it**, (*overwork*) se surmener.

overdose /'əʊvədəʊs/ *n.* dose excessive *f.*

overdraft /'əʊvədrɑːft/ *n.* découvert *m.*

overdraw /əʊvə'drɔː/ *v.t.* (*p.t.* **-drew**, *p.p.* **-drawn**) (*one's account*) mettre à découvert.

overdue /əʊvə'djuː/ *a.* en retard; (*belated*) tardif; (*bill*) impayé.

overestimate /əʊvər'estɪmeɪt/ *v.t.* surestimer.

overflow[1] /əʊvə'fləʊ/ *v.i.* déborder.

overflow[2] /'əʊvəfləʊ/ *n.* (*outlet*) trop-plein *m.*

overgrown /əʊvə'grəʊn/ *a.* (*garden etc.*) envahi par la végétation.

overhang /əʊvə'hæŋ/ *v.t.* (*p.t.* **-hung**) surplomber. —*v.i.* faire saillie.

overhaul[1] /əʊvə'hɔːl/ *v.t.* réviser.

overhaul[2] /'əʊvəhɔːl/ *n.* révision *f.*

overhead[1] /əʊvə'hed/ *adv.* au-dessus; (*in sky*) dans le ciel.

overhead[2] /'əʊvəhed/ *a.* aérien. **~s** *n. pl.* frais généraux *m. pl.*

overhear /əʊvə'hɪə(r)/ *v.t.* (*p.t.* **-heard**) surprendre, entendre.

overjoyed /əʊvə'dʒɔɪd/ *a.* ravi.

overland *a.* /'əʊvəlænd/, *adv.* /əʊvə'lænd/ par voie de terre.

overlap /əʊvə'læp/ *v.t./i.* (*p.t.* **-lapped**) (se) chevaucher.

overleaf /əʊvə'liːf/ *adv.* au verso.

overload /əʊvə'ləʊd/ *v.t.* surcharger.

overlook /əʊvə'lʊk/ *v.t.* oublier, négliger; (*of window, house*) donner sur; (*of tower*) dominer.

overly /'əʊvəlɪ/ *adv.* excessivement.

overnight /əʊvə'naɪt/ *adv.* (pendant) la nuit; (*instantly*: *fig.*) du jour au lendemain. —*a.* /'əʊvənaɪt/ (*train etc.*) de nuit; (*stay etc.*) d'une nuit; (*fig.*) soudain.

overpay /əʊvə'peɪ/ *v.t.* (*p.t.* **-paid**) (*person*) surpayer.

overpower /əʊvə'paʊə(r)/ *v.t.* subjuguer; (*opponent*) maîtriser; (*fig.*) accabler. **~ing** *a.* irrésistible; (*heat, smell*) accablant.

overpriced /əʊvə'praɪst/ *a.* trop cher.

overrate /əʊvə'reɪt/ *v.t.* surestimer. **~d** /-ɪd/ *a.* surfait.

overreact /əʊvərɪ'ækt/ *v.i.* réagir excessivement.

overreach /əʊvə'riːtʃ/ *v. pr.* **~ o.s.**, trop entreprendre.

overrid|e /əʊvə'raɪd/ *v.t.* (*p.t.* **-rode**, *p.p.* **-ridden**) passer outre à. **~ing** *a.* prépondérant; (*importance*) majeur.

overripe /'əʊvəraɪp/ *a.* trop mûr.

overrule /əʊvə'ruːl/ *v.t.* rejeter.

overrun /əʊvə'rʌn/ *v.t.* (*p.t.* **-ran**, *p.p.* **-run**, *pres. p.* **-running**) envahir; (*a limit*) aller au-delà de.

overseas /əʊvə'siːz/ *a.* d'outremer, étranger. —*adv.* outre-mer, à l'étranger.

oversee /əʊvə'siː/ v.t. (p.t. -**saw**, p.p. -**seen**) surveiller. ~**r** /'əʊvəsɪə(r)/ n. contremaître m.

overshadow /əʊvə'ʃædəʊ/ v.t. (darken) assombrir; (fig.) éclipser.

overshoot /əʊvə'ʃuːt/ v.t. (p.t. -**shot**) dépasser.

oversight /'əʊvəsaɪt/ n. omission f.

oversleep /əʊvə'sliːp/ v.i. (p.t. -**slept**) se réveiller trop tard.

overstep /əʊvə'step/ v.t. (p.t. -**stepped**) dépasser.

overt /'əʊvɜːt/ a. manifeste.

overtake /əʊvə'teɪk/ v.t./i. (p.t. -**took**, p.p. -**taken**) dépasser; (vehicle) doubler, dépasser; (surprise) surprendre.

overtax /əʊvə'tæks/ v.t. (strain) fatiguer; (taxpayer) surimposer.

overthrow /əʊvə'θrəʊ/ v.t. (p.t. -**threw**, p.p. -**thrown**) renverser.

overtime /'əʊvətaɪm/ n. heures supplémentaires f. pl.

overtone /'əʊvətəʊn/ n. nuance f.

overture /'əʊvətjʊə(r)/ n. ouverture f.

overturn /əʊvə'tɜːn/ v.t./i. (se) renverser.

overweight /əʊvə'weɪt/ a. be ~, peser trop, excéder le poids normal.

overwhelm /əʊvə'welm/ v.t. accabler; (defeat) écraser; (amaze) bouleverser. ~**ing** a. accablant; (victory) écrasant; (urge) irrésistible.

overwork /əʊvə'wɜːk/ v.t./i. (se) surmener. —n. surmenage m.

ow|e /əʊ/ v.t. devoir. ~**ing** a. dû. ~**ing to**, à cause de.

owl /aʊl/ n. hibou m.

own[1] /əʊn/ a. propre. a **house**/etc. of one's ~, sa propre maison/etc., une maison/etc. à soi. **get one's ~ back**, (fam.) prendre sa revanche. **hold one's ~**, bien se défendre. **on one's ~**, tout seul.

own[2] /əʊn/ v.t. posséder. ~ **up (to)**, (fam.) avouer. ~**er** n. propriétaire m./f. ~**ership** n. possession f. (of, de); (right) propriété f.

ox /ɒks/ n. (pl. **oxen**) bœuf m.

oxygen /'ɒksɪdʒən/ n. oxygène m.

oyster /'ɔɪstə(r)/ n. huître f.

P

pace /peɪs/ n. pas m. —v.t. (room etc.) arpenter. —v.i. ~ (**up and down**), faire les cent pas. **keep** ~ **with**, suivre.

Pacific /pə'sɪfɪk/ a. pacifique. —n. ~ (**Ocean**), Pacifique m.

pacifist /'pæsɪfɪst/ n. pacifiste m./f.

pacify /'pæsɪfaɪ/ v.t. (country) pacifier; (person) apaiser.

pack /pæk/ n. paquet m.; (mil.) sac m.; (of hounds) meute f.; (of thieves) bande f.; (of lies) tissu m. —v.t. emballer; (suitcase) faire; (box, room) remplir; (press down) tasser. —v.i. ~ (**one's bags**), faire ses valises. ~ **into**, (cram) (s')entasser dans. ~ **off**, expédier. **send** ~**ing**, envoyer promener. ~**ed** a. (crowded) bondé. ~**ed lunch**, repas froid m. ~**ing** n. (action, material) emballage m.

package /'pækɪdʒ/ n. paquet m. —v.t. empaqueter. ~ **deal**, marché global m., ensemble de propositions (à accepter) m. ~ **tour**, voyage organisé m.

packet /'pækɪt/ n. paquet m.

pact /pækt/ n. pacte m.

pad[1] /pæd/ n. bloc(-notes) m.; (for ink) tampon m. (**launching**) ~, rampe (de lancement) f. —v.t. (p.t. **padded**) rembourrer; (text: fig.) délayer. ~**ding** n. rembourrage m.; délayage m.

pad[2] /pæd/ v.i. (p.t. **padded**) (walk) marcher les pas feutrés.

paddle[1] /'pædl/ n. pagaie f. —v.t. ~ **a canoe**, pagayer. ~**-steamer** n. bateau à roues m.

paddle[2] /'pædl/ v.i. barboter, se mouiller les pieds.

paddock /'pædək/ n. paddock m.

paddy(-field) /'pædɪ(fiːld)/ n. rizière f.

padlock /'pædlɒk/ n. cadenas m. —v.t. cadenasser.

paediatrician /piːdɪə'trɪʃn/ n. pédiatre m./f.

pagan /'peɪɡən/ a. & n. païen(ne) (m. (f.)).

page[1] /peɪdʒ/ n. (of book etc.) page f.

page[2] /peɪdʒ/ n. (in hotel) chasseur m. —v.t. (faire) appeler.

pageant /'pædʒənt/ n. spectacle (historique) m. ~**ry** n. pompe f.

pagoda /pə'ɡəʊdə/ n. pagode f.

paid /peɪd/ see **pay**. —a. **put** ~ **to**, (fam.) mettre fin à.

pail /peɪl/ n. seau m.

pain /peɪn/ n. douleur f. ~**s**, efforts m. pl. —v.t. (grieve) peiner. **be in** ~, souffrir. **take** ~**s to**, se donner du mal pour. ~**-killer** n. analgésique m. ~**less** a. indolore.

painful /'peɪnfl/ a. douloureux; (laborious) pénible.

painstaking /'peɪnzteɪkɪŋ/ a. assidu, appliqué.

paint /peɪnt/ n. peinture f. ~**s**, (in tube, box) couleurs f. pl. —v.t./i. peindre. ~**er** n. peintre m. ~**ing** n. peinture f.

paintbrush /'peɪntbrʌʃ/ n. pinceau m.

pair /peə(r)/ n. paire f.; (of people) couple m. **a** ~ **of trousers**, un pantalon. —v.i. ~ **off**, (at dance etc.) former un couple.

pajamas /pə'dʒɑːməz/ n.pl. (Amer.) pyjama m.

Pakistan /pɑːkɪ'stɑːn/ n. Pakistan m. ~**i** a. & n. pakistanais(e) (m.(f.)).

pal /pæl/ n. (fam.) cop|ain, -ine m., f.

palace /'pælɪs/ n. palais m.

palat|e /'pælət/ n. (of mouth) palais m. ~**able** a. agréable au goût.

palatial /pə'leɪʃl/ a. somptueux.

palaver /pə'lɑːvə(r)/ n. (fuss: fam.) histoire(s) f. (pl.).

pale[1] /peɪl/ a. (-er, -est) pâle. —v.i. pâlir. ~**ness** n. pâleur f.

pale[2] /peɪl/ n. (stake) pieu m.

Palestin|e /'pælɪstaɪn/ n. Palestine f. ~**ian** /-'stɪnɪən/ a. & n. palestinien(ne) (m. (f.)).

palette /'pælɪt/ n. palette f.

pall /pɔːl/ v.i. devenir insipide.

pallid /'pælɪd/ a. pâle.

palm /pɑːm/ n. (of hand) paume f.; (tree) palmier m.; (symbol) palme f. —v.t. ~ **off**, (thing) refiler, coller (on, à); (person) coller. **P~ Sunday**, dimanche des Rameaux m.

palmist /'pɑːmɪst/ n. chiromancien(ne) m. (f.).

palpable /'pælpəbl/ a. manifeste.

palpitat|e /'pælpɪteɪt/ v.i. palpiter. ~**ion** /-'teɪʃn/ n. palpitation f.

paltry /'pɔːltrɪ/ *a.* (**-ier, -iest**) dérisoire, piètre.

pamper /'pæmpə(r)/ *v.t.* dorloter.

pamphlet /'pæmflɪt/ *n.* brochure *f.*

pan /pæn/ *n.* casserole *f.*; (*for frying*) poêle *f.*; (*of lavatory*) cuvette *f.* —*v.t.* (*p.t.* **panned**) (*fam.*) critiquer.

panacea /pænə'sɪə/ *n.* panacée *f.*

panache /pə'næʃ/ *n.* panache *m.*

pancake /'pænkeɪk/ *n.* crêpe *f.*

pancreas /'pæŋkrɪəs/ *n.* pancréas *m.*

panda /'pændə/ *n.* panda *m.* **~ car,** voiture pie (de la police) *f.*

pandemonium /pændɪ'məʊnɪəm/ *n.* tumulte *m.*, chaos *m.*

pander /'pændə(r)/ *v.i.* **~ to,** (*person, taste*) flatter bassement.

pane /peɪn/ *n.* carreau *m.*, vitre *f.*

panel /'pænl/ *n.* (*of door etc.*) panneau *m.*; (*jury*) jury *m.*; (*speakers: TV*) invités *m. pl.* (**instrument**) **~,** tableau de bord *m.* **~ of experts,** groupe d'experts *m.* **~led** *a.* lambrissé. **~ling** *n.* lambrissage *m.* **~list** *n.* (*TV*) invité(e) (de tribune) *m.* (*f.*).

pang /pæŋ/ *n.* pincement au cœur *m.* **~s,** (*of hunger, death*) affres *f. pl.* **~s of conscience,** remords *m.pl.*

panic /'pænɪk/ *n.* panique *f.* —*v.t./i.* (*p.t.* **panicked**) (s')affoler, paniquer. **~-stricken** *a.* pris de panique, affolé.

panorama /pænə'rɑːmə/ *n.* panorama *m.*

pansy /'pænzɪ/ *n.* (*bot.*) pensée *f.*

pant /pænt/ *v.i.* haleter.

panther /'pænθə(r)/ *n.* panthère *f.*

panties /'pæntɪz/ *n. pl.* (*fam.*) slip *m.*, culotte *f.* (*de femme*).

pantomime /'pæntəmaɪm/ *n.* (*show*) spectacle de Noël *m.*; (*mime*) pantomime *f.*

pantry /'pæntrɪ/ *n.* office *m.*

pants /pænts/ *n. pl.* (*underwear: fam.*) slip *m.*; (*trousers: fam. & Amer.*) pantalon *m.*

papacy /'peɪpəsɪ/ *n.* papauté *f.*

papal /'peɪpl/ *a.* papal.

paper /'peɪpə(r)/ *n.* papier *m.*; (*newspaper*) journal *m.*; (*exam*) épreuve *f.*; (*essay*) exposé *m.* —*v.t.* (*room*) tapisser. **on ~,** par écrit. **~-clip** *n.* trombone *m.*

paperback /'peɪpəbæk/ *a. & n.* **~** (**book**), livre broché *m.*

paperweight /'peɪpəweɪt/ *n.* presse-papiers *m. invar.*

paperwork /'peɪpəwɜːk/ *n.* paperasserie *f.*

paprika /'pæprɪkə/ *n.* paprika *m.*

par /pɑː(r)/ *n.* **be below ~,** ne pas être en forme. **on a ~ with,** à égalité avec.

parable /'pærəbl/ *n.* parabole *f.*

parachut|e /'pærəʃuːt/ *n.* parachute *m.* —*v.i.* descendre en parachute. **~ist** *n.* parachutiste *m./f.*

parade /pə'reɪd/ *n.* (*procession*) défilé *m.*; (*ceremony, display*) parade *f.*; (*street*) avenue *f.* —*v.i.* défiler. —*v.t.* faire parade de.

paradise /'pærədaɪs/ *n.* paradis *m.*

paradox /'pærədɒks/ *n.* paradoxe *m.* **~ical** /-'dɒksɪkl/ *a.* paradoxal.

paraffin /'pærəfɪn/ *n.* pétrole (lampant) *m.*; (*wax*) paraffine *f.*

paragon /'pærəgən/ *n.* modèle *m.*

paragraph /'pærəgrɑːf/ *n.* paragraphe *m.*

parallel /'pærəlel/ *a.* parallèle. —*n.* (*line*) parallèle *f.*; (*comparison & geog.*) parallèle *m.* —*v.t.* (*p.t.* **paralleled**) être semblable à.

paralyse /'pærəlaɪz/ *v.t.* paralyser.

paraly|sis /pə'ræləsɪs/ *n.* paralysie *f.* **~tic** /pærə'lɪtɪk/ *a. & n.* paralytique (*m./f.*).

parameter /pə'ræmɪtə(r)/ *n.* paramètre *m.*

paramount /'pærəmaʊnt/ *a.* primordial, fondamental.

paranoia /pærə'nɔɪə/ *n.* paranoïa *f.*

parapet /'pærəpɪt/ *n.* parapet *m.*

paraphernalia /pærəfə'neɪlɪə/ *n.* attirail *m.*, équipement *m.*

paraphrase /'pærəfreɪz/ *n.* paraphrase *f.* —*v.t.* paraphraser.

parasite /'pærəsaɪt/ *n.* parasite *m.*

parasol /'pærəsɒl/ *n.* ombrelle *f.*; (*on table, at beach*) parasol *m.*

paratrooper /'pærətruːpə(r)/ *n.* (*mil.*) parachutiste *m./f.*

parcel /'pɑːsl/ *n.* colis *m.*, paquet *m.* —*v.t.* (*p.t.* **parcelled**). **~ out,** diviser en parcelles.

parch /pɑːtʃ/ *v.t.* dessécher. **be ~ed,** (*person*) avoir très soif.

parchment /'pɑːtʃmənt/ *n.* parchemin *m.*

pardon /'pɑːdn/ *n.* pardon *m.*; (*jurid.*) grâce *m.* —*v.t.* (*p.t.* **pardoned**) pardonner (**s.o. for sth.,** qch. à qn.); gracier. **I beg your ~,** pardon.

pare /peə(r)/ *v.t.* (*clip*) rogner; (*peel*) éplucher.

parent /'peərənt/ *n.* père *m.*, mère *f.* **~s,** parents *m. pl.* **~al** /pə'rentl/ *a.* des parents. **~hood** *n.* paternité *f.*, maternité *f.*

parenthesis /pə'renθəsɪs/ *n.* (*pl.* -theses /-siːz/) parenthèse *f.*

Paris /'pærɪs/ *n.* Paris *m.|f.* ~**ian** /pə'rɪzɪən, *Amer.* pə'riːʒn/ *a.* & *n.* parisien(ne) (*m.* (*f.*)).

parish /'pærɪʃ/ *n.* (*relig.*) paroisse *f.*; (*municipal*) commune *f.* ~**ioner** /pə'rɪʃənə(r)/ *n.* paroissien(ne) *m.* (*f.*).

parity /'pærətɪ/ *n.* parité *f.*

park /pɑːk/ *n.* parc *m.* —*v.t.|i.* (se) garer; (*remain parked*) stationner. ~**ing-lot** *n.* (*Amer.*) parking *m.* ~**ing-meter** *n.* parcmètre *m.*

parka /'pɑːkə/ *n.* parka *m.|f.*

parliament /'pɑːləmənt/ *n.* parlement *m.* ~**ary** /-'mentrɪ/ *a.* parlementaire.

parlour /'pɑːlə(r)/ *n.* salon *m.*

parochial /pə'rəʊkɪəl/ *a.* (*relig.*) paroissial; (*fig.*) borné, provincial.

parody /'pærədɪ/ *n..* parodie *f.* —*v.t.* parodier.

parole /pə'rəʊl/ *n.* on ~, en liberté conditionnelle.

parquet /'pɑːkeɪ/ *n.* parquet *m.*

parrot /'pærət/ *n.* perroquet *m.*

parry /'pærɪ/ *v.t.* (*sport*) parer; (*question etc.*) esquiver. —*n.* parade *f.*

parsimonious /pɑːsɪ'məʊnɪəs/ *a.* parcimonieux.

parsley /'pɑːslɪ/ *n.* persil *m.*

parsnip /'pɑːsnɪp/ *n.* panais *m.*

parson /'pɑːsn/ *n.* (*fam.*) pasteur *m.*

part /pɑːt/ *n.* partie *f.*; (*of serial*) épisode *m.*; (*of machine*) pièce *f.*; (*theatre*) rôle *m.*; (*side in dispute*) parti *m.* —*a.* partiel. —*adv.* en partie. —*v.t.|i.* (*separate*) (se) séparer. in ~, en partie. on the ~ of, de la part de. ~-**exchange** *n.* reprise *f.* ~ of speech, catégorie grammaticale *f.* ~-time *a.* & *adv.* à temps partiel. ~ with, se séparer de. these ~s, cette région, ce coin.

partake /pɑː'teɪk/ *v.i.* (*p.t.* -took, *p.p.* -taken) participer (in, à).

partial /'pɑːʃl/ *a.* partiel; (*biased*) partial. be ~ to, avoir une prédilection pour. ~**ity** /-ɪ'ælətɪ/ *n.* (*bias*) partialité *f.*; (*fondness*) prédilection *f.* ~**ly** *adv.* partiellement.

particip|ate /pɑː'tɪsɪpeɪt/ *v.i.* participer (in, à). ~**ant** *n.* participant(e) *m.* (*f.*). ~**ation** /-'peɪʃn/ *n.* participation *f.*

participle /'pɑːtɪsɪpl/ *n.* participe *m.*

particle /'pɑːtɪkl/ *n.* particule *f.*

particular /pə'tɪkjʊlə(r)/ *a.* particulier; (*fussy*) difficile; (*careful*) méticu-

leux. that ~ man, cet homme-là en particulier. ~**s** *n. pl.* détails *m. pl.* in ~, en particulier. ~**ly** *adv.* particulièrement.

parting /'pɑːtɪŋ/ *n.* séparation *f.*; (*in hair*) raie *f.* —*a.* d'adieu.

partisan /pɑːtɪ'zæn, *Amer.* 'pɑːtɪzn/ *n.* partisan(e) *m.* (*f.*).

partition /pɑː'tɪʃn/ *n.* (*of room*) cloison *f.*; (*pol.*) partage *m.*, partition *f.* —*v.t.* (*room*) cloisonner; (*country*) partager.

partly /'pɑːtlɪ/ *adv.* en partie.

partner /'pɑːtnə(r)/ *n.* associé(e) *m.* (*f.*); (*sport*) partenaire *m.|f.* ~**ship** *n.* association *f.*

partridge /'pɑːtrɪdʒ/ *n.* perdrix *f.*

party /'pɑːtɪ/ *n.* réception *f.*; (*informal*) surprise-partie *f.*; (*for birthday*) fête *f.*; (*group*) groupe *m.*, équipe *f.*; (*pol.*) parti *m.*; (*jurid.*) partie *f.* ~ **line**, (*telephone*) ligne commune *f.*

pass /pɑːs/ *v.t.|i.* (*p.t.* passed) passer; (*overtake*) dépasser; (*in exam*) être reçu (à); (*approve*) accepter, autoriser; (*remark*) faire; (*judgement*) prononcer; (*law, bill*) voter. ~ (by), (*building*) passer devant; (*person*) croiser. —*n.* (*permit*) laissez-passer *m. invar.*; (*ticket*) carte (d'abonnement) *f.*; (*geog.*) col *m.*; (*sport*) passe *f.* ~ (**mark**), (*in exam*) moyenne *f.* make a ~ at, (*fam.*) faire des avances à. ~ away, mourir. ~ out or round, distribuer. ~ out, (*faint: fam.*) s'évanouir. ~ over, (*overlook*) passer sur. ~ up, (*forego: fam.*) laisser passer.

passable /'pɑːsəbl/ *a.* (*adequate*) passable; (*road*) praticable.

passage /'pæsɪdʒ/ *n.* (*way through, text, etc.*) passage *m.*; (*voyage*) traversée *f.*; (*corridor*) couloir *m.*

passenger /'pæsɪndʒə(r)/ *n.* passag|er, -ère *m.*, *f.*; (*in train*) voyageu|r, -se *m.*, *f.*

passer-by /pɑːsə'baɪ/ *n.* (*pl.* passers-by) passant(e) *m.* (*f.*).

passing /'pɑːsɪŋ/ *a.* (*fleeting*) fugitif, passager.

passion /'pæʃn/ *n.* passion *f.* ~**ate** *a.* passionné. ~**ately** *adv.* passionnément.

passive /'pæsɪv/ *a.* passif. ~**ness** *n.* passivité *f.*

Passover /'pɑːsəʊvə(r)/ *n.* Pâque *f.*

passport /'pɑːspɔːt/ *n.* passeport *m.*

password /'pɑːswɜːd/ *n.* mot de passe *m.*

past /pɑːst/ *a.* passé; (*former*) ancien.

—*n.* passé *m.* —*prep.* au-delà de; (*in time*) plus de; (*in front of*) devant. —*adv.* devant. **the ~ months,** ces derniers mois.

pasta /'pæstə/ *n.* pâtes *f. pl.*

paste /peɪst/ *n.* (*glue*) colle *f.*; (*dough*) pâte *f.*; (*of fish, meat*) pâté *m.*; (*jewellery*) strass *m.* —*v.t.* coller.

pastel /'pæstl/ *n.* pastel *m.* —*a.* pastel *invar.*

pasteurize /'pæstʃəraɪz/ *v.t.* pasteuriser.

pastiche /pæ'sti:ʃ/ *n.* pastiche *m.*

pastille /'pæstɪl/ *n.* pastille *f.*

pastime /'pɑ:staɪm/ *n.* passe-temps *m. invar.*

pastoral /'pɑ:stərəl/ *a.* pastoral.

pastry /'peɪstrɪ/ *n.* (*dough*) pâte *f.*; (*tart*) pâtisserie *f.*

pasture /'pɑ:stʃə(r)/ *n.* pâturage *m.*

pasty[1] /'pæstɪ/ *n.* petit pâté *m.*

pasty[2] /'peɪstɪ/ *a.* pâteux.

pat /pæt/ *v.t.* (*p.t.* **patted**) tapoter. —*n.* petite tape *f.* —*adv.* & *a.* à propos; (*ready*) tout prêt.

patch /pætʃ/ *n.* pièce *f.*; (*over eye*) bandeau *m.*; (*spot*) tache *f.*; (*of vegetables*) carré *m.* —*v.t.* ~ **up,** rapiécer; (*fig.*) régler. **bad ~,** période difficile *f.* **not be a ~ on,** ne pas arriver à la cheville de. **~y** *a.* inégal.

patchwork /'pætʃwɜ:k/ *n.* patchwork *m.*

pâté /'pæteɪ/ *n.* pâté *m.*

patent /'peɪtnt/ *a.* patent. —*n.* brevet (d'invention) *m.* —*v.t.* breveter. ~ **leather,** cuir verni *m.* **~ly** *adv.* manifestement.

paternal /pə'tɜ:nl/ *a.* paternel.

paternity /pə'tɜ:nətɪ/ *n.* paternité *f.*

path /pɑ:θ/ *n.* (*pl.* **-s** /pɑ:ðz/) sentier *m.*, chemin *m.*; (*in park*) allée *f.*; (*of rocket*) trajectoire *f.*

pathetic /pə'θetɪk/ *a.* pitoyable.

pathology /pə'θɒlədʒɪ/ *n.* pathologie *f.*

pathos /'peɪθɒs/ *n.* pathétique *m.*

patience /'peɪʃns/ *n.* patience *f.*

patient /'peɪʃnt/ *a.* patient. —*n.* malade *m.*/*f.*, patient(e) *m.* (*f.*). **~ly** *adv.* patiemment.

patio /'pætɪəʊ/ *n.* (*pl.* **-os**) patio *m.*

patriot /'pætrɪət, 'peɪtrɪət/ *n.* patriote *m.*/*f.* **~ic** /-'ɒtɪk/ *a.* patriotique; (*person*) patriote. **~ism** *n.* patriotisme *m.*

patrol /pə'trəʊl/ *n.* patrouille *f.* —*v.t.*/*i.* patrouiller (dans).

patron /'peɪtrən/ *n.* (*of the arts etc.*) protec|teur, -trice *m.*, *f.*; (*customer*)

client(e) *m.* (*f.*). ~ **saint,** saint(e) patron(ne) *m.* (*f.*).

patron|age /'pætrənɪdʒ/ *n.* clientèle *f.*; (*support*) patronage *m.* **~ize** *v.t.* être client de; (*fig.*) traiter avec condescendance.

patter[1] /'pætə(r)/ *n.* (*of steps*) bruit *m.*; (*of rain*) crépitement *m.*

patter[2] /'pætə(r)/ *n.* (*speech*) baratin *m.*

pattern /'pætn/ *n.* motif *m.*, dessin *m.*; (*for sewing*) patron *m.*; (*procedure, type*) schéma *m.*; (*example*) exemple *m.*

paunch /pɔ:ntʃ/ *n.* panse *f.*

pauper /'pɔ:pə(r)/ *n.* indigent(e) *m.* (*f.*), pauvre *m.*, pauvresse *f.*

pause /pɔ:z/ *n.* pause *f.* —*v.i.* faire une pause; (*hesitate*) hésiter.

pav|e /peɪv/ *v.t.* paver. **~e the way,** ouvrir la voie (**for,** à). **~ing-stone** *n.* pavé *m.*

pavement /'peɪvmənt/ *n.* trottoir *m.*; (*Amer.*) chaussée *f.*

pavilion /pə'vɪljən/ *n.* pavillon *m.*

paw /pɔ:/ *n.* patte *f.* —*v.t.* (*of animal*) donner des coups de patte à; (*touch: fam.*) tripoter.

pawn[1] /pɔ:n/ *n.* (*chess & fig.*) pion *m.*

pawn[2] /pɔ:n/ *v.t.* mettre en gage. —*n.* **in ~,** en gage. **~-shop** *n.* mont-de-piété *m.*

pawnbroker /'pɔ:nbrəʊkə(r)/ *n.* prêteur sur gages *m.*

pay /peɪ/ *v.t.*/*i.* (*p.t.* **paid**) payer; (*yield: comm.*) rapporter; (*compliment, visit*) faire. —*n.* salaire *m.*, paie *f.* **in the ~ of,** à la solde de. ~ **back,** rembourser. ~ **for,** payer. ~ **homage,** rendre hommage (**to,** à). ~ **in,** verser (**to,** à). ~ **off** *or* **out** *or* **up,** payer. ~ **off,** (*succeed: fam.*) être payant. **~-off** *n.* (*sl.*) règlement de comptes *m.*

payable /'peɪəbl/ *a.* payable.

payment /'peɪmənt/ *n.* paiement *m.*; (*reward*) récompense *f.*

payroll /'peɪrəʊl/ *n.* registre du personnel *m.* **be on the ~ of,** être membre du personnel de.

pea /pi:/ *n.* (petit) pois *m.* **~shooter** *n.* sarbacane *f.*

peace /pi:s/ *n.* paix *f.* ~ **of mind,** tranquillité d'esprit *f.* **~able** *a.* pacifique.

peaceful /'pi:sfl/ *a.* paisible; (*intention, measure*) pacifique.

peacemaker /'pi:smeɪkə(r)/ *n.* concilia|teur, -trice *m.*, *f.*

peach /piːtʃ/ n. pêche f.

peacock /'piːkɒk/ n. paon m.

peak /piːk/ n. sommet m.; (of mountain) pic m.; (maximum) maximum m. ~ hours, heures de pointe f. pl. ~ed cap, casquette f.

peaky /'piːkɪ/ a. (pale) pâlot; (puny) chétif; (off colour) patraque.

peal /piːl/ n. (of bells) carillon m.; (of laughter) éclat m.

peanut /'piːnʌt/ n. cacahuète f. ~s, (money: sl.) une bagatelle.

pear /peə(r)/ n. poire f.

pearl /pɜːl/ n. perle f. ~y a. nacré.

peasant /'peznt/ n. paysan(ne) m. (f.).

peat /piːt/ n. tourbe f.

pebble /'pebl/ n. caillou m.; (on beach) galet m.

peck /pek/ v.t./i. (food etc.) picorer; (attack) donner des coups de bec (à). —n. coup de bec m.

peckish /'pekɪʃ/ a. be ~, (fam.) avoir faim.

peculiar /pɪ'kjuːlɪə(r)/ a. (odd) bizarre; (special) particulier (to, à). ~ity /-'ærətɪ/ n. bizarrerie f.; (feature) particularité f.

pedal /'pedl/ n. pédale f. —v.i. pédaler.

pedantic /pɪ'dæntɪk/ a. pédant.

peddle /'pedl/ v.t. colporter.

pedestal /'pedɪstl/ n. piédestal m.

pedestrian /pɪ'destrɪən/ n. piéton m. —a. (precinct, street) piétonnier; (fig.) prosaïque. ~ crossing, passage pour piétons m.

pedigree /'pedɪɡriː/ n. (of person) ascendance f.; (of animal) pedigree m. —a. (cattle etc.) de race.

pedlar /'pedlə(r)/ n. camelot m.; (door-to-door) colporteu|r, -se m., f.

peek /piːk/ v.i. & n. = peep¹.

peel /piːl/ n. épluchure(s) f. (pl.); (of orange) écorce f. —v.t. (fruit, vegetables) éplucher. —v.i. (of skin) peler; (of paint) s'écailler. ~ings n. pl. épluchures f. pl.

peep¹ /piːp/ v.i. jeter un coup d'œil (furtif) (at, à). —n. coup d'œil (furtif) m. ~-hole n. judas m. P~ing Tom, voyeur m.

peep² /piːp/ v.i. (chirp) pépier.

peer¹ /pɪə(r)/ v.i. ~ (at), regarder attentivement, scruter.

peer² /pɪə(r)/ n. (equal, noble) pair m. ~age n. pairie f.

peeved /piːvd/ a. (sl.) irrité.

peevish /'piːvɪʃ/ a. grincheux.

peg /peɡ/ n. cheville f.; (for clothes)

pince à linge f.; (to hang coats etc.) patère f.; (for tent) piquet m. —v.t. (p.t. pegged) (prices) stabiliser. buy off the ~, acheter en prêt-à-porter.

pejorative /pɪ'dʒɒrətɪv/ a. péjoratif.

pelican /'pelɪkən/ n. pélican m. ~ crossing, passage clouté (avec feux de signalisation) m.

pellet /'pelɪt/ n. (round mass) boulette f.; (for gun) plomb m.

pelt¹ /pelt/ n. (skin) peau f.

pelt² /pelt/ v.t. bombarder (with, de). —v.i. pleuvoir à torrents.

pelvis /'pelvɪs/ n. (anat.) bassin m.

pen¹ /pen/ n. (for sheep etc.) enclos m.; (for baby, cattle) parc m.

pen² /pen/ n. stylo m.; (to be dipped in ink) plume f. —v.t. (p.t. penned) écrire. ~-friend n. correspondant(e) m. (f.). ~-name n. pseudonyme m.

penal /'piːnl/ a. pénal. ~ize v.t. pénaliser; (fig.) handicaper.

penalty /'penltɪ/ n. peine f.; (fine) amende f.; (sport) pénalité f.

penance /'penəns/ n. pénitence f.

pence /pens/ see penny.

pencil /'pensl/ n. crayon m. —v.t. (p.t. pencilled) crayonner. ~-sharpener n. taille-crayon(s) m.

pendant /'pendənt/ n. pendentif m.

pending /'pendɪŋ/ a. en suspens. —prep. (until) en attendant.

pendulum /'pendjʊləm/ n. pendule m.; (of clock) balancier m.

penetrat|e /'penɪtreɪt/ v.t. (enter) pénétrer dans; (understand, permeate) pénétrer. —v.i. pénétrer. ~ing a. pénétrant. ~ion /-'treɪʃn/ n. pénétration f.

penguin /'peŋɡwɪn/ n. manchot m., pingouin m.

penicillin /penɪ'sɪlɪn/ n. pénicilline f.

peninsula /pə'nɪnsjʊlə/ n. péninsule f.

penis /'piːnɪs/ n. pénis m.

peniten|t /'penɪtənt/ a. & n. pénitent(e) (m. (f.)). ~ce n. pénitence f.

penitentiary /penɪ'tenʃərɪ/ n. (Amer.) prison f., pénitencier m.

penknife /'pennaɪf/ n. (pl. -knives) canif m.

pennant /'penənt/ n. flamme f.

penniless /'penɪlɪs/ a. sans le sou.

penny /'penɪ/ n. (pl. pennies or pence) penny m.; (fig.) sou m.

pension /'penʃn/ n. pension f.; (for retirement) retraite f. —v.t. ~ off, mettre à la retraite. ~able a. qui a droit à une retraite. ~er n. (old-age)

~er, retraité(e) *m.* (*f.*)., personne âgée *f.*

pensive /'pensɪv/ *a.* pensif.

Pentecost /'pentɪkɒst/ *n.* Pentecôte *f.*

penthouse /'penthaʊs/ *n.* appartement de luxe *m.* (*sur le toit d'un immeuble*).

pent-up /pent'ʌp/ *a.* refoulé.

penultimate /pen'ʌltɪmət/ *a.* avant-dernier.

people /'piːpl/ *n. pl.* gens *m. pl.*, personnes *f. pl.* —*n.* peuple *m.* —*v.t.* peupler. **English**/*etc.* ~, les Anglais/ *etc. m. pl.* ~ **say,** on dit.

pep /pep/ *n.* entrain *m.* ~ **talk,** discours d'encouragement *m.*

pepper /'pepə(r)/ *n.* poivre *m.*; (*vegetable*) poivron *m.* —*v.t.* (*culin.*) poivrer. ~**y** *a.* poivré.

peppermint /'pepəmɪnt/ *n.* (*plant*) menthe poivrée *f.*; (*sweet*) bonbon à la menthe *m.*

per /pɜː(r)/ *prep.* par. ~ **annum,** par an. ~ **cent,** pour cent. ~ **kilo**/*etc.*, le kilo/*etc.* **ten km.** ~ **hour,** dix km à l'heure.

perceive /pə'siːv/ *v.t.* percevoir; (*notice*) s'apercevoir de. ~ **that,** s'apercevoir que.

percentage /pə'sentɪdʒ/ *n.* pourcentage *m.*

perceptible /pə'septəbl/ *a.* perceptible.

percept|ion /pə'sepʃn/ *n.* perception *f.* ~**ive** /-tɪv/ *a.* pénétrant.

perch /pɜːtʃ/ *n.* (*of bird*) perchoir *m.* —*v.i.* (se) percher.

percolat|e /'pɜːkəleɪt/ *v.t.* passer. —*v.i.* filtrer. ~**or** *n.* cafetière *f.*

percussion /pə'kʌʃn/ *n.* percussion *f.*

peremptory /pə'remptərɪ/ *a.* péremptoire.

perennial /pə'renɪəl/ *a.* perpétuel; (*plant*) vivace.

perfect[1] /'pɜːfɪkt/ *a.* parfait. ~**ly** *adv.* parfaitement.

perfect[2] /pə'fekt/ *v.t.* parfaire, mettre au point. ~**ion** /-kʃn/ *n.* perfection *f.* **to** ~**ion,** à la perfection. ~**ionist** /-kʃənɪst/ *n.* perfectionniste *m.*/*f.*

perforat|e /'pɜːfəreɪt/ *v.t.* perforer. ~**ion** /-'reɪʃn/ *n.* perforation *f.*; (*line of holes*) pointillé *m.*

perform /pə'fɔːm/ *v.t.* exécuter, faire; (*a function*) remplir; (*mus., theatre*) interpréter, jouer. —*v.i.* jouer; (*behave, function*) se comporter. ~**ance** *n.* exécution *f.*; interprétation *f.*; (*of car, team*) performance *f.*; (*show*)

représentation *f.*; séance *f.*; (*fuss*) histoire *f.* ~**er** *n.* artiste *m.*/*f.*

perfume /'pɜːfjuːm/ *n.* parfum *m.*

perfunctory /pə'fʌŋktərɪ/ *a.* négligent, superficiel.

perhaps /pə'hæps/ *adv.* peut-être.

peril /'perəl/ *n.* péril *m.* ~**ous** *a.* périlleux.

perimeter /pə'rɪmɪtə(r)/ *n.* périmètre *m.*

period /'pɪərɪəd/ *n.* période *f.*, époque *f.*; (*era*) époque *f.*; (*lesson*) cours *m.*; (*gram.*) point *m.*; (*med.*) règles *f. pl.* —*a.* d'époque. ~**ic** /-'ɒdɪk/ *a.* périodique. ~**ically** /-'ɒdɪklɪ/ *adv.* périodiquement.

periodical /pɪərɪ'ɒdɪkl/ *n.* périodique *m.*

peripher|y /pə'rɪfərɪ/ *n.* périphérie *f.* ~**al** *a.* périphérique; (*of lesser importance: fig.*) accessoire.

periscope /'perɪskəʊp/ *n.* périscope *m.*

perish /'perɪʃ/ *v.i.* périr; (*rot*) se détériorer. ~**able** *a.* périssable. ~**ing** *a.* (*cold: fam.*) glacial.

perjur|e /'pɜːdʒə(r)/ *v. pr.* ~**e o.s.,** se parjurer. ~**y** *n.* parjure *m.*

perk[1] /pɜːk/ *v.t.*/*i.* ~ **up,** (*fam.*) (se) remonter. ~**y** *a.* (*fam.*) gai.

perk[2] /pɜːk/ *n.* (*fam.*) avantage *m.*

perm /pɜːm/ *n.* permanente *f.* —*v.t.* **have one's hair** ~**ed,** se faire faire une permanente.

permanen|t /'pɜːmənənt/ *a.* permanent. ~**ce** *n.* permanence *f.* ~**tly** *adv.* à titre permanent.

permeable /'pɜːmɪəbl/ *a.* perméable.

permeate /'pɜːmɪeɪt/ *v.t.* imprégner, se répandre dans.

permissible /pə'mɪsəbl/ *a.* permis.

permission /pə'mɪʃn/ *n.* permission *f.*

permissive /pə'mɪsɪv/ *a.* tolérant, laxiste. ~**ness** *n.* laxisme *m.*

permit[1] /pə'mɪt/ *v.t.* (*p.t.* **permitted**) permettre (**s.o. to,** à qn. de), autoriser (**s.o. to,** qn. à).

permit[2] /'pɜːmɪt/ *n.* permis *m.*; (*pass*) laissez-passer *m. invar.*

permutation /pɜːmjuː'teɪʃn/ *n.* permutation *f.*

pernicious /pə'nɪʃəs/ *a.* nocif, pernicieux; (*med.*) pernicieux.

peroxide /pə'rɒksaɪd/ *n.* eau oxygénée *f.*

perpendicular /pɜːpən'dɪkjʊlə(r)/ *a.* & *n.* perpendiculaire (*f.*).

perpetrat|e /'pɜːpɪtreɪt/ *v.t.* perpétrer. ~**or** *n.* auteur *m.*

perpetual /pə'petʃʊəl/ *a.* perpétuel.

perpetuate /pə'petʃʊeɪt/ *v.t.* perpétuer.

perplex /pə'pleks/ *v.t.* rendre perplexe. ~**ed** *a.* perplexe. ~**ing** *a.* déroutant. ~**ity** *n.* perplexité *f.*

persecut|e /'pɜːsɪkjuːt/ *v.t.* persécuter. ~**ion** /-'kjuːʃn/ *n.* persécution *f.*

persever|e /pɜːsɪ'vɪə(r)/ *v.i.* persévérer. ~**ance** *n.* persévérance *f.*

Persian /'pɜːʃn/ *a.* & *n.* (*lang.*) persan (*m.*).

persist /pə'sɪst/ *v.i.* persister (**in doing**, à faire). ~**ence** *n.* persistance *f.* ~**ent** *a.* (*cough, snow, etc.*) persistant; (*obstinate*) obstiné; (*continual*) continuel. ~**ently** *adv.* avec persistance.

person /'pɜːsn/ *n.* personne *f.* **in** ~, en personne. ~**able** *a.* beau.

personal /'pɜːsənl/ *a.* personnel; (*hygiene, habits*) intime; (*secretary*) particulier. ~**ly** *adv.* personnellement.

personality /pɜːsə'næləti/ *n.* personnalité *f.*; (*on TV*) vedette *f.*

personify /pə'sɒnɪfaɪ/ *v.t.* personnifier.

personnel /pɜːsə'nel/ *n.* personnel *m.*

perspective /pə'spektɪv/ *n.* perspective *f.*

perspir|e /pə'spaɪə(r)/ *v.i.* transpirer. ~**ation** /-ə'reɪʃn/ *n.* transpiration *f.*

persua|de /pə'sweɪd/ *v.t.* persuader (**to**, de). ~**sion** /-eɪʒn/ *n.* persuasion *f.*

persuasive /pə'sweɪsɪv/ *a.* (*person, speech, etc.*) persuasif. ~**ly** *adv.* d'une manière persuasive.

pert /pɜːt/ *a.* (*saucy*) impertinent; (*lively*) plein d'entrain. ~**ly** *adv.* avec impertinence.

pertain /pə'teɪn/ *v.i.* ~ **to**, se rapporter à.

pertinent /'pɜːtɪnənt/ *a.* pertinent. ~**ly** *adv.* pertinemment.

perturb /pə'tɜːb/ *v.t.* troubler.

Peru /pə'ruː/ *n.* Pérou *m.* ~**vian** *a.* & *n.* péruvien(ne) (*m.* (*f.*)).

perus|e /pə'ruːz/ *v.t.* lire (attentivement). ~**al** *n.* lecture *f.*

perva|de /pə'veɪd/ *v.t.* imprégner, envahir. ~**sive** *a.* envahissant.

pervers|e /pə'vɜːs/ *a.* (*stubborn*) entêté; (*wicked*) pervers. ~**ity** *n.* perversité *f.*

perver|t[1] /pə'vɜːt/ *v.t.* pervertir. ~**sion** *n.* perversion *f.*

pervert[2] /'pɜːvɜːt/ *n.* perverti(e) *m.* (*f.*), dépravé(e) *m.*(*f.*).

peseta /pə'seɪtə/ *n.* peseta *f.*

pessimis|t /'pesɪmɪst/ *n.* pessimiste *m.*/*f.* ~**m** /-zəm/ *n.* pessimisme *m.* ~**tic** /-'mɪstɪk/ *a.* pessimiste. ~**tically** /-'mɪstɪklɪ/ *adv.* avec pessimisme.

pest /pest/ *n.* insecte *or* animal nuisible *m.*; (*person: fam.*) enquiquineu|r, -se *m.*, *f.*

pester /'pestə(r)/ *v.t.* harceler.

pesticide /'pestɪsaɪd/ *n.* pesticide *m.*, insecticide *m.*

pet /pet/ *n.* animal (domestique) *m.*; (*favourite*) chouchou(te) *m.* (*f.*). —*a.* (*tame*) apprivoisé. —*v.t.* (*p.t.* **petted**) caresser; (*sexually*) peloter. ~ **hate**, bête noire *f.* ~ **name**, diminutif *m.*

petal /'petl/ *n.* pétale *m.*

peter /'piːtə(r)/ *v.i.* ~ **out**, (*supplies*) s'épuiser; (*road*) finir.

petite /pə'tiːt/ *a.* (*woman*) menue.

petition /pɪ'tɪʃn/ *n.* pétition *f.* —*v.t.* adresser une pétition à.

petrify /'petrɪfaɪ/ *v.t.* pétrifier; (*scare: fig.*) pétrifier de peur.

petrol /'petrəl/ *n.* essence *f.* ~ **station**, station-service *f.*

petroleum /pɪ'trəʊlɪəm/ *n.* pétrole *m.*

petticoat /'petɪkəʊt/ *n.* jupon *m.*

petty /'petɪ/ *a.* (**-ier, -iest**) (*minor*) petit; (*mean*) mesquin. ~ **cash**, petite monnaie *f.*

petulan|t /'petjʊlənt/ *a.* irritable. ~**ce** *n.* irritabilité *f.*

pew /pjuː/ *n.* banc (d'église) *m.*

pewter /'pjuːtə(r)/ *n.* étain *m.*

phallic /'fælɪk/ *a.* phallique.

phantom /'fæntəm/ *n.* fantôme *m.*

pharmaceutical /fɑːmə'sjuːtɪkl/ *a.* pharmaceutique.

pharmac|y /'fɑːməsɪ/ *n.* pharmacie *f.* ~**ist** *n.* pharmacien(ne) *m.* (*f.*).

pharyngitis /færɪn'dʒaɪtɪs/ *n.* pharyngite *f.*

phase /feɪz/ *n.* phase *f.* —*v.t.* ~ **in/out**, introduire/retirer progressivement.

pheasant /'feznt/ *n.* faisan *m.*

phenomen|on /fɪ'nɒmɪnən/ *n.* (*pl.* **-ena**) phénomène *m.* ~**al** *a.* phénoménal.

phew /fjuː/ *int.* ouf.

phial /'faɪəl/ *n.* fiole *f.*

philanderer /fɪ'lændərə(r)/ *n.* coureur (de femmes) *m.*

philanthrop|ist /fɪ'lænθrəpɪst/ *n.* philanthrope *m.*/*f.* ~**ic** /-ən'θrɒpɪk/ *a.* philanthropique.

philatel|y /fɪˈlætəlɪ/ *n.* philatélie *f.*
~**ist** *n.* philatéliste *m.|f.*

philharmonic /fɪlɑːˈmɒnɪk/ *a.* philharmonique.

Philippines /ˈfɪlɪpiːnz/ *n. pl.* the ~, les Philippines *f. pl.*

philistine /ˈfɪlɪstaɪn, *Amer.* ˈfɪlɪstiːn/ *n.* philistin *m.*

philosoph|y /fɪˈlɒsəfɪ/ *n.* philosophie *f.* ~**er** *n.* philosophe *m.|f.*
~**ical** /-əˈsɒfɪkl/ *a.* philosophique; (*resigned*) philosophe.

phlegm /flem/ *n.* (*med.*) mucosité *f.*

phlegmatic /flegˈmætɪk/ *a.* flegmatique.

phobia /ˈfəʊbɪə/ *n.* phobie *f.*

phone /fəʊn/ *n.* téléphone *m.* —*v.t.* (*person*) téléphoner à; (*message*) téléphoner. —*v.i.* téléphoner. ~ **back**, rappeler. ~ **book**, annuaire *m.* ~ **box**, ~ **booth**, cabine téléphonique *f.* ~ **call**, coup de fil *m.*

phonetic /fəˈnetɪk/ *a.* phonétique.

phoney /ˈfəʊnɪ/ *a.* (**-ier**, **-iest**) (*sl.*) faux. —*n.* (*person*: *sl.*) charlatan *m.* **it is a** ~, (*sl.*) c'est faux.

phosphate /ˈfɒsfeɪt/ *n.* phosphate *m.*

phosphorus /ˈfɒsfərəs/ *n.* phosphore *m.*

photo /ˈfəʊtəʊ/ *n.* (*pl.* **-os**) (*fam.*) photo *f.*

photocopy /ˈfəʊtəʊkɒpɪ/ *n.* photocopie *f.* —*v.t.* photocopier.

photogenic /fəʊtəʊˈdʒenɪk/ *a.* photogénique.

photograph /ˈfəʊtəɡrɑːf/ *n.* photographie *f.* —*v.t.* photographier. ~**er** /fəˈtɒɡrəfə(r)/ *n.* photographe *m.|f.*
~**ic** /-ˈɡræfɪk/ *a.* photographique. ~**y** /fəˈtɒɡrəfɪ/ *n.* (*activity*) photographie *f.*

phrase /freɪz/ *n.* expression *f.*; (*idiom* & *gram.*) locution *f.* —*v.t.* exprimer, formuler. ~**-book** *n.* recueil de locutions *m.*

physical /ˈfɪzɪkl/ *a.* physique. ~**ly** *adv.* physiquement.

physician /fɪˈzɪʃn/ *n.* médecin *m.*

physicist /ˈfɪzɪsɪst/ *n.* physicien(ne) *m.* (*f.*).

physics /ˈfɪzɪks/ *n.* physique *f.*

physiology /fɪzɪˈɒlədʒɪ/ *n.* physiologie *f.*

physiotherap|y /fɪzɪəʊˈθerəpɪ/ *n.* kinésithérapie *f.* ~**ist** *n.* kinésithérapeute *m.|f.*

physique /fɪˈziːk/ *n.* constitution *f.*; (*appearance*) physique *m.*

pian|o /pɪˈænəʊ/ *n.* (*pl.* **-os**) piano *m.*
~**ist** /ˈpɪənɪst/ *n.* pianiste *m.|f.*

piazza /pɪˈætsə/ *n.* (*square*) place *f.*

pick[1] /pɪk/ (*tool*) *n.* pioche *f.*

pick[2] /pɪk/ *v.t.* choisir; (*flower etc.*) cueillir; (*lock*) crocheter; (*nose*) se curer; (*pockets*) faire. ~ (**off**), enlever. —*n.* choix *m.*; (*best*) meilleur(e) *m.* (*f.*). ~ **a quarrel with**, chercher querelle à. ~ **holes in**, relever les défauts de. ~ **on**, harceler. ~ **out**, choisir; (*identify*) distinguer. ~ **up** *v.t.* ramasser; (*sth. fallen*) relever; (*weight*) soulever; (*habit, passenger, speed, etc.*) prendre; (*learn*) apprendre; *v.i.* s'améliorer. ~**-me-up** *n.* remontant *m.* ~**-up** *n.* partenaire de rencontre *m.|f.*; (*truck, stylus-holder*) pick-up *m.*

pickaxe /ˈpɪkæks/ *n.* pioche *f.*

picket /ˈpɪkɪt/ *n.* (*single striker*) gréviste *m.|f.*; (*stake*) piquet *m.* ~ (**line**), piquet de grève *m.* —*v.t.* (*p.t.* **picketed**) mettre un piquet de grève devant.

pickings /ˈpɪkɪŋz/ *n. pl.* restes *m. pl.*

pickle /ˈpɪkl/ *n.* vinaigre *m.*; (*brine*) saumure *f.* ~**s**, pickles *m. pl.*; (*Amer.*) concombres *m.pl.* —*v.t.* conserver dans du vinaigre *or* de la saumure. **in a** ~, (*fam.*) dans le pétrin.

pickpocket /ˈpɪkpɒkɪt/ *n.* (*thief*) pickpocket *m.*

picnic /ˈpɪknɪk/ *n.* pique-nique *m.*
—*v.i.* (*p.t.* **picnicked**) pique-niquer.

pictorial /pɪkˈtɔːrɪəl/ *a.* illustré.

picture /ˈpɪktʃə(r)/ *n.* image *f.*; (*painting*) tableau *m.*; (*photograph*) photo *f.*; (*drawing*) dessin *m.*; (*film*) film *m.*; (*fig.*) description *f.*, tableau *m.* —*v.t.* s'imaginer; (*describe*) dépeindre. **the** ~**s**, (*cinema*) le cinéma.

picturesque /pɪktʃəˈresk/ *a.* pittoresque.

piddling /ˈpɪdlɪŋ/ *a.* (*fam.*) dérisoire.

pidgin /ˈpɪdʒɪn/ *a.* ~ **English**, pidgin *m.*

pie /paɪ/ *n.* tarte *f.*; (*of meat*) pâté en croûte *m.*

piebald /ˈpaɪbɔːld/ *a.* pie *invar.*

piece /piːs/ *n.* morceau *m.*; (*of currency, machine, etc.*) pièce *f.*
—*v.t.* ~ (**together**), (r)assembler. **a** ~ **of advice/furniture/***etc.*, un conseil/meuble/*etc.* ~**-work** *n.* travail à la pièce *m.* **take to** ~**s**, démonter.

piecemeal /ˈpiːsmiːl/ *a.* par bribes.

pier /pɪə(r)/ n. (*promenade*) jetée f.

pierc|e /pɪəs/ v.t. percer. ~**ing** a. perçant; (*cold*) glacial.

piety /'paɪətɪ/ n. piété f.

piffl|e /'pɪfl/ n. (sl.) fadaises f. pl. ~**ing** a. (sl.) insignifiant.

pig /pɪg/ n. cochon m. ~**headed** a. entêté.

pigeon /'pɪdʒən/ n. pigeon m. ~**hole** n. casier m.

piggy /'pɪgɪ/ a. porcin; (*greedy*: fam.) goinfre. ~**back** adv. sur le dos. ~ **bank,** tirelire f.

pigment /'pɪgmənt/ n. pigment m. ~**ation** /-en'teɪʃn/ n. pigmentation f.

pigsty /'pɪgstaɪ/ n. porcherie f.

pigtail /'pɪgteɪl/ n. natte f.

pike /paɪk/ n. invar. (*fish*) brochet m.

pilchard /'pɪltʃəd/ n. pilchard m.

pile /paɪl/ n. pile f., tas m.; (*of carpet*) poils m.pl. —v.t. ~ (**up**), (*stack*) empiler. —v.i. ~ **into,** s'empiler dans. ~ **up,** (*accumulate*) (s')accumuler. **a** ~ **of,** (fam.) un tas de. ~-**up** n. (*auto*) carambolage m.

piles /paɪlz/ n. pl. hémorroïdes f. pl.

pilfer /'pɪlfə(r)/ v.t. chaparder. ~**age** n. chapardage m.

pilgrim /'pɪlgrɪm/ n. pèlerin m. ~**age** n. pèlerinage m.

pill /pɪl/ n. pilule f.

pillage /'pɪlɪdʒ/ n. pillage m. —v.t. piller. —v.i. se livrer au pillage.

pillar /'pɪlə(r)/ n. pilier m. ~-**box** n. boîte à or aux lettres f.

pillion /'pɪljən/ n. siège arrière m. **ride** ~, monter derrière.

pillory /'pɪlərɪ/ n. pilori m.

pillow /'pɪləʊ/ n. oreiller m.

pillowcase /'pɪləʊkeɪs/ n. taie d'oreiller f.

pilot /'paɪlət/ n. pilote m. —a. pilote. —v.t. (p.t. **piloted**) piloter. ~-**light** n. veilleuse f.

pimento /pɪ'mentəʊ/ n. (pl. -os) piment m.

pimp /pɪmp/ n. souteneur m.

pimpl|e /'pɪmpl/ n. bouton m. ~**y** a. boutonneux.

pin /pɪn/ n. épingle f.; (*techn.*) goupille f. —v.t. (p.t. **pinned**) épingler, attacher; (*hold down*) clouer. **have** ~**s and needles,** avoir des fourmis. ~ **s.o. down,** (fig.) forcer qn. à se décider. ~**point** v.t. repérer, définir. ~ **up,** afficher. ~-**up** n. (fam.) pin-up f. invar.

pinafore /'pɪnəfɔː(r)/ n. tablier m.

pincers /'pɪnsəz/ n. pl. tenailles f. pl.

pinch /pɪntʃ/ v.t. pincer; (*steal*: sl.) piquer. —v.i. (*be too tight*) serrer. —n. (*mark*) pinçon m.; (*of salt*) pincée f. **at a** ~, au besoin.

pincushion /'pɪnkʊʃn/ n. pelote à épingles f.

pine[1] /paɪn/ n. (*tree*) pin m.

pine[2] /paɪn/ v.i. ~ **away,** dépérir. ~ **for,** languir après.

pineapple /'paɪnæpl/ n. ananas m.

ping /pɪŋ/ n. bruit métallique m.

ping-pong /'pɪŋpɒŋ/ n. ping-pong m.

pink /pɪŋk/ a. & n. rose (m.).

pinnacle /'pɪnəkl/ n. pinacle m.

pint /paɪnt/ n. pinte f. (*imperial* = 0.57 *litre; Amer.* = 0.47 *litre*).

pioneer /paɪə'nɪə(r)/ n. pionnier m. —v.t. être le premier à faire, utiliser, étudier, etc.

pious /'paɪəs/ a. pieux.

pip[1] /pɪp/ n. (*seed*) pépin m.

pip[2] /pɪp/ n. (*sound*) top m.

pipe /paɪp/ n. tuyau m.; (*of smoker*) pipe f.; (*mus.*) pipeau m. —v.t. transporter par tuyau. ~**cleaner** n. curepipe m. ~ **down,** se taire. ~-**dream** n. chimère f.

pipeline /'paɪplaɪn/ n. pipeline m. **in the** ~, en route.

piping /'paɪpɪŋ/ n. tuyau(x) m. (pl.). ~ **hot,** très chaud.

piquant /'piːkənt/ a. piquant.

pique /piːk/ n. dépit m.

pira|te /'paɪərət/ n. pirate m. ~**cy** n. piraterie f.

pistachio /pɪ'stæʃɪəʊ/ n. (pl. -os) pistache f.

pistol /'pɪstl/ n. pistolet m.

piston /'pɪstən/ n. piston m.

pit /pɪt/ n. fosse f., trou m.; (*mine*) puits m.; (*quarry*) carrière f.; (*of stomach*) creux m.; (*of cherry etc.*: Amer.) noyau m. —v.t. (p.t. **pitted**) trouer; (fig.) opposer. ~ **o.s. against,** se mesurer à.

pitch[1] /pɪtʃ/ n. (*tar*) poix f. ~**black** a. d'un noir d'ébène.

pitch[2] /pɪtʃ/ v.t. lancer; (*tent*) dresser. —v.i. (*of ship*) tanguer. —n. degré m.; (*of voice*) hauteur f.; (*mus.*) ton m.; (*sport*) terrain m. ~**ed battle,** bataille rangée f. ~ **in,** (fam.) contribuer. ~ **into,** (fam.) s'attaquer à.

pitcher /'pɪtʃə(r)/ n. cruche f.

pitchfork /'pɪtʃfɔːk/ n. fourche à foin f.

piteous /'pɪtɪəs/ *a.* pitoyable.
pitfall /'pɪtfɔːl/ *n.* piège *m.*
pith /pɪθ/ *n.* (*of orange*) peau blanche *f.*; (*essence: fig.*) moelle *f.*
pithy /'pɪθɪ/ *a.* (-ier, -iest) (*terse*) concis; (*forceful*) vigoureux.
piti|ful /'pɪtɪfl/ *a.* pitoyable. ~less *a.* impitoyable.
pittance /'pɪtns/ *n.* revenu *or* salaire dérisoire *m.*
pity /'pɪtɪ/ *n.* pitié *f.*; (*regrettable fact*) dommage *m.* —*v.t.* plaindre. **take ~ on**, avoir pitié de.
pivot /'pɪvət/ *n.* pivot *m.* —*v.i.* (*p.t.* **pivoted**) pivoter.
pixie /'pɪksɪ/ *n.* lutin *m.*
pizza /'piːtsə/ *n.* pizza *f.*
placard /'plækɑːd/ *n.* affiche *f.*
placate /plə'keɪt, *Amer.* 'pleɪkeɪt/ *v.t.* calmer.
place /pleɪs/ *n.* endroit *m.*, lieu *m.*; (*house*) maison *f.*; (*seat, rank, etc.*) place *f.* —*v.t.* placer; (*an order*) passer; (*remember*) situer. **at** *or* **to my ~**, chez moi. **be ~d**, (*in race*) se placer. **~-mat** *n.* set *m.*
placid /'plæsɪd/ *a.* placide.
plagiar|ize /'pleɪdʒəraɪz/ *v.t.* plagier. ~ism *n.* plagiat *m.*
plague /pleɪg/ *n.* peste *f.*; (*nuisance: fam.*) fléau *m.* —*v.t.* harceler.
plaice /pleɪs/ *n. invar.* carrelet *m.*
plaid /plæd/ *n.* tissu écossais *m.*
plain /pleɪn/ *a.* (-er, -est) clair; (*candid*) franc; (*simple*) simple; (*not pretty*) sans beauté; (*not patterned*) uni. —*adv.* franchement. —*n.* plaine *f.* **in ~ clothes**, en civil. **~ly** *adv.* clairement; franchement; simplement. **~ness** *n.* simplicité *f.*
plaintiff /'pleɪntɪf/ *n.* plaignant(e) *m.* (*f.*).
plaintive /'pleɪntɪv/ *a.* plaintif.
plait /plæt/ *v.t.* tresser, natter. —*n.* tresse *f.*, natte *f.*
plan /plæn/ *n.* projet *m.*, plan *m.*; (*diagram*) plan *m.* —*v.t.* (*p.t.* **planned**) prévoir, projeter; (*arrange*) organiser; (*design*) concevoir; (*economy, work*) planifier. —*v.i.* faire des projets. **~ to do**, avoir l'intention de faire.
plane[1] /pleɪn/ *n.* (*tree*) platane *m.*
plane[2] /pleɪn/ *n.* (*level*) plan *m.*; (*aeroplane*) avion *m.* —*a.* plan.
plane[3] /pleɪn/ *n.* (*tool*) rabot *m.* —*v.t.* raboter.

planet /'plænɪt/ *n.* planète *f.* ~ary *a.* planétaire.
plank /plæŋk/ *n.* planche *f.*
planning /'plænɪŋ/ *n.* (*pol., comm.*) planification *f.* **family ~**, planning familial *m.*
plant /plɑːnt/ *n.* plante *f.*; (*techn.*) matériel *m.*; (*factory*) usine *f.* —*v.t.* planter; (*bomb*) (dé)poser. ~ation /-'teɪʃn/ *n.* plantation *f.*
plaque /plɑːk/ *n.* plaque *f.*
plasma /'plæzmə/ *n.* plasma *m.*
plaster /'plɑːstə(r)/ *n.* plâtre *m.*; (*adhesive*) sparadrap *m.* —*v.t.* plâtrer; (*cover*) tapisser (**with**, de). **~ of Paris**, plâtre à mouler *m.* ~er *n.* plâtrier *m.*
plastic /'plæstɪk/ *a.* en plastique; (*art, substance*) plastique. —*n.* plastique *m.* **~ surgery**, chirurgie esthétique *f.*
Plasticine /'plæstɪsiːn/ *n.* (P.) pâte à modeler *f.*
plate /pleɪt/ *n.* assiette *f.*; (*of metal*) plaque *f.*; (*gold or silver dishes*) vaisselle plate *f.*; (*in book*) gravure *f.* —*v.t.* (*metal*) plaquer. ~ful *n.* (*pl.* -fuls) assiettée *f.*
plateau /'plætəʊ/ *n.* (*pl.* -eaux /-əʊz/) plateau *m.*
platform /'plætfɔːm/ *n.* (*in classroom, hall, etc.*) estrade *f.*; (*for speaking*) tribune *f.*; (*rail.*) quai *m.*; (*of bus & pol.*) plate-forme *f.*
platinum /'plætɪnəm/ *n.* platine *m.*
platitude /'plætɪtjuːd/ *n.* platitude *f.*
platonic /plə'tɒnɪk/ *a.* platonique.
platoon /plə'tuːn/ *n.* (*mil.*) section *f.*
platter /'plætə(r)/ *n.* plat *m.*
plausible /'plɔːzəbl/ *a.* plausible.
play /pleɪ/ *v.t./i.* jouer; (*instrument*) jouer de; (*game*) jouer à; (*opponent*) jouer contre; (*match*) disputer. —*n.* jeu *m.*; (*theatre*) pièce *f.* **~-act** *v.i.* jouer la comédie. **~ down**, minimiser. **~-group**, **~-school** *ns.* garderie *f.* **~ on**, (*take advantage of*) jouer sur. **~ on words**, jeu de mots *m.* **~ed out**, épuisé. **~-pen** *n.* parc *m.* **~ safe**, ne pas prendre de risques. **~ up**, (*fam.*) créer des problèmes (à). **~ up to**, flatter. ~er *n.* joueu|r, -se *m.,f.*
playboy /'pleɪbɔɪ/ *n.* play-boy *m.*
playful /'pleɪfl/ *a.* enjoué; (*child*) joueur. **~ly** *adv.* avec espièglerie.
playground /'pleɪɡraʊnd/ *n.* cour de récréation *f.*

playing /'pleɪɪŋ/ *n.* jeu *m.* ~-**card** *n.* carte à jouer *f.* ~-**field** *n.* terrain de sport *m.*

playmate /'pleɪmeɪt/ *n.* camarade *m.|f.*, cop|ain, -ine *m., f.*

plaything /'pleɪθɪŋ/ *n.* jouet *m.*

playwright /'pleɪraɪt/ *n.* dramaturge *m.|f.*

plc *abbr.* (*public limited company*) SA.

plea /pliː/ *n.* (*entreaty*) supplication *f.*; (*reason*) excuse *f.*; (*jurid.*) défense *f.*

plead /pliːd/ *v.t.|i.* (*jurid.*) plaider; (*as excuse*) alléguer. ~ **for**, (*beg for*) implorer. ~ **with**, (*beg*) implorer.

pleasant /'pleznt/ *a.* agréable. ~ly *adv.* agréablement.

please /pliːz/ *v.t.|i.* plaire (à), faire plaisir (à). *—adv.* s'il vous *or* te plaît. ~ **o.s.**, **do as one** ~s, faire ce qu'on veut. ~**d** *a.* content (**with**, de). **pleasing** *a.* agréable.

pleasur|e /'pleʒə(r)/ *n.* plaisir *m.* ~**able** *a.* très agréable.

pleat /pliːt/ *n.* pli *m.* *—v.t.* plisser.

plebiscite /'plebɪsɪt/ *n.* plébiscite *m.*

pledge /pledʒ/ *n.* (*token*) gage *m.*; (*fig.*) promesse *f.* *—v.t.* promettre; (*pawn*) engager.

plentiful /'plentɪfl/ *a.* abondant.

plenty /'plentɪ/ *n.* abondance *f.* ~ (**of**), (*a great deal*) beaucoup (de); (*enough*) assez (de).

pleurisy /'plʊərəsɪ/ *n.* pleurésie *f.*

pliable /'plaɪəbl/ *a.* souple.

pliers /'plaɪəz/ *n. pl.* pince(s) *f.* (*pl.*).

plight /plaɪt/ *n.* triste situation *f.*

plimsoll /'plɪms(ə)l/ *n.* chaussure de gym *f.*

plinth /plɪnθ/ *n.* socle *m.*

plod /plɒd/ *v.i.* (*p.t.* **plodded**) avancer péniblement *or* d'un pas lent; (*work*) bûcher. ~**der** *n.* bûcheu|r, -se *m., f.* ~**ding** *a.* lent.

plonk /plɒŋk/ *n.* (*sl.*) pinard *m.*

plot /plɒt/ *n.* complot *m.*; (*of novel etc.*) intrigue *f.* ~ (**of land**), terrain *m.* *—v.t.|i.* (*p.t.* **plotted**) comploter; (*mark out*) tracer.

plough /plaʊ/ *n.* charrue *f.* *—v.t.|i.* labourer. ~ **into**, rentrer dans. ~ **through**, avancer péniblement dans.

plow /plaʊ/ *n. & v.t.|i.* (*Amer.*) = **plough**.

ploy /plɔɪ/ *n.* (*fam.*) stratagème *m.*

pluck /plʌk/ *v.t.* cueillir; (*bird*) plumer; (*eyebrows*) épiler. *—n.* courage *m.* ~ **up courage**, prendre

son courage à deux mains. ~**y** *a.* courageux.

plug /plʌg/ *n.* (*of cloth, paper, etc.*) tampon *m.*; (*for sink etc.*) bonde *f.*; (*electr.*) fiche *f.*, prise *f.* *—v.t.* (*p.t.* **plugged**) (*hole*) boucher; (*publicize*: *fam.*) faire du battage autour de. *—v.i.* ~ **away**, (*work*: *fam.*) bosser. ~ **in**, brancher. ~-**hole** *n.* vidange *f.*

plum /plʌm/ *n.* prune *f.* ~ **job**, travail en or *m.* ~ **pudding**, (plum-)pudding *m.*

plumb /plʌm/ *adv.* tout à fait. *—v.t.* (*probe*) sonder.

plumb|er /'plʌmə(r)/ *n.* plombier *m.* ~**ing** *n.* plomberie *f.*

plume /pluːm/ *n.* plume(s) *f.* (*pl.*).

plummet /'plʌmɪt/ *v.i.* (*p.t.* **plummeted**) tomber, plonger.

plump /plʌmp/ *a.* (**-er, -est**) potelé, dodu. *—v.i.* ~ **for**, choisir. ~**ness** *n.* rondeur *f.*

plunder /'plʌndə(r)/ *v.t.* piller. *—n.* (*act*) pillage *m.*; (*goods*) butin *m.*

plunge /plʌndʒ/ *v.t.|i.* (*dive, thrust*) plonger; (*fall*) tomber. *—n.* plongeon *m.*; (*fall*) chute *f.*

plunger /'plʌndʒə(r)/ *n.* (*for sink etc.*) ventouse *f.*, débouchoir *m.*

plural /'plʊərəl/ *a.* pluriel; (*noun*) au pluriel. *—n.* pluriel *m.*

plus /plʌs/ *prep.* plus. *—a.* (*electr. & fig.*) positif. *—n.* signe plus *m.*; (*fig.*) atout *m.* **ten** ~, plus de dix.

plush(y) /'plʌʃ(ɪ)/ *a.* somptueux.

ply /plaɪ/ *v.t.* (*tool*) manier; (*trade*) exercer. *—v.i.* faire la navette. ~ **s.o. with drink**, offrir continuellement à boire à qn.

plywood /'plaɪwʊd/ *n.* contreplaqué *m.*

p.m. /piː'em/ *adv.* de l'après-midi *or* du soir.

pneumatic /njuː'mætɪk/ *a.* pneumatique.

pneumonia /njuː'məʊnɪə/ *n.* pneumonie *f.*

PO *abbr. see* **Post Office.**

poach /pəʊtʃ/ *v.t.|i.* (*steal*) braconner; (*culin.*) pocher. ~**er** *n.* braconnier *m.*

pocket /'pɒkɪt/ *n.* poche *f.* *—a.* de poche. *—v.t.* empocher. **be £5 in/out of** ~, avoir empoché/ déboursé £5. ~-**book** *n.* (*notebook*) carnet *m.*; (*purse*: *Amer.*) porte-monnaie *m. invar.*; (*handbag*: *Amer.*) sac à main *m.* ~-**money** *n.* argent de poche *m.*

pock-marked /'pɒkmɑːkt/ *a.* (*face etc.*) grêlé.

pod /pɒd/ *n.* cosse *f.*

podgy /'pɒdʒɪ/ *a.* (-ier, -iest) dodu.

poem /'pəʊɪm/ *n.* poème *m.*

poet /'pəʊɪt/ *n.* poète *m.* **~ic** /-'etɪk/ *a.* poétique.

poetry /'pəʊɪtrɪ/ *n.* poésie *f.*

poignant /'pɔɪnjənt/ *a.* poignant.

point /pɔɪnt/ *n.* point *m.*; (*tip*) pointe *f.*; (*decimal point*) virgule *f.*; (*meaning*) sens *m.*, intérêt *m.*; (*remark*) remarque *f.* **~s**, (*rail.*) aiguillage *m.* —*v.t.* (*aim*) braquer; (*show*) indiquer. —*v.i.* indiquer du doigt (**at** *or* **to s.o.**, qn.). **good ~s**, qualités *f. pl.* **on the ~ of**, sur le point de. **~-blank** *a.* & *adv.* à bout portant. **~ in time**, moment *m.* **~ of view**, point de vue *m.* **~ out**, signaler. **to the ~**, pertinent. **what is the ~?**, à quoi bon?

pointed /'pɔɪntɪd/ *a.* pointu; (*remark*) lourd de sens.

pointer /'pɔɪntə(r)/ *n.* (*indicator*) index *m.*; (*dog*) chien d'arrêt *m.*; (*advice*: *fam.*) tuyau *m.*

pointless /'pɔɪntlɪs/ *a.* inutile.

poise /pɔɪz/ *n.* équilibre *m.*; (*carriage*) maintien *m.*; (*fig.*) assurance *f.* **~d** *a.* en équilibre; (*confident*) assuré. **~d for**, prêt à.

poison /'pɔɪzn/ *n.* poison *m.* —*v.t.* empoisonner. **~ous** *a.* (*substance etc.*) toxique; (*plant*) vénéneux; (*snake*) venimeux.

poke /pəʊk/ *v.t./i.* (*push*) pousser; (*fire*) tisonner; (*thrust*) fourrer. —*n.* (petit) coup *m.* **~ about**, fureter. **~ fun at**, se moquer de. **~ out**, (*head*) sortir.

poker[1] /'pəʊkə(r)/ *n.* tisonnier *m.*

poker[2] /'pəʊkə(r)/ *n.* (*cards*) poker *m.*

poky /'pəʊkɪ/ *a.* (-ier, -iest) (*small*) exigu; (*slow*: *Amer.*) lent.

Poland /'pəʊlənd/ *n.* Pologne *f.*

polar /'pəʊlə(r)/ *a.* polaire. **~ bear**, ours blanc *m.*

polarize /'pəʊləraɪz/ *v.t.* polariser.

pole[1] /pəʊl/ *n.* (*fixed*) poteau *m.*; (*rod*) perche *f.*; (*for flag*) mât *m.*

pole[2] /pəʊl/ *n.* (*geog.*) pôle *m.*

Pole /pəʊl/ *n.* Polonais(e) *m.* (*f.*).

polemic /pə'lemɪk/ *n.* polémique *f.*

police /pə'liːs/ *n.* police *f.* —*v.t.* faire la police dans. **~ state**, état policier *m.* **~ station**, commissariat de police *m.*

police|man /pə'liːsmən/ *n.* (*pl.* -men) agent de police *m.* **~woman** (*pl.* -women) femme-agent *f.*

policy[1] /'pɒlɪsɪ/ *n.* politique *f.*

policy[2] /'pɒlɪsɪ/ *n.* (*insurance*) police (d'assurance) *f.*

polio(myelitis) /'pəʊlɪəʊ(maɪə'laɪtɪs)/ *n.* polio(myélite) *f.*

polish /'pɒlɪʃ/ *v.t.* polir; (*shoes, floor*) cirer. —*n.* (*for shoes*) cirage *m.*; (*for floor*) encaustique *f.*; (*for nails*) vernis *m.*; (*shine*) poli *m.*; (*fig.*) raffinement *m.* **~ off**, finir en vitesse. **~ up**, (*language*) perfectionner. **~ed** *a.* raffiné.

Polish /'pəʊlɪʃ/ *a.* polonais. —*n.* (*lang.*) polonais *m.*

polite /pə'laɪt/ *a.* poli. **~ly** *adv.* poliment. **~ness** *n.* politesse *f.*

political /pə'lɪtɪkl/ *a.* politique.

politician /pɒlɪ'tɪʃn/ *n.* homme politique *m.*, femme politique *f.*

politics /'pɒlətɪks/ *n.* politique *f.*

polka /'pɒlkə, *Amer.* 'pəʊlkə/ *n.* polka *f.* **~ dots**, pois *m. pl.*

poll /pəʊl/ *n.* scrutin *m.*; (*survey*) sondage *m.* —*v.t.* (*votes*) obtenir. **go to the ~s**, aller aux urnes. **~ing-booth** *n.* isoloir *m.*

pollen /'pɒlən/ *n.* pollen *m.*

pollut|e /pə'luːt/ *v.t.* polluer. **~ion** /-ʃn/ *n.* pollution *f.*

polo /'pəʊləʊ/ *n.* polo *m.* **~ neck**, col roulé *m.*

polygamy /pə'lɪgəmɪ/ *n.* polygamie *f.*

polytechnic /pɒlɪ'teknɪk/ *n.* institut universitaire de technologie *m.*

polythene /'pɒlɪθiːn/ *n.* polythène *m.*, polyéthylène *m.*

pomegranate /'pɒmɪgrænɪt/ *n.* (*fruit*) grenade *f.*

pomp /pɒmp/ *n.* pompe *f.*

pompon /'pɒmpɒn/ *n.* pompon *m.*

pomp|ous /'pɒmpəs/ *a.* pompeux. **~osity** /-'pɒsətɪ/ *n.* solennité *f.*

pond /pɒnd/ *n.* étang *m.*; (*artificial*) bassin *m.*; (*stagnant*) mare *f.*

ponder /'pɒndə(r)/ *v.t./i.* réfléchir (à), méditer (sur).

ponderous /'pɒndərəs/ *a.* pesant.

pong /pɒŋ/ *n.* (*stink*: *sl.*) puanteur *f.* —*v.i.* (*sl.*) puer.

pony /'pəʊnɪ/ *n.* poney *m.* **~-tail** *n.* queue de cheval *f.*

poodle /'puːdl/ *n.* caniche *m.*

pool[1] /puːl/ *n.* (*puddle*) flaque *f.*; (*pond*) étang *m.*; (*of blood*) mare *f.*; (*for swimming*) piscine *f.*

pool[2] /puːl/ *n.* (*fund*) fonds commun *m.*, (*of ideas*) réservoir *m.*; (*of typists*) pool *m.*; (*snooker*) billard américain *m.* ~**s,** pari mutuel sur le football *m.* —*v.t.* mettre en commun.

poor /pʊə(r)/ *a.* (-**er,** -**est**) pauvre; (*not good*) médiocre, mauvais. ~**ly** *adv.* mal; *a.* malade.

pop¹ /pɒp/ *n.* (*noise*) bruit sec *m.* —*v.t./i.* (*p.t.* **popped**) (*burst*) crever; (*put*) mettre. ~ **in/out/off,** entrer/sortir/partir. ~ **over,** faire un saut (**to see s.o.,** chez qn.). ~ **up,** surgir.

pop² /pɒp/ *n.* (*mus.*) musique pop *f.* —*a.* pop *invar.*

popcorn /'pɒpkɔːn/ *n.* pop-corn *m.*

pope /pəʊp/ *n.* pape *m.*

poplar /'pɒplə(r)/ *n.* peuplier *m.*

poppy /'pɒpɪ/ *n.* pavot *m.*; (*wild*) coquelicot *m.*

popular /'pɒpjʊlə(r)/ *a.* populaire; (*in fashion*) en vogue. **be** ~ **with,** plaire à. ~**ity** /-'lærətɪ/ *n.* popularité *f.* ~**ize** *v.t.* populariser. ~**ly** *adv.* communément.

populat|e /'pɒpjʊleɪt/ *v.t.* peupler. ~**ion** /-'leɪʃn/ *n.* population *f.*

populous /'pɒpjʊləs/ *a.* populeux.

porcelain /'pɔːsəlɪn/ *n.* porcelaine *f.*

porch /pɔːtʃ/ *n.* porche *m.*

porcupine /'pɔːkjʊpaɪn/ *n.* (*rodent*) porc-épic *m.*

pore¹ /pɔː(r)/ *n.* pore *m.*

pore² /pɔː(r)/ *v.i.* ~ **over,** étudier minutieusement.

pork /pɔːk/ *n.* (*food*) porc *m.*

pornograph|y /pɔː'nɒgrəfɪ/ *n.* pornographie *f.* ~**ic** /-ə'græfɪk/ *a.* pornographique.

porous /'pɔːrəs/ *a.* poreux.

porpoise /'pɔːpəs/ *n.* marsouin *m.*

porridge /'pɒrɪdʒ/ *n.* porridge *m.*

port¹ /pɔːt/ *n.* (*harbour*) port *m.* ~ **of call,** escale *f.*

port² /pɔːt/ *n.* (*left: naut.*) bâbord *m.*

port³ /pɔːt/ *n.* (*wine*) porto *m.*

portable /'pɔːtəbl/ *a.* portatif.

portal /'pɔːtl/ *n.* portail *m.*

porter¹ /'pɔːtə(r)/ *n.* (*carrier*) porteur *m.*

porter² /'pɔːtə(r)/ *n.* (*door-keeper*) portier *m.*

portfolio /pɔːt'fəʊlɪəʊ/ *n.* (*pl.* -**os**) (*pol., comm.*) portefeuille *m.*

porthole /'pɔːthəʊl/ *n.* hublot *m.*

portico /'pɔːtɪkəʊ/ *n.* (*pl.* -**oes**) portique *m.*

portion /'pɔːʃn/ *n.* (*share, helping*) portion *f.*; (*part*) partie *f.*

portly /'pɔːtlɪ/ *a.* (-**ier,** -**iest**) corpulent (et digne).

portrait /'pɔːtrɪt/ *n.* portrait *m.*

portray /pɔː'treɪ/ *v.t.* représenter. ~**al** *n.* portrait *m.*, peinture *f.*

Portug|al /'pɔːtjʊgl/ *n.* Portugal *m.* ~**uese** /-'giːz/ *a.* & *n. invar.* portugais(e) (*m.* (*f.*)).

pose /pəʊz/ *v.t./i.* poser. —*n.* pose *f.* ~ **as,** (*expert etc.*) se poser en.

poser /'pəʊzə(r)/ *n.* colle *f.*

posh /pɒʃ/ *a.* (*sl.*) chic *invar.*

position /pə'zɪʃn/ *n.* position *f.*; (*job, state*) situation *f.* —*v.t.* placer.

positive /'pɒzətɪv/ *a.* (*test, help, etc.*) positif; (*sure*) sûr, certain; (*real*) réel, vrai. ~**ly** *adv.* positivement; (*absolutely*) complètement.

possess /pə'zes/ *v.t.* posséder. ~**ion** /-ʃn/ *n.* possession *f.* **take** ~**ion of,** prendre possession de. ~**or** *n.* possesseur *m.*

possessive /pə'zesɪv/ *a.* possessif.

possib|le /'pɒsəbl/ *a.* possible. ~**ility** /-'bɪlətɪ/ *n.* possibilité *f.*

possibly /'pɒsəblɪ/ *adv.* peut-être. **if I** ~ **can,** si cela m'est possible. **I cannot** ~ **leave,** il m'est impossible de partir.

post¹ /pəʊst/ *n.* (*pole*) poteau *m.* —*v.t.* ~ (**up**), (*a notice*) afficher.

post² /pəʊst/ *n.* (*station, job*) poste *m.* —*v.t.* poster; (*appoint*) affecter.

post³ /pəʊst/ *n.* (*mail service*) poste *f.*; (*letters*) courrier *m.* —*a.* postal. —*v.t.* (*put in box*) poster; (*send*) envoyer (par la poste). **keep** ~**ed,** tenir au courant. ~-**box** *n.* boîte à *or* aux lettres *f.* ~-**code** *n.* code postal *m.* **P**~ **Office,** postes *f. pl.*; (*in France*) Postes et Télécommunications *f. pl.* ~ **office,** bureau de poste *m.*, poste *f.*

post /pəʊst/ *pref.* post-.

postage /'pəʊstɪdʒ/ *n.* tarif postal *m.*, frais de port *m.pl.*

postal /'pəʊstl/ *a.* postal. ~ **order,** mandat *m.* ~ **worker,** employé(e) des postes *m.*(*f.*)

postcard /'pəʊstkɑːd/ *n.* carte postale *f.*

poster /'pəʊstə(r)/ *n.* affiche *f.*

posterior /pɒ'stɪərɪə(r)/ *n.* postérieur *m.*

posterity /pɒ'sterətɪ/ *n.* postérité *f.*

postgraduate /pəʊst'grædʒʊət/ *n.* étudiant(e) de troisième cycle *m.*(*f.*).

posthumous /'pɒstjʊməs/ *a.* posthume. ~**ly** *adv.* à titre posthume.

postman /'pəʊstmən/ *n.* (*pl.* -**men**) facteur *m.*

postmark /'pəʊstmɑːk/ *n.* cachet de la poste *m.*

postmaster /'pəʊstmɑːstə(r)/ *n.* receveur des postes *m.*

post-mortem /pəʊst'mɔːtəm/ *n.* autopsie *f.*

postpone /pə'spəʊn/ *v.t.* remettre. ~**ment** *n.* ajournement *m.*

postscript /'pəʊsskrɪpt/ *n.* (*to letter*) post-scriptum *m. invar.*

postulate /'pɒstjʊleɪt/ *v.t.* postuler.

posture /'pɒstʃə(r)/ *n.* posture *f.* —*v.i.* (*affectedly*) poser.

post-war /'pəʊstwɔː(r)/ *a.* d'après-guerre.

pot /pɒt/ *n.* pot *m.*; (*for cooking*) marmite *f.*; (*drug: sl.*) mariejeanne *f.* **go to** ~, (*sl.*) aller à la ruine. ~-**belly** *n.* gros ventre *m.* **take** ~ **luck,** tenter sa chance. **take a** ~-**shot at,** faire un carton sur.

potato /pə'teɪtəʊ/ *n.* (*pl.* -**oes**) pomme de terre *f.*

poten|t /'pəʊtnt/ *a.* puissant; (*drink*) fort. ~**cy** *n.* puissance *f.*

potential /pə'tenʃl/ *a.* & *n.* potentiel (*m.*). ~**ly** *adv.* potentiellement.

pot-hol|e /'pɒthəʊl/ *n.* (*in rock*) caverne *f.*; (*in road*) nid de poule *m.* ~**ing** *n.* spéléologie *f.*

potion /'pəʊʃn/ *n.* potion *f.*

potted /'pɒtɪd/ *a.* (*plant etc.*) en pot; (*preserved*) en conserve; (*abridged*) condensé.

potter[1] /'pɒtə(r)/ *n.* potier *m.* ~**y** *n.* (*art*) poterie *f.*; (*objects*) poteries *f. pl.*

potter[2] /'pɒtə(r)/ *v.i.* bricoler.

potty /'pɒtɪ/ *a.* (-**ier**, -**iest**) (*crazy: sl.*) toqué.

pouch /paʊtʃ/ *n.* poche *f.*; (*for tobacco*) blague *f.*

pouffe /puːf/ *n.* pouf *m.*

poultice /'pəʊltɪs/ *n.* cataplasme *m.*

poult|ry /'pəʊltrɪ/ *n.* volaille *f.* ~**erer** *n.* marchand de volailles *m.*

pounce /paʊns/ *v.i.* bondir (**on,** sur). —*n.* bond *m.*

pound[1] /paʊnd/ *n.* (*weight*) livre *f.* (= 454 *g.*); (*money*) livre *f.*

pound[2] /paʊnd/ *n.* (*for dogs, cars*) fourrière *f.*

pound[3] /paʊnd/ *v.t.* (*crush*) piler; (*bombard*) pilonner. —*v.i.* frapper fort; (*of heart*) battre fort; (*walk*) marcher à pas lourds.

pour /pɔː(r)/ *v.t.* verser. —*v.i.* couler, ruisseler (**from,** de); (*rain*) pleuvoir à torrents. ~ **in/out,** (*people*) arriver/ sortir en masse. ~ **off** *or* **out,** vider. ~**ing** **rain,** pluie torrentielle *f.*

pout /paʊt/ *v.t./i.* ~ (**one's lips**), faire la moue. —*n.* moue *f.*

poverty /'pɒvətɪ/ *n.* misère *f.*, pauvreté *f.*

powder /'paʊdə(r)/ *n.* poudre *f.* —*v.t.* poudrer. ~**ed** *a.* en poudre. ~**y** *a.* poudreux.

power /'paʊə(r)/ *n.* puissance *f.*; (*ability, authority*) pouvoir *m.*; (*energy*) énergie *f.*; (*electr.*) courant *m.* ~ **cut,** coupure de courant *f.* ~**ed by,** fonctionnant à; (*jet etc.*) propulsé par. ~**less** *a.* impuissant. ~-**station** *n.* centrale électrique *f.*

powerful /'paʊəfl/ *a.* puissant. ~**ly** *adv.* puissamment.

practicable /'præktɪkəbl/ *a.* praticable.

practical /'præktɪkl/ *a.* pratique. ~ **joke,** farce *f.*

practically /'præktɪklɪ/ *adv.* pratiquement.

practice /'præktɪs/ *n.* pratique *f.*; (*of profession*) exercice *m.*; (*sport*) entraînement *m.*; (*clients*) clientèle *f.* **be in** ~, (*doctor, lawyer*) exercer. **in** ~, (*in fact*) en pratique; (*well-trained*) en forme. **out of** ~, rouillé. **put into** ~, mettre en pratique.

practis|e /'præktɪs/ *v.t./i.* (*musician, typist, etc.*) s'exercer (à); (*sport*) s'entraîner (à); (*put into practice*) pratiquer; (*profession*) exercer. ~**ed** *a.* expérimenté. ~**ing** *a.* (*Catholic etc.*) pratiquant.

practitioner /præk'tɪʃənə(r)/ *n.* praticien(ne) *m.* (*f.*).

pragmatic /præg'mætɪk/ *a.* pragmatique.

prairie /'preərɪ/ *n.* (*in North America*) prairie *f.*

praise /preɪz/ *v.t.* louer. —*n.* éloge(s) *m.* (*pl.*), louange(s) *f.* (*pl.*).

praiseworthy /'preɪzwɜːðɪ/ *a.* digne d'éloges.

pram /præm/ *n.* voiture d'enfant *f.*, landau *m.*

prance /prɑːns/ *v.i.* caracoler.

prank /præŋk/ *n.* farce *f.*

prattle /'prætl/ *v.i.* jaser.

prawn /prɔːn/ *n.* crevette rose *f.*

pray /preɪ/ *v.i.* prier.

prayer /preə(r)/ *n.* prière *f.*

pre /priː/ *pref.* pré-.

preach /priːtʃ/ *v.t./i.* prêcher. ~ at *or* to, prêcher. ~er *n.* prédicateur *m.*

preamble /priːˈæmbl/ *n.* préambule *m.*

pre-arrange /priːəˈreɪndʒ/ *v.t.* fixer à l'avance.

precarious /prɪˈkeərɪəs/ *a.* précaire.

precaution /prɪˈkɔːʃn/ *n.* précaution *f.* ~ary *a.* de précaution.

preced|e /prɪˈsiːd/ *v.t.* précéder. ~ing *a.* précédent.

precedence /ˈpresɪdəns/ *n.* priorité *f.*; (*in rank*) préséance *f.*

precedent /ˈpresɪdənt/ *n.* précédent *m.*

precept /ˈpriːsept/ *n.* précepte *m.*

precinct /ˈpriːsɪŋkt/ *n.* enceinte *f.*; (*pedestrian area*) zone *f.*; (*district*: *Amer.*) circonscription *f.*

precious /ˈpreʃəs/ *a.* précieux. —*adv.* (*very*: *fam.*) très.

precipice /ˈpresɪpɪs/ *n.* (*geog.*) à-pic *m.* *invar.*; (*fig.*) précipice *m.*

precipitat|e /prɪˈsɪpɪteɪt/ *v.t.* (*person, event, chemical*) précipiter. ~ion /-ˈteɪʃn/ *n.* précipitation *f.*

précis /ˈpreɪsiː/ *n. invar.* précis *m.*

precis|e /prɪˈsaɪs/ *a.* précis; (*careful*) méticuleux. ~ely *adv.* précisément. ~ion /-ˈsɪʒn/ *n.* précision *f.*

preclude /prɪˈkluːd/ *v.t.* (*prevent*) empêcher; (*rule out*) exclure.

precocious /prɪˈkəʊʃəs/ *a.* précoce.

preconc|eived /priːkənˈsiːvd/ *a.* préconçu. ~eption *n.* préconception *f.*

pre-condition /priːkənˈdɪʃn/ *n.* condition requise *f.*

predator /ˈpredətə(r)/ *n.* prédateur *m.* ~y *a.* rapace.

predecessor /ˈpriːdɪsesə(r)/ *n.* prédécesseur *m.*

predicament /prɪˈdɪkəmənt/ *n.* mauvaise situation *or* passe *f.*

predict /prɪˈdɪkt/ *v.t.* prédire. ~able *a.* prévisible. ~ion /-kʃn/ *n.* prédiction *f.*

predispose /priːdɪˈspəʊz/ *v.t.* prédisposer (**to do**, à faire).

predominant /prɪˈdɒmɪnənt/ *a.* prédominant. ~ly *adv.* pour la plupart.

predominate /prɪˈdɒmɪneɪt/ *v.i.* prédominer.

pre-eminent /priːˈemɪnənt/ *a.* prééminent.

pre-empt /priːˈempt/ *v.t.* acquérir d'avance.

preen /priːn/ *v.t.* (*bird*) lisser. ~ **o.s.**, (*person*) se bichonner.

prefab /ˈpriːfæb/ *n.* (*fam.*) bâtiment préfabriqué *m.* ~ricated /-ˈfæbrɪkeɪtɪd/ *a.* préfabriqué.

preface /ˈprefɪs/ *n.* préface *f.*

prefect /ˈpriːfekt/ *n.* (*pupil*) élève chargé(e) de la discipline *m./f.*; (*official*) préfet *m.*

prefer /prɪˈfɜː(r)/ *v.t.* (*p.t.* **preferred**) préférer (**to do**, faire). ~able /ˈprefrəbl/ *a.* préférable.

preferen|ce /ˈprefrəns/ *n.* préférence *f.* ~tial /-əˈrenʃl/ *a.* préférentiel.

prefix /ˈpriːfɪks/ *n.* préfixe *m.*

pregnan|t /ˈpregnənt/ *a.* (*woman*) enceinte; (*animal*) pleine. ~cy *n.* (*of woman*) grossesse *f.*

prehistoric /priːhɪˈstɒrɪk/ *a.* préhistorique.

prejudge /priːˈdʒʌdʒ/ *v.t.* préjuger de; (*person*) juger d'avance.

prejudice /ˈpredʒʊdɪs/ *n.* préjugé(s) *m.* (*pl.*); (*harm*) préjudice *m.* —*v.t.* (*claim*) porter préjudice à; (*person*) prévenir. ~d *a.* partial; (*person*) qui a des préjugés.

preliminar|y /prɪˈlɪmɪnərɪ/ *a.* préliminaire. ~ies *n. pl.* préliminaires *m. pl.*

prelude /ˈpreljuːd/ *n.* prélude *m.*

pre-marital /priːˈmærɪtl/ *a.* avant le mariage.

premature /ˈpremətjʊə(r)/ *a.* prématuré.

premeditated /priːˈmedɪteɪtɪd/ *a.* prémédité.

premier /ˈpremɪə(r)/ *a.* premier. —*n.* premier ministre *m.*

première /ˈpremɪeə(r)/ *n.* première *f.*

premises /ˈpremɪsɪz/ *n. pl.* locaux *m. pl.* **on the ~**, sur les lieux.

premiss /ˈpremɪs/ *n.* prémisse *f.*

premium /ˈpriːmɪəm/ *n.* prime *f.* **be at a ~**, faire prime.

premonition /priːməˈnɪʃn/ *n.* prémonition *f.*, pressentiment *m.*

preoccup|ation /priːɒkjʊˈpeɪʃn/ *n.* préoccupation *f.* ~ied /-ˈɒkjʊpaɪd/ *a.* préoccupé.

prep /prep/ *n.* (*work*) devoirs *m. pl.* ~ **school** = **preparatory school**.

preparation /prepəˈreɪʃn/ *n.* préparation *f.* ~s, préparatifs *m. pl.*

preparatory /prɪˈpærətrɪ/ *a.* préparatoire. ~ **school**, école primaire privée *f.*; (*Amer.*) école secondaire privée *f.*

prepare /prɪˈpeə(r)/ *v.t./i.* (se) préparer (**for**, à). **be ~d for**, (*expect*) s'attendre à. ~**d to**, prêt à.

prepay /priːˈpeɪ/ *v.t.* (*p.t.* **-paid**) payer d'avance.

preponderance /prɪ'pɒndərəns/ *n.* prédominance *f.*

preposition /prepə'zɪʃn/ *n.* préposition *f.*

preposterous /prɪ'pɒstərəs/ *a.* absurde, ridicule.

prerequisite /priː'rekwɪzɪt/ *n.* condition préalable *f.*

prerogative /prɪ'rɒgətɪv/ *n.* prérogative *f.*

Presbyterian /prezbɪ'tɪərɪən/ *a.* & *n.* presbytérien(ne) (*m.* (*f.*)).

prescri|be /prɪ'skraɪb/ *v.t.* prescrire. **~ption** /-ɪpʃn/ *n.* prescription *f.*; (*med.*) ordonnance *f.*

presence /'prezns/ *n.* présence *f.* **~ of mind**, présence d'esprit *f.*

present[1] /'preznt/ *a.* présent. —*n.* présent *m.* **at ~**, à présent. **for the ~**, pour le moment.

present[2] /'preznt/ *n.* (*gift*) cadeau *m.*

present[3] /prɪ'zent/ *v.t.* présenter; (*film, concert, etc.*) donner. **~ s.o. with**, offrir à qn. **~able** *a.* présentable. **~ation** /prezn'teɪʃn/ *n.* présentation *f.*

presently /'prezntlɪ/ *adv.* bientôt; (*now*: *Amer.*) en ce moment.

preservative /prɪ'zɜːvətɪv/ *n.* (*culin.*) agent de conservation *m.*

preserv|e /prɪ'zɜːv/ *v.t.* préserver; (*maintain & culin.*) conserver. —*n.* réserve *f.*; (*fig.*) domaine *m.*; (*jam*) confiture *f.* **~ation** /prezə'veɪʃn/ *n.* conservation *f.*

preside /prɪ'zaɪd/ *v.i.* présider. **~ over**, présider.

presiden|t /'prezɪdənt/ *n.* président(e) *m.* (*f.*). **~cy** *n.* présidence *f.* **~tial** /-'denʃl/ *a.* présidentiel.

press /pres/ *v.t./i.* (*button etc.*) appuyer (sur); (*squeeze, urge*) presser; (*iron*) repasser; (*pursue*) poursuivre. —*n.* (*newspapers, machine*) presse *f.*; (*for wine*) pressoir *m.* **be ~ed for**, (*time etc.*) manquer de. **~ conference/cutting**, conférence/coupure de presse *f.* **~ on**, continuer (**with sth.**, qch.). **~-stud** *n.* bouton-pression *m.* **~-up** *n.* traction *f.*

pressing /'presɪŋ/ *a.* pressant.

pressure /'preʃə(r)/ *n.* pression *f.* —*v.t.* faire pression sur. **~cooker** *n.* cocotte-minute *f.* **~ group**, groupe de pression *m.*

pressurize /'preʃəraɪz/ *v.t.* (*cabin etc.*) pressuriser; (*person*) faire pression sur.

prestige /pre'stiːʒ/ *n.* prestige *m.*

prestigious /pre'stɪdʒəs/ *a.* prestigieux.

presumably /prɪ'zjuːməblɪ/ *adv.* vraisemblablement.

presum|e /prɪ'zjuːm/ *v.t.* (*suppose*) présumer. **~e to**, (*venture*) se permettre de. **~ption** /-'zʌmpʃn/ *n.* présomption *f.*

presumptuous /prɪ'zʌmptʃʊəs/ *a.* présomptueux.

pretence /prɪ'tens/ *n.* feinte *f.*, simulation *f.*; (*claim*) prétention *f.*; (*pretext*) prétexte *m.*

pretend /prɪ'tend/ *v.t./i.* faire semblant (**to do**, de faire). **~ to**, (*lay claim to*) prétendre à.

pretentious /prɪ'tenʃəs/ *a.* prétentieux.

pretext /'priːtekst/ *n.* prétexte *m.*

pretty /'prɪtɪ/ *a.* (**-ier, -iest**) joli. —*adv.* assez. **~ much**, presque.

prevail /prɪ'veɪl/ *v.i.* prédominer; (*win*) prévaloir. **~ on**, persuader.

prevalen|t /'prevələnt/ *a.* répandu. **~ce** *n.* fréquence *f.*

prevent /prɪ'vent/ *v.t.* empêcher (**from doing**, de faire). **~able** *a.* évitable. **~ion** /-enʃn/ *n.* prévention *f.* **~ive** *a.* préventif.

preview /'priːvjuː/ *n.* avant-première *f.*; (*fig.*) aperçu *m.*

previous /'priːvɪəs/ *a.* précédent, antérieur. **~ to**, avant. **~ly** *adv.* précédemment, auparavant.

pre-war /'priːwɔː(r)/ *a.* d'avant-guerre.

prey /preɪ/ *n.* proie *f.* —*v.i.* **~ on**, faire sa proie de; (*worry*) préoccuper. **bird of ~**, rapace *m.*

price /praɪs/ *n.* prix *m.* —*v.t.* fixer le prix de. **~less** *a.* inestimable; (*amusing*: *sl.*) impayable.

pricey /'praɪsɪ/ *a.* (*fam.*) coûteux.

prick /prɪk/ *v.t.* (*with pin etc.*) piquer. —*n.* piqûre *f.* **~ up one's ears**, dresser l'oreille.

prickl|e /'prɪkl/ *n.* piquant *m.*; (*sensation*) picotement *m.* **~y** *a.* piquant; (*person*) irritable.

pride /praɪd/ *n.* orgueil *m.*; (*satisfaction*) fierté *f.* —*v. pr.* **~ o.s. on**, s'enorgueillir de. **~ of place**, place d'honneur *f.*

priest /priːst/ *n.* prêtre *m.* **~hood** *n.* sacerdoce *m.* **~ly** *a.* sacerdotal.

prig /prɪg/ *n.* petit saint *m.*, pharisien(ne) *m.*(*f.*). **~gish** *a.* hypocrite.

prim /prɪm/ a. (**primmer, primmest**) guindé, méticuleux.

primar|y /'praɪmərɪ/ a. (*school, elections, etc.*) primaire; (*chief, basic*) premier, fondamental. ∼**ily** /*Amer.* -'merɪlɪ/ adv. essentiellement.

prime[1] /praɪm/ a. principal, premier; (*first-rate*) excellent. **P**∼ **Minister**, Premier Ministre m. **the** ∼ **of life**, la force de l'âge.

prime[2] /praɪm/ v.t. (*pump, gun*) amorcer; (*surface*) apprêter. ∼**r**[1] /-ə(r)/ n. (*paint etc.*) apprêt m.

primer[2] /'praɪmə(r)/ n. (*schoolbook*) premier livre m.

primeval /praɪ'miːvl/ a. primitif.

primitive /'prɪmɪtɪv/ a. primitif.

primrose /'prɪmrəʊz/ n. primevère (jaune) f.

prince /prɪns/ n. prince m. ∼**ly** a. princier.

princess /prɪn'ses/ n. princesse f.

principal /'prɪnsəpl/ a. principal. —n. (*of school etc.*) direc|teur, -trice m., f. ∼**ly** adv. principalement.

principle /'prɪnsəpl/ n. principe m. **in/on** ∼, en/par principe.

print /prɪnt/ v.t. imprimer; (*write in capitals*) écrire en majuscules. —n. (*of foot etc.*) empreinte f.; (*letters*) caractères m. pl.; (*photograph*) épreuve f.; (*engraving*) gravure f. **in** ∼, disponible. **out of** ∼, épuisé. ∼**-out** n. listage m. ∼**ed matter**, imprimés m. pl.

print|er /'prɪntə(r)/ n. (*person*) imprimeur m.; (*computer device*) imprimante f. ∼**ing** n. impression f.

prior[1] /'praɪə(r)/ a. précédent. ∼ **to**, prep. avant (de).

prior[2] /'praɪə(r)/ n. (*relig.*) prieur m. ∼**y** n. prieuré m.

priority /praɪ'ɒrətɪ/ n. priorité f.

prise /praɪz/ v.t. forcer. ∼ **open**, ouvrir en forçant.

prism /'prɪzəm/ n. prisme m.

prison /'prɪzn/ n. prison f. ∼**er** n. prisonn|ier, -ière m., f. ∼ **officer**, gardien(ne) de prison m. (f.).

pristine /'prɪstiːn/ a. primitif; (*condition*) parfait.

privacy /'praɪvəsɪ/ n. intimité f., solitude f.

private /'praɪvɪt/ a. privé; (*confidential*) personnel; (*lessons, house, etc.*) particulier; (*ceremony*) intime. —n. (*soldier*) simple soldat m. **in** ∼, en privé; (*of ceremony*) dans l'intimité. ∼**ly** adv. en privé; dans l'intimité; (*inwardly*) intérieurement.

privet /'prɪvɪt/ n. (*bot.*) troène m.

privilege /'prɪvəlɪdʒ/ n. privilège m. ∼**d** a. privilégié. **be** ∼**d to**, avoir le privilège de.

privy /'prɪvɪ/ a. ∼ **to**, au fait de.

prize /praɪz/ n. prix m. —a. (*entry etc.*) primé; (*fool etc.*) parfait. —v.t. (*value*) priser. ∼**-fighter** n. boxeur professionnel m. ∼**-winner** n. lauréat(e) m.(f.); (*in lottery etc.*) gagnant(e) m. (f.).

pro /prəʊ/ n. **the** ∼**s and cons**, le pour et le contre.

pro- /prəʊ/ pref. pro-.

probab|le /'prɒbəbl/ a. probable. ∼**ility** /-'bɪlətɪ/ n. probabilité f. ∼**ly** adv. probablement.

probation /prə'beɪʃn/ n. (*testing*) essai m.; (*jurid.*) liberté surveillée f. ∼**ary** a. d'essai.

probe /prəʊb/ n. (*device*) sonde f.; (*fig.*) enquête f. —v.t. sonder. —v.i. ∼ **into**, sonder.

problem /'prɒbləm/ n. problème m. —a. difficile. ∼**atic** /-'mætɪk/ a. problématique.

procedure /prə'siːdʒə(r)/ n. procédure f.

proceed /prə'siːd/ v.i. (*go*) aller, avancer; (*pass*) passer (to, à); (*act*) procéder. ∼ (**with**), (*continue*) continuer. ∼ **to do**, se mettre à faire. ∼**ing** n. procédé m.

proceedings /prə'siːdɪŋz/ n. pl. (*discussions*) débats m. pl.; (*meeting*) réunion f.; (*report*) actes m. pl.; (*jurid.*) poursuites f. pl.

proceeds /'prəʊsiːdz/ n. pl. (*profits*) produit m., bénéfices m. pl.

process /'prəʊses/ n. processus m.; (*method*) procédé m. —v.t. (*material, data*) traiter. **in** ∼, en cours. **in the** ∼ **of doing**, en train de faire.

procession /prə'seʃn/ n. défilé m.

procl|aim /prə'kleɪm/ v.t. proclamer. ∼**amation** /prɒklə'meɪʃn/ n. proclamation f.

procrastinate /prə'kræstɪneɪt/ v.i. différer, tergiverser.

procreation /prəʊkrɪ'eɪʃn/ n. procréation f.

procure /prə'kjʊə(r)/ v.t. obtenir.

prod /prɒd/ v.t./i. (*p.t.* **prodded**) pousser. —n. poussée f., coup m.

prodigal /'prɒdɪgl/ a. prodigue.

prodigious /prə'dɪdʒəs/ a. prodigieux.

prodigy /'prɒdɪdʒɪ/ *n*. prodige *m*.

produc|e[1] /prə'dju:s/ *v.t./i*. produire; (*bring out*) sortir; (*show*) présenter; (*cause*) provoquer; (*theatre, TV*) mettre en scène; (*radio*) réaliser. ~**er** *n*. metteur en scène *m*.; réalisateur *m*. ~**tion** /-'dʌkʃn/ *n*. production *f*.; mise en scène *f*.; réalisation *f*.

produce[2] /'prɒdju:s/ *n*. (*food etc.*) produits *m. pl*.

product /'prɒdʌkt/ *n*. produit *m*.

productiv|e /prə'dʌktɪv/ *a*. productif. ~**ity** /prɒdʌk'tɪvətɪ/ *n*. productivité *f*.

profan|e /prə'feɪn/ *a*. sacrilège; (*secular*) profane. ~**ity** /-'fænətɪ/ *n*. (*oath*) juron *m*.

profess /prə'fes/ *v.t*. professer. ~ **to do,** prétendre faire.

profession /prə'feʃn/ *n*. profession *f*. ~**al** *a*. professionnel; (*of high quality*) de professionnel; (*person*) qui exerce une profession libérale; *n*. professionnel(le) *m*. (*f*.).

professor /prə'fesə(r)/ *n*. professeur (titulaire d'une chaire) *m*.

proficien|t /prə'fɪʃnt/ *a*. compétent. ~**cy** *n*. compétence *f*.

profile /'prəʊfaɪl/ *n*. profil *m*.

profit /'prɒfɪt/ *n*. profit *m*., bénéfice *m*. —*v.i*. (*p.t*. profited). ~ **by,** tirer profit de. ~**able** *a*. rentable.

profound /prə'faʊnd/ *a*. profond. ~**ly** *adv*. profondément.

profus|e /prə'fju:s/ *a*. abondant. ~**e in,** (*lavish in*) prodigue de. ~**ely** *adv*. en abondance. ~**ion** /-ʒn/ *n*. profusion *f*.

progeny /'prɒdʒənɪ/ *n*. progéniture *f*.

program /'prəʊgræm/ *n*. (*Amer.*) = programme. (computer) ~, programme *m*. —*v.t*. (*p.t*. programmed) programmer. ~**mer** *n*. programmeu|r, -se *m*., *f*. ~**ming** *n*. (*on computer*) programmation *f*.

programme /'prəʊgræm/ *n*. programme *m*.; (*broadcast*) émission *f*.

progress[1] /'prəʊgres/ *n*. progrès *m*. (*pl*.). in ~, en cours.

progress[2] /prə'gres/ *v.i*. (*advance, improve*) progresser. ~**ion** /-ʃn/ *n*. progression *f*.

progressive /prə'gresɪv/ *a*. progressif; (*reforming*) progressiste. ~**ly** *adv*. progressivement.

prohibit /prə'hɪbɪt/ *v.t*. interdire (**s.o. from doing,** à qn. de faire).

prohibitive /prə'hɪbətɪv/ *a*. (*price etc.*) prohibitif.

project[1] /prə'dʒekt/ *v.t*. projeter. —*v.i*. (*jut out*) être en saillie. ~**ion** /-kʃn/ *n*. projection *f*.; saillie *f*.

project[2] /'prɒdʒekt/ *n*. (*plan*) projet *m*.; (*undertaking*) entreprise *f*.

projectile /prə'dʒektaɪl/ *n*. projectile *m*.

projector /prə'dʒektə(r)/ *n*. (*cinema etc.*) projecteur *m*.

proletari|at /prəʊlɪ'teərɪət/ *n*. prolétariat *m*. ~**an** *a*. prolétarien; *n*. prolétaire *m*./*f*.

proliferat|e /prə'lɪfəreɪt/ *v.i*. proliférer. ~**ion** /-'reɪʃn/ *n*. prolifération *f*.

prolific /prə'lɪfɪk/ *a*. prolifique.

prologue /'prəʊlɒg/ *n*. prologue *m*.

prolong /prə'lɒŋ/ *v.t*. prolonger.

promenade /prɒmə'nɑːd/ *n*. promenade *f*. —*v.t./i*. (se) promener.

prominen|t /'prɒmɪnənt/ *a*. (*projecting*) proéminent; (*conspicuous*) bien en vue; (*fig.*) important. ~**ce** *n*. proéminence *f*.; importance *f*. ~**tly** *adv*. bien en vue.

promiscu|ous /prə'mɪskjʊəs/ *a*. de mœurs faciles. ~**ity** /prɒmɪ'skju:ətɪ/ *n*. liberté de mœurs *f*.

promis|e /'prɒmɪs/ *n*. promesse *f*. —*v.t./i*. promettre. ~**ing** *a*. prometteur; (*person*) qui promet.

promot|e /prə'məʊt/ *v.t*. promouvoir. ~**ion** /-'məʊʃn/ *n*. (*of person, sales, etc.*) promotion *f*.

prompt /prɒmpt/ *a*. rapide; (*punctual*) à l'heure, ponctuel. —*adv*. (*on the dot*) pile. —*v.t*. inciter; (*cause*) provoquer; (*theatre*) souffler (son rôle) à. ~**er** *n*. souffleu|r, -se *m*., *f*. ~**ly** *adv*. rapidement; ponctuellement. ~**ness** *n*. rapidité *f*.

prone /prəʊn/ *a*. couché sur le ventre. ~ **to,** prédisposé à.

prong /prɒŋ/ *n*. (*of fork*) dent *f*.

pronoun /'prəʊnaʊn/ *n*. pronom *m*.

pron|ounce /prə'naʊns/ *v.t*. prononcer. ~**ouncement** *n*. déclaration *f*. ~**unciation** /-ʌnsɪ'eɪʃn/ *n*. prononciation *f*.

pronounced /prə'naʊnst/ *a*. (*noticeable*) prononcé.

proof /pru:f/ *n*. (*evidence*) preuve *f*.; (*test, trial copy*) épreuve *f*.; (*of liquor*) teneur en alcool *f*. —*a*. ~ **against,** à l'épreuve de.

prop[1] /prɒp/ *n*. support *m*. —*v.t*. (*p.t*. propped). ~ **(up),** (*support*) étayer; (*lean*) appuyer.

prop[2] /prɒp/ *n.* (*theatre, fam.*) accessoire *m.*

propaganda /prɒpə'gændə/ *n.* propagande *f.*

propagat|e /'prɒpəgeɪt/ *v.t./i.* (se) propager. ~**ion** /-'geɪʃn/ *n.* propagation *f.*

propel /prə'pel/ *v.t.* (*p.t.* **propelled**) propulser.

propeller /prə'pelə(r)/ *n.* hélice *f.*

proper /'prɒpə(r)/ *a.* correct, bon; (*seemly*) convenable; (*real*) vrai; (*thorough*: *fam.*) parfait. ~ **noun**, nom propre *m.* ~**ly** *adv.* correctement, comme il faut; (*rightly*) avec raison.

property /'prɒpətɪ/ *n.* propriété *f.*; (*things owned*) biens *m. pl.*, propriété *f.* —*a.* immobilier, foncier.

prophecy /'prɒfəsɪ/ *n.* prophétie *f.*

prophesy /'prɒfɪsaɪ/ *v.t./i.* prophétiser. ~ **that**, prédire que.

prophet /'prɒfɪt/ *n.* prophète *m.* ~**ic** /prə'fetɪk/ *a.* prophétique.

proportion /prə'pɔːʃn/ *n.* (*ratio, dimension*) proportion *f.*; (*amount*) partie *f.* ~**al**, ~**ate** *adjs.* proportionnel.

proposal /prə'pəʊzl/ *n.* proposition *f.*; (*of marriage*) demande en mariage *f.*

propos|e /prə'pəʊz/ *v.t.* proposer. —*v.i.* ~**e to**, faire une demande en mariage à. ~**e to do**, se proposer de faire. ~**ition** /prɒpə'zɪʃn/ *n.* proposition *f.*; (*matter*: *fam.*) affaire *f.*; *v.t.* (*fam.*) faire des propositions malhonnêtes à.

propound /prə'paʊnd/ *v.t.* (*theory etc.*) proposer.

proprietor /prə'praɪətə(r)/ *n.* propriétaire *m./f.*

propriety /prə'praɪətɪ/ *n.* (*correct behaviour*) bienséance *f.*

propulsion /prə'pʌlʃn/ *n.* propulsion *f.*

prosaic /prə'zeɪɪk/ *a.* prosaïque.

proscribe /prə'skraɪb/ *v.t.* proscrire.

prose /prəʊz/ *n.* prose *f.*; (*translation*) thème *m.*

prosecut|e /'prɒsɪkjuːt/ *v.t.* poursuivre. ~**ion** /-'kjuːʃn/ *n.* poursuites *f. pl.* ~**or** *n.* procureur *m.*

prospect[1] /'prɒspekt/ *n.* perspective *f.*; (*chance*) espoir *m.*

prospect[2] /prə'spekt/ *v.t./i.* prospecter. ~**or** *n.* prospecteur *m.*

prospective /prə'spektɪv/ *a.* (*future*) futur; (*possible*) éventuel.

prospectus /prə'spektəs/ *n.* prospectus *m.*; (*univ.*) guide *m.*

prosper /'prɒspə(r)/ *v.i.* prospérer.

prosper|ous /'prɒspərəs/ *a.* prospère. ~**ity** /-'sperətɪ/ *n.* prospérité *f.*

prostitut|e /'prɒstɪtjuːt/ *n.* prostituée *f.* ~**ion** /-'tjuːʃn/ *n.* prostitution *f.*

prostrate /'prɒstreɪt/ *a.* (*prone*) à plat ventre; (*submissive*) prosterné; (*exhausted*) prostré.

protagonist /prə'tægənɪst/ *n.* protagoniste *m.*

protect /prə'tekt/ *v.t.* protéger. ~**ion** /-kʃn/ *n.* protection *f.* ~**or** *n.* protec|teur, -trice *m.,f.*

protective /prə'tektɪv/ *a.* protecteur; (*clothes*) de protection.

protégé /'prɒtɪʒeɪ/ *n.* protégé *m.* ~**e** *n.* protégée *f.*

protein /'prəʊtiːn/ *n.* protéine *f.*

protest[1] /'prəʊtest/ *n.* protestation *f.* **under** ~, en protestant.

protest[2] /prə'test/ *v.t./i.* protester. ~**er** *n.* (*pol.*) contestataire *m./f.*

Protestant /'prɒtɪstənt/ *a. & n.* protestant(e) (*m.* (*f.*)).

protocol /'prəʊtəkɒl/ *n.* protocole *m.*

prototype /'prəʊtətaɪp/ *n.* prototype *m.*

protract /prə'trækt/ *v.t.* prolonger, faire traîner.

protractor /prə'træktə(r)/ *n.* (*for measuring*) rapporteur *m.*

protrude /prə'truːd/ *v.i.* dépasser.

proud /praʊd/ *a.* (**-er, -est**) fier, orgueilleux. ~**ly** *adv.* fièrement.

prove /pruːv/ *v.t.* prouver. —*v.i.* ~ (**to be**) **easy**/*etc.*, se révéler facile/*etc.* ~ **o.s.**, faire ses preuves. ~**n** *a.* prouvé.

proverb /'prɒvɜːb/ *n.* proverbe *m.* ~**ial** /prə'vɜːbɪəl/ *a.* proverbial.

provide /prə'vaɪd/ *v.t.* fournir (**s.o. with sth.**, qch. à qn.). —*v.i.* ~ **for**, (*allow for*) prévoir; (*guard against*) parer à; (*person*) pourvoir aux besoins de.

provided /prə'vaɪdɪd/ *conj.* ~ **that**, à condition que.

providence /'prɒvɪdəns/ *n.* providence *f.*

providing /prə'vaɪdɪŋ/ *conj.* = **provided**.

provinc|e /'prɒvɪns/ *n.* province *f.*; (*fig.*) compétence *f.* ~**ial** /prə'vɪnʃl/ *a. & n.* provincial(e) (*m.*(*f.*)).

provision /prə'vɪʒn/ *n.* (*stock*) provision *f.*; (*supplying*) fourniture *f.*; (*stipulation*) disposition *f.* ~**s**, (*food*) provisions *f. pl.*

provisional /prə'vɪʒənl/ *a.* provisoire. ~**ly** *adv.* provisoirement.

proviso /prə'vaɪzəʊ/ n. (pl. -os) condition f., stipulation f.

provo|ke /prə'vəʊk/ v.t. provoquer. **~cation** /prɒvə'keɪʃn/ n. provocation f. **~cative** /-'vɒkətɪv/ a. provocant.

prow /praʊ/ n. proue f.

prowess /'praʊɪs/ n. prouesse f.

prowl /praʊl/ v.i. rôder. —n. be on the **~**, rôder. **~er** n. rôdeu|r, -se m., f.

proximity /prɒk'sɪmətɪ/ n. proximité f.

proxy /'prɒksɪ/ n. by **~**, par procuration.

prud|e /pruːd/ n. prude f. **~ish** a. prude.

pruden|t /'pruːdnt/ a. prudent. **~ce** n. prudence f. **~tly** adv. prudemment.

prune[1] /pruːn/ n. pruneau m.

prune[2] /pruːn/ v.t. (cut) tailler.

pry[1] /praɪ/ v.i. être indiscret. **~ into**, fourrer son nez dans.

pry[2] /praɪ/ v.t. (Amer.) = **prise**.

psalm /sɑːm/ n. psaume m.

pseudo /'sjuːdəʊ/ pref. pseudo-.

pseudonym /'sjuːdənɪm/ n. pseudonyme m.

psychiatr|y /saɪ'kaɪətrɪ/ n. psychiatrie f. **~ic** /-ɪ'ætrɪk/ a. psychiatrique. **~ist** n. psychiatre m./f.

psychic /'saɪkɪk/ a. (phenomenon etc.) métapsychique; (person) doué de télépathie.

psychoanalys|e /saɪkəʊ'ænəlaɪz/ v.t. psychanalyser. **~t** /-ɪst/ n. psychanalyste m./f.

psychoanalysis /saɪkəʊə'næləsɪs/ n. psychanalyse f.

psycholog|y /saɪ'kɒlədʒɪ/ n. psychologie f. **~ical** /-ə'lɒdʒɪkl/ a. psychologique. **~ist** n. psychologue m./f.

pyschopath /'saɪkəʊpæθ/ n. psychopathe m./f.

pub /pʌb/ n. pub m.

puberty /'pjuːbətɪ/ n. puberté f.

public /'pʌblɪk/ a. public; (library etc.) municipal. in **~**, en public. **~ house**, pub m. **~ school**, école privée f.; (Amer.) école publique f. **~ servant**, fonctionnaire m./f. **~-spirited** a. dévoué au bien public. **~ly** adv. publiquement.

publican /'pʌblɪkən/ n. patron(ne) de pub m.(f.).

publication /pʌblɪ'keɪʃn/ n. publication f.

publicity /pʌb'lɪsətɪ/ n. publicité f.

publicize /'pʌblɪsaɪz/ v.t. faire connaître au public.

publish /'pʌblɪʃ/ v.t. publier. **~er** n. éditeur m. **~ing** n. publication f. (of, de); (profession) édition f.

puck /pʌk/ n. (ice hockey) palet m.

pucker /'pʌkə(r)/ v.t./i. (se) plisser.

pudding /'pʊdɪŋ/ n. dessert m.; (steamed) pudding m. **black ~**, boudin m. **rice ~**, riz au lait m.

puddle /'pʌdl/ n. flaque d'eau f.

pudgy /'pʌdʒɪ/ a. (-ier, -iest) dodu.

puerile /'pjʊəraɪl/ a. puéril.

puff /pʌf/ n. bouffée f. —v.t./i. souffler. **~ at**, (cigar) tirer sur. **~ out**, (swell) (se) gonfler.

puffy /'pʌfɪ/ a. gonflé.

pugnacious /pʌg'neɪʃəs/ a. batailleur, combatif.

pug-nosed /'pʌgnəʊzd/ a. camus.

pull /pʊl/ v.t./i. tirer; (muscle) se froisser. —n. traction f.; (fig.) attraction f.; (influence) influence f. **give a ~**, tirer. **~ a face**, faire une grimace. **~ one's weight**, faire sa part du travail. **~ s.o.'s leg**, faire marcher qn. **~ away**, (auto.) démarrer. **~ back** or **out**, (withdraw) (se) retirer. **~ down**, baisser; (building) démolir. **~ in**, (enter) entrer; (stop) s'arrêter. **~ off**, enlever; (fig.) réussir. **~ out**, (from bag etc.) sortir; (extract) arracher; (auto.) déboîter. **~ over**, (auto.) se ranger. **~ round** or **through**, s'en tirer. **~ o.s. together**, se ressaisir. **~ up**, remonter; (uproot) déraciner; (auto.) (s')arrêter.

pulley /'pʊlɪ/ n. poulie f.

pullover /'pʊləʊvə(r)/ n. pull(-over) m.

pulp /pʌlp/ n. (of fruit) pulpe f.; (for paper) pâte à papier f.

pulpit /'pʊlpɪt/ n. chaire f.

pulsate /pʌl'seɪt/ v.i. battre.

pulse /pʌls/ n. (med.) pouls m.

pulverize /'pʌlvəraɪz/ v.t. (grind, defeat) pulvériser.

pummel /'pʌml/ v.t. (p.t. **pummelled**) bourrer de coups.

pump[1] /pʌmp/ n. pompe f. —v.t./i. pomper; (person) soutirer des renseignements à. **~ up**, gonfler.

pump[2] /pʌmp/ n. (plimsoll) tennis m.; (for dancing) escarpin m.

pumpkin /'pʌmpkɪn/ n. potiron m.

pun /pʌn/ n. jeu de mots m.

punch[1] /pʌntʃ/ v.t. donner un coup de poing à; (perforate) poinçonner; (a *hole*) faire. —*n.* coup de poing *m.*; (*vigour: sl.*) punch *m.*; (*device*) poinçonneuse *f.* ∼-**drunk** *a.* sonné. ∼-**up** *n.* (*fam.*) bagarre *f.*

punch² /pʌntʃ/ *n.* (*drink*) punch *m.*

punctual /'pʌŋktʃʊəl/ *a.* à l'heure; (*habitually*) ponctuel. ∼**ity** /-'æləti/ *n.* ponctualité *f.* ∼**ly** *adv.* à l'heure; ponctuellement.

punctuat|e /'pʌŋktʃʊeɪt/ *v.t.* ponctuer. ∼**ion** /-'eɪʃn/ *n.* ponctuation *f.*

puncture /'pʌŋktʃə(r)/ *n.* (*in tyre*) crevaison *f.* —*v.t./i.* crever.

pundit /'pʌndɪt/ *n.* expert *m.*

pungent /'pʌndʒənt/ *a.* âcre.

punish /'pʌnɪʃ/ *v.t.* punir (**for sth.**, de qch.). ∼**able** *a.* punissable (**by**, de). ∼**ment** *n.* punition *f.*

punitive /'pjuːnɪtɪv/ *a.* punitif.

punk /pʌŋk/ *n.* (*music, fan*) punk *m.*; (*person: Amer., fam.*) salaud *m.*

punt¹ /pʌnt/ *n.* (*boat*) bachot *m.*

punt² /pʌnt/ *v.i.* (*bet*) parier.

puny /'pjuːnɪ/ *a.* (**-ier**, **-iest**) chétif.

pup(py) /'pʌp(ɪ)/ *n.* chiot *m.*

pupil /'pjuːpl/ *n.* (*person*) élève *m./f.*; (*of eye*) pupille *f.*

puppet /'pʌpɪt/ *n.* marionnette *f.*

purchase /'pɜːtʃəs/ *v.t.* acheter (**from s.o.**, à qn.). —*n.* achat *m.* ∼**r** /-ə(r)/ *n.* acheteu|r, -se *m.*, *f.*

pur|e /pjʊə(r)/ *a.* (**-er**, **-est**) pur. ∼**ely** *adv.* purement. ∼**ity** *n.* pureté *f.*

purgatory /'pɜːɡətrɪ/ *n.* purgatoire *m.*

purge /pɜːdʒ/ *v.t.* purger (**of**, de). —*n.* purge *f.*

purif|y /'pjʊərɪfaɪ/ *v.t.* purifier. ∼**ication** /-ɪ'keɪʃn/ *n.* purification *f.*

purist /'pjʊərɪst/ *n.* puriste *m./f.*

puritan /'pjʊərɪtən/ *n.* puritain(e) *m.* (*f.*). ∼**ical** /-'tænɪkl/ *a.* puritain.

purple /'pɜːpl/ *a.* & *n.* violet (*m.*).

purport /pə'pɔːt/ *v.t.* ∼ **to be**, (*claim*) prétendre être.

purpose /'pɜːpəs/ *n.* but *m.*; (*fig.*) résolution *f.* **on** ∼, exprès. ∼**built** *a.* construit spécialement. **to no** ∼, sans résultat.

purposely /'pɜːpəslɪ/ *adv.* exprès.

purr /pɜː(r)/ *n.* ronronnement *m.* —*v.i.* ronronner.

purse /pɜːs/ *n.* porte-monnaie *m. invar.*; (*handbag: Amer.*) sac à main *m.* —*v.t.* (*lips*) pincer.

pursue /pə'sjuː/ *v.t.* poursuivre. ∼**r** /-ə(r)/ *n.* poursuivant(e) *m.* (*f.*).

pursuit /pə'sjuːt/ *n.* poursuite *f.*; (*fig.*) activité *f.*, occupation *f.*

purveyor /pə'veɪə(r)/ *n.* fournisseur *m.*

pus /pʌs/ *n.* pus *m.*

push /pʊʃ/ *v.t./i.* pousser; (*button*) appuyer sur; (*thrust*) enfoncer. —*n.* poussée *f.*; (*effort*) gros effort *m.*; (*drive*) dynamisme *m.* **be** ∼**ed for**, (*time etc.*) manquer de. **be** ∼**ing thirty**/*etc.*, (*fam.*) friser la trentaine/ *etc.* **give the** ∼ **to**, (*sl.*) flanquer à la porte. ∼ **back**, repousser. ∼-**chair** *n.* poussette *f.* ∼ **off**, (*sl.*) filer. ∼ **on**, continuer. ∼ **up**, (*lift, increase*) relever. ∼-**up** *n.* (*Amer.*) traction *f.*

pushing /'pʊʃɪŋ/ *a.* arriviste.

puss /pʊs/ *n.* (*cat*) minet(te) *m./f.*).

put /pʊt/ *v.t./i.* (*p.t.* put, *pres. p.* **putting**) mettre, placer, poser; (*say*) dire; (*estimate*) évaluer; (*question*) poser. ∼ **across**, communiquer. ∼ **away**, ranger; (*fig.*) enfermer. ∼ **back**, remettre; (*delay*) retarder. ∼ **by**, mettre de côté. ∼ **down**, (dé)poser; (*write*) inscrire; (*pay*) verser; (*suppress*) réprimer. ∼ **in**, (*insert*) introduire; (*submit*) soumettre. ∼ **in for**, faire une demande de. ∼ **off**, (*postpone*) renvoyer à plus tard; (*disconcert*) déconcerter. ∼ **s.o. off sth.**, dégoûter qn. de qch. ∼ **on**, (*clothes, light, radio*) mettre; (*speed, accent*) prendre. ∼ **out**, sortir; (*stretch*) (é)tendre; (*extinguish*) éteindre; (*disconcert*) déconcerter; (*inconvenience*) déranger. ∼ **up**, lever, remonter; (*building*) construire; (*notice*) mettre; (*price*) augmenter; (*guest*) héberger; (*offer*) offrir. ∼-**up job**, coup monté *m.* ∼ **up with**, supporter.

putrefy /'pjuːtrɪfaɪ/ *v.i.* se putréfier.

putt /pʌt/ *n.* (*golf*) putt *m.*

putter /'pʌtə(r)/ *v.i.* (*Amer.*) bricoler.

putty /'pʌtɪ/ *n.* mastic *m.*

puzzle /'pʌzl/ *n.* énigme *f.*; (*game*) casse-tête *m. invar.* —*v.t.* rendre perplexe. —*v.i.* se creuser la tête.

pygmy /'pɪɡmɪ/ *n.* pygmée *m.*

pyjamas /pə'dʒɑːməz/ *n. pl.* pyjama *m.*

pylon /'paɪlɒn/ *n.* pylône *m.*

pyramid /'pɪrəmɪd/ *n.* pyramide *f.*

Pyrenees /pɪrə'niːz/ *n. pl.* **the** ∼, les Pyrénées *f. pl.*

python /'paɪθn/ *n.* python *m.*

Q

quack[1] /kwæk/ n. (of duck) coin-coin m. invar.

quack[2] /kwæk/ n. charlatan m.

quad /kwɒd/ (fam.) = **quadrangle, quadruplet.**

quadrangle /ˈkwɒdræŋgl/ (of college) n. cour f.

quadruped /ˈkwɒdrʊped/ n. quadrupède m.

quadruple /kwɒˈdruːpl/ a. & n. quadruple (m.). —v.t./i. quadrupler. ~ts /-plɪts/ n. pl. quadruplé(e)s m. (f.) pl.

quagmire /ˈkwægmaɪə(r)/ n. (bog) bourbier m.

quail /kweɪl/ n. (bird) caille f.

quaint /kweɪnt/ a. (-er, -est) pittoresque; (old) vieillot; (odd) bizarre. ~ness n. pittoresque m.

quake /kweɪk/ v.i. trembler. —n. (fam.) tremblement de terre m.

Quaker /ˈkweɪkə(r)/ n. quaker(esse) m. (f.).

qualification /kwɒlɪfɪˈkeɪʃn/ n. diplôme m.; (ability) compétence f.; (fig.) réserve f., restriction f.

qualif|y /ˈkwɒlɪfaɪ/ v.t. qualifier; (modify; fig.) mettre des réserves à; (statement) nuancer. —v.i. obtenir son diplôme (as, de); (sport) se qualifier; (fig.) remplir les conditions requises. ~ied a. diplômé; (able) qualifié (to do, pour faire); (fig.) conditionnel; (success) modéré.

qualit|y /ˈkwɒlətɪ/ n. qualité f. ~ative /-ɪtətɪv/ a. qualitatif.

qualm /kwɑːm/ n. scrupule m.

quandary /ˈkwɒndərɪ/ n. embarras m., dilemme m.

quantit|y /ˈkwɒntətɪ/ n. quantité f. ~ative /-ɪtətɪv/ a. quantitatif.

quarantine /ˈkwɒrəntiːn/ n. (isolation) quarantaine f.

quarrel /ˈkwɒrəl/ n. dispute f., querelle f. —v.i. (p.t. quarrelled) se disputer. ~some a. querelleur.

quarry[1] /ˈkwɒrɪ/ n. (prey) proie f.

quarry[2] /ˈkwɒrɪ/ n. (excavation) carrière f.

quart /kwɔːt/ n. (approx.) litre m.

quarter /ˈkwɔːtə(r)/ n. quart m.; (of year) trimestre m.; (25 cents: Amer.) quart de dollar m.; (district) quartier m. ~s, logement(s) m. (pl.). —v.t.

diviser en quatre; (mil.) cantonner. **from all** ~s, de toutes parts. ~**final** n. quart de finale m. ~**ly** a. trimestriel; adv. trimestriellement.

quartermaster /ˈkwɔːtəmɑːstə(r)/ n. (mil.) intendant m.

quartet /kwɔːˈtet/ n. quatuor m.

quartz /kwɔːts/ n. quartz m. —a. (watch etc.) à quartz.

quash /kwɒʃ/ v.t. (suppress) étouffer; (jurid.) annuler.

quasi /ˈkweɪsaɪ/ pref. quasi-.

quaver /ˈkweɪvə(r)/ v.i. trembler, chevroter. —n. (mus.) croche f.

quay /kiː/ n. (naut.) quai m. ~**side** n. (edge of quay) quai m.

queasy /ˈkwiːzɪ/ a. (stomach) délicat. **feel** ~, avoir mal au cœur.

queen /kwiːn/ n. reine f.; (cards) dame f. ~ **mother**, reine mère f.

queer /kwɪə(r)/ a. (-er, -est) étrange; (dubious) louche; (ill) patraque. —n. (sl.) homosexuel m.

quell /kwel/ v.t. réprimer.

quench /kwentʃ/ v.t. éteindre; (thirst) étancher; (desire) étouffer.

query /ˈkwɪərɪ/ n. question f. —v.t. mettre en question.

quest /kwest/ n. recherche f.

question /ˈkwestʃən/ n. question f. —v.t. interroger; (doubt) mettre en question, douter de. **in** ~, en question. **no** ~ **of**, pas question de. **out of the** ~, hors de question. ~ **mark**, point d'interrogation m.

questionable /ˈkwestʃənəbl/ a. discutable.

questionnaire /kwestʃəˈneə(r)/ n. questionnaire m.

queue /kjuː/ n. queue f. —v.i. (pres. p. queuing) faire la queue.

quibble /ˈkwɪbl/ v.i. ergoter.

quick /kwɪk/ a. (-er, -est) rapide. —adv. vite. —n. **cut to the** ~, piquer au vif. **be** ~, (hurry) se dépêcher. **have a** ~ **temper**, s'emporter facilement. ~**ly** adv. rapidement, vite.

quicken /ˈkwɪkən/ v.t./i. (s')accélérer.

quicksand /ˈkwɪksænd/ n. ~(s), sables mouvants m. pl.

quid /kwɪd/ n. invar. (sl.) livre f.

quiet /ˈkwaɪət/ a. (-er, -est) (calm, still)

tranquille; (*silent*) silencieux; (*gentle*)
doux; (*discreet*) discret. —*n.* tranquillité *f*. **keep** ∼, se taire. **on the** ∼,
en cachette. ∼**ly** *adv.* tranquille-
ment; silencieusement; doucement;
discrètement. ∼**ness** *n.* tranquillité *f*.
quieten /ˈkwaɪətn/ *v.t./i.* (se) calmer.
quill /kwɪl/ *n.* plume (d'oie) *f*.
quilt /kwɪlt/ *n.* édredon *m.* (**continental**) ∼, couette *f*. —*v.t.* matelasser.
quinine /ˈkwɪniːn, *Amer.* ˈkwaɪnaɪn/ *n.*
quinine *f*.
quintet /kwɪnˈtet/ *n.* quintette *m*.
quintuplets /kwɪnˈtjuːplɪts/ *n. pl.*
quintuplé(e)s *m.* (*f.*) *pl.*
quip /kwɪp/ *n.* mot piquant *m*.
quirk /kwɜːk/ *n.* bizarrerie *f*.
quit /kwɪt/ *v.t.* (*p.t.* **quitted**) quitter.
—*v.i.* abandonner; (*resign*) démissionner. ∼ **doing,** (*cease*: *Amer.*)
cesser de faire.
quite /kwaɪt/ *adv.* tout à fait, vrai-

ment; (*rather*) assez. ∼ (**so**)!, parfaitement! ∼ **a few,** un assez grand
nombre (de).
quits /kwɪts/ *a.* quitte (**with,** envers).
call it ∼, en rester là.
quiver /ˈkwɪvə(r)/ *v.i.* trembler.
quiz /kwɪz/ *n.* (*pl.* **quizzes**) test *m.*;
(*game*) jeu-concours *m.* —*v.t.* (*p.t.*
quizzed) questionner.
quizzical /ˈkwɪzɪkl/ *a.* moqueur.
quorum /ˈkwɔːrəm/ *n.* quorum *m*.
quota /ˈkwəʊtə/ *n.* quota *m*.
quotation /kwəʊˈteɪʃn/ *n.* citation *f.*;
(*price*) devis *m.*; (*stock exchange*) cota-
tion *f.* ∼ **marks,** guillemets *m. pl.*
quote /kwəʊt/ *v.t.* citer; (*reference*:
comm.) rappeler; (*price*) indiquer;
(*share price*) coter. —*v.i.* ∼ **from,**
citer. —*n.* (*fam.*) = **quotation. in** ∼**s,**
(*fam.*) entre guillemets.
quotient /ˈkwəʊʃnt/ *n.* quotient *m*.

R

rabbi /'ræbaɪ/ *n.* rabbin *m.*

rabbit /'ræbɪt/ *n.* lapin *m.*

rabble /'ræbl/ *n.* (*crowd*) cohue *f.* the ∼, (*pej.*) la populace.

rabid /'ræbɪd/ *a.* enragé.

rabies /'reɪbiːz/ *n.* (*disease*) rage *f.*

race[1] /reɪs/ *n.* course *f.* —*v.t.* (*horse*) faire courir; (*engine*) emballer. ∼ (**against**), faire la course à. —*v.i.* courir; (*rush*) foncer. ∼**-track** *n.* piste *f.*; (*for horses*) champ de courses *m.* **racing** *n.* courses *f. pl.* **racing car,** voiture de course *f.*

race[2] /reɪs/ *n.* (*group*) race *f.* —*a.* racial; (*relations*) entre les races.

racecourse /'reɪskɔːs/ *n.* champ de courses *m.*

racehorse /'reɪshɔːs/ *n.* cheval de course *m.*

racial /'reɪʃl/ *a.* racial.

racis|t /'reɪsɪst/ *a. & n.* raciste (*m./f.*). ∼**m** /-zəm/ *n.* racisme *m.*

rack[1] /ræk/ *n.* (*shelf*) étagère *f.*; (*pigeon-holes*) casier *m.*; (*for luggage*) porte-bagages *m. invar.*; (*for dishes*) égouttoir *m.*; (*on car roof*) galerie *f.* —*v.t.* ∼ **one's brains,** se creuser la cervelle.

rack[2] /ræk/ *n.* **go to** ∼ **and ruin,** aller à la ruine; (*building*) tomber en ruine.

racket[1] /'rækɪt/ *n.* raquette *f.*

racket[2] /'rækɪt/ *n.* (*din*) tapage *m.*; (*dealings*) combine *f.*; (*crime*) racket *m.* ∼**eer** /-ə'tɪə(r)/ *n.* racketteur *m.*

racy /'reɪsɪ/ *a.* (**-ier, -iest**) fougueux, piquant; (*Amer.*) risqué.

radar /'reɪdɑː(r)/ *n.* radar *m.* —*a.* (*system etc.*) radar *invar.*

radian|t /'reɪdɪənt/ *a.* rayonnant. ∼**ce** *n.* éclat *m.* ∼**tly** *adv.* avec éclat.

radiat|e /'reɪdɪeɪt/ *v.t.* dégager. —*v.i.* rayonner (**from,** de). ∼**ion** /-'eɪʃn/ *n.* rayonnement *m.*; (*radioactivity*) radiation *f.*

radiator /'reɪdɪeɪtə(r)/ *n.* radiateur *m.*

radical /'rædɪkl/ *a.* radical. —*n.* (*person: pol.*) radical(e) *m.(f.).*

radio /'reɪdɪəʊ/ *n.* (*pl.* **-os**) radio *f.* —*v.t.* (*message*) envoyer par radio; (*person*) appeler par radio.

radioactiv|e /reɪdɪəʊ'æktɪv/ *a.* radioactif. ∼**ity** /-'tɪvətɪ/ *n.* radioactivité *f.*

radiographer /reɪdɪ'ɒgrəfə(r)/ *n.* radiologue *m./f.*

radish /'rædɪʃ/ *n.* radis *m.*

radius /'reɪdɪəs/ *n.* (*pl.* **-dii** /-dɪaɪ/) rayon *m.*

raffish /'ræfɪʃ/ *a.* libertin.

raffle /'ræfl/ *n.* tombola *f.*

raft /rɑːft/ *n.* radeau *m.*

rafter /'rɑːftə(r)/ *n.* chevron *m.*

rag[1] /ræg/ *n.* lambeau *m.*, loque *f.*; (*for wiping*) chiffon *m.*; (*newspaper*) torchon *m.* **in** ∼**s,** (*person*) en haillons; (*clothes*) en lambeaux.

rag[2] /ræg/ *v.t.* (*p.t.* **ragged**) (*tease: sl.*) taquiner. —*n.* (*univ., sl.*) carnaval *m.*

ragamuffin /'rægəmʌfɪn/ *n.* va-nu-pieds *m. invar.*

rage /reɪdʒ/ *n.* rage *f.*, fureur *f.* —*v.i.* rager; (*storm, battle*) faire rage. **be all the** ∼, faire fureur. **raging** *a.* (*storm, fever, etc.*) violent.

ragged /'rægɪd/ *a.* (*clothes, person*) loqueteux; (*edge*) déchiqueté.

raid /reɪd/ *n.* (*mil.*) raid *m.*; (*by police*) rafle *f.*; (*by criminals*) hold-up *m. invar.* —*v.t.* faire un raid *or* une rafle *or* un hold-up dans. ∼**er** *n.* (*person*) bandit *m.*, pillard *m.* ∼**ers** *n. pl.* (*mil.*) commando *m.*

rail /reɪl/ *n.* (*on balcony*) balustrade *f.*; (*stairs*) main courante *f.*, rampe *f.*; (*for train*) rail *m.*; (*for curtain*) tringle *f.* **by** ∼, par chemin de fer.

railing /'reɪlɪŋ/ *n.* ∼(**s**), grille *f.*

railroad /'reɪlrəʊd/ *n.* (*Amer.*) = **railway.**

railway /'reɪlweɪ/ *n.* chemin de fer *m.* ∼**man** *n.* (*pl.* **-men**) cheminot *m.* ∼ **station,** gare *f.*

rain /reɪn/ *n.* pluie *f.* —*v.i.* pleuvoir. ∼**-storm** *n.* trombe d'eau *f.* ∼**-water** *n.* eau de pluie *f.*

rainbow /'reɪnbəʊ/ *n.* arc-en-ciel *m.*

raincoat /'reɪnkəʊt/ *n.* imperméable *m.*

rainfall /'reɪnfɔːl/ *n.* précipitation *f.*

rainy /'reɪnɪ/ *a.* (**-ier, -iest**) pluvieux; (*season*) des pluies.

raise /reɪz/ *v.t.* lever; (*breed, build*) élever; (*question etc.*) soulever; (*price etc.*) relever; (*money etc.*) obtenir; (*voice*) élever. —*n.* (*Amer.*) augmentation *f.*

raisin /'reɪzn/ *n.* raisin sec *m.*

rake[1] /reɪk/ *n.* râteau *m.* —*v.t.*
(*garden*) ratisser; (*search*) fouiller
dans. ~ **in,** (*money*) amasser. ~**-off**
n. (*fam.*) profit *m.* ~ **up,** (*memories,
past*) remuer.

rake[2] /reɪk/ *n.* (*man*) débauché *m.*

rally /'rælɪ/ *v.t./i.* (se) rallier; (*strength*)
reprendre. —*n.* rassemblement *m.*;
(*auto.*) rallye *m.*

ram /ræm/ *n.* bélier *m.* —*v.t.* (*p.t.*
rammed) (*thrust*) enfoncer; (*crash
into*) emboutir, percuter.

rambl|e /'ræmbl/ *n.* randonnée *f.* —*v.i.*
faire une randonnée. ~**e on,** parler
(sans cesse), divaguer. ~**ing** *a.*
(*speech*) décousu.

ramification /ræmɪfɪ'keɪʃn/ *n.* ramification *f.*

ramp /ræmp/ *n.* (*slope*) rampe *f.*; (*in
garage*) pont de graissage *m.*

rampage[1] /ræm'peɪdʒ/ *v.i.* se livrer à
des actes de violence, se déchaîner.

rampage[2] /'ræmpeɪdʒ/ *n.* **go on the** ~
= **rampage**[1].

rampant /'ræmpənt/ *a.* **be** ~, (*disease
etc.*) sévir, être répandu.

rampart /'ræmpɑːt/ *n.* rempart *m.*

ramshackle /'ræmʃækl/ *a.* délabré.

ran /ræn/ *see* **run.**

ranch /rɑːntʃ/ *n.* ranch *m.*

rancid /'rænsɪd/ *a.* rance.

rancour /'ræŋkə(r)/ *n.* rancœur *f.*

random /'rændəm/ *a.* fait, pris, *etc.* au
hasard. —*n.* **at** ~, au hasard.

randy /'rændɪ/ *a.* (**-ier, -iest**) (*fam.*)
lascif, voluptueux.

rang /ræŋ/ *see* **ring**[2].

range /reɪndʒ/ *n.* (*distance*) portée *f.*;
(*of aircraft etc.*) rayon d'action *m.*;
(*series*) gamme *f.*; (*scale*) échelle *f.*;
(*choice*) choix *m.*; (*domain*) champ
m.; (*of mountains*) chaîne *f.*; (*stove*)
cuisinière *f.* —*v.i.* s'étendre; (*vary*)
varier.

ranger /'reɪndʒə(r)/ *n.* garde forestier
m.

rank[1] /ræŋk/ *n.* rang *m.*; (*grade*: mil.)
grade *m.*, rang *m.* —*v.t./i.* ~ **among,**
compter parmi. **the** ~ **and file,** les
gens ordinaires.

rank[2] /ræŋk/ *a.* (**-er, -est**) (*plants: pej.*)
luxuriant; (*smell*) fétide; (*complete*)
absolu.

ransack /'rænsæk/ *v.t.* (*search*) fouiller; (*pillage*) saccager.

ransom /'rænsəm/ *n.* rançon *f.* —*v.t.*
rançonner; (*redeem*) racheter. **hold
to** ~, rançonner.

rant /rænt/ *v.i.* tempêter.

rap /ræp/ *n.* petit coup sec *m.* —*v.t./i.*
(*p.t.* **rapped**) frapper.

rape /reɪp/ *v.t.* violer. —*n.* viol *m.*

rapid /'ræpɪd/ *a.* rapide. ~**ity** /rə'pɪdətɪ/
n. rapidité *f.* ~**s** *n. pl.* (*of river*) rapides
m. pl.

rapist /'reɪpɪst/ *n.* violeur *m.*

rapport /ræ'pɔː(r)/ *n.* rapport *m.*

rapt /ræpt/ *a.* (*attention*) profond. ~
in, plongé dans.

raptur|e /'ræptʃə(r)/ *n.* extase *f.* ~**ous**
a. (*person*) en extase; (*welcome etc.*)
frénétique.

rar|e[1] /reə(r)/ *a.* (**-er, -est**) rare. ~**ely**
adv. rarement. ~**ity** *n.* rareté *f.*

rare[2] /reə(r)/ *a.* (**-er, -est**) (*culin.*) saignant.

rarefied /'reərɪfaɪd/ *a.* raréfié.

raring /'reərɪŋ/ *a.* ~ **to,** (*fam.*) impatient de.

rascal /'rɑːskl/ *n.* coquin(e) *m.(f.).*

rash[1] /ræʃ/ *n.* (*med.*) éruption *f.*, rou-
geurs *f. pl.*

rash[2] /ræʃ/ *a.* (**-er, -est**) imprudent.
~**ly** *adv.* imprudemment. ~**ness** *n.*
imprudence *f.*

rasher /'ræʃə(r)/ *n.* tranche (de lard)
f.

rasp /rɑːsp/ *n.* (*file*) râpe *f.*

raspberry /'rɑːzbrɪ/ *n.* framboise *f.*

rasping /'rɑːspɪŋ/ *a.* grinçant.

rat /ræt/ *n.* rat *m.* —*v.i.* (*p.t.* **ratted**).
~ **on,** (*desert*) lâcher; (*inform on*)
dénoncer. ~ **race,** jungle *f.*, course
au bifteck *f.*, lutte acharnée pour réussir *f.*

rate /reɪt/ *n.* (*ratio, level*) taux *m.*;
(*speed*) allure *f.*; (*price*) tarif *m.* ~**s,**
(*taxes*) impôts locaux *m. pl.* —*v.t.*
évaluer; (*consider*) considérer; (*de-
serve: Amer.*) mériter. **at any** ~, en
tout cas. **at the** ~ **of,** (*on the basis of*)
à raison de.

rateable /'reɪtəbl/ *a.* ~ **value,** valeur
locative imposable *f.*

ratepayer /'reɪtpeɪə(r)/ *n.* contribuable *m./f.*

rather /'rɑːðə(r)/ *adv.* (*by preference*)
plutôt; (*fairly*) assez, plutôt; (*a little*)
un peu. **I would** ~ **go,** j'aimerais
mieux partir.

ratif|y /'rætɪfaɪ/ *v.t.* ratifier. ~**ication**
/-ɪ'keɪʃn/ *n.* ratification *f.*

rating /'reɪtɪŋ/ *n.* classement *m.*;

(*sailor*) matelot *m.* (*number*) indice *m.*; (*TV*) popularité *f.*

ratio /'reɪʃɪəʊ/ *n.* (*pl.* **-os**) proportion *f.*

ration /'ræʃn/ *n.* ration *f.* —*v.t.* rationner.

rational /'ræʃənl/ *a.* rationnel; (*person*) raisonnable.

rationalize /'ræʃənəlaɪz/ *v.t.* donner une explication rationnelle à; (*organize*) rationaliser.

rattle /'rætl/ *v.i.* faire du bruit; (*of bottles*) cliqueter. —*v.t.* secouer; (*sl.*) déconcerter. —*n.* bruit (de ferraille) *m.*; cliquetis *m.*; (*toy*) hochet *m.* ~ **off**, débiter en vitesse.

rattlesnake /'rætlsneɪk/ *n.* serpent à sonnette *m.*, crotale *m.*

raucous /'rɔːkəs/ *a.* rauque.

raunchy /'rɔːntʃɪ/ *a.* (**-ier**, **-iest**) (*Amer.*, *sl.*) grossier, cochon.

ravage /'rævɪdʒ/ *v.t.* ravager. ~**s** /-ɪz/ *n. pl.* ravages *m. pl.*

rav|e /reɪv/ *v.i.* divaguer; (*in anger*) tempêter. ~**e about**, s'extasier sur. ~**ings** *n. pl.* divagations *f. pl.*

raven /'reɪvn/ *n.* corbeau *m.*

ravenous /'rævənəs/ *a.* vorace. **I am** ~, je meurs de faim.

ravine /rə'viːn/ *n.* ravin *m.*

raving /'reɪvɪŋ/ *a.* ~ **lunatic**, fou furieux *m.*, folle furieuse *f.*

ravioli /rævɪ'əʊlɪ/ *n.* ravioli *m. pl.*

ravish /'rævɪʃ/ *v.t.* (*rape*) ravir. ~**ing** *a.* (*enchanting*) ravissant.

raw /rɔː/ *a.* (**-er**, **-est**) cru; (*not processed*) brut; (*wound*) à vif; (*immature*) inexpérimenté. **get a** ~ **deal**, être mal traité. ~ **material**, matière première *f.*

ray /reɪ/ *n.* (*of light etc.*) rayon *m.* ~ **of hope**, lueur d'espoir *f.*

raze /reɪz/ *v.t.* (*destroy*) raser.

razor /'reɪzə(r)/ *n.* rasoir *m.*

re /riː/ *prep.* concernant.

re- /riː/ *pref.* re-, ré-, r-.

reach /riːtʃ/ *v.t.* atteindre, arriver à; (*contact*) joindre; (*hand over*) passer. —*v.i.* s'étendre. —*n.* portée *f.* ~ **for**, tendre la main pour prendre. **within** ~ **of**, à portée de; (*close to*) à proximité de.

react /rɪ'ækt/ *v.i.* réagir.

reaction /rɪ'ækʃn/ *n.* réaction *f.* ~**ary** *a. & n.* réactionnaire (*m./f.*).

reactor /rɪ'æktə(r)/ *n.* réacteur *m.*

read /riːd/ *v.t./i.* (*p.t.* **read** /red/) lire; (*fig.*) comprendre; (*study*) étudier; (*of instrument*) indiquer. —*n.* (*fam.*) lec-

ture *f.* ~ **about s.o.**, lire un article sur qn. ~**able** *a.* agréable *or* facile à lire. ~**ing** *n.* lecture *f.*; indication *f.* ~**ing-lamp** *n.* lampe de bureau *f.*

reader /'riːdə(r)/ *n.* lec|teur, -trice *m.*, *f.* ~**ship** *n.* lecteurs *m. pl.*

readily /'redɪlɪ/ *adv.* (*willingly*) volontiers; (*easily*) facilement.

readiness /'redɪnɪs/ *n.* empressement *m.* **in** ~, prêt (**for**, à).

readjust /riːə'dʒʌst/ *v.t.* rajuster. —*v.i.* se réadapter (**to**, à).

ready /'redɪ/ *a.* (**-ier**, **-iest**) prêt; (*quick*) prompt. —*n.* **at the** ~, tout prêt. ~-**made** *a.* tout fait. ~ **money**, (argent) liquide *m.* ~ **reckoner**, barème *m.*

real /rɪəl/ *a.* vrai, véritable, réel. —*adv.* (*Amer.*, *fam.*) vraiment. ~ **estate**, biens fonciers *m. pl.*

realis|t /'rɪəlɪst/ *n.* réaliste *m./f.* ~**m** /-zəm/ *n.* réalisme *m.* ~**tic** /-'lɪstɪk/ *a.* réaliste. ~**tically** /-'lɪstɪklɪ/ *adv.* avec réalisme.

reality /rɪ'ælətɪ/ *n.* réalité *f.*

realiz|e /'rɪəlaɪz/ *v.t.* se rendre compte de, comprendre; (*fulfil, turn into cash*) réaliser; (*price*) atteindre. ~**ation** /-'zeɪʃn/ *n.* prise de conscience *f.*; réalisation *f.*

really /'rɪəlɪ/ *adv.* vraiment.

realm /relm/ *n.* royaume *m.*

reap /riːp/ *v.t.* (*crop, field*) moissonner; (*fig.*) récolter.

reappear /riːə'pɪə(r)/ *v.i.* réapparaître, reparaître.

reappraisal /riːə'preɪzl/ *n.* réévaluation *f.*

rear[1] /rɪə(r)/ *n.* arrière *m.*, derrière *m.* —*a.* arrière *invar.*, de derrière.

rear[2] /rɪə(r)/ *v.t.* (*bring up, breed*) élever. —*v.i.* (*horse*) se cabrer. ~ **one's head**, dresser la tête.

rearguard /'rɪəɡɑːd/ *n.* (*mil.*) arrière-garde *f.*

rearm /riː'ɑːm/ *v.t./i.* réarmer.

rearrange /riːə'reɪndʒ/ *v.t.* réarranger.

reason /'riːzn/ *n.* raison *f.* —*v.i.* raisonner. ~ **with**, raisonner. **within** ~, avec modération. ~**ing** *n.* raisonnement *m.*

reasonable /'riːznəbl/ *a.* raisonnable.

reassur|e /riːə'ʃʊə(r)/ *v.t.* rassurer. ~**ance** *n.* réconfort *m.*

rebate /'riːbeɪt/ *n.* remboursement (partiel) *m.*; (*discount*) rabais *m.*

rebel[1] /'rebl/ *n. & a.* rebelle (*m./f.*).

rebel[2] /rɪ'bel/ *v.i.* (*p.t.* **rebelled**) se

rebeller. ∼**lion** *n.* rébellion *f.* ∼**lious** *a.* rebelle.

rebound /rɪˈbaʊnd/ *v.i.* rebondir. ∼ **on**, (*backfire*) se retourner contre. —*n.* /ˈriːbaʊnd/ *n.* rebond *m.*

rebuff /rɪˈbʌf/ *v.t.* repousser. —*n.* rebuffade *f.*

rebuild /riːˈbɪld/ *v.t.* reconstruire.

rebuke /rɪˈbjuːk/ *v.t.* réprimander. —*n.* réprimande *f.*, reproche *m.*

rebuttal /rɪˈbʌtl/ *n.* réfutation *f.*

recall /rɪˈkɔːl/ *v.t.* (*to s.o., call back*) rappeler; (*remember*) se rappeler. —*n.* rappel *m.*

recant /rɪˈkænt/ *v.i.* se rétracter.

recap /ˈriːkæp/ *v.t./i.* (*p.t.* **recapped**) (*fam.*) récapituler. —*n.* (*fam.*) récapitulation *f.*

recapitulat|e /riːkəˈpɪtʃʊleɪt/ *v.t./i.* récapituler. ∼**ion** /-ˈleɪʃn/ *n.* récapitulation *f.*

recapture /riːˈkæptʃə(r)/ *v.t.* reprendre; (*recall*) recréer.

reced|e /rɪˈsiːd/ *v.i.* s'éloigner. **his hair is** ∼**ing**, son front se dégarnit. ∼**ing** *a.* (*forehead*) fuyant.

receipt /rɪˈsiːt/ *n.* (*written*) reçu *m.*; (*receiving*) réception *f.* ∼**s**, (*money*: *comm.*) recettes *f. pl.*

receive /rɪˈsiːv/ *v.t.* recevoir. ∼**r** /-ə(r)/ *n.* (*of stolen goods*) receleu|r, -se *m.*, *f.*; (*telephone*) récepteur *m.*

recent /ˈriːsnt/ *a.* récent. ∼**ly** *adv.* récemment.

receptacle /rɪˈseptəkl/ *n.* récipient *m.*

reception /rɪˈsepʃn/ *n.* réception *f.* ∼**ist** *n.* réceptionniste *m./f.*

receptive /rɪˈseptɪv/ *a.* réceptif.

recess /rɪˈses/ *n.* (*alcove*) renfoncement *m.*; (*nook*) recoin *m.*; (*holiday*) vacances *f. pl.*; (*schol., Amer.*) récréation *f.*

recession /rɪˈseʃn/ *n.* récession *f.*

recharge /riːˈtʃɑːdʒ/ *v.t.* recharger.

recipe /ˈresəpɪ/ *n.* recette *f.*

recipient /rɪˈsɪpɪənt/ *n.* (*of honour*) récipiendaire *m.*; (*of letter*) destinataire *m./f.*

reciprocal /rɪˈsɪprəkl/ *a.* réciproque.

reciprocate /rɪˈsɪprəkeɪt/ *v.t.* offrir en retour. —*v.i.* en faire autant.

recital /rɪˈsaɪtl/ *n.* récital *m.*

recite /rɪˈsaɪt/ *v.t.* (*poem, lesson, etc.*) réciter; (*list*) énumérer.

reckless /ˈreklɪs/ *a.* imprudent. ∼**ly** *adv.* imprudemment.

reckon /ˈrekən/ *v.t./i.* calculer; (*judge*) considérer; (*think*) penser. ∼ **on/**

with, compter sur/avec. ∼**ing** *n.* calcul(s) *m.* (*pl.*).

reclaim /rɪˈkleɪm/ *v.t.* (*seek return of*) réclamer; (*land*) défricher; (*flooded land*) assécher.

reclin|e /rɪˈklaɪn/ *v.i.* être étendu. ∼**ing** *a.* (*person*) étendu.

recluse /rɪˈkluːs/ *n.* reclus(e) *m.* (*f.*), ermite *m.*

recognition /rekəɡˈnɪʃn/ *n.* reconnaissance *f.* **beyond** ∼, méconnaissable. **gain** ∼, être reconnu.

recognize /ˈrekəɡnaɪz/ *v.t.* reconnaître.

recoil /rɪˈkɔɪl/ *v.i.* reculer.

recollect /rekəˈlekt/ *v.t.* se souvenir de, se rappeler. ∼**ion** /-kʃn/ *n.* souvenir *m.*

recommend /rekəˈmend/ *v.t.* recommander. ∼**ation** /-ˈdeɪʃn/ *n.* recommandation *f.*

recompense /ˈrekəmpens/ *v.t.* (ré)compenser. —*n.* récompense *f.*

reconcil|e /ˈrekənsaɪl/ *v.t.* (*people*) réconcilier; (*facts*) concilier. ∼**e o.s. to,** se résigner à. ∼**iation** /-sɪlɪˈeɪʃn/ *n.* réconciliation *f.*

recondition /riːkənˈdɪʃn/ *v.t.* remettre à neuf, réviser.

reconn|oitre /rekəˈnɔɪtə(r)/ *v.t.* (*pres. p.* -**tring**) (*mil.*) reconnaître. ∼**aissance** /rɪˈkɒnɪsns/ *n.* reconnaissance *f.*

reconsider /riːkənˈsɪdə(r)/ *v.t.* reconsidérer. —*v.i.* se déjuger.

reconstruct /riːkənˈstrʌkt/ *v.t.* reconstruire; (*crime*) reconstituer.

record[1] /rɪˈkɔːd/ *v.t./i.* (*in register, on tape, etc.*) enregistrer; (*in diary*) noter. ∼ **that,** rapporter que. ∼**ing** *n.* enregistrement *m.*

record[2] /ˈrekɔːd/ *n.* (*report*) rapport *m.*; (*register*) registre *m.*; (*mention*) mention *f.*; (*file*) dossier *m.*; (*fig.*) résultats *m. pl.*; (*mus.*) disque *m.*; (*sport*) record *m.* (**criminal**) ∼, casier judiciaire *m.* —*a.* record *invar.* **off the** ∼, officieusement. ∼**-player** *n.* électrophone *m.*

recorder /rɪˈkɔːdə(r)/ *n.* (*mus.*) flûte à bec *f.*

recount /rɪˈkaʊnt/ *v.t.* raconter.

re-count /riːˈkaʊnt/ *v.t.* recompter.

recoup /rɪˈkuːp/ *v.t.* récupérer.

recourse /rɪˈkɔːs/ *n.* recours *m.* **have** ∼ **to,** avoir recours à.

recover /rɪˈkʌvə(r)/ *v.t.* récupérer. —*v.i.* se remettre; (*med.*) se rétablir;

(*economy*) se redresser. ∼**y** *n.* récupération *f.*; (*med.*) rétablissement *m.*

recreation /rekrɪ'eɪʃn/ *n.* récréation *f.* ∼**al** *a.* de récréation.

recrimination /rɪkrɪmɪ'neɪʃn/ *n.* contre-accusation *f.*

recruit /rɪ'kruːt/ *n.* recrue *f.* —*v.t.* recruter. ∼**ment** *n.* recrutement *m.*

rectang|le /'rektæŋgl/ *n.* rectangle *m.* ∼**ular** /-'tæŋgjʊlə(r)/ *a.* rectangulaire.

rectif|y /'rektɪfaɪ/ *v.t.* rectifier. ∼**ication** /-ɪ'keɪʃn/ *n.* rectification *f.*

recuperate /rɪ'kjuːpəreɪt/ *v.t.* récupérer. —*v.i.* (*med.*) se rétablir.

recur /rɪ'kɜː(r)/ *v.i.* (*p.t.* **recurred**) revenir, se répéter.

recurren|t /rɪ'kʌrənt/ *a.* fréquent. ∼**ce** *n.* répétition *f.*, retour *m.*

recycle /riː'saɪkl/ *v.t.* recycler.

red /red/ *a.* (**redder, reddest**) rouge; (*hair*) roux. —*n.* rouge *m.* **in the** ∼, en déficit. ∼ **carpet,** réception solennelle *f.* **R∼ Cross,** Croix-Rouge *f.* ∼**-handed** *a.* en flagrant délit. ∼ **herring,** fausse piste *f.* ∼**-hot** *a.* brûlant. **R∼ Indian,** Peau-Rouge *m./f.* ∼ **light,** feu rouge *m.* ∼ **tape,** paperasserie *f.*, bureaucratie *f.*

redd|en /'redn/ *v.t./i.* rougir. ∼**ish** *a.* rougeâtre.

redecorate /riː'dekəreɪt/ *v.t.* (*repaint etc.*) repeindre, refaire.

redeem /rɪ'diːm/ *v.t.* racheter. ∼**ing quality,** qualité qui rachète les défauts *f.* **redemption** *n.* /rɪ'dempʃn/ rachat *m.*

redeploy /riːdɪ'plɔɪ/ *v.t.* réorganiser; (*troops*) répartir.

redirect /riːdaɪə'rekt/ *v.t.* (*letter*) faire suivre.

redness /'rednɪs/ *n.* rougeur *f.*

redo /riː'duː/ *v.t.* (*p.t.* **-did**, *p.p.* **-done**) refaire.

redouble /rɪ'dʌbl/ *v.t.* redoubler.

redress /rɪ'dres/ *v.t.* (*wrong etc.*) redresser. —*n.* réparation *f.*

reduc|e /rɪ'djuːs/ *v.t.* réduire; (*temperature etc.*) faire baisser. ∼**tion** /rɪ'dʌkʃn/ *n.* réduction *f.*

redundan|t /rɪ'dʌndənt/ *a.* superflu; (*worker*) mis au chômage. ∼**cy** *n.* mise au chômage *f.*; (*word, phrase*) pléonasme *m.*

reed /riːd/ *n.* (*plant*) roseau *m.*; (*mus.*) anche *f.*

reef /riːf/ *n.* récif *m.*, écueil *m.*

reek /riːk/ *n.* puanteur *f.* —*v.i.* ∼ (**of**), puer.

reel /riːl/ *n.* (*of thread*) bobine *f.*; (*of film*) bande *f.*; (*winding device*) dévidoir *m.* —*v.i.* chanceler. —*v.t.* ∼ **off,** réciter.

refectory /rɪ'fektərɪ/ *n.* réfectoire *m.*

refer /rɪ'fɜː(r)/ *v.t./i.* (*p.t.* **referred**). ∼ **to,** (*allude to*) faire allusion à; (*concern*) s'appliquer à; (*consult*) consulter; (*submit*) soumettre à; (*direct*) renvoyer à.

referee /refə'riː/ *n.* arbitre *m.*; (*for job*) répondant(e) *m.* (*f.*). —*v.t.* (*p.t.* **refereed**) arbitrer.

reference /'refrəns/ *n.* référence *f.*; (*mention*) allusion *f.*; (*person*) répondant(e) *m.* (*f.*). **in** *or* **with** ∼ **to,** en ce qui concerne; (*comm.*) suite à. ∼ **book,** ouvrage de référence *m.*

referendum /refə'rendəm/ *n.* (*pl.* **-ums**) référendum *m.*

refill[1] /riː'fɪl/ *v.t.* remplir (à nouveau); (*pen etc.*) recharger.

refill[2] /'riːfɪl/ *n.* (*of pen, lighter, lipstick*) recharge *f.*

refine /rɪ'faɪn/ *v.t.* raffiner. ∼**d** *a.* raffiné. ∼**ment** *n.* raffinement *m.*; (*techn.*) raffinage *m.* ∼**ry** /-ərɪ/ *n.* raffinerie *f.*

reflate /riː'fleɪt/ *v.t.* relancer.

reflect /rɪ'flekt/ *v.t.* refléter; (*of mirror*) réfléchir, refléter. —*v.i.* réfléchir (**on,** à). ∼ **on s.o.,** (*glory etc.*) (faire) rejaillir sur qn. ∼**ion** /-kʃn/ *n.* réflexion *f.*; (*image*) reflet *m.* ∼**or** *n.* réflecteur *m.*

reflective /rɪ'flektɪv/ *a.* réfléchi.

reflex /'riːfleks/ *a.* & *n.* réflexe (*m.*).

reflexive /rɪ'fleksɪv/ *a.* (*gram.*) réfléchi.

reform /rɪ'fɔːm/ *v.t.* réformer. —*v.i.* (*person*) s'amender. —*n.* réforme *f.* ∼**er** *n.* réforma|teur, -trice *m.*, *f.*

refract /rɪ'frækt/ *v.t.* réfracter.

refrain[1] /rɪ'freɪn/ *n.* refrain *m.*

refrain[2] /rɪ'freɪn/ *v.i.* s'abstenir (**from,** de).

refresh /rɪ'freʃ/ *v.t.* rafraîchir; (*of rest etc.*) ragaillardir, délasser. ∼**ing** *a.* (*drink*) rafraîchissant; (*sleep*) réparateur. ∼**ments** *n. pl.* rafraîchissements *m. pl.*

refresher /rɪ'freʃə(r)/ *a.* (*course*) de perfectionnement.

refrigerat|e /rɪ'frɪdʒəreɪt/ *v.t.* réfrigérer. ∼**or** *n.* réfrigérateur *m.*

refuel /riː'fjuːəl/ *v.t./i.* (*p.t.* **refuelled**) (se) ravitailler.

refuge /'refjuːdʒ/ n. refuge m. **take ~,** se réfugier.

refugee /refjʊ'dʒiː/ n. réfugié(e) m. (f.).

refund /rɪ'fʌnd/ v.t. rembourser. —n. /'riːfʌnd/ remboursement m.

refurbish /riː'fɜːbɪʃ/ v.t. remettre à neuf.

refus|e[1] /rɪ'fjuːz/ v.t./i. refuser. **~al** n. refus m.

refuse[2] /'refjuːs/ n. détritus m. pl.

refute /rɪ'fjuːt/ v.t. réfuter.

regain /rɪ'geɪn/ v.t. retrouver; (lost ground) regagner.

regal /'riːgl/ a. royal, majestueux.

regalia /rɪ'geɪlɪə/ n. pl. (insignia) insignes (royaux) m. pl.

regard /rɪ'gɑːd/ v.t. regarder, considérer. —n. considération f., estime f. **~s,** amitiés f. pl. **in this ~,** à cet égard. **as ~s, ~ing** prep. en ce qui concerne.

regardless /rɪ'gɑːdlɪs/ adv. quand même. **~ of,** sans tenir compte de.

regatta /rɪ'gætə/ n. régates f. pl.

regenerate /rɪ'dʒenəreɪt/ v.t. régénérer.

regen|t /'riːdʒənt/ n. régent(e) m. (f.). **~cy** n. régence f.

regime /reɪ'ʒiːm/ n. régime m.

regiment /'redʒɪmənt/ n. régiment m. **~al** /-'mentl/ a. d'un régiment. **~ation** /-en'teɪʃn/ n. discipline excessive f.

region /'riːdʒən/ n. région f. **in the ~ of,** environ. **~al** a. régional.

regist|er /'redʒɪstə(r)/ n. registre m. —v.t. enregistrer; (vehicle) immatriculer; (birth) déclarer; (letter) recommander; (indicate) indiquer; (express) exprimer. —v.i. (enrol) s'inscrire; (fig.) être compris. **~er office,** bureau d'état civil m. **~ration** /-'streɪʃn/ n. enregistrement m.; inscription f.; (vehicle document) carte grise f. **~ration (number),** (auto.) numéro d'immatriculation m.

registrar /redʒɪ'strɑː(r)/ n. officier de l'état civil m.; (univ.) secrétaire général m.

regret /rɪ'gret/ n. regret m. —v.t. (p.t. **regretted**) regretter (**to do,** de faire). **~fully** adv. à regret. **~table** a. regrettable, fâcheux. **~tably** adv. malheureusement; (small, poor, etc.) fâcheusement.

regroup /riː'gruːp/ v.t./i. (se) regrouper.

regular /'regjʊlə(r)/ a. régulier;

(usual) habituel; (thorough: fam.) vrai. —n. (fam.) habitué(e) m. (f.). **~ity** /-'lærətɪ/ n. régularité f. **~ly** adv. régulièrement.

regulat|e /'regjʊleɪt/ v.t. régler. **~ion** /-'leɪʃn/ n. réglage m.; (rule) règlement m.

rehabilitat|e /riːə'bɪlɪteɪt/ v.t. réadapter; (in public esteem) réhabiliter. **~ion** /-'teɪʃn/ n. réadaptation f.; réhabilitation f.

rehash[1] /riː'hæʃ/ v.t. remanier.

rehash[2] /'riːhæʃ/ n. réchauffé m.

rehears|e /rɪ'hɜːs/ v.t./i (theatre) répéter. **~al** n. répétition f.

reign /reɪn/ n. règne m. —v.i. régner (over, sur).

reimburse /riːɪm'bɜːs/ v.t. rembourser.

rein /reɪn/ n. rêne f.

reindeer /'reɪndɪə(r)/ n. invar. renne m.

reinforce /riːɪn'fɔːs/ v.t. renforcer. **~ment** n. renforcement m. **~ments** n. pl. renforts m. pl.

reinstate /riːɪn'steɪt/ v.t. réintégrer, rétablir.

reiterate /riː'ɪtəreɪt/ v.t. réitérer.

reject[1] /rɪ'dʒekt/ v.t. (offer, plea, etc.) rejeter; (book, goods, etc.) refuser. **~ion** /-kʃn/ n. rejet m.; refus m.

reject[2] /'riːdʒekt/ n. (article de) rebut m.

rejoic|e /rɪ'dʒɔɪs/ v.i. se réjouir. **~ing** n. réjouissance f.

rejoin /rɪ'dʒɔɪn/ v.t. rejoindre.

rejuvenate /rɪ'dʒuːvəneɪt/ v.t. rajeunir.

relapse /rɪ'læps/ n. rechute f. —v.i. rechuter. **~ into,** retomber dans.

relate /rɪ'leɪt/ v.t. raconter; (associate) rapprocher. —v.i. **~ to,** se rapporter à; (get on with) s'entendre avec. **~d** /-ɪd/ a. (ideas etc.) lié. **~d to s.o.,** parent(e) de qn.

relation /rɪ'leɪʃn/ n. rapport m.; (person) parent(e) m. (f.). **~ship** n. lien de parenté m.; (link) rapport m.; (affair) liaison f.

relative /'relətɪv/ n. parent(e) m. (f.). —a. relatif; (respective) respectif. **~ly** adv. relativement.

relax /rɪ'læks/ v.t./i. (se) relâcher; (fig.) (se) détendre. **~ation** /riːlæk'seɪʃn/ n. relâchement m.; détente f. **~ing** a. délassant.

relay[1] /'riːleɪ/ n. relais m. **~ race,** course de relais f.

relay[2] /rɪˈleɪ/ *v.t.* relayer.

release /rɪˈliːs/ *v.t.* libérer; (*bomb*) lâcher; (*film*) sortir; (*news*) publier; (*smoke*) dégager; (*spring*) déclencher. —*n.* libération *f.*; sortie *f.*; (*record*) nouveau disque *m.*

relegate /ˈrelɪɡeɪt/ *v.t.* reléguer.

relent /rɪˈlent/ *v.i.* se laisser fléchir. **~less** *a.* impitoyable.

relevan|t /ˈreləvənt/ *a.* pertinent. **be ~t to,** avoir rapport à. **~ce** *n.* pertinence *f.*, rapport *m.*

reliab|le /rɪˈlaɪəbl/ *a.* sérieux, sûr; (*machine*) fiable. **~ility** /-ˈbɪlətɪ/ *n.* sérieux *m.*; fiabilité *f.*

reliance /rɪˈlaɪəns/ *n.* dépendance *f.*; (*trust*) confiance *f.*

relic /ˈrelɪk/ *n.* relique *f.* **~s,** (*of past*) vestiges *m. pl.*

relief /rɪˈliːf/ *n.* soulagement *m.* (**from,** à); (*assistance*) secours *m.*; (*outline, design*) relief *m.* **~ road,** route de délestage *f.*

relieve /rɪˈliːv/ *v.t.* soulager; (*help*) secourir; (*take over from*) relayer.

religion /rɪˈlɪdʒən/ *n.* religion *f.*

religious /rɪˈlɪdʒəs/ *a.* religieux.

relinquish /rɪˈlɪŋkwɪʃ/ *v.t.* abandonner; (*relax hold of*) lâcher.

relish /ˈrelɪʃ/ *n.* plaisir *m.*, goût *m.*; (*culin.*) assaisonnement *m.* —*v.t.* savourer; (*idea etc.*) aimer.

relocate /riːləʊˈkeɪt/ *v.t.* muter. —*v.i.* se déplacer, déménager.

reluctan|t /rɪˈlʌktənt/ *a.* fait, donné, *etc.* à contrecœur. **~t to,** peu disposé à. **~ce** *n.* répugnance *f.* **~tly** *adv.* à contrecœur.

rely /rɪˈlaɪ/ *v.i.* **~ on,** compter sur; (*financially*) dépendre de.

remain /rɪˈmeɪn/ *v.i.* rester. **~s** *n. pl.* restes *m. pl.*

remainder /rɪˈmeɪndə(r)/ *n.* reste *m.*; (*book*) invendu soldé *m.*

remand /rɪˈmɑːnd/ *v.t.* mettre en détention préventive. —*n.* **on ~,** en détention préventive.

remark /rɪˈmɑːk/ *n.* remarque *f.* —*v.t.* remarquer. —*v.i.* **~ on,** faire des commentaires sur. **~able** *a.* remarquable.

remarry /riːˈmærɪ/ *v.i.* se remarier.

remed|y /ˈremədɪ/ *n.* remède *m.* —*v.t.* remédier à. **~ial** /rɪˈmiːdɪəl/ *a.* (*class etc.*) de rattrapage; (*treatment*: *med.*) curatif.

rememb|er /rɪˈmembə(r)/ *v.t.* se souvenir de, se rappeler. **~er to do,**

ne pas oublier de faire. **~rance** *n.* souvenir *m.*

remind /rɪˈmaɪnd/ *v.t.* rappeler (**s.o. of sth.,** qch. à qn.). **~ s.o. to do,** rappeler à qn. qu'il doit faire. **~er** *n.* (*letter, signal*) rappel *m.*

reminisce /remɪˈnɪs/ *v.i.* évoquer ses souvenirs. **~nces** *n. pl.* réminiscences *f. pl.*

reminiscent /remɪˈnɪsnt/ *a.* **~ of,** qui rappelle, qui évoque.

remiss /rɪˈmɪs/ *a.* négligent.

remission /rɪˈmɪʃn/ *n.* rémission *f.*; (*jurid.*) remise (de peine) *f.*

remit /rɪˈmɪt/ *v.t.* (*p.t.* **remitted**) (*money*) envoyer; (*debt*) remettre. **~tance** *n.* paiement *m.*

remnant /ˈremnənt/ *n.* reste *m.*, débris *m.*; (*trace*) vestige *m.*; (*of cloth*) coupon *m.*

remorse /rɪˈmɔːs/ *n.* remords *m.* (*pl.*). **~ful** *a.* plein de remords. **~less** *a.* implacable.

remote /rɪˈməʊt/ *a.* (*place, time*) lointain; (*person*) distant; (*slight*) vague. **~ control,** télécommande *f.* **~ly** *adv.* au loin; vaguement. **~ness** *n.* éloignement *m.*

removable /rɪˈmuːvəbl/ *a.* (*detachable*) amovible.

remov|e /rɪˈmuːv/ *v.t.* enlever; (*lead away*) emmener; (*dismiss*) renvoyer; (*do away with*) supprimer. **~al** *n.* enlèvement *m.*; renvoi *m.*; suppression *f.*; (*from house*) déménagement *m.* **~er** *n.* (*for paint*) décapant *m.*

remunerat|e /rɪˈmjuːnəreɪt/ *v.t.* rémunérer. **~ion** /-ˈreɪʃn/ *n.* rémunération *f.*

rename /riːˈneɪm/ *v.t.* rebaptiser.

rend /rend/ *v.t.* (*p.t.* **rent**) déchirer.

render /ˈrendə(r)/ *v.t.* (*give, make*) rendre; (*mus.*) interpréter. **~ing** *n.* interprétation *f.*

rendezvous /ˈrɒndeɪvuː/ *n.* (*pl.* **-vous** /-vuːz/) rendez-vous *m. invar.*

renegade /ˈrenɪɡeɪd/ *n.* renégat(e) *m.* (*f.*).

renew /rɪˈnjuː/ *v.t.* renouveler; (*resume*) reprendre. **~able** *a.* renouvelable. **~al** *n.* renouvellement *m.*; reprise *f.*

renounce /rɪˈnaʊns/ *v.t.* renoncer à; (*disown*) renier.

renovat|e /ˈrenəveɪt/ *v.t.* rénover. **~ion** /-ˈveɪʃn/ *n.* rénovation *f.*

renown /rɪ'naʊn/ *n.* renommée *f.* **~ed** *a.* renommé.

rent[1] /rent/ *see* rend.

rent[2] /rent/ *n.* loyer *m.* —*v.t.* louer. **~al** *n.* prix de location *m.*

renunciation /rɪnʌnsɪ'eɪʃn/ *n.* renonciation *f.*

reopen /ri:'əʊpən/ *v.t./i.* rouvrir. **~ing** *n.* réouverture *f.*

reorganize /ri:'ɔ:gənaɪz/ *v.t.* réorganiser.

rep /rep/ *n.* (*comm.*, *fam.*) représentant(e) *m.* (*f.*).

repair /rɪ'peə(r)/ *v.t.* réparer. —*n.* réparation *f.* **in good/bad ~,** en bon/mauvais état.

repartee /repɑ:'ti:/ *n.* repartie *f.*

repatriat|e /ri:'pætrɪeɪt/ *v.t.* rapatrier. **~ion** /-'eɪʃn/ *n.* rapatriement *m.*

repay /ri:'peɪ/ *v.t.* (*p.t.* **repaid**) rembourser; (*reward*) récompenser. **~ment** *n.* remboursement *m.*; récompense *f.*

repeal /rɪ'pi:l/ *v.t.* abroger, annuler. —*n.* abrogation *f.*

repeat /rɪ'pi:t/ *v.t./i.* répéter; (*renew*) renouveler. —*n.* répétition *f.*; (*broadcast*) reprise *f.* **~ itself, ~ o.s.,** se répéter.

repeatedly /rɪ'pi:tɪdlɪ/ *adv.* à maintes reprises.

repel /rɪ'pel/ *v.t.* (*p.t.* **repelled**) repousser. **~lent** *a.* repoussant.

repent /rɪ'pent/ *v.i.* se repentir (**of,** de). **~ance** *n.* repentir *m.* **~ant** *a.* repentant.

repercussion /ri:pə'kʌʃn/ *n.* répercussion *f.*

repertoire /'repətwɑ:(r)/ *n.* répertoire *m.*

repertory /'repətrɪ/ *n.* répertoire *m.* **~ (theatre),** théâtre de répertoire *m.*

repetit|ion /repɪ'tɪʃn/ *n.* répétition *f.* **~ious** /-'tɪʃəs/, **~ive** /rɪ'petətɪv/ *adjs.* plein de répétitions.

replace /rɪ'pleɪs/ *v.t.* remettre; (*take the place of*) remplacer. **~ment** *n.* remplacement *m.* (**of,** de); (*person*) remplaçant(e) *m.* (*f.*); (*new part*) pièce de rechange *f.*

replay /'ri:pleɪ/ *n.* (*sport*) match rejoué *m.*; (*recording*) répétition immédiate *f.*

replenish /rɪ'plenɪʃ/ *v.t.* (*refill*) remplir; (*renew*) renouveler.

replete /rɪ'pli:t/ *a.* (*with food*) rassasié. **~ with,** rempli de.

replica /'replɪkə/ *n.* copie exacte *f.*

reply /rɪ'plaɪ/ *v.t./i.* répondre. —*n.* réponse *f.*

report /rɪ'pɔ:t/ *v.t.* rapporter, annoncer (**that,** que); (*notify*) signaler; (*denounce*) dénoncer. —*v.i.* faire un rapport. **~ (on),** (*news item*) faire un reportage sur. **~ to,** (*go*) se présenter chez. —*n.* rapport *m.*; (*in press*) reportage *m.*; (*schol.*) bulletin *m.*; (*sound*) détonation *f.* **~edly** *adv.* selon ce qu'on dit.

reporter /rɪ'pɔ:tə(r)/ *n.* reporter *m.*

repose /rɪ'pəʊz/ *n.* repos *m.*

repossess /ri:pə'zes/ *v.t.* reprendre possession de.

represent /reprɪ'zent/ *v.t.* représenter. **~ation** /-'teɪʃn/ *n.* représentation *f.* **~ations** /-'teɪʃnz/ *n. pl.* remontrances *f. pl.*

representative /reprɪ'zentətɪv/ *a.* représentatif, typique (**of,** de). —*n.* représentant(e) *m.* (*f.*).

repress /rɪ'pres/ *v.t.* réprimer. **~ion** /-ʃn/ *n.* répression *f.* **~ive** *a.* répressif.

reprieve /rɪ'pri:v/ *n.* (*delay*) sursis *m.*; (*pardon*) grâce *f.* —*v.t.* accorder un sursis à; gracier.

reprimand /'reprɪmɑ:nd/ *v.t.* réprimander. —*n.* réprimande *f.*

reprint /'ri:prɪnt/ *n.* réimpression *f.*; (*offprint*) tiré à part *m.*

reprisals /rɪ'praɪzlz/ *n. pl.* représailles *f. pl.*

reproach /rɪ'prəʊtʃ/ *v.t.* reprocher (**s.o. for sth.,** qch. à qn.). —*n.* reproche *m.* **~ful** *a.* de reproche, réprobateur. **~fully** *adv.* avec reproche.

reproduc|e /ri:prə'dju:s/ *v.t./i.* (se) reproduire. **~tion** /-'dʌkʃn/ *n.* reproduction *f.* **~tive** /-'dʌktɪv/ *a.* reproducteur.

reptile /'reptaɪl/ *n.* reptile *m.*

republic /rɪ'pʌblɪk/ *n.* république *f.* **~an** *a.* & *n.* républicain(e) (*m.* (*f.*)).

repudiate /rɪ'pju:dɪeɪt/ *v.t.* répudier; (*treaty*) refuser d'honorer.

repugnan|t /rɪ'pʌgnənt/ *a.* répugnant. **~ce** *n.* répugnance *f.*

repuls|e /rɪ'pʌls/ *v.t.* repousser. **~ion** /-ʃn/ *n.* répulsion *f.* **~ive** *a.* repoussant.

reputable /'repjʊtəbl/ *a.* honorable, de bonne réputation.

reputation /repjʊ'teɪʃn/ *n.* réputation *f.*

repute /rɪ'pju:t/ *n.* réputation *f.* **~d**

/-ɪd/ *a.* réputé. ~**dly** /-ɪdlɪ/ *adv.* d'après ce qu'on dit.

request /rɪ'kwest/ *n.* demande *f.* −*v.t.* demander (**of, from,** à). ~ **stop,** arrêt facultatif *m.*

requiem /'rekwɪem/ *n.* requiem *m.*

require /rɪ'kwaɪə(r)/ *v.t.* (*of thing*) demander; (*of person*) avoir besoin de; (*demand, order*) exiger. ~**d** *a.* requis. ~**ment** *n.* exigence *f.*; (*condition*) condition (require) *f.*

requisite /'rekwɪzɪt/ *a.* nécessaire. −*n.* chose nécessaire *f.* ~**s,** (*for travel etc.*) articles *m. pl.*

requisition /rekwɪ'zɪʃn/ *n.* réquisition *f.* −*v.t.* réquisitionner.

re-route /riː'ruːt/ *v.t.* dérouter.

resale /'riːseɪl/ *n.* revente *f.*

rescind /rɪ'sɪnd/ *v.t.* annuler.

rescue /'reskjuː/ *v.t.* sauver. −*n.* sauvetage *m.* (**of,** de); (*help*) secours *m.* ~**r** /-ə(r)/ *n.* sauveteur *m.*

research /rɪ'sɜːtʃ/ *n.* recherche(s) *f.* (*pl.*). −*v.t./i.* faire des recherches (sur). ~**er** *n.* chercheu|r, -se *m., f.*

resembl|e /rɪ'zembl/ *v.t.* ressembler à. ~**ance** *n.* ressemblance *f.*

resent /rɪ'zent/ *v.t.* être indigné de, s'offenser de. ~**ful** *a.* plein de ressentiment, indigné. ~**ment** *n.* ressentiment *m.*

reservation /rezə'veɪʃn/ *n.* réserve *f.*; (*booking*) réservation *f.*; (*Amer.*) réserve (indienne) *f.*

reserve /rɪ'zɜːv/ *v.t.* réserver. −*n.* (*reticence, stock, land*) réserve *f.*; (*sport*) remplaçant(e) *m.* (*f.*). **in** ~, en réserve. **the** ~**s,** (*mil.*) les réserves *f. pl.* ~**d** *a.* (*person, room*) réservé.

reservist /rɪ'zɜːvɪst/ *n.* (*mil.*) réserviste *m.*

reservoir /'rezəvwɑː(r)/ *n.* (*lake, supply, etc.*) réservoir *m.*

reshape /riː'ʃeɪp/ *v.t.* remodeler.

reshuffle /riː'ʃʌfl/ *v.t.* (*pol.*) remanier. −*n.* (*pol.*) remaniement (ministériel) *m.*

reside /rɪ'zaɪd/ *v.i.* résider.

residen|t /'rezɪdənt/ *a.* résidant. **be** ~**t,** résider. −*n.* habitant(e) *m.* (*f.*); (*foreigner*) résident(e) *m.* (*f.*); (*in hotel*) pensionnaire *m.*|*f.* ~**ce** *n.* résidence *f.*; (*of students*) foyer *m.* **in** ~**ce,** (*doctor*) résidant; (*students*) au foyer.

residential /rezɪ'denʃl/ *a.* résidentiel.

residue /'rezɪdjuː/ *n.* résidu *m.*

resign /rɪ'zaɪn/ *v.t.* abandonner; (*job*) démissionner de. −*v.i.* démissionner. ~ **o.s. to,** se résigner à. ~**ation** /rezɪg'neɪʃn/ *n.* résignation *f.*; (*from job*) démission *f.* ~**ed** *a.* résigné.

resilien|t /rɪ'zɪlɪənt/ *a.* élastique; (*person*) qui a du ressort. ~**ce** *n.* élasticité *f.*; ressort *m.*

resin /'rezɪn/ *n.* résine *f.*

resist /rɪ'zɪst/ *v.t./i.* résister (à). ~**ance** *n.* résistance *f.* ~**ant** *a.* (*med.*) rebelle; (*metal*) résistant.

resolut|e /'rezəluːt/ *a.* résolu. ~**ion** /-'luːʃn/ *n.* résolution *f.*

resolve /rɪ'zɒlv/ *v.t.* résoudre (**to do,** de faire). −*n.* résolution *f.* ~**d** *a.* résolu (**to do,** à faire).

resonan|t /'rezənənt/ *a.* résonnant. ~**ce** *n.* résonance *f.*

resort /rɪ'zɔːt/ *v.i.* ~ **to,** avoir recours à. −*n.* (*recourse*) recours *m.*; (*place*) station *f.* **in the last** ~, en dernier ressort.

resound /rɪ'zaʊnd/ *v.i.* retentir (**with,** de). ~**ing** *a.* retentissant.

resource /rɪ'sɔːs/ *n.* (*expedient*) ressource *f.* ~**s,** (*wealth etc.*) ressources *f. pl.* ~**ful** *a.* ingénieux. ~**fulness** *n.* ingéniosité *f.*

respect /rɪ'spekt/ *n.* respect *m.*; (*aspect*) égard *m.* −*v.t.* respecter. **with** ~ **to,** à l'égard de, relativement à. ~**ful** *a.* respectueux.

respectab|le /rɪ'spektəbl/ *a.* respectable. ~**ility** /-'bɪlətɪ/ *n.* respectabilité *f.* ~**ly** *adv.* convenablement.

respective /rɪ'spektɪv/ *a.* respectif. ~**ly** *adv.* respectivement.

respiration /respə'reɪʃn/ *n.* respiration *f.*

respite /'resp(a)ɪt/ *n.* répit *m.*

resplendent /rɪ'splendənt/ *a.* resplendissant.

respond /rɪ'spɒnd/ *v.i.* répondre (**to,** à). ~ **to,** (*react to*) réagir à.

response /rɪ'spɒns/ *n.* réponse *f.*

responsib|le /rɪ'spɒnsəbl/ *a.* responsable; (*job*) qui comporte des responsabilités. ~**ility** /-'bɪlətɪ/ *n.* responsabilité *f.* ~**ly** *adv.* de façon responsable.

responsive /rɪ'spɒnsɪv/ *a.* qui réagit bien. ~ **to,** sensible à.

rest[1] /rest/ *v.t./i.* (se) reposer; (*lean*) (s')appuyer (**on,** sur); (*be buried, lie*) reposer. −*n.* (*repose*) repos *m.*; (*support*) support *m.*

rest[2] /rest/ *v.i.* (*remain*) demeurer. −*n.* (*remainder*) reste *m.* (**of,** de).

the ~ (of the), (*others*, *other*) les autres. it ~s with him to, il lui appartient de.

restaurant /'restərɒnt/ *n.* restaurant *m.*

restful /'restfl/ *a.* reposant.

restitution /restɪ'tjuːʃn/ *n.* (*for injury*) compensation *f.*

restive /'restɪv/ *a.* rétif.

restless /'restlɪs/ *a.* agité. ~ly *adv.* avec agitation, fébrilement.

restor|e /rɪ'stɔː(r)/ *v.t.* rétablir; (*building*) restaurer. ~ation /restə'reɪʃn/ *n.* rétablissement *m.*

restrain /rɪ'streɪn/ *v.t.* contenir. ~ s.o. from, retenir qn. de. ~ed *a.* (*moderate*) mesuré; (*in control of self*) maître de soi. ~t *n.* contrainte *f.*; (*moderation*) retenue *f.*

restrict /rɪ'strɪkt/ *v.t.* restreindre. ~ion /-kʃn/ *n.* restriction *f.* ~ive *a.* restrictif.

restructure /riː'strʌktʃə(r)/ *v.t.* restructurer.

result /rɪ'zʌlt/ *n.* résultat *m.* —*v.i.* résulter. ~ in, aboutir à.

resum|e /rɪ'zjuːm/ *v.t./i.* reprendre. ~ption /rɪ'zʌmpʃn/ *n.* reprise *f.*

résumé /'rezjuːmeɪ/ *n.* résumé *m.*

resurgence /rɪ'sɜːdʒəns/ *n.* réapparition *f.*

resurrect /rezə'rekt/ *v.t.* ressusciter. ~ion /-kʃn/ *n.* résurrection *f.*

resuscitate /rɪ'sʌsɪteɪt/ *v.t.* réanimer.

retail /'riːteɪl/ *n.* détail *m.* —*a.* & *adv.* au détail. —*v.t./i.* (se) vendre au détail. ~er *n.* détaillant(e) *m.* (*f.*).

retain /rɪ'teɪn/ *v.t.* (*hold back*, *remember*) retenir; (*keep*) conserver.

retainer /rɪ'teɪnə(r)/ *n.* (*fee to lawyer etc.*) provision *f.*

retaliat|e /rɪ'tælieɪt/ *v.i.* riposter. ~ion /-'eɪʃn/ *n.* représailles *f. pl.*

retarded /rɪ'tɑːdɪd/ *a.* arriéré.

retch /retʃ/ *v.i.* avoir un haut-le-cœur.

retentive /rɪ'tentɪv/ *a.* (*memory*) fidèle. ~ of, qui retient.

rethink /riː'θɪŋk/ *v.t.* (*p.t.* rethought) repenser.

reticen|t /'retɪsnt/ *a.* réticent. ~ce *n.* réticence *f.*

retina /'retɪnə/ *n.* rétine *f.*

retinue /'retmjuː/ *n.* suite *f.*

retire /rɪ'taɪə(r)/ *v.i.* (*from work*) prendre sa retraite; (*withdraw*) se retirer; (*go to bed*) se coucher. —*v.t.* mettre à la retraite. ~d *a.* retraité. ~ment *n.* retraite *f.*

retiring /rɪ'taɪərɪŋ/ *a.* réservé.

retort /rɪ'tɔːt/ *v.t./i.* répliquer. —*n.* réplique *f.*

retrace /riː'treɪs/ *v.t.* revenir sur.

retract /rɪ'trækt/ *v.t./i.* (se) rétraiter.

retrain /riː'treɪn/ *v.t./i.* (se) recycler.

retreat /rɪ'triːt/ *v.i.* (*mil.*) battre en retraite. —*n.* retraite *f.*

retrial /riː'traɪəl/ *n.* nouveau procès *m.*

retribution /retrɪ'bjuːʃn/ *n.* châtiment *m.*; (*vengeance*) vengeance *f.*

retriev|e /rɪ'triːv/ *v.t.* (*recover*) récupérer; (*restore*) rétablir; (*put right*) réparer. ~al *n.* récupération *f.*; (*of information*) recherche documentaire *f.* ~er *n.* (*dog*) chien d'arrêt *m.*

retrograde /'retrəgreɪd/ *a.* rétrograde —*v.i.* rétrograder.

retrospect /'retrəspekt/ *n.* in ~, rétrospectivement.

return /rɪ'tɜːn/ *v.i.* (*come back*) revenir; (*go back*) retourner; (*go home*) rentrer. —*v.t.* (*give back*) rendre; (*bring back*) rapporter; (*send back*) renvoyer; (*put back*) remettre. —*n.* retour *m.*; (*yield*) rapport *m.* ~s, (*comm.*) bénéfices *m. pl.* in ~ for, en échange de. ~ match, match retour *m.* ~ ticket, aller et retour *m.*

reunion /riː'juːnɪən/ *n.* réunion *f.*

reunite /riːjuː'naɪt/ *v.t.* réunir.

rev /rev/ *n.* (*auto.*, *fam.*) tour *m.* —*v.t./i.* (*p.t.* revved). ~ (up), (*engine*: *fam.*) (s')emballer.

revamp /riː'væmp/ *v.t.* rénover.

reveal /rɪ'viːl/ *v.t.* révéler; (*allow to appear*) laisser voir. ~ing *a.* révélateur.

revel /'revl/ *v.i.* (*p.t.* revelled) faire bombance. ~ in, se délecter de. ~ry *n.* festivités *f. pl.*

revelation /revə'leɪʃn/ *n.* révélation *f.*

revenge /rɪ'vendʒ/ *n.* vengeance *f.*; (*sport*) revanche *f.* —*v.t.* venger.

revenue /'revənjuː/ *n.* revenu *m.*

reverberate /rɪ'vɜːbəreɪt/ *v.i.* (*sound*, *light*) se répercuter.

revere /rɪ'vɪə(r)/ *v.t.* révérer. ~nce /'revərəns/ *n.* vénération *f.*

reverend /'revərənd/ *a.* révérend.

reverent /'revərənt/ *a.* respectueux.

reverie /'revərɪ/ *n.* rêverie *f.*

revers|e /rɪ'vɜːs/ *a.* contraire, inverse. —*n.* contraire *m.*; (*back*) revers *m.*, envers *m.*; (*gear*) marche arrière *f.* —*v.t.* (*situation*, *bucket*, *etc.*) renverser; (*order*) inverser; (*decision*) annuler. —*v.i.* (*auto.*) faire marche arrière. ~**al** *n.* renversement *m.*; (*of view*) revirement *m.*

revert /rɪ'vɜːt/ *v.i.* ~ **to**, revenir à.

review /rɪ'vjuː/ *n.* (*inspection, magazine*) revue *f.*; (*of book etc.*) critique *f.* —*v.t.* passer en revue; (*situation*) réexaminer; faire la critique de. ~**er** *n.* critique *m.*

revile /rɪ'vaɪl/ *v.t.* injurier.

revis|e /rɪ'vaɪz/ *v.t.* réviser. ~**ion** /-ɪʒn/ *n.* révision *f.*

revitalize /riː'vaɪtəlaɪz/ *v.t.* revitaliser, revivifier.

reviv|e /rɪ'vaɪv/ *v.t./i.* ressusciter, (se) ranimer. ~**al** *n.* (*resumption*) reprise *f.*; (*of faith*) renouveau *m.*

revoke /rɪ'vəʊk/ *v.t.* révoquer.

revolt /rɪ'vəʊlt/ *v.t./i.* (se) révolter. —*n.* révolte *f.*

revolting /rɪ'vəʊltɪŋ/ *a.* dégoûtant.

revolution /revə'luːʃn/ *n.* révolution *f.* ~**ary** *a.* & *n.* révolutionnaire (*m./f.*). ~**ize** *v.t.* révolutionner.

revolv|e /rɪ'vɒlv/ *v.i.* tourner. ~**ing door**, tambour *m.*

revolver /rɪ'vɒlvə(r)/ *n.* revolver *m.*

revulsion /rɪ'vʌlʃn/ *n.* dégoût *m.*

reward /rɪ'wɔːd/ *n.* récompense *f.* —*v.t.* récompenser. ~**ing** *a.* rémunérateur; (*worthwhile*) qui (en) vaut la peine.

rewrite /riː'raɪt/ *v.t.* récrire.

rhapsody /'ræpsədɪ/ *n.* rhapsodie *f.*

rhetoric /'retərɪk/ *n.* rhétorique *f.* ~**al** /rɪ'tɒrɪkl/ *a.* (de) rhétorique; (*question*) de pure forme.

rheumati|c /ruː'mætɪk/ *a.* (*pain*) rhumatismal; (*person*) rhumatisant. ~**sm** /'ruːmətɪzəm/ *n.* rhumatisme *m.*

rhinoceros /raɪ'nɒsərəs/ *n.* (*pl.* -**oses**) rhinocéros *m.*

rhubarb /'ruːbɑːb/ *n.* rhubarbe *f.*

rhyme /raɪm/ *n.* rime *f.*; (*poem*) vers *m. pl.* —*v.t./i.* (faire) rimer.

rhythm /'rɪðəm/ *n.* rythme *m.* ~**ic(al)** /'rɪðmɪk(l)/ *a.* rythmique.

rib /rɪb/ *n.* côte *f.*

ribald /'rɪbld/ *a.* grivois.

ribbon /'rɪbən/ *n.* ruban *m.* **in** ~**s**, (*torn pieces*) en lambeaux.

rice /raɪs/ *n.* riz *m.*

rich /rɪtʃ/ *a.* (-**er**, -**est**) riche. ~**es** *n. pl.* richesses *f. pl.* ~**ly** *adv.* richement. ~**ness** *n.* richesse *f.*

rickety /'rɪkətɪ/ *a.* branlant.

ricochet /'rɪkəʃeɪ/ *n.* ricochet *m.* —*v.i.* (*p.t.* **ricocheted** /-ʃeɪd/) ricocher.

rid /rɪd/ *v.t.* (*p.t.* **rid**, *pres. p.* **ridding**) débarrasser (**of**, de). **get** ~ **of,** se débarrasser de.

riddance /'rɪdns/ *n.* **good** ~**!**, bon débarras!

ridden /'rɪdn/ *see* **ride**. —*a.* ~ **by**, plein de; (*fear*) hanté par. **debt-**~ *a.* criblé de dettes.

riddle[1] /'rɪdl/ *n.* énigme *f.*

riddle[2] /'rɪdl/ *v.t.* ~ **with**, (*bullets*) cribler de; (*mistakes*) bourrer de.

ride /raɪd/ *v.i.* (*p.t.* **rode**, *p.p.* **ridden**) aller (à bicyclette, à cheval, *etc.*); (*in car*) rouler. ~ (**a horse**), (*go riding as sport*) monter (à cheval). —*v.t.* (*a particular horse*) monter; (*distance*) parcourir. —*n.* promenade *f.*, tour *m.*; (*distance*) trajet *m.* ~**r** /-ə(r)/ *n.* caval|ier, -ière *m.*, *f.*; (*cyclist*) cycliste *m./f.*; (*in document*) annexe *f.*

ridge /rɪdʒ/ *n.* arête *f.*, crête *f.*

ridicule /'rɪdɪkjuːl/ *n.* ridicule *m.* —*v.t.* ridiculiser.

ridiculous /rɪ'dɪkjʊləs/ *a.* ridicule.

riding /'raɪdɪŋ/ *n.* équitation *f.*

rife /raɪf/ *a.* **be** ~, être répandu, sévir. ~ **with**, abondant en.

riff-raff /'rɪfræf/ *n.* canaille *f.*

rifle /'raɪfl/ *n.* fusil *m.* —*v.t.* (*rob*) dévaliser.

rift /rɪft/ *n.* (*crack*) fissure *f.*; (*between people*) désaccord *m.*

rig[1] /rɪg/ *v.t.* (*p.t.* **rigged**) (*equip*) équiper. —*n.* (*for oil*) derrick *m.* ~ **out**, habiller. ~**out** *n.* (*fam.*) tenue *f.* ~ **up**, (*arrange*) arranger.

rig[2] /rɪg/ *v.t.* (*p.t.* **rigged**) (*election, match, etc.*) truquer.

right /raɪt/ *a.* (*correct*) exact, juste; (*morally*) bon; (*fair*) juste; (*not mistaken*) bon, qu'il faut; (*not left*) droit. **be** ~, (*person*) avoir raison (**to**, de). —*n.* (*entitlement*) droit *m.*; (*not left*) droite *f.*; (*not evil*) le bien. —*v.t.* (*a wrong, sth. fallen, etc.*) redresser. —*adv.* (*not left*) à droite; (*directly*) tout droit; (*exactly*) bien, juste; (*completely*) tout (à fait). **be in the** ~, avoir raison. **put** ~, arranger, rectifier. ~ **angle**, angle droit *m.* ~ **away**, tout de suite. ~-**hand** *a.* à *or* de droite. ~-**hand man**, bras droit *m.* ~-**handed** *a.* droitier. ~ **of way**, (*auto.*) priorité *f.* ~-**wing** *a.* (*pol.*) de droite.

righteous /'raɪtʃəs/ *a.* (*person*) vertueux; (*cause, anger*) juste.

rightful /'raɪtfl/ *a.* légitime. ~**ly** *adv.* à juste titre.

rightly /'raɪtlɪ/ adv. correctement; (with reason) à juste titre.

rigid /'rɪdʒɪd/ a. rigide. **~ity** /rɪ'dʒɪdətɪ/ n. rigidité f.

rigmarole /'rɪgmərəʊl/ n. charabia m.; (procedure) comédie f.

rig|our /'rɪgə(r)/ n. rigueur f. **~orous** a. rigoureux.

rile /raɪl/ v.t. (fam.) agacer.

rim /rɪm/ n. bord m.; (of wheel) jante f. **~med** a. bordé.

rind /raɪnd/ n. (on cheese) croûte f.; (on bacon) couenne f.; (on fruit) écorce f.

ring[1] /rɪŋ/ n. anneau m.; (on finger, with stone) bague f.; (circle) cercle m.; (boxing) ring m.; (arena) piste f. —v.t. entourer; (word in text etc.) entourer d'un cercle.

ring[2] /rɪŋ/ v.t./i. (p.t. rang, p.p. rung) sonner; (of words etc.) retentir. —n. sonnerie f.; (fam.) coup de téléphone m. **~ the bell,** sonner. **~ back,** rappeler. **~ off,** raccrocher. **~ up,** téléphoner (à). **~ing** n. (of bell) sonnerie f. **~ing tone,** tonalité f.

ringleader /'rɪŋliːdə(r)/ n. chef m.

rink /rɪŋk/ n. patinoire f.

rinse /rɪns/ v.t. rincer. **~ out,** rincer. —n. rinçage m.

riot /'raɪət/ n. émeute f.; (of colours) orgie f. —v.i. faire une émeute. **run ~,** se déchaîner. **~er** n. émeut|ier, -ière m., f.

riotous /'raɪətəs/ a. turbulent.

rip /rɪp/ v.t./i. (p.t. ripped) (se) déchirer. —n. déchirure f. **let ~,** (not check) laisser courir. **~ off,** (sl.) rouler. **~-off** n. (sl.) vol m.

ripe /raɪp/ a. (-er, -est) mûr. **~ness** n. maturité f.

ripen /'raɪpən/ v.t./i. mûrir.

ripple /'rɪpl/ n. ride f., ondulation f.; (sound) murmure m. —v.t./i. (water) (se) rider.

rise /raɪz/ v.i. (p.t. rose, p.p. risen) (go upwards, increase) monter, s'élever; (stand up, get up from bed) se lever; (rebel) se soulever; (sun, curtain) se lever. —n. (slope) pente f.; (of curtain) lever m.; (increase) hausse f.; (in pay) augmentation f.; (progress, boom) essor m. **give ~ to,** donner lieu à. **~r** /-ə(r)/ n. **be an early ~r,** se lever tôt.

rising /'raɪzɪŋ/ n. (revolt) soulèvement m. —a. (increasing) croissant; (price) qui monte; (tide) montant; (sun) le-

vant. **~ generation,** nouvelle génération f.

risk /rɪsk/ n. risque m. —v.t. risquer. **at ~,** menacé. **~ doing,** (venture) se risquer à faire. **~y** a. risqué.

rissole /'rɪsəʊl/ n. croquette f.

rite /raɪt/ n. rite m. **last ~s,** derniers sacrements m. pl.

ritual /'rɪtʃʊəl/ a. & n. rituel (m.).

rival /'raɪvl/ n. rival(e) m. (f.). —a. rival; (claim) opposé. —v.t. (p.t. rivalled) rivaliser avec. **~ry** n. rivalité f.

river /'rɪvə(r)/ n. rivière f.; (flowing into sea & fig.) fleuve m. —a. (fishing, traffic, etc.) fluvial.

rivet /'rɪvɪt/ n. (bolt) rivet m. —v.t. (p.t. riveted) river, riveter. **~ing** a. fascinant.

Riviera /rɪvɪ'eərə/ n. the (French) **~,** la Côte d'Azur.

road /rəʊd/ n. route f.; (in town) rue f.; (small) chemin m. **the ~ to,** (glory etc.: fig.) le chemin de. **~hog** n. chauffard m. **~-map** n. carte routière f. **~-works** n. pl. travaux m. pl.

roadside /'rəʊdsaɪd/ n. bord de la route m.

roadway /'rəʊdweɪ/ n. chaussée f.

roadworthy /'rəʊdwɜːðɪ/ a. en état de marche.

roam /rəʊm/ v.i. errer. —v.t. (streets, seas, etc.) parcourir.

roar /rɔː(r)/ n. hurlement m.; rugissement m.; grondement m. —v.t./i. hurler; (of lion, wind) rugir; (of lorry, thunder) gronder.

roaring /'rɔːrɪŋ/ a. (trade, success) très gros. **~ fire,** belle flambée f.

roast /rəʊst/ v.t./i. rôtir. —n. (roast or roasting meat) rôti m. —a. rôti. **~ beef,** rôti de bœuf m.

rob /rɒb/ v.t. (p.t. robbed) voler (s.o. of sth., qch. à qn.); (bank, house) dévaliser; (deprive) priver (of, de). **~ber** n. voleu|r, -se m., f. **~bery** n. vol m.

robe /rəʊb/ n. (of judge etc.) robe f.; (dressing-gown) peignoir m.

robin /'rɒbɪn/ n. rouge-gorge m.

robot /'rəʊbɒt/ n. robot m.

robust /rəʊ'bʌst/ a. robuste.

rock[1] /rɒk/ n. roche f.; (rock face, boulder) rocher m.; (hurled stone) pierre f.; (sweet) sucre d'orge m. **on the ~s,** (drink) avec des glaçons; (marriage) en crise. **~-bottom** a. (fam.) très bas.

rock[2] /rɒk/ v.t./i. (se) balancer; (shake)

(faire) trembler; (*child*) bercer. —*n.* (*mus.*) rock *m.* ~**ing-chair** *n.* fauteuil à bascule *m.*

rockery /'rɒkərɪ/ *n.* rocaille *f.*

rocket /'rɒkɪt/ *n.* fusée *f.*

rocky /'rɒkɪ/ *a.* (**-ier, -iest**) (*ground*) rocailleux; (*hill*) rocheux; (*shaky*: *fig.*) branlant.

rod /rɒd/ *n.* (*metal*) tige *f.*; (*for curtain*) tringle *f.*; (*wooden*) baguette *f.*; (*for fishing*) canne à pêche *f.*

rode /rəʊd/ *see* **ride.**

rodent /'rəʊdnt/ *n.* rongeur *m.*

rodeo /rəʊ'deɪəʊ, *Amer.* 'rəʊdɪəʊ/ *n.* (*pl.* **-os**) rodéo *m.*

roe[1] /rəʊ/ *n.* œufs de poisson *m. pl.*

roe[2] /rəʊ/ *n.* (*pl.* **roe** *or* **roes**) (*deer*) chevreuil *m.*

rogu|e /rəʊg/ *n.* (*dishonest*) bandit, voleu|r, -se *m.*; (*mischievous*) coquin(e) *m.* (*f.*). ~**ish** *a.* coquin.

role /rəʊl/ *n.* rôle *m.*

roll /rəʊl/ *v.t./i.* rouler. ~ (**about**), (*child, dog*) se rouler. —*n.* rouleau *m.*; (*list*) liste *f.*; (*bread*) petit pain *m.*; (*of drum, thunder*) roulement *m.*; (*of ship*) roulis *m.* be ~**ing** (**in money**), (*fam.*) rouler sur l'or. ~**call** *n.* appel *m.* ~**ing-pin** *n.* rouleau à pâtisserie *m.* ~ **over**, (*turn over*) se retourner. ~ **up** *v.t.* (*sleeves*) retrousser; *v.i.* (*fam.*) s'amener.

roller /'rəʊlə(r)/ *n.* rouleau *m.* ~**coaster** *n.* montagnes russes *f. pl.* ~**-skate** *n.* patin à roulettes *m.*

rollicking /'rɒlɪkɪŋ/ *a.* exubérant.

rolling /'rəʊlɪŋ/ *a.* onduleux.

Roman /'rəʊmən/ *a.* & *n.* romain(e) (*m.* (*f.*)). ~ **Catholic** *a.* & *n.* catholique (*m./f.*). ~ **numerals,** chiffres romains *m. pl.*

romance /rə'mæns/ *n.* roman d'amour *m.*; (*love*) amour *m.*; (*affair*) idylle *f.*; (*fig.*) poésie *f.*

romantic /rə'mæntɪk/ *a.* (*of love etc.*) romantique; (*of the imagination*) romanesque. ~**ally** *adv.* (*behave*) en romantique.

Romania /rəʊ'meɪnɪə/ *n.* Roumanie *f.* ~**n** *a.* & *n.* roumain(e) (*m.* (*f.*)).

romp /rɒmp/ *v.i.* s'ébattre; (*fig.*) réussir. —*n.* ébats *m. pl.*

roof /ruːf/ *n.* (*pl.* **roofs**) toit *m.*; (*of tunnel*) plafond *m.*; (*of mouth*) palais *m.* —*v.t.* recouvrir. ~**ing** *n.* toiture *f.* ~**-rack** *n.* galerie *f.* ~**-top** *n.* toit *m.*

rook[1] /rʊk/ *n.* (*bird*) corneille *f.*

rook[2] /rʊk/ *n.* (*chess*) tour *f.*

room /ruːm/ *n.* pièce *f.*; (*bedroom*) chambre *f.*; (*large hall*) salle *f.*; (*space*) place *f.* ~**s,** meublé *m.* ~**y** *a.* spacieux; (*clothes*) ample.

roost /ruːst/ *n.* perchoir *m.* —*v.i.* percher. ~**er** /'ruːstə(r)/ *n.* coq *m.*

root[1] /ruːt/ *n.* racine *f.*; (*source*) origine *f.* —*v.t./i.* (s')enraciner. ~ **out**, extirper. **take** ~, prendre racine. ~**less** *a.* sans racines.

root[2] /ruːt/ *v.i.* ~ **about**, fouiller. ~ **for**, (*Amer., fam.*) encourager.

rope /rəʊp/ *n.* corde *f.* —*v.t.* attacher. **know the** ~**s,** être au courant. ~ **in,** (*person*) enrôler.

rosary /'rəʊzərɪ/ *n.* chapelet *m.*

rose[1] /rəʊz/ *n.* (*flower*) rose *f.*; (*colour*) rose *m.*; (*nozzle*) pomme *f.*

rose[2] /rəʊz/ *see* **rise.**

rosé /'rəʊzeɪ/ *n.* rosé *m.*

rosette /rəʊ'zet/ *n.* (*sport*) cocarde *f.*; (*officer's*) rosette *f.*

roster /'rɒstə(r)/ *n.* liste (de service) *f.*, tableau (de service) *m.*

rostrum /'rɒstrəm/ *n.* (*pl.* **-tra**) tribune *f.*; (*sport*) podium *m.*

rosy /'rəʊzɪ/ *a.* (**-ier, -iest**) rose; (*hopeful*) plein d'espoir.

rot /rɒt/ *v.t./i.* (*p.t.* **rotted**) pourrir. —*n.* pourriture *f.*; (*nonsense*: *sl.*) bêtises *f. pl.*, âneries *f. pl.*

rota /'rəʊtə/ *n.* liste (de service) *f.*

rotary /'rəʊtərɪ/ *a.* rotatif.

rotat|e /rəʊ'teɪt/ *v.t./i.* (faire) tourner; (*change round*) alterner. ~**ion** /-ʃn/ *n.* rotation *f.*

rote /rəʊt/ *n.* **by** ~, machinalement.

rotten /'rɒtn/ *a.* pourri; (*tooth*) gâté; (*bad*: *fam.*) mauvais, sale.

rotund /rəʊ'tʌnd/ *a.* rond.

rouge /ruːʒ/ *n.* rouge (à joues) *m.*

rough /rʌf/ *a.* (**-er, -est**) rude; (*to touch*) rugueux; (*ground*) accidenté; (*violent*) brutal; (*bad*) mauvais; (*estimate etc.*) approximatif; (*diamond*) brut. —*adv.* (*live*) à la dure; (*play*) brutalement. —*n.* (*ruffian*) voyou *m.* —*v.t.* ~ **it,** vivre à la dure. ~**-and-ready** *a.* (*solution etc.*) grossier (mais efficace). ~**-and-tumble** *n.* mêlée *f.* ~ **out,** ébaucher. ~ **paper,** papier brouillon *m.* ~**ly** *adv.* rudement; (*approximately*) à peu près. ~**ness** *n.* rudesse *f.*; brutalité *f.*

roughage /'rʌfɪdʒ/ *n.* fibres (alimentaires) *f. pl.*

roulette /ruː'let/ *n.* roulette *f.*

round /raʊnd/ *a.* (**-er, -est**) rond.

—*n.* (*circle*) rond *m.*; (*slice*) tranche *f.*;
(*of visits, drinks*) tournée *f.*; (*mil.*)
ronde *f.*; (*competition*) partie *f.*,
manche *f.*; (*boxing*) round *m.*; (*of
talks*) série *f.* —*prep.* autour de.
—*adv.* autour. —*v.t.* (*object*) arrondir;
(*corner*) tourner. go *or* come ~ to, (*a
friend etc.*) passer chez. ~ about,
(*near by*) par ici; (*fig.*) à peu près. ~
of applause, applaudissements *m. pl.*
~ off, terminer. ~ the clock, vingt-
quatre heures sur vingt-quatre. ~
up, rassembler. ~-up *n.* rassemblement *m.*; (*of suspects*) rafle *f.*

roundabout /ˈraʊndəbaʊt/ *n.* manège
m.; (*for traffic*) rond-point (à sens
giratoire) *m.* —*a.* indirect.

rounders /ˈraʊndəz/ *n.* sorte de base-
ball *f.*

roundly /ˈraʊndlɪ/ *adv.* (*bluntly*) franchement.

rous|e /raʊz/ *v.t.* éveiller. be ~ed,
(*angry*) être en colère. ~ing *a.*
(*speech, music*) excitant; (*cheers*)
frénétique.

rout /raʊt/ *n.* (*defeat*) déroute *f.* —*v.t.*
mettre en déroute.

route /ruːt/ *n.* itinéraire *m.*, parcours
m.; (*naut., aviat.*) route *f.*

routine /ruːˈtiːn/ *n.* routine *f.* —*a.* de
routine. daily ~, travail quotidien
m.

rov|e /rəʊv/ *v.t./i.* errer (dans). ~ing
a. (*life*) vagabond.

row[1] /rəʊ/ *n.* rangée *f.*, rang *m.* in a
~, (*consecutive*) consécutif.

row[2] /rəʊ/ *v.i.* ramer. —*v.t.* faire aller à
la rame. ~ing *n.* canotage *m.* ~(ing)-
boat *n.* bateau à rames *m.*

row[3] /raʊ/ *n.* (*noise: fam.*) tapage *m.*;
(*quarrel: fam.*) engueulade *f.* —*v.i.*
(*fam.*) s'engueuler.

rowdy /ˈraʊdɪ/ *a.* (-ier, -iest) tapageur. —*n.* voyou *m.*

royal /ˈrɔɪəl/ *a.* royal. ~ly *adv.* (*treat,
live, etc.*) royalement.

royalty /ˈrɔɪəltɪ/ *n.* famille royale *f.*;
(*payment*) droits d'auteur *m. pl.*

rub /rʌb/ *v.t./i.* (*p.t.* rubbed) frotter.
—*n.* friction *f.* ~ it in, insister là-
dessus. ~ off on, déteindre sur. ~
out, (s')effacer.

rubber /ˈrʌbə(r)/ *n.* caoutchouc *m.*;
(*eraser*) gomme *f.* ~ band, élastique
m. ~ stamp, tampon *m.* ~-stamp *v.t.*
approuver. ~y *a.* caoutchouteux.

rubbish /ˈrʌbɪʃ/ *n.* (*refuse*) ordures *f.*

pl.; (*junk*) saletés *f. pl.*; (*fig.*) bêtises *f.*
pl. ~y *a.* sans valeur.

rubble /ˈrʌbl/ *n.* décombres *m. pl.*

ruby /ˈruːbɪ/ *n.* rubis *m.*

rucksack /ˈrʌksæk/ *n.* sac à dos *m.*

rudder /ˈrʌdə(r)/ *n.* gouvernail *m.*

ruddy /ˈrʌdɪ/ *a.* (-ier, -iest) coloré,
rougeâtre; (*damned: sl.*) fichu.

rude /ruːd/ *a.* (-er, -est) impoli, grossier; (*improper*) indécent; (*shock,
blow*) brutal. ~ly *adv.* impoliment.
~ness *n.* impolitesse *f.*; indécence *f.*;
brutalité *f.*

rudiment /ˈruːdɪmənt/ *n.* rudiment *m.*
~ary /-ˈmentrɪ/ *a.* rudimentaire.

rueful /ˈruːfl/ *a.* triste.

ruffian /ˈrʌfɪən/ *n.* voyou *m.*

ruffle /ˈrʌfl/ *v.t.* (*hair*) ébouriffer;
(*clothes*) froisser; (*person*) contrarier. —*n.* (*frill*) ruche *f.*

rug /rʌg/ *n.* petit tapis *m.*

Rugby /ˈrʌgbɪ/ *n.* ~ (football), rugby
m.

rugged /ˈrʌgɪd/ *a.* (*surface*) rude, rugueux; (*ground*) accidenté; (*character, features*) rude.

ruin /ˈruːɪn/ *n.* ruine *f.* —*v.t.* (*destroy*)
ruiner; (*damage*) abîmer; (*spoil*)
gâter. ~ous *a.* ruineux.

rule /ruːl/ *n.* règle *f.*; (*regulation*) règlement *m.*; (*pol.*) gouvernement *m.*
—*v.t.* gouverner; (*master*) dominer;
(*decide*) décider. —*v.i.* régner. as a ~,
en règle générale. ~ out, exclure. ~d
paper, papier réglé *m.* ~r /-ə(r)/ *n.*
dirigeant(e) *m.* (*f.*), gouvernant *m.*;
(*measure*) règle *f.* ruling *a.* (*class*)
dirigeant; *n.* décision *f.*

rum /rʌm/ *n.* rhum *m.*

rumble /ˈrʌmbl/ *v.i.* gronder; (*stomach*) gargouiller. —*n.* grondement *m.*;
gargouillement *m.*

rummage /ˈrʌmɪdʒ/ *v.i.* fouiller.

rumour /ˈruːmə(r)/ *n.* bruit *m.*, rumeur *f.* —*v.t.* it is ~ed that, le bruit
court que.

rump /rʌmp/ *n.* (*of horse etc.*) croupe
f.; (*of fowl*) croupion *m.*

rumpus /ˈrʌmpəs/ *n.* (*uproar: fam.*)
chahut *m.*

run /rʌn/ *v.i.* (*p.t.* ran, *p.p.* run, *pres.
p.* running) courir; (*flow*) couler;
(*pass*) passer; (*function*) marcher;
(*melt*) fondre; (*extend*) s'étendre; (*of
bus etc.*) circuler; (*of play*) se jouer;
(*last*) durer; (*of colour in washing*)
déteindre; (*in election*) être candidat. —*v.t.* (*manage*) diriger; (*risk,*

race) courir; (*house*) tenir; (*blockade*) forcer; (*temperature, errand*) faire; (*drive*) conduire, transporter; (*pass*) passer; (*present*) présenter. —*n.* course *f.*; (*journey*) parcours *m.*; (*outing*) promenade *f.*; (*rush*) ruée *f.*; (*series*) série *f.*; (*in cricket*) point *m.* **have the ~ of**, avoir à sa disposition. **in the long ~**, avec le temps. **on the ~**, en fuite. **~ across**, rencontrer par hasard. **~ away**, s'enfuir. **~ down**, descendre en courant; (*of vehicle*) renverser; (*belittle*) dénigrer. **be ~ down**, (*weak etc.*) être sans forces *or* mal fichu. **~ in**, (*vehicle*) roder. **~ into**, (*hit*) heurter. **~ off**, (*copies*) tirer. **~of-the-mill** *a.* ordinaire. **~ out**, (*be used up*) s'épuiser; (*of lease*) expirer. **~ out of**, manquer de. **~ over**, (*of vehicle*) écraser. **~ up**, (*bill*) laisser accumuler. **the ~-up to**, la période qui précède.

runaway /'rʌnəweɪ/ *n.* fugiti|f, -ve *m.*, *f.* —*a.* fugitif; (*horse, vehicle*) fou; (*inflation*) galopant.

rung[1] /rʌŋ/ *n.* (*of ladder*) barreau *m.*
rung[2] /rʌŋ/ *see* **ring**[2].

runner /'rʌnə(r)/ *n.* coureu|r, -se *m.*, *f.* **~ bean**, haricot (grimpant) *m.* **~-up** *n.* second(e) *m.* (*f.*).

running /'rʌnɪŋ/ *n.* course *f.* —*a.* (*commentary*) suivi; (*water*) courant. **be in the ~**, avoir des chances de réussir. **four days**/*etc.* **~**, quatre jours/*etc.* de suite.

runny /'rʌnɪ/ *a.* (*nose*) qui coule.
runt /rʌnt/ *n.* avorton *m.*
runway /'rʌnweɪ/ *n.* piste *f.*
rupture /'rʌptʃə(r)/ *n.* (*breaking, breach*) rupture *f.*; (*med.*) hernie *f.* —*v.t./i.* (se) rompre. **~ o.s.**, se donner une hernie.
rural /'rʊərəl/ *a.* rural.
ruse /ruːz/ *n.* (*trick*) ruse *f.*
rush[1] /rʌʃ/ *n.* (*plant*) jonc *m.*
rush[2] /rʌʃ/ *v.i.* (*move*) se précipiter; (*be in a hurry*) se dépêcher. —*v.t.* faire, envoyer, *etc.* en vitesse; (*person*) bousculer; (*mil.*) prendre d'assaut. —*n.* ruée *f.*; (*haste*) bousculade *f.* **in a ~**, pressé. **~hour** *n.* heure de pointe *f.*
rusk /rʌsk/ *n.* biscotte *f.*
russet /'rʌsɪt/ *a.* roussâtre, roux.
Russia /'rʌʃə/ *n.* Russie *f.* **~n** *a.* & *n.* russe (*m./f.*); (*lang.*) russe *m.*
rust /rʌst/ *n.* rouille *f.* —*v.t./i.* rouiller. **~-proof** *a.* inoxydable. **~y** *a.* (*tool, person, etc.*) rouillé.
rustic /'rʌstɪk/ *a.* rustique.
rustle /'rʌsl/ *v.t./i.* (*leaves*) (faire) bruire; (*steal: Amer.*) voler. **~ up**, (*food etc.: fam.*) préparer.
rut /rʌt/ *n.* ornière *f.* **be in a ~**, rester dans l'ornière.
ruthless /'ruːθlɪs/ *a.* impitoyable. **~ness** *n.* cruauté *f.*
rye /raɪ/ *n.* seigle *m.*; (*whisky*) whisky *m.* (*à base de seigle*).

S

sabbath /'sæbəθ/ *n.* (*Jewish*) sabbat *m.*; (*Christian*) dimanche *m.*

sabbatical /sə'bætɪkl/ *a.* (*univ.*) sabbatique.

sabot|age /'sæbətɑːʒ/ *n.* sabotage *m.* —*v.t.* saboter. **~eur** /-'tɜː(r)/ *n.* saboteu|r, -se *m.*, *f.*

saccharin /'sækərɪn/ *n.* saccharine *f.*

sachet /'sæʃeɪ/ *n.* sachet *m.*

sack¹ /sæk/ *n.* (*bag*) sac *m.* —*v.t.* (*fam.*) renvoyer. **get the ~,** (*fam.*) être renvoyé. **~ing** *n.* toile à sac *f.*; (*dismissal*: *fam.*) renvoi *m.*

sack² /sæk/ *v.t.* (*plunder*) saccager.

sacrament /'sækrəmənt/ *n.* sacrement *m.*

sacred /'seɪkrɪd/ *a.* sacré.

sacrifice /'sækrɪfaɪs/ *n.* sacrifice *m.* —*v.t.* sacrifier.

sacrileg|e /'sækrɪlɪdʒ/ *n.* sacrilège *m.* **~ious** /-'lɪdʒəs/ *a.* sacrilège.

sacrosanct /'sækrəʊsæŋkt/ *a.* sacrosaint.

sad /sæd/ *a.* (**sadder, saddest**) triste. **~ly** *adv.* tristement; (*unfortunately*) malheureusement. **~ness** *n.* tristesse *f.*

sadden /'sædn/ *v.t.* attrister.

saddle /'sædl/ *n.* selle *f.* —*v.t.* (*horse*) seller. **~ s.o. with,** (*task, person*) coller à qn. **in the ~,** bien en selle. **~-bag** *n.* sacoche *f.*

sadis|t /'seɪdɪst/ *n.* sadique *m.*/*f.* **~m** /-zəm/ *n.* sadisme *m.* **~tic** /sə'dɪstɪk/ *a.* sadique.

safari /sə'fɑːrɪ/ *n.* safari *m.*

safe /seɪf/ *a.* (-er, **~est**) (*not dangerous*) sans danger; (*reliable*) sûr; (*out of danger*) en sécurité; (*after accident*) sain et sauf; (*wise*: *fig.*) prudent. —*n.* coffre-fort *m.* **in ~ keeping,** en sécurité. **~ conduct,** sauf-conduit *m.* **~ from,** à l'abri de. **~ly** *adv.* sans danger; (*in safe place*) en sûreté.

safeguard /'seɪfgɑːd/ *n.* sauvegarde *f.* —*v.t.* sauvegarder.

safety /'seɪftɪ/ *n.* sécurité *f.* **~-pin** *n.* épingle de sûreté *f.* **~-valve** *n.* soupape de sûreté *f.*

saffron /'sæfrən/ *n.* safran *m.*

sag /sæg/ *v.i.* (*p.t.* **sagged**) s'affaisser, fléchir. **~ging** *a.* affaissé.

saga /'sɑːgə/ *n.* saga *f.*

sage¹ /seɪdʒ/ *n.* (*herb*) sauge *f.*

sage² /seɪdʒ/ *a.* & *n.* sage (*m.*).

sago /'seɪgəʊ/ *n.* (*pl.* -os) sagou *m.*

said /sed/ *see* say.

sail /seɪl/ *n.* voile *f.*; (*journey*) tour en bateau *m.* —*v.i.* naviguer; (*leave*) partir; (*sport*) faire de la voile; (*glide*) glisser. —*v.t.* (*boat*) piloter. **~ing-boat, ~ing-ship** *ns.* bateau à voiles *m.*

sailor /'seɪlə(r)/ *n.* marin *m.*

saint /seɪnt/ *n.* saint(e) *m.* (*f.*). **~ly** *a.* (*person, act, etc.*) saint.

sake /seɪk/ *n.* **for the ~ of,** pour, pour l'amour de.

salad /'sæləd/ *n.* salade *f.* **~-dressing** *n.* sauce de salade *f.*

salami /sə'lɑːmɪ/ *n.* salami *m.*

salar|y /'sælərɪ/ *n.* traitement *m.*, salaire *m.* **~ied** *a.* salarié.

sale /seɪl/ *n.* vente *f.* **~s,** (*at reduced prices*) soldes *m. pl.* **for ~,** à vendre. **on ~,** en vente; (*at a reduced price*: *Amer.*) en solde.

saleable /'seɪləbl/ *a.* vendable.

sales|man /'seɪlzmən/ *n.* (*pl.* -men) (*in shop*) vendeur *m.*; (*traveller*) représentant *m.* **~woman** *n.* (*pl.* -women) vendeuse *f.*; représentante *f.*

salient /'seɪlɪənt/ *a.* saillant.

saliva /sə'laɪvə/ *n.* salive *f.*

sallow /'sæləʊ/ *a.* (-er, -est) (*complexion*) jaunâtre.

salmon /'sæmən/ *n. invar.* saumon *m.*

salon /'sælɒn/ *n.* salon *m.*

saloon /sə'luːn/ *n.* (*on ship*) salon *m.*; (*bar*: *Amer.*) bar *m.*, saloon *m.* **~ (car),** berline *f.*

salt /sɔːlt/ *n.* sel *m.* —*a.* (*culin.*) salé. —*v.t.* saler. **~-cellar** *n.* salière *f.* **~y** *a.* salé.

salutary /'sæljʊtrɪ/ *a.* salutaire.

salute /sə'luːt/ *n.* (*mil.*) salut *m.* —*v.t.* saluer. —*v.i.* faire un salut.

salvage /'sælvɪdʒ/ *n.* sauvetage *m.*; (*of waste*) récupération *f.*; (*goods*) objets sauvés *m. pl.* —*v.t.* sauver; (*for re-use*) récupérer.

salvation /sæl'veɪʃn/ *n.* salut *m.*

salvo /'sælvəʊ/ *n.* (*pl.* -oes) salve *f.*

same /seɪm/ *a.* même (**as,** que). —*pron.* **the ~,** le *or* la même, les mêmes. **at**

the ~ time, en même temps. the ~ (thing), la même chose.

sample /'sɑːmpl/ *n.* échantillon *m.* —*v.t.* essayer; (*food*) goûter.

sanatorium /sænə'tɔːrɪəm/ *n.* (*pl.* -iums) sanatorium *m.*

sanctify /'sæŋktɪfaɪ/ *v.t.* sanctifier.

sanctimonious /sæŋktɪ'məʊnɪəs/ *a.* (*person*) bigot; (*air, tone*) de petit saint.

sanction /'sæŋkʃn/ *n.* sanction *f.* —*v.t.* sanctionner.

sanctity /'sæŋktətɪ/ *n.* sainteté *f.*

sanctuary /'sæŋktʃʊərɪ/ *n.* (*relig.*) sanctuaire *m.*; (*for animals*) réserve *f.*; (*refuge*) asile *m.*

sand /sænd/ *n.* sable *m.* ~s, (*beach*) plage *f.* —*v.t.* sabler. ~castle *n.* château de sable *m.*

sandal /'sændl/ *n.* sandale *f.*

sandpaper /'sændpeɪpə(r)/ *n.* papier de verre *m.* —*v.t.* poncer.

sandwich /'sænwɪdʒ/ *n.* sandwich *m.* —*v.t.* ~ed between, pris en sandwich entre.

sandy /'sændɪ/ *a.* sablonneux, de sable; (*hair*) blond roux *invar.*

sane /seɪn/ *a.* (-er, -est) (*view etc.*) sain; (*person*) sain d'esprit. ~ly *adv.* sainement.

sang /sæŋ/ *see* **sing**.

sanitary /'sænɪtrɪ/ *a.* (*clean*) hygiénique; (*system etc.*) sanitaire.

sanitation /sænɪ'teɪʃn/ *n.* hygiène (publique) *f.*; (*drainage etc.*) système sanitaire *m.*

sanity /'sænətɪ/ *n.* santé mentale *f.*; (*good sense: fig.*) bon sens *m.*

sank /sæŋk/ *see* **sink**.

Santa Claus /'sæntəklɔːz/ *n.* le père Noël *m.*

sap /sæp/ *n.* (*of plants*) sève *f.* —*v.t.* (*p.t.* **sapped**) (*undermine*) saper.

sapphire /'sæfaɪə(r)/ *n.* saphir *m.*

sarcas|m /'sɑːkæzəm/ *n.* sarcasme *m.* ~tic /sɑː'kæstɪk/ *a.* sarcastique.

sardine /sɑː'diːn/ *n.* sardine *f.*

Sardinia /sɑː'dɪnɪə/ *n.* Sardaigne *f.*

sardonic /sɑː'dɒnɪk/ *a.* sardonique.

sash /sæʃ/ *n.* (*on uniform*) écharpe *f.*; (*on dress*) ceinture *f.*

sat /sæt/ *see* **sit**.

satanic /sə'tænɪk/ *a.* satanique.

satchel /'sætʃl/ *n.* cartable *m.*

satellite /'sætəlaɪt/ *n.* & *a.* satellite (*m.*).

satiate /'seɪʃɪeɪt/ *v.t.* rassasier.

satin /'sætɪn/ *n.* satin *m.*

satir|e /'sætaɪə(r)/ *n.* satire *f.* ~ical /sə'tɪrɪkl/ *a.* satirique.

satiri|ze /'sætəraɪz/ *v.t.* faire la satire de. ~st /-ɪst/ *n.* écrivain satirique *m.*

satisfactor|y /sætɪs'fæktərɪ/ *a.* satisfaisant. ~ily *adv.* d'une manière satisfaisante.

satisf|y /'sætɪsfaɪ/ *v.t.* satisfaire; (*convince*) convaincre. ~action /-'fækʃn/ *n.* satisfaction *f.* ~ying *a.* satisfaisant.

satsuma /sæt'suːmə/ *n.* mandarine *f.*

saturat|e /'sætʃəreɪt/ *v.t.* saturer. ~ed *a.* (*wet*) trempé. ~ion /-'reɪʃn/ *n.* saturation *f.*

Saturday /'sætədɪ/ *n.* samedi *m.*

sauce /sɔːs/ *n.* sauce *f.*; (*impudence: sl.*) toupet *m.*

saucepan /'sɔːspən/ *n.* casserole *f.*

saucer /'sɔːsə(r)/ *n.* soucoupe *f.*

saucy /'sɔːsɪ/ *a.* (-ier, -iest) impertinent; (*boldly smart*) coquin.

Saudi Arabia /saʊdɪə'reɪbɪə/ *n.* Arabie Séoudite *f.*

sauerkraut /'saʊəkraʊt/ *n.* choucroute *f.*

sauna /'sɔːnə/ *n.* sauna *m.*

saunter /'sɔːntə(r)/ *v.i.* flâner.

sausage /'sɒsɪdʒ/ *n.* saucisse *f.*; (*pre-cooked*) saucisson *m.*

savage /'sævɪdʒ/ *a.* (*fierce*) féroce; (*wild*) sauvage. —*n.* sauvage *m./f.* —*v.t.* attaquer férocement. ~ry *n.* sauvagerie *f.*

sav|e /seɪv/ *v.t.* sauver; (*money, time*) économiser, épargner; (*keep*) garder; (*prevent*) éviter (from, de). —*n.* (*football*) arrêt *m.* —*prep.* sauf. ~er *n.* épargnant(e) *m.* (*f.*). ~ing *n.* (*of time, money*) économie *f.* ~ings *n. pl.* économies *f. pl.*

saviour /'seɪvɪə(r)/ *n.* sauveur *m.*

savour /'seɪvə(r)/ *n.* saveur *f.* —*v.t.* savourer. ~y *a.* (*tasty*) savoureux; (*culin.*) salé.

saw[1] /sɔː/ *see* **see**[1].

saw[2] /sɔː/ *n.* scie *f.* —*v.t.* (*p.t.* **sawed**, *p.p.* **sawn** /sɔːn/ *or* **sawed**) scier.

sawdust /'sɔːdʌst/ *n.* sciure *f.*

saxophone /'sæksəfəʊn/ *n.* saxophone *m.*

say /seɪ/ *v.t./i.* (*p.t.* **said** /sed/) dire; (*prayer*) faire. —*n.* **have a ~**, dire son mot; (*in decision*) avoir voix au chapitre. **I ~!**, dites donc!

saying /'seɪɪŋ/ *n.* proverbe *m.*

scab /skæb/ *n.* (*on sore*) croûte *f.*; (*blackleg: fam.*) jaune *m.*

scaffold /'skæfəʊld/ n. (gallows) échafaud m. ~ing /-əldɪŋ/ n. (for workmen) échafaudage m.

scald /skɔːld/ v.t. (injure, cleanse) ébouillanter. —n. brûlure f.

scale[1] /skeɪl/ n. (of fish) écaille f.

scale[2] /skeɪl/ n. (for measuring, size, etc.) échelle f.; (mus.) gamme f. —v.t. (climb) escalader. ~ down, réduire (proportionnellement).

scales /skeɪlz/ n. pl. (for weighing) balance f.

scallop /'skɒləp/ n. coquille Saint-Jacques f.

scalp /skælp/ n. cuir chevelu m. —v.t. (mutilate) scalper.

scalpel /'skælp(ə)l/ n. scalpel m.

scamp /skæmp/ n. coquin(e) m.(f.).

scamper /'skæmpə(r)/ v.i. courir, trotter. ~ away, détaler.

scampi /'skæmpɪ/ n. pl. grosses crevettes f. pl., gambas f. pl.

scan /skæn/ v.t. (p.t. scanned) scruter; (quickly) parcourir; (poetry) scander; (of radar) balayer.

scandal /'skændl/ n. (disgrace, outrage) scandale m.; (gossip) cancans m. pl. ~ous a. scandaleux.

scandalize /'skændəlaɪz/ v.t. scandaliser.

Scandinavia /skændɪ'neɪvɪə/ n. Scandinavie f. ~n a. & n. scandinave (m./f.).

scant /skænt/ a. insuffisant.

scant|y /'skæntɪ/ a. (-ier, -iest) insuffisant; (clothing) sommaire. ~ily adv. insuffisamment. ~ily dressed, à peine vêtu.

scapegoat /'skeɪpgəʊt/ n. bouc émissaire m.

scar /skaː(r)/ n. cicatrice f. —v.t. (p.t. scarred) marquer d'une cicatrice; (fig.) marquer.

scarc|e /skeəs/ a. (-er, -est) rare. **make o.s.** ~e, (fam.) se sauver. ~ity n. rareté f., pénurie f.

scarcely /'skeəslɪ/ adv. à peine.

scare /skeə(r)/ v.t. faire peur à. —n. peur f. **be** ~d, avoir peur. **bomb** ~, alerte à la bombe f.

scarecrow /'skeəkrəʊ/ n. épouvantail m.

scaremonger /'skeəmʌŋgə(r)/ n. alarmiste m./f.

scarf /skaːf/ n. (pl. scarves) écharpe f.; (over head) foulard m.

scarlet /'skaːlət/ a. écarlate. ~ fever, scarlatine f.

scary /'skeərɪ/ a. (-ier, -iest) (fam.) qui fait peur, effrayant.

scathing /'skeɪðɪŋ/ a. cinglant.

scatter /'skætə(r)/ v.t. (throw) éparpiller, répandre; (disperse) disperser. —v.i. se disperser. ~brain n. écervelé(e) m. (f.).

scatty /'skætɪ/ a. (-ier, -iest) (sl.) écervelé, farfelu.

scavenge /'skævɪndʒ/ v.i. fouiller (dans les ordures). ~r /-ə(r)/ n. (vagrant) personne qui fouille dans les ordures f.

scenario /sɪ'naːrɪəʊ/ n. (pl. -os) scénario m.

scene /siːn/ n. scène f.; (of accident, crime) lieu(x) m. (pl.).; (sight) spectacle m.; (incident) incident m. **behind the** ~s, en coulisse.

scenery /'siːnərɪ/ n. paysage m.; (theatre) décor(s) m. (pl.).

scenic /'siːnɪk/ a. pittoresque.

scent /sent/ n. (perfume) parfum m.; (trail) piste f. —v.t. flairer; (make fragrant) parfumer.

sceptic /'skeptɪk/ n. sceptique m./f. ~al a. sceptique. ~ism /-sɪzəm/ n. scepticisme m.

sceptre /'septə(r)/ n. sceptre m.

schedule /'ʃedjuːl, Amer. 'skedʒʊl/ n. programme m., horaire m. —v.t. prévoir. **behind** ~, en retard. **on** ~, (train) à l'heure; (work) à jour.

scheme /skiːm/ n. plan m.; (dishonest) combine f.; (fig.) arrangement m. —v.i. intriguer. ~r /-ə(r)/ n. intrigant(e) m. (f.).

schism /'sɪzəm/ n. schisme m.

schizophrenic /skɪtsəʊ'frenɪk/ a. & n. schizophrène (m./f.).

scholar /'skɒlə(r)/ n. érudit(e) m. (f.) ~ly a. érudit. ~ship n. érudition f.; (grant) bourse f.

scholastic /skə'læstɪk/ a. scolaire.

school /skuːl/ n. école f.; (of university) faculté f. —a. (age, year, holidays) scolaire. —v.t. (person) éduquer; (animal) dresser. ~ing n. (education) instruction f.; (attendance) scolarité f.

school|boy /'skuːlbɔɪ/ n. écolier m. ~girl n. écolière f.

school|master /'skuːlmaːstə(r)/, ~mistress, ~teacher ns. (primary) institu|teur, -trice m., f.; (secondary) professeur m.

schooner /'skuːnə(r)/ n. goélette f.

sciatica /saɪ'ætɪkə/ n. sciatique f.

scien|ce /'saɪəns/ n. science f. ~ce

fiction, science-fiction *f.* ~**tific** /-'tɪfɪk/ *a.* scientifique.

scientist /'saɪəntɪst/ *n.* scientifique *m./f.*

scintillate /'sɪntɪleɪt/ *v.i.* scintiller; (*person: fig.*) briller.

scissors /'sɪzəz/ *n. pl.* ciseaux *m. pl.*

sclerosis /sklə'rəʊsɪs/ *n.* sclérose *f.*

scoff[1] /skɒf/ *v.i.* ~ **at,** se moquer de.

scoff[2] /skɒf/ *v.t.* (*eat: sl.*) bouffer.

scold /skəʊld/ *v.t.* réprimander. ~**ing** *n.* réprimande *f.*

scone /skɒn/ *n.* petit pain au lait *m.*, galette *f.*

scoop /skuːp/ *n.* (*for grain, sugar*) pelle (à main) *f.*; (*for food*) cuiller *f.*; (*news*) exclusivité *f.* —*v.t.* (*pick up*) ramasser. ~ **out,** creuser.

scoot /skuːt/ *v.i.* (*fam.*) filer.

scooter /'skuːtə(r)/ *n.* (*child's*) trottinette *f.*; (*motor cycle*) scooter *m.*

scope /skəʊp/ *n.* étendue *f.*; (*competence*) compétence *f.*; (*opportunity*) possibilité(s) *f.* (*pl.*).

scorch /skɔːtʃ/ *v.t.* brûler, roussir. ~**ing** *a.* brûlant, très chaud.

score /skɔː(r)/ *n.* score *m.*; (*mus.*) partition *f.* —*v.t.* marquer; (*success*) remporter. —*v.i.* marquer un point; (*football*) marquer un but; (*keep score*) compter les points. **a** ~ (**of**), (*twenty*) vingt. **on that** ~, à cet égard. ~ **out,** rayer. ~**r** /-ə(r)/ *n.* (*sport*) marqueur *m.*

scorn /skɔːn/ *n.* mépris *m.* —*v.t.* mépriser. ~**ful** *a.* méprisant. ~**fully** *adv.* avec mépris.

scorpion /'skɔːpɪən/ *n.* scorpion *m.*

Scot /skɒt/ *n.* Écossais(e) *m.* (*f.*). ~**tish** *a.* écossais.

Scotch /skɒtʃ/ *a.* écossais. —*n.* whisky *m.*, scotch *m.*

scotch /skɒtʃ/ *v.t.* mettre fin à.

scot-free /skɒt'friː/ *a. & adv.* sans être puni; (*gratis*) sans payer.

Scotland /'skɒtlənd/ *n.* Écosse *f.*

Scots /skɒts/ *a.* écossais. ~**man** *n.* Écossais *m.* ~**woman** *n.* Écossaise *f.*

scoundrel /'skaʊndrəl/ *n.* vaurien *m.*, bandit *m.*, gredin(e) *m.*(*f.*).

scour[1] /'skaʊə(r)/ *v.t.* (*pan*) récurer. ~**er** *n.* tampon à récurer *m.*

scour[2] /'skaʊə(r)/ *v.t.* (*search*) parcourir.

scourge /skɜːdʒ/ *n.* fléau *m.*

scout /skaʊt/ *n.* (*mil.*) éclaireur *m.* —*v.i.* ~ (**for**), chercher.

Scout /skaʊt/ *n.* (*boy*) scout *m.*, éclaireur *m.* ~**ing** *n.* scoutisme *m.*

scowl /skaʊl/ *n.* air renfrogné *m.* —*v.i.* se renfrogner.

scraggy /'skrægɪ/ *a.* (-**ier**, -**iest**) décharné, efflanqué.

scram /skræm/ *v.i.* (*sl.*) se tirer.

scramble /'skræmbl/ *v.i.* (*clamber*) grimper. —*v.t.* (*eggs*) brouiller. —*n.* bousculade *f.*, ruée *f.* ~ **for,** se bousculer pour avoir.

scrap[1] /skræp/ *n.* petit morceau *m.* ~**s,** (*of metal, fabric, etc.*) déchets *m. pl.*; (*of food*) restes *m. pl.* —*v.t.* (*p.t.* **scrapped**) mettre au rebut; (*plan etc.*) abandonner. ~-**book** *n.* album *m.* ~-**iron** *n.* ferraille *f.* ~-**paper** *n.* brouillon *m.* ~**py** *a.* fragmentaire.

scrap[2] /skræp/ *n.* (*fight: fam.*) bagarre *f.*, dispute *f.*

scrape /skreɪp/ *v.t.* racler, gratter; (*graze*) érafler. —*v.i.* (*rub*) frotter. —*n.* raclement *m.*; éraflure *f.*; (*fig.*) mauvais pas *m.* ~ **through,** réussir de justesse. ~ **together,** réunir. ~**r** /-ə(r)/ *n.* racloir *m.*

scratch /skrætʃ/ *v.t./i.* (se) gratter; (*with claw, nail*) griffer; (*graze*) érafler. —*n.* éraflure *f.* **start from** ~, partir de zéro. **up to** ~, au niveau voulu.

scrawl /skrɔːl/ *n.* gribouillage *m.* —*v.t./i.* gribouiller.

scrawny /'skrɔːnɪ/ *a.* (-**ier**, -**iest**) décharné, émacié.

scream /skriːm/ *v.t./i.* crier, hurler. —*n.* cri (perçant) *m.*

screech /skriːtʃ/ *v.i.* (*scream*) hurler; (*of brakes*) grincer. —*n.* hurlement *m.*; grincement *m.*

screen /skriːn/ *n.* écran *m.*; (*folding*) paravent *m.* —*v.t.* masquer; (*protect*) protéger; (*film*) projeter; (*candidates*) filtrer.

screw /skruː/ *n.* vis *f.* —*v.t.* visser. ~ **up,** (*eyes*) plisser; (*ruin: sl.*) bousiller.

screwdriver /'skruːdraɪvə(r)/ *n.* tournevis *m.*

screwy /'skruːɪ/ *a.* (-**ier**, -**iest**) (*crazy: sl.*) cinglé.

scribble /'skrɪbl/ *v.t./i.* griffonner. —*n.* griffonnage *m.*

scribe /skraɪb/ *n.* scribe *m.*

script /skrɪpt/ *n.* écriture *f.*; (*of film*) scénario *m.*; (*of play*) texte *m.* ~-**writer** *n.* scénariste *m./f.*

Scriptures /'skrɪptʃəz/ *n. pl.* **the** ~, l'Écriture (sainte) *f.*

scroll /skrəʊl/ n. rouleau m.
scrounge /skraʊndʒ/ v.t. (meal) se faire payer; (steal) chiper. —v.i. (beg) quémander. ~ **money from,** taper. ~**r** /-ə(r)/ n. parasite m.; (of money) tapeu|r, -se m., f.
scrub¹ /skrʌb/ n. (land) broussailles f. pl.
scrub² /skrʌb/ v.t./i. (p.t. **scrubbed**) nettoyer (à la brosse), frotter. —n. nettoyage m.
scruff /skrʌf/ n. **by the ~ of the neck,** par la peau du cou.
scruffy /ˈskrʌfɪ/ a. (-ier, -iest) (fam.) miteux, sale.
scrum /skrʌm/ n. (Rugby) mêlée f.
scruple /ˈskruːpl/ n. scrupule m.
scrupulous /ˈskruːpjʊləs/ a. scrupuleux. ~**ly** adv. scrupuleusement. ~**ly clean,** impeccable.
scrutin|y /ˈskruːtɪnɪ/ n. examen minutieux m. ~**ize** v.t. scruter.
scuff /skʌf/ v.t. (scratch) érafler.
scuffle /ˈskʌfl/ n. bagarre f.
sculpt /skʌlpt/ v.t./i. (fam.) sculpter. ~**or** n. sculpteur m. ~**ure** /-tʃə(r)/ n. sculpture f.; v.t./i. sculpter.
scum /skʌm/ n. (on liquid) écume f.; (people: pej.) racaille f.
scurf /skɜːf/ n. pellicules f. pl.
scurrilous /ˈskʌrɪləs/ a. grossier, injurieux, venimeux.
scurry /ˈskʌrɪ/ v.i. courir (for, pour chercher). ~ **off,** filer.
scurvy /ˈskɜːvɪ/ n. scorbut m.
scuttle¹ /ˈskʌtl/ v.t. (ship) saborder.
scuttle² /ˈskʌtl/ v.i. ~ **away,** se sauver, filer.
scythe /saɪð/ n. faux f.
sea /siː/ n. mer f. —a. de (la) mer, marin. **at ~,** en mer. **by ~,** par mer. ~-**green** a. vert glauque invar. ~-**level** n. niveau de la mer m. ~ **shell,** coquillage m. ~**shore** n. rivage m.
seaboard /ˈsiːbɔːd/ n. littoral m.
seafarer /ˈsiːfeərə(r)/ n. marin m.
seafood /ˈsiːfuːd/ n. fruits de mer m. pl.
seagull /ˈsiːgʌl/ n. mouette f.
seal¹ /siːl/ n. (animal) phoque m.
seal² /siːl/ n. sceau m.; (with wax) cachet m. —v.t. sceller; cacheter; (stick down) coller. ~**ing-wax** n. cire à cacheter f. ~ **off,** (area) boucler.
seam /siːm/ n. (in cloth etc.) couture f.; (of coal) veine f.
seaman /ˈsiːmən/ n. (pl. -**men**) marin m.

seamy /ˈsiːmɪ/ a. ~ **side,** côté sordide m.
seance /ˈseɪɑːns/ n. séance de spiritisme f.
seaplane /ˈsiːpleɪn/ n. hydravion m.
seaport /ˈsiːpɔːt/ n. port de mer m.
search /sɜːtʃ/ v.t./i. fouiller; (study) examiner. —n. fouille f.; (quest) recherche(s) f. (pl.). **in ~ of,** à la recherche de. ~ **for,** chercher. ~-**party** n. équipe de secours f. ~**ing** a. (piercing) pénétrant.
searchlight /ˈsɜːtʃlaɪt/ n. projecteur m.
seasick /ˈsiːsɪk/ a. **be ~,** avoir le mal de mer.
seaside /ˈsiːsaɪd/ n. bord de la mer m.
season /ˈsiːzn/ n. saison f. —v.t. assaisonner. ~**able** a. qui convient à la saison. ~**al** a. saisonnier. ~**ing** n. assaisonnement m. ~-**ticket** n. carte d'abonnement f.
seasoned /ˈsiːznd/ a. expérimenté.
seat /siːt/ n. siège m.; (place) place f.; (of trousers) fond m. —v.t. (put) placer; (have seats for) avoir des places assises pour. **be ~ed, take a ~,** s'asseoir. ~-**belt** n. ceinture de sécurité f.
seaweed /ˈsiːwiːd/ n. algues f. pl.
seaworthy /ˈsiːwɜːðɪ/ a. en état de naviguer.
sece|de /sɪˈsiːd/ v.i. faire sécession. ~**ssion** /-eʃn/ n. sécession f.
seclu|de /sɪˈkluːd/ v.t. isoler. ~**ded** a. isolé. ~**sion** /-ʒn/ n. solitude f.
second¹ /ˈsekənd/ a. deuxième, second. —n. deuxième m./f., second(e) m. (f.); (unit of time) seconde f. ~**s,** (goods) articles de second choix m. pl. —adv. (in race etc.) en seconde place. —v.t. (proposal) appuyer. ~-**best** a. de second choix, numéro deux invar. ~-**class** a. de deuxième classe. **at ~ hand,** de seconde main. ~-**hand** a. d'occasion; n. (on clock) trotteuse f. ~-**rate** a. médiocre. **have ~ thoughts,** avoir des doutes, changer d'avis. **on ~ thoughts,** (Amer.) **on ~ thought,** à la réflexion. ~**ly** adv. deuxièmement.
second² /sɪˈkɒnd/ v.t. (transfer) détacher (to, à).
secondary /ˈsekəndrɪ/ a. secondaire. ~ **school,** lycée m., collège m.
secrecy /ˈsiːkrəsɪ/ n. secret m.
secret /ˈsiːkrɪt/ a. secret. —n. secret m. **in ~,** en secret. ~**ly** adv. en secret, secrètement.

secretariat /sekrə'teəriət/ *n.* secrétariat *m.*

secretar|y /'sekrətrı/ *n.* secrétaire *m.*/*f.* **S~y of State,** ministre *m.*; (*Amer.*) ministre des Affaires étrangères *m.* **~ial** /-'teəriəl/ *a.* (*work etc.*) de secrétaire.

secret|e /sɪ'kri:t/ *v.t.* (*med.*) sécréter. **~ion** /-ʃn/ *n.* sécrétion *f.*

secretive /'si:krətɪv/ *a.* cachottier.

sect /sekt/ *n.* secte *f.* **~arian** /-'teəriən/ *a.* sectaire.

section /'sekʃn/ *n.* section *f.*; (*of country, town*) partie *f.*; (*in store*) rayon *m.*; (*newspaper column*) rubrique *f.*

sector /'sektə(r)/ *n.* secteur *m.*

secular /'sekjulə(r)/ *a.* (*school etc.*) laïque; (*art, music, etc.*) profane.

secure /sɪ'kjuə(r)/ *a.* (*safe*) en sûreté; (*in mind*) tranquille; (*firm*) solide; (*window etc.*) bien fermé. —*v.t.* attacher; (*obtain*) s'assurer; (*ensure*) assurer. **~ly** *adv.* solidement; (*safely*) en sûreté.

security /sɪ'kjuərətɪ/ *n.* (*safety*) sécurité *f.*; (*for loan*) caution *f.*

sedate[1] /sɪ'deɪt/ *a.* calme.

sedat|e[2] /sɪ'deɪt/ *v.t.* donner un sédatif à. **~ion** /-ʃn/ *n.* sédation *f.*

sedative /'sedətɪv/ *n.* sédatif *m.*

sedentary /'sedntrɪ/ *a.* sédentaire.

sediment /'sedɪmənt/ *n.* sédiment *m.*

sedition /sɪ'dɪʃn/ *n.* sédition *f.*

seduce /sɪ'dju:s/ *v.t.* séduire. **~r** /-ə(r)/ *n.* séduc|teur, -trice *m.*, *f.*

seduct|ion /sɪ'dʌkʃn/ *n.* séduction *f.* **~ive** /-tɪv/ *a.* séduisant.

see[1] /si:/ *v.t.*/*i.* (*p.t.* **saw,** *p.p.* **seen**) voir; (*escort*) (r)accompagner. **~ about** *or* **to,** s'occuper de. **~ through,** (*task*) mener à bonne fin; (*person*) deviner (le jeu de). **~ (to it) that,** veiller à ce que. **~ing that,** vu que.

see[2] /si:/ *n.* (*of bishop*) évêché *m.*

seed /si:d/ *n.* graine *f.*; (*collectively*) graines *f. pl.*; (*origin: fig.*) germe *m.*; (*tennis*) tête de série *f.* **go to ~,** (*plant*) monter en graine; (*person*) se laisser aller. **~ling** *n.* plant *m.*

seedy /'si:dɪ/ *a.* (**-ier, -iest**) miteux.

seek /si:k/ *v.t.* (*p.t.* **sought**) chercher. **~ out,** aller chercher.

seem /si:m/ *v.i.* sembler. **~ingly** *adv.* apparemment.

seemly /'si:mlɪ/ *adv.* convenable.

seen /si:n/ *see* **see**[1].

seep /si:p/ *v.i.* (*ooze*) suinter. **~ into,**

s'infiltrer dans. **~age** *n.* suintement *m.*; infiltration *f.*

see-saw /'si:sɔ:/ *n.* bascule *f.*

seethe /si:ð/ *v.i.* **~ with,** (*anger*) bouillir de; (*people*) grouiller de.

segment /'segmənt/ *n.* segment *m.*

segregat|e /'segrɪgeɪt/ *v.t.* séparer. **~ion** /-'geɪʃn/ *n.* ségrégation *f.*

seize /si:z/ *v.t.* saisir; (*take possession of*) s'emparer de. —*v.i.* **~ on,** (*chance etc.*) saisir. **~ up,** (*engine etc.*) se gripper.

seizure /'si:ʒə(r)/ *n.* (*med.*) crise *f.*

seldom /'seldəm/ *adv.* rarement.

select /sɪ'lekt/ *v.t.* choisir, sélectionner. —*a.* choisi; (*exclusive*) sélect. **~ion** /-kʃn/ *n.* sélection *f.*

selective /sɪ'lektɪv/ *a.* sélectif.

self /self/ *n.* (*pl.* **selves**) (*on cheque*) moi-même. **the ~,** le moi *m. invar.* **your good ~,** vous-même.

self- /self/ *pref.* **~-assurance** *n.* assurance *f.* **~-assured** *a.* sûr de soi. **~-catering** *a.* où l'on fait la cuisine soi-même. **~-centred** *a.* égocentrique. **~-confidence** *n.* confiance en soi *f.* **~-confident** *a.* sûr de soi. **~-conscious** *a.* gêné, timide. **~-contained** *a.* (*flat*) indépendant. **~-control** *n.* maîtrise de soi *f.* **~-defence** *n.* légitime défense *f.* **~-denial** *n.* abnégation *f.* **~-employed** *a.* qui travaille à son compte. **~-esteem** *n.* amour-propre *m.* **~-evident** *a.* évident. **~-government** *n.* autonomie *f.* **~-indulgent** *a.* qui se permet tout. **~-interest** *n.* intérêt personnel *m.* **~-portrait** *n.* autoportrait *m.* **~-possessed** *a.* assuré. **~-reliant** *a.* indépendant. **~-respect** *n.* respect de soi *m.*, dignité *f.* **~-righteous** *a.* satisfait de soi. **~-sacrifice** *n.* abnégation *f.* **~-satisfied** *a.* content de soi. **~-seeking** *a.* égoïste. **~-service** *n.* & *a.* libre-service (*m.*). **~-styled** *a.* soidisant. **~-sufficient** *a.* indépendant. **~-willed** *a.* entêté.

selfish /'selfɪʃ/ *a.* égoïste; (*motive*) intéressé. **~ness** *n.* égoïsme *m.*

selfless /'selflɪs/ *a.* désintéressé.

sell /sel/ *v.t.*/*i.* (*p.t.* **sold**) (se) vendre. **be sold out of,** n'avoir plus de. **~ off,** liquider. **~-out,** *n.* trahison *f.* **it was a ~-out,** on a vendu tous les billets. **~ up,** vendre son fonds, sa maison, *etc.* **~er** *n.* vendeu|r, -se *m.*, *f.*

Sellotape /'seləuteɪp/ *n.* (P.) scotch *m.* (P.).

semantic /sɪ'mæntɪk/ a. sémantique. ~s n. sémantique f.

semaphore /'seməfɔː(r)/ n. signaux à bras m. pl.; (*device*: *rail.*) sémaphore m.

semblance /'sembləns/ n. semblant m.

semen /'siːmən/ n. sperme m.

semester /sɪ'mestə(r)/ n. (*univ.*, *Amer.*) semestre m.

semi /'semɪ/ *pref.* semi-, demi-.

semibreve /'semɪbriːv/ n. (*mus.*) ronde f.

semicirc|le /'semɪsɜːkl/ n. demi-cercle m. ~ular /-'sɜːkjʊlə(r)/ a. en demi-cercle.

semicolon /semɪ'kəʊlən/ n. point-virgule m.

semi-detached /semɪ'dɪtætʃt/ a. ~ **house**, maison jumelle f.

semifinal /semɪ'faɪnl/ n. demi-finale f.

seminar /'semɪnɑː(r)/ n. séminaire m.

seminary /'semɪnərɪ/ n. séminaire m.

semiquaver /'semɪkweɪvə(r)/ n.(*mus.*) double croche f.

Semit|e /'siːmaɪt, *Amer.* 'semaɪt/ n. Sémite m./f. ~ic /sɪ'mɪtɪk/ a. sémite; (*lang.*) sémitique.

semolina /semə'liːnə/ n. semoule f.

senat|e /'senɪt/ n. sénat m. ~or /-ətə(r)/ n. sénateur m.

send /send/ v.t./i. (*p.t.* **sent**) envoyer. ~ **away**, (*dismiss*) renvoyer. ~ (**away** *or* **off**) **for**, commander (par lettre). ~ **back**, renvoyer. ~ **for**, (*person, help*) envoyer chercher. ~-**off** n. adieux chaleureux m. pl. ~ **up**, (*fam.*) parodier. ~**er** n. expédi|teur, -trice m., f.

senil|e /'siːnaɪl/ a. sénile. ~**ity** /sɪ'nɪlətɪ/ n. sénilité f.

senior /'siːnɪə(r)/ a. plus âgé (**to**, que); (*in rank*) supérieur; (*teacher*, *partner*) principal. —n. aîné(e) m. (f.); (*schol.*) grand(e) m. (f.). ~ **citizen**, personne âgée f. ~**ity** /-'ɒrətɪ/ n. priorité d'âge f.; supériorité f.; (*in service*) ancienneté f.

sensation /sen'seɪʃn/ n. sensation f. ~**al** a. (*event*) qui fait sensation; (*wonderful*) sensationnel.

sense /sens/ n. sens m.; (*sensation*) sensation f.; (*mental impression*) sentiment m.; (*common sense*) bon sens m. ~**s**, raison f. —v.t. (pres)sentir. **make** ~, avoir du sens. **make** ~ **of**, comprendre. ~**less** a. stupide; (*med.*) sans connaissance.

sensibilit|y /sensə'bɪlətɪ/ n. sensibilité f. ~**ies**, susceptibilité f.

sensible /'sensəbl/ a. raisonnable, sensé; (*clothing*) fonctionnel.

sensitiv|e /'sensətɪv/ a. sensible (**to**, à); (*touchy*) susceptible. ~**ity** /-'tɪvətɪ/ n. sensibilité f.

sensory /'sensərɪ/ a. sensoriel.

sensual /'senʃʊəl/ a. sensuel. ~**ity** /-'ælətɪ/ n. sensualité f.

sensuous /'senʃʊəs/ a. sensuel.

sent /sent/ *see* **send**.

sentence /'sentəns/ n. phrase f.; (*decision*: *jurid.*) jugement m., condamnation f.; (*punishment*) peine f. —v.t. ~ **to**, condamner à.

sentiment /'sentɪmənt/ n. sentiment m.

sentimental /sentɪ'mentl/ a. sentimental. ~**ity** /-'tælətɪ/ n. sentimentalité f.

sentry /'sentrɪ/ n. sentinelle f.

separable /'sepərəbl/ a. séparable.

separate[1] /'seprət/ a. séparé, différent; (*independent*) coordonnés m. pl. ~**ly** adv. séparément.

separat|e[2] /'sepəreɪt/ v.t./i. (se) séparer. ~**ion** /-'reɪʃn/ n. séparation f.

September /sep'tembə(r)/ n. septembre m.

septic /'septɪk/ a. (*wound*) infecté. ~ **tank**, fosse septique f.

sequel /'siːkwəl/ n. suite f.

sequence /'siːkwəns/ n. (*order*) ordre m.; (*series*) suite f.; (*of film*) séquence f.

sequin /'siːkwɪn/ n. paillette f.

serenade /serə'neɪd/ n. sérénade f. —v.t. donner une sérénade à.

seren|e /sɪ'riːn/ a. serein. ~**ity** /-enətɪ/ n. sérénité f.

sergeant /'sɑːdʒənt/ n. (*mil.*) sergent m.; (*policeman*) brigadier m.

serial /'sɪərɪəl/ n. (*story*) feuilleton m. —a. (*number*) de série.

series /'sɪərɪz/ n. *invar.* série f.

serious /'sɪərɪəs/ a. sérieux; (*very bad, critical*) grave, sérieux. ~**ly** adv. sérieusement, gravement. **take** ~**ly**, prendre au sérieux. ~**ness** n. sérieux m.

sermon /'sɜːmən/ n. sermon m.

serpent /'sɜːpənt/ n. serpent m.

serrated /sɪ'reɪtɪd/ a. (*edge*) en dents de scie.

serum /'sɪərəm/ n. (*pl.* **-a**) sérum m.

servant /'sɜːvənt/ *n.* domestique *m.*/*f.*; (*of God etc.*) serviteur *m.*

serve /sɜːv/ *v.t.*/*i.* servir; (*undergo, carry out*) faire; (*of transport*) desservir. —*n.* (*tennis*) service *m.* ~ **as**/**to**, servir de/à. ~ **its purpose**, remplir sa fonction.

service /'sɜːvɪs/ *n.* service *m.*; (*maintenance*) révision *f.* ~**s**, (*mil.*) forces armées *f. pl.* —*v.t.* (*car etc.*) réviser. **of** ~ **to**, utile à. ~ **area**, (*auto.*) aire de services *f.* ~ **charge**, service *m.* ~ **station**, station-service *f.*

serviceable /'sɜːvɪsəbl/ *a.* (*usable*) utilisable; (*useful*) commode; (*durable*) solide.

serviceman /'sɜːvɪsmən/ *n.* (*pl.* -**men**) militaire *m.*

serviette /sɜːvɪ'et/ *n.* serviette *f.*

servile /'sɜːvaɪl/ *a.* servile.

session /'seʃn/ *n.* séance *f.*; (*univ.*) année (universitaire) *f.*; (*univ., Amer.*) semestre *m.*

set /set/ *v.t.* (*p.t.* **set**, *pres. p.* **setting**) mettre; (*put down*) poser, mettre; (*limit etc.*) fixer; (*watch, clock*) régler; (*example, task*) donner; (*in plaster*) plâtrer. —*v.i.* (*of sun*) se coucher; (*of jelly*) prendre. —*n.* (*of chairs, stamps, etc.*) série *f.*; (*of knives, keys, etc.*) jeu *m.*; (*of people*) groupe *m.*; (*TV, radio*) poste *m.*; (*style of hair*) mise en plis *f.*; (*theatre*) décor *m.*; (*tennis*) set *m.*; (*mathematics*) ensemble *m.* —*a.* fixe; (*in habits*) régulier; (*opposed*) opposé; (*meal*) à prix fixe; (*book*) au programme. **be** ~ **on doing**, être résolu à faire. ~ **about** *or* **to**, se mettre à. ~ **back**, (*delay*) retarder; (*cost: sl.*) coûter. ~-**back** *n.* revers *m.* ~ **fire to**, mettre le feu à. ~ **in**, (*take hold*) s'installer, commencer. ~ **off** *or* **out**, partir. ~ **off**, (*mechanism, activity*) déclencher; (*bomb*) faire éclater. ~ **out**, (*state*) exposer; (*arrange*) disposer. ~ **sail**, partir. ~ **square**, équerre *f.* ~ **to**, (*about to*) sur le point de. ~-**to** *n.* querelle *f.* ~ **up**, (*establish*) fonder, établir; (*launch*) lancer. ~-**up** *n.* (*fam.*) affaire *f.*

settee /se'tiː/ *n.* canapé *m.*

setting /'setɪŋ/ *n.* cadre *m.*

settle /'setl/ *v.t.* (*arrange, pay*) régler; (*date*) fixer; (*nerves*) calmer. —*v.i.* (*come to rest*) se poser; (*live*) s'installer. ~ **down**, se calmer; (*become orderly*) se ranger. ~ **for**, accepter.

~ **up (with)**, régler. ~**r** /-ə(r)/ *n.* colon *m.*

settlement /'setlmənt/ *n.* règlement *m.* (**of**, de); (*agreement*) accord *m.*; (*place*) colonie *f.*

seven /'sevn/ *a. & n.* sept (*m.*). ~**th** *a. & n.* septième (*m.*/*f.*).

seventeen /sevn'tiːn/ *a. & n.* dix-sept (*m.*). ~**th** *a. & n.* dix-septième (*m.*/*f.*).

sevent|**y** /'sevntɪ/ *a. & n.* soixante-dix (*m.*). ~**ieth** *a. & n.* soixante-dixième (*m.*/*f.*).

sever /'sevə(r)/ *v.t.* (*cut*) couper; (*relations*) rompre. ~**ance** *n.* (*breaking off*) rupture *f.*

several /'sevrəl/ *a. & pron.* plusieurs.

sever|**e** /sɪ'vɪə(r)/ *a.* (-**er**, -**est**) sévère; (*violent*) violent; (*serious*) grave. ~**ely** *adv.* sévèrement; gravement. ~**ity** /sɪ'verətɪ/ *n.* sévérité *f.*; violence *f.*; gravité *f.*

sew /səʊ/ *v.t.*/*i.* (*p.t.* **sewed**, *p.p.* **sewn** *or* **sewed**) coudre. ~**ing** *n.* couture *f.* ~**ing-machine** *n.* machine à coudre *f.*

sewage /'sjuːɪdʒ/ *n.* eaux d'égout *f. pl.*, vidanges *f. pl.*

sewer /'sjuːə(r)/ *n.* égout *m.*

sewn /səʊn/ *see* **sew**.

sex /seks/ *n.* sexe *m.* —*a.* sexuel. **have** ~, avoir des rapports (sexuels). ~ **maniac**, obsédé(e) sexuel(le) *m.*(*f.*). ~**y** *a.* sexy *invar.*

sexist /'seksɪst/ *a. & n.* sexiste (*m.*/*f.*).

sextet /seks'tet/ *n.* sextuor *m.*

sexual /'sekʃʊəl/ *a.* sexuel. ~ **intercourse**, rapports sexuels *m. pl.* ~**ity** /-'ælətɪ/ *n.* sexualité *f.*

shabb|**y** /'ʃæbɪ/ *a.* (-**ier**, -**iest**) (*place, object*) minable, miteux; (*person*) pauvrement vêtu; (*mean*) mesquin. ~**ily** *adv.* (*dress*) pauvrement; (*act*) mesquinement.

shack /ʃæk/ *n.* cabane *f.*

shackles /'ʃæklz/ *n. pl.* chaînes *f. pl.*

shade /ʃeɪd/ *n.* ombre *f.*; (*of colour, opinion*) nuance *f.*; (*for lamp*) abat-jour *m.*; (*blind: Amer.*) store *m.* **a** ~ **bigger**/*etc.*, légèrement plus grand/ *etc.* —*v.t.* (*of person etc.*) abriter; (*of tree*) ombrager.

shadow /'ʃædəʊ/ *n.* ombre *f.* —*v.t.* (*follow*) filer. **S**~ **Cabinet**, cabinet fantôme *m.* ~**y** *a.* ombragé; (*fig.*) vague.

shady /'ʃeɪdɪ/ *a.* (-**ier**, -**iest**) ombragé; (*dubious: fig.*) louche.

shaft /ʃɑːft/ *n.* (*of arrow*) hampe *f.*; (*axle*) arbre *m.*; (*of mine*) puits *m.*

shaggy /'ʃægɪ/ a. (-ier, -iest) (beard) hirsute; (hair) broussailleux; (animal) à longs poils.

shake /ʃeɪk/ v.t. (p.t. **shook,** p.p. **shaken**) secouer; (bottle) agiter; (house, belief, etc.) ébranler. —v.i. trembler. —n. secousse f. ~ **hands with,** serrer la main à. ~ **off,** (get rid of) se débarrasser de. ~ **one's head,** (in refusal) dire non de la tête. ~ **up,** (disturb, rouse, mix contents of) secouer. ~**up** n. (upheaval) remaniement m.

shaky /'ʃeɪkɪ/ a. (-ier, -iest) (hand, voice) tremblant; (table etc.) branlant; (weak: fig.) faible.

shall /ʃæl, unstressed ʃ(ə)l/ v. aux. I ~ **do,** je ferai. **we** ~ **do,** nous ferons.

shallot /ʃə'lɒt/ n. échalote f.

shallow /'ʃæləʊ/ a. (-er, -est) peu profond; (fig.) superficiel.

sham /ʃæm/ n. comédie f.; (person) imposteur m.; (jewel) imitation f. —a. faux; (affected) feint. —v.t. (p.t. **shammed**) feindre.

shambles /'ʃæmblz/ n. pl. (mess: fam.) désordre m., pagaille f.

shame /ʃeɪm/ n. honte f. —v.t. faire honte à. **it is a** ~, c'est dommage. ~**ful** a. honteux. ~**fully** adv. honteusement. ~**less** a. éhonté.

shamefaced /'ʃeɪmfeɪst/ a. honteux.

shampoo /ʃæm'puː/ n. shampooing m. —v.t. faire un shampooing à, shampooiner.

shandy /'ʃændɪ/ n. panaché m.

shan't /ʃɑːnt/ = **shall not.**

shanty /'ʃæntɪ/ n. (shack) baraque f. ~ **town,** bidonville m.

shape /ʃeɪp/ n. forme f. —v.t. (fashion, mould) façonner; (future etc.: fig.) déterminer. —v.i. ~ **up,** (plan etc.) prendre tournure or forme; (person etc.) faire des progrès. ~**less** a. informe.

shapely /'ʃeɪplɪ/ a. (-ier, -iest) (leg, person) bien tourné.

share /ʃeə(r)/ n. part f.; (comm.) action f. —v.t./i. partager. ~**out** n. partage m.

shareholder /'ʃeəhəʊldə(r)/ n. actionnaire m./f.

shark /ʃɑːk/ n. requin m.

sharp /ʃɑːp/ a. (-er, -est) (knife etc.) tranchant; (pin etc.) pointu; (point) aigu; (acute) vif; (sudden) brusque; (dishonest) peu scrupuleux. —adv. (stop) net. **six o'clock**/etc. ~, six heures/etc. pile. —n. (mus.) dièse m. ~**ly** adv. (harshly) vivement; (suddenly) brusquement.

sharpen /'ʃɑːpən/ v.t. aiguiser; (pencil) tailler. ~**er** n. (for pencil) taille-crayon(s) m.

shatter /'ʃætə(r)/ v.t./i. (glass etc.) (faire) voler en éclats, (se) briser; (upset, ruin) anéantir.

shav|e /ʃeɪv/ v.t./i. (se) raser. —n. **have a** ~**e,** se raser. ~**en** a. rasé. ~**er** n. rasoir électrique m. ~**ing-brush** n. blaireau m. ~**ing-cream** n. crème à raser f.

shaving /'ʃeɪvɪŋ/ n. copeau m.

shawl /ʃɔːl/ n. châle m.

she /ʃiː/ pron. elle. —n. femelle f.

sheaf /ʃiːf/ n. (pl. **sheaves**) gerbe f.

shear /ʃɪə(r)/ v.t. (p.p. **shorn** or **sheared**) (sheep etc.) tondre.

shears /ʃɪəz/ n. pl. cisaille(s) f. (pl.).

sheath /ʃiːθ/ n. (pl. -s /ʃiːðz/) gaine f., fourreau m.; (contraceptive) préservatif m.

sheathe /ʃiːð/ v.t. rengainer.

shed[1] /ʃed/ n. remise f.

shed[2] /ʃed/ v.t. (p.t. **shed,** pres. p. **shedding**) perdre; (light, tears) répandre.

sheen /ʃiːn/ n. lustre m.

sheep /ʃiːp/ n. invar. mouton m. ~**dog** n. chien de berger m.

sheepish /'ʃiːpɪʃ/ a. penaud. ~**ly** adv. d'un air penaud.

sheepskin /'ʃiːpskɪn/ n. peau de mouton f.

sheer /ʃɪə(r)/ a. pur (et simple); (steep) à pic; (fabric) très fin. —adv. à pic, verticalement.

sheet /ʃiːt/ n. drap m.; (of paper) feuille f.; (of glass, ice) plaque f.

sheikh /ʃeɪk/ n. cheik m.

shelf /ʃelf/ n. (pl. **shelves**) rayon m., étagère f. **on the** ~, (person) laissé pour compte.

shell /ʃel/ n. coquille f.; (on beach) coquillage m.; (of building) carcasse f.; (explosive) obus m. —v.t. (nut etc.) décortiquer; (peas) écosser; (mil.) bombarder.

shellfish /'ʃelfɪʃ/ n. invar. (lobster etc.) crustacé(s) m. (pl.); (mollusc) coquillage(s) m. (pl.).

shelter /'ʃeltə(r)/ n. abri m. —v.t./i. (s')abriter; (give lodging to) donner asile à. ~**ed** a. (life etc.) protégé.

shelve /ʃelv/ v.t. (plan etc.) laisser en suspens, remettre à plus tard.

shelving /'ʃelvɪŋ/ *n.* (*shelves*) rayonnage(s) *m.* (*pl.*).

shepherd /'ʃepəd/ *n.* berger *m.* —*v.t.* (*people*) guider. ~ess /-'des/ *n.* bergère *f.* ~'s **pie**, hachis Parmentier *m.*

sherbet /'ʃɜːbət/ *n.* jus de fruits *m.*; (*powder*) poudre acidulée *f.*; (*water-ice*: *Amer.*) sorbet *m.*

sheriff /'ʃerɪf/ *n.* shérif *m.*

sherry /'ʃerɪ/ *n.* xérès *m.*

shield /ʃiːld/ *n.* bouclier *m.*; (*screen*) écran *m.* —*v.t.* protéger.

shift /ʃɪft/ *v.t./i.* (se) déplacer, bouger; (*exchange*, *alter*) changer de. —*n.* changement *m.*; (*workers*) équipe *f.*; (*work*) poste *m.* **make** ~, se débrouiller.

shiftless /'ʃɪftlɪs/ *a.* paresseux.

shifty /'ʃɪftɪ/ *a.* (**-ier, -iest**) louche.

shilling /'ʃɪlɪŋ/ *n.* shilling *m.*

shilly-shally /'ʃɪlɪʃælɪ/ *v.i.* hésiter, balancer.

shimmer /'ʃɪmə(r)/ *v.i.* chatoyer. —*n.* chatoiement *m.*

shin /ʃɪn/ *n.* tibia *m.*

shine /ʃaɪn/ *v.t./i.* (*p.t.* **shone** /ʃɒn/) (faire) briller. —*n.* éclat *m.*, brillant *m.* ~ **one's torch** *or* **the light (on)**, éclairer.

shingle /'ʃɪŋɡl/ *n.* (*pebbles*) galets *m. pl.*; (*on roof*) bardeau *m.*

shingles /'ʃɪŋɡlz/ *n. pl.* (*med.*) zona *m.*

shiny /'ʃaɪnɪ/ *a.* (**-ier, -iest**) brillant.

ship /ʃɪp/ *n.* bateau *m.*, navire *m.* —*v.t.* (*p.t.* **shipped**) transporter; (*send*) expédier; (*load*) embarquer. ~**ment** *n.* cargaison *f.*, envoi *m.* ~**per** *n.* expéditeur *m.* ~**ping** *n.* (*ships*) navigation *f.*, navires *m. pl.*

shipbuilding /'ʃɪpbɪldɪŋ/ *n.* construction navale *f.*

shipshape /'ʃɪpʃeɪp/ *adv.* & *a.* parfaitement en ordre.

shipwreck /'ʃɪprek/ *n.* naufrage *m.* ~**ed** *a.* naufragé. **be** ~**ed**, faire naufrage.

shipyard /'ʃɪpjɑːd/ *n.* chantier naval *m.*

shirk /ʃɜːk/ *v.t.* esquiver. ~**er** *n.* tire-au-flanc *m. invar.*

shirt /ʃɜːt/ *n.* chemise *f.*; (*of woman*) chemisier *m.* **in** ~**sleeves**, en bras de chemise.

shiver /'ʃɪvə(r)/ *v.i.* frissonner. —*n.* frisson *m.*

shoal /ʃəʊl/ *n.* (*of fish*) banc *m.*

shock /ʃɒk/ *n.* choc *m.*, secousse *f.*; (*electr.*) décharge *f.*; (*med.*) choc *m.*

—*a.* (*result*) choc *invar.*; (*tactics*) de choc. —*v.t.* choquer. **be a** ~**er**, (*fam.*) être affreux. ~**ing** *a.* choquant; (*bad*: *fam.*) affreux. ~**ingly** *adv.* (*fam.*) affreusement.

shodd|y /'ʃɒdɪ/ *a.* (**-ier, -iest**) mal fait, mauvais. ~**ily** *adv.* mal.

shoe /ʃuː/ *n.* chaussure *f.*, soulier *m.*; (*of horse*) fer (à cheval) *m.*; (*in vehicle*) sabot (de frein) *m.* —*v.t.* (*p.t.* **shod** /ʃɒd/, *pres. p.* **shoeing**) (*horse*) ferrer. **be well shod**, être bien chaussé. **on a** ~**string**, avec très peu d'argent.

shoehorn /'ʃuːhɔːn/ *n.* chausse-pied *m.*

shoelace /'ʃuːleɪs/ *n.* lacet *m.*

shoemaker /'ʃuːmeɪkə(r)/ *n.* cordonnier *m.*

shone /ʃɒn/ *see* **shine**.

shoo /ʃuː/ *v.t.* chasser.

shook /ʃʊk/ *see* **shake**.

shoot /ʃuːt/ *v.t.* (*p.t.* **shot**) (*gun*) tirer un coup de; (*missile*, *glance*) lancer; (*kill*, *wound*) tuer, blesser (d'un coup de fusil, de pistolet, *etc.*); (*execute*) fusiller; (*hunt*) chasser; (*film*) tourner. —*v.i.* tirer (**at**, sur). —*n.* (*bot.*) pousse *f.* ~ **down**, abattre. ~ **out**, (*rush*) sortir en vitesse. ~ **up**, (*spurt*) jaillir; (*grow*) pousser vite. ~**ing-range** *n.* stand de tir *m.*

shop /ʃɒp/ *n.* magasin *m.*, boutique *f.*; (*workshop*) atelier *m.* —*v.i.* (*p.t.* **shopped**) faire ses courses. ~ **around**, comparer les prix. ~ **assistant**, vendeu|r, -se *m.*, *f.* ~**-floor** *n.* (*workers*) ouvriers *m. pl.* ~**per** *n.* acheteu|r, -se *m.*, *f.* ~**-soiled**, (*Amer.*) ~**-worn** *adjs.* abîmé. ~ **steward**, délégué(e) syndical(e) *m.* (*f.*). ~ **window**, vitrine *f.*

shopkeeper /'ʃɒpkiːpə(r)/ *n.* commerçant(e) *m.* (*f.*).

shoplift|er /'ʃɒplɪftə(r)/ *n.* voleu|r, -se à l'étalage *m.*, *f.* ~**ing** *n.* vol à l'étalage *m.*

shopping /'ʃɒpɪŋ/ *n.* (*goods*) achats *m. pl.* **go** ~, faire ses courses. ~ **bag**, sac à provisions *m.* ~ **centre**, centre commercial *m.*

shore /ʃɔː(r)/ *n.* rivage *m.*

shorn /ʃɔːn/ *see* **shear**. —*a.* ~ **of**, dépouillé de.

short /ʃɔːt/ *a.* (**-er, -est**) court; (*person*) petit; (*brief*) court, bref; (*curt*) brusque. **be** ~ (**of**), (*lack*) manquer (de). —*adv.* (*stop*) net. —*n.* (*electr.*) court-circuit *m.* ~**s**, (*trousers*) short *m.* **he is called**

Tom for ~, son diminutif est Tom. **in ~,** en bref. **~-change** *v.t.* (*cheat*) rouler. **~ circuit,** court-circuit *m*. **~-circuit** *v.t.* court-circuiter. **~ cut,** raccourci *m*. **~-handed** *a.* à court de personnel. **~ list,** liste des candidats choisis *f*. **~-lived** *a.* éphémère. **~-sighted** *a.* myope. **~ story,** nouvelle *f*. **~ wave,** ondes courtes *f. pl.*

shortage /ˈʃɔːtɪdʒ/ *n.* manque *m*.

shortbread /ˈʃɔːtbred/ *n.* sablé *m*.

shortcoming /ˈʃɔːtkʌmɪŋ/ *n.* défaut *m*.

shorten /ˈʃɔːtn/ *v.t.* raccourcir.

shorthand /ˈʃɔːthænd/ *n.* sténo (graphie) *f*. **~ typist,** sténodactylo *f*.

shortly /ˈʃɔːtlɪ/ *adv.* bientôt.

shot /ʃɒt/ *see* **shoot.** —*n.* (*firing, attempt, etc.*) coup *m*.; (*person*) tireur *m*.; (*bullet*) balle *f*.; (*photograph*) photo *f*.; (*injection*) piqûre *f*. **like a ~,** comme une flèche. **~-gun** *n.* fusil de chasse *m*.

should /ʃʊd, *unstressed* ʃəd/ *v. aux.* devoir. **you ~ help me,** vous devriez m'aider. **I ~ have stayed,** j'aurais dû rester. **I ~ like to,** j'aimerais bien. **if he ~ come,** s'il vient.

shoulder /ˈʃəʊldə(r)/ *n.* épaule *f*. —*v.t.* (*responsibility*) endosser; (*burden*) se charger de. **~-blade** *n.* omoplate *f*.

shout /ʃaʊt/ *n.* cri *m*. —*v.t./i.* crier. **~ at,** engueuler. **~ down,** huer.

shove /ʃʌv/ *n.* poussée *f*. —*v.t./i.* pousser; (*put*: *fam.*) ficher. **~ off,** (*depart*: *fam.*) se tirer.

shovel /ˈʃʌvl/ *n.* pelle *f*. —*v.t.* (*p.t.* **shovelled**) pelleter.

show /ʃəʊ/ *v.t.* (*p.t.* **showed,** *p.p.* **shown**) montrer; (*of dial, needle*) indiquer; (*put on display*) exposer; (*film*) donner; (*conduct*) conduire. —*v.i.* (*be visible*) se voir. —*n.* démonstration *f*.; (*ostentation*) parade *f*.; (*exhibition*) exposition *f*., salon *m*.; (*theatre*) spectacle *m*.; (*cinema*) séance *f*. **for ~,** pour l'effet. **on ~,** exposé. **~-down** *n.* épreuve de force *f*. **~-jumping** *n.* concours hippique *m*. **~ in,** faire entrer. **~ off** *v.t.* étaler; *v.i.* poser, crâner. **~-off** *n.* poseu|r, -se *m*., *f*. **~-piece** *n.* modèle du genre *m*. **~ up,** (faire) ressortir; (*appear*: *fam.*) se montrer. **~ing** *n.* performance *f*.; (*cinema*) séance *f*.

shower /ˈʃaʊə(r)/ *n.* (*of rain*) averse *f*.; (*of blows etc.*) grêle *f*.; (*for washing*) douche *f*. —*v.t.* **~ with,** couvrir de. —*v.i.* se doucher. **~y** *a.* pluvieux.

showerproof /ˈʃaʊəpruːf/ *a.* imperméable.

showmanship /ˈʃəʊmənʃɪp/ *n.* art de la mise en scène *m*.

shown /ʃəʊn/ *see* **show.**

showroom /ˈʃəʊrʊm/ *n.* salle d'exposition *f*.

showy /ˈʃəʊɪ/ *a.* (-ier, -iest) voyant; (*manner*) prétentieux.

shrank /ʃræŋk/ *see* **shrink.**

shrapnel /ˈʃræpn(ə)l/ *n.* éclats d'obus *m. pl.*

shred /ʃred/ *n.* lambeau *m*.; (*least amount*: *fig.*) parcelle *f*. —*v.t.* (*p.t.* **shredded**) déchiqueter; (*culin.*) râper.

shrew /ʃruː/ *n.* (*woman*) mégère *f*.

shrewd /ʃruːd/ *a.* (-er, -est) astucieux. **~ness** *n.* astuce *f*.

shriek /ʃriːk/ *n.* hurlement *m*. —*v.t./i.* hurler.

shrift /ʃrɪft/ *n.* **give s.o. short ~,** traiter qn. sans ménagement.

shrill /ʃrɪl/ *a.* strident, aigu.

shrimp /ʃrɪmp/ *n.* crevette *f*.

shrine /ʃraɪn/ *n.* (*place*) lieu saint *m*.; (*tomb*) châsse *f*.

shrink /ʃrɪŋk/ *v.t./i.* (*p.t.* **shrank,** *p.p.* **shrunk**) rétrécir; (*lessen*) diminuer. **~ from,** reculer devant. **~age** *n.* rétrécissement *m*.

shrivel /ˈʃrɪvl/ *v.t./i.* (*p.t.* **shrivelled**) (se) ratatiner.

shroud /ʃraʊd/ *n.* linceul *m*. —*v.t.* (*veil*) envelopper.

Shrove /ʃrəʊv/ *n.* **~ Tuesday,** Mardi gras *m*.

shrub /ʃrʌb/ *n.* arbuste *m*.

shrug /ʃrʌg/ *v.t.* (*p.t.* **shrugged**). **~ one's shoulders,** hausser les épaules. —*n.* haussement d'épaules *m*.

shrunk /ʃrʌŋk/ *see* **shrink. ~en** *a.* rétréci; (*person*) ratatiné.

shudder /ˈʃʌdə(r)/ *v.i.* frémir. —*n.* frémissement *m*.

shuffle /ˈʃʌfl/ *v.t.* (*feet*) traîner; (*cards*) battre. —*v.i.* traîner les pieds. —*n.* démarche traînante *f*.

shun /ʃʌn/ *v.t.* (*p.t.* **shunned**) éviter, fuir.

shunt /ʃʌnt/ *v.t.* (*train*) aiguiller.

shush /ʃʊʃ/ *int.* (*fam.*) chut.

shut /ʃʌt/ *v.t./i.* (*pres. p.* **shut, pres. p. shutting**) fermer. —*v.i.* se fermer; (*of shop, bank, etc.*) fermer. **~ down** *or* **up,**

fermer. **∼-down** n. fermeture f. **∼ in** or up, enfermer. **∼ up** v.i. (fam.) se taire; v.t. (fam.) faire taire.

shutter /'ʃʌtə(r)/ n. volet m.; (photo.) obturateur m.

shuttle /'ʃʌtl/ n. (bus etc.) navette f. —v.i. faire la navette. —v.t. transporter. **∼ service**, navette f.

shuttlecock /'ʃʌtlkɒk/ n. (badminton) volant m.

shy /ʃaɪ/ a. (-er, -est) timide. —v.i. reculer. **∼ness** n. timidité f.

Siamese /saɪə'miːz/ a. siamois.

sibling /'sɪblɪŋ/ n. frère m., sœur f.

Sicily /'sɪsɪlɪ/ n. Sicile f.

sick /sɪk/ a. malade; (humour) macabre. **be ∼**, (vomit) vomir. **be ∼ of**, en avoir assez or marre de. **feel ∼**, avoir mal au cœur. **∼room** n. chambre de malade f.

sicken /'sɪkən/ v.t. écœurer. —v.i. be **∼ing for**, (illness) couver.

sickle /'sɪkl/ n. faucille f.

sickly /'sɪklɪ/ a. (-ier, -iest) (person) maladif; (taste, smell, etc.) écœurant.

sickness /'sɪknɪs/ n. maladie f.

side /saɪd/ n. côté m.; (of road, river) bord m.; (of hill) flanc m.; (sport) équipe f. —a. latéral. —v.i. **∼ with**, se ranger du côté de. **on the ∼**, (extra) en plus; (secretly) en catimini. **∼ by side**, côte à côte. **∼-car** n. side-car m. **∼effect** n. effet secondaire m. **∼-saddle** adv. en amazone. **∼-show** n. petite attraction f. **∼-step** v.t. (p.t. -stepped) éviter. **∼-track** v.t. faire dévier de son sujet. **∼whiskers** n. pl. favoris m. pl.

sideboard /'saɪdbɔːd/ n. buffet m. **∼s**, (whiskers: sl.) pattes f. pl.

sideburns /'saɪdbɜːnz/ n. pl. pattes f. pl., rouflaquettes f. pl.

sidelight /'saɪdlaɪt/ n. (auto.) veilleuse f., lanterne f.

sideline /'saɪdlaɪn/ n. activité secondaire f.

sidewalk /'saɪdwɔːk/ n. (Amer.) trottoir m.

side|ways /'saɪdweɪz/, **∼long** adv. & a. de côté.

siding /'saɪdɪŋ/ n. voie de garage f.

sidle /'saɪdl/ v.i. avancer furtivement (up to, vers).

siege /siːdʒ/ n. siège m.

siesta /sɪ'estə/ n. sieste f.

sieve /sɪv/ n. tamis m.; (for liquids) passoire f. —v.t. tamiser.

sift /sɪft/ v.t. tamiser. —v.i. **∼ through**, examiner.

sigh /saɪ/ n. soupir m. —v.t./i. soupirer.

sight /saɪt/ n. vue f.; (scene) spectacle m.; (on gun) mire f. —v.t. apercevoir. **at** or **on ∼**, à vue. **catch ∼ of**, apercevoir. **in ∼**, visible. **lose ∼ of**, perdre de vue.

sightsee|ing /'saɪtsiːɪŋ/ n. tourisme m. **∼r** /-ə(r)/ n. touriste m./f.

sign /saɪn/ n. signe m.; (notice) panneau m. —v.t./i. signer. **∼ on** or **up**, (s')enrôler.

signal /'sɪɡnəl/ n. signal m. —v.t. (p.t. signalled) communiquer (par signaux); (person) faire signe à. **∼-box** n. poste d'aiguillage m.

signalman /'sɪɡnəlmən/ n. (pl. -men) (rail.) aiguilleur m.

signatory /'sɪɡnətrɪ/ n. signataire m./f.

signature /'sɪɡnətʃə(r)/ n. signature f. **∼ tune**, indicatif musical m.

signet-ring /'sɪɡnɪtrɪŋ/ n. chevalière f.

significan|t /sɪɡ'nɪfɪkənt/ a. important; (meaningful) significatif. **∼ce** n. importance f.; (meaning) signification f. **∼tly** adv. (much) sensiblement.

signify /'sɪɡnɪfaɪ/ v.t. signifier.

signpost /'saɪnpəʊst/ n. poteau indicateur m.

silence /'saɪləns/ n. silence m. —v.t. faire taire. **∼r** /-ə(r)/ n. (on gun, car) silencieux m.

silent /'saɪlənt/ a. silencieux; (film) muet. **∼ly** adv. silencieusement.

silhouette /sɪluː'et/ n. silhouette f. — v.t. **be ∼d against**, se profiler contre.

silicon /'sɪlɪkən/ n. silicium m. **∼ chip**, microplaquette f.

silk /sɪlk/ n. soie f. **∼en**, **∼y** adjs. soyeux.

sill /sɪl/ n. rebord m.

silly /'sɪlɪ/ a. (-ier, -iest) bête, idiot. **∼(-billy)** n. (fam.) idiot(e) m. (f.).

silo /'saɪləʊ/ n. (pl. -os) silo m.

silt /sɪlt/ n. vase f.

silver /'sɪlvə(r)/ n. argent m.; (silverware) argenterie f. —a. en argent, d'argent. **∼ wedding**, noces d'argent f. pl. **∼y** a. argenté; (sound) argentin.

silversmith /'sɪlvəsmɪθ/ n. orfèvre m.

silverware /'sɪlvəweə(r)/ n. argenterie f.

similar /'sɪmɪlə(r)/ a. semblable (to, à). **∼ity** /-ə'lærətɪ/ n. ressemblance f. **∼ly** adv. de même.

simile /'sɪmɪlɪ/ n. comparaison f.

simmer /'sɪmə(r)/ v.t./i. (soup etc.) mijoter; (water) (laisser) frémir; (smoulder: fig.) couver. ~ **down,** se calmer.

simpl|e /'sɪmpl/ a. (-er, -est) simple. ~**e-minded** a. simple d'esprit. ~**icity** /-'plɪsətɪ/ n. simplicité f. ~**y** adv. simplement; (absolutely) absolument.

simpleton /'sɪmpltən/ n. niais(e) m. (f.).

simplif|y /'sɪmplɪfaɪ/ v.t. simplifier. ~**ication** /-ɪ'keɪʃn/ n. simplification f.

simulat|e /'sɪmjʊleɪt/ v.t. simuler. ~**ion** /-'leɪʃn/ n. simulation f.

simultaneous /sɪml'teɪnɪəs, Amer. saɪml'teɪnɪəs/ a. simultané. ~**ly** adv. simultanément.

sin /sɪn/ n. péché m. —v.i. (p.t. sinned) pécher.

since /sɪns/ prep. & adv. depuis. —conj. depuis que; (because) puisque. ~ **then,** depuis.

sincer|e /sɪn'sɪə(r)/ a. sincère. ~**ely** adv. sincèrement. ~**ity** /-'serətɪ/ n. sincérité f.

sinew /'sɪnjuː/ n. tendon m. ~**s,** muscles m. pl.

sinful /'sɪnfl/ a. (act) coupable, qui constitue un péché; (shocking) scandaleux. ~ **person,** péch|eur, -eresse m.,f.

sing /sɪŋ/ v.t./i. (p.t. sang, p.p. sung) chanter. ~**er** n. chanteu|r, -se m.,f.

singe /sɪndʒ/ v.t. (pres. p. singeing) brûler légèrement, roussir.

single /'sɪŋgl/ a. seul; (not double) simple; (unmarried) célibataire; (room, bed) pour une personne; (ticket) simple. —n. (ticket) aller simple m.; (record) 45 tours m. invar. ~**s,** (tennis) simple m. —v.t. ~ **out,** choisir. ~**handed** a. sans aide. ~**-minded** a. tenace. **singly** adv. un à un.

singlet /'sɪŋglɪt/ n. maillot de corps m.

singsong /'sɪŋsɒŋ/ n. **have a** ~, chanter en chœur. —a. (voice) monotone.

singular /'sɪŋgjʊlə(r)/ n. singulier m. —a. (uncommon & gram.) singulier; (noun) au singulier. ~**ly** adv. singulièrement.

sinister /'sɪnɪstə(r)/ a. sinistre.

sink /sɪŋk/ v.t./i. (p.t. sank, p.p. sunk) (faire) couler; (of ground, person) s'affaisser; (well) creuser; (money) investir. —n. (in kitchen) évier m.; (wash-basin) lavabo m. ~ **in,** (fig.)

être compris. ~ **into** v.t. (thrust) enfoncer dans; v.i. (go deep) s'enfoncer dans.

sinner /'sɪnə(r)/ n. péch|eur, -eresse m.,f.

sinuous /'sɪnjʊəs/ a. sinueux.

sinus /'saɪnəs/ n. (pl. -uses) (anat.) sinus m.

sip /sɪp/ n. petite gorgée f. —v.t. (p.t. sipped) boire à petites gorgées.

siphon /'saɪfn/ n. siphon m. —v.t. ~ **off,** siphonner.

sir /sɜː(r)/ n. monsieur m. **S~,** (title) Sir m.

siren /'saɪərən/ n. sirène f.

sirloin /'sɜːlɔɪn/ n. faux-filet m., aloyau m.; (Amer.) romsteck m.

sissy /'sɪsɪ/ n. personne efféminée f.; (coward) dégonflé(e) m. (f.).

sister /'sɪstə(r)/ n. sœur f.; (nurse) infirmière en chef f. ~**-in-law** (pl. ~**s-in-law**) belle-sœur f. ~**ly** a. fraternel.

sit /sɪt/ v.t./i. (p.t. sat, pres. p. sitting) (s')asseoir; (of committee etc.) siéger. ~ **(for),** (exam) se présenter à. **be** ~**ting,** être assis. ~ **around,** ne rien faire. ~ **down,** s'asseoir. ~**-in** n. sit-in m. invar. ~**ting** n. séance f.; (in restaurant) service m. ~**ting-room** n. salon m.

site /saɪt/ n. emplacement m. **(building)** ~, chantier m. —v.t. placer, construire, situer.

situat|e /'sɪtʃʊeɪt/ v.t. situer. **be** ~**ed,** être situé. ~**ion** /-'eɪʃn/ n. situation f.

six /sɪks/ a. & n. six (m.). ~**th** a. & n. sixième (m./f.).

sixteen /sɪk'stiːn/ a. & n. seize (m.). ~**th** a. & n. seizième (m./f.).

sixt|y /'sɪkstɪ/ a. & n. soixante (m.). ~**ieth** a. & n. soixantième (m./f.).

size /saɪz/ n. dimension f.; (of person, garment, etc.) taille f.; (of shoes) pointure f.; (of sum, salary) montant m.; (extent) ampleur f. —v.t. ~ **up,** (fam.) jauger, juger. ~**able** a. assez grand.

sizzle /'sɪzl/ v.i. grésiller.

skate[1] /skeɪt/ n. invar. (fish) raie f.

skat|e[2] /skeɪt/ n. patin m. —v.i. patiner. ~**er** n. patineu|r, -se m., f. ~**ing** n. patinage m. ~**ing-rink** n. patinoire f.

skateboard /'skeɪtbɔːd/ n. skateboard m., planche à roulettes f.

skelet|on /'skelɪtən/ n. squelette m. ~**on crew** or **staff,** effectifs minimums m. pl. ~**al** a. squelettique.

sketch /sketʃ/ *n.* esquisse *f.*, croquis *m.*; (*theatre*) sketch *m.* —*v.t.* (*portrait, idea, etc.*) esquisser. —*v.i.* faire des esquisses.

sketchy /'sketʃɪ/ *a.* (**-ier, -iest**) sommaire, incomplet.

skew /skjuː/ *n.* **on the ~**, de travers. **~-whiff** *a.* (*fam.*) de travers.

skewer /'skjʊə(r)/ *n.* brochette *f.*

ski /skiː/ *n.* (*pl.* **-is**) ski *m.* —*v.i.* (*p.t.* **ski'd** *or* **skied**, *pres. p.* **skiing**) skier; (*go skiing*) faire du ski. **~er** *n.* skieu|r, -se *m.*, *f.* **~ing** *n.* ski *m.*

skid /skɪd/ *v.i.* (*p.t.* **skidded**) déraper. —*n.* dérapage *m.*

skilful /'skɪlfl/ *a.* habile.

skill /skɪl/ *n.* habileté *f.*; (*craft*) métier *m.* **~s**, aptitudes *f. pl.* **~ed** *a.* habile; (*worker*) qualifié.

skim /skɪm/ *v.t.* (*p.t.* **skimmed**) écumer; (*milk*) écrémer; (*pass or glide over*) effleurer. —*v.i.* **~ through**, parcourir.

skimp /skɪmp/ *v.t./i.* lésiner (sur).

skimpy /'skɪmpɪ/ *a.* (**-ier, -iest**) (*clothes*) étriqué; (*meal*) chiche.

skin /skɪn/ *n.* peau *f.* —*v.t.* (*p.t.* **skinned**) (*animal*) écorcher; (*fruit*) éplucher. **~-diving** *n.* plongée sousmarine *f.*

skinflint /'skɪnflɪnt/ *n.* avare *m.*/*f.*

skinny /'skɪnɪ/ *a.* (**-ier, -iest**) maigre, maigrichon.

skint /skɪnt/ *a.* (*sl.*) fauché.

skip[1] /skɪp/ *v.i.* (*p.t.* **skipped**) sautiller; (*with rope*) sauter à la corde. —*v.t.* (*page, class, etc.*) sauter. —*n.* petit saut *m.* **~ping-rope** *n.* corde à sauter *f.*

skip[2] /skɪp/ *n.* (*container*) benne *f.*

skipper /'skɪpə(r)/ *n.* capitaine *m.*

skirmish /'skɜːmɪʃ/ *n.* escarmouche *f.*, accrochage *m.*

skirt /skɜːt/ *n.* jupe *f.* —*v.t.* contourner. **~ing-board** *n.* plinthe *f.*

skit /skɪt/ *n.* sketch satirique *m.*

skittle /'skɪtl/ *n.* quille *f.*

skive /skaɪv/ *v.i.* (*sl.*) tirer au flanc.

skivvy /'skɪvɪ/ *n.* (*fam.*) boniche *f.*

skulk /skʌlk/ *v.i.* (*move*) rôder furtivement; (*hide*) se cacher.

skull /skʌl/ *n.* crâne *m.* **~-cap** *n.* calotte *f.*

skunk /skʌŋk/ *n.* (*animal*) mouffette *f.*; (*person: sl.*) salaud *m.*

sky /skaɪ/ *n.* ciel *m.* **~-blue** *a.* & *n.* bleu ciel *a.* & *m. invar.*

skylight /'skaɪlaɪt/ *n.* lucarne *f.*

skyscraper /'skaɪskreɪpə(r)/ *n.* gratteciel *m. invar.*

slab /slæb/ *n.* plaque *f.*, bloc *m.*; (*of paving-stone*) dalle *f.*

slack /slæk/ *a.* (**-er, -est**) (*rope*) lâche; (*person*) négligent; (*business*) stagnant; (*period*) creux. —*n.* **the ~**, (*in rope*) du mou —*v.t./i.* (se) relâcher.

slacken /'slækən/ *v.t./i.* (se) relâcher; (*slow*) (se) ralentir.

slacks /slæks/ *n. pl.* pantalon *m.*

slag /slæg/ *n.* scories *f. pl.*

slain /sleɪn/ *see* **slay.**

slake /sleɪk/ *v.t.* étancher.

slalom /'slɑːləm/ *n.* slalom *m.*

slam /slæm/ *v.t./i.* (*p.t.* **slammed**) (*door etc.*) claquer; (*throw*) flanquer; (*criticize: sl.*) critiquer. —*n.* (*noise*) claquement *m.*

slander /'slɑːndə(r)/ *n.* diffamation *f.*, calomnie *f.* —*v.t.* diffamer, calomnier. **~ous** *a.* diffamatoire.

slang /slæŋ/ *n.* argot *m.* **~y** *a.* argotique.

slant /slɑːnt/ *v.t./i.* (faire) pencher; (*news*) présenter sous un certain jour. —*n.* inclinaison *f.*; (*bias*) angle *m.* **be ~ing**, être penché.

slap /slæp/ *v.t.* (*p.t.* **slapped**) (*strike*) donner une claque à; (*face*) gifler; (*put*) flanquer. —*n.* claque *f.*; gifle *f.* —*adv.* tout droit. **~happy** *a.* (*carefree: fam.*) insouciant; (*dazed: fam.*) abruti. **~-up meal,** (*sl.*) gueuleton *m.*

slapdash /'slæpdæʃ/ *a.* négligent.

slapstick /'slæpstɪk/ *n.* grosse farce *f.*

slash /slæʃ/ *v.t.* (*cut*) taillader; (*sever*) trancher; (*fig.*) réduire (radicalement). —*n.* taillade *f.*

slat /slæt/ *n.* (*in blind*) lamelle *f.*

slate /sleɪt/ *n.* ardoise *f.* —*v.t.* (*fam.*) critiquer, éreinter.

slaughter /'slɔːtə(r)/ *v.t.* massacrer; (*animals*) abattre. —*n.* massacre *m.*; abattage *m.*

slaughterhouse /'slɔːtəhaʊs/ *n.* abattoir *m.*

Slav /slɑːv/ *a.* & *n.* slave (*m.*/*f.*). **~onic** /slə'vɒnɪk/ *a.* (*lang.*) slave.

slave /sleɪv/ *n.* esclave *m.*/*f.* —*v.i.* trimer. **~-driver** *n.* négr|ier, -ière *m.*, *f.* **~ry** /-ərɪ/ *n.* esclavage *m.*

slavish /'sleɪvɪʃ/ *a.* servile.

slay /sleɪ/ *v.t.* (*p.t.* **slew**, *p.p.* **slain**) tuer.

sleazy /'sliːzɪ/ *a.* (**-ier, -iest**) (*fam.*) sordide, miteux.

sledge /sledʒ/ *n.* luge *f.*; (*horse-drawn*)

traîneau *m.* ~**-hammer** *n.* marteau de forgeron *m.*

sleek /sliːk/ *a.* (-er, -est) lisse, brillant; (*manner*) onctueux.

sleep /sliːp/ *n.* sommeil *m.* —*v.i.* (*p.t.* **slept**) dormir; (*spend the night*) coucher. —*v.t.* loger. **go to ~**, s'endormir. ~**er** *n.* dormeu|r, -se *m.*, *f.*; (*beam: rail.*) traverse *f.*; (*berth*) couchette *f.* ~**ing-bag** *n.* sac de couchage *m.* ~**less** *a.* sans sommeil. ~**-walker** *n.* somnambule *m.*/*f.*

sleep|y /'sliːpɪ/ *a.* (-ier, -iest) somnolent. **be ~y**, avoir sommeil. ~**ily** *adv.* à moitié endormi.

sleet /sliːt/ *n.* neige fondue *f.*; (*coat of ice: Amer.*) verglas *m.* —*v.i.* tomber de la neige fondue.

sleeve /sliːv/ *n.* manche *f.*; (*of record*) pochette *f.* **up one's ~**, en réserve. ~**less** *a.* sans manches.

sleigh /sleɪ/ *n.* traîneau *m.*

sleight /slaɪt/ *n.* **~ of hand**, prestidigitation *f.*

slender /'slendə(r)/ *a.* mince, svelte; (*scanty: fig.*) faible.

slept /slept/ *see* sleep.

sleuth /sluːθ/ *n.* limier *m.*

slew[1] /sluː/ *v.i.* (*turn*) virer.

slew[2] /sluː/ *see* slay.

slice /slaɪs/ *n.* tranche *f.* —*v.t.* couper (en tranches).

slick /slɪk/ *a.* (*unctuous*) mielleux; (*cunning*) astucieux. —*n.* (**oil**) ~, nappe de pétrole *f.*, marée noire *f.*

slide /slaɪd/ *v.t.*/*i.* (*p.t.* **slid**) glisser. —*n.* glissade *f.*; (*fall: fig.*) baisse *f.*; (*in playground*) toboggan *m.*; (*for hair*) barrette *f.*; (*photo.*) diapositive *f.* **~ into**, (*go silently*) se glisser dans. **~-rule** *n.* règle à calcul *f.* **sliding** *a.* (*door, panel*) à glissière, à coulisse. **sliding scale**, échelle mobile *f.*

slight /slaɪt/ *a.* (-er, -est) petit, léger; (*slender*) mince; (*frail*) frêle. —*v.t.* (*insult*) offenser. —*n.* affront *m.* ~**est** *a.* moindre. ~**ly** *adv.* légèrement, un peu.

slim /slɪm/ *a.* (**slimmer**, **slimmest**) mince. —*v.i.* (*p.t.* **slimmed**) maigrir. ~**ness** *n.* minceur *f.*

slim|e /slaɪm/ *n.* boue (visqueuse) *f.*; (*on river-bed*) vase *f.* ~**y** *a.* boueux; vaseux; (*sticky, servile*) visqueux.

sling /slɪŋ/ *n.* (*weapon, toy*) fronde *f.*; (*bandage*) écharpe *f.* —*v.t.* (*p.t.* **slung**) jeter, lancer.

slip /slɪp/ *v.t.*/*i.* (*p.t.* **slipped**) glisser.

—*n.* faux pas *m.*; (*mistake*) erreur *f.*; (*petticoat*) combinaison *f.*; (*paper*) fiche *f.* **give the ~ to**, fausser compagnie à. **~ away**, s'esquiver. ~**cover** *n.* (*Amer.*) housse *f.* **~ into**, (*go*) se glisser dans; (*clothes*) mettre. **~ of the tongue**, lapsus *m.* ~**road** *n.* bretelle *f.* ~ **s.o.'s mind**, échapper à qn. **~ up**, (*fam.*) gaffer. ~**up** *n.* (*fam.*) gaffe *f.*

slipper /'slɪpə(r)/ *n.* pantoufle *f.*

slippery /'slɪpərɪ/ *a.* glissant.

slipshod /'slɪpʃɒd/ *a.* (*person*) négligent; (*work*) négligé.

slit /slɪt/ *n.* fente *f.* —*v.t.* (*p.t.* **slit**, *pres. p.* **slitting**) couper, fendre.

slither /'slɪðə(r)/ *v.i.* glisser.

sliver /'slɪvə(r)/ *n.* (*of cheese etc.*) lamelle *f.*; (*splinter*) éclat *m.*

slob /slɒb/ *n.* (*fam.*) rustre *m.*

slobber /'slɒbə(r)/ *v.i.* baver.

slog /slɒg/ *v.t.* (*p.t.* **slogged**) (*hit*) frapper dur. —*v.i.* (*work*) trimer. —*n.* (*work*) travail dur *m.*; (*effort*) gros effort *m.*

slogan /'sləʊgən/ *n.* slogan *m.*

slop /slɒp/ *v.t.*/*i.* (*p.t.* **slopped**) (se) répandre. ~**s** *n. pl.* eaux sales *f. pl.*

slop|e /sləʊp/ *v.t.*/*i.* être en pente; (*of handwriting*) pencher. —*n.* pente *f.*; (*of mountain*) flanc *m.* ~**ing** *a.* en pente.

sloppy /'slɒpɪ/ *a.* (-ier, -iest) (*ground*) détrempé; (*food*) liquide; (*work*) négligé; (*person*) négligent; (*fig.*) sentimental.

slosh /slɒʃ/ *v.t.* (*fam.*) répandre; (*hit: sl.*) frapper. —*v.i.* patauger.

slot /slɒt/ *n.* fente *f.* —*v.t.*/*i.* (*p.t.* **slotted**) (s')insérer. ~**-machine** *n.* distributeur automatique *m.*; (*for gambling*) machine à sous *f.*

sloth /sləʊθ/ *n.* paresse *f.*

slouch /slaʊtʃ/ *v.i.* avoir le dos voûté; (*move*) marcher le dos voûté.

slovenl|y /'slʌvnlɪ/ *a.* débraillé. ~**iness** *n.* débraillé *m.*

slow /sləʊ/ *a.* (-er, -est) lent. —*adv.* lentement. —*v.t.*/*i.* ralentir. **be ~**, (*clock etc.*) retarder. **in ~ motion**, au ralenti. ~**ly** *adv.* lentement. ~**ness** *n.* lenteur *f.*

slow|coach /'sləʊkəʊtʃ/, (*Amer.*) ~**poke** *ns.* lambin(e) *m.* (*f.*).

sludge /slʌdʒ/ *n.* gadoue *f.*, boue *f.*

slug /slʌg/ *n.* (*mollusc*) limace *f.*; (*bullet*) balle *f.*; (*blow*) coup *m.*

sluggish /'slʌgɪʃ/ *a.* lent, mou.

sluice /sluːs/ n. (gate) vanne f.

slum /slʌm/ n. taudis m.

slumber /ˈslʌmbə(r)/ n. sommeil m. —v.i. dormir.

slump /slʌmp/ n. effondrement m.; baisse f.; (in business) marasme m. —v.i. (collapse, fall limply) s'effondrer; (decrease) baisser.

slung /slʌŋ/ see sling.

slur /slɜː(r)/ v.t./i. (p.t. slurred) (spoken words) mal articuler. —n. bredouillement m.; (discredit) atteinte f. (on, à).

slush /slʌʃ/ n. (snow) neige fondue f. ~ fund, fonds servant à des pots-de-vin m. ~y a. (road) couvert de neige fondue.

slut /slʌt/ n. (dirty) souillon f.; (immoral) dévergondée f.

sly /slaɪ/ a. (slyer, slyest) (crafty) rusé; (secretive) sournois. —n. on the ~, en cachette. ~ly adv. sournoisement.

smack¹ /smæk/ n. tape f.; (on face) gifle f. —v.t. donner une tape à; gifler. —adv. (fam.) tout droit.

smack² /smæk/ v.i. ~ of sth., (have flavour) sentir qch.

small /smɔːl/ a. (-er, -est) petit. —n. ~ of the back, creux des reins m. —adv. (cut etc.) menu. ~ness n. petitesse f. ~ talk, menus propos m. pl. ~-time a. petit, peu important.

smallholding /ˈsmɔːlhəʊldɪŋ/ n. petite ferme f.

smallpox /ˈsmɔːlpɒks/ n. variole f.

smarmy /ˈsmɑːmɪ/ a. (-ier, -iest) (fam.) obséquieux, patelin.

smart /smɑːt/ a. (-er, -est) élégant; (clever) astucieux, intelligent; (brisk) rapide. —v.i. (of wound etc.) brûler. ~ly adv. élégamment. ~ness n. élégance f.

smarten /ˈsmɑːtn/ v.t./i. ~ (up), embellir. ~ (o.s.) up, se faire beau; (tidy) s'arranger.

smash /smæʃ/ v.t./i. (se) briser, (se) fracasser; (opponent, record) pulvériser. —n. (noise) fracas m.; (blow) coup m.; (fig.) collision f.

smashing /ˈsmæʃɪŋ/ a. (fam.) formidable, épatant.

smattering /ˈsmætərɪŋ/ n. connaissances vagues f. pl.

smear /smɪə(r)/ v.t. (stain) tacher; (coat) enduire; (discredit: fig.) entacher. —n. tache f.

smell /smel/ n. odeur f.; (sense) odorat

m. —v.t./i. (p.t. smelt or smelled) sentir. ~ of, sentir. ~y a. malodorant.

smelt¹ /smelt/ see smell.

smelt² /smelt/ v.t. (ore) fondre.

smil|e /smaɪl/ n. sourire. —v.i. sourire. ~ing a. souriant.

smirk /smɜːk/ n. sourire affecté m.

smite /smaɪt/ v.t. (p.t. smote, p.p. smitten) (old use) frapper.

smith /smɪθ/ n. forgeron m.

smithereens /smɪðəˈriːnz/ n. pl. to or in ~, en mille morceaux.

smitten /ˈsmɪtn/ see smite. —a. (in love) épris (with, de).

smock /smɒk/ n. blouse f.

smog /smɒg/ n. brouillard mélangé de fumée m., smog m.

smoke /sməʊk/ n. fumée f. —v.t./i. fumer. have a ~, fumer. ~less a. (fuel) non polluant. ~r /-ə(r)/ n. fumeu|r, -se m., f. ~-screen n. écran de fumée m.; (fig.) manœuvre de diversion f. smoky a. (air) enfumé.

smooth /smuːð/ a. (-er, -est) lisse; (movement) régulier; (manners, cream) onctueux. —v.t. lisser. ~ out, (fig.) faire disparaître. ~ly adv. facilement, doucement.

smother /ˈsmʌðə(r)/ v.t. (stifle) étouffer; (cover) couvrir.

smoulder /ˈsməʊldə(r)/ v.i. (fire, discontent, etc.) couver.

smudge /smʌdʒ/ n. tache f. —v.t./i. (se) salir, (se) tacher.

smug /smʌg/ a. (smugger, smuggest) suffisant. ~ly adv. avec suffisance. ~ness n. suffisance f.

smuggl|e /ˈsmʌgl/ v.t. passer (en contrebande). ~er n. contreband|ier, -ière m., f. ~ing n. contrebande f.

smut /smʌt/ n. saleté f. ~ty a. sale.

snack /snæk/ n. casse-croûte m. invar. ~-bar n. snack(-bar) m.

snag /snæg/ n. difficulté f., inconvénient m.; (in cloth) accroc m.

snail /sneɪl/ n. escargot m. at a ~'s pace, à un pas de tortue.

snake /sneɪk/ n. serpent m.

snap /snæp/ v.t./i. (p.t. snapped) (whip, fingers, etc.) (faire) claquer; (break) (se) casser net; (say) dire sèchement. —n. claquement m.; (photograph) instantané m.; (press-stud: Amer.) bouton-pression m. —a. soudain. ~ at, (bite) happer. ~ up, (buy) sauter sur.

snappy /ˈsnæpɪ/ a. (-ier, -iest) (brisk:

fam.) prompt, rapide. **make it ~,** (*fam.*) se dépêcher.

snapshot /'snæpʃɒt/ *n.* instantané *m.*, photo *f.*

snare /sneə(r)/ *n.* piège *m.*

snarl /snɑ:l/ *v.i.* gronder (en montrant les dents). —*n.* grondement *m.*

snatch /snætʃ/ *v.t.* (*grab*) saisir; (*steal*) voler. **~ from s.o.,** arracher à qn. —*n.* (*theft*) vol *m.*; (*short part*) fragment *m.*

sneak /sni:k/ *v.i.* aller furtivement. —*n.* (*schol., sl.*) rapporteu|r, -se *m., f.* **~y** *a.* sournois.

sneakers /'sni:kəz/ *n. pl.* (*shoes*) tennis *m. pl.*

sneaking /'sni:kɪŋ/ *a.* caché.

sneer /snɪə(r)/ *n.* ricanement *m.* —*v.i.* ricaner.

sneeze /sni:z/ *n.* éternuement *m.* —*v.i.* éternuer.

snide /snaɪd/ *a.* (*fam.*) narquois.

sniff /snɪf/ *v.t./i.* renifler. —*n.* reniflement *m.*

snigger /'snɪgə(r)/ *n.* ricanement *m.* —*v.i.* ricaner.

snip /snɪp/ *v.t.* (*p.t.* **snipped**) couper. —*n.* morceau coupé *m.*; (*bargain: sl.*) bonne affaire *f.*

snipe /snaɪp/ *v.i.* canarder. **~r** /-ə(r)/ *n.* tireur embusqué *m.*

snippet /'snɪpɪt/ *n.* bribe *f.*

snivel /'snɪvl/ *v.i.* (*p.t.* **snivelled**) pleurnicher.

snob /snɒb/ *n.* snob *m./f.* **~bery** *n.* snobisme *m.* **~bish** *a.* snob *invar.*

snooker /'snu:kə(r)/ *n.* (*sorte de*) jeu de billard *m.*

snoop /snu:p/ *v.i.* (*fam.*) fourrer son nez partout. **~ on,** espionner.

snooty /'snu:tɪ/ *a.* (-**ier,** -**iest**) (*fam.*) snob *invar.*, hautain.

snooze /snu:z/ *n.* petit somme *m.* —*v.i.* faire un petit somme.

snore /snɔ:(r)/ *n.* ronflement *m.* —*v.i.* ronfler.

snorkel /'snɔ:kl/ *n.* tuba *m.*

snort /snɔ:t/ *n.* grognement *m.* —*v.i.* (*person*) grogner; (*horse*) s'ébrouer.

snout /snaʊt/ *n.* museau *m.*

snow /snəʊ/ *n.* neige *f.* —*v.i.* neiger. **be ~ed under with,** être submergé de. **~-drift** *n.* congère *f.* **~-plough** *n.* chasse-neige *m. invar.* **~y** *a.* neigeux.

snowball /'snəʊbɔ:l/ *n.* boule de neige *f.*

snowdrop /'snəʊdrɒp/ *n.* perceneige *m./f. invar.*

snowfall /'snəʊfɔ:l/ *n.* chute de neige *f.*

snowflake /'snəʊfleɪk/ *n.* flocon de neige *m.*

snowman /'snəʊmæn/ *n.* (*pl.* -**men**) bonhomme de neige *m.*

snowstorm /'snəʊstɔ:m/ *n.* tempête de neige *f.*

snub /snʌb/ *v.t.* (*p.t.* **snubbed**) (*person*) snober; (*offer*) repousser. —*n.* rebuffade *f.*

snub-nosed /'snʌbnəʊzd/ *a.* au nez retroussé.

snuff[1] /snʌf/ *n.* tabac à priser *m.*

snuff[2] /snʌf/ *v.t.* (*candle*) moucher.

snuffle /'snʌfl/ *v.i.* renifler.

snug /snʌg/ *a.* (**snugger, snuggest**) (*cosy*) confortable; (*tight*) bien ajusté; (*safe*) sûr.

snuggle /'snʌgl/ *v.i.* se pelotonner.

so /səʊ/ *adv.* si, tellement; (*thus*) ainsi. —*conj.* donc, alors. **~ am I,** moi aussi. **~ does he,** lui aussi. **that is ~,** c'est ça. **I think ~,** je pense que oui. **five or ~,** environ cinq. **~-and-so** *n.* un(e) tel(le) *m.* (*f.*). **~ as to,** de manière à. **~-called** *a.* soi-disant *invar.* **~ far,** jusqu'ici. **~ long!,** (*fam.*) à bientôt! **~ many, ~ much,** tant (de). **~-so** *a.* & *adv.* comme ci comme ça. **~ that,** pour que.

soak /səʊk/ *v.t./i.* (faire) tremper (**in,** dans). **~ in** *or* **up,** absorber. **~ing** *a.* trempé.

soap /səʊp/ *n.* savon *m.* —*v.t.* savonner. **~ opera,** feuilleton mélo *m.* **~ powder,** lessive *f.* **~y** *a.* savonneux.

soar /sɔ:(r)/ *v.i.* monter (en flèche).

sob /sɒb/ *n.* sanglot *m.* —*v.i.* (*p.t.* **sobbed**) sangloter.

sober /'səʊbə(r)/ *a.* qui n'est pas ivre; (*serious*) sérieux; (*colour*) sobre. —*v.t./i.* **~ up,** dessoûler.

soccer /'sɒkə(r)/ *n.* (*fam.*) football *m.*

sociable /'səʊʃəbl/ *a.* sociable.

social /'səʊʃl/ *a.* social; (*gathering, life*) mondain. —*n.* réunion (amicale) *f.*, fête *f.* **~ly** *adv.* socialement; (*meet*) en société. **~ security,** aide sociale *f.*; (*for old age: Amer.*) pension (de retraite) *f.* **~ worker,** assistant(e) social(e) *m.* (*f.*).

socialis|t /'səʊʃəlɪst/ *n.* socialiste *m./f.* **~m** /-zəm/ *n.* socialisme *m.*

socialize /'səʊʃəlaɪz/ *v.i.* se mêler aux autres. **~ with,** fréquenter.

society /sə'saɪətɪ/ *n.* société *f.*

sociolog|y /ˌsəʊsɪˈɒlədʒɪ/ *n.* sociologie *f.* **~ical** /-əˈlɒdʒɪkl/ *a.* sociologique. **~ist** *n.* sociologue *m./f.*

sock¹ /sɒk/ *n.* chaussette *f.*

sock² /sɒk/ *v.t.* (*hit: sl.*) flanquer un coup (de poing) à.

socket /ˈsɒkɪt/ *n.* cavité *f.*; (*for lamp*) douille *f.*; (*wall plug*) prise de courant *f.*; (*of tooth*) alvéole *f.*

soda /ˈsəʊdə/ *n.* soude *f.* **~(-pop)**, (*Amer.*) soda *m.* **~(-water)**, soda *m.*, eau de Seltz *f.*

sodden /ˈsɒdn/ *a.* détrempé.

sodium /ˈsəʊdɪəm/ *n.* sodium *m.*

sofa /ˈsəʊfə/ *n.* sofa *m.*

soft /sɒft/ *a.* (**-er, -est**) (*gentle, lenient*) doux; (*not hard*) doux, mou; (*heart, wood*) tendre; (*silly*) ramolli; (*easy: sl.*) facile. **~ drink**, boisson non alcoolisée *f.* **~ly** *adv.* doucement. **~ness** *n.* douceur *f.* **~ spot**, faible *m.*

soften /ˈsɒfn/ *v.t./i.* (se) ramollir; (*tone down, lessen*) (s')adoucir.

software /ˈsɒftweə(r)/ *n.* (*for computer*) logiciel *m.*

soggy /ˈsɒgɪ/ *a.* (**-ier, -iest**) détrempé; (*bread etc.*) ramolli.

soil¹ /sɔɪl/ *n.* sol *m.*, terre *f.*

soil² /sɔɪl/ *v.t./i.* (se) salir.

solar /ˈsəʊlə(r)/ *a.* solaire.

sold /səʊld/ *see* **sell.** —*a.* **~ out**, épuisé.

solder /ˈsɒldə(r), *Amer.* ˈsɒdə(r)/ *n.* soudure *f.* —*v.t.* souder.

soldier /ˈsəʊldʒə(r)/ *n.* soldat *m.* —*v.i.* **~ on**, (*fam.*) persévérer.

sole¹ /səʊl/ *n.* (*of foot*) plante *f.*; (*of shoe*) semelle *f.*

sole² /səʊl/ *n.* (*fish*) sole *f.*

sole³ /səʊl/ *a.* unique, seul. **~ly** *adv.* uniquement.

solemn /ˈsɒləm/ *a.* (*formal*) solennel; (*not cheerful*) grave. **~ity** /səˈlemnətɪ/ *n.* solennité *f.* **~ly** *adv.* solennellement; gravement.

solicit /səˈlɪsɪt/ *v.t.* (*seek*) solliciter. —*v.i.* (*of prostitute*) racoler.

solicitor /səˈlɪsɪtə(r)/ *n.* avoué *m.*

solid /ˈsɒlɪd/ *a.* solide; (*not hollow*) plein; (*gold*) massif; (*mass*) compact; (*meal*) substantiel. —*n.* solide *m.* **~s**, (*food*) aliments solides *m. pl.* **~ity** /səˈlɪdətɪ/ *n.* solidité *f.* **~ly** *adv.* solidement.

solidarity /sɒlɪˈdærətɪ/ *n.* solidarité *f.*

solidify /səˈlɪdɪfaɪ/ *v.t./i.* (se) solidifier.

soliloquy /səˈlɪləkwɪ/ *n.* monologue *m.*, soliloque *m.*

solitary /ˈsɒlɪtrɪ/ *a.* (*alone, lonely*) solitaire; (*only, single*) seul.

solitude /ˈsɒlɪtjuːd/ *n.* solitude *f.*

solo /ˈsəʊləʊ/ *n.* (*pl.* **-os**) solo *m.* —*a.* (*mus.*) solo *invar.*; (*flight*) en solitaire. **~ist** *n.* soliste *m./f.*

solstice /ˈsɒlstɪs/ *n.* solstice *m.*

soluble /ˈsɒljʊbl/ *a.* soluble.

solution /səˈluːʃn/ *n.* solution *f.*

solv|e /sɒlv/ *v.t.* résoudre. **~able** *a.* soluble.

solvent /ˈsɒlvənt/ *a.* (*comm.*) solvable. —*n.* (dis)solvant *m.*

sombre /ˈsɒmbə(r)/ *a.* sombre.

some /sʌm/ *a.* (*quantity, number*) du, de l'*, de la, des; (*unspecified, some or other*) un(e), quelque; (*a little*) un peu de; (*a certain*) un(e) certain(e), quelque; (*contrasted with others*) quelques, certain(e)s. —*pron.* quelques-un(e)s; (*certain quantity of it or them*) en; (*a little*) un peu. —*adv.* (*approximately*) quelque. **pour ~ milk**, versez du lait. **he wants ~**, il en veut. **~ book (or other)**, un livre (quelconque), quelque livre.

somebody /ˈsʌmbədɪ/ *pron.* quelqu'un. —*n.* **be a ~**, être quelqu'un.

somehow /ˈsʌmhaʊ/ *adv.* d'une manière ou d'une autre; (*for some reason*) je ne sais pas pourquoi.

someone /ˈsʌmwʌn/ *pron.&n.* = **somebody.**

somersault /ˈsʌməsɔːlt/ *n.* culbute *f.* —*v.i.* faire la culbute.

something /ˈsʌmθɪŋ/ *pron.* & *n.* quelque chose (*m.*). **~ good**/*etc.*, quelque chose de bon/*etc.* **~ like**, un peu comme.

sometime /ˈsʌmtaɪm/ *adv.* un jour. —*a.* (*former*) ancien.

sometimes /ˈsʌmtaɪmz/ *adv.* quelquefois, parfois.

somewhat /ˈsʌmwɒt/ *adv.* quelque peu, un peu.

somewhere /ˈsʌmweə(r)/ *adv.* quelque part.

son /sʌn/ *n.* fils *m.* **~-in-law** *n.* (*pl.* **~s-in-law**) beau-fils *m.*, gendre *m.*

Sonar /ˈsəʊnɑː(r)/ *n.* sonar *m.*

sonata /səˈnɑːtə/ *n.* sonate *f.*

song /sɒŋ/ *n.* chanson *f.* **going for a ~**, à vendre pour une bouchée de pain.

sonic /ˈsɒnɪk/ *a.* **~ boom,** bang supersonique *m.*

sonnet /ˈsɒnɪt/ *n.* sonnet *m.*

sonny /ˈsʌnɪ/ *n.* (*fam.*) fiston *m.*

soon /suːn/ adv. (-er, -est) bientôt; (early) tôt. **I would ~er stay**, j'aimerais mieux rester. **~ after**, peu après. **~er or later**, tôt ou tard.

soot /sʊt/ n. suie f. **~y** a. couvert de suie.

sooth|e /suːð/ v.t. calmer. **~ing** a. (remedy, words, etc.) calmant.

sophisticated /səˈfɪstɪkeɪtɪd/ a. raffiné; (machine etc.) sophistiqué.

sophomore /ˈsɒfəmɔː(r)/ n. (Amer.) étudiant(e) de seconde année m. (f.).

soporific /sɒpəˈrɪfɪk/ a. soporifique.

sopping /ˈsɒpɪŋ/ a. trempé.

soppy /ˈsɒpɪ/ a. (-ier, -iest) (fam.) sentimental; (silly: fam.) bête.

soprano /səˈprɑːnəʊ/ n. (pl. -os) (voice) soprano m.; (singer) soprano m./f.

sorcerer /ˈsɔːsərə(r)/ n. sorcier m.

sordid /ˈsɔːdɪd/ a. sordide.

sore /ˈsɔː(r)/ a. (-er, -est) douloureux; (vexed) en rogne (**at, with**, contre). —n. plaie f.

sorely /ˈsɔːlɪ/ adv. fortement.

sorrow /ˈsɒrəʊ/ n. chagrin m. **~ful** a. triste.

sorry /ˈsɒrɪ/ a. (-ier, -iest) (regretful) désolé (**to, de**; **that**, que); (wretched) triste. **feel ~ for**, plaindre. **~!**, pardon!

sort /sɔːt/ n. genre m., sorte f., espèce f.; (person: fam.) type m. —v.t. **~ (out)**, (classify) trier. **be out of ~s**, ne pas être dans son assiette. **~ out**, (tidy) ranger; (arrange) arranger; (problem) régler.

soufflé /ˈsuːfleɪ/ n. soufflé m.

sought /sɔːt/ see **seek**.

soul /səʊl/ n. âme f.

soulful /ˈsəʊlfl/ a. plein de sentiment, très expressif.

sound[1] /saʊnd/ n. son m., bruit m. —v.t./i. sonner; (seem) sembler (**as if**, que). **~ a horn**, klaxonner. **~ barrier**, mur du son m. **~ like**, sembler être. **~-proof** a. insonorisé; v.t. insonoriser.

sound[2] /saʊnd/ a. (-er, -est) solide; (healthy) sain; (sensible) sensé. **~ asleep**, profondément endormi. **~ly** adv. solidement; (sleep) profondément.

sound[3] /saʊnd/ v.t. (test) sonder.

soup /suːp/ n. soupe f., potage m. **in the ~**, (sl.) dans le pétrin.

sour /ˈsaʊə(r)/ a. (-er, -est) aigre. —v.t./i. (s')aigrir.

source /sɔːs/ n. source f.

south /saʊθ/ n. sud m. —a. sud invar., du sud. —adv. vers le sud. **S~ Africa/America**, Afrique/Amérique du Sud f. **S~ African** a. & n. sud-africain(e) (m. (f.)). **S~ American** a. & n. sud-américain(e) (m. (f.)). **~-east** n. sud-est m. **~erly** /ˈsʌðəlɪ/ a. du sud. **~ward** a. au sud. **~wards** adv. vers le sud. **~-west** n. sud-ouest m.

southern /ˈsʌðən/ a. du sud. **~er** n. habitant(e) du sud m. (f.).

souvenir /suːvəˈnɪə(r)/ n. (thing) souvenir m.

sovereign /ˈsɒvrɪn/ n. & a. souverain(e) (m. (f.)). **~ty** n. souveraineté f.

Soviet /ˈsəʊvɪət/ a. soviétique. **the ~ Union**, l'Union soviétique f.

sow[1] /səʊ/ v.t. (p.t. **sowed**, p.p. **sowed** or **sown**) (seed etc.) semer; (land) ensemencer.

sow[2] /saʊ/ n. (pig) truie f.

soya /ˈsɔɪə/ n. **~ bean**, graine de soja f.

spa /spɑː/ n. station thermale f.

space /speɪs/ n. espace m.; (room) place f.; (period) période f. —a. (research etc.) spatial. —v.t. **~ (out)**, espacer. **space|craft** /ˈspeɪskrɑːft/ n. invar., **~ship** n. engin spatial m.

spacesuit /ˈspeɪss(j)uːt/ n. scaphandre m.

spacious /ˈspeɪʃəs/ a. spacieux.

spade[1] /speɪd/ n. (large, for garden) bêche f.; (child's) pelle f.

spade[2] /speɪd/ n. (cards) pique m.

spadework /ˈspeɪdwɜːk/ n. (fig.) travail préparatoire m.

spaghetti /spəˈgetɪ/ n. spaghetti m. pl.

Spa|in /speɪn/ n. Espagne f. **~niard** /ˈspænɪəd/ n. Espagnol(e) m. (f.). **~nish** /ˈspænɪʃ/ a. espagnol; n. (lang.) espagnol m.

span[1] /spæn/ n. (of arch) portée f.; (of wings) envergure f.; (of time) durée f. —v.t. (p.t. **spanned**) enjamber; (in time) embrasser.

span[2] /spæn/ see **spick**.

spaniel /ˈspænɪəl/ n. épagneul m.

spank /spæŋk/ v.t. donner une fessée à. **~ing** n. fessée f.

spanner /ˈspænə(r)/ n. (tool) clé (plate) f.; (adjustable) clé à molette f.

spar /spɑː(r)/ v.i. (p.t. **sparred**) s'entraîner (à la boxe).

spare /speə(r)/ v.t. épargner; (do without) se passer de; (afford to give) donner, accorder; (use with restraint) ménager. —*a.* (*surplus*) de trop; (*tyre, shoes, etc.*) de rechange; (*room, bed*) d'ami. —*n.* ~ (**part**), pièce de rechange *f.* ~ **time**, loisirs *m. pl.*

sparing /'speərɪŋ/ *a.* frugal. ~ **of**, avare de. ~**ly** *adv.* frugalement.

spark /spɑːk/ *n.* étincelle *f.* —*v.t.* ~ **off**, (*initiate*) provoquer. ~(**ing**)-**plug** *n.* bougie *f.*

sparkle /'spɑːkl/ *v.i.* étinceler. —*n.* étincellement *m.*

sparkling /'spɑːklɪŋ/ *a.* (*wine*) mousseux, pétillant.

sparrow /'spærəʊ/ *n.* moineau *m.*

sparse /spɑːs/ *a.* clairsemé. ~**ly** *adv.* (*furnished etc.*) peu.

spartan /'spɑːtn/ *a.* spartiate.

spasm /'spæzəm/ *n.* (*of muscle*) spasme *m.*; (*of coughing, anger, etc.*) accès *m.*

spasmodic /spæz'mɒdɪk/ *a.* intermittent.

spastic /'spæstɪk/ *n.* handicapé(e) moteur *m.* (*f.*).

spat /spæt/ *see* **spit**[1].

spate /speɪt/ *n.* **a** ~ **of**, (*letters etc.*) une avalanche de.

spatter /'spætə(r)/ *v.t.* éclabousser (**with**, de).

spatula /'spætjʊlə/ *n.* spatule *f.*

spawn /spɔːn/ *n.* frai *m.*, œufs *m. pl.* —*v.t.* pondre. —*v.i.* frayer.

speak /spiːk/ *v.i.* (*p.t.* **spoke**, *p.p.* **spoken**) parler. —*v.t.* (*say*) dire; (*language*) parler. ~ **up**, parler plus fort.

speaker /'spiːkə(r)/ *n.* (*in public*) orateur *m.*; (*loudspeaker*) haut-parleur *m.* **be a French**/**a good**/ *etc.* ~, parler français/bien/ *etc.*

spear /spɪə(r)/ *n.* lance *f.*

spearhead /'spɪəhed/ *n.* fer de lance *m.* —*v.t.* (*lead*) mener.

spearmint /'spɪəmɪnt/ *n.* menthe verte *f.* —*a.* à la menthe.

spec /spek/ *n.* **on** ~, (*as speculation*: *fam.*) à tout hasard.

special /'speʃl/ *a.* spécial; (*exceptional*) exceptionnel. ~**ity** /-ɪ'ælətɪ/ *n.* spécialité *f.* ~**ly** *adv.* spécialement. ~**ty** *n.* spécialité *f.*

specialist /'speʃəlɪst/ *n.* spécialiste *m.*/*f.*

specialize /'speʃəlaɪz/ *v.i.* se spécialiser (**in**, en). ~**d** *a.* spécialisé.

species /'spiːʃiːz/ *n. invar.* espèce *f.*

specific /spə'sɪfɪk/ *a.* précis, explicite. ~**ally** *adv.* explicitement; (*exactly*) précisément.

specif|**y** /'spesɪfaɪ/ *v.t.* spécifier.

~**ication** /-ɪ'keɪʃn/ *n.* spécification *f.*; (*details*) prescriptions *f. pl.*

specimen /'spesɪmɪn/ *n.* spécimen *m.*, échantillon *m.*

speck /spek/ *n.* (*stain*) (petite) tache *f.*; (*particle*) grain *m.*

speckled /'spekld/ *a.* tacheté.

specs /speks/ *n. pl.* (*fam.*) lunettes *f. pl.*

spectacle /'spektəkl/ *n.* spectacle *m.* ~**s**, lunettes *f. pl.*

spectacular /spek'tækjʊlə(r)/ *a.* spectaculaire.

spectator /spek'teɪtə(r)/ *n.* specta|teur, -trice *m.*, *f.*

spectre /'spektə(r)/ *n.* spectre *m.*

spectrum /'spektrəm/ *n.* (*pl.* **-tra**) spectre *m.*; (*of ideas etc.*) gamme *f.*

speculat|**e** /'spekjʊleɪt/ *v.i.* s'interroger (**about**, sur); (*comm.*) spéculer. ~**ion** /-'leɪʃn/ *n.* conjectures *f. pl.*; (*comm.*) spéculation *f.* ~**or** *n.* spécula|teur, -trice *m.*, *f.*

speech /spiːtʃ/ *n.* (*faculty*) parole *f.*; (*diction*) élocution *f.*; (*dialect*) langage *m.*; (*address*) discours *m.* ~**less** *a.* muet (**with**, de).

speed /spiːd/ *n.* (*of movement*) vitesse *f.*; (*swiftness*) rapidité *f.* —*v.i.* (*p.t.* **sped** /sped/) aller vite; (*p.t.* **speeded**) (*drive too fast*) aller trop vite. ~ **up**, accélérer; (*of pace*) s'accélérer. ~**ing** *n.* excès de vitesse *m.*

speedometer /spiː'dɒmɪtə(r)/ *n.* compteur (de vitesse) *m.*

speedway /'spiːdweɪ/ *n.* piste pour motos *f.*; (*Amer.*) autodrome *m.*

speed|**y** /'spiːdɪ/ *a.* (**-ier**, **-iest**) rapide. ~**ily** *adv.* rapidement.

spell[1] /spel/ *n.* (*magic*) charme *m.*, sortilège *m.*; (*curse*) sort *m.*

spell[2] /spel/ *v.t.*/*i.* (*p.t.* **spelled** *or* **spelt**) écrire; (*mean*) signifier. ~ **out**, épeler; (*explain*) expliquer. ~**ing** *n.* orthographe *f.*

spell[3] /spel/ *n.* (courte) période *f.*

spend /spend/ *v.t.* (*p.t.* **spent**) (*money*) dépenser (**on**, pour); (*time, holiday*) passer; (*energy*) consacrer (**on**, à). —*v.i.* dépenser.

spendthrift /'spendθrɪft/ *n.* dépens|ier, -ière *m.*, *f.*

spent /spent/ *see* **spend**. —*a.* (*used*) utilisé; (*person*) épuisé.

sperm /spɜːm/ *n.* (*pl.* **sperms** *or* **sperm**) (*semen*) sperme *m.*; (*cell*) spermatozoïde *m.*

spew /spjuː/ *v.t.*/*i.* vomir.

sphere /sfɪə(r)/ *n.* sphère *f.*
spherical /'sferɪkl/ *a.* sphérique.
sphinx /sfɪŋks/ *n.* sphinx *m.*
spic|e /spaɪs/ *n.* épice *f.*; (*fig.*) piquant *m.* ~y *a.* épicé; piquant.
spick /spɪk/ *a.* ~ **and span,** impeccable, d'une propreté parfaite.
spider /'spaɪdə(r)/ *n.* araignée *f.*
spik|e /spaɪk/ *n.* (*of metal etc.*) pointe *f.* ~y *a.* garni de pointes.
spill /spɪl/ *v.t.* (*p.t.* **spilled** *or* **spilt**) renverser, répandre. —*v.i.* se répandre. ~ **over,** déborder.
spin /spɪn/ *v.t./i.* (*p.t.* **spun,** *pres. p.* **spinning**) (*wool, web, of spinner*) filer; (*turn*) (faire) tourner; (*story*) débiter. —*n.* (*movement, excursion*) tour *m.* ~**-drier** *n.* essoreuse *f.* ~**ning-wheel** *n.* rouet *m.* ~**-off** *n.* avantage accessoire *m.*; (*by-product*) dérivé *m.*
spinach /'spɪnɪdʒ/ *n.* (*plant*) épinard *m.*; (*as food*) épinards *m. pl.*
spinal /'spaɪnl/ *a.* vertébral. ~ **cord,** moelle épinière *f.*
spindl|e /'spɪndl/ *n.* fuseau *m.* ~y *a.* filiforme, grêle.
spine /spaɪn/ *n.* colonne vertébrale *f.*; (*prickle*) piquant *m.*
spineless /'spaɪnlɪs/ *a.* (*fig.*) sans caractère, mou, lâche.
spinster /'spɪnstə(r)/ *n.* célibataire *f.*; (*pej.*) vieille fille *f.*
spiral /'spaɪərəl/ *a.* en spirale; (*staircase*) en colimaçon. —*n.* spirale *f.* —*v.i.* (*p.t.* **spiralled**) monter (en spirale).
spire /'spaɪə(r)/ *n.* flèche *f.*
spirit /'spɪrɪt/ *n.* esprit *m.*; (*boldness*) courage *m.* ~**s,** (*morale*) moral *m.*; (*drink*) spiritueux *m. pl.* —*v.t.* ~ **away,** faire disparaître. ~**-lamp** *n.* lampe à alcool *f.* ~**level** *n.* niveau à bulle *m.*
spirited /'spɪrɪtɪd/ *a.* fougueux.
spiritual /'spɪrɪtʃʊəl/ *a.* spirituel. —*n.* (*song*) (negro-)spiritual *m.*
spiritualis|t /'spɪrɪtʃʊəlɪst/ *n.* spirite *m./f.* ~**m** /-zəm/ *n.* spiritisme *m.*
spit[1] /spɪt/ *v.t./i.* (*p.t.* **spat** *or* **spit,** *pres. p.* **spitting**) cracher; (*of rain*) crachiner. —*n.* crachat(s) *m.* (*pl.*). **the** ~**ting image of,** le portrait craché *or* vivant de.
spit[2] /spɪt/ *n.* (*for meat*) broche *f.*
spite /spaɪt/ *n.* rancune *f.* —*v.t.* contrarier. **in** ~ **of,** malgré. ~**ful** *a.* méchant, rancunier. ~**fully** *adv.* méchamment.

spittle /'spɪtl/ *n.* crachat(s) *m.* (*pl.*).
splash /splæʃ/ *v.t.* éclabousser. —*v.i.* faire des éclaboussures. ~ (**about**), patauger. —*n.* (*act, mark*) éclaboussure *f.*; (*sound*) plouf *m.*; (*of colour*) tache *f.*
spleen /spli:n/ *n.* (*anat.*) rate *f.*
splendid /'splendɪd/ *a.* magnifique, splendide.
splendour /'splendə(r)/ *n.* splendeur *f.*, éclat *m.*
splint /splɪnt/ *n.* (*med.*) éclisse *f.*
splinter /'splɪntə(r)/ *n.* éclat *m.*; (*in finger*) écharde *f.* ~ **group,** groupe dissident *m.*
split /splɪt/ *v.t./i.* (*p.t.* **split,** *pres. p.* **splitting**) (se) fendre; (*tear*) (se) déchirer; (*divide*) (se) diviser; (*share*) partager; (*of friends*) rompre. —*n.* fente *f.*; déchirure *f.*; (*share: fam.*) part *f.*, partage *m.*; (*quarrel*) rupture *f.*; (*pol.*) scission *f.* **a** ~ **second,** un rien de temps. ~ **one's sides,** se tordre (de rire).
splurge /splɜ:dʒ/ *v.i.* (*fam.*) faire de folles dépenses.
splutter /'splʌtə(r)/ *v.i.* crachoter; (*stammer*) bafouiller; (*engine*) tousser; (*fat*) crépiter.
spoil /spɔɪl/ *v.t.* (*p.t.* **spoilt** *or* **spoiled**) (*pamper*) gâter; (*ruin*) abîmer; (*mar*) gâcher, gâter. —*n.* ~(**s**), (*plunder*) butin *m.* ~**-sport** *n.* trouble-fête *m./f. invar.*
spoke[1] /spəʊk/ *n.* rayon *m.*
spoke[2], **spoken** /spəʊk, 'spəʊkən/ *see* **speak.**
spokesman /'spəʊksmən/ *n.* (*pl.* **-men**) porte-parole *m. invar.*
sponge /spʌndʒ/ *n.* éponge *f.* —*v.t.* éponger. —*v.i.* ~ **on,** vivre aux crochets de. ~**-cake** *n.* gâteau de Savoie *m.* ~**r** /-ə(r)/ *n.* parasite *m.* **spongy** *a.* spongieux.
sponsor /'spɒnsə(r)/ *n.* personne qui assure le patronage *f.*; (*surety*) garant *m.*; (*for membership*) parrain *m.*, marraine *f.* —*v.t.* patronner; (*member*) parrainer. ~**ship** *n.* patronage *m.*; parrainage *m.*
spontane|ous /spɒn'teɪnɪəs/ *a.* spontané. ~**ity** /-tə'ni:ətɪ/ *n.* spontanéité *f.* ~**ously** *adv.* spontanément.
spoof /spu:f/ *n.* (*fam.*) parodie *f.*
spooky /'spu:kɪ/ *a.* (**-ier, -iest**) (*fam.*) qui donne des frissons.
spool /spu:l/ *n.* bobine *f.*
spoon /spu:n/ *n.* cuiller *f.* ~**-feed** *v.t.*

(*p.t.* **-fed**) nourrir à la cuiller; (*help*: *fig.*) mâcher la besogne à. ∼**ful** *n.* (*pl.* **-fuls**) cuillerée *f.*

sporadic /spə'rædɪk/ *a.* sporadique.

sport /spɔːt/ *n.* sport *m.* (**good**) ∼, (*person*: *sl.*) chic type *m.* —*v.t.* (*display*) exhiber, arborer. ∼**s car/coat**, voiture/veste de sport *f.* ∼**y** *a.* (*fam.*) sportif.

sporting /'spɔːtɪŋ/ *a.* sportif. **a ∼ chance**, une assez bonne chance.

sports|man /'spɔːtsmən/ *n.* (*pl.* **-men**) sportif *m.* ∼**manship** *n.* sportivité *f.* ∼**woman** *n.* (*pl.* **-women**) sportive *f.*

spot /spɒt/ *n.* (*mark, stain*) tache *f.*; (*dot*) point *m.*; (*in pattern*) pois *m.*; (*drop*) goutte *f.*; (*place*) endroit *m.*; (*pimple*) bouton *m.* —*v.t.* (*p.t.* **spotted**) (*fam.*) apercevoir. **a ∼ of**, (*fam.*) un peu de. **be in a ∼**, (*fam.*) avoir des problèmes. **on the ∼**, sur place; (*without delay*) sur le coup. ∼ **check**, contrôle à l'improviste *m.* ∼**ted** *a.* tacheté; (*fabric*) à pois. ∼**ty** *a.* (*skin*) boutonneux.

spotless /'spɒtlɪs/ *a.* impeccable.

spotlight /'spɒtlaɪt/ *n.* (*lamp*) projecteur *m.*, spot *m.*

spouse /spaʊz/ *n.* époux *m.*, épouse *f.*

spout /spaʊt/ *n.* (*of vessel*) bec *m.*; (*of liquid*) jet *m.* —*v.i.* jaillir. **up the ∼**, (*ruined*: *sl.*) fichu.

sprain /spreɪn/ *n.* entorse *f.*, foulure *f.* —*v.t.* ∼ **one's wrist**/*etc.*, se fouler le poignet/*etc.*

sprang /spræŋ/ *see* **spring.**

sprawl /sprɔːl/ *v.i.* (*town, person, etc.*) s'étaler. —*n.* étalement *m.*

spray[1] /spreɪ/ *n.* (*of flowers*) gerbe *f.*

spray[2] /spreɪ/ *n.* (*water*) gerbe d'eau *f.*; (*from sea*) embruns *m. pl.*; (*device*) bombe *f.*, atomiseur *m.* —*v.t.* (*surface, insecticide*) vaporiser; (*plant etc.*) arroser.

spread /spred/ *v.t./i.* (*p.t.* **spread**) (*stretch, extend*) (s')étendre; (*news, fear, etc.*) (se) répandre; (*illness*) (se) propager; (*butter etc.*) (s')étaler. —*n.* propagation *f.*; (*paste*) pâte à tartiner *f.* ∼**-eagled** *a.* bras et jambes écartés.

spree /spriː/ *n.* **go on a ∼**, (*have fun*: *fam.*) faire la noce.

sprig /sprɪg/ *n.* (*shoot*) brin *m.*; (*twig*) brindille *f.*

sprightly /'spraɪtlɪ/ *a.* (**-ier, -iest**) alerte, vif.

spring /sprɪŋ/ *v.i.* (*p.t.* **sprang**, *p.p.* **sprung**) bondir. —*v.t.* faire, an-

noncer, *etc.* à l'improviste (**on**, à). —*n.* bond *m.*; (*device*) ressort *m.*; (*season*) printemps *m.*; (*of water*) source *f.* ∼**-clean** *v.t.* nettoyer de fond en comble. ∼ **from**, provenir de. ∼ **up**, surgir.

springboard /'sprɪŋbɔːd/ *n.* tremplin *m.*

springtime /'sprɪŋtaɪm/ *n.* printemps *m.*

springy /'sprɪŋɪ/ *a.* (**-ier, -iest**) élastique.

sprinkle /sprɪŋkl/ *v.t.* (*with liquid*) arroser (**with**, de); (*with salt, flour*) saupoudrer (**with**, de). ∼ **sand**/*etc.*, répandre du sable/*etc.*

sprinkling /'sprɪŋklɪŋ/ *n.* (*amount*) petite quantité *f.*

sprint /sprɪnt/ *v.i.* (*sport*) sprinter. —*n.* sprint *m.* ∼**er** *n.* sprinteu|r, -se *m.*, *f.*

sprite /spraɪt/ *n.* lutin *m.*

sprout /spraʊt/ *v.t./i.* pousser. —*n.* (*on plant etc.*) pousse *f.* (**Brussels**) ∼**s**, choux de Bruxelles *m. pl.*

spruce[1] /spruːs/ *a.* pimpant. —*v.t.* ∼ **o.s. up**, se faire beau.

spruce[2] /spruːs/ *n.* (*tree*) épicéa *m.*

sprung /sprʌŋ/ *see* **spring.** —*a.* (*mattress etc.*) à ressorts.

spry /spraɪ/ *a.* (**spryer, spryest**) alerte, vif.

spud /spʌd/ *n.* (*sl.*) patate *f.*

spun /spʌn/ *see* **spin.**

spur /spɜː(r)/ *n.* (*of rider, cock, etc.*) éperon *m.*; (*stimulus*) aiguillon *m.* —*v.t.* (*p.t.* **spurred**) éperonner. **on the ∼ of the moment**, sous l'impulsion du moment.

spurious /'spjʊərɪəs/ *a.* faux.

spurn /spɜːn/ *v.t.* repousser.

spurt /spɜːt/ *v.i.* jaillir; (*fig.*) accélérer. —*n.* jet *m.*; (*fig.*) élan *m.*

spy /spaɪ/ *n.* espion(ne) *m.* (*f.*). —*v.i.* espionner. —*v.t.* apercevoir. ∼ **on**, espionner. ∼ **out**, reconnaître.

squabble /'skwɒbl/ *v.i.* se chamailler. —*n.* chamaillerie *f.*

squad /skwɒd/ *n.* (*of soldiers etc.*) escouade *f.*; (*sport*) équipe *f.*

squadron /'skwɒdrən/ *n.* (*mil.*) escadron *m.*; (*aviat.*) escadrille *f.*; (*naut.*) escadre *f.*

squal|id /'skwɒlɪd/ *a.* sordide. ∼**or** *n.* conditions sordides *f. pl.*

squall /skwɔːl/ *n.* rafale *f.*

squander /'skwɒndə(r)/ *v.t.* (*money, time, etc.*) gaspiller.

square /skweə(r)/ *n.* carré *m.*; (*open*

space in town) place *f.*; (*instrument*) équerre *f.* —*a.* carré; (*honest*) honnête; (*meal*) solide. (all) ~, (*quits*) quitte. —*v.t.* (*settle*) régler. —*v.i.* (*agree*) s'accorder. ~ **up to**, faire face à. ~**ly** *adv.* carrément.

squash /skwɒʃ/ *v.t.* écraser; (*crowd*) serrer. —*n.* (*game*) squash *m.*; (*marrow*: *Amer.*) courge *f.* **lemon** ~, citronnade *f.* **orange** ~, orangeade *f.* ~**y** *a.* mou.

squat /skwɒt/ *v.i.* (*p.t.* **squatted**) s'accroupir. —*a.* (*dumpy*) trapu.

squatter /ˈskwɒtə(r)/ *n.* squatter *m.*

squawk /skwɔːk/ *n.* cri rauque *m.* —*v.i.* pousser un cri rauque.

squeak /skwiːk/ *n.* petit cri *m.*; (*of door etc.*) grincement *m.* —*v.i.* crier; grincer. ~**y** *a.* grinçant.

squeal /skwiːl/ *n.* cri aigu *m.* —*v.i.* pousser un cri aigu. ~ **on**, (*inform on*: *sl.*) dénoncer.

squeamish /ˈskwiːmɪʃ/ *a.* (trop) délicat, facilement dégoûté.

squeeze /skwiːz/ *v.t.* presser; (*hand, arm*) serrer; (*extract*) exprimer (**from**, de); (*extort*) soutirer (**from**, à). —*v.i.* (*force one's way*) se glisser. —*n.* pression *f.*; (*comm.*) restrictions de crédit *f. pl.*

squelch /skweltʃ/ *v.i.* faire flic flac. —*v.t.* (*suppress*) supprimer.

squid /skwɪd/ *n.* calmar *m.*

squiggle /ˈskwɪɡl/ *n.* ligne onduleuse *f.*

squint /skwɪnt/ *v.i.* loucher; (*with half-shut eyes*) plisser les yeux. —*n.* (*med.*) strabisme *m.*

squire /ˈskwaɪə(r)/ *n.* propriétaire terrien *m.*

squirm /skwɜːm/ *v.i.* se tortiller.

squirrel /ˈskwɪrəl, *Amer.* ˈskwɜːrəl/ *n.* écureuil *m.*

squirt /skwɜːt/ *v.t./i.* (faire) jaillir. —*n.* jet *m.*

stab /stæb/ *v.t.* (*p.t.* **stabbed**) (*with knife etc.*) poignarder. —*n.* coup (de couteau) *m.*

stabilize /ˈsteɪbəlaɪz/ *v.t.* stabiliser.

stab|le[1] /ˈsteɪbl/ *a.* (-er, -est) stable. ~**ility** /stəˈbɪlətɪ/ *n.* stabilité *f.*

stable[2] /ˈsteɪbl/ *n.* écurie *f.* ~**-boy** *n.* lad *m.*

stack /stæk/ *n.* tas *m.* —*v.t.* ~ (**up**), entasser, empiler.

stadium /ˈsteɪdɪəm/ *n.* stade *m.*

staff /stɑːf/ *n.* personnel *m.*; (*in school*) professeurs *m. pl.*; (*mil.*) état-major

m.; (*stick*) bâton *m.* —*v.t.* pourvoir en personnel.

stag /stæɡ/ *n.* cerf *m.* ~**-party** *n.* réunion d'hommes *f.*

stage /steɪdʒ/ *n.* (*theatre*) scène *f.*; (*phase*) stade *m.*, étape *f.*; (*platform in hall*) estrade *f.* —*v.t.* mettre en scène; (*fig.*) organiser. **go on the** ~, faire du théâtre. ~**-coach** *n.* (*old use*) diligence *f.* ~ **fright**, trac *m.*

stagger /ˈstæɡə(r)/ *v.i.* chanceler. —*v.t.* (*shock*) stupéfier; (*holidays etc.*) étaler. ~**ing** *a.* stupéfiant.

stagnant /ˈstæɡnənt/ *a.* stagnant.

stagnat|e /stæɡˈneɪt/ *v.i.* stagner. ~**ion** /-ʃn/ *n.* stagnation *f.*

staid /steɪd/ *a.* sérieux.

stain /steɪn/ *v.t.* tacher; (*wood etc.*) colorer. —*n.* tache *f.*; (*colouring*) colorant *m.* ~**ed glass window**, vitrail *m.* ~**less steel**, acier inoxydable *m.*

stair /steə(r)/ *n.* marche *f.* ~**s**, escalier *m.*

stair|case /ˈsteəkeɪs/, ~**way** *ns.* escalier *m.*

stake /steɪk/ *n.* (*post*) pieu *m.*; (*wager*) enjeu *m.* —*v.t.* (*area*) jalonner; (*wager*) jouer. **at** ~, en jeu. ~ **a claim to**, revendiquer.

stale /steɪl/ *a.* (-er, -est) pas frais; (*bread*) rassis; (*smell*) rance; (*news*) vieux. ~**ness** *n.* manque de fraîcheur *m.*

stalemate /ˈsteɪlmeɪt/ *n.* (*chess*) pat *m.*; (*fig.*) impasse *f.*

stalk[1] /stɔːk/ *n.* (*of plant*) tige *f.*

stalk[2] /stɔːk/ *v.i.* marcher dignement. —*v.t.* (*prey*) traquer.

stall /stɔːl/ *n.* (*in stable*) stalle *f.*; (*in market*) éventaire *m.* ~**s**, (*theatre*) orchestre *m.* —*v.t./i.* (*auto.*) caler. ~ (**for time**), temporiser.

stallion /ˈstæljən/ *n.* étalon *m.*

stalwart /ˈstɔːlwət/ *n.* (*supporter*) partisan(e) fidèle *m.* (*f.*).

stamina /ˈstæmɪnə/ *n.* résistance *f.*

stammer /ˈstæmə(r)/ *v.t./i.* bégayer. —*n.* bégaiement *m.*

stamp /stæmp/ *v.t./i.* ~ (**one's foot**), taper du pied. —*v.t.* (*letter etc.*) timbrer. —*n.* (*for postage, marking*) timbre *m.*; (*mark*: *fig.*) sceau *m.* ~**-collecting** *n.* philatélie *f.* ~ **out**, supprimer.

stampede /stæmˈpiːd/ *n.* fuite désordonnée *f.*; (*rush*: *fig.*) ruée *f.* —*v.i.* s'enfuir en désordre; se ruer.

stance /stæns/ *n.* position *f.*

stand /stænd/ *v.i.* (*p.t.* **stood**) être *or* se tenir (debout); (*rise*) se lever; (*be situated*) se trouver; (*rest*) reposer; (*pol.*) être candidat (**for**, à). —*v.t.* mettre (debout); (*tolerate*) supporter. —*n.* position *f.*; (*mil.*) résistance *f.*; (*for lamp etc.*) support *m.*; (*at fair*) stand *m.*; (*in street*) kiosque *m.*; (*for spectators*) tribune *f.*; (*jurid., Amer.*) barre *f.* **~ a chance,** avoir une chance. **~ back,** reculer. **~ by** *or* **around,** ne rien faire. **~ by,** (*be ready*) se tenir prêt; (*promise, person*) rester fidèle à. **~-by** *a.* de réserve; *n.* **be a ~-by,** être de réserve. **~ down,** se désister. **~ for,** représenter; (*fam.*) supporter. **~ in for,** remplacer. **~-in** *n.* remplaçant(e) *m.* (*f.*). **~ in line,** (*Amer.*) faire la queue. **~-offish** *a.* (*fam.*) distant. **~ out,** (*be conspicuous*) ressortir. **~ to reason,** être logique. **~ up,** se lever. **~ up for,** défendre. **~ up to,** résister à.

standard /'stændəd/ *n.* norme *f.*; (*level*) niveau (voulu) *m.*; (*flag*) étendard *m.* **~s,** (*morals*) principes *m. pl.* —*a.* ordinaire. **~ lamp,** lampadaire *m.* **~ of living,** niveau de vie *m.*

standardize /'stændədaɪz/ *v.t.* standardiser.

standing /'stændɪŋ/ *a.* debout *invar.*; (*army, offer*) permanent. —*n.* position *f.*, réputation *f.*; (*duration*) durée *f.*

standpoint /'stændpɔɪnt/ *n.* point de vue *m.*

standstill /'stændstɪl/ *n.* **at a ~,** immobile. **bring/come to a ~,** (s')immobiliser.

stank /stæŋk/ *see* **stink.**

stanza /'stænzə/ *n.* strophe *f.*

staple[1] /'steɪpl/ *n.* agrafe *f.* —*v.t.* agrafer. **~r** /-ə(r)/ *n.* agrafeuse *f.*

staple[2] /'steɪpl/ *a.* principal, de base. —*n.* (*comm.*) article de base *m.*

star /stɑː(r)/ *n.* étoile *f.*; (*famous person*) vedette *f.* —*v.t.* (*p.t.* **starred**) (*of film*) avoir pour vedette. —*v.i.* **~ in,** être la vedette de. **~dom** *n.* célébrité *f.*

starboard /'stɑːbəd/ *n.* tribord *m.*

starch /stɑːtʃ/ *n.* amidon *m.*; (*in food*) fécule *f.* —*v.t.* amidonner. **~y** *a.* féculent; (*stiff*) guindé.

stare /steə(r)/ *v.i.* **~ at,** regarder fixement. —*n.* regard fixe *m.*

starfish /'stɑːfɪʃ/ *n.* étoile de mer *f.*

stark /stɑːk/ *a.* (**-er, -est**) (*desolate*) désolé; (*severe*) austère; (*utter*) complet; (*fact etc.*) brutal. —*adv.* complètement.

starling /'stɑːlɪŋ/ *n.* étourneau *m.*

starlit /'stɑːlɪt/ *a.* étoilé.

starry /'stɑːrɪ/ *a.* étoilé. **~-eyed** *a.* naïf, (*trop*) optimiste.

start /stɑːt/ *v.t./i.* commencer; (*machine*) (se) mettre en marche; (*fashion etc.*) lancer; (*leave*) partir; (*cause*) provoquer; (*jump*) sursauter; (*of vehicle*) démarrer. —*n.* commencement *m.*, début *m.*; (*of race*) départ *m.*; (*lead*) avance *f.*; (*jump*) sursaut *m.* **~ to do,** commencer *or* se mettre à faire. **~er** *n.* (*auto.*) démarreur *m.*; (*runner*) partant *m.*; (*culin.*) entrée *f.*

startle /'stɑːtl/ *v.t.* (*make jump*) faire tressaillir; (*shock*) alarmer.

starv|e /stɑːv/ *v.i.* mourir de faim. —*v.t.* affamer; (*deprive*) priver. **~ation** /-'veɪʃn/ *n.* faim *f.*

stash /stæʃ/ *v.t.* (*hide*: *sl.*) cacher.

state /steɪt/ *n.* état *m.*; (*pomp*) apparat *m.* **S~,** (*pol.*) État *m.* —*a.* d'État, de l'État; (*school*) public. —*v.t.* affirmer (**that,** que); (*views*) exprimer; (*fix*) fixer.

stateless /'steɪtlɪs/ *a.* apatride.

stately /'steɪtlɪ/ *a.* (**-ier, -iest**) majestueux. **~ home,** château *m.*

statement /'steɪtmənt/ *n.* déclaration *f.*; (*of account*) relevé *m.*

statesman /'steɪtsmən/ *n.* (*pl.* **-men**) homme d'État *m.*

static /'stætɪk/ *a.* statique. —*n.* (*radio, TV*) parasites *m. pl.*

station /'steɪʃn/ *n.* station *f.*; (*rail.*) gare *f.*; (*mil.*) poste *m.*; (*rank*) condition *f.* —*v.t.* poster, placer. **~ed at** *or* **in,** (*mil.*) en garnison à.

stationary /'steɪʃənrɪ/ *a.* immobile, stationnaire; (*vehicle*) à l'arrêt.

stationer /'steɪʃnə(r)/ *n.* papet|ier, -ière *m.*, *f.* **~'s shop,** papeterie *f.* **~y** *n.* papeterie *f.*

statistic /stə'tɪstɪk/ *n.* statistique *f.* **~s,** statistique *f.* **~al** *a.* statistique.

statue /'stætʃuː/ *n.* statue *f.*

statuesque /stætʃʊ'esk/ *a.* sculptural.

stature /'stætʃə(r)/ *n.* stature *f.*

status /'steɪtəs/ *n.* (*pl.* **-uses**) situation *f.*, statut *m.*; (*prestige*) standing *m.* **~ quo,** statu quo *m.*

statut|e /'stætʃuːt/ *n.* loi *f.* **~es,** (*rules*) statuts *m. pl.* **~ory** /-ʊtrɪ/ *a.* statutaire; (*holiday*) légal.

staunch /stɔːntʃ/ a. (-er, -est) (friend etc.) loyal, fidèle.

stave /steɪv/ n. (mus.) portée f. —v.t. ～ **off**, éviter, conjurer.

stay /steɪ/ v.i. rester; (spend time) séjourner; (reside) loger. —v.t. (hunger) tromper. —n. séjour m. ～ **away from**, (school etc.) ne pas aller à. ～ **in**, rester à la maison. ～ **up (late)**, veiller, se coucher tard.

stead /sted/ n. **in my**/**your**/etc. ～, à ma/votre/etc. place.

steadfast /'stedfɑːst/ a. ferme.

stead|y /'stedɪ/ a. (-ier, -iest) stable; (hand, voice) ferme; (regular) régulier; (staid) sérieux. —v.t. maintenir, assurer; (calm) calmer. ～**ily** adv. fermement; régulièrement.

steak /steɪk/ n. steak m., bifteck m.

steal /stiːl/ v.t./i. (p.t. **stole**, p.p. **stolen**) voler (from s.o., à qn.).

stealth /stelθ/ n. **by** ～, furtivement. ～**y** a. furtif.

steam /stiːm/ n. vapeur f.; (on glass) buée f. —v.t. (cook) cuire à la vapeur; (window) embuer. —v.i. fumer. ～**engine** n. locomotive à vapeur f. ～**y** a. humide.

steam|er /'stiːmə(r)/, ～**ship** ns. (bateau à) vapeur m.

steamroller /'stiːmrəʊlə(r)/ n. rouleau compresseur m.

steel /stiːl/ n. acier m. —v. pr. ～ **o.s.**, s'endurcir, se cuirasser. ～ **industry**, sidérurgie f.

steep[1] /stiːp/ v.t. (soak) tremper. ～**ed in**, (fig.) imprégné de.

steep[2] /stiːp/ a. (-er, -est) raide, rapide. (price: fam.) excessif. ～**ly** adv. **rise** ～**ly**, (slope, price) monter rapidement.

steeple /'stiːpl/ n. clocher m.

steeplechase /'stiːpltʃeɪs/ n. (race) steeple(-chase) m.

steer[1] /stɪə(r)/ n. (ox) bouvillon m.

steer[2] /stɪə(r)/ v.t. diriger; (ship) gouverner; (fig.) guider. —v.i. (in ship) gouverner. ～ **clear of**, éviter. ～**ing** n. (auto.) direction f. ～**ing-wheel** n. volant m.

stem[1] /stem/ n. tige f. —v.i. (p.t. **stemmed**). ～ **from**, provenir de.

stem[2] /stem/ v.t. (p.t. **stemmed**) (check, stop) endiguer, contenir.

stench /stentʃ/ n. puanteur f.

stencil /'stensl/ n. pochoir m.; (for typing) stencil m. —v.t. (p.t. **stencilled**) (document) polycopier.

stenographer /ste'nɒɡrəfə(r)/ n. (Amer.) sténodactylo f.

step /step/ v.i. (p.t. **stepped**) marcher, aller. —v.t. ～ **up**, augmenter. —n. pas m.; (stair) marche f.; (of train) marchepied m.; (action) mesure f. ～**s**, (ladder) escabeau m. **in** ～, au pas; (fig.) conforme (**with**, à). ～ **down**, (resign) démissionner. ～ **in**, (intervene) intervenir. ～**-ladder** n. escabeau m. ～**ping-stone** n. (fig.) tremplin m.

step|brother /'stepbrʌðə(r)/ n. demi-frère m. ～**daughter** n. belle-fille f. ～**father** n. beau-père m. ～**mother** n. belle-mère f. ～**sister** n. demi-sœur f. ～**son** n. beau-fils m.

stereo /'steriəʊ/ n. (pl. -os) stéréo f.; (record-player) chaîne stéréo f. —a. stéréo invar. ～**phonic** /-ə'fɒnɪk/ a. stéréophonique.

stereotype /'steriətaɪp/ n. stéréotype m. ～**d** a. stéréotypé.

steril|e /'steraɪl, Amer. 'sterəl/ a. stérile. ～**ity** /stə'rɪlətɪ/ n. stérilité f.

steriliz|e /'steralaɪz/ v.t. stériliser. ～**ation** /-'zeɪʃn/ n. stérilisation f.

sterling /'stɜːlɪŋ/ n. livre(s) sterling f. (pl.). —a. sterling invar.; (silver) fin; (fig.) excellent.

stern[1] /stɜːn/ a. (-er, -est) sévère.

stern[2] /stɜːn/ n. (of ship) arrière m.

stethoscope /'steθəskəʊp/ n. stéthoscope m.

stew /stjuː/ v.t./i. cuire à la casserole. —n. ragoût m. ～**ed fruit**, compote f. ～**ed tea**, thé trop infusé m. ～**-pan** n. cocotte f.

steward /stjʊəd/ n. (of club etc.) intendant m.; (on ship etc.) steward m. ～**ess** /-'des/ n. hôtesse f.

stick[1] /stɪk/ n. bâton m.; (for walking) canne f.

stick[2] /stɪk/ v.t. (p.t. **stuck**) (glue) coller; (thrust) enfoncer; (put: fam.) mettre; (endure: sl.) supporter. —v.i. (adhere) coller, adhérer; (to pan) attacher; (remain: fam.) rester; (be jammed) être coincé. **be stuck with s.o.**, (fam.) se farcir qn. ～**-in-the-mud** n. encroûté(e) m. (f.). ～ **out** v.t. (head etc.) sortir; (tongue) tirer; v.i. (protrude) dépasser. ～ **to**, (promise etc.) rester fidèle à. ～ **up for**, (fam.) défendre. ～**ing-plaster** n. sparadrap m.

sticker /'stɪkə(r)/ n. autocollant m.

stickler /'stɪklə(r)/ *n.* be a ~ for, insister sur.

sticky /'stɪkɪ/ *a.* (-ier, -iest) poisseux; (*label, tape*) adhésif.

stiff /stɪf/ *a.* (-er, -est) raide; (*limb, joint*) ankylosé; (*tough*) dur; (*drink*) fort; (*price*) élevé; (*manner*) guindé. ~ neck, torticolis *m.* ~ness *n.* raideur *f.*

stiffen /'stɪfn/ *v.t./i.* (se) raidir.

stifle /'staɪfl/ *v.t./i.* étouffer.

stigma /'stɪgmə/ *n.* (*pl.* -as) stigmate *m.* ~tize *v.t.* stigmatiser.

stile /staɪl/ *n.* échalier *m.*

still[1] /stɪl/ *a.* immobile; (*quiet*) calme, tranquille. —*n.* silence *m.* —*adv.* encore, toujours; (*even*) encore; (*nevertheless*) tout de même. ~ life, nature morte *f.*

still[2] /stɪl/ *n.* (*apparatus*) alambic *m.*

stillborn /'stɪlbɔːn/ *a.* mort-né.

stilted /'stɪltɪd/ *a.* guindé.

stilts /stɪlts/ *n. pl.* échasses *f. pl.*

stimul|ate /'stɪmjʊleɪt/ *v.t.* stimuler. ~ant *n.* stimulant *m.* ~ation /-'leɪʃn/ *n.* stimulation *f.*

stimulus /'stɪmjʊləs/ *n.* (*pl.* -li /-laɪ/) (*spur*) stimulant *m.*

sting /stɪŋ/ *n.* piqûre *f.*; (*organ*) dard *m.* —*v.t./i.* (*p.t.* **stung**) piquer. ~ing *a.* (*fig.*) cinglant.

stingy /'stɪndʒɪ/ *a.* (-ier, -iest) avare (with, de).

stink /stɪŋk/ *n.* puanteur *f.* —*v.i.* (*p.t.* **stank** *or* **stunk**, *p.p.* **stunk**). ~ (of), puer. —*v.t.* ~ out, (*room etc.*) empester.

stinker /'stɪŋkə(r)/ *n.* (*thing: sl.*) vacherie *f.*; (*person: sl.*) vache *f.*

stint /stɪnt/ *v.i.* ~ on, lésiner sur. —*n.* (*work*) part de travail *f.*

stipend /'staɪpend/ *n.* (*of clergyman*) traitement *m.*

stipulat|e /'stɪpjʊleɪt/ *v.t.* stipuler. ~ion /-'leɪʃn/ *n.* stipulation *f.*

stir /stɜː(r)/ *v.t./i.* (*p.t.* **stirred**) (*move*) remuer; (*excite*) exciter. —*n.* agitation *f.* ~ up, (*trouble etc.*) provoquer.

stirrup /'stɪrəp/ *n.* étrier *m.*

stitch /stɪtʃ/ *n.* point *m.*; (*in knitting*) maille *f.*; (*med.*) point de suture *m.* —*v.t.* coudre. be in ~es, (*fam.*) avoir le fou rire.

stoat /stəʊt/ *n.* hermine *f.*

stock /stɒk/ *n.* réserve *f.*; (*comm.*) stock *m.*; (*financial*) valeurs *f. pl.*; (*family*) souche *f.*; (*soup*) bouillon *m.* —*a.* (*goods*) courant. —*v.t.* (*shop etc.*) approvisionner; (*sell*) vendre.

—*v.i.* ~ up, s'approvisionner (with, de). ~-car *n.* stock-car *m.* S~ Exchange, ~ market, Bourse *f.* ~ phrase, cliché *m.* ~-taking *n.* (*comm.*) inventaire *m.* take ~, (*fig.*) faire le point.

stockbroker /'stɒkbrəʊkə(r)/ *n.* agent de change *m.*

stocking /'stɒkɪŋ/ *n.* bas *m.*

stockist /'stɒkɪst/ *n.* stockiste *m.*

stockpile /'stɒkpaɪl/ *n.* stock *m.* —*v.t.* stocker; (*arms*) amasser.

stocky /'stɒkɪ/ *a.* (-ier, -iest) trapu.

stodg|e /stɒdʒ/ *n.* (*fam.*) aliment(s) lourd(s) *m.* (*pl.*). ~y *a.* lourd.

stoic /'stəʊɪk/ *n.* stoïque *m./f.* ~al *a.* stoïque. ~ism /-sɪzəm/ *n.* stoïcisme *m.*

stoke /stəʊk/ *v.t.* (*boiler, fire*) garnir, alimenter.

stole[1] /stəʊl/ *n.* (*garment*) étole *f.*

stole[2], **stolen** /stəʊl, 'stəʊlən/ *see* **steal.**

stolid /'stɒlɪd/ *a.* flegmatique.

stomach /'stʌmək/ *n.* estomac *m.*; (*abdomen*) ventre *m.* —*v.t.* (*put up with*) supporter. ~-ache *n.* mal à l'estomac *or* au ventre *m.*

ston|e /stəʊn/ *n.* pierre *f.*; (*pebble*) caillou *m.*; (*in fruit*) noyau *m.*; (*weight*) 6.350 kg. —*a.* de pierre. —*v.t.* lapider; (*fruit*) dénoyauter. ~y *a.* pierreux. ~y-broke *a.* (*sl.*) fauché.

stone- /stəʊn/ *pref.* complètement.

stonemason /'stəʊnmeɪsn/ *n.* maçon *m.*, tailleur de pierre *m.*

stood /stʊd/ *see* **stand.**

stooge /stuːdʒ/ *n.* (*actor*) comparse *m./f.*; (*fig.*) fantoche *m.*, laquais *m.*

stool /stuːl/ *n.* tabouret *m.*

stoop /stuːp/ *v.i.* (*bend*) se baisser; (*condescend*) s'abaisser. —*n.* have a ~, être voûté.

stop /stɒp/ *v.t./i.* (*p.t.* **stopped**) (s')arrêter; (*prevent*) empêcher (from, de); (*hole, leak, etc.*) boucher; (*of pain, noise, etc.*) cesser; (*stay: fam.*) rester. —*n.* arrêt *m.*; (*full stop*) point *m.* ~-(over), halte *f.*; (*port of call*) escale *f.* ~-light *n.* (*on vehicle*) stop *m.* ~-watch *n.* chronomètre *m.*

stopgap /'stɒpgæp/ *n.* bouchetrou *m.* —*a.* intérimaire.

stoppage /'stɒpɪdʒ/ *n.* arrêt *m.*; (*of work*) arrêt de travail *m.*; (*of pay*) retenue *f.*

stopper /'stɒpə(r)/ *n.* bouchon *m.*

storage /'stɔːrɪdʒ/ *n.* (*of goods, food, etc.*) emmagasinage *m.*

store /stɔː(r)/ *n.* réserve *f.*; (*warehouse*) entrepôt *m.*; (*shop*) grand magasin *m.*; (*Amer.*) magasin *m.* —*v.t.* (*for future*) mettre en réserve; (*in warehouse, mind*) emmagasiner. **have in ~ for,** réserver à. **set ~ by,** attacher du prix à. **~-room** *n.* réserve *f.*

storey /'stɔːrɪ/ *n.* étage *m.*

stork /stɔːk/ *n.* cigogne *f.*

storm /stɔːm/ *n.* tempête *f.*, orage *m.* —*v.t.* prendre d'assaut. —*v.i.* (*rage*) tempêter. **~y** *a.* orageux.

story /'stɔːrɪ/ *n.* histoire *f.*; (*in press*) article *m.*; (*storey: Amer.*) étage *m.* **~-teller** *n.* conteu|r, -se *m.*, *f.*; (*liar: fam.*) menteu|r, -se *m.*, *f.*

stout /staʊt/ *a.* (**-er, -est**) corpulent; (*strong*) solide. —*n.* bière brune *f.* **~ness** *n.* corpulence *f.*

stove /stəʊv/ *n.* (*for cooking*) cuisinière *f.*; (*heater*) poêle *m.*

stow /stəʊ/ *v.t.* **~ away,** (*put away*) ranger; (*hide*) cacher. —*v.i.* voyager clandestinement.

stowaway /'stəʊəweɪ/ *n.* passag|er, -ère clandestin(e) *m.*, *f.*

straddle /'strædl/ *v.t.* être à cheval sur, enjamber.

straggle /'strægl/ *v.i.* (*lag behind*) traîner en désordre. **~r** /-ə(r)/ *n.* traînard(e) *m.* (*f.*).

straight /streɪt/ *a.* (**-er, -est**) droit; (*tidy*) en ordre; (*frank*) franc. —*adv.* (*in straight line*) droit; (*direct*) tout droit. —*n.* ligne droite *f.* **~ ahead** *or* **on,** tout droit. **~ away,** tout de suite. **~ face,** visage sérieux *m.* **~ off,** (*fam.*) sans hésiter.

straighten /'streɪtn/ *v.t.* (*nail, situation, etc.*) redresser; (*tidy*) arranger.

straightforward /streɪt'fɔːwəd/ *a.* honnête; (*easy*) simple.

strain[1] /streɪn/ *n.* (*breed*) race *f.*; (*streak*) tendance *f.*

strain[2] /streɪn/ *v.t.* (*rope, ears*) tendre; (*limb*) fouler; (*eyes*) fatiguer; (*muscle*) froisser; (*filter*) passer; (*vegetables*) égoutter; (*fig.*) mettre à l'épreuve. —*v.i.* fournir des efforts. —*n.* tension *f.*; (*fig.*) effort *m.* **~s,** (*tune: mus.*) accents *m. pl.* **~ed** *a.* forcé; (*relations*) tendu. **~er** *n.* passoire *f.*

strait /streɪt/ *n.* détroit *m.* **~s,** détroit *m.*; (*fig.*) embarras *m.* **~-jacket** *n.* camisole de force *f.* **~-laced** *a.* collet monté *invar.*

strand /strænd/ *n.* (*thread*) fil *m.*, brin *m.*; (*lock of hair*) mèche *f.*

stranded /'strændɪd/ *a.* (*person*) en rade; (*ship*) échoué.

strange /streɪndʒ/ *a.* (**-er, -est**) étrange; (*unknown*) inconnu. **~ly** *adv.* étrangement. **~ness** *n.* étrangeté *f.*

stranger /'streɪndʒə(r)/ *n.* inconnu(e) *m.* (*f.*).

strangle /'stræŋgl/ *v.t.* étrangler.

stranglehold /'stræŋglhəʊld/ *n.* **have a ~ on,** tenir à la gorge.

strap /stræp/ *n.* (*of leather etc.*) courroie *f.*; (*of dress*) bretelle *f.*; (*of watch*) bracelet *m.* —*v.t.* (*p.t.* **strapped**) attacher.

strapping /'stræpɪŋ/ *a.* costaud.

stratagem /'strætədʒəm/ *n.* stratagème *m.*

strategic /strə'tiːdʒɪk/ *a.* stratégique.

strategy /'strætədʒɪ/ *n.* stratégie *f.*

stratum /'strɑːtəm/ *n.* (*pl.* **strata**) couche *f.*

straw /strɔː/ *n.* paille *f.*

strawberry /'strɔːbrɪ/ *n.* fraise *f.*

stray /streɪ/ *v.i.* s'égarer; (*deviate*) s'écarter. —*a.* perdu; (*isolated*) isolé. —*n.* animal perdu *m.*

streak /striːk/ *n.* raie *f.*, bande *f.*; (*trace*) trace *f.*; (*period*) période *f.*; (*tendency*) tendance *f.* —*v.t.* (*mark*) strier. **~y** *a.* strié.

stream /striːm/ *n.* ruisseau *m.*; (*current*) courant *m.*; (*flow*) flot *m.*; (*in schools*) classe (de niveau) *f.* —*v.i.* ruisseler (**with,** de).

streamer /'striːmə(r)/ *n.* (*of paper*) serpentin *m.*; (*flag*) banderole *f.*

streamline /'striːmlaɪn/ *v.t.* rationaliser. **~d** *a.* (*shape*) aérodynamique.

street /striːt/ *n.* rue *f.* **~ lamp,** réverbère *m.*

streetcar /'striːtkɑː(r)/ *n.* (*Amer.*) tramway *m.*

strength /streŋθ/ *n.* force *f.*; (*of wall, fabric, etc.*) solidité *f.* **on the ~ of,** en vertu de.

strengthen /'streŋθn/ *v.t.* renforcer, fortifier.

strenuous /'strenjʊəs/ *a.* énergique; (*arduous*) ardu; (*tiring*) fatigant. **~ly** *adv.* énergiquement.

stress /stres/ *n.* accent *m.*; (*pressure*) pression *f.*; (*med.*) stress *m.* —*v.t.* souligner, insister sur.

stretch /stretʃ/ *v.t.* (*pull taut*) tendre; (*arm, leg*) étendre; (*neck*) tendre; (*clothes*) étirer; (*truth etc.*) forcer. —*v.i.* s'étendre; (*of person, clothes*)

s'étirer. —*n.* étendue *f.*; (*period*)
période *f.*; (*of road*) tronçon *m.* —*a.*
(*fabric*) extensible. **at a ~,** d'affilée.
stretcher /'stretʃə(r)/ *n.* brancard *m.*
strew /struː/ *v.t.* (*p.t.* **strewed,** *p.p.*
strewed *or* **strewn**) (*scatter*) répandre; (*cover*) joncher.
stricken /'strɪkən/ *a.* **~ with,** frappé
or atteint de.
strict /strɪkt/ *a.* (**-er, -est**) strict. **~ly**
adv. strictement. **~ness** *n.* sévérité *f.*
stride /straɪd/ *v.i.* (*p.t.* **strode,** *p.p.*
stridden) faire de grands pas. —*n.*
grand pas *m.*
strident /'straɪdnt/ *a.* strident.
strife /straɪf/ *n.* conflit(s) *m.* (*pl.*).
strike /straɪk/ *v.t.* (*p.t.* **struck**)
frapper; (*blow*) donner; (*match*)
frotter; (*gold etc.*) trouver; (*of clock*)
sonner. —*v.i.* faire grève; (*attack*) attaquer. —*n.* (*of workers*) grève *f.*;
(*mil.*) attaque *f.*; (*find*) découverte *f.*
on ~, en grève. **~ off** *or* **out,** rayer.
~ up a friendship, lier amitié (**with,**
avec).
striker /'straɪkə(r)/ *n.* gréviste *m/f.*;
(*football*) buteur *m.*
striking /'straɪkɪŋ/ *a.* frappant.
string /strɪŋ/ *n.* ficelle *f.*; (*of violin,
racket, etc.*) corde *f.*; (*of pearls*) collier
m.; (*of lies etc.*) chapelet *m.* —*v.t.*
(*p.t.* **strung**) (*thread*) enfiler. **pull
~s,** faire jouer ses relations. **~ out,**
(s')échelonner. **~ed** *a.* (*instrument*) à
cordes.
stringent /'strɪndʒənt/ *a.* rigoureux,
strict.
stringy /'strɪŋɪ/ *a.* filandreux.
strip[1] /strɪp/ *v.t./i.* (*p.t.* **stripped**) (*undress*) (se) déshabiller; (*machine*) dé-
monter; (*deprive*) dépouiller. **~per** *n.*
stripteaseuse *f.*; (*solvent*) décapant *m.*
~-tease *n.* strip-tease *m.*
strip[2] /strɪp/ *n.* bande *f.* **comic ~,**
bande dessinée *f.*
stripe /straɪp/ *n.* rayure *f.*, raie *f.* **~d**
a. rayé.
strive /straɪv/ *v.i.* (*p.t.* **strove,** *p.p.*
striven) s'efforcer (**to,** de).
strode /strəʊd/ *see* **stride.**
stroke[1] /strəʊk/ *n.* coup *m.*; (*of pen*)
trait *m.*; (*swimming*) nage *f.*; (*med.*)
attaque *f.*, congestion *f.*
stroke[2] /strəʊk/ *v.t.* (*with hand*) caresser. —*n.* caresse *f.*
stroll /strəʊl/ *v.i.* flâner. —*n.* petit tour
m. **~ in/***etc.*, entrer/*etc.* tranquil-
lement.

strong /strɒŋ/ *a.* (**-er, -est**) fort; (*shoes,
fabric, etc.*) solide. **be fifty/** *etc.* **~,**
être au nombre de cinquante/*etc.* **~-
box** *n.* coffre-fort *m.* **~ language,**
propos grossiers *m. pl.* **~-minded** *a.*
résolu. **~room** *n.* chambre forte *f.*
~ly *adv.* (*greatly*) fortement; (*with
energy*) avec force; (*deeply*) profondément.
stronghold /'strɒŋhəʊld/ *n.* bastion *m.*
strove /strəʊv/ *see* **strive.**
struck /strʌk/ *see* **strike.** —*a.* **~ on,**
(*sl.*) impressionné par.
structur|e /'strʌktʃə(r)/ *n.* (*of cell,
poem, etc.*) structure *f.*; (*building*) construction *f.* **~al** *a.* structural; de (la)
construction.
struggle /'strʌgl/ *v.i.* lutter, se battre. —*n.* lutte *f.*; (*effort*) effort *m.* **have
a ~ to,** avoir du mal à.
strum /strʌm/ *v.t.* (*p.t.* **strummed**)
(*banjo etc.*) gratter de.
strung /strʌŋ/ *see* **string.** —*a.* **~ up,**
(*tense*) nerveux.
strut /strʌt/ *n.* (*support*) étai *m.* —*v.i.*
(*p.t.* **strutted**) se pavaner.
stub /stʌb/ *n.* bout *m.*; (*of tree*) souche
f.; (*counterfoil*) talon *m.* —*v.t.* (*p.t.*
stubbed). **~ out,** écraser.
stubble /'stʌbl/ *n.* (*on chin*) barbe de
plusieurs jours *f.*; (*remains of wheat*)
chaume *m.*
stubborn /'stʌbən/ *a.* opiniâtre, obstiné. **~ly** *adv.* obstinément. **~ness**
n. opiniâtreté *f.*
stubby /'stʌbɪ/ *a.* (**-ier, -iest**) (*finger*)
épais; (*person*) trapu.
stuck /stʌk/ *see* **stick**[2]. —*a.* (*jammed*)
coincé; (*in difficulties*) en panne. **~-
up** *a.* (*sl.*) prétentieux.
stud[1] /stʌd/ *n.* clou *m.*; (*for collar*)
bouton *m.* —*v.t.* (*p.t.* **studded**)
clouter. **~ded with,** parsemé de.
stud[2] /stʌd/ *n.* (*horses*) écurie *f.* **~
(-farm)** *n.* haras *m.*
student /'stjuːdnt/ *n.* (*univ.*) étu-
diant(e) *m.* (*f.*); (*schol.*) élève *m./f.*
—*a.* (*restaurant, life, residence*) universitaire.
studied /'stʌdɪd/ *a.* étudié.
studio /'stjuːdɪəʊ/ *n.* (*pl.* **-os**) studio *m.*
~ flat, studio *m.*
studious /'stjuːdɪəs/ *a.* (*person*) stu-
dieux; (*deliberate*) étudié. **~ly** *adv.*
(*carefully*) avec soin.
study /'stʌdɪ/ *n.* étude *f.*; (*office*) bureau
m. —*v.t./i.* étudier.
stuff /stʌf/ *n.* substance *f.*; (*sl.*) chose(s)

f. (*pl.*). —*v.t.* rembourrer; (*animal*) empailler; (*cram*) bourrer; (*culin.*) farcir; (*block up*) boucher; (*put*) fourrer. ~**ing** *n.* bourre *f.*; (*culin.*) farce *f.*

stuffy /'stʌfɪ/ *a.* (**-ier, -iest**) mal aéré; (*dull: fam.*) vieux jeu *invar.*

stumbl|e /'stʌmbl/ *v.i.* trébucher. ~**e across** *or* **on**, tomber sur. ~**ing-block** *n.* pierre d'achoppement *f.*

stump /stʌmp/ *n.* (*of tree*) souche *f.*; (*of limb*) moignon *m.*; (*of pencil*) bout *m.*

stumped /stʌmpt/ *a.* (*baffled: fam.*) embarrassé.

stun /stʌn/ *v.t.* (*p.t.* **stunned**) étourdir; (*bewilder*) stupéfier.

stung /stʌŋ/ *see* **sting**.

stunk /stʌŋk/ *see* **stink**.

stunning /'stʌnɪŋ/ *a.* (*delightful: fam.*) sensationnel.

stunt[1] /stʌnt/ *v.t.* (*growth*) retarder. ~**ed** *a.* (*person*) rabougri.

stunt[2] /stʌnt/ *n.* (*feat: fam.*) tour de force *m.*; (*trick: fam.*) truc *m.*

stupefy /'stjuːpɪfaɪ/ *v.t.* abrutir; (*amaze*) stupéfier.

stupendous /stjuː'pendəs/ *a.* prodigieux, formidable.

stupid /'stjuːpɪd/ *a.* stupide, bête. ~**ity** /-'pɪdətɪ/ *n.* stupidité *f.* ~**ly** *adv.* stupidement, bêtement.

stupor /'stjuːpə(r)/ *n.* stupeur *f.*

sturd|y /'stɜːdɪ/ *a.* (**-ier, -iest**) robuste. ~**iness** *n.* robustesse *f.*

sturgeon /'stɜːdʒən/ *n. invar.* (*fish*) esturgeon *m.*

stutter /'stʌtə(r)/ *v.i.* bégayer. —*n.* bégaiement *m.*

sty[1] /staɪ/ *n.* (*pigsty*) porcherie *f.*

sty[2] /staɪ/ *n.* (*on eye*) orgelet *m.*

styl|e /staɪl/ *n.* style *m.*; (*fashion*) mode *f.*; (*sort*) genre *m.*; (*pattern*) modèle *m.* —*v.t.* (*design*) créer. **in** ~**e**, (*live etc.*) dans le luxe. ~**e s.o.'s hair**, coiffer qn. ~**ist** *n.* (*of hair*) coiffeu|r, -se *m., f.*

stylish /'staɪlɪʃ/ *a.* élégant.

stylized /'staɪlaɪzd/ *a.* stylisé.

stylus /'staɪləs/ *n.* (*pl.* **-uses**) (*of record-player*) saphir *m.*

suave /swɑːv/ *a.* (*urbane*) courtois; (*smooth: pej.*) doucereux.

sub /sʌb/ *pref.* sous-, sub-.

subconscious /sʌb'kɒnʃəs/ *a. & n.* subconscient (*m.*).

subcontract /sʌbkən'trækt/ *v.t.* sous-traiter.

subdivide /sʌbdɪ'vaɪd/ *v.t.* subdiviser.

subdue /səb'djuː/ *v.t.* (*feeling*) maîtriser; (*country*) subjuguer. ~**d** *a.* (*weak*) faible; (*light*) tamisé.

subject[1] /'sʌbdʒɪkt/ *a.* (*state etc.*) soumis. —*n.* sujet *m.*; (*schol., univ.*) matière *f.*; (*citizen*) ressortissant(e) *m.* (*f.*), sujet(te) *m.* (*f.*). ~**-matter** *n.* contenu *m.* ~ **to**, soumis à; (*liable to*) sujet à.

subject[2] /səb'dʒekt/ *v.t.* soumettre. ~**ion** /-kʃn/ *n.* soumission *f.*

subjective /səb'dʒektɪv/ *a.* subjectif.

subjunctive /səb'dʒʌŋktɪv/ *a. & n.* subjonctif (*m.*).

sublimate /'sʌblɪmeɪt/ *v.t.* (*emotion etc.*) sublimer.

sublime /sə'blaɪm/ *a.* sublime.

submarine /sʌbmə'riːn/ *n.* sous-marin *m.*

submerge /səb'mɜːdʒ/ *v.t.* submerger. —*v.i.* plonger.

submissive /səb'mɪsɪv/ *a.* soumis.

submi|t /səb'mɪt/ *v.t./i.* (*p.t.* **submitted**) (se) soumettre (**to**, à). ~**ssion** *n.* soumission *f.*

subordinate[1] /sə'bɔːdɪnət/ *a.* subalterne; (*gram.*) subordonné. —*n.* subordonné(e) *m.* (*f.*).

subordinate[2] /sə'bɔːdɪneɪt/ *v.t.* subordonner (**to**, à).

subpoena /səb'piːnə/ *n.* (*pl.* **-as**) (*jurid.*) citation *f.*, assignation *f.*

subscribe /səb'skraɪb/ *v.t./i.* verser (de l'argent) (**to**, à). ~ **to**, (*loan, theory*) souscrire à; (*newspaper*) s'abonner à, être abonné à. ~**r** /-ə(r)/ *n.* abonné(e) *m.* (*f.*). **subscription** /-ɪpʃn/ *n.* souscription *f.*; abonnement *m.*; (*membership dues*) cotisation *f.*

subsequent /'sʌbsɪkwənt/ *a.* (*later*) ultérieur; (*next*) suivant. ~**ly** *adv.* par la suite.

subside /səb'saɪd/ *v.i.* (*land etc.*) s'affaisser; (*flood, wind*) baisser. ~**nce** /-əns/ *n.* affaissement *m.*

subsidiary /səb'sɪdɪərɪ/ *a.* accessoire. —*n.* (*comm.*) filiale *f.*

subsid|y /'sʌbsədɪ/ *n.* subvention *f.* ~**ize** /-ɪdaɪz/ *v.t.* subventionner.

subsist /səb'sɪst/ *v.i.* subsister. ~**ence** *n.* subsistance *f.*

substance /'sʌbstəns/ *n.* substance *f.*

substandard /sʌb'stændəd/ *a.* de qualité inférieure.

substantial /səb'stænʃl/ *a.* considérable; (*meal*) substantiel. ~**ly** *adv.* considérablement.

substantiate /səb'stænʃɪeɪt/ *v.t.* justifier, prouver.

substitut|e /'sʌbstɪtjuːt/ *n.* succédané *m.*; (*person*) remplaçant(e) *m.* (*f.*). —*v.t.* substituer (**for**, à). ∼**ion** /-'tjuːʃn/ *n.* substitution *f.*

subterfuge /'sʌbtəfjuːdʒ/ *n.* subterfuge *m.*

subterranean /sʌbtə'reɪnɪən/ *a.* souterrain.

subtitle /'sʌbtaɪtl/ *n.* sous-titre *m.*

subtle /'sʌtl/ *a.* (**-er, -est**) subtil. ∼**ty** *n.* subtilité *f.*

subtotal /sʌb'təʊtl/ *n.* total partiel *m.*

subtract /səb'trækt/ *v.t.* soustraire. ∼**ion** /-kʃn/ *n.* soustraction *f.*

suburb /'sʌbɜːb/ *n.* faubourg *m.*, banlieue *f.* ∼**s**, banlieue *f.* ∼**an** /sə'bɜːbən/ *a.* de banlieue.

suburbia /sə'bɜːbɪə/ *n.* la banlieue *f.*

subversive /səb'vɜːsɪv/ *a.* subversif.

subver|t /səb'vɜːt/ *v.t.* renverser. ∼**sion** /-ʃn/ *n.* subversion *f.*

subway /'sʌbweɪ/ *n.* passage souterrain *m.*; (*Amer.*) métro *m.*

succeed /sək'siːd/ *v.i.* réussir (**in doing**, à faire). —*v.t.* (*follow*) succéder à. ∼**ing** *a.* suivant.

success /sək'ses/ *n.* succès *m.*, réussite *f.*

successful /sək'sesfl/ *a.* réussi, couronné de succès; (*favourable*) heureux; (*in exam*) reçu. **be** ∼ **in doing**, réussir à faire. ∼**ly** *adv.* avec succès.

succession /sək'seʃn/ *n.* succession *f.* **in** ∼, de suite.

successive /sək'sesɪv/ *a.* successif. **six** ∼ **days**, six jours consécutifs.

successor /sək'sesə(r)/ *n.* successeur *m.*

succinct /sək'sɪŋkt/ *a.* succinct.

succulent /'sʌkjʊlənt/ *a.* succulent.

succumb /sə'kʌm/ *v.i.* succomber.

such /sʌtʃ/ *a. & pron.* tel(le), tel(le)s; (*so much*) tant (de). —*adv.* si. ∼ **a book**/*etc.*, un tel livre/*etc.* ∼ **books**/ *etc.*, de tels livres/*etc.* ∼ **courage**/ *etc.*, tant de courage/*etc.* ∼ **a big house**, une si grande maison. ∼ **as**, comme, tel que. ∼**-and-such** *a.* tel ou tel.

suck /sʌk/ *v.t.* sucer. ∼ **in** *or* **up**, aspirer. ∼**er** *n.* (*rubber pad*) ventouse *f.*; (*person: sl.*) dupe *f.*

suckle /'sʌkl/ *v.t.* allaiter.

suction /'sʌkʃn/ *n.* succion *f.*

sudden /'sʌdn/ *a.* soudain, subit. **all of a** ∼, tout à coup. ∼**ly** *adv.* subite-

ment, brusquement. ∼**ness** *n.* soudaineté *f.*

suds /sʌdz/ *n. pl.* (*froth*) mousse de savon *f.*

sue /s(j)uː/ *v.t.* (*pres. p.* **suing**) poursuivre (en justice).

suede /sweɪd/ *n.* daim *m.*

suet /'suːɪt/ *n.* graisse de rognon *f.*

suffer /'sʌfə(r)/ *v.t./i.* souffrir; (*loss, attack, etc.*) subir. ∼**er** *n.* victime *f.*, malade *m./f.* ∼**ing** *n.* souffrance(s) *f.* (*pl.*).

suffice /sə'faɪs/ *v.i.* suffire.

sufficient /sə'fɪʃnt/ *a.* (*enough*) suffisamment de; (*big enough*) suffisant. ∼**ly** *adv.* suffisamment.

suffix /'sʌfɪks/ *n.* suffixe *m.*

suffocat|e /'sʌfəkeɪt/ *v.t./i.* suffoquer. ∼**ion** /-'keɪʃn/ *n.* suffocation *f.*; (*med.*) asphyxie *f.*

suffused /sə'fjuːzd/ *a.* ∼ **with**, (*light, tears*) baigné de.

sugar /'ʃʊɡə(r)/ *n.* sucre *m.* —*v.t.* sucrer. ∼**y** *a.* sucré.

suggest /sə'dʒest/ *v.t.* suggérer. ∼**ion** /-tʃn/ *n.* suggestion *f.*

suggestive /sə'dʒestɪv/ *a.* suggestif. **be** ∼ **of**, suggérer.

suicid|e /'s(j)uːɪsaɪd/ *n.* suicide *m.* **commit** ∼**e**, se suicider. ∼**al** /-'saɪdl/ *a.* suicidaire.

suit /s(j)uːt/ *n.* complet *m.*, costume *m.*; (*woman's*) tailleur *m.*; (*cards*) couleur *f.* —*v.t.* convenir à; (*of garment, style, etc.*) aller à; (*adapt*) adapter. ∼**ability** *n.* (*of action etc.*) à-propos *m.*; (*of candidate*) aptitude(s) *f.* (*pl.*). ∼**able** *a.* qui convient (**for**, à), convenable. ∼**ably** *adv.* convenablement. ∼**ed** *a.* (**well**) ∼**ed**, (*matched*) bien assorti. ∼**ed to**, fait pour, apte à.

suitcase /'s(j)uːtkeɪs/ *n.* valise *f.*

suite /swiːt/ *n.* (*rooms, retinue*) suite *f.*; (*furniture*) mobilier *m.*

suitor /'s(j)uːtə(r)/ *n.* soupirant *m.*

sulk /sʌlk/ *v.i.* bouder. ∼**y** *a.* boudeur, maussade.

sullen /'sʌlən/ *a.* maussade. ∼**ly** *adv.* d'un air maussade.

sulphur /'sʌlfə(r)/ *n.* soufre *m.* ∼**ic** /-'fjʊərɪk/ *a.* ∼**ic acid**, acide sulfurique *m.*

sultan /'sʌltən/ *n.* sultan *m.*

sultana /sʌl'tɑːnə/ raisin de Smyrne *m.*, raisin sec *m.*

sultry /'sʌltrɪ/ *a.* (**-ier, -iest**) étouffant, lourd; (*fig.*) sensuel.

sum /sʌm/ *n.* somme *f.*; (*in arithmetic*)

calcul *m.* —*v.t./i.* (*p.t.* **summed**). ~
up, résumer, récapituler; (*assess*)
évaluer.

summar|y /'sʌmərɪ/ *n.* résumé *m.* —*a.*
sommaire. ~**ize** *v.t.* résumer.

summer /'sʌmə(r)/ *n.* été *m.* —*a.* d'été.
~**-time** *n.* été *m.* ~**y** *a.* estival.

summit /'sʌmɪt/ *n.* sommet *m.* ~ **conference**, (*pol.*) conférence au sommet
f.

summon /'sʌmən/ *v.t.* appeler; (*meeting, s.o. to meeting*) convoquer. ~ **up**,
(*strength, courage, etc.*) rassembler.

summons /'sʌmənz/ *n.* (*jurid.*) assignation *f.* —*v.t.* assigner.

sump /sʌmp/ *n.* (*auto.*) carter *m.*

sumptuous /'sʌmptʃʊəs/ *a.* somptueux, luxueux.

sun /sʌn/ *n.* soleil *m.* —*v.t.* (*p.t.*
sunned). ~ **o.s.**, se chauffer au soleil.
~**-glasses** *n. pl.* lunettes de soleil *f.
pl.* ~**-tan** *n.* bronzage *m.* ~**-tanned**
a. bronzé.

sunbathe /'sʌnbeɪð/ *v.i.* prendre un
bain de soleil.

sunburn /'sʌnbɜːn/ *n.* coup de soleil
m. ~**t** *a.* brûlé par le soleil.

Sunday /'sʌndɪ/ *n.* dimanche *m.* ~
school, catéchisme *m.*

sundial /'sʌndaɪəl/ *n.* cadran solaire
m.

sundown /'sʌndaʊn/ *n.* = **sunset**.

sundr|y /'sʌndrɪ/ *a.* divers. ~**ies** *n. pl.*
articles divers *m. pl.* **all and** ~**y,** tout
le monde.

sunflower /'sʌnflaʊə(r)/ *n.* tournesol
m.

sung /sʌŋ/ *see* **sing**.

sunk /sʌŋk/ *see* **sink**.

sunken /'sʌŋkən/ *a.* (*ship etc.*) submergé; (*eyes*) creux.

sunlight /'sʌnlaɪt/ *n.* soleil *m.*

sunny /'sʌnɪ/ *a.* (-**ier, -iest**) (*room,
day, etc.*) ensoleillé.

sunrise /'sʌnraɪz/ *n.* lever du soleil *m.*

sunset /'sʌnset/ *n.* coucher du soleil
m.

sunshade /'sʌnʃeɪd/ *n.* (*lady's*) ombrelle *f.*; (*awning*) parasol *m.*

sunshine /'sʌnʃaɪn/ *n.* soleil *m.*

sunstroke /'sʌnstrəʊk/ *n.* insolation *f.*

super /'suːpə(r)/ *a.* (*sl.*) formidable.

superb /suːˈpɜːb/ *a.* superbe.

supercilious /suːpəˈsɪlɪəs/ *a.* hautain,
dédaigneux.

superficial /suːpəˈfɪʃl/ *a.* superficiel.
~**ity** /-ɪˈælətɪ/ *n.* caractère superficiel
m. ~**ly** *adv.* superficiellement.

superfluous /suːˈpɜːflʊəs/ *a.* superflu.

superhuman /suːpəˈhjuːmən/ *a.* surhumain.

superimpose /suːpərɪmˈpəʊz/ *v.t.*
superposer (**on,** à).

superintendent /suːpərɪnˈtendənt/ *n.*
direc|teur, -trice *m.,f.*; (*of police*) com-
missaire *m.*

superior /suːˈpɪərɪə(r)/ *a.* & *n.* su-
périeur(e) (*m.* (*f.*)). ~**ity** /-ˈɒrətɪ/ *n.*
supériorité *f.*

superlative /suːˈpɜːlətɪv/ *a.* suprême. —*n.* (*gram.*) superlatif *m.*

superman /'suːpəmæn/ *n.* (*pl.* -**men**)
surhomme *m.*

supermarket /'suːpəmɑːkɪt/ *n.* supermarché *m.*

supernatural /suːpəˈnætʃrəl/ *a.* surnaturel.

superpower /'suːpəpaʊə(r)/ *n.* superpuissance *f.*

supersede /suːpəˈsiːd/ *v.t.* remplacer,
supplanter.

supersonic /suːpəˈsɒnɪk/ *a.* supersonique.

superstiti|on /suːpəˈstɪʃn/ *n.* super-
stition *f.* ~**ous** *a.* superstitieux.

supertanker /'suːpətæŋkə(r)/ *n.* pétrolier géant *m.*

supervis|e /'suːpəvaɪz/ *v.t.* surveiller,
diriger. ~**ion** /-ˈvɪʒn/ *n.* surveillance
f. ~**or** *n.* surveillant(e) *m.* (*f.*); (*shop*)
chef de rayon *m.*; (*firm*) chef de service *m.* ~**ory** /-ˈvaɪzərɪ/ *a.* de surveillance.

supper /'sʌpə(r)/ *n.* dîner *m.*; (*late at
night*) souper *m.*

supple /'sʌpl/ *a.* souple.

supplement[1] /'sʌplɪmənt/ *n.* supplément *m.* ~**ary** /-ˈmentrɪ/ *a.* supplémentaire.

supplement[2] /'sʌplɪment/ *v.t.* compléter.

supplier /səˈplaɪə(r)/ *n.* fournisseur *m.*

suppl|y /səˈplaɪ/ *v.t.* fournir; (*equip*)
pourvoir; (*feed*) alimenter (**with,**
en). —*n.* provision *f.*; (*of gas etc.*)
alimentation *f.* ~**ies,** (*food*) vivres *m.
pl.*; (*material*) fournitures *f. pl.*

support /səˈpɔːt/ *v.t.* soutenir; (*family*)
assurer la subsistance de; (*endure*)
supporter. —*n.* soutien *m.*, appui *m.*;
(*techn.*) support *m.* ~**er** *n.* partisan(e)
m. (*f.*).; (*sport*) supporter *m.*

suppos|e /səˈpəʊz/ *v.t./i.* supposer. **be
~ed to do**, être censé faire, devoir
faire. ~**ition** /sʌpəˈzɪʃn/ *n.* supposition *f.*

supposedly /sə'pəʊzɪdlɪ/ *adv.* soi-disant, prétendument.

suppress /sə'pres/ *v.t.* (*put an end to*) supprimer; (*restrain*) réprimer; (*stifle*) étouffer. **~ion** /-ʃn/ *n.* suppression *f.*; répression *f.*

suprem|e /suː'priːm/ *a.* suprême. **~acy** /-eməsɪ/ *n.* suprématie *f.*

surcharge /'sɜːtʃɑːdʒ/ *n.* prix supplémentaire *m.*; (*tax*) surtaxe *f.*; (*on stamp*) surcharge *f.*

sure /ʃʊə(r)/ *a.* (**-er, -est**) sûr. *—adv.* (*Amer.*, *fam.*) pour sûr. **make ~ of,** s'assurer de. **~ly** *adv.* sûrement.

surety /'ʃʊərətɪ/ *n.* caution *f.*

surf /sɜːf/ *n.* (*waves*) ressac *m.* **~-riding** *n.* surf *m.*

surfboard /'sɜːfbɔːd/ *n.* planche de surf *f.*

surface /'sɜːfɪs/ *n.* surface *f. —a.* superficiel. *—v.t.* revêtir. *—v.i.* faire surface; (*fig.*) réapparaître. **~ mail,** courrier maritime *m.*

surfeit /'sɜːfɪt/ *n.* excès *m.* (**of,** de).

surge /sɜːdʒ/ *v.i.* (*of crowd*) déferler; (*of waves*) s'enfler; (*increase*) monter. *—n.* (*wave*) vague *f.*; (*rise*) montée *f.*

surgeon /'sɜːdʒən/ *n.* chirurgien *m.*

surg|ery /'sɜːdʒərɪ/ *n.* chirurgie *f.*; (*office*) cabinet *m.*; (*session*) consultation *f.* **~ical** *a.* chirurgical.

surly /'sɜːlɪ/ *a.* (**-ier, -iest**) bourru.

surmise /sə'maɪz/ *v.t.* conjecturer. *—n.* conjecture *f.*

surmount /sə'maʊnt/ *v.t.* (*overcome, cap*) surmonter.

surname /'sɜːneɪm/ *n.* nom de famille *m.*

surpass /sə'pɑːs/ *v.t.* surpasser.

surplus /'sɜːpləs/ *n.* surplus *m. —a.* en surplus.

surpris|e /sə'praɪz/ *n.* surprise *f. —v.t.* surprendre. **~ed** *a.* surpris (**at,** de). **~ing** *a.* surprenant. **~ingly** *adv.* étonnamment.

surrealism /sə'rɪəlɪzəm/ *n.* surréalisme *m.*

surrender /sə'rendə(r)/ *v.i.* se rendre. *—v.t.* (*hand over*) remettre; (*mil.*) rendre. *—n.* (*mil.*) reddition *f.*; (*of passport etc.*) remise *f.*

surreptitious /sʌrəp'tɪʃəs/ *a.* subreptice, furtif.

surround /sə'raʊnd/ *v.t.* entourer; (*mil.*) encercler. **~ing** *a.* environnant. **~ings** *n. pl.* environs *m. pl.*; (*setting*) cadre *m.*

surveillance /sɜː'veɪləns/ *n.* surveillance *f.*

survey[1] /sə'veɪ/ *v.t.* (*review*) passer en revue; (*inquire into*) enquêter sur; (*building*) inspecter. **~or** *n.* expert (géomètre) *m.*

survey[2] /'sɜːveɪ/ *n.* (*inquiry*) enquête *f.*; inspection *f.*; (*general view*) vue d'ensemble *f.*

survival /sə'vaɪvl/ *n.* survie *f.*; (*relic*) vestige *m.*

surviv|e /sə'vaɪv/ *v.t./i.* survivre (à). **~or** *n.* survivant(e) *m.* (*f.*).

susceptib|le /sə'septəbl/ *a.* sensible (**to,** à). **~le to,** (*prone to*) prédisposé à. **~ility** /-'bɪlətɪ/ *n.* sensibilité *f.*; prédisposition *f.*

suspect[1] /sə'spekt/ *v.t.* soupçonner; (*doubt*) douter de.

suspect[2] /'sʌspekt/ *n. & a.* suspect(e) (*m.* (*f.*)).

suspen|d /sə'spend/ *v.t.* (*hang, stop*) suspendre; (*licence*) retirer provisoirement. **~sion** *n.* suspension *f.*; retrait provisoire *m.* **~sion bridge,** pont suspendu *m.*

suspender /sə'spendə(r)/ *n.* jarretelle *f.* **~s,** (*braces*: *Amer.*) bretelles *f. pl.*

suspense /sə'spens/ *n.* attente *f.*; (*in book etc.*) suspense *m.*

suspicion /sə'spɪʃn/ *n.* soupçon *m.*; (*distrust*) méfiance *f.*

suspicious /səs'pɪʃəs/ *a.* soupçonneux; (*causing suspicion*) suspect. **be ~ of,** (*distrust*) se méfier de. **~ly** *adv.* de façon suspecte.

sustain /səs'teɪn/ *v.t.* supporter; (*effort etc.*) soutenir; (*suffer*) subir.

sustenance /'sʌstɪnəns/ *n.* (*food*) nourriture *f.*; (*quality*) valeur nutritive *f.*

swab /swɒb/ *n.* (*pad*) tampon *m.*

swagger /'swægə(r)/ *v.i.* (*walk*) se pavaner, parader.

swallow[1] /'swɒləʊ/ *v.t./i.* avaler. **~ up,** (*absorb, engulf*) engloutir.

swallow[2] /'swɒləʊ/ *n.* hirondelle *f.*

swam /swæm/ *see* **swim.**

swamp /swɒmp/ *n.* marais *m. —v.t.* (*flood, overwhelm*) submerger. **~y** *a.* marécageux.

swan /swɒn/ *n.* cygne *m.* **~-song** *n.* (*fig.*) chant du cygne *m.*

swank /swæŋk/ *n.* (*behaviour*: *fam.*) épate *f.*, esbroufe *f.*; (*person*: *fam.*) crâneu|r, -se *m.*, *f. —v.i.* (*show off*: *fam.*) crâner.

swap /swɒp/ *v.t./i.* (*p.t.* **swapped**)

(*fam.*) échanger. —*n.* (*fam.*) échange *m.*

swarm /swɔ:m/ *n.* (*of insects, people*) essaim *m.* —*v.i.* fourmiller. ∼ **into** *or* **round**, (*crowd*) envahir.

swarthy /'swɔ:ðɪ/ *a.* (-**ier**, -**iest**) noiraud; (*complexion*) basané.

swastika /'swɒstɪkə/ *n.* (*Nazi*) croix gammée *f.*

swat /swɒt/ *v.t.* (*p.t.* **swatted**) (*fly etc.*) écraser.

sway /sweɪ/ *v.t./i.* (se) balancer; (*influence*) influencer. —*n.* balancement *m.*; (*rule*) empire *m.*

swear /sweə(r)/ *v.t./i.* (*p.t.* **swore**, *p.p.* **sworn**) jurer (**to sth.**, de qch.). ∼ **by** **sth.**, (*fam.*) ne jurer que par qch. ∼-**word** *n.* juron *m.*

sweat /swet/ *n.* sueur *f.* —*v.i.* suer. ∼**y** *a.* en sueur.

sweater /'swetə(r)/ *n.* pull-over *m.*

swede /swi:d/ *n.* rutabaga *m.*

Swed|e /swi:d/ *n.* Suédois(e) *m.* (*f.*). ∼**en** *n.* Suède *f.* ∼**ish** *a.* suédois; *n.* (*lang.*) suédois *m.*

sweep /swi:p/ *v.t./i.* (*p.t.* **swept**) balayer; (*go*) aller rapidement *or* majestueusement; (*carry away*) emporter, entraîner. —*n.* coup de balai *m.*; (*curve*) courbe *f.*; (*mouvement*) geste *m.*, mouvement *m.* ∼**ing** *a.* (*gesture*) large; (*action*) qui va loin; (*statement*) trop général.

sweet /swi:t/ *a.* (-**er**, -**est**) (*not sour*, *pleasant*) doux; (*not savoury*) sucré; (*charming: fam.*) gentil. —*n.* bonbon *m.*; (*dish*) dessert *m.*; (*person*) chéri(e) *m.* (*f.*). **have a** ∼ **tooth**, aimer les sucreries. ∼ **shop**, confiserie *f.* ∼**ly** *adv.* gentiment. ∼**ness** *n.* douceur *f.*; goût sucré *m.*

sweeten /'swi:tn/ *v.t.* sucrer; (*fig.*) adoucir. ∼**er** *n.* édulcorant *m.*

sweetheart /'swi:thɑ:t/ *n.* petit(e) ami(e) *m.* (*f.*).; (*term of endearment*) chéri(e) *m.* (*f.*).

swell /swel/ *v.t./i.* (*p.t.* **swelled**, *p.p.* **swollen** *or* **swelled**) (*increase*) grossir; (*expand*) (se) gonfler; (*of hand*, *face*) enfler. —*n.* (*of sea*) houle *f.* —*a.* (*fam.*) formidable. ∼**ing** *n.* (*med.*) enflure *f.*

swelter /'sweltə(r)/ *v.i.* étouffer.

swept /swept/ *see* **sweep**.

swerve /swɜ:v/ *v.i.* faire un écart.

swift /swɪft/ *a.* (-**er**, -**est**) rapide. —*n.* (*bird*) martinet *m.* ∼**ly** *adv.* rapidement. ∼**ness** *n.* rapidité *f.*

swig /swɪg/ *v.t.* (*p.t.* **swigged**) (*drink*: *fam.*) lamper. —*n.* (*fam.*) lampée *f.*, coup *m.*

swill /swɪl/ *v.t.* rincer; (*drink*) lamper. —*n.* (*pig-food*) pâtée *f.*

swim /swɪm/ *v.i.* (*p.t.* **swam**, *p.p.* **swum**, *pres. p.* **swimming**) nager; (*be dizzy*) tourner. —*v.t.* traverser à la nage; (*distance*) nager. —*n.* baignade *f.* ∼**mer** *n.* nageu|r, -se *m.*, *f.* ∼**ming** *n.* natation *f.* ∼**ming-bath**, ∼**ming-pool** *ns.* piscine *f.* ∼-**suit** *n.* maillot (de bain) *m.*

swindle /'swɪndl/ *v.t.* escroquer. —*n.* escroquerie *f.* ∼**r** /-ə(r)/ *n.* escroc *m.*

swine /swaɪn/ *n. pl.* (*pigs*) pourceaux *m. pl.* —*n. invar.* (*person: fam.*) cochon *m.*

swing /swɪŋ/ *v.t./i.* (*p.t.* **swung**) (se) balancer; (*turn round*) tourner; (*of pendulum*) osciller. —*n.* balancement *m.*; (*seat*) balançoire *f.*; (*of opinion*) revirement *m.*; (*mus.*) rythme *m.* **be in full** ∼, battre son plein. ∼ **round**, (*of person*) se retourner.

swingeing /'swɪndʒɪŋ/ *a.* écrasant.

swipe /swaɪp/ *v.t.* (*hit: fam.*) frapper; (*steal: fam.*) piquer. —*n.* (*hit: fam.*) grand coup *m.*

swirl /swɜ:l/ *v.i.* tourbillonner. —*n.* tourbillon *m.*

swish /swɪʃ/ *v.i.* (*hiss*) siffler, cingler l'air. —*a.* (*fam.*) chic *invar.*

Swiss /swɪs/ *a.* suisse. —*n. invar.* Suisse(sse) *m.* (*f.*).

switch /swɪtʃ/ *n.* bouton (électrique) *m.*, interrupteur *m.*; (*shift*) changement *m.*, revirement *m.* —*v.t.* (*transfer*) transférer; (*exchange*) échanger (**for**, contre); (*reverse positions of*) changer de place. ∼ **trains**/*etc.*, (*change*) changer de train/*etc.* —*v.i.* (*go over*) passer. ∼ **off**, éteindre, fermer. ∼ **on**, mettre, allumer.

switchback /'swɪtʃbæk/ *n.* montagnes russes *f. pl.*

switchboard /'swɪtʃbɔ:d/ *n.* (*telephone*) standard *m.*

Switzerland /'swɪtsələnd/ *n.* Suisse *f.*

swivel /'swɪvl/ *v.t./i.* (*p.t.* **swivelled**) (faire) pivoter.

swollen /'swəʊlən/ *see* **swell**.

swoon /swu:n/ *v.i.* se pâmer.

swoop /swu:p/ *v.i.* (*bird*) fondre; (*police*) faire une descente, foncer. —*n.* (*police raid*) descente *f.*

sword /sɔ:d/ *n.* épée *f.*

swore /swɔ:(r)/ *see* **swear**.

sworn /swɔːn/ *see* **swear.** —*a.* (*enemy*) juré; (*ally*) dévoué.

swot /swɒt/ *v.t./i.* (*p.t.* **swotted**) (*study*: *sl.*) bûcher. —*n.* (*sl.*) bûcheu|r, -se *m., f.*

swum /swʌm/ *see* **swim.**

swung /swʌŋ/ *see* **swing.**

sycamore /'sɪkəmɔː(r)/ *n.* (*maple*) sycomore *m.*; (*Amer.*) platane *m.*

syllable /'sɪləbl/ *n.* syllabe *f.*

syllabus /'sɪləbəs/ *n.* (*pl.* -**uses**) (*schol.*, *univ.*) programme *m.*

symbol /'sɪmbl/ *n.* symbole *m.* ~**ic(al)** /-'bɒlɪk(l)/ *a.* symbolique. ~**ism** *n.* symbolisme *m.*

symbolize /'sɪmbəlaɪz/ *v.t.* symboliser.

symmetr|y /'sɪmətrɪ/ *n.* symétrie *f.* ~**ical** /sɪ'metrɪkl/ *a.* symétrique.

sympathize /'sɪmpəθaɪz/ *v.i.* ~ **with**, (*pity*) plaindre; (*fig.*) comprendre les sentiments de.

sympath|y /'sɪmpəθɪ/ *n.* (*pity*) compassion *f.*; (*fig.*) compréhension *f.*; (*solidarity*) solidarité *f.*; (*condolences*) condoléances *f. pl.* **be in** ~**y with**, comprendre, être en accord avec. ~**etic** /-'θetɪk/ *a.* compatissant; (*fig.*) compréhensif. ~**etically** /-'θetɪklɪ/ *adv.* avec compassion; (*fig.*) avec compréhension.

symphon|y /'sɪmfənɪ/ *n.* symphonie *f.* —*a.* symphonique. ~**ic** /-'fɒnɪk/ *a.* symphonique.

symposium /sɪm'pəʊzɪəm/ *n.* (*pl.* -**ia**) symposium *m.*

symptom /'sɪmptəm/ *n.* symptôme *m.* ~**atic** /-'mætɪk/ *a.* symptomatique (**of**, de).

synagogue /'sɪnəgɒg/ *n.* synagogue *f.*

synchronize /'sɪŋkrənaɪz/ *v.t.* synchroniser.

syncopat|e /'sɪŋkəpeɪt/ *v.t.* syncoper. ~**ion** /-'peɪʃn/ *n.* syncope *f.*

syndicate /'sɪndɪkət/ *n.* syndicat *m.*

syndrome /'sɪndrəʊm/ *n.* syndrome *m.*

synonym /'sɪnənɪm/ *n.* synonyme *m.* ~**ous** /sɪ'nɒnɪməs/ *a.* synonyme.

synopsis /sɪ'nɒpsɪs/ *n.* (*pl.* -**opses** /-siːz/) résumé *m.*

syntax /'sɪntæks/ *n.* syntaxe *f.*

synthesis /'sɪnθəsɪs/ *n.* (*pl.* -**theses** /-siːz/) synthèse *f.*

synthetic /sɪn'θetɪk/ *a.* synthétique.

syphilis /'sɪfɪlɪs/ *n.* syphilis *f.*

Syria /'sɪrɪə/ *n.* Syrie *f.* ~**n** *a.* & *n.* syrien(ne) (*m.* (*f.*)).

syringe /sɪ'rɪndʒ/ *n.* seringue *f.*

syrup /'sɪrəp/ *n.* (*liquid*) sirop *m.*; (*treacle*) mélasse raffinée *f.* ~**y** *a.* sirupeux.

system /'sɪstəm/ *n.* système *m.*; (*body*) organisme *m.*; (*order*) méthode *f.* ~**s analyst**, analysteprogrammeu|r, -se *m., f.*

systematic /sɪstə'mætɪk/ *a.* systématique.

T

tab /tæb/ *n.* (*flap*) languette *f.*, patte *f.*; (*loop*) attache *f.*; (*label*) étiquette *f.*; (*Amer.*, *fam.*) addition *f.* keep ~s on, (*fam.*) surveiller.

tabernacle /'tæbənækl/ *n.* tabernacle *m.*

table /'teɪbl/ *n.* table *f.* —*v.t.* présenter; (*postpone*) ajourner. at ~, à table. lay or set the ~, mettre la table. ~-cloth *n.* nappe *f.* ~-mat *n.* dessous-de-plat *m. invar.* ~ of contents, table des matières *f.* ~ tennis, ping-pong *m.*

tablespoon /'teɪblspuːn/ *n.* cuiller à soupe *f.* ~ful *n.* (*pl.* ~fuls) cuillerée à soupe *f.*

tablet /'tæblɪt/ *n.* (*of stone*) plaque *f.*; (*drug*) comprimé *m.*

tabloid /'tæblɔɪd/ *n.* tabloïd *m.*

taboo /təˈbuː/ *n.* & *a.* tabou (*m.*).

tabulator /'tæbjʊleɪtə(r)/ *n.* (*on typewriter*) tabulateur *m.*

tacit /'tæsɪt/ *a.* tacite.

taciturn /'tæsɪtɜːn/ *a.* taciturne.

tack /tæk/ *n.* (*nail*) broquette *f.*; (*stitch*) point de bâti *m.*; (*course of action*) voie *f.* —*v.t.* (*nail*) clouer; (*stitch*) bâtir; (*add*) ajouter. —*v.i.* (*naut.*) louvoyer.

tackle /'tækl/ *n.* équipement *m.*, matériel *m.*; (*football*) plaquage *m.* —*v.t.* (*problem etc.*) s'attaquer à; (*football player*) plaquer.

tacky /'tækɪ/ *a.* (-ier, -iest) poisseux, pas sec; (*shabby*, *mean*: *Amer.*) moche.

tact /tækt/ *n.* tact *m.* ~ful *a.* plein de tact. ~fully *adv.* avec tact. ~less *a.* qui manque de tact. ~lessly *adv.* sans tact.

tactic /'tæktɪk/ *n.* tactique *f.* ~s *n.* & *n. pl.* tactique *f.* ~al *a.* tactique.

tactile /'tæktaɪl/ *a.* tactile.

tadpole /'tædpəʊl/ *n.* têtard *m.*

tag /tæg/ *n.* (*label*) étiquette *f.*; (*end piece*) bout *m.*; (*phrase*) cliché *m.* —*v.t.* (*p.t.* tagged) étiqueter; (*join*) ajouter. —*v.i.* ~ along, (*fam.*) suivre.

tail /teɪl/ *n.* queue *f.*; (*of shirt*) pan *m.* ~s, (*coat*) habit *m.* ~s!, (*tossing coin*) pile! —*v.t.* (*follow*) filer. —*v.i.* ~ away or off, diminuer. ~-back *n.* (*traffic*) bouchon *m.* ~-end *n.* fin *f.*, bout *m.*

tailcoat /'teɪlkəʊt/ *n.* habit *m.*

tailor /'teɪlə(r)/ *n.* tailleur *m.* —*v.t.*

(*garment*) façonner; (*fig.*) adapter. ~-made *a.* fait sur mesure. ~made for, (*fig.*) fait pour.

tainted /'teɪntɪd/ *a.* (*infected*) infecté; (*decayed*) gâté; (*fig.*) souillé.

take /teɪk/ *v.t./i.* (*p.t.* took, *p.p.* taken) prendre; (*carry*) (ap)porter (to, à); (*escort*) accompagner, amener; (*contain*) contenir; (*tolerate*) supporter; (*prize*) remporter; (*exam*) passer; (*choice*) faire; (*precedence*) avoir. be ~n by or with, être impressionné par. be ~n ill, tomber malade. it ~s time to, il faut du temps pour. ~ after, ressembler à. ~ away, (*object*) emporter; (*person*) emmener; (*remove*) enlever (from, à). ~ back, reprendre; (*return*) rendre; (*accompany*) raccompagner; (*statement*) retirer. ~ down, (*object*) descendre; (*notes*) prendre. ~ in, (*object*) rentrer; (*include*) inclure; (*cheat*) tromper; (*grasp*) saisir. ~ it that, supposer que. ~ off *v.t.* enlever; (*mimic*) imiter. *v.i.* (*aviat.*) décoller. ~-off *n.* imitation *f.*; (*aviat.*) décollage *m.* ~ on, (*task*, *staff*, *passenger*, *etc.*) prendre. ~ out, sortir; (*stain etc.*) enlever. ~ over *v.t.* (*factory*, *country*, *etc.*) prendre la direction de; (*firm*: *comm.*) racheter; *v.i.* (*of dictator*) prendre le pouvoir. ~ over from, (*relieve*) prendre la relève de; (*succeed*) prendre la succession de. ~-over *n.* (*pol.*) prise de pouvoir *f.*; (*comm.*) rachat *m.* ~ part, participer (in, à). ~ place, avoir lieu. ~ sides, prendre parti (with, pour). ~ to, se prendre d'amitié pour; (*activity*) prendre goût à. ~ to doing, se mettre à faire. ~ up, (*object*) monter; (*hobby*) se mettre à; (*occupy*) prendre; (*resume*) reprendre. ~ up with, se lier avec.

takings /'teɪkɪŋz/ *n. pl.* recette *f.*

talcum /'tælkəm/ *n.* talc *m.* ~ powder, talc *m.*

tale /teɪl/ *n.* conte *m.*; (*report*) récit *m.*; (*lie*) histoire *f.*

talent /'tælənt/ *n.* talent *m.* ~ed *a.* doué, qui a du talent.

talk /tɔːk/ *v.t./i.* parler; (*say*) dire; (*chat*) bavarder. —*n.* conversation *f.*, entretien *m.*; (*words*) propos *m. pl.*;

(*lecture*) exposé *m.* ~ **into doing,** persuader de faire. ~ **over,** discuter (de). ~**er** *n.* causeu|r, -se *m.*, *f.* ~**ing-to** *n.* (*fam.*) réprimande *f.*

talkative /'tɔːkətɪv/ *a.* bavard.

tall /tɔːl/ *a.* (**-er, -est**) (*high*) haut; (*person*) grand. ~ **story,** (*fam.*) histoire invraisemblable *f.*

tallboy /'tɔːlbɔɪ/ *n.* commode *f.*

tally /'tælɪ/ *v.i.* correspondre (**with,** à), s'accorder (**with,** avec).

tambourine /tæmbə'riːn/ *n.* tambourin *m.*

tame /teɪm/ *a.* (**-er, -est**) apprivoisé; (*dull*) insipide. —*v.t.* apprivoiser; (*lion*) dompter. ~**r** /-ə(r)/ *n.* dompteu|r, -se *m.*, *f.*

tamper /'tæmpə(r)/ *v.i.* ~ **with,** toucher à, tripoter; (*text*) altérer.

tampon /'tæmpən/ *n.* (*med.*) tampon hygiénique *m.*

tan /tæn/ *v.t.*/*i.* (*p.t.* **tanned**) bronzer; (*hide*) tanner. —*n.* bronzage *m.* —*a.* marron clair *invar.*

tandem /'tændəm/ *n.* (*bicycle*) tandem *m.* **in** ~, en tandem.

tang /tæŋ/ *n.* (*taste*) saveur forte *f.*; (*smell*) odeur forte *f.*

tangent /'tændʒənt/ *n.* tangente *f.*

tangerine /tændʒə'riːn/ *n.* mandarine *f.*

tangible /'tændʒəbl/ *a.* tangible.

tangle /'tæŋgl/ *v.t.* enchevêtrer. —*n.* enchevêtrement *m.* **become** ~**d,** s'enchevêtrer.

tango /'tæŋgəʊ/ *n.* (*pl.* **-os**) tango *m.*

tank /tæŋk/ *n.* réservoir *m.*; (*vat*) cuve *f.*; (*for fish*) aquarium *m.*; (*mil.*) char *m.*, tank *m.*

tankard /'tæŋkəd/ *n.* chope *f.*

tanker /'tæŋkə(r)/ *n.* camion-citerne *m.*; (*ship*) pétrolier *m.*

tantaliz|e /'tæntəlaɪz/ *v.t.* tourmenter. ~**ing** *a.* tentant.

tantamount /'tæntəmaʊnt/ *a.* **be** ~ **to,** équivaloir à.

tantrum /'tæntrəm/ *n.* crise de colère *or* de rage *f.*

tap[1] /tæp/ *n.* (*for water etc.*) robinet *m.* —*v.t.* (*p.t.* **tapped**) (*resources*) exploiter; (*telephone*) mettre sur table d'écoute.

tap[2] /tæp/ *v.t.*/*i.* (*p.t.* **tapped**) frapper (doucement). —*n.* petit coup *m.* **on** ~, (*fam.*) disponible. ~**-dance** *n.* claquettes *f. pl.*

tape /teɪp/ *n.* ruban *m.*; (*sticky*) ruban adhésif *m.* (**magnetic**) ~, bande

(*magnétique*) *f.* —*v.t.* (*tie*) attacher; (*stick*) coller; (*record*) enregistrer. ~-**measure** *n.* mètre (à) ruban *m.* ~ **recorder,** magnétophone *m.*

taper /'teɪpə(r)/ *n.* (*for lighting*) bougie *f.* —*v.t.*/*i.* (s')effiler. ~ **off,** (*diminish*) diminuer. ~**ed,** ~**ing** *adjs.* (*fingers etc.*) effilé, fuselé; (*trousers*) étroit du bas.

tapestry /'tæpɪstrɪ/ *n.* tapisserie *f.*

tapioca /tæpɪ'əʊkə/ *n.* tapioca *m.*

tar /tɑː(r)/ *n.* goudron *m.* —*v.t.* (*p.t.* **tarred**) goudronner.

tardy /'tɑːdɪ/ *a.* (**-ier, -iest**) (*slow*) lent; (*belated*) tardif.

target /'tɑːgɪt/ *n.* cible *f.*; (*objective*) objectif *m.*

tariff /'tærɪf/ *n.* (*charges*) tarif *m.*; (*on imports*) tarif douanier *m.*

Tarmac /'tɑːmæk/ *n.* (P.) macadam (goudronné) *m.*; (*runway*) piste *f.*

tarnish /'tɑːnɪʃ/ *v.t.*/*i.* (se) ternir.

tarpaulin /tɑː'pɔːlɪn/ *n.* bâche goudronnée *f.*

tarry /'tærɪ/ *v.i.* (*old use*) s'attarder.

tart[1] /tɑːt/ *a.* (**-er, -est**) acide.

tart[2] /tɑːt/ *n.* tarte *f.*; (*prostitute: sl.*) poule *f.* —*v.t.* ~ **up,** (*pej., sl.*) embellir (sans le moindre goût).

tartan /'tɑːtn/ *n.* tartan *m.* —*a.* écossais.

tartar /'tɑːtə(r)/ *n.* tartre *m.* ~ **sauce,** sauce tartare *f.*

task /tɑːsk/ *n.* tâche *f.*, travail *m.* **take to** ~, réprimander. ~ **force,** détachement spécial *m.*

tassel /'tæsl/ *n.* gland *m.*, pompon *m.*

taste /teɪst/ *n.* goût *m.* —*v.t.* (*eat, enjoy*) goûter; (*try*) goûter à; (*perceive taste of*) sentir le goût de. —*v.i.* ~ **of** *or* **like,** avoir un goût de. **have a** ~ **of,** (*experience*) goûter de. ~**less** *a.* sans goût; (*fig.*) de mauvais goût.

tasteful /'teɪstfl/ *a.* de bon goût. ~**ly** *adv.* avec goût.

tasty /'teɪstɪ/ *a.* (**-ier, -iest**) délicieux, savoureux.

tat /tæt/ *see* **tit**[2].

tatter|s /'tætəz/ *n. pl.* lambeaux *m. pl.* ~**ed** /-əd/ *a.* en lambeaux.

tattoo[1] /tə'tuː/ *n.* (*mil.*) spectacle militaire *m.*

tattoo[2] /tə'tuː/ *v.t.* tatouer. —*n.* tatouage *m.*

tatty /'tætɪ/ *a.* (**-ier, -iest**) (*shabby:* *fam.*) miteux, minable.

taught /tɔːt/ *see* **teach.**

taunt /tɔːnt/ v.t. railler. —n. raillerie f. ~ing a. railleur.

taut /tɔːt/ a. tendu.

tavern /'tævn/ n. taverne f.

tawdry /'tɔːdrɪ/ a. (-ier, -iest) (showy) tape-à-l'œil invar.

tax /tæks/ n. taxe f., impôt m.; (on income) impôts m. pl. —v.t. imposer; (put to test: fig.) mettre à l'épreuve. ~able a. imposable. ~ation /-'seɪʃn/ n. imposition f.; (taxes) impôts m. pl. ~-collector n. percepteur m. ~ing a. (fig.) éprouvant.

taxi /'tæksɪ/ n. (pl. -is) taxi m. —v.i. (p.t. taxied, pres. p. taxiing) (aviat.) rouler au sol. ~-cab n. taxi m. ~rank, (Amer.) ~ stand, station de taxi f.

taxpayer /'tækspeɪə(r)/ n. contribuable m./f.

tea /tiː/ n. thé m.; (snack) goûter m. ~bag n. sachet de thé m. ~-break n. pause-thé f. ~-leaf n. feuille de thé f. ~-set n. service à thé m. ~-shop n. salon de thé m. ~-towel n. torchon m.

teach /tiːtʃ/ v.t. (p.t. taught) apprendre (s.o. sth., qch. à qn.); (in school) enseigner (s.o. sth., qch. à qn.). —v.i. enseigner. ~er n. professeur m.; (primary) institu|teur, -trice m., f.; (member of teaching profession) enseignant(e) m. (f.). ~ing n. enseignement m.; a. pédagogique; (staff) enseignant.

teacup /'tiːkʌp/ n. tasse à thé f.

teak /tiːk/ n. (wood) teck m.

team /tiːm/ n. équipe f.; (of animals) attelage m. —v.i. ~ up, faire équipe (with, avec). ~work n. travail d'équipe m.

teapot /'tiːpɒt/ n. théière f.

tear[1] /teə(r)/ v.t./i. (p.t. tore, p.p. torn) (se) déchirer; (snatch) arracher (from, à); (rush) aller à toute vitesse. —n. déchirure f.

tear[2] /tɪə(r)/ n. larme f. in ~s, en larmes. ~-gas n. gaz lacrymogène m.

tearful /'tɪəfl/ a. (voice) larmoyant; (person) en larmes. ~ly adv. en pleurant, les larmes aux yeux.

tease /tiːz/ v.t. taquiner. —n. (person: fam.) taquin(e) m. (f.).

teaser /'tiːzə(r)/ n. (fam.) colle f.

teaspoon /'tiːspuːn/ n. petite cuiller f. ~ful n. (pl. -fuls) cuillerée à café f.

teat /tiːt/ n. (of bottle, animal) tétine f.

technical /'teknɪkl/ a. technique. ~ity /-'kælətɪ/ n. détail technique m. ~ly adv. techniquement.

technician /tek'nɪʃn/ n. technicien(ne) m. (f.).

technique /tek'niːk/ n. technique f.

technolog|y /tek'nɒlədʒɪ/ n. technologie f. ~ical /-ə'lɒdʒɪkl/ a. technologique.

teddy /'tedɪ/ a. ~ bear, ours en peluche m.

tedious /'tiːdɪəs/ a. fastidieux.

tedium /'tiːdɪəm/ n. ennui m.

tee /tiː/ n. (golf) tee m.

teem[1] /tiːm/ v.i. (swarm) grouiller (with, de).

teem[2] /tiːm/ v.i. ~ (with rain), pleuvoir à torrents.

teenage /'tiːneɪdʒ/ a. (d')adolescent. ~d a. adolescent. ~r /-ə(r)/ n. adolescent(e) m. (f.).

teens /tiːnz/ n. pl. in one's ~, adolescent.

teeny /'tiːnɪ/ a. (-ier, -iest) (tiny: fam.) minuscule.

teeter /'tiːtə(r)/ v.i. chanceler.

teeth /tiːθ/ see tooth.

teeth|e /tiːð/ v.i. faire ses dents. ~ing troubles, (fig.) difficultés initiales f. pl.

teetotaller /tiː'təʊtlə(r)/ n. personne qui ne boit pas d'alcool f.

telecommunications /telɪkəmjuːnɪ'keɪʃnz/ n. pl. télécommunications f. pl.

telegram /'telɪgræm/ n. télégramme m.

telegraph /'telɪgrɑːf/ n. télégraphe m. —a. télégraphique. ~ic /-'græfɪk/ a. télégraphique.

telepath|y /tɪ'lepəθɪ/ n. télépathie f. ~ic /telɪ'pæθɪk/ a. télépathique.

telephone /'telɪfəʊn/ n. téléphone m. —v.t. (person) téléphoner à; (message) téléphoner. —v.i. téléphoner. ~ book, annuaire m. ~ box n., ~ booth, cabine téléphonique f. ~ call, coup de téléphone m.

telephonist /tɪ'lefənɪst/ n. (in exchange) téléphoniste m./f.

telescop|e /'telɪskəʊp/ n. télescope m. —v.t./i. (se) télescoper. ~ic /-'skɒpɪk/ a. télescopique.

televise /'telɪvaɪz/ v.t. téléviser.

television /'telɪvɪʒn/ n. télévision f. ~ set, poste de télévision m.

telex /'teleks/ n. télex m. —v.t. envoyer par télex.

tell /tel/ v.t. (p.t. told) dire (s.o. sth,

qch. à qn.); (*story*) raconter; (*distinguish*) distinguer. —*v.i.* avoir un effet; (*know*) savoir. ~ **of**, parler de. ~ **off**, (*fam.*) gronder. ~**-tale** *n.* rapporteu|r, -se *m.,f.* ~ **tales**, rapporter.

teller /'telə(r)/ *n.* (*in bank*) caiss|ier, -ière *m., f.*

telling /'telɪŋ/ *a.* révélateur.

telly /'telɪ/ *n.* (*fam.*) télé *f.*

temerity /tɪ'merətɪ/ *n.* témérité *f.*

temp /temp/ *n.* (*temporary employee*: *fam.*) intérimaire *m.|f.*

temper /'tempə(r)/ *n.* humeur *f.*; (*anger*) colère *f.* —*v.t.* (*metal*) tremper; (*fig.*) tempérer. **lose one's** ~, se mettre en colère.

temperament /'temprəmənt/ *n.* tempérament *m.* ~**al** /-'mentl/ *a.* capricieux; (*innate*) inné.

temperance /'tempərəns/ *n.* (*in drinking*) tempérance *f.*

temperate /'tempərət/ *a.* tempéré.

temperature /'temprətʃə(r)/ *n.* température *f.* **have a** ~, avoir (de) la fièvre *or* de la température.

tempest /'tempɪst/ *n.* tempête *f.*

tempestuous /tem'pestʃʊəs/ *a.* (*meeting etc.*) orageux.

template /'templ(e)ɪt/ *n.* patron *m.*

temple[1] /'templ/ *n.* temple *m.*

temple[2] /'templ/ *n.* (*of head*) tempe *f.*

tempo /'tempəʊ/ *n.* (*pl.* **-os**) tempo *m.*

temporal /'tempərəl/ *a.* temporel.

temporar|y /'temprərɪ/ *a.* temporaire, provisoire. ~**ily** *adv.* temporairement, provisoirement.

tempt /tempt/ *v.t.* tenter. ~ **s.o. to do**, donner envie à qn. de faire. ~**ation** /-'teɪʃn/ *n.* tentation *f.* ~**ing** *a.* tentant.

ten /ten/ *a.* & *n.* dix (*m.*).

tenable /'tenəbl/ *a.* défendable.

tenac|ious /tɪ'neɪʃəs/ *a.* tenace. ~**ity** /-æsətɪ/ *n.* ténacité *f.*

tenancy /'tenənsɪ/ *n.* location *f.*

tenant /'tenənt/ *n.* locataire *m.|f.*

tend[1] /tend/ *v.t.* s'occuper de.

tend[2] /tend/ *v.i.* ~ **to**, (*be apt to*) avoir tendance à.

tendency /'tendənsɪ/ *n.* tendance *f.*

tender[1] /'tendə(r)/ *a.* tendre; (*sore, painful*) sensible. ~**ly** *adv.* tendrement. ~**ness** *n.* tendresse *f.*

tender[2] /'tendə(r)/ *v.t.* offrir, donner. —*n.* (*comm.*) soumission *f.* **be legal** ~, (*money*) avoir cours.

tendon /'tendən/ *n.* tendon *m.*

tenement /'tenəmənt/ *n.* maison de

rapport *f.*, H.L.M. *m.|f.*; (*slum*: *Amer.*) taudis *m.*

tenet /'tenɪt/ *n.* principe *m.*

tenfold /'tenfəʊld/ *a.* décuple. —*adv.* au décuple.

tenner /'tenə(r)/ *n.* (*fam.*) billet de dix livres *m.*

tennis /'tenɪs/ *n.* tennis *m.*

tenor /'tenə(r)/ *n.* (*meaning*) sens général *m.*; (*mus.*) ténor *m.*

tense[1] /tens/ *n.* (*gram.*) temps *m.*

tense[2] /tens/ *a.* (**-er, -est**) tendu. —*v.t.* (*muscles*) tendre, raidir. —*v.i.* (*of face*) se crisper. ~**ness** *n.* tension *f.*

tension /'tenʃn/ *n.* tension *f.*

tent /tent/ *n.* tente *f.*

tentacle /'tentəkl/ *n.* tentacule *m.*

tentative /'tentətɪv/ *a.* provisoire; (*hesitant*) timide. ~**ly** *adv.* provisoirement; timidement.

tenterhooks /'tentəhʊks/ *n. pl.* **on** ~, sur des charbons ardents.

tenth /tenθ/ *a.* & *n.* dixième (*m.|f.*).

tenuous /'tenjʊəs/ *a.* ténu.

tenure /'tenjʊə(r)/ *n.* (*in job, office*) (période de) jouissance *f.*

tepid /'tepɪd/ *a.* tiède.

term /tɜːm/ *n.* (*word, limit*) terme *m.*; (*of imprisonment*) temps; (*in school etc.*) trimestre *m.*; (*Amer.*) semestre *m.* ~**s**, conditions *f. pl.* —*v.t.* appeler. **on good/bad** ~**s**, en bons/mauvais termes. ~ **of office**, (*pol.*) mandat *m.*

terminal /'tɜːmɪnl/ *a.* terminal, final. —*n.* (*oil, computer*) terminal *m.*; (*rail.*) terminus *m.*; (*electr.*) borne *f.* (*air*) ~, aérogare *f.*

terminat|e /'tɜːmɪneɪt/ *v.t.* mettre fin à. —*v.i.* prendre fin. ~**ion** /-'neɪʃn/ *n.* fin *f.*

terminology /tɜːmɪ'nɒlədʒɪ/ *n.* terminologie *f.*

terminus /'tɜːmɪnəs/ *n.* (*pl.* **-ni** /-naɪ/) (*station*) terminus *m.*

terrace /'terəs/ *n.* terrasse *f.*; (*houses*) rangée de maisons contiguës *f.* **the** ~**s**, (*sport*) les gradins *m. pl.*

terrain /te'reɪn/ *n.* terrain *m.*

terrestrial /tɪ'restrɪəl/ *a.* terrestre.

terribl|e /'terəbl/ *a.* affreux, atroce. ~**y** *adv.* affreusement; (*very*) terriblement.

terrier /'terɪə(r)/ *n.* (*dog*) terrier *m.*

terrific /tə'rɪfɪk/ *a.* (*fam.*) terrible. ~**ally** /-klɪ/ *adv.* (*very*: *fam.*) terriblement; (*very well*: *fam.*) terriblement bien.

terrif|y /'terɪfaɪ/ *v.t.* terrifier. **be ~ied of,** avoir très peur de.

territorial /terɪ'tɔːrɪəl/ *a.* territorial.

territory /'terɪtərɪ/ *n.* territoire *m.*

terror /'terə(r)/ *n.* terreur *f.*

terroris|t /'terərɪst/ *n.* terroriste *m./f.* **~m** /-zəm/ *n.* terrorisme *m.*

terrorize /'terəraɪz/ *v.t.* terroriser.

terse /tɜːs/ *a.* concis, laconique.

test /test/ *n.* examen *m.*, analyse *f.*; (*of goods*) contrôle *m.*; (*of machine etc.*) essai *m.*; (*in school*) interrogation *f.*; (*of strength etc.: fig.*) épreuve *f.* —*v.t.* examiner, analyser; (*check*) contrôler; (*try*) essayer; (*pupil*) donner une interrogation à; (*fig.*) éprouver. **~ match,** match international *m.* **~ tube** *n.* éprouvette *f.*

testament /'testəmənt/ *n.* testament *m.* **Old/New T~,** Ancien/Nouveau Testament *m.*

testicle /'testɪkl/ *n.* testicule *m.*

testify /'testɪfaɪ/ *v.t./i.* témoigner (**to,** de). **~ that,** témoigner que.

testimonial /testɪ'məʊnɪəl/ *n.* recommendation *f.*

testimony /'testɪmənɪ/ *n.* témoignage *m.*

testy /'testɪ/ *a.* grincheux.

tetanus /'tetənəs/ *n.* tétanos *m.*

tetchy /'tetʃɪ/ *a.* grincheux.

tether /'teðə(r)/ *v.t.* attacher. —*n.* **at the end of one's ~,** à bout.

text /tekst/ *n.* texte *m.*

textbook /'tekstbʊk/ *n.* manuel *m.*

textile /'tekstaɪl/ *n.* & *a.* textile (*m.*).

texture /'tekstʃə(r)/ *n.* (*of paper etc.*) grain *m.* (*of fabric*) texture *f.*

Thai /taɪ/ *a.* & *n.* thaïlandais(e) (*m.* (*f.*)). **~land** *n.* Thaïlande *f.*

Thames /temz/ *n.* Tamise *f.*

than /ðæn, *unstressed* ðən/ *conj.* que, qu'*; (*with numbers*) de. **more/less ~ ten,** plus/moins de dix.

thank /θæŋk/ *v.t.* remercier. **~s** *n. pl.* remerciements *m. pl.* **~ you!,** merci! **~s!,** (*fam.*) merci! **~s to,** grâce à. **T~sgiving (Day),** (*Amer.*) jour d'action de grâces *m.* (*fête nationale*).

thankful /'θæŋkfl/ *a.* reconnaissant (**for,** de). **~ly** *adv.* (*happily*) heureusement.

thankless /'θæŋklɪs/ *a.* ingrat.

that /ðæt, *unstressed* ðət/ *a.* (*pl.* **those**) ce *or* cet*, cette. **those,** ces. —*pron.* ce *or* c'*, cela, ça. **~ (one),** celui-là, celle-là. **those (ones),** ceux-là, celles-là. —*adv.* si, aussi. —*rel. pron.* (*sub-*

ject) qui; (*object*) que, qu'*. —*conj.* que, qu'*. **~ boy,** ce garçon; (*with emphasis*) ce garçon-là. **~ is,** c'est. **~ is (to say),** c'est-à-dire. **after ~,** après ça *or* cela. **the day ~,** le jour où. **~ much,** autant que ça.

thatch /θætʃ/ *n.* chaume *m.* **~ed** *a.* en chaume. **~ed cottage,** chaumière *f.*

thaw /θɔː/ *v.t./i.* (faire) dégeler; (*snow*) (faire) fondre. —*n.* dégel *m.*

the /*before vowel* ðɪ, *before consonant* ðə, *stressed* ðiː/ *a.* le *or* l'*, la *or* l'*, *pl.* les. **of ~, from ~,** du, de l'*, de la, *pl.* des. **to ~, at ~,** au, à l'*, à la, *pl.* aux.

theatre /'θɪətə(r)/ *n.* théâtre *m.*

theatrical /θɪ'ætrɪkl/ *a.* théâtral.

theft /θeft/ *n.* vol *m.*

their /ðeə(r)/ *a.* leur, *pl.* leurs.

theirs /ðeəz/ *poss. pron.* le *or* la leur, les leurs.

them /ðem, *unstressed* ðəm/ *pron.* les; (*after prep.*) eux, elles. **(to) ~,** leur. **I know ~,** je les connais.

theme /θiːm/ *n.* thème *m.* **~ song,** (*in film etc.*) chanson principale *f.*

themselves /ðəm'selvz/ *pron.* eux-mêmes, elles-mêmes; (*reflexive*) se; (*after prep.*) eux, elles.

then /ðen/ *adv.* alors; (*next*) ensuite, puis; (*therefore*) alors, donc. —*a.* d'alors. **from ~ on,** dès lors.

theolog|y /θɪ'ɒlədʒɪ/ *n.* théologie *f.* **~ian** /θɪə'ləʊdʒən/ *n.* théologien(ne) *m.* (*f.*).

theorem /'θɪərəm/ *n.* théorème *m.*

theor|y /'θɪərɪ/ *n.* théorie *f.* **~etical** /-'retɪkl/ *a.* théorique.

therapeutic /θerə'pjuːtɪk/ *a.* thérapeutique.

therapy /'θerəpɪ/ *n.* thérapie *f.*

there /ðeə(r)/ *adv.* là; (*with verb*) y; (*over there*) là-bas. —*int.* allez. **he goes ~,** il y va. **on ~,** là-dessus. **~ is, ~ are,** il y a; (*pointing*) voilà. **~, ~!,** allons, allons! **~abouts** *adv.* par là. **~after** *adv.* par la suite. **~by** *adv.* de cette manière.

therefore /'ðeəfɔː(r)/ *adv.* donc.

thermal /'θɜːml/ *a.* thermique.

thermometer /θə'mɒmɪtə(r)/ *n.* thermomètre *m.*

thermonuclear /θɜːməʊ'njuːklɪə(r)/ *a.* thermonucléaire.

Thermos /'θɜːməs/ *n.* (P.) thermos *m./f. invar.* (P.).

thermostat /'θɜːməstæt/ *n.* thermostat *m.*

thesaurus /θɪˈsɔːrəs/ *n.* (*pl.* **-ri** /-raɪ/) dictionnaire de synonymes *m.*

these /ðiːz/ *see* **this.**

thesis /ˈθiːsɪs/ *n.* (*pl.* **theses** /-siːz/) thèse *f.*

they /ðeɪ/ *pron.* ils, elles; (*emphatic*) eux, elles; (*people in general*) on.

thick /θɪk/ *a.* (-**er**, -**est**) épais; (*stupid*) bête; (*friends: fam.*) très lié. —*adv.* = **thickly.** —*n.* in the ~ of, au plus gros de. ~**ly** *adv.* (*grow*) dru; (*spread*) en couche épaisse. ~**ness** *n.* épaisseur *f.* ~-**skinned** *a.* peu sensible.

thicken /ˈθɪkən/ *v.t./i.* (s')épaissir.

thickset /θɪkˈset/ *a.* trapu.

thief /θiːf/ *n.* (*pl.* **thieves**) voleu|r, -se *m., f.*

thiev|e /θiːv/ *v.t./i.* voler. ~**ing** *a.* voleur.

thigh /θaɪ/ *n.* cuisse *f.*

thimble /ˈθɪmbl/ *n.* dé (à coudre) *m.*

thin /θɪn/ *a.* (**thinner, thinnest**) mince; (*person*) maigre, mince; (*sparse*) clairsemé; (*fine*) fin. —*adv.* = **thinly.** —*v.t./i.* (*p.t.* **thinned**) (*liquid*) (s')éclaircir. ~ **out,** (*in quantity*) (s')éclaircir. ~**ly** *adv.* (*slightly*) légèrement. ~**ness** *n.* minceur *f.*; maigreur *f.*

thing /θɪŋ/ *n.* chose *f.* ~**s,** (*belongings*) affaires *f. pl.* **the best** ~ **is to,** le mieux est de. **the** (**right**) ~, ce qu'il faut (**for s.o.,** à qn.).

think /θɪŋk/ *v.t./i.* (*p.t.* **thought**) penser (**about, of,** à); (*carefully*) réfléchir (**about, of,** à). ~ **better of it,** se raviser. ~ **nothing of,** trouver naturel de. ~ **of,** (*hold opinion of*) penser de. ~ **over,** bien réfléchir à. ~-**tank** *n.* comité d'experts *m.* ~ **up,** inventer. ~**er** *n.* penseu|r, -se *m., f.*

third /θɜːd/ *a.* troisième. —*n.* troisième *m./f.*; (*fraction*) tiers *m.* ~**ly** *adv.* troisièmement. ~-**rate** *a.* très inférieur. **T**~ **World,** Tiers Monde *m.*

thirst /θɜːst/ *n.* soif *f.* ~**y** *a.* be ~**y,** avoir soif. **make** ~**y,** donner soif à.

thirteen /θɜːˈtiːn/ *a. & n.* treize (*m.*). ~**th** *a. & n.* treizième (*m./f.*).

thirt|y /ˈθɜːtɪ/ *a. & n.* trente (*m.*). ~**ieth** *a. & n.* trentième (*m./f.*).

this /ðɪs/ *a.* (*pl.* **these**) ce *or* cet*, cette. **these,** ces. —*pron.* ce *or* c'*, ceci. ~ (**one**), celui-ci, celle-ci. **these** (**ones**), ceux-ci, celles-ci. ~ **boy,** ce garçon; (*with emphasis*) ce garçon-ci. ~ **is,** c'est. **after** ~, après ceci.

thistle /ˈθɪsl/ *n.* chardon *m.*

thorn /θɔːn/ *n.* épine *f.* ~**y** *a.* épineux.

thorough /ˈθʌrə/ *a.* consciencieux; (*deep*) profond; (*cleaning, washing*) à fond. ~**ly** *adv.* (*clean, study, etc.*) à fond; (*very*) tout à fait.

thoroughbred /ˈθʌrəbred/ *n.* (*horse etc.*) pur-sang *m. invar.*

thoroughfare /ˈθʌrəfeə(r)/ *n.* grande artère *f.*

those /ðəʊz/ *see* **that.**

though /ðəʊ/ *conj.* bien que. —*adv.* (*fam.*) cependant.

thought /θɔːt/ *see* **think.** —*n.* pensée *f.*; (*idea*) idée *f.*

thoughtful /ˈθɔːtfl/ *a.* pensif; (*considerate*) attentionné. ~**ly** *adv.* pensivement; avec considération.

thoughtless /ˈθɔːtlɪs/ *a.* étourdi. ~**ly** *adv.* étourdiment.

thousand /ˈθaʊznd/ *a. & n.* mille (*m. invar.*). ~**s of,** des milliers de.

thrash /θræʃ/ *v.t.* rosser; (*defeat*) écraser. ~ **out,** discuter à fond.

thread /θred/ *n.* (*yarn & fig.*) fil *m.*; (*of screw*) pas *m.* —*v.t.* enfiler. ~ **one's way,** se faufiler.

threadbare /ˈθredbeə(r)/ *a.* râpé.

threat /θret/ *n.* menace *f.*

threaten /ˈθretn/ *v.t./i.* menacer. ~**ingly** *adv.* d'un air menaçant.

three /θriː/ *a. & n.* trois (*m.*). ~**fold** *a.* triple; *adv.* trois fois (autant).

thresh /θreʃ/ *v.t.* (*corn etc.*) battre.

threshold /ˈθreʃəʊld/ *n.* seuil *m.*

threw /θruː/ *see* **throw.**

thrift /θrɪft/ *n.* économie *f.* ~**y** *a.* économe.

thrill /θrɪl/ *n.* émotion *f.*, frisson *m.* —*v.t.* transporter (de joie). —*v.i.* frissonner (de joie). **be** ~**ed,** être ravi. ~**ing** *a.* excitant.

thriller /ˈθrɪlə(r)/ *n.* livre *or* film à suspense *m.*

thriv|e /θraɪv/ *v.i.* (*p.t.* **thrived** *or* **throve,** *p.p.* **thrived** *or* **thriven**) prospérer. **he** ~**es on it,** cela lui réussit. ~**ing** *a.* prospère.

throat /θrəʊt/ *n.* gorge *f.* **have a sore** ~, avoir mal à la gorge.

throb /θrɒb/ *v.i.* (*p.t.* **throbbed**) (*wound*) causer des élancements; (*heart*) palpiter; (*fig.*) vibrer. —*n.* (*pain*) élancement *m.*; palpitation *f.* ~**bing** *a.* (*pain*) lancinant.

throes /θrəʊz/ *n. pl.* in the ~ of, au milieu de, aux prises avec.

thrombosis /θrɒmˈbəʊsɪs/ *n.* thrombose *f.*

throne /θrəʊn/ *n*. trône *m*.

throng /θrɒŋ/ *n*. foule *f*. —*v.t.* (*streets etc.*) se presser dans. —*v.i.* (*arrive*) affluer.

throttle /'θrɒtl/ *n*. (*auto.*) accélérateur *m*. —*v.t.* étrangler.

through /θru:/ *prep.* à travers; (*during*) pendant; (*by means or way of, out of*) par; (*by reason of*) grâce à, à cause de. —*adv.* à travers; (*entirely*) jusqu'au bout. —*a*. (*train etc.*) direct. **be ~**, (*finished*) avoir fini. **come** or **go ~**, (*cross, pierce*) traverser.

throughout /θru:'aʊt/ *prep.* **~ the** country/*etc.*, dans tout le pays/*etc.* **~ the day**/*etc.*, pendant toute la journée/*etc.* —*adv.* (*place*) partout; (*time*) tout le temps.

throw /θrəʊ/ *v.t.* (*p.t.* **threw**, *p.p.* **thrown**) jeter, lancer; (*baffle: fam.*) déconcerter. —*n*. jet *m*.; (*of dice*) coup *m*. **~ a party**, (*fam.*) donner une réception. **~ away**, jeter. **~-away** *a*. à jeter. **~ off**, (*get rid of*) se débarrasser de. **~ out**, jeter; (*person*) expulser; (*reject*) rejeter. **~ over**, (*desert*) plaquer. **~ up**, (*one's arms*) lever; (*resign from*) abandonner; (*vomit*) vomir.

thrush /θrʌʃ/ *n*. (*bird*) grive *f*.

thrust /θrʌst/ *v.t.* (*p.t.* **thrust**) pousser. —*n*. poussée *f*. **~ into**, (*put*) enfoncer dans, mettre dans. **~ upon**, (*force on*) imposer à.

thud /θʌd/ *n*. bruit sourd *m*.

thug /θʌɡ/ *n*. voyou *m*., bandit *m*.

thumb /θʌm/ *n*. pouce *m*. —*v.t.* (*book*) feuilleter. **~ a lift**, faire de l'auto-stop. **~-index**, répertoire à onglets *m*.

thumbtack /'θʌmtæk/ *n*. (*Amer.*) punaise *f*.

thump /θʌmp/ *v.t./i.* cogner (sur); (*of heart*) battre fort. —*n*. grand coup *m*. **~ing** *a*. (*fam.*) énorme.

thunder /'θʌndə(r)/ *n*. tonnerre *m*. —*v.i.* (*weather, person, etc.*) tonner. **~ past**, passer dans un bruit de tonnerre. **~y** *a*. orageux.

thunderbolt /'θʌndəbəʊlt/ *n*. coup de foudre *m*.; (*event: fig.*) coup de tonnerre *m*.

thunderstorm /'θʌndəstɔ:m/ *n*. orage *m*.

Thursday /'θɜ:zdɪ/ *n*. jeudi *m*.

thus /ðʌs/ *adv*. ainsi.

thwart /θwɔ:t/ *v.t.* contrecarrer.

thyme /taɪm/ *n*. thym *m*.

thyroid /'θaɪrɔɪd/ *n*. thyroïde *f*.

tiara /tɪ'ɑ:rə/ *n*. diadème *m*.

tic /tɪk/ *n*. tic (nerveux) *m*.

tick[1] /tɪk/ *n*. (*sound*) tic-tac *m*.; (*mark*) coche *f*.; (*moment: fam.*) instant *m*. —*v.i.* faire tic-tac. —*v.t.* **~ (off)**, cocher. **~ off**, (*sl.*) réprimander. **~ over**, (*engine, factory*) tourner au ralenti.

tick[2] /tɪk/ *n*. (*insect*) tique *f*.

ticket /'tɪkɪt/ *n*. billet *m*.; (*for bus, cloakroom, etc.*) ticket *m*.; (*label*) étiquette *f*. **~-collector** *n*. contrôleu|r, -se *m., f*. **~-office** *n*. guichet *m*.

tickle /'tɪkl/ *v.t.* chatouiller; (*amuse: fig.*) amuser. —*n*. chatouillement *m*.

ticklish /'tɪklɪʃ/ *a*. chatouilleux.

tidal /'taɪdl/ *a*. qui a des marées. **~ wave**, raz-de-marée *m. invar*.

tiddly-winks /'tɪdlɪwɪŋks/ *n*. (*game*) jeu de puce *m*.

tide /taɪd/ *n*. marée *f*.; (*of events*) cours *m*. —*v.t.* **~ over**, dépanner.

tidings /'taɪdɪŋz/ *n. pl*. nouvelles *f. pl*.

tid|y /'taɪdɪ/ *a*. (**-ier**, **-iest**) (*room*) bien rangé; (*appearance, work*) soigné; (*methodical*) ordonné; (*amount: fam.*) joli. —*v.t./i.* ranger. **~y o.s.**, s'arranger. **~ily** *adv*. avec soin. **~iness** *n*. ordre *m*.

tie /taɪ/ *v.t.* (*pres. p.* **tying**) attacher, nouer; (*a knot*) faire; (*link*) lier. —*v.i.* (*darts etc.*) finir à égalité de points; (*football*) faire match nul; (*in race*) être ex aequo. —*n*. attache *f*.; (*necktie*) cravate *f*.; (*link*) lien *m*.; égalité (de points) *f*.; match nul *m*. **~ in with**, être lié à. **~ up**, attacher; (*money*) immobiliser; (*occupy*) occuper. **~-up** *n*. (*link*) lien *m*.; (*auto., Amer.*) bouchon *m*.

tier /tɪə(r)/ *n*. étage *m*., niveau *m*.; (*in stadium etc.*) gradin *m*.

tiff /tɪf/ *n*. petite querelle *f*.

tiger /'taɪɡə(r)/ *n*. tigre *m*.

tight /taɪt/ *a*. (**-er**, **-est**) (*clothes*) étroit, juste; (*rope*) tendu; (*lid*) solidement fixé; (*control*) strict; (*knot, collar, schedule*) serré; (*drunk: fam.*) ivre. —*adv*. (*hold, sleep, etc.*) bien; (*squeeze*) fort. **~ corner**, situation difficile *f*. **~-fisted** *a*. avare. **~ly** *adv*. bien; (*squeeze*) fort.

tighten /'taɪtn/ *v.t./i.* (se) tendre; (*bolt etc.*) (se) resserrer; (*control etc.*) renforcer. **~ up on**, se montrer plus strict à l'égard de.

tightrope /'taɪtrəʊp/ *n.* corde raide *f.* ~ **walker,** funambule *m.|f.*

tights /taɪts/ *n. pl.* collant *m.*

tile /taɪl/ *n.* (*on wall, floor*) carreau *m.*; (*on roof*) tuile *f.* —*v.t.* carreler; couvrir de tuiles.

till[1] /tɪl/ *v.t.* (*land*) cultiver.

till[2] /tɪl/ *prep. & conj.* = **until.**

till[3] /tɪl/ *n.* caisse (enregistreuse) *f.*

tilt /tɪlt/ *v.t./i.* pencher. —*n.* (*slope*) inclinaison *f.* **(at) full** ~, à toute vitesse.

timber /'tɪmbə(r)/ *n.* bois (de construction) *m.*; (*trees*) arbres *m. pl.*

time /taɪm/ *n.* temps *m.*; (*moment*) moment *m.*; (*epoch*) époque *f.*; (*by clock*) heure *f.*; (*occasion*) fois *f.*; (*rhythm*) mesure *f.* ~**s,** (*multiplying*) fois *f. pl.* —*v.t.* choisir le moment de; (*measure*) minuter; (*sport*) chronométrer. **behind the** ~**s,** en retard sur son temps. **for the** ~ **being,** pour le moment. **from** ~ **to time,** de temps en temps. **have a good** ~, s'amuser. **in no** ~, en un rien de temps. **in** ~, à temps; (*eventually*) avec le temps. **on** ~, à l'heure. ~ **bomb,** bombe à retardement *f.* ~-**honoured** *a.* consacré (par l'usage). ~-**lag** *n.* décalage *m.* ~ **off,** du temps libre. ~ **zone,** fuseau horaire *m.*

timeless /'taɪmlɪs/ *a.* éternel.

timely /'taɪmlɪ/ *a.* à propos.

timer /'taɪmə(r)/ *n.* (*techn.*) minuterie *f.*; (*culin.*) compte-minutes *m. invar.*; (*with sand*) sablier *m.*

timetable /'taɪmteɪbl/ *n.* horaire *m.*

timid /'tɪmɪd/ *a.* timide; (*fearful*) peureux. ~**ly** *adv.* timidement.

timing /'taɪmɪŋ/ *n.* (*measuring*) minutage *m.*; (*moment*) moment *m.*; (*of artist*) rythme *m.*

tin /tɪn/ *n.* étain *m.*; (*container*) boîte *f.* ~(**plate**), fer-blanc *m.* —*v.t.* (*p.t.* **tinned**) mettre en boîte. ~ **foil,** papier d'aluminium *m.* ~**ny** *a.* métallique. ~-**opener** *n.* ouvre-boîte(s) *m.*

tinge /tɪndʒ/ *v.t.* teinter (**with,** de). —*n.* teinte *f.*

tingle /'tɪŋgl/ *v.i.* (*prickle*) picoter. —*n.* picotement *m.*

tinker /'tɪŋkə(r)/ *n.* rétameur *m.* —*v.i.* ~ (**with**), bricoler.

tinkle /'tɪŋkl/ *n.* tintement *m.*; (*fam.*) coup de téléphone *m.*

tinsel /'tɪnsl/ *n.* cheveux d'ange *m. pl.*, guirlandes de Noël *f. pl.*

tint /tɪnt/ *n.* teinte *f.*; (*for hair*) shampooing colorant *m.* —*v.t.* (*glass, paper*) teinter.

tiny /'taɪnɪ/ *a.* (-**ier,** -**iest**) minuscule, tout petit.

tip[1] /tɪp/ *n.* bout *m.* ~**ped cigarette,** cigarette (à bout) filtre *f.*

tip[2] /tɪp/ *v.t./i.* (*p.t.* **tipped**) (*tilt*) pencher; (*overturn*) (faire) basculer; (*pour*) verser; (*empty*) déverser. —*n.* (*money*) pourboire *m.*; (*advice*) tuyau *m.*; (*for rubbish*) décharge *f.* ~ **off,** prévenir. ~-**off** *n.* tuyau *m.* (*pour prévenir*).

tipple /'tɪpl/ *v.i.* (*drink*) picoler.

tipsy /'tɪpsɪ/ *a.* un peu ivre, gris.

tiptoe /'tɪptəʊ/ *n.* **on** ~, sur la pointe des pieds.

tiptop /'tɪptɒp/ *a.* (*fam.*) excellent.

tir|e[1] /'taɪə(r)/ *v.t./i.* (se) fatiguer. ~**e of,** se lasser de. ~**eless** *a.* infatigable. ~**ing** *a.* fatigant.

tire[2] /'taɪə(r)/ *n.* (*Amer.*) pneu *m.*

tired /'taɪəd/ *a.* fatigué. **be** ~ **of,** en avoir assez de.

tiresome /'taɪəsəm/ *a.* ennuyeux.

tissue /'tɪʃuː/ *n.* tissu *m.*; (*handkerchief*) mouchoir en papier *m.* ~-**paper** *n.* papier de soie *m.*

tit[1] /tɪt/ *n.* (*bird*) mésange *f.*

tit[2] /tɪt/ *n.* **give** ~ **for tat,** rendre coup pour coup.

titbit /'tɪtbɪt/ *n.* friandise *f.*

titillate /'tɪtɪleɪt/ *v.t.* exciter.

title /'taɪtl/ *n.* titre *m.* ~-**deed** *n.* titre de propriété *m.* ~-**role** *n.* rôle principal *m.*

titled /'taɪtld/ *a.* (*person*) titré.

tittle-tattle /'tɪtltætl/ *n.* commérages *m. pl.*, potins *m. pl.*

titular /'tɪtjʊlə(r)/ *a.* (*ruler etc.*) nominal.

to /tuː, *unstressed* tə/ *prep.* à; (*towards*) vers; (*of attitude*) envers. —*adv.* **push or pull** ~, (*close*) fermer. ~ **France** /*etc.*, en France/*etc.* ~ **town,** en ville. ~ **Canada**/*etc.*, au Canada/*etc.* ~ **the baker's**/*etc.*, chez le boulanger/*etc.* **the road/door**/*etc.* ~, la route/porte /*etc.* de. ~ **me/ her**/*etc.*, me/lui/*etc.* **do/sit**/*etc.*, faire/s'asseoir/*etc.* **ten** ~ **six,** (*by clock*) six heures moins dix. **go** ~ **and fro,** aller et venir. **husband**/*etc.* ~-**be** *n.* mari/*etc.* futur *m.* ~-**do** *n.* (*fuss*) chichi(s) *m.* (*pl.*).

toad /təʊd/ *n.* crapaud *m.*

toadstool /'təʊdstuːl/ *n.* champignon (vénéneux) *m.*

toast /təʊst/ *n.* pain grillé *m.*, toast *m.*; (*drink*) toast *m.* —*v.t.* (*bread*) faire

griller; (*drink to*) porter un toast à; (*event*) arroser. ~**er** *n*. grille-pain *m*. *invar*.

tobacco /tə'bækəʊ/ *n*. tabac *m*.

tobacconist /tə'bækənɪst/ *n*. marchand(e) de tabac *m*. (*f*.). ~'s **shop**, tabac *m*.

toboggan /tə'bɒgən/ *n*. toboggan *m*., luge *f*.

today /tə'deɪ/ *n*. & *adv*. aujourd'hui (*m*.).

toddler /'tɒdlə(r)/ *n*. tout(e) petit(e) enfant *m./f*.

toddy /'tɒdɪ/ *n*. (*drink*) grog *m*.

toe /təʊ/ *n*. orteil *m*.; (*of shoe*) bout *m*. —*v.t*. ~ **the line**, se conformer. **on one's** ~**s**, vigilant. ~**-hold** *n*. prise (précaire) *f*.

toff /tɒf/ *n*. (*sl*.) dandy *m*., aristo *m*.

toffee /'tɒfɪ/ *n*. caramel *m*. ~**-apple** *n*. pomme caramélisée *f*.

together /tə'geðə(r)/ *adv*. ensemble; (*at same time*) en même temps. ~ **with**, avec. ~**ness** *n*. camaraderie *f*.

toil /tɔɪl/ *v.i*. peiner. —*n*. labeur *m*.

toilet /'tɔɪlɪt/ *n*. toilettes *f. pl*.; (*grooming*) toilette *f*. ~**-paper** *n*. papier hygiénique *m*. ~**-roll** *n*. rouleau de papier hygiénique *m*. ~ **water**, eau de toilette *f*.

toiletries /'tɔɪlɪtrɪz/ *n. pl*. articles de toilette *m. pl*.

token /'təʊkən/ *n*. témoignage *m*., marque *f*.; (*voucher*) bon *m*.; (*coin*) jeton *m*. —*a*. symbolique.

told /təʊld/ *see* **tell.** —*a*. **all** ~, (*all in all*) en tout.

tolerabl|e /'tɒlərəbl/ *a*. tolérable; (*not bad*) passable. ~**y** *adv*. (*work, play, etc*.) passablement.

toleran|t /'tɒlərənt/ *a*. tolérant (**of**, à l'égard de). ~**ce** *n*. tolérance *f*. ~**tly** *adv*. avec tolérance.

tolerate /'tɒləreɪt/ *v.t*. tolérer.

toll[1] /təʊl/ *n*. péage *m*. **death** ~, nombre de morts *m*. **take its** ~, (*of age*) faire sentir son poids.

toll[2] /təʊl/ *v.i*. (*of bell*) sonner.

tom /tɒm/, ~**-cat** *n*. matou *m*.

tomato /tə'mɑːtəʊ, *Amer*. tə'meɪtəʊ/ *n*. (*pl*. ~**oes**) tomate *f*.

tomb /tuːm/ *n*. tombeau *m*.

tombola /tɒm'bəʊlə/ *n*. tombola *f*.

tomboy /'tɒmbɔɪ/ *n*. garçon manqué *m*.

tombstone /'tuːmstəʊn/ *n*. pierre tombale *f*.

tomfoolery /tɒm'fuːlərɪ/ *n*. âneries *f. pl*., bêtises *f. pl*.

tomorrow /tə'mɒrəʊ/ *n*. & *adv*. demain (*m*.). ~ **morning/night**, demain matin/soir.

ton /tʌn/ *n*. tonne *f*. (= *1016 kg*.). (**metric**) ~, tonne *f*. (= *1000 kg*.). ~**s of**, (*fam*.) des masses de.

tone /təʊn/ *n*. ton *m*.; (*of radio, telephone, etc*.) tonalité *f*. —*v.t*. ~ **down**, atténuer. —*v.i*. ~ **in**, s'harmoniser (**with**, avec). ~**-deaf** *a*. qui n'a pas d'oreille. ~ **up**, (*muscles*) tonifier.

tongs /tɒŋz/ *n. pl*. pinces *f. pl*.; (*for sugar*) pince *f*.; (*for hair*) fer *m*.

tongue /tʌŋ/ *n*. langue *f*. ~**-tied** *a*. muet. ~**-twister** *n*. phrase difficile à prononcer *f*. **with one's** ~ **in one's cheek**, ironiquement.

tonic /'tɒnɪk/ *n*. (*med*.) tonique *m*. —*a*. (*effect, water, accent*) tonique.

tonight /tə'naɪt/ *n*. & *adv*. cette nuit (*f*.); (*evening*) ce soir (*m*.).

tonne /tʌn/ *n*. (*metric*) tonne *f*.

tonsil /'tɒnsl/ *n*. amygdale *f*.

tonsillitis /tɒnsɪ'laɪtɪs/ *n*. angine *f*.

too /tuː/ *adv*. trop; (*also*) aussi. ~ **many** *a*. trop de; *n*. trop. ~ **much** *a*. trop de; *adv*. & *n*. trop.

took /tʊk/ *see* **take.**

tool /tuːl/ *n*. outil *m*. ~**-bag** *n*. trousse à outils *f*.

toot /tuːt/ *n*. coup de klaxon *m*. —*v.t./i*. ~ **(the horn)**, klaxonner.

tooth /tuːθ/ *n*. (*pl*. **teeth**) dent *f*. ~**less** *a*. édenté.

toothache /'tuːθeɪk/ *n*. mal de dents *m*.

toothbrush /'tuːθbrʌʃ/ *n*. brosse à dents *f*.

toothcomb /'tuːθkəʊm/ *n*. peigne fin *m*.

toothpaste /'tuːθpeɪst/ *n*. dentifrice *m*., pâte dentifrice *f*.

toothpick /'tuːθpɪk/ *n*. cure-dent *m*.

top[1] /tɒp/ *n*. (*highest point*) sommet *m*.; (*upper part*) haut *m*.; (*upper surface*) dessus *m*.; (*lid*) couvercle *m*.; (*of bottle, tube*) bouchon *m*.; (*of beer bottle*) capsule *f*.; (*of list*) tête *f*. —*a*. (*shelf etc*.) du haut; (*in rank*) premier; (*best*) meilleur; (*distinguished*) éminent; (*maximum*) maximum. —*v.t*. (*p.t*. **topped**) (*exceed*) dépasser. **from** ~ **to bottom**, de fond en comble. **on** ~ **of**, sur; (*fig*.) en plus de. ~ **hat**, haut-de-forme *m*. ~**-heavy** *a*. trop lourd du haut. ~**-notch** *a*. excellent. ~ **secret**, ultra-secret. ~ **up**, remplir.

~**ped with,** surmonté de; (*cream etc.: culin.*) nappé de.

top[2] /tɒp/ *n.* (*toy*) toupie *f.*

topic /'tɒpɪk/ *n.* sujet *m.*

topical /'tɒpɪkl/ *a.* d'actualité.

topless /'tɒplɪs/ *a.* aux seins nus.

topple /'tɒpl/ *v.t./i.* (faire) tomber, (faire) basculer.

topsy-turvy /tɒpsɪ'tɜːvɪ/ *adv.* & *a.* sens dessus dessous.

torch /tɔːtʃ/ *n.* (*electric*) lampe de poche *f.*; (*flaming*) torche *f.*

tore /tɔː(r)/ *see* **tear**[1].

torment[1] /'tɔːmənt/ *n.* tourment *m.*

torment[2] /tɔː'ment/ *v.t.* tourmenter; (*annoy*) agacer.

torn /tɔːn/ *see* **tear**[1].

tornado /tɔː'neɪdəʊ/ *n.* (*pl.* -oes) tornade *f.*

torpedo /tɔː'piːdəʊ/ *n.* (*pl.* -oes) torpille *f.* —*v.t.* torpiller.

torrent /'tɒrənt/ *n.* torrent *m.* ~**ial** /tə'renʃl/ *a.* torrentiel.

torrid /'tɒrɪd/ *a.* (*climate etc.*) torride; (*fig.*) passionné.

torso /'tɔːsəʊ/ *n.* (*pl.* -os) torse *m.*

tortoise /'tɔːtəs/ *n.* tortue *f.*

tortoiseshell /'tɔːtəʃel/ *n.* (*for ornaments etc.*) écaille *f.*

tortuous /'tɔːtʃʊəs/ *a.* tortueux.

torture /'tɔːtʃə(r)/ *n.* torture *f.*, supplice *m.* —*v.t.* torturer. ~**r** /-ə(r)/ *n.* tortionnaire *m.*

Tory /'tɔːrɪ/ *n.* tory *m.* —*a.* tory (*f. invar.*).

toss /tɒs/ *v.t.* jeter, lancer; (*shake*) agiter. —*v.i.* s'agiter. ~ **a coin,** ~ **up,** tirer à pile ou face (**for,** pour).

tot[1] /tɒt/ *n.* petit(e) enfant *m./f.*; (*glass: fam.*) petit verre *m.*

tot[2] /tɒt/ *v.t.* (*p.t.* **totted**). ~ **up,** (*fam.*) additionner.

total /'təʊtl/ *a.* total. —*n.* total *m.* —*v.t.* (*p.t.* **totalled**) (*find total of*) totaliser; (*amount to*) s'élever à. ~**ity** /-'tælətɪ/ *n.* totalité *f.* ~**ly** *adv.* totalement.

totalitarian /təʊtælɪ'teərɪən/ *a.* totalitaire.

totter /'tɒtə(r)/ *v.i.* chanceler.

touch /tʌtʃ/ *v.t./i.* toucher; (*of ends, gardens, etc.*) se toucher; (*tamper with*) toucher à. —*n.* (*sense*) toucher *m.*; (*contact*) contact *m.*; (*of colour*) touche *f.*; (*football*) touche *f.* **a ~ of,** (*small amount*) un peu de. **get in ~ with,** contacter. ~**-and-go** *a.* douteux. ~ **down,** (*aviat.*) atterrir. ~**line** *n.* (ligne de) touche *f.* ~ **off,**

(*explode*) faire partir; (*cause*) déclencher. ~ **on,** (*mention*) aborder. ~ **up,** retoucher.

touching /'tʌtʃɪŋ/ *a.* touchant.

touchstone /'tʌtʃstəʊn/ *n.* pierre de touche *f.*

touchy /'tʌtʃɪ/ *a.* susceptible.

tough /tʌf/ *a.* (**-er, -est**) (*hard, difficult*) dur; (*strong*) solide; (*relentless*) acharné. —*n.* ~ (**guy**), dur *m.* ~ **luck!,** (*fam.*) tant pis! ~**ness** *n.* dureté *f.*; solidité *f.*

toughen /'tʌfn/ *v.t.* (*strengthen*) renforcer; (*person*) endurcir.

toupee /'tuːpeɪ/ *n.* postiche *m.*

tour /tʊə(r)/ *n.* voyage *m.*; (*visit*) visite *f.*; (*by team etc.*) tournée *f.* —*v.t.* visiter. **on ~,** en tournée.

tourism /'tʊərɪzəm/ *n.* tourisme *m.*

tourist /'tʊərɪst/ *n.* touriste *m./f.* —*a.* touristique. ~ **office,** syndicat d'initiative *m.*

tournament /'tɔːnəmənt/ *n.* (*sport & medieval*) tournoi *m.*

tousle /'taʊzl/ *v.t.* ébouriffer.

tout /taʊt/ *v.i.* ~ (**for**), racoler. —*v.t.* (*sell*) revendre. —*n.* racoleu|r, -se *m.f.*; revendeu|r, -se *m.*, *f.*

tow /təʊ/ *v.t.* remorquer. —*n.* remorque *f.* **on ~,** en remorque. ~ **away,** (*vehicle*) (faire) enlever. ~**-path** *n.* chemin de halage *m.*

toward(s) /tə'wɔːd(z), *Amer.* tɔːd(z)/ *prep.* vers; (*of attitude*) envers.

towel /'taʊəl/ *n.* serviette *f.*; (*tea-towel*) torchon *m.* ~**ling** *n.* tissu-éponge *m.*

tower /'taʊə(r)/ *n.* tour *f.* —*v.i.* ~ **above,** dominer. ~ **block,** tour *f.*, immeuble *m.* ~**ing** *a.* très haut.

town /taʊn/ *n.* ville *f.* **go to ~,** (*fam.*) mettre le paquet. ~ **council,** conseil municipal *m.* ~ **hall,** hôtel de ville *m.*

toxic /'tɒksɪk/ *a.* toxique.

toxin /'tɒksɪn/ *n.* toxine *f.*

toy /tɔɪ/ *n.* jouet *m.* —*v.i.* ~ **with,** (*object*) jouer avec; (*idea*) caresser.

toyshop /'tɔɪʃɒp/ *n.* magasin de jouets *m.*

trace /treɪs/ *n.* trace *f.* —*v.t.* suivre *or* retrouver la trace de; (*draw*) tracer; (*with tracing-paper*) décalquer; (*relate*) retracer.

tracing /'treɪsɪŋ/ *n.* calque *m.* ~**paper** *n.* papier-calque *m. invar.*

track /træk/ *n.* (*of person etc.*) trace *f.*, piste *f.*; (*path, race-track & of tape*) piste *f.*; (*of rocket etc.*) trajectoire *f.*;

(*rail.*) voie *f.* —*v.t.* suivre la trace *or* la trajectoire de. **keep ~ of,** suivre. **~ down,** (*find*) retrouver; (*hunt*) traquer. **~ suit,** survêtement *m.*

tract[1] /trækt/ *n.* (*land*) étendue *f.*; (*anat.*) appareil *m.*

tract[2] /trækt/ *n.* (*pamphlet*) tract *m.*

tractor /'træktə(r)/ *n.* tracteur *m.*

trade /treɪd/ *n.* commerce *m.*; (*job*) métier *m.*; (*swap*) échange *m.* —*v.i.* faire du commerce. —*v.t.* échanger. **~ in,** (*used article*) faire reprendre. **~-in** *n.* reprise *f.* **~ mark,** marque de fabrique *f.* **~ on,** (*exploit*) abuser de. **~ union,** syndicat *m.* **~-unionist** *n.* syndicaliste *m.*/*f.* **~r** /-ə(r)/ *n.* négociant(e) *m.* (*f.*), commerçant(e) *m.* (*f.*).

tradesman /'treɪdzmən/ *n.* (*pl.* **-men**) commerçant *m.*

trading /'treɪdɪŋ/ *n.* commerce *m.* **~ estate,** zone industrielle *f.*

tradition /trə'dɪʃn/ *n.* tradition *f.* **~al** *a.* traditionnel.

traffic /'træfɪk/ *n.* trafic *m.*; (*on road*) circulation *f.* —*v.i.* (*p.t.* **trafficked**) trafiquer (**in,** de). **~ circle,** (*Amer.*) rond-point *m.* **~ jam,** embouteillage *m.* **~-lights** *n. pl.* feux (de circulation) *m. pl.* **~ warden,** contractuel(le) *m.* (*f.*).

tragedy /'trædʒədɪ/ *n.* tragédie *f.*

tragic /'trædʒɪk/ *a.* tragique.

trail /treɪl/ *v.t.*/*i.* traîner; (*of plant*) ramper; (*track*) suivre. —*n.* (*of powder etc.*) traînée *f.*; (*track*) piste *f.*; (*beaten path*) sentier *m.*

trailer /'treɪlə(r)/ *n.* remorque *f.*; (*caravan: Amer.*) caravane *f.*; (*film*) bande-annonce *f.*

train /treɪn/ *n.* (*rail.*) train *m.*; (*procession*) file *f.*; (*of dress*) traîne *f.* —*v.t.* (*instruct, develop*) former; (*sportsman*) entraîner; (*animal*) dresser; (*ear*) exercer; (*aim*) braquer. —*v.i.* recevoir une formation; s'entraîner. **~ed** *a.* (*skilled*) qualifié; (*doctor etc.*) diplômé. **~er** *n.* (*sport*) entraîneu|r, -se *m.*, *f.* **~ing** *n.* formation *f.*; entraînement *m.*; dressage *m.*

trainee /treɪ'niː/ *n.* stagiaire *m.*/*f.*

traipse /treɪps/ *v.i.* (*fam.*) traîner.

trait /treɪ(t)/ *n.* trait *m.*

traitor /'treɪtə(r)/ *n.* traître *m.*

tram /træm/ *n.* tram(way) *m.*

tramp /træmp/ *v.i.* marcher (d'un pas lourd). —*v.t.* parcourir. —*n.* pas lourds *m. pl.*; (*vagrant*) clochard(e)

m. (*f.*); (*Amer., sl.*) dévergondée *f.*; (*hike*) randonnée *f.*

trample /'træmpl/ *v.t.*/*i.* **~ (on),** piétiner; (*fig.*) fouler aux pieds.

trampoline /'træmpəliːn/ *n.* (*canvas sheet*) trampoline *m.*

trance /trɑːns/ *n.* transe *f.*

tranquil /'træŋkwɪl/ *a.* tranquille. **~lity** /-'kwɪlətɪ/ *n.* tranquillité *f.*

tranquillizer /'træŋkwɪlaɪzə(r)/ *n.* (*drug*) tranquillisant *m.*

transact /træn'zækt/ *v.t.* traiter. **~ion** /-kʃn/ *n.* transaction *f.*

transatlantic /trænzət'læntɪk/ *a.* transatlantique.

transcend /træn'send/ *v.t.* transcender. **~ent** *a.* transcendant.

transcri|be /træn'skraɪb/ *v.t.* transcrire. **~ption** /-ɪpʃn/ *n.* transcription *f.*

transcript /'trænskrɪpt/ *n.* (*written copy*) transcription *f.*

transfer[1] /træns'fɜː(r)/ *v.t.* (*p.t.* **transferred**) transférer; (*power*) faire passer. —*v.i.* être transféré. **~ the charges,** (*telephone*) téléphoner en PCV.

transfer[2] /'trænsfɜː(r)/ *n.* transfert *m.*; (*of power*) passation *f.*; (*image*) décalcomanie *f.*

transform /træns'fɔːm/ *v.t.* transformer. **~ation** /-ə'meɪʃn/ *n.* transformation *f.* **~er** *n.* (*electr.*) transformateur *m.*

transfusion /træns'fjuːʒn/ *n.* (*of blood*) transfusion *f.*

transient /'trænzɪənt/ *a.* transitoire, éphémère.

transistor /træn'zɪstə(r)/ *n.* (*device, radio set*) transistor *m.*

transit /'trænsɪt/ *n.* transit *m.*

transition /træn'zɪʃn/ *n.* transition *f.* **~al** *a.* transitoire.

transitive /'trænsətɪv/ *a.* transitif.

transitory /'trænsɪtərɪ/ *a.* transitoire.

translat|e /trænz'leɪt/ *v.t.* traduire. **~ion** /-ʃn/ *n.* traduction *f.* **~or** *n.* traduc|teur, -trice *m.*, *f.*

translucent /trænz'luːsnt/ *a.* translucide.

transmi|t /trænz'mɪt/ *v.t.* (*p.t.* **transmitted**) (*pass on etc.*) transmettre; (*broadcast*) émettre. **~ssion** *n.* transmission *f.*; émission *f.* **~tter** *n.* émetteur *m.*

transparen|t /træns'pærənt/ *a.* transparent. **~cy** *n.* transparence *f.*; (*photo.*) diapositive *f.*

transpire /træn'spaɪə(r)/ *v.i.* s'avérer; (*happen*: *fam.*) arriver.

transplant[1] /træns'plɑːnt/ *v.t.* transplanter; (*med.*) greffer.

transplant[2] /'trænsplɑːnt/ *n.* transplantation *f.*; greffe *f.*

transport[1] /træn'spɔːt/ *v.t.* (*carry*, *delight*) transporter. **~ation** /-'teɪʃn/ *n.* transport *m.*

transport[2] /'trænspɔːt/ *n.* (*of goods*, *delight, etc.*) transport *m.*

transpose /træn'spəʊz/ *v.t.* transposer.

transverse /'trænzvɜːs/ *a.* transversal.

transvestite /trænz'vestaɪt/ *n.* travesti(e) *m.* (*f.*).

trap /træp/ *n.* piège *m.* —*v.t.* (*p.t.* **trapped**) (*jam*, *pin down*) coincer; (*cut off*) bloquer; (*snare*) prendre au piège. **~per** *n.* trappeur *m.*

trapdoor /træp'dɔː(r)/ *n.* trappe *f.*

trapeze /trə'piːz/ *n.* trapèze *m.*

trappings /'træpɪŋz/ *n. pl.* (*fig.*) signes extérieurs *m. pl.*, apparat *m.*

trash /træʃ/ *n.* (*junk*) saleté(s) *f.* (*pl.*); (*refuse*) ordures *f. pl.*; (*nonsense*) idioties *f. pl.* **~-can** *n.* (*Amer.*) poubelle *f.* **~y** *a.* qui ne vaut rien, de mauvaise qualité.

trauma /'trɔːmə/ *n.* traumatisme *m.* **~tic** /-'mætɪk/ *a.* traumatisant.

travel /'trævl/ *v.i.* (*p.t.* **travelled**, *Amer.* **traveled**) voyager; (*of vehicle*, *bullet, etc.*) aller. —*v.t.* parcourir. —*n.* voyage(s) *m.* (*pl.*). **~ler** *n.* voyageu|r, -se *m.*, *f.* **~ler's cheque**, chèque de voyage *m.* **~ling** *n.* voyage(s) *m.* (*pl.*).

travesty /'trævəstɪ/ *n.* parodie *f.*, simulacre *m.* —*v.t.* travestir.

trawler /'trɔːlə(r)/ *n.* chalutier *m.*

tray /treɪ/ *n.* plateau *m.*; (*on office desk*) corbeille *f.*

treacherous /'tretʃərəs/ *a.* traître. **~ly** *adv.* traîtreusement.

treachery /'tretʃərɪ/ *n.* traîtrise *f.*

treacle /'triːkl/ *n.* mélasse *f.*

tread /tred/ *v.i.* (*p.t.* **trod**, *p.p.* **trodden**) marcher. —*v.t.* parcourir (à pied); (*soil*: *fig.*) fouler. —*n.* pas *m.*; (*of tyre*) chape *f.* **~ sth. into**, (*carpet*) étaler qch. sur (avec les pieds).

treason /'triːzn/ *n.* trahison *f.*

treasure /'treʒə(r)/ *n.* trésor *m.* —*v.t.* attacher une grande valeur à; (*store*) conserver. **~r** /-ə(r)/ *n.* trésor|ier, -ière *m.*, *f.*

treasury /'treʒərɪ/ *n.* trésorerie *f.* **the T~**, le ministère des Finances.

treat /triːt/ *v.t.* traiter; (*consider*) considérer. —*n.* (*pleasure*) plaisir *m.*, régal *m.*; (*present*) gâterie *f.*; (*food*) régal *m.* **~ s.o. to sth.**, offrir qch. à qn.

treatise /'triːtɪz/ *n.* traité *m.*

treatment /'triːtmənt/ *n.* traitement *m.*

treaty /'triːtɪ/ *n.* (*pact*) traité *m.*

trebl|e /'trebl/ *a.* triple. —*v.t./i.* tripler. —*n.* (*voice*: *mus.*) soprano *m.* **~y** *adv.* triplement.

tree /triː/ *n.* arbre *m.* **~-top** *n.* cime (d'un arbre) *f.*

trek /trek/ *n.* voyage pénible *m.*; (*sport*) randonnée *f.* —*v.i.* (*p.t.* **trekked**) voyager (péniblement); (*sport*) faire une randonnée.

trellis /'trelɪs/ *n.* treillage *m.*

tremble /'trembl/ *v.i.* trembler.

tremendous /trɪ'mendəs/ *a.* énorme; (*excellent*: *fam.*) fantastique. **~ly** *adv.* fantastiquement.

tremor /'tremə(r)/ *n.* tremblement *m.* (**earth**) **~**, secousse (sismique) *f.*

trench /trentʃ/ *n.* tranchée *f.*

trend /trend/ *n.* tendance *f.*; (*fashion*) mode *f.* **~-setter** *n.* lanceu|r, -se de mode *m.*, *f.* **~y** *a.* (*fam.*) dans le vent.

trepidation /trepɪ'deɪʃn/ *n.* (*fear*) inquiétude *f.*

trespass /'trespəs/ *v.i.* s'introduire sans autorisation (**on**, dans). **~er** *n.* intrus(e) *m.* (*f.*).

trestle /'tresl/ *n.* tréteau *m.* **~-table** *n.* table à tréteaux *f.*

tri /traɪ/ *pref.* tri-.

trial /'traɪəl/ *n.* (*jurid.*) procès *m.*; (*test*) essai *m.*; (*ordeal*) épreuve *f.* **go on ~**, passer en jugement. **~ and error**, tâtonnements *m. pl.*

triang|le /'traɪæŋgl/ *n.* triangle *m.* **~ular** /-'æŋgjʊlə(r)/ *a.* triangulaire.

trib|e /traɪb/ *n.* tribu *f.* **~al** *a.* tribal.

tribulation /trɪbjʊ'leɪʃn/ *n.* tribulation *f.*

tribunal /traɪ'bjuːnl/ *n.* tribunal *m.*; (*mil.*) commission *f.*

tributary /'trɪbjʊtərɪ/ *n.* affluent *m.*

tribute /'trɪbjuːt/ *n.* tribut *m.* **pay ~ to**, rendre hommage à.

trick /trɪk/ *n.* astuce *f.*, ruse *f.*; (*joke*, *feat of skill*) tour *m.*; (*habit*) manie *f.* —*v.t.* tromper. **do the ~**, (*fam.*) faire l'affaire.

trickery /'trɪkərɪ/ *n.* ruse *f.*

trickle /'trɪkl/ v.i. dégouliner; (*fig.*) arriver *or* partir en petit nombre. —n. filet m.; (*fig.*) petit nombre m.

tricky /'trɪkɪ/ a. (*crafty*) rusé; (*problem*) délicat, difficile.

tricycle /'traɪsɪkl/ n. tricycle m.

trifle /'traɪfl/ n. bagatelle f.; (*cake*) diplomate m. —v.i. ~ **with,** jouer avec. **a** ~, (*small amount*) un peu.

trifling /'traɪflɪŋ/ a. insignifiant.

trigger /'trɪgə(r)/ n. (*of gun*) gâchette f., détente f. —v.t. ~ (**off**), (*initiate*) déclencher.

trilby /'trɪlbɪ/ n. (*hat*) feutre m.

trilogy /'trɪlədʒɪ/ n. trilogie f.

trim /trɪm/ a. (**trimmer, trimmest**) net, soigné. —v.t. (*p.t.* **trimmed**) (*cut*) couper légèrement; (*hair*) rafraîchir. —n. (*cut*) coupe légère f.; (*decoration*) garniture f. **in** ~, en bon ordre; (*fit*) en forme. ~ **with,** (*decorate*) orner de. ~**ming(s)** n. (*pl.*) garniture(s) f. (*pl.*).

Trinity /'trɪnətɪ/ n. (*feast*) Trinité f. **the** ~, (*dogma*) la Trinité.

trinket /'trɪŋkɪt/ n. colifichet m.

trio /'triːəʊ/ n. (*pl.* -**os**) trio m.

trip /trɪp/ v.t./i. (*p.t.* **tripped**) (faire) trébucher; (*go lightly*) marcher d'un pas léger. —n. (*journey*) voyage m.; (*outing*) excursion f.; (*stumble*) faux pas m.

tripe /traɪp/ n. (*food*) tripes f. pl.; (*nonsense*: *sl.*) bêtises f. pl.

triple /'trɪpl/ a. triple. —v.t./i. tripler. ~**ts** /-plɪts/ n. pl. triplé(e)s m. (f.) pl.

triplicate /'trɪplɪkət/ n. **in** ~, en trois exemplaires.

tripod /'traɪpɒd/ n. trépied m.

tripper /'trɪpə(r)/ n. (*on day trip etc.*) excursionniste m./f.

trite /traɪt/ a. banal.

triumph /'traɪəmf/ n. triomphe m. —v.i. triompher (**over,** de). ~**al** /-'ʌmfl/ a. triomphal. ~**ant** /-'ʌmfənt/ a. triomphant, triomphal. ~**antly** /-'ʌmfəntlɪ/ adv. en triomphe.

trivial /'trɪvɪəl/ a. insignifiant. ~**ity** /-'ælətɪ/ n. insignifiance f.

trod, trodden /trɒd, 'trɒdn/ *see* **tread.**

trolley /'trɒlɪ/ n. chariot m. (**tea-**)~, table roulante f. ~-**bus** n. trolleybus m.

trombone /trɒm'bəʊn/ n. (*mus.*) trombone m.

troop /truːp/ n. bande f. ~**s,** (*mil.*) troupes f. pl. —v.i. ~ **in/out,** entrer/sortir en bande. ~**er** n. soldat de

cavalerie m. ~**ing the colour,** le salut au drapeau.

trophy /'trəʊfɪ/ n. trophée m.

tropic /'trɒpɪk/ n. tropique m. ~**s,** tropiques m. pl. ~**al** a. tropical.

trot /trɒt/ n. trot m. —v.i. (*p.t.* **trotted**) trotter. **on the** ~, (*fam.*) de suite. ~ **out,** (*produce*: *fam.*) sortir; (*state*: *fam.*) formuler.

trouble /'trʌbl/ n. ennui(s) m. (*pl.*), difficulté(s) f. (*pl.*); (*pains, effort*) mal m., peine f. ~(**s**), (*unrest*) conflits m. pl. —v.t./i. (*bother*) (se) déranger; (*worry*) ennuyer. **be in** ~, avoir des ennuis. ~**d** a. inquiet; (*period*) agité. ~-**maker** n. provoca|teur, -trice m., f.

troublesome /'trʌblsəm/ a. ennuyeux, pénible.

trough /trɒf/ n. (*drinking*) abreuvoir m.; (*feeding*) auge f. ~ (**of low pressure**), dépression f.

trounce /traʊns/ v.t. (*defeat*) écraser; (*thrash*) rosser.

troupe /truːp/ n. (*theatre*) troupe f.

trousers /'traʊzəz/ n. pl. pantalon m. **short** ~, culotte courte f.

trousseau /'truːsəʊ/ n. (*pl.* -**s** /-əʊz/) (*of bride*) trousseau m.

trout /traʊt/ n. invar. truite f.

trowel /'traʊəl/ n. (*garden*) déplantoir m.; (*for mortar*) truelle f.

truan|t /'truːənt/ n. absentéiste m./f.; (*schol.*) élève absent(e) sans permission m./f. **play** ~**t,** sécher les cours. ~**cy** n. absentéisme m.

truce /truːs/ n. trève f.

truck /trʌk/ n. (*lorry*) camion m.; (*cart*) chariot m.; (*rail.*) wagon m., plateforme f. ~-**driver** n. camionneur m.

truculent /'trʌkjʊlənt/ a. agressif.

trudge /trʌdʒ/ v.i. marcher péniblement, se traîner.

true /truː/ a. (-**er,** -**est**) vrai; (*accurate*) exact; (*faithful*) fidèle.

truffle /'trʌfl/ n. truffe f.

truly /'truːlɪ/ adv. vraiment; (*faithfully*) fidèlement; (*truthfully*) sincèrement.

trump /trʌmp/ n. atout m. —v.t. ~ **up,** inventer. ~ **card,** atout m.

trumpet /'trʌmpɪt/ n. trompette f.

truncheon /'trʌntʃən/ n. matraque f.

trundle /'trʌndl/ v.t./i. rouler bruyamment.

trunk /trʌŋk/ n. (*of tree, body*) tronc m.; (*of elephant*) trompe f.; (*box*) malle *f.*; (*auto.*, *Amer.*) coffre *m.* ~s, (*for swimming*) slip de bain *m.* ~-**call** *n.* communication interurbaine *f.* ~-**road** *n.* route nationale *f.*

truss /trʌs/ *n.* (*med.*) bandage herniaire *m.* —*v.t.* (*fowl*) trousser.

trust /trʌst/ *n.* confiance *f.*; (*association*) trust *m.* —*v.t.* avoir confiance en. —*v.i.* ~ **in** *or* **to**, s'en remettre à. **in** ~, en dépôt. **on** ~, de confiance. ~ **s.o. with**, confier à qn. ~**ed** *a.* (*friend etc.*) éprouvé, sûr. ~**ful**, ~**ing** *adjs.* confiant. ~**y** *a.* fidèle.

trustee /trʌsˈtiː/ *n.* administra|teur, -trice *m.*, *f.*

trustworthy /ˈtrʌstwɜːðɪ/ *a.* digne de confiance.

truth /truːθ/ *n.* (*pl.* -s /truːðz/) vérité *f.* ~**ful** *a.* (*account etc.*) véridique; (*person*) qui dit la vérité. ~**fully** *adv.* sincèrement.

try /traɪ/ *v.t./i.* (*p.t.* **tried**) essayer; (*be a strain on*) éprouver; (*jurid.*) juger. —*n.* (*attempt*) essai *m.*; (*Rugby*) essai *m.* ~ **on** *or* **out**, essayer. ~ **to do**, essayer de faire. ~**ing** *a.* éprouvant.

tsar /zɑː(r)/ *n.* tsar *m.*

T-shirt /ˈtiːʃɜːt/ *n.* tee-shirt *m.*

tub /tʌb/ *n.* baquet *m.*, cuve *f.*; (*bath: fam.*) baignoire *f.*

tuba /ˈtjuːbə/ *n.* tuba *m.*

tubby /ˈtʌbɪ/ *a.* (-**ier**, -**iest**) dodu.

tub|e /tjuːb/ *n.* tube *m.*; (*railway: fam.*) métro *m.* ~**ing** *n.* tubes *m. pl.*

tuberculosis /tjuːbɜːkjʊˈləʊsɪs/ *n.* tuberculose *f.*

tubular /ˈtjuːbjʊlə(r)/ *a.* tubulaire.

tuck /tʌk/ *n.* (*fold*) rempli *m.*, (re)pli *m.* —*v.t.* (*put away, place*) ranger; (*hide*) cacher. —*v.i.* ~ **in** *or* **into**, (*eat: sl.*) attaquer. ~ **in**, (*shirt*) rentrer; (*blanket, person*) border. ~-**shop** *n.* (*schol.*) boutique à provisions *f.*

Tuesday /ˈtjuːzdɪ/ *n.* mardi *m.*

tuft /tʌft/ *n.* (*of hair etc.*) touffe *f.*

tug /tʌg/ *v.t.* (*p.t.* **tugged**) tirer fort (sur). —*v.i.* tirer fort. —*n.* (*boat*) remorqueur *m.*

tuition /tjuːˈɪʃn/ *n.* cours *m. pl.*; (*fee*) frais de scolarité *m. pl.*

tulip /ˈtjuːlɪp/ *n.* tulipe *f.*

tumble /ˈtʌmbl/ *v.i.* (*fall*) dégringoler. —*n.* chute *f.* ~-**drier** *n.* séchoir à linge (à air chaud) *m.* ~ **to**, (*realize: fam.*) piger.

tumbledown /ˈtʌmbldaʊn/ *a.* délabré, en ruine.

tumbler /ˈtʌmblə(r)/ *n.* gobelet *m.*

tummy /ˈtʌmɪ/ *n.* (*fam.*) ventre *m.*

tumour /ˈtjuːmə(r)/ *n.* tumeur *f.*

tumult /ˈtjuːmʌlt/ *n.* tumulte *m.* ~**uous** /-ˈmʌltʃʊəs/ *a.* tumultueux.

tuna /ˈtjuːnə/ *n. invar.* thon *m.*

tune /tjuːn/ *n.* air *m.* —*v.t.* (*engine*) régler; (*mus.*) accorder. —*v.i.* ~ **in (to)**, (*radio, TV*) écouter. **be in** ~/**out of** ~, (*instrument*) être accordé/désaccordé; (*singer*) chanter juste/faux. ~**ful** *a.* mélodieux.

tuning-fork *n.* diapason *m.*

tunic /ˈtjuːnɪk/ *n.* tunique *f.*

Tunisia /tjuːˈnɪzɪə/ *n.* Tunisie *f.* ~**n** *a. & n.* tunisien(ne) (*m.* (*f.*)).

tunnel /ˈtʌnl/ *n.* tunnel *m.* —*v.i.* (*p.t.* **tunnelled**) creuser un tunnel (**into**, dans).

turban /ˈtɜːbən/ *n.* turban *m.*

turbine /ˈtɜːbaɪn/ *n.* turbine *f.*

turbulen|t /ˈtɜːbjʊlənt/ *a.* turbulent. ~**ce** *n.* turbulence *f.*

tureen /tjʊˈriːn/ *n.* soupière *f.*

turf /tɜːf/ *n.* (*pl.* **turf** *or* **turves**) gazon *m.* —*v.t.* ~ **out**, (*sl.*) jeter dehors. **the** ~, (*racing*) le turf.

turgid /ˈtɜːdʒɪd/ *a.* (*speech, style*) boursouflé, ampoulé.

Turk /tɜːk/ *n.* Turc *m.*, Turque *f.* ~**ey** *n.* Turquie *f.* ~**ish** *a.* turc; *n.* (*lang.*) turc *m.*

turkey /ˈtɜːkɪ/ *n.* dindon *m.*, dinde *f.*; (*as food*) dinde *f.*

turmoil /ˈtɜːmɔɪl/ *n.* trouble *m.*, chaos *m.* **in** ~, en ébullition.

turn /tɜːn/ *v.t./i.* tourner; (*of person*) se tourner; (*change*) (se) transformer (**into**, en); (*become*) devenir; (*deflect*) détourner. —*n.* tour *m.*; (*in road*) tournant *m.*; (*of mind, events*) tournure *f.*; (*illness: fam.*) crise *f.* **do a good** ~, rendre service. **in** ~, à tour de rôle. **speak out of** ~, commettre une indiscrétion. **take** ~s, se relayer. ~ **against**, se retourner contre. ~ **away** *v.i.* se détourner; *v.t.* (*avert*) détourner; (*refuse*) refuser; (*send back*) renvoyer. ~ **back** *v.i.* (*return*) retourner; (*vehicle*) faire demi-tour; *v.t.* (*fold*) rabattre. ~ **down**, refuser; (*fold*) rabattre; (*reduce*) baisser. ~ **in**, (*go to bed: fam.*) se coucher. ~ **off**, (*light etc.*) éteindre, fermer; (*tap*) fermer; (*of driver*) tourner. ~ **on**, (*light etc.*) mettre, allumer; (*tap*) ouvrir. ~ **out** *v.t.* (*light*) éteindre; (*empty*) vider; (*produce*) produire; *v.i.*

(*transpire*) s'avérer; (*come*: *fam.*) venir. **~-out** *n.* assistance *f.* **~ round,** (*person*) se retourner. **~ up** *v.i.* arriver; (*be found*) se retrouver; *v.t.* (*find*) déterrer; (*collar*) remonter. **~-up** *n.* (*of trousers*) revers *m.*

turning /'tɜːnɪŋ/ *n.* rue (latérale) *f.*; (*bend*) tournant *m.* **~-point** *n.* tournant *m.*

turnip /'tɜːnɪp/ *n.* navet *m.*

turnover /'tɜːnəʊvə(r)/ *n.* (*pie, tart*) chausson *m.*; (*money*) chiffre d'affaires *m.*

turnpike /'tɜːnpaɪk/ *n.* (*Amer.*) autoroute à péage *f.*

turnstile /'tɜːnstaɪl/ *n.* (*gate*) tourniquet *m.*

turntable /'tɜːnteɪbl/ *n.* (*for record*) platine *f.*, plateau *m.*

turpentine /'tɜːpəntaɪn/ *n.* térébenthine *f.*

turquoise /'tɜːkwɔɪz/ *a.* turquoise *invar.*

turret /'tʌrɪt/ *n.* tourelle *f.*

turtle /'tɜːtl/ *n.* tortue de mer *f.* **~- neck** *a.* à col montant, roulé.

tusk /tʌsk/ *n.* (*tooth*) défense *f.*

tussle /'tʌsl/ *n.* bagarre *f.*, lutte *f.*

tutor /'tjuːtə(r)/ *n.* précep|teur, -trice *m., f.*; (*univ.*) direc|teur, -trice d'études *m.,f.*

tutorial /tjuːˈtɔːrɪəl/ *n.* (*univ.*) séance d'études *or* de travaux pratiques *f.*

tuxedo /tʌkˈsiːdəʊ/ *n.* (*pl.* -os) (*Amer.*) smoking *m.*

TV /tiːˈviː/ *n.* télé *f.*

twaddle /'twɒdl/ *n.* fadaises *f. pl.*

twang /twæŋ/ *n.* (*son: mus.*) pincement *m.*; (*in voice*) nasillement *m.* —*v.t./i.* (faire) vibrer.

tweed /twiːd/ *n.* tweed *m.*

tweezers /'twiːzəz/ *n. pl.* pince (à épiler) *f.*

twel|ve /twelv/ *a. & n.* douze (*m.*). **~fth** *a. & n.* douzième (*m./f.*).

twent|y /'twentɪ/ *a. & n.* vingt (*m.*). **~ieth** *a. & n.* vingtième (*m./f.*).

twerp /twɜːp/ *n.* (*sl.*) idiot(e) *m.* (*f.*).

twice /twaɪs/ *adv.* deux fois.

twiddle /'twɪdl/ *v.t./i.* **~ (with),** (*fiddle with*) tripoter.

twig[1] /twɪg/ *n.* brindille *f.*

twig[2] /twɪg/ *v.t./i.* (*p.t.* **twigged**) (*understand: fam.*) piger.

twilight /'twaɪlaɪt/ *n.* crépuscule *m.* —*a.* crépusculaire.

twin /twɪn/ *n. & a.* jum|eau, -elle (*m., f.*). —*v.t.* (*p.t.* **twinned**) jumeler. **~ning** *n.* jumelage *m.*

twine /twaɪn/ *n.* ficelle *f.* —*v.t./i.* (*wind*) (s')enlacer.

twinge /twɪndʒ/ *n.* petite douleur aiguë *f.*; (*remorse*) remords *m.*

twinkle /'twɪŋkl/ *v.i.* (*star etc.*) scintiller; (*eye*) pétiller. —*n.* scintillement *m.*; pétillement *m.*

twirl /twɜːl/ *v.t./i.* (faire) tournoyer.

twist /twɪst/ *v.t.* tordre; (*weave together*) entortiller; (*roll*) enrouler; (*distort*) déformer. —*v.i.* (*rope etc.*) s'entortiller; (*road*) zigzaguer. —*n.* torsion *f.*; (*in rope*) tortillon *m.*; (*in road*) tournant *m.*; (*of events*) tournure *f.*, tour *m.*

twit /twɪt/ *n.* (*fam.*) idiot(e) *m.* (*f.*).

twitch /twɪtʃ/ *v.t./i.* (se) contracter nerveusement. —*n.* (*tic*) tic *m.*; (*jerk*) secousse *f.*

two /tuː/ *a. & n.* deux (*m.*). **in** *or* **of ~ minds,** indécis. **~-faced** *a.* hypocrite. **~fold** *a.* double; *adv.* au double. **~-piece** *n.* (*garment*) deux-pièces *m. invar.*

twosome /'tuːsəm/ *n.* couple *m.*

tycoon /taɪˈkuːn/ *n.* magnat *m.*

tying /'taɪɪŋ/ *see* tie.

type /taɪp/ *n.* (*example*) type *m.*; (*kind*) genre *m.*, sorte *f.*; (*person: fam.*) type *m.*; (*print*) caractères *m. pl.* —*v.t./i.* (*write*) taper (à la machine).

typescript /'taɪpskrɪpt/ *n.* manuscrit dactylographié *m.*

typewrit|er /'taɪpraɪtə(r)/ *n.* machine à écrire *f.* **~ten** /-ɪtn/ *a.* dactylographié.

typhoid /'taɪfɔɪd/ *n.* **~ (fever),** typhoïde *f.*

typhoon /taɪˈfuːn/ *n.* typhon *m.*

typhus /'taɪfəs/ *n.* typhus *m.*

typical /'tɪpɪkl/ *a.* typique. **~ly** *adv.* typiquement.

typify /'tɪpɪfaɪ/ *v.t.* être typique de.

typing /'taɪpɪŋ/ *n.* dactylo(graphie) *f.*

typist /'taɪpɪst/ *n.* dactylo *f.*

tyrann|y /'tɪrənɪ/ *n.* tyrannie *f.* **~ical** /tɪˈrænɪkl/ *a.* tyrannique.

tyrant /taɪərənt/ *n.* tyran *m.*

tyre /'taɪə(r)/ *n.* pneu *m.*

U

ubiquitous /juː'bɪkwɪtəs/ *a.* omniprésent, qu'on trouve partout.

udder /'ʌdər/ *n.* pis *m.*, mamelle *f.*

ugl|y /'ʌglɪ/ *a.* (-ier, -iest) laid. ~iness *n.* laideur *f.*

UK *abbr. see* **United Kingdom.**

ulcer /'ʌlsə(r)/ *n.* ulcère *m.*

ulterior /ʌl'tɪərɪə(r)/ *a.* ultérieur. ~ **motive,** arrière-pensée *f.*

ultimate /'ʌltɪmət/ *a.* dernier, ultime; (*definitive*) définitif; (*basic*) fondamental. ~ly *adv.* à la fin; (*in the last analysis*) en fin de compte.

ultimatum /ʌltɪ'meɪtəm/ *n.* (*pl.* -ums) ultimatum *m.*

ultra- /'ʌltrə/ *pref.* ultra-.

ultraviolet /ʌltrə'vaɪələt/ *a.* ultraviolet.

umbrella /ʌm'brelə/ *n.* parapluie *m.*

umpire /'ʌmpaɪə(r)/ *n.* (*sport*) arbitre *m.* —*v.t.* arbitrer.

umpteen /'ʌmptiːn/ *a.* (*many: sl.*) un tas de. ~th *a.* (*sl.*) énième.

un- /ʌn/ *pref.* in-, dé(s)-, non, peu, mal, sans.

unabated /ʌnə'beɪtɪd/ *a.* non diminué, aussi fort qu'avant.

unable /ʌn'eɪbl/ *a.* incapable (**to do,** de faire).

unabridged /ʌnə'brɪdʒd/ *a.* (*text*) intégral.

unacceptable /ʌnək'septəbl/ *a.* inacceptable, inadmissible.

unaccountable /ʌnə'kaʊntəbl/ *a.* (*strange*) inexplicable.

unaccustomed /ʌnə'kʌstəmd/ *a.* inaccoutumé. ~ **to,** peu habitué à.

unadulterated /ʌnə'dʌltəreɪtɪd/ *a.* (*pure, sheer*) pur.

unaided /ʌn'eɪdɪd/ *a.* sans aide.

unanim|ous /juː'nænɪməs/ *a.* unanime. ~ity /-ə'nɪmətɪ/ *n.* unanimité *f.* ~ously *adv.* à l'unanimité.

unarmed /ʌn'ɑːmd/ *a.* non armé.

unashamed /ʌnə'ʃeɪmd/ *a.* éhonté. ~ly /-ɪdlɪ/ *adv.* sans vergogne.

unassuming /ʌnə'sjuːmɪŋ/ *a.* modeste, sans prétention.

unattached /ʌnə'tætʃt/ *a.* libre.

unattainable /ʌnə'teɪnəbl/ *a.* inaccessible.

unattended /ʌnə'tendɪd/ *a.* (laissé) sans surveillance.

unattractive /ʌnə'træktɪv/ *a.* peu séduisant, laid; (*offer*) peu intéressant.

unavoidabl|e /ʌnə'vɔɪdəbl/ *a.* inévitable. ~y *adv.* inévitablement.

unaware /ʌnə'weə(r)/ *a.* be ~ of, ignorer. ~s /-eəz/ *adv.* au dépourvu.

unbalanced /ʌn'bælənst/ *a.* (*mind, person*) déséquilibré.

unbearable /ʌn'beərəbl/ *a.* insupportable.

unbeat|able /ʌn'biːtəbl/ *a.* imbattable. ~en *a.* non battu.

unbeknown(st) /ʌnbɪ'nəʊn(st)/ *a.* ~(st) to, (*fam.*) à l'insu de.

unbelievable /ʌnbɪ'liːvəbl/ *a.* incroyable.

unbend /ʌn'bend/ *v.i.* (*p.t.* unbent) (*relax*) se détendre.

unbiased /ʌn'baɪəst/ *a.* impartial.

unblock /ʌn'blɒk/ *v.t.* déboucher.

unborn /ʌn'bɔːn/ *a.* futur, à venir.

unbounded /ʌn'baʊndɪd/ *a.* illimité.

unbreakable /ʌn'breɪkəbl/ *a.* incassable.

unbridled /ʌn'braɪdld/ *a.* débridé.

unbroken /ʌn'brəʊkən/ *a.* (*intact*) intact; (*continuous*) continu.

unburden /ʌn'bɜːdn/ *v. pr.* ~ o.s., (*open one's heart*) s'épancher.

unbutton /ʌn'bʌtn/ *v.t.* déboutonner.

uncalled-for /ʌn'kɔːldfɔː(r)/ *a.* injustifié, superflu.

uncanny /ʌn'kænɪ/ *a.* (-ier, -iest) étrange, mystérieux.

unceasing /ʌn'siːsɪŋ/ *a.* incessant.

unceremonious /ʌnserɪ'məʊnɪəs/ *a.* sans façon, brusque.

uncertain /ʌn'sɜːtn/ *a.* incertain. be ~ **whether,** ne pas savoir exactement si (**to do,** on doit faire). ~ty *n.* incertitude *f.*

unchang|ed /ʌn'tʃeɪndʒd/ *a.* inchangé. ~ing *a.* immuable.

uncivilized /ʌn'sɪvɪlaɪzd/ *a.* barbare.

uncle /'ʌŋkl/ *n.* oncle *m.*

uncomfortable /ʌn'kʌmftəbl/ *a.* (*thing*) peu confortable; (*unpleasant*) désagréable. **feel** *or* **be** ~, (*person*) être mal à l'aise.

uncommon /ʌn'kɒmən/ *a.* rare. ~ly *adv.* remarquablement.

uncompromising /ʌn'kɒmprə-maɪzɪŋ/ *a.* intransigeant.

unconcerned /ʌnkən'sɜːnd/ *a.* (*indifferent*) indifférent (**by**, à).

unconditional /ʌnkən'dɪʃənl/ *a.* inconditionnel.

unconscious /ʌn'kɒnʃəs/ *a.* sans connaissance, inanimé; (*not aware*) inconscient (**of**, de). **~ly** *adv.* inconsciemment.

unconventional /ʌnkən'venʃənl/ *a.* peu conventionnel.

uncooperative /ʌnkəʊ'ɒpərətɪv/ *a.* peu coopératif.

uncork /ʌn'kɔːk/ *v.t.* déboucher.

uncouth /ʌn'kuːθ/ *a.* grossier.

uncover /ʌn'kʌvə(r)/ *v.t.* découvrir.

unctuous /'ʌŋktʃʊəs/ *a.* onctueux.

undecided /ʌndɪ'saɪdɪd/ *a.* indécis.

undefinable /ʌndɪ'faɪnəbl/ *a.* indéfinissable.

undeniable /ʌndɪ'naɪəbl/ *a.* indéniable, incontestable.

under[1] /'ʌndə(r)/ *prep.* sous; (*less than*) moins de; (*according to*) selon. *—adv.* au-dessous. **~ age**, mineur. **~-side** *n.* dessous *m.* **~ way**, (*in progress*) en cours; (*on the way*) en route.

under[2] /'ʌndə(r)/ *pref.* sous-.

undercarriage /'ʌndəkærɪdʒ/ *n.* (*aviat.*) train d'atterrissage *m.*

underclothes /'ʌndəkləʊðz/ *n. pl.* sous-vêtements *m. pl.*

undercoat /'ʌndəkəʊt/ *n.* (*of paint*) couche de fond *f.*

undercover /ʌndə'kʌvə(r)/ (*agent, operation*) *a.* secret.

undercurrent /'ʌndəkʌrənt/ *n.* courant (profond) *m.*

undercut /ʌndə'kʌt/ *v.t.* (*p.t.* **undercut**, *pres. p.* **undercutting**) (*comm.*) vendre moins cher que.

underdog /'ʌndədɒg/ *n.* (*pol.*) opprimé(e) *m.* (*f.*); (*socially*) déshérité(e) *m.* (*f.*).

underdone /'ʌndədʌn/ *a.* pas assez cuit; (*steak*) saignant.

underestimate /ʌndə'restɪmeɪt/ *v.t.* sous-estimer.

underfed /'ʌndəfed/ *a.* sousalimenté.

underfoot /ʌndə'fʊt/ *adv.* sous les pieds.

undergo /ʌndə'gəʊ/ *v.t.* (*p.t.* **-went**, *pp.* **-gone**) subir.

undergraduate /ʌndə'grædʒʊət/ *n.* étudiant(e) (qui prépare la licence) *m.* (*f.*).

underground[1] /ʌndə'graʊnd/ *adv.* sous terre.

underground[2] /'ʌndəgraʊnd/ *a.* souterrain; (*secret*) clandestin. *—n.* (*rail*) métro *m.*

undergrowth /'ʌndəgrəʊθ/ *n.* sous-bois *m. invar.*

underhand /'ʌndəhænd/ *a.* (*deceitful*) sournois.

under|lie /ʌndə'laɪ/ *v.t.* (*p.t.* **-lay**, *p.p.* **-lain**, *pres. p.* **-lying**) soustendre. **~lying** *a.* fondamental.

underline /ʌndə'laɪn/ *v.t.* souligner.

undermine /ʌndə'maɪn/ *v.t.* (*cliff, society, etc.*) miner, saper.

underneath /ʌndə'niːθ/ *prep.* sous. *—adv.* (en) dessous.

underpaid /ʌndə'peɪd/ *a.* souspayé.

underpants /'ʌndəpænts/ *n. pl.* (*man's*) slip *m.*

underpass /'ʌndəpɑːs/ *n.* (*for cars, people*) passage souterrain *m.*

underprivileged /ʌndə'prɪvəlɪdʒd/ *a.* défavorisé.

underrate /ʌndə'reɪt/ *v.t.* sous-estimer.

undersized /ʌndə'saɪzd/ *a.* trop petit; (*stunted, puny*) chétif.

understand /ʌndə'stænd/ *v.t./i.* (*p.t.* **-stood**) comprendre. **~able** *a.* compréhensible. **~ing** *a.* compréhensif; *n.* compréhension *f.*; (*agreement*) entente *f.*

understatement /'ʌndəsteɪtmənt/ *n.* affirmation au-dessous de la vérité *f.*

understudy /'ʌndəstʌdɪ/ *n.* (*theatre*) doublure *f.*

undertak|e /ʌndə'teɪk/ *v.t.* (*p.t.* **-took**, *p.p.* **-taken**) entreprendre; (*responsibility*) assumer. **~e to**, s'engager à. **~ing** *n.* (*task*) entreprise *f.*; (*promise*) promesse *f.*

undertaker /'ʌndəteɪkə(r)/ *n.* entrepreneur de pompes funèbres *m.*

undertone /'ʌndətəʊn/ *n.* **in an ~**, à mi-voix.

undervalue /ʌndə'væljuː/ *v.t.* sous-évaluer.

underwater /ʌndə'wɔːtə(r)/ *a.* sous-marin. *—adv.* sous l'eau.

underwear /'ʌndəweə(r)/ *n.* sous-vêtements *m. pl.*

underweight /'ʌndəweɪt/ *a.* (*person*) qui ne pèse pas assez.

underwent /ʌndə'went/ *see* **undergo**.

underworld /'ʌndəwɜːld/ *n.* (*of crime*) milieu *m.*, pègre *f.*

undeserved /ʌndɪ'zɜːvd/ *a.* immérité.

undesirable /ˌʌndɪ'zaɪərəbl/ a. peu souhaitable; (*person*) indésirable.

undies /'ʌndɪz/ n. pl. (*female underwear*: *fam*.) dessous m. pl.

undignified /ʌn'dɪgnɪfaɪd/ a. qui manque de dignité, sans dignité.

undisputed /ˌʌndɪ'spjuːtɪd/ a. incontesté.

undistinguished /ˌʌndɪ'stɪŋgwɪʃt/ a. médiocre.

undo /ʌn'duː/ v.t. (*p.t.* -**did**, *p.p.* -**done** /-dʌn/) défaire, détacher; (*a wrong*) réparer. leave ~ne, ne pas faire.

undoubted /ʌn'daʊtɪd/ a. indubitable. ~ly adv. indubitablement.

undreamt /ʌn'dremt/ a. ~ of, insoupçonné, inimaginable.

undress /ʌn'dres/ v.t./i. (se) déshabiller. get ~ed, se déshabiller.

undue /ʌn'djuː/ a. excessif. ~ly adv. excessivement.

undulate /'ʌndjʊleɪt/ v.i. onduler.

undying /ʌn'daɪŋ/ a. éternel.

unearth /ʌn'ɜːθ/ v.t. déterrer.

unearthly /ʌn'ɜːθlɪ/ a. mystérieux. ~ hour, (*fam*.) heure indue f.

uneasy /ʌn'iːzɪ/ a. (*ill at ease*) mal à l'aise; (*worried*) inquiet; (*situation*) difficile.

uneducated /ʌn'edʒʊkeɪtɪd/ a. (*person*) inculte; (*speech*) populaire.

unemploy|ed /ˌʌnɪm'plɔɪd/ a. en chômage. ~ment n. chômage m.

unending /ʌn'endɪŋ/ a. interminable, sans fin.

unequal /ʌn'iːkwəl/ a. inégal. ~led a. inégalé.

unerring /ʌn'ɜːrɪŋ/ a. infaillible.

uneven /ʌn'iːvn/ a. inégal.

unexpected /ˌʌnɪk'spektɪd/ a. inattendu. ~ly adv. subitement; (*arrive*) à l'improviste.

unfailing /ʌn'feɪlɪŋ/ a. constant, continuel; (*loyal*) fidèle.

unfair /ʌn'feə(r)/ a. injuste. ~ness n. injustice f.

unfaithful /ʌn'feɪθfl/ a. infidèle.

unfamiliar /ˌʌnfə'mɪlɪə(r)/ a. inconnu, peu familier. be ~ with, ne pas connaître.

unfasten /ʌn'fɑːsn/ v.t. défaire.

unfavourable /ʌn'feɪvərəbl/ a. défavorable.

unfeeling /ʌn'fiːlɪŋ/ a. insensible.

unfinished /ʌn'fɪnɪʃt/ a. inachevé.

unfit /ʌn'fɪt/ a. (*med*.) peu en forme; (*unsuitable*) impropre (for, à). ~ to, (*unable*) pas en état de.

unflinching /ʌn'flɪntʃɪŋ/ a. (*fearless*) intrépide.

unfold /ʌn'fəʊld/ v.t. déplier; (*expose*) exposer. —v.i. se dérouler.

unforeseen /ˌʌnfɔː'siːn/ a. imprévu.

unforgettable /ˌʌnfə'getəbl/ a. inoubliable.

unforgivable /ˌʌnfə'gɪvəbl/ a. impardonnable, inexcusable.

unfortunate /ʌn'fɔːtʃʊnət/ a. malheureux; (*event*) fâcheux. ~ly adv. malheureusement.

unfounded /ʌn'faʊndɪd/ a. (*rumour etc.*) sans fondement.

unfriendly /ʌn'frendlɪ/ a. peu amical, froid.

ungainly /ʌn'geɪnlɪ/ a. gauche.

ungodly /ʌn'gɒdlɪ/ a. impie. ~ hour, (*fam*.) heure indue f.

ungrateful /ʌn'greɪtfl/ a. ingrat.

unhapp|y /ʌn'hæpɪ/ a. (-ier, -iest) malheureux, triste; (*not pleased*) mécontent (with, de). ~ily adv. malheureusement. ~iness n. tristesse f.

unharmed /ʌn'hɑːmd/ a. indemne, sain et sauf.

unhealthy /ʌn'helθɪ/ a. (-ier, -iest) (*climate etc.*) malsain; (*person*) en mauvaise santé.

unheard-of /ʌn'hɜːdɒv/ a. inouï.

unhinge /ʌn'hɪndʒ/ v.t. (*person, mind*) déséquilibrer.

unholy /ʌn'həʊlɪ/ a. (-ier, -iest) (*person, act, etc.*) impie; (*great*: *fam*.) invraisemblable.

unhook /ʌn'hʊk/ v.t. décrocher; (*dress*) dégrafer.

unhoped /ʌn'həʊpt/ a. ~ for, inespéré.

unhurt /ʌn'hɜːt/ a. indemne.

unicorn /'juːnɪkɔːn/ n. licorne f.

uniform /'juːnɪfɔːm/ n. uniforme m. —a. uniforme. ~ity /-'fɔːmətɪ/ n. uniformité f. ~ly adv. uniformément.

unif|y /'juːnɪfaɪ/ v.t. unifier. ~ication /-ɪ'keɪʃn/ n. unification f.

unilateral /juːnɪ'lætrəl/ a. unilatéral.

unimaginable /ˌʌnɪ'mædʒɪnəbl/ a. inimaginable.

unimportant /ˌʌnɪm'pɔːtnt/ a. peu important.

uninhabited /ˌʌnɪn'hæbɪtɪd/ a. inhabité.

unintentional /ˌʌnɪn'tenʃənl/ a. involontaire.

uninterest|ed /ʌn'ɪntrəstɪd/ a. indifférent (in, à). ~ing a. peu intéressant.

union /'juːnɪən/ n. union f.; (*trade*

union) syndicat *m*. ~**ist** *n*. syndiqué(e) *m*. (*f*.). **U**~ **Jack**, drapeau britannique *m*.

unique /juːˈniːk/ *a*. unique. ~**ly** *adv*. exceptionnellement.

unisex /ˈjuːnɪseks/ *a*. unisexe.

unison /ˈjuːnɪsn/ *n*. **in** ~, à l'unisson.

unit /ˈjuːnɪt/ *n*. unité *f*.; (*of furniture etc*.) élément *m*., bloc *m*.

unite /juːˈnaɪt/ *v.t./i.* (s')unir. **U**~**d Kingdom**, Royaume-Uni *m*. **U**~**d States** (**of America**), États-Unis (d'Amérique) *m. pl*.

unity /ˈjuːnətɪ/ *n*. unité *f*.; (*harmony*: *fig*.) harmonie *f*.

universal /juːnɪˈvɜːsl/ *a*. universel.

universe /ˈjuːnɪvɜːs/ *n*. univers *m*.

university /juːnɪˈvɜːsətɪ/ *n*. université *f*. —*a*. universitaire; (*student, teacher*) d'université.

unjust /ʌnˈdʒʌst/ *a*. injuste.

unkempt /ʌnˈkempt/ *a*. négligé.

unkind /ʌnˈkaɪnd/ *a*. pas gentil, méchant. ~**ly** *adv*. méchamment.

unknowingly /ʌnˈnəʊɪŋlɪ/ *adv*. sans le savoir, inconsciemment.

unknown /ʌnˈnəʊn/ *a*. inconnu. —*n*. **the** ~, l'inconnu *m*.

unleash /ʌnˈliːʃ/ *v.t.* déchaîner.

unless /ənˈles/ *conj*. à moins que.

unlike /ʌnˈlaɪk/ *a*. (*brothers etc*.) différents. —*prep*. à la différence de; (*different from*) très différent de.

unlikel|y /ʌnˈlaɪklɪ/ *a*. improbable. ~**ihood** *n*. improbabilité *f*.

unlimited /ʌnˈlɪmɪtɪd/ *a*. illimité.

unload /ʌnˈləʊd/ *v.t.* décharger.

unlock /ʌnˈlɒk/ *v.t.* ouvrir.

unluck|y /ʌnˈlʌkɪ/ *a*. (**-ier, -iest**) malheureux; (*number*) qui porte malheur. ~**ily** *adv*. malheureusement.

unmarried /ʌnˈmærɪd/ *a*. célibataire, qui n'est pas marié.

unmask /ʌnˈmɑːsk/ *v.t.* démasquer.

unmentionable /ʌnˈmenʃənəbl/ *a*. dont il ne faut pas parler; (*shocking*) innommable.

unmistakable /ʌnmɪˈsteɪkəbl/ *a*. (*voice etc*.) facilement reconnaissable; (*clear*) très net.

unmitigated /ʌnˈmɪtɪɡeɪtɪd/ *a*. (*absolute*) absolu.

unmoved /ʌnˈmuːvd/ *a*. indifférent (**by,** à), insensible (**by,** à).

unnatural /ʌnˈnætʃrəl/ *a*. pas naturel, anormal.

unnecessary /ʌnˈnesəsərɪ/ *a*. inutile; (*superfluous*) superflu.

unnerve /ʌnˈnɜːv/ *v.t.* troubler.

unnoticed /ʌnˈnəʊtɪst/ *a*. inaperçu.

unobtrusive /ʌnəbˈtruːsɪv/ *a*. (*person, object*) discret.

unofficial /ʌnəˈfɪʃl/ *a*. officieux.

unorthodox /ʌnˈɔːθədɒks/ *a*. peu orthodoxe.

unpack /ʌnˈpæk/ *v.t.* (*suitcase etc*.) défaire; (*contents*) déballer. —*v.i.* défaire sa valise.

unpalatable /ʌnˈpælətəbl/ *a*. (*food, fact, etc*.) désagréable.

unparalleled /ʌnˈpærəleld/ *a*. incomparable.

unpleasant /ʌnˈpleznt/ *a*. désagréable (**to,** avec).

unplug /ʌnˈplʌɡ/ *v.t.* (*electr*.) débrancher; (*unblock*) déboucher.

unpopular /ʌnˈpɒpjʊlə(r)/ *a*. impopulaire.

unprecedented /ʌnˈpresɪdəntɪd/ *a*. sans précédent.

unpredictable /ʌnprɪˈdɪktəbl/ *a*. imprévisible.

unprepared /ʌnprɪˈpeəd/ *a*. non préparé; (*person*) qui n'a rien préparé. **be** ~ **for,** (*not expect*) ne pas s'attendre à.

unpretentious /ʌnprɪˈtenʃəs/ *a*. sans prétention(s).

unprincipled /ʌnˈprɪnsəpld/ *a*. sans scrupules.

unprofessional /ʌnprəˈfeʃənl/ *a*. (*work*) d'amateur; (*conduct*) contraire au code professionnel.

unpublished /ʌnˈpʌblɪʃt/ *a*. inédit.

unqualified /ʌnˈkwɒlɪfaɪd/ *a*. non diplômé; (*success etc*.) total. **be** ~ **to,** ne pas être qualifié pour.

unquestionabl|e /ʌnˈkwestʃənəbl/ *a*. incontestable. ~**y** *adv*. incontestablement.

unravel /ʌnˈrævl/ *v.t.* (*p.t.* **unravelled**) démêler, débrouiller.

unreal /ʌnˈrɪəl/ *a*. irréel.

unreasonable /ʌnˈriːznəbl/ *a*. déraisonnable, peu raisonnable.

unrecognizable /ʌnrekəɡˈnaɪzəbl/ *a*. méconnaissable.

unrelated /ʌnrɪˈleɪtɪd/ *a*. (*facts*) sans rapport (**to,** avec).

unreliable /ʌnrɪˈlaɪəbl/ *a*. peu sérieux; (*machine*) peu fiable.

unrelieved /ʌnrɪˈliːvd/ *a*. perpétuel; (*colour*) uniforme.

unreservedly /ʌnrɪ'zɜːvɪdlɪ/ *adv.* sans réserve.

unrest /ʌn'rest/ *n.* troubles *m. pl.*

unrivalled /ʌn'raɪvld/ *a.* sans égal, incomparable.

unroll /ʌn'rəʊl/ *v.t.* dérouler.

unruffled /ʌn'rʌfld/ *a.* (*person*) qui n'a pas perdu son calme.

unruly /ʌn'ruːlɪ/ *a.* indiscipliné.

unsafe /ʌn'seɪf/ *a.* (*dangerous*) dangereux; (*person*) en danger.

unsaid /ʌn'sed/ *a.* **leave** ∼, passer sous silence.

unsatisfactory /ʌnsætɪs'fæktərɪ/ *a.* peu satisfaisant.

unsavoury /ʌn'seɪvərɪ/ *a.* désagréable, répugnant.

unscathed /ʌn'skeɪðd/ *a.* indemne.

unscrew /ʌn'skruː/ *v.t.* dévisser.

unscrupulous /ʌn'skruːpjʊləs/ *a.* sans scrupules, malhonnête.

unseemly /ʌn'siːmlɪ/ *a.* inconvenant, incorrect, incongru.

unseen /ʌn'siːn/ *a.* inaperçu. *—n.* (*translation*) version *f.*

unsettle /ʌn'setl/ *v.t.* troubler. ∼**d** *a.* (*weather*) instable.

unshakeable /ʌn'ʃeɪkəbl/ *a.* (*person, belief, etc.*) inébranlable.

unshaven /ʌn'ʃeɪvn/ *a.* pas rasé.

unsightly /ʌn'saɪtlɪ/ *a.* laid.

unskilled /ʌn'skɪld/ *a.* inexpert; (*worker*) non qualifié.

unsociable /ʌn'səʊʃəbl/ *a.* insociable, farouche.

unsophisticated /ʌnsə'fɪstɪkeɪtɪd/ *a.* simple.

unsound /ʌn'saʊnd/ *a.* peu solide. **of** ∼ **mind,** fou.

unspeakable /ʌn'spiːkəbl/ *a.* indescriptible; (*bad*) innommable.

unspecified /ʌn'spesɪfaɪd/ *a.* indéterminé.

unstable /ʌn'steɪbl/ *a.* instable.

unsteady /ʌn'stedɪ/ *a.* (*step*) chancelant; (*ladder*) instable; (*hand*) mal assuré.

unstuck /ʌn'stʌk/ *a.* décollé. **come** ∼, (*fail: fam.*) échouer.

unsuccessful /ʌnsək'sesfl/ *a.* (*result, candidate*) malheureux; (*attempt*) infructueux. **be** ∼, ne pas réussir (**in doing,** à faire).

unsuit|able /ʌn's(j)uːtəbl/ *a.* qui ne convient pas (**for,** à), peu approprié. ∼**ed** *a.* inapte (**to,** à).

unsure /ʌn'ʃʊə(r)/ *a.* incertain.

unsuspecting /ʌnsə'spektɪŋ/ *a.* qui ne se doute de rien.

untangle /ʌn'tæŋgl/ *v.t.* démêler.

unthinkable /ʌn'θɪŋkəbl/ *a.* impensable, inconcevable.

untid|y /ʌn'taɪdɪ/ *a.* (**-ier, -iest**) désordonné; (*clothes, hair*) mal soigné. ∼**ily** *adv.* sans soin.

untie /ʌn'taɪ/ *v.t.* (*knot, parcel*) défaire; (*person*) détacher.

until /ən'tɪl/ *prep.* jusqu'à. **not** ∼, pas avant. *—conj.* jusqu'à ce que; (*before*) avant que.

untimely /ʌn'taɪmlɪ/ *a.* inopportun; (*death*) prématuré.

untold /ʌn'təʊld/ *a.* incalculable.

untoward /ʌntə'wɔːd/ *a.* fâcheux.

untrue /ʌn'truː/ *a.* faux.

unused[1] /ʌn'juːzd/ *a.* (*new*) neuf; (*not in use*) inutilisé.

unused[2] /ʌn'juːst/ *a.* ∼ **to,** peu habitué à.

unusual /ʌn'juːʒʊəl/ *a.* exceptionnel; (*strange*) insolite, étrange. ∼**ly** *adv.* exceptionnellement.

unveil /ʌn'veɪl/ *v.t.* dévoiler.

unwanted /ʌn'wɒntɪd/ *a.* (*useless*) superflu; (*child*) non souhaité.

unwelcome /ʌn'welkəm/ *a.* fâcheux; (*guest*) importun.

unwell /ʌn'wel/ *a.* indisposé.

unwieldy /ʌn'wiːldɪ/ *a.* difficile à manier.

unwilling /ʌn'wɪlɪŋ/ *a.* peu disposé (**to,** à); (*victim*) récalcitrant. ∼**ly** *adv.* à contrecœur.

unwind /ʌn'waɪnd/ *v.t./i.* (*p.t.* **unwound** /ʌn'waʊnd/) (se) dérouler; (*relax: fam.*) se détendre.

unwise /ʌn'waɪz/ *a.* imprudent.

unwittingly /ʌn'wɪtɪŋlɪ/ *adv.* involontairement.

unworkable /ʌn'wɜːkəbl/ *a.* (*plan etc.*) irréalisable.

unworthy /ʌn'wɜːðɪ/ *a.* indigne.

unwrap /ʌn'ræp/ *v.t.* (*p.t.* **unwrapped**) ouvrir, défaire.

unwritten /ʌn'rɪtn/ *a.* (*agreement*) verbal, tacite.

up /ʌp/ *adv.* en haut, en l'air; (*sun, curtain*) levé; (*out of bed*) levé, debout; (*finished*) fini. **be** ∼, (*level, price*) avoir monté. *—prep.* (*a hill*) en haut de; (*a tree*) dans; (*a ladder*) sur. *—v.t.* (*p.t.* **upped**) augmenter. **come** *or* **go** ∼, monter. ∼ **to,** jusqu'à; (*task*) à la hauteur de. **it is** ∼ **to you,** ça dépend de vous (**to,** de). **be** ∼ **to sth.,** (*do*) faire qch.; (*plot*) préparer qch. **be ~ to,** (*in book*) en être à. **be ~ against,** faire face à. **be ~ in,** (*fam.*) s'y connaître en. **feel ~ to doing,** (*able*) être de taille à faire. **have ~s and downs,** connaître des hauts et des bas. **~ to date,** moderne; (*news*) récent.

upbringing /ˈʌpbrɪŋɪŋ/ *n.* éducation *f.*

update /ʌpˈdeɪt/ *v.t.* mettre à jour.

upgrade /ʌpˈgreɪd/ *v.t.* (*person*) promouvoir; (*job*) revaloriser.

upheaval /ʌpˈhiːvl/ *n.* bouleversement *m.*

uphill /ʌpˈhɪl/ *a.* qui monte; (*fig.*) difficile. —*adv.* **go ~,** monter.

uphold /ʌpˈhəʊld/ *v.t.* (*p.t.* **upheld**) maintenir.

upholster /ʌpˈhəʊlstə(r)/ *v.t.* (*pad*) rembourrer; (*cover*) recouvrir. **~y** *n.* (*in vehicle*) garniture *f.*

upkeep /ˈʌpkiːp/ *n.* entretien *m.*

upon /əˈpɒn/ *prep.* sur.

upper /ˈʌpə(r)/ *a.* supérieur. —*n.* (*of shoe*) empeigne *f.* **have the ~ hand,** avoir le dessus. **~ class,** aristocratie *f.* **~most** *a.* (*highest*) le plus haut.

upright /ˈʌpraɪt/ *a.* droit. —*n.* (*post*) montant *m.*

uprising /ˈʌpraɪzɪŋ/ *n.* soulèvement *m.*, insurrection *f.*

uproar /ˈʌprɔː(r)/ *n.* tumulte *m.*

uproot /ʌpˈruːt/ *v.t.* déraciner.

upset[1] /ʌpˈset/ *v.t.* (*p.t.* **upset,** *pres. p.* **upsetting**) (*overturn*) renverser; (*plan, stomach*) déranger; (*person*) contrarier, affliger.

upset[2] /ˈʌpset/ *n.* dérangement *m.*; (*distress*) chagrin *m.*

upshot /ˈʌpʃɒt/ *n.* résultat *m.*

upside-down /ʌpsaɪdˈdaʊn/ *adv.* (*in position, in disorder*) à l'envers, sens dessus dessous.

upstairs /ʌpˈsteəz/ *adv.* en haut. —*a.* (*flat etc.*) d'en haut.

upstart /ˈʌpstɑːt/ *n.* (*pej.*) parvenu(e) *m.* (*f.*).

upstream /ʌpˈstriːm/ *adv.* en amont.

upsurge /ˈʌpsɜːdʒ/ *n.* recrudescence *f.*; (*of anger*) accès *m.*

uptake /ˈʌpteɪk/ *n.* **be quick on the ~,** comprendre vite.

uptight /ˈʌptaɪt/ *a.* (*tense*: *fam.*) crispé; (*angry*: *fam.*) en colère.

upturn /ˈʌptɜːn/ *n.* amélioration *f.*

upward /ˈʌpwəd/ *a. & adv.,* **~s** *adv.* vers le haut.

uranium /jʊˈreɪnɪəm/ *n.* uranium *m.*

urban /ˈɜːbən/ *a.* urbain.

urbane /ɜːˈbeɪn/ *a.* courtois.

urchin /ˈɜːtʃɪn/ *n.* garnement *m.*

urge /ɜːdʒ/ *v.t.* conseiller vivement (**to do,** de faire). —*n.* forte envie *f.* **~ on,** (*impel*) encourager.

urgen|t /ˈɜːdʒənt/ *a.* urgent; (*request*) pressant. **~cy** *n.* urgence *f.*; (*of request, tone*) insistance *f.* **~tly** *adv.* d'urgence.

urinal /jʊəˈraɪnl/ *n.* urinoir *m.*

urin|e /ˈjʊərɪn/ *n.* urine *f.* **~ate** *v.i.* uriner.

urn /ɜːn/ *n.* urne *f.*; (*for tea, coffee*) fontaine *f.*

us /ʌs, *unstressed* əs/ *pron.* nous. (**to**) **~,** nous.

US *abbr. see* **United States.**

USA *abbr. see* **United States of America.**

usable /ˈjuːzəbl/ *a.* utilisable.

usage /ˈjuːsɪdʒ/ *n.* usage *m.*

use[1] /juːz/ *v.t.* se servir de, utiliser; (*consume*) consommer. **~ up,** épuiser. **~r** /-ə(r)/ *n.* usager *m.*

use[2] /juːs/ *n.* usage *m.*, emploi *m.* **in ~,** en usage. **it is no ~ shouting**/*etc.,* ça ne sert à rien de crier/*etc.* **make ~ of,** se servir de. **of ~,** utile.

used[1] /juːzd/ *a.* (*second-hand*) d'occasion.

used[2] /juːst/ *p.t.* **he ~ to do,** il faisait (autrefois), il avait l'habitude de faire. —*a.* **~ to,** habitué à.

use|ful /ˈjuːsfl/ *a.* utile. **~fully** *adv.* utilement. **~less** *a.* inutile; (*person*) incompétent.

usher /ˈʌʃə(r)/ *n.* (*in theatre, hall*) placeur *m.* —*v.t.* **~ in,** faire entrer. **~ette** *n.* ouvreuse *f.*

USSR *abbr.* (*Union of Soviet Socialist Republics*) URSS *f.*

usual /ˈjuːʒʊəl/ *a.* habituel, normal. **as ~,** comme d'habitude. **~ly** *adv.* d'habitude.

usurp /juːˈzɜːp/ *v.t.* usurper.

utensil /juːˈtensl/ *n.* ustensile *m.*

uterus /ˈjuːtərəs/ *n.* utérus *m.*

utilitarian /juːtɪlɪˈteərɪən/ *a.* utilitaire.

utility /juːˈtɪlətɪ/ *n.* utilité *f.* (**public**) **~,** service public *m.*

utilize /ˈjuːtɪlaɪz/ *v.t.* utiliser.

utmost /ˈʌtməʊst/ *a.* (*furthest, most intense*) extrême. **the ~ care**/*etc.,* (*greatest*) le plus grand soin/*etc.* —*n.* **do one's ~,** faire tout son possible.

Utopia /juːˈtəʊpɪə/ *n.* utopie *f.* **~n** *a.* utopique.

utter[1] /'ʌtə(r)/ *a.* complet, absolu. ~ly *adv.* complètement.

utter[2] /'ʌtə(r)/ *v.t.* proférer; (*sigh, shout*) pousser. ~ance *n.* déclaration *f.* give ~ance to, exprimer.

U-turn /'juːtɜːn/ *n.* demi-tour *m.*

V

vacan|t /'veɪkənt/ *a.* (*post*) vacant; (*seat etc.*) libre; (*look*) vague. **~cy** *n.* (*post*) poste vacant *m.*; (*room*) chambre disponible *f.*

vacate /və'keɪt, *Amer.* 'veɪkeɪt/ *v.t.* quitter.

vacation /veɪ'keɪʃn/ *n.* (*Amer.*) vacances *f. pl.*

vaccinat|e /'væksɪneɪt/ *v.t.* vacciner. **~ion** /-'neɪʃn/ *n.* vaccination *f.*

vaccine /'væksiːn/ *n.* vaccin *m.*

vacuum /'vækjʊəm/ *n.* (*pl.* -**cuums** *or* -**cua**) vide *m.* **~ cleaner**, aspirateur *m.* **~ flask**, bouteille thermos *f.* (P.).

vagabond /'vægəbɒnd/ *n.* vagabond(e) *m.* (*f.*).

vagina /və'dʒaɪnə/ *n.* vagin *m.*

vagrant /'veɪɡrənt/ *n.* vagabond(e) *m.* (*f.*), clochard(e) *m.* (*f.*).

vague /veɪɡ/ *a.* (**-er, -est**) vague; (*outline*) flou. **be ~ about,** ne pas préciser. **~ly** *adv.* vaguement.

vain /veɪn/ *a.* (**-er, -est**) (*conceited*) vaniteux; (*useless*) vain. **in ~,** en vain. **~ly** *adv.* en vain.

valentine /'væləntaɪn/ *n.* (*card*) carte de la Saint-Valentin *f.*

valet /'vælɪt, 'væleɪ/ *n.* (*manservant*) valet de chambre *m.*

valiant /'væliənt/ *a.* courageux.

valid /'vælɪd/ *a.* valable. **~ity** /və'lɪdətɪ/ *n.* validité *f.*

validate /'vælɪdeɪt/ *v.t.* valider.

valley /'vælɪ/ *n.* vallée *f.*

valuable /'væljʊəbl/ *a.* (*object*) de valeur; (*help etc.*) précieux. **~s** *n. pl.* objets de valeur *m. pl.*

valuation /væljʊ'eɪʃn/ *n.* expertise *f.*; (*of house*) évaluation *f.*

value /'væljuː/ *n.* valeur *f.* —*v.t.* (*appraise*) évaluer; (*cherish*) attacher de la valeur à. **~ added tax**, taxe à la valeur ajoutée *f.*, TVA *f.* **~r** /-ə(r)/ *n.* expert *m.*

valve /vælv/ *n.* (*techn.*) soupape *f.*; (*of tyre*) valve *f.*; (*radio*) lampe *f.*

vampire /'væmpaɪə(r)/ *n.* vampire *m.*

van /væn/ *n.* (*vehicle*) camionnette *f.*; (*rail.*) fourgon *m.*

vandal /'vændl/ *n.* vandale *m./f.* **~ism** /-əlɪzəm/ *n.* vandalisme *m.*

vandalize /'vændəlaɪz/ *v.t.* abîmer, détruire, saccager.

vanguard /'vænɡɑːd/ *n.* (*of army, progress, etc.*) avant-garde *f.*

vanilla /və'nɪlə/ *n.* vanille *f.*

vanish /'vænɪʃ/ *v.i.* disparaître.

vanity /'vænətɪ/ *n.* vanité *f.* **~ case,** mallette de toilette *f.*

vantage-point /'vɑːntɪdʒpɔɪnt/ *n.* (*place*) excellent point de vue *m.*

vapour /'veɪpə(r)/ *n.* vapeur *f.*

vari|able /'veərɪəbl/ *a.* variable. **~ation** /-'eɪʃn/ *n.* variation *f.* **~ed** /-ɪd/ *a.* varié.

variance /'veərɪəns/ *n.* **at ~,** en désaccord (**with,** avec).

variant /'veərɪənt/ *a.* différent. —*n.* variante *f.*

varicose /'værɪkəʊs/ *a.* **~ veins,** varices *f. pl.*

variety /və'raɪətɪ/ *n.* variété *f.*; (*entertainment*) variétés *f. pl.*

various /'veərɪəs/ *a.* divers. **~ly** *adv.* diversement.

varnish /'vɑːnɪʃ/ *n.* vernis *m.* —*v.t.* vernir.

vary /'veərɪ/ *v.t./i.* varier.

vase /vɑːz, *Amer.* veɪs/ *n.* vase *m.*

vast /vɑːst/ *a.* vaste, immense. **~ly** *adv.* infiniment, extrêmement. **~ness** *n.* immensité *f.*

vat /væt/ *n.* cuve *f.*

VAT /viːeɪ'tiː, væt/ *abbr.* (*value added tax*) TVA *f.*

vault¹ /vɔːlt/ *n.* (*roof*) voûte *f.*; (*in bank*) chambre forte *f.*; (*tomb*) caveau *m.*; (*cellar*) cave *f.*

vault² /vɔːlt/ *v.t./i.* sauter. —*n.* saut *m.*

vaunt /vɔːnt/ *v.t.* vanter.

veal /viːl/ *n.* (*meat*) veau *m.*

veer /vɪə(r)/ *v.i.* tourner, virer.

vegan /'viːɡən/ *n.* végétaliste *m./f.*, végétarien(ne) *m.* (*f.*).

vegetable /'vedʒtəbl/ *n.* légume *m.* —*a.* végétal. **~ garden,** (jardin) potager *m.*

vegetarian /vedʒɪ'teərɪən/ *n.* végétarien(ne) *m.* (*f.*).

vegetate /'vedʒɪteɪt/ *v.i.* végéter.

vegetation /vedʒɪ'teɪʃn/ *n.* végétation *f.*

vehement /'viːəmənt/ *a.* véhément. **~ly** *adv.* avec véhémence.

vehicle /'viːɪkl/ n. véhicule m.

veil /veɪl/ n. voile m. —v.t. voiler.

vein /veɪn/ n. (in body, rock) veine f.; (mood) esprit m.

velocity /vɪ'lɒsətɪ/ n. vélocité f.

velvet /'velvɪt/ n. velours m.

vendetta /ven'detə/ n. vendetta f.

vending-machine /'vendɪŋməʃiːn/ n. distributeur automatique m.

vendor /'vendə(r)/ n. vendeu|r, -se m., f.

veneer /və'nɪə(r)/ n. placage m.; (appearance: fig.) vernis m.

venerable /'venərəbl/ a. vénérable.

venereal /və'nɪərɪəl/ a. vénérien.

venetian /və'niːʃn/ a. ~ blind, jalousie f.

vengeance /'vendʒəns/ n. vengeance f. with a ~, furieusement.

venison /'venɪzn/ n. venaison f.

venom /'venəm/ n. venin m. ~ous /'venəməs/ a. venimeux.

vent[1] /vent/ n. (in coat) fente f.

vent[2] /vent/ n. (hole) orifice m.; (for air) bouche d'aération f. —v.t. (anger) décharger (on, sur). give ~ to, donner libre cours à.

ventilat|e /'ventɪleɪt/ v.t. ventiler. ~ion /-'leɪʃn/ n. ventilation f. ~or n. ventilateur m.

ventriloquist /ven'trɪləkwɪst/ n. ventriloque m./f.

venture /'ventʃə(r)/ n. entreprise (risquée) f. —v.t./i. (se) risquer.

venue /'venjuː/ n. lieu de rencontre or de rendez-vous m.

veranda /və'rændə/ n. véranda f.

verb /vɜːb/ n. verbe m.

verbal /'vɜːbl/ a. verbal.

verbatim /vɜː'beɪtɪm/ adv. textuellement, mot pour mot.

verbose /vɜː'bəʊs/ a. verbeux.

verdict /'vɜːdɪkt/ n. verdict m.

verge /vɜːdʒ/ n. bord m. —v.i. ~ on, friser, frôler. on the ~ of doing, sur le point de faire.

verif|y /'verɪfaɪ/ v.t. vérifier. ~ication /-ɪ'keɪʃn/ n. vérification f.

vermicelli /vɜːmɪ'selɪ/ n. vermicelle(s) m. (pl.).

vermin /'vɜːmɪn/ n. vermine f.

vermouth /'vɜːməθ/ n. vermouth m.

vernacular /və'nækjʊlə(r)/ n. langue f.; (regional) dialecte m.

versatil|e /'vɜːsətaɪl, Amer. 'vɜːsətl/ a. (person) aux talents variés; (mind) souple. ~ity /-'tɪlətɪ/ n. sou-

plesse f. her ~ity, la variété de ses talents.

verse /vɜːs/ n. strophe f.; (of Bible) verset m.; (poetry) vers m. pl.

versed /vɜːst/ a. ~ in, versé dans.

version /'vɜːʃn/ n. version f.

versus /'vɜːsəs/ prep. contre.

vertebra /'vɜːtɪbrə/ n. (pl. -brae /-briː/) vertèbre f.

vertical /'vɜːtɪkl/ a. vertical. ~ly adv. verticalement.

vertigo /'vɜːtɪgəʊ/ n. vertige m.

verve /vɜːv/ n. fougue f.

very /'verɪ/ adv. très. —a. (actual) même. the ~ day/etc., le jour/etc. même. at the ~ end, tout à la fin. the ~ first, le tout premier. ~ much, beaucoup.

vessel /'vesl/ n. (duct, ship) vaisseau m.

vest /vest/ n. tricot de corps m.; (waistcoat: Amer.) gilet m.

vested /'vestɪd/ a. ~ interests, droits acquis m. pl., intérêts m. pl.

vestige /'vestɪdʒ/ n. vestige m.

vestry /'vestrɪ/ n. sacristie f.

vet /vet/ n. (fam.) vétérinaire m./f. —v.t. (p.t. vetted) (candidate etc.) examiner (de près).

veteran /'vetərən/ n. vétéran m. (war) ~, ancien combattant m.

veterinary /'vetərɪnərɪ/ a. vétérinaire. ~ surgeon, vétérinaire m./f.

veto /'viːtəʊ/ n. (pl. -oes) veto m.; (right) droit de veto m. —v.t. mettre son veto à.

vex /veks/ v.t. contrarier, irriter. ~ed question, question controversée f.

via /'vaɪə/ prep. via, par.

viable /'vaɪəbl/ a. (baby, plan, firm) viable.

viaduct /'vaɪədʌkt/ n. viaduc m.

vibrant /'vaɪbrənt/ a. vibrant.

vibrat|e /vaɪ'breɪt/ v.t./i. (faire) vibrer. ~ion /-ʃn/ n. vibration f.

vicar /'vɪkə(r)/ n. pasteur m. ~age n. presbytère m.

vicarious /vɪ'keərɪəs/ a. (emotion) ressenti indirectement.

vice[1] /vaɪs/ n. (depravity) vice m.

vice[2] /vaɪs/ n. (techn.) étau m.

vice /vaɪs/ pref. vice-.

vice versa /'vaɪsɪ 'vɜːsə/ adv. vice versa.

vicinity /vɪ'sɪnətɪ/ n. environs m. pl. in the ~ of, aux environs de.

vicious /'vɪʃəs/ a. (spiteful) méchant; (violent) brutal. ~ circle, cercle vicieux *m*. ∼ly *adv*. méchamment; brutalement.

victim /'vɪktɪm/ *n*. victime *f*.

victimiz|e /'vɪktɪmaɪz/ *v.t*. persécuter, martyriser. ∼ation /-'zeɪʃn/ *n*. persécution *f*.

victor /'vɪktə(r)/ *n*. vainqueur *m*.

Victorian /vɪk'tɔːrɪən/ *a*. & *n*. victorien(ne) (*m*. (*f*.)).

victor|y /'vɪktərɪ/ *n*. victoire *f*. ∼ious /-'tɔːrɪəs/ *a*. victorieux.

video /'vɪdɪəʊ/ *a*. vidéo *invar*. —*n*. (*fam*.) magnétoscope *m*.

videotape /'vɪdɪəʊteɪp/ *n*. bande vidéo *f*. ∼ recorder, magnétoscope *m*.

vie /vaɪ/ *v.i*. (*pres. p*. vying) rivaliser (with, avec).

view /vjuː/ *n*. vue *f*. —*v.t*. regarder; (*house*) visiter. in my ∼, à mon avis. in ∼ of, compte tenu de. on ∼, exposé. with a ∼ to, dans le but de. ∼er *n*. (*TV*) téléspecta|teur, -trice *m*., *f*.

viewpoint /'vjuːpɔɪnt/ *n*. point de vue *m*.

vigil /'vɪdʒɪl/ *n*. veille *f*.; (*over sick person, corpse*) veillée *f*.

vigilan|t /'vɪdʒɪlənt/ *a*. vigilant. ∼ce *n*. vigilance *f*.

vig|our /'vɪgə(r)/ *n*. vigueur *f*. ∼orous *a*. vigoureux.

vile /vaɪl/ *a*. (*base*) infâme, vil; (*bad*) abominable, exécrable.

vilify /'vɪlɪfaɪ/ *v.t*. diffamer.

villa /'vɪlə/ *n*. villa *f*., pavillon *m*.

village /'vɪlɪdʒ/ *n*. village *m*. ∼r /-ə(r) / *n*. villageois(e) *m*. (*f*.).

villain /'vɪlən/ *n*. scélérat *m*., bandit *m*.; (*in story etc*.) traître *m*. ∼y *n*. infamie *f*.

vindicat|e /'vɪndɪkeɪt/ *v.t*. justifier. ∼ion /-'keɪʃn/ *n*. justification *f*.

vindictive /vɪn'dɪktɪv/ *a*. vindicatif.

vine /vaɪn/ *n*. vigne *f*.

vinegar /'vɪnɪgə(r)/ *n*. vinaigre *m*.

vineyard /'vɪnjəd/ *n*. vignoble *m*.

vintage /'vɪntɪdʒ/ *n*. (*year*) année *f*., millésime *m*. —*a*. (*wine*) de grand cru; (*car*) d'époque.

vinyl /'vaɪnɪl/ *n*. vinyle *m*.

viola /vɪ'əʊlə/ *n*. (*mus*.) alto *m*.

violat|e /'vaɪəleɪt/ *v.t*. violer. ∼ion /-'leɪʃn/ *n*. violation *f*.

violen|t /'vaɪələnt/ *a*. violent. ∼ce *n*. violence *f*. ∼tly *adv*. violemment, avec violence.

violet /'vaɪələt/ *n*. (*bot*.) violette *f*.; (*colour*) violet *m*. —*a*. violet.

violin /vaɪə'lɪn/ *n*. violon *m*. ∼ist *n*. violoniste *m*./*f*.

VIP /viːaɪ'piː/ *abbr*. (*very important person*) personnage de marque *m*.

viper /'vaɪpə(r)/ *n*. vipère *f*.

virgin /'vɜːdʒɪn/ *n*. (*woman*) vierge *f*. —*a*. vierge. be a ∼, (*woman, man*) être vierge. ∼ity /və'dʒɪnətɪ/ *n*. virginité *f*.

viril|e /'vɪraɪl, *Amer*. 'vɪrəl/ *a*. viril. ∼ity /vɪ'rɪlətɪ/ *n*. virilité *f*.

virtual /'vɜːtʃʊəl/ *a*. vrai. a ∼ failure /*etc*., pratiquement un échec/*etc*. ∼ly *adv*. pratiquement.

virtue /'vɜːtʃuː/ *n*. (*goodness, chastity*) vertu *f*.; (*merit*) mérite *m*. by *or* in ∼ of, en raison de.

virtuos|o /vɜːtʃʊ'əʊsəʊ/ *n*. (*pl*. -si /-siː/) virtuose *m*./*f*. ∼ity /-'ɒsətɪ/ *n*. virtuosité *f*.

virtuous /'vɜːtʃʊəs/ *a*. vertueux.

virulent /'vɪrʊlənt/ *a*. virulent.

virus /'vaɪərəs/ *n*. (*pl*. -uses) virus *m*.

visa /'viːzə/ *n*. visa *m*.

viscount /'vaɪkaʊnt/ *n*. vicomte *m*.

viscous /'vɪskəs/ *a*. visqueux.

vise /vaɪs/ *n*. (*Amer*.) étau *m*.

visib|le /'vɪzəbl/ *a*. (*discernible, obvious*) visible. ∼ility /-'bɪlətɪ/ *n*. visibilité *f*. ∼ly *adv*. visiblement.

vision /'vɪʒn/ *n*. vision *f*.

visionary /'vɪʒənərɪ/ *a*. & *n*. visionnaire (*m*./*f*.).

visit /'vɪzɪt/ *v.t*. (*p.t*. visited) (*person*) rendre visite à; (*place*) visiter. —*v.i*. être en visite. —*n*. (*tour, call*) visite *f*.; (*stay*) séjour *m*. ∼or *n*. visiteu|r, -se *m*., *f*.; (*guest*) invité(e) *m*. (*f*.); (*in hotel*) client(e) *m*. (*f*.).

visor /'vaɪzə(r)/ *n*. visière *f*.

vista /'vɪstə/ *n*. perspective *f*.

visual /'vɪʒʊəl/ *a*. visuel. ∼ly *adv*. visuellement.

visualize /'vɪʒʊəlaɪz/ *v.t*. se représenter; (*foresee*) envisager.

vital /'vaɪtl/ *a*. vital. ∼ statistics, (*fam*.) mensurations *f. pl*.

vitality /vaɪ'tælətɪ/ *n*. vitalité *f*.

vitally /'vaɪtəlɪ/ *adv*. extrêmement.

vitamin /'vɪtəmɪn/ *n*. vitamine *f*.

vivac|ious /vɪ'veɪʃəs/ *a*. plein d'entrain, animé. ∼ity /-æsətɪ/ *n*. vivacité *f*., entrain *m*.

vivid /'vɪvɪd/ *a*. vif; (*graphic*) vivant. ∼ly *adv*. vivement; (*describe*) de façon vivante.

vivisection /vɪvɪ'sekʃn/ n. vivisection f.

vocabulary /və'kæbjʊlərɪ/ n. vocabulaire m.

vocal /'vəʊkl/ a. vocal; (person: fig.) qui s'exprime franchement. ~ cords, cordes vocales f. pl. ~ist n. chanteu|r, -se m., f.

vocation /və'keɪʃn/ n. vocation f. ~al a. professionnel.

vociferous /və'sɪfərəs/ a. bruyant.

vodka /'vɒdkə/ n. vodka f.

vogue /vəʊg/ n. (fashion, popularity) vogue f. **in** ~, en vogue.

voice /vɔɪs/ n. voix f. —v.t. (express) formuler.

void /vɔɪd/ a. vide (of, de); (not valid) nul. —n. vide m.

volatile /'vɒlətaɪl, Amer. 'vɒlətl/ a. (person) versatile; (situation) variable.

volcan|o /vɒl'keɪnəʊ/ n. (pl. -oes) volcan m. ~ic /-ænɪk/ a. volcanique.

volition /və'lɪʃn/ n. **of one's own** ~, de son propre gré.

volley /'vɒlɪ/ n. (of blows etc.) volée f.; (of gunfire) salve f.

volt /vəʊlt/ n. (electr.) volt m. ~age n. voltage m.

voluble /'vɒljʊbl/ a. volubile.

volume /'vɒljuːm/ n. volume m.

voluntar|y /'vɒləntərɪ/ a. volontaire; (unpaid) bénévole. ~ily /-trəlɪ, Amer. -'terəlɪ/ adv. volontairement.

volunteer /vɒlən'tɪə(r)/ n. volontaire m./f. —v.i. s'offrir (**to do**, pour faire); (mil.) s'engager comme volontaire. —v.t. offrir.

voluptuous /və'lʌptʃʊəs/ a. voluptueux.

vomit /'vɒmɪt/ v.t./i. (p.t. **vomited**) vomir. —n. vomi(ssement) m.

voracious /və'reɪʃəs/ a. vorace.

vot|e /vəʊt/ n. vote m.; (right) droit de vote m. —v.t./i. voter. ~ (**in**), (person) élire. ~**er** n. élec|teur, -trice m., f. ~**ing** n. vote m. (**of**, de); (poll) scrutin m.

vouch /vaʊtʃ/ v.i. ~ **for,** se porter garant de, répondre de.

voucher /'vaʊtʃə(r)/ n. bon m.

vow /vaʊ/ n. vœu m. —v.t. (loyalty etc.) jurer (**to**, à). ~ **to do,** jurer de faire.

vowel /'vaʊəl/ n. voyelle f.

voyage /'vɔɪɪdʒ/ n. voyage (par mer) m.

vulgar /'vʌlgə(r)/ a. vulgaire. ~**ity** /-'gærətɪ/ n. vulgarité f.

vulnerab|le /'vʌlnərəbl/ a. vulnérable. ~**ility** /-'bɪlətɪ/ n. vulnérabilité f.

vulture /'vʌltʃə(r)/ n. vautour m.

W

wad /wɒd/ *n.* (*pad*) tampon *m.*; (*bundle*) liasse *f.*

wadding /'wɒdɪŋ/ *n.* rembourrage *m.*, ouate *f.*

waddle /'wɒdl/ *v.i.* se dandiner.

wade /weɪd/ *v.i.* ~ **through,** (*mud etc.*) patauger dans; (*book*: *fig.*) avancer péniblement dans.

wafer /'weɪfə(r)/ *n.* (*biscuit*) gaufrette *f.*; (*relig.*) hostie *f.*

waffle[1] /'wɒfl/ *n.* (*talk*: *fam.*) verbiage *m.* —*v.i.* (*fam.*) divaguer.

waffle[2] /'wɒfl/ *n.* (*cake*) gaufre *f.*

waft /wɒft/ *v.i.* flotter. —*v.t.* porter.

wag /wæg/ *v.t./i.* (*p.t.* **wagged**) (*tail*) remuer.

wage[1] /weɪdʒ/ *v.t.* (*campaign*) mener. ~ **war,** faire la guerre.

wage[2] /weɪdʒ/ *n.* (*weekly, daily*) salaire *m.* ~**s,** salaire *m.* ~**earner** *n.* salarié(e) *m.* (*f.*).

wager /'weɪdʒə(r)/ *n.* (*bet*) pari *m.* —*v.t.* parier (**that,** que).

waggle /'wægl/ *v.t./i.* remuer.

wagon /'wægən/ *n.* (*horse-drawn*) chariot *m.*; (*rail.*) wagon (de marchandises) *m.*

waif /weɪf/ *n.* enfant abandonné(e) *m./f.*

wail /weɪl/ *v.i.* (*utter cry or complaint*) gémir. —*n.* gémissement *m.*

waist /weɪst/ *n.* taille *f.*

waistcoat /'weɪskəʊt/ *n.* gilet *m.*

wait /weɪt/ *v.t./i.* attendre. —*n.* attente *f.* ~ **for,** on, servir. ~**ing-list** *n.* liste d'attente *f.* ~**ing-room** *n.* salle d'attente *f.*

wait|er /'weɪtə(r)/ *n.* garçon *m.*, serveur *m.* ~**ress** *n.* serveuse *f.*

waive /weɪv/ *v.t.* renoncer à.

wake[1] /weɪk/ *v.t./i.* (*p.t.* **woke,** *p.p.* **woken**). ~ (**up**), (se) réveiller.

wake[2] /weɪk/ *n.* (*track*) sillage *m.* **in the ~ of,** (*after*) à la suite de.

waken /'weɪkən/ *v.t./i.* (se) réveiller, (s')éveiller.

Wales /weɪlz/ *n.* pays de Galles *m.*

walk /wɔːk/ *v.i.* marcher; (*not ride*) aller à pied; (*stroll*) se promener. —*v.t.* (*streets*) parcourir; (*distance*) faire à pied; (*dog*) promener. —*n.* promenade *f.*, tour *m.*; (*gait*) (dé)marche *f.*; (*pace*) marche *f.*, pas *m.*; (*path*) allée *f.* ~ **of life,** condition sociale *f.* ~ **out,** (*go away*) partir; (*worker*) faire grève. ~**-out** *n.* grève surprise *f.* ~ **out on,** abandonner. ~**over** *n.* victoire facile *f.*

walker /'wɔːkə(r)/ *n.* (*person*) marcheu|r, -se *m.*, *f.*

walkie-talkie /wɔːkɪ'tɔːkɪ/ *n.* talkie-walkie *m.*

walking /'wɔːkɪŋ/ *n.* marche (à pied) *f.* —*a.* (*corpse, dictionary*: *fig.*) vivant. ~**-stick** *n.* canne *f.*

wall /wɔːl/ *n.* mur *m.*; (*of tunnel, stomach, etc.*) paroi *f.* —*a.* mural. —*v.t.* (*city*) fortifier. **go to the ~,** (*firm*) faire faillite.

wallet /'wɒlɪt/ *n.* portefeuille *m.*

wallflower /'wɔːlflaʊə(r)/ *n.* (*bot.*) giroflée *f.*

wallop /'wɒləp/ *v.t.* (*p.t.* **walloped**) (*hit*: *sl.*) taper sur. —*n.* (*blow*: *sl.*) grand coup *m.*

wallow /'wɒləʊ/ *v.i.* se vautrer.

wallpaper /'wɔːlpeɪpə(r)/ *n.* papier peint *m.* —*v.t.* tapisser.

walnut /'wɔːlnʌt/ *n.* (*nut*) noix *f.*; (*tree*) noyer *m.*

walrus /'wɔːlrəs/ *n.* morse *m.*

waltz /wɔːls/ *n.* valse *f.* —*v.i.* valser.

wan /wɒn/ *a.* pâle, blême.

wand /wɒnd/ *n.* baguette (magique) *f.*

wander /'wɒndə(r)/ *v.i.* errer; (*stroll*) flâner; (*digress*) s'écarter. ~**er** *n.* vagabond(e) *m.* (*f.*).

wane /weɪn/ *v.i.* décroître. —*n.* **on the ~,** (*strength, fame, etc.*) en déclin; (*person*) sur son déclin.

wangle /'wæŋgl/ *v.t.* (*obtain*: *sl.*) se débrouiller pour avoir.

want /wɒnt/ *v.t.* vouloir (**to do,** faire); (*need*) avoir besoin de; (*ask for*) demander. —*v.i.* ~ **for,** manquer de. —*n.* (*need, poverty*) besoin *m.*; (*desire*) désir *m.*; (*lack*) manque *m.* **for ~ of,** faute de. ~**ed** *a.* (*criminal*) recherché par la police.

wanting /'wɒntɪŋ/ *a.* **be ~,** manquer (**in,** de).

wanton /'wɒntən/ *a.* (*cruelty*) gratuit; (*woman*) impudique.

war /wɔː(r)/ *n.* guerre *f.* **at ~,** en guerre. **on the ~-path,** sur le sentier de la guerre.

ward /wɔːd/ *n.* (*in hospital*) salle *f.*; (*minor*: *jurid.*) pupille *m.*/*f.*; (*pol.*) division électorale *f.* —*v.t.* ~ **off,** (*danger*) prévenir; (*blow*, *anger*) détourner.

warden /'wɔːdn/ *n.* direc|teur, -trice *m.*, *f.*; (*of park*) gardien(ne) *m.* (*f.*). (*traffic*) ~, contractuel(le) *m.* (*f.*).

warder /'wɔːdə(r)/ *n.* gardien (de prison) *m.*

wardrobe /'wɔːdrəʊb/ *n.* (*place*) armoire *f.*; (*clothes*) garde-robe *f.*

warehouse /'weəhaʊs/ *n.* (*pl.* -s /-haʊzɪz/) entrepôt *m.*

wares /weəz/ *n. pl.* (*goods*) marchandises *f. pl.*

warfare /'wɔːfeə(r)/ *n.* guerre *f.*

warhead /'wɔːhed/ *n.* ogive *f.*

warily /'weərɪlɪ/ *adv.* avec prudence.

warm /wɔːm/ *a.* (-**er,** -**est**) chaud; (*hearty*) chaleureux. **be** *or* **feel** ~, avoir chaud. **it is** ~, il fait chaud. —*v.t.*/*i.* ~ (**up**), (se) réchauffer; (*food*) chauffer; (*liven up*) (s')animer. ~-**hearted** *a.* chaleureux. ~**ly** *adv.* (*wrap up etc.*) chaudement; (*heartily*) chaleureusement. ~**th** *n.* chaleur *f.*

warn /wɔːn/ *v.t.* avertir, prévenir. ~ **s.o. off sth.,** (*advise against*) mettre qn. en garde contre qch.; (*forbid*) interdire qch. à qn. ~**ing** *n.* avertissement *m.*; (*notice*) avis *m.* **without** ~**ing,** sans prévenir.

warp /wɔːp/ *v.t.*/*i.* (*wood etc.*) (se) voiler; (*pervert*) pervertir.

warrant /'wɒrənt/ *n.* (*for arrest*) mandat (d'arrêt) *m.*; (*comm.*) autorisation *f.* —*v.t.* justifier.

warranty /'wɒrəntɪ/ *n.* garantie *f.*

warring /'wɔːrɪŋ/ *a.* en guerre.

warrior /'wɒrɪə(r)/ *n.* guerr|ier, -ière *m.*, *f.*

warship /'wɔːʃɪp/ *n.* navire de guerre *m.*

wart /wɔːt/ *n.* verrue *f.*

wartime /'wɔːtaɪm/ *n.* **in** ~, en temps de guerre.

wary /'weərɪ/ *a.* (-**ier,** -**iest**) prudent.

was /wɒz, *unstressed* wəz/ *see* **be.**

wash /wɒʃ/ *v.t.*/*i.* (se) laver; (*flow over*) baigner. —*n.* lavage *m.*; (*clothes*) lessive *f.*; (*of ship*) sillage *m.* **have a** ~, se laver. ~-**basin** *n.* lavabo *m.* ~-**cloth** *n.* (*Amer.*) gant de toilette *m.* ~ **down,** (*meal*) arroser. ~ **one's hands of,** se laver les mains de. ~ **out,** (*cup etc.*) laver; (*stain*)

enlever. ~-**out** *n.* (*sl.*) fiasco *m.* ~-**room** *n.* (*Amer.*) toilettes *f. pl.* ~ **up,** faire la vaisselle; (*Amer.*) se laver. ~**able** *a.* lavable. ~**ing** *n.* lessive *f.* ~**ing-machine** *n.* machine à laver *f.* ~**ing-powder** *n.* lessive *f.* ~**ing-up** *n.* vaisselle *f.*

washed-out /wɒʃt'aʊt/ *a.* (*faded*) délavé; (*tired*) lessivé; (*ruined*) anéanti.

washer /'wɒʃə(r)/ *n.* rondelle *f.*

wasp /wɒsp/ *n.* guêpe *f.*

wastage /'weɪstɪdʒ/ *n.* gaspillage *m.* **some** ~, (*in goods, among candidates, etc.*) du déchet.

waste /weɪst/ *v.t.* gaspiller; (*time*) perdre. —*v.i.* ~ **away,** dépérir. —*a.* superflu; (*product*) de rebut. —*n.* gaspillage *m.*; (*of time*) perte *f.*; (*rubbish*) déchets *m. pl.* ~ (**land,** (*desolate*) terre désolée *f.*; (*unused*) terre inculte *f.*; (*in town*) terrain vague *m.* ~ **paper,** vieux papiers *m. pl.* ~-**paper basket,** corbeille (à papier) *f.*

wasteful /'weɪstfl/ *a.* peu économique; (*person*) gaspilleur.

watch /wɒtʃ/ *v.t.*/*i.* regarder, observer; (*guard, spy on*) surveiller; (*be careful about*) faire attention à. —*n.* surveillance *f.*; (*naut.*) quart *m.*; (*for telling time*) montre *f.* **be on the** ~, guetter. ~**dog** *n.* chien de garde *m.* ~ **out,** (*be on the look-out*) guetter; (*take care*) faire attention (**for,** à). ~**tower** *n.* tour de guet *f.* ~**ful** *a.* vigilant.

watchmaker /wɒtʃmeɪkə(r)/ *n.* horlog|er, -ère *m.*, *f.*

watchman /'wɒtʃmən/ *n.* (*pl.* -**men**) (*of building*) gardien *m.*

water /'wɔːtə(r)/ *n.* eau *f.* —*v.t.* arroser. —*v.i.* (*of eyes*) larmoyer. **my**/**his**/*etc.* **mouth** ~**s,** l'eau me/lui/*etc.* vient à la bouche. **by** ~, en bateau. ~-**closet** *n.* waters *m. pl.* ~-**colour** *n.* couleur pour aquarelle *f.*; (*painting*) aquarelle *f.* ~ **down,** couper (d'eau); (*tone down*) édulcorer. ~-**ice** *n.* sorbet *m.* ~-**lily** *n.* nénuphar *m.* ~-**main** *n.* canalisation d'eau *f.* ~-**melon** *n.* pastèque *f.* ~-**pistol** *n.* pistolet à eau *m.* ~ **polo,** water-polo *m.* ~-**power** *n.* énergie hydraulique *f.* ~-**skiing** *n.* ski nautique *m.*

watercress /'wɔːtəkres/ *n.* cresson (de fontaine) *m.*

waterfall /'wɔːtəfɔːl/ *n.* chute d'eau *f.*, cascade *f.*

watering-can /'wɔːtərɪŋkæn/ n. arrosoir m.

waterlogged /'wɔːtəlɒgd/ a. imprégné d'eau; (land) détrempé.

watermark /'wɔːtəmɑːk/ n. (in paper) filigrane m.

waterproof /'wɔːtəpruːf/ a. (material) imperméable.

watershed /'wɔːtəʃed/ n. (in affairs) tournant décisif m.

watertight /'wɔːtətaɪt/ a. étanche.

waterway /'wɔːtəweɪ/ n. voie navigable f.

waterworks /'wɔːtəwɜːks/ n. (place) station hydraulique f.

watery /'wɔːtəri/ a. (colour) délavé; (eyes) humide; (soup) trop liquide; (tea) faible.

watt /wɒt/ n. watt m.

wav|e /weɪv/ n. vague f.; (in hair) ondulation f.; (radio) onde f.; (sign) signe m. —v.t. agiter. —v.i. faire signe (de la main); (of flag, hair, etc.) onduler. ~y a. (line) onduleux; (hair) ondulé.

wavelength /'weɪvleŋθ/ n. (radio & fig.) longueur d'ondes f.

waver /'weɪvə(r)/ v.i. vaciller.

wax[1] /wæks/ n. cire f.; (for skis) fart m. —v.t. cirer; farter; (car) astiquer. ~en, ~y adjs. cireux.

wax[2] /wæks/ v.i. (of moon) croître.

waxwork /'wækswɜːk/ n. (dummy) figure de cire f.

way /weɪ/ n. (road, path) chemin m. (to, de); (distance) distance f.; (direction) direction f.; (manner) façon f.; (means) moyen m.; (particular) égard m. ~s, (habits) habitudes f. pl. —adv. (fam.) loin. **be in the** ~, bloquer le passage; (hindrance: fig.) gêner (qn.). **be on one's** or **the** ~, être en route. **by the** ~, à propos. **by the** ~side, au bord de la route. **by** ~ **of**, comme; (via) par. **go out of one's** ~ **to**, se donner du mal pour. **in a** ~, dans un sens. **that** ~, par là. **this** ~, par ici. ~ **in**, entrée f. ~ **out**, sortie f. ~-**out** a. (strange: fam.) original.

wayfarer /'weɪfeərə(r)/ n. voyageu|r, -se m., f.

waylay /'weɪleɪ/ v.t. (p.t. -laid) (assail, stop) assaillir.

wayward /'weɪwəd/ a. capricieux.

WC /dʌb(ə)ljuːˈsiː/ n. w.-c. m. pl.

we /wiː/ pron. nous.

weak /wiːk/ a. (-er, -est) faible; (delicate) fragile. ~ly adv. faiblement; a.

faible. ~ness n. faiblesse f.; (fault) point faible m. **a** ~ness for, (liking) un faible pour.

weaken /'wiːkən/ v.t. affaiblir —v.i. s'affaiblir, faiblir.

weakling /'wiːklɪŋ/ n. gringalet m.

wealth /welθ/ n. richesse f.; (riches, resources) richesses f. pl.; (quantity) profusion f.

wealthy /'welθi/ a. (-ier, -iest) riche. —n. **the** ~, les riches m. pl.

wean /wiːn/ v.t. (baby) sevrer.

weapon /'wepən/ n. arme f.

wear /weə(r)/ v.t. (p.t. **wore**, p.p. **worn**) porter; (put on) mettre; (expression etc.) avoir. —v.i. (last) durer. ~ **(out)**, (s')user. —n. usage m.; (damage) usure f.; (clothing) vêtements m. pl. ~ **down**, user. ~ **off**, (colour, pain) passer. ~ **on**, (time) passer. ~ **out**, (exhaust) épuiser. ~er n. ~er of, personne vêtue de f.

wear|y /'wɪəri/ a. (-ier, -iest) fatigué, las; (tiring) fatigant. —v.i. ~y of, se lasser de. ~ily adv. avec lassitude. ~iness n. lassitude f., fatigue f.

weasel /'wiːzl/ n. belette f.

weather /'weðə(r)/ n. temps m. —a. météorologique. —v.t. (survive) réchapper de or à. **under the** ~, patraque. ~-**beaten** a. tanné. ~-**vane** n. girouette f.

weathercock /'weðəkɒk/ n. girouette f.

weave /wiːv/ v.t./i. (p.t. **wove**, p.p. **woven**) tisser; (basket etc.) tresser; (move) se faufiler. —n. (style) tissage m. ~r /-ə(r)/ n. tisserand(e) m. (f.).

web /web/ n. (of spider) toile f.; (fabric) tissu m.; (on foot) palmure f. ~**bed** a. (foot) palmé. ~**bing** n. (in chair) sangles f. pl.

wed /wed/ v.t. (p.t. **wedded**) épouser. —v.i. se marier. ~**ded to**, (devoted to: fig.) attaché à.

wedding /'wedɪŋ/ n. mariage m. ~-**ring** n. alliance f.

wedge /wedʒ/ n. coin m.; (under wheel etc.) cale f. —v.t. caler; (push) enfoncer; (crowd) coincer.

wedlock /'wedlɒk/ n. mariage m.

Wednesday /'wenzdɪ/ n. mercredi m.

wee /wiː/ a. (fam.) tout petit.

weed /wiːd/ n. mauvaise herbe f. —v.t./i. désherber. ~-**killer** n. désherbant m. ~ **out**, extirper. ~y a. (person: fig.) faible, maigre.

week /wiːk/ n. semaine f. **a** ~ **today**/

tomorrow, aujourd'hui/demain en huit. ∼**ly** *adv.* toutes les semaines; *a.* & *n.* (*periodical*) hebdomadaire (*m.*).

weekday /'wi:kdeɪ/ *n.* jour de semaine *m.*

weekend /wi:k'end/ *n.* week-end *m.*, fin de semaine *f.*

weep /wi:p/ *v.t./i.* (*p.t.* **wept**) pleurer (*for s.o.*, qn.). ∼**ing willow,** saule pleureur *m.*

weigh /weɪ/ *v.t./i.* peser. ∼ **anchor,** lever l'ancre. ∼ **down,** lester (avec un poids); (*bend*) faire plier; (*fig.*) accabler. ∼ **up,** (*examine: fam.*) calculer.

weight /weɪt/ *n.* poids *m.* —*v.t.* ∼ **down** = **weigh down.** ∼**-lifting** *n.* haltérophilie *f.* ∼**y** *a.* lourd; (*subject etc.*) de poids.

weighting /'weɪtɪŋ/ *n.* indemnité *f.*

weir /wɪə(r)/ *n.* barrage *m.*

weird /wɪəd/ *a.* (**-er, -est**) mystérieux; (*strange*) bizarre.

welcome /'welkəm/ *a.* agréable; (*timely*) opportun. **be** ∼, être le *or* la bienvenu(e), être les bienvenu(e)s. **you're** ∼!, (*after thank you*) il n'y a pas de quoi! ∼ **to do,** libre de faire. —*int.* soyez le *or* la bienvenu(e), soyez les bienvenu(e)s. —*n.* accueil *m.* —*v.t.* accueillir; (*as greeting*) souhaiter la bienvenue à; (*fig.*) se réjouir de.

weld /weld/ *v.t.* souder. —*n.* soudure *f.* ∼**er** *n.* soudeur *m.* ∼**ing** *n.* soudure *f.*

welfare /'welfeə(r)/ *n.* bien-être *m.*; (*aid*) aide sociale *f.* **W**∼ **State,** État-providence *m.*

well[1] /wel/ *n.* (*for water, oil*) puits *m.*; (*of stairs*) cage *f.*

well[2] /wel/ *adv.* (**better, best**) bien. —*a.* bien *invar.* **be** ∼, (*healthy*) aller bien. —*int.* eh bien; (*surprise*) tiens. **do** ∼, (*succeed*) réussir. ∼**behaved** *a.* sage. ∼**being** *n.* bien-être *m.* ∼**disposed** *a.* bien disposé. ∼**done!,** bravo! ∼**heeled** *a.* (*fam.*) nanti. ∼**known** *a.* (bien) connu. ∼**meaning** *a.* bien intentionné. ∼ **off,** aisé, riche. ∼**read** *a.* instruit. ∼**spoken** *a.* qui parle bien. ∼**to-do** *a.* riche. ∼**wisher** *n.* admira|teur, -trice *m.,f.*

wellington /'welɪŋtən/ *n.* (*boot*) botte de caoutchouc *f.*

Welsh /welʃ/ *a.* gallois. —*n.* (*lang.*) gallois *m.* ∼**man** *n.* Gallois *m.* ∼**rabbit,** croûte au fromage *f.* ∼**woman** *n.* Galloise *f.*

welsh /welʃ/ *v.i.* ∼ **on,** (*debt, promise*) ne pas honorer.

welterweight /'weltəweɪt/ *n.* poids mi-moyen *m.*

wench /wentʃ/ *n.* (*old use*) jeune fille *f.*

wend /wend/ *v.t.* ∼ **one's way,** se diriger, aller son chemin.

went /went/ *see* **go.**

wept /wept/ *see* **weep.**

were /wɜː(r), *unstressed* wə(r)/ *see* **be.**

west /west/ *n.* ouest *m.* **the W**∼, (*pol.*) l'Occident *m.* —*a.* d'ouest. —*adv.* vers l'ouest. **W**∼ **Germany,** Allemagne de l'Ouest *f.* **W**∼ **Indian** *a.* & *n.* antillais(e) (*m.* (*f.*)). **the W**∼ **Indies,** les Antilles *f. pl.* ∼**erly** *a.* d'ouest. ∼**ern** *a.* de l'ouest; (*pol.*) occidental; *n.* (*film*) western *m.* ∼**erner** *n.* occidental(e) *m.* (*f.*). ∼**ward** *a.* à l'ouest. ∼**wards** *adv.* vers l'ouest.

westernize /'westənaɪz/ *v.t.* occidentaliser.

wet /wet/ *a.* (**wetter, wettest**) mouillé; (*damp, rainy*) humide. —*v.t.* (*p.t.* **wetted**) mouiller. —*n.* **the** ∼, l'humidité *f.*; (*rain*) la pluie *f.* ∼ **blanket,** rabat-joie *m. invar.* ∼**ness** *n.* humidité *f.*

whack /wæk/ *n.* (*fam.*) grand coup *m.* —*v.t.* (*fam.*) taper sur.

whacked /wækt/ *a.* (*fam.*) claqué.

whacking /'wækɪŋ/ *a.* énorme.

whale /weɪl/ *n.* baleine *f.*

wham /wæm/ *int.* vlan.

wharf /wɔːf/ *n.* (*pl.* **wharfs**) (*for ships*) quai *m.*

what /wɒt/ *a.* (*in questions*) quel(le), quel(le)s. —*pron.* (*in questions*) qu'est-ce qui; (*object*) (qu'est-ce) que *or* qu'*; (*after prep.*) quoi; (*that which*) ce qui; (*object*) ce que, ce qu'*. —*int.* quoi, comment. ∼ **a fool**/*etc.*, quel idiot/*etc.* ∼ **about me/him**/*etc.*?, et moi/lui/*etc.*? ∼ **about doing?,** si on faisait? ∼ **for?,** pourquoi? ∼ **is it?,** qu'est-ce que c'est? ∼ **you need,** ce dont vous avez besoin.

whatever /wɒt'evə(r)/ *a.* ∼ **book**/*etc.*, quel que soit le livre/ *etc.* —*pron.* (*no matter what*) quoi que, quoi qu'*; (*anything that*) tout ce qui; (*object*) tout ce que *or* qu'*. **nothing** ∼, rien du tout.

whatsoever /wɒtsəʊ'evər/ *a.* & *pron.* = **whatever.**

wheat /wi:t/ *n.* blé *m.*, froment *m.*

wheedle /'wiːdl/ *v.t.* cajoler.
wheel /wiːl/ *n.* roue *f.* —*v.t.* pousser. —
v.i. tourner. **at the ~,** (*of vehicle*) au
volant; (*helm*) au gouvernail. **~ and
deal,** (*Amer.*) faire des combines.
wheelbarrow /'wiːlbærəʊ/ *n.* brouette
f.
wheelchair /'wiːltʃeə(r)/ *n.* fauteuil
roulant *m.*
wheeze /wiːz/ *v.i.* siffler (en respi-
rant). —*n.* sifflement *m.*
when /wen/ *adv.* & *pron.* quand.
—*conj.* quand, lorsque. **the day/
moment ~,** le jour/moment où.
whenever /wen'evə(r)/ *conj.* & *adv.*
(*at whatever time*) quand; (*every time
that*) chaque fois que.
where /weə(r)/ *adv.*, *conj.*, & *pron.*
où; (*whereas*) alors que; (*the place
that*) là où. **~abouts** *adv.* (à peu
près) où; *n.* **s.o.'s ~abouts,** l'endroit
où se trouve qn. **~by** *adv.* par quoi.
~upon *adv.* sur quoi.
whereas /weər'æz/ *conj.* alors que.
wherever /weər'evə(r)/ *conj.* & *adv.*
où que; (*everywhere*) partout où;
(*anywhere*) (là) où; (*emphatic where*)
où donc.
whet /wet/ *v.t.* (*p.t.* **whetted**) (*appetite,
desire*) aiguiser.
whether /'weðə(r)/ *conj.* si. **not know
~,** ne pas savoir si. **~ I go or not,**
que j'aille ou non.
which /wɪtʃ/ *a.* (*in questions*) quel(le),
quel(le)s. —*pron.* (*in questions*) lequel, laquelle, lesquel(le)s; (*the one or
ones that*) celui (celle, ceux, celles)
qui; (*object*) celui (celle, ceux, celles)
que *or* qu'*; (*referring to whole sentence,* = *and that*) ce qui; (*object*) ce
que, ce qu'*; (*after prep.*) lequel/*etc.*
—*rel. pron.* qui; (*object*) que, qu'*.
the bird ~ flies, l'oiseau qui vole.
the hat ~ he wears, le chapeau qu'il
porte. **~ one,** lequel/*etc.* **of ~, from
~,** duquel/*etc.* **to ~, at ~,** auquel/*etc.*
the book of ~, le livre dont *or*
duquel. **after ~,** après quoi.
whichever /wɪtʃ'evə(r)/ *a.* **~ book/**
etc., quel que soit le livre/*etc.* que *or*
qui. **take ~ book you wish,** prenez
le livre que vous voulez. —*pron.* celui
(celle, ceux, celles) qui *or* que.
whiff /wɪf/ *n.* (*puff*) bouffée *f.*
while /waɪl/ *n.* moment *m.* —*conj.*
(*when*) pendant que; (*although*) bien
que; (*as long as*) tant que. —*v.t.* **~
away,** (*time*) passer.

whilst /waɪlst/ *conj.* = **while.**
whim /wɪm/ *n.* caprice *m.*
whimper /'wɪmpə(r)/ *v.i.* geindre,
pleurnicher. —*n.* pleurnichement *m.*
whimsical /'wɪmzɪkl/ *a.* (*person*)
capricieux; (*odd*) bizarre.
whine /waɪn/ *v.i.* gémir, se plaindre.
—*n.* gémissement *m.*
whip /wɪp/ *n.* fouet *m.* —*v.t.* (*p.t.* **whip-
ped**) fouetter; (*culin.*) fouetter, battre;
(*seize*) enlever brusquement. —*v.i.*
(*move*) aller en vitesse. **~-round** *n.*
(*fam.*) collecte *f.* **~ out,** (*gun etc.*)
sortir. **~ up,** exciter; (*cause*) provoquer; (*meal: fam.*) préparer.
whirl /wɜːl/ *v.t./i.* (faire) tourbillonner. —*n.* tourbillon *m.*
whirlpool /'wɜːlpuːl/ *n.* (*in sea etc.*)
tourbillon *m.*
whirlwind /'wɜːlwɪnd/ *n.* tourbillon
(de vent) *m.*
whirr /wɜː(r)/ *v.i.* vrombir.
whisk /wɪsk/ *v.t.* (*snatch*) enlever
or emmener brusquement; (*culin.*)
fouetter. —*n.* (*culin.*) fouet *m.*;
(*broom, brush*) petit balai *m.* **~ away,**
(*brush away*) chasser.
whisker /'wɪskə(r)/ *n.* poil *m.* **~s,**
(*man's*) barbe *f.*, moustache *f.*; (*side-
boards*) favoris *m. pl.*
whisky /'wɪskɪ/ *n.* whisky *m.*
whisper /'wɪspə(r)/ *v.t./i.* chuchoter.
—*n.* chuchotement *m.*; (*rumour:
fig.*) rumeur *f.*, bruit *m.*
whistle /'wɪsl/ *n.* sifflement *m.*; (*instrument*) sifflet *m.* —*v.t./i.* siffler. **~ at** *or*
for, siffler.
Whit /wɪt/ *a.* **~ Sunday,** dimanche de
Pentecôte *m.*
white /waɪt/ *a.* (**-er, -est**) blanc. —*n.*
blanc *m.*; (*person*) blanc(he) *m.* (*f.*).
~ coffee, café au lait *m.* **~collar
worker,** employé(e) de bureau *m.* (*f.*).
~ elephant, objet, projet, *etc.* inutile
m. **~ lie,** pieux mensonge *m.* **W~
Paper,** livre blanc *m.* **~ness** *n.* blancheur *f.*
whiten /'waɪtn/ *v.t./i.* blanchir.
whitewash /'waɪtwɒʃ/ *n.* blanc de
chaux *m.* —*v.t.* blanchir à la chaux;
(*person: fig.*) blanchir.
whiting /'waɪtɪŋ/ *n. invar.* (*fish*)
merlan *m.*
Whitsun /'wɪtsn/ *n.* la Pentecôte *f.*
whittle /'wɪtl/ *v.t.* **~ down,** tailler (au
couteau); (*fig.*) réduire.
whiz /wɪz/ *v.i.* (*p.t.* **whizzed**) (*through
air*) fendre l'air; (*hiss*) siffler; (*rush*)

aller à toute vitesse. ~**-kid** *n*. jeune prodige *m*.

who /huː/ *pron.* qui.

whodunit /huːˈdʌnɪt/ *n*. (*story*: *fam.*) roman policier *m*.

whoever /huːˈevə(r)/ *pron.* (*no matter who*) qui que ce soit qui *or* que; (*the one who*) quiconque.

whole /həʊl/ *a*. entier; (*intact*) intact. **the ~ house**/*etc.*, toute la maison/ *etc.* —*n*. totalité *f*.; (*unit*) tout *m*. **on the ~,** dans l'ensemble. ~**-hearted** *a*., ~**heartedly** *adv.* sans réserve.

wholemeal /ˈhəʊlmiːl/ *a*. ~ **bread**, pain complet *m*.

wholesale /ˈhəʊlseɪl/ *n*. gros *m*. —*a*. (*firm*) de gros; (*fig.*) systématique. —*adv.* (*in large quantities*) en gros; (*buy or sell one item*) au prix de gros; (*fig.*) en masse. ~**r** /-ə(r)/ *n*. grossiste *m*./*f*.

wholesome /ˈhəʊlsəm/ *a*. sain.

wholewheat /ˈhəʊlhwiːt/ *a*. (*Amer.*) = **wholemeal**.

wholly /ˈhəʊlɪ/ *adv.* entièrement.

whom /huːm/ *pron.* (*that*) que, qu'*; (*after prep. & in questions*) qui. **of ~,** dont. **with ~,** avec qui.

whooping cough /ˈhuːpɪŋkɒf/ *n*. coqueluche *f*.

whopping /ˈwɒpɪŋ/ *a*. (*sl.*) énorme.

whore /hɔː(r)/ *n*. putain *f*.

whose /huːz/ *pron. & a*. à qui, de qui. ~ **hat is this?,** ~ **is this hat?,** à qui est ce chapeau? ~ **son are you?,** de qui êtes-vous le fils? **the man ~ hat I see,** l'homme dont *or* de qui je vois le chapeau.

why /waɪ/ *adv.* pourquoi. —*int.* eh bien, ma parole, tiens.

wick /wɪk/ *n*. (*of lamp etc.*) mèche *f*.

wicked /ˈwɪkɪd/ *a*. méchant, mauvais, vilain. ~**ly** *adv.* méchamment. ~**ness** *n*. méchanceté *f*.

wicker /ˈwɪkə(r)/ *n*. osier *m*. ~**work** *n*. vannerie *f*.

wicket /ˈwɪkɪt/ *n*. guichet *m*.

wide /waɪd/ *a*. (**-er, -est**) large; (*ocean etc.*) vaste. —*adv.* (*fall etc.*) loin du but. **open ~,** ouvrir tout grand. ~ **awake,** éveillé. ~**ly** *adv.* (*spread, space*) largement; (*travel*) beaucoup; (*generally*) généralement; (*extremely*) extrêmement.

widen /ˈwaɪdn/ *v.t.*/*i*. (s')élargir.

widespread /ˈwaɪdspred/ *a*. très répandu.

widow /ˈwɪdəʊ/ *n*. veuve *f*. ~**ed** *a*.

(*man*) veuf; (*woman*) veuve. **be ~ed,** (*become widower or widow*) devenir veuf *or* veuve. ~**er** *n*. veuf *m*.

width /wɪdθ/ *n*. largeur *f*.

wield /wiːld/ *v.t.* (*axe etc.*) manier; (*power*: *fig.*) exercer.

wife /waɪf/ *n*. (*pl.* **wives**) femme *f*., épouse *f*. ~**ly** *a*. d'épouse.

wig /wɪg/ *n*. perruque *f*.

wiggle /ˈwɪgl/ *v.t.*/*i*. remuer; (*hips*) tortiller; (*of worm*) se tortiller.

wild /waɪld/ *a*. (**-er, -est**) sauvage; (*sea, enthusiasm*) déchaîné; (*mad*) fou; (*angry*) furieux. —*adv.* (*grow*) à l'état sauvage. ~**s** *n. pl.* régions sauvages *f. pl.* **run ~,** (*free*) courir en liberté. ~**-goose chase,** fausse piste *f*. ~**ly** *adv.* violemment; (*madly*) follement.

wildcat /ˈwaɪldkæt/ *a*. ~ **strike,** grève sauvage *f*.

wilderness /ˈwɪldənɪs/ *n*. désert *m*.

wildlife /ˈwaɪldlaɪf/ *n*. faune *f*.

wile /waɪl/ *n*. ruse *f*., artifice *m*.

wilful /ˈwɪlfl/ *a*. (*intentional, obstinate*) volontaire.

will[1] /wɪl/ *v. aux.* **he ~ do**/**you ~ sing**/*etc.*, (*future tense*) il fera/ tu chanteras/*etc.* ~ **you have a coffee?,** voulez-vous prendre un café?

will[2] /wɪl/ *n*. volonté *f*.; (*document*) testament *m*. —*v.t.* (*wish*) vouloir. **at ~,** quand *or* comme on veut. ~**-power** *n*. volonté *f*. ~ **o.s. to do,** faire un effort de volonté pour faire.

willing /ˈwɪlɪŋ/ *a*. (*help, offer*) spontané; (*helper*) bien disposé. ~ **to,** disposé à. ~**ly** *adv.* (*with pleasure*) volontiers; (*not forced*) volontairement. ~**ness** *n*. empressement *m*. (**to do,** à faire); (*goodwill*) bonne volonté *f*.

willow /ˈwɪləʊ/ *n*. saule *m*.

willowy /ˈwɪləʊɪ/ *a*. (*person*) svelte.

willy-nilly /wɪlɪˈnɪlɪ/ *adv.* bon gré mal gré.

wilt /wɪlt/ *v.i.* (*plant etc.*) dépérir.

wily /ˈwaɪlɪ/ *a*. (**-ier, -iest**) rusé.

win /wɪn/ *v.t.*/*i*. (*p.t.* **won,** *pres. p.* **winning**) gagner; (*victory, prize*) remporter; (*fame, fortune*) acquérir, trouver. —*n*. victoire *f*.

winc|**e** /wɪns/ *v.i.* se crisper, tressaillir. **without ~ing,** sans broncher.

winch /wɪntʃ/ *n*. treuil *m*. —*v.t.* hisser au treuil.

wind[1] /wɪnd/ n. vent m.; (breath) souffle m. get ∼ of, avoir vent de. in the ∼, dans l'air. ∼-cheater, (Amer.) ∼breaker ns. blouson m. ∼ instrument, instrument à vent m. ∼-swept a. balayé par les vents.

wind[2] /waɪnd/ v.t./i. (p.t. **wound**) (s')enrouler; (of path, river) serpenter. ∼ (up), (clock etc.) remonter. ∼ up, (end) (se) terminer. ∼ing a. (path) sinueux.

windfall /'wɪndfɔːl/ n. fruit tombé m.; (money: fig.) aubaine f.

windmill /'wɪndmɪl/ n. moulin à vent m.

window /'wɪndəʊ/ n. fenêtre f.; (in vehicle, train) vitre f.; (in shop) vitrine f.; (counter) guichet m. ∼-box n. jardinière f. ∼-dresser n. étalagiste m./f. ∼-ledge n. rebord de (la) fenêtre m. ∼-shopping n. lèche-vitrines m. ∼-sill n. (inside) appui de (la) fenêtre m.; (outside) rebord de (la) fenêtre m.

windpipe /'wɪndpaɪp/ n. trachée f.

windscreen /'wɪndskriːn/ n. parebrise m. invar.

windshield /'wɪndʃiːld/ n. (Amer.) pare-brise m. invar.

windy /'wɪndɪ/ a. (-ier, -iest) venteux. it is ∼, il y a du vent.

wine /waɪn/ n. vin m. ∼-cellar n. cave (à vin) f. ∼-grower n. viticulteur m. ∼-growing n. viticulture f.; a. viticole. ∼ list, carte des vins f. ∼-tasting n. dégustation de vins f. ∼ waiter, sommelier m.

wineglass /'waɪnglɑːs/ n. verre à vin m.

wing /wɪŋ/ n. aile f. ∼s, (theatre) coulisses f. pl. under one's ∼, sous son aile. ∼ed a. ailé. ∼er n. (sport) ailier m.

wink /wɪŋk/ v.i. faire un clin d'œil; (light, star) clignoter. —n. clin d'œil m.; clignotement m.

winner /'wɪnə(r)/ n. (of game) gagnant(e) m. (f.); (of fight) vainqueur m.

winning /'wɪnɪŋ/ see **win**. —a. (number, horse) gagnant; (team) victorieux; (smile) engageant. ∼s n. pl. gains m. pl.

wint|er /'wɪntə(r)/ n. hiver m. —v.i. hiverner. ∼ry a. hivernal.

wipe /waɪp/ v.t. essuyer. —v.i. ∼ up, essuyer la vaisselle. —n. coup de torchon or d'éponge m. ∼ off or out,

essuyer. ∼ out, (destroy) anéantir; (remove) effacer. ∼r /-ə(r)/ n. (for windscreen: auto.) essuie-glace m. invar.

wir|e /'waɪə(r)/ n. fil m. ∼e netting, grillage m. ∼ing n. (electr.) installation électrique f.

wireless /'waɪəlɪs/ n. radio f.

wiry /'waɪərɪ/ a. (-ier, -iest) (person) nerveux et maigre.

wisdom /'wɪzdəm/ n. sagesse f.

wise /waɪz/ a. (-er, -est) prudent, sage; (look) averti. ∼ guy, (fam.) petit malin m. ∼ man, sage m. ∼ly adv. prudemment.

wisecrack /'waɪzkræk/ n. (fam.) mot d'esprit m., astuce f.

wish /wɪʃ/ n. (specific) souhait m., vœu m.; (general) désir m. —v.t. souhaiter, vouloir, désirer (to do, faire); (bid) souhaiter. —v.i. ∼ for, souhaiter. best ∼es, (in letter) amitiés f. pl.; (on greeting card) meilleurs vœux m. pl.

wishful /'wɪʃfl/ a. it is ∼ thinking, on se fait des illusions.

wishy-washy /'wɪʃɪwɒʃɪ/ a. fade.

wisp /wɪsp/ n. (of smoke) volute f.

wistful /'wɪstfl/ a. mélancolique.

wit /wɪt/ n. intelligence f.; (humour) esprit m.; (person) homme d'esprit m., femme d'esprit f. be at one's ∼'s or ∼s' end, ne plus savoir que faire.

witch /wɪtʃ/ n. sorcière f. ∼craft n. sorcellerie f.

with /wɪð/ prep. avec; (having) à; (because of) de; (at house of) chez. the man ∼ the beard, l'homme à la barbe. fill/etc. ∼, remplir/etc. de. pleased/shaking/etc. ∼, content/ frémissant/etc. de. ∼ it, (fam.) dans le vent.

withdraw /wɪð'drɔː/ v.t./i. (p.t. **withdrew**, p.p. **withdrawn**) (se) retirer. ∼al n. retrait m. ∼n a. (person) renfermé.

wither /'wɪðə(r)/ v.t./i. (se) flétrir. ∼ed a. (person) desséché.

withhold /wɪð'həʊld/ v.t. (p.t. **withheld**) refuser (de donner); (retain) retenir; (conceal, not tell) cacher (from, à).

within /wɪ'ðɪn/ prep. & adv. à l'intérieur (de); (in distances) à moins de. ∼ a month, (before) avant un mois. ∼ sight, en vue.

without /wɪ'ðaʊt/ prep. sans.

withstand /wɪð'stænd/ v.t. (p.t. **withstood**) résister à.

witness /'wɪtnɪs/ *n.* témoin *m.*; (*evidence*) témoignage *m.* —*v.t.* être le témoin de, voir; (*document*) signer. **bear ~ to,** témoigner de.

witticism /'wɪtɪsɪzəm/ *n.* bon mot *m.*

witt|y /'wɪtɪ/ *a.* (-**ier**, -**iest**) spirituel. **~iness** *n.* esprit *m.*

wives /waɪvz/ *see* **wife.**

wizard /'wɪzəd/ *n.* magicien *m.*; (*genius*: *fig.*) génie *m.*

wizened /'wɪznd/ *a.* ratatiné.

wobbl|e /'wɒbl/ *v.i.* (*of jelly, voice, hand*) trembler; (*stagger*) chanceler; (*of table, chair*) branler. **~y** *a.* tremblant; branlant.

woe /wəʊ/ *n.* malheur *m.*

woke, woken /wəʊk, 'wəʊkən/ *see* **wake**[1].

wolf /wʊlf/ *n.* (*pl.* **wolves**) loup *m.* —*v.t.* (*food*) engloutir. **cry ~,** crier au loup. **~-whistle** *n.* sifflement admiratif *m.*

woman /'wʊmən/ *n.* (*pl.* **women**) femme *f.* **~ doctor,** femme médecin *f.* **~ driver,** femme au volant *f.* **~ friend,** amie *f.* **~hood** *n.* féminité *f.* **~ly** *a.* féminin.

womanize /'wʊmənaɪz/ *v.i.* courir le jupon *or* les femmes.

womb /wuːm/ *n.* utérus *m.*

women /'wɪmɪn/ *see* **woman.**

won /wʌn/ *see* **win.**

wonder /'wʌndə(r)/ *n.* émerveillement *m.*; (*thing*) merveille *f.* —*v.t.* se demander (**if,** si). —*v.i.* s'étonner (**at,** de); (*reflect*) songer (**about,** à). **it is no ~,** ce *or* il n'est pas étonnant (**that,** que).

wonderful /'wʌndəfl/ *a.* merveilleux. **~ly** *adv.* merveilleusement; (*work, do, etc.*) à merveille.

won't /wəʊnt/ = **will not.**

woo /wuː/ *v.t.* (*woman*) faire la cour à; (*please*) chercher à plaire à.

wood /wʊd/ *n.* bois *m.* **~ed** *a.* boisé. **~en** *a.* en *or* de bois; (*stiff*: *fig.*) raide, comme du bois.

woodcut /'wʊdkʌt/ *n.* gravure sur bois *f.*

woodland /'wʊdlənd/ *n.* région boisée *f.*, bois *m. pl.*

woodpecker /'wʊdpekə(r)/ *n.* (*bird*) pic *m.*, pivert *m.*

woodwind /'wʊdwɪnd/ *n.* (*mus.*) bois *m. pl.*

woodwork /'wʊdwɜːk/ *n.* (*craft, objects*) menuiserie *f.*

woodworm /'wʊdwɜːm/ *n.* (*larvae*) vers (de bois) *m. pl.*

woody /'wʊdɪ/ *a.* (*wooded*) boisé; (*like wood*) ligneux.

wool /wʊl/ *n.* laine *f.* **~len** *a.* de laine. **~lens** *n. pl.* lainages *m. pl.* **~ly** *a.* laineux; (*vague*) nébuleux; *n.* (*garment*: *fam.*) lainage *m.*

word /wɜːd/ *n.* mot *m.*; (*spoken*) parole *f.*, mot *m.*; (*promise*) parole *f.*; (*news*) nouvelles *f. pl.* —*v.t.* rédiger. **by ~ of mouth,** de vive voix. **have a ~ with,** parler à. **in other ~s,** autrement dit. **~ processor,** machine de traitement de texte *f.* **~ing** *n.* termes *m. pl.*

wordy /'wɜːdɪ/ *a.* verbeux.

wore /wɔː(r)/ *see* **wear.**

work /wɜːk/ *n.* travail *m.*; (*product, book, etc.*) œuvre *f.*, ouvrage *m.*; (*building etc. work*) travaux *m. pl.* **~s,** (*techn.*) mécanisme *m.*; (*factory*) usine *f.* —*v.t./i.* (*of person*) travailler; (*shape, hammer, etc.*) travailler; (*techn.*) (faire) fonctionner, (faire) marcher; (*land, mine*) exploiter; (*of drug etc.*) agir. **~ s.o.,** (*make work*) faire travailler qn. **~ in,** (s')introduire. **~ off,** (*get rid of*) se débarrasser de. **~ out** *v.t.* (*solve*) résoudre; (*calculate*) calculer; (*elaborate*) élaborer; *v.i.* (*succeed*) marcher; (*sport*) s'entraîner. **~-to-rule** *n.* grève du zèle *f.* **~ up** *v.t.* développer; *v.i.* (*to climax*) monter vers. **~ed up,** (*person*) énervé.

workable /'wɜːkəbl/ *a.* réalisable.

workaholic /wɜːkə'hɒlɪk/ *n.* (*fam.*) bourreau de travail *m.*

worker /'wɜːkə(r)/ *n.* travailleu|r, -se *m.*, *f.*; (*manual*) ouvri|er, -ière *m.*, *f.*

working /'wɜːkɪŋ/ *a.* (*day, lunch, etc.*) de travail. **~s** *n. pl.* mécanisme *m.* **~ class,** classe ouvrière *f.* **~-class** *a.* ouvrier. **in ~ order,** en état de marche.

workman /'wɜːkmən/ *n.* (*pl.* -**men**) ouvrier *m.* **~ship** *n.* maîtrise *f.*

workshop /'wɜːkʃɒp/ *n.* atelier *m.*

world /wɜːld/ *n.* monde *m.* —*a.* (*power etc.*) mondial; (*record etc.*) du monde. **a ~ of,** énormément de. **~-wide** *a.* universel.

worldly /'wɜːldlɪ/ *a.* de ce monde, terrestre. **~-wise** *a.* qui a l'expérience du monde.

worm /wɜːm/ *n.* ver *m.* —*v.t.* **~ one's way into,** s'insinuer dans. **~-eaten** *a.* (*wood*) vermoulu; (*fruit*) véreux.

worn /wɔːn/ *see* **wear.** —*a.* usé. ∼**-out** *a.* (*thing*) complètement usé; (*person*) épuisé.

worr|y /'wʌrɪ/ *v.t./i.* (s')inquiéter. —*n.* souci *m.* ∼**ied** *a.* inquiet. ∼**ier** *n.* inqu|iet, -iète *m.*,*f.*

worse /wɜːs/ *a.* pire, plus mauvais. —*adv.* plus mal. —*n.* pire *m.*

worsen /'wɜːsn/ *v.t./i.* empirer.

worship /'wɜːʃɪp/ *n.* (*adoration*) culte *m.* —*v.t.* (*p.t.* **worshipped**) adorer. —*v.i.* faire ses dévotions. ∼**per** *n.* (*in church*) fidèle *m.*/*f.*

worst /wɜːst/ *a.* pire, plus mauvais. —*adv.* (**the**) ∼, (*sing etc.*) le plus mal. —*n.* **the** ∼ (**one**), (*person, object*) le *or* la pire. **the** ∼ (**thing**), le pire (**that**, **que**). **get the** ∼ **of it**, (*be defeated*) avoir le dessous.

worth /wɜːθ/ *a.* **be** ∼, valoir. **it is** ∼ **waiting**/*etc.*, ça vaut la peine d'attendre/*etc.* —*n.* valeur *f.* **ten pence** ∼ **of**, (pour) dix pence de. **it is** ∼ (**one's**) **while**, ça (en) vaut la peine. ∼**less** *a.* qui ne vaut rien.

worthwhile /wɜːθ'waɪl/ *a.* qui (en) vaut la peine.

worthy /'wɜːðɪ/ *a.* (-**ier**, -**iest**) digne (**of**, **de**); (*laudable*) louable. —*n.* (*person*) notable *m.*

would /wʊd, *unstressed* wəd/ *v. aux.* **he** ∼ **do**/**you** ∼ **sing**/*etc.*, (*conditional tense*) il ferait/tu chanterais/*etc.* **he** ∼ **have done**, il aurait fait. **I** ∼ **come every day**, (*used to*) je venais chaque jour. ∼ **you come here?**, voulez-vous venir ici? ∼**-be** *a.* soi-disant.

wound[1] /wuːnd/ *n.* blessure *f.* —*v.t.* blesser. **the** ∼**ed**, les blessés *m. pl.*

wound[2] /waʊnd/ *see* **wind**[2].

wove, woven /wəʊv, 'wəʊvn/ *see* **weave.**

wow /waʊ/ *int.* mince (alors).

wrangle /'ræŋgl/ *v.i.* se disputer. —*n.* dispute *f.*

wrap /ræp/ *v.t.* (*p.t.* **wrapped**). ∼ (**up**), envelopper. —*v.i.* ∼ **up**, (*dress warmly*) se couvrir. —*n.* châle *m.* ∼**ped up in**, (*engrossed*) absorbé par. ∼**per** *n.* (*of book*) jaquette *f.*; (*of sweet*) papier *m.* ∼**ping** *n.* emballage *m.*

wrath /rɒθ/ *n.* courroux *m.*

wreak /riːk/ *v.t.* ∼ **havoc**, (*of storm etc.*) faire des ravages.

wreath /riːθ/ *n.* (*pl.* -**s** /-ðz/) (*of flowers, leaves*) couronne *f.*

wreck /rek/ *n.* (*sinking*) naufrage

m.; (*ship, remains, person*) épave *f.*; (*vehicle*) voiture accidentée *or* délabrée *f.* —*v.t.* détruire; (*ship*) provoquer le naufrage de. ∼**age** *n.* (*pieces*) débris *m. pl.*

wren /ren/ *n.* roitelet *m.*

wrench /rentʃ/ *v.t.* (*pull*) tirer sur; (*twist*) tordre; (*snatch*) arracher (**from**, à). —*n.* (*tool*) clé *f.*

wrest /rest/ *v.t.* arracher (**from**, à).

wrestl|e /'resl/ *v.i.* lutter, se débattre (**with**, contre). ∼**er** *n.* lutteu|r, -se *m.*, *f.*; catcheu|r, -se *m.*, *f.* ∼**ing** *n.* lutte *f.* (**all-in**) ∼**ing**, catch *m.*

wretch /retʃ/ *n.* malheureu|x, -se *m.*, *f.*; (*rascal*) misérable *m.*/*f.*

wretched /'retʃɪd/ *a.* (*pitiful, poor*) misérable; (*bad*) affreux.

wriggle /'rɪgl/ *v.t./i.* (se) tortiller.

wring /rɪŋ/ *v.t.* (*p.t.* **wrung**) (*twist*) tordre; (*clothes*) essorer. ∼ **out of**, (*obtain from*) arracher à. ∼**ing wet**, trempé (jusqu'aux os).

wringer /'rɪŋə(r)/ *n.* essoreuse *f.*

wrinkle /'rɪŋkl/ *n.* (*crease*) pli *m.*; (*on skin*) ride *f.* —*v.t./i.* (se) rider.

wrist /rɪst/ *n.* poignet *m.* ∼**-watch** *n.* montre-bracelet *f.*

writ /rɪt/ *n.* acte judiciaire *m.*

write /raɪt/ *v.t./i.* (*p.t.* **wrote**, *p.p.* **written**, écrire. ∼ **back**, répondre. ∼ **down**, noter. ∼ **off**, (*debt*) annuler; (*vehicle*) considérer bon pour la casse. ∼**-off** *n.* perte totale *f.* ∼ **up**, (*from notes*) rédiger. ∼**-up** *n.* compte rendu *m.*

writer /'raɪtə(r)/ *n.* auteur *m.*, écrivain *m.* ∼ **of**, auteur de.

writhe /raɪð/ *v.i.* se tordre.

writing /'raɪtɪŋ/ *n.* écriture *f.* ∼(**s**), (*works*) écrits *m. pl.* **in** ∼, par écrit. ∼**-paper** *n.* papier à lettres *m.*

written /'rɪtn/ *see* **write.**

wrong /rɒŋ/ *a.* (*incorrect, mistaken*) faux, mauvais; (*unfair*) injuste; (*amiss*) qui ne va pas; (*clock*) pas à l'heure. **be** ∼, (*person*) avoir tort (**to**, de); (*be mistaken*) se tromper. —*adv.* mal. —*n.* injustice *f.*; (*evil*) mal *m.* —*v.t.* faire (du) tort à. **be in the** ∼, avoir tort. **go** ∼, (*err*) se tromper; (*turn out badly*) mal tourner; (*vehicle*) tomber en panne. **it is** ∼ **to**, (*morally*) c'est mal de. **what is** ∼ **with you?**, qu'est-ce que vous avez? ∼**ly** *adv.* mal; (*blame etc.*) à tort.

wrongful /'rɒŋfl/ *a.* injustifié, injuste. ∼**ly** *adv.* à tort.
wrote /rəʊt/ *see* **write.**
wrought /rɔːt/ *a.* ∼ **iron,** fer forgé *m.*

wrung /rʌŋ/ *see* **wring.**
wry /raɪ/ *a.* (**wryer, wryest**) (*smile*) désabusé, forcé. ∼ **face,** grimace *f.*

X

xerox /'zɪərɒks/ *v.t.* photocopier.
Xmas /'krɪsməs/ *n.* Noël *m.*
X-ray /'eksreɪ/ *n.* rayon X *m.*; (*photo-*

graph) radio(graphie) *f.* —*v.t.* radio-graphier.
xylophone /'zaɪləfəʊn/ *n.* xylophone *m.*

Y

yacht /jɒt/ *n.* yacht *m.* ∼**ing** *n.* yachting *m.*
yank /jæŋk/ *v.t.* tirer brusquement. —*n.* coup brusque *m.*
Yank /jæŋk/ *n.* (*fam.*) Américain(e) *m.* (*f.*), Amerloque *m./f.*
yap /jæp/ *v.i.* (*p.t.* **yapped**) japper.
yard[1] /jɑːd/ *n.* (*measure*) yard *m.* (= 0.9144 metre).
yard[2] /jɑːd/ *n.* (*of house etc.*) cour *f.*; (*garden: Amer.*) jardin *m.*; (*for storage*) chantier *m.*, dépôt *m.*
yardstick /'jɑːdstɪk/ *n.* mesure *f.*
yarn /jɑːn/ *n.* (*thread*) fil *m.*; (*tale: fam.*) (longue) histoire *f.*
yawn /jɔːn/ *v.i.* bâiller. —*n.* bâillement *m.* ∼**ing** *a.* (*gaping*) béant.
year /jɪə(r)/ *n.* an *m.*, année *f.* **school/tax**/*etc.* ∼, année scolaire/fiscale/*etc.* **be ten**/*etc.* ∼**s old,** avoir dix/*etc.* ans. ∼**-book** *n.* annuaire *m.* ∼**ly** *a.* annuel; *adv.* annuellement.
yearn /jɜːn/ *v.i.* avoir bien *or* très envie (**for, to,** de). ∼**ing** *n.* envie *f.*
yeast /jiːst/ *n.* levure *f.*

yell /jel/ *v.t./i.* hurler. —*n.* hurlement *m.*
yellow /'jeləʊ/ *a.* jaune; (*cowardly: fam.*) froussard. —*n.* jaune *m.*
yelp /jelp/ *n.* (*of dog etc.*) jappement *m.* —*v.i.* japper.
yen /jen/ *n.* (*desire*) grande envie *f.*
yes /jes/ *adv.* oui; (*as answer to negative question*) si. —*n.* oui *m. invar.*
yesterday /'jestədɪ/ *n.* & *adv.* hier (*m.*).
yet /jet/ *adv.* encore; (*already*) déjà. —*conj.* pourtant, néanmoins.
yew /juː/ *n.* (*tree, wood*) if *m.*
Yiddish /'jɪdɪʃ/ *n.* yiddish *m.*
yield /jiːld/ *v.t.* (*produce*) produire, rendre; (*profit*) rapporter; (*surrender*) céder. —*v.i.* (*give way*) céder. —*n.* rendement *m.*
yoga /'jəʊgə/ *n.* yoga *m.*
yoghurt /'jɒgət, *Amer.* 'jəʊgərt/ *n.* yaourt *m.*
yoke /jəʊk/ *n.* joug *m.*
yokel /'jəʊkl/ *n.* rustre *m.*
yolk /jəʊk/ *n.* jaune (d'œuf) *m.*
yonder /'jɒndə(r)/ *adv.* là-bas.
you /juː/ *pron.* (*familiar form*) tu, *pl.*

vous; (*polite form*) vous; (*object*) te, t'*, *pl.* vous; (*polite*) vous; (*after prep.*) toi, *pl.* vous; (*polite*) vous; (*indefinite*) on; (*object*) vous. (**to**) ∼, te, t'*, *pl.* vous; (*polite*) vous. **I know** ∼, je te connais; je vous connais.

young /jʌŋ/ *a.* (**-er, -est**) jeune. —*n.* (*people*) jeunes *m. pl.*; (*of animals*) petits *m. pl.* ∼**er** *a.* (*brother etc.*) cadet. ∼**est** *a.* **my** ∼**est brother,** le cadet de mes frères.

youngster /'jʌŋstə(r)/ *n.* jeune *m./f.*

your /jɔ:(r)/ *a.* (*familiar form*) ton, ta, *pl.* tes; (*polite form, & familiar form pl.*) votre, *pl.* vos.

yours /jɔ:z/ *poss. pron.* (*familiar form*) le tien, la tienne, les tien(ne)s; (*polite*

form, & familiar form pl.*) le *or* la vôtre, les vôtres.

yoursel|f /jɔ:'self/ *pron.* (*familiar form*) toi-même; (*polite form*) vous-même; (*reflexive & after prep.*) te, t'*; vous. ∼**ves** *pron. pl.* vous-mêmes; (*reflexive*) vous.

youth /ju:θ/ *n.* (*pl.* **-s** /-ðz/) jeunesse *f.*; (*young man*) jeune *m.* ∼ **club,** centre de jeunes *m.* ∼ **hostel,** auberge de jeunesse *f.* ∼**ful** *a.* juvénile, jeune.

yo-yo /'jəʊjəʊ/ *n.* (*pl.* **-os**) (P.) yo-yo *m. invar.* (P.).

Yugoslav /'ju:gəslɑ:v/ *a. & n.* Yougoslave (*m./f.*). ∼**ia** /-'slɑ:vɪə/ *n.* Yougoslavie *f.*

Z

zany /'zeɪnɪ/ *a.* (**-ier, -iest**) farfelu.

zeal /zi:l/ *n.* zèle *m.*

zealous /'zeləs/ *a.* zélé. ∼**ly** *adv.* avec zèle.

zebra /'zebrə, 'zi:brə/ *n.* zèbre *m.* ∼ **crossing,** passage pour piétons *m.*

zenith /'zenɪθ/ *n.* zénith *m.*

zero /'zɪərəʊ/ *n.* (*pl.* **-os**) zéro *m.* ∼ **hour,** l'heure H *f.*

zest /zest/ *n.* (*gusto*) entrain *m.*; (*spice: fig.*) piment *m.*; (*of orange or lemon peel*) zeste *m.*

zigzag /'zɪgzæg/ *n.* zigzag *m.* —*a. & adv.* en zigzag. —*v.i.* (*p.t.* **zigzagged**) zigzaguer.

zinc /zɪŋk/ *n.* zinc *m.*

Zionism /'zaɪənɪzəm/ *n.* sionisme *m.*

zip /zɪp/ *n.* (*vigour*) allant *m.* ∼ (**-fastener**), fermeture éclair *f.* (P.). —*v.t.* (*p.t.* **zipped**) fermer avec une

fermeture éclair (P.). —*v.i.* aller à toute vitesse. **Z**∼ **code,** (*Amer.*) code postal *m.*

zipper /'zɪpə(r)/ *n.* (*Amer.*) = **zip** (**-fastener**).

zither /'zɪðə(r)/ *n.* cithare *f.*

zodiac /'zəʊdɪæk/ *n.* zodiaque *m.*

zombie /'zɒmbɪ/ *n.* mort(e) vivant(e) *m.* (*f.*); (*fam.*) automate *m.*

zone /zəʊn/ *n.* zone *f.*

zoo /zu:/ *n.* zoo *m.*

zoolog|y /zəʊ'ɒlədʒɪ/ *n.* zoologie *f.* ∼**ical** /-ə'lɒdʒɪkl/ *a.* zoologique. ∼**ist** *n.* zoologiste *m./f.*

zoom /zu:m/ *v.i.* (*rush*) se précipiter. ∼ **lens,** zoom *m.* ∼ **off** *or* **past,** filer (comme une flèche).

zucchini /zu:'ki:nɪ/ *n. invar.* (*Amer.*) courgette *f.*